BUSINESS
SPANISH
DICTIONARY

Spanish-English
English-Spanish

español-inglés
inglés-español

BUSINESS
SPANISH
DICTIONARY

Spanish-English
English-Spanish

español-inglés
inglés-español

PETER COLLIN PUBLISHING

Editorial Team
P.H.Collin
Lourdes Melcion
Jorge Díaz-Cintas
Maite Echart
Robert Sutcliffe

Readers
Fernanda Chicharro Bernat
Cris Sanders

Adviser
Alfonso Torrens dels Prats

This paperback edition first published 1998

Reprinted 2000

Hardback edition first published 1993
Revised second edition first publised in Great Britain 1997
by Peter Collin Publishing Ltd
1 Cambridge Road, Teddington, Middx, TW11 8DT - UK
© P.H.Collin & Peter Collin Publishing Ltd 1993, 1997, 1998

British Library Cataloguing in Publication Data
A catalogue record for this book is available from the British Library

ISBN 1-901659-23-2

Text typeset by Tradespools Ltd, Frome
Printed by WS Bookwell, Finland

PREFACE

The aim of this dictionary is to give the user a basic business vocabulary in Spanish and English, with translations into the other language.

The vocabulary covers the main areas of day-to-day business usage, including office practice, sales and purchases, shops, banking, invoices, credit control, international communications; these are the situations in which the user may frequently require translations from one language to the other.

The dictionary covers not only usage current in Britain, the USA and Spain, but also includes words and expressions from other English- or Spanish-speaking areas.

The dictionary gives many examples of usage, both to show how the words are used in context and how they can be translated; these examples are supplemented by short quotations in both languages from newspapers and magazines from all over the world: these show the worldwide applications of the two languages.

PREFACIO

El objetivo de este diccionario es ofrecer al usuario el vocabulario esencial del lenguaje económico y comercial en inglés y español con sus respectivas traducciones.

El vocabulario cubre el lenguaje actual de los negocios y abarca la terminología propia de los distintos campos relacionados con el mundo de la economía y las finanzas. Recoge no sólo términos que se usan diariamente dentro de la oficina, la empresa, la banca o la bolsa; sino también términos específicos del lenguaje informático, financiero y de gestión que frecuentemente requieren traducción de una lengua a otra.

El diccionario cubre, además del uso corriente de la lengua en Gran Bretaña, EE UU y España, palabras y expresiones utilizadas en otros países de habla inglesa y castellana.

Una innovación importante en el diccionario es la introducción de innumerables ejemplos y su correcta traducción en un contexto determinado. Estos ejemplos vienen acompañados, además, de citas cortas extraídas de periódicos y revistas de actualidad en inglés y español que permiten ilustrar el uso de la palabra en los dos idiomas

COMO USAR ESTE DICCIONARIO

Este diccionario presenta una estructura clara y fácil de manejar.
Las palabras principales aparecen en negrita.
Las palabras derivadas vienen precedidas de un rombo .
Las funciones gramaticales se introducen mediante números: 1, 2, etc..
Las letras (a), (b), etc. introducen una división semántica seguida de una explicación en cursiva y entre paréntesis.

Las abreviaturas se han mantenido a un mínimo y a continuación se ofrece una lista de las que aparecen:

abrev	abreviatura	abbreviation
adj	adjetivo	adjective
adv	adverbio	adverb
EE UU	Estados Unidos	United States
f	femenino	feminine
GB	Gran Bretaña	Great Britain
inv	invariable	invariable
m	masculino	masculine
n	nombre	noun
nf	nombre femenino	feminine noun
nfpl	nombre femenino plural	plural feminine noun
nm	nombre masculino	masculine noun
nmf	nombre masculino o femenino	masculine or feminine noun
nmpl	nombre masculino plural	plural masculine noun
pl	plural	plural
pp	participio pasado	past participle
vi	verbo intransitivo	intransitive verb
vr	verbo reflexivo	reflexive verb
vt	verbo transitivo	transitive verb
vt/i	verbo transitivo o intransitivo	transitive or intransitive verb
US	Estados Unidos	United States

USING THE DICTIONARY

The Dictionary aims to provide a clear layout which will help the user find the required translation as easily as possible. Each entry is formed of a headword in bold type, with clearly numbered divisions showing different parts of speech, or lettered divisions showing differences of meaning. Words which are derived from the main entry word are listed under that word, each time preceded by a lozenge

As far as is possible, abbreviations are not used in the dictionary, apart from the following:

abrev	abreviatura	abbreviation
adj	adjetivo	adjective
adv	adverbio	adverb
EE UU	Estados Unidos	United States
f	femenino	feminine
GB	Gran Bretaña	Great Britain
inv	invariable	invariable
m	masculino	masculine
n	nombre	noun
nf	nombre femenino	feminine noun
nfpl	nombre femenino plural	plural feminine noun
nm	nombre masculino	masculine noun
nmf	nombre masculino o femenino	masculine or feminine noun
nmpl	nombre masculino plural	plural masculine noun
pl	plural	plural
pp	participio pasado	past participle
vi	verbo intransitivo	intransitive verb
vr	verbo reflexivo	reflexive verb
vt	verbo transitivo	transitive verb
vt/i	verbo transitivo o intransitivo	transitive or intransitive verb
US	Estados Unidos	United States

DICCIONARIO ESPAÑOL-INGLÉS
SPANISH-ENGLISH DICTIONARY

Aa

A1, A2, A3, A4, A5 *(tamaño de papel)* **tenemos que pedir más papel con membrete, tamaño A4** = we must order some more A4 headed notepaper

abajo *adv* down *o* below *o* under; **más abajo** = further down; **abajo firmante** = undersigned; **nosotros, los abajo firmantes** = we, the undersigned; *(proyecto)* **venirse abajo** = to fall through *o* to collapse

abanderar *vt* to register (a ship)

◊ **abanderamiento** *nm* registry; **abanderamiento de un barco** = registration *o* registering of a ship

abandonado, -da 1 *adj* abandoned *o* neglected **2** *pp de* ABANDONAR

abandonar *vt* **(a)** *(plan, idea)* to abandon *o* to scrap *o* to drop; **abandonamos la idea de abrir una sucursal en Nueva York** = we abandoned the idea of setting up a New York office; **abandonar los planes de expansión** = to scrap plans for expansion; **el programa de desarrollo se tuvo que abandonar cuando los fondos de la compañía se agotaron** = the development programme had to be abandoned when the company ran out of cash; **el proyecto se abandonó** = the project was scrapped **(b)** *(alguien o algo)* to abandon *o* to leave someone *o* something; **la tripulación abandonó el barco que se hundía** = the crew abandoned the sinking ship **(c)** *(dimitir)* **abandonar el trabajo** = to resign *o* to quit one's job; **abandonó el trabajo y se compró una granja** = he left his job and bought a farm; **abandonar el puesto de trabajo** = to walk off the job; **la totalidad del personal abandonó el trabajo en señal de protesta** = the whole workforce walked out in protest; **los contratistas abandonaron la obra porque dijeron que era demasiado peligrosa** = the builders walked off the site because they said it was too dangerous

abandono *nm* abandonment; **abandono de un barco** = abandonment of a ship; *(agricultura)* **abandono de tierras** = set-aside system

abanico *nm (bolsa)* spread; *(variedad)* **abanico de productos** = product line *o* range of products

abaratar *vt* to make cheaper *o* to lower the price

> se anuncian movilizaciones contundentes
> si el gobierno abarata el despido
> **El País**

> a pesar de las críticas, la liberalización
> introducida en el suelo lo abaratará, y si
> se logra una reducción de plazos
> administrativos, los costes disminuirán
> **El País**

abarcar *vt* to extend; **la compañía ha querido abarcar demasiado** = the company overextended itself

abarrotar *vt* to overstock *o* to overcrowd; **el mercado estaba abarrotado de gente** = the market was overcrowded

abastecedor, -ra *n (suministrador)* supplier; *(de comidas preparadas)* caterer; **son abastecedores importantes de repuestos para la industria del automóvil** = they are major suppliers of spare parts to the car industry; **es un abastecedor que se preocupa de la calidad del producto** = he is a supplier who is concerned about the quality of his product

abastecer *vt* to provide *o* to supply *o* to cater for; **abastecer el mercado** = to supply the market

◊ **abastecido, -da** *adj y pp* supplied *o* stocked

◊ **abastecimiento** *nm* supply *o* provision; **abastecimiento de aguas** = water supply

abierto, -ta 1 *adj* **(a)** *(cuenta, billete)* open; **billete abierto** = open ticket; **crédito abierto** = open credit; **cuenta abierta** = open account; **sobre abierto** = unsealed envelope; *(no cruzado)* **cheque abierto** = open cheque **(b)** *(horario de trabajo)* open; **está abierto al público todos los días de la semana** = they are open for business every day of the week; **abierto tarde** *o* **por la noche** = late opening *o* late-night opening **(c)** *(susceptible de modificaciones)* open-ended; **acuerdo abierto** = open-ended agreement; **oferta abierta** = open bid **(d) abierto a todos los aspirantes** = open to all applicants **2** *pp de* ABRIR

abogacía *nf* the legal profession

abogado, -da *n* GB lawyer; solicitor; barrister *o* counsel; *US* attorney; **ejercer de abogado** *o* **como abogado** = to practise as a solicitor *o* as a barrister *o* as a lawyer; **Colegio de Abogados** = *GB* Bar Council *o* Law Society; *US* American Bar Association; **ingresar en el Colegio de Abogados** = to be called to the bar; **otorgaron poder judicial a su abogado** = his solicitor was granted power of attorney; **confió su testamento a su abogado** = he deposited his will with his solicitor; **dar instrucciones a un abogado para que proceda judicialmente** *o* **contratar a un abogado** = to instruct a solicitor; **abogado auxiliar** = junior (counsel); **abogado defensor** = defence counsel; **abogado del diablo** = devil's advocate; **abogado de oficio** = duty solicitor; **abogado de la parte demandante** = prosecution counsel *o* counsel for the prosecution; **abogado especialista en derecho internacional** = international lawyer; **abogado especialista en derecho mercantil** = commercial lawyer *o* company lawyer; **abogado especializado en derecho marítimo** = maritime lawyer; **abogado especializado en derecho fiscal** = tax lawyer; **pasante de abogado** = articled clerk

abonable *adj* payable *o* debitable

abonado, -da 1 *n* **(a)** *(suscrito)* subscriber; **abonado a una revista** = subscriber to a magazine *o* magazine subscriber; **el número extra se envía gratuitamente a todos los abonados** = the extra issue is sent free to all subscribers; **abonado telefónico** = telephone subscriber **(b)** *(teatro o transporte)* season-ticket holder **2** *adj* credited *o* paid **3** *pp de* ABONAR

abonar *vt* to pay *o* to credit; **abonar en cuenta** = to credit an account; **abonar 20.000 ptas. en cuenta a alguien** = to enter 20,000 pesetas to someone's credit; **el banco tardó diez días en abonar el cheque a cuenta** = the cheque took ten days to clear *o* the bank took ten days to clear the cheque; **cuente con que el cheque tardará seis días en abonarse en cuenta** = you should allow six days for cheque clearance

◇ **abonarse** *vr* to subscribe (to)

◇ **abono** *nm* **(a)** *(suscripción)* subscription; **¿te acordaste de pagar el abono a la revista de ordenadores?** = did you remember to pay the subscription to the computer magazine? **(b)** *(crédito)* credit *o* credit entry; **nota de abono** = credit note **(c)** *(pago)* payment

abordaje *nm* boarding

abordar *vt* **(a)** *(barco)* to board a ship **(b) abordar un tema** = to address a subject

> el informe está estructurado en 12 capítulos, en los que se aborda el tema de la cooperación desde distintas perspectivas
>
> **El País**

abreviado, -da 1 *adj* brief *o* short *o* shortened; **en versión abreviada** = abridged version **2** *pp de* ABREVIAR

abreviar 1 *vt* to shorten *o* to abridge **2** *vi* to be brief; **para abreviar** = in short

abrir 1 *vt* **(a)** to open; **abrir la correspondencia** = to open the mail; **abrir una cuenta bancaria** = to open a bank account; **abrir una línea de crédito** = to open a line of credit; **abrir nuevos mercados** = to open up new markets **(b)** *(empezar)* to start *o* to set up; **abrir un negocio** = to open a business *o* to set up in business; **la empresa va a abrir una oficina en Nueva York el año próximo** = the firm is going to open an office in New York next year **(c)** *(extender)* to issue; **abrir una carta de crédito** = to issue a letter of credit **2** *vi* to open; **la oficina abre a las 9 de la mañana** = the office opens at 9 a.m.; **abrimos al público los domingos** = we open for business on Sundays; **la tienda abre los domingos por la mañana** = the store is open on Sunday mornings; **nuestras oficinas abren de 9 a 6** = our offices are open from 9 to 6; **volver a abrir** = to reopen; **la oficina volverá a abrir próximamente después de las reformas** = the office will reopen soon after its refit

absentismo *nm* absenteeism; **el absentismo es elevado durante la semana anterior a las Navidades** = absenteeism is high in the week before Christmas; **el índice de absentismo siempre aumenta con el buen tiempo** = the rate of absenteeism *o* the absenteeism rate always increases in fine weather

◇ **absentista** *nmf* absentee

absolución *nf* acquittal

absoluto, -ta *adj* absolute *o* outright *o* unconditional; **de un modo absoluto** = absolutely *o* outright; **monopolio absoluto** = absolute monopoly; **la empresa tiene el monopolio absoluto de la importación de vino francés** = the company has an absolute monopoly of imports of French wine; **propietario absoluto** = ground landlord

absorber *vt* to absorb; *(empresa)* to take over; **absorber un excedente** = to absorb a surplus; **absorber gastos generales** = to absorb overheads; **los gastos generales nos han absorbido todos los beneficios** = overheads have absorbed all our profits; **absorber las pérdidas de una filial** = to absorb a loss by a subsidiary; **una empresa que ha sido absorbida por un competidor** = a business which has been taken over *o* absorbed by a competitor

absorción *nf* absorption *o* takeover; **cálculo de costes de absorción** = absorption costing; **coeficiente de absorción** = absorption rate

abstenerse *vr* to hold back *o* to refrain; **se abstuvo de firmar el contrato de arrendamiento hasta que hubo verificado los detalles** = he held back from signing the lease until he had checked the details

abstracto, -ta *adj* abstract; **en abstracto** = notional *o* in the abstract

abundancia *nf* abundance

◇ **abundante** *adj* abundant *o* plentiful *o* bumper (crop)

abuso *nm* abuse; **abuso de confianza** = breach of trust; **abuso de poder** *o* **de autoridad** = abuse of power *o* abuse of a position of authority

acabado, -da 1 *adj* complete *o* finished **2** *nm* finish; **el producto tiene un acabado atractivo** = the product has an attractive finish **3** *pp de* ACABAR

acabar *vt/i* to complete *o* to finish; **el nuevo director de finanzas acabó con los gastos de representación** = the new finance director put a stop to the reps' expense claims

◇ **acabarse** *vr* to finish *o* to run out; **se nos acabó el papel con membrete** = we have run out of headed notepaper

acaparado, -da 1 *adj* cornered; **mercado acaparado** = cornered market **2** *pp de* ACAPARAR

acaparador, -ra *n* **(a)** *(que acumula)* hoarder **(b)** *(agiotista)* profiteer

◇ **acaparamiento** *nm* hoarding; **acaparamiento de mercancías** = hoarding of goods *o* commodities

acaparar *vt* **(a)** *(monopolizar)* to corner *o* to capture; **la empresa ha acaparado el mercado de diccionarios especializados** = the firm has cornered the market in specialist dictionaries; **acaparar un 10% del mercado** = to capture 10% of the market **(b)** *(acumular)* to hoard

acarreo *nm* trucking

acatamiento *nm* respect

acatar *vt* to respect (someone) *o* to obey (an order, the law)

acaudalado, -da 1 *adj* wealthy *o* affluent **2** *pp de* ACAUDALAR

acaudalar *vt* to accumulate wealth

acceder *vi* to agree (to do something); **accedió a trabajar con nosotros** = he agreed to work with us; **se ha accedido a que el arrendamiento dure 25**

años = it has been agreed that the lease will run for 25 years

accesible *adj* **(a)** accessible *o* available; **un lugar accesible** = an accessible spot **(b)** *(persona)* (easily) approachable

◊ **acceso** *nm* **(a)** access; **tener acceso a algo** = to have access to something; **tiene acceso a grandes cantidades de capital riesgo** = he has access to large amounts of venture capital **(b)** *(informática)* **acceso directo** = direct access; **acceso secuencial** = sequential access; **acceso único** *o* **en paralelo** = single access *o* parallel access; **almacenamiento de acceso rápido** = quick access storage; **tiempo de acceso** = access time **(c)** *(entrada)* entrance *o* entry; **prohibido el acceso** = no admittance

accesorio, -ria **1** *adj* **gastos accesorios** = incidental costs **2** *nm* **accesorios** = fittings *o* accessories; **accesorios para automóviles** = car accessories; **instalaciones fijas y accesorios** = fixtures and fittings (f. & f.)

accidente *nm* accident; *(avión)* crash; **después del accidente los dos coches fueron declarados siniestro total** = the two cars were written off after the accident; **accidente de trabajo** *o* **accidente laboral** = industrial accident; **lesiones sufridas en un accidente laboral** = industrial injuries; **una póliza de accidentes** = an accident policy; **seguro de accidentes** = accident insurance

acción *nf* **(a)** *(acto)* action; **acción directa** = direct action **(b)** *(legal)* **acción legal** = legal action *o* lawsuit; **acción criminal** = criminal action; **acción penal** = trial; **desistir de una acción** = to abandon an action **(c)** *(comercial)* share *o* stock; **acciones en cartera** = treasury stocks; **acciones de clase 'A' (con derecho de voto limitado)** = 'A' shares; **acciones de clase 'B' (con derecho de voto especial, normalmente propiedad del fundador y su familia)** = 'B' shares; **acciones en compañías norteamericanas** = dollar stocks; **acciones cotizables en bolsa** = listed securities; **acciones con derecho a dividendo en último lugar** = deferred shares; **acción con derecho a voto** = voting share *o* stock; **valores convertibles en acciones en una fecha futura** = convertible loan stock; **acciones por encima** *o* **por debajo de la par** = shares above par *o* below par; **acción especulativa** = speculative share; **acción fraccionada** = fractional share; **acciones de fundador** = founder's shares; **acciones con garantía** = qualifying shares; **acciones liberadas** *o* **cubiertas** = fully-paid shares; **acciones no liberadas totalmente** = partly-paid up shares; **acción líder** = bellwether; **acciones nominativas** = registered shares; **acción nueva** = new share; **acciones ordinarias** = ordinary shares *o* equities; *US* common stock; **acciones poco corrientes** = funny money; **acciones preferentes** = preference shares; *US* preferred stock; **acción preferente acumulativa** = cumulative preferred stock; **acción prima** *o* **gratuita** *o* **liberada** = bonus share *o* stock dividend; **acciones de tesorería** = Treasury stocks *o* bonds; **acciones de valor a la par** = shares at par; **asignación de acciones** = share allocation *o* share allotment; **asignar acciones** = to allot shares; **capital en acciones** = share capital *o* equity capital; **emisión de acciones** = share issue; **emisión gratuita de acciones** = scrip *o* rights issue; **emitir acciones a la par** = to issue shares at par; **paquete de acciones** = block of shares; **compró un paquete**

de acciones de la Telefónica = he bought a block of shares in la Telefónica; **sociedad por acciones** = joint stock company; **suscripción de acciones** = share subscription *o* application for shares; **tenedor de acciones de una compañía** = holder of stock *o* of shares in a company; **título** *o* **certificado de una acción** = share certificate; **las acciones bajaron en el mercado madrileño** = shares fell on the Madrid market; **la compañía ofreció 1,8 millones de acciones en el mercado** = the company offered 1.8m shares on the market

> los beneficios netos por acción han subido de 57, 2 pesetas a 1. 200 este año
> **España Económica**

> deseaba invertir en España por un camino diferente del tradicional, fuera de la mera compra de acciones cotizadas en bolsa
> **España Económica**

> en una semana se llegaron a mover en bolsa casi 25. 000 acciones de la compañía, más que durante los dos pasados años, con un precio actual de 9. 200 pesetas
> **El País**

accionar *vt* to trigger

accionista *nmf* shareholder *o* member; *US* stockholder; **accionista de una compañía** = holder of stock *o* of shares in a company; **un accionista mayoritario** = a majority shareholder; **la compañía está controlada por el accionista mayoritario** = the company is controlled by the majority shareholder; **accionista minoritario** = minority shareholder; **el abogado que actúa en nombre de los accionistas minoritarios** = the solicitor acting on behalf of the minority shareholders; **pequeños accionistas** = small shareholders; **capital de los accionistas** = shareholders' equity; **convocar una junta general de accionistas** = to call a shareholders' meeting; **liquidación** *o* **disolución de una sociedad por los mismos accionistas** = members' voluntary winding up

> la oferta de CVNE a los accionistas de Bilbaínas era de 8. 800 pesetas por título
> **El País**

> el consejo estaba reducido a cuatro miembros tras la tumultuosa junta de accionistas
> **El País**

aceite *nm* oil; **aceite de motor** = engine oil; **la exportación de aceite de oliva al Reino Unido ha aumentado este año** = olive oil exports to the UK have increased this year

aceleración *nf* acceleration; **coeficiente de aceleración** = acceleration coefficient *o* ratio

> no se puede olvidar la aceleración creciente que han experimentado los préstamos financieros, desde la supresión del depósito del 30%, en el Banco de España
> **Mercado**

acelerado, -da *adj* accelerated *o* fast *o* rapid; **amortización acelerada** = accelerated depreciation; **curso de formación profesional**

acelerada = intensive training course **2** *pp de* ACELERAR

> el desarrollo económico español ha sido
> más acelerado que el de otros países
> **Tiempo**

acelerar *vt* to accelerate *o* to speed up; **pretendemos acelerar nuestros plazos de entrega** = we are aiming to speed up our delivery times; **las ventas comenzaron despacio, pero se aceleraron más tarde** = sales got off to a slow start, but picked up later

acentuar *vt* to emphasize *o* to stress *o* to accentuate; **las preocupaciones del mercado se vieron acentuadas por la noticia de la subida de las tarifas de electricidad** = market worries were increased by news of an increase in electricity charges

aceptable *adj* acceptable; **la oferta no es aceptable para ambas partes** = the offer is not acceptable to both parties; **la compañía en realidad está obteniendo unos beneficios aceptables** = the company is really making an acceptable profit; **precio aceptable** = fair price *o* acceptable price

◊ **aceptación** *nf* **(a)** *(admisión)* acceptance; **aceptación de una oferta** = acceptance of an offer; **dar una aceptación condicional a una oferta** = to accept an offer conditionally *o* to give an offer a conditional acceptance; **aceptación incondicional de la oferta por parte de la junta** = unconditional acceptance of the offer by the board; **muestra de aceptación** = acceptance sampling; **nivel de aceptación de un producto** = level of acceptability of a product *o* market acceptability of a product **(b)** *(comercio internacional)* bill of acceptance; **presentar una letra a la aceptación** = to present a bill for acceptance

◊ **aceptado, -da 1** *adj* accepted; **no aceptado** = overruled; **letra aceptada** = due bill *o* accepted bill; **letra no aceptada** = dishonoured bill **2** *pp de* ACEPTAR

aceptar *vt* **(a)** *(admitir)* to accept; **aceptar una letra** = to accept a bill; **aceptar la entrega de mercancías** = to accept delivery of a shipment *o* to take delivery of goods; **aceptó la oferta de un puesto de trabajo en Australia** = she accepted the offer of a job in Australia; **aceptó sus precios** = he has accepted *o* agreed your prices; **aceptó 200.000 ptas. por el coche** = he accepted 200,000 pesetas for the car; **hemos recibido una carta suya aceptando la oferta** = we have his letter of acceptance **(b)** *(aprobar)* to allow *o* to honour; **aceptar una demanda** *o* **una apelación** = to allow a claim *o* an appeal; **aceptar una firma** = to honour a signature **(c)** *(consentir)* to agree; **aceptar condicionalmente** = to give a conditional acceptance; **aceptar hacer algo** = to agree to do something; **aceptamos los términos del contrato con tal de que sea ratificado por nuestra junta general** = we accept the terms of the contract, on the understanding that it has to be ratified by our main board; **no aceptar** = to refuse *o* to decline (to do something); **se negó a aceptar algunas de las condiciones del contrato** = he refused to agree to some of the terms of the contract **(d)** *(asumir)* to take (on); **ha aceptado mucho trabajo extra** = he has taken on a lot of extra work

acerca *prep* **acerca de** = about *o* concerning *o* relating to

acercar *vt* to bring closer; **acerca tu silla** = bring your chair closer

◊ **acercarse** *vr* to approach *o* to come near to *o* to border on; **acercarse a la edad de jubilación** = to approach *o* to be coming up to retirement age

acertado, -da 1 *adj* correct; *(consejo)* wise *o* sound; *(plan)* well conceived *o* good; **nos dio un consejo muy acertado** = he gave us some very sound advice **2** *pp de* ACERTAR

acertar 1 *vt* to get right *o* to guess correctly; **acertó los resultados de las quinielas** = he guessed the results of the football pools correctly **2** *vi* to be right; **acertó en la elección de su carrera profesional** = he chose the right career

acervo *nm* common property *o* total assets of an estate

aclaración *nf* explanation; **una aclaración al margen** = a note in the margin

acogerse *vr* to join; **todo el personal se ha acogido al plan de pensiones de la empresa** = all the staff have joined the company pension plan

acomodado, -da 1 *adj* well-off **2** *pp de* ACOMODAR

acomodar *vt* to arrange

◊ **acomodo** *nm* arrangement *o* understanding

acompañar *vt* **(a)** *(a alguien)* to accompany; **el presidente vino a la reunión acompañado del director de finanzas** = the chairman came to the meeting accompanied by the finance director **(b)** *(en carta)* to enclose *o* to attach

aconsejar *vt* to advise *o* to counsel; **aconsejar en contra** = to advise against; **nos aconsejan que llevemos la compañía naviera a los tribunales** = we are advised to take the shipping company to court; **el contable nos aconsejó que enviáramos los documentos a la policía** = the accountant advised us to send the documents to the police; **mi agente de bolsa aconseja no comprar esas acciones** = my stockbroker has advised against buying those shares; **el director del banco nos aconsejó que no cerráramos la cuenta** = the bank manager advised against closing the account

acopiar *vt* to gather *o* to stock *o* to stockpile

◊ **acopio** *nm* stock

acoplador *nm* coupler; **acoplador acústico** = acoustic coupler

acoplamiento *nm* **(a)** *(conexión)* connection *o* connexion **(b)** *(informática)* interface

acordado, -da 1 *adj* agreed; **en las condiciones acordadas** = on agreed terms **2** *pp de* ACORDAR

acordar *vt* to agree *o* to come to an agreement *o* to resolve; **las dos partes interesadas acordaron las cifras** = the figures were agreed between the two parties

> los países de la UE han acordado la puesta
> en circulación de la moneda única para el
> año 2002
> **El País**

◊ **acordarse** *vr* **(a)** *(recordar)* to remember; **se acordó de que había visto el artículo en el catálogo de un proveedor** = she remembered seeing the item in a supplier's catalogue **(b)** *(ponerse de acuerdo)* to agree *o* to come to an agreement; **se acordó la reunión para el jueves** = the meeting was agreed for Thursday

acortar *vt* to shorten *o* to reduce

acotación *nf* limit

acotar *vt* to set limits

ACP *sigla (Países de Africa, del Caribe y del Pacífico con tratamiento comercial preferente en la UE)* = ACP countries

acre *nm* acre

acrecentar *vt* to increase *o* to augment

◊ **acrecentarse** *vr* to increase *o* to grow; **la subida en la cotización de las acciones se vio acrecentada por los rumores de una oferta de adquisición** = the rise in the share price was fuelled by rumours of a takeover bid

acreditado, -da 1 *adj* accredited *o* reputable; **agente acreditado** = recognized agent; **una empresa de contables acreditada** = a reputable firm of accountants; **empleamos solamente transportistas acreditados** = we only use reputable carriers **2** *pp de* ACREDITAR

> es decir, no todos los concesionarios de la marca nipona pueden vender Lexus, sólo los más acreditados y que cuenten con unas instalaciones especializadas para la venta
>
> **Blanco y Negro**

acreditar *vt* to credit *o* to vouch for; **acreditar una firma** = to vouch for a signature

acreedor, -ra 1 *adj* **saldo acreedor** = credit balance; **mi cuenta arroja todavía un saldo acreedor** = my bank account is still in the black; **cuenta con saldo acreedor** = account in credit **2** *n* creditor; **acreedor asegurado** *o* **con garantía** = secured creditor; **acreedores comerciales** = trade creditors; **acreedor común** *o* **sin garantía** = unsecured creditor; **acreedor hipotecario** = mortgagee *o* mortgage creditor; **acreedor preferente** = preferred *o* preferential creditor; **junta de acreedores** = creditors' meeting

> siempre llega un momento en el que los acreedores se niegan a prestar más o exigen intereses crecientes
>
> **Cambio 16**

acta *nf* **(a)** *(de una reunión)* minutes *o* proceedings; **levantar acta** = to take the minutes (of a meeting); **constar en acta** = to be minuted; **no quiero que éso conste en acta** = I do not want that to be put in the minutes *o* to be minuted *o* I want that not to be minuted; **acta de la junta general** = proceedings of the general meeting; **el presidente firmó el acta de la última reunión** = the chairman signed the minutes of the last meeting **(b)** **actas de un congreso** = conference proceedings **(c)** *(legal)* **acta notarial** = affidavit **(d)** **Acta de Navegación** = Navigation Act; **Acta Unica Europea** = Single European Act

actitud *nf* attitude *o* position

activador *nm* trigger

activar *vt* to activate *o* to speed up; *(mercado)* to stimulate

actividad *nf* **(a)** activity; **actividad comercial** = business; **la actividad es intensa** = business is brisk; **la actividad comercial es baja** = business is slow; **tasa de actividad** = activity rate; **un nivel reducido de actividad comercial** = a low level of business activity; **el verano es la temporada de mayor actividad para los hoteles** = summer is the busy season for hotels; **enero es siempre un periodo de baja actividad** *o* **de poca actividad comercial** = January is always a slack period *o* business is always slow in January; **cubrimos gastos en los dos primeros meses de actividad** = we broke even in our first two months of trading; **quebró después de dos años de actividad empresarial** = he went bankrupt after two years in business; **un día de gran actividad en la bolsa** = a very active day on the Stock Exchange; **había mucha actividad en el mercado de acciones petrolíferas** = oil shares were very active *o* there was a lot of activity in oil shares; **es una empresa en plena actividad** = it is a going concern; **gráfico de actividades** = activity chart; **informe mensual de actividades** = monthly activity report; **ampliar las actividades de un negocio** *o* **ampliar un negocio a otras actividades** = to branch out; **las actividades de la empresa se están reduciendo en preparación del cierre** = the company is being run down **(b)** *(profesional)* occupation; **su actividad principal es la construcción de casas** = his main occupation is house building

◊ **actividades** *nfpl (en una conferencia)* **programa de actividades** = schedule of events; **resumen de actividades** = agenda

> si la actividad económica es inferior a la prevista y el déficit público mucho mayor, el control monetario pasa a ser mucho más necesario, evitando que la expansión monetaria financie inflación en vez de crecimiento económico
>
> **Mercado**

> con una actividad constructora que está tocando techo es difícil que los precios sigan subiendo
>
> **España Económica**

> la disminución de la actividad económica en muchos sectores ha llevado a las empresas a invertir menos dinero en sus presupuestos publicitarios
>
> **Tiempo**

> para que el peso del ajuste no recaiga especialmente sobre la actividad y el empleo, hay que incrementar la competitividad
>
> **España Económica**

activo, -va 1 *adj* active; *(enérgico)* brisk; **mano de obra** *o* **población activa** = active labour force *o* workforce; **población económicamente activa (pea)** = economically active population; **mercado poco activo** = easy market; **el precio de las acciones bajó ligeramente en un mercado poco activo** = shares drifted lower in a dull market; **el mercado de acciones petrolíferas se muestra especialmente activo** = the market in oil shares is particularly brisk; **socio activo** = active partner **2** *nm* asset; **tiene**

solamente un activo de 640.000 ptas. frente a un pasivo de 24.000.000 de ptas. = her assets are only 640,000 pesetas as against liabilities of 24m pesetas; **activo de caja** = *(empresa)* cash reserves; *(banca)* bank reserves; **activo circulante** = current assets; **activo congelado** = frozen assets; **activo consumible** = wasting asset; **activo(s) ficticio(s)** = ficticious assets; **activo fijo** = capital assets *o* fixed assets; **activos fijos intangibles** = intangible fixed assets; **activo financiero** = financial asset; **activo inmaterial** *o* **intangible** = intangible assets; **activo invisible** = invisible assets; **activo líquido** = liquid assets; **activo líquido en manos del público (ALPs)** = liquid assets held by the public *o* money supply (M3); **activo neto** = net worth; **activo y pasivo** = assets and liabilities; **su activo supera el pasivo** = he has an excess of assets over liabilities; **activo realizable** = realizable assets; **activo tangible** = tangible assets; **depreciación de un activo** = writedown of an asset; **liquidar el activo** = to realize one's assets *o* to go liquid; **liquidación de activo** *o* **de activos** = realization of assets *o* asset stripping; **valor de activo** = asset value

◊ **activamente** *adv* actively

> pensó en adquirir la famosa firma de automóviles, pero le pidieron dos millones de dólares, cuando el único activo que tenían estaba valorado en apenas 100.000 dólares
> **España Económica**

> el activo líquido por excelencia, el dinero y las divisas tienen un precio, pero no suelen tener barreras de entrada y mucho menos en el marco europeo con la libertad de movimientos de capitales
> **Mercado**

> con unos activos de 118.200 millones de dólares, estos dos bancos del sureste pasaron a ocupar el tercer lugar del ranking el pasado 23 de julio
> **El País**

acto *nm* **(a)** act *o* action; **en el acto** = immediately; **acto administrativo** = administrative action; **acto ilegal** = malfeasance **(b) acto de clausura** = closing ceremony; **salón de actos** = assembly hall

actuación *nf* behaviour *o* performance; **medir la actuación del gobierno** = to measure the government's performance; **la compañía tuvo** *o* **las acciones tuvieron una mala actuación** = the company *o* the shares performed badly

actual *adj* current *o* present *o* up to date *o* going; **las acciones son demasiado caras al precio actual** = the shares are too expensive at their present price; **¿cuál es la dirección actual de la compañía?** = what is the present address of the company?; **los precios vigentes en el momento actual** = current prices *o* prices which are ruling at the moment; **valor actual** = present value

◊ **actualización** *nf* update; updating; **curso de actualización** = refresher course

> la actualización de balances aumentará el valor de las empresas que se acojan voluntariamente a esta medida
> **El País**

◊ **actualmente** *adv* currently *o* at present *o* at the moment; **actualmente estamos negociando un** préstamo con el banco = we are currently negotiating with the bank for a loan; **actualmente es el director gerente de García S.A., pero antes trabajaba para Torres** = he is currently managing director of García S.A., but formerly he worked for Torres

◊ **actualizar** *vt* to update *o* to bring something up to date

actuar *vi* to act; **los abogados están actuando según nuestras instrucciones** = the lawyers are acting on our instructions; **actuar como representante de una empresa** = to act as an agent for a company; *(representar a alguien)* **actuar en nombre de alguien** = to act for someone *o* to act on someone's behalf *o* to represent someone; **actuar como fiador de alguien** = to stand surety for someone; **actuar como sustituto de alguien** = to stand in for someone *o* to act as deputy for someone *o* to act as someone's deputy; *(mediar en un conflicto)* **actuar de juez** = to adjudicate *o* to mediate in a dispute

actuarial *adj* actuarial; **las primas se determinan según cálculos actuariales** = the premiums are worked out according to actuarial calculations; **tablas actuariales** = actuarial tables

◊ **actuario** *nm* actuary; **actuario de seguros** = insurance actuary

acuerdo *nm* **(a)** *(convenio)* agreement *o* arrangement *o* understanding; **acuerdo abierto** *o* **susceptible de modificaciones** = open-ended agreement; **acuerdo bilateral** = bilateral agreement; **acuerdo entre caballeros** = gentleman's agreement; **acuerdo de comercialización** = a marketing agreement; **acuerdo (por) escrito** = written agreement; **acuerdo no escrito** *o* **acuerdo verbal** = unwritten *o* verbal agreement; **acuerdo general** = omnibus agreement; **acuerdo sobre precios** = pricing agreement *o* agreement on prices *o* price fixing agreement; **acuerdo preventivo** = scheme of arrangement; **acuerdo que prohibe la huelga** = no-strike agreement; **acuerdo recíproco** = reciprocal agreement; **acuerdo de representación exclusiva** = exclusive agreement; **acuerdo sindical** = union agreement; **acuerdo solemne y obligatorio** = solemn and binding agreement; **acuerdo unilateral** = one-sided agreement; **mientras el acuerdo esté vigente** = during the life of the agreement; **los delegados de los sindicatos hicieron objeciones al texto del acuerdo** = the union delegates raised an objection to the wording of the agreement; **alcanzar un acuerdo** = to come to an agreement *o* to reach an agreement; **se ha alcanzado un acuerdo** = an agreement has been reached *o* concluded *o* come to; **concertar un acuerdo** = to make an agreement; **llegar a un acuerdo** = to come to an agreement *o* to strike a bargain with someone *o* to hammer out an agreement; **llegar a un acuerdo sobre los precios** *o* **salarios** = to reach an agreement on prices *o* salaries; **llegar a un acuerdo con los acreedores** = to reach an accommodation with creditors; **llegaron a un acuerdo provisional sobre la propuesta** = they reached a tentative agreement over the proposal; **esperamos finalizar el acuerdo mañana** = we hope to finalize the agreement tomorrow; **negarse a cumplir un acuerdo** = to repudiate an agreement; **poner término a un acuerdo** = to terminate an agreement; **romper un acuerdo** = to break an agreement **(b)** *(negocio)* deal;

el acuerdo se firmará mañana = the deal will be signed tomorrow; **llegaron a un acuerdo con una línea aérea estadounidense** = they did a deal with a US airline; **suspender** *o* **anular** *o* **cancelar un acuerdo** = to call off a deal; **cuando el presidente se enteró del acuerdo lo suspendió** = when the chairman heard about the deal he called it off; **acuerdo de conjunto** *o* **acuerdo global** = blanket agreement *o* package deal; **llegaron a un acuerdo de conjunto, que incluye la construcción de la fábrica, la formación del personal y la compra del producto** = they agreed a package deal, which involves the construction of the factory, training of staff and purchase of the product **(c)** *(después de un conflicto)* settlement; **se llegó a un acuerdo amistoso** = a settlement was reached out of court; **llevar a un acuerdo a las dos partes** *o* **poner de acuerdo a dos partes** = to effect a settlement between two parties; **esperan alcanzar un acuerdo amistoso** = they are hoping to reach an out-of-court settlement; **las dos partes llegaron a un acuerdo extrajudicialmente** = a settlement was reached out of court *o* the two parties reached an out-of-court settlement **(d) de acuerdo con** = in accordance with *o* under **(e) acuerdo con fines ilegales** = concert **(f)** *(contrato comercial)* treaty; **acuerdo comercial** = commercial treaty; **Acuerdo General sobre Aranceles Aduaneros y Comercio (GATT)** = General Agreement on Tariffs and Trade (GATT); *ver también* OMC **Acuerdo General sobre Préstamos** = General Arrangements to Borrow (GAB); **vender una casa por acuerdo privado** = to sell a house by private treaty

una cosa es propiciar el acuerdo entre sindicatos y patronal y otra muy distinta sentar a la mesa de negociación al Gobierno con el Presupuesto debajo del brazo

España Económica

acumulación *nf* **(a)** *(gradual)* accrual; **acumulación de interés** = accrual of interest; **permitir la acumulación de dividendos** = to allow dividends to accumulate **(b)** *(acaparamiento)* stocking; **acumulación de provisiones** = hoarding of supplies; **tener una acumulación excesiva de existencias de piezas de recambio** = to be overstocked with spare parts **(c) acumulación de trabajo atrasado** = backlog of work; **mi secretaria no puede hacer frente a la acumulación de trabajo administrativo atrasado** = my secretary can't cope with the backlog of paperwork

acumulado, -da 1 *adj* accumulated *o* accrued; **beneficio acumulado** = accumulated profit; **deudas acumuladas** *o* **pasivo acumulado** = accrued liabilities *o* accruals; **dividendo acumulado** = accrued dividend **2** *pp de* ACUMULAR

acumular *vt* **(a)** *(cantidad)* to stock up *o* to hoard; **acumularon papel de ordenador** = they stocked up with computer paper; **acumular un exceso de existencias** = to be overstocked **(b)** *(reservas)* to stockpile; **acumular materias primas** = to stockpile raw materials

◊ **acumularse** *vr* **(a)** *(interés, beneficio)* to accrue *o* to accumulate **(b)** *(amontonarse)* to pile up; **las facturas se acumulaban sobre la mesa** = the invoices were piling up on the table

acumulativo, -va *adj* cumulative; **interés**

acumulativo = cumulative interest; **acción preferente de dividendo acumulable** = cumulative preference share; *US* cumulative preferred stock

acuñación *nf* coinage *o* minting

◊ **acuñar** *vt* to coin *o* to mint

acusación *nf* **(a)** *(cargo)* charge *o* indictment; **formular una acusación** = to prefer a charge; **negar una acusación** = to deny a charge; **retirar una acusación** = to withdraw charges **(b)** *(parte acusadora)* prosecution; **testigo de la acusación** = witness for the prosecution

◊ **acusado, -da** *n* defendant **2** *adj* noticeable **3** *pp de* ACUSAR

◊ **acusadamente** *adv* sharply; **el precio de las acciones subió acusadamente** = the share price rose sharply; **las acciones reaccionaron acusadamente ante la caída del tipo de cambio** = shares reacted sharply to the fall in the exchange rate

acusador, -ra 1 *adj* **parte acusadora** = prosecution **2** *n* accuser

acusar *vt* **(a)** *(culpar)* to accuse; **la acusaron de robar dinero de la caja** = she was accused of stealing from the petty cash box; **se le acusó de espionaje industrial** = he was accused of industrial espionage **(b)** *(jurídico)* to charge; **se le acusó de malversar fondos de sus clientes** = he was charged with embezzling his clients' money; **compareció ante el tribunal acusado de malversación de fondos** = he appeared in court charged with embezzlement *o* he appeared in court on a charge of embezzlement **(c)** *(correos)* **acusar recibo** = to acknowledge receipt; **todavía no ha acusado recibo de mi carta del día 24** = he has still not acknowledged my letter of the 24th

◊ **acusarse** *vr* to get stronger *or* to become more noticeable; **se acusa una tendencia inflacionista** = there is a clear inflationary trend

acuse *nm* **acuse de recibo** = acknowledgement (of receipt); **ella envió un acuse de recibo** *o* **una carta de acuse de recibo** = she sent an acknowledgement of receipt *o* a letter of acknowledgement; **correo certificado con acuse de recibo** = recorded delivery; **enviamos los documentos por correo certificado con acuse de recibo** = we sent the documents (by) recorded delivery

ad valorem *frase* ad valorem; **derechos ad valorem** = ad valorem duty; **impuesto ad valorem** = ad valorem tax; **tarifa ad valorem** = ad valorem tariff *o* duty

adaptar *vt* to adapt *o* to tailor; **comunicados de prensa adaptados a los intereses de los lectores de distintos periódicos** = press releases tailored to the reader interests of different newspapers

adecuado, -da *adj* suitable *o* adequate; **una persona adecuada para el trabajo** = a suitable person for the job; **lo más adecuado** = the best *o* the most appropriate; **precio adecuado** = keen prices

◊ **adecuadamente** *adv* suitably

adelantado, -da 1 *adj* advanced *o* forward; **ir adelantado** = to be ahead of schedule; **por**

adelantado = in advance; **pago por adelantado** = money paid in advance *o* money up front; **poner fecha adelantada** = to postdate; **pagar por adelantado** = to pay in advance; **flete pagadero por adelantado** = freight payable in advance **2** *pp de* ADELANTAR

adelantar *vt* **(a)** *(anticipar)* to bring forward *o* to advance; **adelantar la fecha de reembolso** = to bring forward the date of repayment; **la fecha de la próxima reunión se ha adelantado a marzo** = the date of the next meeting has been advanced to March **(b)** *(avanzar)* to speed up **(c)** *(dinero)* to advance

adelante *adv* forward *o* ahead; **sacar adelante un negocio** = to carry on a business

◊ **adelanto** *nm* **(a)** *(dinero)* advance *o* cash advance; **los vendedores reciben un adelanto de 1.000 ptas. cada uno para gastos menores** = the sales reps have a float of 1000 pesetas each **(b)** *(progreso)* advance *o* progress *o* step forward; **los últimos adelantos técnicos** = the latest technical advances *o* the latest technology

además *adv* **además de** = in addition to *o* further to; **hay que enviar doce cartas certificadas además de este paquete** = there are twelve registered letters to be sent in addition to this packet

adeudable *adj* debitable

adeudar *vt* **(a)** *(deber)* to owe **(b)** *(cargar)* to debit *o* to charge; **adeude esta partida en mi cuenta** = please charge this consignment to my account

◊ **adeudarse** *vr* to get into debt; **nos hemos adeudado en 20 millones de ptas.** = we are in debt to the tune of 20m pesetas

◊ **adeudo** *nm* charge *o* debit; **asiento de adeudo** = debit entry; **nota de adeudo** = debit note

adhesión *nf* adhesion *o* adherence; **Tratado de adhesión (a la UE)** = Treaty of Accession (to the EU)

adhesivo, -va 1 *adj* adhesive *o* sticky; **papel adhesivo** = adhesive paper; **precintó el paquete con cinta adhesiva** = he sealed the parcel with adhesive tape **2** *nm* adhesive *o* glue; **tiene un tubo de adhesivo en el cajón de su escritorio** = she has a tube of adhesive in the drawer of her desk

adición *nf* addition

◊ **adicional** *adj* additional *o* further *o* supplementary *o* extra; **beneficios adicionales** = fringe benefits; **cargos adicionales** = additional charges; **cláusula adicional** = additional clause *o* extra clause *o* rider; **pedir cobertura adicional** = to ask for additional cover; **costes adicionales** = additional costs; **gastos adicionales** = extraordinary charges; **habrá que pagar un impuesto adicional** = additional duty will have to be paid; **los pedidos adicionales serán atendidos por nuestra oficina de Barcelona** = further orders will be dealt with by our Barcelona office

adiestramiento *nm* training; **adiestramiento profesional en el trabajo** = on the job training; **adiestramiento profesional fuera del lugar de trabajo** = off-the job training

adivinar *vt* to guess (at) something

adj. *abrev de* ADJUNTO enc *o* encl

adjudicación *nf* adjudication

adjudicación de servicios complementarios al transporte por ferrocarril en la terminal de Irún **El País**

adjudicar *vt* **(a)** *(asignar)* to award; **adjudicar un contrato a alguien** = to award a contract to someone **(b)** *(jurídico)* to assign; **adjudicar un derecho a alguien** = to assign a right to someone **(c)** *(subasta)* to knock down; **adjudicar algo a un postor** = to knock something down to a bidder

◊ **adjudicarse** *vr* to appropriate; **el contrato se adjudicará a la oferta más baja** = the tender will go to the lowest bidder

◊ **adjudicatario, -ria** *n* **(a)** *(contrato, premio)* person who receives an award **(b)** *(subasta)* successful bidder

adjuntar *vt* to attach *o* to enclose; **adjuntar una factura a una carta** = to enclose an invoice with a letter; **adjunto una copia del contrato** = I am enclosing a copy of the contract; **adjunto a la presente una copia de mi carta del 24 de junio** *o* **de mi carta anterior** = please find attached a copy of my letter of June 24th *o* of my previous letter; **adjunto el cheque a la presente** = please find the cheque enclosed herewith

◊ **adjunto, -ta 1** *adj* attached *o* enclosed; **remitir adjunto** = to enclose; **carta adjunta** *o* **documento adjunto** = enclosure; **carta con documentos adjuntos** = letter with enclosures; **le envío adjunto el cheque** = please find the cheque enclosed herewith; **adjunto remito mi currículum vitae** = please find enclosed my CV **2** *n* deputy; **presidente adjunto** = deputy chairman; **director adjunto** = associate director; **director general adjunto** = deputy managing director; **cedió el puesto a su adjunto** = he handed over to his deputy; **en ausencia del presidente presidió su adjunto** = in the absence of the chairman his deputy took the chair

administración *nf* **(a)** *(oficial o del Estado)* administration *o* government; **la Administración Central** = central government; **Administración de aduanas** = customs administration; **Administración local** = local government; **la plantilla de la Administración local** = local government staff; **la Administración pública** = the civil service; **tiene un trabajo en la Administración** = he has a job in the civil service; **Administración tributaria** = tax administration **(b)** *(gestión)* management; **administración de empresas** = business administration *o* management; **la sección de administración dice que necesita el informe inmediatamente** = admin say they need the report immediately; **los gastos de administración** = administrative expenses *o* administration expenses; **un licenciado en administración de empresas** = a management graduate *o* a graduate in management; **su hijo está cursando un Master en administración de empresas en los EE UU** = her son is doing a Master's course in Business Administration in the States; **administración del personal** = personnel management; **administración de valores** *o* **de patrimonios** *o* **de carteras** = portfolio management;

reservado a la administración = for office use only; consejo de administración = board of directors

> durante varios años, la redacción de la Ley de Comercio constituyó una de las cuestiones más polémicas abordadas por la Administración anterior
>
> **El País**

administrador, -ra n administrator o manager o manageress; **administrador fiduciario** = trustee; **administrador judicial (de la quiebra)** = official receiver; **la compañía está en manos del administrador judicial** = the company is in the hands of the receiver; **el tribunal nombró un administrador judicial para la liquidación de la compañía** = the court appointed a receiver for the company; **el administrador judicial celebrará una subasta del activo de la compañía** = the receiver will hold an auction of the company's assets; **nombramiento de administrador judicial o de un administrador testamentario** = letters of administration **(c) administrador de fincas** = land agent o estate manager

administrar vt to administer o to manage; **administrar mal** = to mismanage; **administra un importante fondo de pensiones** = he administers a large pension fund; **administrar una propiedad** = to manage a property

administrativo, -va 1 adj administrative o managerial; **delitos administrativos** = white-collar crime; **detalles administrativos** = administrative details; **gastos administrativos** = administration expenses o administration expenses; **el personal administrativo** = managerial staff; **auxiliar administrativo** = office junior o junior clerk **2** n office worker o white-collar worker

admisible adj allowable o admissible o acceptable; **deducción admisible** = allowable deduction; **su conducta no es admisible** = his behaviour is not acceptable

◊ **admisión** nf **(a)** (entrada) entrance o entry; **examen de admisión** = entrance exam; **condiciones de admisión** = conditions of entry **(b)** (aceptación) admission o acceptance

admitir vt to admit o to accept; **no se admiten propinas** = tips are not accepted o tipping is not allowed

adolecer vi to suffer from something; **los productos de la empresa adolecen de un mal diseño** = the company's products suffer from bad design

adoptar vt to adopt; **adoptar una decisión o resolución** = to reach a decision; **adoptar una moción** = to pass o to adopt a resolution

adquirente nmf acquirer o purchaser o buyer

adquirir vt **(a)** (comprar) to acquire o to buy o to purchase; **adquirir una compañía** = to acquire a company o to take over a company; **la empresa ha sido adquirida por su principal suministrador** = the company has been bought by its leading supplier; **la compañía fue adquirida por una gran multinacional** = the company was taken over by a large multinational **(b)** (ganar) to gain; **adquirió** cierta experiencia práctica trabajando en un banco = he gained some useful experience working in a bank; **adquirió la mayor parte de su experiencia en el Extremo Oriente** = he gained most of his experience in the Far East

adquisición nf **(a)** (cosa adquirida) acquisition o takeover; **adquisición apalancada** = leveraged buyout (LBO); **adquisición de una empresa por sus propios directivos** = management buyout (MBO); **la fábrica de chocolate es su última adquisición** = the chocolate factory is his latest acquisition; **oferta de adquisición disputada** = contested takeover; **oferta pública de adquisición (OPA)** = takeover bid; **hacer una oferta de adquisición de una compañía** = to make a takeover bid for a company; **retirar una oferta de adquisición** = to withdraw a takeover bid; **la compañía rechazó la oferta de adquisición** = the company rejected the takeover bid **(b)** (acción de adquirir) acquisition; **adquisición de datos** = data acquisition o acquisition of data **(c)** (materias primas) procurement

> una vez que pudo contar con una compañía que cotizaba en bolsa, y que se podía usar como un 'holding', se dedicó a buscar buenas adquisiciones
>
> **España Económica**

adquisitivo, -va adj **poder adquisitivo** = buying power o purchasing power o spending power; **el descenso del poder adquisitivo de la peseta** = the decline in the purchasing power of the peseta; **el poder adquisitivo de la peseta ha bajado durante los últimos diez años** = the purchasing power of the peseta has fallen over the last ten years

adscribir vt to appoint o to assign to; **el director para Europa está adscrito a nuestra sucursal de Londres** = the European manager is based in our London office; **adscribir el personal a una clase de trabajo diferente** = to redeploy personnel; **cerramos el departamento de diseño y adscribimos el personal a los departamentos de publicidad y ventas** = we closed the design department and redeployed the workforce in the publicity and sales departments

aduana nf customs; **pasar la aduana** = to go through customs; **pasar algo por la aduana sin declararlo** = to take something through customs without declaring it; **pasamos la aduana sin problemas** = we passed through customs easily; **fue detenido en la aduana** = he was stopped by customs; **le registraron el coche en la aduana** = her car was searched by customs; **Aduanas y Arbitrios (administración de aduanas e impuestos sobre el consumo)** = Customs and Excise o Excise Department; **agente de aduanas** = customs broker; **certificado de aduana** = clearance certificate; **declaración de aduana** = customs declaration; **derecho de aduana** = customs duty; **bienes sujetos a derechos de aduana** = dutiable goods o dutiable items; **funcionarios de aduanas** = customs officers o customs officials; **los funcionarios de la aduana sellaron los documentos** = the documents were stamped by the customs officials; **rellenar una declaración de aduana** = to fill in a customs (declaration) form; **ha perdido los documentos de la aduana** = he has lost the customs papers

aduanero, -ra 1 adj customs; **arancel aduanero**

= customs tariff; **mercancías en depósito aduanero** = goods (held) in bond; **retirar mercancías del depósito aduanero** = to take goods out of bond; **despacho aduanero** = customs clearance; **esperar para efectuar el despacho aduanero** = to wait for customs clearance; **inspección aduanera** = customs examination; **formalidades aduaneras** = customs formalities; **pasar por un puesto aduanero** = to pass a customs entry point; **unión aduanera** = customs union **2** *n* customs officer *o* customs official

adverso, -sa *adj* unfavourable *o* adverse; **una situación adversa** = an unfavourable position

advertencia *nf* **(a)** *(aviso)* warning *o* advice *o* caveat; **se colocaron letreros** *o* **carteles de advertencia por toda la obra** = warning notices were put up around the construction site; **hacer una advertencia** = to enter a caveat **(b)** *(recordatorio)* reminder

advertir *vt* to advise *o* to warn; **le advertí que no fuera a la reunión** = I warned him not to go to the meeting

AELC = ASOCIACION EUROPEA DE LIBRE COMERCIO European Free Trade Area (EFTA) (NOTA: más frecuente **EFTA**)

aéreo, -rea *adj* correo aéreo = air mail; **el precio del correo aéreo ha aumentado en un 15%** = air mail charges have risen by 15%; **etiqueta de correo aéreo** = airmail sticker; **enviar cartas** *o* **paquetes por correo aéreo** = to airmail letters *o* parcels; **enviamos un documento a Nueva York por correo aéreo** = we airmailed a document to New York; **carga aérea** *o* **flete aéreo** = air cargo; **línea aérea** = airline; **la línea aérea tiene una flota de diez aviones comerciales** = the airline has a fleet of ten commercial aircraft; **tráfico aéreo** = air traffic; **transporte aéreo** = transport by air *o* air transport; **empresa de transporte aéreo** = air carrier; **servicio de transportes aéreos** = airline service; **despachar por carga aérea** *o* **enviar por transporte aéreo** = to airfreight; **sobretasa aérea** = air surcharge; **vía aérea** = by air; **envío por vía aérea** = air forwarding; **mandar una carta** *o* **un envío por vía aérea** = to send a letter *o* a shipment by air

aerograma *nm GB* air letter; *US* aerogramme

aerolínea *nf* airline

aeronavegabilidad *nf* airworthiness; **certificado de aeronavegabilidad** = certificate of airworthiness

aeropuerto *nm* airport; **salimos del aeropuerto de Barajas a las 10.00** = we leave from Madrid Airport at 10.00; **O'Hare es el aeropuerto principal de Chicago** = O'Hare Airport is the main airport for Chicago; **autobús del aeropuerto** = airport bus; **carrito de aeropuerto** = airport trolley; **tasas de aeropuerto** = airport tax; **terminal del aeropuerto** = airport terminal *o* terminal building

afán *nm* enthusiasm; **afán de lucro** = profit motive

afectar *vt* **(a)** *(influir)* to affect; **la nueva reglamentación oficial no nos afecta** = the new government regulations do not affect us **(b)** *(dañar)* to hurt *o* to hit; **la caída de los tipos de cambio afectó gravemente a la compañía** = the company

was badly hit by the falling exchange rate; **la venta de ropa de verano se vio afectada por el mal tiempo** = sales of summer clothes were hurt by the bad weather

◊ **afectado, -da** *pp* affected; **los beneficios de las principales compañías aéreas se han visto afectados por la subida de precios del combustible** = profits of major airlines have been affected by the rise in fuel prices

afectuosamente *adv (en carta)* Yours (ever)

affaire *nm* scandal *o* affair

su implicación en el 'affaire' de Renfe será difícil de conocer en toda su extensión ya que nunca firmó un documento
Cambio 16

Afganistán *nm* Afghanistan

◊ **afgano, -na** *o* **afgani** *adj* Afghan
NOTA: capital: **Kabul**; moneda: **afgani (Af)** = afghani

afianzamiento *nm* **(a)** *(consolidación)* strengthening; **el afianzamiento de los precios** = a hardening of prices **(b)** *(aval)* guarantee

afianzar *vt* **(a)** *(consolidar)* to strengthen **(b)** *(avalar)* to guarantee

◊ **afianzarse** *vr* to strengthen *o* to firm; **las acciones se afianzaron a 1.500 ptas.** = the shares firmed at 1,500 pesetas

afiliación *nf* affiliation *o* membership; **afiliación sindical** = union membership

◊ **afiliado, -da 1** *adj* affiliated *o* associate(d); **compañía afiliada** = associate company *o* affiliate; **la compañía Ferrer S.A. y su empresa afiliada, García Hnos** = Ferrer S.A. and its associated company, García Brothers **2** *n* associate member; **afiliado a un sindicato** = union member **3** *pp de* AFILIAR

afiliar *vt* to affiliate

◊ **afiliarse** *vr* to join; **muchos empleados se han afiliado al sindicato** = a good many staff members have joined the union

afín *adj* related; **cuestiones afines en el orden del día** = related items on the agenda

afirmación *nf* statement *o* assertion; **contradecir una afirmación** = to contradict a statement

afirmar *vi* **(a)** *(confirmar)* to state *o* to declare *o* to claim; **afirma no haber recibido las mercancías** = he claims he never received the goods **(b)** *(consolidar)* to make firm *o* to strengthen; **afirmar un acuerdo** = to strengthen an agreement

afirmativo, -va *adj* affirmative; **la respuesta fue afirmativa** = the answer was in the affirmative *o* the answer was yes

aflojar *vt* to slack *o* to slacken *o* to loosen; **aflojar el paso** = to slow down

afluencia *nf* **(a)** *(flujo)* stream *o* rush; **horas de mayor afluencia** = rush hour *o* peak hours *o* peak period; **tuvimos una gran afluencia de clientes en el primer día de liquidación** = we had a stream of customers on the first day of the sale **(b)** *(entrada)* influx *o* inflow *o* afflux; **la afluencia de capitales al**

país = inflow of capital into the country; **la afluencia de divisas al país** = the influx of foreign currency into the country; **la afluencia de mano de obra barata a las ciudades** = the influx of cheap labour into the cities

afortunado, -da *adj* lucky *o* successful

Africa del Sur *ver* SUDAFRICA

afueras *nfpl* outskirts

agencia *nf* agency *o* bureau; **agencia de alquiler de viviendas** = letting agency; **agencia de empleo** *o* **de colocación** = employment agency *o* employment bureau *o* employment office; **agencia filial** = branch office; **agencia de informes comerciales** = credit agency; *US* credit bureau; **agencia inmobiliaria** = estate agent; **agencia de noticias** *o* **agencia de prensa** = news agency *o* press office; **agencia de publicidad** = advertising agency; **agencia de recortes (de prensa)** = press cutting agency; **agencia de trabajo temporal** = temp agency; **agencia de transportes** = shipping agent *o* road haulier; **agencia de venta de localidades de teatro** = ticket agency; **agencia de viajes** = travel agency; **agencia de viajes mayorista** = tour operator; **jefe de agencia** = agent; **encargamos todo el trabajo de mecanografía a una agencia local** = we farm out the office typing to a local bureau

las agencias de viajes, que han percibido el reto, proponen, sobre todo en invierno, una solución muy atractiva y particular para sus clientes: los viajes a la carta destinados a satisfacer los hobbies del viajero

agenda *nf* (a) *(en una reunión)* agenda (b) *(dietario)* diary *o* appointments book; **agenda de bolsillo** = pocket diary; **agenda electrónica** = electronic *o* personal organizer; **anotó la cita en su agenda** = she noted the appointment in her engagements diary

agente *nmf* (a) *(economía)* agent **ser agente de** = to be the agent for *o* to represent; **nuestro distribuidor francés también es el agente de varias empresas competidoras** = our French distributor represents several other competing firms; **agente acreditado** = recognized agent; **agente de bolsa** *o* **agente bursátil** = stockbroker; **llamó a su agente de bolsa** = he rang (up) his stockbroker; **agente de bolsa no oficial** = street jobber; **agente de cambio** = foreign exchange dealer; **agente cobrador de morosos** = debt collector; **agente comercial** = broker; **agente comisionado** = commission agent *o* factor; **agente comprador de deudas** = debt factor; **agente del credere** = del credere agent; **agente expedidor** = (freight) forwarder *o* shipping clerk; **agente de finanzas** = financial intermediary; **agente inmobiliario** *o* **agente de la propiedad inmobiliaria** = estate agent; *US* realtor; **agente de letras** = bill broker; **agente marítimo** = ship broker; **agentes mediadores** = intermediaries; **agente de negocios** = middleman; **agente de prensa** = press officer; **agente de publicidad** *o* **agente publicitario** = advertising agent *o* adman; **agente de seguros** = insurance agent; **se estableció como agente (libre) de seguros** = he set up in business as an insurance broker; **agente de transporte** = forwarding agent; **comisión del agente** = agent's commission (b)

(política) **agente electoral** = canvasser (c) *(viajes)* agent *o* operator; **agente de viajes** = travel agent; **agente de viajes organizados** = tour operator

lleva más de veinte años trabajando en este país como agente bursátil

agilizar *vt* to expedite

agio *nm* (a) *(especulación)* agio (b) *(cargo adicional)* extra charge *o* premium; **agio del cambio** = exchange premium (c) *(México)* usury

◊ **agiotaje** *nm* speculation

◊ **agiotista** *nmf* speculator *o* jobber *o* profiteer

agitado, -da 1 *adj* (i) agitated *o* hectic; (ii) jumpy *o* nervous; **los agentes de bolsa estaban muy agitados** = stockbrokers were very nervous **2** *pp de* AGITAR

agitar *vt* (a) *(sacudir)* to shake (b) *(inquietar)* to surprise *o* to disturb

agobiado, -da *adj* burdened *o* overwhelmed; **estar agobiado de deudas** = to be burdened with debt

agotado, -da 1 *adj* (a) *(existencias)* out of stock *o* sold out *o* depleted *o* unavailable *o* exhausted; **estos discos están temporalmente agotados** = those records are temporarily out of stock; **hace semanas que están pedidos varios artículos agotados** = several out-of-stock items have been on order for weeks; **este producto se ha agotado** = this item has sold out (b) *(publicaciones)* out of print (c) *(personas)* exhausted *o* worn out; **las dependientas están agotadas después del frenesí de las Navidades** = shop assistants are worn out *o* exhausted after the Christmas rush **2** *pp de* AGOTAR

agotar *vt* to empty *o* to drain *o* to exhaust; **los recursos de capital de la compañía se han agotado** = the company's capital resources have drained away; **agotar las existencias** = to sell out (one's stock) *o* to run out of stock; **agotar las existencias de un artículo** = to sell out of an item; **agotar las existencias de una gama de productos** = to sell out of a product line; **hemos agotado las existencias de máquinas de escribir** = we have sold out of typewriters

◊ **agotarse** *vr* to be used up *o* to sell out *o* to run out; **este producto se ha agotado rápidamente** = this item sold out rapidly *o* has been a sellout

agradecer *vt* to thank *o* to appreciate; **el cliente siempre agradece el buen servicio** = the customer always appreciates efficient service; **les agradecemos su carta del 15 de junio** = thank you for your letter of June 15th; **el comité agradeció al presidente saliente la labor realizada** = the committee thanked the retiring chairman for his work

◊ **agradecimiento** *nm* thanks *o* gratitude; **palabras de agradecimiento** = speech of thanks *o* vote of thanks

agrario, -ria *adj* agricultural; **el sector agrario** =

the agricultural sector; **reforma agraria** = land reform o agrarian reform

agravio nm insult o offence; (jurídico) tort; **alegar agravios** = to allege an offence

agregado, -da 1 n attaché; **agregado comercial** = commercial attaché **2** pp de AGREGAR

◊ **agregaduría** nf (embajada) commercial section (in an embassy)

agregar vt to add; **han agregado dos nuevos productos a su gama** = they have added two new products to their range; **exponemos varios productos que hemos agregado a nuestra gama habitual** = we are exhibiting several additions to our usual product line

agresivo, -va adj aggressive o vigorous o forceful; **publicidad agresiva** = knocking copy; **venta agresiva** = hard selling o hard sell

agrícola adj agricultural; **cooperativa agrícola** = agricultural co-operative; **economista agrícola** = agricultural economist; **explotación agrícola** = farm o agribusiness; **los recintos de la feria agrícola** = the agricultural exhibition grounds; **peón agrícola** = agricultural labourer; **Política Agrícola Común (PAC)** = Common Agricultural Policy (CAP); **trabajador agrícola** = farm worker

◊ **agricultor, -ra** n farmer

◊ **agricultura** nf agriculture; **agricultura y ganadería** = agriculture and stockbreeding

agroindustria nf agribusiness

◊ **agroindustrial** adj agro-industrial

agrónomo nm agronomist; **ingeniero agrónomo** = agricultural expert

agropecuario, -ria adj agricultural o farming; **riqueza agropecuaria** = agricultural wealth; **política agropecuaria** = farming policy

agrupación nf (a) (grupo) group o grouping (b) (bienes) consolidation (c) (personas) association; **hacerse socio de una agrupación** = to join an association; **agrupación sectorial** = trade association; **agrupación temporal de empresas** = joint venture

agrupar vt (a) (lotes) to batch (together); **agrupar facturas o cheques por lotes** = to batch invoices o cheques (b) (grupos) to bracket together o to group together; **los países europeos están todos agrupados en los informes de ventas** = in the sales reports, all the European countries are bracketed together (c) (carga) to consolidate; **agrupar envíos** = to consolidate shipments

◊ **agruparse** vr to group together; **las ventas de seis agencias diferentes se han agrupado bajo el título de 'ventas europeas'** = sales from six different agencies are grouped together under the heading 'European sales'

agua nf (a) water; **agua corriente** = running water; **agua potable** = drinking water; **aguas residuales** = sewage o waste water; **aguas territoriales o jurisdiccionales** = territorial waters; **fuera de las aguas territoriales o jurisdiccionales** = outside territorial waters; **contador de agua** = water meter; **estar con el agua al cuello** = to be in an awkward

position; **estar entre dos aguas** = to be undecided o to sit on the fence (b) (poner la cubierta en un edificio en construcción) **cubrir aguas** = to top out

aguantar 1 vt to stand o to support **2** vi to hold out o to resist o to last

◊ **aguante** nm patience o endurance; **tiene mucho aguante** = he is very patient

aguardar vt to wait for o to expect; **a la compañía le aguarda un periodo de reducción de gastos** = the company is in for a period of retrenchment

agudo, -da adj keen o sharp

ahorrador, -ra 1 adj thrifty **2** n saver

la inversión en productos que no sean financieros ni inmobiliarios es una alternativa cada vez más atractiva para determinado tipo de ahorradores
El País

ahorrar vt (a) (dinero) to save o to put (money) aside o to save up (for); **está tratando de ahorrar dinero yendo al trabajo a pie** = he is trying to save money by walking to work; **ahorra 5.000 ptas. cada semana para comprarse un coche** = he is putting 5000 pesetas aside each week to pay for his car; **están ahorrando para ir de vacaciones a los EE UU o para comprar una casa** = they are saving up for a holiday in the USA o to buy a house (b) (economizar) to save; **ahorrar tiempo** = to save time; **la dirección está muy interesada en ahorrar tiempo** = the management is keen on time saving; **nos proponemos ahorrar un 10% en combustible** = we are aiming for a 10% saving in fuel; **un mecanismo o dispositivo para ahorrar energía o trabajo** = an energy-saving o labour-saving device; **el gobierno está alentando a las empresas para que ahorren energía** = the government is encouraging companies to save energy

◊ **ahorrarse** vr to save oneself; **ahorrarse molestias** = to save oneself the effort o to save oneself bother

otro de los fraudes que están siendo investigados consiste en la compraventa fraudulenta de terrenos, con el fin de ahorrarse buena parte del pago de los impuestos
Cambio 16

ahorrativo, -va adj thrifty

ahorro nm (a) (economía) economy o saving; **ahorro de tiempo** = saving time; **ahorro de energía** = saving energy; **la compañía está introduciendo medidas de ahorro de energía** = the company is introducing energy-saving measures (b) (dinero) savings o thrift; **plan de ahorro ajustado a las exigencias de los particulares** = savings plan made to suit the requirements of the individual; **bono de ahorro** = savings certificate; US savings bond; **cuenta de ahorro** = savings account

◊ **ahorros** nmpl (a) (dinero) savings; **puso todos sus ahorros en una cuenta a plazo fijo** = he put all his savings into a deposit account; **invirtió todos sus ahorros en títulos del Estado** = he invested all his savings in government securities (b) (banco) **caja de ahorros** = savings bank; US thrift; **Caja Postal de Ahorros** = Post Office Savings Bank; **tiene 100.000 ptas. en su cuenta de ahorros** = she has 100,000 pesetas in her savings bank account

existe un fuerte plan de ahorro, 350 millones de dólares, realizado a base de suprimir empleos, integrando los sistemas informáticos y áreas operativas y eliminando las duplicidades operativas
El País

los cambios demográficos en los principales países industriales tendrán un impacto sustancial sobre el ahorro y la inversión a nivel mundial
Mercado

aire *nm* air; **aire acondicionado** = air-conditioning; **al aire libre** = in the open air

airear *vt* **(a)** *(ventilar)* to ventilate **(b)** *(publicar)* to make public *o* to bring out into the open; **la prensa aireó los resultados sin confirmar** = the newspapers published the results without confirming them

aislado, -da *adj* isolated

ajetreado, -da *adj* hectic *o* busy; **un día ajetreado en la bolsa** = a hectic day on the Stock Exchange

ajustable *adj* adjustable

◊ **ajustado, -da 1** *adj* adjusted *o* linked; **pensiones ajustadas al coste de vida** = index-linked pensions; **las pensiones de los funcionarios están ajustadas al coste de vida** = civil service pensions are index-linked; **utilizamos programas de ordenador ajustados a las necesidades del cliente** = we use tailor-made *o* customized computer software **2** *pp de* AJUSTAR

ajustar *vt* **(a)** *(adaptar)* to adjust *o* to link *o* to gear; **los precios están ajustados a la inflación** = prices are adjusted for inflation; **los tipos de interés bancario están ajustados a los tipos de interés americanos** = bank interest rates are geared to American interest rates; **salario ajustado al coste de vida** = salary adjusted *o* linked *o* geared to the cost of living; **ajustar las pensiones a la inflación** = to link pensions to inflation; **su salario está ajustado al coste de vida** = his salary is linked to the cost of living **(b)** *(máquinas)* to adjust *o* to regulate **(c)** *(saldar)* to settle; *US* to square; **ajustar cuentas** = (i) to make up accounts *o* to balance accounts; (ii) to get even

◊ **ajustarse** *vr* **(a)** *(corresponder)* to fit; **la verdad es que el producto no se ajusta al mercado** = the fact of the matter is that the product does not fit the market; **el papel no se ajusta a la impresora** = the paper doesn't fit the printer **(b)** *(atenerse a)* to hold to; **intentaremos que se ajuste al contrato** = we will try to hold him to the contract

ajuste *nm* adjustment; **ajuste por cierre del ejercicio** = year-end adjustment; **ajuste estacional** = seasonal adjustment; **ajuste estructural** = structural adjustment; **ajuste financiero** = financial settlement; **ajuste fino** = fine tuning; **ajuste fiscal** *o* **ajuste impositivo** = tax adjustment; **ajuste fiscal en frontera** = border tax adjustment; **ajuste de precios (en la Bolsa)** = technical correction; **ajuste salarial** = wage adjustment; **acuerdo** *o* **convenio de ajuste salarial sobre el coste de vida** = index-linked wage agreement; **coeficiente de ajuste salarial** = wage differentials; **proceso de ajuste** = process of adjustment

en una economía con los graves desequilibrios que padece la española - paro, inflación, déficit exterior - hablar como si el ajuste no fuera necesario es demagogia o torpeza
España Económica

ALALC = ASOCIACION LATINOAMERICANA DE LIBRE COMERCIO Latin American Free Trade Association (LAFTA)

albacea *nmf* administrator *o* executor (NOTA: femenino: **executrix**) **albacea testamentario** = executor *o* trustee; **se le comunicó al albacea que el testamento era válido** = the executor was granted probate; **le nombraron albacea testamentario de su hermano** = he was named executor of his brother's will

Albania *nf* Albania

◊ **albanés, -esa** *adj y n* Albanian
NOTA: capital: **Tirana**; moneda: **lek albanés** = new lek

albarán *nm* delivery note; **albarán de entrada** = receipt for goods

alcance *nm* **(a)** *(accesible)* reach; **estar al alcance** = to be within reach **(b)** *(importancia)* scope; **trabajamos en un proyecto de gran alcance** = we are working on a wide-ranging project

alcanzar *vt* to reach *o* to achieve; **alcanzamos todos nuestros objetivos en 1995** = we achieved all our objectives in 1995; **hemos alcanzado nuestros objetivos de exportación** = we have hit our export targets; **esperan alcanzar un acuerdo amistoso** = they are hoping to reach an out-of-court settlement; **alcanzar el punto máximo** *o* **más alto** = to reach a ceiling; **la producción ha alcanzado su nivel más alto** = output has reached a ceiling; **alcanzar el punto mínimo** *o* **más bajo** = to reach rock bottom *o* to bottom (out)

el beneficio después de impuestos ha pasado de 93 millones de pesetas en 1986 a 1.200 este año y se prevé que la cifra alcance los 1.577 millones en 1990
España Económica

alcista 1 *adj* bull *o* bullish *o* rising *o* upward; **tendencia alcista** = upward trend; **mercado alcista** = bull market **2** *nm* speculator; **alcista de bolsa** = bull

aleatorio, -ria *adj* random; **muestra aleatoria** = random sample; **muestreo aleatorio** = random sampling

alegar *vt* **(a)** *(jurídico)* to allege *o* to affirm *o* to plead; **alegar agravios** = to allege an offence **(b)** *(afirmar)* to claim *o* to state; **alegar razones** = to put forward reasons; **para disculparse de la tardanza en contestar, alegó que había estado en viaje de negocios** = as an excuse for the delay in replying, he said he had been on a business trip

Alemania *nf* Germany; **República Federal de Alemania (RFA)** = Federal Republic of Germany (FRG)

◊ **alemán, -ana** *adj y n* German
NOTA: capital: **Berlín** (= Berlin); moneda: **marco alemán** = Deutschmark *o* D-mark

alentar *vt* to encourage; **el gobierno está**

alentando a las empresas para que mantengan los precios bajos = the government is encouraging firms to keep prices low

alfabético, -ca *adj* alphabetical *o* alphabetic

◊ **alfanumérico, -ca** *adj* alphanumeric *o* alphanumerical

alfiler *nm* pin; **sujetó los papeles con un alfiler** = she pinned the papers together

alguien *pron* someone *o* somebody; anyone *o* anybody

alguno, -na *adj y pron* (NOTA: **algún** delante nms) anyone *o* someone *o* somebody

◊ **algunos, -nas** *adj y pron pl* some *o* several *o* a number of; **algunos de nuestros productos se venden bien en Japón** = several of our products sell well in Japan; **algunos de nuestros vendedores tienen un Mercedes** = some of our salesmen drive Mercedes

aliento *nm* **(a)** *(impulso)* encouragement; **el apoyo del director fue un gran aliento para todos nosotros** = the support of the manager was a great encouragement for all of us **(b)** *(respiración)* breath; **hagamos una pausa para tomar aliento** = let's take a break to get our breath back

aligerar *vt* to lighten; **aligerar la carga impositiva** = to lighten the tax burden

alimentación *nf* **(a)** *(alimentos)* food; **el negocio de alimentación** = the food industry *o* the catering trade **(b)** *(informática)* feed; **alimentación de hojas sueltas** = sheet feed; **alimentación de papel continuo** = continuous feed; **cable de alimentación eléctrica** = input lead

◊ **alimentador** *nm* feed; **alimentador de papel** = paper feed; **el alimentador del papel se ha atascado** = the paper feed has jammed

alimentar *vt* **(a)** *(proveer)* to supply **(b)** *(informática)* to feed

◊ **alimento** *nm* food

alivio *nm* reassurance *o* relief; **la partida del jefe de personal fue un alivio para todos** = the departure of the personnel manager was a great relief to everyone *o* everyone was relieved when the personnel manager left

almacén *nm* **(a)** *(tienda)* store *o* big shop; *(de efectos navales)* ship chandler's *o* chandlery; **almacén de bricolaje** = do-it-yourself (DIY) store; **almacén al por mayor** = wholesale store; *US* discount house; **grandes almacenes** = department store; *US* general store; **unos grandes almacenes de ropa** = a big clothing store; **una cadena de grandes almacenes** = a chain of department stores *o* a department store chain; **sucursal de una cadena de grandes almacenes** = chain store *o* multiple store **(b)** *(depósito)* storeroom *o* stockroom *o* warehouse *o* depository; *(en Extremo Oriente)* godown; **hemos abierto nuestro nuevo almacén** = we have opened our new warehouse; **el almacén está situado cerca de la autopista** = the warehouse is located near to the motorway; **almacén frigorífico** = cold store; **en almacén** = in stock; **tenemos 2.000 productos en almacén** = to hold 2,000 lines in stock; **capacidad de almacén** = warehouse capacity; **ficha de**

almacén = stock control card *o* bin card; **jefe de almacén** = stock controller; **precio franco en almacén** *o* **precio puesto en almacén** = price ex warehouse

almacenaje *nm* **(a)** *(almacenamiento)* storage *o* storing *o* warehousing; **almacenaje frigorífico** = cold storage; **capacidad de almacenaje** = storage capacity; **coste de almacenaje** = storage (charge); **los costes de almacenaje están aumentando vertiginosamente** = warehousing costs are rising rapidly; **nos deshicimos de las existencias ya que el coste de almacenaje representaba el 10% de su valor** = storage was 10% of value, so we scrapped the stock; **empresa de almacenaje** = storage company; **instalaciones de almacenaje** = storage facilities; **unidad de almacenaje** = storage unit **(b)** *(informática)* storage; **un disco con una capacidad de almacenaje de 10Mb** = disk with a storage capacity of 10Mb

◊ **almacenamiento** *nm* storing *o* storage; **instalaciones de almacenamiento** = storage facilities; *(informática)* **almacenamiento en disco** = disc storage; **almacenamiento de reserva** = back-up storage; **almacenamiento principal** = primary *o* main storage; **almacenamiento secundario** = secondary storage; **almacenamiento temporal** = temporary storage

almacenar *vt* to put into stock *o* to store *o* to warehouse; **almacenar mercancías durante seis meses** = to store goods for six months

◊ **almacenero, -ra** *n* storekeeper *o* warehouse keeper *o* storeman *o* warehouseman

almohadilla *nf* pad; **la máquina está protegida por almohadillas de caucho** = the machine is protected by rubber pads

almuerzo *nm* lunch; **hora del almuerzo** = lunch hour *o* lunchtime; **almuerzo de negocios** = business lunch; **la oficina está cerrada durante la hora del almuerzo** = the office is closed during the lunch hour *o* at lunchtimes

alojamiento *nm* accommodation *o* lodging; **buscar alojamiento** = to look for somewhere to stay; **dar alojamiento a alguien** = to put someone up *o* to take someone in; **los turistas tienen dificultades para encontrar alojamiento durante el verano** = visitors have difficulty in finding hotel accommodation during the summer

alojar *vt* to accommodate *o* to house

◊ **alojarse** *vr* to stay **alojarse en hoteles de primera categoría** = to stay in first-class hotels; **el presidente se aloja en el Hotel Ritz** = the chairman is staying at the Ritz

ALP = ACTIVO LÍQUIDO EN MANOS DEL PÚBLICO money supply

alquilar *vt* **(a)** *(arrendatario)* to hire *o* to rent *o* to charter *o* to lease; **alquilar un coche** = to hire *o* to rent a car; **alquiló un camión para trasladar los muebles** = he hired a truck to move his furniture; **alquilar una grúa** = to hire a crane; **alquilar una oficina** = to rent an office; **alquila una oficina en el centro de la ciudad** = he rents an office in the centre of town; **alquilaron la oficina por un corto periodo de tiempo** = they took the office on a short let; **autobús alquilado** = hired bus *o* chartered bus;

conducían un coche alquilado cuando la policía les detuvo = they were driving a rented car when they were stopped by the police; **todos los coches de nuestra empresa son alquilados** = all our company cars are leased **(b)** *(propietario)* to rent (out) *o* to let; **alquilar coches** *o* **equipos** = to hire out cars *o* equipment; **alquilar material** = to lease equipment; **alquilar una oficina** = to let an office; **tenemos 3.500 metros cuadrados de superficie útil para alquilar** = we have 3,500 square metres of floor space to let; **alquilamos parte del edificio a una empresa norteamericana** = we rented part of the building to an American company; **vivienda amueblada** *o* **local amueblado para alquilar** = furnished lettings

◊ **alquilarse** *vr* to be let; **el piso se alquila a un precio económico** = the flat is let at an economic rent; *(acto)* **'se alquila'** = 'for hire'

> la empresa catalana había logrado que el selecto Metropolitan Museum of Art accediera a alquilar sus salones para una cena privada
>
> **Cambio 16**

alquiler *nm* **(a)** *(arrendamiento)* hire *o* rental *o* chartering; **alquiler de camiones** = truck hire; **alquiler de coches** *o* **de automóviles** = car hire; **alquiler de un medio de transporte** = charter; **agencia de alquiler de viviendas** = letting agency; **la empresa ha extendido sus actividades al alquiler de coches** = the company has branched out into car leasing; **lleva un negocio de alquiler de automóviles** = he runs a car-hire business; **empresa de alquiler de coches** *o* **empresa de alquiler de equipo especializado** = car hire firm *o* equipment hire firm; **coche de alquiler** = hire car; **tuvo el accidente conduciendo un coche de alquiler** = he was driving a hire car when the accident happened; **oficinas de alquiler** = offices to let **(b)** *(precio)* rent; **alquiler anual de una propiedad** = annual rent; **alquiler atrasado** = back rent; **alquiler barato** = low rent; **alquiler elevado** = high rent; **alquiler exorbitante** = rack rent; **alquiler simbólico** = peppercorn rent; **los alquileres en el centro de la ciudad son caros** = rents are high in the centre of the town; **los alquileres del centro no están a nuestro alcance** = we cannot afford to pay High Street rents; **pagar tres meses de alquiler por adelantado** = to pay three months' rent in advance; **cobrador de alquileres** = rent collector; **control de alquileres** = rent control; **controlar los alquileres** = to control rents; **la factura del alquiler del teléfono sube a más de 10.000 ptas. al trimestre** = the telephone rental bill comes to over 10,000 pesetas a quarter; **ingresos por alquiler** = rental income *o* income from rentals **(c)** *(acto)* **'alquiler sin chófer'** = 'self-drive' **(d)** *periodo de alquiler* = let

> se ha producido un incremento de los alquileres, mientras que algunos sostienen que ha disminuido el parque de viviendas
>
> **España Económica**

> en la actualidad, el 22,3% de todo el parque nacional de viviendas de alquiler se rige por el decreto que entró en vigor en mayo de 1985
>
> **España Económica**

alrededor 1 *adv* around; **alrededor de** = around *o*

about *o* in the region of; **percibía un salario de alrededor de 250.000 ptas.** = he was earning a salary in the region of 250,000 pesetas **2** *nmpl* outskirts; **los alrededores de Madrid** = the outskirts of Madrid

alternativa *nf* alternative *o* option; **¿hay una alternativa que no sea despedir a la mitad del personal?** = what is the alternative to firing half the staff?; **no hay otra alternativa** = we have no alternative

◊ **alternativo, -va** *adj* **(a)** *(opción)* alternative **(b)** **movimiento alternativo** = swing

altibajos *nmpl* ups and downs

> la industria soporta un mayor aumento del paro que los servicios, donde se dan altibajos de contratación según la evolución económica
>
> **El País**

alto, alta 1 *adj* **(a)** *(elevado)* high; **imposición alta** = high taxation; **ventas altas** = high sales; **los precios altos disuaden a los clientes** = high prices put customers off; **prevén un nivel de gastos alto** = they are budgeting for a high level of expenditure; **inversiones que proporcionan una alta tasa de rendimiento** = investments which bring in a high rate of return; **los altos tipos de interés están arruinando a las pequeñas empresas** = high interest rates are killing small businesses; **alta calidad** = best quality *o* premium quality; **nuestra especialidad es la importación de mercancías de alta calidad** = we specialize in top quality imported goods; **un oficial** *o* **delegado** *o* **representante de alta categoría** = a high-ranking official; **alta dirección** = top management; **la delegación se entrevistó con un alto funcionario del Ministerio de Comercio** = the delegation met a highly-placed *o* a high-ranking official in the Department of Trade and Industry; **las altas finanzas** = high finance; **alto nivel** = high-level; **una reunión de alto nivel** = a high-level meeting; **una delegación comercial de alto nivel** = a high-grade trade delegation; **una decisión de alto nivel** = a high-level decision; **una decisión tomada al más alto nivel** = a decision taken at the highest level; *(informática)* **lenguaje de programación de alto nivel** = high-level computer language; **gasolina de alto octanaje** = high-grade petrol *o* 'super'; **alta presión** = high pressure; **acciones de alto rendimiento** = high-income shares; **el volumen de ventas ha alcanzado la cifra más alta jamás registrada** = sales volume has reached an all-time high **(b)** *(dimensión)* high *o* tall; **las estanterías tienen 30 cm de alto** = the shelves are 30 cm high; **la puerta no es lo bastante alta como para permitir la entrada de máquinas en el edificio** = the door is not high enough to let us get machines into the building **(c)** **plataforma petrolífera en alta mar** = off-shore oil platform **2** *nm* **(a)** stop *o* halt **(b)** **pasar por alto** = to overlook; **esta vez pasaremos por alto el retraso** = in this instance we will overlook the delay; **pujar más alto** = to outbid **3** *nf* **(a)** high; **las altas y bajas de la bolsa** = the highs and lows on the Stock Exchange **(b)** *(certificado médico)* discharge; **dar a uno de alta** = (i) to give someone permission to return to work after illness; (ii) to discharge a patient from hospital **(c)** *(propiedad, negocio)* **dar de alta** = to register

◊ **altamente** *adv* highly

altamente   16   ampliar

> lo normal sería que la entidad que da el
> alta, dé la baja
> **El País**

altura *nf* height; **midió la altura de la habitación desde el suelo hasta el techo** = he measured the height of the room from floor to ceiling

aludir *vt* to mention; **el presidente aludió a la obra del director gerente con ocasión de su jubilación** = the chairman mentioned the work of the retiring managing director

alza *nf* rise; **alza de precios** = rise in prices *o* advance in prices; **el comercio está en alza** = business is expanding; **una acción en fuerte alza** = a boom share

◊ **alzado, -da** *adj* raised *o* elevated; *(precio)* fixed; **tanto alzado** = flat rate *o* fixed price; **se le paga un tanto alzado de 450 ptas. por mil** = he is paid a flat rate of 450 pesetas per thousand

ama *nf* landlady *o* proprietress *o* boss; **ama de casa** = housewife

amañar *vt* to fiddle; **intentó amañar su declaración de la renta** = he tried to fiddle his tax returns; **sorprendieron al vendedor amañando su cuenta de gastos** = the salesman was caught fiddling his expense account

amarradero *nm* berth *o* mooring

amarrar *vt* to tie up; **el barco estaba amarrado en el muelle** = the ship was tied up to the quay

amasar *vt (dinero)* to amass (money) *o* to rake it in

ambiente *nm* atmosphere; **el medio ambiente** = the environment; **cambió de trabajo porque no le gustaba el ambiente de la oficina** = she changed jobs because she didn't like the atmosphere in the office

ámbito *nm* range *o* scope *o* area; **esto entra dentro del ámbito de actividades de la compañía** = this falls within the company's range of activities; **dentro del ámbito legal** = within the law; **de ámbito nacional** = nationwide; **el nuevo coche se lanzará con una campaña de ventas de ámbito nacional** = the new car is being launched with a nationwide sales campaign

ambulante *adj* **trabajador ambulante** = itinerant worker; **vendedor, -ra ambulante** = hawker *o* pedlar

América *nf* America; **América Central** = Central America; **América Latina** = Latin America; **América del Norte** = North America; **América del Sur** = South America

◊ **americano, -na** *adj y n* American

amo *nm* boss *o* landlord *o* proprietor

amontonar *vt* to pile *o* to stack; **amontonó los papeles sobre la mesa** = he piled the papers on his desk

◊ **amontonarse** *vr* to pile up; **se están amontonando reclamaciones sobre el servicio de posventa** = complaints are piling up about the after-sales service

amortiguador *nm* **(a)** *(máquina)* shock abosorber **(b)** *(dinero)* cushion

amortizable *adj* amortizable *o* redeemable; **el costo del capital es amortizable a lo largo de un periodo de diez años** = the capital cost is amortizable over a period of ten years; **no amortizable** = irredeemable

◊ **amortización** *nf* **(a)** *(depreciación)* depreciation; *(liquidación)* amortization; **amortización acelerada** = accelerated depreciation; **amortización anticipada** = early repayment *o* redemption before due date; **amortización anual uniforme** *o* **lineal** = straight line depreciation; **amortización por anualidades** = annual depreciation; **amortización de una deuda** = redemption *o* amortization of a debt; **amortización fiscal** = capital allowances; **amortización de una hipoteca** = redemption of a mortgage; **fecha de amortización** = redemption date; **tasa de amortización** = depreciation rate **(b)** **amortizaciones** = capital allowances

> la amortización de la inversión que estaba
> dispuesto a hacer hubiera tardado 30 años,
> según la contabilidad del propio grupo
> **Cambio 16**

> los diferentes importes destinados a
> amortizaciones y saneamientos, se sitúan
> por encima de los 20.000 millones de
> pesetas
> **Actualidad Económica**

amortizar *vt* **(a)** *(liquidar)* to amortize *o* to redeem; **el costo del capital se amortiza en cinco años** = the capital cost is amortized over five years; **amortizar una hipoteca** = to redeem a mortgage **(b)** *(depreciar)* to depreciate; **amortizamos los coches de la empresa en tres años** = we depreciate our company cars over three years

> hoy su tasa de rentabilidad es de un 15% y
> las inversiones, como la de la red TGV-
> Atlántico que costó 18.000 millones de
> francos, están a punto de ser amortizadas
> antes de lo previsto
> **Cambio 16**

amparo *nm* protection *o* shelter; **amparo fiscal** = tax shelter

ampliación *nf* **(a)** *(aumento)* expansion *o* increase *o* extension; **ampliación de capital** = capital increase; *(bolsa)* **ampliación de capital en curso** = rights issue; **ampliación de inversiones en activo fijo** = increase in capital expenditure; **ampliación de un plazo** = extension of a time limit **(b)** *(fotografía)* enlargement *o* photocopy enlargement **(c)** **ampliación de póliza** = endorsement to a policy

> la Comisión de la Unión Europea le
> concedió la autorización para realizar
> una ampliación de capital durante el año
> pasado por valor de 87.000 millones de
> pesetas
> **El País**

ampliar *vt* **(a)** *(agrandar)* to expand *o* to increase; **hemos tenido que ampliar nuestro personal de ventas** = we have had to expand our sales force; **ampliar el negocio a una nueva rama** = to branch out; **la empresa amplió su negocio de venta de coches a la rama de alquiler** = from car retailing, the company branched out into car leasing **(b)** *(fotografía)* to enlarge

◊ **amplio, -a** *adj* broad *o* wide *o* extensive *o* comprehensive

amueblar *vt* to furnish; **amuebló su oficina con sillas y mesas de segunda mano** = he furnished his office with secondhand chairs and desks; **la compañía gastó 2.000.000 ptas. en amueblar la oficina del presidente** = the company spent 2m pesetas on furnishing the chairman's office; **piso amueblado** = furnished flat *o* apartment; **casa amueblada** = furnished house

análisis *nm* analysis *o* review; **análisis de costes** = cost analysis; **análisis coste-beneficio** = cost-benefit analysis; **análisis estadístico** = statistical analysis; **análisis de medios de comunicación** = media analysis *o* media research; **análisis de mercado** = market analysis *o* market research; **análisis de las operaciones** = operations review; **análisis de un puesto de trabajo** = job analysis; **análisis de sistemas** = systems analysis; **análisis de vencimientos** = aged debtors analysis; **análisis de ventas** = sales analysis; **llevar a cabo un análisis de la situación de las ventas** = to do a break-down *o* an analysis of the sales position; **hacer un análisis de los distribuidores** = to conduct a review of distributors; **realizar un análisis del potencial del mercado** = to carry out an analysis of the market potential

◊ **analista** *nmf* analyst; **analista de bolsa** = chartist; **analista de mercado** = market analyst; **analista de sistemas** = systems analyst; **analista financiero** = financial analyst

analizar *vt* to analyse *o* analyze; **analizar un estado de cuentas** = to analyse a statement of account; **analizar las posibilidades de mercado** = to analyse the market potential; **datos sin analizar** = raw data

anaquel *nm* shelf

ancho, -cha 1 *adj* wide **2** *nm* width

andar *vi* **(a)** *(personas)* to walk *o* to go; **va a la oficina andando todas las mañanas** = he walks to the office every morning; **¿cómo andas de trabajo?** = how are you placed for work?; **andar escaso** = to be short of **(b)** *(funcionar)* to run; **el negocio anda mal** = business is going badly *o* is not doing well

andén *nm* platform; **el tren para Toledo sale del andén 12** = the train for Toledo leaves from platform 12; **la taquilla está en el andén 2** = the ticket office is on platform 2

Andorra *nf* Andorra

◊ **andorrano, -na** *adj y n* Andorran
NOTA: capital: **Andorra la Vella**; moneda: **franco francés (F), peseta (ptas.)** = French franc (F), peseta (ptas)

anexo *nm* enclosure *o* annexe *o* appendix

animado, -da 1 *adj (activo)* brisk *o* busy; **un mercado de acciones petrolíferas muy animado** = a brisk market in oil shares **2** *pp de* ANIMAR

◊ **animador** *nm* **animador de ventas** = sales promoter

animar *vt* **(a)** *(discusión)* to liven up **(b)** *(persona)* to encourage; **me animó a que solicitara el puesto** = he encouraged me to apply for the job

◊ **animarse** *vr* **(a)** *(recuperarse)* to go up *o* to pick up; **las ventas se animaron después de la publicidad en televisión** = sales picked up after the TV commercials **(b)** *(persona)* to feel encouraged

ánimo *nm* encouragement; **dar ánimos** = to give encouragement *o* to encourage; **sin ánimos** = discouraged; **tener ánimos para hacer algo** = to feel like doing something

anónimo, -ma *adj* anonymous; **sociedad anónima** = corporation *o* company *o* public company

anotación *nf* entry *o* record *o* recording; **anotación en cuenta** = account entry; **anotación de un pedido** *o* **de una queja** = noting *o* recording of an order *o* of a complaint

anotar *vt* **(a)** *(tomar nota)* to log *o* to minute *o* to record *o* to note; **anotar algo** = to take note of something; **anotar las llamadas recibidas** = to log phone calls **(b)** *(contabilidad)* to enter *o* to put down (a figure); **anotar una cifra de gastos** = to put down a figure for expenses; **anotar una compra** = to charge a purchase; **anotar una contrapartida** *o* **un contraasiento** = to contra an entry; **el empleado anotó los intereses en mi libreta** = the clerk entered the interest in my bank book

ansioso, -sa *adj* eager *o* keen; **nuestros vendedores están ansiosos por ver la nueva gama de productos** = our salesmen are eager to see the new product range

antecedentes *nmpl* **(a)** *(general)* background *o* track record; **tiene buenos antecedentes como vendedor de coches de segunda mano** = he has a good track record as a secondhand car salesman; **¿cuáles son sus antecedentes?** *o* **¿sabe Vd. algo de sus antecedentes?** = what is his background? *o* do you know anything about his background?; **estamos investigando los antecedentes del nuevo proveedor** = we are inquiring into the background of the new supplier **(b)** *(jurídico)* **antecedentes penales** = criminal record

antecesor, -ra *n* predecessor; **utiliza la misma oficina que su antecesora** = she is using the same office as her predecessor

antedatar *vt* to antedate *o* to backdate; **antedate su factura al 1 de abril** = backdate your invoice to April 1st

antelación *nf* advance; **con antelación** = in advance; **hay que avisar con siete días de antelación que se van a retirar fondos de la cuenta** = you must give seven days' advance notice of withdrawals from the account

antemano *adv* **de antemano** = beforehand *o* in advance

antepasado, -da 1 *adj* previous *o* before last; **la semana antepasada** *o* **el mes antepasado** *o* **el año antepasado** = the week *o* month *o* year before last **2** *n* ancestor

anteproyecto *nm* draft project

anterior 1 *adj* former *o* previous; **el**

anterior presidente se ha puesto a trabajar para la competencia = the former chairman has taken a job with a rival company; las cifras del año pasado fueron malas, pero fueron mejores que las del año anterior = last year's figures were bad, but they were an improvement on those of the year before last **2** *adv* anterior a = before

◊ **anteriormente** *adv* previously *o* formerly *o* before

antes *adv* (a) *(primero)* first *o* before *o* once (b) *(preferencia)* sooner *o* rather (c) *(anteriormente)* before; tengo que darme prisa para sacar dinero antes que cierren los bancos = I'm in a hurry to get some money before the banks close

◊ **antes de** *prep* before *o* previous to; una venta antes del inventario = a pre-stocktaking sale; el periodo justo antes de Navidad siempre es muy activo = the pre-Christmas period is always very busy; no es necesario que vengas antes de las 10 = there is no need for you to come before 10 o'clock

anti- *prefijo* anti-

anticipado, -da 1 *adj* advanced *o* early; por anticipado = beforehand *o* early; gastos anticipados = prepaid expenses; gracias por anticipado = thanks in advance; indicador anticipado = leading indicator; pago anticipado = payment in advance **2** *pp de* ANTICIPAR

anticipar *vt* (a) *(adelantar)* to bring forward; anticipar una fecha = to bring a date forward (b) *(prever)* to anticipate *o* to foresee; anticipamos que nuestro plan tendrá una fuerte oposición = we expect a lot of opposition to our plan (c) *(dinero)* to advance; anticipar contra una letra nominativa = to make an advance against a draft

◊ **anticiparse** *vr* to be ahead of *o* to be sooner than expected; se anticiparon a sus competidores en el lanzamiento del nuevo modelo = they were ahead of their competitors in launching the new model first

anticipo *nm* (a) *(trabajo)* retainer; le pagamos un anticipo (sobre los honorarios) de 10.000 ptas. = we pay him a retainer of 10,000 pesetas (b) *(compra)* deposit (c) *(préstamo o sueldo)* advance; un anticipo a cuenta = an advance on account; ¿puede darme un anticipo de 50.000 ptas. sobre el sueldo del mes próximo? = can I have an advance of 50,000 pesetas against next month's salary?

anticonstitucional *adj* anticonstitutional; la reelección del presidente es anticonstitucional = the reelection of the chairman is not constitutional

anticuado, -da *adj* (a) *(obsoleto)* obsolete; cuando se equipó la oficina con ordenadores las máquinas de escribir quedaron anticuadas = when the office was equipped with word-processors the typewriters became obsolete (b) *(viejo)* out of date *o* old-fashioned; su sistema informático está muy anticuado = their computer system is very out of date; sigue utilizando una máquina de escribir anticuada = he still uses an old-fashioned typewriter

antieconómico, -ca *adj* uneconomic *o* wasteful

antiestatutario, -ria *adj* anticonstitutional; la

reelección del presidente es antiestatutaria = the reelection of the chairman is not constitutional

antigüedad *nf* seniority *o* length of service; los nombres de los directores aparecían por orden de antigüedad = the managers were listed in order of seniority; socio de menor antigüedad = junior partner

antiguo, -gua *adj* (a) *(viejo)* old *o* old-established (b) *(de hace tiempo o de muchos años)* (i) long-standing; (ii) former *o* ex-; más antiguo = senior; cliente antiguo = long-standing customer *o* customer of long standing; antiguo alumno = former student *o* ex-student

antiinflacionario, -ria *adj* anti-inflationary; medidas antiinflacionarias = anti-inflationary measures

◊ **antiinflacionista** *adj* anti-inflationary

antimonopolista *adj* anti-trust; ley *o* legislación antimonopolista = anti-trust laws *o* legislation

antirreglamentario, -ria *adj* against the rules

anual *adj* yearly *o* annual; expresado en base anual = annualized; el término medio anual es del 10% = it averages out at 10% per annum; calendario de trabajo anual *o* planificador anual = year planner; crecimiento anual del 5% = annual growth of 5%; las cuentas anuales = the annual accounts; la declaración anual de renta = annual statement of income; informe anual = annual report; ingresos anuales *o* renta anual = annual income; pago anual = yearly payment; prima anual de 5.000 ptas. = yearly premium of 5,000 pesetas

◊ **anualidad** *nf* annuity; comprar *o* suscribir una anualidad = to buy *o* to take out an annuity; anualidad vitalicia = annuity for life *o* life annuity; anualidad reversible = reversionary annuity

◊ **anualmente** *adv* annually *o* on an annual basis; las cifras se actualizan anualmente = the figures are updated annually; las cifras se revisan anualmente = the figures are revised on an annual basis; salario que aumenta anualmente en 50.000 ptas. = salary which rises in annual increments of 50,000 pesetas

◊ **anuario** *nm* yearbook

anulación *nf* annulling *o* cancellation *o* invalidation *o* nullification; anulación de un contrato = annulling *o* annulment of a contract; anulación de un acuerdo = cancellation of an agreement

anular *vt* to annul *o* to cancel *o* to invalidate *o* to nullify *o* to rescind; anular un contrato = to cancel *o* to void a contract; se sintió obligado a anular el contrato = he felt obliged to cancel the contract; el contrato fue anulado por el tribunal = the contract was annulled by the court; como la empresa ha cambiado de dueño el contrato ha sido anulado = the contract has been invalidated because the company has changed hands; anular un cheque = to cancel a cheque; anular una decisión = to render a decision null; anular una partida contable = to write off an entry; anular un pedido = to cancel an order; anular una sentencia = to annul a judgment;

el fallo del árbitro se anuló en la apelación = the arbitrator's award was set aside on appeal

◊ **anulativo, -va** *adj* annulling; **cláusula anulativa** = annulling clause

anunciante *nmf* advertiser; **el catálogo contiene una lista de anunciantes** = the catalogue gives a list of advertisers

> televisando una ópera en todo el mundo se puede conseguir, por poco dinero, una audiencia de alto poder adquisitivo que resulta muy atractiva para los anunciantes
> **Actualidad Económica**

anunciar *vt* **(a)** *(poner un anuncio)* to advertise; **anunciar una vacante** = to advertise a vacancy; **anunciar un puesto de secretaria** = to advertise for a secretary **(b)** *(comunicar)* to announce; **anunciar un aumento** = to post an increase; **anunciar un déficit** = to report a loss; **anunciar un programa de inversiones** = to announce a programme of investment **(c)** *(avisar)* to warn; **el gobierno anunció que podrían aplicarse aranceles a la importación** = the government warned of possible import duties

anuncio *nm* **(a)** *(publicidad)* advertisement *o* ad; **anuncio aislado** = solus (advertisement); **anuncio con impreso de solicitud de información** = coupon ad; **anuncios breves** = small ads; **anuncios clasificados** *o* **por palabras** = classified advertisements; **contestar a un anuncio del periódico** = to answer an advertisement in the paper; **encontró trabajo a través de un anuncio en el periódico** = he found his job through an ad in the paper; **poner un anuncio en el periódico** = to put an advertisement *o* an ad in a paper; **nuestro anuncio se publicó en la primera página del periódico** = our ad appeared on the front page of the newspaper; **mire los anuncios por palabras para ver si alguien vende un ordenador** = look in the small ads to see if anyone has a computer for sale; **tonadilla de un anuncio** = advertising jingle *o* publicity jingle **(b)** *(televisión)* commercial; **tarifa de anuncios publicitarios** = rate card; **vamos a presentar una serie de anuncios en la televisión durante las próximas tres semanas** = we are running a series of TV spots over the next three weeks; **emitieron seis anuncios que recomendaban las vacaciones en España** = they ran six commercials plugging holidays in Spain **(c)** *(aviso)* announcement *o* notice; **anuncio del nombramiento de un nuevo director gerente** = announcement of the appointment of a new managing director; **anuncio de un recorte de gastos** = announcement of a cutback in expenditure; **tablón de anuncios** = noticeboard *o* message board

añadir *vt* **(a)** *(sumar)* to add; **añadir los intereses al capital** = to add interest to the capital; **hemos añadido un 10% a nuestra previsión de costes para imprevistos** = we have built 10% for contingencies into our cost forecast **(b)** *(incorporar)* to add *o* to supplement; **añadiremos seis empleados eventuales al personal del almacén durante la campaña de Navidad** = we will supplement the warehouse staff with six temporary workers during the Christmas rush; **si no entran todas las cuentas en la hoja, puedes añadir otra al final** = if the paper is too short to take all the accounts, you can join an extra piece on the bottom

año *nm* year; **el año antepasado** = the year before last; **año civil** = calendar year; **los años de escasez** *o* **los años de las vacas flacas** = the lean years; **año fiscal** = financial year *o* fiscal year *o* tax year; **el año pasado** = last year; **las cifras del año pasado fueron malas, pero fueron mejores que las del año antepasado** = last year's figures were bad, but they were an improvement on those of the year before last; **fin de año** = year end; **mejor año** = best year *o* peak year; **tenemos que partir del supuesto de que las ventas no se duplicarán el próximo año** = we have to go on the assumption that sales will not double next year; **el año empezó lleno de incertidumbres** = the year got off to a shaky start

◊ **al año** *adv* per annum; **una vez el año** = once a year; **¿cuál es su volumen de ventas al año?** = what is their turnover per annum?

> en diciembre, entre fiestas y puentes, quedan menos de 15 días laborables y además coincide con el cierre del año fiscal de la mayoría
> **Datamation**

apagado, -da *adj* dull *o* lifeless; *(luz o motor)* switched off **2** *pp de* APAGAR

apagar *vt* to switch off *o* to turn off

apalancamiento *nm* leverage *o* gearing; **apalancamiento financiero** = financial gearing

aparato *nm* **(a)** *(política)* machinery; **aparato estatal** = the government machinery; **aparato estatal local** = the local government machinery **(b)** *(maquinaria)* device; **inventó un aparato para enroscar el tapón a las botellas** = he invented a device for screwing tops on bottles

aparcamiento *nm* car park

aparcar 1 *vt/i (coche)* to park; **el representante aparcó el coche enfrente de la tienda** *o* **oficina** = the rep parked his car outside the shop *o* the office; **no se puede aparcar aquí en las horas punta** = you cannot park here during the rush hour; **es difícil aparcar en el centro de la ciudad** = parking is difficult in the centre of the city **2** *vt (proyecto o idea)* to shelve *o* to put on the back burner

aparejador, -ra *n* quantity surveyor

apartado 1 *adj* isolated *o* remote; **mantenerse apartado** = to stay in the background **2** *nm* **(a)** *(correspondencia)* box; **apartado de Correos** = Post Office box *o* P.O. box number **(b)** *(parte de un informe)* paragraph *o* section; **mire la cifra en el apartado de 'Costes 89-90'** = look at the figure under the heading 'Costs 89-90'

> los interesados deberán enviar su currículum vitae, así como pretensiones, al apartado 35.298 de Barcelona, C.P. 08025, indicando en el sobre la Ref. Ingeniero Proyectos
> **Actualidad Económica**

> enviar currículum vitae debidamente justificado al apartado de Correos 60.546 de Madrid, indicando en la referencia 'Analista'. Se realizará una selección previa por currículum
> **Actualidad Económica**

aparte 1 *adv* **(a)** *(por separado)* separately *o* apart;

(no está incluido) **el servicio es aparte** = service is extra; **enviar por correo aparte** = to send something under separate cover **(b)** *(además)* besides **2** *prep* **aparte de** = apart from

apelación *nf* appeal; **la apelación en contra de la decisión de planificación será examinada durante el mes próximo** = the appeal against the planning decision will be heard next month; **perdió la apelación por daños y perjuicios contra la compañía** = he lost his appeal for damages against the company; **ganó la causa en apelación** = she won her case on appeal; **Tribunal de Apelación** = Appeal Court *o* Court of Appeal

apelar *vi* to appeal; **la empresa apeló contra la decisión de los planificadores** = the company appealed against the decision of the planning officers

apellido *nm* surname

apenas *adv* **(a)** barely; **apenas tuvo tiempo de llamar a su abogado** = she barely had time to call her lawyer **(b)** as soon as; **apenas llegó se puso a leer las actas de la última reunión** = as soon as he arrived he started to read the minutes of the last meeting

apéndice *nm* appendix

apertura *nf* **(a)** *(comienzo)* opening; **apertura de un mercado** = a market opening; **la apertura de un nuevo mercado** *o* **de una nueva red de distribución** = the opening of a new market *o* of a new distribution network **(b)** *(contabilidad)* **asiento de apertura** = opening entry **(c)** *(bolsa)* **precio** *o* **cotización de apertura** = opening price

> la apertura de los mercados aumentará nuestro nivel de vida porque intensificará el comercio, fomentará la eficacia de la economía estadounidense y aumentará la expansión estimulando la innovación e inversión
> **Mercado**

> la apertura del mercado interior supondrá un fuerte aumento de la competencia en el negocio bancario al por mayor, pero no dejará de incidir en la banca al por menor
> **Mercado**

apilar *vt* to pile *o* to stack; **las cajas están apiladas en el almacén** = the boxes are stacked in the warehouse

aplazado, -da 1 *adj* deferred *o* postponed; **aplazado hasta la próxima reunión** = held over to the next meeting; **pago aplazado** = deferred payment **2** *pp de* APLAZAR; **el proyecto ha sido aplazado** = the project has been postponed *o* has been put on the back burner

◊ **aplazamiento** *nm* **(a)** *(prórroga)* adjournment *o* deferment *o* postponement; **aplazamiento de una decisión** = deferment of a decision; **aplazamiento de una sentencia** = stay of execution; **aplazamiento de pago** = deferment of payment; **propuso el aplazamiento de la reunión** = he proposed the adjournment of the meeting; **tuve que cambiar mis citas por el aplazamiento de la reunión del consejo** = I had to change my appointments because of the postponement of the board meeting **(b)** *(de un plan, de un proyecto)*

putting off *o* shelving; **el aplazamiento del proyecto ha ocasionado seis despidos** = the shelving of the project has resulted in six redundancies

aplazar *vt* to adjourn *o* to defer *o* to hold over *o* to postpone *o* to put back *o* to put off *o* to shelve *o* to put (something) on ice; **aplazar una reunión** = to adjourn a meeting; **el presidente aplazó la reunión hasta las tres** = the chairman adjourned the meeting until three o'clock; **la decisión ha sido aplazada hasta la próxima reunión** = the decision has been deferred until the next meeting; **la discusión del punto 4 quedó aplazada hasta la reunión siguiente** = discussion of item 4 was held over until the next meeting; **se aplazó el proyecto de inversiones en su totalidad** = the whole investment programme was put on ice; **preguntaron si podían aplazar el pago hasta que la situación de caja fuera mejor** = they asked if they could postpone payment until the cash situation was better; **preguntó si podíamos aplazar la visita hasta mañana** = he asked if we could put the visit off until tomorrow; **la reunión se aplazó dos horas** = the meeting was put back (by) two hours; **la reunión fue aplazada dos semanas** = the meeting was put off for two weeks; **el proyecto fue aplazado** = the project was shelved; **aplazar el examen de una moción** = to put off discussion of a motion; *US* to table a motion; **aplazar un plan indefinidamente** = to put a plan into cold storage

aplicación *nf* enforcement *o* implementation; **la aplicación de nuevas reglas** = the implementation of new rules; **aplicación de los términos de un contrato** = enforcement of the terms of a contract

aplicar *vt* to implement; **aplicar un impuesto** = to impose a tax

◊ **aplicarse** *vr* to apply oneself *o* to work hard; **la secretaria se aplicó en el estudio y aprobó el examen** = the secretary worked hard at her course and passed the exam

apoderado, -da *n* **(a)** *(representante)* nominee; **cuenta administrada por un apoderado** = nominee account; **apoderado, -da general** = authorized signatory **(b)** *(poderhabiente)* proxy; **actuar como apoderado de alguien** = to act as proxy for someone

aportación *nf* contribution; **plan de pensiones con aportaciones del trabajador** = contributory pension plan *o* scheme

apostar *vt* to bet; **apostó 1.000 ptas. por el resultado de las elecciones** = he bet 1000 pesetas on the result of the election; **te apuesto 5.000 ptas. a que el dólar subirá con relación a la peseta** = I bet you 5,000 pesetas the dollar will rise against the peseta

apoyar *vt* to support *o* to back (someone) up; **el director gerente se había negado a apoyarle en su conflicto con el departamento de administración del IVA** = the managing director refused to back him up in his argument with the VAT office; **espera que los demás miembros del comité la apoyen** = she hopes the other members of the committee will support her; **apoyar una moción** = to second a motion; **no hubo nadie que apoyara la moción por lo que no fue sometida a votación** = there was no seconder for the motion so it was not put to the vote; **el banco le apoya con un préstamo de 100.000**

ptas. = the bank is backing him with a loan of 100,000 pesetas

apoyo *nm* support *o* backing; **el presidente tiene el apoyo del comité** = the chairman has the support of the committee; **apoyo del Estado** = government support; **con apoyo estatal** *o* **del gobierno** = government-backed; **apoyo financiero** = financial backing; **no recibimos ningún apoyo financiero de los bancos** = we have no financial support from the banks; **¿de dónde procede el apoyo financiero del proyecto?** = who is providing the backing for the project *o* where does the backing for the project come from?; **la empresa tendrá éxito únicamente si cuenta con el debido apoyo financiero** = the company will succeed only if it has sufficient backing; **consiguió el apoyo de un grupo australiano** = he secured the backing of an Australian group

apreciación *nf* **(a)** *(estimación)* estimate; **según una apreciación prudente** = at a conservative estimate; **su volumen de negocios ha aumentado un 20% como mínimo en el último año y se trata de una apreciación prudente** = their turnover has risen by at least 20% in the last year, and that is a conservative estimate **(b)** *(revaluación)* appreciation

◊ **apreciar** *vt* to appreciate

◊ **apreciarse** *vr* to appreciate

◊ **aprecio** *nm* appreciation *o* estimation

apremiante *adj* **(a)** *(insistente)* **vendedor apremiante** = high-pressure salesman **(b)** *(urgente)* urgent *o* pressing; **tengo un trabajo apremiante** = I have an urgent job *o* some urgent work to do

apremiar *vt* to urge *o* to chase (payment); **apremiaremos al departamento de producción para que atienda a su pedido** = we will chase your order with the production department

◊ **apremio** *nm* pressure; **vía de apremio** = legal means for collection

aprendiz, -za *n* **(a)** *(en un oficio)* apprentice; **ser aprendiz de alguien** *o* **estar de aprendiz con alguien** = to be apprenticed to someone; **trabajó de aprendiz para un contratista** = he was apprenticed *o* indentured to a builder **(b)** *(en prácticas)* trainee; **empleamos a un aprendiz de cocinero para ayudar cuando hay mucho trabajo** = we employ a trainee cook to help at peak periods

◊ **aprendizaje** *nm* traineeship *o* training; apprenticeship; **persona en aprendizaje** = trainee; **contrato de aprendizaje** = indenture; **contratar a una persona para hacer su aprendizaje** = to indenture someone; **realizó un aprendizaje de seis años en la acería** = he served a six-year apprenticeship in the steel works

> tanto los profesionales como las propias organizaciones deben seguir un proceso continuo de aprendizaje
>
> **El País**

apresurado, -da *adj* hurried *o* rushed *o* hasty; **una venta apresurada de la libra** = a run on the pound

apretado, -da 1 *adj* busy; **el director tiene un** horario muy apretado hoy, no puede aceptar más citas = the manager has a very tight schedule today - he cannot fit in any more appointments **2** *pp de* APRETAR

apretar *vt* to tighten *o* to squeeze; **apretarse el cinturón** = to tighten one's belt

aprobación *nf* approval; **presentar un presupuesto para su aprobación** = to submit a budget for approval; **certificado de aprobación** = certificate of approval

aprobar *vt* **(a)** *(autorizar)* to agree to *o* to approve of; **aprobar sin debate** *o* **automáticamente** = to approve automatically *o* to rubber stamp; **la junta directiva aprobó el acuerdo sin debate previo** = the board simply rubber stamped the agreement; **aprobar con carácter definitivo** = to finalize; **el presidente aprueba el nuevo membrete de la compañía** = the chairman approves of the new company letter heading; **los auditores han aprobado las cuentas** = the auditors have agreed the accounts; **los auditores han aprobado las cuentas con reservas** = the auditors have qualified the accounts; **el director financiero tiene que aprobar las facturas antes de su envío** = the finance director has to pass an invoice before it is sent out; **todos aprobamos el plan** = we all agreed on the plan; **aprobar los términos de un contrato** = to approve the terms of a contract; **no se han aprobado todavía los términos del contrato** = terms of the contract are still to be agreed; **hemos aprobado los presupuestos del año próximo** = we have agreed the budgets for next year; **el consejo de administración aprobó un presupuesto de 1,2 millones para el proyecto de expansión** = the board sanctioned the expenditure of 1.2m on the development project **(b)** *(adoptar)* **aprobar una moción** = to pass a resolution; **la moción fue aprobada** = the motion was carried; **el préstamo ha sido aprobado por la junta** = the loan has been passed by the board; **la reunión aprobó una propuesta para congelar los salarios** = the meeting passed a proposal that salaries should be frozen **(c)** *(exámenes)* to pass; **aprobó todos los exámenes y ahora tiene el título de contable** *o* **el título de ingeniero** = she has passed all her exams and now is a qualified accountant *o* a qualified engineer

apropiación *nf* appropriation; **apropiación ilícita** = misappropriation

apropiado, -da 1 *adj* **(a)** *(adecuado)* appropriate *o* suitable; **el miércoles es el día más apropiado para reuniones del consejo de administración** = Wednesday is the most suitable day for board meetings **(b)** *(pertinente)* relevant *o* fitting; **una observación apropiada** = a relevant comment **2** *pp de* APROPRIAR

apropiar *vt* to adapt *o* to fit; **apropiar las leyes a las costumbres** = to adapt laws to local customs

◊ **apropiarse** *vr* to take *o* to convert; **apropiarse ilícitamente de fondos en provecho propio** = to convert funds to one's own use

aprovechado, -da 1 *adj* *(trabajador)* industrious *o* hard-working **2** *n* opportunist **3** *pp de* APROVECHAR

aprovechar *vt* to take advantage of *o* to capitalize

on *o* to exploit *o* to cash in on; **aprovechar el valor de su posición en el mercado** = to capitalize on one's market position; **la compañía aprovecha sus contactos en el Ministerio de Comercio** = the company is exploiting its contacts in the Ministry of Trade; **la empresa aprovecha el interés que existe por los juegos de ordenador** = the company is cashing in on the interest in computer games

aprovisionamiento *nm* supply *o* procurement

◊ **aprovisionar** *vt* to supply

aproximación *nf* approximation; **aproximación de los gastos** = approximation of expenditure; **la cifra final no es más que una aproximación** = the final figure is only an approximation

aproximado, -da *adj* approximate *o* rough; **cálculo aproximado** = rough calculation *o* rough estimate; **hice unos cálculos aproximados al dorso de un sobre** = I made some rough calculations on the back of an envelope; **la sección de ventas ha hecho una previsión aproximada de los gastos** = the sales division has made an approximate forecast of expenditure

◊ **aproximadamente** *adv* approximately *o* roughly; **los gastos son aproximadamente un 10% inferiores a los del trimestre anterior** = expenditure is approximately 10% down on the previous quarter ; **el volumen de ventas es aproximadamente el doble del correspondiente al año pasado** = the turnover is roughly twice last year's; **su sueldo es de aproximadamente 6.800.000 de ptas.** = his salary is around 6,800,000 pesetas

aptitud *nf* aptitude; **tiene una aptitud especial para los negocios** = he has a particular capacity for business; **certificado de aptitud** = proficiency certificate *o* test; **tiene un certificado de aptitud en inglés** = she has a certificate of proficiency in English; **prueba de aptitud** = aptitude test *o* proficiency test; **para conseguir el trabajo tuvo que pasar una prueba de aptitud** = to get the job he had to pass a proficiency test

apto, -ta *adj* suitable *o* qualified

apuesta *nf* bet

apuntado, -da 1 *adj* noted *o* registered 2 *pp de* APUNTAR

apuntar *vt* **(a)** to log *o* to record *o* to enter *o* to note; **apuntar un éxito** = to score a success **(b)** to point at

◊ **apuntarse** *vr* to sign up

apuro *nm* financial need *o* hardship; **tenía grandes apuros financieros** = he was under considerable financial pressure

Arabia Saudita *o* **Arabia Saudí** *nf* Saudi Arabia

◊ **árabe saudita** *o* **árabe saudí** *adj y n* Saudi (Arabian)
NOTA: capital: **Riyadh**; moneda: **riyal árabe saudita (SRls)** = Saudi Arabian riyal

arancel *nm* tariff *o* duty; **imponer un arancel a las importaciones de artículos de lujo** = to levy a duty on the import of luxury items; **aranceles**

aduaneros = customs tariffs; **Acuerdo General sobre Aranceles Aduaneros y Comercio** = General Agreement on Tariffs and Trade (GATT)

◊ **arancelario, -ia** *adj* tariff; **barreras arancelarias** = tariff barriers

arbitraje *nm* **(a)** *(juicio de un árbitro)* arbitration; **conciliación y arbitraje de conflictos laborales** = conciliation and arbitration of industrial disputes; **someter** *o* **confiar un conflicto a arbitraje** = to submit *o* to take a dispute to arbitration; **remitir un asunto a arbitraje** = to refer a question to arbitration; **recurrir al arbitraje** = to go to arbitration; **comisión de arbitraje** *o* **tribunal de arbitraje** = arbitration board *o* arbitration tribunal; **tribunal de arbitraje laboral** = industrial arbitration tribunal; **aceptar la decisión de la comisión de arbitraje** = to accept the ruling of the arbitration board **(b)** *(operación bancaria, de bolsa)* arbitrage; **arbitraje de riesgos** = risk arbitrage; **sindicato de arbitraje** = arbitrage syndicate

arbitrar *vi* to arbitrate; **arbitrar en un conflicto** *o* **una disputa** = to arbitrate in a dispute; **arbitrar un litigio** = to adjudicate in a dispute

arbitrario, -ria *adj* arbitrary

árbitro, -ra *n* arbitrator *o* adjudicator; **árbitro laboral** = industrial arbitrator; **aceptar** *o* **rechazar la decisión del árbitro** = to accept *o* to reject the arbitrator's ruling; **árbitro en un conflicto laboral** = adjudicator in an industrial dispute; **ser árbitro en un conflicto** = to adjudicate in a dispute

árbol *nm* tree; **árbol de decisión** = decision tree

arca *nf* safe; bin

archivador, -ra 1 *adj* filing **2** *n (persona)* filing clerk **3** *nm* **(a)** *(mueble para archivar documentos)* filing cabinet; **este archivador contiene facturas clasificadas por fechas** = this filing cabinet contains invoices ordered by date; **la correspondencia del año pasado está en el último cajón del archivador** = last year's correspondence is in the bottom drawer of the filing cabinet **(b)** *(caja archivadora)* box file; **archivador de anillas** = ring binder

archivar *vt* **(a)** *(guardar en un archivo)* to file; **archivar algo** = to file something *o* to place something on file; **archivar documentos** = to file documents; **tener el nombre de alguien archivado** = to keep someone's name on file; **bandeja de documentos para archivar** = filing tray *o* filing basket; **el director ojeó los documentos archivados durante la semana para ver qué cartas se habían enviado** = the manager looked through the week's filing to see what letters had been sent **(b)** *(informática)* to save

◊ **archivero, -ra** *n* filing clerk

archivo *nm* **(a)** *(registro)* file *o* register; **sistema de archivo** = filing system; **hay mucho trabajo de archivo por hacer al final de la semana** = there is a lot of filing to do at the end of the week; **ponga estas cartas en el archivo de clientes** = put these letters in the customer file; **copia de archivo** = file copy **(b)** *(informática)* computer file; **¿cómo podemos proteger los archivos del ordenador?** = how can we protect our computer files? **(c)** *(carpeta)* archive box **(d)** *(plural)* archives; **los archivos de la**

compañía se remontan al año de su fundación en 1892 = the company's archives go back to its foundation in 1892

área *nf* **(a)** *(superfície)* area; **buscamos una tienda con un área de ventas de unos 100 metros cuadrados** = we are looking for a shop with a sales area of about 100 square metres **(b)** *(zona)* region *o* area; **área deprimida** = depressed area *o* depressed region; **área del dolar** *o* **área de la libra esterlina** = dollar area *o* sterling area; **área de libre comercio** = free trade area; *EC* **área aduanera exenta** = free zone *o* free port; **muestreo por áreas** = area sampling **(c)** *(tema)* subject *o* area (of study)

Argelia *nf* Algeria

◊ **argelino, -na** *adj y n* Algerian
NOTA: capital: **Argel** (= Algiers); moneda: **dinar argelino (DA)** = Algerian dinar (ALD)

Argentina *nf* Argentina

◊ **argentino, -na** *adj y n* Argentinian
NOTA: capital: **Buenos Aires**; moneda: **peso argentino** = Argentinian peso

argumento *nm* **(a)** argument *o* reasoning **(b)** **argumento de venta** = unique selling proposition

armario *nm* cabinet *o* cupboard *o* bookcase

armonización *nf* harmonization; **armonización de los tipos del IVA** = harmonization of VAT rates

armonizar *vt* to harmonize *o* to fine-tune; **armonizar los tipos del IVA** = to harmonize VAT rates

arranque *nm* starting; **punto de arranque** = trigger point

arreglado, -da 1 *adj* **(a)** *(ordenado y de buen gusto)* smart; **su oficina está muy bien arreglada** = his office is very smart **(b)** *(razonable)* reasonable; **nos han vendido el coche a un precio muy arreglado** = they sold us the car at a very reasonable price **2** *pp de* ARREGLAR

arreglar *vt* **(a)** *(reparar)* to fix *o* to mend *o* to repair; **los técnicos van a venir a arreglar la centralita de teléfonos** = the technicians are coming to fix the telephone switchboard; **¿puedes arreglar la fotocopiadora?** = can you mend the photocopier?; **no lo hagas arreglar - sólo vale 5.000 ptas.** = don't get it repaired - it is worth only 5,000 pesetas **(b)** *(organizar)* to arrange *o* to organize *o* to sort out; **arreglaron una cita con el nuevo cliente** = they arranged a meeting with the new client; **arreglar papeles** = to tidy up *o*; *US* to square away; **tengo que arreglar los papeles del despacho** = I have to sort out the papers in the office **(c)** to settle; **el jefe de personal arreglará este asunto** = the personnel officer will settle this matter

◊ **arreglarse** *vr* to work out *o* to be solved; **todo se arregló cuando llegó el presidente a la reunión** = everything was sorted out when the president arrived at the meeting

◊ **arreglárselas** *locución* to manage *o* to cope *o* to get along; **el nuevo director adjunto se las arregló muy bien cuando el director se fue de vacaciones** = the new assistant manager coped very well when the manager was on holiday; **se las arregló para anotar seis pedidos y atender a tres**

llamadas en dos minutos = she managed to write six orders and take three phone calls all in two minutes; **nos las estamos arreglando bastante sólo con la mitad del personal** = we are getting along quite well with only half the staff

arreglo *nm* **(a)** *(acomodo)* understanding; **llegar a un arreglo sobre el reparto del mercado** = to come to an understanding about dividing the market **(b)** *(acuerdo)* settlement; **llegar a un arreglo** = to settle; **llegar a un arreglo amistoso** = to settle out of court; **la disputa se resolvió mediante un arreglo amistoso** = a settlement was reached out of court *o* the two parties reached an out-of-court settlement

arrendador, -ra *n* (i) lessor; (ii) landlord, landlady

> tampoco es bueno para nadie que el arrendador se comprometa de por vida con el arrendatario
> **España Económica**

arrendamiento *nm* **(a)** *(arriendo)* lease *o* headlease; **arrendamiento financiero** = leasing; **utilizar una multicopista en virtud de un contrato de arrendamiento financiero** = to run a copier under a leasing arrangement; **propiedad en régimen de arrendamiento** = leasehold property; **realizar una operación de cesión-arrendamiento** = to lease back; **vendieron el edificio de oficinas y siguieron ocupándolo en virtud de un contrato de arrendamiento suscrito con el comprador** = they sold the office building and then took it back under a lease-back arrangement; **se cede arrendamiento** = lease for sale; **no conseguimos vender el arrendamiento** = we had no success in selling the lease; **renta por arrendamiento** = rental income *o* income from rentals; **arrendamiento a largo plazo** *o* **arrendamiento a corto plazo** = long lease *o* short lease; **el arrendamiento tiene una duración de veinte años** *o* **expira en 1999** = the lease runs for twenty years *o* the lease expires *o* runs out in 1999 **(b)** *(foro)* leasehold; **la compañía tiene arrendamientos valiosos** = the company has some valuable leaseholds **(c)** *(alquiler)* tenancy *o* let

> la nueva ley de arrendamientos urbanos tendrá un carácter más proteccionista para con el inquilino
> **España Económica**

> el leasing o arrendamiento financiero permite financiar el 100% de cualquier tipo de maquinaria o equipo industrial
> **El País**

arrendar *vt* **(a)** *(propietario)* to let *o* to lease; **arrendar equipo** = to lease equipment; **arrendar oficinas a empresas pequeñas** = to lease offices to small firms; **propiedad arrendada** = leasehold property **(b)** *(tomar en arriendo)* to rent *o* to lease *o* to hire; **arrendar una oficina a una compañía de seguros** = to lease an office from an insurance company; **vendieron el edificio de oficinas para obtener dinero en efectivo y luego lo arrendaron por veinticinco años** = they sold the office building to raise cash, and then leased it back for twenty-five years

◊ **arrendatario, -ria** *n* (i) leaseholder *o* lessee; (ii) tenant; (iii) hirer

tampoco es bueno para nadie que el arrendador se comprometa de por vida con el arrendatario
España Económica

arriba *adv* above; **los arriba mencionados** = the above-mentioned; **(hacia) arriba** = upwards

arriendo *nm* lease; **arriendo con opción a compra** = leasing (with option to purchase); **en arriendo** = leasehold; **propiedad en arriendo** = leasehold property; **comprar una propiedad en arriendo** = to buy a property leasehold; **ceder en arriendo** = to lease (to someone); **tomar en arriendo** = to lease (from someone); **tomar un edificio de oficinas en arriendo a largo plazo** = to take an office building on a long lease; **el arriendo de nuestros locales actuales es a corto plazo** = we have a short lease on our current premises; **alquilar un espacio para oficinas con un arriendo de veinte años** = to rent office space on a twenty-year lease; **cuando expire el arriendo** = on expiration of the lease

arriesgado, -da 1 *adj* risky; **perdió todo su dinero en unos negocios arriesgados en América del Sur** = he lost all his money in some risky ventures in South America **2** *pp de* ARRIESGAR

el mundo del dinero despide el primer semestre del año con un balance general positivo. Ganan más los inversores arriesgados, en tanto que a los timoratos se les deshincha la rentabilidad
El País

arriesgar *vt* to risk money *o* to venture; **arriesgar dinero en algo** = to risk *o* to stake money on something

◊ **arriesgarse** *vr* to take a risk; **la empresa se arriesga seriamente al fabricar 25 millones de unidades sin haber hecho un estudio de mercado** = the company is taking a considerable risk in manufacturing 25m units without doing any market research

arrojar *vt* to throw *o* to project; **arrojar una ganancia** *o* **una pérdida** = to show a profit *o* a loss

arruinar *vt* to bankrupt *o* to ruin; **la recesión arruinó a mi padre** = the recession bankrupted my father; **consiguieron arruinar a sus competidores** = they succeeded in putting their rivals out of business

◊ **arruinarse** *vr* to be ruined

arte 1 *nm* art *o* skill; **arte de vender** = salesmanship **2** *nfpl* **artes gráficas** = graphic arts

artesanía *nf* craft *o* handicraft; **productos de artesanía** = handicrafts

◊ **artesano, -na** *n* craftsman *o* artisan; *US* tradesman

artículo *nm* **(a)** *(comercio)* article *o* item (for sale); **artículo clave** = flagship; **artículos defectuosos** = defective merchandise *o* rejects; **artículo sin existencias** = out-of-stock item *o* stockout; **artículos de fantasía** = fancy goods; **artículo invendible** = unsaleable item; *(informal)* dog; **artículo de lanzamiento** *o* **reclamo** = loss-leader; **artículo-líder** = leading item; **mercado negro de**

artículos de lujo = black market in luxury articles; **artículos de marca** = branded goods; **artículo de mayor venta** = best-seller *o* money-spinner; **artículo de primera necesidad** = staple commodity; **artículos rebajados** = knockdown goods; **artículo vendido en buen estado** = item sold in good condition; **artículos de venta al contado** = cash items; **adjunto le envío un pedido de los siguientes artículos de su catálogo** = please find enclosed an order for the following items from your catalogue; **tenemos pedidos de artículos agotados** = we are holding orders for out of stock items; **seguimos recibiendo pedidos de este artículo aunque dejó de fabricarse hace dos años** = we keep on receiving orders for this item although it was discontinued two years ago **(b)** *(contrato)* article; **véase el artículo 8 del contrato** = see article 8 of the contract **(c)** *(prensa)* article; **se refirió a un artículo que había visto en 'El País'** = he referred to an article which he had seen in 'El País'; **artículo de fondo** = editorial

asalariado, -da 1 *adj* salaried *o* paid; **la población asalariada** = the wage-earning population **2** *n* salaried person *o* wage-earner; **la empresa tiene 250 asalariados** = the company has 250 salaried staff

la proporción de las remuneraciones de los asalariados en la renta nacional ha disminuido del 53,2% en 1983 al 49,9% en 1988
España Económica

asamblea *nf* **(a)** *(reunión)* meeting *o* conference; **asamblea de personal** = staff meeting; **la asamblea general anual terminó en una pelea generalizada entre los accionistas** = the AGM ended in a fight among the shareholders **(b)** *(corporación)* assembly; **Asamblea General de las Naciones Unidas** = the United Nations General Assembly; **asamblea nacional constituyente** = constituent national assembly

el pasado 13 de diciembre se celebró una asamblea general informativa en la que se presentaron los estatutos sociales y el reglamento del régimen interior de la asociación
Chip

ascendente 1 *adj* upward **2** *adv* upwards

ascender 1 *vt* to promote *o* to upgrade; **fue ascendido de vendedor a director de ventas** = he was promoted from salesman to sales manager **2** *vi* **(a)** *(subir)* to go up **(b)** *(cifrarse)* **ascender a** = to amount to *o* to run into *o* to add up to; **los gastos ascendieron a miles de pesetas** = costs ran into thousands of pesetas; **el gasto total asciende a más de 100.000 ptas.** = the total expenditure adds up to more than 100,000 pesetas; **sus deudas ascienden a más de 1 millón de pesetas** = their debts amount to over 1m pesetas; **sus ingresos ascienden a más de 1.000.000 de ptas.** = he has an income running into millions

en lo que va de año, las deudas de las suspensiones de pagos ascienden a 375.668 millones
El País

ascenso *nm* promotion; **oportunidades de ascenso** = promotion chances *o* promotion prospects; **perdió su oportunidad de ascenso**

cuando se peleó con el director gerente = he ruined his chances of promotion when he argued with the managing director; **ganarse el ascenso** = to earn promotion; **escala de ascenso** = promotion ladder; **subió varios grados en la escala de ascenso al ser nombrado director de ventas** = by being appointed sales manager, he moved several rungs up the promotion ladder

ascensor *nm* lift; *US* elevator; **tomó el ascensor hasta el piso 27** = he took the lift to the 27th floor; **los empleados no pudieron entrar en la oficina al averiarse el ascensor** = the staff could not get into the office because the lift had broken down

asegurable *adj* insurable

asegurado, -da 1 *adj* insured *o* assured; **no asegurado** = uninsured; **la persona asegurada** *o* **la vida asegurada** = the life assured; **la cantidad asegurada** = the sum insured **2** *n* the insured person; **el asegurado deberá pagar el total** = the total must be paid by the insured person **3** *pp de* ASEGURAR

asegurador, -ra 1 *adj* insurance *o* insuring; **compañía aseguradora** = insurance company; **consorcio asegurador** = underwriting syndicate **2** *n* *(persona)* insurer *o* underwriter; *(compañía)* assurer *o* assuror; **asegurador de Lloyd** = Lloyd's underwriter; **asegurador de riesgos marítimos** = marine underwriter

asegurar *vt* **(a)** *(propiedad)* to insure (something); **sin asegurar** *o* **no asegurado** = uninsured; **asegurar una casa contra incendios** = to insure a house against fire; **asegurar el equipaje contra robos y pérdidas** = to insure baggage against loss **(b)** *(la vida)* to assure; **asegurar la vida de alguien** = to assure someone's life; **estaba asegurado por 10.000.000 ptas.** = he was insured for 10,000,000 pesetas; **ha pagado las primas para asegurar la vida de su esposa** = he has paid the premiums to have his wife's life assured **(c)** *(garantizar)* to underwrite

◊ **asegurarse** *vr* to take out an insurance *o* to insure oneself; **asegurarse contra el mal tiempo** = to insure against bad weather; **asegurarse contra la pérdida de ingresos** = to insure against loss of earnings

asequible *adj* available *o* attainable; **precio asequible** = price within one's budget *o* reasonable price

asesor, -ra 1 *adj* advisory; **comisión asesora** = advisory committee; **técnico asesor** = consulting engineer **2** *n* adviser *o* advisor *o* consultant; **actúa en calidad de asesor** = he is acting in an advisory capacity *o* as an advisor; **asesor de empresas** = management consultant; **asesor financiero** = financial adviser; **asesor fiscal** = tax adviser *o* tax consultant; **se estableció como asesor fiscal** = he set himself up as a tax adviser; **asesor jurídico** = legal adviser; **ha consultado al asesor jurídico de la empresa** = he has consulted the company's legal adviser; **asesor técnico** = engineering consultant

◊ **asesoramiento** *nm* advice *o* counselling; **asesoramiento de deudas** = debt counselling; **asesoramiento jurídico** = legal advice; **tuvimos que pedir asesoramiento jurídico sobre el contrato a nuestro abogado** = we had to ask our lawyer for professional advice on the contract; **la compañía perdió mucho tiempo buscando asesoramiento profesional** = the company lost a great deal of time looking for expert advice

◊ **asesorar** *vt* to counsel *o* to advise *o* to act as a consultant

◊ **asesorarse** *vr* to consult *o* to take advice; **asesorarse jurídicamente** = to take legal advice

◊ **asesoría** *nf* consultancy; **una asesoría** = a consultancy firm

asiento *nm* entry; **hacer un asiento** = to enter *o* to make an entry *o* to post an entry; **asiento en un libro mayor** = to enter up an item in a ledger *o* to make an entry in a ledger; **asiento en el debe** *o* **asiento de débito** = debit entry; **asiento de apertura** *o* **inicial** = opening entry

asignación *nf* **(a)** *(asignar algo a alguien)* assignment *o* allocation *o* apportionment *o* appropriation; **asignación de sueldo** = assignment of salary; **la empresa obtuvo la asignación del proyecto** = the company was the successful tenderer for the project; **asignación de capital** *o* **de fondos a un proyecto** = allocation of capital *o* of funds to a project; **asignación de fondos a las reservas** = appropriation of funds to the reserve; **cuenta de asignación** = appropriation account **(b)** *(distribución)* assignation *o* allotment; **asignación de acciones** = assignation of shares *o* share allotment *o* share allocation *o* allocation of shares; **notificación de asignación de acciones** = letter of allotment *o* allotment letter **(d)** *(subsidio)* allowance; **asignación por kilometraje** = mileage allowance

asignar *vt* **(a)** *(ajudicar)* to allot *o* to assign; **asignar acciones** = to allot shares; **asignar acciones a alguien** = to assign shares to someone; **le asignaron la tarea de revisar las cifras de ventas** = he was assigned the job of checking the sales figures; **asignar personal** = to appoint staff to do something; **asignar personal para una exposición** = to man an exhibition **(b)** *(fondos)* to allocate *o* to earmark *o* to appropriate; **asignamos el 10% de los ingresos a la publicidad** = we allocate 10% of revenue to publicity; **se asignaron 250.000 ptas. para comprar muebles de oficina** = 250,000 pesetas were allocated for the purchase of office furniture; **asignar fondos a un proyecto** = to earmark funds for a project *o* to commit funds to a project; **asignar fondos a un proyecto de inversión** = to allocate funds to an investment project **(c)** *(bienes)* to settle on; **asignó sus bienes a sus hijos** = he settled his property on his children

asistencia *nf* **(a)** *(ayuda)* assistance; **asistencia médica** = medical assistance **(b)** *(número de asistentes)* attendance; **asistencia insuficiente** = inquorate; **la asistencia a la reunión es obligatoria** = attendance at the meeting is compulsory **(c)** *(consejos)* counsel

asistenta *nf* **(a)** *(en la casa)* domestic help *o* cleaning lady **(b)** *(en la oficina)* assistant

asistente *nmf* **(a)** *(ayudante)* assistant **(b)** *(en una reunión)* **los asistentes** = people present *o* people taking part *o* the public

asistido, -da 1 *adj* assisted *o* manned; **asistido por ordenador** = computer-assisted; **trabajo editorial asistido por ordenador** = desk-top publishing (DTP) **2** *pp de* ASISTIR

asistir 1 *vi (acudir a)* **asistir a** = to attend *o* to be present; **el presidente ha pedido que todos los consejeros asistan a la reunión** = the chairman has asked all managers to attend the meeting; **ningún accionista asistió a la junta general anual** = none of the shareholders attended the AGM; **tuvo que asistir a una sesión de reciclaje** = he had to attend a training session **2** *vt (ayudar)* to assist (someone); **mi secretaria me asiste en mi trabajo** = my secretary helps me with my work

asociación *nf* association *o* institute; **hacerse socio de una asociación** = to join an association *o* a group; **asociación comercial** *o* **profesional** *o* **asociación de comerciantes y empresarios** = trade association; **García S.A. ha solicitado ingresar en la asociación de comerciantes** = García S.A. has applied to join the trade association; **asociación de consumidores** = consumer association; **Asociación Europea de Libre Comercio (AELC)** = European Free Trade Association (EFTA); **asociación de fabricantes** = manufacturers' association; **Asociación Latinoamericana de Libre Comercio (ALALC)** = Latin American Free Trade Association (LAFTA); **asociación patronal** = employers' association; **Asociación de Transporte Aéreo Internacional (IATA)** = International Air Transport Association (IATA)

asociado, -da 1 *adj* associate *o* associated **2** *n* partner *o* member **3** *pp de* ASOCIAR

asociar *vt* to associate

◊ **asociarse** *vr* to join *o* to combine; **los trabajadores y la dirección se asociaron para hacer frente al intento de adquisición** = the workforce and management combined to fight the takeover bid; **asociarse con alguien** = to join forces with someone *o* to go into partnership with someone; **asociarse con un amigo** = to enter into a partnership with a friend

aspirante *nmf* candidate; **hay seis aspirantes al puesto de director adjunto** = there are six candidates for the post of assistant manager

aspirar *vi* **aspirar a algo** = to aim to *o* to aspire to *o* to have aspirations (towards); **aspiraba a ser presidente** = he aspired to be president *o* he hoped to be president; **cada vendedor tiene que aspirar a duplicar las ventas del año anterior** = each salesman must aim to double his previous year's sales; **la compañía aspira a crecer** = the company is aiming for growth

astillero *nm* dockyard *o* shipyard

astuto , -ta *adj* sharp *o* keen *o* sly *o* clever; **los inversores astutos han obtenido mucho dinero con las acciones** = clever investors have made a lot of money on the share deal

asumir *vt* **(a)** *(responsabilidad)* to assume; **asumir todos los riesgos** = to assume all risks; **ha asumido la responsabilidad de la comercialización** = he has taken on *o* assumed responsibility for marketing; **asumió la tarea de preparar las declaraciones del IVA** = she took on the job of preparing the VAT returns; **el comprador asume el pasivo de la compañía** = the buyer takes over the company's

liabilities **(b)** *(suponer)* to assume *o* to take for granted

asunción *nf* assumption; **asunción de riesgos** = assumption of risks

asunto *nm* **(a)** *(cuestión)* question *o* problem *o* matter; **primero examinaremos el asunto de la baja de precios del mes pasado** = we shall consider first the matter of last month's fall in prices; **un asunto problemático** *o* **un asunto preocupante** = a problem area *o* an area of concern; **tuvo que viajar al extranjero por asuntos de negocios** = he had to go abroad on business **(b)** *(negocio)* business *o* affair *o* proposition; **este asunto nunca será un negocio** = this business will never be a commercial proposition; **es un mal asunto** = it is a bad bargain; *(en una reunión)* **otros asuntos** = any other business (A.O.B.); **el asunto principal de la reunión se concluyó antes de las 3 de la tarde** = the main business of the meeting was finished by 3 p.m.; **¿está Vd. involucrado en el asunto de los derechos de autor?** = are you involved in the copyright affair?; **sus asuntos eran tan complicados que los abogados tuvieron que consultar a unos contables** = his affairs were so difficult to understand that the lawyers had to ask accountants for advice

atacar *vt* to attack

en un imprevisto flash surrealista, el presidente de la Comunidad de Madrid ha atacado la devaluación de la peseta en 1967
España económica

atar *vt* to tie (up); **ató el paquete con cuerda gruesa** = he tied the parcel with thick string; **dejó el asunto atado y bien atado** = he sorted out all the problems *o* he didn't leave any loose ends; **sus obligaciones como presidente le atan mucho** = his duties as chairman keep him very busy

atascar *vt* to stop *o* to jam

◊ **atascarse** *vr* to jam *o* to become jammed; **el alimentador de hojas se ha atascado** = the paper feed has jammed

atasco *nm* jam *o* bottleneck; **atasco de coches** = traffic jam; **un atasco en el sistema de suministro** = a bottleneck in the supply system; **hay serios atascos en la cadena de montaje** = there are serious bottlenecks in the production line

atención *nf* **(a)** *(acción de atender)* attention; **prestar atención** = to attend to *o* to pay attention to; **sus pedidos recibirán nuestra máxima atención** = your orders will have our best attention **(b)** *(carta)* **a la atención del Sr. Urbino** = attention: Mr Urbino; **a la atención del director gerente** = for the attention of the Managing Director

atender *vt* **(a)** *(dedicar tiempo a alguien, a algo)* to attend to *o* to provide; **mi agenda está llena, pero trataré de atenderle mañana por la tarde** = my appointments diary is full, but I shall try to fit you in tomorrow afternoon; **el equipo de producción atendió el pedido con rapidez** = the production team dealt with the order very promptly **(b)** *(tienda)* to serve; **atender a un cliente** = to serve a customer **(c)** *(abastecer)* to cater for; **la tienda atiende principalmente a clientes extranjeros** = the store caters mainly for overseas customers

◊ **atendido, -da** *adj y pp* manned; **la centralita está atendida las veinticuatro horas del día** = the switchboard is manned twenty-four hours a day; **el stand de la exposición estaba atendido por tres vendedoras o por nuestro personal de ventas** = the exhibition stand was manned by three salesgirls o by our sales staff

atento, -ta *adj* **(a)** *(cortés)* polite; **estipulamos que las vendedoras sean atentas con los clientes** = we stipulate that our salesgirls must be polite to customers; **recibimos una atenta carta del director gerente** = we had a polite letter from the MD **(b)** *(prestar atención)* attentive o watchful; **estuvo atento a las explicaciones de su jefe** = he listened attentively to his manager's instructions; **los representantes estuvieron muy atentos durante la conferencia** = the reps paid a lot of attention during the sales conference

◊ **atentamente** *adv* *(carta)* **le saluda atentamente** = (i) Yours faithfully o Yours truly; *US* Truly yours; (ii) Yours sincerely; *US* Sincerely yours

aterrizaje *nm* landing; **aterrizaje forzoso** = emergency landing; **aterrizaje suave** = soft landing

◊ **aterrizar** *vi* to land; **el avión aterrizó con diez minutos de retraso** = the plane landed ten minutes late

atesoramiento *nm* hoard o hoarding o accumulation

atesorar *vt* to hoard o to accumulate

átono *adj* *(sin movimiento)* flat; **hoy el mercado se ha mantenido átono** = the market was flat today

atracadero *nm* mooring

atracar *vi* to moor o to berth; *(entrar en dársena)* to dock; **el barco atracó a las 17.00** = the ship docked at 17.00; **el barco atracará en Rotterdam el miércoles** = the ship will berth at Rotterdam on Wednesday; **la mitad de la flota está atracada por la recesión** = half the shipping fleet is laid up by the recession

atractivo, -va **1** *adj* attractive **2** *nm* appeal o attraction; **atractivo para los clientes** = customer appeal; **atractivo para los compradores** = sales appeal

> el principal atractivo del modelo está bajo su capó delantero, donde se encuentra el corazón que lo mueve
>
> **El País**

atraer *vt* to appeal to o to attract; **este compact atrae a los menores de 25 años** = this CD appeals to the under-25 market; **la empresa ofrece vacaciones gratuitas en Inglaterra para atraer clientes** = the company is offering free holidays in England to attract buyers; **tenemos dificultades para atraer personal cualificado a esta parte del país** = we have difficulty in attracting skilled staff to this part of the country; **los depósitos atraen intereses del 15%** = the deposits attract interest at 15%

atrás *adv* behind; **quedarse atrás** = to fall behind; **nos hemos quedado atrás de nuestros competidores** = we have fallen behind our rivals

atrasado, -da **1** *adj* outstanding o overdue o late o in arrears; **ir atrasado** = to be behind schedule; **intereses atrasados** = back interest o arrears of interest; **los vendedores reclaman el pago de las comisiones atrasadas** = the salesmen are claiming for back payment of unpaid commission; **alquiler atrasado** = back rent; **la empresa debe 10 millones de renta atrasada** = the company owes 10m in back rent; **pago atrasado** = back o late payment; **despachar pedidos atrasados** = to deal with overdue orders o to release dues; **el almacén está tratando de atender los pedidos atrasados** = the warehouse is trying to cope with a backlog of orders; **acumulación de trabajo atrasado** = backlog of work; **mi secretaria no puede hacer frente a la acumulación de trabajo atrasado** = my secretary can't cope with the backlog of paperwork **2** *pp de* ATRASAR

atrasar *vt* to delay; **tuvieron que atrasar el vuelo a causa de la huelga de controladores de tráfico aéreo** = their flight was delayed due to a strike of air traffic controllers

◊ **atrasarse** *vr* to fall behind o to be late; **atrasarse en los pagos** = to allow payments to fall into arrears o to be in arrears

atraso *nm* **(a)** *(deuda)* arrears; **atrasos (de sueldo)** = back pay; **salario y atrasos efectivos a partir del 1 de enero** = salary with arrears effective from January 1st; **me deben 50.000 ptas. de atrasos de sueldo** = I am owed 50,000 pesetas in back pay **(b)** **de atraso** = in arrears; **los pagos tienen seis meses de atraso** = the payments are six months in arrears; **lleva seis meses de atraso en el pago del alquiler** = he is six months in arrears with his rent **(c)** *(retraso)* delay; **el tren de la seis lleva media hora de atraso** = the six o'clock train is running half an hour late

atribución *nf* assignation; **atribución de acciones** = share allocation o allocation of shares

◊ **atribuir** *vt* to attribute o to impute

atrio *nm* atrium

audiencia *nf* **(a)** *(jurídico)* court o hearing; **la sesión de la audiencia fue aplazada** = the court proceedings were adjourned **(b)** *(medios de comunicación)* audience; **horas de mayor (índice de) audiencia** = prime time; **tenemos una serie de anuncios en las horas de mayor (índice de) audiencia** = we are putting out a series of prime-time commercials; **nivel de audiencia de los programas televisivos** = ratings; **el programa tiene un alto nivel de audiencia con lo cual atraerá mucha publicidad** = the show is high in the ratings, which means it will attract good publicity

auditar *vt* to audit

◊ **auditor, -ra** *n* auditor; **la junta general anual nombra a los auditores de la compañía** = the AGM appoints the company's auditors; **auditor externo** = external auditor; **auditor interno** = internal auditor; **informe de los auditores** = auditors' report

◊ **auditoría** *nf* audit o auditing; **realizar una auditoría** = to audit; **realizar la auditoría anual** = to carry out the annual audit; **auditoría externa o independiente** = external audit o independent audit; **auditoría interna** = internal audit; **es el director del departamento de auditoría interna** = he is the manager of the internal audit department

> la auditoría fue encargada por iniciativa del cesado presidente del consejo
> **El País**

> se hizo pública la auditoría correspondiente a 1990, en la que el auditor concluía que no puede expresar opinión alguna sobre las cuentas presentadas por la empresa
> **El País**

auge *nm* boom; **auge impulsado por las exportaciones** = export-led boom; **el mercado de los locales comerciales está en auge** = the commercial property market is booming; **la tecnología es un sector de la economía que experimenta un gran auge** = technology is a booming sector of the economy; **industria en pleno auge** = boom industry

aumentar 1 *vt* **(a)** *(agregar)* to add to *o* to increase; **estamos aumentando el personal de ventas** = we are adding to the sales force; **todo esto aumenta los costes de la empresa** = this all adds to the company's costs **(b)** *(precio o producción)* to increase *o* to step up *o* to put up *o* to raise; *US* to hike; **aumentar de precio** = to increase in price; **aumentar los precios** = to raise prices *o* to mark prices up; **se han aumentado estos precios en un 10%** = these prices have been marked up by 10%; **aumentar los precios exageradamente** = to inflate prices; **aumentar proporcionalmente** *o* **a escala** = to scale up; **la empresa ha aumentado la producción de los últimos modelos** = the company has stepped up production of the latest models; **el sindicato aumentó su demanda a 1.500 ptas. la hora** = the union raised its demand to 1,500 pesetas an hour; **esfuerzo para aumentar las ventas** = campaign to increase sales **(c)** *(valor)* to appreciate; **estas acciones han subido un 5%** = these shares have appreciated by 5% **2** *vi* to increase *o* to go up *o* to climb *o* to boom *o* to rise; **las ventas aumentan rápidamente** = sales are booming; **aumentar de tamaño** *o* **valor** = to increase in size *o* in value; **las ventas han aumentado en un 10%** = there is a rise in sales of 10% *o* sales show a rise of 10%; **las exportaciones a Africa han aumentado en más de un 25%** = exports to Africa have increased by more than 25%; **los costes están aumentando con rapidez** = costs are mounting up; **los salarios aumentan para compensar el alza del coste de la vida** = wages are increasing to keep up with the rise in the cost of living; **los beneficios aumentaron rápidamente cuando la nueva dirección redujo los costes** = profits climbed rapidly as the new management cut costs; **los costes administrativos parecen aumentar cada trimestre** = admin costs seem to be rising each quarter

> la deuda exterior española aumentó en un 29% al pasar de los 44.973 millones de dólares a los 58.071 contabilizados a finales de diciembre
> **El País**

aumento *nm* **(a)** *(subida)* increase *o* rise; **anunciar un aumento** = to announce *o* to post an increase; **porcentaje de aumento** = percentage increase; **un aumento fijo de un 10%** = a flat-rate increase of 10%; **los beneficios registraron un aumento del 10% sobre el pasado año** = profits showed a 10% increase *o* an increase of 10% on last year; **habrá un aumento persistente de la publicidad antes del lanzamiento del nuevo modelo** = there will be a big publicity buildup before the launch of the new model; **aumento del coste de la vida** = increase in the cost of living; **aumento impositivo** = increase in tax *o* tax increase; **planear un aumento de los intereses bancarios** = to plan for an increase in bank interest charges; **aumento de precios** = increase in price *o* price increase; **aumento anual de los precios** = annual increase in charges *o* annual price increase; **aumento repentino de precios** *o* **de las cifras de paro** = jump in prices *o* sudden rise in unemployment figures; **aumento de la rentabilidad** = gain in profitability; **los usuarios del tren se quejan del aumento de las tarifas** = rail travellers are complaining about rising fares; **aumento de sueldo** *o* **aumento salarial** = pay increase *o* salary increase *o* rise; *US* raise; **tuvo dos aumentos el año pasado** = he had two increases last year; **pidió un aumento a su jefe** = she asked her boss for a rise; *US* for a raise; **recibió un aumento del 6% en enero** = he had a 6% rise in January; **el gobierno espera que el aumento de los salarios se limite al 3%** = the government hopes to hold wage increases to 3%; **el aumento salarial es retroactivo al 1 de enero** = the pay increase is backdated to January 1st; **aumento de sueldo para compensar el aumento del coste de vida** = cost-of-living increase; **aumento salarial por méritos** = merit increase; **un aumento de las ventas** = a buildup in sales *o* an increase in sales; **hay un aumento de ventas de un 10%** = there is a rise in sales of 10% *o* sales show a rise of 10%; **el aumento de las ventas ha alcanzado un promedio del 15%** = sales increases have averaged out at 15% **(b)** *(valor)* appreciation **(c)** **en aumento** = on the increase; **los robos en las tiendas van en aumento** = stealing in shops is on the increase

> estas cuotas no suponen un aumento tributario respecto a las actuales licencias fiscales
> **Tiempo**

ausencia *nf* absence; **en ausencia de** = in the absence of; **en ausencia del presidente, su adjunto presidió la reunión** = in the absence of the chairman, his deputy took the chair

◊ **ausente 1** *adj* absent; **por estar ausente** = in the absence of; **el director gerente está ausente por motivos de trabajo** = the managing director is away on business; **ausente del trabajo** = away from work *o* off work; **mi secretaria está ausente por enfermedad** = my secretary is off sick **2** *nmf* **(a)** absentee **(b)** *(jurídico)* missing person

Australia *nf* Australia

◊ **australiano, -na** *adj y n* Australian
NOTA: capital: **Canberra**; moneda: **dólar australiano ($A)** = Australian dollar (A$)

Austria *nf* Austria

◊ **austríaco, -ca** *adj y n* Austrian
NOTA: capital: **Viena** (= Vienna); moneda: **chelín austríaco** = Austrian schilling (Sch)

autenticidad *nf* authenticity *o* genuineness; **certificar la autenticidad de una firma** = to certify a signature

◊ **auténtico, -ca** *adj* true *o* genuine *o* real; **un Picasso auténtico** = a genuine Picasso; **el artículo auténtico** = the genuine article; **su maleta es de**

cuero auténtico *o* **tiene una maleta de cuero auténtico** = his case is made of real leather *o* he has a real leather case

autentificar *vt* to authenticate

auto *nm* **(a)** *(legal)* sentence *o* judgement; **auto de embargo** = garnishee order *o* garnishment **(b)** *(coche)* car

auto- *prefijo* self-

◊ **autoadhesivo, -va** *adj* self-adhesive; **etiqueta autoadhesiva** = self-adhesive label

autobús *nm* bus; **empresa de autobuses** = bus company; **va al trabajo en autobús** = he goes to work by bus; **tomó el autobús para ir a la oficina** = she took the bus to go to her office

autoedición *nf* desk-top publishing (DTP)

autoempleo *nm* self-employment

autoexcluirse *vr* to opt out

◊ **autoexclusión** *nf* opt-out; **cláusula de autoexclusión** = opt-out clause

autofinanciación *nf* self-financing

◊ **autofinanciado, -da** *adj* self-supporting *o* self-financing *o* self-financed

autofinanciarse *vr* **la compañía se autofinancia completamente** = the company is completely self-financing *o* is completely self-financed

autolimitarse *vr* to set voluntary limits

automático, -ca *adj* automatic; **ajuste salarial automático** = automatic wage adjustment; **hay un aumento automático de salarios el 1 de enero** = there is an automatic pay increase on January 1st; **cajero automático** = cash dispenser *o* cashpoint *o* automatic telling machine (ATM); *US* automatic teller machine; **distribuidor automático** = automatic dispenser; **máquina expendedora automática** = automatic vending machine; *(informática)* **proceso automático de datos** ∷ automatic data processing

◊ **automáticamente** *adv* automatically; **las facturas se distribuyen automáticamente** = the invoices are sent out automatically; **las direcciones se escriben automáticamente** = addresses are typed in automatically; **se envía automáticamente una reclamación al vencimiento del pago de la factura** = a demand note is sent automatically when the invoice is overdue

automatización *nf* automation

automatizado, -da 1 *adj* automated; **una planta de montaje de automóviles totalmente automatizada** = a fully automated car assembly plant **2** *pp de* AUTOMATIZAR

automatizar *vt* to automate

automóvil *nm* car; **seguro de automóviles** = car insurance *o* motor insurance (NOTA: se abrevia **auto**)

autónomo, -ma *adj (que trabaja por su cuenta)* freelance *o* self-employed; **un trabajador autónomo** = a freelance *o* a freelancer; **los trabajadores autónomos** = the self-employed; **trabajar como autónomo** = to freelance *o* to work freelance

autopropulsado, -da *adj (barcos)* roll on/roll off

autor, -ra *n* **(a)** *(que realiza una acción o una obra)* author; **derechos de autor** = copyright; **ley de los derechos de autor** = copyright act; **nota sobre los derechos de autor** = copyright notice; **registrado con derechos de autor** = copyrighted; **titular de los derechos de autor** = copyright holder; **violación de los derechos de autor** = infringement of copyright *o* copyright infringement; **obra todavía protegida por los derechos de autor** = work still in copyright; **es ilegal fotocopiar una obra protegida por los derechos de autor** = it is illegal to photocopy a copyright work **(b)** *(proponente)* proposer; **autor de una moción** = proposer *o* mover of a motion

autorregulación *nf* self-regulation

◊ **autorregulado, -da** *adj* self-regulatory *o* self-regulated

autoservicio *nm* self-service *o* self-service store; *(gasolinera)* self-service petrol station; **autoservicio mayorista de pago al contado** = cash and carry

autoridad 1 *nf* **(a)** *(poder)* authority; **no tiene autoridad para actuar en nuestro nombre** = he has no authority to act on our behalf; **autoridad local** = local authority **(b)** *(de más tiempo)* seniority **2** *nfpl* **las autoridades** = the authorities; **autoridades portuarias** = port authority; **hay que pasar un periodo de prueba de seis meses para poder obtener una subvención de las autoridades locales** = there is a six-month qualifying period before you can get a grant from the local authority

autorización *nf* **(a)** *(acción de autorizar)* authorization; **dar la autorización a algo** = to authorize something *o* to give something the go-ahead; **¿tiene Vd. autorización para realizar este gasto?** = do you have authorization for this expenditure?; **la junta se negó a dar la autorización al plan de desarrollo** = the board refused to give the go-ahead to the expansion plan **(b)** *(documento oficial)* warrant; **certificado de autorización de salida de un buque** = (ship's) clearance papers

autorizado, -da 1 *adj* authorized *o* approved *o* accredited; **agente autorizado** = authorized dealer; **distribuidor autorizado** = authorized dealer; **emisión autorizada** = authorized capital; **persona autorizada** = authorized person *o* officially designated person; **precio máximo autorizado** = ceiling price; **no autorizado** *o* **desautorizado** = unauthorized; **acceso no autorizado a los archivos de la compañía** = unauthorized access to the company's records; **no está autorizado para**

actuar en nuestro nombre = he has no authorization to act on our behalf **2** *pp de* AUTORIZAR

autorizar *vt* to authorize *o* to empower *o* to give the green light *o* to entitle; **autorizar a alguien para que actúe en nombre de la compañía** = to authorize someone to act on the company's behalf; **autorizar el pago de 10.000 ptas.** = to authorize payment of 10,000 pesetas; **la compañía le autorizó a firmar el contrato** = she was empowered by the company to sign the contract; **dar luz verde a** *o* **autorizar un proyecto** = to give a project the green light

autosuficiencia *nf* self-sufficiency

◊ **autosuficiente** *adj* self-sufficient; **el país es autosuficiente en petróleo** = the country is self-sufficient in oil

auxiliar 1 *adj* auxiliary; **servicios auxiliares** = auxiliary services; **almacenamiento auxiliar** = back-up store; **ejecutivo auxiliar** = junior executive *o* junior manager **2** *nmf* assistant; **auxiliar de vuelo** = steward *o* stewardess *o* air hostess; **auxiliar administrativo** = office assistant *o* junior clerk

aval *nm* guarantee *o* endorsement; **aval bancario** = banker's reference; **aval financiero** = letter of comfort *o* comfort letter; **sin aval** = without guarantee

avalar *vt* **(a)** *(garantizar)* to guarantee; **avalar a alguien** = to stand security for someone *o* to go guarantee for someone; **avalar a una empresa asociada** = to guarantee an associate company; **avalar una deuda** = to guarantee a debt; **avalar una letra** = to back a bill; **avalar una letra de cambio** = to guarantee a bill of exchange **(b)** *(seguros)* to underwrite; **avalar una póliza de seguros** = to underwrite an insurance policy

> según la Confederación Española de Sociedades de Garantía Recíproca (CESGAR) se han avalado en España más de 71.000 pequeñas y medianas empresas por un valor superior a los 395.000 millones de pesetas. Estos avales ha contribuido a generar unos 231.000 nuevos empleos
> *El País*

avance *nm* advance *o* progress; **el director les felicitó por sus numerosos avances en su campo de investigación** = the director congratulated them on their progress in their field of research

> el aumento del desempleo ha echado por tierra en un sólo año los avances para reducir el paro logrados en los cinco ejercios precedentes
> *El País*

avanzar 1 *vt (dinero)* to advance (money) **2** *vi* to advance *o* to go forward *o* to progress; **avanzar lentamente** *o* **poco a poco** = to creep forward *o* to edge forward; **las negociaciones avanzan con normalidad** = negotiations are progressing normally; **el contrato avanza a través de varios departamentos** = the contract is progressing through various departments; **el proyecto avanza de acuerdo con lo previsto** = the project is on schedule

avenirse *vr* to compound (with creditors)

avería *nf* **(a)** *(falta)* damage *o* fault *o* breakdown;

no podemos comunicar con nuestra sucursal en Nigeria debido a la avería en las líneas telefónicas = we cannot communicate with our Nigerian office because of the breakdown of the telephone lines **(b)** *(seguros)* average; **perito de averías** = average adjuster; **avería gruesa** = general average; **avería simple** = particular average

◊ **averiarse** *vr* to break down *o* to get damaged; **se nos averió el coche en la autopista** = we broke down on the motorway *o* we had a breakdown on the motorway; **¿qué hace Vd. cuando se avería su fotocopiadora?** = what do you do when your photocopier breaks down?

avión *nm* plane *o* aircraft; **avión de carga** = cargo plane; **avión chárter** = charter plane; **ir en avión** = to go by plane *o* to fly; **mandar una carta por avión** = to send a letter by air; **fletar un avión** = to charter an aircraft; **éste no es el avión que va a París** = this is not the right plane for Paris; **se trata de una de las empresas norteamericanas más importantes de fabricantes de aviones** = the company is one of the most important American aircraft manufacturers

avisar *vt* to warn *o* to notify; **el director gerente nos avisó que llegaría tarde a la cita** = the MD warned us he would be late for the meeting; **avisó con seis meses de antelación** = he gave six months' notice

aviso *nm* **(a)** *(advertencia)* warning; **aviso de huelga** = strike warning *o* notice of strike action; **aviso de pago** = reminder; **publicar un aviso** = to issue a warning **(b)** **aviso de expedición** *o* **de envío** = advice note *o* notification; **poner un aviso** = to post up a notice; **hasta nuevo aviso** = until further notice; **debe pagar 20.000 ptas. el 30 de cada mes hasta nuevo aviso** = you must pay 20,000 pesetas on the 30th of each month until further notice; **la secretaria de la empresa puso un aviso sobre el programa de pensiones en el tablón de anuncios** = the company secretary put up a notice about the pension scheme

ayuda *nf* help *o* aid *o* assistance *o* relief *o* support; **ayuda financiera** = financial assistance; **ayuda en la oficina** = clerical assistance; **el procesador de textos le resulta de gran ayuda para escribir cartas** = she finds the word-processor a great help in writing letters; **su auxiliar no es de gran ayuda en la oficina - ni sabe escribir a máquina ni conducir** = her assistant is not much help in the office - he cannot type or drive; **ayuda estatal** *o* **del Estado** = *(compañías)* government support; *(individuos)* assistance *o* welfare; **el gobierno ha prestado ayuda a la industria electrónica** = the government has provided support to the electronics industry; **la compañía se fundó con ayuda financiera del Estado** = the company was set up with financial help from the government

> a partir de 1995 se produce un recorte en las ayudas a las empresas públicas
> *El País*

◊ **ayudante** *nmf* assistant; **ayudante a sueldo** = paid assistant

ayudar *vt* to help *o* to assist *o* to support; **él me ayuda a hacer la declaración de la renta** = he helps me with my income tax returns; **ayudó al vendedor a llevar su maleta de muestras** = he helped the salesman carry his case of samples; **esperamos que**

los bancos nos ayuden durante el periodo de expansión = we hope the banks will support us during the expansion period ; el gobierno ayuda a las empresas exportadoras con facilidades de crédito = the government helps exporting companies with easy credit

Ayuntamiento *nm* **(a)** *(edificio)* Town Hall *o* City Hall **(b)** *(corporación)* town council *o* city council

azafata *nf* hostess *o* stewardess; **azafata de congreso** = conference hostess; **azafata de vuelo** = air hostess; *US* airline hostess; **azafata de tierra** = ground hostess

azar *nm* **al azar** = at random; **el presidente eligió al azar los informes de dos vendedores** = the chairman picked out two salesmen's reports at random; **chequeo al azar** = random check

Bb

Bahamas (Las) *nfpl* the Bahamas; **(habitante) de Las Bahamas** = Bahamian
NOTA: capital: **Nassau**; moneda: **dólar de Las Bahamas (B$)** = Bahamian dollar (B$)

baile *nm* **baile de cifras** = number transposition

baja *nf* **(a)** *(precios, bolsa)* decline *o* dip *o* drop *o* fall; **durante el último año los salarios reales** *o* **los resultados de la compañía han experimentado una baja** = the last year has seen a decline in real wages *o* a dip in the company's performance; **la baja del precio del oro** = the fall in the price of gold; **mercado a la baja** = bear market *o* depressed market; **especular a la baja** = to be bearish; **tendencia a la baja** = bearish tendency; **con tendencia a la baja** = falling; **durante el último trimestre la economía tendió a la baja** = the last quarter saw a downturn in the economy **(b)** *(caída repentina)* slump; **baja repentina de beneficios** = slump in profits; **la peseta ha sufrido una baja repentina en los mercados de divisas** = the peseta slumped on the foreign exchange markets **(c)** *(en el trabajo)* leave; **baja por enfermedad** = sick leave; **darse de baja** = to give notice *o* to retire; **darse de baja de una revista** = to cancel a subscription to a magazine; **parte de baja** = doctor's certificate; **baja incentivada** *o* **baja voluntaria con derecho a indemnización** = voluntary redundancy; **baja por maternidad** *o* **paternidad** = maternity *o* paternity leave

> el mercado no ha tenido más remedio que
> ajustarse a la baja

> lo normal sería que la entidad que da el
> alta, dé la baja

bajada *nf* decrease; **bajada de precio** = decrease in price

bajar 1 *vi* **(a)** *(disminuir)* to decrease *o* to dip *o* to drop *o* to ease; **el valor de la peseta ha bajado un 5%** = the value of the peseta has decreased by 5%; **las ventas han bajado un 10%** = sales have dropped by 10% *o* have dropped 10%; **la peseta ha bajado tres puntos con respecto al dólar** = the peseta dropped three points against the dollar; **los precios de las acciones están bajando** = share prices are easier **(b)** *(descender)* to fall *o* to decline; **hoy las acciones bajaron en la bolsa** = shares fell on the market today; **el precio del oro bajó por segundo día consecutivo** = the price of gold fell for the second day running; **el poder adquisitivo de la peseta ha bajado durante los últimos años** = the buying power of the peseta has fallen in recent years; **bajar bruscamente** = to sink *o* to slump; **los precios bajaron bruscamente al hacerse público el cierre de la fábrica** = prices sank at the news of the closure of the factory; **las acciones bajaron fuertemente durante la jornada de ayer** = shares dipped sharply in yesterday's trading; **el precio de las acciones bajó en un mercado inactivo** = shares declined in a weak market **(c) bajar en picado** = to slide *o* to slip (back); **los beneficios bajaron a 300 millones de ptas.** = profits slipped to 300m pesetas; **los precios de la bolsa volvieron a bajar al cierre** = shares slipped back at the close; **bajar ligeramente** = to drift; **el precio de las acciones bajó ligeramente en un mercado poco activo** = shares drifted lower in a dull market; **el índice de cotización de las acciones ha bajado hoy ligeramente** = the share index eased slightly today **(d)** *(valor)* to lose value; **el dólar bajó dos centavos frente al yen** = the dollar lost two cents against the yen; **las acciones de las minas de oro bajaron ayer un 5% en el mercado** = gold shares lost 5% on the market yesterday **2** *vt* **(a)** *(reducir)* to bring down (prices) *o* to reduce to a lower price; **bajar los precios para conseguir una mayor participación en el mercado** = to lower prices to secure a larger market share; **obligar a bajar** *o* **hacer bajar los precios** = to force prices down; **la competencia ha hecho bajar los precios** = competition has forced prices down; **bajar el tipo de interés** = to lower the interest rate; **el banco se ha visto obligado a bajar considerablemente los tipos de interés** = the bank has been forced to slash interest rates **(b) bajar a alguien de categoría profesional** = to demote *o* downgrade someone; **en la reorganización de la empresa se le bajó de categoría** = his job was downgraded in the company reorganization

bajista 1 *adj* **mercado bajista** = bear market; **tendencia bajista** = bearish tendency **2** *nm (en la Bolsa)* bear

bajo, -ja 1 *adj* **(a)** *(precio)* low; **los bajos gastos generales mantienen bajo el coste unitario** = low overhead costs keep the unit cost low; **intentamos mantener bajos nuestros gastos de personal** = we try to keep our wages bill low; **un tipo de interés bajo** = a low rate of interest; **la peseta tiene un tipo de cambio muy bajo frente al dólar** = the peseta is at a very low rate of exchange against the dollar; **el precio más bajo posible** = the lowest price possible; **las acciones están al precio más bajo de los dos últimos años** = shares are at their lowest for two years; **ventas bajas** = low sales; **un volumen de ventas bajo** = low volume of sales; **la oferta más baja** = the lowest bidder; **el contrato se adjudicará a la oferta más baja** = the tender will go to the lowest bidder **(b)** *(calidad)* low; **artículos de baja calidad** = low quality merchandise *o* seconds; **intentaron vendernos acero de baja calidad** = they tried to sell us some low-quality steel; **en una reunión de bajo nivel se decidió aplazar la decisión** = a low-level meeting decided to put off making a decision **2** *prep* **bajo la jurisdicción del tribunal** = within the jurisdiction of the court; **fugarse estando bajo fianza** = to jump bail; **(hacer algo) bajo mano** = under the counter

bala *nf* bale; **2.520 balas de lana quedaron destruidas en el incendio** = 2,520 bales of wool were destroyed in the fire

balance *nm* **(a)** *(contabilidad)* balance; **el balance de la compañía es de 240.000 ptas.** = the company's balance stands at 240,000 pesetas;

balance de comprobación = trial balance; **balance final** *o* **último balance** = final accounts; **balance de resultados** = consolidated profit and loss account **(b)** *(estado de cuentas)* balance sheet *o* statement; **el balance de la compañía para 1995** = the company's balance sheet for 1995; **partidas de un balance** = items on a balance sheet; **el contable ha preparado el balance de situación del primer semestre** = the accountant has prepared the balance sheet for the first half-year; **balance detallado** = itemized statement; **balance general** = financial statement; **el balance general de la compañía para 1995 arroja unas pérdidas considerables** = the company balance sheet for 1995 shows a substantial loss; **el departamento de contabilidad ha preparado un balance general para los accionistas** = the accounts department has prepared a financial statement for the shareholders; **hacer balance** = to balance

balanza *nf* **(a)** *(instrumento)* weighing machine *o* scales **(b)** *(comercio)* **balanza comercial** = balance of trade *o* trade balance; **balanza comercial negativa** *o* **deficitaria** = adverse balance of trade; **balanza comercial desfavorable** *o* **con déficit** = unfavourable *o* negative balance of trade; **balanza comercial favorable** *o* **con superávit** = favourable *o* positive trade balance; **balanza de pagos** = balance of payments *o* current account

> la combinación de altos tipos de interés con una peseta fuerte amenaza directamente la estructura industrial y está creando un problema creciente de balanza de pagos
> **Actualidad Económica**

banca *nf* **la banca** = banking *o* the banking sector; **ha empezado a trabajar en la banca** = she has gone into banking; **está estudiando banca** = he is studying banking; **banca a distancia** = direct banking; **banca electrónica** = electronic banking; **banca telefónica** *o* **banca por teléfono** = phone banking *o* telebanking; **banca privada** = private banks

> la banca a distancia supondrá un gran cambio. El ordenador, el teléfono y la televisión serán un banco para casi todas las operaciones
> **Actualidad Económica**

> la banca telefónica o el empleo del teléfono como canal de distribución de productos y servicios financieros nació a mediados de los setenta en EEUU, de la mano de las grandes corporaciones
> **El País**

> la banca por teléfono hace muy accesible y personal la conexión entre el banco y el cliente, más allá del horario convencional de oficina
> **El País**

bancario, -ria *adj* **las acciones bancarias han atraído poco interés en la bolsa esta semana** = bank shares have attracted little interest *o* have been a neglected sector of the market this week; **cuenta bancaria** = bank account; **abrir una cuenta bancaria** = to open a bank account; **cerrar una cuenta bancaria** = to close a bank account; **tener una cuenta bancaria** = to have a bank account; **¿dónde tiene Vd. su cuenta bancaria?** = where do you have your bank account? *o* where is your bank account? *o* where do you bank?; **¿cuánto dinero tiene Vd. en su cuenta bancaria?** = how much money do you have in your bank account?; **cheque** *o* **talón bancario** = cheque; **crisis bancaria** = banking crisis; **depósitos bancarios** = bank deposits; **gastos bancarios** = bank charges; **giro bancario** = giro *o* banker's draft; **horario bancario** = banking hours; **letra bancaria** = bill of exchange; **transferencia bancaria** = bank transfer *o* bank giro transfer; **pagar por transferencia bancaria** = to pay by bank giro transfer; **orden de domiciliación bancaria** = standing order *o* direct debit; **pago mi suscripción por domiciliación bancaria** = I pay my subscription by standing order *o* by direct debit; **préstamo bancario** = bank loan *o* bank advance *o* bank borrowing; **pidió un préstamo bancario para empezar el negocio** = he asked for a bank loan to start his business; **la nueva fábrica fue financiada con un préstamo bancario** = the new factory was financed by bank borrowing

> la única forma de sobrevivir y superar la crisis bancaria que se extiende en este país de costa a costa es acaparar dinero fresco y en la máxima cantidad posible
> **El País**

bancarrota *nf* bankruptcy; **declararse en bancarrota** = to go bankrupt; **socio en bancarrota** = bankrupt partner

banco *nm* **(a)** bank; **banco por acciones** = joint-stock bank; **banco en casa** = home banking; **banco central** = central bank; **banco de cobros** = collecting agency; **banco comercial** = (i) clearing bank; (ii) acceptance house *o* accepting house; *US* acceptance bank; **banco de descuento** = discount house *o* discounter; **banco emisor** = issuing bank; **banco extraterritorial** *o* **situado en un paraíso fiscal** = off-shore bank; **Banco de España** = Bank of Spain; **Banco Europeo de Inversiones (BEI)** = European Investment Bank; **Banco Europeo de Reconstrucción y Desarrollo (BERD)** = European Bank for Reconstruction and Development; **banco exterior** = foreign trade bank; **Banco Hipotecario de España** = Spanish Mortgage Bank; **Banco de Inglaterra** = Bank of England; **Banco Lloyds** = Lloyds Bank; **el Banco Mundial** = the World Bank; **banco nacional** = national bank; **banco de negocios** *o* **mercantil** = merchant bank; **Banco de Pagos Internacionales (BPI)** = Bank for International Settlements (BIS); **los bancos de la Reserva Federal** = *US* the Federal Reserve Banks; **Banco de Santander** = Bank of Santander; **depósitó todos sus ingresos en el banco** = he put all his earnings in the bank; **tiene el respaldo de un banco australiano** = he has the backing of an Australian bank; **tomó en préstamo 1 millón de ptas. del banco** = he borrowed 1m pesetas from the bank; **billetes de banco** = bank notes; **sacó un montón de billetes de banco usados** = he pulled out a pile of used bank notes; **cajero de un banco** = teller; **director de banco** = bank manager; **horario de oficina de los bancos** = banking hours; **orden de pago domiciliada a través del banco** = banker's order **(b) banco de datos** = data bank

banda *nf* **(a)** *(expresión gráfica de una variable económica)* band; **banda de fluctuación** = exchange rate band; **banda impositiva** = tax band; **banda salarial** = wage scale **(b)** *(tira)* strip; **banda magnética** = magnetic strip

bandeja *nf* **(a)** *(recipiente plano)* tray; **bandeja de documentos para archivar** = filing tray *o* basket; **bandeja de documentos despachados** *o* **bandeja de documentos ya cumplimentados** = out tray; **bandeja de asuntos pendientes** = pending tray; **bandeja de entrada** *o* **de documentos por despachar** = in tray **(b)** *(paleta)* pallet

bandera *nf* flag *o* banner; **embarcación de bandera británica** = a ship flying a British flag

Bangladesh *nm* Bangladesh; **de Bangladesh** = Bangladeshi
NOTA: capital **Dacca**; moneda: **taka de Bangladesh** = Bangladesh taka

banquero, -ra *n* banker; **banquero de negocios** = merchant banker

bar *nm* bar; **los representantes de ventas se reunieron en el bar del hotel** = the sales reps met in the bar of the hotel

barato, -ta 1 *adj* cheap *o* inexpensive *o* economical; **estos artículos son realmente baratos** = these goods are really cheap; **resultan más baratos comprándolos por cajas** = they work out cheaper by the box; **mano de obra barata** = cheap labour; **hemos abierto una fábrica en Extremo Oriente porque la mano de obra es barata** = we have opened a factory in the Far East because of the cheap labour *o* because labour is cheap; **dinero** *o* **crédito barato** = cheap money **2** *adv* cheaply; **comprar algo barato** = to buy something cheap; **vender más barato** = to sell more cheaply *o* to sell cheaper *o* to undercut; **no hay otra compañía que venda más barato** = the company is never undersold; **es más barato viajar en tren que en avión** = rail travel is cheaper than air travel

◊ **baratura** *nf* cheapness

Barbados *nf* Barbados

◊ **(habitante) de Barbados** *adj y n* Barbadian
NOTA: capital: **Bridgetown**; moneda: **dólar de Barbados (BDS$)** = Barbados dollar (BDS$)

barcaza *nf* lighter

barco *nm* boat *o* ship *o* vessel; **barco de carga** = cargo boat *o* ship; **barco de pasajeros** = passenger boat *o* liner; **cogimos el barco de noche para Mallorca** = we took the night boat to Majorca; **todas las mañanas salen** *o* **zarpan barcos para Grecia** = boats for Greece leave every morning; **un barco cargado de hierro** = a ship loaded with iron; **barco fletado** = chartered ship; **barco fletado por el Sr. González** = boat on charter to Sr Gonzalez

baremo *nm* scale; **baremo fijo** = fixed scale of charges; **baremo equitativo de contribuciones** = graduated tax system

barra *nf* **(a)** *(metal)* ingot *o* bar; **barra de oro** = gold bar **(b)** *(teclado)* **barra espaciadora** = space bar **(c)** **diagrama** *o* **gráfico de barras** = bar chart

barrera *nf* barrier; **barrera arancelaria** = custom barrier *o* tariff barrier; **imponer barreras comerciales** *o* **arancelarias a ciertos productos** = to impose trade barriers *o* tariff barriers on certain goods; **los sindicatos han pedido al gobierno que imponga barreras comerciales a la importación de automóviles** = the unions have asked the government to impose trade barriers on foreign cars; **levantar barreras comerciales** *o* **arancelarias a ciertos productos** = to lift trade barriers *o* tariff barriers from certain goods; **suprimir las barreras comerciales a la importación** = to lift trade barriers from imports; **el gobierno ha suprimido las barreras comerciales a la importación de automóviles** = the government has lifted trade barriers from foreign cars; **una barrera contra la inflación** = a hedge against inflation; **barrera de entrada** *o* **de salida** = barriers to entry *o* to exit

barril *nm* *(medida de capacidad)* barrel; **compró veinticinco barriles de vino** = he bought twenty-five barrels of wine; **vender vino por barriles** = to sell wine by the barrel; **el precio del petróleo ha subido a 30 dólares el barril** = the price of oil has reached $30 a barrel

barrio *nm* neighbourhood *o* district *o* suburb; **los barrios bajos** = the slums

basado, -da 1 *adj* based **2** *pp de* BASAR

basar *vt* to base; **basamos nuestros cálculos en la previsión del volumen de ventas** = we based our calculations on the forecast turnover; **basado en** = based on; **basado en las cifras del año pasado** = based on last year's figures; **basado en previsiones de población** = based on population forecasts

◊ **basarse** *vr* to be based on

báscula *nf* weighing machine; **báscula puente** *o* **puente-báscula** = weighbridge

base *nf* **(a)** *(fundamento)* basis; **prevemos el volumen de ventas en base a un aumento del precio de un 6%** = we forecast the turnover on the basis of a 6% price increase; **las cifras de 1992 son su única base de información** = the figures for 1992 are all he has to go on; **el volumen de ventas aumentó el 200%, partiendo sin embargo de una base baja** = turnover increased by 200%, but starting from a low base; **año base** = base year; **expresado en base anual** = annualized; **tipo de interés expresado en base anual** = annualized percentage rate (APR); **base imponible** = tax base; **cálculo de la base impositiva** = tax assessment; **base monetaria** = monetary base; **precio base** = basic price; **rendimiento base** = basic yield; **salario base** *o* **sueldo base** = basic pay *o* basic salary *o* basic wage; *o US* base pay; **tipo base de interés bancario** = bank base rate **(b)** *(normas)* element; **las bases de un acuerdo** = the elements of a settlement **(c)** *(política)* ordinary member; **los afiliados de base del sindicato** = the ordinary trade union members *o* the rank and file of the trade union membership; **la decisión no gustó a las bases** = the decision was not liked by the rank and file **(d)** *(sede)* base; **tiene una oficina en Madrid que emplea como base cuando viaja por el sur de Europa** = he has an office in Madrid which he uses as a base while he is travelling in Southern Europe; **un ejecutivo de ventas con base en Madrid** = a Madrid-based sales executive **(e)** *(informática)* **base de datos** = database; **podemos extraer las listas de clientes potenciales de nuestra base de datos** = we can extract the lists of potential customers from our database

BASIC *nm (lenguaje de programa)* BASIC

básico, -ca *adj* **(a)** *(de primera necesidad)* primary *o* basic; **productos básicos** = primary *o* basic commodities *o* products **(b)** *(normal)* basic; **coste básico de producción** = prime cost; **descuento básico** = basic discount; **necesita un conocimiento básico del mercado para trabajar en la Bolsa** = he needs a basic knowledge of the market to work on the Stock Exchange; **necesita una preparación básica en matemáticas** = you need a basic qualification in maths

◊ **básicamente** *adv* basically

bastante 1 *adj* enough *o* quite a lot; **no tiene bastante tiempo libre** = he has not got very much free time; **la nueva empresa tiene bastantes clientes** = the new firm has quite a lot of clients; **llegan bastantes pedidos antes de la Navidad 2** *adv* fairly *o* quite *o* rather; **es un vendedor bastante bueno** = he is quite a good salesman; **las ventas han sido bastante satisfactorias en el primer trimestre** = sales are pretty satisfactory in the first quarter; **estamos bastante hartos de trabajar los fines de semana** = we are fed up with working at weekends; **andamos bastante escasos de personal en este momento** = we are rather shorthanded at the moment; **está bastante ocupado en este momento** = he is rather tied up at the moment

basura *nf* junk *o* rubbish; *ver* BONOS-BASURA

batería *nf* battery

batir *vt* to beat *o* to smash; **batir todos los records de producción** = to smash all production records; **las ventas han batido todos los records en el primer semestre del año** = sales have smashed all records for the first half of the year

bazar *nm* bazaar *o* market place

Bélgica *nf* Belgium

◊ **belga** *adj y n* Belgian
NOTA: capital: **Bruselas** (= Brussels); moneda: **franco belga (FB)** = Belgian franc (BF)

beca *nf* grant *o* award *o* scholarship; **comisión de becas** = grants committee

benefactor, -ra *adj* beneficient; **estado benefactor** *o* **del bienestar** = welfare state

beneficiar 1 *vt* to benefit; **la inflación no beneficia la economía** = inflation does not help the economy **2** *vi* to be of benefit; **su comportamiento en este asunto no beneficia a nadie** = his attitude on this question is of no help to anyone

◊ **beneficiarse de** *vr* to benefit from *o* to profit from; **las exportaciones se han beneficiado de la caída del tipo de cambio** = exports have benefited from the fall in the exchange rate; **los empleados se han beneficiado del plan de participación en los beneficios** = the employees have benefited from the profit-sharing scheme

beneficiario, -ria *n* beneficiary *o* payee *o* recipient; **los beneficiarios de un testamento** = the beneficiaries of a will; **el beneficiario de un subsidio** = the recipient of an allowance; **beneficiario** *o* **persona beneficiaria de una póliza** = person named in the policy; **beneficiario proindiviso** = joint beneficiary

beneficio *nm* **(a)** benefit *o* profit *o* return; **beneficio bruto** = gross profit; **¿cuál es el beneficio bruto de estos productos?** = what is the gross return on this line?; **obtener unos beneficios brutos** = to make a gross profit *o* to gross; **el grupo obtuvo unos beneficios brutos de 5.000 millones en 1995** = the group grossed 5,000m in 1995; **beneficios complementarios** *o* **extrasalariales** = fringe benefits; **beneficio considerable** = healthy profit; **beneficio de ejercicio** = trading profit; **beneficios de la empresa** = corporate profits; **beneficio de explotación** = operating *o* trading profit; **beneficios extraordinarios** = excess profit; **beneficio hasta la fecha de rescate** = redemption yield; **beneficios imputables** = attributable profits; **beneficio neto** = net profit *o* net income *o* clear profit; **sacamos un beneficio neto de 600.000 ptas. en la transacción** = we made 600,000 pesetas clear profit on the deal; **los beneficios de una venta** = the proceeds of a sale; **baja repentina de beneficios** = slump in profits; **los beneficios han bajado bruscamente** = profits have slumped; **maximizar los beneficios** = to maximize profits; **impuesto sobre los beneficios** = profits tax *o* tax on profits; **impuesto sobre los beneficios extraordinarios** = excess profits tax; **beneficio antes de deducir impuestos** *o* **beneficio sin deducir impuestos** = pretax profit *o* profit before tax; **beneficios después de deducir impuestos** = after-tax profit; **margen de beneficio** = profit margin; **obtener beneficios** = to make a profit; **la compañía trata de conseguir beneficios rápidos de sus inversiones** = the company is looking for quick returns on its investments; **empezar a obtener beneficios** = to move into profit; **la compañía ha cubierto gastos y espera empezar a obtener beneficios en los próximos dos meses** = the company is breaking even now, and expects to move into profit within the next two months; **participación en los beneficios** = profit-sharing; **realizar beneficios** = to take one's profit; **beneficio no realizado** *o* **ficticio** *o* **sobre el papel** = paper profit; **su inversión arroja un beneficio sobre el papel de 5 millones de ptas.** = he is showing a paper profit of 5m pesetas on his investment; **mostrar** *o* **registrar beneficios** = to show a profit; **hemos**

registrado un escaso beneficio en el primer trimestre = we are showing a small profit for the first quarter; vender con beneficio = to sell at a profit; compró dos compañías a bajo precio y las vendió con beneficio = he bought two companies cheap and sold them again at a profit; reducción de la tasa de beneficio = fall in profits o profit squeeze (b) (aumento en ganancia o precio o valor) gain o earning; los valores de las sociedades inmobiliarias registraron unos beneficios del 10% al 15% = property shares put on gains of 10%-15%; beneficios a corto plazo = short-term gains; haber obtenido un beneficio de 25.000 ptas. = to have made 25,000 pesetas o to be 25,000 pesetas in pocket; beneficios no distribuidos = retained earnings o income o undistributed profits; el balance incluye 10.000.000 de ptas. de beneficios no distribuidos = the balance sheet has 10,000,000 pesetas in retained income (c) (ventaja) payoff; uno de los beneficios de las carreras universitarias es que permiten una mayor rentabilidad económica = one of the payoffs of a university degree is increased earning power

◊ **beneficioso, -sa** adj cost-effective o profitable o beneficial

◊ **benéfico, -ca** adj beneficial; sociedad benéfica = friendly society

estimamos que los beneficios anuales para el consumidor superan los 10.000 millones de dólares
Mercado

los beneficios netos por acción han subido de 57,2 pesetas a 1.200 este año
España Económica

Benín nm Benin

◊ **(habitante) de Benín** adj y n Beninois
NOTA: capital: **Porto Novo**; moneda: **franco CFA (FCFA)** = CFA franc (CFAF)

'bestseller' nm (éxito de venta) best-seller

bi- prefijo bi-

bianualmente adv bi-annually

bien 1 nm commodity; bien de primera necesidad = basic necessity; bien económico = economic good **2** adv well o properly; bien pagado, -da = well-paid; un trabajo bien hecho = a job well done

◊ **bienes** nmpl (a) (propiedad) possessions o assets; perdieron todos sus bienes en el incendio = they lost all their possessions in the fire; sus bienes han sido bloqueados por los tribunales = his assets have been frozen by the court; bienes inmuebles o bienes raíces = real estate; bienes muebles = moveable property o personal property; bienes personales = personal assets; bienes raíces = real estate; legado de bienes raíces = devise; legatario de bienes raíces = devisee; bienes tangibles o fijos = tangible assets o property (b) (en una empresa) goods o commodities; bienes de capital = capital goods; desgravación sobre bienes de capital = capital allowances; la compañía se deshizo de sus bienes en los Estados Unidos = the company had divested itself of its assets in the States; bienes de consumo = consumer goods o consumable goods; bienes de consumo duraderos = consumer durables; bienes duraderos = durable goods; bienes de equipo = capital equipment; bienes perecederos

= non-durables o perishable goods; bienes sujetos a derechos de aduana = dutiable goods o dutiable items

las facturas se expiden en forma de venta de bienes o prestación de servicios por personas o sociedades inactivas o en quiebra
Cambio 16

se aprecia una desaceleración en la producción de bienes de inversión
España Económica

bienal adj (cada dos años) biennial

bienestar nm welfare; el presidente está interesado en el bienestar de las familias de los trabajadores = the chairman is interested in the welfare of the workers' families; estado del bienestar = welfare state

la expansión económica a largo plazo es el factor más importante para el éxito o el fracaso de una nación y es, sin duda, la base fundamental del progreso del bienestar de la población en su conjunto
Mercado

bifurcación nf (a) (cambio) change of plan o development (b) (ramificación) branching o junction

es una bifurcación que no ha hecho más que iniciarse y que a medida que se desarrolle tendrá importantes consecuencias
Mercado

bilateral adj bilateral; comercio bilateral = bilateral trade o two-way trade; el ministro firmó un convenio bilateral de comercio = the minister signed a bilateral trade agreement

billete nm (a) (transporte) ticket o fare; billete de abono = season ticket; billete de ida = single ticket; US one-way ticket; quiero dos billetes de ida a Londres = I want two singles to London; billete de ida y vuelta = return ticket; US round-trip ticket; billete en lista de espera = standby ticket; un billete de primera clase o de segunda clase = a first-class o a second-class ticket; billete de tren o de autobús o de avión = train ticket o bus ticket o plane ticket; billete valedero para tres meses = ticket which is valid for three months; máquina expendedora de billetes = ticket machine (b) (papel o etiqueta) ticket; billete de consigna = baggage ticket (c) (nota de banco) billete de banco = bank note o banknote o currency note; US bill; (letra de cambio) bank bill; un billete de 5.000 ptas. = a 5,000 peseta note; un billete de $5 = a $5 bill; cambiar un billete de 10.000 ptas. = to change a 10,000 peseta note

◊ **billetera** nf wallet

billón nm GB billion; US trillion

el fraude fiscal en España puede llegar a dos billones de pesetas
Cambio 16

bimensual adj (quincena) twice-monthly

◊ **bimensualmente** adv (quincenalmente) bi-monthly

bimestral adj (cada dos meses) bi-monthly

Birmania nf Burma

◇ **birmano, -na** *adj y n* Burmese
NOTA: capital: **Rangoon;** moneda: **kyat birmano (K)**
= Burmese kyat (K)

bit *nm (informática)* bit

blanco, -ca 1 *adj* white; **rebajas de ropa blanca**
= white sale **2** *nf (antigua moneda española)* **estar**
sin blanca = to be flat broke **3** *nm* white; **en blanco** =
blank; **un cheque en blanco** = a blank cheque;
espacio en blanco = box *o* blank space (on a form);
rellene los espacios en blanco y devuelva el
formulario a su oficina local = fill in the blanks and
return the form to your local office

blando, -da *adj* soft; **crédito blando** = soft loan;
disco blando = floppy disk

blanquear *vt* **blanquear dinero negro** = to
launder money; **blanquear dinero a través de un**
banco de un paraíso fiscal = to launder money
through an offshore bank

◇ **blanqueo** *nm* **blanqueo de dinero** = money
laundering

bloc *nm* pad; **bloc de notas** = memo pad *o* note pad;
bloc de mesa = desk pad

bloque *nm* block; **tienen en proyecto un bloque**
de oficinas de 30 pisos = they are planning a
30-storey high office block; **reserva en bloque** =
block booking; **la empresa ha hecho una reserva**
en bloque de veinte plazas en el avión *o* **de diez**
habitaciones en el hotel = the company has a block
booking for twenty seats on the plane *o* for ten rooms
at the hotel

bloqueado, -da 1 *adj* blocked *o* frozen;
moneda bloqueada = blocked currency; **la**
empresa tiene una cuenta enorme de rublos
bloqueados = the company has a large account in
blocked roubles **2** *pp de* BLOQUEAR

bloquear *vt* to block *o* to freeze *o* to jam *o* to
deadlock; **el comité de planificación bloqueó el**
plan de reorganización = the planning committee
blocked the redevelopment plan; **sus bienes han**
sido bloqueados por los tribunales = his assets
have been frozen by the court; **bloquear los créditos**
= to freeze credits; **bloquear los dividendos de la**
compañía = to freeze company dividends; **bloquear**
una cuenta = to put an account on stop *o* to block an
account

bloqueo *nm* freezing *o* blocking; **bloqueo**
económico = embargo

bocadillo *nm* sandwich

bodega *nf* **(a)** *(tienda)* wine merchant; *GB* off-
licence; *US* liquor store **(b)** *(almacén de vinos)* cellar
(c) *(barco)* hold

boicot *nm* boycott; **el sindicato organizó un**
boicot contra los coches de importación = the
union organized a boycott against *o* of imported
cars; **el sindicato ha declarado el boicot contra**
una empresa de transporte = the union has blacked
a trucking firm

◇ **boicotear** *vt* to boycott; **estamos boicoteando**
todas las importaciones de aquel país = we are
boycotting all imports from that country; **la**
patronal ha boicoteado la reunión = the
management has boycotted the meeting

boletín *nm* **(a)** *(revista)* journal *o* bulletin; **boletín**
informativo de una empresa = company
newsletter; **boletín interno de una empresa** =
house journal *o* house magazine; **Boletín Oficial del**
Estado (BOE) = Official State Bulletin (in Spain)
(b) *(comercial)* **boletín de inscripción** =
registration form; **boletín de pedido** = application
form; **boletín de respuesta** = reply coupon; **adjuntó**
un boletín de respuesta internacional a su carta =
he enclosed an international reply coupon with his
letter; **boletín de suscripción** = subscription form

Bolivia *nf* Bolivia

◇ **boliviano, -na** *adj y n* Bolivian
NOTA: capital: **La Paz;** moneda: **peso boliviano ($b)**
= Bolivian peso ($b)

bolsa *nf* **(a)** *(lonja)* Stock Exchange; stock market;
la Bolsa de Nueva York = the New York Stock
Exchange; **especular en la bolsa** *o* **jugar a la bolsa**
= to speculate on the Stock Exchange; **opera en la**
bolsa = he deals *o* he is a dealer on the Stock
Exchange; **trabaja en la bolsa** = he works on the
Stock Exchange; **acciones que se cotizan en bolsa** =
quoted shares; **acciones que no se cotizan en bolsa**
o **títulos no cotizados en bolsa** = unlisted securities
o unquoted shares; **las acciones de la compañía se**
cotizan en la bolsa = shares in the company are
traded on the Stock Exchange; **agente** *o* **corredor de**
bolsa = stockbroker; **manipulador de la bolsa** =
stock market manipulator; **periodo de crédito en la**
bolsa = account; **una venta en la bolsa** = a bargain;
agente de bolsa autónomo = independent
stockbroker; *US* stag; **ha ganado mucho dinero en**
la bolsa = he has made a good deal of money on the
stock market; **la bolsa bajó ligeramente ayer** = the
Stock Exchange fell slightly yesterday; **las acciones**
de la compañía se venden raramente en la bolsa =
the company's shares are rarely sold on the Stock
Exchange **(b)** **bolsa de contratación** = commodity
market *o* commodity exchange; **bolsa de trabajo** =
job centre **(c)** *(saco)* bag; **bolsa de la compra** =
shopping bag; **trajo sus documentos en una bolsa**
de El Corte Inglés = he brought his files in a bag
from El Corte Inglés; **bolsa de plástico** = plastic bag
o carrier bag; **regalamos 5.000 bolsas de plástico**
en la exposición = we gave away 5,000 plastic bags
at the exhibition **(d)** *(en periódico)* **Bolsa de la**
Propiedad = Property Section *o* Properties To Let *o*
Properties For Sale **(e)** *(pequeña)* **bolsita** = sachet

bolsillo *nm* pocket; **calculadora** *o* **agenda de**
bolsillo = pocket calculator *o* pocket diary; **edición**
de bolsillo = pocket edition

bolsín *nm* local stock exchange

bombo *nm* *(publicidad)* hype; **hacer publicidad**
con mucho bombo = to hype; **todo el bombo que**
acompaña el lanzamiento del nuevo jabón = all
the hype surrounding the launch of the new soap

bonanza *nf* boom *o* prosperity; **periodo de**

bonanza económica = period of economic prosperity o boom period

> tanto en tiempo de crisis como de bonanza económica, los aspectos comerciales de la venta de productos o servicios no dejan de estar de moda
>
> **El País**

bonificación *nf* **(a)** *(gratificación)* allowance o bonus o weighting; **bonificación de capital** = capital bonus; **cuando se retiró le dieron una bonificación** = when he retired he was given a lump-sum bonus; **bonificación por ausencia de siniestralidad** o **de reclamaciones** = no-claims bonus; **bonificación recibida al concluir un seguro** = terminal bonus **(b)** *(descuento)* discount o rebate

bono *nm* **(a)** *(finanzas)* bond; **los bonos producen un interés del 10%** = the bonds carry interest at 10%; **bonos del Estado** o **bonos del Tesoro** = government bonds o treasury bonds; **bono municipal** o **de la administración local** = municipal bond o local authority bond; **bonos-basura** = junk bonds; **bono de caja** = short-term bond; **vender un bono** = to redeem a bond; **bono de interés fijo** = debenture; **bono hipotecario** = mortgage bond **(b)** *(general)* voucher; **bono de empresa para comida** = luncheon voucher

> las rentabilidades negociadas en la contratación a plazo en los bonos del Estado a tres años experimentaron subidas de más de 0,20 puntos porcentuales
>
> **Mercado**

boom *nm (del inglés)* boom

> la economía de los Estados Unidos dispone del potencial para aumentar el ahorro en cuanto la generación del baby boom envejezca
>
> **Mercado**

> en 1986, primer año del boom económico registramos un superávit del 1,7% del PIB; en 1990 habíamos pasado a un déficit del 3,5%
>
> **Cambio 16**

borde *nm* edge; **se sentó en el borde de la mesa del director** = he sat on the edge of the managing director's desk; **la impresora ha impreso las cifras hasta el borde del papel** = the printer has printed the figures right to the edge of the printout; **al borde de** = on the verge of o on the brink of; **la compañía está al borde de la ruina financiera** = the company is on the brink of financial collapse; **la compañía estaba al borde de la quiebra** = the company was on the verge of bankruptcy

bordo *nm (náutico)* **a bordo** = on board (ship); **franco a bordo** = free on board (f.o.b.); **diario de a bordo** = ship's log o log-book

borrador *nm* **(a)** *(proyecto)* draft; **el departamento de contabilidad hizo el borrador de cuentas a tiempo para la junta** = the accounts department put out the draft accounts in time for the meeting; **el director de finanzas hizo un borrador de un plan de inversiones** = the finance director roughed out a plan of investment; *(impresora)* **calidad borrador** = draft quality **(b)** *(primera versión)* rough copy o first draft; **preparó un borrador del nuevo diseño** = he made a rough draft

of the new design; **borrador de un acuerdo** = draft agreement; **borrador de un contrato** = draft of a contract o draft contract; **el primer borrador del contrato fue corregido por el director gerente** = the first draft of the contract was corrected by the managing director **(c)** *(papel para notas)* notepaper o scribbling pad o day book

> el Gobierno estudia en estos días los primeros borradores del nuevo plan de convergencia económica acordado en la última reunión de presidentes de Estado y de Gobierno
>
> **Tiempo**

borrar *vt* to cross off o to erase o to remove; **podemos borrar su nombre de la lista de destinatarios** = we can remove his name from the mailing list; **cortaron la luz y toda la información se borró del ordenador** = there was a power cut and all the data was wiped off the computer

bosquejo *nm* outline o rough draft

bote *nm* kitty

Botsuana *nm* Botswana; **de Botsuana** = Botswanan
NOTA: capital: **Gaborone**; moneda: **pula** = pula

boutique *nf* boutique; **las boutiques del centro** = the High Street boutiques

bracero *nm (peón agrícola)* day labourer

Brasil *nm* Brazil

◊ **brasileño, -ña** o **brasilero, -ra** *adj y n* Brazilian
NOTA: capital: **Brasilia**; moneda: **real** = real

brazo *nm* arm; *(hombre de confianza)* **brazo derecho** = right-hand man; **cruzarse de brazos** = to sit back and do nothing; **huelga de brazos caídos** = sit-down strike

breve *adj* short o brief; **en breve** = very soon o shortly

bricolaje *nm* do-it-yourself; **revista de bricolaje** = do-it-yourself magazine; **tienda de bricolaje** = do-it-yourself store o hardware store; **la empresa ha gastado millones en introducirse en el mercado del bricolaje** = the company has spent millions trying to enter the do-it-yourself market

británico, -ca *adj y n* British; **es de nacionalidad británica** = he is of British nationality o he is a British national

bronca *nf* **(a)** row o fuss; **armaron una gran bronca en la sección de muebles** = they made a great fuss o they kicked up a row in the furniture department **(b)** **echar una bronca a alguien** = to give someone a ticking-off

brusco,-ca *adj* abrupt o sudden o sharp

◊ **bruscamente** *adverb* abruptly o suddenly o sharply; **bajar bruscamente** = to slump; **los precios bajaron bruscamente al hacerse público el cierre de la fábrica** = prices sank at the news of the closure of the factory

Bruselas *nf* Brussels

bruto, -ta *adj* gross; **beneficio bruto** = gross

profit; **facturación** o **producción bruta** = gross turnover; **ingresos brutos** = gross earnings o gross receipts; **margen bruto** = gross margin; **el margen bruto varía de trimestre en trimestre** = the gross margin varies from quarter to quarter; **nuestra política de precios tiene como objeto que nos quede un 35% de margen bruto** = our pricing policy aims at producing a 35% gross margin; **peso bruto** = gross weight; **producto interior bruto (PIB)** = gross domestic product (GDP); **producto nacional bruto (PNB)** = gross national product (GNP); **rendimiento bruto** = gross yield; **renta bruta** = gross income; **sueldo bruto** = gross salary; **le pagan el sueldo bruto** = his salary is paid gross; **tonelaje bruto** = gross tonnage

bueno, -na adj good; **una buena compra** = a good buy; **comprar algo de buena fe** = to buy something in good faith; **un viaje comercial a Alemania con buenos resultados** = a successful selling trip to Germany (NOTA: se emplea **buen** delante de nm) **un buen número** = a good many; **de buen rendimiento** = efficient; **nos dio muy buen consejo** = he gave us some very sound advice

bufete nm bufete de abogados = firm of solicitors o lawyers' office o barristers' chambers

buhonero nm hawker o street vendor

Bulgaria nf Bulgaria

◊ **búlgaro, -ra** adj y n Bulgarian
NOTA: capital: **Sofía** (= Sofia); moneda: **lev búlgaro** = Bulgarian lev

Bundesbank nm (Banco Central de Alemania) Bundesbank

en el mercado alemán lo más notable esta semana ha sido el mantenimiento de los tipos de interés oficiales del Bundesbank
El País

buque nm ship o vessel; **buque de carga** = cargo ship o cargo vessel o freighter; **buque mercante** = merchant ship o merchant vessel o merchantman; **abastecedor de buques** = ship chandler; **buque cisterna** = tanker; **buque de contenedores** = container ship; **buque en perfectas condiciones** = ship which is A1 at Lloyd's; **buque gemelo (de la misma flota)** = sister ship; **buque para carga a granel** = bulk carrier

burbuja nf bubble; **embalaje de plástico tipo burbuja** = bubble pack o bubble wrap

burocracia nf bureaucracy o red tape

bursátil adj agente bursátil = stockbroker; mercado bursátil = stock exchange o stock market; **valor de las acciones de una compañía a precio de mercado bursátil** = stock market valuation; **sesión bursátil** = trading session

lleva más de veinte años trabajando en este país como agente bursátil
España Económica

Burundi nm Burundi

◊ **(habitante) de Burundi** adj y n Burundian
NOTA: capital: **Bujumbura**; moneda: **franco de Burundi (FBu)** = Burundi franc (BuF)

buscar vt/i to look for o to search for; **está buscando clientes para su peluquería** = he's canvassing for customers for his hairdresser's shop; **buscar en las tiendas** = to shop (for something); **buscó el número de la compañía en la guía telefónica** = he looked up the number of the company in the telephone book; **está buscando un trabajo de responsabilidad en el ámbito del marketing** = he is looking for a responsible job in marketing; **la empresa busca a alguien que haya tenido éxito en la industria electrónica** = the company is looking for someone with a background of success in the electronics industry; **la compañía perdió mucho tiempo buscando asesoramiento profesional** = the company lost a great deal of time seeking expert advice

búsqueda nf search; **búsqueda de clientes** o **de votos** = door-to-door canvassing; **técnicas de búsqueda de clientes** o **de votos** = canvassing techniques; **búsqueda de ejecutivos** o **directivos** = executive search; **búsqueda (de puestos) de trabajo** = job search

buzón nm mail box o letter box; **buzón de sugerencias** = suggestions box

byte nm (informática) byte

Cc

caballero *nm* gentleman; 'caballeros' = 'gentlemen'; **acuerdo entre caballeros** = gentleman's agreement; *US* gentlemen's agreement

cabecera *nf* head; *(de un periódico o documento)* headline *o* heading *o* title

> Grupo Zeta es hoy en día una empresa de medios de comunicación desarrollada, un conglomerado de 27 cabeceras distintas
> **Tiempo**

caber *vi* **(a)** *(entrar)* to fit in *o* to go in; **¿cabrá el ordenador en esa sala tan pequeña?** = will the computer fit into that little room? **(b)** *(contener)* to contain *o* to hold; **en una bolsa caben veinte kilos de azúcar** = a bag can hold twenty kilos of sugar

cabeza *nf* **(a)** *(parte del cuerpo)* head; **meter en la cabeza** = to get through to someone *o* to make someone understand **(b)** *(parte o persona principal)* top; **cabeza de familia** = head of the household *o* householder; **empresa a la cabeza de un sector** = a market leader; **estar a la cabeza** = to head *o* to head up; **está a la cabeza de una misión comercial a China** = he is heading a buying mission to China; **ir en cabeza** = to head *o* to lead *o* to be at the top of; **la empresa va en cabeza de sus competidores en el sector de los ordenadores baratos** = the company leads the market in cheap computers **(c)** **ir de cabeza** = to be busy **(d)** *(transporte)* **cabeza de línea** = railhead

cabina *nf* cabin *o* booth; **cabina telefónica** *o* **cabina de teléfono** *o* **de teléfonos** = call box *o* telephone booth *o* telephone kiosk *o* phone box

cable *nm* cable; **televisión por cable** = cable television

> los optimistas esperan que la competencia entre las emisoras por satélite y las televisiones por cable acabe en una espiral disparatada de ofertas por la retransmisión de acontecimientos deportivos
> **Actualidad Económica**

cabo *nm* end; **al cabo de seis meses** = at the end of six months; **llevar a cabo** = to carry out *o* to implement *o* to effect

cada *adj* each *o* every; **cada dos años** = every two years *o* bi-annually; **cada vez más** = more and more *o* increasingly; **la compañía tiene que depender cada vez más del mercado de exportación** = the company has to depend increasingly on the export market

cadena *nf* **(a)** *(serie)* chain; **cadena de grandes almacenes** = chain of department stores; **una cadena de hoteles** = a chain of hotels *o* a hotel chain; **sucursal de una cadena** = chain store *o* multiple store; **el presidente de una gran cadena de tiendas de bricolaje** = the chairman of a large do-it-yourself chain; **lleva una cadena de zapaterías** = he runs a chain of shoe shops; **compró varias zapaterías y** poco a poco se hizo con una cadena de tiendas = she bought several shoe shops and gradually built up a chain; **tiene una participación mayoritaria en una cadena de supermercados** = he has a majority interest in a supermarket chain **(b)** *(red)* **cadena de televisión** = television network **(c)** *(proceso de producción)* **cadena de montaje** = assembly line *o* production line; **es una obrera de la cadena de montaje** = she is an assembly line worker *o* a production line worker; **trabaja en la cadena de montaje** *o* **es un trabajador de la cadena de montaje de la fábrica de coches** = he works on the assembly line *o* on the production line *o* he is a production line worker in the car factory **(d)** *(legal)* **cadena perpetua** = life sentence *o* life imprisonment

> en España sólo el 15% de los hoteles forman parte de una cadena
> **Tiempo**

> en la cadenas de producción existe un mayor riesgo de siniestralidad laboral
> **El País**

caducado, -da 1 *adj* **(a)** *(expirado)* expired; **su pasaporte está caducado** = his passport has expired; **permiso caducado** = permit that has expired **(b)** *(anticuado)* out-of-date **2** *pp de* CADUCAR

caducar *vi* to lapse *o* to expire *o* to go out of date; **la garantía ha caducado** = the guarantee has lapsed; **dejar caducar una oferta** = to let an offer lapse; **tu pasaporte ha caducado** = your passport is no longer valid

caducidad *nf* obsolescence *o* expiry; **fecha de caducidad** = (i) expiry date; (ii) sell-by date; **caducidad de la fianza** = forfeiture of a bond

caer *vi* **(a)** *(derrumbarse)* to drop *o* to fall; **caer en picado** = to collapse *o* to plummet *o* to plunge *o* to slump *o* to nosedive; **los precios cayeron en picado al registrarse pérdidas en la compañía** = prices collapsed after the company reported a loss; **volver a caer** = to fall back **(b)** *(fecha)* to fall; **la fiesta nacional cae en martes** = the public holiday falls on a Tuesday **(c)** *(lugar)* **el restaurante cae cerca de la oficina** = the restaurant is near the office **(d)** *(divisas)* to lose

cafetería *nf* snack bar *o* coffee shop

caída *nf* collapse *o* fall; **una caída de las ventas** = a drop in sales *o* slump in sales; **una caída de los precios** = a drop in prices; **una caída del tipo de cambio** = a fall in the exchange rate; **una caída acusada de los precios** = a sharp drop in prices; **caída repentina** *o* **caída en picado** = slump; **caída en el valor de la peseta** = slump in the value of the peseta; **la caída de la libra esterlina** = the fall in the value of sterling; **la caída de la libra en los mercados de divisas** = the pound's slump on the foreign exchange markets

tras la fuerte caída del índice Dow Jones el pasado 15 de noviembre, el resto de los mercados internacionales no sufrían el temido pánico generalizado y podían sujetar sus cambios con unas pérdidas razonables

Tiempo

con esta iniciativa, la aerolínea intenta parar la caída en picado que viene sufriendo durante los últimos cinco ejercicios, tanto en resultados como en cuota de mercado

Cinco Días

caja *nf* **(a)** *(para cobros y pagos)* till *o* cash box *o* cashdesk; *(supermercado)* checkout; **caja registradora** = cash register *o* cash till; **pague en caja** = please pay at the desk; **no había mucho dinero en la caja al final del día** = there was not much money in the till at the end of the day **(b)** *(seguridad)* **caja fuerte** *o* **caja de caudales** *o* **caja de seguridad** = safe *o* strongbox *o* safe deposit box; **caja nocturna** = night safe; **caja de pared** = wall safe; **caja protegida contra incendios** = fire-proof safe; **guardamos los documentos en una caja a prueba de incendios** = we keep the papers in a fireproof safe **(c)** *(dinero)* cash; **caja para gastos menores** = petty cash box; **caja de reptiles** *o* **de sobornos** = slush fund; **comprobante de caja** = sales receipt *o* petty cash voucher; **cuenta de caja** = cash account; **efectivo en caja** = cash in hand; **flujo de caja** = cash flow; **fondo de caja** = cash float; **empezamos el día con un fondo de caja de 3.000 ptas.** = we start the day with 3,000 pesetas float in the cash desk; **hacer arqueo de caja** = to count the cash *o* to cash up; **guardamos la caja para gastos menores en la caja de caudales** = we keep the petty cash in the safe; **libro de caja** = cash book; **libro de caja auxiliar** = petty cash book; **presupuesto de caja** = cash budget; **reserva de caja** = cash reserves; **saldo de caja** = cash balance **(d)** *(banco)* **caja de ahorros** = savings bank; **Caja Postal de Ahorros** = Post Office Savings Bank **(e)** *(embalaje)* box *o* case *o* crate; **caja de cuatro unidades** = four-pack; **las mercancías se enviaron en cajas de cartón delgado** *o* **fino** = the goods were sent in thin cardboard boxes; **una caja de embalar** = a packing case; **envíen las películas en una caja hermética** = send the films in an airtight container; **el ordenador está embalado en una caja hermética** = the computer is packed in a watertight case; **los relojes vienen empaquetados en cajas de plástico que permiten su exhibición** = the watches are prepacked in plastic display boxes; **los clips se venden en cajas de doscientos** = paperclips come in boxes of two hundred; **seis cajas de vino** = six cases of wine **(f)** *(archivador)* **caja de registros** = box file **(g)** *(expositor)* **caja de artículos sueltos para la venta** = dump bin

◊ **cajero, -ra** *n* **(a)** *(persona)* cashier; **cajero de un banco** = bank clerk *o* teller **(b)** *(máquina)* **cajero automático** = cash dispenser *o* cashpoint; **tarjeta de cajero** = cash card

la red de cajeros automáticos ha incorporado a su equipo una avanzada tarjeta multifunción, para uso tanto en imposiciones como en reintegros

Micros

la remuneración media ofrecida por bancos y cajas por un depósito a plazo de dos millones de pesetas es ahora del 6%, cuando al inicio del año la ganancia se situaba en el 7,25%

El País

cajetilla *nf* small box *o* packet; **cajetilla de cigarrillos** = packet of cigarettes; **cajetilla de cerillas** = box of matches

cajón *nm* **(a)** *(caja grande)* big box *o* crate *o* case; **un cajón de naranjas** = a crate of oranges **(b)** *(en un mueble)* drawer; **cajón de mesa de despacho** = desk drawer

calco *nm* tracing; *(papel carbón)* **papel de calco** = carbon paper

calculable *adj* calculable *o* computable

◊ **calculadora** *nf* calculator *o* calculating machine; **calculadora de bolsillo** = pocket calculator; **mi calculadora de bolsillo necesita pilas nuevas** = my pocket calculator needs new batteries; **calculó el descuento en su calculadora** = he worked out the discount on his calculator

calcular *vt* **(a)** *(contar)* to calculate *o* to work out *o* to reckon; **máquina de calcular** = calculating machine *o* calculator; **el empleado del banco calculó el tipo de cambio del dólar** = the bank clerk calculated the rate of exchange for the dollar; **calculamos que la pérdida es superior a 1 millón de ptas.** = we reckon the loss to be over 1m pesetas; **calculo que nos quedan existencias para seis meses** = I calculate that we have six months' stock left **(b)** *(anticipar)* to estimate *o* to forecast; **calcular que costará 1 millón de ptas.** = to estimate that it will cost 1m pesetas *o* to estimate costs at 1m pesetas; **calculamos que las ventas actuales suponen sólo el 60% del pasado año** = we estimate current sales at only 60% of last year; **calcular mal** = to miscalculate; **calculó mal el tiempo que se necesitaba para terminar el trabajo** = he miscalculated the amount of time needed to finish the work; **el vendedor calculó mal el descuento, por lo que apenas cubrimos gastos en la transacción** = the salesman miscalculated the discount, so we hardly broke even on the deal **(c)** *(precio)* to quote

cálculo *nm* calculation *o* computation *o* estimate; **hacer un cálculo** = to work out (a sum); **hizo el cálculo del descuento en su calculadora** = she worked out the discount on her calculator; **hay un error de 200.000 ptas. en nuestros cálculos** = we are 200,000 pesetas out in our calculations; **cálculo aproximado** = rough calculation *o* rough estimate; **hice unos cálculos aproximados al dorso de un sobre** = I made some rough calculations on the back of an envelope; **estas cifras son sólo un cálculo aproximado** = these figures are only an estimate; **cálculo aventurado** = rough guess *o* guesstimate; **cálculo de la base impositiva** = tax assessment; **cálculo de costos** = calculation of costs *o* costing; *(informática)* **hoja de cálculo** = spreadsheet

calderilla *nf* small change *o* coppers; **dejó toda la calderilla de propina** = he left all his small change as a tip

miles de personas van a tener la
posibilidad de manejar las tarjetas
inteligentes o monederos electrónicos,
un producto financiero que amenaza con
sustituir al viejo bolsillo de calderilla

El País

calendario *nm* **(a)** *(anuario)* calendar; **por Año Nuevo el garage me envió un calendario con fotos de coches antiguos** = for the New Year the garage sent me a calendar with photographs of old cars **(b)** *(agenda)* timetable *o* time scale; **tiene que ceñirse a un calendario muy exigente** = he is working to a strict timetable **(c)** *(programa de actividades)* planner; **calendario de trabajo** = desk *o* wall planner; **calendario de trabajo anual** = year planner

calibrar *vt* to gauge *o* to grade *o* to measure; **calibrar el carbón** = to grade coal

calidad *nf* **(a)** *(cualidad)* quality; **sólo vendemos productos agrícolas de calidad** = we sell only quality farm produce; **alta calidad** *o* **de calidad superior** *o* **de primera calidad** = premium quality *o* high quality *o* top quality *o* up market; **la compañía ha decidido lanzarse al mercado de artículos de primera calidad** = the company has decided to move up market; **la tienda está especializada en artículos de importación de primera calidad** = the store specializes in high quality imported items; **acero de calidad superior** = high-quality steel; **baja calidad** *o* **calidad inferior** = low-quality *o* poor quality *o* second-rate; **artículos de baja calidad** = seconds; **intentaron vendernos acero de baja calidad** = they tried to sell us some low-quality steel; **nunca compre nada de calidad inferior** = never buy anything second-rate; **buena calidad** *o* **mala calidad** = good quality *o* bad quality; **hay demanda de ordenadores de segunda mano de buena calidad** = there is a market for good quality secondhand computers; **control de calidad** = quality control; **controlar la calidad del producto** = to inspect a product for defects *o* to check the quality of a product; **inspector de calidad** = quality controller; **signo de calidad** = quality label **(b)** *(imprenta)* **calidad borrador** = draft quality; **calidad de semicorrespondencia** = near letter-quality (NLQ) **(c)** *(capacidad)* capacity *o* position; **en calidad de** = in the capacity of *o* as; **en su calidad de presidente** = in his capacity as chairman; **actúa en calidad de asesor** = he is acting in an advisory capacity; **calidad de no disponible** = unavailability; **calidad de miembro** = membership

los agricultores franceses se quejan de
que el paso del tren afecta a la calidad de
los vinos

Cambio 16

caliente *adj* hot; **la máquina de bebidas sirve café, té y sopa caliente** = the drinks machine sells coffee, tea and hot soup; **apaga la máquina si se calienta demasiado** = switch off the machine if it gets too hot; *(especulativo)* **dinero caliente** = hot money

calificado, -da 1 *adj* qualified; **emplean a veintiséis ingenieros sumamente calificados** = they employ twenty-six highly qualified engineers **2** *pp de* CALIFICAR

calificar *vt* to call *o* to describe

los expertos calificaron la nueva medida
como innecesaria y perjudicial para el
mercado

Expansión

calle *nf* street; **calle principal** *o* **calle mayor** = High Street; *US* Main Street; **calle de una sola dirección** *o* **de dirección única** = one-way street

◊ **callejero** *nm* street map *o* street directory

◊ **callejón** *nm* alley *o* alleyway; **callejón sin salida** = cul-de-sac; **llegar a un callejón sin salida** = to reach a deadlock; **las negociaciones han llegado a un callejón sin salida** = the negotiations are deadlocked

calma *nf* quiet period *o* lull; **en calma** = quiet; **después de la agitada actividad comercial de la semana pasada, la calma de esta semana es de agradecer** = after last week's hectic trading this week's lull was welcome

◊ **calmarse** *vr* to calm down; **los mercados de divisas se calmaron después de la declaración del gobierno sobre los tipos de cambio** = currency exchanges were quieter after the government's statement on exchange rates

calumnia *nf* *(oral)* slander; *(escrito)* libel

◊ **calumniar** *vt* **calumniar a alguien** = *(oral)* to slander someone; *(escrito)* to libel someone

cama *nf* bed; **en cama** = in bed *o* laid up; **la mitad de la oficina está en cama con gripe** = half the office is laid up with flu

cámara *nf* **(a)** *(habitación)* room; **cámara acorazada** = strongroom **(b) Cámara de Comercio** = Chamber of Commerce **(c) cámara de compensación** = clearing house **(d)** *(fotografía)* camera; **cámara de vídeo** = video camera

camarera *nf* waitress

◊ **camarero** *nm* waiter; **camarero principal** = head waiter; **ser camarero en un restaurante** = to be a waiter in a restaurant

cambiable *adj* exchangeable

cambiar 1 *vt* **(a)** *(modificar)* to change *o* to alter; **cambiar las condiciones de un contrato** = to alter the terms of a contract **(b)** *(sustituir)* to replace; **cambiar un artículo por otro** = to exchange *o* to swap one article for another; **cambió su coche viejo por una moto nueva** = he swapped his old car for a new motorcycle; **la empresa cambiará cualquier artículo defectuoso gratuitamente** = the company will replace any defective item free of charge; **la fábrica ha cambiado la calefacción y ahora tiene gas** = the factory has switched over to gas for heating **(c)** *(divisas)* **cambiar divisas** *o* **moneda extranjera** = to change foreign currency; **cambiar pesetas por libras** = to exchange pesetas for pounds *o* to change pesetas into pounds; **cambiamos nuestras pesetas por francos suizos** = we converted our pesetas into Swiss francs; **queremos cambiar unos cheques de viaje** = we want to change some traveller's cheques; **cambiar un billete de 10.000 ptas.** = to change a 10,000 peseta note **2** *vi* **(a)** to change *o* to alter; **cambiar de dueño** = to change hands; **cambiar de dirección** = to change direction *o* to turn **(b)**

(trasladar) to move; **cambió de local al ampliar el negocio** = he moved to new premises because his business was expanding

◊ **cambiarse** *vr* to change; **cambiarse a** = to switch over to; **nos hemos cambiado a un suministrador francés** = we have switched over to a French supplier

cambiario, -ria *adj* exchange *o* foreign exchange; **mercado cambiario** = foreign exchange market; **los mercados cambiarios se mostraron muy activos después de la devaluación del dólar** = foreign exchange markets were very active after the dollar devalued; **operaciones cambiarias** = exchange dealings

cambio *nm* **(a)** *(sustitución)* alteration *o* change; **cambio de dirección** *o* **de dueño** = change of management *o* 'under new management'; **hizo algunos cambios en los términos de un contrato** = he made some alterations to the terms of a contract; **el acuerdo se firmó sin cambios** = the agreement was signed without any alterations; **un cambio en la estrategia de comercialización de la empresa** = a shift in the company's marketing strategy; **cambio de fecha** = change of date; **cambio de impresiones** = exchange of ideas *o* of views **(b)** *(intercambio)* exchange; **no se admiten cambios** = we do not exchange goods **(c)** *(monedas)* change *o* loose change *o* small change; **dar a alguien cambio de 1.000 ptas.** = to give someone change for 1000 pesetas; **se equivocó al darme el cambio** = he gave me the wrong change; **máquina de cambio** = change machine; **quédese con el cambio** = keep the (odd) change **(d)** *(finanzas)* exchange; **agio del cambio** = exchange premium; **cambio fijo** = fixed exchange rate; **cambios flotantes** = floating rates of exchange; **cambio de moneda extranjera** = foreign exchange; **control de cambio** = exchange control; **el gobierno tuvo que imponer controles de cambio para detener la compra masiva de dólares** = the government had to impose exchange controls to stop the rush to buy dollars; **letra de cambio** = bill of exchange; **tipo de cambio** = rate of exchange *o* exchange rate; **el tipo de cambio dólar/peseta** = the peseta/dollar exchange rate; **tipo de cambio actual** = current rate of exchange; **¿cuál es el cambio del día** *o* **actual del dólar?** = what is today's rate *o* the current rate for the dollar?; **el tipo de cambio actual es de 200 ptas. la libra** = the current rate of exchange is 200 pesetas to the pound; *(EMS)* **mecanismo de cambio (del SME)** = exchange rate mechanism (ERM); **operaciones de cambio** = foreign exchange dealing; **operador de cambios** = exchange dealer; **una sociedad de agentes de cambio y bolsa** = a stockbroking firm **(e)** *(trueque)* **cambio en especie** = bartering; **a cambio de** = in exchange for

◊ **cambista** *nmf* money changer; *(operador de cambios)* foreign currency dealer *o* foreign exchange broker

Camboya *nf* Cambodia

◊ **camboyano, -na** *adj y n* Cambodian
NOTA: capital: **Phnom Penh;** moneda: **rial** = riel

Camerún *nm* Cameroon

◊ **camerunense** *adj y n* Cameroonian
NOTA: capital: **Yaoundé;** moneda: **franco CFA (FCFA)** = CFA franc (CFAF)

camino *nm* route *o* way *o* path; **en el camino de** *o* **de camino a** = on the way to *o* en route for; **abrir camino** = to open up *o* to pioneer; **la compañía abrió el camino a nuevos adelantos en el campo de la electrónica** = the company pioneered developments in the field of electronics

camión *nm* truck *o* lorry; **cargar un camión** = to load a lorry; **descargar un camión** = to unload a lorry; **camión con remolque** = articulated lorry *o* articulated vehicle; **un camión cargado de cajas** = a truck loaded with boxes; **conduce un camión de cinco toneladas** = he drives a five-ton lorry; **camión pesado** = heavy lorry; **camión de gran tonelaje** = heavy goods vehicle; **carga de un camión** = *(carga)* lorryload *o* truckload; *(género)* load of a lorry; **chófer de camión** = lorry driver *o* truck driver *o* trucker; *US* teamster

◊ **camionada** *nf (carga de un camión)* lorryload *o* truckload; **entregaron seis camionadas de carbón** = they delivered six lorryloads *o* truckloads of coal

◊ **camionero** *nm* lorry driver *o* truck driver *o* trucker; *US* teamster

◊ **camioneta** *nf* van; **camioneta de reparto** = delivery van *o* pickup truck; **camioneta de correos** = Post Office van

campaña *nf* campaign; **campaña para reducir gastos** = economy drive; **campaña publicitaria** = publicity campaign *o* advertising campaign; **campaña de ventas** = sales campaign; **están preparando una campaña para lanzar una nueva marca de jabón** = they are working on a campaign to launch a new brand of soap

campo *nm* **(a)** *(campiña)* country *o* countryside; **cubre principalmente la zona del campo, pero tiene su sede en la ciudad** = his territory is mainly the country, but he is based in the town **(b)** *(terreno)* field; **las vacas están en el campo** = the cows are in the field; **campo de aterrizaje** = landing field; **trabajos de campo** = field work **(c)** *(esfera)* sphere *o* scope; **campo de actividad** = sphere of activity **(d)** *(informática)* **campo de almacenamiento** = storage field **(e)** *(ámbito)* area

```
uno de los campos de mayor crecimiento
potencial del gas es el de la producción de
electricidad, a través de las centrales
llamadas de ciclo combinado, que permiten
un    mayor    rendimiento    que    las
convencionales
                                  El País
```

Canadá *nm* Canada

◊ **canadiense** *adj y n* Canadian
NOTA: capital: **Ottawa;** moneda: **dólar canadiense ($** *o* **Can$)** = Canadian dollar ($ *o* Can$)

canal *nm* **(a)** channel; **abrir nuevos canales de comunicación** = to open up new channels of communication; **canales de distribución** = distribution channels *o* channels of distribution **(b)** **canal de televisión** = TV channel **(c)** **el Canal de la Mancha** = the English Channel

cancelación *nf* cancellation *o* annulment; **cancelación de una deuda** = (i) cancellation of a debt; (ii) redemption of a debt

cancelar *vt* *(anular)* to cancel *o* to annul *o* to

countermand; **cancelar un acuerdo** = to call off a deal; **el acuerdo ha sido cancelado** = the agreement has been cancelled *o* the agreement is off; **cancelar una cita** = to cancel an appointment; **el gobierno ha cancelado el pedido de una flota de autobuses** = the government has cancelled the order for a fleet of buses **(b)** *(deudas)* to write off; **cancelar las deudas incobrables** = to write off bad debts **(c)** *(cuentas)* to pay *o* to settle

candidato, -ta *n* candidate *o* applicant; **candidato propuesto** = nominee; **candidato a un puesto de trabajo** = applicant for a job *o* job applicant; **hemos llamado a tres candidatos para una entrevista** = we have called three candidates for interview

> en cualquier prueba de selección, la persona está en un proceso en el que se descartan y eligen a los candidatos
> **El País**

candidatura *nf* candidature *o* candidacy; **impreso de candidatura** = application form

canje *nm* trade-off *o* exchange; **canje parcial** = part exchange; **aceptaron el coche viejo en canje parcial por el nuevo** = they took the old car in part exchange for the new one

canjear *vt* to exchange; **canjear un artículo por otro** = to exchange one article for another; **las mercancías sólo pueden ser canjeadas mediante la presentación de la factura** = goods can be exchanged only on production of the sales slip

canon *nm* tax *o* royalty; **cánones del petróleo** = oil royalties

cantidad *nf* **(a)** *(cifra)* amount *o* quantity *o* figure; **la cantidad de acciones vendidas** = the number of shares sold; **una cantidad determinada** = a certain quantity; **una gran cantidad de algo** = a lot of *o* a great deal of *o* a good deal of something; **compró una gran cantidad de piezas de recambio** = he bought a large quantity of spare parts; **cantidad de repetición de pedidos** = reorder quantity; **cantidades superiores a veinticinco kilos** = amounts *o* quantities in excess of twenty-five kilos; **una pequeña cantidad de drogas ilegales** = a small amount of illegal drugs; **descuento por grandes cantidades** = quantity discount; **la empresa ofrece un descuento cuando se compra en grandes cantidades** = the company offers a discount for quantity purchase **(b)** *(mucho)* mass; **recibieron gran cantidad de pedidos después de los anuncios en televisión** = they received a mass of orders *o* masses of orders after the TV commercials **(c)** *(dinero)* amount *o* sum; **por una pequeña cantidad** = for a small sum *o* for a small consideration; **rogamos abonen la cantidad de 1.200 ptas.** = please pay the sum of 1,200 pesetas; **perdió grandes cantidades de dinero en la bolsa** = he lost large sums on the Stock Exchange; **una pequeña cantidad invertida en papel del Estado** = a small amount invested in gilt-edged stock; **la cantidad asegurada** = the sum insured

cantina *nf* canteen

canto *nm* corner; **la caja debe tener los cantos especialmente resistentes** = the box has to have specially strong corners; **el canto del cajón sufrió desperfectos** = the corner of the crate was damaged

caos *nm* chaos

> el creciente déficit, los despidos de los trabajadores y las dudas sobre el modelo a seguir están llevando al caos al Ente Público
> **Tiempo**

capacidad *nf* **(a)** *(aptitud)* capacity *o* capability *o* ability *o* aptitude; **tiene una gran capacidad para los negocios** = he has a particular capacity for business **(b)** *(comercial)* **capacidad de carga** = load-carrying capacity; **capacidad de endeudamiento** = borrowing power; **capacidad de ganar dinero** = earning capacity *o* earning power; **capacidad de venta** = saleability **(c)** *(producción)* capacity; **capacidad industrial** *o* **de fabricación** *o* **de producción** = industrial *o* manufacturing *o* production capacity; **trabajar a plena capacidad** = to work at full capacity; **aprovechar** *o* **utilizar la capacidad ociosa** *o* **el exceso de capacidad** = to use up spare *o* excess capacity **(d)** *(espacio)* capacity; **capacidad del almacén** = warehouse capacity; **capacidad de almacenamiento** = storage capacity; **medida de capacidad** = cubic measure **(e)** *(posibilidades)* potential

> el negocio va tan bien que GHS está aumentando la capacidad de producción de Tecfloor en un 500%
> **España Económica**

capacitación *nf* training; **el negocio está cerrado porque el personal está realizando un cursillo de capacitación** = the business is closed for staff training; **capacitación industrial** *o* **capacitación laboral** = industrial training; **capacitación del personal** = staff training; **director** *o* **responsable de la capacitación** = training officer; **programa de capacitación** = training program; **unidad de capacitación** = training unit

> este manual pretende ayudar en la capacitación de los vendedores de tienda
> **El País**

capacitado, -da 1 *adj* qualified; **cada vez es más difícil encontrar personal capacitado para el trabajo** = it's getting increasingly difficult to find qualified staff **2** *pp de* CAPACITAR

capacitar *vt* to train *o* to qualify; **este título me capacita para ejercer la medicina en España** = this diploma qualifies me to practise as a doctor in Spain

capataz *nm* foreman *o* chargehand

◊ **capataza** *nf* forewoman

capaz *adj* capable *o* competent *o* proficient; **el personal de ventas tiene que ser capaz de vender todas las mercancías del almacén** = the sales force must be capable of selling all the stock in the warehouse

capital 1 *nm* **(a)** *(finanzas)* capital; **compañía con un capital de 2 millones de ptas.** = company with 2m peseta capital *o* with a capital of 2m pesetas *o* company capitalized at 2m pesetas; **capital en acciones** = share capital *o* equity capital; **capital de los accionistas** = shareholders' equity *o* equity capital; **capital autorizado** = authorized capital; **capital circulante** *o* **operativo** = circulating capital *o* working capital; **capital desembolsado** *o* **cubierto** = (fully) paid-up capital *o* called up capital;

capital emitido = issued capital; **valor de mercado del capital emitido** = market capitalization; **capital no emitido** = unissued capital; **capital escriturado** = authorized capital *o* shareholders' equity; **capital fijo** = fixed capital; **capital inactivo** = idle capital; **capital nominal** = nominal capital; **capital riesgo** = risk capital *o* venture capital; **capital social** = shareholders' equity *o* equity capital; *(activo fijo)* **bienes de capital** = capital assets *o* capital equipment *o* capital goods; **cuenta de capital** = capital account; **dilución del capital** = dilution of capital; **estructura del capital de una compañía** = capital structure of a company; **evasión** *o* **fuga de capitales** = flight of capital; **ganancias de capital** = capital gains; *(inversión en activo fijo)* **gastos de capital** = capital costs *o* capital expenditure *o* investment *o* outlay; **inmovilizar capital** = to lock up capital; **impuesto sobre el capital** = capital levy; **impuesto sobre las transferencias de capital** = capital transfer tax; **una inyección de capital de 1 millón de ptas.** = a capital injection of 1m pesetas *o* an injection of 1m pesetas capital; **inyectar capital en un negocio** = to inject capital into a business; **mercado de capitales** = capital market; **movimientos** *o* **circulación de capital** = movements of capital *o* capital movements; **pérdidas de capital** = capital loss; **rendimiento de capital** = return on investment *o* on capital employed; **rendimiento del capital utilizado** = return against capital employed; **reservas de capital** = capital reserves **(b)** *(empréstito)* principal; **amortizar el capital y pagar los intereses** = to repay principal and interest **(c)** *(IVA)* **capital invertido** = inputs **2** *nf (ciudad)* capital city

◊ **capitalismo** *nm* capitalism

◊ **capitalista** **1** *adj* capitalist; **una economía capitalista** = a capitalist economy; **el sistema capitalista** = the capitalist system; **los países capitalistas** *o* **el mundo capitalista** = the capitalist countries *o* world **2** *nmf* financier *o* backer *o* capitalist; **cuenta con un capitalista australiano** = he has an Australian backer; **uno de los capitalistas de la compañía se ha retirado** = one of the company's backers has withdrawn

◊ **capitalización** *nf* capitalization; **capitalización bursátil** = stock market capitalization; **compañía con una capitalización bursátil de 200 millones de ptas.** = company with a 200m peseta capitalization; **capitalización de las reservas** = capitalization of reserves

◊ **capitalizar** *vt* to capitalize; **capitalizar los intereses** = to capitalize interest

```
podría resultar rentable el adquirir
empresas privadas que carecieran de una
gestión eficiente o de capital para su
expansión
```

```
a principios de la década de los 80,
trabajó en México capital, donde puso en
marcha un mercado de pagarés de empresa a
tipo de interés flotante
```

cara *nf* face *o* side; **se ruega escribir por una cara del papel solamente** = please write on one side of the paper only; **se encontraron cara a cara** = they met face to face

carácter *nm* **(a)** *(cualidad personal)* character;

tiene buen carácter y se relaciona bien con los clientes = he has a pleasant character and relates well to customers **(b)** *(impresión de escritura)* **escriba su nombre y dirección en caracteres de imprenta** = write your name and address in block letters **(c)** **con carácter comercial** = on a commercial basis

carbón *nm* coal *o* charcoal; **papel carbón** = carbon (paper); **copia carbón** = carbon copy

carburante *nm* fuel

carecer *vi* to lack; **carece de fondos para el proyecto** = he lacks funds for the project; **carece de sentido** = it doesn't make sense; **carece de talento** = he has no talent

```
podría resultar rentable el adquirir
empresas privadas que carecieran de una
gestión eficiente de capital para su
expansión
```

carencia *nf* lack *o* shortage *o* want

carestía *nf* **(a)** *(encarecimiento)* high cost; **carestía de la vida** = cost of living; **plus de carestía de vida** = cost-of-living bonus; **subsidio por aumento del coste de vida** = cost-of-living allowance **(b)** *(escasez)* scarcity

carga *nf* **(a)** *(cargamento)* cargo *o* freight; **carga aérea** = air freight *o* air cargo; **hacer un envío por carga aérea** = to send a shipment by air freight; **gastos** *o* **tarifas de carga aérea** = air freight charges *o* rates; **carga de un barco** = shipload; **carga de un camión** = lorryload *o* truckload; **carga de ida** = outward cargo *o* outward freight; **carga máxima** = maximum load *o* deadweight capacity *o* deadweight tonnage; **carga rentable** = commercial load; **carga de retorno** = cargo homewards; **avión de carga** = cargo plane *o* freight plane; **barco** *o* **buque de carga** = cargo ship *o* freighter; **barco a plena carga** = fully-laden ship; **buque para carga a granel** = bulk carrier; **capacidad de carga** = load-carrying capacity; **muelle de carga** = loading dock; **rampa de carga** = loading ramp; **echar la carga al mar** = to jettison the cargo; **salvaron la carga del naufragio** = they saved the cargo from the wreck; **carga útil** = payload *o* commercial load **(b)** *(trabajo o responsabilidad)* **carga de trabajo** = workload; **tiene dificultades en hacer frente a su pesada carga de trabajo** = he has difficulty in coping with his heavy workload **(c)** *(contribución)* **carga impositiva** = tax burden; **aligerar** *o* **reducir la carga impositiva** = to lighten the tax burden; **cargas sociales** = social security contributions

cargado, -da **1** *adj* laden *o* loaded *o* burdened; **barco cargado por completo** *o* **barco completamente cargado** = fully-laden ship; **un barco cargado de hierro** = a ship loaded with iron; **un camión cargado de cajas** = a truck loaded with boxes; **estar cargado de deudas** = to be burdened with debt **2** *pp de* CARGAR

cargamento *nm* cargo *o* shipment; **el barco está tomando un cargamento de madera** = the ship is loading a cargo of wood

cargar *vt* **(a)** *(barcos)* to load cargo; **cargar un barco** = to load a ship *o* to load cargo onto a ship; **el barco estaba cargando** = the ship was taking on cargo **(b)** *(informática)* to load; **cargue el programa del procesador de textos antes de empezar a teclear** = load the word-processing program before you start keyboarding **(c)** *(cobrar)* to charge; **cargar en exceso** = to overcharge; **no carga el IVA porque pide el pago al contado** = he does not charge VAT because he asks for payment in cash; **cargar un 10% de más por franqueo** = to charge 10% extra for postage; **cargar en cuenta** = to charge an account *o* to debit an account; **cargar una compra en cuenta** = to charge a purchase *o* to put a purchase on one's account **(d)** *(seguros)* **cargar gastos** = to load

cargo *nm* **(a)** *(carga)* load **(b)** *(puesto de trabajo)* post *o* position *o* title; **alto cargo** = high office; **cargos sindicales** = union officials; **cargo de director** = post of manager *o* post of director *o* directorship; **solicitar el cargo de director** = to apply for a position as manager; **le ofrecieron el cargo de consejero en García S.A.** = he was offered a directorship with García S.A.; **tiene** *o* **ocupa el cargo de tesorero** = he holds *o* performs the office of treasurer; **tiene el cargo de 'Director General'** = he has the title 'Chief Executive' **(c)** *(débito)* charge; **cargos en concepto de interés** = interest charges; **cargos excepcionales** = exceptional charges **(d)** *(responsabilidad)* **la compañía se hará cargo de los daños ocasionados** = the company will make good the damage; **los clientes deben hacerse cargo de los objetos que rompan** = customers are expected to pay for breakages; **a cargo** = chargeable to; **las reparaciones corren a cargo del inquilino** = repairs chargeable to the occupier

carguero *nm* *(buque de carga)* freighter; **avión carguero** = cargo plane *o* freight plane; **carguero de graneles** = bulk carrier

carné *nm* card *o* permit; **carné de identidad** = identity card; **carné sindical** = union card; **carné de socio** *o* **miembro** = membership card (NOTA: se escribe también **carnet**)

caro, -ra 1 *adj* dear *o* expensive; **dinero caro** = dear money; **las fincas son muy caras en esta región** = property is very dear in this area; **viajar en avión en primera clase se está poniendo cada vez más caro** = first-class air travel is becoming more and more expensive **2** *adv* dear *o* highly-priced; **vender caro** = to sell at a high price; **estos artículos salen muy caros** = these items work out very expensive

carpeta *nf* **(a)** *(encuadernador)* binder *o* folder; **carpeta de anillas** = ring binder; **ponga todos los documentos en una carpeta para el presidente** = put all the documents in a folder for the chairman **(b)** *(archivador)* file *o* wallet file; **la correspondencia se archiva en la carpeta de reclamaciones** = the correspondence is filed under 'complaints'

carpetazo *nm* *(de un plan o proyecto)* shelving; **se dio carpetazo al plan de expansión** = the whole expansion plan was shelved *o* was pigeonholed

carrera *nf* **(a)** *(competición)* race; **es un gran aficionado a las carreras de caballos** = he is keen on horse-racing **(b)** *(profesión)* career *o* profession **(c)** *(licenciatura)* university degree course; **hacer la carrera de derecho** *o* **de arquitectura** = to study law *o* architecture

carretera *nf* road; **enviar mercancías por carretera** = to send *o* to ship goods by road; **impuesto de carretera** = road tax; **tráfico de carretera** = road traffic; **transporte por carretera** = road haulage; **el precio del transporte por carretera ha subido** = road transport costs have risen

carretilla *nf* truck *o* trolley; **carretilla elevadora (de horquilla)** = fork-lift truck

carro *nm* trolley; **carro** *o* **carrito de la compra** = supermarket trolley; **carro** *o* **carrito del equipaje** = baggage cart

carta *nf* **(a)** *(correspondencia)* letter; **carta de acuse de recibo** = letter of acknowledgement; **enviar una carta de acuse de recibo** = to acknowledge receipt by letter; **acusamos recibo de su carta del 14 de junio** = we acknowledge receipt of your letter of June 14th; **carta adjunta** *o* **explicatoria** = covering letter *o* covering note; **carta por avión** = airmail letter; **carta certificada** = registered letter; **carta comercial** = business letter; **carta con documentos adjuntos** = letter with enclosures; **carta de intención** = letter of intent; **carta personal** = private letter; **carta de presentación** = letter of introduction; **te daré una carta de presentación para el director gerente, es un viejo amigo mío** = I'll give you an introduction to the MD - he is an old friend of mine ; **carta de reclamación** = letter of complaint; **escribió una carta de reclamación inmediatamente** = he wrote an immediate letter of complaint; **enviaron una carta de reclamación, con una factura de indemnización adjunta** = they sent a formal letter of complaint, accompanied by an invoice for damage; **carta de recomendación** = (letter of) reference *o* testimonial; **escribir una carta de recomendación para alguien** = to write someone a reference *o* a testimonial; **carta recordatoria** = chasing letter *o* chaser; **carta de reiteración** *o* **de contestación a otra** = follow-up letter; **carta de solicitud** = letter of application; **carta tipo** *o* **standard** *o* **estándar** *o* **modelo** = standard letter; **carta urgente** = express letter; **echar una carta al correo** = to mail a letter *o* to put a letter in the post; **le agradecemos su carta de fecha 15 de junio (referencia 1234)** = thank you for your letter dated June 15th (reference 1234) **(b) carta blanca** = carte blanche; **carta de crédito** = letter of credit; **carta de crédito irrevocable** = irrevocable letter of credit; **carta de crédito general** = circular letter of credit; **carta de porte** = waybill; *(documento automóvil)* **carta verde** = green card

cartel *nm* **(a)** *(anuncio)* poster; **cartel publicitario** = display advertisement; **carteles que lleva el hombre-anuncio** = sandwich boards; **poner un cartel** = to stick up *o* to post up a notice **(b)** *(grupo industrial, consorcio)* cartel; **cartel de exportación** = export cartel; **cartel industrial** = monopoly *o* trust

cartelera *nf* **(a)** *(valla publicitaria)* advertisement hoarding *o* billboard **(b)** *(en una publicación)* **cartelera de espectáculos** = listings *o* theatre section *o* list of plays *o* list of films *o* entertainments

cartera *nf* **(a)** *(maletín)* briefcase; **metió todos los documentos en su cartera** = he put all the files into his briefcase; **una cartera de cuero legítimo** = a genuine leather purse; **cartera que lleva el nombre o las iniciales** = personalized briefcase **(b)** *(bolsa)* portfolio; **una cartera de valores** = a portfolio of shares; **una cartera de valores de renta elevada** = a high-income portfolio; **cartera de valores vinculada a un índice** = indexed portfolio; **acciones en cartera** = treasury stocks; **administración de una cartera de valores** = portfolio management; **ha vendido toda su cartera del Extremo Oriente** = he has sold all his holdings in the Far East **(c)** *(ministerio)* **ministro sin cartera** = minister without portfolio **(d)** *(comercio)* **cartera de pedidos** = order book; **pagó 100.000 ptas. por la cartera de pedidos de la tienda y 400.000 por las existencias** = he paid 100,000 pesetas for the goodwill of the shop and 400,000 for the stock **(e)** *(para dinero)* wallet

cartilla *nf* pass book; **cartilla de ahorros** = savings book

cartón *nm* **(a)** *(material)* **cartón ondulado** = corrugated cardboard; **caja de cartón** = cardboard box; **una carpeta de cartón** = a cardboard folder *o* a folder made of cardboard **(b)** *(rótulo publicitario)* **reclamo de cartón** = showcard **(c)** *(caja)* box *o* carton; **un cartón de cigarrillos** = a carton of cigarettes

cartucho *nm* cartridge; **cartucho de virador** = toner cartridge

cartulina *nf* thin cardboard *o* card; **hemos imprimido las instrucciones en cartulina blanca** = we have printed the instructions on thin white card

casa 1 *nf* **(a)** *(lugar de residencia)* home; *(de fabricación casera)* **hecho en casa** = homemade **(b)** *(edificio)* house *o* apartment *o* flat; **dueño, o una casa** = householder; **pusieron la casa en venta** = they put their house on the market *o* they offered the house for sale **(c)** *(comercial)* company *o* firm *o* house *o* establishment; **casa comercial** = business *o* firm *o* house; **una casa comercial francesa** = a French business (house); **trabaja para una casa de corretaje** = he works for a broking house; **casa editorial** = publishing house; *(monte de piedad)* **casa de empeños** = pawnshop; **casa exportadora** = export house; **casa matriz** = head office *o* parent company; **casa de la moneda** = mint **(d)** **en la propia casa** = inside (a company); **el personal de la casa** = the in-house staff; **decidimos nombrar a alguien de la casa** = we decided to make an internal appointment

casco *nm* **(a)** *(de protección)* helmet; **todos los visitantes de la obra tienen que llevar el casco de seguridad** = all visitors to the site must wear safety helmets **(b)** *(en una ciudad)* **casco comercial** = business centre; **casco antiguo** *o* **viejo** = the old quarter

casero, -ra 1 *adj* domestic; **de fabricación casera** = homemade; **industria casera** = cottage industry; **mermelada casera** = homemade jam **2** *n* **(a)** *(propietario)* landlord; *(propietaria)* landlady **(b)** *(administrador de una casa)* caretaker **(c)** *(administrador de fincas)* estate agent

casette *nm* cassette; **copie la información del ordenador en un casette** = copy the information from the computer onto a cassette

'cash flow' *nm* cash flow; **cash flow actualizado** = discounted cash flow; **situación de cash flow** = cash flow position; **esperan mejorar la situación de cash flow de la empresa** = they hope to improve the company's cash flow position

casi *adv* almost *o* nearly *o* barely; **casi no queda dinero para pagar al personal** = there is barely enough money left to pay the staff

casillero *nm* pigeonhole

caso *nm* **(a)** case; **estudio de casos** = case studies; **me envió los documentos relacionados con el caso** = he sent me the relevant papers on the case **(b)** **hacer caso omiso** = to ignore; **en este caso pasaremos por alto el retraso** = in this instance we will overlook the delay; **estos productos se devolverán en el caso de que no se vendan** = these goods are all on sale or return

castigo *nm* penalty *o* punishment; **levantar el castigo** = to withdraw the penalty

casualidad *nf* chance *o* coincidence; **dio la casualidad de que el contrato llegó cuando el director estaba de vacaciones** = the contract happened to arrive when the managing director was away on holiday

catalogación *nf* cataloguing

catalogar *vt* to catalogue *o* to index; *US* to catalog

catálogo *nm* catalogue; *US* catalog; **nos enviaron un catálogo de su nueva gama de mesas de oficina** = they sent us a catalogue of their new range of desks; **catálogo de ventas por correo** = mail order catalogue; **le enviaremos nuestro último catálogo** = we will mail you our most recent catalogue; **enumerar los productos en un catálogo** = to list products in a catalogue; **precio de catálogo** = catalogue price *o* list price; **sólo pagó una cuarta parte del precio de catálogo** = he paid only a quarter of the list price

catastral *adj* *(registro de la propiedad)* **registro catastral** = land register *o* land registry

◊ **catastro** *nm* *(registro de la propiedad)* land register *o* land registry

catástrofe *nf* **catástrofe natural** = (i) natural disaster; (ii) act of God

cátedra *nf* *(universidad)* chair

categoría *nf* **(a)** *(calidad)* category; **de primera categoría** = first-class *o* top-flight; **alojarse en hoteles de primera categoría** = to stay in first-class hotels; **es un contable de primera categoría** = he is a first-class accountant; **acciones de primera categoría** = blue chips; **ofrecimos una recepción de categoría a nuestros visitantes** = we laid on VIP treatment for our visitors *o* we gave our visitors a VIP reception; **de segunda categoría** = second-class **(b)** *(clase)* rank; **todos los directores tienen la misma categoría** = all managers are of equal rank *o* all managers rank equally; **su sueldo bajó mucho cuando le rebajaron de categoría** = she lost a lot of salary when she was demoted **(c)** *(posición)* status; **el coche del presidente es un signo externo de su categoría** = the chairman's car is a status symbol; **un funcionario de poca categoría** *o* **de categoría inferior** = a low-grade official; **categoría crediticia** = credit rating

caucho *nm* rubber

caudal *nm* wealth; *(caja fuerte)* **caja de caudales** = safe *o* strongbox

causa *nf* **(a)** *(motivo)* cause *o* reason; **¿cuál fue la causa de la quiebra del banco?** = what was the cause of the bank's collapse?; **la policía intentó encontrar la causa del incendio** = the police tried to find the cause of the fire; **el avión llegó tarde a causa de la niebla** = the plane was late owing to fog **(b)** *(proceso)* court case; **la causa se verá la semana que viene** = the case is being heard next week; **causa criminal** = criminal case

causar *vt* to cause; **la recesión causó cientos de quiebras** = the recession caused hundreds of bankruptcies

cautela *nf* caution

◊ **cauteloso, -sa** *adj* cautious

caza *nf* chase *o* hunt; **dedicarse a la caza de cerebros** *o* **talentos para una empresa** = to headhunt; **lo reclutó una empresa dedicada a la caza de cerebros** = he was headhunted

◊ **cazar** *vt* to chase *o* to hunt; **cazar talentos** = to headhunt

◊ **cazatalentos** *nm* headhunter

CC OO = COMISIONES OBRERAS Workers' Union

cedente *nmf* assignor

ceder 1 *vt* to transfer *o* to surrender *o* to assign *o* to handover *o* to cede; **ceder la casa a los propios hijos** = to make over the house to one's children; **ceder los derechos de una letra** = to assign one's rights to a bill; **ceder una propiedad** = to assign a property **2** *vi* to give in *o* to yield; **el director no cedió a pesar de la presión de los trabajadores** = the director did not give in in spite of being under pressure from the workforce

cédula *nf* register *o* bond; **cédula hipotecaria** = mortgage bond *o* mortgage debenture; **cédula de tesorería** = treasury note

CE = COMUNIDAD EUROPEA EC (European Community); **los ministros de la CE se han reunido hoy en Bruselas** = EC ministers met today in Brussels; **los EE UU están aumentando sus intercambios comerciales con la CE** = the USA is increasing its trade with the EC

◊ **CEE** = COMUNIDAD ECONOMICA EUROPEA EEC (European Economic Community)

celebración *nf* **(a)** *(conmemoración)* celebration **(b)** *(reunión)* holding (of a meeting)

> el Salón Náutico tiene prevista la celebración de un amplio programa de actividades
> **Tiempo**

celebrar *vt* to celebrate; **celebrar una reunión** = to hold a meeting; **el consejo de administración celebrará su próxima reunión en la sala de juntas** = the next board meeting will be held in the boardroom

◊ **celebrarse** *vr* to be held *o* to take place; **la**

feria de ordenadores se celebrará en Madrid el mes próximo = the computer show will be held in Madrid next month; **la junta general anual se celebrará el 24 de marzo** = the AGM will be held on March 24th

célebre *adj* famous

censor, -ra *n* censor **jurado de cuentas** = chartered accountant *o* certified accountant; **colegio de censores públicos** = Institute of Chartered Accountants

centavo *nm* *(moneda)* cent; **venden naranjas a 99 centavos la unidad** = they sell oranges at 99 cents each

centímetro *nm* centimetre; *US* centimeter; **el papel tiene un ancho de quince centímetros** = the paper is fifteen centimetres wide (NOTA: abreviado se escribe: **cm**)

central 1 *adj* central; **banco central** = central bank; **oficina central** *o* **principal** = central office; **oficina central de correos** = main post office **2** *nf* **(a)** *(comercial)* headquarters *o* head office; **central eléctrica** = power station; **central nuclear** = nuclear power station **(b)** *(teléfono)* telephone exchange **(c)** **central sindical** = trade union

◊ **centralita** *nf* **centralita telefónica** = (i) telephone exchange; (ii) telephone switchboard; **está aprendiendo a manejar la nueva centralita de teléfonos** = he is learning to operate the new telephone switchboard

◊ **centralización** *nf* centralization; **centralización de las compras** = centralization of purchasing *o* bulk purchasing; **centralización de datos** = data collection

centralizar *vt* to centralize; **todas las actividades de compra han sido centralizadas en nuestra oficina principal** = all purchasing has been centralized in our main office; **el grupo se beneficia de una estructura organizativa altamente centralizada** = the group benefits from a highly centralized organizational structure

centro *nm* **(a)** *(núcleo)* middle *o* centre; *US* center; **centro comercial** = (i) business centre; (ii) shopping centre *o* shopping arcade *o* shopping precinct *o* shopping mall; **las tiendas del centro** = the High Street shops; **ha comprado una zapatería en el centro de la ciudad** = he has bought a shoe shop in the centre of town **(b)** **Centro de Comercio Internacional (CCI)** = International Trade Center (ITC); **Centro de Documentación de Comercio Exterior (CEDIN)** = (Spanish) Foreign Trade Information Centre; **centro docente** = teaching institution; **centro de investigación** = research centre **(c)** *(ciudad)* **centro industrial** = industrial centre; **centro manufacturero** = manufacturing centre; **el centro de la industria del calzado** = the centre for the shoe industry **(d)** *(contabilidad)* **centro de costes** = cost centre; **centro de beneficios** = profit centre

> la compañía imparte a sus centros cursos de acreditación sobre los últimos avances producidos en el mercado de las tecnologías de la información
> **Micros**

ceñirse *vr* **(a)** *(ajustarse)* to adjust *o* to limit oneself; **tiene que ceñirse a un calendario muy exigente** = he is working to a strict timetable **(b)** *(recortar)* to reduce expenditure

CEOE = CONFEDERACION ESPAÑOLA DE ORGANIZACIONES EMPRESARIALES

cerca *adv* near *o* nearby *o* close; **estamos muy cerca de cumplir nuestros objetivos de ventas** = we are close to meeting our sales targets

◊ **cercanías** *nfpl* outskirts; **tren de cercanías** = commuter train

con los 400 millones que ya se ha gastado el Estado, dicen los sindicatos, el servicio de cercanías madrileño se pondrá a nivel europeo
Cambio 16

cercenar *vt* to retrench

cero *nm* nothing *o* nil *o* zero; **inflación cero** = zero inflation; **empezar un negocio a** *o* **desde cero** = to start a business from cold *o* from scratch; **el código para las conferencias internacionales en España es cero siete (07)** = in Spain, the code for international calls is zero seven (07) ; **un millón se puede escribir '1m' o con un uno seguido de seis ceros** = a million can be written as ' 1m' or as one and six zeros

cerrado, -da 1 *adj* closed *o* shut; **las oficinas estarán cerradas durante las vacaciones de Navidad** = the offices will shut down for the Christmas holiday; **mercado cerrado** = closed market; **sobre cerrado** = sealed envelope; **la información se envió en un sobre cerrado** = the information was sent in a sealed envelope; **ofertas en pliego cerrado** = sealed tenders; **la compañía ha pedido ofertas en pliego cerrado para el almacén** = the company has asked for sealed bids for the warehouse **2** *pp* CERRAR

cerradura *nf* lock; **la cerradura de la caja para gastos menores está rota** = the lock is broken on the petty cash box; **he olvidado la combinación de la cerradura de mi cartera** = I have forgotten the combination of the lock on my briefcase

cerrar *vt* **(a)** *(puerta, tienda)* to shut *o* to close; **los sábados cerramos temprano** = we close early on Saturdays; **cerrar una cuenta bancaria** = to close an account; **cerró su cuenta en la sociedad hipotecaria** = he closed his building society account **(b)** *(liquidar)* to close down *o* to fold (up); **cerrar un negocio** = to close down a business; **cerrar una tienda** *o* **un almacén** = to shut a shop *o* a warehouse; **la empresa va a cerrar su sucursal de Barcelona** = the company is closing down its Barcelona office **(c)** *(negocio)* to clinch *o* to firm up; **ofreció un 5% más para cerrar el trato** = he offered an extra 5% to clinch the deal; **necesitan la confirmación de la junta directiva para poder cerrar el trato** = they need approval from the board before they can clinch *o* firm up the deal **(d)** *(sellar)* to seal; **sobre sin cerrar** = unsealed envelope **(e)** *(con llave)* to lock; **cerrar una tienda** *o* **una oficina** = to lock up a shop *o* an office; **la caja para gastos menores no estaba cerrada con llave** = the petty cash box was not locked; **el director olvidó cerrar con llave la puerta de la sala de ordenadores** = the manager forgot to lock the door of the computer room **2** *vi* **la empresa cerró con deudas superiores a 200**

millones de ptas. = the company folded with debts of over 200m pesetas

certificado, -da 1 *adj* certified *o* registered; **carta certificada** = registered letter; **copia certificada** = certified copy; **correo certificado** = registered post *o* recorded delivery; **enviar documentos por correo certificado** = to send documents by registered mail *o* registered post; **enviamos los documentos por correo certificado** = we sent the documents (by) recorded delivery; **paquete certificado** = registered parcel **2** *nm* certificate *o* testimonial **(a) certificado de aduana** = customs clearance certificate; **certificado de ahorro** = savings certificate; **certificado de aptitud** = (i) proficiency certificate; (ii) certificate of fitness; **certificado de aprobación** = certificate of approval; **certificado de conformidad** = compliance certificate; **certificado de depósito** = certificate of deposit; **certificado médico** = doctor's certificate; **certificado de navegabilidad** = certificate of airworthiness *o* of seaworthiness; **certificado de origen** = certificate of origin; **certificado de registro** = certificate of registration; **certificado de seguro** = insurance certificate **(b) certificado de una acción** = share certificate *o* stock certificate; **certificado de acciones** = stock *o* share certificate *o* share warrant; **certificado que devenga intereses de un 5%** = certificate bearing interest at 5% **3** *pp de* CERTIFICAR

certificar *vt* **(a)** *(dar fe de)* to certify; **certifico que ésta es una copia auténtica** = I certify that this is a true copy; **el documento está certificado como copia auténtica** = the document is certified as a true copy **(b)** *(correo)* to register; **certifiqué la carta porque contenía dinero** = I registered the letter, because it contained some money

cesado, -da 1 *adj* retired *o* former *o* ex- **2** *pp de* CESAR

la auditoría fue encargada por iniciativa del cesado presidente del consejo
El País

cesar *vi* **(a)** *(dejar de producir)* to cease *o* to stop; **el personal cesó de trabajar cuando la empresa no pudo pagar sus salarios** = the workforce stopped work when the company could not pay their wages; **la compañía ha cesado** = the company has stopped trading **(b)** *(dejar una ocupación)* to leave work *o* to retire *o* to quit; **se le ha obligado a cesar** = he was asked to leave *o* he was forced to resign; **el presidente ha cesado en el cargo** = the chairman has quit *o* has resigned

cese *nm* **(a)** *(cierre)* stoppage *o* cessation; **cese de operaciones** = shutdown **(b)** *(abandono de un cargo, de un puesto)* dismissal *o* compulsory retirement; **se le ha pedido el cese** = he was asked to resign; **le dieron el cese** = he was sacked; **va a ser muy difícil conseguir el cese del director general** = the removal of the managing director is going to be very difficult

cesión *nf* assignment *o* cession *o* assignation *o* transfer; **cesión de bienes** = surrender of property; **cesión de una patente** = assignment of a patent; **firmar una escritura de cesión** = to sign a deed of assignment

◊ **cesión-arrendamiento** *nf* lease-back; **realizar una operación de cesión-arrendamiento** = to lease back *o* to arrange a lease-back

◊ **cesionario, -ria** *n* assignee *o* transferee

cesta *nf* basket; **cesta de la compra** = shopping basket; *(moneda o bienes base)* **la peseta ha bajado con relación a una cesta de monedas europeas** = the peseta has fallen against a basket of European currencies

cesto *nm* basket; **un cesto de manzanas** = a basket of apples

Chad *nm* Chad

◊ **chadiano, -na** *adj y n* Chadian
NOTA: capital: **Ndjamena**; moneda: **franco CFA (FCFA)** = CFA franc (CFAF)

chanchullo *nm* fiddle *o* sharp practice; **tiene un chanchullo de venta de billetes a precio reducido** = he runs a cut-price ticket racket; **andar en chanchullos** = to be on the fiddle

chantaje *nm* blackmail *o* racket

◊ **chantajista** *nmf* blackmailer *o* racketeer

chapa *nf* badge *o* pin

chapucear *vt* to do a bad job *o* to botch

◊ **chapucería** *nf (calidad)* shoddiness

◊ **chapucero, -ra 1** *adj* shoddy *o* careless; **un trabajo chapucero** = a shoddy piece of work **2** *n* shoddy worker *o* cowboy; **los que vinieron a pintar la oficina eran un par de chapuceros** = the people we got in to paint the office were a couple of cowboys

◊ **chapuza** *nf* **(a) chapuzas** = odd jobs **(b)** shoddy piece of work *o* cowboy job

> de las chapuzas menores, que se cuentan por cientos, algunas llegaron a los periódicos
> **Cambio 16**

chárter *nm* **vuelo chárter** = charter flight

chatarra *nf* scrap *o* junk; **vender un barco como chatarra** = to sell a ship for scrap; **su valor como chatarra es de 500.000 ptas.** = its scrap value is 500,000 pesetas; **comerciante de chatarra** = scrap dealer *o* scrap merchant

◊ **chatarrero** *nm* scrap dealer

checa (República) *nf* Czech Republic

◊ **checo, -ca** *adj y n* Czech
NOTA: capital: **Praga** (= Prague); moneda: **corona checa** = Czech koruna (Kcs)

chelín *nm (moneda de Austria)* shilling

cheque *nm* cheque; *US* check; **cheque abierto** *o* **no cruzado** *o* **sin cruzar** = open *o* uncrossed cheque; **cheque de banco** = cashier's cheque; **cheque en blanco** = blank cheque; **cheque conformado** = certified cheque; **cheque cruzado** = crossed cheque; **cheque por depositar** = unbanked cheque; **cheque negociable** = negotiable cheque; **cheque nominativo** = cheque made payable to (the name of); **un cheque por 2.000 ptas.** = a cheque for 2,000 pesetas *o* a 2,000 peseta cheque; **el cheque fue enviado ayer a su banco** = the cheque went to your bank yesterday; **el banco devolvió el cheque al librador** = the bank referred the cheque to drawer; **cheque al portador** = cheque to bearer; **cheque en pago de dividendos** = dividend warrant; **cheque sin fondos** = dud cheque *o* cheque which bounces *o* bad cheque; *US* rubber check; **cheque de sueldo** = pay cheque *o* salary cheque; **cheques de viaje** = traveller's cheques; *US* traveler's checks; **cobrar un cheque** = to cash a cheque; **depositar** *o* **ingresar un cheque** = to deposit a cheque *o* to pay a cheque into an account; **ingresó el cheque en cuanto lo recibió** = he banked the cheque as soon as he received it; **detener el pago de un cheque** = to stop a cheque; **endosar un cheque** = to endorse a cheque; **extender un cheque a alguien** = to write out a cheque *o* to make out a cheque to someone; **¿a nombre de quién extiendo el cheque?** = who shall I make the cheque out to?; **firmar un cheque** = to sign a cheque; **el cheque no tiene valor si no está firmado** = the cheque is worthless if it is not signed; **pagar con cheque** = to pay by cheque

chico, -ca 1 *adj* small *o* little **2** *nf* **(a)** *(muchacha)* girl **(b)** *(criada)* maid *o* servant **3** *nm* **(a)** *(muchacho)* boy *o* lad **(b)** *(en la oficina)* **chico de recados** *o* **ordenanza** = office boy *o* messenger boy; **chico para todo** = dogsbody; *US* gofer

Chile *nm* Chile

◊ **chileno, -na** *adj y n* Chilean
NOTA: capital: **Santiago de Chile**; moneda: **peso chileno ($Ch)** = Chilean peso (Chil$)

China *nf* China

◊ **chino, -na** *adj y n* Chinese
NOTA: capital: **Pekín** (= Beijing); moneda: **yuan chino (Y)** = Chinese yuan (Y)

chincheta *nf* drawing pin; **fijaron los carteles con chinchetas en la parte posterior del stand de la exposición** = they pinned the posters up at the back of the exhibition stand; **utilizó chinchetas para colgar el póster en la puerta** = she used drawing pins to pin the poster to the door

'chip' *nm (informática)* (computer) chip

Chipre *nf* Cyprus

◊ **chipriota** *adj y nmf* Cypriot
NOTA: capital: **Nicosia**; moneda: **libra chipriota (£C)** = Cyprus pound (C£)

chisme *nm* **(a)** *(trasto)* gadget *o* gismo; **chismes** = odds and ends **(b)** *(habladuría)* gossip

chocar 1 *vt* **(a)** *(asombrar)* to shock *o* to surprise *o* to startle **(b)** *(saludos)* to shake hands; **¡chócala!** = let's shake hands on it! **2** *vi* **(a)** *(sorprender)* to be odd *o* to be shocking **(b)** *(colisión)* to crash

chófer *nm* **(a)** *(conductor)* driver; **la mercancía se entregará la semana próxima siempre que los chóferes no estén en huelga** = the goods will be delivered next week provided *o* providing the drivers are not on strike **(b)** *(servicio particular)* chauffeur

choque *nm* **(a)** *(accidente)* crash; **el coche sufrió daños en el choque** = the car was damaged in the crash **(b)** *(finanzas)* crash

Cía. = COMPAÑIA Co. (Company)

cíclico, -ca *adj* cyclical; **factores cíclicos** = cyclical factors

ciclo *nm* **(a)** *(periodo)* cycle; **ciclo económico** *o* **ciclo comercial** = economic cycle *o* trade cycle *o* business cycle; **ciclo del producto** = product cycle; **ciclo de trabajo** = work cycle **(b)** *(de conferencias)* course *o* series *o* programme

cien *adj y nm* hundred; **unos cien** = a hundred odd

ciencia *nf* science; **ciencias empresariales** = business studies *o* management science; **tiene un master en ciencias empresariales** = he has a master's degree in business studies

ciento *adj y nm* hundred; *(porcentaje)* **tanto por ciento** = percentage

cierre *nm* **(a)** *(comercial)* **cierre dominical** = Sunday closing; **hora de cierre** = closing time **(b)** *(bolsa)* **cierre de la sesión bursátil** = finish *o* close; **al cierre** = closing; **precio al cierre** = closing price; **al cierre de la sesión las acciones habían bajado un 20%** = at the close of the day's trading the shares had fallen 20%; **las acciones petrolíferas se recuperaron en el momento del cierre** = oil shares rallied at the finish; **el precio de las acciones fue de 1.200 ptas. al cierre** = the shares closed at 1,200 pesetas; **las acciones subieron después del cierre de la sesión** = the shares rose in after-hours trading **(c)** *(cese de operaciones)* closing *o* closure *o* shutdown; **liquidación total por cierre** = closing-down sale; **cierre patronal** = lockout; **declarar el cierre patronal** = to lock out workers; **cierre para impedir la entrada del personal** = shutout **(d)** **cierre de ejercicio** = year end; **ajuste por cierre de ejercicio** = year end adjustment **(e)** *(fecha límite)* deadline

> el cierre de la semana pasada en la Bolsa de Valencia se caracterizó por los descensos casi generalizados y por la escasa actividad en los corros
>
> **Expansión**

cierto, -ta 1 *adj* certain; *(tener razón)* **estar en lo cierto** = to be right; **el presidente estaba en lo cierto al decir que las cifras no cuadraban** = the chairman was right when he said the figures did not add up **2** *adv* of course *o* certainly

CIF = COSTE, SEGURO Y FLETE c.i.f. (cost, insurance and freight)

cifra *nf* **(a)** *(cantidad)* figure; **mire la cifra en la sección de 'Costes 89-90'** = look at the figure under the heading 'Costs 89-90'; **cifra de ventas** *o* **cifra de negocios** *o* **de facturación** = sales figures *o* turnover; **no alcanzaron la cifra propuesta de 400 millones de ventas** = they missed the target figure of 400m turnover; **las cifras del año pasado** = the figures for last year *o* last year's figures; **examinar las cifras de ventas del semestre anterior** = to examine the sales figures *o* the sales statistics for the previous six months; **cifras ajustadas estacionalmente** = seasonally adjusted figures; **cifras reales** = actuals *o* actual figures; **estas son las cifras reales de 1995** = these figures are the actuals for 1995 **(b)** *(dígito)* digit; **un número telefónico de siete cifras** = a seven-digit phone number

> el beneficio después de impuestos ha pasado de 93 millones de pesetas en 1992 a 1.200 este año y se prevé que la cifra alcance los 1.577 millones en 1999
>
> **España Económica**

cima *nf* top *o* height *o* peak

cingalés, -esa *adj y n* Sri Lankan; *ver* SRI LANKA

cinta *nf* **(a)** *(para grabar, medir)* tape; **cinta magnética** = magnetic tape *o* mag tape; **cinta métrica** = measuring tape *o* tape measure; **cinta de ordenador** = computer tape; **cinta de video** = video tape **(b)** *(para imprimir)* ribbon; **cinta de impresora** = printer ribbon; **cinta para máquina de escribir** = typewriter ribbon

circuito *nm* circuit; **circuito cerrado** = closed circuit

circulación *nf* **(a)** *(movimiento de capital)* circulation *o* movement; **circulación de capital** = circulation of capital; **poner dinero en circulación** = to put money into circulation *o* to circulate money; **la cantidad de dinero en circulación aumentó más de lo previsto** = the amount of money in circulation increased more than was expected; **circulación fiduciaria** = fiduciary money; *US* fiat money **(b)** *(tráfico)* traffic

circulante *adj* circulating; **activo circulante** = current assets; **capital circulante** = circulating capital *o* working capital; **oferta circulante** = money supply; **pasivo circulante** = current liabilities

circular 1 *adj* circular; **gráfico circular** = pie chart **2** *nf* *(carta)* circular *o* circular letter; **enviaron una circular a todos los representantes de ventas ofreciendo un descuento del 10%** = they sent out a memo *o* a circular to all the sales representatives offering a 10% discount; **enviaron una circular con una nueva lista de precios a todos los clientes** = they circularized all their customers with a new list of prices **3** *vi* **(a)** *(moverse)* to travel *o* to run; **este tren circula los días laborables** = this train runs on weekdays **(b)** *(dinero)* to circulate; **circular libremente** = to circulate freely

cita *nf* appointment; **acudir a una cita** = to keep an appointment; **cancelar una cita** = to cancel an appointment; **concertar una cita** = to make *o* to fix an appointment; **anotó la cita en su agenda** = she noted the appointment in her engagements diary; **llegó tarde a la cita** = he was late for his appointment; **sin cita previa** = at short notice; **el director del banco no recibirá a nadie sin cita previa** = the bank manager will not see anyone without an appointment

citación *nf* **citación judicial** = *(para dar testimonio)* subpoena; *(para defender un asunto)* summons; **el director de finanzas recibió una citación del fiscal** = the finance director was subpoenaed by the prosecution; **tiró la citación y se marchó de vacaciones a México** = he threw away the summons and went on holiday to Mexico

citar *vt* **(a)** *(en un juicio)* to subpoena *o* to summon **(b)** *(mencionar)* to quote *o* to mention; **citó cifras del informe anual** = he quoted figures from the annual report; **citado a continuación** =

undermentioned **(c)** *(para una reunión)* to arrange to meet *o* to make an appointment

◊ **citarse** *vr* to arrange to meet; **citarse con alguien a las dos** = to make an appointment with someone for two o'clock

ciudad *nf* city; **las principales ciudades de Europa están conectadas por vuelos que salen cada hora** = the largest cities in Europe are linked by hourly flights; **vive en el extrarradio de la ciudad** = he lives in the commuter belt; **en el centro de la ciudad** = in the centre of town; *US* downtown; **ha comprado una zapatería en el centro de la ciudad** = he has bought a shoe shop in the centre of town; **ciudad-factoría** = *US* company town

◊ **ciudadano, -na** *n* citizen

civil 1 *adj* civil; **año civil** = calendar year; **demanda civil** = civil action; **derecho civil** = civil law; **mes civil** = calendar month **2** *nmf (paisano)* civilian

claro, -ra 1 *adj (lenguaje, explicación)* clear *o* plain; **para dejar las cosas en claro** = for the record *o* to put the record straight; **dejó bien claro que quería la dimisión del director** = he made it clear that he wanted the manager to resign **2** *adv* **(a)** *(claramente)* clear *o* clearly; **hablar claro** = to speak plainly; **el director es un hombre que habla muy claro** = the manager is a very plain-spoken man **(b)** *(por supuesto)* of course; **claro que la compañía está interesada en obtener beneficios *o* ganancias** = of course the company is interested in profits **3** *nm* gap *o* space; **hacer un claro en la agenda para ver a un cliente** = to find a gap in one's diary to see a client *o* to fit in a client

◊ **claramente** *adv* clearly; **explicamos claramente al sindicato que el 5% era la última oferta de la dirección** = we made it plain to the union that 5% was the management's final offer; **tendrá que explicar claramente al personal que la productividad está bajando** = you will have to make it clear to the staff that productivity is falling

clase *nf* **(a)** *(categoría)* class; **inversiones de primera clase** = gilt-edged investments **(b)** *(transporte público)* **primera clase** = first-class; *(aviones)* **clase preferente** = business class; **clase económica *o* turista** = economy class *o* tourist class; **segunda clase** = second-class; **viajar en segunda clase** = to travel second-class; **¿cuánto cuesta un viaje en primera clase a Nueva York?** = what is the cost of a first class ticket to New York?; **el precio del billete de segunda clase es la mitad del de uno de primera** = the price of a second-class ticket is half that of a first class; **viajo en clase económica porque es más barato** = I travel economy class because it is cheaper **(c)** *(tipo)* kind *o* sort; **¿qué clase de dividendos devengan estas acciones?** = what level of dividend do these shares earn?; **dedicarse a cierta clase de artículos** = to carry a certain range of items in stock **(d)** *(enseñanza)* lesson *o* class *o* lecture *o* tuition; **dar clases** = to teach *o* to lecture; **se gana la vida dando clases particulares** = she earns money giving private lessons **(e)** *(aula)* classroom **(f)** *(posición social)* **clase alta** = upper class; **clase dirigente** = governing class; **clase media** = middle class; **clase obrera *o* trabajadora** = working class

clasificación *nf* classification *o* rating;

clasificación de puestos de trabajo = job classification; **clasificación crediticia** = credit rating

clasificar *vt* to classify *o* to sort *o* to put in order *o* to index; **está clasificando fichas por orden alfabético** = she is sorting index cards into alphabetical order; **los candidatos están clasificados por orden de aparición** = candidates are ranked in order of appearance; **clasificar mercancías *o* productos** = to grade merchandise

◊ **clasificarse** *vr* to occupy a position *o* to rank

cláusula *nf (contrato)* article *o* clause; **hay diez cláusulas en el contrato** = there are ten clauses in the contract; **según la cláusula seis, los pagos no vencen hasta el año que viene** = according to clause six, payments will not be due until next year; **cláusula anulativa** = annulling clause; **cláusula de excepción *o* cláusula de salvaguardia *o* de escape** = escape clause *o* let-out clause *o* hedge clause; **añadió una cláusula de excepción especificando que los pagos se revisarían si el tipo de cambio bajaba más de un 5%** = he added a let-out clause to the effect that the payments would be revised if the exchange rate fell by more than 5%; **cláusula de exclusión** = exclusion clause; **cláusula penal** = penalty clause; **cláusula que prohibe la huelga** = no-strike clause; **cláusula de rescisión** = cancellation clause; **cláusula resolutoria** = termination clause; **cláusula de revisión de precios *o* salarios** = escalator clause; **cláusula suplementaria** = rider *o* supplementary clause; **añadir una cláusula suplementaria a un contrato** = to add a rider to a contract

clausura *nf* closing *o* closure; **sesión de clausura** = closing session

clausurar *vt (reunión)* to close *o* to adjourn *o* wind up (a meeting); **clausuró la reunión dando las gracias al comité** = he wound up the meeting with a vote of thanks to the committee

clave *nf* key; **artículo clave** = flagship; **factor clave** = key factor; **industria clave** = key industry; **personal clave** = key personnel *o* key staff; **puesto clave** = key post

> la clave consiste en volver a motivar a los ejecutivos que ya existen en la empresa; si se consigue, no es preciso cambiar a toda la dirección
>
> **España Económica**

clavo *nm* nail

cliché *nm (estarcido de multicopista)* stencil

cliente *nmf* client *o* customer *o* patron; **un cliente satisfecho** = a satisfied customer; **cliente privado *o* personal** = private client *o* customer; **la tienda estaba llena de clientes** = the shop was full of customers; **¿puede atender a este cliente en primer lugar, por favor?** = can you serve this customer first please?; **aparcamiento para uso exclusivo de los clientes del hotel** = the car park is for the use of hotel patrons only; **es un cliente de la casa** = he is a regular customer; **cliente antiguo *o* de toda la vida** = long-standing customer *o* customer of long standing; **los vendedores estaban buscando posibles clientes** = the salesmen were on the lookout for possible customers; **departamento de atención al cliente** = customer service department

clientela *nf* clientele *o* goodwill; **perder la clientela** = to lose customers *o* to lose someone's custom; **la empresa ha adoptado una imagen dirigida a una clientela más modesta** = the company has adopted a down-market image

clima *nm* climate; *(entre el público)* **clima de confianza** *o* **clima favorable** *o* **clima de optimismo** = feelgood factor

clip *nm* paperclip *o* clip; **los clips se venden en cajas de doscientos** = paperclips come in boxes of two hundred

club *nm* club; **club del personal** = staff club; **cuota del club** = club subscription; **los socios de un club** = club membership; **el club tiene quinientos socios** = the club has a membership of five hundred; **ha solicitado hacerse socio del club deportivo** = he has applied to join the sports club; **si quiere hablar con el director gerente, puede llamarle a su club** = if you want the managing director, you can phone him at his club

> el presidente del club es uno de los hombres a los que Barcelona debe su denominación olímpica
>
> **Cambio 16**

CM = CENTIMETRO

co- *prefijo* co-; **coacreedor** = co-creditor; **coaseguro** = co-insurance; **codirector** = co-director; **codirector gerente** = joint managing director; **codirección** = joint management; **coparticipación** = copartnership *o* joint participation

cobertura *nf* **(a)** *(protección)* cover *o* coverage; **cobertura (contra los cambios de precio** *o* **contra las variaciones de los precios)** = hedge *o* hedging (against changes in price); **cobertura de paro** = percentage of unemployed people receiving unemployment benefit **(b)** *(seguro)* **cobertura del seguro** = insurance cover; **operar sin cobertura suficiente** = to operate without adequate cover; **pedir cobertura adicional** = to ask for additional cover; **cobertura total** = full cover; **¿tiene Vd. cobertura contra daños por incendio?** = do you have cover against fire damage?; **nota de cobertura** = cover note; *US* binder **(c) cobertura periodística** = media coverage; **conseguimos una buena cobertura periodística para el lanzamiento del nuevo producto** = we got good media coverage for the launch of the new model

> el seguro ofrece cobertura al cliente sobre todas sus tarjetas, tanto sobre la del banco emisor que se le recomendó como todas las demás que posea, incluso sobre las tarjetas sanitarias o de compra o de centros comerciales
>
> **El País**

cobrable *adj* collectable *o* cashable

cobrador, -ra *n* collector; **cobrador de alquileres** = rent collector; **(agente) cobrador de morosos** = debt collector

cobrar *vt* **(a)** *(recibir un pago)* to get (paid) *o* to receive *o* to collect; **cobra 50.000 ptas. a la semana por no hacer nada** = he gets 50,000 pesetas a week for doing nothing; **cobrar un cheque** = to cash a cheque; **un cheque cruzado no se puede cobrar en efectivo en ningún banco** = a crossed cheque is not cashable at any bank; **cobrar a destajo** = to be paid by the job; **cobrar una deuda** = to collect a debt; **cobrar las sumas debidas** = to collect money owing *o* monies due; **cobrar un sueldo** = to draw a salary *o* to be paid a salary; **cobrar por horas** = to be paid by the hour; **cobra 1.200 ptas. por hora** = he charges 1,200 pesetas an hour; **cobrar semanalmente** = to be paid by the week; **sin** *o* **por cobrar** = uncollected; **impuestos sin cobrar** = uncollected taxes; **letras por cobrar** = bills receivable *o* bills for collection; **letras a cobrar en pocos días** = short-dated bills; **suscripciones por cobrar** = uncollected subscriptions **(b)** *(precio, pago)* to charge; **cobrar de menos** = to charge too little *o* to undercharge; **cobrar de más** *o* **en exceso** = to charge too much *o* to overcharge; **pedimos que nos reembolsaran porque nos habían cobrado en exceso** = we asked for a refund because we had been overcharged; **cobrar el embalaje al comprador** = to charge the packing to the customer; **cobrar 1.000 ptas. por la entrega** = to charge 1,000 pesetas for delivery; **cobrar una pequeña cantidad por el alquiler** = to make a small charge for rental; **¿cuánto cobra?** = how much does he charge?

cobro *nm* **(a)** *(acción de cobrar)* collection; **cobro de deudas** *o* **de morosos** = debt collection; **agencia de cobro de deudas** *o* **de morosos** = debt collection agency; **cobro a la entrega** = cash on delivery; **cobro en metálico** = cashing *o* encashment; **cobro por recogida** = collection charges *o* collection rates **(b) cobros anticipados** = accrued income; **cobros diferidos** = deferred income **(c)** *(teléfono)* **telefonear a alguien a cobro revertido** = to reverse the charges; *o US* to call somone collect; **llamada a cobro revertido** = transferred charge call; *o US* collect call

coche *nm* car; **coche alquilado** *o* **de alquiler** = a hired car *o* a rented car; **coche particular** = private car; **utilizará su propio coche** = he will be using private transport; **coche de la empresa** = company car

codificación *nf* coding; **la codificación de facturas** = the coding of invoices; **codificación numérica** = numerical coding *o* coding by numbers

código *nm* **(a)** *(reglas)* code; **código de ética profesional** = code of practice; **código de leyes** = statute book **(b)** *(signos, números o letras con significado)* code; **código de almacenamiento** = stock code; **código de barras** = bar code; **código impositivo** *o* **fiscal** = tax code; **códigos legibles por el ordenador** *o* **para la lectura automática** = machine-readable codes; **código postal** = postcode; *US* zip code; **código de un producto** = product code *o* stock code **(c)** *(teléfono)* **código territorial** = area code *o* dialling code **(d)** *(informática)* **código de función** = function code

coeficiente *nm* coefficient *o* rate *o* factor *o* ratio; **coeficiente de absorción** = absorption rate; **coeficiente de ajuste de precios** = price differential; **coeficiente de ajuste salarial** = wage differentials; **coeficientes bancarios** = banking ratios; **coeficientes bursátiles** = stock exchange ratios; **coeficiente de endeudamiento de una empresa** = leverage; **coeficiente de liquidez** = liquidity ratio *o* acid test ratio; **coeficiente de ocupación** = load factor

cohecho *nm* bribe *o* bribery

el ex presidente, inculpado por cohecho en
el 'caso Sóller'
El País

coincidir *vi* **(a)** to coincide **(b) coincidir con** = to agree with; **los dos grupos de cálculos no coinciden** = the two sets of calculations do not agree

cojín *nm* cushion; **colocó un cojín en la silla porque era demasiado dura** = she put a cushion on her chair as it was too hard

cola *nf* **(a)** *(pegamento)* glue *o* gum; **pegó la etiqueta a la caja con cola** = he stuck the label to the box with glue **(b)** *(fila)* queue; *US* line; **formar una cola** *o* **ponerse en la cola** = to form a queue *o* to join a queue; **se formaron colas en las puertas del banco cuando se divulgó la noticia de su posible quiebra** = queues formed at the doors of the bank when the news spread about its possible collapse; **saltarse la cola** = to jump the queue; **se saltaron la cola de espera y consiguieron la licencia de exportación antes que nosotros** = they jumped the queue and got their export licence before we did; **cola para cobrar el subsidio del paro** = dole queue; **su pedido fue a parar al final de la cola** = his order went to the end of the queue

colaboración *nf* collaboration *o* contribution; **su colaboración en el proyecto fue muy provechosa** = their collaboration on the project was very profitable

◊ **colaborador, -ra** *n* collaborator

colaborar *vi* to collaborate; **colaborar con una empresa francesa en una obra de construcción** = to collaborate with a French firm on a building project; **colaboraron en la construcción de la nueva aeronave** = they collaborated on the new aircraft

colapso *nm* collapse *o* breakdown; **el director sufrió un colapso nervioso y tuvimos que cancelar el proyecto** = the manager suffered a nervous breakdown and we had to cancel the project

el colapso de la producción industrial, el aumento del desempleo y el cierre de empresas desvalorizadas, serán las espoletas de la transformación económica y no los síntomas negativos de un declive económico
Actualidad Económica

colateral *adj* collateral

colectivo, -va 1 *adj* collective *o* joint; **convenio colectivo libre** = free collective bargaining; **firmaron un convenio salarial colectivo** = they signed a collective wage agreement; **granja colectiva** = collective farm; **propiedad colectiva** = collective ownership; **signatario colectivo** = joint signatory **2** *nm* group

este manual pretende ayudar en la capacitación de los vendedores de tienda, un colectivo de profesionales a los que la formación siempre ha postergado debido a las dificultades para su acceso a los canales habituales de la formación
El País

colega *nmf* colleague *o* associate; **cuando se casó, sus colegas le hicieron un regalo** = his colleagues gave him a present when he got married; **conozco a**

Juanjo, fuimos *o* **éramos colegas en mi último trabajo** = I know Juanjo - he was a colleague of mine at my last job; **es una colega** = she's a colleague *o* a business associate of mine

colegiado, -da *adj* contable colegiado = chartered accountant

colegio *nm* **(a)** *(escuela)* school *o* college; **Collegio Mayor** = halls of residence (at a university) **(b)** *(asociación profesional)* association *o* institute; **colegio de abogados** = the Law Society *o* the Bar Association; **colegio de censores públicos** = Institute of Chartered Accountants; **colegio profesional** = professional association

colgar 1 *vt* to hang; **colgó el paraguas en el respaldo de la silla** = he hung his umbrella over the back of his chair **2** *vi* *(teléfono)* to hang up; **no cuelgue** = hold the line please; **cuando le pregunté por la factura, colgó** = when I asked him about the invoice, he hung up

colisión *nf* collision *o* crash *o* clash

colocación *nf* **(a)** *(trabajo)* employment; **agencia de colocación** = employment agency **(b)** *(posicionamiento)* placing *o* placement; **la colocación de una emisión de acciones** = the placing of a share issue

colocar *vt* to place *o* to put *o* to lodge; **colocar dinero en una cuenta** = to place money in an account; **colocar a empleados** = to place staff; **colocar un paquete de acciones** = to place a block of shares

Colombia *nf* Colombia

◊ **colombiano, -na** *adj y n* Colombian
NOTA: capital: **Bogotá** (= Bogota); moneda: **peso colombiano (Col$)** = Colombian peso (Col$)

color *nm* colour; *US* color; **muestra de color** = colour swatch

columna *nf* **(a)** *(periódico)* column; **escribe una columna sobre finanzas personales que se publica en varios periódicos** = he writes a syndicated column on personal finance **(b)** *(lista vertical de cifras)* column; **sumar una columna de cifras** = to add up a column of figures; **ponga el total al pie de la columna** = put the total at the bottom of the column; **columna del haber** = credit column; **columna del debe** = debit column *o* debit side; **el haber es la columna de la derecha de las cuentas** = the credit side is the right-hand column in the accounts

columnista *nmf* columnist

llamó mucho la atención que dentro del mismo semanario convivieran columnistas de prestigio de muy distinta tendencia ideológica
Tiempo

coma *nf* comma; **coma decimal** = decimal point

comandita *nf* sleeping partnership *o* silent partnership; **sociedad en comandita** = limited partnership; **socio en comandita** = sleeping partner *o* silent partner *o* limited partner

◊ **comanditario** *adj* socio comanditario = sleeping partner *o* silent partner *o* limited partner

combatir 1 *vt* to fight *o* to challenge **2** *vi*
combatir contra = to fight against

combinación *nf* **(a)** *(mezcla)* combination; **una**
combinación de problemas de tesorería y del
mercado ocasionó el hundimiento de la compañía
= a combination of cash flow problems and difficult
trading conditions caused the company's collapse
(b) *(de números, cifras)* combination *o* number
permutation; **he olvidado la combinación de la**
cerradura de mi cartera = I have forgotten the
combination of the lock on my briefcase; **la caja**
fuerte de la oficina tiene una cerradura de
combinación = the office safe has a combination
lock

combinar *vt* to combine *o* to mix; **me gusta**
combinar el trabajo con el placer, ¿por qué no
hablamos del asunto mientras almorzamos? = I
like to mix business with pleasure - why don't we
discuss the deal over lunch?

combustible *nm* fuel; **la factura anual de**
combustible de la fábrica se ha duplicado en los
últimos años = the annual fuel bill for the plant has
doubled over the last years

comedor *nm (en el trabajo)* canteen

comentario *nm* comment *o* commentary; **sin**
comentarios = no comment

comenzar *vt* to begin *o* to start; **el presidente**
comenzó la reunión a las 10.30 = the chairman
opened the meeting at 10.30

comerciable *adj* marketable *o* saleable

comercial 1 *adj* commercial *o* business; **la**
ciudad de veraneo se ha hecho tan comercial que
resulta desagradable = the holiday town has
become so commercialized that it is unpleasant; **hay**
siempre poca actividad comercial después de
Navidades = business is always slow after
Christmas; **acreedores comerciales** = trade
creditors; **acuerdo comercial** = trade agreement;
agregado comercial = commercial attaché;
asociación comercial = trade association;
Proyectos González ha solicitado ingresar en la
asociación comercial = Proyectos González has
applied to join the trade association; **atracción**
comercial = sales appeal; **avión comercial** *o*
aviones comerciales = commercial aircraft;
balanza comercial = balance of trade *o* trade
balance; **balanza comercial desfavorable** *o* **con**
déficit *o* **negativa** = adverse balance of trade; **el país**
tuvo una balanza comercial negativa por segundo
mes consecutivo = the country had an adverse
balance of trade for the second month running;
balanza comercial favorable = favourable balance
of trade; **banco comercial** = clearing bank *o*
accepting house *o* acceptance house; **imponer**
barreras comerciales sobre = to impose trade
barriers on; **carta comercial** = business letter;
centro comercial = business centre *o* shopping
centre; **condiciones comerciales desfavorables** =
adverse trading conditions; **convenio comercial** =
trade agreement; **correspondencia comercial** =
business correspondence; **corresponsal comercial**
= business correspondent; **curso comercial** =
commercial course; **estudió un curso comercial**
por correspondencia = he took a commercial
course by correspondence; **déficit comercial** = trade

deficit *o* trade gap; **descripción comercial** = trade
description; **deudores comerciales** = trade debtors;
dirección comercial = business address; **distrito**
comercial = business dictrict *o* commercial district;
estrategia comercial = business strategy; **feria**
comercial = trade fair; **organizar una feria**
comercial = to organize *o* to run a trade fair; **guía**
comercial = commercial directory *o* trade directory;
horario comercial = opening hours; **oficina de**
información comercial = trade bureau; **marca**
comercial = brand name; **misión comercial** = trade
mission; **nombre comercial** = trade name *o*
trademark; **plan comercial** = business plan; **prensa**
comercial = trade press; **progreso comercial** =
advance in trade; **puerto comercial** = commercial
port; **quiebra comercial** = business failure; **ramo**
comercial = line of business *o* line of work; **pedir**
referencias comerciales a una empresa = to ask a
company to supply trade references; **tener**
relaciones comerciales con alguien = to have
dealings with someone; **repertorio comercial** =
trade directory; **sección comercial** = marketing
department; **sociedad comercial** = trading
company; **tratado comercial** = trade agreement;
muestra gratuita - sin valor comercial = sample
only - of no commercial value; **vehículo comercial**
= commercial vehicle; **zona comercial peatonal** =
shopping precinct **2** *nm* commercial

comercialización *nf* marketing *o*
commercialization *o* merchandising;
comercialización a gran escala = mass marketing;
la comercialización de los museos = the
commercialization of museums; **comercialización**
de un producto = marketing *o* merchandising of a
product; **planificar la comercialización de un**
nuevo producto = to plan the marketing of a new
product; **acuerdo de comercialización** = marketing
agreement; **costes de comercialización** = marketing
costs; **departamento de comercialización** =
merchandising department; **director de**
comercialización = marketing manager

> tras la prohibición de comercialización
> de la piel de los animales grandes, la
> industria de la piel se concentró en los
> felinos menores
>   **Ajoblanco**

comercializar *vt* to commercialize *o* to market;
comercializar un producto = to market a product

comercialmente *adv* commercially

comerciante *nmf* dealer *o* merchant *o*
shopkeeper *o* trader *o* merchandiser *o* salesman;
comerciantes = tradespeople; **comerciante al por**
mayor = wholesale dealer *o* wholesaler;
comerciante al por menor *o* **al detall** = retail dealer
o retailer; **comerciante exclusivo** = sole trader;
comerciante de materias primas = commodity
trader; **comerciante de mercancías de segunda**
mano = secondhand dealer; **comerciante de tabaco**
= dealer in tobacco *o* tobacco dealer; **comerciante**
de vinos = wine merchant; **es comerciante de vino**
francés = he trades in French wine; **nación**
comerciante *o* **país comerciante** = trading nation *o*
mercantile country

comerciar *vi* **(a)** *(entre dos personas)* **comerciar**
con alguien = to do business with *o* to deal with
someone *o* to have dealings with someone **(b)** *(entre*
empresas, países) to trade with; **comerciar con otro**

país = to trade with another country **(c)** *(mercancías)* to trade in *o* to deal in; **comerciar en el sector pieles** *o* **cueros** = to deal in leather; **no comerciamos en coches extranjeros** = we do not handle foreign cars; **la empresa comercia con bienes importados** = the company trades in imported goods; **comerciar con bebidas alcohólicas ilícitas** = trade in illicit alcohol

comercio *nm* **(a)** *(transacción comercial)* trade *o* business *o* commerce *o* trading; **comercio bilateral** = bilateral *o* two-way trading; **comercio dominical** = Sunday opening *o* trading; **comercio de exportación** *o* **comercio de importación** = export trade *o* import trade; **comercio exterior** = foreign trade *o* overseas trade *o* external trade; **comercio de futuros** = futures trading; **comercio de importación** = import trade; **comercio interior** *o* **nacional** = domestic trade *o* home trade; **comercio de invisibles** = invisible trade; **comercio justo** = fair trade; **comercio mundial** = world trade; **comercio de ultramar** = overseas trade; **comercio unilateral** = one-way trade; **el comercio está en alza** = business is expanding; **área de comercio** = trading area; **área** *o* **zona de libre comercio** = free trade area; **Cámara de Comercio** = Chamber of Commerce; **costumbres** *o* **usos del comercio** = the customs of the trade; **escuela superior de comercio** = commercial college; **estructura del comercio** = pattern of trade *o* trading pattern; **libre comercio** = free trade; **partidario del libre comercio** = free trader; **prohibir el comercio** = to put an embargo on trade; **reactivación del comercio** = revival of trade **(b)** *(bolsa)* dealing *o* trading; **comercio justo** = fair trading; **corredor de comercio de divisas** = foreign exchange broker

> las inversiones y el comercio con Japón han renovado el panorama económico de toda Asia
>
> **Actualidad Económica**

> no se trata sólo de comprar para ayudar a los necesitados; la filosofía del comercio justo va mucho más allá, es una fórmula comercial en sí
>
> **El País**

> J. R., de 41 años, realizó la carrera de Comercio en la Escuela de Altos Estudios Mercantiles de Barcelona y el MBA en la Escuela Europea de Negocios
>
> **El País**

> el comercio justo promueve la compra de forma directa a los pueblos del sur
>
> **El País**

cometer *vt* to commit; **cometer un error** = to make a mistake *o* to slip up

cometido *nm* task *o* duty *o* remit; **el nuevo director gerente fue nombrado con el cometido de mejorar el rendimiento de la compañía** = the new MD was appointed with the remit to improve the company's performance

comida *nf* food; **comidas preparadas** = convenience foods; **una comida para llevar** = a takeaway meal; **le gusta mucho la comida india** = he is very fond of Indian food; **la comida del restaurante de la empresa es excelente** = the food in the staff restaurant is excellent

comienzo *nm* beginning *o* start *o* starting *o* origin; **fecha de comienzo** = starting date; **comienzo de la puja** = opening *o* starting of the bidding

comisión *nf* **(a)** *(pago)* commission *o* fee; **comisión de corredor de bolsa** = stockbroker's commission *o* brokerage *o* broker's commission; **comisión del credere** *o* **de garantía** = del credere commission; **comisión dividida** = split commission; **cobra** *o* **recibe un 10% de comisión** = he charges *o* he gets 10% commission; **el grupo recibe una comisión por todas las ventas de la compañía** = the group gets a commission on all the company's sales; **representante a comisión** *o* **representante que trabaja a comisión** = commission rep; **trabaja como representante a comisión para dos empresas** = he is a rep for two firms on commission; **venta a comisión** = commission sale *o* sale on commission; *(gastos bancarios)* **comisión bancaria** = bank charges; *US* service charge **(b)** *(comité)* committee *o* commission; **ser miembro de una comisión** = to sit on a committee; **comisión consultiva** = advisory board; **Comisión Europea** = European Commission; **es el presidente de la comisión gubernamental de subsidios a la exportación** = he is the chairman of the government commission on export subsidies; **las conclusiones de una comisión investigadora** = the findings of a commission of enquiry; **comisión negociadora** = negotiating committee; **comisión organizadora** = organizing committee; **es miembro de la comisión organizadora del congreso** = he is a member of the organizing committee for the conference; **Comisiones Obreras (CC OO)** = Workers' Union

◊ **comisionista** *nmf* commission agent; **prima al comisionista** = del credere

> los ingresos de una compañía de gestión son las comisiones que recibe en función de la facturación y rentabilidad del establecimiento
>
> **El País**

comité *nm* committee *o* commission; **ser miembro de un comité** = to be a member of a committee *o* to sit on a committee; **fue elegida miembro del comité** *o* **la nombraron miembro del comité** = she was voted on to the committee *o* she was elected to the committee; **ser presidente de un comité** = to be the chairman of a committee; **es el presidente del comité de planificación** = he is the chairman of the planning committee; **presidir un comité** = to chair a committee; **fue designada para ocupar la vicepresidencia del comité** = she was appointed to the vice-chairmanship of the committee; **el comité agradeció al presidente saliente la labor realizada** = the committee thanked the retiring chairman for his work; **comité de empresa** = works committee *o* works council; **comité de gestión** = management committee; **comité negociador** = negotiating committee; **comité de selección** = selection board *o* selection committee; **el gobierno ha nombrado un comité de investigación para examinar los problemas de los pequeños exportadores** = the government has appointed a commission of inquiry to look into the problems of small exporters

como *adv* as *o* like; **como medida preventiva** = as a precautionary measure; **como un favor** = as a favour; **le pidió un préstamo a la secretaria como**

un favor = he asked the secretary for a loan as a favour

comodidad *nf* comfort *o* convenience; **vive con la mayor comodidad a pesar de su sueldo** = he lives very comfortably in spite of his salary

cómodo, -da *adj* convenient *o* easy *o* handy; **un giro bancario constituye una manera cómoda de enviar dinero al extranjero** = a bank draft is a convenient way of sending money abroad; **el préstamo se devuelve en cómodos plazos** = the loan is repayable in easy payments; **se venden en paquetes de tamaño muy cómodo** = they are sold in handy-sized packs

compañero, -ra *n* companion; **compañero (de trabajo)** = colleague

compañía *nf* **(a)** *(sociedad, empresa)* company; **compañía acreditada** = company of good standing; **compañía afiliada** *o* **asociada** = associate company *o* related company; **compañía cuyas acciones se cotizan en la bolsa** *o* **sociedad registrada** = listed company; **compañía fiable** = reliable company; **compañía fiduciaria** = trust company; **compañía registrada disponible** = off-the-shelf company **(b)** **compañía aérea** = airline; **compañía aseguradora** = insurance company *o* assurer *o* assuror; **compañía naviera** = shipping company; **compañía de seguros** = insurance company; **la compañía de seguros extendió una póliza** = the insurance company made out a policy *o* drew up a policy; **compañía de transporte aéreo** = air carrier **(c)** **accionista de una compañía** = shareholder in a company; **adquirir una compañía** = to take over a company; **los cargos directivos de una compañía** = the company officers *o* the officers of a company; **crear una compañía** = to set up a business *o* company; **financiar una compañía** = to finance *o* to fund a company; **fundación de una compañía** = setting up of a company; **fundar una nueva compañía** = to set up a new company; **el lanzamiento de una nueva compañía** = the flotation of a new company; **liquidar una compañía** = to put a company into liquidation; **adquirió una participación minoritaria de la compañía** = he acquired a minority shareholding in the company; **la reorganización de una compañía** = the reorganization of a company *o* a company reorganization *o* the reconstruction of a company; **sello de la compañía** = common seal *o* company's seal; **la situación financiera de una compañía** = financial situation of a company (NOTA: se abrevia **Cía.**)

> la celebración de la junta de accionistas se saldó con la salida de los representantes de familias tradicionales de la compañía
> **El País**

> las tres compañías europeas con mayor rentabilidad son precisamente las que tienen previsto ahorrar más los próximos años
> **El País**

comparable *adj* comparable; **los dos grupos de cifras no son comparables** = the two sets of figures are not comparable; **escalas de sueldos comparables** = pay comparability

comparación *nf* comparison; **comparación de precios** = price comparison; **en comparación con** = compared with; **el aumento de deudores en comparación con la cifra del último trimestre** = increase in debtors compared with the last quarter's figure; **las ventas han bajado en comparación con el año pasado** = sales are down in comparison with last year; **comparaciones entre países** = comparisons between countries *o* inter-country comparisons

comparar *vt* to compare; **comparar con** = to compare with; **el director de finanzas comparó las cifras del primer y del segundo trimestre** = the finance director compared the figures for the first and second quarters; **no se pueden comparar las ventas en el extranjero con las nacionales** = there is no comparison between overseas and home sales; **comparar precios** = to compare prices *o* to shop around; **deberías comparar precios antes de llevar tu coche a revisar** = you should shop around before getting your car serviced; **vale la pena comparar las opciones antes de solicitar una hipoteca** = it pays to shop around when you are planning to ask for a mortgage

compartir *vt* to divide *o* to share; **compartir la cuenta** = to share the bill *o* to go Dutch; **compartir información** *o* **compartir datos** = to share information *o* to share data; **compartir una oficina** = to share an office; **compartir un teléfono** = to share a telephone; **compartir el tiempo del ordenador** = to share computer time

compasión *nf* sympathy *o* pity; **sin compasión** = merciless

compasivo, -va *adj* sympathetic *o* understanding

compensación *nf* **(a)** *(finanzas)* clearing; **compensación de un cheque** = clearance of a cheque; **cámara de compensación** = clearing house; **Servicio de Compensación y Liquidación de Valores (SCLV)** = share clearing and settlement service **(b)** *(indemnización)* compensation; **compensación por daños y perjuicios** = compensation for damage **(c)** *(a cambio)* **en compensación** = quid pro quo

compensar *vt* **(a)** *(indemnizar)* to compensate *o* to make good *o* to make up (for) *o* to offset *o* to set against; **compensar a un director por pérdida de comisiones** = to compensate a manager for loss of commission; **compensar la pérdida** *o* **la diferencia** = to make up a loss *o* to make up the difference; **compensar un pago insuficiente** *o* **compensar un pago atrasado** = to make up for a short payment *o* to make up for a late payment; **empleamos personal a tiempo parcial para compensar la insuficiencia de plantilla** = we employ part-timers to make up for staff shortages **(b)** *(finanzas)* to clear (a cheque); **tiene que contar con seis días para que el cheque sea compensado** = you should allow six days for the cheque to clear; **compensar dividendos** = to equalize dividends

compensatorio, -ria *adj* compensatory; **derechos compensatorios** = countervailing duties

competencia *nf* **(a)** *(rivalidad)* competition *o* competitiveness; **competencia desleal** = unfair competition; **competencia encarnizada** = cut-throat competition; **competencia intensa** = keen competition; **competencia perfecta** = perfect competition; **fuerte competencia** = keen competition; **nos enfrentamos a la fuerte competencia de los fabricantes europeos** = we are facing some keen competition from European manufacturers; **libre competencia** = free competition; **productos en competencia** = competing products; **el negocio de la confección ha sufrido la competencia extranjera** = the clothing trade has suffered from foreign competition **(b)** *(rival)* **la competencia** = the competition; **hundir a la competencia** = to beat *o* to hammer the competition; **hemos reducido nuestros precios para derrotar a la competencia** = we have lowered our prices to beat the competition; **la competencia ha sacado una nueva gama de productos** = the competition has *o* have brought out a new range of products **(c)** *(aptitud)* expertise *o* qualifications *o* competence; **contratamos al Sr. Iglesias por su competencia en las finanzas** = we hired Sr Iglesias because of his financial expertise **(d)** responsibility; **no es de mi competencia** = it's not my responsibility **(e)** *(jurídico)* competence *o* competency; **el asunto cae dentro de la competencia del tribunal** = the case falls within the competence of the court

> la protección contra la competencia
> extranjera retarda la innovación, sube
> los costes de producción y limita las
> opciones del consumidor
> **Mercado**

> diversos catedráticos, profesores y
> expertos en derecho analizan distintos
> puntos relacionados con el nuevo marco de
> competencia desleal
> **El País**

competente *adj* capable *o* competent *o* proficient; **muy competente** = highly qualified; **es una directora de departamento muy competente** = she is a very capable departmental manager; **tuvimos dificultades para encontrar una secretaria competente** = we had a job to find a qualified secretary

competidor, -ra 1 *adj* competing *o* rival; **una empresa competidora** = a rival company; **estamos analizando las marcas competidoras del mercado** = we are analyzing the rival brands on the market **2** *n* competitor *o* rival; **dos empresas alemanas son nuestros principales competidores** = two German firms are our main competitors

competir *vi* to compete; **competir con alguien** *o* **con una compañía** = to compete with someone *o* with a company; **estaban compitiendo sin éxito con compañías locales en su propia zona** = they were competing unsuccessfully with local companies on their home territory; **las dos empresas compiten por un contrato** = the two companies are competing for a contract; **tenemos que competir con las importaciones a bajo precio del Extremo Oriente** = we have to compete with cheap imports from the Far East

competitividad *nf* competitiveness

> para que el peso del ajuste no recaiga
> especialmente sobre la actividad y el
> empleo, hay que incrementar la
> competitividad
> **España Económica**

> En el caso de Estados Unidos, la
> competitividad internacional se buscará
> mediante una nueva devaluación del dólar
> **Actualidad Económica**

competitivo, -va *adj* competing *o* competitive; **precio competitivo** = competitive price *o* keen price; **con precio competitivo** = competitively priced; **fijación de precios competitivos** = competitive pricing; **nuestros precios son los más competitivos del mercado** = our prices are the keenest on the market; **productos competitivos** = competing products

compilación *nf* compilation

◊ **compilar** *vt* to compile

complejo, -ja 1 *adj* complex; **un sistema complejo de controles de importación** = a complex system of import controls; **las especificaciones de la máquina son muy complejas** = the specifications for the machine are very complex **2** *nm* complex; **un gran complejo industrial** = a large industrial complex

complementario, -ria *adj* complementary *o* additional; **gastos adicionales y complementarios** = extra charges

completar *vt* **(a)** *(hacer completo)* to complete **(b)** *(llenar)* to fill up *o* to top up

completo, -ta *adj* **(a)** *(entero)* complete *o* full; **por completo** = completely; **el pedido está completo y listo para su envío** = the order is complete and ready for sending; **el pedido debe entregarse solamente si está completo** = the order should be delivered only if it is complete; **tres días laborables completos** = three clear days *o* three working days; **a tiempo completo** *o* **a jornada completa** = full-time; **trabajador a tiempo completo** = full-timer; **es uno de nuestros trabajadores a jornada completa** = he is one of our full-time staff; **trabaja a tiempo completo** = she is in full-time work *o* she works full-time *o* she is in full-time employment **(b)** 'completo' = 'no vacancies'; **el hotel** *o* **el vuelo está completo** = the hotel *o* the flight is fully booked *o* is booked up

◊ **completamente** *adv* completely *o* fully; **el proyecto** *o* **la compañía se autofinancia completamente** = the project *o* the company is completely self-financed *o* completely self-financing; **el agua estropeó completamente el cargamento** = the cargo was completely ruined by water; **la fábrica se quemó completamente** = the factory was burnt to the ground

complicación *nf* complication *o* difficulty

◊ **complicar** *vt* to complicate

componedor, -ra *n* **(a)** *(intermediario)* mediator **(b)** *(jurídico o legal: mediador en un conflicto)* **amigable componedor** = arbitrator *o* honest broker; **actuar de amigable componedor** = to play the honest broker

componente *nm* component; **fábrica de componentes** = components factory; *(informática)* **componentes lógicos** = software

componer *vt* to repair; **se dedica a componer relojes** = he repairs watches

◊ **componerse** *vr* to consist of *o* to be made up of; **el equipo de ventas se compone de cinco representantes** = the sales team consists of *o* is made up of five reps

comportamiento *nm* behaviour *o* performance; **como una medida del comportamiento de la empresa** = as a measure of the company's performance; **el comportamiento de los beneficios** = earnings performance; **comportamiento económico** = economic performance

comportarse *vr* **(a)** *(conducirse)* to behave; **no sabe comportarse en situaciones como éstas** = he doesn't know what to do in a situation like this **(b)** *(actuar)* to perform

compra *nf* **(a)** *(adquisición)* purchase *o* acquisition *o* buying *o* procurement; **compra al contado** *o* **compra de entrega inmediata** = buying for cash *o* cash purchase *o* outright purchase *o* spot purchase; **compra de una empresa por ejecutivos** = management buyout; **compra a grandes cantidades** *o* **compra a granel** = bulk buying *o* bulk purchase *o* quantity purchase; **compra febril de azúcar** *o* **dólares** = panic buying of sugar *o* of dollars; **compra impulsiva** = impulse buying; **compra a plazos** = hire purchase (HP); **está comprando un frigorífico a plazos** = he is buying a refrigerator on hire purchase; **firmar un contrato de compra a plazos** = to sign a hire-purchase agreement; **compra al por mayor** = wholesale purchase *o* bulk purchase; **generalmente concedemos un descuento del 25% a las compras al por mayor** = we generally give a 25% discount for trade purchases; **compra al por menor** = retail purchase; **agente de compras** = purchasing officer; **bolsa de la compra** *o* **cesta de la compra** = shopping basket; **el precio medio de la bolsa de la compra ha aumentado en un 6%** = the price of the average shopping basket *o* the market basket has risen by 6%; **carro** *o* **carrito de la compra** = supermarket trolley; **centralización de las compras** = central purchasing; **departamento de compras** = purchasing department *o* buying department; **hacer una compra** = to make a purchase; **impuesto sobre las compras** = purchase tax; **jefe de compras** = purchasing manager *o* head buyer; **es la encargada de compras de calzado para unos grandes almacenes de Barcelona** = she is the shoe buyer for a Barcelona department store; **libro de compras** = purchase book; **libro mayor de compras** = bought ledger *o* purchase ledger; **orden de compra** = purchase order; **no podemos servirle sin el número de orden de compra** = we cannot supply you without a purchase order number; **precio de compra** = purchase price **(b)** *(bolsa)* **compra apalancada** = leveraged buyout (LBO); **compra de futuros** = forward buying *o* buying forward; **opción de compra de acciones** = call option *o* option to purchase; **conceder una opción de compra a alguien** = to give someone first refusal of something **(c)** **buena compra** *o* **mala compra** = good buy *o* bad buy; **aquel reloj fue una buena compra** = that watch was a good buy; **este coche fue una mala compra** = this car was a bad buy; **hacer la compra en el supermercado del barrio** = to do one's shopping in the local supermarket

◊ **compras** *nfpl* shopping; **ir de compras** = to go shopping; **compras al contado** = cash purchases

comprador, -ra *n* **(a)** *(persona que compra)* buyer *o* purchaser; **un posible comprador** = a prospective buyer; **no hubo compradores** = there were no buyers; **no hubo compradores para las nuevas acciones** = there were no takers for the new shares; **mercado favorable a los compradores** = a buyers' market; **el comprador asume el pasivo de la compañía** = the buyer takes over the company's liabilities; **la compañía busca un comprador** = the company is looking for a purchaser; **la compañía ha encontrado un comprador para su almacén** = the company has found a purchaser for its warehouse; **riesgo a cuenta del comprador** = at buyer's risk **(b)** *(en una tienda)* customer *o* shopper *o* buyer; **comprador impulsivo** = impulse buyer; **la tienda está abierta hasta medianoche para atender a los compradores nocturnos** = the store stays open to midnight to cater for late-night shoppers; **la tienda pone estantes con chocolatines junto a las cajas registradoras para tentar al comprador impulsivo** = the store puts racks of chocolates by the checkout to attract the impulse buyer

comprar *vt* to buy *o* to purchase *o* to acquire; **compró un billete a precio íntegro** = he bought a full-price ticket; **compró 10.000 acciones** = he bought 10,000 shares; **comprar algo de buena fe** = to buy something in good faith; **comprar al contado** *o* **en efectivo** = to buy for cash; **comprar a crédito** = to buy on credit; **comprar algo con fines especulativos** = to buy something on spec; **comprar a futuros** = to buy forward; **comprar divisas a futuros** = to buy currency forward; **comprar a granel** = to buy in bulk; **comprar al instante** = to buy something quickly *o* to snap something up; **compró al instante el 15% de las acciones de la compañía** = he snapped up 15% of the company's shares; **comprar a plazos** = to buy in instalments; **comprar un coche a plazos** *o* **un frigorífico a plazos** = to buy a car *o* a refrigerator on hire purchase *o* on HP; *US* on the installment plan; **todos los muebles de la casa se compraron a plazos** = all the furniture in the house was bought on HP; **comprar al por mayor y vender al por menor** = to buy wholesale and to sell retail; **comprar algo a prueba** = to buy something on approval; **comprar algo sin verlo** = to buy something sight unseen; **volver a comprar** = to buy back; **vendió la tienda el año pasado y ahora está intentando volver a comprarla** = he sold the shop last year and is now trying to buy it back

compraventa *nf* buying and selling *o* sale and purchase *o* trading; **se dedica a la compraventa de coches de segunda mano** = he is in the secondhand car trade (NOTA: se escribe también **compra-venta**)

el mercado mundial de compra-venta de
empresas está alcanzando cotas
históricas de auténtico frenesí
España Económica

otro de los fraudes que están siendo
investigados consiste en la compraventa
fraudulenta de terrenos, con el fin de
ahorrarse buena parte del pago de los
impuestos
Cambio 16

comprender *vt/i* **(a)** *(entender)* to understand *o* to realize; **hacer comprender** = to make someone understand *o* to get something across to someone *o* to get through to someone; **el hecho de que el**

presidente comprendiera que iba a perder la votación = the chairman's realization that he was going to be outvoted; **no podía hacerle comprender que tenía que estar en el aeropuerto antes de las 2.15** = I could not get through to her that I had to be at the airport by 2.15; **el director intentó hacer comprender al personal las razones por las que se iba a despedir a algunas personas** = the manager tried to get across to the workforce why some people were being made redundant **(b)** *(incluir)* to include *o* to comprise; **el desayuno está comprendido en el precio** = the price includes breakfast

comprensión *nf* comprehension *o* realization *o* understanding

comprensivo, -va *adj* reasonable *o* sympathetic *o* tolerant; **el encargado de la tienda fue muy comprensivo cuando ella trató de explicar que se había dejado sus tarjetas de crédito en casa** = the manager of the shop was very reasonable when she tried to explain that she had left her credit cards at home

comprobación *nf* check *o* trial *o* verification; **comprobación de las existencias de almacén** = stock control; **comprobación de informes sobre una persona** = checking a person's references *o* reference check; **balance de comprobación** = trial balance; **lista de comprobación** = check list; **muestra de comprobación** = check sample

comprobante *nm* voucher *o* receipt; **comprobante de caja** = sales receipt *o* petty cash voucher; **comprobante de matriz de talonario** = counterfoil; **comprobante de venta** = bill of sale

comprobar *vt* to check *o* to monitor *o* to verify; **comprobar que una factura es correcta** = to check that an invoice is correct; **sin comprobar** *o* **no comprobado, -da** = unchecked; **cifras sin comprobar** = unchecked figures

comprometer *vt* **(a)** *(arriesgar)* to risk; **comprometió la buena reputación de la empresa** = he put the good name of the firm at risk **(b)** *(obligar)* (i) to agree formally; (ii) to bind; **comprometer a alguien a hacer algo** = to engage *o* oblige someone to do something; **el contrato nos compromete a realizar un mínimo de compras anuales** = the contract engages us to a minimum annual purchase

◇ **comprometerse** *vr* to get involved *o* to commit oneself *o* to undertake; **comprometerse por contrato** = to contract (to do something); **comprometerse a suministrar repuestos por contrato** = to contract to supply spare parts *o* to contract for the supply of spare parts; **no quiero comprometerme** = I want to leave my options open; **se han comprometido por escrito a no hacernos la competencia con sus productos** = they have given us a written undertaking not to sell their products in competition with ours; **cada uno se ha comprometido a no comerciar en la zona del otro** = they have all agreed not to trade in each other's area; **se han comprometido a no vender en nuestro territorio** = they have undertaken not to sell into our territory

compromiso *nm* **(a)** *(obligación)* commitment *o* engagement *o* obligation *o* undertaking; **libre de compromiso** *o* **sin compromiso** = without

obligation; **dos semanas de prueba sin compromiso de compra** = two weeks' free trial without obligation; **romper un compromiso** = to break an engagement; **la compañía rompió su compromiso de no vender los productos de nuestro competidor** = the company broke their engagement not to sell our rival's products **(b)** *(citas)* engagements *o* appointments; **no tengo compromisos para el resto del día** = I have no engagements for the rest of the day **(c)** *(promesa)* compromise *o* undertaking *o* agreement; **la empresa faltó a su compromiso** = the company went back on its word; **compromiso verbal** = verbal agreement **(d)** **poner en un compromiso** = to place in a difficult situation; **sacar** *o* **salir de un compromiso** = to get out of a difficult situation *o* of a tight corner

compulsa *nf* certified (true) copy

compulsado, -da 1 *adj* certified as a true copy; **fotocopia compulsada** = authenticated photocopy **2** *pp de* COMPULSAR

compulsar *vt* to certify as a true copy *o* to authenticate

computable *adj* computable

computar *vt* to calculate *o* to compute

cómputo *nm* calculation *o* computation *o* estimate; **¿podría hacerme un cómputo de las horas que se emplearon en el trabajo ?** = can you give me an estimate of how much time was spent on the job?

común *adj* **(a)** *(frecuente)* common **(b)** *(ordinario)* ordinary **(c)** *(comunitario)* **el Mercado Común Europeo** = the European Common Market; **Política Agrícola Común (PAC)** = Common Agricultural Policy (CAP) **(d)** *(conjuntamente)* joint; **en común** = in common *o* jointly; **empresa mixta** *o* **en común** = joint venture; **tener una propiedad en común** = to own a property jointly

comunicación *nf* communication; **después de la inundación se cortaron todas las comunicaciones con el mundo exterior** = after the flood all communications with the outside world were broken; **la comunicación con la oficina principal es más fácil por fax** = communication with the head office is easier by fax; **establecer comunicación con alguien** = to enter into communication with someone; **hemos establecido comunicación con el departamento gubernamental pertinente** = we have entered into communication with the relevant government department; **medios de comunicación** = mass media *o* the media; **el producto atrajo mucho interés en los medios de comunicación** = the product attracted a lot of interest in the media *o* a lot of media interest

comunicado *nm* **(a)** *(escrito)* communication; **hemos recibido un comunicado del inspector fiscal de la zona** = we have had a communication from the local tax inspector **(b)** **comunicado de prensa** = press release *o* communiqué; **la compañía hizo público un comunicado sobre el nuevo director gerente** = the company sent out a news release about the new managing director; **la empresa emitió un comunicado de prensa sobre el lanzamiento del nuevo coche** = the company sent out *o* issued a press release about the launch of the new car

> a una primera guerra de comunicados siguió la de las valoraciones de las empresas, guerra en la bolsa, cruces de auditorías, anuncios en prensa y finalmente se acaba de abrir la posibilidad de contraopa
> **El País**

comunicante *nmf* **(a)** *(por carta)* correspondant **(b)** *(por teléfono)* caller **(c)** *(congreso)* speaker

comunicar *vt* **(a)** *(transmitir información)* to communicate *o* to get through; **desde que instalamos el fax es más rápido comunicar con la oficina principal** = communicating with head office has been quicker since we installed the fax machine; **intenté comunicarme con el departamento de reclamaciones** = I tried to get through to the complaints department **(b)** *(anunciar)* to announce; **comunicar los resultados para 1996** = to announce the results for 1996 **(c)** *(informar)* to inform *o* to report; **tenemos el placer de comunicarle que su oferta ha sido aceptada** = we are pleased to inform you that your offer has been accepted; **el Ministerio de Comercio nos ha comunicado que van a entrar en vigor nuevas tarifas** = we have been informed by the Department of Trade that new tariffs are coming into force; **los vendedores comunicaron que la demanda del producto había aumentado** = the salesmen reported an increased demand for the product; **comunicó que había visto al trabajador ausente en una tienda** = he reported seeing the absentee in a shop **(d)** *(teléfono)* **señal de comunicar** *o* **comunicando** = engaged tone; **estar comunicando** = to be engaged

◊ **comunicarse** *vr* to communicate; **le resulta imposible comunicarse con el personal** = he finds it impossible to communicate with his staff

comunidad *nf* community; **la Comunidad Europea (CE)** = the European Community (EC); **la Comunidad Económica Europea (CEE)** = the European Economic Community (EEC); **los ministros de la Comunidad** = the Community ministers; *ver también* UNION EUROPEA

con *prep* **(a)** with; **con tal que** = on the understanding that *o* provided that *o* providing **(b)** **con cupón** = cum coupon; **con derechos** = cum rights; **con dividendo** = cum dividend

conceder *vt* **(a)** *(otorgar)* to award *o* to grant; **conceder un aumento salarial a alguien** = to award someone a salary increase; **conceder un préstamo** *o* **un subsidio a alguien** = to grant someone a loan *o* a subsidy; **las autoridades locales concedieron un préstamo libre de interés a la compañía para que pusiera en marcha la nueva fábrica** = the local authority granted the company an interest-free loan to start up the new factory; **se le concedió un visado de no residente** = she was granted a non-resident visa **(b)** *(ofrecer)* to allow *o* to offer; **conceder un descuento a alguien** = to allow someone a discount; **conceder un 5% de descuento al personal** = to allow 5% discount to members of staff; **conceder un crédito a un cliente** = to extend credit to a customer; **el banco le concedió un crédito de 100.000 ptas. con su casa como garantía** = the bank advanced

him 100,000 pesetas against the security of his house; **conceder una opción (de compra) a alguien** = to give someone first refusal of something; **conceder una licencia para fabricar piezas de recambio** = to license a company to manufacture spare parts; **conceder una licencia de explotación** *o* **una franquicia** = to grant a franchise *o* to franchise **(c)** **el banco concede mucha importancia a la transacción** = the bank attaches great importance to the deal

> había concedido excesivos préstamos a países en desarrollo a lo largo de los años setenta, que nunca fueron recuperados y que tuvo que reponer en la década siguiente
> **El País**

concepto *nm* concept *o* thought; **tener un gran concepto de una persona** = to rate someone highly; **el director gerente tiene un gran concepto de ella** = she is highly thought of by the managing director

concertación *nf* agreement *o* reconciliation *o* harmonization; **la concertación ente el gobierno y los sindicatos** = the agreement between the government and the unions

> ante la falta de un presupuesto alegre, no parece que la concertación sea practicable
> **España Económica**

concertar *vt* to agree to *o* to arrange *o* to conclude; **concertamos una reunión en sus oficinas** = we arranged to have the meeting in their offices; **concertar un acuerdo con alguien** = to conclude an agreement with someone

concesión *nf* **(a)** *(otorgamiento)* concession; **concesión de un préstamo** = granting of a loan *o* lending; **el trámite para la concesión de contratos estatales** = the machinery for awarding government contracts **(b)** *(agencia exclusiva)* concession *o* dealership; **tiene la concesión de una joyería en unos grandes almacenes** = she runs a jewellery concession in a department store **(c)** *(franquicia)* franchise *o* franchising; **explotación en régimen de concesión** = a franchising operation; **dirige su cadena de venta de bocadillos en régimen de concesión** = he runs his sandwich chain as a franchising operation **(d)** *(derecho de explotación)* concession; **concesión minera** = mining concession; **tener una concesión petrolífera en el Mar del Norte** = to hold an oil lease in the North Sea **(e)** *(en una negociación)* concession

> de vez en cuando hacen concesiones y renuncian a determinadas cosas, pero a cambio obtienen mucho
> **Tiempo**

concesionario, -ria *n* concessionaire *o* franchisee *o* licensee; **nombrar un concesionario en el extranjero** = to appoint an overseas licensee

conciliación *nf* **(a)** conciliation; **conciliación y arbitraje de conflictos laborales** = conciliation and arbitration of industrial disputes **(b)** **conciliación de cuentas** = reconciliation of accounts

concluir *vt* **(a)** *(completar)* to finish *o* to conclude *o* to complete; **la fábrica concluyó el pedido en dos semanas** = the factory completed the order in two weeks **(b)** *(deducir)* to infer *o* to deduce *o* to arrive at (a conclusion)

◊ **concluirse** *vr* to end *o* to conclude

conclusión *nf* conclusion *o* close *o* end *o* completion; **llegar a una conclusión** = to come to a conclusion *o* to conclude; **la policía llegó a la conclusión de que el ladrón había entrado en el edificio por la entrada principal** = the police concluded that the thief had got into the building through the main entrance

concordar 1 *vt* to agree; **concordaron una reunión para el mes próximo** = they agreed a meeting for next month **2** *vi* to agree *o* to be the same *o* to tally; **que no concuerda** = which is at variance with; **las facturas no concuerdan** = the invoices do not tally

concretar *vt* to specify

concreto, -ta *adj* actual *o* definite *o* particular *o* specific *o* concrete

concurso *nm* competition *o* contest; **concurso oposición** = (public) competitive examination *o* open competition (for a job); **concurso público** = tender *o* invitation to tender for a contract; **concurso subasta** = auction by tender

condición *nf* **(a)** *(estado)* condition *o* state; **el sindicato se ha quejado de las malas condiciones de trabajo existentes en la fábrica** = the union has complained about the bad working conditions in the factory; **condiciones comerciales adversas** = adverse trading conditions **(b)** *(salvedad)* proviso *o* condition; **firmamos el contrato con la condición de que los términos puedan ser discutidos de nuevo después de seis meses** = we are signing the contract with the proviso that the terms can be discussed again after six months; **condiciones de empleo** *o* **de servicio** = conditions of employment *o* conditions of service; **condiciones de venta** = conditions of sale **(c) a condición de que** = on condition that *o* provided that *o* providing *o* on the understanding that; **se les concedió el arrendamiento a condición de que pagasen las costas legales** = they were granted the lease on condition that they paid the legal costs **(d) condición jurídica** = legal status

condicionado, -da *adj* conditioned *o* conditional; **venta condicionada** = conditional sale

condicional *adj* conditional; **hizo una oferta condicional** = he made a conditional offer; **la oferta perdió su carácter condicional el jueves pasado** = the offer went unconditional last Thursday

condominio *nm* US condominium *o* joint ownership

conducir *vt* **(a)** *(coche)* to drive; **conduce un coche de la empresa** = she drives a company car **(b) conducir a** = to lead (up) to

◊ **conducirse** *vr* to behave

menos impuestos condujeron a un abultado déficit público y a un recalentamiento de la economía
España Económica

conducta *nf* behaviour *o* conduct; **conducta ilegal** = malfeasance; **normas de conducta** = code of practice

conductor, -ra *n* driver; **presentó una demanda de indemnización de 50.000.000 de ptas. al conductor del otro coche** = she put in a claim for 50m pesetas damages against the driver of the other car

conectar *vt/i* to connect *o* to switch on; **la oficina de ventas está conectada directamente con el ordenador del almacén** = the sales office is on line to the warehouse; **el vuelo de Nueva York conecta con un vuelo a Atenas** = the flight from New York connects with a flight to Athens

conexión *nf* **(a)** *(vinculación)* connection *o* tie-up *o* link **(b)** *(informática)* port *o* jack

confección *nf* making *o* preparation; **de confección** = ready-made *o* ready-to-wear

◊ **confeccionado, -da** *adj* ready-made *o* ready-to-wear

◊ **confeccionar** *vt* to make; **confeccionar una factura** = to make out an invoice; **confeccionar una lista de destinatarios** = to build up a mailing list

confederación *nf* confederation; **Confederación Española de Organizaciones Empresariales (CEOE)** = Confederation of Spanish Employers' Organizations

conferencia *nf* **(a)** *(congreso, asamblea)* conference *o* meeting; **la conferencia se celebra del 12 al 16 de junio** = the conference runs *o* will be held from the 12th to the 16th of June; US from 12 through *o* thru 16 June; **conferencia de prensa** = press conference **(b)** *(telefónica)* long-distance call; **conferencia personal** = person-to-person call **(c)** *(universidad)* lecture

confesar *vt/i* to confess *o* to admit *o* to acknowledge *o* to declare; **el presidente confesó que había robado el dinero de la caja de seguridad de la empresa** = the chairman admitted he had taken the cash from the company's safe; **tuvo que dimitir después de confesar que había pasado información a la competencia** = he had to resign after his admission that he had passed information to the rival company

◊ **confesarse** *vr* to confess *o* to own up

confesión *nf* admission *o* confession

confianza *nf* **(a)** *(fe)* confidence *o* faith; **tener confianza en algo** *o* **alguien** = to have faith in something *o* someone; **el equipo de ventas no tiene mucha confianza en su jefe** = the sales team do not have much faith in their manager; **la junta directiva tiene absoluta confianza en el director gerente** = the board has total confidence in the managing director **(b)** *(acción de confiar algo a alguien)* trust; **cometió un abuso de confianza** = he was guilty of a breach of trust; **tiene un cargo de confianza** = he has a position of trust **(c)** *(fiable)* de confianza = reliable *o* reputable *o* trustworthy; **nuestros cajeros son una confianza absoluta** = our cashiers are completely trustworthy; **solamente empleamos transportistas de confianza** = we only use reputable carriers; **el director de ventas es una persona de absoluta confianza** = the sales manager is completely reliable; **de poca confianza** = unreliable *o* untrustworthy *o* fly-by-night

confiar 1 *vt* **confiar algo a alguien** = to trust someone with something *o* to entrust; **le confiaron las llaves de la caja fuerte de la oficina** = he was entrusted with the keys to the office safe; **confió el testamento a su abogado** = he deposited his will with his solicitor **2** *vi* to trust (in); **confiar en** = to rely on *o* to bank on; **confía en conseguir un préstamo de su padre para iniciar un negocio** = he is banking on getting a loan from his father to set up in business; **el presidente confía en el departamento de finanzas para la información sobre las ventas** = the chairman relies on the finance department for information on sales; **puede confiar en mí** = you can rely on me

confidencial *adj* confidential; **envió un informe confidencial al presidente** = he sent a confidential report to the chairman; **información confidencial** = inside information; **ponga en la carta la mención de 'Confidencial'** = please mark the letter 'Private and Confidential'; **carta con la mención de 'confidencial'** *o* **'privado y confidencial'** = letter marked 'private and confidential'

confidencialidad *nf* confidentiality *o* secret

confirmación *nf* confirmation; **confirmación de una reserva** = confirmation of a booking; **recibió la confirmación del banco de que los títulos** *o* **las escrituras habían sido depositados** = he received confirmation from the bank that the deeds had been deposited

confirmar *vt* to confirm; **confirmar una reserva de hotel** *o* **un billete** *o* **un acuerdo** *o* **una reserva** = to confirm a hotel reservation *o* a ticket *o* an agreement *o* a booking; **confirmar a alguien en su puesto de trabajo** = to confirm someone in a job; **sin confirmar** = unconfirmed; **hay noticias sin confirmar de que nuestro representante ha sido detenido** = there are unconfirmed reports that our agent has been arrested

confiscación *nf* confiscation *o* forfeit *o* repossession

confiscar *vt* **(a)** *(embargar, incautar)* to confiscate *o* to impound *o* to seize *o* to forfeit; **la aduana confiscó el envío de libros** = customs seized the shipment of books; **las mercancías fueron confiscadas** = the goods were impounded *o* were declared forfeit **(b)** *(propiedad)* to sequester *o* to sequestrate *o* to repossess; **confiscar un bien vendido a plazos** = to repossess something bought on hire-purchase; **el banco confiscó su piso por incumplimiento de pago** = when he fell behind with his mortgage payments, the bank repossessed his flat

conflicto *nm* conflict *o* struggle; **conflicto colectivo** = industrial dispute; **conflicto de intereses** = conflict of interest; **conflictos laborales** = labour disputes; **conflicto sobre la delimitación de tareas** = demarcation dispute

conforme 1 *adj* consistent (with); **recibe un sueldo conforme a la experiencia adquirida** = his salary is consistent with his previous experience **2**

prep **conforme a** = in accordance with *o* under; **conforme a sus órdenes hemos depositado el dinero en su cuenta corriente** = in accordance with your instructions we have deposited the money in your current account

conformidad *nf* agreement *o* approval *o* consent *o* compliance; **certificado de conformidad** = compliance certificate; **dio su conformidad para firmar el nuevo contrato** = he agreed to the signing of the new contract; **de conformidad con** = in accordance with *o* under

confuso, -sa *adj* confused; **el presidente se mostró confuso ante las preguntas de los periodistas** = the chairman was confused by the journalists' questions

congelación *nf* freezing; **congelación de créditos** = credit freeze; **congelación de precios y salarios** = wages and prices freeze *o* a freeze on wages and prices

> los recortes presupuestarios últimos y la congelación de algunos proyectos de obra pública previstos pueden suponer además la pérdida de cuantiosas ayudas de la Unión Europea
> **El País**

congelado, -da 1 *adj* frozen; **activo congelado** = frozen assets; **crédito congelado** = frozen credits **2** *pp de* CONGELAR

congelar *vt* to freeze; **hemos congelado los gastos al nivel del año pasado** = we have frozen expenditure at last year's level; **congelar precios y salarios** = to freeze wages and prices; **la empresa congeló los sueldos durante un periodo de seis meses** = the company froze all salaries for a six-month period

conglomerado *nm* conglomerate

> Grupo Zeta es hoy en día una empresa de medios de comunicación desarrollada, un conglomerado de 27 cabeceras distintas
> **Tiempo**

Congo *nm* Congo

◊ **congoleño, -ña** *adj y n* Congolese
NOTA: capital: **Brazzaville**; moneda: **franco CFA (FCFA)** = CFA franc (CFAF)

congreso *nm* **(a)** *(conferencia)* congress *o* conference; **actas de un congreso** = conference proceedings; **programa de un congreso** = conference timetable; **el congreso anual del Sindicato de Electricistas** = the annual conference of the Electricians' Union; **el congreso de la Asociación de Libreros** = the conference of the Booksellers' Association; **la secretaria preparó el orden del día del congreso** = the conference agenda *o* the agenda of the conference was drawn up by the secretary **(b)** **Congreso de los diputados** = Congress of Deputies *o* House of Commons

> el Gobierno ha solicitado al Congreso nuevas facultades para legislar por decreto el sistema tributario
> **Cambio 16**

conjetura *nf* guess *o* conjecture; **sólo podían hacer conjeturas sobre la pérdida total** = they could only guess at the total loss

conjeturar *vt* to guess (at) something

conjuntamente *adv* jointly; **dirigir una empresa conjuntamente** = to manage a company jointly; **son conjuntamente responsables de los daños** = they are jointly liable for damages

conjunto, -ta 1 *adj* joint; **cuenta conjunta** = joint account; **dirección conjunta** = joint management; **empresa conjunta** = joint venture; **negociaciones conjuntas** = joint discussions; **operaciones conjuntas** = combined operations **2** *nm* **(a)** *(mezcla)* mix; **conjunto de medidas** = package (deal); **conjunto de productos de una compañía** = product mix of a company; **conjunto de ventas** = sales mix; **el puesto lleva aparejado un atractivo conjunto de retribuciones** = the job carries an attractive salary package **(b)** *(en total)* whole; **en conjunto** = altogether *o* gross *o* overall; **el personal de las tres empresas del grupo en conjunto asciende a 2.500 empleados** = the staff of the three companies in the group come to 2,500 altogether

> la falta de interés por el trabajo es un problema dramático entre el conjunto de la población, especialmente los más jóvenes
> **España Económica**

conmutar *vt (cambiar)* to exchange *o* to change *o* to commute *o* to convert; **decidió conmutar una parte de su pensión por una cantidad en efectivo** = he decided to commute part of his pension rights into a lump sum payment

conocer *vt* **(a)** *(tener trato)* to know *o* to have contacts with; **conoce muy bien el mercado africano** = he knows the African market very well; **conoce a mucha gente en la ciudad** = he has many contacts in the town **(b)** *(encontrar a alguien por primera vez)* to meet; **¿has conocido ya al nuevo representante?** = have you already met the new sales representative?

◇ **conocido, -da 1** *adj y pp* known *o* well known *o* famous **2** *nmf (persona)* contact *o* acquaintance

conocimiento *nm* **(a)** *(saber)* knowledge *o* understanding; **no tenía conocimiento de la existencia del contrato** = he had no knowledge of the contract **(b)** **conocimiento de embarque** = bill of lading *o* advice note; **conocimiento de embarque defectuoso** = foul bill of lading

◇ **conocimientos** *nmpl* knowledge; **conocimientos básicos** = basic knowledge; **conocimientos especiales** = expert knowledge; **conocimientos científicos** *o* **técnicos** = scientific *o* technical know-how; **conocimientos de electrónica** = electronic know-how; **adquirir conocimientos de informática** = to acquire computer know-how

conquistar *vt* to conquer *o* to win; **conquistar un mercado** = to open up a market

consecuencia *nf* consequence *o* outcome *o* result; **en consecuencia** = accordingly *o* as a result; **hemos recibido su carta y hemos modificado el contrato en consecuencia** = we have received your letter and have altered the contract accordingly

> aunque los especialistas señalan las consecuencias positivas que hay en la jornada intensiva para los empleados, sin embargo, existen algunos riesgos que no siempre son resaltados suficientemente
> **El País**

consecutivo, -va *adj* consecutive; **la compañía ha obtenido beneficios durante seis años consecutivos** = the company has made a profit for six years running

conseguir *vt* **(a)** **conseguir algo** = to obtain *o* to get something; **que se puede conseguir** = obtainable; **imposible de conseguir** = unobtainable; **extremarse en conseguir algo** = to go to great lengths to get something; **los precios bajan cuando las materias primas pueden conseguirse fácilmente** = prices fall when raw materials are easily obtainable; **¿puede conseguirme una habitación para mañana por la noche?** = can you get me a room *o* fix me up with a room for the night?; **conseguir suministros del extranjero** = to obtain supplies from abroad; **conseguir un requerimiento judicial contra una empresa** = to obtain an injunction against a company; **conseguir un 20% de las acciones de una compañía** = to acquire 20% of a company's shares **(b)** *(tener éxito)* to win *o* to succeed; **conseguir un contrato** = to win a contract; **la empresa anunció que había conseguido un contrato por un valor de 5.000 millones para suministrar autobuses y camiones** = the company announced that it had won a contract worth 5,000m to supply buses and trucks **(c)** *(obtener dinero, préstamos)* to get money *o* a loan *o* to raise money; **conseguir fondos** = to secure funds; **la compañía está intentando conseguir capital para financiar su programa de expansión** = the company is trying to raise the capital to fund its expansion programme; **¿de dónde conseguirá el dinero para empezar su negocio?** = where will he raise the money to start up his business?

consejero, -ra *n* **(a)** *(asesor)* adviser *o* advisor *o* consultant; **consejero técnico** = technical adviser; **consejero de publicidad** = advertising consultant **(b)** *(en una compañía)* director *o* member of the board; **le ofrecieron el cargo de consejero en Hnos. Martínez S.A.** = he was offered a directorship with Hnos. Martínez S.A.

> el consejero del TAV por CCOO, prevé un déficit diario de 50 millones de pesetas, tirando por lo bajo
> **Cambio 16**

> los estatutos de la empresa establecen que se necesita un mínimo de ocho consejeros para lograr el quorum necesario
> **El País**

> estos consejeros, de talante renovador, querían poner en marcha un plan estratégico que modernizara la gestión de la compañía
> **El País**

consejo *nm* **(a)** *(asesoramiento)* advice; **consejo legal** = counsel; **dar un consejo** = to give a piece of advice *o* to advise; **pedir consejo a un abogado** = to seek legal advice; **pendiente del consejo de nuestros abogados** = pending advice from our lawyers; **siguiendo el consejo del contable enviamos los documentos a la policía** = we took the accountant's advice and sent the documents to the police **(b)** *(junta)* board *o* council; **consejo de administración** = board of directors *o* management; **consejo asesor** = advisory board; **informe** *o* **memoria del consejo de administración** = directors' report; **los miembros del consejo son partidarios de que Hnos. Martínez S.A. participe en el proyecto** = the board members all favour Hnos. Martínez S.A. as partners in the project; **forma parte del consejo de administración de dos compañías** = she is on the boards of two companies; **someter una propuesta al consejo** = to put a proposal to the board **(c) consejo del consumidor** = consumer council; **Consejo de Europa** = Council of Europe; **Consejo Europeo** = European Council; **Consejo Nórdico** = Nordic Council; **Consejo de Ministros de la UE** = EU Council of Ministers; **consejo de redacción** = editorial board; **Consejo de Seguridad de las Naciones Unidas** = UN Security Council; **Consejo Superior Bancario** = Banking Control Council **(d)** meeting; **Consejo de Ministros** = cabinet (meeting)

> la auditoría fue encargada por iniciativa del cesado presidente del consejo
> **El País**

> el consejo estaba reducido a cuatro miembros tras la tumultuosa junta de accionistas
> **El País**

consentir *vt* to agree; **el banco nunca consentirá prestar 5 millones de pesetas a la compañía** = the bank will never agree to lend the company 5 million pesetas

conserje *nm* porter *o* caretaker; *(EE.UU)* janitor; **conserje jefe** = head porter; **ve a pedirle al conserje que cambie la bombilla** = go and ask the caretaker to replace the light bulb

◊ **conserjería** *nf* porter's office

conservación *nf* conservation *o* keeping *o* maintenance; **periodo de conservación de un producto** = shelf life of a product

conservar *vt* to maintain *o* to keep *o* to hold; **conservar el puesto de trabajo** = to hold down a job

considerable *adj* considerable; **vendemos nuestros productos a Africa en cantidades considerables** = we sell considerable quantities of our products to Africa; **perdieron una considerable cantidad de dinero en la bolsa de contratación** = they lost a considerable amount of money on the commodity market

◊ **considerablemente** *adv* considerably *o* largely; **el volumen de ventas es considerablemente mayor que el del año pasado** = sales are considerably higher than they were last year; **los costos de introducir información en un ordenador han subido considerablemente** = keyboarding costs have risen a great deal *o* a lot *o* considerably; **se han retirado considerablemente del mercado estadounidense** = they have largely pulled out of the American market

consideración *nf* consideration; **tomar en consideración** = to consider; **la dirección no tomará en consideración ninguna sugerencia de los representantes de los sindicatos** = the management will not entertain any suggestions from the union representatives; **piden un pago por adelantado de 200.000 ptas. antes de tomar el asunto en consideración** = they are asking for an advance (payment) of 200,000 pesetas before they will consider the deal

considerando *nm (jurídico)* whereas

considerar *vt (juzgar)* to consider; **consideró que era hora de terminar las conversaciones** = he considered *o* felt *o* judged it was time to call an end to the discussions; **estamos considerando la posibilidad de trasladar la oficina central a Galicia** = we are considering *o* giving consideration to moving the head office to Galicia; **consideran que el precio del seguro es demasiado alto** = they reckon that the insurance costs are too high

consigna *nf* **(a)** *(en estación, aeropuerto)* checkroom *o* left luggage office *o* baggage room; **consigna automática** = left-luggage lockers **(b)** *(publicidad)* slogan **(c)** *(orden)* instruction

consignación *nf* **(a)** *(envío)* consignment; **talón de consignación** = consignment note; **bienes en consignación** = goods on consignment **(b)** *(cantidad)* appropriation *o* sum which has been earmarked

consignador, -ra *n* consignor

consignar *vt* **(a)** *(enviar)* to send *o* to consign *o* to dispatch; **consignar mercancías a alguien** = to consign goods to someone **(b)** *(dinero)* to assign *o* to appropriate *o* to earmark (funds); **consignar una cantidad mensual para papel con membrete** = to assign a certain amount each month for headed paper

consignatario, -ria *n* consignee; **consignatario (marítimo)** = ship broker *o* shipping agent

consistir *vi* **consistir en** = to consist of

consolidación *nf* consolidation; **consolidación de deuda** = funding; **consolidación de un préstamo** = restructuring of a loan

consolidado, -da *adj* consolidated *o* funded; **capital consolidado a largo plazo** = long-term funded capital; **deuda consolidada** = funded debt **2** *pp de* CONSOLIDAR

consolidar *vt* **(a)** *(reafirmar)* to consolidate *o* to strengthen **(b)** *(deuda)* to fund

consorcio *nm* syndicate *o* consortium *o* trust *o* copartnership; **consorcio asegurador** = underwriting syndicate; **un consorcio de compañías canadienses** *o* **un consorcio canadiense** = a consortium of Canadian companies *o* a Canadian consortium; **un consorcio de empresas españolas y británicas se propone fabricar el nuevo avión** = a consortium of Spanish and British companies is planning to construct the new aircraft; **un consorcio financiero alemán** = a German finance syndicate

constante *adj* **(a)** *(invariable)* constant *o* steady *o* regular; **las cifras están expresadas en pesetas constantes** = the figures are in constant pesetas; **un aumento constante de los beneficios** = steady increase in profits; **hay una demanda constante de ordenadores** = there is a steady demand for computers; **la empresa ha experimentado un**

aumento constante de su cuota de mercado = the company has steadily increased its market share **(b)** *(que se repite)* recurrent; **un gasto constante** = a recurrent item of expenditure *o* a recurrent expense; **hay un problema constante en el suministro de esta pieza de repuesto** = there is a recurrent problem in supplying this part **(c)** *(persona)* **es un hombre constante en su trabajo** = he's a steady worker

◊ **constantemente** *adv* steadily; **la producción aumentó constantemente durante los dos últimos trimestres** = output has increased steadily over the last two quarters

constar *vi* **(a)** to be on record *o* to be kept on record; **para que conste** = for the record *o* to keep the record straight; **el nuevo modelo no consta en el catálogo actual** = the new model is not listed in the current catalogue **(b) constar de** = to consist of; **el pedido consta de varios artículos no especificados** = the order consists of several unspecified items

constatar *vt* to confirm *o* to observe *o* to note

la OCDE ha constatado que el crecimiento del producto interior bruto (PIB) de España fue del 2,5%, el índice más bajo desde el año 1985
El País

constitución *nf* **(a)** constitution; **constitución de una sociedad** = incorporation (of a company); **escritura de constitución** = memorandum (and articles) of association *o* articles of incorporation **(b) constitución de existencias** = building up stocks

◊ **constitucional** *adj* constitutional; **derecho costitucional** = constitutional law

constituido, -da 1 *adj* incorporated; **sociedad constituida legalmente** = incorporated company; **una sociedad constituida en los EE UU** = a company incorporated in the USA **2** *pp de* CONSTITUIR

constituir *vt* **(a)** to create *o* to form *o* to set up **(b)** **no constituye ningún problema para nosotros** = it's not a problem for us **(c) constituir en sociedad** = to set up *o* to incorporate (a company)

◊ **constituirse** *vr* to organize *o* to establish (oneself) *o* to set oneself up; **constituirse parte civil** = to bring a civil action

construcción *nf* construction *o* building; **para la construcción de la pared se utilizaron diez toneladas de hormigón** = ten tons of concrete were used in the making of the wall; **la empresa ha presentado una oferta para la construcción del nuevo aeropuerto** = the company has tendered for the contract to construct the new airport; **estamos terminando una obra de construcción en el norte de África** = we are just completing a construction project in North Africa; **empresa de construcción** = construction company; **en construcción** = under construction; **el aeropuerto está en construcción** = the airport is under construction; **permiso de construcción** = planning permission; **denegarle a alguien el permiso de construcción** = to refuse someone planning permission; **estamos esperando el permiso de construcción antes de empezar las obras** = we are waiting for planning permission before we can start building

constructivo, -va *adj* constructive; **hizo unas** sugerencias constructivas para mejorar las relaciones entre la dirección y los obreros = she made some constructive suggestions for improving management-worker relations; **crítica constructiva** = constructive criticism

constructor, -ra 1 *adj* construction *o* building; **empresa constructora** = construction company **2** *n* builder *o* constructor; **constructor especulativo** = speculative builder

construir *vt* **(a)** to build *o* to construct **(b)** to develop; **construir un polígono industrial** = to develop an industrial estate **(c)** to make; **los obreros se pasaron tres días construyendo la mesa** = the workmen spent three days making the table

consuetudinario, -ria *adj* consuetudinary; **derecho consuetudinario** = common law

consultar *vt* to consult; **consultar a un abogado** = to take legal advice; **consultó a su contable en lo referente a sus impuestos** = he consulted his accountant about his tax

consultor, -ra *n* consultant

consultivo, -va *adj* advisory; **junta consultiva** = advisory board

consultoría *nf* consultancy

◊ **consultorio** *nm* information bureau *o* consulting room

consumible *adj* consumable; **activo consumible** = wasting asset

consumidor, -ra *n* consumer; **consejo del consumidor** = consumer council; **equipo de consumidores** = consumer panel; **gastos del consumidor** = consumer spending; **protección al consumidor** = consumer protection; **resistencia del consumidor** = consumer resistance; **las últimas subidas de precios han generado una resistencia considerable por parte de los consumidores** = the latest price increases have produced considerable consumer resistance; **los consumidores de gas protestan por el aumento de los precios** = gas consumers are protesting at the increase in prices; **la fábrica es una gran consumidora de agua** = the factory is a heavy consumer of water; **índice de precios al consumidor (IPC)** = retail price index (RPI); *US* consumer price index

tanto las empresas como la confianza de los consumidores mejorarán después de los escándalos y traumas financieros del año anterior
Actualidad Económica

consumir *vt* to use *o* to consume; **la fábrica consume mucho carbón** = the factory uses a lot of coal; **el plan de expansión ha consumido todos nuestros beneficios** = the expansion plan has used up *o* drained all our profits; **el coche consume unos 11 litros por 100 kilómetros** *o* **unos 11 litros por cien km.** = the car does 9 kilometres to the litre

consumo *nm* consumption; **un coche con bajo consumo de gasolina** = a car with low petrol consumption; **consumo doméstico** *o* **interior** *o* **nacional** = home consumption *o* domestic consumption; **consumo per cápita** = per capita consumption; **consumo privado** = private consumption; **bienes de consumo** = consumer goods; **bienes de consumo duraderos** = consumer durables; **crédito al consumo** = consumer credit; **gastos de consumo** = consumer spending; **impuesto sobre el consumo** = tax on consumption; **índice de precios al consumo (IPC)** = retail price index (RPI); *US* consumer price index; **investigación sobre el consumo** = consumer research; **periodo de gran consumo** *o* **de menor consumo** = peak period *o* off-peak period; **propensión al consumo** = propensity to consume; **sociedad de consumo** = consumer society

```
otro ejemplo claro de despilfarro de
productos, sobre los que el Estado
practica una política de precios
subvencionados, es el consumo de energía
                          España Económica
```

```
los efectos deflacionarios a largo plazo de
unos impuestos más altos y un gasto
público menor serán más que compensados
por una demanda del consumo creciente
                          Actualidad Económica
```

contabilidad *nf* **(a)** *(hacer cuentas)* accountancy *o* accounting; **contabilidad de costes actuales** = current cost accounting; **contabilidad a costes históricos** = historic cost accounting; **contabilidad de costes** *o* **contabilidad analítica** = cost accounting; **contabilidad cosmética** = creative accounting; **contabilidad electrónica** *o* **mecanizada** = computerized bookkeeping; **contabilidad falsa** *o* **fraudulenta** = false accounting; **contabilidad del grupo** = group accounts; **departamento de contabilidad** = accounts department; **es estudiante de contabilidad** = he is an accountancy student; **estudió contabilidad** = he trained as an accountant *o* he studied accountancy; **jefe de contabilidad** = accounts manager *o* head of the accounts department; **métodos** *o* **procedimientos de contabilidad** = accounting methods *o* accounting procedures; **sistema de contabilidad** = accounting system **(b)** *(teneduría de libros)* bookkeeping; **contabilidad por partida doble** = double-entry bookkeeping; **contabilidad por partida simple** *o* **por partida única** = single-entry bookkeeping; **asistió a un curso de reciclaje en contabilidad** = he went on a refresher course in bookkeeping

```
el autor del informe no pudo encontrar la
contabilidad adecuada para ratificar que
todas las transacciones realizadas por la
empresa estaban recogidas en las cuentas
anuales
                          El País
```

contabilizar *vt* to enter in the accounts

```
la deuda exterior española aumentó en un
29% al pasar de los 44.973 millones de
dólares a los 58.071 contabilizados a
finales de diciembre
                          El País
```

contable 1 *adj* accounting; **periodo contable** = accounting period; **valor contable** = book value **2** *nmf* accountant *o* bookkeeper; *(Oriente)* shroff; **contable de costes** = cost accountant; **contable colegiado** *o* **contable público titulado** = chartered accountant; *US* certified public accountant; **contable de gestión** = management accountant; **contable titulado** = certified accountant; **Director contable** = chief accountant; **experto contable** =

qualified accountant; **ha sacado el título de contable** = she has qualified as an accountant; **transmito todas las dudas que tengo sobre impuestos a mi contable** = I send all my income tax queries to my accountant; **el contable aconsejó enviar los documentos a la policía** = the accountant's advice was to send the documents to the police

```
la empresa no estaba en condiciones de
explicar las diferencias existentes
entre los extractos de las cuentas y el
saldo contable
                          El País
```

contactar *vt/i* to contact

contacto *nm* contact *o* connection **(a)** *(persona)* **tenemos un contacto en el departamento de producción de la competencia que nos da información muy útil** = we have a contact inside our rival's production department who gives us very useful information **(b)** *(relación)* **estar en contacto** = to be in touch; **poner en contacto** = to put in touch; **me puso en contacto con un buen abogado** = he put me in contact with a good lawyer; **intentó ponerse en contacto con su oficina por teléfono** = he tried to contact his office by phone; **¿puede Vd. ponerse en contacto con el director gerente en su club?** = can you contact the managing director at his club?; **perder el contacto** = to lose contact; **he perdido el contacto con ellos** = I have lost contact with them **(c)** *(publicidad)* **grado de contacto (GRC)** = gross rating point (GRP)

contado, -da 1 *adj* numbered **2** *nm* **operaciones al contado** = cash settlements; **'pago al contado'** = 'pay cash' *o* cash payment *o* spot cash; **rebajó el precio en 2.000 ptas. por pago al contado** = he knocked 2,000 pesetas off the price for cash **3** *pp de* CONTAR

contador *nm* meter; **contador de agua** = water meter; **contador eléctrico** = electricity meter

contante *adj* **dinero contante y sonante** = ready cash *o* cash

contar *vt/i* to count *o* to calculate; **contar con** = to count on *o* to rely on *o* to reckon on *o* to bank on; **puede contar con el apoyo del director gerente** = he can reckon on the support of the managing director; **cuente con un plazo de 28 días para la entrega** = allow 28 days for delivery; **no cuente con un préstamo del banco para iniciar su negocio** = do not count on a bank loan to start your business; **cuentan con que se les adjudique el contrato** = they reckon on being awarded the contract

contenedor *nm* container; **contenedor pequeño** = minicontainer; **buque de contenedores** = container ship; **carga de un contenedor** = container-load; **muelle de contenedores** = container berth; **poner en contenedores** = to containerize; **puerto de contenedores** = container port; **terminal de contenedores** = container terminal; **enviar mercancías en contenedores** = to ship goods in containers

contener *vt* **(a)** *(tener)* to contain *o* to hold; **cada cajón contiene dos ordenadores y sus unidades periféricas** = each crate contains two computers and their peripherals; **un barril contiene 250 litros** = a barrel contains *o* holds 250 litres; **hemos perdido un**

archivo que contiene documentos importantes = we have lost a file containing important documents; la caja contiene veinte paquetes = the carton holds twenty packets; cada caja contiene 250 hojas de papel = each box holds 250 sheets of paper (b) *(mantener bajo)* to keep down *o* to hold down *o* to check; contener la inflación = to check *o* to curb inflation

◇ contenido, -da 1 *adj y pp* controlled *o* kept in check 2 *nm* content *o* contents; el contenido de la carta = the contents of the letter; el contenido de la botella se derramó por el suelo = the contents of the bottle poured out onto the floor; los aduaneros registraron el contenido del cajón = the customs officials inspected the contents of the crate; ¿cuál es el contenido del paquete? = what are the contents of the parcel?; puso el contenido de la caja para gastos menores en su cartera = he emptied the contents of the petty cash box into his briefcase

contento, -ta *adj* happy

contestación *nf* answer *o* reply; no recibí contestación a mi carta *o* no hubo contestación a mi carta = my letter got no answer *o* there was no answer to my letter; escribo en contestación a su carta del 24 = I am writing in reply to your letter of the 24th; servicio de contestación = answering service; se ruega contestación (s.r.c.) = RSVP

contestador *nm* contestador automático = answering machine *o* answerphone; cuando llamé no estaba y por eso dejé un mensaje en el contestador = he wasn't in when I called so I left a message on his answerphone

contestar *vt* to answer *o* to reply; contestar a una carta = to answer a letter *o* to reply to a letter; contestar el teléfono = to answer the telephone; se demoraron en contestar a las quejas del cliente = they were slow to reply *o* slow at replying to the customer's complaints; intenté llamar a su oficina pero no me contestaron = I tried to phone his office but there was no answer; ¿cuándo vas a contestar a mi carta? = when are you going to answer my letter?

contingencia *nf* contingency; planes de contingencia = emergency plans *o* standby arrangements; prever todas las contingencias = to provide for all eventualities

contingente *nm* import *o* export quota

continuación *nf* continuation; a continuación = below *o* next; citado a continuación = undermentioned; no disponemos en este momento de los artículos de su pedido que se indican a continuación = the following items on your order are temporarily unavailable

continuar 1 *vi* to carry on *o* to continue; el presidente continuó hablando durante dos horas a pesar del barullo que armaban los accionistas = the chairman went on speaking for two hours in spite of the noise from the shareholders; las negociaciones continuarán el próximo lunes = negotiations will continue next Monday; las negociaciones continúan lentamente = the negotiations are proceeding slowly 2 *vt* to continue *o* to go on with

continuo, -nua *adj* continual *o* continuous; la producción avanzó lentamente debido a las continuas interrupciones = production was slow because of continual breakdowns; alimentación continua = continuous feed; cadena de montaje continua = continuous production line; papel continuo = continuous stationery

◇ continuamente *adv* continually; la fotocopiadora se avería continuamente = the photocopier is continually breaking down

contra 1 *adv* en contra = against; votar en contra = to vote against 2 *prep* against *o* facing *o* opposite; proceder contra alguien = to proceed against someone; seguro contra terceros = third party insurance *o* third party policy; ¿tiene Vd. cobertura contra daños por incendio? = do you have coverage against fire damage?; caja protegida contra incendios = fire-proof safe; contra reembolso = cash on delivery (c.o.d.); el avión se estrelló contra el monte = the plane crashed into the mountain

contra- *prefijo* counter-

◇ contraasiento *nm* contra entry; anotar un contraasiento = to contra an entry

◇ contrapartida *nf* contra entry; anotar una contrapartida = to contra an entry

contrabandista *nmf* smuggler

◇ contrabando *nm* smuggling *o* contraband (goods); hizo su fortuna en el contrabando de armas = he made his money in arms smuggling; tuvieron que pasar los repuestos en el país de contrabando = they had to smuggle the spare parts into the country

contracción *nf* shrinkage *o* contraction; dejar un margen por posibles contracciones = to allow for shrinkage

contractual *adj* contractual; responsabilidad contractual = contractual liability; cumplir las obligaciones contractuales = to fulfill your contractual obligations

contradecir *vt* to contradict

contraer *vt* (a) *(deudas)* to incur *o* to run up; contraer deudas = to incur debts *o* to get into debt; contrajo rápidamente una deuda de 250.000 ptas = he quickly ran up a bill for 250,000 pesetas (b) *(encoger)* to contract *o* to shrink

◇ contraerse *vr* to shrink *o* to get smaller; el mercado se ha contraído en un 20% = the market has shrunk by 20%

contramaestre *nm* foreman

contraoferta *nf* counterbid *o* counter-offer; cuando ofrecí 4.000 ptas. él hizo una contraoferta de 5.000 ptas. = when I bid 4,000 pesetas he put in a counterbid of 5,000; F.C.I. S.A. hizo una oferta de 200 millones por la propiedad, y Bayer respondió con una contraoferta de 280 millones = F.C.I. S.A. made an offer of 200m for the property, and Bayer replied with a counter-offer of 280m

contraopa *nf* counterbid *o* rival bid (to a takeover)

la reciente ampliación del plazo de
finalización de la OPA deja la puerta
abierta a que la compañía estudie una
nueva defensa y los expertos no descartan
que llegue a presentar una contraopa
El País

contrapartida *nf (asiento)* balancing item

contraproducente *adj* counter-productive; **el
incremento de pago de horas extras fue
contraproducente ya que los trabajadores
trabajaban más despacio** = increasing overtime
pay was counter-productive, the workers simply
worked more slowly

contrario, -ria 1 *adj* contrary *o* opposite *o*
opposed; **sostener opiniones contrarias** = to hold
differing opinions; **es contrario a la OPA** = he is
opposed to the takeover bid **2** *nm* **lo contrario** = the
contrary *o* the opposite; **al contrario** = on the
contrary; **el presidente no estaba enfadado con su
asistente; por el contrario, le ofreció un ascenso** =
the chairman was not annoyed with his assistant - on
the contrary, he promoted him

contrarrestar *vt* to counteract *o* to offset *o* to
cancel out; **los costos han contrarrestado los
ingresos de las ventas** = costs have cancelled out the
sales revenue

contraseña *nf* password

contraste *nm* **(a)** *(oposición)* contrast; **en
contraste con** = in contrast to; **contraste de
opiniones** = difference of opinion; **contraste de
imagen** = picture contrast **(b)** *(marca)* hallmark;
una cucharilla con el sello de contraste = a
hallmarked spoon

contrata *nf* contract; **trabajo a contrata** =
contract work

contratación *nf* **(a)** *(de personal)* hiring (of
staff) *o* recruitment *o* recruiting; **contratación de
nuevo personal** = the recruitment of new staff; **la
dirección ha suspendido la contratación de nuevo
personal** = the management has stopped all
additions to the staff; **la contratación de nuevo
personal ha sido interrumpida** = hiring of new
personnel has been stopped; **contratación de
personal graduado** *o* **titulado** = graduate
recruitment **(b)** **lonja** *o* **bolsa de contratación** =
commodity market *o* commodity exchange **(c)**
(sacar a licitación) invitation to tender for a contract

existe la posibilidad de que en el próximo
ejercicio se registren incrementos
salariales mayores a la productividad y
por lo tanto descensos en la contratación
salarial
Mercado

contratar *vt* **(a)** *(personal)* to contract *o* to hire;
contratar personal = to recruit *o* to engage *o* to
appoint (new staff) *o* to hire staff; **volver a
contratar a personal** = to re-engage *o* to rehire
staff; **tener dificultades en contratar personal
para la fábrica** = to have difficulty in staffing the
factory; **estamos contratando personal para
nuestro nuevo almacén** = we are recruiting staff for
our new store; **contratar a un abogado para que
represente a una compañía** = to retain a lawyer to
act for a company; **hemos contratado al mejor
abogado mercantilista para que nos represente** =

we have engaged the best commercial lawyer to
represent us; **la empresa ha contratado a veinte
nuevos vendedores** = the company has taken on
twenty new salesmen **(b)** **contratar en régimen de
aprendizaje** = to indenture **(c)** *(trabajo)* to put out to
contract; **contrataron a una pequeña empresa
para pintar las oficinas** = they hired a small firm to
paint the offices; **contrata a varias oficinas de la
localidad para el trabajo de mecanografía de la
oficina** = she farms out the office typing to various
local bureaux; **contratar a otra empresa para la
realización de un trabajo** = to put work out to
contract **(d)** *(jurídico)* **contratar a un abogado** = to
instruct a solicitor

contratista *nmf* contractor; **contratista del
Estado** = government contractor; **contratista de
obras** = building contractor *o* builder; **pedir a un
constratista un presupuesto para la construcción
del almacén** = to ask a builder for an estimate for
building the warehouse; **contratista de transporte
por carretera** = haulage contractor

contrato *nm* contract *o* agreement; **contrato de
aprendizaje** = indentures *o* articles of indenture;
contrato de bolsa = contract note; **contrato de
corta duración** = short-term contract; **contrato de
empleo** = contract of employment; **contrato en
exclusiva** = exclusive agreement; **contrato de
opción** = option contract; **contrato a plazo fijo** =
fixed-term contract; **contrato a plazos** *o* **de futuros**
= futures contract; **por contrato privado** = by
private contract; **un contrato de representación** =
an agency agreement; **contrato sellado** = contract
under seal; **contrato de servicios** = service contract;
contrato de suministro de repuestos = contract for
the supply of spare parts; **el contrato de suministro
de repuestos fue adjudicado a Hnos. Martínez
S.A.** = the supply of spare parts was contracted out to
Hnos. Martínez S.A.; **contrato de trabajo** =
contract of employment; **contrato de venta a plazos**
= hire purchase agreement; **se pasaron dos horas
hablando de los detalles del contrato** = they spent
two hours discussing the details of the contract; **el
contrato tiene fuerza jurídica** = the contract is
legally binding; **intentaremos que se atenga al
contrato** = we will try to hold him to the contract;
adjudicación del contrato = contract award;
adjudicar un contrato = to place a contract;
cuentan con que se les adjudique el contrato =
they reckon on being awarded the contract; **anular
un contrato** = to void a contract; **se sintió obligado
a anular el contrato** = he felt obliged to cancel the
contract; **concertar** *o* **firmar un contrato** = to sign a
contract *o* agreement; **firmar un contrato de
suministro de repuestos por valor de dos millones
de pesetas** = to sign a contract for 2m pesetas' worth
of spare parts; **actuar de testigo en la firma de un
contrato** = to witness an agreement; **ofrecer un
contrato a una empresa** *o* **firmar un contrato con
una compañía** = to award a contract to a company *o*
to place a contract with a company; **licitar para un
contrato** *o* **presentar un oferta para un contrato** =
to tender for a contract; **sacar un contrato a
licitación** *o* **concurso** = to invite tenders for a
contract; **el contrato obliga a las dos partes** = the
contract is binding on both parties; **condiciones del
contrato** = conditions of contract *o* contract
conditions; **se negó a aceptar algunas de las
condiciones del contrato** = he refused to agree to
some of the terms of the contract; **oponerse a una**

cláusula del contrato = to object to a clause in a contract; **prorrogar el contrato a alguien** = to renew someone's contract; **redactar un contrato** = to draw up *o* to draft an agreement *o* a contract; **incumplimiento** *o* **violación de contrato** = breach of contract; **la compañía** *o* **la empresa no ha cumplido el contrato** = the company is in breach of contract; **intercambio de contratos** = exchange of contracts; **rescisión de un contrato** = release from a contract; **realización de un contrato** = completion of a contract; **nuestros socios australianos se han retirado del contrato** = our Australian partners pulled out of the contract; **bajo** *o* **según los términos del contrato** *o* **de conformidad con el contrato** = under contract; **según los términos del contrato, la empresa debe entregar las mercancías antes de noviembre** = the firm is under contract to deliver the goods by November; **por contrato** = contractual

> en la nueva ley figuran puntos como la posibilidad de desgravar por una vivienda alquilada y poder fijar duraciones de contratos y actualizaciones de los incrementos de las ventas
> **España Económica**

> los contratos laborales temporales suponen un tercio de la contratación total en España
> **El País**

contribución *nf* contribution *o* tax; **contribución de capital** = contribution of capital; **contribución municipal** = council tax (formerly, the rates); **contribución territorial rústica** = land tax; **contribución territorial urbana** = urban land tax; **contribución sobre la renta** = personal income tax

contribuir *vt* to contribute; **contribuir con el 10% de los beneficios** = to contribute 10% of the profits; **la caída de los tipos de cambio ha sido un factor que ha contribuido a la pérdida de rentabilidad de la empresa** = falling exchange rates have been a contributory factor in *o* to the company's loss of profits

contribuyente *nmf* taxpayer; **contribuyente municipal** = ratepayer; **contribuyente que paga el impuesto básico** = basic taxpayer *o* taxpayer at the basic rate

control *nm* **(a)** *(inspección)* control *o* check; **control de alquileres** = rent control; **control de equipajes** = baggage check; **bajo control** = under control; **los gastos están sometidos a un control riguroso** = expenses are kept under tight control; **de control** = supervisory; **fuera de control** = out of control; **control de calidad** = quality control; **control de crédito** = credit control; **control de divisas** = exchange controls; **control de existencias** = stock control; **control de inventario** = inventory control; **control de pasaportes** = passport inspection; **control de precios** = price controls; **control presupuestario** = budgetary control; **grupo de control** = control group; **los directivos asistieron a la presentación del nuevo sistema de control de existencias** = the managers saw the new stock control system being demonstrated **(b)** *(dominio)* control; **la compañía está bajo el control de tres accionistas** = the company is under the control of three shareholders; **lograr el control de un negocio** = to gain control of a business; **perder el control de un negocio** = to lose control of a

business; **liberalización** *o* **supresión de control** = decontrol *o* decontrolling; **suprimir el control de salarios** = to decontrol wages; **sujeto a control estatal** = state-controlled; **televisión sujeta a control estatal** = state-controlled television **(c)** *(informática)* **sistemas de control** = control systems **(d)** *(electrónica)* **control remoto** = remote control; **por control remoto** = by remote control

> el presidente explicó a lo largo de su intervención la dificultad que existe en los delitos económicos que tienen una incidencia internacional y señaló que los movimientos de dinero son muy rápidos y en divisas, lo que dificulta su control
> **El País**

controlado, -da 1 *adj* controlled; **controlado por el gobierno** *o* **por el Estado** = government-controlled *o* state-controlled; **mercado controlado** = closed market; **no controlado** = uncontrolled; **precio controlado** = administered price **2** *pp de* CONTROLAR

controlador, -ra *n* controller; **controlador de créditos** = credit controller; **controlador de tráfico aéreo** = air traffic controller

controlar *vt* **(a)** *(dominar)* to control; **el gobierno está luchando por controlar la inflación** = the government is fighting to control inflation; **controlar un negocio** = to control a business; **el negocio está controlado por una compañía con sede en Luxemburgo** = the business is controlled by a company based in Luxemburg; **tener suficientes acciones para controlar una compañía** = to have a controlling interest in a company **(b)** *(inspeccionar)* to monitor *o* to check *o* to control; **controlar los alquileres** = to control rents; **controlar la calidad del producto** = to check the quality of the product *o* to inspect the product for defects; **controla la marcha de las ventas** = he is monitoring the progress of sales; **¿cómo controla Vd. el rendimiento de los representantes?** = how do you monitor the performance of the sales reps?

convalidación *nf* validation; **convalidación de título** = recognition of qualifications

◊ **convalidar** *vt* to check *o* to validate; **el documento fue convalidado por el banco** *o* **el banco convalidó el doumento** = the document was validated by the bank

convencer *vt* to convince *o* to persuade

convenido, -da 1 *adj* agreed; **una cantidad convenida** = an agreed amount; **vender algo a precio convenido** = to sell at an agreed price **2** *pp de* CONVENIR

conveniente *adj* suitable *o* convenient; **¿le parece las 9.30 una hora conveniente para la reunión?** = is 9.30 a convenient time for the meeting?

convenio *nm* agreement *o* covenant; **convenio colectivo (libre)** = (free) collective bargaining; **convenio comercial** = trade agreement; **un convenio internacional de comercio** = an international agreement on trade; **convenio de nivel crítico** = threshold agreement; **un convenio salarial colectivo** = collective wage agreement; **escritura de convenio** = deed of covenant; **firmar un convenio** = to sign an agreement *o* a deal

convenir *vt/i* to agree; **convenir en pagar 2.000 ptas. al año** = to agree to pay 2,000 pesetas per annum; **convenir un precio** = to agree a price *o* to arrive at a price

conversión *nf* conversion; **precio de conversión** = conversion price; **tasa de conversión** = conversion rate; **conversión de divisas** = currency conversion; **conversión de un préstamo** = refunding *o* restructuring of a loan

convertibilidad *nf* convertibility

◇ **convertible** *adj* convertible (currency); **empréstito convertible en acciones** = convertible loan stock; **estas mercancías deben pagarse en moneda convertible** = these goods must be paid for in hard currency; **moneda no convertible** = soft *o* weak currency; **obligación convertible** = convertible debenture

convertir *vt* to convert *o* to transform *o* to turn; **convirtió la compañía en una empresa rentable en menos de un año** = he turned the company round in less than a year; **convertir en dinero** = to turn something into cash

◇ **convertirse** *vr* to become *o* to turn into

convocar *vt* to call *o* to convene; **el sindicato convocó una huelga** = the union called a strike; **convocar una reunión** = to call *o* to convene a meeting; **convocar una reunión de accionistas** = to convene a meeting of shareholders

> en la protesta convocada el pasado viernes, los trabajadores demostraron su capacidad de movilización a través de un paro general y una manifestación con más de 15.000 asistentes
> *El País*

coopción *nf* co-option; **nombrar por coopción** = to co-opt someone onto a committee

cooperación *nf* co-operation; **con la cooperación de los trabajadores, el proyecto se llevó a cabo antes de lo previsto** = the project was completed ahead of schedule with the co-operation of the workforce

> el informe está estructurado en 12 capítulos, en los que se aborda el tema de la cooperación desde distintas perspectivas y realiza un amplio recorrido por los distintos organismos multilaterales de cooperación, con especial atención a la política de cooperación comunitaria
> *El País*

cooperar *vi* to co-operate; **los gobiernos cooperan en la lucha contra la piratería** = the governments are co-operating in the fight against piracy; **las dos empresas han cooperado en el proyecto informático** = the two firms have co-operated on the computer project; **el personal no ha cooperado debidamente en el plan de productividad de la empresa** = the workforce has not been co-operative over the management's productivity plan

cooperativa *nf* co-operative; **cooperativa agrícola** = agricultural co-operative; **crear una cooperativa de trabajadores** = to set up a workers' co-operative; **cooperativa de crédito** = credit union

cooperativo, -va *adj* co-operative; **sociedad cooperativa** = co-operative society

copar *vt* **copar el mercado** = to corner the market; *(Mex)* to monopolize

coparticipación *nf* copartnership *o* joint participation

copia *nf* copy *o* duplicate; **copia de archivo** = file copy; **copia auténtica** *o* **copia certificada** = certified copy; **copia carbón** = carbon copy; **me envió la copia del contrato** = he sent me the duplicate of the contract; **déme el original y archive la copia** = give me the original, and file the copy; **copia exacta** = true copy; **certifico que esta es una copia exacta** = I certify that this is a true copy; **copia falsa** = forgery; **copia fotostática** = photostat; **hacer una copia fotostática** = to photostat; **copia impresa** = hard copy; *(impresión de ordenador)* computer printout; **el director de ventas pidió una copia impresa de las comisiones de los representantes** = the sales director asked for a printout of the agents' commissions; **copia en limpio** = fair copy *o* final copy; **copia maestra de un fichero** = master copy of a file; **copia de reserva** *o* **de seguridad** = backup copy; **con copia** = two-part; **error de copia** = clerical error; **facturas con copia** = two-part invoices; **papel de escribir con copia** = two-part stationery

copiadora *nf* photocopier *o* copier *o* photocopying machine; **tenemos que pedir más papel para la copiadora** = we must order some more paper for the photocopier

copiar *vt* **(a)** *(repetir)* to copy; **copiar una factura** = to duplicate an invoice *o* to make a copy of an invoice; **copió el informe de la compañía por la noche y se lo llevó a casa** = he copied the company report at night and took it home **(b)** *(informática)* to back up

copropiedad *nf* **(a)** *(acción)* co-ownership *o* joint ownership *o* part-ownership; timeshare **(b)** *(cosa poseída)* coproperty **(c)** *(multipropiedad)* jointly owned property

◇ **copropietario, -ria** *n* co-owner *o* coproprietor *o* part-owner *o* joint owner; **las dos hermanas son copropietarias** = the two sisters are co-owners of the property; **es copropietario del restaurante** = he is part-owner of the restaurant

Corea del Norte *nf* North Korea

◇ **coreano, -na (del norte)** *o* **norcoreano, -na** *adj y n* North Korean
NOTA: capital: **Pyongyang**; moneda: **won coreano (W)** = Korean won (W)

Corea del Sur *nf* South Korea

◇ **coreano, -na (del sur)** *o* **surcoreano, -na** *adj y n* South Korean
NOTA: capital: **Seúl** (= Seoul); moneda: **won coreano (W)** = Korean won (W)

corona *nf* *(moneda de Dinamarca y Noruega)* krone; *(moneda de Suecia e Islandia)* krona

corporación *nf* corporation *o* guild

corrección *nf* correction *o* adjustment; **corrección inflacionaria** = adjustment for inflation

correcto, -ta *adj* accurate *o* correct *o* right; **el**

departamento de ventas hizo una previsión correcta de las ventas = the sales department made an accurate forecast of sales; **las cuentas publicadas no dan una visión correcta de la situación financiera de la compañía** = the published accounts do not give a correct picture of the company's financial position

◇ **correctamente** *adv* accurately *o* correctly

corrector, -ra 1 *n* corrector; **corrector de pruebas** = proofreader; **corrector de estilo** = editor **2** *adj* **líquido corrector** = correction fluid

corredor, -ra *n* broker; **corredor de bolsa** = stockbroker; **corredor de fincas** = estate agent; *US* realtor; **corredor de seguros** = insurance broker

> lleva más de veinte años trabajando en este país como agente bursátil, intermediario de inversiones y corredor de materias primas
> **España Económica**

correduría *nf* brokerage; **correduría de bolsa** = stockbroking

corregir *vt* to correct *o* to revise; **tendrá que corregir todos estos errores de mecanografía antes de enviar la carta** = you will have to correct all these typing errors before you send the letter

correo *nm* **(a)** *(servicio postal)* mail *o* post; **correo aéreo** = airmail; **el precio del correo aéreo ha aumentado en un 15%** = airmail charges have risen by 15%; **etiqueta de correo aéreo** = airmail sticker; **sobre de correo aéreo** = airmail envelope; **correo certificado (con acuse de recibo)** = recorded delivery; **correo electrónico** = electronic mail *o* e-mail; **enviar una respuesta a vuelta de correo** = to send a reply by return of post; **echar una carta al correo** = to post *o* to mail a letter *o* to put a letter in the post *o* in the mail; **la factura se envió por correo ayer** = the invoice was put in the mail yesterday; **lista de correos** = poste restante *o* general delivery; **creemos que el cheque** *o* **su encargo se ha perdido en el correo** = we are afraid the cheque *o* your order has been lost in the post; **el correo a algunas de las islas del Pacífico puede tardar seis semanas en llegar** = mail to some of the islands in the Pacific can take six weeks; **oficina de clasificación del correo** *o* **despacho de distribución del correo** = post room *o* mail room **(b) por correo** = by mail *o* by post; **enviar una factura por correo** = to send an invoice by post; **propaganda enviada por correo** = mail shot *o* mailing shot; **publicidad por correo** = direct-mail advertising; **venta por correo** = mail-order; **catálogo de ventas por correo** = mail-order catalogue; **la empresa dirige un próspero negocio de venta por correo** = the company runs a successful direct-mail operation; **estas calculadoras solamente se venden por correo** = these calculators are sold only by direct mail; **enviar cartas** *o* **paquetes por correo aéreo** = to airmail *o* to send a package by airmail; **recibir una muestra por correo aéreo** = to receive a sample by air mail; **enviar documentos por correo certificado** = to send documents by registered mail *o* registered post; **enviar un paquete por correo ordinario** *o* **por correo marítimo** = to send a package by surface mail *o* by sea mail; **enviar por correo urgente** = to send by express mail *o* to express **(c)** *(correspondencia)* **¿ha llegado ya el correo?** = has the post arrived yet?; **correo entrante** = incoming

mail; **su cheque llegó en el correo de ayer** = your cheque arrived in yesterday's post *o* mail; **el recibo estaba en el correo de la mañana** = the receipt was in this morning's mail **(d)** *(persona)* (motorcycle *o* cycle) courier *o* postman

◇ **Correos** *nmpl* the Post Office (the GPO); **Oficina Central de Correos** = main post office *o* central post office *o* General Post Office (GPO); **estafeta de correos** = sub-post office; **apartado de Correos** = Post Office box *o* P.O. box number; **nuestra dirección es: apartado de correos número 12.345, Madrid** = our address is: P.O. Box 12.345, Madrid

> enviar currículum vitae debidamente justificado al apartado de Correos 60.546 de Madrid, indicando en el sobre la referencia 'Analista'. Se realizará una selección previa por currículum
> **Actualidad Económica**

correr *vi* to run; **correr con** = to meet; **correr con los gastos** = to meet expenses *o* to foot the bill; **la empresa correrá con sus gastos** = the company will meet your expenses; **el director corrió con los gastos de la fiesta de Navidad del departamento** = the director paid for the department's Christmas party

correspondencia *nf* **(a)** *(cartas)* correspondence; **mantener correspondencia con alguien** = to be in correspondence with someone; **empleado encargado de la correspondencia** = correspondence clerk; **¿ha llegado ya la correspondencia?** = has the post *o* the mail arrived yet?; **abrir la correspondencia** = to open the mail *o* the post; **mi secretaria me abre la correspondencia en cuanto llega** = my secretary opens my mail as soon as it arrives; **la correspondencia se archiva en la carpeta de reclamaciones** = the correspondence is filed under 'complaints'; **correspondencia comercial** *o* **de negocios** = business correspondence; **correspondencia recibida** = incoming mail; **correspondencia de salida** *o* **correspondencia despachada** = outgoing mail; **negocios** *o* **empresa de ventas por correspondencia** = mail-order business *o* mail-order firm *o* mail-order house **(b)** *(enlace)* connection; **el vuelo de Nueva York tiene correspondencia con un vuelo a Atenas** = the flight from New York connects with a flight to Athens; **pregunta en el mostrador de helicópteros por los vuelos de correspondencia al centro de la ciudad** = check at the helicopter desk for connecting flights to the city centre

corresponder *vi* **(a)** *(coincidir)* to agree; **corresponder a algo** = to correspond with something; **corresponder con** = to agree with **(b)** **nos ofrecieron la representación exclusiva de sus coches y nosotros correspondimos ofreciéndoles la representación de nuestros autobuses** = they offered us an exclusive agency for their cars and we reciprocated with an offer of the agency for our buses

◇ **corresponderse** *vr* to correspond *o* to agree; **los dos grupos de cálculos no se corresponden** = the two sets of calculations do not agree; **las cifras de los auditores no se corresponden con las de la sección de contabilidad** = the auditors' figures do not agree with those of the accounts department

corresponsal *nmf* **(a)** *(prensa)* correspondent; **es el corresponsal de 'El País' en Londres** = he is the London correspondent of 'El País'; **un corresponsal financiero** = a financial correspondent; **la corresponsal comercial del 'Times'** = the 'Times' business correspondent **(b)** *(cartas)* correspondent; **corresponsal comercial** = business correspondent

corretaje *nm* **(a)** *(correduría)* (stock)broking; **corretaje marítimo** = shipbroking **(b)** *(comisión)* brokerage *o* broker's commission

corriente 1 *adj* **(a)** *(actual)* current; **activo corriente** = current assets; **gastos corrientes** *o* **costes corrientes de una empresa** = running costs *o* running expenses *o* current costs of running a business; **cuenta corriente** = current account; **depositar dinero en una cuenta corriente** = to pay money into a current account; **precio corriente** = current price *o* the going rate; **el precio corriente de las oficinas es de 6.000 ptas. por metro cuadrado** = the going rate for offices is 6,000 pesetas per square metre; **haremos las facturas a los precios corrientes** = we will invoice at ruling prices; **¿cuál es el precio corriente de los SEAT de segunda mano?** = what is the going price for secondhand SEATs?; **rendimiento corriente** = current yield; **pagamos a las mecanógrafas la tarifa corriente** = we pay the going rate for typists *o* we pay our typists the going rate **(b)** *(común)* common *o* frequent *o* ordinary *o* normal; **poco corriente** = odd; **acciones poco corrientes** = funny money; **poner el papel carbón al revés es un error corriente** = putting the carbon paper in the wrong way round is a common mistake; **tallas poco corrientes** = odd sizes **2** *nm* **(a)** **estar al corriente de una situación** = to be informed *o* to be aware of what is going on **(b)** *(actual)* current month; **de los corrientes** = instant *o* inst; **nuestra carta del 6 del corriente** *o* **de los corrientes** = our letter of the 6th instant *o* of the 6th inst **3** *nf* course *o* tendency

nuestro déficit corriente continúa su marcha hacia la cota nunca vista de los millones de dólares
España Económica

corro *nm* ring of dealers on the stock exchange *o* pit

en nuestro país, el mercado de corros ha sido el sistema de contratación tradicional de la Bolsa
El País

corrupción *nf* corruption *o* bribery; **es difícil controlar la corrupción y los sobornos** = bribery and corruption are difficult to control

corrupto, -ta *adj* corrupt

cortar *vt* to cut *o* to chop

corte 1 *nm* cut; **ha habido un corte del suministro eléctrico esta mañana, por lo que los ordenadores no han podido funcionar** = the electricity was cut off this morning, so the computers could not work **2** *nfpl* **Cortes** = Spanish Parliament; **Cortes constituyentes** = constituent assembly

cortés *adj* polite

◇ **cortesía** *nf* courtesy *o* politeness; **contestó con**

cortesía a las preguntas de los clientes = she politely answered the customers' questions

corto, -ta *adj* short; **a corto plazo** = short-term *o* in the short term; **crédito a corto plazo** = short *o* short-term credit; **tomar un préstamo a corto plazo** = to take out a short-term loan; **ha sido nombrado para un periodo corto** = he has been appointed on a short-term basis

cortocircuito *nm* short circuit

cosa *nf* thing *o* object; **poner las cosas difíciles a alguien** = to make things difficult for someone; **en cosa de unos meses** = it's a matter of a few months; **no vale gran cosa** = it's not worth much

cosecha *nf* crop *o* harvest; **una cosecha extraordinaria de maíz** = a bumper crop of corn

cosechar *vt* to gather *o* to harvest

costa *nf* **(a)** *(finanzas)* cost *o* price; **a costa de** = at the expense of; **a toda costa** = at all costs **(b)** *(litoral)* coast *o* shore

◇ **costas** *nfpl* *(jurídico)* costs; **pagar las costas** = to pay costs; **el juez impuso el pago de costas al demandado** *o* **las costas correrán a cargo de la parte demandada** = the judge awarded costs to the defendant *o* costs of the case will be borne by the prosecution; **la compañía pagó las costas de ambas partes** = the company bore the legal costs of both parties

Costa de Marfil *nf* Ivory Coast *o* Côte d'Ivoire

◇ **marfileño, -ña** *adj y n* Ivorien *o* Ivorian
NOTA: capital: **Abidjan;** moneda: **franco CFA (FCFA)** = CFA franc (CFAF)

Costa Rica *nf* Costa Rica

◇ **costarricense** *o* **costarriqueño, -ña** *adj y n* Costa Rican
NOTA: capital: **San José** (= San Jose); moneda: **colón costarricense (C)** = Costa Rican colon (C)

costar *vt* to cost; **¿cuánto cuesta la máquina?** = how much does the machine cost?; **la alfombra cuesta más de 100.000 ptas.** = the carpet costs over 100,000 pesetas; **cuesta mucho trabajo** = it takes a lot of work; **cueste lo que cueste** = at all costs

coste *nm* **(a)** *(importe)* cost; **coste, seguro y flete (cif)** = cost, insurance and freight (c.i.f.); **los costes de los ordenadores descienden cada año** = computer costs are falling each year; **los costes de la exposición los pagará la empresa** = the costs of the exhibition will be borne by the company; **no nos pudimos permitir el coste de dos teléfonos** = we could not afford the cost of two telephones; **calcular el coste de un producto** = to calculate the cost of a product *o* to cost a product; **no podemos calcular el coste hasta que no tengamos los pormenores de todos los gastos de producción** = we cannot do the costing until we have details of all the production expenditure; **los cálculos de costes nos dieron un precio al por menor de 236 ptas.** = the costings gave us a retail price of 236 pesetas; **coste básico de producción** = prime cost; **costes de comercialización** = marketing costs; **costes corrientes de una empresa** = running expenses *o* costs of running a business; **costes directos** = direct costs; **costes de explotación**

= operating costs o running costs; **costes fijos** = fixed costs; **costes indirectos** = indirect costs; **coste inicial** o **histórico** = historic(al) cost; **costes de investigación y desarrollo** = research and development costs; **coste de mantenimiento** o de **entretenimiento** = upkeep o maintenance costs; **coste marginal** = marginal cost; **fijación de precios según el coste marginal** = marginal pricing; **coste de materiales** = materials cost; **costes de personal** o **de mano de obra** = labour costs; **costes de producción** o **de fabricación** = manufacturing costs o production costs; **coste de reposición** = replacement cost o cost of replacement; **coste total** o **coste global** = total cost o full cost; **costes variables** = variable costs; **coste de ventas** = cost of sales; **análisis de costes** = cost analysis; **centro de costes** = cost centre; **contabilidad de costes** = cost accounting; **contable de costes** = cost accountant; **precio de coste** = cost price; **vender a precio de coste** = to sell at cost **(b)** (cargo) charge; **coste de manipulación** = handling charge **(c) coste de vida** = cost of living; **ajustado al coste de vida** = index-linked; **índice del coste de vida** = cost-of-living index; **subsidio por aumento del coste de la vida** = cost-of-living allowance

> la protección contra la competencia extranjera retarda la innovación, sube los costes de producción y limita las opciones del consumidor
> **Mercado**

> para luchar contra el fraude fiscal, Hacienda ha puesto en marcha este año una campaña, fundamentalmente en televisión y prensa escrita, cuyo coste global es de 400 millones de pesetas
> **El País**

costear vt to pay for; **costear los gastos de alguien** = to pay someone's expenses

◊ **costearse** vr to afford; **cuando se está sin empleo es difícil costearse incluso las necesidades básicas** = being unemployed makes it difficult to afford even the basic necessities

costo nm cost; **costo más honorarios** = cost-plus; **costo de expedición** = shipping charges

costoso, -sa adj costly o dear o expensive

costumbre nf custom o practice o routine; **su costumbre era llegar al trabajo a las 7.30 y empezar a contar la caja** = his practice was to arrive at work at 7.30 and start counting the cash; **desviarse de la costumbre** = to depart from normal practice; **como de costumbre** = as usual

cota nf **(a)** (cifra) figure **(b)** (altitud) height

> la actividad económica está ahora como en una plataforma, donde los indicadores presentan todavía tasas elevadas de aumento sobre las cotas de hace un año
> **España Económica**

cotejar vt to check o to compare; **cotejó la impresión del ordenador con las facturas para ver si la cifras coincidían** = he checked the computer printout against the invoices to see if the figures agreed; **cotejar la letra** = to compare handwriting; **cotejar firmas** = to compare signatures

cotidiano, -na adj daily o day-to-day; **organiza la gestión cotidiana de la compañía** = he organizes the day-to-day running of the company

cotizable adj **acciones cotizables** = listed securities

cotización nf **(a)** (valoración) price o quotation; **cotización del día** = today's price o current price; **cotización en el mercado bursátil** = stock market price o price on the stock market; **las acciones salieron ayer a cotización sin dividendos** = the shares went ex dividend yesterday; **el índice de cotización de acciones ha bajado un 10% desde su máxima de enero** = the share index has fallen 10% since the peak in January; **aceptamos la cotización más baja** = we accepted the lowest quotation; **cotización de la bolsa** = quotation on the Stock Exchange o Stock Exchange quotation; **buscamos una cotización en el mercado de valores** = we are seeking a stock market quotation **(b)** (contribución) contribution; **cotizaciones a la Seguridad Social** = National Insurance contributions

> las cotizaciones se han movido a lo largo de esta semana con un margen muy estrecho, delimitado por el poco riesgo asumido por los inversores y las expectativas que a medio plazo despiertan los tipos de interés
> **El País**

cotizar vt **(a)** (valorar) to quote; **cotizar los precios en pesetas** = to quote prices in pesetas o to quote peseta prices; **cotizar el precio para el suministro de ordenadores** = to give someone a quote for supplying computers **(b)** (contribuir) to contribute; **cotizó al fondo de pensiones durante 10 años** = he contributed to the pension fund for 10 years **(c)** **derecho a cotizar en la bolsa** = Stock Exchange listing

◊ **cotizarse** vr to be quoted o to sell for; **sus precios siempre se cotizan en dólares** = their prices are always quoted in dollars; **la empresa va a cotizarse en la bolsa** = the company is going to be quoted on the Stock Exchange; **la compañía intenta conseguir que sus acciones se coticen en la bolsa** = the company is planning to obtain a Stock Exchange listing; **las acciones de la compañía se cotizan en la Bolsa de Nueva York** = the company's shares are traded on the New York Stock Exchange

> deseaba invertir en España por un camino diferente del tradicional, fuera de la mera compra de acciones cotizadas en bolsa
> **España Económica**

> todos los sectores que cotizaron en la Bolsa de Valencia sufrieron retrocesos, excepto el inmobiliario y el de energía y aguas
> **Expansión**

coyuntura nf situation o prevailing conditions; **la coyuntura económica** = the economic situation; **perspectivas de la coyuntura** = economic prospects; **cambio en la coyuntura** = a change in economic trends

> en momentos de tensión suele pasarse revista a la coyuntura en un tono más negativo que el habitual
> **El País**

CP = CAJA POSTAL, CODIGO POSTAL

crac *nm (bolsa)* crash; *(empresa)* bankruptcy; **crac financiero** = financial crash; **la empresa hizo un crac** = the company went bankrupt; **la industria textil hizo un crac el año pasado** = the textile industry collapsed last year (NOTA: se usa también el término inglés **crash**)

> con el peligro de 'crash' bursátil y de enfriamiento financiero ya superado, los profetas nipones están confundidos
> **Actualidad Económica**

creación *nf* creation; **plan de creación de empleo** *o* **puestos de trabajo** = job creation scheme

crear *vt* to create *o* to establish *o* to set up; **a través de adquisiciones de pequeñas empresas no rentables pronto creó un gran grupo manufacturero** = by acquiring small unprofitable companies he soon created a large manufacturing group; **el plan del gobierno pretende crear nuevos empleos para los jóvenes** = the government scheme aims at creating new jobs for young people; **los hermanos han creado una nueva sociedad** = the brothers have formed a new company; **crear un grupo de trabajo** = to set up a working party

crecer *vi* to expand *o* to grow *o* to increase; **la empresa está creciendo rápidamente** = the company is expanding fast; **el volumen de ventas está creciendo a un ritmo del 15% anual** = turnover is growing at a rate of 15% per annum; **la compañía aspira a crecer** = the company is aiming for growth; **los beneficios han crecido más que la tasa de inflación** = profits have increased faster than the rate of inflation

creciente *adj* increasing *o* rising; **beneficios crecientes** = increasing profits; **rendimiento creciente** = increasing returns; **la sociedad tiene una creciente participación en el mercado** = the company has an increasing share of the market; **dimitió ante la creciente presión de los accionistas** = he resigned in the face of mounting pressure from the shareholders

crecimiento *nm* growth; **crecimiento económico** = economic growth; **crecimiento externo** *o* **exterior** = external growth; **un área de crecimiento** = a growth area; **industria de rápido crecimiento** = boom industry; **tasa de crecimiento** = growth rate

> no existe crecimiento económico indefinido en ningún sector
> **Tiempo**

> aunque los más optimistas apuntan a un crecimiento real del 3,4% para 1992; otros consideran que el aumento real del PIB no llegará al 3%
> **Actualidad Económica**

crediticio, -cia *adj* credit; **clasificación crediticia** = credit rating; **política crediticia** = credit policy; **techo crediticio** = credit ceiling; **unión crediticia** = credit union

crédito *nm* **(a)** *(préstamo)* credit *o* advance *o* facility; **conceder un crédito con garantía a alguien** = to pay someone an advance against a security; **crédito abierto** = open credit; **crédito de apoyo** *o* **standby** *o* **contingente** = standby credit;

crédito bancario = bank credit; **retirada del crédito bancario** = closing of an account; **crédito barato** *o* **caro** = cheap money *o* dear money; **crédito blando** = soft loan; **crédito a corto plazo** = short credit; **crédito a largo plazo** = long credit *o* extended credit; **crédito libre de interés** *o* **sin intereses** = interest-free credit; **crédito puente** = bridging loan; **crédito renovable** = revolving credit; **crédito tope** = credit ceiling; **a crédito** = on credit *o* on account; **vivir a crédito** = to live on credit; **todos los muebles de la casa se compran a crédito** = all the furniture in the house is bought on credit; **conceder seis meses de crédito a alguien** = to give someone six months' credit; **banco de crédito** = credit bank; **carta de crédito** = letter of credit; **carta de crédito irrevocable** = irrevocable letter of credit; **congelación** *o* **restricción del crédito** = credit freeze *o* credit squeeze; **control de crédito** = credit control; **controlador de créditos** = credit controller; **cooperativa de crédito** = credit union; **cuenta de crédito** = charge account *o* credit account; **abrir una cuenta de crédito** = to open a credit account; **facilidades de crédito** = credit facilities; **Instituto de Crédito Oficial (ICO)** = Official Credit Institute; **límite** *o* **techo de crédito** = credit limit; **ha sobrepasado el límite de su crédito** = he has exceeded his credit limit; **abrir una línea de crédito** = to open a line of credit *o* a credit line; **la empresa se equivocó con el envío y tuvo que emitir una nota de crédito** = the company sent the wrong order and so had to issue a credit note; **sociedad de crédito inmobiliario** *o* **de crédito hipotecario** = *GB* building society; *US* savings and loan (association); **recibir un crédito del banco** = to receive an advance from the bank; **refinanciar un crédito** = to roll over credit; **retirar el crédito** = to stop an account; **tarjeta de crédito** = credit card *o* charge card; *(fig)* plastic money; **vender con buenas condiciones de crédito** = to sell on good credit terms; **lo compramos todo con créditos a sesenta días** = we buy everything on sixty days credit; **la compañía se mantiene gracias a los créditos de sus acreedores** = the company exists on credit from its suppliers; **vendemos a Argentina con créditos a largo plazo** = we sell to Argentina on extended credit **(b)** *(confianza)* trust; **su palabra no merece crédito** = he cannot be trusted to keep his word; **es una persona digna de crédito** = she is reliable *o* she can be trusted

> el porcentaje de crecimiento para el crédito interno a las empresas y familias se fijó entre el 10,5% y el 11%
> **Mercado**

> al darse cuenta de que podían dar crédito en cualquier parte del mundo a través de la pantalla de sus ordenadores, los bancos se lanzaron a una carrera desenfrenada
> **Actualidad Económica**

> el fuerte peso del crédito hipotecario en el conjunto de la inversión crediticia (41,57%) asegura una inversión de los fondos invertidos
> **Actualidad Económica**

cría *nf* breeding *o* farming; **cría de pollos** = chicken farming

criado, -da *n* servant

criba *nf* screening *o* selection (of candidates); **pasar por la criba** = to screen

crimen *nm* crime

criminal *adj* criminal; **causa criminal** = criminal action *o* case

crisis *nf* crisis; **crisis bancaria** = banking crisis; **crisis económica** = economic crisis *o* slump; **la crisis económica mundial de 1929 - 1933** = the Depression *o* the Slump (of 1929 to 1933); **crisis financiera** = financial crisis; **crisis internacional** = international crisis; **crisis de la peseta** = peseta crisis

> tras una década de desarrollo continuado del sector, éste está padeciendo ahora las repercusiones de la crisis en otros sectores
>
> **Tiempo**

> en los periodos de crisis económicas los Bancos de emisión desarrollan una enorme actividad
>
> **España Económica**

criterio *nm* judgement *o* opinion; **el consejo tiene confianza en el criterio del director gerente** = the board has faith in the managing director's judgement

criticar *vt* to criticize; **el director gerente criticó al director de ventas por no haber aumentado el volumen de ventas** = the managing director criticized the sales manager for not improving the volume of sales; **el diseño del nuevo catálogo ha sido criticado** = the design of the new catalogue has been criticized

crítico, -ca 1 *adj* critical; **la compañía está atravesando una etapa crítica** = the company is going through a critical period; **convenio de nivel crítico** = threshold agreement **2** *n* critic; **crítico de arte** *o* **de cine** = art critic *o* film critic

Croacia *nf* Croatia

◊ **croata** *adj y n* Croat *o* Croatian
NOTA: capital: **Zagreb**; moneda: **corona croata** = (Croatian) kuna

crónico, -ca *adj* chronic; **tenemos una escasez crónica de personal cualificado** = we have a chronic shortage of skilled staff

crudo, -da 1 *adj* (*sin refinar*) raw **2** *nm* crude (oil); **el precio del crudo árabe ha bajado** = the price for Arabian crude has fallen

cruzado, -da 1 *adj* **cheque cruzado** = crossed cheque; **cheque no cruzado** = uncrossed cheque **2** *pp de* CRUZAR

cruzar *vt* (a) (*atravesar*) to go across *o* to cross; **el Concorde solamente tarda tres horas en cruzar el Atlántico** = Concorde only takes three hours to cross the Atlantic; **para llegar al banco tiene que torcer a la izquierda y cruzar la calle a la altura de la oficina de correos** = to get to the bank, you turn left and cross the street at the post office (b) **cruzar un cheque** = to cross a cheque; **cheque sin cruzar** = uncrossed cheque

cuaderno *nm* notebook

cuadrado, -da 1 *adj* square; **las dimensiones de la oficina son de diez metros por doce - su área es de ciento veinte metros cuadrados** = the office is ten metres by twelve - its area is one hundred and twenty square metres **2** *nm* square; **el papel cuadriculado presenta una serie de cuadrados pequeños** = graph paper is drawn with a series of small squares

cuadrar 1 *vt* to balance *o* to reconcile; **cuadrar las cuentas** = to reconcile the accounts; **he acabado de cuadrar las cuentas de marzo** = I have finished balancing the accounts for March; **cuadrar una cuenta con otra** = to reconcile one account with another; **el departamento de contabilidad intentó hacer cuadrar las cifras** = the accounts department tried to make the figures tally **2** *vi* to agree *o* to tally; **el balance de las cuentas de febrero no cuadra** = the February accounts do not balance; **los dos grupos de cálculos no cuadran** = the two sets of calculations do not agree; **las cifras no cuadran** = the figures do not add up

cuadrícula *nf* grid

◊ **cuadriculado, -da** *adj* squared; **papel cuadriculado** = graph paper *o* squared paper

cuadro *nm* (a) (*pintura*) picture (b) (*tabla*) table *o* chart; **cuadro estadístico** = statistical table; **cuadro de financiamiento anual** = chart of annual financial changes (c) (*tablero*) **cuadro de mandos** = control panel *o* switchboard (d) (*personal*) staff; **cuadros intermedios** = middle management *o* middle managers

> todos los especialistas coinciden en la necesidad de dominar, al menos, un idioma en niveles ejecutivos, cuadros intermedios y, por supuesto, en la alta dirección
>
> **El País**

cuadruplicado, -da *adj* quadruplicate; **por cuadruplicado** = in quadruplicate; **las facturas se imprimen por cuadruplicado** = the invoices are printed in quadruplicate

cuadruplicar *vt* to quadruple; **los beneficios de la compañía se han cuadruplicado en los últimos cinco años** = the company's profits have quadrupled over the last five years

cualificación *nf* qualification; **cualificación profesional** = professional qualifications

◊ **cualificado, -da 1** *adj* skilled; **no cualificado** = unskilled; **obreros cualificados** *o* **mano de obra cualificada** = skilled workers *o* skilled labour; **sumamente cualificado** = highly qualified; **todos nuestros empleados están sumamente cualificados** = all our staff are highly qualified; **la compañía sólo emplea electricistas cualificados** = the company only employs trained electricians **2** *pp de* CUALIFICAR

◊ **cualificar** *vt* to qualify; **mano de obra sin cualificar** = unskilled labour *o* unskilled workforce *o* unskilled workers

> la nación debe enfrentarse al desafío de aumentar la productividad de su mano de obra, que, a su vez, depende de las cualificaciones cada vez más desarrolladas de los trabajadores, y de poner a su disposición un capital más elevado y una tecnología más avanzada
>
> **Mercado**

antes, llegar a ser licenciado era una
meta a la que muchos se aferraban porque
abría las puertas al mundo laboral
'cualificado'

El País

cuantificable *adj* quantifiable; **el efecto de las alteraciones en la estructura del descuento no es cuantificable** = the effect of the change in the discount structure is not quantifiable *o* cannot be quantified

cuantificar *vt* to quantify; **es imposible cuantificar el efecto que la nueva legislación tendrá sobre nuestro volumen de negocios** = it is impossible to quantify the effect of the new legislation on our turnover

cuanto, -ta *adj y pron* (a) all that *o* as much as; **en cuanto a** = regarding; **¿puedes telefonear en cuanto consigas la información?** = can you phone as soon as you get the information? **(b)** *(en interrogación o exclamación)* **¿cuánto, cuánta?** = how much?; **¿cuánto cuesta la máquina?** = how much does the machine cost?; **¿cuánto le deben todavía los deudores a la compañía?** = how much is still owing to the company by its debtors?; **¿cuántos, cuántas?** = how many?; **¿cuántas personas se necesitan?** = how many people are needed?

cuartil *nm* quartile

cuarto, -ta 1 *adj* fourth; **cuarta parte** = quarter; **tres cuartas partes** = three quarters; **cuarto trimestre** = fourth quarter **2** *nm* **(a)** *(habitación)* room **(b)** *(una cuarta parte)* quarter; **un cuarto de hora** = a quarter of an hour; **un cuarto de litro** = a quarter of a litre *o* a quarter litre; **tres cuartos** = three quarters

cuasi *prefijo* quasi-

Cuba *nm* Cuba

◇ **cubano, -na** *adj y n* Cuban
NOTA: capital: **La Habana** (= Havana); moneda: **peso cubano ($)** = Cuban peso ($)

cúbico, -ca *adj* cubic; **la caja tiene una capacidad de seis metros cúbicos** = the crate holds six cubic metres

cubierta *nf* **(a)** *(de un libro)* cover **(b)** *(de un barco)* deck; **carga en cubierta** = deck cargo; **marinero de cubierta** = deck hand **(c)** *(impresora)* acoustic hood

cubierto 1 *adj* covered; **cheque no cubierto** = bad *o* uncovered cheque **2** *nm* **(a)** *(en restaurante)* cover charge **(b)** place setting *o* set of cutlery **3** *pp de* CUBRIR

cubo *nm* **(a)** *(matemáticas)* cube **(b)** *(recipiente)* bin *o* bucket

cubrir *vt* **(a)** *(proteger)* to cover *o* to insure (against loss); **cubrir un riesgo** = to cover a risk; **estar cubierto contra todo riesgo** = to be fully covered; **¿está Vd. cubierto contra robo?** = do you have cover against theft?; **el seguro cubre incendio, robo y pérdida de empleo** = the insurance covers fire, theft and loss of work; **el seguro cubrió los daños** = the damage was covered by the insurance **(b)** **cubrir un puesto** *o* **una vacante** = to fill a post *o*

a vacancy; **cubrir los puestos del turno** = to man a shift; **su solicitud llegó demasiado tarde - el puesto ya ha sido cubierto** = your application arrived too late - the post has already been filled **(c)** *(compensar)* to meet; **cubrir una compra a plazo** = to cover a position; **cubrir gastos** = to cover costs *o* to break even; **cubrir los gastos** = to meet the expenses; **no vendemos lo suficiente para cubrir los gastos de la tienda** = we do not sell enough to cover the expense of running the shop; **el umbral de rentabilidad se alcanza cuando las ventas cubren todos los costes** = breakeven point is reached when sales cover all costs **(d)** *(tapar)* to cover *o* to put a cover on; **no olvide cubrir su ordenador antes de marcharse** = don't forget to cover your computer before you go home

◇ **cubrirse** *vr* to cover oneself; **cubrirse contra el riesgo de la inflación** = to hedge against inflation; **compró oro para cubrirse contra las pérdidas en el cambio** = he bought gold to cover himself *o* as a hedge against exchange losses

cuenta *nf* **(a)** *(banco)* account; **cuenta bancaria** = bank account; *US* banking account; **cuenta de caja de ahorros** = savings bank account; **cuenta de caja postal de ahorro** = Girobank account; **una cuenta en el Banco de Santander** = Banco de Santander account; **tengo una cuenta en el Banco Zaragozano** *o* = I bank at *o* with the Banco Zaragozano *o* I have an account with the Banco Zaragozano; **¿dónde tiene Vd. su cuenta bancaria?** = where do you bank?; **cuenta de ahorro** = savings account; **cuenta bloqueada** = frozen account; **cuenta de caja** = cash account; **cuenta conjunta** *o* **en participación** = joint account; **cuenta corriente** = current account *o* cheque account; *US* checking account; **cuenta de depósito** *o* **a plazo** = deposit account; **cuenta discrecional** = discretionary account; **cuenta en divisas** = foreign currency account; **cuenta inactiva** = dormant *o* dead *o* inactive account; **cuenta numerada** = numbered account; **cuenta presupuestaria** = budget account; **cuenta en regla** = clear account; **cuenta de no residente** = external account; **cuenta con saldo deudor** *o* **cuenta al descubierto** = overdrawn account; **nuestra cuenta quedó al descubierto el mes pasado** = our bank balance went into the red last month; **he recibido una carta de mi banco advirtiéndome que mi cuenta está al descubierto** = I have had a letter from my bank telling me my account is overdrawn; **número de cuenta** = bank account number; **cuenta que devenga un interés del 10 %** = account which earns interest at 10%; **abrir una cuenta** = to open an account; **abrió una cuenta en la Caja Postal de Ahorros** = she opened an account with the Caja Postal de Ahorros; **cerrar una cuenta** = to close an account; **cerró su cuenta en el Banco de Santander** = he closed his account with the Banco de Santander; **ingresar un talón en una cuenta** = to pay a cheque into an account; **ingresó 5.000 ptas. en su cuenta** = she put 5,000 pesetas into her account; **ingresar dinero en su cuenta** = to put money in(to) your account; **sacar** *o* **retirar dinero de su cuenta** = to take money out of your account *o* to withdraw money from your account; **cargaron 5.000 ptas. a su cuenta** = his account was debited with the sum of 5,000 pesetas; **cuenta con saldo positivo** = account in credit **(b)** *(empresas)* **cuentas anuales** = annual accounts; **cuentas por cobrar** = accounts receivable; **cuenta compensada** = contra account; **cuentas**

consolidadas = consolidated accounts; **las cuentas de una empresa** = the accounts of a business *o* a company's accounts; **cuenta de explotación** *o* **de ejercicio** = trading account; **cuentas de gestión** = management accounts; **cuentas del grupo** = group accounts; **cuentas por pagar** = accounts payable; **cuenta de pérdidas y ganancias** = profit and loss account; **cuenta de resultados** = income statement; **libro de cuentas** = account book; **llevar las cuentas** = to keep the accounts of a business; **pasar a cuenta nueva** = carry forward; **revisar las cuentas** = to audit the accounts; **saldar a cuenta nueva** = bring forward; **saldo a cuenta nueva** = balance carried forward; **saldo a cuenta nueva: 73.030 ptas.** = balance brought forward: 73,030 pesetas; **el trabajo del contable consiste en registrar en las cuentas todo el dinero recibido** = the accountant's job is to enter all the money received in the accounts **(c)** *(en una tienda)* account; **tener una cuenta** *o* **una cuenta abierta** *o* **una cuenta de crédito en el Corte Inglés** = to have an account *o* a charge account *o* a credit account with el Corte Inglés; **cárguelo en mi cuenta** = put it on my account *o* charge it to my account; **bloquear una cuenta** = to put an account on stop *o* to block an account; **liquidar una cuenta** = to settle an account **(d) a cuenta** = on account; **anticipo a cuenta** = advance on account; **pagar a cuenta** = to pay money on account; **pago a cuenta** = interim payment *o* down payment; **pagos a cuenta** = progress payments **(e)** *(control de existencias)* tally; **llevar la cuenta del movimiento de existencias** *o* **de gastos** = to keep a tally of stock movements *o* of expenses **(f)** *(en restaurante)* bill; *US* check; **¿me puede traer la cuenta, por favor?** = can I have the bill please?; **la cuenta asciende a 4.000 ptas., servicio incluido** = the bill comes to 4,000 pesetas including service; **¿está el servicio incluido en la cuenta?** = does the bill include service? **(g)** *(aviso de pago)* account; **sírvase enviarnos su cuenta** *o* **una cuenta detallada** *o* **pormenorizada** = please send us your account *o* a detailed *o* an itemized account; **pagamos la cuenta cada seis meses** = we pay the account half-yearly; **cuenta (de gastos) de representación** = expense account; **cargó la factura del hotel en su cuenta de gastos** = he charged his hotel bill to his expense account **(h)** *(facturas)* bill; **cuentas por pagar** = bills payable; **cuentas por cobrar** = bills receivable **(i)** *(independientemente)* **que trabaja por su cuenta** *o* **por cuenta propia** = self-employed *o* freelance; **trabaja en una oficina de contabilidad, pero lleva una empresa de construcción por su cuenta** = he works in an accountant's office, but he runs a construction company on the side; **trabaja por su cuenta y por eso no tiene unos ingresos fijos** = she works freelance so she does not have a regular income; **trabajó en un banco durante diez años pero ahora trabaja por cuenta propia** = he worked in a bank for ten years but now is self-employed **(j) tener en cuenta** = to take into account *o* to take account of *o* to allow for; **tener en cuenta la inflación** = to take account of inflation *o* to take inflation into account; **tener en cuenta el dinero pagado por adelantado** = to allow for money paid in advance; **sin tener en cuenta** = regardless of *o* exclusive of; **el presidente amuebló su oficina sin tener en cuenta el gasto** = the chairman furnished his office regardless of expense; **darse cuenta** = to realize; **los pequeños comerciantes se dieron cuenta de que el hipermercado les quitaría una parte de su mercado** = the small shopkeepers realized that the hypermarket would take away some of their trade

> no le cobramos por domiciliar sus pagos en cuentas a la vista
> **España Económica**

> la empresa cliente paga el supuesto servicio o la supuesta venta con un talón nominativo a nombre de la empresa inactiva, que es entregado en un banco donde ésta tiene una cuenta, controlada por el falsificador
> **Cambio 16**

> todas las transacciones realizadas por la empresa estaban recogidas en las cuentas anuales
> **El País**

> se hizo pública la auditoría correspondiente a 1990, en la que el auditor concluía que no puede expresar opinión alguna sobre las cuentas presentadas por la empresa
> **El País**

cuerpo *nm* **(a) cuerpo estatal** = public body; **cuerpo legislativo** = legislative body **(b)** *(personas)* body; **cuerpo de bomberos** = fire brigade; **cuerpo diplomático** = diplomatic corps; **cuerpo de inspectores** = inspectorate; **cuerpo de inspectores de fábricas** = the factory inspectorate

cuestión *nf* question *o* issue *o* matter (for discussion); **la cuestión más importante del orden del día** = the most important matter on the agenda; **cuestiones afines en el orden del día** = related items on the agenda; **la junta debatió la cuestión de las indemnizaciones por despido** = the board discussed the question of redundancy payments; **el comité trató la cuestión de los derechos de importación de los automóviles** = the committee discussed the issue of import duties on cars

cuestionar 1 *vt* to question (someone) **2** *vi* to argue *o* to dispute

cuestionario *nm* questionnaire; **enviar un cuestionario para analizar la opinión de los usuarios del sistema** = to send out a questionnaire to get the opinion of users of the system; **contestar** *o* **rellenar un cuestionario sobre vacaciones en el extranjero** = to answer *o* to fill in a questionnaire about holidays abroad

culminar *vi* to culminate *o* to reach a peak

culpa *nf* **(a)** *(falta)* blame *o* fault; **echaron la culpa a los vendedores por las bajas cifras de ventas** = the sales staff got the blame for the poor sales figures; **si el almacén se queda sin existencias la culpa es del encargado del inventario** = it is the stock controller's fault if the warehouse runs out of stock **(b)** *(jurídico)* **culpa penal** = criminal negligence

culpable 1 *adj* guilty; **se le declaró culpable de difamación** = he was found guilty of libel; **la compañía fue culpable de no informar a los auditores sobre las ventas** = the company was guilty of not reporting the sales to the auditors **2** *nmf* the offender *o* the guilty party

culpar *vt* to blame *o* to accuse; **el sindicato culpa a la dirección de las malas relaciones laborales** =

the union is blaming the management for poor industrial relations

cultivar *vt* to farm; **cultiva una extensión de 150 hectáreas** = he farms 150 hectares

cultivo *nm* **(a)** *(cosecha)* crop **(b)** *(labranza)* cultivation *o* farming; **cultivo intensivo** = intensive farming

cumbre *nf* **(a)** *(cima)* top *o* summit *o* peak *o* height **(b)** *(reunión)* summit (meeting)

la cumbre de Lisboa tendrá también que elegir nuevo presidente para la Comisión Europea, que empezará su mandato a principios del próximo año
Actualidad Económica

cumplidor,-ra *adj* reliable *o* trustworthy

cumplimiento *nm* execution *o* fulfilment; **en el cumplimiento de sus funciones como director** = in discharge of his duties as director

cumplir *vt* **(a)** *(condición, promesa, contrato)* to carry out *o* to execute *o* to fulfil; *US* to fulfill; **cumplir las instrucciones** = to carry out the instructions; **cumplir las instrucciones de una carta** = to act on a letter; **cumplir uno sus obligaciones** = to discharge one's liabilities; **cumplir con los requisitos** = to meet requirements; **la cláusula referente a los pagos no se ha cumplido** = the clause regarding payments has not been fulfilled; **hacer cumplir** = to enforce; **hacer cumplir los términos de un contrato** = to enforce the terms of a contract; **negarse a cumplir un acuerdo** = to repudiate an agreement **(b)** *(ser puntual)* **cumplir un plazo establecido** = to meet a deadline; **cumplir los plazos** = to be on schedule; **no consiguieron cumplir el plazo establecido** = they failed to meet the deadline; **no pudimos cumplir el plazo del 1 de octubre** = we've missed our October 1st deadline **(c)** **la compañía cumplirá 125 años el año próximo** = the company is 125 years old next year

cuota *nf* **(a)** *(precio)* fee *o* rate *o* allowance *o* contribution; **cuota de depreciación** = allowance for depreciation; **cuota de entrada** = entrance fee *o* admission fee; **pagamos una cuota fija de luz cada trimestre** = we pay a flat rate for electricity each quarter; **cuotas de flete** = freight rates; **cuota patronal** = employer's contribution **(b)** *(cupo)* quota; **cuota de importación** = import quota **(c)** *(suscripción)* subscription; **pagar la cuota de socio** = to pay your club membership *o* your membership fees; **olvidó renovar su cuota del club** = he forgot to renew his club subscription; **cuota sindical** *o* **cuota de inscripción sindical** = union dues *o* union subscription **(d)** *(proporción)* share; **su cuota de mercado ha subido en un 10%** = their share of the market has gone up by 10%; **la empresa ha experimentado un aumento constante de su cuota de mercado** = the company has steadily increased its market share; **la empresa sufrió una pérdida de su cuota de mercado** = the company lost market share *o* suffered a loss of market penetration

ha podido reducir o aumentar las cuotas del plan de pensiones o jubilación según su deseo y el paso del tiempo
España Económica

Hacienda ha publicado ya en el Boletín Oficial del Estado (BOE) las tarifas y correspondientes cuotas a pagar por cada una de las actividades económicas o de negocio
Tiempo

cupo *nm* quota; **cupo de importación** = import quota; **el gobierno ha impuesto un cupo de importación de coches** = the government has imposed a quota on the importation of cars; **el cupo de coches de importación ha sido suprimido** = the quota on imported cars has been lifted; **cupo de ventas** = sales quota; **sistema de cupo** = quota system; **organizar la distribución por un sistema de cupo** = to arrange distribution through a quota system

cupón *nm* coupon; **cupón de anuncio** = coupon ad; **cupón de interés** = interest coupon; **con cupón de interés** = cum coupon; **sin cupón de interés** = ex coupon; **cupón-respuesta internacional** = international (postal) reply coupon; **remitió un cupón-respuesta internacional en su carta** = he enclosed an international reply coupon with his letter; **acciones cotizadas sin cupón** = shares quoted ex dividend; **obligación con cupón cero** = zero-coupon bond; **cupón con prima** = trading stamp

currículum (vitae) *nm* curriculum vitae; *US* résumé; **los aspirantes deben enviar al encargado de personal una carta de solicitud con el currículum** = candidates should send a letter of application with a curriculum vitae to the personnel officer; **se ruega hacer la solicitud por escrito, adjuntando un currículum (vitae) actualizado** = please apply in writing, enclosing a current CV

enviar currículum vitae debidamente justificado al apartado de Correos 60.546 de Madrid, indicando en el sobre la referencia 'Analista'. Se realizará una selección previa por currículum
Actualidad Económica

los interesados deberán enviar su currículum vitae, así como pretensiones, al apartado 35.298 de Barcelona, C.P.08025, indicando en el sobre la Ref. Ingeniero Proyectos
Actualidad Económica

cursar *vt* **(a)** *(enviar)* to send **(b) cursar pedidos** = to order; **el departamento ha cursado un pedido para comprar un nuevo ordenador** = the department has ordered *o* has placed an order for a new computer **(c)** *(estudios)* to study

curso *nm* **(a)** *(estudio)* course; **curso de actualización** *o* **reciclaje** = refresher course; **curso de secretariado** = secretarial course; **curso de formación en el empleo** = on-the-job training course; **la mayor parte de los vendedores ha seguido un curso de formación en el empleo** = most salesmen have had a course of on-the-job training; **la empresa le ha pagado un curso de formación de gestión comercial** = the company has paid for her to attend a training course in sales management; **el director adjunto de ventas asiste a un curso en jornada laboral** = the junior sales manager is attending a day release course **(b) en curso** = in progress; **negociaciones en curso** = negotiations in progress; **trabajo en curso** = work in progress **(c) moneda de curso legal** = legal tender;

dinero de curso forzoso = fiat money **(d)** *(jurídico)* **el curso seguido por la Justicia** = the due processes of the law

curva *nf* curve; **curva del aprendizaje** = learning curve; **curva de Laffer** = Laffer curve; **curva de ventas** = sales curve; **el gráfico muestra una curva ascendente** = the graph shows an upward curve

custodia *nf* safe keeping; **fondo de custodia** = trust fund

Dd

dama *nf* lady; **¡Damas y Caballeros!** = Ladies and Gentlemen!

dañado, -da 1 *adj* damaged; **mercancías dañadas en el transporte** = goods damaged in transit; **mercancías dañadas por un incendio** = fire-damaged goods; **existencias dañadas por el agua** = stock which has been damaged by water **2** *pp de* DAÑAR

dañar *vt* **(a)** *(objeto)* to damage *o* to spoil *o* to cause damage (to); **la tormenta dañó la carga** = the storm damaged the cargo; **algunas de las mercancías fueron dañadas en el tránsito** = some of the goods were damaged in transit **(b)** *(persona)* to harm *o* to hurt *o* to injure

◊ **dañarse** *vr* **(a)** *(objeto)* to get damaged *o* to be damaged **(b)** *(persona)* to get hurt *o* to be hurt

daño *nm* **(a)** *(perjuicio)* damage *o* harm; **daños por incendio** = fire damage; **el incendio causó daños calculados en 20.000.000 de ptas.** = the fire caused damage estimated at 20m pesetas; **daños por tormenta** = storm damage; **sufrir daños** = to suffer damage; **estamos intentando calcular los daños que sufrió el envío durante el transporte** = we are trying to assess the damage which the shipment suffered in transit; **inspección de daños** *o* **de avería** = damage survey; **la recesión ha hecho mucho daño a las exportaciones** = the recession has done a lot of harm to export sales; **daños y perjuicios** = damages; **indemnización por daños y perjuicios** = compensation for damages *o* damages indemnification; **obtener daños y perjuicios del conductor del coche** = to recover damages from the driver of the car; **pagar** *o* **reclamar 200.000 ptas. por daños y perjuicios** = to pay *o* to claim 200,000 pesetas in damages; **presentar una demanda por daños y perjuicios** = to bring an action for damages against someone; **ser responsable de los daños y perjuicios** = to be liable for damages

dar 1 *vt* **(a)** *(ofrecer)* to give; **le dieron dos meses de sueldo en lugar del aviso de despido** = she was given two months' salary in lieu of notice; **le dimos un vale para un regalo por su aniversario** = we gave her a gift token for her birthday; **¿me puede dar información sobre el nuevo sistema informático?** = can you give me some information about the new computer system?; **dar a alguien cambio de 10.000 ptas.** = to give someone change for 10,000 pesetas; **la empresa dio una fiesta en un barco para anunciar su nuevo sistema de descuentos** = the company gave a party on a boat to publicize its new discount system **(b)** *(precio)* to quote; **dar un precio para el suministro de material de oficina** = to quote a price for supplying stationery **(c)** *(beneficio)* to yield **(d)** *(impresión)* to cause *o* to produce **(e) dar la autorización** = to authorize *o* to give the go-ahead; **dar carpetazo a algo** = to pigeonhole; **dar la casualidad** = to happen to; **dar encargos** *o* **dar instrucciones** = to instruct *o* to brief; **dar instrucciones a alguien para que haga algo** = to instruct someone to do something; **dar una entrada** = to put money down; **dar una entrada**

para la compra de una casa = to put down money on a house; **dar poderes a alguien** = to nominate someone as proxy; **dar a algo prioridad absoluta** = to give something top priority; **dar una propina** = to give a tip *o* to tip; **dar un recado** = to deliver a message; **dar publicidad** = to publicize *o* to plug; **dar un salto** = to jump; **los valores de las acciones dieron un salto en la bolsa** = share values jumped on the Stock Exchange **2** *vi* **(a)** *(posición)* **dar a** = to overlook *o* to face; **la habitación del hotel da al jardín** = the hotel room looks out onto the garden; **la oficina del director gerente da a la fábrica** = the MD's office overlooks the factory **(b) dar de sí** = to be very productive **(c) dar con** = to meet *o* to run into

◊ **darse** *vr* **darse cuenta** = to realize; **los pequeños comerciantes se dieron cuenta de que el hipermercado les quitaría una parte de su clientela** = the small shopkeepers realized that the hypermarket would take away some of their trade; **darse la mano** = to shake hands; **darse por vencido** = to give in *o* to give up

datar *vi* to date; **el pedido data del mes pasado** = the order dates back to last month

dato *nm* **(a)** *(información)* fact *o* piece of information; **el presidente pidió que se examinaran todos los datos sobre la reclamación del impuesto sobre la renta** = the chairman asked to see all the facts on the income tax claim; **el director de ventas le puede proporcionar los datos exactos sobre la operación africana** = the sales director can give you the facts and figures about the African operation **(b)** *(informática)* datos = data; **los datos están en discos flexibles de 5,25 pulgadas** = the data is on 5¼ inch floppies; **los datos están siendo procesados por nuestro ordenador** = the data is being processed by our computer; **banco de datos** = data bank *o* bank of data; **hoja de datos** = fact sheet; **introducir** *o* **pasar datos al ordenador** = to input information *o* to key in data; **procesamiento** *o* **proceso de datos** = data processing; **proceso electrónico de datos** = electronic data processing (EDP); **efectuamos todo el proceso de datos en la empresa** = we do all our data processing in-house; **recopilación de datos** = data acquisition *o* data collection; **recuperación de datos** = information retrieval; **toma de datos** = data capture; **datos sin analizar** = raw data; **datos de salida** = computer output

> digan lo que digan los datos oficiales de paro, en ciertos sectores y regiones se está llegando a situaciones muy próximas al pleno empleo
> **España Económica**

> los datos de la economía real indican que, tras el ajuste monetario, el 'aterrizaje' real se está produciendo
> **España Económica**

debajo *adv* under *o* below *o* beneath *o* less than; **por debajo de** = under; **acciones que se cotizan por debajo de su valor nominal** = shares which stand at a discount; **el tipo de interés está por debajo del 10%** = the interest rate is less than 10%; **la**

contabilidad de la compañía presenta unos beneficios por debajo de los reales = the company accounts understate the real profit; las ventas están un 10% por debajo del año pasado = sales show a 10% decrease on last year; los beneficios han permanecido por debajo del 10% durante dos años = profits have stayed below 10% for two years

debate *nm* discussion *o* argument *o* debate; tras un debate de diez minutos el consejo de administración aceptó los aumentos salariales = after ten minutes' discussion the board agreed the salary increases; aprobar sin debate = to agree without discussing *o* to rubber stamp; la junta directiva aprobó el acuerdo sin debate previo = the board simply rubber stamped the agreement

debe *nm* debit *o* debit side *o* debit balance; debe y haber = debits and credits; columna del debe = debit column

deber 1 *vt* to owe; deber dinero = to owe money *o* to be in debt; debe al banco 50.000.000 de ptas. = he owes the bank 50m pesetas; debe a la empresa las mercancías que compró = he owes the company for the stock he purchased; dinero que se debe a los consejeros = money owing to the directors; ¿cuánto le deben todavía los deudores a la compañía? = how much is still owed to the company by its debtors? **2** *vi (obligación)* to have to; debe fotocopiar la hoja de cálculos en papel A3 = you must photocopy the spreadsheet on A3 paper; debe hacerlo antes de salir de la oficina = he has to do it before he leaves the office **3** *nm* duty *o* obligation *o* remit

◊ **debido, -da** *adj y pp* (a) owing *o* due; porte debido = carriage forward *o* freight forward (b) debido a = owing to *o* due to; sentimos no poder servirle el pedido a tiempo debido a la cantidad de trabajo acumulado = I am sorry that owing to pressure of work, we cannot supply your order on time; los suministros se han retrasado debido a una huelga en la fábrica = supplies have been delayed due to a strike at the manufacturers (c) en buena y debida forma = in due form *o* duly; contrato redactado en la debida forma = contract drawn up in due form

◊ **debidamente** *adv* duly; representante debidamente autorizado = duly authorized representative

débil *adj* weak *o* slack *o* frail; mercado débil = weak market; moneda débil = weak *o* soft currency

◊ **debilidad** *nf* weakness *o* slackness *o* failing; el presidente tiene una debilidad - se duerme durante las juntas = the chairman has one failing - he goes to sleep at board meetings

debilitar *vt* to weaken *o* to slacken

◊ **debilitarse** *vr* to slacken *o* to become weak; el mercado se debilitó = the market weakened *o* slackened

débito *nm* charge *o* debit; débito flotante *o* variable = floating charge; aparece en las cuentas como débito = it appears as a charge on the accounts; asiento de débito = debit entry; débito directo = direct debit; pago la factura de la luz por

débito directo = I pay my electricity bill by direct debit; tarjeta de débito = debit card

decaer *vi* to slacken off; la actividad comercial ha decaído = trade has slackened off

decidir 1 *vt* (a) *(tomar una decisión)* to decide *o* to resolve; decidimos nombrar a alguien de la casa = we decided to make an internal appointment; la junta decidió no pagar dividendos = the meeting resolved that a dividend should not be paid; decidir recurrir a los tribunales = to decide to go to court (b) *(acordar)* to rule; la comisión de investigación decidió que la compañía había incumplido el contrato = the commission of inquiry ruled that the company was in breach of contract **2** *vi* to decide on *o* to choose *o* to determine; tuvo que decidir entre los candidatos = he had to choose between the applicants

◊ **decidirse** *vr* to make up one's mind; la empresa no se decide a montar una nueva fábrica de ordenadores = the company can't make up its mind *o* is hesitating about starting up a new computer factory; tiene que darle tiempo al cliente para que se decida = you must give the customer time to make up his mind; decidirse por la opción más fácil = to take the soft option

decila *nf* decile

decimal *adj y n* decimal; coma decimal = decimal point

◊ **decimalización** *nf* decimalization

decimalizar *vt* to decimalize

decir *vt/i* (a) to say *o* to mention; siento decir que llevamos tres meses de retraso = I am sorry to say that we are three months behind schedule; su secretaria llamó para decir que él llegaría tarde = his secretary phoned to say he would be late; ¿puede decirle a la secretaria que se ha cambiado la fecha de la próxima reunión? = can you mention to the secretary that the date of the next meeting has been changed?; la sección de administración dice que necesita el informe inmediatamente = admin say they need the report immediately; cuando le preguntaron qué pensaba hacer la compañía, el presidente volvió a decir 'nada' = when asked what the company planned to do, the chairman repeated 'Nothing'; el presidente ha dicho oficialmente que las ganancias van a aumentar = the chairman has stated that profits are set to rise (b) es decir = that is *o* i.e.; la mayor empresa, es decir Durán y Durán, tuvo un primer trimestre muy bueno = the largest company, i.e. Durán y Durán, had a very good first quarter

◊ **decirse** *vr* se dice en el mundo financiero que han vendido la compañía = they say in the City that the company has been sold

decisión *nf* decision *o* ruling; árbol de decisión = decision tree; llegar a una decisión *o* tomar una decisión = to come to a decision *o* to reach a decision; en una reunión de bajo nivel se decidió aplazar la decisión = a low-level meeting decided to put off making a decision; estamos esperando una decisión del tribunal = we are awaiting a decision of the court; toma de decisiones = decision making; procesos de toma de decisiones = decision-making processes; decisión mayoritaria = majority vote *o* majority decision; anular una

decisión = to annul a decision *o* to render a decision null

◇ **decisivo, -va** *adj* decisive; **un acontecimiento decisivo** = a decisive event

◇ **decisorio, -ria** *adj* **procesos decisorios** = decision-making processes

declaración *nf* **(a)** *(anuncio)* announcement *o* statement; **declaración oficial** = official statement; **el director gerente hizo una declaración al personal** = the managing director made an announcement to the staff **(b) declaración oficial** = official return; **declaración de ingresos nulos** = nil return; **declaración de siniestro** = insurance claim; **formulario de declaración de siniestro** = claim form; **declaración de quiebra** = declaration of bankruptcy; **declaración judicial de quiebra** = adjudication order *o* adjudication of bankruptcy; **presentar una declaración de quiebra** = to file a petition in bankruptcy; **declaración de renta** = declaration of income *o* income statement; **declaración a Hacienda** *o* **declaración fiscal** = *(individuo)* tax return; *(empresa)* tax declaration; **declaración de aduana** = customs declaration; **declaración del IVA** = VAT declaration *o* VAT return; **hacer una declaración falsa** = to make a false statement **(c)** *(evidencia)* evidence; **la secretaria prestó declaración a favor** *o* **en contra de su anterior patrono** = the secretary gave evidence *o* against her former employer **(d)** *(testimonio)* affidavit

declarado, -da 1 *adj* declared; **valor declarado** = declared value **2** *pp de* DECLARAR

declarar *vt* **(a)** *(hacer una declaración)* to declare *o* to state *o* to return; **declarar unos ingresos de 3 millones de pesetas al fisco** = to return income of 3 million pesetas to the tax authorities; **declarar a alguien en quiebra** = to declare someone bankrupt; **se le declaró en quiebra** = he was adjudicated bankrupt; **declarar un dividendo del 10%** = to declare a dividend of 10%; **declarar mercancías en la aduana** = to declare goods to customs; **los funcionarios de aduanas le preguntaron si tenía algo que declarar** = the customs officials asked him if he had anything to declare ; **declarar una participación en una compañía** = to declare an interest in a company **(b) declarar el cierre patronal** = to lock out workers; **declarar una huelga de solidaridad** = to strike in sympathy **(c)** *(jurídico)* to find; **el tribunal declaró culpables a ambas partes** = the tribunal found that both parties were at fault

◇ **declararse** *vr* **(a)** *(manifestarse)* to state one's opinion; **declararse en huelga** = to strike *o* to come out on strike *o* to walk out; **declararse en huelga para conseguir aumentos salariales** *o* **una reducción de la jornada laboral** = to strike for higher wages *o* for shorter working hours; **declararse en quiebra** = to file a petition in bankruptcy; **declararse culpable** = to plead guilty **(b)** *(incendio)* to break out; **el envío resultó dañado en el incendio que se declaró a bordo del carguero** = the shipment was damaged in the fire on board the cargo boat

declinar *vi* to decline *o* to refuse; **declinar cualquier responsabilidad** = to refuse to take on any responsibility *o* to decline all responsibility; **declinar una invitación** = to turn down an invitation

decomisar *vt* to seize *o* to confiscate *o* to forfeit

◇ **decomiso** *nm* forfeit *o* forfeiture *o* confiscation; **decomiso de mercancías no declaradas** = seizure of undeclared goods

◇ **decomisoria** *adj* **cláusula decomisoria** = forfeit clause

decoración *nf* decoration; **decoración de escaparates** = window dressing *o* display

decreciente *adj* falling *o* decreasing *o* regressive; **imposición decreciente** = regressive taxation

◇ **decrecimiento** *nm* decrease

decreto *nm* decree *o* order; *(parlamento)* **decreto-ley** = decree *o* order in council

dedicar *vt* **(a)** *(a un fin determinado)* to dedicate *o* to devote **(b)** *(tiempo, personas, esfuerzo)* to spend; **los empleados de la empresa dedican muchas horas de trabajo a reuniones** = the company spends hundreds of man-hours on meetings

◇ **dedicarse** *vr* to take up *o* to devote oneself to; **¿a qué se dedica?** = what is his line of business? *o* what does he do?; **dedicarse a** = to be engaged in; **dedicarse a los negocios** = to be in business; **se dedica a la venta de automóviles** = he sells cars for a living; **la compañía se dedica al comercio con Africa** = the company is engaged in trade with Africa

deducción *nf* allowance *o* deduction *o* (tax) abatement; **deducciones fiscales** *o* **impositivas** = tax deductions; **deducciones personales** = personal allowances; **deducciones en origen** = deductions at source; **deducciones salariales** *o* **deducciones del salario** = salary deductions *o* deductions from salary *o* stoppage(s) (from a worker's pay packet)

deducible *adj* deductible; **gastos deducibles** = allowable expenses; *o US* itemized tax deductions

deducir *vt* **(a)** *(cantidad)* to deduct *o* to take away *o* to subtract *o* to set against *o* to offset; **el salario neto es el salario bruto después de deducir los impuestos y la cotización a la seguridad social** = net salary is salary after deduction of tax and social security; **deducir una cantidad por gastos** = to deduct a sum for expenses; **después de deducir los costes el margen neto es de sólo el 23%** = after deducting costs the net margin is only 23%; **faltan todavía por deducir los gastos** = expenses are still to be deducted; **impuestos deducidos en origen** = tax deducted at source; **deducir las pérdidas de los impuestos** = to offset losses against tax; **¿puedes deducir los gastos de la cantidad imponible?** = can you set the expenses against tax?; **si deducimos las ventas nacionales, el volumen de negocios total ha bajado** = if you take away the home sales, the total turnover is down; **antes de deducir los impuestos** = before tax *o* before deducting tax *o* pretax; **beneficio antes de deducir los impuestos** = pretax profit; **el dividendo total pagado es equivalente a un cuarto de los ingresos antes de deducir impuestos** = the total dividend paid is equivalent to one quarter of the pretax profits; **beneficios después de deducir los impuestos** = after-tax profit; **deducir algo del sueldo** = to dock someone's pay; **le dedujeron 4.000 ptas. de su sueldo por llegar tarde** = he had 4,000 pesetas docked from his pay for being late; **tendremos que deducirle algo del sueldo si llega de nuevo tarde al trabajo** = we will have to stop some of his pay if he is late for work again **(b)** *(derivar)* to deduce *o* to infer

◊ **deducirse** *vr* to follow *o* to infer

> el impuesto de la renta, que se deduce directamente del salario, será aproximadamente de un 7%
> *España Económica*

defectivo, -va *adj* imperfect *o* incomplete *o* defective

defecto *nm* **(a)** *(deficiencia, falta)* defect *o* imperfection *o* flaw; **un defecto del ordenador** = a computer defect *o* a defect in the computer; **controlar defectos en un lote** = to check a batch for imperfections; **en su defecto** = failing that; **por defecto** = by default **(b)** *(programa de informática)* **parámetro** *o* **valor por defecto** = default setting *o* value

defectuoso, -sa *adj* **(a)** *(imperfecto)* faulty *o* imperfect; **artículos defectuosos** *o* **material defectuoso** = seconds; **venta de artículos defectuosos** = sale of imperfect items; **la tienda hace una liquidación de artículos defectuosos** = the shop has a sale of seconds; **controlar un lote para detectar productos defectuosos** = to check a batch for imperfect products **(b)** *(que no funciona)* defective *o* faulty; **equipo defectuoso** = faulty equipment; **instalaron programas de ordenador defectuosos** = they installed faulty computer programs; **la máquina se averió debido a un sistema de refrigeración defectuoso** = the machine broke down because of a defective cooling system **(c)** *(sin validez)* defective; **conocimiento de embarque defectuoso** = foul bill of lading

defender *vt* to defend *o* to plead (for); **defender una causa ante un tribunal** = to defend a lawsuit

◊ **defenderse** *vr* to defend oneself (against); **la compañía se está defendiendo de la oferta de adquisición** = the company is defending itself against the takeover bid; **contrató a los mejores abogados para defenderse del fisco** = he hired the best lawyers to defend him against the tax authorities

defensa *nf* **(a)** *(jurídico)* defence; *US* defense; **conceder la palabra a la defensa** = to ask the defence to speak **(b)** *(protección)* defence; *US* defense; **el banco de negocios organiza la defensa de la compañía frente al intento de adquisición** = the merchant bank is organizing the company's defence against the takeover bid

◊ **defensor, -ra** *n* **(a)** *(que defiende)* defender *o* protector; **defensor del pueblo** = ombudsman; **abogado defensor** = defence counsel **(b)** *(de un título)* champion

deficiencia *nf* deficiency; **cubrir una deficiencia** = to make up a deficiency

deficiente *adj* *(de baja calidad)* bad *o* poor; **servicio deficiente** = poor service

déficit *nm* deficit *o* shortfall; **déficit de la balanza de pagos** *o* **de la balanza comercial** = balance of payments deficit *o* trade deficit; **déficit comercial** = trade gap *o* deficit; **déficit presupuestario** = budget

deficit; **anunciar un déficit** = to report a loss; **balanza comercial con déficit** = adverse balance of trade; **la compañía entró en déficit en 1995** = the company went into the red in 1995; **las cuentas arrojan un déficit** = the accounts show a deficit; **cubrir un déficit** = to make good a deficit

◊ **deficitario, -ria** *adj* in deficit; **balanza comercial deficitaria** = adverse *o* unfavourable balance of trade; **organización deficitaria** = loss-making organization

> los precios empezaron a subir y el déficit hizo su aparición aproximadamente al mismo tiempo
> *España Económica*

> el déficit público de más de cinco por ciento del Producto Interior Bruto (PIB) es sensiblemente más alto que el 'record' conseguido en el año anterior
> *Actualidad Económica*

> cuando tengamos una inflación similar y un similar déficit exterior podremos llegar a la unidad plena
> *Tiempo*

definir *vt* to define *o* to explain *o* to determine

definitivo, -va *adj* definitive *o* final *o* ultimate; **el proyecto definitivo** = the final plan; **aprobar con carácter definitivo** = to finalize; **en definitiva** = finally *o* to sum up

◊ **definitivamente** *adv* definitively *o* finally

deflación *nf* deflation; **deflación de los precios** = price deflation

◊ **deflacionario, -ria** *adj* deflationary; **medidas deflacionarias** = deflationary measures

> los efectos deflacionarios a largo plazo de unos impuestos más altos y un gasto público menor serán más que compensados por una demanda del consumo creciente
> *Actualidad Económica*

deflacionista *adj* deflationary; **el gobierno ha introducido algunas medidas deflacionistas en el presupuesto** = the government has introduced some deflationary measures in the budget

deflactar *vt* to deflate (the economy)

◊ **deflactación** *nf (S. América)* deflation

deformar *vt* to deform *o* to distort; **deformar los hechos** = to misrepresent

◊ **deformarse** *vr* to get distorted

defraudación *nf* fraud *o* defrauding; **defraudación fiscal** = tax evasion

defraudar *vt* **(a)** *(estafar)* to cheat *o* to defraud; **defraudó a Hacienda de miles de pesetas** = he cheated the Income Tax out of thousands of pesetas **(b)** *(decepcionar)* to disappoint; **estaba defraudado por los resultados de la compañía** = he was disappointed with the company's results

> los propietarios originales de los terrenos habrían defraudado a Hacienda interponiendo a unos falsos compradores para eludir el pago de plusvalías
> *Cambio 16*

defunción *nf* decease *o* death; **certificado de defunción** = death certificate

DEG = DERECHOS ESPECIALES DE GIRO special drawing rights (SDRs)

degradación *nf* **(a)** *(pérdida de categoría profesional)* demotion **(b)** *(calidad)* impoverishment *o* decline; **la degradación del suelo provocará una grave crisis agrícola en la región** = impoverishment of the soil will cause a serious agricultural crisis in the region

degradar *vt* to downgrade *o* to demote; **de director, le degradaron al puesto de vendedor** = he was demoted from manager to salesman

dejar 1 *vt* **(a)** *(abandonar)* to leave *o* to resign *o* to quit; **dejar un negocio** = to go out of business; **dejar atrás** = to leave behind; **dejar la habitación** = to leave the room; *(hotel)* to check out; **dejar el empleo** *o* **dejar el puesto vacante** = to give up one's job; **dejó el trabajo después de una discusión con el director gerente** = he quit after an argument with the managing director; **tengo entendido que ha dejado la oficina (b)** = I gather he has left the office **(b)** **dejar constancia** = to leave on record; **para dejar las cosas en claro** = for the record *o* to keep the record straight; **quisiera dejar constancia de estas cifras de ventas consignándolas en el acta** = for the record, I would like these sales figures to be noted in the minutes **(c)** *(empeñar)* **dejar algo en prenda** = to pawn something **(d)** **dejar una cuenta al descubierto** = to overdraw an account; **dejar un margen** = to allow for; **dejar un margen de un 10% para embalaje** = to allow 10% for packing **(e)** **dejar una señal** = to pay money down *o* to leave a deposit **(f)** *(legar)* **dejó su propiedad en fideicomiso para ser entregada a sus nietos** = he left his property in trust for his grandchildren **2** *vi* **(a)** **dejar de hacer algo** = to stop doing something; **dejar de trabajar** = to stop working; **el personal dejó de trabajar cuando la empresa no pudo pagar sus salarios** = the workforce stopped work when the company could not pay their wages; **la fábrica no dejó de trabajar a pesar del incendio** = the factory kept on working in spite of the fire; **hemos dejado de suministrar a Solana y Cía.** = we have stopped supplying Solana y Cía.; **no dejar de hacer algo** = to keep on doing something **(b)** *(embrollar)* **dejar confuso** = to confuse

◊ **dejarse** *vr* **dejarse llevar por los demás** = to be led by others

delante *adv* ahead; **delante de** = in front of; **pusieron el cartel 'en venta' delante de la fábrica** = they put up a 'for sale' sign in front of the factory; **la empresa tiene mucho trabajo por delante si quiere aumentar su participación en el mercado** = the company has a lot of work ahead of it if it wants to increase its market share

delegación *nf* **(a)** *(comité)* delegation; **una delegación comercial china** = a Chinese trade delegation; **la dirección se reunió con una delegación sindical** = the management met a union delegation **(b)** *(acto de pasar responsabilidades a otros)* delegation; **delegación de poderes** = delegation of powers **(c)** *(comercio)* branch office *o* local office; **tendrá que reclamar directamente a la delegación de Hacienda** = you will have to send your claim to your local tax office **(d)** *(parlamento)* devolution

delegado, -da 1 *n* delegate *o* representative *o* deputy; **delegado de personal** = worker director; **la dirección se negó a reunirse con los delegados sindicales** = the management refused to meet the trade union representatives; **delegado sindical** = shop steward *o* union delegate; **delegado de un sindicato local** = local union official; *US* business agent **2** *pp de* DELEGAR

delegar *vt* to delegate; **delegar la autoridad** = to delegate authority; **no sabe delegar** = he can't delegate; **delegar trabajo** = to farm out work

delictivo *adj* criminal; **la malversación de fondos constituye un acto delictivo** = misappropriation of funds is a criminal act

delimitación *nf* delimitation *o* demarcation; **la producción del nuevo automóvil fue retrasada debido a conflictos sobre la delimitación de tareas entre los obreros** = production of the new car was held up by demarcation disputes

delito *nm* crime *o* offence; **los delitos en los supermercados han aumentado en un 25%** = supermarket crime has risen by 25%; **delitos administrativos** *o* **de oficinistas** = white-collar crime; **delito por omisión** = non-feisance; **delito penal** = criminal offence

demanda *nf* **(a)** *(comercio)* demand; **demanda efectiva** = effective demand; **gran demanda** = keen demand; **hay una gran demanda de ordenadores personales** = there is a keen demand for PCs; **una gran demanda de acciones petrolíferas** = an active demand for oil shares; **este libro tiene mucha demanda** *o* **hay mucha demanda de este libro** = this book is in great demand *o* there is a great demand for this book; **oferta y demanda** = supply and demand; **ley de la oferta y la demanda** = law of supply and demand; **precio de demanda** = demand price; **periodo de demanda máxima** = time of peak demand; **satisfacer la demanda** *o* **satisfacer una demanda** = to keep up with the demand *o* to meet the demand *o* to fill a demand *o* to satisfy a demand; **la fábrica tuvo que aumentar la producción para satisfacer la demanda adicional** = the factory had to increase production to meet the extra demand; **la empresa de limpieza de oficinas no puede satisfacer la demanda de sus servicios** = the office cleaning company cannot keep up with the demand for its services; **reducción de la demanda** = reduction in demand; **la fábrica tuvo que reducir la producción cuando bajó la demanda** = the factory had to cut production when demand slackened; **no hay mucha demanda de este artículo** = there is not much demand for this item **(b)** *(formular una protesta o queja)* representation; **los directores presentaron una demanda a la junta directiva en nombre del personal pagado por horas** = the managers made representations to the board on behalf of the hourly-paid members of staff **(c)** *(solicitud, pregunta)* request *o* inquiry; **ref.: su demanda de información del 29 de mayo** = re your inquiry of May 29th **(d)** *(jurídico)* action; **demanda civil** = civil action; **demanda por daños y perjuicios** = action for damages; **demanda por difamación** = libel action *o* slander action *o* action for libel *o* for slander; **presentar una demanda** = to sue; **ha presentado una demanda de 5.000.000 de ptas. contra la compañía** = he is suing the company for 5m pesetas in compensation **(e)** *(petición)* request *o* claim; **demanda de compras** = purchase requisition; **demanda de pago** = request for payment; *(bolsa)* call

la mayor demanda chocó con la rigidez de la oferta de este mercado
España Económica

la demanda alemana de productos españoles será particularmente boyante; muchas empresas alemanas establecerán fuertes lazos de unión con España
Actualidad Económica

demandado, -da 1 *adj y n* defendant; **abogado de la parte demandada** = defence counsel **2** *pp de* DEMANDAR

demandante *nmf* claimant *o* plaintiff; **abogado de la parte demandante** = prosecution counsel *o* counsel for the prosecution *o* counsel for the plaintiff

demandar *vt* **(a)** *(pedir)* to demand *o* to ask for *o* to request **(b)** *(entablar un pleito)* to sue; **demandar judicialmente a alguien** = to bring a lawsuit against someone; **demandar a alguien por daños y perjuicios** = to sue someone for damages; **no existe ningún fundamento por el cual podamos ser demandados** = there are no grounds on which we can be sued

demás *adj & pron* the rest *o* the others; **el presidente se marchó a casa, pero los demás consejeros se quedaron en la sala de juntas** = the chairman went home, but the rest of the directors stayed in the boardroom; **por lo demás** = apart from that

demasiado *adj y adv* too much *o* excessively; **nuestro personal se queja demasiado** = our staff complain too much

demográfico, -ca *adj* demographic; **crecimiento demográfico** = population growth; **tendencias demográficas** = population trends

demora *nf* **(a)** delay; **sin demora** = without delay; **lamentamos la demora en servirles el pedido** *o* **en contestar a su carta** = we are sorry for the delay in supplying your order *o* in replying to your letter **(b)** **gastos de demora** = demurrage; **sanción de demora** = penalty for delay

demorar *vt/i* to delay

◇ **demorarse** *vr* to be slow *o* to take a long time to do something; **se demoraron en contestar a las quejas del cliente** = they were slow to reply *o* slow at replying to the customer's complaints

demostración *nf* **(a)** *(presentación)* demonstration *o* show *o* display **(b)** *(prueba)* proof *o* evidence

demostrar *vt* to demonstrate *o* to show

denegación *nf* denial *o* refusal

denegar *vt* to deny *o* to refuse *o* to reject; *(reclamación de seguros)* to disallow; **reclamó 400.000 ptas. en concepto de daños por incendio, pero la reclamación fue denegada** = he claimed 400,000 pesetas for fire damage, but the claim was disallowed; **pidió un aumento de sueldo pero le fue denegado** = he asked for a rise but it was refused; **el préstamo fue denegado por el banco** = the loan was refused by the bank; **denegar un pago** = to refuse payment

denominación *nf* **(a)** denomination; *(producción vinícola)* **denominación de origen** = appellation contrôlée; **las botellas deben llevar una etiqueta con la denominación de origen** = bottles should carry a label specifying the appellation contrôlée **(b)** *(Mex.)* **denominación social** = corporate name

dentro 1 *adv* inside *o* indoors **2** *prep* **dentro de** = inside *o* within; **dentro de una semana** = within a week; **dentro de la caja** = inside the box; **no había nada dentro del contenedor** = there was nothing inside the container

departamental *adj* departmental; **un asunto departamental** = a departmental matter

departamento *nm* **(a)** *(oficina)* division *o* department *o* section; **departamento de comercialización** = marketing division; **departamento de contabilidad** = accounts department; **departamento de diseño** = design department; **departamento de emisión de nuevas acciones** = new issues department; **departamento de exportación** = export department; **departamento de facturación** = invoicing department; **departamento de Investigación Económica** = Department of Economic Research; **departamento de marketing** = marketing department; **departamento de personal** = personnel department; **departamento de producción** = production department; **departamento de reclamaciones** = claims department; **director de departamento** *o* **jefe de departamento** = head of department *o* department head; *(en oficina)* department manager *o* departmental manager; **dirigir un departamento** = to be in charge of *o* to head a department **(b)** *(sección de tienda o almacén)* department **(c)** **departamento jurídico** = legal section

nuestro departamento de investigación y desarrollo crea tecnologías que contribuyen a mejorar la vida de la gente en todas las partes del mundo
Tiempo

dependencia *nf* **(a)** **estar bajo la dependencia de** = to be dependent on **(b)** *(sucursal)* branch *o* branch office *o* section; **trabaja en la misma oficina que yo, pero en distinta dependencia** = he works in the same office as me, but in a different section

depender *vi* **(a)** *(estar subordinado)* to depend; **depender de** = to depend on *o* to rely on *o* conditional on; **la empresa depende del buen servicio de sus proveedores** = the company depends on efficient service from its suppliers; **dependemos de los subsidios del Estado para pagar los salarios** = we depend on government grants to pay the salary bill; **el éxito del lanzamiento dependerá de la publicidad** = the success of the launch will depend on the publicity; **la oferta depende de la aceptación del consejo de administración** = the offer is conditional on the board's acceptance **(b)** *(rendir cuentas)* **depender de alguien** = to be under someone *o* to report to someone

dependiente, -ta 1 *adj* dependent **2** *nm* shop assistant *o* salesman; *US* salesclerk; **es el jefe de**

dependientes de la sección de alfombras = he is the head salesman in the carpet department; **ser dependiente en una tienda 3** *nf* salesgirl *o* saleslady *o* shop assistant

deponer *vt* to remove; **dos consejeros fueron depuestos de su cargo en la junta anual** = two directors were removed from the board at the AGM

depositante *nmf* depositor

depositar *vt* to deposit *o* to place *o* to leave for safe keeping *o* to lodge; **depositar acciones en un banco** = to deposit shares with a bank; **depositar dinero** = to make a deposit; **depositar dinero a corto plazo** = to place money on short-term deposit; **hemos depositado la escritura de la casa en un banco** = we have deposited the deeds of the house with the bank; **depositar 20.000 ptas. en una cuenta corriente** = to deposit 20,000 pesetas in a current account; **depositar valores como garantía prendaria** = to lodge securities as collateral; **las mercancías se depositan aquí por cuenta y riesgo del propietario** = goods left here are at owner's risk

◊ **depositario, -ria** *n* depository *o* depositary; trustee

depósito *nm* **(a)** *(dinero)* deposit *o* down payment; **hizo un depósito de 10.000 ptas. y el resto lo pagó en plazos mensuales** = he paid 10,000 pesetas down and the rest in monthly instalments **(b)** *(en un banco)* **certificado de depósito** = certificate of deposit; **cuenta de depósito** = deposit account; **nota** *o* **recibo de depósito** = deposit slip; **depósitos bancarios** = bank deposits; **los depósitos bancarios han alcanzado un nivel sin precedentes** = bank deposits are at an all-time high; **depósitos que devengan intereses** = interest-bearing deposits; **depósito en caja fuerte** = safe deposit; **depósito a plazo fijo** = fixed deposit; **depósito a la vista** = demand deposit; **depósito con preaviso de 7 días** = deposit at 7 days' notice **(c)** *(almacén)* (i) storeroom *o* stockroom; (ii) warehouse *o* depot; **almacén de depósitos** = depository; **guardamos los muebles en depósito** = we put our furniture into storage; **depósito aduanero** = bonded warehouse; **depósito de mercancías** = goods depot; **depósito central de petróleo** = oil storage depot; **depósito de transporte por carretera** = road haulage depot **(d)** **en depósito** = (i) sale or return; (ii) in escrow; **documento guardado en depósito** = document held in escrow **(e)** *(líquidos)* tank *o* cistern

depreciación *nf* **(a)** *(pérdida de valor)* depreciation; **depreciación de un activo** = depreciation of an asset *o* asset writedown; **depreciación por desuso** = obsolescence; **la depreciación de la libra esterlina** = the fall in the value of the sterling; **la depreciación de la peseta respecto al dólar** = the depreciation of the peseta against the dollar; **cuota de depreciación** = allowance for depreciation; **tasa de depreciación** = depreciation rate **(b)** *(de bienes)* write-off; **reservar una partida para depreciación en las cuentas anuales** = to allow for write-offs in the yearly accounts

depreciar 1 *vi* to depreciate; **la peseta se ha depreciado en un 5% respecto al dólar** = the peseta has depreciated by 5% against the dollar **2** *vt* to write off *o* to write down; **depreciar el valor de un activo** = to write down an asset; **el valor del**

coche está depreciado en los libros de la compañía = the car is written off in the company's books

depresión *nf* **(a)** depression; **una depresión económica** = an economic depression *o* a slump; **la Gran Depresión** = the Great Depression; **estamos viviendo una situación de depresión económica** = we are experiencing slump conditions **(b)** **depresión nerviosa** = nervous breakdown

como consecuencia de la crisis económica de 1929, se originó un periodo de depresión que se propagó durante la década de 1930, alcanzando cifras de paro muy elevadas

España Económica

deprimido, -da 1 *adj* depressed; **mercado deprimido** = depressed market; **zona deprimida** = depressed area **2** *pp de* DEPRIMIR

deprimir *vt* to depress

deprisa *adv* fast; **más deprisa** = faster; **hacer algo más deprisa** = to hurry up

depurar *vt (eliminar errores)* to debug

Hacienda depurará los datos con la ayuda de los ayuntamientos

Tiempo

derecho, -cha 1 *adj (mano, lado)* right; **el haber está en el lado derecho de la página** = the credits are on the right side of the page **2** *adv* directly *o* straight to; **todo derecho** = straight on **3** *nf* right side *o* right-hand side; **a** *o* **de la derecha** = right-hand; **guarda la lista de direcciones en el cajón de la derecha de su mesa de trabajo** = he keeps the address list in the right-hand drawer of his desk **4** *nm* **(a)** *(título, privilegio)* entitlement *o* right *o* claim *o* title; **tiene derecho a un descuento** = he is entitled to a discount; **derechos exclusivos para la comercialización de un producto** = exclusive right to market a product; **derechos de explotación** = mineral rights; **derecho de huelga** = right to strike; **derecho de paso** = (i) right of way; (ii) easement; **derecho a una pensión** *o* **jubilación** = pension entitlement; **derecho de renovación de un contrato** = right of renewal of a contract; **derecho de retención** = lien; **derecho de usufructo** = beneficial interest; **derecho a vacaciones** = holiday entitlement; **derechos de venta en el extranjero** = foreign rights; **derecho a voto** = right to vote *o* voting right; **acciones sin derecho a voto** = non-voting shares; **dar derecho a** = to entitle (to); **ejercer el derecho de opción** = to take up an option *o* to exercise an option; **tiene derecho a la propiedad** = she has a right to the property; **tiene justo derecho a la propiedad** = he has a good title to the property; **no tiene derecho de propiedad** = she has no title to the property; **el personal tiene derecho a conocer la marcha de la empresa** = the staff have a right to know how the company is doing; **no ha agotado todavía las vacaciones a que tiene derecho** = she has not used up all her holiday entitlement; **no tiene derechos sobre la patente** = he has no right to the patent **(b)** **con derecho a** = eligible for *o* with a right to *o* having a right to; **con derecho a devolución** = on approval **(c)** *(tributos)* duty; **derecho aduanero** = customs duty; **derecho de sucesión** = estate duty *o* death duty; **derecho del timbre** = stamp duty **(d)** *(jurídico)* law; **derecho**

civil = civil law; **derecho de contratos** = contract law *o* the law of contract; **derecho consuetudinario** = common law; **derecho habiente** = rightful claimant; **derecho internacional** = international law; **derecho laboral** = labour laws *o* labour legislation; **derecho marítimo** = maritime law *o* the law of the sea; **derecho mercantil** = commercial law; **derecho de obligaciones** = contract law *o* law of contract; **derecho penal** = criminal law **(e)** *(bolsa)* **emisión de derechos (a comprar acciones a un precio inferior)** = rights issue

◊ **derechos** *nmpl* fee(s) *o* duty; **derechos ad valorem** = ad valorem duty; **derechos de aduana** *o* **arancelarios** = customs duty; **derechos de autor** = royalties *o* copyright; **titular de los derechos de autor** = copyright holder; **derechos compensatorios** = countervailing duty; **derechos de importación** = import duty; **derechos de matrícula** = registration fee; **derechos de dársena** *o* **derechos portuarios** = dock dues *o* port dues *o* harbour dues; **derechos de muelle** = wharfage; **derechos especiales de giro (DEG)** = special drawing rights (SDRs); **derechos preferentes** = prior charge

derivar *vi* **derivar de** = to result from

◊ **derivados** *nmpl* *(títulos, productos)* derivatives

> hay que tener en cuenta que los derivados son instrumentos altamente apalancados, en los que con una pequeña cantidad se mueve un valor nominal decenas de veces superior
> **El País**

derrochar *vt* to waste; **derrochar fondos públicos** = to waste public funds

◊ **derroche** *nm* waste

derrota *nf* defeat; **el presidente ofreció su dimisión después de la derrota sufrida por su propuesta en la junta general anual** = the chairman offered to resign after the defeat of the proposal at the AGM; **en la votación para presidente del sindicato sufrió una gran derrota** = he was heavily defeated in the ballot for union president

derrotar *vt* to beat *o* to defeat

derrumbamiento *nm* collapse; **derrumbamiento bancario** = bank failure *o* crash *o* collapse

derrumbarse *vr* to collapse *o* to slump *o* to plunge *o* to plummet

desacato *nm* contempt of court

desacelerar *vi* to slow down

◊ **desaceleración** *nf* deceleration *o* slowing down *o* slowdown

> se aprecia una desaceleración en la producción de bienes de inversión
> **España Económica**

desaconsejar *vt* to advise against

desacreditar *vt* to discredit; **este producto desacredita a nuestra empresa** = this product is no credit to our firm *o* does our firm no credit at all

desacuerdo *nm* disagreement *o* variance; **hay un desacuerdo general entre los representantes de cada sección** = there is general disagreement between the representatives of each section

desagüe *nm (dinero)* drain

desahucio *nm* eviction

desajuste *nm* maladjustment *o* disagreement

> si logramos evitar un desajuste grave en la balanza comercial, si podemos seguir financiando nuestro actual déficit y si las tensiones inflacionistas se controlan no hay razón para hablar de ajuste duro
> **España Económica**

desalojar *vt* **(a)** *(inquilino)* to evict (someone) **(b)** *(abandonar)* to abandon *o* to vacate *o* to move out of; **desalojar los locales** = to vacate the premises

desaparecer 1 *vi* to disappear *o* to peter out *o* to wear off; **hacer desaparecer** = to phase out **2** *vt* to make (something) disappear

◊ **desaparecido, -da** *adj y pp* missing *o* unaccounted for; **hubo veinte desaparecidos en el naufragio** = twenty people were missing when the ship sank

desarrollar *vt* **(a)** *(ampliar)* to expand **(b)** *(dar mayor importancia)* to develop; **Japón es un mercado poco desarrollado para nuestros productos** = Japan is an underdeveloped market for our products

◊ **desarrollarse** *vr* to grow; **la industria de ordenadores se desarrolló rápidamente en la década de los 80** = the computer industry grew fast in the 1980s

◊ **desarrollo** *nm* development *o* growth *o* expansion; **desarrollo demográfico** = population growth; **desarrollo económico** = economic development; **desarrollo industrial** = industrial development; **área** *o* **región de desarrollo** = development area *o* development zone; **capacidad de desarrollo** = growth potential; **costes de desarrollo** = growth potential; **costes de investigación y desarrollo** = research and development costs; **una economía en desarrollo** = a developing *o* an expanding economy; **Fondo Europeo de Desarrollo Regional (FEDER)** = European Regional Development Fund (ERDF); **investigación y desarrollo (I+D)** = research and development (R & D); **país en vías de desarrollo** = developing country *o* developing nation; **zona de desarrollo industrial** *o* **comercial** = enterprise zone

> tras una década de desarrollo continuado del sector, éste está padeciendo ahora las repercusiones de la crisis en otros sectores
> **Tiempo**

> el desarrollo económico español ha sido más acelerado que el de otros países
> **Tiempo**

> un nivel mínimo de desarrollo económico es condición necesaria, aunque no suficiente, para la democracia
> **Mercado**

desastre *nm* **(a)** *(accidente)* disaster; **diez personas murieron en el desastre aéreo** = ten people died in the air disaster; **desastre provocado**

por una tormenta en la costa sur = a storm disaster on the south coast **(b)** *(finanzas)* disaster; **la campaña de publicidad fue un desastre** = the advertising campaign was a disaster

◊ **desastroso, -sa** *adj* disastrous; **la empresa sufrió una caída desastrosa de las ventas** = the company suffered a disastrous drop in sales; **ambos fueron igualmente responsables del desastroso lanzamiento** = they were both equally responsible for the disastrous launch

desautorizado, -da 1 *adj* unauthorized **2** *pp de* DESAUTORIZAR

desautorizar *vt* **(a)** to remove authority from *o* to deprive someone of authority **(b) desautorizar una declaración** = to discredit a statement

desbloquear *vt* to unblock *o* to unfreeze; **desbloquear las negociaciones** = to break a deadlock

desbordar 1 *vi* to flood *o* to overflow **2** *vt* to pass *o* to go beyond; *(sentido figurativo)* to flood; **el departamento de ventas está desbordado de pedidos** *o* **de reclamaciones** = the sales department is flooded with orders *o* with complaints

◊ **desbordarse** *vr* to overflow

descalificación *nf* disqualification

◊ **descalificar** *vt* to disqualify

descansar *vi* to rest; **tuvo que pedirle permiso para descansar** = she had to ask him for permission to take a break

◊ **descanso** *nm (pausa)* break *o* rest; **descanso durante el trabajo** = coffee break *o* tea break; **descanso publicitario** = commercial break

descapitalizado, -da *adj* undercapitalized; **la compañía está muy descapitalizada** = the company is severely undercapitalized

descarga *nf* unloading; **no hay instalaciones de descarga para los barcos portacontenedores** = there are no unloading facilities for container ships; **gastos de descarga** = landing charges

descargar *vt* **(a)** *(depositar)* to unload; **el barco está descargando en Hamburgo** = the ship is unloading at Hamburg; **necesitamos un vehículo con carretilla elevadora de horquilla para descargar el camión** = we need a fork-lift truck to unload the lorry; **descargamos las piezas de recambio en Lagos** = we unloaded the spare parts at Lagos; **el cargamento fue descargado tarde** = the shipment was landed late **(b) descargar mercancías en un puerto** = to land goods at a port; **coste descargado** = landed costs **(c)** *(jurídico)* to acquit *o* to clear (someone) **(d)** *(residuos)* to dump

descender 1 *vi* to drop *o* to fall (off); **las ventas han descendido** = sales are down; **la tasa de inflación está descendiendo gradualmente** = the inflation rate is gradually coming down; **las acciones de las minas de oro descendieron un 10%** *o* **descendieron 45 pesetas en la bolsa** = gold shares fell 10% *o* fell 45 pesetas on the Stock Exchange ; **las acciones descendieron de nuevo un mercado poco activo** = shares fell back in light trading; **las reservas hoteleras han descendido desde que terminó la temporada turística** = hotel

bookings have fallen away since the tourist season ended **2** *vt* to lower *o* to bring down

descenso *nm* decline *o* decrease *o* downturn *o* fall; **un descenso en la bolsa** = a fall on the Stock Exchange; **un descenso en el precio del mercado** = a downturn in the market price; **el descenso del valor de la peseta** = the decline in the value of the peseta; **los beneficios registraron un descenso del 10%** = profits showed a 10% fall

descentralización *nf* decentralization; **la descentralización de los departamentos de compras** = the decentralization of the buying departments

descentralizar *vt* to decentralize *o* to hive off; **el nuevo director general ha descentralizado las secciones de venta al por menor** = the new managing director hived off the retail sections of the company

descolgar *vt* **descolgar el teléfono** *o* **el receptor** = to pick up the phone *o* the receiver; **no podemos llamarles porque tienen el teléfono descolgado** = we cannot get hold of them because they left the phone off the hook

desconcertar *vt (personas)* to confuse *o* to surprise *o* to shock *o* to upset; *(objetos)* to disturb *o* to disarrange

◊ **desconcertarse** *vr (objetos)* to develop a fault; *(personas)* to get upset *o* to get confused

desconectado, -da *adj* off-line

desconfiar *vi* to mistrust; **desconfíe de las imitaciones** = beware of imitations

descongelar *vt* to unfreeze *o* to unblock

desconocer *vt* to be unaware of; **desconozco su paradero** = I don't know where he is *o* I don't know his whereabouts

descontable *adj* bankable *o* discountable; **efecto descontable** = a bankable paper

◊ **descontado, -da 1** *adj* discounted; **flujo de caja descontado** = discounted cash flow (DCF); **precio descontado** = discounted price; **valor descontado** = discounted value **2** *pp de* DESCONTAR

descontar *vt* **(a)** *(reducir)* to discount *o* to deduct *o* to dock; **descontar dinero del salario de alguien** = to stop someone's wages; **le descontamos 5.000 ptas. del salario por llegar siempre tarde** = we stopped 5,000 pesetas from his pay because he was always late; **descontar 600 ptas. del precio** = to deduct 600 pesetas from the price; **descontar facturas** = to discount invoices; **descontar letras de cambio** = to discount bills of exchange **(b)** *(tener en cuenta)* to allow for

ni tan siquiera descontó en su totalidad el efecto del encarecimiento de los productos petrolíferos del ejercicio anterior
                                                    Tiempo

desconvocar *vt* to call off; **el sindicato ha desconvocado la huelga** = the union has called off the strike

describir *vt* to describe; **el folleto describe los**

servicios que ofrece la compañía = the leaflet describes the services which the company offers *o* the services offered by the company

descripción *nf* description; **descripción engañosa del contenido** = false description of contents; **descripción del puesto de trabajo** = job description *o* specification; **descripción comercial** = trade description

descubierto, -ta 1 *adj* exposed *o* open **2** *nm* **(a)** *(banco)* overdraft; **el banco me ha permitido un descubierto de 1.000.000 de ptas.** = the bank has allowed me an overdraft of 1m pesetas; **línea de descubierto** = overdraft facilities; **al descubierto** = overdrawn *o* in the red; **girar en descubierto** = to overdraw one's account; **mi cuenta bancaria está** *o* **quedó al descubierto** = my bank account is in the red *o* went into the red; **su cuenta está al descubierto** = your account is overdrawn *o* you are overdrawn **(b)** *(bolsa)* **vender al descubierto** = to sell short; **venta al descubierto** = short selling *o* selling short **3** *pp de* DESCUBRIR

descubrir *vt* **(a)** *(enterarse)* to discover; **los auditores descubrieron algunos errores en las cuentas** = the auditors discovered some errors in the accounts **(b)** *(revelar)* to disclose *o* to reveal; **la empresa descubrió finalmente sus planes** = the company finally revealed its plans; **al descubrirse la existencia de una oferta de adquisición, se disparó el precio de las acciones** = the disclosure of the takeover bid raised share prices

descuento *nm* **(a)** *(comercial)* discount *o* rebate *o* reduction in price; **descuento básico** = basic discount; **ofrecemos un 25% de descuento básico, pero podemos añadir un 5% por pago en efectivo** = we give 25% as a basic discount, but can add 5% for cash payment; **descuento al por mayor** = wholesale *o* bulk discount; **ofrecer un descuento por las ventas al por mayor** *o* **en grandes cantidades** = to give a discount on bulk purchases; **descuento para comerciantes del sector** *o* **del ramo** = trade discount *o* trade terms; **descuento por cantidad** = quantity discount; **descuento de un 10% por compras en grandes cantidades** = 10% discount for quantity purchases; **descuento por pago al contado** *o* **por pronto pago** = discount for cash *o* cash discount; **vender mercancías con descuento** = to sell goods at a discount *o* at a discount price; **tendremos mucho gusto en ofrecerles un descuento del 25%** = we will be happy to supply you at 25% discount; **ofrecer un descuento del 10% sobre determinadas mercancías** = to offer a 10% rebate on selected goods; **ofrecemos un descuento del 10% sobre nuestros precios normales** = we give 10% off our normal prices; **tiene derecho a un descuento** = he is entitled to a discount; **precio de descuento** = discount price; **calculó el descuento aplicando un 15%** = he worked out the discount at 15% **(b)** **descuentos impositivos** = tax credits **(c)** **banco de descuentos** = discount house *o* discounter; **tipo de descuento** = discount rate; **estas letras no pueden presentarse al descuento** = these bills are not discountable

descuidado, -da 1 *adj* **(a)** *(abandonado)* neglected; **negocio descuidado** = neglected business **(b)** *(negligente)* careless *o* negligent **2** *pp de* DESCUIDAR

desechable *adj* disposable; **envases desechables** = non-returnable empties; **tazas desechables** = disposable cups

desecho *nm* waste; **materiales de desecho** = waste materials

deseconomías de escala *nfpl* diseconomies of scale

desembarcado, -da 1 *adj* **(a)** *(personas)* landed **(b)** *(mercancías)* unloaded **2** *pp de* DESEMBARCAR

desembarcadero *nm* quay

desembarcar *vt/i* **(a)** *(personas)* to land *o* to disembark; **desembarcar pasajeros en un aeropuerto** = to land passengers at an airport; **desembarcamos a las 10** = we land at 10 o'clock **(b)** *(mercancías)* to unload

◊ **desembarco** *nm* disembarkation

◊ **desembarque** *nm* disembarkation; **tarjeta de desembarque** = landing card *o* disembarkation card

desembolsar *vt* to spend *o* to pay out *o* to disburse; **hemos desembolsado la mitad de nuestros beneficios en dividendos** = we have paid out half our profits in dividends; **capital no desembolsado totalmente** = partly-paid capital

desembolso *nm* expenditure *o* disbursement; **haremos un desembolso inicial de 2.000.000 de pesetas y el saldo les llegará dentro de seis meses** = we will pay 2m pesetas down, with the balance to follow in six months' time

◊ **desembolsos** *nmpl* outgoings *o* outlay

desempeñar *vt* **(a)** *(casa de empeños)* to take out of pawn **(b)** *(cargo)* to occupy *o* to hold; **desempeñar un cargo muy importante** = to hold a very important position

desempleado, -da 1 *adj* unemployed; **estar desempleado** = to be unemployed *o* to be out of a job; **inscribirse como desempleado** = to sign on for the dole; **tenemos la intención de ofrecer puestos de trabajo a 250 jóvenes desempleados** = we intend to offer jobs to 250 unemployed young people **2** *n* unemployed person *o* person without any work; **los desempleados** = the unemployed *o* the jobless; **desempleados de larga duración** = long-term unemployed

desempleo *nm* unemployment; **desempleo estacional** = seasonal unemployment; **desempleo de larga duración** = long-term unemployment; **cobrar el desempleo** = to be on the dole; **subsidio de desempleo** = unemployment pay; **tasa de desempleo** = rate of unemployment *o* unemployment rate

la tasa de cobertura del desempleo es de sólo 35%

España Económica

el desempleo es hoy un problema social más que un desequilibrio del mercado de trabajo

Tiempo

el colapso de la producción industrial, el
aumento del desempleo y el cierre de
empresas desvalorizadas, serán las
espoletas de la transformación económica
y no los síntomas negativos de un declive
económico
                                Actualidad Económica

desencadenar *vt* to trigger

desenvolver *vt* **(a)** *(paquetes)* to unwrap **(b)**
(ideas) to explain

◊ **desenvolverse** *vr (en el trabajo)* to get on *o*
to be confident; **¿qué tal se desenvuelve la nueva
secretaria?** = how is the new secretary getting on?

deseoso, -sa *adj* eager *o* keen; **la dirección está
deseosa de introducirse en los mercados de
Extremo Oriente** = the management is eager to get
into the Far Eastern markets

desequilibrado, -da *adj* unbalanced

◊ **desequilibrio** *nm* imbalance; **el
desequilibrio entre la oferta y la demanda** = the
imbalance between supply and demand

en una economía con los graves
desequilibrios que padece la española -
paro, inflación, déficit exterior - hablar
como si el ajuste no fuera necesario es
demagogia o torpeza
                                España Económica

desfalcador, -ra *n* embezzler

desfalcar *vt* to embezzle

◊ **desfalco** *nm* embezzlement *o* defalcation;
estuvo en la cárcel seis meses por desfalco = he
was sent to prison for six months for embezzlement

desfasado, -da *adj* badly adjusted; **desfasado
con respecto a** = out of step with; **los salarios están
desfasados con respecto al coste de la vida** =
wages are out of step with the cost of living; **la
peseta estaba desfasada con respecto a las demás
monedas europeas** = the peseta was out of step with
other European currencies

desfavorable *adj* unfavourable; **balanza
comercial desfavorable** = unfavourable *o* adverse
balance of trade; **tipo de cambio desfavorable** =
unfavourable exchange rate; **el tipo de cambio
desfavorable asestó un golpe a las exportaciones
del país** = the unfavourable exchange rate hit the
country's exports; **nos enfrentamos a una
situación desfavorable para el comercio** = we are
facing adverse trading conditions

desgastar *vt* to erode *o* to wear down

desgaste *nm* wear and tear; **desgaste natural** *o*
normal = fair wear and tear; **la póliza de seguros
cubre la mayoría de los daños, pero no el desgaste
natural de la máquina** = the insurance policy
covers most damage but not fair wear and tear to the
machine

desglosar *vt* to itemize *o* to break down;
desglosamos los gastos en costes fijos y variables =
we broke the expenditure down into fixed and
variable costs; **¿puede desglosar esta factura en
repuestos y mano de obra?** = can you break down
this invoice into spare parts and labour?

◊ **desglose** *nm* breakdown; **desglose por**

conceptos = itemized breakdown; **desglose del
presupuesto** = itemized budget

desgravable *adj* tax-deductible; **estos gastos no
son desgravables** = these expenses are not tax-
deductible

desgravación *nf* allowance *o* concession *o*
rebate; **desgravación sobre bienes de capital** =
capital allowances; **desgravación fiscal** *o*
desgravación impositiva = tax concession *o* tax
relief; **consiguió una desgravación fiscal a fin de
año** = he got a tax rebate at the end of the year;
desgravación tributaria = tax allowance *o*
allowance against tax; **desgravación fiscal de los
intereses de la hipoteca** = mortgage interest relief;
**la desgravación fiscal de los intereses
hipotecarios es total** = there is full tax relief on
mortgage interest payments; **desgravación
impositiva por gastos** = tax-deductible expenses

desgravar *vt* **(a)** *(reducir impuestos)* to reduce
tax *o* to lighten the tax burden **(b)** *(eximir de
impuestos)* to exempt from tax

en la nueva ley figuran puntos como la
posibilidad de desgravar por una vivienda
alquilada y poder fijar duraciones de
contratos y actualizaciones de los
incrementos de las ventas
                                España Económica

desguace *nm* **(a)** *(acto)* scrapping **(b)** *(local)*
scrapyard *o* junkyard

desguazar *vt* to scrap

deshabitado , -da 1 *adj* empty *o* vacant; **piensa
convertir este local deshabitado en oficinas 2** *pp*
de DESHABITAR

deshabitar *vt* to move out of *o* to leave

deshacer *vt* to undo *o* to ruin

◊ **deshacerse de** *vr* deshacerse de algo = to
dispose of *o* to get rid of something *o* to throw
something out *o* to divest oneself of something;
deshacerse de existencias sobrantes = to dispose of
excess stock *o* to offload excess stock; **la empresa
está intentando deshacerse de todas las
existencias antiguas** = the company is trying to get
rid of all its old stock; **el departamento ha recibido
órdenes de deshacerse de veinte empleados** = our
department has been told to get rid of twenty staff; **la
compañía se deshizo de sus bienes en los Estados
Unidos** = the company had divested itself of its US
interests

deshinchar *vt* to deflate *o* to let down;
deshinchar la economía = to deflate the economy

deshonesto, -ta *adj* dishonest

designación *nf* nomination *o* appointment

◊ **designar** *vt* to appoint *o* to nominate; **designar
un representante** = to appoint an agent; **designar
por su nombre** = to name

desigual *adj* unequal *o* irregular *o* one-sided

desinflación *nf* disinflation

desinversión *nf* disinvestment

desinvertir *vi* to disinvest

desistimiento *nm* *(jurídico)* waiver *o* disclaimer; **desistimiento de la acción** = abandonment of a suit

◊ **desistir** *vi* to stop *o* to give up *o* to waive; **desistir de una acción** = to abandon an action

desleal *adj* disloyal *o* unfair; **prácticas desleales** = unfair practices

desmandado, -da *adj y pp* out of control; **los costes se han desmandado** = costs have got out of control

◊ **desmandarse** *vr* to get out of control

desmonetización *nf* demonetization; **desmonetización del oro** = demonetization of gold

◊ **desmonetizar** *vt* to demonetize *o* to depreciate

desmontar *vt* to dismantle; **llegó tarde porque tuvo que ayudarles a desmontar la exposición** = she arrived late because she had to stay and help them dismantle the exhibition

desnacionalización *nf* denationalization; **la desnacionalización de la industria aeronáutica** = the denationalization of the aircraft industry

◊ **desnacionalizar** *vt* to denationalize; **el gobierno se propone desnacionalizar la industria siderúrgica** = the government has plans to denationalize the steel industry

desocupado, -da *adj* **(a)** *(inmueble)* unoccupied *o* vacant; **propiedad desocupada** = vacant possession **(b)** **estar desocupado** = to be unemployed

◊ **desocupar** *vt* to vacate

despachado, -da 1 *adj* practical *o* resourceful **2** *pp de* DESPACHAR

despachar 1 *vt* **(a)** *(ocuparse de)* to deal with *o* to complete; **despachar un pedido** = to deal with an order; **bandeja de documentos por despachar** = in tray **(b)** *(enviar)* to dispatch *o* to send; **podemos despachar pedidos de hasta 15.000 unidades** = we can handle orders for up to 15,000 units; **tenemos tan poco personal que no podemos despachar más pedidos antes de Navidad** = we are so understaffed that we cannot fulfil any more orders before Christmas; **despachar pedidos atrasados** *o* **pendientes** = to release dues *o* to clear a backlog of orders; **la fábrica tardó seis semanas en despachar los pedidos atrasados** = it took the factory six weeks *o* the factory took six weeks to clear the backlog *o* of orders; **hemos tomado nota de su pedido y lo despacharemos en cuanto tengamos existencias** = your order has been noted and will be dispatched as soon as we have stock; **despachar un envío a México por carga aérea** = to airfreight a consignment to Mexico **2** *vi* to do business; *(en una tienda)* to serve *o* to attend to; **ahora mismo le despacho** = I'll attend to you straight away

◊ **despacharse** *vr* to finish things off quickly *o* to hurry

despacho *nm* **(a)** *(envío)* dispatch; **despacho de pedidos** = order fulfilment; **despacho de aduanas** = customs clearance; **efectuar el despacho aduanero** = to effect customs clearance; **despacho de mercancías de la aduana** = release of goods from customs; **despacho de mercancías por la aduana** = clearing of goods through the customs; *(S América)* **tramitar el despacho de aduanas de una mercancía** = to clear goods through customs **(b)** *(taquilla)* **despacho de billetes** *o* **pasajes** = booking office; **despacho de localidades** = box office **(c)** *(oficina)* office; **tiene un despacho de dimensiones medias** = he has an average-sized office; **el despacho del presidente está al final del pasillo** = the chairman's room is at the end of the corridor; **entre en mi despacho** = come into my office; **mesa de despacho** = office desk **(d)** *(de un juez)* chambers; **el juez vio la causa en su despacho** = the judge heard the case in chambers

> un prestigioso despacho de abogados apoya la acción de un grupo de artistas que pretenden convertir una ruina municipal en un dinámico centro cultural
>
> **Ajoblanco**

desparejado, -da *adj* odd; **un zapato desparejado** = an odd shoe

despacio *adv* slowly; **repitió su dirección despacio para que la vendedora pudiera apuntarla** = he repeated his address slowly so that the salesgirl could write it down; **las ventas comenzaron despacio, pero se aceleraron más tarde** = the sales started slowly *o* got off to a slow start, but picked up later

despedido, -da *adj y pp* dismissed *o* discharged; **estar despedido** = to be sacked

despedir *vt* to dismiss *o* to discharge; *(informal)* to chop *o* to fire *o* to axe; **despedir a un empleado** = to dismiss an employee; **fue despedido por llegar tarde** = he was dismissed for being late; **contratar y despedir a empleados** = to hire and fire; **despedir del trabajo a alguien** = to fire someone *o* to sack someone *o* to pay someone off *o* to axe; **le despidieron después de llegar tarde al trabajo** = he was sacked after being late for work; **van a despedir a varios miles de empleados** = several thousand jobs are to be axed; **el nuevo director gerente despidió a la mitad del personal de ventas** = the new managing director fired half the sales force; **siento tener que despedir a tanto personal** = I regret having to make so many staff redundant; **despedir temporalmente a los trabajadores** = to lay off workers; **la fábrica despidió temporalmente a la mitad de sus obreros por falta de pedidos** = the factory laid off half its workers because of lack of orders; **cuando la compañía fue adquirida, despidieron al director de ventas con una indemnización de 5.000.000 de ptas.** = when the company was taken over, the sales director was made redundant and received 5m pesetas in compensation

◊ **despedirse** *vr* **(a)** *(de alguien)* to say goodbye **(b)** *(del trabajo)* to give up one's job

> el nuevo banco contará con 600 sucursales, de las que cerrará 60, y 45.000 empleados, de los que espera despedir a 6.200.
>
> **El País**

despegar 1 *vi* *(avión)* to take off; **el avión para Madrid acaba de despegar** = the plane for Madrid has just taken off **2** *vt* to detach *o* to unstick

◇ **despegarse** *vr* to come unstuck *o* to come loose; **la etiqueta se ha despegado de la botella** = the label has become detached from the bottle

◇ **despegue** *nm* take-off; **despegue económico** = economic lift-off

desperdiciar *vt* to waste; **desperdiciar el papel** *o* **la electricidad** = to waste paper *o* electricity; **comprar ese ordenador es desperdiciar el dinero** = that computer is a waste of money

desperdicio *nm* waste *o* wastage

desperfecto *nm* damage *o* flaw *o* breakages

despido *nm* dismissal *o* sacking *o* redundancy; **indemnización por despido** = redundancy payment; **despido injusto** *o* **improcedente** = unfair dismissal *o* wrongful dismissal; **expediente de despido** *o* **trámites de despido** = dismissal procedures; **su despido provocó una huelga** = his sacking led to a strike; **el sindicato protestó por los despidos** = the union protested against the sackings; **despido con una compensación en metálico** *o* **con indemnización** = golden handshake; **despido temporal** *o* **despido laboral** = lay-off; **la recesión ha provocado cientos de despidos temporales en la industria del automóvil** = the recession has caused hundreds of lay-offs in the car industry; **paquete de indemnización por despido** = redundancy package

> el creciente déficit, los despidos de los trabajadores y las dudas sobre el modelo a seguir están llevando al caos al Ente Público
>
> **Tiempo**

despilfarrar *vt* **despilfarrar el dinero** = to waste money

◇ **despilfarro** *nm* waste *o* squandering

> otro ejemplo claro de despilfarro de productos, sobre los que el Estado practica una política de precios subvencionados, es el consumo de energía
>
> **España Económica**

despistado, -da *adj* absent-minded *o* confused

desplazamiento *nm* **(a)** *(viaje)* travelling; **gastos de desplazamiento** = travelling expenses **(b)** *(movimiento, cambio)* movement *o* shift

desplazar *vt* **(a)** *(trasladar)* to relocate; **con el traslado de la sede, la compañía tuvo que desplazar a 1.500 personas** = when the company moved its headquarters, 1,500 people had to be relocated **(b)** *(informática)* to scroll

despliegue *nm* *(informática)* **unidad de despliegue visual (UDV)** = visual display unit (VDU)

desplome *nm* collapse; **el desplome del dólar en los mercados de divisas** = the collapse of the dollar on the foreign exchange markets

despreciable *adj* negligible; **nada despreciable** = not negligible

desregulación *nf* deregulation

> las rebajas de impuestos y la desregulación de algunos mercados tiene un coste para la hacienda pública y ese coste tendrá graves repercusiones para el déficit del sector público
>
> **El País**

destacado, -da **1** *adj* *(excepcional)* outstanding; **índice** *o* **precio destacado** = leading rate; **varios empresarios destacados opinan que el final de la recesión está cerca** = leading industrialists feel the end of the recession is near **2** *pp de* DESTACAR

destacar *vt* to emphasize *o* to highlight

destajo *nm* piecework; **tarifa a destajo** = piece rate; **cobrar a destajo** = to earn piece rates; **producción** *o* **trabajo a destajo** = piecework *o* contract work; **pago a destajo** = payment for work done *o* payment by results

destinar *vt* **(a)** *(designar)* to destine *o* to assign *o* to earmark *o* to allocate; **destinar fondos** = to fund; **la beca está destinada al desarrollo de sistemas informáticos** = the grant is earmarked for computer systems development; **la campaña está destinada a divulgar los servicios de la junta de turismo** = the campaign is intended to publicize the services of the tourist board **(b)** *(persona)* to appoint to; **le han destinado a la oficina central** = they have appointed him to head office

destinatario, -ria *n* addressee *o* consignee *o* recipient; **el destinatario del envío** = the consignee *o* receiver of the shipment; **remítase al destinatario** = please forward *o* to be forwarded

destino *nm* destination; **el barco tardará diez semanas en llegar a su destino** = the ship will take ten weeks to reach its destination; **destino final** = final destination *o* ultimate destination; **el vuelo de Madrid termina en Nueva York - para destinos ulteriores hay que tomar un vuelo del interior** = the flight from Madrid terminates in New York - for further destinations you must change to internal flights

destitución *nf* *(despido)* dismissal *o* sacking *o* removal

destituir *vt* to sack *o* to dismiss *o* to remove (someone) from a job; **le destituyeron de su cargo** = they sacked him

destreza *nf* skill *o* workmanship

destruir *vt* to destroy; **el almacén quedó totalmente destruido por un incendio** = the warehouse was completely destroyed by fire; **todos los archivos de la empresa se perdieron cuando las oficinas quedaron destruidas por un incendio** = the company records were all lost when the offices were burnt down

desusado, -da *adj* obsolete *o* out of date

desuso *nm* disuse; **caer en desuso** = to become neglected *o* obsolete; **depreciación por desuso** = obsolescence

desvalorización *nf* devaluation

desvalorizar *vt* to devalue

desventaja *nf* disadvantage *o* drawback

desviación *nf* **(a) desviación de la norma** = departure from normal practice **(b)** *(en carretera)* deviation

detall, detal *adv* retail; **venta al detall** = retail sale

detallado, -da 1 *adj* detailed *o* in detail; **balance detallado** = itemized statement; **cuenta detallada** = itemized account; **factura detallada** = itemized invoice *o* detailed account; **el departamento de personal puede proporcionar información detallada sobre las direcciones y los teléfonos de los trabajadores** = details of staff addresses and phone numbers can be supplied by the personnel staff **2** *pp de* DETALLAR

detallar *vt* **(a)** *(describir con detalle)* to detail; **el catálogo detalla la modalidad de pago para los compradores extranjeros** = the catalogue details the payment arrangements for overseas buyers; **los términos de la licencia están detallados en el contrato** = the terms of the licence are detailed in the contract **(b)** *(pormenorizar)* to break down (into items) *o* to itemize; **detallar los ingresos y los gastos** = to itemize receipts and expenditure; **detallar las cifras de ventas nos llevará unos dos días** *o* **supondrá unos diez días de trabajo** = itemizing the sales figures will take about two days *o* will entail about ten days' work

detalle *nm* **(a)** detail *o* breakdown (into items); **déme el detalle de los costes de inversión** = give me a breakdown of investment costs; **el catálogo da todos los detalles de nuestra gama de productos** = the catalogue gives all the details of our product range; **estamos preocupados por algunos detalles del contrato** = we are worried by some of the details in the contract; **en detalle** = in detail; **el catálogo indica todos los productos con detalle** = the catalogue lists all the products in detail **(b) venta al detalle** = retail sale; **tiendas al detalle** = retail outlets

◊ **detalles** *nmpl* details *o* particulars; **el inspector pidió los detalles del coche desaparecido** = the inspector asked for particulars of the missing car; **los detalles de los gastos de los directivos no se revelan a los accionistas** = the actual figures for directors' expenses are not shown to the shareholders; **se pasaron dos horas hablando de los detalles del contrato** = they spent two hours discussing the details of the contract

◊ **detallista** *nmf* retailer; **precio al detallista** = trade price

detener *vt* **(a)** *(frenar)* to stop; **hizo uso de su voto de calidad para detener la propuesta** = he used his casting vote to block the motion; **el envío fue detenido por la aduana** = the shipment was stopped by customs **(b)** *(jurídico)* to arrest; **hay noticias sin confirmar de que nuestro representante ha sido detenido** = there are unconfirmed reports that our agent has been arrested

detenidamente *adv* thoroughly; **examinar detenidamente** = to examine thoroughly *o* to go into; **el banco quiere examinar detenidamente los detalles de los préstamos entre sociedades** = the bank wants to go into the details of the inter-company loans

deteriorado, -da *adj* spoiled *o* damaged; **géneros deteriorados por haber estado expuestos en una tienda** = shop-soiled articles **2** *pp de* DETERIORAR

deteriorar *vt* to spoil *o* to damage

◊ **deteriorarse** *vr* to deteriorate *o* to get worse; **la situación se ha deteriorado** = the situation has got worse

◊ **deterioro** *nm* deterioration *o* wear and tear

determinación *nf* determination; **determinación de los daños** = assessment of damages

determinado, -da 1 *adj* particular *o* a certain; **un número determinado** *o* **una cantidad determinada** = a certain number *o* a certain quantity **2** *pp de* DETERMINAR

determinar *vt* to determine *o* to decide on; **determinar los precios** *o* **las cantidades** = to decide on prices *o* quantities; **condiciones todavía por determinar** = conditions still to be determined

detonante *nm* trigger

> el detonante de la creación de esta sociedad ha sido la construcción de la autopista Éibar-Vitoria. Un proyecto de unos 100.000 millones de pesetas cuya financiación se reparten al 50% la iniciativa pública y la privada
>
> **El País**

detrás (de) *adv* behind; **cuelga tu abrigo en el perchero detrás de la puerta** = hang your coat on the hook behind the door; **nos hemos quedado por detrás de nuestros competidores** = we have fallen behind our rivals

detrimento *nm* prejudice; **actuar en detrimento de una demanda** = to act to the prejudice of a claim

deuda *nf* **(a)** *(dinero debido)* debt *o* indebtness; **deudas acumuladas** = accrued liabilities *o* accruals; **deuda consolidada** = funded debt; **deuda exterior** = foreign debt; **deuda garantizada** = secured debt; **deuda no garantizada** = unsecured debt; **deuda incobrable** = bad debt *o* write-off; **la compañía ha dado por perdidos 6.000.000 de ptas. de deudas incobrables** = the company has written off 6m pesetas in bad debts; **deuda a largo** *o* **a corto plazo** = long-term *o* short-term debt; **deuda morosa** = bad debt *o* outstanding debt; **deudas por pagar** = debts due; **deudas prioritarias** = senior debts; **la deuda pública** = the National Debt; **títulos de la deuda pública** = GB gilts; US Treasury bonds; **la sociedad suspendió sus operaciones con una deuda de más de 1 millón de pesetas** = the company stopped trading with debts of over 1 million pesetas; **la deuda de la compañía se ha duplicado** = the company's borrowings have doubled; **tiene una deuda de 50.000 ptas.** = he is in debt to the tune of 50,000 pesetas; **la compañía ya no tiene deudas** = the company is out of debt; **asesoramiento de deudas** = debt counselling; **avalar una deuda** = to guarantee a debt; **cobro de deudas** = debt collection; **contraer deudas** = to get into debt *o* to incur debts; **devolver una deuda** = to pay back a debt; **impago de una deuda** = non-payment of a debt; **liquidación de una deuda** = liquidation of a debt; **liquidar** *o* **pagar una deuda** = to clear a debt *o* to pay off a debt; **pagar los intereses de una deuda** = to service a debt; **reembolso de una deuda** = debt repayment; **refinanciar una deuda** = to roll over a debt; **situación de deudas** = state of indebtedness **(b)** *(obligación)* obligation; **pagar las deudas propias** = to meet one's obligations

> el saldo vivo de deuda del Estado negociable ha ascendido en 1, 3 billones de pesetas
> **El País**

deudor, -ra *adj* indebted; **nación deudora** = debtor nation; **saldo deudor** = debit balance **2** *n* debtor *o* defaulter; **solicitó el archivo sobre los deudores del año 1994** = he asked for the file on 1994 debtors; **¿cuánto le deben todavía los deudores a la compañía?** = how much is still owing to the company by its debtors?; **deudores comerciales** = trade debtors; **deudor hipotecario** = mortgager *o* mortgagor

devaluación *nf* devaluation; **la devaluación de la peseta** = the devaluation of the peseta; **las cotizaciones de las acciones cayeron ante la noticia de la devaluación** = share prices fell on the news of the devaluation; **los mercados cambiarios se mostraron muy activos después de la devaluación del dólar** = foreign exchange markets were very active after the dollar devalued

> en un imprevisto flash surrealista, el presidente de la Comunidad de Madrid ha atacado la devaluación de la peseta en 1967
> **España económica**

> En el caso de Estados Unidos, la competitividad internacional se buscará mediante una nueva devaluación del dólar
> **Actualidad Económica**

devaluar *vt* to devalue; **devaluar una moneda** = to devalue a currency; **el gobierno ha devaluado la peseta en un 7%** = the government has devalued the peseta by 7%

> dentro del SME los países temen devaluar sus monedas por miedo a perder votos
> **España Económica**

> el Gobierno reafirmará su compromiso para no devaluar la peseta, optando por el mecanismo de la banda estrecha que sólo permite fluctuaciones del 2,25%
> **Actualidad Económica**

devengar *vt* **(a)** *(acumularse)* to accrue; **los intereses se devengan a partir de principios de mes** = interest accrues from the beginning of the month; **el interés devengado se añade cada tres meses** = accrued interest is added quarterly **(b)** **devengar intereses** *o* **dividendos** = to bear *o* to yield (interest *o* dividends); **títulos del Estado que devengan poco interés** = government stocks which yield a low interest; **depósitos que devengan intereses** = interest-bearing deposits

devolución *nf* return *o* repayment *o* payback *o* refund *o* clawback *o*; **exigir la devolución de dinero** = to claim money back; **devolución de impuestos** = tax refund

devolver *vt* **(a)** *(dinero)* to pay back *o* to repay; **devolver de menos** = to short-change; **les devolvió de menos** = he short-changed them; **devolver el**

importe cargado en exceso = to pay back an overcharge; **devolver un préstamo** = to pay back a loan; **nunca me ha devuelto el dinero que me pidió prestado** = he has never paid me back for the money he borrowed **(b)** *(objetos)* to return *o* to take back *o* to send back; **cuando el reloj se estropeó, lo devolvió a la tienda** = when the watch went wrong, he took it back to the shop; **la tienda devolvió el cheque por un error de fecha** = the store sent back the cheque because the date was wrong; **si el color no te gusta, puedes devolverlo y cambiarlo** = if you do not like the colour, you can take it back and exchange it; **devolver existencias no vendidas al mayorista** = to return unsold stock to the wholesaler; **devolver una carta al remitente** = to return a letter to sender; **en caso de no efectuarse la entrega, devuélvase** *o* **sírvanse devolver a** = if undelivered, please return to; **hemos tomado 4.000 artículos que podemos devolver si no vendemos** = we have taken 4,000 items on sale or return; **envases devueltos** = returned empties; **productos devueltos (al suministrador sin vender)** = returns **(c)** *(teléfono)* **devolver una llamada** = to return a call **(d)** **devolver una letra** = to dishonour a bill

día *nm* **(a)** *(periodo de 24 horas)* day; **junio tiene treinta días** = there are thirty days in June; **día festivo** = bank holiday *o* public holiday; **el primer día del mes es festivo** = the first day of the month is a public holiday; **el día de Año Nuevo es festivo** = New Year's Day is a bank holiday; **días hábiles** = clear days; **avisar con una antelación de diez días hábiles** = to give ten clear days' notice; **cuente con un margen de cuatro días hábiles para que el cheque sea abonado en cuenta** = allow four clear days for the cheque to be paid into the bank; **días inhábiles** = *GB* vacation **(b)** *(jornada laboral)* day; **mañana es el día libre de la secretaria** = it is the secretary's day off tomorrow; **se tomó dos días de descanso** = she took two days off; **damos cuatro días libres por Navidad a los empleados** = we give the staff four days off at Christmas; **trabaja tres días sí y dos no** = he works three days on, two days off; **turno de día** = day shift; **hay 150 obreros que trabajan durante el turno de día** = there are 150 men on the day shift; **día laborable** = working day *o* weekday; **día de pago** = pay day; **día de trabajo** = workday *o* working day **(c)** *(bolsa)* **día de liquidación** = settlement day; **día del reporte** = contango day **(d)** **al día** = (i) every day *o* per day (ii) state-of-the-art; **hay diez aviones al día de Londres a Madrid** = there are ten planes a day from London to Madrid; **estar al día** = to be up to date; **mantener al día** = to keep up to date; **poner algo al día** = to bring something up to date *o* to update something; **debemos mantener nuestra lista de destinatarios al día** = we must keep our mailing list up to date **(e)** *(en un restaurante)* **menú del día** = set menu *o* today's menu

> el nuevo ministro responsable de Transportes ha requerido ya la puesta al día de una situación complicada también en este momento por los cambios administrativos que se preparan
> **El País**

diagrama *nm* diagram; **diagrama de barras** = bar chart; **diagrama de flujos** *o* **de secuencias** = flow diagram; **diagrama que muestra los lugares de venta** = diagram showing sales locations; **diagrama de planificación** = desk *o* wall planner;

dibujó un diagrama para mostrar el funcionamiento del proceso de toma de decisiones = he drew a diagram to show how the decision-making processes work

diálogo nm dialogue o talks; **restablecer el diálogo** = to break a deadlock

diario, -ria 1 adj daily o day-to-day; **consumo diario** = daily consumption; **informes diarios de ventas** = daily sales returns; **producción diaria de automóviles** = daily car production; **registro diario de entradas y salidas** = daybook; **las ventas apenas cubren los gastos diarios** = sales only just cover the day-to-day expenses **2** nm (periódico) **un diario** = a daily newspaper o a daily

dictado 1 nm dictation; **escribir al dictado** = to take dictation; **la secretaria tomaba el dictado** o **estaba escribiendo al dictado las palabras del director gerente** = the secretary was taking dictation from the managing director; **mecanógrafo, -fa de dictado** = audio-typist; **velocidad de dictado** = dictation speed **2** pp de DICTAR

dictáfono nm dictating machine o dictaphone; **estaba grabando órdenes en su dictáfono de bolsillo** = he was dictating orders into his pocket dictating machine

dictamen nm opinion o verdict; **los abogados emitieron su dictamen** = the lawyers gave their opinion; **dictamen de los auditores** = auditors' report

dictaminar vi (jurídico) to rule o to give an opinion; **el juez dictaminó que los documentos debían depositarse ante el tribunal** = the judge ruled that the documents had to be deposited with the court

dictar vt to dictate; **dictar una carta a una secretaria** = to dictate a letter to a secretary

diestro, -tra adj (a) (hábil) skilful (b) (derecho) right

dieta nf allowance o subsistence allowance; **dieta para gastos de viaje** = travel allowance o travelling allowance; **dietas para gastos de representación** = entertainment allowance

difamación nf slander o libel; **demanda por difamación** = action for libel o libel action o action for slander o slander action

diferencia nf (a) (diferenciación) difference; **¿cuál es la diferencia entre estos dos productos?** = what is the difference between these two products?; **¿qué diferencia existe entre las ventas de este año y las del año pasado?** = how do the sales this year compare with last year's?; **diferencia de precios** = price difference; **diferencias de precio** = differences in price o price differences; **diferencias salariales** = wage differentials (b) (discrepancia) discrepancy o shortfall; **tuvimos que tomar un préstamo para cubrir la diferencia entre los gastos y los ingresos** = we had to borrow money to cover the shortfall between expenditure and

revenue; **partir la diferencia** = to split the difference (c) **diferencia entre valor contable y de mercado** = hidden asset

diferenciado, -da adj differential; **tarifas diferenciadas** = differential tariffs

diferencial 1 adj differential; **cálculo diferencial** = differential calculus; **tarifas diferenciales** = differential tariffs **2** nm differential o spread; **diferencial de inflación** = price differential; **diferencial de salarios** = wage drift

el viernes comenzó la negociación en el mercado español de futuros financieros (MEFF Renta Fija) de los nuevos contratos denominados sobre el diferencial o 'spread' entre las cotizaciones de tres de los principales futuros sobre Bonos a 10 años existentes en Europa

El País

diferenciar vt to differentiate

diferente adj different

diferido, -da 1 adj deferred; **acciones diferidas** = deferred stock; **acreedor diferido** = deferred creditor **2** pp de DIFERIR

diferir 1 vt to defer o to postpone; **diferir el pago** = to defer payment **2** vi to differ; **que difiere** = at variance with

difícil adj (a) (dificultoso) difficult o hard o awkward; **a la empresa le resultó difícil vender en el mercado europeo** = the company found it difficult to sell into the European market; **estas máquinas de escribir son difíciles de vender** = these typewriters are hard to sell; **es difícil conseguir gente buena a sueldo bajo** = it is hard to get good people to work on low salaries; **el período de relevo es siempre difícil** = the take-over period is always difficult (b) (persona) difficult; **es un hombre difícil** = he's a difficult man (c) (prueba) hard o stiff; **tuvo que pasar una prueba difícil para sacar el título** = he had to take a stiff test before he qualified (d) (poco probable) unlikely; **es difícil que vaya a la reunión** = I am not likely to go to the meeting

dificultad nf (a) (inconveniente) difficulty; **tuvieron muchas dificultades para vender en el mercado europeo** = they had a lot of difficulty selling into the European market (b) (problemas) trouble; **hubo dificultades en el almacén cuando el director fue despedido** = there was some trouble in the warehouse after the manager was fired; **la compañía tiene grandes dificultades financieras** = the company is in financial trouble

difusión nf circulation o spread; **la empresa está intentando mejorar la difusión de información entre los departamentos** = the company is trying to improve the circulation of information between departments

las televisiones competitivas empezarán a distraer dinero de la emisión de acontecimientos de gran difusión, como los Juegos Olímpicos, para dedicarlo a otros programas de difusión limitada, como los de arte

Actualidad Económica

dígito nm digit o figure; **hemos experimentado**

una inflación de dos dígitos durante unos años = we have had double-figure inflation for some years; **dígito de control** = check digit

digno, -na *adj* worthy; **una persona digna de confianza** = trustworthy *o* safe person; **tenemos información digna de crédito sobre las ventas de nuestro competidor** = we have reliable information about our rival's sales

diligencia *nf* **(a)** diligence **(b) hacer diligencias** = (i) to take steps; (ii) to do business; **haremos las diligencias necesarias** = we'll take all necessary steps

◇ **diligente** *adj* industrious

dilución *nf* **dilución de las acciones** = dilution of equity *o* of shareholding

dimensión *nf* **(a)** *(tamaño)* size; **¿cuáles son las dimensiones del contenedor?** = what is the size of the container?; **tiene un despacho de dimensiones medias** = he has an average-sized office **(b)** *(plural)* **dimensiones** = measurements; **las dimensiones de un paquete** = the measurements of a parcel

dimisión *nf* resignation; **presentar la dimisión** = to hand in *o* to give in *o* to send in *o* to tender one's resignation; **ha presentado su dimisión con efectos a partir del 1 de julio** = he has resigned with effect from July 1st; **entregó su dimisión** = she gave in *o* handed in her notice

dimitir *vi* to resign; **dimitió de su cargo de tesorero** = he resigned from his post as treasurer; **dimitió de su cargo de directora de finanzas** = she resigned *o* she quit as finance director; **dimitió después de una discusión con el director gerente** = he quit after an argument with the managing director; **dimitió por motivos de salud** = he resigned for medical reasons

Dinamarca *nf* Denmark

◇ **danés, -esa** *n* Dane

◇ **danés, -esa** *o* **dinamarqués, -esa** *adj* Danish
NOTA: capital: **Copenhague** (= Copenhagen); moneda: **corona danesa (DKr)** = Danish krone (DKr)

dinámica *nf* dynamics; **dinámica de grupo** = group dynamics

◇ **dinámico, -ca** *adj* dynamic *o* go-ahead; **trabaja para una empresa de confección dinámica** = she works for a go-ahead clothing company

◇ **dinamismo** *nm* energy; **le falta dinamismo para ser un buen vendedor** = he hasn't the energy to be a good salesman

dinero *nm* **(a)** *(moneda)* money; **dinero ajeno** = other people's money (OPM); **dinero barato** = cheap money; **dinero caliente** *o* **especulativo** = hot money; **dinero caro** = dear money; **dinero de curso forzoso** = fiat money; **dinero en efectivo** = cash; **dinero escaso** = tight money; **dinero fácil** = easy money; **vender seguros es ganar dinero fácil** = selling insurance is easy money; **dinero inactivo** = money lying idle *o* idle money; **dinero líquido** = ready money; **dinero en metálico** = hard cash; **dinero pagadero a petición** *o* **dinero a la vista** = money at call *o* money on call *o* call money; **dinero de plástico** = plastic money; **dinero suelto** = change; **dinero que se debe a la compañía** *o* **a los consejeros** = money owing to the company *o* to the directors; **¿cuánto dinero se debe?** = what is the amount outstanding?; **arriesgar dinero en algo** = to stake money on something; **confiar dinero a alguien** = to lodge money with someone *o* to leave money in trust with someone; **depositar dinero** = to deposit money *o* to make a deposit; **ganar** *o* **hacer dinero** = to earn money *o* to make money; **ganar mucho dinero** = to make a lot of money; **ha ganado mucho dinero en la bolsa** *o* **hizo mucho dinero en la bolsa** = he made a great deal of money on the stock market; **invertir dinero en un negocio** = to put money into a business; **invirtió todo el dinero recibido como indemnización por despido en una tienda** = he put all his redundancy money into a shop; **hacer dinero fácilmente** = to make a quick buck; **oferta de dinero** = money supply; **perder dinero** = to lose money; **la compañía ha estado perdiendo dinero durante meses** = the company has been losing money for months; **en esta transacción he perdido dinero** = I lost money on the deal; **recuperar el dinero** = to get your money back; **sin dinero** = broke; **la compañía está sin dinero** = the company is broke; **superabundancia de dinero** = glut of money; **tipos de interés del dinero** = money rates; **cuando contamos el dinero nos faltaron 2.000 ptas.** = when we cashed up we were 2,000 pesetas short; **vendió su casa e invirtió el dinero en su totalidad** = she sold her house and invested the money as a lump sum; **¿quién aportó el dinero para la tienda?** = who put up the money for the shop?; **valen mucho dinero** = they are worth a lot of money **(b)** *(en efectivo)* cash; **tarjeta dinero** *o* **tarjeta de cajero automático** = cash card

los inversores entregaban su dinero sin saber para qué se iba a utilizar
España Económica

con el enorme número de cajeros que existen, todavía muchos usuarios primero extraen el dinero en efectivo y después acuden a comercios donde admiten tarjeta
Actualidad Económica

bancos y cajas detallan los límites por los que deben responder los usuarios del dinero de plástico
El País

diplomado, -da 1 *adj* qualified *o* having a diploma **2** *n* graduate *o* person with qualifications

diplomático, -ca 1 *adj* diplomatic; **inmunidad diplomática** = diplomatic immunity; **invocó la inmunidad diplomática para evitar ser detenido** = he claimed diplomatic immunity to avoid being arrested; **conceder estatus diplomático a alguien** = to grant someone diplomatic status **2** *n* diplomat *o* diplomatist

dique *nm* dock; **dique seco** = dry dock

dirección 1 *nf* **(a)** *(domicilio)* address; **dirección comercial** = business address; **dirección postal** = accommodation address; **dirección privada** = home address; **dirección de reenvío** = forwarding address; **dirección telegráfica** = cable address; **mi dirección profesional y el número de teléfono están indicados en la tarjeta** = my business address and phone number are printed on the card; **indique**

su nombre, apellidos y dirección = give your full name and address *o* give your name and address in full; **libro de direcciones** = address book; **lista de direcciones** = address list; **mantenemos una lista de dos mil direcciones en Europa** = we keep a list of two thousand addresses in Europe; **el paquete llevaba una dirección incorrecta** *o* **equivocada** = the package was incorrectly addressed; **poner la dirección a un sobre** = to address an envelope **(b)** *(sentido)* direction *o* way; **calle de una sola dirección** *o* **de dirección única** = one-way street **(c)** *(consejo de administración)* management *o* the directors; **cambio de dirección** = change of management *o* under new management; **alta dirección** = top management; **decisiones tomadas por la dirección** = decisions taken at managerial level; **la dirección ha decidido conceder un aumento general de sueldo** = the management has decided to give an overall pay increase **(d)** *(comercial)* management; **dirección por objetivos** = management by objectives; **técnicas de dirección de empresas** = management techniques; **asumió la dirección de un grupo multinacional** = he took over the management of a multinational group; **después de seis años le ofrecieron la dirección de una sucursal en Escocia** = after six years, he was offered the managership of a branch in Scotland **(e)** *(política)* leadership; **la dirección del partido** = the party leaders *o* the leaders of the party *o* the leadership of the party

la clave consiste en volver a motivar a los ejecutivos que ya existen en la empresa; si se consigue, no es preciso cambiar a toda la dirección
España Económica

las propuestas de las centrales sindicales han sido rechazadas por la dirección del partido
España Económica

directivo, -va *adj* managerial; **ser nombrado para un puesto directivo** = to be appointed to a managerial position; **equipo directivo** = management team; **junta directiva** = board of directors; **la junta directiva discutirá el aumento de salarios en la próxima reunión** = the board will discuss wage rises at its next meeting; **tres encargados representan al personal en las negociaciones con la junta directiva** = three managers represent the workforce in discussions with the directors

◊ **directiva** *nf* **(a)** board of directors *o* directorate *o* governing body **(b)** *(directriz)* directive *o* guideline

◊ **directivo** *nm* manager *o* director; **búsqueda de directivos** = executive search; **los directivos asistieron a la presentación del nuevo sistema de control de existencias** = the managers attended the demonstration of the new stock control system; **adquisición** *o* **compra de una empresa por sus propios directivos** = management buyout (MBO)

es demasiado tarde para producir y ejecutar directivas extraordinarias sobre servicios de inversión, seguros y fondos de jubilación, antes de finales de año
Actualidad Económica

la banca es el sector que mejor retribuye a los directivos en España
Cinco Días

directo, -ta *adj* **(a)** *(inmediato)* direct; **acción directa** = direct action; **costes directos** = direct costs; **débito directo** = direct debit; **pago la factura de la luz por débito directo** = I pay my electricity bill by direct debit; **envío directo** = drop shipment; **imposición directa** = direct taxation; **el gobierno obtiene más ingresos de los impuestos directos que de los indirectos** = the government raises more money by direct taxation than by indirect; **llamada internacional directa** = international direct dialling; **marketing directo** = direct marketing; **venta directa** = direct selling; **vuelo directo** = non-stop flight **(b)** *(televisión)* **en directo** = live; **transmitir en directo** = to broadcast live

◊ **directamente** *adv* directly *o* direct; **pagamos el impuesto sobre la renta directamente al Estado** = we pay income tax direct to the government; **puedes llamar directamente (sin operadora)** = you can dial direct; **puede llamar a Nueva York desde Madrid directamente si quiere** = you can dial New York direct from Madrid if you want; **los vendedores dependen directamente del director de ventas** = the salesmen report directly to the sales director; **la oficina de ventas está conectada directamente con el ordenador del almacén** = the sales office is linked direct to the warehouse; **obtenemos nuestros datos directamente del departamento de control de existencias** = we get our data on line from the stock control department

director, -ra 1 *adj* leading *o* directing *o* controlling **2** *n* **(a)** *(empresa)* manager *o* director; **director adjunto** = deputy manager; **director de capacitación** = training officer; **es una directora competente** = she is a competent manager; **director de departamento** *o* **sección** = department *o* departmental manager; **director de empresa** = company director; **director, directora de una fábrica** *o* **taller** = manager, manageress of a factory *o* workshop; **director financiero** = financial controller; **director general** = general manager; **director interino** *o* **en funciones** *o* **provisional** = acting manager; **director de personal** = personnel manager; **director de planta** = floor manager; **director de producción** = production manager; **director de reclamaciones** = claims manager; **director regional** = area manager; **director suplente** = alternate director; **director de ventas** = sales manager; **las cifras que el director de ventas presentó a la reunión eran incorrectas** = the sales director reported the wrong figures to the meeting; **cuando le nombraron director** = when he was appointed manager *o* on his appointment as manager **(b)** *(banco, tienda)* manager; **director del Banco de Inglaterra** = Governor of the Bank of England; **director de sucursal** = branch manager; **director de una sucursal bancaria** = bank manager; **el Sr. Luque es el director de nuestra sucursal del Banco de Santander** = Sr Luque is the manager of our local Banco de Santander; **el director de nuestra sucursal de Londres está en Madrid para asistir a una serie de reuniones** = the manager of our London branch is in Madrid for a series of meetings **(c)** *(miembro de una junta)* director; **director adjunto** = associate director; **director ejecutivo** = executive director; **director no ejecutivo** = non-executive director; **director**

externo = outside director; **director gerente** = managing director (MD); **presidente y director gerente** = chairman and managing director; **un director de sección** = a divisional director; **¿accederá el director financiero a dimitir?** = will the finance director agree to resign?; **¿conoce al Sr. Solá, nuestro nuevo director de ventas?** = do you know Sr Solá, our new sales director?; **el director está de vacaciones** = the director is on holiday **(d)** *(de una organización)* director *o* head; **director del instituto estatal de investigaciones** = the director *o* the head of the government research institute ; **fue nombrada directora de la organización** = she was appointed director of the organization **(e)** *(de un periódico)* editor; **el director de 'El País'** = the editor of 'El País'

haciendo una previsión del panorama nacional de arrendamientos el director general de Vivienda permanece tranquilo

directorio *nm* directory; **directorio comercial** = commercial *o* trade directory; **directorio comercial por secciones** = classified directory

empresas y profesionales disponen desde hace unos días de un amplio directorio de empresas con sede en Cataluña que recoge datos sobre 12.000 sociedades de diversos sectores

directriz *nf* directive *o* guideline; **el gobierno ha publicado directrices sobre los aumentos de rentas y precios** = the government has issued directives on increases in incomes and prices; **el aumento de los precios al consumidor contraviene *o* va en contra de las directrices del gobierno** = the increase in retail price breaks *o* goes against the government guidelines

dirigente *nmf* **(a)** *(en un club o sociedad)* officer; **la elección de los dirigentes de una asociación** = the election of officers of an association **(b)** *(persona)* leader; **el dirigente del sindicato obrero de la construcción** = the leader of the construction workers' union *o* the construction workers' leader

los reveses en las urnas han crispado los nervios de los dirigentes y militantes del partido

dirigir *vt* **(a)** *(encabezar)* to direct *o* to lead *o* to superintend *o* to manage *o* to run *o* to channel; **dirige una compañía multimillonaria** = he is running a multimillion-dollar company; **dirigir un departamento** = to manage a department *o* to be the manager of a department *o* to head a department; **dirigir una empresa conjuntamente** = to manage a company jointly; **dirigir erróneamente** = to misdirect; **dirigir mal** = to mismanage; **dirigir una sucursal de oficina** = to manage a branch office; **dirige las ventas de la empresa en el extranjero** = he superintends the company's overseas sales; **estuvo dirigiendo la sección de desarrollo hasta el año pasado** = she was director of the development unit until last year; **dirige nuestras actividades en el sureste de Asia** = he heads our South-East Asian operations; **la compañía está dirigida por el accionista mayoritario** = the company is controlled by the majority shareholder; **ha sido nombrado para dirigir nuestra organización europea** = he has been appointed to head up our European organization; **dirigen los fondos de investigación al desarrollo de sistemas de comunicación europeos** = they are channelling their research funds into developing European communication systems **(b)** *(negociaciones)* to conduct; **el presidente dirigió las negociaciones muy eficazmente** = the chairman conducted the negotiations very efficiently **(c)** *(por carta)* to address; **por favor dirija sus peticiones al director** = please address your enquiries to the manager; **una carta dirigida al director gerente** = a letter addressed to the managing director **(d)** *(tener como objetivo)* to aim at *o* to target; **producto dirigido a un mercado popular** = product aimed at the popular market *o* which targets the popular market *o* down market product

◊ **dirigirse** *vr* **(a)** *(ir a)* dirigirse hacia = to head for; **el petrolero naufragó cuando se dirigía al Golfo** = the tanker sank when she was en route to the Gulf; **se dirigía al trabajo en coche cuando oyó las noticias por la radio** = he was driving to work when he heard the news on the car radio **(b)** *(hacer una propuesta)* to approach; **se dirigió al banco para pedir un préstamo** = he approached the bank with a request for a loan **(b)** *(hablar)* to address; **dirigirse a los asistentes de una reunión** = to address a meeting

disciplinar *vt* to discipline *o* to train

disco *nm* disk; **disco flexible** *o* **blando** = floppy disk; **disco duro** *o* **fijo** *o* **rígido** = hard disk

puede gestionar como cualquier controladora normal dos discos duros configuardos como las unidades C: y D:

discográfico, -ca *adj* **casa discográfica** = record company; **novedades discográficas** = new record releases

discontinuar *vt* to discontinue *o* to drop *o* to cease

discreción *nf* discretion; **a discreción** = on a discretionary basis; **se lo dejo a su discreción** = I leave it to your discretion; **a discreción de alguien** = at the discretion of someone; **la afiliación es a discreción del comité** = membership is at the discretion of the committee

discrecional *adj* discretionary; **cuenta discrecional** = discretionary account; **los poderes discrecionales del ministro** = the minister's discretionary powers

discrepancia *nf* discrepancy *o* variance; **discrepancia estadística** = statistical discrepancy; **hay una discrepancia en las cuentas** = there is a discrepancy in the accounts; **explicar una discrepancia de números** = to account for a discrepancy

discriminación *nf* discrimination; **discriminación sexual** = sexual discrimination *o* sex discrimination *o* discrimination on grounds of sex; **discriminación de precios** = price discrimination

disculpa *nf* apology *o* excuse; **escribir una carta de disculpa** = to write a letter of apology

disculpar *vt* to excuse; **adjunto un cheque de**

2.000 ptas. rogando me disculpe la demora en contestarle = I enclose a cheque for 2,000 pesetas with apologies for the delay in answering your letter

◊ **disculparse** *vr* to excuse oneself *o* to apologize; **disculparse por la demora en contestar** = to apologize for the delay in answering

discurrir *vi* to flow; **la producción discurre ahora normalmente después de la huelga** = production is now flowing normally after the strike

discusión *nf* **(a)** *(disputa)* argument *o* dispute; **se enzarzaron en una discusión sobre los documentos con los aduaneros** = they got into an argument with the customs officials over the documents; **le despidieron tras una discusión con el director gerente** = he was sacked after an argument with the managing director; **las conversaciones condujeron a una fuerte discusión entre la patronal y el sindicato** = the discussions led to a big argument between the management and the union **(b)** *(debate)* discussion

discutir *vt/i* to discuss *o* to argue about *o* to haggle; **discutir los detalles de un contrato** = to haggle about *o* over the details of a contract; **discutieron sobre el precio** = they argued over *o* about the price; **precio a discutir** = price negotiable; **el coche está a la venta por 400.000 ptas. - precio a discutir** = the car is for sale at 400,000 pesetas or near offer; **pasamos horas discutiendo con el director gerente sobre el emplazamiento de la nueva fábrica** = we spent hours arguing with the managing director about the site for the new factory; **la junta directiva discutirá el aumento de salarios en la próxima reunión** = the board will discuss wage rises at its next meeting

diseñador, -ra *n* designer; **es la diseñadora del nuevo ordenador** = she is the designer of the new computer; **trabaja independientemente como diseñador** = he works freelance as a designer

diseñar *vt* to design; **diseña muebles de jardín** = she designs garden furniture

◊ **diseño** *nm* **(a)** *(técnico)* design; **diseño industrial** = industrial design; **diseño de productos** = product design; **agencia** *o* **taller de diseño** = design studio; **departamento de diseño** = design department; **hacemos todo el diseño en la propia empresa** = we do all our design work inside (the company) **(b)** *(dibujo)* pattern

el show fue un éxito y ha dado origen a un concurso internacional de diseñadores de ropa

Ajoblanco

disminución *nf* decrease *o* lowering *o* abatement; **disminución de valor** = decrease in value; **disminución de las importaciones** = decrease in imports; **una disminución del poder adquisitivo** = a decline in purchasing power; **disminución de las ventas** = drop in sales

disminuir 1 *vi* to decline *o* to decrease *o* to diminish *o* to fall off; **las exportaciones** *o* **las importaciones han disminuido durante el último año** = exports *o* imports have fallen *o* have declined over the last year; **nuestra cuota de mercado ha disminuido durante los últimos años** = our share of the market has diminished over the last few years; **las ventas han disminuido desde que terminó la**

temporada turística = sales have fallen off since the tourist season ended **2** *vt* to reduce; **hemos disminuido los gastos** = we have reduced expenditure

disolución *nf* dissolution *o* demerger

disolver *vt* **(a)** *(por completo)* to dissolve; **disolver una sociedad** = to dissolve a partnership *o* to liquidate a company **(b)** *(en varias partes)* to demerge

◊ **disolverse** *vr* to demerge

disparador *nm* trigger

◊ **disparar** *vt* to trigger

dispararse *vr* to go up fast *o* to soar *o* to shoot up; **precios que se disparan** = rocketing prices; **durante la huelga los precios se han disparado** = prices have shot up during the strike; **los precios de los alimentos se dispararon durante el periodo de frío** = food prices soared during the cold weather; **los precios de las acciones se dispararon al hacerse pública la noticia de la oferta de adquisición** = share prices soared on the news of the takeover bid *o* the news of the takeover bid sent share prices soaring

dispensar *vt* to exempt

disponer 1 *vt* to arrange *o* to lay out; **la oficina está dispuesta en un espacio abierto con unas salas pequeñas aparte para reuniones** = the office is arranged as an open-plan area with small separate rooms for meetings **2** *vi* **(a)** *(tener disponible)* to have available; **no disponemos del tiempo suficiente para llevar a cabo el proyecto** = we do not have enough time to carry out the plan **(b)** *(tener en existencia)* to keep; **siempre disponemos de este artículo** = we always keep this item in stock

disponibilidad *nf* availability; **oferta sujeta a la disponibilidad de las existencias** = offer subject to stock availability

disponible *adj* **(a)** *(accesible)* available; **capital disponible** = available capital; **ha invertido su capital disponible en una tienda de informática** = he has invested his spare capital in a computer shop; **existencias disponibles** = stock in hand; **fondos disponibles para inversión en empresas pequeñas** = funds which have been made available for investment in small businesses; **renta personal disponible** = personal disposable income; **no disponible** = unavailable; **artículo no disponible** = item no longer available; **artículos disponibles sólo por encargo** = items available to order only **(b)** *(inmueble)* vacant

disposición *nf* **(a)** *(arreglo)* provision *o* arrangement *o* disposition; **tomar disposiciones** = to make provision for; **hemos tomado disposiciones al respecto** = we have made provision to this effect; **(b)** *(normas)* order *o* regulation; **disposiciones sobre la importación y exportación** = regulations concerning imports and exports; **las nuevas disposiciones gubernamentales sobre la normalización de viviendas** = the new government regulations on housing standards

dispositivo *nm* device; **dispositivo de alarma** = warning device

dispuesto, -ta 1 *adj* arranged *o* disposed; **estar**

dispuesto a hacer algo = to be prepared to do something; **no está dispuesto a cambiar de oficina** = he is reluctant to move to another office **2** *pp de* DISPONER

disputa *nf* **(a)** dispute *o* argument; **disputa entre sindicatos sobre la delimitación de tareas** = demarcation dispute **(b) sin disputa** = without any doubt

disputar *vt* to dispute; **disputó la cuenta** = he disputed the bill

◊ **disputarse** *vr* to compete; **las dos empresas se disputan una cuota de mercado** = the two companies are competing for a market share

disquete *nm* diskette

◊ **disquetera** *nf* disk drive

distancia *nf* distance; **de gran distancia** = long-haul; **vuelo de larga distancia** = long-haul flight

distinguir *vt* to distinguish *o* to recognize

◊ **distinguirse** *vr* to be distinguished *o* to differ; **empresa que se distingue por la calidad de sus servicios** = company with a reputation for quality of service

distintivo *nm* badge; **los visitantes deben inscribirse en recepción donde se les dará un distintivo** = visitors have to sign in at reception, and will be given visitors' badges

distinto, -ta *adj* different; **ser distinto** = to be different *o* to differ; **nuestra gama de productos tiene un diseño totalmente distinto del de nuestros competidores** = our product range is quite different in design from that of our rivals; **ofrecemos diez modelos, cada uno en seis colores distintos** = we offer ten models each in six different colours; **los dos productos son bastante distintos - uno lleva un motor eléctrico, el otro funciona con gasolina** = the two products differ considerably - one has an electric motor, the other runs on petrol

distorsión *nf* distortion; **distorsión de los precios** = price distortion

distorsionar *vt* to distort

> su presencia distorsiona el mercado al introducir intereses ajenos a la comunicación
>
> *Tiempo*

distribución *nf* **(a)** *(reparto)* distribution; **distribución exclusiva** = sole distributorship; **distribución normal** = normal distribution; **distribución de la renta** = income distribution; **la distribución es difícil en las regiones rurales** = distribution is difficult in country areas; **canales de distribución** = channels of distribution *o* distribution channels; **costes de distribución** = distribution costs; **jefe de distribución** = distribution manager; **lista** *o* **nota de distribución** = distribution slip; **red de distribución** = distribution network **(b)** *(trazado)* layout; **han modificado la distribución de las oficinas** = they have altered the layout of the offices; **oficina de distribución modificable** = open-plan office **(c) una distribución de los beneficios** = a shareout of the profits **(d)** *(reparto proporcional)* apportionment; **distribución de créditos** = apportionment of appropriations

distribuible *adj* distributable *o* available for distribution; **beneficios distribuibles** = distributable profit

distribuido, -da 1 *adj* distributed; **beneficios distribuidos** = distributed profits; **beneficios no distribuidos** = retained earnings; **gastos no distribuidos** = undistributed expenses **2** *pp de* DISTRIBUIR

distribuidor, -ra *n* **(a)** *(persona)* distributor *o* stockist; **distribuidor autorizado** *o* **oficial** = authorized dealer; **distribuidor exclusivo** = sole distributor; **una red de distribuidores** = a network of distributors; **Hnos Martínez S.A. es la distribuidora de varias pequeñas empresas** = Martínez S.A. distributes for several smaller companies **(b)** *(máquina)* **distribuidor de toallas** = towel dispenser; **distribuidor automático** *o* **distribuidora automática** = automatic vending machine

distribuir *vt* **(a)** *(repartir)* to distribute *o* to deliver **(b) distribuir un dividendo** = to pay a dividend **(c) distribuir los pagos a lo largo de varios meses** = to spread payments over several months

distributivo, -va *adj* distributive; **comercios de repartimiento** = distributive trades

distrito *nm* district *o* area *o* zone; *US* precinct; **la oficina está en el distrito comercial de la ciudad** = the office is in the commercial area of the town; **distrito de Madrid con impuestos municipales elevados** = highly-rated part of Madrid; **distrito postal** = (i) postal code *o* post code; *US* zip code; (ii) postal district

disuadir *vi* to deter *o* to discourage; **para disuadir a los eventuales evasores fiscales** = as a disincentive to potential tax evaders; **los precios altos disuaden a los clientes** = high prices put customers off

diversificación *nf* diversification; **diversificación de productos** = product diversification *o* diversification into new products

diversificarse *vr* to diversify; **diversificarse hacia nuevos produtos** = to diversify into new products

diverso, -sa *adj* diverse *o* different; **géneros diversos** *o* **artículos diversos** = sundries

dividendo *nm* dividend; **dividendo por acción** = earnings per share *o* earnings yield; **estas acciones producen un dividendo de 300 ptas.** = these shares pay a dividend of 300 pesetas; **dividendo final** = final dividend; **dividendo pronosticado** = forecast dividend *o* prospective dividend; **dividendo provisional** = interim dividend; **aumentar el dividendo** = to raise *o* to increase the dividend; **la compañía incrementó su dividendo en un 10%** = the company raised its dividend by 10%; **cheque en pago de dividendos** = dividend warrant; **cobertura del dividendo** = dividend cover; **distribuir un dividendo** = to pay a dividend; **mantener el dividendo** = to maintain the dividend; **no declarar dividendo** *o* **omitir el pago de un dividendo** = to pass a dividend; **los dividendos se pagan a prorrata** = dividends are paid pro rata; **pronóstico del dividendo** = dividend forecast; **advirtió a los accionistas que el dividendo podía ser recortado**

= he warned the shareholders that the dividend might be cut; **el dividendo está cubierto cuatro veces (por las ganancias)** = the dividend is covered four times; **rentabilidad del dividendo** = dividend yield; **con dividendo** = cum dividend; **sin dividendo** = ex dividend; **acciones cotizadas sin dividendo** = shares quoted ex dividend; **las acciones se cotizan sin dividendo** = the shares are quoted ex dividend

> el Banco ha acordado distribuir, a todas las acciones en circulación números 1 al 231.000.000, un tercer dividendo a cuenta con cargo a los resultados del ejercicio
> **El País**

dividido, -da *adj* split; **comisión dividida** = split commission; **pago dividido** = split payment

dividir *vt* to divide *o* to break up *o* to separate; **dividir acciones** = to split shares; **dividir en zonas** = to divide into zones *o* to zone (land); **la compañía fue dividida y se vendió cada parte por separado** = the company was broken up and separate divisions sold off; **el país está dividido en seis áreas de venta** = the country is divided into six sales areas

divisa *nf* (foreign) currency; **divisas de reserva** = reserve currency; **divisa fuerte** = strong currency; **la afluencia de divisas al país** = the influx of foreign currency into the country; **control de divisas** = exchange control; **la compañía tiene más de 1 millón de ptas. en divisas** = the company has more than 1m pesetas in foreign exchange; **mercados de divisas** = foreign exchange markets; **operaciones en divisas** = exchange dealings; **operación en múltiples divisas** = multicurrency operation; **préstamo en múltiples divisas** = multicurrency loan; **reordenación de divisas** = realignment of currencies *o* currency realignment; **reordenar las divisas** = to realign currencies; **reservas de divisas** = currency reserves; **tipos de divisas a plazo** = forward (exchange) rate

> ante la dificultad de repatriar las divisas, exige como único sistema de pago las tarjetas de crédito
> **España Económica**

> se han creado empresas mixtas tan irrelevantes como una para la venta de productos extranjeros, exclusivamente a extranjeros y en divisa convertible
> **España Económica**

división *nf* **(a)** *(parte de una compañía)* division; **la sede de la división** = the divisional headquarters; **Pascual Hermanos es ahora una división del grupo de compañías La Olivera** = Pascual Hermanos is now a division of the Olivera group of companies **(b)** *(acuerdos, partidas)* split

> la división de interiorismo se está convirtiendo en una importante fuerza en el mercado empresarial de Madrid
> **España Económica**

divulgación *nf* disclosure; **la divulgación de la oferta de adquisición hizo subir el precio de las acciones** = the disclosure of the takeover bid raised the price of the shares

divulgar *vt* **(a)** *(publicar)* to release; **la empresa divulgó información sobre la nueva mina de Australia** = the company released information about the new mine in Australia **(b)** *(anunciar)* to publicize; **la campaña está destinada a divulgar los servicios de la junta de turismo** = the campaign is intended to publicize the services of the tourist board

◊ **divulgarse** *vr* to leak out

DNI = DOCUMENTO NACIONAL DE IDENTIDAD identity card *o* ID card

doblar 1 *vt* **(a)** *(duplicar)* to double **(b)** to fold *o* to double over; **dobló la carta de forma que la dirección quedara claramente visible** = she folded the letter so that the address was clearly visible **(c)** *(cine, TV)* to dub **2** *vi (dirección)* to turn *o* to go round; **al doblar la esquina encontrará Vd. la farmacia** = you will see the chemist as you turn the corner

◊ **doblarse** *vr* to double

doble 1 *adj* double; **contabilidad por partida doble** = double-entry bookkeeping; **doble imposición** = double taxation; **tratado de doble imposición** = double taxation agreement; **recibir paga doble** *o* **cobrar tarifa doble por trabajar en días festivos** = to be on double time **2** *nm* double; **el volumen de sus ventas es el doble del nuestro** = their turnover is twice as big as ours

doce *adj* twelve; *(UE hasta 1995)* **los Doce** = the Twelve

docena *nf* dozen; **vender por lotes de una docena** = to sell in lots of one dozen

documentación *nf* documentation *o* papers *o* literature; **sírvase enviarme la documentación completa referente a la venta** = please send me the complete documentation concerning the sale ; **documentación sobre una nueva gama de productos** = literature about a new product range

documental *adj* documentary; **prueba documental** = documentary proof; **pruebas documentales** = documentary evidence

◊ **documentalista** *nmf (empleado de información)* documentalist

documento *nm* document; **documento falso** = forgery; **documento financiero** = financial instrument; **documento legal** = legal document; **este documento no tiene fuerza jurídica** = this document is not legally binding; **documento nacional de identidad (DNI)** = identity card *o* ID card; **documento negociable** = negotiable instrument; **documento no negociable** = non-negotiable instrument; **fotocopiar un documento** = to photocopy *o* to xerox a document; **el documento presenta un organigrama de la compañía** = the paper gives a diagram of the company's organizational structure; **necesitamos comprobar sus documentos** = we need to check your papers

dólar *nm (unidad monetaria en los EE UU, Canadá, Australia y otros países)* dollar; *(en lenguaje coloquial)* US greenback *o* buck; **dólar (norte)americano** = American dollar; **el dólar norteamericano subió el 2%** = the US dollar rose 2%; **cincuenta dólares canadienses** *o* **dólares australianos** = fifty Canadian *o* Australian dollars; **billete de cinco dólares** = five dollar bill; **mil dólares** = one thousand dollars *o* one grand; **le ofrecieron cincuenta mil dólares por la información** = they offered him fifty thousand dollars for the information; **¿a cuánto está el dólar?** = what's the exchange rate for the dollar?; **¿cuántos dólares son diez mil pesetas?** = what are ten thousand pesetas worth in dollars?; **crisis del dólar** = dollar crisis; **déficit de dólares** *o* **escasez de dólares** = dollar gap *o* dollar shortage; **reservas en dólares que tiene un país** = dollar balances *o* dollar reserves; **zona del dólar** = dollar area

doloso *adj* fraudulent *o* deceitful; **engaño doloso** = fraudulent misrepresentation

doméstico, -ca *adj* domestic; **ahora se dedica solamente a las tareas domésticas** = all she does now is housework; **enseres domésticos** = household goods

domiciliación   *nf*   automatic   payment; **domiciliación bancaria** = standing order *o* direct debit; **paga su subscripción por domiciliación bancaria** = he pays his subscription by standing order

domiciliado, -da *adj* **(a)** domiciled; **letras domiciliadas en España** = bills domiciled in Spain **(b) orden de pago domiciliado** = standing order *o* direct debit

domicilio *nm* domicile *o* residence; **domicilio particular** = home address; **le ruego me envíe la carta a mi domicilio particular, no a la oficina** = please send the letter to my home address, not my office; **tiene su domicilio en Dinamarca** = he is domiciled in Denmark *o* he lives in Denmark; **domicilio social** = registered office; **trabajador a domicilio** = homeworker *o* outside worker; **vendedor a domicilio** = door-to-door salesman; **ventas a domicilio** = door-to-door selling

domingo *nm* Sunday

◊ **dominical** *adj* Sunday *o* dominical; **comercio dominical** = Sunday opening *o* trading

Dominicana (República) *nf* Dominican Republic

◊ **dominicano, -na** *adj y n* Dominican
NOTA: capital: **Santo Domingo**; moneda: **peso domicano** = Dominican peso

dominio *nm* domain *o* territory; **dominio público** = public domain; **obra cuyos derechos de autor son del dominio público** = work which is out of copyright

donación *nf* bequest; **donación inter vivos** = gift inter vivos

dorso *nm* back; **escriba su dirección al dorso del sobre** = write your address on the back of the envelope; **las condiciones de venta figuran al dorso de la factura** = the conditions of sale are printed on the back of the invoice ; **sírvase firmar el cheque al dorso** = please endorse the cheque on the back

dos *adj* two; **se suspendió la reunión del consejo de administración por estar enfermos dos de los directores** = two of the directors were ill, so the board meeting was cancelled

dosificar *vt* to ration

dotación *nf* **(a)** allowance *o* endowment; **dotación de divisas** = foreign currency allowance

(b) dotación de personal = staffing *o* manning; **niveles de dotación de personal** = manning levels; **acuerdo sobre dotación de personal** = manning agreement *o* agreement on manning

dotado, -da 1 *adj* **(a)** *(persona)* gifted *o* talented; **una persona bien dotada** = a gifted person **(b)** *(maquinaria, etc.)* equipped; **acaban de instalar un laboratorio dotado con los últimos adelantos técnicos** = they have just installed a lab equipped with the latest technology **2** *pp de* DOTAR

dotal *adj* **póliza dotal** = endowment insurance *o* endowment policy

dotar *vt* to endow *o* to equip

dracma *nf (moneda de Grecia)* drachma

drástico, -ca *adj* drastic; **hacer rebajas drásticas de precios** = to make drastic cuts in prices *o* to slash prices

dudoso, -sa *adj* doubtful; **préstamo dudoso** = doubtful loan

dueño, -ña *n* owner; **cambio de dueño** = under new management

todos ellos tienen como características comunes el ser dueños de empresas familiares en las que una o dos familias tienen la mayoría del poder en el accionariado y además participan en la dirección
Cambio 16

'dumping' *nm (vender en el extranjero a un precio inferior al coste de producción)* dumping; **practicar el 'dumping'** = to dump goods on a market

este crecimiento de las importaciones de productos desde terceros países constituye un grave atentado contra los intereses   de   los   agricultores comunitarios, al tiempo que no suponen un apoyo a las rentas de los campesinos de esos países que están sometidos a condiciones   de   'dumping'   social   y económico
El País

duplicación *nf* duplicating *o* duplication; **duplicación del trabajo** = duplication of work

duplicado *nm* duplicate; **por duplicado** = in duplicate; **factura por duplicado** *o* **duplicado de una factura** = duplicate receipt *o* duplicate of a receipt; **imprimir una factura por duplicado** = to print an invoice in duplicate; **recibo por duplicado** = receipt in duplicate

duplicar *vt* to duplicate *o* to double; **el personal se ha duplicado durante los últimos dos años** = the size of the staff has doubled in the last two years; **este año hemos duplicado nuestros beneficios** = we have doubled our profits this year

◊ **duplicarse** *vr* to double; **este año nuestros beneficios se han duplicado** = our profits have doubled this year; **la deuda de la compañía se ha duplicado** = the company's borrowings have doubled

duración *nf* duration *o* term *o* life; **contrato de corta duración** = short-term contract; **el**

arrendamiento tiene una duración de veinte años = the lease runs for twenty years; **la duración de un préstamo** = the life of a loan

durante *adv* during *o* while *o* for *o* in the meantime *o* in the course of; **durante la vigencia del acuerdo** = during the life of the agreement; **durante su mandato como presidente** = during his term of office as chairman; **durante el último semestre los beneficios se duplicaron** = over the last half of the year profits doubled; **las acciones han bajado un poco durante la jornada de hoy** = shares are slightly down on the day; **las discusiones se prolongaron incesantemente durante horas** = the discussions continued for hours on end

durar *vi* (a) *(perdurar)* to last; **el 'boom' empezó en los años 70 y duró hasta principios de los años 80** = the boom started in the 1970s and lasted until the early 1980s; **la reunión empezó a las 10 de la mañana y duró hasta las 6 de la tarde** = the meeting started at 10 a.m. and continued until 6 p.m.; **las conversaciones sobre la reducción de plantilla duraron todo el día** = the discussions over

redundancies lasted all day (b) *(extenderse)* to run; **la película dura dos horas** = the film runs for two hours

duro, -ra 1 *adj* (a) *(fuerte)* hard; **disco duro** = hard disk; **negocio duro** = hard bargain; **tras semanas de duras negociaciones** = after weeks of hard bargaining; **ser duro en los negocios** *o* **ser un negociador duro** *o* **imponer duras condiciones** = to drive a hard bargain; **es un duro negociador** = he drives a hard bargain; **adoptar una línea dura en las negociaciones sindicales** = to take a hard line in trade union negotiations (b) *(difícil)* stiff *o* hard; **competencia dura** = stiff competition **2** *nm* five peseta coin; **vale cinco duros** = it costs twenty-five pesetas; **no puede pagar el nuevo coche porque no tiene un duro** = he cannot pay for the new car because he is broke

```
los 471 kilómetros de vía entre Madrid y
Sevilla han dejado a Renfe sin un duro
mientras  la  mayor  parte  de  la  red
ferroviaria      (12.700      kilómetros)
languidece obsoleta y abandonada
```
Cambio 16

Ee

echar *vt* **(a)** *(tirar)* to throw (out); **echar la carga al mar** = to jettison cargo **(b) echar un discurso** = to give a speech **(c) echar mano de** = to get some help; **echar una mano a alguien** = to lend someone a hand *o* to give someone help; **echar mano de las reservas en efectivo** = to fall back on cash reserves **(d) echar un vistazo** = to look through; **el contable echó un vistazo rápido al montón de facturas** = the accountant quickly looked through the pile of invoices **(e) echar al correo** = to post *o* to put in the post; **echar una carta** = to post a letter **(f) echar algo abajo** = to demolish **(g) echar a alguien del trabajo** = to sack someone *o* to fire someone; **le echaron del trabajo porque siempre llegaba tarde** = he was fired because he was always late to work **(h) echar de menos** = to miss **(i) echar la culpa** = to blame

◊ **echarse** *vr* **echarse atrás** = to go back; **prometió firmar el contrato esta mañana, pero a última hora se ha echado atrás** = he promised that he would sign the contract this morning, but he has gone back on his word at the last minute; **echarse a perder** = to be spoiled *o* spoilt; **los resultados de la compañía se echaron a perder por un último trimestre desastroso** = the company's results were spoiled by a disastrous last quarter

echazón *nm* **pecios y echazón** = flotsam and jetsam

ecológico, -ca *adj* ecological

economato *nm* (i) company store; (ii) cooperative store

econometría *nf* econometrics

economía *nf* **(a)** *(sistema económico)* economy; **el estado general de la economía** = the general state of the economy; **la economía del país está en ruina** = the country's economy is in ruins; **los efectos de la huelga sobre la economía se harán sentir durante mucho tiempo** = the strike will have durable effects on the economy; **inflar la economía** = to inflate the economy; **economía capitalista** = capitalist economy; **economía dirigida** = controlled economy; **economía de (libre) mercado** = free market economy; **economía madura** = mature economy; **economía de mínima intervención estatal** = laissez-faire economy; **economía mixta** = mixed economy; **economía negra** *o* **economía sumergida** = black economy; **economía de oferta** = supply side economics; **economía planificada** = planned economy; **una economía próspera** = a thriving economy **(b)** *(aspectos, estudios)* economics; **la economía de la planificación urbana** = the economics of town planning; **no entiendo la economía de la industria del carbón** = I do not understand the economics of the coal industry **(c)** *(ahorro)* saving *o* economy; **economías de escala** = economies of scale; **a la compañía le aguarda un periodo de economías** = the company is in for a period of retrenchment

económico, -ca *adj* **(a)** *(relativo a la economía)* economic; **bloqueo económico** = embargo; **ciclo económico** = economic cycle *o* trade cycle *o* business cycle; **la Comunidad Económica Europea (CEE)** = the European Economic Community (EEC); **crecimiento económico** = economic growth; **el país disfrutó de un periodo de crecimiento económico en la década de los 80** = the country enjoyed a period of economic growth in the eighties; **crisis económica** = economic crisis *o* economic depression; **el gobierno ha impuesto controles a la importación para solucionar la actual crisis económica** = the government has introduced import controls to solve the current economic crisis; **desarrollo económico** = economic development; **el desarrollo económico de la región ha cambiado totalmente desde que se encontró petróleo** = the economic development of the region has totally changed since oil was discovered there; **ejercicio económico** = financial *o* fiscal *o* tax year; **Espacio Económico Europeo (EEE)** = European Economic Area (EEA); **indicadores económicos** = economic indicators; **plan económico** = business plan; **planificación económica** = economic planning; **planificador económico** = economic planner; **la política económica del gobierno** = the government's economic policy; **pronosticador económico** *o* **especialista en previsiones económicas** = economic forecaster; **sanciones económicas** = economic sanctions; **las naciones occidentales impusieron sanciones económicas al país** = the western nations imposed economic sanctions on the country; **el sistema económico de la nación** = the country's economic system; **la situación económica** = the economic situation; **tendencias económicas** = economic trends **(b)** *(de bajo consumo)* economical; **un coche económico** = an economical car; **utilización económica de los recursos** = economical use of resources **(c)** inexpensive *o* cheap *o* economical; **precios económicos** = budget prices; **tamaño económico** = economy size **(d)** *(viaje)* **clase económica** = economy class; **viajar en clase económica** = to travel economy class **(e)** *(rentable)* economic; **el piso se alquila a un precio económico** = the flat is let at an economic rent; **no resulta económico que la empresa tenga su propio almacén** = it is hardly economic for the company to run its own warehouse

◊ **económicamente** *adv* **(a)** *(comercialmente)* economically *o* from a commercial point of view; **no viable económicamente** = not commercially viable **(b)** *(barato)* cheaply; **el representante vivía económicamente en su casa y reclamaba unos gastos de hotel elevados** = the salesman was living cheaply at home and claiming a high hotel bill on his expenses

economista *nmf* economist; **economista agrícola** = agricultural economist

economizar *vt* to economize (on) *o* to cut down (on) *o* to save on; **la oficina intenta economizar en el consumo de electricidad** = the office is trying to cut down on electricity consumption; **economizar en gasolina** = to economize on petrol

ECU *o* **ecu** *nm (unidad monetaria europea)* ecu *o* ECU; **un ecu** = one ecu

> Esta compensación será la misma para todos los cereales, excepto el trigo duro, en donde se establece una ayuda suplementaria de trescientos ecus por hectárea
> **Actualidad Económica**

Ecuador *nm* Ecuador

◊ **ecuatoriano, -na** *adj y n* Ecuadorian
NOTA: capital: **Quito;** moneda: **sucre ecuatoriano (S/.)** = Ecuadorian sucre (S/.)

edad *nf* age; **límite de edad** *o* **edad máxima** = age limit; **existe un límite de edad de treinta y cinco años para el puesto de comprador** = there is an age limit of thirty-five on the post of buyer; **mayor de edad** = adult; **alcanzar la mayoría de edad** = to come of age; **menor de edad** = young *o* under age; **de mediana edad** = middle-aged

edición *nf* **(a)** *(publicación)* publication *o* edition; **anunciaremos el puesto en la edición de la mañana** = we shall advertise the post in the morning edition; **he comprado la edición de bolsillo (b)** *(acción de editar)* publishing

edificación *nf* construction *o* building; **terreno para la edificación** = building site; **el terreno ha de venderse con el permiso de edificación** = the land is to be sold with planning permission

edificar *vt* to build; **terreno para edificar** = building site

edificio *nm* building *o* premises *o* property *o* unit; **un edificio de oficinas** = a block of offices *o* an office block; **edificio público** = public building; **el edificio se terminó antes de lo previsto** = the building was completed ahead of schedule; **han renovado el entorno del viejo edificio comercial** = they have redeveloped the site of the old office building; **te esperaré enfrente del edificio de la Cámara de Comercio** = I'll meet you in front of the Chamber of Commerce Building; **siempre hay un médico en el edificio** = there is a doctor on the premises at all times; **tenemos varios edificios en venta en el centro de la ciudad** = we have several properties for sale in the centre of the town; **ocupación de un edificio** = occupation of a building; **dado el aumento de producción, nos hemos trasladado a un edificio más grande en el mismo polígono** = as production has increased, we have moved to a larger unit on the same estate

editar *vt* to publish; **la compañía edita seis revistas para el mercado empresarial** = the company publishes six magazines for the business market

editor, -ra *n* publisher *o* editor

editorial 1 *adj* editorial **2** *nf* publishing house *o* publisher; **trabaja para una editorial conocida** = she works for a well-known publishing house *o* for a well-known publisher **3** *nm (en un periódico, revista)* editorial *o* leading article

> puso sobre la mesa hasta 60.000 millones de pesetas por el 30% de nuestra editorial
> **Cambio 16**

educado, -da 1 *adj* polite **2** *pp de* EDUCAR

educar *vt* to educate

EEE = ESPACIO ECONOMICO EUROPEO European Economic Area (EEA)

EE UU = ESTADOS UNIDOS DE AMERICA United States of America (USA)

efectivo, -va 1 *adj* **(a)** *(real)* effective; actual; **hacer efectivo** = (i) to carry something out; (ii) to cash; **los plazos se harán efectivos al final de cada trimestre** = the instalments are payable at the end of each quarter; **la renta del primer trimestre se hará efectiva por adelantado** = the first quarter's rent is payable in advance; **control efectivo de una compañía** = effective control of a company; **rendimiento efectivo** = effective yield **(b)** *(moneda)* real *o* actual; **dinero efectivo** = hard cash **(c)** *(eficaz)* effective **2** *nm* cash *o* specie; **efectivo en caja** = cash in hand; **en efectivo** = in cash; **hacer una oferta en efectivo** *o* **ofrecer pago en efectivo** = to make a cash offer *o* bid *o* to offer to pay cash; **pagar en efectivo** = to pay cash down; **pago en efectivo** = cash payment *o* settlement in cash *o* cash settlement; **venta en efectivo** = cash sale *o* cash transaction; **tenemos 2.000.000 de ptas. en efectivo** = we have 2m pesetas in hand

efecto *nm* **(a)** *(consecuencia, resultado)* effect; **efecto indirecto** = spinoff; **uno de los efectos indirectos del programa de investigación ha sido el desarrollo del automóvil eléctrico** = one of the spinoffs of the research programme has been the development of the electric car; **efecto secundario** = knock-on effect *o* side effect; **la subida de sueldos tuvo como efecto un aumento en la productividad** = the effect of the pay increase was to raise productivity levels; **cuantificar el efecto de algo** = to quantify the effect of something **(b)** *(entrar en vigor)* **en efecto** = in fact; **surtir efecto** = to come into effect *o* to take effect; **los términos del contrato surten efecto a partir del 1 de enero** = the terms of the contract take effect *o* come into effect from January 1st; **los precios suben un 10% con efecto a partir del 1 de enero** = prices are increased 10% with effect from January 1st; **se fechó la factura con efecto retroactivo al 1 de enero** = the invoice was antedated to January 1st **(c)** *(bienes)* **efectos personales** = personal effects *o* property **(d)** **efectos** = bills *o* securities; **efectos de favor** = accommodation bills; **efectos por cobrar** = receivables; **efectos por pagar** = bills payable; **efectos públicos** = government bonds; **efectos redescontables** = eligible bill *o* paper

> ni tan siquiera descontó en su totalidad el efecto del encarecimiento de los productos petrolíferos del ejercicio anterior debido a la crisis del Golfo
> **Tiempo**

efectuar *vt* to carry out *o* to effect; **el pago no se efectuará hasta que el contrato haya sido firmado** = payment will not be made *o* will be held back until the contract has been signed

eficacia *nf* effectiveness *o* efficiency; **dudo de la eficacia de la publicidad en televisión** = I doubt the effectiveness of television advertising; **con un alto grado de eficacia** = highly effective; **un experto en eficacia** = an efficiency expert

eficaz *adj* effective *o* efficient; **la manera más eficaz de vender** = the most effective way of selling

eficiencia *nf* effectiveness *o* efficiency; **exposición de eficiencia comercial** = business efficiency exhibition

◊ **eficiente** *adj* **(a)** *(eficaz)* efficient; **necesita una secretaria eficiente que lo atienda** = he needs an efficient secretary to look after him; **el eficiente funcionamiento de un sistema** = the efficient working of a system **(b)** *(rápido)* rapid *o* streamlined

◊ **eficientemente** *adv* efficiently; **organizó la reunión de ventas muy eficientemente** = she organized the sales conference very efficiently

podría resultar rentable el adquirir
empresas privadas que carecieran de una
gestión eficiente de capital para su
expansión
España Económica

Egipto *nm* Egypt

◊ **egipcio, -cia** *adj y n* Egyptian
NOTA: capital: **El Cairo** (= Cairo); moneda: **libra egipcia (LE)** = Egyptian pound (E£)

ej. = EJEMPLO e.g.; **el contrato tiene validez en algunos países (ej. Francia y Bélgica) pero en otros no** = the contract is valid in some countries (e.g. France and Belgium) but not in others

ejecución *nf* **(a)** *(aplicación)* enforcement *o* execution *o* implementation; **ejecución de un pedido** = execution of an order; **aplazamiento de la ejecución de una sentencia** = stay of execution **(b)** **trabajo en curso de ejecución** = work in progress

ejecutar *vt* to execute *o* to implement; **hacer ejecutar** = to enforce; **ejecutar una hipoteca** = to foreclose on a mortgaged property

ejecutivo, -va 1 *adj* executive; **comisión ejecutiva** = executive committee; **director ejecutivo** *o* **consejero ejecutivo** = executive director; **poder ejecutivo** = executive powers **2** *n* executive; **ejecutivo auxiliar** *o* **ejecutivo subalterno** = junior executive *o* junior manager; **ejecutivo en formación** = management trainee; **ejecutivo principal** = senior executive *o* senior manager; **ejecutivo de ventas** = sales executive; **búsqueda de ejecutivos** = executive search; **jefe ejecutivo** = chief executive **3** *nm* *(política)* the Executive

en países de honda tradición democrática
existen a veces conflictos entre la
autoridad monetaria y señaladas áreas del
ejecutivo
España Económica

el 90% de las normas vigentes han sido
elaboradas por el ejecutivo
Cambio 16

la clave consiste en volver a motivar a los
ejecutivos que ya existen en la empresa;
si se consigue, no es preciso cambiar a
toda la dirección
España Económica

ejemplar 1 *adj* model *o* exemplary **2** *nm* **(a)** *(ejemplo)* example **(b)** *(publicaciones)* copy; **ejemplar gratuito** = free copy; **lo leí en el ejemplar del 'Fortune' de la oficina** = I read it in the office copy of 'Fortune'; **¿dónde está mi ejemplar de la guía telefónica?** = where is my copy of the telephone directory?

ejemplo *nm* example *o* instance; **por ejemplo** = for example; **el gobierno quiere animar las exportaciones y, por ejemplo, concede créditos libres a los exportadores** = the government wants to encourage exports, and, for example, it gives free credit to exporters

ejercer *vt* **(a)** *(ejercitar)* to exercise *o* to practise; **ejercer el derecho de opción** = to exercise an option; **la presidenta ejerció su derecho de veto para bloquear la moción** = the chairwoman exercised her veto to block the motion **(b)** **ejercer una profesión** = to practise a profession; **ejercer un negocio** = to run *o* to manage a business

ejercicio *nm* exercise; **ejercicio del derecho de opción** = exercise of an option; **ejercicio económico** *o* **ejercicio financiero** = financial year *o* fiscal year *o* tax year; **ejercicio fiscal** = tax year; **cierre del ejercicio** = year end; **el departamento de contabilidad ha empezado a trabajar en las cuentas de cierre del ejercicio** = the accounts department has started work on the year-end accounts; **cuenta de ejercicio** = trading account; **pérdida de ejercicio** = trading loss

en el primer trimestre del presente
ejercicio se produjo una pérdida de
empleos del 2,7% en el sector industrial
Mercado

es de esperar una recuperación lenta y
pausada que empiece a alegrar de nuevo a la
parroquia inversora, aunque sin grandes
alardes, por lo menos hasta bien entrado
el próximo ejercicio
Tiempo

ejercitar *vt* to exercise

El Salvador *nm* El Salvador

◊ **salvadoreño, -ña** *adj y n* Salvadorian
NOTA: capital: **San Salvador;** moneda: **colón salvadoreño (C)** = Salvadorian colon (C)

elaboración *nf* **(a)** *(preparación)* making **(b)** *(informática)* processing; **elaboración de datos** = data processing

elaborar *vt* **(a)** *(fabricar)* to make *o* to produce *o* to manufacture *o* to work **(b)** *(informática)* to process; **elaborar cifras** = to process figures; **nuestro departamento de contabilidad está elaborando las cifras de ventas** = the sales figures are being processed by our accounts department **(c)** *(materia prima)* to process (raw materials)

elasticidad *nf* elasticity; **elasticidad de la oferta y la demanda** = elasticity of supply and demand

elástico, -ca *adj* elastic

elección *nf* **(a)** *(selección)* election; **la elección de los directivos de una asociación** = the election of officers of an association; **la elección de consejeros por parte de los accionistas** = the election of directors by the shareholders; **vencer en una**

elección = to win an election **(b)** *(política)*
elecciones generales = general election **(c)** choice;
elección de un momento *o* **de una fecha** = choosing
of a time *o* of a date

> se equivocan los que piensan que el
> gobierno tomará una serie de medidas
> económicas después de las elecciones
> **España Económica**

electo, -ta *adj* -elect; **es la presidenta electa** =
she is the president-elect

electricidad *nf* electricity; **nuestra factura de
electricidad ha subido considerablemente este
trimestre** = our electricity bill has increased
considerably this quarter; **los gastos de electricidad
son una parte importante de nuestros gastos
generales** = electricity costs are an important factor
in our overheads

eléctrico, -ca *adj* electric *o* electrical; **contador
eléctrico** = electricity meter; **una máquina de
escribir eléctrica** = an electric typewriter; **los
ingenieros están tratando de reparar un fallo
eléctrico** = the engineers are trying to repair an
electrical fault; **suministro eléctrico** = electricity
supply; **ha habido un corte del suministro
eléctrico esta mañana, por lo que los ordenadores
no han podido funcionar** = the electricity was cut
off this morning, so the computers could not work

electrodoméstico 1 *adj* household *o*
electrical; **aparatos electrodomésticos** = electrical
appliances *o* labour-saving devices **2** *nmpl*
electrodomésticos = household appliances *o* white
goods

electrónica *nf* electronics; **un especialista** *o* **un
experto en electrónica** = an electronics specialist *o*
expert

electrónico, -ca *adj* electronic; **agenda
electrónica** = electronic *o* personal organizer; **la
industria electrónica** = the electronics industry;
ingeniero electrónico = electronics engineer;
monedero electrónico = plastic money

elegibilidad *nf* eligibility

elegir *vt* **(a)** *(escoger)* to choose *o* to select *o* to
pick; **elija a su gusto** = take your pick; **había
buenos aspirantes entre los que elegir** = there were
several good candidates to choose from; **eligieron a
la única mujer que solicitó el cargo de director de
ventas** = they chose the only woman applicant as
sales director; **el presidente le eligió para un
ascenso** = he was picked out for promotion by the
chairman; **tiene que dar a los clientes tiempo
suficiente para elegir** = you must give the
customers plenty of time to choose; **la asociación ha
elegido Barcelona para su próxima reunión** = the
Association has selected Barcelona for its next
meeting; **el consejo de administración eligió al
director financiero como sucesor del director
gerente** = the board picked the finance director to
succeed the retiring MD **(b)** *(votación)* to elect;
elegir a los directivos de una asociación = to elect
the officers of an association; **fue elegida
presidenta** = she was elected president

elemento *nm* **(a)** *(cosa)* element *o* factor;
elementos esenciales = essentials **(b)** *(persona)*
individual; **cuenta con buenos elementos como
colaboradores** = his collarorators are good people

elevado, -da *adj* high; **precios elevados** =
inflated prices; **los gastos generales elevados
aumentan el precio unitario** = high overhead costs
increase the unit price

elevar *vt* to lift *o* to raise; **elevar el tipo de interés**
= to raise the rate of interest

◊ **elevarse** *vr* to rise *o* to go up *o* to amount to; **el
total se eleva a** = the total amounts to *o* comes to

eliminar *vt* **(a)** *(excluir)* to eliminate; **eliminar
defectos del sistema** = to eliminate defects in the
system; **el uso de un ordenador debería eliminar
toda posibilidad de error** = using a computer
should eliminate all possibility of error **(b)** *(anular)*
to write off **(c)** *(informática)* **eliminar errores** = to
debug

eludir *vt* to avoid *o* to escape; **eludir un acuerdo** *o*
un contrato = avoidance of an agreement *o* of a
contract; **eludir una prohibición** = to beat a ban

elusión *nf* avoidance *o* evasion; **elusión de
impuestos** *o* **elusión fiscal** = tax avoidance

embalado, -da *adj* wrapped; **embalado al vacío**
= shrink-wrapped

embalador, -ra *n* packer

embalaje *nm* **(a)** *(acción)* packing *o* packaging;
embalaje al vacío = shrink-wrapping *o* vacuum
wrapping; **gastos de embalaje** = packing charges;
(gastos de) franqueo y embalaje = postage and
packing (p & p); **material de embalaje** = packaging
material; **¿cuánto cuesta el embalaje?** = what is the
cost of the packing?; **el embalaje está incluido en el
precio** = packing is included in the price **(b)**
(material) pack *o* packaging; **embalaje de cartón** =
mailer; **embalaje de exposición** = display pack;
embalaje defectuoso = faulty packaging; **embalaje
hermético** = airtight packaging; **embalaje plano
(de muebles para montar)** = flat pack; **embalaje de
plástico tipo burbuja** = blister pack *o* bubble pack;
embalaje no retornable = non-returnable packing;
embalaje vacío *o* **ficticio (para exposición)** =
dummy pack

embalar *vt* to pack *o* to bale *o* to wrap; **volver a
embalar** *o* **embalar de nuevo** = to repack;
embalado herméticamente = packed in airtight
packing; **embalar mercancías** = to package goods;
embalar mercancías en cajas de cartón = to pack
goods into cartons; **el ordenador se embala en
poliestireno expandido antes de ser expedido** =
the computer is packed in expanded polystyrene
before being shipped; **caja de embalar** = packing
case

embandejar *vt* to palletize; **cajas de cartón
embandejadas** = palletized cartons

embarazoso, -sa *adj* awkward *o* embarrassing;
**el consejo de administración está intentando
resolver el embarazoso problema del hijo del
director gerente** = the board is trying to solve the
awkward problem of the managing director's son

embarcadero *nm* wharf *o* pier *o* quay;
trabajador *o* **administrador del embarcadero** =
wharfinger

embarcar *vt* *(personas)* to embark; *(mercancías)*
to ship

◊ **embarcarse** *vr* **(a)** *(avión, barco)* to board *o* to embark *o* to go on board; **los pasajeros se embarcaron en Bilbao** = the passengers embarked at Bilbao **(b) embarcarse en** = to embark on; **la compañía se ha embarcado en un programa de expansión** = the company has embarked on an expansion programme

embargado, da *n* garnishee

embargador, -ra *n* sequestrator

embargar *vt* **(a)** *(frenar)* to restrain **(b)** *(prohibir)* to embargo **(c)** *(confiscar)* to impound *o* to seize *o* to sequester *o* to sequestrate *o* to distress; **embargar un bien hipotecado (por impago)** = to foreclose (on a mortgaged property)

embargo *nm* **(a)** *(bloqueo económico)* embargo; **imponer un embargo comercial a un país** = to lay *o* put an embargo on trade with a country; **levantar un embargo** = to lift an embargo; **el ministro ha levantado el embargo a la venta de equipos informáticos** = the minister has lifted *o* removed the embargo on the sale of computer equipment **(b)** *(retención)* sequestration *o* distress; **auto** *o* **sentencia de embargo** = garnishee order *o* garnishment; **orden de embargo** = distress warrant; **el tribunal ordenó el embargo de los fondos de la compañía** = the court ordered the company's funds to be seized

embarque *nm* **(a)** *(acción de embarcar)* embarkation *o* boarding; **puerto de embarque** = port of embarkation; **sala de embarque** = departure lounge; **tarjeta de embarque** = boarding card *o* boarding pass *o* embarkation card **(b)** *(carga)* lading; **conocimiento de embarque** = bill of lading

embaucar *vt* to trick *o* to fiddle

emblema *nm* emblem *o* symbol; **su emblema publicitario es un oso** = their advertising symbol is a bear

embolsar *vt* to pocket; **embolsamos una buena suma** = we pocketed a considerable amount of money *o* a tidy sum

◊ **embolsarse** *vr* to pocket; **se embolsó una gran parte del dinero de la compañía** = he pocketed a great deal of the company's money

embotellamiento *nm* **(a)** *(circulación)* traffic jam **(b)** *(sistema productivo)* bottleneck

embrollar *vt* to confuse *o* to muddle; **plantear el problema del IVA no hará más que embrollar el asunto** = to introduce the problem of VAT will only confuse the issue

emergencia *nf* **(a)** *(urgencia)* emergency; **tomar medidas de emergencia** = to take emergency measures *o* to take crisis measures; **la compañía tuvo que tomar medidas de emergencia para no perder más dinero** = the company had to take emergency measures to stop losing money; **planes de emergencia** = contingency plans **(b) salida** *o* **escalera de emergencia** = fire escape

Emiratos Arabes Unidos (EAU) *nmpl* United Arab Emirates (UAE)
NOTA: capital: **Abu Dhabi;** moneda: **dirham EAU (Dh)** = UAE dirham (Dh)

emisión *nf* **(a)** *(finanzas)* issue; **emisión de acciones** = share issue; **emisión de nuevas acciones** = issue of new shares; **departamento de emisión de nuevas acciones** = new issues department; **suscribir una nueva emisión de acciones** = to subscribe to a new share issue; **emisión de derechos** = rights issue; **emisión gratuita** = bonus issue *o* scrip issue; **emisión de obligaciones** = issue of debentures *o* debenture issue; **emisión de títulos del Estado** = issue of gilt-edged stock; *UK* tap stock; **precio de emisión** = issue price **(b)** *(comunicaciones)* broadcast *o* broadcasting; **emisión publicitaria** = commercial

las televisiones competitivas empezarán a distraer dinero de la emisión de acontecimientos de gran difusión para dedicarlo a otros programas de difusión limitada
Actualidad Económica

emisor, -ra 1 *adj* issuing; **banco emisor** *o* **casa emisora** = issuing bank *o* issuing house **2** *nm* transmitter **3** *nf* radio station *o* broadcasting station

los optimistas esperan que la competencia entre las emisoras por satélite y las televisiones por cable acabe en una espiral disparatada de ofertas por la retransmisión de acontecimientos deportivos
Actualidad Económica

emitir *vt* **(a)** to issue; **emitir acciones de una nueva sociedad** = to issue shares in a new company; **emitir un empréstito** = to float a loan; **emitir de nuevo** = to reissue **(b) emitieron seis espacios publicitarios que recomendaban las vacaciones en España** = they ran six commercials plugging holidays in Spain

emolumento *nm* emoluments *o* fee *o* honorarium; **emolumento de los directivos** = director's fees

empacar *vt* to pack *o* to bale

empadronar *vt* to register taxpayers *o* to register in a census

empaquetado, -da *adj* wrapped; **empaquetado al vacío** = shrink-wrapped

empaquetador, -ra *n* packer

empaquetar *vt* to pack *o* to parcel (up); **volver a empaquetar** *o* **empaquetar de nuevo** = to repack; **empaquetar una partida de libros** = to parcel up a consignment of books; **empaquetar mercancías** = to package goods *o* to parcel goods *o* to do up goods into parcels; **empaquetar previamente para la venta** = to prepack *o* to prepackage; **la fruta viene ya empaquetada en bandejas de plástico** = the fruit are prepacked *o* prepackaged in plastic trays

empeñar *vt* to pawn *o* to pledge; **empeñar un reloj** = to pawn a watch

◊ **empeñarse** *vr* **(a)** *(endeudarse)* to get into debt; **tuvo que empeñarse para comenzar el negocio** = he had to borrow money to start his business **(b)** *(insistir en algo)* to insist *o* to persist; **se ha empeñado en abrir una tienda de objetos de segunda mano** = he is determined to open a second-hand shop

empeño *nm* **(a)** *(prenda)* pledge; **papeleta de**

empeño = pawn ticket **(b)** *(insistencia)* determination

empeorar 1 *vt* to make worse **2** *vi* to get worse *o* to decline; **la economía empeoró con el último gobierno** = the economy declined during the last government; **la situación está empeorando** = the situation is getting worse

◊ **empeorarse** *vr* to get worse

empezar *vt/i* to begin *o* to start; **empezar un negocio desde cero** = to start a business from cold *o* from scratch; **empezar a producir** = to start to produce *o* to come on stream; **la empresa empezó a perder su cuota de mercado** = the company began to lose its market share; **empezó a redactar el informe que los accionistas habían pedido** = he began to draft the report which the shareholders had asked for; **el informe empieza con la lista de los directores y las acciones que posee cada uno** = the report begins with a list of the directors and their shareholdings; **'buenos días señores, si están todos presentes, puede empezar la reunión'** = 'good morning, gentlemen, if everyone is here, the meeting can start'

emplazamiento *nm* **(a)** *(sitio)* site *o* location; **emplazamineto de difícil acceso** = an awkward site *o* location; **emplazamiento de una obra** = work site; **emplazamiento de un anuncio** = ad position *o* position of an ad **(b)** *(citación judicial)* summons

empleado, -da 1 *n* **(a)** *(trabajador)* employee *o* worker *o* member of the staff; **empleado, -da a tiempo completo** = full-time employee *o* full-timer; **empleado, -da a tiempo parcial** = part-time employee *o* part-timer; **contratar nuevos empleados** = to take on new employees; **despedir a un empleado** = to dismiss an employee; **empleados y patronos** = employees and employers; **las relaciones entre la dirección y los empleados han mejorado** = relations between management and employees have improved; **ser un empleado fijo** = to be on the staff *o* to be a member of staff *o* a staff member; **los empleados son en su mayoría chicas de veinte a treinta años de edad** = the staff are mostly girls between twenty and thirty years of age; **programa de oferta de acciones a los empleados** = employee share ownership programme (ESOP); **los empleados de la empresa tienen derecho a tomar parte en un plan de participación en los beneficios** = employees of the firm are eligible to join a profit-sharing scheme **(b)** *(empleado de oficina)* = office worker *o* clerical worker *o* white-collar worker; **empleado de banco** = bank clerk **2** *pp de* EMPLEAR

> el empleado del banco, al recibir el talón, entrega a cambio varios talones bancarios al portador por la suma del talón que recibe
> **Cambio 16**

emplear *vt* **(a)** *(incorporar a la plantilla)* to employ *o* to take on (staff) *o* to hire; **emplear de nuevo** = to re-employ; **emplear más personal** = to take on more staff; **tiene tendencia a emplear chicas jóvenes** = he tends to employ young girls; **volver a emplear a obreros despedidos** = to take back dismissed workers; **emplear a alguien a prueba** = to take someone on probation; **emplear a veinte personas** *o* **a veinte nuevos empleados** = to employ twenty staff *o* twenty new staff; **emplean a**

trabajadores independientes para la mayor parte de su trabajo = they use freelancers for most of their work **(b)** *(dedicar)* to spend; **empleamos mucho tiempo en mantener nuestra lista de direcciones al día** = we spend a lot of time keeping our mailing list up to date; **tuvimos que emplear la mitad del presupuesto de caja para equipar la nueva fábrica** = we had to spend half our cash budget on equipping the new factory **(c)** *(usar)* to use; **emplearon el dinero para arreglar la oficina** = they used the money to refurbish the office

empleo *nm* **(a)** *(uso)* use *o* utilization; **empleo de la capacidad** = capacity utilization; *(instrucciones)* **modo de empleo** = directions for use **(b)** *(trabajo)* **empleo estacional** = seasonal employment employment *o* work; **empleo eventual** = temporary employment; **empleo fijo** *o* **permanente** = permanent employment *o* staff appointment *o* secure job; **tiene un empleo fijo** = she is in permanent employment; **tener un empleo a jornada completa** = to be in full-time employment; **no tener empleo** = to be out of work; **formación en el empleo** = on-the-job training; **facilitar otro empleo a alguien** = to find someone alternative employment; **sin empleo** = out of work; **su empleo se terminó** = his employment was terminated; **empleo remunerado** = paid work *o* gainful employment; **que ejerce un empleo remunerado** = gainfully employed; **no tiene un empleo remunerado** = he is not gainfully employed; **su empleo le exige viajar mucho** = his work involves a lot of travelling; **agencia de empleo** *o* **oficina de empleo** = job centre *o* employment office *o* bureau *o* agency; **pleno empleo** = full employment; **programa de creación de empleo** = job creation scheme; **seguridad de empleo** *o* **empleo asegurado** = security of employment; **solicitud de empleo** = job application *o* application for a job **(c)** *(puesto)* job *o* post *o* appointment; **buscar empleo** = to look for a job; **está buscando empleo en la industria de ordenadores** = he is looking for a job in the computer industry; **dejar un empleo** = to give up one's job; **rechazó tres empleos antes de aceptar el que le ofrecimos** = she turned down three places before accepting the one we offered; **perdió su empleo cuando la fábrica cerró** = he lost his job when the factory closed

> digan lo que digan los datos oficiales de paro, en ciertos sectores y regiones se está llegando a situaciones muy próximas al pleno empleo
> **España Económica**

> en España, el 36,2% de los más de dos millones de parados lleva más de dos años buscando empleo
> **Tiempo**

> su actividad da empleo directamente a más de 5.000 personas, y la reinversión de su beneficio es aprovechada, de un modo u otro, por todos los ciudadanos de la región
> **Actualidad Económica**

> habrá poca creación de empleo, pues no hay que olvidar que el paro nunca ha disminuido con tasas de crecimiento del PIB inferiores al 3%
> **Actualidad Económica**

emprendedor, -ra 1 *adj* enterprising *o* go-ahead; **es un tipo muy emprendedor** = he is a very go-ahead type **2** *nm* entrepreneur

emprender *vt* **(a)** *(negocio)* to undertake; **emprendió un negocio en sociedad con su hijo** = she went into business in partnership with her son **(b)** *(viaje)* to set out on

empresa *nf* **(a)** *(compañía)* company *o* business *o* enterprise *o* firm; **empresa asociada** = associated company; **empresa comercial** = commercial undertaking; **una empresa editorial importante** = an important publishing firm; **empresa estatal** = a state enterprise; **los altos cargos de las empresas estatales son nombrados por el gobierno** = bosses of state enterprises are appointed by the government; **empresa familiar** = family company; **empresa fantasma** = dummy corporation *o* firm; **empresa inmobiliaria** = property company; **empresa manufacturera** = manufacturing firm; **empresa mediana** = medium-sized company; **empresa pequeña** = small company; **empresa privada** = private enterprise; **el proyecto está financiado en su totalidad por la empresa privada** = the project is completely funded by private enterprise; **trabaja para una empresa de relaciones públicas** = he works for a PR company; **empresa subsidiaria** = subsidiary company; **es dueño de una pequeña empresa de reparación de coches** = he owns a small car repair business; **una empresa de tractores *o* aviones *o* chocolate** = a tractor *o* aircraft *o* chocolate company; **empresa de transportes** = freight company *o* freighter; **beneficios de la empresa** = corporate profits; **un coche de la empresa** = company car; **todos los coches de nuestra empresa son alquilados** = all our company cars are leased; **comité de empresa** = works committee *o* works council; **las grandes empresas** = big business; **las pequeñas empresas** = small businesses; **libre empresa** = free enterprise; **plan de pensiones de la empresa** = occupational pension scheme; **entrar *o* ingresar en una empresa** = to join a firm; **dirige una empresa desde su casa** = she runs a business from her home; **me han dicho que la empresa está en venta** = I hear the company has been put on the market **(b)** *(negocio con riesgo)* venture; **ha lanzado una nueva empresa - una tienda de ordenadores** = she has started a new venture - a computer shop; **empresa conjunta *o* mixta** = joint venture

la empresa española no tiene el tamaño adecuado para competir en la Europa única
España Económica

se han creado empresas mixtas tan irrelevantes como una para la venta de productos extranjeros, exclusivamente a extranjeros y en divisa convertible
España Económica

empresarial *adj* managerial *o* entrepreneurial; **una decisión empresarial** = an entrepreneurial decision; **escuela de (estudios) empresariales** = business school; **organización empresarial** = employers' organization *o* association; **planificación empresarial** = corporate planning; **el sector empresarial** = the business sector; **quebró después de dos años de actividad empresarial** = he went bankrupt after two years in business

el mundo empresarial español más combativo ha vivido con la sensación de que el país está en venta
Cambio 16

empresario, -ria *n* (i) employer; (ii) businessman, -woman; **es una buena empresaria** = she's a good businesswoman; **un pequeño empresario** = a small businessman

en todas las encuestas que dentro o fuera del país se vienen realizando en estos años, los empresarios españoles muestran una auténtica obsesión por agruparse o fusionarse
España Económica

empréstito *nm* loan; **empréstito convertible en acciones** = convertible loan stock; **empréstito estatal** = government loan; **rescate de un empréstito** = redemption (of a loan)

empuje *nm* push *o* drive

encabezamiento *nm* head *o* heading; **encabezamiento de factura** = billhead

encabezar *vt* **(a)** *(dirigir)* to lead; **encabezará la misión comercial a Nigeria** = she will lead the trade mission to Nigeria **(b)** *(ir en cabeza)* to head *o* to be at the top of a list; **el nombre del presidente encabeza la lista del personal** = the chairman's name comes first on the staff list; **las dos principales compañías petrolíferas encabezan la lista del mercado de valores** = the two largest oil companies head the list of stock market results

encajar *vt/i* to fit *o* to match *o* to correspond to; **el informe anual no encaja con los datos recibidos** = the annual report doesn't match the information received

encajonado, -da *adj* boxed

encarecer *vt* to make more expensive *o* to put the price up

◊ **encarecerse** *vr* to become dearer *o* more expensive

◊ **encarecimiento** *nm* price increase *o* rise in price

encargado, -da 1 *adj* commissioned; **aún no se ha terminado el trabajo encargado** = the work which was commissioned has not been completed yet **2** *n* person in charge *o* foreman *o* forewoman *o* manager; **encargado de la facturación** = invoice clerk **3** *pp de* ENCARGAR

encargar *vt* **(a)** *(confiar)* to commission; **encargar algo a alguien** = to entrust someone with something *o* to entrust something to someone; **encargar trabajo a trabajadores autónomos** = to put work out to freelancers; **encargamos trabajo a varios especialistas independientes** = we freelance work out to several specialists; **encargamos todo el trabajo de mecanografía a una agencia** = we put all our typing out to a bureau **(b)** *(pedir)* to order; **encargaron un nuevo Mercedes para el director gerente** = they ordered a new Mercedes for the managing director

◊ **encargarse de** *vr* to undertake *o* to handle; **encargarse de algo** = to manage *o* to look after something; **¿puedes encargarte de cobrar las**

facturas? = can you collect the bills?; **se encargó de la nueva máquina** = he looked after the new machine; **el grupo sigue una política de compras descentralizadas por la que cada departamento se encarga de sus propias compras** = the group has a policy of decentralized purchasing where each division is responsible for its own purchasing

encargo *nm* **(a)** *(cometido)* job; **el astillero acometerá un gran encargo en agosto** = the shipyard has a big job starting in August **(b)** *(pedido)* order; **artículos disponibles sólo por encargo** = items available to order only; **creemos que su encargo se ha perdido en el correo** = we are afraid your order has been lost in the post

encarte *nm* insert; **encarte dentro de una revista** = an insert in a magazine mailing *o* a magazine insert

encauzar *vt* to channel *o* to canalize

encendedor *nm* lighter

encender *vt* to switch on

enchufar *vt* to plug (in); **el ordenador no estaba enchufado** = the computer was not plugged in

◊ **enchufe** *nm* **(a)** *(dispositivo eléctrico)* plug; **la impresora va provista de un enchufe** = the printer is supplied with a plug **(b)** *(influencia)* contact; **consiguió el trabajo a través de un enchufe** = he got the job through contacts

encierro *nm (manifestación)* sit-in

encogimiento *nm* shrinkage

encolado, -da *adj* gummed

encontrar *vt* to find; **encontrar apoyo para un proyecto** = to find backing for a project; **encontrar tiempo** = to find time; **tenemos que encontrar tiempo para visitar el nuevo club de deportes del personal** = we must find time to visit the new staff sports club; **el presidente nunca encuentra tiempo suficiente para jugar al golf** = the chairman never finds enough time to play golf; **el presidente trata de encontrar tiempo para una partida de golf todas las tardes** = the chairman tries to fit in a game of golf every afternoon; **encontrar una laguna fiscal** = to find a tax loophole

◊ **encontrarse** *vr* to meet; **encontrarse con** = to run into; **no encontrarse con** = to miss; **los dos estaban en la misma ciudad pero no se encontraron** = both of them were in the same town but they missed each other

encuadernador, -ra *n* binder

encuadrador, -ra *n (informática)* spreadsheet

encubrimiento *nm* concealment; **encubrimiento de activos** = concealment of assets

encuentro *nm* encounter *o* meeting; **un encuentro fortuito** = a chance meeting

encuesta *nf* **(a)** *(formulario)* questionnaire **(b)**

(investigación) survey **(c)** *(sondeo de opinión)* opinion poll; **antes de empezar el nuevo servicio, la compañía realizó encuestas de opinión por todo el país** = before starting the new service, the company carried out nationwide opinion polls

> en todas las encuestas que dentro o fuera del país se vienen realizando en estos años, los empresarios españoles muestran una auténtica obsesión por agruparse o fusionarse
>
> *España Económica*

endémico, -ca *adj* chronic *o* endemic; **situación de paro endémico** = chronic unemployment

endeudado, -da *adj* indebted; **estar endeudado con** = to be in debt to *o* indebted to; **está fuertemente endeudado** = he is heavily in debt; **país endeudado** = debtor nation

endeudamiento *nm* borrowing *o* indebtedness

> tiene un fuerte endeudamiento de más de 2.000 millones de pesetas, y ha venido experimentando un descenso considerable de sus beneficios
>
> *El País*

> su nivel de endeudamiento con respecto a sus recursos propios es muy conservador, y tiene una amplia esfera de expansión
>
> *España Económica*

endeudarse *vr* to get *o* to run into debt

endosante *nmf* endorser *o* backer of a bill

endosar *vt* to endorse *o* to back; **endosar una letra** *o* **un cheque** = to endorse a bill *o* a cheque

endosatario, -ia *n* endorsee

endoso *nm* endorsement; *US* indorsement; **póliza ampliada por endoso** = policy extended by endorsement; **endoso condicional** = qualified endorsement

energía *nf* **(a)** *(vigor)* energy *o* drive; **no tiene energía para ser un buen vendedor** = he hasn't the energy to be a good salesman; **desperdiciaron sus energías intentando vender coches en el mercado alemán** = they wasted their energy on trying to sell cars in the German market; **tiene mucha energía** = he has a lot of drive **(b)** *(electricidad, etc.)* energy; **energía eléctrica** = electricity; **energía eólica** = wind energy; **energía nuclear** = nuclear energy; **energía solar** = solar energy; **apagamos las luces cuando las habitaciones están vacías para ahorrar energía** = we try to save energy by switching off the lights when the rooms are empty

enérgico, -ca *adj* vigorous *o* energetic; **estamos proyectando una enérgica campaña publicitaria** = we are planning a vigorous publicity campaign

enfermedad *nf* sickness; **licencia de enfermedad** *o* **baja por enfermedad** = sick leave; **estar de baja por enfermedad** = to be away on sick leave; **seguro de enfermedad** = health insurance; **seguro de enfermedad privado** = private health insurance; **subsidio de enfermedad** = (i) sick pay; (ii) sickness benefit; **el subsidio de enfermedad se paga mensualmente** = the sickness benefit is paid monthly; **enfermedad profesional** = occupational disease

enfermo, -ma 1 *adj* sick 2 *n* sick person *o* a patient

enfiteusis *nf* ground lease

◊ **enfiteuta** *nmf* ground lessee; **renta que paga el enfiteuta al propietario absoluto** = ground rent

enfrentarse *vr* to face *o* to confront; **la compañía se enfrenta con deudas cada vez mayores** = the company is faced with mounting debts

> los países en vías de desarrollo tendrán que enfrentarse a una competencia creciente
> **Actualidad Económica**

engañar *vt* to deceive *o* to trick *o* to con; **consiguieron engañar al banco para que les prestara 5.000.000 de ptas. sin garantías** = they conned the bank into lending them 5m pesetas with no security

engaño *nm* deceit *o* fraud *o* trick; **engaño doloso** = fraudulent misrepresentation; **fue encarcelado por obtener dinero con engaños** = he was sent to prison for obtaining money by false pretences

engomado, -da *adj* gummed; **etiqueta engomada** = gummed label

enhorabuena *nf* congratulations; **dar la enhorabuena** = to congratulate

enjuiciar *vt* (i) to judge; (ii) to prosecute; **enjuiciar un caso** = to judge a case

enlace *nm* (a) *(conexión)* link *o* tie-up; **la empresa tiene enlace con un distribuidor alemán** = the company has a tie-up with a German distributor (b) *(persona)* **enlace sindical** = shop steward *o* union representative

enmendar *vt* (a) *(ley)* to amend (b) *(texto)* to correct

enmienda *nf* amendment *o* change; **proponer una enmienda a la constitución** = to propose an amendment to the constitution; **hacer enmiendas a un contrato** = to make amendments to a contract

enredar *vt* (a) *(complicar)* to confuse *o* to complicate; **enredó aún más las cosas cuando sacó el documento** = he complicated matters when he produced the document (b) *(engañar)* to deceive; **nos enredó a todos** = he decieved us all

enriquecerse *vr* to get rich

◊ **enriquecimiento** *nm* enrichment

enrollar *vt* to scroll

ensamblaje *nm* assembly

ensayo *nm* test *o* trial; **muestra de ensayo** = trial sample; **pedido de ensayo** = trial order

enseguida *adv* as soon as possible (asap) *o* at once *o* immediately

enseñanza *nf* education *o* teaching; **enseñanza para adultos** = adult education; **se dedica a la enseñanza para adultos desde hace dos años** = he has been teaching adults for two years

enseñar *vt* (a) *(profesión, actividad)* to teach *o* to instruct (b) *(mostrar)* to show; **si espera un momento le enseñaré el catálogo** = if you wait a minute I will show you the catalogue; **después de la comida les enseñaron la fábrica a los visitantes** = after lunch the visitors were shown round the mill

enseres *nmpl* equipment; **enseres domésticos** = household goods; **mobiliario y enseres** = furniture and fittings; **muebles y enseres** = goods and chattels

entablar *vt* (a) *(legal, pleitos, etc.)* to institute *o* to start; **entablar un proceso contra alguien** = to institute proceedings against someone; **entablar un pleito** = to take legal action (b) *(empezar)* to begin *o* to open; **entablar negociaciones** = to open negotiations

ente *nm* (a) entity; **un ente público** = a public body (b) **el Ente Público** = the public sector

> el creciente déficit, los despidos de los trabajadores y las dudas sobre el modelo a seguir están llevando al caos al Ente Público
> **Tiempo**

entender 1 *vt* to understand 2 *vi* **entender de** = to be an expert on; **entiende mucho de ordenadores** = he is an expert on computers

enteramente *adv* fully *o* completely *o* entirely

enterarse *vr* to discover *o* to find out; **nos enteramos de que nuestro agente vendía los productos de nuestro competidor al mismo precio que los nuestros** = we discovered that our agent was selling our rival's products at the same price as ours

entero, -ra 1 *adj* entire *o* whole; **invitó a la plantilla entera** = he invited the entire staff 2 *nm* *(bolsa)* point; **las acciones han bajado dos enteros** = shares have gone down two points

entidad *nf* entity *o* body *o* organization; **entidades financieras** = financial institutions

> en 1991, Andalucía cuenta por fin con una entidad financiera a la altura de su importancia
> **Actualidad Económica**

> los datos del mes de junio refuerzan la tendencia a la expansión de los depósitos de las entidades financieras
> **Mercado**

> cuando se produce el extravío o robo de una tarjeta, tanto de débito como de crédito, el titular de la misma únicamente responde ante la entidad por el importe equivalente a 150 ecus
> **El País**

entorno *nm* environment *o* setting; **es muy importante trabajar en un entorno agradable** *o* **saludable** = it is very important to work in a pleasant *o* healthy environment

> la compra de terrenos en el entorno del nuevo trazado lo realizó Renfe en el más estricto secreto
> **Cambio 16**

entrada 1 *nf* (a) *(admisión)* admission *o* admittance *o* entrance; **la entrada cuesta 200 ptas.** = there is a 200 peseta admission charge; **la entrada**

cuesta 300 ptas. para adultos y 200 para niños = entrance is 300 pesetas for adults and 200 pesetas for children; **entrada gratuita los domingos** *o* **al presentar esta tarjeta** = free admission on Sundays *o* on presentation of this card; **prohibida la entrada** = no admittance **(b)** *(espectáculo)* ticket; **entrada de teatro** *o* **cine** = theatre *o* cinema ticket; **entrada de favor** = complimentary ticket **(c)** *(puerta de acceso)* entrance; **el taxi le dejará en la entrada principal** = the taxi will drop you at the main entrance; **las entregas deben efectuarse por la entrada de la calle Pelayo** = deliveries should be made to the Pelayo Street entrance; **el personal tiene prohibido utilizar la entrada principal** = the staff are forbidden to use the main entrance **(d)** *(ingreso)* entry; **segunda** *o* **nueva entrada** = re-entry; **entrada de mercancías en el depósito aduanero** = entry of goods under bond; **precio de entrada** = entry charge; **reembolsamos el precio de la entrada por la compra mínima de 1.000 ptas.** = the entrance fee is refundable if you purchase 1,000 pesetas' worth of goods; **visado de entrada** = entry visa; **visado de entrada múltiple** = multiple entry visa **(e)** *(asistentes a un partido de fútbol)* gate; **hubo una entrada de 50.000 en la final de fútbol** = there was a gate of 50,000 at the football final **(f)** *(informática)* input; **entrada de información** = input of information *o* computer input **(g)** *(cantidad inicial)* (i) down payment; (ii) money up front; **dar una entrada** = to put money down; **dio una entrada de 25.000 ptas. y pagó el resto a plazos** = he made a down payment of 25,000 pesetas and paid the rest in instalments; **tuvo que dar una entrada para poder cerrar el trato** = he had to put money up front before he could clinch the deal **(h)** *(diccionario)* entry **2** *pp de* ENTRAR

la apertura del mercado español abre, efectivamente, importantes oportunidades de negocio y la entrada en él de un gigante del sector, como SCI, puede provocar una auténtica convulsión
El País

entrar *vi* **(a)** *(introducirse en)* to enter *o* to go in; **todos se levantaron cuando el presidente entró en la sala** = they all stood up when the chairman entered the room; **entrar en dársena** = to dock; **entrar en una empresa** = to join a firm; **entró el 1 de enero** = he joined on January 1st; **entrar en vigor** = to start to operate *o* to come into force; **la compañía entró en déficit en 1995** = the company went into the red in 1995 **(b)** *(informática)* to access; **entró en el archivo de direcciones del ordenador** = she accessed the address file on the computer

entre *prep* between *o* among *o* inter-; **comparaciones entre compañías** = inter-company comparisons; **operaciones entre compañías** = inter-company dealings; **tres empresas se reparten el mercado entre ellas** = three companies share the market between them; **busco algo que cueste entre 400 y 600 ptas.** = I am looking for something in the 400 - 600 peseta price range

entrega *nf* delivery; **entrega contra reembolso** *o* **cobro a la entrega** = cash on delivery; **entrega a domicilio** = home delivery; **entrega extraordinaria** = special delivery; **entrega gratuita** = free delivery *o* delivery free; **entrega inmediata** = immediate delivery *o* spot delivery; **compra de entrega inmediata** = spot delivery purchase; **mercado de entrega inmediata del petróleo** = the spot market in oil; **precio** *o* **tarifa de entrega inmediata** = spot price *o* spot rate; **entrega de mercancías** = delivery of goods; **aceptar la entrega de mercancías** = to take delivery of goods; **entrega de mercancías gratuita** = goods delivered free *o* free delivered goods; **entrega no incluida** *o* **los gastos de entrega no están incluidos** = delivery is not allowed for *o* is not included; **en caso de no efectuarse la entrega, sírvanse a devolver a** = if undelivered, please return to; **recibimos tres entregas al día** = we get three deliveries a day; **la empresa anda retrasada en sus entregas** = the company has fallen behind with its deliveries; **faltaban cuatro artículos en la última entrega** = there were four items missing in the last delivery; **las entregas normales se realizan los martes y los viernes** = normal deliveries are made on Tuesdays and Fridays; **fecha de entrega** = delivery date; **paquetes en espera de entrega** = parcels awaiting delivery; **plazo de entrega** = delivery time; **entrega en el plazo de 28 días** = delivery within 28 days; **hablamos de los plazos de entrega con nuestros proveedores** = we discussed delivery schedules with our suppliers; **precio de entrega** = delivered price

entregar *vt* to deliver *o* to hand in; **mercancías entregadas a bordo** = goods delivered on board; **entregó los documentos al abogado** = she handed over the documents to the lawyer; **pedido por entregar** = unfulfilled order

entrenamiento *nm* training; **periodo de entrenamiento** = training period

entretanto *adv* meanwhile *o* in the interim *o* in the meantime

entretener *vt* **(a)** *(mantener ocupado)* to keep busy *o* to entertain *o* to distract; **tuve que entretener al cliente mientras le preparaban el pedido** = I had to keep the customer busy while his order was being made up **(b)** *(retrasar)* to delay

◇ **entretenerse** *vr* to delay; **me entretuve demasiado en el aeropuerto y perdí el autobús** = I took too long at the airport and missed the bus

entretenimiento *nm* upkeep *o* maintenance; **coste de entretenimiento** = maintenance cost

entrevista *nf* interview; **llamamos a seis personas para la entrevista** = we called six people for interview; **tengo una entrevista la semana que viene** = I have an interview next week *o* I am going for an interview next week

◇ **entrevistado, -da** **1** *n* interviewee **2** *pp de* ENTREVISTAR

◇ **entrevistador, -ra** *n* interviewer

entrevistar *vt* **(a)** *(trabajo)* to interview; **entrevistamos a diez candidatos pero no encontramos a ninguno apropiado** = we interviewed ten candidates, but did not find anyone suitable **(b)** *(radio o TV)* to interview

entrometerse *vr* to interfere; **no consiento que nadie se entrometa en mis asuntos** = I don't let anyone interfere in my business

enumerar *vt* to enumerate *o* to list; **el catálogo enumera veintitrés modelos de lavadoras** = the catalogue lists twenty-three models of washing machines

envasar *vt* to pack; **envasado al vacío** = vacuum-packed

envase *nm* **(a)** *(contenedor)* container; **el gas es transportado en envases metálicos resistentes** = the gas is shipped in strong metal containers **(b)** *(acción)* packing *o* packaging **(c)** *(mercancías)* package; **las mercancías deben enviarse en envases herméticos** = the goods are to be sent in airtight packages **(d)** *(material)* packing *o* packaging; **envase no retornable** = non-returnable packing; **envases vacíos** = empties; **envases (vacíos) devueltos** = returned empties

enviar *vt* **(a)** *(mandar)* to send; **la compañía le envía a Argentina en calidad de director general de la sucursal de Buenos Aires** = the company is sending him to Argentina to be general manager of the Buenos Aires office; **enviar algo a alguien** = to forward *o* to send something to someone; **enviar una carta** *o* **un pedido** *o* **un cargamento** = to send a letter *o* an order *o* a shipment; **enviamos una carta solicitando el nuevo catálogo** = we sent away for the new catalogue; **enviar una circular** = to send a circular *o* to circularize; **el comité ha acordado enviar una circular a todos sus miembros** = the committee has agreed to circularize the members; **enviar una solicitud** = to send an application *o* to apply; **enviar por fax** = to fax; **enviar por télex** = to telex; **envió su dimisión** = he sent in his resignation; **se ruega enviar los pagos al tesorero** = please send remittances to the treasurer **(b)** *(expedir)* to dispatch *o* to ship; **enviar mercancías** = to ship goods; **enviamos toda nuestra mercancía por ferrocarril** = we ship all our goods by rail

◊ **enviarse** *vr* to be sent *o* to be shipped; **las muestras se enviarán posteriormente por correo ordinario** = the samples will follow by ordinary mail

envío *nm* **(a)** *(acción)* dispatch *o* shipment *o* consignment; **envío agrupado de mercancías** = consolidated shipment; **envío de grandes cantidades** *o* **envío a granel** = bulk shipment; **envío por correo** = mailing; **envío por transporte aéreo** = air forwarding; **costes de envío** = shipping charges *o* shipping costs; **gastos de envío no incluidos** = delivery is not included; **instrucciones de envío** = shipping instructions *o* forwarding instructions *o* instructions for forwarding; **instrucciones relativas al envío de mercancías a Africa** = instructions regarding the shipment of goods to Africa; **nota de envío** = dispatch note *o* shipping note; **la huelga retrasó el envío unas cuantas semanas** = the strike held up dispatch for several weeks; **solicitar el envío de algo** = to ask for something to be sent *o* to send off for something **(b)** *(mercancías)* shipment *o* consignment; **ha llegado un envío de mercancías** = a consignment of goods has arrived; **estamos esperando un envío de coches de Japón** = we are expecting a consignment of cars from Japan; **un envío de ordenadores sufrió daños** = a shipment of computers was damaged; **el envío semanal salió ayer** = the weekly dispatch went off yesterday; **hacemos dos envíos semanales a Francia** = we make two shipments a week to France

envoltorio *nm* wrapper; **las galletas están empaquetadas** *o* **se presentan en envoltorios de plástico** = the biscuits are packed in plastic wrappers

◊ **envoltura** *nf* wrapper; **envoltura exterior** *o* **externa** = outer wrapper

envolver *vt* to wrap (up); **envolver un obsequio con papel de regalo** = to gift-wrap a present; **envolvió el paquete con papel verde** = he wrapped (up) the parcel in green paper; **los relojes vienen envueltos en cajas atractivas** = the watches are prepacked in attractive display boxes

epígrafe *nm* epigraph; **epígrafe de un acuerdo** = heads of agreement

equilibrar *vt* to balance *o* to equalize; **el presidente se propone adoptar un presupuesto equilibrado** = the president is planning for a balanced budget

equilibrio *nm* balance *o* equilibrium; **guardar** *o* **mantener el equilibrio** = to balance; **equilibrio de mercado** = market equilibrium

equipaje *nm* baggage *o* luggage; **equipaje de mano** = hand luggage *o* cabin luggage; **facturar el equipaje** = to check baggage in; **equipaje no reclamado** = unclaimed baggage; **el equipaje no reclamado se subastará a los seis meses** = unclaimed property *o* unclaimed baggage will be sold by auction after six months; **carro del equipaje** = baggage cart; **franquicia de equipaje** = free baggage allowance

equipamiento *nm* equipping *o* fitting; **equipamiento de una tienda** = fitting out of a shop

equipar *vt* to equip *o* to fit out; **equipar una fábrica con nueva maquinaria** = to equip a factory with new machinery; **equiparon la fábrica con ordenadores** = they fitted out the factory with computers; **equiparon la tienda a un costo de 2.000.000 de ptas.** = the shop was fitted out at a cost of 2,000,000 pesetas

equiparación *nf* comparison

equiparar *vt* to compare (with)

equipo *nm* **(a)** *(personas)* team; **equipo de consumidores** = consumer panel; **equipo directivo** = management team; **trabaja para un equipo financiero** = he works for a finance group; **equipo de promoción** = promotion team; **llamaron a un equipo de relaciones públicas** = they called in a public relations firm; **equipo de ventas** = sales team; **jefe de equipo de ventas** = field sales manager; **el equipo de ventas no ha conseguido sus objetivos** = the sales team has missed its sales targets **(b)** *(objetos)* equipment; **equipos domésticos** *o* **artículos de equipo** = consumer durables; **equipo informático** = computer system; **equipos de oficina** = office equipment *o* business equipment; **equipo pesado** = heavy equipment; **arrendar equipo** = to lease equipment; **una empresa de alquiler de equipos** = an equipment-leasing company; **bienes de equipo** = capital goods *o* equipment

la banca europea tendrá que destinar entre 10.000 y 15.000 millones de euros en seis años para adecuar sus equipos informáticos a la moneda única

El País

equitativo, -va *adj* fair *o* equitable *o* equal

equivalencia *nf* equivalence

equivalente *adj* equivalent; **ser equivalente a** = to be equivalent to; **el dividendo repartido es equivalente a una cuarta parte de los beneficios antes de deducir los impuestos** = the dividend paid is equivalent to one quarter of the pretax profit

equivocación *nf* error *o* mistake; **cometer una equivocación** = to make a mistake; **por equivocación** = by mistake

equivocado, -da 1 *adj* wrong; **cometieron un error en la tienda y mandaron los artículos equivocados** = the shop made a mistake and sent the wrong items; **el total de la última columna está equivocado** = the total in the last column is wrong **2** *pp de* EQUIVOCAR

◇ **equivocadamente** *adv* wrongly

equivocar *vt* to mistake *o* to confuse one thing with another

◇ **equivocarse** *vr* to miscalculate *o* to miscount *o* to be out; **el tendero se equivocó en la cuenta** = the shopkeeper miscounted; **intenté llamar pero me equivoqué de número** = I tried to phone, but I got the wrong number; **nos hemos equivocado de 4.000.000 de ptas. en nuestros cálculos** = we are 4m pesetas out in our calculations

erario *nm* Treasury funds; **erario público** = Treasury

ergonomía *nf* ergonomics

◇ **ergonómico, -ca** *adj* ergonomic

> se persigue un objetivo ergonómico, es decir, la posibilidad de sentarse en posición correcta, de estar cómodo y de tener todo a mano
>
> **España Económica**

erosionar *vt* to erode

◇ **erosionarse** *vr* to be eroded

errar 1 *vt* to miss **2** *vi* to be wrong *o* to make a mistake

erróneo, -nea *adj* wrong *o* incorrect

◇ **erróneamente** *adv* wrongly *o* incorrectly; **facturó erróneamente a García S.A. por un valor de 500.000 ptas.**, **cuando hubiera tenido que abonarles la misma cantidad** = he wrongly invoiced García S.A. for 500,000 pesetas, when he should have credited them with the same amount

error *nm* **(a)** *(equivocación, falta)* error *o* mistake; **error aleatorio** = random error; **error de cálculo** = miscalculation *o* computational error; **error de copia** *o* **de oficina** = clerical error; **error de mecanografía** *o* **de impresión** = typing error; **error de muestreo** = sampling error; **error de ordenador** = computer error; **error relativo** = relative error; **error de suma** = miscount; **el saldo tiene un error de 2.000 ptas.** = the balance is 2,000 pesetas out; **había un error en la dirección** = there was a mistake in the address; **coeficiente de errores** = error rate; **cometer un error** = to make a mistake *o* an error; **cometió un error al calcular el total** = he made an error in calculating the total; **cometió un error al escribir la dirección de la carta** = she made a mistake in addressing the letter; **cometimos un grave error al no firmar el acuerdo con la empresa china** = we made a bad mistake *o* we

slipped up badly in not signing the agreement with the Chinese company; **hizo un par de errores al calcular el descuento** = he made a couple of slips in calculating the discount; **margen de error** = margin of error; **salvo error u omisión** = errors and omissions excepted **(b) por error** = by mistake *o* in error *o* by error; **la carta fue enviada a la oficina de Londres por error** = the letter was sent to the London office in error; **puso mi carta en un sobre para el presidente por error** = she put my letter into an envelope for the chairman by mistake **(c)** *(programa de ordenador)* bug *o* malfunction; **eliminar errores** = to debug

esbozar *vt* to rough out *o* to sketch

esbozo *nm* outline

escala *nf* **(a)** *(gradación)* scale; **deseconomías de escala** = diseconomies of scale; **economías de escala** = economies of scale; **gran escala** *o* **pequeña escala** = large scale *o* small scale; **reducciones de plantilla a gran escala en la industria de la construcción** = large scale redundancies in the construction industry; **empresa a pequeña escala** = small-scale enterprise; **iniciar actividades comerciales a pequeña escala** = to start in business on a small scale; **a escala nacional** = nationwide; **ofrecemos un servicio de distribución** *o* **entrega a escala nacional** = we offer a nationwide delivery service **(b) escala de derechos** = scale of charges; **escalas impositivas** = tax bands *o* tax schedules; **escala de precios** = scale of prices; **fabricamos zapatos dentro de una amplia escala de precios** = we make shoes in a wide range of prices; **escala de precios fija** = fixed scale of charges; **escala de rendimiento** = earning capacity; **escala de salarios** *o* **escala salarial** = scale of salaries *o* salary scale; **le dieron el puesto con una asignación máxima en la escala de salarios** = he was appointed at the top end of the salary scale; **escala móvil de salarios** = incremental scale *o* sliding wage scale; **escalas de sueldos comparables** = pay comparability **(c)** *(escalera)* ladder; **escala de ascenso** = promotion ladder **(d)** *(viaje en avión, barco)* stopover *o* port of call; **hacer escala** = to stop over; **vuelo sin escala** = non-stop flight

> ahora puede volar directamente, sin escalas, de Madrid a los Angeles en Boeing 747
>
> **El País**

escalada *nf* escalation; **escalada de precios** = escalation of price increases

escalafón *nm* promotion ladder; **subir en el escalafón** = to work one's way up the promotion ladder

escalar *vi* to climb *o* to rise *o* to escalate

escalera *nf* **(a)** *(de mano)* ladder; **necesitarás una escalera de mano para examinar la máquina** = you will need a ladder to look into the machine **(b)** *(en un inmueble)* staircase; **escalera de incendios** *o* **de emergencia** = fire scape

escalonado, -da 1 *adj* staggered **2** *pp de* ESCALONAR

escalonar *vt* to stagger *o* to space out; **las vacaciones escalonadas ayudan a la industria del turismo** = staggered holidays help the tourist industry; **tenemos que escalonar la hora del almuerzo para que siempre haya alguien en la centralita de teléfonos** = we have to stagger the lunch hour so that there is always someone on the switchboard; **los pagos pueden escalonarse durante un periodo de diez años** = payments can be spaced out over a period of ten years

escándalo *nm* **(a)** *(asunto)* scandal *o* affair; *US* scam **(b)** *(ruido)* row

escáner *nm* scanner

escapar *vi* to escape; **dejó escapar una oportunidad** = he let an opportunity slip

◊ **escaparse** *vr* to run away *o* to get away

escaparate *nm* shop window; **mirar los escaparates** *o* **ir de escaparates** = to go window shopping; **decoración de escaparates** = window dressing *o* display; **objetos expuestos en un escaparate** = window display; **escaparate de exposición** = display unit

escape *nm* escape; **cláusula de escape** = escape clause *o* let-out clause

escasez *nf* lack *o* scarceness *o* scarcity *o* shortage; **hay escasez de personal cualificado** = there is a scarcity of trained staff; **escasez de mano de obra** = labour shortage *o* shortage of labour *o* manpower shortage *o* shortage of manpower; **escasez de dólares** = dollar gap; **valor de escasez** = scarcity value

> en Japón, el peligro vendrá de la escasez de trabajadores, cada vez más preocupante
> **Actualidad Económica**

escaso, -sa *adj* scarce *o* in short supply; **la balanza comercial experimentó una escasa mejora** = there was a slight improvement in the balance of trade; **escaso de personal** = shorthanded *o* understaffed; **el personal cualificado fiable es escaso** = reliable trained staff are scarce; **dinero escaso** = tight money; **política de dinero escaso** = tight money policy; **materias primas escasas** = scarce raw materials; **peso escaso** = false weight; **los repuestos son escasos debido a la huelga** = spare parts are in short supply because of the strike

escatimar *vt* **escatimar (en) el peso** = to give short weight; **no escatimar gastos** *o* **esfuerzos** = to spare no expense *o* no effort

escisión *nf* split *o* division *o* break-up; **la escisión de la sociedad ha dejado sin trabajo a la mitad del personal** = the break-up of the company has left half the staff without a job

escoger *vt* to pick *o* to select; *(lista de candidatos)* to shortlist; **escoja el que quiera** = take your pick

◊ **escogido, -da** *adj y pp* chosen *o* choice *o* selected; **está en la lista de candidatos escogidos** = he is on the shortlist for the job

escondidas *nfpl* **a escondidas** = (i) on the quiet *o* secretly; (ii) behind someone's back

escribiente *nm* office junior *o* clerk

escribir *vt/i* **(a)** *(apuntar, redactar)* to write; **el número de teléfono está escrito al pie de la nota** = the telephone number is written at the bottom of the notepaper; **escribir con todas las letras** = to write out in full; **escriba su nombre y dirección en mayúsculas** = fill in your name and address in block capitals; **escribir a alguien** = to write to someone *o* to correspond with someone; **escribió una carta de reclamación al director** = she wrote a letter of complaint to the manager; **escribir al dictado** = to take dictation; **escribir a mano** = to write out by hand; **las solicitudes deben escribirse a mano y enviarse al jefe de personal** = applications should be written in longhand and sent to the personnel officer **(b)** **escribir a máquina** = to type; **envió una solicitud de trabajo escrita a máquina** = he sent in a typewritten job application; **escribe a máquina bastante deprisa** = she can type quite fast; **le llevará toda la mañana escribir mis cartas** = it will take her all morning to do my letters; **máquina de escribir** = typewriter **(c)** *(deletrear)* to spell; **¿cómo se escribe esta palabra?** = how do you spell this word? *o* how is this word spelt?

◊ **escribirse** *vr* to correspond with *o* to write to

escrito, -ta 1 *adj* written *o* stated; **escrito a mano** = handwritten *o* in longhand; **escrito a máquina** = typewritten *o* typed **2** *nm* writing *o* document *o* text *o* (legal) brief; **por escrito** = in writing; **escrito difamatorio** = libel; **difamar por escrito a alguien** = to libel someone; **poner por escrito** = to put in writing; **poner el acuerdo por escrito** = to put the agreement in writing **3** *pp de* ESCRIBIR

escritor, -ra *n* writer

escritorio *nm* desk; **un escritorio con tres cajones** = a three-drawer desk; **objetos de escritorio** = stationery

escritura *nf* **(a)** *(título)* deed; **escritura de cesión** = deed of assignment; **escritura de constitución** = memorandum *o* articles of association *o* articles of incorporation; **escritura de convenio** = deed of covenant; **escritura de propiedad** = title deeds; **escritura de sociedad** = deed of partnership; **escritura de transferencia** = deed of transfer **(b)** **escritura (a mano)** = writing *o* handwriting *o* longhand

escudo *nm* *(moneda de Portugal)* escudo

escuela *nf* college *o* school; **escuela empresarial** *o* **escuela de negocios** *o* **escuela superior de comercio** = business college *o* business school *o* commercial college; **escuela de secretariado** = secretarial college

> existen algunos centros y escuelas de negocios en donde el perfil del profesor tiene una vertiente claramente internacional y el intercambio se produce durante todo el año académico
> **El País**

esencial *adj* essential; **a la compañía le faltan piezas de recambio esenciales** = the factory is lacking essential spare parts; **recordar lo esencial** = to get back to basics

esfera *nf* sphere *o* field; **esfera de influencia** = sphere of influence; **altas esferas** = high circles; **esfera de actividad** = field of action; **es el mejor en su esfera profesional** = he's the best in his field

esfuerzo *nm* effort *o* endeavour; **con mucho**

esfuerzo = with a lot of hard work *o* with much effort; **los vendedores hicieron grandes esfuerzos para aumentar las ventas** = the salesmen made great efforts to increase sales; **sin esfuerzo** = effortlessly *o* without any effort; **su trabajo no le exige un esfuerzo al máximo** = he is not fully stretched; **gracias a los esfuerzos del departamento de finanzas se han reducido los gastos generales** = thanks to the efforts of the finance department, overheads have been reduced; **con un esfuerzo más podremos despachar los pedidos atrasados** = if we make one more effort, we should clear the backlog of orders; **si todos los empleados hacen un esfuerzo el pedido puede estar listo a tiempo** = if all the workforce works hard, the order should be completed on time

eslogan *nm* publicity slogan; **empleamos el mismo eslogan en toda nuestra publicidad** = we are using the same slogan on all our publicity

Eslovaquia *o* República Eslovaca *nf* Slovakia

◊ **eslovaco, -ca** *adj y n* Slovakian
NOTA: capital: **Bratislava;** moneda: **corona eslovaca** = koruna

Eslovenia *nf* Slovenia

◊ **esloveno, -na** *adj y n* Slovene
NOTA: capital: **Ljubljana;** moneda: **tolar** = tolar

espaciado, -da 1 *adj* spaced-out; **el nombre de la compañía está escrito en letras espaciadas** = the company name is written in spaced-out letters **2** *pp de* ESPACIAR

espaciar *vt* to space out *o* to expand; **espaciar los pagos** = to space out payments

espacio *nm* **(a)** *(área)* space; **Espacio Económico Europeo (EEE)** = European Economic Area (EEA); **espacio para oficinas** = office space; **estamos buscando espacio adicional para nuestro nuevo departamento de contabilidad** = we are looking for extra office space for our new accounts department **(b) espacio publicitario** = advertising space; **espacio publicitario en un periódico** = advertising space *o* advertisement panel (in a newspaper); **contratar espacio publicitario en un periódico** = to take advertising space in a newspaper; **espacio publicitario en la televisión** = a commercial *o* a TV spot **(c)** *(hueco)* space (on form); **rellene los espacios en blanco y devuelva el formulario a su oficina local** = fill in the blanks and return the form to your local office; **si necesita un recibo marque el espacio indicado con 'R'** = tick the box marked 'R' if you require a receipt **(d)** *(extensión)* room; **los archivadores ocupan mucho espacio** = the filing cabinets take up a lot of room **(e)** *(ordenadores)* **espacio disponible** = workspace; **no hay más espacio en el archivo del ordenador** = there is no more room in the computer file

España *nf* Spain

◊ **español, -ola 1** *adj* Spanish **2** *n* Spaniard
NOTA: capital: **Madrid;** moneda: **peseta (pta.)** = Spanish peseta (pta)

especial *adj* **(a)** *(particular)* special; **en especial** = specially *o* in particular *o* especially; **tiene una aptitud especial para los negocios** = he has a particular capacity for business; **nos ofreció condiciones especiales** = he offered us special terms; **la fotocopiadora sólo funciona con un tipo especial de papel** = the photocopier only works with a particular type of paper; **el coche se ofrece a un precio especial** = the car is being offered at a special price; **promoción especial** = special promotion; **reparto especial** = special delivery; **resolución especial** = special resolution **(b) depósitos especiales** = special deposits; **derechos especiales de giro (DEG)** = special drawing rights (SDRs)

◊ **especialmente** *adv* in particular *o* specially *o* especially; **las mercancías frágiles, especialmente los vasos, precisan un embalaje especial** = fragile goods, in particular glasses, need special packing

especialidad *nf* **(a)** *(especialización)* speciality *o* specialty; **su especialidad son los programas de ordenadores** = their speciality is computer programs **(b)** *(actividad profesional)* field

especialista *nmf* specialist; **especialista en ergonomía** = ergonomist; **tienes que consultar a un especialista en informática** = you should go to a specialist in computers *o* to a computer specialist for advice; **especialista en previsiones económicas** = economic forecaster

> los especialistas coinciden en que la tendencia para los próximos años es que este tipo de fraude se incremente
>
> **El País**

especialización *nf* specialization; **su especialización es en el campo de programas de contabilidad para empresas pequeñas** = the company's area of specialization is accounts packages for small businesses

especializado, -da *adj* **(a)** *(que se especializa en algo)* specialized; **la empresa está especializada en componentes electrónicos** = the company specializes in electronic components; **tienen una gama de productos especializados** = they have a specialized product line; **vende equipos muy especializados para la industria electrónica** = he sells very specialized equipment for the electronics industry; **tienda especializada** = *US* specialty store **(b)** *(cualificado)* skilled; **mano de obra especializada** = skilled labour

especializarse *vr* to specialize (in); **se ha especializado en 'marketing'** = he specializes in marketing

especificación *nf* specification; **detallar las especificaciones de un sistema informático** = to detail the specifications of a computer system; **el trabajo no cumple con nuestras especificaciones** = the work is not up to specification *o* does not meet our specifications

especificar *vt* to itemize *o* to specify

específico, -ca 1 *adj* specific **2** *nm* patent medicine

espécimen *nm* specimen *o* sample; **dar espécimen de firmas de una orden bancaria** = to give specimen signatures on a bank mandate

espectáculo *nm* *(función para invitados)* entertainment

especulación *nf* speculation; **perdió todo su**

dinero en especulaciones bursátiles = she lost all her money in Stock Exchange speculations

◇ **especulador, -ra** *n* speculator; **especulador de acciones** = bull; **un especulador en bolsa** = a speculator on the Stock Exchange *o* a Stock Exchange speculator; **un especulador en divisas** = a currency speculator; **un especulador inmobiliario** = a property speculator

◇ **especular** *vi* to speculate; **especular en la bolsa** = to speculate on the Stock Exchange; **especular a la baja** = to bear *o* to speculate on a fall

◇ **especulativo, -va** *adj* **(a)** *(que sirve para especular)* speculative; **compró la compañía con fines especulativos** = he bought the company as a speculation **(b)** *(teórico)* notional

> se forjó como experto inmobiliario en la especulación urbanística de la Costa del Sol durante los años 70
> **Cambio 16**

espera *nf* period of waiting; **se saltaron el turno de espera y consiguieron la licencia de exportación antes que nosotros** = they jumped the queue and got their export licence before we did; **lista de espera** = waiting list; **tarifa de billete en lista de espera** = standby fare; **sala de espera** = waiting room

esperado, -da 1 *adj* expected; **la casa se vendió a un precio más alto que el esperado** = the house was sold for more than the expected price **2** *pp de* ESPERAR

esperanza *nf* expectation *o* hope; **esperanza de vida** = life expectancy; **tener esperanza de éxito** = to hope for success

esperar *vt* **(a)** *(aguardar)* to expect *o* to await; **el agente está esperando nuestras órdenes** = the agent is awaiting our instructions; **esperamos que llegue a las 10.45** = we are expecting him to arrive at 10.45; **esperan recibir un cheque de su representante la semana próxima** = they are expecting a cheque from their agent next week; **los inversores están esperando la presentación del presupuesto** = investors are holding back until after the Budget **(b)** *(teléfono)* to wait *o* to hang on *o* to hold on; **el presidente está hablando por la otra línea - ¿quiere esperar?** = the chairman is on the other line - will you hold?; **si espera un momento, el presidente pronto terminará por la otra línea** = if you hang on a moment, the chairman will be off the other line soon **(c)** *(contar con)* to hope *o* to count on; **esperamos poder enviar el pedido la semana próxima** = we hope to be able to dispatch the order next week; **espera poder introducirse en el mercado de los EE UU** = he is hoping to break into the US market; **creyeron que la publicidad en la televisión les ayudaría a aumentar las ventas** = they had hoped the TV commercials would help sales

espionaje *nm* espionage; **espionaje industrial** = industrial espionage

espiral *nf* spiral; **espiral salarios-precios** = wage-price spiral; **la economía está en una espiral inflacionaria** *o* **en la espiral salarios-precios** = the economy is in an inflationary spiral *o* a wage-price spiral; **un periodo de subida en espiral de los precios** = a period of spiralling prices

esquema *nf* scheme *o* outline *o* plan; **esquema de presupuesto** = outline budget; **esquema económico** = economic pattern

esquina *nf* corner; **la oficina de correos está en la esquina de la calle Mayor y la calle Balmes** = the Post Office is on the corner of the calle Mayor and the calle Balmes

esquirol *nm* strikebreaker *o* scab *o* blackleg; *US* fink

estabilidad *nf* **(a)** *(equilibrio)* stability; **un periodo de estabilidad económica** = a period of economic stability **(b)** *(firmeza)* steadiness *o* firmness; **estabilidad de los precios** = price stability; **la estabilidad de los mercados de divisas** = the stability of the currency markets; **la estabilidad de los mercados se debe a la intervención del gobierno** = the steadiness of the markets is due to the government's intervention

estabilización *nf* stabilization; **estabilización de la economía** = stabilization of the economy

estabilizador, -ra 1 *adj* stabilizing; **tener un efecto estabilizador en la economía** = to have a stabilizing effect on the economy; **las cifras oficiales tuvieron un efecto estabilizador sobre el tipo de cambio** = the government's figures had a steadying influence on the exchange rate **2** *nm* stabilizer; **estabilizador automático** = automatic stabilizer

estabilizar *vt* to stabilize; **estabilizar los precios** = to stabilize prices

◇ **estabilizarse** *vr* **(a)** *(equilibrarse)* to level off *o* to level out; **los beneficios se han estabilizado en los últimos años** = profits have levelled off over the last few years; **los precios se están estabilizando** = prices are levelling out **(b)** *(fijarse)* to steady *o* to become stable; **los precios se han estabilizado** = prices have stabilized; **los precios de los mercados de materias primas se estabilizaron** = prices steadied on the commodity markets

estable *adj* permanent *o* stable *o* steady *o* firm; **el mercado se mantuvo estable** = the market stayed steady; **economía estable** = stable economy; **moneda estable** = stable currency; **precios estables** = stable prices; **tipos de cambio estables** = stable exchange rates

establecer *vt* to establish *o* to set up; **la subasta estableció un récord de precios** = the auction set a record for high prices; **establecer una estructura de ventas** = to build a sales structure; **establecieron un negocio en el centro de la ciudad** = they set up a business in the centre of town

◇ **establecerse** *vr* to establish oneself *o* to set up; **establecerse por cuenta propia** = to set oneself up as a freelancer *o* to become self-employed; **establecerse en un negocio** = to establish oneself in business

◇ **establecido, -da** *adj* established; *(en marcha)* in progress *o* on-going; **conforme a lo establecido en el contrato** = according to the provisions of the contract

establecimiento *nm* **(a)** *(comercio)* establishment; **fidelidad a un establecimiento** = customer loyalty; **dirige un establecimiento**

tipográfico importante = he runs an important printing establishment **(b)** *(personas y propiedad de una empresa)* establishment; **gastos de primer establecimiento** = establishment charges

estación *nf* **(a)** *(temporada)* season; **el verano es la estación de mayor actividad para los hoteles** = summer is the busy season for hotels **(b)** *(transporte)* station; **estación de autobuses** = coach *o* bus station *o* bus depot; **estación terminal** = terminus *o* railhead; **las mercancías se enviarán a la estación terminal por camión** = the goods will be sent to the railhead by lorry; **el tren sale de la estación central a las 14.15** = the train leaves the Central Station at 14.15; **estación de mercancías** = freight depot; **el cargamento tiene que ser entregado en el depósito de la estación de mercancías** = the shipment has to be delivered to the freightliner depot **(c)** *(informática)* **estación de trabajo** = workstation

> Ahora, IBM le ofrece una nueva solución ATM a 25 Mbps que integra adaptadores para su estación de trabajo, y que aumentará inmediatamente el ancho de banda disponible, asegurando la capacidad de crecimiento futuro
> **PC Week**

estacional *adj* seasonal; **ajustes estacionales** = seasonal adjustments; **demanda estacional** = seasonal demand; **empleo estacional** = seasonal employment; **paro** *o* **desempleo estacional** = seasonal unemployment; **la demanda de este artículo es muy estacional** = the demand for this item is very seasonal

estacionamiento *nm* car park

estacionar *vt* to park; **si el aparcamiento está lleno, puede estacionar en la calle durante treinta minutos** = if the car park is full, you can park in the street for thirty minutes

◇ **estacionarse** *vr* to park

estadística *nf* **(a)** *(cifras, números)* statistics; **estadística demográfica** = population statistics; **las estadísticas oficiales muestran un aumento de las importaciones** = government trade statistics show an increase in imports **(b)** *(ciencia)* statistics

> según la estadística oficial de la empresa, en la ruta Madrid-Sevilla viajaron 384.283 personas: 1.052 al día.
> **Cambio 16**

> en España, las estadísticas muestran que se mantiene un ritmo de crecimiento medio anual del 54% en el mercado de ordenadores personales
> **Micros**

estadístico, -ca 1 *adj* statistical; **análisis estadístico** = statistical analysis; **discrepancia estadística** = statistical discrepancy; **información estadística** = statistical information **2** *n* statistician

estado *nm* **(a)** *(condición)* state *o* condition; **artículo vendido en buen estado** = item sold in good condition; **¿en qué estado estaba el coche cuando se vendió?** = what was the condition of the car when it was sold?; **máquina en perfecto estado de funcionamiento** = machine in full working order; **el estado general de la economía** = the general state of the economy **(b)** *(país)* state; **estado asistencial** *o* **de bienestar** = welfare state **(c)**

(gobierno) government *o* state; **está trabajando en un proyecto subvencionado por el Estado para ayudar a la pequeña empresa** = he is working in a government-sponsored scheme to help small businesses; **la industria de ordenadores depende de la ayuda del Estado** = the computer industry relies on government support **(d)** **estado de cuenta** *o* **de cuentas** = (i) bank statement *o* bank balance; (ii) financial statement; **estado de cuentas mensual** *o* **trimestral** = monthly *o* quarterly statement; **estado de flujo de fondos** = cash flow statement

> el intervencionismo del Estado fue aumentando poco a poco, apoyado en la teoría de los fallos del mercado
> **España Económica**

Estados Unidos de América (EE UU) *nm* United States of America (USA)

◇ **estadounidense 1** *adj* American **2** *nmf* American *o* American citizen

NOTE: capital: **Washington;** moneda: **dólar EE UU ($** *o* **$US)** = US dollar ($ *o* $US)

estafa *nf* **(a)** *(timo)* confidence trick **(b)** *(fraude)* fraud *o* false pretences; **tomó posesión de la propiedad por medio de estafas** = he got possession of the property by fraud; **fue encarcelado por obtener dinero por medio de estafas** = he was sent to prison for obtaining money by false pretences

◇ **estafador, -ra** *n* confidence trickster *o* conman

estafar *vt* to trick *o* to con *o* to cheat *o* to defraud; **se le acusó de estafar a clientes que acudían en busca de consejo** = she was accused of cheating clients who came to ask her for advice; **estafó 20.000.000 de ptas. a la compañía financiera** = he conned the finance company out of 20m pesetas

estafeta *nf* estafeta de correos = sub-post office

estampilla *nf* stamp

estancado, -da 1 *adj* stagnant; **una economía estancada** = a stagnant economy; **la economía está estancada** = the economy is stagnating; **mercado estancado** = static market **2** *pp de* ESTANCAR

estancamiento *nm* **(a)** stagnation; **el país entró en una fase de estancamiento** = the country entered a period of stagnation; **estancamiento económico** = economic stagnation; **estancamiento con inflación** = stagflation **(b)** **estancamiento temporal** = blip

estancar *vt* to hold up *o* to stop progress

◇ **estancarse** *vr* to be held up *o* to stagnate; **después de seis horas las negociaciones se estancaron** = after six hours the talks were stagnating; **el volumen de ventas se estancó durante el primer trimestre del año** = turnover was stagnant for the first half of the year

estancia *nf* stay; **los turistas estuvieron en la ciudad sólo durante una breve estancia** = the tourists were in town only for a short stay

estándar *adj* standard; **carta estándar** = standard letter; **un modelo de coche estándar** = a standard model car

◇ **estandarización** *nf* standardization;

estandarización del diseño = standardization of design

◊ **estandarizar** *vt* to standardize *o* to normalize

> uno de los primeros trabajos de Equal será establecer unos estándares europeos de calidad similares a los ya existentes en las otras cuatro asociaciones nacionales
> **El País**

estanflación *nf* stagflation

estante *nm* rack *o* shelf; **estante de exposición** = display rack; **estante de revistas** = magazine rack; **estante de tarjetas** = card rack; **espacio en los estantes** = shelf space

estantería *nf* rack *o* shelf *o* shelving; **estantería aparte** = bin; **instalamos estanterías metálicas en el departamento de enseres** = we installed metal shelving in the household goods department

estar *vi* to be; **las negociaciones están paralizadas desde hace diez días** = talks have been deadlocked for ten days; **las normas están en vigor desde 1946** = the rules have been in force since 1946; **estar de acuerdo** = to agree with; **estar sin fondos** = to bounce; **estar seguro** = to be sure; **estar situado** = to to be sited *o* to be located; **estar vigente** = to be in force

◊ **estarse** *vr* to remain *o* to stay

estatal *adj (del gobierno)* state; **con apoyo estatal** = government-backed; **empresa estatal** = state enterprise; **los jefes de las empresas estatales son nombrados por el gobierno** = the bosses of state industries are appointed by the government; **una industria estatal** = a state-owned industry; **intervención estatal** = state intervention; **propiedad estatal** = state ownership

estático, -ca *adj* static; **mercado estático** = static market

estatutario, -ria *adj* constitutional *o* statutory; **disposiciones estatutarias** = statutory provisions

estatuto *nm* **(a)** *(ley)* statute *o* constitution *o* rule; **Estatuto de Autonomía** = statute of autonomy **(b)** *(de una asociación)* **estatutos** = articles of association *o* articles of incorporation *o* bylaws (USA); **estatutos sociales** = memorandum (and articles) of association; **consejero nombrado conforme a los estatutos de la sociedad** = director appointed under the articles of the company; **los estatutos no permiten que los cargos de la asociación reciban una remuneración** = payments to officers of the association are not allowed by the constitution; **este procedimiento no está permitido por los estatutos de la compañía** = this procedure is not allowed under the articles of association of the company

> los estatutos de la empresa establecen que se necesita un mínimo de ocho consejeros para lograr el quorum necesario
> **El País**

> el pasado 13 de diciembre se celebró una asamblea general informativa en la que se presentaron los estatutos sociales y el reglamento del régimen interior de la asociación
> **Chip**

estenógrafo, -fa *n* stenographer

estibador, -ra *n* stevedore

estilo *nm* style; **estilo de la vivienda** = house style; **un nuevo estilo de producto** = a new style of product

estimación *nf* **(a)** *(cálculo aproximado)* estimate *o* guess; **estimación baja** = underestimate; **la cifra de un volumen de negocios de 10.000.000 de ptas. fue una estimación muy baja** = the figure of 10m pesetas turnover was a considerable underestimate; **la previsión de ventas es sólo una estimación** = the forecast of sales is only a guess; **hizo una estimación de los beneficios brutos** = he made a guess at the pretax profits **(b)** *(valoración)* valuation

estimado, -da 1 *adj* **(a)** *(según cálculo aproximado)* estimated; **cifras estimadas** = estimated figures; **hora estimada de llegada** = estimated time of arrival (ETA); **ventas estimadas** = estimated sales **(b)** *(en carta)* 'Estimado Señor' = 'Dear Sir'; 'Estimados Señores' = 'Dear Sirs' **2** *pp de* ESTIMAR

estimador, -ra *n* estimator *o* valuer

estimar *vt* to estimate *o* to reckon; **estimar los costes en 250.000 ptas.** = to reckon the costs at 250,000 pesetas; **el director de ventas trató de estimar el volumen de ventas de la sección de Extremo Oriente** = the sales director tried to guess the turnover of the Far East division

◊ **estimarse** *vr* to be estimated *o* valued

estimular *vt* **(a)** *(impulsar)* to stimulate *o* to boost *o* to promote *o* to encourage; **estimular la economía** = to stimulate the economy; **estimular el comercio con el Oriente Medio** = to stimulate trade with the Middle East; **esperamos que nuestra campaña publicitaria estimule las ventas en un 25%** = we expect our publicity campaign to boost sales by 25%; **los planes de incentivo están estimulando la producción** = incentive schemes are boosting production; **la empresa trata de estimular las ventas ofreciendo grandes descuentos** = the company is trying to encourage sales by giving large discounts **(b)** *(instigar)* to challenge

estímulo *nm* **(a)** *(ánimo)* encouragement; **los diseñadores crearon un producto muy comercial, gracias al estímulo del director de ventas** = the designers produced a very marketable product, thanks to the encouragement of the sales director **(b)** *(impulso)* stimulus *o* boost; **el gobierno pretende dar un estímulo al desarrollo industrial** = the government hopes to give a boost to industrial development

estipulación *nf* stipulation *o* provision; **estipulación claramente definida** = clearly stated stipulation; **estipulaciones del convenio** = provisions *o* articles of an agreement

estipulado, -da 1 *adj* stipulated; **pagar los gastos estipulados** = to pay the stipulated charges **2** *pp de* ESTIPULAR

estipular *vt* **(a)** *(convenir o pactar)* to provide *o* to provide for; **se han estipulado 5.000.000 de ptas. de gastos en el presupuesto** = 5,000,000 pesetas have been provided for expenses in the budget **(b)** *(ordenar o regular)* to stipulate; **estipular que el**

contrato tenga una validez de cinco años = to stipulate that the contract should run for five years; **el contrato estipula que el vendedor pagará los gastos jurídicos del comprador** = the contract stipulates that the seller pays the buyer's legal costs

estirado, -da *adj* tight *o* stretched

estraperlo *nm* black market

estratagema *nf* stratagem *o* device

estrategia *nf* strategy; **estrategia comercial** = business strategy; **estrategia de comercialización** = marketing strategy; **estrategia de la compañía** = company strategy; **estrategia financiera** = financial strategy; **estrategia a plazo medio** = medium-term strategy

estratégico, -ca *adj* strategic; **planificación estratégica** = strategic planning

> estos consejeros, de talante renovador, querían poner en marcha un plan estratégico que modernizara la gestión de la compañía
>
> **El País**

estrella *nf* star; **hotel de cuatro estrellas** = four star hotel

estrellarse *vr* to crash; **el camión se estrelló contra la oficina de correos** = the lorry crashed into the post office; **el avión se estrelló contra el monte** = the plane crashed into the mountain

estrés *nm* stress; **medidas para combatir el estrés** = stress management; **personas en puestos de responsabilidad sufren enfermedades producidas por el estrés** = people in positions of responsability suffer from stress- related illnesses

> los trabajoadictos provienen casi siempre de una situación de estrés
>
> **Tiempo**

◊ **estresante** *adj* stressful

estricto, -ta *adj* strict; **en el sentido estricto de la palabra** = in the strict sense of the word

◊ **estrictamente** *adv* strictly; **estrictamente confidencial** = strictly confidential; **lo estrictamente necesario** = whatever is strictly necessary

estropear *vt* to harm *o* to spoil

◊ **estropearse** *vr* to break down; **la fotocopiadora se ha estropeado** = the photocopier has broken down

estructura *nf* structure; **estructura de capital de una compañía** = a comapny's capital structure; **estructura del comercio** = pattern of trade *o* trading pattern; **estructura cuadricular** = grid structure; **estructura de precios en el mercado de automóviles utilitarios** = the price structure in the small car market; **la estructura profesional dentro de la corporación** = the career structure within a corporation; **la estructura de salarios** *o* **la**

estructura salarial de la empresa = the company's salary structure; **establecer una estructura de ventas** = to build a sales structure

> la combinación de altos tipos de interés con una peseta fuerte amenaza directamente la estructura industrial y está creando un problema creciente de balanza de pagos
>
> **Actualidad Económica**

estructural *adj* structural; **hacer cambios estructurales en una compañía** = to make structural changes in a company; **Fondos Estructurales** = Structural Funds; **paro estructural** = structural unemployment

estructurar *vt* to structure *o* to arrange

estudiar *vt* **(a)** *(examinar)* to consider *o* to examine; **está estudiando las diferentes posibilidades de envase para la presentación de la nueva línea de productos** = he is engaged in research into the packaging of the new product line; **estudiar las condiciones de un contrato** = to consider the terms of a contract; **estamos estudiando la posibilidad de establecer una sucursal en Nueva York** = we are looking into the possibility of setting up an office in New York; **el gobierno estudió las propuestas del comité durante dos meses** = the government studied the committee's proposals for two months; **tendrá que estudiar el mercado cuidadosamente antes de decidir el diseño del producto** = you will need to study the market carefully before deciding on the design of the product **(b)** *(cursar estudios)* to study; **está estudiando banca** = he is studying banking; **estudiar ciencias empresariales** = to study management science

estudio *nm* **(a)** *(investigación)* study *o* investigation *o* research; **estudio sobre el comportamiento del consumidor** = consumer research; **estudio de desplazamientos y tiempos** = time and motion study; **estudio de mercado** = market research; **la empresa ha pedido a los asesores que preparen un estudio de la nuevas técnicas de producción** = the company has asked the consultants to prepare a study of new production techniques; **llevar a cabo un estudio de viabilidad** *o* **factibilidad de un proyecto** = to carry out a feasibility study on a project; **ha leído el estudio del gobierno sobre las posibilidades de venta** = he has read the government study on sales opportunities **(b)** *(lugar de trabajo)* studio; **estudio de diseño** = design studio; **estudio insonorizado** = soundproof studio; **estudios de televisión** = TV studios

> el impacto en el paro de un descenso en el ritmo de crecimiento económico ha sido cuantificado en un estudio interno de la CE
>
> **El País**

etapa *nf* **(a)** stage; **las distintas etapas del proceso de producción** = the different stages of the production process; **el contrato está todavía en la etapa de preparación** = the contract is still in the drafting stage **(b)** **por etapas** = in stages; **la compañía ha acordado devolver el préstamo por etapas** = the company has agreed to repay the loan in stages; **pagos por etapas** = staged payments

etc. = ETCETERA etc.

etcétera *adv* etcetera *o* and so on; **hay que pagar**

derechos de aduana por los artículos de lujo como coches, relojes etc. = the import duty is to be paid on luxury items including cars, watches, etc.

Etiopía *nf* Ethiopia

◇ **etíope** *adj y n* Ethiopian
NOTA: capital: **Addis Ababa;** moneda: **dólar etíope** *o* **birr (Br)** = Ethiopian birr (Br)

etiqueta *nf* **(a)** *(para objetos o paquetes)* label *o* tag; **etiqueta adhesiva** = sticker; **etiqueta autoadhesiva** = sticky label *o* self-sticking label *o* self-adhesive label; **etiqueta colgante** = tie-on label; **etiqueta engomada** = gummed label; **etiqueta de correo aéreo** = airmail sticker; **etiqueta de precio** = price tag *o* price label *o* price ticket; **etiqueta de señas** = address label; **poner etiqueta a** = to label *o* to stick a label on *o* to sticker; **ató dos etiquetas al paquete** = she tied two labels on to the parcel **(b)** *(formal)* etiquette *o* formality

etiquetado **1** *nm* labelling; **departamento de etiquetado** = labelling department **2** *pp de* ETIQUETAR

etiquetar *vt (poner etiqueta a)* to label *o* to sticker

euro *nm* euro

la banca europea tendrá que destinar entre 10.000 y 15.000 millones de euros en seis años para adecuar sus equipos informáticos a la moneda única
El País

el diseño del billete de 100 euros, que empezará a circular cuando entre en vigor la última fase de la Unión Monetaria Europea, es español
El País

euro- *prefijo* Euro-

◇ **eurobono** *nm* Eurobond; **el mercado de eurobonos** = the Eurobond market

◇ **eurocheque** *nm* Eurocheque

◇ **eurodivisa** *nf* Eurocurrency; **un crédito en eurodivisas** = a Eurocurrency loan; **el mercado de eurodivisas** = the Eurocurrency market

◇ **eurodiputado, -da** *n* Euro MP *o* member of the European Parliament (MEP)

◇ **eurodólar** *nm* Eurodollar; **un crédito en eurodólares** = a Eurodollar loan; **el mercado de eurodólares** = the Eurodollar market

◇ **euromercado** *nm* Euromarket

Europa *nf* Europe; **la mayoría de los países de Europa Occidental son miembros de la Unión Europea** = most of the countries of Western Europe are members of the European Union; **las exportaciones estadounidenses a Europa han aumentado un 25%** = American exports to Europe have risen by 25%; **representa a una empresa norteamericana de automóviles en Europa** = he represents an American car firm in Europe; **las ventas del Reino Unido a Europa han aumentado este año** = UK sales to Europe have increased this year

◇ **europeo, -pea** *adj* European; **Asociación Europea de Libre Comercio (AELC)** = European Free Trade Association (EFTA); **Comisión Europea** = European Commission; **la Comunidad Económica Europea (la CE** *o* **CEE)** = the European Economic Community (the EC *o* EEC); **Espacio Económico Europeo (EEE)** = European Economic Area (EEA); **el Mercado Común Europeo** = the European Common Market; **el Sistema Monetario Europeo (el SME)** = the European Monetary System (the EMS); **Unión Europea (UE)** = European Union (EU)

europeísta **1** *adj* communautaire **2** *nmf* proeuropean

Eurotúnel *nm* the Channel Tunnel

Euskadi *nm* Basque Country

evadir *vt* to evade *o* to avoid; **evadir impuestos** = to evade tax

◇ **evadirse** *vr* to escape

evaluación *nf* assessment *o* appraisal *o* evaluation; **evaluación de personal** = staff assessments; **evaluación del rendimiento** = performance measurement *o* measurement of performance; **evaluación de la rentabilidad** = measurement of profitability

evaluar *vt* to evaluate *o* to value *o* to assess *o* to appraise; **evaluar los costes** = to evaluate costs; **evaluar una situación** = to take stock of a situation

evasión *nf* **(a)** *(elusión)* evasion; **evasión de impuestos** *o* **fiscal** = tax evasion; **el gobierno está intensificando el control de la evasión de impuestos** = the government is tightening up on tax evasion **(b)** *(fuga)* flight *o* escape; **evasión de capitales** = flight of capital; **la evasión de capitales de Europa a los EE UU** = the flight of capital from Europe into the USA

eventual *adj* **(a)** *(temporero)* temporary *o* casual; **empleo eventual** = temporary employment; **tiene un empleo eventual en una empresa de construcción** = he has a temporary post with a construction company; **personal eventual** = temporary staff; **mano de obra eventual** = casual labour; **obrero** *o* **trabajador eventual** = casual labourer *o* casual worker; **trabajo eventual** = casual work; **tiene trabajo eventual como archivero** = he has a temporary job as a filing clerk *o* he has a job as a temporary filing clerk; **hacer trabajo eventual** = to temp; **puede ganar más en un trabajo eventual que en un trabajo a tiempo completo** = she can earn more money temping than from a full-time job **(b)** *(potencial)* prospective *o* potential; **cliente eventual** = prospective customer; **para disuadir a los eventuales evasores fiscales** = as a disincentive to potential tax evaders

eventualidad *nf* contingency *o* eventuality; **reserva para eventualidades** = provision for contingencies; **una parte de los beneficios brutos se reserva para eventualidades** = a proportion of the pre-tax profit is set aside for contingencies

evidente *adj* evident *o* plain *o* obvious *o* clear

evitación *nf* avoidance *o* prevention; **evitación de impuestos** = tax avoidance

evitar *vt* **(a)** *(prevenir)* to avoid; **la compañía está intentando evitar la quiebra** = the company is trying to avoid bankruptcy; **mi objetivo es evitar**

pagar demasiados impuestos = my aim is to avoid paying too much tax; **queremos evitar la competencia directa con García Hermanos S.A.** = we want to avoid direct competition with García Hermanos S.A. **(b)** *(impedir)* to prevent; **debemos intentar evitar la oferta pública de adquisición** = we must try to prevent the takeover bid

evolución *nf* development *o* change; **evolución del mercado** = market trends

evolucionar *vi* **(a)** *(actuar)* to perform; **¿cómo evolucionaron las acciones?** = how did the shares perform? **(b)** *(desarrollarse)* to evolve

ex *prefijo* ex- *o* former; **la secretaria fue a visitar al ex director en el hospital** = the secretary visited the ex-director in hospital; **pago ex-gratia** = an ex gratia payment

exactitud *nf* accuracy; **con exactitud** = accurately; **la disminución de las ventas del segundo trimestre fue pronosticada con exactitud por el ordenador** = the second quarter's drop in sales was accurately forecast by the computer

exacto, -ta *adj* exact *o* accurate *o* strict; **los diseñadores hicieron una copia exacta del plan** = the designers produced an accurate copy of the plan; **la vendedora me preguntó si tenía el importe exacto ya que no tenían cambio en la tienda** = the salesgirl asked me if I had the exact sum, since the shop had no change

◇ **exactamente** *adv* exactly *o* accurately *o* strictly; **el coste total fue exactamente de 1.250.000 ptas.** = the total cost was exactly 1.25m pesetas; **son exactamente las 10.27** = it is exactly 10.27 *o* the exact time is 10.27

exagerado, -da 1 *adj* exaggerated; **precios exagerados** = inflated prices; **previsión de beneficios exagerados** = inflated profit forecast **2** *pp de* EXAGERAR

exagerar *vt* to exaggerate; **sin exagerar** = conservatively

examen *nm* **(a)** *(inspección)* inspection *o* review; **examen general** = general review; **someter a un examen riguroso** = to examine carefully *o* to vet **(b)** *(prueba)* examination *o* exam *o* test; **examen para obtener el carnet de conducir** = driving test; **aprobó el examen de contabilidad** = he passed his accountancy examinations; **sacó la mejor nota de la clase en el examen de final de curso** = she came first in the final examination for the course; **suspendió el examen de aptitud por lo que tuvo que dejar su trabajo** = he failed his proficiency examination and so had to leave his job

examinar *vt* **(a)** *(estudiar)* to examine *o* to inspect *o* to consider; **examinar detenidamente** = to examine thoroughly *o* to go into; **el banco quiere examinar detenidamente los detalles de los préstamos entre sociedades** = the bank wants to go into the details of the inter-company loans; **examinar rigurosamente** = to examine carefully *o* to vet; **todos los candidatos tienen que ser rigurosamente examinados por el director gerente** = all candidates have to be vetted by the managing director; **la policía está examinando los documentos de la caja fuerte del director** = the police are examining the papers from the managing director's safe **(b)** *(examen)* to examine *o* to test

◇ **examinarse** *vr* to take an examination

excedencia *nf* leave of absence; **con respecto a su solicitud de excedencia** = with regard to your request for unpaid leave

excedente *nm* surplus *o* excess; **excedente laboral** = overmanning; **excedente de plantilla** = redundancy; **equipos excedentes del estado** = surplus government equipment; **los excedentes de mantequilla están a la venta en las tiendas** = surplus butter is on sale in the shops; **los gobiernos están buscando la manera de eliminar los excedentes agrícolas en la Unión Europea** = governments are trying to find ways of reducing the agricultural surpluses in the European Union

exceder *vt/i* **(a)** *(sobrepasar)* to exceed *o* to cap; **el año pasado los costes excedieron por primera vez al 20% de los ingresos** = last year costs exceeded 20% of income for the first time **(b)** **estos artículos exceden a nuestras necesidades** = these items are surplus to our requirements

excelente *adj* excellent *o* top quality *o* first class; **la calidad de los productos de la empresa es excelente, pero no tiene suficiente personal de ventas** = the quality of the firm's products is excellent, but its sales force is not large enough; **1995 fue un año excelente para la venta de ordenadores** = 1995 was an excellent year *o* a bumper year for computer sales

◇ **Excelentísimo, -ma** *n (título de cortesía)* Excellency

excepción *nf* **(a)** *(proviso)* exception; **con excepción de** = except *o* excluding; **todos los vendedores, con excepción de los que viven en Barcelona, pueden reclamar los gastos de asistencia a la reunión de ventas** = all salesmen, excluding those living in Barcelona, can claim expenses for attending the sales conference; **cláusula de excepción** = escape clause **(b)** *(emergencia)* emergency; **estado de excepción** = state of emergency; **el gobierno declaró el estado de excepción** = the government declared a state of emergency **(c)** *(renuncia)* waiver; **si quiere trabajar sin permiso, deberá solicitar una excepción** = if you want to work without a permit, you will have to apply for a waiver **(d) de excepción** = exceptional *o* very unusual; **una obra de excepción** = an exceptional piece of work

◇ **excepcional** *adj* exceptional *o* rare *o* very unusual; **cargos excepcionales** = exceptional charges; **partidas excepcionales** = exceptional items; **es excepcional encontrar una empresa pequeña con una buena situación de flujo de caja** = it is rare to find a small business with good cash flow

excepto *adv* except *o* excluding *o* unless; **excepto cuando se indique lo contrario** = unless otherwise stated

exceptuar *vt* to exclude *o* to leave out

excesivo, -va *adj* **(a)** *(desmesurado)* excessive *o* too high; **costes excesivos** = excessive costs; **oferta excesiva** oversupply; **precio excesivo** = overcharge **(b)** *(sobrante)* redundant

exceso *nm* **(a)** *(sobrante)* surplus *o* excess; **exceso de capacidad** = excess capacity; **exceso de**

equipaje = excess baggage; **un exceso de los gastos sobre los ingresos** = an excess of expenditure over revenue; **exceso de personal** = overmanning; **despedir a un trabajador por exceso de plantilla** = to make someone redundant; **personal despedido por exceso de plantilla** = redundant staff **(b) en exceso** = in excess *o* too much; **importe cargado en exceso** = overcharge; **devolver el importe cargado en exceso** = to pay back an overcharge; **pedimos que nos reembolsaran el dinero que nos habían cobrado en exceso** = we asked for a refund because we had been overcharged; **capitalizado en exceso** = overcapitalized; **pagado en exceso** = overpaid **(c) exceso de existencias**; overstocks; **tendremos que liquidar el exceso de existencias para hacer sitio en el almacén** = we will have to sell off the overstocks to make room in the warehouse **(d)** *(superabundancia)* glut

excluir *vt* to exclude; **los cargos en concepto de interés han sido excluidos del documento** = the interest charges have been excluded from the document; **los daños por incendio están excluidos de la póliza** = fire damage is excluded from the policy

exclusión *nf* exclusion; **cláusula de exclusión** = exclusion clause; **con exclusión de** = excluding *o* to the exclusion of

exclusiva *nf* exclusivity *o* sole rights *o* sole agency; **contrato en exclusiva** = exclusive agreement; **tener la exclusiva** = to have sole rights to *o* to be the sole agent for; **trabajar en exclusiva para una empresa** = to work exclusively for a firm

exclusividad *nf* exclusivity; **firmaron un acuerdo de exclusividad con una empresa egipcia** = they signed a closed market agreement with an Egyptian company

exclusivo, -va *adj* exclusive *o* sole; **comerciante exclusivo** = sole trader; **distribuidor exclusivo** = sole distributor; **representación exclusiva** = sole agency *o* exclusive representation; **tiene la representación exclusiva de los automóviles Ford** = he has the sole agency for Ford cars; **representante** *o* **concesionario exclusivo** = sole agent; **derechos exclusivos para la comercialización de un producto** = exclusive right to market a product

Excmo, -ma = EXCELENTISIMO, -MA

excusa *nf* apology *o* excuse; **presentó sus excusas por llegar tarde** = she apologized for being late; **su excusa por no venir a la reunión fue que sólo se lo habían comunicado el día anterior** *o* **con un día de antelación** = his excuse for not coming to the meeting was that he had been told about it only the day before; **el director gerente rechazó las excusas del director comercial por las bajas ventas registradas** = the managing director refused to accept the sales manager's excuses for the poor sales

excusar *vt* to excuse

◊ **excusarse** *vr* to excuse oneself *o* to apologize; **se excusó por llegar tarde** = he apologized for being late

exención *nf* allowance *o* exemption; **exención fiscal** = allowance(s) against tax *o* tax allowance(s); **al ser una organización sin fines de lucro Vds.**

pueden reclamar la exención fiscal = as a non-profit-making organization you can claim tax exemption; **exenciones tributarias** = exemption from tax *o* tax exemption

exento, -ta *adj* exempt *o* free; **exento de alquileres** = rent-free; **exento de impuestos** = exempt from tax *o* tax-exempt *o* non-taxable *o* duty-free; **como somos una organización sin fines lucrativos estamos exentos del pago de impuestos** = as a non-profit-making organization we are exempt from tax; **los productos alimenticios están exentos del impuesto sobre la venta** = food is exempted from sales tax; **importar vino exento de derechos de aduana** = to import wine free of duty *o* duty-free; **productos** *o* **servicios exentos del IVA** = exempt supplies

exhibición *nf* exhibition *o* show *o* display; **sala de exhibición de automóviles** = car showroom

◊ **exhibidor, -ra** *n* demonstrator

exhibir *vt* to display *o* to exhibit; **los aduaneros me pidieron que exhibiera el pasaporte** = customs officials asked me to show my passport

exigente *adj* demanding

exigible *adj* enforceable; *(dinero)* at call; **exigible legalmente** = legally enforceable *o* enforceable by law; **crédito exigible en cualquier momento** = money at call *o* money on call *o* call money

exigir *vt* **(a)** *(reclamar, pedir)* to claim *o* to demand; **exigió a su compañía de seguros el pago de las reparaciones del coche** = she claimed against her insurance company for repairs to the car; **exigieron que el Estado invirtiera más en nuevas industrias** = they called for more government investment in new industries; **exigió un reembolso** = she demanded a refund; **los proveedores exigen el pago de sus facturas pendientes** = the suppliers are demanding immediate payment of their outstanding invoices **(b)** *(requerir)* to require; **exigir una explicación detallada de los gastos** = to require a full explanation of expenditure; **exigir el pago de una deuda** = to call a loan; **la ley exige declarar todos los ingresos a las autoridades fiscales** = the law requires you to declare all income to the tax authorities; **el programa de inversiones ha exigido la máxima utilización de los recursos de la compañía** = the investment programme has stretched the company's resources

eximir *vt* to exempt; **el gobierno eximió de impuestos a los fideicomisos** = the government exempted trusts from tax

existencias *nfpl* **(a)** stock; *US* inventory; **tener muchas existencias** = to carry high stocks *o* a high inventory; **tratar de reducir las existencias** = to aim to reduce stocks *o* inventory; **tener excesivas existencias de piezas de recambio** = to be overstocked with spare parts; **el almacén se quemó totalmente y todas las existencias quedaron destruidas** = the warehouse burnt down and all the stock was destroyed **(b) existencias agotadas** = out of stock; **existencias disponibles** = in stock *o* stock in hand; **se agotaron las existencias del producto poco antes de Navidades pero estuvo disponible de nuevo durante la primera semana de enero** = the item went out of stock just before Christmas but came back into stock in the first week of January; **no**

nos quedan más existencias de este producto y estamos esperando reposiciones = we are out of stock of this item and are waiting for replacements **(c) existencias iniciales** = opening stock; **existencias finales** = closing stock; **existencias físicas** = physical stock; **existencias reguladoras** = buffer stocks; **control de existencias** = stock control; **control de existencias físicas** = physical stock check o physical stocktaking; **depreciación de las existencias por almacenaje** = stock depreciation; **inventario de existencias** = stock figures; **hacer un inventario de existencias** = to take stock; **nivel de existencias** = stock level; **nivel de existencias que justifica nuevos pedidos** = reorder level; **nivel de existencias mínimo** = minimum stock level; **tratamos de mantener bajos los niveles de existencias durante el verano** = we try to keep stock levels low during the summer; **rotación de existencias** = stock turn o stock turnround o stock turnover; **valoración de existencias** = stock valuation; **comprar una tienda con las existencias según valoración** = to buy a shop with stock at valuation; **comprar existencias según valoración** = to purchase stock at valuation; **liquidar las existencias** = to liquidate stock o to sell off stock; **tenemos una liquidación de existencias sobrantes** = we are holding a sale of surplus stock; **se vendieron todas las existencias en subasta pública** = all the stock was auctioned off; **existencias a la venta** = stock-in-trade

existir vi to exist; **no creo que el documento exista - creo que lo quemaron** = I do not believe the document exists - I think it has been burnt

éxito nm success; **el lanzamiento del nuevo modelo fue un gran éxito** = the launch of the new model was a great success; **con éxito** = (i) successful; (ii) successfully; **sin éxito** = (i) unsuccessful; (ii) unsuccessfully; **el proyecto era caro y no tuvo éxito** = the project was expensive and unsuccessful; **tener éxito** = to be successful; **su negocio ha tenido más éxito de lo que esperaba** = his business has succeeded more than he had expected; **la empresa ha tenido un gran éxito en el mercado japonés** = the company has had great success in the Japanese market; **artículo con gran éxito de venta** = best-seller

exorbitante adj exorbitant; **precios exorbitantes** = exorbitant prices o fancy prices

expandir vt to expand o to extend; **poliestireno expandido** = expanded polystyrene

expansión nf expansion; **la expansión del mercado interior** = the expansion of the domestic market; **una economía en expansión** = an expanding economy; **en fuerte expansión** = booming; **una industria en expansión** o **un mercado en expansión** = a growth industry o a growth market; **una industria** o **empresa en fuerte expansión** = a booming industry o company; **programa de expansión** = expansion programme; **la compañía tuvo dificultades para financiar su programa de expansión actual** = the company had difficulty in financing its current expansion programme; **proyecto de expansión comercial** = business expansion scheme

el ritmo medio de expansión económica se acelerará, pasando del escaso 1,1 por ciento conseguido en 1991 a una previsión de crecimiento que ronda el tres por ciento.

la expansión económica a largo plazo es el factor más importante para el éxito o el fracaso de una nación y es, sin duda, la base fundamental del progreso del bienestar de la población en su conjunto

expedición nf shipping o dispatching o forwarding; **aviso de expedición** = advice note; **nota de expedición** = dispatch note; **orden de expedición** = delivery order

expedidor, -ra n sender o forwarding agent o shipper o dispatcher; **agente expedidor** = shipping clerk

expediente nm **(a)** (carpeta que contiene documentos) file o dossier; **número de expediente** = registration number **(b)** (documentos en una casa) records o documents **(c)** (jurídico) proceedings o case; **abrir un expediente** = to start proceedings **(d)** **cubrir el expediente** = (i) to keep staff numbers to the minimum; (ii) to do the minimum required

El Gobierno rechazó la pretensión de su ministro de Economía de eliminar la autorización administrativa previa en los expedientes de regulación de empleo

expedir vt **(a)** (enviar) to send off o to dispatch; **expedir algo a alguien** = to forward o to send something to someone; **expedir un envío a Africa a toda prisa** = to rush a shipment to Africa **(b)** (en barco) to ship

expendedor, -ra 1 n **expendedor automático** = (automatic) vending machine **2** adj **máquina expendedora** = (i) (automatic) vending machine; (ii) dispenser

experiencia nf experience o background o skill; **este trabajo requiere cierta experiencia** = some experience is required for this job; **basarse en la experiencia acumulada** = to build on past experience; **es un hombre que tiene una gran experiencia** = he is a man of considerable experience; **su experiencia procede de la industria siderúrgica** = his background is in the steel industry; **tiene experiencia en el mundo editorial** = she has a publishing background; **adquirió la mayor parte de su experiencia en el Extremo Oriente** = he gained most of his experience in the Far East; **la empresa no tiene experiencia en el mercado de ordenadores** = the company has no track record in the computer market

experimentado, -da 1 adj experienced; **es el negociador más experimentado que conozco** = he is the most experienced negotiator I know **2** pp de EXPERIMENTAR

experimental adj experimental o pilot; **la compañía introdujo un plan** o **programa experimental para comprobar si el sistema de fabricación propuesto era eficaz** = the company set up a pilot project to see if the proposed manufacturing system was efficient

experimentar vt to experience; **experimentar**

una recuperación = to stage a recovery; **la compañía, que se encontraba al borde de la quiebra, ha experimentado una fuerte recuperación** = the company has staged a strong recovery from a point of near bankruptcy; **estas acciones han experimentado una subida del 10%** = these shares show an appreciation of 10%

experto, -ta 1 *adj* expert *o* proficient *o* experienced; **es bastante experta en inglés** = she is quite proficient in English **2** *n* expert *o* professional; **experto en el campo de la electrónica** *o* **experto en electrónica** = an expert in the field of electronics *o* an electronics expert; **la compañía pidió asesoramiento a un experto en finanzas** = the company asked a financial expert for advice *o* asked for expert financial advice

> diversos catedráticos, profesores y expertos en derecho analizan distintos puntos relacionados con el nuevo marco de competencia desleal
>
> **El País**

expiración *nf* expiration *o* expiry *o* termination; **la expiración de una póliza de seguros** = expiration of an insurance policy; **pagar antes de la expiración del periodo establecido** = to repay before the expiration of the stated period

expirar *vi* to expire; **el arriendo** *o* **contrato de arrendamiento expira en 1999** = the lease expires in 1999; **al expirar el arriendo** = on expiration of the lease

explicación *nf* explanation; **el inspector del IVA pidió una explicación de las facturas** = the VAT inspector asked for an explanation of the invoices; **en la junta general anual, el presidente dio una explicación de los altos intereses pagados** = at the AGM, the chairman gave an explanation for the high level of interest payments

explicar *vt* to explain; **explicar una pérdida** *o* **una diferencia de números** = to account for a loss *o* a discrepancy; **explicó a los funcionarios de aduanas que los dos ordenadores eran regalos de unos amigos** = he explained to the customs officials that the two computers were presents from friends; **explicó su magnífico plan para la reorganización del solar de la fábrica** = he explained his grand plan for redeveloping the factory site; **¿puede Vd. explicar por qué las ventas del primer trimestre son tan altas?** = can you explain why the sales in the first quarter are so high?

explícito, -ta *adj* explicit *o* express; **el contrato tiene una condición explícita que prohibe vender en Africa** = the contract has an express condition forbidding sale in Africa

◇ **explícitamente** *adv* expressly *o* explicitly

explorar *vt* to explore *o* to investigate; **explorar el terreno** = to examine the situation *o* to see how the land lies; **tendremos que explorar el terreno antes de tomar una decisión** = we shall examine the situation carefully before taking a decision

explotación *nf* **(a)** *(aprovechamiento)* exploitation; **beneficios de explotación** = operating profit *o* trading profit; **costes de explotación** = operating costs *o* operational costs; **cuenta de explotación** = trading account; **gastos de explotación** = running costs *o* running expenses *o*

costs of running a business *o* business expenses *o* operating expenses; **margen de explotación** = operating margin; **pérdidas de explotación** = operating loss; **presupuesto de explotación** = operating budget *o* operational budget; **la creación de sindicatos puso fin a la explotación de los trabajadores agrícolas inmigrantes** = the exploitation of migrant farm workers was only stopped when they became unionized **(b)** **explotación agrícola** = farm *o* farm business *o* agribusiness; **derechos de explotación** = mineral rights; **explotación en régimen de concesión** = a franchising operation; **conceder una licencia de explotación** = to franchise **(c)** *(realización de ganancias excesivas)* profiteering

> durante el primer año de explotación, en 1982, el TGV transportó más de seis millones de personas. En 1990, 33 millones
>
> **Cambio 16**

explotar *vt* to exploit *o* to run *o* to operate; **esperamos explotar los recursos petrolíferos en el mar de China** = we hope to exploit the oil resources in the China Sea

exponer *vt* **(a)** *(describir)* to describe *o* to set out; **exponer los detalles en un informe** = to set out the details in a report; **exponer a grandes rasgos** = to outline; **el presidente expuso a grandes rasgos los planes de la compañía para el año próximo** = the chairman outlined the company's plans for the coming year; **el director general expuso los problemas de la compañía en materia de flujo de caja** = the managing director described the company's difficulties with cash flow **(b)** *(exhibir)* to exhibit *o* to display; **la empresa exponía tres nuevos modelos en el Salón del Automóvil** = the company was displaying three new car models at the show; **pidió en la oficina de información los detalles de las empresas que exponían en el Salón del Automóvil** = he asked the information office for details of companies exhibiting at the Motor Show; **los compradores admiraron los objetos expuestos en nuestro stand** = the buyers admired the exhibits on our stand **(c)** **exponer una queja** = to air a grievance; **el comité de gestión es útil porque permite a los obreros exponer sus quejas** = the management committee is useful because it allows the workers' representatives to air their grievances

exportación *nf* **(a)** *(acción)* export *o* exportation; **exportación de importaciones** = entrepot trade; **aranceles** *o* **derechos** *o* **tarifas de exportación** = export duty; **auge impulsado por las exportaciones** = export-led boom; **el comercio de exportación** = the export trade; **departamento de exportación** = export department; **director de exportación** = export manager; **licencia** *o* **permiso de exportación** = export licence; **el gobierno ha denegado una licencia de exportación para piezas de recambio de ordenadores** = the government has refused an export licence for computer parts **(b)** *(mercancías)* **exportaciones** = exports; **las exportaciones a Africa han aumentado el 25%** = exports to Africa have increased by 25%

> la política económica no ayudará a la inversión empresarial y las exportaciones tirarán del crecimiento en 1992
>
> **Actualidad Económica**

exportador, -ra 1 *adj* exporting; **el mercado exportador** = the export market; **la Organización de los Países Exportadores de Petróleo (OPEP)** = Organization of Petroleum Exporting Countries (OPEC) **2** *n* exporter; **un importante exportador de muebles** = a major furniture exporter; **Venezuela es un importante exportador de petróleo** = Venezuela is an important exporter of oil *o* an important oil exporter

exportar *vt* to export; **exportamos el 50% de nuestra producción** = we export 50% of our production *o* 50% of our production is exported; **la compañía importa materias primas y exporta productos acabados** = the company imports raw materials and exports the finished products

exposición *nf* **(a)** *(exhibición)* display *o* exhibition *o* show; **la exposición tiene lugar en el palacio de congresos** = the exhibition is being staged in the conference centre; **el gobierno ha patrocinado una exposición de diseño** = the government has sponsored a design exhibition; **una exposición atractiva de aparatos de cocina** = an attractive display of kitchen equipment; **embalaje** *o* **caja de exposición** = display pack *o* display box; **los relojes se presentan empaquetados en cajas de exposición de plástico** = the watches are prepacked in plastic display boxes; **escaparate de exposición** = display unit; **estantería** *o* **vitrina de exposición** = display stand *o* display unit; **local de exposición** = exhibition stand; **material de exposición** = display material; **salón** *o* **sala de exposiciones** = exhibition room *o* hall; **stand de exposición** = exhibition stand; *US* exhibition booth; **tenemos un stand en la Exposición del Hogar Ideal** = we have a stand at the Ideal Home Exhibition; **exposición comercial** = trade fair; **exposición itinerante** = travelling exhibition **(b)** *(stand en una feria)* exhibit *o* stand; **la Exposición Comercial Española en la Feria Internacional de Ordenadores** = the Spanish Trade Exhibit at the International Computer Fair

expositor, -ra 1 *n* exhibitor; **la feria atrae a muchos expositores extranjeros** = the fair attracts many foreign exhibitors **2** *nm* *(vitrina)* showcase; **colocamos el expositor en el centro de la tienda** = we have placed the showcase in the middle of the shop

expresar *vt* to express *o* to show; **este gráfico muestra las ventas nacionales expresadas como porcentaje del volumen total de ventas** = this chart shows home sales expressed as a percentage of total turnover

expresión *nf* expression *o* record; **el presidente firmó el acta como expresión fiel de la última reunión** = the chairman signed the minutes as a true record of the last meeting

expreso, -sa *adj* express; **por orden expresa de** = by express order of

◊ **expresamente** *adv* expressly *o* on purpose; **el contrato prohibe expresamente la venta en los Estados Unidos** = the contract expressly forbids sales to the United States; **conduce un Mercedes fabricado expresamente para él** = he drives a custom-built Mercedes

expropiación *nf* expropriation; **expropiación forzosa** = compulsory purchase

expulsar *vt* to expel *o* to throw out *o* to evict; **la junta general anual expulsó al antiguo consejo de administración** = the AGM threw out the old board of directors

◊ **expulsión** *nf* expulsion

ext (a) = EXTERIOR **(b)** = EXTENSION

extender *vt* **(a)** *(prolongar, conceder)* to extend **(b)** *(ampliar)* to extend *o* to stretch *o* to expand; **extender las actividades de un negocio** = to branch out; **la empresa ha extendido sus actividades al alquiler de coches** = the company has branched out into car leasing **(c)** **extender un mandato judicial contra alguien** = to issue a writ against someone; **extender un cheque** = to write out a cheque; **extender un cheque a nombre de alguien** = to make out a cheque to someone

◊ **extenderse** *vr* to extend *o* to spread *o* to range *o* to reach

extensión *nf* **(a)** *(teléfono)* extension; **¿puede ponerme con la extensión 21?** = can you get me extension 21?; **el director de ventas está hablando por la extensión 53** = the sales manager is on extension 53 **(b)** *(ampliación, prolongación)* extension; **extensión de garantía** = extended guarantee *o* warranty

extensivo, -va *adj* extensive

extenso, -sa *adj* extensive *o* widespread *o* large; **una extensa red de ventas** = an extensive network of sales outlets

exterior 1 *adj* **(a)** *(de un país)* outside *o* external; **comercio exterior** = foreign trade *o* overseas trade *o* external trade; **crecimiento exterior** = external growth; **inversiones exteriores** = foreign investments; **Ministerio de Asuntos Exteriores** = Foreign Ministry; *GB* Foreign Office; *US* State Department; **el servicio exterior** = the overseas division **(b)** *(de una compañía)* outside *o* external; **línea exterior** = outside line; **se marca el 9 para obtener la línea exterior** = you dial 9 to get an outside line **2** *nm* **(a)** *(de un país)* foreign countries; **el comercio con el exterior** = foreign trade *o* overseas trade **(b)** *(de una compañía)* exterior *o* outside

> para abordar fusiones en el exterior con cierta dignidad, resulta imprescindible conseguir antes una cierta dimensión de respetabilidad en el interior
> **España Económica**

externo, -na *adj* external *o* outside; **auditor** *o* **interventor externo** = external auditor; **auditoría externa** = external audit; **consejero externo** = outside director; **crecimiento externo** = external growth

extintor *nm* fire extinguisher

extirpar *vt* to cut out *o* to eradicate *o* to excise

extra 1 *adj* extra; **beneficios extras** = fringe benefits; **horas extras** = overtime; **tarifa de horas extras** = overtime pay; **prohibición de realizar horas extras** = overtime ban; **tenía una paga extra de 5.000 ptas. por trabajar los domingos** = he had 5,000 pesetas extra pay for working on Sunday **2** *nm* **(a)** *(cosa añadida)* extra item **(b)** *(suma adicional)* overs; **el precio incluye un 10% extra para la**

indemnización de daños eventuales = the price includes 10% overs to compensate for damage **3** *prefijo* extra-; **beneficios extrasalariales** = fringe benefits

extracto *nm* extract; **extracto de cuenta** = statement of account *o* bank statement; **me envió un extracto de las cuentas** = he sent me a statement (of account)

extraer *vt* **(a)** *(sacar)* to extract *o* to take out **(b)** *(obtener)* to mine; **la compañía extrae carbón en el sur del país** = the company is mining coal in the south of the country

```
según los datos facilitados por la Bolsa
de Madrid y extraídos del registro de caja
del Banco de España, los extranjeros
realizaron compras en las bolsas
españolas por un valor de 1,6 billones de
ptas.
                                    El País
```

extranjero, -ra 1 *adj* foreign *o* overseas; **moneda extranjera** = foreign currency; **los mercados extranjeros** = overseas markets; **productos extranjeros** = foreign goods; **los coches extranjeros han inundado nuestro mercado** = foreign cars have flooded our market; **estamos aumentando nuestro comercio con los países extranjeros** = we are increasing our trade with foreign countries **2** *nm* abroad *o* overseas; **una llamada al** *o* **del extranjero** = an overseas call; **en el** *o* **al extranjero** = abroad; **los beneficios obtenidos en el extranjero son mucho mayores que los del mercado interior** = the profits from overseas are far higher than those of the home division; **los automóviles fueron enviados al extranjero la semana pasada** = the consignment of cars was shipped abroad last week **3** *n* foreigner

extraoficial *adj (no oficial)* unofficial; **hizo unas observaciones extraoficiales referentes a las desastrosas cifras de las ventas nacionales** = he made some remarks off the record about the disastrous home sales figures

◊ **extraoficialmente** *adv* **(a)** *(que no es oficial)* unofficially *o* informally *o* off-the-record; **la delegación de Hacienda le dijo extraoficialmente a la compañía que sería procesada** = the tax office told the company unofficially that it would be prosecuted **(b)** *(por cuenta propia)* on the side **(c)** *(en privado)* off the record

extraordinario, -ria *adj* **(a)** extraordinary; **beneficios extraordinarios** = excess profit; **impuesto sobre los beneficios extraordinarios** = windfall tax; **horas extraordinarias** = overtime; **la tarifa de las horas extraordinarias es una vez y media la tarifa normal** = the overtime rate is one and a half times normal pay; **Junta General Extraordinaria** = Extraordinary General Meeting; **convocar una Junta General Extraordinaria** = to call an Extraordinary General Meeting; **partidas extraordinarias** = extraordinary items; **los auditores advirtieron varias partidas extraordinarias en las cuentas** = the auditors noted several extraordinary items in the accounts **(b)** **una cosecha extraordinaria de maíz** = an exceptionally large corn crop *o* a bumper crop of corn

extraterritorial *adj* extraterritorial; **banco extraterritorial** = off-shore bank

extremadamente *adv* extremely; **es extremadamente difícil introducirse en el mercado estadounidense** = it is extremely difficult to break into the US market

extremarse *vr* **extremarse en conseguir algo** = to go to great lengths to get something

Ff

FA = FUSIONES Y ADQUISICIONES

fábrica *nf* factory *o* works *o* plant; **cerraron seis fábricas en el norte del país** = they closed down six factories in the north of the country; **fábrica de acero** = steel works; **fábrica de calzado** = shoe factory; **fábrica de coches** = car factory *o* car plant; **piensan construir una fábrica de coches cerca del río** = they are planning to build a car factory near the river; **fábrica de construcción de máquinas** *o* **de maquinaria** = an engineering works; **fábrica industrial** = an industrial works; **fábrica de tejidos de algodón** = cotton mill; **director de fábrica** = the works manager; **le nombraron director de la fábrica** = he was appointed works manager; **inspector de fábrica** = factory inspector *o* inspector of factories; **cuerpo de inspectores de fábricas** = the factory inspectorate; **obrero** *o* **trabajador de fábrica** = factory worker; **precio en fábrica** *o* **franco en fábrica** *o* **vendido en fábrica** = price ex works *o* factory price *o* price ex factory; **tienda de fábrica** = factory outlet

fabricación *nf* manufacture *o* manufacturing *o* making; **de fabricación casera** = homemade; **productos de fabricación extranjera** = products of foreign manufacture; **capacidad de fabricación** = manufacturing capacity; **costes de fabricación** = manufacturing costs; **gastos generales de fabricación** = manufacturing overheads; **procesos de fabricación** = manufacturing *o* industrial processes; **unidad de fabricación** = factory unit

fabricante *nmf* maker *o* manufacturer *o* producer; **fabricante de coches** = car maker *o* producer; **un importante fabricante de coches** = a major car maker; **fabricante de coches deportivos** = sports car manufacturer; **fabricantes extranjeros** = foreign manufacturers; **un fabricante de muebles** = a furniture maker; **fabricante de tejidos de algodón** = (cotton) textile manufacturer; **todas las máquinas de escribir - un 20% de descuento sobre el precio recomendado por el fabricante** = all typewriters - 20% off the manufacturer's recommended price

fabricar *vt* to manufacture *o* to make *o* to produce; **fabricar un coche** *o* **fabricar un ordenador** = to make a car *o* to make a computer; **fabricar un nuevo producto** = to develop a new product; **la empresa fabrica piezas de recambio para coches** = the company manufactures spare parts for cars; **fabricado en Japón** = made in Japan *o* Japanese-made; **fabricar en serie** *o* **a gran escala** = to mass-produce; **fabricar coches a gran escala** = to mass-produce cars

◊ **fabricarse** *vr* to be made; **estas alfombras ya no se fabrican** = these carpets are not made any more *o* are a discontinued line

fachada *nf* front; **fachada de la tienda** = shopfront; **la fachada de las oficinas da a La Calle Mayor** = the front of the office building is on the Calle Mayor

fácil *adj* easy; **fácil de usar** *o* **fácil para el usuario** *o* **de fácil manejo** = user-friendly; **dinero fácil** = easy money; **artículos de venta fácil** = fast-selling

items; **algunos diccionarios no son fáciles de vender** = some dictionaries are not fast-moving stock

◊ **fácilmente** *adv* easily

facilidad *nf* facility; **facilidades de crédito** = credit facilities; **facilidad de venta** = saleability *o* marketability; **pagar algo con facilidades de crédito** *o* **con facilidades de pago** = to pay for something on easy terms; **ofrecemos facilidades de pago** = we offer credit terms

factibilidad *nf* feasibility; **informe de factibilidad** = feasibility report; **llevar a cabo un estudio de la factibilidad de un proyecto** = to carry out a feasibility study on a project

factor *nm* (a) factor; **la caída de las ventas es un factor importante en la reducción de los beneficios de la empresa** = the drop in sales is an important factor in the company's lower profits; **factor del coste** = cost factor; **factores cíclicos** = cyclical factors; **factor decisivo** = deciding factor; **factor negativo** = minus factor; **factores de producción** = factors of production; **factor de riesgo** = risk factor *o* downside factor (b) **por un factor de diez** = by a factor of ten

factoría *nf* factory *o* plant; **ciudad-factoría** = company town; **factoría de construcción naval** = shipyard

factura *nf* (a) invoice *o* bill; **su factura del 10 de noviembre** = your invoice dated November 10th; **llamó** *o* **telefoneó para hablar de la factura de enero** = he phoned about the January invoice; **hacer duplicado de** *o* **copiar una factura** = to copy *o* to duplicate an invoice; **descontar facturas** = to discount invoices; **envío de facturas** = invoicing; **el contratista envió su factura** = the builder sent in his bill; **hacer una factura** = to make out an invoice; **el vendedor hizo la factura por un importe de 50.000 ptas.** = the salesman wrote out the bill for 50,000 pesetas; **la factura está dirigida** *o* **extendida a nombre de García S.A.** = the bill is made out to García S.A.; **pasar factura** = to invoice; **le pasamos la factura el 10 de noviembre** = we invoiced you on November 10th; **preparar una factura** = to prepare an invoice *o* to raise an invoice; **presentaron la factura con seis semanas de retraso** = they sent in their invoice six weeks late; **el contratista le presentó una factura por las reparaciones hechas en la casa de su vecino** = the builders billed him for the repairs to his neighbour's house; **saldar** *o* **pagar una factura** = to settle *o* to pay an invoice; **pago de la factura presentada** = payment for account rendered; **en la factura pone 'pagado'** = the invoice is marked 'paid'; **impago de una factura** = non-payment of a bill; **facturas impagadas** = unpaid invoices *o* bills; **se desprende de nuestros libros que la factura número 1234 no ha sido pagada** = we find from our records that our invoice number 1234 has not been paid; **importe pagadero en el plazo de treinta días a partir de la fecha de la factura** = the total is payable within thirty days of invoice; **factura con el IVA incluido**

o **desglosado** = VAT invoice; **¿está incluido el IVA en la factura?** = does the bill include VAT?; **el IVA no está incluido en la factura** = the invoice is exclusive of VAT; **la factura incluye el 15% de IVA** = the invoice includes VAT at 15%; **factura conforme** = receipt in due form; **valor total de factura** = total invoice value **(b) según factura** = as per invoice **(c) facturas en cuatro partes** = four-part invoices; **factura pro forma** = pro forma (invoice); **nos enviaron una factura pro forma** = they sent us a pro forma

> Más de 600 empresas públicas y privadas están implicadas en la compra de facturas falsas, utilizadas para pagar menos impuestos
>
> **Cambio 16**

facturación *nf* **(a)** *(factura)* invoicing *o* billing; **nuestra facturación se realiza por ordenador** = our invoicing is done by the computer; **facturación con IVA incluido** = VAT invoicing; **facturación por triplicado** = invoicing in triplicate; **departamento de facturación** = invoicing department; **encargado de la facturación** = invoice clerk **(b) (cifra de) facturación** *o* **volumen de facturación** = turnover; **facturación bruta** = gross turnover; **facturación neta** = net turnover **(c)** *(equipaje) (aeropuerto)* check-in; *(estación)* registration

> en un año considerado malo para el sector, nuestro volumen de facturación ha seguido creciendo
>
> **Tiempo**

> la empresa tiene 90 trabajadores en plantilla y una facturación de 3.600 millones de pesetas
>
> **El País**

> Iberia y sus compañías participadas van a unir sus actividades combinando tanto la facturación y emisión de billetes como la utilización de la sala VIP para pasajeros de clase preferente y gran clase
>
> **Tiempo**

facturar *vt* **(a)** *(pasar factura)* to invoice *o* to bill; **facturar a un cliente** = to invoice a customer **(b) facturar el equipaje** = *(aeropuerto)* to check baggage in; *(estación)* to register luggage

◊ **facturado, -da** *adj y pp* registered *o* invoiced; **precio facturado** = invoice price

facultad *nf* **(a)** *(habilidad)* faculty *o* ability; **tiene la facultad de aprender idiomas fácilmente** = he has the ability to learn languages easily **(b)** *(autoridad)* power; **el presidente tiene facultad para nombrar a los consejeros** = the chairman has the power to appoint directors **(c)** *(universidad)* faculty *o* school; **Facultad de Filosofía y Letras** *o* **de Derecho** = Faculty of Letters *o* of Law

> el Gobierno ha solicitado al Congreso nuevas facultades para legislar por decreto el sistema tributario
>
> **Cambio 16**

facultativo, -va *adj* optional

faena *nf* job *o* task; **tener faena** = to be busy

fallar *vi* **(a)** *(fracasar)* to fail; **el prototipo falló en su primera prueba** = the prototype failed its first test **(b)** *(jurídico)* to find *o* to rule; **el juez falló a**

favor del demandado = the judge found for the defendant

fallecimiento *nm* death *o* demise *o* decease; **indemnización por fallecimiento** = death benefit; **indemnización por fallecimiento de un trabajador** = compensation for death in service *o* death in service compensation

fallo *nm* **(a)** *(defecto)* defect *o* mistake *o* fault; **los técnicos están intentando corregir un fallo del programa** = the technicians are trying to correct a programming fault **(b)** *(jurídico)* award *o* ruling *o* judgement; **el fallo del árbitro se anuló tras la apelación** = the arbitrator's award was set aside on appeal; **el tribunal pronunció el fallo sobre la causa** = the inquiry gave a ruling on the case; **según el fallo del tribunal, el contrato era ilegal** = according to the ruling of the court, the contract was illegal **(c)** *(informática)* malfunction; **se perdió la información debido a un fallo del programa** = the data was lost due to a software malfunction

falsear *vt* to falsify *o* to forge; *(informal)* to fiddle (accounts)

falsedad *nf* falseness; **falsedad fraudulenta** = fraudulent misrepresentation

falsificación *nf* falsification *o* forgery *o* fake; **falsificación de documentos** = forgery; **fue a la cárcel por falsificación de documentos** = he was sent to prison for forgery

> el sistema de falsificación de facturas, que afecta al IVA y al Impuesto sobre Sociedades se realiza de distintas formas
>
> **Cambio 16**

falsificado, -da 1 *adj* counterfeit *o* fake *o* forged; **se demostró que la firma era falsificada** = the signature was proved to be a forgery **2** *pp de* FALSIFICAR

falsificador, -ra *n* forger *o* counterfeiter

> la empresa cliente paga el supuesto servicio o la supuesta venta con un talón nominativo a nombre de la empresa inactiva, que es entregado en un banco donde ésta tiene una cuenta, controlada por el falsificador
>
> **Cambio 16**

falsificar *vt* **(a)** *(falsear)* to fake *o* to falsify *o* to forge; **falsificó los resultados de la prueba** = he faked the results of the test; **falsificar las cuentas** = to falsify the accounts *o* to fiddle the accounts **(b)** *(dinero)* to counterfeit

falso, -sa 1 *adj* **(a)** *(falsificado)* false *o* counterfeit; *(informal)* dud; **el billete de 10.000 ptas. era falso** = the 10,000 peseta note was a dud; **contabilidad falsa** = false accounting; **documento falso** = faked document *o* forgery; **peso falso** = false weight; **intentó entrar en el país con documentación falsa** = he tried to enter the country with forged documents; **anotar una partida falsa en el balance de situación** = to make a false entry in the balance sheet **(b)** *(perjurar)* **dar falso testimonio** = to perjure yourself **2** *adv* **en falso** = falsely; **jurar en falso** = to commit perjury

falta *nf* **(a)** *(fallo)* fault *o* failure **(b)** *(carencia)* lack *o* shortage *o* want; **no hay falta de asesoramiento**

sobre inversiones = there is no shortage of investment advice *o* no lack of advice for investors; **falta de datos** *o* **falta de información** = lack of data *o* lack of information; **falta de entrega** = non-delivery; **falta de fondos** = lack of funds; **el proyecto fue cancelado por falta de fondos** = the project was cancelled because of lack of funds; **el control a las importaciones ha provocado la falta de repuestos** = the import controls have resulted in the shortage of spare parts **(c) a falta de** *o* **por falta de** = for lack of *o* failing; **a falta de pago** = in default of payment; **fue elegido a falta de otro candidato** = he was elected by default; **a falta de instrucciones al contrario** = failing instructions to the contrary; **la decisión se ha aplazado por falta de información actualizada** = the decision has been put back for lack of up-to-date information

faltar *vi* to be lacking; **faltarle a uno algo** = to lack; **nos falta dinero** = we are short of money; **nos falta bastante personal en este momento** = we are rather short-staffed at the moment; **faltan diez de los obreros porque tienen gripe** = ten of the workers are absent with flu; **hacer una lista de cosas que faltan** = to draw up a wants list; **faltan 2.000 ptas. en la caja para gastos menores** = the petty cash is 2,000 pesetas short; **faltaban tres artículos en el envío** = the shipment was three items short; **a la empresa le faltan nuevas ideas** = the company is short of new ideas; **a la compañía le falta capital** = the company lacks capital; **la fotocopiadora no funciona - le falta un repuesto** = the photocopier will not work - it needs a spare part

falto, -ta *adj* short *o* lacking; **falto de personal** = short-staffed *o* undermanned; **falto de recursos** = without resources

fama *nf* reputation *o* standing; **tener fama de** = to be famous for *o* to have a reputation for; **tiene fama de ser muy difícil en las negociaciones** = he has a reputation for being difficult to negotiate with; **tiene fama de moroso** = he is well known as a slow payer

familiar *adj* family *o* familiar; **marca familiar** = household name

familiarizar *vt* to familiarize

◊ **familiarizarse** *vr* **familiarizarse con** = to familiarize oneself with

famoso, -sa *adj* famous; **la sociedad posee unos grandes almacenes muy famosos en el centro de Madrid** = the company owns a famous department store in the centre of Madrid

fase *nf* phase *o* stage; **la primera fase del programa de expansión** = the first phase of the expansion programme

```
la primera fase del proyecto finalizará en
el plazo de año y medio, y una vez finalizado
será    puesto    a    prueba    en    los    más
prestigiosos    centros    sanitarios    de
Europa
                                          Micros
```

favor *nm* **(a) saldo a favor** = credit balance **(b)** favour; **a favor de** = in favour of; **seis miembros de la junta están a favor de la propuesta, y tres en contra** = six members of the board are in favour of the proposal, and three are against it; **como un favor (especial)** = as a favour **(c) en favor de** = on behalf of

◊ **favorable** *adj* favourable; **balanza comercial favorable** = favourable balance of trade; **en condiciones favorables** = on favourable terms; **negociar para obtener condiciones más favorables** = to negotiate for better terms

◊ **favorablemente** *adv* favourably; **el mercado reaccionó favorablemente ante la noticia de la decisión del gobierno** = the market reacted favourably to the news of the government's decision

favorecer *vt* to benefit *o* to favour; **una reducción de la inflación favorece el tipo de cambio** = a fall in inflation benefits the exchange rate; **le acusaron de utilizar su cargo en el consejo para favorecer sus propios intereses** = he was accused of using his membership of the board to further his own interests

◊ **favorecido, -da** *adj y pp* favoured; **cláusula de la nación más favorecida** = most-favoured-nation clause

favorito, -ta *adj* favourite

fax *nm* **(a)** *(sistema de envío, documento)* fax; **enviar un fax** *o* **enviar por fax** *o* **mandar un fax** *o* **mandar por fax** = to fax; **enviaremos el proyecto por fax** = we will send a fax of the design plan; **recibimos un fax del pedido esta mañana** = we received a fax of the order this morning; **¿puede confirmar la reserva por fax?** = can you confirm the booking by fax?; **he mandado los documentos por fax a nuestra oficina de Caracas** = I've faxed the documents to our Caracas office; **nada más oír la noticia envió un fax a su oficina** = as soon as he heard the news he immediately faxed his office **(b)** *(máquina)* fax machine; **número de fax** = fax number; **papel para el fax** = fax paper; **rollo de papel para el fax** = fax roll

fe *nf* faith; **de buena fe** = bona fide; **comprar algo de buena fe** = to buy something in good faith; **dar fe de** = to certify; **tener fe en alguien** *o* **algo** = to have faith in someone *o* something

febril *adj* **compra febril** = panic buying

fecha *nf* **(a)** date; **fecha de amortización** *o* **de rescate** = redemption date; **fecha de caducidad** = (i) sell-by date (ii) expiry date; **fecha de entrada en vigor** = effective date; **fecha de entrega** = delivery date; **fecha inicial** = starting date; **fecha de liquidación** = settlement date; **fecha de recepción** = date of receipt; **fecha tope** *o* **límite** = closing date *o* deadline; **fecha de vencimiento** = maturity date *o* date of maturity; *(de pago)* final date for payment; **fecha de vencimiento del IVA** = tax point; **fecha de vencimiento de una letra** = date of bill; **cantidad a pagar en la fecha de vencimiento** = amount payable on maturity; **con fecha de** = dated; **he recibido su carta con fecha de ayer** = I have received your letter of yesterday's date; **le agradecemos su carta de fecha 15 de junio** = thank you for your letter dated June 15th; **se olvidó poner la fecha en el cheque** = you forgot to date the cheque; **poner una fecha adelantada en un cheque** = to date a cheque forward; **nos mandó un cheque con una fecha futura** = he sent us a postdated cheque; **valores convertibles en acciones en una fecha futura** = convertible loan stock; **sello de fecha** = date stamp **(b) hasta la fecha** = to date; **intereses hasta la fecha** = interest to date

◇ **fechador** *nm (sello de fecha)* date stamp

fechar *vt* to date; **el cheque estaba fechado el 24 de marzo** = the cheque was dated March 24th

FED = FONDO EUROPEO DE DESARROLLO European Development Fund (EDF)

FEDER = FONDO EUROPEO DE DESARROLLO REGIONAL European Regional Development Fund (ERDF)

federación *nf* federation; **federación patronal** = employers' federation; **federación de sindicatos** = trade union federation

federal *adj* federal; **Reserva Federal** = Federal Reserve; *(EE.UU)* **la mayoría de las oficinas federales están en Washington** = most federal offices are in Washington

felicitación *nf* congratulations; **recibió felicitaciones del personal por su ascenso** = the staff congratulated him on his promotion

felicitar *vt* to congratulate; **el director de ventas felicitó a los vendedores por haber duplicado las ventas** = the sales director congratulated the salesmen on doubling sales; **quiero felicitarle por su ascenso** = I want to congratulate you on your promotion

feliz *adj* happy

feria *nf* show *o* fair; **feria del automóvil** = motor show; **feria comercial** = trade fair; **la Feria de la Informática se celebra del 1 al 6 de abril** = the Computer Fair *o* Computer Show runs from April 1st to 6th; **la feria está abierta de 9 a 5** = the fair is open from 9 a.m. to 5 p.m.; **organizar** *o* **dirigir una feria comercial** = to organize *o* to run a trade fair; **los recintos de la feria agrícola** = the agricultural exhibition grounds

ferretería *nf* **(a)** *(tienda)* hardware shop **(b)** *(herramientas)* hardware

ferrocarril *nm* rail *o* railway; *US* railroad; **enviamos todas las mercancías por ferrocarril** = we ship all our goods by rail; **estación de ferrocarril** = railway station; **línea de ferrocarril** = railway line; **la red nacional de ferrocarriles** = the national railway network; *ver también* RENFE

ferry *nm* ferry; **ferry con acceso directo para vehículos** *o* **con embarque y desembarque por propulsión propia** = roll on/roll off ferry

FF.CC. = FERROCARRILES railway

FGD = FONDO DE GARANTÍA DE DEPOSITOS Deposit Guarantee Fund

FGS = FONDO DE GARANTÍA SALARIAL Wages Guarantee Fund

fiabilidad *nf* reliability; **el producto ha pasado las pruebas de fiabilidad** = the product has passed its reliability tests

fiable *adj* reliable; **tenemos información fiable sobre las ventas de nuestro competidor** = we have reliable information about our rival's sales; **poco fiable** = unreliable; **el servicio de correos es muy poco fiable** = the postal service is very unreliable

fiador, -ra *n* **(a)** *(garante)* guarantor *o* warrantor;

ser fiador de = to guarantee; **actuar como fiador de alguien** = to stand surety for someone; **se presentó como fiador de su hermano** = he stood guarantor for his brother *(jurídico)* **ser fiador de alguien por 600.000 ptas.** = to stand bail of 600,000 pesetas for someone

fianza *nf* **(a)** *(para estar en libertad)* bail; **fue puesto en libertad bajo fianza de 300.000 ptas.** *o* **le pusieron en libertad bajo fianza de 300.000 ptas.** = he was released on bail of 300,000 pesetas *o* he was released on payment of 300,000 pesetas bail; **fugarse estando bajo fianza** = to jump bail **(b)** *(garantía)* security *o* guarantee; **el banco le prestó 4.000.000 de ptas. sin fianza** = the bank lent him 4m pesetas without security

fiar 1 *vt* **(a)** *(dejar en posesión de otro)* to entrust; **nos fiaron la fotocopiadora por dos meses** = they entrusted us with the photocopier for two months **(b)** *(vender sin cobrar inmediatamente)* to sell on credit **2** *vi* to trust; **ser de fiar** = to be trustworthy; **poco de fiar** = untrustworthy *o* unreliable; **quiero un contratista de confianza no una de esas empresas que son poco de fiar** = I want a reputable builder, not one of these shady outfits

◇ **fiarse** *vr* to trust *o* to rely on someone *o* something; **no me fío de él** = I don't trust him; **nos fiamos de sus afirmaciones** = we took his statement on trust

ficha *nf* index card *o* filing card; *US* file card; **ficha para activar el reloj de control de asistencia del personal** = clock card; **ficha de almacén** = stock control card *o* bin card

fichar *vt/i* to file *o* to index; **fichar a la entrada al trabajo** = to clock in *o* to clock on; **fichar a la salida del trabajo** = to clock out *o* to clock off

fichero *nm* **(a)** *(clasificador)* file *o* filing cabinet; **fichero de tarjetas** = card-index file; **pasar información a un fichero** = to card-index; **paso de información a un fichero** = card-indexing; **mire en el fichero de 'ventas en Canarias'** = look in the file marked 'Canaries sales'; **fotocopió todo el fichero** = she photocopied all the file; **tarjeta de fichero** = index card *o* filing card; *US* file card **(b)** *(informática)* file *o* computer file; **copia maestra de un fichero** = master copy of a file

ficticio, -cia *adj* fictitious; **activo(s) ficticio(s)** = fictitious assets

fidelidad *nf* loyalty; **fidelidad a la marca** = brand loyalty

fideicomiso *nm* trust; **establecieron un fideicomiso familiar para sus nietos** = they set up a family trust for their grandchildren; **dejó su propiedad en fideicomiso para ser entregada a sus nietos** = he left his property in trust for his grandchildren; **contrato de fideicomiso** = trust deed; **fondo de fideicomiso** = trust fund

fiduciario, -ria 1 *adj* fiduciary; **los directores tienen la obligación fiduciaria de actuar en beneficio de la compañía** = directors have fiduciary duty to act in the best interests of the company **2** *nm* fiduciary *o* trustee

fiesta *nf* **(a)** *(días festivos)* holiday *o* festival; **fiesta oficial** *o* **nacional** = public holiday *o* bank holiday *o* legal holiday; **hacer fiesta** = to take time off work **(b)** *(festejo, celebración)* party

figurar 1 *vt (significar)* to represent; **estas cuatro paredes figuran el despacho** = these four walls represent the office **2** *vi (incluirse)* to be in *o* to appear; **sin figurar** = unaccounted for; **su nombre figura en mi informe** = his name appears in my report

◊ **figurarse** *vr* to imagine *o* to think; **se figuró que te habían despedido** = he thought you had been sacked

> en la nueva ley figuran puntos como la posibilidad de desgravar por una vivienda alquilada y poder fijar duraciones de contratos y actualizaciones de los incrementos de las ventas
> *España Económica*

fijación *nf* fixing *o* establishing; **fijación del interés de la hipoteca** = fixing of the mortgage rate; **fijación de precios** = pricing *o* price fixing; **fijación colectiva de precios** = common pricing; **fijación de precios competitivos** = competitive pricing; **fijación de tarifas** = fixing of charges

fijar *vt* **(a)** to fix *o* to set; **fijar una fecha** = to fix a date; **todavía no se ha fijado la fecha** = the date has still to be fixed; **fijar los aumentos salariales conforme al índice del coste de la vida** = to peg wage increases to the cost-of-living index; **el interés de la hipoteca ha quedado fijado en el 11%** = the mortgage rate has been fixed at 11%; **las cuentas fijan el valor de las existencias en 2.000.000 de ptas.** = the accounts put the stock value at 2m pesetas; **fijar precios** = to fix prices *o* to price; **el precio del oro se fijó en $300** = the price of gold was fixed at $300; **tenemos que fijar un precio para el nuevo ordenador** = we have to set a price for the new computer; **fijar un presupuesto** = to fix a budget; **fijar una reunión** = to fix a meeting **(b)** **fijar en la pared con chinchetas** = to pin up **(c)** **fijar daños y perjuicios** = to award damages; **fijar los daños en 200.000 ptas.** = to assess damages at 200,000 pesetas

> la ley fijará un férreo control de los bancos de datos privados
> *El País*

fijo, -ja *adj* fixed *o* permanent *o* set; **activo fijo** = fixed assets; **activos fijos intangibles** = intangible fixed assets; **un aumento fijo de un 10%** = a flat-rate increase of 10%; **bienes fijos** = tangible assets *o* property; **capital fijo** = fixed capital; **contrato a plazo fijo** = fixed-term contract; **costes fijos** = fixed costs; **depósito a plazo fijo** = fixed deposit; **empleo** *o* **trabajo fijo** = permanent job *o* staff appointment *o* secure job; **tiene un empleo fijo** = she is in permanent employment; **ha encontrado un puesto fijo** = he has found a permanent job; **gastos fijos** = fixed costs; **hacer fijo a alguien en un**

trabajo = to confirm someone in a job; **ingreso fijo** = regular income; **interés fijo** = fixed interest; **inversiones de interés fijo** = fixed-interest investments; **lista de precios fijos** = fixed scale of charges; **personal fijo** = permanent staff *o* regular staff; **porcentaje fijo** *o* **cuota fija** = flat rate; **precio fijo** = set price; **renta fija** = fixed income; **títulos** *o* **valores de interés fijo** = fixed-interest securities; **se le paga una cuota fija de 400 ptas. por mil** = he is paid a flat rate of 400 pesetas per thousand; **pagamos una cuota fija por la electricidad cada trimestre** = we pay a flat rate for electricity each quarter; **trabaja por su cuenta y por eso no tiene unos ingresos fijos** = she works freelance so she does not have a regular income

filial 1 *adj* affiliated; **una de nuestras sociedades filiales** = one of our affiliated companies **2** *nf* subsidiary company *o* subsidiary; **una filial propiedad total de la empresa** *o* **filial en propiedad absoluta** = wholly-owned subsidiary

> de hecho tenemos ya empresas filiales en México y Argentina
> *Tiempo*

Filipinas *nfpl* Philippines

◊ **filipino, -na** *adj y n* Filipino
NOTA: capital **Manila**; moneda: **peso filipino (p)** = Philippine peso (PP)

filtrar *vt* to leak; **descubrieron que el director gerente filtraba información a la competencia** = they discovered the MD was leaking information to the competition

◊ **filtrarse** *vr* to leak; **la información sobre el contrato se filtró a la prensa** = information on the contract was leaked to the press

fin *nm* **(a)** *(final)* close *o* end *o* ending; **fin de año** = year end; **fin de mes** = month end; **cuentas de fin de mes** = month-end accounts; **al fin** = in the end; **llegar a su fin** = to come to an end; **nuestro acuerdo de distribución llega a su fin el próximo mes** = our distribution agreement comes to an end next month; **por fin** = finally; **ayer se firmó por fin el contrato** = the contract was finally signed yesterday **(b)** *(objetivo)* aim; **con fines especulativos** = on spec; **con fines de lucro** = profit-orientated

final 1 *adj* final *o* ultimate; **balance final** = final accounts; **consumidor final** = end user; **demanda final** = final demand; **dividendo final** = final dividend; **oferta final** = closing bid *o* final offer; **producto final** = end product *o* final product; **reembolso final** = final discharge; **saldo final** = closing balance; **usuario final** = end user; **después de seis meses de producción experimental, el producto final todavía no es aceptable** = after six months' trial production, the end product is still not acceptable; **dar los toques finales a un documento** = to put the final details on a document **2** *nm* **(a)** *(espacio)* end; **el despacho del presidente está al final del pasillo** = the chairman's room is at the end of the corridor **(b)** *(tiempo, acción)* end *o* conclusion; **al final del periodo de contrato** = at the end of the contract period; **final del periodo de crédito en la bolsa** = account end; **los precios de las acciones subieron al final del periodo de crédito** = share prices rose at the end of the account *o* the account end; **las acciones habían subido ligeramente al final de la sesión** = shares were up slightly at the end of the day **(c)** *(como conclusión)* **al final** = in the end; **al final la compañía tuvo que salirse del mercado estadounidense** = in the end the company had to pull out of the US market; **al final acabaron firmando el contrato en el aeropuerto** = in the end they signed the contract at the airport; **al final la empresa tuvo que llamar a la policía** = in the end the company had to call in the police

◊ **finalmente** *adv* finally *o* in the end *o* lastly *o* ultimately; **finalmente, la dirección tuvo que acceder a las demandas del sindicato** = ultimately, the management had to agree to the demands of the union

finalidad *nf* aim *o* purpose; **finalidad lucrativa** = profit motive

finalización *nf* completion *o* termination *o* conclusion; **fecha de finalización** = completion date

finalizar 1 *vi* to end *o* to come to an end; **el acuerdo de distribución finaliza en julio** = the distribution agreement ends in July **2** *vt* to finalize; **esperamos finalizar el acuerdo mañana** = we hope to finalize the agreement tomorrow

◊ **finalizarse** *vr* to end *o* to finish

> la primera fase del proyecto finalizará en el plazo de año y medio, y una vez finalizado será puesto a prueba en los más prestigiosos centros sanitarios de Europa
>
> **Micros**

financiación *nf* financing; **financiación del déficit presupuestario** = deficit financing; **financiación inicial** = start-up financing; **financiación retroactiva** = back financing; **renovar la financiación** = to refinance

◊ **financiamiento** *nm* financing

◊ **financiar** *vt* to finance *o* to fund; **financiar una compañía** = to fund a company; **financiar una operación** = to finance an operation; **el proyecto fue financiado por dos bancos internacionales** = the financing of the project was done by two international banks; **el banco financia el lanzamiento del nuevo producto** = the bank is providing the funding for the new product launch; **la compañía no tiene recursos suficientes para financiar su programa de expansión** = the company does not have enough resources to fund its expansion programme

> desde el punto de vista económico, no hay obstáculos de ningún tipo para financiar la profesionalización progresiva de las Fuerzas Armadas
>
> **España Económica**

> la expansión vertiginosa de nuestra empresa ha sido posible gracias a las acertadas disposiciones que sobre financiación de la exportación fueron promulgadas en el año 1963
>
> **España Económica**

financiero, -ra 1 *adj* financial; **apoyo** *o* **respaldo financiero** = financial backing; **¿de dónde procede el apoyo financiero del proyecto?** = who is providing the backing for the project *o* where does the backing for the project come from?; **asesor financiero** = financial adviser; **ayuda financiera** = financial assistance; **corresponsal financiero** = financial correspondent; **director financiero** = finance director *o* financial controller; **ejercicio financiero** = financial year; **estado financiero** = financial statement; **el departamento de cuentas ha preparado un estado financiero para los accionistas** = the accounts department has prepared a financial statement for the shareholders; **instrumento** *o* **documento financiero** = financial instrument; **mercado financiero** = finance market; **préstamos financieros** = loans *o* borrowings; **recursos financieros** = financial resources; **una compañía con grandes recursos financieros** = a company with strong financial resources; **riesgo financiero** = financial risk; **situación financiera** = financial position; **debe pensar en su situación financiera** = he must think of his financial position; **sociedad financiera** = finance company *o* finance corporation *o* finance house **2** *nm* financier

◊ **financieramente** *adv* financially; **compañía financieramente sólida** = company which is financially sound

finanzas *nfpl* **(a)** finance *o* finances; **agente de finanzas** = financial intermediary; **altas finanzas** = high finance; **director de finanzas** = finance director; *US* treasurer; **el mal estado de las finanzas de la compañía** = the bad state of the company's finances **(b)** **ministro de finanzas** = finance minister; **los ministros de finanzas de la Unión Europea** = the European Union finance ministers; **el mundo de las finanzas** = the world of finance

finca *nf* property *o* land *o* real estate *o* lot; **administrador de una finca** = land agent

fingir *vt* to pretend; **finge trabajar** *o* **finge que trabaja** = he's pretending to work; **fingió tener gripe y se tomó el día libre** = she pretended she had 'flu and took the day off

finiquito *nm* settlement (of accounts)

Finlandia *nf* Finland

◊ **finés, -esa** *o* **finlandés, -esa** *adj & n* Finnish *n* Finn
NOTA: capital: **Helsinki**; moneda: **marco finlandés (Fmk)** = Finnish markka (Fmk)

fino, -na *adj* **(a)** *(calidad)* fine *o* excellent **(b)** *(delgado)* thin **(c)** *(liso)* smooth **(d)** *(agudo)* sharp **(e)** *(persona)* shrewd; polite; refined

firma *nf* **(a)** *(empresa)* firm *o* company; **es socio de una firma de abogados** = he is a partner in a law firm **(b)** *(rúbrica)* signature; **aceptar una firma** = to honour a signature; **un montón de cartas pendientes de la firma del director gerente** = a pile of letters waiting for the managing director's signature; **firma de un contrato** = signature *o* completion of a contract

> a través de su división de distribución de maquinaria para obras públicas y de limpieza vial, es también una de las firmas más destacadas del país
>
> **España Económica**

firmante *nmf* signatory; **si quieres cambiar las condiciones, tienes que conseguir el permiso de todos los firmantes del acuerdo** = you have to get the permission of all the signatories to the agreement if you want to change the terms; **el abajo firmante** =

the undersigned; **nosotros, los abajo firmantes** = we, the undersigned

firmar *vt* **(a)** *(poner la firma)* to sign; **firmar una carta** *o* **un contrato** *o* **un documento** *o* **un cheque** *o* **un convenio** = to sign a letter *o* a contract *o* a document *o* a cheque *o* a deal; **la carta está firmada por el director gerente** = the letter is signed by the managing director; **el jefe de almacén firmó la entrada** *o* **la recepción de las mercancías** *o* **la salida de las mercancías** = the warehouse manager signed the goods in *o* signed for the goods *o* signed the goods out; **firmó al pie de la factura** = he signed his name at the bottom of the invoice; **firmar con las iniciales** = to initial; **firmar la carta por procuración** *o* **por poder** = to p.p. the letter; **la secretaria firmó la carta por poderes mientras el director estaba almorzando** = the secretary p.p.'d the letter while the manager was at lunch **(b) firmar como testigo** = to witness (a document); **firmar como testigo de un acuerdo** *o* **de una firma** = to witness an agreement *o* a signature

firme *adj* **(a)** *(fuerte)* strong; **la compañía necesita un presidente firme** = the company needs a strong chairman **(b)** *(sólido)* **en firme** = firm; **hacer una oferta en firme** = to make a firm offer for something; **hacer un pedido en firme de dos aviones** = to place a firm order for two aircraft; **enviar un pedido en firme** = to place a firm order *o* to send a formal order; **ofrecen un precio firme de 250 ptas. por unidad** = they are quoting a firm price of 250 pesetas per unit; **venta en firme** = firm sale **(c)** *(estable)* firm *o* steady; **la peseta se mostró más firme en los mercados de divisas** = the peseta was firmer on the foreign exchange markets; **las acciones se mantuvieron firmes** = shares remained firm

firmeza *nf* firmness; **la firmeza de la peseta** = the firmness of the peseta; **firmeza del mercado** = hardness of the market

fiscal 1 *adj* fiscal; **amortización fiscal** = capital allowances; **amparo fiscal** = tax shelter; **año fiscal** *o* fiscal year *o* financial year *o* tax year; **asesor fiscal** = tax adviser *o* tax consultant; **se estableció como asesor fiscal** = he set himself up as a tax adviser; **desgravación fiscal** = tax relief; **ejercicio fiscal** = tax year *o* fiscal year; **evasión fiscal** = tax evasion; **franquicia fiscal** = tax holiday; **laguna fiscal** = tax loophole; **encontrar una laguna fiscal** = to find a tax loophole; **medidas fiscales** = fiscal measures; **método fiscal de retención directa** = pay as you earn (PAYE); *US* pay-as-you-go; **paraíso fiscal** = tax haven; **fondos colocados en un paraíso fiscal** = off-shore fund; **la política fiscal del gobierno** = the government's fiscal policies; **sistema fiscal** = tax system **2** *nmf (jurídico)* prosecutor; *US* district attorney

el panorama se complica, si, además, tiene usted la suerte de que algunos de sus proveedores fundamentales, sean de los que cierran el año fiscal en junio o en septiembre
Datamation

la presión fiscal, pese a haber crecido más que en la CEE, sigue varios puntos por debajo y ha descendido incluso 0,3 puntos del PIB en 1988
España Económica

fisco *nm (gobierno)* treasury *o* tax office; *GB* the Exchequer *o* the Inland Revenue; *US* the Internal Revenue Service; **necesitamos la factura para la declaración al fisco** = we need the invoice for the purpose of declaration to the tax authorities

físico, -ca *adj* physical; **control de existencias físicas** = physical stock check *o* physical stocktaking; **existencias físicas** = physical stock; **inventario físico** = physical inventory

flaco, -ca *adj* thin *o* lean; **los años de las vacas flacas** = the lean years

fletado 1 *adj* chartered; **avión fletado** = chartered plane **2** *pp de* FLETAR

fletador *nm* freighter *o* charterer

fletamento *nm* **(a)** *(mercancías)* freight *o* freightage **(b)** *(alquiler)* chartering **(c)** *(Mex.)* charter

fletar *vt* **(a)** *(cargar)* to take on freight; **fletar mercancías** = to freight goods **(b)** *(alquilar)* to charter; **fletar un avión** *o* **un barco** = to charter a plane *o* a boat

flete *nm* **(a)** *(precio)* freight; **flete contra reembolso** = freight forward; **costes de flete** = freight costs; **cuotas de flete** *o* **tarifas de flete** = freight charges *o* freight rates; **las cuotas de flete han subido mucho este año** = freight charges have gone up sharply this year; **coste, seguro y flete (cif)** = cost, insurance and freight (c.i.f.) **(b)** *(carga)* freight; **flete de ida** = outward freight; **flete de vuelta** = homeward freight; **flete aéreo** = air freight *o* air cargo; **hacer un envío por flete aéreo** = to send a shipment by air freight

flexibilidad *nf* flexibility; **no existe flexibilidad en la política de precios de la empresa** = there is no flexibility in the company's pricing policy

una fuente clave del dinamismo y de la elasticidad de la economía estadounidense es la flexibilidad que se deriva de su confianza en los mercados
Mercado

flexible *adj* flexible; **disco flexible** = floppy disk; **horario de trabajo flexible** = flexible working hours *o* flexitime; **tenemos un horario de trabajo flexible** = we work flexible hours *o* we work flexitime; **la empresa estableció el horario de trabajo flexible hace dos años** = the company introduced flexitime working two years ago; **precios flexibles** = flexible prices; **política de precios flexibles** = flexible pricing policy; **presupuesto flexible** = flexible budget

flojo, -ja *adj* slack *o* loose *o* weak; **la actividad comercial es floja durante el fin de semana** = business is slack at the end of the week; **los precios de las acciones se mantuvieron flojos** = share prices remained weak

'floppy' *nm* floppy disk

florecer *vi* to flourish

◊ **floreciente** *adj* flourishing; **comercio floreciente** = flourishing trade; **dirige un floreciente negocio de calzado** = he runs a flourishing shoe business

florín *nm (moneda de los Países Bajos)* guilder *o* florin

flota *nf* fleet; **flota de vehículos** = fleet (of cars); **la flota de coches de representantes de una empresa** = a company's fleet of representatives' cars; **la línea aérea tiene una flota de diez aviones comerciales** = the airline has a fleet of ten commercial aircraft

flotación *nf* float *o* flotation *o* floating; **flotación de divisas** = currency flotation; **la flotación de la libra** = the floating of the pound; **flotación libre** = clean float; **flotación sucia** *o* **dirigida** = dirty *o* managed float

◊ **flotante** *adj* floating; **débito flotante** = floating charge; **la libra flotante** = the floating pound; **tipo flotante** = floating rate; **tipos de cambio flotantes** = floating exchange rates

flotar *vt/i* to float; **el gobierno ha decidido dejar flotar** *o* **ha dejado flotar la libra** = the government has decided to float the pound *o* has let sterling float

fluctuación *nf* fluctuation; **fluctuaciones cambiarias** = exchange rate fluctuations *o* differences; **fluctuación estacional** = seasonal variation; **las fluctuaciones de la peseta** = the fluctuations of the peseta; **las fluctuaciones de los tipos de cambio** = exchange rate fluctuations; **fluctuaciones de los precios** = price fluctuations *o* price movements

◊ **fluctuante** *adj* fluctuating; **el precio fluctuante del dólar** = the fluctuating value of the dollar; **tipo de cambio fluctuante** = fluctuating exchange rate

> los tipos de interés seguirán relativamente elevados y con resistencia a la baja, mientras que la peseta se mantendrá en la zona alta de la banda de fluctuación
> **Actualidad Económica**

> el Gobierno reafirmará su compromiso para no devaluar la peseta, optando por el mecanismo de la banda estrecha que sólo permite fluctuaciones del 2,25%
> **Actualidad Económica**

fluctuar *vi* to fluctuate; **la libra fluctuó durante todo el día en los mercados de divisas** = the pound fluctuated all day on the foreign exchange markets

fluir *vi* to flow *o* to run

flujo *nm* **(a)** *(movimiento; transacción financiera)* stream *o* flow; **el flujo de inversiones hacia Japón** = the flow of investments into Japan **(b)** flujo de caja = cash flow; **flujo de caja descontado** = discounted cash flow; **flujo negativo de efectivo** = negative cash flow; **flujo neto de efectivo** = net cash flow; **flujo positivo de efectivo** = positive cash flow; **estado de flujo de fondos** = cash flow statement; **la empresa tiene dificultades de flujo de caja** = the company is suffering from cash flow problems **(c)** *(organigrama)* **diagrama de flujo** = flow chart *o* flow diagram

FMI = FONDO MONETARIO INTERNACIONAL International Monetary Fund (IMF)

foliar *vt* to number pages *o* to folio

folio *nm* folio; **la carta estaba escrita en seis folios** = the letter was on six sheets of foolscap

folleto *nm* folleto (publicitario) = leaflet *o* pamphlet *o* prospectus *o* sales sheet *o* brochure *o* publicity handout; **el restaurante emplea a chicas que distribuyen folletos publicitarios en la calle** = the restaurant has girls handing out prospectuses in the street; **folleto publicitario por correo** = mailing piece

fomentar *vt* to encourage; **el aumento general de los sueldos fomenta el consumo** = the general rise in wages encourages consumer spending

fondeadero *nm* mooring *o* anchorage

fondo *nm* **(a)** *(dinero, caudal)* fund; **fondo de amortización** = sinking fund; **fondo de caja** = cash float; **empezamos el día con un fondo de caja de 4.000 ptas.** = we start the day with a 4,000 peseta float in the cash desk; **fondo común** = common fund; **Fondo Europeo de Desarrollo (FED)** = European Development Fund (EDF); **Fondo Europeo de Desarrollo Regional (FEDER)** = European Regional Development Fund (ERDF); **Fondo Europeo de Orientación y Garantía Agrícola (FEOGA)** = European Agricultural Guidance and Guarantee Fund (EAGGF); **fondo de especulación de acciones** = performance fund; **fondo de fideicomiso** *o* **fondo de custodia** = trust fund; **Fondo de Garantía de Depósitos en Establecimientos Bancarios (FGD)** = Deposit Guarantee Fund; **Fondo de Garantía Salarial (FGS)** = Wages Guarantee Fund; **fondo para gastos menores** = petty cash; **fondo para imprevistos** = contingency fund; **fondo indicador** = index fund; **fondo de pensiones** = pension fund; **los administradores del fondo de pensiones** = the trustees of the pension fund; **fondo de protección** = hedge fund; **fondo de regulación** = buffer stocks **(b)** **el Fondo Monetario Internacional (FMI)** = the International Monetary Fund (the IMF) **(c)** **fondo de comercio** = goodwill **(d)** **tocar fondo** = to bottom (out); **el mercado ha tocado fondo** = the market has bottomed out; **las ventas han tocado fondo** = sales have reached rock bottom

◊ **fondos** *nmpl* **(a)** *(recursos, dinero del que se puede disponer)* finance *o* funds; **Fondos Estructurales** = Structural Funds; **¿dónde conseguirán los fondos necesarios para el proyecto?** = where will they get the necessary finance for the project?; **la compañía no tiene fondos para financiar el programa de investigación** = the company has no funds to pay for the research programme; **la compañía solicitó más fondos** = the company called for extra funds; **fondos de inversión** = unit trust; **fondos para invertir** = capital for investment; **fondos para la provisión de asesoramiento y preparación técnica** = know-how fund **(b)** *(reservas)* **los fondos públicos** = public funds; **el coste se pagó con cargo a los fondos públicos** = the cost was paid for out of public funds; **agotar los fondos** = to run out of funds; **apropiación indebida de fondos** = conversion of funds; **apropiarse indebidamente de fondos en beneficio propio** = to convert funds to one's own use; **asignar fondos** = to fund; **asignación de fondos** = funding; **desviar fondos a otros fines** = to convert funds to another purpose; **sin fondos**

suficientes = non-sufficient funds; **cheque sin fondos** = dud cheque *o* bad cheque *o* cheque which bounces **(c) gestión de fondos** = fund management; **gestor de fondos** = fund manager; **fondo de inversión controlado** *o* **dirigido** = managed fund *o* fund of funds *o* managed unit trust

> el fuerte peso del crédito hipotecario en el conjunto de la inversión crediticia (41,57%) asegura una inversión de los fondos invertidos
> **Actualidad Económica**

forastero, -ra *n* foreigner

'forfaiting' *nm* forfaiting

> el forfaiting o la necesidad de financiar las exportaciones puede definirse como un descuento sin recurso, y consiste en la compra por el forfaiteur al exportador de los efectos representativos de su venta al exterior
> **El País**

forma *nf* form *o* shape; **en buena y debida forma** *o* **en la debida forma** = in due form

formación *nf* **(a)** *(creación)* formation *o* forming; **la formación de una nueva compañía** = the formation of a new company **(b)** *(preparación profesional)* training; **formación en el empleo** *o* **formación en el puesto de trabajo** = in-house training *o* on-the-job training; **formación fuera del empleo** = off-the-job training; **formación laboral** = industrial training; **formación de mandos** = management training; **formación del personal** = staff training; **ejecutivo en formación** = management trainee; **periodo de formación** = training period; **hay un periodo de formación de diez semanas para el personal de nueva contratación** = there is a ten-week training period for new staff

> Renovarse o morir. La formación permanente es el antídoto necesario para no quedarse anclado en el puesto de trabajo
> **El País**

formal *adj* formal; **las cartas comerciales son generalmente muy formales** = business letters are usually very formal; **contrato formal** = formal contract

◊ **formalmente** *adv* formally

formalidad *nf* formality; **formalidades aduaneras** = customs formalities; **formalidades burocráticas** = bureaucratic formalities *o* red tape

formar *vt* **(a)** *(crear, constituir)* to form; **la delegación de comercio está formada por los directores de ventas de diez empresas importantes** = the trade mission is made up of *o* consists of the sales directors of ten major companies **(b)** *(educar)* to train

◊ **formarse** *vr* *(educarse)* to train

formulario *nm* form; **formulario de declaración de la renta** = tax return *o* tax form; **formulario de declaración de siniestro** *o* **de reclamaciones** = claim form; **formulario de pedido** = order form; **un bloc de formularios de pedido** = a pad of order forms; **formulario de solicitud** = application form; **rellenar un formulario** = to fill in a form

foro *nm* **(a)** *(arrendamiento)* leasehold **(b)** *(reunión)* forum **(c)** *(abogacía)* the legal profession; **forma parte del foro de abogados** = he is in the legal profession

> la asociación pretende convertirse en un foro donde compartir conocimientos, potenciar la formación, la promoción de sus asociados y su participación en convocatorias internacionales
> **El País**

fortuna *nf* **(a)** *(capital)* fortune; **hizo una fortuna invirtiendo en acciones petrolíferas** = he made a fortune from investing in oil shares **(b)** *(patrimonio)* estate *o* fortune; **dejó su fortuna a sus tres hijos** = she left her fortune to her three children

forzar *vt* to force; **la competencia ha forzado a la empresa a bajar sus precios** = competition has forced the company to lower its prices; **forzar a bajar** = to force down; **forzar a subir** = to force up

forzoso, -sa *adj* compulsory; **trabajo forzoso** = compulsory work *o* forced labour; **liquidación forzosa** = compulsory liquidation; **orden forzosa de liquidación** = compulsory winding up order

foso *nm* pit

fotocopia *nf* **(a)** *(reproducción de un impreso)* photocopy; **fotocopia compulsada** = authenticated photocopy; **hacer una fotocopia de una carta** = to photocopy a letter *o* to make a photocopy of a letter; **haga seis fotocopias del contrato** = make six photocopies of the contract; **enviar una fotocopia del contrato a la otra parte** = to send the other party a copy of the contract; **hemos mandado fotocopias a cada uno de los representantes** = we have sent photocopies to each of the agents; **hay un montón de fotocopias por hacer** = there is a mass of photocopying to be done **(b)** *(acto)* photocopying; **los costes de las fotocopias aumentan cada año** = photocopying costs are rising each year; **despacho que ofrece el servicio de fotocopias** = photocopying bureau

◊ **fotocopiadora** *nf* copier *o* photocopier; **esta fotocopiadora gasta mucho papel** = this photocopier is very wasteful of paper; **hay que comprar una fotocopiadora nueva** = the photocopier needs replacing; **la fotocopiadora se avería con frecuencia** = the photocopier is often breaking down; **papel de fotocopiadora** = copier paper

◊ **fotocopiaje** *nm* photocopying

fotocopiar *vt* to photocopy; **fotocopió el contrato** *o* **todo el fichero** = she photocopied the contract *o* all the file

fotostatar *vt* *(hacer una copia fotostática)* to photostat

◊ **fotostática** *adj* **copia fotostática** = photostat; **hacer una copia fotostática** = to make a photostat *o* to photostat

◊ **fotostato** *nm* *(copia fotostática)* photostat

fracasado, -da 1 *adj* failed *o* unsuccessful; **un proyecto fracasado** = an unsuccessful project **2** *n* failure; **es un fracasado** = he's a failure **3** *pp de* FRACASAR

fracasar 1 *vi* to fail *o* to flop *o* to be unsuccessful *o* to fall through *o* to collapse; **la compañía fracasó por la mala administración del presidente** = the company failed because of the chairman's mismanagement **2** *vt* to wreck *o* to damage; **los sindicatos hicieron fracasar las negociaciones** = the negotiations were wrecked by the unions

fracaso *nm* **(a)** *(actividad)* failure *o* flop; **el fracaso de las negociaciones** = the failure of the negotiations; **el nuevo modelo fue un fracaso** = the new model was a flop **(b)** *(negocio)* collapse

fraccionamiento *nm* split; **fraccionamiento de acciones** = share split; **la compañía propone el fraccionamiento de las acciones en cinco partes** = the company is proposing a five for one split

fraccionario, -ria *adj* fractional; **certificado fraccionario** = fractional certificate; **moneda fraccionaria** = small change

frágil *adj* fragile; **hay una prima extra para asegurar el transporte de mercancías frágiles** = there is an extra premium for insuring fragile goods in shipment

Francia *nf* France

◊ **francés, -esa 1** *adj* French **2** *nmf* Frenchman, Frenchwoman; **los franceses** = the French NOTA: capital: **París** (= Paris); moneda: **franco** *o* **franco francés (F)** = French franc (F *o* Fr)

franco, -ca 1 *adj* **(a)** free *o* exempt; **franco a bordo** = free on board (f.o.b.); **franco de porte** = carriage free; **franco sobre vagón** *o* **franco vagón FF.CC.** = free on rail; **puerto franco** = free port *o* free trade zone **(b)** *(precio)* franco en almacén = price ex warehouse **2** *nm* *(moneda de Francia, Bélgica, Suiza y otros países)* franc; **francos franceses** *o* **francos belgas** *o* **francos suizos** = French francs *o* Belgian francs *o* Swiss francs; **cuenta en francos** = franc account

franqueadora *nf* *(correos)* **máquina franqueadora** = franking machine

franquear *vt* *(correos)* to frank *o* to stamp; **envíe un sobre franqueado con sus señas para recibir más información y el catálogo** = send a stamped addressed envelope for further details and catalogue

franqueo *nm* postage; **franqueo concertado** = postpaid *o* postage paid *o* carriage paid; **el precio es 1.190 ptas. con el franqueo concertado** = the price is 1,190 pesetas postpaid; **franqueo pagado** = freepost; **tarjeta de respuesta con el franqueo pagado** = prepaid reply card; **(gastos de) franqueo y embalaje** = postage & packing (p & p)

franquicia *nf* **(a)** *(exención, privilegio)* exemption; **franquicia arancelaria** = exemption from customs duties; **franquicia de equipaje** = free baggage allowance; **franquicia fiscal** = tax holiday **(b)** *(concesión)* franchise *o* franchising; dealership; **su bar de bocadillos tuvo tanto éxito que decidió conceder franquicias** = his sandwich bar was so successful that he decided to franchise it

◊ **franquiciado, -da** *n* franchisee

◊ **franquiciador** *nm* franchiser

la franquicia se establece, normalmente, entre dos empresas independientes, tanto económica como jurídicamente
El País

la franquicia comercial mueve 600.000 millones de pesetas anuales en España
El País

la guía de franquicias aporta toda la información y requisitos que necesita conocer el futuro franquiciado
El País

franquiciar *vt* to franchise

fraude *nm* deceit *o* deception *o* fraud; *US* scam; **fraude fiscal** = tax evasion; **fue acusado de fraude de divisas** = he was accused of frauds relating to foreign currency; **brigada contra el fraude** = fraud squad

el fraude fiscal en España puede llegar a dos billones de pesetas
Cambio 16

los especialistas coinciden en que la tendencia para los próximos años es que este tipo de fraude se incremente
El País

el volumen de fraude en relación con las transacciones que se hacen es muy pequeño
Actualidad Económica

fraudulento, -ta *adj* fraudulent; **contabilidad fraudulenta** = false accounting; **falsedad fraudulenta** = fraudulent misrepresentation; **medios fraudulentos** = false pretences; **fue encarcelado por obtener dinero por medios fraudulentos** = he was sent to prison for obtaining money by false pretences; **negocio fraudulento** = racket; **una transacción fraudulenta** = a fraudulent transaction

◊ **fraudulentamente** *adv* fraudulently; **mercancías importadas fraudulentamente** = goods imported fraudulently; **obtener dinero fraudulentamente** = to obtain money by fraud; **obtuvo 2.000.000 de ptas. fraudulentamente** = he obtained 2m pesetas by deception

frecuencia *nf* frequency; **con frecuencia** = frequently; **la fotocopiadora se avería con frecuencia** = the photocopier is often breaking down; **con poca frecuencia** = rarely; **¿con qué frecuencia salen aviones para Barcelona?** = how frequent are the planes to Barcelona? *o* how often is there a plane to Barcelona?

frecuente *adj* frequent; **poco frecuente** = infrequent *o* rare; **hay un servicio frecuente de transbordador a Inglaterra** = there is a frequent ferry service to England; **los vendedores con experiencia son poco frecuentes hoy en día** = experienced salesmen are rare these days

◊ **frecuentemente** *adv* frequently; **visitamos frecuentemente nuestras oficinas en Madrid** = we visit our Madrid offices frequently

frenar *vt* to curb *o* to restrain *o* to plug; **frenar la expansión** = to cut back *o* to retrench; **frenar la inflación** = to curb *o* to check inflation; **la empresa está intentando frenar la sangría de las reservas de caja** = the company is trying to plug the drain on cash reserves; **la caída del tipo de cambio se está frenando** = the fall in the exchange rate is slowing down

frenesí *nm* frenzy

◊ **frenético, -ca** *adj* hectic; **después de las frenéticas transacciones comerciales de la semana pasada, esta semana ha sido muy tranquila** = after last week's hectic trading, this week has been very calm

freno *nm* restraint *o* check; **la empresa intenta poner freno a sus gastos generales** = the company is trying to keep its overheads under control

frío, fría 1 *adj* cold; **la máquina de café también despacha bebidas frías** = the coffee machine also sells cold drinks **2** *nm* cold weather; **hacía tanto frío en la oficina que el personal empezó a quejarse** = the office was so cold that the staff started complaining; **las máquinas funcionan mal con el frío** = the machines work badly in cold weather

fructífero, -ra *adj* fruitful; **conversaciones fructíferas** = productive discussions

frugal *adj* thrifty

frustrar *vt* to frustrate

fuego *nm* fire; **prender fuego a** = to set on fire

fuente *nf* source; **fuente de ingresos** = source of income; **se tienen que declarar todas las fuentes de ingresos al fisco** = you must declare income from all sources to the tax office

> la mayor fuente de ingresos de los medios de comunicación es la publicidad
>
> *Tiempo*

fuera *adv* **(a)** away *o* out; **el Sr. Robles telefoneó mientras Vd. estaba fuera y pidió que le llamara** = Sr Robles called while you were out and asked if you would phone him back **(b) fuera de** = outside; **fuera de horas de oficina** = outside office hours; **encargar trabajo fuera (de la empresa)** = to send work to be done outside (the office); **hacemos todo el proceso de datos fuera de la empresa** = we do all our data processing out of the office **(c) fuera de actas** = off-the-record; **fuera de serie** = one-off

fuerte *adj* **(a)** *(firme)* strong; **fuerte competencia** = strong *o* keen competition; **nos encontramos ante una fuerte competencia de los fabricantes europeos** = we are facing some keen competition from European manufacturers; **una fuerte demanda de ordenadores personales** = a strong demand for home computers; **la empresa se aprovechó de la fuerte demanda de ordenadores personales** = the company took advantage of the strength of the demand for home computers; **caja fuerte** = strong box *o* safe; **divisas fuertes** = hard currency; **libra fuerte** = strong pound **(b)** *(repentino)* sharp **(c)** *(vertiginoso)* steep; **un fuerte aumento de los cargos en concepto de interés** = a steep increase in interest charges; **una acción en fuerte alza** = a boom share

◊ **fuertemente** *adv* severely *o* sharply *o* strongly *o* heavily; **las acciones bajaron fuertemente durante la jornada de ayer** = shares dipped sharply in yesterday's trading

fuerza *nf* strength *o* force *o* power; **fuerzas del mercado** = market forces; **el contrato tiene fuerza jurídica** = the contract is legally binding; **este documento no tiene fuerza jurídica** = this document is not legally binding; **fuerza mayor** = force majeure *o* act of God

> la división de interiorismo se está convirtiendo en una importante fuerza en el mercado empresarial de Madrid
>
> *España Económica*

fuga *nf* flight *o* escape; **fuga de capitales** = flight of capital; **fuga de la peseta al dólar** = the flight from the peseta into the dollar

función *nf* **(a)** *(cargo)* function; **función directiva** = management function *o* function of management **(b)** *(plural)* duties; **entrar en funciones** = to take office; **hacer las funciones de otro** = to act as someone's deputy; **presidente en funciones** = acting president **(c)** *(informática)* función; **código de función** = function code; **tecla de función** = function key; **el ordenador tenía autocorrector** *o* **deletreador ortográfico pero no llevaba incorporada la función para editar textos** = the word-processor had a spelling-checker function but no built-in text-editing function **(d)** *(espectáculo)* entertainment

funcionamiento *nm* **(a)** *(de una máquina)* operating *o* run; **manual de funcionamiento** = operating manual; **mostrar el funcionamiento de algo** = to demonstrate something *o* to show how something works **(b)** *(rendimiento)* performance; **el eficiente funcionamiento de un sistema** = the efficient working of a system **(c) en funcionamiento** = in use *o* in operation; **el ordenador está en funcionamiento las veinticuatro horas del día** = the computer is in use twenty-four hours a day; **poner una máquina en funcionamiento** = to put a machine into service; **ponerse en funcionamiento** = to become operative; **el sistema entró en funcionamiento el 1 de junio** = the system became operational on June 1st; **el sistema estará en funcionamiento para junio** = the system will be in operation by June **(d)** *(informática)* **mal funcionamiento** = malfunction

funcionar *vi* **(a)** *(trabajar, andar)* to function *o* to work; **hacer funcionar** = to use *o* to run; **hacer funcionar una máquina** = to operate a machine *o* to work a machine; **la campaña publicitaria está funcionando perfectamente** = the advertising campaign is functioning smoothly; **el nuevo sistema funciona desde el 1 de junio** = the new system has been operative since June 1st; **la nueva estructura directiva no parece que funcione muy bien** = the new management structure does not seem to be functioning very well; **el ordenador funciona las veinticuatro horas del día** = the computer is in use twenty-four hours a day; **'no funciona'** = 'out of order'; **la fotocopiadora no funciona - tenemos que cambiarle una pieza** = the photocopier isn't working - we need to replace a part *o* a part needs replacing **(b)** *(informática)* **funcionar mal** = to malfunction; **el teclado empieza a tener teclas que funcionan mal** = some of the keys on the keyboard have started to malfunction

funcionariado *nm* civil service

funcionario, -ria *n* official *o* civil servant; **funcionario de aduanas** = customs officer *o* customs official; **funcionarios de Correos** = Post Office officials *o* officials of the Post Office; **funcionario público** = civil servant *o* government employee; **el cuerpo de funcionarios del Estado** = the civil service; **para ser funcionario del Estado tiene que pasar una oposición** = you have to pass an examination to get a job in the civil service *o* to get a civil service job; **las pensiones de los funcionarios están ajustadas al coste de vida** = civil service pensions are index-linked; **funcionario de hacienda** = tax official *o* taxman; **alto funcionario** = high official *o* top official; **es el funcionario más importante de la delegación** = he is the top-ranking official in the delegation; **funcionario subalterno** *o* **de poca categoría** = minor official; **los funcionarios del aeropuerto inspeccionaron el cargamento** = airport officials inspected the shipment; **funcionarios del gobierno suspendieron la licencia de importación** = government officials stopped the import licence

> la desastrosa gestión del personal de la Administración al servicio del fisco, ha enfrentado al Ministerio con sus funcionarios
> **España Económica**

funda *nf* **(a)** *(cubierta)* cover *o* case; **ponga la funda al ordenador cuando salga de la oficina** = put the cover over your computer when you leave the office; **funda de la tarjeta de crédito** = credit card holder **(b)** *(impresora)* acoustic hood

fundador, -ra *n* **(a)** *(creador)* founder (of a company); **acciones de fundador** = founder's shares; **obtuvo el control al comprar las acciones del fundador** = he obtained control by buying the founder's shareholding; **todos los fundadores de la compañía fallecieron ya** = the founders of the company are all dead **(b)** *(empresario)* company promoter

> la acertada política comercial del fundador de la empresa hizo que uno de sus principales clientes se convirtiera pronto en socio
> **Micros**

fundamental *adj* fundamental *o* basic; **hay una diferencia fundamental entre los objetivos de los dos consejeros** = there is a fundamental difference between the objectives of the two directors

◊ **fundamento** *nm* **(a)** *(base, motivo)* basis *o* foundation *o* grounds; **no existe ningún fundamento por el cual podamos ser demandados** = there are no grounds on which we can be sued **(b) fundamentos** = basics; **ha estudiado los fundamentos del comercio de divisas** = he has studied the basics of foreign exchange dealing

fundar *vt* to establish *o* to start; **fundar una compañía** = to set up a company *o* to float a company; **fundar una nueva compañía** = (i) to found a new company; (ii) to promote a new company; **la empresa fue fundada en Asturias en 1823** = the business was established in Asturias in 1823

furgoneta *nf* van; **furgoneta de reparto** = delivery van *o* pickup truck

fusión *nf* merger; **fusión por absorción** = takeover merger; **fusiones y adquisiciones (FA)** = mergers and acquisitions (MA); **como resultado de la fusión, la compañía es la más grande del sector** = as a result of the merger, the company is the largest in the field

> el 84% de los empresarios españoles desean la fusión para poder competir en Europa, aunque parecen incapaces de abordarla
> **España Económica**

> los grandes bancos de Estados Unidos inician el proceso de fusiones como única salida a la crisis que atraviesan
> **El País**

> para abordar fusiones en el exterior con cierta dignidad, resulta imprescindible conseguir antes una cierta dimensión de respetabilidad en el interior
> **España Económica**

fusionar *vt* to merge *o* to amalgamate; **fusionar acciones** = to merge shares

◊ **fusionarse** *vr* to merge *o* to amalgamate; **las dos compañías se han fusionado** = the two companies have merged; **la firma se fusionó con su mayor competidor** = the firm merged with its main competitor

futuro, -ra 1 *adj* future; **entrega futura** = future delivery; **tipos de cambio futuros** = forward (exchange) rate **2** *nm* future; **industrias del futuro** = sunrise industries; **en el futuro** = in the future *o* hereafter; **trata de ser más cuidadoso en el futuro** = try to be more careful in future; **en el futuro todos los informes deberán enviarse a Australia por avión** = in future all reports must be sent to Australia by air; **en fecha futura** = forward

◊ **futuros** *nmpl* **(a)** *(contrato de entrega futura)* futures; **compra de futuros** = forward buying *o* buying forward; **contrato de futuros** = futures contract; **futuros financieros** = financial futures; **mercado de futuros** = forward market *o* futures market; **mercado de futuros financieros** = financial futures market; **ayer el oro** *o* **la plata subió un 5% en el mercado de futuros** = gold *o* silver rose 5% on the commodity futures market yesterday; **café cotizado en el mercado de futuros** = coffee futures; **materias primas cotizadas en el mercado de futuros** = commodity futures; **transacciones de futuros** = forward dealings; **venta de futuros** = forward sales *o* forward selling **(b) vender divisas a futuros** = to sell forward; **comprar divisas a futuros** = to buy forward

> el viernes comenzó la negociación en el mercado español de futuros financieros (MEFF Renta Fija) de los nuevos contratos denominados sobre el diferencial o 'spread' entre las cotizaciones de tres de los principales futuros sobre Bonos a 10 años existentes en Europa
> **El País**

Gg

Gabón *nm* Gabon

◊ **gabonés, -esa** *adj y n* Gabonese
NOTA: capital: **Libreville;** moneda: **franco CFA (FCFA)** = CFA franc (CFAF)

gaje *nm* perk; **gajes del oficio** = occupational hazard

galería *nf* gallery; **galería comercial** = shopping arcade

galón *nm* gallon

gama *nf* **(a)** *(surtido)* range; **una gama de mercancías de primera categoría** = a select range of merchandise; **nuestra gama de modelos es la más moderna del mercado** = we have the most modern range of models *o* model range on the market; **gama de precios** = price range; **gama de productos** = product line; **vender bien una gama de productos** = to do a good trade in a range of products; **su gama de productos es demasiado limitada** = their range of products *o* product range is too narrow; **no tratamos** *o* **no vendemos esa gama de productos** = we do not stock that line; **fabrican una interesante gama de herramientas de jardinería** = they produce an interesting line in garden tools **(b) tiene una amplia gama de inversiones** *o* **de intereses** = he has a wide spread of investments *o* of interests

Gambia *nf* Gambia

◊ **gambiano, -na** *adj y n* Gambian
NOTA: capital: **Banjul;** moneda: **dalasi** = dalasi

ganadería *nf* cattle *o* livestock *o* stock farm; **agricultura y ganadería** = agriculture

ganancia *nf* **(a)** *(beneficio)* profit *o* return *o* earning capacity *o* earning power; **ganancia inesperada** = windfall; **ganancia neta** = clear profit; **sacar una ganancia neta del 10%** *o* **de 500.000 ptas. en la operación** = to clear 10% *o* 500,000 pesetas on the deal; **sacamos unos 6.000 dólares de ganancia neta en la venta** = we made $6,000 clear profit on the sale; **producir una ganancia rápida** = to bring in a quick return **(b)** *(comisión)* commission; **ganancias del corredor de bolsa** = stockbroker's commission

◊ **ganancias** *nfpl* earnings *o* proceeds; **las acciones petrolíferas registraron ganancias en la bolsa** = oil shares showed gains on the Stock Exchange; **vendió la tienda e invirtió las ganancias en un negocio de reparación de ordenadores** = he sold his shop and invested the proceeds in a computer repair business; **cuenta de pérdidas y ganancias** = profit and loss account

ganar *vt* **(a)** *(dinero)* to earn; **ganar 10.000 ptas. a la semana** = to earn 10,000 pesetas a week; **gana 10.000.000 de ptas. al año** *o* **5.000 ptas. a la hora** = he earns *o* makes 10m pesetas a year *o* 5,000 pesetas an hour; **gana 200.000 ptas. al mes** *o* **gana unas 200.000 ptas. al mes** = he earns 200,000 ptas. a month *o* he makes about 200,000 ptas. per month; **nuestro representante en París no se gana su comisión de ninguna manera** = our agent in Paris certainly does not earn his commission; **ganar mucho dinero** = to earn a lot of money; **capacidad de ganar dinero** = earning capacity *o* earning power; **vender materias primas para ganar divisas convertibles** = to sell raw materials to earn hard currency **(b)** *(aumentar)* to gain; **el dólar ganó seis puntos en los mercados de divisas** = the dollar gained six points on the foreign exchange markets; **las acciones ganaron 292 ptas. en las operaciones de hoy** = the shares made 292 pesetas in today's trading **(c)** *(obtener)* to get *o* to obtain *o* to gain **(d)** *(lograr)* to win

gandul, -la *adj y n* lazy *o* idle

ganga *nf* bargain; *(informal)* snip; **ese coche es una ganga por 100.000 ptas.** = that car is a (real) bargain at 100,000 pesetas; **estas máquinas de escribir son una ganga a 10.000 ptas.** = these typewriters are a snip at 10,000 pesetas; **persona que busca gangas** = bargain hunter

garante 1 *adj* responsible; **salir garante de** = to stand surety for **2** *nmf* (i) guarantor *o* warrantor; (ii) backer

garantía *nf* **(a)** *(seguridad)* collateral *o* cover; **¿tiene Vd. suficiente garantía para este préstamo?** = do you have sufficient cover for this loan?; **cuenta de garantía bloqueada** = escrow account **(b)** *(documento legal)* guarantee *o* warranty; **certificado de garantía** = certificate of guarantee *o* guarantee certificate; **garantía adicional** *o* **a largo plazo** *o* **extensión de garantía** = extended guarantee *o* warranty; **la garantía dura dos años** = the guarantee lasts for two years; **el producto tiene una garantía de doce meses** = the product is guaranteed for twelve months; **el coche se vende con una garantía de doce meses** = the car is sold with a twelve-month warranty; **el coche está todavía bajo garantía** = the car is still under warranty; **todas las piezas de repuesto tienen garantía** = all the spare parts are guaranteed; **la garantía cubre las piezas de recambio pero no los costes de la mano de obra** = the warranty covers spare parts but not labour costs; **violación de garantía** = breach of warranty; **garantía de indemnización** = letter of indemnity **(c)** *(fianza)* security *o* pledge; **hacer un préstamo con garantía** = to make a loan against a security; **dejar certificados de acciones como garantía** = to leave share certificates as security; **dar una casa en garantía de un préstamo** = to use a house as security for a loan; **acreedor sin garantía** = unsecured creditor; **préstamo sin garantía** = unsecured loan **(d)** endorsement

> precisamente la garantía y el servicio posventa era algo que se les criticaba a estas compañías ensambladoras, pero algunas empiezan a ofrecer buenas ofertas
> **El País**

garantizar *vt* **(a)** *(asegurar)* to underwrite; **garantizar el pago** = to underwrite payment;

garantizar una emisión de acciones = to underwrite a share issue; **la emisión fue garantizada por tres empresas aseguradoras** = the issue was underwritten by three underwriting companies; **el gobierno ha garantizado el pago de los costes de desarrollo del proyecto** = the government has underwritten the development costs of the project **(b)** *(avalar)* to guarantee; **garantizar una deuda** = to give something as security for a debt; **deudas garantizadas** = secured debts; **garantizar un préstamo** = to secure a loan

gasolina *nf* petrol *o* fuel; *US* gasoline *o* gas; **gasolina súper** *o* **de alto octanaje** = four-star petrol *o* top-grade petrol; **el coche consume poca gasolina** = the car is very economic on petrol; **ha comprado un coche que consume poca gasolina** = he has bought a car with low fuel consumption *o* low petrol consumption; **el precio de la gasolina ha bajado** = the price of petrol has gone down

◊ **gasolinera** *nf* filling station

gastar *vt* **(a)** *(dinero)* to spend; **gastaron todos sus ahorros en comprar la tienda** = they spent all their savings on buying the shop; **la compañía gasta miles de libras en investigación** = the company spends thousands of pounds on research; **gastar excesivamente** = to overspend; **gastar más de lo presupuestado** = to overspend one's budget; **gastar menos** = to underspend **(b)** *(usar)* to use; **gasta la marca más cara del mercado** = he is using the most expensive brand in the market

gasto *nm* expenditure *o* expense; **un gasto constante** = a recurrent item of expenditure; **el programa actual de gastos de la empresa** = the company's current expenditure programme; **gran parte de nuestro gasto actual se va en almuerzos de trabajo** = expense account lunches form a large part of our current expenditure; **gasto excesivo** = overspending; **la junta decidió limitar el gasto excesivo de los servicios de producción** = the board decided to limit the overspending by the production departments; **el gasto es demasiado elevado dado el estado de mi cuenta bancaria** = the expense is too much for my bank balance; **con mucho gasto** = at great expense; **gran gasto** = heavy expenditure; **grandes gastos en bienes de equipo** = heavy expenditure on equipment; **con poco gasto** = inexpensive *o* cheap *o* inexpensively; **amuebló la oficina sin escatimar gastos** = he furnished the office with no expense spared; **partida de gasto** = item of expenditure; **permitirse un gasto** = to afford; **no podemos permitirnos el gasto de dos teléfonos** = we cannot afford the cost of two telephones

◊ **gastos** *nmpl* **(a)** *(coste)* charge; **gastos aparte** = extras; **gastos bancarios** = bank charges; *US* service charge; **gastos a cobrar a la entrega** = charges forward; **los gastos de envío no están incluidos** = delivery is not included *o* packing and postage are extras; **gastos de franqueo** = postal charges; **sin gastos de franqueo** = post free; **los gastos de franqueo subirán un 10% en septiembre** = postal charges are going up by 10% in September; **gastos de mantenimiento** = operating costs *o* running costs; **gastos de tramitación** = handling charges **(b)** *(en contabilidad)* expenditure *o* expenses *o* outlay; **gastos accesorios** = petty expenses *o* incidental expenses; **gastos adicionales** = extraordinary charges; **gastos anticipados** =

prepaid expenses; **gastos de capital** = capital expenditure *o* capital outlay; **gastos deducibles de impuestos** = allowable expenses (against tax); **estos gastos no son desgravables** = these expenses are not tax-deductible; **gastos de explotación** = business expenses; **gastos fijos** = fixed expenditure; **gastos generales** *o* **de producción** = general expenses *o* running expenses *o* overhead costs *o* expenses *o* overheads; *US* overhead; **presupuesto de gastos generales** = overhead budget; **gastos del hogar** = household expenses; **gastos imprevistos** = contingent expenses *o* incidentals; **gastos judiciales** = legal expenses; **gastos menores** *o* **varios** = incidental expenses *o* petty expenses; **caja para gastos menores** = petty cash; **gastos no autorizados** = unauthorized expenditure; **gastos pagados** = expenses paid; **gastos reembolsables** = out-of-pocket expenses; **gastos de representación** = entertainment expenses; **gastos de viaje** = travelling expenses; **absorver gastos generales** = to absorb overheads; **los detalles de los gastos de los directivos no se revelan a los accionistas** = the actual figures for directors' expenses are not shown to the shareholders; **el salario ofrecido es de 2.000.000 de ptas. más gastos** = the salary offered is 2m pesetas plus expenses; **los costes de producción más los gastos generales son superiores a los ingresos** = production costs plus overheads are higher than revenue; **todos los representantes reciben un adelanto de 20.000 ptas. para gastos menores** = the sales reps have a float of 20,000 pesetas each to cover incidental expenses; **la compañía le envió a San Francisco con todos los gastos pagados** = the company sent him to San Francisco all expenses paid; **dietas para gastos de representación** = entertainment allowance **(c)** **cubrir gastos** = to cover expenses *o* to break even; **el año pasado la compañía apenas cubrió gastos** = last year the company only just broke even; **sólo cubrimos los gastos** = we cleared only our expenses; **los ingresos por las ventas cubren los costes de fabricación pero no los gastos generales** = the sales revenue covers the manufacturing costs but not the overheads; **cubrimos gastos en los dos primeros meses de actividad** = we broke even in our first two months of trading; **los ingresos por ventas apenas cubren los gastos de publicidad** *o* **de fabricación** = the sales revenue barely covers the costs of advertising *o* the manufacturing costs; **correr con los gastos** = to foot the bill; **correr con los gastos de alguien** = to meet someone's expenses; **cuenta de gastos** = expense account; **recorte de gastos** = reduction of expenditure; **pagar los gastos** = to foot the bill *o* to pay expenses; **reducir gastos** = to cut down on expenses *o* to reduce expenditure *o* to retrench; **reembolso de gastos** = reimbursement of expenses; **relación de gastos** = statement of expenses **(d)** *(consumo)* spending; **gastos de los consumidores** = consumer spending; **gastos en efectivo** = cash spending; **gastos en tarjetas de crédito** = credit card spending; **dinero para gastos** = spending money **(e)** *(publicidad)* **gastos de publicidad incluidos** = above the line **(f)** *(seguro)* **gastos deducidos de los beneficios** = back-end loaded; **gastos iniciales** *o* **degresivos** = front-end loaded

GATT = ACUERDO GENERAL SOBRE ARANCELES ADUANEROS Y COMERCIO

general *adj* **(a)** *(universal)* general *o* across-the-board *o* comprehensive *o* overall *o* global; **Acuerdo General sobre Aranceles Aduaneros y Comercio (GATT)** = the General Agreement on Tariffs and Trade (GATT); **un aumento general de precios** = an across-the-board price increase; **la compañía anunció que había registrado una baja general de los beneficios** = the company reported an overall fall in profits; **comercio general** = general trading; **el director gerente ordenó una revisión general de las condiciones de crédito** = the MD ordered a full-scale review of credit terms; **la dirección propuso una revisión general de los salarios** = the management proposed a global review of salaries; **total general** = grand total **(b)** *(que abarca todo y todos)* general; **auditoría general** = general audit; **balance general** = balance sheet; **director general** = general manager; **elecciones generales** = general election; **gastos generales** = general expenses; **huelga general** = general strike; **junta general** = general meeting; **junta general anual** = Annual General Meeting (AGM); **junta general extraordinaria** = Extraordinary General Meeting (EGM); **media general** = overall average; **negativa general** = blanket refusal; **oficina general** = general office; **plan general** = overall plan; **seguro general** = general insurance **(c) por lo general** *o* **en general** = generally; **la oficina cierra en general entre Navidad y Año Nuevo** = the office is generally closed between Christmas and the New Year

◇ **generalmente** *adv* generally

género *nm* **(a)** stock; **¿cuándo espera recibir más género?** = when do you expect to get more stock?; **mercancías de buen género** = good quality stock **(b) géneros** = articles *o* merchandise; **géneros diversos** = sundries *o* sundry items

generoso, -sa *adj* generous; **el personal contribuyó con una generosa cantidad para el regalo de jubilación del director** = the staff contributed a generous sum for the retirement present for the manager

genuino, -na *adj* genuine *o* real

gerente *nmf* manager *o* manageress *o* director; **codirector gerente** = joint managing director; **director gerente** = managing director (MD); **gerente de línea** = line manager

gestión *nf* **(a)** *(administración)* management; **gestión eficaz** = efficient management; **gestión ineficaz** = inefficient management; **gestión de productos** = product management; **buena gestión** = good management; **comité de gestión** = management committee; **contable de gestión** = management accountant; **cuentas de gestión** = management accounts; **curso de gestión empresarial** = management course; **mala gestión** = bad management; **el grupo se ve perjudicado por una mala gestión** = the group suffers from bad management; **personal de gestión** = managerial staff; **técnicas de gestión anticuadas** = old-style management techniques **(b)** *(negociación)* negotiation; **entrar en gestión** = to negotiate **(c)** *(medidas)* measures *o* steps (taken); **se han hecho gestiones** = some steps have been taken **(d) gestión de deudas con descuento** = factoring

gestionar *vt* **(a)** *(administrar)* to manage **(b)** *(negociar)* to negotiate (a deal); **gestionar deudas con descuento** = to factor

gestor, -ra *n* business agent *o* manager; **gestor de cuentas** = account manager

◇ **gestoría** *nf* agency

Ghana *nm* Ghana

◇ **ghanés, -esa** *adj y n* Ghanaian
NOTA: capital: **Accra**; moneda: **cedi ghanés (C)** = Ghanaian cedi

Gibraltar *nm* Gibraltar

◇ **gibraltareño, -ña** *adj y n* Gibraltarian
NOTA: capital: **Gibraltar**; moneda: **libra de Gibraltar (£)** = Gibraltar pound (£)

gira *nf* tour; **el ministro efectuó una gira de inspección por la región** = the minister went on a fact-finding tour of the region

girar 1 *vt* *(cambiar de sentido)* to turn **2** *vi* **(a)** *(comerciar)* to trade; **la empresa gira a razón de Gil y Gil** = the firm trades under the name Gil & Gil **(b)** *(librar)* to draw; **girar en descubierto** = to overdraw (one's account)

giro *nm* **(a)** *(pago)* draft *o* remittance; **la familia vive de un giro semanal que les envía el padre desde los EE UU** = the family lives on a weekly remittance from their father in the USA; **giro bancario** = bank draft *o* banker's draft *o* bank giro; **realizar un giro bancario** = to make a draft on a bank; **nos envió un giro librado contra el Banco de Santander** = he sent us an order on the Banco de Santander; **giro postal** = money order; **giro postal internacional** = foreign money order *o* international money order *o* overseas money order; **giro telegráfico** = telegraphic transfer; **la oficina le envió un giro telegráfico de 200.000 ptas. para cubrir sus gastos** = the office cabled him 200,000 pesetas to cover his expenses; **giro a la vista** = sight draft *o* demand bill **(b) derechos especiales de giro (DEG)** = special drawing rights (SDRs)

global *adj* global *o* across-the-board *o* overall *o* all-in *o* comprehensive; **acuerdo global** = blanket agreement; **planificación global** = comprehensive planning; **producto global** = aggregate output; **rechazo global** = blanket refusal; **se trata de una oferta global que incluye el sistema completo de ordenadores, la formación del personal y el**

mantenimiento del equipo = we are offering a package deal which includes the whole office computer system, staff training and hardware maintenance

globo *nm* balloon; **préstamo globo** = balloon (loan); **hipoteca globo** = balloon mortgage

gnomo *nm* gnome; *(banqueros suizos)* 'los gnomos de Zurich' = the gnomes of Zurich

gobernador, -ra *n* governor

gobernar *vt* to govern; **el país está gobernado por un grupo de dirigentes militares** = the country is governed by a group of military leaders

gobierno *nm* **(a)** *(gobernación)* government; **gobierno de una provincia** *o* **de un estado** = provincial government *o* state government; **con apoyo del gobierno** = government-backed; **intervención del gobierno** = government intervention; **medidas expansionistas de un gobierno** = government measures to expand the economy; **medir la actuación del gobierno** = to measure the government's performance; **la política del gobierno está resumida en el folleto (b)** *(dirección)* control; **llevar el gobierno de una empresa** = to manage a company

golpe *nm* blow *o* knock; **golpe de Estado** = coup d'état; **un golpe maestro** = a master stroke; **asestar un duro golpe a la competencia** = to knock the competition; **subir de golpe** = to jump

golpear *vt* to hit *o* to knock; **se golpeó la cabeza contra el archivador** = she knocked her head on the filing cabinet

goma *nf* **(a)** *(de pegar)* glue *o* gum; **la goma del sobre no pega muy bien (b)** *(de borrar)* rubber *o* eraser; **(c)** *(elástica)* rubber band; **sujete las fichas con una goma para que no se mezclen** = put a band round the filing cards to stop them getting mixed up

góndola *nf* gondola *o* island display unit

grabadora *nf* recorder; **grabadora de vídeo** = video recorder

grabar *vt* to tape *o* to record; **grabar en vídeo** = to video

gracia *nf* grace *o* favour; **conceder a un acreedor un periodo de gracia** = to give a creditor a period of grace

◊ **gracias** *nfpl* thanks; **voto de gracias** = vote of thanks; **gracias a** = thanks to; **la compañía pudo continuar gracias a un préstamo del banco** = the company was able to continue trading thanks to a loan from the bank

grado *nm* **(a)** *(temperatura)* degree; **a 0 grados** = 0 degrees; **grado de alcohol** = alcohol proof **(b)** *(universidad)* degree **(c)** *(categoría)* grade *o* rank; **de grado máximo** = top-grade; **funcionario de grado máximo** = top grade civil servant *o* high-level civil servant; **alcanzar el grado máximo en la administración pública** = to reach the top grade in the civil service; **de grado inferior** = low-grade *o* low-level; **de grado superior** *o* **de alto grado** = high-grade **(d)** grado de rendimiento = earning capacity *o* earning power

graduado, -da 1 *adj* graduated **2** *n* graduate; **programa de formación para graduados** = graduate training scheme **3** *pp de* GRADUAR

gradual *adj* gradual; **en 1996 tuvo lugar un restablecimiento gradual de la rentabilidad** = 1996 saw a gradual return to profits; **su currículum vitae muestra su ascensión gradual al puesto de presidente de la compañía** = his CV describes his gradual rise to the position of company chairman

◊ **gradualmente** *adv* gradually; **aprendió gradualmente los detalles del comercio de importación-exportación** = she gradually learnt the details of the import-export business; **prescindiremos gradualmente de García S.A. como proveedor de piezas de recambio** = García S.A. will be phased out as a supplier of spare parts; **el nuevo sistema de facturación será introducido gradualmente en los próximos dos meses** = the new invoicing system will be phased in over the next two months

graduar *vt* to grade *o* to classify

◊ **graduarse** *vr* to graduate

gráfico, -ca 1 *adj* graphic; **artes gráficas** = graphic arts; **en forma gráfica** = in diagrammatic form; **el cuadro mostraba el patrón de ventas en forma gráfica** = the chart showed the sales pattern in diagrammatic form **2** *nf* graph *o* diagram **3** *nm* chart *o* diagram *o* graph; **gráfico de barras** = bar chart; **gráfico circular** *o* **sectorial** = pie chart; **gráfico lineal** = line chart *o* line graph; **gráfico de organización** = organization chart; **gráfico de ventas** = sales chart; **el gráfico de las ventas muestra un aumento constante** = the sales graph shows a steady rise; **el documento contiene** *o* **presenta un gráfico de la estructura organizativa de la compañía** = the paper gives a diagram of the company's organizational structure; **exponer los resultados en un gráfico** = to set out the results in a graph; **trazar un gráfico que muestre la creciente rentabilidad** = to draw a graph showing the rising profitability

◊ **gráficamente** *adv* diagrammatically; **la figura muestra la evolución de ventas gráficamente** = the chart shows the sales pattern in the form of a diagram

gramo *nm* gram *o* gramme

gran *adj* *(contracción de 'grande' delante de un nombre singular)* grand *o* great *o* large; **gran cantidad** = a lot *o* many *o* a great deal of; **la empresa es una gran consumidora de acero** *o* **de electricidad** = the company is a heavy user of steel *o* a heavy consumer of electricity; **gran demanda** = keen demand; **una gran demanda de acciones petrolíferas** = an active demand for oil shares; **hay una gran demanda de ordenadores personales** = there is a heavy demand for PCs; **los vendedores tienen gran fe en el producto** = the salesmen have great faith in the product; **gran gasto** = heavy expenditure; **gran plan** = grand plan; **los años de gran prosperidad** = the boom years; **persona de gran talento** = highly talented person; **gran volumen de ventas** = high volume of sales

Gran Bretaña *nf* Great Britain

◊ **británico, -ca** *adj y n* British
NOTA: capital: **Londres** (= London); moneda: **libra esterlina (£)** = pound sterling (£)

grande *adj* **(a)** *(cantidad)* great *o* high *o* large; **un pedido muy grande** = an outsize order; **un programa de grandes inversiones en el extranjero** = a programme of heavy investment overseas; **sufrió grandes pérdidas en la bolsa** = he had heavy losses on the Stock Exchange; **grandes costes** = heavy costs **(b) grandes almacenes** = department store

granel *nm* bulk; **carguero de graneles** = bulk carrier; **a granel** = in bulk *o* loose; **envíos a granel** = bulk shipments; **vender café a granel** = to sell coffee loose *o* in beans

◊ **granelero** *nm* bulk carrier

granja *nf* farm; **granja colectiva** = collective farm; **granja mixta** = mixed farm

grapa *nf* staple; **empleó unas tijeras para quitar** *o* **desprender las grapas de los documentos** = he used a pair of scissors to take the staples out of the documents

◊ **grapadora** *nf* stapler

grapar *vt* to staple; **grapar papeles** = to staple papers together

gratificación *nf* bonus *o* reward *o* gratuity *o* perk

gratis *adv* free of charge *o* without paying; **entramos en la exposición gratis** = we got into the exhibition free

gratuito, -ta *adj* free *o* free of charge; **solicite catálogo gratuito** = catalogue sent free on request; **emisión gratuita** = bonus issue; **recibir una entrada gratuita para una exposición** = to be given a free ticket to the exhibition; **muesta gratuita** = free sample; **periódico gratuito** = free paper *o* freesheet *o* giveaway paper; **prueba gratuita** = free trial; **ofrecemos un servicio posventa gratuito a los clientes** = we offer a free after-sales service to customers; **el transporte de mercancías es gratuito** = goods are delivered free

◊ **gratuitamente** *adv* free *o* free of charge

> la familia obtiene servicio médico gratuito y si lo requiere, también enseñanza gratuita
> **España Económica**

gravamen *nm* tax *o* tax burden *o* countervailing duty; *(derecho de retención)* lien; **gravamen a las importaciones** = import levy

gravar *vt* to impose *o* to levy (a tax); **gravar con un impuesto** = to tax; **gravar el tabaco con un impuesto** = to put a duty on cigarettes; **gravar las empresas con un impuesto del 50%** = to tax businesses at 50%; **gravar las bicicletas con un impuesto** = to impose a tax on bicycles; **el gobierno gravó el petróleo con unos derechos de aduana especiales** = the government imposed a special duty on oil; **el gobierno ha decidido gravar los coches de importación con un impuesto** = the government has decided to levy a tax on imported cars

grave *adj* serious *o* very bad *o* severe; **la tormenta produjo daños graves** = the storm caused serious damage; **los daños en el ordenador no fueron muy graves** = the damage to the computer was not very serious

◊ **gravemente** *adv* severely *o* seriously; **la carga resultó gravemente dañada por el agua** = the cargo was seriously damaged by water

gravoso, -sa *adj* costly *o* heavy

> heredar una empresa familiar resulta con las nuevas medidas fiscales menos gravoso
> **El País**

Grecia *nf* Greece

◊ **griego, -ga** *adj y n* Greek
NOTA: capital: **Atenas** (= Athens); moneda: **dracma (Dr)** = drachma (Dr)

gremio *nm* guild; **el gremio de panaderos** = the guild of master bakers

gris *adj* grey; **mercado gris** = grey market

grúa *nf* crane; **tuvieron que alquilar una grúa para colocar la máquina en la fábrica** = they had to hire a crane to get the machine into the factory

grueso, -sa 1 *adj* thick *o* bulky **2** *nm* **(a)** *(espesor)* thickness **(b)** *(parte principal)* main part *o* bulk; **el grueso del pedido se ha enviado** = the bulk of the order has been dispatched **3** *nf* gross; **encargó cuatro gruesas de plumas estilográficas** = he ordered four gross of pens; **contrato a la gruesa** = bottomry

grupo *nm* **(a)** *(negocios)* group; **el grupo Banesto** = the Banesto group; **grupo industrial** = industrial group *o* combine; **un grupo industrial alemán** = a German industrial combine; **cuentas** *o* **contabilidad del grupo** = group accounts; **el presidente del grupo** = the group chairman *o* the chairman of the group; **los resultados del grupo** = group results; **el volumen de negocios del grupo** = group turnover *o* turnover for the group; **el grupo obtuvo unos beneficios brutos de 5.000 millones de pesetas en 1995** = the group grossed 5,000m pesetas in 1995 **(b)** *(personas)* group; **un grupo de empleados ha enviado una nota al presidente quejándose por el ruido de la oficina** = a group of the staff has sent a memo to the chairman complaining about noise in the office; **grupo de expertos** = panel of experts *o* think tank; **grupo de presión** = lobby *o* pressure group; **grupo de presión para el ahorro de energía** = the energy-saving lobby; **grupo de trabajo** = working party; **el gobierno ha creado un grupo de trabajo para estudiar los problemas de los residuos industriales** = the government has set up a working party to study the problems of industrial waste; **lo mejor del grupo** = the pick of the group; **es la encargada de un grupo de jóvenes contables** = she is responsible for a group of junior accountants **(c)** *(en una cuenta)* **grupo de partidas** = centre

> Grupo Zeta es hoy en día una empresa de medios de comunicación desarrollada, un conglomerado de 27 cabeceras distintas
> **Tiempo**

Grupo de los Cinco (G5) Group of Five (G5): France, Germany, Japan. UK and the USA

Grupo de los Siete (G7) Group of Seven (G7): France, Germany, Japan, UK, Canada, Italy and the USA

Grupo de los Diez (G10) Group of Ten (G10): Belgium, Canada, France, Germany, Italy, Japan, Netherlands, Sweden, Switzerland, UK and the USA

guarda *nm* caretaker *o* guard *o* keeper

guardamuebles *nm* furniture depository *o* furniture storage

guardapolvo *nm* dust cover

guardar *vt* **(a)** *(conservar)* to keep *o* to store; **guardamos nuestra información sobre salarios en el ordenador** = we store our pay records on computer; **los nombres de los clientes se guardan en los archivos de la compañía** = the names of customers are kept in the company's records **(b)** *(retener)* to hold (onto); **deberías guardar estas acciones - es probable que suban** = you should hold these shares - they look likely to rise; **te guardaremos el puesto hasta que hayas aprobado el examen de conducir** = we will keep the job open for you until you have passed your driving test **(c)** *(informática)* to save; **no olvides guardar tus archivos cuando los hayas pasado al ordenador** = do not forget to save your files when you have finished keyboarding them

guardarropa *nm* cloakroom

guardia *nf* duty; **guardia de noche** = night duty

Guatemala *nf* Guatemala

◊ **guatemalteco, -ca** *adj y n* Guatemalan
NOTA: capital: **Ciudad de Guatemala** (= Guatemala City); moneda: **quetzal guatemalteco (Q)** = Guatemalan quetzal (Q)

Guayana *nf* Guyana

◊ **guayanés, -esa** *adj y n* Guyanese
NOTA: capital: **Cayenne;** moneda: **dólar de Guayana ($G)** = Guyana dollar (G$)

gubernamental *adj* governmental

gubernativo, -iva *adj* governmental

guerra *nf* war; **los precios del petróleo han subido desde que empezó la guerra** = oil prices have jumped since the war started; **material de guerra** = military hardware; **guerra comercial** = trade war; **guerra de precios** = price war; **guerra de tarifas** = tariff war

Aviaco, la filial para vuelos del grupo Iberia, se ha embarcado en una guerra de precios sin precedentes en el mercado aéreo nacional español
Cinco Días

guía 1 *nf* directory *o* handbook; **guía del estudiante** = student's guide; **guía telefónica** = phone book *o* telephone directory; **busque su dirección en la guía telefónica** = look up his address in the phone book; **buscar un número en la guía telefónica** = to look up a number in the telephone directory; **buscó el número de la compañía en la guía** = he looked up the number of the company in the telephone book; **su número está en la guía de Lérida** = his number is in the Lérida directory; **su número no figura en la guía telefónica** = his number is not in the phone book *o* his number is ex-directory; **guía urbana** = street directory **2** *nmf (persona)* guide; **excursión con guía** = guided tour *o* conducted tour; **guía de turismo** = tourist guide *o* (tourist) courier

◊ **guiar** *vt* to guide

guillotina *nf* guillotine

guión *nm* script *o* explanatory text

Guinea *nf* Guinea

◊ **guineano, -ana** *adj y n* Guinean
NOTA: capital: **Conakry;** moneda: **franco guineano (FG)** = Guinean franc (GF)

Guinea Ecuatorial *nf* Equatorial Guinea

◊ **guineano, -ana ecuatorial** *adj y n* Equatorial Guinean
NOTA: capital: **Bata;** moneda: **franco CFA (FCFA)** = CFA franc (CFAF)

gustar *vi* to like *o* to appreciate; **a los turistas no les gusta que les hagan esperar mucho tiempo en los bancos** = tourists do not appreciate long delays at banks

gusto *nm* **(a)** taste *o* style; **a gusto del cliente** = to suit the customer **(b)** to have a liking for; **tengo el gusto de presentarles** = I have the pleasure to introduce to you; **con gusto te ayudaría** = I'd gladly help you; **¡Mucho gusto!** = pleased to meet you!

Hh

Ha = HECTAREA hectare (ha)

haber 1 *vt* to have **2** *v aux* **he visitado el banco esta mañana** = I went to the bank this morning **3** *v impersonal* **hay** = there is *o* there are; **no hay dinero en la caja** = there's no money in the box; **hay 10 personas esperando** = there are ten people waiting; **hay que** = it is necessary to; **¿qué hay?** = what's the matter? **4** *nm (en contabilidad)* credit side *o* credit balance; **columna del haber** = credit column; **deber y haber** = debit and credit

habiente *adj* **derecho habiente** = rightful claimant

hábil *adj* **(a)** *(listo)* clever; **es muy hábil para encontrar gangas** = he is very clever at spotting a bargain **(b)** *(diestro)* skilful; **ser hábil para cualquier trabajo** = to be skilful (at doing something) **(c) día hábil** = working day

◊ **habilidad** *nf* **(a)** *(destreza)* skill *o* workmanship; **tiene una gran habilidad para los negocios** = she has great business skills **(b)** *(competencia)* expertise **(c)** *(capacidad)* capacity

habilitar *vt* to qualify

habitación *nf* room; *(vivienda)* accommodation; **quiero una habitación con baño para dos noches** = I want a room with bath for two nights; **habitación doble** = double room; **habitación individual** = single room; **habitaciones libres** = hotel vacancies; **servicio de habitaciones de un hotel** = room service; **debe dejar libre la habitación a las 12.00** = checkout time is 12.00 *o* please leave the room by 12.00; **dejaremos la habitación antes del desayuno** = we will check out before breakfast

habitante *nmf* **(a)** *(país)* inhabitant *o* resident **(b)** *(casa)* occupant *o* tenant

hábito *nm* habit *o* custom

> los hábitos de consumo, en general, y de la
> información, en particular, están
> cambiando muy rápidamente en todo el mundo
> **Tiempo**

habitual *adj* usual *o* routine; **cliente habitual** = regular customer

hablar *vt/i* to speak *o* to talk; **le ofrecieron la plaza porque habla dos idiomas** = they offered her the job because she speaks two languages; **¿habla español?** = do you speak Spanish?; **telefonear para hablar de algo** = to phone about something; **hablemos de negocios** = let's talk business

hacer *vt* **(a)** *(producir, fabricar, construir)* to make; **hacer chapuzas** *o* **hacer pequeños trabajos** = to do odd jobs; **hacer dinero** = to make money; **hacer una llamada telefónica** = to make a phone call; **hacer negocios** = to do business *o* to transact business; **hacer una oferta** = to make a bid for something; **hágalo Vd. mismo** = do-it-yourself (DIY) **(b)** **hacer una advertencia** = to warn; **hacer un análisis de los distribuidores** = to conduct a review of distributors; **hacer un asiento** = to post an entry; **hacer un asiento complementario** *o* **compensatorio** = to contra an entry; **hacer un balance** = to balance; **hacer un balance de costes y ventas** = to set the costs against the sales; **hacer un borrador** = to draft *o* to rough out; **hacer contrabando** = to smuggle; **hacer una declaración de renta** = to fill in a tax return; **hacer escala** = to stop (at) *o* to call (at); **hacer fotocopias** = to photocopy; **hacer horas extraordinarias** *o* **extras** = to work overtime; **hacer un inventario** = to take stock *o* to inventory; **hacer una lista** = to list; **hacer una objeción a algo** = to raise an objection to something; **hacer objeciones** = to object to something; **hacer un plan** = to plan; **hacer un trato** = to make a deal; **hacer un viaje** = to travel; **hacer un vídeo** **(c)** = to video; **hacer algo más deprisa** = to hurry up; **aceptar hacer algo** = to agree to do something; **no decidirse a hacer algo** = to hesitate; **tiene Vd. que hacer algo si quiere que la gente deje de engañarle** = you must take action if you want to stop people cheating you; **obligar a alguien a hacer algo** = to force someone to do something; **estar obligado a hacer algo** = to be obliged to do something; **hacer bajar los precios** = to force prices down; **hacer flotar una divisa** = to float a currency; **hacer subir los precios** = to force prices up **(e) hacer cola** = to queue; **cuando los alimentos estaban racionados la gente tenía que hacer cola para el pan** = when food was rationed, people had to queue for bread **(f) hacer frente a** = to meet; **no pudo hacer frente a sus deudas** *o* **a los pagos de la hipoteca** = he was not able to meet his liabilities *o* his mortgage repayments; **el almacén está intentando hacer frente a los pedidos atrasados** = the warehouse is trying to cope with the backlog of orders **(g) hicieron falta seis hombres y una grúa para instalar el ordenador en la oficina** = it took six men and a crane to get the computer into the office; **hicieron todo lo posible por guardar en secreto el volumen de ventas** = they went to considerable lengths to keep the turnover secret; **tres empresas han hecho presupuestos para el mobiliario de las oficinas** = three firms estimated for the fitting of the offices

◊ **hacerse** *vr* **(a)** to become; **piensa hacerse abogado** = he is intending to become a lawyer; **hacerse socio de una asociación** = to join an association *o* a group *o* to become a member **(b)** **hacerse cargo** = *(darse cuenta)* to realize; *(aceptar responsabilidad)* to accept responsibility; **los clientes deben hacerse cargo de los objetos que rompan** = customers are expected to pay for breakages; **me hago cargo de su difícil situación** = I realize he is in a difficult situation **(c) hacerse un seguro** = to take out an insurance policy; **hacerse un seguro contra robo** = to take out insurance against theft **(d) hacerse pasar por alguien** = to pretend to be someone else; **entró haciéndose pasar por técnico de teléfonos** = he got in by pretending to be a telephone engineer

hacia *prep* towards *o* to; **hacia abajo** = downwards *o* down; **hacia adelante** = forwards; **hacia arriba** = upwards *o* up; **hacia atrás** = backwards

hacienda *nf* property *o* estate; **Hacienda Pública** = *GB* the Inland Revenue; *US* Internal Revenue Service (IRS); **hacer una declaración a Hacienda** = to make a return to the tax office *o* to make an income tax return; **recibió una carta de Hacienda** = he received a letter from the Inland Revenue

> Hacienda fija la cuota a pagar, los ayuntamientos la pueden aumentar y las autonomías también obtienen beneficios
> **Tiempo**

> las rebajas de impuestos y la desregulación de algunos mercados tiene un coste para la hacienda pública y ese coste tendrá graves repercusiones para el déficit del sector público
> **El País**

Haití *nm* Haiti

◇ **haitiano, -na** *adj y n* Haitian
NOTA: capital: **Port-au-Prince;** moneda: **gourde haitiano (G)** = Haitian gourde (G)

hallar *vt* to find *o* to discover

◇ **hallarse** *vr* **(a) hallarse sin dinero** = to have no money **(b)** to be situated; **¿dónde se hallan las islas que mencionaste?** = where are the islands you mentioned?

'hardware' *nm* hardware

hasta *prep* up to *o* until *o* as far as; **compraremos hasta un precio máximo de 5.000 ptas.** = we will buy at prices up to 5,000 pesetas; **sumó las ventas de los seis meses hasta diciembre** = he counted up the sales for the six months to December

hecho, -cha 1 *adj* made *o* finished; **hecho a medida** *o* **a la orden** = made to order *o* custom-built *o* custom-made; **hecho a mano** = handmade; **escribe todas sus cartas en papel hecho a mano** = he writes all his letters on handmade paper **2** *nm* fact; **los hechos hablan por sí solos** = the facts speak for themselves; **volviendo otra vez a los hechos** = getting back to the matter in hand **3 de hecho** = in fact *o* really; **el edificio de oficinas pertenece de hecho al padre del presidente** = the office building really belongs to the chairman's father **4** *pp de* HACER

hectárea *nf* hectare (NOTA: se abrevia **Ha)**

> se concederán ayudas directas, de seis mil pesetas por tonelada, a los agricultores con extensiones superiores a las 36,8 hectáreas que dejen en barbecho el 15% de sus tierras
> **Actualidad Económica**

helicóptero *nm* helicopter; **pista de helicópteros** = helipad; **tomó el helicóptero desde el aeropuerto hasta el centro de la ciudad** = he took the helicopter from the airport to the centre of town

helipuerto *nm* heliport

heredado, -da 1 *adj* inherited; **impuesto sobre patrimonio heredado** = tax on inherited wealth *o* estate duty **2** *pp de* HEREDAR

heredar *vt* to inherit; **cuando murió su padre, ella heredó la tienda** = when her father died she inherited the shop; **heredó 2.000.000 de ptas. de su**

abuelo = he inherited 2m pesetas from his grandfather

◇ **heredero, -ra** *n* heir; **sus herederos se repartieron la herencia** = his heirs split the estate between them

◇ **herencia** *nf* estate *o* inheritance *o* legacy; **impuesto sobre la herencia** = estate duty *o* death duty; **después de pagar varios legados el resto de la herencia se dividió entre sus hijos** = after paying various bequests the residue of his estate was split between his children

> heredar una empresa familiar resulta con las nuevas medidas fiscales menos gravoso
> **El País**

herida *nf* injury *o* wound

◇ **herido, -da 1** *adj* injured **2** *n* injured person **3** *pp de* HERIR

herir *vt* to injure; **dos trabajadores resultaron heridos en el incendio** = two workers were injured in the fire

hermético, -ca *adj* airtight; **las mercancías están embaladas en contenedores herméticos** = the goods are packed in airtight containers; **el ordenador está embalado en una caja hermética** = the computer is packed in a watertight case

herramienta *nf* tool *o* implement; **máquinas-herramienta** = machine tools; **proveedor de herramientas** = tool supplier; *(informática)* software utilities supplier

> la contabilidad es una herramienta valiosa pero es limitada porque mide los beneficios pero olvida otras realidades
> **El País**

> su estrategia futura parte de la necesidad de asegurar su posición como proveedor de herramientas y soluciones para la gestión de entornos abiertos
> **PC Week**

hindú *adj y n* Indian; *ver* INDIA

hiper *prefijo* hyper-

◇ **hiperinflación** *nf* hyperinflation

◇ **hipermercado** *nm* hypermarket *o* megastore *o* superstore

> una de las cuestiones más polémicas abordadas por la Administración anterior fue el grado de enfrentamiento que se produjo entre las cadenas de hipermercados con el resto de la distribución y la industria alimentaria
> **El País**

hipoteca *nf* mortgage; **hipoteca de inversión** = endowment mortgage; **hipoteca ampliable** = open-end mortgage; **hipoteca globo** = balloon mortgage; **amortización de una hipoteca** = redemption of a mortgage; **comprar una casa con una hipoteca** = to buy a house with a mortgage; **escasez de hipotecas** = mortgage famine; **lista de espera de hipotecas** = mortgage queue; **ejecución de una hipoteca** = foreclosure; **pagos de la hipoteca** = mortgage payments *o* repayment mortgage; **no pudo hacer frente a los pagos de la hipoteca** = he was unable to meet his mortgage repayments; **se retrasó en el pago de la hipoteca** = he fell behind with his mortgage repayments; **primera hipoteca** = first mortgage; **redimir una hipoteca** = to pay off a mortgage; **segunda hipoteca** = second mortgage; **título garantizado por hipoteca** = mortgage debenture

◊ **hipotecado, -da 1** *adj* mortgaged; **la casa está hipotecada** = the house is mortgaged; **embargar una propiedad hipotecada** = to foreclose on a mortgaged property **2** *pp de* HIPOTECAR

hipotecar *vt* to mortgage; **hipotecar una casa** = to take out a mortgage on a house; **hipotecó la casa para establecer un negocio** = he mortgaged his house to set up his business

◊ **hipotecario, -ria** *adj* mortgage; **cédula hipotecaria** = mortgage debenture *o* mortgage bond; **crédito hipotecario** = mortgage loan; **juicio hipotecario** = foreclosure; **entablar juicio hipotecario** = to foreclose; **sociedad hipotecaria** = building society

> el fuerte peso del crédito hipotecario en el conjunto de la inversión crediticia (41,57%) asegura una inversión de los fondos invertidos
> **Actualidad Económica**

hispano, -na *adj* Spanish *o* Hispanic

◊ **Hispanoamérica** *nf* Latin America

◊ **hispanoamericano, -na** *adj y n* Latin American

historial *nm* record; **el historial del vendedor** = the salesman's record of service *o* service record; **el historial de la empresa en el campo de las relaciones laborales** = the company's record in industrial relations; **la empresa tiene un historial de malas relaciones laborales** = the company has a history of bad labour relations

histórico, -ca *adj* historic *o* historical; **cifras históricas** = historical figures; **coste histórico** = historic(al) cost

hobby *nm* hobby

> Golf, museos, óperas, caza o deportes de riesgo son los hobbies que están provocando la aparición de agencias especializadas
> **Tiempo**

> las agencias de viajes, que han percibido el reto, proponen, sobre todo en invierno, una solución muy atractiva y particular para sus clientes: los viajes a la carta destinados a satisfacer los hobbies del viajero
> **Tiempo**

hogar *nm* home; *(unidad familiar)* household; **gastos del hogar** = household expenses; **sin hogar** = homeless

hoja *nf* leaf *o* sheet *o* page; **hoja de asistencia** = time sheet; **hoja de cálculo** = spreadsheet; **hoja de datos** = fact sheet; **hoja de papel** = sheet of paper

Holanda *nf (= los Países Bajos)* Holland *o* the Netherlands

◊ **holandés, -esa** *adj y n* Dutch; **los holandeses** = the Dutch

NOTA: capital: **Amsterdam;** moneda: **florín neerlandés (fl)** = Dutch guilder (fl)

'holding' *nm (sociedad que controla a otras compañías)* holding company

> una vez que pudo contar con una compañía que cotizaba en bolsa, y que se podía usar como un 'holding', se dedicó a buscar buenas adquisiciones
> **España Económica**

> en 1983 Boyer iniciaba el acoso y derribo de Ruiz Mateos y su holding de empresas, Rumasa
> **Tiempo**

holgazán, -ana 1 *adj* lazy **2** *n* lazy person *o* loafer

holograma *nm* hologram

hombre *nm* man; **el hombre de la calle** = the man in the street; **hombre de confianza** = right-hand man; **hombre de negocios** = businessman; **un hombre de negocios fracasado** = an unsuccessful businessman; **un próspero hombre de negocios** = a successful businessman; **hombre que sirve para todo** *o* **que hace pequeños trabajos** = odd-job-man; **hombre de paja** = front man; **hombre-anuncio** = sandwich man

homólogo, -ga 1 *adj* equivalent **2** *n* counterpart *o* opposite number; **Juan es mi homólogo en la sociedad Pereira** = Juan is my counterpart *o* my opposite number in Pereira's

Honduras *nf* Honduras

◊ **hondureño, -eña** *adj y n* Honduran
NOTA: capital: **Tegucigalpa;** moneda: **lempira hondureño (L)** = Honduras lempira (L)

honesto, -ta *adj* honest

honor *nm* **(a)** honour; **hombre de honor** = man of honour *o* honourable man **(b) de honor** = honorary

honorario, -ria *adj* honorary; **miembro honorario** = honorary member

◊ **honorarios** *nmpl* (i) honorarium; (ii) salary *o* fee; **cobramos unos pequeños honorarios por nuestros servicios** = we charge a small fee for our services; **los honorarios del asesor** = the consultant's fee; **los honorarios de un consejero** = director's fees

honrado, -da *adj* honest

◊ **honradamente** *adv* honestly

hora *nf* **(a)** *(parte del día)* hour; **hora local** = local time; **llega allí a las 4 de la tarde, hora local** = she gets there at 4 pm local time; **hora media de Greenwich** = Greenwich Mean Time; **horas de oficina** = office hours *o* business hours; **no telefonee en horas de oficina** = do not telephone during office hours; **trabajamos ocho horas al día** *o* **treinta y cinco horas a la semana** = we work an eight-hour day *o* a thirty-five hour week; **cada hora** = every hour *o* hourly; **un cuarto de hora** = a quarter of an hour; **fuera de horas** = after working hours; **no se puede sacar dinero de un banco fuera de las horas de oficina** = you cannot get money out of a bank outside banking hours; **trabajó en las cuentas fuera de las horas de oficina** = he worked on the accounts out of hours; **gana 800 ptas. a la hora** = he earns 800 pesetas an hour; **pagar por horas** = to pay by the hour; **obreros pagados a la hora** = hourly-paid workers; **pagamos 1.200 ptas. la hora** = we pay 1,200 pesetas an hour; **salario por horas** = hourly wage; **trabajar a horas intempestivas *o* fuera de horas normales** = to work unsocial hours **(b)** (*horario*) time; **hora de apertura *o* hora de cierre** = opening time *o* closing time; **hora de comer *o* del almuerzo** = lunch hour *o* lunchtime; **hora estimada de llegada** = estimated time of arrival (ETA); **horas extraordinarias *o* extras** = overtime; **la hora de llegada está indicada en la pantalla** = the time of arrival *o* the arrival time is indicated on the screen; **hora normal** = Standard Time; **hora punta *o* horas punta** = rush hour *o* peak period; **hora de verano** = Summer Time *o* Daylight Saving Time; **tuvo una reunión en el aeropuerto a última hora de la noche** = he had a late-night meeting at the airport; **llegar a la hora** = to arrive on time **(c)** (*momento*) **a la hora de pagar, se dio cuenta que no llevaba dinero** = when he was going to pay he realized he didn't have any money

◊ **hora-hombre** *nf* man-hour; **se perdió un millón de horas-hombre por las huelgas** = one million man-hours were lost through industrial action

◊ **horario** *nm* **(a)** (*programa*) schedule *o* timetable; **preparar un horario** = to timetable; **según el horario debería haber un tren para Madrid a las 10.22** = according to the timetable, there should be a train to Madrid at 10.22; **la compañía de autobuses ha sacado su horario de invierno** = the bus company has brought out its winter timetable; **el horario de salida lleva quince minutos de retraso** = departure times are delayed by up to fifteen minutes **(b)** horario de banca = banking hours; **horario comercial *o* horario de taquillas** = business hours *o* opening hours; **horario flexible** = flexitime; **horario intensivo** = working day without a lunch break; **horario partido** = split-shift working; **horario de oficina** = office hours; **horario de oficina de los bancos** = banking hours; **fuera del horario de trabajo** = outside hours *o* out of hours; **tenemos un horario de trabajo flexible** = we work flexitime

> asumimos el horario intensivo y concentramos todas las gestiones con los fabricantes por la mañana
>
> *Datamation*

> la jornada intensiva conlleva normalmente un adelanto en la hora de entrada al trabajo y, por otro lado, una ausencia del tiempo de descanso que se produce con el almuerzo en una jornada de mañana y tarde
>
> *El País*

horizontal *adj* horizontal; **comunicación horizontal** = horizontal communication; **integración horizontal** = horizontal integration

hostelería *nf* (**el sector de**) **hostelería** = the hotel trade *o* the catering trade *o* business

hostil *adj* hostile; **oferta pública de adquisición hostil (OPAH)** = hostile takeover

hotel *nm* hotel; **dejó su coche en el aparcamiento del hotel** = he left his car in the hotel car park; **el hotel suministra los uniformes del personal** = staff

uniforms are provided by the hotel; **hotel homologado** = graded hotel; **cadena de hoteles** = hotel chain *o* chain of hotels; **director de hotel** = hotel manager; **factura de hotel** = hotel bill; **gastos de hotel** = hotel expenses; **habitaciones de hotel** = hotel accommodation; **todas las habitaciones del hotel han sido reservadas para la exposición** = all hotel accommodation has been booked up for the exhibition; **personal del hotel** = hotel staff

◊ **hotelero, -ra** *adj* hotel; **cadena hotelera** = hotel chain *o* chain of hotels; **capacidad hotelera** = amount of hotel accommodation; **negocio hotelero *o* el sector hotelero** = the hotel trade *o* the catering trade *o* business **2** *n* hotelier *o* hotel manager *o* hotel manageress

> la palabra marketing es un vocablo anglosajón, de reciente introducción en el sector hotelero español
>
> *Tiempo*

hucha *nf* **(a)** (*arca*) bin **(b)** (*para guardar ahorros*) money box *o* piggy bank

hueco, -ca **1** *adj* empty *o* hollow **2** *nm* gap *o* hole; **un hueco en el mercado** = niche *o* gap in the market; **buscar un hueco en el mercado** = to look for a gap in the market; **encontrar un hueco en el mercado** = to find a gap in the market; **un hueco en la ley** = a loophole in the law

huelga *nf* **(a)** strike *o* walk-out *o* industrial action; **huelga de brazos caídos** = sit-down strike; **huelga de celo** = go-slow *o* work-to-rule; **hacer huelga de celo** = to go slow *o* to work to rule; **huelga general** = general strike; **huelga ilegal** = unofficial strike; **huelga no autorizada por los cargos sindicales** = unofficial strike; **huelga oficial** = official strike; **huelga de protesta** = protest strike; **hacer huelga en protesta por las malas condiciones laborales** = to strike in protest against bad working conditions; **huelga salvaje** = wildcat strike; **huelga simbólica** = token strike; **huelga de solidaridad** = sympathy strike; **declarar una huelga de solidaridad** = to strike in sympathy; **huelga técnica** = work-to-rule; **huelga total** = all-out strike; **el sindicato convocó una huelga total** = the union called for an all-out strike; **la huelga tendrá consecuencias persistentes para la economía** = the strike will have durable effects on the economy; **durante la huelga los precios se han disparado** = prices have shot up during the strike **(b)** **acuerdo que prohibe la huelga** = no-strike agreement; **aviso de huelga** = strike warning *o* notice of strike action; **convocar una huelga** = to call a strike; **convocatoria de huelga *o* llamada a la huelga** = strike call; **los delegados sindicales convocaron al personal a una huelga** = the shop stewards called the workforce out on strike; **desconvocaron la huelga** = they called the strike off; **fondo de huelga** = strike fund; **el sindicato llamó a sus afiliados a la huelga** = the union called its members out on strike; **votación para decidir si se hace huelga** = strike ballot *o* strike vote **(c)** **en huelga** = on strike; **declararse en huelga *o* ir a la huelga** = to strike *o* to come out on strike *o* to go on strike *o* to take strike action *o* to walk out *o* to take industrial action; **declararse en huelga para conseguir aumentos salariales *o* una reducción de la jornada laboral** = to strike for higher wages *o* for shorter working hours; **los obreros están en huelga desde hace cuatro semanas** = the workers have been out on strike for four weeks **(d)** **paralizado por**

la huelga = strikebound; **seis barcos están paralizados en el puerto debido a la huelga** = six ships are strikebound in the docks

◊ **huelguista** *nmf* striker

huir *vi* to flee *o* to escape *o* to run away; **huir estando bajo fianza** = to jump bail

humano, na *adj* human; **recursos humanos** = human resources

hundimiento *nm* collapse; **el hundimiento del mercado de la plata** = the collapse of the market in silver; **consiguió salvar algunas de sus inversiones en el hundimiento de la compañía** = he managed to save some of his investment from the wreck of the company

hundir *vt* to sink; **la política europea ha hundido la agricultura** = European politics have ruined agriculture; **la falta de dinero hundió nuestros** planes definitivamente = lack of money ruined our plans for good

◊ **hundirse** *vr* **(a)** *(barco)* to sink; **el barco se hundió con la tormenta y se perdió toda la carga** = the ship sank in the storm and all the cargo was lost **(b)** *(negocio)* to collapse *o* to sink; **las empresas se hunden** = firms are going bust *o* are going bankrupt **(c)** *(economía)* to slump; **el comercio se ha hundido en los últimos meses** = trade has slumped over the last months

Hungría *nf* Hungary

◊ **húngaro, -ra** *o* **magiar** *adj y n* Hungarian NOTA: capital: **Budapest**; moneda: **forint húngaro (Ft)** = Hungarian forint (Ft)

hurtado, -da 1 *adj* stolen **2** *pp de* HURTAR

hurtar *vt* to steal

◊ **hurto** *nm* theft; **hurto en las tiendas** = shoplifting; **pequeño hurto** = pilferage *o* pilfering

Ii

ICO = INSTITUTO DE CREDITO OFICIAL

I+D = INVESTIGACION Y DESARROLLO Research and Development (R & D); **I+DT (investigación y desarrollo técnico)** = technical R & D

ida *nf* departure; **viaje de ida** = outward journey; **quiero dos billetes de ida a Madrid** = I want two singles to Madrid; **billete de ida y vuelta** = *GB* return; *US* round-trip ticket; **en el viaje de ida el barco hará escala en las Antillas** = on the outward voyage the ship will stop at *o* call in at the West Indies

idea *nf* idea; **uno de los vendedores tuvo la idea de cambiar el color del producto** = one of the salesmen had the idea of changing the product colour; **el presidente piensa que sería una buena idea pedir a todos los consejeros que detallen sus gastos** = the chairman thinks it would be a good idea to ask all directors to itemize their expenses; **tormenta** *o* **torbellino de ideas** = brainstorming

ideal *adj* ideal; **este es el lugar ideal para un nuevo supermercado** = this is the ideal site for a new supermarket

identidad *nf* identity; **carné de identidad** = identity card *o* ID Card; **identidad corporativa** = corporate identity

identificación *nf* identification; **número de identificación fiscal (NIF)** = tax number

idioma *nm* (foreign) language; **el director gerente dirigió las negociaciones en tres idiomas** = the managing director conducted the negotiations in three languages

> todos los especialistas coinciden en la necesidad de dominar, al menos, un idioma en niveles ejecutivos, cuadros intermedios y, por supuesto, en la alta dirección
>
> **El País**

idóneo, -nea *adj* suitable; **tuvimos que volver a convocar la plaza porque no se presentó ningún candidato idóneo** = we had to readvertise the job because there were no suitable candidates

igual 1 *adj* **(a)** *(equitativo)* equal; **igual salario** = equal pay; **los obreros y las obreras ganan igual salario** = male and female workers have equal pay; **por partes iguales** *o* **a partes iguales** = half and half *o* fifty-fifty; **ir a partes iguales** = to go fifty-fifty *o* to pay half each **(b)** *(invariable)* unchanged **(c)** **ser igual a** = to be the same as *o* to equal; **estar igual a** = (i) to stay unchanged; (ii) to be square; **las cosas siguen igual con el nuevo director** = things have stayed the same under the new manager **(d)** **dar igual** = to be indifferent to; **todo le da igual** = he doesn't care about anything **2** *nmf* **(a)** *(con relación a otros)* equal; **él** *o* **ella es mi igual** = he *o* she is my equal; **la trataron de igual a igual** = they treated her as an equal **(b)** **por igual** = equally *o* on an equal footing; **los costes se distribuirán por igual entre las dos partes** = costs will be shared equally between the two parties; **sin igual** = exceptional **3** *nm* equals sign

igualar *vt* to equalize *o* to equal *o* to match; **la producción de este mes iguala la de nuestro mejor mes hasta la fecha** = production this month has equalled our best month ever; **igualaremos cualquier oferta que reciba** = we shall match any offer you receive

◇ **igualdad** *nf* equality *o* parity; **el personal femenino quiere igualdad de condiciones con los hombres** = the female staff want parity with the men; **programa de igualdad de oportunidades de empleo** = equal opportunities programme

◇ **igualmente** *adv* equally; **todos los candidatos serán tratados igualmente** = all candidates will be treated equally

ilegal *adj* illegal *o* unlawful; **la importación de armas en el país es ilegal** = the importation of arms into the country is illegal

◇ **ilegalidad** *nf* illegality

◇ **ilegalmente** *adv* illegally; **fue acusado de importar armas ilegalmente** = he was accused of illegally importing arms into the country; **los diseños para la nueva colección de vestidos se copiaron ilegalmente en Extremo Oriente** = the designs for the new dress collection were pirated in the Far East

ilegítimo, -ma *adj* unlawful *o* illegitimate

ilícito, -ta *adj* illicit *o* unlawful; **venta ilícita de bebidas alcohólicas** = illicit sale of alcohol; **negocio ilícito** = unlawful business

ilimitado, -da *adj* unlimited; **el banco le ofreció un crédito ilimitado** = the bank offered him unlimited credit; **responsabilidad ilimitada** = unlimited liability

ilíquido, -da *adj* illiquid

imagen *nf* image; **imagen pública de una empresa** = corporate image; **promocionar la imagen pública de una empresa** = to promote a corporate image; **están gastando mucho dinero en publicidad para mejorar la imagen de la compañía** = they are spending a lot of advertising money to improve the company's image; **imagen de marca** = brand image

◇ **imágenes** *nfpl* illustrations

imitación *nf* imitation *o* copy; **desconfíe de las imitaciones** = beware of imitations; **imitación fraudulenta** = fraudulent copy

imitar *vt* to imitate *o* to copy; **imitan todos nuestros trucos comerciales** = they imitate all our sales gimmicks; **imitar un producto patentado** = to copy a patented product *o* to infringe a patent

impaciente *adj* impatient *o* anxious *o* eager; **estoy impaciente por ver el muestrario nuevo** = I am anxious to see the new book of samples

impacto *nm* impact; **el impacto de la nueva**

tecnología sobre el comercio del algodón = the impact of new technology on the cotton trade; **el nuevo diseño ha causado poco impacto entre los compradores** = the new design has made little impact on the buying public

> el impacto en el paro de un descenso en el ritmo de crecimiento económico ha sido cuantificado en un estudio interno de la CE
> **El País**

impagado, -da *adj* unpaid; **facturas impagadas** = unpaid invoices; **letras impagadas** = dishonoured bills

◇ **impago** *nm* non-payment; **impago de una factura** = failure to pay a bill *o* non-payment of a bill

impar *adj* odd *o* uneven; **números impares** = odd numbers

impedimento *nm* impediment; **actuamos sin ningún impedimento** = we were totally free to act

impedir *vt* **(a)** *(obstruir)* to block *o* to obstruct; **los huelguistas impidieron el paso a la fábrica** = the strikers blocked the way to the factory **(b)** *(imposibilitar)* to prevent *o* to stop; **unos funcionarios le impidieron que abandonara el país** = government officials prevented him leaving the country; **la policía impidió que nadie saliera del edificio** = the police prevented anyone from leaving the building; **los consejeros organizaron la compra de la sociedad con el fin de impedir una oferta pública de adquisición** = they staged a management buyout to prevent *o* to pre-empt a takeover bid

imperfección *nf* imperfection *o* fault *o* defect

◇ **imperfecto, -ta** *adj* imperfect *o* faulty *o* defective

impermeable *adj* waterproof; **las piezas se envían en paquetes impermeables** = the parts are sent in waterproof packing

impersonal *adj* impersonal; **un estilo de gestión impersonal** = an impersonal style of management

ímpetu *nm* momentum *o* impetus

implementación *nf* implementation

implicar *vt* **(a)** *(significar)* to imply; **la palabra 'permiso' no implica aprobación** = the word 'permission' does not imply approval **(b)** *(mezclar)* to involve; **todos sabían que el secretario estaba implicado en ello** = they all knew that the secretary was involved in it

imponer *vt* **(a)** *(impuestos, sanciones)* to impose; **imponer barreras arancelarias** *o* **barreras comerciales a un producto** = to impose tariff barriers *o* trade barriers on a product; **el gobierno impuso controles financieros rigurosos** = the government imposed severe financial restrictions; **el gobierno impuso elevados impuestos a los artículos de lujo** = the government imposed a heavy tax on luxury goods; **imponer un límite a un presupuesto** = to fix a ceiling to a budget; **intentaron imponer la prohibición de fumar** = they tried to impose a ban on smoking; **imponer restricciones a las importaciones** = to impose import restrictions; **imponer sanciones económicas a un país** = to impose economic sanctions on a

country; **el juez impuso el pago de las costas al demandado** = the judge awarded costs to the defendant **(b)** *(depositar)* to deposit; **imponer dinero en un banco** = to deposit money in a bank **(c)** *(gravar)* to levy; **imponer un arancel a las importaciones de artículos de lujo** = to levy a duty on the import of luxury items

◇ **imponerse** *vr* **(a)** to impose one's authority on; **la empresa necesita un gerente que se imponga** = the firm needs a strong manager *o* a manager who can impose his authority on the staff **(b)** **imponerse la necesidad** = to be necessary; **se impone la necesidad de convocar a todos los accionistas** = it is necessary to call all the shareholders to a meeting

◇ **imponible** *adj* taxable; **no imponible** = non-taxable; **base imponible** = tax base; **valor imponible** = assessed value

importación *nf* **(a)** import *o* importing *o* importation; **el gobierno ha prohibido la importación de armas** = the government has banned arms imports; **el sindicato organizó un boicot contra los coches de importación** = the union organized a boycott of imported cars; **aranceles** *o* **derechos de importación** = import duties *o* tariffs; **el gobierno anunció que podrían aplicarse aranceles a la importación** = the government warned of possible import duties; **comercio de importación** = import trade; **cuota de importación** *o* **cupo de importación** = import quota; **el gobierno ha impuesto un cupo de importación a los coches** = the government has imposed an import quota on cars; **exportación de importaciones** = entrepot trade; **licencia de importación** = import licence *o* import permit; **recargo** *o* **sobretasa a la importación** = import surcharge **(b)** **importaciones** = imports; **importaciones de bienes** = visible imports; **las importaciones de Polonia han aumentado a 1m de dólares por año** = imports from Poland have risen to $1m a year; **las importaciones están disminuyendo** = imports are decreasing; **importaciones y exportaciones invisibles** = invisible imports and exports; **gravamen a las importaciones** = import levy; **restricciones a la importación** = import restrictions; **imponer restricciones a las importaciones** = to retrict imports *o* to put restrictions on imports

◇ **importación-exportación** *nf* import-export; **comercio de importación-exportación** = import-export trade; **se dedica a la importación-exportación** = he is in import-export

importador, -ra 1 *adj* importing; **países importadores de petróleo** = oil-importing countries; **una empresa importadora** = an importing company **2** *n* importer; **un importador de puros** = a cigar importer; **la compañía es una gran importadora de coches extranjeros** = the company is a big importer of foreign cars

importancia *nf* **(a)** *(de gran significado)* importance *o* significance; **el banco da mucha importancia a la transacción** = the bank attaches great importance to the deal; **quitar importancia** = to understate; **las acciones sin derecho a voto tienen tanta importancia como las que tienen derecho a voto** = the non-voting shares rank equally with the voting shares; *(insignificante)* **de poca importancia** = petty; **una pérdida de poca**

importancia = a loss of minor importance; **en orden de importancia** = in order of importance **(b)** *(negocio)* volume (of sales)

importante *adj* important *o* large *o* major *o* leading; **poco importante** = unimportant *o* low-level; **se dejó un montón de papeles importantes en el taxi** = he left a pile of important papers in the taxi; **tiene una cita importante a las 10.30** = she has an important meeting at 10.30; **fue ascendido a un puesto más importante** = he was promoted to a more important job; **es nuestro cliente más importante** = he is our largest customer; **es el funcionario más importante de la delegación** = he is the top-ranking official in the delegation; **una delegación poco importante visitó el ministerio** = a low-level delegation visited the ministry; **accionista importante** = major shareholder; **adquirir una parte importante de las acciones de la compañía** = to acquire a substantial interest in the company; **dirige una imprenta importante** = he runs an important printing firm

importar 1 *vt* to import; **prohibición de importar** = import ban; **este coche se importó de Francia** = this car was imported from France; **la compañía importa aparatos de televisión de Japón** = the company imports television sets from Japan **2** *vi* to matter *o* to be important; **¿importa que las ventas de un mes sean bajas?** = does it matter if one month's sales are down?

importe *nm* **(a)** *(dinero)* amount; **importe amortizado** = amount written off; **importe debido** = amount owing; **importe deducido** = amount deducted; **importe pagado** = amount paid **(b)** **hasta el importe máximo de 5.000 ptas.** = up to a maximum of 5,000 pesetas *o* not exceeding 5,000 pesetas **(c)** *(precio)* cost *o* value; **el importe de la mano de obra** = the cost of labour *o* labour cost; **importe nominal** = nominal value

cuando se produce el extravío o robo de una tarjeta, tanto de débito o crédito, el titular de la misma únicamente responde ante la entidad por el importe equivalente a 150 ecus

El País

imposibilidad *nf* impossibility; **el presidente se vio en la imposibilidad de asistir a la reunión** = the chairman was unable to come to the meeting

◊ **imposible** *adj* impossible; **es imposible proteger completamente la oficina contra incendios** = it is impossible to make the office completely fireproof; **la reglamentación oficial nos hace imposible la exportación** = government regulations make it impossible for us to export; **los aduaneros les están haciendo la vida imposible a los narcotraficantes** = customs officials are making life difficult for drug smugglers; **imposible de conseguir** = unobtainable

imposición *nf* **(a)** *(impuestos)* taxation; **imposición decreciente** = degressive taxation; **imposición directa** = direct taxation; **imposición indirecta** = indirect taxation; **imposición progresiva** *o* **proporcional** = progressive *o* graduated taxation; **imposición regresiva** = regressive taxation; **doble imposición** = double taxation; **acuerdo de doble imposición** = double taxation agreement; **imposición del 0% de IVA** = zero-rating of VAT **(b)** *(obligación)* imposition **(c)** *(depósito)* deposit; **imposición a plazos** = time deposit; **imposición de efectivo** = cash deposit

la red de cajeros automáticos ha incorporado a su equipo una avanzada tarjeta multifunción, para uso tanto en imposiciones como en reintegros

Micros

impositivo, -va *adj* tax; **carga impositiva** = tax burden; **descuentos impositivos** = tax credits; **escalas impositivas** = tax schedules; **tramo inferior** *o* **superior de la escala impositiva** = lower *o* upper income bracket *o* lowest *o* highest tax bracket

impositor, -ra *n* depositor

imprenta *nf* printing firm *o* printing works; **letras de imprenta** = block capitals *o* block letters; **escriba su nombre y dirección en caracteres de imprenta** = write your name and address in block capitals

imprescindible *adj* essential *o* indispensable

impresión *nf* **(a)** *(de imprenta)* printing; **impresión electrónica** = electronic printing; **impresión deficiente** = faulty printing; **error de impresión** = typing error **(b)** *(copia impresa)* printout; **impresión de ordenador** = computer printout

◊ **impreso, -sa 1** *adj* printed; **acuerdo impreso** = printed agreement; **copia impresa** = printed copy *o* printout; **el director de ventas pidió una copia impresa de las comisiones de los representantes** = the sales director asked for a printout of the agents' commissions; **material impreso** = printed matter; **reglamentación impresa** = printed regulations **2** *nm* **(a)** form; **tiene que rellenar el impreso A20** = you have to fill in form A20; **impreso de declaración de aduana** = customs declaration form; **impreso de inscripción** = application form; **impreso de solicitud** = application form **(b)** pamphlet **3** *pp de* IMPRIMIR

◊ **impresor, -ra 1** *n* *(persona)* printer **2** *nf* *(informática)* printer; **impresora láser** = laser printer; **impresora de líneas** = computer printer *o* line printer; **impresora por puntos** *o* **de matriz de puntos** = dot-matrix printer; **impresora de rueda de margarita** = daisy-wheel printer; **cinta de impresora** = printer ribbon; **papel de impresora** = computer paper *o* listing paper; **se ha terminado el papel de la impresora** = the printer has run out of paper

imprevisto, -ta 1 *adj* unexpected *o* unforeseen **2** *nmpl* **imprevistos** = incidental expenses; **fondo** *o* **reserva para imprevistos** = contingency fund *o* contingency reserve; **añadir un 10% para imprevistos** = to add on 10% to provide for contingencies; **hemos incluido en nuestra previsión de costes un 10% para imprevistos** = we have built 10% for contingencies into our cost forecast; **póliza para imprevistos** = contingent policy

imprimir *vt* to print; *(ordenadores)* to print out

improductivo, -va *adj* unproductive *o* idle; **capital improductivo** = unproductive capital *o* capital lying idle; **dinero improductivo** = money lying idle *o* idle money

imprudencia *nf* **(a)** *(jurídico)* criminal

negligence; **imprudencia temeraria** = gross negligence **(b)** *(error)* **cometer una imprudencia** = to commit a faux-pas

impuesto *nm* **(a)** tax; **impuesto adicional** = surtax; **impuesto ad valorem** = ad valorem tax; **impuesto atrasado** = back tax; **impuesto básico** = basic tax; **impuesto de carretera** = road tax; **impuesto al consumo** *o* **impuesto sobre la venta** = sales tax *o* tax on consumption; **impuesto directo** = direct tax; **impuesto encubierto** = hidden tax; **impuesto indirecto** = indirect tax; **el gobierno obtiene más ingresos de los impuestos indirectos que de los directos** = the government raises more money by indirect than by direct taxation; **impuesto no incluido** = exclusive of tax; **impuesto progresivo** = graded tax; **impuesto proporcional** = proportional tax; **impuesto regresivo** = regressive tax; **impuesto retenido en el origen** = tax deducted at source; **impuesto sobre beneficios extraordinarios** = excess profits tax; **impuesto sobre beneficios de las sociedades** = corporation tax; **impuesto sobre el capital** = capital levy; **impuesto sobre la plusvalía** *o* **las plusvalías** = capital gains tax; **impuesto sobre la renta** = income tax; **Impuesto sobre la Renta de las Personas Físicas (IRPF)** = personal income tax; **tasa máxima del impuesto sobre la renta** = the top income tax bracket; **impuesto sobre sociedades** = corporation tax; **impuesto sobre sociedades anticipado** = Advanced Corporation Tax (ACT); **impuesto sobre sociedades corriente** = mainstream corporation tax; **impuesto sobre sucesiones** = inheritance tax; **impuesto del timbre** = stamp duty; **impuesto sobre las transferencias de capital** = capital transfer tax; **impuesto sobre la venta** = sales tax; **impuesto sobre el volumen de negocios** = turnover tax; **necesitamos la factura por razones de impuestos** = we need the invoice for tax purposes; **todos los pagos son sin impuestos** = all payments are exclusive of tax **(b) establecer un impuesto** = to levy a tax *o* to impose a tax; **el gobierno ha establecido un impuesto del 15% sobre la gasolina** = the government has imposed a 15% tax on petrol; **gravar con un impuesto** = to tax *o* to put a tax on; **gravar el tabaco con un impuesto** = to put a duty on cigarettes; **gravar las empresas con un impuesto del 50%** = to tax businesses at 50%; **suprimir un impuesto** = to lift a tax; **suprimir los impuestos sobre el alcohol** = to take the duty off alcohol; **el impuesto sobre los beneficios de las sociedades ha sido suprimido** = the tax on company profits has been lifted; **la renta tiene un impuesto del 25%** = income is taxed at 25%; **crédito por impuestos pagados** = tax credit; **elusión de impuestos** = tax avoidance; **recaudador de impuestos** = tax collector; **compró un reloj libre de impuestos en el aeropuerto** *o* **compró el reloj libre de impuestos** = he bought a duty-free watch at the airport *o* he bought the watch duty-free; **sujeto a impuesto** = taxable; **artículos sujetos a impuesto** = taxable items; **las mercancías están sujetas al impuesto del timbre** = the goods are liable to stamp duty; **los artículos de lujo están sujetos a un impuesto elevado** = luxury items are heavily taxed **(c) impuesto sobre el valor añadido (IVA)** = value added tax (VAT)

hacienda se enfrenta a los que no pagan y a los que no quieren pagar: el fraude del IVA y el rechazo al Impuesto sobre Actividades Económicas

el nuevo Impuesto sobre Sociedades intentará terminar con las prácticas habituales de ventas de empresas en pérdidas para compensar beneficios y no pagar impuestos
Cambio 16

impulsar *vt* to boost; **la empresa espera impulsar su participación en el mercado** = the company hopes to boost its market share

impulsivo, -va *adj* impulsive *o* done on impulse; **compra impulsiva** = impulse purchase; **comprador impulsivo** = impulse buyer

impulso *nm* **(a)** *(interés)* impulse; **hacer algo obedeciendo a un impulso momentáneo** = to do something on impulse **(b)** *(estímulo)* boost; **esta publicidad dará un impulso a las ventas** = this publicity will give sales a boost **(c)** *(ímpetu)* momentum; **ganar** *o* **perder impulso** = to gain *o* to lose momentum; **la huelga está cobrando impulso** = the strike is gaining momentum

imputable *adj* attributable; **cantidades imputables a la reserva** = sums chargeable to the reserve

inaceptable *adj* unacceptable; **los términos del contrato son totalmente inaceptables** = the terms of the contract are quite unacceptable

inactividad *nf* inactivity *o* dullness; **la inactividad del mercado** = the dullness of the market

◊ **inactivo, -va** *adj* **(a)** *(parado)* inactive *o* dead *o* dull; **cuenta inactiva** = dead *o* dormant *o* inactive account; **mercado inactivo** = dull market *o* inactive market; **tiempo inactivo** = idle time **(b)** *(sin cambios)* flat

inadecuado, -da *adj* inadequate *o* unsuitable *o* ineligible

inadvertido, -da *adj* unseen

inalcanzable *adj* unobtainable

inalterado, -da *adj* unchanged

inamovible *adj* immovable

inauguración *nf* opening; **la inauguración de una nueva sucursal** = the opening of a new branch

◊ **inaugural** *adj* inaugural *o* opening

incapacidad *nf* **(a)** *(incompetencia)* incapacity *o* incompetence *o* inefficiency; **incapacidad laboral** = incapacity to work; **la incapacidad de la mano de obra** = the inefficiency of the workforce **(b)** *(física)* disability; **incapacidad total** = total disability; **incapacidad transitoria** = temporary disability

incapaz *adj* **(a)** *(que no puede)* incapable *o* unable **(b)** *(inadecuado)* incompetent; **es un hombre totalmente incapaz** = he is totally incompetent

incautación *nf* attachment *o* seizure; **el tribunal ordenó la incautación del envío** *o* **de los fondos de**

la compañía = the court ordered the seizure of the shipment *o* of the company's funds

incautarse *vr* to impound *o* to seize; **la aduana se incautó de la totalidad del cargamento** = the customs impounded the whole cargo

incendiarse *vr* to catch fire

incendio *nm* fire; **daños (causados) por incendio** = fire damage; **el almacén quedó totalmente destruido por un incendio** = the warehouse was completely destroyed by fire; **reclamó 50.000 ptas. en concepto de daños por incendio** = he claimed 50,000 pesetas for fire damage; **mercancías dañadas en un incendio** = fire-damaged goods; **escalera de incendios** = fire escape; **liquidación por incendio** = fire sale; **peligro de incendio** = fire hazard; **riesgo de incendio** = fire risk; **ese almacén lleno de papel constituye un peligro de incendio** = that warehouse full of paper is a fire hazard; **prevención de incendios** = fire safety; **puerta de incendios** = fire door; **seguro contra incendios** = fire insurance; **responsable de la seguridad contra incendios** = fire safety officer

incentivo *nm* incentive *o* inducement; **incentivos ofrecidos al personal** = staff incentives; **prima de incentivo** = incentive bonus *o* incentive payment; **programa de incentivos** = incentive scheme; **los programas de incentivos están estimulando la producción** = incentive schemes are boosting production; **le ofrecieron un coche de la empresa como incentivo para que se quedara** = they offered him a company car as an inducement to stay

incertidumbre *nf* uncertainty *o* doubt; **el año empezó lleno de incertidumbres** = the year got off to a doubtful *o* shaky start

incidencia *nf* impact; **la huelga tuvo escasa incidencia** = the strike had little impact; **la incidencia de la publicidad se muesta en las ventas** = the effect of advertising is shown in the sales

la política presupuestaria se configura en la actualidad como el factor de mayor incidencia sobre la evolución de los tipos de interés en los mercados financieros
Mercado

incidental *adj* incidental

incidente 1 *adj* incidental **2** *nm* incident; **un incidente fatal** = a fatal incident; **el incidente se produjo cuando salía del trabajo** = the incident took place as he was leaving work

incitar *vt* to encourage *o* to instigate; **si dejas tus tarjetas de crédito sobre la mesa del despacho incitas a la gente a robar** *o* **incitas al robo** = leaving your credit cards on your desk encourages people to steal *o* encourages stealing

incluido, -da *adj* inclusive; **impuestos incluidos** = inclusive of tax; **impuestos no incluidos** = exclusive of tax; **IVA no incluido** = not inclusive of VAT; **el IVA no está incluido en la factura** = the invoice is exclusive of VAT; **precio todo incluido** = inclusive sum *o* inclusive charge *o* all-in price; **el total asciende a 200.000 ptas. incluido el flete** = the total comes to 200,000 pesetas including freight; **¿está el servicio incluido en la cuenta?** = does the bill include a service charge?; **el servicio no está**

incluido = service is not included; **los ingresos de la adquisición de 1995 están incluidos en las cuentas** = income from the 1995 acquisition is incorporated into the accounts

incluir *vt* to include; **el precio incluye el IVA** = the charge includes VAT; **el precio incluye el reparto** *o* **la entrega** = the price includes free delivery; **el total asciende a 28.000 ptas. sin incluir ni seguro ni flete** = the total is 28,000 pesetas not including insurance and freight; **incluir un plus de carestía de vida en los salarios** = to include a cost-of-living bonus in wages; **el viaje completo incluye el billete de avión, seis noches en un hotel de lujo, todas las comidas y visitas a lugares de interés** = the holiday package consists of air travel, six nights in a luxury hotel, all meals and visits to places of interest

◊ **inclusive** *adj* inclusive; **el congreso se celebrará del 12 al 16 ambos inclusive** = the conference runs from the 12th to the 16th inclusive; *US* from 12 through 16; **la cuenta cubre los servicios prestados hasta el mes de junio inclusive** = the account covers services up to and including the month of June

incoar *vt* to start *o* to institute; **incoar un proceso** *o* **un expediente contra alguien** = to start *o* to institute proceedings against someone

incobrable *adj* irrecoverable; **deuda incobrable** = irrecoverable debt *o* bad debt *o* write-off

incombustible *adj* fireproof

incómodo, -da *adj* uncomfortable *o* awkward *o* inconvenient; **cuando solicitó el préstamo, el banco empezó a hacerle preguntas muy incómodas** = when he asked for the loan the bank started to ask some very awkward questions

incompetencia *nf* incompetence *o* inefficiency; **incompetencia de jurisdicción** = lack of competence (to deal with a case)

◊ **incompetente** *adj* incompetent *o* inefficient; **necesitamos una nueva secretaria porque la que tenemos es incompetente** = we need a new secretary because the one we have is inefficient; **el director de ventas es bastante incompetente** = the sales manager is quite incompetent

incompleto, -ta *adj* unfinished *o* incomplete; **hemos recibido el pedido incompleto** = we have received the order but it was not complete

incondicional *adj* unconditional; **aceptación incondicional de la oferta por parte de la junta** = unconditional acceptance of the offer by the board

◊ **incondicionalmente** *adv* unconditionally; **la oferta fue aceptada incondicionalmente por el sindicato** = the offer was accepted unconditionally by the trade union

inconstitucional *adj* unconstitutional; **el presidente decidió que la reunión era inconstitucional** = the chairman ruled that the meeting was unconstitutional

incontrolable *adj* uncontrollable; **inflación incontrolable** = uncontrollable inflation

inconveniente *nm* drawback; **uno de los inconvenientes del plan es que se necesitarán seis años para llevarlo a cabo** = one of the main drawbacks of the scheme is that it will take six years to complete

inconvertible *adj* inconvertible *o* non-convertible *o* irredeemable; **moneda inconvertible** = non-convertible currency

incorporación *nf* incorporation *o* inclusion *o* addition; **incorporación de reservas** = capitalization of reserves

incorporado, -da 1 *adj* built-in; **el sistema contable tiene incorporada toda una serie de controles** = the accounting system has a series of built-in checks **2** *pp de* INCORPORAR

incorporar *vt* to incorporate *o* to take into *o* to build into; **incorporar artículos a las existencias** *o* **al almacén** = to take items into stock *o* into the warehouse; **debe incorporar todas las previsiones en el presupuesto** = you must build all the forecasts into the budget

◊ **incorporarse** *vr* to join; **el director de comercialización es la última persona incorporada al consejo de administración** = the marketing director is the latest addition to the board

incorrecto, -ta *adj* incorrect *o* wrong; **el acta de la reunión era incorrecta y tuvo que ser modificada** = the minutes of the meeting were incorrect and had to be changed; **las cifras que el director de ventas presentó a la reunión eran incorrectas** = the sales director reported the wrong figures to the meeting; **un paquete con la dirección incorrecta** = an wrongly addressed package

◊ **incorrectamente** *adv* incorrectly *o* wrongly

Incoterms *npl* Incoterms

incremental *adj* incremental *o* marginal; **coste incremental** = incremental cost *o* marginal cost

incrementar *vt* to increase; **la compañía incrementó su dividendo en un 10%** = the company raised its dividend by 10%

◊ **incremento** *nm* increase *o* rise *o* mark up; **incremento salarial** = increment; **incremento salarial anual** = annual increment

un crecimiento más lento de la mano de obra va acompañado de un incremento en la productividad laboral
Mercado

el incremento salarial medio hasta finales de junio se situó en el 7,79%
Mercado

incumplimiento *nm* **(a)** *(violación)* breach; **incumplimiento de contrato** = breach of contract **(b)** *(no cumplir)* non-compliance *o* default; **incumplimiento de pago** = failure to pay *o* default; **incumplimiento de las normas** = failure to comply with regulations

incumplir *vt* to fail to obey; **incumplir los pagos** = to default on payments; **incumplir el pago de una letra** = to dishonour a bill

incurrir *vi* to incur; **incurrir en un error** = to make a mistake; **incurrir en gastos** = to incur costs; **la empresa ha incurrido en grandes gastos para poner en práctica el programa de expansión** = the company has incurred heavy costs to implement the

expansion programme (NOTA: seguido de la prep. **en**)

indagación *nf* investigation *o* inquiry; **equipo de indagación** = fact-finding team; **trabajo de indagación** = fact-finding mission

indagar *vt* to investigate *o* to inquire

indebido, -da *adj* incorrect *o* unlawful; **uso indebido de fondos** *o* **de los bienes** = misuse of funds *o* of assets

indecisión *nf* indecision

◊ **indeciso, -sa** *adj* hesitant *o* uncertain

indemnidad *nf* indemnity *o* immunity

indemnización *nf* indemnification *o* indemnity; **indemnización por cese** *o* **despido en el cargo** = compensation for loss of office; **indemnización por daños y perjuicios** = compensation for damage; **pidió una indemnización de 20.000.000 de ptas. a la empresa de limpieza** = he claimed 20m pesetas damages against the cleaning firm; **indemnización por despido** = redundancy payment *o* severance pay; **indemnización por fallecimiento** *o* **defunción** = death benefit; **indemnización por pérdida de ingresos** = compensation for loss of earnings; **cuando la compañía fue adquirida, despidieron al director de ventas con una indemnización de 5.000.000 de ptas.** = when the company was taken over, the sales director received a golden handshake of 5m pesetas; **tuvo que pagar una indemnización de 20.000 ptas.** = he had to pay an indemnity of 20,000 pesetas; **pedir una indemnización** = to put in a claim for damage; **recibió la cantidad de 100.000 ptas. como indemnización** = she received the sum of 100,000 pesetas in compensation; **enviaron una carta de reclamación, con una factura de indemnización adjunta** = they sent a formal letter of complaint, accompanied by an invoice for damage

indemnizar *vt* to compensate *o* to indemnify; **indemnizar a alguien por una pérdida** = to indemnify someone for a loss; **nos indemnizaron los daños** = we received compensation for damages; **indemnizar un siniestro** = to settle a claim

independiente *adj* **(a)** *(libre)* independent; **auditoría independiente** = external audit *o* independent audit; **compañía independiente** = independent company; **comerciante independiente** = independent trader **(b)** *(autónomo)* freelance *o* self-employed; **un ingeniero independiente** = a self-employed engineer; **un trabajador independiente** = a freelance *o* a freelancer; **los trabajadores independientes** = the self-employed; **trabajar como independiente** = to work freelance *o* to freelance; **trabaja como periodista independiente para los periódicos locales** = she freelances for the local newspapers

indeterminado, -da *adj* indeterminate *o* vague

indexación *nf* indexation

◊ **indexar** *vt* to index; **pensión indexada** = index-linked pension *o* inflation-proof pension

India *nf* India

◊ **indio, -dia** *o* **hindú** *adj y n* Indian
NOTA: capital: **Nueva Delhi** (= New Delhi); moneda: **rupia india (Rs)** = Indian rupee (Rs)

indicación *nf* **(a)** *(señal)* sign **(b)** *(sugerencia)* suggestion; **presento la reclamación de indemnización por daños y perjuicios por indicación de nuestros asesores jurídicos** = I am submitting the claim for damages in accordance with the advice of our legal advisers

indicador, -ra 1 *adj* indicating; **fondo indicador** = index fund **2** *nm* **(a)** *(señal)* indicator; **indicador anticipado** = leading indicator; **los indicadores económicos oficiales** = government economic indicators; **indicador de confianza** = feelgood factor **(b)** *(informática)* flag

> destaca como claro indicador de que la inflación no está totalmente controlada, el incremento de la inflación subyacente (6,2%) que rompe la tendencia descendente registrada durante todo el año
> **Tiempo**

> el indicador de confianza ha mejorado en los cuatro primeros meses, al igual que los salarios reales
> **El País**

indicar *vt* **(a)** *(señalar)* to indicate *o* to mark *o* to show; **indicar un aumento** *o* **una baja** = to show a gain *o* a fall; **las últimas cifras indican una caída de la tasa de inflación** = the latest figures indicate a fall in the inflation rate; **nuestras ventas en 1995 indican una desviación del mercado interior hacia las exportaciones** = our sales for 1995 indicate a move from the home market to exports; **indicar en un producto 'sólo para la exportación'** = to mark a product 'for export only'; **no incluir el IVA en la factura a menos que se indique** = do not include VAT on the invoice unless specified; **el documento indica que todo ingreso tiene que ser declarado al fisco** = the document states that all revenue has to be declared to the tax office **(b)** *(citar)* to quote; **sírvanse indicar este número al contestar** = in reply please quote this number; **cuando haga una reclamación, indique siempre el número del lote que figura en la caja** = when making a complaint always quote the batch number printed on the box

indicativo, -va 1 *adj* indicative **2** *nm* *(telecomunicación)* area code; **indicativo telefónico para llamar al extranjero** = international dialling code

índice *nm* **(a)** *(relación)* index *o* index number; **índice de la bolsa de Madrid** = Madrid Stock Exchange Index; **índice del coste de la vida** = cost-of-living index; **índice de crecimiento** = growth index; **el índice Dow Jones subió diez puntos** = the Dow Jones Average rose ten points; **índice del 'Financial Times'** = the Financial Times Index; **índice ponderado** = weighted index; **índice de precios al consumo** *o* **al consumidor (IPC)** = retail price index; *US* consumer price index; **índice de precios al por mayor** = wholesale price index; **índice de producción industrial (IPI)** = industrial production index; **el índice de cotización de acciones ha bajado un 10% desde su máxima de enero** = the share index has fallen 10% since the peak in January; **vincular a un índice** = to index; **cartera de valores vinculada a un índice** = indexed portfolio **(b)** **letra** *o* **número del índice** = index letter *o* number; **índice de materias** = contents *o* table of contents **(c)** *(tasa)* rate; **índice destacado** = leading rate; **el índice de absentismo siempre**

aumenta con el buen tiempo = the rate of absenteeism always increases in fine weather; **el índice de natalidad** = birth rate

> el índice general de la Bolsa de Madrid continúa con su mala racha
> **Tiempo**

> la OCDE ha constatado que el crecimiento del producto interior bruto (PIB) de España fue del 2,5%, el índice más bajo desde el año 1985.
> **El País**

indiciación *nf* indexation

indirecto, -ta *adj* indirect; **gastos** *o* **costes indirectos** = indirect expenses *o* costs; **costes laborales indirectos** = indirect labour costs; **imposición indirecta** = indirect taxation

indispensable *adj* indispensable *o* essential; **es indispensable llegar a un acuerdo antes de final de mes** = it is essential that an agreement be reached before the end of the month

indisponibilidad *nf* unavailability

◇ **indisponible** *adj* unavailable

indispuesto, -ta *adj* indisposed; **el director no acudió a la reunión porque se encontraba indispuesto** = the director could not attend the meeting because he was ill

individual *adj* individual; **plan de pensiones ajustado a las exigencias individuales de cada persona** = a pension plan designed to meet each person's individual requirements; **plan de jubilación individual** = personal pension plan; *US* Individual Retirement Account (IRA)

individuo *nm* individual

industria *nf* **(a)** industry; **industrias de alta tecnología** *o* **del futuro** = sunrise industries; **industria básica** = basic industry; **industria casera** = cottage industry; **industrias crepusculares** = sunset industries; **una industria en expansión** = a boom industry *o* a growth industry; **industria ligera** = light industry; **terreno asignado para la industria ligera** = land zoned for light industrial use; **industrias manufactureras** = manufacturing industries; **industria nacionalizada** = nationalized industry; **industria pesada** = heavy *o* smokestack industry; **industria principal** = staple industry; **una industria propiedad del Estado** = a state-owned industry; **industria terciaria** *o* **industria de los servicios** = tertiary sector *o* service sector; **industria con un alto coeficiente de mano de obra** = labour-intensive industry; **industria con un alto coeficiente de capital** = capital-intensive industry **(b)** **la industria aeronáutica** = the aircraft industry; **la industria alimentaria** = the food processing industry; **la industria del automóvil** = the car industry; **la industria de la construcción** = the building industry; **la industria minera** = the mining industry; **la industria petrolífera** = the petroleum industry; **la industria del turismo** = the tourist industry; **la industria del vestido** = the clothing industry; *(informal)* the rag trade; **es muy conocida en la industria del vestido** = she is very well known in the clothing trade **(c)** **la industria se está recuperando después de la recesión** = industry is reviving after the recession; **todos los sectores de la**

industria han registrado aumentos de la producción = all sectors of industry have shown rises in output; **las altas esferas de la industria** = the upper echelons of industry; **tiene contactos útiles en la industria** = he has useful connections in industry; **está buscando empleo en la industria de ordenadores** = he is looking for a job in the computer industry **(d) el Ministerio de Industria, Comercio y Turismo** = the Department of Trade and Industry o the Board of Trade

tras la prohibición de comercialización de la piel de los animales grandes, la industria de la piel se concentró en los felinesmenores
Ajoblanco

industrial 1 *adj* industrial; **capacidad industrial** = industrial capacity; **centro industrial** = industrial centre; **diseño industrial** = industrial design; **espionaje industrial** = industrial espionage; **expansión industrial** = industrial expansion; **polígono industrial** = industrial park o industrial estate; **procesos industriales** = industrial processes; **sociedades industriales** = industrialized societies; **zona industrial** = industrial estate o trading estate **2** *nmf* industrialist o manufacturer

industrialización *nf* industrialization

industrializar *vt* to industrialize

inédito *adj* unpublished o new; **sus obras están todavía inéditas** = her works are still unpublished

ineficacia o **ineficiencia** *nf* inefficiency; **la ineficacia de este producto ya ha sido demostrada** = the inefficiency of this product has already been shown; **el informe criticaba la ineficiencia del personal de ventas** = the report criticized the inefficiency of the sales staff

◊ **ineficaz** *adj* inefficient; **es una secretaria ineficaz** = she is not an efficient secretary

inelegible *adj* ineligible

INEM = INSTITUTO NACIONAL DE EMPLEO

inercia *nf* inertia

inestabilidad *nf* instability; **periodo de inestabilidad en los mercados monetarios** = period of instability in the money markets

◊ **inestable** *adj* unstable o unsettled; **equilibrio inestable** = unstable balance; **precios inestables** = fluctuating prices; **tipos de cambio inestables** = unstable exchange rates; **el mercado es inestable** = the market is unsettled

inevitable *adj* unavoidable; **los vuelos están sujetos a retrasos inevitables** = flights are subject to unavoidable delays

inexacto, -ta *adj* incorrect

inexperto, -ta *adj* inexperienced o unskilled

inexplicado, -da *adj* unaccounted for

inferior *adj* **(a)** *(calidad)* inferior o lower; **productos inferiores** o **productos de inferior calidad** = inferior products o products of lower quality **(b)** *(cantidad)* less; **no concedemos crédito por sumas inferiores a 10.000 ptas.** = we do not grant credit for sums of less than 10,000 pesetas; **los ingresos son inferiores a los del año pasado en el mismo periodo** = receipts are less than those of the same period last year

inflación *nf* inflation; **inflación de costes** = cost-push inflation; **inflación en espiral** = spiralling inflation; **inflación galopante** = galloping inflation o runaway inflation; **la inflación alcanza el 15%** = inflation is running at 15%; **inflación provocada por la demanda excesiva** = demand-led inflation; **contener la inflación** = to curb o to check inflation; **a prueba de inflación** = inflation proof; **tasa de inflación** = rate of inflation o inflation rate; **tomar medidas para reducir la inflación** = to take measures to reduce inflation; **los tipos de interés altos tienden a disminuir la inflación** = high interest rates tend to decrease inflation; **la inflación está subiendo sin parar** = the inflation rate is going up steadily

◊ **inflacionario, -ria** *adj* inflationary; **medidas antiinflacionarias** = anti-inflationary measures; **la economía está en una espiral inflacionaria** = the economy is in an inflationary spiral

◊ **inflacionista** *adj* inflationary; **moneda inflacionista** = inflated currency; **tendencias inflacionistas de la economía** = inflationary trends in the economy

la inflación permanecerá en torno al 5 ó 6 por ciento, como consecuencia del énfasis del Presupuesto en el consumo y de la presión sobre los precios del sector protegido de la economía española, fundamentalmente los servicios
Actualidad Económica

el éxito de cualquier política monetaria es conseguir que la inflación baje hasta que desaparezca
España Económica

la inflación creció en el mes de octubre un 0,6%, por lo que la tasa interanual se sitúa en el 5,5%
Tiempo

el peligro estriba en hacer que el sector real pague la contención inflacionaria, es decir que haya una recesión
España Económica

inflar *vt* to inflate; **inflar la economía** = to inflate the economy; **precios inflados** = inflated prices

influencia *nf* influence; **el precio del petróleo tiene una notable influencia sobre el precio de los productos manufacturados** = the price of oil has a marked influence on the price of manufactured goods; **estamos padeciendo la influencia de un tipo de cambio alto** = we are suffering from the influence of a high exchange rate; **su decisión tuvo una gran influencia sobre Bruselas** = his decision had a great impact on Brussels; **no tiene influencia sobre el presidente** = he has no influence o no leverage over the chairman

influenciar *vt* to influence

influir 1 *vt* to influence o to affect; **el consejo de administración tomó una decisión influida por el memorandum de los directores** = the board was influenced in its decision by the memo from the managers **2** *vi* to have influence; **el precio del**

petróleo ha **influido** sobre el precio de los productos **manufacturados** = the price of oil has influenced the price of manufactured goods; **la alta inflación influye sobre nuestra rentabilidad** = high inflation is having an effect on *o* is influencing our profitability

información *nf* **(a)** *(informe)* information; **una información** = a piece of information; **una información confidencial acerca de la bolsa** = a stock market tip; **información engañosa** = misrepresentation; **escribe la información financiera del periódico** = she writes the City column in the newspaper; *(bolsa)* **información privada** *o* **confidencial** *o* **privilegida** = inside information *o* insider dealing; **información publicitaria** = sales literature; **información turística** = tourist information; **información de vuelos** = flight information; **información sobre vuelos a Nueva York** = please send me information on *o* about flights to New York; **las cifras de 1994 son su única base de información** = the figures for 1994 are all he has to go on; **¿tiene Vd. información sobre las cuentas de depósito?** = have you any information on *o* about deposit accounts?; **dar una información completa sobre algo** = to give full particulars of something; **no deis ninguna información a la policía** = do not give any details to the police **(b)** *(informática)* **entrada de información** = input of information *o* computer input; **unidad de información** = bit **(c)** **oficina de información** = information bureau *o* information office; **para su información** = for your information; **responsable del servicio de información** = information officer; **le remito este folleto adjunto para su información** = I enclose this leaflet for your information; **para más información diríjase a la sección 27** = for further information, please write to Department 27; **contestar a una solicitud de información** = to answer a request for information; **para obtener información diríjanse al secretario** = all inquiries should be addressed to the secretary; **ocultar información a alguien** = to keep back information from someone; **pidió información sobre el tipo de interés de la hipoteca** = she inquired about the mortgage rate; **revelar una información** = to disclose a piece of information; **revelación de información confidencial** = disclosure of confidential information; **descubrieron que el director gerente pasaba información a una empresa competidora** = they discovered the managing director was passing information to a rival company

la información es fundamental en cualquier sistema democrático
Tiempo

escuchar, utilizar la información, tener una referencia permanente de lo que ocurre en el entorno son herramientas tan necesarias hoy como los resultados financieros
El País

informar *vt* **(a)** *(dar información)* to inform *o* to report; **lamento tener que informarle que su oferta no ha sido aceptada** = I regret to inform you that your tender was not acceptable; **le pedimos al banco que nos informara de su situación financiera** = we asked the bank to report on his financial status; **el director gerente informó al consejo de administración sobre la evolución de**

las negociaciones = the managing director briefed the board on the progress of the negotiations **(b)** **nos informan de que el envío llegará la semana que viene** = we are advised that the shipment will arrive next week; **informar erróneamente** = to give wrong information *o* to misdirect **(c)** *(abogado)* to brief

◊ **informarse** *vr* to find out *o* to be informed; **para más detalles infórmese en nuestras oficinas** = for further details, ask at our offices

informático, -ca **1** *adj* **equipo informático** = computer hardware; **sistema informático** = computer system **2** *nf* computing *o* computer science; **informática de gestión** = business data processing; **departamento de informática** = computer department; **oficina de informática** = computer bureau; **servicios de informática** = computer services; **tecnología informática** = information technology (IT)

existe un fuerte plan de ahorro, 350 millones de dólares, realizado a base de suprimir empleos, integrando los sistemas informáticos y áreas operativas y eliminando las duplicidades operativas
El País

en estos tiempos de crisis, todo en informática baja de precios
PC Actual

informativo, -va *adj* informative; **medios informativos** = mass media; **todos los vendedores tienen que asistir a una sesión informativa sobre el nuevo producto** = all salesmen have to attend a sales briefing on the new product

informatizado, -da **1** *adj* computerized; **oficina informatizada** = paperless office; **sistema de facturación informatizado** = a computerized invoicing system; **nuestro control de existencias ha sido totalmente informatizado** = our stock control has been completely computerized **2** *pp de* INFORMATIZAR

informatizar *vt* to computerize

informe *nm* **(a)** *(información)* report *o* memorandum *o* statement; **el informe anual de la compañía** = the company's annual report; **informe de los auditores** = auditors' report; **informe de auditoría con salvedades** = auditors' qualification *o* qualified audit report; **informe confidencial** = confidential report; **el informe del consejo de administración** = the directors' report; **informe a favor** = letter of comfort; **informe financiero** = financial report; **informe sobre la marcha de una situación** = progress report; **el informe del presidente** = the chairman's report; **informe provisional** = interim report; **el informe del tesorero** = the treasurer's report; **informe (diario *o* semanal *o* trimestral) de ventas** = (daily *o* weekly *o* quarterly) sales return; **informe de viabilidad** = feasibility report **(b)** **enviar un informe** = to send in a report; **hacer un informe** = to make a report; **presentar un informe** = to present a report; **redactar un informe** = to draft a report; **el director de ventas lee todos los informes de su equipo de vendedores** = the sales director reads all the reports from the sales team; **el presidente ha recibido un informe de la compañía de seguros** = the chairman has received a report from the insurance company; **le**

mostraré el informe en secreto = I will show you the report in confidence; **el informe de los auditores empezaba con una explicación de los principios generales adoptados** = the auditors' report began with a description of the general principles adopted **(c)** *(declaración oficial)* report; *(del gobierno)* White Paper; **el gobierno ha publicado un informe sobre los problemas crediticios de los exportadores** = the government has issued a report on the credit problems of exporters **(d)** *(datos)* survey; **hemos pedido al departamento de ventas que haga un informe de los productos competidores** = we have asked the sales department to produce a survey of competing products **(e)** *(declaración escrita)* record

◊ **informes** *nmpl* **(a)** *(detalles)* information; **pedir informes** = to ask for information *o* to make inquiries *o* to inquire; **ref.: su petición de informes del 29 de mayo** = re your inquiry of May 29th **(b)** *(referencias)* references; **envíe su solicitud adjuntando informes** = send in your application and enclose references

> se trata, por el momento, de un informe confidencial, al encontrarse todavía en revisión y no existir de la nueva ley más que un texto de criterios generales
> **España Económica**

> el pasado octubre la Comisión Europea presentó su informe anual sobre la evolución económica de los quince países miembros
> **España Económica**

> el autor del informe revela que una de cada cuatro empresas familiares ha considerado la posibilidad de vender acciones o de no continuar
> **Cambio 16**

> el informe está estructurado en 12 capítulos, en los que se aborda el tema de la cooperación desde distintas perspectivas
> **El País**

infra- *prefijo* infra *o* under

◊ **infracapitalizado, -da** *adj* undercapitalized

◊ **infraestructura** *nf* infrastructure; **la infraestructura del país** = the country's infrastructure; **la infraestructura de la compañía** = the company's infrastructure

◊ **infraocupación** *nf* underemployment; **la infraocupación preocupa mucho a las autoridades** = underemployment is a matter of concern to the authorities

◊ **infrautilizado, -da** *adj* underemployed *o* underutilized

◊ **infravaloración** *nf* undervaluation *o* underestimate

◊ **infravalorado, -da 1** *adj* undervalued; **las propiedades están infravaloradas en el balance de situación** = the properties are undervalued on the balance sheet; **el dólar está infravalorado en los mercados de divisas** = the dollar is undervalued on the foreign exchanges **2** *pp de* INFRAVALORAR

infravalorar *vt* to underestimate; **infravaloramos su potencial** = we underestimated her potential

infracción *nf* infringement; **infracción aduanera** = infringement of customs regulations; **infracción fiscal** = tax offence; **infracción del código de circulación** = traffic offence

infringir *vt* to infringe *o* to break; **la empresa ha infringido el contrato** *o* **acuerdo** = the company has broken the contract *o* the agreement; **infringir los derechos de autor** = to infringe a copyright

infructuosamente *adv* unsuccessfully

ingeniería *nf* engineering; **ingeniería civil** = civil engineering; **ingeniería financial** = financial management

> las operaciones de la Corporación abarcan todas las áreas financieras: bolsa, renta fija, deuda pública, mercado monetario e ingeniería financiera
> **Tiempo**

ingeniero, -ra *n* engineer; **ingeniero asesor** = engineering consultant *o* consulting engineer; **ingeniero civil** *o* **de caminos** = civil engineer; **ingeniero electrónico** = electronic engineer; **ingeniero de obra** = site engineer; **ingeniero de producto** = product engineer; **ingeniero de programación** = programming engineer; **ingeniero de proyectos** = project engineer

Inglaterra *nf* England

◊ **inglés, -esa 1** *adj* English **2** *n* Englishman, Englishwoman; **los ingleses** = the English
NOTA: capital: **Londres** (= London); moneda: **libra esterlina (£)** = pound sterling (£)

ingresar 1 *vi* to go in; **ingresar en una empresa** = to join a firm **2** *vt* **(a)** *(money)* to credit *o* to deposit; **ingresar un cheque** = to pay a cheque into your account; **ingresar dinero en el banco** = to put money into the bank *o* to deposit money in the bank; **se han ingresado 30.000 ptas. en su cuenta** = 30,000 pesetas have been credited to your account *o* have been deposited in your account **(b) la tienda ingresa en caja 400.000 ptas. a la semana** = the shop takes 400,000 pesetas a week

ingreso *nm* **(a)** *(entrada)* entry *o* admission; **condiciones de ingreso** = conditions of membership; **¿va a solicitar Islandia el ingreso en la Unión Europea?** = is Iceland going to apply for membership of the European Union? **(b)** *(dinero)* income *o* revenue; **ingreso fijo** = regular income **(c)** *(banco)* deposit

◊ **ingresos** *nmpl* **(a)** *(dinero recibido)* earnings *o* income *o* receipts; **ingresos por alquiler** = income from rents *o* rent income; **ingresos anuales** = annual income; **ingresos brutos** = gross earnings; **ingresos libres de impuestos** = non-taxable income; **ingresos marginales** = marginal revenue; **ingresos de un negocio** *o* **de una tienda** = takings; **ingresos por operaciones invisibles** = invisible earnings; **ingresos profesionales** *o* **ingresos percibidos** = earned income; **el hospital tiene grandes ingresos procedentes de donaciones** = the hospital has a large income from gifts; **ingresos procedentes de intereses y dividendos** = unearned income; **ingresos por publicidad** = revenue from advertising *o* advertising revenue; **ingresos teóricos** = notional income; **los ingresos por las ventas de petróleo han subido con el alza del dólar** = oil revenues have risen with the rise in the dollar **(b) de**

altos ingresos = high-income; **contabilidad de ingresos** = revenue accounts; **declaración de ingresos nulos** = nil return; **indemnización por pérdida de ingresos** = compensation for loss of earnings; **personas de ingresos medios** = people in the middle-income bracket

> para ilustrar lo que podría ser el valor real de una moneda puede ser útil describir los ingresos y gastos de una familia normal
>
> **España Económica**

> el nuevo Chemical Banking goza de una situación privilegiada en el mercado de préstamos a pequeñas y medianas empresas (aquellas que obtienen menos de 100 millones de dólares de ingresos anuales)
>
> **El País**

INI = INSTITUTO NACIONAL DE INDUSTRIA

iniciación *nf* **(a)** *(comienzo)* beginning *o* start; **iniciación de negociaciones** = start of negotiations; **iniciación de programa** = loading of the program *o* bootstrap; **desde la iniciación del proyecto** = since the project began *o* since the start of the project **(b)** *(introducción)* induction; **cursos de iniciación** = induction courses *o* induction training

◊ **iniciado, -da 1** *adj y n* initiated **2** *pp de* INICIAR

◊ **inicial** *adj* initial *o* opening *o* starting; **capital inicial** = initial capital; **coste inicial** = historic(al) cost; **existencias iniciales** = opening stock; **fecha inicial** = starting date; **financiación inicial**= start-up financing; **comenzó el negocio con unos gastos iniciales** *o* **una inversión inicial de 100.000 ptas.** = he started the business with an initial expenditure *o* initial investment of 100,000 pesetas; **oferta inicial** = opening bid; **pago inicial** = down payment; **la reacción inicial a la publicidad en televisión ha sido muy buena** = the initial response to the TV advertising has been very good; **salario inicial** = starting salary; **saldo inicial** = opening balance; **ventas iniciales** = initial sales

◊ **iniciales** *nfpl* initials; **poner las iniciales a un documento** = to initial a document; **le ruego firme con sus iniciales el acuerdo en el lugar señalado con una X** = please initial the agreement at the place marked with an X; **marcar con las iniciales una enmienda de un contrato** = to initial an amendment to a contract; **el presidente marcó con sus iniciales todas las modificaciones efectuadas en el contrato que firmó** = the chairman wrote his initials by each alteration in the contract he was signing; **con las iniciales de la persona** = personalized *o* with someone's initials

iniciar *vt* *(comenzar)* to start *o* to initiate *o* to pioneer; **iniciar conversaciones** = to initiate *o* to open discussions; **inició los debates con una descripción del producto** = he opened the discussions with a description of the product; **iniciar una investigación** = to set up an enquiry; **iniciar negociaciones** = to enter into negotiations; **iniciar un negocio** = to start a business

> los grandes bancos de Estados Unidos inician el proceso de fusiones como única salida a la crisis que atraviesan
>
> **El País**

iniciativa *nf* initiative; **seguir una iniciativa** = to follow up an initiative; **tomar la iniciativa** = to take the initiative

> entre las nuevas iniciativas, esta empresa montará una guardería para que los más pequeños manejen ordenadores mientras el padre compra
>
> **El País**

inicio *nm* beginning *o* start *o* startup; **inicio del año** = beginning of the year; *(informática)* **inicio de texto** = start of text

ininflamable *adj* fire-resistant

injerencia *nf* interference; **el departamento de ventas se quejó de la continua injerencia del departamento de contabilidad** = the sales department complained of continual interference from the accounts department

injusticia *nf* injustice; *(agravio)* tort

inmediato, -ta *adj* immediate *o* prompt; **respuesta inmediata a una carta** = prompt reply to a letter; **el mercado de entrega inmediata del petróleo** = the spot market in oil

◊ **inmediatamente** *adv* immediately *o* at once *o* promptly; **partió para el aeropuerto inmediatamente después de recibir el mensaje teléfonico** = he left for the airport directly after receiving the telephone message; **atenderemos su pedido inmediatamente** = your order will receive immediate attention; **tienes que hacer algo inmediatamente si quieres evitar los robos** = you must take immediate action if you want to stop thefts

inmobiliario, -ria 1 *adj* property; **mercado inmobiliario** = property market; **una sociedad inmobiliaria ha comprado la oficina** = the office has been bought by a property company; **ganó dinero durante los años 70 en transacciones inmobiliarias** = he made his money from property deals *o* real estate in the 1970s **2** *nf* **(a)** *(sociedad)* real estate company *o* property company; **acciones de inmobiliarias** = property shares **(b)** *(agencia)* estate agency

> se forjó como experto inmobiliario en la especulación urbanística de la Costa del Sol durante los años 70
>
> **Cambio 16**

inmóvil *adj* immovable; **permanecer inmóvil** = to remain motionless

inmovilización *nf* typing up *o* immobilization; **la inmovilización de dinero en acciones** = the locking up of money in shares

◊ **inmovilizado, -da 1** *adj* frozen **2** *pp de* INMOVILIZAR

inmovilizar *vt* *(dinero)* to tie up; **inmovilizar capital** = to lock up capital; **la empresa tiene 500.000 ptas. inmovilizadas en existencias que nadie quiere comprar** = the company has 500,000 pesetas tied up in stock which no one wants to buy

inmueble *nm* *(edificio)* building *o* property; **inmuebles residenciales** = house property *o* residential properties; **bienes inmuebles** = property *o* real estate

inmunidad *nf* immunity; **inmunidad**

diplomática = diplomatic immunity; **se le concedió inmunidad judicial** = he was granted immunity from prosecution

innecesario, -ria *adj* unnecessary *o* redundant; **cláusula innecesaria de un contrato** = redundant clause in a contract; **debido a la nueva ley la cláusula 6 resulta innecesaria** = the new legislation has made clause 6 redundant

innovación *nf* innovation

◊ **innovador, -ra 1** *adj* innovative **2** *n* innovator

◊ **innovar 1** *vt* to make new; **se han aplicado nuevas medidas para innovar la gestión de la empresa** = new measures have been introduced to modernize the management of the company **2** *vi* to innovate

> las innovaciones llegan hasta el sector de seguros, que se ha caracterizado siempre por una rigidez importante
> **El País**

inoperante *adj* unworkable *o* out of use

inoportuno, -na *adj* inopportune *o* inconvenient *o* inappropriate; **su llegada diez minutos después de que acabara la reunión fue muy inoportuna** = his arrival ten minutes after the meeting finished was very bad timing

'input' *nm* (*entrada de información*) input of information *o* computer input

inquietud *nf* anxiety *o* worry *o* concern

inquilino, -na *n* tenant *o* lessee *o* occupant; **inquilino en posesión** = sitting tennant; **el inquilino ha de pagar los gastos de electricidad** = electricity charges are payable by the tenant; **el inquilino es responsable de las reparaciones** *o* **las reparaciones corren a cargo del inquilino** = the tenant is liable for repairs *o* repairs are chargeable to the occupier; **libre de inquilinos** = with vacant possession

> la nueva ley de arrendamientos urbanos tendrá un carácter más proteccionista para con el inquilino
> **España Económica**

inscribir *vt* (**a**) (*registrar*) to write in *o* to enrol *o* to register; **inscribir una compañía en un registro** = to register a company (**b**) (*anotar*) to enter; **inscribir un punto al orden del día** = to put an item on the agenda

◊ **inscribirse** *vr* to enrol *o* to register

inscripción *nf* registration *o* registering *o* enrolment; **tienes que rellenar el boletín de inscripción** = you have to fill in the registration form *o* the enrolment form; **certificado de inscripción** = certificate of registration *o* registration certificate; **cuota de inscripción** = registration fee; **cuota de inscripción sindical** = union dues; **impreso de inscripción** = registration form; **número de inscripción** = registration number

inseguro, -ra *adj* insecure *o* unsafe *o* uncertain *o* shaky; **no se puede confiar en él porque es un hombre muy inseguro** = you can't rely on him because he is very insecure

insertar *vt* to insert; **insertar un anuncio en una**

revista = to insert a publicity piece into a magazine mailing

inservible *adj* useless; **la fotocopiadora está inservible, necesitamos una nueva** = the photocopier is useless, we need a new one

insignia *nf* badge

insignificante *adj* negligible *o* trivial *o* petty

insistencia *nf* insistence *o* persistence; **en ese negocio hubo que proceder con mucha insistencia** = a lot of hard selling went into that deal

insistir *vi* (**a**) (*reiterar*) to insist *o* to persist; **insistir en** = to insist on *o* to hold out for; **deberíais insistir en un aumento de sueldo del 10%** = you should hold out for a 10% pay rise (**b**) (*presionar*) to press; **insistir en que alguien pague** *o* **conteste** = to press someone for payment *o* for an answer

insolvencia *nf* bankruptcy *o* insolvency; **estaba en situación de insolvencia** = he was in a state of insolvency

◊ **insolvente** *adj* bankrupt *o* insolvent; **se le declaró insolvente** = he was declared insolvent; **compañía insolvente** = insolvent company

inspección *nf* (**a**) (*control*) inspection *o* check *o* checking; **inspección aduanera** = customs examination; **inspección de equipajes** = baggage check; **inspección del IVA** = VAT inspection; **inspección sanitaria** = medical inspection; **los auditores realizaron una inspección del libro de caja** = the auditors carried out checks on the petty cash book; **una inspección rutinaria del equipo contra incendios** = a routine check of the fire equipment; **los inspectores encontraron algunos defectos durante la inspección del edificio** = the inspectors found some defects during their inspection of the building (**b**) **dar una orden de inspección** = to issue an inspection order; **efectuar una inspección** *o* **llevar a cabo una inspección de una instalación** = to make an inspection *o* to carry out an inspection of an installation; **llevar a cabo** *o* **hacer una visita de inspección** = to carry out a tour of inspection; **muestra de inspección** = check sample; **sello de inspección** = inspection stamp (**c**) (*examen profesional*) survey; **inspección de daños** *o* **de avería** = damage survey; **hemos pedido una inspección de la casa antes de comprarla** = we have asked for a survey of the house before buying it; **la compañía de seguros está llevando a cabo una inspección de los daños** = the insurance company is carrying out a survey of the damage

inspeccionar *vt* (**a**) (*revisar*) to inspect; **inspeccionar una instalación** = to inspect an installation (**b**) (*examinar*) to survey; **han inspeccionado la casa** = the house has been surveyed

inspector, -ra *n* inspector; **inspector de fábricas** = inspector of factories *o* factory inspector; **inspector de Hacienda** = inspector of taxes *o* tax inspector; **inspector del IVA** = VAT inspector; **inspector de obra** = surveyor; **inspector de pesos y medidas** = inspector of weights and measures

instalación *nf* (**a**) (*acción*) installation; **supervisar la instalación de nuevo equipo** = to supervise the installation of new equipment; **se ha**

producido una avería en la instalación eléctrica = there is a fault in the wiring **(b) instalaciones** = facilities *o* installations; **no hay instalaciones de descarga** = there are no facilities for unloading *o* there are no unloading facilities; **instalaciones fijas** = fixtures; **instalaciones fijas y accesorios** = fixtures and fittings (f. & f.); **instalaciones portuarias** = harbour installations *o* harbour facilities; **el incendio causó graves daños a las instalaciones petrolíferas** = the fire seriously damaged the oil installations

instalar *vt* **(a)** *(establecer)* to set up *o* to establish; **la compañía ha instalado una sucursal en Argentina** = the company has established a branch in Argentina **(b)** *(montar)* to install; **instalar nueva maquinaria** = to install new machinery; **nos van a instalar una nueva fotocopiadora mañana** = we are having a new photocopier installed tomorrow

◊ **instalarse** *vr* to install oneself *o* to set oneself up; **se instalaron en Madrid** = they settled in Madrid

instancia *nf* **(a)** *(petición)* request *o* petition; **en última instancia** = as a last resort; **a instancia de** = at the request of; **presentaron una instancia para que las autoridades locales reconsideraran su decisión** = they presented a petition asking the local authorities to reconsider their decision **(b)** *(solicitud)* application form; **sírvanse enviar las instancias por duplicado** = please send the applications in duplicate **(c)** *(jurídico)* instance; **tribunal** *o* **juzgado de primera instancia** = court of first instance; **tribunal** *o* **juzgado de segunda instancia** = court of appeal

instantáneo, -nea *adj* instant; **crédito instantáneo** = instant credit

instante *nm* instant *o* moment; **al instante** = immediately *o* instantly; **compró al instante el 15% de las acciones de la compañía** = he snapped up 15% of the company's shares

instar *vi* to urge; **instar a alguien a hacer algo con rapidez** *o* **de forma inmediata** = to press someone to do something; **fue instado a dar una respuesta inmediata** = he was pressed to give a quick answer

institución *nf* institution; **institución financiera** = financial institution

◊ **institucional** *adj* institutional; **compra** *o* **venta institucional** = institutional buying *o* selling; **inversores institucionales** = institutional investors

instituto *nm* institute; **instituto de investigación** = research institute; **Instituto Nacional de Empleo (INEM)** = National Employment Institute; **Instituto Nacional de Industria (INI)** = National Industrial Institute; **Instituto de la Salud (Insalud)** = National Health Service (NHS)

instrucción *nf* **(a)** *(enseñanza)* education *o* instruction; **instrucción pública** = state education **(b)** *(conocimiento)* knowledge; **tiene poca instrucción en la materia** = he knows very little about the subject

◊ **instrucciones** *nfpl* instructions *o* directions for use; **instrucciones de envío** = shipping *o* forwarding instructions; **instrucciones de uso** = operating manual *o* directions for use; **esperar instrucciones** = to await instructions; **dar**

instrucciones = to issue instructions; *(abogado)* to brief; **dio instrucciones a su agente de bolsa para que vendiera las acciones inmediatamente** = he gave instructions to his stockbroker to sell the shares immediately; **dio instrucciones al director de ventas a crédito para que tomara medidas** = he instructed the credit controller to take action; **los vendedores recibieron instrucciones relativas al nuevo producto** = the salesmen were briefed on the new product; **según las instrucciones recibidas** = in accordance with *o* according to instructions received; **salvo instrucciones contrarias** = failing instructions to the contrary

instructor, -ra *n* instructor

instrumento *nm* **(a)** *(herramienta)* instrument *o* tool; **el técnico trajo instrumentos para medir la potencia eléctrica generada** = the technician brought instruments to measure the output of electricity; **su actuación sirvió de instrumento para lograr los objetivos** = his action served as a means to meet their objectives **(b)** *(documento)* instrument; **instrumento financiero** = financial instrument; **instrumento negociable** = negotiable instrument; **instrumento de venta** = bill of sale

> hay que tener en cuenta que los derivados son instrumentos altamente apalancados, en los que con una pequeña cantidad se mueve un valor nominal decenas de veces superior
>
> **El País**

insuficiencia *nf* lack *o* shortage *o* shortfall; **insuficiencia de personal** *o* **mano de obra** = undermanning *o* shortage of staff

◊ **insuficiente** *adj* **(a)** *(menos de lo necesario)* insufficient *o* inadequate; **asistencia insuficiente** = inquorate; **saldo insuficiente** = insufficient funds **(b)** *(poco, pequeño)* short; **esta cantidad es insuficiente para cubrir los gastos** = this amount is too small to cover expenses

◊ **insuficientemente** *adv* insufficiently; **el personal está insuficientemente utilizado debido al recorte sufrido en la producción** = the staff is underemployed because of the cutback in production

intacto, -ta *adj* intact *o* unbroken *o* safe; **el paquete llegó intacto** = the parcel arrived intact

intangible *adj* intangible; **activos fijos intangibles** = intangible fixed assets; **activo intangible** = intangible assets

integración *nf* integration; **integración horizontal** = horizontal integration; **integración vertical** = vertical integration

> la convertibilidad del rublo y las posibilidades de integración de la economía soviética son una quimera mientras no se realicen transformaciones del mismo sistema
>
> **España Económica**

integrar *vt* to integrate; **integraron al nuevo equipo sin ninguna dificultad** = the new team was integrated without any difficulty; **la sociedad está integrada por varias empresas pequeñas** = the company is made up of several small firms

íntegro, -ra *adj* complete *o* whole; **precio**

íntegro = full price; **compró un billete a precio íntegro** = he bought a full-price ticket

intelectual *adj* intellectual; **propiedad intelectual** = intellectual property

inteligente *adj* intelligent *o* clever; **tarjeta inteligente** = smart card

> miles de personas van a tener la posibilidad de manejar las tarjetas inteligentes o monederos electrónicos, un producto financiero que amenaza con sustituir al viejo bolsillo de calderilla
> **El País**

intención *nf* effect *o* intent; **habló con esa intención** = he spoke to that effect; **carta de intención** = letter of intent; **tener la intención de hacer algo** = to intend to do something; **el gobierno tiene la intención de aumentar el IVA al 17,5%** = the government is proposing to increase VAT to 17.5%

intensamente *adv* actively *o* intensely; **la empresa está buscando intensamente nuevo personal** = the company is actively recruiting new personnel

intensificar *vt* to intensify *o* to increase; **intensificar la huelga** = to step up industrial action; **tenemos que intensificar el control de los gastos de los representantes** = we must tighten up on the reps' expenses

> al intensificarse la competencia internacional puede ser necesario que muchos empleadores eviten los costes de una plantilla de personal fijo
> **El País**

intensivo, -va *adj* intensive; **tendrá que realizar un curso intensivo de preparación para el nuevo puesto** = he will have to take an intensive course in preparation for the new job; **horario intensivo** *o* **jornada intensiva** = working day without a lunch break

◊ **intensivamente** *adv* intensively; **industria que usa intensivamente mano de obra** = labour-intensive industry

intentar *vt* to attempt *o* to try; **el director de ventas intentó explicar la repentina caída de las ventas** = the sales director tried to explain the sudden drop in sales; **la empresa está intentando introducirse en el mercado turístico** = the company is attempting to get into the tourist market; **intentó conseguir que el director de ventas fuera despedido** = he attempted to have the sales director sacked

◊ **intento** *nm* attempt; **fue detenido por intento de robo** = he was arrested on a charge of attempted robbery; **la empresa realizó un intento para introducirse en el mercado alemán** = the company made an attempt to break into the German market; **todos sus intentos por conseguir trabajo han fracasado** = all his attempts to get a job have failed

inter 1 inter; **donación inter vivos** = gift inter vivos **2** *prefijo* inter-; **interestatal** = interstate; **interurbano** = inter-city

intercalar *vt* to insert

intercambiable *adj* interchangeable *o* exchangeable; **piezas intercambiables** = interchangeable parts

intercambiar *vt* to exchange *o* to swap; **intercambiaron trabajos** = they swapped jobs; **intercambiar contratos** = to exchange contracts

◊ **intercambio** *nm* exchange *o* swap; **intercambio de contratos** = exchange of contracts; **los EE UU están aumentando sus intercambios comerciales con la UE** = the USA is increasing its trade with the EU

interés *nm* **(a)** *(dar importancia a algo)* interest; **el director gerente no se toma ningún interés por el club de los empleados** = the MD takes no interest in the staff club; **los compradores mostraron un gran interés por nuestra nueva gama de productos** = the buyers showed a lot of interest in our new product range **(b)** *(participación)* interest; **interés mayoritario** = majority shareholding *o* majority interest; **tiene un interés mayoritario en la compañía** = he has a controlling interest in the company; **interés minoritario** = minority shareholding *o* minority interest; **interés personal** *o* **intereses creados** = vested interest; **tiene un interés personal en que el negocio siga funcionando** = she has a vested interest in keeping the business working; **interés usufructuario** = beneficial interest; **declarar un interés** = to declare an interest **(c)** *(finanzas)* interest; **interés acumulado** *o* **devengado** = accrued interest; **interés atrasado** = back interest; **interés compuesto** = compound interest; **interés elevado** *o* **bajo** = high *o* low interest; **interés fijo** = fixed interest; **inversiones a interés fijo** = fixed-interest investment; **interés simple** = simple interest; **el banco paga un 10% de interés sobre las imposiciones a plazo fijo** = the bank pays 10% interest on deposits; **recibir un interés del 5%** = to receive interest at 5%; **el préstamo paga un 5% de interés** = the loan pays 5% interest; **los bonos producen un interés del 10%** = the bonds carry interest at 10%; **depósitos con interés** = interest-bearing deposits; **bonos del Estado que devengan un 5% de interés** = government bonds which bear 5% interest; **cuenta que devenga un interés del 10%** = account which earns interest at 10% *o* which earns 10% interest; **depósito que devenga un 5% de interés** = deposit which bears 5% interest **(d)** **acumulación de interés** = accrual of interest; **cargos en concepto de interés** = interest charges; **sin interés** = interest-free; **crédito** *o* **préstamo sin interés** = interest-free credit *o* soft loan; **la compañía concede a sus empleados préstamos sin interés** = the company gives its staff interest-free loans; **tipo** *o* **tasa de interés** = interest rate *o* rate of interest; **tipo de interés vigente** = standard rate

> la falta de interés por el trabajo es un problema dramático entre el conjunto de la población, especialmente entre los más jóvenes
> **España Económica**

> los tipos de interés se resisten a bajar en un contexto de actividad débil
> **Actualidad Económica**

> los tipos de interés seguirán relativamente elevados y con resistencia a la baja, mientras que la peseta se mantendrá en la zona alta de la banda de fluctuación
> **Actualidad Económica**

su presencia distorsiona el mercado al
introducir intereses ajenos a la
comunicación

Tiempo

interesado, -da 1 *adj* interested; **parte interesada** = interested party; **interesado en** = interested in; **el director gerente sólo está interesado en aumentar la rentabilidad** = the managing director is interested only in increasing profitability **2** *n* applicant; **todos los interesados pueden solicitar el puesto** = the job is open to all applicants **3** *pp de* INTERESAR

interesante *adj* interesting; **nos hicieron una oferta muy interesante por la fábrica** = they made us a very interesting offer for the factory; **fabrican una interesante gama de herramientas de jardinería** = they produce an interesting line in garden tools; **precios interesantes** = attractive prices; **salario interesante** = attractive salary

interesar *vt* to interest *o* to appeal (to); **intentó interesar a varias compañías en su nuevo invento** = he tried to interest several companies in his new invention

interestatal *adj* interstate; **Comisión de Comercio Interestatal** = *US* Interstate Commerce Commission

interface *o* **interfaz** *nm (informática)* interface

el usuario dispone de un interface que le permite grandes facilidades como la utilización de ratón

PC Actual

interferir *vt* to interfere; **no quisieron interferir en la toma de decisión** = they did not want to interfere in the decision-making process

ínterin *nm* **en el ínterin** = in the interim

◊ **interino, -na** *adj* temporary *o* acting *o* provisional; **director interino** = acting manager

interior 1 *adj* **(a)** *(en un país)* internal *o* domestic *o* inland; **comercio interior** = internal *o* domestic trade; **consumo interior** = domestic consumption; **el consumo interior de petróleo ha caído estrepitosamente** = domestic consumption of oil has fallen sharply; **correo interior** = inland postage; **coste del flete interior** = inland freight charges; **mercado interior** = domestic market *o* home market; **producción interior** = domestic production; **Producto Interior Bruto (PIB)** = Gross Domestic Product (GDP); **transportista del interior** = inland carrier; **ventas en el mercado interior** = home sales *o* sales in the home market; **sus ventas se sitúan principalmente en el mercado interior** = their sales are mainly in the home market **(b)** *(en una compañía)* internal **2** *nm* **(a)** *(en un país)* interior (of a country); **en el interior y en el extranjero** = at home and abroad; **las normas se aplican a los servicios postales del interior** = the rules operate on inland postal services; **vuelo del interior** = an internal flight; **Ministerio del Interior** = Ministry of the Interior; *GB* Home Office **(b)** *(en una compañía)* **en el interior de la empresa** = internally

para abordar fusiones en el exterior con cierta dignidad, resulta imprescindible conseguir antes una cierta dimensión de respetabilidad en el interior

España Económica

intermediario, -ria 1 *adj* intermediary **2** *n* intermediary *o* middleman *o* mediator; **se negó a desempeñar el papel de intermediario entre los dos consejeros** = he refused to act as an intermediary between the two directors; **vendemos directamente de la fábrica al cliente y así suprimimos al intermediario** = we sell direct from the factory to the customer and cut out the middleman; **servir de intermediario** = to act as intermediary *o* to mediate; **sirve de intermediario entre el director y sus empleados** = he is mediating between the manager and his staff

lleva más de veinte años trabajando en este país como agente bursátil, intermediario de inversiones y corredor de materias primas

España Económica

internacional *adj* international; **comercio internacional** = international trade; **cupón-respuesta internacional** = international (postal) reply coupon; **remitió un cupón-respuesta internacional en su carta** = he enclosed an international reply coupon with his letter; **derecho internacional** = international law; **Fondo Monetario Internacional (FMI)** = the International Monetary Fund (IMF); **llamada internacional** = international telephone call; **código de llamadas internacionales** = international dialling code; **Organización Internacional del Trabajo (OIT)** = International Labour Organization (ILO)

◊ **internacionalización** *nf* internationalization

Sol Meliá ha apostado por la internacionalización de actividades como fórmula de expansión, explotando zonas turísticas con un alto potencial de crecimiento, como América

El País

interno, -na *adj* **(a)** *(interior)* internal *o* inside *o* inward; **el micro tiene un reloj interno** = the micro has a built-in clock; **conocimiento de embarque interno** = inward bill **(b)** *(en una compañía)* internal *o* in-house; **auditor interno** = internal auditor; **auditoría interna** = internal audit; **departamento de auditoría interna** = internal audit department; **teléfono interno** = house phone *o* internal telephone

◊ **internamente** *adv* internally

interpretar *vt* to interpret; **interpretó mal lo que le dije** = he misinterpreted what I said

◊ **intérprete** *nmf* interpreter; **mi secretaria actuará de intérprete** = my secretary will act as interpreter; **mi ayudante sabe griego, así que nos servirá de intérprete** = my assistant knows Greek, so he will interpret for us

interrogar *vt* to interrogate *o* to question; **la policía interrogó a los empleados de la sección de contabilidad durante cuatro horas** = the police interrogated the accounts staff for four hours; **interrogó al presidente sobre la política de inversiones de la empresa** = she questioned the chairman on the company's investment policy

interrumpir *vt* to interrupt *o* to break off *o* to discontinue *o* to stop; **interrumpimos las conversaciones a medianoche** = we broke off the discussion at midnight; **la producción ha sido interrumpida por la huelga de los trabajadores** = production has been held up by the workers' strike

◊ **interrumpirse** *vr* to stop *o* to come to a stop *o* to come to a halt; **el trabajo se interrumpió cuando la empresa no pudo pagar los salarios de los obreros** = work came to a halt when the company could not pay the workers' wages

interrupción *nf* **(a)** *(alto)* interruption *o* stop; **trabajó cinco horas sin interrupción** = she worked for five hours without interruption **(b)** *(negociaciones)* failure

interurbano, -na *adj* **(a)** *(tren)* inter-city; **los servicios de trenes interurbanos son buenos** = the inter-city rail services are good; **los servicios interurbanos de tren son muchas veces más rápidos que los aviones** = inter-city train services are often quicker than going by air **(b)** **llamada interurbana** = long-distance call

intervención *nf* **(a)** *(participación)* intervention; **intervención estatal** *o* **del gobierno** = state intervention *o* government intervention; **economía de mínima intervención estatal** = laissez-faire economy; **la intervención del gobierno en el conflicto laboral** *o* **en los mercados de divisas** = the government's intervention in the labour dispute *o* in the foreign exchange markets; **la intervención del banco central en la crisis bancaria** = the central bank's intervention in the banking crisis; *(en la UE)* **precio de intervención** = intervention price **(b)** *(cuentas)* audit

◊ **intervencionismo** *nm* interventionism

> el intervencionismo del Estado fue aumentando poco a poco, apoyado en la teoría de los fallos del mercado
> **España Económica**

intervenir 1 *vi* to intervene; **intervenir en una disputa** *o* **conflicto** = to intervene in a dispute; **el banco central intervino para respaldar el dólar** = the central bank intervened to support the dollar **2** *vt* **intervenir una cuenta** = to audit an account

interventor, -ra *n* controller *o* comptroller; **interventor de cuentas** = auditor; **interventor externo** = external auditor

intestado, -da *adj* intestate *o* without leaving a will; **morir intestado** = to die intestate

◊ **ab intestato** *adv* intestate; **morir ab intestato** = to die intestate

intranquilo, -la *adj* anxious *o* restless

introducción *nf* **(a)** *(presentación)* introduction; **la introducción de nueva tecnología** = the introduction of new technology **(b)** *(iniciación)* induction; **cursos de introducción** = induction courses *o* induction training

introducir *vt* **(a)** *(colocar, poner en uso)* to introduce; **se han introducido nuevas medidas de seguridad en la oficina** = we have adopted new safety measures in the office; **introducir gradualmente** = to introduce gradually *o* to phase in; **el nuevo sistema de facturación será**

introducido gradualmente en los próximos dos meses = the new invoicing system will be phased in over the next two months; **introducir una cláusula en un contrato** = to insert a clause into a contract **(b)** *(informática)* **introducir datos al ordenador** = to input information *o* to key in data

◊ **introducirse** *vr* to enter; **espera poder introducirse en el mercado de los EE UU** = he is hoping to get into the US market; **la compañía intentó introducirse sin éxito en el mercado sudamericano** = the company unsuccessfully tried to break into the South American market

intromisión *nf* interference; **no toleraremos su intromisión en nuestros asuntos** = we won't tolerate his interference in our affairs

inundación *nf* flood; **daños debidos a una inundación catastrófica** = flood disaster damage

inundar *vt* to flood; **inundar el mercado** = to flood the market; **el mercado se inundó de imitaciones baratas** = the market was flooded with cheap imitations; **estamos inundados de pedidos** = we are flooded with orders *o* we have received a flood of orders

inútil *adj* useless

invalidación *nf* invalidation; **invalidación de testamento** = invalidation of a will

invalidar *vt* to invalidate; **invalidar un contrato** = to void a contract

◊ **invalidez** *nf* **(a)** *(nulidad)* invalidity; **invalidez de una reclamación** = invalidity of a claim **(b)** *(personas)* disability; **pensión de invalidez** = disability pension; **invalidez total** *o* **parcial** = total *o* partial disability

◊ **inválido, -da** *adj* invalid *o* void

invariable *adj* invariable *o* unchanged *o* constant

invención *nf* invention; **patente de invención** = letters patent; **recibe regalías por su invención** = he is receiving royalties from his invention

inventar *vt* to invent; **inventó un nuevo tipo de terminal de ordenadores** = she invented a new type of computer terminal; **¿quién inventó la taquigrafía?** = who invented shorthand?; **el contable jefe ha inventado un nuevo sistema para archivar las cuentas de los clientes** = the chief accountant has invented a new system of customer filing

inventariar *vt* to draw up an inventory *o* to inventory

inventario *nm* **(a)** *(lista o catálogo)* inventory *o* stocklist; **inventario contable** = book stock *o* book inventory; **inventario final** = closing stock; **inventario físico** = physical inventory; **inventario de posición (en almacén)** = picking list; **hacer un inventario** = to draw up an inventory *o* to inventory; **hacer un inventario de las instalaciones fijas** = to draw up an inventory of fixtures; **control de inventario** = inventory control; **estar de acuerdo con el inventario** = to agree the inventory **(b)** *(acción)* stocktaking; **hacer un inventario** = to take stock *o* to do the stock-take; **el almacén está cerrado para hacer el inventario anual** = the warehouse is closed for the annual stocktaking; **hay**

varios miles de unidades que no figuran en el inventario = several thousand units are unaccounted for in the stocktaking; **liquidación de inventario** = stocktaking sale

invento *nm* invention; **intentó vender su último invento a un fabricante de coches estadounidense** = he tried to sell his latest invention to a US car manufacturer

◊ **inventor, -ra** *n* inventor; **es el inventor del coche fabricado enteramente de plástico** = he is the inventor of the all-plastic car

inversión *nf* **(a)** *(capital invertido)* investment *o* capital expenditure; **inversión inmobiliaria** = investment in real estate; **inversiones a interés fijo** = fixed-interest investments; **inversión a largo plazo** *o* **inversión a corto plazo** = long-term investment *o* short-term investment; **inversión segura** = safe investment; **inversiones en valores de la máxima confianza** = blue-chip investments; **hacer inversiones en compañías petrolíferas** = to make investments in oil companies; **planificar las inversiones** = to plan investments; **intenta proteger sus inversiones** = he is trying to protect his investments **(b)** **asesor de inversiones** = investment adviser; **ayudas** *o* **incentivos a la inversión** = investment grants; **fondos de inversión** = unit trust; **rendimiento de la inversión** = return on investment (ROI) *o* on capital employed; **renta de inversiones** = investment income; **sociedad de inversión** *o* **sociedad de inversiones** = investment company *o* investment trust **(c)** *(IVA)* inputs

la apertura de los mercados aumentará nuestro nivel de vida porque intensificará el comercio, fomentará la eficacia de la economía estadounidense y aumentará la expansión estimulando la innovación e inversión
Mercado

la inversión debería ser la variable estratégica a preservar, porque es el vehículo de incorporación del progreso técnico y de la creación de empleo
España Económica

la posibilidad de unas elecciones anticipadas podrían llegar a frenar planes de inversión a corto plazo, como lo haría una mayor protesta sindical
Actualidad Económica

inversionista *nmf* investor

inversor, -ra *n* investor; **el pequeño inversor** *o* **el inversor privado** = the small investor *o* the private investor; **el inversor institucional** = the institutional investor; **los inversores perdieron millones de pesetas en el hundimiento de la compañía** = investors lost millions of pesetas in the collapse *o* in the wreck of the company

los inversores entregaban su dinero sin saber para qué se iba a utilizar
España Económica

invertido, -da 1 *adj* **(a)** *(capital)* invested; **tener dinero invertido en un negocio** = to have money invested in a business *o* to have a stake in a business **(b)** *(con sentido opuesto)* reverse *o* reversed; **orden invertido** = reverse order **2** *pp de* INVERTIR

invertir *vt* **(a)** *(capital)* to invest *o* to pump;

invertir en el extranjero = to invest abroad; **invertir en un negocio** = to put money into a business; **invertir los beneficios en la propia empresa** = to plough back profits into the company; **los bancos han ido invirtiendo dinero en la compañía para mantenerla a flote** = the banks have been pumping money into the company to keep it afloat; **invirtió todo su dinero en una empresa de ingeniería** = he invested all his money in an engineering business; **invertir capital en una fábrica nueva** *o* **dinero en nueva maquinaria** = to invest capital in a new factory *o* to invest money in new machinery; **invirtió todos sus ahorros en títulos del Estado** = he invested all his savings in government securities; **vendió la casa e invirtió el dinero en su totalidad** = she sold her house and invested the money as a lump sum; **invertir de nuevo** = to reinvest **(b)** *(tiempo o esfuerzo)* to spend; **invirtieron más de un mes en el proyecto** = they spent over a month completing the project

los inversores extranjeros invirtieron un total de 240.636 millones de pesetas en el conjunto de las cuatro bolsas españolas durante el año pasado
El País

investigación *nf* **(a)** *(indagación)* investigation; **dirigir una investigación sobre posibles irregularidades en la venta de acciones** = to conduct an investigation into irregularities in share dealings; **hacer investigaciones sobre algo** = to inquire into *o* to investigate something; **iniciar una investigación** = to set up an inquiry **(b)** *(estudio)* research; **la investigación científica** = scientific research; **departamento de investigación** = research department; **un instituto** *o* **centro de investigación** = a research institute *o* organization; **trabajos de investigación** = research work; **la compañía está llevando a cabo trabajos de investigación para hallar una medicina que cure el resfriado** = the company is carrying out research into finding a medicine to cure colds; **unidad de investigación** = research unit **(c)** **de investigación** = fact-finding; **un trabajo** *o* **una misión de investigación** = a fact-finding mission **(d)** **investigación y desarrollo (I+D)** = research and development (R & D); **investigación y desarrollo técnico (I+DT)** = technical R & D; **la compañía gasta millones en investigación y desarrollo** = the company spends millions on research and development *o* on R & D; **costes de investigación y desarrollo** = research and development costs; **el departamento de investigación y desarrollo** = the R & D department **(e)** **investigación de mercados** = market research; **hacer una investigación de mercado para un producto** = to research the market for a product

◊ **investigador, -ra** *n* investigator *o* researcher; **investigador oficial** = government investigator; **trabajo como investigador** = I am doing research

investigar *vt* **(a)** *(indagar)* to investigate *o* to inquire into; **estamos investigando los antecedentes del nuevo proveedor** = we are inquiring into the background of our new supplier **(b)** *(examinar)* to explore *o* to examine; **estamos investigando la posibilidad de abrir una oficina en Londres** = we are exploring the possibility of opening an office in London **(c)** *(estudiar)* to research

el papel del mercado en el impulso de la I+DT empresarial fue profundamente analizado en una de las mesas del encuentro, ya que es la parcela clave para la supervivencia en los entornos de alta competitividad actuales

PC Week

invisible *adj* invisible; **importaciones y exportaciones invisibles** = invisibles; **ingresos invisibles** *o* **ingresos por exportaciones invisibles** = invisible earnings

invitación *nf* invitation; **extender una invitación a alguien para que forme parte del consejo de administración** = to issue an invitation to someone to join the board; **invitación gratuita** = complimentary ticket

invitar *vt* to invite; **invitar a alguien a una entrevista** = to invite someone to an interview; **invitar a alguien a formar parte del consejo** = to invite someone to join the board; **invitar a los accionistas a suscribir nuevas acciones** = to invite shareholders to subscribe a new issue

IPC = INDICE DE PRECIOS AL CONSUMO *o* AL CONSUMIDOR Retail Price Index (RPI)

IPI = INDICE DE PRODUCCION INDUSTRIAL

ir *vi* **(a)** to go; **ir a buscar** = to fetch; **ir contracorriente** = to buck the trend; **ir con** = to belong with; **esos documentos van con los informes de ventas (b)** ir en primer lugar = to lead

◊ **irse** *vr* to go away *o* to leave; **se va de la empresa** = he is leaving the company

Irán *nm* Iran

◊ **iraní** *o* **persa** *adj y nmf* Iranian
NOTA: capital: **Teherán** (= Tehran); moneda: **rial iraní (RIs)** = Iranian rial (RIs)

Iraq *nm* Iraq

◊ **iraquí** *adj y nmf* Iraqi
NOTA: capital: **Bagdad** (= Baghdad); moneda: **dinar iraquí (ID)** = Iraqi dinar (ID)

Irlanda *nf* Ireland

◊ **irlandés, -esa 1** *adj* Irish **2** *n* Irishman, Irishwoman; **los irlandeses** = the Irish
NOTA: capital: **Dublín** (= Dublin); moneda: **libra irlandesa (£Ir)** = Irish pound *o* punt (£Ir)

IRPF = IMPUESTO SOBRE LA RENTA DE LAS PERSONAS FISICAS personal income tax

irrecuperable *adj* irrecoverable

irredimible *adj* (*no amortizable*) irredeemable; **obligación irredimible** = irredeemable bond

irregular *adj* irregular; **documentación irregular** = irregular documentation; **este procedimiento es muy irregular** = this procedure is highly irregular

irregularidad *nf* **(a)** irregularity; **la irregularidad del reparto de correo** = the irregularity of the postal deliveries **(b)** **irregularidades** = irregularities; **investigar irregularidades en la venta de acciones** = to investigate irregularities in the share dealings

irrevocable *adj* irrevocable; **aceptación irrevocable** = irrevocable acceptance; **carta de crédito irrevocable** = irrevocable letter of credit

Islandia *nf* Iceland

◊ **islandés, -esa 1** *adj* Icelandic **2** *n* Icelander
NOTA: capital: **Reykjavik**; moneda: **corona islandesa (Isk)** = Icelandic krona (Isk)

Italia *nf* Italy

◊ **italiano, -na** *adj y n* Italian
NOTA: capital: **Roma** (= Rome); moneda: **lira italiana (Lit)** = Italian lira (Lit)

itinerario *nm* itinerary; **el itinerario de un vendedor** = a salesman's itinerary

IVA = IMPUESTO SOBRE EL VALOR AÑADIDO Value Added Tax (VAT); **factura con el IVA incluido** = VAT invoice; **facturación con IVA incluido** = VAT invoicing; **pregúntale a la vendedora si la factura incluye el IVA** = ask the salesgirl if the bill includes VAT; **¿está incluido el IVA en la factura?** = does the bill include VAT?; **el IVA no está incluido en la factura** = the invoice is exclusive of VAT; **la factura incluye el 15% de IVA** = the invoice includes VAT at 15%; **inspección del IVA** = VAT inspection; **productos *o* servicios exentos del IVA** = exempt supplies

el sistema de falsificación de facturas, que afecta al IVA y al Impuesto sobre Sociedades se realiza de distintas formas

Cambio 16

hacienda se enfrenta a los que no pagan y a los que no quieren pagar: el fraude del IVA y el rechazo al Impuesto sobre Actividades Económicas

Cambio 16

izquierdo, -da *adj* **(a)** left; **los números figuran en el lado izquierdo de la página** = the numbers run down the left side of the page; **ponga los débitos en la columna izquierda** = put the debits in the left column **(b)** **de la izquierda** = left-hand; **los débitos figuran en la columna de la izquierda de las cuentas** = the debits are in the left-hand column in the accounts; **guarda los expedientes del personal en el cajón de la izquierda de su mesa de despacho** = he keeps the personnel files in the left-hand drawer of his desk

Jj

Jamaica *nf* Jamaica

◊ **jamaicano, -na** *adj y n* Jamaican
NOTA: capital: **Kingston**; moneda: **dólar jamaicano (J$)** = Jamaican dollar (J$)

Japón *nm* Japan

◊ **japonés, -esa** *o* **nipón, -ona** *adj y n* Japanese
NOTA: capital: **Tokio** (= Tokyo); moneda: **yen japonés** = Japanese yen

jefe, -fa *n* **(a)** *(persona que dirige)* head *o* chief; *(informal)* boss; **jefe de almacén** = stock controller; **jefe de comedor** *o* **camareros** = head waiter; **jefe de compras** = head buyer; **¿conseguiste ver al jefe de compras?** = did you manage to see the head buyer?; **jefe de departamento** = head of department *o* department head; **jefe ejecutivo** = chief executive *o* chief executive officer (CEO); **jefe de oficina** = chief clerk *o* head clerk; **jefe de porteros** = head porter; **jefe de sanidad municipal** = medical officer of health; **jefe de sección** = head of department *o* department head; **le nombraron consejero cuando se casó con la hija del jefe** = he became a director when he married the boss's daughter; **siguieron trabajando incluso cuando el jefe les dijo que pararan** = they kept working, even when the boss told them to stop; **contable jefe** = chief accountant; **es el contable jefe de un grupo industrial** = he is the chief accountant of an industrial group; **vendedor en jefe** = head salesman **(b)** *(director, gerente)* manager; **jefe de contabilidad** = accounts manager; **jefe de equipo de ventas** = field sales manager; **jefe de personal** = personnel manager *o* officer; **jefe de publicidad** = advertising manager **(c)** *(en cabeza)* leader; **es la jefa de la misión comercial a Nigeria** = she is the leader of the trade mission to Nigeria

el director de recursos humanos, antes
jefe de personal, sigue ejerciendo su
función como un burócrata
El País

jerárquico, -ca *adj* hierarchic(al); **orden jerárquico** = line of command *o* line management *o* line organization; **por vía jerárquica** = through official channels

Jordania *nf* Jordan

◊ **jordano, -na** *adj y n* Jordanian
NOTA: capital: **Ammán** = Amman; moneda: **dinar jordano (JD)** = Jordanian dinar (JD)

jornada *nf* day's work *o* working day; **trabajar a jornada completa** = to work full-time; **jornada intensiva** = working day without a lunch break; **jornada partida** = split shift; **jornada reducida** = short time *o* part-time; **trabajar a jornada reducida** = to be on short time; **está buscando trabajo a jornada reducida** = he is trying to find part-time work; **la empresa ha tenido que reducir la jornada por falta de pedidos** = the company has had to introduce short-time working because of lack of orders

aunque los especialistas señalan las
consecuencias positivas que hay en la
jornada intensiva para los empleados, sin
embargo, existen algunos riesgos que no
siempre son resaltados suficientemente
El País

la jornada intensiva conlleva
normalmente un adelanto en la hora de
entrada al trabajo y, por otro lado, una
ausencia del tiempo de descanso que se
produce con el almuerzo en una jornada de
mañana y tarde
El País

jornal *nm* (daily) wage; **jornal acumulado** = accrual of wages; **trabajar a jornal** = to be paid by the day

◊ **jornalero, -ra** *n* day labourer *o* day worker

jubilación *nf* superannuation *o* retirement (pension); **con derecho a jubilación** = entitled to a pension *o* pensionable; **jubilación anticipada** *o* **prematura** = early retirement; **tomar la jubilación anticipada** *o* **prematura** = to take early retirement; **edad de jubilación** = pensionable age *o* retirement age; **pensión de jubilación** = retirement pension; **cotizaciones a la pensión de jubilación** = pension contributions

ha podido reducir o aumentar las cuotas
del plan de pensiones o jubilación según
su deseo y el paso del tiempo
España Económica

jubilado, -da 1 *adj* retired; **la tienda es propiedad de un policía jubilado** = the shop is owned by a retired policeman **2** *n* retired person *o* old age pensioner (OAP); **la entrada para los jubilados es a mitad de precio** = old age pensioners are admitted at half price **3** *pp de* JUBILAR

jubilar *vt* **jubilar a alguien** = to pension someone off; **decidieron jubilar a todo el personal de más de 50 años** = they decided to retire all staff over 50

◊ **jubilarse** *vr* to retire (from one's job); **jubilarse anticipadamente** *o* **prematuramente** = to take early retirement; **el fundador de la compañía se jubiló a los 85 años con una pensión de 1.200.000 ptas.** = the founder of the company retired at the age of 85 with a 1.2m peseta pension; **varios empleados se jubilarán este año** = a number of the staff will be retiring this year

judice *ver* SUB JUDICE

judicial *adj* judicial *o* legal; **costas judiciales** = legal costs *o* legal charges *o* legal expenses; **mandato judicial** *o* **requerimiento judicial** = injunction; **orden judicial** = court order; **procedimientos judiciales** = judicial processes; **proceso judicial** = legal proceedings; **recurrir a la vía judicial** = to take legal action

◊ **judicialmente** *adv* judicially *o* legally; **la compañía fue intervenida judicialmente por**

quiebra = the company went into receivership; **secuestro judicial de salario** = attachment of earnings

juego *nm* **(a) impuesto sobre el juego** = betting tax **(b)** *(conjunto)* set; **juego de herramientas** *o* **juego de accesorios** = set of tools *o* set of equipment

juez *nmf* **(a)** *(magistrado)* judge; **el juez lo encarceló por desfalco** = the judge sent him to prison for embezzlement **(b)** *(árbitro)* adjudicator; **actuar de juez en un conflicto** = to adjudicate in a dispute

jugador, -ra *n* gambler

jugar *vt* to gamble; **jugar a la Bolsa** = to play the stock market

juicio *nm* **(a)** *(facultad que permite valorar las cosas)* judgement *o* judgment; **emitió un juicio negativo sobre el proyecto** = he judged the project negatively **(b)** *(opinión)* opinion; **a mi juicio** = in my opinion; **dejó la decisión a mi juicio** = he left me to decide **(c)** *(razón)* reason **(d)** *(proceso)* lawsuit; **suspender un juicio indefinidamente** = to adjourn a case sine die; **la parte acusadora pagará las costas del juicio** = the costs of the case will be borne by the prosecution **(e) juicio de faltas** = grievance procedure

junta *nf* **(a)** *(asamblea)* meeting; **los consejeros fueron de prisa a la junta** = the directors hurried into the meeting; **junta de accionistas** = meeting of shareholders *o* shareholders' meeting; **junta de dirección** = management meeting; **junta general** = general meeting; **junta general anual** = Annual General Meeting (AGM); **junta general extraordinaria** = Extraordinary General Meeting (EGM) **(b)** *(consejo)* **junta directiva** = board (of directors); **le ofrecieron formar parte de la junta** = he was asked to join the board

el consejo estaba reducido a cuatro miembros tras la tumultuosa junta de accionistas
El País

la celebración de la junta de accionistas se saldó con la salida de los representantes de familias tradicionales de la compañía
El País

juntar *vt* to join *o* to assemble; **juntaron las oficinas abriendo una puerta en la pared** = the offices were joined together by making a door in the wall; **juntaron suficiente capital para comprar la fábrica** = they raised enough money to buy the factory

◊ **juntarse** *vr* to meet *o* to assemble *o* to associate with someone; **se juntaron para discutir el problema** = they met to discuss the problem

junto, -ta 1 *adj* united *o* joined *o* together; **trabajan juntos** = they work together **2** *adv* near *o* close; **la fábrica se encuentra en un paraje muy agradable junto al mar** = the factory is in a very pleasant situation by the sea **3** *prep* **junto con** = together with

jurado, -da 1 *adj* chartered; **censor jurado de cuentas** = chartered accountant **2** *nm* jury

juramento *nm* oath; **había prestado juramento** *o* **estaba bajo juramento** = he was under oath

jurídico, -ca *adj* legal; **consultar a un asesor jurídico** = to take legal advice; **asesor jurídico** = legal adviser; **asesoría jurídica** *o* **departamento jurídico** = legal department *o* legal section; **pretensión con fundamento jurídico** = legal claim

jurisdicción *nf* **(a)** *(autoridad que da un cargo)* jurisdiction; **caer bajo la jurisdicción de** = to fall under the jurisdiction of **(b)** *(distrito)* district

jurista *nmf* legal expert

justicia *nf* justice; **tribunales de justicia** = law courts; **el Ministerio de Justicia** = the Ministry of Justice; *US* the Justice Department

justificante *nm* receipt

justificar *vt* to justify *o* to account for; **los representantes tienen que justificar sus gastos al director de ventas** = the reps have to account for all their expenses to the sales manager; **el volumen comercial que la empresa tiene con los EE UU no justifica los seis viajes anuales a Nueva York realizados por el director de ventas** = the company's volume of trade with the USA does not justify six trips a year to New York by the sales director

justo, -ta *adj* **(a)** *(que actúa con justicia)* fair *o* honest; **comercio justo** = fair trading; **trato justo** = fair deal *o* fair dealing; **los trabajadores creen que no recibieron un trato justo por parte de la dirección** = the workers feel they did not get a fair deal from the management; **prácticas comerciales justas** = fair practice; *US* fair trading *o* fair dealing; **precio justo** = fair price; **valor justo de venta** *o* **mercado** = fair market value **(b)** *(exacto)* exact *o* right; **me dieron el cambio** *o* **el dinero justo** = they gave me the exact change *o* the right money; **en el momento justo** = at the precise moment; **justo a tiempo** = just in time

el comercio justo promueve la compra de forma directa a los pueblos del sur
El País

juzgado *nm* tribunal *o* court; **juzgado de paz** = magistrates' court; **juzgado de primera instancia** = court of first instance; **juzgado de segunda instancia** = court of appeal

el juzgado de Primera Instancia número 21 de Barcelona admitió ayer a trámite el recurso presentado por el consejo
Expansión

juzgar *vt* to adjudicate *o* to judge; **juzgar una demanda** = to adjudicate a claim

Kk

Kenia *nf* Kenya

◊ **keniano, -na** *adj y n* Kenyan
NOTA: capital: **Nairobi**; moneda: **chelín keniano (KSh)** = Kenyan shilling (Ksh)

kilo *nm* (a) kilo *o* kilogram; **vender naranjas por kilos** = to sell oranges by the kilo; **un kilo de naranjas** = a kilo of oranges; **las naranjas cuestan 150 ptas. el kilo** = oranges cost 150 pesetas a kilo (b) *(informal)* one million pesetas

kilocteto *nm (= 1.024 bytes)* kilobyte (KB)

kilogramo *nm* kilogram *o* kilo (NOTA: se abrevia **kg**)

kilómetro *nm* kilometre; *US* kilometer; **el coche gasta un litro por cada quince kilómetros** = the car does fifteen kilometres to the litre (NOTA: se abrevia: **km**)

◊ **kilometraje** *nm* distance in kilometres *o* mileage

Kuwait *nm* Kuwait

◊ **kuwaití** *adj y nmf* Kuwaiti
NOTA: moneda: **dinar kuwaití (KD)** = Kuwaiti dinar (KD)

Ll

l = LITRO

labor *nf* labour *o* work *o* job; **felicitaron al presidente saliente por la labor realizada** = the outgoing president was congratulated for the work which had been done

◊ **labores** *nfpl* occupations *o* tasks; **profesión: sus labores** = profession: housewife

◊ **laborable** *adj* working; **día laborable** = working day *o* weekday; **los días laborables** = (on) weekdays

◊ **laboral** *adj* occupational; **accidente laboral** = industrial accident *o* occupational accident; **lesiones sufridas en un accidente laboral** = industrial injuries; **conflictos laborales** = industrial disputes; **derecho laboral** = labour laws *o* labour legislation; **formación laboral** = industrial training; **productividad laboral** = productivity; **riesgo laboral** = occupational hazard; **satisfacción laboral** = job satisfaction; **tregua laboral** = cooling off period

> un crecimiento más lento de la mano de obra va acompañado de un incremento en la productividad laboral
> **Mercado**

> la siniestrabilidad laboral ha aumentado en 45% entre 1987 y 1988 por causa de la generalización del trabajo precario
> **España Económica**

laboratorio *nm* laboratory; **el producto fue perfeccionado en los laboratorios de la empresa** = the product was developed in the company's laboratories; **todos los productos se someten a prueba en nuestros propios laboratorios** = all products are tested in our own laboratories

labranza *nf* farming

labrar *vt* to farm

lado *nm* side; **el lado del haber** = the credit side of the account; **dejar de lado** = to set aside

laguna *nf* loophole; **encontrar una laguna en la ley** = to find a loophole in the law; **encontrar una laguna fiscal** = to find a tax loophole

lamentar *vt* to regret; **lamentamos la demora en responder a su carta** = we regret the delay in answering your letter; **lamentamos informarles de la muerte del presidente** = we regret to inform you of the death of the chairman

lanzamiento *nm* **(a)** *(de un nuevo producto o modelo)* launch *o* launching; **artículo de lanzamiento** = loss-leader; **costes de lanzamiento** = launching costs; **fecha de lanzamiento** = launching date; **la dirección ha decidido que la fecha del lanzamiento sea en septiembre** = the management has decided that the launch will be in September *o* has decided on a September launch date; **fiesta de lanzamiento** = launching party; **oferta de lanzamiento** = promotional offer; **el lanzamiento del nuevo modelo se ha retrasado tres meses** = the launch of the new model has been put back three months; **la empresa está preparada para el lanzamiento de la nueva marca de jabón** = the company is geared up for the launch of the new brand of soap; **ambos fueron igualmente responsables del desastroso lanzamiento** = they were both equally responsible for the disastrous launch **(b)** *(de una compañía)* float *o* flotation; **el lanzamiento de una nueva compañía *o* de una sociedad** = floating *o* flotation of a new company; **el lanzamiento de la nueva empresa fue un fracaso total** = the float of the new company was a complete failure

lanzar *vt* **(a)** *(dar a conocer)* to launch; **lanzar un producto al mercado** = to bring out (a new product) *o* to bring a new product onto the market; **el nuevo modelo fue lanzado con éxito el mes pasado** = the new model was successfully launched last month; **van a lanzar un nuevo modelo del coche para el Salón del Automóvil** = they are bringing out a new model of the car for the Motor Show; **la empresa está gastando miles de libras para lanzar una nueva marca de jabón** = the company is spending thousands of pounds to launch a new brand of soap; **Pereira S.A. tiene la gran ventaja de ser la primera en lanzar al mercado un coche eléctrico de calidad** = Pereira S.A. has a great advantage in being first in the field with a reliable electric car **(b)** *(una compañía)* to float

Laos *nm* Laos

◊ **laosiano, -na** *adj y n* Laotian
NOTA: capital: **Vientiane**; moneda: **kip laosiano (KL)** = Laotian kip (KL)

lápiz *nm* pencil *o* pen; **lápiz luminoso *o* óptico *o* fotosensible** = light pen

lapso *nm* lapse of time *o* period of time

largo, -ga 1 *adj* long; **los beneficios de la compañía han descendido a lo largo de los últimos años** = the company's profits have moved downwards over the last few years; **desempleados de larga duración** = long-term unemployed; **desempleo *o* paro de larga duración** = long-term unemployment; **a largo plazo *o* a la larga** = in the long term; **crédito a largo plazo** = long credit; **garantía a largo plazo** = extended guarantee; **hacer proyectos a largo plazo** = to take the long view; **trenes de largo recorrido** = long-distance trains *o* inter-city trains; **a lo largo y ancho del país** = nationwide **2** *nm* length; **una mesa de 3m de largo** = a table 3 metres in length; **la mesa tiene 1,80 m. de largo** = the table is 1.8m long

láser *nm* laser; **impresora láser** = laser printer

lastre *nm* ballast

lealtad *nf* loyalty; **lealtad de marca** = brand loyalty

'leasing' *nm* (NOTA: del inglés) *(arriendo con opción de compra)* leasing

> el leasing o arrendamiento financiero permite financiar el 100% de cualquier tipo de maquinaria o equipo industrial
> **El País**

leer *vt* to read; **las condiciones se imprimen en letra muy pequeña para que sean difíciles de leer** = the terms and conditions are printed in very small letters so that they are difficult to read; **¿puede el ordenador leer esta información?** = can the computer read this information?; **¿ha leído el director gerente tu informe sobre las ventas en la India?** = has the managing director read your report on sales in India?

legado *nm* bequest *o* legacy; **legado de bienes raíces** = devise; **hizo varios legados a sus empleados** = he made several bequests to his staff

legal *adj* **(a)** *(lícito)* legal *o* lawful *o* judicial; **comercio legal** = lawful trade; **práctica legal** = lawful practice; **la actuación de la compañía fue completamente legal** = the company's action was completely legal; **moneda de curso legal** = legal currency *o* legal tender; **reclamación** *o* **derecho legal** = legal claim **(b)** *(estatutario)* statutory

◊ **legalmente** *adv* lawfully *o* legally; *(dentro de la ley)* inside the law *o* within the law; **sociedad constituida legalmente** = incorporated company

legalidad *nf* legality; **estar en la legalidad** = to be within the law; **existen dudas sobre la legalidad de la actuación de la compañía al despedirlo** = there is doubt about the legality of the company's action in dismissing him

legalización *nf* **(a)** *(legitimación)* legalization **(b)** *(testamento)* probate; **solicitar la legalización de un testamento** = to apply for probate

legalizar *vt* to authenticate *o* to legalize

legar *vt* to bequeath *o* to devise

legatario, -ria *n* legatee; **legatario de bienes raíces** = devisee; **legatario universal** = general legatee

legible *adj* legible *o* readable; **el aviso es perfectamente legible desde aquí** = the notice can be read easily from here; **su letra no es fácilmente legible** = his handwriting is hardly legible; **códigos legibles por la máquina** *o* **legibles por el ordenador** = machine-readable codes *o* computer-readable codes; **los datos deben presentarse en forma legible por el ordenador** = the data has to be presented in computer-readable form

legislación *nf* legislation; **legislación antidumping** = anti-dumping legislation; **legislación laboral** = labour legislation

legitimación *nf* legitimation *o* legalization

legitimar *vt* to legalize *o* to legitimize

◊ **legítimo, -ma** *adj* **(a)** *(verdadero)* genuine *o* real; **un monedero de cuero legítimo** = a genuine leather purse **(b)** *(que tiene derecho legal)* rightful; **propietario legítimo** = rightful owner; **no tiene derecho legítimo alguno sobre la propiedad** = he has no legal claim to the property

lejos *adj* far; **más lejos** = further

lengua *nf* language; **lengua materna** = native language

◊ **lenguaje** *nm* language; **lenguaje administrativo** = officialese; **lenguaje de** **programación** = programming language; **lenguaje de programación de bajo nivel** = low-level computer language; **¿con qué lenguaje funciona el programa?** = what language does the program run on?

lento, -ta *adj* slow; **un comienzo lento de las operaciones del día** = a slow start to the day's trading; **el consejo de administración es lento en tomar decisiones** = the board is slow to come to a decision; **hubo una lenta mejora en las ventas durante el primer semestre del año** = there was a slow improvement in sales in the first half of the year

◊ **lentamente** *adv* slowly; **las ventas de la empresa mejoraron lentamente** = the company's sales slowly improved; **estamos aumentando lentamente nuestra participación en el mercado** = we are slowly increasing our market share; **hoy las acciones han ido subiendo lentamente** = prices on the stock market edged upwards today

lesión *nf* injury; **indemnización por lesiones** = injury benefit; **lesiones laborales** = industrial injuries; **lesión de trabajo** = occupational injury

Letonia *nf* Latvia

◊ **letón, -ona** *adj y n* Latvian
NOTA: capital: **Riga**; moneda: **lats** = lats

letra *nf* **(a)** *(escritura)* writing *o* handwriting; **de puño y letra** = in one's handwriting *o* handwritten; **en fe de lo cual firmo de mi puño y letra** = in witness whereof I sign *o* set my hand; **le cuesta leer mi letra** = he has difficulty in reading my writing; **¿reconoces la letra de la carta?** = do you recognize the handwriting on the letter? **(b)** *(grafía, tipo de imprenta)* letter; **letras impresas** *o* **letras mayúsculas** *o* **letras de imprenta** = capital letters *o* block capitals *o* block letters; **escriba su nombre y dirección con letras mayúsculas** = write your name and address in block letters *o* in capital letters; **letras pequeñas** = fine print *o* small print *o* fine type; **leer la letra pequeña de un contrato** = to read the small print *o* the fine print on a contract; **¿leíste la letra menuda** *o* **pequeña al dorso del contrato?** = did you read the small type on the back of the contract? **(c)** *(comercial)* bill *o* draft; **letra bancaria** = bank bill; **letra de cambio** = bill of exchange; **letras de cambio de primera clase** = prime bills; **letras del tesoro** = treasury bills; **letras por cobrar** = bills receivable; **letra de complacencia** *o* **de favor** = accommodation bill; **letras no negociables** = ineligible bills; **letras por pagar** *o* **pagaderas** = bills payable; **letra pagadera a la vista** = bill payable at sight; **aceptar una letra** = to accept a bill; **agente de letras** = bill broker; **avalar una letra** = to back a bill; **descontar una letra** = to discount a bill; **devolver una letra** = to dishonour a bill; **endosar una letra** = to endorse a bill; **protestar una letra** = to protest a bill; **letra que vence el 1 de mayo** = bill due on May 1st

los perdedores del semestre son los productos bancarios y las letras del Tesoro, como consecuencia de los recortes en el precio del dinero practicados por el Banco de España

El País

letrero *nm* notice *o* sign; **el letrero dice 'se prohibe fumar'** = the notice says 'no smoking'; **letreros luminosos** = neon signs

levantar *vt* **(a)** *(aplazar)* to adjourn; **levantar una sesión** = to adjourn *o* to close a meeting; **¡se levanta la sesión!** = the meeting is adjourned **(b)** *(suprimir)* to lift *o* to remove; **levantar barreras comerciales** = to lift trade barriers; **levantar barreras arancelarias a un producto** = to lift tariff barriers from a product; **levantar un embargo** = to lift an embargo; **el ministro ha levantado el embargo a la exportación de ordenadores a los países de Europa del Este** = the minister has lifted the embargo on the export of computers to East European countries; **el gobierno ha levantado el embargo sobre la importación de productos japoneses** = the government has removed the ban on imports from Japan **(c)** *(en una reunión)* **levantar acta** = to take the minutes (of a meeting)

◊ **levantarse** *vr* to get up *o* to stand up; **todos se levantaron cuando el presidente entró en la sala** = they all stood up when the chairman entered the room

ley *nf* **(a)** *(derecho)* law; **ley de la oferta y la demanda** = law of supply and demand; **ley de Parkinson** = Parkinson's law; **ley de prescripción** = statute of limitations; **ley de rendimientos decrecientes** = law of diminishing returns **(b)** **ley sobre la propiedad intelectual** = copyright law; **ley de sociedades anónimas** = company law; **dentro de la ley** = inside the law *o* within the law; **fuera de la ley** = against *o* outside the law; **la empresa está actuando fuera de la ley** = the company is operating outside the law; **encontrar una laguna en la ley** = to find a loophole in the law; **infringir la ley** = to break the law; **infringirás la ley si intentas sacar este ordenador fuera del país sin una licencia de exportación** = you will be breaking the law if you try to take that computer out of the country without an export licence; **los consejeros son responsables ante la ley** = the directors are legally responsible **(c)** *(parlamento)* act (of Parliament); **el gobierno ha promulgado una ley 'anti-dumping'** = the government has passed anti-dumping legislation; **Ley bancaria** = National Bank Act; **Ley de expansión industrial** = Industrial Expansion Act; **ley de Pareto** = Pareto's law; **Ley presupuestaria** = Finance Act; **Ley de seguridad vial** = Road Safety Act; **Ley de la Seguridad Social** = Social Security Act; **Ley de servicios financieros** = Financial Services Act; **Ley de sociedades anónimas** = Companies Act; **Ley de sociedades de inversión** = Investment Companies Act; **Ley de transportes** = Transport Act; **código de leyes** = statute book

el Gobierno ha identificado con acierto la falta de competencia en el sector de servicios como causa de la inflación y está preparando nuevas leyes para incrementar su potencia

Actualidad Económica

la ley considera que la residencia habitual se encuentra situada en territorio español cuando la persona vive en él más de 183 días al año o tiene en el mismo la base principal de sus actividades profesionales o empresariales

El País

Líbano *nm* Lebanon

◊ **libanés, -esa** *adj y n* Lebanese
NOTA: capital: **Beirut**; moneda: **libra libanesa (LL)** = Lebanese pound (LL)

libelo *nm* libel

liberación *nf* release; **liberación de derechos** = release of rights

liberado, -da 1 *adj* paid-up; **acciones liberadas** = paid-up shares **2** *pp de* LIBERAR

liberalización *nf* deregulation *o* decontrol *o* liberalization; **la liberalización de las compañías aéreas** = the deregulation of the airlines; **liberalización de precios** = decontrol

la liberalización de las líneas aéreas ha sido un gran éxito porque los precios al consumidor han bajado sustancialmente

Mercado

liberalizar *vt* to decontrol *o* to deregulate; **liberalizar el precio de la gasolina** = to decontrol the price of petrol; **el gobierno de EE.UU liberalizó el sector bancario en los años 80** = the US government deregulated the banking sector in the 1980's

liberar *vt* to free *o* to release; **liberar a alguien de una deuda** = to release someone from a debt; **la decisión del gobierno ha liberado millones de libras para la inversión** = the government's decision to free millions of pounds for investment

Liberia *nf* Liberia

◊ **liberiano, -na** *adj y n* Liberian
NOTA: capital: **Monrovia**; moneda: **dólar liberiano** = Liberian dollar

libertad *nf* liberty *o* freedom; **obtener la libertad de alguien bajo fianza** = to bail someone out; **libertad de elección** = freedom of choice

Libia *nf* Libya

◊ **libio, -bia** *adj y n* Libyan
NOTA: capital: **Trípoli** (= Tripoli); moneda: **dinar libio (LD)** = Libyan dinar (LD)

libra *nf* **(a)** *(moneda)* pound; *(informal)* quid; **la libra abandonó el patrón-oro** = the pound came off the gold standard; **libra esterlina** = pound sterling; **área de la libra esterlina** = sterling area; **libra irlandesa** = Irish pound *o* punt; **un billete de cinco libras** = a five pound note; **una moneda de una libra** = a pound coin; **la caída de la libra en los mercados de divisas** = the pound's slump on the foreign exchange markets; **la libra cayó frente a otras monedas europeas** = the pound fell against other European currencies; **cuesta seis libras** = it costs six pounds; **crisis de la libra** = sterling crisis; **la flotación de la libra** = the floating of the pound **(b)** *(medida de peso = 0.45 kilos)* pound

librado, -da 1 *adj* **pagó la factura con un cheque librado contra un banco egipcio** = he paid the invoice with a cheque drawn on an Egyptian bank **2** *n* drawee **3** *pp de* LIBRAR

librador, -ra *n* drawer; **el banco devolvió el cheque al librador** = the bank returned the cheque to drawer; **'remitir al librador'** = 'refer to drawer'

libramiento *nm* order for payment *o* bank draft *o* bank mandate

librar *vt* **(a)** *(de una situación difícil)* to free *o* to rescue **(b)** *(expedir)* to draw (a cheque)

libre *adj* **(a)** *(desocupado)* free; **¿hay mesas libres en el restaurante?** = are there any free tables in the restaurant?; **estaré libre en unos minutos** = I shall be free in a few minutes **(b)** *(sin restricciones)* free; **libre comercio** *o* **cambio** = free trade; **el gobierno adoptó una política de libre comercio** = the government adopted a free trade policy; **área de libre comercio** = free trade area; **partidario del libre comercio** = free trader; **libre competencia** = free competition; **libre empresa** = free enterprise; **libre de impuestos** = free of tax *o* tax-free; **le dieron un total de 5.000.000 de ptas. libres de impuestos cuando le despidieron** = he was given a tax-free sum of 5m pesetas when he was made redundant; **interés libre de impuestos** = interest free of tax *o* tax-free interest; **libre de derechos de aduana** *o* **de impuestos** = free of duty *o* duty-free; **agente libre de seguros** = insurance broker; **se estableció como agente libre de seguros** = he set up in business as an insurance broker; **convenio colectivo libre** = free collective bargaining; **flotación libre** = clean float; **mercado libre** = open market; **moneda de libre circulación** = free currency; **de venta libre** = over the counter **(c)** *(vacante)* vacant; **libre de inquilinos** = with vacant possession; **la casa está en venta y libre de inquilinos** = the house is for sale with vacant possession; **la propiedad ha de venderse libre de inquilinos** = the property is to be sold with vacant possession **(d)** *(independientemente)* **por libre** = freelance; **tenemos a tres personas trabajando por libre** = we have three people working on a freelance basis **(e)** **tiempo libre** = spare time; **tomarse el día libre** = to take the day off; **mañana es el día libre de la secretaria** = it is the secretary's day off tomorrow

◊ **librecambista** *nmf* *(partidario del libre comercio)* free trader

◊ **libremente** *adv* freely; **el dinero debería circular libremente dentro de la Unión Europea** = money should circulate freely within the European Market

librería *nf* bookshop; *US* bookstore

librero, -ra 1 *n* bookseller **2** *nm* bookcase

libreta *nf* booklet *o* notebook; **libreta de ahorros** = bank book; **libreta de depósitos** *o* **libreta de depósitos bancarios** = passbook *o* paying-in book

libro *nm* **(a)** book; **libro de hojas sueltas** = loose-leaf book; **libro de muestras** = pattern book **(b)** **los libros de una compañía** = a company's books; **llevar los libros de una empresa** = to keep the books of a company *o* to keep a company's books **(c)** **libro de actas** = minutebook; **libro de caja** = cash book; **libro de caja auxiliar** *o* **para gastos menores** = petty cash book; **libro de compras** = purchase book; **encargado del libro de compras** = bought ledger clerk; **libro de contabilidad** = account book; **libro de cuentas** = account book; **libro diario** = journal; **libro diario de ventas** = sales journal *o* sales day book; **libro de direcciones** = address book; **libro de inventario** = stock ledger; **libro mayor** = ledger; **libro mayor de compras** = bought ledger *o* purchase ledger; **libro mayor de resultados** = nominal ledger; **libro mayor de salarios** = payroll ledger; **libro mayor de ventas** = sales ledger; **libro de pedidos** = order book; **la empresa tiene el libro de pedidos completo** = the company has a full order book; **libro de ventas** = sales book; **encargado del libro de ventas** = sales ledger clerk

licencia *nf* **(a)** *(permiso)* permit *o* licence; *US* license; *(Latinoamérica)* **licencia de conducir** = driving licence; *US* driver's license; **licencia de exportación** = export licence *o* export permit; **licencia de importación** = import licence *o* import permit; **licencia de obras** = building permit; **licencia de venta de armamentos** = licence to sell arms; **conceder una licencia** = to license; **mercancías fabricadas bajo licencia** = goods manufactured under licence; **persona que tiene una licencia** = licensee; **tiene licencia para dirigir una agencia de colocación** = she is licensed to run an employment agency **(b)** *(franquicia)* franchise *o* franchising *o* licensing; **ha comprado una licencia para imprimir** = he has bought a printing franchise; **un contrato de licencia** = a licensing agreement; **persona que concede franquicias** = franchiser **(c)** *(permiso de estar ausente)* leave; **licencia por enfermedad** = sick leave; **licencia por maternidad** = maternity leave; **licencia por paternidad** = paternity leave

licenciado, -da *n* graduate; **licenciado en prácticas** = graduate trainee

licenciatario *nm* franchisee

licitación *nf* tendering; **para tener éxito hay que seguir el procedimiento de licitación que se explica en los documentos** = to be successful, you must follow the tendering procedure as laid out in the documents

◊ **licitador, -ra** *n* tenderer *o* bidder

lícito, -ta *adj* lawful *o* legal; **medio lícito** = legal means

líder 1 *adj* leading; **empresa líder del sector** *o* **artículo líder** = a market leader; **somos la empresa líder en el mercado de ordenadores personales** = we are the market leader in home computers **2** *nmf* *(persona)* leader

◊ **liderazgo** *o* **liderato** *nm* leadership

> es normal que el líder del banco emisor proclame sus ideas sobre política económica
> **España Económica**

> con toda Asia dispuesta a concentrarse en el desarrollo económico, Japón se convierte en el líder natural de Asia
> **Actualidad Económica**

> a pesar del liderazgo de las multinacionales y de los grandes grupos nacionales en el sector de empresas de trabajo temporal se están manteniendo también compañías de fuerte implantación local y regional
> **El País**

Liechtenstein *nm* Liechtenstein
NOTA: capital: **Vaduz**; moneda: **franco suizo** = Swiss franc

ligero, -ra *adj* **(a)** *(no pesado)* light; **industria ligera** = light industry **(b)** *(pequeño)* slight *o* small; **comprobamos un ligero aumento de las ventas en febrero** = we saw a slight increase in sales in February **(c)** *(locución)* **hacer algo a la ligera** = to do something superficially

◇ **ligeramente** *adv* a little *o* slightly; **las ventas bajaron ligeramente durante el segundo semestre** = sales fell slightly in the second quarter

limitación *nf* limit *o* limitation *o* restriction; **limitación de la responsabilidad** = limitation of liability; **el contrato impone limitaciones al número de coches que pueden importarse** = the contract imposes limits on the number of cars which can be imported

limitado, -da 1 *adj* limited; **no limitado** = unlimited *o* open-ended; **tenemos solamente un número limitado de posibles proveedores** = we have only a limited choice of suppliers; **mercado limitado** = limited market; **vender en un mercado limitado** = to sell into a restricted market; **sociedad de responsabilidad limitada (S.R.L.)** = limited liability company; **sociedad limitada (S.L.)** = private limited company; **sociedad personal de responsabilidad limitada** = limited partnership **2** *pp de* LIMITAR

limitar *vt* to limit *o* to restrict *o* to cap; **limitar el crédito** = to restrict credit; **los bancos han limitado su crédito** = the banks have limited their credit; **limitar el capital destinado a la inversión** = to ration investment capital *o* to ration funds for investment; **limitar las importaciones** = to set limits to imports *o* to impose import limits; **limitar los fondos disponibles para hipotecas** = to ration mortgages; **el tamaño de nuestras oficinas nos obliga a limitar la plantilla a veinte empleados** = we are restricted by the size of our offices to twenty staff; **el gobierno espera limitar las subidas salariales al 5%** = the government hopes to restrict *o* to hold wage increases to 5%; **limitar el alza del coste de la vida** = to control the rise in the cost of living; **limitar el presupuesto municipal** = to cap a local authority's budget

limitativo, -va *adj* limiting; **la corta temporada de vacaciones es un factor limitativo del negocio hotelero** = the short holiday season is a limiting factor on the hotel trade

límite *nm* limit; **límite de caja** = cash limit; **límite de crédito** = credit limit *o* lending limit; **ha excedido su límite de crédito** = he has exceeded his credit limit; **límite de descubierto** = overdraft facility; **límite de edad** = age limit; **cada representante tiene un límite de veinticinco unidades** = each agent is limited to twenty-five units; **plazo de tiempo límite** = time limitation; **exceder el límite de velocidad** = to go over the speed limit

limpio, -pia 1 *adj* clean *o* tidy; **juego limpio** = fair play; **manos limpias** = clean hands **2** *nm* **copia en limpio** = fair copy; **pasó a limpio sus notas de las actas de la reunión** = she wrote out the minutes of the meeting from her notes

línea *nf* **(a)** *(raya)* line; **impresora de líneas** = line printer; **línea de puntos** = dotted line; **firme por favor en la línea de puntos** = please sign on the dotted line; **no escriba nada por debajo de la línea de puntos** = do not write anything below the dotted line; **leer entre líneas** = to read between the lines **(b)** *(cadena)* line; **línea de montaje** = assembly line; **línea de productos** = product line **(c)** **conceder** *o* **abrir una línea de crédito** = to open a line of credit *o* a credit line **(d)** **línea de carga** *o* **de flotación** =

load line **(e)** *(telecomunicación)* **línea telefónica** = telephone line; **cruce de líneas** = a crossed line; **señal de línea** = dialling tone; **la línea está ocupada** = the line is engaged; **el presidente está hablando por la otra línea** = the chairman is on the other line; **se cortó la línea telefónica** = the line went dead; **línea exterior** = outside line **(f)** *(vía de transporte)* **línea aérea** = (i) airline; (ii) air route; **línea marítima** = shipping company *o* shipping line; *(ferroviaria)* **cabeza de línea** = railhead **(g)** *(informática)* **en línea** = on line *o* online **(h)** *(electricidad)* cable **(i) por encima de la línea** *o* **sobre la línea** = above the line; **las partidas excepcionales se anotan sobre la línea en las cuentas de la compañía** = exceptional items are notes above the line in company accounts

◇ **lineal** *adj* **(a)** *(relacionado con la línea)* linear; **dibujo lineal** = technical drawing *o* line drawing; **función lineal** = linear function; **gráfico lineal** = line chart *o* line graph **(b)** *(global)* across-the-board; **aumento lineal** = across-the-board pay increase **(c) gestión lineal** *o* **organización lineal** = line management *o* line organization

lingote *nm* ingot; **mercado de lingotes** = bullion market

lío *nm* mix-up *o* problem; **hacer un lío** = to get mixed up; **está metido en un gran lío** = he has got himself in a big mix-up; **el director tiene líos serios** = the manager has serious problems

liquidación *nf* **(a)** *(negocio)* winding up *o* liquidation; **liquidación de activo** = realization of assets; **liquidación de una deuda** = liquidation *o* clearing of a debt; **liquidación forzosa** = compulsory liquidation; **una orden forzosa de liquidación** = a compulsory winding-up order; **liquidación voluntaria** = voluntary liquidation; **sociedad entró en liquidación** = the company went into liquidation; **la compañía está en liquidación** = the company is in the hands of the receiver **(b)** *(bolsa)* **día de liquidación** = settlement day; **fecha de liquidación** = settlement date **(c)** sale *o* bargain sale *o* clearance sale *o* fire sale; **liquidación total por cierre** = closing-down sale; *US* close-out sale; **tenemos una liquidación de existencias sobrantes** = we are holding a sale of surplus stock; **la tienda hace una liquidación de artículos defectuosos** = the shop has a sale of seconds; **'liquidación de modelos de demostración'** = 'demonstration models to clear'

liquidar *vt* **(a)** *(saldar)* to settle *o* to pay; **liquidar una deuda** = to liquidate *o* to clear a debt; **la compañía ha liquidado sus deudas por primera vez desde 1990** = the company is out of the red for the first time since 1990; **liquidar una reclamación** = to settle a claim **(b)** *(vender)* to liquidate *o* to realize; **liquidar el activo** = to realize one's assets *o* to go liquid; **liquidar las existencias** = to liquidate stock; **liquidar las existencias de artículos defectuosos** = to sell off reject stock; **liquidamos el exceso de existencias** = we are holding a sale of surplus stock; **liquidar propiedades** = to realize property; **no le gustó el informe anual, así que liquidó su participación antes de que la empresa se viniera abajo** = he didn't like the annual report, so he got out before the company collapsed **(c)** *(eliminar)* **liquidar la competencia** = to freeze out competition **(d)** *(negocio)* to sell out; **liquidar una sociedad** = to wind up a company *o* to put a company into liquidation; **liquidar un negocio con todas sus existencias** = to sell up

liquidez *nf* liquidity; **coeficiente de liquidez** = liquidity ratio *o* acid test ratio; **crisis de liquidez** = liquidity crisis; **liquidez secundaria** = secondary reserves

líquido, -da 1 *adj* liquid; **saldo líquido** = balance in hand *o* cash in hand **2** *nm* **(a) líquido corrector** = correction fluid **(b) líquido imponible** = taxable earnings

lira *nf (moneda de Italia)* lira; **el libro costó 2.700 liras** = the book cost 2,700 lira *o* L2,700

liso, -sa *adj* simple *o* plain *o* flat; **el diseño del paquete es a cuadros lisos azules y blancos** = the design of the package is in plain blue and white squares; **un acabado liso** = a smooth finish; **superficie lisa** = flat surface

lista *nf* **(a)** *(relación de nombres, artículos)* list; **lista adjunta** = attached list *o* schedule; **véase la lista adjunta** *o* **según la lista adjunta** = see the attached list *o* as per the attached schedule; **lista de comprobación** = checklist; **lista de contenidos** *o* **lista del contenido de un paquete** = packing list *o* packing slip; **lista de correos** = poste restante *o* General Delivery; **lista de direcciones** *o* **destinatarios** = address list *o* mailing list; **su nombre está en nuestra lista de destinatarios** = his name is on our mailing list; **comprar una lista de destinatarios** = to buy a mailing list; **confeccionar una lista de destinatarios** = to build up a mailing list; **lista de distribución** = distribution slip; **lista de espera** = waiting list; **billete en lista de espera** = standby ticket; **lista de existencias** = stocklist; **lista negra** = black list; **poner en la lista negra** = to blacklist; **el gobierno puso a su empresa en la lista negra** = his firm was blacklisted by the government; **lista de pasajeros** = passenger list *o* manifest; **hacer una lista** = to list *o* to make a list; **hacer una lista de productos por categorías** = to list products by category; **hacer una lista de representantes por zonas** = to list representatives by area; **está en la lista de candidatos escogidos** = he is on the shortlist for the job; **añadir un artículo a una lista** = to add an item to a list; **tachar un artículo de una lista** = to cross an item off a list; **lista de suscriptores de valores** = subscription list; **lista de territorios en los que tiene validez un contrato** = schedule of territories to which a contract applies **(b)** *(catálogo)* **lista de precios** = price list; **adjuntamos nuestra lista de precios** = please find enclosed our price list *o* our schedule of charges; **distribuyeron una nueva lista de precios a todos los clientes** = they circulated a new list of prices to all their customers; **lista de productos** = list of products *o* product list **(c)** *(informática)* **lista de opciones** = menu

◊ **listado** *nm (informática)* listing *o* printout

listo, -ta *adj* **(a)** *(inteligente)* clever **(b)** *(preparado)* ready; **listo para vender** = off-the-shelf; **el pedido estará listo para su entrega la**

semana que viene = the order will be ready for delivery next week

litigio *nm* litigation; **litigio internacional** = international dispute; **en litigio** = in dispute

litro *nm* litre; *US* liter; **el coche consume unos 7 litros por 100 kilómetros** = the car does fifteen kilometres to the litre *o* fifteen kilometres per litre; **un cuarto de litro** = a quarter of a litre *o* a quarter litre (NOTA: abreviado es: **l**)

llamada *nf* **(a)** *(teléfono)* call; **llamada a cobro revertido** = reverse charge call *o* transferred charge call; *US* collect call; **llamada de fuera** = incoming call; **llamada internacional** = overseas call *o* international call; **llamada internacional directa** = international direct dialling; **llamada interurbana** = trunk call *o* long-distance call; **llamada local** = local call; **llamada telefónica** = phone call; **llamadas telefónicas gratuitas** = freephone *o* freefone; **devolver una llamada** = to phone back; **hacer una llamada (telefónica)** = to make a (phone) call; **recibir una llamada** = to take a call **(b)** **llamada a la huelga** = strike call

llamar *vt* **(a)** *(nombrar)* to name *o* to call **(b)** *(teléfono)* to phone *o* to call *o* to dial; **llamar a Nueva York** *o* **a Juan** = to telephone New York *o* to phone Juan; **no me llames, ya te llamaré yo** = don't phone me, I'll phone you; **llamar por teléfono** = to call *o* to phone *o* to ring; **le llamaré mañana a su oficina** = I'll call you at your office tomorrow; **llamó a su agente de bolsa** = he rang (up) his stockbroker; **llamar a la telefonista** = to call the operator *o* to dial the operator; **puede llamar a Nueva York desde Madrid marcando directamente el número** = you can dial New York direct from Madrid; **llamar para pedir algo** = to phone for something; **volver a llamar** = to call back *o* to ring back; **el presidente está en una reunión, ¿puede Vd. volver a llamar dentro de una media hora?** = the chairman is in a meeting, can you phone back in about half an hour?; **llamó el director gerente ¿puedes devolverle la llamada?** = the managing director rang - can you ring him back? **(c)** *(dirigirse a alguien)* to send for; **mandó llamar al jefe de contabilidad** = he sent for the chief accountant **(d)** *(convocar)* **llamar a la huelga** = to call a strike

llave *nf* key; **llave maestra** = master key; **hemos perdido las llaves del cuarto de ordenadores** = we have lost the keys to the computer room; **'llave en mano'** = with vacant possession; **una operación llaves en mano** = turnkey operation; **la llave del éxito** = the key to success

llegada *nf* **(a)** arrival; **esperar la llegada** = 'to await arrival'; **esperamos la llegada de un envío de repuestos** = we are waiting for the arrival of a consignment of spare parts; **hora estimada de llegada** = estimated time of arrival (ETA); **se les notificó la llegada del envío** = they were notified of the arrival of the shipment **(b)** *(aeropuerto)* **llegadas** = arrivals

llegar *vi* **(a)** **llegar a** = to arrive at *o* to reach *o* to get (to); **su secretaria llamó por teléfono para decir que llegaría tarde** = his secretary telephoned to say he would be late; **el envío todavía no ha llegado** = the consignment has still not arrived; **el envío llegó sin documentación alguna** = the shipment arrived without any documentation; **el cargamento llegó a**

Argentina con seis semanas de retraso = the shipment got to *o* reached Argentina six weeks late; **llegó por fin a la oficina a las 10.30** = she finally got to the office at 10.30; **haremos un desembolso inicial de 2.000.000 de ptas. y el resto les llegará a los seis meses** = we will pay 2m pesetas down, with the balance to follow in six months' time **(b)** *(convenir)* **llegar a** = to arrive at *o* to reach; **llegar a un acuerdo** = to come to an agreement *o* to reach an agreement *o* to strike a bargain with someone *o* to hammer out an agreement; **se ha llegado a un acuerdo entre la dirección y los sindicatos** = an agreement has been reached between the management and the trade unions; **llegar a un arreglo** = to compromise; **llegar a una conclusión** = to reach a conclusion **(c) hacer llegar el dinero** *o* **el sueldo** = to make ends meet

llenar *vt* **(a)** to fill (up) *o* to top up; **llenó de gasolina el depósito del coche** = he filled up the car with petrol; **el departamento de fabricación ha llenado el almacén de artículos invendibles** = the production department has filled the warehouse with unsellable products; **llenar un vacío** = to fill a gap; **la nueva gama de coches pequeños llena un vacío en el mercado** = the new range of small cars fills a gap in the market; **este ordenador ha venido a llenar una necesidad que existía en el mercado** = this computer has filled a real gap in the market **(b)** *(poner dentro de sobres, cajas)* to stuff *o* to fill; **pagamos a los trabajadores eventuales 400 ptas. la hora por llenar sobres** = we pay casual workers 400 pesetas an hour for stuffing envelopes *o* for envelope stuffing

lleno, -na *adj* full; **¿está ya lleno el contenedor** *o* **el recipiente?** = is the container full yet?; **enviamos un camión lleno de piezas de recambio a nuestro almacén** = we sent a lorry full of spare parts to our warehouse; **mi agenda está completamente llena** = my appointments book is completely filled up; **cuando el disco esté lleno, no te olvides de hacer una copia de reserva** = when the disk is full, don't forget to make a backup copy

llevar *vt* **(a)** *(de un lugar a otro)* to transport *o* to carry *o* to take; **llevaremos a los visitantes a la fábrica en autocar** = we'll take the visitors to the factory by coach; **el tren llevaba un contingente de automóviles para la exportación** = the train was carrying a consignment of cars for export; **una comida para llevar** = a takeaway meal; **venta de comidas para llevar** = sales of food to take away **(b) llevar a** = to lead (up) to; **llevar a un acuerdo a las dos partes** = to effect a settlement between two parties; **llevar a alguien ante los tribunales** = to take someone to court **(c)** *(tener)* to bear *o* to carry; **el cheque lleva la firma del secretario de la compañía** = the cheque bears the signature of the company secretary; **una carta que lleva la fecha de ayer** = a letter bearing yesterday's date; **el certificado de las acciones lleva su nombre** = the share certificate bears his name **(d)** *(dirigir)* to manage *o* to run; **lleva un negocio de venta por correo desde su domicilio** = she runs a mail-order business from home; **llevar los libros** *o* **la contabilidad de una empresa** = to keep the books of a company *o* to keep a company's books; **llevar negociaciones** = to conduct negotiations **(e)** *(cumplir)* **llevar a cabo** = to implement **(f)** *(transcurso de tiempo)* to have been *o* to take; **la tienda lleva abierta seis años** = the shop has been

open (for) six years; **le llevará toda la mañana escribir mis cartas** = it will take her all morning to do my letters

◊ **llevarse** *vr* **(a)** to take away *o* to remove; **la policía se llevó montones de documentos de la oficina** = the police took away piles of documents from the office **(b) llevarse bien** = to get on with; **no se lleva bien con su nuevo jefe** = she does not get on with her new boss

local 1 *adj* local; **administración local** = local government; **autoridad local** = local authority; **hora local** = local time; **llamada local** = local call; **mano de obra local** = local labour **2** *nm* premises; **en el local** = on the premises; **local comercial** = business premises *o* commercial premises; **local de una oficina** *o* **de una tienda** = office premises *o* shop premises; **local de exposición** = exhibition stand; **local con vivienda incorporada** = business premises with living accommodation; **local sin vivienda incorporada** = lock-up premises

◊ **localidad** *nf* **(a)** *(local)* locality *o* place; **de la localidad** = local *o* locally; **los empresarios de la localidad** = the local business community **(b)** *(cine o teatro)* seat *o* place; **venta de localidades** = sale of tickets

◊ **localización** *nf* location *o* situation; **localización geográfica** = geographical location

◊ **localmente** *adv* locally

'lock-out' *nm* lockout

lógico, -ca 1 *adj* **(a)** *(natural)* logical *o* natural; **es lógico que quiera cambiar de trabajo, le pagan muy mal** = it's only natural that he should want to change jobs as he is very badly paid **(b)** *(informática)* **componentes lógicos** = software **2** *nf* lógica = logic *o* rationale; **no entiendo la lógica de la decisión de vender el almacén** = I do not understand the rationale behind the decision to sell the warehouse; **una decisión sin lógica** = a stupid decision; **es un argumento sin lógica** = the argument is faulty

logotipo *nm* logo

> hay que reconocer que nuestro logotipo es todo un acierto. Es más fácil para el cliente recordar únicamente un número y una letra que el nombre
>
> **El País**

lograr *vt* **(a)** *(alcanzar)* to achieve; **la empresa ha logrado grandes éxitos en el Extremo Oriente** = the company has achieved great success in the Far East **(b)** *(adquirir)* to get *o* to gain; **lograr el control de un negocio** = to gain control of a business

logro *nm* achievement; **logros técnicos** = technical achievements

longitud *nf* length; **las pulgadas y los centímetros son medidas de longitud** = inches and centimetres are measurements of length; **la mesa de la sala de juntas tiene 3m 50cm de longitud** = the boardroom table is 3.5m long

lonja *nf* market *o* mart; **lonja de contratación** = commodity exchange *o* commodity market

lote *nm* **(a)** *(parte de un conjunto)* lot; **pujar por el lote 23** = to bid for lot 23; **al terminar la subasta la**

mitad de los lotes quedaron sin vender = at the end of the auction half the lots were unsold; **vender acciones en lotes pequeños** = to sell shares in small lots **(b)** *(grupo)* batch *o* pack; **lote de artículos** = pack of items; **lote de artículos varios** = job lot *o* odd lot; **este lote de zapatos lleva el número de serie 25-02** = this batch of shoes has the serial number 25-02 **(c)** *(ordenadores)* **procesamiento por lotes** = batch processing

lotería *nf* lottery

lucha *nf* fight *o* struggle *o* battle; **luchas en el seno del consejo de administración** = boardroom battles

lucrativo, -va *adj* lucrative *o* profitable *o* profit-making *o* money-making; **finalidad lucrativa** = profit motive; **no lucrativo** = unprofitable; **sin fines lucrativos** = non profit-making; **las organizaciones sin fines lucrativos están exentas de impuestos** = non profit-making organizations are exempt from tax

◊ **lucrativamente** *adv* profitably

lucro *nm* profit; **lucro cesante** = loss of profit; **afán de lucro** = profit motive; **empresa con fines de lucro** = profit-oriented company

luego *adv* then *o* later; **desde luego** = of course; **hasta luego** = see you later

lugar *nm* **(a)** *(sitio)* place *o* point *o* spot *o* site; **lugar de operaciones** = dealing *o* trading floor; **lugar de reunión** = meeting place; **hemos cambiado el lugar de la reunión** = we have changed the venue for the conference; **lugar seguro** = safe keeping; **lugar de trabajo** = place of work *o* workplace; **tenemos un representante en el lugar para ocuparse de cualquier problema que surja en la obra** = we have a man on the spot to deal with any problems which happen on the building site; **¿dónde tiene lugar la exposición?** = what is the venue for the exhibition? **(b)** *(posición)* place; **tres empresas luchan por el primer lugar en el mercado nacional de ordenadores** = three companies are fighting for first place in the home computer market;

ocupar el lugar de alguien temporalmente = to take someone's place temporarily; **ponerse en lugar de alguien** = to put oneself in someone's place; **en lugar de** = instead of *o* in lieu of; **en lugar de ir al trabajo se fue a comprar** = instead of going to work he went shopping; **le dieron dos meses de sueldo en lugar del aviso de despido** = she was given two months' salary in lieu of notice; **en primer lugar** = primarily *o* in the first place **(c) dar lugar** = to result in; **tener lugar** = to take place; **la reunión tendrá lugar en nuestras oficinas** = the meeting will take place in our offices; **la exposición tiene lugar en el palacio de congresos** = the exhibition is being staged in the conference centre

lujo *nm* luxury; **artículos de lujo** = luxury items *o* luxury goods; **un mercado negro en artículos de lujo** = a black market in luxury articles; **impuesto sobre los artículos de lujo** = tax on luxury items; **los artículos de lujo están sujetos a un impuesto elevado** = luxury items are heavily taxed; **el gobierno impuso elevados impuestos a los artículos de lujo** = the government imposed a heavy tax on luxury goods

◊ **lujoso, -sa** *adj* luxurious *o* luxury

luminoso, -sa *adj* bright *o* luminous; **idea luminosa** = bright idea; **lápiz luminoso** = light pen; **letreros luminosos** = neon signs

lusitano, -na *o* **luso, -sa** *adj y n* Portuguese

lustro *nm* five-year period

> parece que ahora hay menos nubes en el horizonte económico japonés que el último lustro
>
> **Actualidad Económica**

Luxemburgo *nm* Luxembourg

◊ **luxemburgués, -esa** *adj & n* Luxembourgois *o* Luxembourger *o* Luxemburger moneda: **franco luxemburgués (FLux)** = Luxembourg franc (LuxF)

luz *nf* light; **luz verde** = green light

Mm

m = METRO

macro *prefijo* macro-

◇ **macroeconomía** *nf* macro-economics

Madagascar *nm* Madagascar

◇ **malgache** *adj y n* Madagascan
NOTA: capital: **Antananarivo;** moneda: **franco malgache (FMG)** = Malagasy franc (FMG)

madrina *nf (de fundación o asociación)* patron; *(de candidato)* sponsor

madrugada *nf* early morning; **el avión llega a Madrid a las 4.00 de la madrugada** = the plane arrives in Madrid at 04.00 a.m.

maduro, -ra *adj* **(a)** *(fruta)* ripe **(b)** *(experimentado)* mature; **economía madura** = mature economy; **edad madura** = maturity

magiar *adj y nmf* Hungarian

magistrado, -da *n* magistrate *o* judge

magistratura *nf* **(a) magistratura de trabajo** = industrial tribunal **(b) la magistratura del país** = the country's legal profession **(c) durante su magistratura** = during his period in office

magnate *nm* magnate *o* tycoon; **magnate de la industria naviera** = a shipping magnate

> hace unos años al magnate recientemente fallecido le dieron calabazas en sus merodeos por el mercado español
> **Cambio 16**

magnético, -ca *adj* magnetic; **banda magnética** = magnetic strip; **tarjeta magnética** = magnetic card

magnífico, -ca *adj* magnificent; **explicó su magnífico plan para la reorganización del solar de la fábrica** = he explained his grand plan for redeveloping the factory site

mal 1 *adj (apócope de malo delante de nms)* bad; **es un mal asunto** = it is a bad bargain *o* nasty business; **es mal momento para hacer negocios** = it's the wrong time to do business **2** *adv* badly *o* poorly; **las oficinas están mal distribuidas** = the offices are poorly laid out; **mal equipado** = badly equipped *o* underequipped; **el plan se presentó mal** = the plan was poorly presented; **mal pagado** = badly paid *o* underpaid; **personal mal pagado** = poorly-paid staff; **preguntó si algo iba mal** = he inquired if anything was wrong; *(teléfono)* **se oye mal** = the line is bad

Malasia *nf* Malaysia

◇ **malasio, -sia** *adj* Malaysian
NOTA: capital: **Kuala Lumpur;** moneda: **ringgit malasio (M$)** = Malaysian ringgit (M$)

Malawi *nm* Malawi

◇ **malawiano, -na** *adj y n* Malawian
NOTA: capital: **Lilongwe;** moneda: **kwacha malawiano (Mk)** = Malawi kwacha (Mk)

malentendido *nm* misunderstanding; **hubo un malentendido con mis entradas** = there was a misunderstanding over my tickets

maleta *nf* **(a)** case *o* suitcase; **el funcionario de la aduana le hizo abrir sus tres maletas** = the customs officer made him open his three suitcases; **tenía una maleta pequeña que llevó en el avión** = she had a small case which she carried onto the plane **(b) maletas** = luggage *o* baggage; **hacer las maletas** = to pack one's bags *o* to pack up

maletín *nm* attaché case *o* briefcase

malgastar *vt* to waste; **malgastar dinero** = to waste money

Mali *nm* Mali

◇ **maliense** *adj y n* Malian
NOTA: capital: **Bamako;** moneda: **franco CFA (FCFA)** = CFA franc (CFAF)

malo, -la *adj* bad *o* poor (quality); **ni bueno ni malo** = mixed *o* middling; **mala administración** *o* **dirección** *o* **gestión** = maladministration *o* mismanagement; **el grupo se ve perjudicado por una mala gestión** *o* **administración** = the group suffers from bad management; **mala calidad** = poor quality; **una mala compra** = a bad buy; **un mal negocio** = a bad bargain

Malta *nf* Malta

◇ **maltés, -esa** *adj y n* Maltese
NOTA: capital: **Valletta;** moneda: **lira maltesa (Lm)** = Maltese lira (Lm)

malversación *nf* embezzlement *o* misappropriation; **malversación de fondos** = misappropriation of funds

◇ **malversador, -ra** *n* embezzler

malversar *vt* to embezzle *o* to misappropriate; **estuvo en la cárcel seis meses por malversar fondos de sus clientes** = he was sent to prison for six months for embezzling his clients' money

Malvinas, Islas *nfpl* Falkland Islands

◇ **malvino, -na 1** *adj* of *o* from the Falkland Islands **2** *n* Falkland Islander

Mancha, el Canal de la *nm* the English Channel

mancomunado, -da *adj* joint; **propiedad mancomunada** = joint ownership; **signatario mancomunado** = joint signatory

mandamiento *nm* **(a)** *(mandato)* order *o* mandate **(b)** *(documento legal)* writ *o* warrant; **notificar un mandamiento judicial a alguien** = to serve someone with a writ *o* to serve a writ on someone

mandante *nmf* principal; **el mandatario ha venido a Londres a ver a sus mandantes** = the agent has come to London to see his principals

mandar *vt* **(a)** *(dar órdenes)* to order *o* to instruct;

me mandó hacerlo = he ordered me to do it **(b)** *(enviar)* to send; **mandar por correo** = to send by post *o* to post *o* to mail; **mandar una carta** = to post a letter; **mandamos nuestro pedido por correo el miércoles pasado** = we mailed our order last Wednesday **(c)** *(encargos)* to send for; **mandó llamar al jefe de contabilidad** = he sent for the chief accountant; **mandó buscar los documentos del contrato** = she sent for the papers on the contract

mandarín *nm* **los mandarines de la prensa** = the press barons

mandatario, -ria *n* **(a)** *(representante)* agent *o* representative; **el mandatario ha venido a Madrid a ver a sus mandantes** = the agent has come to Madrid to see his principals **(b)** *(de un país)* **el primer mandatario** = head of state

mandato *nm* **(a)** *(orden)* order *o* mandate **(b)** *(instrucciones)* terms of reference *o* brief; **conforme a su mandato, el comité no puede investigar quejas del público** = under its terms of reference, the committee cannot investigate complaints from the public; **las exportaciones no se incluyen en el mandato del comité** = the committee's terms of reference do not cover exports **(c)** *(documento legal)* writ; **mandato judicial** = injunction; **consiguió un mandato judicial para impedir que la empresa vendiera su coche** = he got an injunction preventing the company from selling his car **(d)** *(periodo en que se ejerce el mando)* tenure *o* term of office; **durante su mandato como presidente** = during his tenure of the office of chairman *o* while he was chairman; **el tesorero termina su mandato en el consejo a los seis años** = the treasurer retires from the council after six years **(e)** *(tarea)* remit

mando *nm* command *o* control; **mandos intermedios** = middle management; **mando a distancia** = remote control

manejable *adj* manageable *o* handy *o* easy to use; **es un trabajo manejable** = it's a manageable job *o* it's a job that can be done

manejar *vt* **manejar una máquina** = to operate a machine *o* to work a machine; **está aprendiendo a manejar la nueva centralita de teléfonos** = he is learning to operate the new telephone switchboard

◊ **manejo** *nm* handling; **manejo de materiales** = materials handling; **de fácil manejo** = user-friendly

manera *nf* manner *o* way *o* method

manifestación *nf* demonstration

en la protesta convocada el pasado viernes, los trabajadores demostraron su capacidad de movilización a través de un paro general y una manifestación con más de 15.000 asistentes
El País

los sindicatos anuncian ya nuevas manifestaciones y presiones más radicales si el Gobierno no modifica sus planes
El País

manifiesto *nm* manifest; **poner de manifiesto** = to show; **manifiesto de carga** = waybill

manila *nf* **papel de manila** = manilla (paper)

maniobra *nf* **(a)** manoeuvre; **maniobra hábil** = clever manoeuvre **(b)** **maniobra manual** = manual operation

manipulación *nf* handling; **costes de manipulación** = handling charges; **manipulación del mercado bursátil** = stock market manipulation; **manipulación de votos** *o* **de elecciones** = rigging of ballots *o* ballot-rigging

manipular *vt* to rig; **manipular las cuentas** = to manipulate the accounts *o* to fix the accounts; **intentaron manipular la elección de los dirigentes de la compañía** = they tried to rig the election of officers; **manipular el mercado** = to rig *o* to manipulate the market

mano *nf* **(a)** hand; **manos limpias** = clean hands; **dar la mano** *o* **estrechar la mano** = to shake hands with someone; **las dos parte negociadoras se dieron la mano y a continuación se sentaron a la mesa de conferencias** = the two negotiating teams shook hands and sat down at the conference table; **cerrar un trato con un apretón de manos** = to shake hands on a deal; **echar mano de** = to fall back on **(b)** **a mano** = (i) by hand *o* manually; (ii) handy; **tengo la factura a mano** = I have the invoice to hand; **estos zapatos están hechos a mano** = these shoes are hand-made; **accionado a mano** = hand-operated; **una máquina accionada a mano** = a hand-operated machine; **escrito a mano** = handwritten; **las solicitudes deben escribirse a mano y enviarse al jefe de personal** = applications should be written in longhand and sent to the personnel officer; **se han tenido que hacer las facturas a mano porque el ordenador se ha averiado** = invoices have had to be made out manually because the computer has broken down; **votación a mano alzada** = show of hands; **la moción se llevó a cabo en una votación a mano alzada** = the motion was carried on a show of hands **(c)** **en mano** = by hand; **entregar una carta en mano** = to send a letter by hand; **operación llaves en mano** = turnkey operation; **trabajo entre manos** = work in hand; **los documentos están en sus manos** = the documents are in his possession **(d)** **de primera** *o* **segunda mano** = first-hand *o* secondhand; **se compró un coche de segunda mano** = he bought a secondhand car; **mercadillo de objetos de segunda mano** = flea market

◊ **mano de obra** *nf* **(a)** labour *o* labour force *o* manpower *o* work force; **mano de obra activa** = active labour force *o* workforce; **mano de obra barata** = cheap labour; **hemos abierto una fábrica en Extremo Oriente porque la mano de obra es barata** = we have opened a factory in the Far East because of the cheap labour *o* because labour is cheap; **mano de obra cualificada** *o* **especializada** = skilled labour; **mano de obra sin cualificar** = unskilled labour *o* unskilled workforce *o* unskilled workers; **mano de obra eventual** = casual labour; **mano de obra local** = local labour; **industria con un alto coeficiente de mano de obra** = labour-intensive industry **(b)** **costes de la mano de obra** = labour costs *o* labour charges; **escasez de mano de obra** = manpower shortage *o* shortage of manpower *o* labour shortage; **la producción de la empresa se ve afectada por la falta de mano de obra en la cadena de montaje** = the company's production is affected by undermanning on the assembly line; **necesidades de mano de obra** = manpower requirements; **planificación de la mano de obra** = manpower planning; **previsión de mano de obra** = manpower forecasting

> se persigue un objetivo ergonómico, es decir, la posibilidad de sentarse en posición correcta, de estar cómodo y de tener todo a mano
> **España Económica**

> la mano de obra soviética está muy mal pagada, pero esto no quiere decir que sea barata
> **España Económica**

> el proyecto ofrecía un nuevo mercado de casi 300 millones de personas, materias primas abundantes y mano de obra barata
> **España Económica**

mantener vt (a) (sostener) to keep up o to maintain; **mantener buenas relaciones con los clientes** = to maintain good relations with one's customers; **mantener contacto con un mercado exterior** = to maintain contact o to keep in contact with an overseas market; **mantener un dividendo** = to maintain a dividend; **mantener el tipo de interés al 5%** = to maintain the interest rate at 5%; **debemos mantener el volumen de ventas a pesar de la recesión** = we must keep up the turnover in spite of the recession; **mantuvo el ritmo de sesenta palabras por minuto durante varias horas** = she kept up a rate of sixty words per minute for several hours **(b)** (a un mismo nivel) to keep; **mantener algo al día** = to keep something up to date; **debemos mantener nuestra lista de destinatarios al día** = we must keep our mailing list up to date; **mantener los gastos al mínimo** = to keep spending to a minimum; **el precio del petróleo ha mantenido la libra alta** = the price of oil has kept the pound at a high level; **mantener bajo** = to hold down o to keep down; **la escasa demanda de máquinas de escribir ha mantenido los precios bajos** = lack of demand for typewriters has kept prices down; **estamos recortando los márgenes para mantener los precios bajos** = we are cutting margins to hold our prices down

◊ **mantenerse** vr (a) to stay up o to keep up o to hold up; **las cotizaciones de las acciones se han mantenido bien** = share prices have held up well; **las ventas se mantuvieron durante la temporada turística** = sales held up during the tourist season **(b)** **mantenerse en vigor** = to remain in effect

mantenimiento nm **(a)** maintenance; **mantenimiento del precio de venta** = resale price maintenance; **mantenimiento de relaciones** = maintenance of contacts; **mantenimiento de suministros** = maintenance of supplies **(b)** **contrato de mantenimiento** = maintenance contract; **contrato de mantenimiento del material informático** = hardware maintenance contract; **coste de mantenimiento** = maintenace cost o upkeep; **manual de mantenimiento** = service handbook o service manual; **servicio de mantenimiento** = maintenance service; **ofrecemos un servicio de mantenimiento completo** = we offer a full maintenance service

> la compañía suministrará mantenimiento y soporte a los usuarios de su sistema a través de los centros de telediagnóstico
> **Chip**

manual 1 adj manual; (accionado a mano) hand-operated; **trabajo manual** = manual labour o manual work; **obrero manual** = manual labourer **2** nm handbook o manual; **manual de funcionamiento** = operating manual; **manual de mantenimiento** = service handbook o service manual; **el manual no indica cómo se abre la fotocopiadora** = the handbook does not say how you open the photocopier

> este manual pretende ayudar en la capacitación de los vendedores de tienda
> **El País**

◊ **manualmente** adv (a mano) manually

manufacturado, -da 1 adj manufactured o made; **productos manufacturados** = manufactured goods **2** pp de MANUFACTURAR

manufacturar vt to manufacture o to make o to produce

◊ **manufacturero, -ra** adj manufacturing; **industrias manufactureras** = manufacturing industries

manuscrito, -ta 1 adj handwritten o manuscript **2** nm manuscript

manutención nf **(a)** (persona) maintenance o upkeep; **la manutención de una familia** = the maintenance of a family **(b)** (conservación) upkeep

manzana nf block (of buildings); **quieren renovar una manzana en el centro de la ciudad** = they want to redevelop a block in the centre of the town; **la oficina está unas manzanas más abajo en la Calle Mayor** = the office is a few blocks further down the Calle Mayor

maña nf skill o knack; **tener maña para todo** = to be skilful

mañana 1 nf morning; **de la mañana** = a.m.; **el vuelo sale a las 9.20 de la mañana** = the flight leaves at 9.20 a.m.; **antes de las 6 de la mañana las llamadas telefónicas se cobran a tarifa reducida** = telephone calls before 6 a.m. are charged at the cheap rate **2** adv tomorrow; **el día de mañana** = in the future

maqueta nf model o mock-up; **nos mostró una maqueta del nuevo edificio de oficinas** = he showed us a model of the new office building

máquina nf **(a)** machine; **máquina accionada a mano** = hand-operated machine; **máquina de buen rendimiento** = efficient machine; **máquina de cambio** = change machine; **máquina de escribir** = typewriter; **máquina de escribir portátil** = portable typewriter; **máquina de escribir electrónica** = electronic typewriter; **máquina expendedora** = automatic vending machine; **máquina de imprimir direcciones** = addressing machine; **máquina perforadora** = punch; **máquina de sacar copias** = copying machine o duplicating machine; **máquina de sumar** o **máquina sumadora** = adding machine; **la máquina está sujeta al suelo para que no pueda desplazarse** = the machine is attached to the floor so it cannot be moved **(b)** **encargado de una máquina** = machine operator o machinist; **escribir** o **pasar a máquina** = to type o to type out; **escrito a máquina** = typewritten; **envió una solicitud de trabajo escrita a máquina** = he sent in a typewritten job application; **las demás secretarias se quejan de que canta mientras escribe a máquina** = the other secretaries complain that she keeps singing when she is typing; **hecho a máquina** = machine-made *o* machine-produced; **prueba de una máquina** = test run (of a machine) **(c)** *(ordenador)* **código de máquina** *o* **lenguaje máquina** = machine code *o* machine language

◊ **máquinas-herramienta** *nfpl* machine tools

◊ **maquinaria** *nf* **(a)** *(máquinas)* machinery; **instalar la maquinaria en una fábrica** = to install machinery in a factory *o* to tool up; **siguen empleando maquinaria anticuada** = they are still using out-of-date machinery; **maquinaria parada** = idle machinery *o* machinery lying idle **(b)** *(equipo)* plant; **empresa de alquiler de maquinaria** = plant-hire firm

◊ **maquinista** *nmf* **(a)** *(encargado de una máquina)* machinist **(b)** *(operador)* operative

mar *nmf* sea; **los yacimientos petrolíferos del mar del Norte** = the North Sea oil fields

maravillas *nfpl* wonders; **hacer maravillas** = to do wonders

la Expo de Sevilla guarda un riguroso orden tecnológico, hecho de fibra óptica y bioclimatización por agua micronizada y otras modernas maravillas
Cambio 16

marca *nf* **(a)** *(modelo)* brand *o* make; **marca blanca** = unbranded product; **marca conocida** *o* **familiar** = household name; **marca de fabricación** *o* **marca comercial** = brand name *o* trademark *o* trade name; **¿de qué marca es el nuevo ordenador?** = what make is the new computer *o* what is the make of the new computer?; **la empresa va a lanzar una nueva marca de jabón** = the company is launching a new brand of soap; **marcas japonesas de coches** = Japanese makes of cars; **marca líder** = brand leader *o* leading brand; **marca propia** = own brand; **productos de marca propia** = own brand goods *o* own label goods; **marca registrada** = registered trademark; **no puede llamar a sus camas 'Pikolín', es una marca registrada** = you cannot call your beds 'Pikolín' - it is a registered trademark; **de marca registrada** = proprietary; **marca X** = brand X; **fidelidad a la marca** = brand loyalty; **imagen de marca** = brand image; **reconocimiento de marca** = brand recognition **(b)** *(señal)* mark *o* stamp **(c)** *(señal en un papel)* tick; **hacer una marca** = to tick; *US* to check; **haga una marca en la casilla 'R'** = make a tick in the box marked 'R'

◊ **marcador** *nm* marker pen *o* highlighter

las dos bodegas tienen marcas de calidad en el mercado y se encuentran en un sector que ha sido calificado de 'diamante' cara al futuro
El País

y, por si los problemas fueran pocos, los industriales deben hacer frente a las marcas blancas importadas de terceros países y a una nueva distribución con los precios a la baja como principal reclamo, el descuento duro
El País

marcar *vt* **(a)** *(poner una señal)* to mark; **marcó la página hasta donde había llegado con un bolígrafo rojo** = she marked her place in the text with a red pen; **artículo marcado a 150 ptas.** = article marked at 150 pesetas; **estas alfombras se venden con un descuento del 25% sobre el precio marcado** = these carpets are sold at 25% off the marked price **(b)** *(teléfono)* to dial; **marcar un número** = to dial a number; **marcar el número directamente** = to dial direct; **señal de marcar** = dialling tone **(c)** *(en un papel)* to tick; *US* to check

marcha *nf* **(a)** *(progreso)* progress; **la marcha de los negocios** *o* **acontecimientos** = the course of business *o* of events; **lo pensaré sobre la marcha** = I'll think about it as I go along; **hacer un informe sobre la marcha del trabajo** = to make a progress report; **informar sobre la marcha del trabajo** *o* **de las negociaciones** = to report on the progress of the work *o* of the negotiations; **dar marcha al trabajo** = to speed up work; **hacer marcha atrás** = to go back on one's word *o* to reverse; **poner en marcha** = to start **(b)** **a toda marcha** = speedily; **los obreros trabajaron a toda marcha durante semanas seguidas para servir el pedido a tiempo** = the workforce worked at top speed for weeks on end to finish the order on time **(c)** **en marcha** = in progress *o* working *o* ongoing; **costes de puesta en marcha** = start-up costs; **vender un negocio en marcha** = to sell a business as a going concern

para luchar contra el fraude fiscal, Hacienda ha puesto en marcha este año una campaña, fundamentalmente en televisión y prensa escrita, cuyo coste global es de 400 millones de pesetas
El País

marcharse *vr* to go away *o* to leave; **varios de los directores se marchan para establecer su propia empresa** = several of the managers are quitting to set up their own company

marfileño, -ña *ver* COSTA DE MARFIL

marco *nm* **(a)** *(moneda alemana)* Deutschmark *o* mark; **el precio es de 25 marcos** = the price is 25DM *o* 25 marks; **el marco subió frente al dólar** = the mark rose against the dollar **(b)** *(límites en que se sitúa una cuestión)* framework; **marco legal** = legal framework **(c)** **en un marco adecuado** = in an appropriate setting

margen *nm* **(a)** *(beneficio)* margin; **margen de beneficio** = profit margin *o* mark-up; **trabajamos con un margen de beneficio de 3 veces y media** *o* **con un margen de beneficio del 350%** = we work to a 3.5 times mark-up *o* to a 350% mark-up; **nuestros márgenes se han visto reducidos por la competencia** = our margins have been squeezed by the competition; **margen bruto** = gross margin; **margen de cobertura** = backwardation; **margen neto** = net margin **(b)** *(ventaja)* edge; **la oficina local nos proporciona un margen competitivo** = the local office gives us a competitive edge **(c)** *(cálculo previsible)* margin; **margen de error** = margin of error; **margen de explotación** = operating margin; **margen de seguridad** = safety margin *o* margin of safety; **dejar un margen** = to allow for; **deje un margen de 28 días para la entrega** = allow 28 days for delivery; **dejar un margen de un 10% para embalaje** = to allow 10% for packing; **cuente con un margen de tres días hábiles para el depósito**

del cheque en el banco = allow three clear days for the cheque to be paid into the bank; **hay margen para mejorar nuestras ventas** = there is scope for improvement in our sales performance **(d)** *(borde)* border; **mantenerse** *o* **quedar al margen de un asunto** = not to get involved in something *o* to stay on the sidelines

las cotizaciones se han movido a lo largo de esta semana con un margen muy estrecho, delimitado por el poco riesgo asumido por los inversores y las expectativas que a medio plazo despiertan los tipos de interés

El País

marginal *adj* marginal; **coste marginal** = marginal cost *o* incremental cost; **rendimiento marginal de la inversión** = marginal return on investment; **tipo de impuesto marginal** = marginal tax rate

marino, -na 1 *adj* marine; **asegurador de riesgos marinos** = marine underwriter **2** *nf* **(a)** navy *o* marine; **marina mercante** = merchant navy *o* merchant marine **(b)** sea *o* shore *o* coast **3** *nm* sailor *o* seaman

marítimo, -ma *adj* maritime; **comercio marítimo** = maritime trade; **derecho marítimo** = maritime law; **abogado especializado en derecho marítimo** = maritime lawyer; **seguro marítimo** = marine insurance; **transporte marítimo** = sea transport; **correo por vía marítima** = sea mail; **enviar algo por vía marítima** = to send something by sea

marketing *nm* marketing; **marketing directo** = direct marketing; **departamento de marketing** = marketing department; **está buscando un trabajo de responsabilidad en el ámbito del marketing** = he is looking for a responsible job in marketing

la palabra marketing es un vocablo anglosajón, de reciente introducción en el sector hotelero español

Tiempo

Marruecos *nm* Morocco

◊ **marroquí** *adj y nmf* Moroccan
NOTA: capital: **Rabat**; moneda: **dirham marroquí (DH)** = Moroccan dirham (DH)

martillar *o* **martillear** *vt* to hammer; **me martilla los oídos con sus quejas** = he's always complaining *o* pestering me with his complaints

◊ **martillo** *nm* hammer; **martillo del subastador** = auctioneer's hammer

más 1 *adj y adv* **(a)** *(comparación)* more *o* more than; **gastar más de lo presupuestado** = to spend more than one's budget *o* to overspend one's budget; **más adelante** = further on; **pujar más alto que** = to bid more than *o* to outbid; **las ventas fueron más bajas en diciembre que en noviembre** = sales were lower in December than in November **(b)** *(superlativo)* most; **el más popular** = the most popular; **lo más caro del mercado** = the most expensive item on the market; **nación más favorecida** = most favoured nation; **más vendido** = best-selling *o* top-selling; **las marcas de pasta dentífrica más vendidas** = top-selling brands of toothpaste; **los ordenadores no son uno de los artículos que más vendemos** = computers are not

one of our best-selling lines **(c)** *(extra)* further *o* more; **necesitamos más secretarias para que se ocupen de los envíos por correo** = we need extra secretarial help to deal with the mailings; **pedir más detalles** = to ask for further details *o* particulars; **pidió seis semanas más para pagar** = he asked for a further six weeks to pay **(d)** **más de** = more than; **más de una vez** = more than once; **su sueldo asciende a más de 250.000 ptas.** = his salary comes to more than 250,000 pesetas; **casas valoradas en más de 100.000 ptas.** = houses valued at 100,000 pesetas plus; **tienda dedicada especialmente a las personas de más de sesenta años** = shop which caters to the over-60s **(e)** **cobrar de más** = to charge too much *o* to overcharge; **nos cobraron de más por las comidas** = they overcharged us for meals; **tener de más** = to have too much **2** *nm* plus *o* plus sign

masa *nf* **(a)** *(gente)* mass; **producto destinado a un mercado de masas** = mass market product **(b)** *(volumen o cantidad)* mass *o* bulk; **comprar en masa** = to buy in bulk; **producción en masa** = mass production; **producir en masa** = to produce masses of *o* to churn out

masivo, -va *adj* massive *o* in mass; **paro masivo** = mass unemployment

master *nm* master's degree *o* M.A.; **está haciendo un master en administración de empresas en los EE UU** = he is taking a Master's (degree) *o* an M.A. in Business Administration (MBA) in the States

se trata de un programa con el contenido de un master tradicional que se cursa en tres instituciones docentes de tres países distintos

Mercado

matasellos *nm* postmark; **la carta llevaba el matasellos de Nueva York** = the letter was postmarked New York; **el sobre lleva el matasellos de Lérida** = the envelope has a Lérida postmark

materia *nf* **(a)** matter; **entrar en materia** = to get down to business **(b)** **materias primas** = raw materials

hay abundancia de materias primas, pero fundamentalmente están inexplotadas por falta de recursos

España Económica

material 1 *adj* material; **daños materiales** = damage to property *o* property damage **2** *nm* **(a)** material *o* equipment; **material de construcción** = building materials; **material de exposición** = display material; **material impreso** = printed matter; **material militar** *o* **de guerra** = military hardware; **material de oficina** = office equipment *o* business equipment *o* office supplies; **catálogo de material de oficina** = office equipment catalogue; **proveedor de material de oficina** = office equipment supplier *o* stationery supplier; **material de promoción** = promotional material; **los técnicos publicitarios utilizan globos como material de promoción** = the publicity people *o* the admen are using balloons as promotional material; **material de publicidad** = publicity matter; **el envío de material publicitario por correo** = the mailing of publicity material; **material rodante** = rolling stock; **materiales sintéticos** = synthetic materials **(b)** **alquilar material** = to lease equipment; **cobrar los materiales y la mano de obra** = to charge for materials and labour; **control de materiales** = materials control; **coste de materiales** = materials cost; **manejo de materiales** = materials handling

maternidad *nf* maternity; **está de baja por maternidad** = she is away on maternity leave; **licencia** *o* **baja por maternidad** = maternity leave; **subsidio de maternidad** = maternity benefit

matrícula *nf* registration; **cuota de matrícula** = registration fee; **número de matrícula** = registration number

matriz *nf* **(a) impresora de matriz de puntos** = dot-matrix printer **(b)** *(de un talonario)* cheque stub **(c) casa matriz** = head office; **sociedad matriz** = parent company

Mauricio *nf* Mauritius

◊ **mauricio, -cia** *adj y n* Mauritian
NOTA: capital: **Port-Louis;** moneda: **rupia mauricia (MauRs)** = Mauritian rupee (MauRs)

maximización *nf* maximization; **maximización de beneficios** = profit maximization *o* maximization of profit

maximizar *vt* to maximize

máximo, -ma 1 *adj* maximum *o* all-out *o* top *o* highest; **máximo tipo de impuesto** = maximum income tax rate *o* top rate of tax; **carga máxima** = maximum load; **de grado máximo** = top-grade; **niveles máximos de producción** = maximum production levels; **aumentar la producción al máximo** = to increase production to the maximum level; **peso máximo** = maximum weight *o* weight limit; **precio máximo** = maximum price; **punto máximo** = highest point *o* peak; **rendimiento máximo** = peak output **2** *nm* **(a)** maximum; **hasta un máximo de 10 cajas** = up to a maximum of 10 boxes; **es lo máximo que pagará la compañía de seguros** = it is the most the insurance company will pay; **las acciones alcanzaron su máximo en enero** = the shares reached their peak in January **(b) al máximo** = to the maximum; **llevar algo al máximo** = to maximize; **la productividad llegó al máximo en enero** = productivity peaked in January; **aumentar las exportaciones al máximo** = to increase exports to the maximum; **estamos reduciendo nuestros márgenes al máximo** = we are cutting our margins very fine

mayor *adj* **(a)** main *o* most important *o* major; **Calle Mayor** = High Street; *US* Main Street **(b)** *(en comparaciones)* bigger *o* larger *o* largest; **¿por qué tiene ella una oficina mayor que la mía?** = why has she got an office which is larger than mine?; **las pérdidas por el cambio de divisas son mucho mayores que los beneficios obtenidos en el mercado interior** = foreign exchange losses are much larger than the profits in the domestic market; **la mayor sociedad financiera de Londres** = the largest London finance house; **nuestra empresa es una de las mayores proveedoras de ordenadores del gobierno** = our company is one of the largest suppliers of computers to the government; **a la mayor brevedad** = at your earliest convenience **(c)** *(persona)* senior *o* older *o* elder **(d) al por mayor** = wholesale; **comerciante al por mayor** = wholesale

dealer *o* wholesaler; **descuento al por mayor** = wholesale *o* bulk discount

> la apertura del mercado interior supondrá un fuerte aumento de la competencia en el negocio bancario al por mayor, pero no dejará de incidir en la banca al por menor
> **Mercado**

mayoría *nf* majority *o* most; **en su mayoría** = mostly; **la mayoría de los accionistas** = the majority of the shareholders; **la junta aceptó la propuesta por una mayoría de tres contra dos** = the board accepted the proposal by a majority of three to two; **la mayoría del personal es licenciado** = most of the staff are graduates; **la mayoría de nuestros clientes viven cerca de la fábrica** = most of our customers live near the factory; **la mayoría de los pedidos llegan al principio del año** = most of the orders come in the early part of the year

◊ **mayorista** *nmf* wholesale dealer *o* wholesaler; **precio de mayorista** = wholesale price

mayúscula *nf* **letras mayúsculas** = capital letters *o* block capitals *o* block letters *o* caps; **escriba su nombre con letras mayúsculas en la parte superior del formulario** = write your name in block capitals at the top of the form *o* please print your name and address on the top of the form

mecánico, -ca 1 *adj* mechanical; **bomba mecánica** = a mechanical pump; **taller mecánico** = machine shop **2** *nm* mechanic *o* repairer *o* repair man *o* service engineer; **ha llegado el mecánico para reparar la fotocopiadora** = the repair man has come to mend the photocopier; **mecánico de coches** = car mechanic **3** *nf* mechanics; **mecánica de precisión** = precision engineering

mecanismo *nm* machinery *o* mechanism; **mecanismo administrativo** = administrative machinery; **mecanismo para frenar la inflación** = mechanism to slow down inflation

mecanización *nf* mechanization; **la mecanización agrícola** = farm mechanization *o* the mechanization of farms

mecanizar *vt* to mechanize; **el país se propone mecanizar la industria agrícola** = the country is aiming to mechanize its farming industry

mecanografía *nf* typing; **mecanografía de copias** *o* **mecanografía de originales** = copy typing; **mecanografía de dictado** = audio-typing; **error de mecanografía** = typing error; **el secretario tiene que haber hecho un error de mecanografía** = the secretary must have made a typing error; **servicio de mecanografía** = typing pool

◊ **mecanografiado, -da 1** *adj* typed *o* typewritten; **todos sus informes son mecanografiados en su máquina portátil** = all his reports are typed on his portable typewriter **2** *pp de* MECANOGRAFIAR

mecanografiar *vt* to type

◊ **mecanógrafo, -fa** *n* typist; **mecanógrafo de dictado** = audio-typist; **mecanógrafo de originales a mano** = copy typist

mechera *nf (ladrona)* shoplifter

media *nf* mean *o* average; **media ponderada** =

weighted avarage; **hacer** *o* **hallar la media** = to work out *o* to find the average; *ver también* MEDIO

> la aportación actual del gas en la balanza energética es por término medio del 7,5%, muy por debajo del 18%, que es la media europea
> **El País**

mediación *nf* mediation; **los empresarios rechazaron una oferta de mediación del gobierno** = the employers refused an offer of government mediation; **el conflicto se resolvió a través de la mediación de los cargos sindicales** = the dispute was ended through the mediation of union officials

◊ **mediador, -ra** *n* mediator; **mediador de conflictos laborales** = troubleshooter; **mediador del gobierno** = official mediator

mediados *adj* middle *o* mid-; **desde mediados de 1995** = from mid-1995; **a mediados de mes** = in the middle of the month; **cuentas de mediados de mes** = mid-month accounts; **la fábrica está cerrada hasta mediados de julio** = the factory is closed until mid-July; **a mediados de semana** = mid-week

mediano, -na 1 *adj* average *o* medium; **empresa mediana** = medium-sized company; **de tamaño mediano** = middle-sized; **la empresa es de tamaño mediano** = the company is of medium size; **una empresa mediana de ingeniería** = a medium-sized engineering company **2** *nf* median

◊ **medianamente** *adv* moderately *o* fairly

mediar *vi* to mediate *o* to intervene; **mediar en favor de alguien** = to intervene on someone's behalf; **mediar en un conflicto** = to adjudicate *o* to mediate in a dispute; **el gobierno se ofreció a mediar en la disputa** = the government offered to mediate in the dispute

medicamento *nm* (*medicina*) medicine *o* drug

medicina *nf* **(a)** (*ciencia*) medicine **(b)** (*medicamento*) medicine *o* drug

medición *nf* measurement *o* survey; **medición de la rentabilidad** = measurement of profitability

médico, -ca 1 *adj* medical; **parte médico de baja** = medical certificate; **reconocimiento médico** *o* **revisión médica** = medical examination *o* medical; **seguro médico** = medical insurance **2** *n* doctor; **médico de empresa** = company doctor; **todo el personal está obligado a ir al médico de la empresa una vez al año** = the staff are all sent to see the company doctor once a year

medida *nf* **(a)** (*efecto de medir*) measure *o* measurement; **medida de áridos** = dry measure; **medida de capacidad** = cubic measure; **medida del rendimiento de la empresa** = measure of the company's performance; **medida de superficie** = square measure; **medida de volumen** = cubic measure; **hecho a la medida** = made to measure; **se hace la ropa a la medida** = he has his clothes made to measure; **inspector de pesos y medidas** = inspector of weights and measures; **anotar las medidas de un paquete** = to write down the measurements of a package; **tomar las medidas de un paquete** = to measure the size of a package **(b)** (*disposición*) action *o* measure *o* step; **una medida de ahorro** = an economy measure; **medidas fiscales**

= fiscal measures; **medidas preventivas** = precautionary measures; **medidas reflacionarias** = reflationary measures; **medidas de seguridad** = safety measures *o* safety precautions; **medidas de seguridad de un aeropuerto** = airport security; **medidas de seguridad en una oficina** = office security; **introducir en el sistema medidas para reducir gastos** = to introduce economies *o* economy measures into the system; **tomar medidas** = to take action *o* to take measures *o* to make provision for; **la primera medida tomada por el nuevo gerente fue analizar todos los gastos** = the first step taken by the new MD was to analyse all the expenses; **tomar medidas de emergencia** = to take emergency measures; **tomar medidas preventivas** *o* **tomar medidas para evitar que algo ocurra** = to take steps *o* measures to prevent something happening; **tomar medidas provisionales** = to take temporary measures

> el gobierno no tiene prevista ninguna medida de ajuste sino todo lo contrario
> **España Económica**

> se equivocan los que piensan que el gobierno tomará una serie de medidas económicas después de las elecciones
> **España Económica**

medio, -dia 1 *adj* **(a)** (*promedio*) average *o* mean *o* medium *o* middle; **aumento anual medio** = mean annual increase; **las cifras medias de los últimos tres meses** = the average figures for the last three months; **clase media** = middle class; **el costo unitario medio** = average cost per unit; **estrategia a plazo medio** = medium-term strategy; **a plazo medio** = medium term; **precio medio** = average price *o* mean price; **préstamo a plazo medio** = medium-term loan; **la subida media de precios** = the average increase in prices; **de tamaño medio** = middle-sized; **por término medio** = on the average; **ser por término medio** = to average (out); **el término medio anual es del 10%** = it averages out at 10% per annum; **es un trabajador medio** = he is an average worker; **ventas medias por representante** = average sales per representative **(b)** (*mitad*) half; **los domingos cobra paga y media más** = he is paid time and a half on Sundays; **anuncio de media página** = half-page ad; **media docena** = half a dozen *o* a half-dozen; **el medio por ciento** = half a per cent *o* a half per cent; **su comisión en el negocio es del doce y medio por ciento** = his commission on the deal is twelve and a half per cent **2** *nfpl* **a medias** = half and half *o* fifty-fifty; **ir a medias** = to share half and half *o* to go fifty-fifty **3** *nm* **(a)** (*manera*) means *o* way; **el transporte aéreo es el medio más rápido para enviar mercancías a Sudamérica** = air freight is the fastest means of getting stock to South America; **¿tenemos algún medio para copiar todos estos documentos rápidamente?** = do we have any means of copying all these documents quickly?; **medios de producción** = means of production; **medios de transporte** = means of transport **(b)** **los medios informativos** *o* **de comunicación** = the (mass) media; **el producto atrajo mucho interés en los medios de comunicación** = the product attracted a lot of interest in the media *o* a lot of media interest **(c)** medio publicitario = advertising medium; **los agentes publicitarios utilizan globos como medio de promoción** = the admen are using balloons as promotional material **(d)** **medios fraudulentos** =

false pretences; **fue encarcelado por obtener dinero por medios fraudulentos** = he was sent to prison for obtaining money by false pretences **(e) el medio ambiente** = the environment

◇ **medios** *nmpl (recursos económicos)* means; **este nivel de inversión está por encima de los medios de una pequeña empresa privada** = such a level of investment is beyond the means of a small private company

> el sector de medios de información es uno de los más dinámicos del mercado
> **Tiempo**

> en España, las estadísticas muestran que se mantiene un ritmo de crecimiento medio anual del 54% en el mercado de ordenadores personales
> **Micros**

mediocre *adj* mediocre *o* low-quality

mediodía *nm* midday *o* noon; **el avión llega a Hong Kong a mediodía** = the plane reaches Hong Kong at midday

medir *vt/i* to measure *o* to meter; **un paquete que mide 10cm por 25 cm** = a package which measures 10cm by 25cm *o* a package measuring 10cm by 25cm

mega- *prefijo* mega-

◇ **megabyte** *o* **megaocteto** *nm* megabyte (MB)

mejicano, -na *ver* MEXICO

mejor *adj* best *o* better *o* superior *o* improved; **compararemos los precios de otros lugares para ver si son mejores** = we will shop around to see if we can get a better price; **el banco suizo ofrece condiciones un poco mejores** = the Swiss bank is offering slightly better terms; **venden más porque tienen un servicio de distribución mejor** = their sales are higher because of their superior distribution service; **mejor año** = best year *o* peak year; **1995 fue el mejor año en la historia de la compañía** = 1995 was the company's best year ever; **los resultados de este año son mejores que los del año pasado** = this year's results are better than last year's; **lo mejor** = the best; **lo mejor del grupo** = the pick of the group; **el sindicato rechazó la mejor oferta de la dirección** = the union rejected the management's improved offer; **el mejor postor** = the highest bidder

mejora *nf* improvement; *(economía)* upturn; **mejora de una oferta** = improvement on an offer

◇ **mejorado, -da** **1** *adj* improved **2** *pp de* MEJORAR

◇ **mejoramiento** *nm* improvement; **mejoramiento de la calidad** = improvement of quality *o* quality upgrading

mejorar *vt* to improve *o* to improve on; **mejorar el nivel de vida** = to raise the standard of living; **estamos intentando mejorar nuestra imagen con una serie de anuncios publicitarios en televisión** = we are trying to improve our image with a series of TV commercials; **esperan mejorar la situación de cash flow de la empresa** = they hope to improve the company's cash flow position; **las exportaciones han mejorado mucho durante el primer**

trimestre = export trade has improved sharply during the first quarter; **la bolsa bajó por la mañana, pero mejoró durante la tarde** = the stock market fell in the morning, but recovered during the afternoon; **se negó a mejorar su oferta anterior** = he refused to improve on his previous offer

mejoría *nf* **(a)** *(mejora)* improvement; **las ventas registran una gran mejoría con respecto al año pasado** = sales are showing a sharp improvement over last year **(b)** *(economía)* recovery; **la economía experimentó una mejoría** = the economy staged a recovery

membrete *nm* letterhead *o* letter heading *o* heading on notepaper; **papel con membrete** = *GB* headed notepaper; *US* letterhead

memorandum *nm* memorandum

memoria *nf* **(a)** *(informe)* report; **la memoria anual de la compañía** = the company's annual report **(b)** *(informática)* memory; **memoria de acceso al azar** = random access memory; **memoria de lectura solamente** = read only memory; **memoria de un ordenador para trabajos temporales** = workspace; **memoria de reserva** = extended memory storage

mención *nf* mention; **hacer mención** = to mention

mencionar *vt* to mention *o* to refer to; **mencionado más abajo** = undermentioned

menor 1 *adj* **(a)** *(pequeño)* minor *o* less important; **gastos menores** = minor expenditure; **fondo *o* dinero para gastos menores** = petty cash; **tribunal de demandas de menor cuantía** = small claims court; **de menor consumo *o* de menor tráfico** = off-peak **(b)** *al por menor* = retail; **comerciante al por menor** = retail dealer; **ventas al por menor** = retail sales *o* goods sold over the counter **2** *nmf* **menor de edad** = minor; **legislación sobre trabajo de menores** = child labour laws; **tribunal de menores** = juvenile court

◇ **menorista** *nmf* *(Latinoamérica)* = MINORISTA retail dealer

> la apertura del mercado interior supondrá un fuerte aumento de la competencia en el negocio bancario al por mayor, pero no dejará de incidir en la banca al por menor
> **Mercado**

menos *adj y adv* **(a)** *(en comparación)* less *o* fewer *o* the least; **menos de** = less than *o* under; **lo vendió por menos de lo que había pagado por él** = he sold it for less than he had paid for it; **ha gastado menos de lo que había previsto** = he has underspent his budget; **menos de la mitad de los accionistas aceptaron la oferta** = under half of the shareholders accepted the offer; **menos de diez** = under ten *o* in single figures; **cobrar de menos** = to charge too little *o* to undercharge; **menos que** = less than **(b)** *(indica exclusión)* minus *o* less; **el salario neto es el salario bruto menos los impuestos y las deducciones de la seguridad social** = net salary is gross salary minus tax and National Insurance deductions; **el beneficio bruto equivale a las ventas menos los costes de**

producción = gross profit is sales minus production costs; **el precio de compra menos el 15% de descuento** = purchase price less 15% discount; **el interés menos la comisión bancaria** = interest less bank charges

menospreciar *vt* to minimize *o* to underestimate *o* to underrate

mensaje *nm* message; **mensaje telegráfico** = telemessage; **enviar un mensaje** = to send a message; **dice que no recibió el mensaje** = he says he never received the message

◊ **mensajero, -ra** *n* messenger *o* courier; **lo mandamos a través de un mensajero porque el correo es demasiado lento** = we are sending it by messenger because the post is too slow

mensual *adj* monthly; **billete mensual** = monthly ticket; **estado de cuentas mensual** = monthly statement; **pagos mensuales** = monthly payments; **está pagando el coche en plazos mensuales** = he is paying for his car by monthly instalments; **revista** *o* **publicación mensual** = a monthly; **el cheque de mi sueldo mensual lleva retraso** = my monthly salary cheque is late

◊ **mensualmente** *adv* monthly; **pagar mensualmente** = to pay monthly; **se abona en cuenta mensualmente** = the account is credited monthly; **los intereses se calculan mensualmente** = interest is added monthly

mensualidad *nf* monthly payment; **deberá pagar una entrada de 25.000 ptas. y el resto en mensualidades de 20.000 ptas.** = to pay 25,000 pesetas down and monthly instalments of 20,000 pesetas

menú *nm* **(a)** *(comida)* menu; **menú del día** = set menu *o* today's menu **(b)** *(informática)* menu; **menú de programa** = program menu; **menú de selección** = pop-up *o* pull down menu

menudo, -da **1** *adj* small *o* little; **leer la letra menuda en un contrato** = to read the small print on a contract **2** *adv* **a menudo** = frequently; **enviamos un telefax a nuestra oficina de Nueva York muy a menudo - cuatro veces al día como mínimo** = we fax our New York office very frequently - at least four times a day

mercadería *nf* merchandise *o* goods; **mercadería de reventa** = goods for resale; **mercadería en venta** = goods for sale; **mercadería en viaje** = goods in transit

mercadillo *nm* flea market

mercado *nm* **(a)** *(lonja)* market; **mercado al aire libre** = open-air market; **mercado de coches** = car mart; **mercado de flores** = flower market; **aquí están los precios de mercado de las ovejas esta semana** = here are this week's market prices for sheep; **mercado de pescado** = fish market; **mercado de subastas** = auction rooms *o* auction mart; **día de mercado** = market day; **el martes es día de mercado, por lo que las calles están cerradas al tráfico** = Tuesday is market day, so the streets are closed to traffic; **cuota por un puesto en el mercado** = market dues **(b)** *(comercio)* market; **mercado cautivo** = captive market; **mercado cerrado** *o* **controlado** = closed market; **mercado deprimido** *o* **a la baja** = depressed market;

mercado estático *o* **estancado** = static market; **un mercado en expansión** = a growth market; **mercado favorable al comprador** = a buyer's market; **mercado favorable al vendedor** = a seller's market; **mercado interior** *o* **nacional** = home *o* domestic market; **ventas en el mercado interior** = home sales *o* sales in the home market; **las ventas en el mercado interior subieron un 22%** = sales in the home market rose by 22%; **sus ventas se sitúan principalmente en el mercado interior** = their sales are mainly in the home market; **mercado libre** = open market *o* free market; **comprar acciones en el mercado libre** = to buy shares in the open market; **mercado limitado** = narrow market; **mercado de masas** = mass market; **mercado perfecto** = perfect market; **mercado popular** = mass market *o* down market; **mercado selecto** = high-class market *o* up market; **dirigir la actividad comercial a un mercado selecto** *o* **un mercado popular** = to go up market *o* to go down market; **la empresa ha decidido dedicarse a un mercado más popular** = the company has decided to go down market **(c)** **el mercado negro** = the black market; **ventas en el mercado negro** = black market sales *o* under-the-counter sales; **pagar precios de mercado negro** = to pay black market prices; **se pueden comprar monedas de oro en el mercado negro** = you can buy gold coins on the black market; **existe un floreciente mercado negro de piezas de recambio para coches** = there is a flourishing black market in spare parts for cars **(d)** **análisis de mercado** = market analysis; **copar el mercado** = to corner the market; **cuota de mercado** = market share; **esperamos que nuestra nueva gama de productos aumente nuestra cuota** *o* **participación en el mercado** = we hope our new product range will increase our market share; **economía de (libre) mercado** = free market economy; **economista de mercado** = market economist; **estudio** *o* **investigación de mercado** = market research; **emprender una investigación del mercado** = to research a market *o* to undertake an investigation of the market; **las fuerzas del mercado** = market forces; **manipular el mercado** = to manipulate the market; **objetivo de mercado** = target market; **oportunidades de mercado** = market opportunities; **penetrar** *o* **introducirse en un mercado** = to penetrate a market; **penetración** *o* **participación en el mercado** = market penetration *o* market share; **precio de mercado** = market price; **previsión de mercado** = market forecast; **salir al mercado** = to come on to the market; **nos salimos del mercado sudamericano** = we got out of the South American market; **tarifa de mercado** = market rate; **pagamos a las secretarias la tarifa del mercado** = we pay the market rate for secretaries *o* we pay secretaries the market rate **(e)** *(bolsa)* **mercado alcista** = bull market; **mercado animado** = lively market; **el mercado de acciones petrolíferas estuvo muy activo** = the market in oil shares was very active *o* there was a brisk market in oil shares; **mercado bajista** = bear market; **mercados cambiarios** = foreign exchange markets; **mercado de capitales** = capital market; **mercados de divisas** = foreign exchange markets; **mercado financiero** = finance market; **mercado de futuros** = forward market *o* futures market; **la plata subió ayer un 5% en el mercado de futuros** = silver rose 5% on the commodity futures market yesterday; **mercado gris** = grey market; **mercado de materias primas** = commodity market; **mercado monetario** = money market; **mercado de valores** = stock market; **las altas y bajas del mercado de valores** = the highs and lows on the stock market; **cotización en el mercado bursátil** = stock market price *o* price on the stock market; **manipulación del mercado bursátil** = stock market manipulation; **tendencias del mercado** = market trends; **valor de mercado** = market value; **valor de mercado del capital emitido** = market capitalization **(f) mercado inmobiliario** = property market; **el mercado de ordenadores personales ha bajado bruscamente** = the market for home computers has fallen sharply; **tenemos el 20% del mercado de automóviles español** = we have 20% of the Spanish car market; **el mercado de los locales comerciales está en auge** = the commercial property market is booming; **mercado de propiedad comercial** = commercial property market; **el mercado de trabajo** = the labour market; **25.000 licenciados han ingresado en el mercado de trabajo** = 25,000 graduates have come on to the labour market **(g)** *(lugar donde se vende)* marketplace; **nuestros vendedores piensan que es difícil trabajar en el mercado** = our salesmen find life difficult in the marketplace; **¿cuál es la reacción del mercado hacia el nuevo coche?** = what is the reaction to the new car in the marketplace? *o* what is the marketplace reaction to the new car? **(h) el Mercado Común (Europeo)** = the (European) Common Market; **el Mercado Único Europeo** = the Single European Market; **los ministros del Mercado Común** = the Common Market ministers; **la política agrícola del Mercado Común** = the Common Market agricultural policy

> el proyecto ofrecía un nuevo mercado de casi 300 millones de personas, materias primas abundantes y mano de obra barata
> **España Económica**

> el mercado es dinámico y cambiante
> **Tiempo**

> la división de interiorismo se está convirtiendo en una importante fuerza en el mercado empresarial de Madrid
> **España Económica**

> la apertura del mercado interior supondrá un fuerte aumento de la competencia en el negocio bancario al por mayor, pero no dejará de incidir en la banca al por menor
> **Mercado**

> el valor del rublo en el mercado negro es 15 veces inferior a su valor oficial
> **España Económica**

mercadotecnia *nf* marketing *o* merchandising

mercancía *nf* commodity; **mercancías** = goods *o* merchandise *o* freight; **las mercancías se envían a través de dos puertos** = the merchandise is shipped through two ports; **las mercancías están sujetas al impuesto del timbre** = the goods are liable to stamp duty; **no venderán mercancías producidas por otras empresas** = they will not handle goods produced by other firms; **mercancías no vendidas** = goods left on hand; **mercancías en depósito aduanero** = goods in bond; **mercancías en tránsito** = goods in transit; **depósito** *o* **almacén** *o* **estación de mercancías** = goods depot *o* freight depot; **tren de mercancías** = goods train *o* freight train; **vagón de mercancías** = freight wagon; *US* freight car

mercante *adj* **barco mercante** = merchant ship *o* merchant vessel; **marina mercante** = merchant marine *o* merchant navy

mercantil *adj* mercantile; **banco mercantil** = merchant bank; **derecho mercantil** = commercial law *o* mercantile law; **périto mercantil** = chartered accountant; **registrador mercantil** = Registrar of Companies *o* the Company Registrar; **Registro Mercantil** = Companies House; **Oficina del Registro Mercantil** = Companies Registration Office

mercería *nf* haberdashery; **artículos de mercería** = dry goods

mérito *nm* merit; **gratificación por méritos** = merit award *o* merit bonus; **aumento de sueldo por méritos** = merit increase; **valoración de méritos** = merit rating; **méritos (profesionales)** = professional qualifications

merma *nf* leakage *o* waste *o* loss; **merma natural** = natural wastage

mermar *vt* to shrink

mes *nm* month; **mes civil** = calendar month; **mes corriente** = current month; **letras que vencen a finales del mes corriente** = bills due at the end of the current month; **cuentas de mediados de mes** = mid-month accounts; **del presente mes** = of the current month *o* 'instant'; **conceder a un cliente dos meses de crédito** = to give a customer two months' credit; **le presté 5.000 ptas. y prometió devolvérmelas en un mes** = I lent him 5,000 pesetas and he promised to pay me back in a month; **pagado por meses** = paid by the month; **la empresa le paga 100.000 ptas. al mes** = the firm pays him 100,000 pesetas a month

mesa *nf* **(a)** table; **la mesa tiene 1,80 m. de largo** = the table is 1.8m long; **quiero reservar una mesa para cuatro personas** = I want to reserve a table for four people; **mesa de la máquina de escribir** = typing table; **mesa redonda** = round table; **mesa vitrina** = display case **(b) mesa de despacho** = office desk; **una mesa de despacho con tres cajones** = a three-drawer desk; **agenda de mesa** = desk diary; **bloc de mesa** = desk pad; **lámpara de mesa** = desk light; **guarda la lista de direcciones en el cajón de la derecha de su mesa de trabajo** = he keeps the address list in the right-hand drawer of his desk

meta *nf* target *o* goal; **alcanzar una meta** = to hit a target *o* to meet one's target; **no alcanzar una meta** = to miss a target

metálico *nm* cash *o* hard cash; **pagó 20.000 ptas. en metálico por la silla** = he paid out 20,000 pesetas in cash for the chair

método *nm* method *o* technique; **un nuevo método de fabricación** *o* **de hacer algo** = a new method of making something *o* of doing something; **sus métodos de fabricación** *o* **producción figuran entre los más modernos del país** = their manufacturing methods *o* production methods are among the most modern in the country; **la empresa ha inventado un método nuevo para la elaboración del acero** = the company has developed a new technique for processing steel; **sus métodos organizativos son anticuados** = his organizing methods are out of date; **estudio de tiempos y métodos** = time and method study; **método de muestreo** = sampling method; **método de tanteo** = trial and error method

métrico, -ca *adj* metric; **tonelada métrica** = metric ton *o* tonne; **el sistema métrico** = the metric system

metro *nm* **(a)** *(longitud)* metre; *US* meter; **mi oficina tiene 3m. por 3,60m.** = my office is 3m by 3.6m; **metro cuadrado** *o* **cúbico** = square metre *o* cubic metre (NOTA: se abrevia **m**) **(b)** *(transporte)* **el metro** = the underground

México *nm* Mexico

◊ **mexicano, -na** *o* **mejicano, -na** *adj y n* Mexican
NOTA: capital: **México City** (= Mexico City); moneda: **peso mexicano ($Mex)** = Mexican peso (Mex$)

mezcla *nf* mix *o* mixture

◊ **mezclado, -da** 1 *adj* mixed 2 *pp de* MEZCLAR

mezclar *vt* to mix

mg = MILIGRAMO

mibor *nm* international money price (in Madrid)

micro- *prefijo* micro-

◊ **microficha** *nf* microfiche; **guardamos nuestros registros en microfichas** = we hold our records on microfiche

◊ **microfilm** *nm* microfilm; **guardamos nuestros registros en microfilmes** = we hold our records on microfilm

microfilmar *vt* to microfilm; **mande la correspondencia de 1990 para que sea microfilmada** = send the 1990 correspondence to be microfilmed *o* for microfilming

◊ **microordenador** *nm* microcomputer

◊ **microprocesador** *nm* microprocessor

miembro *nmf* **(a)** *(persona)* member; **miembros de una comisión** = members of a committee *o* committee members; **los eligieron miembros del consejo de administración** = they were elected members of the board; **fue elegida miembro del comité** = she was voted on to the committee; **el tesorero es miembro del comité financiero por razón de su cargo** = the treasurer is ex officio a member *o* an ex officio member of the finance committee; **miembro honorario** = honorary member; **carné de miembro** = membership card **(b)** *(organización)* member; **los países miembros de la UE** = the member countries of the EU; **los miembros de las Naciones Unidas** = the members of the United Nations; **las empresas miembros de una asociación comercial** = the member companies of a trade association

mil *adj y n* thousand; **mil millones** = billion

◊ **miligramo** *nm* milligram (NOTA: se abrevia **mg)**

◊ **mililitro** *nm* millilitre; *US* milliliter (NOTA: se abrevia **ml)**

◊ **milímetro** *nm* millimetre; *US* millimeter (NOTA: se abrevia **mm)**

militante 1 *adj* militant 2 *nmf* **(a)** militant **(b)** *(política)* active party member

milla *nf* mile

millón *nm* **(a)** million; **la compañía perdió 2 millones el año pasado y 4 millones este año, lo que supone 6 millones en total para los dos años** = the company lost 2m last year and 4m this year, making 6m altogether for the two years; **nuestro volumen de ventas ha subido a 13,4 millones de pesetas** = our turnover has risen to 13.4 million pesetas; **se perdió un millón de horas-hombre por las huelgas** = one million man-hours were lost through industrial action **(b) de varios millones** = multimillion; **firmaron un trato de varios millones** = they signed a multimillion deal

◊ **millonario, -ria** *n* millionaire; **millonario en acciones** = paper millionaire; **millonario en dólares** = dollar millionaire

mina *nf* mine *o* pit; **se han cerrado las minas a causa de una huelga** = the mines have been closed by a strike; **mina de oro** = goldmine; **esa tienda es una pequeña mina de oro** = that shop is a little goldmine

mineral 1 *adj* mineral; **recursos minerales** = mineral resources 2 *nm* mineral

mini- *prefijo* mini-

◊ **miniordenador** *nm* minicomputer

minimizar *vt* to minimize; **no minimice los posibles riesgos** = do not minimize the risks involved; **tiene tendencia a minimizar la dificultad del proyecto** = he tends to minimize the difficulty of the project

mínimo, -ma 1 *adj* minimum *o* minimal; **cantidad mínima** = minimum quantity; **el lote presentaba una cantidad mínima de imperfecciones** = there was a minimal quantity of imperfections in the batch; **la oficina principal ejerce un control mínimo sobre las sucursales** = the head office exercises minimal control over the branch offices; **dividendo mínimo** = minimum dividend; **nivel de existencias mínimo** = minimum stock level; **pago mínimo** = minimum payment; **precio mínimo** = lowest price *o* rock-bottom price *o* floor price; **punto mínimo** = lowest point *o* bottom; **salario mínimo** = minimum wage; **no gana el salario mínimo vital** = he does not earn a living wage 2 *nm* minimum *o* low; **las ventas han alcanzado un nuevo mínimo** = sales have reached a new low; **mantener los gastos a** *o* **al mínimo** = to keep spending to a minimum *o* to the minimum; **reducir el riesgo de pérdidas a un mínimo** = to reduce the risk of a loss to a minimum

> muchos valores se encuentran ya por debajo
> de los mínimos alcanzados en la crisis del
> Golfo Pérsico
> **Tiempo**

ministerio *nm* ministry *o* (government) department; **Ministerio de Asuntos Exteriores** = Foreign Ministry *o* Ministry of Foreign Affairs; *GB* Foreign Office; *US* State Department; **Ministerio de Economía y Hacienda** = Finance Ministry *o* Ministry of Finance *o* Treasury; *GB* Exchequer; **Ministerio de Educación y Ciencia** = Department of Education and Science; **Ministerio de Industria, Comercio y Turismo** = Department of Trade and Industry *o* the Board of Trade; **el Ministerio del Interior** = the Ministry of the Interior; *GB* the Home Office; **el Ministerio de Justicia** = the Ministry of Justice; *US* the Justice Department; **Ministerio de la Seguridad Social** = Department of Health and Social Security; **Ministerio de Trabajo** = Department of Employment (DoE); **¿a qué ministerio concierne?** = which is the relevant government department?; **un funcionario del ministerio** = a ministry official *o* an official from the ministry; **trabaja en el ministerio de Hacienda** = he works in the Ministry of Finance *o* the Finance Ministry

> los técnicos del Ministerio de Economía
> trabajan en estos días un nuevo plan
> económico cuatrienal
> **Tiempo**

ministro, -tra *n* minister; *GB* Secretary of State; **un ministro del gobierno** = a government minister; *(presidente del Gobierno)* **primer ministro** *o* **primera ministra** = Prime Minister; **el primer ministro español** = the Spanish Prime Minister *o* the Prime Minister of Spain; **el ministro de Asuntos Exteriores** = the Minister of Foreign Affairs *o* the Foreign Minister; *GB* the Foreign Secretary; *US* the Secretary of State; **el ministro de Comercio** = the Minister of Trade *o* the Trade Minister; **ministro de Economía y Hacienda** = the Finance Minister; *GB* the Chancellor of the Exchequer; *US* the Secretary of the Treasury; **el ministro de Educación** = the Education Secretary; **los ministros de la UE se han reunido hoy en Bruselas** = EU ministers met today in Brussels

minoría *nf* minority; **una minoría de los miembros del consejo de administración se opuso al presidente** = a minority of board members opposed the chairman; **en minoría** = in the minority; **los buenos vendedores están en minoría en nuestro equipo de ventas** = good salesmen are in the minority in our sales team

minorista *nmf* retailer *o* retail trader; **comercio de minorista** = retail store

minúscula *nf* small letter *o* lower case letter

minusvalía *nf* capital loss *o* depreciation

minuta *nf* **(a)** *(cuenta)* lawyer's bill **(b)** **minuta de un contrato** *o* **testamento** *o* **documento** = draft of a contract *o* a will *o* a deed

minuto *nm* minute; **sólo puedo dedicarte diez minutos** = I can see you for ten minutes only; **si no le importa esperar, el Sr. López estará libre en unos veinte minutos** = if you do not mind waiting, Sr López will be free in about twenty minutes' time

misceláneo, nea *adj* miscellaneous

misión *nf* mission *o* assignment; **misión comercial** = trade mission; **dirigió una misión comercial a China** = he led a trade mission to China; **misión investigadora** *o* **misión de investigación** = a fact-finding mission

mismo, -ma *adj* same; **el mismo** = the same; **uno mismo** *o* **una misma** = oneself; **al mismo tiempo** = at the same time

mitad *nf* half; **mitad y mitad** = half and half *o* fifty-fifty; **nos repartimos los beneficios mitad y mitad** = we share the profits half and half; **rebajas a mitad de precio** = half-price sale; **la mitad de las existencias quedaron destruidas en el incendio del almacén** = half the stock was destroyed in the warehouse fire

mixto, -ta *adj* mixed *o* joint; **comisión mixta de investigación** = joint commission of inquiry *o* joint committee; **economía mixta** = mixed economy; **empresa mixta** = joint venture; **granja mixta** = mixed farm

ml = MILILITRO

mm = MILIMETRO

mobiliario *nm* furniture; **mobiliario y enseres** = furniture and fittings; **una tienda de mobiliario de oficina** = an office furniture store; **tres empresas han hecho presupuestos para el mobiliario de las oficinas** = three firms estimated for the furnishing of the offices

moción *nf* motion; **autor de una moción** = mover *o* proposer of a motion; **persona que apoya una moción** = seconder of a motion; **presentar una moción** = to table a motion; **proponer una moción** = to propose *o* to move a motion; **se votó la moción en la reunión** = the meeting voted on the motion; **hablar en contra** *o* **a favor de una moción** = to speak against *o* for a motion; **la moción fue aprobada por 220 votos a favor y 196 en contra** *o* **fue rechazada por 220 votos en contra y 196 a favor** = the motion was carried *o* was defeated by 220 votes to 196; **la moción se aprobó a mano alzada** = the motion was carried on a show of hands; **una minoría de miembros del consejo se opuso a la moción** = a minority of board members opposed the motion

modelo 1 *adj* model; **un acuerdo modelo** = a model agreement; **una empresa modelo** = a model company **2** *nm* **(a)** *(estilo)* model *o* design *o* pattern; **un modelo de equipo estándar** = a standard make of equipment; **éste es el último modelo** = this is the latest model; **el modelo expuesto es el del año pasado** = the model on display is last year's; **conduce un Ford modelo 1994** = he drives a 1994 model Ford; **modelo de prueba** = demonstration model; **modelo económico** = economic model **(b)** *(persona)* model **(c)** **modelo a escala** = scale model *o* mock-up

módem *nm* *(informática)* modem

moderación *nf* moderation; **moderación salarial** = pay restraint *o* wage restraint

moderado, -da 1 *adj* *(prudente)* moderate *o* conservative; **su previsión de gastos es muy moderada** = his forecast of expenditure is very conservative; **el sindicato presentó unas reivindicaciones moderadas** = the trade union made a moderate claim; **el gobierno propuso un**

aumento moderado del tipo de impuesto = the government proposed a moderate increase in the tax rate **(b)** *(razonable)* reasonable; **el restaurante ofrece buena comida a precios moderados** = the restaurant offers good food at reasonable prices **2** *pp de* MODERAR

moderador, -ra *n* chairman *o* chairwoman *o* chairperson; **actuar de moderador** = to take the chair

moderar *vt* to moderate; **el sindicato se vio obligado a moderar sus pretensiones** = the union was forced to moderate its claim

◊ **moderarse** *vr* to restrain oneself *o* to hold back

modernización *nf* modernization *o* updating; **la modernización del taller** = the modernization of the workshop

modernizar *vt* to modernize *o* to update; **modernizó toda la gama de productos** = he modernized the whole product range

moderno, -na *adj* modern *o* up-to-date; **un sistema informático moderno** = an up-to-date computer system; **es un invento bastante moderno - tan sólo se patentó en los años 70** = it is a fairly modern invention - it was patented only in the 1970s

modesto, -ta *adj* modest; **las acciones petroliferas alcanzaron una modesta alza durante la semana** = oil shares showed modest gains over the week's trading

módico, -ca *adj* reasonable *o* moderate; **puede visitar el museo por un precio módico** = you can see the museum for a very reasonable price

modificable *adj* modifiable; **acuerdo modificable** = open-ended agreement

modificación *nf* modification; **hacer *o* llevar a cabo modificaciones del plan** = to make *o* to carry out modifications to the plan; **el nuevo modelo presenta modificaciones importantes** = the new model has had several important modifications

◊ **modificado, -da 1** *adj* modified; **éste es el nuevo acuerdo modificado** = this is the new modified agreement **2** *pp de* MODIFICAR

modificar *vt* to modify; **la dirección modificó sus propuestas** = the management modified its proposals; **el coche tendrá que ser modificado para pasar las pruebas oficiales** = the car will have to be modified to pass the government tests; **pedimos que se modificara el contrato** = we asked for modifications to the contract

modo *nm* **(a)** *(método)* method *o* way; **modo de empleo** = instructions (for use); **modo de pago** = method of payment *o* way of paying; **¿cuál es el mejor modo de pago?** = what is the best method of payment?; **de ningún modo** = under no circumstances **(b)** *(manera)* manner *o* way; **¿de que modo?** = in what way ? *o* how? **(c)** *(modales)* **modos** = manners; **es buen secretario pero tiene unos modos reprochables** = he's a good secretary but his manners leave a lot to be desired

modular 1 *adj* modular **2** *vt* to modulate

módulo *nm* module *o* unit; **módulos intercambiables** = interchangeable units

molestia *nf* bother; **ahorrarse molestias** = to save oneself the effort *o* to save oneself the bother; **ocasionar molestias** = to be a nuisance

Mónaco *nm* Monaco

◊ **monegasco, -ca** *adj y n* Monegasque *o* Monacan
NOTA: moneda: **franco francés (F)** = French franc (F)

moneda *nf* **(a)** *(dinero)* coin; **monedas sueltas** *o* **moneda suelta** = small change *o* cash *o* loose coins; **necesito monedas de 25 ptas. para el teléfono** = I need some 25 peseta coins for the telephone; **papel moneda** = paper money **(b)** *(divisa)* currency; **moneda convertible** *o* **moneda fuerte** = convertible currency *o* strong currency *o* hard currency; **pagar las importaciones en moneda convertible** = to pay for imports in hard currency; **una transacción en moneda convertible** = a hard currency deal; **moneda no convertible** *o* **moneda débil** = weak currency; **moneda corriente** = currency in circulation; **moneda de curso legal** *o* de **curso forzoso** = legal tender; **moneda extranjera** = foreign currency; **cambio de moneda extranjera** = foreign exchange; **moneda falsa** = false currency; **moneda fuerte** = strong currency; **moneda inflacionista** = inflated currency; **moneda única** = single currency; **Casa de la Moneda** = Mint; **sostener una moneda** = to support a currency

> por iniciativa de la Fábrica Nacional de Moneda y Timbre de España, 400 millones de iberoamericanos podrán usar una moneda de curso casi continental
>
> **Cambio 16**

> la banca europea tendrá que destinar entre 10.000 y 15.000 millones de euros en seis años para adecuar sus equipos informáticos a la moneda única
>
> **El País**

monedero *nm* **monedero electrónico** = plastic money

> los monederos electrónicos llegan al mundo de la educación
>
> **El País**

> miles de personas van a tener la posibilidad de manejar las tarjetas inteligentes o monederos electrónicos un producto financiero que amenaza con sustituir al viejo bolsillo de calderilla.
>
> **El País**

monetario, -ria *adj* monetary; **el Fondo Monetario Internacional (FMI)** = the International Monetary Fund (IMF); **mercados monetarios** = money markets; **objetivos monetarios** = monetary targets; **oferta monetaria** = money supply; **patrón monetario** = monetary standard; **la política monetaria del gobierno** = the government's monetary policy; **reserva monetaria de respaldo** = currency backing; **el sistema monetario internacional** = the international monetary system; **el Sistema Monetario Europeo (SME)** = the European Monetary System (EMS); **unidad monetaria** = monetary unit

> la política monetaria ortodoxa está muy
> bien, pero corre el riesgo de convertirse
> en una tecnocracia si se parte de
> situaciones distintas
> **Tiempo**

> el éxito de cualquier política monetaria
> es conseguir que la inflación baje hasta
> que desaparezca
> **España Económica**

monetarismo *nm* monetarism

◊ **monetarista** **1** *adj* monetarist; **teorías monetaristas** = monetarist theories **2** *nmf* monetarist

monitor, -ra 1 *n (persona)* instructor **2** *nm (pantalla)* monitor

monopolio *nm* monopoly; **estar en una situación de monopolio** = to be in a monopoly situation; **tener el monopolio de la venta de bebidas alcohólicas** = to have the monopoly of alcohol sales; **la compañía tiene el monopolio absoluto de las importaciones de vino francés** = the company has an absolute monopoly of imports of French wine; **monopolio público** *o* **estatal** = public monopoly *o* state monopoly

◊ **monopolización** *nf* monopolization

monopolizar *vt* to monopolize

monótono, -na *adj* monotonous *o* routine

montacargas *nm* goods lift *o* freight elevator

montaje *nm* **(a)** *(acoplamiento)* assembly; **no hay instrucciones de montaje para las estanterías** = there are no assembly instructions to show how to put the shelves together; **en montaje** = in the course of assembly *o* being assembled; **planta de montaje de automóviles** = car assembly plant; **cadena de montaje** = assembly line *o* production line; **trabaja en la cadena de montaje de la fábrica de coches** = he works on the production line in the car factory; **es una obrera de la cadena de montaje** = she is a production line worker; **línea de montaje** = assembly line **(b)** *(cine)* editing

montante *nm* amount *o* total sum

montaña *nf* mountain

montar *vt* to assemble *o* to build; **los motores se fabrican en Zaragoza, la carrocería en Valladolid y los coches se montan en Barcelona** = the engines are made in Zaragoza and the bodies in Valladolid, and the cars are assembled in Barcelona; **montar un negocio rentable** = to build up a profitable business

monte *nm* mountain; **Monte de Piedad** = pawnshop

monto *nm* total amount *o* sum; **monto a pagar por un deudor** = sum due from a debtor

montón *nm* heap *o* pile *o* stack; **un montón de facturas** = a pile of invoices; **tengo un montón de cosas para pasar a máquina** = I have mountains of typing to do *o* piles of things to type; **hay un montón de facturas en la mesa de despacho del director de ventas** = there is a heap of invoices on the sales manager's desk; **sacó un montón de billetes de banco usados** = he pulled out a pile of used bank notes

MOPU = MINISTERIO DE OBRAS PUBLICAS Ministry of Works

moratoria *nf* moratorium; **los bancos pidieron una moratoria en materia de pagos** = the banks called for a moratorium on payments

morir *vi* to die; **todos los pasajeros murieron en el accidente de aviación** = all the passengers were killed in the plane crash

moroso, -sa 1 *adj* slow; **deudor moroso** = slow payer; **la compañía es morosa** = the company is in default; **cobrador de morosos** = debt collector; **cobro de morosos** = debt collection; **agencia de cobro de morosos** = debt collection agency *o* collecting agency **2** *n* slow payer *o* defaulter

> entrar en un fichero de morosos no es
> difícil, no pagar una letra de la lavadora
> o la televisión es suficiente
> **El País**

mostrador *nm* counter; *(aeropuerto)* **mostrador de facturación** = check-in *o* check-in counter *o* check-in desk; **el mostrador de facturación está en el primer piso** = the check-in is on the first floor; **mostrador de recepción** = reception desk

> tradicionalmente, el hotelero ha visto
> llegar a sus clientes, desde la atalaya
> del mostrador de recepción, atraídos la
> mayoría de las veces por decisión de los
> touroperadores o los agentes de viaje
> **Tiempo**

mostrar *vt* **(a)** *(indicar)* to show; *(exponer)* to display; **mostrar beneficios** = to show a profit; **mostrar el funcionamiento de algo** = to demonstrate how something works **(b)** *(presentar)* to produce

motivación *nf* motivation; **al personal de ventas le falta motivación** = the sales staff lack motivation

◊ **motivado, -da 1** *adj* motivated; **personal de ventas muy motivado** = highly motivated sales staff **2** *pp de* MOTIVAR

motivar *vt* to motivate

motivo *nm* motive *o* reason *o* cause; **el jefe de personal le preguntó el motivo de su nuevo retraso** = the personnel officer asked him for the reason why he was late again; **el presidente está de viaje por Holanda por motivos de trabajo** = the chairman is absent in Holland on business; **¿tiene motivos fundados para quejarse?** = does he have good grounds for complaint?

motor *nm* motor *o* engine; **un coche con un motor pequeño es más económico que uno con uno grande** = a car with a small engine is more economic than one with a large one; **el motor del ascensor se ha averiado de nuevo - tendremos que subir andando hasta el 4° piso** = the lift motor has broken down again - we shall just have to walk up to the 4th floor

mover *vt* to move *o* to shift; **la empresa se está moviendo para contratar nuevo personal** = the company is busy recruiting new staff

◊ **moverse** *vr* to move

◊ **movible** *adj* mobile *o* moveable

◊ **movido, -da 1** *adj* agitated; **un mercado muy movido** = a nervous market **2** *pp de* MOVER

◊ **móvil** *adj* mobile *o* moveable; **escala móvil de derechos** = a sliding scale of charges; **escala móvil de salarios** = sliging scale of salaries *o* incremental salary scale; **mano de obra móvil** = mobile workforce; **piquete móvil** = flying pickets; **promedio móvil** = moving average

movilidad *nf* mobility; **movilidad de la mano de obra** = mobility of labour *o* labour mobility

movilizar *vt* to mobilize; **movilizar capital** = to mobilize capital; **movilizar recursos para defenderse de una oferta de adquisición** = to mobilize resources to defend a takeover bid

◊ **movilización** *nf (trabajadores)* action *o* protest

> el paquete de medidas aprobado por el Gobierno contribuye a movilizar recursos sin dañar los ingresos fiscales y la estabilidad de precios
> **El País**

movimiento *nm* **(a)** *(actividad)* movement *o* flow *o* motion; **sin movimiento** = motionless *o* flat (market); **un movimiento ascendente** = an upward movement; **durante el periodo de menor movimiento** = during the off-peak period; **las acciones bajaron en un día de poco movimiento** = shares fell back in light trading; **los movimientos de los mercados monetarios** = movements in the money markets; **movimientos de capital** = movements of capital *o* capital movements; **el movimiento de capitales hacia el país** = the flow of capital into a country; **movimientos cíclicos del comercio** = cyclical movements of trade; **movimientos de existencias** = stock movements; **el ordenador anota** *o* **registra todos los movimientos de existencias** = all stock movements are logged by the computer **(b)** *(personas)* movement; **el movimiento obrero** = the labour movement; **el movimiento en pro del libre comercio** = the free trade movement

> el presidente explicó a lo largo de su intervención la dificultad que existe en los delitos económicos que tienen una incidencia internacional y señaló que los movimientos de dinero son muy rápidos y en divisas, lo que dificulta su control
> **El País**

Mozambique *nm* Mozambique

◊ **mozambiqueño, -ña** *adj y n* Mozambiquan NOTA: capital: **Maputo;** moneda: **metical de Mozambique (Mt)** = Mozambique metical (Mt)

muchedumbre *nf* crowd *o* mass (of people)

mucho, -cha 1 *adj* a lot of *o* a great deal of *o* a good deal of; **mucha demanda** = a large demand; **la oficina de correos comunicó que había mucha demanda de los nuevos sellos** = the Post Office reported a heavy demand for *o* a run on the new stamps **2** *pron* many *o* a lot of; **¿te queda mucho por hacer todavía?** = do you still have a lot to do? **3** *adv* a lot *o* very much; **viaja mucho por su trabajo** = his job involves a lot of travelling

mudanza *nf* removal; **empresa de mudanzas** = removal *o* removals company

mudar *vt* to move; **le han mudado de oficina** = they have moved him to another office

◊ **mudarse** *vr* to move; **mudarse de edificio** = to move to another building

mueble 1 *adj* **bienes muebles** = moveable property **2** *nm* piece of furniture; **muebles** = furniture; **una tienda de muebles** = a furniture store; **muebles y enseres** = goods and chattels; **muebles de oficina** = office furniture; **tiene un negocio de muebles de oficina de segunda mano** = he deals in secondhand office furniture

muellaje *nm (derechos de muelle)* wharfage

muelle *nm* wharf *o* berth *o* dock *o* quay; **muelle de carga** = loading dock; **precio puesto en muelle** *o* **franco en muelle** = price ex quay; **tenemos que ir a buscar las mercancías del muelle** = we have to fetch the goods from the docks; **derechos de muelle** = wharfage

muerte *nf* death *o* demise; **después de su muerte la propiedad pasó a su hija** = on his death the estate passed to his daughter

muerto, -ta *adj* dead; **seis personas resultaron muertas a consecuencia del accidente** = six people were dead as a result of the accident **2** *pp de* MORIR

muestra *nf* **(a)** *(espécimen)* specimen *o* sample; **muestra de aceptación** = acceptance sampling; **muestra de firma** = specimen signature; **muestra de color** = colour sample *o* colour swatch; **muestra de control** = check sample; **muestra gratuita** = free sample; **muestra de inspección** *o* **comprobación** = check sample; **muestra pequeña** = little sample; **muestra de prueba** *o* **ensayo** = trial sample; **una muestra de la tela** = a sample of the cloth *o* a cloth sample; **libro de muestras** = sample book *o* book of samples; **según muestra** = as per sample **(b)** *(encuesta)* sample; **una muestra aleatoria** = a random sample; **sondear a una muestra de la población** = to poll a sample of the population; **toma de muestras** = sampling; **entrevistamos a una muestra de clientes potenciales** = we interviewed a sample of potential customers **(c)** *(modelo)* pattern

◊ **muestrario** *nm* sample book *o* pattern book

◊ **muestreo** *nm* sampling; **muestreo aleatorio** = random sampling; **muestreo de productos de la Unión Europea** = sampling of European Union produce; **error de muestreo** = sampling error

mujer *nf* woman; **mujer de negocios** = businesswoman

multa *nf* fine *o* penalty; **le pusieron una multa de 25.000 ptas.** = he was asked to pay a 25,000 peseta fine; **tuvimos que pagar una multa por aparcamiento indebido** = we had to pay a parking fine; **correr el riesgo de que le pongan a uno una multa** = to incur the risk of a penalty; **expuesto a una multa** = liable to a fine

multar *vt* to fine *o* to penalize; **multar a alguien con 500.000 ptas. por obtener dinero fraudulentamente** = to fine someone 500,000 pesetas for obtaining money by false pretences

multi- *prefijo* multi-

◊ **multicopista** *nf* duplicator *o* copying machine *o* duplicating machine; **papel de multicopista** = duplicating paper; **estarcido de multicopista** = stencil

◊ **multilateral** *adj* multilateral; **un acuerdo multilateral** = a multilateral agreement; **comercio multilateral** = multilateral trade

◊ **multilingüe** *adj* multilingual; **un contrato multilingüe** = a multilingual contract *o* a contract in several languages

◊ **multimillonario, -ria** *n* multimillionaire

◊ **multinacional 1** *adj* multinational; **compañía** *o* **empresa multinacional** = multinational *o* trans-national corporation **2** *nf* *(compañía)* multinational; **la empresa ha sido comprada por una de las grandes multinacionales** = the company has been bought by one of the big multinationals

> el pedazo más grande del pastel se lo reparten dos multinacionales norteamericanas que controlan entre ambas la mitad del mercado
>
> **Micros**

múltiple *adj* multiple; **operación en múltiples divisas** = multicurrency operation; **préstamo en múltiples divisas** = muticurrency loan; **visado de entradas múltiples** = multiple entry visa

multiplicación *nf* multiplication

multiplicar *vt* to multiply; **signo de multiplicar** = multiplication sign; **multiplicar doce por tres** = to multiply twelve by three; **las medidas de superficie se calculan multiplicando la longitud por la anchura** = square measurements are calculated by multiplying length by width; **los beneficios se multiplicaron en los años de prosperidad** = profits multiplied in the boom years

multipropiedad *nf* time share *o* time sharing

multitud *nf* crowd *o* mass

mundial *adj* worldwide *o* global; **el mercado mundial del acero** = the world market for steel; **la compañía tiene una red mundial de distribuidores** = the company has a worldwide network of distributors; **ofrecemos un servicio de reparto a domicilio mundial las 24 horas del día** = we offer a 24-hour global delivery service; **las ventas mundiales han superado la cifra de dos millones de unidades** = worldwide sales *o* sales worldwide have topped two million units

◊ **mundialmente** *adv* worldwide; **los Riojas**

son vinos conocidos **mundialmente** = Rioja wines are famous worldwide

mundo *nm* **(a)** *(universo)* world; **en todo el mundo** = worldwide; **esta marca de ordenadores se vende en todo el mundo** = this make of computer is available worldwide **(b)** *(en sentido figurado: oficio)* world; **el mundo de los abogados** = the world of lawyers *o* the legal world; **el mundo de las editoriales** = the world of publishing *o* the publishing world; **el mundo de los grandes negocios** = the world of big business

> el trabajo fijo para toda la vida, antes panacea de burócratas y asalariados, ha dejado de ser una moneda común en el actual complejo mundo de los negocios
>
> **El País**

municipal *adj* municipal; **concejo municipal** = town council; **contribuyente municipal** = ratepayer; **impuestos municipales** = municipal taxes; **oficinas municipales** = municipal offices; **jefe de sanidad municipal** = medical officer of health

◊ **municipio** *nm* town hall

◊ **municipalidad** *nf* local authority

mutualidad *nf* mutuality *o* friendly society

mutuo, -tua 1 *adj* mutual; **sociedad mutua (de seguros)** = mutual (insurance) company; **fondos mutuos** = unit trust; *US* mutual fund **2** *nf* mutual (insurance) company

muy *adv* **(a)** *(mucho)* very *o* much *o* quite; **los precios están muy altos** = prices are running high; **muy conocido** = well-known; **crédito en condiciones muy favorables** = loan given on very favourable terms; **es muy probable que la compañía se venda** = the company is very probably going to be sold; **estos bonos son muy sólidos** = these bonds are very safe **(b)** **muy bien** = very well *o* greatly *o* highly; **ese restaurante está muy bien de precios** = that restaurant gives value for money; **muy bien pagado** = highly-paid; **muy bien situado** = highly-placed; **las ventas van muy bien** = sales are going well; **que se vende muy bien** = best-selling; **a mi hijo le va muy bien - acaba de ser ascendido** = my son is getting on well - he has just been promoted

Nn

nación *nf* nation; **nación deudora** = debtor nation; **nación más favorecida** = most favoured nation; **cláusula de la nación más favorecida** = most-favoured-nation clause; **Organización de las Naciones Unidas (la ONU)** = the United Nations (the UN)

◊ **nacional** *adj* (a) *(relacionado a la nación)* national; **de ámbito nacional** = nationwide; **banco nacional** = national bank; **campaña nacional** = national campaign; **a escala nacional** = on a national scale *o* nationwide; **el sindicato convocó una huelga a escala nacional** = the union called for a nationwide strike; **publicidad a escala nacional** = national advertising; **fiesta nacional** = public holiday; **los periódicos nacionales** *o* **la prensa nacional** = national newspapers *o* the national press; **Producto Nacional Bruto (PNB)** = gross national product (GNP); **renta nacional** = national income (b) *(interior)* domestic *o* home *o* inland; **comercio nacional** = domestic trade; **producen mercancías para el mercado nacional** = they produce goods for the domestic market; **productos nacionales** = home-produced products; **transportista nacional** = inland carrier; **ventas nacionales** = domestic sales; **volumen de ventas nacionales** = domestic turnover

◊ **nacionalidad** *nf* nationality *o* citizenship; **es de nacionalidad española** = he is of Spanish nationality *o* he is a Spanish national

◊ **nacionalización** *nf* nationalization

nacionalizar *vt* to nationalize; **el gobierno tiene el proyecto de nacionalizar la banca** = the government is planning to nationalize the banking system

nada 1 *nf* nil *o* nothing *o* nought; **de nada** = don't mention it *o* you're welcome; **nada más** = that's all; **no sirve para nada** = it's useless **2** *pron* nothing; **no ha dicho nada interesante** = he hasn't said anything interesting **3** *adv* at all; **no es nada fácil** = it isn't at all easy; **no es nada servicial** = he's not at all helpful

naira *nf (moneda de Nigeria)* naira

Namibia *nf* Namibia; **de Namibia** = Namibian NOTA: capital: **Windhoek**; moneda: **rand surafricano** = South African rand

natural 1 *adj* (a) *(que no es producido por el hombre)* natural; **fibras naturales** = natural fibres; **gas natural** = natural gas; **recursos naturales** = natural resources (b) *(normal)* natural; **era natural que el tendero se sintiera molesto cuando el hipermercado se instaló cerca de su tienda** = it was natural for the shopkeeper to feel annoyed when the hypermarket was set up close to his shop; **desgaste natural** = fair wear and tear **2** *nmf* native *o* inhabitant

◊ **naturaleza** *nf* nature

◊ **naturalmente** *adv* naturally *o* of course

naufragar *vi* to be wrecked *o* to sink; **están intentando salvar el petrolero que naufragó** = they are trying to salvage the wrecked tanker; **el petrolero naufragó cuando se dirigía al Golfo** = the tanker sank when she was en route to the Gulf

◊ **naufragio** *nm* shipwreck *o* wreck; **restos de un naufragio** = wreckage

nave *nf* (a) *(barco)* ship *o* vessel (b) *(de una fábrica o almacén)* **nave de carga** = loading bay; **nave industrial** = factory premises *o* industrial premises

navegar *vt/i* to sail

necesario, -ria *adj* necessary; **¿es realmente necesario que el presidente tenga seis ayudantes?** = is it really necessary for the chairman to have six personal assistants?; **debe reunir toda la documentación necesaria para poder solicitar una subvención** = you must have all the necessary documentation before you apply for a subsidy; **menos de lo necesario** = not enough; **tenemos menos personal del necesario** = we are short of staff

necesidad *nf* (a) necessity *o* need *o* want; **alimentos de primera necesidad** = essential foodstuffs; **artículo** *o* **producto de primera necesidad** = staple commodity (b) **necesidades** = requirements; **necesidades básicas** = basic necessities; **satisfacer las necesidades de un cliente** = to meet a customer's requirements; **las necesidades de un mercado** = the requirements of a market *o* market requirements; **necesidades presupuestarias** = budgetary requirements; **necesidades de la mano de obra** = manpower requirements

◊ **necesitado, -da 1** *adj* (a) *(falto de recursos)* poor *o* needy; **la empresa trata de ayudar a los empleados más necesitados con préstamos sin interés** = the company tries to help the poorest members of staff with soft loans (b) **necesitado de** = in need of **2** *pp de* NECESITAR

necesitar *vt* to need *o* to require; **para redactar el programa se necesita un especialista en informática** = to write the program requires a computer specialist

neerlandés, -esa *adj y n* Dutch; *ver* PAISES BAJOS

negar *vt* (a) *(rechazar)* to refuse *o* to deny; **le negaron el crédito** = they refused him credit (b) *(la existencia de algo)* to deny; **negó los hechos** = he denied the facts

◊ **negarse** *vr* to refuse to; **se negaron a pagar** = they refused to pay; **se negó a aceptar algunas de las condiciones del contrato** = he refused to agree to some of the terms of the contract; **la dirección se negó a negociar con el sindicato** = the management refused to negotiate with the union; **el gobierno se ha negado a ayudar a las compañías en dificultades económicas** = the government has refused to help companies which are in difficulty

negativo, -va 1 *adj* negative; **la respuesta fue**

negativa = the answer was in the negative; **balanza comercial negativa** = negative *o* adverse balance of trade; **factor negativo** = minus factor; **la pérdida de ventas en el mejor trimestre del año es un factor negativo para el equipo de ventas** = to have lost sales in the best quarter of the year is a minus factor for the sales team; **flujo de caja negativo** = negative cash flow; **las cuentas arrojan un saldo negativo** = the accounts show a minus figure **2** *nf* refusal; **me contestó con la negativa** = he replied in the negative; **negativa general** = general refusal *o* blanket refusal

negligencia *nf* negligence

◊ **negligente** *adj* negligent

negociable *adj* negotiable; **cheque negociable** = negotiable cheque; **documento negociable** = negotiable instrument; **letras no negociables** = ineligible bills

negociación *nf* negotiations *o* bargaining; **negociaciones salariales** = pay negotiations *o* wage negotiations; **poder de negociación** = bargaining power; **entablar negociaciones** = to enter into negotiations *o* to start negotiations; **llevar a cabo negociaciones** = to conduct negotiations; **después de seis horas se interrumpieron las negociaciones** = negotiations broke down after six hours; **reanudar las negociaciones** = to resume negotiations; **romper las negociaciones** = to break off negotiations

> el resultado del proceso de negociación salarial definirá el margen para el descenso de los tipos de interés, así como del tipo de cambio de la peseta
> **Actualidad Económica**

negociado, -da 1 *nm* department *o* section; **negociado de asuntos generales** = service department; **jefe de negociado** = head of department **2** *pp de* NEGOCIAR

negociador, -ra 1 *adj* negotiating; **postura negociadora** = bargaining position **2** *n* negotiator; **un negociador sindical experimentado** = an experienced union negotiator; **es un negociador duro** = he's a tough negotiator

negociante *nmf* **(a)** *(comerciante)* businessman *o* businesswoman *o* business person *o* dealer *o* merchant; **negociante de carbón** = coal merchant; **negociante de coches** = car dealer; **negociante de tabaco** = tobacco merchant **(b)** **negociante de arbitraje** = arbitrager *o* arbitrageur

negociar 1 *vt* to negotiate; **negociar las condiciones** *o* **negociar un contrato** = to negotiate terms and conditions *o* to negotiate a contract; **negoció un préstamo de 250.000 ptas. con el banco** = he negotiated a 250,000 peseta loan with the bank; **negoció con éxito un nuevo contrato con los sindicatos** = he successfully negotiated a new contract with the unions; **contrato que está siendo negociado** = contract under negotiation; **un asunto que debe ser negociado** = a matter for negotiation **2** *vi* **(a)** to negotiate *o* to deal; **negociar con alguien** = to negotiate with someone; **la dirección se negó a negociar con el sindicato** = the management refused to negotiate with the union; **negociar para obtener condiciones más favorables** = to negotiate for better terms **(b)** to trade; **negociar en bolsa** = to trade on the Stock Exchange

negocio *nm* **(a)** *(actividad comercial)* business; **negocio hotelero** = the hotel trade; **negocio ilícito** = illicit trade; **negocio lucrativo** = profitable business; **negocio en marcha** = going concern; **su negocio marcha bien** = his business is a going concern; **negocio en participación** = joint venture; **negocio sucio** = shady deal; **negocio suplementario** = secondary business *o* sideline; **lleva un rentable negocio suplementario de venta de postales a turistas** = he runs a profitable sideline selling postcards to tourists; **el negocio cerró en diciembre** = the business folded up last December; **el negocio de la confección ha sufrido la competencia extranjera** = the ready-to-wear trade has suffered from foreign competition **(b)** **abrir un negocio** = to open a business; **dedicarse a los negocios** = to go into business; **se dedicó al negocio de venta de automóviles** = he went into business as a car dealer; **emprender un negocio** *o* **iniciar un negocio** = to go into business *o* to open a business; **invertir en un negocio** = to invest in a business *o* to put money into a business; **inyectar capital en un negocio** = to inject capital into a business; **llevar un negocio** = to carry on a business; **poner un negocio** = to set up in business; **vender el negocio propio** = to dispose of one's business *o* to sell up; **vendió su negocio y se retiró a la costa** = he sold up and retired to the seaside **(c)** **agente de negocios** = middleman; **banco de negocios** = merchant bank; **banquero de negocios** = merchant banker; **cifra de negocios** = turnover; **hombre** *o* **mujer de negocios** = businessman *o* businesswoman; **un hombre de negocios fracasado** = an unsuccessful businessman; **un próspero hombre de negocios** = a successful businessman; **su negocio está en pleno funcionamiento** = his business is a going concern; **ingresos de un negocio** = takings of a business; **volumen de negocios** = turnover **(d)** *(trato)* deal; **el director de ventas consiguió firmar un negocio de varios millones de dólares** = the sales director managed to sign a deal worth several million dollars; **en ese negocio hubo que proceder con mucha insistencia** = a lot of hard selling went into that deal

> el negocio va tan bien que GHS está aumentando la capacidad de producción de Tecfloor en un 500%
> **España Económica**

> el año que viene será bueno para los negocios y mejor aún para la política
> **Actualidad Económica**

negro, -gra *adj* black; **economía negra** = black economy; **lista negra** = black list; **mercado negro** = black market; **un próspero mercado negro de radios para automóviles** = thriving black market in car radios

Nepal *nm* Nepal

◊ **nepalés, -esa** *adj y n* Nepalese *o* Nepali
NOTA: capital: **Katmandú** (= Katmandu); moneda: **rupia nepalesa (NRs)** = Nepalese rupee (NRs)

nervioso, -sa *adj* nervous *o* jumpy; **depresión nerviosa** = nervous breakdown

neto, -ta *adj* net; **activo neto** = net assets *o* net worth; **beneficio neto** = net profit; **beneficio neto sin descontar los impuestos** = net profit before tax; **facturación** *o* **producción neta** = net turnover; **flujo neto de caja** = net cash flow; **ganancias netas** = net earnings *o* net income; **ingresos netos** = net income *o* net receipts; **margen neto** = net margin; **pérdida neta** = net loss; **peso neto** = net weight; **precio neto** = net price; **rendimiento neto** = net yield; **salario neto** *o* **sueldo neto** = net income *o* net salary *o* take-home pay; **valor neto en los libros de la compañía** = net book value; **ventas netas** = net sales

neutralizar *vt* to cancel out *o* to neutralize; **los impuestos altos neutralizarán los aumentos de sueldo** = high taxes will cancel out wage increases

◊ **neutralizarse** *vr* to cancel each other out; **las dos cláusulas se neutralizan mutuamente** = the two clauses cancel each other out

Nicaragua *nf* Nicaragua

nicaragüense *adj y nmf* Nicaraguan
NOTA: capital: **Managua;** moneda: **córdoba nicaragüense ($C)** = Nicaraguan cordoba (C$)

nicho *nm* **nicho de mercado** = niche

el tráfico mercantil actual ha permitido el
florecimiento de un nuevo nicho de mercado,
el de la información 'on line'
         El País

NIF = NUMERO DE IDENTIFICACION FISCAL tax number

Níger *nm* Niger

◊ **nigeriano, -na** *adj y n* Nigerien
NOTA: capital: **Niamey;** moneda: **franco CFA (FCFA)** = CFA franc (CFAF)

Nigeria *nf* Nigeria

◊ **nigeriano, -na** *adj y n* Nigerian
NOTA: capital: **Abuja;** moneda: **naira nigeriana (N)** = Nigerian naira (N)

nipón, -ona *ver* JAPON

nivel *nm* **(a)** level; **aumentar el nivel de los subsidios de los empleados** = to raise the level of employee benefits; **reducir el nivel de los préstamos** = to lower the level of borrowings; **niveles de dotación de personal** *o* **de plantilla** = manning levels *o* staffing levels; **nivel de audiencia de los programas televisivos** = TV ratings; **decisiones tomadas a nivel de dirección** = decisions taken at managerial level; **alto nivel de inversión** = high level of investment; **la producción ha alcanzado su nivel más alto** = output has reached a ceiling; **niveles bajos de productividad** = low levels of productivity *o* low productivity levels **(b) de alto nivel** = (i) high-level; (ii) of a high standard; **una reunión** *o* **delegación de alto nivel** = a high-level meeting *o* delegation; **una delegación comercial de alto nivel** = a high-grade trade delegation; **una decisión de alto nivel** = a high-level decision; **una reunión de alto nivel** = a high-level meeting; **lenguaje de programación de alto nivel** = high-level computer language; **de bajo nivel** = low-level; **en una reunión de bajo nivel se decidió aplazar la decisión** = a low-level meeting decided to put off making a decision **(c) nivel de vida** = standard of living *o* living standards; **el nivel de vida descendió a medida que aumentaba el paro** =

living standards fell as unemployment rose; **este lote no alcanza el debido nivel** = this batch is not up to standard *o* does not meet our standards

los sindicatos se han distanciado de un
Gobierno socialista moderado cuyo pacto
de competitividad han rechazado temiendo
que acarreara un descenso del nivel de
vida
      Actualidad Económica

nivelar *vt* to level out *o* to balance

◊ **nivelarse** *vr* to level off *o* to level out; **los precios se han nivelado** = prices have levelled off

no *adv* **(a)** *(negación)* no *o* not; **no aceptación** = non-acceptance; **no archivado** = unrecorded; **no asegurado** = uninsured; **no autorizado** = unauthorized *o* unlicensed; **no confirmado** = unconfirmed; **no disponible** = not available; **no reembolsable** = non-refundable; **depósito no reembolsable** = non-refundable deposit; **no residente** = non-resident; **tiene una cuenta bancaria de no residente** = he has a non-resident bank account; **no solicitado** = unsolicited; **no usado** = unused; **no verificado** = unaudited **(b) no pagar** = to default

noche *nf* night; **el ordenador estuvo preparando facturas toda la noche** = the computer was running invoices all night; **turno de noche** = night shift; **hay treinta trabajadores en el turno de noche** = there are thirty men on the night shift; **turno** *o* **guardia de noche** = night duty; **trabaja en el turno de noche** = he works nights *o* he works the night shift; **de la noche** = at night; **11 de la noche** = 11 p.m.; **abierto por la noche** = late-night opening

nocturno, -na *adj* nocturnal *o* evening *o* late-night

nombrado, -da 1 *adj* appointed *o* designate; **el presidente nombrado** = the chairman designate; **nombrado para la candidatura** = nominated as a candidate; **nombrado a continuación** = hereinafter mentioned **2** *pp de* NOMBRAR

nombramiento *nm* nomination *o* appointment; **nuevo nombramiento** = reappointment; **notificación del nombramiento para un puesto** = letter of appointment *o* letter appointing someone to a post; **nombramiento de administrador judicial** = letters of administration

nombrar *vt* **(a)** *(escoger)* to appoint; **nombrar director a José Martínez** = to appoint José Martínez (to the post of) manager; **hemos nombrado un nuevo director de distribución** = we have appointed a new distribution manager; **cuando le nombraron director** = when he was appointed manager *o* on his appointment as manager; **decidimos nombrar a alguien de la casa** = we decided to make an internal appointment; **nombrar por coopción** = to co-opt someone (onto a committee); **le nombraron de nuevo presidente por otro periodo de tres años** = he was reappointed chairman for a further three-year period; **nombrar candidatos** = to nominate candidates **(b)** *(mencionar)* to mention; **nombrar un lugar** *o* **una fecha** = to mention a place *o* a date

nombre *nm* **(a)** name; **su nombre está en nuestra lista de destinatarios** = his name is on our mailing list; **no puedo recordar el nombre del director**

general de la empresa Sopasa S.A. = I cannot remember the name of the managing director of Sopasa S.A.; **su nombre de pila es Juan pero no estoy seguro de sus apellidos** = his first name is Juan but I am not sure of his other names; **indique su nombre, apellidos y dirección** = give your full name and address o your name and address in full; **la factura está dirigida a nombre de García y Hnos.** = the bill is made out to García y Hnos.; *(razón social)* **nombre comercial** = (i) corporate name ; (ii) trademark o trade name; **con el nombre de** = under the name of; **productos vendidos con el nombre de 'La Mejor Comida'** = trading under the name of 'La Mejor Comida' **(b) actuar en nombre de** = to act on behalf of; **actúa en mi nombre** = she is acting on my behalf; **en nombre de** = on behalf of; **escribo en nombre de los accionistas minoritarios** = I am writing on behalf of the minority shareholders

nómina *nf* payroll; **impuesto sobre la nómina** = payroll tax; **tenemos 250 personas en nómina** = we have 250 people on the payroll; **el departamento de contabilidad está organizando un nuevo programa de nóminas** = the accounts department is running a new payroll program

nominal *adj* nominal o in name only; **coste nominal** = nominal cost; **valor nominal** = nominal value o par value

nominativo, -va *adj* nominative o nominal; **acciones nominativas** = registered shares; **cheque nominativo** = cheque made out to

norcoreano, -na *adj y n* North Korean

nórdico, -ca *adj* nordic; **Consejo Nórdico** = Nordic Council

norma *nf* **(a)** *(regla)* rule; **conforme a la norma** = according to the rule; **actua conforme a la norma 23 de los estatutos del sindicato** = he is acting under rule 23 of the union constitution; **normas estatutorias** = statutory regulations; **según la norma vigente** = under current regulations; **normas de la empresa** = company rules; **normas de conducta** = code of practice; **es norma de la empresa que no se fume en las oficinas** = it is a company rule that smoking is not allowed in the offices; **va en contra de las normas de la compañía conceder más de treinta días de crédito** = it is against company policy to give more than thirty days' credit **(b)** *(patrón)* norm o standard; **normas de producción** = production standards; **la producción de esta fábrica está muy por encima de la norma de este sector industrial** = the output from this factory is well above the norm for the industry o well above the industry norm; **este lote no cumple nuestras normas** = this batch is not up to standard o does not meet our standards **(c)** *(por regla general)* **por norma** = as a rule; **tenemos por norma que la asesoría jurídica examine todos los contratos** = our policy is to submit all contracts to the legal department

algunos mercados no son perfectos, y es posible que hagan falta regulaciones y normas para alcanzar algunos de nuestros objetivos
Mercado

la obra comenzó en vísperas de que entraran en vigor las estrictas normas europeas de protección al medio ambiente
Cambio 16

el 90% de las normas vigentes han sido elaboradas por el ejecutivo
Cambio 16

normal *adj* **(a)** *(corriente)* normal o usual o standard; **lo normal es que el contrato sea firmado por el director gerente** = the usual practice is to have the contract signed by the MD; **el horario normal de trabajo es de 9 a 7** = the usual hours of work are from 9 to 7; **en condiciones normales** = under normal conditions; **en condiciones normales un paquete llega a Copenhague en dos días** = under normal conditions a package takes two days to get to Copenhagen; **nuestras condiciones normales son treinta días de crédito** = our usual terms o usual conditions are thirty days' credit; **tasa de impuesto normal** = standard rate of tax; **tamaño normal** = regular size; **tarifa normal** = full fare; **nuestro precio normal es de 2.500 ptas. la sesión de media hora** = we have a standard charge of 2,500 pesetas for a thirty-minute session; **el precio normal es de 195 ptas. pero los ofrecemos a 95** = the regular price is 195 pesetas, but we are offering them at 95 **(b)** *(ordinario)* ordinary o common; **un día normal** = an ordinary day; **el coche funciona mejor con gasolina normal** = the car runs best on ordinary petrol

normalización *nf* standardization; **normalización de medidas** = standardization of measurements; **normalización de productos** = standardization of products

normalizar *vt* to standardize

normativa *nf* regulations; **la normativa vigente** = current regulations

el proceso liberalizador español sea cual sea la normativa final de la Administración, no impedirá que Gas Natural culmine prácticamente en solitario la gasificación de España, un proceso que acaba de empezar
El País

Norteamérica *nf* North America

◊ **norteamericano, -na** *adj y n* North American

Noruega *nf* Norway

◊ **noruego, -ga** *adj y n* Norwegian
NOTA: capital: **Oslo**; moneda: **corona noruega (NKr)** = Norwegian krone (NKr)

nota *nf* **(a)** *(escrito informal)* note o memo; **enviar una nota a alguien** = to send someone a note; **le envié al director gerente una nota sobre su reclamación** = I sent the managing director a memo about your complaint; **escribir una nota al director financiero** = to write a memo to the finance director; **dejé una nota sobre su mesa de despacho** = I left a note on his desk **(b)** *(documento)* note; **nota de abono** o **crédito** = credit note; **nota de cargo** o **adeudo** = debit note; **cobramos de menos al Sr Pereira y tuvimos que mandarle una nota de cargo por la cantidad extra** o **adicional** = we undercharged Sr Pereira and had to send him a debit note for the extra amount; **nota de cobertura** = cover note; *US* binder; **nota de envío** o **expedición** = advice note o dispatch note; **según nota de expedición** = as per advice **(c)** *(papel o recibo)* slip; **nota de copyright** o **sobre los derechos de autor** =

copyright notice; **nota de depósito** = deposit slip *o* paying-in slip; **nota de distribución** = distribution slip **(d) tomar nota** = to note; **tomamos nota que la mercancía fue entregada en malas condiciones** = we note that the goods were delivered in bad condition; **hemos tomado nota de su queja** *o* **de su reclamación** = your complaint has been noted; **hemos tomado nota de su pedido y lo despacharemos en cuanto tengamos existencias** = your order has been noted and will be dispatched as soon as we have stock **(e) nota a pie de página** = footnote

notable *adj* exceptional *o* outstanding

notar *vt* to notice *o* to see

notario, -ria *n GB* solicitor; *US* notary public

noticia *nf* **(a)** *(comunicación)* item *o* piece of news; **tener noticias de alguien** = to hear from someone; **esperamos tener noticias de los abogados dentro de unos días** = we hope to hear from the lawyers within a few days; **no hemos tenido noticias suyas desde hace algún tiempo** = we have not heard from them for some time; **las cotizaciones de las acciones cayeron en picado ante la noticia de la devaluación** = share prices plummeted *o* plunged on the news of the devaluation; **la noticia de la devaluación causó conmoción en los mercados financieros** = financial markets were shocked by the news of the devaluation **(b)** *(en un periódico)* **noticias** = news; **noticias financieras** = financial news; **la sección de noticias comerciales** = the business section

◊ **noticiario** *nm* the news

notificación *nf* **(a)** *(aviso)* notification; **notificación de rescisión de contrato** *o* **de modificación de condiciones** = official notice that a contract is going to end *o* that new conditions will be introduced; **notificación del nombramiento para un puesto** = letter of appointment *o* letter appointing someone to a post; **al recibir la notificación, la compañía presentó una apelación** = on receipt of the notification, the company lodged an appeal **(b)** **notificación de despido** = notice; **exigimos una notificación previa de tres meses** = we require three months' notice

notificar *vt* to report *o* to notify; **notificó los daños a la compañía de seguros** = he reported the damage to the insurance company; **notificar algo a alguien** = (i) to notify someone of something; (ii) to serve notice on someone; **notificar el desahucio a un inquilino** = to give a tenant notice to quit; **se les notificó la llegada del envío** = they were notified of the arrival of the shipment

novedad *nf* novelty *o* new development *o* new departure; **la venta de discos será una novedad para la librería local** = selling records will be a departure for the local bookshop; **sin novedad** = no change *o* nothing new

n/ref = NUESTRA REFERENCIA

nudo *nm* knot

Nueva Zelanda *nf* New Zealand

◊ **neocelandés, -esa** *o* **neozelandés, -esa 1** *adj* New Zealand **2** *n* New Zealander
NOTA: capital: **Wellington**; moneda: **dólar neocelandés ($NZ)** = New Zealand dollar ($NZ)

nuevo, -va *adj* **(a)** *(que acaba de salir)* new; **nueva edición** = new edition; **nueva emisión (de acciones)** = new issue; **departamento de nuevas emisiones** = new issues department; **suscribir una nueva emisión de acciones** = to subscribe to a new share issue; **nuevo embalaje** = repacking; **nuevo examen** = re-examination; **no podemos hacer nada hasta que no hayamos recibido nuevas instrucciones** = nothing can be done until we have new instructions; **nuevo nombramiento** = reappointment; **nueva solicitud** = reapplication; **nueva tecnología** = new technology; **completamente nuevo** = brand new; **los vendedores recibieron instrucciones relativas al nuevo producto** = the salesmen were briefed on the new product; **se mató cuando estaba demostrando el funcionamiento del nuevo tractor** = he was demonstrating a new tractor when he was killed; **el nuevo reglamento entrará en vigor el 1 de enero** = the new regulations will come into force on January 1st **(b)** *(persona)* new *o* incoming *o* newly-elected *o* newly-appointed; **el nuevo consejo de administración** = the incoming board of directors; **el nuevo presidente** = the incoming chairman *o* president; **se pidió a los socios que votaran al nuevo presidente** = the membership was asked to vote for the new president; **¿conoce al Sr. Pereira, nuestro nuevo director de ventas?** = do you know Sr Pereira, our new sales director?; **nombrar de nuevo** = to reappoint; **le nombraron de nuevo presidente por otro periodo de tres años** = he was reappointed chairman for a further three-year period **(c)** *(no usado)* new *o* unused; **estamos intentando vender tres máquinas de escribir nuevas** = we are trying to sell off three unused typewriters

nulidad *nf* invalidity; **la nulidad del contrato** = the invalidity of the contract

nulo, -la *adj* **(a)** *(inválido)* invalid *o* null *o* void; **demanda declarada nula** = claim which has been declared invalid; **el contrato fue declarado nulo y sin valor** = the contract was declared null and void; **permiso nulo** = permit that is invalid **(b)** *(nada)* **hacer una declaración de ingresos nulos** = to make a nil return

numerar *vt* to number; **numerar un pedido** = to number an order

numérico, -ca *adj* numeric *o* numerical; **datos numéricos** = numeric data; **en orden numérico** = in numerical order; **archive estas facturas por orden numérico** = file these invoices in numerical order; **teclado numérico** = numeric keypad

número 1 *nm* **(a)** *(cifra escrita)* number; **número de apartado de correos** = P.O. box number; **nuestra dirección es: apartado de correos número 12.345, Madrid** = our address is P.O. Box 12345, Madrid; **número de cheque** = cheque number; **número de cuenta** = account number; **número de factura** = invoice number; **referente a su factura número 1234** = I refer to your invoice numbered 1234; **números impares** = odd numbers; **los edificios con números impares están en el lado sur de la calle** = odd-numbered buildings *o* buildings with odd numbers are on the south side of the street; **número de lote** = batch number; **número de matrícula** *o* **de inscripción** *o* **de registro** = registration number; **número de página** = page number; **números pares** = even numbers; **número de pedido** = order number; **número personal de**

identificación (NPI) = personal identification number (PIN); **número de serie** = serial number; **este lote de zapatos lleva el número de serie 25-02** = this batch of shoes has the serial number 25-02; **¿cuál es el número de su última solicitud oficial?** = what is the number of your latest order?; **número de teléfono** = phone number *o* telephone number; **su número no figura en la guía telefónica** = he has an ex-directory number; **mi cuenta bancaria está en números rojos** = my bank account is in the red; **asignar un número a** *o* **poner número a** = to number; **asignar un número a un pedido** = to number an order; **en números redondos** = in round figures **(b)** *(cantidad)* number; **un número determinado** = a certain number; **el número de personas en nómina aumentó durante el pasado año** = the number of staff on the payroll has increased over the last year; **el número de días perdidos por huelgas ha disminuido** = the number of days lost through strikes has fallen; **tenemos solamente un número limitado de posibles proveedores** = we have only a limited choice of suppliers **(c)** *(revista o periódico)* copy; **¿ha guardado Vd. el número de 'El País' de ayer?** = have you kept yesterday's copy of 'El País'

◇ **numeroso, -sa** *adj* numerous *o* large; **familia numerosa** = large family; **en numerosas ocasiones** = on many occasions

numerario, -ria 1 *adj* **(a)** *(empleado)* permanent *o* tenured; **profesor no numerario** = lecturer without tenure **(b) miembro numerario** = full member **2** *nm (efectivo)* cash *o* money

Oo

obediencia *nf* obedience *o* compliance

◇ **obediente** *adj* obedient

objeción *nf* objection; **hacer objeciones** = to object (to); **los delegados de los sindicatos hicieron objeciones al texto del acuerdo** = the union delegates objected *o* raised objections to the wording of the agreement

objetivo, -va 1 *adj* objective; **hay que ser objetivo al evaluar el rendimiento del personal** = you must be objective in assessing the performance of the staff; **llevar a cabo un estudio objetivo del mercado** = to carry out an objective survey of the market **2** *nm* objective *o* target *o* aim *o* goal *o* purpose; **objetivo a largo plazo** *o* **objetivo a corto plazo** = long-term objective *o* short-term objective; **objetivos monetarios** = monetary targets; **objetivo de producción** = production target; **objetivo de ventas** = sales target; **cumplir un objetivo** = to reach a target; **no cumplir un objetivo** = to miss a target; **dirección por objetivos** = management by objectives; **fijar objetivos** = to set targets; **fijamos ciertos objetivos al personal de ventas** = we set the sales force certain objectives; **uno de nuestros objetivos es mejorar la calidad de nuestros productos** = one of our aims is to increase the quality of our products; **la compañía ha alcanzado todos sus objetivos** = the company has achieved all its aims; **nuestro objetivo es cubrir gastos en nueve meses** = our goal is to break even within nine months

> uno de los objetivos más urgentes que debe tener el nuevo Gobierno es reconstruir nuestro sistema fiscal, sumido en el caos y la inseguridad más completa
> **España Económica**

objeto *nm* (a) *(cosa)* thing *o* object; **objeto expuesto** = exhibit; **liquidación de objetos salvados de una inundación** = a sale of flood salvage items; **la dirección no se hace responsable de los objetos personales dejados en las habitaciones del hotel** = the management is not responsible for personal property left in the hotel rooms (b) *(objetivo)* purpose *o* aim; **esto tiene por objeto** = the purpose of this is; **necesitamos la factura con el objeto de declarar al fisco** = we need the invoice for the purpose of declaration to the tax authorities; **objeto de una OPA** = takeover target *o* target of a takeover

obligación *nf* (a) *(deber)* obligation *o* duty; **tener la obligación de hacer algo** = to be under an obligation to do something; **no tiene obligación contractual de comprar** *o* **no tiene obligación de comprar según el contrato** = he is under no contractual obligation to buy; **cumplir las obligaciones contractuales** = to fulfill one's contractual obligations; **no poder cumplir con las obligaciones** = not to be able to meet one's commitments (b) **obligaciones** = responsibilities *o* commitments; **las obligaciones de su cargo como director gerente le parecen excesivas** = he finds the responsibilities of being managing director too heavy (c) *(finanzas)* bond *o* obligation; **obligaciones**

= equities *o* securities *o* debenture stock *o* liabilities; **obligaciones a corto plazo** = current liabilities; **obligación convertible** = convertible debenture; **obligación con cupón cero** = zero-coupon bond; **obligación con interés fijo** = debenture *o* loan stock; **obligaciones del Estado** = Treasury bonds; **obligaciones garantizadas** = debenture capital *o* debenture stock; **obligación no hipotecaria** = debenture bond; **obligación que ha llegado a su vencimiento** = bond due for repayment; **obligaciones indexadas** = index-linked savings bonds; **obligación perpetua** = irredeemable bond; **obligación redimible** = callable bond; **tenedor de obligaciones** = debenture holder *o* bondholder; **los tenedores de obligaciones tienen prioridad sobre los tenedores de acciones ordinarias** = debenture holders have priority over ordinary shareholders; **derecho de obligaciones** = contract law *o* law of contract

◇ **obligacionista** *nmf* *(tenedor de obligaciones)* debenture holder *o* bondholder

> se pone en conocimiento de los señores obligacionistas de esta sociedad que durante el próximo mes de febrero se efectuará el pago de los intereses correspondientes a las emisiones de obligaciones
> **Expansión**

obligar *vt* (a) *(forzar)* to force; **obligar a alguien a hacer algo** = to force *o* to oblige someone to do something; **obligar a bajar** = to force down; **obligar a subir** = to force up; **los pedidos adicionales obligaron a todo el personal de la fábrica a hacer horas extraordinarias** = the extra orders made it necessary for all the factory staff to work overtime (b) *(atar)* to bind; **la compañía está obligada a respetar sus estatutos** = the company is bound by its articles of association; **la empresa está obligada por contrato a pagar sus gastos** = the company is contractually bound to pay his expenses; **no estar obligado a hacer algo** = to be under no obligation to do something; **no se considera obligado al acuerdo firmado por su predecesor** = he does not consider himself bound by the agreement which was signed by his predecessor

◇ **obligatorio, -ia** *adj* binding *o* obligatory *o* compulsory; **el acuerdo es obligatorio para todas las partes** = the agreement is binding on all parties; **todas las personas deben someterse a una revisión médica obligatoria** = every person has to pass an compulsory medical examination; **acuerdo solemne y obligatorio** = solemn and binding agreement; **no es obligatorio comprar** = there is no obligation to buy

obra *nf* (a) *(trabajo)* work *o* piece of work; **es ilegal fotocopiar una obra protegida por los derechos de autor** = it is illegal to photocopy a copyright work; **obra benéfica** = charity; **obra en curso** = work in progress; **Ministerio de Obras Públicas (MOPU)** = Ministry of Works (b) *(construcción)* building site *o* construction site; **es obligatorio llevar casco en la obra** = safety helmets must be worn on the construction site (c) **mano de obra** =

labour force *o* workforce **(d)** *(proyecto)* project; **una obra de gran envergadura** = a large-scale project

> en Alemania piensan que se debe invertir el 7% del presupuesto de una obra para conseguir un nivel de daños cero
> **Cambio 16**

> la obra comenzó en vísperas de que entraran en vigor las estrictas normas europeas de protección al medio ambiente
> **Cambio 16**

obrar *vt* to act *o* to behave; **obrar de común acuerdo** = to act in concert

obrero, -ra 1 *adj* working; **el movimiento obrero** = the labour movement; **sindicato obrero** = blue-collar union **2** *n* labourer *o* worker; **obrero diurno** = day worker; **obrero especializado** = skilled worker; **obrero de fábrica** = factory worker *o* factory hand; **obrero manual** = manual worker *o* manual labourer *o* blue-collar worker; **obrero pagado a la hora** = part-time worker *o* hourly-paid worker; **obreros semicualificados** = semi-skilled workers; **obreros sindicados** = organized labour; **todos los obreros volvieron al trabajo ayer** = all the men went back to work yesterday; **la opinión entre los obreros es que el director no conoce su oficio** = the feeling on the shop floor is that the manager does not know his job

obsequiar *vt* to give someone something *o* to present someone with something

◇ **obsequio** *nm* gift *o* giveaway *o* present; **obsequio ofrecido como publicidad** = free gift *o* freebie; **obsequio publicitario** = premium offer; **cupones-obsequio** = trading stamps

obsolescencia *nf* obsolescence; **obsolescencia planificada** = built-in obsolescence *o* planned obsolescence

◇ **obsolescente** *adj* obsolescent

◇ **obsoleto, -ta** *adj* obsolete

> los 471 kilómetros de vía entre Madrid y Sevilla han dejado a Renfe sin un duro mientras la mayor parte de la red ferroviaria (12.700 kilómetros) languidece obsoleta y abandonada
> **Cambio 16**

obstáculo *nm* obstacle *o* hindrance *o* bar; **la legislación oficial es un obstáculo para el comercio exterior** = government legislation is a bar to foreign trade

obstrucción *nf* obstruction *o* impediment

obtener *vt* to get *o* to obtain; *(crédito o préstamo)* to raise (a loan); **obtener unos beneficios brutos** = to produce gross profits *o* to gross; **obtener un beneficio neto de 2.000.000** = to net a profit of 2m; **obtener una patente de invención** = to take out a patent for an invention; **nos resulta difícil obtener estos artículos** = we find these items very difficult to obtain; **obtener daños y perjuicios del conductor del coche** = to recover damages from the driver of the car; **pagó una fianza de 600.000 ptas. para obtener su libertad** = she paid 600,000 pesetas to bail him out; **obtuvieron un préstamo de 5.000.000 dando la fábrica como garantía** = they borrowed 5m against the security of the factory; **obtuvo una**

revisión del sueldo el pasado abril = she had a salary review last April

◇ **obtenible** *adj* obtainable

ocasión *nf* **(a)** *(oportunidad)* occasion *o* chance *o* opportunity; **presentarse la ocasión** = to have the opportunity; **perder una ocasión** = to miss an opportunity *o* to miss a chance **(b) de ocasión** = bargain *o* secondhand; **oferta de ocasión** = bargain offer *o* special offer; **estas alfombras se venden a precios de ocasión** = these carpets are for sale at bargain prices; **el coche vale 1.200.000 ptas. en el mercado de ocasión** = the car is worth 1.2m pesetas on the secondhand market

◇ **ocasional** *adj* occasional

ocasionar *vt* to cause; **el aplazamiento del proyecto ha ocasionado seis despidos** = the shelving of the project has resulted in six redundancies

OCDE = ORGANIZACION DE COOPERACION Y DESARROLLO ECONOMICO Organization for Economic Cooperation and Development (OECD)

ocio *nm* leisure; **tiempo de ocio** = leisure time

octanaje *nm* octane rating; **gasolina de alto octanaje** = four-star petrol *o* top-grade petrol

octavilla *nf* *(folleto)* flyer *o* pamphlet *o* leaflet; **repartieron octavillas publicitarias fuera de la tienda** = advertising flyers were handed out outside the shop

octeto *nm* byte

ocultar *vt* to hide *o* to conceal; **ocultó el dinero en un lugar seguro** = he kept the money in a safe place; **ocultar información** *o* **ocultar algo a alguien** = to keep back information *o* to keep something back from someone; **le ocultó su verdadero plan** = he didn't tell him what his real plan was

◇ **ocultarse** *vr* to hide *o* to keep out of sight

◇ **oculto, -ta** *adj* hidden; **reservas ocultas** = hidden reserves; **defecto oculto del programa** = hidden defect in the program

ocupación *nf* **(a)** *(empleo)* employment *o* occupation; **ocupación temporal** = temporary employment **(b)** *(propiedad)* occupancy; **de ocupación inmediata** = with immediate occupancy; **índice de ocupación** *o* **ocupancy rate; durante los meses de invierno el índice de ocupación bajó al 50%** = during the winter months the occupancy rate was down to 50%; **ocupación de un edificio** = occupation of a building **(c)** *(en los medios de transporte público)* **coeficiente de ocupación** = load factor **(d)** *(cargo)* tenure

ocupado, -da 1 *adj* **(a)** *(persona)* busy; **estar ocupado en algo** = to be engaged in; **está bastante ocupado en este momento** = he is fairly busy *o* rather tied up at the moment; **está ocupado con la preparación de las cuentas anuales** = he is busy preparing the annual accounts **(b)** *(teléfono)* busy *o* engaged; **la línea está ocupada** = the line is busy; **no puede hablar con el director en este momento - su línea está ocupada** = you cannot speak to the manager - his line is engaged; **la extensión 21 está ocupada** = extension 21 is engaged **(c)** *(edificio o* *sala)* occupied *o* in use; **la sala de reuniones estará ocupada hasta las 3 en punto** = the boardroom will be in use until 3 o'clock **2** *pp de* OCUPAR

ocupante *nmf* occupant *o* occupier; **los ocupantes del autobus** = the bus passengers

ocupar *vt* to fill *o* to occupy; **todas las habitaciones del hotel están ocupadas** = all the rooms in the hotel are full *o* taken; **todos los sitios están ocupados** = all seats are taken; **la compañía ocupa tres pisos de un edificio de oficinas** = the company occupies three floors of an office block; **ocupar un puesto** = to occupy a post

◊ **ocuparse** *vr* **ocuparse de** = to attend to *o* to deal (with) *o* to handle; **déjelo para el archivero; él se ocupará de eso** = leave it to the filing clerk - he'll deal with it; **el departamento de contabilidad se ocupa de la caja** = the accounts department handles all the cash; **el director gerente se ocupará personalmente de su queja** = the managing director will attend to your complaint personally; **hemos contratado a expertos para que se ocupen del problema de la instalación del nuevo ordenador** = we have brought in experts to handle the problem of installing the new computer

OECE = ORGANIZACION EUROPEA DE COOPERACION ECONOMICA Organization of European Economic Cooperation (OEEC)

oferta *nf* **(a)** *(promesa)* offer; **una oferta seria** = serious offer *o* a bona fide offer; **la dirección ha mejorado la oferta a los empleados** = the management has made an increased offer to all employees; **se trata de una oferta global que incluye el sistema completo de ordenadores, la formación del personal y el mantenimiento del equipo** = we are offering a package deal which includes the whole office computer system, staff training and hardware maintenance; **hizo la oferta más baja por el trabajo** = he made the lowest bid for the job; **presentar una oferta por algo** = to put in a bid for something *o* to enter a bid for something; **solicitaremos ofertas a subcontratistas para la instalación eléctrica** = we will subcontract the electrical work *o* we will put the electrical work out to subcontract **(b)** *(compra o venta)* offer; **hacer una oferta de compra** = to offer to buy something *o* to make a bid for something; **oferta de venta** = offer for sale; **hizo una oferta por la casa** = he made a bid for the house; **hacer una oferta por una empresa** = to make an offer for a company; **hizo una oferta de 2.000 ptas. por acción** = he made an offer of 2,000 pesetas a share; **hicimos una oferta por la casa por escrito** = we made a written offer for the house; **aceptar una oferta** = to accept an offer; **se ha hecho una oferta por la casa** = the house is under offer; **la compañía admite ofertas por la fábrica vacía** = the company is open to offers for the empty factory; **admitimos toda clase de ofertas** = we are open to offers; **se han recibido varias ofertas por la casa** = several people made offers for the house **(c)** *(empleo)* **ofertas de trabajo** = appointments vacant *o* job vacancies; **recibió seis ofertas de trabajo** = he received six offers of jobs *o* six job offers **(d)** *(ganga)* **oferta especial** = special offer *o* premium offer; **tenemos un surtido de camisas de caballero en oferta especial** = we have a range of men's shirts on special offer; **oferta de lanzamiento** = introductory offer; **oferta de ocasión** = bargain offer *o* special offer; **oferta de la semana: 30% de**

rebaja en todas las alfombras = this week's bargain offer - 30% off all carpet prices; **la oferta termina el 31 de julio** = the offer ends on July 31st **(e)** *(en bolsa)* **oferta para suscribir nuevas acciones** = invitation to subscribe a new issue; **la compañía hizo una oferta por la empresa competidora** = the company made a bid for its rival; **oferta pública de adquisición de acciones (OPA)** = takeover bid; **oferta pública de adquisición hostil (OPAH)** = hostile takeover bid; **hacer o retirar una oferta de adquisición de acciones de una compañía** = to make *o* to withdraw a takeover bid for a company; **la compañía rechazó la oferta de adquisición de acciones** = the company rejected the takeover bid; **oferta pública de venta (OPV)** = offer for sale; *US* public offering; **oferta pública inicial (OPI)** = initial offer for sale; *US* initial public offering **(f)** *(en una subasta)* bid; **oferta en metálico** = cash offer; **oferta final** = closing bid; **oferta inicial** = opening bid; **hacer una oferta** = to bid for something *o* to make a bid for something; **hacer una oferta en efectivo** *o* **ofrecer pago en efectivo** = to make a cash bid **(g)** *(cálculo)* quotation *o* quote; **su oferta fue mucho más baja que todas las demás** = his quotation was much lower than all the others; **aceptamos la oferta más baja** = we accepted the lowest quote **(h)** *(presupuesto)* tender *o* tendering; **solicitaron ofertas para el suministro de repuestos** = they asked for tenders *o*; *US* they asked for bids for the supply of spare parts; **oferta aceptada** *o* **oferta no aceptada** = a successful tender *o* an unsuccessful tender; **presentar una oferta** = to put in a tender *o* to submit a tender; **presentar una oferta para la construcción de un hospital** = to tender for the construction of a hospital; **subastar acciones invitando ofertas por escrito** = to sell shares by tender; **ofertas cerradas (i)** *(economía)* supply; **oferta circulante** *o* **monetaria** = money supply; **precio de oferta** = supply price; **oferta y demanda** = supply and demand; **oferta excesiva** = oversupply; **la ley de la oferta y la demanda** = the law of supply and demand **(j)** *(propuesta)* proposition

> la mayor demanda chocó con la rigidez de la oferta de este mercado
> **España Económica**

> con esta norma se pretenden eliminar las trabas con el objetivo de incrementar la oferta
> **España Económica**

> en esta ocasión la oferta había sido la más tentadora que nadie les había hecho jamás
> **Cambio 16**

> los optimistas esperan que la competencia entre las emisoras por satélite y las televisiones por cable acabe en una espiral disparatada de ofertas por la retransmisión de acontecimientos deportivos
> **Actualidad Económica**

> la situación de su propio banco no le permitía lanzar ofertas públicas de adquisición contra sus competidores
> **El País**

'offshore' *adj y adv* off-shore

oficial 1 *adj* **(a)** *(formal)* official *o* formal; **en**

asuntos oficiales = on official business; **hablando con carácter oficial** = speaking in an official capacity; **recibió una carta oficial explicatoria** = she received an official letter of explanation; **distribuidor oficial** = authorized dealer; **se dejó documentos oficiales en el coche** = he left official documents in his car; **la huelga es oficial** = the strike is official; **no oficial** = unofficial; **esto debe ser un pedido oficial - está escrito en el papel de la empresa** = this must be an official order - it is written on the company's notepaper; **precios** _o_ **tarifas oficiales** = scheduled prices _o_ scheduled charges; **presentar una solicitud oficial** = to make a formal application; **actuar por la vía oficial** = to go through the official channels **(b)** _(del gobierno)_ official; **declaración oficial** = official return; **fiesta oficial** = legal holiday _o_ bank holiday; **una investigación oficial sobre el crimen organizado** = a government investigation into organized crime; **un organismo oficial** = a government organization; **un organismo semi oficial** = a quasi-official body; **tipo oficial de cambio** = the official exchange rate; **el tipo oficial de cambio es de diez por dólar, pero puedes conseguir el doble en el mercado negro** = the official exchange rate is ten to the dollar, but you can get twice that on the black market; **las disposiciones oficiales establecen que deben pagarse derechos de aduana por los artículos de lujo** = government regulations state that import duty has to be paid on luxury items **2** _nmf (administrativo)_ official; **oficial cesante** = lame duck **(b)** _(en taller)_ skilled worker **(c)** _(militar)_ officer

◊ **oficialmente** _adv_ formally _o_ officially; **hablando oficialmente** = speaking in an official capacity; **hemos solicitado oficialmente el permiso para la planificación de la nueva zona comercial** = we have formally applied for planning permission for the new shopping precinct; **el presidente ha dicho oficialmente que las ganancias van a aumentar** = the chairman is on record as saying that profits are set to rise

oficina _nf_ **(a)** _(lugar de trabajo)_ office _o_ bureau; **oficina de cambio** = bureau de change; **oficina central** = head office _o_ headquarters (HQ); **oficina central de correos** = main post office; **oficina comercial** = trade bureau; **oficina de correos** = post office; **oficina de empleo** _o_ **de colocación** = employment bureau _o_ job centre; **oficina de expedición** _o_ **de envío** = dispatch department; **oficina general** = general office; **oficina de información** = information office _o_ information bureau _o_ inquiry office; **oficina de informática** = computer bureau; **oficina informatizada** = paperless office; **oficina del IVA** = VAT office; **oficina principal** = main office; **oficina de recepción** = receiving office; **oficina de reclamaciones** = complaints department; **Oficina del Registro Mercantil** = Companies Registration Office; **oficina técnica** = technical department _o_ engineering department; **oficina de turismo** = tourist office; **oficina de visitantes** = visitors' bureau **(b)** _(despacho)_ office; **oficina con una distribución modificable** = open-plan office; **venga a mi oficina** = come into my office; **la oficina del director está en el tercer piso** = the manager's office is on the third floor; **el director gerente está en su oficina** = the MD is in his office; **oficina independiente** = self-contained office **(c) artículos de oficina** = office supplies; **una empresa de artículos de oficina** = an office supplies firm;

artículos de papelería para oficina = office stationery; **edificio de oficinas** = office block _o_ a block of offices; **empleado de oficina** = office worker _o_ clerk; **equipo de oficina** = office equipment _o_ business equipment; **espacio para oficinas** = office space _o_ office accommodation; **horario de oficina** _o_ **horas de oficina** = = office hours _o_ business hours; **abierto en horas normales de oficina** = open during normal office hours; **la oficina cierra a las 5.30** = the office closes at 5.30; **puede hablar con el director en su casa fuera de las horas de oficina** = the manager can be reached at home out of office hours; **local para oficinas** = office space _o_ office accommodation; **estamos buscando más locales para oficinas** = we are looking for extra office space; **hemos abierto una oficina en Madrid** = we have opened an office in Madrid; **personal de oficinas** = office staff; **recadista de oficina** = office messenger; **tiene un trabajo de oficina** = he has a white-collar job

◊ **oficinista** _nmf_ office worker _o_ clerk _o_ clerical worker _o_ white-collar; _(Escocia)_ clerkess; **es oficinista** = he works in an office _o_ he has an office job; **delitos de oficinistas** = white-collar crime

oficio _nm_ **(a)** _(profesión)_ profession _o_ occupation; **apender un oficio** = to learn a trade; **no tener ni oficio ni beneficio** = to be without a job **(b) de oficio** = ex officio; **turno de oficio** _o_ **abogado de oficio** = court-appointed counsel

oficioso, -sa _adj (no oficial)_ unofficial

◊ **oficiosamente** _adv_ unofficially; **oficialmente no sabe nada del problema, pero oficiosamente nos ha dado buenos consejos** = officially he knows nothing about the problem, but unofficially he has given us a lot of advice about it

ofrecer _vt_ **(a)** _(ofrecer o facilitar)_ to offer; **ofrecer un trabajo a alguien** = to offer someone a job; **ofrecemos un 5% de descuento por pago al contado** = we offer 5% discount for rapid settlement **(b)** _(comprar)_ to offer; **ofrecer menos que** = to bid less than _o_ to underbid; **ofrecer a alguien 10 millones por su casa** = to offer someone 10 million for his house; **200.000 ptas. es lo más que puedo ofrecer** = 200,000 pesetas is the best offer I can make _o_ is the most I can offer; **ofreció 2.000 ptas. por acción** = he offered 2,000 pesetas a share; **ofrecer pago en efectivo** = to make a cash bid; **ofrecer a cambio** = to trade in **(c)** _(vender)_ to offer; **ofrecer una mercancía a distintos clientes** = to offer something to various customers _o_ to hawk something round

oír _vt_ to hear; **se oye la impresora de la oficina de al lado** = you can hear the printer in the next office; **el tráfico hace tanto ruido que no oigo el teléfono** = the traffic makes so much noise that I cannot hear my phone ringing

OIT = ORGANIZACION INTERNACIONAL DEL TRABAJO International Labour Organization (ILO)

oleada _nf_ big wave; **oleadas de turistas llenaron los hoteles** = floods of tourists filled the hotels

olvidar _vt_ to forget; **olvidó poner el sello al sobre** = she forgot to put a stamp on the envelope; **no te olvides de que mañana almorzamos juntos** = don't forget we're having lunch together tomorrow

Omán _nm_ Oman

◇ **omaní** *adj y nmf* Omani
NOTA: capital: **Muscat;** moneda: **rial omaní (RO)** = Omani rial (RO)

OMC = ORGANIZACION MUNDIAL DEL COMERCIO World Trade Organization (WTO)

omisión *nf* omission; **salvo error u omisión (s.e.u.o.)** = errors and omissions excepted (e. & o. e.)

omiso *pp de* OMITIR **hacer caso omiso** = to ignore *o* to overlook

omitir *vt* to omit *o* to leave out *o* to fail to do something; **omitió poner la fecha en la carta** = she forgot to put the date on the letter *o* she left out the date on the letter; **el contrato omite todos los detalles sobre disposiciones comerciales** = the contract leaves out all details of marketing arrangements; **omitió decirle al director gerente que había perdido los documentos** = he omitted to tell the managing director that he had lost the documents; **la compañía omitió notificar a la delegación de Hacienda su cambio de dirección** = the company failed to notify the tax office of its change of address

oneroso, -sa *adj* onerous *o* burdensome; **las condiciones de pago son especialmente onerosas** = the repayment terms are particularly onerous

ONU *o* **Onu** = ORGANIZACION DE LAS NACIONES UNIDAS United Nations Organization (UN)

> aunque la Onu cumplía muchas funciones útiles, necesitaba un cambio drástico que se ha producido con el fin de la guerra fría
> **Actualidad Económica**

onza *nf (medida de peso = 28 gramos)* ounce; **onza troy** = troy ounce

opa *o* **OPA** *nf* = OFERTA PUBLICA DE ADQUISICION takeover bid; **objeto de una OPA** = takeover target; **hacer** *o* **retirar una OPA de una compañía** = to make *o* to withdraw a takeover bid for a company; **la compañía rechazó la OPA** = the company rejected the takeover bid

◇ **OPAH** = OFERTA PUBLICA DE ADQUISICION HOSTIL hostile takeover bid

> calificaba la opa de hostil, y cifraba en 20.000 pesetas el valor real de sus acciones según una valoración de 1988
> **El País**

> la reciente ampliación del plazo de finalización de la OPA deja la puerta abierta a que la compañía estudie una nueva defensa e, incluso los expertos no descartan que llegue a presentar una contraopa
> **El País**

opción *nf* **(a)** *(alternativa)* option; **concederle a alguien una opción de seis meses sobre la representación** *o* **la fabricación de un producto** = to grant someone a six-month option on a product; **ejerció su derecho de opción para adquirir los derechos exclusivos de comercialización del producto** = he exercised his option *o* he took up his option to acquire sole marketing rights to the product **(b)** **decidirse por la opción más fácil** = to take the soft option; **vale la pena comparar las opciones**

antes de solicitar una hipoteca = it pays to shop around when you are planning to ask for a mortgage **(c)** *(bolsa)* **operaciones de opción** = option dealing *o* option trading; **opción-bono** *o* **opción de compra de acciones por los empleados de una compañía** = stock option; **opción de venta** = put option; **opción de compra** = call option **(d)** *(informática)* **lista de opciones** = menu

◇ **opcional** *adj* optional; **el seguro es opcional** = the insurance cover is optional; **extras opcionales** = optional extras

OPEP = ORGANIZACION DE LOS PAISES EXPORTADORES DE PETROLEO Organization of Petroleum Exporting Countries (OPEC)

operación *nf* operation *o* deal; *(con riesgo)* venture; **operaciones bancarias electrónicas** = electronic banking; **operación bursátil** *o* **operación de bolsa** = Stock Exchange operation *o* a transaction on the Stock Exchange; **operaciones en bolsa** = stock exchange deals *o* dealing; **el periódico publica una lista diaria de las operaciones de bolsa** = the paper publishes a daily list of Stock Exchange transactions; **operación al contado** = cash transaction; **operación de divisas** = exchange transaction; **operación fraudulenta** = fraudulent transaction; **operación llaves en mano** = turnkey operation; **operación mercantil** = business transaction; **operación en múltiples divisas** = multicurrency operation; **operaciones de opción** = option dealing *o* option trading; **lugar de operaciones** = dealing *o* trading floor; **revisión de las operaciones** = operations review; **dirige las operaciones en el norte de Europa** = he heads up the operations in Northern Europe; **perdió dinero en varias operaciones de importación** = he lost money on several import ventures

◇ **operacional** *adj* operational

> las operaciones de la Corporación abarcan todas las áreas financieras: bolsa, renta fija, deuda pública, mercado monetario e ingeniería financiera
> **Tiempo**

> este nuevo cambio no se aplica a las operaciones comerciales con el extranjero
> **España Económica**

operador, -ra *n* **(a)** *(de una máquina)* operator; **operador de teclado** = keyboard operator *o* keyboarder; **operador de télex** = a telex operator **(b)** *(telefonista)* switchboard operator **(c)** *(cambista)* **operador de cambios** = foreign exchange dealer *o* broker

operar *vi* to operate *o* to transact; **la compañía opera bajo el nombre de 'Pikolín'** = the company trades under the name 'Pikolín'; **opera en la Bolsa** = he deals on the Stock Exchange

operario, -ria *n* worker *o* operative *o* hand; **contratar a diez operarios más** = to take on ten more hands

operativo, -va *adj* operational *o* operative; **investigación operativa** = operational research; **planificación operativa** = operational planning; **sistema operativo** = operating system; **sistema operativo de redes** = networked system *o* network operating system

OPI = OFERTA PUBLICA INICIAL initial offer for sale; *US* initial public offering

opinión *nf* opinion *o* view; **opinión pública** = public opinion; **dar una opinión** = to give an opinion; **pedir una opinión** = to ask for an opinion; **preguntamos al director de ventas su opinión sobre la reorganización de las zonas de los representantes** = we asked the sales manager for his views on the reorganization of the reps' territories; **el presidente es de la opinión que el crédito no debería sobrepasar nunca los treinta días** = the chairman takes the view that credit should never be longer than thirty days; **sondear la opinión pública** = to canvass *o* to conduct an opinion poll; **sondeo de opinión** = opinion poll *o* canvassing *o* market research; **los sondeos de opinión mostraron que el público prefería la mantequilla a la margarina** = opinion polls showed that the public preferred butter to margarine; **antes de empezar el servicio la empresa realizó encuestas de opinión por todo el país** = before starting the service the company carried out a nationwide opinion poll

oponer *vt* to oppose

◇ **oponerse** *vr* to oppose *o* to object (to); **todos nos oponemos a la adquisición** = we are all opposed to the takeover; **oponerse a una cláusula del contrato** = to object to a clause in a contract

oportunamente *adv* duly; **hemos recibido oportunamente su carta del 21 de octubre** = we duly received your letter of 21st October

oportunidad *nf* **(a)** *(ocasión)* opportunity *o* chance; **está esperando la oportunidad de ver al director gerente** = she is waiting for a chance to see the managing director; **tuvo la oportunidad de ascender cuando dimitió el director adjunto de finanzas** = he had his chance of promotion when the finance director's assistant resigned; **oportunidades de empleo** *o* **oportunidades de trabajo** = employment opportunities *o* job opportunities; **el aumento de pedidos de exportación ha creado cientos de oportunidades de empleo** = the increase in export orders has created hundreds of job opportunities; **oportunidades de inversión** *o* **oportunidades de ventas** = investment opportunities *o* sales opportunities; **una oportunidad de mercado** = a market opportunity; **oportunidad de oro** = golden opportunity **(b)** *(tienda)* **sección de oportunidades** = bargain basement *o* bargain counter

oposición *nf* **concurso oposición** = (public) competitive examination *o* open competition (for a job)

◇ **opositor, -tora** *n* candidate

optar *vi* to decide *o* to resolve (to do something); **optar por una línea de conducta** = to decide on a course of action; **la junta optó por no pagar dividendos** = the meeting resolved that a dividend should not be paid

◇ **optativo, -va** *adj* optional

optimismo *nm* optimism; **el optimismo del mercado** = market optimism

◇ **optimista** *adj* optimistic; **tiene una visión optimista del tipo de cambio** = he takes an optimistic view of the exchange rate; **es muy optimista sobre las posibilidades de ventas en el Extremo Oriente** = he has considerable optimism about sales possibilities in the Far East

óptimo, -ma *adj* optimal *o* optimum; **el mercado ofrece condiciones óptimas para las ventas** = the market offers optimum conditions for sales; **vendemos solamente productos en óptimas condiciones** = we sell only goods in top condition

opuesto, -ta 1 *adj* opposed; reverse **2** *pp de* OPONER

opulento, -ta *adj* affluent; **vivimos en una sociedad opulenta** = we live in an affluent society

OPV = OFERTA PUBLICA DE VENTA offer for sale; *US* public offering

orden 1 *nf* **(a)** *(documento legal)* order *o* writ *o* warrant; **orden de embargo** = distress warrant; **orden judicial** = court order; **el tribunal dictó una orden para impedir que el sindicato fuera a la huelga** = the court issued a writ to prevent the trade union from going on strike; **obedecer una orden del tribunal** = to comply with a court order **(b)** *(mandato o instrucciones)* instruction *o* order; **el agente está esperando nuestras órdenes** = the agent is awaiting our instructions; **orden de expropiación forzosa** = compulsory purchase order; **orden de liquidación forzosa** = compulsory winding up order **(c)** *(pago)* order; **orden bancaria** = banker's order; **páguese a la orden del Sr. Ramos** = pay to the order of Sr Ramos; **pagar en efectivo al Sr. Ramos o según sus órdenes** = pay to Sr Ramos or order; **orden de pago** = order for payment *o* bank draft *o* money order *o* bank mandate; **orden de pago domiciliado en el banco** = banker's order; **paga su suscripción por orden de pago domiciliado en el banco** = he pays his subscription by banker's order **(d)** *(pedidos)* **orden de compra** = purchase order; **cursó una orden de compra de una nueva partida de jabón** = he put in an order for a new stock of soap; **orden de expedición** = delivery order **2** *nm* **(a)** *(clasificación)* order; **orden alfabético** = alphabetical order; **los ficheros están clasificados por orden alfabético** = the files are arranged in alphabetical order; **orden cronológico** = chronological order; **los informes están archivados por orden cronológico** = the reports are filed in chronological order; **en orden de importancia** = in order of importance *o* in rank order; **orden jerárquico** = line of command; **orden numérico** = numerical order; **coloque estas facturas por o en orden numérico** = put these invoices in numerical order **(b)** **orden del día** = agenda; **el orden del día de la conferencia** *o* **del congreso** = the conference agenda *o* the agenda of the conference; **transcurridas dos horas todavía discutíamos el primer punto del orden del día** = after two hours we were still discussing the first item on the agenda; **el secretario puso las finanzas como asunto prioritario del orden del día** = the secretary put finance at the top of the agenda; **el presidente quiere que se eliminen dos puntos del orden del día** = the chairman wants two items removed from *o* taken off the agenda

> la Expo de Sevilla guarda un riguroso orden tecnológico, hecho de fibra óptica y bioclimatización por agua micronizada y otras modernas maravillas
>
> **Cambio 16**

ordenador *nm* computer; **los ordenadores y la informática** = computers and IT; **ordenador analógico** = analog computer; **ordenador digital** = digital computer; **ordenador de empresa** = business computer; **ordenador fácil de usar** = user-friendly computer; **ordenador personal (PC)** = personal computer (PC) *o* home computer; **ordenador portátil** = portable computer *o* laptop; **ordenador principal** = mainframe; **no faltan posibles compradores para el ordenador** = there is no shortage of prospective buyers for the computer; **no sé cómo funciona un ordenador** = I do not know how a computer works; **códigos legibles por el ordenador** = computer-readable codes; **departamento de ordenadores** *o* **informática** = computer department; **error de ordenador** = computer error; **lenguaje de ordenador** = computer language; **listado de ordenador** = computer listing; **programa de ordenador** = computer program; **programador de ordenadores** = computer programmer; **publicación ayudada por ordenador** = desk-top publishing (DTP); **para compilar todos esos informes de ventas se invierte mucho tiempo de ordenador** = running all those sales reports costs a lot in computer time; **velocidad del ordenador** = computing speed

> la palabra saturación comienza a escucharse con relativa frecuencia en el mercado europeo de ordenadores personales
>
> **Micros**

> al darse cuenta de que podían dar crédito en cualquier parte del mundo a través de la pantalla de sus ordenadores, los bancos se lanzaron a una carrera desenfrenada
>
> **Actualidad Económica**

ordenar *vt* **(a)** *(clasificar)* to arrange *o* to sort; **los archivos están ordenados por orden alfabético** = the files are arranged in alphabetical order; **la lista de direcciones está ordenada por países** = the address list is ordered by country **(b)** *(mandar)* to instruct *o* to order; **nos ordenaron que viniéramos a trabajar más temprano** = we were told to come to work earlier

ordinario, -ria *adj* ordinary *o* regular; **acciones ordinarias** = ordinary shares; *US* common stock; **tenedor de acciones ordinarias** = ordinary shareholder; **por correo ordinario** = by ordinary mail; **miembro ordinario** = ordinary member *o* rank-and-file member; **resolución ordinaria** = ordinary resolution; **de ordinario** = usually *o* regularly

organigrama *nm* *(gráfico de organización)* organization chart; *(diagrama de flujo)* flow chart *o* flow diagram; **organigrama de procesos decisorios** = decision tree; **el documento presenta un organigrama de la compañía** = the paper gives a diagram of the company's organizational structure

organización *nf* **(a)** *(organismo)* organization; **Organización de Cooperación y Desarrollo Económico (OCDE)** = Organization for Economic Cooperation and Development (OECD); **Organización Europea de Cooperación Económica (OECE)** = Organization for European Economic Cooperation (OEEC); **Organización Internacional del Trabajo (OIT)** = International Labour Organization (ILO); **Organización Mundial del Comercio (OMC)** = World Trade Organization (WTO); **Organización de las Naciones Unidas (ONU)** = United Nations Organization (UNO *o* UN); **la Organización de los Países Exportadores de Petróleo (OPEP)** = the Organization of Petroleum Exporting Countries (OPEC); **una organización patronal** = an employers' organization; **una organización de turismo** = a travel organization **(b)** *(acción de organizar)* organization *o* organizing; **el presidente se ocupa de la organización de la junta general anual** = the chairman handles the organization of the AGM; **la organización del grupo está demasiado centralizada para ser eficaz** = the organization of the group is too centralized to be efficient; **la organización de la oficina principal en departamentos** = the organization of the head office into departments; **organización y métodos** = organization and methods; **organización lineal** = line organization; **gráfico de organización** = organization chart **(c)** *(negocio)* setup; **costes de organización** = setup costs

◊ **organizado, -da 1** *adj* organized; **viaje organizado (con todos los gastos incluidos)** = package holiday *o* package tour **2** *pp de* ORGANIZAR

◊ **organizador, -ra** *n* organizer *o* convenor; **organizador de viajes** = travel agent *o* tour operator

organizar *vt* to organize *o* to arrange; **organizó un coche para que le recogiera en el aeropuerto** = she arranged for a car to meet him at the airport; **organizar un equipo de vendedores** = to build up a team of salesmen; **el grupo está organizado en zonas de venta** = the group is organized by sales areas

◊ **organizativo, -va** *adj* organizational

órgano *nm* body *o* unit *o* organism; **órganos administrativos** = administrative bodies

orientado, -da 1 *adj* oriented *o* orientated; **empresa orientada hacia la exportación** = export-oriented company **2** *pp de* ORIENTAR

orientar *vt* **(a)** *(dirigir)* to direct *o* to give directions to **(b)** *(guiar)* to guide; **me orientó en el asunto** = I was guided by him in the matter

origen *nm* origin *o* source; **ingreso sujeto a retención en el origen** = income which is taxed at source; **piezas de recambio de origen europeo** = spare parts of European origin; **certificado de origen** = certificate of origin; **país de origen** = country of origin *o* home country; **hacia el país de origen** = homewards

original 1 *adj* **(a)** *(primero)* original; **enviaron una copia de la factura original** = they sent a copy of the original invoice; **se guardó el recibo original para sus archivos** = he kept the original receipt for reference **(b) coste original** = historic(al) cost **(c)** *(inédito)* **presentó una idea original** = she introduced an original idea **2** *nm* master *o* original *o* top copy; **haga un original y dos copias con papel carbón** = make a top copy and two carbons; **mande el original y archive dos copias** = send the original and file two copies

originariamente *adv* originally

oro *nm* **(a)** gold; **oro fino** = fine gold; **oro de 14 quilates** = 14-carat gold; **comerciar con oro** = to deal in gold; **comprar oro** = to buy gold; **oro en lingotes** = gold bullion; **el precio del oro en lingotes se fija diariamente** = the price of bullion is fixed daily; **precio del día en el mercado londinense del oro** = the London gold fixing; **monedas de oro** = gold coins; **reservas de oro y divisas** = gold and foreign exchange reserves; **las reservas de oro del país** = the country's gold reserves; **el patrón-oro** = the gold standard; **punto oro** = gold point; **tarjeta oro** = gold card **(b) de oro** = golden; **oportunidad de oro** = golden opportunity

oscilación *nf* fluctuation; **oscilación de los precios** = price fluctuation; **oscilaciones cíclicas** = cyclical fluctuations *o* fluctuations in the business cycle

oscilar *vi* to fluctuate *o* to swing *o* to range; **los precios oscilan entre 220 y 250 ptas.** = prices fluctuate between 220 and 250 pesetas; **la escala salarial de la empresa oscila entre las 50.000 ptas.**

para un aprendiz y las 500.000 para el director gerente = the company's salary scale ranges from 50,000 pesetas for a trainee to 500,000 for the managing director

> el número de pobres oscila, según diversos estudios, entre 8 y 11 millones de personas
>
> **España Económica**

otomano, -na *ver* TURQUIA

otorgar *vt* to grant *o* to confer; **el contrato de suministro de repuestos fue otorgado a Ibersum S.A.** = the contract for the supply of spare parts was awarded to Ibersum S.A.

otro, -tra 1 *adj y pron* **(a)** *(distinto)* other; **el otro día** = the other day; **encontrar otro empleo para alguien** = to find someone another job *o* alternative employment **(b)** *(adicional)* further; **había pedido prestadas 100.000 ptas. y luego intentó pedir otras 25.000** = he had borrowed 100,000 pesetas and then tried to borrow a further 25,000 **2** *pron* another; **los otros** *o* **las otras** = the others

'outsourcing' *nm (subcontratar a especialistas)* outsourcing

> el 'outsourcing' surgió a mediados de los ochenta
>
> **El País**

> los expertos confían encontrar soluciones a los errores cometidos con el 'outsourcing'
>
> **El País**

Pp

pabellón *nm* **(a)** *(bandera)* flag; **barco que navega con pabellón de conveniencia** = ship sailing under a flag of convenience **(b)** *(informática)* flag **(c)** *(de exposición)* pavilion; **el pabellón canadiense en la Expo** = the Canadian pavilion at the Expo

> toda esa acumulación de pabellones más o menos indistintos y resueltamente timoratos acaba formando un gran desorden
> **Cambio 16**

> el símbolo arquitectónico del Pabellón de España es una sala cúbica de 576 metros cuadrados de superficie utilizable
> **Cambio 16**

PAC = POLITICA AGRICOLA COMUN Common Agricultural Policy (CAP)

paca *nf* bale; **una paca de algodón** = a bale of cotton

pactar *vt* to covenant *o* to agree; **las dos partes pactaron las condiciones del contrato** = both parties agreed on the terms of the contract

◊ **pacto** *nm* pact *o* covenant; **pacto con fines ilegales** = concert; **pacto de retorventa** = repurchase agreement

padecer *vi* to suffer from (something); **la empresa padece una mala gestión** = the company suffers from bad management

padrino *nm* sponsor

paga *nf* pay; **sobre de paga** = wage packet; **paga extraordinaria de Navidad** = Christmas bonus; **paga por horas extras** = overtime pay

pagadero, -ra *adj* payable; **pagadero a sesenta días** = payable at sixty days; **pagadero al orden de** = payable to the order of; **talón pagadero al portador** = cheque made payable to bearer; **pagadero por adelantado** = payable in advance; **pagadero a la entrega** = payable on delivery; **pagadero a la vista** = payable on demand *o* at sight; **acciones pagaderas en el momento de la suscripción** = shares payable on application

◊ **pagado, -da 1** *adj* paid *o* paid-up; **en la factura pone 'pagado'** = the invoice is marked 'paid'; **no pagado** = unpaid; **pagado por adelantado** = prepaid; **pagado en exceso** = overpaid; **impuesto pagado** = tax paid; **letras pagadas** = paid bills; **porte pagado** = carriage paid *o* carriage prepaid *o* postpaid *o* postage paid *o* post free; **el fabricante envía el juego con porte pagado** = the game is obtainable post free from the manufacturer; **vacaciones pagadas** = paid holidays **2** *pp de* PAGAR

◊ **pagador, -ra** *n* payer; **pagador puntual** = prompt payer

pagar *vt* **(a)** *(abonar)* to pay *o* to pay out *o* to repay; **pagar por adelantado** = to pay in advance *o* to prepay; **tuvimos que pagar por adelantado para que nos instalaran la nueva red telefónica** = we had to pay in advance to have the new telephone system installed; **pagar el capital y los intereses** = to repay principal and interest; **pagar con un cheque** *o* **talón** = to pay by cheque; **a pagar en cómodos plazos** = repayable in easy payments; **pagar al contado** *o* **en efectivo** = to pay cash; **pagar una cuenta** = to pay a bill; *(EE.UU)* to square a bill; **pagar derechos sobre las importaciones** = to pay duty on imports; **pagar una deuda** = to pay off a debt *o* to clear off a debt; **pagó por fin la deuda, pero con seis meses de retraso** = he finally paid up six months late; **pagar una factura** = (i) to pay an invoice; (ii) to honour a bill; **pagar impuestos** = to pay tax; **pagar intereses** = to pay interest; **pagar los intereses de una deuda** = to pay interest on a debt *o* to service a debt; **pagar una letra** = to pay a bill; **pagar más de la cuenta** *o* **demasiado** = to overpay; **pagamos 5.000 ptas. más de la cuenta** = we overpaid the invoice by 5,000 pesetas; **pagar a plazos** = to pay in instalments; **estamos pagando el ordenador en plazos mensuales de 10.000 ptas.** = we are paying for the computer by instalments of 10,000 pesetas a month; **pagar puntualmente** = to pay on time *o* on the dot on the nail; **pagar una reclamación** = to settle a claim; **pagar con tarjeta de crédito** = to pay by credit card; **pagar todas las deudas propias** = to discharge one's liabilities in full; **pagar a la vista** = to pay on demand *o* at sight; **paga su subscripción por domiciliación bancaria** = he pays his subscription by banker's order; **la compañía no pagó en la fecha establecida por el contrato** = the company failed to pay on the date stipulated in the contract; **pagar 1.000.000 de ptas. por un coche** = to pay 1,000,000 pesetas for a car; **¿cuánto pagaste por limpiar la oficina?** = how much did you pay to have the office cleaned? **(b)** *(salarios o sueldos)* to pay; **no se ha pagado al personal desde hace tres semanas** = the workforce has not been paid for three weeks; **pagamos buenos sueldos a los trabajadores especializados** = we pay good wages for skilled workers; **¿cuánto te pagan por hora?** = how much do they pay you per hour?; **pagar a alguien a prorrata** = to pay someone pro rata; **claro que la empresa es rentable - paga muy mal a los obreros** = of course the firm makes a profit - it pays its workers badly **(c)** **por pagar** = due *o* payable; **cuentas por pagar** = accounts payable; **efectos por pagar** = bills payable; **sin pagar** = (i) free *o* gratis; (ii) unpaid; **abandonó el país sin pagar sus deudas** = he left the country without paying his bills

pagaré *nm* **(a)** *(vale)* IOU (= I owe you); **hacer efectivos un montón de pagarés** = to pay a pile of IOUs **(b)** *(letra al propio cargo)* note of hand *o* promissory note; **pagaré de empresa** = debenture bond; **el banco es tenedor de un pagaré de la empresa** = = the bank holds a debenture on the company; **pagaré de tesorería** = treasury note **(c)** *(efecto de favor)* accommodation bill

> a principios de la década de los 80, trabajó en México capital, donde puso en marcha un mercado de pagarés de empresa a tipo de interés flotante
> **España Económica**

> el recorte de tipos de interés ha dejado casi paralizado el mercado de pagarés de empresa. Los inversores están demostrando que antes de acudir al papel privado, prefieren refugiarse en la deuda pública, menos arriesgada y con mayor liquidez, aunque eso sí, también algo menos rentable
>
> **El País**

página *nf* page; **páginas amarillas** = yellow pages; **página siguiente** = next page *o* continuation page

paginar *vt* to number pages *o* to paginate

pago *nm* (a) *(reintrego)* paying *o* payment; **pago por adelantado** = prepayment; **pedir el pago de honorarios por adelantado** = to ask for prepayment of a fee; **pago anticipado** = advance payment; **pagos aplazados** = deferred payments; **la compañía acordó aplazar los pagos durante tres meses** = the company agreed to defer payments for three months; **pago atrasado** = back *o* late payment; **pago dividido** = split payment; **pago en exceso** = overpayment; **pago íntegro** = full payment *o* payment in full; **pago parcial** = part payment; *o US* partial payment; **un pago a prorrata** = a pro rata payment; **pago simbólico** = token payment; **hay un pago simbólico por la calefacción** = a token charge is made for heating; **pago total** = full payment *o* payment in full; **pago único** = lump sum (b) **pago de acciones a plazo** = rolling settlement; **pago de una cuenta** = settlement; **pago de una deuda** = payment *o* paying of a debt *o* clearing of a debt; **pago total de una deuda** = full discharge of a debt; **en pago total de una deuda** = in full discharge of a debt; **se ha retrasado en el pago de los plazos de la hipoteca** = he has fallen behind with his mortgage repayments; **pago de intereses** = payment of interest *o* interest payment; **pago contra presentación de la factura** = payment on invoice; **pago de la factura presentada** = payment for account rendered; **pagos que vencen** = payments which fall due; **el pago del préstamo vence el año que viene** = the loan is due for repayment next year (c) **aviso de pago** = reminder; **efectuar un pago** = to make a payment; **realizar un pago** = to effect a payment; **supeditar el pago de bonificaciones a la productividad** = to link bonus payments to productivity; **condiciones de pago** = terms of payment *o* payment terms; **facilidades de pago** = easy terms; **pronto pago** = rapid settlement *o* prompt payment; **hacemos un descuento del 5% por pronto pago** = we give 5% off for quick settlement; **nuestro descuento normal es de un 20% pero ofrecemos un 5% adicional por pronto pago** = our basic discount is 20% but we offer an extra 5% for rapid settlement; **el quinto pago a cuenta debe hacerse en marzo** = the fifth progress payment is due in March; **último requerimiento de pago** = final demand; **entregar el coche antiguo como pago parcial de uno nuevo** = to give the old car as a trade-in (d) **pago a cuenta** = payment on account; **pago al contado** *o* **en efectivo** *o* **en metálico** = payment in cash *o* cash payment *o* settlement in cash *o* cash settlement; **condiciones de pago al contado** = cash price *o* cash terms; **ofrecemos un 5% de descuento por pago al contado** = we offer 5% discount for cash settlement; **pago mediante cheque** *o* **talón** = payment by cheque; **el banco tardó diez días en tramitar el pago del cheque** = the cheque took ten days to clear

o the bank took ten days to clear the cheque; **pago en especie** = payment in kind (e) **día de pago** = pay day; **pago según resultados** *o* **según producción** *o* **a destajo** = payment by results (f) **sociedad sujeta al pago de impuestos** = corporate taxpayer; **resultado después del pago de impuestos** = profit after tax; **las organizaciones sin fines de lucro** *o* **no lucrativas están exentas del pago de impuestos** = non-profit-making organizations are exempted from tax; **cheque en pago de dividendos** = dividend warrant (g) *(comercio internacional)* **balanza de pagos** = balance of payments *o* current account

país *nm* (a) *(nación)* country; **país desarrollado** = developed country; **país endeudado** = debtor nation; **país de origen** = country of origin *o* home country; **hacia el país de origen** = homewards; **países subdesarrollados** = underdeveloped countries; **país en vías de desarrollo** = developing country *o* developing nation; **el contrato comprende la distribución en todos los países de la Unión Europea** = the contract covers distribution in the countries of the European Union; **algunos países de Africa exportan petróleo** = some African countries export oil; **la Organización de Países Exportadores de Petróleo (OPEP)** = the Organization of Petroleum Exporting Countries (OPEC); **el director gerente está fuera del país** = the managing director is out of the country (b) **del país** *o* **creado en el país** = local *o* home-produced *o* homegrown; **una industria de ordenadores creada en el país** = a local computer industry; **productos del país** = home-produced products

> este crecimiento de las importaciones de productos desde terceros países constituye un grave atentado contra los intereses de los agricultores comunitarios, al tiempo que no suponen un apoyo a las rentas de los campesinos de esos países que están sometidos a condiciones de 'dumping' social y económico
>
> **El País**

los Países Bajos *nmpl* *(informal)* **Holanda** the Netherlands

◊ **neerlandés, -esa** *adj y n* Dutch
NOTA: capital: **Amsterdam**; moneda: **florín neerlandés (fl)** = Dutch guilder (fl)

Pakistán *o* **Paquistán** *nm* Pakistan

◊ **pakistaní** *o* **paquistaní** *adj y nmf* Pakistani
NOTA: capital: **Islamabad**; moneda: **rupia paquistaní (PRs)** = Pakistan rupee (PRs)

palabra *nf* word; **palabras de agradecimiento** = vote of thanks; **palabra clave** = (i) keynote speech; (ii) keyword

paleta *nf* pallet

paliza *nf* beating *o* hammering; **les dimos una paliza** = we gave them a hammering

Panamá *nm* Panama

◊ **panameño, -ña** *adj y n* Panamanian
NOTA: capital: **Panamá** = Panama City; moneda: **balboa panameño (B)** = Panamanian balboa (B)

pancarta *nf* sign *o* banner; **pancarta publicitaria** = advertising hoarding

panel *nm* (a) *(tablero)* panel; **panel de control** =

control panel **(b)** *(tribunal)* **panel de consumidores** = consumer panel

pánico *nm* panic; **compra motivada por el pánico** = panic buying

pantalla *nf* screen; **una pantalla de televisión** = a TV screen; **proyectó los datos en la pantalla** = he brought up the information on the screen

papel *nm* **(a)** *(hoja)* paper; **papel de calco** *o* **papel carbón** = carbon paper; **papel de cartas** = notepaper; **papel con membrete de la compañía** = office stationery *o* company notepaper; **papel continuo** = continuous stationery; **papel cuadriculado** = graph paper; **papel de envolver** = wrapping paper; **papel para escribir a máquina** = typing paper; **papel de estraza** = brown paper; **papel para el fax** = fax paper; **papel de fotocopiadora** = copier paper; **papel de impresora** = listing paper; **papel manila** = manilla (paper); **papel con membrete** *o* **papel timbrado** = headed notepaper; **papel de multicopista** = duplicating paper; **papel rayado** = lined paper; **papel sin rayar** = unlined paper; **papel reciclado** = recycled paper; **papel de regalo** = gift-wrapping paper; **debe fotocopiar la hoja de cálculos en papel A3** = you must photocopy the spreadsheet on A3 paper; **papel tamaño folio** = foolscap paper **(b)** **alimentador de papel** = sheet feed; **bolsa de papel** = paper bag **(c)** *(documentos)* **papeles** = documents *o* papers; **la oficina pide los papeles del IVA** = the office is asking for the VAT papers; **la mesa del director gerente está cubierta de papeles** = the managing director's desk is covered with piles of paper **(d)** **beneficio sobre el papel** = paper profit; **pérdida sobre el papel** = paper loss; **papel moneda** = paper money *o* paper currency; **papel del Estado** = government bonds

◊ **papeleo** *nm* paperwork *o* red tape; **exportar a Rusia implica una gran cantidad de papeleo** = exporting to Russia involves a large amount of paperwork

◊ **papelera** *nf* **(a)** *(fábrica de papel)* paper mill **(b)** *(cesto)* bin *o* waste paper basket; *US* wastebasket

◊ **papelería** *nf* stationery *o* stationer's (shop)

paquete *nm* **(a)** *(artículos empaquetados para la venta)* packet *o* pack; **paquete de cigarrillos** = pack *o* packet of cigarettes; **paquete de fichas** = packet of filing cards; **paquete de galletas** = pack *o* packet of biscuits; **paquete plano** = flat pack; **paquete de sobres** = pack of envelopes; **el paquete lleva las instrucciones impresas** = instructions for use are printed on the package; **artículo vendido en paquetes de 20 unidades** *o* **artículos vendidos en paquetes de 200 unidades** = item sold in packets of 20 *o* items sold in packs of 200; **faltan veinte gramos en el paquete** = the pack is twenty grams underweight **(b)** *(bulto)* parcel *o* package; **paquete postal** = parcel *o* postal packet; **atar un paquete** = to tie up a parcel; **oficina de paquetes** = parcels office; **servicio de entrega de paquetes** = parcel delivery service; **servicio de paquetes postales** = parcel post; **enviar una caja por el servicio de paquetes postales** = to send a box by parcel post; **tarifas de paquetes** = parcel rates; **la oficina de correos no acepta paquetes voluminosos** = the Post Office does not accept bulky packages **(c)** **paquete de acciones** = block *o* parcel of shares; **vender un paquete de acciones** = to sell a block *o*

lot of shares; **las acciones se ofrecen en paquetes de 50** = the shares are on offer in parcels of 50; **compró un paquete de 6.000 acciones** = he bought a block of 6,000 shares **(d)** *(acuerdo o transacción global)* package deal; **paquete de indemnización por despido** = redundancy package; **paquete de medidas económicas** = package of financial measures; **paquete de negociación** = negotiating package; **paquete de retribuciones** = pay package *o* salary package; *US* compensation package **(e)** *(informática)* **paquete de autoedición** = desk-top publishing package

Paquistán *ver* PAKISTAN

par 1 *adj* equal *o* even; **números pares** = even numbers **2** *nf* **(a)** **a la par** = at par; **valor a la par** = par value; **acciones (de valor) a la par** = shares at par; **emitir acciones a la par** = to issue shares at par; **acciones por encima de la par** *o* **por debajo de la par** = shares above par *o* below par; **acciones vendidas por encima de la par** = shares sold above par *o* at a premium; **el dólar está por encima de la par** = the dollar is at a premium; **la libra quedó a la par con el dólar después de su caída** = the pound fell to parity with the dollar **(b)** *(al mismo ritmo)* **a la par que** = in step with; **la libra subió a la par con el dólar** = the pound rose in step with the dollar **3** *nm* couple *o* pair; **tenemos existencias solamente para un par de semanas** = we only have enough stock for a couple of weeks; **las negociaciones duraron alrededor de un par de horas** = the negotiations lasted a couple of hours

para *prep* for *o* in order to; *(en una carta)* **Sr. P.Rosales, para entregar a Herr Schmidt** = Herr Schmidt, care of Sr P.Rosales

parado, -da 1 *adj* unemployed *o* not working; **maquinaria parada** = idle machinery *o* machines lying idle; **hay mucha gente parada** = lots of people are out of work; **seis fábricas han estado paradas durante este mes** = six factories have shut down this month **2** *n* unemployed person; **los parados** = the unemployed *o* the jobless **3** *nf* stop *o* stopover; **el billete permite dos paradas entre Madrid y Tokio** = the ticket allows you two stopovers between Madrid and Tokyo **4** *pp de* PARAR

Paraguay *nm* Paraguay

◊ **paraguayo, -ya** *adj y n* Paraguayan
NOTA: capital: **Asunción** (= Asuncion); moneda: **guaraní paraguayo** = Paraguayan guarani (G)

paraíso *nm* paradise; **paraíso fiscal** = tax haven;

blanquear dinero a través de un banco de un paraíso fiscal = to launder money through an offshore bank

paralización *nf* paralysis *o* standstill; **la huelga provocó la paralización de la fábrica** = the strike brought the factory to a standstill; **la paralización de las negociaciones** = deadlock in negotiations

◊ **paralizado, -da 1** *adj* paralyzed; **la producción está paralizada** = production is at a standstill **2** *pp de* PARALIZAR

paralizar *vt* **(a)** to paralyze; **seis barcos están paralizados en el puerto debido a la huelga** = six ships are strikebound in the docks; **las negociaciones han estado paralizadas durante diez días** = talks have been deadlocked for ten days; **la huelga paralizó el sistema de ferrocariles** = the strike closed down the railway system **(b)** to deadlock

parámetro *nm* parameter; **el director financiero fija los parámetros del presupuesto** = the budget parameters are fixed by the finance director; **el gasto de cada departamento tiene que ajustarse a determinados parámetros** = spending by each department has to fall within certain parameters

parar *vt/i* **(a)** *(cesar)* to stop; **sin parar** = non-stop *o* on end; **escribió a máquina sin parar durante dos horas** = she typed for two hours without a break; **la inflación está subiendo sin parar** = the inflation rate is going up steadily; **trabajaron sin parar para terminar la revisión de cuentas a tiempo** = they worked non-stop to finish the audit on time **(b)** **parar el trabajo** = to strike *o* to walk out *o* to walk off; **parar una fábrica** = to shut down a factory

◊ **pararse** *vr* to stop; **no nos paramos en detalles** = we did not go into details

parcela *nf* piece of ground; **división en parcelas** = parcelling out of land; **venta de parcelas** = land for sale; **compramos una parcela cerca de la playa** = we bought a piece of land near the sea; **parcela para construir** = building plot

parcelar *vt* to divide up (land)

parcial *adj* **(a)** *(una parte)* partial; **obtuvo una indemnización parcial por los daños sufridos** = he got partial compensation for damage; **canje parcial** = part exchange; **entrega parcial** = part delivery; **envío parcial** = part shipment; **pago parcial** = part payment; *US* partial payment; **se negaron a aceptar el coche viejo en pago parcial del nuevo** = they refused to take my old car as part exchange for the new one; **pedido parcial** = part order; **pérdida parcial** = partial loss; **trabaja a tiempo parcial** = she works part-time; **estamos buscando personal para trabajar con nuestros ordenadores a tiempo parcial** = we are looking for part-time staff to work our computers **(b)** *(partidario)* one-sided *o* biased; **una opinión muy parcial** = a very biased opinion

◊ **parcialmente** *adv* partly *o* partially

parecer 1 *nm* view; **sin pedir nuestro parecer** = without asking for our opinion; **al parecer** = apparently; **según el parecer de** = according to **2** *vi* to appear *o* to seem; **la empresa parecía estar en buena situación** = the company appeared to be doing well; **el director gerente parece dominar la situación** = the managing director appears to be in control; **parece ser que** = it would seem that

◊ **parecerse** *vr* to look alike

pared *nf* wall; **pared divisoria** = room divider

paridad *nf* parity *o* equivalence; **paridad del poder adquisitivo (PPA)** = purchasing power parity; **paridad de consumo** = par rate of exchange

> la teoría conocida como la paridad del poder adquisitivo (PPA) postula que a largo plazo una divisa con tasas superiores de inflación tiende a depreciarse frente a otra con tasas de inflación menores, de forma que mantenga su competitividad
>
> **El País**

'parking' *nm* car park

paro *nm* **(a)** *(desempleo)* unemployment; **paro estacional** = seasonal unemployment; **paro de larga duración** = long-term unemployment; **paro masivo** = mass unemployment; **subsidio de paro** = unemployment pay *o* unemployment benefit; *US* unemployment compensation; **tiene derecho al subsidio de paro** = she qualifies for unemployment pay; **tasa de paro** = unemployment rate; **estar en paro** = to be unemployed *o* to be out of work; **darse de alta en el paro** = to sign on for the dole; **oficinistas en paro** = unemployed office workers **(b)** *(huelga)* strike *o* walk-out *o* shutdown; **paro general** = general strike; **paro técnico** = work-to-rule; **estar en paro técnico** = to work to rule **(c)** *(interrupción)* stoppage; **las entregas se retrasarán debido a los paros de la cadena de producción** = deliveries will be late because of stoppages on the production line

> como consecuencia de la crisis económica de 1929, se originó un periodo de depresión que se propagó durante la década de 1930, alcanzando cifras de paro muy elevadas
>
> **España Económica**

> habrá poca creación de empleo, pues no hay que olvidar que el paro nunca ha disminuido con tasas de crecimiento del PIB inferiores al 3%
>
> **Actualidad Económica**

> en la protesta convocada el pasado viernes, los trabajadores demostraron su capacidad de movilización a través de un paro general y una manifestación con más de 15.000 asistentes
>
> **El País**

parque *nm* **(a)** park; **parque tecnológico** = science park; **parque nacional** = national park **(b)** **parque de viviendas** = housing stock

> ha disminuido notablemente el parque de viviendas de alquiler, de 2.000.000 en 1981 a 1.365.000 viviendas en la actualidad
>
> **España Económica**

parqué *nm* *(bolsa)* trading *o* dealing floor

párrafo *nm* paragraph; **el primer párrafo de la carta** = the first paragraph of the letter *o* paragraph one of the letter; **consulte el párrafo del contrato sobre 'instrucciones de envío'** = please refer to the paragraph in the contract on 'shipping instructions'

parte 1 *nf* **(a)** *(sección)* part *o* section; **se estropeó**

una parte del cargamento = part of the shipment was damaged; **una parte del personal hace horas extraordinarias** = part of the workforce is on overtime; **se reembolsará una parte de los gastos** = part of the expenses will be refunded; **la primera parte del acuerdo es aceptable** = the first part *o* section of the agreement is acceptable; **pequeña parte** = small part *o* fraction; **se suscribió tan sólo una pequeña parte de la nueva emisión de acciones** = only a fraction of the new share issue was subscribed; **parte principal** = main part; **parte superior** = top (part); **cuarta parte** = quarter; **tercera parte** = third; **contribuir a parte de los costes** *o* **pagar una parte de los costes** = to contribute in part to the costs *o* to pay the costs in part **(b) formar parte de** = to be part of; **entrar a formar parte de** = to become part of; **le pidieron que formara parte del consejo de administración** = she was asked to join the board **(c) en parte** = in part **(d) parte de comisión** = cut *o* share of commission; **presenta a nuevos clientes y recibe una parte de la comisión del vendedor** = he introduces new customers and gets a cut of the salesman's commission **(e)** *(participante)* party; **parte en una acción concertada** = concert party; **una de las partes litigantes ha muerto** = one of the parties to the suit has died; **la compañía no es parte en el acuerdo** = the company is not a party to the agreement; **parte acusadora** = prosecution; **la parte acusadora pagará las costas del juicio** = the costs of the case will be borne by the prosecution; **parte contratante** = contracting party; **parte demandada** = defendant; **parte demandante** = claimant; **parte perjudicada** = injured party **2** *nm* report *o* message; **dar parte** = to inform; **parte de baja** = doctor's certificate; **ha estado enfermo en casa durante diez días y todavía no ha enviado el parte de baja** = he has been off sick for ten days and still has not sent in a doctor's certificate

participación *nf* **(a)** *(colaboración)* participation; **participación de los trabajadores en la gestión de la empresa** = worker participation; **no tratamos las relaciones entre la dirección y los trabajadores como un proceso de participación en la gestión** = we do not treat management-worker relations as a participative process **(b)** *(parte)* share; **participación en el mercado** = market share *o* share of the market; **la empresa espera aumentar su participación en el mercado** = the company hopes to boost its market share; **participación en los beneficios** = profit-sharing; **la empresa tiene un plan** *o* **un programa de participación en los beneficios** = the company runs *o* operates a profit-sharing scheme **(c)** *(interés)* interest; **participación de beneficios** = equity *o* shareholding; **participaciones en otras empresas** = investments in other companies; **adquirir una participación en un negocio** = to acquire a stake in a business; **adquirió una participación de un 25% en el negocio** = he acquired a 25% stake in the business; **participación mayoritaria (de las acciones)** = majority shareholding *o* majority interest; **tiene una participación mayoritaria en la cadena de supermercados** = he has a controlling interest *o* a majority interest in a supermarket chain; **participación minoritaria (en las acciones)** = minority shareholding *o* minority interest; **declarar una participación en una compañía** = to declare an interest

participar 1 *vt* to inform *o* to notify **2** *vi* to take part *o* to participate; **participar en** = to have a share in; **participar en las decisiones de la dirección** = to have a share in *o* to participate in management decisions

participativo, -va *adj* participative

particular 1 *adj* particular *o* private; **inversor particular** = private investor; **coche particular** = private car *o* private transport; **irá en** *o* **utilizará coche particular** = he will be using private transport; **clases particulares** = private tuition **2** *nm* **(a)** *(persona)* individual *o* person; **venta a particulares** = for sale; **lo compró un particular, no una compañía** = it was bought by a private individual, not by a company **(b)** *(asunto)* matter; **en ese particular la decisión corresponde al director** = it is a matter which is left to the director's discretion **(c)** *(correspondencia)* **sin otro particular, le saluda atentamente** = looking forward to hearing from you

partida *nf* **(a)** *(remesa)* lot *o* consignment *o* shipment; **adeude esta partida en mi cuenta** = please debit my account with this consignment *o* please charge this consignment to my account; **la partida le fue adjudicada por 100.000 ptas.** = the lot was knocked down to him for 100,000 pesetas; **¿dónde está la última partida de pedidos?** = where is the last batch of orders? **(b)** *(asiento)* entry *o* item; **partidas de un balance** = items on a balance sheet; **anular una partida contable** = to write off an entry; **partida de gasto** = item of expenditure; **partidas excepcionales** = exceptional items; **partidas extraordinarias** = extraordinary items *o* non-recurring items; **contabilidad por partida doble** = double entry bookkeeping; **contabilidad por partida simple** *o* **por partida única** = single entry bookkeeping **(c)** *(registro)* certificate; **partida de nacimiento** = birth certificate **(d)** *(salida)* departure; **punto de partida** = starting point; **la partida del jefe de personal fue un alivio para todos** = the departure of the personnel manager was a great relief to everyone

partido *nm* *(política)* party

◊ **partidario, -ria** *n* supporter; **ser partidario** = to favour *o* to be in favour of; **se mostró partidario al voto** = he supported the vote

partir 1 *vt* to divide; **partir la diferencia** = to split the difference **2** *vi* to depart *o* to leave; **partir de cero** = to start from scratch; **partiendo de una base** = starting from a base *o* on the basis of; **a partir de** = starting from; **a partir de una fecha** = from a given date *o* starting from a certain date

pasado, -da 1 *adj* **(a)** *(tiempo)* past *o* previous; **la semana pasada** *o* **el mes pasado** *o* **el año pasado** = last week *o* last month *o* last year; **se ha pedido a los**

directores comerciales que informen sobre el descenso de las ventas del mes pasado = the sales managers have been asked to report on last month's drop in unit sales; **el negocio cerró en diciembre pasado** = the business folded up last December **(b) pasado de moda** = old-fashioned *o* out of fashion **2** *nm* the past **3** *pp de* PASAR

pasaje *nm* **(a)** *(viaje)* fare; **pasaje de ida** = *GB* single; *US* one-way fare; **pasaje de ida y vuelta** = return fare **(b)** *(lugar)* arcade; **pasaje comercial** = shopping arcade

◊ **pasajero, -ra 1** *adj* temporary; **dificultades pasajeras** = temporary difficulties **2** *n* passenger; **pasajero de a pie** = foot passenger; **pasajero de transbordo** = transfer passenger; **terminal de pasajeros** = passenger terminal; **tren de pasajeros** = passenger train

pasante *nm* assistant *o* junior clerk; **pasante de abogado** = articled clerk

pasaporte *nm* passport; **tuvimos que enseñar el pasaporte en la aduana** = we had to show our passports at the customs post; **su pasaporte ha caducado** *o* **está caducado** = his passport has expired *o* is out of date *o* is no longer valid; **el funcionario de pasaportes selló mi pasaporte** = the passport officer stamped my passport; **llevaba un pasaporte en regla** = he was carrying a valid passport

pasar 1 *vt* **(a)** *(de un lugar a otro)* to pass; **descubrieron que el director gerente pasaba información a una empresa competidora** = they discovered the managing director was passing information to a rival company **(b) hacer pasar una cosa por otra** = to pass something off as something else; **intentó hacer pasar el vino por español, cuando en realidad era de fuera de la UE** = he tried to pass off the wine as Spanish, when in fact it came from outside the EU **(c)** *(tiempo)* to spend; **el presidente pasó la tarde de ayer con los auditores** = the chairman spent yesterday afternoon with the auditors **(d)** *(cuentas)* **pasar factura** = to invoice; **pasar a cuenta nueva** = to carry forward *o* to carry over (a balance); **pasar el saldo anterior a cuenta nueva** = to carry over a balance **(e) pasar modelos** = to model (clothes) **(f)** *(informática)* **pasar datos al ordenador** = to input information *o* to key in data **2** *vi* **(a)** *(atravesar)* to pass *o* to go; **pasar por un puesto aduanero** = to pass a customs entry point **(b)** *(exceder)* **paquetes que no pasen de los 200 gramos** = packages not over 200 grams **(c)** *(tener lugar)* to happen; **¿qué ha pasado con eso?** = what has happened to it?; **la empresa que empezó como un pequeño taller de reparaciones ha pasado a ser una gran empresa multinacional de electrónica** = the company has grown from a small repair shop to a multinational electronics business

◊ **pasarse** *vr* to switch over to; **nos hemos pasado a un suministrador francés** = we have switched over to a French supplier

pase *nm* **(a)** *(permiso)* pass; **para entrar en las oficinas del ministerio hace falta un pase** = you need a pass to enter the ministry offices; **todos los empleados deben mostrar su pase** = all members of staff must show a pass **(b) pase de modelos** = fashion show; **pase publicitario** = advertising slot

pasivo, -va 1 *adj* passive *o* inactive **2** *nm* liabilities; **pasivo acumulado** = accrued liabilities *o* accruals; **pasivo circulante** = current liabilities; **pasivo contingente** *o* **para imprevistos** = contingent liability; **pasivo a largo plazo** = long-term liabilities; **en el pasivo** = on the debit side; **el balance general muestra el activo y el pasivo de la sociedad** = the balance sheet shows the company's assets and liabilities

paso *nm* step; **ser nombrado ayudante del director gerente es un paso hacia adelante en la escalera de promoción** = becoming assistant to the MD is a step up the promotion ladder; **preferencia de paso** = right of way

patentado, -da 1 *adj* patented; **producto farmacéutico patentado** = proprietary drug; **imitar un producto patentado** = to infringe a patent **2** *pp de* PATENTAR

patentar *vt* to patent; **patentar un invento** = to patent an invention

◊ **patente** *nf* patent; **patente de invención** = patent *o* letters patent; **patente solicitada** *o* **en tramitación** = patent applied for *o* patent pending; **agente de patentes y marcas** = patent agent; **derechos de patente** = patent rights; **obtener una patente de invención** = to take out a patent for an invention; **oficina de patentes y marcas** = patent office; **perder el derecho de patente** = to forfeit a patent; **perder una patente** = to forfeit a patent; **sacar una patente para un nuevo tipo de bombilla** = to take out a patent for a new type of light bulb; **solicitar una patente** = to apply for a patent *o* to file a patent application; **violación de patente** = infringement of patent *o* patent infringement; **violar una patente** = to infringe a patent

patio *nm* **patio de cargo** = freight yard *o* loading area; *(bolsa)* **patio de operaciones** = trading floor

patrimonio *nm* fortune *o* wealth; **impuesto sobre el patrimonio** = wealth tax; **impuesto sobre el patrimonio heredado** = estate duty; **patrimonio neto** = net worth; **patrimonio social** = shareholders' equity

> no es fácil determinar con qué nivel de renta o de patrimonio uno puede ser considerado rico
>
> **El País**

patrocinado, -da 1 *adj* sponsored; **patrocinado por el Estado** = government-sponsored; **una feria comercial patrocinada por el gobierno** = a government-sponsored trade exhibition **2** *pp de* PATROCINAR

patrocinador, -ra *n* sponsor

patrocinar *vt* to sponsor; **patrocinar un programa de televisión** = to sponsor a television programme; **el gobierno ha patrocinado una exposición de diseño** = the government has sponsored a design exhibition

◊ **patrocinio** *nm* sponsorship; **patrocinio gubernamental de misiones comerciales en el extranjero** = government sponsorship of overseas trade missions

patrón *nm* **(a)** *(jefe)* employer *o* boss; **si quieres un aumento de sueldo, ve a hablar con tu patrón** =

if you want a pay rise, go and talk to your boss **(b)** *(modelo)* standard; **patrón monetario** = monetary standard; **patrón oro** = gold standard

◊ **patrona** *nf* employer *o* boss

◊ **patronal 1** *adj* **cierre patronal** = lockout; **cuota patronal** = employer's contribution; **organización patronal** = employers' organization *o* association **2** *nf* the management; **los sindicatos y la patronal** = unions and management

◊ **patrono, -na** *n* **(a)** *(patrocinador)* sponsor **(b)** *(jefe)* employer

paulatinamente *adv* gradually; **la compañía se ha hecho paulatinamente más rentable** = the company has gradually become more profitable; **compró varias zapaterías y paulatinamente fue creando una cadena** = he bought several shoe shops and gradually built up a chain

pausa *nf* break *o* pause; **pausa publicitaria** = commercial break; **tras una breve pausa continuaron con la reunión** = after a short break they they went on with the meeting

> la necesidad de pausas breves durante las horas del trabajo se acepta cada día más y, aunque normalmente no están prescritas por ley, son a menudo objeto de regulación en los convenios colectivos
> **El País**

pauta *nf* pattern; **pauta económica** = economic pattern; **servir de pauta** = to act as a model

paz *nf* peace; **ahora estamos en paz** = now we're square

PC (NOTA: del inglés) *(ordenador personal)* personal computer (PC)

peaje *nm* toll; **tuvimos que cruzar un puente de peaje para llegar a la isla** = we had to cross a toll bridge to get to the island

peatonal *adj* pedestrian; **zona peatonal** *o* **zona comercial peatonal** = pedestrian precinct *o* shopping precinct

pecios *nm* **pecios y echazón** = flotsam and jetsam

pecuniario, -ria *adj* pecuniary; **resursos pecuniarios** = financial resources; **no sacó ninguna ventaja pecuniaria** = he gained no pecuniary advantage

pedazo *nm* piece; **a pedazos** = in bits; **hacer pedazos** = to smash to pieces

pedestal *nm* pedestal; **servir de pedestal** = to be a stepping stone

pedido, -da *adj* ordered *o* on order; **este artículo está agotado, pero está pedido** = this item is out of stock, but is on order **2** *nm* **(a)** *(encargo)* order; **pedidos atrasados** = back orders *o* backlog of orders; **el almacén está intentando hacer frente a los pedidos atrasados** = the warehouse is trying to cope with the backlog of orders; **pedido cursado al viajante** = journey order; **pedido de dimensiones óptimas** = economic order quantity; **pedidos pendientes** = outstanding orders; **pedido permanente** = regular order; **pedidos por servir** = unfulfilled orders; **pedidos por teléfono** = telephone orders; **desde que enviamos el catálogo por correo**

hemos recibido un gran número de pedidos por teléfono = since we mailed the catalogue we have had a large number of telephone orders; **pedido suplementario** *o* **nuevo pedido** = repeat order *o* new order; **el producto ha estado a la venta solamente durante diez días y ya estamos desbordados con pedidos suplementarios** = the product has been on the market only ten days and we are already flooded with repeat orders; **pedido urgente** = rush order **(b)** **cursar un pedido** = to place an order; **despachar un pedido** = to fill *o* to fulfil *o* to deal with an order; **no podemos despachar más pedidos antes de Navidad** = we cannot fulfil any more orders before Christmas; **despacho de pedidos** = order fulfilment; **hacer un pedido** = to place an order with someone; **condiciones: el pago se efectuará al hacer el pedido** = terms: cash with order; **preparación de pedidos** = order processing; **renovar un pedido** = to repeat an order; **servir un pedido** = to deal with *o* to supply an order; **servir un pedido de veinte archivadores** = to supply an order for twenty filing cabinets; **el pedido debe ser entregado en nuestro almacén** = the order should be delivered to our warehouse; **no disponemos en este momento de los artículos de su pedido que se indican a continuación** = the following items on your order are temporarily unavailable; **atenderemos su pedido inmediatamente** = your order will receive immediate attention **(c)** **un bloc de hojas de pedido** = a pad of order forms; **cartera de pedidos** = order book; **la empresa tiene el libro de pedidos completo** = the company has a full order book; **pérdida de un pedido** = loss of an order **3** *pp de* PEDIR

> las empresas deben realizar sus pedidos con años de antelación
> **España Económica**

pedir *vt* **(a)** *(solicitar)* to ask *o* to ask for *o* to request; **¿se acordó de pedir a la centralita que me pasara las llamadas a la sala de juntas?** = did you remember to ask the switchboard to put my calls through to the boardroom?; **los aduaneros me pidieron que exhibiera el pasaporte** = customs officials asked me to show my passport; **pedir ayuda al Estado** = to request assistance from the government; **llamar para pedir algo** = to phone for something; **llamó para pedir un taxi** = he telephoned for a taxi; **pedir cobertura adicional** = to ask for additional cover; **pedir el desembolso de capital** = to call up capital; **pedir una indemnización** = to put in a claim for damage; **pedir información** = to ask for information *o* to inquire; **pedir licitaciones** = to invite tenders; **pedir prestado** = to borrow **(b)** *(encargar)* to order; **pedir mercancías** = to order goods; **diga a la secretaria que pida más papel para la fotocopiadora** = tell the secretary to order some more photocopying paper; **¿has pedido el vino?** = have you ordered the wine? **(c)** **pedir el reembolso de un préstamo** = to call in (a loan)

pegamento *nm* glue *o* gum; **puso un poco de pegamento en la parte posterior del cartel para pegarlo a la pared** = she put some glue on the back of the poster to fix it to the wall

pegar *vt* **(a)** *(adherir)* to attach *o* to stick on *o* to glue; **pegó la etiqueta a la caja** = he glued the label to the box; **pegar un sello a una carta** = to stick a stamp on a letter; **pegaron un cartel en la puerta** = they stuck a poster on the door; **pegar etiquetas** = to put stickers on *o* to sticker; **tuvimos que pegar etiquetas en todas las existencias** = we had to sticker all the stock **(b)** *(golpe)* to hit *o* to knock; **el nuevo modelo pega fuerte en el mercado juvenil** = the new model is a great hit among young people

peligro *nm* danger; **la maquinaria vieja constituye un peligro para el personal** = there is danger to the workforce in the old machinery; **peligro de incendio** = fire hazard *o* fire risk; **ese almacén lleno de madera y papel supone un peligro de incendio** = that warehouse full of wood and paper is a fire hazard; **correr peligro** = to be in danger; **la compañía corre el peligro de ser adquirida** = the company is in danger of being taken over; **sin peligro** = safely *o* without danger

◊ **peligroso, -sa** *adj* dangerous *o* risky; **trabajo peligroso** = dangerous job; **los obreros han dejado de trabajar para reivindicar una prima por trabajo peligroso** = the workforce has stopped work and asked for danger money

pena *nf* **(a)** *(castigo, multa)* penalty *o* punishment **(b)** ¡**qué pena!** = what a shame! *o* what a pity! **(c)** **vale** *o* **merece la pena** = it's worth it

◊ **penal** *adj* penal; **antecedentes penales** = criminal record; **cláusula penal** = penalty clause; **el contrato contiene una cláusula penal que multa a la sociedad con un 1% por cada semana que se atrase en la fecha de cumplimiento** = the contract contains a penalty clause which fines the company 1% for every week's delay in completing the work

penalizar *vt* to penalize

pendiente 1 *adj* **(a)** *(en espera)* pending; **bandeja de asuntos pendientes** = pending tray; **asuntos pendientes de la reunión anterior** = matters outstanding from the previous meeting; **puso la carta en el montón de cartas pendientes de firma** = she put the letter on the pile of letters waiting to be signed; **pendiente de repuesta** = pending a reply; **pendiente del consejo de nuestros abogados** = pending advice from our lawyers **(b)** *(por pagar, por servir)* outstanding *o* unpaid; **deudas pendientes** = outstanding debts; **pedidos pendientes** = outstanding orders *o* back orders; **después de la huelga la fábrica tardó seis semanas en despachar todos los pedidos pendientes** = after the strike it took the factory six weeks to clear all the accumulated back orders **2** *nf* slope; **remontar la pendiente** = to climb back up

penique *nm GB* penny

pensión *nf* **(a)** *(anualidad)* pension *o* annuity; **pensiones ajustadas al coste de vida** = index-linked pensions; **pensión estatal** = government pension *o* state pension; **recibe una pensión del Estado** = he has a government annuity *o* an annuity from the government; **pensión calculada en función del salario** = earnings-related pension; **pensión laboral** = occupational pension; **cotizaciones a la pensión de jubilación** = pension contributions; **pensión indexada** = inflation-proof pension; **pensión de retiro** = retirement pension *o* old age pension; **pensión vitalicia** = life annuity *o* annuity for life; **pensión de viudedad** = widow's pension; **derecho a pensión** = pension entitlement;

fondo de pensiones = pension fund **(b)** **plan de pensiones** = pension plan *o* pension scheme; **plan** *o* **programa de pensiones de la empresa** = occupational *o* company pension scheme; **plan de pensiones con aportación del trabajador** = contributory pension scheme; **programa de pensiones sin aportación del trabajador** = non-contributory pension scheme; **el programa de pensiones está totalmente financiado por la empresa** = the company pension scheme is non-contributory; **plan de pensiones personal** = personal pension plan; **decidió apuntarse al programa de pensiones de la empresa** = he decided to join the company's pension scheme; **programa de pensiones proporcionales** = graduated pension scheme **(c)** *(casa de huéspedes)* boarding house *o* guest house **(d)** *(hospedaje)* **pensión completa** = full board; **media pensión** = half board

◊ **pensionista** *nmf* **(a)** *(rentista)* annuitant **(b)** *(persona que recibe una pensión de jubilación)* pensioner *o* old age pensioner (OAP)

el 72% de las pensiones están por debajo del salario mínimo interprofesional
España Económica

pequeño, -ña *adj* small *o* little *o* slight *o* minor; **pequeños comerciantes** = small shopkeepers; **pequeñas empresas** = small businesses; **pequeñas y medianas empresas (PYMEs)** = small and medium-sized businesses; **pequeño empresario** = small businessman; **pequeño hurto** = petty thefts *o* pilferage *o* pilfering; **el pequeño inversionista** = the small investor; **pequeño supermercado** = minimarket; **pequeño teclado** = keypad; **pequeños accionistas** = small shareholders; **billetes de pequeño valor** = small denomination banknotes; **empresa pequeña** = small company

el sector público controla aún el 3,8% del capital, mientras que el resto está repartido entre 18.000 pequeños accionistas
El País

per cápita *adv* per capita; **consumo per cápita** = per capita consumption; **la renta media per cápita** = average income per capita *o* per capita income; **el gasto per cápita** = per capita expenditure

percentil *nm* percentile

percibir *vt* to earn *o* to receive *o* to get; **trabajar sin percibir sueldo** = to do voluntary work

perder *vt* **(a)** to lose; **perder clientes** = to lose customers; **tienen un servicio tan lento que han ido perdiendo clientes** = their service is so slow that they have been losing customers; **perder el control de una compañía** = to lose control of a company; **perder la posesión de algo** = to lose possession of something *o* to forfeit something; **perder un depósito** *o* **una entrada** = to forfeit a deposit; **perder dinero** = to lose (money); **perdió 2.000.000 de ptas. en la empresa de ordenadores de su padre** = he lost 2m pesetas in his father's computer company; **perder un pedido** = to lose an order; **durante la huelga, la empresa perdió seis pedidos que fueron a los competidores estadounidenses** = during the strike, the company lost six orders to American competitors; **perdió su trabajo cuando la fábrica cerró** = she lost her job when the factory closed; **perdieron todos sus bienes en el incendio** =

they lost all their possessions in the fire **(b) perder el tiempo** = to waste time; **al director gerente no le gusta que le hagan perder el tiempo con pequeños detalles** = the MD does not like people wasting their time on minor details **(c) perder valor** = to lose value *o* to depreciate; **la libra ha perdido valor** = the pound has lost value; **acción que ha perdido el 10% de su valor durante el año** = share which has depreciated by 10% over the year **(d) la mitad del envío se echó a perder por culpa del agua** = half the shipment was spoiled by water **(e)** *(salir perdiendo)* to lose out; **la empresa ha salido perdiendo al precipitarse a fabricar ordenadores baratos** = the company has lost out in the rush to make cheap computers **(f) perder el tren** *o* **avión** = to miss the train *o* the plane; **perdió el último avión** *o* **vuelo a Berlín** = he missed the last plane to Berlin; **perder la oportunidad de hacer algo** = to miss the chance of doing something; **llegué tarde, así que me perdí la mayor parte del debate** = I arrived late, so missed most of the discussion

◊ **perderse** *vr* **(a)** *(extraviarse)* to get lost **(b)** to miss

pérdida *nf* **(a)** *(acción de perder)* loss; **pérdidas de capital** = capital losses; **pérdida de clientela** = loss of customers; **pérdida a efectos fiscales** = tax loss; **pérdida de ejercicio** *o* **de explotación** = trading loss; **pérdida de un pedido** = loss of an order; **pérdida de peso** = loss in weight; **pérdida de puestos de trabajo** = job losses; **pérdidas razonables** = acceptable losses; **pérdida sobre el papel** = paper loss; **pérdida total** = dead loss *o* write-off; **se declaró la pérdida total del cargamento** = the cargo was written off as a total loss **(b)** *(reducción de beneficios)* loss; **cuenta de pérdidas y ganancias** = profit and loss account; **las acciones experimentaron pérdidas en la bolsa de hasta un 5%** = shares showed losses of up to 5% on the Stock Exchange; **la compañía sufrió una pérdida** = the company made a loss; **la compañía anunció que había sufrido pérdidas por valor de 1 millón de pesetas en el primer año** = the company reported a loss of 1m pesetas in the first year's trading; **deducir las pérdidas de los impuestos** = to offset losses against tax; **la empresa ya no tiene pérdidas** = the company has moved into the black; **reducir las pérdidas** = to cut one's losses; **tasador de pérdidas** = loss adjuster **(c) con pérdidas** = at a loss *o* out of pocket; **la compañía trabaja con pérdidas** = the company is trading at a loss; **vendió la tienda con pérdidas** = he sold the shop at a loss; **nos retiramos con pérdidas de 25.000 ptas.** = in the end, we lost 25,000 pesetas *o* we ended up 25,000 pesetas out of pocket **(d)** *(cosas que se pierden)* **pérdidas** = leakage *o* wastage; **contar con un 10% de material de más para pérdidas** = to allow 10% extra material for wastage; **pérdida natural (durante el transporte)** = loss in transport **(e)** *(jurídico)* forfeiture

el nuevo Impuesto sobre Sociedades intentará terminar con las prácticas habituales de ventas de empresas en pérdidas para compensar beneficios y no pagar impuestos
Cambio 16

tras la fuerte caída del índice Dow Jones el pasado 15 de noviembre, el resto de los mercados internacionales no sufrían el temido pánico generalizado y podían sujetar sus cambios con unas pérdidas razonables
Tiempo

perdonar *vt* to excuse *o* to forgive; **se le puede perdonar que no sepa cómo se dice 'photocopier' en español** = she can be excused for not knowing the Spanish for 'photocopier'

perecedero, -ra *adj* perishable *o* non-durable; **mercancías perecederas** *o* **artículos perecederos** *o* **carga perecedera** = perishable goods *o* items *o* cargo; **bienes no perecederos** = durable goods *o* durables

perezoso, -sa *adj* lazy; **es demasiado perezosa para hacer horas extraordinarias** = she is too lazy to do any overtime; **es tan perezoso que ni siquiera presenta a tiempo sus justificantes de gastos** = he is so lazy he does not even send in his expense claims on time

perfeccionar *vt* to perfect; **perfeccionó el proceso para fabricar acero de alta calidad** = he perfected the process for making high grade steel

perfecto, -ta *adj* perfect; **competencia perfecta** = perfect competition; **mercado perfecto** = perfect market; **examinamos cada lote para asegurarnos de que es perfecto** = we check each batch to make sure it is perfect; **hizo un examen de mecanografía perfecto** = she did a perfect typing test

◊ **perfectamente** *adv* perfectly; **mecanografió la carta perfectamente** = she typed the letter perfectly; **es perfectamente capaz de llevar el departamento solo** = he is quite capable of running the department by himself

perfil *nm* profile; **perfil del consumidor** = consumer profile; **perfil de ventas** = sales contour; **solicitó un perfil de las compañías que podrían asociarse en una empresa conjunta** = he asked for a company profile of the possible partners in the joint venture; **el perfil del cliente muestra que nuestro comprador medio es varón, de 25 a 40 años de edad y empleado del sector servicios** = the customer profile shows our average buyer to be male, aged 25-40, and employed in the service industries

perfilar *vt* to outline

◊ **perfilarse** *vpr* **se perfila como el próximo presidente** = he is tipped to be come the next chairman

perforar *vt* to perforate *o* to punch

◊ **perforador, -ra** *adj* punching; **máquina perforadora** = punch

pericia *nf* expertise *o* proficiency; **pericia natural** = natural skill

◊ **pericial** *adj* skilled *o* expert; **informe pericial** = expert's report

periferia *nf* periphery

◊ **periférico, -ca 1** *adj* marginal **2** *nm* **(a)** *(latinoamérica)* ringroad **(b)** *(informática)* **periféricos** = peripherals

periódico, -ca 1 *adj* periodic *o* periodical *o* routine; **una revisión periódica del rendimiento de la empresa** = a periodic review of the company's performance; **un examen periódico del equipo contra incendios** = a routine check of the fire equipment **2** *nm* paper *o* newspaper; **periódico gratuito** = free paper *o* giveaway paper *o* freesheet; **pusimos un anuncio en el periódico** = we put an ad in the paper; **nuestro anuncio se publicó en la primera página del periódico** = our ad appeared on the front page of the newspaper; **contestó a un anuncio del periódico** = she answered an ad in the paper; **encontró su trabajo a través de un anuncio en el periódico** = he found his job through an ad in the paper; **reportaje de un periódico** = a report in a newspaper *o* a newspaper report; **sección de un periódico** = section of a newspaper; **escribe la crónica** *o* **información financiera del periódico** = she writes the City column in the newspaper

◊ **periodista** *nmf* journalist; **es una periodista que trabaja por su cuenta** = she is a freelance journalist; **trabaja como periodista independiente para los periódicos locales** = she freelances for the local newspapers

◊ **periodístico, -ca** *adj* journalistic; **cobertura periodística** = media coverage

periodo *nm* **(a)** *(espacio de tiempo)* period *o* (a lapse of) time; **periodo de tiempo** = a period of time; **durante un periodo de meses** *o* **durante un periodo de seis años** = for a period of months *o* for a six-year period; **las ventas efectuadas durante un periodo de tres meses** *o* **durante el periodo de vacaciones** = sales over a period of three months *o* over the holiday period; **el periodo del año de mayor actividad en las tiendas es la semana anterior a las Navidades** = the busiest time of year for stores is the week before Christmas; **los pagos pueden escalonarse durante un periodo de diez años** = payments can be spaced out over a period of ten years; **fue trasladado al Ministerio de Comercio por un periodo de dos años** = he was seconded to the Department of Trade for two years; **un periodo de precios que suben en espiral** = a period of spiralling prices **(b)** *(curso legal o universitario)* term **(c) periodo de arrendamiento** = term of a lease; **periodo de conservación de un producto** = shelf life of a product; **periodo contable** = accounting period; **periodo de demanda máxima** = time of peak demand; **periodo de espera** = waiting period; **periodo de formación** = qualifying period *o* period of qualification; **periodo medio de pago (PMG)** = average payment period; **periodo de preaviso** = period of notice; **periodo de prueba** = probation period *o* period of qualification; **está en periodo de prueba de tres meses** = he is on three months' probation **(d)** *(jurídico)* **periodo de prácticas** = articles (NOTA: también se escribe **período)**

perito, -ta 1 *adj* skilled **2** *n* **(a)** *(experto)* expert **(b)** *(tasador)* valuer *o* adjuster; **perito de averías** = average adjuster **(c)** *(título técnico, comercial)* **perito mercantil** = chartered accountant; **perito electricista** = qualified electrician

perjudicar *vt* **(a)** *(dañar)* to affect *o* to harm *o* to hurt; **parte perjudicada** = injured party; **las ventas de la empresa en el Extremo Oriente se vieron seriamente perjudicadas por el embargo** = the company's sales in the Far East were seriously affected by the embargo; **la mala publicidad ha perjudicado la reputación de la empresa** = the bad publicity has harmed the company's reputation; **la recesión no ha perjudicado a nuestra compañía** = the company has not been hurt by the recession; **las pequeñas empresas han sido las más perjudicadas por la nueva legislación** = the new legislation has hit the small companies hardest **(b) perjudicar los intereses** *o* **las pretensiones de alguien** = to prejudice someone's interests *o* claims

perjuicio *nm* **(a)** *(daño)* harm *o* prejudice; **demanda por daños y perjuicios** = action for damages; **entablar una demanda contra alguien por daños y perjuicios** = to bring an action for damages against someone **(b) en perjuicio de** = to the prejudice of; **sin perjuicio** = 'without prejudice'

perjurar *vi* *(dar falso testimonio)* to perjure oneself

◊ **perjurio** *nm* perjury; **lo encarcelaron por cometer perjurio** = he was sent to prison for perjury; **compareció ante los tribunales acusada de cometer perjurio** = she appeared in court on a perjury charge

permanecer *vi* to remain *o* to stay; **los beneficios han permanecido por debajo del 10% durante dos años** = profits have stayed below 10% for two years

permanencia *nf* **(a)** *(estancia)* stay **(b)** *(duración)* permanency; **seguridad de permanencia en el empleo** = security of employment

permanente *adj* permanent; **comisión permanente** = standing committee; **servicio permanente** = 24-hour service; **la empresa tiene problemas permanentes de flujo de caja** = the company has chronic cash flow problems

◊ **permanentemente** *adv* permanently

permisible *adj* allowable; **tiempo permisible** = allowed time

permiso *nm* **(a)** *(autorización)* permission; **permiso por escrito** = written permission; **permiso verbal** *o* **de palabra** = verbal permission; **dar permiso a alguien para hacer algo** = to give someone permission to do something; **solicitó permiso al director para tomarse un día libre** = he asked the manager's permission to take a day off; **necesitará el permiso de las autoridades locales para derribar el edificio de oficinas** = you will need the permission of the local authorities before you can knock down the office block **(b) permiso de construcción** = planning permission; **les denegaron el permiso de construcción** = they were refused planning permission; **permiso para edificar** = building permit; **permiso provisional para edificar** = outline planning permission **(c)** *(licencia)* permit *o* licence; **conceder un permiso** = to license; **permiso de conducir** = driving licence; *US* driver's license; **los candidatos deben tener un permiso de conducir válido** = applicants should hold a valid driving licence; **permiso de descarga** = landing order; **permiso de residencia** = residence permit; (US) green card; **permiso de trabajo** = work permit **(d)** (en el trabajo) leave; **pidió permiso para visitar a su madre en el hospital** = he asked for leave of absence to visit his mother in hospital; **disfrutar de un permiso laboral** o **estar de permiso** = to go on leave o to be on leave

permitir vt to allow o to permit; **este documento le permite exportar veinticinco sistemas informáticos** = this document permits you to export twenty-five computer systems; **el billete permite la entrada de tres personas a la exposición** = the ticket allows three people to the exhibition; **la compañía permite que todo el personal tome seis días de vacaciones en Navidades** = the company allows all members of staff to take six days' holiday at Christmas; **este sistema permite cambios de última hora** = this system allows for last-minute changes; **no está permitida la entrada de personas no autorizadas en el laboratorio** = unauthorized persons are not allowed o no unauthorized persons are allowed into the laboratory; **no se permite fumar en el edificio** = smoking is not allowed in the building; **permítame que le recuerde** = may I remind you

◊ **permitirse** vr to afford; **se permitió el lujo de cambiar de coche** = he could afford to buy a new car; **por fin nos podemos permitir unas vacaciones** = at last we can afford to go on holiday; **no nos pudimos permitir el coste de dos teléfonos** = we could not afford the cost of two telephones

persa adj y nmf Iranian

perseguir vt to chase; **perseguir un mercado determinado** = to target a market

persistente adj persistent; **consecuencias persistentes** = durable effects; **la huelga tendrá consecuencias persistentes para la economía** = the strike will have durable effects on the economy

persona nf person; **llamada telefónica de persona a persona** = person-to-person call; **persona ambiciosa** = ambitious person o high flyer; **persona embargada** = garnishee; **persona física** = individual; **persona jurídica** = legal entity; **persona nombrada** = appointee; **persona que solicita votos** = canvasser; **persona que toma decisiones** = decision maker; **¿quién es su persona de confianza en el ministerio?** = who is your contact in the ministry?; **póliza de seguros que protege a la persona mencionada** = insurance policy which covers a named person; **las personas mencionadas en el contrato** = the persons named in the contract; **en persona** = in person o personally; **este importante paquete debe ser entregado al presidente en persona** = this important package is to be delivered to the chairman in person; **por persona** = per person o per head; **los representantes cuestan una media de 5.000.000 de ptas. por persona y año** = representatives cost on average 5m pesetas per head per annum

personal 1 adj **(a)** (propio de una persona) personal; **bienes personales** = personal assets o personal effects o personal property; **comunicación personal** = personal call; **deducciones personales** = personal allowances; **efectos personales** = personal assets o personal effects o personal property; **interés personal** = vested interest; **llamada personal** = personal call; **ordenador personal** = personal

computer (PC); **además de las acciones familiares, tiene una participación personal en la sociedad** = apart from the family shares, he has a personal shareholding in the company; **renta personal** = personal income; **secretario personal** = personal assistant; **el coche es para su uso personal** = the car is for his personal use **(b)** (privado) private o personal; **cliente personal** = private client o customer; **quiero ver al director por un asunto personal** = I want to see the director on a personal matter **2** nm **(a)** personnel o staff; **personal administrativo** = clerical staff o administrative staff o office staff; **el personal del almacén** = the personnel o the warehouse o the warehouse personnel o the warehouse staff; **personal de atención al público** = counter staff; **personal capacitado** = qualified staff; **el personal de la casa** = the in-house staff; **personal de contabilidad** = accounts staff; **personal de Correos** = Post Office staff; **personal fijo** = regular staff; **personal de gestión** = managerial staff; **personal de mayor categoría** o **antigüedad** o **de más edad** = senior staff; **personal de menor categoría** o **antigüedad** o **de menos edad** = junior staff; **personal de oficina** = office staff o clerical staff; **personal de ventas** = sales force; **personal de ventas muy motivado** = highly motivated sales staff; **el personal de ventas no se ocupa de la limpieza de la tienda** = the sales staff are not concerned with the cleaning of the store; **el hotel suministra los uniformes del personal** = staff uniforms are provided by the hotel; **los delegados sindicales convocaron al personal a una huelga** = the shop stewards called the workforce out on strike; **tres cuartas partes del personal tiene menos de treinta años** = three quarters of the staff are less than thirty years old; **falto** o **escaso de personal** = understaffed o undermanned o shorthanded; **andamos bastante escasos de personal en este momento** = we are rather shorthanded at the moment; **reducciones de personal** = staff cuts o reductions **(b) agencia de personal administrativo** = staff agency; **asociación del personal de una empresa** = staff association; **capacitación** o **formación de personal** = staff training; **delegado de personal** = worker director; **el departamento de personal** = the personnel department; **dirección de personal** = personnel management; **director de personal** = personnel manager; **evaluación de personal** = staff assessments; **jefe de personal** = head of personnel o personnel officer; **la Sra. Balea es la jefa de personal** = Sra Balea is the personnel officer; **reclutar personal** = to recruit new staff; **suministro de personal** = staffing; **trasladar personal** = to redeploy staff

◊ **personalizado, -da** adj personalized

◊ **personalmente** adv personally o in person; **me escribió personalmente** = she wrote to me personally; **vino a verme personalmente** = he came to see me in person

perspectiva nf **(a)** (visión) perspective o outlook; **perspectiva industrial** = industrial outlook; **las perspectivas económicas no son buenas** = the economic outlook is not good; **las**

perspectivas del mercado de valores son inquietantes = the stock market outlook is worrying (b) *(expectativa)* prospects; perspectivas de inversión = investment prospects; sus perspectivas de trabajo son buenas = his job prospects are good; las perspectivas de mercado son peores que las del año pasado = prospects for the market *o* market prospects are worse than those of last year

persuadir *vt* to persuade *o* to convince; tras una discusión de diez horas, persuadieron al director gerente a que dimitiera = after ten hours of discussion, they persuaded the MD to resign; no pudimos persuadir a la empresa francesa para que firmara el contrato = we could not persuade the French company to sign the contract

◊ persuadirse *vr* to be convinced

pertenecer *vi* to belong to; la compañía pertenece a una vieja familia de banqueros norteamericanos = the company belongs to an old American banking family; la patente pertenece al hijo del inventor = the patent belongs to the inventor's son

◊ pertenencia *nf* ownership; pertenencias = possessions

pertinente *adj* relevant; ¿puedes darme los documentos pertinentes? = can you give me the relevant papers?

perturbado, -da 1 *adj* unsettled; el mercado se vió perturbado por la noticia del fracaso de la OPA = the market was unsettled by the news of the failure of the takeover bid 2 *pp de* PERTURBAR

perturbar *vt* to disturb *o* to surprise *o* to shock; los mercados se vieron perturbados por los resultados de la compañía = the markets were shaken by the company's results

Perú *nm* Peru

◊ peruano, -na *adj y n* Peruvian
NOTA: capital: **Lima**; moneda: **inti peruano (I/.)** = Peruvian inti (I/.)

pesado, -da 1 *adj* heavy; la oficina de correos se negó a aceptar el paquete porque era demasiado pesado = the Post Office refused to handle the package because it was too heavy; excesivamente pesado = overweight; industria pesada = heavy *o* smokestack industry; maquinaria pesada = heavy machinery 2 *pp de* PESAR

pesar *vt* (a) *(medir)* to weigh; el paquete pesa 125 gramos = the packet weighs 125 grams; pesó el paquete en la oficina de correos = he weighed the packet at the post office (b) *(valorar)* to weigh; pesar el pro y el contra = to weigh the pros and the cons (c) *(ser una carga)* le pesa la responsabilidad de su cargo = he finds the responsibilities of his job a burden (d) *(influir)* las consideraciones económicas pesaron mucho en mi decisión = economic considerations played an important part in my decision

peseta *nf* peseta; billete de 1.000 ptas. = 1,000 peseta note; cambiar pesetas a dólares = to change

pesetas into dollars; cuenta en pesetas = peseta account; cuesta 200.000 ptas. = it costs 200,000 pesetas

los tipos de interés seguirán relativamente elevados y con resistencia a la baja, mientras que la peseta se mantendrá en la zona alta de la banda de fluctuación
Actualidad Económica

la oferta de CVNE a los accionistas de Bilbaínas era de 8.800 pesetas por título
El País

pesimismo *nm* pessimism; pesimismo en el mercado = market pessimism *o* pessimism on the market; reina un gran pesimismo sobre las posibilidades de encontrar trabajo = there is considerable pessimism about job opportunities

◊ pesimista *adj* pessimistic; tiene una visión pesimista del tipo de cambio = he takes a pessimistic view of the exchange rate

peso *nm* (a) *(medida)* weight; peso bruto = gross weight; peso falso *o* peso escaso = short weight *o* false weight; de peso insuficiente = underweight; peso máximo = weight limit; peso muerto = deadweight; peso neto = net weight; pesos y medidas = weights and measures; peso troy = troy weight; el paquete tiene un exceso de peso de sesenta gramos = the package is sixty grams overweight; escatimar en el peso = to give short weight; vender fruta a peso = to sell fruit by weight (b) *(moneda en ciertos países de Sudamérica)* peso; 200 pesos mexicanos = 200 Mexican pesos

petición *nf* (a) *(demanda)* request; petición de informes = inquiry; petición de informes sobre crédito = status inquiry; petición de patente = patent application; petición de propuestas = call for tenders; petición de quiebra = petition in bankruptcy *o* bankruptcy petition; petición de votos = canvassing; con referencia a su petición del 25 de mayo = I refer to your inquiry of May 25th; rechazaron su petición *o* su petición fue rechazada = his request was turned down *o* met with a refusal (b) a petición = on request; enviaremos muestras a petición *o* muestras disponibles a petición de los interesados = we will send samples on request *o* samples available on request; dinero pagadero a petición = money at call *o* money on call *o* call money

petrodólar *nm* petrodollar

petróleo *nm* (a) oil *o* petroleum; petróleo crudo = crude oil; petróleo derramado en el naufragio del petrolero = discharge of oil from the wreck of the tanker; tenemos grandes reservas de petróleo = we have large stocks of oil (b) cánones del petróleo = oil royalties; países exportadores de petróleo = oil-exporting countries *o* petroleum-exporting countries; países importadores de petróleo = oil-importing countries; países productores de petróleo = oil-producing countries; precio del petróleo = oil price; los precios del petróleo han subido desde que empezó la guerra = oil prices have jumped since the war started; pozo de petróleo = oil well; productos derivados del petróleo = petroleum products; renta del petróleo = petroleum revenues

◊ petrolero *nm* tanker; un petrolero con una

carga de petróleo del Golfo = a tanker carrying oil from the Gulf; **el petrolero se hundió durante el viaje al Golfo** = the tanker sank when she was en route to the Gulf

◊ **petrolífero, -ra** *adj* **acciones petrolíferas** = oil shares; **industria petrolífera** = petroleum industry; **plataforma petrolífera** = oil platform *o* oil rig; **yacimiento petrolífero** = oil field

PIB = PRODUCTO INTERIOR BRUTO Gross Domestic Product (GDP)

> habrá poca creación de empleo, pues no hay que olvidar que el paro nunca ha disminuido con tasas de crecimiento del PIB inferiores al 3%
> **Actualidad Económica**

> el saldo externo seguirá en torno al 3% del PIB, sin grandes expectativas de mejora
> **Actualidad Económica**

picado *adj* **caída en picado** = slump *o* sharp fall

> con esta iniciativa, la aerolínea intenta parar la caída en picado que viene sufriendo durante los últimos cinco ejercicios, tanto en resultados como en cuota de mercado
> **Cinco Días**

pie *nm* **(a)** *(parte del cuerpo humano)* foot; **a pie** = on foot; **andar** *o* **recorrer a pie** = to walk *o* to go on foot; **pasajero de a pie** = foot passanger; **los visitantes recorrieron la fábrica a pie** = the visitors walked round the factory; **los representantes hacen la mayoría de sus visitas dentro de Madrid a pie** = the reps make most of their calls in central Madrid on foot **(b)** *(medida de longitud = 30cm)* foot **(c)** **a pie de página** = at the foot of the page; **nota a pie de página** = footnote

pieza *nf* **(a)** *(unidad)* piece; **el precio es de 50 ptas. por pieza** = the price is 50 pesetas each *o* the piece; **tarifa por pieza unitaria** = piece rate; **cobrar por pieza a destajo** = to earn piece rates **(b)** *(parte)* component; **la cadena de montaje se paró por el retraso del suministro de una pieza** = the assembly line stopped because supply of a component was delayed; **pieza de recambio** *o* **repuesto** = spare part; **la fotocopiadora no funciona - tenemos que cambiarle una pieza** = the photocopier will not work - we need to replace a part *o* a part needs replacing

pignorar *vt* to pawn; **pignorar acciones** = to pledge share certificates

pila *nf* **(a)** *(montón)* pile; **tengo una pila de cosas por hacer** = I have a pile of things to do; **una pila de cajas** = a pile of boxes **(b)** *(batería)* battery; **la calculadora necesita una pila nueva** = the calculator needs a new battery; **una calculadora de pilas** *o* **accionada por pilas** = a battery-powered calculator

pilotar *vt* to pilot

piloto 1 *adj* *(prueba)* pilot; **casa piloto** *o* **piso piloto** = show house *o* show flat; **la fábrica piloto ha sido construida para probar los nuevos procesos productivos** = the pilot factory has been built to test the new production processes; **está dirigiendo un programa piloto para formar a jóvenes desempleados** = he is directing a pilot scheme for training unemployed young people **2** *nmf* *(persona)* pilot

PIN = PRODUCTO INTERIOR NETO Net Domestic Product

pinta *nf* *(medida de capacidad; = 0,568 litro en el Reino Unido ó 0,473 litro en EE UU)* pint

pionero, -ra 1 *adj* pioneering; **proyecto pionero** *o* **desarrollo pionero** = pioneer project *o* pioneer development **2** *n* pioneer

piquete *nm* picket; **piquete de huelga** = strike picket; **formar piquetes a la entrada de una fábrica** = to picket a factory; **formación de piquetes huelgistas** = mass picketing; **piquete de vigilancia a la entrada de una fábrica** = picket line; **estar en el piquete de vigilancia a la entrada de una fábrica** = to man a picket line *o* to be on the picket line

pirata 1 *adj* pirate; **copia pirata de un libro** = a pirate copy of a book; **edición pirata de un libro** *o* **diseño pirata** = a pirated book *o* a pirated design; **hacer una edición pirata** = to pirate **2** *nmf* pirate

piratear *vt* *(hacer una edición pirata)* to pirate

◊ **piratería** *nf* piracy

piscicultura *nf* fish farming

◊ **piscifactoría** *nf* fish farm

piso *nm* **(a)** *(apartamento)* flat; *US* apartment; **tiene un piso en el centro de la ciudad** = he has a flat in the centre of town; **va a comprarse un piso cerca de la oficina** = she is buying a flat close to her office; **viven en un piso amueblado** = they are living in furnished accommodation *o* in a furnished flat **(b)** *(planta)* floor; **la sección de calzado está en el primer piso** = the shoe department is on the first floor; **su oficina está en el piso 26** = her office is on the 26th floor; **tome el ascensor hasta el piso 26** = take the elevator to the 26th floor; **un nuevo edificio de 20 pisos** = a new 20-storey building

plan *nm* **(a)** *(proyecto)* plan *o* scheme *o* blueprint; **plan comercial** *o* **económico** = business plan; **plan de emergencia** = contingency plan; **plan general** = overall plan; **plan magnífico** *o* **grandioso** *o* **extraordinario** *o* **gran plan** = grand plan; **plan periódicamente actualizado** = rolling plan; **un plan quinquenal** = a Five-Year Plan; **un plan remunerativo** = a money-making plan; **hacer un plan** = to plan; **aplazar un plan indefinidamente** = to put a plan into cold storage; **se dio carpetazo al plan de expansión** = the whole expansion plan was shelved; **el plan se vino abajo en el último momento** = the plan fell through at the last moment; **trazaron el esquema del plan** = they drew up an outline plan *o* the outline of a plan **(b)** **plan de ahorro** = savings plan *o* savings scheme; **plan de ahorro ajustado a las exigencias personales** = customized savings plan; **plan de bonificación** = bonus scheme; **plan de inversiones** = investment plan; **plan de pensiones** = pension scheme *o* pension plan; **plan de pensiones de la empresa** = occupational pension scheme

estos consejeros, de talante renovador, querían poner en marcha un plan estratégico que modernizara la gestión de la compañía

El País

la posibilidad de unas elecciones anticipadas podría llegar a frenar planes de inversión a corto plazo, como lo haría una mayor protesta sindical

Actualidad Económica

planear *vt* to plan; **planear un aumento de los intereses bancarios** = to plan for an increase in bank interest charges

planificación *nf* planning; **planificación económica** = economic planning; **planificación empresarial** = corporate planning; **planificación a largo plazo** *o* **planificación a corto plazo** = long-term planning *o* short-term planning; **planificación de la mano de obra** = manpower planning; **planificación de viaje** = journey planning; **diagrama de planificación** = desk planner *o* wall planner; **departamento de planificación urbana** = the city planning department

◊ **planificador, -ra 1** *adj* planning **2** *n* planner; **planificador anual** = year planner; **los planificadores económicos del gobierno** = the government's economic planners

planificar *vt* to plan *o* to take the long view; **planificar las inversiones** = to plan investments

plano 1 *nm* **(a)** *(mapa)* plan; **plano de la ciudad** = street plan *o* town plan; **los delineantes nos enseñaron los primeros planos de las nuevas oficinas** = the designers showed us the first plans for the new offices **(b)** **poner en primer plano** = to bring to the forefront **2** *adj* flat; **paquete** *o* **embalaje plano** = flat pack

planta *nf* **(a)** *(fábrica)* plant; **instalar una nueva planta** = to set up a new plant; **planta depuradora** = purifying plant; **planta industrial** = factory *o* industrial plant; **planta de montaje** = assembly plant **(b)** *(piso)* floor; **director de planta** = floor manager; **planta baja** = ground floor; **la sección de caballeros está en la planta baja** = the men's department is on the ground floor; **tiene una oficina en la planta baja** = he has a ground-floor office **(c)** *(plano de un piso)* floor plan

plante *nm* walk-out *o* stoppage

planteado, -da *adj y pp* raised; **en relación a las cuestiones planteadas por el Señor García** = in answer to the questions raised by Sr García

plantear *vt* to bring up *o* to raise; **plantear una cuestión** *o* **un asunto en una reunión** = to raise a question *o* a point at a meeting; **el presidente intentó evitar que se planteara la cuestión de los despidos** = the chairman tried to prevent the question of redundancies being raised; **el presidente planteó la cuestión de las indemnizaciones por despido** = the chairman brought up the question of redundancy payments

plantilla *nf* **(a)** *(nómina)* list of personnel *o* staff (list) *o* payroll; **la empresa tiene una plantilla de 250 empleados** = the company has 250 on the payroll; **estar en plantilla** = to be on the staff *o* to be a staff member *o* to be on the payroll; **excedente de**

plantilla = redundancy; **forma parte de nuestra plantilla de personal** = she is on our full-time staff; **miembro de la plantilla permanente** = member of the permanent staff *o* permanent staff member; *US* staffer; **niveles de plantilla** = staffing levels; **reducción de plantilla** = downsizing **(b)** *(cliché o estarcido)* **plantilla de multicopista** = stencil **(c)** *(patrón)* model *o* pattern *o* template

la empresa tiene 90 trabajadores en plantilla y una facturación de 3.600 millones de pesetas

El País

plata *nf* **(a)** *(metal precioso)* silver; **moneda de plata** = silver coin; **plata ley** = real silver **(b)** *(Latinoamérica) (dinero)* money; **tiene mucha plata** = he has a lot of money; **estar sin plata** = to be broke

plataforma *nf* platform; **plataforma petrolífera** = oil platform *o* oil rig; **plataforma petrolífera en alta mar** = off-shore oil platform

plaza *nf* **(a)** *(espacio rodeado de edificios)* square **(b)** **plaza del mercado** = market *o* marketplace **(c)** *(asiento)* place *o* seat; **¿puede pedir a su secretaria que me reserve una plaza en el tren de Badajoz?** = can you ask your secretary to reserve a seat for me on the train to Badajoz?; **no pudo conseguir una plaza en el avión del martes y por eso tuvo que esperar hasta el miércoles** = he could not get a seat on Tuesday's plane, so he had to wait until Wednesday **(d)** *(vacante)* vacancy *o* job *o* position; **se han anunciado dos plazas esta semana** = two vacancies have been advertised this week; **solicitar una plaza** = to apply for a vacancy **(e)** *(en la localidad)* **en plaza** = on the spot *o* locally; **contratamos a todos nuestros empleados en plaza** = we recruit all our staff locally

plazo *nm* **(a)** *(tiempo)* time *o* period *o* term; **el plazo de un arrendamiento** = the term of a lease; **el plazo de amortización del préstamo es de quince años** = the term of the loan is fifteen years; **obtener un préstamo por un plazo de quince años** = to have a loan for a term of fifteen years; **¿cuáles son los cambios a plazo para la libra?** = what are the forward rates for the pound?; **plazo de entrega** = delivery time; **hablamos de los plazos de entrega con nuestros proveedores** = we discussed delivery schedules with our suppliers; **entrega en el plazo de 28 días** = delivery within 28 days; **plazo de espera** = lead time; **el plazo de espera para este artículo es de más de seis semanas** = the lead time on this item is more than six weeks; **depositar dinero a plazo fijo** = to deposit money for a fixed period; **préstamo a plazo fijo** = term loan; **plaza de preaviso** = term of notice; **contrato a plazo** = futures contract; **depósito a plazo** = term deposit *o* time deposit **(b)** *(término)* time limit; **cumplir el plazo estipulado** = to keep within the time limits *o* within the time schedule; **no pudimos cumplir el plazo del 1 de octubre** = we've missed our October 1st deadline; **terminar antes de plazo** = to meet a deadline; **plazo de tiempo límite** = time limitation; **a corto plazo** = short-term; **a largo plazo** = long-term; **contrato a plazo fijo** = fixed-term contract; **plazo medio** = medium-term; **estrategia a plazo medio** = medium-term strategy; **préstamo a plazo medio** = medium-term loan **(c)** *(fecha tope)* (i) closing date; (ii) notice; **a corto plazo** = at short notice; **tiene que dar un plazo de siete días para sacar dinero** = you must give seven days' notice of withdrawal **(d)** *(pago)* instalment; *US* installment; **el primer plazo se paga al firmar el contrato** = the first instalment is payable on signature of the agreement; **el último plazo ha vencido ya** = the final instalment is now due; **no pagar** *o* **saltarse un plazo** = to miss an instalment; **dio una entrada de 5.000 ptas. y pagó el resto en plazos mensuales** = he paid 5,000 pesetas down and the rest in monthly instalments; **comprar un coche a plazos** = to buy a car on hire purchase; *US* on the installment plan

la expansión económica a largo plazo es el factor más importante para el éxito o el fracaso de una nación y es, sin duda, la base fundamental del progreso del bienestar de la población en su conjunto
Mercado

el programa sindical recopila las reivindicaciones a medio y largo plazo
Tiempo

la reciente ampliación del plazo de finalización de la OPA deja la puerta abierta a que la compañía estudie una nueva defensa e, incluso los expertos no descartan que llegue a presentar una contraopa
El País

los efectos deflacionarios a largo plazo de unos impuestos más altos y un gasto público menor serán más que compensados por una demanda del consumo creciente
Actualidad Económica

plegar *vt* to fold

pleito *nm* lawsuit *o* litigation; **entablar un pleito** = to take legal action; **poner** *o* **ponerle un pleito a alguien** = to bring a lawsuit against someone *o* to institute proceedings against someone

pleno, -na 1 *adj* full; **pleno empleo** = full employment; **plenos poderes** = full powers; **es difícil encontrar habitaciones de hotel en plena temporada turística** = it is difficult to find hotel rooms at the height of the tourist season; **estamos trabajando a plena capacidad** *o* **a pleno rendimiento** = we are working at full capacity **2** *nm* plenary meeting; **ayer hubo pleno del consejo de administración** = yesterday the board held a plenary meeting

digan lo que digan los datos oficiales de paro, en ciertos sectores y regiones se está llegando a situaciones muy próximas al pleno empleo
España Económica

pluma *nf* pen

pluri- *prefijo* pluri- *o* several

◇ **pluriempleado, -da** *n* moonlighter

◇ **pluriempleo** *nm* moonlight *o* moonlighting; **practicar** *o* **ejercer el pluriempleo** = to moonlight

plus *nm* extra *o* bonus *o* perk; **plus de carestía de vida** = cost-of-living bonus; **plus de peligrosidad** = danger money

plusvalía *nf* **(a)** capital gains **(b) plusvalía municipal** = local property tax

los propietarios originales de los terrenos habrían defraudado a Hacienda interponiendo a unos falsos compradores para eludir el pago de plusvalías
Cambio 16

PMG = PERIODO MEDIO DE PAGO

PNB = PRODUCTO NACIONAL BRUTO Gross National Product (GNP)

PNN = PRODUCTO NACIONAL NETO Net National Product

población *nf* population; **Valencia tiene una población de más de un millón de habitantes** = Valencia has a population of over one million; **la población activa** = the working population; **la población asalariada** = the wage-earning population; **población flotante** = floating population; **sondear a una muestra de la población** = to poll a sample of the population; **tasa anual de crecimiento de la población** = annual population increase rate

pobre 1 *adj* **(a)** *(sin dinero)* poor; **es uno de los países más pobres del mundo** = it is one of the poorest countries in the world **(b)** *(calidad)* poor; **este producto tiene un diseño pobre** = this product is poorly designed **2** *nmf* **los pobres** = the poor *o* poor people

el número de pobres oscila, según diversos estudios, entre 8 y 11 millones de personas
España Económica

pobreza *nf* poverty

al contrario de la pobreza, un mal estudiado abundantemente por economistas y sociólogos, la riqueza es un tema virgen desde el punto de vista científico
El País

poco, -ca 1 *adj y pron* **(a)** *(escaso)* few; **unos pocos** *o* **unas pocas** = a few; **recibimos muy pocos pedidos entre Navidad y Año Nuevo** = we get very few orders in the period from Christmas to the New Year; **son pocos los empleados que permanecen en la empresa más de seis meses** = few of the staff stay with us more than six months; **de poca confianza** = unreliable **(b) un poco** = a little *o* slightly; **las acciones han bajado un poco durante la jornada** = shares are slightly down on the day **2** *adv* **(a)** *(apenas)* not much; **acciones poco buscadas en la bolsa** = neglected shares; **tallas poco corrientes** = odd sizes; **poco desarrollado** = underdeveloped; **métodos poco escrupulosos** = sharp practice; **poco de fiar** = unreliable; **poco rentable** = uneconomic; **es una proposición** *o* **propuesta poco rentable** = it is an uneconomic proposition; **empresa poco fiable** *o* **poco de fiar** = cowboy outfit *o* fly-by-night firm **(b) poco a poco** = little by little; **las cifras de ventas bajaron poco a poco en enero** = sales figures edged downwards in January; **los huelguistas están volviendo al trabajo poco a poco** = strikers are drifting back to work

poder 1 *nm* **(a)** *(fuerza)* power; **poder adquisitivo** = purchasing power *o* buying power; **el poder adquisitivo del mercado estudiantil** *o* **del**

mercado escolar = the spending power of the student market *o* of the school market; **el poder adquisitivo de la peseta ha bajado durante los últimos cinco años** = the purchasing power of the peseta has fallen over the last five years; **poder ejecutivo** = executive power; **fue nombrado director gerente con plenos poderes ejecutivos para la operación europea** = he was made managing director with full executive powers over the European operation; **poder de negociación** = bargaining power; **poder reglamentario** = regulatory power; **dar poder** = to give authority *o* to empower; **el poder de un grupo de consumidores** = the power of a consumer group **(b) poder notarial** = power of attorney; **su abogado recibió poder notarial** = his solicitor was granted power of attorney **(c)** proxy; **firmar por poderes** = to sign by proxy; **voto por poderes** = proxy vote; **todos los votos por poderes eran a favor de la recomendación del consejo** = the proxy votes were all in favour of the board's recommendation **2** *vi* to be able to; **¿puedo pasar?** = can I come in?; **sin poder salir** = unable to go out; **el presidente no pudo asistir a la reunión** = the chairman was unable to come *o* couldn't come to the meeting; **poder con** = to cope

◊ **poderhabiente** *nmf* proxy

descontando la inflación, la ganancia del poder adquisitivo alcanzó un 1,59%
Mercado

televisando una ópera en todo el mundo se puede conseguir, por poco dinero, una audiencia de alto poder adquisitivo que resulta muy atractiva para los anunciantes
Actualidad Económica

polemizar *vi* to argue

policultivo *nm* mixed farming

poliestireno *nm* polystyrene; **poliestireno expandido** = expanded polystyrene; **el ordenador se entrega embalado en poliestireno expandido** = the computer is delivered packed in expanded polystyrene

política *nf* **(a)** *(arte de gobernar)* politics; **la política ya no interesa a la gente** = people are no longer interested in politics **(b)** *(programa de gobierno)* policy; **Política Agrícola Común (PAC)** = Common Agricultural Policy (CAP); **la política salarial del gobierno** = government policy on wages *o* government wages policy; **la política gubernamental de precios** *o* **de rentas** = the government's prices policy *o* incomes policy; **la política económica del país** = the country's economic policy; **política fiscal** = fiscal policy; **política monetaria** = monetary policy; **política monetaria expansiva** = easy money policy; **política presupuestaria** = budgetary policy; **el gobierno hizo una declaración de política** = the government made a policy statement *o* made a statement of policy **(c)** *(programa de actividad comercial)* **política de una empresa** = company policy; **la política comercial de una empresa** = a company's trading policy; **¿cuál es la política de la empresa en materia de crédito?** = what is the company policy on credit?; **la política de personal de la empresa** = the company's staffing policy; **política de precios** = pricing policy

otro ejemplo claro de despilfarro de productos, sobre los que el Estado practica una política de precios subvencionados, es el consumo de energía
España Económica

la versión actual de la política agrícola común está en vías de desaparición
Actualidad Económomica

político, -ca 1 *adj* political; **contribución política** *o* **impuesto político** = political levy; **partido político** = political party **2** *n* politician

póliza *nf* **(a)** *(seguros)* insurance policy *o* insurance certificate; **póliza de accidentes** = accident policy; **póliza dotal** = endowment policy; **póliza general** *o* **integral** = blanket policy; **póliza para imprevistos** = contingent policy; **póliza provisional** = cover note; *US* binder; **póliza de seguros** = insurance policy; **póliza de seguros nominativa** = insurance policy which covers a named person; **póliza de seguro de la vivienda** = household insurance policy; **póliza a todo riesgo** = all-risks policy; **extender una póliza** = to issue a policy; **tenedor** *o* **titular de una póliza de seguros** = holder of an insurance policy *o* policy holder **(b)** *(préstamo)* **póliza de crédito** = loan agreement

Polonia *nf* Poland

◊ **polaco, -ca 1** *adj* Polish **2** *n* Pole

◊ **polonés, -esa** *adj* Polish
NOTA: capital: **Varsovia** (= Warsaw); moneda: **zloty polaco (Zl)** = Polish zloty (Zl)

ponderado, -da *adj* weighted; **promedio ponderado** *o* **media ponderada** = weighted average

poner *vt* **(a)** *(colocar)* to put *o* to place; **poner en circulación** = to put into circulation *o* to circulate; **poner en contenedores** = to put into containers *o* to containerize **(b)** **poner algo en venta** = to put something on the market; **cuando se retiró, decidió poner en venta su piso de la ciudad** = when he retired he decided to put his town flat up for sale; **ponga su nombre y dirección en mayúsculas** = fill in your name and address in block capitals; **la fecha se pone en la parte superior de la carta** = the date goes at the top of the letter; **poner al día** = to update; **poner en duda** = to question *o* to query; **poner etiqueta a** = to label; **poner en libertad** = to free; **poner límite** = to limit *o* to cap; **poner en marcha** = to start; **poner el matasellos** = to postmark; **poner un negocio** = to set up in business; **poner número a** = to number; **poner el precio a algo** = to mark the price on something; **poner el sello** = to stamp; **poner término a** = to end *o* to terminate; **poner término a un acuerdo** = to terminate an agreement; **poner un término para la aceptación de una oferta** = to set a time limit for acceptance of the offer; **poner a la venta** = to put on sale *o* to release **(c)** **poner de acuerdo a dos partes** = to effect a settlement between two parties

◊ **ponerse** *vr* **(a)** *(hacerse)* to become; **ponerse caro** = to become expensive; **el mercado de exportación se ha puesto muy difícil después del alza del dólar** = the export market has become very difficult since the rise in the dollar **(b)** **ponerse de acuerdo** = to come to an agreement *o* to reach an agreement; **las dos partes se han puesto de acuerdo** = the two sides have reached an agreement;

ponerse a trabajar = to set to work; **ponerse en venta** = to come on to the market; **este jabón acaba de ponerse en venta** = this soap has just come on to the market; **los precios se han puesto por las nubes** = prices have rocketed

popular *adj* popular; **éste es nuestro modelo más popular** = this is our most popular model; **la costa del sur es la zona más popular para las vacaciones** = the South Coast is the most popular area for holidays; **producto dirigido a un mercado popular** = market aimed at the popular market *o* which targets the popular market *o* down market product; **precios populares** = popular prices

por *prep* **por adelantado** = in advance *o* up front; **por ciento** = per cent; **por debajo de** = below; **por favor** = please; **por igual** = equally; **al por mayor** = wholesale; **al por menor** = retail; **por el momento** *o* **por ahora** = for the time being *o* pro tem; **por poder(es)** = per pro *o* per procurationem; **por la presente** = hereby; **por término medio** = on the average; **por su cuenta** = freelance

> la apertura del mercado interior supondrá un fuerte aumento de la competencia en el negocio bancario al por mayor, pero no dejará de incidir en la banca al por menor
> **Mercado**

porcentaje *nm* percentage *o* rate; **porcentaje de aumento** = percentage increase; **porcentaje de comisión** = cost plus; **porcentaje de descuento** = percentage discount; **porcentaje fijo** = flat rate *o* fixed rate; **porcentaje de suscripción** = take up rate; **porcentaje de habitaciones no ocupadas** = vacancy rate; **cobramos los costos más un porcentaje** = we are charging for the work on a cost plus basis

porción *nf* portion; **servimos helado en porciones individuales** = we serve ice cream in individual portions

pormenor *nm* detail; **pormenores** = particulars; **hoja que da los pormenores de los artículos en venta** = sheet which gives particulars of the items for sale

◊ **pormenorizar** *vtr* to break down *o* to itemize *o* to detail

porquería *nf* junk

portacontenedor *nm* container ship

portador, -ra *n* holder *o* bearer; payee; **el cheque es pagadero al portador** = the cheque is payable to bearer

> el empleado del banco, al recibir el talón, entrega a cambio varios talones bancarios al portador por la suma del talón que recibe
> **Cambio 16**

portapapeles *nm* copyholder

portarse *vr* to behave

portátil *adj* portable; **ordenador portátil** = portable computer *o* laptop; **máquina de escribir portátil** = portable typewriter; **todos sus informes son mecanografiados en su máquina portátil** = all his reports are typed on his portable typewriter

portavoz *nmf* spokesperson

porte *nm* carriage *o* freight *o* transport (charge); **porte debido** = carriage forward *o* freight forward; **porte pagado** = postpaid *o* carriage paid; **el fabricante envía el juego con porte pagado** = the game is obtainable post free from the manufacturer; **en una subasta, el comprador paga los portes** = at an auction, the buyer pays the freight; **dejar un margen del 10% para el porte** = to allow 10% for carriage; **franco de porte** = carriage free

portero, -ra *n* porter *o* caretaker; *(US)* janitor; **portero automático** = entryphone

pórtico *nm* arcade

portillo *nm* gate

portorriqueño, -ña *ver* PUERTO RICO

portuario, -ria *adj* port *o* harbour; **autoridades portuarias** = port authority; **derechos portuarios** = harbour dues; **instalaciones portuarias** = harbour installations *o* harbour facilities *o* port installations; **trabajador portuario** = dock worker *o* docker

Portugal *nm* Portugal

◊ **portugués, -esa** *adj y n* Portuguese
NOTA: capital: **Lisboa** (= Lisbon); moneda: **escudo portugués (Esc)** = Portuguese escudo (Esc)

pos(t)- *prefijo* post-; **servicio de post-venta** *o* **posventa** = after-sales service

posdata *nf* P.S. *o* postscript; **¿leyó la posdata al final de la carta?** = did you read the P.S. at the end of the letter?

poseedor, -ra *n* owner *o* holder; **poseedor de patente** = patentee *o* patent holder

poseer *vt* to own *o* to possess; **posee el 50% de las acciones** = he owns 50% of the shares; **la compañía posee propiedades en el centro de la ciudad** = the company possesses property in the centre of the town; **perdió todo lo que poseía en el hundimiento de su empresa** = he lost all he possessed in the collapse of his company

posesión *nf* **(a)** *(tenencia)* possession **(b)** *(de puesto)* tenure; **tener la posesión de un cargo** = to hold an office; **tomar posesión** = to take over; **el nuevo presidente toma posesión el 1 de julio** = the new chairman takes over on July 1st; **la toma de posesión resultó en 250 despidos** = the takeover caused 250 redundancies

posfechar *vt* *(poner fecha posterior a la del día)* to postdate

posibilidad *nf* **(a)** *(oportunidad)* possibility *o* chance; **tiene pocas posibilidades de ascenso** = his promotion chances are small; **existe la posibilidad de que el avión llegue antes de la hora** = there is a possibility that the plane will be early; **la empresa tiene grandes posibilidades de conseguir el contrato** = the company has a good chance of winning the contract; **hay grandes posibilidades de extender las actividades al mercado de exportación** = there is considerable scope for expansion into the export market **(b)** **posibilidades** = potential; **acción con posibilidades de mejorar su precio** = share with a growth potential *o* with a potential for growth; **producto con grandes posibilidades de ventas** = product with considerable sales potential

posible 1 *adj* possible; **posible cliente** = prospective customer; **un posible comprador** = a prospective buyer; **lo antes posible** *o* **en cuanto sea posible** = as soon as possible (asap) *o* at the earliest; **tan pronto como le sea posible** = at your earliest convenience; **el 25 y el 26 son las fechas posibles para nuestra próxima reunión** = the 25th and 26th are possible dates for our next meeting; **es posible que la producción se vea interrumpida por la huelga** = it is possible that production will be held up by industrial action; **hay dos posibles candidatos para el puesto** = there are two possible candidates for the job; **dentro de lo posible** = as far as possible; **hicieron todo lo posible por guardar el secreto del volumen de ventas** = they went to considerable lengths to keep the turnover secret; **los vendedores están haciendo todo lo posible, pero no pueden vender la mercancía a ese precio** = the salesmen are doing their best, but the stock simply will not sell at that price **2** *nmpl* means *o* funds

posición *nf* **(a)** position *o* status; **pérdida de posición** = loss of status **(b)** **inventario de posición (en almacén)** = picking list

positivo, -va *adj* **(a)** positive *o* constructive; **recibimos una propuesta positiva de una empresa distribuidora italiana** = we had a constructive proposal from a distribution company in Italy **(b)** **un factor positivo para la compañía es que el mercado es mucho mayor de lo que en un principio se había creído** = a plus factor for the company is that the market is much larger than they had originally thought; **el consejo de administración dio una respuesta positiva** = the board gave a positive reply; **flujo de caja positivo** = positive cash flow; **cuenta con saldo positivo** = account in credit **(c)** **por el lado positivo** = on the plus side

posponer *vt* to postpone; **posponer algo** = to put something on ice

post- *prefijo* post-; **servicio de post-venta** = after-sales service

postal *adj* postal; **gastos postales** = postal charges; **giro postal** = postal order *o* money order; **tarifas postales** = postal rates *o* postage; **¿cuál es la tarifa postal para Nigeria?** = what is the postage to Nigeria?

postor, -ra *n* bidder; **adjudicar algo a un postor** = to knock something down to a bidder; **el mejor postor** = (i) highest bidder; (ii) lowest bidder; **la propiedad se vendió al mejor postor** = the property was sold to the highest bidder; **el contrato se adjudicará al mejor postor** = the tender will go to the lowest bidder

post scriptum *frase latina & nm* post scriptum

postura *nf* **(a)** *(posición)* attitude *o* position; **postura negociadora** = bargaining position; **postura intransigente** = hard line **(b)** *(subasta)* bid price *o* bidding

posventa *nf* **servicio posventa** = after-sales service; **ofrecemos un servicio posventa gratuito a los clientes** = we offer a free backup service to customers

potencia *nf* power *o* strength; **en potencia** = potential; **mercado en potencia** = potential market; **es un director gerente en potencia** = he is a potential managing director

potencial 1 *adj* potential; **clientes potenciales** = potential customers; **no hay escasez de clientes potenciales para el ordenador** = there is no shortage of potential customers for the computer; **mercado potencial** = potential market; **el producto tiene unas ventas potenciales de 100.000 unidades** = the product has potential sales of 100,000 units **2** *nm* potential; **analizar el potencial del mercado** = to analyze the market potential; **potencial negativo** = downside potential; **potencial positivo** = upside potential; **potencial de rentabilidad** = earning potential; **infravaloramos su potencial** = we underestimated her potential

potenciar *vt* **(a)** *(hacer posible)* to make something possible **(b)** *(dar fuerza)* to give more power to something **(c)** *(fomentar)* to encourage; **potenciar las inversiones** = to encourage investment

potente *adj* powerful

PPA = PARIDAD DEL PODER ADQUISITIVO purchasing power parity

práctico, -ca 1 *adj* practical *o* handy; **esta pequeña maleta es muy práctica para viajar** = this small case is handy for use when travelling **2** *nf* **(a)** *(experiencia)* experience *o* practice; **poner en práctica** = to put into practice *o* to implement; **poner en práctica un acuerdo** = to implement an agreement; **puesta en práctica** = putting into practice *o* implementation; **periodo de prácticas** = training period; **algunos universitarios hacen un periodo de prácticas en el laboratorio al terminar su carrera** = graduate trainees come to work in the laboratory when they have finished their courses at university; **prácticas de trabajo** = placement **(b)** **en la práctica** = in practice; **el plan de marketing parece muy interesante, ¿pero qué costará en la práctica?** = the marketing plan seems very interesting, but what will it cost in practice? **(c)** *(acción)* **prácticas comerciales leales** *o* **justas** = fair dealing; **prácticas desleales** = unfair practices; **prácticas industriales** *o* **prácticas comerciales** = industrial practices *o* trade practices; **prácticas restrictivas** = restrictive practices

pre- *prefijo* pre-

◊ **preaviso** *nm* notice; **plazo de preaviso** = term of notice

precario, -ria *adj* precarious *o* uncertain

> la siniestrabilidad laboral ha aumentado
> en 45% entre 1987 y 1988 por causa de la
> generalización del trabajo precario
> **España Económica**

precaución *nf* precaution; **tomar precauciones para evitar robos en la oficina** = to take precautions to prevent thefts in the office; **la empresa no tomó las debidas precauciones contra incendios** = the company did not take proper fire precautions

precintar *vt* to seal *o* to seal off; **los discos del ordenador fueron enviados en un paquete precintado** = the computer disks were sent in a sealed container; **la aduana precintó el envío** = the customs sealed the shipment

◊ **precinto** *nm* seal; **precinto de aduana** = customs seal

precio *nm* **(a)** *(coste)* price *o* rate *o* cost; **precio acordado** = agreed price; **precio actual** = current price; **precio en almacén** = price ex works *o* ex factory; **precio anunciado** = asking price; **precio bajo** = cheap price *o* low price; **el bajo precio de su producto juega a su favor** = the cheapness of their product is a plus; **compró dos compañías a bajo precio y las vendió a beneficio** = he bought two companies cheap and sold them again at a profit; **precio de catálogo** = catalogue price *o* list price; **precio de chatarra** = scrap value *o* salvage value; **precio competitivo** = competitive price *o* keen price; **precio al contado** = cash price; **precio controlado** = administered price; **precio convenido** = agreed price; **precio de coste** = cost price; **precio descontado** *o* **rebajado** = discounted price; **precio de descuento** = discount price; **precio sin descuento** = full price; **precio destacado** = leading rate; **precio definitivo** = firm price; **precio a discutir** = negotiable price; **precios exagerados** = inflated prices; **precios exorbitantes** = exorbitant prices *o* fancy prices; **precio de fábrica** *o* **precio en fábrica** = factory price *o* price ex factory *o* price ex works; **precio facturado** = invoice price; **precio fijo** *o* **en firme** = firm price; **cotizan un precio en firme de 123 ptas. por unidad** = they are quoting a firm price of 123 pesetas a unit; **precio franco en almacén** = price ex warehouse; **precio fuerte** = full price *o* retail price; **precios inflados** = inflated prices; **precio íntegro** = full price; **precios interesantes** = attractive prices; **precios irrisorios** *o* **de saldo** = distress prices; **precio justo** = fair price; **precio máximo autorizado** = ceiling price; **precio de mercado** = market price; **precio mínimo** = minimum price *o* rock-bottom price *o* floor price; *(en una subasta)* **precio mínimo aceptable** = reserve (price); **el cuadro fue retirado de la subasta por no alcanzar el precio mínimo** = the painting was withdrawn when it did not reach its reserve; **precio neto** = net price; **el precio normal** *o* **vigente** = the going rate *o* usual price; **el precio normal de las oficinas es de 1.000 ptas. por metro cuadrado** = the going rate for offices is 1,000 pesetas per square metre; **precio de ocasión** = bargain price; **lo vendo a precio de ocasión** = I'm selling this at a bargain price; **precio de oferta** = asking price; **precios oficiales** = scheduled prices *o* scheduled charges; **el precio pedido es de 5.000.000 de ptas.** = the asking price is 5m pesetas; **precio al por mayor** = wholesale price; **precio al por menor** = retail price; **precio razonable** = fair *o* sensible price; **precio**

reducido = reduced rate; **gasolina a precio reducido** = cut-price petrol; **precios reventados** = rock-bottom prices; **precio simbólico** = token charge; **cobramos un precio simbólico por nuestros servicios** = we make a nominal charge for our services; **precio 'spot'** *o* **de entrega inmediata** = spot price; **precio de entrega inmediata del petróleo en las bolsas de contratación** = the spot price of oil on the commodity markets; **precio de subvención** = support price; **precio todo incluido** = all-in price *o* all-in rate; **precio tope** = ceiling price *o* price ceiling; **precio total** = all-in price *o* all-in rate; **precio de venta** = selling price; **precio de venta al público (PVP)** = full price *o* retail price *o* recommended retail price; **vender mercancías a mitad de precio** = to sell goods off at half price; **índice de precios al consumo (IPC)** = retail price index; **el precio es de 595 ptas. con el franqueo concertado** = the price is 595 pesetas postpaid; **el precio de la gasolina ha bajado** = the price of petrol has gone down; **el precio de las acciones en bolsa se recuperó** = shares staged a rally on the Stock Exchange; **el precio del oro en lingotes se fija diariamente** = the price of bullion is fixed daily; **la oferta pública de adquisición de la compañía hizo subir su precio a 2 millones de dólares** = the takeover bid put a $2m price tag on the company **(b)** **acuerdo sobre precios** = price fixing; **aumentar un precio** = to reprice; **buen precio** = good value (for money); **compre ese ordenador ahora - tiene un buen precio** = buy that computer now - it is very good value; **control de precios** = price control; **diferencia de precios** = price differential; **etiqueta de precio** = price label *o* price tag *o* price ticket; **gama de precios** = price range; **coches en la gama de precios de 1 a 2 millones de ptas.** = cars in the 1-2 million peseta price range; **guerra de precios** = price war *o* price-cutting war; **límite de precios** = price ceiling; **lista de precios** *o* **tarifa de precios** = price list **(c)** **bajar los precios** = to cut prices; **cambiar el precio (de un artículo)** = to change the price of an item *o* to reprice an item; **convenir un precio** = to arrive at a price *o* to agree a price; **deflación de los precios** = price deflation; **fijación de precios** = price fixing; **fijar un precio** = to fix a price *o* to price; **fijar un nuevo precio** = to reprice; **liberalización de precios** = decontrol (of prices); **liberalizar el precio de la gasolina** = to decontrol the price of petrol; **reducir los precios** = to lower prices *o* to reduce prices; **subir** *o* **aumentar los precios** = to increase prices *o* to raise prices; **subir** *o* **aumentar de precio** = to increase in price; **la gasolina ha subido de precio** *o* **el precio de la gasolina ha subido** = petrol has increased in price *o* the price of petrol has increased; **intentaremos ajustarnos a su precio** = we will try to meet your price **(d)** *(en la Bolsa)* **precio al cierre** = closing price; **precio de apertura** *o* **de primer curso** = opening price; **precio de emisión** = issued price; **precio solicitado** = asking price; **relación precio-ganancias** *o* **precio-beneficios** = price/earnings ratio *o* P/E ratio **(e)** *(tarifa)* tariff *o* charge; **precio de la entrada** = admission charge *o* entry charge; **precio todo incluido** = inclusive charge **(f)** *(estimación de costes)* quotation *o* quote *o* estimate; **pedir precios para renovar el mobiliario de la tienda** = to ask for quotations for refitting the shop; **hemos pedido precios para renovar el mobiliario de la tienda** = we have asked for quotes for refitting the shop; **¿puede darnos el precio para el suministro de 20.000 sobres?** = can you quote for supplying 20,000 envelopes?; **me dio un precio de 1.026 ptas.** = he quoted me a price of 1,026 pesetas

---

en una semana se llegaron a mover en bolsa casi 25.000 acciones de la compañía, más que durante los dos pasados años, con un precio actual de 9.200 pesetas

El País

---

el alto precio de esta técnica ha conducido a su abandono

España Económica

---

los precios empezaron a subir y el déficit hizo su aparición aproximadamente al mismo tiempo

España Económica

---

con una actividad constructora que está tocando techo es difícil que los precios sigan subiendo

España Económica

---

precipitarse *vr* to rush; **no os precipitéis** = don't rush

precisar *vt* to specify; **precisar con todo detalle los artículos pedidos** = to specify full details of the goods ordered

precisión *nf* accuracy; **todos ponemos en duda la precisión de las copias impresas del ordenador** = we all question how accurate the computer printout is; **mecánica de precision** = precision engineering

predecesor, -ra *n* predecessor; **sustituyó a su predecesor el pasado mes de mayo** = he took over from his predecessor last May

predecir *vt* to forecast *o* to predict

preempaquetar *vt* to prepack *o* to prepackage

preferencia *nf* preference *o* choice; **recibir tratamiento de preferencia** = to get preferential treatment; **mostrar preferencia por algo** *o* **alguien** = to show preference for something *o* someone; **consiguió dos entradas de preferencia para la sesión de esta noche** = he managed to get two seats in the reserved section for tonight's performance

◊ **preferencial** *adj* preferential; **tarifa preferencial** = preferential duty *o* preferential tariff; **tipo preferencial de interés bancario** = prime rate *o* prime; **trato preferencial** = preferential terms *o* preferential treatment

◊ **preferente** *adj* preferential; **acciones preferentes** = preference shares; *US* preferred stock; **tenedores de acciones preferentes** = preference shareholders; **acción preferente acumulativa** = cumulative preference share; *US* cumulative preferred stock; **acreedor preferente** = preferential creditor; *(en aviones)* **clase preferente** = business class; **tarifa preferente** = preferential duty *o* preferential tariff; **términos preferentes** = preferential terms; **las empresas filiales obtienen un trato preferente cuando hay que dar trabajo a contrata** = subsidiary companies get preferential treatment when it comes to subcontracting work

◊ **preferido, -da 1** *adj* favourite; **esta marca de chocolate es una de las preferidas por los niños** = this brand of chocolate is a favourite with children **2** *pp de* PREFERIR

preferir *vt* to prefer; **preferimos la pequeña**

tienda del barrio al gran supermercado = we prefer the small corner shop to the large supermarket; **la mayoría de los clientes prefieren escoger la ropa ellos mismos a seguir el consejo del dependiente** = most customers prefer to choose clothes themselves, rather than take the advice of the sales assistant

prefijo *nm (teléfono)* area code *o* dialling code; **el prefijo del área central de Madrid es el 91** = the area code for central Madrid is 91; **¿cuál es el prefijo de Barcelona?** = what is the code for Barcelona?

prefinanciación *nf* pre-financing

pregunta *nf* query *o* question *o* inquiry; **el director gerente se negó a contestar preguntas sobre despidos** = the managing director refused to answer questions about redundancies; **el equipo de investigación de mercados preparó una serie de preguntas para analizar las reacciones del público al color y al precio** = the market research team prepared a series of questions to test the public's reactions to colour and price

preguntar *vt* to ask *o* to inquire; **preguntar por** = to ask for; **hay un hombre en la recepción que pregunta por el Señor Pons** = there is a man in reception asking for Sr Pons

preliminar *adj* **(a)** *(inicial)* preliminary; **conversaciones preliminares** = preliminary discussions; **trabajo preliminar** = preparatory work **(b)** *(inacabado)* rough; **proyecto** *o* **modelo preliminar** = rough plan *o* rough model

premio *nm* prize *o* award *o* reward

prenda *nf* **(a)** pledge; **rescatar una prenda** = to redeem a pledge; **prenda no rescatada** *o* **sin desempeñar** = unredeemed pledge; **dejar algo en prenda** = to put something in pawn **(b)** **prenda de vestir** = item of clothing

◊ **prendario, -ria** *adj* collateral; **depositar valores como garantía prendaria** = to lodge securities as collateral

prensa *nf* press; **la prensa amarilla** = the tabloids; **prensa comercial** = trade press; **la prensa local** = the local press; **la prensa nacional** = the national press; **se ha hecho publicidad del nuevo coche en la prensa nacional** = the new car has been advertised in the national press; **la prensa no mencionó el nuevo producto** = the press didn't mention the new product *o* there was no mention of the new product in the press; **agencia de prensa** = news agency *o* press office; **agente de prensa** = press officer; **cobertura en la prensa** = press coverage; **comunicado de prensa** = press release; **la empresa emitió un comunicado de prensa sobre el lanzamiento del nuevo coche** = the company sent out a press release about the launch of the new car; **conferencia de prensa** = press conference; **publicidad en la prensa** = press publicity *o* press advertising; **recorte de prensa** = press cutting; **agencia de recortes (de prensa)** = press cutting agency; **servicio de recortes de prensa** = clipping service; **hemos archivado los recortes de prensa sobre el nuevo coche** = we have kept a file of press cuttings about the new car; **tenemos un archivo de recortes de prensa sobre los productos de nuestros rivales** = we have a file of press cuttings on our rivals' products; **reportaje en la prensa** = press coverage; **nos decepcionó mucho el reportaje de la prensa sobre el nuevo coche** = we were very disappointed by the press coverage of the new car

preocupación *nf* worry *o* concern; **la dirección no manifestó ninguna preocupación por la seguridad de los trabajadores** = the management showed no concern at all for the workers' safety

preparación *nf* preparation *o* drafting; **preparación de pedidos** = order processing; **preparación de presupuestos** = budgeting; **la preparación del contrato duró seis semanas** = the drafting of the contract took six weeks

◊ **preparado, -da** 1 *adj* ready; **el conductor tuvo que esperar porque la mercancía no estaba preparada** = the driver had to wait because the shipment was not ready 2 *pp de* PREPARAR

preparar *vt* to get ready *o* to prepare *o* to draw up *o* to process; **los pedidos se preparan en nuestro almacén** = orders are processed in our warehouse; **preparar una factura** = to raise an invoice

◊ **prepararse** *vr* to get ready *o* to gear up; **prepararse para dar un impulso a las ventas** = to gear up for a sales drive; **la empresa se está preparando para la expansión en el mercado africano** = the company is gearing itself up for expansion into the African market

preparativo *nm* preparation *o* arrangement; **la secretaria de la compañía está haciendo los preparativos para la junta general anual** = the company secretary is making all the arrangements for the AGM

◊ **preparatorio, -ria** *adj* preparatory

prescribir *vt* to prescribe

prescripción *nf* prescription; **ley de prescripción** = statute of limitations

prescrito, -ta 1 *adj* prescribed *o* specified; **una vez transcurrido el tiempo prescrito** = after the specified time; **según lo prescrito en la cláusula 1** = as laid down *o* set out in clause 1 2 *pp de* PRESCRIBIR

preselección *nf* shortlist; **hacer una preselección** = to draw up a shortlist

preseleccionar *vt* to shortlist; **cuatro candidatos han sido preseleccionados** = four candidates have been shortlisted; **los candidatos preseleccionados serán convocados para una entrevista** = shortlisted candidates will be asked for an interview

presentación *nf* (a) *(acción de presentar)* presentation *o* production; **cheque pagadero a su presentación** = cheque payable on presentation; **mediante la presentación de** = on production of; **la mercancía se puede cambiar sólo mediante la presentación del recibo de venta** = goods can be exchanged only on production of the sales slip (b) *(exposición)* presentation *o* demonstration; **el fabricante hizo la presentación de su nueva gama de productos a posibles clientes** = the manufacturer made a presentation of his new product line to possible customers; **asistimos a la presentación de un nuevo modelo de fax** = we went to a

demonstration of a new fax machine; **la empresa distribuidora hizo la presentación de los servicios que podía ofrecer** = the distribution company gave a presentation of the services they could offer (c) *(en el aeropuerto)* **horario de presentación** = check-in time (d) *(personas)* introduction; **el director hizo las presentaciones debidas antes de empezar la reunión** = the MD introduced everyone before the meeting

presentar *vt* (a) *(entregar)* to submit *o* to present; **presentar una declaración en la delegación de Hacienda** = to file a return to the tax office; **presentar la dimisión** = to tender one's resignation; **presentó su dimisión** = he handed in his notice *o* he handed in his resignation; **presentar excusas** = to apologize; **presentar una propuesta al comité** = to submit a proposal to the committee; **presentó una reclamación a los aseguradores** = he submitted a claim to the insurers; **se ruega a los representantes que presenten las notas de gastos una vez al mes** = the reps are asked to submit their expenses claims once a month; **presentar una solicitud de patente** = to file an application for a patent; **presentar una reconvención** = to counter-claim (b) *(mostrar)* to present *o* to show; **hemos pedido a dos empresas de relaciones públicas que nos presenten sus proyectos de campaña publicitaria** = we have asked two PR firms to make presentations of proposed publicity campaigns; **presentaron el nuevo modelo en el Salón del Automóvil** = they showed their new model at the Motor Show (c) *(persona, cosa desconocida)* to introduce; **presentar a un cliente** = to introduce a client; **presentar un nuevo producto en el mercado** = to introduce a new product on the market (d) *(en una reunión)* to present *o* to table; **se presentó el informe del comité de finanzas** = the report of the finance committee was tabled; **presentar una moción** = to table a motion (e) *(documentos)* to produce *o* to present; **presentar una factura** = to present a bill *o* to bill; **presentar una letra para su aceptación** = to present a bill for acceptance; **presentar una letra al pago** = to present a bill for payment; **presentar el presupuesto de algo** = to put in an estimate for something; **presentó documentos para justificar su reclamación** = he produced documents to prove his claim; **los negociadores presentaron las nuevas cifras** = the negotiators produced a new set of figures; **el aduanero le pidió que presentara los documentos pertinentes** = the customs officer asked him to produce the relevant documents (f) **al presentar** = on production of; **entrada gratuita al presentar la tarjeta** = free admission on presentation of the card; **la aduana devolverá la maleta al presentar los documentos pertinentes** = the case will be released by the customs on production of the relevant documents

◊ **presentarse** *vr* (a) *(comparecer)* to attend *o* to report; **presentarse a una entrevista** = to report for an interview (b) *(aeropuerto)* to check in (c) **estas letras no pueden presentarse al descuento** = these bills are not discountable (d) *(puesto de trabajo o candidatura)* to apply for; **cuando vio que el puesto de trabajo no había sido asignado todavía, volvió a presentarse** = when he saw that the job had still not been filled, he reapplied for it; **presentarse como candidato** = to stand as a candidate; **tiene derecho a presentarse a la reelección** = she can stand for re-election *o* she is eligible for re-election **(e)** *(darse a conocer)* to introduce oneself

> la actividad económica está ahora como en una plataforma, donde los indicadores presentan todavía tasas elevadas de aumento sobre las cotas de hace un año
> **España Económica**

presente 1 *adj* **(a)** present; **sólo estuvieron presentes seis consejeros en la reunión del consejo** = only six directors were present at the board meeting **(b) del presente mes** = of the current month *o* instant **(c) por el presente documento revocamos el acuerdo del 1 de enero de 1982 2** *nf* **en fe de lo cual, firmo la presente** = in witness whereof, I set my hand

presidencia *nf* chair *o* chairmanship; **el comité se reunió bajo la presidencia del Sr. Pons** = the committee met under the chairmanship of Sr Pons; **estar en la presidencia** = to be in the chair; **dirigirse a la presidencia** = to address the chair; **dirija sus observaciones a la presidencia, por favor** = please address your remarks to the chair

◊ **presidenta** *nf* **(a)** *(comité)* chairwoman; **fue elegida presidenta** = she was voted into the chair *o* she was elected chairwoman *o* chairperson **(b)** *(de un país)* President

◊ **presidente** *nmf* **(a)** *(de un país)* President; **Presidente del Gobierno** = Prime Minister **(b)** *(club)* chairman *o* chairperson *o* president; **fue elegido presidente del club deportivo** = he was elected president of the sports club; **ella aceptó ser presidente** = she agreed to be chairman *o* chairperson; **en su calidad de presidente** = in his capacity as chairman **(c)** *(comité)* chairman; **el Sr. Martín fue presidente** *o* **actuó como presidente** = Sr Martín was chairman *o* acted as chairman; **señor presidente** *o* **señora presidenta** = Mr Chairman *o* Madam Chairman; **se pidió a los socios que votaran al nuevo presidente** = the membership was asked to vote for the new president; **el presidente firmó el acta de la última reunión** = the chairman signed the minutes of the last meeting **(d)** *(curso)* convenor **(e)** *(de una compañía)* chairman *o* president; **el presidente de la junta** *o* **del consejo** *o* **de la compañía** = the chairman of the board *o* the company chairman; **el Sr. Díaz ha sido nombrado presidente de la compañía** = Sr Díaz has been appointed chairman *o* president of the company; **el informe anual del presidente** = the chairman's report; **las observaciones del presidente sobre los auditores se hicieron constar en acta** = the chairman's remarks about the auditors were minuted; **presidente honorario** = honorary president; **se perfila como el próximo presidente** = he is tipped to become the next chairman; **sustituyó al presidente, que estaba resfriado** = he deputized for the chairman who had a cold; **el presidente está en Holanda en viaje de negocios** = the chairman is in Holland on business; **¿cómo reaccionará el presidente cuando le informemos de la noticia?** = how will the chairman react when we tell him the news?; **el presidente en funciones** = the acting chairman; **el presidente en funciones enseñó la fábrica a los visitantes japoneses** = the acting chairman showed the Japanese visitors round the factory; **el presidente ha salido para almorzar** =

the chairman is out at lunch; **el presidente no cobra sueldo** = the chairman does not draw a salary; **el presidente quedó confuso con las preguntas de los periodistas** = the chairman was confused by all the journalists' questions; **el presidente saliente** = the outgoing chairman *o* the outgoing president; **el comité agradeció al presidente saliente la labor realizada** = the committee thanked the retiring chairman for his work; **el presidente salió derrotado en la votación** = the chairman was outvoted; **el Sr. Balea, ex presidente de la compañía** = Sr Balea, the ex-chairman of the company; **la reelección del presidente es anticonstitucional** *o* **antiestatutaria** = the reelection of the chairman is not constitutional

presidir *vt* to chair *o* to preside (over) *o* to take the chair; **presidir una reunión** = to chair a meeting *o* to preside over a meeting; **la reunión se celebró en la sala de juntas y fue presidida por el Sr. Balea** = the meeting was held in the committee room, Sr Balea presiding *o* in the chair

presión *nf* pressure; **trabajar bajo una gran presión** = to work under high pressure; **grupo de presión** = pressure group; **ejercer presión** = to press for *o* to put pressure on *o* to lobby; **el grupo ejerció presión sobre los presidentes de todos los comités** = the group lobbied the chairmen of all the committees; **dimitió ante la creciente presión de los accionistas** = he resigned in the face of mounting pressure from the shareholders

presionar *vt* to lobby *o* to put pressure on *o* to press; **presionar a alguien para que haga algo** = to put pressure on someone to do something; **el grupo intentó presionar al gobierno para que actuara** = the group tried to put pressure on the government to act; **los bancos presionaron a la compañía para que redujera sus préstamos** = the banks put pressure on the company to reduce its borrowings

prestación *nf* benefit (payment); **prestación por baja laboral** = statutory sick pay (SSP); **prestación por desempleo** = unemployment benefit; **prestación de servicios** = rendering of services; **prestaciones de la seguridad social** = social security benefits; **prestaciones sociales** = social benefits

> los países vienen dedicando una parte de su gasto público a prestaciones por desempleo
> **Tiempo**

prestado, -da 1 *adj* borrowed; **dar prestado** = to lend; **tomar prestado** = to borrow; **dinero prestado** = loan *o* borrowed money; **el contable presentó su factura por los servicios profesionales prestados** = the accountant sent in his bill for professional services **2** *pp de* PRESTAR

prestamista *nmf* lender *o* moneylender *o* pawnbroker; *(banco central)* **prestamista en última instancia** = lender of the last resort

préstamo *nm* loan *o* borrowing; **préstamo de ahorro-vivienda** = home loan; **préstamo bancario** = bank loan *o* bank advance *o* bank borrowing; **la nueva fábrica se financió con préstamos bancarios** = the new factory was financed by bank borrowing; **los préstamos bancarios han aumentado** = bank borrowings have increased; **préstamo a corto plazo** = short-term loan;

préstamo dudoso = doubtful loan; **préstamos financieros** = borrowings; **préstamo garantizado** = secured loan; **préstamo globo** = balloon; **préstamo interbancario** = inter-bank loan; **préstamo a largo plazo** = long-term loan; **préstamo en múltiples divisas** = multicurrency loan; **préstamo a plazo medio** = medium-term loan; **préstamo respaldado** *o* **subsidiario** = back-to-back loan; **préstamo sin garantía** = unsecured loan; **préstamo sin interés** = interest-free *o* soft loan; **el préstamo paga un 5% de interés** = the loan pays 5% interest; **conceder un préstamo** = to open a loan; **la duración de un préstamo** = the life of a loan; **después de seis semanas de negociaciones el préstamo fue aprobado definitivamente ayer** = after six weeks of negotiations the loan was finalized yesterday; **hacer un préstamo de 10.000 ptas. a alguien** = to lend someone 10,000 pesetas *o* to make an advance of 10,000 pesetas to someone; **reembolsará el préstamo en plazos mensuales** = he will pay back the money in monthly instalments; **solicitó un préstamo al director del banco** = he asked his bank manager for a loan; **pedir** *o* **tomar a préstamo** *o* **en préstamo** = to borrow; **sacó un préstamo de 10.000.000 de ptas. del banco** = he borrowed 10m pesetas from the bank; **la compañía tuvo que pedir grandes préstamos para pagar a sus proveedores** = the company had to borrow heavily to pay its suppliers; **los préstamos tomados por la compañía se han duplicado** = the company's borrowings have doubled

> había concedido excesivos préstamos a países en desarrollo a lo largo de los años setenta, que nunca fueron recuperados y que tuvo que reponer en la década siguiente
> **El País**

> el nuevo Chemical Bank goza de una situación privilegiada en el mercado de préstamos a pequeñas y medianas empresas (aquellas que obtienen menos de 100 millones de dólares de ingresos anuales)
> **El País**

> no se puede olvidar la aceleración creciente que han experimentado los préstamos financieros, desde la supresión del depósito del 30%, en el Banco de España
> **Mercado**

prestar *vt* **(a)** *(dinero)* to lend *o* to loan *o* to advance; **prestar algo a alguien** = to lend something to someone *o* to lend someone something; **el banco le prestó 5 millones para poner en marcha su negocio** = the bank lent him 5 million to start his business; **tendrán dificultad en conseguir prestado el dinero que necesitan para su programa de expansión** = they will have a job to borrow the money they need for the expansion programme; **prestar dinero con garantía** = to lend money against security; **prestó dinero a la compañía** = he lent the company money *o* he lent money to the company; **el banco se negó a prestar más dinero a la compañía** = the bank refused to lend the company any more money; **el banco le prestó 10 millones de pesetas tomando su casa como garantía** = the bank advanced him 10 million pesetas against the security of his house **(b)** *(apoyo)* **prestar ayuda a alguien** = to help someone *o* to give someone help; **prestar un servicio a alguien** = to do someone a service

◊ **prestatario, -ria** *n* borrower; **los prestatarios pagan un 12% de interés al banco** = borrowers from the bank pay 12% interest

> siempre llega un momento en el que los acreedores se niegan a prestar más o exigen intereses crecientes
> **Cambio 16**

prestigio *nm* prestige; **oficinas de prestigio** = prestige offices

◊ **prestigioso, -sa** *adj* prestigious; **producto prestigioso** = prestige product

> llamó mucho la atención que dentro del mismo semanario convivieran columnistas de prestigio de muy distinta tendencia ideológica
> **Tiempo**

presunción *nf* presumption *o* assumption

presupuestar *vt* to budget *o* to estimate cost; **hemos presupuestado la campaña en 800.000 ptas.** = we have estimated the cost of the campaign at 800,000 pesetas; **gastar más de lo presupuestado** = to spend more than has been budgeted for *o* to spend more than one's budget *o* to overspend one's budget

◊ **presupuestario, -ria** *adj* budgetary; **control presupuestario** = budgetary control; **cuenta presupuestaria** = budget account; **déficit presupuestario** = budget deficit; **Ley presupuestaria** = Finance Act; **política presupuestaria** = budgetary policy; **requisitos presupuestarios** = budgetary requirements; **superávit presupuestario** = budget surplus

presupuesto *nm* **(a)** *(conjunto de gastos e ingresos)* budget; **presupuesto actualizado periódicamente** = rolling budget; **presupuesto de caja** = cash budget; **presupuesto de costes** *o* **de gastos** = estimate of costs *o* of expenditure; **antes de poder conceder la subvención debemos tener un presupuesto del total de los costes comprendidos** = before we can give the grant we must have an estimate of the total costs involved; **presupuesto de explotación** = operational budget; **presupuesto de gastos generales** = overhead budget; **presupuesto principal** = master budget; **presupuesto de promoción** = promotion budget; **presupuesto de publicidad** = publicity budget *o* advertising budget; **el presupuesto de publicidad ha sido suprimido** = the advertising budget has been reduced to zero; **presupuesto de ventas** = sales budget; **preparar un presupuesto** = to draw up a budget; **estamos haciendo un presupuesto de ventas de 9.000.000 de ptas. para el año próximo** = we are budgeting for 9m pesetas of sales next year; **hemos aprobado los presupuestos para el año próximo** = we have agreed the budgets for next year **(b)** *(cálculo anticipado)* estimate *o* quote *o* quotation; **pedir a un contratista un presupuesto para la construcción del almacén** = to ask a builder for an estimate for building the warehouse; **hacer un presupuesto de materiales y mano de obra** = to carry out a quantity survey; **hacer el presupuesto de un trabajo** *o* **de una obra** = to estimate for a job; **presentar el presupuesto de algo** = to put in an estimate for something; **tres empresas presentaron presupuestos de la obra** *o* **del trabajo** = three firms put in estimates for the job; **presentaron su presupuesto para el trabajo** = they sent in their quotation for the job **(c)** *(gobierno)* **el presupuesto del Estado** *o* **presupuesto nacional** = the Budget; **el ministro propuso un presupuesto destinado a reactivar la economía** = the minister put forward a budget aimed at boosting the economy; **presupuesto equilibrado** = balanced budget; **el presidente proyecta un presupuesto equilibrado** = the president is planning for a balanced budget; **presupuesto no equilibrado** *o* **desequilibrado** = unbalanced budget; **equilibrar el presupuesto** = to balance the budget; **reducción** *o* **recortes de presupuesto** = budget cuts; **reducción general de los presupuestos** = sweeping cuts in budget **(d)** **presupuesto sobre emisión de acciones** = prospectus

> una cosa es propiciar el acuerdo entre sindicatos y patronal y otra muy distinta sentar a la mesa de negociación al Gobierno con el Presupuesto debajo del brazo
>
> **España Económica**

> ante la falta de un presupuesto alegre, no parece que la concertación sea practicable
>
> **España Económica**

> la disminución de la actividad económica en muchos sectores ha llevado a las empresas a invertir menos dinero en sus presupuestos publicitarios
>
> **Tiempo**

> los Presupuestos Generales del Estado para el próximo año no ayudarán a resolver los principales problemas macroeconómicos del país
>
> **Actualidad Económica**

pretender *vt* **(a)** *(alegar)* to claim; **pretende no haber recibido nunca las mercancías** = he claims he never received the goods; **pretende que las acciones son de su propiedad** = she claims that the shares are her property **(b)** *(Latinoamérica)* **pretender al puesto** = to apply for the job

◊ **pretensión** *nf* claim; **pretensión con fundamento jurídico** = legal claim

prevención *nf* precaution *o* prevention; **prevención de incendios** = fire prevention

prevenir *vt* **(a)** *(impedir)* to prevent; **tomar medidas para prevenir que algo ocurra** = to take steps to prevent something happening **(b)** *(adelantarse a los acontecimientos)* to pre-empt; **prevenir una OPA** = to pre-empt a takeover bid

◊ **preventivo, -va** *adj* preventive; **acuerdo preventivo** = scheme of arrangement; **tomar medidas preventivas contra robos** = to take preventive measures against theft

prever *vt* to foresee *o* to forecast *o* to anticipate; **ha gastado menos de lo que había previsto** = he has spent less than he forecast *o* he has underspent his budget; **el contrato prevé un aumento anual de los gastos** = the contract provides for an annual increase in charges; **está previsto que el edificio se termine en mayo** = the building is scheduled for completion in May; **no se ha previsto ningún aparcamiento en los planos del edificio de oficinas** = there is no

provision for *o* no provision has been made for car parking in the plans for the office block

> el beneficio después de impuestos ha pasado de 93 millones de pesetas a 1.200 este año y se prevé que la cifra alcance los 1.577 millones en dos años
>
> **España Económica**

previo, -ia **1** *adj* **(a)** *(anterior)* previous *o* prior; **no pudo aceptar la invitación porque tenía un compromiso previo** = he could not accept the invitation because he had a previous engagement; **acuerdo previo** = prior agreement; **sin previo aviso** = without warning; **sin conocimiento previo** = without prior knowledge **(b)** *(preliminar)* preliminary; **una reunión previa** = a preliminary meeting **(c)** **previo a** = before *o* previous to; **habrá una reunión del Consejo de Administración previa a la junta general anual** = there will be a pre-AGM board meeting *o* there will be a board meeting before the AGM

◊ **previamente** *adv* previously

previsión *nf* **(a)** forecast *o* projection *o* forecasting; **previsión de beneficios exagerada** = inflated profit forecast; **previsión a corto plazo** = short-term forecast *o* short-range forecast; **previsión a largo plazo** = long-term forecast *o* long-range forecast; **una previsión económica a largo plazo** = a long-range economic forecast; **la previsión de beneficios para los próximos tres años** = projection of profits for the next three years; **previsión de 'cash flow'** = cash flow forecast; **previsión demográfica** = population forecast; **previsión de mano de obra** = manpower forecasting; **previsión a plazo medio** = medium-term forecast; **previsión de ventas** = sales forecast; **se pidió al director de ventas que elaborara previsiones de ventas para los próximos tres años** = the sales manager was asked to draw up sales projections for the next three years; **la empresa se ha equivocado de nuevo en su previsión de ventas** = the company has missed its sales forecast again **(b)** **previsión social** = social security; **fondo de previsión** = a provident fund

◊ **previsor, -ra** *adj* provident

> las previsiones de las autoridades apuntan hacia una reducción de un punto en la tasa de crecimiento de la economía en el periodo 1992-95
>
> **Mercado**

> haciendo una previsión del panorama nacional de arrendamientos el director general de Vivienda permanece tranquilo
>
> **España Económica**

previsto, -ta **1** *adj* **(a)** projected; **según lo previsto** = as planned *o* as forecast; **basamos nuestros cálculos en el volumen de ventas previsto** = we based our calculations on the forecast turnover; **el edificio se terminó antes de lo previsto** = the building was completed ahead of schedule; **ventas previstas** = projected sales; **las ventas previstas en Europa para el próximo año deberían superar el millón de pesetas** = projected sales in Europe next year should be over 1m pesetas **(b)** **mercado previsto** = target market **2** *pp de* PREVER

prima *nf* **(a)** *(bonificación)* bonus; **prima de**

incentivo = incentive bonus; **prima de producción** = incentive payment; **prima de productividad** = productivity bonus; **los obreros han dejado de trabajar para reivindicar una prima por trabajo peligroso** = the workforce has stopped work and asked for danger money; **acción con prima** = bonus share **(b)** *(seguros)* premium; **prima de riesgo** = risk premium; **prima de seguros** = insurance premium; **se paga o bien una prima anual de 3.600 ptas. o bien doce primas mensuales de 320** = you pay either an annual premium of 3,600 pesetas or twelve monthly premiums of 320 **(c)** *(bolsa)* **prima de opción a vender** = put option

> la prima de riesgo para invertir en España cae al mínimo en 26 meses
>

primario, -ria *adj* primary; **productos primarios** = primary products *o* primary commodities; **sector primario** = primary industry *o* primary sector

primer *adj (apócope de 'primero')* first *o* top; **la empresa ha conseguido el primer puesto en el mercado** = the company has climbed to number one position in the market; **primer trimestre** = first quarter; **primer semestre** = first half *o* first half-year; **el primer semestre del año** = the first half-year

primero, -ra 1 *adj* **(a)** first *o* top; **es la primera empresa del sector** = they are the leading company in the field **(b) primera clase** = first class; **de primera categoría** *o* **clase** = first-class *o* top-flight *o* top-ranking; **los directores de primera clase pueden ganar sueldos muy elevados** = top-flight managers can earn very high salaries **2** *n* the first; **nuestra empresa fue una de las primeras en vender en el mercado europeo** = our company was one of the first to sell into the European market; *(en contabilidad)* **primeras entradas, primeras salidas** = first in, first out (FIFO)

primitivo, -va *adj* primitive *o* original; **mi oferta primitiva** = my first offer *o* my original offer

primo, -ma *adj* raw; **materias primas** = (i) primary commodities; (ii) raw materials

◊ **primordial** *adj* basic *o* fundamental

principal 1 *adj* principal *o* main *o* chief *o* most important *o* master; **director principal** = senior manager *o* senior executive; **edificio principal** = main building; **industria principal** = staple industry; **oficina principal** = main office; **parte principal** = main part; **presupuesto principal** = master budget; **producto principal** = main product *o* staple product; **los principales productos del país son el papel y la madera** = the country's principal products are paper and wood; **socio principal** = senior partner; **es el delegado o representante principal de la delegación** = he is the top-ranking *o* the senior-ranking official in the delegation; **los principales accionistas solicitaron una reunión** = the principal shareholders asked for a meeting; **los principales accionistas obligaron a modificar la política directiva** = leading shareholders in the company forced a change in management policy; **uno de nuestros principales clientes** = one of our main customers **2** *nm (préstamo)* principal *o* capital (of a loan)

◊ **principalmente** *adv* mainly *o* mostly;

trabaja principalmente en la oficina de Madrid = he works mostly in the Madrid office

principio *nm* **(a)** *(regla general)* principle; **por principio** = on principle; **acuerdo de principio** = agreement in principle; **principios contables (b)** *(provisional)* **en principio** = tentatively; **sugerimos el miércoles en principio como fecha para nuestra próxima reunión** = we tentatively suggested Wednesday as the date for our next meeting **(c)** *(cabecera)* head; **escriba el nombre de la compañía al principio de la lista** = write the name of the company at the head of the list **(d)** *(comienzo)* beginning *o* start; **al principio** = at first; **principio de texto** = start of text

prioridad *nf* priority; **la reducción de los gastos generales tiene prioridad sobre el aumento del volumen de negocios** = reducing overheads takes priority over increasing turnover

prisa *nf* **(a)** hurry *o* rush; **las cifras no corren prisa, no las necesitamos hasta la semana próxima** = there is no hurry for the figures, we do not need them until next week; **darse prisa** = to hurry **(b) de prisa** = in a hurry; **sin prisa** = slowly; **el director de ventas quiere el informe de prisa** = the sales manager wants the report in a hurry; **los consejeros fueron de prisa a la junta** = the directors hurried into the meeting; **¿puede hacer este pedido más de prisa? - el cliente lo quiere en seguida** = can you hurry up that order? - the customer wants it immediately

privado, -da *adj* **(a)** private; **cliente privado** = private client *o* private customer; **empresa privada** = private enterprise; **el proyecto está financiado por la empresa privada** = the project is funded by private enterprise; **propiedad privada** = private property; **renta privada** = private income; **el sector privado** = the private sector; **seguro de enfermedad privado** = a private health scheme; **sociedad anónima privada** = private limited company **(b) en privado** = in private *o* privately *o* (speaking) off the record; **el trato se negoció en privado** = the deal was negotiated privately; **solicitó ver al director gerente en privado** = he asked to see the managing director in private; **en público dijo que la compañía pronto cubriría gastos, pero en privado fue menos optimista** = in public he said the company would break even soon, but in private he was less optimistic; **información privada** = inside information

◊ **privadamente** *adv* privately

> la inversión privada permite sostener la actividad y reducir el déficit, pero encarece las infraestructuras y en algún caso podría ser incompatible con determinadas ayudas de la UE
>

privatización *nf* privatization

privatizar *vt* to denationalize *o* to privatize

privilegio *nm* privilege; **las nuevas acciones tendrán los mismos privilegios que las ya existentes** = the new shares will have the same privileges *o* will rank pari passu with the existing ones

pro 1 *nm* pro; **examinemos los pros y los contras antes de tomar la decisión final** = let's analyse the pros and cons before taking our final decision **2** *prep* **en pro** = for *o* on behalf of *o* pro **3** *prefijo* pro-; **pro-europeo** = pro-European

◊ **pro forma** *nf* pro forma; **factura pro forma** = pro forma *o* pro forma invoice; **suministramos esa cuenta únicamente con factura pro forma** = we only supply that account on pro forma; **¿puede mandar una factura pro forma para este pedido?** can you pro forma this order?

probabilidad *nf* probability *o* chance *o* prospect; **no existen probabilidades de que las negociaciones finalicen pronto** = there is no prospect of negotiations coming to an end soon

◊ **probable** *adj* probable; **está intentando evitar el probable hundimiento de la compañía** = he is trying to prevent the probable collapse of the company

◊ **probablemente** *adv* probably; **el director gerente se retirará probablemente el año próximo** = the MD is probably going to retire next year; **esta tienda ofrece probablemente el mejor servicio de la ciudad** = this shop gives probably the best service in town

probar *vt* to test *o* to sample; **probar un sistema de ordenador** = to test a computer system; **probar un producto antes de comprarlo** = to sample a product before buying it; **hicieron un muestreo entre 2.000 personas escogidas al azar para probar la nueva bebida** = they sampled 2,000 people at random to test the new drink

problema *nm* problem *o* question *o* trouble; **sin problemas** = easily; **tenemos algunos problemas con el ordenador** = we are having some computer trouble *o* some problems with the computer; **la compañía tiene problemas de flujo de caja** *o* **problemas laborales** = the company suffers from cash flow problems *o* staff problems ; **planteó el problema del traslado a oficinas menos caras** = he raised the question of moving to less expensive offices; **es un problema que preocupa a los miembros del comité** = it is a matter of concern to the members of the committee; **el problema principal es el del coste** = the main question is that of cost; **resolver** *o* **solucionar un problema** = to solve a problem; **el crédito resolverá algunos de nuestros problemas a corto plazo** = the loan will solve some of our short-term problems; **la prueba de un buen director es su capacidad para resolver problemas** = problem solving is a test of a good manager; **¿solucionaste el problema de las cuentas con los auditores?** = did you sort out the accounts problem with the auditors?

◊ **problemático, -ca** *adj* problematical; **el sector de ventas al extranjero es uno de los más problemáticos en nuestra compañía** = overseas sales is one of our biggest problem areas

procedimiento *nm* procedure *o* proceedings; **procedimientos de contabilidad** = accounting procedures; **procedimiento disciplinario** = disciplinary procedure; **procedimientos industriales** = industrial processes; **procedimiento legal** = legal proceedings; **procedimiento de reclamación** = complaints procedure *o* grievance procedure; **procedimiento de selección** = selection procedure; **seguir el procedimiento adecuado** = to follow the proper procedure; **el sindicato ha**

seguido el procedimiento correcto para presentar reclamaciones = the trade union has followed the correct complaints procedure; **este procedimiento es muy irregular** = this procedure is very irregular

procesador *nm* processor; **procesador de textos** = word-processor

◊ **procesamiento** *nm* **(a)** *(informática)* processing; **procesamiento de datos** = data processing *o* information processing **(b)** *(fabricación)* **procesamiento por lotes** = batch processing **(c)** *(legal)* prosecution; **su procesamiento por desfalco** = his prosecution for embezzlement

procesar *vt* **(a)** *(elaborar)* to process; **los datos están siendo procesados por nuestro ordenador** = data is being processed by our computer **(b)** *(legal)* to prosecute; **fue procesado por desfalco** = he was prosecuted for embezzlement; **está procesado por malversación** = he is on trial *o* is standing trial for embezzlement

◊ **proceso** *nm* **(a)** *(elaboración)* processing; **proceso de datos** = data processing *o* information processing; **proceso electrónico de datos** = electronic data processing (EDP); **efectuamos todo nuestro proceso de datos en la empresa** = we do all our data processing in-house **(b)** *(legal)* lawsuit *o* trial *o* court case; **proceso judicial** = legal proceedings; **entablar un proceso contra alguien** = to institute proceedings against someone **(c)** *(industria)* **proceso de fabricación** *o* **de producción** = manufacturing processes

> finalmente, la innovación para la empresa supone la introducción en la misma de una nueva tecnología o proceso de producción. Este último concepto de innovación es el que más difícilmente se subvenciona
>
> **El País**

procuración *nf* **(a)** proxy *o* power of attorney **(b)** **firmar la carta por procuración** = to sign a letter on behalf of someone *o* to p.p. a letter

◊ **procurador, -ra** *n* attorney

producción *nf* **(a)** *(acción de producir)* production; **producción bruta** = gross turnover; **producción industrial** = industrial production; **producción interior** *o* **nacional** = domestic production; **producción por lotes** = batch production; **producción modernizada** *o* **racionalizada** = lean production; **producción neta** = net turnover; **producción en serie** *o* **a gran escala** = mass production; **producción de coches** *o* **de calculadoras en serie** = mass production of cars *o* of calculators; **la producción se verá probablemente interrumpida por la huelga** = production will probably be held up by industrial action; **esperamos acelerar la producción instalando nueva maquinaria** = we are hoping to speed up production by installing new machinery; **coste de producción** = production cost; **departamento de producción** = production department; **director de producción** = production manager; **prima de producción** = incentive payment; **reducir la producción** = to cut (back) production; **ritmo de producción** = rate of production *o* production rate; **unidad de producción** = production unit; **una serie de huelgas de celo redujeron la producción** = a series of go-slows reduced production **(b)** *(rendimiento)* output; **la producción ha aumentado un 10% =**

output has increased by 10%; **el 25% de nuestra producción se exporta** = 25% of our output is exported; **producción por hora** = output per hour; **plus por aumento de producción** = output bonus

---

el índice de la producción industrial ha aumentado en agosto un 2, 3%, sobre agosto del año anterior, y un 0, 9% sobre julio
España Económica

---

el colapso de la producción industrial, el aumento del desempleo y el cierre de empresas desvalorizadas, serán las espoletas de la transformación económica y no los síntomas negativos de un declive económico
Actualidad Económica

producido, -da 1 *adj* produced; **las cifras producidas** = published figures; **impuesto sobre los bienes** *o* **servicios producidos** = output tax **2** *pp de* PRODUCIR

producir *vt* **(a)** *(inversiones)* to produce *o* to yield; **las acciones producen una renta pequeña** = the shares bring in a small amount; **los bonos producen un interés del 10%** = the bonds carry interest at 10%; **inversiones que producen un 10% anual aproximadamente** = investments which produce about 10% per annum **(b)** *(fabricar)* to make *o* to manufacture *o* to produce; **producir en exceso** = to overproduce; **producir coches** *o* **motores** *o* **libros** = to produce cars *o* engines *o* books; **producir en masa** = to churn out; **producir en serie** *o* **a gran escala** = to mass produce; **la fábrica produce cincuenta unidades al día** = the factory turns out *o* makes fifty units per day **(c)** *(informática)* to output; **la impresora producirá gráficos en color** = the printer will output colour graphics; **ésta es la información producida por el ordenador** = that is the information outputted from the computer **(d)** *(resultar)* to produce *o* to have as a result; **la duplicación del personal de ventas produjo un aumento de las ventas** = the doubling of the sales force resulted in increased sales

◊ **producirse** *vr* to happen; **se ha producido un error** = a mistake has been made; **se ha producido un accidente** = there has been an accident

productividad *nf* productivity; **el pago de bonificaciones va unido a la productividad** = bonus payments are linked to productivity; **la compañía se propone aumentar la productividad** = the company is aiming to increase productivity; **la productividad ha bajado** *o* **aumentado desde que la nueva dirección tomó el mando de la compañía** = productivity has fallen *o* risen since the company was taken over; **acuerdo de productividad** = productivity agreement; **impulso a la productividad** = productivity drive; **prima de productividad** = productivity bonus; **la productividad llegó al máximo en enero** = productivity peaked in January

◊ **productivo, -va** *adj* productive *o* profitable; **capacidad productiva** = producing capacity; **capital productivo** = productive capital; **inversiones productivas** = profitable investments

◊ **productivamente** *adv* productively *o* profitably

---

entre las causas de la ralentización económica se encuentra la posibilidad de que en el próximo ejercicio se registren incrementos salariales mayores a la productividad y por lo tanto descensos en la contratación salarial
Mercado

---

la nación debe enfrentarse al desafío de aumentar la productividad de su mano de obra, que, a su vez, depende de las cualificaciones cada vez más desarrolladas de los trabajadores
Mercado

producto *nm* **(a)** *(cosa producida)* product; **producto acabado** *o* **producto final** = end product *o* final product *o* finished product; **productos acabados** = finished goods; **producto de alta rentabilidad** = cash cow; **producto básico** *o* **de primera necesidad** = basic product *o* staple commodity; **productos en competencia** = competing products; **producto defectuoso** = reject; **productos manufacturados** = manufactured goods; **productos de marca propia** = own brand *o* own label goods; **productos del país** *o* **productos nacionales** = home-produced products; **productos perecederos** = perishable goods *o* perishables *o* non-durables; **producto primario** = commodity *o* primary product; **producto principal** = staple product; **producto secundario** = by-product; **productos semiacabados** = semi-finished products; **producto sensible a los cambios de precio** = price-sensitive product; **productos terminados** = finished goods **(b)** **análisis de productos** = product analysis; **anuncio del producto** = product advertising; **código de un producto** = stock code *o* product code; **conjunto de productos de una compañía** = product mix; **desarrollo de productos** = product development; **dirección de producto** = product management; **diseño de productos** = product design; **gama** *o* **línea de productos** = product line *o* product range; **no tratamos** *o* **no vendemos esa gama de productos** = we do not stock that line; **ingeniero de productos** = product engineer; **promoción de un producto** = promotion of a product; **tenemos 2.000 productos en almacén** = to hold 2,000 lines in stock; **el producto se anunció en las publicaciones del ramo** = the product was advertised through the medium of the trade press; **enumerar los productos en un catálogo** = to list products in a catalogue; **lanzar un nuevo producto al mercado** = to launch a new article on the market; **estos productos se devolverán en el caso de que no se vendan** = these goods are on sale or return; **los vendedores tienen gran fe en el producto** = the salesmen have great faith in the product; **nuestros productos pueden adquirirse en todas las tiendas de ordenadores** = our products are obtainable in all computer shops **(c)** *(artículo)* article *o* item (of stock); **este producto se ha agotado** = this item has sold out **(d)** **productos agrícolas** = (agricultural) produce *o* farm produce; **productos agrícolas nacionales** = home produce; **muestreo de productos del Mercado Común** = sampling of Common Market produce **(e)** *(economía)* **producto global** = aggregate output; **Producto Interior Bruto (PIB)** = Gross Domestic Product (GDP); **Producto Interior Neto (PIN)** = Net Domestic Product; **Producto Nacional Bruto (PNB)** = Gross National Product (GNP); **Producto Nacional Neto (PNN)** = Net National Product

◊ **productor, -ra 1** *adj* producing; **un país productor de relojes de gran calidad** = country which produces high quality watches; **país productor de petróleo** = oil-producing country **2** *n* producer

proeuropeo, -pea *adj* communautaire *o* proeuropean

profesión *nf* **(a)** *(oficio)* profession *o* career *o* occupation; **la profesión médica** = the medical profession; **su profesión ha sido la electrónica** = he made his career in electronics; **¿cuál es su profesión?** = what is her occupation? **(b) de profesión** = by profession *o* by trade; **es médico de profesión** = she's a doctor by profession; **es músico de profesión** = he is a professional musician

profesional 1 *adj* **(a)** *(laboral)* professional *o* vocational *o* occupational; **capacitación** *o* **formación profesional** = vocational training; **código de ética profesional** = code of practice; **enfermedad profesional** = occupational disease; **impuesto profesional** = business tax; *GB* uniform business rate (UBR); **orientación profesional** = vocational guidance; **ramo profesional** = line of business *o* line of work; **riesgos profesionales** = occupational hazards; **los ataques de corazón son uno de los riesgos profesionales de los consejeros** = heart attacks are one of the occupational hazards of directors; **el contable presentó su factura por los servicios profesionales prestados** = the accountant sent in his bill for professional services **(b)** *(experto)* professional; **su trabajo es muy profesional** = his work is very professional; **hicieron un trabajo muy profesional** = they did a very professional job **(c)** *(de profesión)* professional; **un tenista profesional** = a professional tennis player; **hemos nombrado a un diseñador profesional para que supervise el proyecto de la nueva fábrica** = we have appointed a qualified designer to supervise the new factory project; **es un mediador profesional de conflictos laborales** = he is a professional troubleshooter **2** *nmf* professional; **un profesional** = a professional man; **una profesional** = a professional woman; **los profesionales** = people in professional occupations

◊ **profesionalización** *nf* making something more professional

desde el punto de vista económico, no hay obstáculos de ningún tipo para financiar la profesionalización progresiva de las Fuerzas Armadas
España Económica

profundizar *vt* to deepen; **profundizar un tema** = to study a subject in depth; **profundizar en un asunto** = to examine a matter thoroughly

programa *nm* **(a)** *(plan)* programme *o* plan *o* scheme; **programa de ahorro de la Caja Postal** = National Savings scheme; **programa de desarrollo** = development programme; **programa de formación** = training programme; **elaborar un programa de inversión** = to draw up a programme of investment *o* an investment programme; **programa de investigación** = research programme; **programa de ventas** = sales plan **(b)** *(horario)* schedule *o* timetable *o* time scale; **según nuestro programa, todo el trabajo debe terminarse antes de finales de agosto** = our time scale is that all work should be completed by the end of August; **el director gerente tiene un programa de visitas muy apretado** = the

managing director has a busy schedule of appointments; **el director tiene un programa muy apretado y dudo que pueda recibirle hoy** = the manager has a very full timetable, so I doubt if he will be able to see you today; **programa de un congreso** = conference timetable **(c)** *(informática)* **programa informático** = software; **programa de ordenador** = computer program

el programa sindical recopila las reivindicaciones a medio y largo plazo
Tiempo

China cuenta con un presupuesto militar en pleno crecimiento y un amplio programa de ventas de armamentos al tercer mundo
Actualidad Económica

programable *adj* programmable

◊ **programación** *nf* **(a)** *(programa)* scheduling; **programación de pedidos** = order scehduling **(b)** *(informática)* programming; **lenguaje de programación** = programming language; **programación de ordenadores** = computer programming

◊ **programador, -ra** *n* computer programmer

programar *vt* **(a)** *(planificar)* to plan **(b)** *(informática)* to program; **programar un ordenador** = to program a computer; **el ordenador está programado para imprimir etiquetas** = the computer is programmed to print labels **(c)** *(horario)* to schedule; **volver a programar** = to reschedule; **perdió el avión y todas las reuniones tuvieron que volver a ser programadas** = he missed his plane, and all the meetings had to be reschedule

progresar *vi* to progress *o* to make progress

progresivo, -va *adj* progressive *o* gradual *o* graduated; **imposición progresiva** = progressive *o* graduated taxation; **impuesto progresivo** = progressive *o* graduated tax; **impuesto progresivo sobre la renta** = graduated income tax; **tributación progresiva** = progressive taxation

progreso *nm* progress; **progreso comercial** = advance in trade; **progreso técnico** = technical progress; **hacer progreso** = to make progress

prohibición *nf* ban *o* embargo; **prohibición de fumar** = ban on smoking; **levantar la prohibición de fumar** = to lift the ban on smoking; **prohibición de importar** = import ban; **una prohibición del gobierno sobre la importación de armas** = a government ban on the import of arms; **prohibición sobre la exportación de programas de ordenador** = a ban on the export of computer software; **prohibición de realizar horas extraordinarias** = overtime ban; **eludir una prohibición** = to beat the ban on something

tras la prohibición de comercialización de la piel de los animales grandes, la industria de la piel se concentró en los felinos menores
Ajoblanco

prohibido, -da 1 *adj* banned *o* forbidden *o* prohibited; **estar prohibido** = to be prohibited *o* under an embargo; **la importación de armas en el país está prohibida** = the importation of arms into the country is forbidden; **prohibida la entrada** = no admittance; **prohibido fumar** = no smoking **2** *pp de* PROHIBIR

prohibir *vt* to ban *o* to embargo *o* to prohibit *o* to disallow; **prohibir la entrada en el país** = to refuse entry into the country; **el gobierno ha prohibido la importación de armas** *o* **la exportación de ordenadores** = the government has imposed an import ban on arms *o* has put an embargo on the export of computers; **el gobierno ha prohibido la venta de bebidas alcohólicas** = the government has banned the sale of alcohol; **prohibir el comercio** = to forbid trade *o* to ban trade *o* to put an embargo on trade; **prohibir el comercio con un país** = to ban trade *o* to embargo trade *o* to lay an embargo on trade with a country; **el gobierno ha prohibido el comercio con los países del Este** = the government has banned trade with the Eastern countries; **prohibir fumar** = to ban smoking *o* to impose a ban on smoking; **'se prohibe fumar'** = smoking is forbidden *o* 'no smoking'

prohibitivo, -va *adj* prohibitive; **el coste de desarrollar de nuevo el producto es prohibitivo** = the cost of redeveloping the product is prohibitive

proindiviso *adv (expresión jurídica)* undivided (right); **beneficiario proindiviso** = joint beneficiary

prolongación *nf* extension; **le hemos concedido una prolongación del plazo de entrega** = we have granted him an extension of the delivery term

promedio *nm* average *o* mean; **promedio móvil** = moving average; **alcanzar un promedio de** = to average (out); **el promedio de los últimos tres meses** = the average for the last three months *o* the last three months' average; **nuestros representantes hacen un promedio de seis visitas al día** = our reps make on average six calls a day; **promedio de ventas** = sales average *o* average of sales; **el promedio de ventas por representante** = the average sales per representative; **el aumento de las ventas ha alcanzado un promedio del 15%** = sales increases have averaged out at 15%; **el número de unidades vendidas sobrepasa el promedio del primer trimestre** = unit sales are over the mean for the first quarter *o* above the first quarter mean

promesa *nf* promise *o* undertaking; **una promesa de pago** = a promise to pay; **cumplir una promesa** = to keep a promise; **dice que pagará la próxima semana, pero nunca cumple sus promesas** = he says he will pay next week, but he never keeps his promises; **faltar a una promesa** = to go back on a promise; **la dirección faltó a su promesa de aumentar el sueldo a nivel general** = the management went back on its promise to increase salaries across the board

prometer *vt* to promise; **prometieron pagar el último plazo la próxima semana** = they promised to pay the last instalment next week; **el director de personal prometió que estudiaría las quejas del personal de oficinas** = the personnel manager promised he would look into the grievances of the office staff

promoción *nf* promotion; **promoción de ventas** = sales promotion *o* drive; **de promoción** *o* **en promoción** = promotional

promocionar *vt* to promote; **promocionar un nuevo producto** = to promote a new product; **hicimos publicidad en todo el país para promocionar nuestro nuevo servicio a domicilio las 24 horas del día** = we took national advertising to promote our new 24-hour home delivery service

promotor, -ra *n* company promoter; **promotor inmobiliario** *o* **de construcciones** = property developer

promover *vt* to promote; **promover el comercio internacional** = to promote international trade; **la propuesta promovió un fuerte debate en la reunión de ventas** = the proposal started a lively discussion at the sales meeting

pronosticador, -ra *n* forecaster; **pronosticador económico** = economic forecaster

pronosticar *vt* to forecast *o* to predict *o* to tip; **pronostica unas ventas de 2 millones de pesetas** = he is forecasting sales of 2m pesetas; **los economistas han pronosticado un descenso del tipo de cambio** = economists have forecast a fall in the exchange rate

◊ **pronóstico** *nm* forecast *o* scenario; **pronóstico del dividendo** = dividend forecast; **basamos nuestros cálculos en los pronósticos del volumen de ventas** = we based our calculations on the forecast turnover; **ya hemos rebasado nuesto pronóstico de ventas** = we are already ahead of our sales forecast

pronto 1 *adj* early *o* prompt; **muy pronto** = at an early date; **pronto pago** = prompt payment; **nuestro descuento base es de un 20% pero ofrecemos un 5% más por pronto pago** = our basic discount is 20%, but we offer 5% extra for rapid settlement **2** *adv* promptly *o* soon; **esperamos que las negociaciones se reanuden pronto** = we hope for an early resumption of negotiations; **tan pronto como** = as soon as; **tan pronto como le sea posible** = as soon as possible *o* at your earliest convenience; **intentamos deshacernos de nuestras acciones tan pronto como la sociedad hizo públicas sus cuentas** = we tried to unload our shareholding as soon as the company published its accounts

propaganda *nf* advertising *o* publicity; **hacer propaganda** = to advertise; **propaganda enviada por correo** = mail shot *o* mailing shot

propensión *nf* propensity *o* tendency; **propensión al consumo** = propensity to consume; **propensión al ahorro** = propensity to save

propicio, -cia *adj* favourable; **las condiciones actuales son propicias** = the present conditions are favourable

propiedad *nf* **(a)** *(pertenencia)* ownership; **propiedad colectiva** = common *o* collective ownership; **propiedad conjunta** = multiple ownership; **la propiedad intelectual** = intellectual property *o* copyright; **ley sobre la propiedad intelectual** = copyright law; **propiedad en común** = joint ownership; **propiedad privada** *o* **particular** =

(i) private ownership *o* property; (ii) personal property; **la tormenta causó numerosos daños materiales a la propiedad privada** = the storm caused considerable damage to personal property; **propiedad pública** *o* **estatal** = public ownership *o* state ownership; **de propiedad pública** = state-owned; **la propiedad de la compañía ha pasado a los bancos** = the ownership of the company has passed to the banks; **filial en propiedad absoluta** = wholly-owned subsidiary **(b)** *(edificio o tierra)* property; **propiedad amueblada para alquilar** = furnished property to let; **propiedad desocupada** = vacant possession; **propiedad inmobiliaria** = real estate *o* realty; **agente de la propiedad inmobiliaria** = estate agent; *US* realtor; **administrar una propiedad** = to manage property; **catastro** *o* **registro de la propiedad** *o* **registro catastral** = land registry *o* land registration *o* land register; **impuesto sobre la propiedad** = property tax; **el mercado de propiedad comercial** = the commercial property market; **registrar una propiedad** = to register a property; **su título de propiedad tiene vicios jurídicos** = his title to the property is defective; **valor imponible de la propiedad** = rateable value

propietaria *nf* owner *o* proprietress; *(vivienda)* landlady; **la propietaria de una empresa asesora en publicidad** = the owner of an advertising consultancy

propietario, -ria 1 *adj* proprietary **2** *nm* **(a)** owner *o* proprietor; *(vivienda)* landlord; **el propietario de un hotel** = the proprietor of a hotel *o* a hotel proprietor; **propietario único** = sole owner; **propietario de su vivienda** = homeowner; **propietario ocupante de una vivienda** = owner-occupier **(b) propietario absoluto de un inmueble** = freeholder; **nudo propietario** *o* **propietario absoluto** = ground landlord; **el nudo propietario de nuestra vivienda es una compañía de seguros** = our ground landlord is an insurance company

los propietarios originales de los terrenos habrían defraudado a Hacienda interponiendo a unos falsos compradores para eludir el pago de plusvalías
Cambio 16

propina *nf* gratuity *o* tip; **dar propina** = to tip *o* to give a tip to; **el personal no está autorizado a aceptar propinas** = the staff are not allowed *o* are instructed not to accept tips *o* gratuities; **le di una propina de 100 pesetas al taxista** = I gave the taxi driver a 100 peseta tip *o* I tipped the taxi driver 100 pesetas

propio, -pia *adj* own; **trabaja en beneficio propio** = he works for himself *o* for his own benefit; **tiene su propia oficina** = she has her own office; **productos de marca propia** = own-brand goods

proponente *nmf* proposer

proponer *vt* **(a)** *(presentar, sugerir)* to suggest *o* to propose; **proponer la candidatura** = to nominate; **proponer a alguien para un puesto** = to nominate someone to a post; **proponer a alguien para presidente** = to propose someone as president; **propusimos al Señor Pereira para el puesto de tesorero** = we suggested Sr Pereira for the post of treasurer **(b) proponer una moción** = to propose a motion; **propuso que se aprobaran las cuentas** = he moved that the accounts be agreed; **propongo**

que la reunión se suspenda durante diez minutos = I move that the meeting should adjourn for ten minutes

◊ **proponerse** *vr* to propose to *o* to aim to; **me propongo devolver el préstamo pagando 25.000 ptas. al mes** = I propose to repay the loan at 25,000 pesetas a month; **nos proponemos ser el número uno del mercado dentro de dos años** = we aim to be number one in the market within two years

proporción *nf* proportion; **reducir a proporción** = to scale down; **en proporción con** = in proportion to; **las ventas en Europa son pequeñas en proporción con las de EE UU** = our sales in Europe are small in proportion to those in the USA; **las acciones se dividieron en una proporción de cinco a una** = the shares were split five for one; **la proporción de artículos imperfectos es de aproximadamente veinticinco por mil** = the rate of imperfect items is about twenty-five per thousand

◊ **proporcional** *adj* proportional *o* graduated; **imposición proporcional** = progressive *o* graduated taxation; **el aumento de los beneficios es proporcional a la reducción de los gastos generales** = the increase in profit is proportional to the reduction in overheads; **impuesto proporcional sobre la renta** = graduated income tax; **programa de pensiones proporcionales** = graduated pension scheme

◊ **proporcionalmente** *adv* proportionately; **los beneficios aumentaron proporcionalmente a la reducción de los gastos generales** = profits went up in proportion to the fall in overhead costs

proporcionar *vt* to provide *o* to give; **proporcionar algo a alguien** = to provide someone with something *o* to supply someone with something *o* to fix (someone) up with something; **proporcionar beneficios** = to carry benefits; **mi secretaria me proporcionó un coche en el aeropuerto** = my secretary fixed me up with a car at the airport; **el tener una oficina local nos proporciona un margen competitivo sobre García S.A.** = having a local office gives us a competitive edge over García S.A.; **a cada representante se le proporciona un coche de la empresa** = each rep is provided with a company car; **al presentar las solicitudes, se ruega indicar los nombres de tres personas que puedan proporcionar referencias** = when applying please give the names of three people who can supply references

proposición *nf* proposal *o* proposition; **proposición contraria** = counterproposal; **proposición no rentable** = not a commercial proposition; **proposición de seguro** = insurance proposal

propósito *nm* effect *o* purpose; **a propósito de** = with regard to *o* regarding; **con este propósito** = to this end; **hacer algo a propósito** = to do something on purpose; **cláusula con el propósito de** = clause to the effect that; **tener el propósito de hacer algo** = to intend to do something

propuesto, -ta 1 *adj* intended *o* suggested *o* proposed; **cifra propuesta** = target figure; **no alcanzaron la cifra propuesta de 2 millones de pesetas de ventas** = they missed the target figure of 2m pesetas turnover; **el plan propuesto** = the suggested plan *o* the plan put forward *o* the proposal **2** *nf* proposal *o* suggestion; **hacer una propuesta** = to make a proposal to; **la empresa hizo una propuesta a la cadena de supermercados** = the company made an approach to the supermarket chain; **someter una propuesta a votación** = to put a proposal to the vote; **someter** *o* **presentar una propuesta a la junta** = to make a proposal *o* to put forward a proposal to the board; **el comité rechazó la propuesta** = the committee turned down the proposal; **la propuesta fue aprobada por el consejo de administración** = the proposal was approved by the board; **el consejo de administración rechazó todas las propuestas de fusión** = the board turned down all approaches on the subject of mergers

prorrata *nf* share *o* quota; **a prorrata** = pro rata; **los dividendos se pagan a prorrata** = dividends are paid pro rata; **un pago a prorrata** = a pro rata payment

prorratear *vt* to share *o* to apportion; **los costes se prorratean de acuerdo con los ingresos previstos** = costs are apportioned according to projected revenue

◊ **prorrateo** *nm* apportionment; **a prorrateo** = pro rata

prórroga *nf* **(a)** *(prolongación)* extension **(b)** *(renovación)* renewal; **prórroga de un arrendamiento** = renewal of a lease **(c)** *(aplazamiento)* deferment; **conseguir una prórroga del crédito** = to get an extension of credit; **prórroga del contrato** = extension of a contract; **conceder a un acreedor dos semanas de prórroga** = to give a creditor two weeks' grace

prorrogar *vt* to renew; **prorrogar un arrendamiento** = to renew a lease; **habrá que prorrogar el arrendamiento el mes que viene** = the lease is up for renewal next month; **prorrogar un contrato por dos años** = to extend a contract for two years

proseguir *vt/i* to continue *o* to proceed with; **proseguiremos la reunión mañana** = we will continue the meeting tomorrow; **proseguir con la tarea** = to go on with one's job

prospecto *nm* leaflet *o* prospectus *o* flyer; **prospecto publicitario** = publicity leaflet; *US* broadside; **enviar prospectos por correo** *o* **distribuir prospectos publicitarios** = to mail leaflets *o* to hand out leaflets; **enviaron prospectos por correo a 20.000 direcciones** = they made a leaflet mailing to 20,000 addresses

prosperar *vi* **(a)** *(florecer)* to boom *o* to flourish *o* to prosper; **los negocios prosperan** = business is booming; **la compañía prospera** *o* **está prosperando** = the company is flourishing; **la empresa prospera a pesar de la recesión** = the company is thriving in spite of the recession; **el comercio con Argentina prosperó** = trade with Argentina flourished **(b)** *(tener éxito)* to succeed; **la idea no ha prosperado** = the idea came to nothing

prosperidad *nf* **(a)** *(general)* prosperity; **en tiempos de prosperidad** = in times of prosperity; **los años de gran prosperidad** = the boom years **(b)** *(negocios)* bonanza

próspero, -ra *adj* prosperous *o* flourishing *o*

booming; **un próspero comerciante** = a prosperous shopkeeper; **una ciudad próspera** = a prosperous town; **un próspero hombre de negocios** = a successful businessman; **el año pasado fue un año próspero** = last year was a boom year; **tiene un negocio muy próspero de reparación de coches** = he does a thriving business in repairing cars; **un próspero mercado negro de radios para automóviles** = thriving black market in car radios

protección *nf* **(a)** *(amparo)* protection; **la legislación no ofrece protección a los trabajadores a jornada parcial** = the legislation offers no protection to part-time workers; **protección al consumidor** = consumer protection; **protección del trabajo** = employment protection **(b)** *(cobertura contra los cambios de precio)* hedge *o* hedging; **fondo de protección** = hedge fund **(c)** *(seguros)* coverage

◊ **proteccionismo** *nm* protectionism

◊ **proteccionista** *adj* protectionist; **arancel proteccionista** = protective tariff; **política proteccionista** = protectionist policy

protector, -ra 1 *adj* protective; **funda protectora** = protective cover **2** *nm* **(a)** *(que protege)* protector **(b)** *(impresora)* acoustic hood

proteger *vt* to protect *o* to safeguard *o* to cover; **la legislación estatal protege a los trabajadores contra el despido injusto** = the workers are protected from unfair dismissal by government legislation; **el ordenador está protegido por una funda de plástico** = the computer is protected by a plastic cover; **la funda es para proteger a la máquina del polvo** = the cover is supposed to protect the machine from dust; **proteger una industria imponiendo barreras arancelarias** = to protect an industry by imposing tariff barriers; **proteger los intereses de los accionistas** = to safeguard the interests of the shareholders

◊ **protegido, -da** *pp* protected; **protegido contra incendios** = fire-proofed

protesta *nf* protest; **hacer una protesta contra los precios altos** = to make a protest against high prices; **en protesta por** = in protest at; **el personal ocupó las oficinas en protesta por los bajos sueldos** = the staff occupied the offices in protest at the low pay; **actuar bajo protesta** = to do something under protest

---

en la protesta convocada el pasado viernes, los trabajadores demostraron su capacidad de movilización a través de un paro general y una manifestación con más de 15.000 asistentes

El País

---

protestar 1 *vt* **protestar una letra** = to protest a bill **2** *vi* to make a fuss; **protestar contra algo** = to protest against something; *o US* to protest something; **los importadores protestan contra la prohibición de importar artículos de lujo** = the importers are protesting against the ban on luxury goods

◊ **protesto** *nm* protest; **documento** *o* **certificado de protesto** = certificate of protest

prototipo *nm* **(a)** *(modelo)* prototype; **prototipo de coche** *o* **prototipo de avión** = prototype car *o* prototype plane; **la empresa presenta el prototipo**

del nuevo modelo en la exposición = the company is showing the prototype of the new model at the exhibition **(b) prototipo de un contrato** = model agreement

provechoso, -sa *adj* profitable *o* beneficial; **un negocio provechoso** = a profitable business

proveedor, -ra *n* supplier; **proveedor puntual** = prompt supplier; **proveedor de comidas preparadas** = caterer; **proveedor de efectos navales** = ship chandler; **proveedor de herramientas** = tool supplier; *(informática)* software utilities supplier; **prescindiremos gradualmente de Comilsa S.A. como proveedora de piezas de recambio** = Comilsa S.A. will be phased out as a supplier of spare parts; **estamos investigando los antecedentes del nuevo proveedor** = we are inquiring into the background of the new supplier; **nuestra empresa es una de las mayores proveedoras de ordenadores del gobierno** = our company is one of the largest suppliers of computers to the government

> su estrategia futura parte de la necesidad de asegurar su posición como proveedor de herramientas y soluciones para la gestión de entornos abiertos
>
> **PC Week**

proveer *vt* to equip *o* to supply; **la oficina está plenamente provista de procesadores de textos** = the office is fully equipped with word-processors; **proveer directamente** = to supply direct; **proveer fondos** = to provide funds

providente *adj* provident

provincia *nf* province; **las provincias** = the provinces; **hay menos establecimientos al por menor en las provincias que en la capital** = there are fewer retail outlets in the provinces than in the capital

◊ **provincial** *adj* provincial; **un gobierno provincial** = a provincial government; **sucursal provincial de un banco nacional** = a provincial branch of a national bank

provisión *nf* provision *o* supply; **provisión de fondos** = provision *o* reserve; **provisión de clientes dudosos** *o* **provisión para insolvencias** = provision for doubtful accounts; **el banco ha hecho una provisión de fondos de 200 millones de pesetas para deudas incobrables** = the bank has made a 200m peseta provision for bad debts

◊ **provisional** *adj* **(a)** *(no definitivo)* provisional *o* tentative; **mandaron por fax su aceptación provisional del contrato** = they faxed their provisional acceptance of the contract; **llegaron a un acuerdo provisional sobre la propuesta** = they reached a tentative agreement over the proposal; **sugerimos el miércoles 10 de mayo como fecha provisional para la próxima reunión** = we suggested Wednesday May 10th as a tentative date for the next meeting; **director provisional** = acting manager; **informe provisional** = interim report; **permiso provisional para edificar** = outline planning permission; **presupuesto provisional** = provisional budget; **previsión provisional de ventas** = provisional sales forecast **(b)** *(seguros)* **póliza provisional** = cover note; *US* binder

◊ **provisionalmente** *adv* provisionally *o* tentatively; **el contrato ha sido aceptado**

provisionalmente = the contract has been accepted provisionally; **sugerimos el miércoles provisionalmente como fecha para nuestra próxima reunión** = we tentatively suggested Wednesday as the date for our next meeting

próximo, -ma *adj* **(a)** next; **la próxima vez** = the next time; **se perfila como el próximo presidente** = he is tipped to become the next chairman; **tenemos que partir del supuesto de que las ventas no se duplicarán el próximo año** = we have to go on the assumption that sales will not double next year **(b)** *(cercano)* close to **(c)** *(muy pronto)* **en fecha próxima** = at an early date

proyectado, -da 1 *adj* projected **2** *pp de* PROYECTAR

proyectar *vt* **(a)** *(diseñar)* to design; **proyectó una nueva fábrica de automóviles** = he designed a new car factory **(b)** *(planificar)* to plan *o* to schedule; **tenemos que proyectar sobre el futuro** = we need to plan for the future *o* to plan ahead

◊ **proyectista** *nmf* designer *o* planner

proyecto *nm* **(a)** *(plan)* plan *o* project *o* blueprint; **los proyectos económicos del gobierno** = the government's economic plans; **ha elaborado un proyecto para crear nuevos mercados en Europa** = he has drawn up a project for developing new markets in Europe; **la compañía tiene en proyecto abrir una oficina en Nueva York el próximo año** = the company intends to open an office in New York next year **(b)** *(obra)* project; **la empresa empezará a trabajar en el proyecto el mes próximo** = the company will start work on the project next month; **los miembros del consejo son partidarios de que Roldán S.A. participe en el proyecto** = the board members all favour Roldán S.A. as partners in the project; **análisis de proyectos** = project analysis; **director de proyecto** = project manager; **ingeniero de proyectos** = project engineer; **realizar un proyecto** = to carry through a project; **sacar un proyecto a contrata** *o* **a licitación** *o* **a concurso** = to put a project out to tender *o* to ask for *o* to invite tenders for a project **(c)** *(borrador)* draft; **redactó el proyecto del acuerdo al dorso de un sobre** = he drew up the draft agreement on the back of an envelope **(d)** *(propuesta)* proposal; **presentar un proyecto a la junta** = to make a proposal *o* to put forward a proposal to the board; **el comité rechazó el proyecto** = the committee turned down the proposal **(e)** *(parlamento)* **proyecto de ley** = bill

> teóricamente el proyecto ofrecía muchas ventajas al capital extranjero
>
> **España Económica**

> tenemos varios proyectos más para los dos próximos años, aunque sería prematuro el desvelarlos ahora
>
> **Tiempo**

> la primera fase del proyecto finalizará en el plazo de año y medio, y una vez finalizada será puesto a prueba en los más prestigiosos centros sanitarios de Europa
>
> **Micros**

prudencia *nf* prudence *o* caution; **con prudencia** = cautiously

◊ **prudente** *adj* **(a)** *(juicioso)* wise; **una decisión**

prudente = a wise decision **(b)** *(moderado)* conservative; **una estimación de ventas prudente** = a conservative estimate of sales

◊ **prudentemente** *adv* conservatively; **calculando prudentemente** = at a conservative estimate; **las ventas totales están prudentemente calculadas en 2,3 millones** = the total sales are conservatively estimated at 2.3m

prueba *nf* **(a)** *(testimonio)* proof *o* evidence; **prueba documental** *o* **documentada** = documentary proof *o* evidence **(b)** *(examen)* test *o* testing *o* trial; **prueba de aptitud** = aptitude *o* proficiency test; **prueba a ciegas** = blind test *o* testing; **prueba gratuita** = free trial; **prueba de mercado** = market test; **prueba de selección** = selection test; **prueba de viabilidad** *o* **de factibilidad** = feasibility test; **durante la prueba del sistema se rectificaron algunos defectos** = during the testing of the system several defects were corrected; **someter a prueba** = to test; **someter un coche a una prueba de carretera** = to test-drive a car; **someter un producto a una prueba de mercado** = to test the market for a product *o* to test market a product; **muestra de prueba** = trial sample; **periodo de prueba** = trial period **(c)** **a prueba** = (i) on approval; (ii) on trial; **el producto está siendo sometido a prueba en nuestros laboratorios** = the product is on trial in our laboratories; **comprar algo a prueba** = to buy something on approval *o* on appro; **comprar una fotocopiadora a prueba** = to buy a photocopier on approval; **emplear a alguien a prueba** = to take someone on probation; **poner un proyecto a prueba** = to pilot **(d)** *(protegido)* **a prueba de** = proof against *o* -proof; **a prueba de incendios** = fireproof; **guardamos los documentos en una caja a prueba de incendios** = we packed the papers in a fireproof safe; **a prueba de inflación** = inflation-proof **(e)** *(probatorio)* **de prueba** = probationary; **un periodo de prueba de tres meses** = a probationary period of three months; **después del periodo de prueba la compañía decidió ofrecerle un contrato a jornada completa** = after the probationary period the company decided to offer him a full-time contract

en cualquier prueba de selección, la persona está en un proceso en el que se descartan y eligen a los candidatos
El País

ptas. *abrev ver* PESETAS

publicación *nf* **(a)** *(acción de publicar)* publication *o* publishing; **la publicación de las últimas cifras comerciales** = the publication of the latest trade figures **(b)** *(obra publicada)* publication *o* magazine *o* newspaper; **pidió en la biblioteca una lista de las publicaciones del gobierno** = he asked the library for a list of government publications; **publicación comercial** = business publication *o* trade paper; **la compañía edita seis publicaciones comerciales** = the company has six business publications; **publicación periódica** = periodical; **publicaciones profesionales** *o* **del ramo** = trade press

publicar *vt* to publish *o* to issue; **el gobierno publicó un informe sobre el tráfico de Madrid** = the government issued a report on Madrid's traffic; **la sociedad publica su lista de socios anualmente** = the society publishes its list of members annually; **el gobierno no ha publicado las cifras en las que se basa su propuesta** = the government has not published the figures on which its proposals are based; **no se pueden publicar anuncios en los periódicos gubernamentales** = advertisements cannot be placed in the government-controlled newspapers; **escribe una columna sobre finanzas personales que se publica en varios periódicos** = he writes a syndicated column on personal finance *o* a column on personal finance which is published in various magazines

publicidad *nf* **(a)** publicity *o* advertising *o* exposure; **trabaja en publicidad** = she works in advertising; **tiene un empleo en publicidad** = he has a job in advertising; **agencia de publicidad** = advertising agency *o* publicity agency *o* publicity bureau; **agente de publicidad** = advertising agent *o* adman; **campaña de publicidad intensiva** = saturation advertising; **dar publicidad** = to publicize; **estamos intentando dar publicidad a nuestros productos por medio de anuncios en los autobuses** = we are trying to publicize our products by advertisements on buses; **departamento de publicidad** = publicity department; **director de publicidad** = publicity manager; **gastos de publicidad** = advertising expenditure *o* publicity expenditure; **gastos de publicidad no incluidos** = below-the-line advertising; **hacer publicidad de un nuevo producto** = to advertise a new product; **jefe de publicidad** = advertising manager; **material de publicidad** = publicity matter; **presupuesto de publicidad** = advertising budget *o* publicity budget; **el presupuesto de publicidad ha sido suprimido** = the advertising budget has been reduced to zero; **nuestra campaña ha recibido más publicidad desde que decidimos anunciarla a escala nacional** = our company has achieved more exposure since we decided to advertise nationally; **habían esperado que la publicidad en la televisión les ayudaría a aumentar las ventas** = they had hoped the TV commercials would help sales **(b)** **publicidad colectiva** = association advertising; **publicidad agresiva** = knocking copy; **publicidad por correo** = direct-mail advertising; **publicidad exagerada** = hype; **publicidad en el punto de venta** = point of sale material; **publicidad subliminar** = subliminal advertising

hay deportes de gran interés televisivo, como el atletismo, que pueden obtener miles de millones de dólares por publicidad estática en el campo y por derechos de retransmisión
Actualidad Económica

los españoles que no quieran recibir publicidad por correo en sus domicilios podrán inscribirse a partir de ahora en una lista creada por la Asociación Española de Marketing Directo AEMD
El País

publicitario, -ria 1 *adj* **agencia publicitaria** = publicity agency *o* publicity bureau *o* advertising agency; **campaña publicitaria** = advertising campaign *o* publicity campaign; **descanso publicitario** *o* **pausa publicitaria** = commercial break; **espacio publicitario** = advertising space; **adquirir espacio publicitario en un periódico** = to take advertising space in a paper; **material publicitario** = publicity matter; **presupuesto**

publicitario = advertising budget *o* publicity budget; **tarifas publicitarias** = advertising rates; **texto publicitario** = blurb *o* advertorial; **valla publicitaria** = advertisement hoarding *o* billboard **2** *n (agente de publicidad)* publicist *o* advertising executive

público, -ca 1 *adj* **(a)** public; **finanzas públicas** = public finance; **fondos públicos** = public funds; **gasto público** = public expenditure; **imagen pública** = public image; **el ministro está intentando mejorar su imagen pública** = the minister is trying to improve his public image; **propiedad pública** = public ownership; **relaciones públicas (RP)** = public relations (PR); **departamento de relaciones públicas** = public relations department *o* PR department; **teléfono público** = public telephone *o* pay phone; **transporte público** = public transport **(b) el sector público** = public sector; **un informe sobre los aumentos de sueldo en el sector público** *o* **los acuerdos salariales del sector público** = a report on wage rises in the public sector *o* on public sector wage settlements; **servicio público** = utility **(c) en público** = in public; **en público dijo que la compañía pronto tendría beneficios pero en privado fue menos optimista** = in public he said that the company would soon be in profit, but in private he was less optimistic **2** *nm* **(a) el público (en general)** = the public *o* the general public; **la sociedad va a ofrecer sus acciones al público** = the company is going public; **los sondeos de opinión mostraron que el público prefería la mantequilla a la margarina** = opinion polls showed that the public preferred butter to margarine **(b)** audience

> por lo que se refiere al Sector Público, la tasa de crecimiento del crédito interno al mismo es prácticamente nula desde diciembre último
>
> **Mercado**

pucherazo *nm (manipulación de votos)* ballot-rigging

puente *nm* **(a)** bridge; **puente colgante** = suspension bridge; **báscula puente** *o* **puente-báscula** = weighbridge **(b) puente aéreo** = air shuttle **(c)** *(día laboral entre dos días festivos)* (i) extra day off between two public holidays; (ii) long weekend; **haremos puente ya que el jueves es fiesta** = we'll have a long weekend since Thursday is a bank holiday

> en diciembre, entre fiestas y puentes, quedan menos de 15 días laborables y además coincide con el cierre del año fiscal de la mayoría
>
> **Datamation**

puerta *nf* **(a)** door; **llamó a la puerta y entró** = he knocked on the door and went in; **el director de finanzas llamó a la puerta del presidente y entró** = the finance director knocked on the chairman's door and walked in; **el director de ventas tiene su nombre en la puerta** = the sales manager's name is on his door; **cuelga tu abrigo en el perchero detrás de la puerta** = hang your coat on the hook behind the door; **la tienda abrió sus puertas el 1 de junio** = the store opened its doors on June 1st **(b) de puerta en puerta** = door-to-door *o* house-to-house; **sondeo de puerta en puerta** = house-to-house canvassing; **vender de puerta en puerta** = to sell from door to door; **vendedor de puerta en puerta** = door-to-door

salesman **(c)** *(aeropuerto)* gate; **salida del vuelo IB270 por la puerta 23** = flight IB270 is now boarding at Gate 23 **(d) el trabajo fue anunciado de puertas adentro** = the job was advertised internally; **política de puertas abiertas** = open door policy

puerto *nm* port *o* harbour; **el puerto** = the docks; **el puerto de Rotterdam** = the port of Rotterdam; **los aduaneros subieron al barco atracado en el puerto** = customs officials boarded the ship in the harbour; **arribar** *o* **hacer escala en un puerto** = to call at a port; **puerto comercial** = commercial port; **puerto distribuidor** = entrepot port; **puerto de embarque** = port of embarkation; **puerto de escala** *o* **de arribada** = port of call; **puerto franco** = free port; **puerto interior** = inland port; **puerto marítimo** = seaport; **puerto pesquero** = fishing port; **el director del puerto** = the dock manager

Puerto Rico *nm* Puerto Rico

◊ **portorriqueño, -ña** *o* **puertorriqueño, -ña** *adj y n* Puerto Rican

NOTA: capital: **San Juan**; moneda: **dólar USA (US$)** = US dollar (US$)

puesta *nf* putting *o* placing; **costes de puesta en marcha** = start-up costs

puesto, -ta 1 *nm* **(a)** *(cargo)* job *o* place *o* position *o* post; **pérdida de puestos de trabajo** = job losses; **proponer a alguien para un puesto** = to nominate someone to a post; **cedió el puesto a su adjunto** = he handed over to his deputy; **le ofrecieron un puesto en una compañía de seguros** = he was offered a place with an insurance company; **tenemos varios puestos vacantes** = we have several positions vacant; **todos los puestos vacantes han sido cubiertos** = all the vacant positions have been filled; **tiene un puesto clave** = he is in a key position; **ha encontrado un puesto fijo** = he has found a permanent job; **solicitar un puesto de cajero** = to apply for a post as cashier; **anunciamos tres puestos en 'El País'** = we advertised three posts in 'El País' **(b)** *(posición)* position; **la empresa ha conseguido el primer puesto en el mercado** = the company has climbed to number one position in the market **(c)** *(espacio)* **puesto en el mercado** = market stall; *(exposición)* **puesto de exposición** = stand *o* place; US booth **(d)** *(operador de informática)* **puesto de trabajo** = workstation **(e) puesto aduanero** = customs entry point *o* customs post **2** *pp de* PONER

> como señalan las empresas de selección, el conocimiento del inglés se utiliza como filtro discriminatorio para descartar candidatos ante la gran cantidad de solicitantes a un determinado puesto de trabajo
>
> **El País**

pugna *nf* conflict

> la pugna que hoy se vive en Europa enfrenta a monetaristas (bancos centrales) con fiscalistas (o ministerios de Economía, aunque con excepciones)
>
> **Tiempo**

puja *nf* bidding; **la puja culminó con 250.000 ptas.** = the bidding stopped at 250,000 pesetas

pujar *vt* to bid; **pujar más alto** = to outbid; **ofrecimos 100.000 ptas. por el almacén, pero otra**

sociedad pujó más alto = we offered 100,000 pesetas for the warehouse, but another company bid more than we did *o* outbid us

pulgada *nf (medida* = *2,54cm)* inch; **disco de 3,5 pulgadas** = 3½ inch disk

punta *nf* **(a)** end *o* tip **(b) horas punta** = peak period *o* peak time; **el taxi se retrasó por el tráfico de la hora punta** = the taxi was delayed in the rush hour traffic; **fuera de horas punta** = outside peak hours *o* off-peak; **tarifa fuera de horas punta** = off-peak tariff

punto *nm* **(a)** *(sitio)* point; **punto más alto** = highest point *o* peak *o* ceiling; **alcanzar el punto más alto** = to peak; **punto de arranque** = trigger point; **punto más bajo** = lowest point *o* bottom *o* trough; **las ventas han llegado a su punto más bajo** = sales have reached rock bottom; **punto culminante** = peak *o* high point; **punto muerto** = deadlock; **las negociaciones han llegado a un punto muerto** = the negotiations have reached a deadlock; **punto de equilibrio** = breakeven point; **punto de partida** = starting point; **punto de vencimiento del IVA** = tax point; **punto de venta** = point of sale (p.o.s *o* POS); **publicidad en el punto de venta** = point of sale material **(b)** *(señal)* dot *o* point; **recorte el boletín de pedido por la línea de puntos** = the order form should be cut off along the dotted line; **punto porcentual** = percentage point;

medio punto porcentual = half a percentage point; **el dólar ganó dos puntos** = the dollar gained two points; **el cambio bajó diez puntos** = the exchange fell ten points; **punto de referencia** = benchmark **(c)** *(asunto)* item; **discutiremos ahora el punto cuatro del orden del día** = we will now take item four on the agenda; **inscribir un punto en el orden del día** = to put an item on the agenda **(d) punto débil** = failing *o* weak point **(e) estar a punto** = to be ready

puntual *adj* punctual *o* prompt *o* on time; **ser puntual** = to be punctual *o* to be on schedule *o* to be on time; **proveedor puntual** = prompt supplier; **es un pagador puntual** = he's a prompt payer

◊ **puntualidad** *nf* punctuality *o* promptness; **recibió una advertencia por falta de puntualidad** = he was warned for bad time-keeping

◊ **puntualmente** *adv* punctually; **pagar puntualmente** = to pay on time

PVP = PRECIO DE VENTA AL PUBLICO

PYME *o* **PYMEs** *nf* = PEQUEÑAS Y MEDIANAS EMPRESAS small and medium-sized enterprises (SME)

la pyme es la gran apuesta del nuevo Gobierno para reactivar la economía y, sobre todo, para la creación de empleo
El País

Qq

quebrado, -da 1 *adj* broken 2 *n* bankrupt; **rehabilitar a un quebrado** = to discharge a bankrupt; **quebrado rehabilitado** = discharged bankrupt; **quebrado no rehabilitado** = undischarged bankrupt; **rehabilitación del quebrado** = discharge in bankruptcy 3 *pp de* QUEBRAR

quebrar *vi* to go bankrupt *o* to collapse *o* to fail; *(informal)* to go bust *o* to crash; **la compañía quebró** = the company failed; **la compañía quebró el mes pasado** = the company went bust last month; **la compañía quebró dejando deudas de más de 20 millones de pesetas** = the company crashed *o* collapsed with debts of over 20m pesetas; **perdió todo su dinero cuando el banco quebró** = he lost all his money when the bank failed; **la empresa quebró durante la recesión** = the firm went out of business during the recession

quedar *vi* **(a)** *(permanecer)* to remain *o* to stay; **no queda nada por decir** = there is nothing else to talk about; **quedar atrás** = to stay behind; **nos quedamos una semana en Valencia** = we stayed a week in Valencia; **liquidaremos las existencias viejas a mitad de precio y tiraremos lo que quede** = we will sell off the old stock at half price and anything remaining will be thrown away; **las habitaciones deben quedar libres antes de las 12.00** = rooms must be vacated before 12.00; **el volumen de sus ventas ha subido por lo menos un 20% en el último año, y probablemente me quedo corto** = their turnover has risen by at least 20% in the last year, and that is probably an understatement; **mi cuenta bancaria quedó al descubierto** = my bank account went into the red **(b)** *(acordar)* **quedamos para mañana a las 9 en la oficina** = let's meet in the office tomorrow morning at 9 **(c)** **quedar bien** *o* **mal** = to make a good *o* bad impression; **intentó quedar bien con todos y no quedó bien con nadie** = he tried to please everyone and ended up by pleasing nobody **(d)** *(en una carta)* **'quedamos a su disposición'** *o* **'quedamos a la espera de su respuesta'** = looking forward to hearing from you

◇ **quedarse** *vr* to remain *o* to stay; **se quedó en la oficina después de las 6.30 para terminar el trabajo** = she remained behind at the office after 6.30 to finish her work; **2.000 empleados se quedaron sin trabajo por la recesión** = 2,000 employees were made idle by the recession; **las ventas se han quedado fijas en 2 millones de pesetas durante los últimos dos años** = sales have stuck at 2m pesetas for the last two years; **quedarse con** = to keep back; **quedarse con 2.000 ptas. del salario de alguien** = to keep 2,000 pesetas back from someone's salary; **quedarse atrás** = to fall behind; **nos hemos quedado atrás de nuestros competidores** = we have fallen behind our rivals

queja *nf* complaint *o* grievance; **presentar una queja contra alguien** = to make *o* lodge a complaint against someone; **procedimiento de tramitación de quejas** = complaints procedure *o* grievance procedure

◇ **quejarse** *vr* to complain; **hace tanto frío en la oficina que el personal ha empezado a quejarse** = the office is so cold the staff have started complaining; **se quejó del servicio** = she complained about the service; **se quejan de que nuestros precios son demasiado elevados** = they are complaining that our prices are too high; **los usuarios del tren se quejan del aumento de las tarifas** = rail travellers are complaining about rising fares; **si quiere quejarse, escriba al director** = if you want to complain, write to the manager; **recuperé mi dinero después de quejarme al director** = I got my money back after I had complained to the manager; **¿tiene motivos fundados para quejarse?** = does he have good grounds for complaint?

quemar *vt* to burn; **el contable jefe quemó los documentos antes de que llegara la policía** = the chief accountant burnt the documents before the police arrived

◇ **quemarse** *vr* **(a)** to burn *o* to be burnt; **quemarse totalmente** = to burn down; **el almacén se quemó totalmente y todas las existencias quedaron destruidas** = the warehouse burnt down and all the stock was destroyed **(b)** *(incendiarse)* to catch fire; **los papeles de la papelera se quemaron** = the papers in the waste paper basket caught fire

querella *nf* **(a)** *(queja)* complaint **(b)** *(demanda)* charge

◇ **querellante** *nmf* plaintiff

querido, -da *adj* *(en carta)* **Querido Jaime** *o* **Querida Julia** = Dear James *o* Dear Julia

quiebra *nf* **(a)** *(bancarrota)* bankruptcy *o* failure; **quiebra comercial** = commercial failure; **la recesión ha provocado miles de quiebras** = the recession has caused thousands of bankruptcies; **perdió todo su dinero en la quiebra del banco** = he lost all his money in the bank failure; **declaración (judicial) de quiebra** *o* **presentación de quiebra** = adjudication of bankruptcy *o* declaration of bankruptcy *o* adjudication order; **presentar una declaración de quiebra** *o* **declararse en quiebra** = to file a petition in bankruptcy; **la compañía fue intervenida judicialmente por quiebra** = the company went into receivership; **rehabilitación de quiebra** = discharge (in bankruptcy); **transacción previa a la quiebra** = scheme of arrangement; **en quiebra** = bankrupt; **un promotor inmobiliario en quiebra** = a bankrupt property developer; **fue declarado en quiebra** = he was adjudicated bankrupt **(b)** *(economía)* crash *o* slump *o* collapse

las facturas se expiden en forma de venta de bienes o prestación de servicios por personas o sociedades inactivas o en quiebra

Cambio 16

quilate *nm* carat; **un anillo de oro de 22 quilates** = a 22-carat gold ring; **un diamante de 5 quilates** = a 5-carat diamond

quincalla *nf* **(a)** *(ferretería)* hardware **(b)** *(baratija)* trinket

quince 1 *adj* fifteen *o* fifteenth; *(dos semanas)* **quince días** = two weeks *o* a fortnight; **lo vi hace quince días** = I saw him a fortnight ago **2** *nm* fifteen; *(UE)* **Los Quince** = the Fifteen

◊ **quincena** *nf (dos semanas)* fortnight; **estaremos de vacaciones durante la última quincena de julio** = we will be on holiday during the last fortnight of July

◊ **quincenalmente** *adv* fortnightly *o* every two weeks *o* bi-monthly

quinquenio *nm* five year period

> al término del presente ejercicio, los beneficios de explotación de la Compañía se habrán multiplicado por cuatro en el último quinquenio
> **España Económica**

quiosco *nm* kiosk; **quiosco de periódicos** = a newspaper kiosk *o* news stand; **quiosco de libros** = bookstall

quitar *vt* **(a)** *(sacar)* to remove *o* to take away; **hemos quitado el télex con la intención de reducir los costes** = we have taken out the telex in order to try to cut costs **(b)** *(ropa)* to take off **(c)** **quitar importancia a un asunto** = to play down a matter

quórum *nm* quorum; **haber quórum** = to have a quorum; **¿hay quórum?** = do we have a quorum?; **con suficiente quórum** = quorate

> los estatutos de la empresa establecen que se necesita un mínimo de ocho consejeros para lograr el quórum necesario
> **El País**

Rr

ración *nf* portion

racionalización *nf* rationalization *o* streamlining; **la racionalización industrial es fundamental para el desarrollo del país** = industrial rationalization is essential for the country's development

◊ **racionalizado, -da 1** *adj* rationalized *o* streamlined; **producción racionalizada** = streamlined production **2** *pp de* RACIONALIZAR

racionalizar *vt* to streamline *o* to rationalize; **racionalizar el sistema de contabilidad** = to streamline the accounting system; **racionalizar los servicios de distribución** = to streamline distribution services; **la compañía de ferrocarriles está intentando racionalizar su servicio de carga** = the rail company is trying to rationalize its freight services

racionamiento *nm* rationing; **es posible que este invierno haya un periodo de racionamiento de víveres** = there may be a period of food rationing this winter

racionar *vt* to ration

raíz *nf* root; **a raíz de** = as a result of; **bienes raíces** = real estate; **legado de bienes raíces** = devise; **legatario de bienes raíces** = devisee

ralentización *nf* deceleration *o* slowing down

◊ **ralentizar** *vt* to slow down

> entre las causas de la ralentización económica se encuentra la posibilidad de que en el próximo ejercicio se registren incrementos salariales mayores a la productividad y por lo tanto descensos en la contratación salarial
> **Mercado**

> la ralentización que vive la economía desde finales del año pasado ha originado que pocas empresas hayan decidido emprender grandes planes de inversión
> **El País**

rama *nf* division *o* branch *o* department

> por ramas de actividad, el mayor aumento (8,14%) correspondió al sector servicios
> **Mercado**

ramificarse *vr* to branch out *o* to ramify

> el menor de los cuatro hermanos dirige el imperio que empezó en los perfumes y hoy se ramifica en varios sectores
> **Cambio 16**

ramo *nm* sector; **el ramo de la hostelería** = the catering sector

rampa *nf* ramp; **rampa de acceso** = access ramp; **rampa de carga** = loading ramp

rand *nm* (*moneda de Sudáfrica y Namibia*) rand

rango *nm* rank; **se reunió con unos funcionarios de alto rango** = he had a meeting with some high-ranking officials

> las normas que regulen este mercado no deben tener un rango inferior sino el rango que confiera al sector la importancia que merece
> **España Económica**

'ránking' *o* **'ranking'** *nm* ranking *o* classification

> con unos activos de 118.200 millones de dólares, estos dos bancos del sureste pasaron a ocupar el tercer lugar del ránking el pasado 23 de julio
> **El País**

> cuando anunciaron la operación, el pasado 15 de julio, se situaban en el segundo lugar del ranking bancario norteamericano
> **El País**

> Japón sigue siendo la tercera del 'ranking' mundial por gasto militar
> **Actualidad Económica**

ranura *nf* slot

rapidez *nf* speed *o* rapidity; **con rapidez** = fast *o* rapidly; **despachar un pedido con rapidez** = to rush an order; **los costes están aumentando con rapidez** = costs are mounting up rapidly

rápido, -da *adj* fast *o* quick *o* rapid *o* express; **el tren es el medio más rápido para llegar a la fábrica de nuestros proveedores** = the train is the fastest way of getting to our supplier's factory; **está buscando un beneficio rápido de sus inversiones** = he is looking for a quick return on his investments; **una recuperación rápida de la bolsa** = a sharp rally on the stock market; **la empresa tuvo una recuperación rápida** = the company made a quick recovery; **servicio rápido** = prompt service; **esperamos realizar una venta rápida** = we are hoping for a quick sale

◊ **rápidamente** *adv* fast *o* quickly *o* rapidly *o* promptly; **los ordenadores individuales se venden rápidamente antes de las Navidades** = home computers sell fast in the pre-Christmas period; **la venta de la compañía se realizó rápidamente** = the sale of the company went through quickly; **la compañía contrajo rápidamente deudas de más de 1 millón de pesetas** = the company rapidly ran up debts of over 1m pesetas; **las ventas han subido rápidamente durante los últimos meses** = sales have risen sharply in the course of the last few months

raro, -ra *adj* rare *o* strange *o* odd

◊ **raramente** *adv* rarely *o* not often; **el presidente está raramente en su oficina los viernes por la tarde** = the chairman is rarely in his office on Friday afternoons

rastrear *vt* to search

rastro *nm* (a) (*mercadillo*) flea market (b) (*señal*) trace; **sin dejar rastro** = without a trace *o* leaving no trace

ratero, -ra *n* pickpocket *o* small-time thief; **ratero de tiendas** = shoplifter

ratificación *nf* ratification; **el convenio tiene que obtener la ratificación del consejo de administración** = the agreement has to go to the board for ratification

ratificar *vt* to ratify; **el convenio tiene que ser ratificado por el consejo de administración** = the agreement has to be ratified by the board

rato *nm* short period of time *o* a while; **¿puedes esperar un rato, por favor?** could you wait a short while, please?

ratón *nm (informática)* mouse

raya *nf* line; **prefiero el papel de cartas sin rayas** = I prefer notepaper without any lines; **raya azul** *o* **tenue** = thin blue line *o* feint

◊ **rayado, -da 1** *adj* lined; **papel rayado** = lined paper *o* paper with thin blue lines; **prefiere papel rayado para tomar apuntes** = he prefers lined paper for writing notes **2** *pp de* RAYAR

rayar (a) *(marcar con una línea)* to line *o* to mark with lines **(b) rayar en** = to come near to *o* to border on; **la herencia raya en los 40 millones** = the estate comes to nearly 40 million

razón *nf* **(a)** *(motivo)* reason *o* grounds; **le pidieron al presidente que expusiera sus razones para el cierre de la fábrica** = the chairman was asked for his reasons for closing the factory; **'razón aquí'** = 'inquire within' **(b)** *(estar en lo cierto)* **tener razón** = to be right **(c)** *(relación)* ratio; **a razón de** = by a ratio of; **nuestro producto se vende más que el suyo a razón de dos a uno** = our product outsells theirs by a ratio of two to one; **el gobierno ayuda a la industria electrónica a razón de 20 millones de pesetas al año** = the government is supporting the electronics industry to the tune of 20m pesetas per annum **(d) razón social** = business name *o* trade name *o* registered name

◊ **razonable** *adj* **(a)** *(bueno, seguro)* reasonable; **se acepta cualquier oferta razonable** = no reasonable offer refused **(b)** *(sólido)* sound; **siempre nos da consejos razonables** = she always gives us sound advice **(c) precios razonables** = sensible prices

re- *prefijo* re-

reacción *nf* reaction *o* response *o* feedback; **la reacción de las acciones ante la noticia de la oferta de adquisición** = the reaction of the shares to the news of the takeover bid; **nuestros folletos de propaganda a domicilio no produjeron ninguna reacción** = there was no response to our mailing shot; **¿le han comunicado ya los vendedores la reacción de los clientes ante el nuevo modelo?** = have you any feedback from the sales force about the customers' reaction to the new model?

reaccionar *vi* to react; **reaccionar ante** = to react to; **el mercado reaccionó favorablemente ante la noticia de la decisión del gobierno** = the market reacted favourably to the news of the government's decision

reacio, -cia *adj* reluctant *o* opposed *o* difficult; **se muestra reacio a concedernos otro crédito** = he is being very awkward about giving us further credit

---

el Bundesbank se muestra más bien reacio a la puesta en práctica de los planes del euro, y rechaza estrictamente una relajación de los criterios

El País

reactivación *nf* **(a)** *(mejoría)* recovery *o* upturn; **reactivación del comercio** = revival of trade; **una reactivación de la economía** = an upturn in the economy; **la reactivación de la economía después de una recesión** = the recovery of the economy after a slump; **una reactivación del mercado** = an upturn in the market **(b)** *(volver a ser rentable)* turnround **(c)** *(inversión en un nuevo proyecto)* pump priming

---

las medidas de reactivación, choque o liberalización del Gobierno suscitan una duda razonable y de inesquivable gravedad

El País

readmisión *nf* reinstatement

readmitir *vt* to reinstate; **el sindicato exigió que los trabajadores despedidos fueran readmitidos** = the union demanded that the sacked workers should be reinstated

reajustar *vt* to adjust *o* to readjust; **reajustar los precios para tener en cuenta la inflación** = to adjust prices to take account of inflation; **reajustar los precios para tener en cuenta el aumento del costo de materias primas** = to readjust prices to take account of the rise in the costs of raw materials

◊ **reajustarse** *vr* to readjust; **los precios de las acciones se reajustaron rápidamente ante la noticia de la devaluación** = share prices readjusted quickly to the news of the devaluation

◊ **reajuste** *nm* readjustment *o* adjustment; **reajuste de averías** = average adjustment; **reajuste impositivo** = tax adjustment; **un reajuste de precios** = a readjustment in pricing; **reajuste de precios por aumento de costes** = adjustment of prices to take account of rising costs; **hacer un reajuste de salarios** = to make an adjustment to salaries; **después de la devaluación hubo un periodo de reajuste de los tipos de cambio** = after the devaluation there was a period of readjustment in the exchange rates

real 1 *adj* **(a)** *(verdadero, efectivo)* real *o* actual; **¿cuál es el coste real por unidad?** = what is the actual cost per unit?; **ingreso real** *o* **salarios reales** = real income *o* real wages; **en términos reales** = in real terms; **los salarios han subido un 3% pero con una inflación del 5% supone un deterioro en términos reales** = wages have gone up by 3% but with inflation running at 5% that is a fall in real terms **(b)** *(informática)* **tiempo real (de ordenador)** = real time; **sistema de ordenador a tiempo real** = real-time system **2** *nm (moneda brasileña)* Brazilian rial

◊ **realmente** *adv* really; **estos artículos son realmente baratos** = these goods are really cheap

realidad *nf* reality *o* fact; **en realidad** = in fact *o* really *o* in real terms; **el presidente culpó al director financiero de las pérdidas sufridas cuando en realidad era él el responsable** = the chairman blamed the finance director for the loss when in fact he was responsible for it himself; **la tienda es en realidad una librería, aunque también vende algunos discos** = the shop is really a bookshop, though it does carry some records

realizable *adj* realizable; **activo realizable** = current assets *o* liquid assets

realización *nf* **(a)** realization *o* fulfilment *o* implementation; **el plan avanzó hacia su realización cuando se firmaron los contratos** = the plan moved a stage nearer realization when the contracts were signed; **realización de un proyecto** = the realization of a project **(b) realización de beneficios** = realization of assets *o* profit-taking

realizar *vt* **(a)** *(activos o bienes)* to realize (assets) **(b)** *(llevar a cabo)* to carry out *o* to effect; **realizar un acuerdo entre dos partes** = to effect a settlement between two parties; **realizar un pago** = to make a payment; **realizar un proyecto** *o* **un plan** = to carry out a project *o* a plan

reanimar *vt* to revive; **el gobierno está introduciendo medidas para reanimar el comercio** = the government is introducing measures to revive trade

reanudación *nf* resumption; **esperamos una pronta reanudación de las negociaciones** = we expect an early resumption of negotiations

reanudar *vt* to resume *o* to start again; **ahora que la huelga ha terminado esperamos reanudar el servicio normal lo antes posible** = now that the strike is over we hope to resume normal service as soon as possible

reapertura *nf* reopening; **la reapertura del almacén después de las reformas** = the reopening of the store after refitting

reasegurador, -ra *n* reinsurer

reasegurar *vt* to reinsure *o* to underwrite *o* to lay off risks

◊ **reaseguro** *nm* reinsurance; **contrato** *o* **póliza de reaseguro** = reinsurance policy

reasignación *nf* reassignment

reasignar *vt* to reassign

rebaja *nf* **(a)** *(reducción)* reduction *o* cut; **rebaja de precios** = price cuts *o* cuts in prices; **la rebaja de los precios ha aumentado el volumen de ventas** = reduced prices have increased sales; **porcentaje de rebaja** = mark-down *o* rebate; **hemos aplicado una rebaja del 30% para fijar el precio de venta** = we have used a 30% mark-down to fix the sale price; **ciertos artículos tienen una rebaja del 25%** = selected items are reduced by 25% **(b)** *(oferta de ocasión)* bargain offer; **oferta de la semana: 30% de rebaja en todas las alfombras** = this week's bargain offer - 30% off all carpet prices

◊ **rebajas** *nfpl* sale *o* sales; **la tienda ha organizado unas rebajas para liquidar las existencias antiguas** = the shop is having a sale to clear old stock; **hemos reducido todos los artículos en un 30% para las rebajas** = we have marked all prices down by 30% for the sale; **compré esto en las rebajas** *o* **en las rebajas de enero** = I bought this in the sales *o* at the sales *o* in the January sales; **rebajas**

de precios = price reductions *o* price cutting; **hacer rebajas drásticas de precios** *o* **de condiciones de crédito** = to slash prices *o* credit terms; **rebajas a mitad de precio** *o* **al 50%** = half-price sale; **tienda de rebajas** = discount store; *(US)* discount house

◊ **rebajado, -da 1** *adj* reduced; **artículos rebajados** = knockdown goods; **precio rebajado** = discounted price; **el precio rebajado es el 50% del precio normal** = the sale price is 50% of the normal price **2** *pp de* REBAJAR

rebajar *vt* to reduce *o* to cut (prices) *o* to mark down; **rebajar un precio** = to reduce a price *o* to mark down a price; **hemos rebajado los precios de todos los modelos** = we are cutting prices on all our models; **rebajó el precio a la mitad** = he took 50% off the price; **rebajó el precio en un 10% por pago al contado** = he knocked 10% off the price for cash; **esta línea ha sido rebajada a 2.499 ptas.** = this range has been marked down to 2,499 pesetas; **el precio de las alfombras ha sido rebajado de 10.000 a 5.000 ptas.** = carpets are reduced from 10,000 to 5,000 pesetas

rebasar *vt* to overrun *o* to exceed *o* to surpass; **la compañía rebasó el plazo establecido para terminar la fábrica** = the company overran the time limit set to complete the factory; **he rebasado el límite de mi crédito** = I have gone over my credit limit

rebotar *vi* to rebound

recadero *o* **recadista** *nm* messenger *o* deliveryman; **recadista de oficina** = office messenger

◊ **recado** *nm* message; **le dejaré un recado a su secretaria** = I will leave a message with his secretary; **¿puede darle al director un recado de su esposa?** = can you give the director a message from his wife?

recalentamiento *nm* overheating

menos impuestos condujeron a un abultado déficit público y a un recalentamiento de la economía
España Económica

recambio *nm* **(a)** *(repuesto)* spare; **piezas de recambio** = spare parts; **compró una gran cantidad de piezas de recambio** = he bought a large quantity of spare parts **(b)** *(cartucho)* cartridge

recargar *vt* to increase prices *o* to mark up

◊ **recargo** *nm* surcharge *o* mark-up; **recargo a la importación** = import surcharge; **en junio aplicamos un recargo del 10% a todos los precios** = we put into effect a 10% price increase in June; **no hay recargo por la calefacción** = there is no extra charge for heating

recaudación *nf* collection; **recaudación de impuestos** = tax collection *o* collection of tax; **recaudación tributaria** = tax revenue; **oficina de recaudación** = tax office

las medidas fiscales adoptadas por el Ejecutivo suponen, a priori, un descenso de la recaudación que no va a ayudar a reducir el déficit público
El País

◊ **recaudado, -da 1** *adj* collected; **no recaudado** = uncollected; **impuestos no recaudados** = uncollected taxes **2** *pp de* RECAUDAR

◊ **recaudador, -ra** *n* collector; **recaudador de impuestos** = collector of taxes *o* tax collector *o* excise officer *o* exciseman

recaudar *vt* **(a)** *(impuesto)* to collect (a tax) **(b)** *(deuda)* to recover (a debt)

recaudo *nm* precaution; **estar a buen recaudo** = to be in safekeeping

recepción *nf* **(a)** *(acogida)* reception; **ofrecimos una recepción de categoría a nuestros visitantes** = we laid on VIP treatment for our visitors *o* we gave our visitors a VIP reception **(b)** *(empresa)* reception *o* reception desk; **recepción de mercancías** = receiving *o* reception (of goods); **oficina de recepción** = receiving office; **servicio de recepción** = receiving department **(c)** *(hotel)* reception; *(aeropuerto)* check-in; **mostrador de recepción** = reception desk *o* check-in counter

◊ **recepcionista** *nmf* **(a)** *(hotel)* receptionist; **le dio 500 ptas. de propina al** *o* **a la recepcionista** = he tipped the receptionist 500 pesetas **(b)** *(mercancías)* receiving clerk

◊ **receptor, -ra** *n* **(a)** *(persona)* recipient **(b)** *(aparato)* receiver

> tradicionalmente, el hotelero ha visto llegar a sus clientes, desde la atalaya del mostrador de recepción, atraídos la mayoría de las veces por decisión de los touroperadores o los agentes de viaje
> **Tiempo**

recesión *nf* recession; **la recesión ha dejado sin trabajo a millones de personas** *o* **ha reducido los beneficios de muchas compañías** = the recession has put millions out of work *o* has reduced profits in many companies; **varias empresas han cerrado sus fábricas debido a la recesión** = several firms have closed factories because of the recession; **debemos mantener el volumen de ventas a pesar de la recesión** = we must keep up the turnover in spite of the recession

> el peligro estriba en hacer que el sector real pague la contención inflacionaria, es decir que haya una recesión
> **España Económica**

receso *nm* **(a)** *(descanso)* break **(b) receso económico** = recession *o* downturn in the economy

rechazar *vt* to defeat *o* to reject *o* to turn down *o* to refuse *o* to disallow; **rechazar rotundamente** = to refuse totally *o* to give a flat refusal; **la propuesta fue rechazada por 10 votos a favor y 23 en contra** = the proposal was defeated by 23 votes to 10; **el sindicato rechazó las propuestas de la dirección** = the union rejected the management's proposals; **la compañía rechazó la oferta de adquisición** = the company rejected the takeover bid; **hemos recibido varias propuestas pero las hemos rechazado todas** = we have been approached several times but have turned down all offers; **el banco rechazó su solicitud de préstamo** = the bank turned down their request for a loan; **el comité de planificación rechazó la propuesta** = the proposal was thrown out by the planning committee; **el consejo de**

administración rechazó el proyecto de contrato propuesto por el sindicato = the board threw out the draft contract submitted by the union

> El Gobierno rechazó la pretensión de su ministro de Economía de eliminar la autorización administrativa previa en los expedientes de regulación de empleo
> **El País**

rechazo *nm* rejection *o* refusal; **rechazo global** = total refusal *o* blanket refusal

recibir *vt* **(a)** *(cobrar)* to get *o* to receive; **'recibí'** = 'received with thanks'; **poner el sello de 'recibí' en una factura** = to stamp an invoice 'Paid'; **esta mañana hemos recibido una carta del abogado** = we got a letter from the solicitor this morning; **recibimos el pago hace diez días** = we received the payment ten days ago; **recibimos la mercancía en nuestro almacén el día 25** = we took delivery of the stock into our warehouse on the 25th; **las mercancías se entregarán en el plazo de treinta días después de haber recibido el pedido** = goods will be supplied within thirty days of receipt of order; **las mercancías se recibieron en buen estado** = the goods were received in good condition; **al recibir la notificación, la compañía presentó una apelación** = on receipt of the notification, the company lodged an appeal **(b) recibir a clientes** = to entertain clients **(c)** *(teléfono)* to take; **recibir una llamada** = to take a call

recibo *nm* **(a)** *(acto de recibir)* receipt; **acusar recibo de una carta** = to acknowledge receipt of a letter; **acusamos recibo de su carta del día 15** = we acknowledge receipt of your letter of the 15th; **las facturas son pagaderas en el plazo de treinta días a partir de la fecha de recibo** = invoices are payable within thirty days of receipt **(b)** *(comprobante)* receipt *o* purchase slip *o* sales slip *o* sales receipt; **libro de recibos** = receipt book *o* book of receipts; **recibo de aduana** = customs receipt; **recibo del alquiler** = rent receipt; **recibo de compra** = receipt for items purchased; **los artículos pueden cambiarse solamente si se presenta el recibo** = goods can be exchanged only on production of a sales slip; **en caso de que quiera cambiar los artículos comprados se ruega presentar el recibo** = please produce your receipt if you want to exchange items; **recibo de depósito** = deposit slip *o* paying-in slip

reciclado, -da 1 *adj* recycled; **papel reciclado** = recycled paper; **el cartón está hecho de papel reciclado** = cardboard is made from recycled waste paper **2** *nm* recycling **3** *pp de* RECICLAR

reciclaje *nm* **(a)** *(papel, etc.)* recycling **(b)** *(personal)* retraining *o* training; **reciclaje profesional** = professional retraining; **curso de reciclaje** = refresher course; **la tienda está cerrada por reciclaje del personal** = the shop is closed for staff training

reciclar *vt* **(a)** *(papel)* to recycle **(b)** *(personal)* to retrain

recién *adv* recently; **recién salido de fábrica** = brand new

◊ **reciente** *adj* recent; **la reciente adquisición por parte de la compañía de una cadena de zapaterías** = the company's recent acquisition of a chain of shoe shops; **su reciente nombramiento al consejo de administración** = his recent appointment to the board; **más reciente** = latest

◊ **recientemente** *adv* recently; **decidieron recientemente cerrar la sucursal de Bilbao** = they recently decided to close the branch office in Bilbao

recinto *nm* site; **recinto ferial** *o* **recinto de la exposición** = exhibition site

> el Salón Náutico Internacional de Barcelona se celebrará entre el 30 de noviembre y 8 de diciembre en el recinto ferial de Montjuich
>
> **Tiempo**

recipiente *nm* container; **el recipiente se rompió durante el transporte** = the container burst during shipping

reciprocidad *nf* reciprocity

recíproco, -ca *adj* reciprocal; **acuerdo recíproco** = reciprocal agreement; **comercio recíproco** = reciprocal trade; **contrato recíproco** = reciprocal contract; **tenencia recíproca de acciones** = reciprocal holdings

reclamación *nf* **(a)** *(de pago)* claim *o* demand *o* request for payment; **liquidar** *o* **pagar una reclamación** = to settle a claim; **la compañía de seguros rehusó pagar su reclamación de daños causados por la tormenta** = the insurance company refused to settle his claim for storm damage **(b)** *(queja)* complaint; **hemos tomado nota de su reclamación** = your complaint has been noted; **escribió una carta de reclamación inmediatamente** = he wrote an immediate letter of complaint; **envió su carta de reclamación al director gerente** = she sent her letter of complaint to the managing director; **nuestras reclamaciones tuvieron muy poca acogida** = we got very little response to our complaints; **reclamación recíproca por daños y perjuicios** = counter-claim; **presentar una reclamación** = to counter-claim

> la UCE contabilizó en su departamento de vivienda la mayor cantidad de reclamaciones respecto al total que se presentaron a lo largo de todo el pasado año
>
> **España Económica**

reclamado, -da 1 *adj* claimed; **no reclamado** = unclaimed; **equipaje no reclamado** = unclaimed baggage; **los objetos no reclamados se venderán** *o* **el equipaje no reclamado se venderá a los seis meses en una subasta** = unclaimed property *o* unclaimed baggage will be sold by auction after six months **2** *pp de* RECLAMAR

reclamar *vt* **(a)** *(propiedad)* to claim *o* to reclaim *o* to put in a claim; **reclama la propiedad de la casa** = he is claiming possession of the house; **nadie reclamó el paraguas aparecido en mi oficina** = no one claimed the umbrella found in my office; **sin reclamar** = unclaimed **(b)** *(exigir)* to ask for *o* to demand; **reclamamos una subida salarial** = we are asking for a pay rise

> los ciudadanos podrán reclamar que no se les envíe publicidad por correo a casa
>
> **El País**

reclamo *nm* call *o* advertisement *o* slogan;

reclamo de cartón publicitario = showcard; **artículo de reclamo** = loss-leader; **utilizamos estas películas baratas como artículos de reclamo** = we use these cheap films as a loss-leader

> y, por si los problemas fueran pocos, los industriales deben hacer frente a las marcas blancas importadas de terceros países y a una nueva distribución con los precios a la baja como principal reclamo, el descuento duro
>
> **El País**

reclasificar *vt* to reclassify; **su puesto de trabajo ha sido reclasificado dentro de la categoría de gerente principal** = his job has been upgraded to senior manager level

reclutamiento *nm* recruitment *o* recruiting

reclutar *vt* to recruit; **reclutar personal** = to recruit new staff

recobrar *vt* to recover *o* to get back; **recobrar las fuerzas** = to regain strength

recobro *nm* repossession; **el recobro de la propiedad ha aumentado dada la dificultad que la gente tiene en pagar las hipotecas** = repossessions are increasing as people find it difficult to meet mortgage repayments

recoger *vt* **(a)** *(reunir)* to gather; **recogió sus papeles antes de que empezara la reunión** = he gathered his papers together before the meeting started **(b)** *(ir a buscar)* to collect; **tenemos que recoger la mercancía del almacén** = we have to collect the stock from the warehouse; **¿puede Vd. recoger mis cartas del servicio de mecanografía?** = can you collect my letters from the typing pool?; **la mercancía está en el almacén esperando ser recogida** = the stock is in the warehouse awaiting collection *o* waiting to be collected; **se recogen las cartas dos veces al día** = letters are collected twice a day; **recoger viajeros** = to pick up passengers

◊ **recogerse** *vr* to withdraw *o* to retire

recogida *nf* **(a)** *(mercancías)* collection; **servicio de recogida y reparto** = pickup and delivery service **(b)** *(cosecha)* harvest

recomendación *nf* recommendation *o* reference; **le nombramos por recomendación de su antiguo jefe** = we appointed him on the recommendation of his former employer; **recomendación no solicitada** = unsolicited testimonial; **adjuntó cartas de recomendación de sus dos jefes anteriores** = he enclosed letters of reference from his two previous employers

recomendado, -da 1 *adj* recommended; **precio recomendado por el fabricante para la venta al por menor** = manufacturer's recommended price (MRP) *o* recommended retail price (RRP); **'para todas las máquinas de escribir - descuento del 20% sobre el precio recomendado'** = 'all typewriters - 20% off MRP' **2** *pp de* RECOMENDAR

recomendar *vt* **(a)** *(sugerir)* to recommend *o* to suggest; **el asesor de inversiones recomendó comprar acciones de compañías aeronáuticas** = the investment adviser recommended buying shares in aircraft companies; **no recomendamos las acciones de los bancos como una inversión segura** = we do not recommend bank shares as a safe investment; **el consejo de administración recomendó repartir un dividendo de 200 ptas. por acción** = the board meeting recommended a dividend of 200 pesetas a share **(b)** *(dar informes)* to recommend; **recomendó una zapatería en la Calle Mayor** = he recommended a shoe shop in the Calle Mayor; **yo nunca recomendaría a la señorita García para el trabajo** = I certainly would not recommend Miss García for the job; **¿puedes recomendar un buen hotel en Amsterdam?** = can you recommend a good hotel in Amsterdam?

recompensa *nf* reward *o* payoff

reconciliación *nf* reconciliation; **estado de reconciliación** = reconciliation statement

reconocer *vt* **(a)** *(distinguir)* to recognize; **reconocí su voz antes de que dijera quién era** = I recognized his voice before he said who he was **(b)** *(aceptar)* **reconocer una firma** = to honour a signature; **reconocer a un sindicato** = to recognize a union *o* to grant a trade union recognition; **aunque todo el personal se había afiliado al sindicato, la patronal se negó a reconocerlo** = although all the staff had joined the union, the management refused to recognize it

reconocimiento *nm* **(a)** *(agradecimiento)* appreciation *o* recognition; **le aumentaron el sueldo en reconocimiento de su excelente trabajo** = he was given a rise in appreciation of his excellent work **(b)** *(aceptación)* **reconocimiento de un sindicato** = union recognition **(c)** *(inspección)* **reconocimiento médico** = medical examination *o* check-up **(d)** **reconocimiento de deuda** = acknowledgement of a debt; **reconocimiento de marca** = brand recognition

reconstrucción *nf* reconstruction; **la reconstrucción económica de una zona después de una catástrofe** = the economic reconstruction of an area after a disaster

reconvención *nf* counter-claim

reconvenir *vt* *(jurídico)* to counter-claim

reconversión *nf* reconversion; **reconversión industrial** = industrial rationalization; **reconversión profesional** = industrial retraining

> la situación cambiante de la economía, las reconversiones sectoriales o la marcha de la propia empresa, son circunstancias por las que ningún profesional o ejecutivo puede estar seguro de que permanecerá en la compañía por tiempo indeterminado
> **El País**

recopilar *vt* to gather; **ha estado recopilando información de varias fuentes sobre los controles a la importación** = she has been gathering information on import controls from various sources

récord *o* **record** 1 *adj* record-breaking; **estamos orgullosos de nuestros beneficios récord** = we are proud of our record-breaking profits; **el año pasado fue un año récord para la compañía** = last year was a record year for the company 2 *nm* **(a)** high point; **las cotizaciones de las acciones han bajado el 10% desde el récord registrado el 2 de enero** =

share prices have dropped by 10% since the high of January 2nd **(b)** record; **récord de ventas** *o* **récord de pérdidas** *o* **récord de ganancias** = record sales *o* record losses *o* record profits; **las ventas en 1996 igualaron el récord de 1992** = sales for 1996 equalled the record of 1992; **nuestro mejor vendedor ha establecido un nuevo récord de ventas por visita** = our top salesman has set a new record for sales per call; **hemos batido nuestro récord de junio** = we broke our record for June

> el déficit público de más de cinco por ciento del Producto Interior Bruto (PIB) es sensiblemente más alto que el 'récord' conseguido en el año anterior
> **Actualidad Económica**

> el TGV ha cambiado el paisaje francés, ha aumentado el tráfico ferroviario y ha batido tres veces el récord de velocidad
> **Cambio 16**

recordar *vt* **(a)** *(algo a alguien)* to remind; **tengo que recordar a mi secretaria que haga una reserva en el vuelo a Nueva York** = I must remind my secretary to book the flight for New York; **recordó al presidente que la reunión tenía que terminar a las 6.30** = he reminded the chairman that the meeting had to finish at 6.30 **(b)** *(acordarse)* to remember; **he perdido el hilo y no puedo recordar hasta dónde había archivado** = I have lost my place and cannot remember where I have reached in my filing; **no recuerdo la marca de la fotocopiadora que nos dijo era tan buena** = I cannot remember the make of photocopier which he said was so good; **¿recuerdas el nombre del director gerente de Pereda S.A.?** = do you remember the name of the Managing Director of Pereda S.A.?

◊ **recordatorio** *nm* reminder; **enviar a alguien un recordatorio** = to send someone a reminder

recorrer *vt* to go round; **le resulta difícil recorrer toda su región en una semana** = he finds it difficult to cover all his area in a week; **los visitantes recorrieron la fábrica a pie** = the visitors walked round the factory

recorrido *nm* journey *o* distance travelled; **recorrido en kilómetros** = distance in kilometres; **vuelo de corto recorrido** = short-haul flight; **trenes de largo recorrido** = long distance trains *o* inter-city trains

recortar *vt* to axe; *o US* to ax *o* to cut *o* to reduce; **recortar gastos** = to cut *o* to axe expenditure; **la empresa ha recortado su producción debido a la caída de la demanda** = the company reduced output because of a fall in demand; **estamos recortando los márgenes para mantener los precios bajos** = we are cutting margins to hold our prices down; **advirtió a los accionistas que el dividendo podía ser recortado** = he warned the shareholders that the dividend might be cut

◊ **recorte** *nm* **(a)** *(reducción)* cut *o* cutback; **recorte de gastos** = reduction of expenditure; **recortes en los gastos del Estado** = cutbacks in government spending; **recortes presupuestarios** *o* **de presupuesto** = budget cuts; **recorte salarial** *o* **recortes de salario** = salary cut *o* cut in salary *o* cuts in salaries; **recibió un recorte salarial** *o* **aceptó un recorte de sueldo** = he took a cut in salary **(b)** *(prensa)* cuttings; **recortes** = press cuttings;

---

tenemos un archivo de recortes de prensa sobre los productos de nuestros rivales = we have a file of press cuttings on our rivals' products

> los recortes presupuestarios últimos y la congelación de algunos proyectos de obra pública previstos pueden suponer además la pérdida de cuantiosas ayudas de la Unión Europea
> **El País**

rectificación *nf* correction *o* rectification; **hizo algunas rectificaciones al texto de su discurso** = he made some corrections to the text of the speech

rectificar *vt* to amend *o* to correct *o* to rectify; **por favor rectifique su copia del contrato en consecuencia** = please amend your copy of the contract accordingly; **el departamento de facturación ha rectificado la factura** = the accounts department have corrected the invoice; **rectificar un asiento** = to rectify an entry

recuperable *adj* recoverable; **gastos no recuperables** = non-recoverable expenses

recuperación *nf* **(a)** *(mejora)* rally *o* recovery; **después de una breve recuperación, las acciones descendieron a sus precios más bajos** = after a brief rally shares fell back to a new low; **experimentar una recuperación** = to stage a recovery **(b)** *(rescate)* recovery *o* retrieval; **nuestro objetivo es la recuperación total del dinero invertido** = we are aiming for the complete recovery of the money invested; **iniciar un proceso para la recuperación de bienes** = to start an action for recovery of property **(c)** *(informática)* **recuperación de datos** = data retrieval *o* information retrieval; **sistema de recuperación** = retrieval system **(d)** *(volver a ser rentable)* turnround **(e)** *(bienes y propiedad)* repossession

> es de esperar una recuperación lenta y pausada que empiece a alegrar de nuevo a la parroquia inversora, aunque sin grandes alardes, por lo menos hasta bien entrado el próximo ejercicio
> **Tiempo**

> el mercado americano vuelve a evitar una recuperación, al menos técnica, de nuestra Bolsa, provocando que la desconfianza inversora prosiga
> **Tiempo**

recuperar *vt* **(a)** *(rescatar)* to recover *o* to get back *o* to retrieve; **recuperé el dinero después de quejarme al director** = I got my money back after I complained to the manager; **nunca recuperó su dinero** = he never recovered his money; **recuperar una pérdida** *o* **las pérdidas** = to recoup a loss *o* one's losses; **la inversión inicial nunca fue recuperada** = the initial investment was never recovered; **recuperó su inversión inicial en dos meses** = he got his initial investment back in two months; **la empresa está luchando para recuperar su cuota de mercado** = the company is fighting to regain its market share; **iniciar un proceso judicial para recuperar unos bienes** = to start a court action to recover property; **no podemos recuperar nuestras cifras de ventas del mes pasado dado que toda la información se borró accidentalmente del ordenador** = all of the information was accidentally wiped off the computer so we cannot retrieve our sales figures for

the last month **(b)** **recuperar la rentabilidad de una empresa** = to turn a company round

◇ **recuperarse** *vr* to recover *o* to pick up *o* to rally; **el mercado no se ha recuperado de la subida de los precios del petróleo** = the market has not recovered from the rise in oil prices; **la industria se está recuperando después de la recesión** = industry is reviving after the recession; **las acciones se recuperaron en la Bolsa al anunciarse los últimos resultados del gobierno** = shares rallied *o* staged a rally on the Stock Exchange on the news of the latest government figures; **el negocio** *o* **el comercio se está recuperando** = business *o* trade is picking up

recurrir *vi* **(a)** **recurrir a los tribunales** = to appeal **(b)** to resort to; *(echar mano de)* to fall back on; **recurrir a alguien** = to appeal to *o* to turn to someone

recurso *nm* **(a)** *(apelación)* appeal; **recurso de arbitraje** = appeal to arbitration **(b)** **recursos** = resources *o* means; **recursos económicos** *o* **recursos financieros** = financial resources; **los recursos financieros de la compañía no son lo suficientemente fuertes como para soportar el coste del programa de investigación** = the company's financial resources are not strong enough to support the cost of the research programme; **recursos minerales** = mineral resources; **recursos naturales** = natural resources; **el país es rico en recursos naturales** = the country is rich in natural resources; **buscamos un paraje con grandes recursos de agua** = we are looking for a site with good water resources; **recursos propios** = private means; **la empresa tiene recursos para lanzar el nuevo producto** = the company has the means to launch the new product; **nuestros recursos son más que suficientes para pagar el coste del nuevo proyecto** = the cost of the new project is easily within our resources; **aplicaremos todos los recursos que nos ofrece la ley para recuperar la posesión de nuestra propiedad** = we will apply the full power of the law to get possession of our property again **(c)** *(personal)* **recursos humanos** = human resources

> su nivel de endeudamiento con respecto a sus recursos propios es muy conservador, y tiene una amplia esfera de expansión
> **España Económica**

> hay abundancia de materias primas, pero fundamentalmente están inexplotadas por falta de recursos
> **España Económica**

> el volumen de recursos generados, agregación de beneficios y de los diferentes importes destinados a amortizaciones y saneamientos, se sitúa por encima de los 20.000 millones de pesetas
> **Actualidad Económica**

> el director de recursos humanos, antes jefe de personal, sigue ejerciendo su función como un burócrata
> **El País**

red *nf* network; **una red de distribuidores** *o* **una red de distribución** = a network of distributors *o* a distribution network; **red de ordenadores** = computer network; **nos instalaron una nueva red**

telefónica la semana pasada = we had a new phone system installed last week

> el nuevo equipo puede ser utilizado tanto como sistema personal o como estación de trabajo conectada a una red
>
> **Datamation**

> hoy su tasa de rentabilidad es de un 15% y las inversiones, como la de la red TGV-Atlántico que costó 18.000 millones de francos, están a punto de ser amortizadas antes de lo previsto
>
> **Cambio 16**

> nos sentimos particularmente satisfechos del desarrollo de los trabajos relativos a la integración operativa de nuestra amplia red de centros y oficinas
>
> **Actualidad Económica**

redacción *nf* (a) *(documento)* writing *o* drafting (b) *(equipo de redactores)* editorial office *o* editorial staff; **consejo de redacción** = editorial board; **jefe de redacción** = editor (c) *(texto)* wording; **la redacción de los términos de un contrato** = the wording of a contract

redactar *vt* (a) *(escribir)* to draw up *o* to put in writing; **redactar un contrato** *o* **un convenio** = to draw up a contract *o* an agreement; **contrato redactado con los requisitos debidos** = contract drawn up in due form; **redactar los estatutos de una asociación** *o* **compañía** = to draw up a company's articles of association; **redactar actas** = to take the minutes (of a meeting) (b) *(preparar)* to draft; **redactar una carta** *o* **un contrato** = to draft a letter *o* contract

◇ **redactor, -ra** *n* (a) *(persona)* person who draws up (a document) *o* drafter; **la redactora del documento** = the person who drafted the document *o* the drafter of the document (b) *(prensa)* **redactor jefe** = editor; **el redactor jefe de la sección financiera** = the editor of the financial section; *GB* the City editor

redimir *vt* to pay off *o* to redeem; **redimir una hipoteca** = to pay off a mortgage

redistribuir *vt* to redistribute; **el gobierno pretende redistribuir la riqueza a través de impuestos a los ricos y subsidios a los pobres** = the government aims to redistribute wealth by taxing the rich and giving grants to the poor; **los pedidos han sido redistribuidos entre las fábricas de la compañía** = the orders have been redistributed among the company's factories

rédito *nm* interest

redondear *vt* to round off; **redondear por defecto** = to round down; **redondear por exceso** = to round up; **redondear las cifras por exceso** = to round up the figures

◇ **redondo, -da** *adj* round; **en números redondos** = in round figures; **tienen una plantilla de 2.500 empleados en números redondos** = they have a workforce of 2,500 in round figures; **un negocio redondo** = a successful operation

reducción *nf* reduction *o* cutback *o* cut *o* shrinkage *o* cutting *o* decrease; **reducción de costes** = cost-cutting; **hemos despedido a tres secretarias dentro de nuestro plan de reducción de costes** =

we have made three secretaries redundant as part of our cost-cutting programme; **reducción de la demanda** = reduction in demand; **reducción de empleos** = job cuts; **reducción de gastos** = reduction in expenditure; **a la compañía le aguarda un periodo de reducción de gastos** = the company is in for a period of retrenchment; **reducción general de los presupuestos** = sweeping cuts in budget; **reducción de los impuestos** = tax reductions; **la reducción de la oferta de dinero trae como consecuencia la disminución de la demanda de bienes de consumo** = reducing the money supply has the effect of depressing demand for consumer goods; **reducción de plantilla** = downsizing; **reducción de precios** = lowering of prices; **reducción de presupuesto** = budget cuts; **esperamos conseguir unos precios bajos sin reducir la calidad** = we hope to achieve low prices with no lowering of quality; **una reducción de la expansión de la compañía** = a slowdown in the company's expansion; **reducción de un tipo impositivo** = reduction in tax *o* tax abatement

reducido, -da 1 *adj* (a) *(rebajado)* reduced; **los precios han bajado como consecuencia de una demanda reducida de los artículos** = prices have fallen due to a reduced demand for the goods (b) *(matemáticas)* **reducido a tres decimales** = correct to three places of decimals **2** *pp de* REDUCIR

reducir *vt* to reduce *o* to cut *o* to bring down *o* to chop; **reducir la carga impositiva** = to lighten the tax burden; **reducir la demanda** = to damp down demand; **reducir las diferencias salariales** = to erode wage differentials; **reducir drásticamente** = to slash; **los precios han sido drásticamente reducidos en todos los departamentos** = prices have been slashed in all departments; **reducir gastos** = to reduce expenditure *o* to cut down on expenses *o* to retrench; **el gobierno está reduciendo los gastos de la seguridad social** = the government is cutting down on welfare expenditure; **reducir gradualmente** = to run down *o* to phase out; **reducir los impuestos** = to reduce taxes; **reducir las pérdidas** = to cut one's losses; **reducir un precio** = to reduce a price *o* to mark down; **los precios han sido reducidos en un 15%** = prices have been reduced by 15%; **reducir la plantilla** *o* **el personal** = to reduce staff; **la empresa se vió obligada a reducir la plantilla** = the company was forced to make job cuts *o* to cut staff; **reducir el empleo** *o* **los puestos de trabajo** = to cut jobs; **reducir el plazo de un crédito** = to shorten credit terms; **reducir la producción** = to cut (back) production; **la dirección decidió reducir la tasa de producción** = the management decided to slow down production; **reducir a proporción** = to scale down; **hemos instalado un procesador de textos para reducir el papeleo** = we have installed a word-processor to cut down on paperwork; **nuestros márgenes se han reducido mucho** = our margins have been squeezed; **la política del gobierno es reducir la inflación al 5%** = the government's policy is to reduce inflation to 5%; **la inflación sigue siendo alta a pesar de los esfuerzos del gobierno por reducirla** = inflation has stayed high in spite of the government's efforts to bring it down

◇ **reducirse** *vr* to diminish *o* to fall; **dejar que las existencias se reduzcan gradualmente** = to let stocks run down; **la inflación se está reduciendo** = inflation is slowing down

el aumento del desempleo ha echado por tierra en un sólo año los avances para reducir el paro logrados en los cinco ejercios precedentes

El País

redundante *adj* redundant *o* more than is needed

reedición *nf* reprint *o* reissue

reeditar *vt* to reprint *o* to reissue; **la empresa reeditó su catálogo con una nueva lista de precios** = the company reissued its catalogue with a new price list

reelección *nf* re-election; **la reelección del presidente saliente está asegurada** = the outgoing chairman is certain to be re-elected; **tiene derecho a presentarse a reelección** = she is eligible to stand for re-election; **dos directores salientes se presentan a reelección** = two retiring directors offer themselves for re-election; **la reelección del presidente es anticonstitucional** *o* **antiestatutaria** = the reelection of the chairman is unconstitutional

reelegir *vt* to re-elect; **fue reelegido presidente** = he was re-elected chairman

reembolsable *adj* refundable *o* repayable; **depósito reembolsable** = refundable deposit; **gastos reembolsables** = out-of-pocket expenses; **un préstamo reembolsable en diez años** = loan which is repayable over ten years

reembolsar *vt* **(a)** *(préstamo, deuda)* to pay back *o* to repay; **reembolsar una deuda** = to repay money owed; **la compañía tuvo que recortar los gastos para reembolsar sus deudas** = the company had to cut back on expenditure in order to repay its debts; **reembolsar un préstamo** = to pay off a loan; **pidieron más tiempo para reembolsar el préstamo** = they asked for more time to repay the loan; **me reembolsó íntegramente** = he repaid me in full **(b)** *(gastos)* to reimburse *o* to pay back; **reembolsarle los gastos a alguien** = to pay back someone's expenses *o* to reimburse someone his expenses; **se le reembolsarán sus gastos** *o* **sus gastos serán reembolsados** = you will be reimbursed for your expenses *o* your expenses will be reimbursed; **reembolsar los gastos de correo** = to refund the cost of postage **(c)** *(reclamación)* to refund; **en caso de que el producto no resulte satisfactorio se reembolsará el importe íntegro** = all money will be refunded if the goods are not satisfactory; **le reembolsaron el importe total cuando se quejó del servicio** = he got a full refund when he complained about the service

◊ **reembolsarse** *vr* to take back *o* to claw back; **del millón asignado al proyecto, el Estado se reembolsó 100.000 ptas. en impuestos** = of the 1m allocated to the project, the government clawed back 100,000 pesetas in taxes

reembolso *nm* **(a)** *(pago)* pay; **entrega contra reembolso** = cash on delivery (c.o.d.); **cláusula de reembolso** = payback clause; **periodo de reembolso** = payback period **(b)** *(devolución)* refund *o* repayment *o* clawback *o* rebate; **exigir el reembolso** = to ask for a refund; **reembolso final** = final discharge; **reembolsos fiscales** = tax refunds;

reembolso de gastos = reimbursement of expenses; **reembolso anticipado de un préstamo** = early repayment of a loan *o* repayment of a loan before it is due; **reembolso total** = full refund *o* refund in full

reemplazar *vt* to replace; **el Sr. Prats reemplazará al Sr. Zubiri en el cargo de presidente** = Sr Prats will replace Sr Zubiri as chairman; **las piezas viejas deben reemplazarse con nuevas** = old parts need to be replaced with new ones

◊ **reemplazo** *nm* replacement

reempleo *nm* re-employment

reestructuración *nf* restructuring; **la reestructuración de la compañía** = the restructuring of the company

reestructurar *vt* **(a)** *(empresa)* to restructure **(b)** *(crédito)* to reschedule; **algunos países del Tercer Mundo pidieron que se les reestructuraran los préstamos** = some Third World countries asked for their loans to be rescheduled

reexaminar *vt* to re-examine

reexportación *nf* re-export; **comercio de reexportación** = re-export trade; **el valor de las reexportaciones ha subido** = the value of re-exports has increased

reexportar *vt* to re-export; **importamos lana para reexportarla** = we import wool for re-export

ref. *abrev de* REFERENCIA re; **ref.: orden del día de la junta anual** = re: the agenda for the AGM

referencia *nf* **(a)** *(relación)* reference; **con referencia a** = with reference to *o* re; **con referencia a su carta** *o* **a su petición del 25 de mayo** = with reference to your letter *o* to your inquiry of May 25th; **con referencia a nuestra carta del 21** = further to our letter of the 21st; **nuestra referencia (n/ref.)** = our reference *o* our ref.; **nuestra referencia: PC/MS 1234** = our reference: PC/MS 1234; **su referencia (s/ref.)** = your reference *o* your ref.; **sírvanse indicar esta referencia en su correspondencia** = please quote this reference in all correspondence **(b)** *(recomendación)* reference; **dar el nombre de alguien que pueda proporcionar una referencia** = to give someone's name as a reference *o* as a referee; **dio el nombre de su jefe como referencia** = she gave the name of her boss as a referee; **dar referencias a alguien** = to write someone a reference *o* to give someone a reference; **puedes dar mi nombre como referencia, si quieres** = please use me as a reference if you wish; **pedir a los solicitantes que proporcionen referencias** = to ask applicants to supply references; **al presentar las solicitudes, se ruega indicar los nombres de tres personas que puedan proporcionar referencias** = when applying please give the names of three referees; **pedirle a una empresa referencias comerciales** *o* **referencias bancarias** = to ask a company for trade references *o* for bank references

referente *adj* referente a = in relation to *o* in connection with *o* further to *o* with regard to; **llenó el cuestionario referente a la utilización del ordenador** = he filled in a questionnaire concerning computer utilization

referir *vt* to report *o* to refer

◊ **referirse** *vr* to refer; **referirse a** = to concern *o* to refer to; **nos referimos a su estimación del 26 de mayo** = we refer to your estimate of May 26th; **me refiero a su factura número 1234** = I refer to your invoice numbered 1234; **esta cláusula se refiere solamente a las transacciones fuera de la UE** = this clause applies only to deals outside the EU

refinanciación *nf* refinancing of a loan

refinanciar *vt* to refinance

reflación *nf* reflation

reflacionar *vt* to reflate; **reflacionar la economía** = to reflate the economy; **los esfuerzos del gobierno para reflacionar la economía no tuvieron éxito** = the government's attempts to reflate the economy were not successful

reflexión *nf* reflection; *(en un contrato de venta a plazos)* **periodo de reflexión** = cooling off period

reforma *nf* **(a)** *(renovación)* reform; **reforma agraria** = agricultural reform *o* land reform; **reforma fiscal** = tax reform **(b)** *(reparación)* refit; **reformas** = refitting; **la reapertura de una tienda después de reformas** = the reopening of a store after a refit

reformar *vt* **(a)** *(renovar)* to reform *o* to change *o* to improve **(b)** *(reparar)* to refit

reforzar *vt* to tighten *o* to reinforce; **el departamento de contabilidad está reforzando su control sobre los presupuestos departamentales** = the accounts department is tightening its control over departmental budgets

```
los datos del mes de junio refuerzan la
tendencia a la expansión de los depósitos
de las entidades financieras
                                      Mercado
```

refrendar *vt* to countersign; **todos los cheques tienen que estar refrendados por el director financiero** = all cheques have to be countersigned by the finance director; **el director de ventas refrenda todos mis pedidos** = the sales director countersigns all my orders

refrendo *nm* counter-signature *o* endorsement

refugio *nm* haven *o* shelter; **refugio tributario** = tax shelter

regalar *vt* to give *o* to give away; **regalamos una calculadora de bolsillo por cada 10.000 ptas. de compra** = we are giving away a pocket calculator with each 10,000 pesetas of purchases; **la oficina le regaló un reloj cuando se jubiló** = the office gave him a clock when he retired; **cuando cumplió veinticinco años de servicio en la compañía le regalaron un reloj** = he was presented with a watch on completing twenty-five years' service in the company

regalía *nf* royalty

regalo *nm* **(a)** *(obsequio)* gift *o* present; **estas calculadoras son un buen regalo** = these calculators make good presents; **la oficina le hizo un regalo cuando se casó** = the office gave her a present when she got married; **vale** *o* **cupón de**

regalo = gift coupon *o* gift token *o* gift voucher; **le dimos un vale de regalo para su cumpleaños** = we gave her a gift token for her birthday; **un regalo no solicitado** = an unsolicited gift; **papel de regalo** *o* **de envolver regalos** = gift-wrapping paper; **envolver con papel de regalo** = to gift-wrap; **¿quiere que le envuelva el libro en papel de regalo?** = do you want this book gift-wrapped?; **tienda de regalos (b)** *(oferta)* free gift *o* giveaway; **se ofrece un regalo por valor de 2.000 ptas. a todo cliente que compre una lavadora** = there is a free gift worth 2,000 pesetas to any customer buying a washing machine

regatear *vt* to bargain *o* to haggle; **se pasaron dos horas regateando** = they spent two hours bargaining about *o* over the price; **tendrá que regatear con el vendedor si quiere conseguir una rebaja** = you will have to bargain with the dealer if you want a discount

◊ **regateo** *nm* haggling *o* bargaining *o* horse trading; **después de dos días de regateo se firmó el contrato** = after two days' haggling the contract was signed

régimen *nm* rule *o* system of rules; regime

```
el pasado 13 de diciembre se celebró una
asamblea general informativa en la que se
presentaron los estatutos sociales y el
reglamento del régimen interior de la
asociación
                                         Chip
```

región *nf* region *o* district; **región de desarrollo** = development zone *o* enterprise zone

◊ **regional** *adj* regional; **director regional** = district manager *o* area manager; **Fondo Europeo de Desarrollo Regional (FEDER)** = European Regional Development Fund (ERDF); **planificación regional** = regional planning

regir 1 *vt* to rule *o* to govern; **fluctuaciones en la ley de la oferta y la demanda rigen los cambios del mercado** = fluctuations in supply and demand control changes in the market **2** *vi (estar en vigor)* to be in force *o* to apply; **esta ley ya no rige** = this law is no longer in force; **las condiciones que rigen** = prevailing conditions; **los precios que rigen** = current prices

registrado, -da 1 *adj* registered; **no registrado** = unregistered; **marca registrada** = registered trademark; **ventas registradas** = book sales **2** *pp de* REGISTRAR

```
las ventas de los caldos de Rioja superan
en un 20% a las registradas en el mismo
periodo del ejercicio anterior
                                      El País
```

registrador, -ra *n* registrar

registrar *vt* **(a)** *(inscribir en un registro)* to register *o* to record; **registrar como propiedad literaria** = to copyright (a book); **sin registrar** = unregistered; **el ordenador registra todos los movimientos de las existencias** = all stock movements are logged by the computer; **la empresa ha registrado en otro año consecutivo un aumento de ventas** = the company has recorded another year of increased sales; **registrar una marca comercial** = to register a trademark;

registrar una propiedad = to register a property; **registrar una venta** = to register a sale **(b)** *(revisar)* to examine; **los funcionarios de aduanas quisieron registrar el interior del coche** = the customs officials asked to examine the inside of the car **(c) registrar un cambio** = to change; **registrar una mejoría** = to improve; **registrar una subida** = to increase *o* to go up; **se ha registrado un ligero aumento en el consumo** = consumption has increased slightly

◇ **registrarse** *vr* **(a)** *(hotel)* to register *o* to check in; **se registró a las 12.15** = he checked in at 12.15; **se registraron en el hotel con el apellido Gutiérrez** = they registered at the hotel under the name of Gutiérrez **(b)** *(aeropuerto)* to check in

registro *nm* **(a)** *(relación de datos)* register *o* record; **registro diario de entradas y salidas** = daybook; **registro diario de ventas** = sales journal *o* sales day book; **registro de compañías** = companies' register *o* register of companies; **registros contables** = accounting records; **registro de horas trabajadas** = time sheet; **el registro de Lloyd's** = Lloyd's register; **barco que está en condiciones óptimas según el registro Lloyd's** = ship which is A1 at Lloyd's; **registro de nóminas** = payroll ledger; **registro de obligacionistas** = debenture register *o* register of debentures; **registro de la propiedad** = land register; **registro de títulos** = register of debentures *o* debenture register; **anotar algo en un registro** = to enter something in a register; **inscribir en un registro** = to register *o* to record; **libro de registro** = register; **libro registro de accionistas** *o* **acciones** = register of shareholders *o* share register; **mantener actualizado un registro** = to keep a register up to date; **número de registro** = registration number; **Oficina del Registro Mercantil** = Companies Registration Office **(b)** *(asiento)* entry **(c)** *(acto)* registration *o* recording; **registro de una marca comercial** *o* **de una transacción de acciones** = registration of a trademark *o* of a share transaction; **oficina del registro civil** = registry office; **puerto de registro** = port of registry **(d)** *(inspección)* examination *o* inspection **(e)** **registro automático** = comptometer

regla *nf* **(a)** *(reglamento)* rule *o* regulation *o* order; **regla empírica** = rule of thumb; **en regla** = in order; **¿está toda la documentación en regla?** = is all the documentation in order?; **llevaba un pasaporte en regla** = he was carrying a valid passport; **por regla general** = as a rule; **por regla general no damos descuentos por encima del 20%** = as a rule, we do not give discounts over 20% **(b)** *(listón para trazar rayas)* ruler

reglamentación *nf* regulation; **reglamentación bancaria** = banking regulations; **reglamentación de salarios** = wage regulations

reglamentar *vt* to regulate

◇ **reglamentario, -ria** *adj* statutory *o* regulatory; **hay un periodo reglamentario de prueba de trece semanas** = there is a statutory period of probation of thirteen weeks; **poder reglamentario** = statutory power; **vacaciones reglamentarias** = statutory holidays; **seguir el conducto reglamentario** = to go through official channels

◇ **reglamento** *nm* **(a)** *(regla)* rules *o* regulations; **reglamento sobre incendios** = fire regulations; **reglamentos de un sindicato** = rulebook; **reglamento vigente** = regulations in force *o* current regulations; **el reglamento no permite fumar en la sala de ordenadores** = smoking is forbidden in the computer room *o* it is against the rules to smoke in the computer room **(b)** *(estatuto)* UK articles of association; US bylaws

el pasado 13 de diciembre se celebró una asamblea general informativa en la que se presentaron los estatutos sociales y el reglamento del régimen interior de la asociación
                                                              Chip

regresar *vi* to go back *o* to return

regresivo, -va *adj* regressive; **imposición regresiva** = regressive taxation; **impuesto regresivo** = regressive tax; **tarifas publicitarias regresivas** = graded advertising rates

regreso *nm* return; **viaje de regreso** = return journey *o* homeward journey

regulación *nf* regulation; **la regulación de las prácticas comerciales** = the regulation of trading practices; **fondo de regulación** = buffer stocks

algunos mercados no son perfectos, y es posible que hagan falta regulaciones y normas para alcanzar algunos de nuestros objetivos
                                                           Mercado

regulado, -da 1 *adj* regulated; **precio regulado por el gobierno** = government-regulated price **2** *pp de* REGULAR

regulador, -ra *adj* regulatory

regular 1 *adj* **(a)** *(normal o habitual)* regular *o* ordinary *o* standard; **vuelo regular** = scheduled flight; **partió para Helsinki en un vuelo regular** = he left for Helsinki on a scheduled flight; **el vuelo regular para Atenas sale a las 06.00** = the regular flight to Athens leaves at 06.00 **(b)** *(ordinario)* average *o* ordinary; **el resultado de la compañía ha sido sólo regular** = the company's performance has been only average **2** *vt* to regulate *o* to control; **los precios se regulan por la oferta y la demanda** = prices are regulated by supply and demand **3** *adv* so-so; **¿Cómo estás? - Regular** = How are you? - Can't complain *o* so-so

◇ **regularidad** *nf* regularity; **con regularidad** = regularly

rehabilitación *nf* rehabilitation *o* reinstatement; **rehabilitación de quiebra** *o* **rehabilitación del quebrado** = discharge in bankruptcy

◇ **rehabilitado, -da 1** *adj* rehabilitated; **quebrado rehabilitado** = discharged bankrupt; **quebrado no rehabilitado** = undischarged bankrupt **2** *pp de* REHABILITAR

rehabilitar *vt* to rehabilitate *o* to restore; **rehabilitar a un quebrado** = to discharge a bankrupt

rehusar *vt* to refuse *o* to decline; **el cliente rehusó aceptar las mercancías** = the customer refused the goods *o* refused to accept the goods ; **rehusar rotundamente** = to refuse totally *o* to give a flat refusal

reimportación *nf* reimport *o* reimportation

reimportar *vt* to reimport

reincidencia *nf* relapse *o* repetition

Reino Unido *nm* United Kingdom (UK)

◊ **británico, -ca** *adj y n* British; **los británicos** = the British; *ver también* INGLATERRA, INGLES NOTA: capital: **Londres** (= London); moneda: **libra esterlina (£)** = pound sterling (£)

reintegrar *vt* to reinstate; **le reintegraron en su puesto de trabajo** = he was reinstated in his job *o* he got his job back

reintegro *nm* **(a)** *(reembolso)* refund *o* repayment; **reintegros de préstamos** = loan repayments **(b)** *(cuenta bancaria)* withdrawal; **ha efectuado 10 reintegros de su cuenta esta semana** = she has made 10 withdrawals from her account this week

la red de cajeros automáticos ha incorporado a su equipo una avanzada tarjeta multifunción, para uso tanto en imposiciones como en reintegros
Micros

reinversión *nf* reinvestment

su actividad da empleo directamente a más de 5.000 personas, y la reinversión de su beneficio es aprovechada, de un modo u otro, por todos los ciudadanos de la región
Actualidad Económica

reinvertir *vt* to reinvest; **reinvirtió el dinero en títulos del Estado** = he reinvested the money in government stocks

reivindicación *nf* claim; **reivindicación salarial** = wage claim; **el sindicato presentó una reivindicación salarial del 6%** = the union put in a 6% wage claim

reivindicar *vt* to claim; **el sindicato reivindicó un aumento salarial de un 6%** = the union put in a 6% wage claim

relación *nf* **(a)** *(vínculo)* connection; **¿hay alguna relación entre su discusión con el director y su traslado repentino a encargado de almacén?** = is there a connection between his argument with the director and his sudden move to become warehouse manager?; **hay una relación entre la empresa y el gobierno porque el padre del presidente es ministro** = the company is connected to the government because the chairman's father is a minister **(b) en relación con** = in relation to; **con relación a** = further to; **con relación a su carta del 25 de mayo** = further to *o* with reference to your letter of May 25th **(c) relaciones laborales** = industrial relations; **buenas relaciones laborales** = good industrial relations; **relaciones públicas (RP)** = public relations (PR); **es un relaciones públicas** = he is a public relations man *o* a PR man; **responsable de relaciones públicas** = public relations officer; **una empresa de relaciones públicas se ocupa de toda nuestra publicidad** = a public relations firm *o* a PR firm is handling all our publicity; **el equipo de relaciones públicas distribuyó 100.000 globos** = the PR people *o* the PR team gave away 100,000 balloons; **una campaña de relaciones públicas** = a public relations exercise **(d)** *(razón)* ratio; **la relación entre éxitos y fracasos** = the ratio of successes to failures; **relación precio-ganancias** *o* **precio-beneficios** = price/earnings ratio *o* P/E ratio; **el precio de las acciones implica una relación precio-ganancias de 7** = the share price gives a P/E ratio of 7 **(e)** *(contacto)* contact; **entablar relaciones con alguien** = to enter into relations with someone; **establecer relaciones con una compañía** = to enter into relations with a company; **romper las relaciones con alguien** = to break off relations with someone **(f)** *(lista)* list; **relación de directivos de una empresa** = register of directors; **relación de gastos** = statement of expenses

◊ **relacionado, -da 1** *adj* related; **relacionado con** = related to; **todo lo relacionado con el mundo de los negocios** = everything concerning the business world **2** *pp de* RELACIONAR

relacionar *vt* to connect

◊ **relacionarse** *vr* to get to know people *o* to make contacts; **tiene buen carácter y se relaciona bien con los clientes** = he has a pleasant character and gets on well with the customers

relativo, -va *adj* **(a)** relative; **error relativo** = relative error; **valor relativo** = relative value **(b) relativo a** = regarding *o* relating to

◊ **relativamente** *adv* relatively *o* fairly; **hemos nombrado a una empresa de relaciones públicas relativamente nueva para dirigir nuestra publicidad** = we have appointed a relatively new PR firm to handle our publicity

relevar *vt (reemplazar)* to remove; **dos consejeros fueron relevados del consejo de administración en la junta general anual** = two directors were removed from the board at the AGM

rellenar *vt* **(a)** to fill in *o* to fill up *o* to fill out; **para hacer el despacho de aduanas hay que rellenar tres impresos** = to get customs clearance you must fill out three forms; **hay que rellenar debidamente el formulario para no tener dificultades en la aduana** = it is necessary to fill in the form correctly if you are not to have difficulty at the customs; **rellenó el impreso y lo envió al banco** = he filled out the form and sent it to the bank **(b) rellenar un sobre** = to address a letter

reloj *nm* clock *o* watch; **el reloj de la oficina adelanta** = the office clock is fast; **el ordenador tiene un reloj interno** = the computer has a built-in clock; **reloj digital** = digital clock

rematar *vt* to knock down

remesa *nf* batch; **la remesa de pedidos de hoy** = today's batch of orders; **procesamiento por remesas** = batch processing

remite *nm* return address *o* sender's name and address

remitente *nmf* sender *o* shipper *o* consignor; **'devolver al remitente'** = 'return to sender'; **sobre con sello y la dirección del remitente** = stamped addressed envelope

remitir *vt* **(a)** *(enviar)* to send *o* to remit; **remitir por cheque** = to remit by cheque; **remitió la carta a su hermano** = he sent the letter on to his brother **(b)**

(referir) to refer; **remitir una cuestión a un comité** = to refer a question to a committee; **hemos remitido su queja a nuestro suministrador** = we have referred your complaint to our supplier **(c)** *(devolver)* **'remitir al librador'** = 'refer to drawer'; **el banco remitió el cheque al librador** = the bank referred the cheque to drawer

◊ **remitirse** *vr* to refer to; **me remito a las cifras publicadas** = I am quoting the published figures

remontarse *vr* to soar

remoto, -ta *adj* remote; **control remoto** = remote control; **por control remoto** = by remote control

remuneración *nf* remuneration; **recibe una remuneración mensual de 80.000 ptas.** = her monthly salary is 80,000 pesetas

remunerado, -da 1 *adj* paid; **trabajo bien remunerado** = well-paid job **2** *pp de* REMUNERAR

◊ **remunerador, -ra** *adj* remunerative

remunerar *vt* to pay *o* to remunerate; **remunerar a alguien por sus servicios** = to pay someone *o* to remunerate someone for their services

◊ **remunerativo, -va** *adj* remunerative *o* money-making; **tiene un trabajo muy remunerativo** = he is in a very remunerative job; **un plan remunerativo** = a money-making plan

rendimiento *nm* **(a)** *(actuación)* performance *o* throughput; **rendimiento del personal frente a los objetivos marcados** = performance of personnel against objectives; **rendimiento de un trabajo** = job performance; **revisión del rendimiento en el trabajo** = performance review; **de buen rendimiento** = efficient; **una máquina de buen rendimiento** = an efficient machine; **trabajar a pleno rendimiento** = to work at full capacity; **esperamos aumentar nuestro rendimiento mediante la instalación de dos nuevas máquinas** = we hope to increase our throughput by putting in two new machines; **el bajo rendimiento de las acciones en la bolsa** = the poor performance of the shares on the stock market; **el año pasado se produjo una baja en el rendimiento de la empresa** = last year saw a dip in the company's performance **(b)** *(producción)* capacity *o* output **(c)** *(beneficios)* return (on an investment) *o* yield; **rendimiento bruto** = gross yield; **rendimiento del capital utilizado** = return against capital employed; **rendimiento corriente** = current yield; **rendimiento efectivo** = effective yield; **rendimiento fijo** = fixed yield; **rendimiento de la inversión** *o* **de capital** = return on investment (ROI) *o* return on capital employed (ROCE); **rendimiento máximo** = peak output; **acciones de alto rendimiento** = high-income shares; **acción con un rendimiento corriente del 5%** = share with a current yield of 5%; **escala de rendimiento** = earning power; **grado de rendimiento** = earning capacity

rendir 1 *vt* **(a)** *(producir)* to yield *o* to produce; **acciones que rinden un 10%** = shares which yield 10% **(b) rendir cuentas a alguien** = to report to someone; **que tiene que rendir cuentas a alguien** = responsible to someone; **rinde cuentas directamente al director gerente** = he reports direct to *o* he is directly responsible to the managing

director **2** *vi* to be profitable; **tuvimos que cerrar la fábrica porque no rendía** = we had to close the factory because it wasn't profitable

RENFE = RED NACIONAL DE LOS FERROCARRILES ESPAÑOLES Spanish railways

renovación *nf* renewal; **renovación de una suscripción** *o* **de una letra** = renewal of a subscription *o* of a bill; **¿cuál es la fecha de renovación de la letra?** = when is the renewal date of the bill?; **notificación de renovación** = renewal notice; **prima de renovación** = renewal premium; **renovación de existencias** = restocking; **renovación urbana** = urban redevelopment *o* urban renewal; **el plan de renovación urbana fue rechazado por la comisión de planificación** = the redevelopment plan was rejected by the planning committee

renovar *vt* **(a)** *(reanudar, prorrogar)* to renew; **renovar una letra de cambio** = to renew a bill of exchange; **renovar un pedido** = to repeat an order *o* to reorder; **renovar una póliza de seguros** = to renew an insurance policy; **renovar una suscripción** *o* **un abono** = to renew a subscription **(b) renovar existencias** = to restock; **renovar existencias después de las rebajas de Navidad** = to restock after the Christmas sales **(c) renovar la financiación** = to refinance

> las inversiones y el comercio con Japón han renovado el panorama económico de toda Asia
>
> **Actualidad Económica**

renta *nf* **(a)** *(ingresos)* income; **renta por alquiler** = income from rents *o* rent income; **renta anual** = annual income; **renta bruta** = gross income; **renta disponible** = disposable income; **renta elevada** = high income; **renta fija** = fixed income; **renta imponible** = taxable income; **renta nacional** = public revenue *o* national income; **renta neta** = net income; **renta percibida** = earned income; **renta personal** = personal income; **renta privada** = private income; **renta salarial** = earned income; **renta no salarial** = private income *o* unearned income; **renta del trabajo** = earned income; **desgravación de la renta del trabajo** = earned income allowance; **renta vitalicia** = life annuity *o* annuity for life *o* life interest; **la política de rentas del gobierno** = the government's incomes policy; **está en el grupo de contribuyentes que pagan renta por el tramo más alto** = he comes into the higher income bracket; **declaración de renta** = tax return *o* tax declaration; **formulario de declaración de la renta** = tax form; **impuesto sobre la renta** = income tax; **impreso para la declaración del impuesto sobre la renta** = income tax form; **declaración del impuesto sobre la renta** = declaration of income *o* income tax return; **la renta tiene un impuesto del 25%** = income is taxed at 25% **(b)** *(alquiler)* rent; **renta que no llega a cubrir los costes** = uneconomic rent; **renta nominal** = nominal rent; **renta de la tierra** *o* **del terreno** *o* **subsuelo** = ground rent; **control de rentas** = rent control; **renta simbólica** = token rent; **pagan una renta simbólica** = they are paying a nominal rent; **renta teórica** = notional rent

la proporción de las remuneraciones de los asalariados en la renta nacional ha disminuido del 53,2% en 1983 al 49,9% en 1988

España Económica

en 1870, la renta per cápita en Italia representaba sólo un 40% de la renta per cápita en el Reino Unido

Mercado

rentabilidad *nf* **(a)** *(condición de rentable)* cost-effectiveness; **(coeficiente de) rentabilidad** = profitability; **medición** *o* **evaluación de la rentabilidad** = measurement of profitability; **producto** *o* **subsidiario de alta rentabilidad** = cash cow; **umbral de rentabilidad** = breakeven point; **recuperar la rentabilidad de una empresa** = to make a company profitable again *o* to turn a company round; **¿podemos calcular la rentabilidad del transporte aéreo en comparación con el transporte marítimo?** = can we calculate the cost-effectiveness of air freight against shipping by sea? **(b)** *(rendimiento)* yield; **rentabilidad del dividendo** = dividend yield; **potencial de rentabilidad** = earning potential; **tasa de rentabilidad** = rate of return

las rentabilidades negociadas en la contratación a plazo en los bonos del Estado a tres años experimentaron subidas de más de 0,20 puntos porcentuales

Mercado

hoy su tasa de rentabilidad es de un 15% y las inversiones, como la de la red TGV-Atlántico que costó 18.000 millones de francos, están a punto de ser amortizadas antes de lo previsto

Cambio 16

rentable *adj* profitable *o* commercial *o* cost-effective; **no rentable** = unprofitable; **poco rentable** = not very profitable *o* uneconomic; **es un negocio rentable** = it is a profitable business; **carga rentable** = commercial load; **propuesta no rentable** = not a commercial proposition; **no es una propuesta rentable** = it is not a paying proposition; **nos resulta muy rentable insertar publicidad en los periódicos del domingo** = we find advertising in the Sunday newspapers very cost-effective; **se esperaba que todo el proyecto fuera rentable al cabo de un año** = the whole project was expected to be profit-making by the end of the year

◊ **rentablemente** *adv* profitably

rentista *nmf* annuitant

renuncia *nf* **(a)** *(abandon, dimisión)* renunciation *o* resignation; **carta de renuncia** = letter of renunciation; **escribió su carta de renuncia al presidente del Consejo** = he wrote his letter of resignation to the chairman **(b)** *(en un contrato)* disclaimer *o* waiver; **cláusula de renuncia** = waiver clause

renunciar *vt* **(a)** *(desistir)* to renounce *o* to waive; **renunció a su derecho a la herencia** = he waived his claim to the estate; **renunciar a un pago** = to waive a payment **(b)** *(abandonar un plan o una idea)* to abandon *o* to give up; **renunciamos al proyecto cuando vimos que hacía falta una gran inversión** = we gave up the project when we realized that it needed a lot of investment

reordenación *nf* realignment; **reordenación de divisas** = realignment of currencies *o* currency realignment

reordenar *vt* to realign; **reordenar las divisas** = to realign currencies

reorganización *nf* reorganization *o* reconstruction; **la reorganización de una compañía** = the reorganization of a company *o* a company reorganization *o* the reconstruction of a company; **una reorganización de la alta dirección** = a shakeout in the top management; **reorganización total** = thorough reorganization *o* complete shakeout; **el director gerente ordenó una reorganización total de los servicios de ventas** = the managing director ordered a shakeup of the sales departments; **después de la reorganización del mercado de ordenadores solamente quedaron tres empresas** = only three companies were left after the shakeout in the computer market

reorganizar *vt* to reorganize

reparación *nf* repair; **hacer reparaciones a la maquinaria** = to carry out repairs to the machinery; **la fotocopiadora está en reparación** = the photocopier is being repaired; **centro de reparaciones** = service centre; **reparaciones y conservación** = repairs and maintenance

◊ **reparador, -ra** *n* repairer *o* repair man

reparar *vt* to repair; **su coche está en el garage para que lo reparen** = his car is in the garage for repair

repartir *vt* **(a)** *(distribuir)* to distribute *o* to share (out); **los beneficios fueron repartidos entre los accionistas** = profits were distributed among the shareholders; **repartir los beneficios entre los directivos** = to share the profits among the senior executives; **el mercado está repartido entre tres empresas** = three companies share the market; **repartir un riesgo** = to spread a risk **(b)** *(entregar)* to deliver; **reparte folletos de puerta en puerta** = he delivers leaflets door-to-door; **'se reparte a domicilio'** = 'home delivery service'

◊ **repartirse** *vr* to share out; **las dos empresas acordaron repartirse el mercado entre ellas** = the two companies agreed to divide the market between them

◊ **reparto** *nm* **(a)** *(participación)* shareout *o* sharing **(b)** *(pago total por reparto)* = payment in full on allotment **(c)** *(entrega)* delivery; **reparto a domicilio** = home delivery service; **reparto especial** = special delivery; **reparto de mercancías** = delivery of goods; **reparto urgente** = express delivery; **camioneta** *o* **furgoneta de reparto** = delivery van *o* pickup truck; **servicio de recogida y reparto** = pickup and delivery service; **la tienda tiene un servicio de reparto a todas las partes de la ciudad** = the store has a delivery service to all parts of the town **(d)** *(proporcional)* **reparto de mercados** = apportionment of markets

repentino, -na *adj* sudden; **el consejo de administración adoptó una decisión repentina** = the board came to a snap decision

repercusión *nf* **(a)** *(consecuencias)* repercussion; **el gobierno ha anunciado unas medidas económicas de amplia repercusión** = the government announced some far-reaching economic measures **(b)** *(efecto secundario)* after-effect

> las rebajas de impuestos y la desregulación de algunos mercados tiene un coste para la hacienda pública y ese coste tendrá graves repercusiones para el déficit del sector público
>
> **El País**

repercutir *vi* **repercutir en** = to affect *o* to have an effect (on); **la huelga de funcionarios de aduanas ha repercutido en la producción de coches al retrasar las exportaciones** = the strike by customs officers has had a knock-on effect on car production by slowing down exports of cars; **la noticia de la decisión del gobierno repercutió favorablemente en el mercado** = the market shot up on the news of the government's decision

repertorio *nm (compilación)* list *o* index; *(guía comercial)* **repertorio comercial** = commercial directory *o* trade directory

repetir *vt* to repeat; **repitió su dirección despacio para que la vendedora pudiera apuntarla** = he repeated his address slowly so that the salesgirl could write it down

repleto, -ta *adj* full up; **las estanterías del supermercado estaban repletas de artículos antes de las aglomeraciones de las Navidades** = the shelves in the supermarket were full of items before the Christmas rush

reponer *vt* to replace

reportaje *nm* news item *o* coverage; **reportaje periodístico** *o* **en la prensa** = press coverage; **nos decepcionó mucho el reportaje de la prensa sobre el nuevo coche** = we were very disappointed by the press coverage of the new car; **la empresa fue objeto de amplios reportajes periodísticos con ocasión del lanzamiento de su nuevo modelo** = the company had good media coverage for the launch of its new model

reposición *nf* replacement; **coste de reposición** = replacement cost; **el coste de reposición de las existencias dañadas es muy elevado** = the cost of replacing damaged stock is very high; **el ordenador está asegurado por su valor de reposición** = the computer is insured at its replacement value

representación *nf* **(a)** *(agencia)* representation *o* dealership; **representación exclusiva** = sole agency; **les ofrecimos la representación exclusiva en Europa** = we offered them exclusive representation in Europe; **tiene la representación exclusiva de los automóviles Ford** = he has the sole agency for Ford cars; **representación del personal en el consejo de administración** = worker representation on the board; **los accionistas minoritarios quieren tener representación en el consejo de administración** = the minority shareholders want representation on the board; **no tienen representación en los EE UU** = they have no representation in the USA; **firmaron un acuerdo** *o* **contrato de representación** = they signed an agency agreement *o* an agency contract; **gastos de representación** = entertainment expenses; **dietas para gastos de representación** = entertainment allowance **(b) firmar por representación** = to sign by proxy **(c)** *(informática)* **representación visual** = visual display

representante *nmf* **(a)** *(agente comercial)* agent; **ser el representante de IBM** = to be the agent for IBM *o* the IBM agent; **representante exclusivo** = sole agent; **es el representante exclusivo de los automóviles Ford** = he is the sole agent for Ford cars *o* he has the sole agency for Ford cars **(b)** *(comerciante)* salesman *o* representative *o* rep; **tenemos seis representantes en Europa** = we have six representatives in Europe; **necesitan representantes para visitar clientes en el norte del país** = they have vacancies for representatives to call on accounts in the north of the country; **nuestros representantes visitan a sus clientes principales una vez al mes** = our salesmen call on their best customers once a month; **representante a comisión** = commission rep; **trabaja como representante a comisión para dos empresas** = he works as a commission rep *o* he reps for two firms on commission **(c)** *(delegado)* representative; **el consejo de administración se negó a reunirse con los representantes del personal** = the board refused to meet the representatives of the workforce; **representante sindical** = shop steward

representar *vt* to represent; **representa a una empresa norteamericana de automóviles en Europa** = he represents an American car firm in Europe; **tres encargados representan al personal en las negociaciones con la junta directiva** = three managers represent the workforce in discussions with the directors; **envió a su abogado y a su contable para que le representaran en la reunión** = he sent his solicitor and accountant to represent him at the meeting

representativo, -va *adj* representative; **presentamos una selección representativa de nuestra gama de productos** = we displayed a representative selection of our product range; **la muestra elegida no era representativa de la totalidad del lote** = the sample chosen was not representative of the whole batch

reprochar *vt* to blame *o* to reproach; **el director gerente reprochó al jefe de contabilidad que no le hubiese advertido de las pérdidas** = the managing director blamed the chief accountant for not warning him of the loss

reprogramar *vt* to reschedule

reptil *nm* reptile; **caja de reptiles** = slush fund

repudiar *vt* to repudiate

◊ **repudio** *nm* repudiation

repuesto *nm* spare part; **piezas de repuesto** = spare parts; **la fotocopiadora no funciona - le falta un repuesto** = the photocopier will not work - it needs a spare part

reputación *nf* reputation *o* standing; **la reputación financiera de la compañía** = the financial standing of a company

◊ **reputado, -da** *adj* reputable

requerimiento *nm* **(a)** *(legal)* **requerimiento judicial** = injunction; **la empresa solicitó un requerimiento judicial para evitar que su competidor**

comerciara con un producto similar = the company applied for an injunction to stop their rival from marketing a similar product **(b)** *(reclamación)* **requerimiento de pago** = demand *o* request for payment

requerir *vt* **(a)** *(pedir)* to request *o* to requisition *o* to demand **(b)** *(necesitar)* to need *o* to require; **el documento requiere un examen cuidadoso** = the document requires careful study *o* needs to be studied carefully

requisito *nm* requirement; **satisfacer los requisitos** = to meet the requirements *o* to qualify for; **la compañía no satisface los requisitos para obtener una subvención del Estado** = the company does not qualify for a government grant; **requisitos para ser miembro** = membership requirements; **si nos facilitan la lista de sus requisitos, veremos si les podemos satisfacer** = if you will supply us with a list of your requirements, we shall see if we can meet them

> la guía de franquicias aporta toda la información y requisitos que necesita conocer el futuro franquiciado
> **El País**

resarcir *vt* to make good *o* to repay; **la empresa resarce a los representantes de todos sus gastos** = the company covers all the reps' expenses

◇ **resarcirse** *vr* to be compensated for *o* to claw back; **con el impuesto sobre la renta el Estado se resarce del 25% de lo que paga en pensiones** = income tax claws back 25% of pensions paid out by the government

rescatable *adj* redeemable

rescatador *nm* **rescatador de empresas** = white knight

rescatar *vt* **(a)** *(salvar)* to rescue *o* to bail out; **la compañía estaba al borde de la ruina, pero fue rescatada por los bancos** = the company nearly collapsed, but was rescued by the banks; **rescatar una finca hipotecada** = to redeem a mortgaged property **(b)** *(seguros)* **rescatar una póliza** = to surrender a policy **(c)** *(volver a comprar)* to buy back; **rescató la tienda que había vendido el año anterior** = he bought back the shop he had sold the previous year

◇ **rescate** *nm* **(a)** *(salvamento)* rescue *o* salvage; **rescate financiero** = financial rescue; **operación de rescate (de una compañía)** = rescue operation *o* lifeboat operation; **los bancos planearon una operación de rescate de la compañía** = the banks planned a rescue operation for the company **(b)** *(seguros)* surrender; **valor de rescate** = surrender value *o* redemption value; **rescate anticipado** = redemption before due date; **fecha de rescate** = redemption date; **beneficio hasta la fecha de rescate** = redemption yield

rescindible *adj* annullable

rescindir *vt* to annul *o* to rescind *o* to cancel; **rescindir un acuerdo** = to rescind an agreement; **rescindir un contrato** = to rescind *o* to void a contract

◇ **rescisión** *nf* annulling *o* annulment *o* cancellation; **rescisión de un contrato** = (i) annulment of a contract; (ii) release from a contract; **cláusula de rescisión** = cancellation clause

reserva *nf* **(a)** *(hotel, vuelo)* reservation *o* booking; **reserva anticipada** = advance booking; **reserva en bloque** = block booking; **la empresa ha hecho una reserva en bloque de veinte plazas en el avión** *o* **de diez habitaciones en el hotel** = the company has a block booking for twenty seats on the plane *o* for ten rooms at the hotel; **hacerle a alguien la reserva en un hotel** *o* **un vuelo** = to book someone into a hotel *o* onto a flight; **le hicieron la reserva en el vuelo de las 9 de la mañana a Zurich** = he was booked on the 09.00 flight to Zurich; **las reservas en los hoteles han bajado después de la temporada turística** = hotel bookings have fallen since the end of the tourist season; **confirmar una reserva** = to confirm a booking; **doble reserva** = double booking; **¿puede ponerme con el departamento de reservas?** = can you put me through to reservations? **(b)** *(deducción)* allowance; **reserva para pérdidas en el cambio** = allowance for exchange loss **(c)** *(fondos de precisión)* **reservas** = reserves; **reservas bancarias** = bank reserves; **Reserva Federal** = *(US)* Federal Reserve; **los bancos de la Reserva Federal** = *US* the Federal Reserve Banks; **la Junta de la Reserva Federal** = *US* the Federal Reserve Board; **reservas de caja** *o* **de efectivo** = cash reserves; **reservas de capital** = capital reserves; **reserva para deudas incobrables** = reserve for bad debts; **reservas de divisas** = currency reserves *o* foreign currency reserves; **las reservas de divisas de un país** = a country's foreign currency reserves; **reservas de libras esterlinas** = sterling balances; **las reservas de oro y de dólares de España bajaron $200 millones durante el trimestre** = Spain's gold and dollar reserves fell by $200 million during the quarter; **reservas de efectivo** = cash reserves; **la compañía se vio obligada a recurrir a sus reservas de efectivo** = the company was forced to fall back on its cash reserves; **reservas para emergencias** *o* **para imprevistos** = contingency reserve *o* emergency reserves; **reservas ocultas** = hidden reserves; **reserva de respaldo monetario** = currency backing; **tener que recurrir a las reservas para pagar el dividendo** = to have to draw on reserves to pay the dividend; **cantidades imputables a la reserva** *o* **a cargo de la reserva** = sums chargeable to the reserve; **capitalización de reservas** = capitalization of reserves; **divisa de reserva** = reserve currency; **fondo de reserva** = reserve fund **(d)** **en reserva** = in reserve *o* in hand; **guardar algo en reserva** = to keep something in reserve; **guardamos nuestro nuevo producto en reserva hasta la fecha de lanzamiento** = we are keeping our new product in reserve until the launch date **(e)** **con reservas** = with reservations *o* qualified *o* conditional; **aceptación de un contrato con reservas** = qualified acceptance of a contract; **el plan obtuvo la aprobación con reservas de la junta** = the plan received qualified approval from the board; **cuentas aceptadas con reservas** = qualified accounts; *US* qualified audit report; **los auditores han aprobado las cuentas con reservas** = the auditors have qualified the accounts; **sin reserva** = without reservation *o* in full; **aceptó todas nuestras condiciones sin reservas** = he accepted all our conditions in full **(f)** *(mercancías)* stock *o* store *o* stockpile *o* reserves; **siempre guardo una reserva**

de sobres disponibles en mi mesa = I always keep a store of envelopes ready in my desk; **a la fábrica se le están acabando las reservas de carbón** = the factory is running short of supplies of coal; **nuestras reservas de combustible bajaron durante el invierno** = our reserves of fuel fell during the winter; **las reservas nacionales de mantequilla** *o* **azúcar** = the country's stocks of butter *o* sugar; **las reservas de gas del país son muy grandes** = the country's reserves of gas *o* gas reserves are very large; **reserva de materias primas** = a stockpile of raw materials **(g)** *(informática)* **copia de reserva** = backup copy **(h)** *(personas)* pool; **una reserva de mano de obra desempleada** *o* **de conocimientos técnicos** = a pool of unemployed labour *o* of expertise

reservado, -da 1 *adj* booked *o* reserved; **el restaurante tiene todas las mesas reservadas para el periodo de Navidades** = the restaurant is booked up over the Christmas period; **reservado el derecho de admisión** = the management reserves the right to refuse admission; **'reservados todos los derechos'** = 'all rights reserved' **2** *pp de* RESERVAR

reservar *vt* **(a)** *(hotel, vuelo)* to book; **reservar una habitación en un hotel** *o* **una mesa en un restaurante** *o* **una plaza en un avión** = to book a room in a hotel *o* a table at a restaurant *o* a ticket on a plane; **quiero reservar plaza en el tren de Sevilla de mañana por la tarde** = I want to make a reservation on the train to Seville tomorrow evening; **quiero reservar una mesa para cuatro personas** = I want to book a table for four people **(b)** *(retener)* to reserve *o* to keep *o* to retain *o* to earmark; **la compañía ha reservado 10.000.000 de ptas. de los beneficios como provisión para deudas incobrables** = out of the profits, the company has retained 10m pesetas as provision against bad debts; **se reserva una cantidad fija para deudas incobrables** = a fixed amount is provided against bad debts

◊ **reservarse** *vr* to keep for oneself; **el presidente siempre se reserva la tarde del viernes para jugar una partida de bridge** = the chairman always keeps Friday afternoon free for a game of bridge; **me reservo mi opinión** = I shall keep my opinions to myself

resguardo *nm* receipt *o* slip

residencia *nf* **(a)** *(casa)* residence; **tiene una residencia en el campo donde pasa los fines de semana** = he has a country residence where he spends his weekends **(b) permiso de residencia** = residence permit; *(US)* green card; **ha solicitado un permiso de residencia** = he has applied for a residence permit; **se le concedió un permiso de residencia de un año** = she was granted a residence permit for one year

◊ **residencial** *adj* residential; **inmuebles residenciales** = house property *o* residential property; **zona residencial** = residential area

◊ **residente** *nmf* resident; **no residente** = non-resident; **se le concedió un visado de no residente** = she was granted a non-resident visa; **tiene una cuenta de no residente en un banco español** = he has a non-resident account with a Spanish bank

residir *vi* to reside *o* to be resident; **la compañía reside en España** = the company is resident in Spain

residual *adj* residual; **aguas residuales** = sewage; **valor residual** = salvage value

residuo *nm* residue; **la empresa fue multada por echar residuos industriales al río** = the company was fined for putting industrial waste into the river

◊ **residuos** *nmpl* waste

resistencia *nf* resistance; **hubo mucha resistencia al nuevo plan por parte de los accionistas** = there was a lot of resistance from the shareholders to the new plan; **la propuesta del presidente provocó una gran resistencia por parte de los bancos** = the chairman's proposal met with strong resistance from the banks; **resistencia por parte del consumidor** = consumer resistance; **el nuevo producto no encontró ninguna resistencia por parte de los consumidores a pesar de su elevado precio** = the new product met no consumer resistance even though the price was high

resistir 1 *vt* to resist *o* to stand up to; **el presidente resistió todas las presiones para obligarle a dimitir** = the chairman resisted all attempts to make him resign **2** *vi* to resist *o* to hold on; **los accionistas de la compañía deberían resistir y esperar una oferta mejor** = the company's shareholders should hold on and wait for a better offer

◊ **resistirse** *vr* to fight against; **la compañía se resiste a la oferta de adquisición** = the company is resisting the takeover bid

resolución *nf* resolution; **resolución especial** = special resolution; **resolución ordinaria** = ordinary resolution; **proponer una resolución a una reunión** = to put a resolution to a meeting; **la asamblea aprobó la resolución de iniciar una huelga** = the meeting passed *o* adopted a resolution to go on strike; **la reunión rechazó la resolución** *o* **la resolución fue rechazada, por diez votos a favor y veinte en contra** = the meeting rejected the resolution *o* the resolution was defeated by ten votes to twenty

resolutorio, -ria *adj* **cláusula resolutoria** = termination clause

resolver *vt* **(a)** *(solucionar)* to solve; **resolver un problema** = to solve a problem; **el crédito resolverá algunos de nuestros problemas a corto plazo** = the loan will solve some of our short-term problems; **la prueba definitiva de un buen director es su capacidad para resolver problemas** = problem solving is a test of a good manager; **dificultades que todavía pueden resolverse** = difficulties which are still manageable *o* which can still be overcome; **los problemas son demasiado grandes para ser**

resueltos fácilmente = the problems are too large to be manageable **(b)** *(decidirse)* to determine *o* to decide **(c)** *(jurídico)* to adjudicate; **resolver una demanda** = to adjudicate a claim

◊ **respaldado, -da** *adj* **préstamo respaldado** = back-to-back loan

respaldar *vt* to back (up); **respaldar a alguien** = to back someone; **el banco le respalda con 200.000 ptas.** = the bank is backing him to the tune of 200,000 pesetas; **está buscando a alguien que respalde su proyecto** = he is looking for someone to back his project; **trajo consigo un expediente de documentos para respaldar su reclamación** = he brought along a file of documents to back up his claim; **¿quién respalda el proyecto?** = who is providing the backing for the project?

◊ **respaldo** *nm* backing *o* support; **respaldo financiero** = financial backing; **reserva de respaldo monetario** = currency backing

> el informe de la OCDE es poco crítico con la política económica del Gobierno socialista español y respalda la tesis que el ministro de Economía estableció en el plan de convergencia con Europa
> El País

respectivamente *adv* respectively; **el señor Pereira y el señor Palos son director gerente y director comercial de Pereira S.A., respectivamente** = Sr Pereira and Sr Palos are respectively MD and Sales Director of Pereira S.A.

respecto *nm* **con respecto a** = concerning *o* with respect to *o* with regard to *o* in connection with; **con respecto a su solicitud de excedencia** = with regard to your request for unpaid leave; **quiero hablar con el director gerente con respecto a las previsiones de ventas** = I want to speak to the managing director in connection with the sales forecasts

respetar *vt* to respect; **respetar una cláusula de un acuerdo** = to respect a clause in an agreement; **la empresa no ha respetado los términos del contrato** = the company has not respected the terms of the contract

responder *vt* to answer *o* to reply; **no respondí porque no recibí su carta** = I did not reply because your letter never reached me; **la compañía ha respondido a la oferta de adquisición ofreciendo a los accionistas unos dividendos superiores** = the company has replied to the takeover bid by offering the shareholders higher dividends; **responder de** = to account for *o* to justify *o* to answer for

responsabilidad *nf* **(a)** responsibility *o* liability *o* accountability; **responsabilidad contractual** = contractual liability; **responsabilidad por producto defectuoso** = product liability; **seguro de responsabilidad empresarial** = employers' liability insurance; **responsabilidad limitada** = limited liability; **sociedad de responsabilidad limitada (S.R.L.)** = limited liability company (Ltd) *o* limited partnership; **un trabajo de responsabilidad** = a responsible job; **aceptar la responsabilidad de algo** = to accept liability for something; **rechazar la responsabilidad de algo** = to refuse liability for something; **la empresa no asume ninguna responsabilidad por la pérdida de los objetos de los clientes** = there is no responsibility on the company's part for loss of

customers' property; **la dirección no acepta ninguna responsabilidad por la pérdida de las mercancías en depósito** = the management accepts no responsibility for loss of goods in storage **(b)** **responsabilidades** = responsibilities *o* commitments *o* duties

responsabilizar *vt* to blame

◊ **responsabilizarse** *vr* to take the responsibility; **se responsabilizó de la pérdida de las facturas** = she took responsibility for losing the invoices

responsable 1 *adj* **(a)** responsible; **responsable de** = liable for *o* responsible for; **ser responsable de los daños** = to stand liable for damages; **el cliente será responsable de los desperfectos** = the customer is liable for breakages; **el presidente era personalmente responsable de las deudas de la compañía** = the chairman was personally liable for the company's debts; **es responsable de todas las ventas** = he is responsible for all sales **(b)** **los vendedores son directamente responsables ante el director de ventas** = the salesmen report directly to the sales director **2** *nmf* person in charge *o* manager; **responsable del progreso de un trabajo** = progress chaser; **responsable de relaciones públicas** = public relations officer; **responsable del servicio de información** = information officer; **responsable sindical** = convenor

> el nuevo ministro responsable de Transportes ha requerido que la puesta al día de una situación complicada también en este momento por los cambios administrativos que se preparan
> El País

respuesta *nf* *(reacción)* answer *o* reply *o* response *o* feedback; **hemos recibido un montón de respuestas a nuestro anuncio** = we received a stack of replies to our advertisement; **enviar las respuestas al apartado de correos nº 209** = please reply to Box No. 209; **en respuesta a su carta del 6 de octubre** = I am writing in answer to your letter of October 6th; **no hubo respuesta a mi carta** *o* **a mi llamada telefónica** = there was no reply to my letter *o* to my phone call; **la respuesta de la compañía a la oferta de adquisición** = the company's reply to the takeover bid; **boletín de respuesta** = reply coupon; **boletín de respuesta internacional** = international postal reply coupon; **tarjeta postal** *o* **carta a franquear en destino** = reply paid card *o* letter

resta *nf* subtraction

restablecer *vt* to re-establish *o* to restore; **restablecer el diálogo** = to break a deadlock; **restablecer el equilibrio** = to redress the balance

restar *vt* to subtract *o* to take away; **si se restan los beneficios de las operaciones en el Extremo Oriente, se verá que el grupo no ha sido rentable en el mercado europeo** = if the profits from the Far Eastern operations are subtracted, you will see that the group has not been profitable in the European market

restaurador, -ra *n* restorer; **restaurador de muebles** = furniture restorer

restaurante *nm* restaurant; **dirige un restaurante español en Nueva York** = he runs a Spanish restaurant in New York; **ese restaurante**

está muy bien de precios = that restaurant gives value for money

restaurar *vt* to restore; **restaurar el valor de una moneda** = to restore the value of a currency

restitución *nf* (a) *(readmisión)* reinstatement (b) *(devolver)* restitution; **el tribunal decretó la restitución de los bienes a la compañía** = the court ordered the restitution of assets to the company (c) *(UE)* **restitución a la exportación** = export restitution

restituir *vt* (a) *(readmitir)* to reinstate (b) *(devolver)* to return *o* to give back *o* to restore; **le restituyeron el dinero que le habían robado** = they gave him back the money they had stolen

resto *nm* (a) *(saldo)* rest *o* balance; **puede pagar un depósito de 10.000 ptas. y el resto dentro de 60 días** = you can pay 10,000 pesetas deposit and the balance within 60 days; **vendimos la mayor parte de las existencias antes de Navidades y esperamos liquidar el resto con las rebajas** = we sold most of the stock before Christmas and hope to clear the rest in a sale; **el resto del dinero está invertido en bonos del Estado** = the rest of the money is invested in gilts; **el resto de las existencias se liquidará a mitad de precio** = the remainder of the stock will be sold off at half price; **dio una entrada de dos mil pesetas y pagó el resto a plazos** = he paid 2,000 pesetas down and the rest in instalments (b) **venta de restos de serie** = sale of remnants *o* remnant sale; **restos de edición** = remainders; **comerciante de restos de edición** = remainder merchant; **la librería estaba llena de restos de edición** = the shop was full of piles of remaindered books (c) *(jurídico)* residue; **después de pagar varios legados el resto de la herencia se dividió entre sus hijos** = after paying various bequests the residue of his estate was split between his children

restricción *nf* (a) **restricción comercial** = restraint of trade restriction *o* restraint; **restricciones de crédito** = credit restrictions *o* credit squeeze; **imponer restricciones al crédito** *o* **a las importaciones** = to impose credit restrictions *o* restrictions on imports; **levantar las restricciones de crédito** = to lift credit restrictions (b) *(limitación)* limitation; **restricciones a la importación** = import restrictions

> el tipo de ajuste buscado por el Banco de España se observa en las restricciones monetarias aplicadas desde entonces y la entrada de la peseta en el SME
> **España Económica**

restrictivo, -va *adj* restrictive *o* limiting; **cláusula restrictiva en un contrato** = a limiting clause in a contract; **prácticas comerciales restrictivas** = restrictive trade practices

restringir *vt* *(limitar)* to restrict *o* to cap; **restringir el flujo de comercio** = to restrict the flow of trade; **restringir los márgenes** *o* **beneficios** *o* **el crédito** = to squeeze margins *o* profits *o* credit; **restringir la producción** = to run down production

resucitar *vt* to revive

resultado 1 *nm* (a) *(beneficios o pérdidas)* result *o* balance; **los resultados de la compañía en 1995** = the company's results for 1995; **cuenta de**

resultados = income statement; **resultado después del pago de impuestos** = profit after tax; **balance de resultados consolidados** = consolidated profit and loss account (P&L account) (b) *(consecuencia)* result; **con resultados positivos** = with positive results *o* successful; **tener por** *o* **como resultado** = to result in; **en el resultado final** = in the final analysis; **sin resultado** = without any result *o* unsuccessfully *o* to no effect; **ha estado buscando trabajo durante seis meses, pero sin resultado** = he has been looking for a job for six months, but with no success; **¿cuál fue el resultado de la investigación de precios?** = what was the result of the price investigation?; **la empresa duplicó su personal de ventas con el resultado de un aumento en las ventas del 26%** = the company doubled its sales force with the result that sales rose by 26%; **el programa de expansión ha dado buenos resultados** = the expansion programme has produced results; **pago según resultados** = payment by results **2** *pp de* RESULTAR

> el de los medios de comunicación es un sector cuya eficacia debe medirse tanto por la cuenta de resultados como por su servicio a la sociedad
> **Tiempo**

resultar *vi* (a) *(tener como resultado)* to result in; **resultar de** = to result from (b) *(hacerse)* to become; **la empresa resultó muy rentable en poco tiempo** = the company became very profitable in a short time; **resultan más baratos comprándolos por cajas** = they work out cheaper by the box

> los sistemas de subvención, que pueden resultar muy sofisticados, pueden introducir a veces distorsiones notables en la cuantificación de las cifras
> **El País**

resumen *nm* summary *o* abstract; **hacer un resumen de las cuentas de la compañía** = to make an abstract of the company accounts; **el presidente presentó un resumen de sus negociaciones con la delegación comercial alemana** = the chairman gave a summary of his discussions with the German trade delegation; **la sección de ventas ha presentado un resumen de las ventas del primer semestre en Europa** = the sales department has given a summary of sales in Europe for the first six months

retal *nm* remnant *o* oddment; **venta de retales** = remnant sale *o* sale of remnants

retención *nf* *(sueldo)* **retención salarial** = stoppage *o* deduction (from pay)

retener *vt* to retain *o* to withhold *o* to hold back *o* to hold up; **el envío ha sido retenido en la aduana** = the shipment has been held up at the customs

retirada *nf* withdrawal; **retirada de fondos anticipada** = early withdrawal; **retirada masiva de fondos de un banco** = run on a bank; **retirada del crédito bancario** = closing of an account; **retirada de fondos sin recargo siempre que se avise con siete días de antelación** = withdrawal without penalty at seven days' notice; **dar aviso de retirada de fondos con siete días de antelación** = to give seven days' notice of withdrawal

retirar *vt* (a) *(sacar)* to take away *o* to withdraw;

retirar el crédito = to stop an account; **retirar gradualmente** = to phase out; **tuvimos que retirarle los encargos al proveedor porque la calidad era mala** = we had to take the work away from the supplier because the quality was so bad; **retirar una oferta** = to withdraw an offer; **uno de los capitalistas de la sociedad ha retirado su apoyo** = one of the company's backers has withdrawn (his support); **el presidente le pidió que retirara las observaciones que había hecho sobre el director financiero** = the chairman asked him to withdraw the remarks he has made about the finance director **(b)** *(productos defectuosos)* to recall; **retiraron 10.000 lavadoras porque tenían una conexión eléctrica defectuosa** = they recalled 10,000 whasing machines because of a faulty electrical connection

◊ **retirarse** *vr* **(a)** *(abandonar)* to back out *o* to stand down; **el banco se retiró del contrato** = the bank backed out of the contract; **tuvimos que abandonar el proyecto cuando nuestros socios alemanes se retiraron** = we had to cancel the project when our German partners backed out **(b)** *(teléfono)* **no se retire** = hold the line please **(c)** *(jubilarse)* **retirarse de un empleo** = to retire from one's job *o* to retire; **no hay ninguna posibilidad de que el presidente se retire antes de Navidad** = there is no possibility of the chairman retiring before next Christmas

retiro *nm* **(a)** *(retirada)* withdrawal **(b)** *(jubilación)* retirement *o* pension; **con derecho a retiro** = eligible for a pension *o* pensionable; **edad de retiro** = retirement age; **pensión de retiro** = retirement pension

reto *nm* challenge

ése es el reto del Gobierno para que la
provincia española no sea el pariente
pobre
                                        Tiempo

retornable *adj* returnable; **estas botellas no son retornables** = these bottles are not returnable

retractar *vt* to withdraw

◊ **retractarse** *vr* to go back on; **dos meses después se retractaron del acuerdo** = two months later they went back on the agreement

retrasado, -da **1** *adj* backward *o* underdeveloped; **estar retrasado** *o* **andar retrasado** = to be behind *o* to lag behind; **la empresa anda retrasada en sus entregas** = the company has fallen behind with its deliveries; **pago retrasado** = overdue payment **2** *pp de* RETRASAR

retrasar *vt* to delay *o* to set back; **la empresa ha retrasado el pago de todas las facturas** = the company has delayed payment of all invoices; **la huelga retrasará los envíos por algunas semanas** = the strike will hold up dispatch for some weeks

◊ **retrasarse** *vr* to be delayed *o* to fall behind *o* to lag behind; **se retrasó en el pago de la hipoteca** = he fell behind with his mortgage repayments; **se retrasó porque su taxi tuvo un accidente** = he was delayed because his taxi had an accident; **la compañía se ha retrasado en las entregas** = the company has fallen behind with its deliveries

◊ **retraso** *nm* delay *o* hold-up; **con retraso** = late;

la junta general anual empezó con treinta minutos de retraso = there was a delay of thirty minutes before the AGM started *o* the AGM started after a thirty minute delay; **el proyecto sufrió un retraso de seis semanas debido al mal tiempo** = the project was set back six weeks by bad weather; **la huelga ocasionó retrasos en el despacho de mercancías** = the strike caused hold-ups in the dispatch of goods; **siento decir que llevamos tres meses de retraso** = I am sorry to say that we are three months behind schedule; **el avión llevaba dos horas de retraso** = the plane was two hours late; **les pedimos disculpas por el retraso de la llegada del avión de Amsterdam** = we apologize for the late arrival of the plane from Amsterdam

retribución *nf* pay *o* remuneration *o* fee *o* consideration; **retribución fija** = fixed payment; **por una pequeña retribución** = for a small consideration

◊ **retribuir** *vt* to pay *o* to remunerate

la banca es el sector que mejor retribuye a
los directivos en España
                                    Cinco Días

retroactivo, -va *adj* retroactive; **aumento retroactivo de salarios** = retroactive pay rise; **recibieron un aumento de sueldo con efecto retroactivo al mes de enero pasado** = they got a pay rise retroactive to last January; **el aumento salarial es retroactivo al 1 de enero** = the pay increase is backdated to January 1st

◊ **retroactivamente** *adv* retroactively

retrotraer *vt* to antedate

reunión *nf* meeting *o* assembly; **lugar *o* punto de reunión** = meeting place *o* venue for a meeting; **hemos cambiado el lugar de la reunión** = we have changed the venue for the conference; **reunión del consejo de administración** = board meeting; **reunión de personal** = staff meeting; **reunión plenaria** = plenary meeting; **reunión de ventas** = sales conference; **celebrar una reunión** = to hold a meeting; **la reunión se celebrará en la sala de la comisión** = the meeting will be held in the committee room; **celebrar una reunión de representantes** = to hold a reps' meeting; **estar en una reunión** = to be in a meeting *o* to be in conference; **estructurar una reunión** = to structure a meeting; **tomar la palabra en una reunión** = to address a meeting; **dirigir *o* presidir una reunión** = to take the chair at a meeting *o* to chair *o* to conduct a meeting; **el Sr. Gallardo presidió la reunión** = Sr Gallardo took the chair; **pedir en una reunión que se vote una propuesta** = to put a resolution to a meeting; **acta de la reunión** = the minutes of the meeting; **el presidente firmó el acta de la última reunión** = the chairman signed the minutes of the last meeting; **esto no constará en el acta de la reunión** = this will not appear in the minutes of the meeting

reunir *vt* to gather; **reunir recursos** = to pool resources; **reunir los requisitos** = to fulfil the requirements; **reunir las condiciones necesarias para un puesto de trabajo** = to be the right person for a job

◊ **reunirse** *vr* **(a)** *(con alguien)* to meet *o* to assemble; **las dos partes se reunieron en el despacho del abogado** = the two sides met in the lawyer's office **(b) reunirse con** = to meet; *US* to meet with; **reunirse con una comisión negociadora** = to meet a negotiating committee; **reunirse con un representante en su hotel** = to meet an agent at his hotel; **espero reunirme con él en Nueva York** = I hope to meet with him in New York

revalorización *nf* appreciation *o* revaluation

revaluación *nf* revaluation *o* reassessment; **el balance de situación tiene en cuenta la revaluación de las propiedades de la compañía** = the balance sheet takes into account the revaluation of the company's properties; **la revaluación del dólar frente a la peseta** = the revaluation of the dollar against the peseta

revaluar *vt* to revalue *o* to reassess; **las propiedades de la compañía han sido revaluadas** = the company's properties have been revalued; **el dólar se ha revaluado frente a todas las demás monedas** = the dollar has been revalued against all the other currencies

revelación *nf* disclosure; **la revelación de la oferta de adquisición hizo subir el precio de las acciones** = the disclosure of the takeover bid raised share prices

revelar *vt* to reveal *o* to disclose; **el banco no tiene derecho a revelar los detalles de mi cuenta a la delegación de Hacienda** = the bank has no right to disclose details of my account to the tax office; **el director gerente no reveló el contrato al resto del consejo de administración** = the MD kept the contract secret from the rest of the board; **el gobierno se ha negado a revelar las cifras sobre el número de mujeres en paro** = the government has refused to release figures for the number of unemployed women

revendedor, -ra *n* seller *o* retailer *o* reseller; **rebaja al revendedor** = trade discount

revender *vt* to resell; **el contrato prohibe revender las mercancías a los EE UU** = the contract forbids resale of the goods to the USA; **comprar algo para revenderlo** = to purchase something for resale

reventa *nf* resale; **el contrato prohibe la reventa de las mercancías a los EE UU** = the contract forbids resale of the goods to the USA; **precio de reventa** = resale price

reventado, -da *adj* **estar reventado** = to be exhausted; **me vendió el coche por un precio reventado** = he sold me the car at a knockdown price

reversión *nf* reversion

reverso *nm* reverse *o* back; **calculó los costes en el reverso de un sobre** = he worked out the costs on the back of an envelope

revertible *adj* **anualidad revertible** = reversionary annuity

revertido, -da 1 *adj* **llamada a cobro revertido** = reverse charge call *o* transferred charge call; *US* collect call; **llamar a cobro revertido** = to reverse the charges; *US* to call collect 2 *pp de* REVERTIR

revertir *vi* to reverse *o* to return; **revertir en beneficio del comprador** = to benefit the purchaser

revés *nm* reversal *o* setback; **la empresa sufrió un revés (de fortuna) en el Extremo Oriente** *o* **una serie de reveses en 1995** = the company suffered a reversal in the Far East *o* a series of setbacks in 1995; **las acciones sufrieron un revés en la bolsa** = the shares had a setback on the Stock Exchange

los reveses en las urnas han crispado los nervios de los dirigentes y militantes del partido

Cambio 16

revisar *vt* **(a)** *(cuentas)* to audit *o* to check *o* to inspect; **revisar las cuentas** = (i) to inspect the accounts; (ii) to audit the accounts; **las cuentas no han sido revisadas todavía** = the accounts have not yet been audited **(b)** *(examinar)* to review *o* to examine; **revisar descuentos** = to review discounts; **revisar los salarios** = to review salaries; **su salario se revisará a fin de año** = his salary will be reviewed at the end of the year **(c)** *(corregir)* to revise; **las previsiones de ventas se revisan todos los años** = sales forecasts are revised annually; **el presidente está revisando su discurso para la junta general anual** = the chairman is revising his speech to the AGM **(d)** *(mecánica)* **revisar una máquina** = (i) to inspect a machine; (ii) to service a machine; **el ordenador ha sido devuelto al fabricante para que sea revisado** = the computer has gone back to the manufacturer for servicing

revisión *nf* **(a)** *(de una máquina)* service; **la máquina ha sido entregada para una revisión** = the machine has been sent in for service; **el coche necesita una revisión cada seis meses** = the car needs to be serviced every six months; **la revisión periódica del equipo** = the routine service of equipment; **centro de revisión** = service centre **(b)** *(inspección)* examination; **revisión financiera** = financial review; **revisión general** = general review; **revisión médica** = medical (examination); **revisión de salarios** = wage review *o* salary review; **la empresa ha decidido hacer una revisión de la remuneración de los trabajadores autónomos en vista del aumento del coste de la vida** = the company has decided to review freelance payments in the light of the rising cost of living **(c)** *(cuentas)* audit

revisor, -ra *n* **(a)** **revisor de cuentas** = auditor **(b)** *(transportes)* ticket collector

revista *nf* **(a)** magazine *o* review; **revista de bricolaje** = do-it-yourself magazine; **revista de informática** = computer magazine; **revista mensual** = monthly magazine *o* a monthly; **revista para mujeres** = women's magazine; **revista de una profesión** *o* **ramo** = trade journal *o* trade magazine *o* trade paper *o* trade publication; **revista semanal** = weekly magazine *o* a weekly; **revista de viajes** = travel magazine **(b)** **suscribirse a una revista** = to subscribe to a magazine *o* to take out a subscription to a magazine; **darse de baja de una revista** = to cancel a subscription to a magazine; **encarte publicitario de una revista** = magazine insert; **insertar un folleto publicitario en una revista especializada** = to insert a leaflet in a specialist magazine; **envío de revistas por correo** = magazine mailing

revocación *nf* *(cambio completo)* revoking *o* reversal; **revocación de crédito** = refusal of credit; **revocación de una orden** = revoking of an order

revocar *vt* to reverse *o* to revoke *o* to countermand; **el comité revocó su decisión sobre las cuotas de importación** = the committee reversed its decision on import quotas; **revocar una cláusula de un acuerdo** = to revoke a clause in an agreement; **la cuota de los artículos de lujo ha sido revocada** = the quota on luxury items has been revoked; **revocar una orden** = to countermand an order

rezagarse *vr* to fall behind

riada *nf* flood; **una riada de pedidos** = a flood of orders

rico, -ca 1 *adj* (a) rich *o* wealthy; **un agente de bolsa rico** = a rich stockbroker; **una empresa petrolífera rica** = a rich oil company (b) **rico en** = rich in; **el país es rico en minerales** = the country is rich in minerals; **un territorio rico en petróleo** = oil-rich territory **2** *n* rich person *o* wealthy person; **los ricos** = the rich

riesgo *nm* (a) *(peligro)* danger *o* risk; **correr un riesgo** = to run a risk; **no hay riesgo de que el personal de ventas se vaya** = there is no danger of the sales force leaving; **corre el riesgo de ser despedida** = she is in danger of being made redundant; **corre el riesgo de rebasar su presupuesto de promoción** = he is running the risk of overspending his promotion budget; **correr el riesgo de que le pongan a uno una multa** = to incur the risk of a penalty; **riesgo de incendio** = fire risk *o* fire hazard; **riesgo laboral** *o* **profesional** = occupational hazard; **los ataques cardíacos son uno de los riesgos laborales de los directores** = heart attacks are one of the occupational hazards of directors; **por cuenta y riesgo del comprador** = at the purchaser's risk *o* caveat emptor; **por cuenta y riesgo del propietario** = at owner's risk; **mercancías enviadas por cuenta y riesgo del cliente** = goods sent at owner's risk; **póliza a todo riesgo** = all-risks policy; **riesgo a cuenta del comprador** = at buyer's risk; **seguro a todo riesgo** = all-risks insurance *o* comprehensive insurance *o* full cover (b) **es una persona que presenta un bajo riesgo** *o* **gran riesgo** = he is a good *o* bad risk (c) **riesgo bancario** = bank exposure; **riesgo financiero** = financial risk; **no existe riesgo financiero en vender a crédito a Sudamérica** = there is no financial risk in selling to South American countries on credit; **intenta cubrir sus riesgos en el mercado inmobiliario** = he is trying to cover his exposure in the property market; **capital riesgo** = venture capital; **repartir un riesgo** = to spread a risk

> aunque los especialistas señalan las consecuencias positivas que hay en la jornada intensiva para los empleados, sin embargo, existen algunos riesgos que no siempre son resaltados suficientemente
>
> *El País*

> las cotizaciones se han movido a lo largo de esta semana con un margen muy estrecho, delimitado por el poco riesgo asumido por los inversores y las expectativas que a medio plazo despiertan los tipos de interés
>
> *El País*

riguroso, -sa *adj* strict; **por riguroso orden de**

antigüedad = in strict order of seniority; **los gastos están sujetos a un control riguroso** = expenses are kept under tight control

◊ **rigurosamente** *adv* strictly; **la empresa exige al personal que observe rigurosamente los trámites de compra** = the company asks all staff to follow strictly the buying procedures

rincón *nm* corner

riqueza *nf* wealth; **redistribución de la riqueza** = redistribution of wealth

> al contrario de la pobreza, un mal estudiado abundantemente por economistas y sociólogos, la riqueza es un tema virgen desde el punto de vista científico
>
> *El País*

ritmo *nm* rythm *o* rate; **al mismo ritmo** = at the same rate *o* pari passu; **ritmo de crecimiento** = growth rate; **ritmo de trabajo** = work rate; **ritmo de ventas** = rate of sales

rival 1 *nmf* rival; **vender a precio más bajo que un rival** = to sell at a lower price than a rival *o* to undercut a rival **2** *adj* rival; **empresas rivales** = rival firms *o* competing firms

rivalizar *vi* to compete

robar *vt* to steal *o* to rob; **la empresa competidora nos robó nuestros mejores clientes** = the rival company stole our best clients; **robaron de la caja los ingresos de la semana** = the week's takings were stolen from the cash desk

robo *nm* theft; **hacerse un seguro contra robo** = to take out insurance against theft; **medidas contra robos en una oficina** = office security; **robo en las tiendas** = shoplifting; **hemos empleado guardias de seguridad para proteger la tienda contra los robos** = we have brought in security guards to protect the store against theft; **están intentando reducir sus pérdidas por robo** = they are trying to cut their losses from theft; **uno de nuestros mayores problemas son los robos en la sección de objetos de regalo** = one of our biggest problems is stealing in the gifts department

> cuando se produce el extravío o robo de una tarjeta, tanto de débito o crédito, el titular de la misma únicamente responde ante la entidad por el importe equivalente a 150 ecus
>
> *El País*

robot *nm* robot; **el coche está fabricado por robots** = the car is made by robots

◊ **robótica** *nf* robotics

rodado, -da *adj* **circulación rodada** = road traffic; **transporte rodado** = road haulage

rojo, -ja 1 *adj (color)* red; **mi cuenta bancaria está en números rojos** = my bank account is in the red; **ponerse rojo** = to go red *o* to blush **2** *n* red; **estar al rojo vivo** = to be very hot *o* very excited

rollo *nm* (a) *(material enrollado)* roll; **rollo de papel para el fax** = fax roll; **¿puedes hacer un pedido de rollos de papel para el fax?** can you order some more rolls of fax paper?; **la calculadora de mesa lleva un rollo de papel** = the desk calculator uses a roll of paper (b) *(pesado y* *aburrido*) **estas reuniones son un rollo** = these meetings are terribly boring *o* dull; **rollo publicitario** = sales pitch

romper *vt* to break; **romper un compromiso** = to break an engagement; **la empresa espera poder romper el contrato** = the company is hoping to be able to break the contract; **romper las relaciones con alguien** = to break off relations with someone; **la dirección rompió las negociaciones con el sindicato** = management broke off negotiations with the union

◊ **romperse** *vr* to break down

◊ **rompehuelgas** *nmf* strikebreaker

ronda *nf* round; **una ronda de negociaciones salariales** = a round of pay negotiations; **ronda salarial** = pay round

ropa *nf* clothes *o* clothing; **ropa blanca** = white goods *o* linen; **rebajas de ropa blanca** = white sale

rotación *nf* (a) *(turno)* rotation; **dos consejeros terminan su mandato por rotación** = two directors retire by rotation (b) *(producción)* turnover; **rotación de personal** = staff turnover *o* turnover of staff; **rotación de existencias** = stock turnover *o* stock turn *o* stock turnround; **la empresa tiene una tasa de rotación de existencias del 6,7** = the company has a stock turn of 6.7

> la plantilla, en constante crecimiento y compuesta por 1.788 trabajadores tiene una rotación de personal muy baja
> **El País**

rotulador *nm* marker pen *o* felt pen

rótulo *nm* sign; **han solicitado permiso para colocar un gran rótulo rojo a la entrada de la tienda** = they have asked for planning permission to put up a large red shop sign; **rótulo publicitario** = showcard

rotundamente *adv* **rechazar rotundamente** = to refuse completely *o* flat out; **rechazó la oferta rotundamente** = he turned down the offer flat

rotura *nf* breaking; **roturas** = breakages; **en el caso de rotura o extravío** = in the event of breakage or loss

RP = RELACIONES PUBLICAS

Ruanda *nm* Rwanda

◊ **ruandés, -esa** *adj y n* Rwandan
NOTA: capital: **Kigeli**; moneda: **franco ruandés (FR)** = Rwanda franc (RF)

rublo *nm* *(moneda rusa)* rouble; *US* ruble

rubricar *vt* *(firmar con las iniciales)* to initial; **firmado y rubricado** = signed and sealed

rueda *nf* wheel; **rueda de prensa** = press conference

ruego *nm* *(petición)* request; **ruegos y preguntas** = any other business (AOB)

ruina *nf* ruin; **la compañía va a la ruina** = the company is heading for disaster *o* is on a disaster course; **edificio en ruinas** = derelict building

> un prestigioso despacho de abogados apoya la acción de un grupo de artistas que pretenden convertir una ruina municipal en un dinámico centro cultural
> **Ajoblanco**

Rumania *nf* Romania

◊ **rumano, -na** *adj y n* Romanian
NOTA: capital: **Bucarest** (= Bucharest); moneda: **leu** *o* **lei rumano** = Romanian leu *o* lei

rumbo *nm* route *o* direction; **rumbo a** = bound for *o* heading for; **sin rumbo** = drifting; **moverse sin rumbo** = to edge *o* to drift

rumor *nm* rumour *o* report; **¿puede confirmar el rumor según el cual la compañía tiene la intención de cerrar la fábrica?** = can you confirm the report that the company is planning to close the factory?

rupia *nf* *(moneda de uso en India y otros países)* rupee

ruptura *nf* (a) *(en las negociaciones)* breakdown; **una ruptura de las negociaciones salariales** = a breakdown in wage negotiations; **hubo una ruptura de las negociaciones después de seis horas** = negotiations broke down after six hours (b) *(excisión)* split; **una ruptura entre los accionistas pertenecientes a una familia** = a split in the family shareholders

Rusia *nf* Russia

◊ **ruso, rusa** *adj y n* Russian
NOTA: capital: **Moscú** (= Moscow); moneda: **rublo (Rub)** = rouble (Rub)

ruta *nf* route; **ruta del autobús** = bus route; **ruta habitual** = regular route; **las compañías fueron advertidas de que las rutas marítimas normales eran peligrosas debido a la guerra** = companies were warned that normal shipping routes were dangerous because of the war

rutina *nf* routine; **sigue una rutina cotidiana - toma el tren de las 8.15 a Barcelona luego el autobús a su oficina, y regresa siguiendo la misma ruta por la tarde** = he follows a daily routine - he takes the 8.15 train to Barcelona then the bus to his office, and returns by the same route in the evening; **las reformas de la sala de juntas han perturbado la rutina de la oficina** = refitting the conference room has disturbed the office routine

◊ **rutinario, -ria** *adj* routine; **llamada rutinaria** = routine call; **trabajo rutinario** = routine work

Ss

S.A. = SOCIEDAD ANONIMA

saber 1 *nm* knowledge **2** *vt/i* to know; **la secretaria del director gerente no sabe dónde está él** = the managing director's secretary does not know where he is; **cuando entró en la oficina del director no sabía que iba a ser ascendida** = when she went into the manager's office she did not realize she was going to be promoted; **saber de alguien** = to hear from someone; **nadie lo sabe** = it is anyone's guess

sacapuntas *nm* pencil sharpener

sacar *vt* **(a)** *(retirar)* to take out *o* to withdraw; **sacar dinero del banco** *o* **de una cuenta** *o* **de la cuenta propia** = to withdraw money from the bank *o* from an account *o* from your account **(b)** *(ganar)* to get out *o* to make; **sacar una ganancia neta del 10%** *o* **de 500.000 ptas.** en la operación = to make 10% *o* 500,000 pesetas net on the deal; **saca mucho dinero al año gracias al pluriempleo** = he makes a lot of money each year from moonlighting **(c)** sacar algo = to get out; **sacar de apuros** = to bail out; **sacar un contrato a licitación** *o* **a concurso** = to invite tenders for a contract; **sacar un proyecto** **a contrata** *o* **a licitación** *o* **a concurso** = to put a project out to tender *o* to ask for *o* to invite tenders for a project; **sacar partido de algo** = to take advantage of something; **sacar provecho** = to cash in on; **sacar el título de** = to qualify as; **máquina de sacar copias** = copier *o* copying machine **(d)** sacar algo a subasta = to put something up for auction

saco *nm* bag *o* sack; **un saco de patatas** = a sack of potatoes; **vendemos cebollas por sacos** = we sell onions by the sack

sala *nf* **(a)** *(habitación)* room; **¿cabrá el ordenador en esa sala tan pequeña?** = will the computer fit into that little room?; **sala de conferencias** = conference room; **sala de embarque** = departure lounge; **sala de exposición** *o* **de exhibición** = showroom *o* exhibition hall; **sala de exhibición de automóviles** = car showroom; **sala de juntas** *o* **de reuniones** = boardroom *o* conference room; **sala de subastas** = auction room *o* saleroom; **sala de tránsito** = transit lounge **(b)** *(juzgado)* **sala de apelación** = court of appeal

el símbolo arquitectónico del Pabellón de España es una sala cúbica de 576 metros cuadrados de superficie utilizable
Cambio 16

salarial *adj* **ajustes salariales** = wage adjustments; **deducciones salariales** = salary deductions; **diferencias salariales** *o* **coeficiente de ajuste salarial** = wage differentials; **negociaciones salariales** = pay negotiations *o* pay talks *o* wage negotiations; **política salarial** = wages policy; **reivindicación salarial** = wage claim; **renta salarial** = earned income; **renta no salarial** = private income *o* unearned income; **ronda salarial** = pay round; **una ronda de negociaciones salariales** = a round of pay negotiations

el incremento salarial medio hasta finales de junio se situó en el 7,79%
Mercado

el resultado del proceso de negociación salarial definirá el margen para el descenso de los tipos de interés, así como del tipo de cambio de la peseta
Actualidad Económica

las dos organizaciones preparan un nuevo proceso de negociación colectiva, en la que se va a plantear una subida salarial del 8%
Tiempo

salario *nm* **(a)** *(sueldo)* salary *o* pay *o* wage; **salario base** = basic pay *o* basic salary *o* basic wage; **el salario base es de 22.000 ptas. a la semana** se puede ganar más con horas extras = the basic wage is 22,000 pesetas a week, but you can expect to earn more than that with overtime; **salario garantizado** = guaranteed wage; **salario inicial** = starting salary; **salario interesante** = attractive salary; **salario líquido** = take-home pay; **salario mínimo** = minimum wage *o* basic wage; **salario mínimo interprofesional** = guaranteed minimum wage; **no gana el salario mínimo vital** = he does not earn a living wage; **salario neto** = take-home pay; **su salario neto es de 50.000 ptas. a la semana** = his take-home pay is *o* he takes home 50,000 pesetas a week; **salario por hora** = hourly wage *o* wage per hour; **percibía un salario de alrededor de 95.000 ptas.** = he was earning a salary in the region of 95,000 pesetas; **salario con incrementos anuales de 50.000 ptas.** = salary which rises in annual increments of 50,000 pesetas **(b)** **congelación de salarios** = wage freeze *o* freeze on wages; **escala de salarios** = wage scale; **hoja de salario** = pay slip; **igual salario** = equal pay; **niveles de salarios** = wage levels

el 72% de las pensiones están por debajo del salario mínimo
España Económica

el descenso de la inflación debería llevar a salarios más bajos que, a su vez, rebajarían la inflación
Actualidad Económica

saldar *vt* **(a)** *(liquidar)* to pay *o* to liquidate *o* to settle *o* to balance; **saldar una cuenta** = to settle an account; **saldar una deuda** = to pay *o* to settle *o* to liquidate a debt; **saldar las deudas propias** = to meet one's obligations **(b)** **saldar las cuentas** = to make up accounts *o* to close the accounts; **saldar a cuenta nueva** = bring forward

saldo *nm* **(a)** *(resultado)* balance *o* balance brought down; **saldo acreedor** *o* **a favor** *o* **positivo** = credit balance; **la cuenta arroja un saldo acreedor de 20.000 ptas.** = the account has a credit balance of 20,000 pesetas; **mi cuenta arroja todavía un saldo acreedor** = my bank account is still in credit *o* still in the black; **cuenta con saldo positivo** = account in credit; **la cuenta tiene un saldo positivo de 200.000 ptas.** = the account has a credit balance of 200,000 pesetas; **saldo a nuestro favor** = balance in our favour *o* balance due to us; **saldo de caja** = cash balance; **saldo de cuenta bancaria** = bank balance; **saldo deudor** *o* **en contra** *o* **negativo** = debit balance; **debido a los elevados pagos a proveedores, la cuenta arroja un saldo deudor de 200.000 ptas.** = because of large payments to suppliers, the account has a debit balance of 200,000 pesetas; **las cuentas arrojan un saldo negativo** = the accounts show a minus figure; **saldo disponible** = balance in hand; **saldo inicial** = opening balance; **saldo: 75.000 ptas.** = balance brought down: 75,000 pesetas; **saldo anterior** = balance brought forward; **saldo a cuenta nueva** = balance carrried forward; **pasar el saldo anterior a cuenta nueva** = to carry over a balance; **saldo final** = closing balance *o* bottom line; **al jefe sólo le interesa el saldo final** = the boss is interested only in the bottom line; **saldo líquido** = balance in hand *o* cash in hand; **el saldo tiene un error de 2.000 ptas.** = the balance is 2,000 pesetas out; **¿cuál es el saldo a pagar?** = what is the amount outstanding? **(b) saldo de una deuda** = liquidation of a debt **(c)** *(rebajas)* **saldos** = sale *o* bargain sale; **precios de saldo** = knockdown prices

salida *nf* **(a)** *(lugar y acto de salir)* exit *o* way out; **los clientes se abalanzaron hacia las salidas** = the customers all rushed towards the exits; **salida de incendios** *o* **de urgencia** = fire exit *o* emergency exit; **fichar a la salida del trabajo** = to clock out *o* clock off **(b)** *(transporte)* departure; **'salidas'** = 'departures'; **lugar de salida** = place of departure; **la salida del avión se retrasó dos horas** = the plane's departure was delayed by two hours; **no hay salidas a España debido a la huelga** = there are no sailings to Spain because of the strike **(c) permitir la salida** = to release; **permitir la salida de mercancías de la aduana** = to release goods from customs; **la aduana permitió la salida de las mercancías previo pago de una multa** = customs released the goods against payment of a fine **(d) dar salida a un producto** = to find an outlet *o* a market for a product **(e)** *(de capital)* outflow; **salida de capital de un país** = outflow of capital from a country

saliente *adj* retiring; **dos directores salientes se presentan a la reelección** = two retiring directors are offering themselves for re-election

salir *vi* **(a)** *(de un lugar)* to go *o* to depart *o* to leave; **el vuelo sale de Madrid a las 11.15** = the plane departs from Madrid at 11.15; **el tren sale de Barcelona a las 9.20 de la mañana y llega a Valencia cuatro horas después** = the train leaves Barcelona at 09.20 and arrives at Valencia four hours later; **salió de la oficina temprano para ir a la reunión** = he left his office early to go to the meeting **(b) salir perdiendo** = to lose out **(c) salir caro** *o* **barato** = to work out expensive *o* cheap

◊ **salirse** *vr* **salirse uno con la suya en los negocios** = to get one's way *o* to strike a hard bargain

salón *nm* **(a)** *(habitación)* lounge *o* room; **salón de reuniones** = conference room; **salón VIP** *o* **salón de personalidades** = VIP lounge **(b)** hall; **salón de exposiciones** = exhibition hall **(c)** *(feria)* **Salón del Automóvil** = Motor Show; **Salón Naútico** = Boat Show

saltar *vi* to jump

◊ **saltarse** *vr* to jump; **saltarse las reglas** = to break the rules; **se saltaron la cola y consiguieron la licencia de exportación antes que nosotros** = they jumped the queue and got their export licence before we did

◊ **salto** *nm* jump; **dar un salto** = to jump; **los valores de las acciones dieron un salto en la bolsa** = share values jumped on the Stock Exchange

salud *nf* health; **dimitió por motivos de salud** = he resigned for medical reasons

saludar *vt* to greet; *(en carta)* **le saluda atentamente** = (i) yours faithfully *o* Yours truly; *US* Truly yours; (ii) Yours sincerely; *US* Sincerely yours

saludo *nm* **(a) tarjeta de saludo** = compliments slip **(b)** *(en carta)* best wishes; **un saludo afectuoso** = yours sincerely; **mis mejores saludos** = best wishes *o* kind regards

Salvador, El *nm* El Salvador

◊ **salvadoreño, -ña** *adj y n* Salvadorian
NOTA: capital: **San Salvador**; moneda: **colón salvadoreño (C)** = Salvadorian colon (C)

salvaguardia *nf* safeguard; **cláusula de salvaguardia** = escape *o* hedge clause

salvamento *nm* salvage; **buque de salvamento** = salvage vessel; **lancha de salvamento** = lifeboat; **premio de salvamento** = salvage money

salvar *vt* **(a)** *(rescatar)* to rescue *o* to salvage; **estamos liquidando un almacén lleno de objetos salvados de un siniestro** = we are selling off a warehouse full of salvaged goods; **la compañía está intentando salvar su reputación después del encarcelamiento del director gerente por fraude** = the company is trying to salvage its reputation after the managing director was sent to prison for fraud; **el administrador judicial consiguió salvar algo de la ruina de la compañía** = the receiver managed to salvage something from the collapse of the company **(b)** *(ordenador)* to save (a file)

◊ **salvedad** *nf* **(a)** *(excepción)* proviso *o* exception; **me temo que no puedo hacer una**

salvedad a su favor = I am afraid I cannot make an exception in your case **(b)** qualification; **informe con salvedades** = qualified report

salvo, -va 1 *adj* safe **2** *adv* y *prep* except (for) *o* excepted *o* barring; **salvo error u omisión (s.e.u.o.)** = errors and omissions excepted (e. & o.e.); **las ventas están aumentando en todos los mercados salvo en el Extremo Oriente** = sales are rising in all markets except the Far East; **salvo instrucciones** *o* **órdenes al contrario** = failing instructions to the contrary; **salvo pronto pago** = failing prompt payment

sanción *nf* sanction; **sanción de demora** = penalty for delay; **sanciones económicas** = economic sanctions; **imponer sanciones económicas a un país** = to impose economic sanctions on a country

> los registradores dicen que la subida de las sanciones ayudará a que las empresas se lo piensen más a la hora de incumplir la ley, pero destacan que la medida realmente efectiva es el cierre del registro
>
> **El País**

sancionar *vt* to penalize; **sancionar a un proveedor por entregas tardías** = to penalize a supplier for late deliveries; **fueron sancionados por prestar un mal servicio** = they were penalized for bad service

saneamiento *nm (industria)* reorganization *o* restructuring *o* improvement; **saneamiento de las finanzas** = financial reorganization; **tendencia al saneamiento** = tendency to get better *o* to improve

> la balanza comercial presentó durante el transcurso del año pasado una ligera tendencia al saneamiento, ya que la tasa de cobertura ascendió al 20,6%
>
> **Tiempo**

> el volumen de recursos generados, agregación de beneficios y de los diferentes importes destinados a amortizaciones y saneamientos, se sitúa por encima de los 20.000 millones de pesetas
>
> **Actualidad Económica**

sangrado *nm* indent

sangrar *vt* to indent; **sangra tres espacios en la primera línea** = indent the first line three spaces

◊ **sangría** *nf* drain; **los costes de la sucursal de Badajoz son una sangría para los recursos financieros de la compañía** = the costs of the Badajoz office are a drain on the company's financial resources

satisfacción *nf* satisfaction; **satisfacción del cliente** = customer satisfaction; **satisfacción en el trabajo** *o* **laboral** = job satisfaction

satisfacer *vt* to satisfy *o* to meet (needs); **satisfacer a un cliente** = to satisfy a client; **satisfacer las exigencias de un cliente** = to meet a customer's requirements; **satisfacer la demanda** = to keep up with the demand; **satisfacer una demanda** = to satisfy a demand; **satisfacer la demanda de un nuevo producto** = to meet the demand for a new product; **no podemos producir carbón suficiente para satisfacer la demanda** =

we cannot produce enough coal to satisfy the demand for the product; **satisfacer una deuda** = to pay a debt; **satisfacer los requisitos** = to qualify for

◊ **satisfactorio, -ria** *adj* satisfactory; **los resultados de las pruebas del producto fueron satisfactorios** = the results of the tests on the product were satisfactory

◊ **satisfecho, -cha** *adj* y *pp* satisfied; **el director gerente no se mostró nada satisfecho cuando llegaron las cifras de ventas** = the MD was not at all happy when the sales figures came in

saturación *nf* saturation; **saturación del mercado** = saturation of the market *o* market saturation; **el mercado ha llegado al punto de saturación** = the market has reached saturation point; **saturación de producto** = a glut of produce

> la palabra saturación comienza a escucharse con relativa frecuencia en el mercado europeo de ordenadores personales
>
> **Micros**

saturar *vt* to saturate; **saturar el mercado** = to saturate the market; **el mercado de ordenadores personales está saturado** = the market for home computers is saturated; **la centralita estaba saturada de llamadas** = the switchboard was jammed with calls

SCLV = SERVICIO DE COMPENSACION Y LIQUIDACION DE VALORES

secante *nm* correction fluid

sección *nf* **(a)** *(apartado)* section; **mire la cifra en la sección de 'Costes 90-92'** = look at the figure under the heading 'Costs 90-92' **(b)** *(de una compañía)* department *o* division *o* branch; **sección de ventas al por menor** = retail division; **la sección de pinturas** = the paints division; **es jefe de una de las mayores secciones de la compañía** = he is in charge of one of the major divisions of the company; **nuestra sección internacional está radicada en las Bahamas** = our overseas branch is based in the Bahamas; **sección comercial** = marketing department; **sección de mecanografía** = typing pool; **intenté telefonear a la sección de reclamaciones pero estaba comunicando** = I tried to phone the complaints department but got only the engaged tone **(c)** *(de grandes almacenes)* department; **encontrará camas en la sección de muebles** = you will find beds in the furniture department; **sección de empaquetado para regalos** = gift-wrapping department; **sección (de tienda) de oportunidades** = bargain basement *o* bargain counter; **sección de guantes** = glove counter **(d)** *(de prensa)* desk; **la sección de noticias comerciales** = the business section *o* the business pages **(e)** de sección = divisional *o* departmental; **un director de sección** = a divisional director *o* a section head

seco, -ca *adj* dry; **dique seco** = dry dock

secretaría *nf* **(a)** *(secretaridad)* secretariat; **trabajo de secretaría** = secretarial work; **está buscando trabajo de secretaría** = he is looking for secretarial work **(b)** *(oficina)* secretary's office

◊ **secretariado** *nm* secretariat; **escuela de secretariado** = secretarial college; **está haciendo un curso de secretariado** = she is taking a secretarial course

◊ **secretario, -ria** *n* secretary; **mi secretaria se ocupa de los pedidos recibidos** = my secretary deals with incoming orders; **su secretaria llamó para decir que él llegaría tarde** = his secretary phoned to say he would be late; **secretario adjunto** = assistant secretary; **secretario y ayudante personal** = secretary and personal assistant; **secretaria eventual** = temporary secretary *o* temp; **tenemos dos secretarias eventuales trabajando en la oficina esta semana para despachar las cartas atrasadas** = we have two temps working in the office this week to clear the backlog of letters; **secretario de una compañía** = company secretary *o* registrar; **Secretario General (de las Naciones Unidas)** = United Nations Secretary-General; **secretario honorario** *o* **secretaria honoraria** = honorary secretary *o* hon sec; **fue elegida secretaria del comité** = she was elected secretary of the committee *o* committee secretary; **secretario particular** = private secretary; **secretaria personal** = personal assistant

el nuevo secretario general tendrá que tener las cualidades apropiadas y disfrutar de confianza; pero poco podrá hacer si no tiene respaldo político y económico

Actualidad Económica

secreto, -ta 1 *adj* secret; **firmaron un acuerdo secreto con sus principales competidores** = they signed a secret deal with their main rivals **2** *nm* secret; **guardar un secreto** = to keep a secret; **en secreto** = in confidence *o* in secret *o* secretly; **le mostraré el informe en secreto** = I will show you the report in confidence; **transfirió su cuenta bancaria a Suiza en secreto** = he transferred his bank account to Switzerland on the quiet; **desveló el secreto de las discusiones** = he broke the confidentiality of the discussions; **secreto profesional** = professional secret

sector *nm* sector; **todos los sectores de la economía se vieron afectados por la caída del tipo de cambio** = all sectors of the economy suffered from the fall in the exchange rate; **la tecnología es un sector de la economía en alza** = technology is a booming sector of the economy; **sector especial** = niche; **sector primario** = primary sector *o* primary industry; **sector privado** = private sector; **la expansión está totalmente financiada por el sector privado** = the expansion is funded completely by the private sector; **los salarios en el sector privado han subido con más rapidez que en el público** = salaries in the private sector have increased faster than in the public sector; **sector público** = public sector; **necesidad de préstamos del sector público** = public sector borrowing requirement (PSBR); **sector secundario** = secondary industry *o* secondary sector; **sector (de los) servicios** *o* **sector terciario** = service industry *o* tertiary industry *o* tertiary sector

el de los medios de comunicación es un sector cuya eficacia debe medirse tanto por la cuenta de resultados como por su servicio a la sociedad

Tiempo

por lo que se refiere al Sector Público, la tasa de crecimiento del crédito interno al mismo es prácticamente nula desde diciembre último

Mercado

la palabra marketing es un vocablo anglosajón, de reciente introducción en el sector hotelero español

Tiempo

secuencia *nf* sequence; **diagrama de secuencia** = flow chart

secuestrar *vt* to seize *o* to confiscate *o* to sequester *o* to sequestrate; *(un avión)* to hijack

secundario, -ria *adj* **(a)** *(no esencial)* incidental; **actividad secundaria** = sideline **(b)** *(de menor importancia)* secondary *o* minor *o* subsidiary; **estaban de acuerdo con la mayoría de las condiciones del contrato pero plantearon dudas sobre una o dos cuestiones secundarias** = they agreed to most of the conditions in the contract but queried one or two subsidiary items; **efecto secundario** = side-effect *o* knock-on effect; **producto secundario** = by-product **(c)** **industria secundaria** = secondary industry; **sector secundario** = secondary industry *o* secondary sector

sede *nf* base *o* head office (HQ) *o* main office; **la compañía tiene su sede en Madrid y sucursales en todos los países europeos** = the company has its base in Madrid and branches in all European countries; **la sede de la compañía está en Nueva York** = the company's headquarters are in New York; **la sede de la división** = the divisional headquarters

empresas y profesionales disponen desde hace unos días de un amplio directorio de empresas con sede en Cataluña que recoge datos sobre 12.000 sociedades de diversos sectores

El País

seducir *vt* to attract; **le sedujo la idea de trabajar seis meses en Australia** = the idea of working in Australia for six months appealed to her

segmentación *nf* segmentation

◊ **segmento** *nm* segment

seguido, -da 1 *adj* **(a)** *(sin interrupción)* continuous *o* successive; **los obreros trabajaron a toda marcha durante semanas seguidas para servir el pedido a tiempo** = the workforce worked flat out for weeks on end to finish the order on time **(b)** *(direcciones)* **todo seguido** = straight on **2** *nf* **en seguida** = straight away **3** *pp de* SEGUIR

seguir 1 *vi (continuar)* to carry on *o* to go on; **seguir con algo** = to proceed with something; **¿podemos seguir con la reunión de la comisión?** = shall we proceed with the committee meeting?; **seguir haciendo algo** = to carry on doing something *o* to get on with something; **el personal siguió trabajando a pesar del incendio** = the staff carried on *o* went on working in spite of the fire; **el personal siguió trabajando y terminó el pedido a tiempo** = the staff got on with the work and finished the order on time **2** *vt* **seguir el conducto reglamentario** = to go through official channels; **seguir una iniciativa** = to follow up an initiative

según *adv y prep* according to *o* under *o* depending on; **el ordenador se instaló según las instrucciones del fabricante** = the computer was installed according to the manufacturer's instructions; **según sea el presupuesto**

publicitario, **el nuevo producto se lanzará por radio o por televisión** = depending on the advertising budget, the new product will be launched on radio or on TV; **según contrato** = according to the contract *o* as per contract *o* contractually; **según los términos del contrato, la compañía es responsable de todos los daños causados a la propiedad** = by *o* under the terms of the contract, the company is responsible for all damage to the property; **según los términos del acuerdo, la mercancía debe ser entregada en octubre** = under the terms of the agreement, the goods should be delivered in October; **según factura** = as per invoice; **según muestra** = as per sample; **según nota de expedición** = as per advice; **según su pedido anterior** = as per previous order

segundo, -da *adj* second; **segundo anuncio** = readvertisement; **segunda hipoteca** = second mortgage; **segundo semestre** = second half-year; **segundo trimestre** = second quarter

◊ **de segunda mano** *adj y adv* secondhand; **comprar algo de segunda mano** = to buy something secondhand; **comerciante de mercancías de segunda mano** = secondhand dealer; **el mercado de coches de segunda mano** = the secondhand car market *o* the market in secondhand cars

seguridad *nf* **(a)** *(protección)* safety; security; **la seguridad en esta oficina es nula** = security in this office is nil; **caja de seguridad** = safe deposit box; **con seguridad** = safely; **copia de seguridad** = backup copy; **dispositivos de seguridad** = machinery guards; **guardia de seguridad** = security guard; **margen de seguridad** = safety margin *o* margin of safety; **para mayor seguridad** = for safety; **guardamos los documentos en el banco para mayor seguridad** = we put the documents into the bank for safe keeping; **hacer una copia del disco para mayor seguridad** = to take a copy of the disk for safety; **medidas de seguridad** = safety precautions; **medidas de seguridad de un aeropuerto** = airport security; **medidas de seguridad en una oficina** = office security; **tomar medidas de seguridad** = to take safety precautions *o* safety measures; **normas de seguridad** = safety regulations; **responsable de la seguridad contra incendios** = fire safety officer; **por razones de seguridad** = for safety **(b)** **la Seguridad Social** = social security; *GB* National Insurance; **cotizaciones a la Seguridad Social** = National Insurance contributions; **vive de las prestaciones de la seguridad social** = he lives on social security payments **(c)** *(certeza)* **seguridad de empleo** = job security; **seguridad de permanencia en el empleo** = security of employment

> París, con más de nueve millones de habitantes, una buena parte de ellos inmigrantes, cubre todas sus necesidades de seguridad
>
> *Cambio 16*

seguro, -ra 1 *adj* **(a)** *(protegido)* safe *o* secure; **poco seguro** = unreliable *o* unsafe; **ponga los documentos en el armario para que estén seguros** = put the documents in the cupboard for safety; **guarde los documentos en un lugar seguro** = keep the documents in a safe place; **la empresa fabrica un producto muy seguro** = the company makes a very reliable product; **empleo seguro** = secure job;

inversión segura = secure *o* safe investment; **lugar seguro** = safe keeping **(b)** *(cierto)* certain *o* confident *o* sure; **el presidente está seguro de que sobrepasaremos el nivel de ventas del año pasado** = the chairman is certain we will pass last year's total sales; **estoy seguro de que el volumen de ventas aumentará rápidamente** = I am confident the turnover will increase rapidly; **¿está Vd. seguro de que el equipo de ventas es capaz de vender este producto?** = are you confident the sales team is capable of handling this product? **(c)** *(firme)* **venta segura** = firm sale **2** *nm* insurance **(a)** **seguro de accidentes** = accident insurance; **seguro de automóviles** = car insurance *o* motor insurance; **seguro corriente de vida** = whole-life insurance; **seguro de enfermedad** = health insurance; **seguro general** = general insurance; **seguro contra incendios** = fire insurance; **hacerse un seguro contra incendios** = to take out an insurance against fire; **seguro marítimo** = marine insurance; **seguro médico** = medical insurance; **seguro a todo riesgo** = full cover *o* comprehensive insurance; **seguro temporal** = term insurance; **firmó un seguro temporal de diez años** = he took out a ten-year term insurance; **seguro contra terceros** = third party insurance *o* third party policy; **seguro total** *o* **mixto** = endowment insurance; **seguro de vida** = life assurance *o* life insurance; **seguro de la vivienda** = house insurance; **suscribió un seguro de vida** *o* **un seguro de su casa** = she took out a life assurance policy *o* a house insurance policy; **póliza de seguro de la vivienda** = household insurance policy **(b)** **agente de seguros** = insurance agent *o* insurance broker; **certificado de seguro** = insurance certificate; **cobertura del seguro** = insurance cover; **compañía de seguros** = insurance company *o* assurance company; **contrato de seguros** = insurance contract; **corredor de seguros** = insurance agent *o* insurance broker; **póliza de seguros** = insurance policy *o* assurance policy; **póliza de seguros de la propia vivienda o contra los riesgos del hogar** = homeowner's insurance policy; **prima de seguros** = insurance premium; **sin seguro** = uninsured **(c)** **hacerse un seguro** = to take out an insurance policy; **hacer un seguro de la casa** = to take out an insurance on the house; **hacerse un seguro contra robo** = to take out insurance against theft; **los daños están cubiertos por el seguro** = the damage is covered by the insurance; **el seguro se hará cargo de las reparaciones** = repairs will be paid for by the insurance; **pagar el seguro de un coche** = to pay the insurance on a car

selección *nf* **(a)** *(elección)* selection; **selección de candidatos** = screening of candidates; **selección y formación del personal** = recruitment and training of personnel **(b)** *(muestreo)* sample; **selección al azar** = random sampling

seleccionar *vt* to select; **seleccionar candidatos** = to screen candidates

selectivo, -va *adj* selective; **huelgas selectivas** = selective strikes

selecto, -ta *adj* select *o* choice; **nuestros clientes son muy selectos** = our customers are very select; **alimentación selecta** = choice foodstuffs; **carne selecta** = choice meat; **vinos selectos** = choice wines

sellar *vt* to seal *o* to stamp; **los documentos fueron**

sellados por los funcionarios de la aduana = the documents were stamped by the customs officials

sello *nm* stamp; *(Extremo Oriente)* chop; *(timbre)* rubber stamp; **sello de correos** = a postage stamp; **un sello de 45 ptas.** = a 45 peseta stamp; **poner el sello** = to stamp; **estampó la factura con el sello de 'Pagado'** = he stamped the invoice 'Paid'; **la factura lleva el sello de 'recibí'** *o* **'pagado'** *o* **'cobrado'** = the invoice has the stamp 'Received with thanks' on it; **el funcionario de aduanas le miró los sellos del pasaporte** = the customs officer looked at the stamps in his passport; **sello de la compañía** = common seal *o* company's seal; **sello de contraste** = assay mark *o* hallmark

semana *nf* week; **gana 50.000 ptas. a la semana** *o* **por semana** = he earns 50,000 pesetas a week *o* per week; **trabaja treinta y cinco horas por semana** = she works thirty-five hours per week *o* she works a thirty-five-hour week; **pedimos a los representantes que se presenten todos los viernes para informarnos de las ventas de la semana** = we ask the reps to call in every Friday to report the weeks' sales; **tenemos dos secretarias eventuales trabajando en la oficina esta semana para despachar las cartas atrasadas** = we have two temps working in the office this week to clear the backlog of letters; **a mediados de semana** = mid-week; **la semana pasada** = last week; **la empresa cerró la semana pasada** = the firm went out of business last week; **la semana que viene** = next week; **la causa se verá la semana que viene** = the case is being heard next week; **semana laboral** = working week *o* workweek; **semana laboral normal** = the normal working week

◊ **semanal** *adj* weekly; **el sueldo semanal por el trabajo es de 25.000 ptas.** = the weekly rate for the job is 25,000 pesetas; **revista semanal** = a weekly magazine *o* a weekly

◊ **semanalmente** *adj* weekly; **cobrar semanalmente** = to be paid by the week

◊ **semanario** *nm* weekly (magazine)

> llamó mucho la atención que dentro del mismo semanario convivieran columnistas de prestigio de muy distinta tendencia ideológica
> **Tiempo**

semestral *adj (dos veces al año)* half-yearly *o* bi-annually; **cuentas semestrales** = half-yearly accounts; **estado de cuentas semestral** = half-yearly statement; **pagos semestrales** = half-yearly payment; **una reunión semestral** = a half-yearly meeting

◊ **semestralmente** *adv (cada seis meses)* bi-annually *o* half-yearly

semestre *nm* **(a)** *(seis meses)* half-year; **primer semestre** *o* **segundo semestre** = first half-year *o* second half-year; **comunicar los resultados del primer semestre** = to announce the first half-year's results *o* the results for the half-year to June 30th; **esperamos mejoras en el segundo semestre** = we look forward to improvements in the second half-year; **los contables prepararon un balance de situación del primer semestre** = the accountants prepared a balance sheet for the first half-year **(b)** *(universidad)* semester

semi- *prefijo* semi-; **productos semiacabados** = semi-finished products; **un organismo semi oficial** = a quasi-official body; **trabajos semicualificados** = semi-skilled jobs; *(imprenta)* **calidad semicorrespondencia** = near letter-quality (NLQ)

sencillo, -lla *adj* **(a)** *(billete de ida)* single; **tarifa** *o* **billete** *o* **pasaje sencillo** = one-way fare *o* ticket **(b)** *(simple)* plain; **queremos que los modelos baratos tengan un diseño sencillo** = we want the cheaper models to have a plain design

Senegal *nm* Senegal

◊ **senegalés, -esa** *adj y n* Senegalese
NOTA: capital: **Dakar;** moneda: **franco CFA (FCFA)** = CFA franc (CFAF)

sensible *adj* sensitive; **el mercado es muy sensible al resultado de las elecciones** = the market is very sensitive to the result of the elections; **producto sensible a los cambios de precio** = price-sensitive product

sentada *nf (protesta de brazos caídos)* sit-down protest; **los trabajadores organizaron una sentada en protesta por las malas condiciones de trabajo** = the workers organized a sit-down protest against bad working conditions

sentencia *nf* award *o* judgement *o* judgment; **sentencia de embargo** = garnishee order *o* garnishment; **pronunciar sentencia** = to pronounce judgement; **una sentencia de la magistratura de trabajo** = an award by an industrial tribunal; **deudor por sentencia firme** = judgment debtor; **aplazamiento de la ejecución de una sentencia** = stay of execution

sentido *nm* **(a)** sense; **no tiene ningún sentido** = it doesn't make any sense; **en cierto sentido** = in a sense; **sin sentido** = meaningless **(b)** effect; **hemos tomado disposiciones en este sentido** = we have made provision to this effect **(c)** *(dirección)* direction; **cambio de sentido** = U-turn *o* change of direction; **sentido único** = one way

sentir *vt* **(a)** to feel *o* to sense **(b)** to regret; **siento tener que despedir a tanto personal** = I regret having to make so many staff redundant

señal *nf* **(a)** *(marca)* mark *o* tick; **ponga una señal en el espacio indicado con 'R'** *o* **marque la casilla indicada con una 'R'** = put a tick in the box marked 'R' **(b)** *(dinero)* deposit; **dejar una señal para un reloj** = to leave a deposit on a watch; **dejar una señal de 2.000 ptas.** = to leave 2,000 pesetas as deposit; **dejar una señal** = to pay money down **(c)** *(teléfonos)* **señal de comunicar** = engaged tone; **señal de línea** = dialling tone **(d)** *(informática)* flag

señalar *vt* to mark *o* to point out; **el informe señala los errores cometidos por la compañía durante el año pasado** = the report points out the mistakes made by the company over the last year; **señaló que los resultados eran mejores que en años anteriores** = he pointed out that the results were better than in previous years

señalizar *vt* **(a)** *(ruta)* to signpost **(b)** *(informática)* to flag

señas *nfpl* address; **etiqueta de señas** = address label

Señor *nm* **(a)** man *o* Mister *o* Mr *o* Sir; **'Muy señor**

mío *o* **nuestro'** = 'Dear Sir'; **Estimado Señor** = Dear Sir; **Estimado Señor García** = Dear Mr García; **'Estimados Señores'** *o* **'Muy Señores míos** *o* **nuestros'** = 'Dear Sirs' **(b)** *(hombre)* **'señores'** = 'gentlemen'; **'señoras y señores'** = 'ladies and gentlemen'; **'bien, señores, todos hemos leído el informe de nuestra oficina australiana'** = 'well, gentlemen, we have all read the report from our Australian office'

Señora *nf* lady *o* Madam *o* Mrs; **Estimada Señora** = Dear Madam; **Estimada Señora García** = Dear Mrs García; **Señora Presidenta** = Madam Chairman; **'señoras y señores'** = 'ladies and gentlemen'

◊ **Señorita** *nf* young lady *o* Miss; **Estimada Señorita García** = Dear Miss García; **la señorita García es nuestra directora de ventas** = Miss García is our sales manager

separado, -da **1** *adj (aparte)* separate; **por separado** = severally *o* separately; **enviar algo por separado** = to send something under separate cover; **cada trabajo se facturó por separado** = each job was invoiced separately; **son responsables en grupo y por separado** = they are jointly and severally liable **2** *pp de* SEPARAR

◊ **separadamente** *adv* separately *o* severally

separar *vt* to separate; **no pudo separar las páginas porque los documentos estaban grapados** = he could not separate the pages, because the documents were stapled together

ser *vi* **(a)** to be; **ser el primero** = to lead; **es la primera empresa en el mercado de ordenadores baratos** = the company leads the market in cheap computers **(b)** **o sea que** = that is *o* i.e.; **las restricciones a la importación se aplican a los artículos caros, o sea artículos que cuestan más de 250.000 ptas.** = the import restrictions apply to expensive items, i.e. items costing more than 250,000 pesetas

Serbia *nf* Serbia

◊ **serbio, -bia** *adj y n* Serbian
NOTA: capital: **Belgrado** = (Belgrade); moneda: **dinar** = dinar

serie *nf* **(a)** series; **producción en serie** = mass production; **una serie de adquisiciones favorables hicieron de la compañía una de las más grandes del sector** = a series of successful takeovers made the company one of the largest in the trade; **el contable firmó una serie de cheques** = the accountant signed a batch of cheques; **despachamos los pedidos por series de cincuenta** = we deal with the orders in batches of fifty; **una serie de huelgas de celo redujeron la producción** = a series of go-slows reduced production; **una serie de cheques procesados por el ordenador** = a cheque run **(b)** **fuera de serie** = one-off

serio, -ria *adj* serious; **la dirección está haciendo un intento serio para mejorar las condiciones de trabajo** = the management is making serious attempts to improve working conditions; **en serio** = seriously; **tomamos la amenaza de los competidores muy en serio** = we are taking the threat from our competitors very seriously

◊ **seriamente** *adv* seriously

serpiente *nf (UE)* serpiente monetaria = (monetary) snake

servicio *nm* **(a)** *(trabajo)* service *o* duty; **de servicio** = on duty; **estar de servicio** = to be on duty; **la telefonista está de servicio de las 6 a las 9** = the switchboard operator is on duty from 6 to 9 **(b)** *(departamento)* ofrece un servicio de asesoramiento = he offers a consultancy service; **sección de servicios administrativos** = service department; **servicio de contestación** = answering service; **servicio médico** = health service; **servicio permanente** = 24-hour service; **servicio de recepción** = receiving department **(c)** **industria de servicios** = service industry *o* service sector; **oficina de servicios** = service bureau **(d)** *(al cliente)* **el servicio en ese restaurante es extremadamente lento** = the service in that restaurant is extremely slow; **le reembolsaron totalmente cuando se quejó del servicio** = he got a full refund when he complained about the service **(e)** *(propina)* **suplemento por el servicio** = service charge; **se añade un 10% por el servicio** = a 10% service charge is added; **la cuenta incluye el servicio** = the bill includes service; **¿está el servicio incluido en la cuenta?** = is the service included? *o* does the bill include a service charge?; **el servicio no está incluido** = service is extra; **el camarero ha añadido un 10% por el servicio** = the waiter has added 10% to the bill for the service; **el servicio no se cobra** = there is no charge for service *o* no charge is made for service **(f)** *(maquinaria)* service *o* maintenance; **servicio de asistencia técnica** = support service; **servicio de mantenimiento** = service department; **contrato de servicio de mantenimiento** = service contract *o* maintenance contract; **manual de servicio** = service manual; **servicio posventa** = after-sales service; **ofrecemos un servicio posventa gratuito a los clientes** = we offer a free backup service to customers; **estación de servicio** = service station **(g)** *(organización pública)* service; **servicio público** (i) public service (ii) utility; **Servicio de Compensación y Liquidación de Valores (SCLV)** = share clearing and settlement service; **el servicio de correos es eficiente** = the postal service is efficient; **servicio de cartas postales** *o* **de paquetes postales** = letter post *o* parcel post **(h)** *(medio de transporte)* **el servicio de autobuses es muy irregular** = the bus service is very irregular; **no existen servicios para pasajeros** = there are no facilities for passengers; **tenemos un buen servicio de trenes a Sevilla** = we have a good train service to Seville **(i)** *(condiciones de trabajo)* service; **condiciones de servicio** = terms of employment *o* of service; **las nuevas condiciones de servicio entrarán en vigor a partir del 1 de enero** = the new terms of service will operate from January 1st **(j)** **la compañía tiene problemas para pagar el servicio de sus deudas** = the company is having problems in servicing its debts

◊ **servicios** *nmpl* toilets

la familia obtiene servicio médico gratuito y si lo requiere, también enseñanza gratuita

España Económica

servidumbre *nf* easement; **servidumbre de paso** = right of way

servir *vt* **(a)** to serve; **servir un pedido** = to deal with an order; **pedido no servido** = unfulfilled order;

tardan mucho en servir un pedido = they take a long time to dispatch an order; **sírvase Vd. mismo** = serve yourself; **sírvase sentarse** = please sit down **(b) servir un pago** = to meet a payment

sesión *nf* **(a)** *(asamblea)* meeting *o* session; **sesión de apertura** = opening session; **sesión de clausura** = closing session; **sesión plenaria** = plenary meeting *o* plenary session; **abrir la sesión** = to open a meeting; **levantar una sesión** = to close a meeting; **la sesión de la mañana** *o* **de la tarde tendrá lugar en la sala de reuniones** = the morning session *o* the afternoon session will be held in the conference room; **tuvo que asistir a una sesión de reciclaje** = he had to attend a retraining session **(b)** *(bolsa)* **sesión bursátil** = trading session; **las acciones habían subido ligeramente al final de la sesión** = shares were up slightly at the end of the day; **las acciones subieron después del cierre de la sesión** = the shares rose in after-hours trading **(c)** *(jurídico)* hearing; **la sesión de la audiencia fue aplazada** = the court proceedings were adjourned

s.e.u.o. = SALVO ERROR U OMISION errors and omissions excepted (e.& o.e.)

severo, -ra *adj* severe *o* strict; **tenemos un jefe muy severo** = our boss is strict

◊ **severamente** *adv* severely; **los servicios de trenes han sido severamente afectados por la nieve** = train services have been severely affected by snow

'show' *nm* show

> el show fue un éxito y ha dado origen a un concurso internacional de diseñadores de ropa
>
> **Ajoblanco**

siempre 1 *adv* always; **como siempre** = as usual; **para siempre** = for ever **2** *conj* **siempre que** = provided that *o* providing; **la mercancía se entregará la semana próxima siempre que los conductores no estén en huelga** = the goods will be delivered next week provided *o* providing the drivers are not on strike

Sierra Leona *nf* Sierra Leone; **de Sierra Leona** = Sierra Leonean
NOTA: capital: **Freetown**; moneda: **leone de Sierra Leona (Le)** = Sierra Leonean leone (Le)

sigilosamente *adv* on the quiet

sigla *nf* initial *o* abbreviation; **¿qué significan las siglas FMI?** = what do the initials FMI stand for?

signatario, -ria *adj y n* signatory

significar *vt* to mean; **¿qué significan estas cifras?** = what do these figures mean?

silencioso, -sa *adj* silent

simbólico, -ca *adj* nominal *o* token; **pago simbólico** = token payment; **hay un pago simbólico por la calefacción** = a token charge is made for heating; **arrendar una propiedad por una renta simbólica** = to lease a property for *o* at a peppercorn rent

símbolo *nm* symbol; **tienen un oso como símbolo publicitario** = they use a bear as their advertising symbol; **símbolos de posición social** = status symbols

simple *adj* plain *o* simple; **avería simple** = particular average; **interés simple** = simple interest

sin *prep* without; **sin cobrar** = uncashed; **cheques sin cobrar** = uncashed cheques; **impuestos sin cobrar** = uncollected taxes; **sin condiciones** = unconditional; **sin fecha** = undated; **intentó hacer efectivo un cheque sin fecha** = he tried to cash an undated cheque; **sin papel carbón** = carbonless; **sin problema** = no problem; **sin riesgo** = risk-free *o* riskless; **una inversión sin riesgo** = a risk-free investment; **sin trabajo** = jobless *o* without a job; **2.000 empleados se quedaron sin trabajo por la recesión** = 2,000 employees were made idle by the recession; **sin valor** = worthless

sindicado, -da *adj* unionized; **empresa que contrata a trabajadores no sindicados** = firm using non-union labour

sindical *adj* syndical; **cargos sindicales** = union officials; **cuota sindical** *o* **cuota de inscripción sindical** = union dues *o* union subscription; **delegado** *o* **enlace** *o* **representante sindical** = shop steward *o* union representative *o* union delegate

◊ **sindicalista** *nmf* trade unionist *o* unionist

> el programa sindical recopila las reivindicaciones a medio y largo plazo
>
> **Tiempo**

> la posibilidad de unas elecciones anticipadas podría llegar a frenar planes de inversión a corto plazo, como lo haría una mayor protesta sindical
>
> **Actualidad Económica**

> las propuestas de las centrales sindicales han sido rechazadas por la dirección del partido
>
> **España Económica**

sindicato *nm* **(a)** *(asociación de trabajadores)* trade union *o* trades union; *US* labor union; **sindicato obrero** = blue-collar union; **los sindicatos y la patronal** = unions and management; **están afiliados a un sindicato** *o* **son miembros del sindicato** = they are members of a trades union *o* they are trade union members; **ha solicitado la afiliación a un sindicato** = he has applied for trade union membership *o* he has applied to join a trades union; **está actuando conforme a la norma 23 de los estatutos del sindicato** = he is acting under rule 23 of the union constitution; **el sindicato pide a la dirección que emplee solamente a trabajadores sindicados** = the union is asking the management to agree to a closed shop; **reconocimiento de un sindicato** = union recognition; **reglamentos de un sindicato** = rulebook **(b)** *(consorcio)* syndicate; **sindicato de arbitraje** = arbitrage syndicate; **sindicato bancario** = bank syndicate

> los sindicatos se han distanciado de un Gobierno socialista moderado cuyo pacto de competitividad han rechazado temiendo que acarreara un descenso del nivel de vida
>
> **Actualidad Económica**

> los sindicatos anuncian ya nuevas manifestaciones y presiones más radicales si el Gobierno no modifica sus planes
>
> **El País**

síndico *nm* **(a)** *(quiebra)* liquidator *o* official receiver; **síndicos de la quiebra** = trustees in bankruptcy **(b)** *(bolsa)* **síndico presidente** = Chairman of the Stock Exchange Council

sinergia *nf* synergy

Singapur *nm* Singapore; **de Singapur** = Singaporean
NOTA: capital: **Singapur** (= Singapore); moneda: **dólar de Singapur (S$)** = Singapore dollar (S$)

siniestro *nm* accident *o* disaster; **declaración de siniestro** = insurance claim; **el coche fue declarado siniestro total** = the car was a write-off *o* the car was written off as a total loss

sintético, -ca *adj* synthetic; **fibras sintéticas** *o* **materiales sintéticos** = synthetic fibres *o* synthetic materials

Siria *nf* Syria

◊ **sirio, -ria** *adj y n* Syrian
NOTA: capital: **Damasco** (= Damascus); moneda: **libra siria (LS)** = Syrian pound (LS)

sirviente, -ta *n* servant

sistema *nm* **(a)** *(organización)* system; **sistema de clasificación** = filing system; **el sistema de descuentos concedidos por la empresa** = the company's discount structure; **la compañía está modificando su sistema de descuentos** = the company is reorganizing its discount structure; **sistema fiscal** = tax system; **el sistema de organización de la oficina** = the setup in the office; **sistema de tiempo real** = real-time system; **nuestro sistema de contabilidad ha funcionado bien a pesar del gran aumento de pedidos** = our accounting system has worked well in spite of the large increase in orders; **utilizar un sistema de cupo** = to operate a quota system; **organizamos nuestra distribución según un sistema de cupo - cada representante recibe solamente un número determinado de unidades** = we arrange our distribution using a quota system - each agent is allowed only a certain number of units; **sistema decimal** = decimal system; **el sistema de ferrocarriles** = the railway system **(b)** *(informática)* **sistema de ordenador compuesto de un microprocesador y seis terminales** = computer system consisting of a microprocessor and six terminals; **un sistema informático moderno** = an up-to-date computer system; **quitamos los teléfonos viejos e instalamos un sistema informatizado** = we threw out the old telephones and installed a computerized system; **sistema operativo** = operating system; **sistema operativo del disco** = disk operating system (DOS); **sistema operativo de redes** = network operating system; **análisis de sistemas** = systems analysis; **analista de sistemas** = systems analyst

◊ **Sistema Monetario Europeo (SME)** *nm* European Monetary System (EMS)

sistemático, -ca *adj* systematic; **pidió un informe sistemático sobre el servicio de distribución** = he ordered a systematic report on the distribution service

sitio *nm* site *o* place *o* location; **hay mucho sitio** = there is plenty of room; **cualquier sitio** = anywhere

sito, -ta *adj* located; **la empresa Cintas S.A., sita en Albacete** = Cintas S.A., located in Albacete

situación *nf* situation *o* position; **evaluar una situación** = to take stock of a situation; **situación de endeudamiento** = state of indebtedness; **la situación financiera de una compañía** = financial situation of a company; **¿cuál es la situación de caja?** = what is the cash position?; **balance de situación** = balance sheet; **los contables prepararon un balance de situación del primer semestre** = the accountants prepared a balance sheet for the first half-year; **estamos viviendo una situación de depresión económica** = we are experiencing slump conditions

situado, -da 1 *adj* situated *o* located; **estar situado** = to be located; **la fábrica estará situada cerca de la autopista** = the factory will be sited near the motorway; **el almacén está situado en las afueras de la ciudad** = the warehouse is located on the edge of the town **2** *pp de* SITUAR

situar *vt* **(a)** to place *o* to set up **(b)** to invest

◊ **situarse** *vr* to get a job *o* a position; **su hijo está bien situado en la empresa familiar** = their son has a good position in the family business

S.L. = SOCIEDAD LIMITADA

SME = SISTEMA MONETARIO EUROPEO

soberano *nm* *(moneda de oro)* sovereign

sobornar *vt* to bribe; **tuvimos que sobornar a la secretaria del ministro para que nos permitiera ver a su jefe** = we had to bribe the minister's secretary before she would let us see her boss

◊ **soborno** *nm* bribe *o* kickback; *(informal)* backhander; **el ministro fue destituido por aceptar sobornos** = the minister was dismissed for taking bribes; **dinero para sobornos** = slush fund

sobrante 1 *adj* spare; **estamos tratando de alquilar el espacio sobrante del almacén** = we are trying to let surplus capacity in the warehouse; **capital sobrante** = spare capital *o* redundant capital **2** *nm* excess *o* surplus

sobre 1 *nm* envelope; **impresora de sobres** = addressing machine; **sobre cerrado** = sealed envelope; **enviar la información en sobre cerrado** = to send the information in a sealed envelope; **sobre abierto** *o* **sobre sin cerrar** = unsealed envelope; **sobre para avión** *o* **para correo aéreo** = airmail envelope; **enviar una revista en un sobre corriente** = to send a magazine under plain cover; **sobre con ventanilla** = aperture envelope *o* window envelope; **un sobre franqueado con la dirección del destinatario** = a stamped addressed envelope; **si desea más información junto con nuestro último catálogo envíe un sobre franqueado con su dirección** = please send a stamped addressed envelope for further details and our latest catalogue; **sobre de paga** = wage packet **2** *prep* **(a)** against; **¿**

puede darme un anticipo sobre el sueldo del mes próximo? = can I have an advance against next month's salary? **(b)** on *o* about *o* over; **las observaciones del presidente sobre los auditores se hicieron constar en acta** = the chairman's remarks about the auditors were minuted; **los tenedores de obligaciones tienen prioridad sobre los tenedores de acciones ordinarias** = debenture holders have priority over ordinary shareholders; **no hay insuficiencia de asesoramiento sobre las inversiones** = there is no shortage of investment advice; **telefonear sobre algo** = to telephone about something; **impuesto sobre la plusvalía** = capital gains tax; **suprimir los impuestos sobre el alcohol** = to take the duty off alcohol; **sobre el terreno** = in the field; **tenemos dieciséis representantes sobre el terreno** = we have sixteen reps in the field **(c) sobre todo** = mainly *o* mostly; **estamos interesados sobre todo en comprar artículos de regalo para niños** = we are interested mainly in buying children's gift items **3** *prefijo* super- *o* over-

◊ **sobrecapacidad** *nf* overcapacity; **la sobrecapacidad de la empresa crea problemas de almacenaje** = the company's overcapacity creates problems for the warehouse

◊ **sobrecapitalizado, -da** *adj* overcapitalized

◊ **sobrecarga** *nf* surcharge; **pagamos una sobrecarga por exceso de equipaje** = we paid an excess baggage charge

◊ **sobrecargar** *vt* to overcharge

◊ **sobrecargo** *nm* overcharge

◊ **sobrecontratación** *nm* overbooking; **la sobrecontratación de los hoteles el verano pasado motivó una avalancha de reclamaciones en las agencias de viaje** = overbooking of hotels last summer caused a flood of complaints to travel agents

◊ **sobregiro** *nm* overdraft

sobrepagar *vt* to outbid

sobrepasar *vt* to exceed *o* to cap; **descuento que no sobrepasa el 15%** = discount not exceeding 15%; **hemos sobrepasado nuestro límite de crédito** = we have exceeded our overdraft facilities

◊ **sobreprima** *nf* additional *o* extra premium; **tuve que pagar una sobreprima para cubrir el seguro de viajes** = I had to pay an extra premium to cover travel insurance

◊ **sobreproducción** *nf* overproduction

sobrepujar *vt (pujar más alto)* to outbid

◊ **sobresaliente** *adj* outstanding *o* excellent

sobrestimar *vt* to overestimate *o* to overvalue *o* to overrate; **no se puede sobrestimar el efecto del dólar sobre el comercio europeo** = the effect of the dollar on European trade cannot be overestimated

◊ **sobretasa** *nf* surcharge; **sobretasa a la importación** = import surcharge; **sobretasa postal** = additional postage *o* postal surcharge

◊ **sobrevalorado, -da 1** *adj* **(a)** *(sobrestimado)* overrated *o* overvalued; **moneda sobrevalorada** = overvalued currency; **a 300 ptas., estas acciones están sobrevaloradas** = these shares are overvalued at 300 pesetas; **la peseta está sobrevalorada con**

relación al dólar = the peseta is overvalued against the dollar; **su 'servicio de primera clase' está muy sobrevalorado** = their 'first-class service' is very overrated **(b)** *(bolsa)* overbought; **el mercado está sobrevalorado** = the market is overbought **2** *pp de* SOBREVALORAR

sobrevalorar *vt* to overestimate *o* to overvalue; **sobrevaloró el tiempo necesario para equipar la fábrica** = he overestimated the amount of time needed to fit out the factory

social *adj* **(a)** *(que se aplica a la sociedad)* social; **bienestar** *o* **asistencia social** = welfare; **costes sociales** = social costs; **el informe examina los costes sociales de la construcción de la fábrica en el centro de la ciudad** = the report examines the social costs of building the factory in the middle of the town; **seguridad social** = social security; **recibe un subsidio semanal de la seguridad social** = he gets weekly social security payments; **el sistema social** = the social system **(b)** *(que se aplica a una compañía)* corporate; **beneficio social** = corporate income; **capital social** = a company's capital; **denominación social** = company name *o* corporate name; **domicilio social** = registered office; **razón social** = trade name

sociedad *nf* **(a)** *(población)* society; **sociedad de consumo** = consumer society; **la sociedad opulenta** = the affluent society **(b)** *(asociación o club)* society; **sociedad cooperativa** = cooperative society; **se ha afiliado a una sociedad de informática** = he has joined a computer society **(c)** *(compañía)* company *o* corporation; **sociedad anónima (S.A.)** = public limited company (plc); **ley de sociedades anónimas** = company law; **sociedad de cartera** = holding company *o* proprietary company; **sociedad constituida legalmente** = an incorporated company; **una sociedad constituida en los EE UU** = a company incorporated in the USA; **sociedad cotizada en bolsa** = listed company *o* quoted company; **sociedad limitada (S.L.)** *o* **sociedad de responsabilidad limitada (S.R.L.)** = limited (liability) company (Ltd); **sociedad matriz** = parent company; **sociedad de seguros mutuos** = provident society; **sociedad de socorro mutuo** = friendly society; **constitución de una sociedad** = incorporation of a company; **disolver una sociedad** = to wind up a company; **lanzamiento de una sociedad** = floating of a company; **liquidar una sociedad** = to wind up a company; **el tribunal ordenó que se liquidara la sociedad** = the court ordered the company to be wound up **(d) sociedad de crédito inmobiliario** *o* **sociedad hipotecaria** *o* **de crédito hipotecario** = building society; *US* savings and loan (association); **sociedad financiera** = finance company *o* finance corporation *o* financial intermediary; **la mayor sociedad financiera de Madrid** = the largest Madrid finance house; **sociedad inmobiliaria** = property company; **sociedad de inversión** *o* **de inversiones** = investment trust *o* investment company; **los inversores perdieron miles de libras en el hundimiento de la sociedad de inversiones** = investors lost thousands of pounds in the wreck of the investment company; **sociedad mercantil** = finance corporation **(e)** *(sociedad colectiva)* partnership; **sociedad en comandita** *o* **de responsabilidad limitada** = limited partnership; **formar una sociedad colectiva con alguien** = to join with someone to form a partnership; **proponer**

una sociedad a alguien = to offer someone a partnership; **disolver una sociedad** = to dissolve a partnership

> Más de 600 empresas públicas y privadas están implicadas en la compra de facturas falsas, utilizadas para pagar menos impuestos, emitidas por 52 sociedades, la mayoría inactivas, con las que han ocultado a Hacienda más de 105.000 millones de pesetas
> **Cambio 16**

> las facturas se expiden en forma de venta de bienes o prestación de servicios por personas o sociedades inactivas o en quiebra
> **Cambio 16**

socio, -cia n (a) (de una empresa, asociación) associate o partner; **es socia mía en el negocio** = she is a business associate of mine; **pasó a ser socio de un bufete de abogados** = he became a partner in a firm of solicitors; **tomar a alguien como socio** = to take someone into partnership with you; **socio activo** o **socio que trabaja** = active partner o working partner; **socio comanditario** o **en comandita** = sleeping o limited o silent partner; **socio principal** = senior partner; **socio subalterno** o **de menor antigüedad** = junior partner (b) (de un club) member; **los socios** = the members o the membership; **hacerse socio de una asociación** = to join an association o a group; **carné de socio** = membership card

> la acertada política comercial del fundador de la empresa hizo que uno de sus principales clientes se convirtiera pronto en socio
> **Micros**

socioeconómico, -ca adj socio-economic; **el sistema socioeconómico en los países capitalistas** = the socio-economic system in capitalist countries; **grupos socioeconómicos** = socio-economic groups

solar nm site; **solar para edificar** = building site o land for building; **hemos elegido el solar para la nueva fábrica** = we have chosen a site for the new factory; **el supermercado se va a construir en un solar cerca de la estación** = the supermarket is to be built on a site near the station; **solar inmobiliario** = land bank

solicitación nf requesting; **solicitación de votos** = canvassing

solicitante nmf applicant o petitioner; **los solicitantes deberán adjuntar el currículum vitae** = applicants should enclose a curriculum vitae

> como señalan las empresas de selección, el conocimiento del inglés se utiliza como filtro discriminatorio para descartar candidatos ante la gran cantidad de solicitantes a un determinado puesto de trabajo
> **El País**

solicitar vt (a) (pedir algo) to ask for o to request o to requisition; **solicitó el archivo de los deudores de 1995** = he asked for the file on 1995 debtors; **solicitó un préstamo al director del banco** = he asked his bank manager for a loan; **solicitar algo por escrito** = to write to ask for something o to send away for something; **solicitamos el envío del nuevo** catálogo o **enviamos una carta solicitando el nuevo catálogo** = we sent away for the new catalogue; **le envío el catálogo que había solicitado** = I am sending a catalogue as requested; **solicitar una entrevista** = to ask to see someone; **solicitó una entrevista con el ministro** = she sought an interview with the minister; **solicitar pedidos** o **votos** = to canvass (b) (pedir acciones, un trabajo) to apply; **solicitar acciones** = to apply for shares; **solicitar por escrito** = to apply in writing; **miles de personas solicitaron acciones de la nueva compañía** = there were thousands of applicants for shares in the new company; **solicitó una pensión especial al gobierno** = he petitioned the government for a special pension; **solicitar personalmente** = to apply in person; **solicitar un trabajo** o **un empleo en una oficina** = to apply for a job in an office; **acciones pagaderas al ser solicitadas** = shares payable on application; **volver a solicitar** = to reapply (c) (presentar una solicitud) to petition

solicitud nf application o request o petition; **presentar una solicitud** = to present a petition o to petition; **solicitud de acciones** = application for shares; **adjuntar el cheque al formulario de solicitud de acciones** = attach the cheque to the share application form; **solicitud de empleo** o **solicitud de trabajo** = application for a job o job application; **carta de solicitud** = letter of application; **impreso** o **formulario de solicitud** = application form; **rellenar un formulario** o **impreso de solicitud** = to fill in an application (form) for a job o a job application (form); **tiene que rellenar una solicitud de empleo** = you have to fill in a job application form; **solicitud oficial** = official order o requisition; **¿cuál es el número de su última solicitud oficial?** = what is the number of your latest requisition?; **presentaron una solicitud para conseguir una subvención estatal** = they put in a request for a government subsidy; **su solicitud de préstamo fue rechazada por el banco** = his request for a loan was turned down by the bank; **explicó las bases de la solicitud** = he explained the background of the claim

solidariamente adv jointly; **son responsables solidariamente** = they are jointly liable

solidaridad nf solidarity; **los trabajadores de correos se declararon en huelga y los ingenieros de teléfonos declararon una huelga de solidaridad** = the postal workers went on strike and the telephone engineers came out in sympathy

solidez nf soundness o solidity; **solidez financiera** = financial soundness o healthy state of finances

> su fusión con el Security Pacific no sólo ha garantizado la solidez de su propio banco, sino que se ha convertido en una de las más ambiciosas y mejor estructuradas fusiones bancarias de la historia
> **El País**

sólido, -da adj solid o sound; **la situación financiera de la compañía es muy sólida** = the company's financial situation is very sound

solución nf solution; **buscar una solución a los problemas financieros** = to look for a solution to the financial problems; **el programador sugirió una solución al problema de los sistemas** = the programmer came up with a solution to the systems problem; **creemos que hemos encontrado la**

solución para resolver el problema de la falta de personal cualificado = we think we have found a solution to the problem of getting skilled staff

solucionar *vt* **solucionar un problema** = to solve *o* to sort out a problem; **¿solucionaste el problema de las cuentas con los auditores?** = did you sort out the accounts problem with the auditors?

> prisionera de su propia historia, la empresa ha solucionado el problema que le planteó la salida, por razones de causa mayor, de su anterior presidente y artífice del proceso de la reconversión
> **El País**

solvencia *nf* solvency *o* creditworthiness

◊ **solvente** *adj* solvent *o* creditworthy; **la compañía apenas era solvente cuando la compró** = when he bought the company it was barely solvent

> la ley permite figurar en los ficheros con información de carácter negativo sobre la solvencia económica de un particular durante seis años aun en el caso más desfavorable
> **El País**

Somalia *nf* Somalia

◊ **somalí** *adj y nmf* Somali
NOTA: capital: **Mogadisio** (= Mogadishu); moneda: **chelín somalí (So. Sh.)** = Somali shilling (SoSh)

someter *vt* **(a)** *(informes)* to present *o* to submit **(b) someter a** = to subject to; **someter a voto una propuesta** = to put a resolution to the vote

◊ **someterse** *vr* to give in

sondear *vt* to sound out *o* to canvass; **sondear la opinión pública** = to canvass public opinion; **sondear a los miembros de un club sobre una cuestión** = to canvass *o* to poll the members of the club on an issue

sondeo *nm* survey; **técnicas de sondeo** = canvassing techniques; **sondeo de opinión** = opinion survey; **hemos hecho un sondeo de opinión entre el personal para ver si se pueden aumentar los precios de la cantina** = we have canvassed the staff about raising the prices in the staff restaurant

soportar *vt* to bear *o* to support; **soportar una pérdida** = to bear a loss; **el mercado no soportará otra subida de precios** = the market will not support another price increase

> la industria soporta un mayor aumento del paro que los servicios, donde se dan altibajos de contratación según la evolución económica
> **El País**

soporte *nm* **(a)** *(apoyo)* support *o* holder; **soporte del mensaje** = message holder; **soporte publicitario** = advertising medium **(b)** *(informática)* **soporte físico (de ordenador)** = computer hardware **(c)** *(estanterías)* bracket

sorteo *nm* draw *o* ballot; **elegido por sorteo** = chosen by ballot; **la subscripción de acciones se cubrió con exceso, por lo que hubo que proceder a un sorteo** = the share issue was oversubscribed, so there was a ballot for the shares

soslayar *vt* to get round; **intentamos soslayar el embargo enviando el cargamento desde Canadá** = we tried to get round the embargo by shipping from Canada

sospechoso, -sa *adj* shady *o* suspect

sostener *vt* **(a)** *(apoyar)* to support *o* to keep up; **sostener una moneda** = to support a currency **(b)** *(mantener)* to claim *o* to maintain; **sostiene que las acciones son de su propiedad** = she claims the shares are her property

◊ **sostenerse** *vr* to keep going *o* to keep up; **los negocios tan sólo se sostienen** = business is just ticking over

sótano *nm* basement

'spot' *nm* **(a)** *(anuncio)* **spot publicitario** = TV commercial **(b)** **precio 'spot'** = spot price; **el mercado 'spot' del petróleo** = the spot market in oil

Sr = SEÑOR

Sra = SEÑORA Mrs *o* Ms; **la Sra García ocupó la presidencia** = the chair was taken by Mrs García; **la Sra García es la jefa de personal** = Ms García is the personnel officer

s.r.c. = SE RUEGA CONTESTACION RSVP

s/ref = SU REFERENCIA

Sres = SEÑORES Messrs; **Sres Casals y García** = Messrs Casals and García

Sri Lanka *nm* Sri Lanka

◊ **cingalés, -esa** *adj y n* Sri Lankan
NOTA: capital: **Colombo**; moneda: **rupia de Sri Lanka (SL Rs)** = Sri Lanka rupee (SL Rs)

S.R.L. = SOCIEDAD DE RESPONSABILIDAD LIMITADA

'stand' *nm* *(exposición)* (exhibition) stand; *US* booth; (floor) stand *o* island site; **los compradores admiraron los objetos expuestos en nuestro stand** = the buyers admired the exhibits on our stand; **el 'stand' británico en la Feria Internacional de Informática** = the British trade exhibit at the International Computer Fair

statu quo *nm* status quo; **el contrato no cambia el statu quo** = the contract does not alter the status quo

status *nm* status

'streamer' *nm* *(informática)* (tape) streamer

suave *adj* soft; **aterrizaje suave** = soft landing

sub- *prefijo* sub-

◊ **subagencia** *nf* sub-agency

◊ **subagente** *nmf* sub-agent

◊ **subalterno, -na** *adj* office junior; **no se permite al personal subalterno la utilización del ascensor del presidente** = junior members of staff are not allowed to use the chairman's lift

◊ **subarrendador, -ra** *n* sublessor

◊ **subarrendamiento** *nm* sublease *o* underlease

subarrendar *vt* to sublet *o* to sublease; **hemos subarrendado una parte de nuestra oficina a una asesoría financiera** = we have sublet part of our office to a financial consultancy; **subarrendaron una pequeña oficina en el centro de la ciudad** = they subleased a small office in the centre of town

◊ **subarrendatario, -ria** *n* sublessee *o* subtenant

◊ **subarriendo** *nm* underlease *o* sublease; subtenancy

subasta *nf* auction; **la subasta empezó con una oferta de 10.000 ptas.** the bidding started at 10,000 pesetas; **el subastador empezó la subasta al precio tipo de 10.000 ptas.** = the auctioneer started the bidding at 10,000 pesetas; **el administrador judicial celebrará una subasta del activo de la compañía** = the receiver will hold an auction of the company's assets; **los objetos no reclamados se venderán** *o* **el equipaje no reclamado se venderá a los seis meses en una subasta** = unclaimed property *o* unclaimed baggage will be sold by auction after six months; **sala de subastas** = auction room *o* saleroom; **sacar a subasta** = to put something up for auction; **venta en subasta** = sale by auction; **venderse en pública subasta** = to go under the hammer; **cerraron la fábrica y vendieron la maquinaria en pública subasta** = the factory was closed and the machinery was auctioned off; **subasta a la baja** = Dutch auction; **subasta por licitación** *o* **concurso subasta** = auction by tender

◊ **subastador, -ra** *n* auctioneer

subastar *vt* to auction *o* to sell goods by auction; *US* at auction

subcomité *nm* subcommittee; **la cuestión siguiente del orden del día trata sobre el informe del subcomité de finanzas** = the next item on the agenda is the report of the finance subcommittee

subcontratar *vt* to subcontract; **subcontratar trabajo** = to put work out to contract *o* to farm out work; **las instalación eléctrica ha sido subcontratada a Electricil S.A.** = the electrical work has been subcontracted to Electricil S.A.

◊ **subcontratista** *nmf* subcontractor; **solicitaremos ofertas a subcontratistas para la instalación eléctrica** = we will ask subcontractors to tender for the electrical work *o* we will put the electrical work out to subcontract

◊ **subcontrato** *nm* subcontract; **les han concedido el subcontrato para toda la instalación eléctrica del nuevo edificio** = they have been awarded the subcontract for all the electrical work in the new building

subdesarrollado, -da *adj* underdeveloped; **área subdesarrollada** = depressed area; **países subdesarrollados** = underdeveloped countries

> la Unión Europea considera que el mercado español de gas está 'subdesarrollado' y que en los próximos años se asistirá a una expansión importante de la demanda
> **El País**

subdirector, -ra *n* assistant manager *o* deputy manager

súbdito, -ta *n* subject *o* national; **los súbditos extranjeros tuvieron que abandonar el país** = foreign nationals had to leave the country

subdivisión *nf* subdivision

subempleado, -da *adj* underemployed; **capital subempleado** = underemployed capital

◊ **subempleo** *nm* underemployment

subestimación *nf* underestimate

◊ **subestimado, -da** *adj* **1** underestimated **2** *pp de* SUBESTIMAR

subestimar *vt* to underestimate *o* to underrate *o* to minimize; **no subestime el poder de la competencia en el mercado europeo** = do not underrate the strength of the competition in the European market; **el poder del yen está subestimado** = the power of the yen is underrated; **subestimaron los efectos de la huelga en las ventas** = they underestimated the effects of the strike on their sales

subida *nf* rise *o* increase; **subida de precios** = price increase *o* price rise; **subida del precio de las materias primas** = rise in the price of raw materials; **la subida de los precios del petróleo produjo una recesión del comercio mundial** = oil price rises brought about a recession in world trade; **la subida reciente de los tipos de interés ha encarecido las hipotecas** = the recent rise in interest rates has made mortgages dearer; **subida de sueldo** = increase in pay *o* pay increase; **la subida del dólar en relación a la peseta** = the appreciation of the dollar against the peseta; **estas acciones han experimentado una subida del 10%** = these shares have risen by 10% *o* show an appreciation of 10%

subir 1 *vi* **(a)** *(precios o impuestos)* to rise *o* to go up *o* to increase; **subir en espiral** = to spiral; **subir de precio** = to increase in price; **el precio del petróleo subió dos veces la semana pasada** = the price of oil has increased twice in the past week; **los billetes de avión subirán el 1 de junio** = air fares will go up *o* will be raised on June 1st; **hacer subir los precios** = to force prices up; **la guerra ha hecho subir el precio del petróleo** = the war forced up the price of oil; **subir rápidamente** = to shoot up *o* to rocket; **los precios suben más deprisa que la inflación** = prices are rising faster than inflation; **los tipos de interés han subido al 15%** = interest rates have risen to 15%; **el mercado subió una vez conocidas las noticias del presupuesto** = the market moved upwards after the news of the budget **(b)** *(valor)* to increase in value *o* to appreciate; **el dólar ha subido en relación al yen** = the dollar has appreciated in terms of the yen; **estas acciones han subido un 5%** = these shares have appreciated by 5%; **las acciones inmobiliarias subieron del 10% al 15%** = property shares put on gains of 10%-15% **(c)** *(subir a un avión o barco o tren)* to go on board *o* to board a plane *o* ship *o* train; **los aduaneros subieron al barco atracado en el puerto** = customs officials boarded the ship in the harbour **2** *vt* to increase *o* to raise; **la tienda ha subido un 5% todos sus precios** = the shop has put up all its prices by 5%; **el gobierno ha subido los impuestos** = the government has raised tax levels; **después de subir sus precios, la empresa perdió la mitad de su**

participación en el mercado = when the company raised its prices, it lost half of its share of the market

> los beneficios netos por acción han subido de 57,2 pesetas a 1.200 este año
> **España Económica**

sub judice *adj* (*en manos de los tribunales*) sub judice; **los periódicos no pueden informar sobre el asunto porque está todavía sub judice** = the papers cannot report the case because it is still sub judice

subliminar   *adj*   subliminal;   **publicidad subliminar** = subliminal advertising

subordinado, -da   **1**   *adj*   (*de menor importancia*) subordinate; **subordinado a** = subordinate to **2** *n* subordinate; **a sus subordinados les resulta difícil trabajar con él** = his subordinates find him difficult to work with

subproducto *nm* (*producto secundario*) by-product

subsidiario, -ria 1 *adj* (*de menor importancia*) subsidiary *o* secondary; **compañía subsidiaria** = subsidiary company; **piquete subsidiario** = secondary picketing **2** *nm* **subsidiario de alta rentabilidad** = cash cow

subsidio *nm* **(a)** (*ayuda*) benefit; **recibe semanalmente 25.000 ptas. como subsidio de paro** = she receives 25,000 pesetas a week as unemployment benefit; **el subsidio de enfermedad se paga mensualmente** = the sickness benefit is paid monthly; **subsidio por aumento del coste de vida** *o* **de carestía de vida** = cost-of-living allowance; **subsidio complementario** = supplementary benefit; **subsidio gremial** = strike pay; **subsidio de paro** = unemployment pay *o* unemployment benefit *o* the dole; **está cobrando el subsidio de paro** = he is receiving unemployment benefit *o* he is on the dole; **subsidio de vejez** = old age pension **(b)** (*subvención*) subsidy *o* grant; **sin subsidio** = unsubsidized; **el gobierno ha aumentado su subsidio a la industria del automóvil** = the government has increased its subsidy to the car industry; **subsidio del Estado** *o* **subsidio estatal** = government subsidy; **la industria existe gracias a los subsidios del Estado** = the industry exists on government subsidies

subsistencia *nf* subsistence; **vivir a nivel de subsistencia** = to live at subsistence level

substancial *adj* essential; **es el punto substancial del problema** = it's the essential point of the problem; *ver también* SUSTANCIAL

substituto, -ta *n ver también* SUSTITUTO

subvención *nf* grant *o* subsidy; **el laboratorio tiene una subvención estatal para cubrir el coste del programa de desarrollo** = the laboratory has a government grant to cover the cost of the development programme; **el Estado ha asignado subvenciones para sufragar los costes del proyecto** = the government has allocated grants towards the costs of the scheme; **la compañía existe gracias a las subvenciones del gobierno** = the company exists on handouts *o* grants from the government; **subvención a fondo perdido** = outright grant; **la subvención a la mantequilla** = the subsidy on butter *o* the butter subsidy; (*en la UE*) **precio de subvención** = support price

◊ **subvencionado, -da 1** *adj* subsidized; **no subvencionado** = unsubsidized; **proyecto subvencionado** = subsidized *o* grant-aided scheme; **vivienda subvencionada** = subsidized accommodation **2** *pp de* SUBVENCIONAR

> otro ejemplo claro de despilfarro de productos, sobre los que el Estado practica una política de precios subvencionados, es el consumo de energía
> **España Económica**

subvencionar *vt* to subsidize; **el gobierno se ha negado a subvencionar a la industria del automóvil** = the government has refused to subsidize the car industry

suceder *vt/i* **(a)** (*seguir*) to succeed *o* to follow; **el Señor Pascual sucedió al Señor García en el cargo de presidente** = Sr García was succeeded as chairman by Sr Pascual **(b)** (*tener lugar*) to happen *o* to occur; **¿qué sucedió?** = what happened?

sucesión *nf* succession *o* inheritance; **derecho de sucesión** = estate duty *o* death duty; **impuesto sobre sucesiones** = inheritance tax

sucesivo, -va *adj* successive

sucesor, -ra *n* successor; **el sucesor del Señor Pascual en el cargo de presidente será el Señor García** = Sr Pascual's successor as chairman will be Sr García

sucio, -cia *adj* dirty; **flotación sucia** = dirty *o* managed float

sucursal *nf* branch *o* division; **sucursal filial** = branch office; **sucursal local** = local branch; **director de sucursal** = branch manager; **el director de nuestra sucursal de Lagos** = the manager of our branch in Lagos *o* of our Lagos branch; **el banco** *o* **la tienda tiene sucursales en la mayoría de las ciudades del sur del país** = the bank *o* the store has branches in most towns in the south of the country; **la compañía de seguros cerró sus sucursales sudamericanas** = the insurance company has closed its branches in South America; **hemos decidido abrir una sucursal en Chicago** = we have decided to open a branch office in Chicago

> el nuevo banco contará con 600 sucursales, de las que cerrará 60, y 45.000 empleados, de los que espera despedir a 6.200.
> **El País**

Sudáfrica *nf* South Africa

◊ **sudafricano, -na** *adj y n* South African
NOTA: capital: **Pretoria**; moneda: **rand sudafricano (R)** = South African rand (R)

Sudamérica *nf* South America

◊ **sudamericano, -na** *adj y n* South American

Sudán *nm* Sudan

◊ **sudanés, -esa** *adj y n* Sudanese
NOTA: capital: **Jartum** (= Khartoum); moneda: **libra sudanesa (LSd)** = Sudanese pound (LSd)

Suecia *nf* Sweden

◊ **sueco, -ca 1** *adj* Swedish **2** *n* Swede
NOTA: capital: **Estocolmo** (= Stockholm); moneda: **corona sueca (SKr)** = Swedish krona (SKr)

sueldo *nm* **(a)** *(salario)* earnings *o* pay *o* salary; *(semanal)* wage; **su sueldo es de aproximadamente 85.000 ptas.** = his salary is around 85,000 pesetas; **le dimos tres meses de sueldo en vez de preaviso** = we gave him three months' salary in lieu of notice; **la empresa congeló los sueldos durante un periodo de seis meses** = the company froze all salaries for a six-month period; **su sueldo bajó mucho cuando le rebajaron de categoría** = she lost a lot of pay when she was demoted; **sueldo base** = basic salary *o* basic pay *o* basic wage; **sueldo bruto** = gross salary; **le pagan el sueldo bruto** = his salary is paid gross; **sueldo de los directores** = directors' salaries; **sueldo inicial** = starting salary; **le nombraron con un sueldo inicial de 100.000 ptas.** = he was appointed at a starting salary of 100,000 pesetas; **sueldo neto** = net salary **(b)** **atrasos de sueldo** = back pay; **aumento de sueldo** = pay rise; **recibió un aumento de sueldo en junio** = she got a salary increase in June; **¿en qué se basa la reclamación de un aumento de sueldo?** = what are the grounds for the demand for a pay rise?; **cobrar un sueldo** = to draw a salary; **el presidente no cobra sueldo** = the chairman does not draw a salary; **tener un buen sueldo** = to earn a good salary *o* to earn good money; **gana un buen sueldo en el supermercado** = she is earning a good salary *o* good wages in the supermarket; **pensión proporcional al sueldo** = earnings-related pension; **cheque de sueldo** = pay cheque *o* salary cheque; **hoja de sueldo** = pay slip; **revisión de sueldos** = salary review; **su sueldo fue objeto de una revisión el pasado abril** = she had a salary review last April *o* her salary was reviewed last April; **sobre del sueldo** = pay packet; **subida de sueldo** = pay rise *o* increase **(c) a sueldo** = paid *o* salaried; **ayudante a sueldo** = paid assistant

suelo *nm* **(a)** *(tierra)* ground *o* soil; **suelo poco fértil** = poor soil **(b)** *(piso)* floor; **la máquina está sujeta al suelo para que no pueda desplazarse** = the machine is attached to the floor so it cannot be moved; **los precios están por los suelos** = prices are rock-bottom

suelto, -ta 1 *adj* **(a)** *(a granel)* loose; **dinero suelto** = change; **artículos que se venden sueltos** = items sold separately **(b)** *(que no forma parte de un grupo)* odd; **nos quedan unas pocas cajas sueltas** = we have a few odd boxes left **2** *nm* change; **¿tienes suelto?** = do you have change?

suficiente *adj* sufficient *o* enough; **la compañía tiene fondos suficientes para financiar su programa de expansión** = the company has sufficient funds to pay for its expansion programme; **actuar sin cobertura suficiente** = to operate without adequate cover

sufragar *vt* to defray *o* to pay; **la empresa acordó sufragar los costes de la exposición** = the company agreed to pay the costs of the exhibition

sufrir *vt/i* to suffer *o* to experience; **sin sufrir daños** = safely *o* without suffering any damage; **las exportaciones han sufrido durante los últimos seis meses** = exports have suffered during the last six months; **la empresa sufrió una pérdida de su cuota de mercado** = the company suffered a loss of market penetration

sugerencia *nf* suggestion; **buzón de sugerencias** = suggestion box

sugerir *vt* to suggest; **sugirió una nueva idea para vender los artículos** = she suggested *o* put forward a new idea for selling the goods

Suiza *nf* Switzerland

◇ **suizo, -za** *adj y n* Swiss
NOTA: capital: **Berna** (= Bern); moneda: **franco suizo (FS)** = Swiss franc (SwF)

sujetapapeles *nm* paperclip *o* clip; **tablilla con sujetapapeles** = clipboard

sujetar *vt* to attach *o* to hold; **sujete su cheque a la solicitud con una grapa** = pin your cheque to the application form; **sujetó el cartel en la puerta con chinchetas** = she used drawing pins to pin the poster to the door; **sujetó los papeles con un alfiler** = she pinned the papers together; **el paquete está sujeto con un cordel** = the parcel is tied up with string

◇ **sujeto, -ta** *adj y pp* **(a) sujeto a** = subject to *o* liable to; **sujeto a cambios** = suject to change; **sujeto a la aprobación** = subject to approval; **el contrato está sujeto a la aprobación del gobierno** = the contract is subject to government approval; **acuerdo sujeto a** *o* **venta sujeta a contrato** = agreement *o* sale subject to contract; **productos sujetos a derechos de aduana** *o* **impuestos** = goods which are liable to duty; **sujeto a impuesto** = taxable; **estos artículos están sujetos al impuesto sobre las importaciones** = these articles are subject to import tax **(b)** *(atado)* **el paquete está sujeto con una cuerda** = the parcel is tied up with string **2** *n* individual *o* person

suma *nf* **(a)** *(dinero)* sum (of money); **suma global** = lump sum; **por una modesta suma** = for a modest outlay; **la compañía tuvo que pagar una fuerte suma por el solar del edificio** = the company had to pay a large sum *o* a good deal for the building site **(b)** *(matemáticas)* total *o* sum *o* addition; **no hace falta una calculadora para hacer una simple suma** = you don't need a calculator to do simple addition; **suma total** = grand total **(c) suma y sigue** = amount brought forward *o* carried forward

◇ **sumamente** *adv* extremely *o* highly; **su equipo directivo es sumamente eficiente** = their management team is extremely efficient

sumar *vt* to add (up) *o* to total; **sumó las ventas de los seis meses anteriores a diciembre** = he totted up *o* he counted up the sales for the six months to December; **costes que suman más de 25.000 ptas.** = costs totalling more than 25,000 pesetas; **sumar una columna de cifras** = to add up a column of figures

sumario *nm* **(a)** *(resumen)* summary **(b)** *(jurídico)* indictment **(c)** *(de un libro)* contents

sumergido, -da *adj* hidden *o* submerged; **economía sumergida** = black economy

suministrador, -ra *n* supplier; **suministrador de equipos de oficina** = office equipment supplier; **nos hemos cambiado a un suministrador francés** = we have switched over to a French supplier

suministrar *vt* **suministrar algo a alguien** = to supply *o* to provide someone with something; **suministrar repuestos a una fábrica** = to supply a factory with spare parts; **el departamento de finanzas suministró las cifras al comité** = the finance department supplied the committee with the figures

◊ **suministro** *nm* supply *o* sourcing; **¿puede darnos el precio para el suministro de 20.000 sobres?** = can you quote for supplying 20,000 envelopes?; **suministro eléctrico** = power supply *o* electricity supply; **los suministros de carbón han sido reducidos** = supplies of coal have been reduced; **suministro de personal** = staffing; **el suministro de piezas de repuesto puede diversificarse fuera de Europa** = the sourcing of spare parts can be diversified to suppliers outside Europe

```
los ingresos de una compañía de gestión
son las comisiones que recibe en función
de la facturación y rentabilidad del
establecimiento. La segunda fuente de
ingresos es la que se deriva del
suministro de servicios
                                    El País
```

sumisión *nf* compliance *o* submission

'súper' *nm* gasolina 'súper' = top-grade petrol *o* four-star petrol; **el coche marcha solamente con gasolina 'súper'** = the car only runs on four-star petrol

superabundancia *nf* glut (of produce); **una superabundancia de café** = a coffee glut *o* a glut of coffee

superar *vt* **(a)** *(vencer)* to beat; **superar en las ventas** = to outsell; **han superado a sus competidores, relegándoles al segundo lugar en el mercado de ordenadores** = they have beaten their rivals into second place in the computer market **(b)** *(alcanzar un máximo)* to go higher *o* to be higher; **las ventas superaron 1 millón de pesetas durante el primer trimestre** = sales topped 1m pesetas in the first quarter; **ha superado el límite del crédito** = he has exceeded his credit limit **(c)** *(éxito en examen)* to pass; **consiguió superar la prueba de taquigrafía** = she succeeded in passing her shorthand test **(d)** *(exceder)* to cap

```
el déficit público supera con creces lo que
hasta hace poco era el objetivo oficial
                              Actualidad Económica
```

```
las ventas de los caldos de Rioja superan
en un 20% a las registradas en el mismo
periodo del ejercicio anterior
                                    El País
```

superávit *nm* surplus; **un superávit presupuestario** = a budget surplus; **absorber un superávit** = to absorb a surplus; **balanza comercial con superávit** = favourable trade balance

```
en 1986, primer año del boom económico
registramos un superávit del 1,8% del PIB;
en 1990 habíamos pasado a un déficit del
3,5%
                                    Cambio 16
```

superficie *nf* surface *o* area; **medida de superficie** = square measure; **la superficie de esta oficina es de 1.000 metros cuadrados** = the area of this office is 1,000 square metres; **superficie útil** =

floor space; **tenemos 3.500 metros cuadrados de superficie útil para alquilar** = we have 3,500 square metres of floor space to let

superintendente *nmf* superintendent *o* supervisor

superior 1 *adj* **(a)** *(en cantidad)* higher; **superior a** = higher than *o* in excess of; **las cifras del segundo trimestre son superiores al año anterior** = the figures for the second half are higher than *o* are up on those for last year; **cantidades superiores a veinticinco kilos** = quantities in excess of twenty-five kilos **(b)** *(en calidad)* superior; **nuestro producto es superior a todos los de la competencia** = our product is superior to all competing products; **calidad superior** = top quality; **acero de calidad superior** = high-quality steel **2** *nm* superior *o* line manager; **cada director de sección es responsable de dar información exacta sobre las ventas a su superior** = each manager is responsible to his superior for accurate reporting of sales

superioridad *nf* *(en el trabajo)* seniority

supermercado *nm* supermarket; **las ventas en los supermercados representan la mitad del valor de las ventas de la empresa** = sales in supermarkets *o* supermarket sales account for half the company's turnover; **carrito de supermercado** = supermarket trolley; *US* shopping cart

superpetrolero *nm* supertanker

superproducción *nf* overproduction

supervisar *vt* to supervise; **la mudanza a las nuevas oficinas fue supervisada por el director administrativo** = the move to the new offices was supervised by the administrative manager; **supervisa a seis chicas jóvenes en el departamento de contabilidad** = she supervises six girls in the accounts department

supervisión *nf* **(a)** supervision; **el nuevo personal trabaja bajo supervisión durante los primeros tres meses** = new staff work under supervision for the first three months; **tiene mucha experiencia y puede trabajar sin supervisión** = she is very experienced and can be left to work without any supervision; **el dinero se contó bajo la supervisión del director de finanzas** = the cash was counted under the supervision of the finance manager **(b)** **de supervisión** = supervisory; **personal de supervisión** = supervisory staff

◊ **supervisor, -ra** *n* supervisor *o* superintendent *o* comptroller; **trabaja en calidad de supervisor** = he works in a supervisory capacity

suplementario, -ria *adj* additional *o* supplementary *o* extra; **cláusulas suplementarias de un contrato** = additional clauses to a contract; **la compañía ha pedido crédito suplementario** = the company is asking for further credit; **tenemos que hacer un pedido suplementario de estos artículos porque las existencias están bajando** = we must reorder these items because stock is getting low

suplemento *nm* **(a)** *(cantidad adicional)* supplement; **la empresa le concede un suplemento a su pensión** = the company gives him a supplement to his pension; **suplemento por el servicio** = service charge **(b)** *(billete)* excess fare **(c)** *(seguros)* **suplemento de póliza** = endorsement to a policy

suplente *nmf* substitute *o* deputy; **director suplente** = alternate director

suponer *vt* **(a)** to presume *o* to assume; **suponiendo que** = assuming that; **supongo que la cuenta ha sido pagada** = I presume the account has been paid; **suponemos que el envío ha sido robado** = we assume the shipment has been stolen; **se supone que la empresa es todavía solvente** = the company is presumed to be still solvent **(b)** *(significar)* to mean; **el aumento del paro supone un déficit presupuestario mayor** = the rise in unemployment means that the budget deficit will increase

suposición *nf* supposition *o* presumption *o* assumption

suprimir *vt* to delete *o* to remove *o* to drop; **quieren suprimir del contrato todo lo que hace referencia a las condiciones de crédito** = they want to delete all references to credit terms from the contract; **hemos suprimido estos artículos del catálogo porque se venden poco desde hace tiempo** = we have dropped these items from the catalogue because they've been losing sales steadily for some time; **los abogados han suprimido la cláusula dos** = the lawyers have deleted clause two; **rogamos supriman en las actas todas las referencias a la huelga** = please excise all references to the strike in the minutes; **el gobierno ha suprimido la prohibición a las importaciones de Japón** = the government has lifted the ban on imports from Japan; **suprimir barreras comerciales** = to lift trade barriers; **suprimir el control de salarios** = to decontrol wages; **suprimir los impuestos sobre el alcohol** = to take the duty off alcohol

supuesto *nm* assumption

surcoreano, -na *adj y n* South Korean

Surinam *nm* Surinam; **de Surinam** = Surinamese
NOTA: capital: **Paramaribo**; moneda: **florín de Surinam** = Surinam guilder

surtido *nm* range *o* selection *o* choice; **surtido básico** = basic assortment; **un surtido de nuestra línea de productos** = a selection of our product line; **ofrecemos un amplio surtido de tallas** *o* **una amplia gama de estilos** = we offer a wide range of sizes *o* range of styles; **la tienda tiene un gran surtido de papel** = the shop carries a wide choice of paper

surtirse *vr* to source

suscribir *vt* to subscribe; **suscribir una opción** = to take up an option; **suscribir acciones** = to subscribe for shares; **la mitad de la emisión no fue suscrita por los accionistas** = half the rights issue was not taken up by the shareholders; **suscribió un seguro de vida** *o* **un seguro de su casa** = she took out a life insurance policy *o* a house insurance policy

◊ **suscribirse** *vr* to subscribe to something; **deberíamos suscribirnos a una revista de actualidad** = we should take out a subscription for a current magazine

◊ **suscripción** *nf* subscription; **tarifas de suscripción** = subscription rates; **suscripción de acciones** = application for shares

◊ **suscriptor, -ra** *n (de una revista)* subscriber; *(de seguros)* underwriter; **suscriptor de una emisión de acciones** = subscriber to a share issue

suspender *vt* **(a)** *(interrumpir)* to suspend *o* to stop *o* to cancel *o* to discontinue; **el gobierno ha suspendido la importación de automóviles** = the government has stopped the import of cars; **se han suspendido las salidas en barco hasta que el tiempo mejore** = sailings have been suspended until the weather gets better; **el convenio fue suspendido en el último momento** = the deal was called off at the last moment; **las obras del proyecto de construcción han sido suspendidas** = work on the construction project has been suspended; **la dirección decidió suspender las negociaciones** = the management decided to suspend negotiations; **suspender una cita** *o* **una reunión** = to cancel an appointment *o* a meeting; **suspender una cuenta** = to stop an account; **suspender el pago de un cheque** = to stop a cheque; *US* to stop payment on a check; **suspender pagos** = to stop payments; **hemos suspendido pagos a la espera de noticias de nuestro agente** = we have suspended payments while we are waiting for news from our agent **(b)** *(retraso)* to delay *o* to hold up; **el pago se suspenderá hasta que se firme el contrato** = payment will be held up until the contract has been signed **(c)** *(de un cargo)* **suspender a alguien** = to suspend someone; **le suspendieron de empleo durante la investigación policial** = he was suspended on full pay while the police investigations were going on **(d)** *(jurídico)* **suspender un juicio indefinidamente** = to adjourn a case sine die **(e)** *(en un examen)* to fail

suspensión *nf* suspension *o* stopping *o* stoppage; **suspensión de entregas** = suspension *o* stoppage of deliveries; **suspensión de pagos** = suspension of payments *o* stopping payment; **suspensión de trabajo** = lay-off

las deudas declaradas en suspensiones de pagos alcanzaron en julio un récord histórico

El País

sustancial *adj* large *o* substantial; **adquirir una participación sustancial en la compañía** = to acquire a substantial interest in a company

◊ **sustancioso, -sa** *adj* large *o* substantial; **recibió una indemnización sustanciosa** = she was awarded substantial damages

sustento *nm* support *o* maintenance; **se gana el sustento trabajando para un periódico local** = she earns her living working for a local newspaper

sustituir *vt* to replace *o* to stand in for *o* to substitute for *o* to deputize for *o* to take over from; **sustituir a alguien** = to deputize for someone; **la Señorita Torres sustituyó al Señor Balea el 1 de mayo** = Srta Torres took over from Sr Balea on May 1st; **estamos sustituyendo a todos nuestros trabajadores asalariados por colaboradores autónomos** = we are replacing all our salaried staff with freelancers; **el Señor Pereira sustituye al presidente que está enfermo** = Sr Pereira is standing in for the chairman, who is ill

◊ **sustituto, -ta** *n* deputy *o* substitute *o* replacement; **mi secretaria se marcha la semana que viene, por lo que hemos puesto un anuncio para buscar una sustituta** = my secretary leaves us next week, so we are advertising for a replacement; **actuar como sustituto de alguien** = to act as deputy for someone *o* to act as someone's deputy

sustracción *nf* subtraction

sustraer *vt* to take away

Tt

tabla *nf* **(a)** *(listado o cuadro)* table; **tabla de mortalidad** = actuarial tables; **en forma de tabla** = in tabular form; **disponer datos en forma de tabla** = to lay out data in tabular form *o* to tabulate data **(b)** *(tablero)* board

◊ **tablero** *nm* **(a)** *(panel)* panel; **tablero de control** = control panel *o* switchboard; **tablero de exposición** = display panel; **tablero de hojas sueltas** = flip chart **(b)** *(tabla)* board

◊ **tablilla** *nf* **con sujeta papeles** = clipboard

tablón *nm* board; **tablón de anuncios** = noticeboard *o* message board; **¿viste la nueva lista de precios en el tablón de anuncios?** = did you see the new list of prices on the noticeboard?

tabulación *nf* tabulation; **tabulación de datos** = tabulation of data

tabulador *nm* tabulator *o* tab key

tabular *vt* to tabulate

tachar *vt* to cross off *o* to cross out; **tachó mi nombre de su lista** = he crossed my name off his list; **puede tacharle de nuestra lista de direcciones** = you can cross him off our mailing list; **tachó las 250 ptas. y escribió 500** = she crossed out 250 pesetas and put in 500

tácito, -ta *adj* tacit; **acuerdo tácito a una propuesta** = tacit agreement to a proposal; **aprobación tácita** = tacit approval

taco *nm* pad; **un taco de billetes** = a wad of banknotes

tacógrafo *nm* tachograph

táctica *nf* tactic *o* tactics; **su táctica habitual es comprar acciones de una compañía, organizar una oferta de adquisición, y luego venderlas con beneficios** = his usual tactic is to buy shares in a company, then mount a takeover bid, and sell out at a profit; **los directores decidieron su táctica antes de ir a la reunión con los resprentantes del sindicato** = the directors planned their tactics before going into the meeting with the union representatives

Tailandia *nf* Thailand

◊ **tailandés, -esa** *adj y n* Thai
NOTA: capital: **Bangkok;** moneda: **baht tailandés (B)** = Thai baht (B)

tajada *nf (informal)* rake-off; **sacar tajada** = to get a rake-off; **el grupo saca una tajada de todas las ventas de la compañía** = the group gets a rake-off on all the company's sales

talla *nf* size; **talla corriente** = stock size; **talla grande** = large size; **talla muy grande** *o* **talla extra** = very large size *o* extra large size *o* outsize (OS); **talla mediana** = medium size; **talla pequeña** = small size

taller *nm* **(a)** *(estudio)* studio *o* workshop; **taller mecánico** = machine shop; **taller de reparaciones** = repair shop **(b) fábrica taller** = factory floor; **en el taller** = on the shop floor

talón *nm* cheque; **ingresar un talón en una cuenta** = to pay a cheque into an account; **enviaron un talón sin fondos** = they sent us a bad cheque

◊ **talonario** *nm* book of tickets *o* receipts *o* counterfoils; **talonario de cheques** = cheque book; *US* checkbook; **matriz de un talonario** = cheque stub; **comprobante de matriz de talonario** = counterfoil

> el empleado del banco, al recibir el talón, entrega a cambio varios talones bancarios al portador por la suma del talón que recibe
>
> **Cambio 16**

> la empresa cliente paga el supuesto servicio o la supuesta venta con un talón nominativo a nombre de la empresa inactiva, que es entregado en un banco donde ésta tiene una cuenta, controlada por el falsificador
>
> **Cambio 16**

tamaño *nm* size; **este paquete es del tamaño máximo permitido por correos** = this packet is the maximum size allowed by the post office; **tenemos que pedir más papel con membrete, tamaño A4** = we must order some more A4 headed notepaper; **tamaño corriente** = stock size; **tamaño extra** *o* **de gran tamaño** = king-size; **de tamaño medio** = average-sized; **es una empresa de tamaño medio** = they are an average-sized *o* a middle-sized company

tampón *nm* pad *o* stamp pad; **tampón para entintar** = inking pad

tangible *adj* tangible; **bienes tangibles** = tangible assets *o* property

tantear *vt* **(a)** *(estimar)* to calculate (roughly) **(b)** *(adivinar)* to guess **(c)** *(probar)* to test

◊ **tanteo** *nm* rough calculation *o* guesswork; **método de tanteo** = trial and error method

tanto, -ta 1 *adj* so much *o* so many *o* as much *o* as many; **¿se le puede confiar tanto dinero?** = can he be trusted with all that cash? **2** *adv* so; **no trabajes tanto** = don't work so hard **3** *nm* **(a)** plus; **haber conseguido 1 millón de pesetas de nuevas ventas en menos de seis meses es ciertamente un tanto para el equipo de ventas** = to have achieved 1m pesetas in new sales in less than six months is certainly a plus for the sales team **(b) tanto alzado** = flat rate; **acuerdo** *o* **contrato a tanto alzado** = fixed-price agreement; **tanto por ciento** = percentage

Tanzania *nf* Tanzania

◊ **tanzaniano, -na** *o* **tanzano, -na** *adj y n* Tanzanian

NOTA: capital: **Dodoma;** moneda: **chelín tanzano (TS)** = Tanzanian shilling (TS)

tapa *nf* cover *o* cap; **tapa hermética antipolvo** = dustproof cover

◊ **tapadera** *nf* front; **su restaurante es la tapadera de una organización que trafica en drogas** = his restaurant is a front for a drugs organization

tapón *nm* cap

taquigrafía *nf* shorthand; **secretario con taquigrafía** = shorthand secretary; **tomar taquigrafía** = to take shorthand; **tomó las actas en taquigrafía** = he took down the minutes in shorthand

◊ **taquígrafo, -fa** *n* stenographer

taquilla *nf* ticket counter *o* box office *o* ticket office *o* ticket booth

◊ **taquillero, -ra** *n* booking clerk

taquimecanógrafo, -fa *n* shorthand typist

tara *nf* **(a)** *(defecto)* defect *o* fault; **hay que retirar este lote porque tiene taras** = this batch must be taken out because it is faulty **(b)** *(peso)* tare; **tener en cuenta la tara** = to allow for tare

◊ **tarado, -da** *adj* faulty *o* damaged *o* imperfect

tardar *vi* **(a)** *(llegar tarde)* to be late *o* to delay **(b)** *(transcurrir tiempo)* to take time; **se tarda muy poco desde el centro de la ciudad hasta la fábrica en helicóptero** = it is only a short helicopter flight from the centre of town to the factory; **¿sabe cuánto se tarda en llegar al aeropuerto?** = does he know how long it takes to get to the airport?

tarde 1 *adv* late; **abierto hasta tarde** = late opening; **su secretaria llamó para decir que él llegaría tarde** = his secretary phoned to say he would be late; **el avión llegó tarde a causa de la niebla** = the plane was late owing to fog **2** *nf* afternoon *o* evening; **de la tarde** = p.m.; **las llamadas a Nueva York después de las 6 de la tarde son más baratas** = if you phone New York after 6 p.m. the calls are at a cheaper rate; **el tren sale a las 6.50 de la tarde** = the train leaves at 6.50 p.m.

◊ **tardío, -ía** *adj* late

tarea *nf* job *o* task *o* assignment; **tareas labores** = occupations; **fue nombrado director gerente con la tarea de aumentar la rentabilidad de la empresa** = he was appointed managing director with the assignment to improve the company's profits

tarifa *nf* **(a)** *(transporte público)* fare; **las tarifas de tren han subido un 5%** = train fares have gone up by 5%; **el gobierno pide a las compañías aéreas que no suban las tarifas** = the government is asking the airlines to keep air fares down; **tarifa de ida** *o* **tarifa sencilla** = single fare; *US* one-way fare; **tarifa de ida y vuelta** = return fare; *US* round-trip fare; **tarifa normal** = full fare; **tarifa reducida** = concessionary fare; **tarifa de temporada baja** = off-season tariff *o* rate; **media tarifa** = half fare **(b)** *(precio o tasa)* tariff *o* rate; **tarifa de anuncios publicitarios** = rate card; **tarifa de cartas** *o* **tarifa de paquetes** = letter rate *o* parcel rate; **sale más caro enviar un paquete con tarifa de carta pero llegará**

antes = it is more expensive to send a packet letter rate but it will get there quicker; **tarifas diferenciales** = differential tariffs; **tarifa de flete** = freight rate; **tarifa nocturna** = night rate; **tarifas oficiales** = scheduled prices *o* scheduled charges; **tarifa postal** = postage; **¿cuál es la tarifa postal para Nigeria?** = what is the postage to Nigeria?; **tarifa reducida** = cheap rate; **llamadas telefónicas a tarifa reducida** = cheap rate phone calls; **tarifas de seguros** = insurance rates; **tarifas de suscripción** = subscription rates **(c)** *(empleo)* rate; **pagamos a las mecanógrafas la tarifa corriente** = we pay the going rate for typists; **tarifa horaria** *o* **por horas** = rate per hour *o* hourly rate *o* time rate; **la tarifa es 600 ptas. por hora** = the rate is 600 pesetas per hour; **tarifa de horas extras** = overtime rate *o* pay; **tarifa por pieza unitaria** = piece rate

Hacienda ha elaborado una lista de empleos y a cada cual le aplica una tarifa

Tiempo

tarjeta *nf* **(a)** card; **tarjeta (de visita)** = business card; **tarjeta de cajero automático** *o* **tarjeta dinero** = cash card; **tarjeta comercial** = store card; **tarjeta de crédito** = credit card *o* charge card; *(informal)* plastic money; **titular de una tarjeta de crédito** = credit card holder; **tarjeta de débito** = debit card; **tarjeta de desembarque** = landing card; **tarjeta de embarque** = boarding card *o* disembarkation card *o* boarding pass; **tarjeta de fichero** = filing card; *US* file card; **tarjeta de garantía de cheques** = cheque guarantee card; **tarjeta inteligente** = smart card; **tarjeta magnética** = magnetic card; **tarjeta monedero** = cash card; **tarjeta oro** = gold card; **tarjeta de pago** = debit card; **tarjeta perforada** = punched card; **tarjeta telefónica** = phone card; **tarjeta de viaje** = travelcard **(b)** **tarjeta postal** = postcard; **tarjeta de respuesta con el franqueo pagado** = reply paid card; **tarjeta de saludo** = compliments slip **(c)** **tarjeta de control de entrada** = time-clock card

la red de cajeros automáticos ha incorporado a su equipo una avanzada tarjeta multifunción, para uso tanto en imposiciones como en reintegros

Micros

miles de personas van a tener la posibilidad de manejar las tarjetas inteligentes o monederos electrónicos, un producto financiero que amenaza con sustituir al viejo bolsillo de calderilla.

El País

hay un tramo de transacciones cotidianas como son el pago de peaje en las autopistas, alimentación, etcétera, que está hecho con tarjetas de débito

El País

la organización de tarjetas de pago convive con una tecnología que avanza casi cada minuto y se considera como uno de los pilares fundamentales para que la banca consiga ofrecer calidad de servicio

Actualidad Económica

cuando se debata algo confidencial sobre la tarjeta monedero se hará sólo en un consejo ejecutivo

Actualidad Económica

tasa *nf* **(a)** *(coeficiente)* rate; **tasa de amortización**

o **de depreciación** = depreciation rate; **la tasa de aumento de los despidos** = rate of increase in redundancies; **reducción de la tasa de beneficio** = profit squeeze; **tasa de errores** = error rate; **tasa de inflación** = (rate of) inflation; **la tasa de inflación es de dos cifras** = inflation is in double figures; **tasa de natalidad** = birth rate; **la tasa de natalidad ha bajado a un doce por mil** = the birth rate has fallen to twelve per thousand; **tasa de rentabilidad** *o* **de rendimiento** = rate of return **(b)** *(impuesto)* tax *o* levy; **tasa de aeropuerto** = airport tax; **tasa de importación** = import tax

> la tasa de cobertura del desempleo es de sólo 35%
>
> **España Económica**

> las previsiones de las autoridades apuntan hacia una reducción de un punto en la tasa de crecimiento de la economía en el periodo 1992-95
>
> **Mercado**

> la tasa de inflación no ha caído al ritmo que cabía esperar dado el descenso de la tasa de actividad
>
> **Actualidad Económica**

tasación *nf* valuation *o* rating

◊ **tasador, -ra** *n* valuer *o* appraiser *o* adjuster *o* estimator; **tasador municipal** = rating officer; **tasador de pérdidas** = loss adjuster; **perito tasador** = appraiser

tasar *vt* to value *o* to price; **nos están tasando las joyas para el seguro** = we are having the jewellery valued for insurance; **comprar una tienda con las existencias tasadas** = to buy a shop with stock at valuation

taxi *nm* taxi *o* cab; **cogió un taxi para ir al aeropuerto** = he took a taxi to the airport; **los taxis de Nueva York son muy caros** = taxi fares are very high in New York; **la oficina está a unos minutos de la estación en taxi** = the office is only a short cab ride from the railway station

◊ **taxista** *nmf* taxi driver *o* cab driver *o* cabbie

techo *nm* ceiling *o* roof; cap; **lámpara de techo** = ceiling light; **techo salarial** *o* **crediticio** = wage *o* credit ceiling; **tocar techo** = to reach a ceiling

> la economía española ha tocado techo
>
> **Tiempo**

tecla *nf* key; **tecla de control** = control key; **tecla de función** = function key; **tecla de mayúsculas** = shift key; **hay sesenta y cuatro teclas en el teclado** = there are sixty-four keys on the keyboard

◊ **teclado** *nm* keyboard; **el ordenador tiene un teclado 'qwerty' normal** = the computer has a normal qwerty keyboard; **teclado español** = Spanish keyboard; **teclado numérico** = numeric keypad

teclear *vt* to keyboard; **está tecleando nuestra lista de destinatarios** = he is keyboarding our address list

> las antiguas mecanógrafas también tecleaban, pero cada 50 o 60 golpes cambiaban de postura para mover el carro
>
> **El País**

técnico, -ca 1 *adj* **(a)** technical *o* technological;

el documento explica todos los detalles técnicos del nuevo ordenador = the document gives all the technical details on the new computer; **ajuste técnico** = technical correction; **oficina técnica** *o* **servicio técnico** = technical department *o* engineering department **(b) paro técnico** = work-to-rule; **estar en paro técnico** = to work to rule **2** *nm* technician; **técnico de artes gráficas** = commercial artist; **técnico informático** = computer technician; **técnico de laboratorio** = laboratory technician; **técnico de programas** = programming engineer **3** *nf* **(a)** *(método)* technique; **técnicas de comercialización** = marketing techniques; **técnicas de dirección de empresas** = management techniques; **ha adquirido unas técnicas de gestión de oficinas muy útiles** = she has acquired some very useful office management skills; **técnicas de sondeo** *o* **de búsqueda de clientes** *o* **de votos** = canvassing techniques; **técnicas de venta insistentes** *o* **apremiantes** = high-pressure sales techniques *o* high-pressure selling; **tiene una técnica especial para atender a las quejas de los clientes** = he has a special technique for answering complaints from customers; **tiene que aprender nuevas técnicas si va a dirigir la fábrica** = he will have to learn some new skills if he is going to manage the factory **(b)** *(tecnología)* technology

> el alto precio de esta técnica ha conducido a su abandono
>
> **España Económica**

tecnología *nf* technology; **tecnología informática** = information technology (IT); **tecnología punta** = state-of-the-art technology; **industrias de alta tecnología** = sunrise industries; **la introducción de nueva tecnología** = the introduction of new technology

◊ **tecnológico, -ca** *adj* technological; **investigación tecnológica** = technological research; **parque tecnológico** = science park; **la revolución tecnológica** = the technological revolution

> el TGV se ha convertido en el símbolo de la nueva tecnología y de los ferrocarriles franceses
>
> **Cambio 16**

> la tecnología cumplió su misión con tanto éxito que hoy puede amenazar la movilidad para la que el automóvil fue creado
>
> **Cambio 16**

> la Expo de Sevilla guarda un riguroso orden tecnológico, hecho de fibra óptica y bioclimatización por agua micronizada y otras modernas maravillas
>
> **Cambio 16**

tel. *o* **telef.** = TELEFONO

telecomunicación *nf* telecommunication

teleconferencia *nf* teleconference

telefax *nm* **(a)** *(mensaje)* fax; **enviar un telefax** = to fax; **nada más oír la noticia envió un telefax a su oficina** = as soon as he heard the news he immediately faxed his office **(b)** *(aparato)* fax machine; **número de telefax** = fax number; **papel para el telefax** = fax paper; **enviar por telefax** *o* **mandar por telefax** = to fax; **enviaremos el proyecto por telefax** = we will send a fax of the design plan; **he mandado los documentos por**

telefax a nuestra oficina de Caracas = I've faxed the documents to our Caracas office

telefonear *vi* to phone *o* to call *o* to ring up; **telefonear a alguien** = to phone someone; **volver a telefonear** = to phone back; **telefoneó para pedir un taxi** = he phoned for a taxi; **¿puedes telefonear en cuanto consigas la información?** = can you phone immediately you get the information?

◊ **telefónico, -ca** *adj* telephone; **centralita telefónica** = telephone exchange *o* telephone switchboard

◊ **telefonista** *nmf* switchboard operator; **llamar a la telefonista** = to call the operator *o* to dial the operator; **hacer una llamada a través de la telefonista** = to place a call through *o* via the operator; **la telefonista está de servicio de las 6 a las 9** = the switchboard operator is on duty from 6 to 9; **pidió a la telefonista que le pusiera con un número de Alemania** = he asked the switchboard operator to get him a number in Germany

teléfono *nm* (a) telephone *o* phone; **el teléfono no funciona** = the telephone is out of order; **teléfono celular** *o* **portátil** = cellular telephone; **teléfono inalámbrico** = cordless telephone; **teléfono interno** = house phone; **teléfono público** = public telephone *o* pay phone; **teléfono de tarjeta** = card phone; **cabina de teléfono** = call *o* phone box; **número de teléfono** = telephone number *o* phone number; **tiene una lista de números de teléfono en una pequeña libreta negra** = he keeps a list of phone numbers in a little black book; **el número de teléfono está impreso en el papel de la compañía** = the phone number is on the company notepaper; **¿puede darme su número de teléfono?** = can you give me your phone *o* telephone number?; **contestar al teléfono** = to answer the phone (b) **por teléfono** = by telephone *o* by phone; **hablar por teléfono** = to be on the phone; **ha estado hablando por teléfono toda la mañana** *o* **todo el día** = she has been on the phone all morning *o* all day; **habló por teléfono con el director** = he spoke to the manager on the phone; **llamar a alguien por teléfono** = to phone someone; **pedir algo por teléfono** = to telephone for something *o* to order something by telephone; **hacer un pedido por teléfono** = to place an order by telephone; **pedidos realizados por teléfono** = telephone orders; **después de enviar el catálogo hemos recibido un gran número de pedidos por teléfono** = since we mailed the catalogue we have received a large number of telephone orders; **reservar una habitación por teléfono** = to reserve a room by telephone; **venta por teléfono** = telephone selling

telegrafiar *vt* to cable *o* to telegraph; **telegrafiar a alguien** = to send someone a telegram *o* to wire someone; **telegrafió a la oficina central para decir que se había firmado el trato** = he telegraphed *o* cabled *o* wired the head office to say that the deal had been signed; **telegrafiar un pedido** = to telegraph an order

◊ **telegráfico, -ca** *adj* telegraphic; **dirección telegráfica** = telegraphic address *o* cable address; **la oficina le envió un giro telegráfico de 100.000 ptas. para cubrir sus gastos** = the office cabled him 100,000 pesetas to cover his expenses; **transferencia telegráfica** = telegraphic transfer

◊ **telégrafo** *nm* telegraph; **enviar un mensaje por telégrafo** = to send a message by telegraph; **hacer un pedido por telégrafo** = to telegraph an order; **oficina de telégrafos** = telegraph office

telegrama *nm* telegram *o* cable *o* wire; **enviar o poner un telegrama a alguien** = to send someone a telegram; **enviar un telegrama internacional** = to send an international telegram; **envió un telegrama a su oficina pidiendo que le enviasen más dinero** = he cabled his office to ask them to send more money

teleimpresor, -ra *n* (a) *(persona)* teleprinter operator (b) *(aparato)* teleprinter *o* teletype (TTY)

teletarjeta *nf* phonecard

teletipo *nm* teleprinter

televenta *nf* telephone selling *o* telesales

télex *nm* telex; **enviar información por télex** = to send information by telex; **¿puedes enviar un télex a la sucursal canadiense antes de que abran?** = can you telex the Canadian office before they open?; **el pedido llegó por télex** = the order came by telex; **abonado de télex** = telex subscriber; **línea de télex** = telex line; **no podemos comunicarnos con nuestra oficina de Nigeria porque las líneas de télex están averiadas** = we cannot communicate with our Nigerian office because of the breakdown of the telex lines; **operador de télex** = telex operator

tema *nm* theme *o* subject *o* topic; **tema de actualidad** = current issue; **atenerse al tema** = to keep to the point

temporada *nf* season; **variaciones de temporada en el régimen de ventas** = seasonal variations in sales patterns; **temporada alta** = high season; **temporada baja** = low season *o* off season *o* dead season; **viajar en temporada baja** = to travel in the off season; **los billetes** *o* **los vuelos en avión son más baratos en temporada baja** = air fares are cheaper in the low season *o* the off season; **temporada turística** *o* **temporada de vacaciones** = tourist season *o* holiday season; **las ventas se mantuvieron durante la temporada turística** = sales held up during the tourist season; **es difícil encontrar habitaciones de hotel en plena temporada turística** = it is difficult to find hotel rooms at the height of the tourist season; **temporada de mucha actividad** *o* **de poca actividad** = busy season *o* slack season; **rebajas de fin de temporada** = end of season sale

temporal *adj* (a) temporary; **recibió una licencia temporal de exportación** = he was granted a temporary export licence; **ocupación temporal** = temporary employment (b) **seguro temporal** = term insurance; **firmó un seguro temporal de diez años** = he took out a ten-year term insurance

◊ **temporalmente** *adv* temporarily; **despedir temporalmente a los trabajadores** = to lay off workers

temporero, -ra 1 *adj* casual; **durante la vendimia se encuentra trabajo temporero fácilmente** = you can always find casual work during the grape harvest **2** *n* casual worker

temprano *adv* early; **el correo salió temprano** = the mail left early; **cogió un vuelo que salía temprano para París** = he took an early flight to Paris

tendencia *nf* **(a)** tendency; **tiene tendencia a emplear chicas jóvenes** = he tends to appoint young girls to his staff **(b) tendencias demográficas** = demographic trends *o* population trends; **tendencias económicas** = economic trends; **tendencias del mercado** = market trends; **el mercado mostró una tendencia al estancamiento** = the market showed a tendency to stagnate; **tendencia de los precios** = pattern of prices *o* price pattern; **tendencia de las ventas** = pattern of sales *o* sales pattern; **observamos una tendencia general a vender al mercado estudiantil** = we notice a general trend to sell to the student market; **el informe indica tendencias inflacionarias en la economía** = the report points to inflationary trends in the economy; **una tendencia al alza** *o* **una tendencia alcista** = an upward tendency *o* an upward trend; **una tendencia alcista en las ventas** = an upward trend in sales; **una tendencia a la baja** *o* **una tendencia bajista** = a downward trend *o* tendency; **una tendencia a la baja en las inversiones** = a downward trend in investment

> llamó mucho la atención que dentro del mismo semanario convivieran columnistas de prestigio de muy distinta tendencia ideológica
> **Tiempo**

> son las exigencias de los usuarios - más o menos inducidas - las que decantan las nuevas tendencias del mercado
> **Micros**

tender *vi* to tend to *o* to have a tendency towards; **durante el último trimestre la economía tendió a la baja** = the last quarter saw a downturn in the economy

tendero, -ra *n* tradesman *o* shopkeeper

tenedor, -ra *n* holder *o* bearer; **tenedor de acciones** = shareholder *o* holder of shares in a company; **tenedor de una póliza de seguros** = policy holder; **tenedor de libros** = bookkeeper

◊ **teneduría** *nf* **teneduría de cuentas** *o* **de libros** = bookkeeping

tenencia *nf* **(a)** *(propiedad)* tenure *o* holding; **periodo de tenencia** = holding period **(b) tenencia de acciones** *o* **de valores** = shareholding *o* stockholding *o* shareholdings

tener *vt* **(a)** *(poseer)* to have *o* to possess *o* to own *o* to hold; **tiene el 10% de las acciones de la compañía** = he owns 10% of the company *o* he holds 10% of the company's shares **(b)** *(mantener)* to keep; **tener existencias** = to hold in stock *o* to stock; **tener existencias de 200 productos** *o* **tener 200 productos en almacén** = to stock 200 lines; **tener en existencia** = to keep in stock; **tener el nombre de alguien archivado** = to keep someone's name on file **(c) tener en cuenta** = to take into account; **sin tener en cuenta** = regardless of; **tener cuidado** = to beware; **tener derecho a** = to qualify for; **tener entendido** = to believe *o* to gather; **tener éxito** = to do well *o* to make good *o* to succeed; **tener éxito en un proyecto** = to pull off a project; **tener fe en algo** *o* **alguien** = to have faith in something *o* someone; **tener un negocio** = to carry on a business; **esperamos tener noticias de los abogados dentro de unos días** = we hope to hear from the lawyers within a few days; **tener prioridad sobre algo** = to have priority over *o* to take priority over something; **tener un buen sueldo** = to earn good money **(d) tener que** = to have to

tensión *nf* stress

◊ **tenso, -sa** *adj* tense *o* stressful

tentativa *nf* attempt; **la tentativa de adquisición fue rechazada por el consejo de administración** = the takeover attempt was turned down by the board

tenue *adj* thin; **raya tenue** = thin line

teoría *nf* theory; **en teoría** = in theory *o* on paper; **en teoría el plan debería funcionar** = in theory the plan should work; **en teoría el sistema es ideal, pero tenemos que verlo en funcionamiento antes de firmar el contrato** = on paper the system is ideal, but we have to see it working before we will sign the contract

◊ **teórico, -ca** *adj* theoretical *o* notional

tercer *(contracción de 'tercero')* **Tercer Mundo** = Third World; **vendemos tractores al Tercer Mundo** *o* **a países del Tercer Mundo** = we sell tractors into the Third World *o* to Third World countries; **tercer trimestre** = third quarter

tercero, -ra 1 *adj* third; **vender con un descuento de una tercera parte** = to sell everything at one third off *o* at 33% discount **2** *nm* third party; **seguro contra terceros** = third-party insurance; **el asunto está en manos de un tercero** = the case is in the hands of a third party; **un tercero debería dar fe del documento** = the document should be witnessed by a third person

> la responsabilidad de los titulares principales, adicionales o empresas por utilizaciones fraudulentas realizadas por terceros antes de la denuncia, quedará limitada
> **El País**

tercio *nm* third; **la empresa tiene dos tercios del mercado total** = the company has two thirds of the total market

tergiversación *nf* misrepresentation; **tergiversación fraudulenta** = fraudulent misrepresentation

tergiversar *vt* *(deformar los hechos)* to misrepresent; **los periodistas tergiversaron sus palabras** = the reporters misrepresented what he said

terminable *adj* terminable

terminación *nf* **(a)** *(término)* termination; **terminación de una obra** = completion of works **(b)** *(caducidad)* expiration *o* expiry

terminal *nm* **(a)** terminal; **terminal aérea** *o* **terminal de aeropuerto** = airport terminal *o* terminal building *o* air terminal; **terminal de contenedores** = container terminal; **terminal marítima** = ocean terminal; **estación terminal** = railhead *o* terminus **(b) terminal de ordenador** = computer terminal

terminar 1 *vt* to stop *o* to end *o* to finish; **terminó la prueba antes que los demás candidatos** = she finished the test before all the other candidates; **el**

personal administrativo termina su trabajo a las
5.30 = the office staff stop work at 5.30; ¿cuánto
tiempo le llevará a Vd. terminar el trabajo? =
how long will it take you to complete the job?;
terminar una reunión = to close a meeting; el
presidente terminó la discusión al levantarse y
salir de la sala = the chairman ended the discussion
by getting up and walking out of the meeting 2 *vi* to
stop *o* to come to an end *o* to finish; el pedido se
terminó a tiempo = the order was finished in time;
terminar de trabajar = to finish work; terminar en
= to end in; el contrato termina el mes próximo =
the contract is due to finish next month; la reunión
terminó a las 12.30 = the meeting broke up at 12.30;
terminamos con una factura de 100.000 ptas. =
we ended up with a bill for 100,000 pesetas

◇ **terminarse** *vr* to come to an end *o* to be
finished; la reunión se terminó tarde = the meeting
ended late *o* came to an end late

término *nm* (a) *(terminación)* end; poner
término a = to terminate (b) por término medio =
on an average; por término medio, se roban
artículos por valor de 1.500 ptas. a diario = on an
average, 1,500 pesetas' worth of goods are stolen
every day; ser por término medio = to average
(out); el término medio anual es del 10% = it
averages out at 10% per annum (c) término
municipal = municipal area

◇ **términos** *nmpl* (a) *(condiciones)* terms; según
los términos acordados = on agreed terms; según
los términos del contrato, la compañía es
responsable de todos los daños causados a la
propiedad = under the terms of the contract, the
company is responsible for all damage to the
property; se negó a aceptar los términos del
contrato = he refused to agree to the terms of the
contract (b) *(redacción)* form

terna *nf* shortlist

terrateniente *nmf* landowner

terreno *nm* (a) *(campo)* field; estudio sobre el
terreno = field work (b) terreno para edificar =
plot of building land *o* greenfield site piece of land *o*
ground; concesión de terrenos = ground concession

terrestre *adj* land; correo terrestre = surface
mail; enviar un paquete por correo terrestre = to
send a package by surface mail; transporte
terrestre = ground transportation

territorial *adj* terrirorial; aguas territoriales =
territorial waters; fuera de aguas territoriales =
outside territorial waters

territorio *nm* territory; se han comprometido a
no vender en nuestro territorio = they have
undertaken not to sell into our territory

tesorería *nf* (a) *(puesto)* office *o* post of treasurer
(b) *(oficina)* treasurer's office (c) *(hacienda)*
treasury; cédula *o* pagaré *o* vale de tesorería =
treasury note

◇ **tesorero, -ra** *n* treasurer *o* depository;
tesorero honorario = honorary treasurer

◇ **tesoro** *nm (Hacienda Pública)* The Exchequer;
el Tesoro = the Treasury; bonos del Tesoro (a largo
plazo) = treasury bonds; pagaré del Tesoro (a corto
plazo) = treasury bill; valores del Tesoro = treasury
stocks

---

el Tesoro decide restringir las subastas
de obligaciones, que vuelven a ser
bimensuales

testado, -da *adj* testate

◇ **testador** *nm* testator

◇ **testadora** *nf* testatrix

testaferro *nm* front man

testamentaría *nf* estate *o* inheritance

testamentario, -ria *adj* testamentary;
disposición testamentaria = testamentary
disposition

testamento *nm* will; confió el testamento a su
abogado = he deposited his will with his solicitor;
dejar en testamento = to bequeath; falta de
testamento = intestacy; hizo el testamento en 1964
= he wrote his will in 1964; según el testamento,
todos los bienes pasan a sus hijos = according to
her will, all her property is left to her children;
última voluntad de testamento = last will and
testament

testigo, -ga *n* witness; actuar como testigo de la
veracidad de un documento *o* de una firma = to
act as a witness to a document *o* a signature; el
director gerente firmó como testigo = the MD
signed as a witness; el contrato se ha de firmar en
presencia de *o* ante dos testigos = the contract has
to be signed in front of two witnesses

testimonio *nm* (a) *(declaración)* evidence *o*
affidavit; falso testimonio = false evidence; dar
falso testimonio = to perjure yourself (b)
testimonio no solicitado *o* testimonio espontáneo
= unsolicited testimonial

texto *nm* text *o* wording; texto de un acuerdo *o* de
un contrato = text of an agreement *o* wording of the
contract; escribió notas al margen del texto del
acuerdo = he wrote notes at the side of the text of the
agreement; procesamiento de textos = text
processing; comprar un programa de tratamiento
de textos = to buy a word-processing program; texto
impreso = printed text *o* hard copy; para la
presentación utilizó gráficos y diez páginas de
texto impreso = he made the presentation with
diagrams and ten pages of hard copy; texto
publicitario = blurb *o* advertorial; propuesta de
texto publicitario = publicity copy; escribe textos
publicitarios para una agencia de viajes = she
writes publicity material for a travel firm

---

la AEMD considera que si se aprueba el
texto de la ley, 'todas aquellas empresas
privadas españolas que utilicen ficheros
con datos personales se verán afectadas
gravemente'

---

el texto del proyecto fija condiciones muy
estrictas para la recogida, formación y
cesión de ficheros privados

tfno = TELEFONO

tiburón *nm (negociante poco escrupuloso)*
unscrupulous businessman

tiempo *nm* (a) *(duración de una acción)* time;
tiempo inactivo = idle time; tiempo libre = spare

time; **se construyó un coche en su tiempo libre** = he built himself a car in his spare time; **tiempo muerto** = down time; **tiempo real** = real time; **tiempo de utilización de un ordenador** = computer time; **estudio de desplazamientos y tiempos** = time and motion study; **experto en desplazamientos y tiempos** = time and motion expert; **no hemos tenido noticias suyas desde hace algún tiempo** = we have not heard from them for some time; **tiene que darle tiempo al cliente para que se decida** = you must give the customer time to make up his mind; **la nueva tienda de ropa aumentó sus ventas en poco tiempo** = the new clothes shop rapidly increased sales; **perder el tiempo** = to waste time; **perdimos mucho tiempo discutiendo los preparativos para la junta general anual** = we wasted a good deal of time discussing the arrangements for the AGM **(b)** *(momento oportuno)* **a tiempo** = on time; **el avión llegó a tiempo** = the plane was on time; **tendrás que darte prisa si quieres llegar a tiempo a la reunión** = you will have to hurry if you want to get to the meeting on time *o* if you want to be on time for the meeting; **justo a tiempo** = just in time **(c)** *(jornada laboral)* **a tiempo completo** = full-time; **trabaja a tiempo completo** = she is in full-time work *o* she works full-time *o* she is in full-time employment; **a tiempo parcial** = part-time; **trabaja a tiempo parcial** = she works part-time **(d)** *(clima)* weather

tienda *nf* shop *o* store; **tienda ambulante** = mobile shop; **tienda de artículos eléctricos** = electrical goods shop; **tienda de artículos defectuosos** = reject shop; **la tienda del barrio** *o* **la tienda de la esquina** = the corner shop; *US* convenience store; **tienda de bocadillos** = sandwich bar; **tienda de bricolaje** = do-it-yourself shop *o* store; **una tienda céntrica** = a High Street shop; *US* a downtown store; **tienda de fábrica** = factory outlet *o* factory shop; **una gran tienda de confección** = a big clothing store; **tienda de informática** = computer shop; **tienda libre de impuestos** = duty-free shop; **tienda al por mayor** = wholesale shop; **tienda al por menor** *o* **al detall** = retail shop *o* retail outlet; **una tienda de muebles** = a furniture store; **tienda de precios reducidos** = cut-price store; **tienda de rebajas** = discount store; *US* discount house; **fachada de la tienda** = shopfront; **abrió una tienda de ropa de señora** = she opened a women's wear shop; **todas las tiendas del centro de la ciudad cierran los domingos** = all the shops in the centre of town close on Sundays; **la tienda cambió de dueño** *o* **fue vendida por 10 millones de ptas.** = the shop changed hands for 10 million pesetas; **ir de tiendas** *o* **buscar en las tiendas** = to go shopping *o* to shop for something

tierra *nf* ground *o* land; **azafata de tierra** = ground hostess

timador, -ra *n* confidence trickster *o* racketeer

timbre *nm* stamp; *(sello)* rubber stamp; **impuesto del timbre** = stamp duty

timo *nm* confidence trick *o* con; *(informal)* fiddle; **no es más que un timo** = it's all a fiddle; **su intento de que le pagásemos diez horas extraordinarias no fue nada más que un timo** = trying to get us to pay him for ten hours' overtime was just a con

tinta *nf* ink

tipificación *nf* standardization

tipificar *vt* to standardize

tipo *nm* **(a)** *(letra)* type *o* font **(b)** *(clase)* kind *o* standard; **la impresora realiza dos tipos de impresión** = the printer produces two kinds of printout; **hay tres tipos de sopa en nuestra máquina de bebidas** = our drinks machine has three kinds of soup; **dedicarse a un tipo de mercancía** = to carry a line of goods; **¿a qué tipo de negocios se dedica Vd.?** = what's your line of business?; **no se sabe qué tipo de negocios tiene** = the nature of his business is not known; **carta tipo** = standard letter **(c)** *(tasa)* rate; **tipos base de interés bancario** = bank base rates; **tipo de cambio** = exchange rate *o* rate of exchange; **tipo de cambio actual** = current rate of exchange; **tipos de cambio futuros** = forward (exchange) rates; **el tipo de cambio dólar/peseta** = the peseta/dollar exchange rate; **tipo de cambio vigente** = going rate; **tipo fijo** = fixed rate; **calcular costes tomando como base un tipo de cambio fijo** = to calculate costs on a fixed exchange rate; **tipo de descuento** = discount rate; **tipo flotante** = floating rate; **tipo de interés** = interest rate *o* rate of interest; **tipo de interés vigente** = standard rate; **tipo preferencial de interés bancario** = prime rate *o* prime; **tipo de cambio para operaciones a plazo** = forward rate; **tipo impositivo** *o* **de gravamen** = tax rate; **reducción de un tipo impositivo** = tax abatement **(d)** *(persona)* chap *o* man **(e)** **jugarse el tipo** = to risk one's neck

> el tipo de ajuste buscado por el Banco de España se observa en las restricciones monetarias aplicadas desde entonces y la entrada de la peseta en el SME
> **España Económica**

> a principios de la década de los 80, trabajó en México capital, donde puso en marcha un mercado de pagarés de empresa a tipo de interés flotante
> **España Económica**

> los tipos de interés se resisten a bajar en un contexto de actividad débil
> **Actualidad Económica**

tirado, -da 1 *adj (precio)* **estar tirado** = to be very cheap; **a precios tirados** = dirt cheap *o* at very low prices **2** *nf (periódico)* circulation; **la tirada comprobada de un periódico** = the audited circulation of a newspaper; **el nuevo editor espera aumentar la tirada** = the new editor hopes to improve the circulation **3** *pp de* TIRAR

tirar *vt* **(a)** *(echar)* to throw (out); **tiró la citación y se marchó de vacaciones a Casablanca** = he threw away the summons and went on holiday to Casablanca; **de usar y tirar** = disposable *o* non-returnable; **envases de usar y tirar** = non-returnable empties **(b)** *(desguazar)* to scrap; **tuvieron que tirar 10.000 repuestos** = they had to scrap 10,000 spare parts **(c)** *(arrastrar)* to pull

> la política económica no ayudará a la inversión empresarial y las exportaciones tirarán del crecimiento en 1992
> **Actualidad Económica**

titulado, -da 1 *adj* qualified *o* trained *o* skilled **2** *n* graduate

titular 1 *adj* official **2** *nm (prensa)* headline; **los titulares de los periódicos** = newspaper headlines **3**

nmf holder; **titular de los derechos de autor** = copyright holder; **titular de una patente** = patent holder; **titular de una póliza de seguros** = holder of an insurance policy *o* policy holder; **titular de una tarjeta de crédito** = holder of a credit card *o* credit card holder *o* cardholder

> cuando se produce el extravío o robo de una tarjeta, tanto de débito como de crédito, el titular de la misma únicamente responde ante la entidad por el importe equivalente a 150 ecus
>
> **El País**

título *nm* **(a)** *(derecho)* title; **título de propiedad** = title deeds; **su título de propiedad tiene vicios jurídicos** = his title to the property is defective; **hemos depositado el título de propiedad de la casa en el banco** = we have deposited the deeds of the house in the bank; **transmisión de títulos de propiedad** = conveyancing **(b)** *(dinero)* denomination **(c)** *(finanzas)* bond *o* certificate; **títulos** = equities *o* securities; **título de acción** = share certificate *o* stock certificate; **título al portador** = bearer bond; **títulos de toda confianza** *o* **de la máxima confianza** = blue-chip investments *o* blue-chip shares *o* blue chips; **títulos no cotizados en bolsa** = unlisted securities; **títulos del Estado** *o* **de la deuda pública** *o* **bonos del Tesoro** = gilt-edged securities *o* gilts *o* government securities *o* government stock; **reinvirtió el dinero en títulos del Estado** = he reinvested the money in government stocks; **títulos de interés fijo** = fixed-interest securities; **tenedores de títulos del Estado** = holders of government bonds *o* bondholders; **emisión de títulos del Estado** = tap stock; **títulos negociables** = negotiable paper **(d)** **títulos profesionales** = professional qualifications; **tener los títulos adecuados para el trabajo** = to have the right qualifications for the job; **ha sacado el título de contable** = she has qualified as an accountant; **obtendrá el título de abogado el año próximo** = he will qualify as a solicitor next year; **la compañía ha nombrado a una persona con el título de abogado como director gerente** = the company has appointed a trained lawyer as its managing director **(e)** *(nombre de una obra)* title *o* heading; **los artículos están clasificados por títulos** = items are listed under several headings **(f)** **a título gratuito** = voluntarily *o* without being paid

> la oferta de CVNE a los accionistas de Bilbaínas era de 8.800 pesetas por título
>
> **El País**

todo, -da 1 *adj* all *o* every; **todos los directivos asistieron a la reunión** = all (of) the managers attended the meeting; **el vendedor debería saber los precios de todos los productos que vende** = the salesman should know the prices of all the products he is selling; **todos los días** = every day; **pedimos a los representantes que se presenten todos los viernes para informarnos de las ventas de la semana** = we ask the reps to call in every Friday to report the weeks' sales **2** *nm y pron* all *o* everything; **todo incluido** = including everything *o* all-in (price); **sobre todo** = mainly *o* mostly *o* largely; **chico para todo** = dogsbody; **hombre que sirve para todo** = odd-job-man **3** *npl* all *o* everybody *o* everyone; **todos ponemos en duda la precisión de las copias impresas del ordenador** = we all question how accurate the computer printout is **4** *adv* completely *o* all *o* entirely

Togo *nm* Togo

◊ **togolés, -esa** *adj y n* Togolese
NOTA: capital: **Lomé;** moneda: **franco CFA (FCFA)** = CFA franc (CFAF)

tolerancia *nf* tolerance

◊ **tolerante** *adj* reasonable *o* tolerant

toma *nf* taking; **toma de decisiones** = decision making; **toma de inventario** = stocktaking

tomar *vt* to take *o* to get *o* to accept; **tome el ascensor hasta el piso 26** = take the elevator to the 26th floor; **tomar carga** = to take on cargo *o* to load; **tomar medidas** = to act *o* to take steps; **el consejo de administración tendrá que tomar medidas rápidas para que las pérdidas de la empresa se reduzcan** = the board will have to act quickly if the company's losses are going to be reduced; **tomar medidas provisionales** = to take temporary measures; **tomar nota** = to note *o* to take note of *o* to minute; **hemos tomado nota de su reclamación** = your complaint has been noted; **tomar parte en** = to enter into

◊ **tomarse** *vr* to take; **tomarse tiempo libre durante el trabajo** = to take time off work

tonadilla *nf* **tonadilla de un anuncio** = advertising jingle *o* publicity jingle

tonelada *nf* ton; **tonelada larga** *o* **británica (1016 kilos)** = long ton; **tonelada corta** *o* **norteamericana (907 kilos)** = short ton; **tonelada métrica (1000 kilos)** = metric ton *o* tonne

◊ **tonelaje** *nm* tonnage; **tonelaje bruto** = gross tonnage

tope *nm* **(a)** top *o* limit; **crédito tope** *o* **tope máximo de crédito** = credit ceiling; **plazo** *o* **fecha tope** = deadline; **precio tope** = ceiling price *o* price ceiling **(b)** **a tope** = flat out; **la fábrica trabajó a tope para terminar el pedido a tiempo** = the factory worked flat out to complete the order on time

torre *nf* tower; **torre de perforación** = oil rig

total 1 *adj* total *o* absolute; **activos totales** = total assets; **cantidad total** = total amount; **cobertura total** = full cover; **coste total** = total cost *o* full cost; **gastos totales** = total expenditure; **ingreso total** = total revenue; **pago total** = full payment *o* payment in full; **se declaró la pérdida total del cargamento** = the cargo was written off as a total loss; **precio total** = all-in price *o* all-in rate; **producción total** = total output; **reembolso total** = full refund *o* refund paid in full; **renta total** = total income; **siniestro** *o* **pérdida total** = dead loss *o* write-off; **la carga fue declarada siniestro total** = the cargo was written off as a total loss; **el coche se consideró un siniestro total** = the car was written off as a dead loss *o* a total loss; **suma total** = grand total **2** *nm (cantidad)* total; **el total de los gastos asciende a más de 500.000 ptas.** = the total of the charges comes to more than 500,000 pesetas; **total acumulado** = running total; **total general** *o* **global** = grand total; **total parcial** = subtotal; **en total** = altogether *o* gross

◊ **totalidad** *nf* total; **en su totalidad** = as a whole; **vendió su casa e invirtió el dinero en su totalidad** = she sold her house and invested the money as a lump sum; **la totalidad de los asistentes a la reunión** = all those present at the meeting;

'liquidamos la totalidad de las existencias' = 'clearance sale' o 'all stock to clear'

◊ **totalizar** *vt* to totalize o to total

◊ **totalmente** *adv* totally o absolutely o fully o completely; **la fábrica quedó totalmente destruida por el incendio** = the factory was totally destroyed in the fire; **la carga quedó totalmente estropeada por el agua** = the cargo was totally ruined by water; **dependemos totalmente de los plazos de entrega de nuestros proveedores** = we are absolutely dependent on our suppliers' schedules; **le reembolsaron totalmente cuando se quejó del servicio** = he got a full refund when he complained about the service; **acreedores no asegurados totalmente** = partly-secured creditors

touroperador, -ra o **turoperador, -ra** *n* tour operator

> tradicionalmente, el hotelero ha visto llegar a sus clientes, desde la atalaya del mostrador de recepción, atraídos la mayoría de las veces por decisión de los touroperadores o los agentes de viaje
> **Tiempo**

trabajado, -da 1 *adj* worked; **trabajo pagado por horas trabajadas** = time work **2** *pp de* TRABAJAR

trabajador, -ra 1 *adj* working o industrious; **la población trabajadora de un país** = the working population of a country **2** *n* worker o workman o labourer; **trabajador ambulante** = itinerant worker; **los trabajadores autónomos** = self-employed people o the self-employed; **el personal de la empresa está compuesto de trabajadores cualificados contratados a tiempo parcial** = the business is staffed with skilled part-timers; **trabajador a domicilio** = outside worker o homeworker; **trabajadores no especializados** = unskilled labour o unskilled workforce o unskilled workers; **trabajador eventual** = casual labourer o casual worker; **trabajador independiente** o **por su cuenta** = freelance worker o freelancer; **aunque es un trabajador independiente, trabaja a la semana las horas laborables normales** = even though he is a freelance, he works a normal working week; **trabajador portuario** = a dock worker o docker; **es una gran trabajadora** = she works hard o she's a real worker

> en Japón, el peligro vendrá de la escasez de trabajadores, cada vez más preocupante
> **Actualidad Económica**

trabajar *vi* to work o to have a job; **trabajar conforme a las normas establecidas** = to work to standard specifications; **trabajar horas extraordinarias** = to work overtime; **trabajar una jornada de ocho horas** = to work an eight-hour day; **la fábrica está trabajando duramente para completar el pedido** = the factory is working hard to complete the order; **en este momento, estamos trabajando en seis encargos a la vez** = we are working on six jobs at the moment; **trabajar por cuenta propia** = to freelance o to be self-employed; **trabajó diez años en un banco pero ahora trabaja por su cuenta** = he worked for a bank for ten years but now is self-employed; **una persona que trabaja por su cuenta** = a freelance; **tenemos unos veinte trabajadores independientes que trabajan para nosotros** o **tenemos unas veinte personas que**

trabajan como autónomos para nosotros = we have about twenty freelances working for us o we have about twenty people working for us on a freelance basis; **ahora que ha sido ascendida trabaja mejor** = she works better now that she has been promoted; **trabaja en una oficina** o **en la librería Herder** = she works in an office o at Herder's bookshop; **trabaja de cajero en un supermercado** = he is working as a cashier in a supermarket; **trabajar como dependiente** = to work as a shop assistant; **ha estado sin trabajar durante seis meses** = she has been out of work for six months

trabajo *nm* (a) *(ocupación o empleo)* work o employment o job; **trabajo administrativo** = administrative work o admin work; **todo este trabajo administrativo me lleva mucho tiempo** = all this admin work takes a lot of my time; **trabajo asignado** = workload; **trabajo a destajo** = piecework; **trabajo en equipo** = teamwork; **trabajo estacional** = seasonal employment; **trabajo eventual** = casual work; **hacer trabajo eventual** = to temp; **trabajo fijo** = permanent employment; **trabajo manual** = manual work; **trabajo de oficina** = clerical work; **un trabajo de responsabilidad** = a responsible job; **trabajo a tiempo completo** o **a jornada completa** = full-time work o employment; **trabajo a tiempo parcial** o **de media jornada** = part-time work o employment; **trabajo temporal** = temporary employment o temping; **agencia de trabajo temporal** = temp agency; **trabajo por turnos** = shift work; **el trabajo por turnos nos permite ahorrar combustible** o **energía** = shift working allows us to save on fuel; **todavía está buscando trabajo** = he is still looking for work; **está buscando trabajo de secretaría** = he is looking for secretarial work; **tiene un trabajo en la administración** = he has a job in the civil service **(b)** **accidente de trabajo** = industrial accident o occupational accident; **análisis de un puesto de trabajo** = job analysis; **calendario de trabajo** = desk o wall planner; **carga de trabajo** = workload; **tiene dificultades en hacer frente a su pesada carga de trabajo** = he has difficulty in coping with his heavy workload; **condiciones de trabajo** = (i) conditions of employment ; (ii) working conditions; **contrato de trabajo** = contract of employment o employment contract; **demandas de trabajo** = situations wanted; **garantía de trabajo** = job security; **grupo de trabajo** = working party; **el gobierno creó un grupo de trabajo para que estudiara el problema de los ordenadores en las escuelas** = the government set up a working party to examine the problem of computers in schools; **lugar de trabajo** = place of work o workplace; **magistratura de trabajo** = industrial court o industrial tribunal; **ofertas de trabajo** = situations vacant o appointments vacant; **permiso de trabajo** = work permit; **puesto de trabajo** = job; *(informática)* workstation; **consiguió un puesto de trabajo en una fábrica** = she got a job in a factory; **trabajo de oficina** = office job o white-collar job; **clasificación de puestos de trabajo** = job classification; **descripción del puesto de trabajo** = job description o specification; **formación fuera del puesto de trabajo** = off-the-job training; **perfil o requisitos del puesto de trabajo** = job specification; **valoración de un puesto de trabajo** = job evaluation; **satisfacción en el trabajo** = job satisfaction; **Organización Internacional del**

Trabajo (OIT) = International Labour Organization (ILO) **(c) va al trabajo en autobús** = he goes to work by bus; **nunca llega del trabajo antes de las 8 de la tarde** = she never gets home from work before 8 p.m.; **ofrecer un trabajo a alguien** = to offer someone a job; **sin trabajo** = unemployed; **hay mucha gente sin trabajo** = a lot of people *o* lots of people are out of work; **la recesión ha dejado sin trabajo a millones de personas** = the recession has put millions out of work; **la compañía fue fundada por tres ingenieros que estaban sin trabajo** = the company was set up by three out-of-work engineers **(d) con demasiado trabajo** = overworked; **con poco trabajo** = underworked **(e)** *(faena)* piece of work *o* job; **trabajo en curso** *o* **trabajos en curso de ejecución** = work in progress; **hacer un trabajo** = to do a job of work; **presentaron su presupuesto para el trabajo** = they sent in their quotation for the job; **hacer pequeños trabajos** = to do odd jobs; **nos hace los pequeños trabajos de la casa** = he does odd jobs for us around the house; **trabajo urgente** = rush job **(f)** *(población activa)* **fuerza de trabajo** = workforce; **mercado de trabajo** = labour market; **25.000 jóvenes han acabado su escolarización y entrado a formar parte del mercado de trabajo** = 25,000 young people have left school and have come on to the labour market

◊ **trabajoadicto, -ta** *n* workaholic

> los trabajoadictos provienen casi siempre de una situación de estrés
> **Tiempo**

> a pesar del liderazgo de las multinacionales y de los grandes grupos nacionales en el sector de empresas de trabajo temporal se están manteniendo también compañías de fuerte implantación local y regional
> **El País**

> el trabajo fijo para toda la vida ha dejado de ser una moneda común en el mundo de los negocios
> **El País**

traducción *nf* translation; **entregó la traducción de la carta al departamento de contabilidad** = she passed the translation of the letter to the accounts department; **agencia de traducción** = translation bureau

traducir *vt* to translate; **pidió a su secretaria que tradujera la carta del agente alemán** = he asked his secretary to translate the letter from the German agent; **hemos hecho traducir el contrato del español al japonés** = we have had the contract translated from Spanish into Japanese

◊ **traductor, -ra** *n* translator

traer *vt* **(a)** *(llevar)* to bring; **trajo consigo sus documentos** = he brought his documents with him; **el director de finanzas trajo a su secretaria para que tomara notas de la reunión** = the finance director brought his secretary to take notes of the meeting **(b)** *(ir a buscar)* to fetch; **llevar y traer** = to fetch and carry **(c)** *(conllevar)* **traer consigo** = to entail

traficar *vt* to traffic; **trafican con drogas** = they are trafficking in drugs

tráfico *nm* **(a)** *(circulación)* traffic; **tráfico aéreo** = air traffic; **tráfico de carretera** *o* **vial** = road traffic; **tráfico ferroviario** = rail traffic; **en verano ha disminuido el tráfico de pasajeros en las líneas de cercanías** = passenger traffic on the commuter lines has decreased during the summer; **de menor tráfico** = off-peak; **controlador de tráfico aéreo** = air traffic controller; **embotellamiento del tráfico** = traffic jam **(b)** *(negocio ilegal)* traffic; **tráfico de drogas** = drugs traffic *o* traffic in drugs *o* narcotraffic

> el TGV ha cambiado el paisaje francés, ha aumentado el tráfico ferroviario y ha batido tres veces el récord de velocidad
> **Cambio 16**

> el tráfico de pieles es el responsable de la desaparición de innumerables especies animales salvajes en este siglo
> **Ajoblanco**

tragaperras *nm* slot machine

tramitación *nf* processing; *(gestión)* transaction; **patente en tramitación** = patent pending; **tramitación del pago de un cheque** = clearance of a cheque; **gastos de tramitación** = handling charges; **el banco añade 5% en gastos de tramitación por cambiar cheques de viaje** = the bank adds on a 5% handling charge for changing travellers' cheques; **tramitación de una reclamación al seguro** = the processing of a claim for insurance

tramitar *vt* **(a)** *(despachar)* to process; **el departamento de facturación tramita 6.000 facturas al día** = the invoice department has a throughput of 6,000 invoices a day; **tramitar una reclamación al seguro** = to process an insurance claim; **tramitar el despacho de aduanas de una mercancía** = to clear goods through customs **(b)** *(gestionar)* to negotiate *o* to transact

◊ **trámite** *nm* **(a)** *(fase)* stage **(b)** *(tramitación)* transaction *o* procedure *o* formality; **trámites administrativos** = administrative procedure(s); **trámites de despido** = dismissal procedure(s)

tramo *nm* **(a) tramo de escaleras** = flight of stairs **(b)** bracket; **paga impuestos por el tramo más alto** = he is in the top tax bracket; **tramo inferior** *o* **superior de la escala impositiva** = lower *o* upper income bracket *o* lowest *o* highest tax bracket

trampa *nf* trick *o* trap; *(informal)* fiddle; **intenta hacer trampa** = he's on the fiddle

tranquilizar *vt* to reassure *o* to calm; **los mercados se tranquilizaron después del anuncio del gobierno sobre el tipo de cambio** = the markets were calmer after the government statement on the exchange rate; **el director intentó tranquilizarla, diciéndole que no iba a perder su trabajo** = the manager tried to reassure her that she would not lose her job

tranquilo, -la *adj* calm *o* quiet; **el mercado está muy tranquilo** = the market is very quiet

◊ **tranquilamente** *adv* quietly *o* easily; **pasamos la aduana tranquilamente** = we passed through customs easily

transacción *nf* deal *o* business transaction; **convenir una transacción** = to arrange a deal *o* to set up a deal *o* to do a deal; **transacción en efectivo** = cash deal; **transacción de acciones nominativas**

= registered share transaction; **transacción única** = one-off deal; **en esta transacción he perdido dinero** = the deal has left me out of pocket

> el volumen de fraude en relación con las transacciones que se hacen es muy pequeño
> **Actualidad Económica**

> hay un tramo de transacciones cotidianas como son el pago de peaje en las autopistas, alimentación, etcétera, que está hecho con tarjetas de débito
> **El País**

transatlántico *nm* liner

transbordador *nm* ferry; **transbordador de pasajeros** = passenger ferry; **transbordador de vehículos** = car ferry

transbordar *vt* **(a)** *(traslado)* to transfer; **transbordarán los coches a otro tren antes de pasar la frontera** = they will transfer the cars onto another train before crossing the border **(b)** *(barco)* to tranship; **transbordar mercancías de un barco a otro** = to tranship goods from one boat to another

◊ **transbordo** *nm* transfer; **hacer transbordo** = to transfer *o* to change; **para ir a Granada en avión hay que hacer transbordo** = if you are flying to Granada you will have to change planes; **pasajero de transbordo** = transfer passenger

transcurso *nm* **transcurso del tiempo** = the course of time *o* the lapse of time; **en el transcurso del debate el director gerente explicó los planes de expansión de la compañía** = in the course of the discussion, the managing director explained the company's expansion plans

transferencia *nf* transfer *o* remittance *o* virement; **transferencia bancaria** = bank transfer *o* bank giro; **pagar por transferencia bancaria** = to pay by bank giro transfer; **transferencia por vía aérea** = airmail transfer; **transferencia de divisas** = foreign exchange transfer; **transferencias electrónicas de fondos** = electronic funds transfer (EFT); **transferencias electrónicas de fondos en el punto de venta** = electronic funds transfer at point of sale (EFTPOS); **transferencia de fondos** = credit transfer *o* transfer of funds; **transferencia de propiedad** *o* **de acciones** = transfer of property *o* of shares; **transferencia telegráfica** = telegraphic transfer; **formulario de transferencia de acciones** = stock transfer form; **gasto de transferencia** = handling charge for a bank transfer

> la mayoría de las transferencias son postales (manuales o magnéticas) aunque puede elegirse la vía telegráfica. Las más rápidas suelen ser estas últimas, sin embargo, son las más caras y menos usadas
> **El País**

transferible *adj* transferable; **el billete de abono no es transferible** = the season ticket is not transferable

transferir *vt* to transfer *o* to switch; **el trabajo fue transferido de nuestra fábrica en Valencia a Barcelona** = the job was switched from our Valencia factory to Barcelona; **transfirió sus acciones a un fideicomiso familiar** = he transferred his shares to a family trust; **transfirió su dinero a una cuenta de depósito** = she transferred her money to a deposit account

transformar *vt* to transform

◊ **transformación** *nf* transformation

transición *nf* transition (period); **cuando una empresa cambia de propietario, el periodo de transición es siempre difícil** = when the ownership of a company changes, the handover period is always difficult

transigir *vt* to compromise *o* to agree; **transigiré en el precio pero no en la calidad** = I will come to a compromise over the price but not over the quality

tránsito *nm* transit; **pagar una indemnización por los daños sufridos en tránsito** *o* **por pérdidas en tránsito** = to pay compensation for damage suffered in transit *o* for loss in transit; **mercancías en tránsito** = goods in transit; **sala para pasajeros en tránsito** = transit lounge; **visado** *o* **permiso de tránsito** = transit visa *o* transit permit

◊ **transitorio, -ria** *adj* temporary *o* provisional; **su nombramiento es transitorio** = his apppointment is provisional; **incapacidad transitoria** = temporary incapacity

transmisión *nf* **(a)** *(cesión de bienes)* assignment; **transmisión de una patente** *o* **propiedad intelectual** = assignment of a patent *o* of a copyright; **la transmisión de poderes del antiguo presidente al nuevo se efectuó sin contratiempos** = the handover from the old chairman to the new went very smoothly; **transmisión del título de propiedad** = conveyance; **transmisión de títulos de propiedad** = conveyancing **(b)** *(comunicación)* coverage *o* transmission; **transmisión de un mensaje** = transmission of a message

transmitir *vt* **(a)** *(comunicación)* to transmit *o* to broadcast *o* to network; **transmitir un programa de televisión por toda la red** = to network a television programme **(b)** *(ceder)* to hand over

transportable *adj* transportable

transportar *vt* to transport *o* to carry; **transportar mercancías** = to carry goods *o* to freight goods; **la compañía transporta millones de toneladas de mercancías por tren cada año** = the company transports millions of tons of goods by rail each year; **transportamos mercancías a todos los lugares de los EE UU** = we freight goods to all parts of the USA

transporte *nm* **(a)** *(de personas, mercancías)* transport; **transporte aéreo** *o* **transporte por vía aérea** = air transport *o* transport by air; **transporte por ferrocarril** = rail transport *o* transport by rail; **transporte por carretera** = road transport *o* transport by road *o* road haulage; **contratista de transporte por carretera** = road haulier *o* haulage contractor; **coste de transporte** = carrying cost; **gastos** *o* **tarifas de transporte** = freight charges *o* carrying charges; **costes** *o* **tarifas de transporte por carretera** = haulage costs *o* haulage rates; **el coste del transporte por carretera aumenta un 5% anual** = haulage is increasing by 5% per annum; **transporte en contenedores** = shipping in containers *o* container transport *o* containerization; **transporte de pasajeros** = passenger transport; **los servicios de transporte de pasajeros de la RENFE** = the passenger transport services of RENFE; **la compañía proporcionará el transporte al**

aeropuerto = the company will provide transportation to the airport; **transporte terrestre** = ground transportation; **agencia de transportes** = road haulier; **compañía de transporte** = *(por carretera)* haulage *o* freight company; *(traslado)* haulage business *o* removals firm; **compañía** *o* **empresa de transporte aéreo** = air carrier; **medio de transporte** = means of transport; **medios de transporte** = transport facilities; **¿qué medio de transporte empleará para llegar a la fábrica?** = what means of transport will you use to get to the factory?; **sistema de transporte público** = public transport system; **los visitantes utilizarán el transporte público** = the visitors will be using public transport **(b)** *(porte)* carriage *o* freight; **pagar transporte** = to pay for carriage; **el transporte representa un 15% del coste total** = carriage is 15% of the total cost

◊ **transportista** *nmf* **(a)** shipper *o* carrier; **transportista nacional** *o* **del interior** = inland carrier **(b)** road haulier

> los transportes aunque deficientes, son muy baratos
>
> **España Económica**

trasladar *vt* **(a)** *(mudarse)* to move; **la compañía se va a trasladar de la Gran Vía al centro de la ciudad** = the company is moving from Gran Vía to the centre of town; **hemos decidido trasladar nuestra fábrica a un lugar cercano al aeropuerto** = we have decided to move our factory to a site near the airport; **trasladaron el ordenador a su lugar** = they moved the computer into position **(b)** *(transferir)* to switch *o* to transfer; **trasladar los costes a una empresa filial** = to offload costs onto a subsidiary company; **trasladar fondos de una inversión a otra** = to switch funds from one investment to another **(c)** *(cambiar de sitio, trabajo)* to transfer *o* to relocate; *(adscribir el personal a una clase de trabajo diferente)* to redeploy; **el contable fue trasladado a nuestra sucursal gallega** = the accountant was transferred to our Galician branch; **trasladar temporalmente** *(a otra empresa o departamento)* = to second someone; **fue trasladado al Ministerio de Comercio por un periodo de dos años** = he was seconded to the Department of Trade for two years; **la junta decidió trasladar la compañía a Escocia** = the board decided to relocate the company in Scotland

◊ **trasladarse** *vr* to move; **la empresa se ha trasladado a una nueva dirección** = the company has moved to a new address *o* to a new location

◊ **traslado** *nm* **(a)** *(cambio)* transfer *o* relocation; **solicitó el traslado a nuestra sucursal de Galicia** = he applied for a transfer to our branch in Galicia; **traslado temporal** = temporary assignment *o* secondment; **ha conseguido el traslado a otro colegio por un periodo de tres años** = he is on three years' secondment to another college **(b)** *(mudanza)* removal

traspasar *vt* to transfer *o* to make over; **traspasaron su negocio y ahora viven de rentas** = they sold their business and now live on their private income

◊ **traspaso** *nm* **(a)** *(venta)* transfer *o* sale; **traspaso de bienes** = assignment **(b)** *(pago de entrada de alquiler)* premium *o* key money *o* transfer fee; **piso para alquilar con un traspaso de 2.000.000 de**

ptas. = flat to let with a premium of 2m pesetas; **alquiler anual: 1.600.000, traspaso: 5.000.000** = annual rent: 1.6m, premium: 5m

trastienda *nf (en una tienda)* room at the back of a shop

trasto *nm* junk; **deberías tirar todos esos trastos** = you should throw away all that junk

tratado *nm* treaty *o* agreement; **tratado comercial** = trade agreement; *(UE)* **Tratado de Roma** = Treaty of Rome; **Tratado de la Unión Europea (TUE)** = Treaty of the European Union

tratamiento *nm (informática)* processing; **el tratamiento de la información** *o* **de la estadística** = processing of information *o* of statistics; **tratamiento de textos** = word-processing *o* text processing; **comprar un programa de tratamiento de textos** = to buy a word-processing program; **cargue el programa de tratamiento de textos antes de empezar a teclear** = load the word-processing program before you start keyboarding; **despacho de tratamiento de textos** = word-processing bureau

tratar 1 *vi* **(a)** *(intentar)* to attempt; **tratar de** = (i) to try *o* to endeavour; (ii) to talk about *o* to discuss; **estamos tratando de adquirir una empresa manufacturera** = we are attempting the takeover of a manufacturing company; **en la reunión se trató del resultado de la encuesta** = the outcome of the survey was discussed in the meeting **(b)** **tratar en** = to deal in; **tratar en opciones** = to deal in options **(c)** **tratar con** = to deal with; **tratamos directamente con el fabricante, sin pasar por un mayorista** = we deal directly with the manufacturer, without using a wholesaler **2** *vt* **(a)** *(ocuparse)* to handle; **deberías tratar mejor la nueva máquina** = you should learn how to handle the new machine properly; **la empresa va a dejar de tratar con ordenadores** = the company is getting out of the computer market **(b)** *(cuidar)* to look after; **trata muy bien a los clientes** = he looks after his customers very well **(c)** *(discutir)* to discuss; **el comité trató la cuestión de los derechos de importación de los automóviles** = the committee discussed the question of import duties on cars

trato *nm* bargain *o* deal; **trato justo** = fair deal; **cerrar un trato** = to close a deal *o* to make a bargain *o* to clinch; **conseguir un trato en condiciones muy favorables** = to strike a hard bargain; **deshacer un trato** = to break an agreement; **el trato se negoció en privado** = the deal was negotiated privately; **tiene una gran experiencia en el trato con empresas alemanas** = she has a lot of experience of dealing with German companies

travesía *nf* sea crossing *o* voyage

trayecto *nm* journey *o* distance travelled; **el trayecto de Barcelona a Atenas es muy largo** = it is a long haul from Barcelona to Athens

trazado 1 *nm* design *o* layout *o* sketch **2** *pp de* TRAZAR

trazar *vt* to plan *o* to lay out *o* to draw; **trazó una línea gruesa al final de la columna para indicar la cifra total** = he drew a thick line across the bottom of the column to show which figure was the total

◊ **trazo** *nm* line

tren *nm* train; **tren de cercanías** = local train *o* commuter train; **tren de mercancías** = freight train *o* goods train; **tren de mercancías de contenedores** = freightliner; **enviar mercancías por tren** = to ship goods by train; **tren de pasajeros** = passenger train; **coger el tren** *o* **perder el tren** = to take the train *o* to miss the train; **cogió el tren de las 9.30 para Sevilla** = he took the 09.30 train to Seville; **normalmente viaja en el tren de las 12.45** = his regular train is the 12.45; **el tren sale a las 6.50 de la tarde** = the train leaves at 6.50 p.m.; **los usuarios del tren se quejan del aumento de las tarifas** = rail travellers are complaining about rising fares; **seis millones de personas van al trabajo en tren todos los días** = six million commuters travel to work by rail every day

tribunal *nm* **(a)** *(juzgado)* tribunal *o* court; **tribunal de arbitraje** *o* **arbitral** = arbitration *o* adjudication tribunal; **tribunal de arbitraje laboral** = industrial (arbitration) tribunal; **Tribunal de Cuentas** = Court of Auditors; **tribunales de justicia** = law courts; **tribunal de primera instancia** = trial court; **tribunal de rentas** = rent tribunal; **tribunal sucesorio** *o* **testamentario** = probate court; **llevar a uno ante los tribunales** = to take someone to court; **bajo la jurisdicción del tribunal** = within the jurisdiction of the court; **obedecer una orden del tribunal** = to comply with a court order; **el tribunal ordenó que se liquidara la sociedad** = the court ordered the company to be wound up **(b)** *(universidad)* **tribunal de examinadores** *o* **de examen** = board of examiners *o* exam board

tributario, -ria *adj* tributary *o* tax *o* taxation; **sistema tributario** = tax system; **privilegio tributario** = tax concession

estas cuotas no suponen un aumento tributario respecto a las actuales licencias fiscales
Tiempo

el Gobierno ha solicitado al Congreso nuevas facultades para legislar por decreto el sistema tributario
Cambio 16

trimestral *adj* quarterly; **el banco nos manda un estado de cuentas trimestral** = the bank sends us a quarterly statement

◊ **trimestralmente** *adv* quarterly; **acordamos pagar la renta trimestralmente** = we agreed to pay the rent quarterly *o* on a quarterly basis

trimestre *nm* **(a)** *(legal o universitario)* term **(b)** *(cada tres meses)* quarter; **primer trimestre** *o* **segundo trimestre** *o* **tercer trimestre** = first quarter *o* second quarter *o* third quarter; **cuarto trimestre** *o* **último trimestre** = fourth quarter *o* last quarter; **día de ajuste** *o* **liquidación trimestral** = quarter day; **los gastos de electricidad se cobran por trimestres** = there is a quarterly charge for electricity; **los plazos se harán efectivos al final de cada trimestre** = the instalments are payable at the end of each quarter; **los costes administrativos parecen aumentar cada trimestre** = admin costs seem to be rising each quarter

Trinidad y Tobago *nm* Trinidad & Tobago; **de Trinidad** = Trinidadian

NOTA: capital: **Port of Spain**; moneda: **dólar de Trinidad y Tobago (TT$)** = Trinidad and Tobago dollar (TT$)

triple 1 *adj* threefold *o* triple *o* three times **2** *nm* **el coste del transporte aéreo de las mercancías es el triple de su coste de fabricación** = the cost of airfreighting the goods is triple their manufacturing cost

triplicado 1 *adj* triplicate; **por triplicado** = in triplicate; **imprimir una factura por triplicado** = to print an invoice in triplicate; **facturación por triplicado** = invoicing in triplicate **2** *pp de* TRIPLICAR

triplicar *vt* to treble *o* to triple *o* to multiply by three; **la adquisición de la cadena de tiendas ha triplicado el volumen de ventas del grupo** = the acquisition of the chain of stores has tripled the group's turnover

◊ **triplicarse** *vr* to triple; **los préstamos** *o* **las deudas de la compañía se han triplicado** = the company's borrowings *o* debts have trebled

tríptico *nm* **(a)** *(folleto publicitario)* two-fold leaflet **(b)** *(formulario)* three-part document

tripulación *nf* crew; **el barco lleva una tripulación de 250 personas** = the ship carries a crew of 250

trituradora *nf* shredder

triturar *vt* to shred; **mandaron un montón de facturas viejas para ser trituradas** = they sent a pile of old invoices to be shred; **declaró a la policía que el director le había mandado triturar todos los documentos del archivo** = she told the police that the manager had told her to shred all the documents in the file

triunfar *vi* to triumph *o* to succeed *o* to make good *o* to be successful; **se puede decir que ha triunfado en los negocios** = we can say that he has been successful in business

trocar *vt* to barter *o* to exchange; **acordaron trocar tractores por barriles de vino** = they agreed a deal to barter tractors for barrels of wine

troy *nm* troy; **onza troy** = troy ounce; **peso troy** = troy weight

trozo *nm* piece; **un trozo de papel** = a piece of paper; **en trozos pequeños** = in small pieces

truco *nm* gimmick; **truco publicitario** = a publicity gimmick; **el personal de relaciones públicas ideó este nuevo truco publicitario** = the PR men thought up this new advertising gimmick

trueque *nm* barter *o* bartering; **trueque de divisas** = currency swap; **contrato de trueque** = barter agreement *o* barter arrangement *o* barter deal; **la empresa ha aprobado un contrato de trueque con Bulgaria** = the company has agreed a barter deal with Bulgaria

el sistema del trueque, el más primitivo de los intercambios comerciales asociado ahora al subdesarrollo, se ha consolidado con gran éxito en los mercados europeos y norteamericanos como una auténtica alternativa financiera
El País

túnel *nm* tunnel

Túnez *nf* Tunisia

◊ **tunecino, -na** *adj y n* Tunisian
NOTA: capital: **Túnez** (= Tunis); moneda: **dinar tunecino (D)** = Tunisian dinar (D)

turbio, -bia *adj* shady; **transacción turbia** = shady deal

turismo *nm* **(a)** *(viajes)* tourism *o* tourist trade; **la industria del turismo** = the tourist industry; **oficina de turismo** = tourist bureau *o* tourist information office **(b)** *(coche particular)* private car

◊ **turista** *nmf* tourist; **visado turista** = tourist visa

◊ **turístico, -ca** *adj* tourist; **oficina de información turística** = tourist bureau *o* tourist information office; **clase turística** = tourist class; **siempre viaja en primera clase porque dice que la clase turística es demasiado incómoda** = he always travels first class, because he says tourist class is too uncomfortable

turno *nm* **(a)** shift; **turno de día** = day shift; **turno de noche** = night shift *o* duty; **hay 150 obreros en el turno de día** = there are 150 men on the day shift; **trabaja en el turno de día** *o* **el turno de noche** = he works the day shift *o* night shift; **trabajo por turnos** = shift work; **trabajamos por turnos de 8 horas** = we work by turns of 8 hours; **la dirección va a introducir el trabajo por turnos** = the management is introducing a shift system *o* shift working; **trabajan en turnos dobles** = they work double shifts; **turno de relevo** = relief shift; **cubrir los puestos del turno** = to man a shift **(b)** director en turno = acting manager; **ocupar el cargo de presidente por turno** = to fill the post of chairman by rotation **(c)** **se saltaron el turno de espera y consiguieron la licencia de exportación antes que nosotros** = they jumped the queue and got their export licence before we did **(d)** *(jurídico)* **turno de oficio** = legal aid

turoperador, -ra *n* tour operator

Turquía *nf* Turkey

◊ **turco, -ca** *o* **otomano, -na 1** *adj* Turkish **2** *n* Turk
NOTA: capital: **Ankara**; moneda: **libra turca (LT)** = Turkish lira (LT)

tutear *vt* to address somebody informally *o* to be on first name terms with someone

Uu

ubicación *nf* location *o* whereabouts

Ucrania *nf* Ukraine

◊ **ucraniano, -na** *o* **ucranio, -nia** *adj y n* Ukrainian
NOTA: capital: **Kiev**; moneda: **karbovanets** = karbovanets

UDV = UNIDAD DE DESPLIEGUE VISUAL visual display unit (VDU)

UE = UNION EUROPEA European Union (EU)

Uganda *nf* Uganda

◊ **ugandés, -esa** *adj y n* Ugandan
NOTA: capital: **Kampala**; moneda: **chelín ugandés (U Sh)** = Uganda shilling (U Sh)

UGT = UNION GENERAL DE TRABAJADORES General Workers Trade Union

◊ **ugetista** *nmf* member of UGT

ulterior *adj* further; **el vuelo de Madrid termina en Nueva York - para destinos ulteriores hay que tomar un vuelo del interior** = the flight from Madrid terminates in New York - for further destinations you must change to internal flights

ultimato *nm* (también se escribe: **ultimátum**) ultimatum; **los cargos sindicales discutieron entre ellos sobre la mejor manera de hacer frente al ultimátum de la dirección** = the union officials argued among themselves over the best way to deal with the ultimatum from the management

último, -ma *adj* **(a)** *(final)* last *o* ultimate *o* final; **ésta es la última reunión del consejo de administración antes de trasladarnos a las nuevas oficinas** = this is our last board meeting before we move to our new offices; **terminamos los últimos artículos del pedido justo dos días antes de la fecha de entrega** = we finished the last items in the order just two days before the promised delivery date; **fui el último, de una cola de veinte personas, en ser servido** = out of a queue of twenty people, I was served last; **efectuar el último pago** = to make the final payment; **pagar el último plazo** = to pay the final instalment; **último requerimiento de pago** = final demand; **último trimestre** = last quarter **(b)** *(más reciente)* latest *o* most recent; **siempre conduce el último modelo de coche** = he always drives the latest model of car; **aquí están las últimas cifras de ventas** = here are the latest sales figures; **la última fecha para la firma del contrato** = latest date for signature of the contract; **le enviaremos nuestro último catálogo** = we will mail you our most recent catalogue **(c) por último** = finally

ultra 1 *adj y nmf* extreme *o* extremist **2** *prefijo* ultra *o* extra

ultramar *nm* overseas; **se ocupan de todos nuestros pedidos de ultramar** = they handle all our overseas orders

◊ **ultramarino, -na 1** *adj* overseas **2** *nmpl* *(tienda)* **ultramarinos** = grocer's shop *o* grocery

umbral *nm* threshold; **umbral de rentabilidad** = breakeven point; **el umbral de rentabilidad se alcanza cuando las ventas cubren todos los costes** = breakeven point is reached when sales cover all costs; *(UE)* **precio umbral** = threshold price

unánime *adj* unanimous; **hubo un voto unánime contra la propuesta** = there was a unanimous vote against the proposal; **alcanzaron un acuerdo unánime** = they reached unanimous agreement

◊ **unanimidad** *nf* unanimity; **las propuestas fueron adoptadas por unanimidad** = the proposals were adopted unanimously

único, -ca *adj* **(a)** *(solo)* single *o* sole *o* one-off; **artículo único** = one-off item; **moneda única** = single currency; **pago único** = lump sum; **contabilidad por partida única** = single-entry bookkeeping; **póliza de prima única** = single premium policy; **propietario único** = sole owner **(b)** *(singular)* unique; **único en su género** = unique of its kind **(c) el Acta Unica Europea** = the European Single Act; **el Mercado Unico Europeo** = the European Single Market

unidad *nf* **(a)** *(pieza)* unit *o* piece; **unidad de cuenta** = unit of account; **unidad monetaria** = monetary unit *o* unit of currency; **coste por unidad** = unit cost; **precio por unidad** = unit price; **acordamos un precio de 250 ptas. la unidad** = a deal was struck at 250 pesetas a unit; **vender algo por unidades** = to sell something by the piece **(b)** *(conjunto contable)* unit; **unidad de fabricación** = factory unit; **unidad familiar** = family unit *o* household; **unidad de investigación** = research unit; **unidad de producción** = production unit **(c)** *(informática)* **unidad de despliegue visual (UDV)** *o* **unidad de presentación visual (UPV)** = visual display unit (VDU) *o* visual display terminal (VDT); **unidad de discos** = disk drive; **unidad de información** = bit; **unidad de salida** = output device

unido, -da 1 *adj* **(a) las Naciones Unidas** = the United Nations **(b)** *(junto)* joint *o* joined **2** *pp de* UNIR

uniforme 1 *adj* uniform **2** *nm* uniform

unilateral *adj* unilateral; **acuerdo unilateral** = one-sided agreement; **comercio unilateral** = one-way trade; **tomaron la decisión unilateral de anular el contrato** = they took the unilateral decision to cancel the contract

◊ **unilateralmente** *adv* unilaterally; **anularon el contrato unilateralmente** = they cancelled the contract unilaterally

unión *nf* union; **unión aduanera** = customs union; **Unión General de Trabajadores (UGT)** = General Workers Trade Union

◊ **Unión Europea (UE)** *nf* European Union (EU); **los ministros de la Unión Europea** = the EU ministers

unir *vt* to unite *o* to connect *o* to join *o* to link; **el**

cuerpo directivo se unió a la administración para rechazar la OPA = the directors united with the managers to reject the takeover bid

unitario, -ria *adj* unitary *o* unit; **coste unitario** = unit cost; **precio unitario** = unit price

uno, una 1 *adj* **(a)** *(singular)* one **(b)** *(plural)* **unos, unas** = some *o* about *o* around; **unos años más tarde** = some years later; **el costo de calefacción de la oficina es de unas 400.000 ptas. al año** = the office costs about *o* around 400,000 pesetas a year to heat **2** *pron* one *o* someone *o* somebody

UPV = UNIDAD DE PRESENTACION VISUAL visual display unit (VDU) *o* visual display terminal (VDT)

urbanizar *vt* to develop *o* to build

◊ **urbanización** *nf* urban development; housing estate

urgencia *nf* **(a)** *(prisa)* urgency; **necesitamos las máquinas con urgencia** = we need the machinery urgently **(b)** *(emergencia)* emergency

urgente *adj* urgent *o* express; **una carta urgente** = an express letter; **compromisos urgentes** = pressing engagements; **distribución** *o* **entrega urgente** = express delivery; **envío urgente** = express item; **facturas urgentes** = pressing bills; **pedido urgente** = rush order; **reparto urgente** = express delivery; **trabajo urgente** = rush job; **enviar por transporte urgente** = to send by express mail *o* to express; **enviamos el pedido al almacén del cliente por transporte urgente** = we expressed the order to the customer's warehouse

◊ **urgentemente** *adv* urgently; **hacer algo urgentemente** = to do something urgently

urna *nf* **urna electoral** = ballot box

los reveses en las urnas han crispado los nervios de los dirigentes y militantes del partido
Cambio 16

Uruguay *nm* Uruguay

◊ **uruguayo, -ya** *adj y n* Uruguayan
NOTA: capital: **Montevideo**; moneda: **nuevo peso uruguayo (NUr$)** = new Uruguayan peso (NUr$)

usado, -da 1 *adj* used *o* secondhand; **no usado** = unused; **el mercado de coches usados** = the secondhand car market *o* the market in secondhand cars **2** *pp de* USAR

usar *vt* to use *o* to utilize; **la fotocopiadora se usa continuamente** = the photocopier is being used all the time; **fácil de usar** = user-friendly; **estos programas son realmente fáciles de usar** = these programs are really user-friendly; **ordenador fácil de usar** = user-friendly computer; **sin usar** = unused; **de usar y tirar** = non-returnable *o* disposable

uso *nm* **(a)** *(utilización)* usage *o* use; **uso indebido** = misuse; **terreno destinado a uso industrial** = land zoned for industrial use; **uso de fondos** = application of funds; **usos mercantiles** = business practices =; **artículos de uso personal** = items for personal use; **tiene un coche de la empresa para su uso personal** = he has the use of a company car; **en uso** = in use *o* employed; **instrucciones de uso** = directions for use *o* operating manual; **hacer uso de algo** = to make use of something **(b)** *(desgaste)* wear and tear

usual *adj* usual *o* customary; **el gerente llegó a la hora usual** = the manager arrived at the usual time

usuario, -ria *n* user; **usuario final** = end user; **guía del usuario** = user's guide *o* handbook; **fácil para el usuario** = user-friendly; **la empresa está creando un ordenador pensado para el usuario** = the company is creating a computer with the end user in mind

son las exigencias de los usuarios - más o menos inducidas - las que decantan las nuevas tendencias del mercado
Micros

usufructo vitalicio *nm* life interest

◊ **usufructuario, -ria 1** *adj* **interés usufructuario** = beneficial interest **2** *n* beneficial occupier

usura *nf* usury

◊ **usurero, -ra** *n* usurer *o* loan shark

utensilio *nm* implement *o* utensil; **utensilios de cocina** = kitchen utensils; **utensilios sanitarios** = sanitary ware

útil 1 *adj* useful *o* handy; **carga útil** = commercial load; **día útil** = working day *o* weekday; **superficie útil** = floor space; **vida útil de un producto** = shelf life of a product **2** *nmpl* **útiles** = tools *o* equipment

utilidad *nf* **(a)** *(ventaja)* usefulness *o* advantage; **llegar a la exposición antes de la apertura no tiene ninguna utilidad** = it's no use arriving *o* there is no advantage in arriving at the exhibition before it opens **(b)** **utilidades acumuladas** = retained earnings

utilización *nf* usage; *(de ordenador)* **utilización colectiva** = time-sharing

utilizar *vt* to use *o* to utilize; *(máquina)* to run; **utilizamos el correo aéreo para toda la correspondencia con el extranjero** = we use airmail for all our overseas correspondence; **utilice la salida de emergencia** *o* **urgencia en caso de incendio** = use the emergency exit in case of fire; **utilizar capacidad ociosa** = to use up spare capacity; **el personal está insuficientemente utilizado debido al recorte sufrido en la producción** = the staff is underemployed because of the cutback in production; **fácil de utilizar** = user-friendly

Vv

vacación *nf* vacation; **vacaciones** = holiday *o* leave; *US* vacation; **vacaciones de verano** *o* **de Navidad** = summer holidays *o* Christmas holidays; **la oficina cierra durante las vacaciones de Navidad** = the office is closed for the Christmas holiday; **vacaciones pagadas** = holidays with pay; **vacaciones no pagadas** = unpaid holiday; **vacaciones reglamentarias** *o* **establecidas por ley** = statutory holiday; **tomar vacaciones** *o* **irse** *o* **marcharse de vacaciones** = to take a holiday *o* to go on holiday; **¿cuándo toma las vacaciones el director?** when is the manager taking his holidays?; **el director está de vacaciones** = the director is on holiday; **mi secretaria está de vacaciones mañana** = my secretary is off on holiday tomorrow; **mi secretaria estará de vacaciones durante dos semanas** = my secretary will be away on holiday for two weeks; **el puesto lleva aparejadas cinco semanas de vacaciones** = the job carries five weeks' holiday; **seis semanas de vacaciones al año** = six weeks' annual leave; **no ha agotado todas las vacaciones a que tiene derecho** = she has not used up all her holiday entitlement; **paga** *o* **sueldo de vacaciones** = holiday pay; **¿cobra Vd. durante las vacaciones?** = do you get holiday pay?

vacante 1 *adj* vacant *o* empty *o* unoccupied **2** *nf* *(puesto)* vacancy *o* opening; **vacantes** = job openings; **hemos anunciado una vacante en la prensa local** = we advertised a vacancy in the local press; **conservar una vacante** = to keep a job open; **no hemos podido cubrir la vacante de mecánico especializado** = we have been unable to fill the vacancy for a skilled machinist; **proveer una vacante** = to fill a post; **tienen una vacante de secretaria** = they have a vacancy for a secretary; **tenemos vacantes para personal de oficina** = we have openings for office staff

vaciar *vt* to empty; **vació el archivo y puso las fichas en cajas** = she emptied the filing cabinet and put the files in boxes

vacilar *vi* to hesitate; **vaciló durante algún tiempo antes de aceptar el trabajo** = she hesitated for some time before accepting the job; **sin vacilar** = without hesitation

vacío, -cía 1 *adj* empty; *(sin cargamento)* unladen; **el sobre está vacío** = the envelope is empty; **puedes devolver este archivo al almacén ya que está vacío** = you can take that filing cabinet back to the storeroom as it is empty; **empezar el archivo informático con un espacio vacío** = start the computer file with an empty workspace; **embalaje vacío (para exposición)** = dummy pack **2** *nm* **(a)** *(hueco)* gap **(b)** *(envase)* vacuum; **embalado** *o* **empaquetado** *o* **envasado al vacío** = shrink-wrapped *o* vacuum-packed **(c) hacer el vacío** = to send someone to Coventry

vado *nm* 'vado permanente' = 'keep clear'

vago, -ga *adj* **(a)** *(poco claro)* vague **(b)** *(gandul)* idle *o* lazy

vagón *nm* **(a)** *(mercancías)* wagon *o* railway truck; **vagón cisterna** = tanker; **franco sobre vagón** = free on rail **(b)** *(pasajeros)* carriage; **vagón de primera clase** = first-class carriage

vaivén *nm* constant movement; **los vaivenes bursátiles** = stock market fluctuations

vale *nm* **(a)** *(cupón)* voucher; **vale de caja** = cash voucher; **por cada 2.000 ptas. de compra, el cliente obtiene un vale de caja por un valor de 200 ptas.** = with every 2,000 pesetas of purchases, the customer gets a cash voucher to the value of 200 pesetas; **vale para comprar libros** *o* **flores** = book token *o* flower token; **vale de regalo** = gift voucher *o* gift token *o* gift coupon; **le ofrecimos un vale de regalo por su cumpleaños** = we gave her a gift token for her birthday **(b)** *(pagaré)* IOU **(c) vale de tesorería** = treasury note

valer *vi* to cost *o* to be worth; **esta tela vale 1.000 ptas. el metro** = this cloth costs 1,000 pesetas a metre; **no lo hagas arreglar - sólo vale 2.500 ptas.** = don't get it repaired - it is only worth 2,500 pesetas; **no vale lo que cuesta** = it is not worth the expense

validación *nf* validation

validar *vt* to validate

◊ **validez** *nf* validity; **dar validez a** = to validate; **periodo de validez** = period of validity

◊ **válido, -da** *adj* valid; **ser válido** = to be valid; **no es un argumento válido** *o* **una excusa válida** = that is not a valid argument *o* excuse; **el contrato no es válido si no ha sido firmado por un testigo** = the contract is not valid if it has not been witnessed

valioso, -sa *adj* valuable; **nos reveló una información valiosa** = he disclosed a valuable piece of information

valla *nf* fence; **valla publicitaria** = advertisement hoarding *o* billboard; **las vallas publicitarias cubren la mayor parte de los edificios del centro de la ciudad** = advertising signs cover most of the buildings in the centre of the town

valor *nm* **(a)** *(precio)* value *o* worth; **valor bursátil de un compañía** = stock market valuation; **valor de activo** = asset value (of a company); **valor actual** = present value; **en 1974 la peseta valía cinco veces más que su valor actual** = in 1974 the peseta was worth five times its present value; **valor añadido** = added value *o* value added; **impuesto sobre el valor añadido (IVA)** = Value Added Tax (VAT); **valor contable** = book value; **valor declarado** = declared value; **valor depreciado** = written down value; **valor descontado** = discounted value; **valor de escasez** = scarcity value; **valor justo de mercado** = fair market value; **valor de mercado** = market value; **valor nominal** = face value *o* nominal value; **valor a la par** = par value; **valor de reposición** = replacement value; **valor de rescate** = redemption value *o* surrender value; **valor residual** = scrap value *o* salvage value **(b) aumentar de valor** *o* **perder valor** = to rise in value *o* to fall in value; **el tasador fijó el valor de las existencias en 25 millones** = the valuer put the value of the stock at 25 million; **tener valor** = to be of value; **el cheque no tiene valor si no está firmado** = the cheque is worthless if it is not signed **(c) por valor de** = to the value of; **importó mercancías por valor de 250.000 ptas.** = he imported goods to the value of 250,000 pesetas; **sin valor** = worthless *o* of no value; **el contrato fue declarado nulo y sin valor** = the contract was declared null and void; **'muestra gratuita - sin valor comercial'** = 'sample only - of no commercial value' **(d) billetes de pequeño valor** = small denomination notes; **déme gasolina por valor de 2.000 ptas.** = give me 2,000 pesetas' worth of petrol; **objetos de valor** = valuable property *o* valuables **(e)** *(valentía)* courage; **se armó de valor y se enfrentó al director** = he gathered up courage and confronted the manager

> hay que tener en cuenta que los derivados son instrumentos altamente apalancados, en los que con una pequeña cantidad se mueve un valor nominal decenas de veces superior
>

◊ **ad valorem** *frase* ad valorem; **derechos ad valorem** = ad valorem duty; **impuesto ad valorem** = ad valorem tax; **tarifa ad valorem** = ad valorem tariff *o* duty

◊ **valores** *nmpl* **(a)** *(títulos)* securities; **valores en cartera** = holdings; **valores convertibles en acciones en una fecha futura** = convertible loan stock; **valores cotizables** *o* **bursátiles** *o* **registrados** = listed securities; **valores de interés fijo** = fixed-interest securities; **valores de la máxima confianza** = blue-chip investments; **valores mobiliarios** = stocks and shares; **valores del Tesoro** = treasury stocks; **una cartera de valores** = a portfolio of shares; **cartera de valores vinculada a un índice** = indexed portfolio; **comerciante de valores** = securities trader; **Comisión de Valores y Cambios** = *GB* Securities and Investments Board (SIB); *US* Securities and Exchange Commission (SEC); **Servicio de Compensación y Liquidación de Valores (SCLV)** = share clearing and settlement service; **el mercado** *o* **la bolsa de valores** = the stock market *o* the securities market; **las altas y bajas del mercado de valores** = the highs and lows on the stock market; **lista de suscriptores de valores** = subscription list; **las listas de suscriptores de valores cierran el 24 de septiembre a las 10.00** = the subscription lists close at 10.00 on September 24th; **la empresa tiene valores de sociedades manufactureras alemanas** = the company has holdings in German manufacturing companies **(b) monedas de todos los valores** = coins of all denominations

> el valor del rublo en el mercado negro es 15 veces inferior a su valor oficial
>

> calificaba la opa de hostil, y cifraba en 20.000 pesetas el valor real de sus acciones según una valoración de 1988
>

> para ilustrar lo que podría ser el valor real de una moneda puede ser útil describir los ingresos y gastos de una familia normal
>

> muchos valores se encuentran ya por debajo de los mínimos alcanzados en la crisis del Golfo Pérsico
>

valoración *nf* valuation *o* appraisal *o* assessment *o* estimate *o* rating *o* appreciation *o* evaluation; **solicitar la valoración de una propiedad antes de hacer una oferta** = to ask for a valuation of a property before making an offer for it; **valoración según la cotización en bolsa** = stock market valuation; **valoración de daños** = assessment of damages *o* damage survey; **valoración de existencias** = stock valuation; **valoración de méritos** = merit rating; **valoración del personal** = staff appraisals; **valoración de propiedad** = assessment of property; **valoración de un puesto de trabajo** = job evaluation; **valoración de resultados** = performance rating

valorar *vt* to value *o* to assess *o* to estimate; **casas valoradas en más de 1.000.000 de ptas.** = houses valued at 1m pesetas plus; **valorar una propiedad a efectos del seguro** = to assess a property for the purposes of insurance; **valorar los costes en 1 millón** = to estimate that it will cost 1m *o* to estimate costs at 1m

variabilidad *nf* variability

◊ **variable 1** *adj* variable *o* changeable *o* floating; **costes variables** = variable costs; **débito variable** = floating charge **2** *nf* variable; **variables demográficas** = demographic variables

variación *nf* variance *o* variation; **variación presupuestaria** = budget variance; **variaciones de temporada** *o* **estacionales** = seasonal variations; **variaciones estacionales del consumo** = seasonal variations in consumption

variado, -da 1 *adj* varied *o* miscellaneous; **una caja de piezas variadas** = a box of miscellaneous pieces of equipment **2** *pp de* VARIAR

variar *vi* to vary *o* to range; **el margen bruto varía de trimestre en trimestre** = the gross margin varies from quarter to quarter; **intentamos evitar que varíe el flujo de producción de la fábrica** = we try to prevent variations in the flow of production in the factory

variedad *nf* variety; **la tienda tiene una variedad de mercancías** = the shop stocks a variety of goods; **hoy hemos tenido una gran variedad de visitantes en la oficina** = we had a variety of visitors at the office today

varios, -rias *adj* **(a)** *(variado)* varied *o* miscellaneous *o* sundry; **artículos varios** = miscellaneous items; **gastos varios** = miscellaneous expenditure *o* incidental expenses **(b)** *(algunos)* several *o* a number of; **varios directores se retiran este año** = several managers are retiring this year; **encargamos trabajo a varios especialistas independientes** = we send work out to several freelance specialists; **la tienda tiene varios modelos de automóviles expuestos** = the shop has several models of cars on display

vehículo *nm* **(a)** *(auto)* vehicle; **vehículo de carga pesada** = heavy goods vehicle; **vehículo comercial** *o* **vehículo de mercancías** = commercial vehicle *o* goods vehicle; **los vehículos de mercancías pueden**

aparcar en la nave de carga = goods vehicles can park in the loading bay **(b)** *(uso figurativo)* vehicle *o* means; **como vehículo de comunicación** = as a means of communication

> la inversión debería ser la variable estratégica a preservar, porque es el vehículo de incorporación del progreso técnico y de la creación de empleo
>
> **España Económica**

vejez *nf* old age; **pensión de vejez** *o* **subsidio de vejez** = old age pension

velocidad *nf* speed; **velocidad de dictado** = dictation speed; **velocidad de mecanografiado** = typing speed; **velocidad del ordenador** = computing speed; **a toda velocidad** = as fast as possible *o* at full speed *o* flat out

vencer 1 *vt* to overcome *o* to beat; **vencer en una elección** *o* **votación** = to beat (someone) in an election *o* to outvote (someone) **2** *vi* *(término de plazo)* to expire *o* to fall due *o* to become due *o* to mature; **el plazo para recibir ofertas vence el 1 de mayo** = the closing date for tenders to be received is May 1st; **pagos que vencen** = payments which fall due; **el pago de los intereses venció hace tres semanas** = interest payments are three weeks overdue; **letras que vencen en tres semanas** = bills which mature in three weeks' time

◊ **vencido, -da** *adj y pp* **(a)** *(derrotado)* beaten *o* defeated; **darse por vencido** = to give up **(b)** *(a pagar)* due *o* overdue; **pago vencido** = outstanding payment *o* overdue payment

◊ **vencimiento** *nm* expiration *o* expiry; **el vencimiento de una póliza de seguros** = expiry of an insurance policy; **fecha de vencimiento** = *(caducidad)* expiry date; *(pago)* maturity date *o* final date for payment; **vencimiento medio** *o* **fecha media de vencimiento** = average due date; **obligación que ha llegado a su vencimiento** = bond due for repayment

vendedor *nm* **(a)** *(persona que vende)* seller; **había pocos vendedores en el mercado y por eso los precios se mantuvieron altos** = there were few sellers in the market, so prices remained high; **mercado de vendedores** *o* **favorable a los vendedores** = = seller's market **(b)** *(al público)* salesman; *(en una tienda)* salesman *o* shop assistant; *US* salesclerk; **los vendedores tendrán que trabajar mucho si quieren vender todas esas mercancías para fin de mes** = the salesmen will have to work hard if they want to move all that stock by the end of the month; **vendedor ambulante** = street vendor; **vendedor a domicilio** = door-to-door salesman *o* canvasser; **vendedor insistente** *o* **apremiante** = high-pressure salesman; **vendedor de puerta en puerta** = door-to-door salesman; **vendedor de seguros** = insurance salesman; **tiene buenos antecedentes como vendedor** = he has a good track record as a salesman; **vendedor al por mayor** = wholesaler; **vendedor al por menor** = retailer; **vendedor de coches usados** = a used car *o* a secondhand car salesman; **vendedor de periódicos y revistas** = newsagent **(c)** *(venta de propiedad)* vendor; **el abogado que actúa en nombre del vendedor** = the solicitor acting on behalf of the vendor

◊ **vendedora** *nf* shop assistant *o* salesgirl *o* saleslady *o* saleswoman; **pregúntale a la**

vendedora si la factura incluye el IVA = ask the salesgirl if the bill includes VAT

vender *vt* **(a)** *(comerciar)* to sell *o* to dispose of *o* to handle; **vender algo a crédito** = to sell something on credit; **vender al descubierto** = to sell short; **vender más barato** = to undersell; **vender más barato que un competidor** = to sell cheaper than a competitor *o* to undersell a competitor; **vender al mejor precio posible** = to sell at best; **la empresa vende mucho más que sus competidores** = the company is easily outselling its competitors; **vender más de lo que se puede producir** *o* **vender en exceso** = to oversell; **vender algo con entrega aplazada** *o* **a futuros** = to sell forward; **vender divisas a futuros** = to sell currency forward; **vender al por mayor** = to wholesale (goods); **vender al por menor** = to retail (goods); **compra al por mayor y vende al por menor** = he buys wholesale and sells retail; **vender de puerta en puerta** = to sell from door to door; **vender por las casas** *o* **en la calle** = to peddle; **vender en subasta** = to sell by auction *o* to auction; **venderlo todo** = to sell up; **difícil de vender** = hard *o* difficult to sell; **fácil de vender** = easy to sell; **sin vender** = unsold; **volver a vender** = to resell **(b)** **vender coches** *o* **vender frigoríficos** = to sell cars *o* to sell refrigerators; **han decidido vender su casa** = they have decided to sell their house; **no conseguimos vender el arrendamiento** = we had no success in trying to sell the lease; **vender un paquete de acciones** = to sell a block of shares; **algunos diccionarios no son fáciles de vender** = some dictionaries are not fast-moving stock; **estamos intentando vender seis máquinas de escribir nuevas** = we are trying to sell off six unused typewriters; **vendimos 20.000 artículos en una semana** = we sold 20,000 items in one week; **no venderán mercancías producidas por otras empresas** = they will not handle goods produced by other firms

◊ **venderse** *vr* **(a)** to sell *o* to be sold; *(anuncio)* 'se vende' = 'for sale'; **estos productos se venden bien en el periodo antes de Navidad** = these items sell well in the pre-Christmas period; **este libro siempre se vende bien** = this book is a steady seller; **a devolver si no se vende** = sale or return; **venderse en pública subasta** = to be sold at auction; **este producto se vende en todos los países europeos** = this product is being marketed in all European countries; **las mercancías están empezando a venderse** = the stock is starting to sell *o* to move **(b)** *(por un precio)* to sell for *o* to fetch; **venderse a un precio alto** = to fetch a high price; **estos paquetes se venden a 2.500 ptas. la docena** = those packs sell for 2,500 pesetas a dozen; **estos ordenadores se venden a unos precios muy altos en el mercado negro** = these computers fetch very high prices on the black market; **no se venderá por más de 2.000 ptas.** = it will not fetch more than 2,000 pesetas; **las acciones de la compañía se venden raramente en la bolsa** = the company's shares are rarely sold on the Stock Exchange

◊ **vendible** *adj* sellable *o* saleable *o* marketable

Venezuela *nf* Venezuela

◊ **venezolano, -na** *adj y n* Venezuelan
NOTA: capital: **Caracas**; moneda: **bolívar venezolano (VBO)** = Venezuelan bolivar (VBO)

venta *nf* **(a)** *(acción de vender)* sale *o* selling *o* disposal; **venta agresiva** = hard selling; **venta CIF (coste, seguro y flete)** = cost, insurance and freight sale (CIF); **venta condicionada** = conditional sale; **venta al contado** o cash sale; **venta por correo** = mail-order selling o direct mail; **venta al descubierto** = short selling o selling short; **venta al detalle** o **al detall** = retail sale o retail selling; **venta directa** = direct selling; **venta domiciliaria** = door-to-door selling; **venta forzosa** = forced sale o distress sale; **venta al por mayor** = wholesale sale o wholesale selling; **venta al por menor** = retail sale o retailing; **venta piramidal** = pyramid selling; **venta a plazos** = hire-purchase sale; **contrato de venta a plazos** = hire purchase agreement; **venta de saldos** = end-of-season sale; **venta segura** o **en firme** = firm sale; **venta con tarjeta de crédito** = credit card sale; **venta por teléfono** = telephone selling; **venta de títulos** o **de propiedad** = disposal of securities o sale of property **(b) argumento de venta** = unique selling position; **artículo de gran venta** = best-seller; **artículos de venta fácil** o **rápida** = easy to sell o fast-selling items; **condiciones de venta** = conditions of sale o terms of sale; **condiciones de venta: pago al hacer el pedido** = terms: cash with order; **costes de venta** = selling costs; **cupo de ventas** = sales quota; **documento de venta** = bill of sale; **facilidad de venta** = saleability o marketability; **impuesto sobre la venta** = sales tax o excise duty; **precio de venta** = selling price; **punto de venta electrónico** = electronic point of sale (EPOS); **registrar una venta** = to register a sale **(c) en venta** = for sale; **su tienda está en venta** = his shop is for sale; **en venta en todas las sucursales** = available in all branches; **poner algo en venta** = to offer something for sale o to put something up for sale o to put something on the market; **pusieron la fábrica** o **su casa en venta** = they put the factory o their house up for sale; **arrendamiento** o **negocio en venta** = lease o business for sale o for disposal; **ponerse en venta** = to come on the market; **me he enterado de que la empresa está en venta** = I hear the company has been put on the market; **este jabón acaba de ponerse en venta** = this soap has just come on to the market **(d) a la venta** = on sale; **estos artículos están a la venta en la mayoría de las farmacias** = these items are on sale in most chemists; **estos artículos no están a la venta al público en general** = these items are not for sale to the general public

◊ **ventas** *nfpl* **(a)** *(conjunto de cosas vendidas)* sales; **las ventas han subido durante el primer trimestre** = sales have risen over the first quarter; **las ventas reales difieren de las ventas declaradas por los representantes** = the actual sales are at variance with the sales reported by the reps; **ventas por teléfono** = sales made by telephone o telesales; **ventas en el extranjero** = overseas sales o export sales; **ventas nacionales** = domestic sales o home sales; **ventas a plazo** = forward sales; **ventas registradas** = book sales **(b) análisis de ventas** = sales analysis; **campaña de ventas** = sales campaign; **cifras de ventas** = sales figures; **coste de ventas** = cost of sales; **director de ventas** = sales manager; **ejecutivo responsable de las ventas** = sales executive; **informe mensual de ventas** = monthly sales report; **en los informes de ventas, todos los países europeos se incluyen en una categoría única** = in the sales reports all the European countries are bracketed together; **ingresos de ventas** = sales revenue; **libro de ventas** = sales book; **libro mayor de ventas** = sales ledger; **encargado del libro de ventas** = sales ledger clerk;

personal de ventas = sales force o sales staff o sales people o people from the sales department; **la empresa ha reducido su personal de ventas** = the company has cut back its sales force; **presupuesto de ventas** = sales budget; **previsión de ventas** = sales forecast; **promoción de ventas** = sales drive; **registro diario de ventas** = sales day book; **reunión de ventas** = sales conference o sales meeting; **sección** o **servicio de ventas** = sales department; **volumen de ventas** = turnover o sales volume o volume of sales

ventaja *nf* advantage o edge (over someone); **llevar ventaja a un competidor** = to have the edge on a rival company; **el conocimiento de dos idiomas extranjeros es una ventaja** = knowledge of two foreign languages is an advantage

◊ **ventajoso, -sa** *adj* advantageous; **la tienda se alquila a un precio muy ventajoso** = the shop is let on very favourable terms; **las vacaciones en Italia resultan muy ventajosas por el tipo de cambio** = holidays in Italy are good value because of the exchange rate

ventana *nf* window

◊ **ventanilla** *nf* small window; *(para atender al público)* window o ticket counter; **ventanilla de pagos** = teller's window (in a bank); **sobre de ventanilla** = window envelope

ver *vt* to see; **llegó con diez minutos de retraso y no pudo ver al presidente** = he missed the chairman by ten minutes; **sin ser visto** = unseen

◊ **verse** *vr* **(a)** *(dos personas)* to see each other **(b)** *(encontrarse)* **verse en apuros financieros** = to be in financial difficulties; **el banco se ha visto obligado a bajar considerablemente los tipos de interés** = the bank has been forced to slash interest rates

verbal *adj* verbal; **acuerdo verbal** = verbal agreement; **llegaron a un acuerdo verbal sobre las condiciones y después empezaron a redactar el contrato** = they agreed to the terms verbally, and then started to draft the contract

◊ **verbalmente** *adv* verbally

verdad *nf* truth; **la verdad es que** = the fact of the matter is; **de verdad** = really; **en verdad** = indeed

◊ **verdadero, -ra** *adj* true o genuine o real; **al precio de 30.000 ptas. ese coche es una verdadera ganga** = that car is a real bargain at 30,000 pesetas

verde *adj* green; **billete verde** = 1,000 peseta note; **ecu verde** = green ECU; **luz verde** = green light; **moneda** o **divisa verde** = green currency; **libra**

verde = green pound; **marco verde** = green Deutschmark; **peseta verde** = green peseta

verificación *nf* verification *o* checking; **verificación de cuentas** = audit; **verificación de errores** = error checking

verificar *vt* **(a)** *(comprobar)* to verify *o* to check; **verificar y firmar la aceptación de mercancías** = to check and sign for goods; **se autorizó la entrada del cargamento en el país después de que la aduana verificara los documentos** = the shipment was allowed into the country after verification of the documents by customs **(b)** *(revisar cuentas)* to audit; **cuentas sin verificar** = unaudited accounts

◊ **verificarse** *vr* to happen *o* to take place; **la ceremonia de apertura se verificará mañana** = the opening ceremony will be held tomorrow

versión *nf* version; **versión abreviada** = abridged version *o* short version; **el departamento de finanzas ha aprobado la versión final de las cuentas** = the finance department has passed the final draft of the accounts

verter *vt* to dump

vertical *adj* vertical; **comunicación vertical** = vertical communication; **integración vertical** = vertical integration

vertido *nm* waste *o* spillage

vertiginoso, -sa *adj* steep; **una caída vertiginosa en las ventas en el extranjero** = a steep decline in overseas sales

◊ **vertiginosamente** *adv* steeply; **los costes de almacenaje están aumentando vertiginosamente** = warehousing costs are rising rapidly

vetar *vt* to veto; **vetar una decisión** = to veto a decision

◊ **veto** *nm* veto; **derecho de veto** = right of veto; **poner el veto a** = to veto

vez *nf* **(a)** time; **cuatro veces** = four times *o* four-fold; **el dividendo está cubierto cuatro veces** = the dividend is covered four times; **la demanda de acciones fue seis veces superior al número de acciones emitidas** = the share offer was oversubscribed six times **(b) a veces** = at times; **a la vez** = at the same time; **cada vez más** = more and more; **cada vez menos** = less and less; **de vez en cuando** = from time to time; **otra vez** = once more (NOTA: plural es **veces**)

vía 1 *nf* road *o* route; **vías** = means *o* channel; **país en vías de desarrollo** = developing country **2** *prep* via *o* by way of; **enviaremos nuestro cheque vía nuestra oficina de Nueva York** = we are sending the cheque via our office in New York; **actuar por la vía oficial** = to go through the official channels; **recurrir a la vía judicial** = to take legal action

> los países en vías de desarrollo tendrán que enfrentarse a una competencia creciente
>
> **Actualidad Económica**

viabilidad *nf* viability *o* feasibility; **informar sobre la viabilidad de un proyecto** = to report on the feasibility of a project; **llevar a cabo un estudio de viabilidad de un proyecto** = to carry out a

feasibility study on a project; **sin viabilidad comercial** = not commercially viable

viable *adj* viable; **su proyecto no es viable** = his project is not viable

viajar *vi* to travel; **viajar en primera clase** = to travel first-class; **viajar en primera clase proporciona el mejor servicio** = first-class travel provides the best service; **es más barato viajar en tren que en avión** = rail travel is cheaper than air travel; **su empleo le exige viajar mucho** = his work involves a lot of travelling; **viaja a los Estados Unidos dos veces al año por negocios** = he travels to the States on business twice a year; **viaja todos los días desde el campo hasta su oficina situada en el centro de la ciudad** = he commutes from the country to his office in the centre of town; **en su nuevo trabajo tiene que viajar al extranjero por lo menos diez veces al año** = in her new job, she has to travel abroad at least ten times a year

viaje *nm* **(a)** journey *o* trip *o* tour; **viaje de ida y vuelta** = return *o* round trip; **el barco realiza el viaje de ida** = the ship is outward bound; **viaje por mar** *o* **en barco** = voyage; **viaje de negocios** = business trip; **el presidente está en Holanda en viaje de negocios** = the chairman is in Holland on business; **viaje de regreso** = homeward journey; **viaje de turismo organizado** = package holiday *o* package tour; **planificación de viaje** = journey planning; **organizó el viaje para visitar a todos sus clientes en dos días** = he planned his journey to visit all his accounts in two days; **¿cuánto cuesta un viaje en primera clase a Nueva York?** = what is the cost of a first class ticket to New York?; **vender viajes con todos los gastos incluidos** = to sell package holidays *o* to package holidays; **los viajes de trabajo son una parte importante de nuestros gastos generales** = business travel is a very important part of our overhead expenditure **(b) agencia de viajes** = travel agency; **agencia de viajes organizados** *o* **agente de viajes mayorista** *o* **organizador de viajes** = tour operator; **agente de viajes** = travel agent; **cheques de viaje** = traveller's cheques; *US* traveler's checks; **la industria de los viajes** = the travel industry *o* trade; **revista de viajes** = travel magazine; **tarjeta de viaje** = travelcard **(c) de viaje** = on the road *o* travelling; **los vendedores viajan treinta semanas al año** = the salesmen are on the road thirty weeks a year; **está de viaje de negocios en Londres** = he is on a business visit to London; **el grupo fue de viaje por Italia** = the group went on a tour of Italy

◊ **viajero, -ra** *n* traveller *o* passenger; **viajero diario** = commuter; **viajero de negocios** = business traveller

> las agencias de viajes, que han percibido el reto, proponen, sobre todo en invierno, una solución muy atractiva y particular para sus clientes: los viajes a la carta destinados a satisfacer los hobbies del viajero
>
> **Tiempo**

vial *adj* road; **tráfico vial** = road traffic

vice- *prefijo* vice-

◊ **vicepresidente** *nmf* vice-chairman *o* vice-president; **el vicepresidente principal** *o* **más antiguo** = senior vice-president; **es el vicepresidente de un grupo industrial** = he is the vice-chairman of an industrial group

vida *nf* **(a)** *(vigencia)* life; **hacer la vida imposible** *o* **amargar la vida a alguien** = to make life difficult *o* to make things hot for someone; **los aduaneros les están haciendo la vida imposible a los narcotraficantes** = customs officials are making things hot for the drug smugglers; **de por vida** *o* **para toda la vida** = for life; **su pensión le proporciona un cómodo ingreso de por vida** = his pension gives him a comfortable income for life; **carestía** *o* **coste de la vida** = cost of living; **ajustado al coste de la vida** = index-linked; **plus** *o* **subsidio de carestía de vida** = cost-of-living bonus *o* cost-of-living allowance; **incluir un plus de carestía de vida en los salarios** = to allow for the cost of living in the salaries; **aumento de salario para compensar por el aumento del coste de vida** = cost-of-living increase; **esperanza de vida** = life expectancy; **nivel de vida** = standard of living *o* living standards; **seguro de vida** = life assurance *o* life insurance; **hacer un seguro de vida a alguien** = to insure someone's life **(b) vida útil de un producto** = shelf life of a product

vídeo *nm* video; **cámara de vídeo** = video camera; **cinta de vídeo** = video tape; **grabadora de vídeo** = video recorder; **grabar en vídeo** *o* **hacer un vídeo** = to video

◊ **videocámara** *nf* video camera

◊ **videocasete** *nm* video cassette

◊ **videófono** *nm* videophone

◊ **videograbadora** *nf* video recorder

viejo, -ja *adj* old; **hemos decidido deshacernos del viejo sistema de ordenadores e instalar uno nuevo** = we have decided to get rid of our old computer system and install a new one

Vietnam *nm* Vietnam

◊ **vietnamita** *adj y nmf* Vietnamese
NOTA: capital: **Hanoi**; moneda: **dong vietnamita (D)** = Vietnamese dong (D)

vigencia *nf* **(a)** *(vida)* life (of a contract); **entrar en vigencia** = to take effect; **estar en vigencia** = to be in force; **tener vigencia** = to be valid; **el arrendamiento tiene solamente seis meses más de vigencia** = the lease has only six months to run **(b)** *(periodo)* term

◊ **vigente** *adj* ruling *o* in force *o* prevailing *o* going; **la ley vigente** = the law which is in force; **precio vigente** = ruling price; **seguir vigente** = to remain in effect; **el tipo de cambio vigente** = the going rate

vigilancia *nf* **(a)** vigilance; **piquete de vigilancia** = picket line; **cruzar un piquete de vigilancia a la entrada de una fábrica** = to cross a picket line **(b) personal de vigilancia** = (i) supervisory staff; (ii) security personnel

◊ **vigilante** *nmf* caretaker

vigor *nm* **(a)** *(fuerza)* strength *o* energy; **el vigor de la peseta aumenta la posibilidad de mantener los tipos de interés bajos** = the strength of the peseta increases the possibility of keeping interest rates low

(b) en vigor = in operation; **estar en vigor** = to be in force; **entrar en vigor** = to come into force *o* to operate *o* to become operative; **fecha de entrada en vigor** = effective date; **cláusula que entrará en vigor a partir del 1 de enero** = clause effective as from January 1st; **el nuevo sistema entró en vigor el 1 de junio** = the new system has been operative since June 1st; **el nuevo reglamento entrará en vigor el 1 de enero** = the new regulations will come into force on January 1st; **las nuevas condiciones de servicio entrarán en vigor a partir del 1 de enero** = the new terms of service will operate from January 1st; **las normas han estado en vigor desde 1946** = the rules have been in force since 1946; **mantenerse en vigor** = to remain in effect

vigoroso, -sa *adj* vigorous *o* energetic *o* strong

vinculación *nf* linking *o* tie-up; **vinculación de los aumentos de sueldo al índice del coste de la vida** = indexation of wage increases

◊ **vinculante** *adj* binding; **un contrato vinculante** = a binding contract

vincular *vt* to link *o* to connect; **vincular a un índice** = to index; **cartera de valores vinculada a un índice** = indexed portfolio; **su éxito profesional está muy vinculado al de la empresa** = her professional success is very much linked to that of her company

◊ **vínculo** *nm* **(a)** *(enlace)* connection *o* link **(b)** *(jurídico)* entail

violación *nf* breach *o* infringement; **violación de contrato** = breach of contract; **violación de los derechos de autor** = infringement of copyright *o* copyright infringement; **violación de garantía** = breach of warranty; **violación de patente** = infringement of patent *o* patent infringement

violar *vt* to infringe

VIP *del inglés* VERY IMPORTANT PERSON *(aeropuerto)* **sala VIP** = VIP lounge

Iberia y sus compañías participadas van a unir sus actividades combinando tanto la facturación y emisión de billetes como la utilización de la sala VIP para pasajeros de clase preferente y gran clase

Tiempo

virador *nm* tonner; **se ha acabado el virador de la impresora** = the printer has run out of toner; **cartucho de virador** = toner cartridge

visado *nm* visa; **visado de entrada** = entry visa; **visado de entrada múltiple** = multiple entry visa; **visado turista** = tourist visa; **visado de tránsito** = transit visa; **necesitarás un visado para ir a los EE UU** = you will need a visa before you go to the USA; **rellenó el formulario de solicitud de visado** = he filled in his visa application form

visible *adj* visible; **importaciones** *o* **exportaciones visibles** = visible imports *o* exports

visita *nf* visit *o* call; **visita de negocios** = business call; **los vendedores realizan seis visitas al día** = the salesmen make six calls a day; **estamos esperando una visita de nuestros representantes alemanes** = we are expecting a visit from our German agents; **tuvimos una visita del inspector del IVA** = we had a visit from the VAT inspector;

hacer una visita de inspección = to carry out an inspection *o* a tour of inspection

◊ **visitante** *nmf* visitor *o* caller; **despacho de visitantes** = visitors' bureau; **el presidente enseñó la fábrica a los visitantes japoneses** = the chairman showed the Japanese visitors round the factory

visitar *vt* to visit someone *o* to call on someone; **pasó una semana en Andalucía, visitando a clientes de Sevilla y Granada** = he spent a week in Andalucia, visiting clients in Seville and Granada; **la delegación comercial visitó el Ministerio de Comercio** = the trade delegation visited the Ministry of Trade; **el representante hizo dos visitas durante la semana pasada** = the sales representative called in twice last week

vista *nf* **(a)** *(visión)* sight; **depósito a la vista** = demand deposit; **dinero a la vista** = money at call *o* money on call *o* call money; **letra** *o* **giro a la vista** = demand bill *o* sight bill *o* sight draft; **pagadero a la vista** = payable on demand; **letra pagadera a la vista** = bill payable at sight **(b) en vista de** *o* **a la vista de** = in view of; **en vista de la caída del tipo de cambio, hemos vuelto a hacer nuestro proyecto de previsiones de ventas** = in view of the falling exchange rate, we have redrafted our sales forecasts

visto bueno *nm* approval; **dar el visto bueno a** = to approve *o* to rubber-stamp

visual *adj* visual; **unidad de despliegue visual (UDV)** *o* **unidad de presentación visual (UPV)** = visual display unit (VDU)

vitalicio, -cia *adj* life *o* for life; **anualidad** *o* **renta** *o* **pensión vitalicia** = life annuity *o* annuity for life *o* life interest

vitrina *nf* showcase *o* display cabinet; **mesa vitrina** = display case; **escaparate vitrina de exposición** = display unit

vivienda *nf* home; **local con vivienda incorporada** = business premises with living accommodation; **local sin vivienda incorporada** = lock-up premises; **viviendas de protección oficial** = council housing; **escasez de viviendas** = housing shortage; **estilo de vivienda** = house style; **póliza de seguro de la vivienda** = household insurance policy; **propietario de su vivienda** = homeowner; **seguro de vivienda** = house insurance; **usufructuario de una vivienda** = beneficial occupier; **venta de viviendas nuevas** = new home sales

ha disminuido notablemente el parque de viviendas de alquiler, de 2.000.000 en 1981 a 1.365.000 viviendas en la actualidad
    España Económica

vivir 1 *vi* to live *o* to be alive **2** *vt* to experience; **la empresa vivió un periodo de baja en las ventas** = the company experienced a period of falling sales

vocación *nf* vocation; **siguió su vocación y se hizo contable** = he followed his vocation and became an accountant

vocal *nmf* *(de una asociación o junta)* ordinary member *o* rank-and-file member; **vocal de una comisión** = committee member

volumen *nm* volume *o* bulk; **volumen comercial** *o* **volumen de contratación** *o* **volumen de negocios** = volume of trade *o* volume of business; **volumen de facturación** = turnover *o* sales volume; **la empresa ha mantenido el mismo volumen de negocios a pesar de la recesión** = the company has maintained the same volume of business in spite of the recession; **volumen de producción** = volume of output; **volumen de ventas** = volume of sales *o* sales volume *o* turnover; **el volumen de ventas de la empresa ha aumentado en un 235%** = the company's turnover has increased by 235%; **el aumento del volumen de ventas fue superior al 25%** = the increase in turnover was over 25%; **volumen de ventas alto** *o* **bajo** = low *o* high volume of sales; **tener un volumen de ventas de** = to turn over; **basamos nuestros cálculos en el volumen de ventas previsto** = we based our calculations on the forecast turnover; **descuento por volumen** = bulk discount

en un año considerado malo para el sector, nuestro volumen de facturación ha seguido creciendo
    Tiempo

voluminoso, -sa *adj* bulky; **la oficina de correos no acepta paquetes voluminosos** = the Post Office does not accept bulky packages

voluntad *nf* will; **buena voluntad** = goodwill; **última voluntad y testamento** = last will and testament

voluntario, -ria *adj* **(a)** *(de la propia voluntad)* voluntary; **baja voluntaria con derecho a indemnización** = voluntary redundancy; **liquidación voluntaria** = voluntary liquidation **(b)** *(sin fines lucrativos)* voluntary; **organización voluntaria** = voluntary organization

◊ **voluntariamente** *adv* voluntarily

volver 1 *vi* **(a)** *(regresar)* to return *o* to go back; **tras una pausa volvimos al tema** = we returned to the subject after a break; **volver a lo esencial** = to get back to basics **(b) volver a hacer algo** = to do something again; **volver a abrir** = to reopen; **volver a anunciar** = to readvertise; **volver a anunciar una vacante** = to readvertise a post; **ninguno de los aspirantes superó la prueba, por lo que tendremos que volver a anunciar el puesto** = all the candidates failed the test, so we will just have to readvertise; **volver a comprar** = to buy back *o* to repurchase; **volver a decir** = to repeat; **cuando le preguntaron qué pensaba hacer la compañía, el presidente volvió a decir 'nada'** = when asked what the company planned to do, the chairman repeated 'Nothing'; **volver a emplear a obreros despedidos** = to take back dismissed workers; **volver a llamar** *o* **volver a telefonear** = to call back *o* to phone back *o* to ring back; **volver a nombrar** = to reappoint; **volver a presentarse** *o* **solicitar** = to reapply; **volver a programar** = to reschedule; **perdió el avión y todas las reuniones tuvieron que volver a ser programadas** = he missed his plane, and all the meetings had to be rescheduled; **volver a redactar** = to redraft; **hubo que volver a redactar todo el contrato para incluir las objeciones del presidente** = the whole contract had to be redrafted to take in the objections from the chairman; **volver a vender** = to resell **2** *vt* to turn; **volver una página** = to turn over a page

◇ **volverse** *vr* **(a)** *(persona)* to turn round **(b)** *(hacerse)* to become

votación *nf* vote *o* voting *o* ballot; **someter una propuesta a votación** = to take a vote on a proposal *o* to put a proposal to the vote; **el presidente salió derrotado en la votación** = the chairman was outvoted; **el sindicato está realizando una votación para elegir presidente** = the union is balloting for the post of president; **votación por correo** = postal ballot; **votación a mano alzada** = show of hands; **votación secreta** = secret ballot

◇ **votante** *nmf* voter; **votante inscrito al censo** = registered voter; **votante por poder** = proxy voter

votar *vt/i* to vote (for); **la reunión votó a favor del cierre de la fábrica** = the meeting voted to close the factory; **el 52% de los socios votaron al Sr. Tenas como presidente** = 52% of the members voted for Sr Tenas as chairman; **votar a favor de** *o* **en contra de una propuesta** = to vote for a proposal *o* to vote against a proposal; **en la junta general anual se votó a favor del cese de dos directores** = two directors were voted off the board at the AGM

voto *nm* vote; **voto de calidad** = casting vote; **el presidente tiene derecho al voto de calidad** = the chairman has the casting vote; **utilizó su voto de calidad para bloquear la moción** *o* **para detener la propuesta** = he used his casting vote to block the motion; **voto por correo** = postal vote; **voto mayoritario** = majority vote; **voto por poderes** = proxy vote; **voto por representación** *o* **delegación**

= block vote; **derecho a voto** = right to vote *o* voting right; **acciones sin derecho a voto** = non-voting shares; **papeleta de voto** = ballot paper *o* voting paper; **privar del derecho de voto** = to remove the right to vote *o* to disenfranchise; **la compañía ha intentado privar a los accionistas ordinarios del derecho de voto** = the company has tried to disenfranchise the ordinary shareholders

vuelo *nm* flight; **vuelo chárter** = charter flight; **vuelo de correspondencia** = connecting flight; **vuelo de corto recorrido** = short-haul flight; **vuelo directo** = non-stop flight; **vuelo de larga distancia** = long-haul flight *o* long-distance flight; **vuelo regular** = scheduled flight; **partió para Helsinki en un vuelo regular** = he left for Helsinki on a scheduled flight; **el vuelo IB 267 efectuará su salida de la puerta 46** = flight IB 267 is leaving from Gate 46; **perdió el vuelo** = he missed his flight; **el vuelo de Madrid termina en Nueva York** = the flight from Madrid terminates in New York; **auxiliar de vuelo** = steward

vuelta *nf* **(a)** *(cambio)* change; **quédese con la vuelta** = keep the change **(b)** *(regreso)* return; **respondió a vuelta de correo** = he replied by return of post; **viaje de vuelta** = return journey; **viaje de ida y vuelta** = return *o* round trip; **un billete de ida y vuelta** = a return ticket *o* a return; *US* round-trip ticket; **quiero dos billetes de ida y vuelta a Lérida** = I want two returns to Lerida; **tarifa de ida y vuelta** = return fare *o* round-trip fare **(c)** *(movimiento)* turn; **de vuelta** = back; **de vuelta a casa** = homeward; **flete de vuelta** = homeward freight

Ww Xx Yy Zz

Wall Street *nf (centro financiero de Nueva York)* Wall Street; **un analista de Wall Street** = a Wall Street analyst; **escribe la columna de Wall Street del periódico** = she writes the Wall Street column in the newspaper

marca X *nf* brand X

yacimiento *nm* deposit; **yacimiento petrolífero submarino** = off-shore oil field

yarda *nf (unidad de medida)* yard

Yemen *nm* Yemen

◊ **yemenita** *adj y nmf* Yemeni
NOTA: capital: **San'a;** moneda: **riyal del Yemen (YRIs)** *o* **dinar yemení (YD)** = Yemeni rial (YRIs) *o* Yemeni dinar (YD)

yen *nm (moneda de Japón)* yen; **el yen cayó en los mercados de divisas** = the yen collapsed on the foreign exchange markets

yuppy *del inglés* YUPPY

> siempre habrá yuppies, en el sentido de que siempre habrá quien prefiera el dinero o el poder al tiempo libre
>
> **Tiempo**

yuán *nm (moneda de China)* yuan

Zaire *nm* Zaire

◊ **zairense** *o* **zaireño, -ña** *adj y n* Zairean
NOTA: capital: **Kinshasa;** moneda: **zaire (Z)** = zaïre (Z)

Zambia *nf* Zambia

◊ **zambiano, -na** *adj y n* Zambian
NOTA: capital: **Lusaka;** moneda: **kwacha zambiano (K)** = Zambian kwacha (K)

zarpar *vt* to sail; **el barco zarpa a las 12.00** = the ship sails at 12.00

Zimbabue *o* **Zimbabwe** *nm* Zimbabwe

◊ **zimbabuo, -bua** *o* **zimbabwense** *adj y n* Zimbabwean
NOTA: capital: **Harare;** moneda: **dólar de Zimbabwe (Z$)** = Zimbabwe dollar (Z$)

zona *nf* **(a)** *(área)* area *o* zone; **su fábrica está en una zona de fácil acceso a las autopistas y a los aeropuertos** = their factory is in a very good area for getting to the motorways and airports; **zona comercial peatonal** = shopping precinct; **zona de desarrollo** *o* **industrial** *o* **comercial** = development zone *o* enterprise zone; **zona franca** = free trade zone; **zona industrial** = industrial estate *o* trading estate *o* business park; **zona de libre comercio** = free trade area **(b) zona de venta** = sales area; **zona de un representante** = a rep's territory; **su zona incluye todo el norte del país** = his territory covers all the north of the country; **su zona comercial es el noroeste** = his sales area is the North-West

ENGLISH-SPANISH DICTIONARY
DICCIONARIO INGLÉS-ESPAÑOL

Aa

AAA ['trɪpl 'eɪ] letras que indican que una acción *or* bono *or* banco es de alta fiabilidad; **these bonds have an AAA rating** = estos bonos son muy sólidos

> COMMENT: the AAA rating is given by Standard & Poor's or by Moody's, and indicates a very high level of reliability for a corporate or municipal bond in the US

> QUOTE the rating concern lowered its rating to single-A from double-A, and its senior debt rating to triple-B from single-A
> **Wall Street Journal**

'A' shares ['eɪ 'ʃeəz] *plural noun* acciones *fpl* de clase 'A' con derecho de voto limitado

A1 ['eɪ 'wɒn] *adjective* **(a)** de primera clase *or* excelente; **we sell only goods in A1 condition** = vendemos solamente productos en óptimas condiciones **(b) ship which is A1 at Lloyd's** = barco de primera clase *or* barco que está en condiciones óptimas según el Registro Lloyd's

◊ A1, A2, A3, A4, A5 [eɪ'wɒn *or* eɪ'tu: *or* eɪ'θri: *or* eɪ'fɔ: *or* eɪ'faɪv] *noun* A1, A2, A3, A4, A5 (tamaños de papel); **you must photocopy the spreadsheet on A3 paper** = debe fotocopiar la hoja de cálculos en papel A3; **we must order some more A4 headed notepaper** = tenemos que pedir más papel con membrete, tamaño A4

abandon [əˈbændən] *verb* **(a)** *(to give up)* abandonar *or* renunciar; **we abandoned the idea of setting up a New York office** = abandonamos la idea de abrir una sucursal en Nueva York; **the development programme had to be abandoned when the company ran out of cash** = el programa de desarrollo se tuvo que abandonar cuando los fondos de la compañía se agotaron; **to abandon an action** = desistir de una acción **(b)** *(to leave)* abandonar (algo); **the crew abandoned the sinking ship** = la tripulación abandonó el barco que se hundía

◊ abandonment [əˈbændənmənt] *noun* abandono *m*; **abandonment of a ship** = abandono de un barco

abatement [əˈbeɪtmənt] *noun* disminución *f or* reducción *f*; **tax abatement** = reducción de un tipo impositivo

ability [əˈbɪlɪti] *noun* facultad *f or* habilidad *f*

about [əˈbaʊt] *preposition* sobre; **the chairman's remarks about the auditors were minuted** = las observaciones del presidente sobre los auditores se hicieron constar en acta

above the line [əˈbʌv ðə ˈlaɪn] *adverb* **(a)** *(companies)* sobre la línea *or* por encima de la línea; **exceptional items are noted above the line in company accounts** = las partidas excepcionales se anotan sobre la línea en las cuentas de la compañía **(b)** *(advertising)* gastos de publicidad incluidos

abridge [əˈbrɪdʒ] *verb* abreviar

◊ abridged [əˈbrɪdʒd] *adjective* abreviado, -da; **abridged version** = en versión abreviada

abroad [əˈbrɔːd] *adverb* en el extranjero; **to go abroad** = ir al extranjero; **the consignment of cars was shipped abroad last week** = los automóviles fueron enviados al extranjero la semana pasada; **the chairman is abroad on business** = el presidente está en el extranjero en viaje de negocios; **half of our profit comes from sales abroad** = la mitad de nuestros beneficios proceden de las ventas en el extranjero

absence ['æbsəns] *noun* ausencia *f*; **in the absence of** = en ausencia de *or* por estar ausente; **in the absence of the chairman, his deputy took the chair** = en ausencia del presidente, su adjunto presidió la reunión; **leave of absence** = excedencia *f*; **he asked for leave of absence to visit his mother in hospital** = pidió permiso para visitar a su madre en el hospital

◊ absent ['æbsənt] *adjective* ausente; **ten of the workers are absent with flu** = faltan diez de los obreros porque tienen gripe; **the chairman is absent in Holland on business** = el presidente está de viaje en Holanda por motivos de trabajo

◊ absentee [æbsənˈtiː] *noun* ausente *mf*

◊ absenteeism [æbsənˈtiːɪzəm] *noun* absentismo *m*; **absenteeism is high in the week before Christmas** = el absentismo es elevado durante la semana anterior a las Navidades; **the rate of absenteeism** *or* **the absenteeism rate always increases in fine weather** = el nivel de absentismo siempre aumenta con el buen tiempo

◊ absent-minded ['æbsənt 'maɪndɪd] *adjective* despistado, -da

> QUOTE the reforms still hadn't fundamentally changed conditions on the shop floor: absenteeism was as high as 20% on some days
> **Business Week**

absolute ['æbsəluːt] *adjective* absoluto, -ta *or* total; **absolute monopoly** = monopolio absoluto; **the company has an absolute monopoly of imports of French wine** = la empresa tiene el monopolio absoluto de la importación de vino francés

◊ absolutely [æbsəˈluːtli] *adverb* totalmente; **we are absolutely tied to our suppliers' schedules** = dependemos totalmente de los plazos de entrega de nuestros proveedores

absorb [əbˈzɔːb] *verb* **(a)** absorver; *(include a proportion of overhead costs into a production cost)* **to absorb overheads** = absorver gastos generales; **overheads have absorbed all our profits** = los gastos generales nos han absorbido todos los beneficios; **to absorb a loss by a subsidiary** = absorber las pérdidas de una filial; **to absorb a surplus** = absorber un excedente **(b) business which has been absorbed by a competitor** = una empresa que ha sido absorbida por un competidor

◇ **absorption** [əbˈzɔːpʃən] *noun* absorción *f*; **absorption costing** = cálculo de costes de absorción; **absorption rate** = coeficiente de absorción

abstract [ˈæbstrækt] **1** *adj* abstracto, -ta **2** *noun* resumen *m* (de un informe *or* documento); **to make an abstract of the company accounts** = hacer un resumen de las cuentas de la compañía

abuse [əˈbjuːs] *noun* abuso *m*; **abuse of a position of authority** *or* **abuse of power** = abuso de poder

a/c *or* **acc** = ACCOUNT *(written on a crossed cheque)* **a/c payee** = cheque cruzado que indica la cuenta en la que debe ser depositado

ACAS [ˈeɪkæs] = ADVISORY, CONCILIATION AND ARBITRATION SERVICE

accelerated [əkˈseləreɪtɪd] *adjective* acelerado, -da; **accelerated depreciation** = amortización acelerada

◇ **acceleration clause** [əkseləˈreɪʃən ˈklɔːz] *noun US* cláusula *f* para el vencimiento anticipado de una deuda (permite a un prestatario reclamar el saldo pendiente si se incumplen otras cláusulas)

accept [əkˈsept] *verb* aceptar; **to accept a bill** = aceptar una letra; **to accept delivery of a shipment** = aceptar la entrega de mercancías; **she accepted the offer of a job in Australia** = aceptó la oferta de un puesto de trabajo en Australia; **he accepted £200 for the car** = aceptó £200 por el coche

◇ **acceptable** [əkˈseptəbl] *adjective* aceptable *or* admisible; **the offer is not acceptable to both parties** = la oferta no es aceptable para ambas partes

◇ **acceptance** [əkˈseptəns] *noun* **(a)** aceptación *f*; **to present a bill for acceptance** = presentar una letra a la aceptación; **acceptance house** *US* **acceptance bank** = ACCEPTING HOUSE **(b)** **acceptance of an offer** = aceptación de una oferta; **to give an offer a conditional acceptance** = dar una aceptación condicional a una oferta; **we have his letter of acceptance** = hemos recibido una carta suya aceptando la oferta; **acceptance sampling** = muestra de aceptación

◇ **accepting house** *or* **acceptance house** [əkˈseptɪŋ haʊs *or* əkˈseptəns haʊs] *noun* banco comercial; **Accepting Houses Committee** = Comité de Bancos Comerciales

access [ˈækses] **1** *noun* **(a)** *(entry)* acceso *m*; **to have access to something** = tener acceso a algo; **he has access to large amounts of venture capital** = tiene acceso a grandes cantidades de capital riesgo **(b)** *(computers)* **direct access** = acceso directo; **sequential access** = acceso secuencial; **single** *or* **parallel access** = acceso único *or* en paralelo; **access time** = tiempo de acceso (NOTE: no plural) **2** *verb* *(computers)* entrar (en); **she accessed the address file on the computer** = entró en el archivo de direcciones del ordenador

◇ **accessible** [əkˈsesəbl] *adjective* accesible

accident [ˈæksɪdənt] *noun* accidente *m*; **industrial accident** = accidente de trabajo *or* accidente laboral; **accident insurance** = seguro de *or* contra accidentes

accommodation [əkɒməˈdeɪʃən] *noun* **(a)** *(money lent)* crédito *m* a corto plazo **(b) to reach an accommodation with creditors** = llegar a un acuerdo con los acreedores **(c) accommodation bill** = pagaré *or* efecto de favor **(d)** *(place to live)* alojamiento *m or* habitación *f or* piso *m*; **visitors have difficulty in finding hotel accommodation during the summer** = los turistas tienen dificultades para encontrar alojamiento durante el verano; **they are living in furnished accommodation** = viven en un piso amueblado; **accommodation address** = dirección postal (NOTE: no plural in GB English, but US English can have **accommodations** for meaning (d))

QUOTE an airline ruling requires airlines to provide a free night's hotel accommodation for full fare passengers in transit
Business Traveller

QUOTE any non-resident private landlord can let furnished or unfurnished accommodation to a tenant
Times

QUOTE the airline providing roomy accommodations at below-average fares
Dun's Business Month

accompany [əˈkʌmpni] *verb* acompañar; **the chairman came to the meeting accompanied by the finance director** = el presidente vino a la reunión acompañado del director de finanzas; **they sent a formal letter of complaint, accompanied by an invoice for damage** = enviaron una carta de reclamación, con una factura de indemnización adjunta (NOTE: accompanied **by** something)

accordance [əˈkɔːdəns] *noun* acuerdo *m*; **in accordance with** = de acuerdo con *or* conforme a *or* de conformidad con; **in accordance with your instructions we have deposited the money in your current account** = conforme a sus órdenes hemos depositado el dinero en su cuenta corriente; **I am submitting the claim for damages in accordance with the advice of our legal advisers** = presento la reclamación de indemnización por daños y perjuicios por indicación de nuestros asesores jurídicos

◇ **according to** [əˈkɔːdɪŋ ˈtʊ] *preposition* según; **the computer was installed according to the manufacturer's instructions** = el ordenador fue instalado según las instrucciones del fabricante

◇ **accordingly** [əˈkɔːdɪŋli] *adverb* en consecuencia; **we have received your letter and have altered the contract accordingly** = hemos recibido su carta y hemos modificado el contrato en consecuencia

QUOTE the budget targets for employment and growth are within reach according to the latest figures
Australian Financial Review

account [əˈkaʊnt] **1** *noun* **(a)** *(notice of payment due)* cuenta *f*; **please send us your account** *or* **a detailed** *or* **an itemized account** = sírvase enviarnos su cuenta *or* una cuenta detallada *or* pormenorizada; **expense account** = cuenta de gastos de representación; **he charged his hotel bill to his expense account** = cargó la factura del hotel en su cuenta de gastos **(b)** *(in a shop)* cuenta; **to have an account** *or* **a charge account** *or* **a credit account**

with Harrods = tener una cuenta *or* una cuenta abierta *or* una cuenta de crédito en Harrods; **put it on my account** *or* **charge it to my account** = cárguelo en mi cuenta; *(of a customer)* **to open an account** = abrir una cuenta; *(of a shop)* **to open an account** *or* **to close an account** = conceder *or* no conceder más crédito a un cliente; **to settle an account** = liquidar una cuenta; **to stop an account** = retirar el crédito **(c) on account** = a crédito; **to pay money on account** = hacer un pago parcial *or* pagar a cuenta; **advance on account** = anticipo a cuenta **(d)** *(regular client)* cliente *m*; **he is one of our largest accounts** = es uno de nuestros clientes más importantes; **our salesmen call on their best accounts twice a month** = nuestros representantes visitan a sus clientes principales una vez al mes; **account executive** = ejecutivo de cuentas; **account manager** = gestor de cuentas **(e)** *(financial balance sheet)* **the accounts of a business** *or* **a company's accounts** = las cuentas de una empresa; **to keep the accounts** = llevar las cuentas; **the accountant's job is to enter all the money received in the accounts** = el trabajo del contable consiste en registrar en las cuentas todo el dinero recibido; **account book** = libro de cuentas; **annual accounts** = cuentas anuales; **management accounts** = cuentas de gestión; **profit and loss account (P & L account)** = cuenta de pérdidas y ganancias (NOTE: the US equivalent is the **profit and loss statement** or **income statement**) **accounts department** = departamento de contabilidad; **accounts manager** = jefe de contabilidad; **accounts payable** = cuentas por pagar; **accounts receivable** = cuentas por cobrar **(f) bank account** *US* **banking account** = cuenta bancaria; **building society account** = cuenta en una entidad de crédito hipotecario; **savings bank account** = cuenta de caja de ahorros *or* libreta de ahorros; **Girobank account** = cuenta de caja postal de ahorro; **Lloyds account** = una cuenta en el Lloyds; **he has an account with Lloyds** = tiene una cuenta en el Lloyds; **I have an account with the Halifax Building Society** = tengo una cuenta en la Halifax Building Society; **to put money in(to) your account** = ingresar dinero en su cuenta; **to take money out of your account** *or* **to withdraw money from your account** = sacar *or* retirar dinero de su cuenta; **budget account** = cuenta presupuestaria; **clear account** = cuenta en regla; **current account** *or* **cheque account** *US* **checking account** = cuenta corriente; **deposit account** = cuenta de depósito; **external account** = cuenta de no residente; **frozen account** = cuenta bloqueada; **joint account** = cuenta conjunta *or* en participación; **most married people have joint accounts so that that they can each take money out when they want it** = la mayoría de los matrimonios tienen una cuenta conjunta para que cada uno pueda sacar dinero cuando lo necesite; **overdrawn account** = cuenta con saldo deudor *or* cuenta al descubierto; **savings account** = cuenta de ahorro; **to open an account** = abrir una cuenta; **she opened an account with the Halifax Building Society** abrió una cuenta en la Halifax Building Society; **to close an account** = cerrar una cuenta; **he closed his account with Lloyds** = cerró su cuenta en el Lloyds **(g)** *(Stock Exchange)* periodo *m* de crédito en la bolsa; **account day** = día de liquidación en la bolsa en el cual hay que pagar las acciones compradas a crédito; **share prices rose at the end of the account** *or* **the account end** = los precios de las acciones subieron al final del periodo de crédito **(h)** *(consideration)* cuenta; **to take account of inflation** *or* **to take inflation into**

account = tener en cuenta la inflación **2** *verb* **to account for** = justificar *or* responder de; **to account for a loss** *or* **a discrepancy** = explicar una pérdida *or* una diferencia de números; **the reps have to account for all their expenses to the sales manager** = los representantes tienen que justificar sus gastos al director de ventas

◊ **accountability** [əkaʊntə'bɪlɪti] *noun* responsabilidad *f*

◊ **accountable** [ə'kaʊntəbl] *adjective* responsable (NOTE: you are accountable **to** someone **for** something)

◊ **accountancy** [ə'kaʊntənsi] *noun* contabilidad *f*; **he is studying accountancy** *or* **he is an accountancy student** = estudia *or* está estudiando contabilidad *or* es estudiante de contabilidad (NOTE: US English uses **accounting** in this meaning)

◊ **accountant** [ə'kaʊntənt] *noun* contable *mf*; **the chief accountant of a manufacturing group** = el director de contabilidad de un grupo industrial; **I send all my income tax queries to my accountant** = transmito todas las dudas que tengo sobre impuestos a mi contable; **certified accountant** = contable titulado; *US* **certified public accountant** = contable público titulado *or* censor jurado de cuentas; **chartered accountant** = contable colegiado *or* censor jurado de cuentas; **cost accountant** = contable de costes; **management accountant** = contable de gestión; **qualified accountant** = experto contable

◊ **accounting** [ə'kaʊntɪŋ] *noun* contabilidad *f*; **accounting machine** = máquina de contabilidad; **accounting methods** *or* **accounting procedures** = métodos *or* procedimientos de contabilidad; **accounting system** = sistema de contabilidad; **accounting period** = periodo contable; **cost accounting** = contabilidad de costes *or* contabilidad analítica; **current cost accounting** = contabilidad de costes actuales (NOTE: the word **accounting** is used in the USA to mean the subject as a course of study, where British English uses **accountancy**)

QUOTE applicants will be professionally qualified and have a degree in Commerce or Accounting
Australian Financial Review

accredited [ə'kredɪtɪd] *adjective* autorizado, -da *or* acreditado, -da

accrual [ə'kruːəl] *noun* **(a)** *(gradual increase by addition)* acumulación *f*; **accrual of interest** = acumulación de interés **(b)** *(accrued expenditure and income)* **accruals** = ACCRUED LIABILITIES

◊ **accrue** [ə'kruː] *verb* acumularse *or* devengar; **interest accrues from the beginning of the month** = los intereses se devengan a partir de principios de mes

◊ **accrued** [ə'kruːd] *pp* devengado, -da; **accrued interest is added quarterly** = el interés devengado se añade cada tres meses; **accrued dividend** = dividendo acumulado; **accrued liabilities** *or* **accruals** = deudas acumuladas *or* pasivo acumulado

acct = ACCOUNT

accumulate [ə'kjuːmjʊleɪt] *verb* acumularse; **to allow dividends to accumulate** = permitir la acumulación de dividendos; **accumulated profit** = beneficio acumulado

accurate ['ækjʊrət] *adjective* exacto, -ta *or* correcto, -ta; **the sales department made an accurate forecast of sales** = el departamento de ventas hizo una previsión correcta de las ventas; **the designers produced an accurate copy of the plan** = los diseñadores hicieron una copia exacta del plan

◊ **accurately** ['ækjʊrətli] *adverb* exactamente *or* correctamente; **the second quarter's drop in sales was accurately forecast by the computer** = la disminución de las ventas del segundo trimestre fue pronosticada con exactitud por el ordenador

accusation [ækju:'zeɪʃn] *noun* acusación *f*; **a serious accusation** = una acusación grave

accuse [ə'kju:z] *verb* acusar; **she was accused of stealing from the petty cash box** = la acusaron de robar dinero de la caja; **he was accused of industrial espionage** = se le acusó de espionaje industrial (NOTE: you accuse someone **of** a crime or **of** doing something)

achieve [ə'tʃi:v] *verb* lograr *or* alcanzar; **the company has achieved great success in the Far East** = la empresa ha triunfado *or* ha tenido un gran éxito en el Extremo Oriente; **he hopes to achieve his aim** = espera lograr su objetivo; **we achieved all our objectives in 1991** = alcanzamos todos nuestros objetivos en 1991

◊ **achievement** [ə'tʃi:vmənt] *noun* logri *m*; **technical achievements** = logros técnicos

> QUOTE the company expects to move to profits of FFr 2m for 1990 and achieve equally rapid growth in following years
> **Financial Times**

acid test ratio ['æsɪd test 'reɪʃɪəʊ] *noun* coeficiente de liquidez

acknowledge [ək'nɒlɪdʒ] *verb* acusar recibo; **he has still not acknowledged my letter of the 24th** = todavía no ha acusado recibo de mi carta del día 24; **we acknowledge receipt of your letter of June 14th** = acusamos recibo de su carta del 14 de junio

◊ **acknowledgement** [ək'nɒlɪdʒmənt] *noun* acuse *m* de recibo; **she sent an acknowledgement of receipt** = envió un acuse de recibo; **they sent a letter of acknowledgement** = enviaron una carta de acuse de recibo

acoustic hood [ə'ku:stɪk 'hʊd] *noun* **(a)** *(cover)* cubierta *f or* protector *m or* funda *f* **(b)** *(telephone)* **acoustic coupler** = acoplador acústico

ACP = AFRICAN, CARIBBEAN AND PACIFIC

acquire [ə'kwaɪə] *verb* adquirir *or* comprar; **to acquire a company** = adquirir una compañía

◊ **acquirer** [ə'kwaɪərə] *noun* adquirente *mf*

◊ **acquisition** [ækwɪ'zɪʃən] *noun* **(a)** *(thing bought)* adquisición *or* compra *f*; **the chocolate factory is his latest acquisition** = la fábrica de chocolate es su última adquisición **(b)** *(act of getting or buying something)* **data acquisition** *or* **acquisition of data** = adquisición de datos

acre ['eɪkə] *noun* acre *m* (= 0.45 hectáreas) (NOTE: the plural is used with figures, except before a noun:

he has bought a farm of 250 acres *or* **he has bought a 250 acre farm** = ha comprado una granja de 250 acres)

across-the-board [ə'krɒsðə'bɔ:d] *adjective* global *or* general *or* lineal; **an across-the-board price increase** = un aumento general de precios

ACT = ADVANCE CORPORATION TAX

act [ækt] **1** *noun* **(a)** ley *f or* decreto *m* GB **Companies Act** = Ley de sociedades anónimas; **Finance Act** = ley presupuestaria; **Financial Services Act** = Ley de Servicios Financieros; **Health and Safety at Work Act** = Ley sobre seguridad e higiene en el trabajo; **Navigation Act** = Acta de Navegación; **Road Safety Act** = Ley de seguridad vial; **Single European Act** = Acta Única Europea; **Social Security Act** = Ley de Seguridad Social **(b)** **act of God** = (i) fuerza mayor; (ii) catástrofe natural **2** *verb* **(a)** *(work)* actuar; **to act as an agent for an American company** = actuar como representante de una empresa americana; **to act for someone** *or* **to act on someone's behalf** = representar a alguien *or* actuar en nombre de alguien **(b)** *(do something)* tomar medidas; **the board will have to act quickly if the company's losses are going to be reduced** = el consejo de administración tendrá que tomar medidas rápidas para que las pérdidas de la empresa se reduzcan; **the lawyers are acting on our instructions** = los abogados están actuando según nuestras instrucciones; **to act on a letter** = cumplir las instrucciones de una carta

◊ **acting** ['æktɪŋ] *adjective* interino, -na *or* en funciones; **acting manager** = director interino *or* en funciones *or* provisional; **the Acting Chairman** = el presidente en funciones

◊ **action** ['ækʃən] *noun* **(a)** *(thing which has been done)* acción *f*; **to take action** = tomar medidas *or* hacer algo; **you must take action if you want to stop people cheating you** = tiene Vd. que hacer algo si quiere que la gente deje de engañarle; **administrative action** = acto administrativo **(b)** *(protest)* movilización *f*; **direct action** = acción directa; **industrial action** = huelga; **to take industrial action** = ir a la huelga *or* hacer huelga **(c)** *(case in a law court)* acción legal; **to take legal action** = entablar un pleito *or* recurrir a la vía judicial; **action for damages** = demanda por daños y perjuicios; **action for libel** *or* **libel action** = querella por difamación; **to bring an action for damages against someone** = entablar una demanda contra alguien por daños y perjuicios; **civil action** = demanda civil; **criminal action** = causa penal *or* acción criminal *or* penal

◊ **activate** ['æktɪveɪt] *verb* activar

◊ **active** ['æktɪv] *adjective* activo, -va; **active partner** = socio activo; **an active demand for oil shares** = una gran demanda de acciones petrolíferas; **oil shares are very active** = hay mucha actividad en el mercado de acciones petrolíferas; **an active day on the Stock Exchange** = un día de gran actividad en la bolsa; **business is active** = la actividad es intensa

◊ **actively** ['æktɪvli] *adverb* intensamente *or* activamente; **the company is actively recruiting new personnel** = la empresa se está moviendo para contratar nuevo personal

◊ **activity** [æk'tɪvəti] *noun* actividad *f*; **a low level** of business activity = un nivel reducido de actividad comercial; **there was a lot of activity on the Stock Exchange** = había mucha actividad en la bolsa; **activity chart** = gráfico de actividades; **monthly activity report** = informe mensual de actividades

QUOTE preliminary indications of the level of business investment and activity during the March quarter will provide a good picture of economic activity in 1990
Australian Financial Review

actual ['ækt∫ʊəl] **1** *adjective* real *or* verdadero, -ra *or* efectivo, -va; **what is the actual cost of one unit?** = ¿cuál es el coste real por unidad?; **the actual figures for directors' expenses are not shown to the shareholders** = los detalles de los gastos de los directivos no se revelan a los accionistas **2** *plural noun* cifras *fpl* reales; **these figures are the actuals for 1990** = estas son las cifras reales del 1990

actuary ['æktjʊəri] *noun* actuario, -ria; **insurance actuary** = actuario de seguros

◇ **actuarial** [æktjʊ'eərıəl] *adjective* actuarial; **the premiums are worked out according to actuarial calculations** = las primas se determinan según cálculos actuariales; **actuarial tables** = tablas actuariales *or* tablas de mortalidad

ad [æd] *noun* = ADVERTISEMENT

add [æd] *verb* **(a)** *(total)* añadir; **to add interest to the capital** = añadir los intereses al capital; **interest is added monthly** = los intereses se calculan mensualmente; **added value** = valor añadido; *see also* VALUE ADDED **(b)** *(large group)* agregar *or* aumentar; **we are adding to the sales force** = estamos aumentando el personal de ventas; **they have added two new products to their range** = han agregado dos nuevos productos a su gama; **this all adds to the company's costs** = todo esto aumenta los costes de la empresa

◇ **add up** ['æd 'ʌp] *verb* sumar; **to add up a column of figures** = sumar una columna de cifras; **the figures do not add up** = las cifras no cuadran

◇ **add up to** ['æd 'ʌp tʊ] *verb* ascender a; **the total expenditure adds up to more than £1,000** = el gasto total asciende a más de £1.000

◇ **adding** ['ædıŋ] *noun* sumar *m*; **an adding machine** = una sumadora *or* una máquina sumadora

◇ **addition** [ə'dı∫ən] *noun* **(a)** *(thing added)* incorporación *f or* suma *f or* adición *f or* agregado *m*; **the management has stopped all additions to the staff** = la dirección ha suspendido la contratación de nuevo personal; **we are exhibiting several additions to our product line** = exponemos varios productos que hemos agregado a nuestra gama habitual; **the marketing director is the latest addition to the board** = el director de comercialización es la última persona incorporada al consejo de administración **(b)** *(in addition to)* además de; **there are twelve registered letters to be sent in addition to this packet** = hay que enviar doce cartas certificadas además de este paquete **(c)** *(calculation)* suma *f*; **you don't need a calculator to do simple addition** = no hace falta una calculadora para hacer una simple suma

◇ **additional** [ə'dı∫ənl] *adjective* adicional *or* suplementario, -ria; **additional costs** = costes adicionales; **additional charges** = cargos

adicionales; **additional clauses to a contract** = cláusulas suplementarias de un contrato; **additional duty will have to be paid** = habrá que pagar un impuesto adicional

address [ə'dres] **1** *noun* dirección *f or* señas *fpl*; **my business address and phone number are printed on the card** = mi dirección profesional y el número de teléfono están indicados en la tarjeta; **accommodation address** = dirección postal; **cable address** = dirección telegráfica; **forwarding address** = dirección de reenvío; **home address** = domicilio particular *or* dirección privada; **please send the documents to my home address** = se ruega enviar los documentos a mi domicilio particular; **address book** = libro de direcciones; **address label** = etiqueta (de señas); **address list** = lista de direcciones; **we keep an address list of two thousand addresses in Europe** = mantenemos una lista de dos mil direcciones en Europa **2** *verb* **(a)** *(write)* dirigir *or* poner la dirección; **to address a letter** *or* **a parcel** = rellenar un sobre *or* poner la dirección en un paquete; **please address your enquiries to the manager** = por favor dirija sus peticiones al director; **a letter addressed to the managing director** = una carta dirigida al director gerente; **an incorrectly addressed package** = un paquete con la dirección incorrecta **(b)** *(speak)* dirigirse; **to address a meeting** = dirigirse a los asistentes a una reunión

◇ **addressee** [ædre'si:] *noun* destinatario, -ria

◇ **addressing machine** [ə'dresıŋ mə'∫i:n] *noun* máquina *f* de imprimir direcciones *or* impresora *f* de sobres

adequate ['ædıkwət] *adjective* **(a)** *(enough)* suficiente; **to operate without adequate cover** = actuar sin cobertura suficiente **(b)** *(satisfactory)* adecuado, -da *or* satisfactorio, -ria; **the results of the tests on the product were adequate** = los resultados de las pruebas del producto fueron satisfactorios

adhesive [əd'hi:zıv] **1** *adjective* adhesivo, -va; **adhesive paper** = papel adhesivo; **he sealed the parcel with adhesive tape** = precintó el paquete con cinta adhesiva **2** *noun (glue)* adhesivo *m*; **she has a tube of adhesive in the drawer of her desk** = tiene un tubo de adhesivo en el cajón de su escritorio

adjourn [ə'dʒɜ:n] *verb* aplazar *or* levantar; **to adjourn a meeting** = aplazar una reunión; **the chairman adjourned the meeting until three o'clock** = el presidente aplazó la reunión hasta las tres; **the meeting adjourned at midday** = la reunión se levantó al mediodía

◇ **adjournment** [ə'dʒɜ:nmənt] *noun* aplazamiento *m*; **he proposed the adjournment of the meeting** = propuso el aplazamiento de la reunión

adjudicate [ə'dʒu:dıkeıt] *verb* decidir *or* juzgar *or* resolver; **to adjudicate a claim** = juzgar una demanda; **to adjudicate in a dispute** = arbitrar un litigio; **he was adjudicated bankrupt** = se le declaró en quiebra

◇ **adjudication** [ədʒu:dı'keı∫ən] *noun* adjudicación *f*; **adjudication order** *or* **adjudication of bankruptcy** = declaración judicial de quiebra; **adjudication tribunal** = tribunal arbitral *or* tribunal de justicia

◇ **adjudicator** [ə'dʒu:dıkeıtə] *noun* árbitro *mf or*

juez *mf*; **an adjudicator in an industrial dispute** = árbitro de un conflicto laboral

adjust [ə'dʒʌst] *verb* ajustar *or* reajustar; **to adjust prices to take account of inflation** = reajustar los precios para tener en cuenta la inflación; **prices are adjusted for inflation** = los precios están ajustados a la inflación

◊ **adjustable** [ə'dʒʌstəbl] *adjective* ajustable

◊ **adjuster** [ə'dʒʌstə] *noun* tasador, -ra *or* perito, -ta; **average adjuster** = perito, -ta de averías; **loss adjuster** = tasador de pérdidas

◊ **adjustment** [ə'dʒʌstmənt] *noun* ajuste *m or* reajuste *m*; **to make an adjustment to salaries** = hacer un reajuste de salarios; **adjustment of prices to take account of rising costs** = reajuste de precios por aumento de costes; **average adjustment** = reajuste de averías; **process of adjustment** = proceso de ajuste; **structural adjustment** = ajuste estructural; **tax adjustment** = reajuste impositivo; **border tax adjustment** = ajuste fiscal en frontera; **wage adjustment** = ajuste salarial

◊ **adjustor** [ə'dʒʌstə] *noun* = ADJUSTER

QUOTE inflation-adjusted GNP moved up at a 1.3% annual rate
Fortune

QUOTE Saudi Arabia will no longer adjust its production to match short-term supply with demand
Economist

QUOTE on a seasonally adjusted basis, output of trucks, electric power, steel and paper decreased
Business Week

adman ['ædmæn] *noun* (*informal*) publicitario *m or* agente *m* de publicidad; **the admen are using balloons as promotional material** = los agentes publicitarios utilizan globos como medio de promoción

admin ['ædmɪn] *noun* (*informal*) **(a)** (*work*) trabajo *m* administrativo; **all this admin work takes a lot of my time** = todo este trabajo administrativo me lleva mucho tiempo; **there is too much admin in this job** = hay demasiadas tareas administrativas en este trabajo; **admin costs seem to be rising each quarter** = los costes administrativos parecen aumentar cada trimestre; **the admin people have sent the report back** = el personal administrativo ha devuelto el informe **(b)** (*staff*) personal administrativo; **admin say they need the report immediately** = la sección de administración dice que necesita el informe inmediatamente (NOTE: no plural; as a group of people it can have a plural verb)

◊ **administer** [əd'mɪnɪstə] *verb* administrar; **he administers a large pension fund** = administra un importante fondo de pensiones; *US* **administered price** = precio controlado

◊ **administration** [ədmɪnɪ'streɪʃən] *noun* **(a)** (*organization*) administración *f or* dirección *f*; **the expenses of the administration** *or* **administration expenses** = los gastos de administración *or* gastos administrativos; **business administration** = administración de empresas; **administration of personnel** = administración del personal **(b)** (*given by a court*) **letters of administration** = nombramiento de administrador judicial

◊ **administrative** [əd'mɪnɪstrətɪv] *adjective* administrativo, -va; **administrative details** = detalles administrativos; **administrative expenses** = gastos administrativos

◊ **administrator** [əd'mɪnɪstreɪtə] *noun* **(a)** administrador, -ra **(b)** (*appointed by a court*) albacea *m* testamentario

admissible [əd'mɪsɪbl] *adjective* aceptable *or* admisible

admission [əd'mɪʃən] *noun* **(a)** (*entry*) entrada *f*; **there is a £1 admission charge** = la entrada cuesta £1; **admission is free on presentation of this card** = la entrada es gratuita al presentar esta tarjeta; **free admission on Sundays** = entrada gratis los domingos **(b)** (*confession*) confesión *f*; **he had to resign after his admission that he had passed information to the rival company** = tuvo que dimitir después de confesar que había pasado información a la competencia

admit [əd'mɪt] *verb* **(a)** (*enter*) permitir la entrada *or* admitir; **children are not admitted to the bank** = no se admiten niños en el banco; **old age pensioners are admitted at half price** = la entrada para los jubilados es a mitad de precio **(b)** (*confess*) confesar; **the chairman admitted he had taken the cash from the company's safe** = el presidente confesó que había robado el dinero de la caja de seguridad de la empresa (NOTE: **admitting - admitted**)

◊ **admittance** [əd'mɪtəns] *noun* entrada *f*; **no admittance except on business** = prohibida la entrada salvo por asuntos de negocios

adopt [ə'dɒpt] *verb* adoptar; **to adopt a resolution** = adoptar una moción; **the proposals were adopted unanimously** = se aceptaron las propuestas por unanimidad

ADR = AMERICAN DEPOSITARY RECEIPT

ad valorem [ædvə'lɔːrəm] *phrase* ad valorem (impuesto calculado con relación al valor de las mercancías); **ad valorem duty** = tarifa ad valorem; **ad valorem tax** = impuesto ad valorem

COMMENT: most taxes are 'ad valorem'; VAT is calculated as a percentage of the charge made, income tax is a percentage of income earned, etc.

advance [əd'vɑːns] **1** *noun* **(a)** (*loan*) préstamo *or* crédito *or* anticipo *or* adelanto *m*; **bank advance** = préstamo bancario; **a cash advance** = adelanto *or* anticipo; **to receive an advance from the bank** = recibir un crédito del banco; **an advance on account** = un anticipo a cuenta; **to make an advance of £100 to someone** = hacer un préstamo de £100 a alguien; **to pay someone an advance against a security** = conceder un crédito con garantía a alguien; **can I have an advance of £50 against next month's salary?** = ¿puede darme un anticipo de £50 sobre el sueldo del mes próximo? **(b)** (*early*) **in advance** = por adelantado *or* de antemano *or* por anticipado; **to pay in advance** = pagar por adelantado; **freight payable in advance** = flete pagadero por adelantado; **price fixed in advance** = precio establecido de antemano; **thank you in advance** = gracias por anticipado **(c)** (*increase*) avance *m*; **advance in trade** = progreso comercial; **advance in prices** = alza de precios **2** *adjective* anticipado, -a *or* adelantado, -a *or* con antelación; **advance booking** = reserva anticipada; **advance payment** = pago anticipado; **you must give seven days' advance notice of withdrawals from the account** = hay que avisar con siete días de antelación que se van a retirar fondos de la cuenta **3** *verb* **(a)** *(to lend)* anticipar *or* prestar; **the bank advanced him £10,000 against the security of his house** = el banco le prestó £10.000 tomando su casa como garantía **(b)** *(to increase)* subir; **prices generally advanced on the stock market** = los precios de la bolsa experimentaron un aumento general **(c)** *(to move forward)* adelantar; **the date of the AGM has been advanced to May 10th** = la fecha de la junta general anual ha sido adelantada al 10 de mayo; **the meeting with the German distributors has been advanced from 11.00 to 09.30** = la reunión con los distribuidores alemanes se ha adelantado de las 11.00 a las 9.30

◇ **Advance Corporation Tax (ACT)** [ə'vɑːns kɔːpə'reɪʃn 'tæks] *noun* pago anticipado sobre el impuesto de sociedades

advantage [əd'vɑːntɪdʒ] *noun* ventaja *f or* utilidad *f;* **fast typing is an advantage in a secretary** = escribir a máquina con rapidez es una ventaja para una secretaria; **knowledge of two foreign languages is an advantage** = el conocimiento de dos idiomas extranjeros es una ventaja; **there is no advantage in arriving at the exhibition before it opens** = llegar a la exposición antes de la apertura no tiene ninguna utilidad; **to take advantage of something** = aprovecharse *or* sacar partido de algo

adverse ['ædvɜːs] *adjective* adverso, -sa *or* desfavorable; **adverse balance of trade** = balanza comercial negativa; **adverse trading conditions** = situación desfavorable para el comercio

advertise ['ædvətaɪz] *verb* anunciar *or* publicar; **to advertise a vacancy** = anunciar una vacante; **to advertise for a secretary** = anunciar un puesto de secretaria; **to advertise a new product** = hacer publicidad de un nuevo producto

◇ **ad** [æd] *noun informal* = ADVERTISEMENT **we put an ad in the paper** = pusimos un anuncio en el periódico; **she answered an ad in the paper** = contestó a un anuncio del periódico; **he found his job through an ad in the paper** = encontró trabajo a través de un anuncio en el periódico; **classified ads** *or* **small ads** *or* **want ads** = anuncios breves *or* clasificados *or* por palabras; **look in the small ads to see if anyone has a computer for sale** = mire en los anuncios breves si alguien vende un ordenador; **coupon ad** = anuncio con impreso de solicitud de información; **display ad** = anuncios *or* pancarta publicitaria

◇ **advert** ['ædvɜːt] *noun GB (informal)* = ADVERTISEMENT **to put an advert in the paper** = poner un anuncio en el periódico; **to answer an advert in the paper** = contestar a un anuncio del periódico; **classified adverts** = anuncios clasificados *or* por palabras; **display advert** = pancarta publicitaria

◇ **advertisement** [əd'vɜːtɪsmənt] *noun* anuncio *m;* **to put an advertisement in the paper** = poner un anuncio en el periódico; **to answer an advertisement in the paper** = contestar a un anuncio del periódico; **classified advertisements** =

anuncios clasificados *or* por palabras; **display advertisement** = pancarta publicitaria; **advertisement manager** = jefe de publicidad

◇ **advertiser** ['ædvətaɪzə] *noun* anunciante *mf;* **the catalogue gives a list of advertisers** = el catálago contiene una lista de anunciantes

◇ **advertising** ['ædvətaɪzɪŋ] *noun* publicidad *f;* **she works in advertising** = trabaja en publicidad; **he has a job in advertising** = tiene un empleo en publicidad; **advertising agency** = agencia de publicidad; **advertising agent** = agente de publicidad; **advertising budget** = presupuesto de publicidad; **advertising campaign** = campaña publicitaria; **advertising manager** = jefe de publicidad; **advertising rates** = tarifas publicitarias; **advertising space** = espacio publicitario; **to take advertising space in a paper** = adquirir espacio publicitario en un periódico

◇ **advertorial** [ædvə'tɔːriəl] *noun* texto publicitario

advice [əd'vaɪs] *noun* **(a)** **advice note** = conocimiento *m* de embarque *or* aviso *m* de expedición *or* nota *f* de envío; **as per advice** = según nota de expedición **(b)** consejo *m;* **legal advice** = asesoramiento jurídico; **to take legal advice** = consultar a un abogado; **the accountant's advice was to send the documents to the police** = el contable aconsejó enviar los documentos a la policía; **we sent the documents to the police on the advice of the accountant** *or* **we took the accountant's advice and sent the documents to the police** = enviamos los documentos a la policía por indicación del contable *or* siguiendo el consejo del contable enviamos los documentos a la policía

advise [əd'vaɪz] *verb* **(a)** *(to inform)* informar *or* advertir; **we are advised that the shipment will arrive next week** = nos informan de que el envío llegará la semana que viene **(b)** *(suggest)* aconsejar; **we are advised to take the shipping company to court** = nos aconsejan que llevemos a la compañía naviera a los tribunales; **the accountant advised us to send the documents to the police** = el contable nos aconsejó que enviáramos los documentos a la policía

◇ **advise against** [əd'vaɪz ə'genst] *verb* desaconsejar *or* aconsejar en contra; **the bank manager advised against closing the account** = el director del banco nos aconsejó que no cerráramos la cuenta; **my stockbroker has advised against buying those shares** = mi agente de bolsa desaconseja la compra de esas acciones

◇ **adviser** *or* **advisor** [əd'vaɪzə] *noun* asesor, -ra *or* consejero, -ra; **he is consulting the company's legal adviser** = ha consultado al asesor jurídico de la empresa; **financial adviser** = asesor financiero *or* fiscal; **technical adviser** = consejero técnico

◇ **advisory** [əd'vaɪzəri] *adjective* consultivo, -va *or* asesor, -ra; **he is acting in an advisory capacity** = actúa en calidad de asesor; **an advisory board** =

junta consultiva; **advisory committee** = comisión asesora; **Advisory, Conciliation and Arbitration Service (ACAS)** = Instituto de Mediación, Arbitraje y Conciliación

aerogramme [ˈeərə(ʊ)græm] *noun* US aerograma *m* (NOTE: GB English is **air letter**)

affair [əˈfeə] *noun* asunto *m or* escándalo *m*; **are you involved in the copyright affair?** = ¿está Vd. involucrado en el asunto de los derechos de autor?; **his affairs were so difficult to understand that the lawyers had to ask accountants for advice** = sus asuntos eran tan complicados que los abogados tuvieron que consultar a unos contables

affect [əˈfekt] *verb* afectar *or* influir *or* perjudicar; **the new government regulations do not affect us** = la nueva reglamentación oficial no nos afecta; **the company's sales in the Far East were seriously affected by the embargo** = las ventas de la empresa en el Extremo Oriente se vieron seriamente perjudicadas por el embargo

QUOTE the dollar depreciation has yet to affect the underlying inflation rate
Australian Financial Review

affidavit [æfɪˈdeɪvɪt] *noun* acta *f* notarial *or* declaración *f* jurada *or* testimonio *m*

affiliate [əˈfɪlieɪt] *verb* afiliar *or* afiliarse

◊ **affiliated** [əˈfɪlieɪtɪd] *adjective* afiliado, -da *or* filial; **one of our affiliated companies** = una de nuestras sociedades filiales

affinity card [əˈfɪnɪti ˈkɑːd] *noun* tarjeta de crédito vinculada a una sociedad benéfica

affirmative [əˈfɜːmətɪv] *adjective* afirmativo, -va; **the answer was in the affirmative** = la respuesta fue afirmativa; US **affirmative action program** = programa de medidas a favor de las minorías para eliminar discriminaciones

affluent [ˈæfluənt] *adjective* opulento, -ta *or* acaudalado, -da; **we live in an affluent society** = vivimos en una sociedad opulenta

afford [əˈfɔːd] *verb* permitirse un gasto *or* tener suficiente dinero *or* tiempo para comprar *or* hacer una cosa; **we could not afford the cost of two telephones** = no nos pudimos permitir el coste de dos teléfonos; **the company cannot afford the time to train new staff** = la empresa no tiene tiempo suficiente para capacitar a nuevo personal (NOTE: only used after **can, cannot, could, could not, able to**)

Afghanistan [æfˈgænɪstæn] *noun* Afganistán *m*

◊ **Afghan** [ˈæfgæn] *noun & adjective* afgano, -na NOTE: capital: **Kabul**; currency: **afghani (Af)** = afgani

AFL-CIO [ˈeɪefˈelˈsiːaɪˈəʊ] = AMERICAN FEDERATION OF LABOR - CONGRESS OF INDUSTRIAL ORGANIZATIONS federación americana de trabajadores - congreso de organizaciones industriales

afraid [əˈfreɪd] *adjective* **(a) to be afraid** = tener miedo **(b)** *(to regret)* sentir; **I am afraid there are no seats left on the flight to Amsterdam** = lo siento, pero no quedan plazas en el vuelo a Amsterdam; **we are afraid your order has been**

lost in the post = creemos que su encargo se ha perdido en el correo

after-hours [ˈɑːftəˈaʊəz] *adjective* **after-hours buying** *or* **selling** *or* **dealing** = operación bursátil después de la hora oficial de cierre de la bolsa

◊ **after-sales service** [ˈɑːftəseɪlz ˈsɜːvɪs] *noun* servicio *m* de post-venta

◊ **after-tax profit** [ˈɑːftətæks ˈprɒfɪt] *noun* beneficios *mpl* después de deducir impuestos

against [əˈgenst] *preposition* contra *or* sobre; **to pay an advance against a security** = hacer un préstamo con garantía; **can I have an advance against next month's salary?** = ¿puede darme un anticipo sobre el sueldo del mes próximo?; **the bank advanced him £10,000 against the security of his house** = el banco le concedió un crédito de £10.000 con su casa como garantía; **against the rules** = antirreglamentario, -ria; **it is against the rules to smoke in the computer room** *or* **smoking in the computer room is against the rules** = el reglamento no permite fumar en la sala de ordenadores *or* no está permitido fumar en la sala de ordenadores

QUOTE investment can be written off against the marginal rate of tax
Investors Chronicle

QUOTE the index for the first half of 1985 shows that the rate of inflation went down by about 12.9 per cent against the rate as at December last year
Business Times (Lagos)

aged debtors analysis *or* **ageing schedule** [eɪdʒd ˈdetəz əˈnæləsɪs *or* ˈeɪdʒɪŋ ˈʃedjuːl] *noun* análisis de vencimientos (NOTE: US spelling is **aging**)

COMMENT: an ageing schedule shows all the debtors of a company and lists (usually in descending order of age) all the debts that are outstanding

agency [ˈeɪdʒənsi] *noun* **(a)** *(office representing another)* agencia *f*; **they signed an agency agreement** *or* **an agency contract** = firmaron un acuerdo *or* contrato de representación; **sole agency** = representación exclusiva; **he has the sole agency for Ford cars** = tiene la representación exclusiva de los automóviles Ford **(b)** *(office working for others)* agencia especializada; **advertising agency** = agencia de publicidad; **credit agency** = agencia de informes comerciales; **employment agency** = agencia de empleo *or* oficina de colocación; **estate agency** = agencia inmobiliaria; **news agency** = agencia de noticias; **travel agency** = agencia de viajes **(c)** US **agency shop** = empresa *f* en la que todos los trabajadores cotizan al sindicato (NOTE: plural is **agencies**)

agenda [əˈdʒendə] *noun* orden *m* del día *or* agenda *f or* resumen *m* de actividades; **the conference agenda** *or* **the agenda of the conference** = el orden del día de la conferencia *or* del congreso; **after two hours we were still discussing the first item on the agenda** = transcurridas dos horas todavía discutíamos el primer punto del orden del día; **the secretary put finance at the top of the agenda** = el secretario puso las finanzas como asunto prioritario; **the chairman wants two items removed from** *or* **taken off the agenda** = el presidente quiere que se eliminen dos puntos del orden del día

agent ['eɪdʒənt] *noun* **(a)** *(representative)* agente *mf or* representante *mf or* mandatario *m*; **to be the agent for IBM** = ser el representante de IBM; **sole agent** = representante exclusivo; **he is the sole agent for Ford cars** = es el representante exclusivo de los automóviles Ford; **agent's commission** = comisión del agente **(b)** *(working in an agency)* jefe de agencia; **advertising agent** = agente de publicidad; **estate agent** = agente inmobiliario *or* corredor de fincas; **travel agent** = agente de viajes; **commission agent** = comisionista *mf* **forwarding agent** = agente de transporte *or* agente expedidor; **insurance agent** = agente de seguros; **land agent** = administrador, -ra de una finca **(c)** *US* **(business) agent** = delegado, -da de un sindicato *or* enlace sindical

aggregate ['ægrɪgət] *adjective* agregado, -da; **aggregate output** = producto global

agio ['ædʒɪəu] *noun* agio *m*

AGM ['eɪdʒi:'em] *noun* = ANNUAL GENERAL MEETING junta *f* anual

agree [ə'gri:] *verb* **(a)** *(approve)* aprobar *or* acordar *or* aceptar; **the auditors have agreed the accounts** = los auditores han aprobado las cuentas; **the figures were agreed between the two parties** = las dos partes interesadas acordaron las cifras; **we have agreed the budgets for next year** = hemos aprobado los presupuestos del año próximo; **we all agreed on the plan** = todos aprobamos el plan; **terms of the contract are still to be agreed** = no se han acordado todavía los términos del contrato; **after some discussion he agreed to our plan** = después de un debate aprobó nuestro plan; **he has agreed your prices** = aceptó sus precios **(b)** *(accept)* acceder *a or* aceptar *or* consentir *or* convenir; **it has been agreed that the lease will run for 25 years** = se ha convenido en que el arrendamiento dure 25 años; **the bank will never agree to lend the company £250,000** = el banco nunca consentirá prestar £250.000 a la compañía (NOTE: to agree **to** *or* **on** a plan) **(c) to agree to do something** = aceptar hacer algo *or* acceder; **she agreed to be chairman** = aceptó ser presidente; **will the finance director agree to resign?** = ¿accederá el director financiero a dimitir? **(d)** *(to be the same as)* corresponder *or* coincidir *or* ponerse de acuerdo *or* cuadrar; **the two sets of calculations do not agree** = los dos grupos de cálculos no se corresponden *or* no coinciden *or* no cuadran

◊ **agree with** [ə'gri: 'wɪð] *verb* **(a)** *(to have the same opinion)* estar de acuerdo; **I agree with the chairman that the figures are lower than normal** = estoy de acuerdo con el presidente en que las cifras son inferiores a las normales **(b)** *(be the same as)* corresponder *or* coincidir con; **the auditors' figures do not agree with those of the accounts department** = las cifras de los auditores no se corresponden con las de la sección de contabilidad

◊ **agreed** [ə'gri:d] *adjective* convenido, -da *or* acordado, -da; **an agreed amount** = una cantidad convenida; **on agreed terms** = en las condiciones acordadas *or* según los términos acordados

◊ **agreement** [ə'gri:mənt] *noun* convenio *m or*

acuerdo *m or* contrato *m or* tratado *m*; **written agreement** = acuerdo (por) escrito; **unwritten** *or* **verbal agreement** = acuerdo no escrito *or* acuerdo verbal; **to draw up** *or* **to draft an agreement** = redactar un contrato; **to break an agreement** = romper un acuerdo; **to sign an agreement** = firmar un convenio *or* acuerdo *or* contrato; **to witness an agreement** = actuar de testigo en la firma de un contrato; **an agreement has been reached** *or* **concluded** = se ha alcanzado un acuerdo; **to reach an agreement** *or* **to come to an agreement on prices** *or* **salaries** = llegar a un acuerdo sobre los precios *or* salarios; **an international agreement on trade** = un convenio internacional de comercio; **collective wage agreement** = un convenio salarial colectivo; **an agency agreement** = un contrato de representación; **a marketing agreement** = acuerdo de comercialización; **bilateral agreement** = acuerdo bilateral; **blanket agreement** = acuerdo global; **exclusive agreement** = acuerdo *or* contrato de representación exclusiva; **gentleman's agreement** *or US* **gentlemen's agreement** = acuerdo entre caballeros; **reciprocal agreement** = acuerdo recíproco

QUOTE after three days of tough negotiations the company has reached agreement with its 1,200 unionized workers

Toronto Star

agribusiness *or* **agrobusiness** ['ægrɪbɪznəs *or* 'ægrəubɪznəs] *noun* agroindustria *f or* explotación *f* agrícola

agriculture ['ægrɪkʌltʃə] *noun* agricultura *f or* agricultura y ganadería *f*; **part-time agriculture** = agricultura a tiempo parcial; **group agriculture** = agricultura de grupo

◊ **agricultural** [ægrɪ'kʌltʃərəl] *adjective* agrícola *or* agropecuario, -ria *or* agrario, -ria; **agricultural co-operative** = cooperativa agrícola; **agricultural economist** = economista agrónomo *or* agrícola; **Common Agricultural Policy (CAP)** = Política Agrícola Común (PAC); **agricultural sector** = sector agrario; **agricultural expert** = ingeniero agrónomo

ahead [ə'hed] *adverb* delante; **we are already ahead of our sales forecast** = ya hemos rebasado nuestro pronóstico de ventas; **the company has a lot of work ahead of it if it wants to increase its market share** = la empresa tiene mucho trabajo por delante si quiere aumentar su participación en el mercado

aim [eɪm] **1** *noun* objetivo *m or* fin *m*; **one of our aims is to increase the quality of our products** = uno de nuestros objetivos es mejorar la calidad de nuestros productos; **the company has achieved all its aims** = la compañía ha alcanzado todos sus objetivos **2** *verb* proponerse *or* aspirar a; **we aim to be No. 1 in the market in two years' time** = nos proponemos ser el número uno del mercado dentro de dos años; **each salesman must aim to double his previous year's sales** = cada vendedor tiene que aspirar a duplicar las ventas del año anterior

air [eə] **1** *noun* aire *m*; **to send a letter** *or* **a shipment by air** = mandar una carta *or* un envío por vía aérea *or* por avión; **air carrier** = empresa de transporte aéreo; **air forwarding** = envío por vía aérea; **air letter** = aerograma *m* (NOTE: US English for this is **aerogramme) air traffic** = tráfico aéreo **2** *verb* **to air a grievance** = exponer una queja; **the management committee is useful because it allows the workers' representatives to air their grievances** = el comité de gestión es útil porque permite a los obreros exponer sus quejas

◊ **air cargo** ['eə 'kɑ:gəʊ] *noun* carga *f* aérea *or* flete *m* aéreo

◊ **aircraft** ['eəkrɑ:ft] *noun* avión *m*; **the airline has a fleet of ten commercial aircraft** = la línea aérea tiene una flota de diez aviones comerciales; **the company is one of the most important American aircraft manufacturers** = se trata de una de las empresas norteamericanas más importantes de fabricantes de aviones; **to charter an aircraft** = fletar un avión (NOTE: no plural: **one aircraft, two aircraft**)

◊ **air freight** ['eə 'freɪt] *noun* carga *f* aérea; **to send a shipment by air freight** = hacer un envío por carga aérea; **air freight charges** *or* **rates** = gastos *or* tarifas de carga aérea

◊ **airfreight** ['eəfreɪt] *verb* enviar por transporte aéreo *or* carga aérea; **to airfreight a consignment to Mexico** = despachar un envío a México por carga aérea; **we airfreighted the shipment because our agent ran out of stock** = efectuamos el envío por transporte aéreo porque se agotaron las existencias de nuestro representante

◊ **airline** ['eəlaɪn] *noun* línea *f* aérea *or* aerolínea *f*

◊ **airmail** ['eəmeɪl] **1** *noun* correo *m* aéreo; **to send a package by airmail** = enviar un paquete por correo aéreo; **airmail charges have risen by 15%** = el precio del correo aéreo ha aumentado en un 15%; **airmail envelope** = sobre de correo aéreo; **airmail sticker** = etiqueta de correo aéreo **2** *verb* enviar cartas *or* paquetes por correo aéreo; **to airmail a document to New York** = enviar un documento a Nueva York por correo aéreo

◊ **airport** ['eəpɔ:t] *noun* aeropuerto *m*; **we leave from London Airport at 10.00** = salimos del aeropuerto de Londres a las 10.00; **O'Hare Airport is the main airport for Chicago** = O'Hare es el aeropuerto principal de Chicago; **airport bus** = autobús del aeropuerto; **airport tax** = tasas de aeropuerto; **airport terminal** = terminal del aeropuerto

◊ **air terminal** ['eə 'tɜ:mɪnl] *noun* terminal *f* de aeropuerto

◊ **airtight** ['eətaɪt] *adjective* hermético, -ca; **the goods are packed in airtight containers** = las mercancías están embaladas en contenedores herméticos

◊ **airworthiness** ['eəwɜ:ðɪnəs] *noun* aeronavegabilidad *f*; **certificate of airworthiness** = certificado de aeronavegabilidad

Albania [æl'beɪnɪə] *noun* Albania *f*

◊ **Albanian** [æl'beɪnɪən] *noun & adjective* albanés, -esa
NOTE: capital: **Tirana**; currency: **Albanian lek** = lek albanés

aleatory ['ælɪətrɪ] *adjective* aleatorio, -ria

Algeria [æl'dʒi:ərɪə] *noun* Argelia *f*

◊ **Algerian** [æl'dʒi:ərɪən] *noun & adjective* argelino, -na

NOTE: capital: **Algiers** (= Argel); currency: **Algerian dinar (ALD)** = dinar argelino (DA)

all [ɔ:l] **1** *pronoun* todo, -da *or* todos, -das **2** *adjective* todo, -da; **all (of) the managers attended the meeting** = todos los directivos asistieron a la reunión; **the salesman should know the prices of all the products he is selling** = el vendedor debería saber los precios de todos los productos que vende

◊ **all-in** ['ɔ:l'ɪn] *adjective* global *or* todo incluido; **all-in price** *or* **rate** = precio todo incluido *or* precio total

allocate ['æləkeɪt] *verb* asignar; **we allocate 10% of revenue to publicity** = asignamos el 10% de los ingresos a la publicidad; **$2,500 was allocated to office furniture** = se asignaron $2.500 para comprar muebles de oficina

◊ **allocation** [ælə'keɪʃən] *noun* **(a)** *(money)* asignación *f*; **allocation of capital** = asignación de capital; **allocation of funds to a project** = asignación de fondos a un proyecto **(b)** **share allocation** *or* **allocation of shares** = asignación *or* atribución *f* de acciones

allot [ə'lɒt] *verb* asignar *or* repartir; **to allot shares** = asignar acciones (NOTE: **allotting - allotted**)

◊ **allotment** [ə'lɒtmənt] *noun* **(a)** *(sharing out)* asignación *f*; **allotment of funds to a project** = asignación de fondos a un proyecto **(b)** *(distribution of share issue)* reparto *m* or asignación *or* distribución *f*; **share allotment** = reparto *or* asignación *or* distribución de acciones; **payment in full on allotment** = pago total por reparto; **letter of allotment** *or* **allotment letter** = notificación de asignación de acciones

all-out ['ɔ:laʊt] *adjective* general *or* máximo, -ma; **the union called for an all-out strike** = el sindicato convocó una huelga general; **the personnel manager has launched an all-out campaign to get the staff to work on Friday afternoons** = el director de personal ha iniciado una campaña intensiva para que el personal trabaje los viernes por la tarde

allow [ə'laʊ] *verb* **(a)** *(permit)* permitir; **junior members of staff are not allowed to use the chairman's lift** = no se permite al personal subalterno la utilización del ascensor del presidente; **the company allows all members of staff to take six days' holiday at Christmas** = la compañía permite que todo el personal tome seis días de vacaciones en Navidades **(b)** *(give)* conceder *or* pagar; **to allow someone a discount** = conceder un descuento a alguien; **to allow 5% discount to members of staff** = conceder un 5% de descuento al personal; **to allow 10% interest on large sums of money** = pagar un 10% de interés sobre grandes cantidades de dinero **(c)** *(allow legally)* aceptar; **to allow a claim** *or* **an appeal** = aceptar una demanda *or* una apelación

◊ **allow for** [ə'laʊ 'fɔ:] *verb* descontar *or* dejar un margen *or* tener en cuenta; **to allow for money paid in advance** = descontar el dinero pagado por adelantado; **to allow 10% for packing** = dejar un margen de un 10% para embalaje; **delivery is not allowed for** = los gastos de entrega no están incluidos; **allow 28 days for delivery** = deje un margen de 28 días para la entrega

◊ **allowable** [ə'laʊəbl] *adjective* admisible *or*

permisible; **allowable deduction** = deducción admisible; **allowable expenses** = gastos deducibles

allowance [ə'laυəns] *noun* **(a)** *(concession or subsidy)* dotación *f or* dieta *f or* bonificación *f*; **travel allowance** *or* **travelling allowance** = dieta para gastos de viaje; **foreign currency allowance** = dotación de divisas; **cost-of-living allowance** = subsidio de carestía de vida *or* por aumento del coste de la vida; **entertainment allowance** = dietas para gastos de representación **(b)** *(tax discount)* exención *f or* desgravación *f*; **capital allowances** = amortización fiscal; **tax allowances** *or* **allowances against tax** = exenciones *or* desgravaciones fiscales; **personal allowances** = deducciones personales **(c)** *(deduction)* reserva *f or* deducción *f*; **allowance for depreciation** = cuota de depreciación; **allowance for exchange loss** = reserva para pérdidas en el cambio

◊ **allowed time** [ə'laυd 'taɪm] *noun* tiempo *m* permitido *or* permisible

> QUOTE most airlines give business class the same baggage allowance as first class
> **Business Traveller**

> QUOTE the compensation plan includes base, incentive and car allowance totalling $50,000+
> **Globe and Mail (Toronto)**

all-risks policy ['ɔ:lrɪsks 'pɒlɪsi] *noun* póliza *f* a todo riesgo

all-time ['ɔ:l'taɪm] *adjective* **all-time high** *or* **all-time low** = el punto máximo *or* mínimo alcanzado hasta el momento; **sales have fallen from their all-time high of last year** = las ventas han descendido desde el año pasado cuando alcanzron su más alto nivel registrado

alphabet ['ælfəbet] *noun* alfabeto *m*

◊ **alphabetical order** [ælfə'betɪkəl 'ɔ:də] *noun* orden *m* alfabético; **the files are arranged in alphabetical order** = los ficheros están clasificados por orden alfabético

◊ **alphanumeric(al)** [ælfənju:'meɪkl] *adjective* alfanumérico, -ca

alter ['ɒltə] *verb* cambiar; **to alter the terms of a contract** = cambiar las condiciones de un contrato

◊ **alteration** [ɒltə'reɪʃən] *noun* cambio *m*; **he made some alterations to the terms of a contract** = hizo algunos cambios en los términos de un contrato; **the agreement was signed without any alterations** = el acuerdo se firmó sin cambios

alternate director [ɒl'tɜ:nɪt dɪ'rektə] *noun* director, -ra suplente

alternative [ɒl'tɜ:nətɪv] **1** *noun* alternativa *f*; **what is the alternative to firing half the staff?** = ¿hay una alternativa que no sea despedir a la mitad del personal?; **we have no alternative** = no hay más remedio *or* no hay otra alternativa **2** *adjective* otro, -tra *or* alternativo, -va; **to find someone alternative employment** = encontrar otro empleo para alguien

altogether [ɒltə'geðə] *adverb* en conjunto *or* en total; **the staff of the three companies in the group come to 2,500 altogether** = el personal de las tres empresas del grupo en conjunto asciende a 2.500

empleados; **the company lost £2m last year and £4m this year, making £6m altogether for the two years** = la compañía perdió £2 millones el año pasado y £4 millones este año, lo que supone £6 millones en total en los dos años

a.m. *or US* **A.M.** ['eɪ'em] *adverb* de la mañana; **the flight leaves at 9.20 a.m.** = el vuelo sale a las 9.20 de la mañana; **telephone calls before 6 a.m. are charged at the cheap rate** = antes de las 6 de la mañana las llamadas telefónicas se cobran a tarifa reducida

amend [ə'mend] *verb* enmendar *or* rectificar; **please amend your copy of the contract accordingly** = rectifique su copia del contrato en consecuencia

◊ **amendment** [ə'men(d)mənt] *noun* enmienda *f*; **to propose an amendment to the constitution** = proponer una enmienda a la Constitución; **to make amendments to a contract** = hacer enmiendas a un contrato

American [ə'merɪkən] **1** *adjective* americano, -na; **the American dollar** = el dólar americano **2** *noun (inhabitant of the USA)* americano, -na *or* estadounidense

◊ **American Depositary Receipt (ADR)** [ə'merɪkən dɪ'pɒzɪtəri rɪ'si:t] *noun* certificados de depósito otorgados por bancos americanos

> COMMENT: these are documents issued by American banks to US citizens, making them unregistered shareholders of companies in foreign countries. Buying and selling ADRs is easier for American investors than buying or selling the actual shares themselves, as it avoids stamp duty and can be carried out in dollars without incurring exchange costs

Amex ['æmeks] *noun informal* = AMERICAN STOCK EXCHANGE; AMERICAN EXPRESS

amortize ['æmɔ:taɪz] *verb* amortizar; **the capital cost is amortized over five years** = el costo del capital se amortiza en cinco años

◊ **amortizable** [æmɔ:'taɪzəbəl] *adjective* amortizable; **the capital cost is amortizable over a period of ten years** = el costo del capital es amortizable a lo largo de un periodo de diez años

◊ **amortization** [əmɔ:taɪ'zeɪʃn] *noun* amortización *f*; **amortization of a debt** = amortización de una deuda

amount [ə'maυnt] **1** *noun (of money)* importe *m or* cantidad *f*; **amount paid** = importe pagado; **amount deducted** = importe deducido; **amount owing** = importe debido; **amount written off** = importe amortizado; **what is the amount outstanding?** = ¿cuál es el saldo a pagar?; **a small amount invested in gilt-edged stock** = una pequeña cantidad invertida en papel del Estado **2** *verb* **to amount to** = ascender a; **their debts amount to over £1m** = sus deudas ascienden a más de £1 millón

analog computer ['ænəlɒg kəm'pju:tə] *noun* ordenador *m* analógico

analyse *or* **analyze** ['ænəlaɪz] *verb* analizar; **to analyse a statement of account** = analizar un estado de cuentas; **to analyse the market potential** = analizar las posibilidades del mercado

◊ **analysis** [ə'næləsɪs] *noun* análisis *m*;

statistical analysis = análisis estadístico; **job analysis** = análisis de un puesto de trabajo; **market analysis** = análisis de mercado; **sales analysis** = análisis de ventas; **to carry out an analysis of the market potential** = realizar un análisis del potencial del mercado; **to write an analysis of the sales position** = llevar a cabo un análisis de la situación de las ventas; **cost analysis** = análisis de costes; **systems analysis** = análisis de sistemas (NOTE: plural is **analyses**)

◊ **analyst** ['ænəlɪst] *noun* analista *mf*; **market analyst** = analista de mercado; **systems analyst** = analista de sistemas

Andorra [æn'dɔːrə] *noun* Andorra *f*

◊ **Andorran** [æn'dɔːrən] *noun & adjective* andorrano, -na
NOTE: capital: **Andorra la Vella;** currency: **French franc (F), Spanish peseta (Ptas.)** = franco francés (F), peseta (pta.)

announce [ə'naʊns] *verb* anunciar *or* comunicar; **to announce the results for 1992** = comunicar los resultados para 1992; **to announce a programme of investment** = anunciar un programa de inversiones

◊ **announcement** [ə'naʊnsmənt] *noun* anuncio *m or* declaración *f*; **announcement of a cutback in expenditure** = anuncio de un recorte de gastos; **announcement of the appointment of a new managing director** = anuncio del nombramiento de un nuevo director gerente; **the managing director made an announcement to the staff** = el director gerente hizo una declaración al personal

annual ['ænjʊəl] *adjective* anual; **annual statement of income** = la declaración anual de renta; **he has six weeks' annual leave** = tiene seis semanas de vacaciones al año; **the annual accounts** = las cuentas anuales; **annual growth of 5%** = crecimiento anual del 5%; **annual report** = informe anual; **annual return** = memoria anual de la compañía; **on an annual basis** = anualmente; **the figures are revised on an annual basis** = las cifras se revisan anualmente

◊ **annual general meeting (AGM)** ['ænjʊəl 'dʒenərəl 'miːtɪŋ] *noun* junta *f* anual (NOTE: the US term is **annual meeting** or **annual stockholders' meeting**)

◊ **annualized** ['ænjʊəlaɪzd] *adjective* expresado, -da en base anual; **annualized percentage rate** = tipo de interés expresado en base anual *or* tasa de interés expresada en base anual

◊ **annually** ['ænjʊəli] *adverb* anualmente; **the figures are updated annually** = las cifras se actualizan anualmente

◊ **Annual Percentage Rate (APR)** ['ænjʊəl pə'sentɪdʒ 'reɪt] *noun* tasa de interés anual

QUOTE real wages have risen at an annual rate of only 1% in the last two years
Sunday Times

QUOTE the remuneration package will include an attractive salary, profit sharing and a company car together with four weeks annual holiday
Times

annuity [ə'njuːəti] *noun* anualidad *f or* pensión *f*;

he has a government annuity *or* an annuity from the government = recibe una pensión del Estado; **to buy** *or* **to take out an annuity** = comprar *or* suscribir una anualidad; **annuity for life** *or* **life annuity** = renta *or* anualidad vitalicia; **reversionary annuity** = anualidad reversible (NOTE: plural is **annuities**)

◊ **annuitant** [ə'njuːɪtənt] *noun* pensionista *mf or* rentista *mf*

annul [ə'nʌl] *verb* anular *or* rescindir; **the contract was annulled by the court** = el contrato fue anulado por el tribunal (NOTE: **annulling - annulled**)

◊ **annullable** [ə'nʌləbl] *adjective* rescindible

◊ **annulling** [ə'nʌlɪŋ] **1** *adjective* que anula; **annulling clause** = una cláusula anulativa **2** *noun* anulación *f or* rescisión *f*; **the annulling of a contract** = la anulación *or* rescisión de un contrato

◊ **annulment** [ə'nʌlmənt] *noun* anulación *f or* rescisión *f*; **annulment of a contract** = la anulación *or* rescisión de un contrato

answer ['ɑːnsə] **1** *noun* respuesta *f or* contestación *f*; **I am writing in answer to your letter of October 6th** = en respuesta a su carta del 6 de octubre; **my letter got no answer** *or* **there was no answer to my letter** = no recibí contestación a mi carta *or* no hubo contestación a mi carta; **I tried to phone his office but there was no answer** = intenté llamar a su oficina pero no me contestaron **2** *verb* responder *or* contestar; **to answer a letter** = contestar a una carta; **to answer the telephone** = contestar el teléfono

◊ **answering machine** ['ɑːnsərɪŋ mə'ʃiːn] *noun* contestador *m* automático

◊ **answering service** ['ɑːnsərɪŋ 'sɜːvɪs] *noun* servicio *m* de contestación

◊ **answerphone** ['ɑːnsəfəʊn] *noun* contestador (automático); **he wasn't in when I called so I left a message on his answerphone** = cuando llamé no estaba y por eso dejé un mensaje en el contestador

antedate ['æntɪdeɪt] *verb* antedatar *or* retrotraer; **the invoice was antedated to January 1st** = se fechó la factura con efecto retroactivo al 1 de enero

anti- ['ænti] *prefix* anti-

◊ **anti-dumping** [ænti'dʌmpɪŋ] *adjective* 'antidumping'; **anti-dumping legislation** = legislación antidumping

◊ **anti-inflationary** [æntɪn'fleɪʃnəri] *adjective* antiinflacionario, -ria *or* antiinflacionista; **anti-inflationary measures** = medidas antiinflacionarias

◊ **anti-trust** [æntɪ'trʌst] *adjective* antimonopolista; **anti-trust laws** *or* **legislation** = ley *or* legislación antimonopolista

anticipate ['æntɪsɪpeɪt] *verb* anticipar *or* prever

any other business (AOB) ['eni 'ʌðə 'bɪznəs] *noun (item at the end of an agenda)* ruegos y preguntas

AOB ['eɪəʊ'biː] = ANY OTHER BUSINESS

aperture ['æpətjʊə] *noun* abertura *f*; **aperture envelope** = sobre con ventanilla

apologize [ə'pɒlədʒaɪz] *verb* disculparse *or* presentar excusas; **to apologize for the delay in answering** = disculparse por la demora en contestar;

she apologized for being late = presentó sus excusas por llegar tarde

◊ **apology** [ə'pɒlədʒi] *noun* disculpa *f or* excusa *f*; **to write a letter of apology** = escribir una carta de disculpa; **I enclose a cheque for £10 with apologies for the delay in answering your letter** = adjunto un cheque de £10 rogando me disculpe la demora en contestarle

appeal [ə'pi:l] **1** *noun* **(a)** *(attraction)* atractivo *m or* interés *m*; **customer appeal** = atractivo para los clientes; **sales appeal** = atracción comercial (NOTE: no plural for this meaning) **(b)** *(against a decision)* apelación *f*; **the appeal against the planning decision will be heard next month** = la apelación en contra de la decisión de planificación será examinada durante el mes próximo; **he lost his appeal for damages against the company** = perdió la apelación por daños y perjuicios contra la compañía; **she won her case on appeal** = ganó la causa en apelación; **Appeal Court** *or* **Court of Appeal** = Tribunal de Apelación **2** *verb* **(a)** *(attract)* atraer *or* interesar; **this CD appeals to the under-25 market** = este compact atrae a los menores de 25 años; **the idea of working in Australia for six months appealed to her** = le sedujo la idea de trabajar seis meses en Australia **(b)** *(against a decision)* apelar; **the company appealed against the decision of the planning officers** = la empresa apeló contra la decisión de los planificadores (NOTE: you appeal **to** a court or a person **against** a decision)

appear [ə'pɪə] *verb* parecer; **the company appeared to be doing well** = la empresa parecía estar en buena situación; **the managing director appears to be in control** = el director gerente parece dominar la situación

appendix [ə'pendɪks] *noun* anexo *m* apéndice *m*

apply [ə'plaɪ] *verb* **(a)** *(ask for)* solicitar; **to apply for a job** = solicitar un trabajo; **to apply for shares** = solicitar acciones; **to apply in writing** = solicitar por escrito; **to apply in person** = solicitar personalmente **(b)** *(affect)* referirse; **this clause applies only to deals outside the EU** = esta cláusula se refiere solamente a las transacciones fuera de la UE

◊ **applicant** ['æplɪkənt] *noun* solicitante *mf or* candidato, -ta; **applicant for a job** *or* **job applicant** = candidato a un puesto de trabajo; **there were thousands of applicants for shares in the new company** = miles de personas solicitaron acciones de la nueva compañía

◊ **application** [æplɪ'keɪʃən] *noun* solicitud *f*; **application for shares** = solicitud de acciones; **shares payable on application** = acciones pagaderas al ser solicitadas; **attach the cheque to the share application form** = adjuntar el cheque al formulario de solicitud de acciones; **application for a job** *or* **job application** = solicitud de trabajo; **application form** = impreso *or* formulario de solicitud; **to fill in an application (form) for a job** *or* **a job application (form)** = rellenar un formulario *or* impreso de solicitud; **letter of application** = carta de solicitud

appoint [ə'pɔɪnt] *verb* nombrar; **to appoint James Smith (to the post of) manager** = nombrar director a James Smith; **we have appointed a new distribution manager** = hemos nombrado un nuevo

director de distribución (NOTE: you appoint a person **to** a job)

◊ **appointee** [əpɔɪn'ti:] *noun* persona *f* nombrada

◊ **appointment** [ə'pɔɪntmənt] *noun* **(a)** *(meeting)* cita *f or* compromiso *m*; **to make** *or* **to fix an appointment for two o'clock** = concertar una cita a las dos; **to make an appointment with someone for two o'clock** = citarse con alguien a las dos; **he was late for his appointment** = llegó tarde a la cita; **she had to cancel her appointment** = tuvo que cancelar la cita; **appointments book** = agenda **(b)** *(to a job)* nombramiento *m*; **on his appointment as manager** = cuando le nombraron director; **letter of appointment** = notificación del nombramiento para un puesto *m*; empleo *m*; **staff appointment** = empleo fijo *or* permanente; **appointments vacant** = ofertas de trabajo

apportion [ə'pɔ:ʃən] *verb* asignar *or* prorratear *or* repartir proporcionalmente; **costs are apportioned according to projected revenue** = los costes se prorratean de acuerdo con los ingresos previstos

◊ **apportionment** [ə'pɔ:ʃənmənt] *noun* asignación *f or* prorrateo *m or* reparto *m* proporcional *or* distribución *f*; **apportionment of appropriations** = distribución de los créditos; **apportionment of markets** = reparto de los mercados

appraise [ə'preɪz] *verb* evaluar

◊ **appraisal** [ə'preɪzəl] *noun* valoración *f or* evaluación *f*; **staff appraisals** = valoración del personal

QUOTE we are now reaching a stage in industry and commerce where appraisals are becoming part of the management culture. Most managers now take it for granted that they will appraise and be appraised

Personnel Management

appreciate [ə'pri:ʃɪeɪt] *verb* **(a)** *(how good something is)* apreciar *or* agradecer *or* gustar; **the customer always appreciates efficient service** = el cliente siempre agradece el buen servicio; **tourists do not appreciate long delays at banks** = a los turistas no les gusta que les hagan esperar mucho tiempo en los bancos **(b)** *(increase in value)* subir (de precio) *or* aumentar (en valor); **the dollar has appreciated in terms of the yen** = el dólar ha subido en relación al yen; **these shares have appreciated by 5%** = estas acciones han subido un 5%

◊ **appreciation** [əpri:ʃɪ'eɪʃən] *noun* **(a)** *(increase)* subida *f or* revaluación *f or* apreciación *f*; **these shares show an appreciation of 10%** = estas acciones han experimentado una subida del 10%; **the appreciation of the dollar against the peseta** = la subida del dólar en relación a la peseta **(b)** *(valuing)* aprecio *m or* estimación *f or* reconocimiento *m or* valoración *f*; **he was given a rise in appreciation of his excellent work** = le aumentaron el sueldo en reconocimiento de su excelente trabajo

QUOTE faced with further appreciation of the yen, Japanese executives are accelerating their efforts to increase efficiency

Nikkei Weekly

apprentice [ə'prentɪs] **1** *noun* aprendiz, -za **2** *verb* **to be apprenticed to someone** = ser aprendiz de alguien

◊ **apprenticeship** [ə'prentɪsʃɪp] *noun* aprendizaje *m*; **he served a six-year apprenticeship in the steel works** = realizó un aprendizaje de seis años en la acería

appro ['æprəʊ] *noun* = APPROVAL **to buy something on appro** = comprar algo a prueba

approach [ə'prəʊtʃ] **1** *noun* propuesta *f or* gestión *f*; **the company made an approach to the supermarket chain** = la empresa hizo una propuesta a la cadena de supermercados; **the board turned down all approaches on the subject of mergers** = el consejo de administración rechazó todas las propuestas de fusión; **we have had an approach from a Japanese company to buy our car division** = hemos recibido de una empresa japonesa una propuesta de compra de nuestra sección de automóviles **2** *verb* **(a)** *(propose)* dirigirse *or* hacer una propuesta; **he approached the bank with a request for a loan** = se dirigió al banco para pedir un préstamo; **the company was approached by an American publisher with the suggestion of a merger** = la compañía recibió una propuesta de fusión de una editorial norteamericana; **we have been approached several times but have turned down all offers** = hemos recibido varias propuestas pero las hemos rechazado todas **(b)** *(get nearer)* acercar *or* acercarse

appropriate [ə'prəʊprɪeɪt] **1** *adjective* apropiado, -da **2** *verb* asignar *or* consignar; **to appropriate a sum of money for a capital project** = asignar fondos a un proyecto de inversión

◊ **appropriation** [əprəʊprɪ'eɪʃən] *noun* asignación *f or* consignación *f*; **appropriation of funds to the reserve** = asignación de fondos a las reservas; **appropriation account** = cuenta de asignación

approve [ə'pruːv] *verb* **(a) to approve of** = aprobar; **the chairman approves of the new company letter heading** = el presidente aprueba el nuevo membrete de la compañía; **the sales staff do not approve of interference from the accounts division** = al personal de ventas no le parece bien la ingerencia del departamento de contabilidad **(b)** *(formally agree to)* aprobar; **to approve the terms of a contract** = aprobar los términos de un contrato; **the proposal was approved by the board** = la propuesta fue aprobada por el consejo de administración

◊ **approval** [ə'pruːvəl] *noun* **(a)** aprobación *f*; **to submit a budget for approval** = presentar un presupuesto para su aprobación; **certificate of approval** = certificado de aprobación **(b) on approval** = a prueba; **to buy a photocopier on approval** = comprar una fotocopiadora a prueba

approximate [ə'prɒksɪmət] *adjective* aproximado, -da; **the sales division has made an approximate forecast of expenditure** = la sección de ventas ha hecho una previsión aproximada de los gastos

◊ **approximately** [ə'prɒksɪmətli] *adverb* aproximadamente; **expenditure is approximately 10% down on the previous quarter** = los gastos son aproximadamente un 10% inferiores a los del trimestre anterior

◊ **approximation** [əprɒksɪ'meɪʃən] *noun* aproximación *f*; **approximation of expenditure** = aproximación de los gastos; **the final figure is only an approximation** = la cifra final no es más que una aproximación

APR = ANNUAL PERCENTAGE RATE

aptitude ['æptɪtjuːd] *noun* aptitud *f or* capacidad *f*; **aptitude test** = prueba de aptitud

arbitrage ['ɑːbɪtreɪdʒ] *noun* **(a)** *(foreign currency)* arbitraje *m* **(b)** *(shares)* **risk arbitrage** = arbitraje de riesgos; **arbitrage syndicate** = sindicato de arbitraje

◊ **arbitrager** *or* **arbitrageur** ['ɑːbɪtreɪdʒə *or* ɑːbɪtrɑ:'ʒɜ:] *noun* negociante *mf* de arbitraje

COMMENT: arbitrageurs buy shares in companies which are potential takeover targets, either to force up the price of the shares before the takeover bid, or simply as a position while waiting for the takeover bid to take place. They also sell shares in the company which is expected to make the takeover bid, since one of the consequences of a takeover bid is usually that the price of the target company rises while that of the bidding company falls. Arbitrageurs may then sell the shares in the target company at a profit, either to one of the parties making the takeover bid, or back to the company itself

arbitrate ['ɑːbɪtreɪt] *verb* arbitrar; **to arbitrate in a dispute** = arbitrar en un conflicto *or* en una disputa

◊ **arbitration** [ɑːbɪ'treɪʃən] *noun* arbitraje *m*; **to submit a dispute to arbitration** = someter un conflicto a arbitraje; **to refer a question to arbitration** = remitir un asunto a arbitraje; **to take a dispute to arbitration** = confiar un conflicto a arbitraje; **to go to arbitration** = recurrir al arbitraje; **arbitration board** *or* **arbitration tribunal** = comisión de arbitraje *or* tribunal de arbitraje; **industrial arbitration tribunal** = tribunal de arbitraje laboral; **to accept the ruling of the arbitration board** = aceptar la decisión de la comisión de arbitraje

◊ **arbitrator** ['ɑːbɪtreɪtə] *noun* árbitro *mf*; **industrial arbitrator** = árbitro laboral; **to accept** *or* **to reject the arbitrator's ruling** = aceptar *or* rechazar la decisión del árbitro

arcade [ɑː'keɪd] *noun* pórtico *m or* pasaje *m*; **shopping arcade** = galería *or* pasaje comercial

archives ['ɑːkaɪvz] *noun* archivos *mpl*; **the company's archives go back to its foundation in 1892** = los archivos de la compañía se remontan al año de su fundación en 1892; **archive box** = archivo

area ['eərɪə] *noun* **(a)** *(surface)* área *f or* superficie *f*; **the area of this office is 3,400 square feet** = la superficie de esta oficina es de 1.000 metros cuadrados; **we are looking for a shop with a sales area of about 100 square metres** = buscamos una tienda con un área de ventas de unos 100 metros cuadrados **(b)** *(geographical)* región *f or* zona *f or* área *f*; **Economic European Area (EEA)** = Espacio

Económico Europeo; **free trade area** = área de libre comercio; **dollar area** *or* **sterling area** = área del dolar *or* área de la libra esterlina **(c)** *(subject)* asunto *m or* campo *m or* ámbito *m*; **a problem area** *or* **an area for concern** = un asunto problemático *or* un asunto preocupante **(d)** *(part of town or country)* distrito *m or* zona *f*; **the office is in the commercial area of the town** = la oficina está en el distrito comercial de la ciudad; **their factory is in a very good area for getting to the motorways and airports** = su fábrica está en una zona de fácil acceso a las autopistas y a los aeropuertos **(e)** *(of a representative)* región *f or* zona *f*; **his sales area is the North-West** = su zona comercial es el Noroeste; **he finds it difficult to cover all his area in a week** = le resulta difícil recorrer toda su región en una semana

◊ **area code** ['eərɪə 'kəʊd] *noun* prefijo *m or* indicativo *m*; **the area code for central London is 0171** = el prefijo del área central de Londres es el 0171

◊ **area manager** ['eərɪə 'mænɪdʒə] *noun* director, -ra *or* gerente *mf* regional

Argentina [ɑːdʒən'tiːnə] *noun* Argentina *f*

◊ **Argentine** *or* **Argentinian** ['ɑːdʒəntaɪn *or* ɑːdʒən'tɪnjən] *adjective & noun* argentino, -na NOTE: capital: **Buenos Aires**; currency: **Argentinian peso** = peso argentino

argue ['ɑːgjuː] *verb* discutir *or* polemizar; **they argued over** *or* **about the price** = discutieron sobre el precio; **we spent hours arguing with the managing director about the site for the new factory** = pasamos horas discutiendo con el director gerente sobre el emplazamiento de la nueva fábrica; **the union officials argued among themselves over the best way to deal with the ultimatum from the management** = los cargos sindicales discutieron entre ellos sobre la mejor manera de responder al ultimátum de la dirección (NOTE: you argue **with** someone **about** *or* **over** something)

◊ **argument** ['ɑːgjʊmənt] *noun* discusión *f*; **they got into an argument with the customs officials over the documents** = se enzarzaron en una discusión sobre los documentos con los aduaneros; **he was sacked after an argument with the managing director** = le despidieron tras una discusión con el director gerente

around [ə'raʊnd] *preposition* alrededor de *or* aproximadamente; **the office costs around £2,000 a year to heat** = el costo de calefacción de la oficina es de unas £2.000 al año; **his salary is around $85,000** = su sueldo es de aproximadamente $85.000

arr. = ARRIVAL

arrange [ə'reɪn(d)ʒ] *verb* **(a)** *(put in order)* ordenar *or* disponer *or* acomodar; **the office is arranged as an open-plan area with small separate rooms for meetings** = la oficina está dispuesta en un espacio abierto con unas salas pequeñas aparte para reuniones; **the files are arranged in alphabetical order** = los archivos están ordenados en orden alfabético; **arrange the invoices in order of their dates** = ordene las facturas por orden de fecha **(b)** *(organize)* organizar *or* concertar; **we arranged to have the meeting in their offices** = concertamos una reunión en sus oficinas; **she arranged for a car to meet him at the**

airport = ella organizó un coche para que le recogiera en el aeropuerto (NOTE: you arrange **for** someone to do something; you arrange **for** something to be done or you arrange **to** do something)

◊ **arrangement** [ə'reɪn(d)ʒmənt] *noun* **(a)** *(organized)* plan *m* preparativos *mpl*; **the company secretary is making all the arrangements for the AGM** = la secretaria de la compañía está haciendo los preparativos para la junta general anual; **arrangement fee** = gastos bancarios de transacciones crediticias **(b)** *(financial settlement)* acuerdo *m or* acomodo *m*; **to come to an arrangement with the creditors** = llegar a un acuerdo con los acreedores; **scheme of arrangement** = arreglo *m* acuerdo *m*

> QUOTE on the upside scenario the outlook is reasonably optimistic, bankers say, the worst scenario being that a scheme of arrangement cannot be achieved, resulting in liquidation
> **Irish Times**

arrears [ə'rɪəz] *plural noun* atrasos *mpl or* vencidos *mpl*; **arrears of interest** = intereses atrasados; **to allow the payments to fall into arrears** = atrasarse en los pagos; **salary with arrears effective from January 1st** = salario y atrasos efectivos a partir del 1 de enero; **in arrears** = atrasado; **the payments are six months in arrears** = los pagos tienen seis meses de atraso; **he is six weeks in arrears with his rent** = lleva seis meses de atraso en el pago del alquiler

arrest [ə'rest] *verb* detener; **our agent has been arrested** = nuestro representante ha sido detenido

arrive [ə'raɪv] *verb* **(a)** llegar; **the consignment has still not arrived** = el envío todavía no ha llegado; **the shipment arrived without any documentation** = el envío llegó sin documentación alguna; **the plane arrives in Sydney at 04.00** = el avión llega a Sydney a las 4.00 de la madrugada; **the train leaves Madrid at 09.20 and arrives at Seville two hours later** = el tren sale de Madrid a las 9.20 de la mañana y llega a Sevilla dos horas después (NOTE: you arrive **at** *or* **in** a place or town, but only **in** a country) **(b)** **to arrive at** = convenir *or* llegar a; **to arrive at a price** = convenir un precio; **after some discussion we arrived at a compromise** = después de un debate llegamos a un compromiso

◊ **arrival** [ə'raɪvəl] *noun* llegada *f*; **we are waiting for the arrival of a consignment of spare parts** = esperamos la llegada de un envío de repuestos; **'to await arrival'** = esperar la llegada; *(in an airport)* **arrivals** = llegadas

article ['ɑːtɪkl] *noun* **(a)** *(for sale)* artículo *m or* producto *m*; **to launch a new article on the market** = lanzar un nuevo producto al mercado; **a black market in luxury articles** = un mercado negro en artículos de lujo **(b)** *(in a legal document)* cláusula *f*; **see article 8 of the contract** = véase el artículo 8 del contrato **(c)** *(document)* **articles of association** = estatutos *mpl* (de asociación) *or* escritura *f* de constitución (NOTE: in the US, called **bylaws**) *US* **articles of incorporation** = estatutos *mpl* (de asociación) *or* escritura *f* de constitución (NOTE: in the UK called **Memorandum of Association**) **director appointed under the articles of the company** = consejero nombrado conforme a los estatutos de la sociedad; **this procedure is not**

allowed under the articles of association of the company = este procedimiento no está permitido por los estatutos de la compañía **(d)** *(of a solicitor)* articles = periodo de prácticas

◊ **articled clerk** ['ɑːtɪkld 'klɑːk] *adjective* pasante *mf* de abogado

articulated lorry *or* **articulated vehicle** [ɑː'tɪkjʊleɪtɪd 'lɒrɪ *or* ɑː'tɪkjʊleɪtɪd 'viːɪkl] *noun* camión *m* con remolque

asap ['æsæp] = AS SOON AS POSSIBLE

aside [ə'saɪd] *adverb* aparte; **to put aside** *or* **to set aside** = ahorrar; **he is putting £50 aside each week to pay for his car** = ahorra £50 cada semana para comprarse un coche

ask [ɑːsk] *verb* **(a)** *(question)* preguntar *or* pedir; **he asked the information office for details of companies exhibiting at the motor show** = pidió en la oficina de información los detalles de las empresas que exponían en el salón del automóvil; **ask the salesgirl if the bill includes VAT** = pregúntale a la vendedora si la factura incluye el IVA **(b)** *(order or request)* pedir; **he asked the switchboard operator to get him a number in Germany** = pidió a la telefonista que le pusiera con un número de Alemania; **she asked her secretary to fetch a file from the managing director's office** = le pidió a su secretario que trajese un archivo de la oficina del director gerente; **the customs officials asked him to open his case** = los aduaneros le pidieron que abriera la maleta

◊ **ask for** ['ɑːsk 'fɔː] *verb* **(a)** *(request)* solicitar *or* pedir *or* preguntar por; **he asked for the file on 1996 debtors** = solicitó el archivo de los deudores del (año) 1996; **they asked for more time to repay the loan** = pidieron más tiempo para reembolsar el préstamo; **there is a man in reception asking for Mr Smith** = hay un hombre en la recepción que pregunta por el señor Smith **(b)** *(as a price)* pedir; **they are asking £24,000 for the car** = piden £24.000 por el coche

◊ **asking price** ['ɑːskɪŋ 'praɪs] *noun* precio *m* anunciado *or* de oferta; **the asking price is £24,000** = se piden £24.000

assay mark [ə'seɪ 'mɑːk] *noun (on gold or silver)* sello *m* de contraste *or* marca *f* de ensaye

assemble [ə'sembl] *verb* **(a)** *(put together)* montar; **the engines are made in Japan and the bodies in Scotland, and the cars are assembled in France** = los motores se fabrican en el Japón, la carrocería en Escocia y los coches se montan en Francia **(b)** *(come together)* reunirse

◊ **assembly** [ə'sembli] *noun* **(a)** *(putting together)* ensamblaje *m or* montaje *m*; **there are no assembly instructions to show you how to put the computer together** = no hay instrucciones de montaje para el ordenador **(b)** *(meeting)* asamblea *f or* reunión *f*; **assembly hall** = salón de actos (NOTE: plural for (b) is **assemblies**)

◊ **assembly line** [ə'sembli 'laɪn] *noun* línea *f* or cadena *f* de montaje; **he works on an assembly line** *or* **he is an assembly line worker** = trabaja en una cadena de montaje *or* es obrero en una cadena de montaje

assess [ə'ses] *verb* fijar *or* valorar; **to assess damages at £1,000** = fijar los daños en £1.000; **to assess a property for the purposes of insurance** = valorar una propiedad a efectos del seguro

◊ **assessment** [ə'sesmənt] *noun* valoración *f*; **assessment of damages** = valoración *or* determinación de daños; **assessment of property** = valoración de propiedad; **tax assessment** = cálculo *m* de la base impositiva; **staff assessments** = evaluación *f* de personal

asset ['æset] *noun* activo *m*; **assets and liabilities** = activo y pasivo; **he has an excess of assets over liabilities** = su activo supera al pasivo; **her assets are only £640 as against liabilities of £24,000** = tiene solamente un activo de £640 frente a un pasivo de £24.000; *(property or machinery which a company owns and uses in its business)* **capital assets** *or* **fixed assets** = activo fijo; *(assets used by a company in its ordinary work)* **current assets** = activo circulante; **financial asset** = activo financiero; **frozen assets** = activo congelado; **intangible assets** = activo inmaterial *or* intangible; **liquid assets** = activo líquido; **personal assets** = bienes *mpl* personales; **tangible assets** = activo tangible; **tangible (fixed) assets** = activo (fijo) tangible; **asset stripper** = persona que compra una compañía para realizar el activo; **asset stripping** = liquidación de activos; **asset value** = valor de activo

assign [ə'saɪn] *verb* **(a)** *(to give legally)* asignar *or* adjudicar; **to assign a right to someone** = adjudicar un derecho a alguien; **to assign shares to someone** = asignar acciones a alguien **(b)** *(to give a job)* asignar *or* nombrar; **he was assigned the job of checking the sales figures** = le asignaron la tarea de revisar las cifras de ventas

◊ **assignation** [æsɪg'neɪʃən] *noun* cesión *f or* asignación *f*; **assignation of shares to someone** = asignación de accciones a alguien; **assignation of a patent** = cesión de una patente

◊ **assignee** [æsaɪ'niː] *noun* cesionario, -ria

◊ **assignment** [ə'saɪnmənt] *noun* **(a)** *(property)* traspaso *m* de bienes *or* cesión *f or* transmisión *f* *(salary)* asignación *f*; **assignment of a patent** *or* **of a copyright** = transmisión de una patente *or* propiedad intelectual; **to sign a deed of assignment** = firmar una escritura de cesión **(b)** *(task)* tarea *f or* misión *f*; **he was appointed managing director with the assignment to improve the company's profits** = fue nombrado director gerente con la tarea de aumentar la rentabilidad de la empresa; **the oil team is on an assignment in the North Sea** = el equipo petrolífero está de misión en el Mar del Norte

◊ **assignor** [æsaɪ'nɔː] *noun* cedente *mf*

assist [ə'sɪst] *verb* ayudar *or* asistir; **can you assist the stock controller in counting the stock?** = ¿puede Vd. ayudar al controlador de existencias a hacer un inventario?; **he assists me with my income tax returns** = él me ayuda a hacer la declaración de la renta (NOTE: you assist someone **in doing** something **or with** something)

◊ **assistance** [ə'sɪstəns] *noun* ayuda *f or*

asistencia *f*; **clerical assistance** = ayuda en la oficina; **financial assistance** = ayuda financiera; **medical assistance** = asistencia médica

◊ **assistant** [ə'sɪstənt] *noun* ayudante *mf or* auxiliar *mf or* asistente, -ta; **personal assistant** = ayudante personal; **shop assistant** = vendedor, -ra *or* dependiente *or* -ta; **assistant manager** = subdirector, -ra

associate [ə'səʊsɪət] **1** *adjective* asociado, -da *or* afiliado, -da; **associate company** = compañía afiliada; **associate director** = director adjunto **2** *noun* socio, -cia *or* colega (de trabajo); **she is a business associate of mine** = es una colega

◊ **associated** [ə'səʊsɪeɪtɪd] *adjective* asociado, -da *or* afiliado, -da; **associated company** = compañía afiliada; **Smith Ltd and its associated company, Jones Brothers** = Smith Ltd y su compañía afiliada, Jones Brothers

◊ **association** [əsəʊsɪ'eɪʃən] *noun* **(a)** *(group of people or companies)* asociación *f or* agrupación *f*; **trade association** = agrupación sectorial *or* asociación de comerciantes y empresarios; **employers' association** = asociación patronal; **manufacturers' association** = asociación de fabricantes; **association advertising** = publicidad colectiva **(b)** *(rules of a company)* **articles of association** = escritura de constitución *or* estatutos (de asociación); **Memorandum of Association** = estatutos *mpl* (de asociación) *or* escritura *f* de constitución (NOTE: in the USA, called **articles of incorporation**)

assume [ə'sjuːm] *verb* **(a)** *(suppose)* suponer; **assuming that** = suponiendo que *or* en el supuesto de que **(b)** *(take on)* asumir; **to assume all risks** = asumir todos los riesgos; **he has assumed responsibility for marketing** = ha asumido la responsabilidad de la comercialización

◊ **assumption** [ə'sʌm(p)ʃən] *noun* **(a)** *(supposition)* supuesto *m or* suposición *f or* presunción *f*; **we have to go on the assumption that sales will not double next year** = tenemos que partir del supuesto de que las ventas no se duplicarán el año que viene **(b)** *(taking on)* asunción *f*; **assumption of risks** = asunción de riesgos

assure [ə'ʃʊə] *verb* asegurar; **to assure someone's life** = asegurar la vida de alguien; **he has paid the premiums to have his wife's life assured** = ha pagado las primas para asegurar la vida de su esposa; **the life assured** = la vida asegurada

◊ **assurance** [ə'ʃʊərəns] *noun* seguro *m*; **assurance company** = compañía de seguros; **assurance policy** = póliza de seguros; **life assurance** = seguro de vida

◊ **assurer** *or* **assuror** [ə'ʃʊərə] *noun* asegurador *m or* compañía *f* aseguradora (NOTE: **assure** and **assurance** are used in Britain for insurance policies relating to something which will certainly happen (such as death) for other types of policy use **insure** and **insurance**)

at best ['æt 'best] *phrase* **sell at best** = vender al mejor precio posible

at par ['æt 'pɑː] *phrase* **shares at par** = acciones a la par

ATM ['eɪtiː'em] *noun* = AUTOMATED TELLER MACHINE cajero automático

atmosphere ['ætməsfɪːə] *noun* ambiente *m*; **she changed jobs because she didn't like the atmosphere in the office** = cambió de trabajo porque no le gustaba el ambiente de la oficina

atrium ['eɪtrɪəm] *noun* atrio *m*

at sight ['æt 'saɪt] *phrase* a la vista; **bill payable at sight** = letra pagadera a la vista

attach [ə'tætʃ] *verb* adjuntar *or* sujetar *or* pegar *or* acompañar; **I am attaching a copy of my previous letter** = adjunto copia de mi carta anterior; **please find attached a copy of my letter of June 24th** = adjunto a la presente copia de mi carta del 24 de junio; **the machine is attached to the floor so it cannot be moved** = la máquina está sujeta al suelo para que no pueda desplazarse; **the bank attaches great importance to the deal** = el banco concede mucha importancia a la transacción

◊ **attaché** [ə'tæʃeɪ] *noun* agregado, -da; **commercial attaché** = agregado comercial; **attaché case** = maletín *m*

◊ **attachment** [ə'tætʃmənt] *noun* **(a)** *(action)* embargo *m or* incautación *f or* decomiso *m*; **attachment of earnings** = secuestro judicial de salario **(b)** *(document)* documento *m* adjunto

attack [ə'tæk] *verb* atacar

attempt [ə'tem(p)t] **1** *noun* tentativa *f or* intento *m*; **the company made an attempt to break into the American market** = la empresa realizó un intento para introducirse en el mercado norteamericano; **the takeover attempt was turned down by the board** = la tentativa de adquisición fue rechazada por el consejo de administración; **all his attempts to get a job have failed** = todos sus intentos por conseguir trabajo han fracasado **2** *verb* intentar *or* tratar; **the company is attempting to get into the tourist market** = la empresa está intentando introducirse en el mercado turístico; **we are attempting the takeover of a manufacturing company** = estamos tratando de adquirir una empresa manufacturera; **he attempted to have the sales director sacked** = intentó conseguir que el director de ventas fuera despedido

attend [ə'tend] *verb* asistir; **the chairman has asked all managers to attend the meeting** = el presidente ha pedido que todos los consejeros asistan a la reunión; **none of the shareholders attended the AGM** = ningún accionista asistió a la junta general anual

◊ **attendance** [ə'tendəns] *noun* asistencia *f*

◊ **attend to** [ə'tend 'tuː] *verb* prestar atención *or* ocuparse de; **the managing director will attend to your complaint personally** el director gerente se ocupará personalmente de su queja; **we have brought in experts to attend to the problem of installing the new computer** = hemos contratado a expertos para que se ocupen del problema de la instalación del nuevo ordenador

◊ **attention** [ə'tenʃən] *noun* atención *f*; **your orders will have our best attention** = sus pedidos recibirán nuestra máxima atención; *(written on a letter to show that a certain person must see it)* **for the attention of (attn** *or* **fao)** = a la atención de; **for the attention of the Managing Director** = a la atención del director gerente; **attention: Mr Smith** = a la atención de Mr. Smith

attitude ['ætɪtjuːd] *noun* actitud *f*

attorney [ə'tɜːni] *noun* **(a)** apoderado, -da *or* procurador, -ra; **power of attorney** = poder notarial; **his solicitor was granted power of attorney** = su abogado recibió poder notarial **(b)** *US* abogado, -da

attract [ə'trækt] *verb* atraer; **the company is offering free holidays in Spain to attract buyers** = la empresa ofrece vacaciones gratuitas en España para atraer clientes; **we have difficulty in attracting skilled staff to this part of the country** = tenemos dificultades para atraer personal cualificado a esta parte del país; **the deposits attract interest at 15%** = los depósitos atraen intereses del 15%

◊ **attractive** [ə'træktɪv] *adjective* atractivo, -va; **attractive prices** = precios interesantes; **attractive salary** = salario interesante

QUOTE airlines offer special stopover rates and hotel packages to attract customers and to encourage customer loyalty
Business Traveller

attribute [ə'trɪbjʊt] *verb* atribuir

◊ **attributable profits** [ə'trɪbjʊtəbl 'prɒfɪts] *noun* beneficios imputables

auction ['ɔːkʃən] **1** *noun* subasta *f*; **sale by auction** = venta en subasta; **auction rooms** = sala de subastas; **to sell goods by auction** *or* **at auction** = subastar; **to put something up for auction** = subastar *or* sacar a subasta; **Dutch auction** = subasta a la baja; **auction by tender** subasta por licitación *or* concurso subasta **2** *verb* vender en subasta; **the factory was closed and the machinery was auctioned off** = cerraron la fábrica y vendieron la maquinaria en pública subasta

◊ **auctioneer** [ɔːkʃə'nɪə] *noun* subastador, -ra

audio-typing ['ɔːdɪəʊ'taɪpɪŋ] *noun* mecanografía *f* de dictado

◊ **audio-typist** ['ɔːdɪəʊ'taɪpɪst] *noun* mecanógrafo, -fa de dictado

audit ['ɔːdɪt] **1** *noun* auditoría *f* *or* censura *f* *or* intervención *f* *or* revisión *f* de cuentas; **to carry out the annual audit** = realizar la auditoría anual; **external audit** *or* **independent audit** = auditoría externa *or* independiente; **internal audit** = auditoría interna; **he is the manager of the internal audit department** = es el director del departamento de auditoría interna **2** *verb* auditar *or* revisar las cuentas *or* realizar una auditoría; **to audit the accounts** = revisar las cuentas; **the books have not yet been audited** = las cuentas no han sido revisadas todavía

◊ **auditing** ['ɔːdɪtɪŋ] *noun* auditoría *f*

◊ **auditor** ['ɔːdɪtə] *noun* auditor, -ra *or* censor, -ra de cuentas *or* interventor, -ra de cuentas; **the AGM appoints the company's auditors** = la junta general anual nombra a los auditores de la compañía; **Court of Auditors (EU)** = Tribunal de Cuentas (UE); **external auditor** = auditor externo; **internal auditor** = auditor interno; **auditors' report** = informe de los auditores

COMMENT: auditors are appointed by the company's directors and voted by the AGM. In the USA, audited accounts are only required by corporations which are registered with the SEC, but in the UK all limited companies with a turnover over a certain limit must provide audited annual accounts. After examining the accounts, the auditors write their report; if they are satisfied, the report certifies that, in their opinion, the accounts give a 'true and fair' view of the company's financial position

augment [ɔːg'ment] *verb* acrecentar

Australia [ɒs'treɪlɪə] *noun* Australia *f*

◊ **Australian** [ɒs'treɪlɪən] *adjective & noun* australiano, -na
NOTE: capital: **Canberra;** currency: **Australian dollar (A$)** = dólar australiano ($A)

Austria ['ɒstrɪə] *noun* Austria *f*

◊ **Austrian** ['ɒstrɪən] *adjective & noun* austriaco, -ca
NOTE: capital: **Vienna** (= Viena); currency: **Austrian schilling (S)** = chelín austriaco (S)

authenticate [ɔː'θentɪkeɪt] *verb* **(a)** *(document)* autentificar *or* legalizar **(b)** *(photocopy)* compulsar

◊ **authenticated photocopy** [ɔː'θentɪkeɪtɪd 'fəʊtəʊkɒpɪ] fotocopia *f* compulsada

◊ **authenticity** [ɔːθə'tɪsɪtɪ] *noun* autenticidad *f*

author ['ɔːθə] *noun* autor, -ora

authority [ɔː'θɒrɪtɪ] *noun* **(a)** autoridad *f*; **he has no authority to act on our behalf** = no tiene autoridad para actuar en nuestro nombre **(b)** **local authority** = autoridad local *or* municipalidad *f*; **the authorities** = las autoridades

authorize ['ɔːθəraɪz] *verb* **(a)** *(give permission)* autorizar (algo); **to authorize payment of £10,000** = autorizar el pago de £10.000 **(b)** *(give authority)* autorizar (a alguien); **to authorize someone to act on the company's behalf** = autorizar a alguien para que actúe en nombre de la compañía

◊ **authorization** [ɔːθəraɪ'zeɪʃən] *noun* autorización *f*; **do you have authorization for this expenditure?** = ¿tiene Vd. autorización para realizar este gasto?; **he has no authorization to act on our behalf** = no está autorizado para actuar en nuestro nombre

◊ **authorized** ['ɔːθəraɪzd] *adjective* autorizado, -da; **authorized capital** = emisión autorizada *or* capital escriturado; **authorized dealer** = agente autorizado

QUOTE in 1934 Congress authorized President Franklin D. Roosevelt to seek lower tariffs with any country willing to reciprocate
Duns Business Month

automate ['ɔːtəmeɪt] *verb* automatizar

◊ **automated** ['ɔːtəmeɪtɪd] *adjective* automatizado, -da; **fully automated car assembly plant** = una planta de montaje de automóviles totalmente automatizada; **automated teller** *or* **telling machine (ATM)** = cajero automático

◊ **automation** [ɔːtə'meɪʃən] *noun* automatización *f*

automatic [ɔːtə'mætɪk] *adjective* automático, -ca; **there is an automatic increase in salaries on January 1st** = hay un aumento automático de salarios el 1 de enero; **automatic data processing** = proceso automático de datos; **automatic telling machine** *or* **Automated Teller Machine (ATM)** = cajero automático; **automatic vending machine** = máquina expendedora automática

◊ **automatically** [ɔːtə'mætɪkəli] *adverb* automáticamente; **the invoices are sent out automatically** = las facturas se distribuyen automáticamente; **addresses are typed in automatically** = las direcciones se escriben automáticamente; **a demand note is sent automatically when the invoice is overdue** = se envía automáticamente una reclamación al vencimiento del pago de la factura

available [ə'veɪləbl] *adjective* disponible *or* accesible; **available in all branches** = en venta en todas las sucursales; **item no longer available** = artículo no disponible; **items available to order only** = artículos disponibles sólo por encargo; **funds which are made available for investment in small businesses** = fondos disponibles para inversión en empresas pequeñas; **available capital** = capital disponible

◊ **availability** [əveɪlə'bɪləti] *noun* disponibilidad *f*; **offer subject to availability** = oferta según disponibilidad *or* sujeta a la disponibilidad de las existencias

average ['ævərɪdʒ] **1** *noun* **(a)** *(calculation)* promedio *m*; **the average for the last three months** *or* **the last three months' average** = el promedio de los últimos tres meses; **moving average** = promedio móvil; **sales average** *or* **average of sales** = promedio de ventas; **weighted average** = promedio ponderado *or* media ponderada; **on (an) average** = por término medio *or* de promedio; **on average, £15 worth of goods are stolen every day** = por término medio, se roban artículos por valor de £15 a diario **(b)** *(insurance)* avería *f*; **average adjuster** = perito, -ta de averías; **general average** = media general *or* avería gruesa; **particular average** = avería simple **2** *adjective* **(a)** *(middle)* medio, -dia; **average cost per unit** = el costo unitario medio; **average price** = precio medio; **average sales per representative** = ventas medias por representante; **the average figures for the last three months** = las cifras medias de los últimos tres meses; **the average increase in prices** = la subida media de precios **(b)** *(not very good)* regular *or* mediano, -na; **the company's performance has been only average** = el resultado de la compañía ha sido sólo regular; **he is an average worker** = es un trabajador medio **3** *verb* ser por término medio *or* alcanzar un promedio de; **price increases have averaged 10% per annum** = la subida de precios es de un promedio anual del 10%; **days lost through sickness have averaged twenty-two over the last four years** = el término medio de días perdidos por enfermedad ha sido de veintidós durante los últimos cuatro años

◊ **average due date** ['ævərɪdʒ 'djuː 'deɪt] *noun* vencimiento *m* medio *or* fecha *f* media de vencimiento

◊ **average out** ['ævərɪdʒ 'aʊt] *verb* ser por término medio *or* alcanzar un promedio de; **it averages out at 10% per annum** = el término medio anual es del 10%; **sales increases have averaged out at 15%** = el aumento de las ventas ha alcanzado un promedio del 15%

◊ **averager** ['ævərɪdʒə] *noun* persona *f* que compra la misma acción en distintos momentos a precios distintos para conseguir un precio medio

◊ **average-sized** ['ævərɪdʒ 'saɪzd] *adjective* de tamaño medio; **they are an average-sized company** = es una empresa de tamaño medio; **he has an average-sized office** = tiene un despacho de dimensiones medias

◊ **averaging** ['ævərɪdʒɪŋ] *noun* compra *f* de acciones en distintos momentos a precios distintos para conseguir un precio medio

> QUOTE a share with an average rating might yield 5 per cent and have a PER of about 10
> **Investors Chronicle**

> QUOTE the average price per kilogram for this season to the end of April has been 300 cents
> **Australian Financial Review**

avoid [ə'vɔɪd] *verb* evitar; **the company is trying to avoid bankruptcy** = la compañía está intentando evitar la quiebra; **my aim is to avoid paying too much tax** = mi objetivo es evitar pagar demasiados impuestos; **we want to avoid direct competition with Smith Ltd** = queremos evitar la competencia directa con Smith Ltd (NOTE: you avoid something or avoid **doing** something)

◊ **avoidance** [ə'vɔɪdəns] *noun* evitación *f* *or* evasión *f* *or* elusión *f*; **avoidance of an agreement** *or* **of a contract** = eludir un acuerdo *or* un contrato; **tax avoidance** = evasión de impuestos

avoirdupois [ævədə'pɔɪz] *noun* sistema *m* de pesos usado en Gran Bretaña (expresado en libras, onzas, etc.); **one ounce avoirdupois** = una onza (avoirdupois)

> COMMENT: avoirdupois weight is divided into drams (16 drams = 1 ounce); ounces (14 ounces = one pound); pounds (100 pounds = 1 hundredweight); hundredweight (20 hundredweight = 1 ton). Avoirdupois weights are slightly heavier than troy weights with the same names: the avoirdupois pound equals 0.45kg, whereas the troy pound equals 0.37kg. See also TROY

await [ə'weɪt] *verb* esperar; **we are awaiting the decision of the planning department** = estamos esperando la decisión del departamento de planificación; **they are awaiting a decision of the court** = están esperando una decisión del tribunal; **the agent is awaiting our instructions** = el agente está esperando nuestras órdenes

award [ə'wɔːd] **1** *noun* **(a)** *(decision)* fallo *m* *or* sentencia *f*; **an award by an industrial tribunal** = una sentencia de la magistratura de trabajo; **the arbitrator's award was set aside on appeal** = el fallo del árbitro se anuló tras la apelación **(b)** *(prize)* premio *m* **2** *verb* conceder *or* adjudicar *or* fijar *or* imponer; **to award someone a salary increase** = conceder un aumento salarial a alguien; **to award damages** = fijar daños y perjuicios; **the judge**

awarded costs to the defendant = el juez impuso el pago de las costas al demandado; **to award a contract to someone** = adjudicar un contrato a alguien

away [ə'weɪ] *adverb* ausente *or* fuera; **the managing director is away on business** = el director gerente está ausente por motivos de trabajo; **my secretary is away sick** = mi secretaria está ausente por enfermedad; **the company is moving away from its down-market image** = la empresa está abandonando su imagen dirigida a un mercado popular

awkward ['ɔːkwəd] *adjective* difícil *or* incómodo, -da *or* embarazoso, -sa; **the board is trying to solve the awkward problem of the managing director's son** = el consejo de administración está intentando resolver el embarazoso problema del hijo del director gerente; **when he asked for the loan the bank started to ask some very awkward questions** = cuando solicitó el préstamo, el banco empezó a hacerle preguntas muy incómodas; **he is being very awkward about giving us further credit** = se muestra muy reacio a concedernos otro crédito

axe, *US* **ax** [æks] **1** *noun* **the project got the axe** = el proyecto se abandonó **2** *verb* recortar *or* despedir; **to axe expenditure** = recortar gastos; **several thousand jobs are to be axed** = van a despedir a varios miles de empleados

Bb

'B' shares ['biː 'ʃeəz] *plural noun* acciones *fpl* de clase 'B' con derechos de voto especiales (muchas veces propiedad del fundador y su familia)

baby bonds ['beɪbɪ 'bɒndz] *plural noun US* bonos *mpl* de bajo valor nominal (p.e. $100)

back [bæk] **1** *noun* dorso *m* or reverso *m*; **write your address on the back of the envelope** = escriba su dirección al dorso del sobre; **the conditions of sale are printed on the back of the invoice** = las condiciones de venta figuran al dorso de la factura; **please endorse the cheque on the back** = sírvase firmar el cheque al dorso **2** *adjective* **(a)** *(pending)* atrasado, -da; **back interest** = intereses atrasados; **back orders** = pedidos pendientes; **after the strike it took the factory six weeks to clear all the accumulated back orders** = después de la huelga la fábrica tardó seis semanas en despachar todos los pedidos pendientes; **back pay** = atrasos de sueldo; **I am owed £500 in back pay** = me deben £500 de atrasos de sueldo; **the salesmen are claiming for back payment of unpaid commission** = los vendedores reclaman el pago de las comisiones atrasadas; **back payments** = pagos atrasados; **back rent** = alquiler atrasado or pendiente de pago; **the company owes £100,000 in back rent** = la empresa debe £100.000 de renta atrasada **(b)** *(backwards)* retroactivo, -va; **back financing** = financiación retroactiva **3** *adverb* de vuelta or atrás or de nuevo; **he will pay back the money in monthly instalments** = reembolsará el préstamo en plazos mensuales; **the store sent back the cheque because the date was wrong** = la tienda devolvió el cheque por un error de fecha; **the company went back on its agreement to supply at £1.50 a unit** = la empresa faltó a su compromiso de vender a £1,50 la unidad **4** *verb* **(a)** *(people)* apoyar or respaldar; **to back someone** = apoyar or avalar or respaldar a alguien; **the bank is backing him to the tune of £10,000** = el banco le respalda con £10.000; **he is looking for someone to back his project** = está buscando a alguien que respalde su proyecto **(b)** *(guarantee)* **to back a bill** = avalar or endosar una letra; **to back a loan** = garantizar un préstamo

◇ **back burner** ['bæk 'bɜːnə] *noun* **the project has been put on the back burner** = el proyecto ha sido aplazado

◇ **backdate** ['bæk 'deɪt] *verb* antedatar; **backdate your invoice to April 1st** = antedate su factura al 1 de abril; **the pay increase is backdated to January 1st** = el aumento salarial es retroactivo al 1 de enero

◇ **backer** ['bækə] *noun* **(a)** garante *mf* or capitalista *mf*; **he has an Australian backer** = cuenta con un capitalista australiano; **one of the company's backers has withdrawn** = uno de los capitalistas de la compañía se ha retirado **(b) backer of a bill** = endosante *mf*

◇ **background** ['bækgraʊnd] *noun* **(a)** *(past experience)* antecedentes *mpl* or experiencia *f*; **his background is in the steel industry** = su experiencia procede de la industria siderúrgica; **the company is looking for someone with a background of success in the electronics industry** = la empresa busca a alguien que haya tenido éxito en la industria electrónica; **she has a publishing background** = tiene experiencia en el mundo editorial; **what is his background** or **do you know anything about his background?** = ¿cuáles son sus antecedentes? or ¿sabe Vd. algo de sus antecedentes? **(b)** *(past details)* antecedentes *mpl* or bases *fpl* or pasado *m*; **he explained the background of the claim** = explicó las bases de la solicitud; **I know the contractual situation as it stands now, but can you fill in the background details?** = entiendo la situación contractual actual, pero ¿puede Vd. incluir los antecedentes?

◇ **backhander** ['bækhændə] *noun (informal)* soborno *m*

◇ **backing** ['bækɪŋ] *noun* **(a)** respaldo *m* or apoyo *m* financiero; **he has the backing of an Australian bank** = tiene el respaldo de un banco australiano; **the company will succeed only if it has sufficient backing** = la empresa tendrá éxito únicamente si cuenta con el debido apoyo financiero; **who is providing the backing for the project** or **where does the backing for the project come from?** = ¿quién respalda el proyecto? or ¿de dónde procede el apoyo financiero del proyecto? **(b) currency backing** = reserva monetaria de respaldo

◇ **backlog** ['bæklɒg] *noun* acumulación *f* de trabajo atrasado; **the warehouse is trying to cope with a backlog of orders** = el almacén está tratando de atender los pedidos atrasados; **my secretary can't cope with the backlog of paperwork** = mi secretaria no puede hacer frente a la acumulación de trabajo administrativo atrasado

◇ **back out** ['bæk 'aʊt] *verb* retirarse; **the bank backed out of the contract** = el banco se retiró del contrato; **we had to cancel the project when our German partners backed out** = tuvimos que abandonar el proyecto cuando nuestros socios alemanes se retiraron

◇ **back-to-back loan** ['bæktəbæk 'ləʊn] *noun* préstamo respaldado or subsidiario

◇ **back up** ['bæk 'ʌp] *verb* **(a)** *(support)* respaldar or apoyar; **he brought along a file of documents to back up his claim** = trajo consigo un expediente de documentos para respaldar su reclamación; **the finance director said the managing director had refused to back him up in his argument with the VAT office** = el director de finanzas dijo que el director gerente se había negado a apoyarle en su conflicto con el departamento de administración del IVA **(b)** *(computers)* copiar or hacer una copia (de un archivo o disco)

◇ **backup** ['bækʌp] *adjective* **(a)** *(supporting)* de apoyo or suplementario, -ria; **we offer a free backup service to customers** = ofrecemos un servicio posventa gratuito a los clientes; **after a series of sales tours by representatives, the sales director sends backup letters to all the contacts** = después de las visitas de los representantes, el director de ventas envía cartas de confirmación a todos los clientes **(b)** *(computers)* **backup copy** = copia de reserva *or* de seguridad; **backup storage** = almacenaje en reserva; **backup unit** = unidad de 'back-up'

◊ **backwardation** [bækwə'deɪʃən] *noun* margen *m* de cobertura

QUOTE the businesses we back range from start-up ventures to established companies in need of further capital for expansion
Times

QUOTE the company has received the backing of a number of oil companies who are willing to pay for the results of the survey
Lloyd's List

bad [bæd] *adjective* malo, -la; **bad bargain** = mal negocio; **bad buy** = mala compra; **bad cheque** = cheque sin fondos; **bad debt** = deuda incobrable; **the company has written off £30,000 in bad debts** = la compañía ha dado por perdidas £30.000 de deudas incobrables

badge [bædʒ] *noun* insignia *f or* distintivo *m or* chapa *f*; **all the staff at the exhibition must wear badges** = todo el personal de la exposición debe llevar insignias; **visitors have to sign in at reception, and will be given visitors' badges** = los visitantes deben inscribirse en recepción donde se les dará un distintivo

bag [bæg] *noun* saco *m or* bolsa *f*; **he brought his files in a Harrods bag** = trajo sus documentos en una bolsa de Harrods; **carrier bag** *or* **plastic bag** = bolsa de plástico; **we gave away 5,000 plastic bags at the exhibition** = regalamos 5.000 bolsas de plástico en la exposición; **shopping bag** = bolsa de la compra

baggage ['bægɪdʒ] *noun* equipaje *m*; **free baggage allowance** = franquicia de equipaje; *US* **baggage cart** = carro *or* carrito del equipaje (NOTE: UK English is **luggage trolley**) *US* **baggage room** = consigna *f* (NOTE: no plural; to show one suitcase, etc., you can say **one item** *or* **a piece of baggage**)

Bahamas (The) [bə'hɑːməz] *noun* Las Bahamas *fpl*

◊ **Bahamian** [bə'heɪmɪən] *adjective & noun* (habitante) de Las Bahamas
NOTE: capital: **Nassau**; currency: **Bahamian dollar (B$)** = dólar de Las Bahamas (B$)

bail [beɪl] *noun* fianza *f*; **to stand bail of £3,000 for someone** = ser fiador de alguien por £3.000; **he was released on bail of $3,000** *or* **he was released on payment of $3,000 bail** = le pusieron en libertad bajo fianza de $3.000; **to jump bail** = fugarse *or* huir estando bajo fianza

◊ **bail out** ['beɪl 'aʊt] *verb* (a) *(financially)* rescatar (de dificultades financieras) *or* sacar de apuros (b) *(a prisoner)* **to bail someone out** = obtener la libertad de alguien bajo fianza; **she paid $3,000 to bail him out** = pagó una fianza de $3.000 para obtener su libertad

◊ **bail-out** ['beɪlaʊt] *noun* rescate *m* financiero

QUOTE the government has decided to bail out the bank which has suffered losses to the extent that its capital has been wiped out
South China Morning Post

balance ['bæləns] **1** *noun* (a) *(accounts)* saldo *m or* resultado *m or* balance *m*; **balance in hand** = saldo disponible; **balance brought down** = saldo; **balance brought forward** *or* **balance carrried forward** = saldo a cuenta nueva (b) *(money still to be paid)* resto *m*; **you can pay £100 deposit and the balance within 60 days** = puede pagar un depósito de £100 y el resto dentro de 60 días; **balance due to us** = saldo deudor *or* saldo a nuestro favor (c) **balance of payments** = balanza *f* de pagos; **balance of trade** *or* **trade balance** = balanza comercial; **adverse** *or* **unfavourable balance of trade** = balanza comercial deficitaria *or* desfavorable; **favourable trade balance** = balanza comercial favorable *or* con superávit (d) **bank balance** = saldo *m* de cuenta bancaria; **credit balance** = haber *m or* saldo acreedor *or* saldo a favor; **debit balance** = debe *m or* saldo deudor; **the account has a credit balance of £100** = la cuenta arroja un saldo acreedor de £100; **because of large payments to suppliers, the account has a debit balance of £1,000** = debido a los elevados pagos a proveedores, la cuenta arroja un saldo deudor de £1.000 **2** *verb* (a) *(accounts)* cuadrar *or* saldar *or* hacer balance; **the February accounts do not balance** = el balance de las cuentas de febrero no cuadra; **I have finished balancing the accounts for March** = he acabado de cuadrar las cuentas de marzo (b) *(a budget)* equilibrar; **the president is planning for a balanced budget** = el presidente se propone adoptar un presupuesto equilibrado

◊ **balance sheet** ['bæləns 'ʃiːt] *noun* balance *m* general *or* de situación; **the company balance sheet for 1992 shows a substantial loss** = el balance general de la compañía para 1992 arroja unas pérdidas considerables; **the accountant has prepared the balance sheet for the first half-year** = el contable ha preparado el balance de situación del primer semestre

COMMENT: the balance sheet shows the state of a company's finances at a certain date; the profit and loss account shows the movements which have taken place since the end of the previous accounting period. A balance sheet must balance, with the basic equation that assets (i.e., what the company owns, including money owed to the company) must equal liabilities (i.e., what the company owes to its creditors) plus capital (i.e., what it owes to its shareholders). A balance sheet can be drawn up either in the horizontal form, with (in the UK) liabilities and capital on the left-hand side of the page (in the USA, it is the reverse) or in the vertical form, with assets at the top of the page, followed by liabilities, and capital at the bottom. Most are usually drawn up in the vertical format, as opposed to the more old-fashioned horizontal style

balancing item ['bælənsɪŋ 'aɪtəm] *noun* contrapartida *f*

bale [beɪl] **1** *noun* bala *f or* paca *f*; **a bale of cotton** = una paca de algodón; **2,520 bales of wool were destroyed in the fire** = 2.520 balas de lana quedaron destruidas en el incendio **2** *verb* embalar

ballast ['bæləst] *noun* lastre *m*

balloon [bəˈluːn] *noun* préstamo *m* globo; *US* **balloon mortgage** = hipoteca globo

ballot [ˈbælət] **1** *noun* **(a)** *(election)* votación *f*; **ballot paper** = papeleta de voto; **ballot box** = urna electoral; **postal ballot** = votación por correo; **secret ballot** = votación secreta **(b)** *(selection at random)* sorteo *m*; **the share issue was oversubscribed, so there was a ballot for the shares** = la subscripción de acciones se cubrió con exceso, por lo que hubo que proceder a un sorteo **2** *verb* invitar a votar; **the union is balloting for the post of president** = el sindicato está realizando una votación para elegir presidente

◊ **ballot-rigging** [ˈbælət ˈrɪɡɪŋ] *noun* pucherazo *m or* manipulación *f* de votos

ballpark figure [ˈbɑːlpɔːk ˈfɪɡə] *noun* *(approximate figure)* cifra aproximada (que se toma como puente de partida en una discusión)

ban [bæn] **1** *noun* prohibición *f*; **a government ban on the import of weapons** = prohibición oficial sobre la importación de armas; **a ban on the export of computer software** = prohibición sobre la exportación de programas de ordenador; **overtime ban** = prohibición de realizar horas extraordinarias; **to impose a ban on smoking** = prohibir fumar; **to lift the ban on smoking** = levantar la prohibición de fumar; **to beat the ban on something** = eludir una prohibición **2** *verb* prohibir; **the government has banned the sale of alcohol** = el gobierno ha prohibido la venta de bebidas alcohólicas (NOTE: **banning - banned)**

band [bænd] *noun* **(a)** *(range of figures between low and high)* banda *f*; **exchange rate band** = banda de fluctuación; **tax band** = banda impositiva **(b)** **rubber band** = goma *f* elástica; **put a band round the filing cards to stop them getting mixed up** = sujete las fichas con una goma elástica para que no se mezclen

Bangladesh [bæŋləˈdeʃ] *noun* Bangladesh

◊ **Bangladeshi** [bæŋləˈdeʃi] *adjective & noun* de Bangladesh
NOTE: capital: **Dacca;** currency: **Bangladeshi taka** = taka de Bangladesh

bank [bæŋk] **1** *noun* **(a)** banco *m*; **Lloyds Bank** = el Banco Lloyds; **The First National Bank** = el Primer Banco Nacional; **he put all his earnings into his bank** = depositó todos sus ingresos en el banco; **I have had a letter from my bank telling me my account is overdrawn** = he recibido una carta de mi banco advirtiéndome que mi cuenta está al descubierto; **bank loan** *or* **bank advance** = préstamo bancario; **he asked for a bank loan to start his business** = pidió un préstamo bancario para empezar el negocio; **bank borrowing** = préstamo bancario; **the new factory was financed by bank borrowing** = la nueva fábrica fue financiada con un préstamo bancario; **bank borrowings have increased** = los préstamos bancarios han aumentado; **bank deposits** = depósitos bancarios; **bank reserves** = activo de caja; **bank transfer** = transferencia bancaria **(b)** **central bank** = banco *m* central; **Bank for International Settlements (BIS)** = Banco de Pagos Internacionales (BPI); **European Investment Bank** = Banco Europeo de Inversiones (BEI); **the Federal Reserve Banks** = los bancos de la Reserva Federal; **the World Bank** = el Banco

Mundial **(c)** **savings bank** = caja *f* de ahorros; **foreign trade bank** = banco exterior; **issuing bank** = banco emisor; **merchant bank** = banco de negocios; **the High Street banks** = los bancos comerciales **(d)** **data bank** = banco *m* de datos **2** *verb* ingresar *or* tener una cuenta bancaria; **he banked the cheque as soon as he received it** = ingresó el cheque en cuanto lo recibió; **where do you bank?** = ¿dónde tiene Vd. su cuenta bancaria? *or* ¿qué banco tiene Vd.?; **I bank at** *or* **with Barclays** = tengo una cuenta en el Barclays

◊ **bankable** [ˈbæŋkəbl] *adjective* descontable; **a bankable paper** = un efecto descontable

◊ **bank account** [ˈbæŋk əˌkaʊnt] *noun* cuenta *f* bancaria; **to open a bank account** = abrir una cuenta bancaria; **to close a bank account** = cerrar una cuenta bancaria; **how much money do you have in your bank account?** = ¿cuánto dinero tiene Vd. en su cuenta bancaria?; **she has £100 in her savings bank account** = tiene £100 en su cuenta de ahorros; **if you let the balance in your bank account fall below £100, you have to pay bank charges** = si deja que el saldo de su cuenta baje a menos de £100 el banco le cargará gastos

◊ **bank balance** [ˈbæŋk ˈbæləns] *noun* estado *m* de cuenta; **our bank balance went into the red last month** = nuestra cuenta quedó al descubierto el mes pasado

◊ **bank bill** [ˈbæŋk ˈbɪl] *noun* **(a)** *GB* letra *f* bancaria *or* giro *m* bancario **(b)** *US* billete *m* de banco

◊ **bank book** [ˈbæŋk ˈbʊk] *noun* libreta *f* de ahorros

◊ **bank charges** [ˈbæŋk ˈtʃɑːdʒɪz] *plural noun* gastos *mpl* bancarios (NOTE: in US English this is **a service charge)**

◊ **bank clerk** [ˈbæŋk ˈklɑːk] *noun* empleado, -da de banco

◊ **bank draft** [ˈbæŋk ˈdrɑːft] *noun* giro *m* bancario *or* letra *f* de cambio

◊ **banker** [ˈbæŋkə] *noun* **(a)** banquero, -ra; **merchant banker** = banquero de negocios **(b)** **banker's bill** = letra bancaria *or* giro bancario; **banker's order** = orden de domiciliación bancaria *or* de pago domiciliada a través del banco; **he pays his subscription by banker's order** = paga su subscripción por domiciliación bancaria

◊ **bank giro** [ˈbæŋk ˈdʒaɪrəʊ] *noun* *GB* giro *m or* transferencia *f* bancaria

◊ **bank holiday** [ˈbæŋk ˈhɒlədi] *noun* día *m* festivo; **New Year's Day is a bank holiday** = el día de Año Nuevo es festivo

◊ **banking** [ˈbæŋkɪŋ] *noun* la banca *f*; **he is studying banking** = está estudiando banca; **she has gone into banking** = ha empezado a trabajar en la banca; **direct banking** = banca a distancia; **electronic banking** = banca electrónica; **home banking** = banco en casa; **phone banking** = banca telefónica *or* banca por teléfono; *US* **banking account** = cuenta bancaria; **banking crisis** = crisis bancaria; **banking hours** = horario bancario *or* de oficina de los bancos; **you cannot get money out of the bank after banking hours** = no se puede sacar dinero del banco fuera de las horas de oficina; **banking system** = la banca

◊ **bank manager** [ˈbæŋk ˈmænɪdʒə] *noun*

director, -ra de banco; **he asked his bank manager for a loan** = solicitó un préstamo al director del banco

◇ **bank note** or **banknote** ['bæŋknəʊt] *noun* billete *m* de banco; **he pulled out a pile of used bank notes** = sacó un montón de billetes de banco usados (NOTE: US English is **bill**)

◇ **Bank of England** ['bæŋk əv 'ɪŋlənd] *noun* el Banco de Inglaterra

| COMMENT: the central British bank, owned by the state, which, together with the Treasury, regulates the nation's finances. The Bank of England issues banknotes (which carry the signatures of its officials). It is the lender of last resort to commercial banks and puts into effect the general financial policies of the government. The Governor of the Bank of England is appointed by the government

◇ **Bank of Spain** ['bæŋk əv 'speɪn] *noun* Banco de España

◇ **bank on** ['bæŋk 'ɒn] *verb* contar con or confiar en or dar por seguro; **he is banking on getting a loan from his father to set up in business** = confía en conseguir un préstamo de su padre para iniciar un negocio; **do not bank on the sale of your house** = no dé por segura la venta de su casa

◇ **bankroll** ['bæŋkrəʊl] *verb (informal)* financiar

◇ **bank statement** ['bæŋk 'steɪtmənt] *noun* estado *m* or extracto *m* de cuentas

bankrupt ['bæŋkrʌpt] **1** *noun* **certificated bankrupt** = quebrado rehabilitado por haberse demostrado su inocencia; **discharged bankrupt** = quebrado rehabilitado; **undischarged bankrupt** = quebrado no rehabilitado **2** *adjective* en bancarrota or en quiebra or insolvente; **he was adjudicated** or **declared bankrupt** = fue declarado en quiebra; **a bankrupt property developer** = un promotor inmobiliario en quiebra; **he went bankrupt after two years in business** = se arruinó después de dos años en el negocio **3** *verb* arruinar; **the recession bankrupted my father** = la recesión arruinó a mi padre

◇ **bankruptcy** ['bæŋkrəp(t)si] *noun* insolvencia *f* or quiebra *f* or bancarrota *f*; **the recession has caused thousands of bankruptcies** = la recesión ha provocado miles de quiebras; **adjudication of bankruptcy** or **declaration of bankruptcy** = declaración de quiebra; **discharge in bankruptcy** = rehabilitación del quebrado; **to file a petition in bankruptcy** = solicitar una declaración de quiebra

| COMMENT: in the UK, 'bankruptcy' is applied only to individual persons, but in the USA the term is also applied to corporations. In the UK, a bankrupt cannot hold public office (for example, he cannot be elected an MP) and cannot be the director of a company. He also cannot borrow money. In the USA, there are two types of bankruptcy: 'involuntary', where the creditors ask for a person or corporation to be made bankrupt; and 'voluntary', where a person or corporation applies to be made bankrupt (in the UK, this is called 'voluntary liquidation')

bar [bɑː] *noun* **(a)** *(pub)* bar *m*; **the sales reps met in the bar of the hotel** = los representantes de ventas se reunieron en el bar del hotel **(b)** sandwich bar = tienda de bocadillos; **snack bar** = cafetería *f* **(c)** *(impediment)* obstáculo *m*; **government legislation is a bar to foreign trade** = la legislación oficial es un obstáculo para el comercio exterior **(d)** *(barristers)* GB la abogacía *f*; GB **Bar Council** or US **American**

Bar Association = Colegio de Abogados; **to be called to the bar** = ingresar en el Colegio de Abogados **(e)** *(metal)* barra *f*

◇ **bar chart** ['bɑː 'tʃɑːt] *noun* gráfico *m* de barras

◇ **bar code** ['bɑː 'kəʊd] *noun* código *m* de barras

Barbados [bɑːˈbeɪdɒs] *noun* Barbados *f*

◇ **Barbadian** [bɑːˈbeɪdiən] *adjective & noun* (habitante) de Barbados
NOTE: capital: **Bridgetown**; currency: **Barbados dollar (BDS$)** = dólar de Barbados (BDS$)

bareboat charter ['beəbəʊt 'tʃɑːtə] *noun* contrato *m* de fletamento de 'casco desnudo' quedando los gastos de navegación por cuenta del fletado

barely ['beəli] *adverb* apenas or casi no; **there is barely enough money left to pay the staff** = casi no queda dinero para pagar al personal; **she barely had time to call her lawyer** = apenas tuvo tiempo de llamar a su abogado

bargain ['bɑːgɪn] **1** *noun* **(a)** *(agreement)* trato *m*; **to make a bargain** = cerrar un trato; **to drive a hard bargain** = imponer duras condiciones or ser un negociador duro; **to strike a hard bargain** = conseguir un trato en condiciones muy favorables; **it is a bad bargain** = no conviene or es un mal asunto **(b)** *(cheaper than usual)* ganga *f* de ocasión; **that car is a (real) bargain at £500** = ese coche es una ganga por £500; **bargain hunter** = persona que busca gangas **(c)** *(Stock Exchange)* una venta en la bolsa; **bargains done** = número de transacciones realizadas en la bolsa durante un día **2** *verb* regatear; **you will have to bargain with the dealer if you want a discount** = tendrá que regatear con el vendedor si quiere conseguir una rebaja; **they spent two hours bargaining about** or **over the price** = se pasaron dos horas regateando (NOTE: you bargain **with** someone **over** or **about** or **for** something)

◇ **bargain basement** ['bɑːgɪn 'beɪsmənt] *noun* sección *f* (de almacén) de oportunidades; **I'm selling this at a bargain basement price** = lo vendo a precio de ocasión

◇ **bargain counter** ['bɑːgɪn 'kaʊntə] *noun* sección *f* (de una tienda) de oportunidades

◇ **bargain offer** ['bɑːgɪn 'ɒfə] *noun* oferta *f* de ocasión or rebaja *f*; **this week's bargain offer - 30% off all carpet prices** = oferta de la semana: 30% de rebaja en todas las alfombras

◇ **bargain price** ['bɑːgɪn 'praɪs] *noun* precio *m* de ocasión; **these carpets are for sale at a bargain price** = estas alfombras se venden a precios de ocasión

◇ **bargain sale** ['bɑːgɪn 'seɪl] *noun* liquidación *f* or saldos *mpl*

◇ **bargaining** ['bɑːgɪnɪŋ] *noun* negociación *f*; **(free) collective bargaining** = convenio colectivo (libre); **bargaining power** = poder de negociación; **bargaining position** = postura negociadora

barrel ['bærəl] *noun* **(a)** barril *m*; **he bought twenty-five barrels of wine** = compró veinticinco barriles de vino; **to sell wine by the barrel** = vender vino por barriles **(b)** barril (medida de capacidad); **the price of oil has reached $30 a barrel** = el precio del petróleo ha subido a $30 el barril

QUOTE if signed, the deals would give effective discounts of up to $3 a barrel on Saudi oil

Economist

QUOTE US crude oil stocks fell last week by nearly 2.6m barrels

Financial Times

QUOTE the average spot price of Nigerian light crude oil for the month of July was 27.21 dollars a barrel

Business Times (Lagos)

barrier ['bærɪə] *noun* barrera *f*; **customs barriers** *or* **tariff barriers** = barreras arancelarias; **to impose trade barriers on certain goods** = imponer barreras comerciales a ciertos productos; **the unions have asked the government to impose trade barriers on foreign cars** = los sindicatos han pedido al gobierno que imponga barreras comerciales a la importación de automóviles; **to lift trade barriers from imports** = suprimir las barreras comerciales a la importación; **the government has lifted trade barriers on foreign cars** = el gobierno ha suprimido las barreras comerciales a la importación de automóviles

QUOTE a senior European Community official has denounced Japanese trade barriers, saying they cost European producers $3 billion a year

Times

QUOTE to create a single market out of the EC member states, physical, technical and tax barriers to free movement of trade between member states must be removed. Imposing VAT on importation of goods from other member states is seen as one such barrier

Accountancy

barrister ['bærɪstə] *noun GB* abogado, -da (que actúa únicamente en el juicio oral)

barter ['bɑːtə] **1** *noun* trueque *m*; **barter agreement** *or* **barter arrangement** *or* **barter deal** = contrato de trueque; **the company has agreed a barter deal with Bulgaria** = la empresa ha aprobado un contrato de trueque con Bulgaria **2** *verb* cambiar *or* trocar; **they agreed a deal to barter tractors for barrels of wine** = acordaron trocar tractores por barriles de vino

◊ **bartering** ['bɑːtərɪŋ] *noun* cambio *m* en especie *or* trueque *m*

QUOTE under the barter agreements, Nigeria will export 175,000 barrels a day of crude oil in exchange for trucks, food, planes and chemicals

Wall Street Journal

base [beɪs] **1** *noun* **(a)** *(initial position)* base *f or* sede *f*; **turnover increased by 200%, but starting from a low base** = el volumen de ventas aumentó el 200%, partiendo sin embargo de una base baja; **bank base rate** = tipo base de interés bancario; **monetary base** = base monetaria; *US* **base pay** = sueldo base; **base year** = año base; *see* DATABASE **(b)** *(centre of operations)* base *or* sede; **the company has its base in London and branches in all European countries** = la compañía tiene su sede en

Londres y sucursales en todos los países europeos; **he has an office in Madrid which he uses as a base while he is travelling in Southern Europe** = tiene una oficina en Madrid que emplea como base cuando viaja por el sur de Europa **2** *verb* **(a)** *(start to calculate from)* basar; **we based our calculations on the forecast turnover** = basamos nuestros cálculos en la previsión del volumen de ventas; **based on** = basado en; **based on last year's figures** = basado en las cifras del año pasado; **based on population forecasts** = basado en previsiones de población **(b)** *(in a place)* adscribir, radicar; **the European manager is based in our London office** = el director de la sección europea está adscrito a nuestra sucursal de Londres; **our overseas branch is based in the Bahamas** = nuestra sección internacional está radicada en las Bahamas; **a London-based sales executive** = un ejecutivo de ventas con base en Londres

◊ **basement** ['beɪsmənt] *noun* sótano *m*; **bargain basement** = sección de oportunidades; **I am selling this at a bargain basement price** = lo vendo a precio de ocasión

QUOTE the base lending rate, or prime rate, is the rate at which banks lend to their top corporate borrowers

Wall Street Journal

QUOTE other investments include a large stake in the Chicago-based insurance company

Lloyd's List

basic ['beɪsɪk] **1** *adjective* **(a)** *(normal)* básico, -ca *or* fundamental; **basic pay** *or* **basic salary** *or* **basic wage** = salario base; **basic discount** = descuento básico; **our basic discount is 20%, but we offer 5% extra for rapid settlement** = nuestro descuento base es de un 20% pero ofrecemos un 5% más por pronto pago **(b)** *(most important)* básico , -ca; **basic commodities** = productos básicos **(c)** *(simple)* básico, -ca; **he needs a basic knowledge of the market to work on the Stock Exchange** = necesita un conocimiento básico del mercado para trabajar en la Bolsa; **you need a basic qualification in maths** = necesita una preparación básica en matemáticas

◊ **basics** ['beɪsɪks] *plural noun* lo básico *or* fundamentos *mpl*; **he has studied the basics of foreign exchange dealing** = ha estudiado los fundamentos del comercio de divisas; **to get back to basics** = volver a lo esencial

◊ **basically** ['beɪsɪkəli] *adverb* básicamente *or* fundamentalmente

◊ **BASIC** ['beɪsɪk] *noun* = BEGINNER'S ALL-PURPOSE SYMBOLIC INSTRUCTION CODE *(programming language)* BASIC *m*

basis ['beɪsɪs] *noun* **(a)** *(for calculations)* base *f*; **we forecast the turnover on the basis of a 6% price increase** = hemos calculado el volumen de ventas en base a un aumento del precio de un 6% **(b)** *(of agreement)* términos *mpl* generales (de un acuerdo); **on a short-term** *or* **long-term basis** = a corto *or* largo plazo; **he has been appointed on a short-term basis** = ha sido nombrado para un periodo corto; **we have three people working on a freelance basis** = tenemos a tres personas trabajando por libre (NOTE: the plural is **bases**)

basket ['bɑːskɪt] *noun* **(a)** *(container)* cesta *f or* cesto *m*; **a basket of apples** = un cesto de manzanas; **filing basket** = bandeja *f* de documentos para archivar; **shopping basket** = cesta de la compra; **waste paper basket** *or* US **wastebasket** = papelera *f* **(b)** *(of goods or currencies)* cesta; **the pound has fallen against a basket of European currencies** la libra ha bajado con relación a una cesta de monedas europeas; **the price of the average shopping basket** US **the market basket has risen by 6%** el precio medio de la bolsa de la compra ha aumentado en un 6% **(c)** *(informal)* **basket case** = compañía en dificultades financieras y sin posibilidad de recuperarse

> QUOTE as a basket of European currencies, the ecu is protected from exchange-rate swings
>
> **Economist**

batch [bætʃ] **1** *noun* **(a)** *(group of items, documents)* lote *m or* serie *f or* remesa *f*; **this batch of shoes has the serial number 25-02** = este lote de zapatos lleva el número de serie 25-02; **today's batch of orders** = la remesa de pedidos de hoy; **the accountant signed a batch of cheques** = el contable firmó una serie de cheques; **we deal with the orders in batches of fifty** = despachamos los pedidos por series de cincuenta; **batch processing** = procesamiento por lotes **(b)** *(pile of documents)* montón *m*; **a batch of invoices** = un montón de facturas **2** *verb* agrupar; **to batch invoices** *or* **cheques** = agrupar facturas *or* cheques por lotes

◊ **batch number** ['bætʃ 'nʌmbə] *noun* número *m* de lote; **when making a complaint always quote the batch number on the packet** = cuando haga una reclamación, indique siempre el número del lote que figura en el paquete

battery ['bætəri] *noun* pila *f or* batería *f*; **the calculator needs a new battery** = la calculadora necesita una pila nueva; **a battery-powered calculator** = una calculadora de pilas *or* accionada por pilas

battle ['bætl] *noun* lucha *f*; **boardroom battles** = luchas en el seno del consejo de administración; **circulation battle** = lucha por alcanzar la mayor tirada (entre periódicos)

bay [beɪ] *noun* **loading bay** = nave *f* de carga

bazaar [bə'zɑː] *noun* bazar *m*

b/d = BARRELS PER DAY, BROUGHT DOWN

bear [beə] **1** *noun* **(a)** oso, osa; **their advertising symbol is a bear** = su emblema publicitario es un oso **(b)** *(Stock Exchange)* bajista *mf*; **bear market** = mercado bajista; **bear sale** = venta a la baja; *see* BULL **2** *verb* **(a)** *(to give interest)* devengar intereses; **government bonds which bear 5% interest** = bonos del Estado que devengan un 5% de interés **(b)** *(to carry)* llevar; **the cheque bears the signature of the company secretary** = el cheque lleva la firma del secretario de la compañía; **envelope which bears a London postmark** = sobre que lleva un matasellos de Londres; **a letter bearing yesterday's date** = una carta que lleva la fecha de ayer; **the share certificate bears his name** = el certificado de las acciones lleva su nombre **(c)** *(to pay costs)* pagar (costes); **the costs of the exhibition will be borne by the company** = los costes de la exposición los pagará la empresa; **the company**

bore the legal costs of both parties = la compañía pagó las costas de ambas partes (NOTE: **bearing - bore - has borne)**

◊ **bearer** ['beərə] *noun* portador, -ra; **the cheque is payable to bearer** = el cheque se paga al portador

◊ **bearer bond** ['beərə 'bɒnd] *noun* título *m* al portador

◊ **bearing** ['beərɪŋ] *adjective* que produce; **certificate bearing interest at 5%** = certificado que devenga intereses de un 5%; **interest-bearing deposits** = depósitos que devengan intereses

beat [biːt] *verb* **(a)** superar; **they have beaten their rivals into second place in the computer market** = han superado a sus competidores, relegándoles al segundo lugar en el mercado de ordenadores **(b)** to beat a ban = eludir una prohibición (NOTE: **beating - beat - has beaten)**

◊ **beaten** ['biːtn] *adjective* vencido, -da

become [bɪ'kʌm] *verb* volverse *or* hacerse *or* ponerse *or* resultar; **to become a member** = hacerse socio; **the export market has become very difficult since the rise in the dollar** = el mercado de exportación se ha puesto muy difícil después del alza del dólar; **the company became very profitable in a short time** = la empresa resultó muy rentable en poco tiempo (NOTE: **becoming - became - has become)**

bed-and-breakfast deal ['bedənd'brekfəst 'diːl] *noun* acuerdo *m* para vender acciones y volverlas a comprar al día siguiente con el fín de mostrar pérdidas o beneficios de cara a la declaración de renta

before [bɪ'fɔː] *adverb* antes; **there is no need for you to come before 10 o'clock** = no hace falta que vengas antes de las 10; **I'm in a hurry to get some cash before the banks close** = tengo que darme prisa para sacar dinero antes que cierren los bancos

◊ **beforehand** [bɪ'fɔːhænd] *adverb* por anticipado *or* de antemano

begin [bɪ'gɪn] *verb* empezar *or* comenzar; **the company began to lose its market share** = la empresa empezó a perder su cuota de mercado; **he began the report which the shareholders had asked for** = empezó a redactar el informe que los accionistas habían pedido; **the auditors' report began with a description of the general principles adopted** = el informe de los auditores empezaba con una explicación de los principios generales adoptados (NOTE: you begin something *or* begin to do something *or* begin with something. Note also: **beginning - began - has begun)**

◊ **beginning** [bɪ'gɪnɪŋ] *noun* comienzo *m*; **the beginning of the report is a list of the directors and their shareholdings** = el informe empieza con la lista de los directores y las acciones que posee cada uno

behalf [bɪ'hɑːf] *noun* **on behalf of** = en nombre de; **I am writing on behalf of the minority shareholders** = escribo en nombre de los accionistas minoritarios; **she is acting on my behalf** = actúa en mi nombre; **solicitors acting on behalf of the American company** = abogados que actúan en nombre de la empresa americana

behave [bɪ'heɪv] *verb* comportarse; **he doesn't**

know how to behave in this sort of situation = no sabe comportarse en situacciones como éstas

◊ **behaviour** [bɪ'heɪvjə] *noun* actuación *f or* comportamiento *m*

behind [bɪ'haɪnd] **1** *preposition* detrás; **the company is No. 2 in the market, about £4m behind their rivals** = la empresa es la número 2 en el mercado, a unos £4 millones por detrás de sus competidores **2** *adverb* atrás *or* detrás de; **we have fallen behind our rivals** = nos hemos quedado atrás de nuestros competidores; **the company has fallen behind with its deliveries** = la empresa anda retrasada en sus entregas

Belgium ['beldʒəm] *noun* Bélgica *f*

◊ **Belgian** ['beldʒən] *adjective & noun* belga
NOTE: capital: **Brussels** (= Bruselas); currency: **Belgian franc (BF)** = franco belga (FB)

believe [bɪ'liːv] *verb* creer *or* tener entendido; **we believe he has offered to buy 25% of the shares** = creemos que ha hecho una oferta de compra del 25% de las acciones; **the chairman is believed to be in South America on business** = tenemos entendido que el presidente está en América del Sur por asuntos de negocios

bellwether ['belwðə] *noun* acción *f* líder

belong [bɪ'lɒŋ] *verb* **(a) to belong to** = pertenecer a; **the company belongs to an old American banking family** = la compañía pertenece a una vieja familia de banqueros norteamericanos; **the patent belongs to the inventor's son** = la patente pertenece al hijo del inventor **(b) to belong with** = pertenecer *or* corresponder a *or* ir con; **those documents belong with the sales reports** = esos documentos van con los informes de ventas

below [bɪ'ləʊ] *preposition* por debajo de; **we sold the property at below the market price** = vendimos la propiedad por debajo del precio de mercado; **you can get a ticket for New York at below £150 from a bucket shop** = se puede comprar un viaje a Nueva York por menos de £150 en una agencia de viajes que venda con descuento *or* a precios reducidos

◊ **below-the-line** [bɪ'ləʊðə 'laɪn] *adjective* **below-the-line advertising** = gastos de publicidad no incluidos; **below-the-line expenditure** = gastos no incluidos en las cuentas normales de una compañía

benchmark ['ben(t)ʃmɑːk] *noun* punto *m* de referencia

QUOTE the US bank announced a cut in its prime, the benchmark corporate lending rate, from 10-% to 10%
Financial Times

QUOTE the dollar dropped below three German marks - a benchmark with more psychological than economic significance - for the first time since October
Fortune

QUOTE the benchmark 11³⁄₄% Treasury due 2003/2007 was quoted at 107 11/32, down 13/32 from Monday
Wall Street Journal

beneficial [benɪ'fɪʃəl] *adjective* beneficial

occupier = usufructuario de una vivienda; **beneficial interest** = interés usufructuario

◊ **beneficiary** [benɪ'fɪʃəri] *noun* beneficiario, -ria; **the beneficiaries of a will** = los beneficiarios de un testamento

QUOTE the pound sterling was the main beneficiary of the dollar's weakness
Business Times (Lagos)

benefit ['benɪfɪt] **1** *noun* **(a)** *(payment by social security)* beneficio *m or* subsidio *m or* prestación *f*; **she receives £20 a week as unemployment benefit** = recive un subsidio de paro semanal de £20; **the sickness benefit is paid monthly** = el subsidio de enfermedad se paga mensualmente; **the insurance office sends out benefit cheques each week** = la oficina de seguros envía los cheques del subsidio *or* de indemnización cada semana; **death benefit** = indemnización por fallecimiento *or* defunción **(b)** *(addition to salary)* **fringe benefits** = beneficios complementarios *or* extrasalariales **2** *verb* **(a)** favorecer; **a fall in inflation benefits the exchange rate** = una reducción de la inflación favorece el tipo de cambio **(b) to benefit from** *or* **by something** = beneficiarse de; **exports have benefited from the fall in the exchange rate** = las exportaciones se han beneficiado de la caída del tipo de cambio; **the employees have benefited from the profit-sharing scheme** = los empleados se han beneficiado del plan de participación en los beneficios

QUOTE the retail sector will also benefit from the expected influx of tourists
Australian Financial Review

QUOTE what benefits does the executive derive from his directorship? Compensation has increased sharply in recent years and fringe benefits for directors have proliferated
Duns Business Month

QUOTE salary is negotiable to £30,000, plus car and a benefits package appropriate to this senior post
Financial Times

QUOTE California is the latest state to enact a program forcing welfare recipients to work for their benefits
Fortune

Benin [be'niːn] *noun* Benín *m*

◊ **Beninois** [benɪn'wɑː] *adjective & noun* (habitante) de Benín
NOTE: capital: **Porto Novo**; currency: **CFA franc (CFAF)** = franco CFA (FCFA)

bequeath [bɪ'kwiːð] *verb* legar *or* dejar en testamento

◊ **bequest** [bɪ'kwest] *noun* legado *m or* donación *f*; **he made several bequests to his staff** = dejó varios legados a sus empleados

berth [bɜːθ] **1** *noun* muelle *m or* amarradero *m* **2** *verb* atracar; **the ship will berth at Rotterdam on Wednesday** = el barco atracará en Rotterdam el miércoles

best [best] **1** *adjective* (el, la) mejor; **his best price is still higher than all the other suppliers** = su mejor precio queda todavía por encima del de todos los demás suministradores; **1990 was the**

company's best year ever = 1990 fue el mejor año en la historia de la compañía 2 *noun* lo mejor *or* lo más adecuado; **the salesmen are doing their best, but the stock simply will not sell at that price** = los vendedores están haciendo todo lo posible, pero no pueden vender la mercancía a ese precio

◊ **best-seller** ['best 'selə] *noun* 'bestseller' *m or* artículo *m* de mayor venta *or* artículo con gran éxito de venta

◊ **best-selling** ['best 'selɪŋ] *adjective* que se vende muy bien; **these computer disks are our best-selling line** = estos discos de ordenador son el artículo que más vendemos

bet [bet] 1 *noun* apuesta *f* 2 *verb* apostar; **he bet £100 on the result of the election** = apostó £100 por el resultado de las elecciones; **I bet you £25 the dollar will rise against the pound** = te apuesto £25 a que el dólar subirá con relación a la libra; **betting tax** = impuesto sobre el juego (NOTE: **betting - bet - has bet)**

better ['betə] *adjective* mejor; **this year's results are better than last year's** = los resultados de este año son mejores que los del año pasado; **we will shop around to see if we can get a better price** = compararemos los precios de otros lugares para ver si son mejores

◊ **Better Business Bureau** ['betə 'bɪznəs 'bjʊərəʊ] *noun US* organización local para la promoción de reformas comerciales

beware [bɪ'weə] *verb* tener cuidado; **beware of imitations** = desconfíe de las imitaciones

b/f = BROUGHT FORWARD

bi- [baɪ] *prefix* bi-

◊ **bi-monthly** ['baɪ 'mʌnθli] 1 *adjective* **(a)** *(twice a month)* bimensual **(b)** *(every two months)* bimestral 2 *adverb* **(a)** *(twice a month)* bimensualmente *or* quincenalmente **(b)** *(every two months)* bimestral *or* cada dos meses

◊ **bi-annually** ['baɪ 'ænjʊəli] 1 *adjective* **(a)** *(twice a year)* semestral **(b)** *(every two years)* bienal 2 *adverb* **(a)** *(twice a year)* semestralmente *or* cada seis meses **(b)** *(every two years)* cada dos años

bid [bɪd] 1 *noun* **(a)** *(offer to buy)* oferta *f*; **to make a bid for something** = hacer una oferta de compra; **he made a bid for the house** = hizo una oferta por la casa; **the company made a bid for its rival** = la compañía hizo una oferta por la empresa competidora; **to make a cash bid** = hacer una oferta en efectivo *or* ofrecer pago en efectivo; **to put in a bid for something** *or* **to enter a bid for something** = ofrecer *or* presentar una oferta por algo **(b)** *(at an auction)* **opening bid** = oferta inicial; **closing bid** = oferta final **(c)** *(offer to do work)* oferta; **he made the lowest bid for the job** = hizo la oferta más baja *or* barata por el trabajo **(d)** *US (offer to sell)* oferta de venta a un precio determinado; **they asked for bids for the supply of spare parts** = solicitaron ofertas para el suministro de repuestos **(e)** **takeover bid** = oferta pública de adquisición *or* OPA; **to make a takeover bid for a company** = hacer una oferta de adquisición de una compañía; **to withdraw a takeover bid** = retirar una oferta de adquisición; **the company rejected the takeover bid** = la compañía rechazó la oferta de adquisición 2 *verb* *(at an*

auction) **to bid for something** = hacer una oferta *or* pujar; **he bid £1,000 for the jewels** = ofreció £1.000 por las joyas (NOTE: **bidding - bid - has bid)**

◊ **bidder** ['bɪdə] *noun* postor *m*; **several bidders made offers for the house** = se han recibido varias ofertas por la casa; **the property was sold to the highest bidder** = la propiedad se vendió al mejor postor; **the tender will go to the lowest bidder** = el contrato se adjudicará a la oferta más baja; **successful bidder** = adjudicatario, -ria

◊ **bidding** ['bɪdɪŋ] *noun* ofertas *fpl or* subasta *f or* puja *f*; **starting of the bidding** = comienzo de la puja; **the bidding started at £1,000** = la subasta empezó con una oferta de £1.000; **the bidding stopped at £250,000** = la puja culminó con £250.000; **the auctioneer started the bidding at £100** = el subastador empezó la subasta al precio tipo de £100

Big Board ['bɪg 'bɔːd] *noun US informal* = NEW YORK STOCK EXCHANGE

```
QUOTE at the close, the Dow Jones
Industrial Average was up 24.25 at
2,559.65, while New York S.E. volume
totalled 180m shares. Away from the Big
Board, the American S.E. Composite
climbed 2.31 to 297.87
                              Financial Times
```

bilateral [baɪ'lætərəl] *adjective* bilateral; **bilateral agreement** = acuerdo bilateral; **the minister signed a bilateral trade agreement** = el ministro firmó un convenio bilateral de comercio

```
QUOTE trade between Japan and China will
probably exceed $30 billion in 1993 to
mark a record high. Ministry of Finance
trade statistics show that bilateral
trade in the first half of 1993 totalled
$16.60 billion, up 29.7% from a year
earlier
                               Nikkei Weekly
```

bill [bɪl] 1 *noun* **(a)** *(invoice)* factura *f or* cuenta *f*; **the salesman wrote out the bill** = el vendedor hizo la factura; **does the bill include VAT?** = ¿está incluido el IVA en la factura?; **the bill is made out to Smith Ltd** = la factura está extendida a nombre de Smith Ltd.; **the builder sent in his bill** = el contratista envió su factura; **he left the country without paying his bills** = abandonó el país sin pagar sus deudas; **to foot the bill** = correr con los gastos **(b)** *(in a restaurant)* cuenta *f*; **can I have the bill please?** = ¿me puede traer la cuenta, por favor?; **the bill comes to £20 including service** = la cuenta asciende a £20, servicio incluido; **does the bill include service?** = ¿está el servicio incluido en la cuenta?; **the waiter has added 10% to the bill for the service** = el camarero ha añadido un 10% por el servicio **(c)** *(written promise to pay)* letra *f*; **bill broker** = agente de letras **(d)** *US* billete *m*; **a $5 bill** = un billete de $5 (GB English for this is **note** *or* **banknote) (e)** *(in Parliament)* proyecto *m* de ley 2 *verb* facturar *or* presentar una factura; **the builders billed him for the repairs to his neighbour's house** = el contratista le presentó una factura por las reparaciones hechas en la casa de su vecino

◊ **billboard** ['bɪlbɔːd] *noun US* cartelera *f or* valla *f* publicitaria; *compare* HOARDING

◊ **billhead** ['bɪlhed] *noun* encabezamiento *m* de factura

◊ **billing** ['bɪlɪŋ] *noun US* facturación *f*

◊ **bill of exchange** ['bɪl əv ɪks'tʃeɪnʒ] *noun* letra de cambio; **accommodation bill** = pagaré *m or* efecto *m* de favor; **bank bill** = letra bancaria; **demand bill** = giro a la vista; **to accept a bill** = aceptar una letra; **accepted** *or* **due bill** = letra aceptada; **to discount a bill** = descontar una letra; **dishonoured bill** = letra no aceptada; **bills payable (B/P)** = cuentas *or* letras a pagar; **bills receivable (B/R)** = cuentas *or* letras al cobro

> COMMENT: a bill of exchange is a document raised by a seller and signed by a purchaser, stating that the purchaser accepts that he owes the seller money, and promises to pay it at a later date. The person raising the bill is the 'drawer', the person who accepts it is the 'drawee'. The seller can then sell the bill at a discount to raise cash. This is called a 'trade bill'. A bill can also be accepted (i.e. guaranteed) by a bank, and in this case it is called a 'bank bill'

◊ **bill of lading** ['bɪl əv 'leɪdɪŋ] *noun* conocimiento *m* de embarque

◊ **bill of sale** ['bɪl əv 'seɪl] *noun* instrumento *m* de venta

billion ['bɪljən] *noun* mil millones *mpl* (NOTE: in the US it has always meant one thousand million, but in GB it formerly meant one million million, and it is still sometimes used with this meaning. With figures it is usually written **bn: $5bn** say 'five billion dollars')

> QUOTE gross wool receipts for the selling season to end June 30 appear likely to top $2 billion
> **Australian Financial Review**

> QUOTE at its last traded price the bank was capitalized at around $1.05 billion
> **South China Morning Post**

bin [bɪn] *noun* (a) *(basket)* papelera *f* (b) *(large container)* hucha *f or* arca *f or* cubo *m*; **dump bin** = caja de artículos sueltos para la venta (c) *(in a warehouse)* estantería *f* aparte; **bin card** = ficha de almacén

bind [baɪnd] *verb* obligar; **the company is bound by its articles of association** = la compañía está obligada a respetar sus estatutos; **he does not consider himself bound by the agreement which was signed by his predecessor** = no se considera obligado al acuerdo firmado por su predecesor (NOTE: **binding - bound**)

◊ **binder** ['baɪndə] *noun* (a) *(cover for papers)* archivador *or* encuadernador *m or* carpeta *f*; **ring binder** = carpeta de anillas *or* archivador de anillas (b) *(temporary insurance cover) US* nota *f* de cobertura *or* póliza *f* de seguros provisional (NOTE: the GB English for this is **cover note**) (c) *US* entrada *f or* depósito *m or* paga y señal (NOTE: the GB English for this is **deposit**)

◊ **binding** ['baɪndɪŋ] *adjective* obligatorio, -ria *or* vinculante; **a binding contract** = un contrato vinculante; **this document is not legally binding** = este documento no tiene fuerza jurídica; **the agreement is binding on all parties** = el acuerdo es obligatorio para todas las partes

BIS = BANK FOR INTERNATIONAL SETTLEMENTS

bit [bɪt] *noun (computer)* unidad *f* de información *or* bit *m*

black [blæk] 1 *adjective* (a) negro, -gra; **black market** = mercado negro *or* estraperlo *m*; **there is a flourishing black market in spare parts for cars** = hay un floreciente mercado negro de repuestos para coches; **you can buy gold coins on the black market** = se pueden comprar monedas de oro en el mercado negro; **to pay black market prices** = pagar precios de mercado negro (b) **black economy** = economía sumergida (c) **in the black** = positivo (saldo); **the company has moved into the black** = la empresa ya no tiene pérdidas; **my bank account is still in the black** = mi cuenta arroja todavía un saldo acreedor 2 *verb* boicotear *or* imponer la prohibición de comerciar; **three firms were blacked by the government** = el gobierno ha impuesto la prohibición de comerciar a tres empresas; **the union has blacked a trucking firm** = el sindicato ha declarado el boicot contra una empresa de transporte

◊ **Black Friday** ['blæk 'fraɪdeɪ] *noun* caída de la Bolsa

> COMMENT: called after the first major collapse of the US stock market on 24th September, 1869

◊ **blackleg** ['blækleg] *noun* esquirol *mf*

◊ **black list** ['blæk 'lɪst] *noun* lista *f* negra

◊ **blacklist** ['blæklɪst] *verb* poner en la lista negra; **his firm was blacklisted by the government** = el gobierno puso a su empresa en la lista negra

blame [bleɪm] 1 *noun* culpa *f*; **the sales staff got the blame for the poor sales figures** = echaron la culpa a los vendedores por las bajas cifras de ventas 2 *verb* culpar *or* echar la culpa *or* responsibilizar *or* reprochar; **the managing director blamed the chief accountant for not warning him of the loss** = el director gerente reprochó al jefe de contabilidad que no le hubiese advertido de las pérdidas; **the union is blaming the management for poor industrial relations** = el sindicato culpa a la dirección de las malas relaciones laborales

blank [blæŋk] 1 *adjective* en blanco; **a blank cheque** = un cheque en blanco 2 *noun* blanco *m or* espacio *m* en blanco; **fill in the blanks and return the form to your local office** = rellene los espacios en blanco y devuelva el formulario a su oficina local

blanket ['blæŋkɪt] *noun* **blanket agreement** = acuerdo global; **blanket insurance** = seguro a todo riesgo; **blanket policy** = póliza general *or* integral; **blanket refusal** = negativa general

blind testing ['blaɪnd 'testɪŋ] *noun* prueba *f* a ciegas

blip [blɪp] *noun* periodo *m* breve de estancamiento *or* estancamiento *m* temporal; **this month's bad trade figures are only a blip** = las cifras negativas de este mes son sólo temporales

blister pack ['blɪstə 'pæk] *noun* embalaje *m* de plástico tipo burbuja

block [blɒk] 1 *noun* (a) *(items)* paquete *m*; **he bought a block of 6,000 shares** = compró un paquete de 6.000 acciones; **block booking** = reserva en bloque; **the company has a block booking for twenty seats on the plane** *or* **for ten rooms at the hotel** = la empresa ha hecho una reserva en bloque de veinte plazas en el avión *or* de diez habitaciones en el hotel; **block vote** = voto por representación (b) *(buildings)* manzana *f*; **they want to redevelop a**

block in the centre of the town = quieren renovar una manzana en el centro de la ciudad; **a block of offices** or **an office block** = un edificio de oficinas **(c)** (letters) **block capitals** or **block letters** = letras mayúsculas or letras de imprenta; **write your name and address in block letters** = escriba su nombre y dirección en caracteres de imprenta **2** verb bloquear or impedir; **he used his casting vote to block the motion** = hizo uso de su voto de calidad para detener la propuesta; **the planning committee blocked the redevelopment plan** = el comité de planificación bloqueó el plan de reorganización

◊ **blocked** [blɒkt] adjective bloqueado, -da; **blocked currency** = moneda bloqueada; **the company has a large account in blocked roubles** = la empresa tiene una cuenta enorme de rublos bloqueados

blue [blu:] adjective **blue-chip investments** or **blue-chip shares** or **blue chips** = inversiones or acciones or títulos de toda confianza; **blue-collar worker** = obrero, -ra; **blue-collar union** = sindicato obrero

QUOTE soaring blue-chips and offshore buying helped Australian shares to a new high yesterday. The market opened higher as hopes of an interest rate cut buoyed sentiment
West Australian

◊ **blueprint** ['blu:prɪnt] noun proyecto m or plan m

blurb [blɜ:b] noun texto m publicitario (especialmente para un libro)

bn ['bɪljən] = BILLION

board [bɔ:d] **1** noun **(a)** see BOARD OF DIRECTORS **(b)** (group of people who administer) junta f; **advisory board** = comisión consultiva; **editorial board** = consejo de redacción; **training board** = organización del Estado para la provisión y coordinación de los programas de formación profesional **(c) on board** = a bordo; **free on board (f.o.b.)** = franco a bordo **(d)** (of wood or card) tabla f or tablón m or tablero m; **clipboard** = tablilla con sujetapapeles; **noticeboard** = tablón de anuncios **2** verb abordar or embarcarse or subir a (avión, tren); **customs officials boarded the ship in the harbour** = los aduaneros embarcaron en el puerto

◊ **boarding card** or **boarding pass** ['bɔ:dɪŋ 'kɑ:d or 'bɔ:dɪŋ 'pɑ:s] noun tarjeta f de embarque

◊ **board of directors** ['bɔ:d əv daɪ'rektəz] noun **(a)** GB consejo m de administración or junta f directiva; **the bank has two representatives on the board** = el banco tiene dos representantes en el consejo de administración; **he sits on the board as a representative of the bank** = es el representante del banco en el consejo de administración; **two directors were removed from the board at the AGM** = dos consejeros fueron depuestos de su cargo en la junta general anual; **she was asked to join the board** = le pidieron que formara parte del consejo de administración; **board meeting** = reunión del consejo de administración **(b)** US consejo de administración

COMMENT: the board of an American company may be made up of a large number of non-executive directors and only one or two executive officers; a British board has more executive directors

◊ **boardroom** ['bɔ:drʊm] noun sala f de juntas; **boardroom battles** = luchas personales entre consejeros

QUOTE a proxy is the written authorization an investor sends to a stockholder meeting conveying his vote on a corporate resolution or the election of a company's board of directors
Barrons

QUOTE CEOs, with their wealth of practical experience, are in great demand and can pick and choose the boards they want to serve on
Duns Business Month

boat [bəʊt] noun barco m; **cargo boat** = barco de carga; **passenger boat** = barco de pasajeros; **we took the night boat to Belgium** = cogimos el barco de noche para Bélgica; **boats for Greece leave every morning** = todas las mañanas salen or zarpan barcos para Grecia

Bolivia [bə'lɪvɪə] noun Bolivia f

◊ **Bolivian** [bə'lɪvɪən] adjective & noun boliviano, -na
NOTE: capital: **La Paz**; currency: **Bolivian peso** = peso boliviano ($b)

bona fide ['bəʊnə 'faɪdi] adjective de buena fe; **a bona fide offer** = una oferta seria

bonanza [bə'nænzə] noun bonanza f or prosperidad f or negocio m lucrativo; **the oil well was a bonanza for the company** = el pozo de petróleo fue una mina de oro para la empresa; **1991 was a bonanza year for the computer industry** = 1991 fue un año muy próspero para la industria de la informática

bond [bɒnd] noun **(a)** (debt of company or government) bono m or título m; **government bonds** or **treasury bonds** = papel or bonos del Estado or del Tesoro or efectos públicos; **municipal bond** or **local authority bond** = bono municipal or de la administración local; **bearer bond** = título al portador; **debenture bond** = obligación or pagaré de empresa; **mortgage bond** = cédula hipotecaria or bono hipotecario; GB **premium bond** = bono del Estado con prima **(b) goods (held) in bond** = mercancías en depósito aduanero; **entry of goods under bond** = entrada de mercancías en depósito; **to take goods out of bond** = retirar mercancías del depósito aduanero

◊ **bonded** ['bɒndɪd] adjective en depósito; **bonded warehouse** = depósito aduanero

◊ **bondholder** ['bɒndhəʊldə] noun obligacionista mf or tenedor, -ra de obligaciones

◊ **bond-washing** ['bɒndwɒʃɪŋ] noun transacciones fpl de bonos para obtener una desgravación fiscal

COMMENT: bonds are in effect another form of long-term borrowing by a company or government. They can carry a fixed interest or a floating interest, but the yield varies according to the price at which they are bought; bond prices go up and down in the same way as share prices

bonus ['bəʊnəs] noun **(a)** (extra payment) prima f or bonificación f; **capital bonus** = bonificación de capital; **cost-of-living bonus** = plus m de carestía de vida; **Christmas bonus** = paga extraordinaria de Navidad; **incentive bonus** = prima de incentivo; **productivity bonus** = prima de productividad **(b) bonus issue** = emisión gratuita; **bonus share** = acción con prima **(c)** *(insurance)* **no-claims bonus** = prima de seguros reducida por no haber declarado ningún siniestro (NOTE: plural is **bonuses)**

book [bʊk] **1** *noun* **(a)** libro *m*; **a company's books** = las cuentas *or* los libros de una compañía; **account book** = libro de contabilidad; **cash book** = libro de caja; **order book** = libro de pedidos; **the company has a full order book** = la empresa tiene el libro de pedidos completo; **purchase book** = libro de compras; **sales book** = libro de ventas; **book sales** = ventas registradas; **book value** = valor contable **(b) bank book** = libreta *f* de ahorros; **cheque book** = talonario *m* de cheques; **pass book** *or* **savings bank book** = cartilla *f or* libreta de ahorros; **phone book** *or* **telephone book** = guía *f* telefónica **2** *verb* reservar; **to book a room in a hotel** *or* **a table at a restaurant** *or* **a ticket on a plane** = reservar una habitación en un hotel *or* una mesa en un restaurante *or* una plaza en un avión; **I booked a table for 7.45** = reservé una mesa para las ocho menos cuarto; **he booked a ticket through to Cairo** = reservó un billete hasta el Cairo; **to book someone into a hotel** *or* **onto a flight** = hacerle a alguien la reserva en un hotel *or* un vuelo; **he was booked on the 09.00 flight to Zurich** = le hicieron la reserva en el vuelo de las 9 de la mañana a Zurich; **the hotel** *or* **the flight is fully booked** *or* **is booked up** = el hotel *or* el vuelo está completo; **the restaurant is booked up over the Christmas period** = el restaurante tiene todas las mesas reservadas para el periodo de Navidades

◊ **booking** ['bʊkɪŋ] *noun* reserva *f*; **hotel bookings have fallen since the end of the tourist season** = las reservas en los hoteles han bajado después de la temporada turística; **booking clerk** = taquillero, -ra; **booking office** = taquilla *or* despacho de billetes *or* pasajes; **block booking** = reserva en bloque; **to confirm a booking** = confirmar una reserva; **double booking** = doble reserva

◊ **bookkeeper** ['bʊkiːpə] *noun* contable *mf or* tenedor, -ra de libros

◊ **bookkeeping** ['bʊkiːpɪŋ] *noun* contabilidad *f or* teneduría *f* de libros; **single-entry bookkeeping** = contabilidad por partida simple; **double-entry bookkeeping** = contabilidad por partida doble

◊ **booklet** ['bʊklət] *noun* libreta *f*

◊ **bookseller** ['bʊksələ] *noun* librero, -ra

◊ **bookshop** ['bʊkʃɒp] *noun* librería *f*

◊ **bookstall** ['bʊkstɔːl] *noun* quiosco *m* de libros

◊ **bookstore** ['bʊkstɔː] *noun* US librería *f*

◊ **bookwork** ['bʊkwɜːk] *noun* teneduría *f* de cuentas

boom [buːm] **1** *noun* 'boom' *m or* auge *m or* bonanza *f*; **a period of economic boom** = un periodo de 'boom' económico *or* de bonanza económica; **the boom of the 1970s** = el 'boom' de los años 70; **boom industry** = industria en pleno auge; **a boom share** = una acción en fuerte alza; **the boom years** = los años de gran prosperidad **2** *verb* prosperar *or* aumentar; **business is booming** = los negocios prosperan *or* el negocio está en auge; **sales are booming** = las ventas aumentan rápidamente

◊ **booming** ['buːmɪŋ] *adjective* próspero, -ra *or* floreciente; **a booming industry** *or* **company** = una industria en plena expansión *or* empresa próspera; **technology is a booming sector of the economy** = la tecnología es un sector de la economía que experimenta un gran auge

boost [buːst] **1** *noun* estímulo *or* impulso *m*; **this publicity will give sales a boost** = esta publicidad dará un impulso a las ventas; **the government hopes to give a boost to industrial development** = el gobierno pretende dar un estímulo al desarrollo industrial **2** *verb* estimular *or* impulsar; **we expect our publicity campaign to boost sales by 25%** = esperamos que nuestra campaña publicitaria estimule las ventas en un 25%; **the company hopes to boost its market share** = la empresa espera impulsar su participación en el mercado; **incentive schemes are boosting production** = los planes de incentivo están estimulando la producción

QUOTE the company expects to boost turnover this year to FFr 16bn from FFr 13.6bn in 1994
                     Financial Times

booth [buːð] *noun* **(a)** cabina *f*; **telephone booth** = cabina telefónica; **ticket booth** = taquilla *f* **(b)** *(at exhibition)* US puesto *m* de exposición *or* 'stand' *m* (NOTE: the GB English for this is **stand)**

borrow ['bɒrəʊ] *verb* pedir *or* tomar prestado *or* a préstamo *or* en préstamo; **he borrowed £1,000 from the bank** = sacó un préstamo de £1000 del banco; **the company had to borrow heavily to repay its debts** = la compañía tuvo que pedir grandes préstamos para pagar sus deudas; **they borrowed £25,000 against the security of the factory** = obtuvieron un préstamo de £25.000 dando la fábrica como garantía; **to borrow short** *or* **long** = tomar en préstamo a corto *or* largo plazo

◊ **borrower** ['bɒrəʊə] *noun* prestatario, -ria; **borrowers from the bank pay 12% interest** = los prestatarios pagan un 12% de interés al banco

◊ **borrowing** ['bɒrəʊɪŋ] *noun* **(a)** préstamo *m*; **the new factory was financed by bank borrowing** = la nueva fábrica se financió con préstamos bancarios; **borrowing power** = capacidad de endeudamiento **(b) borrowings** = deuda *f*; **the company's borrowings have doubled** = la deuda de la compañía se ha duplicado; **bank borrowings** = préstamos bancarios

COMMENT: borrowings are sometimes shown as a percentage of shareholders' funds (i.e. capital and money in reserves); this gives a percentage which is the 'gearing' of the company

boss [bɒs] *noun (informal)* patrón, -ona *or* jefe, -fa *or* amo, -ma; **if you want a pay rise, go and talk to your boss** = si quieres un aumento de sueldo, ve a hablar con tu patrón; **he became a director when he married the boss's daughter** = le nombraron consejero cuando se casó con la hija del jefe

Botswana [bɒts'wɑːnə] *noun* Botswana

◊ **Botswanan** [bɒts'wɑːnən] **1** *adjective* de Botswana **2** *noun* nativo, -va *or* habitante de Botswana
NOTE: capital: **Gaborone;** currency: **pula** = pula

bottleneck ['bɒtlnek] *noun* atasco *m*; **a bottleneck in the supply system** = un atasco en el sistema de suministro; **there are serious bottlenecks in the production line** = hay serios atascos en la cadena de montaje

bottom ['bɒtəm] **1** *noun* fondo *m or* punto *m* más bajo *or* mínimo; **sales have reached rock bottom** = las ventas han tocado fondo; **the bottom has fallen out of the market** = el mercado se ha desplomado; **bottom price** = el precio más bajo; **rock-bottom price** = precio mínimo; **bottom line** = saldo final *or* total; **the boss is interested only in the bottom line** = el patrón se interesa únicamente por el saldo final **2** *verb* **to bottom (out)** = tocar fondo *or* alcanzar el punto mínimo *or* más bajo; **the market has bottomed out** = el mercado ha tocado fondo *or* ya no puede descender más

bottomry ['bɒtəmri] *noun* contrato *m* a la gruesa

bought [bɔ:t] *see* BUY **bought ledger** = libro mayor de compras; **bought ledger clerk** = encargado del libro de compras

bounce [baʊns] *verb (cheque)* devolver por falta de fondos; **he paid for the car with a cheque that bounced** = compró el coche con un cheque sin fondos

boundary ['baʊndri] *noun* acotación *f or* límite *m*

bounty ['baʊnti] *noun* subvención *f*

boutique [bu:'ti:k] *noun* boutique *f*; **a jeans boutique** = una tienda de vaqueros; **a ski boutique** = una tienda de artículos de esquí

box [bɒks] *noun* **(a)** caja *f*; **the goods were sent in thin cardboard boxes** = las mercancías se enviaron en cajas de cartón (delgado); **the watches are prepacked in plastic display boxes** = los relojes vienen empaquetados en cajas de plástico que permiten su exhibición; **paperclips come in boxes of two hundred** = los clips se venden en cajas de doscientos; **box file** = caja de registros *or* archivador **(b) box number** = número de apartado de correos; **please reply to Box No. 209** = enviar las respuestas al apartado de correos nº 209; **our address is: P.O. Box 74209, Edinburgh** = nuestra dirección es: P.O. Box 74209, Edimburgo **(c) cash box** = caja *f*; **letter box** *or* **mail box** = buzón *m*; **call box** = cabina *f* de teléfono; **suggestions box** = buzón de sugerencias

◊ **boxed** [bɒkst] *adjective* encajonado, -da; **boxed set** = juego completo de artículos vendidos en una caja

boycott ['bɔɪkɒt] **1** *noun* boicot *m*; **the union organized a boycott against** *or* **of imported cars** = el sindicato organizó un boicot contra los coches de importación **2** *verb* boicotear; **we are boycotting all imports from that country** = estamos boicoteando todas las importaciones de aquel país; **the management has boycotted the meeting** = la patronal ha boicoteado la reunión

B/P = BILLS PAYABLE

B/R = BILLS RECEIVABLE

bracket ['brækɪt] **1** *noun* **(a)** *(class)* categoría *f or* tramo *m or* clase *f*; **people in the middle-income bracket** = personas de ingresos medios; **he is in the top tax bracket** = paga impuestos por el tramo más alto **(b)** *(for shelves)* soporte *m* **2** *verb* **to bracket**

together = agrupar; **in the sales reports, all the European countries are bracketed together** = los países europeos están todos agrupados en los informes de ventas

brainstorming ['breɪnstɔ:mɪŋ] *noun* tormenta *f or* torbellino *m or* de ideas

branch [brɑ:n(t)ʃ] **1** *noun* **(a)** *(junction)* bifurcación *f* **(b)** *(of store, office)* sucursal *f*; **the bank** *or* **the store has branches in most towns in the south of the country** = el banco *or* la tienda tiene sucursales en la mayoría de las ciudades del sur del país; **the insurance company has closed its branches in South America** = la compañía de seguros cerró sus sucursales sudamericanas; **he is the manager of our local branch of Lloyds bank** = es el director de nuestra sucursal local del banco Lloyds; **we have decided to open a branch office in Chicago** = hemos decidido abrir una sucursal en Chicago; **the manager of our branch in Lagos** *or* **of our Lagos branch** = el director de nuestra sucursal de Lagos; **branch manager** = director *m* de sucursal **2** *verb* **to branch out** = ampliar *or* extender las actividades de un negocio *or* ampliar el negocio a una nueva rama *or* a otras actividades; **from car retailing, the company branched out into car leasing** = la empresa amplió su negocio de venta de coches con otro de alquiler

QUOTE a leading manufacturer of business, industrial and commercial products requires a branch manager to head up its mid-western Canada operations based in Winnipeg
Globe and Mail (Toronto)

brand [brænd] *noun* marca *f or* modelo *m or* tipo *m*; **the top-selling brands of toothpaste** = las marcas de pasta de dientes más vendidas; **the company is launching a new brand of soap** = la empresa va a lanzar una nueva marca de jabón; **brand name** = marca de fabricación *or* nombre comercial de un producto; **brand image** = imagen de marca; **brand leader** = marca líder; **brand loyalty** = fidelidad a la marca *or* lealtad de marca; **brand recognition** = reconocimiento de marca; **Brand X** = marca X (marca anónima utilizada en anuncios televisivos); **own brand** = marca propia

◊ **branded** ['brændɪd] *adjective* **branded goods** = artículos de marca

◊ **brand new** ['bræn(d) 'nju:] *adjective* completamente nuevo, -va *or* recién salido de fábrica

Brazil [brə'zɪl] *noun* Brasil *m*

◊ **Brazilian** [brə'zɪliən] *adjective* & *noun* brasileño, -ña *or* brasilero, -ra
NOTE: capital: **Brasilia**; currency: **Brazilian rial** = real (brasileño)

breach [bri:tʃ] *noun* incumplimiento *m or* violación *f*; **breach of contract** = incumplimiento de contrato; **the company is in breach of contract** = la empresa no ha cumplido el contrato; **breach of warranty** = violación de garantía

break [breɪk] **1** *noun* descanso *m or* receso *m*; **she typed for two hours without a break** = escribió a máquina sin parar durante dos horas; **coffee break** *or* **tea break** = pausa *f or* descanso durante el trabajo **2** *verb* **(a)** *(fail to keep)* infringir; **the company has broken the contract** *or* **the agreement** = la empresa ha infringido el contrato *or* el acuerdo; **to break an engagement to do something** = incumplir *or* romper un compromiso **(b)** *(cancel)* romper; **the company is hoping to be able to break the contract** = la empresa espera poder romper el contrato (NOTE: **breaking - broke - has broken)**

◊ **breakages** ['breɪkɪdʒɪz] *plural noun* roturas *fpl*; **customers are expected to pay for breakages** = los clientes deben hacerse cargo de los desperfectos

◊ **break down** ['breɪk 'daʊn] *verb* **(a)** *(machine)* estropearse *or* averiarse; **the telex machine has broken down** = la máquina de telex se ha estropeado; **what do you do when your photocopier breaks down?** = ¿qué hace Vd. cuando se avería su fotocopiadora? **(b)** *(talks)* romperse; **negotiations broke down after six hours** = hubo una ruptura de las negociaciones después de seis horas **(c)** *(itemize)* desglosar *or* detallar *or* pormenorizar; **we broke the expenditure down into fixed and variable costs** = desglosamos los gastos en costes fijos y variables; **can you break down this invoice into spare parts and labour?** = ¿puede desglosar esta factura en repuestos y mano de obra?

◊ **breakdown** ['breɪkdaʊn] *noun* **(a)** *(mechanical)* avería *f*; **we cannot communicate with our Nigerian office because of the breakdown of the telephone lines** = no podemos comunicar con nuestra sucursal en Nigeria debido a la avería en las líneas telefónicas **(b)** *(talks)* ruptura *f*; **a breakdown in wage negotiations** = una ruptura de las negociaciones salariales **(c)** *(items)* desglose *m or* detalle *m*; **give me a breakdown of investment costs** = déme el detalle de los costes de inversión **(d)** **nervous breakdown** = colapso nervioso *or* depresión nerviosa

◊ **break even** ['breɪk 'iːvən] *verb* cubrir gastos; **last year the company only just broke even** = el año pasado la compañía apenas cubrió gastos; **we broke even in our first two months of trading** = cubrimos gastos en los dos primeros meses de actividad

◊ **breakeven point** [breɪk'iːvn 'pɔɪnt] *noun* punto *m* muerto *or* punto crítico *or* umbral *m* de rentabilidad

◊ **break off** ['breɪk 'ɒf] *verb* romper *or* interrumpir; **we broke off the discussion at midnight** = interrumpimos las conversaciones a medianoche; **management broke off negotiations with the union** = la dirección rompió las negociaciones con el sindicato

◊ **break up** ['breɪk 'ʌp] *verb* **(a)** *(divide)* parcelar *or* dividir; **the company was broken up and separate divisions sold off** = la compañía fue dividida y se vendió cada parte por separado **(b)** *(end)* terminar; **the meeting broke up at 12.30** = la reunión terminó a las 12.30

bribe [braɪb] **1** *noun* soborno *m or* cohecho *m*; **the minister was dismissed for taking bribes** = el ministro fue destituido por aceptar sobornos **2** *verb* sobornar; **we had to bribe the minister's secretary before she would let us see her boss** = tuvimos que sobornar a la secretaria del ministro para que nos permitiera ver a su jefe

◊ **bribery** ['braɪbrɪ] *noun* cohecho *m*

bridging loan *or* US **bridge loan** ['brɪdʒɪŋ 'ləʊn *or* 'brɪdʒ 'ləʊn] *noun* crédito *m* puente

brief [briːf] **1** *adjective* breve **2** *noun* instrucciones *fpl or* mandato *m (legal)* escrito *m* **3** *verb* informar *or* dar instrucciones; **the salesmen were briefed on the new product** = los vendedores recibieron instrucciones relativas al nuevo producto; **the managing director briefed the board on the progress of the negotiations** = el director gerente informó al consejo de administración sobre la evolución de las negociaciones

◊ **briefcase** ['briːfkeɪs] *noun* cartera *f or* maletín *m*; **he put all the files into his briefcase** = metió todos los documentos en su cartera

◊ **briefing** ['briːfɪŋ] *noun* sesión *f* informativa *or* de instrucciones; **all salesmen have to attend a sales briefing on the new product** = todos los vendedores tienen que asistir a una sesión informativa sobre el nuevo producto

bring [brɪŋ] *verb* traer *or* llevar; **he brought his documents with him** = trajo consigo sus documentos; **the finance director brought his secretary to take notes of the meeting** = el director de finanzas trajo a su secretaria para que tomara notas de la reunión; **to bring a lawsuit against someone** = demandar judicialmente a alguien (NOTE: **bringing - brought)**

◊ **bring down** ['brɪŋ 'daʊn] *verb* **(a)** reducir; **oil companies have brought down the price of petrol=** las empresas petrolíferas han reducido el precio de la gasolina **(b)** = BRING FORWARD (b) saldar; **balance brought down: £365.15** = saldo anterior: £365,15

◊ **bring forward** ['brɪŋ 'fɔːwəd] *verb* **(a)** adelantar; **to bring forward the date of repayment** = adelantar la fecha de reembolso; **the date of the next meeting has been brought forward to March** = la fecha de la próxima reunión se ha adelantado a marzo **(b)** saldar a cuenta nueva; **balance brought forward: £365.15** = saldo a cuenta nueva: £365,15

◊ **bring in** ['brɪŋ 'ɪn] *verb* producir; **the shares bring in a small amount** = las acciones producen una renta pequeña

◊ **bring out** ['brɪŋ 'aʊt] *verb* lanzar al mercado; **they are bringing out a new model of the car for the Motor Show** = van a lanzar un nuevo modelo del coche para el salón del automóvil

◊ **bring up** ['brɪŋ 'ʌp] *verb* plantear; **the chairman brought up the question of redundancy payments** = el presidente planteó la cuestión de las indemnizaciones por despido

brisk [brɪsk] *adjective* vigoroso, -sa *or* activo, -va *or* animado, -da; **sales are brisk** = las ventas van muy bien; **the market in oil shares is particularly brisk** = el mercado de acciones petrolíferas se muestra especialmente activo; **a brisk market in oil shares** = un mercado de acciones petrolíferas muy animado *or* activo

Britain, British ['brɪtən *or* 'brɪtɪʃ] *see* GREAT BRITAIN

broadside ['brɔːdsaɪd] *noun* US prospecto *m* publicitario

brochure ['brəʊʃə] *noun* folleto *m* publicitario; **we sent off for a brochure about holidays in Greece** *or* **about postal services** = solicitamos *or* pedimos un folleto sobre vacaciones en Grecia *or* sobre los servicios de correo

broke [brəʊk] *adjective (informal)* sin dinero *or* arruinado, -da; **to be flat broke** = estar sin blanca; **the company is broke** = la compañía está sin dinero; **he cannot pay for the new car because he is broke** = no puede pagar el nuevo coche porque no tiene un duro; **to go broke** = quebrar; **the company went broke last month** = la compañía quebró el mes pasado

broker ['brəʊkə] *noun* **(a)** agente *mf* comercial *or* intermediario, -ria *or* corredor *m*; **foreign exchange broker** = operador de cambios *or* cambista; **insurance broker** = agente libre de seguros *or* corredor de seguros; **ship broker** = consignatario *or* agente marítimo **(b) (stock)broker** = corredor de bolsa **(c)** *see also* HONEST

◊ **brokerage** *or* **broker's commission** ['brəʊkərɪdʒ *or* 'brəʊkəz kə'mɪʃən] *noun* corretaje *m* *or* comisión *f*

◊ **broking** ['brəʊkɪŋ] *noun* corretaje *m*

brought down (b/d) *or* **brought forward (b/f)** ['brɔːt 'daʊn *or* 'brɔːt 'fɔːwəd] *phrase* saldo anterior *or* saldo a cuenta nueva; *(in accounts)* **balance brought down** *or* **forward: £365.15** = saldo anterior *or* a cuenta nueva: £365,15

Brussels ['brʌslz] *noun* Bruselas

bubble ['bʌbl] *noun* burbuja *f*; **bubble envelope** = sobre tipo burbuja; **bubble pack** *or* **bubble wrap** = embalaje *m* de plástico tipo burbuja; *see also* BLISTER PACK

buck [bʌk] **1** *noun* US *(informal)* dólar *m* *or* pasta *f*; **to make a quick buck** = hacer dinero fácilmente **2** *verb* **to buck the trend** = ir contracorriente

bucket shop ['bʌkɪt 'ʃɒp] *noun (informal)* **(a)** agencia *f* de viajes que vende billetes de avión con descuento **(b)** *US* operaciones *fpl* ilegales en la bolsa

budget ['bʌdʒɪt] **1** *noun* **(a)** *(spending and income plan)* presupuesto *m*; **to draw up a budget** = preparar un presupuesto; **we have agreed the budgets for next year** = hemos aprobado los presupuestos para el año próximo; **advertising budget** = presupuesto de publicidad; **cash budget** = presupuesto de caja; **overhead budget** = presupuesto de gastos generales; **publicity budget** = presupuesto de publicidad; **sales budget** = presupuesto de ventas; **budget cuts** = reducción *or* recortes de presupuesto **(b)** *(of Government)* **the Budget** = el presupuesto del Estado; **the minister put forward a budget aimed at boosting the economy** = el ministro propuso un presupuesto destinado a reactivar la economía; **to balance the budget** = equilibrar el presupuesto; **the president is planning for a balanced budget** = el presidente proyecta un presupuesto equilibrado; **budget deficit** = déficit presupuestario **(c)** *(in a bank)* **budget account** = cuenta presupuestaria **(d)** *(in shops)* barato, -ta *or* económico, -ca (en tiendas); **budget prices** = precios económicos **2** *verb* presupuestar; **we are budgeting for £10,000 of sales next year** = estamos haciendo un presupuesto de ventas de £10.000 para el año próximo

◊ **budgetary** ['bʌdʒɪtəri] *adjective* presupuestario, -ria; **budgetary policy** = política presupuestaria; **budgetary control** = control presupuestario; **budgetary requirements** = requisitos presupuestarios

◊ **budgeting** ['bʌdʒɪtɪŋ] *noun* preparación *or* elaboración de presupuestos

buffer stocks ['bʌfə 'stɒks] *noun* fondo *m* de regulación *or* existencias *fpl* reguladoras

bug [bʌg] *noun (in computer program)* error *m* *or* defecto *m*

build [bɪld] *verb* construir *or* montar; urbanizar; **to build a sales structure** = establecer una estructura de ventas; **to build on past experience** = basarse en la experiencia acumulada (NOTE: **building - built**)

◊ **building** ['bɪldɪŋ] *noun* edificio *m*; **they have redeveloped the site of the old office building** = han renovado el entorno del viejo edificio comercial; **the Shell Building** = el edificio de Shell; **building site** = obra *f* *or* solar *m* para edificar

◊ **building and loan association** ['bɪldɪŋ ənd 'ləʊn əsəʊsi'eɪʃən] *noun* US = SAVINGS AND LOAN ASSOCIATION

◊ **building society** ['bɪldɪŋ sə'saɪəti] *noun* GB sociedad *f* hipotecaria *or* de crédito hipotecario; **he put his savings into a building society** *or* **into a building society account** = depositó sus ahorros en una sociedad de crédito hipotecario *or* en una cuenta de una sociedad hipotecaria; **I have an account with the Halifax Building Society** = tengo una cuenta en la Halifax Building Society; **I saw the building society manager to ask for a mortgage** = me entrevisté con el director de la sociedad hipotecaria para solicitar una hipoteca

◊ **build into** ['bɪld 'ɪntʊ] *verb* incorporar *or*

añadir; **you must build all the forecasts into the budget** = debe incorporar todos las previsiones en el presupuesto; **we have built 10% for contingencies into our cost forecast** = hemos añadido un 10% a nuestra previsión de costes para imprevistos

◊ **build up** ['bɪld 'ʌp] *verb* **(a)** *(create)* construir *or* levantar; **he bought several shoe shops and gradually built up a chain** = compró varias zapaterías y paulatinamente fue creando una cadena **(b)** *(expand gradually)* montar *or* organizar; **to build up a profitable business** = montar un negocio rentable; **to build up a team of salesmen** = organizar un equipo de vendedores

◊ **buildup** ['bɪldʌp] *noun* aumento *m*; **a buildup in sales** *or* **a sales buildup** = un aumento de las ventas; **there will be a big publicity buildup before the launch of the new model** = habrá un aumento persistente de la publicidad antes del lanzamiento del nuevo modelo

◊ **built-in** ['bɪlt 'ɪn] *adjective* incorporado, -da; **the micro has a built-in clock** = el micro tiene un reloj interno; **the accounting system has a series of built-in checks** = el sistema contable tiene incorporada toda una serie de controles

Bulgaria [bʌl'geəriə] *noun* Bulgaria *f*

◊ **Bulgarian** [bʌl'geəriən] *adjective & noun* búlgaro, -ra
NOTE: capital: **Sofia**; currency: **Bulgarian lev** = lev búlgaro

bulk [bʌlk] *noun* **(a)** *(large quantity)* volumen *m*; **in bulk** = a granel; **to buy rice in bulk** = comprar arroz a granel; **bulk buying** *or* **bulk purchase** = compra a granel; **bulk carrier** = buque para carga a granel *or* granelero; **bulk discount** = descuento al por mayor; **bulk shipments** = envíos a granel **(b)** *(main part)* grueso *m*; **the bulk of the order has been dispatched** = el grueso del pedido se ha enviado

◊ **bulky** ['bʌlki] *adjective* voluminoso, -sa; **the Post Office does not accept bulky packages** = la oficina de correos no acepta paquetes voluminosos

bull [bʊl] *noun (Stock Exchange)* alcista *mf* de bolsa *or* especulador, -ra de acciones; **bull market** = mercado alcista; *see* BEAR

◊ **bullish** ['bʊlɪʃ] *adjective* alcista

QUOTE lower interest rates are always a bull factor for the stock market
Financial Times

QUOTE another factor behind the currency market's bullish mood may be the growing realisation that Japan stands to benefit from the current combination of high domestic interest rates and a steadily rising exchange rate
Far Eastern Economic Review

bulletin ['bʊlɪtɪn] *noun* boletín *m* *(in Spain)* **Official State Bulletin** = Boletín Oficial del Estado (BOE)

bullion ['bʊljən] *noun* oro *m* *or* plata *f* en lingotes; **gold bullion** = oro en lingotes; **the price of bullion is fixed daily** = el precio del oro en lingotes se fija diariamente; **to fix the bullion price for silver** = fijar el precio de la plata en lingotes (NOTE: no plural in English)

bumper ['bʌmpə] *adjective* abundante *or*

extraordinario *or* record; **a bumper crop of corn** = una cosecha extraordinaria de maíz; **1991 was a bumper year for computer sales** = 1991 fue un año excelente para la venta de ordenadores

bumping ['bʌmpɪŋ] *noun US* situación *f* en la cual un empleado superior toma el lugar de un subalterno (en un restaurante *or* en un trabajo)

Bundesbank ['bʊndəsbæŋk] *noun (German central bank)* Bundesbank *m*

burden ['bɜ:dn] **1** *noun* carga *f*; **tax burden** = carga impositiva *or* gravamen; **to lighten the tax burden** = aligerar *or* reducir la carga impositiva *or* desgravar **2** *verb* **to be burdened with debt** = estar cargado *or* agobiado de deudas

bureau ['bjʊərəʊ] *noun* oficina *f* *or* agencia *f*; **computer bureau** = oficina de informática; *US* **credit bureau** = agencia de informes comerciales; **employment bureau** = agencia de empleo; **information bureau** = oficina de información; **trade bureau** = oficina comercial; **visitors' bureau** = oficina de visitantes; **word-processing bureau** = oficina de tratamiento de textos; **we farm out the office typing to a local bureau** = encargamos todo el trabajo de mecanografía a una agencia local (NOTE: the plural is **bureaux**)

◊ **bureau de change** ['bjʊərəʊ də 'ʃɑːnʒ] *noun* oficina *f* de cambio

Burma ['bɜːmə] *noun* Birmania *f* (NOTE: now called **Myanmar**)

◊ **Burmese** [bɜː'miːz] *adjective & noun* birmano, -na
NOTE: capital: **Rangoon**; currency: **Burmese kyat (K)** = kyat birmano (K)

burn [bɜːn] *verb* quemar; **the chief accountant burnt the documents before the police arrived** = el contable jefe quemó los documentos antes de que llegara la policía (NOTE: **burning - burnt**)

◊ **burn down** ['bɜːn 'daʊn] *verb* quemarse totalmente; **the warehouse burnt down and all the stock was destroyed** = el almacén se quemó totalmente y todas las existencias quedaron destruidas; **the company records were all lost when the offices were burnt down** = todos los archivos de la empresa se perdieron cuando las oficinas quedaron destruidas por un incendio

Burundi [bʊ'rʊndi] *noun* Burundi *m*

◊ **Burundian** [bʊ'rʊndiən] *adjective & noun* (habitante) de Burundi
NOTE: capital: **Bujumbura**; currency: **Burundi franc (BuF)** = franco de Burundi (FBu)

bus [bʌs] *noun* autobús *m*; **he goes to work by bus** = va al trabajo en autobús; **she took the bus to go to her office** = tomó el autobús para ir a la oficina; **bus company** = empresa de autobuses

bushel ['bʊʃl] *noun* medida *f* de áridos (= 56 libras)

business ['bɪznəs] *noun* **(a)** *(commerce)* comercio *m* *or* negocios *mpl* *or* actividad *f* comercial; **business is expanding** = el comercio está en alza; **business is slow** = la actividad comercial es baja; **he does a thriving business in repairing cars** = tiene un negocio muy próspero de reparación de coches;

what's your line of business? = ¿a qué tipo de negocios se dedica Vd.?; **business call** = una visita de negocios; **business centre** = centro comercial; **business class** = clase preferente (en aviones); **business college** *or* **business school** = escuela empresarial *or* escuela de negocios *or* escuela superior de comercio; **business correspondent** = corresponsal comercial; **business cycle** = ciclo económico; **business efficiency exhibition** = exposición de eficiencia comercial; **business hours** = horario comercial; **business letter** = carta comercial; **business lunch** = almuerzo de negocios; **business plan** = plan económico *or* comercial (de una empresa); **business strategy** = estrategia comercial (de una empresa); **business trip** = viaje de negocios; **to be in business** = dedicarse a los negocios; **to go into business** = iniciar un negocio; **he went into business as a car dealer** = inició un negocio de venta de automóviles; **to go out of business** = quebrar; **the firm went out of business during the recession** = la empresa quebró durante la recesión; **on business** = por asuntos de negocios; **he had to go abroad on business** = tuvo que viajar al extranjero por asuntos de negocios; **the chairman is in Holland on business** = el presidente está en Holanda en viaje de negocios **(b)** *(company)* empresa *f*; **he owns a small car repair business** = es dueño de una pequeña empresa de reparación de coches; **she runs a business from her home** = dirige una empresa desde su casa; **he set up in business as an insurance broker** = montó una agencia de seguros; **business address** = dirección comercial; **business card** = tarjeta comercial *or* profesional; **business correspondence** = correspondencia comercial; **business equipment** = equipos de oficina; **business expenses** = gastos de explotación; **big business** = las grandes empresas; **small businesses** = las pequeñas empresas **(c)** *(discussion)* asunto *m*; **the main business of the meeting was finished by 3 p.m.** = el asunto principal de la reunión se concluyó antes de las 3 de la tarde; **any other business (AOB)** = ruegos y preguntas *or* otros asuntos (NOTE: no plural for meanings (a) and (c); (b) has the plural **businesses**)

◊ **business agent** [ˈbɪznəs ˈeɪdʒənt] *noun US* delegado *m* de un sindicato local

◊ **businessman** [ˈbɪznɪsmən] *noun* empresario *m or* hombre de negocios; **a small businessman** = un pequeño empresario

◊ **businesswoman** [ˈbɪznɪswʊmən] *noun* empresaria *f or* mujer de negocios; **she's a good businesswoman** = es una buena empresaria

bust [bʌst] *adjective (informal)* **to go bust** = quebrar

busy [ˈbɪzi] *adjective* ocupado, -da; **he is busy preparing the annual accounts** = está ocupado con la preparación de las cuentas anuales; **the manager is busy at the moment, but he will be free in about fifteen minutes** = el director está ocupado ahora, pero estará libre dentro de unos quince minutos; **the busiest time of year for stores is the week before Christmas** = el periodo del año de mayor actividad en las tiendas es la semana anterior a las Navidades; **summer is the busy season for hotels** = el verano es la temporada de mayor actividad para los hoteles; *(on the telephone)* **the line is busy** = la línea está ocupada

buy [baɪ] **1** *verb* comprar *or* adquirir; **he bought**

10,000 **shares** = compró 10.000 acciones; **the company has been bought by its leading supplier** = la empresa ha sido adquirida por su principal suministrador; **to buy wholesale and sell retail** = comprar al por mayor y vender al por menor; **to buy for cash** = comprar en efectivo *or* al contado; **to buy forward** = comprar a futuros (NOTE: buying - bought) **2** *noun* **good buy** *or* **bad buy** = buena compra *or* mala compra; **that watch was a good buy** = aquel reloj fue una buena compra; **this car was a bad buy** = este coche fue una mala compra

◊ **buy back** [ˈbaɪ ˈbæk] *verb* volver a comprar *or* rescatar; **he sold the shop last year and is now trying to buy it back** = vendió la tienda el año pasado y ahora esta tratando de volver a comprarla

◊ **buyer** [ˈbaɪə] *noun* **(a)** comprador, -ra; **there were no buyers** = no hubo compradores; **a buyers' market** = mercado favorable a los compradores (NOTE: the opposite is a **seller's market**) **impulse buyer** = comprador impulsivo; **at buyer's risk** = a cuenta y riesgo del comprador **(b)** encargado, -da de compras; **head buyer** = jefe de compras; **she is the shoe buyer for a London department store** = es la encargada de compras de calzado para unos grandes almacenes de Londres

◊ **buy in** [ˈbaɪ ˈɪn] *verb (of a seller at an auction)* comprar uno mismo lo que subasta al no obtener el precio deseado

◊ **buyin** [ˈbaɪɪn] *noun* **management buyin** = compra de una empresa por los directores de otra compañía

◊ **buying** [ˈbaɪɪŋ] *noun* compra *f*; **bulk buying** = compra a granel; **forward buying** *or* **buying forward** = compra de futuros; **impulse buying** = compra impulsiva; **panic buying** = compras impulsadas por el pánico; **buying department** = departamento de compras; **buying power** = poder adquisitivo; **the buying power of the pound has fallen over the last five years** = el poder adquisitivo de la libra ha bajado durante los últimos cinco años

◊ **buyout** [ˈbaɪaʊt] *noun* **management buyout (MBO)** = adquisición *f or* compra *f* de una empresa por sus propios directivos; **leveraged buyout (LBO)** = compra *or* adquisición apalancada

QUOTE we also invest in companies whose growth and profitability could be improved by a management buyout
Times

QUOTE in a normal leveraged buyout, the acquirer raises money by borrowing against the assets or cash flow of the target company
Fortune

bylaws [ˈbaɪlɔːz] *plural noun* **(a)** reglamentos que gobiernan los organismos autónomos y la administración local **(b)** *US* reglamento *m* estatutos *mpl* de una asociación (NOTE: in the UK, called **Articles of Association**)

by-product [ˈbaɪprɒdʌkt] *noun* subproducto *m or* producto secundario *m*; **glycerol is a useful by-product of soap manufacture** = el glicerol es un producto aprovechable de la fabricación del jabón

byte [baɪt] *noun* 'byte' *m or* octeto *m*

Cc

cab [kæb] *noun (taxi)* taxi; **he took a cab to the airport** = tomó un taxi para ir al aeropuerto; **the office is only a short cab ride from the railway station** = la oficina está a unos minutos de la estación en taxi; **cab fares are very high in New York** = los taxis de Nueva York son muy caros

◊ **cab driver** *or (informal)* **cabbie** ['kæb 'draɪvə *or* 'kæbɪ] *noun* taxista *mf*

cabinet ['kæbɪnət] *noun* **(a)** *(furniture)* armario *m*; **last year's correspondence is in the bottom drawer of the filing cabinet** = la correspondencia del año pasado está en el último cajón del archivador; **display cabinet** = vitrina *f* **(b)** *(government)* gabinete *m*; **cabinet meeting** = Consejo *m* de Ministros

cable ['keɪbl] **1** *noun* telegrama *m*; **he sent a cable to his office asking for more money** = envió un telegrama a su oficina pidiendo más dinero; **cable address** = dirección telegráfica **2** *verb* telegrafiar; **he cabled his office to ask them to send more money** = envió un telegrama a su oficina pidiendo que le enviasen más dinero; **the office cabled him £1,000 to cover his expenses** = la oficina le envió un giro telegráfico de £1.000 para cubrir sus gastos

◊ **cablegram** ['keɪblɡræm] *noun* telegrama *m*

calculate ['kælkjʊleɪt] *verb* **(a)** *(with numbers)* calcular; **the bank clerk calculated the rate of exchange for the dollar** = el cajero calculó el tipo de cambio del dólar **(b)** *(estimate)* calcular *or* tantear; **I calculate that we have six months' stock left** = calculo que nos quedan existencias para seis meses

◊ **calculating machine** ['kælkjʊleɪtɪŋ mə'ʃiːn] *noun* máquina *f* de calcular *or* calculadora *f*

◊ **calculation** [kælkjʊ'leɪʃən] *noun* cálculo *m*; **rough calculation** = cálculo aproximado *or* tanteo *m*; **I made some rough calculations on the back of an envelope** = hice unos cálculos aproximados al dorso de un sobre; **according to my calculations, we have six months' stock left** = de acuerdo con mis cálculos, nos quedan existencias para seis meses; **we are £20,000 out in our calculations** = hay un error de £20.000 en nuestros cálculos

◊ **calculator** ['kælkjʊleɪtə] *noun* calculadora *f*; **my pocket calculator needs new batteries** = mi calculadora de bolsillo necesita pilas nuevas; **he worked out the discount on his calculator** = calculó el descuento en su calculadora

calendar ['kæləndə] *noun* calendario *m*; **for the New Year the garage sent me a calendar with photographs of old cars** = por Año Nuevo el garage me envió un calendario con fotos de coches antiguos; **calendar month** = mes civil; **calendar year** = año civil

call [kɔːl] **1** *noun* **(a)** *(on telephone)* llamada *f*; **local call** = llamada local; **trunk call** *or* **long-distance call** = llamada *or* conferencia interurbana; **overseas call** *or* **international call** = llamada *or* conferencia internacional; **person-to-person call** = conferencia personal; **transferred charge call** *or* **reverse charge**

call *or US* **collect call** = llamada a cobro revertido; **to make a call** = hacer una llamada; **to take a call** = recibir una llamada; **to log calls** = anotar los detalles de las llamadas recibidas **(b)** *(asking for money)* demanda *f* de pago; **money at call** *or* **money on call** *or* **call money** = dinero pagadero a petición *or* dinero a la vista *or* crédito exigible en cualquier momento **(c)** *(Stock Exchange)* demanda *f* de pago por nuevas acciones; **call option** = opción de compra de acciones a un precio determinado (NOTE: the opposite is **put**) **(d)** *(visit)* visita *f*; **the salesmen make six calls a day** = los vendedores realizan seis visitas al día; **business call** = visita de negocios; **cold call** = visita comercial sin cita previa a un cliente no habitual; **call rate** = frecuencia de visitas de un representante durante un tiempo determinado **2** *verb* **(a)** *(to phone)* llamar (por teléfono); **I'll call you at your office tomorrow** = le llamaré mañana a su oficina **(b)** *(to visit)* **to call on someone** = visitar; **our salesmen call on their best accounts twice a month** = nuestros representantes visitan a sus mejores clientes dos veces por mes **(c)** *(convene)* **to call a meeting** = convocar una reunión; **to call a strike** = llamar a la huelga; **the union called a strike** = el sindicato convocó una huelga **(d)** *(stop at)* hacer escala

◊ **callable bond** ['kɔːləbl 'bɒnd] *noun* obligación *f* redimible

◊ **call-back pay** ['kɔːlbæk 'peɪ] *noun* paga *f* por horas extras

◊ **callbox** ['kɔːlbɒks] *noun* cabina *f* telefónica

◊ **called up capital** ['kɔːld ʌp 'kæpɪtl] *noun* capital *m* desembolsado

◊ **caller** ['kɔːlə] *noun* **(a)** *(phone)* comunicante *mf* **(b)** *(visitor)* visita *f or* visitante *m*

◊ **call in** ['kɔːl 'ɪn] *verb* **(a)** *(visit)* visitar; **the sales representative called in twice last week** = el representante hizo dos visitas durante la semana pasada **(b)** *(phone)* llamar por teléfono; **we ask the reps to call in every Friday to report the weeks' sales** = pedimos a los representantes que nos llamen todos los viernes para informarnos de las ventas de la semana **(c)** *(debt)* pedir el reembolso (de un préstamo) *or* exigir el pago de una deuda

◊ **call off** ['kɔːl 'ɒf] *verb* desconvocar; **the union has called off the strike** = el sindicato ha desconvocado la huelga; **the deal was called off at the last moment** = en convenio fue suspendido en el último momento

◊ **call up** ['kɔːl 'ʌp] *verb* pedir el desembolso de capital

calm [kɑːm] *adjective* tranquilo, -la; **the markets were calmer after the government statement on**

the exchange rate = los mercados se tranquilizaron después del anuncio del gobierno sobre el tipo de cambio

Cambodia [kæm'bəʊdiə] *noun* Camboya

◊ **Cambodian** [kæm'bəʊdiən] *adjective & noun* camboyano, -na
NOTE: capital: **Phnom Penh**; currency: **riel** = riel

Cameroon [kæmə'ruːn] *noun* Camerún *m*

◊ **Cameroonian** [kæmə'ruːniən] *adjective & noun* camerunense
NOTE: capital: **Yaoundé**; currency: **CFA franc (CFAF)** = franco CFA (FCFA)

campaign [kæm'peɪn] *noun* campaña *f*; **sales campaign** = campaña de ventas; **publicity campaign** *or* **advertising campaign** = campaña publicitaria; **they are working on a campaign to launch a new brand of soap** = están preparando una campaña para lanzar una nueva marca de jabón

Canada ['kænədə] *noun* Canadá *m*

◊ **Canadian** [kə'neɪdjən] *adjective & noun* canadiense
NOTE: capital: **Ottawa**; currency: **Canadian dollar ($ or Can$)** = dólar canadiense ($ *or* Can$)

cancel ['kænsəl] *verb* **(a)** cancelar *or* suspender *or* anular; **to cancel an appointment** *or* **a meeting** = suspender una cita *or* una reunión; **to cancel a contract** = anular *or* rescindir un contrato; **the government has cancelled the order for a fleet of buses** = el gobierno ha cancelado el pedido de una flota de autobuses **(b) to cancel a cheque** = anular un cheque (NOTE: GB English: **cancelling - cancelled** but US English: **canceling - canceled**)

◊ **cancellation** [kænsə'leɪʃən] *noun* cancelación *f or* anulación *f*; **cancellation of an appointment** = cancelación de una cita; **cancellation of an agreement** = anulación de un acuerdo; **cancellation clause** = cláusula de rescisión

◊ **cancel out** ['kænsəl 'aʊt] *verb* contrarrestar *or* neutralizar; **the two clauses cancel each other out** = las dos cláusulas se neutralizan mutuamente; **costs have cancelled out the sales revenue** = los costos han contrarrestado los ingresos de las ventas

candidate ['kændɪdət] *noun* candidato, -ta *or* aspirante *mf* (*in public competition*) opositor, -tora; **there are six candidates for the post of assistant manager** = hay seis aspirantes al puesto de director adjunto; **we have called three candidates for interview** = hemos llamado a tres candidatos para una entrevista

canteen [kæn'tiːn] *noun* cantina *f or* comedor *m*

canvass ['kænvəs] *verb* solicitar pedidos *or* votos *or* sondear la opinión pública; **he's canvassing for customers for his hairdresser's shop** = está buscando clientes para su peluquería; **we have canvassed the staff about raising the prices in the staff restaurant** = hemos hecho un sondeo de opinión entre el personal para ver si se pueden aumentar los precios de la cantina

◊ **canvasser** ['kænvəsə] *noun* agente *mf* electoral *or* vendedor, -ra a domicilio *or* persona que solicita votos

◊ **canvassing** ['kænvəsɪŋ] *noun* sondeo *m* de opinión *or* búsqueda *f* de clientes *or* solicitación *f* de votos; **canvassing techniques** = técnicas de sondeo; **door-to-door canvassing** = solicitación *f or* sondeo de puerta en puerta

CAP ['siː 'eɪ 'piː] = COMMON AGRICULTURAL POLICY PAC (= Política Agrícola Común)

cap [kæp] **1** *noun* **(a)** (*lid*) tapa *f or* tapón *m*; **child-proof cap** = tapón de seguridad (a prueba de niños) **(b)** (*capital letters*) **caps** = mayúsculas **2** *verb* **(a)** (*to place an upper limit on something*) limitar *or* restringir *or* poner un límite; **to cap a local authority's budget** = limitar el presupuesto municipal **(b)** (*surpass*) superar *or* sobrepasar *or* exceder (NOTE: **capping - capped**)

capable ['keɪpəbl] *adjective* **(a)** (*able*) **capable of** = capaz; **she is capable of very fast typing speeds** = puede escribir a máquina con increíble rapidez; **the sales force must be capable of selling all the stock in the warehouse** = el personal de ventas tiene que ser capaz de vender toda la mercancía del almacén **(b)** (*efficient*) competente; **she is a very capable departmental manager** = es una directora de departamento muy competente (NOTE: you are capable **of** something or **of doing** something)

capacity [kə'pæsəti] *noun* **(a)** (*production*) capacidad *f or* rendimiento *m*; **industrial** *or* **manufacturing** *or* **production capacity** capacidad industrial *or* de fabricación *or* de producción; **to work at full capacity** = trabajar a pleno rendimiento *or* a plena capacidad; **to use up spare** *or* **excess capacity** = aprovechar la capacidad ociosa *or* el exceso de capacidad **(b)** (*space*) capacidad *f*; **storage capacity** = capacidad de almacenamiento; **warehouse capacity** = capacidad del almacén **(c)** (*ability*) capacidad *f or* aptitud *f or* habilidad *f*; **he has a particular capacity for business** = tiene una aptitud especial para los negocios; **earning capacity** = escala *f or* capacidad *f or* grado *m* de rendimiento **(d)** (*acting as*) **in a capacity** = en calidad de; **in his capacity as chairman** = en su calidad de presidente; **speaking in an official capacity** = hablando con carácter oficial

> QUOTE analysts are increasingly convinced that the industry simply has too much capacity
> **Fortune**

capita ['kæpɪtə] *see* PER CAPITA

capital ['kæpɪtl] *noun* **(a)** (*assets*) capital *m*; **company with £10,000 capital** *or* **with a capital of £10,000** = compañía con un capital de £10.000; **authorized capital** *or* **registered capital** *or* **nominal capital** = emisión autorizada *or* capital escriturado; **circulating capital** = capital circulante; **equity capital** = capital en acciones *or* valor nominal de las acciones de una compañía; **fixed capital** = capital fijo; **issued capital** = capital emitido; **paid-up capital** = capital desembolsado; **risk capital** *or* **venture capital** = capital-riesgo; **share capital** = capital en acciones; **working capital** = capital operativo *or* circulante; **capital account** = cuenta de capital; **capital assets** = bienes de capital *or* activo fijo; **capital bonus** = prima concedida por una compañía de seguros en concepto de plusvalía; **capital equipment** = bienes de equipo; **capital expenditure** *or* **investment** *or* **outlay** = gastos de capital *or* inversión; **capital goods** = bienes de capital *or* equipo; **capital inflow** = entrada *or* afluencia de capital; **capital levy** = impuesto sobre el capital; **capital loss** = pérdidas de capital *or* minusvalías; **capital reserves** = reservas de capital; **capital structure of a company** = estructura del capital de una compañía; **capital transfer tax** = impuesto sobre las transferencias de capital **(b)** *(investment)* fondos *mpl* para invertir; **movements of capital** = movimientos *or* circulación de capital; **flight of capital** = evasión *or* fuga de capitales; **capital market** = mercado de capitales (NOTE: no plural for senses (a) or (b)) **(c)** *(letters)* **capital letters** *or* **block capitals** = letras *fpl* mayúsculas; **write your name in block capitals at the top of the form** = escriba su nombre con letras mayúsculas en la parte superior del formulario

◊ **capital allowances** ['kæpɪtl ə'lauənsɪz] *noun* amortizaciones *fpl or* desgravación *f* sobre bienes de capital

COMMENT: allowances based on the value of fixed assets which may be deducted from a company's profits and so reduce its tax liability. Under current UK law, depreciation is not allowable for tax on profits, whereas capital allowances, based on the value of fixed assets owned by the company, are tax-allowable

◊ **capital gains** ['kæpɪtl 'geɪnz] *noun* ganancias de capital *or* plusvalía; **capital gains tax (CGT)** = impuesto sobre la plusvalía

COMMENT: money made by selling fixed assets or certain other types of property (such as works of art, leases, etc.) for more than their purchase price; if the asset is sold for less than its purchase price, the result is a capital loss. In the UK, capital gains tax is payable on capital gains from the sale of assets, in particular shares and properties, above a certain minimum level

◊ **capitalism** ['kæpɪtəlɪzəm] *noun* capitalismo *m*

◊ **capitalist** ['kæpɪtəlɪst] **1** *noun* capitalista *mf* **2** *adjective* capitalista; **a capitalist economy** = una economía capitalista; **the capitalist system** = el sistema capitalista; **the capitalist countries** *or* **world** = los países capitalistas *or* el mundo capitalista

◊ **capitalize** ['kæpɪtəlaɪz] *verb* capitalizar; **company capitalized at £10,000** = compañía con un capital de £10.000

◊ **capitalize on** ['kæpɪtəlaɪz 'ɒn] *verb* aprovechar; **to capitalize on one's market position** = aprovechar el valor de su posición en el mercado

◊ **capitalization** [kæpɪtəlaɪ'zeɪʃən] *noun* capitalización *f*; **market capitalization** = capitalización bursátil *or* valor de mercado del capital emitido; **company with a £1m capitalization** = compañía con una capitalización bursátil de £1 millón; **capitalization of reserves** = capitalización de las reservas

captive market ['kæptɪv 'maːkɪt] *noun* mercado *m* cautivo

capture ['kæptʃə] *verb* conseguir *or* acaparar; **to capture 10% of the market** = acaparar un 10% del mercado; **to capture 20% of a company's shares** = conseguir un 20% de las acciones de una compañía

car [kaː] *noun* coche *m or* automóvil *m*; **company car** = coche de la empresa; **private car** = coche particular *or* turismo *m*; **car boot sale** = venta de objetos usados expuestos en el maletero de un coche

◊ **car-hire** ['kaː 'haɪə] *noun* alquiler *m* de automóviles; **he runs a car-hire business** = dirige un negocio de alquiler de automóviles

carat ['kærət] *noun* quilate *m* a **22-carat gold ring** = un anillo de oro de 22 quilates; **a 5-carat diamond** = un diamante de 5 quilates (NOTE: no plural in English)

COMMENT: pure gold is 24 carats; most jewellery and other items made from gold are not pure, but between 19 and 22 carats. 22 carat gold has 22 parts of gold to two parts of alloy

carbon ['kaːbən] *noun* **(a)** *(paper)* papel *m* de calco *or* papel carbón **(b)** *(copy)* copia *f* carbón; **make a top copy and two carbons** = haga un original y dos copias

◊ **carbon copy** ['kaːbən 'kɒpi] *noun* copia *f* carbón; **give me the original, and file the carbon copy** = déme el original y archive la copia carbón

◊ **carbonless** ['kaːbənləs] *adjective* sin papel carbón; **our reps use carbonless order pads** = nuestros representantes emplean blocs de pedidos que no necesitan papel carbón *or* que hacen copias sin papel carbón

◊ **carbon paper** ['kaːbən 'peɪpə] *noun* papel *m* carbón; **you put the carbon paper in the wrong way round** = pusiste el papel carbón al revés

card [kaːd] *noun* **(a)** *(stiff paper)* cartulina *f*; **we have printed the instructions on thin white card** = hemos impreso las instrucciones en cartulina blanca (NOTE: no plural in this meaning) **(b)** *(small piece of plastic or stiff paper)* tarjeta *f*; **business card** = tarjeta de visita; **cash card** = tarjeta dinero *or* de cajero automático *or* tarjeta monedero; **charge card** = tarjeta de crédito; **cheque (guarantee) card** = tarjeta de garantía) de cheques; **credit card** = tarjeta de crédito; **debit card** = tarjeta de débito; **filing card** = ficha (de registro); **green card** = permiso de residencia (en EE.UU); **index card** = ficha (de fichero); **punched card** = tarjeta perforada; **smart card** = tarjeta inteligente; **store card** = tarjeta comercial; **identity card** *or* **ID card** = carné de identidad; **membership card** = carné de socio *or* miembro; **union card** = carné sindical **(d)** *(postcard)* postal *f or* tarjeta *f* postal; **reply paid card** = tarjeta de respuesta con el franqueo pagado **(e) to get one's cards** = estar despedido

◇ **cardboard** ['kɑːdbɔːd] *noun* cartón *m*; **cardboard box** = caja de cartón; **corrugated cardboard** = cartón ondulado

◇ **cardholder** [kɑːd'həʊldə] *noun* titular *mf* (de tarjeta de crédito) *or* socio, -cia *or* miembro *mf* (de carné)

QUOTE ever since October, when the banks' base rate climbed to 15 per cent, the main credit card issuers have faced the prospect of having to push interest rates above 30 per cent APR. Though store cards have charged interest at much higher rates than this for some years, 30 per cent APR is something the banks fight shy of
Financial Times Review

card index ['kɑːd 'ɪndeks] *noun* fichero *m*; **card-index file** = fichero de tarjetas

◇ **card-index** ['kɑːd 'ɪndeks] *verb* pasar información a un fichero

◇ **card-indexing** ['kɑːd 'ɪndeksɪŋ] *noun* paso de información a un fichero; **no one can understand her card-indexing system** = nadie puede entender su sistema de fichero de tarjetas

◇ **card phone** ['kɑːd fəʊn] *noun* cabina telefónica *or* teléfono de tarjeta

care of ['keər 'ɒv] *phrase (phrase in an address)* para entregar a; **Herr Schmidt, care of Mr W.Brown** = Mr W. Brown, para entregar a Herr Schmidt

career [kə'rɪə] *noun* carrera *f or* profesión *f*; **he made his career in electronics** = su profesión ha sido la electrónica; **career woman** *or* **girl** = profesional *f or* mujer que ejerce una profesión

caretaker ['keəteɪkə] *noun* portero, -ra *or* conserje *m or* vigilante *m*; **go and ask the caretaker to replace the light bulb** = ve a pedirle al conserje que cambie la bombilla (NOTE: US English is **janitor**)

cargo ['kɑːgəʊ] *noun* carga *f*; **the ship was taking on cargo** = el barco estaba cargando; **to load cargo** = cargar; **air cargo** = carga aérea; **cargo ship** *or* **cargo plane** = barco *or* avión de carga (NOTE: plural is **cargoes)**

carnet ['kɑːneɪ] *noun* certificado *m or* documento *m* de circulación de mercancías

carriage ['kærɪdʒ] *noun* porte *m or* transporte *m*; **to pay for carriage** = pagar transporte; **to allow 10% for carriage** = dejar un margen del 10% para el porte; **carriage is 15% of the total cost** = el transporte cuesta un 15% del coste total; **carriage free** = franco de porte; **carriage paid** = porte pagado *or* franco a domicilio; **carriage forward** = porte debido *or* contra reembolso de flete

carrier ['kærɪə] *noun* **(a)** *(company)* empresa *f* de transportes *or* transportista *mf*; **we only use reputable carriers** = empleamos solamente transportistas acreditados; **air carrier** = compañía *f* de transporte aéreo; **carrier's risk** = riesgo a cuenta del transportista **(b)** *(vehicle)* vehículo *m* de transporte; **bulk carrier** = carguero *m* de graneles *or* granelero *m*

carry ['kærɪ] *verb* **(a)** *(from one place to another)* llevar *or* transportar; **to carry goods** = transportar mercancías; **a tanker carrying oil from the Gulf** = un petrolero con una carga de petróleo del Golfo; **the train was carrying a consignment of cars for export** = el tren llevaba una remesa de automóviles para la exportación **(b)** *(vote or approve)* aprobar; **the motion was carried** = la moción fue aprobada **(c)** *(produce)* producir *or* llevar; **the bonds carry interest at 10%** = los bonos producen un interés del 10% **(d)** *(keep in stock)* dedicarse a cierta clase de artículos *or* tener en existencia; **to carry a line of goods** = dedicarse a un tipo de mercancía; **we do not carry pens** = no vendemos estilográficas

◇ **carry down** *or* **carry forward** ['kærɪ 'daʊn *or* 'kærɪ 'fɔːwəd] *verb* pasar a cuenta nueva; **balance carried forward** *or* **balance c/f** = saldo a cuenta nueva

◇ **carrying** ['kærɪɪŋ] *noun* transporte *m*; **carrying charges** = gastos *or* tarifas de transporte; **carrying cost** = coste de transporte

◇ **carry on** ['kærɪ 'ɒn] *verb* continuar *or* seguir; **the staff carried on working in spite of the fire** = el personal siguió trabajando a pesar del incendio; **to carry on a business** = llevar un negocio

◇ **carry over** ['kærɪ 'əʊvə] *verb* **(a) to carry over a balance** = pasar el saldo anterior a cuenta nueva **(b) to carry over stock** = trasladar un inventario de existencias al periodo siguiente

cart [kɑːt] *noun* US **baggage cart** = carrito *m* de equipajes; **shopping cart** = carrito de supermercado (NOTE: GB English for these are **luggage trolley** and **shopping trolley** *or* **supermarket trolley)**

cartage ['kɑːtɪdʒ] *noun* empresa *f* de transporte por carretera *or* camionero *m*

cartel [kɑː'tel] *noun* cartel *m*

carter ['kɑːtə] *noun* transportista *mf* de transporte por carretera *or* por camion

carton ['kɑːtən] *noun* **(a)** *(material)* cartón *m*; **a folder made of carton** = una carpeta de cartón (NOTE: no plural in this meaning) **(b)** *(box)* caja *f* de cartón; **a carton of cigarettes** = un cartón de cigarrillos

cartridge ['kɑːtrɪdʒ] *noun* cartucho *m or* recambio *m*; **toner cartridge** = cartucho de virador

case [keɪs] **1** *noun* **(a)** *(suitcase)* maleta *f*; **the customs made him open his case** = la aduana le obligó a abrir la maleta; **she had a small case which she carried onto the plane** = tenía una maleta pequeña que llevó en el avión **(b)** *(box)* caja *f*; **six cases of wine** = seis cajas de vino; **a packing case** = caja de embalar **(c)** **display case** = mesa vitrina *f* **(d)** **court case** = proceso *m or* causa *f*; **the case is being heard next week** = la causa se verá la semana que viene **2** *verb* *(put in boxes)* poner en una caja *or* embalar

cash [kæʃ] **1** *noun* **(a)** *(coins and notes)* dinero *m* en efectivo; **cash in hand** *or* US **cash on hand** = efectivo en caja; **hard cash** = dinero en metálico; **petty cash** = caja para gastos menores; **ready cash** = efectivo; **cash account** = cuenta de caja; **cash advance** = anticipo de caja a cuenta; **cash balance** = saldo de caja; **cash book (CB)** = libro de caja; **cash box** = caja; **cash budget** = presupuesto de caja; **cash**

card = tarjeta de dinero or cajero; **cash cow** = producto or subsidiario, -ria de alta rentabilidad; **cash desk** = caja; **cash dispenser** = cajero automático; **cash float** = fondo de caja; **cash limit** = límite de caja; **cash offer** = oferta en metálico; **cash payment** = pago en efectivo; **cash purchases** = compras al contado; **cash register** or **cash till** = caja registradora; **cash reserves** = reservas de caja or de efectivo **(b)** *(using coins and notes)* efectivo; **to pay cash down** = pagar en efectivo or al contado; **cash price** or **cash terms** = precio al contado or condiciones de pago al contado; **settlement in cash** or **cash settlement** = pago en efectivo; **cash sale** or **cash transaction** = venta al contado or en efectivo; **terms: cash with order (CWO)** = condiciones de venta: pago al hacer el pedido; **cash on delivery (COD)** = cobro a la entrega; **cash discount** or **discount for cash** = descuento por pago al contado **2** *verb* **to cash a cheque** = cobrar un cheque

◊ **cashable** ['kæʃəbl] *adjective* que se puede cobrar or hacer efectivo; **a crossed cheque is not cashable at any bank** = un cheque cruzado no se puede cobrar en efectivo en ningún banco

◊ **cash and carry** ['kæʃ ənd 'kæri] *noun* autoservicio *m* mayorista de pago al contado; **cash and carry warehouse** = almacén de venta al por mayor con pago al contado

◊ **cash flow** ['kæʃ 'fləu] *noun* flujo *m* de caja or 'cash flow'; **cash flow forecast** = previsión de 'cash-flow'; **cash flow statement** = estado de flujo de caja; **net cash flow** = flujo neto de efectivo; **negative cash flow** = flujo negativo de efectivo; **positive cash flow** = flujo positivo de efectivo; **the company is suffering from cash flow problems** = la empresa tiene problemas de tesorería

◊ **cashier** [kæ'ʃɪə] *noun* cajero, -ra; *US* **cashier's check** = cheque *m* de banco

◊ **cash in** ['kæʃ 'ɪn] *verb* liquidar or realizar

◊ **cash in on** [kæʃ 'ɪn ɒn] *verb* sacar provecho or aprovechar; **the company is cashing in on the interest in computer games** = la empresa aprovecha el interés que existe por los juegos de ordenador

◊ **cashless society** ['kæʃləs sə'saɪəti] *noun* sociedad que utiliza únicamente tarjetas de crédito

◊ **cashpoint** ['kæʃpɔɪnt] *noun* cajero automático

◊ **cash up** ['kæʃ 'ʌp] *verb* hacer arqueo de caja

cassette [kə'set] *noun* casete or cassette *m*; **copy the information from the computer onto a cassette** = copie la información del ordenador en un casete

casting vote ['kɑːstɪŋ 'vəut] *noun* voto *m* de calidad; **the chairman has the casting vote** = el presidente tiene el voto de calidad; **he used his casting vote to block the motion** = empleó su voto de calidad para bloquear la moción

casual ['kæʒjuəl] *adjective* eventual or temporero, -ra; **casual labour** = mano de obra eventual; **casual work** = trabajo eventual; **casual labourer** or **casual worker** = obrero, -ra or trabajador, -ra eventual

catalogue or *US* **catalog** ['kætəlɒg] **1** *noun* catálogo *m*; **an office equipment catalogue** = un catálogo de equipos de oficina; **they sent us a catalogue of their new range of desks** = nos enviaron un catálogo de su nueva gama de mesas de oficina; **mail order catalogue** = catálogo de ventas por correo; **catalogue price** = precio de catálogo **2** *verb* catalogar

> QUOTE the catalogue, containing card and gift offers, will have been sent to 500,000 people by the end of September
> **Precision Marketing**

category ['kætəgəri] *noun* categoría *f*; **we deal only in the most expensive categories of watches** = vendemos solamente relojes de la categoría más cara

cater for ['keɪtə 'fɔː] *verb* atender a or abastecer; **the store caters mainly for overseas customers** = la tienda atiende principalmente a clientes extranjeros

◊ **caterer** ['keɪtərə] *noun* abastecedor, -ra or proveedor, -ra de comidas preparadas

◊ **catering** ['keɪtərɪŋ] *noun* **(a)** *(food)* servicio *m* de comidas; **the catering trade** = hostelería or negocio de alimentación, especialmente de comida preparada para el consumo **(b)** *(supply)* **catering for** = que abastece a or suministra; **store catering for overseas visitors** = tienda que abastece a los visitantes extranjeros

cause [kɔːz] **1** *noun* causa *f*; **what was the cause of the bank's collapse?** = ¿cuál fue la causa de la quiebra del banco?; **the police tried to find the cause of the fire** = la policía investigó la causa del incendio **2** *verb* causar; **the recession caused hundreds of bankruptcies** = la recesión causó cientos de quiebras

caution ['kɔːʃn] *noun* cautela *f*

◊ **cautious** ['kɔːʃəs] *adjective* cauteloso, -sa

caveat ['kævɪæt] *noun* advertencia *f*; **to enter a caveat** = hacer una advertencia

◊ **caveat emptor** ['kævɪæt 'emptɔː] *Latin phrase* por cuenta y riesgo del comprador

> QUOTE the idea that buyers at a car boot sale should have any rights at all is laughable. Even those who do not understand Latin know that caveat emptor is the rule
> **Times**

CB = CASH BOOK

CBI [siːbiː'aɪ] = CONFEDERATION OF BRITISH INDUSTRY equivalent to Confederación Española de Organizaciones Empresariales (C.E.D.E.)

cc ['kɒpɪz] = COPIES (NOTE: **cc** is put on a letter to show who has received a copy of it)

CCA = CURRENT COST ACCOUNTING

CD [siː'diː] = CERTIFICATE OF DEPOSIT

c/d = CARRIED DOWN

cede [ɒiːd] *verb* ceder

ceiling ['siːlɪŋ] *noun* **(a)** *(in room)* techo *m*; **ceiling light** = lámpara de techo **(b)** *(upper limit)* punto *m* más alto or límite *m* or techo *m*; **output has reached a ceiling** = la producción ha tocado techo; **to fix a ceiling to a budget** = imponer un límite a un presupuesto; **ceiling price** or **price ceiling** = precio tope *or* precio máximo autorizado; **credit ceiling** *or* **wage ceiling** = techo crediticio *or* techo salarial

cent [sent] *noun* **(a)** *(currency)* centavo *m*; **the stores are only a 25-cent bus ride away** = el autobús que lleva a las tiendas cuesta solamente 25 centavos; **they sell oranges at 99 cents each** = venden naranjas a 99 centavos la unidad (NOTE: **cent** is usually written c in prices: 25c, but not when a dollar price is mentioned: $1.25) **(b)** *see* PER CENT

centimetre *or US* **centimeter** ['sentimi:tə] *noun* centímetro *m*; **the paper is fifteen centimetres wide** = el papel tiene un ancho de quince centímetros (NOTE: **centimetre** is usually written cm after figures: 260cm)

central ['sentrəl] *adjective* central; **central bank** = banco central; **central office** = oficina central *or* principal; **central purchasing** = centralización de las compras

Central African Republic ['sentrəl 'æfrikən rɪ'pʌblɪk] *noun* República Centroafricana NOTE: capital: **Bangui**; currency: **CFA franc (CFAF)** = franco CFA (FCFA)

centralization [sentrəlaɪ'zeɪʃən] *noun* centralización *f*

◊ **centralize** ['sentrəlaɪz] *verb* centralizar; **all purchasing has been centralized in our main office** = todas las actividades de compra han sido centralizadas en nuestra oficina principal; **the group benefits from a highly centralized organizational structure** = el grupo se beneficia de una estructura organizativa altamente centralizada

QUOTE the official use of the ecu remains limited, since most interventions by central banks on the market are conducted in dollars
Economist

QUOTE central bankers in Europe and Japan are reassessing their intervention policy
Duns Business Month

centre *or US* **center** ['sentə] *noun* **(a)** *(main part of a town)* centro *m*; **business centre** = centro *m* comercial; **shopping centre** = centro comercial *or* zona *f* de tiendas **(b)** *(important town)* centro (ciudad importante); **industrial centre** = centro industrial; **manufacturing centre** = centro manufacturero; **the centre for the shoe industry** = el centro de la industria del calzado **(c)** *GB (office)* **job centre** = oficina de empleo **(d)** *(items in account)* grupo *m* de partidas en una cuenta; **cost centre** = centro de costes; **profit centre** = centro de beneficios

CEO ['si: i: 'əʊ] = CHIEF EXECUTIVE OFFICER

certain ['sɜːtn] *adjective* **(a)** *(sure)* cierto, -ta *or* seguro, -ra; **the chairman is certain we will pass last year's total sales** = el presidente está seguro de que sobrepasaremos el nivel de ventas del año pasado **(b)** *(vague)* **a certain** = determinado, -da; **a certain number** *or* **a certain quantity** = un número determinado *or* una cantidad determinada

certificate [sə'tɪfɪkət] *noun* certificado *m*; **clearance certificate** = certificado de aduana; **insurance certificate** = certificado de seguro; **savings certificate** = certificado de ahorro; **share**

certificate = título de acción; **certificate of airworthiness** *or* **seaworthiness** = certificado de navegabilidad; **certificate of approval** = certificado de aprobación; **certificate of incorporation** = certificado que autoriza la constitución de una sociedad anónima; **certificate of origin** = certificado de origen; **certificate of proficiency** = certificado de aptitud; **certificate of registration** = certificado de registro

◊ **certificated** [sə'tɪfɪkeɪtɪd] *adjective* titulado, -da *or* diplomado,-da; **certificated bankrupt** = quebrado rehabilitado por haberse demostrado su inocencia

◊ **certificate of deposit (CD)** [sə'tɪfɪkət əv dɪ'pɒzɪt] *noun* certificado de depósito

COMMENT: a CD is a bearer instrument, which can be sold by the bearer. It can be sold at a discount to the value, so that the yield on CDs varies

QUOTE interest rates on certificates of deposit may have little room to decline in August as demand for funds from major city banks is likely to remain strong. After delaying for months, banks are now expected to issue a large volume of CDs. If banks issue more CDs on the assumption that the official discount rate reduction will be delayed, it is very likely that CD rates will be pegged for a longer period than expected
Nikkei Weekly

certify ['sɜːtɪfaɪ] *verb* certificar *or* dar fe de; **I certify that this is a true copy** = certifico que ésta es una copia fiel; **the document is certified as a true copy** = el documento está certificado como copia auténtica; **certified accountant** = censor jurado de cuentas; **certified cheque** *US* **certified check** = cheque conformado

cession ['seʃən] *noun* cesión *f*

c/f = CARRIED FORWARD

CFO ['si: ef 'əʊ] = CHIEF FINANCIAL OFFICER

CGT = CAPITAL GAINS TAX

Chad [tʃæd] *noun* Chad *m*

◊ **Chadian** ['tʃædiən] *adjective & noun* chadiano, -na NOTE: capital: **Ndjamena**; currency: **CFA franc (CFAF)** = franco CFA (FCFA)

chain [tʃeɪn] *noun* cadena *f*; **a chain of hotels** *or* a **hotel chain** = una cadena de hoteles; **the chairman of a large do-it-yourself chain** = el presidente de una gran cadena de tiendas de bricolaje; **he runs a chain of shoe shops** = lleva un cadena de zapaterías; **she bought several shoe shops and gradually built up a chain** = compró varias zapaterías y poco a poco se hizo con una cadena de tiendas

◊ **chain store** ['tʃeɪn 'stɔː] *noun* sucursal *f* de una cadena

QUOTE the giant US group is better known for its chain of cinemas and hotels rather than its involvement in shipping
Lloyd's List

chair [tʃeə] **1** *noun* **(a)** *(of a chairman)* presidencia *f*; **to be in the chair** = estar en la presidencia; **she was voted into the chair** = fue elegida presidenta;

Mr Jones took the chair = el Sr. Jones presidió la reunión; **to address the chair** = dirigirse a la presidencia; **please address your remarks to the chair** = dirija sus observaciones a la presidencia, por favor **(b)** *(university)* cátedra *f* **2** *verb* presidir; **the meeting was chaired by Mrs Smith** = la reunión fue presidida por la Sra. Smith

◊ **chairman** ['tʃeəmən] *noun* **(a)** *(of a committee)* presidente, -ta; **Mr Howard was chairman** *or* **acted as chairman** = el Sr. Howard fue presidente *or* actuó como presidente; **Mr Chairman** *or* **Madam Chairman** = señor presidente *or* señora presidenta **(b)** *(of a company)* presidente; **the chairman of the board** *or* **the company chairman** = el presidente de la junta *or* del consejo *or* el presidente de la compañía; **the chairman's report** = el informe anual del presidente

◊ **chairmanship** ['tʃeəmənʃɪp] *noun* presidencia *f*; **the committee met under the chairmanship of Mr Jones** = el comité se reunió bajo la presidencia del Sr. Jones

◊ **chairperson** ['tʃeəpɜ:sn] *noun* presidente *mf*

◊ **chairwoman** ['tʃeəwʊmən] *noun* presidenta *f* (NOTE: the plurals are **chairmen, chairpersons, chairwomen.** Note also that in a UK company, the chairman is less important than the managing director, although one person can combine both posts. In the US, a company president is less important than the chairman of the board)

QUOTE the corporation's entrepreneurial chairman seeks a dedicated but part-time president. The new president will work a three-day week
Globe and Mail (Toronto)

challenge ['tʃæləndʒ] **1** *noun* reto *m* **2** *verb* **(a)** *(to incite)* estimular **(b)** *(to dispute)* combatir

Chamber of Commerce ['tʃeɪmbər əv 'kɒməs] *noun* Cámara *f* de Comercio

chambers ['tʃeɪmbəz] *plural noun* despacho *m* (de un juez); **the judge heard the case in chambers** = el juez vio la causa en su despacho

chance [tʃɑ:ns] *noun* **(a)** *(possibility)* posibilidad *f*; **the company has a good chance of winning the contract** = la empresa tiene grandes posibilidades de conseguir el contrato; **his promotion chances are small** = tiene pocas posibilidades de ascenso **(b)** *(opportunity)* oportunidad *f* *or* ocasión *f*; **she is waiting for a chance to see the managing director** = está esperando la oportunidad de ver al director gerente; **he had his chance of promotion when the finance director's assistant resigned** = tuvo la oportunidad de ascender cuando dimitió el director adjunto de finanzas (NOTE: you have a chance **of doing** something or **to do** something)

Chancellor of the Exchequer ['tʃɑ:nsələr əv ði: ɪks'tʃekə] *noun GB* ministro, -tra de Economía y Hacienda (NOTE: the US equivalent is the **Secretary of the Treasury)**

chandler ['tʃɑ:ndlə] *noun* proveedor, -ra; **ship chandler** proveedor de efectos navales

◊ **chandlery** ['tʃɑ:ndləri] *noun* almacén *m* de efectos navales

change [tʃeɪn(d)ʒ] **1** *noun* **(a)** *(loose coins)* cambio *m* *or* dinero *m* suelto; **small change** = moneda *f* *or* suelta *or* calderilla *f*; **to give someone change for £10** = dar a alguien cambio de £10; **change machine** = máquina de cambio **(b)** *(in a shop)* cambio *m* *or* vuelta *f*; **he gave me the wrong change** = se equivocó al darme el cambio; **you paid the £5.75 bill with a £10 note, so you should have £4.25 change** = pagaste la cuenta de £5,75 con un billete de £10, por lo que deberían darte £4,25 de vuelta; **keep the change** = quédese con la vuelta **2** *verb* **(a)** *(a large note into smaller coins)* **to change a £10 note** = cambiar un billete de £10 **(b)** *(one currency for another)* cambiar; **to change £1,000 into dollars** = cambiar £1.000 en dólares; **we want to change some traveller's cheques** = queremos cambiar unos cheques de viaje **(c)** *(of a business, property, etc.)* **to change hands** = cambiar de dueño; **the shop changed hands for £100,000** = la tienda fue vendida por £100.000 **(d)** *(train or plane)* hacer transbordo; **when you get to London airport, you have to change to an internal flight** = cuando llegas al aeropuerto de Londres, tienes que hacer transbordo a un vuelo nacional **(e)** *(development)* **change of plan** = bifurcación *f* *or* evolución *f*

◊ **changer** ['tʃeɪn(d)ʒə] *noun* **money changer** = cambista *mf*

channel ['tʃænl] **1** *noun* **(a)** *(means or system)* canal *m*; **to go through the official channels** = actuar por la vía oficial; **to open up new channels of communication** = abrir nuevos canales de comunicación *or* crear nuevas vías de comunicación; **distribution channels** *or* **channels of distribution** = canales de distribución **(b)** *(strait)* **the English Channel** = El Canal de la Mancha; **the Channel Tunnel** = el Eurotúnel **2** *verb* encauzar *or* dirigir; **they are channelling their research funds into developing European communication systems** = dirigen los fondos de investigación al desarrollo de sistemas de comunicación europeos

chapter 11 ['tʃæptə ɪ'levən] *noun US* capítulo 11 (cláusula jurídica)

COMMENT: a section of the US Bankruptcy Reform Act 1978, which allows a corporation to be protected from demands made by its creditors for a period of time, while it is reorganized with a view to paying its debts; the officers of the corporation will negotiate with its creditors as to the best way of reorganizing the business

charge [tʃɑ:dʒ] **1** *noun* **(a)** *(price)* precio *m* *or* coste *m* *or* cargo *m* *or* gastos *mpl*; **to make no charge for delivery** = no cobrar por el reparto; **to make a small charge for rental** = cobrar una pequeña cantidad por el alquiler; **there is no charge for service** *or* **no charge is made for service** = el servicio no se cobra; **admission charge** *or* **entry charge** = precio de entrada; **bank charges** *or US* **service charge** = gastos bancarios; **handling charge** = coste de manipulación *or* gasto de tramitación; *(for a bank transfer)* gasto de transferencia; **inclusive charge** = precio todo incluido; **interest charges** = cargos en concepto de interés; **scale of charges** = lista de precios; *(in restaurant)* **service charge** = suplemento por el servicio; **a 10% service charge is added** = se añade un 10% por el servicio; **does the bill include a service charge?** = ¿está el servicio incluido en la cuenta?; *US (in bank)* **service charge** = gastos bancarios; **charge account** = cuenta abierta *or* de crédito; **charges forward** = gastos a cobrar a la entrega; **a token charge is made for heating** = hay un pago simbólico por la calefacción; **free of charge** = gratuito, -ta *or* gratis **(b)** *(debit)* débito *m*; **floating charge** = débito flotante *or* variable; **it appears as a charge on the accounts** = aparece en las cuentas como débito **(c)** *(in court)* acusación *f or* querella *f*; **he appeared in court on a charge of embezzling** *or* **on an embezzlement charge** = compareció ante el tribunal acusado de malversación de fondos ; **to deny a charge** = negar una acusación; **to prefer a charge** = formular una acusación; **to withdraw charges** = retirar una acusación **2** *verb* cobrar; **to charge the packing to the customer** *or* **to charge the customer with the packing** = cobrar el embalaje al comprador; **to charge £5 for delivery** = cobrar £5 por la entrega; **how much does he charge?** = ¿cuánto cobra?; **he charges £6 an hour** = cobra £6 por hora **(b) to charge a purchase** = cargar una compra en cuenta *or* anotar una compra; **please charge this consignment to my account** = adeude esta partida en mi cuenta **(c)** *(in a court)* acusar; **he was charged with embezzling his clients' money** = se le acusó de malversar fondos de sus clientes

◊ **chargeable** ['tʃɑːdʒəbl] *adjective* a cargo de; **repairs chargeable to the occupier** = las reparaciones corren a cargo del inquilino; **sums chargeable to the reserve** = cantidades imputables a las reservas

◊ **charge card** ['tʃɑːdʒˌkɑːd] *noun* tarjeta *f* de crédito

◊ **chargee** [tʃɑː'dʒiː] *noun* deudor privilegiado

◊ **chargehand** ['tʃɑːdʒhænd] *noun* capataz *m*

chart [tʃɑːt] *noun* gráfico *m or* diagrama *m*; **bar chart** = gráfico de barras; **flow chart** = organigrama *m or* diagrama de flujo *or* de secuencias; **organization chart** = organigrama *or* gráfico de organización; **pie chart** = gráfico circular *or* sectorial; **sales chart** = gráfico de ventas

charter ['tʃɑːtə] **1** *noun* **(a)** *(document)* **bank charter** = documento *m* legal que autoriza la constitución de un banco **(b)** *(hiring)* alquiler *m* de un medio de transporte; **charter flight** = vuelo charter; **charter plane** = avión charter; **boat on charter to Mr Smith** = barco fletado por el Sr. Smith **2** *verb* alquilar *or* fletar; **to charter a plane** *or* **a boat** *or* **a bus** = fletar un avión *or* un barco *or* alquilar un autobús

◊ **chartered** ['tʃɑːtəd] *adjective* **(a) chartered accountant** = censor jurado de cuentas *or* perito mercantil *or* contable colegiado **(b) chartered company** = sociedad fundada antiguamente por cédula (carta) real; **a chartered bank** = banco fundado antiguamente por cédula (carta) real **(c) chartered ship** *or* **bus** *or* **plane** = barco *or* avión fletado *or* autobús alquilado

◊ **charterer** ['tʃɑːtərə] *noun* fletador, -ra

◊ **chartering** ['tʃɑːtərɪŋ] *noun* fletamento *m or* alquiler *m*

chartist ['tʃɑːtɪst] *noun* analista *mf* de bolsa

chase [tʃeɪs] *verb* **(a)** *(run after)* perseguir **(b)**

(speed up) apremiar; **we are trying to chase up the accounts department for the cheque** = hemos metido prisa al departamento de contabilidad para que tramiten el cheque; **we will chase your order with the production department** = apremiaremos al departamento de producción para que atienda a su pedido; **chasing letter** = carta *f* recordatoria

◊ **chaser** ['tʃeɪsə] *noun* **(a) progress chaser** = encargado, -da de seguimiento de los programas de trabajo **(b)** carta *f* recordatoria

chattels ['tʃætlz] *plural noun* **goods and chattels** = bienes *mpl* muebles

cheap [tʃiːp] **1** *adjective* barato, -ta; **cheap labour** = mano de obra barata; **we have opened a factory in the Far East because of the cheap labour** *or* **because labour is cheap** = hemos abierto una fábrica en Extremo Oriente porque allí la mano de obra es barata; **cheap money** = dinero *or* crédito barato; **cheap rate** = tarifa reducida; **cheap rate phone calls** = llamadas telefónicas a tarifa reducida **2** *adverb* barato *or* a bajo precio; **to buy something cheap** = comprar algo barato *or* a bajo precio; **he bought two companies cheap and sold them again at a profit** = compró dos compañías a bajo precio y las vendió a beneficio; **they work out cheaper by the box** = resultan más baratos comprándolos por cajas

◊ **cheaply** ['tʃiːpli] *adverb* barato *or* económicamente; **the salesman was living cheaply at home and claiming a high hotel bill on his expenses** = el representante vivía económicamente en su casa y reclamaba unos gastos de hotel elevados

◊ **cheapness** ['tʃiːpnəs] *noun* precio *m* bajo *or* baratura *f*; **the cheapness of their product is a plus** = el bajo precio de su producto juega a su favor *or* es un tanto a su favor; **the cheapness of the pound means that many more tourists will come to London** = el bajo tipo de cambio de la libra significa que vendrán a Londres muchos más turistas

cheat [tʃiːt] *verb* defraudar *or* estafar; **he cheated the Income Tax out of thousands of pounds** = defraudó a Hacienda de miles de libras; **she was accused of cheating clients who came to ask her for advice** = se le acusó de estafar a clientes que le acudían en busca de consejo

check [tʃek] **1** *noun* **(a)** *(sudden stop)* parada *f or* revés *m or* freno *m*; **to put a check on imports** = imponer restricciones a las importaciones **(b)** *(inspection)* inspección *f or* control *m*; **the auditors carried out checks on the petty cash book** = los auditores realizaron una inspección del libro de caja; **a routine check of the fire equipment** = una inspección rutinaria del equipo contra incendios; **baggage check** = inspección *or* control de equipajes **(c)** *(verification)* comprobación *f*; **reference check** = comprobación de informes sobre una persona; **check sample** = muestra de inspección *or* comprobación **(d)** *US (in restaurant)* cuenta *f* **(e)** *US* = CHEQUE **(f)** *US (sign)* marca *m*; **make a check in the box marked 'R'** = marque con una señal la casilla 'R' (NOTE: GB English is **tick**) **2** *verb* **(a)** *(stop or delay)* parar *or* contener; **to check inflation** = contener la inflación; **to check the entry of contraband into the country** = contener la entrada de contrabando en el país **(b)** *(examine)* comprobar *or* cotejar *or* verificar *or* revisar; **to check that an invoice is correct** = comprobar que una factura es correcta; **to check and sign for goods** = verificar y firmar la aceptación de mercancías; **he checked the computer printout against the invoices** = cotejó la impresión del ordenador con las facturas para ver si la cifras coincidían **(c)** *US (mark with a sign)* hacer una marca; **check the box marked 'R'** = marque con una señal la casilla 'R' (NOTE: GB English is **to tick**)

◊ **checkbook** ['tʃekbʊk] *noun US* = CHEQUE BOOK

◊ **check in** ['tʃek 'ɪn] *verb* **(a)** *(at a hotel)* registrarse; **he checked in at 12.15** = se registró a las 12.15 **(b)** *(at an airport)* presentarse **(c)** **to check baggage in** = facturar el equipaje

◊ **check-in** ['tʃekɪn] *noun* **(A)** *(at a hotel)* recepción *f or* registro *m* **(b)** *(at an airport)* mostrador *m* de facturación; **the check-in is on the first floor** = el mostrador de facturación está en el primer piso; **check-in counter** = mostrador de facturación; **check-in time** = horario de presentación en el aeropuerto

◊ **checking** ['tʃekɪŋ] *noun* **(a)** control *m or* inspección *f*; **the inspectors found some defects during their checking of the building** = los inspectores encontraron algunos defectos durante la inspección del edificio **(b)** *US* **checking account** = cuenta corriente

◊ **checklist** ['tʃeklɪst] *noun* lista *f* de comprobación

◊ **checkoff** ['tʃekɒf] *noun US* deducción *f* automática del salario en concepto de cuota sindical

◊ **check out** ['tʃek 'aʊt] *verb (at a hotel)* pagar la cuenta y marcharse *or* dejar la habitación; **we will check out before breakfast** = dejaremos la habitación antes del desayuno

◊ **checkout** ['tʃekaʊt] *noun* **(a)** *(in a supermarket)* caja *f* **(b)** *(in a hotel)* **checkout time is 12.00** = debe dejar libre la habitación las 12.00

◊ **checkroom** ['tʃekrʊm] *noun US* guardarropa *m or* consigna *f*

cheque *or US* **check** [tʃek] *noun* **(a)** cheque *m*; **a cheque for £10** *or* **a £10 cheque** = un cheque por £10; **cheque account** = cuenta corriente; **cheque to bearer** = cheque al portador; **crossed cheque** = cheque cruzado; **open** *or* **uncrossed cheque** = cheque abierto *or* no cruzado *or* sin cruzar; **blank cheque** = cheque en blanco; **pay cheque** *or* **salary cheque** = cheque de sueldo; **traveller's cheques** = cheques de viaje; **bad cheque** *or* **dud cheque** *or* **bouncing cheque** *or* **cheque which bounces** *or US* **rubber check** = cheque sin fondos; **uncovered cheque** = cheque no cubierto **(b)** **to cash a cheque** = cobrar un cheque; **to endorse a cheque** = endosar un cheque; **to make out a cheque to someone** = extender un cheque a alguien; **who shall I make the cheque out to?** = ¿a nombre de quién extiendo el cheque?; **to pay by cheque** = pagar con cheque; **to pay a cheque into your account** = depositar *or* ingresar un cheque; **the bank referred the cheque to drawer** = el banco devolvió el cheque al librador; **to sign a cheque** = firmar un cheque; **to stop a cheque** = detener el pago de un cheque **(c)** *(control)* control *m*; **baggage check** = control de equipajes

◊ **cheque book** *or US* **checkbook** ['tʃekbʊk] *noun* talonario *m* de cheques

◊ **cheque (guarantee) card** ['tʃek gærən'tiː 'kɑːd] *noun* tarjeta *f* de garantía de cheques

chief [tʃiːf] *adjective* principal *or* jefe; **he is the chief accountant of an industrial group** = es el contable jefe de un grupo industrial; **chief executive** *or* **chief executive officer (CEO)** = jefe ejecutivo *or* director general; **chief financial officer (CFO)** = jefe de la sección de finanzas

Chile ['tʃɪli] *noun* Chile *m*

◊ **Chilean** ['tʃɪliən] *adjective & noun* chileno, -na NOTE: capital: **Santiago;** currency: **Chilean peso (Ch$)** = peso chileno (**$Ch**)

China ['tʃaɪnə] *noun* China *f*

◊ **Chinese** [tʃaɪ'niːz] *adjective & noun* chino, -na NOTE: capital: **Beijing** (= Pekín); currency: **Chinese yuan (Y)** = yuan chino (Y)

Chinese walls ['tʃaɪniːz 'wɔːlz] *plural noun* barrera ficticia entre departamentos de una misma empresa para proteger información confidencial

> COMMENT: these are imaginary barriers between departments in the same organization, set up to avoid insider dealing or conflict of interest (as when a merchant bank is advising on a planned takeover bid, its investment department should not know that the bid is taking place, or they would advise their clients to invest in the company being taken over)

chip [tʃɪp] *noun* **(a)** **a computer chip** = 'chip' *m or* plaqueta *f* de silicona; **chip card** = tarjeta con microchip **(b)** **blue chip** = de primera categoría (acciones)

chit [tʃɪt] *noun* nota *f or* cuenta *f*

choice [tʃɔɪs] **1** *noun* **(a)** *(choosing)* preferencia *f or* elección *f*; **you must give the customer time to make his choice** = tiene que darle tiempo al cliente para que se decida **(b)** *(items to chose from)* surtido *m or* serie *f* de posibilidades; **we have only a limited choice of suppliers** = tenemos solamente un número limitado de posibles proveedores; **the shop carries a good choice of paper** = la tienda tiene un gran surtido de papel **2** *adjective* escogido, -da *or* selecto, -ta; **choice meat** = carne selecta; **choice wines** = vinos selectos; **choice foodstuffs** = alimentación selecta

choose [tʃuːz] *verb* elegir; **there were several good candidates to choose from** = había buenos aspirantes entre los que elegir; **they chose the only woman applicant as sales director** = eligieron a la única mujer que solicitó el cargo de director de ventas; **you must give the customers plenty of time to choose** = tiene que dar a los clientes tiempo suficiente para elegir (NOTE: **choosing - chose - chosen**)

chop [tʃɒp] **1** *noun (in the Far East)* sello *m* **2** *verb* **(a)** *(expenses, budget, etc.)* cortar *or* reducir **(b)** *(people)* despedir

chronic ['krɒnɪk] *adjective* crónico, -ca *or* permanente *or* endémico, -ca; **the company has chronic cash flow problems** = la empresa tiene problemas permanentes de 'cash flow' *or* de flujo de caja; **we have a chronic shortage of skilled staff** = tenemos una escasez crónica de personal cualificado; **chronic unemployment** = situación de paro endémico

chronological order [krɒnəˈlɒdʒɪkəl ˈɔːdə] *noun* orden *m* cronológico; **filed in chronological order** = archivado por orden cronológico

churn out [ˈtʃɜːn ˈaʊt] *verb* producir en masa

◊ **churning** [ˈtʃɜːnɪŋ] *noun (of a stockbroker)* compra y venta de acciones con el fin de atraer corretaje y dar la impresión de actividad

c.i.f. *or* **CIF** [ˈsiːˈaɪˈef] = COST, INSURANCE AND FREIGHT coste, seguro y flete (cif)

circuit [ˈsɜːkɪt] *noun* circuito *m*; **closed circuit** = circuito cerrado; **short circuit** = cortocircuito *m*

circular [ˈsɜːkjʊlə] **1** *adjective* circular; **circular letter of credit** = carta de crédito general **2** *noun* circular *f*; **they sent out a circular offering a 10% discount** = enviaron una circular ofreciendo un descuento del 10%

◊ **circularize** [ˈsɜːkjʊləraɪz] *verb* enviar una circular; **the committee has agreed to circularize the members** = el comité ha acordado enviar una circular a todos sus miembros; **they circularized all their customers with a new list of prices** = enviaron una circular con una nueva lista de precios a todos los clientes

◊ **circulate** [ˈsɜːkjʊleɪt] *verb* **(a)** *(of money)* circular; **to circulate freely** = circular libremente **(b)** *(without restrictions)* poner en circulación; **to circulate money** = poner dinero en circulación **(c)** *(information)* enviar *or* distribuir circulares; **they circulated a new list of prices to all their customers** = distribuyeron una nueva lista de precios a todos los clientes

◊ **circulating capital** [ˈsɜːkjʊleɪtɪŋ ˈkæpɪtəl] *noun* capital circulante

◊ **circulation** [sɜːkjʊˈleɪʃən] *noun* **(a)** *(movement)* circulación *f or* difusión *f*; **the company is trying to improve the circulation of information between departments** = la empresa está tratando de mejorar la difusión de información entre los departamentos; **circulation of capital** = circulación de capital **(b)** **to put money into circulation** = poner dinero en circulación; **the amount of money in circulation increased more than was expected** = la cantidad de dinero en circulación aumentó más de lo previsto **(c)** *(of newspapers)* tirada *f*; **the audited circulation of a newspaper** = la tirada comprobada de un periódico; **the new editor hopes to improve the circulation** = el nuevo editor espera aumentar la tirada; **a circulation battle** = lucha entre publicaciones para conseguir *or* alcanzar la mayor tirada

> QUOTE the level of currency in circulation increased to N4.9 billion in the month of August
> **Business Times (Lagos)**

city [ˈsɪti] *noun* **(a)** *(large town)* ciudad *f*; **the largest cities in Europe are linked by hourly flights** = las principales ciudades de Europa están conectadas por vuelos que salen cada hora; **capital city** = capital; **inter-city** = interurbano *or* intercity *or* tren de largo recorrido; **inter-city train services are often quicker than going by air** = los servicios interurbanos de tren son a menudo más rápidos que los aviones; **city council** = consejo *m* municipal *or* ayuntamiento *m*; **City Hall** = ayuntamiento **(b) the City (of London)** = la 'City' (el centro financiero de

Londres); **he works in the City** *or* **he is in the City** = trabaja en la 'City'; **they say in the City that the company has been sold** = se dice en el mundo financiero que la compañía ha sido vendida; **City desk** = sección de noticias financieras de un periódico; **City editor** = encargado *or* redactor de la sección financiera de un periódico británico

civil [ˈsɪvl] *adjective* civil; **civil action** = demanda civil; **civil law** = derecho civil; **to bring a civil action** = constituirse parte civil

◊ **civil servant** [ˈsɪvl ˈsɜːvənt] *noun* funcionario público *or* funcionaria pública

◊ **civil service** [ˈsɪvl ˈsɜːvɪs] *noun* administración *f* pública *or* cuerpo *m* de funcionarios del Estado; **you have to pass an examination to get a job in the civil service** *or* **to get a civil service job** = para ser funcionario del Estado tiene que pasar una oposición

claim [kleɪm] **1** *noun* **(a)** *(money)* reivindicación *f*; **wage claim** = reivindicación salarial; **the union put in a 6% wage claim** = el sindicato reivindicó un aumento salarial de un 6% **(b) legal claim** = pretensión *f* con fundamento jurídico *or* derecho legal; **he has no legal claim to the property** = no tiene derecho legítimo alguno sobre la propiedad **(c) insurance claim** = reclamación *f* de daños o pérdidas a la compañía de seguros *or* declaración *f* de siniestro; **claims department** = departamento de reclamaciones; **claim form** = formulario de declaración de siniestro; **claims manager** = director de reclamaciones; **no claims bonus** = bonificación *f*; **to put in a claim** = presentar una reclamación *or* una demanda *or* pedir una indemnización; **to put in a claim for repairs to the car** = presentar una demanda por las reparaciones del coche; **she put in a claim for £250,000 damages against the driver of the other car** = presentó una demanda de indemnización de £250.000 al conductor del otro coche; **to settle a claim** = liquidar una reclamación *or* indemnizar un siniestro; **the insurance company refused to settle his claim for storm damage** = la compañía de seguros se negó a pagar su reclamación por los daños de la tormenta **(d) small claims court** = tribunal de demandas de menor cuantía **2** *verb* **(a)** *(money)* exigir *or* pedir *or* reivindicar; **he claimed £100,000 damages against the cleaning firm** = pidió una indemnización de £100.000 a la empresa de limpieza; **she claimed for repairs to the car against her insurance** = exigió a su compañía de seguros el pago de las reparaciones del coche **(b)** *(property)* reclamar; **he is claiming possession of the house** = reclama la propiedad de la casa; **no one claimed the umbrella found in my office** = nadie reclamó el paraguas aparecido en mi oficina **(c)** *(to state)* alegar *or* pretender *or* afirmar *or* mantener; **he claims he never received the goods** = afirma no haber recibido las mercancías; **she claims that the shares are her property** = sostiene que las acciones son de su propiedad; **as an excuse for the delay in replying, he claimed he had been on a business trip** = para disculparse de la tardanza en contestar, alegó que había estado en viaje de negocios

◊ **claimant** [ˈkleɪmənt] *noun* demandante *mf*; **rightful claimant** = demandante legítimo *or* derechohabiente mf

◊ **claim back** [ˈkleɪm ˈbæk] *verb* exigir la devolución de dinero

◊ **claimer** ['kleɪmə] *noun* = CLAIMANT

◊ **claiming** ['kleɪmɪŋ] *noun* reclamación *f*

class [klɑːs] *noun* **(a)** clase *f or* categoría *f*;
first-class = primera clase; **he is a first-class
accountant** = es un contable de primera categoría;
economy class *or* **tourist class** = clase económica *or*
turista; **I travel economy class because it is
cheaper** = viajo en clase económica porque es más
barato; **tourist class travel is less comfortable than
first class** = el viaje en clase turista es menos
cómodo que en primera clase; **he always travels
first class because tourist class is too
uncomfortable** = siempre viaja en primera porque
la clase turista es demasiado incómoda; *GB* **first-
class mail** = servicio de correos de primera clase; **a
first-class letter should get to Scotland in a day** =
una carta enviada por correo de primera clase
debería llegar a Escocia en un día; **second-class
mail** = servicio de correo de segunda clase; **the
letter took three days to arrive because he sent it
second-class** = la carta tardó tres días en llegar
porque la envió por correo de segunda clase **(b)**
governing class = clase dirigente; **upper** *or* **middle
class** = clase alta *or* media; **working class** = clase
obrera *or* trabajadora

classify ['klæsɪfaɪ] *verb* clasificar; **classified
advertisements** = anuncios clasificados *or* por
palabras; **classified directory** = guía alfabética

◊ **classification** [klæsɪfɪ'keɪʃən] *noun*
clasificación *f*; **job classification** = clasificación de
puestos de trabajo

clause [klɔːz] *noun* cláusula *f*; **there are ten
clauses in the contract** = hay diez cláusulas en el
contrato; **according to clause six, payments will
not be due until next year** = según la cláusula seis,
los pagos no vencen hasta el año que viene;
annulling clause = cláusula anulativa; **cancellation
clause** = cláusula de rescisión; **escalator clause** =
cláusula de revisión de precios *or* salarios; **escape
clause** *or* **let-out clause** = cláusula de excepción *or*
cláusula de salvaguardia *or* de escape; **he added a
let-out clause to the effect that the payments
would be revised if the exchange rate fell by more
than 5%** = añadió una cláusula de excepción
especificando que los pagos se revisarían si el tipo de
cambio bajaba más de un 5%; **exclusion clause** =
cláusula de exclusión; **no-strike clause** = cláusula
antihuelga; **penalty clause** = cláusula penal;
supplementary clause = cláusula suplementaria; **to
add a supplementary clause to a contract** = añadir
una cláusula suplementaria a un contrato;
termination clause = cláusula resolutoria

claw back ['klɔː 'bæk] *verb* reembolsarse *or*
resarcirse; **income tax claws back 25% of pensions
paid out by the government** = con el impuesto
sobre la renta, el Estado se resarce del 25% de lo que
paga en pensiones; **of the £1m allocated to the
project, the government clawed back £100,000 in
taxes** = del £1 millón asignado al proyecto, el Estado
se reembolsó £100.000 en impuestos

◊ **clawback** ['klɔːbæk] *noun* devolución *f or*
reembolso *m*

clean bill of lading ['kliːn 'bɪl əv 'leɪdɪŋ] *noun*
conocimiento *m* de embarque sin objeciones *or*
reservas

◊ **clean hands** ['kliːn 'hændz] *noun* manos *fpl*
limpias

clear [klɪə] **1** *adjective* **(a)** *(easily understood)*
claro, -ra; **he made it clear that he wanted the
manager to resign** = dejó bien claro que quería la
dimisión del director; **you will have to make it clear
to the staff that productivity is falling** = tendrá que
explicar claramente al personal que la productividad
está bajando **(b)** **clear account** = cuenta en regla;
clear of all expenses = libre de gastos; **clear profit** =
beneficio neto *or* ganancia neta; **we made $6,000
clear profit on the sale** = sacamos unos $6.000 de
beneficio neto en la venta **(c)** *(whole* *or* *free)*
completo, -ta; **three clear days** = tres días
laborables completos; **allow three clear days for
the cheque to be paid into the bank** = cuente con
un margen de tres días hábiles para el depósito del
cheque en el banco **2** *verb* **(a)** *(sell cheaply)* liquidar
existencias; **'demonstration models to clear'** =
'liquidación de modelos de demostración'; **to clear
a debt** = liquidar una deuda **(b)** **to clear goods
through customs** = tramitar el despacho de aduanas
de una mercancía **(c)** **to clear 10%** *or* **$5,000 on the
deal** = sacar una ganancia neta del 10% *or* de $5.000
en la operación; **we cleared only our expenses** =
sólo cubrimos los gastos **(d)** **to clear a cheque** =
compensar un cheque *or* tramitar un cheque; **the
cheque took ten days to clear** *or* **the bank took ten
days to clear the cheque** = el banco tardó diez días
en abonar el cheque a cuenta

◊ **clearance** ['klɪərəns] *noun* **(a)** **customs
clearance** = despacho de aduanas; **to effect customs
clearance** = efectuar el despacho aduanero;
clearance certificate = certificado de aduana **(b)**
clearance sale = liquidación **(c)** **clearance of a
cheque** = tramitación *f* del pago de un cheque *or*
compensación *f* de un cheque; **you should allow six
days for clearance** = cuente con que el
cheque tardará seis días en abonarse en cuenta

◊ **clearing** ['klɪərɪŋ] *noun* **(a)** **clearing of goods
through the customs** = despacho *m* de mercancías
por la aduana **(b)** **clearing of a debt** = liquidación *f or*
pago *m* de una deuda *or* compensación *f* **(c)** **clearing
bank** = banco comercial (Gran Bretaña); **clearing
house** = cámara de compensación

◊ **clear off** ['klɪər 'ɒf] *verb* **to clear off a debt** =
liquidar *or* pagar (una deuda)

clerical ['klerɪkəl] *adjective* de oficina; **clerical
error** = error de copia; **clerical staff** = personal de
oficina *or* oficinistas; **clerical work** = trabajo de
oficina; **clerical worker** = oficinista *or* empleado de
oficina

clerk [klɑːk] **1** *noun* **(a)** oficinista *mf or* empleado,
-da de oficina; **articled clerk** = pasante *mf* de
abogado; **chief clerk** *or* **head clerk** = jefe de oficina;
filing clerk = archivero, -ra; **invoice clerk** =
encargado, -da de la facturación; **shipping clerk** =
encargado, -da de la expedición **(b)** **bank clerk** =
empleado, -da de banco *or* cajero, -ra; **booking clerk**
= taquillero, -ra; *US* **sales clerk** = vendedor, -ra **2**
verb US trabajar como dependiente

◊ **clerkess** [klɑː'kes] *noun* *(in Scotland)*
oficinista *f*

clever ['klevə] *adjective* inteligente *or* listo, -ta *or*
hábil *or* astuto, -ta; **he is very clever at spotting a
bargain** = es muy hábil para encontrar gangas *or*

tiene un talento especial para encontrar gangas; **clever investors have made a lot of money on the share deal** = los inversores astutos han obtenido mucho dinero con las acciones

client ['klaɪənt] *noun* cliente *mf*

◊ **clientele** [kliːɒn'tel] *noun* clientela *f*

climb [klaɪm] *verb* subir *or* aumentar; **the company has climbed to No. 1 position in the market** = la empresa ha conseguido el primer puesto en el mercado; **profits climbed rapidly as the new management cut costs** = los beneficios aumentaron rápidamente cuando la nueva dirección redujo los costes

> QUOTE more recently, the company climbed back to 10, for a market valuation of $30 million
> **Forbes Magazine**

clinch [klɪn(t)ʃ] *verb* cerrar un trato; **he offered an extra 5% to clinch the deal** = ofreció un 5% más para cerrar el trato; **they need approval from the board before they can clinch the deal** = necesitan la confirmación de la junta directiva para poder cerrar el trato

clip [klɪp] *noun* **paperclip** = sujetapapeles *m* clip *m*

◊ **clipboard** ['klɪpbɔːd] *noun* tablilla *f* con sujetapapeles

clipping service ['klɪpɪŋ 'sɜːvɪs] *noun* servicio *m* de recortes de prensa

cloakroom ['kləʊkrʊm] *noun* guardarropa *m* (*in station*) consigna *f*

clock [klɒk] *noun* reloj *m*; **the office clock is fast** = el reloj de la oficina adelanta; **the micro has a built-in clock** = el micro tiene un reloj interno; **digital clock** = reloj digital

◊ **clock card** ['klɒk 'kɑːd] *noun* ficha *f* para activar el reloj de asistencia del personal

◊ **clock in** *or* **clock on** ['klɒk 'ɪn *or* 'klɒk 'ɒn] *verb* (*of worker*) fichar a la entrada al trabajo

◊ **clock out** *or* **clock off** ['klɒk 'aʊt *or* 'klɒk 'ɒf] *verb* (*of worker*) fichar a la salida del trabajo

◊ **clocking in** *or* **clocking on** ['klɒkɪŋ 'ɪn *or* 'klɒkɪŋ 'ɒn] *noun* control *m* de entrada al trabajo

◊ **clocking out** *or* **clocking off** ['klɒkɪŋ 'aʊt *or* 'klɒkɪŋ 'ɒf] *noun* control *m* de salida del trabajo

close 1 [kləʊz] *noun* fin *m or* conclusión *f or* cierre *m*; **at the close of the day's trading the shares had fallen 20%** = al cierre de la sesión las acciones habían bajado un 20% **2** [kləʊs] *adjective* **close to** = cercano, -na *or* próximo, -ma; **the company was close to bankruptcy** = la compañía estaba al borde de la quiebra; **we are close to meeting our sales targets** = estamos muy cerca de cumplir nuestros objetivos de ventas **3** [kləʊz] *verb* **(a)** (*close or shut*) cerrar; **the office closes at 5.30** = la oficina cierra a las 5.30; **we close early on Saturdays** = los sábados cerramos temprano **(b)** (*come to an end*) **to close (off) the accounts** = saldar las cuentas **(c)** (*stop*) **to close an account** = (i) retirar el crédito comercial de un cliente; (ii) cerrar una cuenta bancaria; **he closed his building society account** = cerró su cuenta en la sociedad hipotecaria **(d)** (*end*) **the shares closed at $15** = el precio de las acciones fue de $15 al cierre

◊ **close company** *or* US **close(d) corporation** ['kləʊs 'kʌmpənɪ *or* 'kləʊs kɔːpə'reɪʃən *or* 'kləʊzd kɔːpə'reɪʃən] *noun* sociedad *f* privada con pequeña participación de accionistas

◊ **closed** [kləʊzd] *adjective* **(a)** (*shut*) cerrado, -da; **the office is closed on Mondays** = la oficina cierra los lunes; **all the banks are closed on the National Day** = todos los bancos cierran el día de la fiesta nacional **(b)** (*restricted*) exclusivo, -va; **closed shop** = empresa que emplea sólo a trabajadores sindicados; **a closed shop agreement** = un acuerdo para emplear exclusivamente a trabajadores sindicados; **the union is asking the management to agree to a closed shop** = el sindicato pide a la dirección que emplee exclusivamente a trabajadores sindicados; **closed market** = mercado cerrado; **they signed a closed market agreement with an Egyptian company** = firmaron un acuerdo de exclusividad con una empresa egipcia

◊ **close down** ['kləʊz 'daʊn] *verb* cerrar; **the company is closing down its London office** = la empresa va a cerrar su sucursal de Londres; **the strike closed down the railway system** = la huelga paralizó el sistema de ferrocariles

◊ **close-out sale** ['kləʊz 'aʊt 'seɪl] *noun* US liquidación *f* total

◊ **closing** ['kləʊzɪŋ] **1** *adjective* **(a)** (*final*) final *or* al cierre; **closing bid** = oferta final; **closing date** = fecha tope *or* fecha límite; **the closing date for tenders to be received is May 1st** = el plazo para recibir ofertas vence el 1 de mayo; **closing price** = precio al cierre **(b)** (*at end of accounting period*) final *or* al cierre; **closing balance** = saldo final; **closing stock** = existencias finales **(c)** **closing ceremony** = acto de clausura **2** *noun* **(a)** (*shutting*) cierre *m*; **Sunday closing** = cierre dominical; **closing time** = hora de cierre; **early closing day** = día en que las tiendas cierran por la tarde (GB) **(b)** (*stopping*) **closing of an account** = retirada del crédito bancario

◊ **closing down sale** ['kləʊzɪŋ daʊn 'seɪl] *noun* liquidación *f* total por cierre

◊ **closure** ['kləʊʒə] *noun* clausura *f or* cierre *m*

> QUOTE Toronto stocks closed at an all-time high, posting their fifth straight day of advances in heavy trading
> **Financial Times**

> QUOTE the best thing would be to have a few more plants close down and bring supply more in line with current demand
> **Fortune**

club [klʌb] *noun* club *m*; **if you want the managing director, you can phone him at his club** = si quiere hablar con el director gerente, puede llamarle a su club; **he has applied to join the sports club** = ha solicitado hacerse socio del club deportivo; **club membership** = los socios de un club; **club subscription** = cuota del club; **staff club** = club del personal

cm = CENTIMETRE cm (= centímetro)

C/N = CREDIT NOTE

c/o ['siː'əʊ] = CARE OF

Co. [kəʊ] = COMPANY Cía. (= Compañía)

co- [kəʊ] *prefix* co

◊ **co-creditor** ['kəʊ 'kredɪtə] *noun* coacreedor, -ra

◊ **co-director** [kəʊdɪ'rektə] *noun* codirector, -ra

◊ **co-insurance** [kəʊɪn'ʃʊərəns] *noun* coaseguro *m*

COD *or* **c.o.d.** [si:əʊ'di:] = CASH ON DELIVERY (cóbrese a la entrega *or* contra reembolso)

code [kəʊd] *noun* **(a)** *(signs, numbers or letters with meaning)* código *m*; **area code** = código territorial *or* prefijo *m*; **what is the code for Edinburgh?** = ¿cuál es el prefijo de Edinburgo?; **bar code** = código de barras; **international dialling code** = indicativo telefónico para llamar al extranjero; **machine-readable codes** = códigos legibles por el ordenador; **post code** *or US* **zip code** = código postal; **stock code** = código de almacenamiento; **tax code** = código impositivo *or* fiscal **(b)** *(set of rules)* código *m*; **code of practice** *or US* **code of ethics** = normas de conducta *or* código de ética profesional

◊ **coding** ['kəʊdɪŋ] *noun* codificación *f*; **the coding of invoices** = la codificación de facturas

coefficient [kəʊɪ'fɪʃənt] *noun* coeficiente *m*

coffee shop ['kɒfi 'ʃɒp] *noun* cafetería *f*

coin [kɔɪn] **1** *noun* moneda *f*; **he gave me two 10-franc coins in my change** = me dio dos monedas de 10 francos con el cambio; **I need some 10p coins for the telephone** = necesito monedas de 10 peniques para el teléfono **2** *verb* acuñar

◊ **coinage** ['kɔɪnɪdʒ] *noun* acuñación *f or* sistema *m* de monedas utilizado en un país

cold [kəʊld] *adjective* **(a)** *(not hot)* frío, fría; **the machines work badly in cold weather** = las máquinas funcionan mal con el frío; **the office was so cold that the staff started complaining** = hacía tanto frío en la oficina que el personal empezó a quejarse; **the coffee machine also sells cold drinks** = la máquina de café también despacha bebidas frías **(b)** *(not prepared)* sin preparar; **cold call** = visita sin cita previa; **cold start** = empezar un negocio a cero

collaborate [kə'læbəreɪt] *verb* colaborar; **to collaborate with a French firm on a building project** = colaborar con una empresa francesa en una obra de construcción; **they collaborated on the new aircraft** = colaboraron en la construcción de la nueva aeronave (NOTE: you collaborate **with** someone **on** something)

◊ **collaboration** [kəlæbə'reɪʃən] *noun* colaboración *f*; **their collaboration on the project was very profitable** = su colaboración en el proyecto fue muy provechosa

◊ **collaborator** [kə'læbəreɪtə] *noun* colaborador, -ra

collapse [kə'læps] **1** *noun* **(a)** *(fall in price)* caída *f or* hundimiento *m or* desplome *m*; **the collapse of the market in silver** = el hundimiento del mercado de la plata; **the collapse of the dollar on the foreign exchange markets** = el desplome del dólar en los mercados de divisas **(b)** *(failure)* colapso *m or* quiebra *f or* ruina *f or* fracaso *m*; **investors lost thousands of pounds in the collapse of the company** = los inversionistas perdieron miles de libras con el fracaso de la compañía **2** *verb* **(a)** *(to fall)* derrumbarse *or* hundirse; **the market collapsed** = el mercado se derrumbó; **the yen collapsed on the foreign exchange markets** = el yen sufrió una caída en los mercados de divisas **(b)** *(to fail)* quebrar *or* fracasar; **the company collapsed with £25,000 in debts** = la compañía quebró dejando deudas de £25.000

collar ['kɒlə] *noun* cuello *m* de una prenda de vestir; **blue-collar worker** = obrero, -ra; **white-collar worker** = oficinista; **he has a white-collar job** = tiene un trabajo de oficina *or* es oficinista

collateral [kɒ'lætərəl] **1** *noun* garantía *f*; **to lodge securities as collateral** = depositar valores como garantía prendaria **2** *adjective* colateral *or* prendario, -a

colleague ['kɒliːg] *noun* colega *mf* compañero, -ra de trabajo; **his colleagues gave him a present when he got married** = cuando se casó, sus colegas le hicieron un regalo; **I know Jane Gray - she was a colleague of mine at my last job** = Conozco a Jane Gray, fuimos *or* éramos colegas en mi último trabajo

collect [kə'lekt] **1** *verb* **(a)** *(money)* cobrar; **to collect a debt** = cobrar una deuda **(b)** *(fetch)* recoger; **we have to collect the stock from the warehouse** = tenemos que recoger la mercancía del almacén; **can you collect my letters from the typing pool?** = ¿puede Vd. recoger mis cartas del servicio de mecanografía?; **letters are collected twice a day** = se recogen las cartas dos veces al día **2** *adverb & adjective US* (llamada de teléfono) a cobro revertido; **to make a collect call** = hacer una llamada a cobro revertido; **he called his office collect** = llamó a su oficina a cobro revertido

◊ **collectable** [kə'lektəbl] *adjective* cobrable

◊ **collecting agency** [kə'lektɪŋ 'eɪdʒənsi] *noun* agencia *f* de morosos

◊ **collection** [kə'lekʃən] *noun* **(a)** *(money)* cobro *m*; **tax collection** *or* **collection of tax** = recaudación de impuestos; **debt collection** = cobro de morosos; **debt collection agency** = agencia de cobro de morosos; **bills for collection** = letras por cobrar **(b)** *(goods)* recogida *f*; **the stock is in the warehouse awaiting collection** = la mercancía está en el almacén esperando ser recogida; **collection charges** *or* **collection rates** = cobro por recogida; **to hand something in for collection** = dejar algo a alguien para que lo recojan **(c)** *(money collected)* **collections** = cobros **(d)** *(of post)* recogida *f*; **there are six collections a day from the letter box** = se recogen las cartas del buzón seis veces al día

◊ **collective** [kə'lektɪv] *adjective* colectivo, -va; **free collective bargaining** = convenio colectivo libre; **collective ownership** = propiedad colectiva;

they signed a collective wage agreement = firmaron un convenio salarial colectivo

◊ **collector** [kə'lektə] *noun* cobrador, -ra *or* recaudador, -ra; **collector of taxes** *or* **tax collector** = recaudador de impuestos; **debt collector** = (agente) cobrador de morosos; **rent collector** = cobrador de alquileres

college ['kɒlɪdʒ] *noun* colegio *m or* escuela *f*; **business college** *or* **commercial college** = escuela empresarial *or* de empresariales; **secretarial college** = escuela de secretariado

Colombia [kə'lʌmbiə] *noun* Colombia *f*

◊ **Colombian** [kə'lʌmbiən] *adjective & noun* colombiano, -na
NOTE: capital: **Bogota**; (= Bogotá); currency: **Colombian peso (Col$)** = peso colombiano (Col$)

column ['kɒləm] *noun* **(a)** *(vertical list of numbers)* columna *f*; **to add up a column of figures** = sumar una columna de cifras; **put the total at the bottom of the column** = ponga el total al pie de la columna; **credit column** = columna del haber; **debit column** = columna del debe **(b)** *(in a newspaper)* columna; **she writes the City column in the newspaper** = escribe la crónica *or* información financiera del periódico; **column-centimetre** = medida en centímetros de la extensión de la columna de un periódico que sirve para calcular el coste de los anuncios

combine 1 ['kɒmbaɪn] *noun* asociación *f or* grupo *m* industrial; **a German industrial combine** = un grupo industrial alemán **2** [kəm'baɪn] *verb* asociarse; **the workforce and management combined to fight the takeover bid** = los trabajadores y la dirección se asociaron para hacer frente a la oferta pública de adquisición

◊ **combination** [kɒmbɪ'neɪʃən] *noun* **(a)** *(mixture)* combinación *f*; **a combination of cash flow problems and difficult trading conditions caused the company's collapse** = una combinación de problemas de tesorería y del mercado ocasionó el hundimiento de la compañía *(lock)* combinación; **I have forgotten the combination of the lock on my briefcase** = he olvidado la combinación de la cerradura de mi cartera; **the office safe has a combination lock** = la caja fuerte de la oficina tiene una cerradura de combinación

comfort ['kʌmfət] *noun* **letter of comfort** *or* **comfort letter** = informe *m* favorable sobre una persona que ha solicitado un préstamo *or* un aval

```
QUOTE comfort letters in the context of a
group of companies can take the form of (a)
an undertaking by a holding company to
provide finance to a subsidiary; (b) an
undertaking to meet the debts and
liabilities of a subsidiary as they fall
due. Comfort letters are encountered in
numerous other situations: where a bank is
to grant finance to a subsidiary company,
it may seek a comfort letter from the
parent to the effect that the parent will
not dispose of its interest in the
subsidiary
                              Accountancy
```

comment ['kɒment] *noun* comentario *m*; **'no comment'** = 'sin comentarios'

commerce ['kɒmɜːs] *noun* comercio *m*;

Chamber of Commerce = Cámara de Comercio; *US* **Department of Commerce** *or* **Commerce Department** = Ministerio de Comercio e Industria

◊ **commercial** [kə'mɜːʃəl] **1** *adjective* **(a)** *(business)* comercial; **commercial aircraft** = avión comercial *or* aviones comerciales; **commercial artist** = técnico, -ca de artes gráficas; **commercial attaché** = agregado, -da comercial; **commercial break** = descanso publicitario *or* pausa publicitaria; **commercial college** = escuela superior de comercio; **commercial course** = curso comercial; **he took a commercial course by correspondence** = estudió un curso comercial por correspondencia; **commercial directory** = guía comercial; **commercial district** = distrito comercial; **commercial law** = derecho mercantil; **commercial load** = carga rentable; **commercial port** = puerto comercial; **commercial traveller** = representante *mf*; **commercial vehicle** = vehículo comercial; **sample only - of no commercial value** = muestra gratuita - sin valor comercial **(b)** *(profitable)* rentable *or* económico, -ca; **not a commercial proposition** = propuesta *or* proposición no rentable **2** *noun (TV, radio)* emisión *f* publicitaria *or* anuncio *m or* comercial *m*

◊ **commercialization** [kəmɜːʃəlaɪ'zeɪʃn] *noun* comercialización *f*; **the commercialization of museums** = la comercialización de los museos

◊ **commercialize** [kə'mɜːʃəlaɪz] *verb* comercializar; **the holiday town has become so commercialized that it is unpleasant** = la ciudad de veraneo se ha hecho tan comercial que resulta desagradable

◊ **commercially** [kə'mɜːʃəli] *adverb* comercialmente; **not commercially viable** = sin viabilidad comercial

commission [kə'mɪʃən] **1** *noun* **(a)** *(money paid to salesman or agent)* comisión *f*; **she gets 10% commission on everything she sells** = recibe un 10% de comisión sobre lo que vende; **he charges 10% commission** = cobra un 10% de comisión; **commission agent** = comisionista; **commission rep** = representante a comisión; **commission sale** *or* **sale on commission** = venta a comisión **(b)** *(group of people)* comisión *or* comité *m*; **the government has appointed a commission of inquiry to look into the problems of small exporters** = el gobierno ha nombrado un comité de investigación para examinar los problemas de los pequeños exportadores; **he is the chairman of the government commission on export subsidies** = es el presidente de la comisión gubernamental de subsidios a la exportación **2** *verb* encargar

commit [kə'mɪt] *verb* **(a)** *(crime)* cometer **(b) to commit funds to a project** = asignar fondos a un proyecto (NOTE: **committing - committed**)

◊ **commitments** [kə'mɪtmənts] *noun* compromisos *mpl or* responsabilidades *fpl* obligaciones *fpl*; **to meet one's commitments** = cumplir con las obligaciones; **not to be able to meet one's commitments** = no poder cumplir con las obligaciones *or* los compromisos

committee [kə'mɪti] *noun* comité *m*; **to be a member of a committee** *or* **to sit on a committee** = ser miembro de un comité; **he was elected to the committee of the staff club** = le nombraron miembro del comité del club del personal; **the new**

plans have to be approved by the committee members = los nuevos planes tienen que ser aprobados por los miembros del comité; **to chair a committee** = presidir un comité; **he is the chairman of the planning committee** = es el presidente del comité de planificación; **she is the secretary of the finance committee** = es la secretaria del comité de finanzas; **management committee** = comité de gestión

commodity [kə'mɒdəti] *noun* mercancía *f or* mercadería *f or* producto *m* primario *or* materias *fpl* primas; **primary** *or* **basic commodities** = productos primarios *or* básicos; **staple commodity** = artículo *m* de primera necesidad; **commodity market** *or* **commodity exchange** = lonja *or* bolsa de contratación; **commodity futures** = materias primas cotizadas en el mercado de futuros; **silver rose 5% on the commodity futures market yesterday** = la plata subió ayer un 5% en el mercado de futuros; **commodity trader** = comerciante de materias primas

COMMENT: commodities are either traded for immediate delivery (as 'actuals' or 'physicals'), or for delivery in the future (as 'futures'). Commodity markets deal either in metals (aluminium, copper, lead, nickel, silver, zinc) or in 'soft' items, such as cocoa, coffee, sugar and oil

common ['kɒmən] *adjective* **(a)** *(frequent)* común *or* corriente *or* normal; **putting the carbon paper in the wrong way round is a common mistake** = poner el papel carbón al revés es un error corriente; **being caught by the customs is very common these days** = ser aprehendido por la aduana es muy corriente hoy día **(b)** *(belonging to everyone)* común; **common carrier** = empresa de transporte público *or* de transporte en común; **common ownership** = propiedad colectiva; **common pricing** = fijación colectiva de precios; *US* **common stock** = acciones ordinarias; *(in the EU)* **Common Agricultural Policy (CAP)** = Política Agrícola Común (PAC)

◊ **common law** ['kɒmən 'lɔ:] *noun* derecho consuetudinario (NOTE: you say **at common law** when referring to something happening according to the principles of common law)

◊ **Common Market** ['kɒmən 'mɑ:kɪt] *noun* **the European Common Market** = el Mercado Común Europeo; **the Common Market finance ministers** = los ministros de finanzas del Mercado Común

communautaire [kəmju:nəʊ'teə] *adjective* europeísta *or* proeuropeo, -pea

communicate [kə'mju:nɪkeɪt] *verb* comunicar *or* comunicarse; **he finds it impossible to communicate with his staff** = le resulta imposible comunicarse con el personal; **communicating with head office has been quicker since we installed the fax** = desde que instalamos el fax es más rápido comunicar con la oficina principal

◊ **communication** [kəmju:nɪ'keɪʃən] *noun* **(a)** *(information)* comunicación *f*; **communication with the head office has been made easier by using the fax** = la comunicación con la oficina principal es más fácil por fax ; **to enter into communication with someone** = establecer comunicación con alguien, generalmente por escrito; **we have entered into communication with** the relevant government department = hemos establecido comunicación con el departamento gubernamental pertinente **(b)** *(message)* comunicado *m*; **we have had a communication from the local tax inspector** = hemos recibido un comunicado del inspector fiscal de la zona **(c)** **communications** = comunicaciones; **after the flood all communications with the outside world were broken** = después de la inundación se cortaron todas las comunicaciones con el exterior

community [kə'mju:nəti] *noun* **(a)** *(group of people)* comunidad *f*; **the local business community** = los empresarios de la localidad **(b)** **the European Economic Community** = la Comunidad Económica Europea; **Community assets** = acervo comunitario; **the Community ministers** = los ministros de la Comunidad Europea

commute [kə'mju:t] *verb* **(a)** *(to travel to work)* viajar diariamente al trabajo; **he commutes from the country to his office in the centre of town** = viaja todos los días desde el campo hasta su oficina situada en el centro de la ciudad **(b)** *(to exchange)* conmutar; **he decided to commute part of his pension rights into a lump sum payment** = decidió conmutar una parte de su pensión por una cantidad en efectivo

◊ **commuter** [kə'mju:tə] *noun* viajero diario *or* viajera diaria; **he lives in the commuter belt** = vive en el extrarradio de la ciudad; **commuter train** = tren de cercanías (para ir al trabajo diariamente); **the train was full of commuters** = el tren iba lleno de viajeros de cercanías *or* de viajeros que iban al trabajo

company ['kʌmpəni] *noun* **(a)** *(business)* compañía *f or* sociedad *f or* empresa *f* **to put a company into liquidation** = liquidar una compañía; **to set up a company** = crear una compañía; **associate company** = compañía afiliada *or* asociada; **family company** = empresa familiar; **holding company** = sociedad de cartera *or* 'holding'; **joint-stock company** = sociedad anónima; **limited (liability) company** = sociedad de responsabilidad limitada (S.R.L.); **listed company** = sociedad *f* registrada *or* compañía que se cotiza en la bolsa; **parent company** = sociedad matriz; **private (limited) company** = sociedad anónima privada; **public limited company (plc)** = sociedad anónima (S.A.); **subsidiary company** = filial *or* empresa subsidiaria **(b)** **finance company** = sociedad financiera; **insurance company** = compañía *f* de seguros; **shipping company** = compañía naviera; **tractor** *or* **aircraft** *or* **chocolate company** = una empresa de tractores *or* de aviones *or* de chocolate **(c)** *GB* **the Companies Act** = ley de sociedades (anónimas); **company car** = coche de la empresa; **company doctor** = *(doctor who works for a company)* médico de empresa; *(specialist who rescues companies)* empresario que se especializa en rescatar compañías en dificultades; **company director** = director, -ra de empresa; **company law** = derecho *m or* ley *f* de sociedades; **company secretary** = secretario, -ria de una empresa; *US* **company town** = ciudad factoría *or* en la que la mayor parte de la población activa trabaja en la misma empresa

◊ **Companies Registration Office (CRO)** *or* **Companies House** ['kʌmpəniz redʒɪs'treɪʃn 'ɒfɪs *or* 'kʌmpəniz 'haʊs] *noun* Sede del Registro Mercantil

COMMENT: a company can be incorporated (with memorandum and articles of association) as a private limited company, and adds the initials 'Ltd' after its name, or as a public limited company, when its name must end in 'Plc'. Unincorporated companies are partnerships such as firms of solicitors, architects, accountants, etc. and they add the initials Co. after their name

compare [kəm'peə] *verb* comparar *or* cotejar; **the finance director compared the figures for the first and second quarters** = el director de finanzas comparó las cifras del primer y del segundo trimestre

◊ **compare with** [kəm,peə'wɪð] *verb* comparar con; **how do the sales this year compare with last year's?** = ¿qué diferencia existe entre las ventas de este año y las del año pasado?; **compared with 1995, last year was a boom year** = comparado con 1995, el año pasado fue un año próspero

◊ **comparable** ['kɒmpərəbl] *adjective* comparable; **the two sets of figures are not comparable** = los dos grupos de cifras no son comparables; **which is the nearest company comparable to this one in size?** = ¿cuál es la compañía más parecida a ésta en importancia?

◊ **comparability** [kɒmpærə'bɪləti] *noun* posibilidad *f* de comparación; **pay comparability** = escalas de sueldos comparables

◊ **comparison** [kəm'pærɪsn] *noun* comparación *f*; **sales are down in comparison with last year** = las ventas han bajado en comparación con el año pasado; **there is no comparison between overseas and home sales** = no se pueden comparar las ventas en el extranjero con las nacionales

compensate ['kɒmpenseɪt] *verb* compensar *or* indemnizar; **to compensate a manager for loss of commission** = compensar a un director por pérdida de comisiones (NOTE: you compensate someone **for** something)

◊ **compensation** [kɒmpen'seɪʃən] *noun* **(a)** *(loss or damage)* compensación *f*; **compensation for damage** = compensación *or* indemnización *f* por daños y perjuicios; **compensation for loss of office** = indemnización por despido *or* por cese en el cargo; **compensation for loss of earnings** = indemnización por pérdida de ingresos **(b)** *(salary)* US salario *m*; **compensation package** = paquete de beneficios ofrecidos con un trabajo

compete [kəm'piːt] *verb* competir *or* hacer la competencia; **to compete with someone** *or* **with a company** = competir con alguien *or* con una compañía; **we have to compete with cheap imports from the Far East** = tenemos que competir con las importaciones a bajo precio del Extremo Oriente; **they were competing unsuccessfully with local companies on their home territory** = estaban compitiendo sin éxito con compañías locales en su propia zona; **the two companies are competing for a market share** *or* **for a contract** = las dos empresas

se disputan una cuota de mercado *or* compiten por un contrato

competent ['kɒmpɪtənt] *adjective* competente

competing [kəm'piːtɪŋ] *adjective* competitivo, -va; **competing firms** = empresas rivales; **competing products** = productos en competencia

◊ **competition** [kɒmpə'tɪʃən] *noun* **(a)** *(with a supplier)* competencia *f*; **free competition** = libre competencia; **keen competition** = competencia intensa; **we are facing keen competition from European manufacturers** = nos enfrentamos a la fuerte competencia de los fabricantes europeos **(b)** *(test)* **open competition (for a job)** = concurso oposición **(c) the competition** = la competencia; **we have lowered our prices to beat the competition** = hemos reducido nuestros precios para derrotar a la competencia; **the competition has** *or* **have brought out a new range of products** = la competencia ha sacado una nueva gama de productos (NOTE: singular, but can take a plural verb)

◊ **competitive** [kəm'petɪtɪv] *adjective* competitivo, -va; **competitive price** = precio competitivo; **competitive pricing** = fijación de precios competitivos; **competitive products** = productos competitivos

◊ **competitively** [kəm'petɪtɪvli] *adverb* **competitively priced** = con precio competitivo

◊ **competitiveness** [kəm'petɪtɪvnəs] *noun* competitividad *f*

◊ **competitor** [kəm'petɪtə] *noun* competidor, -ra; **two German firms are our main competitors** = dos empresas alemanas son nuestros principales competidores

competence *or* **competency** ['kɒmpətəns *or* 'kɒmpətənsi] *noun* aptitud *f or* competencia *f*; **the case falls within the competence of the court** = el asunto cae dentro de la competencia del tribunal

◊ **competent** ['kɒmpətənt] *adjective* **(a)**

(efficient) adecuado, -da *or* capaz; **she is a competent secretary** *or* **a competent manager** = es una secretaria *or* una directora competente **(b)** *(legally able)* competente; **the court is not competent to deal with this case** = este asunto no es de la competencia del tribunal

compile [kəm'paɪl] *verb* compilar

◊ **compilation** [kɒmpɪ'leɪʃn] *noun* compilación *f*

complain [kəm'pleɪn] *verb* quejarse; **the office is so cold the staff have started complaining** = hace tanto frío en la oficina que el personal ha empezado a quejarse; **she complained about the service** = se quejó del servicio; **they are complaining that our prices are too high** = se quejan de que nuestros precios son demasiado elevados; **if you want to complain, write to the manager** = si quiere quejarse, escriba al director

◊ **complaint** [kəm'pleɪnt] *noun* queja *f or* querella *f*; **when making a complaint, always quote the reference number** = al hacer una reclamación, cite siempre el número de referencia; **she sent her letter of complaint to the managing director** = envió su carta de reclamación al director gerente; **to make** *or* **lodge a complaint against someone** = presentar una queja *or* reclamación contra alguien; **complaints department** = departamento de reclamaciones; **complaints procedure** = procedimiento de reclamación

complementary [kɒmplɪ'mentəri] *adjective* complementario, -ria

complete [kəm'pliːt] **1** *adjective* completo, -ta; **the order is complete and ready for sending** = el pedido está completo y listo para su envío; **the order should be delivered only if it is complete** = el pedido debe entregarse solamente si está completo **2** *verb* completar *or* concluir *or* terminar *or* acabar; **the factory completed the order in two weeks** = la fábrica completó el pedido en dos semanas; **how long will it take you to complete the job?** = ¿cuánto tiempo le llevará a Vd. terminar el trabajo?

◊ **completely** [kəm'pliːtli] *adverb* completamente *or* totalmente *or* por completo; **the cargo was completely ruined by water** = el agua estropeó por completo el cargamento; **the warehouse was completely destroyed by fire** = el almacén quedó totalmente destruido por un incendio

◊ **completion** [kəm'pliːʃən] *noun* finalización *f or* conclusión *f*; *(final stage in the sale of a property)* **completion date** = fecha de finalización *or* fecha de entrega; **completion of a contract** = firma de un contrato

complex ['kɒmpleks] **1** *noun* complejo *m*; **a large industrial complex** = un gran complejo industrial (NOTE: plural is **complexes**) **2** *adjective* complejo, -ja; **a complex system of import controls** = un sistema complejo de controles de importación; **the specifications for the machine are very complex** = las especificaciones de la máquina son muy complejas

compliance [kəm'plaɪəns] *noun* sumisión *f or* conformidad *f*; **non-compliance** = incumplimiento

m; **compliance certificate** = certificado de conformidad; **compliance department** = oficina que controla el cumplimiento de las normas establecidas en la Bolsa para proteger a los clientes

complicate ['kɒmplɪkeɪt] *verb* complicar *or* enredar

complimentary [kɒmplɪ'mentəri] *adjective* **complimentary ticket** = entrada de favor *or* invitación gratuita

◊ **compliments slip** ['kɒmplɪmənts 'slɪp] *noun* 'saluda' *m*

comply [kəm'plaɪ] *verb* **to comply with a court order** = obedecer una orden del tribunal

component [kəm'pəʊnənt] *noun* pieza *f or* componente *m*; **the assembly line stopped because supply of a component was delayed** = la cadena de montaje se paró por el retraso del suministro de una pieza; **components factory** = fábrica de componentes

composition [kɒmpə'zɪʃən] *noun* **(a)** *(agreement)* composición *f* **(b)** *(with creditors)* acomodamiento *m or* acuerdo *m* (entre deudores y acreedores)

compound 1 ['kɒmpaʊnd] *adjective* **compound interest** = interés compuesto **2** [kəm'paʊnd] *verb* ponerse de acuerdo *or* avenirse

comprehension [kɒmprɪ'henʃn] *noun* comprensión *f*

comprehensive [kɒmprɪ'hensɪv] *adjective* amplio, -plia *or* general *or* global; **comprehensive insurance** = seguro a todo riesgo

compromise ['kɒmprəmaɪz] **1** *noun* acuerdo *m or* compromiso *m*; **management offered £5 an hour, the union asked for £9, and a compromise of £7.50 was reached** = la dirección ofreció £5 por hora, el sindicato reivindicó £9 y se llegó a un acuerdo de £7,50 **2** *verb* llegar a un arreglo *or* transigir; **he asked £15 for it, I offered £7 and we compromised on £10** = pidió £15 por ello, le ofrecí £7 y llegamos a un precio intermedio de £10

comptometer [kɒmp'tɒmɪtə] *noun* registro *m* automático

comptroller [kən'trəʊlə] *noun* interventor, -ra *or* supervisor, -ra

compulsory [kəm'pʌlsəri] *adjective* obligatorio, -ria; **compulsory liquidation** *or* **compulsory winding up** = liquidación forzosa; **compulsory purchase** = expropiación forzosa; **compulsory purchase order** = orden de expropiación forzosa; **compulsory winding up order** = orden de liquidación forzosa

compute [kəm'pjuːt] *verb* calcular *or* computar

◊ **computable** [kəm'pjuːtəbl] *adjective* calculable *or* computable

◊ **computation** [kɒmpjʊ'teɪʃən] *noun* cálculo *m or* cómputo *m*

◊ **computational** [kɒmpjʊ'teɪʃənl] *adjective* **computational error** = error de cálculo

◊ **computer** [kəm'pjuːtə] *noun* ordenador *m*;

computer **bureau** = oficina de informática; **computer department** = departamento de informática; **computer error** = error de ordenador; **computer file** = archivo *or* fichero; **computer language** = lenguaje de ordenador; **computer listing** = listado de ordenador; **computer manager** = responsable de ordenadores; **computer operator** = operador de teclado; **computer program** = programa de ordenador; **computer programmer** = programador de ordenadores; **computer services** = servicios de informática; **computer system** = equipo informático; **computer time** = tiempo invertido por el ordenador; **running all those sales reports costs a lot in computer time** = para compilar todos esos informes de ventas se invierte tiempo de ordenador; **business computer** = ordenador de empresa; **personal computer (PC)** *or* **home computer** = ordenador personal *or* PC

◊ **computerize** [kəm'pju:təraiz] *verb* informatizar; **our stock control has been completely computerized** = nuestro control de existencias ha sido totalmente informatizado

◊ **computerized** [kəm'pju:təraizd] *adjective* informatizado, -da; **a computerized invoicing system** = un sistema de facturación informatizado

◊ **computer-readable** [kəm'pju:tə 'ri:dəbl] *adjective* legible por ordenador; **computer-readable codes** = códigos legibles por ordenador

◊ **computing** [kəm'pju:tɪŋ] *noun* informática *f*; **computing speed** = velocidad del ordenador

con [kɒn] **1** *noun (informal)* engaño *m or* estafa *f* timo *m*; **trying to get us to pay him for ten hours' overtime was just a con** = su intento de que le pagásemos diez horas extraordinarias no fue nada más que un timo **2** *verb (informal)* engañar *or* estafar; **they conned the bank into lending them £25,000 with no security** = consiguieron engañar al banco para que les prestara £25.000 sin garantías; **he conned the finance company out of £100,000** = estafó £100.000 a la compañía financiera (NOTE: **con - conning - conned)**

concealment [kən'si:lmənt] *noun* encubrimiento *m*; **concealment of assets** = encubrimiento de activos

concern [kən'sɜːn] **1** *noun* **(a)** *(business)* negocio *m or* empresa *f*; **his business is a going concern** = su negocio marcha bien; **sold as a going concern** = vendido como negocio en pleno funcionamiento **(b)** *(worry)* preocupación *f or* inquietud *f*; **the management showed no concern at all for the workers' safety** = la dirección no manifestó ninguna preocupación por la seguridad de los trabajadores **2** *verb* ocuparse de *or* referirse a; **the sales staff are not concerned with the cleaning of the store** = el personal de ventas no se ocupa de la limpieza de la tienda; **he filled in a questionnaire concerning computer utilization** = llenó un cuestionario referente a la utilización del ordenador

concert ['kɒnsət] *noun (of several people)* pacto *m or* acuerdo *m* con fines ilegales; **to act in concert** = obrar de común acuerdo; **concert party** = parte en una acción concertada

concession [kən'seʃn] *noun* **(a)** *(right to exploit)* concesión *f*; **mining concession** = concesión minera **(b)** *(exclusive right to sell)* concesión *or* agencia *f* exclusiva; **she runs a jewellery concession in a**

department store = tiene la concesión de una joyería en unos grandes almacenes **(c)** *(reduction)* desgravación *f*; **tax concession** = desgravación fiscal

◊ **concessionaire** [kənseʃə'neə] *noun* concesionario, -ria

◊ **concessionary fare** [kən'seʃnəri 'feə] *noun* tarifa reducida

conciliation [kənsɪlɪ'eɪʃn] *noun* conciliación *f*; **conciliation and arbitration of industrial disputes** = conciliación y arbitraje de conflictos laborales

conclude [kən'klu:d] *verb* **(a)** *(to complete successfully)* concertar *or* concluir; **to conclude an agreement with someone** = concertar un acuerdo con alguien **(b)** *(to believe from evidence)* concluir *or* deducir; **the police concluded that the thief had got into the building through the main entrance** = la policía dedujo *or* concluyó que el ladrón había entrado en el edificio por la puerta principal

condition [kən'dɪʃn] *noun* **(a)** *(terms)* condición *f*; **conditions of employment** *or* **conditions of service** = condiciones de empleo *or* de servicio; **conditions of entry** = condiciones de admisión; **conditions of sale** = condiciones de venta; **on condition that** = a condición de que; **they were granted the lease on condition that they paid the legal costs** = se les concedió el arrendamiento a condición de que pagasen las costas legales **(b)** *(general state)* condición *or* estado *m*; **item sold in good condition** = artículo vendido en buen estado; **what was the condition of the car when it was sold?** = ¿en qué estado estaba el coche cuando se vendió?; **prevailing conditions** = coyuntura *f*; **adverse trading conditions** = condiciones comerciales adversas; **the union has complained of the bad working conditions in the factory** = el sindicato se ha quejado de las malas condiciones de trabajo existentes en la fábrica

◊ **conditional** [kən'dɪʃnl] *adjective* **(a)** condicional *or* con reservas; **to give a conditional acceptance** = aceptar condicionalmente; **he made a conditional offer** = hizo una oferta condicional; **conditional sale** = venta condicionada **(b)** **conditional on** = depende de; **the offer is conditional on the board's acceptance** = la oferta depende de la aceptación del consejo de administración

condominium [kɒndə'mɪnɪəm] *noun* US condominio *m*

conduct [kən'dʌkt] *verb* llevar *or* mantener *or* dirigir; **to conduct negotiations** = llevar negociaciones; **the chairman conducted the negotiations very efficiently** = el presidente dirigió las negociaciones muy eficazmente

Confederation of British Industry (CBI) [kɒnfedə'reɪʃn əv 'brɪtɪʃ 'ɪndəstri] equivalent to Confederación Española de Organizaciones Empresariales (C.E.O.E.)

conference ['kɒnfərəns] *noun* **(a)** *(small scale)* reunión *f or* asamblea *f or* conferencia *f* (en cuestiones políticas, científicas importantes); **to be in conference** = estar en una reunión; **conference phone** = conferencia telefónica compartida por varias personas; **conference room** = sala de conferencias; **press conference** = conferencia *or* rueda de prensa; **sales conference** = reunión de ventas **(b)** *(large scale)* congreso *m*; **the annual conference of the Electricians' Union** = el congreso anual del Sindicato de Electricistas; **the conference of the Booksellers' Association** = el congreso de la Asociación de Libreros; **the conference agenda** *or* **the agenda of the conference was drawn up by the secretary** = la secretaria preparó el orden del día del congreso

confidence ['kɒnfɪdəns] *noun* **(a)** confianza *f*; **the sales teams do not have much confidence in their manager** = los equipos de ventas no tienen mucha confianza en su jefe; **the board has total confidence in the managing director** = la junta directiva tiene absoluta confianza en el director gerente **(b) in confidence** = en secreto; **I will show you the report in confidence** = le mostraré el informe en secreto

◊ **confidence trick** ['kɒnfɪdəns 'trɪk] *noun* timo *m or* estafa *f*

◊ **confidence trickster** ['kɒnfɪdəns 'trɪkstə] *noun* timador, -ra *or* estafador, -ra

◊ **confident** ['kɒnfɪdənt] *adjective* seguro, -ra; **I am confident the turnover will increase rapidly** = estoy seguro de que el volumen de ventas aumentará rápidamente; **are you confident the sales team is capable of handling this product?** = ¿está Vd. seguro de que el equipo de ventas es capaz de vender este producto?

◊ **confidential** [kɒnfɪ'denʃəl] *adjective* confidencial; **he sent a confidential report to the chairman** = envió un informe confidencial al presidente; **please mark the letter 'Private and Confidential'** = ponga en la carta la mención de 'Confidencial'

◊ **confidentiality** [kɒnfɪdenʃɪ'ælətɪ] *noun* confidencialidad *f*; **he broke the confidentiality of the discussions** = no respetó la confidencialidad de las discusiones

confirm [kən'fɜ:m] *verb* confirmar; **to confirm a hotel reservation** *or* **a ticket** *or* **an agreement** *or* **a booking** = confirmar una reserva de hotel *or* un billete *or* un acuerdo *or* una reserva; **to confirm someone in a job** = hacer fijo a alguien en un trabajo

◊ **confirmation** [kɒnfə'meɪʃən] *noun* confirmación *f*; **confirmation of a booking** = confirmación de una reserva; **he received confirmation from the bank that the deeds had been deposited** = recibió la confirmación del banco de que los títulos habían sido depositados

conflict ['kɒnflɪkt] *noun* pugna *f*; **conflict of interest** = conflicto *m* de intereses

confuse [kən'fju:z] *verb* dejar confuso *or* embrollar *or* enredar; **the chairman was confused by all the journalists' questions** = el presidente se mostró confuso ante las preguntas de los periodistas; **to introduce the problem of VAT will only confuse the issue** = plantear el problema del IVA no hará más que embrollar el asunto

conglomerate [kən'glɒmərət] *noun* conglomerado *m*

Congo ['kɒngəʊ] *noun* Congo *m*

◊ **Congolese** [kɒngə'li:z] *adjective & noun* congoleño, -ña

NOTE: capital: **Brazzaville;** currency: **CFA franc (CFAF)** = franco CFA (FCFA)

congratulate [kən'grætjʊleɪt] *verb* felicitar *or* dar la enhorabuena; **the sales director congratulated the salesmen on doubling sales** = el director de ventas felicitó a los vendedores por haber duplicado las ventas; **I want to congratulate you on your promotion** = quiero felicitarle por su ascenso

◊ **congratulations** [kəngrætjʊ'leɪʃənz] *plural noun* felicitaciones *fpl*; **the staff sent him their congratulations on his promotion** = recibió felicitaciones del personal por su ascenso

conman ['kɒnmæn] *noun* *(informal)* = CONFIDENCE TRICKSTER (NOTE: plural is **conmen)**

connect [kə'nekt] *verb* **(a)** conectar *or* relacionar *or* unir; **the company is connected to the government because the chairman's father is a minister** = hay una relación entre la empresa y el gobierno porque el padre del presidente es ministro **(b) the flight from New York connects with a flight to Athens** = el vuelo de Nueva York conecta con un vuelo a Atenas

◊ **connecting flight** [kə'nektɪŋ 'flaɪt] *noun* vuelo *m* de correspondencia; **check at the helicopter desk for connecting flights to the city centre** = pregunta en el mostrador de helicópteros por los vuelos de correspondencia al centro de la ciudad

◊ **connection** [kə'nekʃən] *noun* **(a)** vínculo *m or* relación *f or* conexión *f*; **is there a connection between his argument with the director and his sudden move to become warehouse manager?** = ¿hay alguna relación entre su discusión con el director y su traslado repentino a encargado de almacén?; **in connection with** = referente a *or* con respecto a; **I want to speak to the managing director in connection with the sales forecasts** = quiero hablar con el director gerente con respecto a las previsiones de ventas **(b) connections** = contactos *mpl*; **he has useful connections in industry** = tiene contactos útiles en la industria

conservative [kən'sɜ:vətɪv] *adjective* prudente *or* moderado, -da; **a conservative estimate of sales** = una estimación de ventas prudente; **his forecast of expenditure is very conservative** = su previsión de gastos es muy moderada; **at a conservative estimate** = calculando prudentemente; **their turnover has risen by at least 20% in the last year, and that is probably a conservative estimate** = el volumen de sus ventas ha subido por lo menos un 20% en el último año, y probablemente me quedo corto

◊ **conservatively** [kən'sɜ:vətlɪ] *adverb* prudentemente *or* sin exagerar; **the total sales are conservatively estimated at £2.3m** = las ventas totales están prudentemente calculadas en £2,3 millones

consider [kən'sɪdə] *verb* considerar *or* estudiar; **to consider the terms of a contract** = estudiar *or* examinar las condiciones de un contrato

◊ **consideration** [kənsɪdə'reɪʃən] *noun* **(a)** *(serious thought)* consideración *f*; **we are giving consideration to moving the head office to Scotland** = estamos considerando la posibilidad de trasladar la oficina central a Escocia **(b)** *(money)* retribución *f*; **for a small consideration** = por una pequeña cantidad *or* retribución

considerable [kən'sɪdərəbl] *adjective* considerable; **we sell considerable quantities of our products to Africa** = vendemos nuestros productos a Africa en cantidades considerables; **they lost a considerable amount of money on the commodity market** = perdieron una considerable cantidad de dinero en la bolsa de contratación

◊ **considerably** [kən'sɪdərəbli] *adverb* considerablemente; **sales are considerably higher than they were last year** = el volumen de ventas es considerablemente mayor que el del año pasado

consign [kən'saɪn] *verb* enviar *or* consignar; **to consign goods to someone** = consignar mercancías a alguien

◊ **consignation** [kɒnsaɪ'neɪʃən] *noun* consignación *f or* partida *f or* envío *m*

◊ **consignee** [kɒnsaɪ'niː] *noun* destinatario, -ria *or* consignatario, -ria *or* receptor, -ra

◊ **consignment** [kən'saɪnmənt] *noun* **(a)** *(sending something)* consignación *f or* envío *m or* expedición *f*; **consignment note** = nota *f* de envío; **goods on consignment** = bienes en consignación *or* en comisión **(b)** *(things sent)* envío *or* remesa *f or* partida *f*; **a consignment of goods has arrived** = ha llegado un envío de mercancías; **we are expecting a consignment of cars from Japan** = estamos esperando un envío de coches del Japón

◊ **consignor** [kən'saɪnə] *noun* consignador, -ra *or* remitente *mf*

| COMMENT: the goods remain the property of the consignor until the consignee sells or pays for them

> QUOTE some of the most prominent stores are gradually moving away from the traditional consignment system, under which manufacturers agree to repurchase any unsold goods, and in return dictate prices and sales strategies and even dispatch staff to sell the products
> **Nikkei Weekly**

consist of [kən'sɪst əv] *verb* consistir en *or* constar de *or* estar formado por; **the trade mission consists of the sales directors of ten major companies** = la delegación de comercio está formada por los directores de ventas de diez empresas importantes; **the package tour consists of air travel, six nights in a luxury hotel, all meals and visits to places of interest** = el viaje incluye el billete de avión, seis noches en un hotel de lujo, todas las comidas y visitas a lugares de interés

consolidate [kən'sɒlɪdeɪt] *verb* **(a)** consolidar **(b) to consolidate shipments** = agrupar envíos

◊ **consolidated** [kən'sɒlɪdeɪtɪd] *adjective* **(a)** consolidado, -da; **consolidated accounts** = cuentas consolidadas **(b) consolidated shipment** = envío agrupado de mercancías

◊ **consolidation** [kənsɒlɪ'deɪʃən] *noun* agrupación *f*

consols ['kɒnsɒlz] *plural noun* GB títulos *m* del gobierno británico sin fecha de vencimiento *or* deuda perpetua

consortium [kən'sɔːtjəm] *noun* consorcio *m*; **a**
consortium of Canadian companies *or* **a Canadian consortium** = un consorcio de compañías canadienses *or* un consorcio canadiense; **a consortium of Spanish and British companies is planning to construct the new aircraft** = un consorcio de empresas españolas y británicas se propone fabricar el nuevo avión (NOTE: plural is **consortia**)

constant ['kɒnstənt] *adjective* constante *or* invariable; **the figures are in constant pesetas** = las cifras están expresadas en pesetas constantes

constitution [kɒnstɪ'tjuːʃən] *noun* constitución *f or* estatuto *m*; **under the society's constitution, the chairman is elected for a two-year period** = conforme a los estatutos de la sociedad, el presidente es elegido por un periodo de dos años; **payments to officers of the association are not allowed by the constitution** = los estatutos no permiten que los cargos de la asociación reciban una remuneración

◊ **constitutional** [kɒnstɪ'tjuːʃnl] *adjective* constitucional *or* estatutario, -ria; **the reelection of the chairman is not constitutional** = la reelección del presidente es anticonstitucional *or* antiestatutaria

construct [kən'strʌkt] *verb* construir; **the company has tendered for the contract to construct the new airport** = la empresa ha presentado una oferta para la construcción del nuevo aeropuerto

◊ **construction** [kən'strʌkʃən] *noun* **(a)** *(being built)* construcción *f*; **construction company** = empresa de construcción; **under construction** = en construcción; **the airport is under construction** = el aeropuerto está en construcción **(b)** *(a building)* edificio *m*

◊ **constructive** [kən'strʌktɪv] *adjective* constructivo, -va *or* positivo, -va; **she made some constructive suggestions for improving management-worker relations** = hizo unas sugerencias constructivas para mejorar las relaciones entre la dirección y los obreros; **we had a constructive proposal from a distribution company in Italy** = recibimos una propuesta de cooperación de una empresa distribuidora italiana; **constructive criticism** = crítica constructiva; **constructive dismissal** = dimisión bajo presión de la dirección

◊ **constructor** [kən'strʌktə] *noun* constructor, -ra

consult [kən'sʌlt] *verb* consultar; **he consulted his accountant about his tax** = consultó a su contable en lo referente a los impuestos

◊ **consultancy** [kən'sʌltənsi] *noun* asesoría *f*; **a consultancy firm** = una asesoría *or* una consultoría; **he offers a consultancy service** = ofrece un servicio de asesoramiento

◊ **consultant** [kən'sʌltənt] *noun* asesor, -ra *or* consejero, -ra *or* consultor, -ra; **advertising consultant** = consejero de publicidad; **engineering consultant** = asesor de ingenería; **management consultant** = asesor, -ra de empresas; **tax consultant** = asesor, -ra fiscal

◊ **consulting** [kən'sʌltɪŋ] *adjective* asesor, -ra; **consulting engineer** = técnico asesor; **consulting room** = consultorio *m*

consumable goods *or* **consumables**

[kən'sjuːməbl 'gʊdz or kən'sjuːməblz] *noun* bienes de consumo

◊ **consumer** [kən'sjuːmə] *noun* consumidor, -ra; **gas consumers are protesting at the increase in prices** = los consumidores de gas protestan por el aumento de los precios; **the factory is a heavy consumer of water** = la fábrica es una gran consumidora de agua; **consumer association** or **council** = asociación de consumidores; **consumer credit** = crédito al consumidor; **Consumer Credit Act, 1974** = ley que regula la información y protección al consumido en las operaciones de crédito; **consumer durables** = bienes de consumo duraderos or equipos domésticos; **consumer goods** = bienes de consumo; **consumer panel** = equipo de consumidores; *US* **Consumer Price Index** = índice de precios al consumo (IPC); **consumer protection** = protección al consumidor; **consumer research** = investigación sobre el consumo or estudio de mercado; **consumer resistance** = resistencia del consumidor; **the latest price increases have produced considerable consumer resistance** = las últimas subidas de precios han generado una resistencia considerable por parte de los consumidores; **consumer society** = sociedad de consumo; **consumer spending** = gastos del consumidor or de consumo

QUOTE forecasting consumer response is one problem which will never be finally solved
Marketing Week

QUOTE companies selling in the UK market are worried about reduced consumer spending as a consequence of higher interest rates and inflation
Business

QUOTE analysis of the consumer price index for the first half of the year shows that the rate of inflation went down by about 12.9 per cent
Business Times (Lagos)

consumption [kən'sʌm(p)ʃən] *noun* consumo *m*; **a car with low petrol consumption** = un coche con bajo consumo de gasolina; **the factory has a heavy consumption of coal** = la fábrica consume mucho carbón; **home consumption** or **domestic consumption** = consumo doméstico

cont or **contd** = CONTINUED

contact 1 ['kɒntækt] *noun* **(a)** *(person)* conocido *m* or relación *f* or contacto *m* or enchufe *m*; **he has many contacts in the city** = conoce a or se relaciona con mucha gente en la 'City'; **who is your contact in the ministry?** = ¿quién es su persona de confianza en el ministerio?; **he got his job through contacts in the business** = consiguió el trabajo a través de enchufes **(b)** *(link)* contacto *m*; **I have lost contact with them** = he perdido el contacto con ellos; **he put me in contact with a good lawyer** = me puso en contacto con un buen abogado **2** ['kɒntækt or kən'tækt] *verb* contactar or ponerse en contacto; **he tried to contact his office by phone** = intentó ponerse en contacto con su oficina por teléfono; **can you contact the managing director at his club?** = ¿puede Vd. ponerse en contacto con el director gerente en su club?

contain [kən'teɪn] *verb* contener; **each crate contains two computers and their peripherals** = cada cajón contiene dos ordenadores y sus unidades periféricas; **a barrel contains 250 litres** = un barril contiene 250 litros; **we have lost a file containing important documents** = hemos perdido un archivo que contiene documentos importantes

◊ **container** [kən'teɪnə] *noun* **(a)** *(box or bottle)* recipiente *m* or envase *m*; **the gas is shipped in strong metal containers** = el gas es transportado en envases metálicos resistentes; **the container burst during shipping** = el recipiente se rompió durante el trasporte **(b)** *(large metal case)* contenedor *m* or 'container' *m*; **container berth** = muelle de contenedores; **container port** = puerto de contenedores; **container ship** = buque de contenedores or portacontenedores; **container terminal** = terminal de contenedores; **to ship goods in containers** = enviar mercancías en contenedores; **a container-load of spare parts is missing** = falta todo un contenedor de repuestos

◊ **containerization** [kənteɪnəraɪ'zeɪʃən] *noun* transporte *m* en contenedores

◊ **containerize** [kən'teɪnəraɪz] *verb* (i) poner en contenedores; (ii) transportar en contenedores

contango [kən'tæŋgəʊ] *noun (Stock Exchange)* reporte *m* (operación de bolsa con prórroga o interés aplazado); **contango day** = día del reporte

contempt of court [kən'temt əv 'kɔːt] *noun* desacato *m*

content ['kɒntent] *noun* contenido *m*; **the content of the letter** = el contenido de la carta

◊ **contents** ['kɒntents] *plural noun* **(a)** contenido *m*; **the contents of the bottle poured out onto the floor** = el contenido de la botella se derramó por el suelo; **the customs officials inspected the contents of the crate** = los aduaneros registraron el contenido del cajón; *(words written)* **the contents of the letter** = el contenido de la carta **(b)** *(of a book)* índice *m* de materias or sumario *m*

contested takeover [kən'testɪd 'teɪkəʊvə] *noun* oferta *f* de adquisición disputada or rebatida

contingency [kən'tɪn(d)ʒənsi] *noun* eventualidad *f* or contingencia *f* or imprevisto *m*; **contingency fund** or **contingency reserve** = fondo or reserva para imprevistos; **contingency plans** = planes de emergencia; **to add on 10% to provide for contingencies** = añadir un 10% para imprevistos; **we have built 10% for contingencies into our cost forecast** = hemos incluido en nuestra previsión de costes un 10% para imprevistos

◊ **contingent** [kən'tɪn(d)ʒənt] *adjective* **(a)** contingente; **contingent expenses** = gastos imprevistos **(b)** **contingent policy** = póliza para imprevistos

◊ **contingent liability** [kən'tɪn(d)ʒənt laɪə'bɪlɪti] *noun* pasivo *m* contingente o para imprevistos

COMMENT: a liability which may or may not occur, but for which provision is made in a company's accounts (as opposed to 'provisions', where money is set aside for an anticipated expenditure)

continue [kən'tɪnjʊ] *verb* continuar or proseguir; **the chairman continued speaking in spite of the noise from the shareholders** = el presidente continuó hablando a pesar del barullo que armaban los accionistas; **the meeting started at 10 a.m. and continued until six p.m.** = la reunión empezó a las 10 de la mañana y duró hasta las 6 de la tarde; **negotiations will continue next Monday** = las negociaciones continuarán el próximo lunes

◊ **continual** [kən'tɪnjʊəl] *adjective* continuo, -nua; **production was slow because of continual breakdowns** = la producción avanzó lentamente debido a las continuas interrupciones

◊ **continually** [kən'tɪnjʊəli] *adverb* continuamente; **the photocopier is continually breaking down** = la fotocopiadora se avería continuamente

◊ **continuation** [kəntɪnjʊ'eɪʃən] *noun* continuación *f*; **continuation sheet** = página siguiente

◊ **continuous** [kən'tɪnjʊəs] *adjective* continuo, -nua; **continuous production line** = cadena de montaje continua; **continuous feed** = alimentación continua; **continuous stationery** = papel continuo

contra ['kɒntrə] **1** *noun (account which offsets another account)* **contra account** = cuenta compensada; **contra entry** = contrapartida *f or* contraasiento *m*; **per contra** *or* **as per contra** = asiento complementario *or* compensatorio **2** *verb* **to contra an entry** = anotar una contrapartida *or* un contraasiento

contraband ['kɒntrəbænd] *noun* contrabando *m*; **contraband goods** = artículos de contrabando

contract 1 ['kɒntrækt] *noun* **(a)** *(legal agreement)* contrato *m*; **to draw up a contract** = redactar un contrato; **to draft a contract** = hacer el borrador de un contrato; **to sign a contract** = firmar un contrato; **the contract is binding on both parties** = el contrato obliga *or* es vinculante a las dos partes; **under contract** = bajo *or* según los términos del contrato *or* de conformidad con el contrato; **the firm is under contract to deliver the goods by November** = según los términos del contrato, la empresa debe entregar las mercancías antes de noviembre; **to void a contract** = anular un contrato; **contract award** = adjudicación del contrato; **contract of employment** = contrato de empleo; **fixed-term contract** = contrato a plazo fijo; **service contract** = contrato de servicios; **exchange of contracts** = intercambio de contratos **(b)** **contract law** *or* **law of contract** = derecho de obligaciones; **by private contract** = por contrato privado; **contract note** = contrato de bolsa **(c)** *(agreement to supply something)* contrato; **contract for the supply of spare parts** = contrato de suministro de repuestos; **to enter into a contract to supply spare parts** = firmar un contrato de suministro de repuestos; **to sign a contract for £10,000 worth of spare parts** = firmar un contrato de suministro de respuestos por valor de £10.000; **to put work out to contract** = subcontratar *or* contratar a otra empresa la realización de un trabajo; **to award a contract to a company** *or* **to place a contract with a company** = ofrecer un contrato a una empresa *or* firmar un contrato con una compañía; **to tender for a contract** = presentar una oferta para un contrato; **conditions of contract** *or* **contract conditions** = condiciones del contrato; **breach of contract** = incumplimiento *m or* violación *f* de contrato; **the company is in breach of contract** = la compañía no ha cumplido el

contrato; **contract work** = trabajo a contrata **2** ['kɒntrækt *or* kən'trækt] *verb* **(a)** *(make legal agreement)* contratar *or* comprometerse por contrato; **to contract to supply spare parts** *or* **to contract for the supply of spare parts** = comprometerse a suministrar repuestos por contrato; **the supply of spare parts was contracted out to Smith Ltd** = el contrato de suministro de repuestos fue adjudicado a Smith Ltd; **to contract out of an agreement** = retirarse de un acuerdo con el consentimiento por escrito de la otra parte contratante

◊ **contracting** [kən'træktɪŋ] *adjective* **contracting party** = parte contratante **(b)** *(shrink)* contraer

◊ **contraction** [kən'trækʃn] *noun* contracción *f*

◊ **contractor** [kən'træktə] *noun* contratista *mf*; **haulage contractor** = contratista de transporte por carretera; **government contractor** = contratista del Estado

◊ **contractual** [kən'træktjʊəl] *adjective* contractual *or* por contrato; **contractual liability** = responsabilidad contractual; **to fulfill your contractual obligations** = cumplir las obligaciones contractuales; **he is under no contractual obligation to buy** = no tiene obligación de comprar según el contrato

◊ **contractually** [kən'træktjʊəli] *adverb* según *or* por contrato; **the company is contractually bound to pay his expenses** = la empresa está obligada por contrato a pagar sus gastos

COMMENT: a contract is an agreement between two or more parties to create legal obligations between them. Some contracts are made 'under seal', i.e. they are signed and sealed by the parties; most contracts are made orally or in writing. The essential elements of a contract are: (a) that an offer made by one party should be accepted by the other; (b) consideration (i.e. payment of money); (c) the intention to create legal relations. The terms of a contract may be express or implied. A breach of contract by one party entitles the other party to sue for damages or to ask for something to be done

contradict [kɒntrə'dɪkt] *verb* contradecir

contrary ['kɒntrəri] *noun* contrario; **failing instructions to the contrary** = a falta de instrucciones al contrario; **on the contrary** = al contrario; **the chairman was not annoyed with his assistant - on the contrary, he promoted him** = el presidente no estaba enfadado con su asistente; por el contrario, le ofreció un ascenso

contrast ['kɒntrɑːst] *noun* contraste *m*; **in contrast to** = en contraste con; **picture contrast** = contraste de imagen

contribute [kən'trɪbjuːt] *verb* contribuir *or* cotizar; **to contribute 10% of the profits** = contribuir con el 10% de los beneficios; **he contributed to the pension fund for 10 years** = cotizó al fondo de pensiones durante 10 años

◊ **contribution** [kɒntrɪ'bjuːʃən] *noun* contribución *f or* colaboración *f*; **contribution of capital** = contribución de capital; **employer's contribution** = cuota patronal; **National Insurance contributions (NIC)** = cotizaciones a la Seguridad Social; **pension contributions** = cotizaciones a la pensión de jubilación

◊ **contributor** [kən'trɪbjʊtə] *noun* **contributor of capital** = contribuyente *mf* de capital

◊ **contributory** [kən'trɪbjʊtəri] *adjective* **(a)** *(with money)* **contributory pension plan** *or* **scheme** = plan de pensiones con aportaciones del trabajador cotizable **(b)** *(with help)* que contribuye; **falling exchange rates have been a contributory factor in** *or* **to the company's loss of profits** = la caída de los tipos de cambio ha sido un factor que ha contribuido a la pérdida de rentabilidad de la empresa

con trick ['kɒn 'trɪk] *noun* *(informal)* = CONFIDENCE TRICK

control [kən'trəʊl] **1** *noun* **(a)** *(domination)* control *m* *or* mando *m*; **the company is under the control of three shareholders** = la compañía está bajo el control de tres accionistas; **the family lost control of its business** = la familia perdió el control de su negocio; **to gain control of a business** = lograr el control de un negocio; **to lose control of a business** = perder el control de un negocio; **remote control** = mando a distancia **(b)** *(check)* control; **under control** = bajo control; **expenses are kept under tight control** = los gastos están sometidos a un control riguroso; **the company is trying to bring its overheads back under control** = la empresa intenta poner freno a sus gastos generales; **out of control** = fuera de control; **costs have got out of control** = los costes se han desmandado; **budgetary control** = control presupuestario; **credit control** = control de crédito; **quality control** = control de calidad; **rent control** = control de alquileres; **stock control** *or* *US* **inventory control** = control de existencias **(c)** **exchange controls** = control de divisas; **the government has imposed exchange controls** = el gobierno ha impuesto el control de divisas; **they say the government is going to lift exchange controls** = dicen que el gobierno va a levantar el control de divisas; **price controls** = control de precios **(d)** **control group** = grupo de control; *(computer)* **control systems** = sistemas de control **2** *verb* **(a)** **to control a business** = dirigir un negocio; **the business is controlled by a company based in Luxemburg** = el negocio está controlado por una compañía con sede en Luxemburgo; **the company is controlled by the majority shareholder** = la compañía está dirigida por el accionista mayoritario **(b)** *(keep in check)* controlar; **to control rents** = controlar los alquileres; **the government is fighting to control inflation** *or* **to control the rise in the cost of living** = el gobierno está luchando por controlar la inflación *or* limitar el alza del coste de la vida (NOTE: **controlling - controlled**)

◊ **controlled** [kən'trəʊld] *adjective* controlado, -da; **government-controlled** = controlado por el Estado *or* gobierno; **controlled economy** = economía dirigida

◊ **controller** [kən'trəʊlə] *noun* **(a)** interventor, -ra *or* inspector, -ra *or* director financiero; **credit controller** = controlador de créditos; **financial controller** = director financiero; **stock controller** = controlador de existencias *or* jefe de almacén **(b)** *US* contable *mf* jefe

◊ **controlling** [kən'trəʊlɪŋ] *adjective* que controla; **to have a controlling interest in a company** = tener un interés mayoritario en una compañía

convene [kən'viːn] *verb* convocar; **to convene a meeting of shareholders** = convocar una reunión de accionistas

◊ **convener** *or* **convenor** [kən'viːnə] *noun* organizador, -ra *or* responsable sindical *or* presidente (de comisión)

convenience [kən'viːnjəns] *noun* **at your earliest convenience** = tan pronto como le sea posible; **convenience foods** = comidas preparadas; **ship sailing under a flag of convenience** = barco que navega con pabellón de conveniencia; *US* **convenience store** = tienda de barrio

◊ **convenient** [kən'viːnjənt] *adjective* cómodo, -da *or* conveniente; **a bank draft is a convenient way of sending money abroad** = un giro bancario constituye una manera cómoda de enviar dinero al extranjero; **is 9.30 a convenient time for the meeting?** = ¿les parece bien reunirse a las 9.30?

conversion [kən'vɜːʃən] *noun* **(a)** *(currency)* conversión *f*; **currency conversion** = conversión de divisas; **conversion price** *or* **conversion rate** = precio de conversión *or* tasa de conversión **(b)** *(crime)* **conversion of funds** = apropiación indebida de fondos

convert [kən'vɜːt] *verb* **(a)** *(currency)* convertir *or* cambiar; **we converted our pounds into Swiss francs** = cambiamos nuestras libras en francos suizos **(b)** *(crime)* **to convert funds to one's own use** = apropiarse ilícitamente de fondos en provecho propio

◊ **convertibility** [kənvɜːtə'bɪləti] *noun* convertibilidad *f*

◊ **convertible** [kən'vɜːtəbl] *adjective* **convertible currency** = moneda convertible; **convertible debentures** *or* **convertible loan stock** = valores convertibles en acciones en una fecha futura

conveyance [kən'veɪəns] *noun* transmisión *f* *or* traspaso *m* del título de propiedad

◊ **conveyancer** [kən'veɪənsə] *noun* notario *mf* especialista en escrituras de traspaso

◊ **conveyancing** [kən'veɪənsɪŋ] *noun* transmisión *f* de títulos de propiedad; **do-it-yourself conveyancing** = redacción de escrituras de traspaso sin participación de un abogado

convince [kən'vɪns] *verb* convencer

cooling off period ['kuːlɪŋ 'ɒf 'pɪəriəd] *noun* (i) tregua laboral (para establecer negociaciones); (ii) periodo de reflexión (en un contrato de venta a plazos)

co-op ['kəʊɒp] *noun* = CO-OPERATIVE

◊ **co-operate** [kəʊ'ɒpəreɪt] *verb* cooperar; **the governments are co-operating in the fight against piracy** = los gobiernos cooperan en la lucha contra la piratería; **the two firms have co-operated on the computer project** = las dos empresas han cooperado en el proyecto informático

◊ **co-operation** [kəʊɒpə'reɪʃən] *noun* cooperación *f*; **the project was completed ahead of schedule with the co-operation of the workforce** = con la cooperación de los trabajadores, el proyecto se cumplió antes de lo previsto

◊ **co-operative** [kəʊ'ɒpərətɪv] **1** *adjective*

cooperativo, -va; **the workforce has not been co-operative over the management's productivity plan** = el personal no ha cooperado debidamente en el plan de productividad de la empresa; **co-operative society** = sociedad cooperativa **2** *noun* cooperativa *f*; **agricultural co-operative** = cooperativa agrícola; **to set up a workers' co-operative** = crear una cooperativa de trabajadores

co-opt [kəʊˈɒpt] *verb* **to co-opt someone onto a committee** = nombrar por coopción

co-owner [kəʊˈəʊnə] *noun* copropietario, -ria; **the two sisters are co-owners of the property** = las dos hermanas son copropietarias

◊ **co-ownership** [kəʊˈəʊnəʃɪp] *noun* copropiedad *f*

copartner [kəʊˈpɑːtnə] *noun* socio, -cia

◊ **copartnership** [kəʊˈpɑːtnəʃɪp] *noun* coparticipación *f or* sistema *m* en que los socios *or* trabajadores tienen acciones en la empresa

cope [kəʊp] *verb* (i) arreglárselas; (ii) hacer frente (a) *or* poder con; **the new assistant manager coped very well when the manager was on holiday** = el nuevo director adjunto se las arregló muy bien cuando el director se fue de vacaciones; **the warehouse is trying to cope with the backlog of orders** = el almacén está intentando hacer frente a los pedidos atrasados

copier [ˈkɒpɪə] *noun* = COPYING MACHINE, PHOTOCOPIER **copier paper** = papel de fotocopiadora

coproperty [kəʊˈprɒpəti] *noun* copropiedad *f*

◊ **coproprietor** [kəʊprəˈpraɪətə] *noun* copropietario, -ria

copy [ˈkɒpi] **1** *noun* **(a)** *(the same as)* copia *f*; **carbon copy** = copia carbón; **certified copy** = compulsa *or* copia auténtica *or* copia certificada; **file copy** = copia de archivo **(b)** *(document)* texto *m or* documento *m*; **fair copy** *or* **final copy** = copia en limpio; **hard copy** = copia impresa; **rough copy** = borrador; **top copy** = original **(c)** **publicity copy** = propuesta de texto publicitario; **she writes copy for a travel firm** = escribe textos publicitarios para una agencia de viajes; **knocking copy** = publicidad que critica los productos de la competencia **(d)** *(book, magazine, newspaper)* ejemplar *m or* número *m*; **have you kept yesterday's copy of the 'Times'?** = ¿ha guardado Vd. el número del 'Times' de ayer?; **I read it in the office copy of 'Fortune'** = lo leí en el ejemplar del 'Fortune' de la oficina; **where is my copy of the telephone directory?** = ¿dónde está mi ejemplar de la guía telefónica? **2** *verb* copiar; **he copied the company report at night and took it home** = copió el informe de la compañía por la noche y se lo llevó a casa

◊ **copier** *or* **copying machine** [ˈkɒpɪə *or* ˈkɒpɪŋ məˈʃiːn] *noun* copiadora *f or* máquina *f* de sacar copias

◊ **copyholder** [ˈkɒpɪhəʊldə] *noun* portapapeles *m or* soporte *m*

◊ **copyright** [ˈkɒpɪraɪt] **1** *noun* derechos *mpl* de autor *or* 'copyright' *m*; **copyright act** = ley de los derechos de autor *or* **copyright holder** = titular de los derechos de autor; **copyright law** = ley sobre la propiedad intelectual; **work which is out of copyright** = obra cuyos derechos de autor son del dominio público; **work still in copyright** = obra todavía protegida por los derechos de autor; **infringement of copyright** *or* **copyright infringement** = violación de los derechos de autor; **copyright notice** = nota de copyright **2** *verb* registrar como propiedad literaria **3** *adjective* protegido, -da por los derechos de autor; **it is illegal to photocopy a copyright work** = es ilegal fotocopiar una obra protegida por los derechos de autor

◊ **copyrighted** [ˈkɒpɪraɪtɪd] *adjective* registrado, -da con derechos de autor

copy typing [ˈkɒpɪ ˈtaɪpɪŋ] *noun* mecanografía *f* de copias

◊ **copy typist** [ˈkɒpɪ ˈtaɪpɪst] *noun* mecanógrafo, -fa de originales a mano

copywriter [ˈkɒpɪraɪtə] *noun* escritor, -ra de textos publicitarios

corner [ˈkɔːnə] **1** *noun* **(a)** esquina *f or* rincón *m*; **the Post Office is on the corner of the High Street and London Road** = la oficina de correos está en la esquina de High Street y London Road; **corner shop** = tienda de barrio *or* de la esquina **(b)** canto *m*; **the box has to have specially strong corners** = la caja debe tener los cantos especialmente resistentes; **the corner of the crate was damaged** = el canto del cajón sufrió desperfectos **(c)** monopolio *m* en un mercado determinado **2** *verb* **to corner the market** = acaparar el mercado *or* copar el mercado; **the syndicate tried to corner the market in silver** = el consorcio intentó conseguir el monopolio de la plata

corp *US* = CORPORATION

corporate [ˈkɔːpərət] *adjective* social *or* de una sociedad en su conjunto; **corporate image** = imagen pública de una empresa; **corporate plan** = plan de trabajo de una empresa; **corporate planning** = planificación empresarial; **corporate profits** = beneficios de la sociedad

◊ **corporation** [kɔːpəˈreɪʃən] *noun* **(a)** *(large company)* corporación *f or* sociedad *f* anónima *or* compañía *f* de capital; **finance corporation** = sociedad financiera; **corporation tax (CT)** = impuesto sobre sociedades; **Advance Corporation Tax (ACT)** = pago anticipado sobre el impuesto de sociedades; **Mainstream Corporation Tax** = impuesto de sociedades corriente **(b)** *US* sociedad *or* compañía *or* empresa *f*; **corporation income tax** = impuesto sobre beneficios de sociedades **(c)** *GB (municipal authority)* ayuntamiento *m*; **corporation loan** = préstamo concedido por el ayuntamiento

COMMENT: a corporation is formed by registration with the Registrar of Companies under the Companies Act (in the case of public and private companies) or other Acts of Parliament (in the case of building societies and charities)

QUOTE the prime rate is the rate at which banks lend to their top corporate borrowers
Wall Street Journal

QUOTE corporate profits for the first
quarter showed a 4 per cent drop from last
year
Financial Times

QUOTE if corporate forecasts are met,
sales will exceed $50 million in 1992
Citizen (Ottawa)

correct [kə'rekt] **1** *adjective* correcto, -ta; **the
published accounts do not give a correct picture
of the company's financial position** = las cuentas
publicadas no dan una visión correcta de la situación
financiera de la compañía **2** *verb* corregir *or*
rectificar; **the accounts department have
corrected the invoice** = el departamento de
facturación ha rectificado la factura; **you will have
to correct all these typing errors before you send
the letter** = tendrá que corregir todos estos errores
de mecanografía antes de enviar la carta

◊ **correction** [kə'rekʃən] *noun* **(a)** *(amendment)*
corrección *f or* rectificación *f;* **he made some
corrections to the text of the speech** = hizo algunas
rectificaciones al texto de su discurso; **correction
fluid** = secante *or* líquido corrector **(b)** *(Stock
Exchange)* **technical correction** = ajuste de precios
(en la Bolsa)

◊ **correctly** [kə'rektli] *adverb* correctamente

correspond [kɒrɪs'pɒnd] *verb* **(a)** *(write letters)*
to correspond with someone = escribir a alguien
(b) *(to fit or to match)* **to correspond with
something** = corresponder a algo

◊ **correspondence** [kɒrɪs'pɒndəns] *noun*
(letter-writing) correspondencia *f;* **business
correspondence** = correspondencia comercial; **to
be in correspondence with someone** = mantener
correspondencia con alguien; **correspondence
clerk** = empleado encargado de la correspondencia

◊ **correspondent** [kɒrɪs'pɒndənt] *noun* **(a)**
(who writes letters) correspondiente *mf* **(b)**
(journalist) corresponsal *mf;* **a financial
correspondent** = un corresponsal financiero; **the
'Times' business correspondent** = la corresponsal
comercial del 'Times'; **he is the Paris
correspondent of the 'Telegraph'** = es el
corresponsal del 'Telegraph' en Paris

corrupt [kə'rʌpt] *noun* **(a)** *(person)* corrupto, -ta
(b) *(faulty data)* defecto *m*

◊ **corruption** [kə'rʌpʃn] *noun* corrupción *f;*
bribery and corruption are difficult to control =
es difícil controlar la corrupción y los sobornos

cost [kɒst] **1** *noun* **(a)** *(money to be paid)* costo *m or*
coste *m or* precio *m or* importe *m;* **at all costs** = cueste
lo que cueste; **what is the cost of a first class ticket
to New York?** = ¿cuánto cuesta un viaje en primera
clase a Nueva York?; **computer costs are falling
each year** = los costes de los ordenadores
descienden cada año; **we cannot afford the cost of
two telephones** = no podemos permitirnos el gasto
de dos teléfonos; **to cover costs** = cubrir gastos; **the
sales revenue barely covers the costs of
advertising** *or* **the manufacturing costs** = los
ingresos por ventas apenas cubren los gastos de
publicidad *or* de fabricación; **to sell at cost** = vender
a precio de coste; **direct costs** = costes directos;
fixed costs = costes fijos; **historic(al) cost** = coste
inicial *or* histórico; **indirect costs** = costes

indirectos; **the cost of labour** = el importe de la
mano de obra; **labour costs** = costes de personal *or*
de mano de obra; **manufacturing costs** *or*
production costs = costes de producción *or* de
fabricación; **operating costs** *or* **running costs** =
costes de explotación *or* gastos de mantenimiento;
variable costs = costes variables **(b)** **cost
accountant** = contable de costes; **cost accounting** =
contabilidad de costes; **cost analysis** = análisis de
costes; **cost centre** = centro de costes; **cost,
insurance and freight (c.i.f.)** = coste, seguro y flete
or cif; **cost price** = precio de coste; **cost of sales** =
coste de ventas **(c)** *(legal costs)* **costs** = costas *fpl*
judiciales; **to pay costs** = pagar las costas; **the judge
awarded costs to the defendant** = el juez asignó las
costas al demandado; **costs of the case will be borne
by the prosecution** = las costas correrán a cargo de
la parte demandante **2** *verb* **(a)** *(to have a price)*
costar *or* valer; **how much does the machine cost?** =
¿cuánto cuesta la máquina?; **this cloth costs £10 a
metre** = esta tela vale £10 el metro **(b)** **to cost a
product** = calcular el coste de un producto

◊ **cost-benefit analysis** ['kɒst 'benɪfɪt
ə'næləsɪs] *noun* análisis coste-beneficio

◊ **cost-cutting** ['kɒst'kʌtɪŋ] *noun* reducción *f*
de costes; **we have taken out the telex as a
cost-cutting exercise** = hemos quitado el télex como
medida de reducción de costes

◊ **cost-effective** ['kɒstɪ'fektɪv] *adjective*
rentable *or* beneficioso, -sa; **we find advertising in
the Sunday newspapers very cost-effective** = nos
resulta muy rentable insertar publicidad en los
periódicos del domingo

◊ **cost-effectiveness** ['kɒstɪ'fektɪvnəs] *noun*
rentabilidad *f;* **can we calculate the cost-
effectiveness of air freight against shipping by
sea?** = ¿podemos calcular la rentabilidad del
transporte aéreo en comparación con el transporte
marítimo?

◊ **costing** ['kɒstɪŋ] *noun* cálculo *m* de costos; **the
costings give us a retail price of $2.95** = los
cálculos de costes nos dieron un precio al por menor
de $2,95; **we cannot do the costing until we have
details of all the production expenditure** = no
podemos calcular el coste hasta que no tengamos los
pormenores de todos los gastos de producción

◊ **costly** ['kɒstli] *adjective* costoso, -sa *or*
gravoso, -sa

◊ **cost of living** ['kɒst əv 'lɪvɪŋ] *noun* carestía *f*
or coste *m* de vida; **to allow for the cost of living in
the salaries** = incluir un plus de carestía de vida en
los salarios; **cost-of-living allowance** = subsidio por
aumento del coste de vida; **cost-of-living bonus** =
plus de carestía de vida; **cost-of-living increase** =
aumento de salario para compensar por el aumento
del coste de vida; **cost-of-living index** = índice del
coste de vida

◊ **cost plus** ['kɒst 'plʌs] *noun* costo *m* más
honorarios *or* porcentaje *m* de comisión; **we are
charging for the work on a cost plus basis** =
cobramos los costes más un porcentaje

◊ **cost-push inflation** ['kɒst 'pʊʃ ɪn'fleɪʃən]
noun inflación *f* de costes

Costa Rica ['kɒstə 'riːkə] *noun* Costa Rica *f*

◊ **Costa Rican** ['kɒstə 'riːkən] *adjective & noun*
costarricense *or* costarriqueño, -ña

NOTE: capital **San Jose;** (= San José); currency: **Costa Rican colon (C)** = colón costarricense

Côte d'Ivoire ['kəʊt dɪ'vwɑ:] *noun* Costa de Marfil

◊ **Ivorian** *or* **Ivoirien** [ɪ'vɔ:rɪən *or* ɪ'vwɑ:rɪən] **1** *adjective* de la Costa de Marfil **2** *noun* marfileño, -ña NOTE: capital: **Abidjan;** currency = **CFA franc** = franco CFA

cottage industry ['kɒtɪdʒ 'ɪndəstri] *noun* industria casera

council ['kaʊnsl] *noun* consejo *m*; **consumer council** = asociación de consumidores; **city council** *or* **town council** = consejo municipal *or* ayuntamiento *m*; **council tax** = contribución municipal; **Council of Europe** = Consejo de Europa; **Council of Ministers (EU)** = Consejo de Ministros; *(UE)* **the European Council (EU)** = el Consejo Europeo; *(UE)* **Nordic Council** = Consejo Nórdico; **UN Security Council** = Consejo de Seguridad de las Naciones Unidas

counsel ['kaʊnsl] **1** *noun* **(a)** *(advice)* asistencia *f* *or* consejo *m* legal **(b)** *(lawyer)* abogado, -da; **defence counsel** = abogado defensor; **prosecution counsel** = fiscal; *GB* **Queen's Counsel** = abogado de la Reina nombrado por el presidente de la Cámara de los Lores y el Ministro de Justicia **2** *verb* asesorar *or* aconsejar

◊ **counselling** *or* *US* **counseling** ['kaʊnsəlɪŋ] *noun* asesoramiento *m*; **debt counselling** = asesoramiento de deudas

count [kaʊnt] *verb* **(a)** *(add up)* contar; **he counted up the sales for the six months to December** = sumó las ventas de los seis meses hasta diciembre **(b)** *(include)* incluir; **did you count my trip to New York as part of my sales expenses?** = ¿incluyó Vd. mi viaje a Nueva York como parte de mis gastos de ventas?

◊ **counting house** ['kaʊntɪŋ 'haʊs] *noun (old-fashioned)* oficina *f* de recuento

◊ **count on** ['kaʊnt 'ɒn] *verb* contar con *or* esperar; **they are counting on getting a good response from the TV advertising** = esperan obtener una buena respuesta a la publicidad de la televisión; **do not count on a bank loan to start your business** = no cuente con un préstamo del banco para iniciar su negocio

counter ['kaʊntə] *noun* mostrador *m or* ventanilla *f*; **over the counter** = de venta libre; **goods sold over the counter** = ventas al por menor; **some drugs are sold over the counter, but others need to be prescribed by a doctor** = algunos medicamentos son de venta libre pero para otros se necesita una receta médica; *(Stock Exchange)* **over-the-counter sales** = venta de acciones que no se cotizan en Bolsa; **under the counter** = bajo mano (ilegal); **under-the-counter sales** = ventas bajo mano *or* en el mercado negro; **bargain counter** = sección (de tienda) de oportunidades; *(in airport)* **check-in counter** = mostrador de facturación; *(in supermarket)* **checkout counter** = caja; **ticket counter** = taquilla; **trade counter** = sección de ventas al por mayor; **glove counter** = sección de guantes; **counter staff** = personal de atención al público

counter- ['kaʊntə] *prefix* contra-

◊ **counterbid** ['kaʊntəbɪd] *noun* contraoferta *f*; **when I bid £20 he put in a counterbid of £25** = cuando ofrecí £20 él hizo una contraoferta de £25

◊ **counter-claim** ['kaʊntəkleɪm] **1** *noun* reconvención *f or* reclamación *f* recíproca por daños y perjuicios; **Jones claimed £25,000 in damages against Smith, and Smith entered a counter-claim of £50,000 for loss of office** = Jones reclamó a Smith £25.000 por daños y perjuicios y Smith presentó una reconvención de £50.000 por pérdida del cargo **2** *verb* reconvenir *or* presentar una reconvención *or* demanda *or* reclamación; **Jones claimed £25,000 in damages and Smith counter-claimed £50,000 for loss of office** = Jones reclamó £25.000 por daños y perjuicios y Smith presentó una reconvención de £50.000 por pérdida del cargo

◊ **counterfeit** ['kaʊntəfɪt] **1** *adjective* falso, -sa *or* falsificado, -da **2** *verb* falsificar dinero

◊ **counterfoil** ['kaʊntəfɔɪl] *noun* comprobante *m or* matriz *f* de talonario

◊ **countermand** ['kaʊntə'mɑ:nd] *verb* revocar *or* cancelar; **to countermand an order** = revocar una orden

◊ **counter-offer** ['kaʊntər 'ɒfə] *noun* contraoferta *f*; **Smith Ltd made an offer of £1m for the property, and Blacks replied with a counter-offer of £1.4m** = Smith Ltd hizo una oferta de £1 millón por la propiedad, y Blacks respondió con una contraoferta de £1,4 millones

QUOTE the company set about paring costs and improving the design of its product. It came up with a price cut of 14%, but its counter-offer - for an order that was to have provided 8% of its workload next year - was too late and too expensive
Wall Street Journal

counterpart ['kaʊntəpɑ:t] *noun* homólogo, -ga; **John is my counterpart in Smith's** = John es mi homólogo en Smith's

◊ **counterparty** ['kaʊntəpɑ:ti] *noun* la otra parte

◊ **counter-productive** [kaʊntəprə'dʌktɪv] *adjective* contraproducente; **increasing overtime pay was counter-productive, the workers simply worked more slowly** = el incremento de pago de horas extras fue contraproducente ya que los trabajadores trabajaban más despacio

◊ **countersign** ['kaʊntəsaɪn] *verb* refrendar; **all cheques have to be countersigned by the finance director** = todos los cheques tienen que estar refrendados por el director financiero; **the sales director countersigns all my orders** = el director de ventas refrenda todos mis pedidos

◊ **countersignature** ['kaʊntəsɪgnətʃə] *noun* refrendo *m*

◊ **countervailing duty** ['kaʊntəveɪlɪŋ 'djʊti] *noun* gravamen *m or* derechos *mpl* compensatorios

country ['kʌntri] *noun* **(a)** *(state)* país *m*; **the contract covers distribution in the countries of the EU** = el contrato comprende la distribución en todos los países de la UE; **some African countries export oil** = algunos países de Africa exportan petróleo; **the Organization of Petroleum Exporting Countries (OPEC)** = la Organización de Países Exportadores de Petróleo (OPEP); **the**

managing director is out of the country = el director gerente está fuera del país **(b)** *(opposite of town)* campo *m*; **distribution is difficult in country areas** = la distribución es difícil en las regiones rurales; **his territory is mainly the country, but he is based in the town** = cubre principalmente la zona del campo, pero tiene su sede en la ciudad

couple ['kʌpl] *noun* par *m*; **we only have enough stock for a couple of weeks** = tenemos existencias solamente para un par de semanas; **a couple of the directors were ill, so the board meeting was cancelled** = se suspendió la reunión del consejo de administración por estar enfermos dos de los directores; **the negotiations lasted a couple of hours** = las negociaciones duraron alrededor de un par de horas

coupon ['ku:pɒn] *noun* **(a)** *(money)* cupón *m*; **gift coupon** = vale *m* de regalo **(b)** *(order form)* formulario *m*; **coupon ad** = cupón *m* de anuncio; **reply coupon** = boletín de respuesta **(c) interest coupon** = cupón de interés; **cum coupon** = con cupón de interés; **ex coupon** = sin cupón de interés

courier ['kʊrɪə] *noun* **(a) motorcycle courier** *or* **(bi)cycle courier** = mensajero, -ra *or* correo **(b)** *(of tour)* guía *mf* de turismo

course [kɔːs] *noun* **(a) in the course of** = en el transcurso de *or* durante; **in the course of the discussion, the managing director explained the company's expansion plans** = en el transcurso del debate el director gerente explicó los planes de expansión de la compañía; **sales have risen sharply in the course of the last few months** = las ventas han subido rápidamente durante los últimos meses **(b)** *(study)* curso *m*; **she has finished her secretarial course** = ha terminado el curso de secretariado; **the company has paid for her to attend a course for trainee sales managers** = la empresa le ha pagado un curso de gestión comercial **(c) of course** = desde luego *or* naturalmente *or* por supuesto *or* claro; **of course the company is interested in profits** = claro que la compañía está interesada en obtener beneficios *or* ganancias; **are you willing to go on a sales trip to Australia? - of course!** = ¿estaría Vd. dispuesto a ir a vender a Australia? ¡Por supuesto!

court [kɔːt] *noun* audiencia *f or* tribunal *m or* juzgado *m*; **court case** = proceso *m*; **court order** = orden judicial; **Appeal Court** *or* **Court of Appeal** = Tribunal de Apelación; **magistrates' court** = juzgado de paz; **to take someone to court** = llevar a uno ante los tribunales; **a settlement was reached out of court** *or* **the two parties reached an out-of-court settlement** = la disputa se resolvió mediante un arreglo amistoso *or* las dos partes llegaron a un acuerdo extrajudicialmente; **court of appeal** = sala de apelación

covenant ['kʌvənənt] **1** *noun* pacto *m or* convenio *m*; **deed of covenant** = escritura de convenio **2** *verb* pactar *or* convenir; **to covenant to pay £10 per annum** = convenir en pagar £10 al año

Coventry ['kɒvəntri] **to send someone to Coventry** = hacer el vacío

cover ['kʌvə] **1** *noun* **(a)** *(protection)* cubierta *f or* funda *f*; **put the cover over your micro when you leave the office** = ponga la funda al microordenador cuando salga de la oficina; **always keep a cover over the typewriter** = ponga siempre la funda a la máquina de escribir **(b) insurance cover** = cobertura *f* del seguro; **do you have cover against theft?** = ¿está Vd. asegurado *or* cubierto contra robo?; **to operate without adequate cover** = operar sin cobertura suficiente; **to ask for additional cover** = pedir cobertura adicional; **full cover** = cobertura total *or* seguro a todo riesgo; **cover note** = póliza provisional *or* nota de cobertura (NOTE: the US English for this is **binder**) **(c)** *(guarantee)* garantía *f*; **do you have sufficient cover for this loan?** = ¿tiene Vd. suficiente garantía para este préstamo? **(d)** *(in restaurant)* **cover charge** = (precio del) cubierto *m* **(e) dividend cover** = relación entre los beneficios y los dividendos **(f) to send something under separate cover** = enviar por correo aparte; **to send a magazine under plain cover** = enviar una revista en un sobre corriente **2** *verb* **(a)** *(protect)* cubrir *or* proteger; **don't forget to cover your micro before you go home** = no olvide cubrir su microordenador antes de marcharse **(b) to cover a risk** = cubrir un riesgo; **to be fully covered** = estar cubierto contra todo riesgo; **the insurance covers fire, theft and loss of work** = el seguro cubre incendio, robo y pérdida de empleo **(c)** *(payment)* cubrir; **the damage was covered by the insurance** = el seguro cubrió los daños; **to cover a position** = cubrir una compra a plazo **(d)** *(expenses)* cubrir (gastos); **we do not make enough sales to cover the expense of running the shop** = no vendemos lo suficiente para cubrir los gastos de la tienda; **breakeven point is reached when sales cover all costs** = el umbral de rentabilidad se alcanza cuando las ventas cubren todos los costes; **the dividend is covered four times** = los beneficios cubren cuatro veces el dividendo

◊ **coverage** ['kʌvərɪdʒ] *noun* **(a)** *(media)* reportaje *m or* circulación *f or* transmisión *f*; **press coverage** *or* **media coverage** = cobertura *f* periodística; **the company had good media coverage for the launch of its new model** = la empresa fue objeto de amplios reportajes periodísticos con ocasión del lanzamiento de su nuevo modelo **(b)** *(insurance)* US cobertura *f or* protección *f*; **do you have coverage against fire damage?** = ¿tiene Vd. cobertura contra daños por incendio?

◊ **covering letter** *or* **covering note** ['kʌvərɪŋ 'letə *or* 'kʌvərɪŋ 'nəʊt] *noun* carta *f* adjunta *or* explicatoria

cowboy ['kaʊbɔɪ] *noun* chapucero, -ra; **the people we got in to repaint the office were a couple of cowboys** = los que vinieron a pintar la oficina eran un par de chapuceros; **cowboy job** = chapuza *f*; **cowboy outfit** = empresa *f* pirata (que utiliza métodos poco ortodoxos)

Cr *or* **CR** = CREDIT

crane [kreɪn] *noun* grúa *f*; **the container slipped as the crane was lifting it onto the ship** = el contenedor se cayó al cargarlo la grúa en el barco;

they had to hire a crane to get the machine into the factory = tuvieron que alquilar una grúa para colocar la máquina en la fábrica

crash [kræʃ] **1** *noun* **(a)** *(accident)* accidente *m or* choque *m or* colisión *f*; **the car was damaged in the crash** = el coche sufrió daños en el choque; **the plane crash killed all the passengers** *or* **all the passengers were killed in the plane crash** = en el accidente de aviación resultaron muertos todos los pasajeros *or* todos los pasajeros murieron en el acidente de aviación **(b)** *(financial)* 'crack' *m or* quiebra *f*; **financial crash** = 'crack' financiero; **he lost all his money in the crash of 1929** = perdió todo su dinero en el 'crack' del año 1929 **2** *verb* **(a)** *(hit)* chocar; **the plane crashed into the mountain** = el avión se estrelló contra el monte; **the lorry crashed into the post office** = el camión se estrelló contra la oficina de correos **(b)** *(fail)* quebrar; **the company crashed with debts of over £1 million** = la compañía quebró con deudas de más de £1 millón

crate [kreɪt] **1** *noun* cajón *m*; **a crate of oranges** = un cajón de naranjas **2** *verb* embalar

create [krɪˈeɪt] *verb* crear; **by acquiring small unprofitable companies he soon created a large manufacturing group** = adquiriendo pequeñas empresas poco rentables no tardó en crear un gran grupo manufacturero; **the government scheme aims at creating new jobs for young people** = el plan del gobierno pretende crear nuevos empleos para los jóvenes

◊ **creation** [krɪˈeɪʃən] *noun* creación *f*; **job creation scheme** = plan de creación de empleo

creative accountancy *or* **creative accounting** [krɪˈeɪtɪv əˈkaʊntənsi *or* əˈkaʊntɪŋ] *noun* contabilidad cosmética (práctica contable que presenta una imagen positiva de la situación financiera de una empresa)

COMMENT: 'creative accounting' is the term used to cover a number of accounting practices which, although legal, may be used to mislead banks, investors and shareholders about the profitability or liquidity of a business

credere [ˈkreɪdəri] *see* DEL CREDERE

credit [ˈkredɪt] **1** *noun* **(a)** *(time limit)* crédito *m*; **to give someone six months' credit** = conceder seis meses de crédito a alguien; **to sell on good credit terms** = vender con buenas condiciones de crédito; **extended credit** = crédito a largo plazo; **interest-free credit** = crédito sin interés; **long credit** = crédito a largo plazo; **open credit** = crédito abierto; **short credit** = crédito a corto plazo **(b)** *(in a shop)* **credit account** = cuenta de crédito; **to open a credit account** = abrir una cuenta de crédito; **credit agency** *US* **credit bureau** = agencia de informes comerciales; **credit bank** = banco de crédito; **credit ceiling** = crédito tope *or* tope máximo de crédito; **credit control** = control de crédito; **credit controller** = controlador de créditos; **credit facilities** = facilidades de crédito; **credit freeze** *or* **credit squeeze** = congelación *or* restricción del crédito; **letter of credit (L/C)** = carta de crédito;

irrevocable letter of credit = carta de crédito irrevocable; **credit limit** = techo *or* límite de crédito; **he has exceeded his credit limit** = ha sobrepasado el límite de su crédito; **to open a line of credit** *or* **a credit line** = abrir una línea de crédito; **credit policy** = política crediticia; **credit rating** = clasificación *or* categoría crediticia; **on credit** = a crédito; **to live on credit** = vivir a crédito; **we buy everything on sixty days credit** = lo compramos todo con créditos a sesenta días; **the company exists on credit from its suppliers** = la compañía se mantiene gracias a los créditos de sus acreedores **(c)** *(amount entered into an account)* abono *m*; **to enter £100 to someone's credit** = abonar £100 en cuenta a alguien; **to pay in £100 to the credit of Mr Smith** = abonar £100 en cuenta al Sr.Smith; **debits and credits** = debe y haber; **credit balance** = saldo acreedor; **the account has a credit balance of £1,000** = la cuenta tiene un saldo positivo de £1.000; **credit column** = columna del haber; **credit entry** = abono; **credit note (C/N)** = nota de abono *or* nota de crédito; **the company sent the wrong order and so had to issue a credit note** = la empresa se equivocó con el envío y tuvo que emitir una nota de crédito; **credit side** = haber; **account in credit** = cuenta con saldo positivo *or* acreedor; **bank credit** = crédito bancario; **tax credits** = descuentos impositivos **2** *verb* abonar *or* acreditar *or* ingresar; **to credit an account with £100** *or* **to credit £100 to an account** = abonar £100 en cuenta

◊ **credit card** [ˈkredɪt ˈkɑːd] *noun* tarjeta *f* de crédito

◊ **creditor** [ˈkredɪtə] *noun* acreedor, -ra; **creditors' meeting** = junta de acreedores; **mortgage creditor** = acreedor hipotecario; **preferred** *or* **preferential creditor** = acreedor preferente; **secured creditor** = acreedor asegurado *or* con garantía; **trade creditors** = acreedores comerciales; **unsecured creditor** = acreedor común *or* sin garantía

◊ **credit union** [ˈkredɪt ˈjuːnjən] *noun US* unión *f* crediticia *or* cooperativa *f* de crédito

◊ **creditworthy** [ˈkredɪtwɜːði] *adjective* solvente

◊ **creditworthiness** [ˈkredɪtwɜːðɪnəs] *noun* solvencia *f*

crew [kruː] *noun* tripulación *f or* equipo *m*; **the ship carries a crew of 250** = el barco lleva una tripulación de 250 personas

crime [kraɪm] *noun* crimen *m or* delito *m*; **crimes in supermarkets have risen by 25%** = los delitos en los supermercados han aumentado en un 25%

◊ **criminal** [ˈkrɪmɪnl] *adjective* delictivo, -va *or* criminal; **misappropriation of funds is a criminal act** = la malversación de fondos constituye un acto delictivo; **criminal action** *or* **criminal case** = acción *or* causa criminal; **criminal record** = antecedentes penales

crisis [ˈkraɪsɪs] *noun* crisis *f*; **international crisis** = crisis internacional; **banking crisis** = crisis bancaria; **financial crisis** = crisis financiera; **crisis management** = dirección *or* administración de emergencia; **to take crisis measures** = tomar medidas de emergencia (NOTE: plural is **crises**)

critic [ˈkrɪtɪk] *noun (art or film critic)* crítico, -ca

critical path analysis ['krɪtɪkəl pɑːθ ə'næləsɪs] *noun* análisis del camino crítico (de un proyecto)

criticize ['krɪtɪsaɪz] *verb* criticar; **the MD criticized the sales manager for not improving the volume of sales** = el director gerente criticó al director de ventas por no haber aumentado el volumen de ventas; **the design of the new catalogue has been criticized** = el diseño del nuevo catálogo ha sido criticado

CRO = COMPANIES REGISTRATION OFFICE

Croatia [krəʊ'eɪʃə] *noun* Croacia

◊ **Croat** *or* **Croatian** ['krəʊæt *or* krəʊ'eɪʃən] *adjective & noun* croata *mf*
NOTE: captial: **Zagreb**; currency: **Croatian dinar** = **corona croata**

crore [krɔː] *noun* (*in India*) diez millones (NOTE: one crore equals 100 lakh)

QUOTE for the year 1989-90, the company clocked a sales turnover of Rs. 7.09 crore and earned a profit after tax of Rs. 10.39 lakh on an equity base of Rs. 14 lakh
Business India

cross [krɒs] *verb* (a) (*to go across*) cruzar; **Concorde only takes three hours to cross the Atlantic** = el Concorde solamente tarda tres horas en cruzar el Atlántico; **to get to the bank, you turn left and cross the street at the post office** = para llegar al banco tiene que torcer a la izquierda y cruzar la calle a la altura de la oficina de correos (b) **to cross a cheque** = cruzar un cheque; **crossed cheque** = cheque cruzado

COMMENT: crossed cheques have the words 'A/C payee' printed in the space between the two vertical lines. This means that the cheque can only be paid into a bank, and only into the account of the person whose name is written on it - it cannot be endorsed to a third party

cross holding ['krɒs 'həʊldɪŋ] *noun* propiedad *f* recíproca de acciones entre dos sociedades

◊ **cross off** ['krɒs 'ɒf] *verb* tachar *or* borrar; **he crossed my name off his list** = tachó mi nombre de su lista; **you can cross him off our mailing list** = puede tacharlo de nuestra lista de direcciones

◊ **cross out** ['krɒs 'aʊt] *verb* tachar; **she crossed out £250 and put in £500** = tachó las £250 y escribió £500

◊ **cross rate** ['krɒs 'reɪt] *noun* tipo *m* de cambio de dos divisas expresado en una tercera

crude (oil) [kruːd(ɔɪl)] *noun* crudo *m*; **the price for Arabian crude has slipped** = el precio del crudo árabe ha bajado

Cuba ['kjuːbə] *noun* Cuba *m*

◊ **Cuban** ['kjuːbn] *adjective & noun* cubano, -na
NOTE: capital: **Havana** (= La Habana); currency: **Cuban peso ($)** = peso cubano ($)

cubic ['kjuːbɪk] *adjective* cúbico, -ca; **the crate holds six cubic metres** = la caja tiene una capacidad de seis metros cúbicos; **cubic measure** = medida de capacidad (NOTE: cubic is written in figures as ³: **6m³** = six cubic metres; **10ft³** = ten cubic feet)

cum [kʌm] *preposition* con; **cum dividend** = con dividendo; **cum coupon** = con cupón

cumulative ['kjuːmjʊlətɪv] *adjective* acumulativo, -va; **cumulative interest** = interés acumulativo; **cumulative preference share** *US* **cumulative preferred stock** = acción preferente de dividendo acumulable

curb [kɜːb] *verb* **to curb inflation** = contener *or* frenar la inflación

currency ['kʌrənsi] *noun* moneda *f*; **convertible currency** = moneda convertible; **foreign currency** = moneda extranjera *or* divisa; **foreign currency account** = cuenta en divisas; **foreign currency reserves** = reservas de divisas; **hard currency** = moneda convertible *or* fuerte; **to pay for imports in hard currency** = pagar las importaciones en moneda convertible; **to sell raw materials to earn hard currency** = vender materias primas para ganar divisas convertibles; **legal currency** = moneda de curso legal; **single currency** = moneda única; **soft currency** = moneda no convertible *or* débil; **currency backing** = reserva monetaria de respaldo; **currency note** = billete de banco (NOTE: currency has no plural when it refers to the money of one country: **he was arrested trying to take currency out of the country**)

QUOTE the strong dollar's inflationary impact on European economies, as national governments struggle to support their sinking currencies and push up interest rates
Duns Business Month

QUOTE today's wide daily variations in exchange rates show the instability of a system based on a single currency, namely the dollar
Economist

QUOTE the level of currency in circulation increased to N4.9 billion in the month of August
Business Times (Lagos)

current ['kʌrənt] *adjective* corriente *or* actual; **current assets** = activo circulante *or* corriente *or* realizable; **current cost accounting (CCA)** = contabilidad a costes actuales; **current liabilities** = pasivo circulante *or* obligaciones a corto plazo; **current price** = cotización del día *or* precio corriente *or* precio actual; **current rate of exchange** = tipo de cambio actual; **current yield** = rendimiento corriente

◊ **current account** ['kʌrənt ə'kaʊnt] *noun* (a) (*in bank*) cuenta corriente; **to pay money into a current account** = depositar dinero en una cuenta corriente (NOTE: US equivalent is **checking account**) (b) (*balance of payments*) balanza de pagos

◊ **currently** ['kʌrəntli] *adverb* actualmente; **we are currently negotiating with the bank for a loan** = actualmente estamos negociando un préstamo con el banco

QUOTE crude oil output plunged during the past month and is likely to remain at its current level for the near future
Wall Street Journal

QUOTE customers' current deposit and current accounts also rose to $655.31 million at the end of December
Hongkong Standard

curriculum vitae [kə'rɪkjʊləm 'viːtaɪ] *noun* currículum (vitae) *m*; **candidates should send a letter of application with a curriculum vitae to the personnel officer** = los aspirantes deben enviar al encargado de personal una carta de solicitud con el currículum (NOTE: the plural is **curriculums** *or* **curricula vitae.** Note also that the US English is **résumé**)

curve [kɜːv] *noun* curva *f*; **the graph shows an upward curve** = el gráfico muestra una curva ascendente; **learning curve** = curva de aprendizaje; **sales curve** = curva de ventas

cushion ['kʊʃən] *noun* (a) cojín *m*; **she put a cushion on her chair as it was too hard** = colocó un cojín en la silla porque era demasiado dura (b) *(money)* amortiguador *m*; **we have sums on deposit which are a useful cushion when cash flow is tight** = tenemos un fondo de reserva que nos permite hacer frente a los problemas de tesorería

custom ['kʌstəm] *noun* (a) clientela *f*; **to lose someone's custom** = perder la clientela; **custom-built** *or* **custom-made** = hecho a medida *or* a la orden; **he drives a custom-built Rolls Royce** = conduce un Rolls Royce fabricado expresamente para él (NOTE: no plural for this meaning) (b) **the customs of the trade** = costumbres *or* usos del comercio

◊ **customer** ['kʌstəmə] *noun* cliente *mf*; **the shop was full of customers** = la tienda estaba llena de clientes; **can you serve this customer first please?** = ¿puede atender a este cliente en primer lugar, por favor?; **he is a regular customer of ours** = es un cliente de la casa; **customer appeal** = atractivo para los clientes; **customer service department** = departamento de atención al cliente

◊ **customize** ['kʌstəmaɪz] *verb* adaptar algo a las necesidades del cliente; **we used customized computer software** = utilizamos programas de ordenador ajustados a las necesidades del cliente

◊ **customs** ['kʌstəmz] *plural noun* aduana *f*; **H.M. Customs and Excise** = Aduanas y Arbitrios (administración de aduanas e impuestos sobre el consumo; **to go through customs** = pasar la aduana; **to take something through customs without declaring it** = pasar algo por la aduana sin declararlo; **he was stopped by customs** = fue detenido en la aduana; **her car was searched by the customs** = le registraron el coche en la aduana; **customs barrier** = barrera arancelaria; **customs broker** = agente de aduanas; **customs clearance** = despacho de aduanas; **to wait for customs clearance** = esperar para efectuar el despacho aduanero; **customs declaration** = declaración de aduana; **to fill in a customs (declaration) form** = rellenar una declaración de aduana; **customs duty** = derecho de aduana; **the crates had to go through a customs examination** = los cajones tuvieron que pasar una inspección aduanera; **customs formalities** = formalidades aduaneras; **customs officers** *or*

customs officials = aduaneros *or* funcionarios de aduanas; **customs tariff** = arancel aduanero; **customs union** = unión aduanera

cut [kʌt] **1** *noun* (a) *(sudden lowering)* recorte *m or* rebaja *f or* reducción *f*; **price cuts** *or* **cuts in prices** = rebaja de precios; **salary cuts** *or* **cuts in salaries** = recortes de salario; **budget cuts** = reducción del presupuesto *or* recortes presupuestarios *or* de presupuesto; **job cuts** = reducción de empleos; **he took a cut in salary** *or* **a salary cut** = recibió un recorte salarial *or* aceptó un recorte de sueldo; **sweeping cuts in budgets** = reducción general de los presupuestos (b) *(share of commission)* parte *f*; **he introduces new customers and gets a cut of the salesman's commission** = presenta a nuevos clientes y recibe una parte de la comisión del vendedor **2** *verb* (a) *(lower suddenly)* rebajar *or* recortar; **we are cutting prices on all our models** = hemos rebajado los precios de todos los modelos; **to cut (back) production** = reducir la producción; **the company has cut back its sales force** = la empresa ha reducido su personal de ventas; **we have taken out the telex in order to try to cut costs** = hemos quitado el télex con la intención de reducir los costes (b) *(reduce)* reducir; **to cut jobs** = reducir los puestos de trabajo; **he cut his losses** = redujo las pérdidas (NOTE: **cutting - cut - has cut**)

◊ **cutback** ['kʌtbæk] *noun* reducción *f or* recorte *m*; **cutbacks in government spending** = recortes en los gastos del Estado

◊ **cut down (on)** ['kʌt 'daʊn (ɒn)] *verb* reducir *or* economizar; **the government is cutting down on welfare expenditure** = el gobierno está reduciendo los gastos de la seguridad social ; **the office is trying to cut down on electricity consumption** = la oficina intenta economizar en el consumo de electricidad; **we have installed a word-processor to cut down on paperwork** = hemos instalado un procesador de textos para reducir el papeleo

◊ **cut in** ['kʌt 'ɪn] *verb (informal)* **to cut someone in on a deal** = hacer participar a alguien de los beneficios de una transacción

◊ **cut-price** [kʌt'praɪs] *adjective* a precio reducido; **cut-price goods** = mercancías a precio reducido; **cut-price petrol** = gasolina a precio reducido; **cut-price store** = tienda de precios reducidos

◊ **cut-throat competition** ['kʌtθrəʊt kɒmpɪ'tɪʃn] *noun* competencia encarnizada

◊ **cutting** ['kʌtɪŋ] *noun* (a) *(cutback)* reducción *f*; **cost cutting** = reducción de costes; **we have made three secretaries redundant as part of our cost-cutting programme** = hemos despedido a tres secretarias dentro de nuestro plan de reducción de costes; **price cutting** = rebajas; **price-cutting war** = guerra de precios (b) *(clippings)* recorte *m*; **press cutting agency** = agencia de recortes (de prensa); **press cuttings** = recortes; **we have a file of press cuttings on our rivals' products** = tenemos un archivo de recortes de prensa sobre los productos de nuestros rivales

QUOTE the US bank announced a cut in its prime from 10- per cent to 10 per cent
Financial Times

QUOTE Opec has on average cut production by one third since 1979
Economist

CV ['si:'vi:] *noun* = CURRICULUM VITAE **please apply in writing, enclosing a current CV** = se ruega hacer la solicitud por escrito, adjuntando un currículum (vitae) actualizado

CWO = CASH WITH ORDER

cwt ['hʌndrədweɪt] = HUNDREDWEIGHT

cycle ['saɪkl] *noun* ciclo *m*; **economic cycle** *or* **trade cycle** *or* **business cycle** = ciclo económico *or* ciclo comercial *or* 'business cycle'; **product cycle** = ciclo del producto

◇ **cyclical** ['sɪklɪkəl] *adjective* cíclico, -a; **cyclical factors** = factores cíclicos

Cyprus ['saɪprəs] *noun* Chipre *f*

◇ **Cypriot** ['sɪprɪət] *adjective & noun* chipriota
NOTE: capital: **Nicosia;** currency: **Cyprus pound (£** *or* **C£)** = libra chipriota (£ *or* £C)

Czech Republic ['tʃek rɪ'pʌblɪk] *noun* República Checa

◇ **Czech** [tʃek] *adjective & noun* checo, -ca
NOTE: capital: **Prague;** (= Praga); currency: **Czech koruna (Kcs)** = corona checa

Dd

daily ['deɪli] *adjective* diario, -ria; **daily consumption** = consumo diario; **daily production of cars** = producción diaria de automóviles; **daily sales returns** = informes diarios de ventas; **a daily newspaper** *or* **a daily** = un periódico *or* diario

daisy-wheel printer ['deɪzi wiːfl 'prɪntə] *noun* impresora *f* de rueda de margarita

damage ['dæmɪdʒ] **1** *noun* **(a)** *(harm)* daño *m*; **fire damage** = daños por incendio; **storm damage** = daños por tormenta; **to suffer damage** = sufrir daños; **we are trying to assess the damage which the shipment suffered in transit** = estamos intentando calcular los daños que sufrió el envío durante el transporte; **to cause damage** = dañar; **the fire caused damage estimated at £100,000** = el incendio causó daños calculados en £100.000; **damage survey** = inspección *or* valoración de daños (NOTE: no plural in English) **(b)** *(legal)* **damages** = daños y perjuicios; **to claim £1000 in damages** = reclamar £1000 por daños y perjuicios; **to be liable for damages** = ser responsable de los daños y perjuicios; **to pay £25,000 in damages** = pagar £25.000 por daños y perjuicios; **to bring an action for damages against someone** = presentar una demanda por daños y perjuicios *or* dañar; **the storm damaged the cargo** = la tormenta dañó la carga; **stock which has been damaged by water** = existencias estropeadas *or* dañadas por el agua

◊ **damaged** ['dæmɪdʒd] *adjective* dañado, -da *or* tarado, -da; **goods damaged in transit** = mercancías dañadas en el transporte; **fire-damaged goods** = mercancías dañadas por un incendio

damp down ['dæmp 'daʊn] *verb* reducir; **to damp down demand for domestic consumption of oil** = reducir la demanda del consumo interno de petróleo

danger ['deɪn(d)ʒə] *noun* peligro *m or* riesgo *m*; **there is danger to the workforce in the old machinery** = la maquinaria vieja constituye un peligro para el personal; **there is no danger of the sales force leaving** = no hay riesgo de que el personal de ventas se vaya; **to be in danger of** = correr el peligro de; **the company is in danger of being taken over** = la compañía corre el peligro de ser adquirida; **she is in danger of being made redundant** = corre el riesgo de ser despedida

◊ **danger money** ['deɪn(d)ʒə 'mʌni] *noun* plus *m* de peligrosidad; **the workforce has stopped work and asked for danger money** = los obreros han dejado de trabajar para reivindicar una prima por trabajo peligroso

◊ **dangerous** ['deɪn(d)ʒərəs] *adjective* peligroso, -sa; **dangerous job** = trabajo peligroso

data ['deɪtə] *noun* datos *mpl*; **data acquisition** = recopilación de datos; **data bank** *or* **bank of data** = banco de datos; **data capture** = toma de datos; **data processing** = elaboración *or* proceso de datos; **business data processing** = informática *f* de gestión (NOTE: **data** is usually singular: **the data is easily available**)

◊ **database** ['deɪtəbeɪs] *noun* base *f* de datos; **we can extract the lists of potential customers from our database** = podemos extraer las listas de clientes potenciales de nuestra base de datos

date [deɪt] **1** *noun* **(a)** *(day, month)* fecha *f*; **I have received your letter of yesterday's date** = he recibido su carta con fecha de ayer; **date stamp** = fechador *m*; **date of receipt** = fecha de recepción; **sell-by date** = fecha de caducidad **(b)** *(current)* **up to date** = actual *or* reciente *or* moderno; **an up-to-date computer system** = un sistema informático moderno; **to bring something up to date** = actualizar; **to keep something up to date** = mantener algo al día; **we spend a lot of time keeping our mailing list up to date** = dedicamos mucho tiempo a poner al día nuestra lista de direcciones **(c)** *(up to now)* **to date** = hasta ahora *or* hasta la fecha; **interest to date** = intereses hasta la fecha **(d)** *(old)* **out of date** = anticuado, -da *or* caducado, -da; **their computer system is years out of date** = su sistema informático *or* ordenadores es muy anticuado; **they are still using out-of-date machinery** = siguen empleando maquinaria anticuada **(e)** **closing date** = fecha de cierre; **maturity date** = fecha de vencimiento; **date of bill** = fecha de vencimiento de una letra **2** *verb* fechar; **the cheque was dated March 24th** = el cheque estaba fechado *or* llevaba la fecha del 24 de marzo; **you forgot to date the cheque** = se olvidó poner la fecha en el cheque; **to date a cheque forward** = poner una fecha adelantada en un cheque

◊ **dated** ['deɪtɪd] *adjective* con fecha de *or* fechado; **thank you for your letter dated June 15th** = le agradecemos su carta de fecha 15 de junio; **long-dated bill** = letra a largo plazo; **short-dated bill** = letra a corto plazo

dawn raid ['dɔːn 'reɪd] *noun* maniobra para asegurar la compra de acciones a primera hora de la mañana

COMMENT: the sudden planned purchase of a large number of a company's shares at the beginning of a day's trading; up to 15% of a company's shares may be bought in this way, and the purchaser must wait for seven days before purchasing any more shares; sometimes a dawn raid is the first step towards a takeover of the target company

day [deɪ] *noun* **(a)** *(period of 24 hours)* día *m*; **there are thirty days in June** = junio tiene treinta días; **the first day of the month is a public holiday** = el primer día del mes es festivo; **settlement day** = día de liquidación; **three clear days** = tres días hábiles; **to give ten clear days' notice** = avisar con una antelación de diez días hábiles; **allow four clear days for the cheque to be paid into the bank** = cuente con un margen de cuatro días hábiles para que el cheque sea abonado en cuenta **(b)** *(working day)* día *or* jornada *f*; **she took two days off** = se tomó dos días de descanso; **he works three days on, two days off** = trabaja tres días sí y dos no; **to work an eight-hour day** = trabajar una jornada de ocho horas; **day shift** = turno de día; **there are 150 men on the day shift** = hay 150 obreros en el turno de día; **he works the day shift** = trabaja en el turno de día;

day release = concesión de un día libre a un empleado para que asista a un curso; **the junior sales manager is attending a day release course** = el director de ventas adjunto asiste a un curso de formación un día a la semana

◇ **day book** ['deɪ 'bʊk] *noun* registro *m* diario de entradas y salidas; **sales day book (SDB)** = libro *or* registro diario de ventas

◇ **day-to-day** ['deɪtə'deɪ] *adjective* cotidiano, -na *or* diario, -ria; **he organizes the day-to-day running of the company** = organiza la gestión cotidiana de la compañía; **sales only just cover the day-to-day expenses** = las ventas apenas cubren los gastos diarios

◇ **day worker** ['deɪ 'wɜːkə] *noun* obrero diurno *or* obrera diurna

D & B = DUN & BRADSTREET

DCF = DISCOUNTED CASH FLOW

dead [ded] *adjective* **(a)** *(not alive)* muerto, -ta; **six people were dead as a result of the accident** = seis personas resultaron muertas a consecuencia del accidente; **the founders of the company are all dead** = todos los fundadores de la compañía fallecieron ya **(b)** *(not working)* inactivo, -va; **dead account** = cuenta inactiva; **the line went dead** = se cortó la línea telefónica; **dead loss** = siniestro *or* pérdida total; **the car was written off as a dead loss** = el coche fue declarado siniestro total; **dead money** = dinero inactivo; **dead season** = temporada baja

◇ **deadline** ['dedlaɪn] *noun* plazo *m or* fecha *f* tope *or* límite *m or* cierre *m*; **to meet a deadline** = cumplir un plazo establecido; **we've missed our October 1st deadline** = no pudimos cumplir el plazo del 1 de octubre

◇ **deadlock** ['dedlɒk] **1** *noun* punto *m* muerto; **the negotiations have reached a deadlock** = las negociaciones han llegado a un callejón sin salida *or* a un punto muerto; **to break a deadlock** = desbloquear las negociaciones *or* restablecer el diálogo **2** *verb* estar en punto muerto *or* bloquear *or* paralizar; **talks have been deadlocked for ten days** = las negociaciones están paralizadas desde hace diez días

◇ **deadweight** ['dedweɪt] *noun* peso *m* muerto; **deadweight cargo** = carga que se mide por peso y no por volumen; **deadweight capacity** *or* **deadweight tonnage** = carga máxima

deal [diːl] **1** *noun* **(a)** *(agreement)* transacción *f or* negocio *m or* acuerdo *m or* trato *m*; **to arrange a deal** *or* **to set up a deal** *or* **to do a deal** = convenir una transacción *or* negociar un acuerdo *or* hacer un trato; **to sign a deal** = firmar un convenio; **the sales director set up a deal with a Russian bank** = el director de ventas negoció un acuerdo con un banco ruso; **the deal will be signed tomorrow** = el acuerdo se firmará mañana; **they did a deal with an American airline** = llegaron a un acuerdo con una línea aérea estadounidense; **to call off a deal** = suspender *or* anular *or* cancelar un acuerdo; **when the chairman heard about the deal he called it off** = cuando el presidente se enteró del acuerdo lo suspendió; **cash deal** = transacción en efectivo; **package deal** = acuerdo global *or* convenio *or* transacción de conjunto *or* paquete; **they agreed a package deal, which involves the construction of**

the factory, training of staff and purchase of the product = llegaron a un acuerdo de conjunto, que incluye la construcción de la fábrica, la capacitación del personal y la compra del producto **(b)** *(quantity)* **a great deal** *or* **a good deal of something** = una gran cantidad de algo *or* mucho; **he has made a good deal of money on the stock market** = ha ganado mucho dinero en la bolsa; **the company lost a great deal of time asking for expert advice** = la compañía perdió mucho tiempo buscando asesoramiento profesional **2** *verb* **(a)** *(to organize)* **to deal with** = ocuparse de *or* despachar; **leave it to the filing clerk - he'll deal with it** = déjelo para el archivero; él se ocupará de eso; **to deal with an order** = servir *or* despachar un pedido **(b)** *(to trade)* comerciar; **to deal with someone** = tratar *or* negociar con alguien; **to deal in leather** = comerciar *or* tratar en el sector pieles *or* cueros; **to deal in options** = comprar y vender opciones; **he deals on the Stock Exchange** = opera en la Bolsa

◇ **dealer** ['diːlə] *noun* comerciante *mf or* negociante *mf or* agente *m* mediador; **car dealer** = negociante en coches; **dealer in tobacco** *or* **tobacco dealer** = comerciante de tabaco; **authorized dealer** = distribuidor autorizado *or* oficial; **foreign exchange dealer** = operador de cambios *or* cambista; **retail dealer** = comerciante al por menor *or* al detall *or* minorista; **wholesale dealer** = comerciante al por mayor *or* mayorista

◇ **dealership** ['diːləʃɪp] *noun* **(a)** *(authorization)* concesión *f or* franquicia *f* **(b)** *(authorized business)* representación *f*

◇ **dealing** ['diːlɪŋ] *noun* **(a)** *(Stock Exchange)* operaciones *fpl* en bolsa; **fair dealing** = prácticas comerciales leales *or* justas; **foreign exchange dealing** = cambio *or* operaciones de cambio; **forward dealings** = transacciones de futuros; **insider dealing** = operaciones de iniciado; **option dealing** = tratar en opciones **(b)** *(buying and selling)* comercio *m*; **to have dealings with someone** = tener relaciones comerciales *or* comerciar con alguien

dear [dɪə] *adjective* **(a)** *(expensive)* caro, -ra *or* costoso, -sa; **property is very dear in this area** = las fincas son muy caras en esta zona; **dear money** = dinero caro **(b)** *(in a letter)* **Dear Sir** *or* **Dear Madam** = Estimado Señor *or* Estimada Señora; **Dear Sirs** = Muy Señores míos; **Dear Mr Smith** *or* **Dear Mrs Smith** *or* **Dear Miss Smith** = Estimado Señor Smith *or* Estimada Señora Smith *or* Estimada Señorita Smith; **Dear James** *or* **Dear Julia** = Querido James *or* Querida Julia

COMMENT: first names are commonly used between business people in the UK; they are less often used in other European countries (France, Spain and Germany, for example, where business letters tend to be more formal)

death [deθ] *noun* muerte *f or* fallecimiento *m*; **death benefit** = indemnización por fallecimiento; **death certificate** = certificado de defunción; **death in service** = indemnización o subsidio por fallecimiento de un familiar durante su trabajo en una empresa; *US* **death duty** *or* **death tax** = impuesto de sucesiones *or* sobre herencia (NOTE: the GB equivalent is **inheritance tax**)

debenture [dɪ'bentʃə] *noun* bono *m or* pagaré *m or* obligación *f* de interés fijo; **the bank holds a debenture on the company** = el banco es tenedor de un pagaré de la empresa; **convertible debenture** =

obligación convertible; **mortgage debenture** = cédula hipotecaria; **debenture issue** *or* **issue of debentures** = emisión de obligaciones garantizada por los activos de la compañía; **debenture bond** = obligación no hipotecaria; **debenture capital** *or* **debenture stock** = obligaciones garantizadas por los activos de la compañía; **debenture holder** = obligacionista; **debenture register** *or* **register of debentures** = registro de obligacionistas

| COMMENT: in the UK, debentures are always secured on the company's assets; in the USA, debenture bonds are not secured

debit ['debit] **1** *noun* débito *m or* debe *m*; **debits and credits** = debe y haber; **debit balance** = saldo negativo *or* saldo deudor; **debit card** = tarjeta de débito *or* de pago; **debit column** = columna del debe; **debit entry** = asiento de débito *or* adeudo; **debit side** = debe; **debit note** = nota de adeudo; **we undercharged Mr Smith and had to send him a debit note for the extra amount** = cobramos de menos al señor Smith y tuvimos que enviarle una nota de adeudo por la cantidad adicional; **direct debit** = domiciliación *f* bancaria; **I pay my electricity bill by direct debit** = he domiciliado los pagos de la electricidad **2** *verb* **to debit an account** = adeudar *or* cargar en cuenta; **his account was debited with the sum of £25** = cargaron a su cuenta £25

◊ **debitable** ['debitəbl] *adjective* adeudable *or* abonable

debt [det] *noun* **(a)** *(money owed)* deuda *f*; **the company stopped trading with debts of over £1 million** = la sociedad suspendió sus operaciones con una deuda de más de £1 millón; **to be in debt** = estar endeudado *or* deber dinero; **he is in debt to the tune of £250** = tiene una deuda de £250; **to get into debt** = endeudarse *or* contraer deudas; **the company is out of debt** = la compañía ya no tiene deudas; **to pay back a debt** = reembolsar *or* devolver una deuda; **to pay off a debt** = liquidar *or* pagar una deuda; **to service a debt** = pagar los intereses de una deuda; **the company is having problems in servicing its debts** = la compañía tiene dificultades para pagar el servicio de su deuda; **bad debt** = deuda morosa *or* incobrable; **the company has written off £30,000 in bad debts** = la compañía ha cancelado £30.000 de deudas incobrables; **secured debts** *or* **unsecured debts** = deuda garantizada *or* deuda no garantizada; **debt collecting** *or* **debt collection** = cobro de morosos; **debt collection agency** = agencia de cobro de morosos; **debt collector** = agente *m* cobrador de morosos; **debt counselling** = asesoramiento de deudas; **debts due** = deudas por pagar; **debt factor** = comprador de deudas **(b)** **funded debt** = deuda consolidada; **the National Debt** = la deuda pública

◊ **debtor** ['detə] *noun* **(a)** *(person)* deudor, -ra; **debtor side** = debe *m*; **debtor nation** = nación deudora *or* país endeudado; **bad debtor** = moroso, -sa **(b)** *(accounting)* **debtors** = deudores *mpl*; **trade debtors** = deudores comerciales

| QUOTE the United States is now a debtor nation for the first time since 1914, owing more to foreigners than it is owed itself
| **Economist**

debug [di:'bʌg] *verb* depurar *or* eliminar errores (NOTE: **debugging - debugged**)

deceit *or* **deception** [dɪ'si:t *or* dɪ'sepʃən] *noun*

fraude *m*; **he obtained £10,000 by deception** = obtuvo £10.000 fraudulentamente

deceleration [di:selə'reɪʃn] *noun* desaceleración *f or* ralentización *f*

decentralize [di:'sentrəlaɪz] *verb* descentralizar; **the group has a policy of decentralized purchasing where each division is responsible for its own purchasing** = el grupo sigue una política de compras descentralizadas por la que cada departamento se encarga de sus propias compras

◊ **decentralization** [di:sentrəlaɪ'zeɪʃn] *noun* descentralización *f*; **the decentralization of the buying departments** = la descentralización de los departamentos de compras

decide [dɪ'saɪd] *verb* decidir *or* optar; **to decide on a course of action** = optar por una línea de conducta; **to decide to appoint a new managing director** = decidir nombrar un nuevo director gerente

◊ **deciding** [dɪ'saɪdɪŋ] *adjective* **deciding factor** = factor decisivo

decile ['desaɪl] *noun* decila *f*

decimal ['desɪml] *noun* decimal; **decimal system** = sistema decimal; **correct to three places of decimals** = reducido a tres decimales

◊ **decimalization** [desɪmlaɪ'zeɪʃn] *noun* decimalización *f*

◊ **decimalize** ['desɪmlaɪz] *verb* decimalizar

◊ **decimal point** ['desɪml 'pɔɪnt] *noun* coma decimal

| COMMENT: the decimal point is used in the UK and USA. In most European countries a comma is used to indicate a decimal, so 4.75% in Spain means 4.75% in the UK

decision [dɪ'sɪʒən] *noun* decisión *f*; **to come to a decision** *or* **to reach a decision** = llegar a una decisión *or* adoptar una decisión; **decision making** = toma de decisiones; **the decision-making processes** = procesos decisorios *or* de toma de decisiones; **decision maker** = persona que toma las decisiones; **decision tree** = organigrama de procesos decisorios *or* árbol de decisión

deck [dek] *noun* cubierta *f*; **deck cargo** = carga en cubierta; **deck hand** = marinero de cubierta

declaration [deklə'reɪʃən] *noun* declaración *f*; **declaration of bankruptcy** = declaración de quiebra; **declaration of income** = declaración de renta; **customs declaration** = declaración de aduana; **VAT declaration** = declaración del IVA

◊ **declare** [dɪ'kleə] *verb* declarar *or* confesar; **to declare someone bankrupt** = declarar a alguien en quiebra; **to declare a dividend of 10%** = declarar un dividendo del 10%; **to declare goods to customs** = declarar mercancías en la aduana; **the customs officials asked him if he had anything to declare** = los funcionarios de aduanas le preguntaron si tenía algo que declarar; **to declare an interest** = declarar un interés

◊ **declared** [dɪ'kleəd] *adjective* declarado, -da; **declared value** = valor declarado

decline [dɪ'klaɪn] **1** *noun* descenso *m or* disminución *f or* baja *f*; **the decline in the value of**

the franc = el descenso del valor del franco; **a decline in buying power** = una disminución del poder adquisitivo; **the last year has seen a decline in real wages** = durante el último año los salarios reales han experimentado una baja **2** *verb* **(a)** *(fall slowly)* bajar *or* disminuir *or* empeorar; **shares declined in a weak market** = el precio de las acciones bajó en un mercado inactivo; **imports have declined over the last year** = las importaciones han disminuido durante el último año; **the economy declined during the last government** = la economía empeoró *or* se debilitó con el último gobierno **(b)** *(refuse)* declinar; **to decline to take any responsibility** = declinar cualquier responsabilidad; **to decline an invitation** = declinar una invitación

QUOTE in 1990 the profits again declined to L185bn from the 1989 figure of L229.7bn
Financial Times

QUOTE Saudi oil production has declined by three quarters to around 2.5m barrels a day
Economist

QUOTE this gives an average monthly decline of 2.15 per cent during the period
Business Times (Lagos)

decontrol ['di:kən'trəʊl] **1** *noun (of prices)* liberalización *f* de precios **2** *verb* liberalizar *or* suprimir controles; **to decontrol the price of petrol** = liberalizar el precio de la gasolina; **to decontrol wages** = suprimir el control de salarios (NOTE: **decontrolling - decontrolled)**

decrease 1 ['di:kri:s] *noun* descenso *m or* disminución *f or* bajada *f*; **decrease in price** = bajada de precio; **decrease in value** = disminución de valor; **decrease in imports** = disminución de las importaciones; **exports have registered a decrease** = las exportaciones han disminuido; **sales show a 10% decrease on last year** = las ventas están un 10% por debajo del año pasado **2** [dɪ'kri:s] *verb* disminuir *or* bajar; **imports are decreasing** = las importaciones están disminuyendo; **the value of the pound has decreased by 5%** = el valor de la libra ha bajado un 5%

◊ **decreasing** [di:'kri:sɪŋ] *adj* decreciente; **the decreasing influence of the finance director** = la influencia cada vez menor del director de finanzas

deduct [dɪ'dʌkt] *verb* deducir *or* descontar; **to deduct £3 from the price** = descontar £3 del precio; **to deduct a sum for expenses** = deducir una cantidad por gastos; **after deducting costs the gross margin is only 23%** = después de deducir los costes el margen bruto es de sólo el 23%; **expenses are still to be deducted** = faltan todavía por deducir los gastos; **tax deducted at source** = impuestos deducidos en origen

◊ **deductible** [dɪ'dʌktəbl] *adjective* deducible; **tax-deductible** = desgravable; **these expenses are not tax-deductible** = estos gastos no son desgravables

◊ **deduction** [dɪ'dʌkʃən] *noun* deducción *f*; **net salary is salary after deduction of tax and social security** = el salario neto es el salario bruto después de deducir los impuestos y la cotización a la seguridad social; **deductions from salary** *or* **salary deductions** *or* **deductions at source** = deducciones

de salario *or* deducciones en origen; **tax deductions** = deducciones fiscales *or* impositivas; *US* gastos deducibles

deed [di:d] *noun* título *m or* escritura *f*; **deed of assignment** = escritura de cesión; **deed of covenant** = escritura de convenio (de subvención anual); **deed of partnership** = escritura de sociedad; **deed of transfer** = escritura de transferencia; **title deeds** = título de propiedad; **we have deposited the deeds of the house in the bank** = hemos depositado el título de propiedad de la casa en el banco

deep discount ['di:p 'dɪskaʊnt] *noun* descuento elevado *or* gran descuento

QUOTE as the group's shares are already widely held, the listing will be via an introduction. It will also be accompanied by a deeply discounted £25m rights issue, leaving the company cash positive
Sunday Times

defalcation [di:fæl'keɪʃən] *noun* desfalco *m*

default [dɪ'fɔ:lt] **1** *noun* **(a)** incumplimiento *m*; **in default of payment** = a falta de pago; **the company is in default** = la compañía es morosa **(b) by default** = por defecto *or* a falta de; **he was elected by default** = fue elegido a falta de otro candidato **(c)** *(computer)* **default setting** *or* **value** = parámetro *or* valor por defecto **2** *verb* incumplir *or* faltar *or* no pagar; **to default on payments** = incumplir los pagos

◊ **defaulter** [dɪ'fɔ:ltə] *noun* moroso, -sa *or* deudor, -ra

defeat [dɪ'fi:t] **1** *noun* derrota *f*; **the chairman offered to resign after the defeat of the proposal at the AGM** = el presidente ofreció su dimisión después de la derrota sufrida por su propuesta en la junta anual **2** *verb* derrotar *or* rechazar; **the proposal was defeated by 10 votes to 23** = la propuesta fue rechazada por 10 votos a favor y 23 en contra; **he was heavily defeated in the ballot for union president** = sufrió una gran derrota en la votación para presidente del sindicato

defect ['di:fekt] *noun* defecto *m or* tara *f*; **a computer defect** *or* **a defect in the computer** = un defecto del ordenador

◊ **defective** [dɪ'fektɪv] *adjective* **(a)** *(not functioning)* defectuoso, -sa; **the machine broke down because of a defective cooling system** = la máquina se averió debido a un sistema de refrigeración defectuoso **(b)** *(not valid)* defectuoso, -sa; **his title to the property is defective** = su título de propiedad tiene vicios jurídicos

defence *or US* **defense** [dɪ'fens] *noun* **(a)** *(protection)* defensa *f*; **the merchant bank is organizing the company's defence against the takeover bid** = el banco mercantil organiza la defensa de la compañía frente al intento de adquisición **(b)** *(in a lawsuit)* defensa; **defence counsel** = abogado defensor *or* de la parte demandada

◊ **defend** [dɪ'fend] *verb* defender; **the company is defending itself against the takeover bid** = la compañía se está defendiendo de la oferta de adquisición; **he hired the best lawyers to defend him against the tax authorities** = contrató a los mejores abogados para defenderse del fisco; **to**

defend a lawsuit = defenderse en juicio contra una demanda o acusación

◊ **defendant** [dɪ'fendənt] *noun* parte demandada *or* demandado, -da *or* acusado, -da

defer [dɪ'fɜː] *verb* aplazar *or* diferir; **to defer payment** = diferir el pago; **the decision has been deferred until the next meeting** = la decisión ha sido aplazada hasta la próxima reunión (NOTE: **deferring - deferred**)

◊ **deferment** [dɪ'fɜːmənt] *noun* aplazamiento *m or* prórroga *f* **deferment of payment** = aplazamiento de pago; **deferment of a decision** = aplazamiento de una decisión

◊ **deferred** [dɪ'fɜːd] *adjective* diferido, -da *or* aplazado, -da; **deferred creditor** = acreedor diferido; **deferred payment** = pago aplazado; **deferred stock** = acciones diferidas

deficiency [dɪ'fɪʃənsi] *noun* falta *f or* deficiencia *f*; **there is a £10 deficiency in the petty cash** = faltan £10 en la caja para gastos menores; **to make up a deficiency** = cubrir una deficiencia

deficit ['defɪsɪt] *noun* déficit *m*; **the accounts show a deficit** = las cuentas arrojan un déficit; **to make good a deficit** = cubrir un déficit; **balance of payments deficit** *or* **trade deficit** = déficit de la balanza de pagos *or* de la balanza comercial; **deficit financing** = financiación del déficit presupuestario

deflate [dɪ'fleɪt] *verb* **to deflate the economy** = deflactar *or* deshinchar la economía *o* seguir una política económica deflacionista

◊ **deflation** [dɪ'fleɪʃən] *noun* deflación *f* **price deflation** = deflación de los precios

◊ **deflationary** [dɪ'fleɪʃnəri] *adjective* deflacionista; **the government has introduced some deflationary measures in the budget** = el gobierno ha introducido algunas medidas deflacionistas en el presupuesto

> QUOTE the strong dollar's deflationary impact on European economies as national governments push up interest rates
> **Duns Business Month**

defraud [dɪ'frɔːd] *verb* estafar *or* defraudar (NOTE: you **defraud** someone **of** something)

defray [dɪ'freɪ] *verb* pagar *or* sufragar; **to defray someone's expenses** = costear los gastos de alguien; **the company agreed to defray the costs of the exhibition** = la empresa acordó sufragar los costes de la exposición

degearing ['diː'ɡɪərɪŋ] *noun* reducción *f* de la relación entre la deuda de una sociedad y el valor de sus acciones

degressive [dɪ'ɡresɪv] *adjective* decreciente; **degressive taxation** = imposición decreciente

delay [dɪ'leɪ] **1** *noun* demora *f or* retraso *m*; **there was a delay of thirty minutes before the AGM started** *or* **the AGM started after a thirty minute delay** = la junta general anual empezó con treinta minutos de retraso; **we are sorry for the delay in supplying your order** *or* **in replying to your letter** = lamentamos la demora en servirles el pedido *or* en contestar a su carta **2** *verb* retrasar *or* demorar *or* atrasar *or* entretener; **he was delayed because his**

taxi had an accident = se retrasó porque su taxi tuvo un accidente; **the company has delayed payment of all invoices** = la empresa ha retrasado el pago de todas las facturas

del credere [del 'kreɪdəri] *noun* prima *f* al comisionista; **del credere agent** = agente del credere *or* agente comisionista que responde del crédito de los comprsdores; **del credere commission** comisión del credere *or* de garantía

delegate ['delɪɡət] **1** *noun* delegado, -da *or* representante *mf*; **the management refused to meet the trade union delegates** = la dirección se negó a reunirse con los delegados sindicales; **union delegate** = delegado *or* enlace *or* representante sindical **2** *verb* delegar; **to delegate authority** = delegar la autoridad; **he cannot delegate** = no sabe delegar

◊ **delegation** [delɪ'ɡeɪʃən] *noun* **(a)** *(group of delegates)* delegación *f*; **a Chinese trade delegation** = una delegación comercial china; **the management met a union delegation** = la dirección se reunió con una delegación sindical **(b)** *(passing responsibility to someone else)* delegación *f*

delete [dɪ'liːt] *verb* suprimir; **they want to delete all references to credit terms from the contract** = quieren suprimir del contrato todo lo que hace referencia a las condiciones de crédito; **the lawyers have deleted clause two** = los abogados han suprimido la cláusula dos

deliver [dɪ'lɪvə] *verb* entregar *or* repartir; **goods delivered free** *or* **free delivered goods** = entrega de mercancías gratuita; **goods delivered on board** = mercancías entregadas a bordo; **delivered price** = precio de entrega

◊ **delivery** [dɪ'lɪvəri] *noun* **(a)** **delivery of goods** = entrega *f or* reparto *m* de mercancías; **parcels awaiting delivery** = paquetes en espera de entrega; **free delivery** *or* **delivery free** = entrega gratuita; **home delivery** = entrega a domicilio; **delivery date** = fecha de entrega; **delivery within 28 days** = entrega en el plazo de 28 días; **allow 28 days for delivery** = cuente con un plazo de 28 días para la entrega; **delivery is not allowed for** *or* **is not included** = entrega no incluida *or* los gastos de envío no están incluidos; **delivery note** = albarán *m or* nota *f* de entrega; **delivery order** = orden de entrega *or* de expedición; **the store has a delivery service to all parts of the town** = la tienda tiene un servicio de reparto que abarca toda la ciudad; **delivery time** = plazo de entrega; **delivery van** = furgoneta de reparto; **express delivery** = reparto urgente; *US* **General Delivery** = lista de correos (NOTE: GB English for this is **poste restante**); **recorded delivery** = correo certificado con acuse de recibo; **we sent the documents (by) recorded delivery** = enviamos los documentos por correo certificado; **cash on delivery (c.o.d.)** = cobro a la entrega *or* contra reembolso; **to take delivery of goods** = aceptar la entrega de mercancías; **we took delivery of the stock into our warehouse on the 25th** = recibimos la mercancía en nuestro almacén el día 25 **(b)** *(goods delivered)* entrega *f*; **we take in three deliveries a day** = recibimos tres entregas al día; **there were four items missing in the last delivery** = faltaban cuatro artículos en la última entrega **(c)** *(transfer of bill of exchange)* transferencia *f or* cesión *f* de una letra de cambio

◊ **deliveryman** [dɪ'lɪvrɪmən] *noun* recadero *m*

demand [dɪ'mɑːnd] **1** *noun* **(a)** *(request for payment)* requerimiento *m* de pago *or* reclamación *f*; **payable on demand** = pagadero a la vista; **demand bill** = giro a la vista; *US* **demand deposit** = depósito a la vista; **final demand** = último requerimiento de pago **(b)** *(need for goods)* demanda *f*; **there was an active demand for oil shares on the stock market** = había una fuerte demanda de acciones petrolíferas en la bolsa; **to meet a demand** *or* **to fill a demand** = satisfacer *or* atender a la demanda; **the factory had to increase production to meet the extra demand** = la fábrica tuvo que aumentar la producción para satisfacer la demanda adicional; **the factory had to cut production when demand slackened** = la fábrica tuvo que reducir la producción cuando bajó la demanda; **the office cleaning company cannot keep up with the demand for its services** = la empresa de limpieza de oficinas no puede satisfacer la demanda de sus servicios; **there is not much demand for this item** = no hay mucha demanda de este artículo; **this book is in great demand** *or* **there is a great demand for this book** = este libro tiene mucha demanda *or* hay mucha demanda de este libro; **effective demand** = demanda efectiva; **demand price** = precio de demanda; **supply and demand** = oferta y demanda; **law of supply and demand** = ley de la oferta y la demanda **2** *verb* exigir *or* reclamar *or* requerir *or* demandar; **she demanded a refund** = exigió un reembolso; **the suppliers are demanding immediate payment of their outstanding invoices** = los proveedores exigen el pago de sus facturas pendientes

◊ **demand-led inflation** [dɪ'mɑːndled ɪn'fleɪʃən] *noun* inflación *f* provocada por la demanda excesiva

> QUOTE spot prices are now relatively stable in the run-up to the winter's peak demand
>
> **Economist**

> QUOTE the demand for the company's products remained strong throughout the first six months of the year with production and sales showing significant increases
>
> **Business Times (Lagos)**

> QUOTE growth in demand is still coming from the private rather than the public sector
>
> **Lloyd's List**

demarcation dispute [diːmɑː'keɪʃən dɪs'pjuːt] *noun* conflicto *m* sobre la delimitación de tareas *or* disputa *f* entre sindicatos; **production of the new car was held up by demarcation disputes** = la producción del nuevo automóvil fue retrasada debido a conflictos sobre la delimitación de tareas entre los obreros

demerge [diː'mɜːdʒ] *verb* disolver(se)

◊ **demerger** [diː'mɜːdʒə] *noun* disolución *f*

demise [dɪ'maɪz] *noun* **(a)** *(death)* muerte *f* *or* fallecimiento *m*; **on his demise the estate passed to his daughter** = después de su muerte la propiedad pasó a su hija **(b)** *(granting property on a lease)* cesión *f*

demonetize [diː'mʌnətaɪz] *verb* desmonetizar

◊ **demonetization** [diː'mʌnɪtaɪ'zeɪʃn] *noun* desmonetización *f*

demonstrate ['demənstreɪt] *verb* demostrar *or* mostrar el funcionamiento de algo; **he was demonstrating a new tractor when he was killed** = se mató cuando estaba mostrando el funcionamiento del nuevo tractor; **the managers saw the new stock control system being demonstrated** = los directivos asistieron a la presentación del nuevo sistema de control de existencias

◊ **demonstration** [deməns'treɪʃən] *noun* **(a)** *(showing)* demostración *f*; **we went to a demonstration of a new fax machine** = asistimos a la presentación de un nuevo modelo de fax *or* facsímil; **demonstration model** = modelo de prueba *or* de demostración **(b)** *(political)* manifestación *f*

◊ **demonstrator** ['demənstreɪtə] *noun* **(a)** *(person)* exhibidor, -ra *or* persona que hace una demostración **(b)** *(political)* manifestante *mf*

demote [dɪ'məʊt] *verb* degradar *or* bajar de categoría profesional; **he was demoted from manager to salesman** = de director, le degradaron al puesto de vendedor; **she lost a lot of salary when she was demoted** = su sueldo bajó mucho cuando le degradaron

◊ **demotion** [dɪ'məʊʃən] *noun* degradación *f* *or* pérdida *f* de categoría profesional; **he was very angry at his demotion** = su degradación le enojó mucho

demurrage [dɪ'mʌrɪdʒ] *noun* gastos *mpl* de demora

denationalize [diː'næʃənəlaɪz] *verb* desnacionalizar *or* privatizar; **the government has plans to denationalize the steel industry** = el gobierno se propone desnacionalizar la industria siderúrgica

◊ **denationalization** ['diːnæʃnəlaɪ'zeɪʃn] *noun* desnacionalización *f*; **the denationalization of the aircraft industry** = la desnacionalización de la industria aeronáutica

Denmark ['denmɑːk] *noun* Dinamarca *f*

◊ **Dane** [deɪn] *noun* Danés, -esa

◊ **Danish** ['deɪnɪʃ] *adjective* danés, -esa *or* dinamarqués, -esa
NOTE: capital: **Copenhagen** (= Copenhague); currency: **Danish krone (DKr)** = corona danesa (DKr)

denomination [dɪnɒmɪ'neɪʃən] *noun* valor *m* nominal *or* denominación *f* *or* título *m*; **coins of all denominations** = monedas de todos los valores; **small denomination notes** = billetes de pequeño valor

deny [dɪ'naɪ] *verb* negar; **he denied the facts** = negó los hechos

dep = DEPARTMENT, DEPARTURE

depart [dɪ'pɑːt] *verb* **(a)** *(to leave)* salir; **the plane departs from Madrid at 11.15** = el vuelo sale de Madrid a las 11.15 **(b)** *(to deviate)* **to depart from normal practice** = desviarse de la costumbre

department [dɪ'pɑːtmənt] *noun* **(a)** *(office)* departamento *m* *or* sección *f*; **accounts department**

= departamento de contabilidad; **complaints department** = oficina de reclamaciones; **design department** = departamento de diseño; **dispatch department** = departamento de expedición; **export department** = departamento de exportación; **legal department** = asesoría jurídica; **marketing department** = departamento de marketing _or_ sección comercial; **new issues department** = departamento de emisión de nuevas acciones; **personnel department** = departamento de personal; **head of department** _or_ **department head** _or_ **department manager** = jefe de sección _or_ departamento **(b)** _(section of large store)_ sección (de tienda); **you will find beds in the furniture department** = encontrará camas en la sección de muebles; **budget department** = sección de oportunidades **(c)** _(government department)_ Departamento del Estado _or_ ministerio; **the Department of Education and Science** = el ministerio de Educación y Ciencia; **Department of Employment (DoE)** = Ministerio de Trabajo; **the Department of Trade and Industry** = el ministerio de Comercio e Industria; _US_ **Commerce Department** _or_ **Department of Commerce** = Ministerio de Comercio e Industria

◇ **department store** [dɪ'pɑ:tmənt 'stɔ:] _noun_ grandes almacenes _mpl_

◇ **departmental** [di:pɑ:t'mentl] _adjective_ departamental; **departmental manager** = director de departamento _or_ sección

departure [dɪ'pɑ:tʃə] _noun_ **(a)** _(going away)_ salida _f_; **the plane's departure was delayed by two hours** = la salida del avión se retrasó dos horas; _(in an airport)_ **departures** = salidas; **departure lounge** = sala de embarque **(b)** _(new venture)_ novedad _f or_ nueva orientación comercial; **selling records will be a departure for the local bookshop** = la venta de discos será una novedad para la librería local **(c)** _(change)_ **a departure from normal practice** = una desviación de la norma

depend [dɪ'pend] _verb_ **(a)** _(need someone or something to exist)_ **to depend on** = depender de; **the company depends on efficient service from its suppliers** = la empresa depende del buen servicio de sus suministradores _or_ proveedores; **we depend on government grants to pay the salary bill** = dependemos de los subsidios del Estado para pagar los salarios **(b)** _(to happen because of something)_ depender de; **the success of the launch will depend on the publicity** = el éxito del lanzamiento dependerá de la publicidad; **depending on** = según; **depending on the advertising budget, the new product will be launched on radio or on TV** = según sea el presupuesto publicitario, el nuevo producto se lanzará por radio o por televisión

◇ **dependent** [dɪ'pendənt] _adjective_ **to be dependent on** = estar bajo la dependencia de

deposit [dɪ'pɒzɪt] **1** _noun_ **(a)** _(savings)_ depósito _m or_ imposición _f or_ ingreso _m_; **certificate of deposit** = certificado de depósito; **bank deposits** = los depósitos bancarios; **bank deposits are at an all-time high** = los depósitos bancarios han alcanzado un nivel sin precedentes; **cash deposit** = imposición en efectivo; **fixed deposit** = depósito a plazo fijo; **time deposit** = imposición a plazos; **deposit account** = cuenta a plazo; **deposit at 7 days' notice** = depósito con preaviso de 7 días; **deposit slip** = nota _or_ recibo de depósito **(b)** _(in bank)_ **safe**

deposit = depósito en caja fuerte; **safe deposit box** = caja de seguridad **(c)** _(money paid in advance)_ depósito _or_ señal _f or (on property)_ entrada _f_; **to pay a deposit on a watch** = dejar una señal para un reloj; **to leave £10 as deposit** = dejar una señal de £10 **2** _verb_ **(a)** _(documents)_ depositar _or_ ingresar; **to deposit shares with a bank** = depositar acciones en un banco; **we have deposited the deeds of the house with the bank** = hemos depositado la escritura de la casa en un banco; **he deposited his will with his solicitor** = confió el testamento a su abogado **(b)** _(money)_ depositar _or_ imponer; **to deposit money in a bank** = imponer _or_ ingresar dinero en un banco; **to deposit £100 in a current account** = depositar £100 en una cuenta corriente

◇ **depositary** [dɪ'pɒzɪtəri] _noun US_ depositario, -ria; _see also_ AMERICAN DEPOSITARY RECEIPT

◇ **depositor** [dɪ'pɒzɪtə] _noun_ impositor, -ra _or_ depositante _mf_

◇ **depository** [dɪ'pɒzɪtəri] _noun_ **(a)** _(storage)_ almacén _m_ de depósitos; **furniture depository** = guardamuebles _m_ **(b)** _(person)_ depositario, -ria _or_ tesorero, -ra

depot ['depəʊ] _noun_ **(a)** _(central warehouse)_ almacén _m_ central; **freight depot** = estación _f_ de mercancías; **goods depot** = depósito _m or_ almacén de mercancías; **oil storage depot** = depósito central de petróleo **(b)** _(centre for transport)_ centro _m_ de transporte; **bus depot** = estación _f_ de autobuses

depreciate [dɪ'pri:ʃeɪt] _verb_ **(a)** _(amortize)_ amortizar _or_ depreciar; **we depreciate our company cars over three years** = amortizamos los coches de la empresa en tres años **(b)** _(lose value)_ depreciarse _or_ perder valor; **share which has depreciated by 10% over the year** = acción que ha perdido el 10% de su valor durante el año; **the pound has depreciated by 5% against the dollar** = la libra se ha depreciado en un 5% respecto al dólar

◇ **depreciation** [dɪpri:ʃɪ'eɪʃən] _noun_ **(a)** _(reducing value)_ amortización _f or_ depreciación _f_; **depreciation rate** = tasa de amortización _or_ depreciacíon; **accelerated depreciation** = amortización acelerada; **annual depreciation** = amortización por anualidades; **straight line depreciation** = amortización anual uniforme **(b)** _(loss of value)_ depreciación _or_ pérdida de valor; **share which has shown a depreciation of 10% over the year** = una acción que ha mostrado una pérdida de valor del 10% a lo largo del año; **the depreciation of the pound against the dollar** = la depreciación de la libra con respecto al dólar

COMMENT: various methods of depreciating assets are used, such as the 'straight line method', where the asset is depreciated at a constant percentage of its cost each year and the 'reducing balance method', where the asset is depreciated at a constant percentage which is applied to the cost of the asset after each of the previous years' depreciation has been deducted

QUOTE this involved reinvesting funds on items which could be depreciated against income for three years
Australian Financial Review

QUOTE buildings are depreciated at two per cent per annum on the estimated cost of construction
Hongkong Standard

depress [dɪ'pres] *verb* disminuir *or* deprimir; **reducing the money supply has the effect of depressing demand for consumer goods** = la reducción de la oferta de dinero trae como consecuencia la disminución de la demanda de bienes de consumo

◊ **depressed** [dɪ'prest] *adjective* **depressed area** = zona deprimida; **depressed market** = mercado deprimido *or* a la baja

◊ **depression** [dɪ'preʃən] *noun* depresión *f*; **an economic depression** = una depresión económica; **the Great Depression** = la Gran Depresión

dept [dɪ'pɑːtmənt] = DEPARTMENT

deputy ['depjʊti] *noun* delegado, -da *or* adjunto, -ta *or* suplente *or* sustituto, -ta *mf*; **to act as deputy for someone** *or* **to act as someone's deputy** = hacer las funciones de otro; **deputy chairman** = presidente adjunto; **deputy manager** = director adjunto *or* subdirector; **deputy managing director** = director general adjunto

◊ **deputize** ['depjʊtaɪz] *verb* **to deputize for someone** = sustituir a alguien; **he deputized for the chairman who had a cold** = sustituyó al presidente, que estaba resfriado

deregulate [diː'regjʊleɪt] *verb* liberalizar; **the US government deregulated the banking sector in the 1980s** = el gobierno de EE.UU liberalizó el sector bancario en los años 80

◊ **deregulation** ['diːregjʊ'leɪʃn] *noun* liberalización *f or* desregulación *f*; **the deregulation of the airlines** = la liberalización de las compañías aéreas

derivatives [dɪ'rɪvətɪvz] *plural noun* (productos *or* títulos) derivados *mpl*

COMMENT: any forms of security, such as option contracts, which are derived from ordinary bonds and shares are derivatives. They can also be called 'derivative instruments', and can be bought or sold on stock exchanges or futures exchanges

describe [dɪ'skraɪb] *verb* describir *or* exponer; **the leaflet describes the services the company can offer** = el folleto describe los servicios que ofrece la compañía; **the managing director described the company's difficulties with cash flow** = el director ·general expuso los problemas de la compañía en materia de flujo de caja

◊ **description** [dɪ'skrɪpʃən] *noun* descripción *f*; **false description of contents** = descripción engañosa del contenido; **job description** = descripción del puesto de trabajo; **trade description** = descripción comercial

design [dɪ'zaɪn] **1** *noun* diseño *m*; **industrial design** = diseño industrial; **product design** = diseño de productos; **design department** = departamento de diseño; **design studio** = agencia *or* taller de diseño **2** *verb* diseñar *or* proyectar; **he designed a new car factory** = proyectó una nueva fábrica de automóviles; **she designs garden furniture** = diseña muebles de jardín

◊ **designer** [dɪ'zaɪnə] *noun* diseñador, -ra *or* proyectista; **she is the designer of the new computer** = es la diseñadora del nuevo ordenador

designate ['dezɪgnət] *adjective* nombrado, -da;

the chairman designate = el presidente nombrado (NOTE: always follows a noun)

desk [desk] *noun* **(a)** *(table)* escritorio *m or* mesa *f* de despacho; **desk diary** = agenda de mesa (de despacho); **desk drawer** = cajón de mesa; **desk light** = lámpara de mesa; **a three-drawer desk** = una mesa despacho *or* un escritorio con tres cajones; **desk pad** = bloc de mesa **(b)** *(to pay)* **cash desk** *or* **pay desk** = caja *f*; **please pay at the desk** = pague en caja **(c)** *(section of a newspaper)* sección de un periódico; **the City desk** = la sección de noticias comerciales

◊ **desk-top publishing (DTP)** ['desktɒp 'pʌblɪʃɪŋ] *noun* autoedición *f or* trabajo editorial asistido por ordenador; **desk-top publishing package** = paquete *m* de autoedición

despatch [dɪ'spætʃ] = DISPATCH

destination [destɪ'neɪʃən] *noun* destino *m*; **the ship will take ten weeks to reach its destination** = el barco tardará diez semanas en llegar a su destino; **final destination** *or* **ultimate destination** = destino final

detail ['diːteɪl] **1** *noun* detalle *m or* pormenor *m*; **the catalogue gives all the details of our product range** = el catálogo da todos los detalles de nuestra gama de productos; **we are worried by some of the details in the contract** = estamos preocupados por algunos detalles del contrato; **in detail** = en detalle *or* detallado; **the catalogue lists all the products in detail** = el catálogo indica todos los productos con detalle **2** *verb* detallar *or* pormenorizar; **the catalogue details the payment arrangements for overseas buyers** = el catálogo detalla la modalidad de pago para los compradores extranjeros; **the terms of the licence are detailed in the contract** = los términos de la licencia están detallados en el contrato

◊ **detailed** ['diːteɪld] *adjective* detallado, -da; **detailed account** = factura *or* cuenta detallada

determination [dɪtɜːmɪ'neɪʃn] *noun* determinación *f or* empeño *m*

determine [dɪ'tɜːmɪn] *verb* determinar *or* resolver *or* decidir; **to determine prices** *or* **quantities** = determinar los precios *or* las cantidades; **conditions still to be determined** = condiciones todavía por determinar

Deutschmark ['dɔɪtʃmɑːk] *noun* marco *m* alemán (NOTE: also called a **mark;** when used with a figure, usually written **DM** before the figure: **DM250:** say 'two hundred and fifty Deutschmarks')

devalue ['diː'væljuː] *verb* devaluar *or* desvalorizar; **the pound has been devalued by 7%** = la libra ha sido devaluada en un 7%; **the government has devalued the pound by 7%** = el gobierno ha devaluado la libra en un 7%

◊ **devaluation** ['diːvæljʊ'eɪʃən] *noun* devaluación *f or* desvalorización *f*; **the devaluation of the peseta** = la devaluación de la peseta

develop [dɪ'veləp] *verb* **(a)** *(plan and produce)* desarrollar *or* fabricar; **to develop a new product** = fabricar un nuevo producto **(b)** *(plan and build)* construir *or* urbanizar; **to develop an industrial estate** = construir un polígono industrial

◊ **developed country** [dɪ'veləpt 'kʌntri] *noun*
país desarrollado

◊ **developer** [dɪ'veləpə] *noun* **a property
developer** = promotor inmobiliario *or* de
construcciones

◊ **developing country** *or* **developing
nation** [dɪ'veləpɪŋ 'kʌntri *or* dɪ'veləpɪŋ 'neɪʃən]
noun país *m* en vías de desarrollo

◊ **development** [dɪ'veləpmənt] *noun* **(a)**
desarrollo *m or* evolución *f*; **research and
development (R & D)** = investigación y desarrollo
(I & D) (b) industrial development = desarrollo
industrial; **urban development** = urbanización *f*;
development area *or* **development zone** = área *or*
región de desarrollo **(c)** *(change of plan)* bifurcación
f

> QUOTE developed countries would gain $135
> billion a year and developing countries,
> such as the former centrally planned
> economies of Eastern Europe, would gain
> $85 billion a year. The study also notes
> that the poorest countries would lose an
> annual $7 billion
>
> **Times**

device [dɪ'vaɪs] *noun* aparato *m or* dispositivo *m or*
estratagema *f*; **he invented a device for screwing
tops on bottles** = inventó un aparato para enroscar el
tapón a las botellas

devise [dɪ'vaɪz] **1** *noun* legado de bienes raíces **2**
verb (give freehold property to someone in a will)
legar

◊ **devisee** [dɪvaɪ'zi:] *noun* legatario, -ria de
bienes raíces

| COMMENT: giving of other types of property in a will
is a bequest

diagram ['daɪəgræm] *noun* diagrama *m or* gráfico
m; **diagram showing sales locations** = diagrama
que muestra los lugares de venta; **he drew a
diagram to show how the decision-making
processes work** = dibujó un diagrama para mostrar
el funcionamiento del proceso de toma de
decisiones; **the paper gives a diagram of the
company's organizational structure** = el
documento presenta un gráfico de la estructura
organizativa de la compañía; **flow diagram** =
diagrama de flujos *or* de secuencias *or* organigrama *m*

◊ **diagrammatic** [daɪəgrə'mætɪk] *adjective* **in
diagrammatic form** = en forma gráfica; **the chart
showed the sales pattern in diagrammatic form** =
el cuadro mostraba el patrón de ventas en forma
gráfica

◊ **diagrammatically** [daɪəgrə'mætɪkəli]
adverb gráficamente; **the chart shows the sales
pattern diagrammatically** = la figura muestra la
evolución de ventas gráficamente

dial ['daɪəl] *verb (telephone)* marcar *or* llamar; **to
dial a number** = marcar un número; **to dial the
operator** = llamar a la telefonista; **to dial direct** =
marcar el número directamente; **you can dial New
York direct from London** = puede llamar a Nueva
York desde Londres marcando directamente el
número (NOTE: GB English is **dialling - dialled,** but
US spelling is **dialing - dialed)**

◊ **dialling** ['daɪəlɪŋ] *noun* acto *m* de marcar;
dialling code = prefijo *m or* código *m* territorial;

dialling tone = señal *f* de línea; **international direct
dialling (IDD)** = llamadas internacionales directas

diary ['daɪəri] *noun* agenda *f*; **desk diary** = agenda
de mesa (de despacho)

dictaphone ['dɪktəfəʊn] *noun* marca *f* de un
modelo de dictáfono

dictate [dɪk'teɪt] *verb* dictar; **to dictate a letter to
a secretary** = dictar una carta a una secretaria;
dictating machine = dictáfono *m*; **he was dictating
orders into his pocket dictating machine** = estaba
grabando órdenes en su dictáfono de bolsillo

◊ **dictation** [dɪk'teɪʃən] *noun* dictado *m*; **to take
dictation** = escribir al dictado; **the secretary was
taking dictation from the managing director** = la
secretaria estaba escribiendo al dictado las palabras
del director gerente; **dictation speed** = velocidad de
dictado

differ ['dɪfə] *verb* diferir *or* ser distinto; **the two
products differ considerably - one has an electric
motor, the other runs on petrol** = los dos productos
son bastante distintos - uno lleva un motor eléctrico,
el otro funciona con gasolina

◊ **difference** ['dɪfrəns] *noun* diferencia *f*; **what
is the difference between these two products?** =
¿cuál es la diferencia entre estos dos productos?;
differences in price *or* **price differences** =
diferencias de precio

◊ **different** ['dɪfrənt] *adjective* distinto, -ta *or*
diferente; **our product range is quite different in
design from that of our rivals** = nuestra gama de
productos tiene un diseño totalmente distinto del de
nuestros competidores; **we offer ten models each in
six different colours** = ofrecemos diez modelos,
cada uno en seis colores distintos

◊ **differential** [dɪfə'renʃəl] **1** *adjective*
diferencial *or* diferenciado, -da; **differential tariffs**
= tarifas diferenciadas **2** *noun* **price differential** =
diferencial *m* de inflación *or* coeficiente *m* de ajuste
de precios; **wage differentials** = diferencias
salariales *or* coeficiente de ajuste salarial; **to erode
wage differentials** = reducir diferencias salariales

differentiate [dɪfə'renʃɪeɪt] *verb* diferenciar

difficult ['dɪfɪkəlt] *adjective* difícil; **the company
found it difficult to sell into the European market**
= a la empresa le resultó difícil vender en el mercado
europeo; **the market for secondhand computers is
very difficult at present** = el mercado de
ordenadores de segunda mano está atravesando un
momento difícil

◊ **difficulty** ['dɪfɪkəlti] *noun* dificultad *f*; **they
had a lot of difficulty selling into the European
market** = tuvieron muchas dificultades para vender
en el mercado europeo; **we have had some
difficulties with the customs over the export of
computers** = hemos tenido algunas dificultades con
la aduana para la exportación de ordenadores

digit ['dɪdʒɪt] *noun* dígito *m or* cifra *f*; **a seven-digit
phone number** = un número telefónico de siete
cifras

◊ **digital** ['dɪdʒɪtl] *adjective* **digital clock** = reloj
digital; **digital computer** = ordenador digital

dilution [daɪ'lu:ʃən] *noun* **dilution of equity** *or* **of
shareholding** = dilución *f* de las acciones

dime [daɪm] *noun US (informal)* moneda *f* de diez centavos

diminish [dɪ'mɪnɪʃ] *verb* disminuir; **our share of the market has diminished over the last few years** = nuestra cuota de mercado ha disminuido durante los últimos años; **law of diminishing returns** = ley de rendimientos decrecientes

dip [dɪp] **1** *noun* baja *f*; **last year saw a dip in the company's performance** = el año pasado los resultados de la compañía experimentaron una baja **2** *verb* bajar de precio; **shares dipped sharply in yesterday's trading** = las acciones bajaron fuertemente durante la jornada de ayer (NOTE: **dipping - dipped)**

diplomat *or* **diplomatist** ['dɪpləmæt *or* dɪ'pləʊmətɪst] *noun* diplomático, -ca

◊ **diplomatic** [dɪplə'mætɪk] *adjective* diplomático, -ca; **diplomatic immunity** = inmunidad diplomática; **he claimed diplomatic immunity to avoid being arrested** = invocó la inmunidad diplomática para evitar ser detenido; **to grant someone diplomatic status** = conceder estatus diplomático a alguien

direct [daɪ'rekt] **1** *verb* dirigir; **he directs our South-East Asian operations** = dirige nuestras actividades en el sureste de Asia; **she was directing the development unit until last year** = estuvo dirigiendo la sección de desarrollo hasta el año pasado **2** *adjective* directo, -ta; **direct action** = acción directa; **direct cost** = coste directo; **direct debit** = domiciliación bancaria; **I pay my electricity bill by direct debit** = he domiciliado los pagos de la electricidad; **direct mail** = venta por correo; **these calculators are only sold by direct mail** = estas calculadoras solamente se venden por correo; **the company runs a successful direct-mail operation** = la empresa dirige un próspero negocio de venta por correo; **direct-mail advertising** = publicidad por correo; **direct selling** = venta directa; **direct taxation** = imposición directa; **the government raises more money by direct taxation than by indirect** = el gobierno obtiene más ingresos de los impuestos directos que de los indirectos **3** *adverb* directamente; **we pay income tax direct to the government** = pagamos el impuesto sobre la renta directamente al Estado; **to dial direct** = llamar directamente (sin operadora); **you can dial New York direct from London if you want** = puede llamar a Nueva York desde Londres directamente si quiere

◊ **direction** [daɪ'rekʃən] *noun* **(a)** *(path)* dirección *f*; **change of direction** = cambio de sentido **(b)** *(managing)* dirección; **he took over the direction of a multinational group** = asumió la dirección de un grupo multinacional **(b) directions for use** = instrucciones *or* modo de empleo

◊ **directive** [daɪ'rektɪv] *noun* directriz *f or* directiva *f or* instrucción *f*; **the government has issued directives on increases in incomes and prices** = el gobierno ha publicado directrices sobre los aumentos de rentas y precios

◊ **directly** [daɪ'rektli] *adverb* **(a)** *(immediately)* inmediatamente; **he left for the airport directly after receiving the telephone message** = partió para el aeropuerto inmediatamente después de recibir el mensaje telefónico **(b)** *(straight)*

directamente; **we deal directly with the manufacturer, without using a wholesaler** = tratamos directamente con el fabricante, sin pasar por un mayorista

◊ **director** [daɪ'rektə] *noun* **(a)** *(of a company)* director, -ra *or* consejero, -ra; **managing director** = director gerente; **chairman and managing director** = presidente y director gerente; **board of directors** = consejo de administración *or* junta directiva; **directors' report** = informe *or* memoria del consejo de administración; **directors' salaries** = sueldo de los directores; **associate director** = director adjunto; **executive director** = director ejecutivo; **non-executive director** = director no ejecutivo; **outside director** = director externo **(b)** *(person in charge)* director, -ra; **the director of the government research institute** = director del instituto estatal de investigaciones; **she was appointed director of the organization** = fue nombrada directora de la organización

◊ **directorate** [daɪ'rektərət] *noun* directiva *f or* dirección *m or* consejo *m* de administración

◊ **directorship** [daɪ'rektəʃɪp] *noun* cargo *m* de director; **he was offered a directorship with Smith Ltd** = le ofrecieron el cargo de consejero en Smith Ltd

COMMENT: directors are elected by shareholders at the AGM, though they are usually chosen by the chairman or chief executive. A board will consist of a chairman (who may be non-executive), a chief executive or managing director, and a series of specialist directors in change of various activities of the company (such as a finance director, production director or sales director). The company secretary will attend board meetings, but need not be a director. Apart from the executive directors, who are in fact employees of the company, there may be several non-executive directors, appointed either for their expertise and contacts, or as representatives of important shareholders such as banks. The board of an American company may be made up of a large number of non-executive directors and only one or two executive officers; a British board has more executive directors

QUOTE after five years of growth, fuelled by the boom in financial services, the direct marketing world is becoming a lot more competitive
Marketing Workshop

QUOTE all of those who had used direct marketing techniques used direct mail, and 79% had used some kind of telephone technique
Precision Marketing

QUOTE the research director will manage and direct a team of business analysts reporting on the latest developments in retail distribution throughout the UK
Times

QUOTE what benefits does the executive derive from his directorship? In the first place compensation has increased sharply in recent years
Duns Business Month

directory [daɪ'rektəri] *noun* guía *f or* anuario *m or* directorio *m*; **classified directory** = directorio comercial por secciones; **commercial directory** *or* **trade directory** = directorio comercial; **street directory** = guía urbana; **phone directory** *or* telephone directory = guía telefónica; **to look up a number in the telephone directory** = buscar un número en la guía telefónica; **his number is in the London directory** = su número está en la guía de Londres

disability [dɪsə'bɪlɪti] *noun* incapacidad *f*; **temporary disability** = incapacidad transitoria; **total disability** = incapacidad total

disallow ['dɪsə'lau] *verb* denegar *or* rechazar *or* prohibir; **he claimed £2,000 for fire damage, but the claim was disallowed** = reclamó £2.000 en concepto de daños por incendio, pero la reclamación fue denegada

disappoint [dɪsə'pɔɪnt] *verb* defraudar; **he was disappointed with the company's results** = estaba defraudato por los resultados de la compañía

disaster [dɪ'zɑːstə] *noun* **(a)** *(bad accident)* desastre *m*; **ten people died in the air disaster** = diez personas murieron en el desastre aéreo **(b)** *(financial)* quiebra *f*; **the company is heading for disaster** *or* **is on a disaster course** = la compañía va a la ruina; **the advertising campaign was a disaster** = la campaña de publicidad fue un desastre **(c)** *(natural accident)* desastre *or* catástrofe *f or* siniestro *m*; **a storm disaster on the south coast** = desastre provocado por una tormenta en la costa sur; **flood disaster damage** = daños debidos a una inundación catastrófica

◇ **disastrous** [dɪ'zɑːstrəs] *adjective* desastroso, -sa; **the company suffered a disastrous drop in sales** = la empresa sufrió una caída desastrosa de las ventas

disburse [dɪs'bɜːs] *verb* desembolsar

◇ **disbursement** [dɪs'bɜːsmənt] *noun* desembolso *m*

discharge [dɪs'tʃɑːdʒ] **1** *noun* **(a) discharge in bankruptcy** = rehabilitación de quiebra **(b)** *(payment of debt)* pago *m or* reembolso *m*; **in full discharge of a debt** = en pago total de una deuda; **final discharge** = reembolso final **(c) in discharge of his duties as director** = en el cumplimiento de sus funciones como director **2** *verb* **(a) to discharge a bankrupt** = rehabilitar a un quebrado **(b) to discharge a debt** *or* **to discharge one's liabilities** = pagar una deuda *or* cumplir uno sus obligaciones **(c)** *(to dismiss)* despedir; **to discharge an employee** = despedir a un empleado

disciplinary procedure [dɪsɪ'plɪnəri prə'siːdʒə] *noun* procedimiento disciplinario

disclaimer [dɪs'kleɪmə] *noun* **(a)** *(legal refusal)* renuncia *f or* abandono *m or* negativa *f* a aceptar una responsabilidad **(b)** *(in a contract)* cláusula de renuncia de responsabilidad

disclose [dɪs'kləuz] *verb* revelar; **the bank has no right to disclose details of my account to the tax office** = el banco no tiene derecho a revelar los detalles de mi cuenta a la delegación de Hacienda

◇ **disclosure** [dɪs'kləuʒə] *noun* divulgación *f or* revelación *f*; **the disclosure of the takeover bid raised the price of the shares** = la divulgación de la

oferta de adquisición hizo subir el precio de las acciones

discontinue ['dɪskən'tɪnjuː] *verb* suspender *or* interrumpir (la venta *or* fabricación); **these carpets are a discontinued line** = estas alfombras ya no se fabrican

discount ['dɪskaunt] **1** *noun* **(a)** *(price reduction)* descuento *m or* bonificación *f*; **to give a discount on bulk purchases** = ofrecer un descuento por las ventas al por mayor *or* en grandes cantidades; **to sell goods at a discount** *or* **at a discount price** = vender mercancías con descuento; **basic discount** = descuento básico; **we give 25% as a basic discount, but can add 5% for cash payment** = ofrecemos un 25% de descuento básico, pero podemos añadir un 5% por pago en efectivo; **bulk discount** *or* **quantity discount** *or* **volume discount** = descuento por cantidad; **10% discount for quantity purchases** = descuento de un 10% por compras en grandes cantidades; **10% discount for cash** *or* **10% cash discount** = un 10% de descuento por pago al contado; **trade discount** = descuento para comerciantes del sector **(b) discount house** = *GB* banco de descuentos; *US* almacén de descuento (al por mayor) *or* tienda de rebajas; **discount price** = precio de descuento; **discount rate** = tipo de descuento; **discount store** = almacén de descuento (al por mayor) **(c) shares which stand at a discount** = acciones que se cotizan por debajo de su valor nominal **2** *verb* **(a)** *(sell at a discount)* descontar; **discounted price** = precio descontado *or* rebajado **(b) to discount bills of exchange** = descontar letras de cambio; **to discount invoices** = descontar facturas; **shares are discounting a rise in the dollar** = los precios de las acciones tienen en cuenta una posible subida del dólar; **discounted value** = valor descontado

◇ **discountable** [dɪs'kauntəbl] *adjective* descontable; **these bills are not discountable** = estas letras no pueden presentarse al descuento

◇ **discounted cash flow (DCF)** [dɪs'kauntɪd 'kæʃfləu] *noun* 'cash flow' actualizado *or* flujo de caja descontado

COMMENT: Discounting cash flow is necessary because it is generally accepted that money held today is worth more than money to be received in the future. The effect of discounting is to reduce future income or expenses to their 'present value'. Once discounted, future cash flows can be compared directly with the initial cost of a capital investment which is already stated in present value terms. If the present value of income is greater than the present value of costs the investment can be said to be worthwhile

◇ **discounter** [dɪs'kauntə] *noun* banco de descuentos *or* almacén de descuento (al por mayor)

QUOTE pressure on the Federal Reserve Board to ease monetary policy and possibly cut its discount rate mounted yesterday
Financial Times

QUOTE banks refrained from quoting forward US/Hongkong dollar exchange rates as premiums of 100 points replaced the previous day's discounts of up to 50 points
South China Morning Post

QUOTE a 100,000 square-foot warehouse generates ten times the volume of a discount retailer; it can turn its inventory over 18 times a year, more than triple a big discounter's turnover
Duns Business Month

QUOTE invoice discounting is an instant finance raiser. Cash is advanced by a factor or discounter against the value of invoices sent out by the client company. Debt collection is still in the hands of the client company, which also continues to run its own bought ledger
Times

discover [dɪs'kʌvə] *verb* descubrir *or* enterarse; **we discovered that our agent was selling our rival's products at the same price as ours** = nos enteramos de que nuestro agente vendía los productos de nuestro competidor al mismo precio que los nuestros; **the auditors discovered some errors in the accounts** = los auditores descubrieron algunos errores en las cuentas

discredit [dɪs'kredɪt] *verb* desautorizar *or* desacreditar

discrepancy [dɪs'krepənsi] *noun* discrepancia *f or* diferencia *f*; **there is a discrepancy in the accounts** = hay una discrepancia en las cuentas; **statistical discrepancy** = discrepancia estadística

discretion [dɪs'kreʃən] *noun* discreción *f*; **I leave it to your discretion** = se lo dejo a su discreción; **at the discretion of someone** = a discreción de alguien; **membership is at the discretion of the committee** = la afiliación es a discreción del comité

◊ **discretionary** [dɪs'kreʃənəri] *adjective* **(a)** discrecional; **the minister's discretionary powers** = los poderes discrecionales del ministro **(b)** *(stockbroking)* **discretionary account** = cuenta discrecional; **on a discretionary basis** = a discreción

discrimination [dɪskrɪmɪ'neɪʃən] *noun* discriminación *f*; **sexual discrimination** *or* **sex discrimination** *or* **discrimination on grounds of sex** = discriminación sexual

discuss [dɪs'kʌs] *verb* discutir *or* tratar *or* hablar de; **they spent two hours discussing the details of the contract** = se pasaron dos horas hablando de los detalles del contrato; **the committee discussed the question of import duties on cars** = el comité trató la cuestión de los derechos de importación de los automóviles; **the board will discuss wage rises at its next meeting** = la junta directiva discutirá el aumento de salarios en la próxima reunión; **we discussed delivery schedules with our suppliers** = hablamos de los plazos de entrega con nuestros proveedores

◊ **discussion** [dɪs'kʌʃən] *noun* discusión *f or* debate *m*; **after ten minutes' discussion the board agreed the salary increases** = tras un debate de diez minutos el consejo de administración aceptó los aumentos salariales; **we spent the whole day in discussions with our suppliers** = nos pasamos el día entero hablando con nuestros suministradores

diseconomies of scale [dɪsiː'kɒnəmiːz əv 'skeɪl] *noun* deseconomías *fpl* de escala

COMMENT: the situation where increased production actually increases unit cost. After having increased production using the existing workforce and machinery, giving economies of scale, the company finds that in order to increase production further it has to employ more workers and buy more machinery, leading to an increase in unit cost

disembark [dɪsɪm'bɑːk] *verb* desembarcar

◊ **disembarkation** [dɪsɪmbɑː'keɪʃn] *noun* desembarque *m or* desembarco *m*; **disembarkation card** = tarjeta de desembarque

disenfranchise [dɪsɪn'fræn(t)ʃaɪz] *verb* privar del derecho de voto; **the company has tried to disenfranchise the ordinary shareholders** = la compañía ha intentado privar a los accionistas ordinarios del derecho de voto

dishonour *or US* **dishonor** [dɪs'ɒnə] *verb* deshonrar *or* negarse a aceptar *or* a pagar; **to dishonour a bill** = devolver una letra *or* incumplir el pago de una letra; **dishonoured cheque** = cheque no pagado por el banco por falta de fondos

disinflation [dɪsɪn'fleɪʃən] *noun* desinflación *f*

disinvest ['dɪsɪn'vest] *verb* desinvertir

◊ **disinvestment** ['dɪsɪn'vestmənt] *noun* desinversión *f*

disk [dɪsk] *noun* disco *m*; **floppy disk** = disco flexible *or* diskette *or* 'floppy'; **hard disk** = disco duro; **disk drive** = disquetera *f*

◊ **diskette** [dɪs'ket] *noun* disquete *or* diskette *m*

dismantle [dɪs'mæntəl] *verb* desmontar; **she had to help them dismantle the exhibition** = tuvo que ayudarles a desmontar la exposición

dismiss [dɪs'mɪs] *verb* despedir; **to dismiss an employee** = despedir a un empleado; **he was dismissed for being late** = fue despedido por llegar tarde

◊ **dismissal** [dɪs'mɪsəl] *noun* despido *m*; **constructive dismissal** = dimisión bajo presión de la dirección; **unfair dismissal** = despido injusto; **wrongful dismissal** = despido injusto; **dismissal procedures** = expediente de despido

dispatch [dɪs'pætʃ] **1** *noun* **(a)** *(action)* despacho *m or* envío *m*; **the strike held up dispatch for several weeks** = la huelga retrasó el envío unas cuantas semanas; **dispatch department** = oficina de expedición *or* de envío; **dispatch note** = nota de envío *or* de expedición; **dispatch rider** = mensajero, -ra **(b)** *(things sent)* envío; **the weekly dispatch went off yesterday** = el envío semanal salió ayer **2** *verb* enviar *or* consignar *or* despachar *or* expedir; **your order has been noted and will be dispatched as soon as we have stock** = hemos tomado nota de su pedido y lo despacharemos en cuanto tengamos existencias

◊ **dispatcher** [dɪs'pætʃə] *noun* **(a)** *(sender of goods)* expedidor, -ra **(b)** *(person who schedules routes of taxis, buses) US* responsable de la organización de rutas y horarios de transporte

◊ **dispatching** [dɪs'pætʃɪŋ] *noun* distribución *f or* expedición *f or* despacho *m* (de las mercancías)

dispenser [dɪs'pensə] *noun* distribuidor *m* automático *or* máquina *f* expendedora; **automatic**

dispenser = distribuidor automático; **towel dispenser** = distribuidor de toallas; **cash dispenser** = cajero automático

display [dɪs'pleɪ] **1** *noun* exposición *f or* exhibición *f*; **the shop has several car models on display** = la tienda tiene varios modelos de automóviles expuestos; **an attractive display of kitchen equipment** = una exposición atractiva de aparatos de cocina; **display advertisement** *or* **display ad** = pancarta publicitaria; **display cabinet** *or* **display case** = vitrina *f*; **display material** = material de exposición; **display pack** *or* **display box** = embalaje de exposición; **the watches are prepacked in plastic display boxes** = los relojes se presentan empaquetados en cajas de exposición de plástico; **display stand** *or* **display unit** = estantería *f or* vitrina *f* de exposición; **visual display unit (VDU)** *or* **visual display terminal** = unidad de representación visual **2** *verb* exhibir *or* exponer; mostrar; **the company was displaying three new car models at the show** = la empresa exponía tres nuevos modelos en el Salón del Automóvil

dispose [dɪs'pəʊz] *verb* **to dispose of** = deshacerse de *or* vender; **to dispose of excess stock** = deshacerse de *or* vender las existencias sobrantes; **to dispose of one's business** = vender el negocio propio

◊ **disposable** [dɪs'pəʊzəbl] *adjective* **(a)** *(throw away)* desechable *or* de usar y tirar; **disposable cups** = tazas desechables **(b)** *(available)* **disposable personal income** = renta personal disponible

◊ **disposal** [dɪs'pəʊzəl] *noun* venta *f*; **disposal of securities** *or* **of property** = venta de títulos *or* de propiedad; **lease** *or* **business for disposal** = arrendamiento *or* negocio en venta

dispute [dɪs'pjuːt] **1** *noun* **industrial disputes** *or* **labour disputes** = conflictos laborales; **to adjudicate** *or* **to mediate in a dispute** = actuar de juez *or* mediar en un conflicto **2** *verb* disputar *or* cuestionar; **he disputed the bill** = disputó la cuenta

disqualify [dɪs'kwɒlɪfaɪ] *verb* descalificar

◊ **disqualification** [dɪskwɒlɪfɪ'keɪʃn] *noun* descalificación *f*

QUOTE Even 'administrative offences' can result in disqualification. A person may be disqualified for up to five years following persistent breach of company legislation in terms of failing to file returns, accounts and other documents with the Registrar

Accountancy

dissolve [dɪ'zɒlv] *verb* disolver; **to dissolve a partnership** *or* **a company** = disolver una sociedad *or* una compañía

◊ **dissolution** [dɪsə'luːʃn] *noun* disolución *f or* liquidación *f*

distrain [dɪ'streɪn] *verb* **to distrain on someone's goods** = embargar a alguien

distress [dɪ'stres] *noun* embargo *m*; *US* **distress merchandise** = efectos *mpl* embargados vendidos a bajo precio; **distress prices** = precios de saldo *or* irrisorios; **distress sale** = venta forzosa *or* remate; **distress warrant** = orden de embargo

distribute [dɪ'strɪbjuːt] *verb* **(a)** *(share out)* distribuir *or* repartir; **profits were distributed among the shareholders** = los beneficios fueron repartidos entre los accionistas **(b)** *(deliver)* distribuir *or* repartir; **Smith Ltd distributes for several smaller companies** = Smith Ltd es la distribuidora de varias pequeñas empresas

◊ **distributable** [dɪ'strɪbjuːtəbl] *adjective* distribuible; **distributable profit** = beneficios distribuibles

◊ **distribution** [dɪstrɪ'bjuːʃn] *noun* **(a)** distribución *f or* reparto *m*; **distribution costs** = costes de distribución; **distribution manager** = jefe de distribución; **channels of distribution** *or* **distribution channels** = canales de distribución; **distribution network** = red de distribución **(b)** **distribution slip** = lista *or* nota de distribución

◊ **distributive** [dɪ'strɪbjʊtɪv] *adjective* distributivo, -va; **distributive trades** = comercios de repartimiento

◊ **distributor** [dɪ'strɪbjʊtə] *noun* distribuidor, -ra; **exclusive distributor** *or* **sole distributor** = distribuidor exclusivo; **a network of distributors** = una red de distribuidores

◊ **distributorship** [dɪ'strɪbjʊtəʃɪp] *noun* distribución *f* exclusiva

district ['dɪstrɪkt] *noun* distrito *m or* región *f*; **district manager** = director regional; **the commercial district** *or* **the business district** = el centro comercial

ditto = THE SAME

diversification [daɪvɜːsɪfɪ'keɪʃn] *noun* diversificación *f*; **product diversification** *or* **diversification into new products** = diversificación de productos

◊ **diversify** [daɪ'vɜːsɪfaɪ] *verb* **(a)** *(business)* diversificar; **to diversify into new products** = diversificarse hacia nuevos produtos **(b)** *(investments)* invertir en distintos tipos de activo para reducir el riesgo

diversion [daɪ'vɜːʃn] *noun* desviación *f*

divest [daɪ'vest] *verb* **to divest oneself of something** = vender *or* deshacerse; **the company had divested itself of its US interests** = la compañía se deshizo de sus bienes en los Estados Unidos

divide [dɪ'vaɪd] *verb* dividir *or* compartir; **the country is divided into six sales areas** = el país está dividido en seis áreas de venta; **the two companies agreed to divide the market between them** = las dos empresas acordaron repartirse el mercado entre ellas

dividend ['dɪvɪdend] *noun* dividendo *m*; **to raise** *or* **to increase the dividend** = aumentar el dividendo; **to maintain the dividend** = mantener el dividendo; **to pass the dividend** = no declarar dividendo; **final dividend** = dividendo final; **forecast dividend** *or* **prospective dividend** = dividendo pronosticado; **interim dividend** = dividendo provisional; **dividend cover** = cobertura del dividendo; **the dividend is covered four times** = el dividendo está cubierto cuatro veces por las ganancias; **dividend forecast** = pronóstico del dividendo; **dividend warrant** = cheque en pago de dividendos; **dividend yield** = rentabilidad del dividendo; **cum dividend** = con dividendo; **ex dividend** = sin dividendo; **the shares are quoted ex dividend** = las acciones se cotizan sin dividendo

divider [dɪ'vaɪdə] *noun* **room divider** = pared *f* divisoria

division [dɪ'vɪʒən] *noun* **(a)** *(part of company)* departamento *m or* sección *f or* rama *f*; **marketing division** = sección *or* departamento de marketing *or* comercialización; **production division** = departamento de producción; **retail division** = sección de ventas al por menor; **the paints division** *or* **the hotel division of a large company** = la sección de pinturas *or* la rama hotelera de una gran compañía; **he is in charge of one of the major divisions of the company** = es jefe de una de las mayores secciones de la compañía **(b)** *(company which is part of a large group)* división *f or* sucursal *f*; **Smith's is now a division of the Brown group of companies** = Smith's es ahora una división del grupo de compañías Brown

◊ **divisional** [dɪ'vɪʒənl] *adjective* divisional *or* de sección *or* de ramo *or* de departamento; **a divisional director** = un director de sección; **the divisional headquarters** = la sede de la división

DIY [ˈdiːaɪˈwaɪ] = DO-IT-YOURSELF

DM *or* **D-mark** = DEUTSCHMARK, MARK

do *or* **ditto** = THE SAME

do [duː] *verb* hacer; **to do something again** = volver a hacer algo; **to do someone a service** = prestar un servicio

dock [dɒk] **1** *noun* muelle *m or* dique *m or* 'dock' *m*; **loading dock** = muelle de carga; **a dock worker** = trabajador portuario; **the dock manager** = el director del puerto; **the docks** = el puerto; **dock dues** = derechos de dársena **2** *verb* **(a)** *(of ship)* entrar en dársena *or* atracar; **the ship docked at 17.00** = el barco atracó a las 17.00 **(b)** *(remove money)* deducir *or* descontar algo del sueldo; **we will have to dock his pay if he is late for work again** = tendremos que deducirle algo del sueldo si llega de nuevo tarde al trabajo; **he had £20 docked from his pay for being late** = le dedujeron £20 del sueldo por llegar tarde

◊ **docker** [ˈdɒkə] *noun* trabajador *m* portuario

◊ **dockyard** [ˈdɒkjɑːd] *noun* astillero *m*

docket [ˈdɒkɪt] *noun* lista *f* del contenido de un paquete

doctor [ˈdɒktə] *noun* médico *mf*; **the staff are all sent to see the company doctor once a year** = todo el personal está obligado a ir al médico de la empresa una vez al año; **doctor's certificate** = parte *m* de baja; **he has been off sick for ten days and still has not sent in a doctor's certificate** = ha estado enfermo en casa durante diez días y todavía no ha enviado el parte de baja; **company doctor** = médico de empresa; *(person who rescues companies)* empresario que se especializa en rescatar compañías en dificultades

document [ˈdɒkjʊmənt] *noun* documento *m*; **legal document** = documento legal; **documents** = expediente *m*

◊ **documentary** [dɒkjʊˈmentəri] *adjective* documental; **documentary evidence** = pruebas

documentales; **documentary proof** = prueba documental

◊ **documentation** [dɒkjʊmenˈteɪʃən] *noun* documentación *f*; **please send me the complete documentation concerning the sale** = sírvase enviarme la documentación completa referente a la venta

DoE = DEPARTMENT OF EMPLOYMENT

dog [dɒg] *noun* *(informal)* *(product that doesn't sell)* artículo *m* invendible

dogsbody [ˈdɒgzbɒdi] *noun* *(informal)* chico, -ca para todo *or* burro de carga *or* mulo de carga

do-it-yourself (DIY) [ˈduːɪtjəˈself] **1** *adjective* hágalo Vd. mismo; **do-it-yourself conveyancing** = redacción del documento de transmisión de la propiedad sin participación de un abogado **2** *noun* bricolaje *m*; **do-it-yourself (DIY) magazine** = revista de bricolaje; **do-it-yourself (DIY) store** = tienda *or* almacén de bricolaje

dole [dəʊl] *noun* subsidio *m* de paro; **to be on the dole** = cobrar el paro *or* cobrar el desempleo; **he is receiving dole payments** *or* **he is on the dole** = está cobrando el subsidio de paro; **dole queue** = cola para cobrar el subsidio de paro

dollar [ˈdɒlə] *noun* **(a)** dólar *m*; **the US dollar rose 2%** = el dólar norteamericano subió el 2%; **fifty Canadian dollars** = cincuenta dólares canadienses; **it costs six Australian dollars** = vale seis dólares australianos; **five dollar bill** = billete de cinco dólares **(b)** *(specifically, the US dollar)* dólar (norteamericano); **dollar area** = zona del dólar; **dollar balances** = reservas en dólares que tiene un país; **dollar crisis** = crisis del dólar; **dollar gap** *or* **dollar shortage** = déficit de dólares *or* escasez de dólares; **dollar stocks** = acciones en sociedades estadounidenses (NOTE: usually written $ before a figure: **$250**. The currencies used in different countries can be shown by the initial letter of the country: **C$** (Canadian dollar) **A$** (Australian dollar), etc.)

domestic [dəˈmestɪk] *adjective* interior *or* nacional; **domestic sales** = ventas nacionales; **domestic turnover** = volumen de ventas nacionales; **domestic consumption** = consumo interior; **domestic consumption of oil has fallen sharply** = el consumo interior de petróleo ha caído estrepitosamente; **domestic market** = mercado interior *or* nacional; **they produce goods for the domestic market** = producen mercancías para el mercado nacional; **domestic production** = producción interior *or* nacional; **domestic trade** = comercio interior *or* nacional

domicile [ˈdɒmɪsaɪl] **1** *noun* domicilio *m* **2** *verb* **he is domiciled in Denmark** = tiene su domicilio en Dinamarca; **bills domiciled in Spain** = letras domiciliadas en España

Dominican Republic [dɒˈmɪnɪkən rɪˈpʌblɪk] *noun* República Dominicana

◊ **Dominican** [dɒˈmɪnɪkən] *adjective* & *noun* dominicano, -na
NOTE: capital: **Santo Domingo**; currency: **Dominican peso** = peso dominicano

door [dɔː] *noun* puerta *f*; **the finance director knocked on the chairman's door and walked in** =

el director de finanzas llamó a la puerta del presidente y entró; **the sales manager's name is on his door** = el director de ventas tiene su nombre en la puerta; **the store opened its doors on June 1st** = la tienda abrió sus puertas el 1 de junio

◇ **door-to-door** ['dɔ:tə'dɔ:] *adjective* de puerta en puerta; **door-to-door canvassing** = búsqueda de clientes *or* de votos *or* sondeo de opinión de puerta en puerta; **door-to-door salesman** = vendedor a domicilio *or* vendedor de puerta en puerta; **door-to-door selling** = venta domiciliaria

dormant account ['dɔ:mənt ə'kaunt] *noun* cuenta inactiva

dossier ['dɒsɪə] *noun* expediente *m*

dot [dɒt] *noun* punto *m*; **the order form should be cut off along the line shown by the row of dots** = recorte el boletín de pedido por la línea de puntos

◇ **dot-matrix printer** ['dɒt 'meɪtrɪks 'prɪntə] *noun* impresora *f* matricial *or* de matriz de puntos

◇ **dotted line** ['dɒtɪd 'laɪn] *noun* línea *f* de puntos; **please sign on the dotted line** = firme por favor en la línea de puntos; **do not write anything below the dotted line** = no escriba nada por debajo de la línea de puntos

double ['dʌbl] **1** *adjective* **(a)** *(twice as large)* doble; **their turnover is double ours** = el volumen de sus ventas es el doble del nuestro; **to be on double time** = recibir paga doble *or* cobrar tarifa doble por trabajar en días festivos; **double-entry bookkeeping** = contabilidad por partida doble; **double taxation** = doble imposición; **double taxation agreement** = tratado de doble imposición **(b) in double figures** = de dos cifras (de 10 a 99); **inflation is in double figures** = la tasa de inflación es de dos cifras; **we have had double-figure inflation for some years** = hemos experimentado una inflación de dos dígitos durante unos años **2** *verb* duplicar(se) *or* doblar(se); **we have doubled our profits this year** *or* **our profits have doubled this year** = este año hemos duplicado nuestros beneficios *or* nuestros beneficios se han duplicado; **the company's borrowings have doubled** = la deuda de la compañía se ha duplicado

◇ **double-book** ['dʌbl'buk] *verb* reservar la misma plaza a dos personas; **we had to change our flight as we were double-booked** = tuvimos que cambiar de vuelo porque habían reservado nuestra plaza dos veces

◇ **double-booking** ['dʌbl'bukɪŋ] *noun* doble reserva *f*

doubtful ['dautfəl] *adjective* dudoso, -sa; **doubtful debt** = deuda dudosa; **doubtful loan** = préstamo dudoso

Dow Jones Index [,dau 'dʒəunz 'ɪndeks] *noun* índice *m* Dow Jones (de la bolsa neoyorquina)

◇ **Dow Jones (Industrial) Average (DJIA)** ['dau 'dʒəunz ɪn'dʌstrɪəl 'ævrɪdʒ] *noun* índice *m* Dow Jones (de valores industriales); **the Dow Jones Average rose ten points** = el índice Dow Jones subió diez puntos; **general optimism showed in the rise on the Dow Jones Average** = el optimismo general se reflejó en la subida del índice Dow Jones

down [daun] **1** *adverb & preposition* abajo *or* hacia

abajo; **the inflation rate is gradually coming down** = la tasa de inflación está descendiendo gradualmente; **shares are slightly down on the day** = las acciones han bajado un poco durante la jornada de hoy; **the price of petrol has gone down** = el precio de la gasolina ha bajado; **to pay money down** = hacer un depósito *or* dar una entrada; **he paid £50 down and the rest in monthly instalments** = dio una entrada de £50 y pagó el resto en plazos mensuales **2** *verb* **to down tools** = dejar de trabajar

◇ **downgrade** [daun'greɪd] *verb* degradar *or* bajar de categoría laboral; **his job was downgraded in the company reorganization** = degradaron su cargo al reorganizar la empresa

◇ **download** [daun'ləud] *verb* *(data onto a computer)* pasar información de un ordenador a otro o de disco duro a disco blando

◇ **down market** ['daun 'mɑːkɪt] *adverb & adjective* dirigido, -da a un mercado popular; **the company has adopted a down-market image** = la empresa ha adoptado una imagen dirigida a una clientela más modesta; **the company has decided to go down market** = la empresa ha decidido dedicarse a un mercado más popular

◇ **down payment** ['daun 'peɪmənt] *noun* entrada *f* *or* pago *m* inicial; **he made a down payment of $100** = dio una entrada de $100

◇ **downside** ['daunsaɪd] *noun* **downside factor** *or* **downside risk** = factor de riesgo (en una inversión); **the sales force have been asked to give downside forecasts** = se ha pedido al personal de ventas que haga previsiones a la baja; **downside potential** = potencial negativo (NOTE: the opposite is **upside)**

◇ **downsizing** ['daunsaɪzɪŋ] *noun* reducción *f* de plantilla

◇ **down time** ['daun 'taɪm] *noun* tiempo *m* muerto

◇ **downtown** ['dauntaun] *noun & adverb* en el centro de la ciudad *or* hacia el centro; **his office is in downtown Miami** = su oficina está en el centro de Miami; **a downtown store** = una tienda céntrica; **they established a business downtown** = establecieron un negocio en el centro de la ciudad

◇ **downturn** ['dauntɜːn] *noun* descenso *m*; **a downturn in the market price** = un descenso en el precio del mercado; **the last quarter saw a downturn in the economy** = durante el último trimestre la economía tendió a la baja

◇ **downward** ['daunwəd] *adjective* hacia abajo

◇ **downwards** ['daunwədz] *adverb* hacia abajo; **the company's profits have moved downwards over the last few years** = los beneficios de la compañía han descendido a lo largo de los últimos años

dozen ['dʌzn] *noun* docena *f*; **to sell in sets of one dozen** = vender por lotes de una docena; **cheaper by the dozen** = más barato comprando por docenas *or* si se compra en docenas

D/P = DOCUMENTS AGAINST PAYMENT

Dr *or* **DR 1** = DEBTOR **2** = DRACHMA

drachma ['drækmə] *noun* *(currency used in Greece)* dracma *m* (NOTE: usually written **Dr** before a figure: **Dr22bn)**

draft [drɑːft] **1** *noun* **(a)** *(payment)* letra *f or* giro *m*; **banker's draft** = giro bancario; **to make a draft on a bank** = realizar un giro bancario; **sight draft** = giro a la vista **(b)** *(rough plan)* borrador *m or* proyecto *m*; **draft of a contract** *or* **draft contract** = borrador de un contrato; **he drew up the draft agreement on the back of an envelope** = redactó el proyecto del acuerdo al dorso de un sobre; **the first draft of the contract was corrected by the managing director** = el primer borrador del contrato fue corregido por el director gerente; **the finance department has passed the final draft of the accounts** = el departamento de finanzas ha aprobado la versión final de las cuentas; **draft plan** = anteproyecto *m*; **rough draft** = bosquejo *m or* borrador *m* **2** *verb* hacer un borrador *or* redactar *or* preparar; **to draft a letter** = redactar una carta; **to draft a contract** = redactar un contrato; **the contract is still being drafted** *or* **is still in the drafting stage** = el contrato está todavía en preparación

◊ **drafter** ['drɑːftə] *noun* redactor, -ra; **the drafter of the agreement** = la redactora del documento

◊ **drafting** ['drɑːftɪŋ] *noun (document)* redacción *f*; *(plan)* preparación *f*; **the drafting of the contract took six weeks** = la preparación del contrato duró seis semanas

drain [dreɪn] **1** *noun* **(a)** *(pipe)* desagüe *m* **(b)** *(of money)* sangría *f*; **the costs of the London office are a continual drain on our resources** = los costes de la oficina de Londres son una sangría continua de nuestros recursos **2** *verb* agotar *or* consumir; **the expansion plan has drained all our profits** = el plan de expansión ha consumido todos nuestros beneficios; **the company's capital resources have drained away** = los recursos de capital de la compañía se han agotado

draw [drɔː] *verb* **(a)** *(money)* sacar; **to draw money out of an account** = sacar dinero de una cuenta; **to draw a salary** = cobrar un sueldo; **the chairman does not draw a salary** = el presidente no cobra sueldo **(b)** *(cheque)* girar; **he paid the invoice with a cheque drawn on an Egyptian bank** = pagó la factura con un cheque librado contra un banco egipcio (NOTE: **drawing - drew - has drawn**)

◊ **drawback** ['drɔːbæk] *noun* **(a)** *(likely to cause problems)* desventaja *f or* inconveniente *m*; **one of the main drawbacks of the scheme is that it will take six years to complete** = uno de los inconvenientes del plan es que se necesitarán seis años para llevarlo a cabo **(b)** *(of customs dues)* reintegro *m* de derechos de aduana por reexportación

◊ **draw down** ['drɔː 'daʊn] *verb (under a credit agreement)* sacar dinero a crédito

◊ **drawee** [drɔː'iː] *noun* librado, -da

◊ **drawer** ['drɔːə] *noun* librador, -ra; **the bank returned the cheque to drawer** = el banco devolvió el cheque al librador

◊ **drawing** ['drɔːɪŋ] *noun* **(a)** **drawing account** = cuenta corriente; *(IMF)* **special drawing rights (SDR)** = derechos especiales de giro (DEG) **(b)** **drawing pin** = chincheta *f*; **she used drawing pins to pin the poster to the door** = utilizó chinchetas para colgar el póster en la puerta

◊ **draw up** ['drɔː 'ʌp] *verb* preparar *or* redactar; **to**

draw up a contract *or* **an agreement** = redactar un contrato *or* un convenio; **to draw up a company's articles of association** = redactar los estatutos de asociación de una compañía

drift [drɪft] *verb* moverse lentamente *or* sin rumbo; **drifting** = sin rumbo; **shares drifted lower in a dull market** = el precio de las acciones bajó ligeramente en un mercado poco activo; **strikers are drifting back to work** = los huelguistas están volviendo al trabajo poco a poco

drive [draɪv] **1** *noun* **(a)** *(energy)* energía *f or* impulso *m or* empuje *m*; **economy drive** = campaña para reducir gastos; **sales drive** = promoción de ventas; **he has a lot of drive** = tiene mucho empuje **(b)** *(part of machine)* motor *m*; *(on computer)* **disk drive** = disquetera *f* **2** *verb* **(a)** conducir; **he was driving to work when he heard the news on the car radio** = se dirigía al trabajo en coche cuando oyó las noticias por la radio; **she drives a company car** = conduce un coche de la empresa **(b)** **he drives a hard bargain** = es un duro negociador *or* es difícil cerrar un trato con él (NOTE: **driving - drove - has driven**)

◊ **driver** ['draɪvə] *noun* conductor *m or* chófer *m*

drop [drɒp] **1** *noun (fall)* caída *f or* baja *f*; **drop in sales** = una disminución de las ventas; **sales show a drop of 10%** = las ventas han disminuido en un 10%; **a drop in prices** = una caída de los precios **2** *verb* **(a)** *(to fall)* descender *or* bajar *or* caer; **sales have dropped by 10%** *or* **have dropped 10%** = las ventas han bajado un 10%; **the pound dropped three points against the dollar** = la libra ha bajado tres puntos con respecto al dólar **(b)** *(not to keep in a product range)* abandonar *or* discontinuar *or* suprimir; **we have dropped these items from the catalogue because they've been losing sales steadily for some time** = hemos suprimido estos artículos del catálogo porque se venden poco desde hace tiempo (NOTE: **dropping - dropped**)

◊ **drop ship** ['drɒp 'ʃɪp] *verb* proveer directamente

◊ **drop shipment** ['drɒp 'ʃɪpmənt] *noun* envío directo

QUOTE while unemployment dropped by 1.6 per cent in the rural areas, it rose by 1.9 per cent in urban areas during the period under review
Business Times (Lagos)

QUOTE corporate profits for the first quarter showed a 4 per cent drop from last year's final three months
Financial Times

QUOTE since last summer American interest rates have dropped by between three and four percentage points
Sunday Times

drug [drʌg] *noun* medicamento *m or* medicina *f*; **a drug on the market** = producto con mercado saturado

dry [draɪ] *adjective* seco, -ca; *US* **dry goods** = artículos de mercería; **dry measure** = medida de áridos

DTI [diːtiː'aɪ] = DEPARTMENT OF TRADE AND INDUSTRY

DTP = DESK-TOP PUBLISHING

duck [dʌk] *see* LAME DUCK

dud [dʌd] *adjective & noun (informal)* falso, -sa; **the £50 note was a dud** = el billete de £50 era falso; **dud cheque** = cheque sin fondos

due [dju:] *adjective* **(a)** *(owed)* vencido, -da *or* por pagar; **sum due from a debtor** = monto *or* cantidad a pagar por un deudor; **bond due for repayment** = obligación que ha llegado a su vencimiento; **to fall due** *or* **to become due** = vencer; **bill due on May 1st** = letra que vence el 1 de mayo; **balance due to us** = saldo a nuestro favor **(b)** *(expected)* esperado, -da *or* que debe llegar; **the plane is due to arrive at 10.30** *or* **is due at 10.30** = el avión debe llegar a las 10.30 **(c)** *(proper)* **in due form** = en buena y debida forma; **receipt in due form** = factura conforme; **contract drawn up in due form** = contrato redactado en la debida forma; **after due consideration of the problem** = después de considerar la cuestión debidamente **(d)** *(caused by)* **supplies have been delayed due to a strike at the manufacturers** = los suministros se han retrasado debido a una huelga en la fábrica; **the company pays the wages of staff who are absent due to illness** = la empresa paga el sueldo del personal que está de baja por enfermedad

◊ **dues** [dju:z] *plural noun* **(a)** *(regular payments)* **dock dues** *or* **port dues** *or* **harbour dues** = derechos *mpl* de dársena *or* portuarios; **union dues** = cuota *f* de inscripción sindical **(b)** *(back orders)* pedidos *mpl* por servir; **to release dues** = despachar pedidos pendientes

dull [dʌl] *adjective* inactivo, -va; **dull market** = mercado inactivo

◊ **dullness** ['dʌlnəs] *noun* inactividad *f*; **the dullness of the market** = la inactividad del mercado

duly ['dju:li] *adverb* **(a)** *(properly)* debidamente; **duly authorized representative** = representante debidamente autorizado **(b)** *(as expected)* oportunamente; **we duly received his letter of 21st October** = hemos recibido oportunamente su carta del 21 de octubre

dummy ['dʌmi] *noun* producto *m* ficticio *or* imitación *f*; **dummy corporation** *or* **firm** = /T empresa fantasma **dummy pack** = embalaje vacío para exposición

dump [dʌmp] *verb* verter *or* descargar; **to dump goods on a market** = practicar el 'dumping' *or* vender en el extranjero a un precio inferior al coste de producción

◊ **dump bin** ['dʌmp 'bɪn] *noun* caja *f* de artículos sueltos para la venta

◊ **dumping** ['dʌmpɪŋ] *noun* 'dumping' *m*; **the government has passed anti-dumping legislation** = el gobierno ha promulgado una ley 'anti-dumping'; **dumping of goods on the European market** = el 'dumping' de productos en el mercado europeo; **panic dumping of sterling** = venta apresurada de la libra esterlina a bajo precio ante una posible devaluación

Dun & Bradstreet (D&B) ['dʌn ən 'brædstri:t] *(organization which produces reports on the financial rating of companies)* organización que produce informes sobre la posición *or* categoría financiera de las compañías

duplicate 1 ['dju:plɪkət] *noun* duplicado *m or* copia *f*; **he sent me the duplicate of the contract** = me envió la copia del contrato; **duplicate receipt** *or* **duplicate of a receipt** = factura por duplicado *or* duplicado de una factura; **in duplicate** = por duplicado; **receipt in duplicate** = recibo por duplicado; **to print an invoice in duplicate** = imprimir una factura por duplicado 2 ['dju:plɪkeɪt] *verb* **(a)** *(bookkeeping)* **to duplicate with another** = hacer un asiento doble **(b)** **to duplicate an invoice** = copiar una factura

◊ **duplicating** ['dju:plɪkeɪtɪŋ] *noun* duplicación *f*; **duplicating machine** = multicopista *f*; **duplicating paper** = papel de multicopista

◊ **duplication** [dju:plɪ'keɪʃən] *noun* duplicación *f*; **duplication of work** = duplicación del trabajo

◊ **duplicator** ['dju:plɪkeɪtə] *noun* multicopista *f*

durable ['djʊərəbl] **1** *adjective* **durable goods** = bienes duraderos; **durable effects** = consecuencias persistentes; **the strike will have durable effects on the economy** = la huelga tendrá consecuencias persistentes para la economía **2** *noun* **consumer durables** = bienes *mpl* de consumo duraderos *or* artículos *mpl* de equipo

dust cover ['dʌst 'kʌvə] *noun* funda *f or* guardapolvo *m*

Dutch [dʌtʃ] **1** *adjective* holandés, -esa; **Dutch auction** = subasta a la baja; **to go Dutch** = pagar su parte *or* compartir la cuenta **2** *plural noun* **the Dutch** = los holandeses

dutiable ['dju:tjəbl] *adjective* **dutiable goods** *or* **dutiable items** = bienes sujetos a derechos de aduana

◊ **duty** ['dju:ti] *noun* **(a)** *(tax)* derechos *mpl* de aduana *or* impuestos *mpl*; **to take the duty off alcohol** = suprimir los impuestos sobre el alcohol; **to put a duty on cigarettes** = gravar el tabaco con un impuesto; **ad valorem duty** = derechos ad valorem; **customs duty** *or* **import duty** = derechos de aduana *or* aranceles *or* derechos de importación; **excise duty** = impuesto sobre el consumo; **goods which are liable to duty** = productos sujetos a derechos de aduana *or* a impuestos; **duty-paid goods** = mercancías con derechos de aduana *or* impuestos pagados; **stamp duty** = derecho *or* impuesto del timbre; **estate duty** *or* US **death duty** = derechos de sucesión *or* impuesto sobre la herencia **(b)** *(work)* obligación *f or* deber *m or* servicio *m*; **night duty** = guardia *or* turno de noche; **to be on duty** = estar de servicio; **duties** = funciones *fpl or* responsabilidad *f*

◊ **duty-free** ['dju:tɪ'fri:] *adjective & adverb* libre de derechos de aduana *or* de impuestos; **he bought a duty-free watch at the airport** *or* **he bought the**

watch duty-free = compró un reloj libre de impuestos en el aeropuerto *or* compró el reloj libre de impuestos; **duty-free shop** = tienda libre de impuestos

QUOTE Canadian and European negotiators agreed to a deal under which Canada could lower its import duties on $150 million worth of European goods
Globe and Mail (Toronto)

QUOTE the Department of Customs and Excise collected a total of N79m under the new advance duty payment scheme
Business Times (Lagos)

dynamic [daɪˈnæmɪk] *adjective* dinámico, -ca

Ee

e.& o.e. = = ERRORS AND OMISSIONS EXCEPTED s.e.u.o.

eager ['i:gə] *adjective* ansioso, -sa *or* deseoso, -sa *or* impaciente; **the management is eager to get into the Far Eastern markets** = la dirección está deseosa de introducirse en los mercados de Extremo Oriente; **our salesmen are eager to see the new product range** = nuestros vendedores están ansiosos por ver la nueva gama de productos

early ['ɜ:li] **1** *adjective* **(a)** *(before the usual time)* temprano, -na *or* pronto, -ta; **early closing day** = día en que las tiendas cierran por la tarde; **at your earliest convenience** = a la mayor brevedad; **at an early date** = muy pronto *or* en fecha próxima; **early retirement** = jubilación anticipada *or* prematura; **to take early retirement** = jubilarse anticipadamente *or* prematuramente; **early withdrawal** = retirada de fondos anticipada **(b)** *(at the beginning of a period of time)* pronto *or* temprano; **he took an early flight to Paris** = cogió un vuelo que salía temprano para París; **we hope for an early resumption of negotiations** = esperamos que las negociaciones se reanuden pronto **2** *adverb* temprano *or* pronto *or* al principio de *or* a principios de; **the mail left early** = el correo salió temprano; **he retired early and bought a house in Cornwall** = se jubiló con anticipación y compró una casa en Cornualles

earmark ['ɪəmɑ:k] *verb* afectar *or* asignar *or* destinar *or* reservar; **to earmark funds for a project** = asignar fondos a un proyecto; **the grant is earmarked for computer systems development** = la beca está destinada al desarrollo de sistemas informáticos

earn [ɜ:n] *verb* **(a)** *(money)* ganar *or* percibir; **to earn £50 a week** = ganar £50 a la semana; **our agent in Paris certainly does not earn his commission** = nuestro representante en Paris no se gana su comisión de ninguna manera; **earned income** = renta percibida *or* ingresos **(b)** *(interest)* devengar intereses *or* dividendos; **what level of dividend do these shares earn?** = ¿qué clase de dividendos devengan estas acciones?; **account which earns interest at 10%** = cuenta que devenga un interés del 10%

◊ **earning** ['ɜ:nɪŋ] *noun* ganancia *f or* rendimiento *m*; **earning capacity** *or* **earning power** = capacidad *f* de ganar dinero *or* de rentabilidad *f* económica *or* escala *f* de rendimiento; **he is such a fine designer that his earning power is very large** = es tan buen diseñador que puede ganar mucho dinero; **earning potential** = potencial *m* de rentabilidad

◊ **earnings** ['ɜ:nɪŋz] *plural noun* **(a)** *(salary)* sueldo *m or* ingresos *mpl or* ganancias *fpl or* beneficios *mpl*; **compensation for loss of earnings** = indemnización por pérdida de ingresos; **invisible earnings** = ingresos por operaciones invisibles; **earnings-related pension** = pensión proporcional al sueldo *or* calculada en función de la renta **(b)** *(interest)* dividendos *mpl or* beneficios *mpl or* rendimiento *m*; **earnings per share** *or* **earnings yield** = dividendo por acción *or* porcentaje que supone el dividendo con respecto al precio de

mercado de la acción; **gross earnings** = ingresos brutos *or* renta bruta; **retained earnings** = beneficios no distribuidos *or* utilidades acumuladas

◊ **price/earnings ratio (P/E ratio)** ['preɪs 'ɜ:nɪŋz 'reɪʃɪəʊ] *noun* relación *f* precio-beneficios; **these shares sell at a P/E ratio of 7** = estas acciones se venden a una relación precio-beneficios de 7; *see also the comment at* PRICE

> QUOTE if corporate forecasts are met, sales will exceed $50 million nest year and net earnings could exceed $7 million
> **Citizen (Ottawa)**

> QUOTE the US now accounts for more than half of our world-wide sales. It has made a huge contribution to our earnings turnaround
> **Duns Business Month**

> QUOTE last fiscal year the chain reported a 116% jump in earnings, to $6.4 million or $1.10 a share
> **Barrons**

earnest ['ɜ:nɪst] **1** *adjective* serio, -ria *or* formal **2** *noun* prenda *f or* señal *f*

ease [i:z] *verb* bajar; **the share index eased slightly today** = el índice de cotización de las acciones ha bajado hoy ligeramente

easement ['i:zmənt] *noun* servidumbre *f or* derecho *m* de paso

easy ['i:zi] *adjective* **(a)** *(not difficult)* fácil *or* cómodo, -da; **easy terms** = facilidades *fpl* de pago; **the shop is let on very easy terms** = la tienda se alquila con una renta baja; **the loan is repayable in easy payments** = el préstamo se devuelve en cómodos plazos; **easy money** = (i) dinero fácil; (ii) dinero barato; **easy money policy** = política monetaria expansiva **(b)** **easy market** = mercado poco activo con tendencia a la baja; **the Stock Exchange was easy yesterday** = la bolsa bajó ligeramente ayer; **share prices are easier** = los precios de las acciones están bajando

◊ **easily** ['i:zɪli] *adverb* **(a)** *(without difficulty)* fácilmente *or* tranquilamente *or* sin problemas; **we passed through customs easily** = pasamos la aduana sin problemas **(b)** *(a lot more)* con gran diferencia *or* con mucho; **he is easily our best salesman** = es con gran diferencia nuestro mejor vendedor; **the firm is easily the biggest in the market** = la empresa es con mucho la mayor del mercado

EBRD ['i:bi:ɑ:'di:] = EUROPEAN BANK FOR RECONSTRUCTION AND DEVELOPMENT Banco Europeo de Reconstrucción y Desarrollo (BERD)

EC ['i:'si:] = EUROPEAN COMMUNITY CE; **EC ministers met today in Brussels** = los ministros de la CE se han reunido hoy en Bruselas; **the USA is increasing its trade with the EC** = los EE UU están aumentando sus intercambios comerciales con la CE (NOTE: now called the **European Union (EU)**)

ECGD [ˈiːsiːdʒiːˈdiː] = EXPORT CREDIT GUARANTEE DEPARTMENT

echelon [ˈeʃəlɒn] *noun* escala *f or* jerarquía *f*; **the upper echelons of industry** = las altas esferas de la industria

econometrics [iːkɒnəˈmetrɪks] *plural noun* econometría *f* (NOTE: takes a singular verb)

economic [iːkəˈnɒmɪk] *adjective* **(a)** *(saving)* económico, -ca; **the flat is let at an economic rent** = el piso se alquila a un precio económico; **it is hardly economic for the company to run its own warehouse** = no resulta económico que la empresa tenga su propio almacén; **economic order quantity (EOQ)** = pedido de dimensiones óptimas **(b)** *(system)* económico, -ca; **economic planner** = planificador económico; **economic planning** = planificación económica; **the government's economic policy** = la política económica del gobierno; **the economic situation** = la situación económica *or* la coyuntura económica; **the country's economic system** = el sistema económico de la nación; **economic trends** = tendencias económicas; **economic crisis** *or* **economic depression** = crisis económica; **the government has introduced import controls to solve the current economic crisis** = el gobierno ha impuesto controles a la importación para solucionar la actual crisis económica; **economic cycle** = ciclo económico; **economic development** = desarrollo económico; **the economic development of the region has totally changed since oil was discovered there** = el desarrollo económico de la región ha cambiado totalmente desde que se encontró petróleo; **economic growth** = crecimiento económico; **the country enjoyed a period of economic growth in the 1980s** = el país disfrutó de un periodo de crecimiento económico en la década de los 80; **economic indicators** = indicadores económicos; **economic sanctions** = sanciones económicas; **the western nations imposed economic sanctions on the country** = las naciones occidentales impusieron sanciones económicas al país; **the European Economic Community (EEC)** = la Comunidad Económica Europea (CEE)

◊ **economical** [iːkəˈnɒmɪkəl] *adjective* económico, -ca; **economical car** = un coche económico *or* de bajo consumo; **economical use of resources** = utilización económica de los recursos

◊ **economically** [iːkəˈnɒmɪkli] *adverb* económicamente

◊ **economics** [iːkəˈnɒmɪks] *plural noun* **(a)** *(science)* economía *f* **(b)** *(economic aspects)* economía *f*; **the economics of town planning** = la economía de la planificación urbana; **I do not understand the economics of the coal industry** = no entiendo la economía de la industria del carbón (NOTE: takes a singular verb)

◊ **economist** [ɪˈkɒnəmɪst] *noun* economista *mf*; **agricultural economist** = economista agrícola

◊ **economize** [ɪˈkɒnəmaɪz] *verb* **to economize on petrol** = economizar en gasolina

◊ **economy** [ɪˈkɒnəmi] *noun* **(a)** *(saving)* economía *f or* ahorro *m*; **an economy measure** = una medida para reducir gastos; **to introduce economies** *or* **economy measures into the system** = introducir en el sistema medidas para reducir gastos; **economies of scale** = economías de escala; **economy car** = coche económico *or* de bajo consumo; **economy class** = clase económica *or* turista; **to travel economy class** = viajar en clase económica; **economy drive** = campaña para reducir gastos; **economy size** = tamaño económico **(b)** *(system)* economía *or* sistema *m* económico; **the country's economy is in ruins** = la economía del país está en ruina; **black economy** = economía negra *or* economía sumergida; **capitalist economy** = economía capitalista; **controlled economy** = economía dirigida; **free market economy** = economía de libre mercado; **mixed economy** = economía mixta; **planned economy** = economía planificada

QUOTE each of the major issues on the agenda at this week's meeting is important to the government's success in overall economic management
Australian Financial Review

QUOTE believers in free-market economics often find it hard to sort out their views on the issue
Economist

QUOTE the European economies are being held back by rigid labor markets and wage structures, huge expenditures on social welfare programs and restrictions on the free movement of goods within the Common Market
Duns Business Month

ecu *or* **ECU** [ˈekjuː] *noun* = EUROPEAN CURRENCY UNIT ecu *or* ECU *m*

COMMENT: the value of the ECU is calculated as a composite of various European currencies in certain proportions. The ECU varies in value as the value of the various currencies change. The ECU is used for internal accounting purposes within the EU; it is available in some countries as a metal coin, but this is not yet legal tender

QUOTE the official use of the ecu remains limited. Since its creation in 1981 the ecu has grown popular because of its stability
Economist

Ecuador [ˈekwədɔː] *noun* Ecuador *m*

◊ **Ecuadorian** [ekwəˈdɔːriən] *adjective & noun* ecuatoriano, -na
NOTE: capital: **Quito**; currency: **Ecuadorian sucre (S/.)** = sucre ecuatoriano (S/.)

edge [edʒ] **1** *noun* **(a)** *(side)* borde *m or* canto *m*; **he sat on the edge of the managing director's desk** = se sentó en el borde de la mesa del director; **the printer has printed the figures right to the edge of the printout** = la impresora ha impreso las cifras hasta el borde del papel **(b)** *(advantage)* margen *m or* ventaja *f*; **having a local office gives us a competitive edge over Smith Ltd** = el tener una oficina local nos proporciona un margen competitivo sobre Smith Ltd; **to have the edge on a rival company** = llevar ventaja a un competidor **2** *verb* avanzar lentamente *or* poco a poco; **prices on the stock market edged upwards today** = hoy las acciones han ido subiendo lentamente; **sales figures edged downwards in January** = las cifras de ventas bajaron poco a poco en enero

edition [ɪ'dɪʃn] *noun* edición *f*

editor ['edɪtə] *noun* (i) redactor, -ra jefe *or* jefe de redacción *or* director, -ra de un periódico; (ii) corrector, -ra de estilo; **the editor of the 'Times'** = el director del 'Times'; **the City editor** = el redactor jefe de la sección financiera

◊ **editorial** [edɪ'tɔːrɪəl] **1** *adjective* editorial; **editorial board** = consejo de redacción **2** *noun* editorial *m* or artículo *m* de fondo

EDP ['iːdiː'piː] = ELECTRONIC DATA PROCESSING

EEA ['iːiː'eɪ] = EUROPEAN ECONOMIC AREA

EEC ['iːiː'siː] = EUROPEAN ECONOMIC COMMUNITY CEE (NOTE: now called the **European Union (EU)**

effect [ɪ'fekt] **1** *noun* **(a)** *(result)* efecto *m*; **the effect of the pay increase was to raise productivity levels** = la subida de sueldos tuvo como efecto un aumento en la productividad; **the terms of the contract take effect** *or* **come into effect from January 1st** = los términos del contrato surten efecto *or* entran en vigor a partir del 1 de enero; **prices are increased 10% with effect from January 1st** = los precios suben un 10% con efecto a partir del 1 de enero; **to remain in effect** = mantenerse en vigor *or* seguir vigente **(b)** *(meaning)* sentido *m* or intención *f* or propósito *m*; **clause to the effect that** = cláusula con el propósito de; **we have made provision to this effect** = hemos tomado disposiciones en este sentido **(c)** **personal effects** = efectos personales **2** *verb* efectuar *or* llevar a cabo *or* realizar; **to effect a payment** = realizar un pago; **to effect customs clearance** = efectuar las formalidades aduaneras *or* el despacho aduanero; **to effect a settlement between two parties** = poner de acuerdo a dos partes *or* realizar un acuerdo entre dos partes

◊ **effective** [ɪ'fektɪv] *adjective* **(a)** *(real)* efectivo, -va; **effective control of a company** = control efectivo *or* real de una compañía; **effective demand** = demanda efectiva; **effective yield** = rendimiento efectivo **(b)** **effective date** = fecha de entrada en vigor; **clause effective as from January 1st** = cláusula que entrará en vigor a partir del 1 de enero **(c)** *(which works)* efectivo, -va *or* eficaz; **advertising in the Sunday papers is the most effective way of selling** = anunciarse en la prensa dominical es la manera más eficaz de vender; *see* COST-EFFECTIVE

◊ **effectiveness** [ɪ'fektɪvnəs] *noun* eficacia *f or* eficiencia *f*; **I doubt the effectiveness of television advertising** = dudo de la eficacia de la publicidad en televisión; *see* COST-EFFECTIVENESS

◊ **effectual** [ɪ'fektʃʊəl] *adjective* eficaz *or* válido, -da

efficiency [ɪ'fɪʃənsi] *noun* eficiencia *f or* eficacia *f*; **with a high degree of efficiency** = con un alto grado de eficiencia; **a business efficiency exhibition** = una exhibición de eficiencia comercial; **an efficiency expert** = un experto en eficacia

◊ **efficient** [ɪ'fɪʃənt] *adjective* eficaz *or* eficiente *or* de buen rendimiento; **the efficient working of a system** = el buen funcionamiento de un sistema; **he needs an efficient secretary to look after him** = necesita una secretaria eficiente que lo atienda; **efficient machine** = una máquina de buen rendimiento

◊ **efficiently** [ɪ'fɪʃəntli] *adverb* eficazmente *or* eficientemente; **she organized the sales conference very efficiently** = organizó la reunión de ventas muy eficazmente

efflux ['eflʌks] *noun* flujo *m or* salida *f or* afluencia *f*; **efflux of capital to North America** = afluencia de capitales a Norteamérica

effort ['efət] *noun* esfuerzo *m*; **the salesmen made great efforts to increase sales** = los vendedores hicieron grandes esfuerzos para aumentar las ventas; **thanks to the efforts of the finance department, overheads have been reduced** = gracias a los esfuerzos del departamento de finanzas se han reducido los gastos generales; **if we make one more effort, we should clear the backlog of orders** = con un esfuerzo más podremos despachar los pedidos atrasados

EFT = ELECTRONIC FUNDS TRANSFER

EFTA ['eftə] = EUROPEAN FREE TRADE ASSOCIATION Asociación Europea de Libre Comercio

EFTPOS ['eft'pɒs] = ELECTRONIC FUNDS TRANSFER AT POINT OF SALE

e.g. ['iː'dʒiː] ej.; **the contract is valid in some countries (e.g. France and Belgium) but not in others** = el contrato tiene validez en algunos países (ej. Francia y Bélgica) pero no en otros

EGM ['iːdʒiː'em] = EXTRAORDINARY GENERAL MEETING

Egypt ['iːdʒɪpt] *noun* Egipto *m*

◊ **Egyptian** [ɪ'dʒɪpʃn] *adjective & noun* egipcio, -cia
NOTE: capital: **Cairo** (= el Cairo); currency: **Egyptian pound (£E)** = libra egipcia (LE)

eighty/twenty rule ['eɪti'twenti 'ruːl] *noun* relación de clientes y ventas según la cual un bajo porcentaje de clientes representa un porcentaje alto de ventas; *see also* PARETO'S LAW

800 number [eɪt'hʌndrəd 'nʌmbə] *US* número telefónico al que se llama gratuitamente (NOTE: GB English is **0800**; the equivalent number in Spain is **009**; note also that the US English is also **toll-free number**)

elastic [ɪ'læstɪk] *adjective* elástico, -ca

◊ **elasticity** [elæs'tɪsəti] *noun* elasticidad *f*; **elasticity of supply and demand** = elasticidad de la oferta y la demanda

elect [ɪ'lekt] *verb* elegir; **to elect the officers of an association** = elegir a los directivos de una asociación; **she was elected president** = fue elegida presidenta

◊ **-elect** [ɪˈlekt] *suffix* electo, -ta; **she is the president-elect** = es la presidenta electa (NOTE: the plural is **presidents-elect)**

◊ **election** [ɪˈlekʃən] *noun* elección *f;* **the election of officers of an association** = la elección de los directivos de una asociación; **the election of directors by the shareholders; the election of consejeros por parte de los accionistas; general election** = elecciones generales

electricity [elekˈtrɪsəti] *noun* electricidad *f;* **the electricity was cut off this morning, so the computers could not work** = ha habido un corte del suministro eléctrico esta mañana, por lo que los ordenadores no han podido funcionar; **our electricity bill has increased considerably this quarter** = nuestra factura de electricidad ha subido considerablemente este trimestre; **electricity costs are an important factor in our overheads** = los gastos de electricidad son una parte importante de nuestros gastos generales

◊ **electric** [ɪˈlektrɪk] *adjective* eléctrico, -ca; **an electric typewriter** = una máquina de escribir eléctrica

◊ **electrical** [ɪˈlektrɪkəl] *adjective* eléctrico, -ca; **the engineers are trying to repair an electrical fault** = los ingenieros están tratando de reparar un fallo eléctrico

electronic [elekˈtrɒnɪk] *adjective* electrónico , -ca; **electronic banking** = banca electrónica; **electronic data processing (EDP)** = proceso electrónico de datos; **electronic engineer** = ingeniero electrónico; **electronic funds transfer (EFT)** = transferencias electrónicas de fondos; **electronic funds transfer at point of sale (EFTPOS)** = transferencias electrónicas de fondos en el puente de venta; **electronic mail** = correo electrónico; **electronic point of sale (EPOS)** = puntos de venta electrónicos

◊ **electronics** [elekˈtrɒnɪks] *plural noun* electrónica *f;* **the electronics industry** = la industria electrónica; **an electronics specialist** *or* **expert** = un especialista *or* un experto en electrónica; **electronics engineer** = ingeniero electrónico (NOTE: takes a singular verb)

element [ˈelɪmənt] *noun* elemento *m or* base *f;* **the elements of a settlement** = las bases de un acuerdo

elevator [ˈelɪveɪtə] *noun* **(a)** *(for goods)* montacargas *m* **(b)** *US* ascensor *m;* **take the elevator to the 26th floor** = tome el ascensor hasta el piso 26

eligible [ˈelɪdʒəbl] *adjective* elegible *or* con derecho a; **she is eligible for re-election** = tiene derecho a presentarse a reelección; **eligible bill** *or* **eligible paper** = efectos redescontables

◊ **eligibility** [elɪdʒəˈbɪləti] *noun* elegibilidad *f;* **the chairman questioned her eligibility to stand for re-election** = el presidente cuestionó su derecho a presentarse a reelección

eliminate [ɪˈlɪmɪneɪt] *verb* eliminar; **to eliminate defects in the system** = eliminar defectos del sistema; **using a computer should eliminate all possibility of error** = el uso de un ordenador debería eliminar toda posibilidad de error

El Salvador [ˈel ˈsælvədɔː] *see* SALVADOR

email *or* **E-mail** [ˈiːmeɪl] = ELECTRONIC MAIL

embargo [emˈbɑːgəʊ] **1** *noun* **(a)** *(ban on trade)* embargo *m or* prohibición *f or* bloqueo *m* económico; **to lay** *or* **put an embargo on trade with a country** = prohibir el comercio con un país *or* imponer un embargo comercial a un país; **the government has put an embargo on the export of computer equipment** = el gobierno ha prohibido la exportación de equipos informáticos; **to lift an embargo** = levantar un embargo; **the government has lifted the embargo on the export of computers** = el gobierno ha levantado el embargo impuesto a la exportación de ordenadores; **to be under an embargo** = estar prohibido **(b)** *(ban on publication of news)* prohibición de publicar ciertas noticias (NOTE: plural is **embargoes) 2** *verb* **(a)** *(ban trade)* prohibir *or* embargar; **the government has embargoed trade with the Eastern countries** = el gobierno ha prohibido el comercio con los países del Este **(b)** *(ban publication of news)* prohibir la publicación de noticias; **the news of the merger has been embargoed until next Wednesday** = la noticia de la fusión no podrá publicarse hasta el miércoles próximo

embark [ɪmˈbɑːk] *verb* **(a)** *(ship)* embarcar; **the passengers embarked at Southampton** = los pasajeros embarcaron en Southampton **(b)** *(to start)* **to embark on** = embarcarse en; *(journey)* emprender; **the company has embarked on an expansion programme** = la compañía se ha embarcado en un programa de expansión

◊ **embarkation** [embɑːˈkeɪʃən] *noun* embarque *m;* **port of embarkation** = puerto de embarque; **embarkation card** = tarjeta de embarque

embezzle [ɪmˈbezl] *verb* desfalcar *or* malversar; **he was sent to prison for six months for embezzling his clients' money** = estuvo en la cárcel seis meses por malversar fondos de sus clientes

◊ **embezzlement** [ɪmˈbezlmənt] *noun* malversación *f or* desfalco *m;* **he was sent to prison for six months for embezzlement** = estuvo en la cárcel seis meses por desfalco

◊ **embezzler** [ɪmˈbezlə] *noun* malversador, -ra *or* desfalcador, -ra

emergency [ɪˈmɜːdʒənsi] *noun* emergencia *f or* excepción *f or* urgencia *f;* **the government declared a state of emergency** = el gobierno declaró el estado de excepción; **to take emergency measures** = tomar medidas de emergencia; **the company had to take emergency measures to stop losing money** = la compañía tuvo que tomar medidas de emergencia para no perder más dinero; **emergency reserves** = reservas para imprevistos

emoluments [ɪˈmɒljʊmənts] *plural noun* emolumentos *mpl* (NOTE: US English uses the singular **emolument)**

employ [ɪmˈplɔɪ] *verb* emplear; **to employ twenty staff** = emplear a veinte personas; **to employ twenty new staff** = emplear a veinte personas más

◊ **employed** [ɪmˈplɔɪd] **1** *adjective* **(a)** *(work)* empleado, -da; **he is not gainfully employed** = no tiene un empleo remunerado; **self-employed** = autónomo, -ma *or* por cuenta propia *or* independiente; **he worked in a bank for ten years but now is self-employed** = trabajó en un banco durante diez años pero ahora trabaja por cuenta propia *(b) (money)* en uso *or* utilizado, -da; **return on capital employed (ROCE)** = rendimiento del capital utilizado **2** *plural noun* empleados *mpl*; **the employers and the employed** = los patronos y los empleados; **the self-employed** = los trabajadores autónomos *or* por cuenta propia *or* independientes

◊ **employee** [emplɔɪˈiː] *noun* empleado, -da *or* trabajador, -ra; **employees of the firm are eligible to join a profit-sharing scheme** = los empleados de la empresa tienen derecho a tomar parte en un plan de participación en los beneficios; **employee share ownership plan (ESOP)** *or* **US employee stock ownership plan** = programa de oferta de acciones a los empleados; **relations between management and employees have improved** = las relaciones entre la dirección y los empleados han mejorado; **the company has decided to take on new employees** = la compañía ha decidido contratar nuevos empleados; **employees and employers** = empleados y patronos

◊ **employer** [ɪmˈplɔɪə] *noun* patrón *m or* patrono, -na *or* empresario, ria; **employers' organization** *or* **association** = organización empresarial *or* patronal; **employer's contribution** = cuota patronal

◊ **employment** [ɪmˈplɔɪmənt] *noun* empleo *m or* ocupación *f or* trabajo *m*; **full employment** = pleno empleo; **full-time employment** = trabajo a tiempo completo *or* a jornada completa; **to be in full-time employment** tener un empleo a jornada completa; **part-time employment** = trabajo a tiempo parcial *or* de media jornada; **seasonal employment** = empleo *or* trabajo estacional; **temporary employment** = ocupación temporal *or* empleo eventual; **to be without employment** = estar desempleado *or* en el paro *or* no tener empleo; **to find someone alternative employment** = facilitar otro empleo a alguien; **conditions of employment** = condiciones de trabajo; **contract of employment** *or* **employment contract** = contrato de trabajo; **security of employment** = seguridad de empleo *or* empleo asegurado; **employment office** *or* **bureau** *or* **agency** = oficina de empleo *or* agencia de colocación

QUOTE 70 per cent of Australia's labour force was employed in service activity
Australian Financial Review

QUOTE the blue-collar unions are the people who stand to lose most in terms of employment growth
Sydney Morning Herald

QUOTE companies introducing robotics think it important to involve individual employees in planning their introduction
Economist

emporium [emˈpɔːrɪəm] *noun* mercado *m or* centro *m* comercial (NOTE: plural is **emporiums** or **emporia**)

empower [ɪmˈpaʊə] *verb* autorizar *or* dar poder; **she was empowered by the company to sign the contract** = la compañía le autorizó a firmar el contrato

emptor [ˈem(p)tə] *see* CAVEAT

empty [ˈem(p)ti] **1** *adjective* vacío, -cía; **the envelope is empty** = el sobre está vacío; **you can take that filing cabinet back to the storeroom as it is empty** = puedes devolver este archivo al almacén ya que está vacío; **start the computer file with an empty workspace** = empezar el archivo informático con un espacio vacío **2** *verb* vaciar; **she emptied the filing cabinet and put the files in boxes** = vació el archivo y puso las fichas en cajas; **he emptied the petty cash box into his briefcase** = puso el contenido de la caja para gastos menores en su cartera

◊ **empties** [ˈem(p)tɪz] *plural noun* envases *mpl* vacíos; **returned empties** = envases devueltos

EMS [ˈiːemˈes] = EUROPEAN MONETARY SYSTEM Sistema Monetario Europeo (SME)

EMU [ˈiːˈemˈjuː] = EUROPEAN MONETARY UNION

enc *or* **encl** = ENCLOSURE

encash [ɪnˈkæʃ] *verb* hacer efectivo *or* cobrar

◊ **encashable** [ɪnˈkæʃəbl] *adjective* cobrable

◊ **encashment** [ɪnˈkæʃmənt] *noun* cobro *m* en metálico

enclose [ɪnˈkləʊz] *verb* adjuntar *or* remitir adjunto *or* acompañar; **to enclose an invoice with a letter** = adjuntar una factura a una carta; **I am enclosing a copy of the contract** = adjunto una copia del contrato; **letter enclosing a cheque** = carta con un cheque adjunto; **please find the cheque enclosed herewith** = le envío adjunto el cheque

◊ **enclosure** [ɪnˈkləʊʒə] *noun* carta *f* adjunta *or* documento *m* adjunto *or* anexo *m*; **letter with enclosures** = carta con documentos adjuntos

encourage [ɪnˈkʌrɪdʒ] *verb* **(a)** *(to make it easier)* incitar *or* estimular *or* fomentar *or* potenciar; **the general rise in wages encourages consumer spending** = el aumento general de los sueldos fomenta el consumo; **to encourage investment** = potenciar las inversiones; **leaving your credit cards on your desk encourages people to steal** *or* **encourages stealing** = si dejas tus tarjetas de crédito sobre la mesa del despacho incitas a la gente a robar *or* incitas al robo; **the company is trying to encourage sales by giving large discounts** = la empresa trata de estimular las ventas ofreciendo grandes descuentos **(b)** *(to inspire)* animar *or* alentar; **he encouraged me to apply for the job** = me animó a que solicitara el puesto; **to feel encouraged** = animarse

◊ **encouragement** [ɪnˈkʌrɪdʒmənt] *noun* ánimo *m or* aliento *m or* estímulo *m*; **the designers produced a very marketable product, thanks to the encouragement of the sales director** = los diseñadores crearon un producto muy comercial, gracias al estímulo del director de ventas

end [end] **1** *noun* **(a)** *(final point, last part)* fin *m or* final *m or* cabo *m*; **at the end of the contract period** = al final del periodo de contrato; **at the end of six months** = al cabo de seis meses; **to come to an end** = llegar a su fin *or* terminarse; **our distribution agreement comes to an end next month** = nuestro acuerdo de distribuición llega a su fin el próximo mes; **account end** = final del periodo de crédito en la bolsa; **month end** = fin de mes; **year end** = fin de año; **end product** = producto final *or* acabado; **after six months' trial production, the end product is still not acceptable** = después de seis meses de producción experimental, el producto final no es todavía aceptable; **end user** = usuario final; **the company is creating a computer with the end user in mind** = la empresa está creando un ordenador pensado para el usuario **(b) in the end** = al final *or* al fin; **in the end the company had to pull out of the US market** = al final la compañía tuvo que salirse del mercado estadounidense; **in the end they signed the contract at the airport** = al final acabaron firmando el contrato en el aeropuerto; **in the end the company had to call in the police** = al final la empresa tuvo que llamar a la policía **(c) on end** = sin parar *or* incesantemente *or* seguido; **the discussions continued for hours on end** = las discusiones se prolongaron incesantemente durante horas; **the workforce worked at top speed for weeks on end to finish the order on time** = los obreros trabajaron a toda marcha durante semanas seguidas para servir el pedido a tiempo **2** *verb* terminar *or* finalizar; **the distribution agreement ends in July** = el acuerdo de distribuición finaliza en julio; **the chairman ended the discussion by getting up and walking out of the meeting** = el presidente terminó la discusión levantándose y saliendo de la sala

◊ **end in** ['end 'ın] *verb* terminar en; **the AGM ended in the shareholders fighting on the floor** = la asamblea general anual terminó en una pelea generalizada entre los accionistas

◊ **end up** ['end 'ʌp] *verb* acabar *or* terminar; **we ended up with a bill for £10,000** = terminamos con una factura de £10.000

endorse [ın'dɔ:s] *verb* endosar; **to endorse a bill** *or* **a cheque** = endosar una letra *or* un cheque

◊ **endorsee** [endɔ:'si:] *noun* endosatario, -ria

◊ **endorsement** [ın'dɔ:smənt] *noun* **(a)** *(act)* endoso *m* **(b)** *(condition)* endoso *m* *or* garantía *f* *or* aval *m*; **endorsement to a policy** = adición *f* a una póliza *or* suplemento *m* *or* ampliación *f* de póliza **(c)** *(countersignature)* refrendo *m*

◊ **endorser** [ın'dɔ:sə] *noun* endosante *mf*

endowment [ın'daʊmənt] *noun* dotación *f*; **endowment insurance** *or* **endowment policy** = póliza mixta *or* póliza dotal; **endowment mortgage** = 'endowment' *m* *or* hipoteca de inversión

COMMENT: the borrower pays interest on the mortgage in the usual way, but does not repay the capital; the endowment assurance (a life insurance) is taken out to cover the total capital sum borrowed, and when the assurance matures the capital is paid off, and a further lump sum is usually available for payment to the borrower; a mortgage where the borrower repays both interest and capital is called a 'repayment mortgage'

endurance [ın'djʊrəns] *noun* aguante *m*

energy ['enədʒi] *noun* **(a)** *(force, strength)* energía *f* *or* vigor *m* *or* dinamismo *m*; **he hasn't the energy to be a good salesman** = le falta dinamismo para ser un buen vendedor; **they wasted their energies on trying to sell cars in the German market** = desperdiciaron sus energías intentando vender coches en el mercado alemán **(b)** *(power from electricity, petrol, etc.)* energía; **nuclear energy** = energía nuclear; **solar energy** = energía solar; **wind energy** = energía eólica; **we try to save energy by switching off the lights when the rooms are empty** = apagamos las luces cuando las habitaciones están vacías para ahorrar energía; **if you reduce the room temperature to eighteen degrees, you will save energy** = si bajas la temperatura de la habitación a dieciocho grados, ahorrarás energía

◊ **energetic** [enə'dʒetık] *adjective* enérgico, -ca *or* vigoroso, -sa

◊ **energy-saving** ['enədʒı'seıvıŋ] **1** *noun* ahorro *m* energético **2** *adjective* que ahorra energía; **the company is introducing energy-saving measures** = la compañía está introduciendo medidas para ahorrar energía

enforce [ın'fɔ:s] *verb* hacer cumplir *or* ejecutar; **to enforce the terms of a contract** = hacer cumplir los términos de un contrato

◊ **enforcement** [ın'fɔ:smənt] *noun* aplicación *f* *or* ejecución *f*; **enforcement of the terms of a contract** = aplicación de los términos de un contrato

engage [ın'geıdʒ] *verb* **(a) to engage someone to do something** = comprometer *or* obligar a alguien a hacer algo; **the contract engages us to a minimum annual purchase** = el contrato nos compromete a realizar un mínimo de compras anuales **(b)** *(to employ)* contratar *or* emplear; **we have engaged the best commercial lawyer to represent us** = hemos contratado al mejor abogado mercantil para que nos represente; **the company has engaged twenty new salesmen** = la empresa ha contratado a veinte nuevos vendedores **(c) to be engaged in** = estar ocupado, -da en algo *or* dedicarse a; **he is engaged in work on computers** = se dedica a la informática; **the company is engaged in trade with Africa** = la compañía se dedica al comercio con Africa

◊ **engaged** [ın'geıdʒd] *adjective* *(telephone)* línea ocupada; **to be engaged** = estar ocupado, -da *or* comunicando; **you cannot speak to the manager - his line is engaged** = no puede hablar con el director en este momento - su línea está ocupada; **engaged tone** = señal de comunicar; **I tried to phone the complaints department but got only the engaged tone** = intenté telefonear a la sección de reclamaciones pero estaba comunicando

◊ **engagement** [ın'geıdʒmənt] *noun* **(a)** *(agreement)* compromiso *m*; **to break an engagement to do something** = romper un compromiso (de hacer algo); **the company broke their engagement not to sell our rival's products** = la compañía rompió su compromiso de no vender los productos de nuestro competidor **(b)** *(meetings)* **engagements** = compromisos *mpl* *or* citas *fpl*; **I have no engagements for the rest of the day** = no tengo compromisos para el resto del día; **she noted the appointment in her engagements diary** = anotó la cita en su agenda

engine ['endʒın] *noun* motor *m* *or* máquina *f*; **a car with a small engine is more economic than one with a large one** = un coche con un motor pequeño es más económico que uno con uno grande; **the lift engine has broken down again - we shall just have to walk up to the 4th floor** = el motor del ascensor se ha averiado de nuevo - tendremos que subir andando hasta el 4º piso

◊ **engineer** [en(d)ʒı'nıə] *noun* ingeniero, -ra; **civil engineer** = ingeniero civil *or* de caminos;

consulting engineer = ingeniero asesor; **product engineer** = ingeniero de producto; **project engineer** = ingeniero de proyectos; **programming engineer** = ingeniero de programación

◊ **engineering** [en(d)ʒɪ'nɪərɪŋ] *noun* ingeniería *f*; **civil engineering** = ingeniería civil; *(in a company)* **the engineering department** = oficina técnica *or* servicio técnico; **an engineering consultant** = un ingeniero asesor

England ['ɪŋglənd] *noun* Inglaterra *f*

◊ **English** ['ɪŋglɪʃ] *adjective & noun* inglés, -esa; **the English** = los ingleses
NOTE: capital: **London** (= Londres); currency: **pound sterling (£)** = libra esterlina (£)

enlarge [ɪn'lɑːdʒ] *verb* ampliar

enquire [ɪn'kwaɪə *or* ɪn'kwaɪəri] = INQUIRE
◊ **enquiry** = INQUIRY

en route ['ɒn 'ruːt] *adverb* en eʰ camino; **the tanker sank when she was en route to the Gulf** = el petrolero naufragó cuando se dirigía al Golfo

entail [ɪn'teɪl] **1** *noun* vínculo *m* **2** *verb* traer consigo *or* implicar *or* suponer; **itemizing the sales figures will entail about ten days' work** = detallar las cifras de ventas supondrá unos diez días de trabajo

enter ['entə] *verb* **(a)** *(go in)* entrar en *or* introducirse en; **they all stood up when the chairman entered the room** = todos se levantaron cuando el presidente entró en la sala; **the company has spent millions trying to enter the do-it-yourself market** = la empresa ha gastado millones en introducirse en el mercado del bricolaje **(b)** *(write in)* inscribir *or* apuntar *or* anotar; **to enter a name on a list** = inscribir *or* apuntar un nombre en una lista; **the clerk entered the interest in my bank book** = el empleado anotó los intereses en mi libreta; **to enter an item in a ledger** = hacer un asiento en un libro mayor; **to enter a bid for something** = hacer una oferta por algo; **to enter a caveat** = hacer una advertencia

◊ **enter into** ['entə 'ɪntuː] *verb* entablar *or* tomar parte en; **to enter into relations with someone** = entablar *or* iniciar relaciones con alguien; **to enter into negotiations with a foreign government** = entablar *or* iniciar negociaciones con un gobierno extranjero; **to enter into a partnership with a friend** = asociarse con un amigo; **to enter into an agreement** *or* **a contract** = concertar *or* firmar un acuerdo *or* un contrato

◊ **entering** ['entərɪŋ] *noun* entrada *f or* inscripción *f*

enterprise ['entəpraɪz] *noun* **(a)** *(business system)* empresa *f*; **free enterprise** = libre empresa; **private enterprise** = empresa privada; **the project is completely funded by private enterprise** = el proyecto está financiado en su totalidad por la empresa privada; **enterprise zone** = zona de desarrollo industrial *or* comercial **(b)** *(a business)* negocio *m or* actividad *f or* empresa; **a small-scale enterprise** = un negocio a pequeña escala; **a state enterprise** = empresa estatal; **bosses of state enterprises are appointed by the government** = los altos cargos de las empresas estatales son nombrados por el gobierno

entertain [entə'teɪn] *verb* **(a)** *(a guest)* recibir a clientes **(b)** *(an idea)* tomar en consideración *or* considerar; **the management will not entertain any suggestions from the union representatives** = la dirección no tomará en consideración ninguna sugerencia de los representantes de los sindicatos **(c)** *(keep busy)* entretener

◊ **entertainment** [entə'teɪnmənt] *noun* función *f or* espectáculo *m or* comida *f* para invitados; **entertainment allowance** = dietas *fpl* para gastos de representación; **entertainment expenses** = gastos *mpl* de representación

entitle [ɪn'taɪtl] *verb* dar derecho a *or* autorizar; **he is entitled to a discount** = tiene derecho a un descuento

◊ **entitlement** [ɪn'taɪtlmənt] *noun* derecho *m*; **holiday entitlement** = derecho a vacaciones; **she has not used up all her holiday entitlement** = no ha agotado todavía las vacaciones a que tiene derecho; **pension entitlement** = derecho a una pensión *or* jubilación

entrance ['entrəns] *noun* entrada *f or* admisión *f*; **the taxi will drop you at the main entrance** = el taxi le dejará en la entrada principal; **deliveries should be made to the London Road entrance** = las entregas deben efectuarse por la entrada de London Road; **entrance (charge)** = entrada *f*; **entrance is £1.50 for adults and £1 for children** = la entrada cuesta £1.50 para adultos y £1 para niños; **entrance examination** = examen de admisión

entrepot ['ɒntrəpəʊ] *noun* **entrepot port** = puerto *m* distribuidor; **entrepot trade** = exportación de importaciones

entrepreneur [ɒntrəprə'nɜː] *noun* empresario, -ria *or* contratista *mf*

◊ **entrepreneurial** [ɒntrəprə'nɜːrɪəl] *adjective* *(taking commercial risks)* empresarial; **an entrepreneurial decision** = una decisión empresarial

entrust [ɪn'trʌst] *verb* confiar; **to entrust someone with something** *or* **to entrust something to someone** = encargar *or* confiar algo a alguien; **he was entrusted with the keys to the office safe** = le confiaron las llaves de la caja fuerte de la oficina

entry ['entri] *noun* **(a)** *(accounts)* asiento *m or* anotación *f or* registro *m*; **credit entry** *or* **debit entry** = abono *or* asiento en el debe; **single-entry bookkeeping** = contabilidad por partida única; **double-entry bookkeeping** = contabilidad por partida doble; **to make an entry in a ledger** = efectuar un asiento en un libro mayor; **contra entry** = contrapartida *or* contraasiento; **to contra an entry** = anotar una contrapartida **(b)** *(going in)* acceso *m or* ingreso *m or* entrada *f*; **to pass a customs entry point** = pasar por un puesto aduanero; **entry of goods under bond** = entrada de mercancías en el depósito aduanero; **entry charge** = precio de entrada; **entry visa** = visado de entrada; **multiple entry visa** = visado de entrada múltiple; **conditions of entry** = condiciones de admisión

envelope ['envələʊp] *noun* sobre *m*; **airmail envelope** = sobre para correo aéreo; **aperture envelope** *or* **window envelope** = sobre de ventanilla; **sealed** *or* **unsealed envelope** = sobre cerrado *or* sobre sin cerrar; **to send the information in a sealed**

envelope = enviar la información en sobre cerrado; **a stamped addressed envelope (s.a.e.)** = un sobre franqueado con la dirección del destinatario; **please send a stamped addressed envelope for further details and our latest catalogue** = si desea más información y nuestro último catálogo envíe un sobre franqueado con su dirección

environment [ɪn'vaɪərənmənt] *noun* ambiente *m*

EOC ['i:'əu'si:] = EQUAL OPPORTUNITIES COMMISSION

EOQ ['i:'əu'kju] = ECONOMIC ORDER QUANTITY

epos *or* **EPOS** ['i:pɒs] = ELECTRONIC POINT OF SALE

equal ['i:kwəl] **1** *adjective* igual *or* igualado, -da *or* equitativo, -va; **Equal Opportunities Commission (EOC)** = organismo oficial para fomentar la igualdad de oportunidades; **equal opportunities programme** = programa de igualdad de oportunidades de empleo; **equal pay** = igual salario; **male and female workers have equal pay** = los obreros y las obreras reciben igual salario **2** *verb* igualar *or* ser igual a; **production this month has equalled our best month ever** = la producción de este mes iguala la de nuestro mejor mes hasta la fecha (NOTE: **equalling - equalled** but US: **equaling - equaled**)

◊ **equalize** ['i:kwəlaɪz] *verb* igualar *or* compensar *or* equilibrar; **to equalize dividends** = compensar dividendos

◊ **equalization** [i:kwəlaɪ'zeɪʃən] *noun* equiparación *f or* compensación *f*

◊ **equally** ['i:kwəli] *adverb* igualmente *or* por igual; **costs will be shared equally between the two parties** = los costes se distribuirán por igual *or* equitativamente entre las dos partes; **they were both equally responsible for the disastrous launch** = ambos fueron igualmente responsables del desastroso lanzamiento

Equatorial Guinea [ekwə'tɔːriəl 'gɪni:] *noun* Guinea Ecuatorial

◊ **Equatorial Guinean** [ekwə'tɔːriəl 'gɪniən] *adjective & noun* guineano, -ana ecuatorial
NOTE: capital: **Bata**; currency: **CFA franc = franco CFA**

equip [ɪ'kwɪp] *verb* equipar *or* proveer *or* dotar; **to equip a factory with new machinery** = equipar una fábrica con nueva maquinaria; **the office is fully equipped with word-processors** = la oficina está plenamente provista de procesadores de textos

◊ **equipment** [ɪ'kwɪpmənt] *noun* equipo *m or* material *m or* útiles *mpl*; **office equipment** *or* **business equipment** = accesorios de oficina *or* material de oficina *or* equipos de oficina; **office equipment supplier** = proveedor de material de oficina; **office equipment catalogue** = catálogo de accesorios de oficina; **capital equipment** = bienes de capital; **heavy equipment** = equipo pesado

equity ['ekwəti] *noun* **(a)** *(share)* beneficios *mpl or* participación *f* de beneficios **(b)** *(capital)* **shareholders' equity** = capital escriturado *or* capital social; *(nominal value of the issued shares in a company)* **equity capital** = capital en acciones *or* valor nominal de las acciones de una sociedad

◊ **equities** ['ekwətɪz] *plural noun* títulos *mpl or* acciones *fpl* ordinarias

COMMENT: 'equity' (also called 'capital' or 'shareholders' equity' or 'shareholders' capital' or 'shareholders' funds') is the current net value of the company including the nominal value of the shares in issue. After several years a company would expect to increase its net worth above the value of the starting capital. 'Equity capital' on the other hand is only the nominal value of the shares in issue

QUOTE in the past three years commercial property has seriously underperformed equities and dropped out of favour as a result
Investors Chronicle

QUOTE investment trusts can raise more capital but this has to be done as a company does it, by a rights issue of equity
Investors Chronicle

equivalence [ɪ'kwɪvələns] *noun* equivalencia *f or* paridad *f*

◊ **equivalent** [ɪ'kwɪvələnt] *adjective* **to be equivalent to** = ser equivalente a *or* equivaler a; **the total dividend paid is equivalent to one quarter of the pretax profits** = el dividendo total pagado es equivalente a un cuarto de los ingresos antes de deducir impuestos

erase [ɪ'reɪz] *verb* borrar

◊ **eraser** [ɪ'reɪzə] *noun* goma *f* (de borrar)

ergonomics [ɜːgə'nɒmɪks] *plural noun* ergonomía *f* (NOTE: takes a singular verb)

◊ **ergonomist** [ɜː'gɒnəmɪst] *noun* especialista *mf* en ergonomía

ERM [i:ɑː'em] = EXCHANGE RATE MECHANISM

erode [ɪ'rəud] *verb* erosionar *or* desgastar *or* reducir; **to erode wage differentials** = reducir las diferencias salariales

error ['erə] *noun* error *m or* equivocación *f*; **he made an error in calculating the total** = cometió un error al calcular el total; **the secretary must have made a typing error** = la secretaria debe de haber cometido un error de mecanografía; **clerical error** = error de copia *or* error de oficina; **computer error** = error de ordenador; **margin of error** = margen de error; **errors and omissions excepted (e.& o.e.)** = salvo error u omisión; **error rate** = coeficiente de errores; **in error** *or* **by error** = por error; **the letter was sent to the London office in error** = la carta fue enviada a la oficina de Londres por error

escalate ['eskəleɪt] *verb* escalar

◊ **escalation** [eskə'leɪʃən] *noun* escalada *f*; **escalation of price increases** = escalada *f* de precios; **escalation clause** = ESCALATOR CLAUSE

◊ **escalator clause** ['eskəleɪtə 'klɔːz] *noun* cláusula *f* de revisión de precios *or* salarios

escape [ɪs'keɪp] **1** *noun* evasión *f or* fuga *f or* escape *m*; **escape clause** = cláusula de excepción *or* de escape *or* de salvaguardia **2** *verb* escapar *or* eludir *or* evadir

escrow ['eskrəu] *noun* **in escrow** = en depósito;

document held in escrow = documento guardado en depósito; *US* **escrow account** = cuenta de garantía bloqueada

escudo [es'kjʊdəʊ] *noun (name of currency used in Portugal)* escudo *m*

ESOP = EMPLOYEE SHARE OWNERSHIP PROGRAMME

espionage [espɪə'nɑ:ʒ] *noun* **industrial espionage** = espionaje *m* industrial

essential [ɪ'senʃəl] *adjective* esencial *or* substancial *or* indispensable *or* imprescindible; **it is essential that an agreement be reached before the end of the month** = es indispensable llegar a un acuerdo antes de final de mes; **the factory is lacking essential spare parts** = a la compañía le faltan piezas de recambio esenciales

◊ **essentials** [ɪ'senʃəlz] *plural noun* elementos *mpl* esenciales

establish [ɪs'tæblɪʃ] *verb* establecer *or* consolidar *or* instalar *or* crear; **the company has established a branch in Australia** = la compañía ha instalado una sucursal en Australia; **the business was established in Scotland in 1823** = la empresa fue fundada en Escocia en 1823; **it is a young company - it has been established for only four years** = es una empresa joven - lleva sólo cuatro años en funcionamiento; **to establish oneself in business** = establecerse en un negocio

◊ **establishment** [ɪs'tæblɪʃmənt] *noun* **(a)** *(commercial business)* establecimiento *m or* casa *f*; **he runs an important printing establishment** = dirige un establecimiento tipográfico importante **(b) establishment charges** = gastos de primer establecimiento **(c)** *(people working in a company)* personal *m or* plantilla *f* **to be on the establishment** = estar en plantilla; **office with an establishment of fifteen** = oficina con quince empleados de plantilla

estate [ɪs'teɪt] *noun* **(a)** real estate = bienes *mpl* inmuebles *or* bienes raíces; **estate agency** = agencia *f* inmobiliaria; **estate agent** = agente *m* inmobiliario **(b) industrial estate** *or* **trading estate** = zona *f* industrial **(c)** fortuna *f or* herencia *f or* testamentaría *f*; **estate duty** = derechos de sucesión *or* impuesto sobre el patrimonio heredado

estimate 1 ['estɪmət] *noun* **(a)** *(approximate calculation)* estimación *f or* cálculo *m or* cómputo *m or* apreciación *f or* valoración *f*; **rough estimate** = cálculo aproximado; **at a conservative estimate** = según una apreciación prudente; **their turnover has risen by at least 20% in the last year, and that is a conservative estimate** = su volumen de negocios ha aumentado un 20% como mínimo en el último año y se trata de una apreciación prudente; **these figures are only an estimate** = estas cifras son sólo un cálculo aproximado; **can you give me an estimate of how much time was spent on the job?** = ¿podría hacerme un cómputo de las horas que se emplearon en el trabajo? **(b)** *(written calculation of cost)* presupuesto *m*; **estimate of costs** *or* **of expenditure** = presupuesto de costes *or* de gastos; **before we can give the grant we must have an estimate of the total costs involved** = antes de poder conceder la subvención debemos tener un presupuesto del total de los costes comprendidos; **to ask a builder for an estimate for building the warehouse** = pedir a un

constratista un presupuesto para la construcción del almacén; **to put in an estimate** = presentar un presupuesto; **three firms put in estimates for the job** = tres empresas presentaron presupuestos de la obra **2** ['estɪmeɪt] *verb* **(a)** calcular *or* valorar *or* estimar; **to estimate that it will cost £1m** *or* **to estimate costs at £1m** = calcular que costará £1 millón *or* valorar los costes en £1 millón; **we estimate current sales at only 60% of last year** = calculamos que las ventas actuales son sólo el 60% respecto al año pasado **(b) to estimate for a job** = hacer el presupuesto de un trabajo; **three firms estimated for the fitting of the offices** = tres empresas han hecho presupuestos para el mobiliario de las oficinas

◊ **estimated** ['estɪmeɪtɪd] *adjective* estimado, -da; **estimated figure** = cifras estimadas; **estimated sales** = ventas estimadas; **estimated time of arrival (ETA)** = hora estimada de llegada

◊ **estimation** [estɪ'meɪʃən] *noun* estimación *f or* valoración *f*

◊ **estimator** ['estɪmeɪtə] *noun* estimador, -ra *or* tasador, -ra

et al. = AND OTHERS

etc. [ɪt'setrə] etc.; **the import duty is to be paid on luxury items including cars, watches, etc.** = hay que pagar derechos de aduana por los artículos de lujo como coches, relojes etc.

Ethiopia [i:θɪ'əʊpɪə] *noun* Etiopía *f*

◊ **Ethiopian** [i:θɪ'əʊpɪən] *adjective & noun* etíope
Note: capital: **Addis Ababa**; currency: **Ethiopian birr (Br)** = dólar etíope *or* birr (Br)

EU ['i:'ju:] = EUROPEAN UNION Unión Europea (UE); **EU ministers met today in Brussels** = los ministros de la UE se han reunido hoy en Bruselas; **the USA is increasing its trade with the EU** = los EE.UU están aumentando sus intercambios comerciales con la UE (NOTE: formerly called the **European Community (EC)**

Euro- ['jʊərəʊ] *prefix* euro

◊ **Eurobond** ['jʊərəʊbɒnd] *noun* eurobono *m*; **the Eurobond market** = el mercado de eurobonos

◊ **Eurocheque** ['jʊərəʊtʃek] *noun* eurocheque *m*

◊ **Eurocurrency** [jʊərəʊ'kʌrənsi] *noun* eurodivisa *f*; **a Eurocurrency loan** = un crédito en eurodivisas; **the Eurocurrency market** = el mercado de eurodivisas

◊ **Eurodollar** ['jʊərəʊdɒlə] *noun* eurodólar *m*; **a Eurodollar loan** = un crédito en eurodólares; **the Eurodollar market** = el mercado de eurodólares

◊ **Euromarket** ['jʊərəʊmɑːkɪt] *noun* euromercado *m*

Europe ['jʊərəp] *noun* Europa *f*; **most of the countries of Western Europe are members of the European Union** = la mayoría de los países de Europa Occidental son miembros de la Unión Europea; **Canadian exports to Europe have risen by 25%** = las exportaciones canadienses a Europa han aumentado un 25%; **UK sales to Europe have increased this year** = las ventas del Reino Unido a Europa han aumentado este año

◊ **European** [juərə'pi:ən] *adjective* europeo, -pea; **Single European Act** = Acta única europea

◊ **European Bank for Reconstruction and Development (EBRD)** Banco Europeo de Reconstrucción y Desarrollo (BERD)

◊ **European Commission** [juərə'pi:ən kə'mıʃn] *noun* Comisión Europea

◊ **European Community (EC)** *or* **European Economic Community (EEC)** [juərə'pi:ən kə'mju:nıti] la Comunidad Económica (la CE) *or* Comunidad Económica Europea (CEE) (NOTE: now called **the European Union**)

European Currency Unit (ECU) [juərə'pi:ən 'kərənsi 'ju:nıt] ecu *or* ECU *m see comment at* ECU

European Economic Area (EEA) [juərə'pi:ən i:kə'nɒmık 'eərıə] Espacio Económico Europeo (EEE)

European Free Trade Association (EFTA) [juərə,pi:ən fri:'treıd əsəʊsı'eıʃn] Asociación Europea de Libre Comercio (AELC)

European Monetary System (EMS) [juərə'pi:ən 'mʌnıtəri 'sıstəm] Sistema Monetario Europeo (SME)

COMMENT: the various currencies in the EMS are linked by their exchange rates, each currency being allowed to move up or down within a certain band. If a currency becomes too strong or too weak to remain inside the band, government intervention by the European central banks will be used to bring the currency back into its accepted place; if this fails, the currency may be revalued or devalued at another level within the EMS, and the other currencies may have their rates changed at the same time

European Regional Development Fund (ERDF) [juərə'pi:ən 'ri:dʒənəl dı'veləpmənt 'fʌnd] Fondo Europeo de Desarrollo Regional (FEDER)

European Union (EU) [juərə'pi:ən 'juniən] Unión Europea (UE)

evade [ı'veıd] *verb* evadir *or* eludir; **to evade tax** = evadir impuestos

evaluate [ı'væljʊeıt] *verb* valorar *or* evaluar *or* calcular; **to evaluate costs** = evaluar los costes

◊ **evaluation** [ıvæljʊ'eıʃn] *noun* evaluación *f or* valoración *f or* cálculo *m*; **job evaluation** = valoración de puestos de trabajo

evasion [ı'veıʒən] *noun* evasión *f or* elusión *f (illegally trying not to pay tax)* **tax evasion** = evasión de impuestos *or* fraude fiscal

evict [ı'vıkt] *verb* desalojar

evidence ['evıdəns] *noun* evidencia *f or* prueba *f or* declaración *f*; **documentary evidence** = prueba documental; **the secretary gave evidence for** *or* **against her former employer** = la secretaria prestó declaración a favor *or* en contra de su anterior patrono

ex- [eks] *preposition* **(a)** *(out of, from)* fuera de *or* sin *or* franco en; **price ex warehouse** = precio *m* franco almacén *or* en almacén; **price ex works** *or* **ex factory** = precio en fábrica *or* en almacén **(b)** *(not including)* **ex coupon** = título *m* sin el cupón

correspondiente al próximo pago; **shares quoted ex dividend** = acciones cotizadas sin dividendos *or* cupón; **the shares went ex dividend yesterday** = las acciones salieron ayer a cotización sin dividendos **(c)** *(formerly)* ex *or* antiguo, -gua *or* cesado, -da; **Mr Smith, the ex-chairman of the company** = el Sr Smith, ex presidente de la compañía **(d)** *(phone number)* **ex-directory** = que no figura en la guía telefónica; **he has an ex-directory number** = su número no figura en la guía telefónica

exact [ıg'zækt] *adjective* exacto, -ta; **the exact time is 10.27** = son exactamente las 10.27; **the salesgirl asked me if I had the exact sum, since the shop had no change** = la vendedora me preguntó si tenía el importe exacto ya que no tenían cambio en la tienda

◊ **exactly** [ıg'zæktli] *adverb* exactamente; **the total cost was exactly £6,500** = el coste total fue exactamente de £6.500

exaggerate [ıg'zædʒəreıt] *verb* exagerar

examine [ıg'zæmın] *verb* **(a)** *(look carefully)* examinar *or* revisar *or* registrar *or* investigar; **the customs officials asked to examine the inside of the car** = los funcionarios de aduanas quisieron registrar el interior del coche; **the police are examining the papers from the managing director's safe** = la policía está examinando los documentos de la caja fuerte del director **(b)** *(test)* examinar

◊ **examination** [ıgzæmı'neıʃn] *noun* **(a)** *(inspection)* examen *m or* registro *m or* revisión *or* inspección *f*; **customs examination** = inspección aduanera **(b)** *(test)* examen; **entrance examination** = examen de admisión; **(public) competitive examination** = concurso oposición; **he passed his accountancy examinations** = aprobó el examen de contabilidad; **she came first in the final examination for the course** = sacó la mejor nota en el examen de final de curso; **he failed his proficiency examination and so had to leave his job** = suspendió el examen de aptitud por lo que tuvo que dejar su trabajo

example [ıg'za:mpl] *noun* ejemplo *m or* ejemplar *m*; **the motor show has many examples of energy-saving cars on display** = en el salón del automóvil se exponen muchos coches de consumo reducido; **for example** = por ejemplo; **the government wants to encourage exports, and, for example, it gives free credit to exporters** = el gobierno quiere animar las exportaciones y, por ejemplo, concede créditos libres a los exportadores

exceed [ık'si:d] *verb* exceder *or* sobrepasar *or* superar; **discount not exceeding 15%** = descuento que no sobrepasa el 15%; **last year costs exceeded 20% of income for the first time** = el año pasado los costes excedieron por primera vez el 20% de los ingresos; **he has exceeded his credit limit** = ha superado el límite del crédito

excellent ['eksələnt] *adjective* excelente; **the quality of the firm's products is excellent, but its sales force is not large enough** = la calidad de los productos de la empresa es excelente, pero no tienen suficiente personal de ventas

except [ık'sept] *preposition & conjunction* excepto *or* salvo *or* exceptuando a *or* con excepción de; **VAT is levied on all goods and services except books, newspapers and children's clothes** = el IVA se impone a todas las mercancías y servicios con excepción de los libros, periódicos y la ropa infantil; **sales are rising in all markets except the Far East** = las ventas están aumentando en todos los mercados salvo en el Extremo Oriente

◊ **excepted** [ɪk'septɪd] *adverb* exceptuado *or* salvo; **errors and omissions excepted (e. & o.e.)**= salvo error u omisión (s.e.u.o.)

exception [ɪk'sepʃn] *noun* excepción *f or* salvedad *f*; **I am afraid I cannot make an exception in your case** = me temo que no puedo hacer una salvedad a su favor

◊ **exceptional** [ɪk'sepʃənl] *adjective* excepcional; **exceptional charges (in accounts)** = cargos excepcionales; **exceptional items** = partidas excepcionales

excess 1 [ɪk'ses] *noun* exceso *m or* excedente *m or* sobrante *m*; **an excess of expenditure over revenue** = un exceso de los gastos sobre los ingresos; **in excess of** = superior a; **quantities in excess of twenty-five kilos** = cantidades superiores a veinticinco kilos **2** ['ekses] *adjective* **excess baggage** = exceso de equipaje; **excess capacity** = exceso de capacidad; **excess fare** = suplemento *m*; **excess profits** = beneficios extraordinarios; **excess profits tax** = impuesto sobre beneficios extraordinarios

◊ **excessive** [ɪk'sesɪv] *adjective* excesivo, -va; **excessive costs** = costes excesivos

QUOTE most airlines give business class the same baggage allowance as first class, which can save large sums in excess baggage
Business Traveller

QUOTE control of materials provides manufacturers with an opportunity to reduce the amount of money tied up in excess materials
Duns Business Month

exchange [ɪks'tʃeɪn(d)ʒ] **1** *noun* **(a)** *(swap)* intercambio *m or* cambio *m or* trueque *m or* canje *m*; **part exchange** = canje parcial; **to take a car in part exchange** = comprar un coche entregando el viejo en canje parcial; **exchange of contracts** = intercambio de contratos **(b)** *(currency)* **foreign exchange** = divisas *or* moneda extranjera; **the company has more than £1m in foreign exchange** = la compañía tiene más de £1 millón en divisas; **foreign exchange broker** = corredor de comercio de divisas; **foreign exchange market** = mercado de divisas *or* cambiario; **he trades on the foreign exchange market** = comercia en el mercado de divisas; **foreign exchange markets were very active after the dollar devalued** = los mercados cambiarios se mostraron muy activos después de la devaluación del dólar; **rate of exchange** *or* **exchange rate** = tipo de cambio; **the current rate of exchange is 200 pesetas to the pound** = el tipo de cambio actual es de 200 pesetas la libra; *(EMS)* **exchange rate mechanism (ERM)** = mecanismo de cambio (del SME); **fixed exchange rate** = cambio fijo; **floating rates of exchange** = cambios flotantes; **exchange control** = control de cambio *or* divisas; **the government had to impose exchange controls to stop the rush to buy dollars** = el gobierno tuvo que

imponer controles de cambio para detener la compra masiva de dólares; **exchange dealer** = cambista *or* operador de cambios; **exchange dealings** = operaciones *fpl* en divisas *or* cambiarias; *GB* **Exchange Equalization Account** = cuenta de compensación de cambios; **exchange premium** = agio del cambio **(c)** **bill of exchange** = letra de cambio **(d)** **telephone exchange** = central *or* centralita telefónica **(e)** **the Stock Exchange** = la bolsa *or* bolsa de valores; **the company's shares are traded on the New York Stock Exchange** = las acciones de la compañía se cotizan en la Bolsa de Nueva York; **he works on the Stock Exchange** = trabaja en la bolsa; **commodity exchange** = lonja *f* de contratación **2** *verb* **(a)** *(swap)* canjear; **to exchange one article for another** = cambiar *or* canjear *or* conmutar un artículo por otro; **he exchanged his motorcycle for a car** = cambió su motocicleta por un coche; **if the trousers are too small you can take them back and exchange them for a larger pair** = si los pantalones le están demasiado pequeños los puede devolver y cambiar por una talla mayor; **goods can be exchanged only on production of the sales slip** = las mercancías sólo pueden ser canjeadas mediante la presentación de la factura **(b)** **to exchange contracts** = intercambiar contratos **(c)** *(currency)* cambiar divisas *or* moneda extranjera; **to exchange francs for pounds** = cambiar francos por libras

◊ **exchangeable** [ɪks'tʃeɪn(d)ʒəbl] *adjective* intercambiable *or* cambiable

◊ **exchanger** [ɪks'tʃeɪn(d)ʒə] *noun* agente *mf* de cambio

QUOTE under the barter agreements, Nigeria will export crude oil in exchange for trucks, food, planes and chemicals
Wall Street Journal

QUOTE can free trade be reconciled with a strong dollar resulting from floating exchange rates
Duns Business Month

QUOTE a draft report on changes in the international monetary system casts doubt on any return to fixed exchange-rate parities
Wall Street Journal

Exchequer [ɪks'tʃekə] *noun GB* **the Exchequer** = ministerio *m* de Economía y Hacienda; **the Chancellor of the Exchequer** = ministro, -tra de Economía y Hacienda

excise 1 ['eksaɪz] *noun* **(a)** **excise duty** = impuesto sobre el consumo *or* la venta; **to pay excise duty on wine** = pagar un impuesto sobre la venta de vino **(b)** **Customs and Excise** *or* **Excise Department** = Aduanas y Arbitrios (administración de aduanas e impuestos sobre el consumo); **Excise officer** = recaudador, -ra de impuestos sobre el consumo **2** [ɪk'saɪz] *verb* extirpar *or* suprimir; **please excise all references to the strike in the minutes** = rogamos supriman en las actas todas las referencias a la huelga

◊ **exciseman** ['eksaɪzmæn] *noun* recaudador de impuestos

QUOTE excise taxes account for 45% of liquor prices but only about 10% of wine and beer prices

Business Week

exclude [ɪksˈkluːd] *verb* excluir; **the interest charges have been excluded from the document** = los cargos en concepto de interés han sido excluidos del documento; **damage by fire is excluded from the policy** = los daños por incendio están excluidos de la póliza

◊ **excluding** [ɪksˈkluːdɪŋ] *preposition* excepto *or* con excepción de *or* exceptuando; **ail salesmen, excluding those living in London, can claim expenses for attending the sales conference** = todos los vendedores, con excepción de los que viven en Londres, pueden reclamar gastos de asistencia a la reunión de ventas

◊ **exclusion** [ɪksˈkluːʒən] *noun* exclusión *f (in an insurance policy)* **exclusion clause** = cláusula de exclusión

◊ **exclusive** [ɪksˈkluːsɪv] *adjective* **(a)** exclusive **agreement** = contrato en exclusiva; **exclusive right to market a product** = derechos exclusivos para la comercialización de un producto **(b)** exclusive of = no incluido *or* sin tener en cuenta; **exclusive of tax** = impuestos no incluidos; **all payments are exclusive of tax** = todos los pagos son sin impuestos; **the invoice is exclusive of VAT** = el IVA no está incluido en la factura

◊ **exclusivity** [ekskluːˈsɪvɪti] *noun* exclusividad *f or* exclusiva *f*

excuse 1 [ɪksˈkjuːs] *noun* excusa *f or* disculpa *f*; **his excuse for not coming to the meeting was that he had been told about it only the day before** = su excusa por no venir a la reunión fue que sólo se lo habían comunicado el día anterior; **the managing director refused to accept the sales manager's excuses for the poor sales** = el director gerente rechazó las excusas del director comercial por las bajas ventas registradas **2** [ɪksˈkjuːz] *verb* excusar *or* disculpar *or* perdonar; **she can be excused for not knowing the Spanish for 'photocopier'** = se le puede perdonar que no sepa cómo se dice 'photocopier' en español

execute [ˈeksɪkjuːt] *verb* ejecutar *or* cumplir

◊ **execution** [eksɪˈkjuːʃən] *noun* ejecución *f or* cumplimiento *m*; **stay of execution** = aplazamiento de una sentencia; **the court granted the company a two-week stay of execution** = el tribunal concedió a la compañía dos semanas de prórroga

◊ **executive** [ɪgˈzekjutɪv] **1** *adjective* ejecutivo, -va; **executive committee** = comisión ejecutiva; **executive director** = director ejecutivo *or* consejero ejecutivo; **executive powers** = poder ejecutivo; **he was made managing director with full executive powers over the European operation** = fue nombrado director gerente con plenos poderes para la operación europea **2** *noun* ejecutivo, -va; **sales executive** = ejecutivo de ventas; **senior *or* junior executive** = ejecutivo principal *or* ejecutivo subalterno; **account executive** = encargado, -da de transmitir las propuestas de los clientes a la empresa; **chief executive** = jefe ejecutivo *or* director general; **executive search** = búsqueda de ejecutivos *or* directivos (de empresa) (NOTE: a more polite term for 'headhunting')

QUOTE one in ten students commented on the long hours which executives worked

Employment Gazette

QUOTE our executives are motivated by a desire to carry out a project to the best of their ability

British Business

executor [ɪgˈzekjʊtə] *noun* albacea *m*; **he was named executor of his brother's will** = le nombraron albacea testamentario de su hermano

exempt [ɪgˈzem(p)t] **1** *adjective* exento, -ta *or* dispensado, -da; **exempt from tax *or* tax-exempt** = exento, -ta de impuestos; **as a non-profit-making organization we are exempt from tax** = como somos una organización sin fines lucrativos estamos exentos del pago de impuestos; *(products or services on which no VAT is charged)* **exempt supplies** = productos *or* servicios exentos del IVA **2** *verb* eximir *or* dispensar *or* desgravar; **non-profit-making organizations are exempted from tax** = las organizaciones sin fines de lucro están exentas del pago de impuestos; **food is exempted from sales tax** = los productos alimenticios están exentos del impuesto sobre la venta; **the government exempted trusts from tax** = el gobierno eximió de impuestos a los fideicomisos

◊ **exemption** [ɪgˈzem(p)ʃən] *noun* exención *f (from customs duties)* franquicia *f*; **exemption from tax *or* tax exemption** = exención fiscal; **as a non-profit-making organization you can claim tax exemption** = al ser una organización sin fines de lucro Vds. pueden reclamar exención fiscal

exercise [ˈeksəsaɪz] **1** *noun* ejercicio *m*; **exercise of an option** = ejercicio del derecho de opción **2** *verb* ejercer *or* ejercitar; **to exercise an option** = ejercer el derecho de opción; **he exercised his option to acquire sole marketing rights for the product** = ejerció su derecho de opción para adquirir los derechos exclusivos de comercialización del producto; **the chairwoman exercised her veto to block the motion** = la presidenta ejerció su derecho de veto para bloquear la moción

ex gratia [ˈeks ˈgreɪʃə] *adjective* **an ex gratia payment** = pago ex-gratia *or* abono de una cantidad sin haber obligación para ello

exhaust [ɪgˈzɔːst] *verb* agotar

◊ **exhausted** [ɪgˈzɔːstɪd] *adjective* **(a)** *(stock)* agotado, -da **(b)** *(tired)* cansado, -da

exhibit [ɪgˈzɪbɪt] **1** *noun* **(a)** *(thing shown)* objeto *m* expuesto; **the buyers admired the exhibits on our stand** = los compradores admiraron los objetos expuestos en nuestro stand **(b)** *(exhibition stand)* exposición *f or* exhibición *f*; **the British trade exhibit at the International Computer Fair** = el 'stand' británico en la Feria Internacional de Informática **2** *verb* **to exhibit at the Motor Show** = exponer en el Salón del Automóvil

◊ **exhibition** [eksɪˈbɪʃən] *noun* exhibición *f or* exposición *f*; **the government has sponsored an exhibition of good design** = el gobierno ha patrocinado una exposición de diseño; **we have a stand at the Ideal Home Exhibition** = tenemos un stand en la Exposición del Hogar Ideal; **the agricultural exhibition grounds** = los recintos de la feria agrícola; **travelling exhibition** = exposición itinerante; **exhibition room** *or* **hall** = salón *m or* sala *f* de exposiciones; **exhibition stand** *or* *US* **exhibition booth** = stand de exposición

◊ **exhibitor** [ɪɡ'zɪbɪtə] *noun* expositor *m*

exist [ɪɡ'zɪst] *verb* existir; **I do not believe the document exists - I think it has been burnt** = no creo que el documento exista - creo que ha sido quemado

exit ['eksɪt] *noun* salida *f*; **the customers all rushed towards the exits** = los clientes se abalanzaron hacia las salidas; **fire exit** = salida de urgencia

ex officio ['eks ɔ'fɪʃɪəʊ] *adjective & adverb* de oficio *or* por razón de su cargo; **the treasurer is ex officio a member** *or* **an ex officio member of the finance committee** = el tesorero es miembro del comité financiero por razón de su cargo

expand [ɪk'spænd] *verb* ampliar *or* desarrollar *or* expandir *or* crecer *or* extender; **an expanding economy** = una economía en expansión *or* en desarrollo; **the company is expanding fast** = la empresa está creciendo rápidamente; **we have had to expand our sales force** = hemos tenido que ampliar nuestro personal de ventas

◊ **expanded polystyrene** [ɪk'spændɪd pɒlɪ'staɪriːn] *noun* poliestireno *m* expandido

◊ **expansion** [ɪk'spænʃən] *noun* expansión *f or* ampliación *f*; **the expansion of the domestic market** = la expansión del mercado interior; **the company had difficulty in financing its current expansion programme** = la compañía tuvo dificultades para financiar su programa de expansión actual; *GB* **business expansion scheme** = proyecto de expansión comercial; **expansion of capital expenditure** = ampliación de inversiones en activo fijo

expect [ɪk'spekt] *verb* esperar; **we are expecting him to arrive at 10.45** = esperamos que llegue a las 10.45; **they are expecting a cheque from their agent next week** = esperan recibir un cheque de su representante la semana próxima; **the house was sold for more than the expected price** = la casa se vendió a un precio más alto que el esperado

◊ **expectancy** [ɪk'spektənsi] *noun* **life expectancy** = esperanza *f* de vida

expedite ['ekspɪdaɪt] *verb* agilizar

expenditure [ɪk'spendɪtʃə] *noun* gasto *m or* desembolso *m*; **below-the-line expenditure** = gastos no incluidos en las cuentas normales; **capital expenditure** = inversión *m* gastos de capital; **the company's current expenditure programme** = el programa actual de gastos de la empresa; **heavy expenditure on equipment** = grandes gastos en bienes de equipo (NOTE: no plural in GB English; US English often uses the plural **expenditures**)

◊ **expense** [ɪk'spens] *noun* **(a)** *(money)* gasto *m*; **at the expense of** = a costa de; **it is not worth the expense** = no vale lo que cuesta; **the expense is too much for my bank balance** = el gasto es demasiado elevado dado el estado de mi cuenta bancaria; **at great expense** = con mucho gasto; **he furnished the office regardless of expense** *or* **with no expense spared** = amuebló la oficina sin escatimar gastos **(b)** **expense account** = cuenta de gastos de representación; **I'll put this lunch on my expense account** = cargaré este almuerzo en mi cuenta de gastos de representación; **expense account lunches form a large part of our current expenditure** = gran parte de nuestro gasto actual se va en almuerzos de trabajo

◊ **expenses** [ɪk'spensɪz] *plural noun* gastos *mpl*; **the salary offered is £10,000 plus expenses** = el salario ofrecido es de £10.000 más gastos; **all expenses paid** = gastos pagados; **the company sent him to San Francisco all expenses paid** = la compañía le envió a San Francisco con todos los gastos pagados; **to cut down on expenses** = reducir gastos; **allowable expenses** = gastos deducibles; **business expenses** = gastos de explotación; **direct expenses** = costes directos; **entertainment expenses** = gastos de representación; **fixed expenses** = gastos fijos; **incidental expenses** = gastos varios *or* menores; **indirect expenses** = costes indirectos; **legal expenses** = gastos *or* costas judiciales; **overhead expenses** *or* **general expenses** *or* **running expenses** = gastos generales *or* gastos de mantenimiento; **travelling expenses** = gastos de desplazamiento

◊ **expensive** [ɪk'spensɪv] *adjective* caro, -ra *or* costoso, -sa; **first-class air travel is becoming more and more expensive** = viajar en avión en primera clase se está poniendo cada vez más caro

experience [ɪk'spɪərɪəns] **1** *noun* experiencia *f or* práctica *f*; **he is a man of considerable experience** = es un hombre que tiene una gran experiencia; **she has a lot of experience of dealing with German companies** = tiene una gran experiencia en el trato con empresas alemanas; **he gained most of his experience in the Far East** = adquirió la mayor parte de su experiencia en el Extremo Oriente; **some experience is required for this job** = este trabajo requiere cierta experiencia **2** *verb* experimentar *or* sufrir *or* vivir; **the company experienced a period of falling sales** = la empresa vivió un periodo de baja en las ventas

◊ **experienced** [ɪk'spɪərɪənst] *adjective* experto, -ta *or* experimentado, -da; **he is the most experienced negotiator I know** = es el negociador más experimentado que conozco; **we have appointed a very experienced woman as sales director** = hemos nombrado directora de ventas a una gran experta

expert ['ekspɜːt] *noun* experto, -ta *or* perito, -ta *m*; **an expert in the field of electronics** *or* **an electronics expert** = experto en el campo de la electrónica *or* experto en electrónica; **the company asked a financial expert for advice** *or* **asked for expert financial advice** = la compañía pidió asesoramiento a un experto en finanzas; **expert's report** = informe pericial *or* de un experto

◊ **expertise** [ekspɜːˈtiːz] *noun* pericia *f or* competencia *f or* conocimientos *mpl or* habilidades *fpl*; **we hired Mr Smith because of his financial expertise** *or* **because of his expertise in the African market** = contratamos al Sr. Smith por su competencia en las finanzas *or* por sus conocimientos del mercado africano

expiration [ekspɪˈreɪʃən] *noun* expiración *f or* terminación *f or* vencimiento *m*; **expiration of an insurance policy** = la expiración de una póliza de seguros; **to repay before the expiration of the stated period** = pagar antes de la expiración del periodo establecido; **on expiration of the lease** = al expirar el arriendo

◊ **expire** [ɪkˈspaɪə] *verb* caducar *or* expirar *or* terminar *or* vencer; **the lease expires in 1999** = el arriendo *or* contrato de arrendamiento expira en 1999; **his passport has expired** = su pasaporte está caducado

◊ **expiry** [ɪkˈspaɪəri] *noun* caducidad *f or* expiración *f or* terminación *f or* vencimiento *m*; **expiry of an insurance policy** = el vencimiento de una póliza de seguros; **expiry date** = fecha de caducidad

explain [ɪkˈspleɪn] *verb* explicar; **he explained to the customs officials that the two computers were presents from friends** = explicó a los funcionarios de aduanas que los dos ordenadores eran regalos de unos amigos; **can you explain why the sales in the first quarter are so high?** = ¿puede Vd. explicar por qué las ventas del primer trimestre son tan altas?; **the sales director tried to explain the sudden drop in unit sales** = el director de ventas intentó explicar la repentina caída de las ventas

◊ **explanation** [ekspləˈneɪʃən] *noun* explicación *f or* aclaración *f*; **the VAT inspector asked for an explanation of the invoices** = el inspector del IVA pidió una explicación de las facturas; **at the AGM, the chairman gave an explanation for the high level of interest payments** = en la junta general anual, el presidente dio una explicación de los altos intereses pagados

exploit [ɪkˈsplɔɪt] *verb* explotar *or* aprovechar; **the company is exploiting its contacts in the Ministry of Trade** = la compañía aprovecha sus contactos en el Ministerio de Comercio; **we hope to exploit the oil resources in the China Sea** = esperamos explotar los recursos petrolíferos en el mar de China

◊ **exploitation** [eksplɔɪˈteɪʃn] *noun* explotación *f*; **the exploitation of migrant farm workers was only stopped when they became unionized** = la creación de sindicatos puso fin a la explotación de los trabajadores agrícolas inmigrantes

explore [ɪkˈsplɔː] *verb* explorar *or* examinar *or* investigar; **we are exploring the possibility of opening an office in London** = estamos investigando la posibilidad de abrir una oficina en Londres

export 1 ['ekspɔːt] *noun* **(a) exports** = exportaciones *fpl*; **exports to Africa have increased by 25%** = las exportaciones a Africa han aumentado el 25% **(b)** *(action of sending goods abroad)* exportación *f or* mercancía *f* exportada; **the export trade** *or* **the export market** = el comercio de exportación *or* mercado exportador; **export department** = departamento de exportación; **export duty** = aranceles *or* derechos *or* tarifas de exportación; **export house** = casa exportadora; **export-led boom** = auge impulsado por las exportaciones; **export licence** = licencia *or* permiso de exportación; **the government has refused an export licence for computer parts** = el gobierno ha denegado la licencia de exportación para piezas de recambio de ordenadores; **export manager** = director de exportación; **Export Credit Guarantee Department (ECGD)** = departamento de garantía de credito a la exportación **2** [ɪkˈspɔːt] *verb* exportar; **50% of our production is exported** = exportamos el 50% de nuestra producción; **the company imports raw materials and exports the finished products** = la compañía importa materias primas y exporta productos acabados

◊ **exportation** [ekspɔːˈteɪʃən] *noun* exportación *f*

◊ **exporter** [eksˈpɔːtə] *noun* exportador, -ra; **a major furniture exporter** = un importante exportador de muebles; **Venezuela is an important exporter of oil** *or* **an important oil exporter** = Venezuela es un importante exportador de petróleo

◊ **exporting** [eksˈpɔːtɪŋ] *adjective* de exportación *or* exportador, -ra; **oil exporting countries** = países exportadores de petróleo

QUOTE in that year, Europe's gross exports of white goods climbed to 2.4 billion, about a quarter of total production
Economist

QUOTE the New Zealand producers are now aiming to export more fresh meat as opposed to frozen which has formed the majority of its UK imports in the past
Marketing

exposition [ekspəˈzɪʃən] *noun US* = EXHIBITION

exposure [ɪkˈspəʊʒə] *noun* **(a)** *(publicity)* publicidad *f*; **our company has achieved more exposure since we decided to advertise nationally** = nuestra compañía ha recibido más publicidad desde que decidimos anunciarla a escala nacional **(b)** *(risk)* riesgo *m*; **he is trying to cover his exposure in the property market** = intenta cubrir sus riesgos en el mercado inmobiliario

COMMENT: exposure can be the amount of money lent to a customer (a bank's exposure to a foreign country) or the amount of money which an investor may lose if his investments collapse (such as his exposure in the stock market)

QUOTE it attributed the poor result to the
bank's high exposure to residential
mortgages, which showed a significant
slowdown in the past few months
South China Morning Post

express [ɪk'spres] **1** *adjective* **(a)** *(fast)* rápido,
-da *or* urgente; **express letter** = una carta urgente;
express delivery = distribución *or* entrega urgente;
express item = envío urgente **(b)** *(explicit)* expreso,
-sa *or* explícito, -ta; **the contract has an express
condition forbidding sale in Africa** = el contrato
tiene una condición explícita que prohibe vender en
Africa **2** *verb* **(a)** *(put into words)* expresar; **this
chart shows home sales expressed as a percentage
of total turnover** = este gráfico muestra las ventas
nacionales expresadas como porcentaje del volumen
total de ventas **(b)** *(send)* enviar por correo *or*
transporte urgente; **we expressed the order to the
customer's warehouse** = enviamos el pedido al
almacén del cliente por transporte urgente

◊ **expressly** [ɪk'spresli] *adverb* expresamente *or*
explícitamente; **the contract expressly forbids
sales to the United States** = el contrato prohibe
expresamente la venta a los Estados Unidos

ext = EXTENSION ext

extend [ɪk'stend] *verb* **(a)** *(grant)* conceder *or*
otorgar *or* extender; **to extend credit to a customer**
= conceder un crédito a un cliente **(b)** *(make longer)*
prolongar *or* prorrogar *or* extender; **to extend a
contract for two years** = prorrogar un contrato por
dos años; **extended guarantee** *or* **warranty** =
garantía adicional *or* garantía a largo plazo *or*
extensión de garantía

◊ **extended credit** ɪk'stendɪd 'kredɪt] *noun*
crédito *m* a largo plazo; **we sell to Australia on
extended credit** = vendemos a Australia con
créditos a largo plazo

◊ **extension** [ɪk'stenʃən] *noun* **(a)** *(of time,
credit)* ampliación *f or* prolongación *f or* prórroga *f*; **to
get an extension of credit** = conseguir una prórroga
del crédito; **extension of a contract** = prórroga del
contrato **(b)** *(in an office)* extensión *f or* teléfono *m*
interno; **can you get me extension 21?** = ¿puede
ponerme con la extensión 21?; **extension 21 is
engaged** = la extensión 21 está ocupada; **the sales
manager is on extension 53** = el director de ventas
está hablando por la extensión 53

◊ **extensive** [ɪk'stensɪv] *adjective* extenso, -sa *or*
extensivo, -va; **an extensive network of sales
outlets** = una extensa red de ventas

QUOTE the White House refusal to ask for an
extension of the auto import quotas
Duns Business Month

external [ɪk'stɜ:nl] *adjective* **(a)** *(foreign)*
exterior; **external account** = cuenta de no residente;
external trade = comercio exterior **(b)** *(outside a
company)* externo, -na; **external audit** = auditoría
externa; **external auditor** = auditor *or* interventor
externo; **external growth** = crecimiento externo *or*
exterior

extinguisher [ɪk'stɪŋgwɪʃə] *noun* **fire
extinguisher** = extintor *m* (de fuegos)

extra ['ekstrə] **1** *adjective* extra *or* de más *or*
suplementario, -ria *or* complementario, -ria; **extra
charges** = gastos adicionales y complementarios;
there is no extra charge for heating = no hay
recargo por la calefacción; **to charge 10% extra for
postage** = cargar un 10% de más por franqueo; **he
had £25 extra pay for working on Sunday** = tenía
una paga extra de £25 por trabajar los domingos;
service is extra = el servicio es aparte *or* no está
incluido **2** *plural noun* **extras** = gastos *mpl or* aparte
or suplementarios *or* adicionales *or* extras *mpl*;
packing and postage are extras = el embalaje y el
franqueo no están incluidos

extract 1 ['ekstrækt] *noun* extracto *m*; **he sent me
an extract of the accounts** = me envió un extracto
de las cuentas **2** [ɪk'strækt] *verb* extraer

extraordinary [ɪk'strɔ:dənəri] *adjective*
extraordinario, -ria; **extraordinary charges (in
accounts)** = gastos adicionales; **Extraordinary
General Meeting (EGM)** = Junta General
Extraordinaria; **to call an Extraordinary General
Meeting** = convocar una junta general
extraordinaria; **extraordinary items** = partidas
extraordinarias; **the auditors noted several
extraordinary items in the accounts** = los
auditores advirtieron varias partidas extraordinarias
en las cuentas

extremely [ɪk'stri:mli] *adverb* extremadamente *or*
sumamente; **it is extremely difficult to break into
the US market** = es extremadamente difícil
introducirse en el mercado estadounidense; **their
management team is extremely efficient** = su
equipo directivo es sumamente eficiente

Ff

f. & f. = FIXTURES AND FITTINGS

face value ['feɪs 'væljuː] *noun* valor *m* nominal

facility [fə'sɪlətɪ] *noun* **(a)** *(ease)* facilidad *f*; **we offer facilities for payment** = ofrecemos facilidades de pago **(b)** *(credit)* crédito *m*; **credit facilities** = facilidades de crédito; **overdraft facility** = límite de descubierto **(c) facilities** = instalaciones *fpl or* medios *mpl*; **harbour facilities** = instalaciones portuarias; **storage facilities** = instalaciones de almacenamiento; **transport facilities** = medios de transporte; **there are no facilities for passengers** = no existen servicios para pasajeros; **there are no facilities for unloading** *or* **there are no unloading facilities** = no hay instalaciones de descarga **(d)** *US* edificio *m or* almacén *m*; **we have opened our new warehouse facility** = hemos abierto nuestro nuevo almacén

facsimile [fæk'sɪmɔlɪ] *noun* **facsimile copy** = (i) fax *m or* telefax *m* ; (ii) facsímil *m see also* FAX

fact [fækt] *noun* **(a)** hecho *m or* dato *m or* realidad *f or* información *f*; **fact sheet** = hoja de datos; **the chairman asked to see all the facts on the income tax claim** = el presidente quiso examinar con detalle los datos de la reclamación del impuesto sobre la renta; **the sales director can give you the facts and figures about the African operation** = el director de ventas le puede proporcionar los datos exactos sobre la operación africana **(b)** **the fact of the matter is** = la verdad es que; **the fact of the matter is that the product does not fit the market** = la verdad es que el producto no se ajusta al mercado **(c)** **in fact** = en realidad *or* de hecho; **the chairman blamed the finance director for the loss when in fact he was responsible for it himself** = el presidente culpó al director financiero de las pérdidas sufridas cuando en realidad era él el responsable

◊ **fact-finding** ['fækt 'faɪndɪŋ] *adjective* de investigación *or* de inspección *or* de indagación; **a fact-finding mission** = una delegación de investigación; **the minister went on a fact-finding tour of the region** = el ministro efectuó una gira de inspección por la región

factor ['fæktə] **1** *noun* **(a)** *(element)* factor *m or* elemento *m or* coeficiente *m*; **the drop in sales is an important factor in the company's lower profits** = la caída de las ventas es un factor importante en la reducción de los beneficios de la empresa; **cost factor** = factor del coste; **cyclical factors** = factores cíclicos; **deciding factor** = factor decisivo; **load factor** = coeficiente de ocupación; **factors of production** = factores de producción **(b) by a factor of ten** = por un factor de diez **(c)** *(person or company)* agente *mf or* comisionista *mf* al por mayor **2** *verb* gestionar deudas con descuento

◊ **factoring** ['fæktərɪŋ] *noun* gestión *f* de deudas

(de otras compañías con descuento); **factoring charges** = coste de la gestión de deudas

factory ['fæktrɪ] *noun* fábrica *f*; **car factory** = fábrica de coches; **shoe factory** = fábrica de calzado; **the factory floor** = fábrica *f or* taller *m*; **factory hand** *or* **factory worker** = obrero *or* trabajador de fábrica; **factory inspector** *or* **inspector of factories** = inspector de fábrica; **the factory inspectorate** = cuerpo de inspectores de fábricas; **factory price** *or* **price ex factory** = precio en fábrica; **factory unit** = unidad de fabricación *or* centro de producción

faculty ['fækəltɪ] *noun* facultad *f or* habilidad *f*

fail [feɪl] *verb* **(a)** *(not to do something)* dejar de *or* omitir; **the company failed to notify the tax office of its change of address** = la compañía omitió notificar a la delegación de Hacienda su cambio de dirección **(b)** *(not to succeed)* fallar *or* fracasar; **the prototype failed its first test** = el prototipo falló en su primera prueba **(c)** *(to go bankrupt)* quebrar; **the company failed** = la compañía quebró; **he lost all his money when the bank failed** = perdió todo su dinero cuando el banco quebró

◊ **failing** ['feɪlɪŋ] **1** *noun* defecto *m or* punto *m* débil *or* debilidad *f*; **the chairman has one failing - he goes to sleep at board meetings** = el presidente tiene un punto débil - se duerme durante las juntas **2** *preposition* a falta de *or* salvo; **failing instructions to the contrary** = salvo instrucciones *or* órdenes al contrario; **failing prompt payment** = salvo pronto pago; **failing that** = en su defecto *or* si eso no funciona; **try the company secretary, and failing that the chairman** = inténtelo con la secretaria y si no lo consigue acuda al presidente

◊ **failure** ['feɪljə] *noun* **(a)** *(breaking down)* fracaso *m or* interrupción *f*; **the failure of the negotiations** = el fracaso de las negociaciones **(b)** **failure to pay a bill** = impago *m* de una factura **(c)** *(bankruptcy)* quiebra *f*; **commercial failure** = quiebra *f* comercial; **he lost all his money in the bank failure** = perdió todo su dinero en la quiebra del banco

fair [feə] **1** *noun* feria *f*; **trade fair** = feria *f* comercial; **to organize** *or* **to run a trade fair** = organizar *or* dirigir una feria comercial; **the fair is open from 9 a.m. to 5 p.m.** = la feria está abierta de 9 a 5; **the Computer Fair runs from April 1st to 6th** = la Feria de la Informática se celebra del 1 al 6 de abril; **there are two trade fairs running in London at the same time - the carpet manufacturers' and the computer dealers'** = en Londres se celebran dos ferias comerciales al mismo tiempo - la de los fabricantes de alfombras y la de los vendedores de ordenadores **2** *adjective* **(a)** *(honest or correct)* justo, -ta *or* equitativo, -va; **fair deal** = trato justo; **the workers feel they did not get a fair deal from the management** = los trabajadores creen que no recibieron un trato justo por parte de la dirección; *(legal buying and selling of shares)* **fair dealing** = trato justo; **fair price** = precio justo *or* razonable; **fair trade** = comercio justo; *US* = RESALE PRICE MAINTENANCE **fair trading** *or* **fair dealing** = comercio justo; *GB* **Office of Fair Trading** = servicio oficial de protección al consumidor; **fair value** *or US* **fair market value** = valor justo de venta *or* de mercado; **fair wear and tear** = desgaste natural; **the insurance policy covers most damage, but not fair wear and tear to the machine** = la póliza de seguros cubre la mayoría de los daños, pero no el desgaste natural de la máquina **(b)** *(clean)* **fair copy** = copia en limpio

◊ **fairly** ['feəli] *adverb* bastante; **the company is fairly close to financial collapse** = la compañía está al borde de la ruina financiera; **she is a fairly fast keyboarder** = maneja el teclado con bastante rapidez

faith [feiθ] *noun* fe *f or* confianza *f*; **to have faith in something** *or* **someone** = tener fe *or* confianza en algo *or* alguien; **the salesmen have great faith in the product** = los vendedores tienen gran fe en el producto; **the sales teams do not have much faith in their manager** = los equipos de vendedores tienen poca confianza en su director; **the board has faith in the managing director's judgement** = el consejo tiene confianza en el criterio del director gerente; **to buy something in good faith** = comprar algo de buena fe

◊ **faithfully** ['feiθfəli] *adverb* *(ending a letter)* **yours faithfully** = le saluda atentamente (NOTE: not used in US English)

fake [feik] **1** *noun* falsificación *f*; **the shipment came with fake documentation** = el envío llegó con documentación falsa **2** *verb* falsificar; **faked document** = documento falso; **he faked the results of the test** = falsificó los resultados de la prueba

Falkland Islands ['fɒlklənd 'ailəndz] *noun* Islas Malvinas *fpl*

◊ **Falkland Islander** ['fɒlklənd 'ailəndə] *noun* malvino, -na
NOTE: capital: **Stanley**; currency: **Falkland Island Pound (£)** = libra de las Islas Malvinas (£)

fall [fɔːl] **1** *noun* caída *f or* baja *f or* descenso *m*; **a fall in the exchange rate** = una caída del tipo de cambio; **fall in the price of gold** = la baja del precio del oro; **a fall on the Stock Exchange** = un descenso en la bolsa; **profits showed a 10% fall** = los beneficios registraron un descenso del 10% **2** *verb* **(a)** *(to drop suddenly)* bajar *or* caer *or* descender; **shares fell on the market today** = hoy las acciones bajaron en la bolsa; **gold shares fell 10%** *or* **fell 45 cents on the Stock Exchange** = las acciones de las minas de oro descendieron un 10% *or* descendieron 45 centavos en la bolsa; **the price of gold fell for the second day running** = el precio del oro bajó por segundo día consecutivo; **the pound fell against other European currencies** = la libra cayó frente a otras monedas europeas **(b)** *(to take place)* caer; **the**

public holiday falls on a Tuesday = la fiesta nacional cae en martes; **payments which fall due** = pagos que vencen (NOTE: **falling - fell - has fallen**)

◊ **fall away** ['fɔːl ə'wei] *verb* descender; **hotel bookings have fallen away since the tourist season ended** = las reservas hoteleras han descendido desde que terminó la temporada turística

◊ **fall back** ['fɔːl 'bæk] *verb* descender de nuevo *or* volver a caer; **shares fell back in light trading** = las acciones descendieron de nuevo en un mercado poco activo

◊ **fall back on** ['fɔːl 'bæk ɒn] *verb* echar mano de *or* recurrir a; **to fall back on cash reserves** = echar mano de las reservas en efectivo

◊ **fall behind** ['fɔːl bi'haind] *verb* **(a)** *(be late)* retrasarse; **he fell behind with his mortgage repayments** = se retrasó en el pago de la hipoteca; **the company has fallen behind with its deliveries** = la compañía se ha retrasado en las entregas **(b)** *(be in a worse position than)* rezagarse *or* quedarse atrás; **we have fallen behind our rivals** = nos hemos quedado atrás de nuestros competidores

◊ **falling** ['fɔːlɪŋ] *adjective* decreciente *or* con tendencia a la baja; **a falling market** = un mercado con tendencia a la baja; **the falling pound** = libra con tendencia a la baja

◊ **fall off** ['fɔːl 'ɒf] *verb* disminuir *or* bajar; **sales have fallen off since the tourist season ended** = las ventas han disminuido desde que terminó la temporada turística

◊ **fall out** ['fɔːl 'aʊt] *verb* **the bottom has fallen out of the market** = el mercado se está hundiendo

◊ **fall through** ['fɔːl 'θruː] *verb* fracasar *or* venirse abajo; **the plan fell through at the last moment** = el plan se vino abajo en el último momento

false [fɔːls] *adjective* falso, -sa *or* falseado, -da; **false accounting** = contabilidad falsa *or* fraudulenta; **to make a false entry in the balance sheet** = anotar una partida falsa en el balance de situación; **false pretences** = estafa *f or* medios fraudulentos; **he was sent to prison for obtaining money by false pretences** = fue encarcelado por obtener dinero por medio de estafas; **false weight** = peso escaso *or* falso

◊ **falsify** ['fɔːlsɪfai] *verb* falsificar; **to falsify the accounts** = falsificar las cuentas

◊ **falsification** [fɔːlsɪfɪ'keiʃən] *noun* falsificación *f*

familiarize [fə'mɪljəraiz] *verb* familiarizar; **to familiarize oneself with** = familiarizarse con

famous ['feiməs] *adjective* famoso, -sa *or* célebre;

the company owns a famous department store in the centre of London = la sociedad posee unos grandes almacenes muy famosos en el centro de Londres

fancy ['fænsı] *adjective* **(a)** fancy goods = artículos de fantasía **(b)** fancy prices = precios exorbitantes; **I don't want to pay the fancy prices they ask in London shops** = no quiero pagar los precios exorbitantes que piden en las tiendas de Londres

fao = FOR THE ATTENTION OF

fare [feə] *noun* billete *m or* pasaje *m or* tarifa *f*; **train fares have gone up by 5%** = las tarifas de tren han subido un 5%; **the government is asking the airlines to keep air fares down** = el gobierno pide a las compañías aéreas que no suban las tarifas; **concessionary fare** = tarifa reducida; **excess fare** = suplemento *m*; **full fare** = tarifa normal; **half fare** = media tarifa; **single fare** *US* **one-way fare** = (precio de) billete *or* sencillo *or* pasaje de ida; **return fare** *US* **round-trip fare** = tarifa de ida y vuelta

farm [fɑːm] **1** *noun* explotación *f* agrícola *or* granja *f*; **collective farm** = granja colectiva; **fish farm** = piscifactoría *f*; **mixed farm** = granja mixta **2** *verb* cultivar *or* explotar *or* labrar; **he farms 150 acres** = cultiva una extensión de 150 acres

◊ **farming** ['fɑːmɪŋ] *noun* labranza *f or* cultivo *m or* cría *f*; **chicken farming** = cría de pollos; **fish farming** = piscicultura *f*; **mixed farming** = policultivo *m*

◊ **farm out** ['fɑːm 'aʊt] *verb* **to farm out work** = subcontratar *or* delegar trabajo; **she farms out the office typing to various local bureaux** = contrata a varias oficinas de la localidad para el trabajo de mecanografía de la oficina

fascia ['feɪʃə] *noun (above shop, exhibition stand)* panel *m*

fast [fɑːst] **1** *adjective* rápido, -da; **the train is the fastest way of getting to our supplier's factory** = el tren es el medio más rápido para llegar a la fábrica de nuestros proveedores **2** *adverb* rápidamente *or* deprisa; **home computers sell fast in the pre-Christmas period** = los ordenadores individuales se venden rápidamente antes de las Navidades

◊ **fast-moving** *or* **fast-selling** ['fɑːst'muːvɪŋ *or* 'fɑːst'selɪŋ] *adjective* **fast-selling items** = artículos de venta rápida *or* fácil; **some dictionaries are not fast-moving stock** = algunos diccionarios no son fáciles de vender

fault [fɔːlt] *noun* **(a)** *(blame)* culpa *f or* falta *f*; **it is the stock controller's fault if the warehouse runs out of stock** = si el almacén se queda sin existencias la culpa es del encargado del inventario; **the chairman said the lower sales figures were the fault of a badly motivated sales force** = el presidente afirmó que las bajas cifras de ventas eran debidas a la falta de motivación de los vendedores **(b)** *(mechanical)* defecto *m or* fallo *m or* tara *f or* avería *f*; **the technicians are trying to correct a programming fault** = los técnicos están intentando corregir un fallo del programa; **we think there is a basic fault in the product design** = creemos que existe un defecto básico en el diseño del producto

◊ **faulty** ['fɔːltɪ] *adjective* defectuoso, -sa *or*

tarado, -da; **faulty equipment** = equipo defectuoso; **they installed faulty computer programs** = instalaron programas de ordenador defectuosos

favour *or US* **favor** ['feɪvə] **1** *noun* **(a)** **as a favour** = como favor especial; **he asked the secretary for a loan as a favour** = le pidió un préstamo a la secretaria como un favor **(b)** **in favour of** = a favor de; **six members of the board are in favour of the proposal, and three are against it** = seis miembros de la junta están a favor de la propuesta, y tres en contra **2** *verb* estar a favor de *or* apoyar *or* ser partidario de; **the board members all favour Smith Ltd as partners in the project** = los miembros del consejo son partidarios de que Smith Ltd participe en el proyecto

◊ **favourable** *or US* **favorable** ['feɪvərəbl] *adjective* favorable *or* propicio, -cia; **favourable balance of trade** = balanza comercial favorable; **on favourable terms** = en condiciones favorables; **the shop is let on very favourable terms** = la tienda se alquila a un precio muy ventajoso

◊ **favourite** *or US* **favorite** ['feɪvərɪt] *adjective* favorito, -ta *or* preferido, -da; **this brand of chocolate is a favourite with the children's market** = esta marca de chocolate es una de las preferidas por los niños

fax *or* **FAX** [fæks] **1** *noun* **(a)** *(system or document)* telefax *m or* fax *m*; **we received a fax of the order this morning** = recibimos un fax del pedido esta mañana; **can you confirm the booking by fax?** = ¿puede confirmar la reserva por fax?; **we will send a fax of the design plan** = enviaremos el proyecto por fax **(b)** **fax (machine)** = fax *m*; **fax paper** = papel para el fax; **fax roll** = rollo de papel para el fax **2** *verb* enviar *or* mandar por fax; **I've faxed the documents to our New York office** = he mandado los documentos por fax a nuestra oficina de Nueva York

feasibility [fiːzə'bɪlətɪ] *noun* viabilidad *f or* factibilidad *f*; **to report on the feasibility of a project** = informar sobre la viabilidad de un proyecto; **feasibility report** = informe de factibilidad; **to carry out a feasibility study on a project** = llevar a cabo un estudio de la factibilidad de un proyecto

federal ['fedərəl] *adjective* federal; **most federal offices are in Washington** = la mayoría de las oficinas federales están en Washington

◊ **the Fed** [ðə 'fed] *noun US (informal)* = FEDERAL RESERVE BOARD

Federal Reserve (System) ['fedərəl rɪ'zɜːv] Reserva Federal (EE.UU)

◊ **Federal Reserve Bank** ['fedərəl rɪ'zɜːv 'bæŋk] *noun US* Banco *m* de la Reserva Federal

◊ **Federal Reserve Board** ['fedərəl rɪ'zɜːv 'bɔːd] *noun US* Junta *f* de la Reserva Federal

COMMENT: the Federal Reserve system is the central bank of the USA. The system is run by the Federal Reserve Board, under a chairman and seven committee members (or 'governors') who are all appointed by the President. The twelve Federal Reserve Banks act as lenders of last resort to local commercial banks. Although the board is appointed by the president, the whole system is relatively independent of the US government

> QUOTE indications of weakness in the US economy were contained in figures from the Fed on industrial production for April
> **Financial Times**

> QUOTE federal examiners will determine which of the privately-insured savings and loans qualify for federal insurance
> **Wall Street Journal**

> QUOTE pressure on the Federal Reserve Board to ease monetary policy mounted yesterday with the release of a set of pessimistic economic statistics
> **Financial Times**

> QUOTE since 1978 America has freed many of its industries from federal rules that set prices and controlled the entry of new companies
> **Economist**

> QUOTE the half-point discount rate move gives the Fed room to reduce the federal funds rate further if economic weakness persists. The Fed sets the discount rate directly, but controls the federal funds rate by buying and selling Treasury securities
> **Wall Street Journal**

federation [fedə'reɪʃən] *noun* federación *f*; **federation of trades unions** = federación de sindicatos; **employers' federation** = federación patronal

fee [fi:] *noun* **(a)** *(for work)* honorarios *mpl or* emolumentos *mpl or* comisión *f*; **we charge a small fee for our services** = cobramos unos pequeños honorarios por nuestros servicios; **director's fees** = los honorarios de un consejero; **consultant's fee** = los honorarios del asesor **(b)** *(for something)* cuota *f or* derechos *mpl or* tasa *f*; **entrance fee *or* admission fee** = cuota de entrada; **registration fee** = matrícula *f or* derechos de matrícula

feed [fi:d] **1** *noun* alimentación *f*; **the paper feed has jammed** = el alimentador del papel se ha atascado; **continuous feed** = alimentación de papel continuo; **sheet feed** = alimentación de hojas sueltas **2** *verb (computer)* alimentar (NOTE: **feeding - fed**)

◇ **feedback** ['fi:dbæk] *noun* reacción *f or* respuesta *f or* información *f*; **have you any feedback from the sales force about the customers' reaction to the new model?** = ¿le han comunicado ya los vendedores la reacción de los clientes ante el nuevo modelo?

> QUOTE the service is particularly useful when we are working in a crisis management area and we need fast feedback from consumers
> **PR Week**

feelgood factor ['fi:lgʊd 'fæktə] *noun* indicador *m* de confianza *or* clima *m* de confianza *or* clima favorable *or* clima de optimismo

feint [feɪnt] *noun* raya *f* azul *or* tenue en un papel

ferry ['feri] *noun* transbordador *m or* 'ferry' *m*; **we**

are going to take the night ferry to Belgium = vamos a coger el transbordador de noche para Bélgica; **car ferry** = transbordador de vehículos; **passenger ferry** = transbordador de pasajeros

fetch [fetʃ] *verb* **(a)** *(go to bring)* ir a buscar *or* ir por *or* traer; **we have to fetch the goods from the docks** tenemos que ir a buscar las mercancías del muelle; **it is cheaper to buy at a cash and carry warehouse, provided you have a car to fetch the goods yourself** = siempre que se tenga un coche para transportar las mercancías, es más barato comprar en un almacén de pago al contado al por mayor **(b)** *(sold for a price)* venderse; **to fetch a high price** = venderse a un precio alto *or* obtener un precio alto; **it will not fetch more than £200** = no se venderá por más de £200; **these computers fetch very high prices on the black market** = estos ordenadores se venden a unos precios muy altos en el mercado negro

few [fju:] *adjective & pronoun* **(a)** *(not many)* pocos, -cas; **we sold so few of this item that we have discontinued the line** = vendimos tan pocos artículos que hemos suprimido la gama; **few of the staff stay with us more than six months** = son pocos los empleados que permanecen en la empresa más de seis meses **(b)** *(some)* **a few** = alguno, una *or* unos, -as *or* unos pocos *or* unas pocas; **we get only a few orders in the period from Christmas to the New Year** = recibimos muy pocos pedidos en el periodo entre Navidad y Año Nuevo; **a few of our salesmen drive Rolls-Royces** = algunos de nuestros vendedores tienen un Rolls-Royce

fiat ['fi:ət] *noun* autorización *f*; **fiat money** = dinero de curso forzoso *or* circulación fiduciaria

fictitious [fɪk'tɪʃəs] *adjective* ficticio, -cia; **fictitious assets** = activo ficticio

fiddle ['fɪdl] **1** *noun (informal)* trampa *f or* timo *m*; **it's all a fiddle** = no es más que un timo; **he's on the fiddle** = hace trampa **2** *verb (informal)* embaucar *or* amañar *or* falsificar *or* falsear; **he tried to fiddle his tax returns** intentó amañar su declaración de la renta; **the salesman was caught fiddling his expense account** = sorprendieron al vendedor amañando su cuenta de gastos

fide *see* BONA FIDE

fiduciary [fɪ'dju:ʃjəri] **1** *adjective* fiduciario, -ria; **fiduciary money** = circulación fiduciaria; **directors have fiduciary duty to act in the best interests of the company** = los directores tienen la obligación fiduciaria de actuar en beneficio de la compañía; **fiduciary deposits** = **2** *noun* fiduciario, -ria

field [fi:ld] *noun* **(a)** *(piece of ground)* campo *m*; **the cows are in the field** = las vacas están en el campo **(b)** *(outside the office)* **in the field** = en *or* sobre el terreno; **we have sixteen reps in the field** = tenemos dieciséis representantes sobre el terreno; **first in the field** = primera (empresa) en lanzar un nuevo producto *or* en introducir un nuevo servicio; **Smith Ltd has a great advantage in being first in the field with a reliable electric car** = Smith Ltd tiene la gran ventaja de ser la primera en lanzar al mercado un coche eléctrico de calidad; **field sales manager** = jefe de equipo de ventas; **field work** = trabajos de campo *or* estudios sobre el terreno; **he had to do a lot of field work to find the right**

market for the product = tuvo que hacer mucho trabajo de campo para encontrar el mercado adecuado para el producto **(c)** *(of activity)* especialidad *f*

FIFO ['faɪfəʊ] = FIRST IN FIRST OUT primeras entradas, primeras salidas

fifteen [fɪf'tiːn] *(EU since 1995)* **the Fifteen** = grupo de los Quince

fifty-fifty ['fɪftɪ 'fɪftɪ] *adjective & adverb* a partes iguales *or* a medias *or* mitad y mitad; **to go fifty-fifty** = ir a partes iguales *or* a medias; **he has a fifty-fifty chance of making a profit** = tiene un 50% de posibilidades de obtener beneficios

figure ['fɪgə] *noun* **(a)** *(number)* cifra *f or* cantidad *f*; **the figure in the accounts for heating is very high** = la cifra de los gastos de calefacción es muy alta; **he put a very low figure on the value of the lease** = calculó muy por debajo *or* infravaloró el valor del arrendamiento **(b)** *(written numbers)* **figures** = cifras *or* números *mpl*; **sales figures** = cifras de ventas; **to work out the figures** = calcular; **his income runs into five figures** *or* **he has a five-figure income** = sus ingresos superan las £10.000; **in round figures** = en números redondos; **they have a workforce of 2,500 in round figures** = tienen una plantilla de 2.500 empleados en números redondos **(c)** *(results)* **figures** = cifras *or* resultados *mpl*; **the figures for last year** *or* **last year's figures** = las cifras del año pasado

file [faɪl] **1** *noun* **(a)** *(with documents)* fichero *m or* archivo *m or* archivador *m (cardboard holder)* carpeta *f*; **put these letters in the customer file** = ponga estas cartas en el archivo de clientes; **look in the file marked 'Scottish sales'** = mire en el fichero de 'ventas en Escocia'; **box file** = caja *f* de registros *or* archivador **(b)** *(documents)* expediente *m*; **to place something on file** = archivar; **to keep someone's name on file** = tener el nombre de alguien archivado; *US* **file card** = ficha de registros (NOTE: GB English is **filing card**) **file copy** = copia de archivo; **card-index file** = fichero de tarjetas **(c)** *(on computer)* archivo; **how can we protect our computer files?** = ¿cómo podemos proteger los archivos del ordenador? **2** *verb* **(a)** *(to keep)* **to file documents** = archivar documentos; **the correspondence is filed under 'complaints'** = la correspondencia se archiva en la carpeta de reclamaciones **(b)** *(to make an official request)* presentar una demanda *or* declaración; **to file a petition in bankruptcy** = presentar una declaración de quiebra *or* declararse en quiebra **(c)** *(to register)* presentar; **to file an application for a patent** presentar una solicitud de patente; **to file a return to the tax office** = presentar una declaración en la delegación de Hacienda

◊ **filing** ['faɪlɪŋ] *noun* **(a)** *(documents to be put in order)* clasificación *m or* archivo *m*; **there is a lot of filing to do at the end of the week** = hay mucho trabajo de archivo por hacer al final de la semana; **the manager looked through the week's filing to see what letters had been sent** = el director ojeó los documentos archivados durante la semana para ver qué cartas se habían enviado; **filing basket** *or* **filing tray** = bandeja de documentos para archivar; **filing cabinet** = archivador *m or* fichero *m*; **filing card** *or US* **file card** = ficha; **filing clerk** = archivero, -ra;

filing system = sistema de archivo *or* clasificación **(b)** *(bankruptcy)* declaración *f or* presentación *f* de quiebra

QUOTE the bankruptcy filing raises questions about the future of the company's pension plan
Fortune

fill [fɪl] **1** *verb* **(a)** llenar *or* ocupar *or* cubrir; **we have filled our order book with orders for Africa** = nuestro libro de pedidos está lleno de pedidos para Africa; **the production department has filled the warehouse with unsellable products** = el departamento de fabricación ha llenado el almacén de artículos invendibles **(b) to fill a gap** = llenar *or* ocupar un vacío; **the new range of small cars fills a gap in the market** = la nueva gama de coches pequeños llena un vacío en el mercado **(c) to fill a post** *or* **a vacancy** = cubrir un puesto *or* una vacante; **your application arrived too late - the post has already been filled** = su solicitud llegó demasiado tarde - el puesto ya ha sido cubierto

◊ **filler** ['fɪlə] *noun* **stocking filler** = pequeño regalo de Navidad; *see also* SHELF FILLER

◊ **fill in** ['fɪl 'ɪn] *verb* rellenar *or* poner; **fill in your name and address in block capitals** = ponga *or* escriba su nombre y dirección en mayúsculas

◊ **filling station** ['fɪlɪŋ 'steɪʃən] *noun* gasolinera *f*; **he stopped at the filling station to get some petrol before going on to the motorway** = paró en la estación de servicio para poner gasolina antes de entrar en la autopista

◊ **fill out** ['fɪl 'aʊt] *verb* rellenar; **to get customs clearance you must fill out three forms** = para hacer el despacho de aduanas hay que rellenar tres impresos

◊ **fill up** ['fɪl 'ʌp] *verb* **(a)** *(completely full)* llenar; **he filled up the car with petrol** = llenó de gasolina el depósito del coche; **my appointments book is completely filled up** = mi agenda está completamente llena **(b)** *(write on a form)* rellenar; **he filled up the form and sent it to the bank** = rellenó el impreso y lo envió al banco

final ['faɪnl] *adjective* último, -ma *or* final; **to pay the final instalment** = pagar el último plazo; **to make the final payment** = efectuar el último pago; **to put the final details on a document** = dar los toques finales a un documento; **final accounts** = balance final *or* último balance; **final date for payment** = fecha de vencimiento (de pago); **final demand** = demanda final; **final discharge** = reembolso final; **final dividend** = dividendo final; **final product** = producto final *or* acabado

◊ **finalize** ['faɪnəlaɪz] *verb* finalizar *or* aprobar con carácter definitivo; **we hope to finalize the agreement tomorrow** = esperamos finalizar el acuerdo mañana; **after six weeks of negotiations the loan was finalized yesterday** = después de seis semanas de negociaciones el préstamo fue aprobado definitivamente ayer

◊ **finally** ['faɪnəli] *adverb* finalmente *or* por último *or* por fin; **the contract was finally signed yesterday** el contrato se firmó por fin ayer; **after weeks of trials the company finally accepted the computer system** = después de semanas de pruebas la empresa aceptó finalmente el sistema de ordenador

finance 1 ['faɪnæns] *noun* **(a)** *(company)* fondos *mpl or* recursos *mpl or* finanzas *fpl*; **where will they get the necessary finance for the project?** = ¿dónde conseguirán los fondos necesarios para el proyecto?; **finance company** *or* **finance corporation** *or* **finance house** = sociedad financiera; **finance director** = director, -ra de finanzas; **finance market** = mercado financiero; **high finance** = altas finanzas **(b)** *(club, local authority, etc.)* finanzas *or* fondos *or* recursos; **she is the secretary of the local authority finance committee** = es la secretaria del comité financiero de la administración local **(c)** *(cash available)* **finances** = finanzas; **the bad state of the company's finances** = el mal estado de las finanzas de la compañía **2** [faɪ'næns] *verb* financiar; **to finance an operation** = financiar una operación

◊ **Finance Act** ['faɪnæns 'ækt] *noun GB* ley *f* presupuestaria

◊ **Finance Bill** ['faɪnæns 'bɪl] *noun GB* proyecto *m* de ley presupuestaria

◊ **financial** [fɪ'nænʃəl] *adjective* financiero, -ra; **financial adviser** = asesor financiero; **financial analyst** = analista financiero; **financial asset** = activo financiero; **financial assistance** = ayuda financiera; **financial correspondent** = corresponsal financiero; **financial instrument** = instrumento *or* documento financiero; **financial intermediary** = agente de finanzas *or* sociedad financiera; **financial needs** = apuros económicos; **financial position** = situación financiera; **he must think of his financial position** = debe pensar en su situación financiera; **financial resources** = recursos financieros; **a company with strong financial resources** = una compañía con grandes recursos financieros; **there is no financial risk in selling to East European countries on credit** = no existe riesgo financiero alguno en vender a los países del este de Europa a crédito; **financial settlement** = ajuste financiero; **financial statement** = estado financiero *or* balance general; **the accounts department has prepared a financial statement for the shareholders** = el departamento de cuentas ha preparado un estado financiero para los accionistas; **financial year** = ejercicio económico *or* año fiscal

◊ **financially** [fɪ'nænʃəli] *adverb* financieramente; **company which is financially sound** = compañía financieramente sólida

◊ **Financial Services Act** [fɪ'nænʃəl 'sɜːvɪsɪz 'ækt] ley de servicios financieros

◊ **Financial Times (FT)** [faɪ'nænʃəl 'taɪmz] periódico inglés de economía y finanzas; **FT All-Share Index** = índice de acciones en el 'Financial Times' (NOTE: also simply called the **All-Share Index**) **Financial Times (Ordinary) index** = índice de cotización bursátil del 'Financial Times' (basado en las acciones de un grupo de sociedades importantes); **FT-Stock Exchange 100 Share Index (FT-SE 100** *or* **Footsie)** = índice de cotización del 'Financial Times' y de la Bolsa de Londres (basado en las acciones de 100 sociedades importantes) *or* índice 'Footsie'

◊ **financier** [faɪ'nænsɪə] *noun* financiero, -ra

◊ **financing** [fɪ'nænsɪŋ] *noun* financiación *f or* financiamiento *m*; **the financing of the project was done by two international banks** = el proyecto fue financiado por dos bancos internacionales; **back**

financing = financiación retroactiva; **deficit financing** = financiación del déficit presupuestario

find [faɪnd] *verb* **(a)** *(not there before)* encontrar *or* hallar; **to find backing for a project** = encontrar apoyo para un proyecto **(b)** *(legal decision)* declarar *or* fallar; **the tribunal found that both parties were at fault** = el tribunal declaró culpables a ambas partes; **the judge found for the defendant** = el juez falló a favor del demandado (NOTE: **finding - found)**

◊ **findings** ['faɪndɪŋz] *plural noun* **the findings of a commission of enquiry** = las conclusiones de una comisión investigadora

◊ **find time** ['faɪnd 'taɪm] *verb* encontrar tiempo; **we must find time to visit the new staff sports club** = tenemos que encontrar tiempo para visitar el nuevo club de deportes del personal; **the chairman never finds enough time to play golf** = el presidente nunca encuentra tiempo suficiente para jugar al golf

fine [faɪn] **1** *noun* multa *f*; **he was asked to pay a $25,000 fine** = le pusieron una multa de $25.000; **we had to pay a $10 parking fine** = tuvimos que pagar una multa de $10 por aparcamiento indebido **2** *verb* multar; **to fine someone £2,500 for obtaining money by false pretences** = multar a alguien con £2.500 por obtener dinero fraudulentamente **3** *adjective* **fine print** = letra pequeña; **did you read the fine print on the back of the agreement?** = ¿leíste la letra pequeña al dorso del contrato? **4** *adverb* **(a)** *(very well)* muy bien; **you are doing fine** = vas muy bien **(b)** *(very small or thin)* en trozos pequeños *or* finos; **we are cutting our margins very fine** = estamos reduciendo nuestros márgenes al máximo

◊ **fine tune** ['faɪn 'tjuːn] *verb* armonizar

◊ **fine-tuning** ['faɪn'tjuːnɪŋ] *noun* ajuste fino

finish ['fɪnɪʃ] **1** *noun* **(a)** *(final appearance)* acabado *m*; **the product has an attractive finish** = el producto tiene un acabado atractivo **(b)** *(closing)* cierre *m* de la sesión bursátil; **oil shares rallied at the finish** = las acciones petrolíferas se recuperaron en el momento del cierre **2** *verb* **(a)** *(complete)* terminar; **the order was finished in time** = el pedido se terminó a tiempo; **she finished the test before all the other candidates** = terminó la prueba antes que los demás candidatos **(b)** *(end)* terminar *or* acabar; **the contract is due to finish next month** = el contrato termina el mes próximo

◊ **finished** ['fɪnɪʃt] *adjective* acabado, -da *or* terminado, -da; **finished goods** = productos acabados *or* terminados

fink [fɪŋk] *noun US (informal)* esquirol *m*

Finland ['fɪnlənd] *noun* Finlandia *f*

◊ **Finn** [fɪn] *noun* finlandés, -esa *or* finés, finesa

◊ **Finnish** ['fInIʃ] *adjective* finlandés, -esa *or* finés, finesa
NOTE: capital: **Helsinki**; currency: **Finnish markka (Fmk)** = marco finlandés (Fmk)

fire ['faIə] **1** *noun* fuego *m or* incendio *m*; **the shipment was damaged in the fire on board the cargo boat** = el envío resultó dañado en el incendio que se declaró a bordo del carguero; **half the stock was destroyed in the warehouse fire** = la mitad de las existencias quedaron destruidas en el incendio del almacén; **to catch fire** = incendiarse *or* quemarse; **the papers in the waste paper basket caught fire** = los papeles de la papelera se incendiaron *or* quemaron; **fire damage** = daños (causados) por incendio; **he claimed £250 for fire damage** = reclamó £250 en concepto de daños por incendio; **fire-damaged goods** = mercancías dañadas en un incendio; **fire door** = puerta de incendios *or* salida de emergencia; **fire escape** = escalera de incendios *or* de emergencia; **fire extinguisher** = extintor *m* (de fuegos); **fire hazard** *or* **fire risk** = riesgo *or* peligro de incendio; **that warehouse full of paper is a fire hazard** = ese almacén lleno de papel constituye un peligro de incendio; **fire insurance** = seguro contra incendios; **fire sale** = (*of fire damaged goods*) liquidación por incendio *or* venta de artículos dañados por el fuego; (*sale at very low price*) liquidación *f* **2** *verb* **to fire someone** = despedir a alguien; **the new managing director fired half the sales force** = el nuevo director gerente despidió a la mitad del personal de ventas; **to hire and fire** = contratar y despedir a empleados

◊ **fireproof** ['faIəpru:f] *adjective* ininflamable *or* a prueba de incendios *or* incombustible; **we packed the papers in a fireproof safe** = guardamos los documentos en una caja a prueba de incendios; **it is impossible to make the office completely fireproof** = es imposible conseguir que la oficina esté completamente a prueba de incendios

firm [fɜ:m] **1** *noun* empresa *f or* firma *f*; **he is a partner in a law firm** = es socio de una firma de abogados; **a manufacturing firm** = una empresa manufacturera; **an important publishing firm** = una empresa editorial importante **2** *adjective* **(a)** (*definitive*) firme *or* en firme *or* sólido, -da; **to make a firm offer for something** = hacer una oferta en firme; **to place a firm order for two aircraft** = hacer un pedido en firme de dos aviones; **they are quoting a firm price of £1.22 per unit** = ofrecen un precio firme de £1.22 por unidad **(b)** (*with no tendency to fall in price*) firme *or* estable; **sterling was firmer on the foreign exchange markets** = la libra esterlina se mostró más firme en los mercados de divisas; **shares remained firm** = las acciones se mantuvieron firmes **3** *verb* afirmar *or* afianzar *or* consolidar; **the shares firmed at £1.50** = las acciones se afianzaron a £1.50

◊ **firmness** ['fɜ:mnəs] *noun* firmeza *f or* estabilidad *f*; **the firmness of the pound** = la estabilidad de la libra

◊ **firm up** ['fɜ:m 'ʌp] *verb* cerrar *or* concluir; **we expect to firm up the deal at the next trade fair** = esperamos cerrar el trato en la próxima feria comercial

COMMENT: strictly speaking, a 'firm' is a partnership or other trading organization which is not a limited company. In practice, it is better to use the term for unincorporated businesses such as 'a firm of accountants' or 'a firm of stockbrokers', rather than for 'a major aircraft construction firm' which is likely to be a plc

QUOTE Toronto failed to mirror New York's firmness as a drop in gold shares on a falling bullion price left the market closing on a mixed note
Financial Times

QUOTE some profit-taking was noted, but underlying sentiment remained firm
Financial Times

first [fɜ:st] **1** *noun* primero, -ra; **our company was one of the first to sell into the European market** = nuestra empresa fue una de las primeras en vender en el mercado europeo **2** *adjective* primero, -ra; **first quarter** = primer trimestre; **first half** *or* **first half-year** = primer semestre
Note: 'primer' is used before a masculine noun.

◊ **first-class** ['fɜ:s(t) 'klɑ:s] *adjective & noun* **(a)** (*top quality*) excelente *or* de primera clase *or* calidad *or* categoría; **he is a first-class accountant** = es un contable de primera categoría **(b)** (*most expensive*) **first-class travel** *or* **hotel** = viaje *or* hotel de primera categoría; **to travel first-class** = viajar en primera clase; **first-class travel provides the best service** = los viajes de primera clase ofrecen el mejor servicio; **a first-class ticket** = un billete de primera clase; **to stay in first-class hotels** = alojarse en hoteles de primera categoría; **first-class mail** = *GB* servicio de correos de primera clase; *US* servicio de correos para cartas y tarjetas postales; **a first-class letter should get to Scotland in a day** = una carta en correo de primera clase debería llegar a Escocia en un día

◊ **first in first out (FIFO)** ['fɜ:st 'In 'fɜ:st 'aʊt] (*redundancy and accounting policy*) primeras entradas, primeras salidas (PEPS)

◊ **first-line management** ['fɜ:st'laIn 'mænIdʒmənt] *noun* dirección operacional

fiscal ['fIskəl] *adjective* fiscal; **the government's fiscal policies** = la política fiscal del gobierno; **fiscal measures** = medidas fiscales; **fiscal year** = año fiscal *or* ejercicio económico

QUOTE the standard measure of fiscal policy - the public sector borrowing requirement - is kept misleadingly low
Economist

QUOTE last fiscal year the chain reported a 116% jump in earnings
Barrons

fit [fIt] *verb* ajustar *or* ajustarse *or* corresponder; **the paper doesn't fit the printer** = el papel no se ajusta a la impresora (NOTE: **fitting - fitted**)

◊ **fit in** ['fIt 'In] *verb* tener *or* encontrar tiempo *or* caber *or* encajar; **will the computer fit into that little room?** = ¿cabrá el ordenador en esa sala tan pequeña?; **the chairman tries to fit in a game of golf every afternoon** = el presidente trata de encontrar tiempo para una partida de golf todas las tardes; **my appointments diary is full, but I shall try to fit you in tomorrow afternoon** = mi agenda está llena, pero trataré de atenderle mañana por la tarde

◊ **fit out** ['fIt 'aʊt] *verb* equipar; **they fitted o' the factory with computers** = equiparon la fáb¹ con ordenadores; **the shop was fitted out at a cost of £10,000** = equiparon la tienda a un costo de £10.000; **fitting out of a shop** = equipamiento de una tienda

◊ **fittings** ['fɪtɪŋz] *plural noun* mobiliario *m or* accesorios *mpl*; **fixtures and fittings (f. & f.)** = instalaciones fijas y accesorios

fix [fɪks] *verb* **(a)** *(to arrange)* fijar; **to fix a budget** = fijar un presupuesto; **to fix a meeting for 3 p.m.** = fijar una reunión para las 3 de la tarde; **the date has still to be fixed** = todavía no se ha fijado la fecha; **the price of gold was fixed at $300** = el precio del oro se fijó en $300; **the mortgage rate has been fixed at 11%** = el interés de la hipoteca ha quedado fijado en el 11% **(b)** *(to mend)* arreglar; **the technicians are coming to fix the telephone switchboard** = los técnicos van a venir a arreglar la centralita de teléfonos; **can you fix the photocopier?** = ¿puedes arreglar la fotocopiadora?

◊ **fixed** [fɪkst] *adjective* fijo, -ja; **fixed assets** = activo fijo; **fixed capital** = capital fijo; **fixed costs** = costes fijos; **fixed deposit** = depósito a plazo fijo; **fixed expenses** = gastos fijos; **fixed income** = renta fija; **fixed-price agreement** = acuerdo *or* contrato a tanto alzado; **fixed scale of charges** = lista de precios fijos; **fixed-term contract** = contrato a plazo fijo

◊ **fixed-interest** ['fɪkst 'ɪntrest] *adjective* de interés fijo; **fixed-interest investments** = inversiones de interés fijo; **fixed-interest securities** = títulos *or* valores de interés fijo

◊ **fixer** ['fɪksə] *noun* **(a)** *(informal)* intermediario, -ria **(b)** *US* casa a precio reducido porque necesita reparación

◊ **fixing** ['fɪksɪŋ] *noun* **(a)** *(arranging)* fijación *f*; **fixing of charges** = fijación de tarifas; **fixing of a mortgage rate** = fijación del interés de la hipoteca **(b)** **price fixing** = acuerdo sobre precios *or* fijación de precios **(c)** **the London gold fixing** = precio del día en el mercado londinense del oro

◊ **fixtures** ['fɪkstʃəz] *plural noun* instalaciones *fpl* fijas; **fixtures and fittings (f. & f.)** = instalaciones fijas y accesorios

◊ **fix up with** ['fɪks ʌp wɪð] *verb* proporcionar; **my secretary fixed me up with a car at the airport** = mi secretaria me proporcionó un coche en el aeropuerto; **can you fix me up with a room for tomorrow night?** = ¿puede conseguirme una habitación para mañana por la noche?

flag [flæg] **1** *noun* **(a)** *(country)* bandera *f or* pabellón *m*; **a ship flying a British flag** = embarcación de bandera británica; **ship sailing under a flag of convenience** = barco que navega con pabellón de conveniencia **(b)** *(computing)* señal *f or* indicador *m*; **2** *verb (computing)* señalizar (NOTE: **flagging - flagged)**

◊ **flagship** ['flægʃɪp] *noun (key product)* artículo clave (con el que se asocia la imagen del productor)

flat [flæt] **1** *adjective* **(a)** *(low demand)* sin movimiento *or* átono, -na *or* inactivo, -va *or* horizontal; **the market was flat today** = el mercado no ha experimentado cambios hoy *or* hoy el mercado se ha mantenido átono **(b)** *(fixed)* fijo, -ja *or* uniforme; **flat rate** = porcentaje fijo *or* tanto alzado *or* cuota fija; **we pay a flat rate for electricity each quarter** = pagamos una cuota fija por la electricidad cada trimestre; **he is paid a flat rate of £2 per thousand** = se le paga un tanto alzado de £2 por mil **2** *noun* piso *m*; **he has a flat in the centre of town** = tiene un piso en el centro de la ciudad; **she is buying a flat close to her office** = va a comprarse un piso cerca de la oficina; **company flat** = piso de la empresa (NOTE: US English is **apartment**) **3** *adverb* rotundamente *or* categóricamente; **he turned down the offer flat** = rechazó la oferta rotundamente

◊ **flat out** ['flæt 'aʊt] *adverb* **(a)** *(at full speed)* a tope *or* a toda velocidad; **the factory worked flat out to complete the order on time** = la fábrica trabajó a tope para terminar el pedido a tiempo **(b)** *US (in a blunt way)* **to refuse flat out** = rehusar *or* negarse rotundamente

◊ **flat pack** ['flæt 'pæk] *noun (of furniture)* paquete *or* embalaje plano (de muebles para montar)

flea market ['fliː 'mɑːkɪt] *noun* rastro *m or* mercadillo *m* de objetos de segunda mano

fleet [fliːt] *noun* flota *f* de vehículos (de una empresa); **a company's fleet of representatives' cars** = la flota de coches de representantes de una empresa; **a fleet car** = un coche de la empresa; **fleet discount** = descuento por compra *or* alquiler de los coches de una empresa; **fleet rental** = alquiler de la flota de vehículos de una empresa a precio reducido

flexible ['fleksəbl] *adjective* flexible; **flexible budget** = presupuesto flexible; **flexible prices** = precios flexibles; **flexible pricing policy** = política de precios flexibles; **flexible working hours** = horario (de trabajo) flexible; **we work flexible hours** = tenemos un horario de trabajo flexible

◊ **flexibility** [fleksə'bɪləti] *noun* flexibilidad *f*; **there is no flexibility in the company's pricing policy** = no existe flexibilidad en la política de precios de la empresa

◊ **flexitime** *or US* **flextime** ['fleksɪtaɪm *or* 'flekstaɪm] *noun* horario *m* (de trabajo) flexible; **we work flexitime** = tenemos un horario de trabajo flexible; **the company introduced flexitime working two years ago** = la empresa estableció el horario de trabajo flexible hace dos años

flier *or* **flyer** ['flaɪə] *noun* **(a)** *(person)* **high flier** = persona ambiciosa *or* de gran talento; *(share)* high

flyer = acción *f* cuyo precio sube rápidamente **(b)** *(advertising leaflet)* prospecto *m or* octavilla *f*

flight [flaɪt] *noun* **(a)** *(aircraft)* vuelo *m*; **charter flight** = vuelo chárter; **flight IB 267 is leaving from Gate 46** = el vuelo IB 267 efectuará su salida de la puerta 46; **he missed his flight** = perdió el vuelo; **I always take the afternoon flight to Rome** = siempre cojo el vuelo de la tarde para Roma; **if you hurry you will catch the six o'clock flight to Paris** = si te das prisa podrás coger el vuelo de las seis para París **(b)** *(money)* fuga *f or* evasión *f*; **the flight of capital from Europe into the USA** = la evasión de capitales de Europa a los EE UU; **the flight from the peseta into the dollar** = fuga de la peseta al dólar *or* conversión de pesetas en dólares **(c)** *(steps)* tramo *m* de escaleras; **top-flight** = de primera categoría *or* clase; **top-flight managers can earn very high salaries** = los directores de primera clase pueden ganar sueldos muy altos

flip chart ['flɪp 'tʃɑːt] *noun* tablero *m* de hojas sueltas

float [fləʊt] **1** *noun* **(a)** *(cash)* cantidad *f or* adelanto *m* para gastos menores; **the sales reps have a float of £100 each** = los representantes reciben un adelanto de £100 cada uno para gastos menores; **cash float** = fondo *m* de caja; **we start the day with a £20 float in the cash desk** = empezamos el día con un fondo de caja de £20 **(b)** *(company)* lanzamiento *m or* flotación *f*; **the float of the new company was a complete failure** = el lanzamiento de la nueva empresa fue un fracaso total **(c)** *(of currency)* flotación de divisas; **clean float** = flotación libre (de divisas); **dirty float** *or* **managed float** = flotación sucia *or* dirigida **2** *verb* **(a)** **to float a company** = fundar una compañía; **to float a loan** = emitir un empréstito **(b)** *(exchange rates)* hacer flotar una divisa *or* flotar; **the government has let sterling float** = el gobierno ha dejado flotar la libra esterlina; **the government has decided to float the pound** = el gobierno ha decidido dejar flotar la libra

◊ **floating** ['fləʊtɪŋ] **1** *noun* **(a)** **floating of a company** = lanzamiento *m* de una sociedad **(b)** **the floating of the pound** = la flotación *f* de la libra **2** *adjective* flotante *or* variable; **floating charge** = débito flotante *or* variable; **floating exchange rates** = tipos de cambio flotantes; **the floating pound** = la libra flotante; **floating rate** = tipo flotante (de interés *or* de cambio)

> QUOTE in a world of floating exchange rates the dollar is strong because of capital inflows rather than weak because of the nation's trade deficit
> **Duns Business Month**

flood [flʌd] **1** *noun* inundación *f or* riada *f*; **we are getting a flood of orders** = estamos inundados de pedidos; **floods of tourists filled the hotels** = oleadas de turistas llenaron los hoteles **2** *verb* inundar *or* desbordar; **the market was flooded with cheap imitations** = el mercado se inundó de imitaciones baratas; **the sales department is flooded with orders** *or* **with complaints** = el departamento de ventas está desbordado de pedidos *or* de reclamaciones

floor [flɔː] *noun* **(a)** *(room)* suelo *m*; **floor space** = superficie útil; **we have 3,500 square metres of floor space to let** = tenemos 3.500 metros cuadrados de superficie útil para alquilar; **floor stand** = 'stand';

the factory floor = fábrica *f or* taller *m*; **on the shop floor** = en el taller *or* fábrica *or* entre los obreros; **the feeling on the shop floor is that the manager does not know his job** = la opinión entre los obreros es que el director no conoce su oficio **(b)** *(building)* piso *m*; **the shoe department is on the first floor** = la sección de calzado está en el primer piso; **her office is on the 26th floor** = su oficina está en el piso 26; *US* **floor manager** = director de planta (NOTE: the numbering of floors is different in GB and the USA. The floor at streeet level is the **ground floor** in GB, but the **first floor** in the USA. Each floor in the USA is one number higher than the same floor in GB) **(c)** *(Stock Exchange)* **dealing floor** *or* **trading floor** = parqué *or* lugar de operaciones **(d)** *(lowest level)* **floor price** = precio mínimo

◊ **floorwalker** ['flɔːwɔːkə] *noun* jefe, -fa de sección *or* de departamento de unos grandes almacenes

flop [flɒp] **1** *noun* fracaso *m*; **the new model was a flop** = el nuevo modelo fue un fracaso **2** *verb* fracasar; **the flotation of the new company flopped badly** = el lanzamiento de la nueva compañía fracasó estrepitosamente (NOTE: **flopping - flopped**)

◊ **floppy** ['flɒpi] **1** *adjective* **floppy disk** = disco flexible *or* diskette *or* 'floppy'; **floppy disk drive** = disketera *f* **2** *noun* disco *m* flexible *or* diskette *m or* 'floppy' *m*; **the data is on 5¼ inch floppies** = los datos están en discos flexibles de 5,25 pulgadas

florin ['flɒrɪn] *noun (Dutch guilder)* florín *m* (NOTE: the abbreviation for the guilder is **fl**)

flotation [fləʊ'teɪʃən] *noun* **the flotation of a new company** = el lanzamiento de una nueva compañía; **currency flotation** = flotación de divisas

flotsam ['flɒtsəm] *noun* **flotsam and jetsam** = restos *mpl* flotantes de un naufragio *or* desechos *mpl* arrojados al mar

flourish ['flʌrɪʃ] *verb* florecer *or* prosperar; **the company is flourishing** = la compañía prospera *or* está prosperando; **trade with Nigeria flourished** = el comercio con Nigeria prosperó

◊ **flourishing** ['flʌrɪʃɪŋ] *adjective* floreciente *or* próspero, -ra; **flourishing trade** = comercio próspero; **he runs a flourishing shoe business** = dirige un floreciente negocio de calzado

flow [fləʊ] **1** *noun* **(a)** *(movement)* flujo *m or* movimiento *m*; **the flow of capital into a country** = el movimiento de capitales hacia el país; **the flow of investments into Japan** = el flujo de inversiones hacia Japón **(b)** **cash flow** = flujo *m* de caja *or* 'cash flow' *m*; **discounted cash flow (DCF)** = 'cash flow' actualizado *or* flujo de caja descontado; **the company is suffering from cash flow problems** = la empresa tiene dificultades de flujo de caja **2** *verb* fluir *or* discurrir *or* circular; **production is now flowing normally after the strike** = la producción discurre ahora normalmente después de la huelga

◊ **flowchart** *or* **flow diagram** ['fləʊtʃɑːt *or* 'fləʊ 'daɪəgræm] *noun* diagrama *m* de flujo *or* de secuencia *or* organigrama *m*

fluctuate ['flʌktjʊeɪt] *verb* fluctuar *or* oscilar; **prices fluctuate between £1.10 and £1.25** = los precios oscilan entre £1.10 y £1.25; **the pound fluctuated all day on the foreign exchange**

markets = la libra fluctuó durante todo el día en los mercados de divisas

◊ **fluctuating** ['flʌktjʊeɪtɪŋ] *adjective* fluctuante; **fluctuating dollar prices** = el precio fluctuante del dólar

◊ **fluctuation** [flʌktjʊ'eɪʃən] *noun* fluctuación *f or* oscilación *f*; **the fluctuations of the peseta** = las fluctuaciones de la peseta; **the fluctuations of the exchange rate** = las fluctuaciones de los tipos de cambio

fly [flaɪ] *verb* volar *or* ir en avión; **the chairman is flying to Germany on business** = el presidente irá en avión a Alemania en viaje de negocios; **the overseas sales manager flies about 100,000 miles a year visiting the agents** = el director de ventas en el extranjero hace unas 100.000 millas *or* unos 160.000 kilómetros al año en avión para visitar a los representantes

◊ **fly-by-night** ['flaɪbaɪnaɪt] *adjective (person or company)* (empresa) poco fiable *or* poco de fiar; **I want a reputable builder, not one of these fly-by-night outfits** = quiero un contratista de confianza no una de esas empresas que desparecen de la noche a la mañana

FOB *or* **f.o.b.** ['efəʊ'biː] = FREE ON BOARD franco a bordo

fold [fəʊld] *verb* **(a)** *(to bend)* doblar *or* plegar; **she folded the letter so that the address was clearly visible** = dobló la carta de forma que la dirección quedara claramente visible **(b)** *(informal)* to fold **(up)** = cerrar *or* liquidar; **the business folded up last December** = el negocio cerró en diciembre; **the company folded with debts of over £1m** = la empresa cerró con deudas superiores a £1m

◊ **-fold** [fəʊld] *suffix* veces; **four-fold** = cuatro veces

QUOTE the company's sales have nearly tripled and its profits have risen seven-fold since 1982

Barrons

folder ['fəʊldə] *noun* carpeta *f*; **put all the documents in a folder for the chairman** = ponga todos los documentos en una carpeta para el presidente

folio ['fəʊliəʊ] **1** *noun* folio *m* **2** *verb* foliar *or* paginar

follow ['fɒləʊ] *verb* seguir; **the samples will follow by surface mail** = las muestras se enviarán posteriormente por correo ordinario; **we will pay £10,000 down, with the balance to follow in six months' time** = haremos un desembolso inicial de £10.000 y el saldo les llegará dentro de seis meses

◊ **follow up** ['fɒləʊ 'ʌp] *verb* profundizar *or* estudiar; **I'll follow up your idea of putting our address list on to the computer** = estudiaré tu idea de poner nuestra lista de direcciones en el ordenador; **to follow up an initiative** = seguir una iniciativa

◊ **follow-up letter** ['fɒləʊʌp 'letə] *noun* carta *f* de reiteración

food [fuːd] *noun* alimento *m or* comida *f*; **he is very fond of Indian food** = le gusta mucho la comida india; **the food in the staff restaurant is excellent** = la comida del restaurante de la empresa es excelente;

US **food stamps** = cupones que el gobierno federal entrega a las personas necesitadas con los que pueden adquirir alimentos a precios subvencionados

◊ **foodstuffs** ['fuːdstʌfs] *plural noun* **essential foodstuffs** = alimentos *mpl* de primera necesidad

foolscap ['fuːlzkæp] *noun (size of writing paper (13½ by 8½ inches)* papel *m* tamaño folio; **the letter was on six sheets of foolscap** = la carta estaba escrita en seis folios; **a foolscap envelope** = sobre para folios

foot [fʊt] **1** *noun* **(a)** *(part of the body)* pie *m*; **on foot** = a pie *or* andando; **the reps make most of their central London calls on foot** = los representantes hacen la mayoría de sus visitas en el centro de Londres a pie; **the rush hour traffic is so bad that it is quicker to go to the office on foot** = hay tanto tráfico en las horas punta que es más rápido ir a la oficina andando **(b)** *(bottom part)* pie *or* parte *f* inferior; **he signed his name at the foot of the invoice** = firmó al pie de la factura **(c)** *(measurement of length, equals 30cm)* pie; **the table is six feet long** = la mesa tiene 1,80 m. de largo; **my office is ten feet by twelve** = mi oficina tiene 3m. por 3,60m. (NOTE: the plural is **feet** for (a) and (c); there is no plural for (b). In measurements, **foot** is usually written **ft** or **'** after figures: **10ft** *or* **10'**) **2** *verb* **(a)** **to foot the bill** = correr con los gastos; **the director footed the bill for the department's Christmas party** = el director corrió con los gastos de la fiesta de Navidad del departamento **(b)** *US* **to foot up an account** = calcular el total de *or* sumar una cuenta

◊ **footnote** ['fʊtnəʊt] *noun* nota *f* a pie de página

◊ **Footsie** ['fʊtsiː] = FINANCIAL TIMES/STOCK EXCHANGE 100 INDEX

FOR ['efəʊ'ɑːr] = FREE ON RAIL

forbid [fə'bɪd] *verb* prohibir; **the contract forbids resale of the goods to the USA** = el contrato prohíbe revender las mercancías a los EE UU; **the staff are forbidden to use the front entrance** = el personal tiene prohibido utilizar la entrada principal (NOTE: **forbidding - forbade - forbidden**)

force [fɔːs] **1** *noun* **(a)** *(strength)* fuerza *f*; **to be in force** = estar en vigor *or* ser vigente *or* regir; **the rules have been in force since 1946** = las normas están en vigor desde 1946; **to come into force** = entrar en vigor; **the new regulations will come into force on January 1st** = el nuevo reglamento entrará en vigor el 1 de enero **(b)** *(group of people)* fuerza *f*; **labour force** *or* **workforce** = mano de obra *or* personal *or* población activa; **the management has made an increased offer to the labour force** = la dirección ha ofrecido un aumento al personal; **we are opening a new factory in the Far East because of the cheap local labour force** = abrimos una nueva fábrica en Extremo Oriente para aprovechar la mano de obra local barata; **sales force** = personal de ventas **(c)** **force majeure** = fuerza mayor **2** *verb* forzar *or* obligar; **competition has forced the company to lower its prices** = la competencia ha forzado a la empresa a bajar sus precios

◊ **forced** [fɔːst] *adjective* a la fuerza; **forced sale** = venta forzosa

◊ **force down** ['fɔːs 'daʊn] *verb* forzar *or* obligar a bajar; **to force prices down** = hacer bajar los precios; **competition has forced prices down** = la competencia ha hecho bajar los precios

◊ **force up** ['fɔːs 'ʌp] *verb* forzar *or* obligar a subir; **to force prices up** = hacer subir los precios; **the war forced up the price of oil** = la guerra ha hecho subir el precio del petróleo

forecast ['fɔːkaːst] **1** *noun* previsión *f or* pronóstico *m*; **the chairman did not believe the sales director's forecast of higher turnover** = el presidente no creyó en la previsión de un mayor volumen de ventas hecha por el director de ventas; **we based our calculations on the forecast turnover** = basamos nuestros cálculos en los pronósticos del volumen de ventas; **cash flow forecast** = previsión de 'cash flow'; **population forecast** = previsión demográfica; **sales forecast** = previsión de ventas **2** *verb* pronosticar *or* prever *or* predecir; **he is forecasting sales of £2m** = pronostica unas ventas de £2m; **economists have forecast a fall in the exchange rate** = los economistas han pronosticado un descenso del tipo de cambio (NOTE: **forecasting - forecast**)

◊ **forecaster** ['fɔːkaːstə] *noun* pronosticador, -ra; **economic forecaster** = pronosticador económico *or* especialista en previsiones económicas

◊ **forecasting** ['fɔːkaːstɪŋ] *noun* previsión *f*; **manpower forecasting** = previsión de mano de obra

foreclose [fɔː'kləʊz] *verb* entablar juicio hipotecario *or* embargar un bien hipotecado (por impago); **to foreclose on a mortgaged property** = ejecutar una hipoteca

◊ **foreclosure** [fɔː'kləʊʒə] *noun* ejecución *f* de una hipoteca *or* juicio *m* hipotecario

foreign ['fɒrən] *adjective* extranjero, -ra; **foreign cars have flooded our market** = los coches extranjeros han inundado nuestro mercado; **we are increasing our trade with foreign countries** = estamos aumentando nuestro comercio con los países extranjeros; **foreign currency** = divisas *or* moneda extranjera; **foreign goods** = productos extranjeros; **foreign investments** = inversiones exteriores; **Foreign Ministry** *GB* **Foreign Office** = Ministerio de Asuntos Exteriores; **foreign money order** = giro postal internacional; **foreign trade** = comercio exterior *or* comercio con el exterior

◊ **foreign exchange** ['fɒrən ɪks'tʃeɪn(d)ʒ] *noun* **(a)** *(action)* cambio *m* de moneda extranjera *or* de divisas **(b)** *(currency)* divisas *fpl or* moneda *f* extranjera; **foreign exchange broker** *or* **dealer** = cambista *or* operador de cambios; **foreign exchange dealing** = operaciones de cambio *or* cambio; **the foreign exchange markets** = mercados de divisas *or* cambiarios; **foreign exchange reserves** = reservas de divisas; **foreign exchange transfer** = transferencia de divisas

◊ **foreigner** ['fɒrənə] *noun* extranjero, -ra *or* forastero, -ra

foreman *or* **forewoman** ['fɔːmən *or* 'fɔːwʊmən] *noun* capataz *m or* contramaestre *m or* encargado, -da (NOTE: plural is **foremen** *or* **forewomen**)

foresee [fɔː'siː] *verb* anticipar

forex *or* **Forex** ['fɔːreks] = FOREIGN EXCHANGE

forfaiting ['fɔːfɪtɪŋ] *noun* 'forfaiting' *m* (operación de crédito financiero para el fomento de las exportaciones)

COMMENT: forfaiting is a means of providing finance for exporters, where an agent (the forfaiter) accepts a bill of exchange from an overseas customer; he buys the bill at a discount, and collects the payments from the customer in due course

forfeit ['fɔːfɪt] **1** *noun* confiscación *f or* decomiso *m*; **forfeit clause** = cláusula decomisoria; **the goods were declared forfeit** = las mercancías fueron confiscadas **2** *verb* decomisar *or* confiscar *or* perder el derecho *or* la posesión de algo; **to forfeit a patent** = perder el derecho de patente; **to forfeit a deposit** = perder una entrada *or* un depósito

◊ **forfeiture** ['fɔːfɪtʃə] *noun* decomiso *m or* pérdida *f or* confiscación *f*

forge [fɔːdʒ] *verb* falsificar *or* falsear; **he tried to enter the country with forged documents** = intentó entrar en el país con documentación falsa

◊ **forgery** ['fɔːdʒəri] *noun* **(a)** *(action)* falsificación *f*; **he was sent to prison for forgery** = fue a la cárcel por falsificación de documentos (NOTE: no plural) **(b)** *(illegal copy)* copia falsa *or* documentos falsos; **the signature was proved to be a forgery** = se demostró que la firma era falsificada *or* falsa

forget [fə'get] *verb* olvidar; **she forgot to put a stamp on the envelope** = olvidó poner el sello al sobre; **don't forget we're having lunch together tomorrow** = no te olvides de que mañana almorzamos juntos (NOTE: **forgetting - forgot - forgotten**)

fork-lift truck ['fɔːklɪft 'trʌk] *noun* carretilla *f* elevadora de horquilla

form [fɔːm] **1** *noun* **(a)** *(legal document)* términos *mpl or* fórmulas *fpl* judiciales; **form of words** = forma *f* de expresar un texto; **receipt in due form** = recibo extendido en debida forma **(b)** *(official printed paper)* impreso *m or* formulario *m*; **you have to fill in form A20** = tiene que rellenar el impreso A20; **customs declaration form** = impreso de declaración de aduana; **a pad of order forms** = un bloc de hojas *or* formularios de pedido; **application form** = *(for job)* impreso *or* formulario de solicitud; *(for membership)* impreso de inscripción; **claim**

form = formulario de reclamaciones; **registration form** = boletín *m* de inscripción **2** *verb* formar *or* crear; **the brothers have formed a new company** = los hermanos han creado una nueva sociedad

◊ **formation** *or* **forming** [fɔ:'meɪʃən *or* 'fɔ:mɪŋ] *noun* formación *f*; **the formation of a new company** = la formación de una nueva compañía

forma ['fɔ:mə] *see* PRO FORMA

formal ['fɔ:məl] *adjective* formal *or* oficial; **to make a formal application** = presentar una solicitud oficial; **to send a formal order** = enviar un pedido en firme

◊ **formality** [fɔ:'mæləti] *noun* trámite *m or* formalidad *f*; **customs formalities** = formalidades aduaneras

◊ **formally** ['fɔ:məli] *adverb* formalmente *or* oficialmente; **we have formally applied for planning permission for the new shopping precinct** = hemos solicitado oficialmente el permiso para la planificación de la nueva zona comercial

former ['fɔ:mə] *adjective* anterior *or* pasado, -da *or* cesado, -da; **the former chairman has taken a job with the rival company** = el anterior presidente se ha puesto a trabajar para la empresa rival

◊ **formerly** ['fɔ:məli] *adverb* anteriormente *or* antes *or* en tiempos pasados; **he is currently managing director of Smith Ltd, but formerly he worked for Jones** = actualmente es el director gerente de Smith Ltd., pero antes trabajaba para Jones

fortnight ['fɔ:tnaɪt] *noun* quince días *mpl or* quincena *f or* dos semanas *fpl*; **I saw him a fortnight ago** = lo ví hace quince días; **we will be on holiday during the last fortnight of July** = estaremos de vacaciones durante la última quincena de julio (NOTE: not used in US English)

fortune ['fɔ:tʃu:n] *noun* **(a)** *(large amount of money)* fortuna *f*; **he made a fortune from investing in oil shares** = hizo una fortuna invirtiendo en acciones petrolíferas **(b)** *(received in a will)* patrimonio *m or* fortuna *f*; **she left her fortune to her three children** = dejó su fortuna a sus tres hijos

forum ['fɔ:rəm] *noun (meeting)* foro *m*

forward ['fɔ:wəd] **1** *adjective* de futuros *or* adelantado, -da *or* a plazo *or* en fecha futura; **forward buying** *or* **buying forward** = compra de futuros *or* especulación; **forward contract** = contrato a plazo fijo; **forward market** = mercado de futuros; **forward (exchange) rate** = tipos de cambio futuros *or* divisas a plazo; **what are the forward rates for the pound?** = ¿cuáles son los cambios a plazo para la libra?; **forward sales** = venta a plazo *or* de futuros **2** *adverb* **(a) to date a cheque forward** = extender un cheque con fecha adelantada; **carriage forward** *or* **freight forward** = porte debido *or* contra reembolso del flete; **charges forward** = gastos a cobrar a la entrega **(b) to buy forward** = comprar divisas a futuros; **to sell forward** = vender divisas a futuros **(c) balance brought forward** *or* **carried forward** = saldo a cuenta nueva **(d) to go forward** = progresar *or* avanzar *or* ir hacia adelante **3** *verb* **to forward something to someone** = enviar *or* expedir algo a alguien; **to forward a consignment to Nigeria** = enviar mercancías a Nigeria; **please forward** *or* **to be forwarded** = remítase al destinatario *or* a las nuevas señas

◊ **(freight) forwarder** [('freɪt)'fɔ:wədə] *noun* agente *m* de transporte

◊ **forwarding** ['fɔ:wədɪŋ] *noun* **(a)** *(shipping)* expedición *f or* envío *m or* transporte *m*; **air forwarding** = envío por transporte aéreo; **forwarding agent** = FORWARDER **forwarding instructions** *or* **instructions for forwarding** = instrucciones de envío **(b) forwarding address** = dirección de reenvío

foul [faʊl] *adjective* **foul bill of lading** = conocimiento de embarque defectuoso

founder ['faʊndə] *noun* fundador, -ra; **founder's shares** = acciones de fundador

four [fɔ:] *number* cuatro; **the four O's** = en marketing se refiere al objeto, objetivo, organización y operación; **the four P's** = en marketing se refiere al producto, precio, promoción y lugar

four-part ['fɔ:'pɑ:t] *adjective* **four-part invoices** = facturas en cuatro partes; **four-part stationery** = papel de oficina (recibos, etc.) en cuatro partes

fourth [fɔ:θ] *adjective* cuarto, -ta; **fourth quarter** = cuarto trimestre

Fr = FRANC Fr *or* F

fraction ['frækʃən] *noun* fracción *f or* pequeña parte *f*; **only a fraction of the new share issue was subscribed** = se suscribió tan sólo una pequeña parte de la nueva emisión de acciones

◊ **fractional** ['frækʃənl] *adjective* fraccionario, -ria; **fractional certificate** = certificado fraccionario *or* acción fraccionada

fragile ['frædʒaɪl] *adjective* frágil; **there is an extra premium for insuring fragile goods in shipment** = hay una prima extra para asegurar el transporte de mercancías frágiles

framework ['freɪmwɜ:k] *noun* marco *m*; **the legal framework** = el marco legal

franc [fræŋk] *noun (currency used in France, Belgium, Switzerland, and other countries)* franco *m*; **French francs** *or* **Belgian francs** *or* **Swiss francs** = francos franceses *or* francos belgas *or* francos suizos; **it costs twenty-five Swiss francs** = cuesta veinticinco francos suizos; **franc account** = cuenta en francos (NOTE: in English usually written **Fr** *or* **F** before the figure: **Fr2,500** (say: 'two thousand, five hundred francs'). Currencies of different countries can be shown by the initial letters of the countries: **FFr** (French francs); **SwFr** (Swiss francs); **BFr** (Belgian francs)

France [frɑ:ns] *noun* Francia *f*

◊ **French** [frentʃ] **1** *adjective* francés, -esa **2** *noun* **the French** = los franceses

◊ **Frenchman, Frenchwoman** ['frentʃmən *or* 'frentʃwʊmən] *noun* francés, -esa
NOTE: capital: **Paris** (= París); currency: **franc** *or* **French franc** (**Fr** *or* **F**) = franco *or* franco francés (F)

franchise ['fræn(t)ʃaɪz] **1** *noun* concesión *f or* licencia *f or* franquicia *f*; **he has bought a printing**

franchise *or* **a hot dog franchise** = ha comprado una licencia para imprimir *or* una concesión de venta de perritos calientes **2** *verb* franquiciar *or* conceder una licencia de explotación; **his sandwich bar was so successful that he decided to franchise it** = su bar de bocadillos tuvo tanto éxito que decidió conceder franquicias *or* licencias de explotación

◊ **franchisee** [fræn(t)ʃaɪˈziː] *noun* franquiciado, -da *or* licenciatario, -ria *or* concesionario, -ria

◊ **franchiser** [ˈfræn(t)ʃaɪzə] *noun* franquiciador, -ra

◊ **franchising** [ˈfræn(t)ʃaɪzɪŋ] *noun* concesión *f* *or* licencia *f*; **he runs his sandwich chain as a franchising operation** = dirige su cadena de venta de bocadillos en régimen de concesión *or* franquicia

◊ **franchisor**   [ˈfræn(t)ʃaɪzə]   *noun*   = FRANCHISER

QUOTE a quarter of a million Britons are seeking to become their own bosses by purchasing franchises
Marketing Week

QUOTE restaurants in a family-style chain that the company operates and franchises throughout most parts of the U.S.
Fortune

franco [ˈfræŋkəʊ] *adverb* franco *or* libre

frank [fræŋk] *verb* franquear; **franking machine** = máquina franqueadora

fraud [frɔːd] *noun* fraude *m* *or* defraudación *f* *or* estafa *f*; **he got possession of the property by fraud** = tomó posesión de la propiedad por medio de estafas; **he was accused of frauds relating to foreign currency** = fue acusado de fraude de divisas; **to obtain money by fraud** = obtener dinero fraudulentamente *or* por medio de fraude o engaños; **fraud squad** = brigada contra el fraude; **Serious Fraud Office (SFO)** = juzgado especial de delitos monetarios

◊ **fraudulent**   [ˈfrɔːdjʊlənt]   *adjective* fraudulento, -ta; **fraudulent misrepresentation** = fraude *m* *or* falsedad *f* fraudulenta; **a fraudulent transaction** = una transacción fraudulenta

◊ **fraudulently**   [ˈfrɔːdjʊləntli]   *adverb* fraudulentamente; **goods imported fraudulently** = mercancías importadas fraudulentamente

free [friː] **1** *adjective & adverb* **(a)** *(without payment)* gratuito, -ta *or* gratuitamente; **to be given a free ticket to the exhibition** = recibir una entrada gratuita para la exposición; **the price includes free delivery** = el precio incluye el reparto *or* la entrega; **goods are delivered free** = el transporte de mercancías es gratuito; **catalogue sent free on request** = solicite catálogo gratuito; **carriage free** = franco de porte; **free gift** = regalo; **there is a free gift worth £25 to any customer buying a washing machine** = se ofrece un regalo por valor de £25 a todo cliente que compre una lavadora; **free paper** *or* **freesheet** = periódico gratuito; **free sample** = muestra gratuita; **free trial** = prueba gratuita; **to send a piece of equipment for two weeks' free trial** = enviar un aparato a prueba gratuita por dos semanas; **free of charge** = gratis; **free on board (FOB)** = franco a bordo; **free on rail (FOR)** = franco sobre vagón **(b)** *(without restrictions)* libre; **free collective**

bargaining = convenio colectivo libre; **free competition** = libre competencia; **free currency** = moneda de libre circulación; **free enterprise** = libre empresa; **free market economy** = economía de (libre) mercado; **free port** *or* **free trade zone** = puerto franco; **free of tax** *or* **tax-free** = libre de impuestos; **he was given a tax-free sum of £25,000 when he was made redundant** = le dieron un total de £25.000 libres de impuestos cuando le despidieron; **interest free of tax** *or* **tax-free interest** = interés libre de impuestos; **interest-free credit** *or* **loan** = crédito *or* préstamo libre de interés *or* sin interés; **free of duty** *or* **duty-free** = libre de derechos de aduana *or* de impuestos; **to import wine free of duty** *or* **duty-free** = importar vino exento de derechos de aduana; **free trade** = libre cambio *or* libre comercio; **the government adopted a free trade policy** = el gobierno adoptó una política de libre comercio; **free trade area** = zona de libre cambio; **free trader** = librecambista *mf* *or* partidario, -ria del libre cambio; **free zone** = área aduanera exenta **(c)** *(not busy or not occupied)* libre; **are there any free tables in the restaurant?** = ¿hay mesas libres en el restaurante?; **I shall be free in a few minutes** = estaré libre en unos minutos; **the chairman always keeps Friday afternoon free for a game of bridge** = el presidente siempre se reserva la tarde del viernes para jugar una partida de bridge **2** *verb* **(a)** *(release)* poner en libertad *or* liberar; **the government's decision has freed millions of pounds for investment** = la decisión del gobierno ha liberado millones de libras para la inversión **(b)** *(rescue)* librar

QUOTE American business as a whole is increasingly free from heavy dependence on manufacturing
Sunday Times

QUOTE can free trade be reconciled with a strong dollar resulting from floating exchange rates?
Duns Business Month

QUOTE free traders hold that the strong dollar is the primary cause of the nation's trade problems
Duns Business Month

◊ **freebie** [ˈfriːbiː] *noun* *(informal)* obsequio *m* ofrecido como publicidad

◊ **freehold property** [ˈfriːhəʊld ˈprɒpəti] *noun* propiedad *f* absoluta de un inmueble (en oposición a 'leasehold', especie de enfiteusis)

◊ **freeholder** [ˈfriːhəʊldə] *noun* propietario absoluto de un inmueble

◊ **freelance** [ˈfriːlɑːns] **1** *noun* trabajador autónomo *or* de libre dedicación; **we have about twenty freelances working for us** *or* **about twenty people working for us on a freelance basis** = tenemos una veintena de colaboradores independientes *or* de trabajadores autónomos **2** *adjective* autónomo, -ma *or* independiente *or* que trabaja por su cuenta; **she is a freelance journalist** = es una periodista independiente *or* que trabaja por su cuenta **3** *adverb* independientemente *or* por su cuenta; **he works freelance as a designer** = trabaja independientemente como diseñador **4** *verb* **(a)** *(person)* trabajar por cuenta propia *or* ir por libre; **she freelances for the local newspapers** = trabaja como periodista independiente para los periódicos locales

(b) *(work)* dar encargos a trabajadores autónomos *or* independientes; **we freelance work out to several specialists** = encargamos trabajo a varios especialistas independientes

◊ **freelancer** ['fri:lɑ:nsə] *noun* trabajador autónomo *or* independiente *or* por libre

◊ **freely** ['fri:li] *adverb* libremente; **money should circulate freely within the European Union** = el dinero debería circular libremente dentro de la Unión Europea

◊ **freephone** *or* **freefone** ['fri:fəʊn] *noun GB* llamadas *fpl* telefónicas gratuitas

◊ **freepost** ['fri:pəʊst] *noun GB* franqueo *m* pagado

◊ **freesheet** ['fri:ʃi:t] *noun* = FREE PAPER

freeze [fri:z] **1** *noun* **credit freeze** = congelación *f* de créditos; **wages and prices freeze** *or* **freeze on wages and prices** = congelación de precios y salarios **2** *verb* congelar *or* bloquear; **we have frozen expenditure at last year's level** = hemos congelado los gastos al nivel del año pasado; **to freeze wages and prices** = congelar precios y salarios; **to freeze credits** = bloquear los créditos; **to freeze company dividends** = bloquear los dividendos de la compañía (NOTE: **freezing - froze - has frozen**)

◊ **freeze out** ['fri:z 'aʊt] *verb* **to freeze out competition** = liquidar la competencia

freight [freɪt] **1** *noun* **(a)** *(carriage)* flete *m or* transporte *m or* porte *m*; **at an auction, the buyer pays the freight** = en una subasta, el comprador paga los portes; **freight charges** *or* **freight rates** = cuotas de flete *or* tarifas de flete; **freight charges have gone up sharply this year** = las cuotas de flete han subido mucho este año; **freight costs** = costes de flete *or* gastos de transporte; **freight forward** = porte debido *or* flete contra reembolso **(b) air freight** = flete aéreo *or* carga aérea; **to send a shipment by air freight** = hacer un envío por flete aéreo; **air freight charges** *or* **rates** = gastos *or* tarifas de carga aérea **(c)** *(goods carried)* carga *f or* mercancías *fpl*; **to take on freight** = fletar *or* cargar; *US* **freight car** = vagón de mercancías; **freight depot** = estación de mercancías; **freight elevator** = montacargas *m*; **freight forwarder** = agente *m* de transporte; **freight plane** = avión carguero *or* de carga; **freight train** = tren de mercancías **2** *verb* **to freight goods** = fletar *or* transportar mercancías; **we freight goods to all parts of the USA** = transportamos mercancías a todos los lugares de los EE UU

◊ **freightage** ['freɪtɪdʒ] *noun* flete *m or* fletamento *m*

◊ **freighter** ['freɪtə] *noun* **(a)** *(aircraft or ship)* carguero *m or* avión *m or* buque *m* de carga **(b)** *(company)* fletador *m or* empresa de transportes

◊ **freightliner** ['freɪtlaɪnə] *noun* tren *m* de mercancías de contenedores; **the shipment has to be delivered to the freightliner depot** = el cargamento tiene que ser entregado en el depósito de la estación de mercancías

frequent ['fri:kwənt] *adjective* frecuente *or* corriente; **there is a frequent ferry service to**

France = hay un servicio frecuente de transbordador a Francia; **we send frequent faxes to New York** = enviamos un fax frecuentemente a Nueva York; **how frequent are the planes to Birmingham?** = ¿con qué frecuencia salen aviones para Birmingham?

◊ **frequently** ['fri:kwəntli] *adverb* a menudo *or* con frecuencia *or* frecuentemente; **the photocopier is frequently out of use** = la fotocopiadora está frecuentemente averiada; **we fax our New York office very frequently - at least four times a day** = enviamos un fax a nuestra oficina de Nueva York muy a menudo - cuatro veces al día como mínimo

friendly society ['frendli sə'saɪəti] *noun* mutualidad *f or* sociedad *f* de ayuda mutua

fringe benefits ['frɪn(d)ʒ 'benɪfɪts] *plural noun* beneficios *mpl* complementarios *or* extrasalariales *or* extras *or* adicionales

front [frʌnt] *noun* **(a)** *(face)* frente *m or* parte *f* delantera; **the front of the office building is on the High Street** = la fachada de las oficinas da a High Street; **the front page of the company report has a photograph of the managing director** = la portada del informe de la compañía lleva una fotografía del director gerente; **our ad appeared on the front page of the newspaper** = nuestro anuncio se publicó en la primera página del periódico **(b) in front of** = delante de; **they put up a 'for sale' sign in front of the factory** = pusieron el cartel de 'en venta' delante de la fábrica; **the chairman's name is in front of all the others on the staff list** = el nombre del presidente encabeza la lista del personal **(c)** *(person or business)* fachada *f or* tapadera *f*; **his restaurant is a front for a drugs organization** = su restaurante es la tapadera de una organización que trafica en drogas **(d) money up front** = pago por adelantado *or* entrada; **they are asking for £10,000 up front before they will consider the deal** = piden un pago por adelantado de £10.000 antes de tomar el asunto en consideración; **he had to put money up front before he could clinch the deal** = tuvo que dar una entrada para poder cerrar el trato

◊ **front-end loaded** ['frʌntend 'ləʊdɪd] *adjective* inversión en la que los gastos de gestión se concentran en el primer año

◊ **front-line management** ['frʌntlaɪn 'mænɪdʒmənt] *noun* dirección operacional

◊ **front man** ['frʌntmæn] *noun* testaferro *m or* hombre *m* de paja

frozen ['frəʊzn] *adjective* bloqueado, -da *or* congelado, -da *or* inmovilizado, -da; **frozen account** = cuenta bloqueada; **frozen assets** = activo congelado; **frozen credits** = crédito congelado; **his assets have been frozen by the court** = sus bienes han sido bloqueados por los tribunales; *see also* FREEZE

frustrate [frʌs'treɪt] *verb* frustrar

ft [fʊt] = FOOT

FT ['ef'ti:] = FINANCIAL TIMES

fuel [fjʊəl] **1** *noun* combustible *m or* carburante *m or* gasolina *f*; **the annual fuel bill for the plant has doubled over the last years** = la factura anual de combustible de la fábrica se ha duplicado en los últimos años; **he has bought a car with low fuel**

consumption = ha comprado un coche que consume poca gasolina **2** *verb* aumentar *or* acentuar *or* acrecentar; **market worries were fuelled by news of an increase in electricity charges** = las preocupaciones del mercado se vieron acentuadas por la noticia de la subida de las tarifas de electricidad; **the rise in the share price was fuelled by rumours of a takeover bid** = la subida de las cotizaciones de acciones fue acrecentada por los rumores de una oferta de adquisición (NOTE: GB spelling is **fuelled - fuelling** but US spelling is **fueled - fueling**)

fulfil *or* US **fulfill** [fʊl'fɪl] *verb* cumplir *or* satisfacer; **the clause regarding payments has not been fulfilled** = la cláusula referente a los pagos no se ha cumplido; **to fulfil an order** = despachar un pedido; **we are so understaffed that we cannot fulfil any more orders before Christmas** = tenemos tan poco personal que no podemos despachar más pedidos antes de Navidad

◊ **fulfilment** *or* US **fulfillment** [fʊl'fɪlmənt] *noun* cumplimiento *m or* realización *f*; **order fulfilment** = despacho *m* de pedidos

full [fʊl] *adjective* **(a)** *(filled)* lleno, -na; **the train was full of commuters** = el tren iba lleno de viajeros de cercanías; **is the container full yet?** = ¿está ya lleno el contenedor *or* recipiente?; **we sent a lorry full of spare parts to our warehouse** = enviamos un camión lleno de piezas de recambio a nuestro almacén; **when the disk is full, don't forget to make a backup copy** = cuando el disco esté lleno, no te olvides de hacer una copia de reserva **(b)** *(complete)* completo, -ta *or* pleno, -na; **we are working at full capacity** = estamos trabajando a plena capacidad *or* a pleno rendimiento; **full costs** = coste total; **full cover** = cobertura total; **full discharge of a debt** = pago total de una deuda; **full employment** = pleno empleo; **full fare** = tarifa normal; **full price** = precio íntegro *or* de venta al público *or* precio fuerte (libros); **he bought a full-price ticket** = compró un billete a precio íntegro **(c)** *(in full)* = completamente *or* enteramente; **give your full name and address** *or* **your name and address in full** = indique su nombre, apellidos y dirección; **he accepted all our conditions in full** = aceptó todas nuestras condiciones sin reservas; **full refund** *or* **refund paid in full** = reembolso total; **he got a full refund when he complained about the service** = le reembolsaron totalmente cuando se quejó del servicio; **full payment** *or* **payment in full** = pago íntegro *or* total

◊ **full-scale** ['fʊl'skeɪl] *adjective* completo, -ta *or* general; **the MD ordered a full-scale review of credit terms** = el director gerente ordenó una revisión general de las condiciones de crédito

◊ **full-service banking** ['fʊl 'sɜːvɪs 'bæŋkɪŋ] *noun* banco que ofrece una gama completa de servicios

◊ **full-time** [fʊl'taɪm] *adjective & adverb* a tiempo completo *or* a jornada completa; **she is in full-time work** *or* **she works full-time** *or* **she is in full-time employment** = trabaja a tiempo completo; **he is one of our full-time staff** = es uno de nuestros empleados a jornada completa

◊ **full-timer** [fʊl'taɪmə] *noun* empleado, -da a tiempo completo

◊ **fully** ['fʊli] *adverb* completamente *or*

enteramente *or* totalmente; **fully-paid shares** = acciones liberadas *or* cubiertas; **fully paid-up capital** = capital desembolsado *or* cubierto

function ['fʌŋ(k)ʃən] **1** *noun* **(a)** *(duty)* función *f*; **management function** *or* **function of management** = función directiva **(b)** *(computer)* función *f*; **the word-processor had a spelling-checker function but no built-in text-editing function** = el ordenador tenía autocorrector *or* deletreador ortográfico pero no llevaba incorporada la función para editar textos; **function code** = código de función; **function key** = tecla de función **2** *verb* funcionar; **the advertising campaign is functioning smoothly** = la campaña publicitaria está funcionando perfectamente; **the new management structure does not seem to be functioning very well** = la nueva estructura directiva no parece que funcione muy bien

fund [fʌnd] **1** *noun* **(a)** *(money set aside)* fondo *m*; **contingency fund** = fondo para imprevistos; **pension fund** = fondo de pensiones; **the International Monetary Fund (the IMF)** = el Fondo Monetario Internacional (FMI) **(b)** *(money invested)* **managed fund** *or* **fund of funds** *or* **managed unit trust** = fondo de inversión dirigido *or* controlado; **fund management** = gestión de fondos; **fund manager** = gestor de fondos **2** *plural noun* **(a)** fondos *mpl or* reservas *fpl*; **the company has no funds to pay for the research programme** = la compañía no tiene fondos para financiar el programa de investigación; **the company called for extra funds** = la compañía solicitó más fondos; **to run out of funds** = agotar los fondos; **public funds** = fondos públicos; **the cost was paid for out of public funds** = el coste se pagó con cargo a los fondos públicos; **conversion of funds** = apropiación indebida de fondos; **to convert funds to another purpose** = desviar fondos a otros fines; **to convert funds to one's own use** = apropiarse indebidamente de fondos en beneficio propio **(b)** *GB* **the Funds** = títulos de estado; *US* **Federal Funds** *or* **Fed Funds** = bonos para la regulación monetaria **3** *verb* destinar *or* asignar fondos *or* financiar; **to fund a company** = financiar una compañía; **the company does not have enough resources to fund its expansion programme** = la compañía no tiene recursos suficientes para financiar su programa de expansión

◊ **funded** ['fʌndɪd] *adjective* consolidado, -da; **long-term funded capital** = capital consolidado a largo plazo; *GB* **funded debt** = deuda consolidada

◊ **funding** ['fʌndɪŋ] *noun* **(a)** *(money)* financiación *f or* asignación *f* de fondos; **the bank is providing the funding for the new product launch** = el banco financia el lanzamiento del nuevo producto; **the capital expenditure programme requires long-term funding** = el programa de gastos de capital exige una financiación a largo plazo **(b)** *(loan)* consolidación *f* de fondos

QUOTE the S&L funded all borrowers' development costs, including accrued interest

Barrons

QUOTE small innovative companies have been hampered for lack of funds

Sunday Times

QUOTE the company was set up with funds totalling NorKr 145m

Lloyd's List

funny money ['fʌni 'mʌni] *noun* acciones poco corrientes

furnish ['fɜːnɪʃ] *verb* (a) *(supply)* suministrar *or* proporcionar *or* abastecer (b) *(with furniture)* amueblar; **he furnished his office with secondhand chairs and desks** = amuebló su oficina con sillas y mesas de segunda mano; **the company spent £10,000 on furnishing the chairman's office** = la compañía gastó £10.000 en amueblar la oficina del presidente; **furnished accommodation** = piso amueblado *or* casa amueblada

furniture ['fɜːnɪtʃə] *noun* muebles *mpl or* mobiliario *m*; **furniture and fittings** = mobiliario y enseres; **office furniture** = muebles de oficina; **he deals in secondhand office furniture** = tiene un negocio de muebles de oficina de segunda mano; **an office furniture store** = una tienda de mobiliario de oficina; **furniture depository** *or* **furniture storage** = guardamuebles *m*

further ['fɜːðə] **1** *adjective* (a) *(distance)* más lejos *or* más allá *or* más abajo; **the office is further down the High Street** = la oficina está unas manzanas más abajo en High Street; **the flight from Madrid terminates in New York - for further destinations you must change to internal flights** = el vuelo de Madrid termina en Nueva York - para destinos ulteriores hay que tomar un vuelo del interior (b) *(more)* otro, -ra *or* adicional *or* suplementario, -ria *or* más; **further orders will be dealt with by our London office** = los pedidos adicionales serán

atendidos por nuestra oficina de Londres; **nothing can be done while we are awaiting further instructions** = no podemos hacer nada hasta que no hayamos recibido nuevas instrucciones; **to ask for further details** *or* **particulars** = pedir más detalles; **he had borrowed £100,000 and then tried to borrow a further £25,000** = había pedido prestadas £100.000 y luego intentó pedir otras £25.000; **the company is asking for further credit** = la compañía ha pedido crédito suplementario; **he asked for a further six weeks to pay** = pidió seis semanas más para pagar (c) **further to** = además de *or* tras *or* con relación a; **further to our letter of the 21st** = con referencia a nuestra carta del 21; **further to your letter of the 21st** = con relación a su carta del 21; **further to our telephone conversation** = con relación a nuestra conversación telefónica **2** *verb* favorecer *or* fomentar; **he was accused of using his membership of the council to further his own interests** = le acusaron de utilizar su cargo en el consejo para favorecer sus propios intereses

fuss [fʌs] *noun* **to make a fuss** = protestar *or* armar una bronca

future ['fjuːtʃə] **1** *adjective* futuro, -ra; **future delivery** = entrega futura **2** *noun* futuro *m*; **try to be more careful in future** = trata de ser más cuidadoso en el futuro; **in future all reports must be sent to Australia by air** = en el futuro todos los informes deberán enviarse a Australia por avión

◊ **futures** ['fjuːtʃəz] *plural noun (shares or commodities)* futuros *mpl*; **coffee futures** = café cotizado en el mercado de futuros; **commodity futures** = bienes cotizados en el mercado de futuros; **gold rose 5% on the commodity futures market yesterday** = ayer el oro subió un 5% en el mercado de futuros; **financial futures** = futuros financieros; **financial futures market** = mercado de futuros financieros; **futures contract** = contrato a plazo *or* de futuros

COMMENT: a futures contract is a contract to purchase; if an investor is bullish, he will buy a contract, but if he feels the market will go down, he will sell one

Gg

g = = GRAM gr

G5, G7, G10 [dʒiː'faɪv or dʒiː'sevn or dʒiː'ten] = GROUP OF FIVE, GROUP OF SEVEN, GROUP OF TEN see GROUP

GAB = GENERAL ARRANGEMENTS TO BORROW Acuerdo general sobre préstamos

Gabon ['gæbɒn] *noun* Gabón *m*

◊ **Gabonese** [gæbə'niːz] *adjective & noun* gabonés, -esa
NOTE: capital: **Libreville**; currency: **CFA franc (CFAF)** = franco CFA (FCFA)

gadget ['gædʒɪt] *noun* chisme *m or* aparato *m*

gain [geɪn] **1** *noun* **(a)** *(becoming larger)* aumento *m*; **gain in profitability** = aumento de la rentabilidad **(b)** *(increase in profit or price or value)* ganancia *f or* beneficio *m*; **oil shares showed gains on the Stock Exchange** = las acciones petrolíferas registraron ganancias en la bolsa; **property shares put on gains of 10%-15%** = los valores de las sociedades inmobiliarias registraron una subida del 10% al 15%; **capital gain** = plusvalía *f*; **capital gains tax** = impuesto sobre la plusvalía; **short-term gains** = beneficios a corto plazo **2** *verb* **(a)** *(get)* ganar *or* adquirir *or* lograr; **he gained some useful experience working in a bank** = adquirió experiencia práctica trabajando en un banco; **to gain control of a business** = lograr el control de un negocio **(b)** *(become bigger)* ganar *or* aumentar; **the dollar gained six points on the foreign exchange markets** = el dólar ganó seis puntos en los mercados de divisas

◊ **gainful** ['geɪnf(ʊ)l] *adjective* **gainful employment** = empleo remunerado

◊ **gainfully** ['geɪnfʊli] *adverb* **gainfully employed** = que ejerce un empleo remunerado

gallon ['gælən] *noun* galón *m* (medida de capacidad equivalente a 4,55 litros en el Reino Unido y 3,79 en EE UU); **the car does twenty-five miles per gallon or the car does twenty-five miles to the gallon** = el coche consume unos 11 litros por cien km. (NOTE: usually written **gal** after figures: **25gal**)

galloping inflation ['gæləpɪŋ ɪn'fleɪʃən] *noun* inflación *f* galopante

(the) Gambia [(ðə) 'gæmbɪə] *noun* Gambia

◊ **Gambian** ['gæmbɪən] *adjective & noun* gambiano, -na *or* de Gambia
NOTE: capital: **Banjul**; currency: **dalasi** = dalasi

gap [gæp] *noun* hueco *m or* vacío *m or* espacio *m*; **gap in the market** = un hueco en el mercado; **to look for or to find a gap in the market** = buscar *or* encontrar un hueco en el mercado; **this computer has filled a real gap in the market** = este ordenador

ha venido a llenar una necesidad que existía en el mercado; **dollar gap** = escasez *f* de dólares; **trade gap** = déficit *m* comercial

garnishee [gɑːnɪ'ʃiː] *noun* embargado, -da *or* persona *f* embargada; **garnishee order,** *US* **garnishment** = auto *or* sentencia de embargo

COMMENT: person who owes money to a creditor and is ordered by a court to pay that money to a creditor of the creditor, and not to the creditor himself

gasoline *or* (informal) **gas** ['gæsəliːn *or* gæs] *noun US* gasolina *f* (NOTE: GB English is **petrol**)

gate [geɪt] *noun* **(a)** *(in a field)* portillo *m* **(b)** *(in an airport)* puerta *f*; **flight IB270 is now boarding at Gate 23** = salida del vuelo IB270 por la puerta 23 **(c)** *(number of people attending a match)* entrada *f*; **there was a gate of 50,000 at the football final** = hubo una entrada de 50.000 en la final de fútbol

gather ['gæðə] *verb* **(a)** *(to collect)* recoger *or* reunir *or* recopilar *or* acopiar; **he gathered his papers together before the meeting started** = recogió sus papeles antes de que empezara la reunión; **she has been gathering information on import controls from various sources** = ha estado recopilando información de varias fuentes sobre los controles a la importación **(b)** *(to understand)* tener entendido *or* enterarse; **I gather he has left the office** = tengo entendido que ha dejado la oficina; **did you gather who will be at the meeting?** = ¿te enteraste de quién iría a la reunión?

GATT [gæt] = GENERAL AGREEMENT ON TARIFFS AND TRADE Acuerdo General sobre Aranceles Aduaneros y Comercio (GATT) (NOTE: now replaced by **World Trade Organization (WTO)**

gazump [gə'zʌmp] *verb* romper un acuerdo de venta de una propiedad para venderla a un precio más alto; **he was gazumped** = ofrecieron más que él *or* hubo un postor mejor que él

◊ **gazumping** [gə'zʌmpɪŋ] *noun* retirada *f* de un contrato *or* rechazo *m* de una oferta de compra de una propiedad cuando aparece una oferta más alta

GDP ['dʒiːdiː'piː] = GROSS DOMESTIC PRODUCT Producto Interior Bruto (PIB)

gear [gɪə] *verb* **(a)** *(to link)* ajustar *or* adaptar; **bank interest rates are geared to American interest rates** = los tipos de interés bancario están ajustados a los tipos de interés americanos; **salary geared to the cost of living** = salario ajustado al coste de la vida **(b)** *(a company which is highly geared or a highly-geared company)* = compañía con una gran deuda en comparación con el capital desembolsado **(c)** *(vehicles)* **gear box** = caja de cambio

◊ **gear up** ['gɪər'ʌp] *verb* prepararse; **to gear up for a sales drive** = prepararse para dar un impulso a las ventas; **the company is gearing itself up for expansion into the African market** = la empresa se está preparando para la expansión en el mercado africano

◊ **gearing** ['gɪərɪŋ] *noun* **(a)** *(ratio)* apalancamiento *m* (razón entre la deuda de una compañía y el capital desembolsado) **(b)** *(borrowing)* financiación de actividades rentables mediante capitales tomados en préstamo

COMMENT: high gearing (when a company is said to be 'highly geared') indicates that the level of borrowings is high when compared to its ordinary share capital; a lowly-geared company has borrowings which are relatively low. High gearing has the effect of increasing a company's profitability when the company's trading is expanding; if the trading pattern slows down, then the high interest charges associated with gearing will increase the rate of slowdown

general ['dʒenərəl] *adjective* **(a)** *(ordinary)* gc.:eral; **general expenses** = gastos generales; **general manager** = director general; **general office** = oficina general **(b)** *(dealing with everything or everybody)* general; **general audit** = auditoría general; **general average** = media general *or* avería gruesa; **general election** = elecciones generales; **general meeting** = junta general; **general strike** = huelga general; **Annual General Meeting (AGM)** = junta general anual; **Extraordinary General Meeting (EGM)** = junta general extraordinaria **(c)** **the General Agreement on Tariffs and Trade** = Acuerdo General sobre Aranceles Aduaneros y Comercio; *(IMF)* **General Arrangements to Borrow (GAB)** = Acuerdo General sobre Prestamos **(d)** **general post offfice** = oficina central de correos; **general trading** = comercio general; **general store** = tienda *f*

◊ **generally** ['dʒenərəli] *adverb* generalmente *or* por lo general *or* en general; **the office is generally closed between Christmas and the New Year** = la oficina cierra en general entre Navidad y Año Nuevo; **we generally give a 25% discount for bulk purchases** = generalmente concedemos un descuento del 25% a las compras al por mayor

generous ['dʒenərəs] *adjective* generoso, -sa; **the staff contributed a generous sum for the retirement present for the manager** = el personal contribuyó con una generosa cantidad para el regalo de jubilación del director

gentleman ['dʒentlmən] *noun* **(a)** 'gentlemen' = 'señores' *or* 'caballeros'; **'good morning, gentlemen, if everyone is here, the meeting can start'** = 'buenos días señores, si están todos presentes, puede empezar la reunión'; **'well, gentlemen, we have all read the report from our Australian office'** = 'bien señores, todos hemos leído el informe de nuestra oficina australiana'; **'ladies and gentlemen'** = 'señoras y señores', 'damas y caballeros' **(b)** *(man)* caballero *m*; **gentleman's agreement** *US* **gentlemen's agreement** = acuerdo entre caballeros; **they have a gentleman's agreement not to trade in each other's area** = cada uno se ha comprometido a no comerciar en la zona del otro

genuine ['dʒenjuɪn] *adjective* verdadero, -ra *or* auténtico, -ca *or* genuino, -na; **a genuine Picasso** = un Picasso auténtico; **a genuine leather purse** = un monedero de cuero legítimo; **the genuine article** = el artículo auténtico; **genuine purchaser** = persona auténticamente interesada en comprar

◊ **genuineness** ['dʒenjuɪnnəs] *noun* autenticidad *f*

Germany ['dʒɜ:məni] *noun* Alemania *f*; **Federal Republic of Germany (FRG)** = República Federal de Alemania (RFA)

◊ **German** ['dʒɜ:mən] *adjective* & *noun* alemán, -ana NOTE: capitals: **Bonn; Berlin** (= Berlín); currency: **Deutschmark** *or* **D-mark (DM)** = marco alemán (DM)

get [get] *verb* recibir *or* obtener *or* cobrar; **we got a letter from the solicitor this morning** = esta mañana hemos recibido una carta del abogado; **when do you expect to get more stock?** = ¿cuándo espera recibir más género?; **he gets £250 a week for doing nothing** = cobra £250 a la semana por no hacer nada; **she got £5,000 for her car** = obtuvo £5.000 por su coche (NOTE: **getting - got - has got** *or US* **gotten**)

◊ **get across** ['get ə'krɒs] *verb* hacer comprender *or* ser comprendido; **the manager tried to get across to the workforce why some people were being made redundant** = el director intentó hacer comprender al personal las razones por las que se iba a despedir a algunas personas

◊ **get along** ['get ə'lɒŋ] *verb* arreglárselas; **we are getting along quite well with only half the staff** = nos las estamos arreglando bastante bien sólo con la mitad del personal

◊ **get back** ['get 'bæk] *verb* recuperar *or* recobrar; **I got my money back after I had complained to the manager** = recuperé el dinero después de quejarme al director; **he got his initial investment back in two months** = recuperó su inversión inicial en dos meses

◊ **get on** ['get 'ɒn] *verb* **(a)** *(to work)* desenvolverse; **how is the new secretary getting on?** = ¿qué tal se desenvuelve la nueva secretaria? **(b)** *(to succeed)* irle bien *or* hacer progresos; **my son is getting on well - he has just been promoted** = a mi hijo le va muy bien - acaba de ser ascendido

◊ **get on with** ['get 'ɒn wɪð] *verb* **(a)** *(to be friendly)* llevarse bien; **she does not get on with her new boss** = no se lleva bien con su nuevo jefe **(b)** *(to go on doing work)* seguir haciendo algo; **the staff got on with the work and finished the order on time** = el personal siguió trabajando y terminó el pedido a tiempo

◊ **get out** ['get 'aʊt] *verb* **(a)** *(to have something to show)* hacer *or* sacar algo; **the accounts department got out the draft accounts in time for the meeting** = el departamento de contabilidad hizo el borrador de cuentas a tiempo para la junta **(b)** *(to stop trading)* liquidar *or* vender; **he didn't like the annual report, so he got out before the company collapsed** = no le gustó el informe anual, así que liquidó su participación antes de que la empresa se viniera abajo

◊ **get out of** ['get 'aʊt əv] *verb* dejar de tratar *or* salir; **the company is getting out of computers** = la empresa va a dejar los ordenadores; **we got out of the South American market** = nos salimos del mercado sudamericano

◊ **get round** ['get 'raʊnd] *verb* soslayar *or* evitar; **we tried to get round the embargo by shipping from Canada** = intentamos soslayar el embargo enviando el cargamento desde Canadá

◊ **get through** ['get 'θruː] *verb* **(a)** *(on the phone)* comunicar; **I tried to get through to the complaints department** = intenté comunicarme con el departamento de reclamaciones **(b)** *(to be successful)* conseguir algo; **he got through his exams, so he is now a qualified engineer** = consiguió aprobar los exámenes, por lo que ya tiene el título de ingeniero **(c)** *(to make someone understand)* meter en la cabeza *or* hacer comprender; **I could not get through to her that I had to be at the airport by 2.15** = no podía hacerle comprender que tenía que estar en el aeropuerto antes de las 2.15

◊ **get to** ['get 'tʊ] *verb* llegar; **the shipment got to Canada six weeks late** = el cargamento llegó a Canadá con seis semanas de retraso; **she finally got to the office at 10.30** = llegó por fin a la oficina a las 10.30

Ghana ['gɑːnə] *noun* Ghana *m*

◊ **Ghanaian** [gɑːˈneɪən] *adjective & noun* ghanés, -esa
NOTE: capital: **Accra**; currency: **Ghanaian cedi (C)** = cedi ghanés

Gibraltar [dʒɪˈbrɔːltə] *noun* Gibraltar *m*

◊ **Gibraltarian** [dʒɪbrɔːlˈteərɪən] *adjective & noun* gibraltareño, -ña
NOTE: capital: **Gibraltar**; currency: **Gibraltar pound (£)** = libra de Gibraltar (£)

gift [gɪft] *noun* regalo *m or* obsequio *m*; **gift coupon** *or* **gift token** *or* **gift voucher** = vale *or* cupón para regalo; **we gave her a gift token for her birthday** = le ofrecimos un vale para regalo por su cumpleaños; **gift shop** = tienda de regalos *or* recuerdos; **gift inter vivos** = donación inter vivos; **free gift** = regalo *or* obsequio

◊ **gift-wrap** ['gɪftræp] *verb* envolver con papel de regalo; **do you want this book gift-wrapped?** = ¿quiere que le envuelva el libro en papel de regalo?

◊ **gift-wrapping** ['gɪftræpɪŋ] *noun* **(a)** *(service)* servicio de paquetes para regalo **(b)** *(paper)* papel de envolver regalos

gilts [gɪlts] *plural noun GB* títulos *mpl* del Estado *or* de la deuda pública *or* bonos *mpl* del Tesoro

◊ **gilt-edged** [gɪlt'edʒd] *adjective* de primera clase; **gilt-edged stock** *or* **securities** = valores *or* títulos de la máxima confianza

gimmick ['gɪmɪk] *noun* truco *m*; **a publicity gimmick** = truco publicitario; **the PR people thought up this new advertising gimmick** = el personal de relaciones públicas ideó este nuevo truco publicitario

giro ['dʒaɪrəʊ] *noun* giro *m* bancario *or* transferencia *f* bancaria **(a)** **the giro system** = sistema de giros (que permite transferir dinero de una cuenta bancaria a otra sin necesidad de emitir un cheque); **bank giro credit** = giro bancario; **to pay by bank giro transfer** = pagar por transferencia bancaria **(b)** *GB* **National Giro** = sistema de giros postales administrado por Correos; **a giro cheque** = (i) un cheque del Girobank; (ii) cheque del subsidio

de paro; **giro account** = cuenta del Girobank; **giro account number** = número de cuenta del Girobank; **she put £25 into her giro account** = ingresó £25 en su cuenta del Girobank

◊ **Girobank** ['dʒaɪrəʊbæŋk] *noun GB* banco que participa en el sistema nacional de giros; **a National Girobank account** = cuenta en un banco que forma parte del sistema nacional de giros

give [gɪv] *verb* **(a)** *(as a gift)* regalar; **the office gave him a clock when he retired** = la oficina le regaló un reloj cuando se jubiló **(b)** *(pass)* dar; **she gave the documents to the accountant** = le dio los documentos al contable; **can you give me some information about the new computer system?** = ¿me puede dar información sobre el nuevo sistema informático?; **do not give any details to the police** = no le deis ninguna información a la policía **(c)** *(organize)* dar *or* organizar; **the company gave a party on a boat to publicize its new discount system** = la empresa dio una fiesta en un barco para anunciar su nuevo sistema de descuentos **(d)** *(support)* **to give help** = prestar ayuda *or* ayudar (NOTE: **giving - gave - has given**)

◊ **give away** ['gɪv əˈweɪ] *verb* regalar; **we are giving away a pocket calculator with each £10 of purchases** = regalamos una calculadora de bolsillo por cada £10 de compra

◊ **giveaway** ['gɪvəweɪ] **1** *adjective* tirado, -da *or* de saldo; **to sell at giveaway prices** = vender a precio de saldo **2** *noun* regalo *m or* obsequio *m*

◊ **give up** ['gɪv 'ʌp] *verb* darse por vencido

global ['gləʊbəl] *adjective* **(a)** *(referring to the whole world)* global *or* mundial; **we offer a 24-hour global delivery service** = ofrecemos un servicio mundial de reparto a domicilio las 24 horas del día **(b)** *(referring to all of something)* general; **the management proposed a global review of salaries** = la dirección propuso una revisión general de los salarios

glue [gluː] **1** *noun* pegamento *m or* cola *f or* goma *f*; **she put some glue on the back of the poster to fix it to the wall** = puso un poco de pegamento en la parte posterior del cartel para pegarlo a la pared; **the glue on the envelope does not stick very well** = la goma del sobre no pega muy bien **2** *verb* pegar; **he glued the label to the box** = pegó la etiqueta a la caja

glut [glʌt] **1** *noun* exceso *m or* superabundancia *f*; **glut of produce** = una superabundancia *or* saturación *f or* exceso *m* de producto; **a coffee glut** *or* **a glut of coffee** = una superabundancia de café; **glut of money** = superabundancia de dinero **2** *verb* inundar el mercado; **the market is glutted with cheap cameras** = el mercado está inundado de máquinas fotográficas baratas (NOTE: **glutting - glutted)**

gm = GRAM gr

gnome [nəʊm] *noun (informal)* **the gnomes of Zurich** = 'los gnomos de Zurich' *or* los banqueros suizos

QUOTE if the Frankfurt gnomes put the interest rate brake on a government too carefree for too long about its debt-ridden fiscal policies, they did so out of concern for Germany's monetary stability
Times

GNP ['dʒiːen'piː] = GROSS NATIONAL PRODUCT Producto Nacional Bruto (PNB)

go [gəʊ] *verb* **(a)** *(move from one place to another)* ir *or* salir; **the cheque went to your bank yesterday** = el cheque fue enviado ayer a su banco; **the plane goes to Frankfurt, then to Rome** = el avión va a Frankfort y luego a Roma; **he is going to our Lagos office** = va a nuestra oficina de Lagos **(b)** *(to be placed)* ponerse *or* ir; **the date goes at the top of the letter** = la fecha se pone en la parte superior de la carta (NOTE: going - went - has gone)

◊ **go-ahead** ['gəʊəhed] **1** *noun* **to give something the go-ahead** = dar la autorización a algo; **his project got a government go-ahead** = su proyecto obtuvo la autorización del gobierno; **the board refused to give the go-ahead to the expansion plan** = la junta se negó a dar la autorización al plan de desarrollo **2** *adjective* emprendedor, -ra *or* activo, -va *or* dinámico, -ca; **he is a very go-ahead type** = es un tipo muy emprendedor; **she works for a go-ahead clothing company** = trabaja para una empresa de confección muy dinámica

◊ **go back on** ['gəʊ 'bæk ɒn] *verb* faltar *or* retractarse; **two months later they went back on the agreement** = dos meses después se retractaron del acuerdo

◊ **going** ['gəʊɪŋ] *adjective* **(a)** *(active)* en marcha *or* establecido, -da; **to sell a business as a going concern** = vender un negocio en marcha; **it is a going concern** = es una empresa en plena actividad **(b)** *(current)* corriente *or* actual *or* vigente; **the going price** = el precio corriente *or* de mercado; **what is the going price for 1995 Opels?** = ¿cuánto piden por un Opel de 1995 de segunda mano?; **the going rate** = tipo de cambio vigente; **we pay the going rate for typists** = pagamos a las mecanógrafas la tarifa corriente; **the going rate for offices is £30 per square metre** = el precio corriente de las oficinas es de £30 por metro cuadrado

◊ **going to** ['gəʊɪŋ 'tuː] *verb* **to be going to do something** = ir a hacer algo; **the firm is going to open an office in New York next year** = la empresa va a abrir una oficina en Nueva York el año próximo; **when are you going to answer my letter?** = ¿cuándo vas a contestar a mi carta?

◊ **go into** ['gəʊ 'ɪntʊ] *verb* **(a)** *(to start)* **to go into business** = dedicarse a los negocios *or* emprender un negocio; **he went into business as a car dealer** = se dedicó al negocio de venta de automóviles; **she went into business in partnership with her son** = emprendió un negocio en sociedad con su hijo **(b)** *(to examine)* examinar detenidamente; **the bank wants to go into the details of the inter-company loans** = el banco quiere examinar detenidamente los detalles de los préstamos entre sociedades

◊ **go on** *verb* **(a)** ['gəʊ 'ɒn] *(to continue)* continuar *or* seguir; **the staff went on working in spite of the fire** = el personal siguió trabajando a pesar del incendio; **the chairman went on speaking for two hours** = el presidente continuó hablando durante dos horas **(b)** ['gəʊ ɒn] *(to work with)* partir de *or* basarse; **the figures for 1990 are all he has to go on** = las cifras de 1990 son su única base de información; **we have to go on the assumption that sales will not double next year** = tenemos que partir del supuesto de que las ventas no se duplicarán el próximo año (NOTE: you go on **doing** something)

◊ **go out** ['gəʊ 'aʊt] *verb* **to go out of business** = dejar *or* cerrar un negocio; **the firm went out of business last week** = la empresa cerró la semana pasada

goal [gəʊl] *noun* objetivo *m or* meta *f*; **our goal is to break even within twelve months** = nuestro objetivo es cubrir gastos en nueve meses; **the company achieved all its goals** = la compañía alcanzó todos sus objetivos

godown ['gəʊdaʊn] *noun* almacén *m* (en Extremo Oriente)

gofer ['gəʊfə] *noun US* chico *m* de recados

gold [gəʊld] *noun* **(a)** *(valuable metal)* oro *m*; **to buy gold** = comprar oro; **to deal in gold** = comerciar con oro; **gold coins** = monedas de oro; **gold bullion** = oro en lingotes **(b)** **the country's gold reserves** = las reservas de oro del país; **the gold standard** = el patrón-oro; **the pound came off the gold standard** = la libra abandonó el patrón-oro **(c)** **gold point** = punto oro **(d)** **gold shares** *or* **golds** = acciones de compañías que explotan minas de oro

◊ **gold card** ['gəʊld 'kɑːd] *noun (superior type of credit card)* tarjeta oro

COMMENT: gold is the traditional hedge against investment uncertainties. People buy gold in the form of coins or bars, because they think it will maintain its value when other investments such as government bonds, foreign currency, property, etc. may not be so safe. Gold is relatively portable, and small quantities can be taken from country to country if an emergency occurs. This view, which is prevalent when the political situation is uncertain, has not been borne out in recent years, and gold has not maintained its value for some time

golden ['gəʊldən] *adjective* de oro *or* de un gran valor; **golden hallo** = prima *f* de enganche (prima para atraerse a un directivo); **golden handcuff** = prima *f* de permanencia (para inducir a un directivo a permanecer en su cargo); **golden handshake** = indemnización a un directivo al cesar en su cargo; **when the company was taken over, the sales director received a golden handshake of £25,000** = cuando la compañía fue adquirida, despidieron al director de ventas con una indemnización de £25.000; **a golden opportunity** = una oportunidad de oro; **golden parachute** = contrato especial a nivel directivo que ofrece una prima en caso de dimisión involuntaria; *(share in a privatized company which is retained by the government)* **golden share** = acción en una sociedad privada retenida por el Estado

goldmine ['gəʊldmaɪn] *noun* mina *f* de oro; **that shop is a little goldmine** = esa tienda es una verdadera mina de oro

gondola ['gɒndələ] *noun* góndola *f* (estantería de supermercado)

good [gʊd] *adjective* **(a)** *(not bad)* bueno, -na; **a good buy** = una buena compra; **to buy something in good faith** = comprar algo de buena fe **(b)** *(many)* **a good deal of** = mucho, -cha; **we wasted a good deal of time discussing the arrangements for the AGM** = perdimos mucho tiempo discutiendo los preparativos para la junta general anual; **the company had to pay a good deal for the building site** = la compañía tuvo que pagar una fuerte suma por el solar del edificio; **a good many** = un buen número *or* muchos, -chas; **a good many staff members have joined the union** = muchos empleados se han afiliado al sindicato

◊ **goods** [gʊdz] *plural noun* **(a)** *(personal possessions)* **goods and chattels** = muebles *mpl* y enseres *mpl* **(b)** *(merchandise)* mercancías *fpl*; **goods in bond** = mercancías en depósito aduanero; **goods in transit** = mercadería en viaje; **goods for sale** *or* **resale** = mercadería en venta *or* de reventa; **capital goods** = bienes de capital; **consumer goods** *or* **consumable goods** = bienes de consumo; *US* **dry goods** = artículos de mercería; **finished goods** = productos acabados *or* terminados; **household goods** = enseres domésticos; **luxury goods** = artículos de lujo; **manufactured goods** = productos manufacturados **(c) goods depot** = depósito *or* almacén de mercancías; **goods train** = tren de mercancías

> QUOTE profit margins in the industries most exposed to foreign competition - machinery, transportation equipment and electrical goods
> **Sunday Times**

> QUOTE the minister wants people buying goods ranging from washing machines to houses to demand facts on energy costs
> **Times**

goodwill ['gʊd'wɪl] *noun (good reputation of a business)* fondo *m* de comercio; clientela *f or* cartera *f* de clientes; **he paid £10,000 for the goodwill of the shop and £4,000 for the stock** = pagó £10.000 por la cartera de clientes de la tienda y £4.000 por las existencias

> COMMENT: goodwill can include the trading reputation, the patents, the trade names used, the value of a 'good site', etc., and is very difficult to establish accurately. It is an intangible asset, and so is not shown as an asset in a company's accounts, unless it figures as part of the purchase price paid when acquiring another company

go-slow ['gəʊ 'sləʊ] *noun* huelga *f* de celo; **a series of go-slows reduced production** = una serie de huelgas de celo redujeron la producción

govern ['gʌvən] *verb* gobernar; **the country is governed by a group of military leaders** = el país está gobernado por un grupo de dirigentes militares

◊ **government** ['gʌvnmənt] *noun* **(a)** *(central administration)* gobierno *m or* administración *f* del Estado; **central government** = el Estado *or* la Administración; **local government** = Administración local; **provincial government** *or* **state government** = gobierno de una provincia *or* de un estado **(b)** *(referring to or coming from)* estatal *or* del gobierno; **government annuity** = subsidio estatal; **government bonds** *or* **government securities** *or* **gilt-edged securities** = títulos *or* valores del Estado *or* efectos públicos; **government contractor** = contratista del Estado; **government employees** = funcionarios del Estado; **local government staff** = plantilla de la administración local; **government intervention** *or* **intervention by the government** = intervención estatal *or* del gobierno; **a government ban on the import of arms** = una prohibición del gobierno sobre la importación de armas; **a government investigation into organized crime** = una investigación oficial

sobre el crimen organizado; **government officials prevented him leaving the country** = (unos) funcionarios le impidieron que abandonara el país; **government policy is outlined in the booklet** = la política del gobierno está resumida en el folleto; **government regulations state that import duty has to be paid on luxury items** = las disposiciones oficiales establecen que deben pagarse derechos de aduana por los artículos de lujo; **he invested all his savings in government securities** = invirtió todos sus ahorros en títulos del Estado; **government support** = ayuda *or* apoyo del Estado; **the computer industry relies on government support** = la industria de ordenadores depende de la ayuda del Estado

◊ **governmental** [gʌvən'mentl] *adjective* gubernamental *or* gubernativo, -va

◊ **government-backed** ['gʌvnmənt 'bækt] *adjective* con apoyo estatal *or* del gobierno

◊ **government-controlled** ['gʌvnmənt kən'trəʊld] *adjective* controlado, -da por el Estado; **advertisements cannot be placed in the government-controlled newspapers** = no se pueden publicar anuncios en los periódicos gubernamentales

◊ **government-regulated** ['gʌvnmənt 'regjʊleɪtɪd] *adjective* regulado, -da por el Estado

◊ **government-sponsored** ['gʌvnmənt 'spɒnsəd] *adjective* patrocinado, -da por el Estado; **he is working in a government-sponsored scheme to help small businesses** = está trabajando en un proyecto subvencionado por el Estado para ayudar a la pequeña empresa

governor ['gʌvnə] *noun* **(a)** *(person in charge of an important institution)* gobernador, -ra *or* director, -ra; **the Governor of the Bank of England** = el director del Banco de Inglaterra (NOTE: the US equivalent is the Chairman of the Federal Reserve Board) **(b)** *US (member of the Federal Reserve Board)* miembro de la junta de gobernadores de la Reserva Federal

GPO = GENERAL POST OFFICE Oficina Central de Correos

grace [greɪs] *noun* gracia *f or* prórroga *f*; **to give a creditor a period of grace** *or* **two weeks' grace** = conceder a un acreedor un periodo de gracia *or* dos semanas de prórroga

grade [greɪd] **1** *noun* grado *m*; **top grade of civil servant** = funcionario de grado máximo; **to reach the top grade in the civil service** = alcanzar el grado máximo en la administración pública; **high-grade** = de grado superior *or* alto grado *or* nivel; **high-grade petrol** = gasolina de alto octanaje *or* 'super'; **a high-grade trade delegation** = una delegación comercial de alto nivel; **low-grade** = de baja calidad *or* categoría inferior *or* ordinario; **a low-grade official from the Ministry of Commerce** = funcionario de categoría inferior del Ministerio de Comercio; **the car runs well on low-grade petrol** = el coche funciona bien con gasolina 'normal'; **top-grade** = excelente *or* superior; **top-grade petrol** = gasolina 'super' **2** *verb* **(a)** *(quality)* clasificar *or* calibrar; **to grade coal** = calibrar el carbón **(b)**

(quantity) graduar; **graded advertising rates** = tarifas publicitarias regresivas; **graded tax** = impuesto progresivo **(c) graded hotel** = hotel homologado

gradual ['grædʒʊəl] *adjective* gradual *or* progresivo, -va; **1996 saw a gradual return to profits** = en 1996 tuvo lugar un restablecimiento gradual de la rentabilidad; **his CV describes his gradual rise to the position of company chairman** = su currículum vitae muestra su ascensión gradual al puesto de presidente de la compañía

◊ **gradually** ['grædʒʊəli] *adverb* gradualmente *or* paulatinamente; **the company has gradually become more profitable** = la compañía se ha hecho paulatinamente más rentable; **she gradually learnt the details of the import-export business** = aprendió gradualmente los detalles del comercio de importación-exportación

graduate ['grædʒʊət] *noun* graduado, -da *or* licenciado, -da *or* diplomado, -da *or* titulado, -da; **graduate entry** = ingreso de diplomados; **the graduate entry into the civil service** = el ingreso de diplomados en la administración pública; **graduate training scheme** = programa de formación para graduados; **graduate trainee** = licenciado en prácticas

◊ **graduated** ['grædʒʊeɪtɪd] *adjective* graduado, -da *or* proporcional *or* progresivo, -va *or* escalonado, -da; **graduated income tax** = impuesto proporcional *or* progresivo sobre la renta; **graduated pension scheme** = programa de pensiones proporcionales; **graduated taxation** = imposición proporcional *or* progresiva; **graduated tax system** = baremo equitativo de contribuciones

gram *or* **gramme** [græm] *noun* gramo m (NOTE: usually written **g** or **gm** with figures: **25g**)

grand [grænd] **1** *adjective* gran *or* importante *or* general; **grand plan** = proyecto importante *or* plan magnífico *or* gran plan; **he explained his grand plan for redeveloping the factory site** = explicó su magnífico plan para la reorganización del solar de la fábrica; **grand total** = total general **2** *noun* *(informal)* mil libras *or* mil dólares; **they offered him fifty grand for the information** = le ofrecieron cincuenta mil libras *or* dólares por la información

grant [grɑːnt] **1** *noun* subsidio m *or* subvención f; **the laboratory has a government grant to cover the cost of the development programme** = el laboratorio tiene una subvención estatal para cubrir el coste del programa de desarrollo; **the government has allocated grants towards the costs of the scheme** = el Estado ha asignado subvenciones para sufragar los costes del proyecto; **grant-aided scheme** = proyecto subvencionado **2** *verb* conceder *or* otorgar; **to grant someone a loan** *or* **a subsidy** = conceder un préstamo a alguien *or* un subsidio; **the local authority granted the company an interest-free loan to start up the new factory** = las autoridades locales concedieron un préstamo libre de interés a la compañía para que pusiera en marcha la nueva fábrica

QUOTE the budget grants a tax exemption for $500,000 in capital gains
Toronto Star

graph [grɑːf] *noun* gráfico m; **to set out the results**

in a graph = exponer los resultados en un gráfico; **to draw a graph showing the rising profitability** = trazar un gráfico que muestre la creciente rentabilidad; **the sales graph shows a steady rise** = el gráfico de las ventas muestra un aumento constante; **graph paper** = papel cuadriculado

gratia ['greɪʃə] *see* EX GRATIA

gratis ['grætɪs] *adverb* gratis *or* sin pagar; **we got into the exhibition gratis** = entramos en la exposición gratis

gratuity [grə'tjuːɪti] *noun* propina f *or* gratificación f; **the staff are instructed not to accept gratuities** = el personal ha recibido instrucciones de no aceptar propinas

great [greɪt] *adjective* grande; **a great deal of** = mucho, -cha *or* una gran cantidad; **he made a great deal of money on the Stock Exchange** = ganó *or* hizo mucho dinero en la bolsa; **there is a great deal of work to be done before the company can be made really profitable** = habrá que trabajar mucho para que la compañía sea verdaderamente rentable

Great Britain ['greɪt 'brɪtən] *noun* Gran Bretaña f

◊ **British** ['brɪtɪʃ] *adjective & noun* británico, -ca
NOTE: capital: **London** (= Londres); currency: **pound sterling (£)** = libra esterlina (£)

Greece [griːs] *noun* Grecia f

◊ **Greek** [griːk] *adjective & noun* griego, -ga
NOTE: capital: **Athens** (= Atenas); currency: **drachma (Dr)** = dracma (Dr)

greenback ['griːnbæk] *noun* US *(informal)* billete m de banco *or* el dólar americano

QUOTE just about a year ago, when the greenback was high, bears were an endangered species. Since then, the currency has fallen by 32% against the Deutschmark and by 30% against the Swiss franc
Financial Weekly

◊ **green card** ['griːn 'kɑːd] *noun* **(a)** *UK (insurance certificate)* carta f verde **(b)** *US (residence permit)* permiso m de residencia (en EE UU)

◊ **green currency** ['griːn 'kʌrənsi] *noun* divisa f *or* moneda f verde; **green Deutschmark** = marco verde; **green ECU** = ecu verde

◊ **greenfield site** ['griːnfiːld 'saɪt] *noun* terreno para edificar

◊ **green light** ['griːn 'laɪt] *noun* luz f verde *or* autorización f; **to give a project the green light** = autorizar un proyecto *or* dar luz verde a un proyecto; **the board refused to give the green light to the expansion plan** = la junta se negó a dar la autorización al plan de desarrollo

◊ **greenmail** ['griːnmeɪl] *noun* negocio m *or* chantaje m consistente en adquirir un gran número de acciones de una sociedad y vendérselas a ésta a un precio elevado por retirar la amenaza de adquisición

QUOTE proposes that there should be a limit on greenmail, perhaps permitting payment of a 20% premium on a maximum of 8% of the stock
Duns Business Month

◇ **Green Paper** ['gri:n 'peɪpə] *noun* libro *m* verde (documento oficial del gobierno británico sobre un proyecto de ley)

◇ **green pound** ['gri:n 'paʊnd] *noun* libra *f* verde (valor de la libra esterlina utilizado para calcular los precios agrícolas y subsidios en la CE)

grey market ['greɪ 'mɑːkɪt] *noun* mercado *m* gris

grid [grɪd] *noun* cuadrícula *f*; **grid structure** = estructura cuadricular

grievance ['gri:vəns] *noun* queja *f*; **grievance procedure** = procedimiento de tramitación de quejas

> QUOTE ACAS has a legal obligation to try and resolve industrial grievances before they reach industrial tribunals
> **Personnel Today**

gross [grəʊs] **1** *noun* gruesa *f*; **he ordered four gross of pens** = encargó cuatro gruesas de plumas estilográficas (NOTE: no plural in this meaning) **2** *adjective* **(a)** *(total)* bruto, -ta; **gross earnings** = ingresos brutos; **gross income** *or* **gross salary** = renta bruta *or* sueldo bruto; **gross margin** = beneficio *or* margen bruto; **gross profit** = beneficio bruto; **gross receipts** = ingresos brutos; **gross turnover** = facturación bruta; **gross yield** = rendimiento bruto **(b) gross domestic product (GDP)** = Producto Interior Bruto (PIB); **gross national product (GNP)** = Producto Nacional Bruto (PNB) **(c) gross tonnage** = tonelaje bruto; **gross weight** = peso bruto **(d)** *(marketing)* **gross rating point (GRP)** = grado *m* de contacto (GRC) **3** *adverb* en total *or* en conjunto; **his salary is paid gross** = le pagan el sueldo bruto **4** *verb* obtener unos beneficios brutos; **the group grossed £25m in 1992** = el grupo obtuvo unos beneficios brutos de £25m en 1992

> QUOTE news that gross national product increased only 1.3% in the first quarter of the year sent the dollar down on foreign exchange markets
> **Fortune**

> QUOTE gross wool receipts for the selling season to end June appear likely to top $2 billion
> **Australian Financial Review**

ground [graʊnd] *noun* **(a)** *(soil)* suelo *m* *or* tierra *f*; **the factory was burnt to the ground** = la fábrica se quemó completamente; **ground hostess** = azafata de tierra; **ground landlord** = propietario absoluto; **ground lease** = enfiteusis *f*; **ground rent** = renta que paga el enfiteuta al propietario absoluto **(b)** *(basic reasons)* **grounds** = fundamento *m* *or* motivo *m* *or* base *f* *or* razón *f*; **does he have good grounds for complaint?** = ¿tiene motivos fundados para quejarse?; **there are no grounds on which we can be sued** = no existe ningún fundamento por el cual podamos ser demandados; **what are the grounds for the demand for a pay rise?** = ¿en qué se basa la reclamación de un aumento de sueldo?

◇ **ground floor** ['graʊnd(d) 'flɔ:] *noun* planta *f* baja; **the men's department is on the ground floor** = la sección de caballeros está en la planta baja; **he has a ground-floor office** = tiene una oficina en la planta baja (NOTE: in the USA this is the **first floor**)

group [gru:p] **1** *noun* **(a)** *(of people)* grupo *m* *or* agrupación *f*; **a group of the staff has sent a memo to the chairman complaining about noise in the**

office = un grupo de empleados ha enviado una nota al presidente quejándose del ruido de la oficina **(b)** *(of businesses)* grupo; **the Banesto group** = el grupo Banesto; **group accounts** = cuentas *or* contabilidad del grupo; **the group chairman** *or* **the chairman of the group** = el presidente del grupo; **group results** = los resultados del grupo; **group turnover** *or* **turnover for the group** = el volumen de negocios del grupo **2** *verb* **to group together** = agrupar *or* agruparse; **sales from six different agencies are grouped together under the heading 'European sales'** = las ventas de seis agencias diferentes se han agrupado bajo el título de 'ventas europeas'

◇ **Group of Five (G5)** ['gru:p əv 'faɪv] Grupo de los Cinco; *(Francia, Alemania, Japón, Reino Unido y EE.UU)*

◇ **Group of Seven (G7)** ['gru:p əv 'sevn] Grupo de los Siete; *(Francia, Alemania, Japón, Reino Unido, EE.UU, Italia y Canadá)*

◇ **Group of Ten (G10)** ['gru:p əv 'ten] Grupo de los Diez; *(Bélgica, Canadá, Francia, Alemania, Italia, Japón, Países Bajos, Suecia, Suiza, Reino Unido y EE.UU.)* (NOTE: also called the **'Paris Club'** because its first meeting was in Paris)

grow [grəʊ] *verb* crecer *or* desarrollarse *or* acrecentarse; **the company has grown from a small repair shop to a multinational electronics business** = la empresa que empezó como un pequeño taller de reparaciones ha pasado a ser una gran empresa multinacional de electrónica; **turnover is growing at a rate of 15% per annum** = el volumen de ventas está creciendo a un ritmo del 15% anual; **the computer industry grew fast in the 1980s** = la industria de ordenadores se desarrolló rápidamente en la década de los 80 (NOTE: **growing - grew - has grown**)

◇ **growth** [grəʊθ] *noun* crecimiento *m* *or* desarrollo *m*; **the company is aiming for growth** = la compañía aspira a crecer; **economic growth** = crecimiento económico; **a growth area** *or* **a growth market** = un área de crecimiento *or* un mercado en expansión; **a growth industry** = una industria en expansión; **growth potential** = capacidad de desarrollo; **growth rate** = tasa de crecimiento; **growth share** *or* **growth stock** = acciones con perspectivas de mejorar el precio

> QUOTE a general price freeze succeeded in slowing the growth in consumer prices
> **Financial Times**

> QUOTE the thrift had grown from $4.7 million in assets in 1980 to $1.5 billion
> **Barrons**

> QUOTE growth in demand is still coming from the private rather than the public sector
> **Lloyd's List**

> QUOTE population growth in the south-west is again reflected by the level of rental values
> **Lloyd's List**

guarantee [gærən'ti:] **1** *noun* **(a)** *(legal document)* garantía *f*; **certificate of guarantee** *or* **guarantee certificate** = certificado de garantía; **the guarantee lasts for two years** = la garantía dura dos años; **it is sold with a twelve-month guarantee** = se vende con una garantía de doce meses; **the car is still under guarantee** = el coche tiene todavía garantía; **extended guarantee** = extensión de garantía *or* garantía adicional (NOTE: also called a **warranty) (b)** *(promise to pay)* aval *m or* afianzamiento *m*; **to go guarantee for someone** = avalar a alguien **(c)** *(thing given as security)* fianza *f*; **to leave share certificates as a guarantee** = dejar certificados de acciones como garantía **2** *verb* **(a)** *(to back up)* avalar *or* ser fiador de *or* garantizar; **to guarantee a debt** = avalar una deuda; **to guarantee an associate company** = avalar a una empresa asociada; **to guarantee a bill of exchange** = avalar una letra de cambio; **guaranteed wage** = salario garantizado; **guaranteed minimum wage** = salario mínimo garantizado **(b)** *(to warrant)* **the product is guaranteed for twelve months** = el producto tiene una garantía de doce meses

◊ **guarantor** [gærən'tɔː] *noun* fiador *m or* garante *mf*; **he stood guarantor for his brother** = se presentó como fiador de su hermano

Guatemala [gwætə'mɑːlə] *noun* Guatemala *f*

◊ **Guatemalan** [gwætə'mɑːlən] *adjective & noun* guatemalteco, -ca
NOTE: capital: **Guatemala City** (= Ciudad de Guatemala); currency: **Guatemalan quetzal (Q)** = quetzal guatemalteco (Q)

guess [ges] **1** *noun* estimación *f or* conjetura *f*; **the forecast of sales is only a guess** = la previsión de ventas es sólo una estimación; **he made a guess at the pretax profits** = hizo una estimación de los beneficios brutos; **it is anyone's guess** = nadie lo sabe **2** *verb* **to guess (at) something** = adivinar *or* conjeturar *or* tantear; **they could only guess at the total loss** = sólo podían hacer conjeturas sobre la pérdida total; **the sales director tried to guess the turnover of the Far East division** = el director de ventas trató de estimar el volumen de ventas de la sección de Extremo Oriente

◊ **guesstimate** ['gestɪmət] *noun* *(informal)* cálculo aventurado

◊ **guesswork** ['geswɜːk] *noun* tanteo *m*

guide [gaɪd] *verb* guiar *or* orientar; **I was guided by him** = me orientó en el asunto

◊ **guideline** ['gaɪdlaɪn] *noun* directriz *f*; **the government has issued guidelines on increases in incomes and prices** = el gobierno ha dado directrices sobre el aumento de rentas y precios; **the increase in retail price breaks** *or* **goes against the government guidelines** = el aumento de los precios al consumidor contraviene *or* va en contra de las directrices del gobierno

guild [gɪld] *noun* gremio *m or* corporación *f*; **trade guild** = gremio *or* corporación; **the guild of master bakers** = el gremio de panaderos

guilder ['gɪldə] *noun* *(currency used in the Netherlands)* florín (f) *m* (NOTE: even though called the **guilder** in English, it is usually written **fl** before or after a figure: **fl25 or 25fl**)

> QUOTE the shares, which eased 1.10 guilders to fl49. 80 earlier in the session, were suspended during the final hour of trading
> **Wall Street Journal**

guillotine ['gɪlətiːn] *noun* guillotina *f*

guilty ['gɪlti] *adjective* culpable; **he was found guilty of libel** = se le declaró culpable de difamación; **the company was guilty of not reporting the sales to the auditors** = la compañía fue culpable de no informar a los auditores sobre las ventas

Guinea ['gɪni] *noun* Guinea *f*

◊ **Guinean** ['gɪniən] *adjective & noun* guineo, -nea *or* guienés, -esa
NOTE: capital: **Conakry;** currency: **Guinean franc (GF)** = franco guineo (FG)

gum [gʌm] *noun* goma (de pegar) *f or* pegamento *m or* cola *f*; **he stuck the label to the box with gum** = pegó la etiqueta a la caja con cola

◊ **gummed** [gʌmd] *adjective* engomado, -da *or* encolado, -da; **gummed label** = etiqueta engomada

Guyana [gaɪ'ænə *or* gaɪ'ɑːnə] *noun* Guayana *f*

◊ **Guyanese** [gaɪə'niːz] *adjective & noun* guayanés, -esa
NOTE: capital: **Cayenne;** currency: **Guyana dollar (G$)** = dólar de Guayana ($G)

Hh

ha = HECTARE hectárea (Ha)

haggle ['hægl] *verb* regatear *or* discutir; **to haggle about** *or* **over the details of a contract** = discutir los detalles de un contrato; **after two days' haggling the contract was signed** = después de dos días de regateo se firmó el contrato

Haiti ['haɪti] *noun* Haití *m*

◊ **Haitian** [hæ'i:ʃən] *adjective & noun* haitiano, -na
NOTE: capital: **Port-au-Prince**; currency: **Haitian gourde (G)** = gourde haitiano (G)

half [hɑ:f] **1** *noun* mitad *f or* parte *f*; **the first half of the agreement is acceptable** = la primera parte del contrato es aceptable; **the first half** *or* **the second half of the year** = el primer semestre *or* el segundo semestre del año; **we share the profits half and half** = nos repartimos los beneficios mitad y mitad *or* por partes iguales (NOTE: plural is **halves**) **2** *adjective* medio, -dia; **half a per cent** *or* **a half per cent** = el medio por ciento; **his commission on the deal is twelve and a half per cent** = su comisión en el negocio es del doce y medio por ciento; **half a dozen** *or* **a half-dozen** = media docena; **to sell goods off at half price** = vender mercancías a mitad de precio; **a half-price sale** = rebajas a mitad de precio *or* al 50%

◊ **half-dollar** ['hɑ:f 'dɒlə] *noun US* medio dólar *m*

◊ **half-year** ['hɑ:f'jɪə] *noun* semestre *m*; **first half-year** *or* **second half-year** = primer semestre *or* segundo semestre; **to announce the results for the half-year to June 30th** *or* **the first half-year's results** = comunicar los resultados del primer semestre; **we look forward to improvements in the second half-year** = esperamos mejoras en el segundo semestre

◊ **half-yearly** ['hɑ:f'jɪəli] **1** *adjective* semestral; **half-yearly accounts** = cuentas semestrales; **half-yearly payment** = pagos semestrales; **half-yearly statement** = estado de cuentas semestral; **a half-yearly meeting** = una reunión semestral **2** *adverb* semestralmente *or* cada seis meses; **we pay the account half-yearly** = pagamos la cuenta cada seis meses

hall [hɔ:l] *noun* **exhibition hall** = salón *m or* sala *f* de exposiciones; **town hall** *or* **city hall** = ayuntamiento *m*

hallmark ['hɔ:lmɑ:k] **1** *noun* marca *f* de contraste (en joyería) *or* sello *m* **2** *verb* poner el sello de contraste; **a hallmarked spoon** = una cucharilla con el sello de contraste

hammer ['hæmə] **1** *noun* martillo *m*; **auctioneer's hammer** = martillo del subastador; **to go under the hammer** = venderse en pública subasta; **all the stock went under the hammer** = se vendieron todas las existencias en subasta pública **2** *verb* martillar *or* martillear; **to hammer the competition** = hundir a la competencia; **to hammer prices** = hacer bajar los precios

◊ **hammered** ['hæməd] *adjective (on the London Stock Exchange) he was hammered* = fue declarado insolvente y expulsado de la bolsa

◊ **hammering** ['hæmərɪŋ] *noun* **(a)** *(beating)* paliza *f or* derrota *f*; **the company took a hammering in Europe** = la compañía tuvo grandes pérdidas en Europa; **we gave them a hammering** = les dimos una paliza **(b)** *(on the London Stock Exchange)* expulsión *f* de un agente de bolsa

◊ **hammer out** ['hæmə 'aʊt] *verb* **to hammer out an agreement** = llegar a un acuerdo; **the contract was finally hammered out** = se llegó por fin a un acuerdo sobre el contrato

hand [hænd] *noun* **(a)** *(part of the body)* mano *f*; **to shake hands with someone** = dar la mano *or* estrechar la mano; **the two negotiating teams shook hands and sat down at the conference table** = las dos parte negociadoras se dieron la mano y a continuación se sentaron a la mesa de conferencias; **to shake hands on a deal** = cerrar un trato con un apretón de manos **(b) by hand** = a mano; **these shoes are made by hand** = estos zapatos están hechos a mano; **to send a letter by hand** = entregar una carta en mano **(c) in hand** = en reserva; **balance in hand** *or* **cash in hand** = saldo líquido *or* efectivo en caja; **we have £10,000 in hand** = tenemos £10.000 en reserva; **work in hand** = trabajo entre manos (NOTE: US English is **work on hand**) **(d) goods left on hand** = mercancías no vendidas; **they were left with half the stock on their hands** = se quedaron con la mitad de las mercancías sin vender **(e) to hand** = a mano *or* aquí; **I have the invoice to hand** = tengo la factura a mano **(f) show of hands** = votación a mano alzada; **the motion was carried on a show of hands** = la moción se llevó a cabo en una votación a mano alzada **(g) to change hands** = cambiar de dueño; **the shop changed hands for £100,000** = la tienda cambió de dueño por £100.000; **first hand** *or* **second hand** = primera mano *or* segunda mano **(h) note of hand** = letra al propio cargo *or* pagaré; **in witness whereof, I set my hand** = en fe de lo cual, firmo la presente **(i)** *(worker)* trabajador, -ra *or* operario, -ria; **to take on ten more hands** = contratar a diez operarios más; **deck hand** = marinero *m* de cubierta; **factory hand** = obrero, -ra de fábrica

◊ **handbill** ['hænbɪl] *noun* prospecto *m or* hoja *f* publicitaria

◊ **handbook** ['hænbʊk] *noun* guía *f or* manual *m*; **the handbook does not say how you open the photocopier** = el manual no indica cómo se abre la fotocopiadora; **look in the handbook to see if it** tells you how to clean the typewriter = consulte el manual para ver si indica cómo hay que limpiar la máquina de escribir; **service handbook** = manual de mantenimiento

◊ **hand in** ['hænd 'ɪn] *verb* presentar *or* entregar; **he handed in his notice** *or* **he handed in his resignation** = presentó su dimisión

◊ **hand luggage** ['hæn(d) 'lʌgɪdʒ] *noun* equipaje *m* de mano

◊ **handmade** ['hænmeɪd] *adjective* hecho, -cha a mano; **he writes all his letters on handmade paper** = escribe todas sus cartas en papel hecho a mano

◊ **hand-operated** ['hænd'ɒpəreɪtɪd] *adjective* accionado, -da a mano *or* manual; **a hand-operated machine** = una máquina accionada a mano

◊ **handout** ['hændaʊt] *noun* **(a)** *(information sheet)* publicity handout = folleto *m* publicitario **(b)** *(free gift)* donación *f or* subvención *f*; **the company exists on handouts from the government** = la compañía existe gracias a las subvenciones del Estado

◊ **hand over** ['hænd 'əʊvə] *verb* entregar *or* ceder *or* transmitir; **she handed over the documents to the lawyer** = entregó los documentos al abogado; **he handed over to his deputy** = cedió el puesto a su adjunto

◊ **handover** ['hændəʊvə] *noun* transmisión *f or* paso *m or* transición *f*; **the handover from the old chairman to the new went very smoothly** = la transmisión de poderes del antiguo presidente al nuevo se efectuó sin contratiempos; **when the ownership of a company changes, the handover period is always difficult** = cuando una empresa cambia de propietario, el periodo de transición es siempre difícil

◊ **handshake** ['hænʃeɪk] *noun* **golden handshake** = indemnización concedida a un ejecutivo que cesa en su cargo; **the retiring director received a golden handshake of £25,000** = el director al jubilarse recibió una indemnización de £25.000

◊ **handwriting** ['hændraɪtɪŋ] *noun* letra *f or* escritura *f*; **send a letter of application in your own handwriting** = envía una carta de solicitud escrita a mano

◊ **handwritten** ['hændrɪtn] *adjective* escrito, -ta a mano *or* manuscrito, -ta; **it is more professional to send in a typed letter rather than a handwritten letter of application** = resulta más profesional enviar una carta de solicitud escrita a máquina que a mano

handle ['hændl] *verb* **(a)** *(to deal or organize)* tratar *or* ocuparse *or* encargarse de *or* despachar; **the accounts department handles all the cash** = el departamento de contabilidad se ocupa de la caja; **we can handle orders for up to 15,000 units** = podemos despachar pedidos de hasta 15.000 unidades; **they handle all our overseas orders** = se ocupan de todos nuestros pedidos de ultramar **(b)** *(to sell or trade)* comerciar *or* vender; **we do not handle foreign cars** = no comerciamos en coches extranjeros; **they will not handle goods produced by other firms** = no venderán mercancías producidas por otras empresas

◊ **handling** ['hændlɪŋ] *noun* manejo *m or*

manipulación *f*; **handling charges** = costes de manipulación *or* gastos de tramitación; **the bank adds on a 5% handling charge for changing travellers' cheques** = el banco añade 5% en gastos de tramitación por cambiar cheques de viaje; **materials handling** = manejo de materiales

> QUOTE shipping companies continue to bear the extra financial burden of cargo handling operations at the ports
> **Business Times (Lagos)**

handy ['hændi] *adjective* útil *or* práctico, -ca *or* manejable *or* cómodo, -da; **they are sold in handy-sized packs** = se venden en paquetes de tamaño muy cómodo; **this small case is handy for use when travelling** = esta pequeña maleta es muy práctica para viajar

hang [hæŋ] *verb* colgar; **hang your coat on the hook behind the door** = cuelga tu abrigo en el perchero detrás de la puerta; **he hung his umbrella over the back of his chair** = colgó el paraguas en el respaldo de la silla (NOTE: **hanging - hung**)

◊ **hang on** ['hæŋ 'ɒn] *verb (while phoning)* esperar; **please hang on** = no cuelgue; **if you hang on a moment, the chairman will be off the other line soon** = si espera un momento, el presidente pronto terminará por la otra línea

◊ **hang up** ['hæŋ 'ʌp] *verb (phone)* colgar; **when I asked him about the invoice, he hung up** = cuando le pregunté por la factura, colgó

happen ['hæpən] *verb* **(a)** dar la casualidad; **the contract happened to arrive when the managing director was away on holiday** = dio la casualidad de que el contrato llegó cuando el director gerente estaba de vacaciones; **he happened to be in the shop when the customer placed the order** = se dio la casualidad que estaba en la tienda cuando el cliente hizo el pedido **(b)** *(occur)* pasar *or* suceder; **what has happened to?** = ¿qué ha pasado con eso?; **what has happened to that order for Japan?** = ¿qué ha pasado con el pedido del Japón?

happy ['hæpi] *adjective* feliz *or* contento, -ta; **we will be happy to supply you at 25% discount** = tendremos mucho gusto en ofrecerles un descuento del 25%; **the MD was not at all happy when the sales figures came in** = el director gerente no se mostró nada satisfecho cuando llegaron las cifras de ventas

harbour *or US* **harbor** ['hɑːbə] *noun* puerto *m*; **harbour dues** = derechos portuarios *or* de dársena; **harbour installations** *or* **harbour facilities** = instalaciones portuarias

hard [hɑːd] **1** *adjective* **(a)** *(strong)* duro, -ra *or* fuerte; **to take a hard line in trade union negotiations** = adoptar una línea dura *or* postura intransigente en las negociaciones sindicales **(b)** *(difficult)* difícil; **these typewriters are hard to sell** = estas máquinas de escribir son difíciles de vender; **it is hard to get good people to work on low salaries** = es difícil conseguir gente buena a sueldo bajo **(c)** *(solid)* duro, -ra *or* sólido, -da; **hard cash** = dinero en metálico *or* efectivo *or* contante y sonante; **he paid out £100 in hard cash for the chair** = pagó £100 en metálico por la silla; **hard copy** = copia impresa; **he made the presentation with diagrams and ten pages of hard copy** = para la pesentación utilizó gráficos y diez páginas de texto impreso; **hard disk** = disco duro **(d) hard bargain** = negocio duro *or* difícil; **to drive a hard bargain** *or* **to strike a hard bargain** = ser un negociador duro *or* imponer duras condiciones; **after weeks of hard bargaining** = tras semanas de duras negociaciones **(e) hard currency** = divisas fuertes *or* moneda convertible; **exports which can earn hard currency for the Soviet Union** = exportaciones que la Unión Soviética puede cobrar en moneda convertible; **these goods must be paid for in hard currency** = estas mercancías deben pagarse en moneda convertible; **a hard currency deal** = una transacción en moneda convertible **2** *adverb* con mucho esfuerzo; **the sales team sold the new product range hard into the supermarkets** = nuestros representantes se esforzaron para vender la nueva gama de productos en los supermercados; **if all the workforce works hard, the order should be completed on time** = si todos los empleados hacen un esfuerzo el pedido puede estar listo a tiempo

◊ **harden** ['hɑːdn] *verb* **prices are hardening** = los precios están subiendo

◊ **hardening** ['hɑːdnɪŋ] *noun* **a hardening of prices** = el afianzamiento de los precios

◊ **hardness** ['hɑːdnəs] *noun* **hardness of the market** = firmeza *f* del mercado

◊ **hard sell** ['hɑːd 'sel] *noun* venta agresiva; **to give a product the hard sell** tratar de vender un producto con mucha insistencia; **he tried to give me the hard sell** = intentó venderme el producto por todos los medios

◊ **hard selling** ['hɑːd 'selɪŋ] *noun* venta agresiva; **a lot of hard selling went into that deal** = en ese negocio hubo que proceder con mucha insistencia

◊ **hardship** ['hɑːdʃɪp] *noun* apuro *m* económico

◊ **hardware** ['hɑːdweə] *noun* **(a) computer hardware** = 'hardware' *m or* equipo *m* soporte físico del ordenador; **hardware maintenance contract** = contrato de mantenimiento del material informático **(b) military hardware** = material *m* militar *or* de guerra **(c)** *(for the house)* quincalla *f or* ferretería *f*; **a hardware shop** = ferretería *f*

◊ **hard-working** [hɑːd'wɜːkɪŋ] *adjective* muy trabajador, -ra

> QUOTE hard disks help computers function more speedily and allow them to store more information
> **Australian Financial Review**

> QUOTE few of the paper millionaires sold out and transformed themselves into hard cash millionaires
> **Investors Chronicle**

harm [hɑːm] **1** *noun* daño *m or* perjuicio *m*; **the recession has done a lot of harm to export sales** = la recesión ha hecho mucho daño a las exportaciones **2** *verb* dañar *or* estropear *or* perjudicar; **the bad publicity has harmed the company's reputation** = la mala publicidad ha perjudicado la reputación de la empresa

harmonization [hɑːmənaɪˈzeɪʃn] *noun* armonización *f or* concertación *f*; **harmonization of VAT rates** = armonización de los tipos del IVA

◊ **harmonize** ['hɑːmənaɪz] *verb* **to harmonize VAT rates** = armonizar los tipos del IVA

hatchet man ['hætʃɪt 'mæn] *noun* encargado de suprimir puestos de trabajo para reducir los gastos de la empresa

haul [hɔːl] *noun* trayecto *m or* recorrido *m*; **it is a long haul from Barcelona to Athens** = el trayecto de Barcelona a Atenas es muy largo; **short-haul flight** = vuelo de corto recorrido; **long-haul flight** = vuelo de larga distancia

◊ **haulage** ['hɔːlɪdʒ] *noun* **(a)** *(moving goods)* **road haulage** = transporte *m* por carretera *or* rodado; **road haulage depot** = depósito de transporte por carretera; **haulage contractor** = contratista de transporte por carretera; **haulage costs** *or* **haulage rates** = costes *or* tarifas de transporte por carretera; **haulage firm** *or* **company** = empresa *or* compañía de transporte por carretera **(b)** *(cost of moving goods)* coste del transporte por carretera *or* transporte rodado; **haulage is increasing by 5% per annum** = el coste del transporte por carretera aumenta un 5% anual (NOTE: no plural)

◊ **haulier** ['hɔːljə] *noun* **road haulier** = contratista de transporte por carretera

haven ['heɪvn] *noun* refugio *m*; **tax haven** = paraíso fiscal

hawk [hɔːk] *verb* vender de puerta en puerta *or* en la calle; **to hawk something round** = ofrecer una mercancía a distintos clientes; **he hawked his idea for a plastic car body round all the major car constructors** = visitó a los principales fabricantes de coches para convencerles de su idea sobre una carrocería de plástico

◊ **hawker** ['hɔːkə] *noun* buhonero *m or* vendedor, -ra ambulante

hazard ['hæzəd] *noun* **fire hazard** = peligro *m or* riesgo *m* de incendio; **that warehouse full of wood and paper is a fire hazard** = ese almacén lleno de madera y papel supone un peligro de incendio; **occupational hazard** = riesgo laboral *or* gajes del oficio; **heart attacks are one of the occupational hazards of directors** = los ataques cardíacos son uno de los riesgos laborales de los directores

head [hed] **1** *noun* **(a)** *(person in charge)* jefe, -fa *or* cabeza *f or* director, -ra; **head of department** *or* **department head** = jefe de sección *or* departamento **(b)** *(most important)* jefe; **head clerk** = jefe de oficina; **head porter** = jefe de porteros *or* conserje jefe; **head salesman** = vendedor en jefe *or* principal; **head waiter** = jefe de comedor *or* camareros; **head buyer** = jefe de compras; **head office** = oficina *or* sede central *or* casa matriz **(c)** *(top part)* parte superior *or* principio *or* encabezamiento; **write the name of the company at the head of the list** = escriba el nombre de la compañía al principio de la lista **(d)** *(person)* persona *f or* cabeza; **representatives cost on average £25,000 per head per annum** = los representantes cuestan una media de £25.000 por persona y año **(e) heads of agreement** = borrador *m* de un acuerdo **2** *verb* **(a)** *(to manage)* dirigir *or* estar a la cabeza de *or* conducir; **to head a department** = dirigir un departamento; **he is heading a buying mission to China** = está a la cabeza de una misión comercial a China **(b)** *(to lead)* encabezar *or* ir en cabeza; **the two largest oil companies head the list of stock market results** = las dos principales compañías petrolíferas encabezan la lista del mercado de valores

◊ **headed paper** ['hedɪd 'peɪpə] *noun* papel con membrete

◊ **head for** ['hed 'fɔ:] *verb* dirigirse hacia *or* ir a; **the company is heading for disaster** = la compañía va a la ruina

◊ **headhunt** ['hedhʌnt] *verb* dedicarse a la caza de cerebros *or* cazar talentos para una empresa; **he was headhunted** = lo reclutó por una empresa dedicada a la caza de cerebros (NOTE: also called **executive search**)

◊ **headhunter** ['hedhʌntə] *noun* cazador, -ra de cerebros *or* cazatalentos *m* (empresa que se dedica a la búsqueda de ejecutivos y expertos para sus clientes)

◊ **heading** ['hedɪŋ] *noun* **(a)** *(of a text)* encabezamiento *f or* título *m or* **items are listed under several headings** = los artículos están clasificados por títulos; **look at the figure under the heading 'Costs 91-92'** = mire la cifra en la sección *or* el apartado de 'Costes 91-92' **(b)** *(of a letter)* **letter heading** *or* **heading on notepaper** = membrete *m*

◊ **headlease** ['hedli:s] *noun* arrendamiento *m*

◊ **headline inflation** ['hedlaɪn ɪn'fleɪʃn] *noun* cifra de inflación británica que incluye los intereses hipotecarios y los impuestos locales

> QUOTE the UK economy is at the uncomfortable stage in the cycle where two years of tight money are having the desired effect on demand: output is falling and unemployment is rising, but headline inflation and earnings are showing no sign of decelerating
> **Sunday Times**

headquarters (HQ) ['hed'kwɔ:təz] *plural noun* oficina *f* central *or* domicilio *m* social *or* sede *f*; **the company's headquarters are in New York** = la sede de la compañía está en Nueva York; **divisional headquarters** = oficina central *or* sede de la división; **to reduce headquarters staff** = reducir el personal de la oficina central

◊ **head up** ['hed 'ʌp] *verb* dirigir *or* estar a la cabeza; **he has been appointed to head up our European organization** = ha sido nombrado para dirigir nuestra organización europea

> QUOTE reporting to the deputy managing director, the successful candidate will be responsible for heading up a team which provides a full personnel service
> **Times**

health [helθ] *noun* **(a)** *(being fit and well)* salud *f* **GB Health and Safety at Work Act** = Ley sobre la seguridad e higiene en el trabajo; **health insurance** = seguro de enfermedad; **a private health scheme** = seguro de enfermedad privado **(b)** *(trading profitably)* **to give a company a clean bill of health** = dictaminar que una compañía se encuentra en una situación saneada

◊ **healthy** ['helθi] *adjective* en buen estado; **a healthy balance sheet** = balance saneado; **the company made some very healthy profits** *or* **a very healthy profit** = la compañía obtuvo grandes beneficios *or* un beneficio muy considerable *or* substancioso

> QUOTE the main US banks have been forced to pull back from international lending as nervousness continues about their financial health
> **Financial Times**

hear [hɪə] *verb* **(a)** *(sound)* oír; **you can hear the printer in the next office** = se oye la impresora de la oficina de al lado; **the traffic makes so much noise that I cannot hear my phone ringing** = el tráfico hace tanto ruido que no oigo sonar el teléfono **(b)** *(from someone)* tener noticias de alguien *or* saber de alguien; **we have not heard from them for some time** = no hemos tenido noticias suyas desde hace algún tiempo; **we hope to hear from the lawyers within a few days** = esperamos tener noticias de los abogados dentro de unos días (NOTE: **hearing - heard**)

heavy ['hevi] *adjective* **(a)** *(important)* grande *or* importante; **a programme of heavy investment overseas** = un programa de grandes inversiones en el extranjero; **he had heavy losses on the Stock Exchange** = sufrió grandes pérdidas en la bolsa; **the company is a heavy user of steel** *or* **a heavy consumer of electricity** = la empresa es una gran consumidora de acero *or* de electricidad ; **the government imposed a heavy tax on luxury goods** = el gobierno impuso elevados impuestos a los artículos de lujo ; **heavy costs** *or* **heavy expenditure** = grandes costes *or* gran gasto **(b)** *(weight)* pesado, -da; **the Post Office refused to handle the package because it was too heavy** = la oficina de correos se negó a aceptar el paquete porque era demasiado pesado; **heavy goods vehicle (HGV)** = vehículo de carga pesada; **heavy industry** = industria pesada; **heavy machinery** = maquinaria pesada **(c)** *(costly)* gravoso, -sa

◊ **heavily** ['hevɪli] *adverb* fuertemente; **he is heavily in debt** = está fuertemente endeudado; **they are heavily into property** = tienen grandes inversiones inmobiliarias; **the company has had to borrow heavily to repay its debts** = la compañía tuvo que pedir grandes préstamos para pagar sus deudas

> QUOTE the steel company had spent heavily on new equipment
> **Fortune**

> QUOTE heavy selling sent many blue chips tumbling in Tokyo yesterday
> **Financial Times**

hectare ['hekteə] *noun* hectárea *f* (NOTE: usually written **ha** after figures: **16ha**)

hectic ['hektɪk] *adjective* agitado, -da *or* ajetreado, -da *or* frenético, -ca; **a hectic day on the Stock Exchange** = un día ajetreado en la bolsa; **after last week's hectic trading, this week has been very calm** = después de las frenéticas transacciones comerciales de la semana pasada, esta semana ha sido muy tranquila

hedge [hedʒ] **1** *noun* protección *f or* barrera *f or* cobertura *f* (contra las variaciones de los precios); **hedge against inflation** = una barrera contra la inflación; **he bought gold as a hedge against exchange losses** = compró oro para cubrirse contra las pérdidas en el cambio; **hedge clause** = cláusula de salvaguardia; **hedge fund** = fondo de protección **2** *verb* **to hedge one's bets** = diversificar uno sus inversiones para protegerse; **to hedge against inflation** = cubrirse contra el riesgo de la inflación

◊ **hedging** ['hedʒɪŋ] *noun* protección *f or* cobertura *f* contra los cambios de precio

QUOTE during the 1970s commercial
property was regarded by investors as an
alternative to equities, with many of the
same inflation-hedge qualities
Investors Chronicle

QUOTE gold and silver, the usual hedges
against inflation and a weak dollar, have
been on the wane
Business Week

QUOTE much of what was described as near
hysteria was the hedge funds trying to
liquidate bonds to repay bank debts after
losing multi-million dollar bets on
speculations that the yen would fall
against the dollar
Times

height [haɪt] *noun* **(a)** *(measurement)* altura *f;* **what is the height of the desk from the floor?** = ¿cuánto mide la mesa del despacho de alto?; **he measured the height of the room from floor to ceiling** = midió la altura de la habitación desde el suelo hasta el techo **(b)** *(highest point)* cumbre *f or* punto *m* culminante *or* cima *f;* **it is difficult to find hotel rooms at the height of the tourist season** = es difícil encontrar habitaciones de hotel en plena temporada turística

heir [eə] *noun* heredero, -ra; **his heirs split the estate between them** = sus herederos se repartieron la herencia

helicopter ['helɪkɒptə] *noun* helicóptero *m;* **he took the helicopter from the airport to the centre of town** = tomó el helicóptero desde el aeropuerto hasta el centro de la ciudad; **it is only a short helicopter flight from the centre of town to the factory** = se tarda muy poco desde el centro de la ciudad hasta la fábrica en helicóptero

◊ **helipad** ['helɪpæd] *noun* pista *f* de helicópteros

◊ **heliport** ['helɪpɔːt] *noun* helipuerto *m*

help [help] **1** *noun* ayuda *f;* **she finds the word-processor a great help in writing letters** = el procesador de textos le resulta de gran ayuda para escribir cartas; **the company was set up with financial help from the government** = la compañía se fundó con ayuda financiera del Estado; **her assistant is not much help in the office - he cannot type or drive** = su auxiliar no es de gran ayuda en la oficina - ni sabe escribir a máquina ni conducir **2** *verb* ayudar; **he helped the salesman carry his case of samples** = ayudó al vendedor a llevar su maleta de muestras; **the computer helps in the rapid processing of orders** *or* **helps us to process orders rapidly** = el ordenador ayuda a tramitar rápidamente los pedidos *or* nos ayuda a tramitar los pedidos con rapidez; **the government helps exporting companies with easy credit** = el gobierno ayuda a las empresas exportadoras con facilidades de crédito (NOTE: **you help someone** *or* **something to do something**)

hereafter [hɪər'ɑːftə] *adverb* de ahora en adelante *or* en el futuro

◊ **hereby** [hɪə'baɪ] *adverb* por la presente; **we hereby revoke the agreement of January 1st 1982** = por el presente documento revocamos el acuerdo del 1 de enero de 1982

◊ **herewith** [hɪə'wɪθ] *adverb* adjunto, -ta; **please find the cheque enclosed herewith** = adjunto el cheque a la presente

hereditament [herɪ'dɪtəmənt] *noun* bienes *mpl or* herencia *f*

hesitate ['hezɪteɪt] *verb* vacilar *or* no decidirse a hacer algo; **the company is hesitating about starting up a new computer factory** = la empresa no se decide a montar una nueva fábrica de ordenadores; **she hesitated for some time before accepting the job** = vaciló durante algún tiempo antes de aceptar el trabajo

HGV ['eɪtʃ'dʒiː'viː] = HEAVY GOODS VEHICLE

hidden ['hɪdn] *adjective* escondido, -da *or* oculto, -ta; **hidden asset** = diferencia entre valor contable y de mercado; **hidden reserves** = reservas ocultas; **hidden defect in the program** = defecto oculto del programa

high [haɪ] **1** *adjective* **(a)** *(tall)* alto, -ta; **the shelves are 30 cm high** = las estanterías tienen 30 cm de alto; **the door is not high enough to let us get the machines into the building** = la puerta no es lo bastante alta como para entrar las máquinas en el edificio; **they are planning a 30-storey high office block** = tienen en proyecto un bloque de oficinas de 30 pisos **(b)** *(large)* alto, -ta *or* elevado, -da *or* grande; **high overhead costs increase the unit price** = los gastos generales elevados aumentan el precio unitario; **high prices put customers off** = los precios altos disuaden a los clientes; **they are budgeting for a high level of expenditure** = prevén un nivel de gastos alto; **investments which bring in a high rate of return** = inversiones que proporcionan una alta tasa de rendimiento; **high interest rates are killing small businesses** los altos tipos de interés están arruinando a las pequeñas empresas; **high finance** = las altas finanzas; **high flier** = *(person)* persona ambiciosa *or* de gran talento; *(share)* acción *f* cuyo precio crece rápidamente; **high sales** = ventas altas; **high taxation** = imposición alta; **highest tax bracket** = tramo superior de la escala impositiva; **high volume (of sales)** = gran volumen de ventas **(c)** **highest bidder** = el mejor postor; **the property was sold to the highest bidder** = la propiedad fue vendida al mejor postor; **a decision taken at the highest level** = la decisión fue tomada al más alto nivel **2** *adverb* **prices are running high** = los precios están muy altos **3** *noun* récord *m or* alta *f;* **share prices have dropped by 10% since the high of January 2nd** = las cotizaciones de las acciones han bajado el 10% desde el récord registrado el 2 de enero; **the highs and lows on the Stock Exchange** = las altas y bajas de la bolsa; **sales volume has reached an all-time high** = el volumen de ventas ha alcanzado la cifra más alta jamás registrada *or* un récord nunca visto

◊ **higher** ['haɪə] *adjective* superior; **the figures for the second half are higher than last year** = las cifras del segundo semestre son superiores al año anterior

◊ **high-grade** ['haɪgreɪd] *adjective* de alto grado *or* nivel *or* de calidad superior; **high-grade petrol** gasolina 'Super' *or* de alto octanaje; **a high-grade trade delegation** = una delegación comercial de alto nivel

◊ **high-income** ['haɪ'ɪnkʌm] *adjective* de altos ingresos *or* de renta elevada; **high-income shares** = acciones de alto rendimiento; **a high-income portfolio** = cartera de valores de renta elevada

◊ **high-level** ['haɪ'levl] *adjective* **(a)** *(very important)* de alto nivel; **a high-level meeting** *or* **delegation** = una reunión *or* delegación de alto nivel; **a high-level decision** = una decisión de alto nivel **(b)** **high-level computer language** = lenguaje de programación de alto nivel

◊ **highlighter** ['haɪlaɪtə] *noun (pen)* marcador *m*

◊ **highly** ['haɪli] *adverb (very)* muy *or* sumamente *or* altamente; **highly-geared company** = sociedad con un gran coeficiente de endeudamiento; **highly-paid** = muy bien pagado; **highly-placed** = muy bien situado *or* de alta categoría; **the delegation met a highly-placed official in the Trade Ministry** = la delegación se entrevistó con un alto funcionario del Ministerio de Comercio; **highly-priced** = caro, -ra; **she is highly thought of by the managing director** = el director gerente la tiene en gran concepto *or* tiene un gran concepto de ella

◊ **high pressure** ['haɪ'preʃə] *noun* alta presión *f*; **working under high pressure** = trabajar bajo una gran presión; **high-pressure salesman** = vendedor insistente *or* apremiante; **high-pressure sales techniques** *or* **high-pressure selling** = técnicas de venta insistentes *or* apremiantes

◊ **high-quality** ['haɪ'kwɒləti] *adjective* de calidad superior *or* de primera calidad; **high-quality goods** = productos de primera calidad; **high-quality steel** = acero de calidad superior

◊ **High Street** ['haɪstriːt] *noun (main shopping street in a British town)* calle *f* mayor *or* principal *or* centro *m* comercial de una ciudad; **the High Street shops** = las tiendas del centro; **a High Street bookshop** = una librería del centro; **the High Street banks** = los bancos comerciales

hike [haɪk] **1** *noun US* aumento *m*; **pay hike** = aumento de sueldo **2** *verb US* aumentar; **the union hiked its demand to $3 an hour** = el sindicato aumentó su demanda a $3 la hora

hire ['haɪə] **1** *noun* **(a)** *(rent)* alquiler *m*; **car hire** =

alquiler de coches; **truck hire** = alquiler de camiones; **car hire firm** *or* **equipment hire firm** = empresa de alquiler de coches *or* empresa de alquiler de equipos; **hire car** = coche de alquiler; **he was driving a hire car when the accident happened** = tuvo el accidente conduciendo un coche de alquiler **(b)** *(sign on taxi)* **'for hire'** = 'libre' **(c)** *US* **for hire contract** = contrato de trabajo independiente; **to work for hire** = trabajar independientemente *or* por cuenta propia **2** *verb* **(a)** *(people)* contratar *or* emplear; **to hire staff** = contratar personal; **to hire and fire** = contratar y despedir a empleados; **we have hired the best lawyers to represent us** = hemos contratado a los mejores abogados para que nos representen; **they hired a small company to paint the offices** = contrataron a una pequeña empresa para pintar las oficinas **(b)** *(things)* alquilar; **to hire a car** *or* **a crane** = alquilar un coche *or* una grúa; **he hired a truck to move his furniture** = alquiló un camión para trasladar los muebles **(c)** **to hire out cars** *or* **equipment** = alquilar coches *or* equipo especializado

◊ **hired** ['haɪəd] *adjective* **a hired car** = coche alquilado *or* de alquiler

◊ **hire purchase (HP)** ['haɪə 'pɜːtʃəs] *noun* compra *f* a plazos; **to buy a refrigerator on hire purchase** = comprar un frigorífico a plazos; **to sign a hire-purchase agreement** = firmar un contrato de compra a plazos; **hire-purchase company** = compañía que financia la compra a plazos; **all the furniture in the house was bought on HP** = todos los muebles de la casa se compraron a plazos (NOTE: US English is **to buy on the installment plan**)

◊ **hiring** ['haɪərɪŋ] *noun* contratación *f*; **hiring of new personnel has been stopped** = la contratación de nuevo personal ha sido interrumpida

COMMENT: an agreement to hire a piece of equipment, etc., involves two parties: the hirer and the owner. The equipment remains the property of the owner while the hirer is using it. Under a hire-purchase agreement, the equipment remains the property of the owner until the hirer has complied with the terms of the agreement (i.e., until he has paid all monies due)

historic *or* **historical** [hɪs'tɒrɪk *or* hɪs'tɒrɪkəl] *adjective (which goes back over a period of time)* histórico, -ca; **historic(al) cost** = coste original *or* inicial; **historical figures** = cifras históricas

COMMENT: by tradition, a company's accounts are usually prepared on the historic(al) cost principle, i.e. that assets are costed at their purchase price; with inflation, such assets are undervalued, and current-cost accounting or replacement-cost accounting may be preferred

hit [hɪt] *verb* **(a)** *(knock)* golpear *or* pegar *or* alcanzar; **we have hit our export targets** = hemos alcanzado nuestros objetivos de exportación **(b)** *(damage)* dañar *or* afectar; **the company was badly hit by the falling exchange rate** = la caída de los tipos de cambio afectó gravemente a la compañía; **our sales of summer clothes have been hit by the bad weather** = nuestras ventas de ropa de verano se han visto afectadas por el mal tiempo; **the new legislation has hit the small companies hardest** =

las pequeñas empresas han sido las más perjudicadas por la nueva legislación (NOTE: **hitting - hit**)

hive off ['haɪv 'ɒf] *verb* descentralizar; **the new managing director hived off the retail sections of the company** = el nuevo director general ha descentralizado las secciones de venta al por menor

hoard [hɔːd] *verb* acumular *or* acaparar *or* atesorar

◊ **hoarder** ['hɔːdə] *noun* acaparador, -ra

◊ **hoarding** ['hɔːdɪŋ] *noun* **(a)** *(keeping large quantities)* acaparamiento *m or* atesoramiento *m*; **hoarding of supplies** = acumulación *f* de provisiones **(b)** *(advertising)* **advertisement hoarding** = valla *f* publicitaria *or* cartelera *f*

> QUOTE as a result of hoarding, rice has become scarce with prices shooting up
> **Business Times (Lagos)**

hold [həʊld] **1** *noun* **(a) to have a hold over someone** = tener influencia sobre alguien **(b)** *(in ship)* bodega *f (in aircraft)* compartimiento *m* de carga **2** *verb* **(a)** *(keep)* tener *or* guardar; **he holds 10% of the company's shares** = tiene el 10% de las acciones de la compañía; **you should hold these shares - they look likely to rise** = deberías guardar estas acciones - es probable que suban **(b)** *(contain)* contener *or* caber; **the carton holds twenty packets** = la caja contiene veinte paquetes; **each box holds 250 sheets of paper** = cada caja contiene 250 hojas de papel; **a bag can hold twenty kilos of sugar** = en una bolsa caben veinte kilos de azúcar **(c)** *(make something happen)* celebrar *or* tener *or* hacer; **to hold a meeting** *or* **a discussion** = celebrar una reunión *or* tener una discusión *or* una charla; **the computer show will be held in London next month** = la feria de ordenadores se celebrará en Londres el mes próximo; **board meetings are held in the boardroom** = las reuniones del consejo de administración se celebran en la sala de juntas; **the AGM will be held on March 24th** = la junta general anual se celebrará el 24 de marzo; **we are holding a sale of surplus stock** = liquidamos el exceso de existencias; **the receiver will hold an auction of the company's assets** = el administrador judicial celebrará una subasta del activo de la compañía; **the accountants held a review of the company's accounting practices** = los contables hicieron un análisis de las prácticas contables de la compañía **(d)** *(on telephone)* esperar; **hold the line please** *or* **please hold** = no se retire *or* no cuelgue; **the chairman is on the other line - will you hold?** = el presidente está hablando por la otra línea - ¿quiere esperar?; **if you hold on a moment, the chairman will be off the other line soon** = si espera un momento, el presidente pronto terminará por la otra línea **(e)** *(post)* desempeñar; **to hold a post** = desempeñar un cargo *or* ocupar un puesto (NOTE: **holding - held**)

◊ **hold back** ['həʊld 'bæk] *verb* esperar *or* abstenerse; **investors are holding back until after the Budget** = los inversores están esperando la presentación del presupuesto; **he held back from signing the lease until he had checked the details** = se abstuvo de firmar el contrato de arrendamiento hasta haber verificado los detalles; **payment will be held back until the contract has been signed** = el pago no se efectuará hasta que el contrato haya sido firmado

◊ **hold down** ['həʊld 'daʊn] *verb* **(a)** *(keep at low level)* mantener bajo *or* contener; **we are cutting margins to hold our prices down** = estamos recortando los márgenes para mantener los precios bajos **(b) to hold down a job** = conservar el puesto de trabajo

◊ **holder** ['həʊldə] *noun* **(a)** *(owner)* poseedor, -ra *or* tenedor *m* portador *m or* titular *mf*; **holders of government bonds** *or* **bondholders** = tenedores de títulos del Estado *or* obligacionistas; **holder of stock** *or* **of shares in a company** = tenedor de acciones *or* accionista de una compañía; **holder of an insurance policy** *or* **policy holder** = titular de una póliza de seguros; **credit card holder** = titular de una tarjeta de crédito; **debenture holder** = obligacionista *mf* **(b)** *(for protection)* soporte *m or* funda *f*; **card holder** = funda de la tarjeta; **credit card holder** = funda *or* billetera para la tarjeta de crédito; **message holder** = soporte del mensaje

◊ **holding** ['həʊldɪŋ] *noun* **(a)** *(shares)* valores *mpl* en cartera; **he has sold all his holdings in the Far East** = ha vendido toda su cartera del Extremo Oriente; **the company has holdings in German manufacturing companies** = la empresa tiene valores de sociedades manufactureras alemanas **(b) cross holdings** = propiedad de acciones recíproca; **the two companies have protected themselves from takeover by a system of cross holdings** = las dos sociedades se han protegido contra la adquisición mediante la tenencia recíproca de acciones

◊ **holding company** ['həʊldɪŋ 'kʌmpni] *noun* 'holding' *m or* sociedad *f* de cartera *or* tenedora; *see also* SUBSIDIARY (NOTE: the US English for this is **proprietary company**)

◊ **hold on** ['həʊld 'ɒn] *verb* resistir *or* aguantar; **the company's shareholders should hold on and wait for a better offer** = los accionistas de la compañía deberían resistir y esperar una oferta mejor

◊ **hold out for** ['həʊld 'aʊt fɔː] *verb (to wait and ask for)* insistir en; **you should hold out for a 10% pay rise** = deberíais insistir en un aumento de sueldo del 10%

◊ **hold over** ['həʊld 'əʊvə] *verb* aplazar; **discussion of item 4 was held over until the next meeting** = se aplazó la discusión del punto 4 hasta la reunión siguiente

◊ **hold to** ['həʊld 'tuː] *verb* atenerse a *or* ajustarse *or* limitar; **we will try to hold him to the contract** = intentaremos que se ajuste al contrato; **the government hopes to hold wage increases to 5%** = el gobierno espera limitar las subidas salariales al 5%

◊ **hold up** ['həʊld 'ʌp] *verb* **(a)** *(stay high)* mantenerse *or* sostenerse; **share prices have held up well** = las cotizaciones de las acciones se han mantenido bien; **sales held up during the tourist season** = las ventas se mantuvieron durante la temporada turística **(b)** *(delay)* retener *or* suspender *or* retrasar; **the shipment has been held up at the customs** = el envío ha sido retenido en la aduana; **payment will be held up until the contract has been signed** = el pago se suspenderá hasta que se firme el contrato; **the strike will hold up dispatch for some weeks** = la huelga retrasará los envíos por algunas semanas

◊ **hold-up** ['hɔʊldʌp] *noun* retraso *m*; **the strike caused hold-ups in the dispatch of goods** = la huelga ocasionó retrasos en el despacho de mercancías

> QUOTE real wages have been held down; they have risen at an annual rate of only 1% in the last two years
> **Sunday Times**

> QUOTE as of last night, the bank's shareholders no longer hold any rights to the bank's shares
> **South China Morning Post**

holiday ['hɒlədeɪ] *noun* **(a)** bank holiday = fiesta *f* oficial *or* día *m* festivo; **New Year's Day is a bank holiday** = el día de Año Nuevo es festivo; **public holiday** = fiesta nacional; **statutory holiday** = vacaciones reglamentarias establecidas por ley; **the office is closed for the Christmas holiday** = la oficina cierra durante las vacaciones de Navidad **(b)** *(rest from work)* vacaciones *fpl*; **to take a holiday** *or* **to go on holiday** = tomar vacaciones *or* irse *or* marcharse de vacaciones; **when is the manager taking his holidays?** = ¿cuándo toma las vacaciones el director?; **my secretary is on holiday tomorrow** = mi secretaria no trabaja mañana *or* tiene el día libre mañana; **he is away on holiday for two weeks** = estará de vacaciones durante dos semanas; **the job carries five weeks' holiday** = el puesto lleva aparejadas cinco semanas de vacaciones; **the summer holidays** = vacaciones de verano; **holiday entitlement** = número de días de vacación a que tiene derecho el trabajador; **she has not used up all her holiday entitlement** = no ha agotado todas las vacaciones a que tiene derecho; **holiday pay** = paga *or* sueldo de vacaciones; **do you get holiday pay?** = ¿cobra Vd. durante las vacaciones? (NOTE: US English is **vacation**) **(c)** tax holiday = exención *f* fiscal concedida a una nueva empresa

Holland ['hɒlənd] *noun* Holanda *f see also* NETHERLANDS

hologram ['hɒləgræm] *noun* holograma *m*

home [həʊm] *noun* **(a)** *(place where one lives)* casa *f or* hogar *m or* vivienda *f*; **please send the letter to my home address, not my office** = le ruego me envíe la carta a mi domicilio particular, no a la oficina; **home banking** = sistema de transacciones bancarias a domicilio **(b)** **home country** = país de origen; **home sales** *or* **sales in the home market** = ventas nacionales *or* en el mercado interior; **home-produced products** = productos del país *or* productos nacionales **(c)** *(house)* casa; **new home sales** = venta de viviendas nuevas; **home loan** = préstamo de ahorro-vivienda

◊ **homegrown** ['həʊm'grəʊn] *adjective* del país *or* creado, -da en el país *or* nacional; **a homegrown computer industry** = una industria de ordenadores creada en el país; **India's homegrown car industry** = la industria india de automóviles

◊ **homemade** ['həʊmmeɪd] *adjective* hecho, -cha en casa *or* de fabricación casera; **homemade jam** = mermelada casera

◊ **homeowner** ['həʊm'əʊnə] *noun* propietario, -ria de su vivienda; **homeowner's insurance policy** = póliza de seguros de la propia vivienda *or* contra los riesgos del hogar

◊ **homeward** ['həʊmwəd] *adjective (going towards the home country)* de regreso *or* de vuelta a casa; **homeward freight** = flete de vuelta; **homeward journey** = viaje de regreso

◊ **homewards** ['həʊmwədz] *adverb* hacia el país de origen; **cargo homewards** = carga de retorno

◊ **homeworker** ['həʊm'wʌkə] *noun* trabajador, -ra a domicilio

hon = HONORARY **hon sec** = secretario honorario *or* secretaria honoraria

Honduras [hɒn'djʊərəs] *noun* Honduras *f*

◊ **Honduran** [hɒn'djʊərən] *adjective & noun* hondureño, -ña
NOTE: capital: **Tegucigalpa**; currency: **Honduras lempira (L)** = lempira hondureño (L)

honest ['ɒnɪst] *adjective* honrado, -da *or* honesto, -ta *or* justo, -ta; **to play the honest broker** = actuar de amigable componedor

◊ **honestly** ['ɒnɪstli] *adverb* honradamente *or* sinceramente

honorarium [ɒnə'reərɪəm] *noun* honorarios *mpl or* emolumentos *mpl* (NOTE: plural is **honoraria**)

◊ **honorary** ['ɒnərəri] *adjective* honorario, -ria *or* de honor; **honorary secretary** = secretario honorario; **honorary president** = presidente honorario; **honorary member** = miembro honorario

honour *or* US **honor** ['ɒnə] *verb* pagar; **to honour a bill** = pagar una factura; **to honour a signature** = aceptar *or* reconocer una firma

hope [həʊp] *verb* esperar; **we hope to be able to dispatch the order next week** = esperamos poder enviar el pedido la semana próxima; **he is hoping to break into the US market** = espera poder introducirse en el mercado de los EE UU; **they had hoped the TV commercials would help sales** = creyeron que la publicidad en la Televisión les ayudaría a aumentar las ventas

horizontal [hɒrɪ'zɒntl] *adjective* horizontal; **horizontal integration** = fusión horizontal; **horizontal communication** = comunicación horizontal

horse trading ['hɔːs 'treɪdɪŋ] *noun* negociación *f* con concesiones *or* regateo *m*

hostess ['həʊstəs] *noun* **(a)** *(general)* anfitriona *f* **(b)** *(airline)* azafata *f*; **air hostess** *or* US **airline hostess** = azafata de vuelo; **ground hostess** = azafata de tierra

hostile ['hɒstaɪl *adjective* hostil; **hostile takeover** = OPAH *or* oferta pública de adquisición hostil

hot [hɒt] *adjective* **(a)** *(very warm)* caliente; **the staff complain that the office is too hot in the summer and too cold in the winter** = el personal se queja de que en la oficina hace demasiado calor en verano y demasiado frío en invierno; **the drinks machine sells coffee, tea and hot soup** = la máquina de bebidas sirve café, té y sopa caliente; **switch off the machine if it gets too hot** = apaga la máquina si se calienta demasiado **(b)** *(not safe)* to **make things hot for someone** = poner las cosas difíciles *or* hacer la vida imposible *or* amargar la vida a alguien; **customs officials are making things hot for the drug smugglers** = los aduaneros les están haciendo la vida imposible a los narcotraficantes; **hot money** = dinero caliente *or* especulativo; **he is in the hot seat** = tiene que dar la cara *or* tiene que tomar las decisiones

hotel [hǝu'tel] *noun* hotel *m*; **hotel bill** = factura de hotel; **hotel expenses** = gastos de hotel; **hotel manager** = director de hotel; **hotel staff** = personal del hotel; **hotel accommodation** = habitaciones de hotel *or* capacidad hotelera; **all hotel accommodation has been booked up for the exhibition** = todas las habitaciones del hotel han sido reservadas para la exposición; **hotel chain** *or* **chain of hotels** = cadena hotelera *or* de hoteles; **the hotel trade** = negocio hotelero *or* hostelería

◊ **hotelier** [hǝu'teliǝ] *noun* hotelero, -ra

hour ['auǝ] *noun* **(a)** *(time)* hora *f*; **we work a thirty-five hour week** = trabajamos treinta y cinco horas a la semana; **we work an eight-hour day** = trabajamos ocho horas al día **(b)** *(work)* hora; **he earns £4 an hour** = gana £4 a la hora; **we pay £6 an hour** = pagamos £6 la hora; **to pay by the hour** = pagar por horas **(c)** *(opening time)* **banking hours** = horario de banca; **you cannot get foreign currency out of a bank outside banking hours** = no se puede cambiar dinero de un banco fuera de las horas de oficina; **office hours** = horario de oficina; **do not telephone during office hours** = no telefonee en horas de oficina; **outside hours** *or* **out of hours** = fuera del horario de trabajo; **he worked on the accounts out of hours** = trabajó en las cuentas fuera de las horas de oficina; **the shares rose in after-hours trading** = las acciones subieron después del cierre de la sesión

◊ **hourly** ['auǝli] *adverb* por hora; **hourly-paid worker** = trabajador por horas; **hourly rate** = tarifa horaria

house [haus] *noun* **(a)** *(building)* casa *f*; **house agent** = agente *mf* inmobiliario; **house insurance** = seguro de la vivienda; **house property** = inmuebles residenciales **(b)** *(company)* casa *f* comercial *or* establecimiento *m or* sociedad *f*; **a French business house** = una casa comercial francesa; **the largest London finance house** = la mayor sociedad financiera de Londres; **he works for a broking house** *or* **a publishing house** = trabaja para una casa de corretaje *or* una editorial; **clearing house** = cámara *f* de compensación; **discount house** = banco *m or* casa de descuento; **export house** = casa exportadora; **house journal** *or* **house magazine** *US* **house organ** = boletín interno de una empresa; **house style** = estilo de la vivienda; **house telephone** = teléfono *m* interno

◊ **household** ['haus(h)ǝuld] *noun* hogar *m or* unidad *f* familiar; **household appliances** = electrodomésticos; **household expenses** = gastos del hogar; **household goods** = enseres domésticos; **household insurance policy** = póliza de seguro de la vivienda; **household name** = marca conocida *or* familiar

◊ **householder** ['haus(h)ǝuldǝ] *noun* dueño, -ña de una casa *or* cabeza de familia

◊ **house starts** *or* **housing starts** ['haus 'sta:ts *or* 'hauzɪŋ 'sta:ts] *plural noun* viviendas *fpl* cuya construcción ha comenzado durante el año

◊ **house-to-house** ['haustǝ'haus] *adjective* de puerta en puerta *or* a domicilio; **house-to-house**

canvassing = búsqueda de clientes *or* votos *or* sondeo de puerta en puerta; **house-to-house salesman;** vendedor a domicilio; **house-to-house selling** = ventas a domicilio

◊ **housing estate** ['hauzɪŋ ɪ'steɪt] *noun* urbanización *f*

HP ['eɪtʃ'pi:] = HIRE PURCHASE **all the furniture in the house was bought on HP** = todos los muebles de la casa se compraron a plazos

HQ ['eɪtʃ'kju:] = HEADQUARTERS

human resources ['hju:mǝn rɪ'sɔ:sɪz] *noun* recursos *mpl* humanos

QUOTE effective use and management of human resources hold the key to future business development and success
Management Today

hundredweight ['hʌndrǝdweɪt] *noun* 112 libras, aproximadamente un quintal *m* (NOTE: usually written **cwt** after figures: **20cwt**)

Hungary ['hʌŋgǝri] *noun* Hungría *f*

◊ **Hungarian** [hʌŋ'geǝriǝn] *adjective & noun* húngaro, -ra *or* magiar
NOTE: capital: **Budapest;** currency: **Hungarian forint (Ft)** = forint húngaro (Ft)

hurry ['hʌri] **1** *noun* prisa *f*; **there is no hurry for the figures, we do not need them until next week** = las cifras no corren prisa, no las necesitamos hasta la semana próxima; **in a hurry** = de prisa; **the sales manager wants the report in a hurry** = el director de ventas quiere el informe de prisa **2** *verb* darse prisa *or* apresurarse; **the production team tried to hurry the order through the factory** = el equipo de producción trató que la fábrica atendiera el pedido con rapidez; **the chairman does not want to be hurried into making a decision** = el presidente no quiere que le obliguen a tomar una decisión precipitadamente ; **the directors hurried into the meeting** = los consejeros fueron de prisa a la junta

◊ **hurry up** ['hʌri 'ʌp] *verb* hacer algo más deprisa; **can you hurry up that order - the customer wants it immediately?** = ¿puede hacer ese pedido más de prisa? - el cliente lo quiere en seguida

hurt [hɜ:t] *verb* dañar *or* perjudicar *or* afectar; **the bad publicity did not hurt our sales** = la mala publicidad no nos perjudicó las ventas; **sales of summer clothes were hurt by the bad weather** = la venta de ropa de verano se vio afectada por el mal tiempo; **the company has not been hurt by the recession** = la recesión no ha perjudicado a la compañía (NOTE: **hurting - hurt**)

hype [haɪp] **1** *noun* bombo *m or* publicitario *or* publicidad *f* exagerada; **all the hype surrounding the launch of the new soap** = todo el bombo que acompaña al lanzamiento del nuevo jabón **2** *verb* hacer publicidad con mucho bombo

hyper- ['haɪpǝ] *prefix meaning* hiper

◊ **hyperinflation** ['haɪpǝrɪn'fleɪʃn] *noun* hiperinflación *f*

◊ **hypermarket** ['haɪpǝma:kɪt] *noun* hipermercado *m*

Ii

ice [aɪs] *noun* hielo *m*; **to put something on ice** = aplazar *or* posponer algo; **the whole investment programme was put on ice** = se aplazó el proyecto de inversiones en su totalidad

Iceland [ˈaɪslənd] *noun* Islandia *f*

◊ **Icelander** [ˈaɪsləndə] *noun* islandés, -esa

◊ **Icelandic** [aɪsˈlændɪk] *adjective* islandés, -esa
NOTE: capital: **Reykjavik**; currency: **Icelandic krona (Isk)** = corona islandesa (Isk)

IDD = INTERNATIONAL DIRECT DIALLING

idea [aɪˈdɪə] *noun* idea *f*; **one of the salesman had the idea of changing the product colour** = uno de los vendedores tuvo la idea de cambiar el color del producto; **the chairman thinks it would be a good idea to ask all directors to itemize their expenses** = el presidente piensa que sería una buena idea pedir a todos los consejeros que detallen sus gastos

ideal [aɪˈdɪəl] *adjective* ideal; **this is the ideal site for a new hypermarket** = este es el lugar ideal para un nuevo hipermercado

◊ **Ideal Home Exhibition** [aɪˈdɪəl ˈhəʊm eksɪˈbɪʃən] *noun* 'Exposición del Hogar Ideal'

idle [ˈaɪdl] *adjective* **(a)** *(lazy)* gandul, -la *or* vago, -ga **(b)** *(not being used)* inactivo, -va *or* desocupado , -da *or* parado, -da; **2,000 employees were made idle by the recession** = 2.000 empleados se quedaron sin trabajo por la recesión; **idle capital** = capital inactivo; **money lying idle** *or* **idle money** = dinero inactivo **(c)** *(not productive)* improductivo, -va; **idle machinery** *or* **machines lying idle** = maquinaria parada; **idle time** = tiempo inactivo

i.e. [ˈaɪˈiː or ˈðæt ˈɪz] es decir *or* o sea; **the largest companies, i.e. Smith's and Brown's, had a very good first quarter** = las mayores empresas, es decir Smith y Brown, tuvieron un primer trimestre muy bueno; **the import restrictions apply to expensive items, i.e. items costing more than $2,500** = las restricciones a la importación se aplican a los artículos caros, o sea artículos que cuestan más de $2.500

ill [ɪl] *adjective* enfermo, -ma *or* indispuesto, -ta

illegal [ɪˈliːgəl] *adjective* ilegal *or* ilícito, -ta

◊ **illegality** [ɪlɪˈgælɪti] *noun* ilegalidad *f*

◊ **illegally** [ɪˈliːgəli] *adverb* ilegalmente; **he was accused of illegally importing arms into the country** = fue acusado de importar armas ilegalmente

illicit [ɪˈlɪsɪt] *adjective* ilícito, -ta; **illicit sale of alcohol** = venta ilícita de bebidas alcohólicas; **trade in illicit alcohol** = comercio de bebidas alcohólicas ilícitas

illiquid [ɪˈlɪkwɪd] *adjective* ilíquido, -da

ILO [ˈaɪelˈəʊ] = INTERNATIONAL LABOUR ORGANIZATION Organización Internacional del Trabajo (OIT)

image [ˈɪmɪdʒ] *noun* imagen *f*; **they are spending a lot of advertising money to improve the company's image** = están gastando mucho dinero en publicidad para mejorar la imagen de la compañía; **the company has adopted a down-market image** = la compañía ha adoptado una imagen dirigida a una clientela popular; **brand image** = imagen de marca; **corporate image** = imagen pública de una empresa; **to promote the corporate image** = promocionar la imagen pública de una empresa

imbalance [ɪmˈbæləns] *noun* desequilibrio *m*; **the imbalance between supply and demand** = el desequilibrio entre la oferta y la demanda

IMF [ˈaɪemˈef] = INTERNATIONAL MONETARY FUND Fondo Monetario Internacional (FMI)

imitate [ˈɪmɪteɪt] *verb* imitar; **they imitate all our sales gimmicks** = imitan todos nuestros trucos comerciales

◊ **imitation** [ˌɪmɪˈteɪʃən] *noun* imitación *f*; **beware of imitations** = desconfíe de las imitaciones

immediate [ɪˈmiːdjət] *adjective* inmediato, -ta; **he wrote an immediate letter of complaint** = escribió una carta de reclamación inmediatamente; **your order will receive immediate attention** = atenderemos su pedido inmediatamente

◊ **immediately** [ɪˈmiːdjətli] *adverb* inmediatamente *or* en el acto; **he immediately placed an order for 2,000 boxes** = hizo un pedido de 2.000 cajas inmediatamente; **as soon as he heard the news he immediately faxed his office** = nada más oir la noticia envió un fax a su oficina; **can you phone immediately you get the information?** = ¿puedes telefonear en cuanto consigas la información?

immovable [ɪˈmuːvəbl] *adjective* inmóvil *or* inamovible; **immovable property** = propiedad inmobiliaria *or* inmuebles *mpl or* bienes raíces

immunity [ɪˈmjuːnəti] *noun* inmunidad *f*; **diplomatic immunity** = inmunidad diplomática; **he was granted immunity from prosecution** = se le concedió inmunidad judicial

impact [ˈɪmpækt] *noun* impacto *m or* incidencia *f*; **the impact of new technology on the cotton trade** = el impacto de la nueva tecnología sobre el comercio del algodón; **the new design has made little impact on the buying public** = el nuevo diseño ha causado poco impacto entre los compradores

imperfect [ɪmˈpɜːfɪkt] *adjective* defectuoso, -sa *or* imperfecto, -ta *or* tarado, -da; **sale of imperfect items** = venta de artículos defectuosos; **to check a batch for imperfect products** = controlar un lote para detectar productos defectuosos

◊ **imperfection** [ˌɪmpəˈfekʃən] *noun* defecto *m or* imperfección *f*; **to check a batch for imperfections** = controlar defectos en un lote

impersonal [ɪmˈpɜːsnl] *adjective* impersonal; **an impersonal style of management** = un estilo de gestión impersonal

implement [ˈɪmplɪmənt] **1** *noun* herramienta *f or* utensilio *m or* instrumento *m* **2** *verb* ejecutar *or* aplicar *or* poner en práctica *or* llevar a cabo; **to implement an agreement** = poner en práctica un acuerdo

◊ **implementation** [ˌɪmplɪmenˈteɪʃən] *noun* realización *f or* ejecución *f or* aplicación *f or* puesta *f* en práctica; **the implementation of new rules** = la aplicación de nuevas reglas

imply [ɪmˈplaɪ] *verb* implicar; **the word 'permission' does not imply approval** = la palabra 'permiso' no implica aprobación

import 1 [ˈɪmpɔːt] *noun* **(a)** importación *f*; **imports** = importaciones *fpl*; **imports from Poland have risen to $1m a year** = las importaciones de Polonia han aumentado a $1m por año; **invisible imports** = importaciones invisibles; **visible imports** = importaciones visibles **(b)** **import ban** = prohibición de importar; **the government has imposed an import ban on arms** = el gobierno ha prohibido la importación de armas; **import duty** = aranceles *or* derechos de importación; **import levy** = gravamen a las importaciones; **import licence** *or* **import permit** = licencia de importación; **import quota** = cuota *or* cupo de importación; **the government has imposed an import quota on cars** = el gobierno ha impuesto un cupo de importación a los coches; **import restrictions** = restricciones a la importación; **import surcharge** = recargo *or* sobretasa a la importación (NOTE: **import** is usually used in the plural, but the singular form is used before another noun) **2** [ɪmˈpɔːt] *verb* importar; **this car was imported from France** = este coche se importó de Francia; **the company imports television sets from Japan** = la compañía importa aparatos de televisión de Japón; **the union organized a boycott of imported cars** = el sindicato organizó un boicot contra los coches de importación

◊ **importation** [ˌɪmpɔːˈteɪʃən] *noun* importación *f*; **the importation of arms is forbidden** = la importación de armas está prohibida

◊ **importer** [ɪmˈpɔːtə] *noun* importador, -ra; **a cigar importer** = un importador de puros; **the company is a big importer of foreign cars** = la compañía es una gran importadora de coches extranjeros

◊ **import-export** [ˈɪmpɔːtˈekspɔːt] *adjective and noun* (de) importación-exportación; **import-export trade** = comercio de importación-exportación; **he is in import-export** = se dedica a la importación-exportación

◊ **importing** [ɪmˈpɔːtɪŋ] **1** *adjective* importador, -ra; **oil-importing countries** = países importadores de petróleo; **an importing company** = una empresa importadora **2** *noun* importación *f*; **the importing of arms into the country is illegal** = la importación de armas en el país es ilegal

importance [ɪmˈpɔːtəns] *noun* importancia *f*; **the bank attaches great importance to the deal** = el banco da mucha importancia a la transacción

◊ **important** [ɪmˈpɔːtənt] *adjective* importante; **he left a pile of important papers in the taxi** = se dejó un montón de papeles importantes en el taxi; **she has an important meeting at 10.30** = tiene una cita importante a las 10.30; **he was promoted to a more important job** = fue ascendido a un puesto más importante

impose [ɪmˈpəʊz] *verb* imponer *or* gravar; **to impose a tax on bicycles** = gravar las bicicletas con un impuesto; **they tried to impose a ban on smoking** = intentaron imponer la prohibición de fumar; **the government imposed a special duty on oil** = el gobierno gravó el petróleo con unos derechos de aduana especiales; **the customs have imposed a 10% tax increase on luxury items** = la aduana ha aumentado en un 10% los aranceles sobre los artículos de lujo; **the unions have asked the government to impose trade barriers on foreign cars** = los sindicatos han pedido al gobierno que imponga barreras comerciales a la importación de coches extranjeros

◊ **imposition** [ˌɪmpəˈzɪʃən] *noun* imposición *f*

impossible [ɪmˈpɒsəbl] *adjective* imposible; **getting skilled staff is becoming impossible** = conseguir personal cualificado se está volviendo imposible; **government regulations make it impossible for us to export** = la reglamentación oficial nos hace imposible la exportación

impound [ɪmˈpaʊnd] *verb* confiscar *or* incautarse *or* embargar; **the customs impounded the whole cargo** = la aduana se incautó de la totalidad del cargamento

◊ **impounding** [ɪmˈpaʊndɪŋ] *noun* confiscación *f*

imprest system [ˈɪmprest ˈsɪstəm] *noun* sistema para mantener un saldo de caja fijo

improve [ɪmˈpruːv] *verb* mejorar; **we are trying to improve our image with a series of TV commercials** = estamos intentando mejorar nuestra imagen con una serie de anuncios publicitarios en televisión; **they hope to improve the company's cash flow position** = esperan mejorar la situación de cash flow de la empresa; **we hope the cash flow position will improve or we will have difficulty in paying our bills** = esperamos que nuestra situación de cash flow mejore o tendremos dificultades para pagar las facturas; **export trade has improved sharply during the first quarter** = las exportaciones han mejorado mucho durante el primer trimestre

◊ **improved** [ɪmˈpruːvd] *adjective* mejor *or* mejorado, -da; **the union rejected the**

management's improved offer = el sindicato rechazó la mejor oferta de la dirección

◊ **improvement** [ɪm'pruːvmənt] *noun* **(a)** *(action of getting better)* mejora *f or* mejoramiento *m or* mejoría *f or*; **there is no improvement in the cash flow situation** = la situación de cash flow no ha mejorado; **sales are showing a sharp improvement over last year** = las ventas registran una gran mejoría respecto al año pasado **(b)** *(thing which is better)* mejora; **improvement on an offer** = mejora de una oferta

◊ **improve on** [ɪm'pruːv 'ɒn] *verb* mejorar; **he refused to improve on his previous offer** = se negó a mejorar su oferta anterior

QUOTE the management says the rate of loss-making has come down and it expects further improvement in the next few years
Financial Times

QUOTE we also invest in companies whose growth and profitability could be improved by a management buyout
Times

impulse ['ɪmpʌls] *noun* impulso *m*; **to do something on impulse** = hacer algo por impulso *or* obedeciendo a un impulso momentáneo; **impulse buyer** = comprador impulsivo; **impulse buying** = compra impulsiva; **the store puts racks of chocolates by the checkout to attract the impulse buyer** = la tienda pone estantes con chocolatines junto a las cajas registradoras para tentar al comprador impulsivo; **impulse purchase** = compra impulsiva

impute [ɪm'pjuːt] *verb* atribuir

IMRO ['ɪmrəʊ] = INVESTMENT MANAGEMENT REGULATORY ORGANIZATION

in = INCH

inactive [ɪn'æktɪv] *adjective* inactivo, -va *or* pasivo, -va; **inactive account** = cuenta inactiva; **inactive market** = mercado inactivo

Inc [ɪŋk *or* ɪn'kɔːpəreɪtɪd] *US* = INCORPORATED Sociedad Anónima (S.A.)

incapable [ɪn'keɪpəbl] *adjective* incapaz *or* incapacitado, -da

◊ **incapacity** [ɪnkə'pæsɪtɪ] *noun* incapacidad *f*

incentive [ɪn'sentɪv] *noun* incentivo *m or* estímulo *m*; **staff incentives** = incentivos ofrecidos al personal; **incentive bonus** *or* **incentive payment** = prima de incentivo *or* de producción; **incentive scheme** = programa *m* de incentivos; **incentive schemes are boosting production** = los programas de incentivos están estimulando la producción

QUOTE some further profit-taking was seen yesterday as investors continued to lack fresh incentives to renew buying activity
Financial Times

inch [ɪn(t)ʃ] *noun (measurement* = 2.54cm) pulgada *f*; **a 3½ inch disk** = un disco de 3,5 pulgadas (NOTE: usually written **in** or **"** after figures: **2in** or **2"**)

incidence ['ɪnsɪdəns] *noun* incidencia *f*

incidental [ɪnsɪ'dentl] **1** *adjective* incidente *or*

incidental; **incidental expenses** = gastos varios *or* menores **2** *noun* **incidentals** = gastos *mpl* imprevistos

include [ɪn'kluːd] *verb* incluir; **the charge includes VAT** = el precio incluye el IVA; **the total comes to £1,000 including freight** = el total asciende a £1.000 incluido el flete; **the total is £140 not including insurance and freight** = el total asciende a £140 sin incluir seguro y flete; **the account covers services up to and including the month of June** = la cuenta cubre los servicios prestados hasta el mes de junio inclusive

◊ **inclusive** [ɪn'kluːsɪv] *adjective* inclusivo, -va *or* inclusive *or* incluido, -da; **inclusive of tax** = impuestos incluidos; **not inclusive of VAT** = IVA no incluido; **inclusive sum** *or* **inclusive charge** = precio todo incluido; **the conference runs from the 12th to the 16th inclusive** = el congreso se celebrará del 12 al 16 ambos inclusive (NOTE: US English is **from 12 through 16**)

income ['ɪnkʌm] *noun* **(a)** *(from a salary)* ingresos *mpl or* renta *f*; **annual income** = ingresos anuales *or* renta anual; **disposable income** = renta disponible; **earned income** = ingresos profesionales *or* ingresos percibidos *or* renta del trabajo; **fixed income** = renta fija; **gross income** = renta bruta *or* ingresos brutos; **net income** = renta neta *or* beneficio neto; **private income** = renta privada *or* no salarial; **personal income** = renta personal; **retained income** = beneficios *m* no distribuidos; **unearned income** = renta no salarial *or* ingresos procedentes de intereses y dividendos; *(for tax purposes)* **lower** *or* **upper income bracket** = tramo inferior *or* superior de la escala impositiva; **he comes into the higher income bracket** = está en el grupo de contribuyentes que pagan renta por el tramo más alto; **income shares** = dividendos acumulados en forma de renta; **income units** = unidades de cuenta **(b) the government's incomes policy** = la política de rentas del gobierno **(c)** *(as gifts or from investments)* ingresos; **the hospital has a large income from gifts** = el hospital tiene grandes ingresos procedentes de donaciones **(d)** *US* **income statement** = cuenta de resultados (NOTE: the UK equivalent is the **profit and loss account**)

◊ **income tax** ['ɪnkʌm 'tæks] *noun* impuesto *m* sobre la renta; **income tax form** = impreso *m* para la declaración del impuesto sobre la renta; **declaration of income** *or* **income tax return** = declaración *f* del impuesto sobre la renta

QUOTE there is no risk-free way of taking regular income from your money much higher than the rate of inflation
Guardian

QUOTE the company will be paying income tax at the higher rate next year
Citizen (Ottawa)

incoming ['ɪnkʌmɪŋ] *adjective* **(a)** *(phone or letter)* **incoming call** = llamada de fuera; **incoming mail** = correo entrante **(b)** *(recently elected or appointed)* nuevo, -va; **the incoming board of directors** = el nuevo consejo de administración; **the incoming chairman** *or* **president** = el nuevo presidente

incompetence [ɪn'kɒmpɪtəns] *noun* incapacidad *f*

◇ **incompetent** [ɪn'kɒmpɪtənt] *adjective* incapaz *or* incompetente; **the sales manager is quite incompetent** = el director de ventas es bastante incompetente; **the company has an incompetent sales director** = la empresa tiene un director de ventas incompetente

inconvertible [ɪnkən'vɜːtəbl] *adjective* inconvertible

incorporate [ɪn'kɔːpəreɪt] *verb* **(a)** *(to bring something in)* incorporar *or* incluir; **income from the 1994 acquisition is incorporated into the accounts** = los ingresos de la adquisición de 1994 están incluidos en las cuentas **(b)** *(to form a company)* constituir en sociedad; **a company incorporated in the USA** = una sociedad constituida en los EE UU; **an incorporated company** = sociedad constituida legalmente

◇ **incorporated** [ɪn'kɔːpəreɪtɪd] *adjective* **J. Doe Incorporated** *or* **J. Doe Inc.** = la sociedad anónima J.Doe

◇ **incorporation** [ɪnkɔːpə'reɪʃən] *noun* constitución *f* de una sociedad

> COMMENT: a corporation (a body which is legally separate from its members) is formed in one of three ways: 1) registration under the Companies Act (the normal method for commercial companies); 2) granting of a royal charter; 3) by a special Act of Parliament. A company is incorporated by drawing up a memorandum and articles of association, which are lodged with Companies House. In the UK, a company is either a private limited company (they print Ltd after their name) or a public limited company (they print Plc after their name). A company must be a Plc to obtain a Stock Exchange listing. In the USA, there is no distinction between private and public companies, and all are called 'corporations'; they put Inc. after their name

incorrect [ɪnkə'rekt] *adjective* incorrecto, -ta *or* inexacto, -ta; **the minutes of the meeting were incorrect and had to be changed** = el acta de la reunión era incorrecta y tuvo que ser modificada

◇ **incorrectly** [ɪnkə'rektli] *adverb* incorrectamente *or* erróneamente; **the package was incorrectly addressed** = el paquete llevaba una dirección incorrecta *or* equivocada

Incoterms ['ɪnkəʊtɜːmz] *noun* incoterms

> COMMENT: standard definition (by the International Chamber of Commerce) of terms (such as 'FOB' or 'cif') used in international trade

increase 1 ['ɪŋkriːs] *noun* **(a)** *(growth)* aumento *m or* subida *f or* ampliación *f or* incremento *m*; **capital increase** *or* **increase in capital** = ampliación de capital; **increase in capital expenditure** = ampliación de inversiones en activo fijo; **increase in tax** *or* **tax increase** = aumento impositivo; **increase in price** *or* **price increase** = aumento de precio; **profits showed a 10% increase** *or* **an increase of 10% on last year** = los beneficios registraron un aumento del 10% sobre el pasado año; **increase in the cost of living** = aumento del coste de la vida **(b)** *(higher salary)* aumento *or* subida *f* salarial; **increase in pay** *or* **pay increase** = subida de sueldo; **increase in salary** *or* **salary increase** = aumento de sueldo; **the government hopes to hold salary increases to 3%** = el gobierno espera que el aumento de los salarios se limite al 3%; **he had two increases last year** = tuvo dos aumentos el año pasado; **cost-of-living increase** = aumento de sueldo para compensar el aumento del coste de vida; **merit increase** = aumento salarial por méritos **(c)** **on the increase** = en aumento; **stealing in shops is on the increase** = los robos en las tiendas van en aumento **2** [ɪn'kriːs] *verb* **(a)** *(to grow bigger)* aumentar *or* ampliar *or* subir *or* acrecentarse; **profits have increased faster than the increase in the rate of inflation** = los beneficios han crecido más que la tasa de inflación; **exports to Africa have increased by more than 25%** = las exportaciones a Africa han aumentado en más de un 25%; **the price of oil has increased twice in the past week** = el precio del petróleo subió dos veces la semana pasada; **to increase in price** = aumentar *or* subir de precio; **to increase in size** *or* **in value** = aumentar de tamaño *or* valor **(b)** **the company increased his salary to £20,000** = la empresa le subió el sueldo a £20.000

◇ **increasing** [ɪn'kriːsɪŋ] *adjective* creciente *or* en aumento; **increasing profits** = beneficios crecientes; **the company has an increasing share of the market** = la sociedad tiene una creciente participación en el mercado

◇ **increasingly** [ɪn'kriːsɪŋli] *adverb* cada vez más; **the company has to depend increasingly on the export market** = la compañía tiene que depender cada vez más del mercado de exportación

> QUOTE competition is steadily increasing and could affect profit margins as the company tries to retain its market share = **Citizen (Ottawa)**

> QUOTE turnover has potential to be increased to over 1 million dollars with energetic management and very little capital
> **Australian Financial Review**

increment ['ɪŋkrɪmənt] *noun* incremento *m* salarial; **annual increment** = incremento salarial anual; **salary which rises in annual increments of £500** = salario con incrementos anuales de £500

◇ **incremental** [ɪŋkrɪ'mentl] *adjective* incremental; **incremental cost** = coste marginal *or* incremental; **incremental increase** = incremento salarial anual; **incremental scale** = escala móvil de salarios

incur [ɪn'kɜː] *verb* incurrir en; **to incur the risk of a penalty** = correr el riesgo de que le pongan a uno una multa; **to incur debts** *or* **costs** = contraer deudas *or* incurrir en gastos; **the company has incurred heavy costs to implement the expansion programme** = la empresa ha incurrido en grandes gastos para poner en práctica el programa de expansión (NOTE: **incurring - incurred**)

> QUOTE the company blames fiercely competitive market conditions in Europe for a £14m operating loss last year, incurred despite a record turnover
> **Financial Times**

indebted [ɪn'detɪd] *adjective* endeudado, -da; **to be indebted to a property company** = estar endeudado con una empresa inmobiliaria

◇ **indebtedness** [ɪn'detɪdnəs] *noun* deuda *f*; **(state of) indebtedness** = situación *f* de deuda

indemnification [ɪndemnɪfɪ'keɪʃən] *noun* indemnización *f*

◊ **indemnify** [ɪnˈdemnɪfaɪ] *verb* indemnizar; **to indemnify someone for a loss** = indemnizar a alguien por una pérdida

◊ **indemnity** [ɪnˈdemnəti] *noun* indemnidad *f or* indemnización *f*; **he had to pay an indemnity of £100** = tuvo que pagar una indemnización de £100; **letter of indemnity** = documento por el que se garantiza el pago de una indemnización

indent 1 [ˈɪndent] *noun* **(a)** *(order)* pedido *m or* orden *f* de compra de una mercancía en el extranjero; **he put in an indent for a new stock of soap** = cursó una orden de compra para importar una nueva partida de jabón **(b)** *(typing)* sangrado *m* **2** [ɪnˈdent] *verb* **(a) to indent for something** = pasar un pedido *or* pedir; **the department has indented for a new computer** = el departamento ha cursado un pedido para comprar un nuevo ordenador **(b)** *(in typing)* sangrar; **indent the first line three spaces** = sangra tres espacios en la primera línea

indenture [ɪnˈdentʃə] **1** *noun* **(a)** *(apprenticeship)* contrato *m* entre dos o más partes; **indentures** *or* **articles of indenture** = contrato *m* de aprendizaje **(b)** *US (document)* escritura de emisión de bonos **2** *verb* contratar a una persona en régimen de aprendizaje; **he was indentured to a builder** = trabajó de aprendiz para un contratista

independent [ɪndɪˈpendənt] *adjective* independiente; **independent company** = compañía independiente; **independent trader** *or* **independent shop** = comerciante *mf or* tienda *f* independiente; **the independents** = tiendas y empresas de propiedad privada

index [ˈɪndeks] **1** *noun* **(a)** *(list)* índice *m or* repertorio *m*; **card index** = fichero *m or* clasificador *m*; **index card** = ficha *or* tarjeta de fichero; **index letter** *or* **number** = letra *or* número del índice **(b)** *(statistical report)* índice *or* relación *f*; **growth index** = índice de crecimiento; **cost-of-living index** = índice del coste de la vida; **retail price index** *or US* **consumer price index** = índice de precios al consumo (IPC); **wholesale price index** = índice de precios al por mayor; **the Financial Times Index (FT index)** = índice del 'Financial Times'; **index fund** = fondo indicador; **index number** = índice (NOTE: plural is **indexes** or **indices**) **2** *verb* **(a)** *(make an index)* catalogar *or* clasificar **(b)** *(link payments to an index)* indexar *or* vincular a un índice; **indexed portfolio** = cartera de valores vinculada a un índice

◊ **indexation** [ɪndekˈseɪʃn] *noun* indexación *f or* indiciación *f*; **indexation of wage increases** = vinculación de los aumentos de sueldo al índice del coste de la vida

◊ **index-linked** [ˈɪndeksˈlɪŋkt] *adjective* ajustado, -da al coste de la vida; **index-linked pensions** = pensiones ajustadas al coste de vida; **his pension is index-linked** = su pensión está ajustada al coste de vida; **index-linked savings bonds** = obligaciones indexadas; **index-linked wage agreement** = acuerdo *or* convenio de ajuste salarial sobre el coste de vida

QUOTE the index of industrial production sank 0.2 per cent for the latest month after rising 0.3 per cent in March
Financial Times

QUOTE an analysis of the consumer price index for the first half of 1985 shows that the rate of inflation went down by 12.9 per cent
Business Times (Lagos)

India [ˈɪndjə] *noun* India *f*

◊ **Indian** [ˈɪndjən] *adjective & noun* indio, -dia *or* hindú
NOTE: capital: **New Delhi** (= Nueva Delhi); currency: **Indian rupee (Rs)** = rupia india (Rs)

indicate [ˈɪndɪkeɪt] *verb* indicar; **the latest figures indicate a fall in the inflation rate** = las últimas cifras indican una caída de la tasa de inflación; **our sales for 1994 indicate a move from the home market to exports** = nuestras ventas en 1994 indican una desviación del mercado interior hacia las exportaciones

◊ **indicator** [ˈɪndɪkeɪtə] *noun* indicador *m*; **government economic indicators** = los indicadores económicos oficiales; **leading indicator** = indicador anticipado

QUOTE it reduces this month's growth in the key M3 indicator from about 19% to 12%
Sunday Times

QUOTE we may expect the US leading economic indicators for April to show faster economic growth
Australian Financial Review

QUOTE other indicators, such as high real interest rates, suggest that monetary conditions are extremely tight
Economist

indictment [ɪnˈdaɪtmənt] *noun* acusación *f or* sumario *m*

indirect [ɪndaɪˈrekt] *adjective* indirecto, -ta; **indirect expenses** *or* **costs** = gastos *or* costes indirectos; **indirect labour costs** = costes laborales indirectos; **indirect taxation** = imposición indirecta; **the government raises more money by indirect taxation than by direct** = el gobierno consigue más dinero con los impuestos indirectos que con los directos

indispensable [ɪndɪˈspensəbl] *adjective* imprescindible *or* indispensable

individual [ɪndɪˈvɪdjʊəl] **1** *noun* individuo *m*; **savings plan made to suit the requirements of the private individual** = plan de ahorro ajustado a las exigencias personales **2** *adjective* individual; **a pension plan designed to meet each person's individual requirements** = plan de pensiones ajustado a las exigencias individuales de cada persona; **we sell individual portions of ice cream** = vendemos helado en porciones; *US* **Individual Retirement Account (IRA)** = plan de jubilación individual *or* privado

inducement [ɪnˈdjuːsmənt] *noun* estímulo *m or* incentivo *m*; **they offered him a company car as an inducement to stay** = le ofrecieron un coche de la empresa como incentivo para que se quedara

induction [ɪnˈdʌkʃən] *noun* iniciación *f or* introducción *f*; **induction courses** *or* **induction training** = cursos de iniciación *or* de introducción

industrious [ɪn'dʌstrɪəs] *adjective* aprovechado, -da *or* trabajador, -ra *or* diligente

industry ['ɪndəstri] *noun* **(a)** *(in general)* industria *f*; **all sectors of industry have shown rises in output** = todos los sectores de la industria han registrado aumentos de la producción; **basic industry** = industria básica; **a boom industry** *or* **a growth industry** = una industria en expansión; **heavy industry** = industria pesada; **light industry** = industria ligera; **primary industry** = sector primario; **secondary industry** = sector secundario; **service industry** *or* **tertiary industry** = sector servicios *or* sector terciario **(b)** *(group of companies)* industria; **the aircraft industry** = la industria aeronáutica; **the building industry** = la industria de la construcción; **the car industry** = la industria del automóvil; **the food processing industry** = la industria alimentaria; **the mining industry** = la industria minera; **the petroleum industry** = la industria petrolífera; **the tourist industry** = la industria del turismo

◊ **industrial** [ɪn'dʌstrɪəl] **1** *adjective* industrial; **industrial accident** = accidente de trabajo *or* laboral; **industrial action** = huelga; **to take industrial action** = hacer huelga *or* ir a la huelga; **industrial capacity** = capacidad industrial; **industrial centre** = centro industrial; *GB* **industrial court** *or* **industrial tribunal** = magistratura del trabajo; **industrial design** = diseño industrial; **industrial disputes** = conflictos colectivos *or* laborales; **industrial espionage** = espionaje industrial; **industrial estate** *or* **industrial park** = zona industrial *or* polígono industrial; **industrial expansion** = expansión industrial; **industrial injuries** = lesiones sufridas en un accidente laboral; **industrial processes** = procesos industriales; **industrial relations** = relaciones laborales; **good industrial relations** = buenas relaciones laborales; **industrial training** = formación *or* capacitación laboral; **land zoned for light industrial use** = terreno dividido en zonas para la industria ligera **2** *noun* **industrials** = industriales (acciones) *fpl*

◊ **industrialist** [ɪn'dʌstrɪəlɪst] *noun* industrial *mf*

◊ **industrialization** [ɪndʌstrɪəlaɪ'zeɪʃən] *noun* industrialización *f*

◊ **industrialize** [ɪn'dʌstrɪəlaɪz] *verb* industrializar; **industrialized societies** = sociedades industriales

inefficiency [ɪnɪ'fɪʃənsi] *noun* ineficacia *f* *or* ineficiencia *f* *or* incompetencia *f* *or* incapacidad *f*; **the report criticized the inefficiency of the sales staff** = el informe criticaba la ineficiencia del personal de ventas

◊ **inefficient** [ɪnɪ'fɪʃənt] *adjective* ineficaz *or* incompetente; **an inefficient sales director** = un director de ventas incompetente

ineligible [ɪn'elɪdʒɪbl] *adjective* *(not eligible)* inelegible *or* inadecuado, -da; **ineligible bills** = letras no negociables

inertia [ɪ'nɜ:ʃjə] *noun* inercia *f*; **inertia selling** = venta que se realiza mediante el envío de un artículo no solicitado para que se devuelva si no interesa

inexpensive [ɪnɪk'spensɪv] *adjective* barato, -ta *or* económico, -ca

◊ **inexpensively** [ɪnɪk'spensɪvli] *adverb* barato *or* con poco gasto

inferior [ɪn'fɪərɪə] *adjective* inferior; **inferior products** *or* **products of inferior quality** = productos inferiores *or* productos de inferior calidad

inflate [ɪn'fleɪt] *verb* **(a)** *(prices)* aumentar; **to inflate prices** = aumentar los precios exageradamente; **tourists don't want to pay inflated London prices** = los turistas no quieren pagar los precios exorbitantes de Londres **(b)** *(economy)* inflar; **to inflate the economy** = inflar la economía (aumentando la masa monetaria)

◊ **inflated** [ɪn'fleɪtɪd] *adjective* **(a)** *(prices)* elevado, -da *or* exagerado, -da; **inflated prices** = precios elevados *or* exagerados; **inflated profit forecast** = previsión de beneficios exagerada **(b)** *(currency)* inflacionista; **inflated currency** = moneda inflacionista

◊ **inflation** [ɪn'fleɪʃən] *noun* inflación *f*; **we have 15% inflation** *or* **inflation is running at 15%** = tenemos una inflación del 15% *or* la inflación alcanza el 15%; **to take measures to reduce inflation** = tomar medidas para reducir la inflación; **high interest rates tend to decrease inflation** = los tipos de interés altos tienden a disminuir la inflación; **rate of inflation** *or* **inflation rate** = tasa de inflación; **galloping inflation** *or* **runaway inflation** = inflación galopante; **spiralling inflation** = inflación en espiral

◊ **inflationary** [ɪn'fleɪʃnəri] *adjective* inflacionario, -ria *or* inflacionista; **inflationary trends in the economy** = tendencias inflacionistas de la economía; **the economy is in an inflationary spiral** = la economía está en una espiral inflacionaria; **anti-inflationary measures** = medidas antiinflacionarias

◊ **inflation-proof** [ɪn'fleɪʃn 'pru:f] *adjective* a prueba de inflación

COMMENT: the inflation rate in the UK is calculated on a series of figures, including prices of consumer items; petrol, gas and electricity; interest rates, etc. This gives the 'underlying' inflation rate which can be compared to that of other countries. The calculation can also include mortgage interest and local taxes which give the 'headline' inflation figure; this is higher than in other countries because of these extra items. Inflation affects businesses, in that as their costs rise, so their profits may fall and it is necessary to take this into account when pricing products

QUOTE inflationary expectations fell somewhat this month, but remained a long way above the actual inflation rate, according to figures released yesterday. The annual rate of inflation measured by the consumer price index has been below 2 per cent for over 18 months
Australian Financial Review

QUOTE the retail prices index rose 0.4 per cent in the month, taking the annual headline inflation rate to 1.7 per cent. The underlying inflation rate, which excludes mortgage interest payments, increased to an annual rate of 3.1 per cent
Times

QUOTE the decision by the government to tighten monetary policy will push the annual inflation rate above the year's previous high
Financial Times

QUOTE when you invest to get a return, you want a 'real' return - above the inflation rate
Investors Chronicle

QUOTE for now, inflation signals are mixed. The consumer price index jumped 0.7% in April; the core rate of inflation, which excludes food and energy, has stayed steady during the past six months
Business Week

inflow ['ɪnfləʊ] *noun* afluencia *f or* entrada *f*; **inflow of capital into the country** = la afluencia de capitales al país

QUOTE the dollar is strong because of capital inflows rather than weak because of the trade deficit
Duns Business Month

influence ['ɪnfluəns] **1** *noun* influencia *f*; **the price of oil has a marked influence on the price of manufactured goods** = el precio del petróleo tiene una notable influencia sobre el precio de los productos manufacturados; **we are suffering from the influence of a high exchange rate** = estamos padeciendo la influencia de un tipo de cambio alto **2** *verb* influir *or* influenciar; **the board was influenced in its decision by the memo from the managers** = el consejo de administración tomó una decisión influida por el memorandum de los directores; **the price of oil has influenced the price of manufactured goods** = el precio del petróleo ha influido en el precio de los productos manufacturados; **high inflation is influencing our profitability** = la alta inflación influye sobre nuestra rentabilidad

influx ['ɪnflʌks] *noun* afluencia *f or* entrada *f*; **an influx of foreign currency into the country** = la afluencia de divisas al país; **an influx of cheap labour into the cities** = la afluencia de mano de obra barata a las ciudades (NOTE: plural is **influxes**)

QUOTE the retail sector will also benefit from the expected influx of tourists
Australian Financial Review

inform [ɪn'fɔːm] *verb* informar *or* comunicar; **I**

regret to inform you that your tender was not acceptable = lamento tener que informarle que su oferta no ha sido aceptada; **we are pleased to inform you that your offer has been accepted** = tenemos el placer de comunicarle que su oferta ha sido aceptada; **we have been informed by the Department of Trade that new tariffs are coming into force** = el Ministerio de Comercio nos ha comunicado que van a entrar en vigor nuevas tarifas

◇ **information** [ɪnfə'meɪʃən] *noun* **(a)** *(details)* información *f*; **please send me information on** *or* **about holidays in the USA** = le ruego me envíe información sobre vacaciones en los EE UU; **have you any information on** *or* **about deposit accounts?** = ¿tiene Vd. información sobre las cuentas de depósito?; **I enclose this leaflet for your information** = le remito este folleto adjunto para su información; **to disclose a piece of information** = revelar una información; **to answer a request for information** = contestar a una solicitud de información; **for further information, please write to Department 27** = para más información escribir a la sección 27; **disclosure of confidential information** = revelación de información confidencial; **flight information** = información de vuelos; **tourist information** = información turística **(b) information technology (IT)** = informática *f*; **information retrieval** = recuperación de datos **(c) information bureau** *or* **information office** = oficina de información; **information officer** = documentalista *or* empleado, -da del servicio de información (NOTE: no plural: for one item say **a piece of information**)

infrastructure ['ɪnfrəstrʌktʃə] *noun* **(a)** *(basic structure)* infraestructura *f*; **the company's infrastructure** = la infraestructura de la compañía **(b)** *(basic services)* infraestructura; **the country's infrastructure** = la infraestructura del país

infringe [ɪn'frɪn(d)ʒ] *verb* infringir *or* violar; **to infringe a copyright** = infringir los derechos de autor; **to infringe a patent** = violar una patente

◇ **infringement** [ɪn'frɪn(d)ʒmənt] *noun* infracción *f or* violación *f*; **infringement of copyright** *or* **copyright infringement** = violación de los derechos de autor; **infringement of customs regulations** = infracción aduanera; **infringement of patent** *or* **patent infringement** = violación de patente

ingot ['ɪŋgət] *noun* lingote *m or* barra *f*

inherit [ɪn'herɪt] *verb* heredar; **when her father died she inherited the shop** = cuando murió su padre, heredó la tienda; **he inherited £10,000 from his grandfather** = heredó £10.000 de su abuelo

◇ **inheritance** [ɪn'herɪtəns] *noun* herencia *f*; **inheritance tax** = impuesto sobre sucesiones

in-house ['ɪnhaʊs] *adverb & adjective* interno, -na *or* de la casa *or* en la empresa; **the in-house staff** = el personal de la casa; **we do all our data processing in-house** = efectuamos todo el proceso de datos en la empresa; **in-house training** = formación en el puesto de trabajo

initial [ɪ'nɪʃəl] **1** *adjective* inicial *or* primero, -ra; **initial capital** = capital inicial; **he started the business with an initial expenditure** *or* **initial investment of £500** = comenzó el negocio con unos gastos iniciales *or* una inversión inicial de £500; **initial sales** = ventas iniciales; **the initial response to the TV advertising has been very good** = la reacción inicial a la publicidad en televisión ha sido muy buena **2** *noun* **initials** = iniciales *fpl or* siglas *fpl*; **what do the initials IMF stand for?** = ¿qué significan las siglas IMF?; **the chairman wrote his initials by each alteration in the contract he was signing** = el presidente marcó con sus iniciales todas las ·modificaciones efectuadas en el contrato que firmó **3** *verb* poner las iniciales a *or* firmar con las iniciales *or* rubricar; **to initial an amendment to a contract** = marcar con las iniciales la enmienda de un contrato; **please initial the agreement at the place marked with an X** = le ruego firme con sus iniciales el acuerdo en el lugar señalado con una X

initiate [ɪ'nɪʃɪeɪt] *verb* iniciar; **to initiate discussions** = iniciar conversaciones

◊ **initiative** [ɪ'nɪʃɪətɪv] *noun* iniciativa *f*; **to take the initiative** = tomar la iniciativa; **to follow up an initiative** = seguir una iniciativa

inject [ɪn'dʒekt] *verb* **to inject capital into a business** inyectar capital en un negocio

◊ **injection** [ɪn'dʒekʃən] *noun* **a capital injection of £100,000** *or* **an injection of £100,000 capital** = una inyección de capital de £100.000

injunction [ɪn'dʒʌŋ(k)ʃən] *noun* mandato *m* judicial *or* requerimiento *m* judicial; **he got an injunction preventing the company from selling his car** = consiguió un mandato judicial para impedir que la empresa vendiera su coche; **the company applied for an injunction to stop their rival from marketing a similar product** = la empresa solicitó un requerimiento judicial para evitar que su competidor comerciara con un producto similar

injure ['ɪn(d)ʒə] *verb* herir *or* dañar; **two workers were injured in the fire** = dos trabajadores resultaron heridos en el incendio

◊ **injured party** ['ɪn(d)ʒəd 'pɑːtɪ] *noun* la parte *f* perjudicada

◊ **injury** ['ɪn(d)ʒərɪ] *noun* herida *f or* lesión *f*; **injury benefit** = indemnización por lesiones; **industrial injuries** = lesiones sufridas en un accidente laboral

injustice [ɪn'dʒʌstɪs] *noun* injusticia *f*

ink [ɪŋk] *noun* tinta *f*

◊ **inking pad** ['ɪŋkɪŋ 'pæd] *noun* tampón *m* para entintar

inland ['ɪnlənd] *adjective* **(a)** *(inside a country)* interior *or* nacional; **inland postage** = correo interior; **inland freight charges** = coste del flete interior; *US* **inland carrier** = transportista del interior *or* nacional **(b)** *GB* **the Inland Revenue** = el

fisco *or* Hacienda *f* Pública; **he received a letter from the Inland Revenue** = recibió una carta de Hacienda (NOTE: US equivalent is **Internal Revenue Service (IRS)**

innovate ['ɪnəveɪt] *verb* innovar

◊ **innovation** [ɪnə'veɪʃən] *noun* innovación *f*

◊ **innovative** ['ɪnəveɪtɪv] *adjective* innovador, -ra

◊ **innovator** ['ɪnəveɪtə] *noun* innovador, -ra

input ['ɪnpʊt] **1** *noun* **(a)** *(putting in)* entrada *f or* 'input' *m*; **input of information** *or* **computer input** = entrada *f* de información *or* 'input' *m*; **input lead** = cable de alimentación eléctrica **(b)** *(VAT regulations)* **inputs** = inversión *f or* capital *m* invertido; **input tax** = IVA (sobre los bienes y servicios adquiridos por una empresa) **2** *verb* **to input information** = introducir datos al ordenador (NOTE: **inputting - inputted**)

inquire [ɪŋ'kwaɪə] *verb* pedir información *or* preguntar; **he inquired if anything was wrong** = preguntó si algo iba mal; **she inquired about the mortgage rate** = pidió información sobre el tipo de interés de la hipoteca; **'inquire within'** = 'razón aquí'

◊ **inquire into** [ɪŋ'kwaɪə 'ɪntʊ] *verb* investigar *or* hacer investigaciones sobre algo; **we are inquiring into the background of the new supplier** = estamos investigando los antecedentes del nuevo proveedor

◊ **inquiry** [ɪŋ'kwaɪərɪ] *noun* petición *f* de informes *or* investigación *f or* pregunta *f*; **I refer to your inquiry of May 25th** = con referencia a su petición del 25 de mayo; **all inquiries should be addressed to the secretary** = para obtener información diríjanse al secretario

inquorate [ɪn'kwɔːreɪt] *adjective* asistencia insuficiente

insert 1 ['ɪnsɜːt] *noun* encarte *m*; **an insert in a magazine mailing** *or* **a magazine insert** = encarte dentro de una revista **2** [ɪn'sɜːt] *verb* insertar *or* introducir *or* intercalar; **to insert a clause into a contract** = introducir una cláusula en un contrato; **to insert a publicity piece into a magazine mailing** = insertar *or* poner un anuncio en una revista

inside [ɪn'saɪd] **1** *adjective & adverb* en la propia empresa *or* casa; **we do all our design work inside** = hacemos todo el diseño en la propia empresa; **inside worker** = empleado de oficina *or* fábrica; **inside information** = información privilegiada **2** *preposition* en *or* dentro de; **there was nothing inside the container** = no había nada dentro del contenedor; **we have a contact inside our rival's production department who gives us very useful information** = tenemos un contacto en el departamento de producción de la competencia que nos da información muy útil

◊ **insider** [ɪn'saɪdə] *noun* iniciado *m*; **insider**

dealings _or_ **insider trading** = información privilegiada (transacciones bursátiles realizadas por un iniciado)

insolvent [ɪn'sɒlvənt] _adjective_ insolvente; **he was declared insolvent** = se le declaró insolvente

◊ **insolvency** [ɪn'sɒlvənsi] _noun_ insolvencia _f_; **he was in a state of insolvency** = estaba en situación de insolvencia

COMMENT: a company is insolvent when its liabilities are higher than its assets; if this happens it must cease trading

inspect [ɪn'spekt] _verb_ inspeccionar _or_ revisar _or_ examinar; **to inspect a machine** _or_ **an installation** = revisar una máquina _or_ inspeccionar una instalación; **to inspect the accounts** = revisar las cuentas; **to inspect products for defects** = controlar la calidad del producto

◊ **inspection** [ɪn'spekʃən] _noun_ inspección _f or_ examen _m_; **to make an inspection** _or_ **to carry out an inspection of a machine** _or_ **an installation** = efectuar una inspección _or_ llevar a cabo la revisión de una máquina _or_ una inspección de una instalación; **inspection of a product for defects** = control de la calidad de un producto; **to carry out a tour of inspection** = llevar a cabo una visita de inspección; **VAT inspection** = inspección del IVA; **to issue an inspection order** = dar una orden de inspección; **inspection stamp** = sello de inspección

◊ **inspector** [ɪn'spektə] _noun_ inspector, -ra; **inspector of factories** _or_ **factory inspector** = inspector de fábricas; **inspector of taxes** _or_ **tax inspector** = inspector de Hacienda; **inspector of weights and measures** = inspector de pesos y medidas

◊ **inspectorate** [ɪn'spektərət] _noun_ cuerpo _m_ de inspectores; **the factory inspectorate** = cuerpo de inspectores de fábricas

inst [ɪnst] = INSTANT **your letter of the 6th inst** = su carta del 6 del corriente _or_ de los corrientes

instability [ɪnstə'bɪlɪti] _noun_ inestabilidad _f_; **period of instability in the money markets** = periodo de inestabilidad en los mercados monetarios

install [ɪn'stɔːl] _verb_ instalar; **to install new machinery** = instalar nueva maquinaria; **to install a new data processing system** = instalar un nuevo sistema de procesamiento de datos

◊ **installation** [ɪnstə'leɪʃən] _noun_ **(a)** _(machine)_ instalación _f_; **harbour installations** = instalaciones portuarias; **the fire seriously damaged the oil installations** = el incendio causó graves daños a las instalaciones petrolíferas **(b)** _(action)_ instalación; **to supervise the installation of new equipment** = supervisar la instalación de nuevo equipo

◊ **instalment** _or US_ **installment** [ɪn'stɔːlmənt] _noun_ plazo _m_; **the first instalment is payable on signature of the agreement** = el primer plazo se paga al firmar el contrato; **the final instalment is now due** = el último plazo ha vencido ya; **to pay £25 down and monthly instalments of £20** = pagar una entrada de £25 y el resto en mensualidades de £20; **to miss an instalment** = no pagar _or_ saltarse un plazo

◊ **installment plan** _or_ **installment sales** _or_ **installment buying** [ɪn'stɔːlmənt 'plæn _or_ 'seɪlz _or_ 'baɪɪŋ] _noun US_ venta _f or_ compra _f_ a plazos; **to**

buy a car on the installment plan = comprar un coche a plazos (NOTE: the British English equivalent is **hire purchase or HP**)

instance ['ɪnstəns] _noun_ ejemplo _m or_ caso _m_; **in this instance we will overlook the delay** = esta vez pasaremos por alto el retraso

instant ['ɪnstənt] _adjective_ **(a)** _(immediately available)_ inmediato, -ta _or_ instantáneo, -nea; **instant credit** = crédito instantáneo **(b)** _(this month)_ del presente mes _or_ de los corrientes _or_ del actual; **our letter of the 6th instant** = nuestra carta del 6 del corriente _or_ de los corrientes

instigate ['ɪnstɪgeɪt] _verb_ incitar

institute ['ɪnstɪtjuːt] **1** _noun_ **(a)** _(official organization)_ instituto _m_; **research institute** = instituto de investigación **(b)** _(professional body)_ asociación _f or_ colegio _m or_ instituto _m_; **Institute of Chartered Accountants** = Colegio de Censores Públicos **2** _verb_ entablar _or_ iniciar _or_ incoar; **to institute proceedings against someone** = entablar un proceso contra alguien _or_ llevar a alguien a juicio

◊ **institution** [ɪnstɪ'tjuːʃən] _noun_ institución _f_; **financial institution** = institución financiera

◊ **institutional** [ɪnstɪ'tjuːʃənl] _adjective_ institucional; **institutional buying** _or_ **selling** = compra _or_ venta institucional; **institutional investors** = inversores institucionales

QUOTE during the 1970s commercial property was regarded by big institutional investors as an alternative to equities
Investors Chronicle

instruct [ɪn'strʌkt] _verb_ **(a)** _(to give an order)_ dar instrucciones _or_ ordenar _or_ mandar; **to instruct someone to do something** = dar instrucciones a alguien para que haga algo; **he instructed the credit controller to take action** = dio instrucciones al director de ventas a crédito para que tomara medidas **(b)** _(teach)_ enseñar **(c)** _(solicitor)_ **to instruct a solicitor** = contratar a un abogado _or_ dar instrucciones al abogado para que proceda judicialmente

◊ **instruction** [ɪn'strʌkʃən] _noun_ instrucción _f or_ consigna _f_; **he gave instructions to his stockbroker to sell the shares immediately** = dio instrucciones a su agente de bolsa para que vendiera las acciones inmediatamente; **to await instructions** = esperar instrucciones; **to issue instructions** = dar instrucciones; **in accordance with** _or_ **according to instructions** = con arreglo a _or_ conforme a _or_ según las instrucciones recibidas; **failing instructions to the contrary** = salvo instrucciones contrarias; **forwarding instructions** = instrucciones de envío; **shipping instructions** = instrucciones de envío

◊ **instructor** [ɪn'strʌktə] _noun_ instructor, -ra _or_ monitor, -ra

instrument ['ɪnstrʊmənt] _noun_ **(a)** _(device)_ instrumento _m_; **the technician brought instruments to measure the output of electricity** = el técnico trajo instrumentos para medir la potencia eléctrica generada **(b)** _(document)_ instrumento _m or_ documento *m* escrito; **financial instrument** = instrumento *or* documento financiero; **negotiable instrument** = instrumento negociable

insufficient [ɪnsə'fɪʃənt] *adjective* insuficiente; **insufficient funds** = saldo insuficiente

insure [ɪn'ʃʊə] *verb* asegurar; **to insure a house against fire** = asegurar una casa contra incendios; **to insure someone's life** = hacer un seguro de vida a alguien; **he was insured for £100,000** = estaba asegurado por £100.000; **to insure baggage against loss** = asegurar el equipaje contra robos y pérdidas; **to insure against bad weather** = asegurarse contra el mal tiempo; **to insure against loss of earnings** = asegurarse contra la pérdida de ingresos

◊ **insurable** [ɪn'ʃʊərəbl] *adjective* asegurable

◊ **insurance** [ɪn'ʃʊərəns] *noun* **(a)** *(premium)* seguro *m*; **to take out an insurance against fire** = hacerse un seguro contra incendios; **to take out an insurance on the house** = hacer un seguro de la casa; **the damage is covered by the insurance** = los daños están cubiertos por el seguro; **repairs will be paid for by the insurance** = el seguro se hará cargo de las reparaciones; **to pay the insurance on a car** = pagar el seguro de un coche **(b) accident insurance** = seguro de accidentes; **car insurance** *or* **motor insurance** = seguro de automóviles; **comprehensive insurance** = seguro a todo riesgo; **endowment insurance** = seguro total *or* mixto; **fire insurance** = seguro contra incendios; **general insurance** = seguro general; **house insurance** = seguro de la vivienda; **life insurance** = seguro de vida; **medical insurance** = seguro médico; **term insurance** = seguro temporal; **third-party insurance** = seguro contra terceros; **whole-life insurance** = seguro de vida ordinario (en oposición al seguro temporal) **(c) insurance agent** *or* **insurance broker** = agente *mf* *or* corredor *m* de seguros; **insurance certificate** = certificado de seguro; **insurance claim** = declaración *f* de siniestro; **insurance company** = compañía *f* de seguros; **insurance contract** = contrato *m* de seguros; **insurance cover** = cobertura *f* del seguro; **insurance policy** = póliza *f* de seguros; **insurance premium** = prima *f* de seguros **(d)** *GB* **National Insurance** = Seguridad *f* Social; **National Insurance contributions (NIC)** = cuotas de la seguridad social

◊ **insured** [ɪn'ʃʊəd] *adjective* asegurado, -da; **the life insured** = la persona asegurada *or* el asegurado *or* la asegurada; **the sum insured** = la cantidad asegurada

◊ **insurer** [ɪn'ʃʊərə] *noun* asegurador, -ra (NOTE: for life insurance, GB English prefers to use **assurance, assure, assurer**)

intangible [ɪn'tæn(d)ʒəbl] *adjective* intangible; **intangible assets** = activo intangible; **intangible fixed assets** = activos fijos intangibles

integrate ['ɪntɪgreɪt] *verb* integrar

◊ **integration** [ɪntɪ'greɪʃən] *noun* integración *f*; **horizontal integration** = integración horizontal; **vertical integration** = integración vertical

intellectual property [ɪnte'lektjʊəl 'prɒpəti] *noun* propiedad intelectual

intend [ɪn'tend] *verb* tener la intención *or* el propósito de hacer algo; **the company intends to open an office in New York next year** = la compañía tiene en proyecto abrir una oficina en Nueva York el próximo año; **we intend to offer jobs to 250 unemployed young people** = tenemos la intención de ofrecer puestos de trabajo a 250 jóvenes desempleados

intensive [ɪn'tensɪv] *adjective* intensivo, -va; **intensive farming** = cultivo intensivo; **capital-intensive industry** = industria con alto coeficiente de capital; **labour-intensive industry** = industria que emplea mucha mano de obra

intent [ɪn'tent] *noun* intención *f*; **letter of intent** = carta *f* de intención

inter- ['ɪntə] *prefix* inter *or* entre; **inter-bank loan** = préstamo interbancario; **the inter-city rail services are good** = los servicios de trenes interurbanos son buenos; **inter-company dealings** = operaciones entre compañías; **inter-company comparisons** = estudios comparativos *or* comparaciones entre compañías

interest ['ɪntrəst] **1** *noun* **(a)** *(special attention)* interés *m*; **the MD takes no interest in the staff club** = el director gerente no se interesa en absoluto *or* no tiene ningún interés por el club de los empleados; **the buyers showed a lot of interest in our new product range** = los compradores mostraron un gran interés por nuestra nueva gama de productos **(b)** *(payment by a borrower)* interés; **simple interest** = interés simple; **compound interest** = interés compuesto; **accrual of interest** = acumulación *f* de interés; **accrued interest** = interés acumulado *or* devengado; **back interest** = interés atrasado; **fixed interest** = interés fijo; **high** *or* **low interest** = interés elevado *or* bajo; **interest charges** = cargos *mpl* en concepto de interés; **interest rate** *or* **rate of interest** = tipo *m* *or* tasa *f* de interés; **interest-free credit** *or* **loan** = crédito *m* *or* préstamo *m* libre de interés *or* sin intereses; **the company gives its staff interest-free loans** = la compañía concede a sus empleados préstamos sin interés **(c)** *(money paid as income on investments)* interés *or* rédito *m*; **the bank pays 10% interest on deposits** = el banco paga un 10% de interés sobre las imposiciones a plazo fijo; **to receive interest at 5%** = recibir un interés del 5%; **the loan pays 5% interest** = el préstamo paga un 5% de interés; **deposit which yields** *or* **gives** *or* **produces** *or* **bears 5% interest** = imposición que rinde *or* da *or* devenga un 5% de interés; **account which earns interest at 10%** *or* **which earns 10% interest** = cuenta que devenga un 10% de interés; **interest-bearing deposits** = depósitos con interés *or* que producen intereses; **fixed-interest investments** = inversiones a interés fijo **(d)** *(money invested)* interés *or* participación *f*; **beneficial interest** = derecho *m* de usufructo; **he has a controlling interest in the company** = tiene un interés mayoritario *or* una participación mayoritaria en la compañía; **life interest** = renta vitalicia; **majority interest** *or* **minority interest** = interés *or* participación mayoritaria *or* minoritaria; **he has a majority interest in a supermarket chain** = tiene una participación mayoritaria en una cadena de supermercados; **to acquire a substantial interest in the company** = adquirir una parte importante de las acciones de la compañía; **to declare an interest** = declarar una participación en una compañía **2** *verb* interesar; **he tried to interest several companies in**

his new invention = intentó interesar a varias compañías en su nuevo invento; **interested in** = interesado, -da en; **the managing director is interested only in increasing profitability** = el director gerente sólo está interesado en aumentar la rentabilidad

◊ **interested party** ['ɪntrestɪd 'pɑ:ti] *noun* parte interesada

◊ **interesting** ['ɪntrəstɪŋ] *adjective* interesante; **they made us a very interesting offer for the factory** = nos hicieron una oferta muy interesante por la fábrica

> QUOTE since last summer American interest rates have dropped by between three and four percentage points
> **Sunday Times**

> QUOTE a lot of money is said to be tied up in sterling because of the interest-rate differential between US and British rates
> **Australian Financial Review**

interface ['ɪntəfeɪs] **1** *noun* superficie *f* de contacto *or* interfaz *m or* acoplamiento *m or* conexión *f* **2** *verb* conectar; **the office micros interface with the mainframe computer at head office** = los microordenadores de la oficina están conectados con la unidad central del ordenador de la oficina principal

interfere [ɪntə'fɪə] *verb* entrometerse *or* interferir

◊ **interference** [ɪntə'fɪərəns] *noun* intromisión *f or* injerencia *f*; **the sales department complained of continual interference from the accounts department** = el departamento de ventas se quejó de la continua injerencia del departamento de contabilidad

interim ['ɪntərɪm] *noun* **interim dividend** = dividendo *m* provisional; **interim payment** = pago *m* a cuenta; **interim report** = informe *m* provisional; **in the interim** = en el ínterin *or* entretanto

> QUOTE the company plans to keep its annual dividend unchanged at Y7.5 per share, which includes a Y3.75 interim payout
> **Financial Times**

interior [ɪn'tɪərɪə] *noun* interior *m*

intermediary [ɪntə'mi:djəri] *noun* intermediario, -ria *or* agente *mf* mediador, -ra; **he refused to act as an intermediary between the two directors** = se negó a desempeñar el papel de intermediario entre los dos consejeros; **financial intermediary** = agente de finanzas *or* sociedad financiera

> COMMENT: any institution which takes deposits or loans from individuals and lends money to clients, or which arranges insurance for a client, but is not itself an insurance company. Banks, building societies, hire purchase companies are all types of financial intermediaries

internal [ɪn'tɜ:nl] *adjective* **(a)** *(inside a company)* interno, -na *or* interior; **we decided to make an internal appointment** = decidimos nombrar a alguien de la casa; **internal audit** = auditoría interna; **internal audit department** = departamento de auditoría interna; **internal auditor** = auditor interno; **internal telephone** = teléfono interno **(b)** *(inside a country)* interior; **an internal flight** = vuelo del interior; *US* **Internal Revenue Service (IRS)** =

fisco *m or* Hacienda Pública *f* (NOTE: the British equivalent is the **Inland Revenue**) **internal trade** = comercio interior

◊ **internally** [ɪn'tɜ:nəli] *adverb* internamente; **the job was advertised internally** = el trabajo fue anunciado de puertas adentro

international [ɪntə'næʃənl] *adjective* internacional; **international call** = llamada internacional; **international dialling code** = código de llamadas internacionales; **international direct dialling (IDD)** = llamada internacional directa; **international law** = derecho internacional; **international (postal) reply coupon** = cupón-respuesta internacional; **he enclosed an international reply coupon with his letter** = remitió un cupón-respuesta internacional en su carta; **international trade** = comercio internacional; **International Trade Centre** = Centro de Comercio internacional

◊ **International Labour Organization (ILO)** [ɪntə'næʃənl 'leɪbə ɔ:gənaɪ'zeɪʃn] *noun* Organización Internacional del Trabajo (OIT)

◊ **International Monetary Fund (IMF)** [ɪntə'næʃənl 'mʌnɪtri 'fʌnd] *noun* Fondo Monetario Internacional (FMI)

◊ **internationalization** [ɪntənæʃənəlaɪ'zeɪʃn] *noun* internacionalización *f*

interpret [ɪn'tɜ:prɪt] *verb* interpretar; **my assistant knows Greek, so he will interpret for us** = mi ayudante sabe griego, así que nos servirá de intérprete

◊ **interpreter** [ɪn'tɜ:prɪtə] *noun* intérprete *mf*; **my secretary will act as interpreter** = mi secretaria actuará de intérprete

interruption [ɪntə'rʌpʃn] *noun* interrupción *f*; **she worked for five hours without interruption** = trabajó cinco horas sin interrupción

interstate ['ɪntəsteɪt] *adjective* interestatal; *US* **Interstate Commerce Commission (ICC)** = Comisión de Comercio Interestatal

intervene [ɪntə'vi:n] *verb* intervenir *or* mediar; **to intervene in a dispute** = intervenir en una disputa *or* conflicto; **the central bank intervened to support the dollar** = el banco central intervino para respaldar el dólar; **to intervene on someone's behalf** = mediar en favor de alguien

◊ **intervention** [ɪntə'venʃn] *noun* intervención *f*; **the government's intervention in the foreign exchange markets** = la intervención del gobierno en los mercados de divisas; **the central bank's intervention in the banking crisis** = la intervención del banco central en la crisis bancaria; **the government's intervention in the labour dispute** = la intervención del gobierno en el conflicto laboral; *(in the EU)* **intervention price** = precio de intervención

interview ['ɪntəvju:] **1** *noun* **(a)** *(for a job)* entrevista *f*; **we called six people for interview** = llamamos a seis personas para la entrevista; **I have an interview next week** *or* **I am going for an interview next week** = tengo una entrevista la semana que viene **(b)** *(opinion poll)* entrevista **2** *verb* **(a)** *(for a job)* entrevistar; **we interviewed ten candidates, but did not find anyone suitable** =

entrevistamos a diez candidatos pero no encontramos a ninguno apropiado **(b)** *(on radio or TV)* entrevistar

◊ **interviewee** ['ɪntəvju:'iː] *noun* entrevistado, -da

◊ **interviewer** ['ɪntəvju:ə] *noun* entrevistador, -ra

inter vivos ['ɪntə 'vaɪvəs] *Latin phrase meaning 'between living people'* **gift inter vivos** = donación *f* inter vivos

intestate [ɪn'testət] *adjective* **to die intestate** = morir intestado *or* ab intestato

◊ **intestacy** [ɪn'testəsi] *noun* falta de testamento

COMMENT: when someone dies intestate, the property automatically goes to the parents or siblings of an unmarried person or, if married, to the surviving partner, unless there are children

in transit ['ɪn 'trænzɪt] *adverb* **goods in transit** = mercancías *fpl* en tránsito

in tray ['ɪntreɪ] *noun* bandeja *f* de entrada *or* de documentos por despachar

introduce [ɪntrə'dju:s] *verb* **(a)** *(put forward)* presentar; **to introduce a client** = presentar a un cliente; **to introduce a new product on the market** = presentar un nuevo producto en el mercado **(b)** *(put in use)* introducir; **the new safety measures were introduced gradually** = las nuevas medidas de seguridad fueron introducidas gradualmente

◊ **introduction** [ɪntrə'dʌkʃən] *noun* **(a)** *(letter)* carta *f* de presentación; **I'll give you an introduction to the MD - he is an old friend of mine** = te daré una carta de presentación para el director gerente, es un viejo amigo mío **(b)** *(bringing into use)* introducción *f* *or* presentación *f*; **the introduction of new technology** = la introducción de nueva tecnología

◊ **introductory** [ɪntrə'dʌktəri] *adjective* de presentación; **introductory offer** = oferta de lanzamiento

invalid [ɪn'vælɪd] *adjective* nulo, -la *or* inválido, -da; **permit that is invalid** = permiso nulo; **claim which has been declared invalid** = demanda declarada nula

◊ **invalidate** [ɪn'vælɪdeɪt] *verb* anular *or* invalidar; **because the company has been taken over, the contract has been invalidated** = como la empresa ha cambiado de dueño el contrato ha sido anulado

◊ **invalidation** [ɪnvælɪ'deɪʃən] *noun* anulación *f* *or* invalidación *f*

◊ **invalidity** [ɪnvə'lɪdəti] *noun* invalidez *f* *or* nulidad *f*; **the invalidity of the contract** = la nulidad del contrato

invent [ɪn'vent] *verb* inventar; **she invented a new type of computer terminal** = inventó un nuevo tipo de terminal de ordenadores; **who invented shorthand?** = ¿quién inventó la taquigrafía?; **the chief accountant has invented a new system of customer filing** = el jefe de contabilidad ha inventado un nuevo sistema de clasificación de clientes

◊ **invention** [ɪn'venʃən] *noun* invento *m* *or*

invención *f*; **he tried to sell his latest invention to a US car manufacturer** = intentó vender su último invento a un fabricante de coches estadounidense

◊ **inventor** [ɪn'ventə] *noun* inventor, -ra; **he is the inventor of the all-plastic car** = es el inventor del coche fabricado enteramente de plástico

inventory ['ɪnvəntri] **1** *noun* **(a)** *(stock)* existencias *fpl*; **to carry a high inventory** = tener muchas existencias; **to aim to reduce inventory** = tratar de reducir las existencias; **inventory control** = control *m* de inventario *or* comprobación *f* de las existencias; **to draw up an inventory** = inventariar *or* hacer un inventario (NOTE: the word 'inventory' is used in the USA where British English uses the word 'stock'. So, the American 'inventory control' is 'stock control' in British English) **(b)** *(list of contents)* inventario *m*; **to draw up an inventory of fixtures** = hacer un inventario de las instalaciones fijas; **to agree the inventory** = estar de acuerdo con el inventario **2** *verb* inventariar *or* hacer un inventario

QUOTE a warehouse needs to tie up less capital in inventory and with its huge volume spreads out costs over bigger sales
Duns Business Month

invest [ɪn'vest] *verb* invertir; **he invested all his money in an engineering business** = invirtió todo su dinero en una empresa de ingeniería; **she was advised to invest in real estate** *or* **in government bonds** = le aconsejaron que invirtiera en bienes inmuebles *or* en títulos de la deuda del Estado; **to invest abroad** = invertir en el extranjero; **to invest money in new machinery** = invertir dinero en nueva maquinaria; **to invest capital in a new factory** = invertir capital en una fábrica nueva

◊ **investment** [ɪn'ves(t)mənt] *noun* **(a)** *(increase in value)* inversión *f*; **they called for more government investment in new industries** = exigieron que el Estado invirtiera más en nuevas industrias; **investment in real estate** = inversión inmobiliaria; **to make investments in oil companies** = hacer inversiones en compañías petrolíferas; **return on investment (ROI)** = rendimiento *m* de la inversión; **long-term investment** *or* **short-term investment** = inversión a largo plazo *or* inversión a corto plazo; **safe investment** = inversión segura; **blue-chip investments** = inversiones en valores de la máxima confianza; **quoted investments** = inversiones en acciones cotizadas en bolsa; **he is trying to protect his investments** = intenta proteger sus inversiones **(b)** **investment adviser** = asesor, -ra de inversiones; **investment company** *or* **investment trust** = sociedad *f* de inversiones; **investment grant** = ayudas *fpl* *or* incentivos *mpl* a la inversión; **investment income** = renta *f* de inversiones

◊ **investor** [ɪn'vestə] *noun* inversor, -ra *or* inversionista *mf*; **the small investor** *or* **the private investor** = el pequeño inversor *or* el inversor privado; **the institutional investor** = el inversor institucional

QUOTE we have substantial venture capital to invest in good projects
Times

> QUOTE investment trusts, like unit trusts, consist of portfolios of shares and therefore provide a spread of investments
>
> **Investors Chronicle**

> QUOTE investment companies took the view that prices had reached rock bottom and could only go up
>
> **Lloyd's List**

investigate [ɪn'vestɪgeɪt] *verb* investigar *or* estudiar

◊ **investigation** [ɪnvestɪ'geɪʃən] *noun* investigación *f or* estudio *m*; **to conduct an investigation into irregularities in share dealings** = dirigir una investigación sobre posibles irregularidades en la venta de acciones

◊ **investigator** [ɪn'vestɪgeɪtə] *noun* investigador, -ra; **government investigator** = investigador oficial

invisible [ɪn'vɪzəbl] **1** *adjective* **invisible assets** = activo invisible; **invisible earnings** = ingresos invisibles *or* por exportaciones invisibles; **invisible imports** *or* **exports** = importaciones y exportaciones invisibles; **invisible trade** = comercio de invisibles **2** *plural noun* **invisibles** = importaciones y exportaciones *fpl* invisibles

invite [ɪn'vaɪt] *verb* invitar; **to invite someone to an interview** = invitar a alguien a una entrevista; **to invite someone to join the board** = invitar a alguien a formar parte del consejo; **to invite shareholders to subscribe a new issue** = invitar a los accionistas a suscribir nuevas acciones; **to invite tenders for a contract** = sacar un contrato a licitación *or* concurso

◊ **invitation** [ɪnvɪ'teɪʃən] *noun* invitación *f*; **invitation card** = tarjeta de invitación; **to issue an invitation to someone to join the board** = extender una invitación a alguien para que forme parte del consejo de administración; **invitation to tender for a contract** = concurso *m* público; **invitation to subscribe a new issue** = oferta para suscribir nuevas acciones

invoice ['ɪnvɔɪs] **1** *noun* **(a)** *(payment)* factura *f*; **your invoice dated November 10th** = su factura del 10 de noviembre; **they sent in their invoice six weeks late** = presentaron la factura con seis semanas de retraso; **to make out an invoice for £250** = hacer una factura por un importe de £250; **to settle** *or* **to pay an invoice** = saldar *or* pagar una factura; **the total is payable within thirty days of invoice** = importe pagadero en el plazo de treinta días a partir de la fecha de la factura; **VAT invoice** = factura con el IVA incluido **(b)** *invoice clerk* = empleado que confecciona las facturas; **invoice price** = precio facturado; **total invoice value** = valor total de factura **2** *verb* facturar *or* pasar factura; **to invoice a customer** = facturar a un cliente; **we invoiced you on November 10th** = le pasamos la factura el 10 de noviembre

◊ **invoicing** ['ɪnvɔɪsɪŋ] *noun* facturación *f or* envío *m* de factura; **our invoicing is done by the computer** = realizamos la facturación por ordenador; **invoicing department** = departamento de facturación; **invoicing in triplicate** = facturación

por triplicado; **VAT invoicing** = facturación con IVA incluido

involve [ɪn'vɒlv] *verb* implicar; **they all knew that the secretary was involved in it** = todos sabían que el secretario estaba implicado en ello

inward ['ɪnwəd] *adjective* interior *or* interno, -na; **inward bill** = conocimiento *m* de embarque interno; **inward mission** = misión comercial extranjera de visita al país

IOU ['aɪəʊ'juː] *noun* = I OWE YOU vale *m or* pagaré *m*; **to pay a pile of IOUs** = hacer efectivos un montón de pagarés

IRA [aɪɑː'eɪ] *US* = INDIVIDUAL RETIREMENT ACCOUNT

Iran [ɪ'rɑːn] *noun* Irán *m*

◊ **Iranian** [ɪ'reɪnjən] *adjective & noun* iraní *or* persa
NOTE: capital: **Tehran** (= Teherán); currency: **Iranian rial (Rls)** = rial iraní (Rls)

Iraq [ɪ'rɑːk] *noun* Iraq *m*

◊ **Iraqi** [ɪ'rɑːki] *adjective & noun* iraquí
NOTE: capital: **Baghdad** (= Bagdad); currency: **Iraqi dinar (ID)** = dinar iraquí (ID)

Ireland ['aɪələnd] *noun* Irlanda *f*

◊ **Irish** ['aɪərɪʃ] **1** *adjective* irlandés, -esa **2** *plural noun* **the Irish** = los irlandeses

◊ **Irishman, Irishwoman** *noun* irlandés, -esa
NOTE: capital: **Dublin** (= Dublín); currency: **Irish pound** *or* **punt (£** *or* **£Ir)** = libra irlandesa (£ *or* £Ir)

irrecoverable [ɪrɪ'kʌvərəbl] *adjective* irrecuperable *or* incobrable; **irrecoverable debt** = una deuda incobrable

irredeemable [ɪrɪ'diːməbl] *adjective* irredimible *or* no amortizable *or* inconvertible; **irredeemable bond** = obligación perpetua

irregular [ɪ'regjʊlə] *adjective* irregular *or* desigual; **irregular documentation** = documentación irregular; **this procedure is highly irregular** = este procedimiento es muy irregular

◊ **irregularity** [ɪregjʊ'lærəti] *noun* **(a)** *(not correct)* irregularidad *f*; **the irregularity of the postal deliveries** = la irregularidad del reparto de correo **(b)** *(not always legal)* **irregularities** = irregularidades; **to investigate irregularities in the share dealings** = investigar irregularidades en la venta de acciones

irrevocable [ɪ'revəkəbl] *adjective* irrevocable; **irrevocable acceptance** = aceptación irrevocable; **irrevocable letter of credit** = carta de crédito irrevocable

IRS [aɪɑː'es] *US* = INTERNAL REVENUE SERVICE

island ['aɪlənd] *noun* *(in shop)* sección *f* de un supermercado; **island display unit** = góndola *f (in exhibition)* **island site** *or* **island display** = 'stand' *or* pabellón de exposición

issue ['ɪʃuː] **1** *noun* **(a)** *(topic)* tema *m*; **current issue** = tema de actualidad **(b)** *(of a magazine)* número *m*; **we have an ad in the January issue of the magazine** = publicamos un anuncio en el número de enero **(c)** *(of shares)* emisión *f*; **bonus issue** *or* **scrip issue** = emisión gratuita; **issue of debentures** *or* **debenture issue** = emisión de obligaciones; **issue of new shares** *or* **share issue** = emisión de nuevas acciones; **rights issue** = emisión de derechos; **new issues department** = departamento *m* de emisión de nuevas acciones; **issue price** = precio *m* de emisión **2** *verb* emitir *or* publicar *or* extender *or* abrir; **to issue a letter of credit** = abrir una carta de crédito; **to issue shares in a new company** = emitir acciones de una nueva sociedad; **to issue a writ against someone** = extender un mandato judicial contra alguien; **the government issued a report on London's traffic** = el gobierno publicó un informe sobre el tráfico de Londres

◇ **issued** ['ɪʃuːd] *adjective* **issued capital** = capital emitido; **issued price** = precio de emisión

◇ **issuing** ['ɪʃʊɪŋ] *noun* emisor, -ra; **issuing bank** *or* **issuing house** = banco emisor *or* casa emisora

QUOTE the rights issue should overcome the cash flow problems
Investors Chronicle

QUOTE the company said that its recent issue of 10.5 per cent convertible preference shares at A\$8.50 a share has been oversubscribed
Financial Times

QUOTE issued and fully paid capital is \$100 million
Hongkong Standard

IT ['aɪ'tiː] = INFORMATION TECHNOLOGY

Italy ['ɪtəli] *noun* Italia *f*

◇ **Italian** [ɪ'tæljən] *adjective & noun* italiano, -na
NOTE: capital: **Rome** (= Roma); currency: **Italian lira (Lit)** = lira italiana (Lit)

ITC = INTERNATIONAL TRADE CENTRE

item ['aɪtəm] *noun* **(a)** *(thing for sale)* artículo *m*; **cash items** = artículos de venta al contado; **we are holding orders for out of stock items** = tenemos pedidos de artículos agotados; **please find enclosed an order for the following items from your catalogue** = tengo el gusto de adjuntar un pedido de los siguientes artículos de su catálogo **(b)** *(entry)* partida *f*; **items on a balance sheet** = partidas de un balance; **exceptional items** *or* **extraordinary items** = partidas excepcionales *or* extraordinarias; **item of expenditure** = partida de gasto **(c)** *(point on a list)* punto *m*; **we will now take item four on the agenda** = discutiremos ahora el punto cuatro del orden del día

◇ **itemize** ['aɪtəmaɪz] *verb* detallar *or* especificar *or* pormenorizar; **itemizing the sales figures will take about two days** = detallar las cifras de ventas nos llevará unos dos días; **itemized account** = cuenta detallada; **itemized invoice** = factura detallada; *US* **itemized deductions** = gastos deducibles de impuestos; **itemized statement** = balance detallado

itinerant worker [ɪ'tɪnərənt 'wɜːkə] *noun* trabajador, -ra ambulante

itinerary [aɪ'tɪnərəri] *noun* itinerario *m*; **a salesman's itinerary** = el itinerario de un vendedor

Ivory Coast ['aɪvəri 'kəʊst] *noun* Costa de Marfil *f*

◇ **Ivorien** *or* **Ivorian** [ɪ'vɔːriən] *adjective & noun* marfileño, -ña
NOTE: capital: **Abidjan;** currency: **CFA franc (CFAF)** = franco CFA (FCFA)

Jj

jam [dʒæm] **1** *noun* atasco *m*; **traffic jam** = embotellamiento *m* **2** *verb* atascar *or* bloquear; **the paper feed has jammed** = el alimentador de hojas se ha atascado; **the switchboard was jammed with calls** = la centralita estaba saturada de llamadas (NOTE: **jamming - jammed**)

Jamaica [dʒə'meɪkə] *noun* Jamaica *f*

◊ **Jamaican** [dʒə'meɪkən] *adjective & noun* jamaicano, -na NOTE: capital: **Kingston**; currency: **Jamaican dollar (J$)** = dólar jamaicano (J$)

janitor ['dʒænɪtə] *noun US* conserje *m or* portero, -ra (NOTE: GB English is **caretaker**)

Japan [dʒə'pæn] *noun* Japón *m*

◊ **Japanese** [dʒæpə'niːz] *adjective & noun* japonés, -esa *or* nipón, -ona NOTE: capital: **Tokyo** (= Tokio); currency: **Japanese yen** = yen japonés

J curve ['dʒeɪ 'kɜːv] *noun (line on a graph)* curva en forma de J

jetsam ['dʒetsəm] *noun* **flotsam and jetsam** = pecios *mpl* y echazón *m or* restos *mpl* flotantes de un naufragio (NOTE: not plural in English)

jettison ['dʒetɪsən] *verb* echar la carga al mar

jingle ['dʒɪŋgl] *noun* **advertising jingle** *or* **publicity jingle** = tonadilla *f* de un anuncio

JIT = JUST-IN-TIME

job [dʒɒb] *noun* **(a)** *(piece of work)* trabajo *m or* tarea *f or* faena *f*; **to do a job of work** = hacer un trabajo; **to do odd jobs** = hacer 'chapuzas' *or* hacer pequeños trabajos; **he does odd jobs for us around the house** = de vez en cuando nos hace pequeños trabajos de la casa; **odd-job-man** = hombre que sirve para todo *or* que hace pequeños trabajos; **to be paid by the job** = cobrar a destajo **(b)** *(order)* encargo *m*; **we are working on six jobs at the moment** = en este momento, estamos trabajando en seis encargos a la vez ; **the shipyard has a big job starting in August** = el astillero acometerá un gran encargo en agosto **(c)** *(regular paid work)* puesto *m* de trabajo *or* empleo *m*; **he is looking for a job in the computer industry** = está buscando empleo en la industria de ordenadores; **he lost his job when the factory closed** = perdió su empleo cuando cerró la fábrica; **she got a job in a factory** = consiguió un puesto de trabajo en una fábrica; **to apply for a job in an office** = solicitar un empleo en una oficina; **office job** *or* **white-collar job** = trabajo de oficina; **to give up one's job** = dejar el empleo; **to look for a job** = buscar empleo; **to retire from one's job** = jubilarse *or* retirarse; **to be out of a job** = estar desempleado **(d)** **job analysis** = análisis de un puesto de trabajo; **job application** *or* **application for a job** = solicitud de empleo; **you have to fill in a job application form** = tiene que rellenar una solicitud de empleo; *GB* **job centre** = oficina de empleo; **job classification** = clasificación de puestos de trabajo; **job creation scheme** = programa de creación de empleo; **job description** *or* **specification** = descripción del puesto de trabajo; **job evaluation** = evaluación *or* valoración de un puesto de trabajo; **job losses** = pérdida de puestos de trabajo; **job satisfaction** = satisfacción laboral (en el trabajo); **job search** = búsqueda de (puestos de) trabajo; **job security** = seguridad en el empleo *or* garantía de trabajo; **job sharing** = compartir un puesto de trabajo *or* empleo a media jornada; **job title** = cargo; **her job title is 'Chief Buyer'** = su cargo es el de 'jefe de compras'; **on-the-job training** = formación en el empleo; **off-the-job training** = formación fuera del puesto de trabajo; **job vacancies** = plazas vacantes **(e)** **job lot** = lote *m*; **he sold the household furniture as a job lot** = vendió el mobiliario de la casa en un solo lote **(f)** *(difficulty)* dificultad *f or* complicación *f*; **they will have a job to borrow the money they need for the expansion programme** = tendrán dificultad para conseguir prestado el dinero que necesitan para su programa de expansión; **we had a job to find a qualified secretary** = tuvimos dificultades para encontrar una secretaria competente

◊ **jobber** ['dʒɒbə] *noun* **(a)** *(formerly London Stock Exchange)* **(stock) jobber** = corredor *m* intermediario en la bolsa *or* agente de bolsa especializado *or* agiotista **(b)** *US* vendedor, -ra al por mayor; **rack jobber** = mayorista que aprovisiona directamente las estanterías en tiendas donde vende sus artículos

◊ **jobbing** ['dʒɒbɪŋ] *noun* **(a)** *(formerly London Stock Exchange)* **(stock) jobbing** = corretaje intermediario en la bolsa **(b)** *(doing small jobs)* que realiza pequeños trabajos; **jobbing gardener** *or* **jobbing printer** = persona *f* que realiza pequeños trabajos como jardinero *or* como impresor

◊ **jobclub** ['dʒɒb'klʌb] *noun* organización *f* que ayuda a encontrar trabajo a sus miembros

◊ **jobless** ['dʒɒbləs] *noun* **the jobless** = los desempleados *or* parados (NOTE: takes a plural verb)

◊ **jobseeker** ['dʒɒbsiːkə] *noun* persona *f* que busca trabajo

join [dʒɔɪn] *verb* **(a)** *(put things together)* juntar *or* unir; **the offices were joined together by making a door in the wall** = abrieron una puerta en la pared para juntar las oficinas; **if the paper is too short to take all the accounts, you can join an extra piece on the bottom** = si no entran todas las cuentas en la hoja, puedes añadir otra al final **(b)** *(to become part of)* **to join a firm** = entrar *or* ingresar en una empresa;

he joined on January 1st = entró el 1 de enero (c) *(to become member)* afiliar *or* afiliarse; to join an association *or* a group = hacerse socio de una asociación *or* de una agrupación; all the staff have joined the company pension plan = todo el personal se ha acogido al plan de pensiones de la empresa; he was asked to join the board = le ofrecieron formar parte de la junta; Smith Ltd has applied to join the trade association = Smith Ltd. ha solicitado ingresar en la asociación de comerciantes

joint [dʒɔɪnt] *adjective* **(a)** *(combined)* unido, -da *or* conjunto, -ta *or* colectivo, -va *or* común *or* mixto, -ta; joint commission of inquiry *or* joint committee = comisión mixta de investigación; joint discussions = negociaciones conjuntas; joint management = dirección conjunta *or* codirección; joint venture = empresa conjunta *or* negocio en participación *or* agrupación temporal de empresas *or* empresa mixta **(b)** joint account = cuenta conjunta *or* en participación; joint-stock bank = banco privado constituido en sociedad anónima *or* banco por acciones; joint-stock company = sociedad anónima **(c)** *(linked)* colectivo, -va *or* conjunto, -ta; joint beneficiary = beneficiario proindiviso; joint managing director = codirector gerente; joint owner = copropietario, -ria; joint ownership = copropiedad *f* condominio *m or* propiedad *f* en común; joint signatory = signatario mancomunado *or* colectivo

◇ jointly ['dʒɔɪntli] *adverb* conjuntamente *or* en común; to own a property jointly = tener una propiedad en común; to manage a company jointly = dirigir una empresa conjuntamente; they are jointly liable for damages = son conjuntamente responsables de los daños

Jordan ['dʒɔːdən] *noun* Jordania *f*

◇ Jordanian [dʒɔː'deɪnɪən] *adjective & noun* jordano, -na
NOTE: capital: **Amman**; currency: **Jordanian dinar (JD)** = dinar jordano (JD)

journal ['dʒɜːnl] *noun* **(a)** *(accounts book)* libro *m* diario; sales journal *or* sales day book = libro *or* registro diario de ventas **(b)** *(magazine)* revista *f or* boletín *m*; house journal = boletín interno de una empresa; trade journal = boletín de una actividad profesional determinada

◇ journalist ['dʒɜːnəlɪst] *noun* periodista *mf*

journey ['dʒɜːni] *noun* viaje *m*; he planned his journey to visit all his accounts in two days = organizó el viaje para visitar a todos sus clientes en dos días; journey order = pedido cursado al viajante; journey planning = planificación de viaje

◇ journeyman ['dʒɜːnɪmən] *noun US* obrero *m* especializado

judge [dʒʌdʒ] 1 *noun* juez *mf*; the judge sent him to prison for embezzlement = el juez lo encarceló por desfalco 2 *verb* juzgar *or* considerar; he judged it was time to call an end to the discussions = consideró que era hora de terminar las conversaciones

◇ judgement *or* judgment ['dʒʌdʒmənt] *noun* juicio *m or* sentencia *f or* fallo *m*; to pronounce judgement *or* to give one's judgement on something = pronunciar sentencia *or* dar su opinión sobre algo; judgment debtor = deudor, -ra judicial *or* por sentencia firme (NOTE: the spelling judgment is used by lawyers)

judicial [dʒʊ'dɪʃəl] *adjective* judicial *or* legal; judicial processes = procedimientos judiciales

jumble sale ['dʒʌmbl 'seɪl] *noun* venta *f* de objetos usados organizada por un club *or* asociación para recaudar fondos (con fines benéficos)

jump [dʒʌmp] 1 *noun* aumento *m or* salto *m*; jump in prices = aumento repentino de precios; jump in unemployment figures = aumento repentino de las cifras de paro 2 *verb* **(a)** *(to go up suddenly)* saltar *or* dar un salto *or* subir de golpe; oil prices have jumped since the war started = los precios del petróleo han subido desde que empezó la guerra; share values jumped on the Stock Exchange = los valores de las acciones dieron un salto en la bolsa **(b)** *(to go away suddenly)* escaparse; to jump bail = fugarse estando bajo fianza; to jump the gun = precipitarse; to jump the queue = saltarse la cola; they jumped the queue and got their export licence before we did = se saltaron la cola *or* el turno de espera y consiguieron la licencia de exportación antes que nosotros; to jump ship = abandonar el barco en el que se estaba enrolado

◇ jumpy ['dʒʌmpi] *adjective* agitado, -da *or* inestable *or* nervioso, -sa; the market is jumpy = el mercado es inestable

junior ['dʒuːnjə] 1 *adjective* más joven *or* subalterno, -na; junior clerk = pasante *mf or* auxiliar *mf* administrativo, -va; junior executive *or* junior manager = ejecutivo auxiliar *or* director más reciente; junior partner = socio subalterno *or* de menor antigüedad; John Smith, Junior = John Smith hijo 2 *noun* **(a)** abogado, -da auxiliar **(b)** *(as barrister)* office junior = subalterno, -na *or* auxiliar administrativo

junk [dʒʌŋk] *noun* porquería *f or* trastos *mpl*; you should throw away all that junk = deberías tirar todos esos trastos; junk bonds = bonos-basura; junk mail = publicidad sin interés enviada por correo

QUOTE the big US textile company is running deep in the red, its junk bonds are trading as low as 33 cents on the dollar
Wall Street Journal

jurisdiction [dʒʊərɪs'dɪkʃ(ə)n] *noun* within the jurisdiction of the court = bajo la jurisdicción del tribunal

just-in-time (JIT) ['dʒʌstɪn'taɪm] *noun* justo a tiempo; just-in-time (JIT) production = producción a tiempo; just-in-time (JIT) purchasing = compra en el momento preciso

Kk

K [keɪ] *abbreviation* mil; **'salary: £25K+ '** = salario superior a £25.000 anuales

Kb = KILOBYTE

KD = KNOCKDOWN

keen [kiːn] *adjective* **(a)** *(eager)* deseoso, -sa *or* ansioso, -sa *or* astuto, -ta; **keen competition** = fuerte competencia; **we are facing some keen competition from European manufacturers** = nos encontramos ante una fuerte competencia de los fabricantes europeos; **keen demand** = gran demanda; **there is a keen demand for home computers** = hay una gran demanda de ordenadores personales **(b) keen prices** = precios competitivos; **our prices are the keenest on the market** = nuestros precios son los más competitivos del mercado

keep [kiːp] *verb* **(a)** *(to go on doing something)* seguir *or* continuar; **they kept working, even when the boss told them to stop** = siguieron trabajando incluso cuando el jefe les dijo que pararan; **the other secretaries complain that she keeps singing when she is typing** = las demás secretarias se quejan de que canta mientras escribe a máquina **(b)** *(to do what is necessary)* cumplir; **to keep an appointment** = acudir a una cita; **to keep the books of a company** *or* **to keep a company's books** = llevar los libros *or* la contabilidad de una empresa **(c)** *(to hold items)* tener *or* reservar *or* disponer *or* guardar; **we always keep this item in stock** = siempre disponemos de este producto; **to keep someone's name on file** = guardar el nombre de alguien en un fichero **(d)** *(to hold things at a certain level)* mantener; **we must keep our mailing list up to date** = debemos mantener nuestra lista de destinatarios al día; **to keep spending to a minimum** = mantener los gastos al mínimo; **the price of oil has kept the pound at a high level** = el precio del petróleo ha mantenido la libra alta; **the government is encouraging firms to keep prices low** = el gobierno está alentando a las empresas para que mantengan los precios bajos; **lack of demand for typewriters has kept prices down** = la escasa demanda de máquinas de escribir ha mantenido los precios bajos; **to keep someone busy** = entretener; **I had to keep the customer busy while his order was being made up** = tuve que entretener al cliente mientras le preparaban el pedido **(e)** *(retain)* quedarse *or* retener; **keep the change** = quédese con el cambio **(f)** *(remain)* **he kept quiet about the new project** = no dijo nada sobre el nuevo proyecto (NOTE: **keeping - kept)**

◊ **keep back** [kiːp 'bæk] *verb* ocultar *or* quedarse con; **to keep back information** *or* **to keep something back from someone** = ocultar información *or* ocultar algo a alguien; **to keep £10 back from someone's salary** = quedarse con £10 del salario de alguien

◊ **keeping** ['kiːpɪŋ] *noun* **safe keeping** = custodia *f or* lugar seguro *or* a buen recaudo; **we put the documents into the bank for safe keeping** = guardamos los documentos en el banco para mayor seguridad

◊ **keep on** [kiːp 'ɒn] *verb* seguir *or* no dejar de; **the factory kept on working in spite of the fire** = la fábrica no dejó de trabajar a pesar del incendio; **we keep on receiving orders for this item although it was discontinued two years ago** = seguimos recibiendo pedidos de este artículo aunque dejó de fabricarse hace dos años

◊ **keep up** [kiːp 'ʌp] *verb* sostener *or* mantener; **we must keep up the turnover in spite of the recession** = debemos mantener el volumen de ventas a pesar de la recesión; **she kept up a rate of sixty words per minute for several hours** = mantuvo el ritmo de sesenta palabras por minuto durante varias horas; **to keep up with the demand** = satisfacer la demanda

Kenya ['kenjə *or* 'kiːnjə] *noun* Kenia *f*

◊ **Kenyan** ['kenjən] *adjective & noun* keniano, -na
NOTE: capital: **Nairobi;** currency: **Kenyan shilling (KSh)** = chelín keniano (KSh)

Keogh plan ['kiːəʊ 'plæn] *noun* US plan *m* Keogh *or* de jubilación privado

key [kiː] **1** *noun* **(a)** *(lock)* llave *f*; **we have lost the keys to the computer room** = hemos perdido las llaves del cuarto de ordenadores; **key money** = traspaso *m* **(b)** *(on computer or typewriter)* tecla *f*; **there are sixty-four keys on the keyboard** = hay sesenta y cuatro teclas en el teclado; **control key** = tecla de control; **shift key** = tecla de mayúsculas **2** *adjective and noun* *(very important)* clave *f*; **key factor** = factor clave; **key industry** = industria clave; **key personnel** *or* **key staff** = personal clave *or* esencial; **key post** = puesto clave **3** *verb* **to key in data** = introducir *or* pasar datos al ordenador

◊ **keyboard** ['kiːbɔːd] **1** *noun* teclado *m*; **qwerty keyboard** = teclado QWERTY (alusión a las letras q-w-e-r-t-y, que suelen figurar por este orden en la primera fila de los teclados de las máquinas de escribir); **the computer has a normal qwerty keyboard** = el ordenador tiene un teclado 'qwerty' normal; **Spanish keyboard** = teclado español **2** *verb* teclear *or* pasar a máquina; **he is keyboarding our address list** = está tecleando nuestra lista de destinatarios

◊ **keyboarder** ['kiːbɔːdə] *noun* operador, -ra de teclado que introduce información en un ordenador

◊ **keyboarding** ['kiːbɔːdɪŋ] *noun* tecleo *m or* tecleado *m* (introducción de datos *or* instrucciones en un ordenador por teclado); **keyboarding costs have risen sharply** = la tarifa de tecleo *or* por pasar información a un ordenador ha subido considerablemente

◊ **keypad** ['kiːpæd] *noun* pequeño teclado *m*; **numeric keypad** = teclado numérico

kg = KILOGRAM kilo *or* kilogramo (kg)

kickback ['kɪkbæk] *noun* comisión *f* ilegal *or* soborno *m*

killing ['kɪlɪŋ] *noun* *(informal)* gran jugada *f or* gran golpe *m or* buena operación *f*; **he made a killing on the stock market** = ganó una gran cantidad en la bolsa

kilo *or* **kilogram** ['kiːləʊ *or* 'kɪləgræm] *noun* kilo *m or* kilogramo *m* (NOTE: usually written **kg** after figures: **25kg**. Note also that in Spanish, the abbreviation **kilo** means 'one million pesetas')

◊ **kilobyte (KB)** ['kɪləbaɪt] *noun* kilocteto *m or* 1.024 bytes *m*

◊ **kilometre** *or* *US***kilometer** [kɪ'lɒmɪtə] *noun* kilómetro *m* (km); **the car does fifteen kilometres to the litre** = el coche gasta un litro por cada quince kilómetros (NOTE: usually written **km** after figures: **70km**)

kind [kaɪnd] *noun* clase *f or* tipo *m*; **the printer produces two kinds of printout** = la impresora realiza dos tipos de impresión; **our drinks machine has three kinds of soup** = hay tres tipos de sopa en nuestra máquina de bebidas; **payment in kind** = pago en especie

king-size ['kɪŋ'saɪz] *adjective* de tamaño extra *or* de gran tamaño

kiosk ['kiːɒsk] *noun* quiosco *m*; **a newspaper kiosk** = quiosco de periódicos; **telephone kiosk** = cabina *f* de teléfonos

kite [kaɪt] **1** *noun* **(a) to fly a kite** = lanzar una propuesta para tantear el terreno; **kite flier** = persona que intenta impresionar con sus propuestas; **kite-flying** = intento de impresionar con grandes propuestas **(b)** *GB* **kite mark** = marca de calidad (que indica que un producto se ajusta a las normas oficiales británicas) **2** *verb* **(a)** *US* obtener dinero *or* crédito con cheques sin fondos **(b)** *GB* utilizar tarjetas de crédito o cheques robados

kitty ['kɪti] *noun* bote *m or* fondo *m* común

km = KILOMETRE kilómetro (km)

knock [nɒk] *verb* **(a)** golpear *or* pegar; **he knocked on the door and went in** = llamó a la puerta y entró; **she knocked her head on the filing cabinet** = se golpeó la cabeza contra el archivador **(b) to knock the competition** = asestar un duro golpe a la competencia; **knocking copy** = publicidad agresiva que critica los productos de la competencia

> QUOTE for some years butter advertising
> tended to knock other fats such as
> magarines
> **Marketing Week**

◊ **knock down** ['nɒk 'daʊn] *verb* **(a)** *(price)* rebajar *or* rematar **(b)** *(auction)* adjudicar en una subasta; **to knock something down to a bidder** = adjudicar algo a un postor; **the stock was knocked down to him for £10,000** = la partida le fue adjudicada por £10.000

◊ **knockdown** ['nɒkdaʊn] *noun* **(a)** **knockdown (KD) goods** = artículos rebajados **(b)** **knockdown prices** = precios mínimos *or* de saldo; **he sold me the car at a knockdown price** = me vendió el coche por un precio reventado

◊ **knock off** ['nɒk 'ɒf] *verb* **(a)** *(to stop work)* terminar de trabajar **(b)** *(reduce price)* rebajar; **he knocked £10 off the price for cash** = rebajó el precio en £10 por pago al contado

◊ **knock-on effect** ['nɒk'ɒn ɪ'fekt] *noun* repercusión *f or* efecto *m* secundario; **the strike by customs officers has had a knock-on effect on car production by slowing down exports of cars** = la huelga de funcionarios de aduanas ha repercutido en la producción de coches al retrasar las exportaciones

knot [nɒt] *noun (measure of speed)* nudo *m*

I COMMENT: one knot is one nautical mile per hour

know [nəʊ] *verb* **(a)** *(to learn)* saber; **I do not know how a computer works** = no sé cómo funciona un ordenador; **does he know how long it takes to get to the airport?** = ¿sabe cuánto se tarda en llegar al aeropuerto?; **the managing director's secretary does not know where he is** = la secretaria no sabe dónde está el director gerente **(b)** *(to meet)* conocer; **do you know Mr Jones, our new sales director?** = ¿conoce al Sr. Jones, nuestro nuevo director de ventas?; **he knows the African market very well** = conoce el mercado africano muy bien (NOTE: **knowing - known**)

◊ **know-how** ['nəʊhaʊ] *noun* conocimientos *mpl* técnicos *or* científicos; **electronic know-how** = conocimientos de electrónica; **to acquire computer know-how** = adquirir conocimientos de informática; **know-how fund** = fondos para la provisión de asesoramiento y preparación técnica

◊ **knowledge** ['nɒlɪdʒ] *noun* conocimiento *m or* saber *m*; **he had no knowledge of the contract** = no tenía conocimiento de la existencia del contrato; **basic knowledge** = conocimientos básicos; **expert knowledge** = conocimientos especiales

Korea [kə'rɪə] *noun* Corea *f*

◊ **Korean** [kə'rɪən] *adjective & noun* coreano, -na NOTE: capital: **Seoul** (= Seúl); currency: **Korean won (W)** = won coreano (W)

krona ['krəʊnə] *noun (currency used in Sweden and Iceland)* corona *f*

krone ['krəʊnə] *noun (currency used in Denmark and Norway)* corona *f*

Kuwait [kʊ'weɪt] *noun* Kuwait *or* Kowait *m*

◊ **Kuwaiti** [kə'weɪtɪ] *adjective & noun* kuwaití NOTE: currency: **Kuwaiti dinar (KD)** dinar kuwaití (KD)

LI

l = LITRE litro (l)

label ['leɪbl] **1** *noun* etiqueta *f;* **gummed label** = etiqueta engomada; **self-sticking label** = etiqueta autoadhesiva; **tie-on label** = etiqueta colgante; **address label** = etiqueta (de señas); **price label** = etiqueta de precio; **quality label** = signo *m* de calidad; **own label goods** = productos *mpl* de marca propia **2** *verb* etiquetar *or* poner etiqueta a; **incorrectly labelled parcel** = paquete con información incorrecta en la etiqueta (NOTE: **labelling - labelled** but US **labeling - labeled**)

◊ **labelling** ['leɪblɪŋ] *noun* etiquetado *m;* **labelling department** = departamento de etiquetado

laboratory [lə'bɒrətrɪ] *noun* laboratorio *m;* **the product was developed in the company's laboratories** = el producto fue perfeccionado en los laboratorios de la empresa; **all products are tested in our own laboratories** = todos los productos son sometidos a prueba en nuestros propios laboratorios

labour *or* US **labor** ['leɪbə] *noun* **(a)** *(work)* trabajo *m;* **manual labour** = trabajo manual; **to charge for materials and labour** = cobrar los materiales y la mano de obra; **labour costs** *or* **labour charges** = costes laborales *or* de la mano de obra; **indirect labour costs** = costes laborales indirectos; **labour is charged at £5 an hour** = la mano de obra se cobra a £5 la hora **(b)** *(workforce)* mano *f* de obra *or* obreros *mpl;* **casual labour** = mano de obra eventual; **cheap labour** = mano de obra barata; **local labour** = mano de obra local; **organized labour** = obreros sindicados; **skilled labour** = mano de obra cualificada *or* especializada; **labour force** = mano de obra *or* población activa; **the management has made an increased offer to the labour force** = la dirección ha ofrecido un aumento al personal; **we are setting up a factory in the Far East because of the cheap labour available** = estamos instalando una nueva fábrica en Extremo Oriente porque allí se dispone de mano de obra barata; **labour market** = mercado de trabajo; **25,000 young people have left school and have come on to the labour market** = 25.000 jóvenes han dejado la escuela y han entrado a formar parte del mercado laboral; **labour shortage** *or* **shortage of labour** = escasez *f* de mano de obra; **labour-intensive industry** = industria con un alto coeficiente de mano de obra **(c)** **labour disputes** = conflictos laborales; **labour laws** *or* **labour legislation** = derecho laboral; **labour relations** = relaciones laborales; US **labor union** = sindicato de trabajadores (NOTE: GB English is **trade union**) **(d)** **International Labour Organization (ILO)** = Organización *f* Internacional del Trabajo (OIT)

◊ **labourer** ['leɪbərə] *noun* trabajador, -ra *or* obrero, -ra; **agricultural labourer** = peón *m* agrícola *or* bracero *m;* **casual labourer** = trabajador eventual; **manual labourer** = obrero, -ra manual

◊ **labour-saving** ['leɪbəseɪvɪŋ] *adjective* que ahorra trabajo; **a labour-saving device** = un mecanismo *or* dispositivo para ahorrar trabajo *or* aparato electrodoméstico

lack [læk] **1** *noun* falta *f or* carencia *f or* escasez *f;* **lack of data** *or* **lack of information** = falta de datos *or* falta de información; **the decision has been put back for lack of up-to-date information** = la decisión se ha aplazado por falta de información actualizada; **lack of funds** = falta de fondos; **the project was cancelled because of lack of funds** = el proyecto fue cancelado por falta de fondos **2** *verb* faltarle algo a uno *or* carecer de; **the company lacks capital** = a la compañía le falta capital; **the sales staff lack motivation** = al personal le falta motivación

ladder ['lædə] *noun* escalera *f* de mano *or* escala *f;* **you will need a ladder to look into the machine** = necesitarás una escalera de mano para examinar la máquina; **promotion ladder** = escala de ascenso *or* escalafón *m;* **by being appointed sales manager, he moved several steps up the promotion ladder** = al ser nombrado director de ventas, subió varios grados en la escala de ascenso

laden ['leɪdn] *adjective* cargado, -da; **fully-laden ship** = barco a plena carga *or* cargado por completo; **ship laden in bulk** = barco con carga a granel

lading ['leɪdɪŋ] *noun* carga *f or* embarque *m;* **bill of lading** = conocimiento *m* de embarque

lady ['leɪdɪ] *noun* señora *f;* **young lady** = señorita *f*

Laffer curve ['læfə 'kɜːv] *noun* curva *f* de Laffer

laissez-faire economy ['leseɪ'feə ɪ'kɒnəmɪ] *noun* economía *f* de mínima intervención estatal

lakh [læk] *noun (in India)* cien mil (NOTE: ten lakh equal one crore)

lame duck ['leɪm 'dʌk] *noun* **(a)** compañía *f* en dificultades económicas *or* insolvente; **the government has refused to help lame duck companies** = el gobierno se ha negado a ayudar a las compañías en dificultades económicas **(b)** **a lame duck president** = presidente cesante

land [lænd] **1** *noun* tierra *f;* **land agent** = administrador, -ra de fincas; **land bank** = solar inmobiliario; **land reform** = reforma agraria; *GB* **land register** = catastro *m or* registro *m* de la propiedad; **land registration** = catastro *or* registro de la propiedad; **land registry** = registro *m* catastral *or* de la propiedad; **land taxes** = contribución *f* territorial rústica **2** *verb* **(a)** desembarcar *or* descargar; **to land goods at a port** = descargar mercancías en un puerto; **to land passengers at an airport** = desembarcar pasajeros en un aeropuerto; **landed costs** = coste descargado **(b)** *(of plane)* aterrizar; **the plane landed ten minutes late** = el avión aterrizó con diez minutos de retraso

◊ **landing** ['lændɪŋ] *noun* **landing card** = tarjeta *f* de desembarque; **landing charges** = gastos *mpl* de descarga; **landing order** = permiso *m* de descarga; **soft landing** = aterrizaje suave; **forced landing** = aterrizaje forzoso

◊ **landlady** ['lænleɪdɪ] *noun* propietaria *f or* ama *f or* casera *f*

◊ **landlord** ['lænlɔːd] *noun* propietario *m or* amo *m or* casero ; **ground landlord** = nudo propietario *or* propietario absoluto; **our ground landlord is an insurance company** = el nudo propietario de nuestra vivienda es una compañía de seguros

◊ **landowner** ['lændɔʊnə] *noun* terrateniente *m*

language ['læŋgwɪdʒ] *noun* lengua *f or* idioma *m or* lenguaje *m*; **the managing director conducted the negotiations in three languages** = el director gerente dirigió las negociaciones en tres idiomas; **programming language** = lenguaje de programación; **what language does the program run on?** = ¿con qué lenguaje funciona el programa?

Laos ['læwɔs] *noun* Laos *m*

◊ **Laotian** [læ'ɔʊʃən] *adjective & noun* laosiano, -na
NOTE: capital: **Vientiane**; currency: **Laotian kip (KL)** = kip laosiano (KL)

lapse [læps] **1** *noun* **a lapse of time** = lapso *m or* periodo *m* de tiempo **2** *verb* caducar *or* prescribir; **the guarantee has lapsed** = la garantía ha caducado; **to let an offer lapse** = dejar caducar una oferta

laptop ['læptɒp] *noun* ordenador *m* portátil

large [lɑːdʒ] *adjective* grande *or* importante; **our company is one of the largest suppliers of computers to the government** = nuestra empresa es una de las mayores proveedoras de ordenadores del gobierno; **he is our largest customer** = es nuestro cliente más importante; **why has she got an office which is larger than mine?** = ¿por qué tiene ella una oficina mayor que la mía?

◊ **largely** ['lɑːdʒlɪ] *adverb* en su mayor parte *or* en gran parte *or* considerablemente; **our sales are largely in the home market** = nuestras ventas corresponden en su mayor parte al mercado interior; **they have largely pulled out of the American market** = se han retirado considerablemente del mercado estadounidense

◊ **large-scale** ['lɑːdʒ 'skeɪl] *adjective* a gran escala; **large-scale investment in new technology** = inversión a gran escala en nueva tecnología; **large-scale redundancies in the construction industry** = reducciones de plantilla a gran escala en la industria de la construcción

laser printer ['leɪzə 'prɪntə] *noun* impresora *f* láser

last [lɑːst] **1** *adverb* el último *or* la última *or* en último lugar *or* por último; **out of a queue of twenty people, I was served last** = fui el último, de una cola

de veinte personas, en ser servido **2** *adjective* **(a)** *(at the end)* último, -ma; **this is our last board meeting before we move to our new offices** = ésta es la última reunión del consejo de administración antes de trasladarnos a las nuevas oficinas; **we finished the last items in the order just two days before the promised delivery date** = terminamos los últimos artículos del pedido justo dos días antes de la fecha de entrega; **last quarter** = último trimestre **(b)** *(most recent)* último, -ma *or* pasado, -da; **where is the last batch of orders?** = ¿dónde está la última partida de pedidos?; **the last ten orders were only for small quantities** = los últimos diez pedidos fueron sólo de cantidades pequeñas; **last week** *or* **last month** *or* **last year** = la semana pasada *or* el mes pasado *or* el año pasado; **last week's sales were the best we have ever had** = las ventas de la semana pasada fueron mejores que nunca; **the sales managers have been asked to report on last month's drop in unit sales** = se ha pedido a los directores comerciales que informen sobre el descenso de las ventas del mes pasado; **last year's accounts have to be ready by the AGM** = las cuentas del año pasado tienen que estar listas para la junta general anual **(c) the week** *or* **month** *or* **year before last** = la semana antepasada *or* el mes antepasado *or* el año antepasado; **last year's figures were bad, but they were an improvement on those of the year before last** = las cifras del año pasado fueron malas, pero fueron mejores que las del año anterior **2** *verb* durar; **the boom started in the 1970s and lasted until the early 1980s** = el 'boom' empezó en los años 70 y duró hasta principios de los años 80; **the discussions over redundancies lasted all day** = las conversaciones sobre la reducción de plantilla duraron todo el día

◊ **last in first out (LIFO)** ['lɑːst 'ɪn 'fɜːst 'aʊt] *noun* **(a)** *(redundancy)* política de reducción de plantilla según la cual los últimos en entrar son los primeros en salir **(b)** *(accounting)* método contable según el cuál las existencias se valoran al precio de las últimas compras

late [leɪt] **1** *adjective* **(a)** *(after the time stated)* tardío, -ía *or* retrasado, -da; **we apologize for the late arrival of the plane from Amsterdam** = les pedimos disculpas por el retraso de la llegada del avión de Amsterdam; **there is a penalty for late delivery** = existe una multa por retraso en la entrega; **late payment** = pago atrasado **(b)** *(last)* último, -ma; **latest date for signature of the contract** = la última fecha para la firma del contrato **(c)** *(most recent)* último, -ma *or* más reciente; **he always drives the latest model of car** = siempre conduce el último modelo de coche; **here are the latest sales figures** = aquí están las últimas cifras de ventas **2** *adverb* tarde *or* con retraso; **the shipment was landed late** = el cargamento fue descargado tarde; **the plane was two hours late** = el avión llevaba dos horas de retraso

◊ **late-night** ['leɪt 'naɪt] *adjective* nocturno, -na *or* a última hora de la noche; **late-night opening** = abierto por la noche; **he had a late-night meeting at the airport** = tuvo una reunión en el aeropuerto a última hora de la noche; **their late-night negotiations ended in an agreement which was signed at 3 a.m.** = sus negociaciones nocturnas terminaron con un acuerdo firmado a las 3 de la madrugada

Latin America ['lætɪn ə'merɪkə] *noun* América Latina *or* Hispanoamérica *or* Latinoamérica

◊ **Latin American** ['lætɪn ə'merɪkən] *adjective & noun* latinoamericano, -na

Latvia ['lætvɪə] *noun* Letonia

◊ **Latvian** ['lætvɪən] *adjective & noun* letón, -ona
NOTE: capital: **Riga**; currency: **lat = lat**

launch [lɔːn(t)ʃ] **1** *verb* lanzar; **they launched their new car model at the motor show** = lanzaron su nuevo modelo de coche en el salón del automóvil; **the company is spending thousands of pounds to launch a new brand of soap** = la empresa está gastando miles de libras para lanzar una nueva marca de jabón **2** *noun* lanzamiento *m*; **the launch of the new model has been put back three months** = el lanzamiento del nuevo modelo se ha retrasado tres meses; **the company is geared up for the launch of the new brand of soap** = la empresa está preparada para el lanzamiento de la nueva marca de jabón; **the management has decided on a September launch date** = la dirección ha decidido que la fecha del lanzamiento sea en septiembre

◊ **launching** ['lɔːn(t)ʃɪŋ] *noun* lanzamiento *m*; **launching costs** = costes de lanzamiento; **launching date** = fecha de lanzamiento; **launching party** = fiesta de lanzamiento

launder ['lɔːndə] *verb* blanquear dinero negro; **to launder money through an offshore bank** = blanquear dinero a través de un banco de un paraíso fiscal

◊ **laundering** ['lɔːndrɪŋ] *noun* **money laundering** = blanqueo *m* de dinero

law [lɔː] *noun* **(a)** *(rule by which a country is governed)* derecho *m or* ley *f*; **laws** = leyes *fpl or* derecho *m*; **labour laws** = derecho laboral **(b)** *(profession, science)* derecho; **civil law** = derecho civil; **commercial law** = derecho mercantil; **company law** = ley de sociedades anónimas; **contract law** *or* **the law of contract** = derecho de contratos; **copyright law** = ley sobre la propiedad intelectual *or* ley sobre los derechos de autor; **criminal law** = derecho penal; **international law** = derecho internacional; **maritime law** *or* **the law of the sea** = derecho marítimo; **law courts** = tribunales de justicia; **to take someone to law** = llevar a alguien ante los tribunales; **inside the law** *or* **within the law** = legalmente *or* dentro de la ley; **against** *or* **outside the law** = fuera de la ley; **the company is operating outside the law** = la empresa está actuando fuera de la ley; **to break the law** = infringir la ley; **he is breaking the law by selling goods on Sunday** = está infringiendo la ley al vender mercancías el domingo; **you will be breaking the law if you try to take that computer out of the country without an export licence** = infringirás la ley si intentas sacar este ordenador fuera del país sin una licencia de exportación **(c)** *(general rule)* ley *or* regla *f or* norma *f*; **law of supply and demand** = ley de la oferta y la demanda; **law of diminishing returns** = ley de rendimientos decrecientes

◊ **lawful** ['lɔːful] *adjective* legal *or* lícito, -ta; **lawful practice** = práctica legal; **lawful trade** = comercio legal

◊ **lawfully** ['lɔːfuli] *adverb* legalmente

◊ **Law Society** ['lɔː sə'saɪəti] *noun* Colegio de Abogados

◊ **lawsuit** ['lɔːsuːt] *noun* pleito *m or* juicio *m or*

proceso *m*; **to bring a lawsuit against someone** = poner un pleito a alguien; **to defend a lawsuit** = defender una causa ante un tribunal

◊ **lawyer** ['lɔːjə] *noun* abogado, -da; **commercial lawyer** *or* **company lawyer** = abogado especialista en derecho mercantil; **international lawyer** = abogado especialista en derecho internacional; **maritime lawyer** = abogado especializado en derecho marítimo

lay [leɪ] *verb* poner; **to lay an embargo on trade with a country** = prohibir el comercio con un país (NOTE: **laying - laid**)

◊ **lay off** ['leɪ 'ɒf] *verb* **(a)** *(work)* despedir (temporalmente) *or* suspender; **to lay off workers** = despedir temporalmente a los trabajadores; **the factory laid off half its workers because of lack of orders** = la fábrica despidió temporalmente a la mitad de sus obreros por falta de pedidos **(b) to lay off risks** = reasegurar

◊ **lay-off** ['leɪɒf] *noun* despido *m* temporal *or* suspensión *m* de trabajo; **the recession has caused hundreds of lay-offs in the car industry** = la recesión ha provocado cientos de despidos en la industria del automóvil

◊ **lay out** ['leɪ 'aʊt] *verb* invertir *or* emplear; **we had to lay out half our cash budget on equipping the new factory** = tuvimos que emplear la mitad del presupuesto de caja para equipar la nueva fábrica

◊ **layout** ['leɪaʊt] *noun* distribución *f or* presentación *f or* trazado *m*; **they have altered the layout of the offices** = han modificado la distribución de las oficinas

◊ **lay up** ['leɪ 'ʌp] *verb* **(a)** atracar; **half the shipping fleet is laid up by the recession** = la mitad de la flota está atracada por la recesión **(b)** *(in bed)* **laid up** = en cama; **half the office is laid up with flu** = la mitad de la oficina está en cama con gripe

QUOTE the company lost $52 million last year, and has laid off close to 2,000 employees
Toronto Star

QUOTE while trading conditions for the tanker are being considered, it is possible that the ship could be laid up
Lloyd's List

lazy ['leɪzi] *adjective* perezoso, -sa *or* holgazán, -ana *or* gandul, -la *or* vago, -ga; **she is too lazy to do any overtime** = es demasiado perezosa para hacer horas extraordinarias; **he is so lazy he does not even send in his expense claims on time** = es tan perezoso que ni siquiera presenta a tiempo sus justificantes de gastos

lb = POUND

LBO = LEVERAGED BUYOUT

L/C = LETTER OF CREDIT

LDT = LICENSED DEPOSIT-TAKER

lead [liːd] *verb* **(a)** *(to be first)* ser el primero *or* ir en primer lugar; **the company leads the market in cheap computers** = es la empresa líder en el mercado de ordenadores baratos **(b)** *(to head)* encabezar *or* dirigir; **she will lead the trade mission to Nigeria** = encabezará la misión comercial a

Nigeria; **the tour of American factories will be led by the minister** = la gira por las fábricas estadounidenses estará encabezada por el ministro (NOTE: **leading - led**)

◊ **leader** ['liːdə] *noun* **(a)** *(person)* dirigente *mf or* jefe, -fa; **the leader of the construction workers' union** *or* **the construction workers' leader** = el dirigente del sindicato obrero de la construcción; **she is the leader of the trade mission to Nigeria** = es la jefa de la misión comercial a Nigeria; **the minister was the leader of the party of industrialists on a tour of American factories** = el ministro era el jefe del grupo de industriales en gira por las fábricas estadounidenses **(b)** *(product)* artículo *m* de mayor venta; *(product or company)* **a market leader** = (i) artículo de mayor venta; (ii) empresa líder *or* a la cabeza de un sector; **loss-leader** = artículo de reclamo *or* de lanzamiento **(c)** *(share)* valor *m* principal de los cotizados en la bolsa

◊ **leadership** ['liːdəʃɪp] *noun* liderazgo *m or* liderato *m*

◊ **leading** ['liːdɪŋ] *adjective* principal *or* primero, -ra *or* importante; **leading industrialists feel the end of the recession is near** = varios empresarios destacados opinan que el final de la recesión está cerca; **leading shares rose on the Stock Exchange** = las acciones favoritas subieron en la bolsa; **leading shareholders in the company forced a change in management policy** = los principales accionistas obligaron a modificar la política directiva; **they are the leading company in the field** = es la primera empresa del sector; **leading indicator** = indicador anticipado; **leading rate** = índice *or* precio destacado

◊ **lead time** ['liːd 'taɪm] *noun* plazo *m* de espera; **the lead time on this item is more than six weeks** = el plazo de espera para este artículo es de más de seis semanas

◊ **lead (up) to** ['liːd '(ʌp) 'tuː] *verb* llevar a *or* conducir a; **the discussions led to a big argument between the management and the union** = las conversaciones condujeron a una fuerte discusión entre la dirección y el sindicato; **we received a series of approaches leading up to the takeover bid** = recibimos una serie de propuestas que llevaron a la oferta de adquisición de la empresa

> QUOTE market leaders may benefit from scale economies or other cost advantages; they may enjoy a reputation for quality simply by being at the top, or they may actually produce a superior product that gives them both a large market share and high profits
> **Accountancy**

leaflet ['liːflət] *noun* folleto *m or* prospecto *m*; **to mail leaflets** *or* **to hand out leaflets describing services** = enviar prospectos por correo *or* distribuir prospectos publicitarios; **they did a leaflet mailing to 20,000 addresses** = enviaron prospectos por correo a 20.000 direcciones

leak [liːk] *verb* filtrar; **information on the contract was leaked to the press** = la información sobre el contrato se filtró a la prensa; **they discovered the managing director was leaking information to a rival company** = descubrieron que el director gerente pasaba información a una empresa competidora

◊ **leakage** ['liːkɪdʒ] *noun* pérdidas *fpl or* mermas *fpl*

lean [liːn] *adjective* **(a)** *(thin)* flaco, -ca; **the lean years** = los años de las vacas flacas *or* los años de escasez **(b)** *(slim and efficient)* **lean management** = sistema de racionalización del equipo directivo para facilitar la toma de decisiones; **lean production** = producción racionalizada *or* modernizada

leap-frogging ['liːpfrɒgɪŋ] *adjective* **leap-frogging pay demands** = demandas de aumento de sueldo en cadena

lease [liːs] **1** *noun* **(a)** *(contract for letting, renting)* arrendamiento *m or* arriendo *m*; **lease for sale** = se cede arrendamiento; **long lease** *or* **short lease** = arrendamiento a largo plazo *or* arrendamiento a corto plazo; **to take an office building on a long lease** = tomar un edificio de oficinas en arriendo a largo plazo; **we have a short lease on our current premises** = el arriendo de nuestros locales actuales es a corto plazo; **to rent office space on a twenty-year lease** = alquilar un espacio para oficinas con un arriendo de veinte años; **full repairing lease** = arrendamiento en el que todas las reparaciones corren por cuenta del arrendatario; **headlease** = arriendo concedido por el nudo propietario; **sublease** *or* **underlease** = subarriendo; **the lease expires** *or* **runs out in 1999** = el arrendamiento expira en 1999; **on expiration of the lease** = cuando expire el arriendo **(b) to hold an oil lease in the North Sea** = tener una concesión petrolífera en el Mar del Norte **2** *verb* **(a)** *(of landlord or owner)* arrendar *or* ceder en arriendo; **to lease offices to small firms** = arrendar oficinas a empresas pequeñas; **to lease equipment** = arrendar equipo *or* alquilar material **(b)** *(of tenant)* arrendar *or* tomar en arriendo; **to lease an office from an insurance company** = arrendar una oficina a una compañía de seguros; **all our company cars are leased** = todos los coches de nuestra empresa son alquilados

◊ **lease back** ['liːs 'bæk] *verb* realizar una operación de cesión-arrendamiento *or* alquilar de nuevo lo que se ha vendido; **they sold the office building to raise cash, and then leased it back for twenty-five years** = vendieron el edificio de oficinas para obtener dinero en efectivo y luego lo arrendaron por veinticinco años

◊ **lease-back** ['liːsbæk] *noun* cesión-arrendamiento *f*; **they sold the office building and then took it back under a lease-back arrangement** = vendieron el edificio de oficinas y siguieron ocupándolo en virtud de un contrato de arrendamiento suscrito con el comprador

◊ **leasehold** ['liːshəʊld] **1** *noun* arrendamiento *m or* foro *m*; **the company has some valuable leaseholds** = la compañía tiene arrendamientos valiosos **2** *adjective* arrendado, -da *or* en arriendo; **leasehold property** = propiedad arrendada *or* en arriendo *or* en régimen de arrendamiento; **to buy a property leasehold** = comprar una propiedad en arriendo

◊ **leaseholder** ['liːshəʊldə] *noun* arrendatario, -ria; *see also* LESSEE

◊ **leasing** ['liːsɪŋ] *noun* arriendo *m* con opción a compra *or* arrendamiento *m* financiero *or* 'leasing' *m*; **the company has branched out into car leasing** = la empresa ha extendido sus actividades al alquiler de coches; **an equipment-leasing company** = una empresa de alquiler de equipos con opción de compra; **to run a copier under a leasing arrangement** = utilizar una multicopista en virtud de un contrato de arrendamiento financiero

leave [liːv] **1** *noun* permiso *m or* licencia *f or* vacaciones *fpl*; **six weeks' annual leave** = seis semanas de vacaciones al año; **leave of absence** = excedencia *f*; **maternity** *or* **paternity leave** = licencia *or* baja por maternidad *or* por paternidad; **sick leave** = licencia *or* baja por enfermedad; **to go on leave** *or* **to be on leave** = disfrutar de un permiso laboral *or* estar de permiso; **she is away on sick leave** *or* **on maternity leave** = está de baja por enfermedad *or* por maternidad **2** *verb* **(a)** *(to go away)* irse *or* marcharse *or* salir *or* abandonar; **he left his office early to go to the meeting** = salió de la oficina temprano para ir a la reunión; **the next plane leaves at 10.20** = el próximo avión sale a las 10.20; **to leave behind** = dejar atrás; **to leave on record** = dejar constancia **(b)** *(to resign)* dimitir *or* abandonar; **he left his job and bought a farm** = abandonó el trabajo y se compró una granja **(c)** *(legacy)* **he left his property in trust for his grandchildren** = dejó su propiedad en fideicomiso para ser entregada a sus nietos (NOTE: **leaving - left**)

◇ **leave out** ['liːv 'aʊt] *verb* omitir; **she left out the date on the letter** = omitió poner la fecha en la carta; **the contract leaves out all details of marketing arrangements** = el contrato omite todos los detalles sobre disposiciones comerciales

Lebanon ['lebənən] *noun* Líbano *m*

◇ **Lebanese** [lebə'niːz] *adjective & noun* libanés, -esa
NOTE: capital: **Beirut**; currency: **Lebanese pound (LL)** = libra libanesa (LL)

-led [led] *suffix* inducido por; **an export-led boom** = auge *or* crecimiento inducido por la exportación; **the consumer-led rise in sales** = incremento de ventas inducido por los consumidores

ledger ['ledʒə] *noun* libro *m* mayor; **bought ledger** *or* **purchase ledger** = libro mayor de compras; **bought ledger clerk** *or* **sales ledger clerk** = encargado del libro de compras *or* del libro de ventas; **nominal ledger** *or* **general ledger** = libro mayor de resultados; **payroll ledger** = registro de nóminas; **sales ledger** = libro mayor de ventas; **stock ledger** = libro de inventario

left [left] *adjective* izquierdo, -da; **the numbers run down the left side of the page** = los números figuran en el lado izquierdo de la página; **put the debits in the left column** = ponga los débitos en la columna izquierda; *see also* LEAVE

◇ **left-hand** ['lefthænd] *adjective* de la izquierda; **the debits are in the left-hand column in the accounts** = los débitos figuran en la columna de la izquierda de las cuentas; **he keeps the personnel files in the left-hand drawer of his desk** = guarda los expedientes del personal en el cajón de la izquierda de su mesa de despacho

left luggage office ['left 'lʌgɪdʒ 'ɒfɪs] *noun* consigna *f* (NOTE: US English is **baggage room** *or* **checkroom**)

legacy ['legəsi] *noun* legado *m or* herencia *f*

legal ['liːgəl] *adjective* **(a)** *(according to the law)* legal *or* lícito, -ta; **the company's action was**

completely legal = la actuación de la compañía fue completamente legal **(b)** *(referring to the law)* jurídico, -ca *or* judicial; **to take legal action** = entablar un pleito; **legal advice** = asesoramiento jurídico; **to take legal advice** = asesorarse jurídicamente *or* consultar a un abogado; **legal adviser** = asesor jurídico; *GB* **legal aid** = asistencia jurídica gratuita *or* turno de oficio; **legal claim** = reclamación *f or* derecho *m* legal; **he has no legal claim to the property** = no tiene derecho legítimo alguno sobre la propiedad; **legal costs** *or* **legal charges** *or* **legal expenses** = costas judiciales; **legal currency** = moneda de curso legal; **legal department** *or* **legal section** = asesoría jurídica; **legal expert** = jurista; **legal holiday** = fiesta oficial; **legal means** = medio lícito; **legal tender** = moneda de curso legal

◇ **legality** [lɪ'gæləti] *noun* legalidad *f*; **there is doubt about the legality of the company's action in dismissing him** = existen dudas sobre la legalidad de la actuación de la compañía al despedirlo

◇ **legalize** ['liːgəlaɪz] *verb* legalizar *or* legitimar

◇ **legalization** [liːgəlaɪ'zeɪʃən] *noun* legalización *f or* legitimación *f*

◇ **legally** ['liːgəli] *adverb* legalmente; **the contract is legally binding** = el contrato tiene fuerza jurídica; **the directors are legally responsible** = los consejeros son responsables ante la ley

legatee [legə'tiː] *noun* legatario, -ria

legislation [ledʒɪs'leɪʃən] *noun* legislación *f*; **labour legislation** = legislación laboral

lend [lend] *verb* prestar; **to lend something to someone** *or* **to lend someone something** = prestar algo a alguien; **he lent the company money** *or* **he lent money to the company** = prestó dinero a la compañía; **to lend money against security** = prestar dinero con garantía; **the bank lent him £50,000 to start his business** = el banco le prestó £50.000 para poner en marcha su negocio (NOTE: **lending - lent**)

◇ **lender** ['lendə] *noun* prestamista *mf*; **lender of the last resort** = prestamista en última instancia (banco central)

◇ **lending** ['lendɪŋ] *noun* concesión *f* de un préstamo; **lending limit** = límite de crédito

length [leŋθ] *noun* **(a)** longitud *f or* largo *m*; **inches and centimetres are measurements of length** = las pulgadas y los centímetros son medidas de longitud; **the boardroom table is twelve feet in length** = la mesa de la sala de juntas tiene 3m 50cm de longitud *or* de largo; **a table 3 metres in length** = una mesa de 3m de largo **(b)** **to go to great lengths to get something** = extremarse en conseguir algo; **they went to considerable lengths to keep the turnover secret** = hicieron todo lo posible por guardar en secreto el volumen de ventas

less [les] **1** *adjective* menos *or* menor *or* inferior; **we do not grant credit for sums of less than £100** = no concedemos crédito por sumas inferiores a £100; **he sold it for less than he had paid for it** = lo vendió por menos de lo que había pagado **2** *preposition* menos; **purchase price less 15% discount** = el precio de compra menos el 15% de descuento; **interest less service charges** = el interés menos la comisión bancaria

lessee [le'si:] *noun* arrendatario, -ria *or* inquilino, -na

◊ **lessor** [le'sɔ:] *noun* arrendador, -ra

let [let] **1** *verb* alquilar *or* arrendar; **to let an office** = alquilar una oficina; **offices to let** = oficinas de alquiler (NOTE: **letting - let**) **2** *noun* (periodo de) alquiler *or* arrendamiento; **they took the office on a short let** = alquilaron la oficina por un corto periodo de tiempo

◊ **let-out clause** ['letaʊt 'klɔ:z] *noun* cláusula *f* de excepción; **he added a let-out clause to the effect that the payments would be revised if the exchange rate fell by more than 5%** = añadió una cláusula de excepción especificando que los pagos se revisarían si el tipo de cambio bajaba más de un 5%

letter ['letə] *noun* (a) carta *f*; **business letter** = carta comercial; **circular letter** = circular *f*; **covering letter** = carta adjunta *or* explicatoria; **follow-up letter** = carta de reiteración *or* de contestación; **private letter** = carta personal; **standard letter** = carta tipo *or* modelo *or* standard *or* estándar (b) **letter of acknowledgement** = carta de acuse de recibo; **letters of administration** = nombramiento *m* de administrador judicial; **letter of allotment** *or* **allotment letter** = notificación *f* de la asignación de acciones en una sociedad; **letter of application** = carta de solicitud; **letter of appointment** = notificación del nombramiento para un puesto; **letter of comfort** = aval *m* *or* informe a favor; **letter of complaint** = carta de reclamación; **letter of indemnity** = garantía *f* de indemnización; **letter of intent** = carta de intención; **letters patent** = patente *f* de invención; **letter of reference** = carta de recomendación (c) **air letter** = aerograma *m*; **airmail letter** = carta por avión; **express letter** = carta urgente; **registered letter** = carta certificada (d) **to acknowledge receipt by letter** = enviar una carta de acuse de recibo (e) *(written or printed sign)* letra *f*; **write your name and address in block letters** *or* **in capital letters** = escriba su nombre y dirección con letras mayúsculas

◊ **letter of credit (L/C)** ['letə əv 'kredɪt] *noun* carta *f* de crédito; **irrevocable letter of credit** = carta de crédito irrevocable

◊ **letterhead** ['letəhed] *noun* (a) *(address at the top of notepaper)* membrete *m* (b) *(paper with printed address)* US papel *m* con membrete (NOTE: GB English is **headed paper**)

letting ['letɪŋ] *noun* **letting agency** = agencia *f* de alquiler de viviendas; **furnished lettings** = vivienda amueblada *or* local amueblado para alquilar

level ['levl] **1** *noun* nivel *m*; **low level of productivity** *or* **low productivity levels** = niveles bajos de productividad; **to raise the level of employee benefits** = aumentar el nivel de los subsidios de los empleados; **to lower the level of borrowings** = reducir el nivel de los préstamos; **high level of investment** = alto nivel de inversión; **a decision taken at the highest level** = una decisión tomada al más alto nivel; **low-level** = de bajo nivel *or* de grado inferior *or* poco importante; **a low-level delegation** = una delegación poco importante;

high-level = de alto nivel; **a high-level meeting** *or* **decision** = una decisión *or* reunión de alto nivel; **decisions taken at managerial level** = decisiones tomadas a nivel de dirección; **manning levels** *or* **staffing levels** = niveles de dotación de personal *or* de plantilla **2** *verb* **to level off** *or* **to level out** = nivelarse *or* estabilizarse; **profits have levelled off over the last few years** = los beneficios se han estabilizado en los últimos años; **prices are levelling out** = los precios se están estabilizando (NOTE: **levelling - levelled** but US **leveling - leveled**)

leverage ['li:vərɪdʒ] *noun* (a) *(influence)* influencia *f* *or* poder *m*; **he has no leverage over the chairman** = no tiene influencia sobre el presidente (b) *(ratio of capital borrowed)* coeficiente de endeudamiento de una empresa (c) *(borrowing to produce more money than the interest rate)* apalancamiento *m* financiero

◊ **leveraged buyout (LBO)** ['li:vərɪdʒd 'baɪaʊt] *noun* compra *or* adquisición apalancada

lever-arch file ['li:vɑ:tʃ 'faɪl] *noun* carpeta-archivo *f* de anillas

levy ['levi] **1** *noun* recaudación *f* de impuestos; **capital levy** = impuesto *m* sobre el capital; **import levy** = gravamen *m* sobre las importaciones; **levies on luxury items** = impuesto sobre los artículos de lujo; **training levy** = impuesto para financiar la formación profesional **2** *verb* imponer *or* recaudar *or* gravar; **the government has decided to levy a tax on imported cars** = el gobierno ha decidido gravar los coches de importación con un impuesto; **to levy a duty on the import of luxury items** = imponer un arancel a las importaciones de artículos de lujo; **to levy members for a new club house** = exigir una contribución a los miembros de un club para construir un nuevo local social

liability [laɪə'bɪlɪti] *noun* (a) *(legally responsible)* responsabilidad *f*; **to accept liability for something** = aceptar la responsabilidad de algo; **to refuse liability for something** = rechazar la responsabilidad de algo; **contractual liability** = responsabilidad contractual; **employers' liability insurance** = seguro de responsabilidad empresarial; **limited liability** = responsabilidad limitada; **limited liability company** = sociedad anónima *or* sociedad de responsabilidad limitada **(b)** *(debts)* **liabilities** = deudas *fpl or* obligaciones *fpl or* pasivo *m*; **the balance sheet shows the company's assets and liabilities** = el balance general muestra el activo y el pasivo de la sociedad; **current liabilities** = pasivo circulante; **long-term liabilities** = pasivo a largo plazo; **he was not able to meet his liabilities** = no pudo hacer frente a sus deudas; **to discharge one's liabilities in full** = pagar todas las deudas propias

◊ **liable** ['laɪəbl] *adjective* **(a) liable for** = responsable de; **liable for damages** = responsable de los daños causados; **the customer is liable for breakages** = el cliente es responsable de los desperfectos; **the chairman was personally liable for the company's debts** = el presidente era personalmente responsable de las deudas de la compañía **(b) liable to** = sujeto, -ta a *or* sometido, -da a *or* expuesto, -ta a; **liable to pay a fine** = expuesto a una multa; **goods which are liable to stamp duty** = mercancías sujetas al impuesto del timbre

libel ['laɪbəl] **1** *noun* libelo *m or* difamación *f or* escrito *m* difamatorio; **action for libel** *or* **libel action** = demanda *f* por difamación **2** *verb* to libel = difamar por escrito a alguien (NOTA: **libelling - libelled** but US **libeling - libeled.** Compare SLANDER)

Liberia [laɪ'bi:rɪə] *noun* Liberia

◊ **Liberian** [laɪ'bi:rɪən] *adjective & noun* liberiano, -na
NOTE: capital: **Monrovia**; currency: **Liberian dollar** = dólar liberiano

Libya ['lɪbjə] *noun* Libia *f*

◊ **Libyan** ['lɪbjən] *adjective & noun* libio, -bia
NOTE: capital: **Tripoli** (= Tripoli); currency: **Libyan dinar (LD)** = dinar libio (LD)

licence *or* US **license** ['laɪsəns] *noun* **(a)** licencia *f or* permiso *m*; **driving licence** *or* US **driver's license** = permiso de conducir; **applicants should hold a valid driving licence** = los candidatos deben tener un permiso de conducir válido; **import licence** *or* **export licence** = licencia de importación *or* licencia de exportación; **liquor licence** = licencia de venta de bebidas alcohólicas; **off licence** = licencia de venta de bebidas alcohólicas para ser consumidas fuera del establecimiento **(b) goods manufactured under licence** = mercancías fabricadas bajo licencia

◊ **license** ['laɪsəns] **1** *noun* US = LICENCE **2** *verb* conceder una licencia *or* un permiso; **licensed to sell beers, wines and spirits** = con licencia para la venta de cerveza, vinos y licores; **to license a company to manufacture spare parts** = conceder una licencia para fabricar piezas de recambio; **she is licensed to run an employment agency** = tiene licencia para dirigir una agencia de colocación; **licensed deposit-taker (LDT)** *or* **licensed institution** = sociedad (bancaria) autorizada para recibir depósitos

◊ **licensee** [laɪsən'si:] *noun* concesionario, -ria

◊ **licensing** ['laɪsənsɪŋ] *noun* licencia *f or* autorización *f*; **a licensing agreement** = un contrato de licencia; **licensing laws** = leyes que regulan la concesión de licencias; *GB* **licensing hours** = horario para la venta de bebidas alcohólicas

Liechtenstein ['lɪxtənʃtaɪn] *noun* Liechtenstein
NOTE: capital: **Vaduz**; currency: **Swiss franc** = franco suizo

lien [li:n] *noun* gravamen *m or* derecho *m* de retención

lieu [lju:] *noun* **in lieu of** = en vez de *or* en lugar de *or* como; **she was given two months' salary in lieu of notice** = le dieron dos meses de sueldo en lugar del aviso de despido

life [laɪf] *noun* **(a)** *(time when a person is alive)* vida *f*; **for life** = de por vida *or* para toda la vida; **his pension gives him a comfortable income for life** = su pensión le proporciona un cómodo ingreso de por vida; **life annuity** *or* **annuity for life** = anualidad *or* renta vitalicia *or* pensión vitalicia; **the life assured** *or* **the life insured** = la persona asegurada; **life assurance** *or* **life insurance** = seguro de vida; **life expectancy** = esperanza *f* de vida; **life interest** = usufructo vitalicio **(b)** *(period of time something exists)* vida *or* vigencia *f or* duración *f*; **the life of a loan** = la duración de un préstamo; **during the life of the agreement** = mientras exista el acuerdo; **shelf life of a product** = periodo de conservación de un producto

◊ **lifeboat** ['laɪfbəʊt] *noun* bote *m* salvavidas *or* lancha *f* de salvamento; **lifeboat operation** = operación de rescate de una empresa

LIFO ['laɪfəʊ] = LAST IN FIRST OUT

lift [lɪft] **1** *noun* ascensor *m*; **he took the lift to the 27th floor** = tomó el ascensor hasta el piso 27; **the staff could not get into their office when the lift broke down** = los empleados no pudieron entrar en la oficina al averiarse el ascensor (NOTE: US English is **elevator**) **2** *verb* levantar *or* suprimir; **the government has lifted the ban on imports from Japan** = el gobierno ha suprimido la prohibición a las importaciones de Japón; **to lift trade barriers** = levantar *or* suprimir barreras comerciales; **the minister has lifted the embargo on the export of computers to East European countries** = el ministro ha levantado el embargo a la exportación de ordenadores a los países de Europa del Este

light [laɪt] *adjective* **(a)** *(not heavy)* ligero, -ra; **shares fell back in light trading** = las acciones bajaron en un día de poco movimiento; **light industry** = industria ligera **(b)** *(lighting)* luminoso, -sa; **light pen** = lápiz óptico *or* fotosensible *or* luminoso

◊ **lighter** ['laɪtə] *noun* **(a)** *(lighting)* encendedor *m* **(b)** *(boat)* barcaza *f or* gabarra *f*

limit ['lɪmɪt] **1** *noun* límite *m or* acotación *f*; **to set limits** = acotar; **to set limits to imports** *or* **to impose import limits** = limitar *or* imponer límites a las importaciones; **to set voluntary limits** = autolimitarse; **age limit** = límite de edad *or* edad máxima; **there is an age limit of thirty-five on the post of buyer** = existe un límite de edad de treinta y cinco años para el puesto de comprador; **credit limit** = límite de crédito; **he has exceeded his credit limit** = ha excedido su límite de crédito; **lending limit** = límite de crédito; **time limit** = plazo *m or* término *m*;

to set a time limit for acceptance of the offer = poner un término para la aceptación de una oferta; **weight limit** = peso máximo **2** *verb* limitar; **the banks have limited their credit** = los bancos han limitado su crédito; **each agent is limited to twenty-five units** = cada representante tiene un límite de veinticinco unidades

◊ **limitation** [lɪmɪ'teɪʃən] *noun* **(a)** limitación *f or* restricción *f*; **limitation of liability** = limitación de la responsabilidad; **time limitation** = plazo *m* de tiempo límite; **the contract imposes limitations on the number of cars which can be imported** = el contrato impone limitaciones al número de coches que pueden importarse **(b) statute of limitations** = ley de prescripción

◊ **limited** ['lɪmɪtɪd] *adjective* limitado, -da; **limited company** *or* **limited liability company** = sociedad de responsabilidad limitada (S.R.L.) (NOTE: shortened to **Ltd**) **public limited company** sociedad anónima (S.A.) (NOTE: written as **Plc**) **private limited company** = sociedad limitada (S.L.); **limited market** = mercado limitado *or* con escaso movimiento; **limited partner** = socio comanditario; **limited partnership** = sociedad en comandita *or* de responsabilidad limitada

◊ **limiting** ['lɪmɪtɪŋ] *adjective* restrictivo, -va *or* limitativo, -va; **a limiting clause in a contract** = cláusula restrictiva en un contrato; **the short holiday season is a limiting factor on the hotel trade** = la corta temporada de vacaciones es un factor limitativo del negocio hotelero

line [laɪn] *noun* **(a)** *(long mark)* línea *f or* raya *f or* trazo *m*; **I prefer notepaper without any lines** = prefiero el papel de cartas sin rayas; **he drew a thick line across the bottom of the column to show which figure was the total** = trazó una línea gruesa al final de la columna para indicar la cifra total **(b)** *(company)* **shipping line** *or* **airline** = compañía naviera *or* compañía aérea; **profits of major airlines have been affected by the rise in fuel prices** = los beneficios de las principales compañías aéreas se han visto afectados por la subida de precios del combustible **(c)** *(type of business)* **line of business** *or* **line of work** = ramo *m* comercial *or* profesional; **what is his line?** = ¿a qué se dedica?; **product line** = gama *f* de productos *or* línea de productos; **we do not stock that line** = no tratamos *or* no vendemos esa gama de productos; **computers are not one of our best-selling lines** = los ordenadores no son uno de los artículos que más vendemos; **they produce an interesting line in garden tools** = fabrican una interesante gama de herramientas de jardinería **(d)** *(row on a page)* línea *or* renglón *m*; **bottom line** = saldo *m* final; **the boss is interested only in the bottom line** = al jefe sólo le interesa el saldo final; **to open a line of credit** *or* **a credit line** = conceder *or* abrir una línea de crédito **(e) assembly line** *or* **production line** = cadena de montaje; **he works on the production line** *or* **he is a production line worker in the car factory** = trabaja en la cadena de montaje *or* es un trabajador de la cadena de montaje de la fábrica de coches **(f) line chart** *or* **line graph** = gráfico *m* lineal; **line printer** = impresora *f* de líneas **(g) line of command** *or* **line management** *or* **line organization** = orden *m* jerárquico *or* gerencia *f* lineal *or* organización *f* lineal **(h) telephone line** = línea telefónica; **the line is bad** = se oye mal; **a crossed line** = cruce *m* de líneas *or* interferencia *f* en la comunicación; **the line is engaged** = la línea está

ocupada; **the chairman is on the other line** = el presidente está hablando por la otra línea; **outside line** = línea exterior **(i)** *(queue)* US cola *f*

◊ **linear** *adjective* lineal; **linear function** = función lineal

◊ **lined** [laɪnd] *adjective* rayado, -da; **he prefers lined paper for writing notes** = prefiere papel rayado para tomar apuntes

◊ **liner** ['laɪnə] *noun* transatlántico *m*

QUOTE the best thing would be to have a few more plants close down and bring supply more in line with current demand
Fortune

QUOTE cash paid for overstocked lines, factory seconds, slow sellers, etc.
Australian Financial Review

link [lɪŋk] **1** *noun* conexión *f or* vínculo *m or* enlace *f* **2** *verb* unir *or* vincular *or* ajustar; **to link pensions to inflation** = ajustar las pensiones a la inflación; **his salary is linked to the cost of living** = su salario está ajustado al coste de la vida; **to link bonus payments to productivity** = supeditar el pago de bonificaciones a la productividad

liquid ['lɪkwɪd] *adjective* **liquid assets** = activo líquido; **to go liquid** = liquidar el activo

◊ **liquidate** ['lɪkwɪdeɪt] *verb* saldar; **to liquidate a company** = liquidar *or* disolver una sociedad; **to liquidate a debt** = liquidar *or* saldar una deuda; **to liquidate stock** = liquidar las existencias

◊ **liquidation** [lɪkwɪ'deɪʃən] *noun* **(a) liquidation of a debt** = liquidación *f or* saldo *m* de una deuda **(b)** liquidación; **the company went into liquidation** = la sociedad entró en liquidación; **compulsory liquidation** = liquidación forzosa; **voluntary liquidation** = liquidación voluntaria

◊ **liquidator** ['lɪkwɪdeɪtə] *noun* síndico *m or* depositario *m*

◊ **liquidity** [lɪ'kwɪdəti] *noun* liquidez *f*; **liquidity crisis** = crisis *f* de liquidez

lira ['lɪərə] *noun (currency used in Italy)* lira *f*; **the book cost 2,700 lira** *or* **L2,700** = el libro costó 2.700 liras (NOTE: **lira** is usually written **L** before figures: **L2,700)**

list [lɪst] **1** *noun* **(a)** *(of items)* lista *f or* relación *f*; **list of products** *or* **product list** = lista de productos; **stock list** = inventario *m*; **to add an item to a list** = añadir un artículo a una lista; **to cross an item off a list** = tachar un artículo de una lista; **address list** *or* **mailing list** = lista de direcciones *or* destinatarios; **black list** = lista negra; **picking list** = inventario de posición (en almacén) **(b)** *(catalogue)* catálogo *m*; **list price** = precio de catálogo; **price list** = lista de precios **2** *verb* **(a)** hacer una lista *or* enumerar; **to list products by category** = hacer una lista de productos por categorías; **to list representatives by area** = hacer una lista de representantes por zonas; **to list products in a catalogue** = enumerar los productos en un catálogo; **the catalogue lists twenty-three models of washing machines** = el catálogo enumera veintitrés modelos de lavadoras **(b) listed company** = sociedad cotizada en bolsa; **listed securities** = valores cotizables *or* registrados

◊ **listing** ['lɪstɪŋ] *noun* **(a)** listado *m*; **Stock**

Exchange listing = derecho a cotizar en la bolsa; **the company is planning to obtain a Stock Exchange listing** = la compañía intenta conseguir que sus acciones se coticen en la bolsa **(b) computer listing** = listado *m* de ordenador; **listing paper** = papel de impresora

literature ['lɪtrətʃə] *noun* documentación *f* or información *f*; **please send me literature about your new product range** = sírvanse enviarme documentación sobre su nueva gama de productos

litigation [lɪtɪ'geɪʃən] *noun* litigio *m* or pleito *m*

litre or US **liter** ['liːtə] *noun* litro *m*; **the car does fifteen kilometres to the litre** or **fifteen kilometres per litre** = el coche consume unos 7 litros por 100 kilómetros (NOTE: usually written l after figures: **25l**)

lively ['laɪvli] *adjective* **lively market** = mercado animado

living ['lɪvɪŋ] *noun* **cost of living** = coste *m* de vida; **cost-of-living index** = índice *m* del coste de vida; **he does not earn a living wage** = no gana el salario mínimo vital; **standard of living** or **living standards** = nivel *m* de vida; **living standards fell as unemployment rose** = el nivel de vida descendió a medida que aumentaba el paro

Lloyd's [lɔɪdz] *noun* Compañía de Seguros Lloyd; **Lloyd's Register** = Registro Marítimo de Lloyd; **ship which is A1 at Lloyd's** = buque en perfectas condiciones

COMMENT: Lloyd's is an old-established insurance market: the underwriters who form Lloyd's are divided into syndicates, each made up of active underwriters who arrange the business and non-working underwriters (called 'names') who stand surety for any insurance claims which may arise

load [ləʊd] **1** *noun* **(a)** *(goods)* carga *f* or cargamento *m* de un barco; **load of a lorry** or **of a container** = carga (género) de un camión or de un contenedor; **lorry-load** or **container-load** = carga (cantidad) de un camión or de un contenedor; **a container-load of spare parts is missing** = falta un contenedor con piezas de recambio; **they delivered six lorry-loads** or **truckloads of coal** = entregaron seis camionadas de carbón; **commercial load** = carga útil; **maximum load** = carga máxima; **load-carrying capacity** = capacidad *f* de carga; **load factor** = coeficiente *m* de ocupación **(b) workload** = carga de trabajo; **he has difficulty in coping with his heavy workload** = tiene dificultades en hacer frente a su pesada carga de trabajo **2** *verb* **(a)** *(cargo)* cargar; **to load a lorry** or **a ship** = cargar un camión or un barco; **to load cargo onto a ship** = cargar un barco; **a truck loaded with boxes** = un camión cargado de cajas; **a ship loaded with iron** = un barco cargado de hierro; **fully loaded ship** = un barco completamente cargado **(b)** *(of ship)* tomar carga; **the ship is loading a cargo of wood** = el barco está tomando un cargamento de madera **(c)** *(computer)* cargar; **load the word-processing program before you start keyboarding** = cargue el programa del procesador de textos antes de empezar a teclear **(d)** *(insurance)* cargar gastos; **back-end loaded** = gastos deducidos de los beneficios; **front-end loaded** = *(on first premium)* gastos iniciales; *(on a sliding scale)* gastos degresivos

◊ **loading** ['ləʊdɪŋ] *noun* **loading bay** = nave *f* de carga; **loading dock** = muelle *m* de carga; **loading ramp** = rampa *f* de carga

◊ **load line** ['ləʊd 'laɪn] *noun (line painted on a ship)* línea *f* de carga or de flotación

loan [ləʊn] **1** *noun* préstamo *m*; **loan capital** = empréstito *m* **loan stock** = obligaciones *fpl* **convertible loan stock** = empréstito convertible en acciones; **bank loan** = préstamo bancario; **bridging loan** = crédito puente; **government loan** = empréstito *m* estatal; **home loan** = préstamo de ahorro-vivienda; **short-term loan** = préstamo a corto plazo; **long-term loan** = préstamo a largo plazo; **soft loan** = crédito blando or prestaciones sin interés; **unsecured loan** = préstamo sin garantía **2** *verb* prestar

QUOTE over the last few weeks, companies raising new loans from international banks have been forced to pay more, and an unusually high number of attempts to syndicate loans among banks has failed
Financial Times

lobby ['lɒbi] **1** *noun* grupo *m* de presión; **the energy-saving lobby** = grupo de presión para el ahorro de energía **2** *verb* ejercer presión or presionar or hacer gestiones; **the group lobbied the chairmen of all the committees** = el grupo ejerció presión sobre los presidentes de todos los comités

local ['ləʊkəl] **1** *adjective* local; **local authority** = autoridad local or municipalidad *f*; **local call** = llamada local; **local government** = administración local; **local labour** = mano de obra local **2** *noun US* sección *f* local de un sindicato

◊ **locally** ['ləʊkəli] *adverb* localmente or de la localidad; **we recruit all our staff locally** = contratamos a todos nuestros empleados en plaza

QUOTE each cheque can be made out for the local equivalent of £100 rounded up to a convenient figure
Sunday Times

QUOTE the business agent for Local 414 of the Store Union said his committee will recommend that the membership ratify the agreement
Toronto Star

QUOTE EEC regulations insist that customers can buy cars anywhere in the EEC at the local pre-tax price
Financial Times

locate [ləʊ'keɪt] *verb* **to be located** = estar situado or encontrarse; **the warehouse is located near to the motorway** = el almacén está situado cerca de la autopista

◊ **located** [ləʊ'keɪtɪd] *adjective* situado, -da or sito, -ta; **Cintas S.A., company located in Albacete** = la empresa Cintas S.A., sita en Albacete

◊ **location** [lə'keɪʃən] *noun* localización *f* or sitio *m* or ubicación *f* or emplazamiento *m*; **the company has moved to a new location** = la empresa se ha trasladado a una nueva dirección

lock [lɒk] **1** *noun* cerradura *f*; **the lock on the petty cash box is broken** = la cerradura de la caja para gastos menores está rota; **I have forgotten the combination of the lock on my briefcase** = he olvidado la combinación de la cerradura de mi cartera **2** *verb* cerrar con llave; **the manager forgot to lock the door of the computer room** = el director olvidó cerrar con llave la puerta de la sala de ordenadores; **the petty cash box was not locked** = la caja para gastos menores no estaba cerrada con llave

◊ **lock out** ['lɒk 'aʊt] *verb* **to lock out workers** = declarar el cierre patronal

◊ **lockout** ['lɒkaʊt] *noun* cierre *m* patronal *or* 'lock-out' *m*

◊ **lock up** ['lɒk 'ʌp] *verb* **to lock up a shop** *or* **an office** = cerrar una tienda *or* una oficina; **to lock up capital** = inmovilizar capital

◊ **locking up** ['lɒkɪŋ 'ʌp] *noun* **the locking up of money in stock** = la inmovilización de dinero en acciones

◊ **lock-up shop** *or* **lock-up premises** ['lɒkʌp 'ʃɒp *or* 'premɪsɪz] *noun* tienda *f* sin vivienda para el comerciante

lodge [lɒdʒ] *verb* depositar *or* colocar; **to lodge a complaint against someone** = presentar una demanda contra alguien; **to lodge money with someone** = confiar dinero a alguien; **to lodge securities as collateral** = depositar valores como garantía prendaria

log [lɒg] *verb* anotar *or* apuntar; **to log phone calls** = anotar las llamadas recibidas; **all stock movements are logged by the computer** = el ordenador registra todos los movimientos de las existencias (NOTE: **logging - logged**)

logical ['lɒdʒɪkl] *adjective* lógico, -ca

logo ['lɒgəʊ] *noun* logotipo *m*

long [lɒŋ] **1** *adjective* largo, -ga; **long credit** = crédito a largo plazo; **in the long term** = a largo plazo *or* a la larga; **to take the long view** = hacer proyectos a largo plazo **2** *noun* **longs** = títulos *mpl* del Estado con un vencimiento superior a los quince años

◊ **long-dated** ['lɒŋ 'deɪtɪd] *adjective* **long-dated bill** = letra a largo plazo

◊ **long-distance** ['lɒŋ 'dɪstəns] *adjective* **a long-distance call** = llamada *or* conferencia interurbana; **long-distance flight** = vuelo de larga distancia *or* de largo recorrido

◊ **longhand** ['lɒŋhænd] *noun* escritura *f* a mano; **applications should be written in longhand and sent to the personnel officer** = las solicitudes deben escribirse a mano y enviarse al jefe de personal

◊ **long-haul** ['lɒŋ 'hɔːl] *adjective* de gran distancia *or* de gran radio de acción; **long-haul flight** = vuelo de larga distancia

◊ **long-range** ['lɒŋ 'reɪn(d)ʒ] *adjective* a largo plazo; **long-range economic forecast** = previsión económica a largo plazo

◊ **long-standing** ['lɒŋ 'stændɪŋ] *adjective* antiguo, -gua *or* de hace tiempo *or* de muchos años; **long-standing agreement** = acuerdo de muchos años; **long-standing customer** *or* **customer of long standing** = cliente antiguo *or* de muchos años

◊ **long-term** ['lɒŋtɜːm] *adjective* a largo plazo; **on a long-term basis** = a largo plazo; **long-term**

debts = deudas a largo plazo; **long-term forecast** = previsión a largo plazo; **long-term loan** = préstamo a largo plazo; **long-term objectives** = objetivos a largo plazo; **the long-term unemployed** = desempleados de larga duración; **long-term unemployment** = desempleo *or* paro de larga duración

> QUOTE land held under long-term leases is not amortized
>
> **Hongkong Standard**

> QUOTE the company began to experience a demand for longer-term mortgages when the flow of money used to finance these loans diminished
>
> **Globe and Mail (Toronto)**

loophole ['luːphəʊl] *noun* escapatoria *f or* laguna *f*; **to find a loophole in the law** = encontrar una escapatoria legal; **to find a tax loophole** = encontrar una laguna fiscal

> QUOTE because capital gains are not taxed but money taken out in profits is taxed, owners of businesses will be using accountants and tax experts to find loopholes in the law
>
> **Toronto Star**

loose [luːs] *adjective* suelto, -ta *or* a granel; **loose change** = cambio *m*; **to sell loose coffee** *or* **to sell coffee loose** = vender café a granel

◊ **loose-leaf book** ['luːsliːf 'bʊk] *noun* libro *m* de hojas sueltas

lorry ['lɒri] *noun* camión *m*; **he drives a five-ton lorry** = conduce un camión de cinco toneladas; **articulated lorry** = camión con remolque; **heavy lorry** = camión pesado; **lorry driver** = conductor *m* de camión *or* camionero *m* (NOTE: US English is **truck**)

lose [luːz] *verb* **(a)** *(not to have anymore)* perder; **to lose an order** = perder un pedido; **during the strike, the company lost six orders to American competitors** = durante la huelga, la empresa perdió seis pedidos que fueron a los competidores estadounidenses; **to lose control of a company** = perder la dirección *or* el control de una compañía; **to lose customers** = perder clientes; **their service is so slow that they have been losing customers** = tienen un servicio tan lento que han ido perdiendo clientes; **she lost her job when the factory closed** = perdió su trabajo cuando cerró la fábrica **(b)** *(to have less money)* perder dinero; **he lost £25,000 in his father's computer company** = perdió £25.000 en la empresa de ordenadores de su padre; **the pound has lost value** = la libra ha perdido valor **(c)** *(to drop to a lower price)* bajar *or* caer; **the dollar lost two cents against the yen** = el dólar bajó dos centavos frente al yen; **gold shares lost 5% on the market yesterday** = las acciones de las minas de oro bajaron ayer un 5% en el mercado (NOTE: **losing - lost**)

◊ **lose out** ['luːz 'aʊt] *verb* perder *or* salir perdiendo; **the company has lost out in the rush to make cheap computers** = la empresa ha salido perdiendo al precipitarse a fabricar ordenadores baratos

loss [lɒs] *noun* **(a)** *(not having anymore)* pérdida *f*; **loss of customers** = pérdida *f* de clientela; **job losses** = pérdida de puestos de trabajo; **loss of an order** =

pérdida de un pedido; **the company suffered a loss of market penetration** = la empresa sufrió una pérdida de su cuota de mercado; **compensation for loss of earnings** = indemnización por pérdida de ingresos; **compensation for loss of office** = indemnización por cese en el cargo **(b)** (*not making a profit*) pérdida; **the company suffered a loss** = la compañía sufrió una pérdida; **to report a loss** = anunciar un déficit; **the company reported a loss of £1m on the first year's trading** = la compañía anunció que había sufrido pérdidas por valor de £1 millón en el primer año; **capital loss** = pérdidas de capital *or* minusvalías; **paper loss** = pérdida sobre el papel; **trading loss** = pérdida de explotación; **at a loss** = con pérdidas; **the company is trading at a loss** = la compañía trabaja con pérdidas; **he sold the shop at a loss** = vendió la tienda con pérdida; **to cut one's losses** = cortar por lo sano *or* reducir las pérdidas **(c)** (*being worth less*) pérdida; **shares showed losses of up to 5% on the Stock Exchange** = las acciones experimentaron pérdidas en la bolsa de hasta un 5% **(d)** loss in weight = pérdida de peso; **loss in transport** = pérdida natural (durante el transporte) **(e)** (*insurance: damage to property*) loss adjuster = tasador de pérdidas; **the car was written off as a dead loss** *or* **a total loss** = el coche se consideró un siniestro total

◊ **loss-leader** ['lɒs 'liːdə] *noun* artículo *m* de reclamo *or* de lanzamiento; **we use these cheap films as a loss-leader** = utilizamos estas películas baratas como artículos de reclamo

QUOTE against losses of FFr 7.7m in 1983, the company made a net profit of FFr 300,000 last year
Financial Times

lot [lɒt] *noun* **(a)** (*large quantity*) gran cantidad *f*; **a lot of people** *or* **lots of people are out of work** = hay mucha gente parada *or* sin trabajo **(b)** (*group of items*) lote *m* *or* partida *f*; **to bid for lot 23** = pujar por el lote 23; **at the end of the auction half the lots were unsold** = al terminar la subasta la mitad de los lotes quedaron sin vender **(c)** (*group of shares*) lote *or* paquete *m*; **to sell a lot of shares** = vender un paquete de acciones; **to sell shares in small lots** = vender acciones en lotes pequeños **(d)** (*piece of land*) *US* parcela *f or* finca *f*

lottery ['lɒtəri] *noun* lotería *f*

lounge [laʊn(d)ʒ] *noun* salón *m*; **departure lounge** = sala *f* de embarque; **transit lounge** = sala *f* de tránsito

low [ləʊ] **1** *adjective* bajo, -ja; **low overhead costs keep the unit cost low** = los gastos generales bajos mantienen bajo el coste unitario; **we try to keep our wages bill low** = intentamos mantener bajos nuestros gastos de personal; **the company offered him a mortgage at a low rate of interest** = la compañía le ofreció una hipoteca a un tipo de interés bajo ; **the pound is at a very low rate of exchange against the dollar** = la libra tiene un tipo de cambio muy bajo frente al dólar; **our aim is to buy at the lowest price possible** = nuestro objetivo es comprar al más bajo precio posible; **shares are at their lowest for two years** = las acciones están al precio más bajo de los dos últimos años; **low sales** = ventas bajas; **low volume of sales** = un volumen de ventas bajo; **the tender will go to the lowest bidder** = el contrato se adjudicará al mejor postor (a la oferta

más baja) **2** *noun* mínimo *m*; **sales have reached a new low** = las ventas han alcanzado un nuevo mínimo; **the highs and lows on the stock market** = las altas y bajas del mercado de valores; **shares have hit an all-time low** = las acciones nunca han estado tan bajas

◊ **lower** ['ləʊə] **1** *adjective* más bajo, -ja *or* inferior; **a lower rate of interest** = un tipo de interés más bajo; **sales were lower in December than in November** = las ventas fueron más bajas en diciembre que en noviembre **2** *verb* bajar; **to lower prices to secure a larger market share** = bajar los precios para conseguir una mayor participación en el mercado; **to lower the interest rate** = bajar el tipo de interés

◊ **lowering** ['ləʊərɪŋ] *noun* disminución *f or* reducción *f*; **lowering of prices** = reducción de precios; **we hope to achieve low prices with no lowering of quality** = esperamos conseguir unos precios bajos sin reducir la calidad

◊ **low-grade** ['ləʊɡreɪd] *adjective* de baja calidad *or* poca categoría *or* grado inferior; **a low-grade official from the Ministry of Commerce** = un funcionario de poca categoría del Ministerio de Comercio; **the car runs best on low-grade petrol** = el coche funciona mejor con gasolina normal

◊ **low-level** ['ləʊ'levl] *adjective* **(a)** (*not important*) de bajo nivel *or* de grado inferior *or* poco importante; **a low-level delegation visited the ministry** = una delegación poco importante visitó el ministerio; **a low-level meeting decided to put off making a decision** = en una reunión de bajo nivel se decidió aplazar la decisión **(b)** (*computer*) low-level computer language = lenguaje de programación poco perfeccionado

◊ **low-pressure** ['ləʊ'preʃə] *adjective* low-pressure sales = ventas sin insistencia

◊ **low-quality** ['ləʊ'kwɒləti] *adjective* de baja calidad *or* mediocre; **they tried to sell us some low-quality steel** = intentaron vendernos acero de baja calidad

QUOTE after opening at 79.1 the index touched a peak of 79.2 and then drifted to a low of 78.8
Financial Times

QUOTE the pound which had been as low as $1.02 earlier this year, rose to $1.30
Fortune

QUOTE Canadian and European negotiators agreed to a deal under which Canada could keep its quotas but lower its import duties
Globe and Mail (Toronto)

QUOTE the trade-weighted dollar chart shows there has been a massive devaluation of the dollar since the mid-'80s and the currency is at its all-time low
Financial Weekly

loyalty ['lɔɪəlti] *noun* brand loyalty = fidelidad *f* a la marca; **customer loyalty** = fidelidad a un establecimiento

Ltd ['lɪmɪtɪd] = LIMITED

lucrative ['luːkrətɪv] *adjective* lucrativo, -va

luggage ['lʌɡɪdʒ] *noun* equipaje *m or* maletas *fpl*;

hand luggage *or* **cabin luggage** = equipaje de mano; **free luggage allowance** = franquicia (de equipaje); **luggage trolley** = carro *or* carrito del equipaje (NOTE: the US for this is **baggage cart**. There is no plural: to show one suitcase, etc., say **a piece of luggage.** Note also that US English prefers to use the word **baggage** instead of **luggage**)

lull [lʌl] *noun* calma *f*; **after last week's hectic trading this week's lull was welcome** = después de la agitada actividad comercial de la semana pasada, la calma de esta semana es de agradecer

lump [lʌmp] *noun* **lump sum** = suma *f* global *or* pago *m* único; **when he retired he was given a lump-sum bonus** = cuando se retiró le dieron una bonificación; **she sold her house and invested the money as a lump sum** = vendió su casa e invirtió el dinero en su totalidad

lunch [lʌn(t)ʃ] *noun* almuerzo *m or* comida *f*; **the hours of work are from 9.30 to 5.30 with an hour off for lunch** = el horario de trabajo es de 9.30 a 5.30 con una hora para el almuerzo; **the chairman is out at lunch** = el presidente ha salido a almorzar; **business lunch** = comida *or* almuerzo de negocios

◊ **lunch hour** *or* **lunchtime** ['lʌn(t)ʃ 'aʊə *or* 'lʌn(t)ʃtaɪm] *noun* hora *f* de comer *or* del almuerzo; **the office is closed during the lunch hour** *or* **at lunchtimes** = la oficina está cerrada durante la hora de comer *or* del almuerzo

◊ **luncheon voucher** ['lʌn(t)ʃən 'vaʊtʃə] *noun* vale *m* para una comida

Luxembourg ['lʌksəmbɜːg] **1** *noun* Luxemburgo *m* **2** *adjective* luxemburgués, -esa

◊ **Luxembourger** *or* **Luxemburger** ['lʌksəmbɜːgə] *noun* luxemburgués, -esa
NOTE: currency: **Luxembourg franc (LuxF)** = franco luxemburgués (FLux)

luxury ['lʌkʃəri] *noun* lujo *m*; **luxury items** *or* **luxury goods** = artículos de lujo; **black market in luxury articles** = mercado negro de artículos de lujo

Mm

m = METRE, MILE, MILLION m

M0, M1, M2, M3 ['em'nɔːt *or* 'em'wʌn *or* 'em'tu: *or* 'em'θriː] definiciones de la oferta monetaria *or* M0, M1, M2, M3 (NOTE: when referring to the British money supply, written **£M3,** say 'sterling M3')

> QUOTE Bank of England calculations of notes in circulation suggest that the main component of the narrow measure of money supply, M0, is likely to have risen by 0.4 per cent after seasonal adjustments
> **Times**

machine [mə'ʃiːn] *noun* **(a)** máquina *f*; **adding machine** = máquina de sumar; **copying machine** *or* **duplicating machine** = máquina de sacar copias *or* multicopista; **dictating machine** = dictáfono *m*; **automatic vending machine** = máquina expendedora *or* distribuidora automática; **machine shop** = taller mecánico; **machine tools** = máquinas-herramienta **(b)** **machine-made** *or* **machine-produced** = hecho, -cha a máquina **(c)** **machine code** *or* **machine language** = código de máquina *or* lenguaje máquina; **machine-readable codes** = códigos legibles por el ordenador

◊ **machinery** [mə'ʃiːnəri] *noun* **(a)** *(machine)* maquinaria *f*; **idle machinery** *or* **machinery lying idle** = maquinaria parada; **machinery guards** = dispositivos protectores *or* de seguridad **(b)** *(system)* mecanismo *m* *or* aparato *m*; **the government machinery** = aparato estatal; **the machinery of local government** = la organización del gobierno local; **administrative machinery** = aparato *or* mecanismo administrativo; **the machinery for awarding government contracts** = el trámite para la concesión de contratos estatales

◊ **machinist** [mə'ʃiːnɪst] *noun* maquinista *mf*

macro- ['mækrə(ʊ)] *prefix* macro; **macro-economics** = macroeconomía *f*

Madam ['mædəm] *noun* Señora *f*; **Dear Madam** = Estimada Señora; **Madam Chairman** = Señora Presidenta

Madagascar [mædə'gæskə] *noun* Madagascar *m*

◊ **Madagascan** [mædə'gæskən] *adjective & noun* malgache
NOTE: capital: **Antananarivo**; currency: **Malagasy franc (FMG)** = franco malgache (FMG)

made [meɪd] *adjective* hecho, -cha *or* fabricado, -da; **made in Japan** *or* **Japanese made** = fabricado en Japón; *see also* MAKE

magazine [mægə'ziːn] *noun* revista *f*; **computer magazine** = revista de informática; **do-it-yourself magazine** = revista de bricolaje; **house magazine** = boletín *m* interno de una empresa; **trade magazine** = revista de una actividad profesional determinada; **travel magazine** = revista de viajes; **women's**

magazine = revista para mujeres; **magazine insert** = encarte publicitario de una revista; **to insert a leaflet in a specialist magazine** = insertar un folleto publicitario en una revista especializada; **magazine mailing** = envío de revistas por correo

magistrate ['mædʒɪstreɪt] *noun* juez *m* *or* magistrado, -da; **Magistrates' Court** = juzgado *m* de paz

magnate ['mægneɪt] *noun* magnate *m*; **a shipping magnate** = magnate de la industria naviera

magnetic [mæg'netɪk] *adjective* magnético, -ca; **magnetic card** = tarjeta magnética; **magnetic strip** = banda magnética

◊ **magnetic tape** *or* **mag tape** [mæg'netɪk 'teɪp *or* 'mæg 'teɪp] *noun* cinta *f* magnética

mail [meɪl] **1** *noun* **(a)** *(postal system)* correo *m*; **to put a letter in the mail** = echar una carta al correo; **the cheque was lost in the mail** = el cheque se perdió en el correo; **the invoice was put in the mail yesterday** = la factura se envió por correo ayer; **mail to some of the islands in the Pacific can take six weeks** = el correo a algunas de las islas del Pacífico puede tardar seis semanas en llegar; **by mail** = por correo; **to send a package by surface mail** = enviar un paquete por correo ordinario; **by sea mail** = por correo marítimo; **to receive a sample by air mail** = recibir una muestra por correo aéreo; **we sent the order by first-class mail** = enviamos el pedido por correo de primera clase; **electronic mail** = correo electrónico **(b)** *(letters sent or received)* correo *m* *or* correspondencia *f*; **has the mail arrived yet?** = ¿ha llegado ya la correspondencia?; **to open the mail** = abrir la correspondencia; **your cheque arrived in yesterday's mail** = su cheque llegó en el correo de ayer; **my secretary opens my mail as soon as it arrives** = mi secretaria me abre la correspondencia en cuanto llega; **the receipt was in this morning's mail** = el recibo estaba en el correo de la mañana; **incoming mail** = correo entrante *or* correspondencia recibida; **outgoing mail** = correspondencia despachada *or* de salida; **mail room** = oficina de clasificación del correo **(c)** **direct mail** = venta por correo; **the company runs a successful direct-mail operation** = la empresa se dedica a la venta por correo con gran éxito; **these calculators are sold only by direct mail** = estas calculadoras sólo se venden por correo; **direct-mail advertising** = publicidad por correo; **mail shot** = propaganda enviada por correo **2** *verb* mandar por correo *or* echar al correo; **to mail a letter** = echar una carta al correo; **we mailed our order last Wednesday** = mandamos nuestro pedido por correo el miércoles pasado

◊ **mail box** ['meɪlbɒks] *noun* buzón *m*

◊ **mailer** ['meɪlə] *noun* embalaje *m* de cartón para proteger el producto enviado

◊ **mailing** ['meɪlɪŋ] *noun* envío *m* por correo; **the mailing of publicity material** = el envío de material publicitario por correo; **direct mailing** = envío de publicidad por correo; **mailing list** = lista de destinatarios; **his name is on our mailing list** = su nombre está en nuestra lista de destinatarios; **to** build up a mailing list = confeccionar una lista de destinatarios; **to buy a mailing list** = comprar una lista de destinatarios; **mailing piece** = folleto publicitario por correo; **mailing shot** = propaganda enviada por correo; **mailing tube** = embalaje tubular para enviar documentos

◊ **mail merge** ['meɪl 'mɜːdʒ] *noun (word-processing program)* fusión *f* de cartas y direcciones por ordenador

◊ **mail-order** ['meɪl'ɔːdə] *noun* pedido *m* efectuado por correo; **mail-order business** *or* **mail-order firm** *or* **mail-order house** = empresa de ventas por correspondencia *or* por correo; **mail-order catalogue** = catálogo de ventas por correo

main [meɪn] *adjective* principal *or* mayor; **main office** = oficina principal; **main building** = edificio principal; **one of our main customers** = uno de nuestros principales clientes; **main part** = grueso *m* *or* parte *f* principal; *US* **Main Street** = Calle Mayor (NOTE: British English is **High Street**)

◊ **mainframe** ['meɪnfreɪm] *noun (computer)* unidad *f* *or* componente *m* principal *or* ordenador *m* principal *or* macrocomputadora *f*; **the office micro interfaces with the mainframe in the head office** = el microordenador de la oficina está conectado con el ordenador central de la oficina principal

◊ **mainly** ['meɪnli] *adverb* principalmente *or* mayormente *or* sobre todo; **their sales are mainly in the home market** = sus ventas se sitúan principalmente en el mercado interior; **we are interested mainly in buying children's gift items** = estamos interesados sobre todo en comprar artículos de regalo para niños

◊ **mainstream corporation tax (MCT)** ['meɪnstriːm kɔːpə'reɪʃn 'tæks] *noun* impuesto *m* de sociedades corriente

maintain [meɪn'teɪn] *verb* **(a)** *(keep going)* mantener *or* sostener; **to maintain good relations with one's customers** = mantener buenas relaciones con los clientes; **to maintain contact with an overseas market** = mantener contacto con un mercado exterior **(b)** *(keep at the same level)* mantener *or* conservar; **the company has maintained the same volume of business in spite of the recession** = la empresa ha mantenido el mismo volumen de negocios a pesar de la recesión; **to maintain an interest rate at 5%** = mantener el tipo de interés al 5%; **to maintain a dividend** = mantener un dividendo

◊ **maintenance** ['meɪntənəns] *noun* **(a)** *(keeping things going)* mantenimiento *m*; **maintenance of contacts** = mantenimiento de relaciones; **maintenance of supplies** = mantenimiento de suministros; **resale price maintenance** = precio de reventa *or* mantenimiento del precio de venta **(b)** *(keeping in working order)* mantenimiento *or* conservación; **maintenance contract** = contrato de mantenimiento; **we offer a full maintenance service** = ofrecemos un servicio de mantenimiento completo **(c)** *(people)* manutención *f*; **the maintenance of a family** = la manutención de una familia

QUOTE responsibilities include the maintenance of large computerized databases
Times

QUOTE the federal administration launched a full-scale investigation into the airline's maintenance procedures
Fortune

majeure [mæ'ʒɜː] *see* FORCE MAJEURE fuerza mayor

major ['meɪdʒə] *adjective* importante; **major shareholder** = accionista importante

QUOTE if the share price sinks much further the company is going to look tempting to any major takeover merchant
Australian Financial Review

QUOTE monetary officials have reasoned that coordinated greenback sales would be able to drive the dollar down against other major currencies
Duns Business Month

QUOTE a client base which includes many major commercial organizations and nationalized industries
Times

majority [mə'dʒɒrəti] *noun* mayoría *f*; **majority of the shareholders** = la mayoría de los accionistas; **the board accepted the proposal by a majority of three to two** = la junta aceptó la propuesta por una mayoría de tres contra dos; **majority vote** *or* **majority decision** = voto mayoritario *or* decisión mayoritaria; **majority shareholding** *or* **majority interest** = participación mayoritaria; **a majority shareholder** = un accionista mayoritario

make [meɪk] **1** *noun* marca *f* *or* modelo *m*; **Japanese makes of cars** = marcas japonesas de coches; **a standard make of equipment** = un modelo de equipo estándar; **what make is the new computer?** *or* **what is the make of the new computer?** = ¿de qué marca es el nuevo ordenador? **2** *verb* **(a)** *(to produce)* hacer *or* producir *or* fabricar *or* construir; **to make a car** *or* **to make a computer** = fabricar un coche *or* fabricar un ordenador; **the workmen spent three days making the table** = los obreros se pasaron tres días construyendo la mesa; **the factory makes three hundred cars a day** = la fábrica produce trescientos coches al día **(b)** *(to agree or to do an action)* hacer *or* concertar *or* celebrar; **to make a deal** *or* **to make an agreement** = hacer un trato *or* concertar un acuerdo; **to make a bid for something** = hacer una oferta; **to make a payment** = efectuar un pago; **to make a deposit** = depositar dinero **(c)** *(to earn)* ganar *or* sacar (dinero); **he makes £50,000 a year** *or* **£25 an hour** = gana £50.000 al año *or* £25 a la hora; **the shares made $2.92 in today's trading** = las acciones ganaron $2.92 en las operaciones de hoy **(d)** *(to make a profit or to make a loss)* = obtener beneficios *or* tener pérdidas; **to make a killing** = hacer un gran negocio (NOTE: **making - made**)

◊ **make good** ['meɪk 'gʊd] *verb* **(a)** *(repair)* indemnizar *or* resarcir *or* compensar; **the company will make good the damage** = la compañía se hará cargo de los daños ocasionados; **to make good a loss** = recuperar una pérdida *or* indemnizar por una pérdida **(b)** *(succeed)* tener éxito *or* triunfar; **a local boy made good** = un chico de la localidad que ha tenido éxito

◊ **make out** ['meɪk 'aʊt] *verb* confeccionar *or* extender; **to make out an invoice** = confeccionar una factura; **the bill is made out to Smith & Co.** = la factura está dirigida a nombre de Smith & Co.; **to make out a cheque to someone** = extender un cheque a nombre de alguien

◊ **make over** ['meɪk 'əʊvə] *verb* ceder *or* traspasar; **to make over the house to one's children** = ceder la casa a los propios hijos

◊ **make up** ['meɪk 'ʌp] *verb* **(a)** compensar; **to make up a loss** *or* **to make up the difference** = compensar la pérdida *or* la diferencia **(b) to make up accounts** = saldar *or* ajustar cuentas

◊ **make up for** ['meɪk 'ʌpf ɔ:] *verb* compensar; **to make up for a short payment** *or* **to make up for a late payment** = compensar un pago insuficiente *or* compensar un pago atrasado

◊ **maker** ['meɪkə] *noun* fabricante *m*; **a major car maker** = un importante fabricante de coches; **a furniture maker** = un fabricante de muebles; **decision maker** = persona que toma decisiones

◊ **making** ['meɪkɪŋ] *noun* fabricación *f or* construcción *f or* elaboración *f*; **ten tons of concrete were used in the making of the wall** = para la construcción de la pared se utilizaron diez toneladas de hormigón; **decision making** = toma *f* de decisiones

maladministration ['mæl əd mɪnɪs'treɪʃən] *noun* mala administración *f*

Malawi [mə'lɑːwi] *noun* Malawi *m*

◊ **Malawian** [mə'lɑːwiən] *adjective & noun* malawiano, -na
NOTE: capital: **Lilongwe**; currency: **Malawi kwacha (Mk)** = kwacha malawiano (Mk)

Malaysia [mə'leɪʒə] *noun* Malasia *f*

◊ **Malaysian** [mə'leɪʒn] *adjective & noun* malasio, -ia
NOTE: capital: **Kuala Lumpur**; currency: **Malaysian ringgit (M$)** = ringgit malasio (M$)

malfeasance [mæl'fiːzəns] *noun* acto *m* ilegal *or* conducta *f* ilegal

malfunction [mæl'fʌŋkʃn] **1** *noun* error *m or* fallo *m or* mal funcionamiento *m*; **the data was lost due to a software malfunction** = se perdió la información debido a un fallo del programa **2** *verb* funcionar mal; **some of the keys on the keyboard have started to malfunction** = el teclado empieza a tener teclas defectuosas *or* que funcionan mal

Mali ['mɑːli] *noun* Mali *m*

◊ **Malian** ['mɑːliən] *adjective & noun* maliense
NOTE: capital: **Bamako**; currency: **CFA franc (CFAF)** = franco CFA (FCFA)

mall [mɔːl] *noun* **shopping mall** = centro *m* comercial *or* galería *f* comercial

Malta ['mɒltə] *noun* Malta *f*

◊ **Maltese** [mɒl'tiːz] *adjective & noun* maltés, -esa
NOTE: capital: **Valletta**; currency: **Maltese lira (Lm)** = lira maltesa (Lm)

man [mæn] **1** *noun* hombre *m*; *(workman)* obrero, -ra; **all the men went back to work yesterday** = todos los obreros volvieron al trabajo ayer; **Man Friday** = ayudante *m* leal **2** *verb* asignar personal para una tarea *or* cubrir puestos; **to man a shift** = cubrir los puestos del turno; **to man an exhibition** = asignar personal para una exposición; **the exhibition stand was manned by three salesgirls** = el stand de la exposición estaba atendido por tres vendedoras; *see also* MANNED, MANNING

manage ['mænɪdʒ] *verb* **(a)** *(be in charge)* dirigir *or* llevar *or* gestionar; **to manage a department** = dirigir un departamento; **to manage a branch office** = dirigir una sucursal de oficina **(b) to manage property** = administrar una propiedad; **managed fund** *or* **managed unit trust** = fondo de inversión dirigido *or* controlado **(c) to manage to** = arreglárselas *or* conseguir; **did you manage to see the head buyer?** = ¿conseguiste ver al jefe de compras?; **she managed to write six orders and take three phone calls all in two minutes** = se las arregló para anotar seis pedidos y atender a tres llamadas en dos minutos

◊ **manageable** ['mænɪdʒəbl] *adjective* manejable *or* que puede resolverse; **difficulties which are still manageable** = dificultades que todavía pueden resolverse; **the problems are too large to be manageable** = los problemas son demasiado grandes para ser resueltos fácilmente

◊ **management** ['mænɪdʒmənt] *noun* **(a)** *(running a business)* dirección *f or* gestión *f or* administración *f*; **to study management** = estudiar (ciencias) empresariales; **good management** *or* **efficient management** = buena gestión *or* gestión eficaz; **bad management** *or* **inefficient management** = mala gestión *or* gestión ineficaz; **a management graduate** *or* **a graduate in management** = un graduado en administración de empresas; **fund management** = gestión de fondos; **lean management** = sistema de racionalización del equipo directivo para facilitar la toma de decisiones; **line management** = gestión lineal; **portfolio management** = administración *f* de valores *or* de patrimonios *or* de carteras; **product management** = gestión de productos; **management accountant** = contable *mf* de gestión; **management accounts** = cuentas *fpl* de gestión; **management committee** = comité *m* de gestión; **management consultant** = asesor, -ra de empresas; **management course** = curso *m* de gestión empresarial; **management by objectives** = dirección por objetivos; **management team** = equipo *m* directivo; **management techniques** = técnicas de dirección de empresas; **management training** = formación *f* de mandos; **management trainee** = ejecutivo, -va en formación **(b)** *(group of managers or directors)* dirección *or* consejo *m* de administración; **the management has decided to give an overall pay increase** = la dirección ha decidido conceder un aumento general de sueldo; **senior management** *or* **top management** = alta dirección; **middle management** = mandos *mpl* intermedios; **management buyin (MBI)** = compra de una empresa por ejecutivos; **management buyout (MBO)** = adquisición *or* compra de una empresa por sus propios directivos; **unions and management** = los sindicatos y la patronal

◊ **manager** ['mænɪdʒə] *noun* **(a)** *(head)* director *m*; **accounts manager** = jefe de contabilidad; **area manager** = director regional; **a department**

manager = un director de departamento *or* sección; **general manager** = director general *or* gerente *mf*; **line manager** = superior *or* gerente de línea; **personnel manager** = director de personal; **production manager** = director de producción; **sales manager** = director de ventas **(b)** *(of a bank)* director; *(of a shop)* gerente *or* encargado, -da; **Mr Smith is the manager of our local Lloyds Bank** = el Sr. Smith es el director de nuestra sucursal del Lloyds Bank; **the manager of our Lagos branch is in London for a series of meetings** = el director de nuestra sucursal de Lagos está en Londres para asistir a una serie de reuniones; **bank manager** = director de una sucursal bancaria; **branch manager** = director de sucursal

◊ **manageress** [ˌmænɪdʒəˈres] *noun* directora *f or* administradora *f or* gerente *f*

◊ **managerial** [mænəˈdʒɪərɪəl] *adjective* **(a)** *(administrative)* directivo, -va *or* administrativo, -va; **managerial staff** = personal administrativo *or* de gestión; **to be appointed to a managerial position** = ser nombrado para un puesto directivo; **decisions taken at managerial level** = decisiones tomadas por la dirección **(b)** *(entrepreneurial)* empresarial

◊ **managership** [ˈmænɪdʒəʃɪp] *noun* dirección *f or* administración *f or* gestión *f*; **after six years, he was offered the managership of a branch in Scotland** = después de seis años le ofrecieron la dirección de una sucursal en Escocia

◊ **managing** [ˈmænɪdʒɪŋ] *adjective* **managing director (MD)** = director gerente; **chairman and managing director** = presidente y director gerente

mandate [ˈmændeɪt] *noun* mandato *m*; **bank mandate** = orden *f* de pago

mandatory meeting [ˈmændətəri ˈmiːtɪŋ] *noun* reunión *f* de asistencia obligada

man-hour [ˈmænaʊə] *noun* hora-hombre *f*; **one million man-hours were lost through industrial action** = se perdió un millón de horas-hombre por las huelgas

manifest [ˈmænɪfest] *noun* manifiesto *m*; **passenger manifest** = lista *f* de pasajeros

manilla [məˈnɪlə] *noun* papel *m* manila; **a manilla envelope** = un sobre de papel manila

manipulate [məˈnɪpjʊleɪt] *verb* manipular *or* manejar; **to manipulate the accounts** = manipular las cuentas; **to manipulate the market** = manipular el mercado

◊ **manipulation** [mənɪpjʊˈleɪʃən] *noun* manipulación *f*; **stock market manipulation** = manipulación del mercado bursátil

◊ **manipulator** [məˈnɪpjʊleɪtə] *noun* manipulador, -ra; **stock market manipulator** = manipulador de la bolsa

manned [mænd] *adjective* asistido, -da *or* atendido, -da; **the switchboard is manned twenty-four hours a day** = la centralita está atendida las veinticuatro horas del día; **the stand was manned by our sales staff** = el stand estaba atendido por nuestro personal de ventas

◊ **manning** [ˈmænɪŋ] *noun* dotación *f* de personal; **manning levels** = niveles de dotación de personal; **manning agreement** *or* **agreement on manning** = acuerdo sobre dotación de personal

manner [ˈmænə] *noun* **(a)** *(way)* modo *m* **(b)** **manners** = modos; **good manners** = buenos modos; **he is a good secretary but his manners leave a lot to be desired** = es un buen secretario pero tiene unos modos reprochables

manpower [ˈmænpaʊə] *noun* mano *f* de obra; **manpower forecasting** = previsión *f* de mano de obra; **manpower planning** = planificación *f* de la mano de obra; **manpower requirements** = necesidades *fpl* de mano de obra; **manpower shortage** *or* **shortage of manpower** = escasez *f* de mano de obra

manual [ˈmænjʊəl] **1** *adjective* manual; **manual labour** *or* **manual work** = trabajo manual; **manual labourer** = obrero, -ra manual; **manual worker** = obrero, -ra **2** *noun* manual *m*; **operating manual** = manual de funcionamiento *or* servicio; **service manual** = manual de mantenimiento

◊ **manually** [ˈmænjʊəli] *adverb* manualmente *or* a mano; **invoices have had to be made manually because the computer has broken down** = se han tenido que hacer las facturas a mano porque el ordenador se ha averiado

manufacture [mænjʊˈfæktʃə] **1** *verb* fabricar *or* manufacturar; **manufactured goods** = productos manufacturados; **the company manufactures spare parts for cars** = la empresa fabrica piezas de recambio para coches **2** *noun* fabricación *f*; **products of foreign manufacture** = productos de fabricación extranjera

◊ **manufacturer** [mænjʊˈfæktʃərə] *noun* fabricante *m*; **foreign manufacturers** = fabricantes extranjeros; **cotton manufacturer** = fabricante de tejidos de algodón; **sports car manufacturer** = fabricante de coches deportivos; **manufacturer's recommended price (MRP)** = precio recomendado por el fabricante para la venta al por menor; **all typewriters - 20% off the manufacturer's recommended price** = todas las máquinas de escribir con un 20% de descuento sobre el precio recomendado por el fabricante

◊ **manufacturing** [mænjʊˈfæktʃərɪŋ] *noun* fabricación *f*; **manufacturing overheads** = gastos generales de fabricación; **manufacturing processes** = procesos de fabricación; **manufacturing capacity** = capacidad *f* de fabricación; **manufacturing costs** = costes *mpl* de fabricación; **manufacturing industries** = industrias *fpl* manufactureras

manuscript [ˈmænjuːskrɪpt] **1** *adjective* manuscrito, -ta **2** *noun* manuscrito *m*

margin [ˈmɑːdʒɪn] *noun* **(a)** *(profit per unit)* margen *m*; **gross margin** = margen bruto; **net margin** = margen neto; **operating margin** = margen de explotación; **profit margin** = margen de beneficio; **we are cutting our margins very fine** = estamos reduciendo nuestros márgenes al máximo; **our margins have been squeezed** = nuestros márgenes se han reducido mucho **(b)** *(extra space or time)* margen; **margin of error** = margen de error; **safety margin** *or* **margin of safety** = margen de seguridad

◊ **marginal** [ˈmɑːdʒɪnəl] *adjective* **(a)** *(limit)* marginal; **marginal cost** = coste marginal *or* incremental; **marginal costing** *or* **marginal pricing** = fijación de precios según el coste marginal; **marginal rate of tax** = tipo de impuesto marginal; **marginal revenue** = ingresos marginales **(b)** *(not very profitable)* marginal; **marginal return on investment** = rendimiento marginal de la inversión; **marginal land** = tierra que produce sólo para cubrir costes; **marginal purchase** = compra que no tiene un gran valor

QUOTE profit margins in the industries most exposed to foreign competition - machinery, transportation equipment and electrical goods - are significantly worse than usual

QUOTE pensioner groups claim that pensioners have the highest marginal rates of tax. Income earned by pensioners above $30 a week is taxed at 62.5 per cent, more than the highest marginal rate
Australian Financial Review

marine [məˈriːn] **1** *adjective* marino, -na; **marine insurance** = seguro marítimo; **marine underwriter** = asegurador, -ra de riesgos marinos **2** *noun* **the merchant marine** = la marina mercante

◊ **maritime** [ˈmærɪtaɪm] *adjective* marítimo, -ma; **maritime law** = derecho marítimo; **maritime lawyer** = abogado especializado en derecho marítimo; **maritime trade** = comercio marítimo

mark [mɑːk] **1** *noun* **(a)** *(on an item)* marca *f or* señal *f*; **assay mark** = sello *m* de contraste *or* marca de ensaye; *GB* **kite mark** = marca de calidad (que indica que un producto se ajusta a las normas oficiales británicas) **(b)** *(currency used in Germany)* marco *m*; **the price is twenty-five marks** = el precio es de 20 marcos; **the mark rose against the dollar** = el marco subió frente al dólar (NOTE: usually written **DM** after a figure: **25DM**. Also called **Deutschmark, D-mark**) **2** *verb* marcar *or* señalar *or* indicar; **to mark a product 'for export only'** = indicar en un producto 'sólo para la exportación'; **article marked at £1.50** = artículo marcado a £1.50; **to mark the price on something** = poner el precio a algo

◊ **mark down** [ˈmɑːk ˈdaʊn] *verb* rebajar; **to mark down a price** = rebajar un precio; **this range has been marked down to $24.99** = esta línea ha sido rebajada a $24.99; **we have marked all prices down by 30% for the sale** = hemos reducido todos los artículos en un 30% para las rebajas

◊ **mark-down** [ˈmɑːkdaʊn] *noun* **(a)** *(reduction of price)* rebaja *f or* reducción *f* **(b)** *(percentage of reduction)* porcentaje *m* de rebaja; **we have used a 30% mark-down to fix the sale price** = hemos aplicado una rebaja del 30% para fijar el precio de venta

◊ **marker pen** [ˈmɑːkə ˈpen] *noun* rotulador *m or* marcador *m*

◊ **mark up** [ˈmɑːk ˈʌp] *verb* aumentar *or* recargar; **to mark prices up** = aumentar los precios; **these prices have been marked up by 10%** = estos precios se han aumentado en un 10%

◊ **mark-up** [ˈmɑːkʌp] *noun* **(a)** *(increase in price)* aumento *m or* recargo *m or* incremento *m*; **we put into effect a 10% mark-up of all prices in June** = en junio aplicaremos un recargo del 10% a todos los precios **(b)** *(profit margin)* margen *m* de beneficio; **we work to a 3.5 times mark-up** *or* **to a 350% mark-up** = trabajamos con un margen de beneficio de de 3 veces y media *or* con un margen de beneficio del 350%

market [ˈmɑːkɪt] **1** *noun* **(a)** *(place)* mercado *m or* plaza *f*; **fish market** = mercado de pescado; **flower market** = mercado de flores; **open-air market** = mercado al aire libre; **here are this week's market prices for sheep** = aquí están los precios de mercado de las ovejas de esta semana; **flea market** = mercadillo *m* de objetos de segunda mano *or* rastro *m*; **market day** = día *m* de mercado; **Tuesday is market day, so the streets are closed to traffic** = el martes es día de mercado, por lo que las calles están cerradas al tráfico; **market dues** = cuota por un puesto en el mercado **(b)** *(EU)* **the Single Market** = el Mercado Único; *(formerly)* **the Common Market** = el Mercado Común; **the Common Market agricultural policy** la política agrícola del Mercado Común; **the Common Market ministers** = los ministros del Mercado Común **(c)** *(area or people)* mercado; **home** *or* **domestic market** = mercado interior *or* nacional *or* interno; **sales in the home market rose by 22%** = las ventas en el mercado interior subieron un 22% **(d)** *(possible sales or demand)* mercado; **the market for home computers has fallen sharply** = el mercado de ordenadores personales ha bajado bruscamente; **we have 20% of the British car market** = tenemos el 20% del mercado de automóviles británico; **there is no market for electric typewriters** = no hay mercado para las máquinas de escribir eléctricas; **a growth market** = un mercado en expansión; **the labour market** = el mercado de trabajo; **25,000 graduates have come on to the labour market** = 25.000 licenciados han ingresado en el mercado de trabajo; **the property market** = el mercado inmobiliario **(e)** **the black market** = el mercado negro; **there is a flourishing black market in spare parts for cars** = existe un floreciente mercado negro de piezas de recambio para coches; **to pay black market prices** = pagar precios de mercado negro **(f)** *(where prices are lower)* **a buyer's market** = mercado favorable al comprador; **a seller's market** = mercado favorable al vendedor **(g)** **closed market** = mercado cerrado *or* mercado controlado; **free market economy** = economía de libre mercado; **open market** = mercado libre **(h)** *(where money or commodities are traded)* **capital market** = mercado de capitales; **commodity market** = lonja de contratación *or* mercado de materias primas *or* bolsa de comercio; **the foreign exchange markets** = los mercados de divisas *or* cambiarios; **forward markets** = mercado de futuros; **money market** *or* **finance market** = mercado monetario *or* financiero **(i)** **stock market** = mercado *or* bolsa de valores; **the market in oil shares was very active** *or* **there was a brisk market in oil shares** = el mercado de acciones petrolíferas estuvo muy activo; **to buy shares in the open market** = comprar acciones en el mercado libre; **over-the-counter market** = mercado de valores que no se cotizan en bolsa; **to come to the market** = solicitar el derecho a cotizar en la Bolsa **(j) market analysis** = análisis de mercado; **market capitalization** = capitalización bursátil *or* valor de mercado del capital emitido; **market economist** = economista de mercado; **market forces** = las fuerzas del mercado; **market forecast** = previsión de mercado; **market leader** = empresa líder del sector *or* mercado líder; **we are the market leader in home computers** = somos la empresa líder en el mercado de ordenadores personales; **market opportunities** = oportunidades de mercado; **market penetration** *or* **market share** = penetración *or* participación en el mercado; **we hope our new product range will increase our market share** = esperamos que nuestra nueva gama de productos aumente nuestra participación en el mercado; **market price** = precio de mercado; **market rate** = precio *or* tarifa de mercado; **we pay the market rate for secretaries** *or* **we pay secretaries the market rate** = pagamos a las secretarias la tarifa del mercado; **market research** = estudio *or* investigación de mercado; **market share** = cuota de mercado *or* participación en el mercado; **market trends** = tendencias del mercado; **market value** = valor de mercado **(k) up market** *or* **down market** = mercado selecto *or* mercado popular; **to go up market** *or* **to go down market** = dirigir la actividad comercial a un mercado selecto *or* un mercado popular **(l) to be in the market for secondhand cars** = dedicarse a la compra-venta de coches de segunda mano; **to come on to the market** = ponerse en venta *or* salir al mercado; **this soap has just come on to the market** = este jabón acaba de ponerse en venta; **to put something on the market** = poner algo en venta; **they put their house on the market** = pusieron su casa en venta; **I hear the company has been put on the market** = me han dicho que la empresa está en venta; **the company has priced itself out of the market** = la empresa ha dejado de vender por fijar los precios demasiado altos **2** *verb* vender; **this product is being marketed in all European countries** = este producto se vende en todos los países europeos

◊ **marketability** [maːkətəˈbɪlɪti] *noun* facilidad de venta

◊ **marketable** [ˈmaːkɪtəbl] *adjective* vendible *or* comerciable

◊ **marketing** [ˈmaːkɪtɪŋ] *noun* comercialización *f or* marketing *m or* mercadotecnia *f*; **marketing agreement** = acuerdo *m* de comercialización; **marketing costs** = costes de comercialización; **marketing department** = departamento de marketing *or* de comercialización; **marketing manager** = director de comercialización *or* de marketing; **marketing policy** *or* **marketing plans** = política de marketing *or* planes de comercialización; **to plan the marketing of a new product** = planificar la comercialización de un nuevo producto; **direct marketing** = marketing directo

◊ **marketmaker** [ˈmaːkɪtˈmeɪkə] *noun* corredor, -ra de bolsa

◊ **marketplace** [ˈmaːkɪtpleɪs] *noun* **(a)** *(open space in middle of town)* plaza *f* del mercado **(b)** *(place where something is sold)* mercado; **our salesmen find life difficult in the marketplace** =

nuestros vendedores piensan que es difícil trabajar en el mercado; **what is the reaction to the new car in the marketplace?** *or* **what is the marketplace reaction to the new car?** = ¿como ha reaccionado el mercado ante el nuevo coche? *or* ¿cuál es la reacción del mercado hacia el nuevo coche?

> QUOTE after the prime rate cut yesterday, there was a further fall in short-term market rates
>
> **Financial Times**

> QUOTE market analysts described the falls in the second half of last week as a technical correction to a market which had been pushed by demand to over the 900 index level
>
> **Australian Financial Review**

> QUOTE our scheme has been running for 12 years, but we have only really had a true marketing strategy since 1989
>
> **Marketing**

> QUOTE reporting to the marketing director, the successful applicant will be responsible for the development of a training programme for the new sales force
>
> **Times**

> QUOTE most discounted fares are sold by bucket shops but in today's competitive marketplace any agent can supply them
>
> **Business Traveller**

> QUOTE market leaders may benefit from scale economies or other cost advantages; they may enjoy a reputation for quality simply by being at the top, or they may actually produce a superior product that gives them both a large market share and high profits
>
> **Accountancy**

mart [maːt] *noun* mercado *m or* lonja *f*; **car mart** = mercado de coches; **auction mart** = mercado de subastas

mass [mæs] *noun* **(a)** *(large group of people)* masa *f or* multitud *f or* muchedumbre *f*; **mass market** = mercado de masas; **mass market product** = producto destinado a un mercado de masas; **mass marketing** = comercialización a gran escala; **mass media** = medios *mpl* de comunicación *or* medios informativos; **mass unemployment** = paro masivo **(b)** *(large number)* cantidad *f*; **we have a mass of letters** *or* **masses of letters to write** = tenemos gran cantidad de cartas por escribir; **they received a mass of orders** *or* **masses of orders after the TV commercials** = recibieron gran cantidad de pedidos después de los anuncios en televisión

◊ **mass-produce** [ˈmæsprəˈdjuːs] *verb* producir *or* fabricar en serie *or* a gran escala; **to mass-produce cars** = fabricar coches a gran escala

◊ **mass production** [ˈmæs prəˈdʌkʃən] *noun* producción *f* en serie *or* a gran escala

master [ˈmaːstə] *noun* **(a)** *(main or original)* original *or* principal *m*; **master copy of a file** = copia maestra de un fichero; **master budget** = presupuesto principal **(b)** *(university)* master's degree = master *m*; **Master's degree in Business Administration (MBA)** = master en administración de empresas

◊ **Mastercard** [ˈmaːstəkaːd] *noun* tarjeta de crédito 'Mastercard'

material [mə'tɪərɪəl] *noun* **(a)** material *m*; **building materials** = materiales de construcción; **raw materials** = materias primas; **synthetic materials** = materiales sintéticos; **materials control** = control de materiales; **materials cost** = coste de materiales; **materials handling** = manejo de materiales **(b) display material** = material de exposición

maternity [mə'tɜːnətɪ] *noun* maternidad *f*; **maternity benefit** = subsidio de maternidad; **maternity leave** = licencia *or* baja por maternidad

matrix ['meɪtrɪks] *see* DOT-MATRIX PRINTER

matter ['mætə] **1** *noun* **(a)** *(problem)* problema *m*; **it is a matter of concern to the members of the committee** = es un problema que preocupa a los miembros del comité **(b) printed matter** = material *m* impreso; **publicity matter** = material de publicidad **(c)** *(question or problem to be discussed)* cuestión *f or* asunto *m*; **the most important matter on the agenda** = la cuestión más importante del orden del día; **we shall consider first the matter of last month's fall in prices** = examinaremos primero el asunto de la baja de precios del mes pasado **2** *verb* importar; **does it matter if one month's sales are down?** = ¿importa que las ventas de un mes sean bajas?

mature [mə'tjʊə] **1** *adjective* **mature economy** = economía *f* madura **2** *verb* vencer; **bills which mature in three weeks' time** = letras que vencen en tres semanas

◊ **maturity** [mə'tjʊərətɪ] *noun* vencimiento *m*; **date of maturity** *or* **maturity date** = fecha *f* de vencimiento; **amount payable on maturity** = cantidad *f* a pagar en la fecha de vencimiento

Mauritius [mɒ'rɪʃəs] *noun* (isla) Mauricio *f*

◊ **Mauritian** [mɒ'rɪʃən] *adjective & noun* mauricio, -cia
NOTE: capital: **Port-Louis;** currency: **Mauritian rupee (MauRs)** = rupia mauricia (MauRs)

max = MAXIMUM

maximization [mæksɪmaɪ'zeɪʃən] *noun* maximización *f*; **profit maximization** *or* **maximization of profit** = maximización de beneficios

◊ **maximize** ['mæksɪmaɪz] *verb* maximizar *or* llevar algo al máximo; **to maximize profits** = maximizar los beneficios

maximum ['mæksɪməm] **1** *noun* máximo *m*; **up to a maximum of £10** = hasta un máximo de £10; **to increase exports to the maximum** = aumentar las exportaciones al máximo; **it is the maximum the insurance company will pay** = es lo máximo que pagará la compañía de seguros (NOTE: plural is **maxima**) **2** *adjective* máximo, -ma; **maximum income tax rate** *or* **maximum rate of tax** = máximo tipo de impuesto; **maximum load** = carga máxima; **maximum production levels** = niveles máximos de producción; **maximum price** = precio máximo; **to increase production to the maximum level** = aumentar la producción al máximo

MB = MEGABYTE

MBA = MASTER IN BUSINESS ADMINISTRATION

MBI = MANAGEMENT BUYIN

MBO = MANAGEMENT BUYOUT

MCT = MAINSTREAM CORPORATION TAX

MD ['em'diː] = MANAGING DIRECTOR **the MD is in his office** = el director gerente está en su oficina; **she was appointed MD of a property company** = la nombraron directora gerente de una sociedad inmobiliaria

mean [miːn] **1** *adjective* medio, -dia; **mean annual increase** = aumento anual medio; **mean price** = precio medio **2** *noun* promedio *m or* media *f*; **unit sales are over the mean for the first quarter** *or* **above the first quarter mean** = el número de unidades vendidas sobrepasa el promedio del primer trimestre **3** *verb* significar *or* suponer

◊ **means** [miːnz] *plural noun* **(a)** *(way of doing something)* medio *m*; **air freight is the fastest means of getting stock to South America** = el transporte aéreo es el medio más rápido para enviar mercancías a Sudamérica; **do we have any means of copying all these documents quickly?** = ¿tenemos algún medio para copiar todos estos documentos rápidamente?; **means of production** = medios de producción **(b)** *(money or resources)* recursos *mpl or* medios *mpl*; **the company has the means to launch the new product** = la empresa tiene recursos para lanzar el nuevo producto; **such a level of investment is beyond the means of a small private company** = este nivel de inversión está por encima de los medios de una pequeña empresa privada; **means test** = comprobación *f* de los recursos económicos de una persona; **he has private means** = tiene recursos propios

measure ['meʒə] **1** *noun* **(a)** *(way of calculating size or quantity)* medida *f*; **cubic measure** = medida de volumen; **dry measure** = medida de áridos; **square measure** = medida de superficie; **inspector of weights and measures** = inspector de pesos y medidas; **as a measure of the company's performance** = como medida del rendimiento de la empresa **(b) made to measure** = hecho, -cha a la medida; **he has his clothes made to measure** = se hace la ropa a la medida **(c) tape measure** = cinta *f* métrica **(d)** *(type of action)* medida; *(steps)* gestión *f*; **to take measures to prevent something happening** = tomar medidas preventivas; **to take crisis** *or* **emergency measures** = tomar medidas de emergencia; **an economy measure** = una medida de ahorro; **fiscal measures** = medidas fiscales; **as a precautionary measure** = como medida preventiva; **safety measures** = medidas de seguridad **2** *verb* **(a)** medir *or* tomar las medidas; **to measure the size of a package** = tomar las medidas de un paquete; **a package which measures 10cm by 25cm** *or* **a package measuring 10cm by 25cm** = un paquete que mide 10cm por 25 cm **(b) to measure the government's performance** = medir la actuación del gobierno

◊ **measurement** ['meʒəmənt] *noun* **(a) measurements** = medidas *fpl or* mediciones *fpl or* dimensiones *fpl*; **to write down the measurements of a package** = anotar las medidas de un paquete **(b)** *(way of judging something)* evaluación *f*; **performance measurement** *or* **measurement of performance** = evaluación del rendimiento; **measurement of profitability** = evaluación de la rentabilidad

◊ **measuring tape** ['meʒərɪŋ 'teɪp] *noun* cinta *f* métrica

mechanic [mɪ'kænɪk] *noun* mecánico *m*; **car mechanic** = mecánico de coches

◊ **mechanical** [mɪ'kænɪkəl] *adjective* mecánico, -ca; **a mechanical pump** = bomba *f* mecánica

◊ **mechanism** ['mekənɪzəm] *noun* mecanismo *m*; **a mechanism to slow down inflation** = mecanismo para frenar la inflación; **the company's discount mechanism** = el sistema de descuentos concedidos por la empresa

◊ **mechanize** ['mekənaɪz] *verb* mecanizar; **the country is aiming to mechanize its farming industry** = el país se propone mecanizar la industria agrícola

◊ **mechanization** [mekənaɪ'zeɪʃən] *noun* mecanización *f*; **farm mechanization** *or* **the mechanization of farms** = la mecanización agrícola

media ['miːdjə] *noun* **the media** *or* **the mass media** = los medios *mpl* de comunicación; **the product attracted a lot of interest in the media** *or* **a lot of media interest** = el producto atrajo mucho interés en los medios de comunicación; **media analysis** *or* **media research** = análisis *m* de medios de comunicación; **media coverage** = cobertura *f* periodística (tiempo dedicado a un asunto por los medios de comunicación); **we got good media coverage for the launch of the new model** = conseguimos una buena cobertura periodística para el lanzamiento del nuevo producto (NOTE: **media** can be followed by a singular or plural verb)

> QUOTE media costs represent a major expense for advertisers
>
>   **Marketing**

median ['miːdjən] *noun* mediana *f*

mediate ['miːdɪeɪt] *verb* mediar (entre *or* en); **to mediate between the manager and his staff** = mediar entre el director y sus empleados; **the government offered to mediate in the dispute** = el gobierno se ofreció a mediar en la disputa

◊ **mediation** [miːdɪ'eɪʃən] *noun* mediación *f*; **the employers refused an offer of government mediation** = los empresarios rechazaron una oferta de mediación del gobierno; **the dispute was ended through the mediation of union officials** = el conflicto se resolvió a través de la mediación de los cargos sindicales

◊ **mediator** ['miːdɪeɪtə] *noun* mediador, -ra *or* intermediario, -ria *or* componedor, -ra; **official mediator** = mediador del gobierno

medical ['medɪkəl] **1** *noun* reconocimiento *m* médico *or* revisión *f* médica **2** *adjective* médico, -ca; **medical certificate** = parte médico de baja; **medical inspection** = inspección sanitaria; **medical insurance** = seguro médico; **medical officer of health** = jefe de sanidad municipal; **he resigned for medical reasons** = dimitió por motivos de salud

medium ['miːdjəm] **1** *adjective* medio, -dia *or* mediano, -na; **the company is of medium size** = la empresa es de tamaño medio **2** *noun* **(a)** medio *m* *or* instrumento *m*; **advertising medium** = medio publicitario; **the product was advertised through**

the medium of the trade press = el producto se anunció en las publicaciones del ramo (NOTE: the plural for (a) is **media**) **(b) mediums** = valores *mpl* del Estado que vencen en un periodo de cinco a quince años

◊ **medium-sized** ['miːdjəm 'saɪzd] *adjective* **(a)** *(neither large nor small)* mediano, -na; **a medium-sized firm** = una empresa mediana; **a medium-sized engineering company** = una empresa mediana de ingeniería **(b)** *(for UK tax purposes)* **medium-sized company** = empresa mediana

> COMMENT: a company with at least two of the following characteristics: a turnover of less than £8m; net assets of less than £3.9m; and not more than 250 staff (companies of this size can file modified accounts with the Registrar of Companies)

◊ **medium-term** ['miːdjəm 'tɜːm] *adjective* a plazo medio; **medium-term forecast** = previsión *f* a plazo medio; **medium-term loan** = préstamo a plazo medio; **medium-term strategy** = estrategia a medio plazo

meet [miːt] *verb* **(a)** *(with someone)* reunirse *or* encontrarse; **to meet a negotiating committee** = reunirse con una comisión negociadora; **to meet an agent at his hotel** = reunirse con un representante en su hotel; **the two sides met in the lawyer's office** = las dos partes se reunieron en el despacho del abogado **(b)** *(to be satisfactory for)* cumplir *or* satisfacer; **to meet a customer's requirements** = satisfacer las exigencias de un cliente; **to meet the demand for a new product** = satisfacer la demanda de un nuevo producto; **we will try to meet your price** = intentaremos ajustarnos a su precio; **they failed to meet the deadline** = no consiguieron cumplir el plazo establecido **(c)** *(to pay for)* cubrir *or* hacer frente a *or* correr con; **to meet someone's expenses** = correr con los gastos de alguien; **the company will meet your expenses** = la empresa correrá con sus gastos; **he was unable to meet his mortgage repayments** = no pudo hacer frente a los pagos de la hipoteca (NOTE: **meeting - met**)

◊ **meet with** ['miːt 'wɪð] *verb* **(a)** *US* reunirse con; **I hope to meet with him in New York** = espero reunirme con él en Nueva York **(b) his request met with a refusal** = su petición fue rechazada

◊ **meeting** ['miːtɪŋ] *noun* **(a)** *(group of people)* reunión *f* *or* junta *f* *or* asamblea *f*; **management meeting** = junta de dirección; **staff meeting** = reunión *or* asamblea de personal; **board meeting** = reunión del consejo de administración; **general meeting** *or* **meeting of shareholders** *or* **shareholders' meeting** = junta general *or* junta de accionistas; **Annual General Meeting (AGM)** = junta general anual (ordinaria); **Extraordinary General Meeting (EGM)** = junta general extraordinaria **(b)** **to hold a meeting** = celebrar una reunión *or* sesión; **the meeting will be held in the committee room** = la reunión se celebrará en la sala de la comisión; **to address a meeting** = tomar la palabra en una reunión; **to open a meeting** = abrir la sesión; **to chair** *or* **to conduct a meeting** = dirigir una reunión *or* sesión; **to close a meeting** = levantar una sesión *or* terminar una reunión; **to put a resolution to a meeting** = someter a voto una propuesta

QUOTE if corporate forecasts are met, sales will exceed $50 million next year
Citizen (Ottawa)

QUOTE in proportion to your holding you have a stake in every aspect of the company, including a vote in the general meetings
Investors Chronicle

megabyte (MB) ['megǝbaɪt] *noun* megabyte *m* or megaocteto *m*

megastore ['megǝstɔ:] *noun* hipermercado *m*

member ['membǝ] *noun* **(a)** *(person belonging to a group)* miembro *m* or socio, -cia; **members of a committee** or **committee members** = miembros de una comisión; **they were elected members of the board** = los eligieron miembros del consejo de administración; **ordinary member** = vocal *mf*; **honorary member** = miembro honorario; **union member** = afiliado, -da a un sindicato **(b)** *(shareholder in a company)* accionista *mf* or socio, -cia; **members' voluntary winding up** = liquidación or disolución de una sociedad por los mismos accionistas **(c)** *(institution belonging to a group)* miembro; **the member countries of the EU** = los países miembros de la UE; **the members of the United Nations** = los miembros de las Naciones Unidas; **the member companies of a trade association** = las empresas miembros de una asociación comercial

◇ **membership** ['membǝʃɪp] *noun* **(a)** *(belonging to a group)* afiliación *f* or calidad *f* de miembro; **union membership** = afiliación sindical; **membership qualifications** = requisitos *mpl* para hacerse socio or ser miembro; **conditions of membership** = condiciones de ingreso; **membership card** = carné *m* de socio or de miembro; **to pay your membership** or **your membership fees** = pagar la cuota de socio; **is Iceland going to apply for membership of the European Union?** = ¿va a solicitar Islandia el ingreso en la Unión Europea **(b)** *(all the members)* los socios or los miembros; **the membership was asked to vote for the new president** = se pidió a los socios que votaran al nuevo presidente; **the club has a membership of five hundred** = el club tiene quinientos socios

QUOTE it will be the first opportunity for party members and trade union members to express their views on the tax package
Australian Financial Review

QUOTE the bargaining committee will recommend that its membership ratify the agreement at a meeting called for June
Toronto Star

QUOTE in 1984 exports to Canada from the member-states of the European Community jumped 38 per cent
Globe and Mail (Toronto)

QUOTE for EMS members, which means all EC countries except Britain, the ecu has performed well
Economist

memo ['memǝʊ] *noun* nota *f* or circular *f*; **to write a memo to the finance director** = escribir una nota al director financiero; **to send a memo to all the**

sales representatives = enviar una circular a todos los representantes de ventas; **according to your memo about debtors** = según su nota sobre los deudores; **I sent the managing director a memo about your complaint** = le envié al director gerente una nota sobre su reclamación

◇ **memo pad** ['memǝʊ 'pæd] *noun* bloc *m* de notas

◇ **memorandum** [memǝ'rændǝm] *noun* memorandum *m* or informe *m* or nota *f*; **memorandum (and articles) of association** = estatutos *mpl* sociales or escritura *f* de constitución

memory ['memǝri] *noun* *(of a computer)* memoria *f*; **random access memory (RAM)** = memoria de acceso al azar; **read only memory (ROM)** = memoria de lectura solamente

mention ['menʃǝn] *verb* mencionar or aludir or decir; **the chairman mentioned the work of the retiring managing director** = el presidente aludió a la obra del director gerente con ocasión de su jubilación; **can you mention to the secretary that the date of the next meeting has been changed?** = ¿puede decirle a la secretaria que se ha cambiado la fecha de la próxima reunión?

menu ['menju:] *noun* **(a)** *(restaurant)* menú *m*; **set menu** or **today's menu** = menú del día **(b)** *(computer)* menú or lista *f* de opciones; **pop-up menu** or **pull-down menu** = menú de selección

mercantile ['mɜ:kǝntaɪl] *adjective* mercantil or comercial; **mercantile country** = país comerciante; **mercantile law** = derecho mercantil; **mercantile marine** = marina mercante

merchandise ['mɜ:tʃǝndaɪs] *noun* género *m* or mercancías *fpl*; **the merchandise is shipped through two ports** = las mercancías se envían a través de dos puertos (NOTE: no plural in English)

◇ **merchandize** ['mɜ:tʃǝndaɪz] *verb* comercializar; **to merchandize a product** = comercializar un producto

◇ **merchandizer** ['mɜ:tʃǝndaɪzǝ] *noun* comerciante *mf*

◇ **merchandizing** ['mɜ:tʃǝndaɪzɪŋ] *noun* comercialización *f* or mercadotecnia *f* or marketing *m*; **merchandizing of a product** = comercialización de un producto; **merchandizing department** = departamento de comercialización

QUOTE fill huge warehouses with large quantities but limited assortments of top-brand, first-quality merchandise and sell the goods at rock-bottom prices
Duns Business Month

merchant ['mɜ:tʃǝnt] *noun* **(a)** negociante *mf* or comerciante *mf*; **coal merchant** = negociante de carbón; **tobacco merchant** = negociante de tabaco; **wine merchant** = comerciante de vinos **(b)** **merchant bank** = banco de negocios or banco mercantil; **merchant banker** = banquero de negocios; **merchant navy** or **merchant marine** = marina mercante; **merchant ship** or **merchant vessel** = buque mercante

◇ **merchantman** ['mɜ:tʃǝntmǝn] *noun* buque *m* mercante

merge [mɜ:dʒ] *verb* fusionar; **the two companies**

have merged = las dos compañías se han fusionado; **the firm merged with its main competitor** = la firma se fusionó con su mayor competidor

◊ **merger** ['mɜːdʒə] *noun* fusión *f*; **as a result of the merger, the company is the largest in the field** = como resultado de la fusión, la compañía es la más grande del sector; **mergers and acquisitions** = fusiones y adquisiciones

merit ['merɪt] *noun* mérito *m*; **merit award** *or* **merit bonus** = gratificación *f* por méritos; **merit increase** = aumento *m* de sueldo por méritos; **merit rating** = valoración *f* de méritos

message ['mesɪdʒ] *noun* mensaje *m or* recado *m*; **to send a message** = enviar un mensaje; **I will leave a message with his secretary** = le dejaré un recado a su secretaria; **can you give the director a message from his wife?** = ¿puede darle al director un recado de su esposa?; **he says he never received the message** = dice que no recibió el mensaje; **message board** = tablón de anuncios

messenger ['mesɪndʒə] *noun* mensajero, -ra; **he sent the package by special messenger** *or* **by motorcycle messenger** = mandó el paquete con un mensajero especial *or* con un mensajero motorizado; **office messenger** = recadista *mf* de oficina; **messenger boy** = chico *m* de recados

Messrs ['mesəz] *noun* Sres; **Messrs White and Smith** = Sres White y Smith

meter ['miːtə] **1** *noun* **(a)** *(device which measures)* contador *m*; **electricity meter** = contador eléctrico; **water meter** = contador de agua **(b)** *US* = METRE **2** *verb (to measure amount)* medir

method ['meθəd] *noun* método *m or* modo *m*; **a new method of making something** *or* **of doing something** = un nuevo método de fabricación *or* hacer algo; **what is the best method of payment?** = ¿cuál es el mejor modo de pago?; **his organizing methods are out of date** = sus métodos organizativos son anticuados; **their manufacturing methods** *or* **production methods are among the most modern in the country** = sus métodos de fabricación *or* producción figuran entre los más modernos del país; **time and method study** = estudio de tiempos y métodos

metre *or US* **meter** ['miːtə] *noun* metro *m* (NOTE: usually written **m** after figures: **the case is 2m wide by 3m long)**

◊ **metric** ['metrɪk] *adjective* métrico, -ca; **metric ton** *or* **metric tonne** = tonelada métrica; **the metric system** = el sistema métrico

Mexico ['meksɪkəʊ] *noun* México *m*

◊ **Mexican** ['meksɪkən] *adjective & noun* mexicano, -na *or* mejicano, -na
NOTE: capital: **Mexico City** (= México City); currency: **Mexican peso (Mex$)** = peso mexicano ($Mex)

MFN = MOST FAVOURED NATION

mg = MILLIGRAM

mi = MILE

micro ['maɪkrəʊ] *noun* microordenador *m*

◊ **micro-** ['maɪkrəʊ] *prefix* micro; **micro-economics** = microeconomía *f*

◊ **microcomputer** ['maɪkrəʊkəm'pjuːtə] *noun* microordenador *m*

◊ **microfiche** ['maɪkrə(ʊ)fɪʃ] *noun* microficha *f*; **we hold our records on microfiche** = guardamos nuestros registros en microfichas

◊ **microfilm** ['maɪkrə(ʊ)fɪlm] **1** *noun* microfilm *m*; **we hold our records on microfilm** = guardamos nuestros registros en microfilmes **2** *verb* microfilmar; **send the 1990 correspondence to be microfilmed** *or* **for microfilming** = mande la correspondencia de 1990 para que sea microfilmada

◊ **microprocessor** [maɪkrə(ʊ)'prəʊsesə] *noun* microprocesador *m*

mid- [mɪd] *prefix* medio, -dia *or* mediados; **from mid-1994** = desde mediados de 1994; **the factory is closed until mid-July** = la fábrica está cerrada hasta mediados de julio

◊ **mid-month accounts** ['mɪd'mʌnθ ə'kaʊnts] *noun* cuentas *fpl* de mediados de mes

◊ **mid-week** ['mɪd'wiːk] *adjective* a mediados de semana; **the mid-week lull in sales** = la calma en las ventas entre semana

middle ['mɪdl] *adjective* medio, -dia; **middle management** = mandos *mpl* intermedios *or* cuadros intermedios

◊ **middle-income** ['mɪdl'ɪŋkʌm] *adjective* **people in the middle-income bracket** = personas de ingresos medios

◊ **middleman** ['mɪdlmæn] *noun* intermediario, -ria *or* agente de negocios; **we sell direct from the factory to the customer and cut out the middleman** = vendemos directamente de la fábrica al cliente y así suprimimos al intermediario (NOTE: plural is **middlemen)**

◊ **middle-sized** ['mɪdlsaɪzd] *adjective* mediano, -na *or* de tamaño mediano *or* medio; **a middle-sized company** = una empresa de tamaño medio

mile [maɪl] *noun (measurement of length = 1.625 kilometres)* milla *f*; **the car does twenty-five miles to the gallon** *or* **twenty-five miles per gallon** = el coche consume unos 11 litros por 100 kilómetros; **three-mile limit** = aguas jurisdiccionales (NOTE: miles per gallon is usually written **mpg** after figures: **the car does 25mpg)**

◊ **mileage** ['maɪlɪdʒ] *noun* distancia *f or* recorrido *m* en millas *or* kilometraje *m*; **mileage allowance** = gastos de viaje por millas recorridas; **the salesman's average annual mileage** = distancia media (en millas) recorrida por un representante al año

mill [mɪl] *noun* fábrica *f*; **after lunch the visitors were shown round the mill** = después de la comida les enseñaron la fábrica a los visitantes; **cotton mill** = fábrica de tejidos de algodón; **paper mill** = papelera *f*

milligram ['mɪlɪgræm] *noun* miligramo *m* (NOTE: usually written **mg** after figures)

◊ **millilitre** *or US* **milliliter** ['mɪlɪ'liːtə] *noun* mililitro *m* (NOTE: usually written **ml** after figures)

◊ **millimetre** *or US* **millimeter** ['mɪlɪ'miːtə] *noun* milímetro *m* (NOTE: usually written **mm** after figures)

million ['mɪljən] *number* millón *m*; **the company lost £10 million in the African market** = la compañía perdió £10 millones en el mercado africano; **our turnover has risen to $13.4 million** = nuestro volumen de ventas ha subido a $13,4 millones (NOTE: can be written **m** after figures: **$5m** (say 'five million dollars')

◊ **millionaire** [mɪljə'neə] *noun* millonario, -ria; **dollar millionaire** = millonario en dólares; **paper millionaire** = millonario en acciones

min = MINUTE, MINIMUM

mine [maɪn] **1** *noun* mina *f*; **the mines have been closed by a strike** = se han cerrado las minas a causa de una huelga **2** *verb* extraer; **the company is mining coal in the south of the country** = la compañía extrae carbón en el sur del país; **mining concession** = concesión minera

mineral ['mɪnərəl] **1** *noun* mineral *m* **2** *adjective* mineral; **mineral resources** = recursos minerales; **mineral rights** = derechos de explotación (del subsuelo)

mini- ['mɪni] *prefix* mini

◊ **minicomputer** ['mɪnɪkəm'pju:tə] *noun* miniordenador *m*

◊ **minicontainer** ['mɪnɪkən'teɪnə] *noun* contenedor *m* pequeño

◊ **minimarket** ['mɪnɪ'mɑːkɪt] *noun* pequeño supermercado *m*

minimal ['mɪnɪməl] *adjective* mínimo, -ma; **there was a minimal quantity of imperfections in the batch** = el lote presentaba una cantidad mínima de imperfecciones; **the head office exercises minimal control over the branch offices** = la oficina principal ejerce un control mínimo sobre las sucursales

◊ **minimize** ['mɪnɪmaɪz] *verb* minimizar *or* subestimar; **do not minimize the risks involved** = no minimice los posibles riesgos; **he tends to minimize the difficulty of the project** = tiene tendencia a minimizar la dificultad del proyecto

◊ **minimum** ['mɪnɪməm] **1** *noun* mínimo *m*; **to keep expenses to a minimum** = mantener los gastos al mínimo; **to reduce the risk of a loss to a minimum** = reducir el riesgo de pérdidas a un mínimo (NOTE: plural is **minima** or **minimums) 2** *adjective* mínimo, -ma; **minimum dividend** = dividendo mínimo; **minimum payment** = pago mínimo; **minimum quantity** = cantidad mínima; **minimum stock level** = nivel de existencias mínimo; **minimum wage** = salario mínimo

minister ['mɪnɪstə] *noun* ministro, -tra; **a government minister** = un ministro del gobierno; **the Minister of Trade** *or* **the Trade Minister** = el ministro de Comercio; **the Minister of Foreign Affairs** *or* **the Foreign Minister** = el ministro de Asuntos Exteriores (NOTE: in the UK and USA, they are called . . . **secretary: the Secretary for Commerce)**

◊ **ministry** ['mɪnɪstri] *noun* ministerio *m*; **he works in the Ministry of Finance** *or* **the Finance Ministry** = trabaja en el ministerio de Hacienda; **he is in charge of the Ministry of Information** *or* **of the Information Ministry** = está al cargo del ministerio de Información; **a ministry official** *or* **an official from the ministry** = un funcionario del ministerio (NOTE: in GB and the USA, important government ministries are called **departments: the Department of Trade and Industry; the Commerce Department)**

minor ['maɪnə] *adjective* menor *or* pequeño, -ña; **minor expenditure** = gastos menores; **minor shareholders** = accionistas pequeños; **a loss of minor importance** = una pérdida de poca importancia

◊ **minority** [maɪ'nɒrəti] *noun* minoría *f*; **a minority of board members opposed the chairman** = una minoría de los miembros del consejo de administración se opuso al presidente; **minority shareholding** *or* **minority interest** = participación minoritaria en las acciones *or* interés minoritario; **minority shareholder** = accionista minoritario; **in the minority** = en minoría; **good salesmen are in the minority in our sales team** = los buenos vendedores están en minoría en nuestro equipo de ventas

mint [mɪnt] **1** *noun* casa *f or* fábrica *f* de la moneda **2** *verb* acuñar

◊ **minting** ['mɪntɪŋ] *noun* acuñación *f*

minus ['maɪnəs] **1** *preposition* menos; **net salary is gross salary minus tax and National Insurance deductions** = el salario neto es el salario bruto menos los impuestos y las deducciones de la seguridad social; **gross profit is sales minus production costs** = el beneficio bruto equivale a las ventas menos los costes de producción **2** *adjective* **the accounts show a minus figure** = las cuentas arrojan un saldo negativo; **minus factor** = factor negativo; **to have lost sales in the best quarter of the year is a minus factor for the sales team** = la pérdida de ventas en el mejor trimestre del año es un factor negativo para el equipo de ventas

minute ['mɪnɪt] **1** *noun* **(a)** *(time)* minuto *m*; **I can see you for ten minutes only** = sólo puedo dedicarte diez minutos; **if you do not mind waiting, Mr Smith will be free in about twenty minutes' time** = si no le importa esperar, el Sr Smith estará libre en unos veinte minutos **(b)** *(in a meeting)* acta *f or* actas *fpl*; **the minutes of the meeting** = el acta de la reunión; **to take the minutes** = redactar actas; **the chairman signed the minutes of the last meeting** = el presidente firmó el acta de la última reunión; **this will not appear in the minutes of the meeting** = esto no constará en las actas de la junta **2** *verb* anotar *or* tomar nota *or* levantar acta; **the chairman's remarks about the auditors were minuted** = las observaciones del presidente sobre los auditores se hicieron constar en acta; **I do not want that to be minuted** *or* **I want that not to be minuted** = no quiero que eso conste en acta

◊ **minutebook** ['mɪnɪtbʊk] *noun* libro *m* de actas

misappropriate ['mɪsə'prəʊprɪeɪt] *verb* malversar

◊ **misappropriation** ['mɪsəprəʊprɪ'eɪʃən] *noun* malversación *f or* apropiación ilícita

misc = MISCELLANEOUS

miscalculate ['mɪs'kælkjʊleɪt] *verb* calcular

mal; **the salesman miscalculated the discount, so we hardly broke even on the deal** = el vendedor calculó mal el descuento, por lo que apenas cubrimos gastos en la transacción

◊ **miscalculation** ['mɪskælkjʊ'leɪʃən] *noun* error *m* de cálculo

miscellaneous [mɪsə'leɪnjəs] *adjective* misceláneo, -nea *or* variado, -da *or* varios, -rias; **miscellaneous items** = artículos varios; **a box of miscellaneous pieces of equipment** = una caja de piezas variadas; **miscellaneous expenditure** = gastos varios

miscount 1 ['mɪskaʊnt] *noun* error *m* de suma **2** [mɪs'kaʊnt] *verb* equivocarse en la cuenta; **the shopkeeper miscounted, so we got twenty-five bars of chocolate instead of two dozen** = el tendero se equivocó en la cuenta con lo que nos llevamos veinticinco barras de chocolate en vez de dos docenas

misdirect [mɪsdaɪ'rekt] *verb* dirigir *or* informar erróneamente

misfeasance [mɪs'fiːzəns] *noun* acto legal realizado ilegalmente

mismanage [mɪs'mænɪdʒ] *verb* dirigir *or* administrar mal

◊ **mismanagement** [mɪs'mænɪdʒmənt] *noun* mala administración *or* dirección; **the company failed because of the chairman's mismanagement** = la compañía fracasó por la mala administración del presidente

misrepresent ['mɪsreprɪ'zent] *verb* tergiversar *or* deformar los hechos

◊ **misrepresentation** [mɪsreprɪzen'teɪʃən] *noun* tergiversación *f or* información *f* engañosa *or* falsificación *f*; **fraudulent misrepresentation** = tergiversación fraudulenta *or* engaño doloso

Miss [mɪs] *noun* señorita *f*; **Miss Smith is our sales manager** = la señorita Smith es nuestra directora de ventas

miss [mɪs] *verb* **(a)** *(not to hit)* errar *or* no dar en *or* no conseguir; **the company has missed its profit forecast again** = una vez más la empresa no ha conseguido los beneficios previstos; **the sales team has missed its sales targets** = el equipo de ventas no ha conseguido sus objetivos **(b)** *(not to meet)* perderse algo *or* no encontrarse con; **I arrived late, so missed most of the discussion** = llegué tarde, así que me perdí la mayor parte del debate; **he missed the chairman by ten minutes** = llegó con 10 minutos de retraso y no pudo ver al presidente **(c)** *(not to catch)* perder (el tren *or* avión); **he missed the last plane to Frankfurt** = perdió el último avión *or* vuelo a Frankfurt

mission ['mɪʃən] *noun* misión *f*; **trade mission** = misión comercial; **he led a trade mission to China** = dirigió una misión comercial a China; **inward mission** = misión comercial extranjera de visita al país; **outward mission** = misión comercial a un país extranjero; **a fact-finding mission** = misión investigadora

mistake [mɪ'steɪk] *noun* equivocación *f or* error *m*; **to make a mistake** = cometer una equivocación *or*

incurrir en un error; **the shop made a mistake and sent the wrong items** = cometieron un error en la tienda y mandaron artículos equivocados; **there was a mistake in the address** = había un error en la dirección; **she made a mistake in addressing the letter** = cometió un error al escribir la dirección de la carta; **by mistake** = por error; **they sent the wrong items by mistake** = enviaron artículos equivocados por error; **she put my letter into an envelope for the chairman by mistake** = por error, puso mi carta en un sobre para el presidente

misunderstanding ['mɪsʌndə'stændɪŋ] *noun* malentendido *m*; **there was a misunderstanding over my tickets** = hubo un malentendido con mis entradas

misuse [mɪs'juːs] *noun* abuso *m or* uso *m* indebido; **misuse of funds** *or* **of assets** = uso indebido de fondos *or* de bienes

mix [mɪks] **1** *noun* mezcla *f or* conjunto *m*; **product mix** = conjunto *m* de productos de una compañía; **sales mix** = conjunto de ventas **2** *verb* mezclar *or* combinar; **I like to mix business with pleasure - why don't we discuss the deal over lunch?** = me gusta combinar el trabajo con el placer, ¿por qué no hablamos del asunto mientras almorzamos?

◊ **mixed** [mɪkst] *adjective* **(a)** *(of different sorts or types together)* mixto, -ta *or* mezclado, -da; **mixed economy** = economía mixta; **mixed farm** = granja mixta **(b)** *(neither good nor bad)* ni bueno ni malo

QUOTE prices closed on a mixed note after a moderately active trading session
Financial Times

ml = MILLILITRE mililitro (ml)

mm = MILLIMETRE milímetro (mm)

MMC = MONOPOLIES AND MERGERS COMMISSION

mobile ['məʊbaɪl] *adjective* móvil *or* movible; **mobile shop** = tienda ambulante; **mobile workforce** = mano de obra móvil

◊ **mobility** [mə'bɪlətɪ] *noun* movilidad *f*; **mobility of labour** = movilidad de la mano de obra

◊ **mobilize** ['məʊbɪlaɪz] *verb* movilizar; **to mobilize capital** = movilizar capital; **to mobilize resources to defend a takeover bid** = movilizar recursos para defenderse de una oferta de adquisición

mock-up ['mɒkʌp] *noun* maqueta *f or* modelo *m* a escala

mode [məʊd] *noun* modo *m*; **mode of payment** = modo de pago

model ['mɒdl] **1** *noun* **(a)** *(small copy)* maqueta *f*; **he showed us a model of the new office building** = nos mostró una maqueta del nuevo edificio de oficinas **(b)** *(style or type of product)* modelo *m*; **this is the latest model** = éste es el último modelo; **the model on display is last year's** = el modelo expuesto es el del año pasado; **he drives a 1992 model Ford** = conduce un Ford modelo 1992; **demonstration model** = modelo para demostraciones **(c)** *(person)* modelo *mf* **(d)** *(on computer)* **economic model** = modelo económico **2** *adjective* ejemplar *or* modelo; **a model agreement** =

prototipo de un contrato *or* un acuerdo modelo **3** *verb* (*clothes*) pasar modelos (NOTE: **modelling - modelled** but US **modeling - modeled**)

modem ['məʊdem] *noun* modem *m*

moderate 1 ['mɒdərət] *adjective* moderado, -da; **the trade union made a moderate claim** = el sindicato presentó unas reivindicaciones moderadas; **the government proposed a moderate increase in the tax rate** = el gobierno propuso un aumento moderado del tipo de impuesto **2** ['mɒdəreɪt] *verb* moderar; **the union was forced to moderate its claim** = el sindicato se vio obligado a moderar sus pretensiones

modern ['mɒdən] *adjective* moderno, -na; **it is a fairly modern invention - it was patented only in the 1980s** = es un invento bastante moderno - tan sólo se patentó en los años 80

◊ **modernize** ['mɒdənaɪz] *verb* modernizar; **he modernized the whole product range** = modernizó toda la gama de productos

◊ **modernization** [mɒdənaɪ'zeɪʃən] *noun* modernización *f*; **the modernization of the workshop** = la modernización del taller

modest ['mɒdɪst] *adjective* modesto, -ta; **oil shares showed modest gains over the week's trading** = las acciones petrolíferas alcanzaron un alza moderada durante la semana

modify ['mɒdɪfaɪ] *verb* modificar; **the management modified its proposals** = la dirección modificó sus propuestas; **this is the new modified agreement** = éste es el nuevo acuerdo modificado; **the car will have to be modified to pass the government tests** = el coche tendrá que ser modificado para pasar las pruebas oficiales; **the refrigerator was considerably modified before it went into production** = el frigorífico fue modificado considerablemente antes de ser fabricado; **modified accounts** = cuentas anuales de PYME que se depositan en el Registro Mercantil

◊ **modification** [mɒdɪfɪ'keɪʃən] *noun* modificación *f*; **to make** *or* **to carry out modifications to the plan** = hacer *or* llevar a cabo modificaciones del plan; **the new model has had several important modifications** = el nuevo modelo presenta modificaciones importantes; **we asked for modifications to the contract** = pedimos que se modificara el contrato

modular ['mɒdjʊlə] *adjective* modular

momentum [mə'mentəm] *noun* impulso *m or* ímpetu *m*; **to gain** *or* **to lose momentum** = ganar *or* perder impulso; **the strike is gaining momentum** = la huelga está cobrando impulso

Monaco ['mɒnəkəʊ] *noun* Mónaco *m*

◊ **Monegasque** *or* **Monacan** [mɒnɪ'gæsk *or* mɒn'ɑːkən] *adjective & noun* monegasco, -ca NOTE: currency: **French franc (F)** = franco francés (F)

monetary ['mʌnɪtəri] *adjective* monetario, -ria; **the government's monetary policy** = la política monetaria del gobierno; **monetary standard** = patrón monetario; **the international monetary system** = el sistema monetario internacional; **the European Monetary System (EMS)** = el Sistema Monetario Europeo (SME); **the International**

Monetary Fund (IMF) = el Fondo Monetario Internacional (FMI); **monetary targets** = objetivos monetarios; **monetary unit** = moneda *or* unidad monetaria

◊ **monetarism** ['mʌnɪtərɪzəm] *noun* monetarismo *m*

◊ **monetarist** ['mʌnɪtərɪst] **1** *noun* monetarista *mf* **2** *adjective* monetarista; **monetarist theories** = teorías monetaristas

money ['mʌni] *noun* **(a)** (*coins and notes*) dinero *m*; **to earn money** = ganar dinero; **to earn good money** = tener un buen sueldo; **to lose money** = perder dinero; **the company has been losing money for months** = la compañía ha estado perdiendo dinero durante meses; **to get your money back** = recuperar el dinero; **to make money** = hacer *or* ganar dinero; **to put money into the bank** = ingresar dinero en el banco; **to put money into a business** = invertir dinero en un negocio; **he put all his redundancy money into a shop** = invirtió el total de su indemnización por despido en una tienda; **to put money down** = dar una entrada; **he put £25 down and paid the rest in instalments** = dio una entrada de £25 y pagó el resto a plazos; **call money** *or* **money at call** = dinero a la vista; **cheap money** = dinero *or* crédito barato; **danger money** = plus *m* de peligrosidad; **dear money** = dinero *or* crédito caro; **easy money** = dinero fácil; **selling insurance is easy money** = vender seguros es ganar dinero fácil; **hot money** = dinero caliente *or* que se mueve de un país a otro para obtener el mejor rendimiento; **paper money** = papel moneda; **plastic money** = dinero de plástico; **ready money** = dinero líquido; **money lying idle** = dinero inactivo; **they are worth a lot of money** = valen mucho dinero **(b)** **money supply** = circulante *m or* oferta monetaria *or* activos líquidos en manos del público (ALPs); **money markets** = mercados monetarios; **the international money markets are nervous** = los mercados monetarios internacionales están nerviosos; **money rates** = tipos de interés del dinero **(c)** **money order** = giro postal; **foreign money order** *or* **international money order** *or* **overseas money order** = giro postal internacional **(d)** **monies** = sumas *fpl or* cantidades *fpl or* dinero *m*; **monies owing to the company** = dinero que se debe a la compañía; **to collect monies due** = cobrar las sumas debidas **(e)** **money laundering** = blanqueo *m* de dinero

◊ **moneybox** ['mʌnɪbɒks] *noun* hucha *f*

◊ **moneylender** ['mʌnɪlendə] *noun* prestamista *mf*

◊ **money-making** ['mʌnɪmeɪkɪŋ] *adjective* lucrativo, -va *or* remunerativo, -va *or* que produce dinero; **a money-making plan** = un plan remunerativo

◊ **money-spinner** ['mʌnɪspɪnə] *noun* artículo *m* que se vende bien

monitor ['mɒnɪtə] **1** *noun (screen)* monitor *m or* pantalla *f* **2** *verb* controlar *or* comprobar; **he is monitoring the progress of sales** = controla la marcha de las ventas; **how do you monitor the performance of the sales reps?** = ¿cómo controla Vd. el rendimiento de los representantes?

monopoly [mə'nɒpəli] *noun* monopolio *m*; **to have the monopoly of alcohol sales** *or* **to have the alcohol monopoly** = tener el monopolio de la venta de bebidas alcohólicas; **to be in a monopoly situation** = estar en una situación de monopolio; **the company has the absolute monopoly of imports of French wine** = la compañía tiene el monopolio absoluto de las importaciones de vino francés; **the factory has the absolute monopoly of jobs in the town** = la fábrica tiene el monopolio absoluto del empleo de la ciudad; **public monopoly** *or* **state monopoly** = monopolio público *or* estatal; *GB* **Monopolies and Mergers Commission (MMC)** = la Comisión de Monopolios (NOTE: **trust** is used more often in US English)

◊ **monopolize** [mə'nɒpəlaɪz] *verb* monopolizar; *(Mex)* copar

◊ **monopolization** [mə'nɒpəlaɪ'zeɪʃən] *noun* monopolización *f*

month [mʌnθ] *noun* mes *m*; **the company pays him £100 a month** = la empresa le paga £100 al mes; **he earns £2,000 a month** = gana £2.000 al mes; **bills due at the end of the current month** = letras que vencen a finales del mes corriente; **calendar month** = mes civil; **paid by the month** = pagado por meses; **to give a customer two months' credit** = conceder a un cliente dos meses de crédito

◊ **month end** ['mʌnθ 'end] *noun* fin de mes; **month-end accounts** = cuentas de fin de mes

◊ **monthly** ['mʌnθli] **1** *adjective* mensual; **monthly statement** = estado de cuenta mensual; **monthly payments** = pagos mensuales; **he is paying for his car by monthly instalments** = está pagando el coche en plazos mensuales; **my monthly salary cheque is late** = el cheque de mi sueldo mensual lleva retraso; **monthly ticket** = billete mensual **2** *adverb* mensualmente; **to pay monthly** = pagar mensualmente; **the account is credited monthly** = se abona en cuenta mensualmente **3** *noun* **a monthly** = revista *f or* publicación *f* mensual

moonlight ['mu:nlaɪt] **1** *noun (informal)* pluriempleo *m*; **to do a moonlight flit** = mudarse a la chita callando **2** *verb (informal)* estar pluriempleado *or* ejercer el pluriempleo

◊ **moonlighter** ['mu:nlaɪtə] *noun* pluriempleado, -da

◊ **moonlighting** ['mu:nlaɪtɪŋ] *noun* pluriempleo *m*; **he makes thousands a year from moonlighting** = saca mucho dinero al año gracias al pluriempleo

mooring(s) ['mʊərɪŋ(z)] *noun* fondeadero *m or* amarradero *m or* atracadero *m*

moratorium [mɒrə'tɔ:rɪəm] *noun* moratoria *f*; **the banks called for a moratorium on payments** =

los bancos pidieron una moratoria en materia de pagos (NOTE: plural is **moratoria** or **moratoriums)**

Morocco [mə'rɒkəʊ] *noun* Marruecos *m*

◊ **Moroccan** [mə'rɒkən] *adjective & noun* marroquí
NOTE: capital: **Rabat**; currency: **Moroccan dirham (DH)** = dirham marroquí (DH)

mortality tables [mɔ:'tælɪtɪ 'teɪblz] *plural noun* tabla *f* de mortalidad

mortgage ['mɔ:gɪdʒ] **1** *noun* hipoteca *f*; **to take out a mortgage on a house** = hacer una hipoteca *or* hipotecar una casa; **to buy a house with a £20,000 mortgage** = comprar una casa con una hipoteca de £20.000; **mortgage payments** = pagos de la hipoteca; **endowment mortgage** = hipoteca amparada por una póliza dotal; **first mortgage** = primera hipoteca; **repayment mortgage** = pago de hipoteca; **second mortgage** = segunda hipoteca; **to pay off a mortgage** = redimir una hipoteca; **mortgage bond** = cédula hipotecaria; **mortgage debenture** = título garantizado por hipoteca; **mortgage famine** = escasez *f* de hipotecas; **mortgage queue** = lista de espera de hipotecas **2** *verb* hipotecar; **the house is mortgaged** = la casa está hipotecada; **he mortgaged his house to set up in business** = hipotecó la casa para establecer un negocio; **to foreclose on a mortgaged property** = embargar una propiedad hipotecada

◊ **mortgagee** [mɔ:gə'dʒi:] *noun* acreedor hipotecario *or* acreedora hipotecaria

◊ **mortgager** *or* **mortgagor** ['mɔ:gɪdʒə] *noun* deudor hipotecario *or* deudora hipotecaria

> QUOTE mortgage money is becoming tighter. Applications for mortgages are running at a high level and some building societies are introducing quotas
>
> **Times**

> QUOTE for the first time since mortgage rates began falling a financial institution has raised charges on homeowner loans
>
> **Globe and Mail (Toronto)**

most [məʊst] **1** *noun* mayoría *f*; **most of the staff are graduates** = la mayoría del personal es licenciado; **most of our customers live near the factory** = la mayoría de nuestros clientes viven cerca de la fábrica; **most of the orders come in the early part of the year** = la mayoría de los pedidos llegan al principio del año **2** *adjective* más *or* la mayor parte de; **most orders are dealt with the same day** = la mayor parte de los pedidos se tramitan el mismo día; **most salesmen have had a course of on-the-job training** = la mayor parte de los vendedores ha seguido un curso de formación en el empleo

◊ **most favoured nation (MFN)** ['məʊst 'feɪvəd 'neɪʃən] *noun* la nación más favorecida; **most-favoured-nation clause** = cláusula *f* de la nación más favorecida

◊ **mostly** ['məʊs(t)li] *adverb* principalmente *or* sobre todo *or* en su mayoría; **the staff are mostly girls of twenty to thirty years of age** = los empleados son en su mayoría chicas de veinte a treinta años de edad; **he works mostly in the London office** = trabaja principalmente en la oficina de Londres

motion ['məʊʃən] *noun* **(a)** *(moving about)* movimiento *m*; **time and motion study** = estudio de desplazamientos y tiempos **(b)** *(proposal in a meeting)* moción *f*; **to propose** *or* **to move a motion** = proponer una moción; **the meeting voted on the motion** = se votó la moción en la reunión; **to speak against** *or* **for a motion** = hablar en contra *or* a favor de una moción; **the motion was carried** *or* **was defeated by 220 votes to 196** = la moción fue aprobada *or* rechazada por 220 votos contra 196; **to table a motion** = presentar una moción

◊ **motivate** ['məʊtɪveɪt] *verb* motivar

◊ **motivated** ['məʊtɪveɪtɪd] *adjective* motivado, -da; **highly motivated sales staff** = personal de ventas muy motivado

◊ **motivation** [məʊtɪ'veɪʃən] *noun* motivación *f*; **the sales staff lack motivation** = al personal de ventas le falta motivación

motive ['məʊtɪv] *noun* motivo *m*; **profit motive** = afán de lucro *or* finalidad lucrativa

motor ['məʊtə] *noun* coche *m* *or* automóvil *m*; **motor insurance** = seguro de automóviles

mountain ['maʊntɪn] *noun* montaña *f or* montón *m*; **I have mountains of typing to do** = tengo un montón de cosas para pasar a máquina; **there is a mountain of invoices on the sales manager's desk** = hay un montón de facturas en la mesa de despacho del director de ventas; **butter mountain** = excedente de mantequilla

◊ **mounting** ['maʊntɪŋ] *adjective* creciente *or* cada vez mayor; **he resigned in the face of mounting pressure from the shareholders** = dimitió ante la creciente presión de los accionistas; **the company is faced with mounting debts** = la compañía se enfrenta con deudas cada vez mayores

◊ **mount up** ['maʊnt 'ʌp] *verb* aumentar con rapidez; **costs are mounting up** = los costes están aumentando con rapidez

mouse [maʊs] *noun (computers)* ratón *m*

> QUOTE you can use a mouse to access pop-up menus and a keyboard for a word-processor
> **Byte**

move [mu:v] *verb* **(a)** *(from one place to another)* trasladar(se) *or* mudarse; **the company is moving from London Road to the centre of town** = la compañía se va a trasladar de London Road al centro de la ciudad; **we have decided to move our factory to a site near the airport** = hemos decidido trasladar nuestra fábrica a un lugar cercano al aeropuerto; **to move out** = desalojar *or* deshabitar **(b)** *(sell)* vender; **the stock is starting to move** = las mercancías están empezando a venderse; **the salesmen will have to work hard if they want to move all that stock by the end of the month** = los vendedores tendrán que trabajar mucho si quieren vender todas esas mercancías para fin de mes **(c)** *(a motion)* proponer; **he moved that the accounts be agreed** = propuso que se aprobaran las cuentas; **I move that the meeting should adjourn for ten minutes** = propongo que la reunión se suspenda durante diez minutos

◊ **movable** *or* **moveable** ['mu:vəbl] **1** *adjective* movible *or* móvil; **moveable property** = bienes muebles **2** *plural noun* **moveables** = bienes *mpl* muebles

◊ **movement** ['mu:vmənt] *noun* **(a)** *(changing position)* movimiento *m*; **movements in the money markets** = movimientos en los mercados monetarios; **cyclical movements of trade** = movimientos cíclicos del comercio; **movements of capital** = movimiento *or* circulación *f* de capital; **stock movements** = movimientos de existencias; **all stock movements are logged by the computer** = el ordenador anota todos los movimientos de existencias **(b)** *(people)* movimiento; **the labour movement** = el movimiento obrero; **the free trade movement** = el movimiento en pro del libre comercio

◊ **mover** ['mu:və] *noun* autor, -ra de una moción

Mozambique [məʊzæm'bi:k] *noun* Mozambique *m*

◊ **Mozambiquan** [məʊzæm'bi:kən] *adjective & noun* mozambiqueño, -ña
NOTE: capital: **Maputo**; currency: **Mozambique metical (Mt)** = metical de Mozambique (Mt)

mpg ['empi:'dʒi:] = MILES PER GALLON

Mr ['mɪstə] *noun* Sr; **Mr Smith is the Managing Director** = el Sr Smith es el director gerente

MRP ['ema:'pi:] = MANUFACTURER'S RECOMMENDED PRICE

Mrs ['mɪsɪz] *noun* Sra; **the chair was taken by Mrs Smith** = la Sra Smith ocupó la presidencia

Ms [məz] *noun* (tratamiento dado a una mujer para no especificar su estado civil); **Ms Smith is the personnel officer** = la Sra Smith es la jefa de personal

multi- ['mʌlti] *prefix* multi

◊ **multicurrency** ['mʌ.tɪ'kʌrənsi] *adjective* **multicurrency loan** = préstamo en múltiples divisas *or* monedas; **multicurrency operation** = operación en multiples divisas

◊ **multilateral** ['mʌltɪ'lætərəl] *adjective* multilateral; **a multilateral agreement** = un acuerdo multilateral; **multilateral trade** = comercio multilateral

◊ **multilingual** ['mʌltɪ'lɪŋwəl] *adjective* multilingüe; **a multilingual contract** = un contrato multilingüe

◊ **multimillion** ['mʌltɪ'mɪljən] *adjective* de varios millones; **they signed a multimillion pound deal** = firmaron un trato de varios millones de libras

◊ **multimillionaire** ['mʌltɪmɪljə'neə] *noun* multimillonario, -ria

◊ **multinational** ['mʌltɪ'næʃənl] *noun* multinacional *f*; **the company has been bought by one of the big multinationals** = la empresa ha sido comprada por una de las grandes multinacionales

> QUOTE factory automation is a multi-billion-dollar business
> **Duns Business Month**

QUOTE the number of multinational firms has mushroomed in the past two decades. As their sweep across the global economy accelerates, multinational firms are posing pressing issues for nations rich and poor, and those in between
Australian Financial Review

multiple ['mʌltɪpl] **1** *adjective* múltiple; **multiple entry visa** = visado de entradas múltiples; **multiple store** = sucursal de una cadena de grandes almacenes; **multiple ownership** = propiedad conjunta **2** *noun* **(a)** *(with a P/E ratio of 5)* **share on a multiple of 5** = acción valorada en múltiplos de 5 **(b)** cadena *f* de almacenes

multiply ['mʌltɪplaɪ] *verb* **(a)** *(calculation)* multiplicar; **to multiply twelve by three** = multiplicar doce por tres; **square measurements are calculated by multiplying length by width** = las medidas de superficie se calculan multiplicando la longitud por la anchura **(b)** *(increase)* multiplicar; **profits multiplied in the boom years** = los beneficios se multiplicaron en los años de prosperidad

◊ **multiplication** [mʌltɪplɪ'keɪʃən] *noun* multiplicación *f*; **multiplication sign** = signo *m* de multiplicar

municipal [mjʊ'nɪsɪpəl] *adjective* municipal; **municipal taxes** = impuestos municipales; **municipal offices** = oficinas municipales

Murphy's law ['mɜːfɪz 'lɔː] *noun* ley de Murphy (según la cual cuando existe la posibilidad de que algo salga mal acaba siempre por salir mal)

mutual ['mjuːtʃʊəl] *adjective* mutuo, -tua; **mutual (insurance) company** = mutua *or* sociedad mutua (de seguros); *US* **mutual fund** = fondos mutuos (NOTE: the UK equivalent is a **unit trust**)

Nn

nail [neɪl] *noun* clavo *m*; **to pay on the nail** = pagar puntualmente

naira [ˈnaɪrə] *noun* naira (moneda de Nigeria) (NOTE: no plural: naira is usually written **N** before figures: **N2,000** (say 'two thousand naira')

name [neɪm] *noun* **(a)** *(thing or person)* nombre *m*; **I cannot remember the name of the managing director of Smith's Ltd** = no recuerdo el nombre del director general de la empresa Smith Ltd; **his first name is John, but I am not sure of his other names** = su nombre de pila es John pero no estoy seguro de sus apellidos; **brand name** = marca *f* comercial *or* conocida; **corporate** *or* **trade name** = razón *f* social *or* nombre comercial; *(Mex)* denominación social; **under the name of** = con el nombre de; **trading under the name of 'Best Foods'** = productos vendidos con el nombre de 'Best Foods' **(b)** *(surname)* apellido *m* **(c)** *(underwriter)* asegurador, -ra

◊ **named** [ˈneɪmd] *adjective* **person named in the policy** = beneficiario, -ria de la póliza

Namibia [nəˈmɪbɪə] *noun* Namibia

◊ **Namibian** [nəˈmɪbɪən] *adjective & noun* de Namibia
NOTE: capital: **Windhoek**; currency: **South African rand** = rand

narrow market [ˈnærəʊ ˈmɑːkɪt] *noun (where few shares are available for sale)* mercado limitado

nation [ˈneɪʃən] *noun* nación *f*; **most favoured nation** = nación más favorecida; **most-favoured-nation clause** = cláusula de la nación más favorecida; **the United Nations (the UN)** = Organización de las Naciones Unidas (NN UU) *or* la ONU

◊ **national** [ˈnæʃənl] **1** *adjective* nacional; **national advertising** = publicidad a escala nacional; **we took national advertising to promote our new 24-hour delivery service** = hicimos publicidad en todo el país para promocionar nuestro nuevo servicio a domicilio de 24 horas al día; *(GB)* **National Audit Office** = Tribunal de Cuentas; *US* **national bank** = banco nacional; **national campaign** = campaña *f* nacional; **the National Debt** = la deuda pública; *GB* **National Health Service** = Seguridad Social *or* Servicio Nacional de Salud *or* Instituto de la Salud (Insalud); **national income** = renta nacional; *GB* **National Insurance** = la Seguridad Social; **National Insurance contributions (NIC)** = cotizaciones a la Seguridad Social; **national newspapers** *or* **the national press** = los periódicos nacionales *or* la prensa nacional; **gross national product (GNP)** = producto nacional bruto (PNB); *GB* **National Savings** = Caja de Ahorros; *US* **National Bank** = banco nacional (banco autorizado por el gobierno federal) **2** *noun* súbdito *m or* ciudadano, -na; **he is a British national** = es de nacionalidad británica

◊ **nationality** [næʃəˈnælɪti] *noun* **he is of British nationality** = es de nacionalidad británica

◊ **nationalize** [ˈnæʃənəlaɪz] *verb* nacionalizar;

the government is planning to nationalize the banking system = el gobierno tiene el proyecto de nacionalizar la banca

◊ **nationalized** [ˈnæʃənəlaɪzd] *adjective* **nationalized industry** = industria nacionalizada

◊ **nationalization** [næʃənəlaɪˈzeɪʃən] *noun* nacionalización *f*

◊ **nationwide** [neɪʃənˈwaɪd] *adjective* de ámbito nacional *or* a escala nacional *or* a lo largo y ancho del país; **the union called for a nationwide strike** = el sindicato convocó una huelga a escala nacional; **we offer a nationwide delivery service** = ofrecemos un servicio de distribución a escala nacional; **the new car is being launched with a nationwide sales campaign** = el nuevo coche será lanzado con una campaña de ventas de ámbito nacional

nature [ˈneɪtʃə] *noun* naturaleza *f or* índole *f or* esencia *f*; **what is the nature of the contents of the parcel?** = ¿cuál es el contenido del paquete?; **the nature of his business is not known** = no se sabe qué tipo de negocios tiene

◊ **natural** [ˈnætʃrəl] *adjective* **(a)** *(found in the earth)* natural; **natural gas** = gas natural; **natural resources** = recursos naturales **(b)** *(not man-made)* natural; **natural fibres** = fibras naturales **(c)** *(normal)* natural; **it was natural for the shopkeeper to feel annoyed when the hypermarket was set up close to his shop** = era natural que el tendero se sintiera molesto cuando el hipermercado se instaló cerca de su tienda; **natural wastage** = reducción del número de trabajadores por jubilación o baja voluntaria; **the company is hoping to avoid redundancies and reduce its staff by natural wastage** = la empresa espera evitar el exceso de plantilla y reducir su personal por jubilación o baja voluntaria

navy [ˈneɪvi] *noun* **merchant navy** = marina *f* mercante

NB [ˈenˈbiː] = NOTE

NBV = NET BOOK VALUE

near letter-quality (NLQ) [ˈnɪə ˈletəˈkwɒlɪti] *noun (printers)* calidad de semicorrespondencia

necessary [ˈnesəsəri] *adjective* necesario, -ria; **it is necessary to fill in the form correctly if you are not to have difficulty at the customs** = hay que rellenar debidamente el formulario para no tener dificultades en la aduana; **is it really necessary for the chairman to have six personal assistants?** = ¿es realmente necesario que el presidente tenga seis ayudantes?; **you must have all the necessary documentation before you apply for a subsidy** = debe reunir la documentación necesaria para poder solicitar una subvención *or* ayuda

◊ **necessity** [nɪˈsesəti] *noun* necesidad *f*; **being unemployed makes it difficult to afford even the basic necessities** = cuando se está sin empleo es difícil costearse incluso las necesidades básicas

need [niːd] *noun* necesidad *f*; **in need of** = necesitado de

◊ **needy** ['niːdi] *adjective* necesitado, -da

negative ['negətɪv] *adjective* negativo, -va; **the answer was in the negative** = la respuesta fue negativa; **negative cash flow** = flujo de caja negativo (NOTE: the opposite is **positive**)

neglected [nɪ'glektɪd] *adjective* descuidado, -da *or* abandonado, -da; **neglected shares** = acciones poco buscadas en la bolsa; **bank shares have been a neglected sector of the market this week** = las acciones bancarias han atraído poco interés en la bolsa esta semana; **neglected business** = negocio descuidado

negligence ['neglɪdʒəns] *noun* negligencia *f*; **criminal negligence** = culpa penal *or* imprudencia; **gross negligence** = imprudencia temeraria

◊ **negligent** ['neglɪdʒnt] *adjective* negligente *or* descuidado, -da

◊ **negligible** ['neglɪdʒəbl] *adjective* insignificante *or* despreciable; **not negligible** = nada despreciable

negotiable [nɪ'gəʊʃəbl] *adjective (cheque)* 'not negotiable' = 'no negociable'; **negotiable cheque** = cheque negociable; **negotiable instrument** = documento negociable

◊ **negotiate** [nɪ'gəʊʃɪeɪt] *verb* negociar *or* gestionar *or* tramitar; **to negotiate with someone** = negociar con alguien; **the management refused to negotiate with the union** = la dirección se negó a negociar con el sindicato; **to negotiate terms and conditions** *or* **to negotiate a contract** = negociar las condiciones y los términos *or* negociar un contrato; **he negotiated a £250,000 loan with the bank** = negoció un préstamo de £250.000 con el banco; **negotiating committee** = comisión negociadora *or* comité negociador

◊ **negotiation** [nɪgəʊʃɪ'eɪʃən] *noun* negociación *f*; **contract under negotiation** = contrato en negociación; **a matter for negotiation** = un asunto que debe ser negociado; **to enter into negotiations** *or* **to start negotiations** = entablar negociaciones; **to resume negotiations** = reanudar las negociaciones; **to break off negotiations** = romper las negociaciones; **to conduct negotiations** = llevar a cabo negociaciones; **negotiations broke down after six hours** = después de seis horas se interrumpieron las negociaciones; **pay negotiations** *or* **wage negotiations** = negociaciones salariales

◊ **negotiator** [nɪ'gəʊʃɪeɪtə] *noun* (a) *(general)* negociador, -ra; **an experienced union negotiator** = un negociador sindical experimentado (b) *(estate agent) GB* empleado, -da de una agencia inmobiliaria

neighbourhood *or US* **neighborhood** ['neɪbəhʊd] *noun* barrio *m*

Nepal [nɪ'pɔːl] *noun* Nepal *m*

◊ **Nepalese** *or* **Nepali** ['nepəliːz *or* nə'pɔːli] *adjective & noun* nepalés, -esa
NOTE: capital: **Katmandu** (= Katmandú); currency: **Nepalese rupee (NRs)** = rupia nepalesa (NRs)

nest egg ['nest 'eg] *noun* ahorros *mpl*

net [net] **1** *adjective* (a) *(after deductions)* neto, -ta; **net asset value (NAV)** *or* **net worth** = activo neto; **net book value (NBV)** = valor neto en los libros de la compañía; **net cash flow** = flujo neto de caja; **net earnings** *or* **net income** = ganancias netas *or* ingresos netos; **net income** *or* **net salary** = salario neto *or* sueldo neto; **net loss** = pérdida neta; **net margin** = margen neto; **net price** = precio neto; **net profit** = beneficio neto; **net profit before tax** = beneficio neto antes de impuestos; **net receipts** = ingresos netos; **net sales** = ventas netas; **net weight** = peso neto; **net yield** = rendimiento neto (b) **terms strictly net** = precio sin reducción posible (NOTE: the spelling **nett** is sometimes used on containers) **2** *verb* obtener; **to net a profit of £10,000** = obtener un beneficio neto de £10.000 (NOTE: **netting - netted**)

Netherlands ['neðələndz] *(informal)* **Holland** ['hɒlənd] *noun* los Países Bajos *mpl or* Holanda *f*

network ['netwɜːk] **1** *noun* red *f*; **a network of distributors** *or* **a distribution network** = una red de distribuidores *or* una red de distribución; **computer network** = red de ordenadores; **television network** = red *or* cadena de televisión **2** *verb* (a) *(TV)* transmitir; **to network a television programme** = transmitir un programa de televisión por toda la red (b) **networked system** = sistema operativo de redes

new [njuː] *adjective* nuevo, -va; **under new management** = cambio de dirección *or* dueño; **new issue** = nueva emisión; **new issues department** = departamento de nuevas emisiones; **new technology** = nueva tecnología

◊ **news** [njuːz] *noun* noticias *fpl (in a newspaper)* **business news** = negocios; **financial news** = noticias financieras; **financial markets were shocked by the news of the devaluation** = la noticia de la devaluación causó conmoción en los mercados financieros; **news agency** = agencia de prensa; **news release** = comunicado *m*; **the company sent out a news release about the new managing director** = la compañía hizo público un comunicado sobre el nuevo director gerente

◊ **newsagent** ['njuːzeɪdʒənt] *noun* vendedor, -ra de periódicos y revistas

◊ **newsletter** ['njuːzletə] *noun* **company newsletter** = boletín *m* informativo de una empresa

New Zealand ['nju: 'zi:lənd] **1** *noun* Nueva Zelanda *f* **2** *adjective* neocelandés, -esa *or* neozelandés, -esa

◊ **New Zealander** ['nju: 'zi:ləndə] *noun* Neozelandés, -esa
NOTE: capital: **Wellington**; currency: **New Zealand dollar ($NZ)** = dólar neocelandés ($NZ)

next [nekst] *adjective (place, order, time)* próximo, -ma; **next time** = la próxima vez; **he is tipped to become the next chairman** = se perfila como el próximo presidente

NIC = NATIONAL INSURANCE CONTRIBUTIONS

Nicaragua [nɪkə'ræɡjuə] *noun* Nicaragua *f*

◊ **Nicaraguan** [nɪkə'ræɡjuən] *adjective & noun* nicaragüense
NOTE: capital: **Managua**; currency: **Nicaraguan cordoba (C$)** = córdoba nicaragüense ($C)

niche [ni:ʃ] *noun* nicho *m* de mercado *or* sector *m* especial *or* hueco *m* de un mercado

nickel ['nɪkl] *noun* US moneda *f* de cinco centavos

Niger [ni:'ʒɜ:] *noun* Níger *m*

◊ **Nigerien** [ni:'ʒɜəriæn] *adjective & noun* nigeriano, -na
NOTE: capital: **Niamey**; currency: **CFA franc (CFAF)** = franco CFA (FCFA)

Nigeria [naɪ'dʒɪəriə] *noun* Nigeria *f*

◊ **Nigerian** [naɪ'dʒɪəriən] *adjective & noun* nigeriano, -na
NOTE: capital: **Abuja**; currency: **Nigerian naira (N)** = naira nigeriana (N)

night [naɪt] *noun* noche *f*; **night safe** = caja nocturna; **night shift** = turno de noche; **there are thirty men on the night shift** = hay treinta trabajadores en el turno de noche; **he works nights** *or* **he works the night shift** = trabaja en el turno de noche

Nikkei Average ['nɪkeɪ 'ævrɪdʒ] índice de precios en la bolsa de Tokio

nil [nɪl] *noun* nada *f or* cero *m*; **to make a nil return** = hacer una declaración de ingresos nulos; **the advertising budget has been cut to nil** = el presupuesto de publicidad ha sido suprimido

NLQ = NEAR LETTER-QUALITY

No. = NUMBER número (Nᵒ)

no-claims bonus [nəʊ'kleɪmz 'bəʊnəs] *noun* bonificación *f or* prima *f* por ausencia de siniestralidad *or* reclamaciones

nominal ['nɒmɪnl] *adjective* **(a)** *(very small payment)* simbólico, -ca (pagos); **we make a nominal charge for our services** = cobramos un precio simbólico por nuestros servicios; **they are paying a nominal rent** = pagan una renta simbólica **(b)** *(in name only)* nominal; **nominal share capital** = capital nominal; **nominal ledger** = libro mayor de resultados; **nominal value** = valor *or* importe nominal

nominate ['nɒmɪneɪt] *verb* designar *or* proponer la candidatura de; **to nominate someone to a post** = proponer a alguien para un puesto; **to nominate someone as proxy** = dar poderes a alguien

◊ **nomination** [nɒmɪ'neɪʃən] *noun* designación *f or* nombramiento *m*

◊ **nominee** [nɒmɪ'ni:] *noun* apoderado, -da *or* candidato,-ta propuesto,-ta; **nominee account** = cuenta administrada por un apoderado

non- [nɒn] *prefix* no

◊ **non-acceptance** ['nɒnək'septəns] *noun* no aceptación

◊ **non-contributory** ['nɒnkən'trɪbjʊtəri] *adjective* **non-contributory pension scheme** = plan *or* programa de pensiones sin aportación del trabajador; **the company pension scheme is non-contributory** = el programa de pensiones está totalmente financiado por la empresa

◊ **non-delivery** ['nɒndɪ'lɪvəri] *noun* falta *f* de entrega

◊ **non-durables** ['nɒn'djʊərəblz] *plural noun* bienes *mpl* perecederos

◊ **non-executive director** ['nɒnɪgzekjʊtɪv dɪ'rektə] *noun* director *m* no ejecutivo

◊ **non-feasance** ['nɒn'fi:zəns] *noun* delito *m* por omisión

◊ **non-negotiable instrument** ['nɒnnɪgəʊʃəbl 'ɪnstrəmənt] *noun* documento *m* no negociable

◊ **non-payment** ['nɒn'peɪmənt] *noun* **non-payment of a debt** = impago *m* de una deuda

◊ **non profit-making organization** *or* US **non-profit corporation** ['nɒn 'profɪtmeɪkɪŋ ɔ:gənaɪ'zeɪʃən *or* 'nɒn'profɪt kɔ:pə'reɪʃən] *noun* sociedad *f* no lucrativa *or* sin fines de lucro; **non-profit-making organizations are exempted from tax** = las organizaciones no lucrativas están exentas del pago de impuestos

◊ **non-recurring items** ['nɒnrɪ'kɜ:rɪŋ 'aɪtəmz] *noun* partidas extraordinarias

◊ **non-refundable** ['nɒnrɪ'fʌndəbl] *adjective* no reembolsable; **non-refundable deposit** = depósito no reembolsable

◊ **non-resident** ['nɒn'rezɪdənt] *noun* no residente; **he has a non-resident bank account** = tiene una cuenta de no residente

◊ **non-returnable** ['nɒnrɪ'tɜ:nəbl] *adjective* sin retorno *or* de usar y tirar; **non-returnable packing** = envase *or* embalaje no retornable

◊ **non-stop** ['nɒn'stɒp] **1** *adverb* sin escalas *or* sin parar; **they worked non-stop to finish the audit on time** = trabajaron sin parar para terminar la revisión de cuentas a tiempo **2** *adjective* directo, -ta; **non-stop flight** = vuelo directo; *compare* DIRECT FLIGHT

◊ **non-sufficient funds** ['nɒnsə'fɪʃənt 'fʌndz] *noun* US cuenta en descubierto *or* sin fondos suficientes

◊ **non-taxable** ['nɒn'tæksəbl] *adjective* libre *or*

exento de impuestos; **non-taxable income** = ingresos libres de impuestos

◊ **non-union** ['nɒn'juːnjən] *adjective* **company using non-union labour** = empresa que contrata a trabajadores no sindicados

◊ **non-voting shares** ['nɒn'vəʊtɪŋ 'ʃeəz] *noun* acciones sin derecho a voto

norm [nɔːm] *noun* norma *f*; **the output from this factory is well above the norm for the industry** *or* **well above the industry norm** = la producción de esta fábrica está muy por encima de la norma de ese sector industrial

◊ **normal** ['nɔːməl] *adjective* normal; **normal deliveries are made on Tuesdays and Fridays** = las entregas normales se realizan los martes y los viernes; **now that the strike is over we hope to resume normal service as soon as possible** = ahora que la huelga ha terminado esperamos reanudar el servicio normal lo antes posible; **under normal conditions** = en condiciones normales; **under normal conditions a package takes two days to get to Copenhagen** = en condiciones normales un paquete llega a Copenhague en dos días *or* tarda dos días en llegar a Copenhagen

Norway ['nɔːweɪ] *noun* Noruega *f*

◊ **Norwegian** [nɔː'wiːdʒən] *adjective & noun* noruego, -ga
NOTE: capital: **Oslo**; currency: **Norwegian krone (NKr)** = corona noruega (NKr)

no-strike ['nəʊ'straɪk] *adjective* **no-strike agreement** *or* **no-strike clause** = acuerdo *m* que prohibe la huelga *or* cláusula *f* que compromete a los sindicatos a no ir a la huelga

nosedive ['nəʊzdaɪv] *verb* (*fall very sharply*) caer en picado; **the share price nosedived after the chairman was arrested** = el precio de la acción cayó en picado tras el arresto del presidente

nostro account ['nɒstrəʊ ə'kaʊnt] *noun* nuestra cuenta; *see also* VOSTRO ACCOUNT

notary public ['nəʊtəri 'pʌblɪk] *noun* notario *m* (NOTE: plural is **notaries public**)

note [nəʊt] **1** *noun* **(a)** (*short document*) nota *f*; **to take note** = tomar nota; **advice note** = aviso *m* de expedición *or* envío; **contract note** = nota en la que se indica que se han comprado o vendido acciones pero que no se han pagado todavía; **cover note** = póliza provisional *or* nota de cobertura; **covering note** = carta adjunta *or* explicatoria; **credit note** = nota de abono *or* crédito; **debit note** = nota de cargo *or* débito; **we undercharged Mr Smith and had to send him a debit note for the extra amount** = le cobramos de menos al señor Smith y tuvimos que mandarle una nota de débito por la cantidad extra; **delivery note** = nota de entrega *or* albarán *m*; **dispatch note** = nota de envío *or* expedición; **note of hand** *or* **promissory note** = pagaré *m* *or* letra *f* al propio cargo **(b)** (*short letter*) nota; **to send someone a note** = enviar una nota a alguien; **I left a note on his desk** = dejé una nota sobre su mesa de despacho; **she left a note for the managing director with his secretary** = dejó una nota para el director gerente a su secretaria; **to take note of something** = anotar algo **(c)** bank note *or* currency note = billete de banco; **a £5 note** = un billete de £5;

he pulled out a pile of used notes = sacó un montón de billetes usados (NOTE: US English for this is **bill**) **2** *verb* (*to write down details*) tomar nota *or* apuntar *or* anotar; **we note that the goods were delivered in bad condition** = tomamos nota que la mercancía fue entregada en malas condiciones; **your order has been noted and will be dispatched as soon as we have stock** = hemos tomado nota de su pedido y lo despacharemos en cuanto tengamos existencias; **your complaint has been noted** = hemos tomado nota de su reclamación

◊ **notebook** ['nəʊtbʊk] *noun* cuaderno *m* *or* libreta *f*

◊ **notepad** ['nəʊtpæd] *noun* bloc *m* de notas

◊ **notepaper** ['nəʊtpeɪpə] *noun* **(a)** papel *m* de cartas **(b)** *US* papel para notas *or* borrador *m*

notice ['nəʊtɪs] *noun* **(a)** (*written information*) letrero *m* *or* anuncio *m* *or* aviso *m* *or* notificación *f*; **the company secretary pinned up a notice about the pension scheme** = la secretaria de la empresa puso un aviso sobre el programa de pensiones en el tablón de anuncios; **copyright notice** = nota *f* de copyright *or* nota sobre los derechos de autor **(b)** (*official warning*) notificación de rescisión de contrato *or* de modificación de condiciones; **until further notice** = hasta nuevo aviso; **you must pay £200 on the 30th of each month until further notice** = debe pagar £200 el 30 de cada mes hasta nuevo aviso **(c)** (*leaving a job*) notificación de despido *or* de baja voluntaria en la empresa; **period of notice** = periodo de preaviso; **we require three months' notice** = exigimos una notificación previa de tres meses; **he gave six months' notice** = avisó con seis meses de antelación; **we gave him three months' wages in lieu of notice** = le dimos tres meses de sueldo en vez de preaviso; **she gave in** *or* **handed in her notice** = presentó su dimisión *or* dimitió; **he is working out his notice** = está trabajando los últimos días que le quedan del contrato **(d)** (*period of time*) plazo *m*; **at short notice** = a corto plazo *or* a última hora; **the bank manager will not see anyone at short notice** = el director del banco no recibirá a nadie sin cita previa; **you must give seven days' notice of withdrawal** = tiene que dar un plazo de siete días para sacar dinero **(e)** (*legal document*) aviso *or* notificación; **to give a tenant notice to quit** = notificar el desahucio a un inquilino; **to serve notice on someone** = dar un ultimatum a alguien *or* notificar algo a alguien (oficialmente)

◊ **noticeable** ['nəʊtɪsəbl] *adjective* acusado, -da; **to be noticeable** = acusarse

◊ **noticeboard** ['nəʊtɪsbɔːd] *noun* tablón *m* de anuncios; **did you see the new list of prices on the noticeboard?** = ¿viste la nueva lista de precios en el tablón de anuncios?

notify ['nəʊtɪfaɪ] *verb* notificar *or* avisar; **to notify someone of something** = notificar algo a alguien; **they were notified of the arrival of the shipment** = se les notificó la llegada del envío

◊ **notification** [nəʊtɪfɪ'keɪʃən] *noun* notificación *f* *or* aviso *m*

notional ['nəʊʃənl] *adjective* especulativo, -va *or* teórico, -ca *or* en abstracto; **notional income** = ingresos teóricos; **notional rent** = renta teórica

nought [nɔːt] *number* nada *f* *or* cero *m*; **a million**

pounds can be written as '£1m' or as one and six noughts = un millón de libras se puede escribir '£1m' o con un uno seguido de seis ceros (NOTE: **nought** is commoner in GB English; in US English, **zero** is more usual)

null [nʌl] *adjective* nulo, -la; **contract was declared null and void** = el contrato fue declarado nulo y sin valor; **to render a decision null** = anular una decisión

◊ **nullification** [nʌlɪfɪˈkeɪʃən] *noun* anulación *f*

◊ **nullify** [ˈnʌlɪfaɪ] *verb* anular

number [ˈnʌmbə] **1** *noun* **(a)** *(quantity)* número *m or* cantidad *f*; **the number of persons on the payroll has increased over the last year** = el número de personas en nómina ha aumentado este último año; **the number of days lost through strikes has fallen** = el número de días perdidos por huelgas ha disminuido; **the number of shares sold** = la cantidad de acciones vendidas; **a number of** = algunos, -as *or* varios, -as; **a number of the staff will be retiring this year** = varios empleados se jubilarán este año **(b)** *(written figure)* número;

account number = número de cuenta; **batch number** = número de lote; **cheque number** = número de cheque; **even numbers** = números pares; **invoice number** = número de factura; **odd numbers** = números impares; **order number** = número de pedido; **page number** = número de página; **serial number** = número de serie; **phone number** *or* **telephone number** = número de teléfono; **box number** = número de apartado de correos; **please reply to Box No. 209** = enviar las respuestas al apartado de correos n° 209; **index number** = (i) índice; (ii) indicador (NOTE: **number** is often written **No.** with figures: **No. 23) 2** *verb* numerar *or* poner número a; **to number an order** = numerar un pedido *or* asignar un número a un pedido; **I refer to your invoice numbered 1234** = me refiero a su factura número 1234; **numbered account** = cuenta numerada

◊ **numeric** *or* **numerical** [njʊˈmerɪk *or* njʊˈmerɪkl] *adjective* numérico, -ca; **in numerical order** = en orden numérico; **file these invoices in numerical order** = archive estas facturas en orden numérico; **numeric data** = datos numéricos; **numeric keypad** = teclado numérico

Oo

O & M = ORGANIZATION AND METHODS

0500 number *or* **0800 number**
[əʊ'faɪv'hʌndrəd 'nʌmbə *or* əʊ'eɪt'hʌndrəd 'nʌmbə] número telefónico al que se llama gratuitamente (NOTE: US English is **800 number;** the equivalent number in Spain is **009)**

OAP [əʊeɪ'piː] = OLD AGE PENSIONER

oath [əʊθ] *noun* juramento *m;* **he was under oath** = había prestado juramento *or* estaba bajo juramento

object 1 ['ɒbdʒekt] *noun* objeto *m or* cosa *f* **2** [əb'dʒekt] *verb* oponerse *or* hacer objeciones; **to object to a clause in a contract** = oponerse a una cláusula del contrato (NOTE: you object **to** something)

◊ **objection** [əb'dʒekʃən] *noun* **to raise an objection to something** = hacer una objeción a algo; **the union delegates raised an objection to the wording of the agreement** = los delegados de los sindicatos hicieron objeciones al texto del acuerdo

objective [əb'dʒektɪv] **1** *noun* objetivo *m;* **the company has achieved its objectives** = la compañía ha logrado sus objetivos; **we set the sales force certain objectives** = fijamos ciertos objetivos al personal de ventas; **long-term objective** *or* **short-term objective** = objetivo a largo plazo *or* objetivo a corto plazo; **management by objectives** = dirección por objetivos **2** *adjective* objetivo, -va; **you must be objective in assessing the performance of the staff** = hay que ser objetivo al evaluar el rendimiento del personal; **to carry out an objective survey of the market** = llevar a cabo un estudio objetivo del mercado

obligate ['ɒblɪgeɪt] *verb* **to be obligated to do something** = estar obligado a hacer algo

◊ **obligation** [ɒblɪ'geɪʃən] *noun* **(a)** *(duty)* obligación *f or* compromiso *m;* **to be under an obligation to do something** = tener la obligación de hacer algo; **there is no obligation to buy** = no es obligatorio comprar; **to be under no obligation to do something** = no estar obligado a hacer algo; **he is under no contractual obligation to buy** = no tiene ninguna obligación contractual de comprar; **to fulfill one's contractual obligations** = cumplir las obligaciones contractuales; **two weeks' free trial without obligation** = dos semanas de prueba sin compromiso de compra **(b)** *(debt)* deuda *f;* **to meet one's obligations** = pagar *or* saldar las deudas propias

◊ **obligatory** [ɒ'blɪgətəri] *adjective* obligatorio, -ria; **each person has to pass an obligatory medical examination** = todas las personas deben someterse a una revisión médica obligatoria

◊ **oblige** [ə'blaɪdʒ] *verb* **(a)** *(force)* obligar *or* forzar; **to oblige someone to do something** = obligar a alguien a hacer algo; **he felt obliged to cancel the contract** = se sintió obligado a anular el contrato **(b)** *(please)* hacer un favor

o.b.o. ['əʊbiː'əʊ] = OR BEST OFFER

obsolescence [ɒbsə'lesəns] *noun* caducidad *f or* obsolescencia *f;* **built-in obsolescence** *or* **planned obsolescence** = obsolescencia planificada

◊ **obsolescent** [ɒbsə'lesənt] *adjective* obsolescente *or* que cae en desuso

◊ **obsolete** ['ɒbsəliːt] *adjective* obsoleto, -ta *or* anticuado, -da; **when the office was equipped with word-processors the typewriters became obsolete** = cuando equiparon la oficina con ordenadores las máquinas de escribir quedaron anticuadas

obtain [əb'teɪn] *verb* obtener *or* conseguir; **to obtain supplies from abroad** = conseguir suministros del extranjero; **we find these items very difficult to obtain** = nos resulta difícil obtener estos artículos; **to obtain an injunction against a company** = conseguir un requerimiento judicial contra una empresa; **he obtained control by buying the founder's shareholding** = obtuvo el control al comprar las acciones del fundador

◊ **obtainable** [əb'teɪnəbl] *adjective* obtenible *or* que se puede conseguir; **prices fall when raw materials are easily obtainable** = los precios bajan cuando las materias primas pueden conseguirse fácilmente; **our products are obtainable in all computer shops** = nuestros productos pueden adquirirse en todas las tiendas de ordenadores

occasion [ə'keɪʒn] *noun* ocasión *f*

◊ **occasional** [ə'keɪʒənl] *adjective* ocasional

occupancy ['ɒkjʊpənsi] *noun* ocupación *f;* **with immediate occupancy** = de ocupación inmediata; **occupancy rate** = índice de ocupación; **during the winter months the occupancy rate was down to 50%** = durante los meses de invierno el índice de ocupación bajó al 50%

◊ **occupant** ['ɒkjʊpənt] *noun* ocupante *mf (of a house)* habitante *mf or* inquilino, -na

---

QUOTE three other projects have been open more than one year yet have occupancy rates of less than 36%

Forbes Magazine

QUOTE while occupancy rates matched those of 1991 in July, August has been a much poorer month than it was the year before

Economist

---

occupation [ɒkjʊ'peɪʃən] *noun* **(a)** occupation of a building = ocupación *f* de un edificio **(b)** *(job or work)* ocupación *or* trabajo *m or* profesión *f or* actividad *f or* oficio *m;* **what is her occupation?** = ¿cuál es su profesión?; **his main occupation is house building** = su actividad principal es la construcción de casas **(c)** **occupations** = tareas *fpl or* labores *fpl;* **people in professional occupations** = profesionales

◊ **occupational** [ɒkjʊ'peɪʃənl] *adjective* profesional *or* laboral; **occupational accident** = accidente laboral *or* de trabajo; **occupational disease** = enfermedad profesional; **occupational hazards** = gajes del oficio *or* riesgos laborales *or* profesionales; **heart attacks are one of the**

occupational hazards of directors = los ataques de corazón son gajes del oficio de director; **occupational pension scheme** = plan de pensiones de la empresa

◊ **occupier** ['ɒkjʊpaɪə] *noun* ocupante *mf*; **beneficial occupier** = usufructuario, -ria; **owner-occupier** = propietario ocupante de una vivienda

◊ **occupy** ['ɒkjʊpaɪ] *verb* **(a)** *(property)* ocupar; **all the rooms in the hotel are occupied** = todas las habitaciones del hotel están ocupadas; **the company occupies three floors of an office block** = la compañía ocupa tres pisos de un edificio de oficinas **(b)** **to occupy a post** = ocupar un puesto *or* desempeñar un cargo

QUOTE employment in professional occupations increased by 40 per cent between 1974 and 1983, while the share of white-collar occupations in total employment rose from 44 per cent to 49 per cent

Sydney Morning Herald

odd [ɒd] *adjective* **(a)** *(number)* impar; **odd numbers** = números impares; **odd-numbered buildings** *or* **buildings with odd numbers are on the south side of the street** = los edificios con números impares están en el lado sur de la calle **(b)** *(approximately)* **a hundred odd** = unos cien; **keep the odd change** = quédese con el cambio **(c)** *(one of a group)* suelto, -ta *or* desparejado, -da; **an odd shoe** = un zapato desparejado; **we have a few odd boxes left** = nos quedan unas pocas cajas sueltas; **odd lot** = lote de artículos varios **(d)** *(not usual)* raro, -ra *or* poco corriente; **odd sizes** = tallas poco corrientes **(e)** *(casual work)* **odd jobs** = chapuzas; **to do odd jobs** = hacer pequeños trabajos

◊ **odd-job-man** [ɒd'dʒɒbmæn] *noun* hombre que sirve para todo *or* que hace pequeños trabajos

◊ **oddments** ['ɒdmənts] *plural noun* mercancías *fpl* sobrantes *or* retales *mpl*

OECD [əʊiːsiː'diː] = ORGANIZATION FOR ECONOMIC CO-OPERATION AND DEVELOPMENT Organización de Cooperación y Desarrollo Económico

QUOTE calling for a greater correlation between labour market policies, social policies and education and training, the OECD warned that long-term unemployment would remain unacceptably high without a reassessment of labour market trends

Australian Financial Review

off [ɒf] **1** *adverb* **(a)** *(cancelled)* cancelado *or* suspendido; **the agreement is off** = el acuerdo ha sido cancelado; **they called the strike off** = desconvocaron la huelga **(b)** *(reduced by)* con descuento; **these carpets are sold at 25% off the marked price** = estas alfombras se venden con un descuento del 25% sobre el precio marcado; **we give 5% off for quick settlement** = ofrecemos un descuento del 5% por pronto pago **2** *preposition* **(a)** **to take 25% off the price** = hacer un descuento del 25% sobre el precio; **we give 10% off our normal prices** = hacemos un descuento del 10% sobre nuestros precios normales **(b)** *(accounting: not included)* **items off balance sheet** *or* **off balance sheet assets** = artículos *or* bienes que no aparecen en el balance de la compañía **(c)** *(away from work)* ausente del trabajo; **to take time off work** = tomarse

tiempo libre durante el trabajo; **we give the staff four days off at Christmas** = damos cuatro días libres por Navidad a los empleados; **it is the secretary's day off tomorrow** = mañana es el día libre de la secretaria

QUOTE its stock closed Monday at $21.875 a share in NYSE composite trading, off 56% from its high last July

Wall Street Journal

QUOTE the active December long gilt contract on the LIFFE slipped to close at 83-12 from the opening 83-24. In the cash market, one long benchmark - the 11³⁻₄ issue of 2003-07 - closed 101¹⁻₂ to yield 11.5 per cent, off more than ¹⁻₄ on the day

Financial Times

offence [ə'fens] *noun* infracción *f*; **tax offence** = infracción fiscal; **traffic offence** = infracción del código de circulación

offer ['ɒfə] **1** *noun* **(a)** *(to buy)* oferta *f*; **to make an offer for a company** = hacer una oferta por una empresa; **he made an offer of £10 a share** = hizo una oferta de £10 por acción; **we made a written offer for the house** = hicimos una oferta por la casa por escrito; **£1,000 is the best offer I can make** = £1.000 es lo más que puedo ofrecer; **to accept an offer of £1,000 for the car** = aceptar una oferta de £1.000 por el coche; **the house is under offer** = se ha hecho una oferta por la casa; **we are open to offers** = admitimos toda clase de ofertas; **cash offer** = oferta en metálico; **or near offer (o.n.o.)** *or* *US* **or best offer (o.b.o.)** = precio a discutir; **the car is for sale at £2,000 or near offer** = el coche está en venta por £2.000 - precio a discutir **(b)** *(to sell)* **offer for sale** = oferta de venta; **offer price** = precio de oferta **(c)** **the management has made an increased offer to all employees** = la dirección ha mejorado la oferta a los empleados; **he received six offers of jobs** *or* **six job offers** = recibió seis ofertas de trabajo **(d)** *(cheap)* **bargain offer** = oferta de ocasión *or* rebaja; **this week's bargain offer - 30% off all carpet prices** = la oferta de ocasión de esta semana - 30% de descuento sobre los precios de todas las alfombras; **introductory offer** = oferta de lanzamiento; **special offer** = oferta especial; **we have a range of men's shirts on special offer** = tenemos un surtido de camisas de caballero en oferta especial **2** *verb* **(a)** **to offer someone a job** = ofrecer un trabajo a alguien; **he was offered a directorship with Smith Ltd** = le ofrecieron el cargo de director en Smith Ltd. **(b)** *(to buy)* ofrecer; **to offer someone £100,000 for his house** = ofrecer a alguien £100.000 por su casa; **he offered £10 a share** = ofreció £10 por acción **(c)** *(to sell)* ofrecer; **we offered the house for sale** = pusimos la casa en venta

office ['ɒfɪs] *noun* **(a)** *(place of work)* oficina *f*; **branch office** = sucursal *f or* agencia *f or* filial *f*; **head office** *or* **main office** = oficina principal *or* sede *f* *GB* **registered office** = domicilio *m* social **(b)** **office block** *or* **a block of offices** = edificio de oficinas; **office boy** = chico de recados *or* ordenanza; **office equipment** = equipo de oficina; **office hours** = horario de oficina; **open during normal office hours** = abierto en horas normales de oficina; **do not telephone during office hours** = no telefonee en horas de oficina; **the manager can be reached at home out of office hours** = puede hablar con el director en su casa fuera de las horas de oficina; **office junior** = escribiente *mf or* auxiliar administrativo, -va; **office space** *or* **office accommodation** = espacio *or* local para oficinas; **we are looking for extra office space** = estamos buscando más locales para oficinas; **office staff** = personal administrativo *or* de oficinas; **office supplies** = material *or* artículos de oficina; **an office supplies firm** = una empresa de material de oficina; **for office use only** = reservado a la administración; **office worker** = empleado, -da de oficina *or* oficinista *mf* **(c)** *(room)* oficina *or* despacho *m* **come into my office** = venga a mi oficina *or* entre en mi despacho; **the manager's office is on the third floor** = la oficina del director está en el tercer piso **(d) booking office** = taquilla *f or* despacho *m* de billetes; **box office** = taquilla; **employment office** = agencia *f* de empleo; **general office** = oficina general; **information office** *or* **inquiry office** = oficina de información; **ticket office** = taquilla; **tourist office** = oficina de turismo **(e)** *GB (government department)* ministerio *m*; **the Foreign Office** = ministerio de Asuntos Exteriores; **the Home Office** = ministerio del Interior; **Office of Fair Trading (OFT)** = departamento de control de prácticas comerciales; **Serious Fraud Office (SFO)** = juzgado especial de delitos monetarios **(f)** *(post or position)* cargo *m*; **he holds** *or* **performs the office of treasurer** = ocupa el cargo de tesorero; **high office** = alto cargo; **compensation for loss of office** = indemnización a un directivo por cese en el cargo

officer ['ɒfɪsə] *noun* **(a)** *(official position)* oficial, -la; **customs officer** = funcionario, -ria de aduanas *or* aduanero, -ra; **fire safety officer** = responsable de la seguridad contra incendios; **information officer** = responsable del servicio de información; **personnel officer** = jefe, -fa de personal; **training officer** = director *or* responsable de la capacitación; **the company officers** *or* **the officers of a company** = los cargos directivos de una compañía **(b)** *(of a club or society)* dirigente *mf*; **the election of officers of an association** = la elección de los dirigentes de una asociación

official [ə'fɪʃəl] **1** *adjective* **(a)** *(government department)* oficial: **the official exchange rate** = tipo oficial de cambio; **the official exchange rate is ten to the dollar, but you can get twice that on the black market** = el tipo oficial de cambio es de diez por dólar, pero puedes conseguir el doble en el mercado negro **(b)** *(done or approved)* oficial; **this must be an official order - it is written on the company's notepaper** = esto debe ser un pedido oficial - está escrito en el papel de la empresa; **the strike has been made official** = la huelga es oficial; **on official business** = en asuntos oficiales; **he left official documents in his car** = se dejó documentos oficiales en el coche; **she received an official letter of explanation** = recibió una carta oficial explicativa; **speaking in an official capacity** = hablando oficialmente; **to go through official channels** = seguir el conducto reglamentario **(c) the official receiver** = síndico *or* administrador judicial **2** *noun* funcionario, -ria; **airport officials inspected the shipment** = los funcionarios del aeropuerto inspeccionaron el cargamento; **government officials stopped the import licence** = funcionarios del gobierno suspendieron la licencia de importación; **customs official** = aduanero, -ra *or* funcionario, -ria de aduanas; **high official** = alto

funcionario; **minor official** = funcionario subalterno *or* de poca categoría; **some minor official tried to stop my request for building permission** = un funcionario de poca categoría intentó bloquear mi solicitud de permiso para construir; **top official** = alto funcionario; **union officials** = cargos *m* sindicales

◊ **officialese** [əfɪʃə'liːz] *noun* lenguaje burocrático *or* administrativo

◊ **officially** [ə'fɪʃəli] *adverb* oficialmente; **officially he knows nothing about the problem, but unofficially he has given us a lot of advice about it** = oficialmente no sabe nada del problema, pero oficiosamente nos ha dado buenos consejos

officio [ə'fɪʃɪəʊ] *see* EX OFFICIO

off-licence ['ɒflaɪsəns] *noun GB* **(a)** *(licence)* licencia *f* de venta de bebidas alcohólicas para ser consumidas fuera del establecimiento **(b)** *(shop)* bodega *f*

off-line [ɒf'laɪn] *adjective* desconectado, da *or* fuera de línea

offload [ɒf'ləʊd] *verb* deshacerse de algo pasándoselo a alguien; **to offload excess stock** = deshacerse del exceso de existencias; **to offload costs onto a subsidiary company** = trasladar los costes a una empresa filial (NOTE: you offload something **from** a thing *or* person **onto** another thing *or* person)

off-peak [ɒf'piːk] *adjective* de menor consumo *or* de menor tráfico *or* fuera de horas punta; **during the off-peak period** = durante el periodo de menor movimiento; **off-peak tariff** *or* **rate** = tarifa fuera de horas punta

off-season **1** [ɒf'siːzn] *adjective* **off-season tariff** *or* **rate** = tarifa de temporada baja **2** ['ɒfsiːzn] *noun* temporada baja; **to travel in the off-season** = viajar en temporada baja; **air fares are cheaper in the off-season** = los billetes de avión son más baratos en la temporada baja

offset [ɒf'set] *verb* compensar; **to offset losses against tax** = deducir las pérdidas de los impuestos; **foreign exchange losses more than offset profits in the domestic market** = las pérdidas por el cambio de divisas son mayores que los beneficios obtenidos en el mercado interior (NOTE: **offsetting - offset**)

off-shore [ɒf'ʃɔː] *adjective & adverb* **(a)** *(in the sea)* a cierta distancia de la costa *or* offshore *or* en aguas territoriales; **off-shore oil field** = yacimiento petrolífero submarino; **off-shore oil platform** = plataforma petrolífera (en alta mar) **(b)** *(on a tax haven island)* en un paraíso fiscal; **off-shore bank** = banco extraterritorial *or* situado en un paraíso fiscal; **off-shore fund** = fondos colocados en un paraíso fiscal

off-the-job training ['ɒfðədʒɒb 'treɪnɪŋ] *noun* formación profesional fuera del trabajo

off-the-record ['ɒf ðə 'rekəd] *adverb* extraoficialmente *or* fuera de actas

off-the-shelf ['ɒfðə'ʃelf] *adjective & adverb* confeccionado, -da *or* listo, -ta para vender; **off-the-shelf company** = sociedad de disponibilidad inmediata

OFT = OFFICE OF FAIR TRADING

oil [ɔɪl] *noun* **(a)** *(petroleum)* petróleo *m*; **oil-exporting countries** = países exportadores de petróleo; **oil field** = yacimiento petrolífero; **the North Sea oil fields** = los yacimientos petrolíferos del mar del Norte; **oil-importing countries** = países importadores de petróleo; **oil-producing countries** = países productores de petróleo; **oil platform** *or* **oil rig** = plataforma petrolífera; **oil price** = precio del crudo *or* del petróleo; **oil shares** = acciones petrolíferas; **oil well** = pozo de petróleo **(b)** *(lubricant, cooking oil, etc.)* aceite *m*; **olive oil exports to the UK have increased this year** = la exportación de aceite de oliva al Reino Unido ha aumentado este año

old [əuld] *adjective* viejo, -ja *or* antiguo, -gua; **the old part** *or* **old quarter of the town** = casco antiguo *or* viejo; **the company is 125 years old next year** = la compañía cumplirá 125 años el año próximo; **we have decided to get rid of our old computer system and install a new one** = hemos decidido deshacernos del viejo sistema de ordenadores e instalar uno nuevo

◊ **old age** ['əuld 'eɪdʒ] *noun* vejez *f*; **old age pension** = pensión de vejez; **old age pensioner (OAP)** = pensionista (persona que recibe una pensión de jubilación)

◊ **old-established** ['əuldɪs'tæblɪʃt] *adjective* antiguo, -gua

◊ **old-fashioned** ['əuld'fæʃənd] *adjective* anticuado, -da *or* pasado, -da de moda; **he still uses an old-fashioned typewriter** = sigue utilizando una máquina de escribir anticuada

Oman [ɒ'mɑ:n] *noun* Omán *m*

◊ **Omani** [ɒ'mɑ:ni] *adjective & noun* omaní
NOTE: capital: **Muscat**; currency: **Omani rial (RO)** = rial omaní (RO)

ombudsman ['ɒmbʊdzmən] *noun* defensor *m* del pueblo (NOTE: plural is **ombudsmen**)

COMMENT: there are in fact several ombudsmen: the main one is the Parliamentary Commissioner, who is a civil servant. The Banking Ombudsman and the Insurance Ombudsman are independent officials who investigate complaints by the public against banks or insurance companies

QUOTE radical changes to the disciplinary system, including appointing an ombudsman to review cases where complainants are not satisfied with the outcome, are proposed in a consultative paper the Institute of Chartered Accountants issued last month
Accountancy

omit [ə(u)'mɪt] *verb* **(a)** *(leave something out)* omitir; **the secretary omitted the date when typing the contract** = la secretaria omitió la fecha al pasar el contrato a máquina **(b)** *(not to do something)* omitir; **he omitted to tell the managing director that he had lost the documents** = omitió decirle al director gerente que había perdido los documentos (NOTE: **omitting - omitted**)

◊ **omission** [ə(u)'mɪʃən] *noun* omisión *f*; **errors and omissions excepted (e. & o. e.)** = salvo error u omisión

omnibus ['ɒmnɪbəs] *noun* **omnibus agreement** = acuerdo general; **omnibus edition** = edición completa

on [ɒn] *preposition* **(a)** *(part of)* en *or* formar parte de *or* ser miembro de; **to sit on a committee** = ser miembro de una comisión; **she is on the boards of two companies** = forma parte del consejo de administración de dos compañías; **we have 250 people on the payroll** = tenemos 250 personas en nómina; **she is on our full-time staff** = forma parte de nuestra plantilla de personal **(b)** *(in a certain way)* en *or* sobre *or* con *or* por *or* a; **on a commercial basis** = con carácter comercial; **to buy something on approval** = comprar algo con derecho a devolución; **on the average** = por término medio; **to buy a car on hire-purchase** = comprar un coche a plazos; **to get a mortgage on easy terms** = conseguir una hipoteca con facilidades de pago **(c)** *(at a certain time)* **on weekdays** = los días laborables; **the shop is closed on Wednesday afternoons** = la tienda cierra los miércoles por la tarde; **on May 24th** = el 24 de mayo **(d)** *(doing something)* **the director is on holiday** = el director está de vacaciones; **she is in the States on business** = está en viaje de negocios por los EE UU; **the switchboard operator is on duty from 6 to 9** = la telefonista está de servicio de 6 a 9

once [wʌns] *adverb* una vez *or* antes

oncosts ['ɒnkɒsts] *plural noun* costes *mpl* fijos

on line *or* **online** [ɒn'laɪn] *adverb* en conexión directa con el ordenador central *or* en línea (conectado); **the sales office is on line to the warehouse** = la oficina de ventas está conectada directamente con el ordenador del almacén; **we get our data on line from the stock control department** = obtenemos nuestros datos directamente del departamento de control de existencias

on-the-job training ['ɒnðədʒɒb 'treɪnɪŋ] *noun* formación profesional en el empleo

one [wʌn] *number* uno, -na

◊ **one-man** ['wʌn'mæn] *adjective* **one-man business** *or* **firm** *or* **company** *or* **operation** *or* **band** = negocio *or* empresa individual

◊ **one-off** ['wʌnɒf] *adjective* único, -ca (fuera de serie); **one-off deal** = transacción única; **one-off item** = artículo único; **one-off advertising operation** = campaña publicitaria única

◊ **one-sided** ['wʌn'saɪdɪd] *adjective* parcial *or* desigual; **one-sided agreement** = acuerdo unilateral

◊ **one-way** ['wʌnweɪ] *adjective* **one-way ticket** = billete de ida; *US* **one-way fare** = (precio de) billete sencillo *or* pasaje de ida; **one-way trade** = comercio unilateral

◊ **one-way street** ['wʌnweɪ 'stri:t] *noun* calle *f* de una sola dirección *or* de dirección única *or* sentido único; **the shop is in a one-way street, which makes it very difficult for parking** = la tienda está en una calle de dirección obligatoria lo cual hace que sea muy difícil aparcar

onerous ['ɒnərəs] *adjective* oneroso, -sa *or* pesado, -da; **the repayment terms are particularly onerous** = las condiciones de pago son especialmente onerosas

o.n.o. ['əuen'əu] = OR NEAR OFFER

OPEC ['əʊpek] = ORGANIZATION OF PETROLEUM EXPORTING COUNTRIES la Organización de los Países Exportadores de Petróleo (OPEP)

open ['əʊpən] **1** *adjective* **(a)** *(at work or not closed)* abierto, -ta; **the store is open on Sunday mornings** = la tienda abre los domingos por la mañana; **our offices are open from 9 to 6** = nuestras oficinas abren de 9 a 6; **they are open for business every day of the week** = está abierto al público todos los días de la semana **(b)** *(available)* abierto, -ta; **the job is open to all applicants** = todos los interesados pueden solicitar el puesto; **we will keep the job open for you until you have passed your driving test** = te guardaremos el puesto hasta que hayas aprobado el examen de conducir; **open to offers** = se admiten ofertas; **the company is open to offers for the empty factory** = la compañía admite ofertas por la fábrica vacía **(c) open account** = cuenta abierta; **open cheque** = cheque abierto *or* no cruzado; **open credit** = crédito abierto; **open market** = mercado libre; **to buy shares on the open market** = comprar acciones en el mercado libre; **open ticket** = billete abierto **2** *verb* **(a)** *(to start a new business working)* emprender *or* abrir un negocio; **she has opened a shop in the High Street** = ha abierto una tienda en el centro *or* la calle mayor; **we have opened an office in London (b)** *(to start work or to be at work)* abrir; **the office opens at 9 a.m.** = la oficina abre a las 9 de la mañana; **we open for business on Sundays** = abrimos al público los domingos **(c)** *(to begin)* comenzar *or* entablar *or* iniciar; **to open negotiations** = entablar negociaciones; **he opened the discussions with a description of the product** = inició los debates con una descripción del producto; **the chairman opened the meeting at 10.30** = el presidente comenzó la reunión a las 10.30 **(d)** *(to start something working)* abrir *or* conceder; **to open a bank account** = abrir una cuenta bancaria; **to open a line of credit** = abrir *or* conceder una línea de crédito; **to open a loan** = conceder un préstamo **(e) the shares opened lower** = la cotización de acciones empezó en un tono más bajo

◊ **open-ended** *or* US **open-end** ['əʊpən'endɪd *or* 'əʊpən'end] *adjective* abierto, -ta *or* modificable *or* variable *or* no limitado, -da; **open-ended agreement** = acuerdo modificable; *US* **open-end mortgage** = hipoteca ampliable

◊ **opening** ['əʊpənɪŋ] **1** *noun* **(a)** *(act)* apertura *f or* inauguración *f*; **the opening of a new branch** = la inauguración de una nueva sucursal; **the opening of a new market** *or* **of a new distribution network** = la apertura de un nuevo mercado *or* de una nueva red de distribución **(b)** *(time)* horario *m* **late opening** *or* **late-night opening** = abierto tarde *or* hasta última hora de la noche **(c)** *(opportunity)* oportunidad *f or* vacante *f or* apertura *f*; **job openings** = vacantes *fpl*; **we have openings for office staff** = tenemos vacantes para personal de oficina; **a market opening** = apertura de un mercado **(d)** *(beginning)* **opening of the bidding** = comienzo *m* de la puja **(e) opening of sealed tenders** = apertura de ofertas en pliego cerrado **2** *adjective* **(a)** inaugural *or* de apertura *or* inicial; **opening balance** = saldo *m* inicial; **opening bid** = oferta inicial; **opening entry** = asiento de apertura *or* inicial; **opening price** = precio *or* cotización de apertura; **opening stock** =

existencias iniciales **(b) opening hours** = horario comercial *or* horario de taquillas

◊ **open-plan office** ['əʊpənplæn 'ɒfɪs] *noun* oficina de distribución modificable

◊ **open up** ['əʊpən 'ʌp] *verb* **to open up new markets** = abrir nuevos mercados

operate ['ɒpəreɪt] *verb* **(a)** *(work)* entrar en vigor *or* aplicarse; **the new terms of service will operate from January 1st** = las nuevas condiciones de servicio entrarán en vigor a partir del 1 de enero; **the rules operate on inland postal services** = las normas se aplican a los servicios postales del interior **(b)** *(machinery)* **to operate a machine** = manejar *or* hacer funcionar una máquina; **he is learning to operate the new telephone switchboard** = está aprendiendo a manejar la nueva centralita de teléfonos

◊ **operating** ['ɒpəreɪtɪŋ] *noun* funcionamiento *m or* explotación *f or* operación *f*; **operating budget** = presupuesto de explotación; **operating costs** *or* **operating expenses** = costes *or* gastos de explotación; gastos de mantenimiento; **operating manual** = instrucciones de uso *or* manual de funcionamiento; **operating margin** = margen de explotación; **operating profit** *or* **operating loss** = beneficios de explotación *or* pérdidas de explotación; **operating system** = sistema operativo

◊ **operation** [ɒpə'reɪʃən] *noun* **(a)** operación *f*; **the company's operations in West Africa** = las operaciones de la compañía en Africa occidental; **he heads up the operations in Northern Europe** = dirige las operaciones en el norte de Europa; **operations review** = análisis *m or* revisión *f* de las operaciones; **a franchising operation** = explotación en régimen de concesión **(b) Stock Exchange operation** = operación bursátil **(c) in operation** = en funcionamiento *or* en vigor; **the system will be in operation by June** = el sistema estará en funcionamiento para junio; **the new system came into operation on June 1st** = el nuevo sistema entró en funcionamiento el 1 de junio

◊ **operational** [ɒpə'reɪʃənl] *adjective* **(a)** *(how something works)* operativo, -va *or* operacional; **operational budget** = presupuesto de explotación; **operational costs** = costes de explotación; **operational planning** = planificación operativa; **operational research** = investigación operativa **(b)** *(when something works)* **the system became operational on June 1st** = el sistema entró en funcionamiento el 1 de junio

◊ **operative** ['ɒpərətɪv] **1** *adjective* operativo, -va; **to become operative** = ponerse en funcionamiento *or* entrar en vigor; **the new system has been operative since June 1st** = el nuevo sistema funciona desde *or* entró en vigor el 1 de junio **2** *noun* operario, -ria *or* maquinista *mf*

◊ **operator** ['ɒpəreɪtə] *noun* **(a)** *(machine)* operador, -ra; **computer operator** *or* **keyboard operator** = operador de teclado; **a telex operator** = operador de telex **(b)** *(switchboard)* **switchboard operator** = telefonista *mf or* operador, -ra; **to call the operator** *or* **to dial the operator** = llamar a la telefonista; **to place a call through** *or* **via the**

operator = hacer una llamada a través de la telefonista **(c)** *(Stock Exchange)* agente *mf or* corredor *m* de bolsa **(d)** *(agent)* agente *mf* **tour operator** = organizador *m or* agente *m* de viajes *or* agencia *f* de viajes organizados

> QUOTE the company blamed over-capacity and competitive market conditions in Europe for a £14m operating loss last year
> **Financial Times**

> QUOTE a leading manufacturer of business, industrial and commercial products requires a branch manager to head up its mid-western Canada operations based in Winnipeg
> **Globe and Mail (Toronto)**

> QUOTE the company gets valuable restaurant locations which will be converted to the family-style restaurant chain that it operates and franchises throughout most parts of the US
> **Fortune**

> QUOTE shares are trading at about seven times operating cash flow, or half the normal multiple
> **Business Week**

> QUOTE a number of block bookings by American tour operators have been cancelled
> **Economist**

opinion [ə'pɪnjən] *noun* **(a)** *(judgement)* opinión *f or* juicio *m*; **public opinion** = opinión pública; **opinion leader** = persona de opinión *or* juicio influyente; **opinion poll** *or* **opinion research** = encuesta *or* sondeo de opinión; **opinion polls showed that the public preferred butter to margarine** = los sondeos de opinión mostraron que el público prefería la mantequilla a la margarina; **before starting the new service, the company carried out nationwide opinion polls** = antes de empezar el nuevo servicio, la compañía realizó encuestas de opinión por todo el país **(b)** *(expert advice)* dictamen *m*; **the lawyers gave their opinion** = los abogados emitieron su dictamen; **to ask an adviser for his opinion on a case** = pedir a un consejero su opinión sobre un caso

OPM [əʊpiː'em] = OTHER PEOPLE'S MONEY

opportunist [ɒpə'tjuːnɪst] *noun* oportunista *or* aprovechado, -da

opportunity [ɒpə'tjuːnəti] *noun* oportunidad *f*; **investment opportunities** *or* **sales opportunities** = oportunidades de inversión *or* oportunidades de ventas; **a market opportunity** = una oportunidad de mercado; **employment opportunities** *or* **job opportunities** = oportunidades de empleo *or* oportunidades de trabajo; **the increase in export orders has created hundreds of job opportunities** = el aumento de pedidos de exportación ha creado cientos de oportunidades de empleo

> QUOTE the group is currently undergoing a period of rapid expansion and this has created an exciting opportunity for a qualified accountant
> **Financial Times**

oppose [ə'pəʊz] *verb* oponerse; **a minority of board members opposed the motion** = una minoría

de miembros del consejo se opuso a la moción; **we are all opposed to the takeover** = todos nos oponemos a la adquisición

opposite ['ɒpəzɪt] *adjective* contrario, -ria; **opposite number** = homólogo, -ga; **John is my opposite number in Smith's** = John es mi homólogo en la sociedad Smith

optimal ['ɒptɪməl] *adjective* óptimo, -ma

◊ **optimism** ['ɒptɪmɪzəm] *noun* optimismo *m*; **he has considerable optimism about sales possibilities in the Far East** = es muy optimista sobre las posibilidades de ventas en el Extremo Oriente; **market optimism** = el optimismo del mercado

◊ **optimistic** [ɒptɪ'mɪstɪk] *adjective* optimista; **he takes an optimistic view of the exchange rate** = tiene una visión optimista del tipo de cambio

◊ **optimum** ['ɒptɪməm] *adjective* óptimo, -ma; **the market offers optimum conditions for sales** = el mercado ofrece condiciones óptimas para las ventas

option ['ɒpʃən] *noun* **(a)** opción *f*; **option to purchase** *or* **to sell** = opción *f* de compra *or* de venta; **first option** = la primera opción; **to grant someone a six-month option on a product** = concederle a alguien una opción de seis meses sobre la representación *or* la fabricación de un producto; **to take up an option** *or* **to exercise an option** = ejercer el derecho de opción; **he exercised his option** *or* **he took up his option to acquire sole marketing rights to the product** = ejerció su derecho de opción para adquirir los derechos exclusivos de comercialización del producto; **I want to leave my options open** = no quiero comprometerme; **to take the soft option** = decidirse por la opción más fácil **(b)** *(Stock Exchange)* **call option** = opción de compra (de acciones); **put option** = opción de venta; **share option** = opción de compra *or* venta de acciones a cierto precio para el futuro; **stock option** = opción de compra de acciones (por los empleados de una compañía) *or* opción-bono; **traded options** = opciones comercializables; **option contract** = contrato de opción; **option dealing** *or* **option trading** = operaciones de opción

◊ **optional** ['ɒpʃənl] *adjective* opcional *or* optativo, -va *or* facultativo, -va; **the insurance cover is optional** = el seguro es opcional; **optional extras** = extras opcionales

opt out ['ɒpt 'aʊt] *verb* autoexcluirse

◊ **opt-out** ['ɒptaʊt] *noun* autoexclusión *f*; **opt-out clause** = cláusula de autoexclusión

order ['ɔːdə] **1** *noun* **(a)** *(records or files)* orden *m*; **alphabetical order** = orden alfabético; **chronological order** = orden cronológico; **the reports are filed in chronological order** = los informes están archivados por orden cronológico; **numerical order** = orden numérico; **put these invoices in numerical order** = coloque estas facturas por *or* en orden numérico **(b)** *(working arrangement)* estado *m or* en regla *f*; **machine in full working order** = máquina en perfecto estado de funcionamiento; **the telephone is out of order** = el teléfono no funciona; **is all the documentation in order?** = ¿está toda la documentación en regla? **(c)** **pay to Mr Smith or order** = pagar en efectivo al Sr

Smith o según sus órdenes; **pay to the order of Mr Smith** = páguese a la orden del Sr Smith **(d)** *(request for goods)* pedido *m*; **to give someone an order** *or* **to place an order with someone for twenty filing cabinets** = hacer un pedido de veinte archivadores a alguien; **to fill** *or* **to fulfil an order** = despachar un pedido; **we are so understaffed we cannot fulfil any more orders before Christmas** = estamos tan faltos de personal que no podemos despachar más pedidos antes de Navidad; **to supply an order for twenty filing cabinets** = servir un pedido de veinte archivadores; **purchase order** = orden de compra; **order fulfilment** = despacho de pedidos; **order processing** = preparación de pedidos; **terms: cash with order** = condiciones: el pago se efectuará al hacer el pedido; **items available to order only** = artículos disponibles sólo por encargo; **on order** = pedido, -da; **this item is out of stock, but is on order** = este artículo está agotado, pero está pedido; **unfulfilled orders** *or* **back orders** *or* **outstanding orders** = pedidos no servidos *or* pedidos por servir *or* pedidos atrasados *or* pedidos pendientes; **order book** = cartera de pedidos; **the company has a full order book** = la empresa tiene el libro de pedidos completo; **telephone orders** = pedidos por teléfono; **since we mailed the catalogue we have had a large number of telephone orders** = desde que enviamos el catálogo por correo hemos recibido un gran número de pedidos por teléfono; **a pad of order forms** = un bloc de hojas *or* formularios de pedido; **the order is to be delivered to our warehouse** = el pedido debe ser entregado en nuestro almacén; **order picking** = selección de artículos para un pedido **(e)** *(instruction)* orden *f* *or* mandato *m* *or* mandamiento *m*; **delivery order** = orden de entrega **(f)** *(finance)* libramiento *m* *or* orden de pago; **he sent us an order on the Chartered Bank** = nos envió un giro librado contra el Chartered Bank; **banker's order** = orden *f* de pago domiciliado en el banco *or* orden bancaria; **standing order** = *(at bank)* domiciliación *f* bancaria; *(commerce)* pedido permanente *or* regular; **he pays his subscription by banker's order** = paga su suscripción por domiciliación bancaria; **money order** = giro *m* postal **2** *verb* **(a)** *(people)* ordenar *or* mandar **(b)** *(goods)* hacer un pedido *or* encargar; **to order twenty filing cabinets to be delivered to the warehouse** = hacer un pedido de veinte archivadores para que sean entregados en el almacén; **they ordered a new Rolls Royce for the managing director** = encargaron un nuevo Rolls Royce para el director gerente **(c)** *(arrange)* ordenar; **the address list is ordered by country** = la lista de direcciones está ordenada por países; **that filing cabinet contains invoices ordered by date** = ese archivador contiene facturas clasificadas por fechas

ordinary ['ɔːdnri] *adjective* ordinario, -ria *or* corriente; **ordinary member** = miembro ordinario *or* vocal; **ordinary resolution** = resolución ordinaria; **ordinary shares** = acciones ordinarias (NOTE: the US term is **common stock**) **ordinary shareholder** = tenedor, -ra de acciones ordinarias

organization [ɔːgənaɪˈzeɪʃən] *noun* **(a)** *(way of arranging something)* organización *f*; **the chairman handles the organization of the AGM** = el presidente se ocupa de la organización de la junta general anual; **the organization of the group is too centralized to be efficient** = la organización del grupo está demasiado centralizada para ser eficaz;

the **organization of the head office into departments** = la organización de la oficina principal en departamentos; **organization and methods (O & M)** = organización y métodos; **organization chart** = organigrama *m* *or* gráfico *m* de organización; **line organization** = organización lineal **(b)** *(group or institution)* organización *or* organismo *m*; **a government organization** = un organismo oficial *or* estatal; **a travel organization** = una organización de turismo; **an employers' organization** = una organización patronal

◊ **Organization for Economic Co-operation and Development (OECD)** Organización de Cooperación y Desarrollo Económico (OCDE)

◊ **Organization of Petroleum Exporting Countries (OPEC)** Organización de los Países Exportadores de Petróleo (OPEP)

◊ **organizational** [ɔːgənaɪˈzeɪʃənl] *adjective* organizativo, -va; **the paper gives a diagram of the company's organizational structure** = el documento contiene un gráfico de la estructura de la empresa

◊ **organize** ['ɔːgənaɪz] *verb* organizar; **the company is organized into six profit centres** = la empresa está organizada en seis centros de explotación independientes; **the group is organized by areas of sales** = el grupo está organizado en zonas de venta; **organized labour** = obreros sindicados

◊ **organizer** ['ɔːgənaɪzə] *noun* organizador, -ra; **electronic organizer** *or* **personal organizer** = agenda electrónica

◊ **organizing committee** ['ɔːgənaɪzɪŋ kəˈmɪti] *noun* comisión organizadora; **he is a member of the organizing committee for the conference** = es miembro de la comisión organizadora del congreso

QUOTE working with a client base which includes many major commercial organizations and nationalized industries
Times

QUOTE we organize a rate with importers who have large orders and guarantee them space at a fixed rate so that they can plan their costs
Lloyd's List

QUOTE governments are coming under increasing pressure from politicians, organized labour and business to stimulate economic growth
Duns Business Month

oriented *or* **orientated** ['ɔːrientid *or* 'ɔːrienteitid] *adjective* orientado, -da; **profit-oriented company** = empresa con fines de lucro; **export-oriented company** = empresa orientada hacia la exportación

origin ['ɒrɪdʒɪn] *noun* **(a)** *(where something comes from)* origen *m*; **spare parts of European origin** = piezas de recambio de origen europeo; **certificate of origin** = certificado de origen; **country of origin** = país de origen **(b)** *(beginning)* comienzo *m*

◊ **original** [əˈrɪdʒənl] **1** *adjective* **(a)** *(first)* original *or* primero, -ra; **they sent a copy of the**

original invoice = enviaron una copia de la factura original; **he kept the original receipt for reference** = se guardó el recibo original para sus archivos **(b)** *(new)* original; **she produced an original idea** = presentó una idea original **2** *noun* original *m*; **send the original and file two copies** = mande el original y archive dos copias

◊ **originally** [ə'rɪdʒənəli] *adverb* originariamente

OS = OUTSIZE

O/S = OUT OF STOCK

other ['ʌðə] *adjective* otro, -ra; **the other day** = el otro día

◊ **other people's money (OPM)** ['ʌðə 'piːplz 'mʌni] *noun* dinero ajeno

ounce [aʊns] *noun (measure of weight = 28 grams)* onza *f* (NOTE: usually written **oz** after figures)

> QUOTE trading at $365 an ounce on May 24, gold has declined $45 or 11% since the beginning of the year
> **Business Week**

out [aʊt] *adverb* **(a)** *(not in)* fuera **(b)** *(on strike)* en huelga; **the workers have been out on strike for four weeks** = los obreros han estado en huelga durante cuatro semanas; **as soon as the management made the offer, the staff came out** = en cuanto el director hizo la oferta, los empleados se declararon en huelga; **the shop stewards called the workforce out** = los delegados sindicales convocaron al personal a una huelga **(c)** *(away from work)* US ausente del trabajo (NOTE: GB English in this meaning is **off**) **(d) to be out** = equivocarse; **the balance is £10 out** = el saldo tiene un error de £10; **we are £20,000 out in our calculations** = nos hemos equivocado de £20.000 en nuestros cálculos

◊ **outbid** [aʊt'bɪd] *verb* pujar más alto *or* sobrepujar; **we offered £100,000 for the warehouse, but another company outbid us** = ofrecimos £100.000 por el almacén, pero otra sociedad pujó más alto (NOTE: **outbidding - outbid**)

◊ **outfit** ['aʊtfɪt] *noun* equipo *m*; **they called in a public relations outfit** = llamaron a un equipo de relaciones públicas; **he works for some finance outfit** = trabaja para un equipo financiero

◊ **outflow** ['aʊtfləʊ] *noun* **outflow of capital from a country** = salida *f* de capital de un país

> QUOTE Nigeria recorded foreign exchange outflow of N972.9 million for the month of June 1985
> **Business Times (Lagos)**

outgoing ['aʊtgəʊɪŋ] *adjective* **(a) outgoing mail** = correspondencia de salida **(b) the outgoing chairman** *or* **the outgoing president** = el presidente saliente

◊ **outgoings** ['aʊt'gəʊɪŋz] *plural noun* desembolsos *mpl*

◊ **out-house** ['aʊthaʊs] *adjective* fuera del edificio *or* de la empresa; **the out-house staff** = el personal que trabaja fuera de las oficinas; **we do all our data processing out-house** = hacemos todo el proceso de datos fuera de la empresa

◊ **outlay** ['aʊtleɪ] *noun* desembolso *m or* gasto *m*; **capital outlay** = gastos de capital *or* inversión; **for a modest outlay** = por una modesta suma

◊ **outlet** ['aʊtlet] *noun* mercado *m*; **factory outlet** = tienda *f* de fábrica; **retail outlets** = tiendas al detall

◊ **outline** ['aʊtlaɪn] **1** *noun* bosquejo *m or* esbozo *m or* perfil *m*; **they drew up the outline of a plan** *or* **an outline plan** = trazaron el esquema del plan; **outline planning permission** = permiso provisional para edificar **2** *verb* perfilar *or* trazar las líneas generales; **the chairman outlined the company's plans for the coming year** = el presidente trazó en líneas generales *or* expuso a grandes rasgos los planes de la compañía para el año próximo

◊ **outlook** ['aʊtlʊk] *noun* perspectivas *fpl*; **the economic outlook is not good** = las perspectivas económicas no son buenas; **the stock market outlook is worrying** = las perspectivas del mercado de valores son inquietantes

> QUOTE American demand has transformed the profit outlook for many European manufacturers
> **Duns Business Month**

out of control [aʊt əv kən'trəʊl] *adjective & adverb* desmandado, -da; **to be out of control** = desmandarse; **costs have got out of control** = los costes se han desmandado

◊ **out of court** ['aʊt əv 'kɔːt] *adverb & adjective* **a settlement was reached out of court** = se llegó a un acuerdo amistoso; **they are hoping to reach an out-of-court settlement** = esperan alcanzar un acuerdo amistoso

◊ **out of date** ['aʊt əv 'deɪt] *adjective & adverb* anticuado, -da *or* caducado, -da; **their computer system is years out of date** = su sistema informático está muy anticuado; **they are still using out-of-date equipment** = siguen usando un equipo anticuado

◊ **out of order** ['aʊt əv 'ɔːdə] *adjective* no funciona

◊ **out of pocket** ['aʊt əv 'pɒkɪt] *adjective & adverb (having paid out money personally)* con pérdidas; **the deal has left me out of pocket** = en esta transacción he perdido dinero; **out-of-pocket expenses** = gastos reemborsables

◊ **out of stock** ['aʊt əv 'stɒk] *adjective & adverb* agotado, -da; **those records are temporarily out of stock** = estos discos están temporalmente agotados; **several out-of-stock items have been on order for weeks** = hace semanas que están pedidos varios artículos agotados

◊ **out of work** ['aʊt əv 'wɜːk] *adjective & adverb* sin empleo *or* sin trabajo; **the recession has put millions out of work** = la recesión ha dejado sin trabajo a millones de personas; **the company was set up by three out-of-work engineers** = la compañía fue fundada por tres ingenieros que estaban sin trabajo

output ['aʊtpʊt] **1** *noun* **(a)** *(yield)* producción *f or* rendimiento *m*; **output has increased by 10%** = la producción ha aumentado un 10%; **25% of our output is exported** = el 25% de nuestra producción se exporta; **output per hour** = producción por hora; **output bonus** = plus por aumento de producción; **output tax** = impuesto sobre los bienes o servicios producidos **(b)** *(computer)* datos *mpl* de salida (NOTE: the opposite is **input**) **2** *verb* producir; **the printer will output colour graphs** = la impresora producirá gráficos en color; **that is the information**

outputted from the computer = ésta es la información producida por el ordenador (NOTE: **outputting - outputted**)

> QUOTE crude oil output plunged during the last month and is likely to remain near its present level for the near future
> **Wall Street Journal**

outright ['aʊtraɪt] **1** *adjective* completo, -ta *or* absoluto, -ta *or* total *or* en su totalidad **2** *adverb* de un modo absoluto; **to purchase something outright** *or* **to make an outright purchase** = comprar algo con todos los derechos inherentes

◊ **outsell** [aʊt'sel] *verb* vender más *or* superar en las ventas; **the company is easily outselling its competitors** = la empresa vende mucho más que sus competidores (NOTE: **outselling - outsold**)

◊ **outside** ['aʊtsaɪd] **1** *adjective* exterior *or* externo, -na; **outside dealer** = corredor *or* agente no perteneciente a la bolsa; **outside director** = consejero externo; **outside line** = línea exterior; **you dial 9 to get an outside line** = se marca el 9 para obtener la línea exterior; **outside worker** = trabajador a domicilio **2** *adverb* fuera de; **outside office hours** = fuera de horas de oficina; **to send work to be done outside** = encargar trabajo fuera de la empresa

◊ **outsize (OS)** ['aʊtsaɪz] *noun* **(a)** *(clothing)* talla *f* muy grande **(b)** **an outsize order** = un pedido muy grande

◊ **outskirts** ['aʊtskɜːts] *plural noun* alrededores *mpl or* afueras *fpl*; **the outskirts of Madrid** = los alrededores de Madrid

◊ **outsourcing** ['aʊtsɔːsɪŋ] *noun* subcontratar (a especialistas) *or* 'outsourcing'

> QUOTE organizations in the public and private sectors are increasingly buying in specialist services - or outsourcing - allowing them to cut costs and concentrate on their core business activities
> **Financial Times**

outstanding [aʊt'stændɪŋ] *adjective* **(a)** *(exceptional)* notable *or* destacado, -da *or* sobresaliente **(b)** *(unpaid)* pendiente; **outstanding debts** = deudas pendientes *or* por pagar; **outstanding orders** = pedidos pendientes; **what is the amount outstanding?** = ¿cuánto dinero se debe?; **matters outstanding from the previous meeting** = asuntos pendientes de la reunión anterior

> COMMENT: note the difference between 'outstanding' and 'overdue'. If a debtor has 30 days' credit, then his debts are outstanding until the end of the 30 days, and they only become overdue on the 31st day

out tray ['aʊt 'treɪ] *noun* bandeja *f* de documentos despachados

◊ **outturn** ['aʊtɜːn] *noun* producción *f or* rendimiento *m* de una compañía

◊ **outvote** [aʊt'vəʊt] *verb* vencer en una elección *or* votación; **the chairman was outvoted** = el presidente salió derrotado en la votación

◊ **outward** ['aʊtwəd] *adjective* de ida *or* de salida *or* al exterior; **the ship is outward bound** = el barco realiza el viaje de ida; **on the outward voyage the ship will call in at the West Indies** = en el viaje de ida el barco hará escala en las Antillas; **outward cargo** *or* **outward freight** = carga de ida *or* flete de ida; **outward mission** = misión comercial a un país extranjero

◊ **outwork** ['aʊtwɜːk] *noun* trabajo *m* realizado fuera de la empresa

◊ **outworker** ['aʊtwɜːkə] *noun* trabajador, -ra a domicilio

over ['əʊvə] **1** *preposition* **(a)** *(more than)* por encima de; **the carpet costs over £100** = la alfombra cuesta por encima de £100; **packages not over 200 grams** = paquetes que no pasen de los 200 gramos; **the increase in turnover was over 25%** = el aumento del volumen de ventas fue superior al 25% **(b)** *(compared with)* en comparación con; **increase in output over last year** = el aumento de producción en comparación con el año pasado; **increase in debtors over the last quarter's figure** = el aumento de deudores en comparación con la cifra del último trimestre **(c)** *(during)* durante; **over the last half of the year profits doubled** = durante el último semestre los beneficios se duplicaron **2** *adverb* **held over to the next meeting** = aplazado, -da hasta la próxima reunión; **to carry over a balance** = pasar a cuenta nueva **3** *plural noun* **overs** = extra *m*; **the price includes 10% overs to compensate for damage** = el precio incluye un 10% extra para la indemnización de daños eventuales

◊ **over-** ['əʊvə] *prefix* más de; **shop which caters to the over-60s** = tienda dedicada especialmente a las personas de más de sesenta años

◊ **overall** [əʊvər'ɔːl] *adjective* global *or* en conjunto *or* general; **although some divisions traded profitably, the company reported an overall fall in profits** = aunque algunos departamentos resultaron rentables, la compañía anunció que había registrado una baja general de los beneficios; **overall plan** = plan general

◊ **overbook** [əʊvə'bʊk] *verb* reservar con exceso; **the hotel** *or* **the flight was overbooked** = había más plazas reservadas que las disponibles en el hotel *or* en el vuelo

◊ **overbooking** [əʊvə'bʊkɪŋ] *noun* 'overbooking' *m or* sobrecontratación *m*

◊ **overborrowed** [əʊvə'bɒrəʊd] *adjective* *(company)* (sociedad) financiada en exceso

◊ **overbought** [əʊvə'bɔːt] *adjective* que ha comprado demasiado *or* en exceso; *(stock market)* **the market is overbought** = el mercado está sobrevalorado *or* hay un exceso de compradores en el mercado

> QUOTE they said the market was overbought when the index was between 860 and 870 points
> **Australian Financial Review**

overcapacity [əʊvəkə'pæsɪti] *noun* sobrecapacidad *f*

> QUOTE with the present over-capacity situation in the airline industry the discounting of tickets is widespread
> **Business Traveller**

overcapitalized [əʊvə'kæpɪtəlaɪzd] *adjective* sobrecapitalizado, -da *or* capitalizado, - da en exceso

◊ **overcharge 1** ['əʊvətʃɑːdʒ] *noun* sobrecargo

m *or* precio *m* excesivo *or* importe *m* cargado en exceso; **to pay back an overcharge** = devolver el importe cargado en exceso **2** [əʊvə'tʃɑːdʒ] *verb* sobrecargar *or* cargar en exceso *or* cobrar de más; **they overcharged us for meals** = nos cobraron de más por las comidas; **we asked for a refund because we had been overcharged** = pedimos que nos reembolsaran el dinero que nos habían cobrado de más

◊ **overcrowd** [əʊvə'kraʊd] *verb* abarrotar; **the market was overcrowded** = el mercado estaba abarrotado de gente

overdraft ['əʊvədrɑːft] *noun* sobregiro *m* *or* descubierto *m*; **the bank has allowed me an overdraft of £5,000** = el banco me ha permitido un descubierto de £5.000; **overdraft facilities** = línea de descubierto; **we have exceeded our overdraft facilities** = hemos sobrepasado nuestro límite de crédito

◊ **overdraw** [əʊvə'drɔː] *verb* girar en descubierto *or* rebasar; **your account is overdrawn** *or* **you are overdrawn** = su cuenta está al descubierto (NOTE: **overdrawing - overdrew - overdrawn)**

overdue [əʊvə'djuː] *adjective* vencido, -da *or* atrasado, -da; **interest payments are three weeks overdue** = el pago de los intereses venció hace tres semanas

◊ **overestimate** [əʊvər'estimeit] *verb* sobrevalorar *or* sobrestimar; **he overestimated the amount of time needed to fit out the factory** = sobrevaloró el tiempo necesario para equipar la fábrica

◊ **overextend** [əʊvərɪk'stend] *verb* the company overextended itself = la compañía ha querido abarcar demasiado

overhead ['əʊvəhed] **1** *adjective* **overhead costs** *or* **expenses** = gastos generales de producción; **overhead budget** = presupuesto de gastos generales **2** *noun* **overheads** *US* **overhead** = gastos generales; **the sales revenue covers the manufacturing costs but not the overheads** = los ingresos por las ventas cubren los costes de fabricación pero no los gastos generales

overlook [əʊvə'lʊk] *verb* **(a)** *(to look out over)* dar a *or* tener vistas a; **the Managing Director's office overlooks the factory** = la oficina del director gerente da a la fábrica **(b)** *(not to pay attention to)* pasar por alto *or* hacer caso omiso; **in this instance we will overlook the delay** = esta vez pasaremos por alto el retraso

◊ **overmanning** [əʊvə'mænɪŋ] *noun* exceso *m* de personal *or* excedente *m* laboral; **to aim to reduce overmanning** = tener el propósito de reducir el exceso de plantilla

overpay [əʊvə'pei] *verb* pagar más de la cuenta *or* pagar demasiado; **we overpaid the invoice by $245** = pagamos 245 dólares más de la cuenta

◊ **overpaid** [əʊvə'peid] *adjective* pagado, -da en exceso; **our staff are overpaid and underworked** = nuestro personal cobra demasiado y tiene poco trabajo

◊ **overpayment** [əʊvə'peimənt] *noun* pago *m* en exceso

overproduce [əʊvəprə'djuːs] *verb* producir en exceso

◊ **overproduction** [əʊvəprə'dʌkʃən] *noun* sobreproducción *f* *or* superproducción *f*

overrated [əʊvə'reitid] *adjective* sobrevalorado, -da *or* sobrestimado, -da; **the effect of the dollar on European business cannot be overrated** = no se puede sobrestimar el efecto del dólar sobre el comercio europeo; **their 'first-class service' is very overrated** = su 'servicio de primera clase' está muy sobrevalorado

overrider *or* **overriding commission** ['əʊvəraidə *or* 'əʊvəraidiŋ kə'miʃən] *noun* comisión *f* extra

◊ **overrun** [əʊvə'rʌn] *verb* rebasar; **the company overran the time limit set to complete the factory** = la compañía rebasó el plazo establecido para terminar la fábrica (NOTE: **overrunning - overran - overrun)**

overseas [əʊvə'siːz] **1** *adjective* (al *or* del) extranjero *or* extranjero, -ra *or* ultramarino, -na; **an overseas call** = una llamada al *or* del extranjero; **the overseas division** = el servicio exterior; **overseas markets** = los mercados extranjeros; **overseas trade** = comercio exterior *or* comercio con el exterior **2** *noun* extranjero *m*; **the profits from overseas are far higher than those of the home division** = los beneficios obtenidos en el extranjero son mucho mayores que los del mercado interior

overseer ['əʊvəsiə] *noun* vigilante *mf* *or* capataz *m* *or* supervisor, -ra

oversell [əʊvə'sel] *verb* vender más de lo que se puede producir *or* vender en exceso; **he is oversold** = se ha comprometido a un exceso de ventas; **the market is oversold** = las acciones han bajado mucho por exceso de vendedores (NOTE: **overselling - oversold)**

overspend [əʊvə'spend] *verb* gastar excesivamente; **to overspend one's budget** = gastar más de lo presupuestado (NOTE: **overspending - overspent)**

◊ **overspending** [əʊvə'spendiŋ] *noun* gasto *m* excesivo; **the board decided to limit the overspending by the production departments** = la junta decidió limitar el gasto excesivo de los servicios de producción

overstaffed [əʊvə'stɑːft] *adjective* con un exceso de personal

◊ **overstock** [əʊvə'stɒk] **1** *verb* acumular un exceso de existencias *or* abarrotar; **to be overstocked with spare parts** = tener existencias excesivas de piezas de recambio **2** *plural noun US* **overstocks** = exceso *m* de existencias; **we will have** to sell off the overstocks to make room in the warehouse = tendremos que liquidar el exceso de existencias para hacer sitio en el almacén

oversubscribe [əʊvəsəb'skraɪb] *verb* **the share offer was oversubscribed six times** = la demanda de acciones fue seis veces superior al número de acciones emitidas

◊ **oversupply** [əʊvəsə'plaɪ] *noun* oferta *f* excesiva

◊ **over-the-counter** [əʊvəðə'kaʊntə] *adjective* **over-the-counter sales** = venta de acciones que no se cotizan en Bolsa; **this share is available on the over-the-counter market** = esta acción puede adquirirse fuera de bolsa *or* en la contratación de valores sin cotización oficial

overtime ['əʊvətaɪm] **1** *noun* horas *fpl* extraordinarias *or* extras; **to work six hours' overtime** = trabajar seis horas extraordinarias; **the overtime rate is one and a half times normal pay** = la tarifa de las horas extraordinarias es una vez y media la tarifa normal; **overtime ban** = prohibición de realizar horas extras; **overtime pay** = tarifa de horas extras **2** *adverb* **to work overtime** = hacer *or* trabajar horas extraordinarias

overtrading [əʊvə'treɪdɪŋ] *noun* déficit comercial debido a un exceso de producción *or* a una expansión demasiado rápida

overvalue [əʊvə'vælju:] *verb* sobrevalorar *or* sobrestimar; **these shares are overvalued at £1.25** = a £1.25, estas acciones están sobrevaloradas; **the pound is overvalued against the dollar** = la libra está sobrevalorada con relación al dólar (NOTE: the opposite is **undervalued**)

◊ **overweight** [əʊvə'weɪt] *adjective* excesivamente pesado; **the package is sixty grams overweight** = el paquete tiene un exceso de peso de sesenta gramos

◊ **overwhelmed** [əʊvə'welmd] *adjective* agobiado, -da

◊ **overworked** [əʊvə'wɜ:kt] *adjective* con demasiado trabajo; **our staff complain of being underpaid and overworked** = nuestro personal se queja de estar mal pagado y tener demasiado trabajo

owe [əʊ] *verb* deber; **he owes the bank £250,000** = debe al banco £250.000; **he owes the company for the stock he purchased** = debe a la empresa las mercancías que compró

◊ **owing** ['əʊɪŋ] *adjective* **(a)** *(not paid back)* debido; **money owing to the directors** = dinero que se debe a los consejeros; **how much is still owing to the company by its debtors?** = ¿cuánto le deben todavía los deudores a la compañía? **(b)** *(because of)* **owing to** = debido a *or* a causa de; **the plane was late owing to fog** = el avión llegó tarde a causa de la niebla; **I am sorry that owing to pressure of work, we cannot supply your order on time** = sentimos no poder servirle el pedido a tiempo debido a la cantidad de trabajo acumulado

own [əʊn] **1** *adjective* propio, -ia; **he has his own office** = tiene su propia oficina **2** *verb* poseer *or* tener; **he owns 50% of the shares** = posee el 50% de las acciones; **a wholly-owned subsidiary** = una filial propiedad total de la empresa; **a state-owned industry** = una industria estatal

◊ **own brand goods** ['əʊn 'brænd 'gʊdz] *noun* productos *mpl* de marca propia

◊ **owner** ['əʊnə] *noun* propietario, -ria *or* dueño, -ña; **sole owner** = propietario único; **owner-occupier** = propietario ocupante de una vivienda; **goods sent at owner's risk** = mercancías enviadas por cuenta y riesgo del cliente

◊ **ownership** ['əʊnəʃɪp] *noun* propiedad *f*; **common** *or* **collective ownership** = propiedad colectiva; **joint ownership** = co-propiedad; **public ownership** *or* **state ownership** = propiedad pública *or* estatal; **private ownership** = propiedad privada; **the ownership of the company has passed to the banks** = la propiedad de la compañía ha pasado a los bancos

◊ **own label goods** ['əʊn 'leɪbl 'gʊdz] *noun* productos de marca propia

oz = OUNCE(S)

Pp

P&L = PROFIT AND LOSS

p & p = POSTAGE AND PACKING franqueo y embalaje

PA ['pi:'eɪ] = PERSONAL ASSISTANT

p.a. = PER ANNUM

pack [pæk] **1** *noun* **pack of items** = lote *m* de artículos; **pack of cigarettes** = paquete *m or* cajetilla *f* de cigarrillos; **pack of biscuits** = paquete de galletas; **pack of envelopes** = paquete de sobres; **items sold in packs of 200** = artículos vendidos en paquetes de 200 unidades; **blister pack** *or* **bubble pack** = embalaje de plástico tipo burbuja; **display pack** = embalaje de exposición; **dummy pack** = embalaje vacío *or* ficticio; **four-pack** *or* **six-pack** = embalaje *or* caja de cuatro *or* seis unidades **2** *verb* embalar *or* envasar *or* empaquetar; **to pack goods into cartons** = embalar mercancías en cajas de cartón; **your order has been packed and is ready for shipping** = su pedido está servido y listo para el envío; **the biscuits are packed in plastic wrappers** = las galletas se presentan en envoltorios de plástico; **the computer is packed in expanded polystyrene before being shipped** = el ordenador se embala en poliestireno expandido antes de ser expedido

◊ **package** ['pækɪdʒ] **1** *noun* **(a)** *(wrapping)* paquete *m or* embalaje *m or* envase *m*; **the Post Office does not accept bulky packages** = la oficina de correos no acepta paquetes voluminosos; **the goods are to be sent in airtight packages** = las mercancías deben enviarse en envases herméticos; **instructions for use are printed on the package** = el paquete lleva las instrucciones impresas **(b)** *(items joined together in one deal)* paquete *m or* conjunto *m* de medidas *or* acuerdo *m* global; **pay package** *or* **salary package** US **compensation package** = paquete *or* conjunto de retribuciones; **the job carries an attractive salary package** = el puesto lleva aparejado un atractivo conjunto de retribuciones; **package deal** = acuerdo *or* transacción global *or* paquete; **we are offering a package deal which includes the whole office computer system, staff training and hardware maintenance** = se trata de una oferta global que incluye el sistema completo de ordenadores, la formación del personal y el mantenimiento del equipo; **package holiday** *or* **package tour** = viaje organizado *or* de turismo; **the travel company is arranging a package trip to the international computer exhibition** = la agencia de viajes está programando un viaje organizado a la feria internacional de ordenadores **2** *verb* **(a)** **to package goods** = embalar mercancías **(b)** **to package holidays** = vender viajes con todos los gastos incluidos

◊ **packaging** ['pækɪdʒɪŋ] *noun* **(a)** *(action)* embalaje *m or* envase *m* **(b)** *(wrapping)* embalaje; **airtight packaging** = embalaje hermético; **packaging material** = material de embalaje

◊ **packer** ['pækə] *noun* embalador, -ra *or* empaquetador, -ra

◊ **packet** ['pækɪt] *noun* paquete *m or* cajetilla *f*; **packet of cigarettes** = paquete *or* cajetilla de cigarrillos; **packet of biscuits** = paquete de galletas; **packet of filing cards** = paquete de fichas; **item sold in packets of 20** = artículo vendido en paquetes de 20; **postal packet** = paquete postal

◊ **packing** ['pækɪŋ] *noun* **(a)** *(action)* embalaje *m or* envase *m*; **what is the cost of the packing?** = ¿cuánto cuesta el embalaje?; **packing is included in the price** = el embalaje está incluido en el precio; **packing case** = caja de embalar; **packing charges** = gastos de embalaje; **packing list** *or* **packing slip** = lista de bultos *or* de contenidos **(b)** *(material)* embalaje; **packed in airtight packing** = embalado herméticamente; **non-returnable packing** = envase no retornable

pad [pæd] *noun* **(a)** *(paper)* taco *m or* bloc *m*; **desk pad** *or* **memo pad** *or* **note pad** = bloc de notas; **phone pad** = bloc que se guarda junto al teléfono para anotar recados **(b)** *(soft material)* almohadilla *f or* cojinete *m*; **the machine is protected by rubber pads** = la máquina está protegida por almohadillas de caucho; **inking pad** = tampón *m* para entintar

paid [peɪd] *adjective* **(a)** *(for work done)* pagado, -da *or* remunerado, -da; **paid assistant** = ayudante a sueldo; **paid holidays** = vacaciones pagadas **(b)** *(which has been settled)* pagado, -da; **carriage paid** = franco a domicilio *or* porte pagado; **tax paid** = impuesto pagado; **paid bills** = letras pagadas; **the invoice is marked 'paid'** = en la factura pone 'pagado'

◊ **paid-up** ['peɪdʌp] *adjective* *(paid in full)* pagado, -da; **paid-up (share) capital** = capital desembolsado; **paid-up shares** = acciones liberadas

Pakistan [pækɪ'stɑːn] *noun* Paquistán *or* Pakistán *m*

◊ **Pakistani** [pækɪ'stɑːni] *adjective & noun* paquistaní
NOTE: capital: **Islamabad**; currency: **Pakistan rupee (PRs)** = rupia paquistaní (PRs)

pallet ['pælət] *noun* bandeja *f or* paleta *f*

◊ **palletize** ['pælətaɪz] *verb* empaletar *or* embandejar; **palletized cartons** = cajas de cartón embandejadas

pamphlet ['pæmflət] *noun* folleto *m or* impreso *m* (*political*) octavilla *f*

Panama [pænə'mɑ:] *noun* Panamá *m*

◇ **Panamanian** [pænə'meɪnɪən] *adjective & noun* panameño, -ña
NOTE: capital: **Panama City** (= Panamá); currency: **Panamanian balboa (B)** = balboa panameño (B)

panel ['pænl] *noun* **(a)** panel *m or* tablero *m*; **display panel** = tablero de exposición; **advertisement panel** = espacio publicitario en un periódico **(b) panel of experts** = grupo *m* de expertos; **consumer panel** = equipo de consumidores; **Panel on Takeovers and Mergers** *or* **Takeover Panel** = tribunal que regula las adquisiciones y fusiones

panic ['pænɪk] *adjective* pánico, -ca; **panic buying** = compra febril *or* motivada por el pánico; **panic buying of sugar** *or* **of dollars** = compra febril de azúcar *or* dólares; **panic selling of sterling** = venta febril de libras

paper ['peɪpə] *noun* **(a)** papel *m*; **adhesive paper** = papel adhesivo; **brown paper** = papel de estraza; **carbon paper** = papel carbón; **she put the carbon paper in the wrong way round** = puso el papel carbón al revés; **duplicating paper** = papel de multicopista; **graph paper** = papel cuadriculado; **headed paper** = papel con membrete; **lined paper** = papel rayado; **typing paper** = papel para escribir a máquina; **wrapping paper** = papel de envolver (NOTE: no plural in this meaning) **(b) paper bag** = bolsa de papel; **paper feed** = alimentador de papel **(c) papers** = documentos *mpl or* papeles *mpl*; **he sent me the relevant papers on the case** = me envió los documentos relacionados con el caso; **he has lost the customs papers** = ha perdido los documentos de la aduana; **the office is asking for the VAT papers** = la oficina pide los papeles del IVA **(d) on paper** = en teoría; **on paper the system is ideal, but we have to see it working before we will sign the contract** = en teoría el sistema es ideal, pero tenemos que verlo en funcionamiento antes de firmar el contrato; **paper loss** = pérdida sobre el papel; **paper profit** = beneficio sobre el papel; **paper millionaire** = millonario, -ria en acciones **(e)** (*documents which can represent money*) valores *mpl or* títulos *mpl*; **bankable paper** = valores aceptados por un banco en garantía de un préstamo; **negotiable paper** = títulos negociables **(f) paper money** *or* **paper currency** = papel moneda **(g)** (*newspaper*) periódico *m*; **trade paper** = publicación comercial *or* sobre una actividad profesional determinada; **free paper** *or* **giveaway paper** = periódico gratuito

◇ **paperclip** ['peɪpəklɪp] *noun* sujetapapeles *m*

◇ **paperless office** ['peɪpələs 'ɒfɪs] *noun* oficina *f* informatizada

◇ **paperwork** ['peɪpəwɜ:k] *noun* papeleo *m or* trabajo administrativo; **exporting to Russia involves a large amount of paperwork** = exportar a Rusia implica una gran cantidad de papeleo

par [pɑ:] *adjective* par; **par value** = valor a la par;

shares at par = acciones de valor a la par; **shares above par** *or* **below par** = acciones por encima de la par *or* por debajo de la par

parachute ['pærəʃu:t] *noun* **golden parachute** = indemnización concedida a un directivo cuando se prescinde de sus servicios

paragraph ['pærəgrɑ:f] *noun* párrafo *m*; **the first paragraph of the letter** *or* **paragraph one of the letter** = el primer párrafo de la carta; **please refer to the paragraph in the contract on 'shipping instructions'** = consulte el párrafo del contrato sobre 'instrucciones de envío'

Paraguay ['pærəgwaɪ] *noun* Paraguay *m*

◇ **Paraguayan** ['pærəgwaɪən] *adjective & noun* paraguayo, -ya
NOTE: capital: **Asuncion** (= Asunción); currency: **Paraguayan guarani (G)** = guaraní paraguayo

parameter [pə'ræmɪtə] *noun* parámetro *m*; **the budget parameters are fixed by the finance director** = el director financiero fija los parámetros del presupuesto; **spending by each department has to fall within certain parameters** = el gasto de cada departamento tiene que ajustarse a determinados parámetros

parastatal [pærə'steɪtl] *noun* (*in Africa*) organización *f* paraestatal

parcel ['pɑ:sl] **1** *noun* **(a)** (*goods wrapped up*) paquete *m*; **to do up goods into parcels** = empaquetar mercancías; **to tie up a parcel** = atar un paquete; **parcel delivery service** = servicio de entrega de paquetes; **parcels office** = oficina de paquetes; **parcel post** = servicio de paquetes postales; **to send a box by parcel post** = enviar una caja por el servicio de paquetes postales; **parcel rates** = tarifas de paquetes **(b) parcel of shares** = paquete de acciones; **the shares are on offer in parcels of 50** = las acciones se ofrecen en paquetes de 50 **2** *verb* empaquetar *or* embalar; **to parcel up a consignment of books** = empaquetar una partida de libros (NOTE: **parcelling - parcelled** but US **parceling - parceled**)

parent company ['peər(ə)nt 'kʌmpnɪ] *noun* sociedad *f or* casa *f* matriz *or* oficina *f* central

Pareto's Law [pə'ri:təʊz 'lɔ:] *noun* ley *f* de Pareto

COMMENT: the theory that a small percentage of a total is responsible for a large proportion of value or resources (also called the 80/20 law, because 80/20 is the normal ratio between majority and minority figures: so 20% of accounts produce 80% of turnover; 80% of GDP enriches 20% of the population, etc.)

pari passu ['pæri 'pæsu:] *phrase* al mismo ritmo *or* en igualdad de condiciones; **the new shares will rank pari passu with the existing ones** = las nuevas acciones tendrán los mismos privilegios que las ya existentes

Paris Club ['pærɪs 'klʌb] = GROUP OF TEN

parity ['pærətɪ] *noun* paridad *f or* igualdad *f*; **the female staff want parity with the men** = el personal femenino quiere igualdad de condiciones con los hombres; **the pound fell to parity with the dollar** = la libra quedo a la par con el dólar después de su caída

QUOTE the draft report on changes in the international monetary system casts doubt about any return to fixed exchange-rate parities

Wall Street Journal

park [pɑːk] **1** *noun* parque *m*; **business park** = zona *f* industrial; **car park** = aparcamiento *m or* estacionamiento *m or* 'parking' *m*; **he left his car in the hotel car park** = dejó su coche en el aparcamiento del hotel; **if the car park is full, you can park in the street for thirty minutes** = si el aparcamiento está lleno, puede estacionar en la calle durante treinta minutos; **industrial park** = polígono *m* industrial; **science park** = parque *m* tecnológico **2** *verb* aparcar; **the rep parked his car outside the shop** = el representante aparcó el coche enfrente de la tienda; **you cannot park here during the rush hour** = no se puede aparcar aquí en las horas punta; **parking is difficult in the centre of the city** = es difícil aparcar en el centro de la ciudad

Parkinson's law [ˈpɑːkɪnsnz ˈlɔː] *noun* ley *f* de Parkinson

part [pɑːt] *noun* **(a)** parte *m*; **main part** = grueso *m or* parte principal; **part of the shipment was damaged** = se estropeó una parte del cargamento; **part of the workforce is on overtime** = una parte del personal hace horas extraordinarias; **part of the expenses will be refunded** = se reembolsará una parte de los gastos **(b) in part** = en parte; **to contribute in part to the costs** *or* **to pay the costs in part** = contribuir a parte de los costes *or* pagar una parte de los costes **(c) spare part** = pieza *f* de recambio *or* repuesto *m*; **the photocopier will not work - we need to replace a part** *or* **a part needs replacing** = la fotocopiadora no funciona - tenemos que cambiarle una pieza **(d) part-owner** = copropietario, -ria; **he is part-owner of the restaurant** = es copropietario del restaurante; **part-ownership** = copropiedad *f* **(e) part exchange** = canje parcial; **they refused to take my old car as part exchange for the new one** = se negaron a aceptar el coche viejo en pago parcial del nuevo; **part payment** *or US* **partial payment** = pago parcial; **I gave him £250 as part payment for the car** = le dí £250 como pago parcial por el coche; **part delivery** *or* **part order** *or* **part shipment** = entrega parcial *or* pedido parcial *or* envío parcial

partial [ˈpɑːʃəl] *adjective* parcial; **partial loss** = pérdida parcial; **he got partial compensation for the damage to his house** = obtuvo una indemnización parcial para cubrir los daños de su casa; *US* **partial payment** = pago parcial (NOTE: British English is **part payment**)

participation [pɑːtɪsɪˈpeɪʃən] *noun* participación *f*; **worker participation** = participación de los trabajadores en la gestión de la empresa

◊ **participative** [pɑːˈtɪsɪpeɪtɪv] *adjective* participativo, -va; **we do not treat management-worker relations as a participative process** = no tratamos las relaciones entre la dirección y los trabajadores como un proceso de participación en la gestión

particular [pəˈtɪkjʊlə] **1** *adjective* particular *or* concreto, -ta *or* determinado, -da; **the photocopier only works with a particular type of paper** = la fotocopiadora sólo funciona con un tipo especial de papel; **particular average** = avería simple **2** *noun* **(a) particulars** = detalles *mpl or* pormenores *mpl*; **sheet which gives particulars of the items for sale** = hoja que da los pormenores de los artículos en venta; **the inspector asked for particulars of the missing car** = el inspector pidió los detalles del coche desaparecido; **to give full particulars of something** = dar una información completa sobre algo **(b) in particular** = en especial *or* especialmente *or* particularmente; **fragile goods, in particular glasses, need special packing** = las mercancías frágiles, especialmente los vasos, precisan un embalaje especial

partly [ˈpɑːtli] *adverb* parcialmente; **partly-paid capital** = capital no desembolsado totalmente; **partly-paid up shares** = acciones no liberadas totalmente; **partly-secured creditors** = acreedores no asegurados totalmente

partner [ˈpɑːtnə] *noun* socio, -cia *or* asociado, -da; **he became a partner in a firm of solicitors** = pasó a ser socio de un bufete de abogados; **active partner** *or* **working partner** = socio activo *or* socio que trabaja; **junior partner** *or* **senior partner** = socio subalterno *or* de menor antigüedad *or* socio principal; **limited partner** = socio comanditario; **sleeping partner** = socio comanditario *or* en comandita

◊ **partnership** [ˈpɑːtnəʃɪp] *noun* **(a)** sociedad colectiva *f*; **to go into partnership with someone** = asociarse con alguien; **to join with someone to form a partnership** = formar una sociedad colectiva con alguien; **to offer someone a partnership** *or* **to take someone into partnership with you** = proponer una sociedad a alguien *or* tomar a alguien como socio; **to dissolve a partnership** = disolver una sociedad **(b) limited partnership** = sociedad en comandita *or* sociedad personal de responsabilidad limitada

part-time [pɑːtˈtaɪm] *adjective & adverb* a tiempo parcial *or* jornada reducida; **she works part-time** = trabaja a tiempo parcial; **he is trying to find part-time work** = está buscando trabajo a jornada reducida; **a part-time worker** = trabajador, -ra a tiempo parcial *or* por horas; **we are looking for part-time staff to work our computers** = estamos buscando personal para trabajar con nuestros ordenadores a tiempo parcial; **part-time work** *or* **part-time employment** = trabajo *or* empleo a tiempo parcial *or* por horas

◊ **part-timer** [pɑːtˈtaɪmə] *noun* trabajador, -ra a tiempo parcial

party [ˈpɑːti] *noun* **(a)** parte *f*; **one of the parties to the suit has died** = una de las partes litigantes ha muerto; **the company is not a party to the agreement** = la compañía no es parte en el acuerdo **(b) third party** = tercero; **third party insurance** *or* **third party policy** = seguro contra terceros **(c) working party** = grupo *m* de trabajo; **the government has set up a working party to study the problems of industrial waste** = el gobierno ha creado un grupo de trabajo para estudiar los problemas de los residuos industriales; **Professor Smith is the chairman of the working party on computers in society** = el profesor Smith es el presidente del grupo de trabajo sobre informática en la sociedad

pass [pɑːs] **1** *noun (permit)* pase *m*; **you need a pass to enter the ministry offices** = para entrar en las oficinas del ministerio hace falta un pase; **all members of staff must show a pass** = todos los empleados deben mostrar su pase **2** *verb* **(a) to pass a dividend** = omitir el pago de un dividendo **(b)** *(to approve)* aprobar; **the finance director has to pass an invoice before it is sent out** = el director financiero tiene que aprobar las facturas antes de su envío; **the loan has been passed by the board** = el préstamo ha sido aprobado por la junta; **to pass a resolution** = aprobar *or* adoptar una moción; **the meeting passed a proposal that salaries should be frozen** = la reunión aprobó una propuesta para congelar los salarios **(c)** *(to be successful)* aprobar; **she has passed all her exams and now is a qualified accountant** = aprobó todos los exámenes y ahora tiene el título de contable

◇ **passbook** ['pɑːsbʊk] *noun* libreta *f* de depósitos

QUOTE instead of customers having transactions recorded in their passbooks, they will present plastic cards and have the transactions printed out on a receipt
Australian Financial Review

pass off ['pɑːs 'ɒf] *verb* **to pass something off as something else** = hacer pasar una cosa por otra; **he tried to pass off the wine as Spanish, when in fact it came from outside the EU** = intentó hacer pasar el vino por español, cuando en realidad era de fuera del UE

passage ['pæsɪdʒ] *noun (sea crossing)* travesía *f*

passenger ['pæsɪn(d)ʒə] *noun* pasajero, -ra *or* viajero, -ra; **passenger terminal** = terminal de pasajeros; **passenger train** = tren de pasajeros; **foot passenger** = pasajero de a pie

passport ['pɑːspɔːt] *noun* pasaporte *m*; **we had to show our passports at the customs post** = tuvimos que enseñar el pasaporte en la aduana; **his passport is out of date** = su pasaporte está caducado; **the passport officer stamped my passport** = el funcionario de pasaportes selló mi pasaporte

password ['pɑːswɜːd] *noun* contraseña *f*

patent ['peɪtənt *or* 'pætənt] **1** *noun* **(a)** patente *f*; **to take out a patent for a new type of light bulb** = sacar una patente para un nuevo tipo de bombilla; **to apply for a patent for a new invention** = solicitar una patente para un nuevo invento; **letters patent** = patente de invención; **patent applied for** *or* **patent pending** = patente solicitada *or* en tramitación; **to forfeit a patent** = perder una patente; **to infringe a patent** = violar una patente; **infringement of patent** *or* **patent infringement** = violación de patente **(b)** **patent agent** = agente de patentes y marcas; **to file a patent application** = solicitar una patente; **patent medicine** = específico *m*; **patent office** = oficina de patentes y marcas; **patent rights** = derechos de patente **2** *verb* **to patent an invention** = patentar un invento

◇ **patented** ['peɪtəntɪd *or* 'pætəntɪd] *adjective* patentado, -da

paternity leave [pə'tɜːnɪtɪ 'liːv] *noun* licencia *f* por paternidad

patron ['peɪtrən] *noun (regular customer)* cliente *mf* (habitual); **the car park is for the use of hotel patrons only** = aparcamiento para uso exclusivo de los clientes del hotel

pattern ['pætən] *noun* **(a)** *(model or sample)* modelo *m or* muestra *f or* diseño *m*; **pattern book** = libro *m* de muestras *or* muestrario **(b)** *(general way in which something happens)* pauta *f or* tendencia *f*; **pattern of prices** *or* **price pattern** = tendencia de los precios; **pattern of sales** *or* **sales pattern** = tendencia de las ventas; **pattern of trade** *or* **trading pattern** = estructura *f* del comercio; **the company's trading pattern shows high export sales in the first quarter and high home sales in the third quarter** = el esquema de actividades comerciales de la empresa muestra una elevada cifra de ventas al extranjero en el primer trimestre y al mercado interior en el tercer trimestre

pavilion [pə'vɪljən] *noun (at exhibition)* pabellón *m*

pawn [pɔːn] **1** *noun* **to put something in pawn** = dejar algo en prenda *or* empeñar; **to take something out of pawn** = desempeñar *or* recuperar algo empeñado; **pawn ticket** = papeleta de empeño **2** *verb* **to pawn a watch** = empeñar un reloj

◇ **pawnbroker** ['pɔːnbrəʊkə] *noun* prestamista *mf*

◇ **pawnshop** ['pɔːnʃɒp] *noun* casa *f* de empeños *or* monte *m* de piedad

pay [peɪ] **1** *noun* **(a)** *(salary or wage)* paga *f or* sueldo *m or* salario *m*; **back pay** = atrasos de sueldo; **basic pay** = salario base; **take-home pay** = salario neto; **holidays with pay** = vacaciones pagadas; **unemployment pay** = subsidio de paro *or* desempleo **(b)** **pay cheque** = cheque de sueldo *or* salario; **pay day** = día *m* de pago; **pay negotiations** *or* **pay talks** = negociaciones salariales; **pay packet** = sobre del sueldo; **pay rise** = aumento de sueldo; **pay round** = ronda salarial *or* de negociaciones salariales; **pay slip** = hoja de liquidación de sueldos *or* salarios **(c)** **pay desk** = caja *f*; **pay phone** = teléfono público **2** *verb* **(a)** *(give money to buy)* pagar *or* abonar *or* retribuir; **to pay £1,000 for a car** = pagar £1.000 por un coche; **how much did you pay to have the office cleaned?** = ¿cuánto pagaste por limpiar la oficina?; **to pay in advance** = pagar por adelantado; **we had to pay in advance to have the new telephone system installed** = tuvimos que pagar la nueva instalación telefónica por adelantado; **to pay in instalments** = pagar a plazos; **we are paying for the computer by paying instalments of £50 a month** = estamos pagando el ordenador en plazos mensuales de £50; **to pay cash** = pagar al contado *or* en efectivo; *(written on cheque)* **'pay cash'** = 'pago al contado'; **to pay by cheque** = pagar con un talón; **to pay by credit card** = pagar con tarjeta de crédito **(b)** **to pay on demand** = pagar a la vista; **please pay the sum of £10** = rogamos abonen la cantidad de £10; **to pay a dividend** = distribuir un dividendo; **these shares pay a dividend of 1.5p** = estas acciones producen un dividendo de 1.5p; **to pay interest** = pagar intereses; **building societies pay an interest of 10%** = las sociedades de crédito hipotecario pagan un interés del 10% **(c)** *(for work done)* pagar; **the workforce has not been paid for three weeks** = no se ha pagado al personal desde hace tres semanas; **we pay good wages for skilled workers** = pagamos buenos sueldos a los trabajadores especializados; **how much do they pay**

you per hour? = ¿cuánto te pagan por hora?; to be paid by the hour = cobrar por horas; to be paid at piece-work rates = cobrar a destajo (d) (to settle) pagar or liquidar or saldar; to pay a bill = pagar una letra or cuenta or factura; to pay a debt = satisfacer une deuda; to pay an invoice = pagar una factura; to pay duty on imports = pagar derechos sobre las importaciones; to pay tax = pagar impuestos (e) to pay a cheque into an account = ingresar un talón en una cuenta (NOTE: paying - paid)

◊ **payable** ['peɪəbl] adjective pagadero, -ra; payable in advance = pagadero por adelantado; payable on delivery = pagadero a la entrega; payable on demand = pagadero a la vista; payable at sixty days = pagadero a sesenta días; cheque made payable to bearer = talón pagadero al portador; shares payable on application = acciones pagaderas en el momento de la suscripción; accounts payable = cuentas a pagar; bills payable = cuentas or efectos por pagar; electricity charges are payable by the tenant = el inquilino ha de pagar los gastos de electricidad

◊ **pay as you earn (PAYE)** ['peɪ əz ju 'ɜːn] GB pay as you earn = método fiscal de retención directa

◊ **pay-as-you-go** ['peɪ əz ju 'gəʊ] (a) US = PAY AS YOU EARN (b) GB método fiscal de retención directa

◊ **pay back** ['peɪ 'bæk] verb devolver or reembolsar; to pay back a loan = devolver un préstamo; I lent him £50 and he promised to pay me back in a month = le presté £50 y prometió devolvérmelas en un mes; he has never paid me back for the money he borrowed = nunca me ha devuelto el dinero que me pidió prestado or que le presté

◊ **payback** ['peɪbæk] noun devolución f or reembolso m; payback clause = cláusula de reembolso; payback period = periodo de reembolso or devolución

◊ **pay-cheque** or USpaycheck ['peɪtʃek] noun cheque m del sueldo

◊ **pay down** ['peɪ 'daʊn] verb to pay money down = hacer un depósito or dar una entrada or dejar una señal; he paid £50 down and the rest in monthly instalments = hizo un depósito de £50 y el resto lo pagó en plazos mensuales

◊ **PAYE** ['piːeɪwaɪ'iː] = PAY AS YOU EARN

◊ **payee** [peɪ'iː] noun portador m or beneficiario, -ria

◊ **payer** ['peɪə] noun pagador, -ra; slow payer = moroso, -sa; he is well known as a slow payer = tiene fama de moroso

◊ **paying** ['peɪɪŋ] 1 adjective rentable; it is a paying business = es un negocio rentable; it is not a paying proposition = no es una propuesta rentable 2 noun pago m; paying of a debt = pago de una deuda; paying-in book = libreta f de depósitos bancarios; paying-in slip = nota f or recibo m de depósito

◊ **payload** ['peɪləʊd] noun carga f útil (mercancías or pasajeros)

◊ **payment** ['peɪmənt] noun (a) (giving money) pago m or retribución f; payment in cash or cash payment = pago en metálico or al contado or en efectivo; payment by cheque = pago mediante cheque or talón; payment of interest or interest payment = pago de intereses; payment on account = pago a cuenta; full payment or payment in full = pago total or íntegro; payment on invoice = pago contra presentación de la factura; payment in kind = pago en especie; payment by results = pago según resultados or según producción or a destajo (b) (money paid) pago; back payment = pago atrasado; deferred payments = pagos aplazados; the company agreed to defer payments for three months = la compañía acordó aplazar los pagos durante tres meses; down payment = entrada f or depósito m; repayable in easy payments = a pagar en cómodos plazos; incentive payments = prima f de producción; balance of payments = balanza f de pagos (c) (benefit) prestación f

◊ **pay off** ['peɪ 'ɒf] verb (a) (money owed) redimir or reembolsar; to pay off a mortgage = redimir una hipoteca; to pay off a loan = reembolsar un préstamo (b) (employment) despedir; when the company changed hands the factory was closed and all the workers were paid off = cuando la empresa cambió de dueño, cerraron la fábrica y despidieron a todos los trabajadores

◊ **payoff** ['peɪɒf] noun (a) (money paid) liquidación f de una deuda (b) (profit or reward) resultado m or recompensa f or rentabilidad f or beneficio m; one of the payoffs of a university degree is increased earning power = uno de los beneficios de las carreras universitarias es que permiten una mayor rentabilidad económica

◊ **pay out** ['peɪ 'aʊt] verb pagar or desembolsar; the company pays out thousands of pounds in legal fees = la sociedad paga miles de libras en honorarios de abogados; we have paid out half our profits in dividends = hemos desembolsado la mitad de nuestros beneficios en dividendos

◊ **payout** ['peɪaʊt] noun subvención f; the company only exists on payouts from the government = la sociedad existe sólo gracias a las subvenciones del gobierno

◊ **payroll** ['peɪrəʊl] noun nómina f or plantilla f; the company has 250 on the payroll = la empresa tiene una plantilla de 250 empleados; payroll ledger = libro mayor de salarios; payroll tax = impuesto sobre la nómina

◊ **pay up** ['peɪ 'ʌp] verb pagar una deuda; the company only paid up when we sent them a letter from our solicitor = la compañía no pagó la deuda hasta que nuestro abogado no les envió una carta; he finally paid up six months late = pagó por fin la deuda, pero con seis meses de retraso

QUOTE the yield figure means that if you buy the shares at their current price you will be getting 5% before tax on your money if the company pays the same dividend as in its last financial year
Investors Chronicle

QUOTE after a period of recession followed by a rapid boost in incomes, many tax payers embarked upon some tax planning to minimize their payouts
Australian Financial Review

pc = PER CENT

PC ['piː'siː] = PERSONAL COMPUTER

PCB = PETTY CASH BOOK

P/E ['piː'iː] *abbreviation* = PRICE/EARNINGS **P/E ratio (price/earnings ratio** *or* **PER)** = relación *f* precio-beneficios; **the shares sell at a P/E ratio of 7** = las acciones se venden a una relación precio-beneficios de 7

peak [piːk] **1** *noun* pico *m or* punta *f or* punto *m* máximo *or* cima *f or* cumbre *f*; **peak period** = horas punta *or* periodo de gran consumo *or* de mayor afluencia; **time of peak demand** = periodo de demanda máxima; **peak output** = rendimiento máximo; **peak year** = mejor año; **the shares reached their peak in January** = las acciones alcanzaron su máxima en enero; **the share index has fallen 10% since the peak in January** = el índice de cotización de acciones ha bajado un 10% desde su máxima de enero **2** *verb* llegar al máximo *or* alcanzar el punto más alto; **productivity peaked in January** = la productividad llegó al máximo en enero; **shares have peaked and are beginning to slip back** = las acciones alcanzaron su punto más alto y ahora están empezando a bajar

pecuniary [pɪ'kjuːnjəri] *adjective* pecuniario, -ria; *(made no profit)* **he gained no pecuniary advantage** = no sacó ninguna ventaja pecuniaria

peddle ['pedl] *verb* vender por las casas *or* en la calle

◊ **pedlar** ['pedlə] *noun* buhonero, -ra *or* vendedor, -ra ambulante (NOTE: also spelled **peddler**)

pedestrian [pə'destriən] *adjective* peatonal *or* de peatones; **pedestrian precinct** = zona de peatones *or* zona (comercial) peatonal

peg [peg] *verb* fijar *or* estabilizar; **to peg prices** = estabilizar los precios; **to peg wage increases to the cost-of-living index** = fijar los aumentos salariales conforme al índice del coste de la vida (NOTE: **pegging - pegged**)

pen [pen] *noun* pluma *f*; **felt pen** = rotulador *m*; **light pen** = lápiz luminoso; **marker pen** = rotulador *or* marcador *m*

penalty ['penlti] *noun* pena *f or* castigo *m or* multa *f*; **penalty clause** = cláusula *f* penal; **the contract contains a penalty clause which fines the company 1% for every week the completion date is late** = el contrato contiene una cláusula penal que multa a la compañía con un 1% por cada semana que se atrase en la fecha de cumplimiento

◊ **penalize** ['piːnəlaɪz] *verb* penalizar *or* sancionar; **to penalize a supplier for late deliveries** = sancionar a un proveedor por entregas tardías; **they were penalized for bad service** = fueron sancionados por prestar un mal servicio

pence [pens] *see* PENNY

pencil ['pensəl] *noun* lápiz *m*; **pencil sharpener** = sacapuntas *m*

pending ['pendɪŋ] **1** *adjective* pendiente; **pending tray** = bandeja de asuntos pendientes; **patent pending** = patente solicitada *or* en tramitación **2** *adverb* **pending advice from our lawyers** = pendiente del consejo de nuestros abogados

penetrate ['penɪtreɪt] *verb* **to penetrate a market** = penetrar *or* introducirse en un mercado

◊ **penetration** [penɪ'treɪʃən] *noun* **market penetration** = penetración *f* en el mercado

penny ['peni] *noun* **(a)** *GB* penique *m* **(b)** *US (informal)* centavo *m* (NOTE: in the UK, it is usually written **p** after a figure: **26p**; the plural is **pence**. In British English say 'pee' for the coin and 'pee' or 'pence' for the amount; in US English say 'pennies' for the coins and 'cents' for the amount)

◊ **penny share** *or US* **penny stock** ['peni 'ʃeə *or* 'peni 'stɒk] *noun* acción *f* con valor inferior a 10p *or* 1 dólar

pension ['penʃən] **1** *noun* **(a)** pensión *f*; **retirement pension** *or* **old age pension** = pensión de retiro *or* subsidio *m* de vejez *or* jubilación *f*; **government pension** *or* **state pension** = pensión estatal; **occupational pension** = pensión laboral; **portable pension** = derecho a pensión que se le reconoce a un trabajador aun cuando cambie de empresa; **pension contributions** = cotizaciones a la pensión de jubilación **(b)** **pension plan** *or* **pension scheme** = plan de pensiones; **company pension scheme** = programa de pensiones de la empresa; **he decided to join the company's pension scheme** = decidió apuntarse al programa de pensiones de la empresa; **contributory pension scheme** = plan de pensiones con aportación del trabajador; **graduated pension scheme** = programa de pensiones proporcionales; **non-contributory pension scheme** = programa de pensiones sin aportación del trabajador; **personal pension plan** = plan de pensiones personal; **portable pension plan** = plan de pensiones por el que se reconoce a un trabajador el derecho a pensión aun cuando cambie de empresa **(c)** **pension entitlement** = derecho a pensión; **pension fund** = fondo de pensiones **2** *verb* **to pension someone off** = jubilar a alguien

◊ **pensionable** ['penʃənəbl] *adjective* con derecho a jubilación *or* retiro; **pensionable age** = edad de jubilación *or* del retiro

◊ **pensioner** ['penʃənə] *noun* pensionista *mf*; **old age pensioner (OAP)** = pensionista *or* jubilado, -da

PEP = PERSONAL EQUITY PLAN

peppercorn rent ['pepəkɔːn 'rent] *noun* alquiler *m* simbólico; **to pay a peppercorn rent** = pagar un alquiler simbólico; **to lease a property for** *or* **at a peppercorn rent** = arrendar una propiedad por una renta simbólica *or* un alquiler mínimo

PER = PRICE/EARNINGS RATIO

per [pɜː] *preposition* **(a)** **as per** = según *or* de acuerdo con; **as per invoice** = según factura; **as per sample** = según muestra; **as per previous order** = según su pedido anterior **(b)** a *or* por; **per hour** *or* **per day** *or* **per week** *or* **per year** = por hora *or* al día *or* por semana *or* al año; **the rate is £5 per hour** = la tarifa es £5 por hora; **he makes about £250 per month** = gana unas £250 al mes; **we pay £10 per hour** = pagamos £10 por hora; **the car was travelling at twenty-five miles per hour** = el coche iba a cuarenta kilómetros por hora; **the earnings per share** = los beneficios por acción; **the average sales per representative** = el promedio de ventas por representante; **per head** = por persona; **allow £15 per head for expenses** = contar con unos gastos de £15 por persona; **representatives cost on average £25,000 per head per annum** = el coste medio de los representantes es de £25.000 anuales por persona y año **(c)** por; **the rate of imperfect items is about twenty-five per thousand** = la proporción de artículos imperfectos es de aproximadamente veinticinco por mil; **the birth rate has fallen to twelve per hundred** = la tasa de natalidad ha bajado a un doce por ciento

◊ **per annum** ['pər 'ænəm] *adverb* al año; **what is their turnover per annum?** = ¿cuál es su volumen de ventas anual *or* al año?

◊ **per capita** ['pə 'kæpɪtə] *adjective & adverb* per cápita; **average income per capita** *or* **per capita income** = la renta media per cápita; **per capita expenditure** = el gasto per cápita

◊ **per cent** ['pə 'sent] *adjective & adverb* por ciento; **10 per cent** = diez por ciento; **what is the increase per cent?** = ¿cuál es el tanto por ciento de aumento?; **fifty per cent of nothing is still nothing** = el cincuenta por ciento de cero sigue siendo cero

◊ **percentage** [pə'sentɪdʒ] *noun* porcentaje *m or* tanto *m* por ciento; **percentage discount** = porcentaje de descuento; **percentage increase** = porcentaje de aumento; **percentage point** = punto porcentual

◊ **percentile** [pə'sentaɪl] *noun* percentil *m*

QUOTE a 100,000 square-foot warehouse generates $600 in sales per square foot of space
Duns Business Month

QUOTE this would represent an 18 per cent growth rate - a slight slackening of the 25 per cent turnover rise in the first half
Financial Times

QUOTE buildings are depreciated at two per cent per annum on the estimated cost of construction
Hongkong Standard

QUOTE state-owned banks cut their prime rates a percentage point to 11%
Wall Street Journal

QUOTE a good percentage of the excess stock was taken up during the last quarter
Australian Financial Review

QUOTE the Federal Reserve Board, signalling its concern about the weakening American economy, cut the discount rate by one-half percentage point to 6.5%
Wall Street Journal

perfect 1 ['pɜːfɪkt] *adjective* perfecto, -ta; **we check each batch to make sure it is perfect** = examinamos cada lote para asegurarnos de que es perfecto; **she did a perfect typing test** = hizo un examen de mecanografía perfecto; *(in economic theory)* **perfect competition** *or* **perfect market** = competencia perfecta *or* mercado perfecto **2** [pə'fekt] *verb* perfeccionar; **he perfected the process for making high grade steel** = perfeccionó el proceso para fabricar acero de alta calidad

◊ **perfectly** ['pɜːfɪkli] *adverb* perfectamente; **she typed the letter perfectly** = mecanografió la carta perfectamente

perform [pə'fɔːm] *verb* actuar *or* comportarse *or* evolucionar; **how did the shares perform?** = ¿cómo evolucionaron las acciones?; **the company** *or* **the shares performed badly** = la compañía *or* las acciones tuvieron una mala actuación

◊ **performance** [pə'fɔːməns] *noun* actuación *f or* comportamiento *m or* funcionamiento *m or* rendimiento *m*; **the poor performance of the shares on the stock market** = el bajo rendimiento de las acciones en la bolsa; **last year saw a dip in the company's performance** = el año pasado se produjo una baja en el rendimiento de la empresa; **as a measure of the company's performance** = como una medida del comportamiento de la empresa; **performance of personnel against objectives** = el rendimiento del personal frente a los objetivos marcados; **performance fund** = fondo de especulación de acciones; **performance-related pay** = pago según rendimiento; **performance review** = revisión del rendimiento en el trabajo; **earnings performance** = el comportamiento de los beneficios; **job performance** = el rendimiento de un trabajo

QUOTE inflation-adjusted GNP edged up at a 1.3% annual rate, its worst performance since the economic expansion began
Fortune

period ['pɪərɪəd] *noun* **(a)** periodo *m or* plazo *m*; **a short period of time** = un rato; **for a period of time** *or* **for a period of months** *or* **for a six-year period** = durante cierto tiempo *or* durante un periodo de meses *or* durante un periodo de seis años; **sales over a period of three months** = las ventas efectuadas durante un periodo de tres meses; **sales over the holiday period** = las ventas efectuadas durante el periodo de vacaciones; **to deposit money for a fixed period** = depositar dinero a plazo fijo **(b)** **accounting period** = periodo contable

◊ **periodic** *or* **periodical** [pɪərɪ'ɒdɪk *or* pɪərɪ'ɒdɪkəl] **1** *adjective* periódico, -ca; **a periodic review of the company's performance** = una revisión periódica del rendimiento de la empresa **2** *noun* **periodical** = publicación *f* periódica *or* revista *f*

peripherals [pə'rɪfərəlz] *plural noun* periféricos *mpl*

perishable ['perɪʃəbl] **1** *adjective* perecedero, -ra; **perishable goods** *or* **items** *or* **cargo** = mercancías perecederas *or* artículos perecederos *or* carga perecedera **2** *plural noun* **perishables** = productos perecederos

perjury ['pɜːdʒəri] *noun* perjurio *m*; **he was sent to prison for perjury** = lo encarcelaron por cometer perjurio; **she appeared in court on a perjury**

charge = compareció ante los tribunales acusada de cometer perjurio

◊ **perjure** ['pɜ:dʒə] *verb* **to perjure yourself** = perjurar *or* dar falso testimonio

perk [pɜ:k] *noun* gratificación *f or* plus *m or* gaje *m*

permanent ['pɜ:mənənt] *adjective* permanente *or* estable; **he has found a permanent job** = ha encontrado un puesto fijo; **she is in permanent employment** = tiene un empleo fijo; **the permanent staff and part-timers** = el personal de plantilla y los empleados a tiempo parcial

◊ **permanency** ['pɜ:mənənsi] *noun* permanencia *f*

◊ **permanently** ['pɜ:mənəntli] *adverb* permanentemente

permission [pə'mɪʃən] *noun* permiso *m or* licencia *f*; **written permission** = permiso por escrito; **verbal permission** = permiso verbal *or* de palabra; **to give someone permission to do something** = dar permiso a alguien para hacer algo; **he asked the manager's permission to take a day off** = solicitó permiso al director para tomarse un día libre

permit 1 ['pɜ:mɪt] *noun* permiso *m or* licencia *f*; **building permit** = permiso para edificar *or* licencia de obras; **export permit** *or* **import permit** = licencia de exportación *or* permiso de importación; **work permit** = permiso de trabajo **2** [pə'mɪt] *verb* permitir; **this document permits you to export twenty-five computer systems** = este documento le permite exportar veinticinco sistemas informáticos; **the ticket permits three people to go into the exhibition** = el billete permite la entrada de tres personas a la exposición

per pro ['pɜ: 'prəʊ] = PER PROCURATIONEM por poder(es); **the secretary signed per pro the manager** = el secretario firmó por poderes del director

per procurationem ['pɜ: prɒkjʊræsi'əʊnəm] *Latin phrase* por poder(es)

perquisites ['pɜ:kwɪzɪts] *plural noun* = PERKS

persistent [pə'sɪstənt] *adjective* persistente *or* continuo, -nua

person ['pɜ:sn] *noun* **(a)** persona *f*; **insurance policy which covers a named person** = póliza de seguros nominativa; **the persons named in the contract** = las personas mencionadas en el contrato; **the document should be witnessed by a third person** = un tercero debería dar fe del documento **(b)** **in person** = en persona; **this important package is to be delivered to the chairman in person** = este importante paquete debe ser entregado al presidente en persona; **he came to see me in person** = vino a verme personalmente

◊ **person-to-person call** ['pɜ:sntə'pɜ:sn 'kɔ:l] *noun* conferencia *f* personal

◊ **personal** ['pɜ:sənl] *adjective* **(a)** *(referring to one person)* personal; **personal allowances** = deducciones personales; **personal assets** = bienes personales; **personal call** = *(private call)* comunicación personal; *(person-to-person call)* llamada telefónica de persona a persona; **staff are not allowed to make personal calls during office hours** = las llamadas personales no están permitidas durante horas de oficina; **personal computer (PC)** = ordenador personal; **personal effects** *or* **personal property** = efectos personales *or* bienes personales; **personal income** = renta personal; **apart from the family shares, he has a personal shareholding in the company** = además de las acciones familiares, tiene una participación personal en la sociedad; **the car is for his personal use** = el coche es para su uso personal **(b)** *(private)* personal; **I want to see the director on a personal matter** = quiero ver al director por un asunto personal; **personal assistant (PA)** = secretario, -ria personal

◊ **Personal Equity Plan (PEP)** ['pɜ:sənl 'ekwɪti 'plæn] *noun* plan de inversión personalizado

◊ **Personal Identification Number (PIN)** ['pɜ:sənl aɪdentɪfɪ'keɪʃn 'nʌmbə] *noun* número personal de identificación (NPI)

◊ **Personal Investment Authority (PIA)** ['pɜ:snl ɪn'vestmənt ɔ:'θɒrɪti] autoridades que regulan la inversión privada

◊ **personalized** ['pɜ:snəlaɪzd] *adjective (with a name or initials)* con el nombre *or* las iniciales de la persona *or* personalizado, -da; **personalized cheques** = cheques con el nombre del librador impreso; **personalized briefcase** = cartera que lleva el nombre *or* las iniciales del propietario

◊ **personally** ['pɜ:snəli] *adverb* personalmente *or* en persona *or* uno mismo; **he personally opened the envelope** = él mismo abrió el sobre; **she wrote to me personally** = me escribió personalmente

personnel [pɜ:sə'nel] *noun* personal *m*; **the personnel of the warehouse** *or* **the warehouse personnel** = el personal del almacén; **the personnel department** = el departamento de personal; **personnel management** = dirección de personal; **personnel manager** *or* **personnel officer** *or* **head of personnel** = director, -ra de personal *or* jefe, -fa de personal

persuade [pə'sweɪd] *verb* persuadir *or* convencer; **after ten hours of discussion, they persuaded the MD to resign** = tras una discusión de diez horas, persuadieron al director gerente a que dimitiera; **we could not persuade the French company to sign the contract** = no pudimos persuadir a la empresa francesa para que firmara el contrato

Peru [pə'ru:] *noun* Perú *m*

◊ **Peruvian** [pə'ru:viən] *adjective & noun* peruano, -na
NOTE: capital: **Lima**; currency: **Peruvian inti (I/.)** = inti peruano (I/.)

peseta [pə'seɪtə] *noun* peseta *f* (NOTE: usually written **Ptas.** *or* **ptas.** after a figure: **2,000 ptas.**)

peso ['peɪsəʊ] *noun (money used in many countries of South America)* peso *m*

pessimism ['pesɪmɪzəm] *noun* pesimismo *m*; **market pessimism** *or* **pessimism on the market** = pesimismo en el mercado; **there is considerable pessimism about job opportunities** = reina un gran pesimismo sobre las posibilidades de encontrar trabajo

◊ **pessimistic** [pesɪ'mɪstɪk] *adjective* pesimista;

he takes a pessimistic view of the exchange rate = tiene una visión pesimista del tipo de cambio

peter out ['piːtə 'aʊt] *verb* agotarse *or* desaparecer

> QUOTE economists believe the economy is picking up this quarter and will do better in the second half of the year, but most expect growth to peter out next year
> **Sunday Times**

Peter principle ['piːtə 'prɪnsəpl] *noun* ley de Peter (según la cual una persona es ascendida hasta ocupar un puesto para el que es incompetente)

> COMMENT: a law, based on wide experience, that people are promoted until they occupy positions for which they are incompetent

petition [pə'tɪʃən] **1** *noun* petición *f or* solicitud *f*; **to file a petition in bankruptcy** = declararse en quiebra *or* presentar una declaración de quiebra **2** *verb* solicitar *or* presentar una solicitud; **he petitioned the government for a special pension** = solicitó una pensión especial al gobierno

petrocurrency ['petrəʊ'kʌrənsi] *noun* divisas obtenidas con la exportación de petróleo

petrodollar ['petrəʊ'dɒlə] *noun* petrodólar *m*

petrol ['petrəl] *noun* gasolina *f*; **the car is very economic on petrol** = el coche consume poca gasolina; **we are looking for a car with a low petrol consumption** = buscamos un coche que consuma poca gasolina (NOTE: no plural for **petrol**; US English is **gasoline** or **gas**)

◊ **petroleum** [pə'trəʊljəm] *noun* petróleo *m*; **crude petroleum** = petróleo crudo; **petroleum exporting countries** = países exportadores de petróleo; **petroleum industry** = industria petrolífera; **petroleum products** = productos derivados del petróleo; **petroleum revenues** = renta del petróleo

petty ['peti] *adjective* insignificante *or* de poca importancia; **petty cash** = fondo *or* dinero para gastos menores; **petty cash book** = libro de caja auxiliar *or* para gastos menores; **petty cash box (PCB)** = caja para gastos menores; **petty cash voucher** = comprobante de caja; **petty expenses** = gastos menores

phase [feɪz] *noun* fase *f*; **the first phase of the expansion programme** = la primera fase del programa de expansión

◊ **phase in** ['feɪz 'ɪn] *verb* introducir gradualmente; **the new invoicing system will be phased in over the next two months** = el nuevo sistema de facturación será introducido gradualmente en los próximos dos meses

◊ **phase out** ['feɪz 'aʊt] *verb* reducir *or* hacer desaparecer *or* retirar gradualmente; **Smith Ltd will be phased out as a supplier of spare parts** = prescindiremos gradualmente de Smith Ltd como proveedor de piezas de recambio

> QUOTE the budget grants a tax exemption for $500,000 in capital gains, phased in over the next six years
> **Toronto Star**

Philippines ['fɪlɪpiːnz] *noun* Filipinas *fpl*

◊ **Filipino** [fɪlɪ'piːnəʊ] *adjective & noun* filipino, -na
NOTE: capital: **Manila**; currency: **Philippine peso (P)** = peso filipino (P)

phoenix syndrome *or* **phoenix company** ['fiːnɪks 'sɪndrəʊm *or* 'fiːnɪks 'kʌmpəni] *noun* síndrome del fénix *or* compañía fénix (término para denotar una empresa que cierra dejando deudas y cuyos consejeros forman otra empresa idéntica con un nombre algo diferente para continuar el negocio)

> QUOTE the prosecution follows recent calls for a reform of insolvency legislation to prevent directors from leaving behind a trail of debt while continuing to trade in phoenix companies - businesses which fold only to rise again, often under a slightly different name in the hands of the same directors and management
> **Financial Times**

phone [fəʊn] **1** *noun* teléfono *m*; **we had a new phone system installed last week** = nos instalaron una nueva red telefónica la semana pasada; **house phone** *or* **internal phone** = teléfono interno; **by phone** = por teléfono; **to place an order by phone** = hacer un pedido por teléfono; **to be on the phone** = hablar por teléfono; **she has been on the phone all morning** = ha estado hablando por teléfono toda la mañana; **he spoke to the manager on the phone** = habló por teléfono con el director; **phone book** = guía telefónica; **look up his address in the phone book** = busque su dirección en la guía telefónica; **phone call** = llamada telefónica; **to make a phone call** = hacer una llamada telefónica; **to answer the phone** *or* **to take a phone call** = contestar al teléfono; **card phone** = teléfono de tarjeta; **cordless phone** = teléfono inalámbrico; **phone number** = número de teléfono; **he keeps a list of phone numbers in a little black book** = tiene una lista de números de teléfono en una pequeña libreta negra; **the phone number is on the company notepaper** = el número de teléfono está impreso en el papel de la compañía; **can you give me your phone number?** = ¿puede darme su número de teléfono? **2** *verb* telefonear *or* llamar por teléfono; **to phone someone** = llamar a alguien por teléfono *or* telefonear a alguien; **don't phone me, I'll phone you** = no me llames, ya te llamaré; **his secretary phoned to say he would be late** = su secretaria llamó para decir que él llegaría tarde; **he phoned the order through to the warehouse** = hizo el pedido al almacén por teléfono; **to phone for something** = telefonear *or* llamar para pedir algo; **he phoned for a taxi** = telefoneó para pedir un taxi; **to phone about something** = telefonear para hablar de algo; **he phoned about the January invoice** = telefoneó para hablar de la factura de enero

◊ **phone back** ['fəʊn 'bæk] *verb* volver a telefonear *or* llamar; **the chairman is in a meeting, can you phone back in about half an hour?** = el presidente está en una reunión, ¿puede Vd. volver a llamar dentro de una media hora?; **Mr Smith called while you were out and asked if you would phone him back** = el Sr. Smith telefoneó mientras Vd. estaba fuera y pidió que le volviera a llamar

◊ **phonecard** ['fəʊnkɑːd] *noun* tarjeta telefónica

photocopier ['fəʊtəʊkɒpɪə] *noun* fotocopiadora *f*

◊ **photocopy** ['fəʊtəʊkɒpi] **1** *noun* fotocopia *f*; **authenticated photocopy** = fotocopia compulsada; **make six photocopies of the contract** = haga seis fotocopias del contrato **2** *verb* fotocopiar *or* hacer fotocopias; **she photocopied the contract** = fotocopió el contrato

◊ **photocopying** ['fəʊtəʊkɒpɪɪŋ] *noun* fotocopiaje *m or* fotocopia *f*; **photocopying costs are rising each year** = los costes de las fotocopias aumentan cada año; **photocopying bureau** = despacho que ofrece el servicio de fotocopias; **there is a mass of photocopying to be done** = hay un montón de fotocopias por hacer

◊ **photostat** ['fəʊtəʊstæt] **1** *noun (trademark for a type of photocopy)* fotostato *m or* copia fotostática **2** *verb* hacer una copia fotostática *or* fotostatar

physical ['fɪzɪkl] *adjective* físico, -ca; **physical inventory** = inventario físico; **physical stock** = existencias físicas; **physical stock check** *or* **physical stocktaking** = control de existencias físicas

PIA = PERSONAL INVESTMENT AUTHORITY

pick [pɪk] **1** *noun* elección *f*; **take your pick** = escoja el que quiera *or* elija a su gusto; **the pick of the group** = lo mejor del grupo **2** *verb* elegir *or* escoger; **the board picked the finance director to succeed the retiring MD** = el consejo de administración eligió al director financiero como sucesor del director gerente; **the Association has picked Barcelona for its next meeting** = la asociación ha elegido Barcelona para su próxima reunión

◊ **picking** ['pɪkɪŋ] *noun* **order picking** = selección *f* de artículos para preparar un pedido; **picking list** = inventario de posición (en almacén)

◊ **pick out** ['pɪk 'aʊt] *verb* escoger *or* elegir; **he was picked out for promotion by the chairman** = el presidente le eligió para un ascenso

◊ **pick up** ['pɪk 'ʌp] *verb* **(a) to pick up the phone** = descolgar *or* contestar el teléfono **(b)** *(do better)* recuperarse *or* mejorar; **business** *or* **trade is picking up** = el negocio *or* el comercio se está recuperando

◊ **pickup** ['pɪkʌp] *noun* **pickup (truck)** = camioneta *f or* furgoneta *f* de reparto; **pickup and delivery service** = servicio de recogida y reparto

picket ['pɪkɪt] **1** *noun* piquete *m* de huelga; **flying pickets** = piquete móvil; **picket line** = piquete de vigilancia a la entrada de una fábrica; **to man a picket line** *or* **to be on the picket line** = estar en el piquete de vigilancia a la entrada de una fábrica; **to cross a picket line** = cruzar un piquete de vigilancia a la entrada de una fábrica **2** *verb* **to picket a factory** = formar piquetes a la entrada de una fábrica

◊ **picketing** ['pɪkɪtɪŋ] *noun* formación *f* de piquetes laborales; **lawful picketing** = formación de piquetes laborales en una huelga legal; **mass picketing** = formación de piquetes de huelga en masa; **peaceful picketing** = formación de piquetes pacíficos; **secondary picketing** = formación de piquetes subsidiarios

piece [pi:s] *noun* pieza *f or* pedazo *m or* trozo *m or*

unidad *f*; **to sell something by the piece** = vender algo por unidades; **the price is 25p the piece** = el precio es de 25p por pieza; **mailing piece** = folleto *m* publicitario enviado por correo

◊ **piece rate** ['pi:s 'reɪt] *noun* tarifa *f* por pieza unitaria *or* a destajo; **to earn piece rates** = cobrar a destajo

◊ **piecework** ['pi:swɜ:k] *noun* trabajo *m* a destajo

pie chart ['paɪ 'tʃɑ:t] *noun* gráfico *m* circular *or* sectorial

pigeonhole ['pɪdʒɪnhəʊl] **1** *noun* casillero *m* **2** *verb* dar carpetazo a algo; **the whole expansion plan was pigeonholed** = se dio carpetazo al plan de expansión

piggybank ['pɪgibæŋk] *noun* hucha *f*

pile [paɪl] **1** *noun* pila *f or* montón *m*; **the Managing Director's desk is covered with piles of paper** = la mesa del director gerente está cubierta de papeles; **she put the letter on the pile of letters waiting to be signed** = puso la carta en el montón de cartas pendientes de firma **2** *verb* apilar *or* amontonar; **he piled the papers on his desk** = amontonó los papeles sobre su mesa

◊ **pile up** ['paɪl 'ʌp] *verb* amontonarse *or* acumularse; **the invoices were piling up on the table** = las facturas se acumulaban sobre la mesa; **complaints are piling up about the after-sales service** = se están amontonando reclamaciones sobre el servicio de posventa

pilferage *or* **pilfering** ['pɪlfərɪdʒ *or* 'pɪlfərɪŋ] *noun* pequeño hurto *m or* robo *m*

pilot ['paɪlət] **1** *noun (person)* piloto *m* **2** *adjective (used as a test)* piloto *or* experimental; **the company set up a pilot project to see if the proposed manufacturing system was efficient** = la compañía introdujo un plan piloto *or* programa experimental para comprobar si el sistema de fabricación propuesto era eficaz; **the pilot factory has been built to test the new production processes** = la fábrica piloto ha sido construida para probar los nuevos procesos productivos; **he is directing a pilot scheme for training unemployed young people** = está dirigiendo un programa piloto para formar a jóvenes desempleados **3** *verb* **(a)** *(to guide a ship into port)* pilotar **(b)** *(to test a project)* pilotar *or* poner un proyecto a prueba

PIN (number) [pɪn ('nʌmbə)] = PERSONAL IDENTIFICATION NUMBER

pin [pɪn] **1** *noun* alfiler *m*; **drawing pin** = chincheta *f*; **she used drawing pins to pin the poster to the door** = sujetó el cartel en la puerta con chinchetas; **pin money** = pequeñas cantidades de dinero para gastos personales **2** *verb* sujetar *or* prender con alfileres; **she pinned the papers together** = sujetó los papeles con un alfiler; **pin your cheque to the application form** = sujete su cheque a la solicitud con una grapa

◊ **pin money** ['pɪn 'mʌni] *noun* dinero *m* para pequeños gastos; **she does some typing at home to earn some pin money** = hace trabajos de mecanografía en casa para ganar un poco de dinero

◊ **pin up** ['pɪn 'ʌp] *verb* fijar en la pared con

chinchetas; **they pinned the posters up at the back of the exhibition stand** = fijaron los carteles con chinchetas en la parte posterior del stand de la exposición

pint [paɪnt] *noun (measure of liquids* = *0.568 of a litre in the UK, or 0.473 of a litre in the USA)* pinta *f*

pioneer [paɪə'nɪə] **1** *noun* pionero, -ra; **pioneer project** *or* **pioneer development** = proyecto pionero *or* desarrollo pionero **2** *verb* iniciar *or* promover *or* abrir camino; **the company pioneered developments in the field of electronics** = la compañía abrió el camino a nuevos adelantos en el campo de la electrónica

pirate ['paɪərət] **1** *noun* pirata *mf*; **a pirate copy of a book** = copia pirata de un libro **2** *verb* piratear *or* hacer una edición pirata de; **a pirated book** *or* **a pirated design** = edición pirata de un libro *or* diseño pirata; **the designs for the new dress collection were pirated in the Far East** = los diseños para la nueva colección de vestidos fueron copiados ilegalmente en Extremo Oriente

◊ **piracy** ['paɪərəsi] *noun* piratería *f*

pit [pɪt] *noun* **(a)** *(mine or hole)* mina *f or* foso *m* **(b)** *(stock exchange) US* patio *m* (de operaciones de la bolsa) *or* corro *m* (NOTE: UK English is **trading floor**)

pitch [pɪtʃ] *noun* **sales pitch** = rollo *m* publicitario

pix [pɪks] *plural noun (informal)* imágenes *fpl*

place [pleɪs] **1** *noun* **(a)** *(site)* lugar *m or* sitio *m*; **to take place** = ocurrir *or* suceder *or* tener lugar; **the meeting will take place in our offices** = la reunión tendrá lugar en nuestras oficinas; **meeting place** = lugar de reunión; **place of work** = lugar de trabajo **(b)** *(position in a competition)* lugar *or* posición *f or* puesto *m*; **three companies are fighting for first place in the home computer market** = tres empresas luchan *or* compiten por el primer lugar en el mercado nacional de ordenadores **(c)** *(job)* puesto *m or* empleo *m*; **he was offered a place with an insurance company** = le ofrecieron un puesto en una compañía de seguros; **she turned down three places before accepting the one we offered** = rechazó tres empleos antes de aceptar el que le ofrecimos **(d)** *(position in a text)* página *f or* punto *m or* lugar *m*; **she marked her place in the text with a red pen** = marcó la página hasta donde había llegado con un bolígrafo rojo; **I have lost my place and cannot remember where I have reached in my filing** = he perdido el hilo y no puedo recordar hasta dónde había archivado **2** *verb* **(a)** poner *or* colocar; **to place money in an account** = colocar dinero en una cuenta; **to place a block of shares** = colocar un paquete de acciones; **to place a contract** = adjudicar un contrato; **to place something on file** = archivar algo **(b)** **to place an order** = cursar un pedido; **he placed an order for 250 cartons of paper** = cursó un pedido de 250 cajas de papel **(c)** **to place staff** = colocar a empleados; **how are you placed for work?** = ¿cómo andas de trabajo?

◊ **placement** ['pleɪsmənt] *noun* **(a)** *(job)* colocación *f* **(b)** *(study)* prácticas *fpl* de trabajo

◊ **placing** ['pleɪsɪŋ] *noun* **the placing of a line of shares** = la colocación de una emisión de acciones

plain [pleɪn] *adjective* **(a)** *(easy to understand)* claro, -ra *or* evidente; **we made it plain to the union**

that 5% was the management's final offer = explicamos claramente al sindicato que el 5% era la última oferta de la dirección; **the manager is a very plain-spoken man** = el director es un hombre que habla muy claro **(b)** *(simple)* simple *or* sencillo, -lla *or* liso, -sa; **the design of the package is in plain blue and white squares** = el diseño del paquete es a cuadros lisos azules y blancos; **we want the cheaper models to have a plain design** = queremos que los modelos baratos tengan un diseño sencillo

◊ **plain cover** ['pleɪn 'kʌvə] *noun* **to send something under plain cover** = enviar algo en un sobre corriente

plaintiff ['pleɪntɪf] *noun* demandante *mf or* querellante *mf*

plan [plæn] **1** *noun* **(a)** *(project)* plan *m or* proyecto *m*; **contingency plan** = plan de emergencia; **the government's economic plans** = los proyectos económicos del gobierno; **a Five-Year Plan** = un plan quinquenal **(b)** *(way of saving or investing money)* plan; **investment plan** = plan de inversiones; **pension plan** = plan de pensiones; **savings plan** = plan de ahorro **(c)** *(drawing)* plano *m*; **the designers showed us the first plans for the new offices** = los delineantes nos enseñaron los primeros planos de las nuevas oficinas; **floor plan** = planta *f*; **street plan** *or* **town plan** = plano de la ciudad **2** *verb* planear *or* proyectar *or* planificar *or* hacer un plan; **to plan for an increase in bank interest charges** = planear un aumento de los intereses bancarios; **to plan investments** = planificar las inversiones (NOTE: **planning - planned**)

◊ **planned** [plænd] *adjective* **planned economy** = economía planificada

◊ **planner** ['plænə] *noun* **(a)** planificador, -ra; **the government's economic planners** = los planificadores económicos del gobierno **(b)** **desk planner** *or* **wall planner** = diagrama *m* de planificación *or* calendario *m* de trabajo

◊ **planning** ['plænɪŋ] *noun* **(a)** planificación *f*; **long-term planning** *or* **short-term planning** = planificación a largo plazo *or* planificación a corto plazo; **economic planning** = planificación económica; **corporate planning** = planificación empresarial; **manpower planning** = planificación de la mano de obra **(b)** *GB* **planning permission** = permiso de construcción; **to refuse someone planning permission** = denegar a alguien la licencia de construcción; **we are waiting for planning permission before we can start building** = estamos esperando el permiso de construcción para empezar las obras; **the land is to be sold with planning permission** = el terreno ha de venderse con licencia de construcción; **the planning department** = departamento de planificación urbana

QUOTE the benefits package is attractive and the compensation plan includes base, incentive and car allowance totalling $50,000+
Globe and Mail (Toronto)

QUOTE buildings are closely regulated by planning restrictions
Investors Chronicle

plane [pleɪn] *noun* avión *m*; **I plan to take the 5**

o'clock plane to New York = pienso coger el avión de Nueva York que sale a las 5; he could not get a seat on Tuesday's plane, so he had to wait until Wednesday = no pudo conseguir una plaza en el avión del martes y por eso tuvo que esperar hasta el miércoles; there are ten planes a day from London to Madrid = hay diez aviones al día entre Londres y Madrid

plant [plɑːnt] *noun* **(a)** *(machinery)* maquinaria *f*; **plant-hire firm** = empresa de alquiler de maquinaria (NOTE: no plural in this meaning) **(b)** *(large factory)* planta *f or* fábrica *f*; **they are planning to build a car plant near the river** = piensan construir una fábrica de coches cerca del río; **to set up a new plant** = instalar una nueva planta; **they closed down six plants in the north of the country** = cerraron seis fábricas en el norte del país; **he was appointed plant manager** = le nombraron director de la fábrica

plastic money [ˈplæstɪk ˈmʌni] *noun* dinero de plástico *or* monedero electrónico *or* tarjeta de crédito

platform [ˈplætfɔːm] *noun* **(a)** *(train)* andén *m*; **the train for Birmingham leaves from Platform 12** = el tren para Birmingham sale del andén 12; **the ticket office is on Platform 2** = la taquilla está en el andén 2 **(b)** **oil platform** = plataforma petrolífera

PLC *or* **plc** [piːelˈsiː] = PUBLIC LIMITED COMPANY Sociedad Anónima (S.A.)

plead [pliːd] *verb* defender *or* alegar

pledge [pledʒ] **1** *noun* prenda *f or* garantía *f or* empeño *m*; **to redeem a pledge** = rescatar una prenda; **unredeemed pledge** = prenda no rescatada *or* sin desempeñar **2** *verb* **to pledge share certificates** = pignorar acciones

plenary meeting *or* **plenary session** [ˈpliːnəri ˈmiːtɪŋ *or* ˈpliːnəri ˈseʃn] *noun* reunión plenaria *or* sesión plenaria

plot [plɒt] *noun* **plot of land** *or* **building plot** = terreno *or* solar para edificar

plough back *or* US **plow back** [plaʊˈbæk] *verb* **to plough back profits into the company** = invertir los beneficios en la propia empresa

plug [plʌg] **1** *noun* **(a)** *(electricity)* enchufe *m*; **the printer is supplied with a plug** = la impresora va provista de un enchufe **(b)** **to give a plug to a new product** = dar publicidad a un nuevo producto **2** *verb* **(a)** *(electricity)* **to plug in** = enchufar; **the computer was not plugged in** = el ordenador no estaba enchufado **(b)** *(advertise)* dar publicidad; **they ran six commercials plugging holidays in Spain** = emitieron seis espacios publicitarios que recomendaban las vacaciones en España **(c)** *(stop)* detener *or* frenar; **the company is trying to plug the drain on cash reserves** = la empresa está intentando frenar la sangría de las reservas de caja (NOTE: **plugging - plugged**)

plummet *or* **plunge** [ˈplʌmɪt *or* plʌn(d)ʒ] *verb* caer en picado; **share prices plummeted** *or* **plunged on the news of the devaluation** = las cotizaciones de las acciones cayeron en picado ante la noticia de la devaluación

plus [plʌs] **1** *preposition* **(a)** *(in addition to)* más; **his salary plus commission comes to more than £25,000** = su sueldo más la comisión asciende a más de £25.000; **production costs plus overheads are higher than revenue** = los costes de producción más los gastos generales son superiores a los ingresos **(b)** *(more than)* más de; **houses valued at £100,000 plus** = casas valoradas en más de £100.000 **2** *adjective* positivo, -va; **a plus factor for the company** is that the market is much larger than they had originally thought = un factor positivo para la compañía es que el mercado es mucho mayor de lo que en un principio se había creído; **the plus side of the account** = el lado del haber; **on the plus side** = por el lado positivo; **on the plus side, we must take into account the new product line** = por el lado positivo, debemos tener en cuenta la nueva gama de productos **3** *noun* tanto *m*; **to have achieved £1m in new sales in less than six months is certainly a plus for the sales team** = haber conseguido £1 millón de nuevas ventas en menos de seis meses es ciertamente un tanto para el equipo de ventas

p.m. *or* US **P.M.** [piːˈem] *adverb* de la tarde *or* de la noche; **the train leaves at 6.50 p.m.** = el tren sale a las 6.50 de la tarde; **if you phone New York after 6 p.m. the calls are at a cheaper rate** = las llamadas a Nueva York después de las 6 de la tarde son más baratas

PO [piːˈəʊ] = POST OFFICE

pocket [ˈpɒkɪt] **1** *noun* bolsillo *m or* bolsa *f*; **pocket calculator** *or* **pocket diary** = calculadora de bolsillo *or* diario de bolsillo; **pocket edition** = edición de bolsillo; **to be £25 in pocket** = haber obtenido un beneficio de £25; **to be £25 out of pocket** = haber perdido £25; **out-of-pocket expenses** = desembolsos efectuados por un empleado de su propio bolsillo **2** *verb* embolsar

point [pɔɪnt] **1** *noun* **(a)** punto *m or* lugar *m*; **point of sale (POS)** = punto de venta; **point of sale material** = publicidad en el punto de venta; **breakeven point** = punto de muerto *or* umbral de rentabilidad; **customs entry point** = puesto *m* aduanero; **starting point** = punto de partida; **tax point** = punto *or* fecha de vencimiento del IVA **(b)** **decimal point** = punto *or* coma decimal; **percentage point** = punto porcentual; **half a percentage point** = medio punto porcentual; **the dollar gained two points** = el dólar ganó dos puntos; **the exchange fell ten points** = el cambio bajó diez puntos **2** *verb* **to point at** = apuntar a; **to point out** = señalar; **the report points out the mistakes made by the company over the last year** = el informe señala los errores cometidos por la compañía durante el año pasado; **he pointed out that the results were better than in previous years** = indicó que los resultados eran mejores que en años anteriores

QUOTE sterling M3, the most closely watched measure, rose by 13% in the year to August - seven percentage points faster than the rate of inflation
Economist

QUOTE banks refrained from quoting forward US/Hongkong dollar exchange rates as premiums as premiums of 100 points replaced discounts of up to 50 points
South China Morning Post

poison pill ['pɔɪzn 'pɪl] *noun* acción *f* tomada por una compañía para desalentar una posible OPA

COMMENT: in some cases, the officers of a company will vote themselves extremely high redundancy payments if a takeover is successful; or a company will borrow large amounts of money and give it away to the shareholders as dividends, so that the company has an unacceptably high level of borrowing

Poland ['pəʊlənd] *noun* Polonia *f*

◊ **Pole** [pəʊl] *noun* polaco, -ca

◊ **Polish** ['pəʊlɪʃ] *adjective* polaco, -ca *or* polonés, -esa
NOTE: capital: **Warsaw** (= Varsovia); currency: **Polish zloty (Zl)** = zloty polaco (Zl)

policy ['pɒlɪsi] *noun* **(a)** política *f*; **government policy on wages** *or* **government wages policy** = la política salarial del gobierno; **the government's prices policy** *or* **incomes policy** = la política gubernamental de precios *or* de rentas; **the country's economic policy** = la política económica del país; **the government made a policy statement** *or* **made a statement of policy** = el gobierno hizo una declaración programática *or* de política; **budgetary policy** = política presupuestaria **(b) company policy** = política *or* normas de una empresa; **a company's trading policy** = la política comercial de una empresa; **what is the company policy on credit?** = ¿cuál es la política de la empresa en materia de crédito?; **it is against company policy to give more than thirty days' credit** = va en contra de las normas de la compañía conceder más de treinta días de crédito; **our policy is to submit all contracts to the legal department** = tenemos por norma que la asesoría jurídica examine todos los contratos **(c) insurance policy** = póliza de seguros; **an accident policy** = una póliza de accidentes; **all-risks policy** = póliza a todo riesgo; **a comprehensive** *or* **an all-in policy** = póliza a todo riesgo; **contingent policy** = póliza para imprevistos; **endowment policy** = póliza dotal; **policy holder** = tenedor, -ra de una póliza de seguros; **to take out a policy** = hacerse un seguro; **she took out a life insurance policy** *or* **a house insurance policy** = suscribió un seguro de vida *or* un seguro de su casa; **the insurance company made out a policy** *or* **drew up a policy** = la compañía de seguros extendió una póliza

polite [pə'laɪt] *adjective* educado, -da *or* cortés *or* atento, -ta; **we stipulate that our salesgirls must be polite to customers** = estipulamos que nuestras vendedoras deben ser atentas con los clientes; **we had a polite letter from the MD** = recibimos una atenta carta del director gerente

◊ **politely** [pə'laɪtli] *adverb* con cortesía *or* con educación *or* atentamente; **she politely answered the customers' questions** = contestó con cortesía a las preguntas de los clientes

political [pə'lɪtɪkəl] *adjective* político, -ca; **political levy** = contribución política *or* impuesto político; **political party** = partido político

politician [pɒlɪ'tɪʃən] *noun* político, -ca

poll [pəʊl] **1** *noun* **opinion poll** = encuesta *f or* sondeo *m* de opinión; **opinion polls showed the public preferred butter to margarine** = los sondeos de opinión mostraron que el público prefería la mantequilla a la margarina; **before starting the service the company carried out a nationwide opinion poll** = antes de empezar el servicio la empresa realizó encuestas de opinión por todo el país **2** *verb* **to poll a sample of the population** = sondear a una muestra de la población; **to poll the members of the club on an issue** = sondear a los miembros de un club sobre una cuestión

◊ **pollster** ['pəʊlstə] *noun* analista *mf* profesional de opinión pública

polystyrene [pɒlɪ'staɪriːn] *noun* **expanded polystyrene** = poliestireno expandido; **the computer is delivered packed in expanded polystyrene** = el ordenador se entrega embalado en poliestireno expandido

pool [puːl] **1** *noun* **(a) typing pool** = sección *f* de mecanografía **(b)** *(unused supply)* reserva *f*; **a pool of unemployed labour** *or* **of expertise** = una reserva de mano de obra desempleada *or* de conocimientos técnicos **2** *verb* **to pool resources** = reunir recursos

poor [pɔː] *adjective* **(a)** *(without much money)* pobre *or* necesitado, -da; **the company tries to help the poorest members of staff with soft loans** = la empresa trata de ayudar a los empleados más necesitados con préstamos sin interés; **it is one of the poorest countries in the world** = es uno de los países más pobres del mundo **(b)** *(not very good)* malo, -la *or* deficiente; **poor quality** = mala calidad; **poor service** = servicio deficiente; **poor turnround time of orders** *or* **poor order turnround time** = retraso en servir pedidos *or* tardar mucho en servir un pedido

◊ **poorly** ['pɔːli] *adverb* mal; **the offices are poorly laid out** = las oficinas están mal distribuidas; **the plan was poorly presented** = el plan se presentó mal; **poorly-paid staff** = personal mal pagado

popular ['pɒpjʊlə] *adjective* popular; **this is our most popular model** = éste es nuestro modelo más popular; **the South Coast is the most popular area for holidays** = la costa del sur es la zona más popular para las vacaciones; **popular prices** = precios populares

population [pɒpjʊ'leɪʃən] *noun* población *f*; **Valencia has a population of over one million** = Valencia tiene una población de más de un millón de habitantes; **the working population** = la población activa; **population statistics** = estadística demográfica; **population trends** = tendencias demográficas; **floating population** = población flotante

port [pɔːt] *noun* **(a)** *(harbour)* puerto *m*; **the port of Rotterdam** = el puerto de Rotterdam; **inland port** =

puerto interior; **to call at a port** = arribar *or* hacer escala en un puerto; **port authority** = autoridades portuarias; **port of call** = puerto de escala *or* de arribada; **port charges** *or* **port dues** = derechos de dársena *or* portuarios; **port of embarkation** = puerto de embarque; **port installations** = instalaciones portuarias; **commercial port** = puerto comercial; **fishing port** = puerto pesquero; **free port** = puerto franco **(b)** *(part of a computer)* conexión *f*

portable ['pɔːtəbl] **1** *adjective* portátil; **a portable computer** *or* **a portable typewriter** = un ordenador portátil *or* una máquina de escribir portátil; **portable pension** = derecho a pensión que se le reconoce a un trabajador aun cuando cambie de empresa **2** *noun* **a portable** = un objeto portátil

QUOTE from 1 July, new provisions concerning portable pensions will come into effect
Personnel Management

porter ['pɔːtə] *noun* conserje *m or* portero *m*

portfolio [pɔːt'fəʊljəʊ] *noun* **a portfolio of shares** = cartera *f* de valores; **portfolio management** = administración de una cartera de valores

portion ['pɔːʃən] *noun* porción *f or* ración *f*; **we serve ice cream in individual portions** = servimos helado en porciones individuales

Portugal ['pɔːtjʊgəl] *noun* Portugal *m*

◊ **Portuguese** [pɔːtjʊ'giːz] *adjective & noun* portugués, -esa *or* lusitano, -na *or* luso, -sa
NOTE: capital: **Lisbon** (= Lisboa); currency: **Portuguese escudo (Esc)** = escudo portugués (Esc)

POS *or* **p.o.s.** ['piːəʊ'es] = POINT OF SALE punto de venta

position [pə'zɪʃən] *noun* **(a)** *(state of affairs)* posición *f or* situación *f or* postura *f or* actitud *f*; **what is the cash position?** = ¿cuál es la situación de caja?; **bargaining position** = postura negociadora; **to cover a position** = reservar dinero para un pago futuro de acciones **(b)** *(job)* puesto *m or* cargo *m or* plaza *f*; **to apply for a position as manager** = solicitar el cargo de director; **we have several positions vacant** = tenemos varios puestos vacantes; **all the vacant positions have been filled** = todos los puestos vacantes han sido cubiertos; **she retired from her position in the accounts department** = se retiró de su cargo del departamento de contabilidad; **he is in a key position** = tiene un puesto clave

positive ['pɒzətɪv] *adjective* positivo, -va; **the board gave a positive reply** = el consejo de administración dio una respuesta positiva; **positive cash flow** = flujo de caja positivo (NOTE: the opposite is **negative**)

QUOTE as the group's shares are already widely held, the listing will be via an introduction. It will also be accompanied by a deeply-discounted £25m rights issue, leaving the company cash positive
Sunday Times

possess [pə'zes] *verb* poseer; **the company possesses property in the centre of the town** = la compañía posee propiedades en el centro de la

ciudad; **he lost all he possessed in the collapse of his company** = perdió todo lo que poseía en el hundimiento de su empresa

◊ **possession** [pə'zeʃən] *noun* **(a)** *(owing)* posesión *f*; **the documents are in his possession** = los documentos están en sus manos; **vacant possession** = desocupado, -da *or* libre de inquilinos; **the property is to be sold with vacant possession** = la propiedad ha de venderse libre de inquilinos (NOTE: no plural) **(b)** **possessions** = propiedades *fpl or* pertenencias *fpl or* bienes *mpl*; **they lost all their possessions in the fire** = perdieron todos sus bienes en el incendio

possible ['pɒsəbl] *adjective* posible; **the 25th and 26th are possible dates for our next meeting** = el 25 y el 26 son las fechas posibles para nuestra próxima reunión; **it is possible that production will be held up by industrial action** = es posible que la producción se vea interrumpida por la huelga; **there are two possible candidates for the job** = hay dos posibles candidatos para el puesto

◊ **possibility** [pɒsə'bɪlətɪ] *noun* posibilidad *f*; **there is a possibility that the plane will be early** = existe la posibilidad de que el avión llegue antes de la hora; **there is no possibility of the chairman retiring before next Christmas** = no hay ninguna posibilidad de que el presidente se retire antes de Navidad

post [pəʊst] **1** *noun* **(a)** *(system of sending letters)* correo *m*; **to send an invoice by post** = enviar una factura por correo; **he put the letter in the post** = echó la carta al correo; **the cheque was lost in the post** = el cheque se perdió en el correo; **to send a reply by return of post** = enviar una respuesta a vuelta de correo; **letter post** *or* **parcel post** = servicio de cartas postales *or* de paquetes postales; **post room** = despacho de distribución del correo (NOTE: US English uses only **mail** where GB English uses both **mail** and **post**) **(b)** *(letters sent or received)* correo; **has the post arrived yet?** = ¿ha llegado ya el correo?; **my secretary opens the post as soon as it arrives** = mi secretaria abre el correo en cuanto llega; **the receipt was in this morning's post** = el recibo estaba en el correo de esta mañana; **the letter did not arrive by first post this morning** = la carta no llegó en el primer correo de esta mañana **(c)** *(job)* puesto *m*; **to apply for a post as cashier** = solicitar un puesto de cajero; **we have three posts vacant** = tenemos tres puestos vacantes; **all our posts have been filled** = todos nuestros puestos han sido cubiertos; **we advertised three posts in the 'Times'** = anunciamos tres puestos en el 'Times' **2** *verb* **(a)** *(to send something by post)* enviar *or* mandar por correo; **to post a letter** *or* **to post a parcel** = mandar una carta *or* enviar un paquete; **to post an entry** = hacer un asiento; **to post up a ledger** = poner al día un libro mayor **(c)** **to post up a notice** = poner un cartel *or* aviso **(d)** **to post an increase** = anunciar un aumento

QUOTE Toronto stocks closed at an all-time high, posting their fifth day of advances in heavy trading
Financial Times

post- [pəʊst] *prefix* post; **post-balance sheet event** = operación posterior al balance

postage ['pəʊstɪdʒ] *noun* franqueo *m or* tarifa *f* postal; **what is the postage to Nigeria?** = ¿cuál es la tarifa postal para Nigeria?; **postage and packing (p & p)** = (gastos de) franqueo y embalaje; **postage paid** = franqueo concertado; **postage stamp** = sello de correos

postal ['pəʊstəl] *adjective* postal; **postal charges** *or* **postal rates** = gastos de franqueo *or* tarifas postales; **postal charges are going up by 10% in September** = los gastos de franqueo subirán un 10% en septiembre; **postal order** = giro postal

postcard ['pəʊskɑːd] *noun* tarjeta *f* postal

postcode ['pəʊskəʊd] *noun* código *m* postal (NOTE: US English is **ZIP code)**

postdate ['pəʊs'deɪt] *verb* posfechar *or* poner fecha adelantada *or* posterior a la del día; **he sent us a postdated cheque** = nos mandó un cheque con una fecha futura; **his cheque was postdated to June** = su cheque llevaba fecha del próximo mes de junio

poster ['pəʊstə] *noun* cartel *m or* 'poster' *m*

poste restante ['pəʊst 'restɒnt] *noun* lista *f* de correos; **send any messages to 'Poste Restante, Athens'** = mande todos los mensajes a 'Lista de Correos, Atenas' (NOTE: US English for this is **General Delivery)**

post free ['pəʊst 'friː] *adverb* con porte pagado *or* sin gastos de franqueo; **the game is obtainable post free from the manufacturer** = el fabricante envía el juego con porte pagado

postmark ['pəʊsmɑːk] **1** *noun* matasellos *m*; **letter with a London postmark** = carta con el matasellos de Londres **2** *verb* poner el matasellos; **the letter was postmarked New York** = la carta llevaba el matasellos de Nueva York

post office ['pəʊst 'ɒfɪs] *noun* (a) oficina *f* de correos; **main post office** = oficina central de correos; **sub-post office** = estafeta *f* de correos (b) **the Post Office (the GPO)** = Correos *m*; **Post Office officials** *or* **officials of the Post Office** = funcionarios de Correos; **Post Office staff** = personal de Correos; **Post Office van** = camioneta de correos; **Post Office box number** *or* **PO box number** = apartado de correos; **our address is PO Box 12345 Madrid** = nuestra dirección es: apartado de correos número 12.345, Madrid

postpaid [pəʊs'peɪd] *adjective* porte pagado *or* franqueo concertado; **the price is £5.95 postpaid** = el precio es £5.95 con el franqueo concertado

postpone [pəʊs'pəʊn] *verb* aplazar *or* posponer; **he postponed the meeting to tomorrow** = aplazó la reunión hasta mañana; **they asked if they could postpone payment until the cash situation was better** = preguntaron si podían aplazar el pago hasta que la situación de caja fuera mejor

◇ **postponement** [pəʊs'pəʊnmənt] *noun* aplazamiento *m*; **I had to change my appointments because of the postponement of the board meeting** = tuve que cambiar mis citas por el aplazamiento de la reunión del consejo

post scriptum *or* **postscript (PS)** ['pəʊs 'skrɪptəm *or* 'pəʊskrɪpt] *Latin phrase & noun* post-scriptum *or* nota adicional al final de una carta

potential [pə'tenʃəl] **1** *adjective* potencial *or* eventual; **potential customers** = clientes potenciales *or* eventuales; **there is no shortage of potential customers for the computer** = no hay escasez de clientes potenciales para el ordenador; **potential market** = mercado potencial *or* en potencia; **the product has potential sales of 100,000 units** = el producto tiene unas ventas potenciales de 100.000 unidades; **he is a potential managing director** = es un director gerente en potencia; **as a disincentive to potential tax evaders** = para disuadir a los eventuales evasores fiscales **2** *noun* potencial *m or* capacidad *f or* posibilidades *fpl*; **share with a growth potential** *or* **with a potential for growth** = acción con posibilidades de mejorar su precio; **product with considerable sales potential** = producto con grandes posibilidades de ventas; **to analyze the market potential** = analizar el potencial del mercado; **earning potential** = potencial de rentabilidad

pound [paʊnd] *noun* (a) *(measure of weight = 0.45 kilos)* libra *f* (medida de peso que equivale a 0.45 kilos); **to sell oranges by the pound** = vender naranjas por libras; **a pound of oranges** = una libra de naranjas; **oranges cost 50p a pound** = las naranjas cuestan 50p la libra (NOTE: usually written **lb** after a figure: **25lb) (b)** *(currency)* libra; **pound sterling** = libra esterlina; **a pound coin** = una moneda de una libra; **a five pound note** = un billete de cinco libras; **it costs six pounds** = cuesta seis libras; **the pound/dollar exchange rate** = el tipo de cambio dólar/libra (NOTE: written **£** before a figure: **£25)**

◇ **poundage** ['paʊndɪdʒ] *noun* (i) comisión *f* por cada libra de peso; (ii) impuesto *m* por cada libra de valor

poverty ['pɒvəti] *noun* pobreza *f*

power ['paʊə] *noun* (a) *(strength or ability)* fuerza *f or* poder *m*; **purchasing power** = poder adquisitivo; **the purchasing power of the school market** = el poder adquisitivo del mercado escolar; **the purchasing power of the pound has fallen over the last five years** = el poder adquisitivo de la libra ha bajado durante los últimos cinco años; **the power of a consumer group** = el poder de un grupo de consumidores; **bargaining power** = poder de negociación; **earning power** = capacidad *f* de ganar dinero *or* escala *f* de rendimiento; **he is such a fine designer that his earning power is very large** = es tan buen diseñador que puede ganar mucho dinero; **borrowing power** = capacidad de endeudamiento (b) *(force or legal right)* poder; **executive power** = poder ejecutivo; **power of attorney** = poder notarial *or* poderes *mpl*; **we will apply the full power of the law to get possession of our property again** = aplicaremos todos los recursos que nos ofrece la ley para recuperar la posesión de nuestra propiedad **(c)** *(authority)* facultad *f*; **the chairman has the power to appoint directors** = el presidente tiene facultad para nombrar a los consejeros

p.p. ['piː'piː] *verb* = PER PROCURATIONEM **to p.p. a letter** = firmar la carta por procuración *or* poderes; **the secretary p.p.'d the letter while the manager was at lunch** = la secretaria firmó la carta por poderes mientras el director estaba almorzando

PR ['piː'ɑː] = PUBLIC RELATIONS **PR man** = persona dedicada a las relaciones públicas; **a PR firm is handling all our publicity** = una empresa de relaciones públicas se ocupa de toda nuestra publicidad; **he is working in PR** = trabaja en relaciones públicas; **the PR people gave away 100,000 balloons** = el equipo de relaciones públicas distribuyó 100.000 globos

practice ['præktɪs] *noun* **(a)** práctica *f or* costumbre *f or* uso *m*; **his practice was to arrive at work at 7.30 and start counting the cash** = su costumbre era llegar al trabajo a las 7.30 y empezar a contar la caja; **business practices** *or* **industrial practices** *or* **trade practices** = usos mercantiles *or* prácticas industriales *or* prácticas comerciales; **restrictive practices** = prácticas restrictivas; **sharp practice** = mañas *fpl or* métodos *mpl* poco escrupulosos *or* deshonestos (pero no ilegales); **code of practice** = normas de conducta *or* código de ética profesional **(b) in practice** = en la práctica *or* en la realidad; **the marketing plan seems very interesting, but what will it cost in practice?** = el plan de marketing parece muy interesante, ¿pero qué costará en la práctica?

QUOTE the EC demanded international arbitration over the pricing practices of the provincial boards
Globe and Mail (Toronto)

pre- [pri] *prefix* pre *or* anterior *or* previo, -via; **a pre-stocktaking sale** = una venta antes del inventario; **there will be a pre-AGM board meeting** *or* **there will be a board meeting pre the AGM** = habrá una reunión del Consejo de Administración previa a la junta general anual; **the pre-Christmas period is always very busy** = el periodo justo antes de Navidad siempre es muy activo

precautionary [prɪ'kɔːʃnərɪ] *adjective* **as a precautionary measure** = como medida preventiva

◊ **precautions** [prɪ'kɔːʃənz] *plural noun* prevención *f or* precauciones *fpl*; **to take precautions to prevent thefts in the office** = tomar precauciones para evitar robos en la oficina; **the company did not take proper fire precautions** = la empresa no tomó las debidas precauciones contra incendios; **safety precautions** = medidas *fpl* de seguridad

precinct ['priːsɪŋ(k)t] *noun* **(a)** *(area)* recinto *m*; **pedestrian precinct** *or* **shopping precinct** = zona *f* de peatones *or* zona (comercial) peatonal **(b)** *(administrative area) US* distrito *m*

predecessor ['priːdɪsesə] *noun* predecesor, -ra *or* antecesor, -ra; **he took over from his predecessor**

last May = sustituyó a su predecesor el pasado mes de mayo; **she is using the same office as her predecessor** = utiliza la misma oficina que su antecesora

predict [prɪ'dɪkt] *verb* predecir

QUOTE lower interest rates are a bull factor for the stock market and analysts predict that the Dow Jones average will soon challenge the 1,300 barrier
Financial Times

pre-empt [prɪ'em(p)t] *verb* adelantarse a los acontecimientos para impedir algo *or* prevenir; **they staged a management buyout to pre-empt a takeover bid** = los consejeros organizaron la compra de la sociedad con el fin de impedir una oferta pública de adquisición

◊ **pre-emptive** [prɪ'em(p)tɪv] *adjective* preventivo, -va; **pre-emptive strike against a takeover bid** = una acción rápida para impedir una oferta pública de adquisición; **a pre-emptive right** = derecho preferente del Estado *or* autoridad local para la compra de una propiedad; *US* derecho de tanteo en la compra de acciones

prefer [prɪ'fɜː] *verb* preferir; **we prefer the small corner shop to the large supermarket** = preferimos la pequeña tienda de la esquina al gran supermercado; **most customers prefer to choose clothes themselves, rather than take the advice of the sales assistant** = la mayoría de los clientes prefieren escoger la ropa ellos mismos a seguir el consejo del dependiente

◊ **preference** ['prefrəns] *noun* preferencia *f*; **the customers' preference for small corner shops** = la preferencia de los clientes por la tienda de la esquina; **preference shares** = acciones preferentes; **preference shareholders** = tenedores de acciones preferentes; **cumulative preference share** = acción preferente acumulativa

◊ **preferential** [prefə'renʃəl] *adjective* preferente *or* preferencial; **preferential creditor** = acreedor preferente; **preferential duty** *or* **preferential tariff** = tarifa preferente *or* preferencial; **preferential terms** *or* **preferential treatment** = términos preferentes *or* trato preferencial; **subsidiary companies get preferential treatment when it comes to subcontracting work** = las empresas filiales obtienen un trato preferente cuando hay que dar trabajo a contrata

◊ **preferred** [prɪ'fɜːd] *adjective* **preferred creditor** = acreedor preferente; **preferred shares** *US* **preferred stock** = acciones preferentes; *US* **cumulative preferred stock** = acción preferente acumulativa

pre-financing ['priːfaɪ'nænsɪŋ] *noun* prefinanciación *f*

prejudice ['predʒʊdɪs] **1** *noun* perjuicio *m or* detrimento *m (on a letter)* 'without prejudice' = sin perjuicio *or* con reserva de derechos; **to act to the prejudice of a claim** = actuar en detrimento *or* perjuicio de una demanda **2** *verb* perjudicar; **to prejudice someone's claim** = perjudicar las pretensiones de alguien

preliminary [prɪ'lɪmɪnərɪ] *adjective* preliminar *or* previo, -via; **preliminary discussion** *or* **a**

preliminary meeting = conversaciones preliminares *or* una reunión previa

premises ['premɪsɪz] *plural noun* local *m or* edificio *m*; **business premises** *or* **commercial premises** = local comercial; **office premises** *or* **shop premises** = local de una oficina *or* de una tienda; **lock-up premises** = local sin vivienda incorporada; **licensed premises** = local con licencia para la venta de bebidas alcohólicas; **on the premises** = en el local *or* edificio; **there is a doctor on the premises at all times** = siempre hay un médico en el edificio

premium ['priːmjəm] *noun* **(a) premium offer** = obsequio *m* publicitario *or* oferta *f* especial **(b) insurance premium** = prima *f* de seguros; **you pay either an annual premium of £360 or twelve monthly premiums of £32** = se paga o bien una prima anual de £360 o bien doce primas mensuales de £32; **additional premium** = sobreprima *f*; **risk premium** = prima de riesgo **(c)** *(lease)* traspaso *m*; **flat to let with a premium of £10,000** = piso para alquilar con un traspaso de £10.000; **annual rent: £8,500, premium: £25,000** = alquiler anual: £8.500, traspaso: £25.000 **(d)** *(extra charge)* agio *m*; **exchange premium** = agio del cambio; **the dollar is at a premium** = el dólar está por encima de la par; **shares sold at a premium** = acciones vendidas por encima de la par (NOTE: the opposite is **shares at a discount**) **(e)** *GB* **premium bonds** = bonos del gobierno con prima **(f) premium quality** = alta calidad

prepack *or* **prepackage** [priː'pæk *or* priː'pækɪdʒ] *verb* preempaquetar *or* empaquetar previamente para la venta; **the fruit are prepacked** *or* **prepackaged in plastic trays** = la fruta viene ya empaquetada en bandejas de plástico; **the watches are prepacked in attractive display boxes** = los relojes vienen envueltos en cajas atractivas

prepaid [priː'peɪd] *adjective* pagado, -da por adelantado; **carriage prepaid** = porte pagado; **prepaid reply card** = tarjeta de respuesta con el franqueo pagado

prepare [prɪ'peə] *verb* preparar

◇ **preparation** [prepə'reɪʃn] *noun* **(a)** preparativo *m* **(b)** preparación *f*

◇ **preparatory** [prɪ'pærətri] *adjective* preparatorio, -ria

prepay [priː'peɪ] *verb* pagar por adelantado (NOTE: **prepaying - prepaid**)

◇ **prepayment** [priː'peɪmənt] *noun* pago *m* por adelantado; **to ask for prepayment of a fee** = pedir el pago de honorarios por adelantado

present 1 ['preznt] *noun* regalo *m or* obsequio *m*; **these calculators make good presents** = estas calculadoras son un buen regalo; **the office gave her a present when she got married** = la oficina le hizo un regalo cuando se casó **2** ['preznt] *adjective* **(a)** *(happening now)* actual; **the shares are too expensive at their present price** = las acciones caras al precio actual; **what is the present address of the company?** = ¿cuál es la dirección actual de la compañía? **(b)** *(being there)* presente; **only six directors were present at the board meeting** = sólo estuvieron presentes seis consejeros en la reunión del consejo **3** [prɪ'zent] *verb* **(a)** *(to give)* regalar *or* obsequiar; **he was presented with a watch on completing twenty-five years' service with the company** = cuando cumplió veinticinco años de servicio en la compañía le regalaron un reloj **(b)** *(to show a document)* presentar; **to present a bill for acceptance** = presentar una letra a aceptación; **to present a bill for payment** = presentar una letra al pago

◇ **presentation** [prezən'teɪʃn] *noun* **(a)** *(showing a document)* presentación *f*; **cheque payable on presentation** = cheque pagadero a la vista *or* a su presentación; **free admission on presentation of the card** = entrada gratuita al presentar la tarjeta **(b)** *(exhibition)* presentación; **the manufacturer made a presentation of his new product line to possible customers** = el fabricante hizo la presentación de su nueva gama de productos a posibles clientes; **the distribution company made a presentation of the services they could offer** = la empresa distribuidora hizo la presentación de los servicios que podía ofrecer; **we have asked two PR firms to make presentations of proposed publicity campaigns** = hemos pedido a dos empresas de relaciones públicas que nos presenten sus proyectos de campaña publicitaria

◇ **present value (PV)** ['preznt 'væljuː] *noun* **(a)** *(value at present)* valor *m* actual; **in 1974 the pound was worth five times its present value** = en 1974 la libra valía cinco veces más que su valor actual **(b)** *(discounted value)* valor actual *or* valor descontado

preside [prɪ'zaɪd] *verb* presidir; **to preside over a meeting** = presidir una reunión; **the meeting was held in the committee room, Mr Smith presiding** = la reunión se celebró en la sala de juntas y fue presidida por el señor Smith

◇ **president** ['prezɪdənt] *noun* presidente, -ta; **he was elected president of the sports club** = fue elegido presidente del club deportivo; **A.B.Smith has been appointed president of the company** = el Sr A.B.Smith ha sido nombrado presidente de la compañía (NOTE: in GB, 'president' is sometimes a title given to a non-executive former chairman of a company; in the USA, the president is the main executive director of a company)

press [pres] **1** *noun* prensa *f*; **the local press** = la prensa local; **the national press** = la prensa nacional; **the new car has been advertised in the national press** = se ha hecho publicidad del nuevo coche en la prensa nacional; **trade press** = prensa comercial; **we plan to give the product a lot of press publicity** = pensamos dar al producto mucha publicidad en la prensa; **there was no mention of the new product in the press** = la prensa no mencionó el nuevo producto; **press conference** =

conferencia de prensa; **press coverage** = cobertura *or* reportaje en la prensa; **we were very disappointed by the press coverage of the new car** = nos decepcionó mucho el reportaje de la prensa sobre el nuevo coche; **press cutting** = recorte de periódico *or* de prensa; **we have kept a file of press cuttings about the new car** = hemos archivado los recortes de prensa sobre el nuevo coche; **press office** = agencia de prensa; **press officer** = agente de prensa; **press release** = comunicado de prensa; **the company sent out a press release about the launch of the new car** = la empresa emitió un comunicado de prensa sobre el lanzamiento del nuevo coche **2** *verb* presionar *or* insistir; **to press someone for payment** *or* **for an answer** = insistir en que alguien pague *or* conteste; **to be pressed for time** = ir apremiado de tiempo *or* tener poco tiempo

◊ **pressing** ['presɪŋ] *adjective* urgente *or* apremiante; **pressing engagements** = compromisos urgentes; **pressing bills** = facturas urgentes

pressure ['preʃə] *noun* presión *f or* apremio *m*; **he was under considerable financial pressure** = tenía grandes apuros financieros; **to put pressure on someone to do something** = presionar a alguien para que haga algo; **the group tried to put pressure on the government to act** = el grupo intentó presionar al gobierno para que actuara; **the banks put pressure on the company to reduce its borrowings** = los bancos presionaron a la compañía para que redujera sus préstamos; **to work under high pressure** = trabajar bajo una gran presión; **high-pressure salesman** = vendedor enérgico *or* que presiona a los clientes; **pressure group** = grupo de presión

prestige [pres'tiːʒ] *noun* prestigio *m*; **prestige advertising** = publicidad en revistas caras; **prestige product** = producto prestigioso; **prestige offices** = oficinas de prestigio

presume [prɪ'zjuːm] *verb* suponer; **I presume the account has been paid** = supongo que la cuenta ha sido pagada; **the company is presumed to be still solvent** = se supone que la empresa es todavía solvente; **we presume the shipment has been stolen** = suponemos que el envío ha sido robado

◊ **presumption** [prɪ'zʌmʃən] *noun* suposición *f or* presunción *f*

pre-tax *or* **pretax** ['priːtæks] *adjective* antes de deducir los impuestos; **pretax profit** = beneficio antes de deducir los impuestos; **the dividend paid is equivalent to one quarter of the pretax profit** = el dividendo repartido es equivalente a una cuarta parte de los beneficios antes de deducir los impuestos

pretences *or* US **pretenses** [prɪ'tensiz] *plural noun* **he was sent to prison for obtaining money by false pretences** = fue encarcelado por obtener dinero por medios fraudulentos *or* con engaños

pretend [prɪ'tend] *verb* fingir; **he's pretending to work** = finge trabajar *or* que trabaja; **he got in by pretending to be a telephone engineer** = entró haciéndose pasar por técnico de teléfonos; **the chairman pretended he knew the final profit** = el presidente fingió que sabía el beneficio final; **she pretended she had flu and took the day off** = fingió tener gripe y se tomó el día libre

prevent [prɪ'vent] *verb* impedir *or* evitar *or* prevenir; **we must try to prevent the takeover bid** = debemos intentar evitar la oferta pública de adquisición; **the police prevented anyone from leaving the building** = la policía impidió que nadie saliera del edificio; **we have changed the locks on the doors to prevent the former MD from getting into the building** = hemos cambiado las cerraduras de las puertas para impedir que el anterior director gerente entre en el edificio

◊ **prevention** [prɪ'venʃn] *noun* prevención *f*

◊ **preventive** [prɪ'ventɪv] *adjective* preventivo, -va; **to take preventive measures against theft** = tomar medidas preventivas contra robos

previous ['priːvjəs] *adjective* previo, -via *or* anterior; **he could not accept the invitation because he had a previous engagement** = no pudo aceptar la invitación porque tenía un compromiso previo

◊ **previously** ['priːvjəsli] *adverb* previamente *or* anteriormente

price [praɪs] **1** *noun* **(a)** *(cost)* precio *m*; **agreed price** = precio acordado *or* convenido; **all-in price** = precio todo incluido; **asking price** = precio pedido *or* de oferta; **bargain price** = precio de ocasión; **catalogue price** *or* **list price** = precio de catálogo; **competitive price** = precio competitivo; **cost price** = precio de coste; **cut price** = a precio reducido; **discount price** = precio con descuento; **factory price** *or* **price ex factory** = precio de fábrica *or* precio en fábrica; **fair price** = precio justo; **firm price** = precio definitivo *or* fijo *or* en firme; **they are quoting a firm price of $1.23 a unit** = cotizan un precio en firme de $1.23 por unidad; **going price** *or* **current price** *or* **usual price** = precio del mercado *or* precio actual *or* precio normal; **to sell goods off at half price** = vender mercancías a mitad de precio; **market price** = precio de mercado; **net price** = precio neto; **retail price** = precio al por menor; **Retail Price(s) Index (RPI)** = índice de precios al consumo; **spot price** = el precio de entrega inmediata; **the spot price of oil on the commodity markets** = precio de entrega inmediata del petróleo en las bolsas de contratación **(b)** **price ceiling** = límite de precios; **ceiling price** = precio máximo autorizado; **price control** = control de precios; **price cutting** = rebajas; **price war** *or* **price-cutting war** = guerra de precios; **price differential** = diferencial de inflación; **price fixing** = acuerdo sobre precios; **price label** *or* **price tag** = etiqueta indicadora del precio *or* precio; **the takeover bid put a $2m price tag on the company** = la oferta pública de adquisición de la compañía hizo subir su precio a $2 millones; **price list** = lista de precios; **price range** = gama de precios; **cars in the £8-9,000 price range** = coches en la gama de precios de £8.000 a £9.000;

price-sensitive product = producto sensible a los cambios de precio **(c) to increase in price** = subir *or* aumentar de precio; **petrol has increased in price** *or* **the price of petrol has increased** = la gasolina ha subido de precio *or* el precio de la gasolina ha subido; **to increase prices** *or* **to raise prices** = subir *or* aumentar los precios; **we will try to meet your price** = intentaremos ajustarnos a su precio; **to cut prices** = bajar los precios; **to lower prices** *or* **to reduce prices** = reducir los precios **(d)** *(on the Stock Exchange)* **asking price** = precio solicitado; **closing price** = precio al cierre; **opening price** = precio de apertura *or* primer curso **2** *verb* poner precio a *or* tasar *or* valorar en; **car priced at £5,000** = coche valorado en £5.000; **competitively priced** = con precio competitivo; **the company has priced itself out of the market** = la empresa ha dejado de vender por fijar los precios demasiado altos

◊ **price/earnings ratio (P/E ratio** *or* **PER)** [ˈpraɪsˈɜːnɪŋz ˈreɪʃəʊ] *noun* relación precio-ganancias

◊ **pricing** [ˈpraɪsɪŋ] *noun* fijación *f* de los precios; **pricing policy** = política de precios; **our pricing policy aims at producing a 35% gross margin** = nuestra política de precios tiene como objeto que nos quede un 35% de margen bruto; **common pricing** = fijación colectiva de precios; **competitive pricing** = fijación de precios competitivos; **marginal pricing** = fijación de precios según el coste marginal

QUOTE after years of relying on low wages for their competitive edge, Spanish companies are finding that rising costs and the strength of the peseta are pricing them out of the market
Wall Street Journal

QUOTE that British goods will price themselves back into world markets is doubtful as long as sterling labour costs continue to rise
Sunday Times

QUOTE in today's circumstances, price cutting is inevitable in an attempt to build up market share
Marketing Week

QUOTE the average price per kilogram for this season has been 300c
Australian Financial Review

QUOTE European manufacturers rely heavily on imported raw materials which are mostly priced in dollars
Duns Business Month

primary [ˈpraɪmərɪ] *adjective* primario, -ria; **primary commodities** = materias primas *or* productos básicos *or* primarios *or* de primera necesidad; **primary industry** *or* **primary sector** = sector primario; **primary products** = productos primarios

◊ **primarily** [ˈpraɪmərəlɪ] *adverb* principalmente *or* en primer lugar

QUOTE farmers are convinced that primary industry no longer has the capacity to meet new capital taxes or charges on farm inputs
Australian Financial Review

prime [praɪm] *adjective* **(a)** *(most important)* principal *or* fundamental *or* primordial; **prime reason** = razón principal; **prime time** = horas de mayor (índice de) audiencia; **we are putting out a series of prime-time commercials** = tenemos una serie de anuncios en las horas de mayor índice de audiencia **(b)** *(basic)* original; **prime bills** = letras de cambio *or* efectos de primera clase; **prime cost** = coste básico de producción

◊ **Prime Minister** [praɪm ˈmɪnɪstə] *noun* primer ministro, primera ministra *or* presidente del Gobierno; **the Australian Prime Minister** *or* **the Prime Minister of Australia** = el primer ministro australiano

◊ **prime rate** *or* **prime** [praɪm ˈreɪt] *noun US* tipo preferencial de interés bancario

◊ **priming** [ˈpraɪmɪŋ] *noun see* PUMP PRIMING

QUOTE the base lending rate, or prime rate, is the rate at which banks lend to their top corporate borrowers
Wall Street Journal

principal [ˈprɪnsəpl] **1** *noun* **(a)** *(person or company)* mandante *m*; **the agent has come to London to see his principals** = el mandatario ha venido a Londres a ver a sus mandantes **(b)** *(money invested or borrowed)* principal *m or* capital *m* de una deuda o préstamo; **to repay principal and interest** = pagar el capital y los intereses **2** *adjective* principal; **the principal shareholders asked for a meeting** = los principales accionistas solicitaron una reunión; **the country's principal products are paper and wood** = los principales productos del país son el papel y la madera

QUOTE the company was set up with funds totalling NorKr 145m with the principal aim of making capital gains on the secondhand market
Lloyd's List

principle [ˈprɪnsəpl] *noun* principio *m*; **in principle** = en principio; **agreement in principle** = acuerdo de principio

print [prɪnt] **1** *noun* letra *f* impresa; **to read the small print** *or* **the fine print on a contract** = leer la letra pequeña de un contrato **2** *verb* **(a)** *(with a machine)* imprimir; **printed agreement** = acuerdo impreso; **printed regulations** = reglamentación impresa **(b)** *(capital letters)* escribir con letras de imprenta *or* con mayúsculas; **please print your name and address on the top of the form** = escriba su nombre con letras mayúsculas en la parte superior del formulario

◊ **printer** [ˈprɪntə] *noun* **(a)** *(machine)* impresora *f*; **computer printer** *or* **line printer** = impresora de líneas; **dot-matrix printer** = impresora modelo matricial; **printer ribbon** = cinta de impresora **(b)** *(firm)* imprenta *f*

◊ **printing** [ˈprɪntɪŋ] *noun* impresión *f*; **electronic printing** = impresión electrónica; **faulty printing** = impresión deficiente; **printing firm** *or* **printing works** = imprenta

◊ **print out** [prɪnt ˈaʊt] *verb* imprimir

◊ **printout** [ˈprɪntaʊt] *noun* impresión *f*; **computer printout** = copia impresa *or* impresión de ordenador; **the sales director asked for a printout of the agents' commissions** = el director de ventas pidió una copia impresa de las comisiones de los representantes

prior ['praɪə] *adjective* anterior *or* previo, -via; **prior agreement** = acuerdo previo; **without prior knowledge** = sin conocimiento previo; **prior charge** = derechos preferentes

◊ **priority** [praɪ'ɒrəti] *noun* prioridad *f*; **to have priority** = tener prioridad; **to have priority over** *or* **to take priority over something** = tener prioridad sobre algo; **reducing overheads takes priority over increasing turnover** = la reducción de los gastos generales tiene prioridad sobre el aumento del volumen de negocios; **debenture holders have priority over ordinary shareholders** = los tenedores de obligaciones tienen prioridad sobre los tenedores de acciones ordinarias; **to give something top priority** = dar a algo prioridad absoluta

private ['praɪvət] *adjective* **(a)** privado, -da *or* particular *or* particular; **letter marked 'private and confidential'** = carta con la mención de 'confidencial' *or* 'privado y confidencial'; **private client** *or* **private customer** = cliente privado *or* personal; **private income** = renta privada *or* no salarial; **private investor** = inversor particular; **private property** = propiedad privada; **he will be using private transport** = irá en su propio coche *or* en un coche particular **(b) in private** = en privado; **he asked to see the managing director in private** = solicitó ver al director gerente en privado; **in public he said the company would break even soon, but in private he was less optimistic** = en público dijo que la compañía pronto cubriría gastos, pero en privado fue menos optimista **(c) private limited company** = sociedad anónima privada **(d) private enterprise** = empresa privada; **the project is funded by private enterprise** = el proyecto está financiado por la empresa privada; **the private sector** = el sector privado

◊ **privately** ['praɪvətli] *adverb* en privado *or* privadamente; **the deal was negotiated privately** = el trato se negoció en privado

◊ **privatization** [praɪvətaɪ'zeɪʃən] *noun* privatización *f*

◊ **privatize** ['praɪvətaɪz] *verb* privatizar

prize [praɪz] *noun* premio *m*

PRO = PUBLIC RELATIONS OFFICER

pro [prəʊ] *preposition* por *or* pro; **per pro** = por poderes; **the secretary signed per pro the manager** = la secretaria firmó por poderes del director; *see also* PRO FORMA, PRO RATA, PRO TEM

probable ['prɒbəbl] *adjective* probable; **he is trying to prevent the probable collapse of the company** = está intentando evitar el probable hundimiento de la compañía

◊ **probably** ['prɒbəbli] *adverb* probablemente; **the MD is probably going to retire next year** = el director gerente se retirará probablemente el año próximo; **this shop is probably the best in town for service** = esta tienda ofrece probablemente el mejor servicio de la ciudad

probate ['prəʊbeɪt] *noun* legalización *f*; **the executor was granted probate** = se le comunicó al albacea que el testamento era válido; **probate court** = tribunal sucesorio *or* testamentario

probation [prə'beɪʃən] *noun* periodo de prueba; **he is on three months' probation** = está en un periodo de prueba de tres meses; **to take someone on probation** = emplear a alguien a prueba

◊ **probationary** [prə'beɪʃənəri] *adjective* de prueba *or* probatorio, -ria; **a probationary period of three months** = un periodo de prueba de tres meses; **after the probationary period the company decided to offer him a full-time contract** = después del periodo de prueba la compañía decidió ofrecerle un contrato a jornada completa

problem ['prɒbləm] *noun* problema *m*; **no problem** = sin problema; **the company suffers from cash flow problems** *or* **staff problems** = la compañía tiene problemas de flujo de caja *or* problemas laborales; **to solve a problem** = solucionar un problema; **problem solving is a test of a good manager** = la prueba de un buen director es su capacidad para resolver problemas; **problem area** = asunto problemático; **overseas sales is one of our biggest problem areas** = el sector de ventas en el extranjero es uno de los más problemáticos en nuestra compañía

procedure [prə'siːdʒə] *noun* procedimiento *m* *or* tramitación *f* *or* trámite *m*; **to follow the proper procedure** = seguir el procedimiento adecuado; **this procedure is very irregular** = este procedimiento es muy irregular; **accounting procedures** = procedimientos de contabilidad; **complaints procedure** *or* **grievance procedure** = procedimiento para presentar reclamaciones *or* juicio de faltas; **the trade union has followed the correct complaints procedure** = el sindicato ha seguido el procedimiento correcto para presentar reclamaciones; **disciplinary procedure** = procedimiento disciplinario; **dismissal procedures** = trámites de despido

proceed [prə'siːd] *verb* seguir *or* continuar; **the negotiations are proceeding slowly** = las negociaciones continúan lentamente; **to proceed against someone** = proceder contra alguien; **to**

proceed with something = seguir con algo; **shall we proceed with the committee meeting?** = ¿podemos seguir con la reunión de la comisión?

◊ **proceedings** [prə'si:dɪŋz] *plural noun* **(a)** conference proceedings = actas *fpl* de un congreso **(b)** legal proceedings = proceso *m* judicial *or* procedimiento *m* legal; **to take proceedings against someone** = ponerle un pleito a alguien; **the court proceedings were adjourned** = la sesión de la audiencia fue aplazada; **to institute proceedings against someone** = entablar un proceso contra alguien; **to start proceedings** = incoar un proceso *or* abrir un expediente

◊ **proceeds** ['prəʊsi:dz] *plural noun* **the proceeds of a sale** = los beneficios de una venta; **he sold his shop and invested the proceeds in a computer repair business** = vendió la tienda e invirtió las ganancias en un negocio de reparación de ordenadores

process ['prəʊses] **1** *noun* **(a)** industrial processes = procedimientos *mpl* industriales *or* proceso *m* de fabricación; **decision-making processes** = procesos de toma de decisiones *or* decisorios **(b) the due processes of the law** = el curso seguido por la Justicia **2** *verb* **(a)** *(raw material)* elaborar (materia prima) **(b) to process figures** = elaborar cifras; **the sales figures are being processed by our accounts department** = las cifras de ventas están siendo elaboradas por nuestro departamento de contabilidad; **data is being processed by our computer** = los datos están siendo procesados por nuestro ordenador **(c)** *(to deal with)* preparar *or* elaborar *or* tramitar; **to process an insurance claim** = tramitar una reclamación al seguro; **orders are processed in our warehouse** = los pedidos se preparan en nuestro almacén

◊ **processing** ['prəʊsesɪŋ] *noun* **(a)** *(computer)* tratamiento *m or* elaboración *f*; **processing of information** *or* **of statistics** = el tratamiento de la información *or* de la estadística; **batch processing** = procesamiento *m* por lotes; **data processing** *or* **information processing** = proceso *or* procesamiento de datos; **word processing** *or* **text processing** = tratamiento de textos **(b)** *(dealing with)* **the processing of a claim for insurance** = tramitación *f* de una reclamación al seguro; **order processing** = preparación *f* de pedidos

◊ **processor** ['prəʊsesə] *noun* **word processor** = procesador *m* de textos

procurement [prə'kjʊəmənt] *noun* compra *f or* adquisición *f or* (de materias primas) *or* aprovisionamiento *m*

produce 1 ['prɒdju:s] *noun* productos *mpl*; **home produce** = productos agrícolas nacionales; **agricultural produce** *or* **farm produce** = productos agrícolas (NOTE: no plural in English) **2** [prə'dju:s] *verb* **(a)** *(to bring out)* presentar *or* mostrar; **he produced documents to prove his claim** = presentó documentos para justificar su reclamación; **the negotiators produced a new set of figures** = los negociadores presentaron las nuevas cifras; **the customs officer asked him to produce the relevant documents** = el aduanero le pidió que presentara los documentos pertinentes **(b)** *(to make)* producir *or* fabricar; **to produce cars** *or* **engines** *or* **books** = producir coches *or* motores *or* libros; **to mass produce** = producir *or* fabricar en serie *or* a gran

escala **(c)** *(to give an interest)* producir *or* dar; **investments which produce about 10% per annum** = inversiones que producen un 10% anual aproximadamente

◊ **producer** [prə'dju:sə] *noun* productor, -ra *or* fabricante *m*; **country which is a producer of high quality watches** = un país productor de relojes de gran calidad; **the company is a major car producer** = es una de las compañías fabricantes de coches más importantes

◊ **producing** [prə'dju:sɪŋ] *adjective* productor, -ra *or* productivo, -va; **producing capacity** = capacidad productiva; **oil-producing country** = país productor de petróleo

product ['prɒdʌkt] *noun* **(a)** *(thing which is made)* producto *m*; **basic product** = producto básico; **by-product** = subproducto; **end product** *or* **final product** *or* **finished product** = producto final *or* acabado **(b)** *(manufactured item for sale)* producto; **product advertising** = anuncio del producto; **product analysis** = análisis de productos; **product design** = diseño de productos; **product development** = desarrollo de productos; **product engineer** = ingeniero, -ra de productos; **product liability** = responsabilidad por producto defectuoso; **product line** *or* **product range** = gama *or* línea *or* abanico de productos; **product management** = dirección de producto; **product mix** = conjunto de productos de una compañía **(c) gross domestic product (GDP)** = producto interior bruto (PIB); **gross national product (GNP)** = producto nacional bruto (PNB)

◊ **production** [prə'dʌkʃən] *noun* **(a)** *(action of showing)* presentación *f*; **on production of** = mediante la presentación de *or* al presentar; **the case will be released by the customs on production of the relevant documents** = la aduana devolverá la maleta al presentar los documentos pertinentes; **goods can be exchanged only on production of the sales slip** = la mercancía se puede cambiar sólo mediante la presentación del recibo de venta **(b)** *(making or manufacturing of goods)* producción *f*; **production will probably be held up by industrial action** = la producción se verá probablemente interrumpida por la huelga; **we are hoping to speed up production by installing new machinery** = esperamos acelerar la producción instalando nueva maquinaria; **batch production** = producción por lotes; **domestic production** = producción interior *or* nacional; **lean production** = producción racionalizada *or* modernizada; **mass production** = producción en serie *or* a gran escala; **mass production of cars** *or* **of calculators** = producción de coches *or* calculadoras en serie; **rate of production** *or* **production rate** = ritmo de producción; **production cost** = coste de producción; **production department** = departamento de producción; **production line** = cadena de montaje; **he works on the production line** = trabaja en la cadena de montaje; **she is a production line worker** = es una obrera de la cadena de montaje; **production manager** = director, -ra de producción; **production unit** = unidad de producción

◊ **productive** [prə'dʌktɪv] *adjective* productivo, -va; **productive capital** = capital productivo; **productive discussions** = conversaciones fructíferas

◊ **productively** [prə'dʌktɪvli]   *adverb*
productivamente

◊ **productivity** [prɒdʌk'tɪvɪti]   *noun*
productividad *f*; **bonus payments are linked to
productivity** = el pago de bonificaciones va unido a
la productividad; **the company is aiming to
increase productivity** = la compañía se propone
aumentar la productividad; **productivity has fallen
or risen since the company was taken over** = la
productividad ha bajado *or* aumentado desde que la
nueva dirección tomó el mando de la compañía;
productivity agreement = acuerdo de
productividad; **productivity bonus** = prima de
productividad; **productivity drive** = impulso a la
productividad

QUOTE though there has been productivity
growth, the absolute productivity gap
between many British firms and their
foreign rivals remains
                                    Sunday Times

proeuropean ['prəʊjʊrə'piːən]   *noun* &
adjective europeísta *or* proeuropeo, -pea

profession [prə'feʃən] *noun* **(a)** *(work)* profesión
f; **the managing director is an accountant by
profession** = el director gerente es contable de
profesión **(b)** *(group of specialized workers)*
profesión *or* oficio *m*; **the legal profession** = la
abogacía; **the medical profession** = la profesión
médica; **she's a doctor by profession** = es médico
de profesión

QUOTE one of the key advantages of an
accountancy qualification is its
worldwide marketability. Other
professions are not so lucky: lawyers, for
example, are much more limited in where
they can work
                                    Accountancy

professional [prə'feʃənl] **1** *adjective* **(a)**
(referring to one of the professions) profesional *or* de
profesión; **the accountant sent in his bill for
professional services** = el contable presentó su
factura por los servicios profesionales prestados; **we
had to ask our lawyer for professional advice on
the contract** = tuvimos que pedir asesoramiento
jurídico a nuestro abogado sobre el contrato; **a
professional man** = un profesional; **professional
qualifications** = títulos profesionales **(b)** *(expert or
skilled)* profesional *or* experto,-ta; **his work is very
professional** = su trabajo es muy profesional; **they
did a very professional job in designing the new
office** = hicieron un trabajo muy profesional al
diseñar la nueva oficina **(c)** *(working for money)*
profesional; **a professional tennis player** = un
tenista profesional; **he is a professional
troubleshooter** = es un mediador profesional de
conflictos laborales **2** *noun* profesional *mf*

proficiency [prə'fɪʃənsi] *noun* pericia *f or* aptitud
f; **she has a certificate of proficiency in English** =
tiene un certificado de aptitud en inglés; **to get the
job he had to pass a proficiency test** = para
conseguir el trabajo tuvo que pasar una prueba de
aptitud

◊ **proficient** [prə'fɪʃənt] *adjective* capaz *or*
competente *or* experto, -ta; **she is quite proficient in
English** = es bastante experta en inglés *or* tiene un
buen nivel de inglés

profile ['prəʊfaɪl] *noun* perfil *m or* descripción *f*; **he
asked for a company profile of the possible
partners in the joint venture** = solicitó un perfil de
las compañías que podrían asociarse en una empresa
conjunta; **the customer profile shows our average
buyer to be male, aged 25-30, and employed in the
service industries** = el perfil del cliente muestra que
nuestro comprador medio es varón, de 25 a 40 años
de edad y empleado del sector servicios

QUOTE the audience profile does vary
greatly by period: 41.6% of the adult
audience is aged 16 to 34 during the
morning period, but this figure drops to
24% during peak viewing time
                                    Marketing Week

profit ['prɒfɪt] *noun* ganancia *f or* beneficio *m*;
clear profit = ganancia neta *or* beneficio neto; **we
made $6,000 clear profit on the deal** = sacamos un
beneficio neto de $6.000 en la transacción; **gross
profit *or* gross trading profit** = beneficio bruto; **net
profit *or* net trading profit** = beneficio neto;
operating profit = beneficio de explotación;
trading profit = beneficio de ejercicio; **profit
margin** = margen de beneficio; **profit motive** = afán
de lucro *or* finalidad lucrativa; **profits tax *or* tax on
profits** = impuesto sobre los beneficios; **profit
before tax *or* pretax profit** = beneficio sin deducir
los impuestos; **profit after tax** = beneficio después
de impuestos *or* resultado después del pago de
impuestos; **to take one's profit** = realizar
beneficios; **to show a profit** = mostrar un beneficio
or registrar beneficios; **we are showing a small
profit for the first quarter** = hemos registrado un
escaso beneficio en el primer trimestre; **to make a
profit** = obtener beneficios; **to move into profit** =
empezar a obtener beneficios; **the company is
breaking even now, and expects to move into
profit within the next two months** = la compañía
está haciendo tablas ahora y espera empezar a
obtener beneficios en los próximos dos meses; **to sell
at a profit** = vender con beneficios; **excess profit** =
beneficios extraordinarios; **excess profits tax** =
impuesto sobre los beneficios extraordinarios;
healthy profit = beneficio considerable; **paper
profit** = beneficio no realizado *or* ficticio *or* sobre el
papel; **he is showing a paper profit of £25,000 on
his investment** = su inversión arroja un beneficio
sobre el papel de £25.000

◊ **profitability** [prɒfɪtə'bɪlɪti] *noun* **(a)** *(ability to
make profit)* rentabilidad *f* **(b)** *(amount of profit
made)* coeficiente *m* de rentabilidad; **measurement
of profitability** = evaluación *or* medición de la
rentabilidad

◊ **profitable** ['prɒfɪtəbl] *adjective* rentable *or*
productivo, -va *or* lucrativo, -va

◊ **profitably** ['prɒfɪtəbli] *adverb* rentablemente
or productivamente *or* lucrativamente

QUOTE because capital gains are not taxed
and money taken out in profits and
dividends is taxed, owners of businesses
will be using accountants and tax experts
to find loopholes in the law
                                    Toronto Star

profit and loss account (P&L account)
['prɒfɪt ənd 'lɒs ə'kaʊnt] *noun* cuenta de pérdidas y
ganancias; **consolidated profit and loss account** =

balance de resultados consolidado (NOTE: the US equivalent is the **profit and loss statement** or **income statement)**

> QUOTE the bank transferred $5 million to general reserve compared with $10 million in 1983 which made the consolidated profit and loss account look healthier
> **Hongkong Standard**

profit centre ['prɒfɪt 'sentə] *noun* centro *m* de beneficios

◊ **profit-making** ['prɒfɪtmeɪkɪŋ] *adjective* rentable *or* lucrativo, -va; **the whole project was expected to be profit-making by the end of the year** = se esperaba que todo el proyecto fuera rentable al cabo de un año; **non profit-making** = sin fines lucrativos; **non profit-making organizations are exempt from tax** = las organizaciones sin fines lucrativos están exentas de impuestos

◊ **profit-sharing** ['prɒfɪtʃeərɪŋ] *noun* participación *f* en los beneficios; **the company runs a profit-sharing scheme** = la compañía tiene un programa de participación en los beneficios

◊ **profit-taking** ['prɒfɪtteɪkɪŋ] *noun* realización *f* de beneficios *or* toma *f* de beneficios; **share prices fell under continued profit-taking** = la continua venta de acciones para obtener beneficios hizo bajar las cotizaciones

> QUOTE some profit-taking was seen yesterday as investors continued to lack fresh incentives to renew buying activity
> **Financial Times**

profiteer [prɒfɪ'tɪə] *noun* agiotista *mf or* acaparador, -ra

◊ **profiteering** [prɒfɪ'tɪərɪŋ] *noun* realización *f* de ganancias excesivas *or* explotación *f*

pro forma ['prəʊ 'fɔːmə] **1** *noun* pro forma *or* pro forma invoice = factura *f* pro forma; **they sent us a pro forma** = nos enviaron una factura pro forma; **we only supply that account on pro forma** = suministramos esa cuenta únicamente con factura pro forma **2** *verb* **can you pro forma this order?** = ¿puede mandar una factura pro forma para este pedido?

program ['prəʊɡræm] **1** *noun* **computer program** = programa *m* de ordenador; **to buy a word-processing program** = comprar un programa de tratamiento de textos; **the accounts department is running a new payroll program** = el departamento de contabilidad está organizando un nuevo programa de nóminas **2** *verb* programar; **to program a computer** = programar un ordenador; **the computer is programmed to print labels** = el ordenador está programado para imprimir etiquetas (NOTE: **programming - programmed)**

◊ **programme** *or US* **program** ['prəʊɡræm] *noun* programa *m*; **development programme** = programa de desarrollo; **research programme** = programa de investigación; **training programme** = programa de formación; **to draw up a programme of investment** *or* **an investment programme** = elaborar un programa de inversión

◊ **programmable** [prəʊ'ɡræməbl] *adjective* programable

◊ **programmer** ['prəʊɡræmə] *noun* **computer programmer** = programador, -ra

◊ **programming** ['prəʊɡræmɪŋ] *noun* **computer programming** = programación *f* de ordenadores; **programming engineer** = técnico, -ca de programas; **programming language** = lenguaje de programación

progress 1 ['prəʊɡres] *noun* progreso *m or* marcha *f or* adelanto *m or* avance *m*; **to report on the progress of the work** *or* **of the negotiations** = informar sobre la marcha del trabajo *or* de las negociaciones; **to make a progress report** = hacer un informe sobre la marcha del trabajo; **in progress** = en curso; **negotiations in progress** = negociaciones en curso; **work in progress** = trabajo *or* obra en curso; **progress payments** = pagos a cuenta; **the fifth progress payment is due in March** = el quinto pago a cuenta debe hacerse en marzo **2** [prə'ɡres] *verb* progresar *or* avanzar; **negotiations are progressing normally** = las negociaciones avanzan con normalidad; **the contract is progressing through various departments** = el contrato avanza a través de varios departamentos

◊ **progress chaser** ['prəʊɡres 'tʃeɪsə] *noun* responsable del progreso de un trabajo

◊ **progressive** [prə'ɡresɪv] *adjective* progresivo, -va; **progressive taxation** = tributación progresiva

prohibitive [prə'hɪbɪtɪv] *adjective* prohibitivo, -va; **the cost of redeveloping the product is prohibitive** = el coste de desarrollar de nuevo el producto es prohibitivo

project ['prɒdʒekt] *noun* **(a)** *(plan)* proyecto *m*; **draft project** = anteproyecto *m*; **he has drawn up a project for developing new markets in Europe** = ha elaborado un proyecto para crear nuevos mercados en Europa **(b)** *(particular job of work)* proyecto *or* obra *f*; **we are just completing a construction project in North Africa** = estamos terminando una obra de construcción en el norte de Africa; **the company will start work on the project next month** = la empresa empezará a trabajar en el proyecto el mes próximo; **project analysis** = análisis de proyectos; **project engineer** = ingeniero, -ra de proyectos; **project manager** = director, -ra de proyecto

◊ **projected** [prə'dʒektɪd] *adjective* proyectado, -da *or* previsto, -ta; **projected sales** = ventas previstas; **projected sales in Europe next year should be over £1m** = las ventas previstas en Europa para el próximo año deberían superar £1 millón

◊ **projection** [prə'dʒekʃən] *noun* previsión *f*; **projection of profits for the next three years** = la previsión de beneficios para los próximos tres años; **the sales manager was asked to draw up sales projections for the next three years** = se pidió al director de ventas que elaborara previsiones de ventas para los próximos tres años

promise ['prɒmɪs] **1** *noun* promesa *f*; **to keep a promise** = cumplir una promesa; **he says he will pay next week, but he never keeps his promises** = dice que pagará la próxima semana, pero nunca cumple sus promesas; **to go back on a promise** = faltar a una promesa; **the management went back on its**

promise to increase salaries across the board = la dirección faltó a su promesa de aumentar el sueldo a nivel general; **a promise to pay** = una promesa de pago *or* un pagaré **2** *verb* prometer; **they promised to pay the last instalment next week** = prometieron pagar el último plazo la próxima semana; **the personnel manager promised he would look into the grievances of the office staff** = el director de personal prometió que estudiaría las quejas del personal de oficinas

◊ **promissory note** [prə'mɪsərɪ 'nəʊt] *noun* pagaré *m or* letra *f* al propio cargo

promote [prə'məʊt] *verb* **(a)** *(to give someone a more important job)* ascender; **he was promoted from salesman to sales manager** = fue ascendido de vendedor a director de ventas **(b)** *(to advertise)* promocionar; **to promote a new product** = promocionar un nuevo producto **(c) to promote a new company** = fundar una nueva compañía

◊ **promoter** [prə'məʊtə] *noun* **company promoter** = promotor, -ra *or* fundador, -ra *or* empresario, -ria; **sales promoter** = animador de ventas

◊ **promotion** [prə'məʊʃən] *noun* **(a)** *(moving up)* ascenso *m*; **promotion chances** *or* **promotion prospects** = oportunidades de ascenso; **he ruined his chances of promotion when he argued with the managing director** = perdió su oportunidad de ascenso cuando se peleó con el director gerente; **to earn promotion** = ganarse el ascenso **(b)** *(publicity)* **promotion of a product** = promoción *f* de un producto; **promotion budget** = presupuesto de promoción *or* gastos de seguimiento; **promotion team** = equipo de promoción; **sales promotion** = promoción de ventas; **special promotion** = promoción especial **(c) promotion of a company** = fundación *f* de una compañía

◊ **promotional** [prə'məʊʃənl] *adjective* de promoción *or* en promoción; **the admen are using balloons as promotional material** = los técnicos publicitarios utilizan globos como material de promoción; **promotional budget** = presupuesto de promoción

QUOTE the simplest way to boost sales is by a heavyweight promotional campaign
Marketing Week

QUOTE finding the right promotion to appeal to children is no easy task
Marketing

prompt [prɒm(p)t] *adjective* pronto, -ta *or* rápido, -da *or* inmediato, -ta; **prompt service** = servicio rápido; **prompt reply to a letter** = respuesta inmediata a una carta; **prompt payment** = pronto pago; **prompt supplier** = proveedor puntual

◊ **promptly** ['prɒm(p)tlɪ] *adverb* pronto *or* rápidamente *or* inmediatamente; **he replied to my letter very promptly** = contestó a mi carta inmediatamente

QUOTE they keep shipping costs low and can take advantage of quantity discounts and other allowances for prompt payment
Duns Business Month

proof [pruːf] *noun* prueba *f*; **documentary proof** = prueba documental *or* documentada

◊ **-proof** [pruːf] *suffix* a prueba de *or* protegida *or*

resistente a; **dustproof cover** = tapa cubierta a prueba de polvo; **inflation-proof pension** = pensión indexada; **soundproof studio** = estudio insonorizado

◊ **proofreader** ['pruːfriːdə] *noun* corrector, -ra de pruebas

propensity [prə'pensɪtɪ] *noun* propensión *f*; **propensity to save** = propensión al ahorro

property ['prɒpətɪ] *noun* **(a) personal property** = efectos *mpl* personales *or* propiedad *f* privada; **the storm caused considerable damage to personal property** = la tormenta causó numerosos daños materiales a la propiedad privada; **the management is not responsible for property left in the hotel rooms** = la dirección no se hace responsable de los objetos personales dejados en las habitaciones del hotel **(b)** *(land and buildings)* propiedad *f or* finca *f*; **property market** = mercado inmobiliario; **the commercial property market** = el mercado de propiedad comercial; **the commercial property market is booming** = el mercado de los locales comerciales está en auge; **damage to property** *or* **property damage** = daños materiales; **the office has been bought by a property company** = una sociedad inmobiliaria ha comprado la oficina; **property developer** = promotor inmobiliario; **property tax** = impuesto sobre la propiedad; **private property** = propiedad privada *or* particular **(c)** *(a building)* inmueble *m or* edificio *m*; **we have several properties for sale in the centre of the town** = tenemos varios edificios en venta en el centro de la ciudad

proportion [prə'pɔːʃən] *noun* parte *f or* proporción *f*; **a proportion of the pre-tax profit is set aside for contingencies** = una parte de los beneficios brutos se reserva para eventualidades *or* imprevistos; **only a small proportion of our sales comes from retail shops** = sólo una pequeña parte de nuestras ventas procede de tiendas al por menor; **in proportion to** = en proporción con; **profits went up in proportion to the fall in overhead costs** = los beneficios aumentaron proporcionalmente a la reducción de los gastos generales; **our sales in Europe are small in proportion to those in the USA** = las ventas de Europa son pequeñas en proporción con las de EE UU

◊ **proportional** [prə'pɔːʃənl] *adjective* proporcional; **the increase in profit is proportional to the reduction in overheads** = el aumento de los beneficios es proporcional a la reducción de los gastos generales

◊ **proportionately** [prə'pɔːʃənətlɪ] *adverb* proporcionalmente

proposal [prə'pəʊzəl] *noun* **(a)** *(suggestion)* proposición *f or* propuesta *f*; **to make a proposal** *or* **to put forward a proposal to the board** = presentar una propuesta a la junta; **the committee turned down the proposal** = el comité rechazó la propuesta **(b)** *(document detailing thing or person to be insured)* propuesta

◊ **propose** [prə'pəʊz] *verb* **(a)** proponer; **to propose a motion** = proponer una moción; **to propose someone as president** = proponer a alguien para presidente **(b) to propose to** = proponerse *or* tener la intención de; **I propose to repay the loan at £20 a month** = me propongo devolver el préstamo a £20 al mes

◇ **proposer** [prə'pəʊzə] *noun* proponente *mf or* autor, -ra

◇ **proposition** [prɒpə'zɪʃən] *noun* asunto *m or* negocio *m or* oferta *f*; **it will never be a commercial proposition** = este asunto nunca será un negocio

proprietary [prə'praɪətəri] *adjective* patentado, -da *or* de marca registrada; **proprietary drug** = específico *m or* producto farmacéutico patentado

◇ **proprietary company** [prə'praɪətri 'kʌmpəni] *noun* **(a)** *US* sociedad *f* de cartera *or* 'holding' *m* (NOTE: GB English for this **holding company**) **(b)** *(in South Africa and Australia)* sociedad limitada

◇ **proprietor** [prə'praɪətə] *noun* propietario *m or* amo *m or* dueño *m*; **the proprietor of a hotel** *or* **a hotel proprietor** = el propietario de un hotel

◇ **proprietress** [prə'praɪətrəs] *noun* propietaria *f or* ama *f or* dueña *f*; **the proprietress of an advertising consultancy** = la propietaria de una empresa asesora en publicidad

pro rata ['prəʊ 'rɑːtə] *adjective & adverb* a prorrata *or* a prorrateo; **a pro rata payment** = un pago a prorrata; **to pay someone pro rata** = pagar a alguien a prorrata; **dividends are paid pro rata** = los dividendos se pagan a prorrata

prosecute ['prɒsɪkjuːt] *verb* procesar *or* enjuiciar; **he was prosecuted for embezzlement** = fue procesado por desfalco

◇ **prosecution** [prɒsɪ'kjuːʃən] *noun* **(a)** *(legal action)* procesamiento *m*; **his prosecution for embezzlement** = su procesamiento por desfalco **(b)** *(people)* parte *f* acusadora *or* acusación *f*; **the costs of the case will be borne by the prosecution** = la parte acusadora pagará las costas del juicio; **prosecution counsel** *or* **counsel for the prosecution** = fiscal *or* abogado de la parte demandante; **prosecution witness** *or* **witness for the prosecution** = testigo de la acusación

prospect ['prɒspekt] *noun* **(a)** **prospects** = perspectivas *fpl*; **his job prospects are good** = sus perspectivas de trabajo son buenas; **prospects for the market** *or* **market prospects are worse than those of last year** = las perspectivas de mercado son peores que las del año pasado **(b)** *(possibility)* posibilidades *fpl or* probabilidades *fpl*; **there is no prospect of negotiations coming to an end soon** = no existen probabilidades de que las negociaciones finalicen pronto **(c)** *(future customer)* posible cliente; **the salesmen were looking out for possible prospects** = los vendedores estaban buscando posibles clientes

◇ **prospective** [prə'spektɪv] *adjective* eventual *or* probable; **a prospective buyer** = un posible comprador; **there is no shortage of prospective buyers for the computer** = no faltan posibles compradores para el ordenador

◇ **prospectus** [prə'spektəs] *noun* **(a)** *(to attract buyers)* prospecto *m or* folleto *m*; **the restaurant has girls handing out prospectuses in the street** = el restaurante emplea a chicas que distribuyen folletos publicitarios en la calle **(b)** *(for new company)* presupuesto *m* sobre emisión de acciones (NOTE: plural is **prospectuses**)

prosper ['prɒspə] *verb* prosperar

◇ **prosperous** ['prɒspərəs] *adjective* próspero, -ra; **a prosperous shopkeeper** = un próspero comerciante; **a prosperous town** = una ciudad próspera

◇ **prosperity** [prɒ'sperɪti] *noun* prosperidad *f or* bonanza *f*; **in times of prosperity** = en tiempos de prosperidad

protect [prə'tekt] *verb* proteger; **the workers are protected from unfair dismissal by government legislation** = la legislación estatal protege a los trabajadores contra el despido injusto; **the computer is protected by a plastic cover** = el ordenador está protegido por una funda de plástico; **the cover is supposed to protect the machine from dust** = la funda es para proteger a la máquina del polvo; **to protect an industry by imposing tariff barriers** = proteger una industria imponiendo barreras arancelarias

◇ **protection** [prə'tekʃən] *noun* protección *f*; **the legislation offers no protection to part-time workers** = la legislación no ofrece protección a los trabajadores a jornada parcial; **consumer protection** = protección del consumidor; **employment protection** = protección del trabajo

◇ **protectionism** [prə'tekʃənɪzm] *noun* proteccionismo *m*

◇ **protective** [prə'tektɪv] *adjective* **(a)** *(commercial)* proteccionista; **protective tariff** = arancel proteccionista **(b)** *(cover)* protector, -ra; **protective cover** = funda protectora

pro tem ['prəʊ 'tem] *adverb* provisionalmente *or* temporalmente

protest 1 ['prəʊtest] *noun* **(a)** *(statement or action)* protesta *f (of workers)* movilización *f*; **to make a protest against high prices** = hacer una protesta contra los precios altos; **sit-down protest** = sentada *f*; **sit-down strike** = huelga *f* de brazos caídos; **in protest at** = en protesta por; **the staff occupied the offices in protest at the low pay** = el personal ocupó las oficinas en protesta por los bajos sueldos; **to do something under protest** = hacer algo forzado *or* actuar bajo protesta **(b)** *(official document)* protesto *m* **2** [prə(ʊ)'test] *verb* **(a)** **to protest against something** = protestar contra algo; **the importers are protesting against the ban on luxury goods** = los importadores protestan contra la prohibición de importar artículos de lujo (NOTE: in this sense, GB English is **to protest against something**, but US English is **to protest something**) **(b)** **to protest a bill** = protestar una letra

prototype ['prəʊtətaɪp] *noun* prototipo *m*; **prototype car** *or* **prototype plane** = prototipo de coche *or* prototipo de avión; **the company is showing the prototype of the new model at the**

exhibition = la empresa presenta el prototipo del nuevo modelo en la exposición

provide [prə'vaɪd] *verb* **(a) to provide for** = estipular *or* prever; **the contract provides for an annual increase in charges** = el contrato prevé un aumento anual de los gastos; **£10,000 of expenses have been provided for in the budget** = se han estipulado £10.000 de gastos en el presupuesto **(b)** *(put money aside)* precaverse *or* reservar dinero para imprevistos; **£25,000 is provided against bad debts** = se reservan £25.000 para deudas incobrables **(c) to provide someone with something** = suministrar *or* proporcionar algo a alguien; **each rep is provided with a company car** = a cada representante se le proporciona un coche de la empresa; **staff uniforms are provided by the hotel** = el hotel suministra los uniformes del personal

◇ **provided that** *or* **providing** [prə'vaɪdɪd 'ðæt *or* prə'vaɪdɪŋ] *conjunction* con tal que *or* a condición de que *or* siempre que; **the goods will be delivered next week provided** *or* **providing the drivers are not on strike** = la mercancía se entregará la semana próxima siempre que los chóferes no estén en huelga

◇ **provident** ['prɒvɪdənt] *adjective* providente *or* previsor, -ra; **a provident fund** = fondo de previsión; **a provident society** = sociedad de seguros mutuos *or* mutualidad *or* mutua

province ['prɒvɪns] *noun* **(a)** *(administrative part of a country)* provincia *f*; **the provinces of Canada** = las provincias de Canadá **(b)** *(not the capital)* **the provinces** = las provincias; **there are fewer retail outlets in the provinces than in the capital** = hay menos establecimientos al por menor en las provincias que en la capital

◇ **provincial** [prə'vɪnʃəl] *adjective* provincial; **a provincial government** = un gobierno provincial; **a provincial branch of a national bank** = sucursal provincial de un banco nacional

provision [prə'vɪʒən] *noun* **(a)** *(arrangement)* disposición *f*; **to make provision for** = tomar disposiciones *or* medidas *or* prever *or* prevenir; **there is no provision for** *or* **no provision has been made for car parking in the plans for the office block** = no se ha previsto ningún aparcamiento en los planos del edificio de oficinas **(b)** *(money put aside)* **provisions** = provisión *f* de fondos *or* reserva *f*; **the bank has made a £2m provision for bad debts** = el banco ha hecho una provisión de fondos de £2 millones para deudas incobrables **(c)** *(legal condition)* disposiciones *fpl or* estipulaciones *fpl*; **we have made provision to this effect** = hemos tomado disposiciones al respecto; **provisions of an agreement** = estipulaciones del convenio **(d)** *(supply)* **provisions** = provisiones *fpl*

◇ **provisional** [prə'vɪʒənl] *adjective* provisional; **provisional forecast of sales** = previsión provisional de ventas; **provisional budget** = presupuesto provisional; **they faxed their provisional acceptance of the contract** = mandaron por fax su aceptación provisional del contrato

◇ **provisionally** [prə'vɪʒnəli] *adverb* provisionalmente; **the contract has been accepted provisionally** = el contrato ha sido aceptado provisionalmente

QUOTE landlords can create short lets of dwellings which will be free from the normal security of tenure provisions
Times

proviso [prə'vaɪzəʊ] *noun* condición *f or* salvedad *f*; **we are signing the contract with the proviso that the terms can be discussed again after six months** = firmamos el contrato con la condición de que los términos puedan ser discutidos de nuevo después de seis meses

proxy ['prɒksi] *noun* **(a)** *(document)* procuración *f or* poder *m or* delegación *m*; **to sign by proxy** = firmar por poderes *or* por representación; **proxy vote** = voto por poderes; **the proxy votes were all in favour of the board's recommendation** = todos los votos por poderes eran a favor de la recomendación del consejo **(b)** *(person)* poderhabiente *mf or* apoderado, -da; **to act as proxy for someone** = actuar como apoderado de alguien

P.S. ['piː'es] *noun* = POST SCRIPTUM posdata *f*; **did you read the P.S. at the end of the letter?** = ¿leyó la posdata al final de la carta?

PSBR = PUBLIC SECTOR BORROWING REQUIREMENT

pt [paɪnt] = PINT

ptas [pə'seɪtəz] = PESETAS ptas

PTE = PRIVATE

Pte *(Singapore)* = PRIVATE LIMITED COMPANY

Pty = PROPRIETARY COMPANY

public ['pʌblɪk] **1** *adjective* **(a)** *(people)* público, -ca; **public holiday** = fiesta oficial *or* nacional; **public image** = imagen pública; **the minister is trying to improve his public image** = el ministro está intentando mejorar su imagen pública; **public transport** = transporte público **(b)** *(referring to the state)* público, -ca; **public expenditure** = gasto público; **public finance** = finanzas públicas; **public funds** = fondos públicos; **public ownership** = propiedad pública **(c)** **the company is going public** = la sociedad va a ofrecer sus acciones al público **2** *noun* **the public** *or* **the general public** = el público *or* el público en general *or* los asistentes; **in public** = en público; **in public he said that the company would soon be in profit, but in private he was less optimistic** = en público dijo que la compañía pronto tendría beneficios pero en privado fue menos optimista

◇ **Public Limited Company (Plc)** *noun* sociedad anónima (S.A.) (NOTE: also called a **Public Company**)

◇ **public relations (PR)** ['pʌblɪk rɪ'leɪʃənz] *plural noun* relaciones públicas; **a public relations man** *or* **a PR man** = persona dedicada a las relaciones públicas; **he works in public relations** = trabaja en relaciones públicas; **a public relations firm** *or* **a PR firm handles all our publicity** = una empresa de relaciones públicas se ocupa de toda nuestra publicidad; **a public relations exercise** = una campaña de relaciones públicas; **public relations officer (PRO)** = responsable de relaciones públicas

◊ **public sector** ['pʌblɪk 'sektə] *noun* el sector público; **a report on wage rises in the public sector** *or* **on public sector wage settlements** = un informe sobre los aumentos de sueldo en el sector público *or* sobre los acuerdos salariales del sector público; **public sector borrowing requirement (PSBR)** = necesidades de endeudamiento del sector público

publication [pʌblɪ'keɪʃən] *noun* **(a)** *(action)* publicación *f*; **the publication of the latest trade figures** = la publicación de las últimas cifras comerciales **(b)** *(printed document)* publicación *or* edición *f*; **he asked the library for a list of government publications** = pidió en la biblioteca una lista de las publicaciones del gobierno; **the company has six business publications** = la compañía edita seis publicaciones comerciales

publicity [pʌb'lɪsəti] *noun* publicidad *f*; **publicity agency** *or* **publicity bureau** = agencia *f* de publicidad *or* publicitaria; **publicity budget** = presupuesto de publicidad *or* publicitario; **publicity campaign** = campaña publicitaria; **publicity copy** = original de un texto publicitario; **publicity department** = departamento de publicidad; **publicity expenditure** = gastos de publicidad; **publicity manager** = director, -ra de publicidad; **publicity matter** = material publicitario

◊ **publicize** ['pʌblɪsaɪz] *verb* dar publicidad *or* divulgar; **the campaign is intended to publicize the services of the tourist board** = la campaña está destinada a divulgar los servicios de la junta de turismo; **we are trying to publicize our products by advertisements on buses** = estamos intentando dar publicidad a nuestros productos por medio de anuncios en los autobuses

publish ['pʌblɪʃ] *verb* publicar *or* editar; **the society publishes its list of members annually** = la sociedad publica su lista de socios anualmente; **the government has not published the figures on which its proposals are based** = el gobierno no ha publicado las cifras en las que se basa su propuesta; **the company publishes six magazines for the business market** = la compañía edita seis revistas para el mercado empresarial

◊ **publisher** ['pʌblɪʃə] *noun* editor, -ra *or* editorial

◊ **publishing** ['pʌblɪʃɪŋ] *noun* edición *f*; **desk-top publishing (DTP)** = autoedición *f*; **desk-top publishing package** = paquete de autoedición

Puerto Rico ['pweətəʊ 'riːkəʊ] *noun* Puerto Rico *m*

◊ **Puerto Rican** *or* **Porto Rican** ['pweətəʊ 'riːkən *or* 'pɔːtəʊ 'riːkən] *adjective & noun* portorriqueño, -ña *or* puertorriqueño, -ña
NOTE: capital: **San Juan**; currency: **US dollar (US$)** = dólar USA (US$)

pull off ['pʊl 'ɒf] *verb (informal)* tener éxito en un proyecto

◊ **pull out** ['pʊl 'aʊt] *verb* salirse; **our Australian partners pulled out of the contract** = nuestros socios australianos se han retirado del contrato

pump [pʌmp] *verb* invertir; **the banks have been pumping money into the company to keep it afloat** = los bancos han ido invirtiendo dinero en la compañía para mantenerla a flote

◊ **pump priming** ['pʌmp 'praɪmɪŋ] *noun* medidas *fpl* expansionistas de un gobierno *or* reactivación *f*

> QUOTE in each of the years 1986 to 1989, Japan pumped a net sum of the order of $100bn into foreign securities, notably into US government bonds
> **Financial Times Review**

punch [pʌnʃ] **1** *noun* máquina *f* perforadora **2** *verb (to make holes)* perforar; **punched card** = tarjeta *f* perforada

punt [pʌnt] **1** *noun (money used in the Irish Republic)* libra *f* irlandesa (NOTE: also called **the Irish pound; written £** before a figure: **£25**; if you want to indicate that it is different from the British pound sterling, then it can be written: **£125.00) 2** *verb* jugar *or* apostar

◊ **punter** ['pʌntə] *noun* jugador, -ra

pup [pʌp] *noun (informal)* objeto sin valor; **I've been sold a pup** = me han vendido una cosa que no vale para nada

purchase ['pɜːtʃəs] **1** *noun* compra *f*; **to make a purchase** = hacer una compra; **purchase book** = libro de compras; **purchase ledger** = libro mayor de compras; **purchase order** = orden de compra; **we cannot supply you without a purchase order number** = no podemos servirle sin el número de orden de compra; **purchase price** = precio de compra; **purchase tax** = impuesto sobre las compras; **bulk purchase** *or* **quantity purchase** = compra a granel *or* en grandes cantidades; **cash purchase** = compra al contado; **hire purchase** = compra a plazos; **he is buying a refrigerator on hire purchase** = ha comprado un frigorífico a plazos; **hire purchase agreement** = contrato de venta a plazos **2** *verb* comprar; **to purchase something for cash** = comprar algo al contado

◊ **purchaser** ['pɜːtʃəsə] *noun* comprador, -ra; **the company is looking for a purchaser** = la compañía busca un comprador; **the company has found a purchaser for its warehouse** = la compañía ha encontrado un comprador para su almacén

◊ **purchasing** ['pɜːtʃəsɪŋ] *noun* compra; **purchasing department** = departamento de compras; **purchasing manager** = jefe, -fa de compras; **purchasing officer** = agente de compras; **purchasing power** = poder adquisitivo; **the decline in the purchasing power of the pound** = el descenso del poder adquisitivo de la libra; **purchasing power parity** = paridad del poder adquisitivo (PPA); **central purchasing** = centralización de las compras

purpose ['pɜːpəs] *noun* propósito *m* *or* objetivo *m*; **we need the invoice for tax purposes** *or* **for the purpose of declaration to the tax authorities** = necesitamos la factura por razones de impuestos *or* para la declaración al fisco

put [pʊt] **1** *noun* **put option** = derecho *m* a vender acciones en una fecha y a un precio determinados **2** *verb* poner *or* fijar; **the accounts put the stock value at £10,000** = las cuentas fijan el valor de las existencias en £10.000; **to put a proposal to the vote** = someter una propuesta a votación; **to put a proposal to the board** = someter una propuesta al consejo (NOTE: **putting - put**)

◊ **put back** ['pʊt 'bæk] *verb* aplazar; **the meeting was put back (by) two hours** = la reunión se aplazó dos horas

◊ **put down** ['pʊt 'daʊn] *verb* **(a)** *(deposit)* dar una entrega; **to put down money on a house** = dar una entrada para la compra de una casa **(b)** *(to write an item in a ledger)* anotar; **to put down a figure for expenses** = anotar una cifra de gastos

◊ **put in** ['pʊt 'ɪn] *verb* **to put an ad in a paper** = poner un anuncio en un periódico; **to put in a bid for something** = presentar una oferta de compra de algo; **to put in an estimate for something** = presentar el presupuesto de algo; **to put in a claim for damage** = presentar una reclamación por daños y perjuicios *or* pedir una indemnización; **the union put in a 6% wage claim** = el sindicato presentó una reivindicación salarial del 6%

◊ **put into** ['pʊt 'ɪntʊ] *verb* **to put money into a business** = invertir en un negocio

◊ **put off** ['pʊt 'ɒf] *verb* aplazar; **the meeting was put off for two weeks** = la reunión fue aplazada dos semanas; **he asked if we could put the visit off until tomorrow** = preguntó si podíamos aplazar la visita hasta mañana

◊ **put on** ['pʊt 'ɒn] *verb* **to put an item on the agenda** = inscribir un punto en el orden del día; **to put an embargo on trade** = prohibir el comercio; **property shares put on gains of 10%-15%** = las acciones inmobiliarias subieron del 10% al 15%

◊ **put out** ['pʊt 'aʊt] *verb* encargar; **to put work out to freelancers** = encargar trabajo a trabajadores autónomos; **we put all our typing out to a bureau** = encargamos todo el trabajo de mecanografía a una agencia; **to put work out to contract** = subcontratar trabajo

◊ **put up** ['pʊt 'ʌp] *verb* **(a)** *(provide or offer)* poner *or* dar; **who put up the money for the shop?** = ¿quién aportó el dinero para la tienda?; **to put something up for sale** = poner algo en venta; **when he retired he decided to put his town flat up for sale** = cuando se retiró, decidió poner en venta su piso en la ciudad **(b)** *(increase or make higher)* subir *or* aumentar; **the shop has put up all its prices by 5%** = la tienda ha subido en un 5% todos sus precios *or* ha añadido un 5% a todos sus precios

PV = PRESENT VALUE

pyramid selling ['pɪrəmɪd 'selɪŋ] *noun* venta *f* piramidal

COMMENT: an illegal way of selling goods or investments to the public, where each selling agent pays for the franchise to sell the product or service, and sells that right on to other agents, so that in the end the person who makes most money is the original franchisor, and sub-agents or investors lose all their investments

Qq

QC ['kjuː'siː] = QUEEN'S COUNSEL

qty ['kwɒntəti] = QUANTITY

quadruple [kwɒ'druːpl] *verb* cuadruplicar; **the company's profits have quadrupled over the last five years** = los beneficios de la compañía se han cuadruplicado en los últimos cinco años

◊ **quadruplicate** [kwɒ'druːplɪkət] *noun* **in quadruplicate** = por cuadruplicado; **the invoices are printed in quadruplicate** = las facturas se imprimen por cuadruplicado

qualification [kwɒlɪfɪ'keɪʃ(ə)n] *noun* **(a)** *(professional title or experience)* calificación *f or* título *m or* competencia *f;* **to have the right qualifications for the job** = tener los títulos adecuados para el trabajo *or* estar capacitado para el puesto de trabajo; **professional qualifications** = títulos profesionales **(b) period of qualification** = periodo *m* de prueba *or* de formación **(c) auditors' qualification** = informe de auditoría con salvedades; *see also* QUALIFIED AUDIT REPORT

◊ **qualify** ['kwɒlɪfaɪ] *verb* **(a)** *(specialize in)* calificar *or* capacitar; **to qualify as** = sacar *or* obtener el título de; **she has qualified as an accountant** = ha sacado el título de contable; **he will qualify as a solicitor next year** = obtendrá el título de abogado el año próximo **(b)** *(have the right qualifications)* **to qualify for** = satisfacer los requisitos *or* tener derecho a; **the company does not qualify for a government grant** = la compañía no satisface los requisitos necesarios para obtener una subvención del Estado; **she qualifies for unemployment pay** = tiene derecho al subsidio de paro **(c)** *(accounts)* **the auditors have qualified the accounts** = los auditores han aprobado las cuentas con reservas

◊ **qualified** ['kwɒlɪfaɪd] *adjective* **(a)** *(in a specialist subject)* cualificado, -da *or* capacitado, -da *or* titulado, -da *or* apto, -ta; **qualified electrician** = périto electricista; **she is a qualified accountant** = es una contable profesional *or* con título; **we have appointed a qualified designer to supervise the new factory project** = hemos nombrado a un diseñador profesional para que supervise el proyecto de la nueva fábrica; **highly qualified** = muy competente *or* sumamente cualificado; **all our staff are highly qualified** = todos nuestros empleados están muy bien cualificados *or* capacitados; **they employ twenty-six highly qualified engineers** = emplean a veintiséis ingenieros sumamente calificados **(b)** *(with reservations)* con reservas; **qualified acceptance of a contract** = aceptación de un contrato con reservas; **the plan received qualified approval from the board** = el plan obtuvo la aprobación con reservas de la junta **(c) qualified auditors' report** *or* **qualified audit report** *US* **qualified opinion** = informe de auditoría con salvedades

◊ **qualifying** ['kwɒlɪfaɪɪŋ] *adjective* **(a) qualifying period** = *(for a job)* periodo de prueba *or* de formación; *(for a subsidy)* periodo de cotización necesario para tener derecho a subsidio estatal; **there is a six-month qualifying period before you can get a grant from the local authority** = hay que cotizar durante seis meses para tener derecho a una subvención de las autoridades locales **(b) qualifying shares** = acciones con garantía *or* número de acciones necesarias para obtener determinados derechos

> QUOTE federal examiners will also determine which of the privately insured savings and loans qualify for federal insurance
> **Wall Street Journal**

> QUOTE applicants will be professionally qualified and ideally have a degree in Commerce and post graduate management qualifications
> **Australian Financial Review**

> QUOTE personnel management is not an activity that can ever have just one set of qualifications as a requirement for entry into it
> **Personnel Management**

quality ['kwɒləti] *noun* **(a)** *(of something)* calidad *f;* **good quality** *or* **bad quality** = buena calidad *or* mala calidad; **we sell only quality farm produce** = sólo vendemos productos agrícolas de calidad; **there is a market for good quality second hand computers** = hay demanda de ordenadores de segunda mano de buena calidad; **high quality** *or* **top quality** = de calidad superior *or* de primera calidad; **the store specializes in high quality imported items** = la tienda está especializada en artículos de importación de primera calidad **(b) quality control** = control de calidad; **quality controller** = inspector, -ra de calidad **(c)** *(printers)* **draft quality** = calidad borrador; **near letter-quality (NLQ)** = calidad de semicorrespondencia

quango ['kwæŋgəʊ] *noun GB* organismo *m* oficial para investigar o tratar un asunto determinado

quantify ['kwɒntɪfaɪ] *verb* **to quantify the effect of something** = cuantificar el efecto de algo; **it is impossible to quantify the effect of the new legislation on our turnover** = es imposible cuantificar el efecto que la nueva legislación tendrá sobre nuestro volumen de negocios

◊ **quantifiable** [kwɒntɪ'faɪəbl] *adjective* cuantificable; **the effect of the change in the discount structure is not quantifiable** = el efecto de las alteraciones en la estructura del descuento no es cuantificable

quantity ['kwɒntəti] *noun* **(a)** *(amount)* cantidad *f;* **a small quantity of illegal drugs** = una pequeña cantidad de drogas ilegales; **he bought a large quantity of spare parts** = compró una gran cantidad de piezas de recambio **(b)** *(large amount)* gran cantidad; **the company offers a discount for quantity purchase** = la empresa ofrece un descuento cuando se compra en grandes cantidades; **quantity discount** = descuento por grandes cantidades **(c) to carry out a quantity survey** = hacer un presupuesto de materiales y mano de obra; **quantity surveyor** = aparejador, -ra

quart [k(w)ɔːt] *noun* (= *1.136 litres*) cuarto *m* de galón

quarter ['k(w)ɔːtə] *noun* **(a)** *(one of four parts)* cuarto *m* *or* cuarta parte *f*; **a quarter of a litre** *or* **a quarter litre** = un cuarto de litro; **a quarter of an hour** = un cuarto de hora; **three quarters** = tres cuartos *or* tres cuartas partes; **three quarters of the staff are less than thirty years old** = tres cuartas partes del personal tiene menos de treinta años; **he paid only a quarter of the list price** = sólo pagó una cuarta parte del precio de catálogo **(b)** *(period of three months)* trimestre *m*; **first quarter** *or* **second quarter** *or* **third quarter** *or* **fourth quarter** *or* **last quarter** = primer trimestre *or* segundo trimestre *or* tercer trimestre *or* cuarto trimestre *or* último trimestre; **the instalments are payable at the end of each quarter** = los plazos se harán efectivos al final de cada trimestre; **the first quarter's rent is payable in advance** = la renta del primer trimestre se hará efectiva por adelantado **(c)** *US & Canada (informal)* moneda de 25 centavos **(d)** *(in a town)* **the old quarter** = el casco antiguo *or* viejo

◊ **quarter day** ['kwɔːtə 'deɪ] *noun* día de ajuste *or* liquidación trimestral (último día del trimestre cuando deben hacerse efectivas determinadas cantidades)

COMMENT: in England, the quarter days are 25th March (Lady Day), 24th June (Midsummer Day), 29th September (Michaelmas Day) and 25th December (Christmas Day)

◊ **quarterly** ['k(w)ɔːtəli] **1** *adjective* trimestral; **there is a quarterly charge for electricity** = los gastos de electricidad se cobran por trimestres; **the bank sends us a quarterly statement** = el banco nos manda un estado de cuentas trimestral **2** *adverb* trimestralmente; **we agreed to pay the rent quarterly** *or* **on a quarterly basis** = acordamos pagar la renta trimestralmente *or* cada tres meses

QUOTE corporate profits for the first quarter showed a 4 per cent drop from last year's final three months
Financial Times

QUOTE economists believe the economy is picking up this quarter and will do better still in the second half of the year
Sunday Times

quartile ['k(w)ɔːtaɪl] *noun* cuartil *m*

quasi- ['kweɪzaɪ] *prefix* cuasi; **a quasi-official body** = un organismo semi oficial

quay [kiː] *noun* muelle *m*; **price ex quay** = precio puesto en muelle *or* franco en muelle

query ['kwɪəri] **1** *noun* pregunta *f*; **the chief accountant had to answer a mass of queries from the auditors** = el contable jefe tuvo que responder a un montón de preguntas de los auditores **2** *verb* poner en duda *or* cuestionar; **the shareholders queried the payments to the chairman's son** = los accionistas cuestionaron los pagos hechos al hijo del presidente

question ['kwestʃ(ə)n] **1** *noun* **(a)** *(enquiry)* pregunta *f*; **the managing director refused to answer questions about redundancies** = el director gerente se negó a contestar preguntas sobre despidos; **the market research team prepared a series of questions to test the public's reactions to colour and price** = el equipo de investigación de mercados preparó una serie de preguntas para analizar las reacciones del público al color y al precio **(b)** *(problem)* problema *m* *or* cuestión *f* *or* asunto *m*; **he raised the question of moving to less expensive offices** = planteó el problema del traslado a oficinas menos caras; **the main question is that of cost** = el problema principal es el del coste; **the board discussed the question of redundancy payments** = la junta debatió la cuestión de las indemnizaciones por despido **2** *verb* **(a)** *(ask)* interrogar; **the police questioned the accounts staff for four hours** = la policía interrogó a los empleados de la sección de contabilidad durante cuatro horas; **she questioned the chairman on the company's investment policy** = interrogó al presidente sobre la política de inversiones de la empresa **(b)** *(query)* cuestionar *or* poner en duda; **we all question how accurate the computer printout is** = todos ponemos en duda la precisión de las copias impresas del ordenador

◊ **questionnaire** [k(w)estʃə'neə] *noun* cuestionario *m* *or* encuesta *f*; **to send out a questionnaire to test the opinions of users of the system** = enviar un cuestionario para analizar la opinión de los usuarios del sistema; **to answer** *or* **to fill in a questionnaire about holidays abroad** = contestar *or* rellenar un cuestionario sobre vacaciones en el extranjero

queue [kjuː] **1** *noun* **(a)** *(line of people)* cola *f*; **to form a queue** *or* **to join a queue** = formar una cola *or* ponerse en la cola; **queues formed at the doors of the bank when the news spread about its possible collapse** = se formaron colas en las puertas del banco cuando se divulgó la noticia de su posible quiebra; **dole queue** = cola de parados *or* del subsidio de paro (NOTE: US English is **line**) **(b)** *(waiting list)* **his order went to the end of the queue** = su pedido fue a parar al final de la cola; **mortgage queue** = lista *f* de espera para obtener una hipoteca **2** *verb* hacer cola; **when food was rationed, people had to queue for bread** = cuando los alimentos estaban racionados la gente tenía que hacer cola para el pan; **we queued for hours to get tickets** = hicimos cola durante horas para conseguir billetes; **a list of companies queueing to be launched on the Stock Exchange** = una lista de sociedades esperando *or* en espera de ser lanzadas en bolsa

quick [kwɪk] *adjective* rápido, -da; **the company made a quick recovery** = la empresa tuvo una recuperación rápida; **he is looking for a quick return on his investments** = está buscando un beneficio rápido de sus inversiones; **we are hoping for a quick sale** = esperamos realizar una venta rápida

◊ **quickly** ['kwɪkli] *adverb* rápidamente; **the sale of the company went through quickly** = la venta de la compañía se realizó rápidamente; **the accountant quickly looked through the pile of invoices** = el contable echó un vistazo rápido al montón de facturas

quid [kwɪd] *noun* *(slang: one pound in money)* libra

quid pro quo ['kwɪd prəʊ 'kwəʊ] *noun* en compensación *f* *or* cambio *m*; **we agreed to a two-week extension of the delivery date and as a quid pro quo the supplier reduced the price by**

10% = aceptamos un retraso de dos semanas en el envío y a cambio el proveedor *or* suministrador redujo el precio en un 10%

quiet ['kwaɪət] *adjective* tranquilo, -la *or* en calma; **the market is very quiet** = el mercado está muy tranquilo; **currency exchanges were quieter after the government's statement on exchange rates** = los mercados de divisas se calmaron después de la declaración del gobierno sobre los tipos de cambio; **on the quiet** = a escondidas *or* sigilosamente; **he transferred his bank account to Switzerland on the quiet** = transfirió su cuenta bancaria a Suiza en secreto

quit [kwɪt] *verb* dejar *or* abandonar el trabajo *or* dimitir; **he quit after an argument with the managing director** = dejó el trabajo *or* dimitió después de una discusión con el director gerente; **several of the managers are quitting to set up their own company** = varios de los directores se marchan para establecer su propia empresa (NOTE: **quitting - quit**)

quite [kwaɪt] *adverb* **(a)** *(more or less)* bastante; **he is quite a good salesman** = es un vendedor bastante bueno; **she can type quite fast** = escribe a máquina bastante de prisa; **sales are quite satisfactory in the first quarter** = las ventas han sido bastante satisfactorias en el primer trimestre **(b)** *(very or completely)* muy *or* perfectamente *or* totalmente; **he is quite capable of running the department alone** = es perfectamente capaz de llevar el departamento solo; **the company is quite possibly going to be sold** = es muy probable que la compañía se venda **(c)** **quite a few** *or* **quite a lot** = bastantes; **quite a few of our sales staff are women** = bastantes de nuestros vendedores son mujeres; **quite a lot of orders come in the pre-Christmas period** = llegan bastantes pedidos en el periodo anterior a la Navidad

quorum ['kwɔːrəm] *noun* quórum *m*; **to have a quorum** = haber quórum; **do we have a quorum?** = ¿hay quórum?

◊ **quorate** ['kwɔːreɪt] *adjective* con suficiente quórum

> COMMENT: if there is a quorum at a meeting, the meeting is said to be 'quorate'; if there aren't enough people present to make a quorum, the meeting is 'inquorate'

quota ['kwɔːtə] *noun* cupo *m or* cuota *f*; **import quota** = cuota *or* cupo de importación; **the government has imposed a quota on the importation of cars** = el gobierno ha impuesto un cupo de importación de coches; **the quota on imported cars has been lifted** = el cupo de coches de importación ha sido suprimido; **quota system** = sistema de cupo; **to arrange distribution through a quota system** = organizar la distribución por un sistema de cupo

> QUOTE Canada agreed to a new duty-free quota of 600,000 tonnes a year
> **Globe and Mail (Toronto)**

quote [kwəʊt] **1** *verb* **(a)** *(to repeat words or a reference number)* citar *or* dar *or* indicar; **he quoted figures from the annual report** = citó cifras del informe anual; **in reply please quote this number** = sírvanse indicar este número al contestar; **when making a complaint please quote the batch number printed on the box** = cuando hagan una reclamación indiquen el número de lote impreso en la caja; **he replied, quoting the number of the account** = contestó indicando el número de la cuenta **(b)** *(to estimate costs)* cotizar *or* calcular *or* ofrecer un precio *or* dar el precio; **to quote a price for supplying stationery** = dar un precio para el suministro de material de oficina; **their prices are always quoted in dollars** = sus precios siempre se cotizan en dólares; **he quoted me a price of £1,026** = me dio un precio de £1.026; **can you quote for supplying 20,000 envelopes?** = ¿puede darnos el precio para el suministro de 20.000 sobres? **2** *noun (informal)* cotización *f or* precio *m or* oferta *f*; **to give someone a quote for supplying computers** = cotizar el precio para el suministro de ordenadores; **we have asked for quotes for refitting the shop** = hemos pedido precios para renovar el mobiliario de la tienda; **his quote was the lowest of three** = su oferta fue la más baja de las tres; **we accepted the lowest quote** = aceptamos la oferta más baja

◊ **quotation** [kwə(ʊ)'teɪʃ(ə)n] *noun* **(a)** *(estimate)* cotización *f or* presupuesto *m or* precio *m or* oferta *f*; **they sent in their quotation for the job** = presentaron su presupuesto para el trabajo; **to ask for quotations for refitting the shop** = pedir precios para renovar el mobiliario de la tienda; **his quotation was much lower than all the others** = su oferta fue mucho más baja que las demás; **we accepted the lowest quotation** = aceptamos la cotización más baja **(b)** **quotation on the Stock Exchange** *or* **Stock Exchange quotation** = cotización de la bolsa; **the company is going for a quotation on the Stock Exchange** = la sociedad ha solicitado entrar en la cotización oficial de la Bolsa; **we are seeking a stock market quotation** = buscamos una cotización en el mercado de valores

◊ **quoted** ['kwəʊtɪd] *adjective* **quoted company** = sociedad cuyas acciones se cotizan en bolsa; **quoted shares** = acciones que se cotizan en bolsa

> QUOTE a Bermudan-registered company quoted on the Luxembourg stock exchange
> **Lloyd's List**

> QUOTE banks operating on the foreign exchange market refrained from quoting forward US/Hongkong dollar exchange rates
> **South China Morning Post**

qwerty *or* **QWERTY** ['kwɜːti] *noun* **qwerty keyboard** = teclado *m* QWERTY (alusión a las letras q-w-e-r-t-y, que suelen figurar por este orden en la primera fila de los teclados de las máquinas de escribir); **the computer has a normal qwerty keyboard** = el ordenador tiene un teclado 'qwerty' normal

Rr

R&D ['ɑːrən'diː] = RESEARCH AND DEVELOPMENT investigación y desarrollo (I+D); **the R&D department** = el departamento de investigación y desarrollo; **the company spends millions on R&D** = la compañía gasta millones en investigación y desarrollo

rack [ræk] *noun* **(a)** estante *m or* estantería *f*; **card rack** = estante de tarjetas; **display rack** = estante de exposición; **magazine rack** = estante de revistas; **rack jobber** = mayorista que aprovisiona directamente las estanterías en tiendas donde vende sus artículos **(b) rack rent** = (i) alquiler exorbitante; (ii) alquiler anual de una propiedad

racket ['rækɪt] *noun* chanchullo *m or* negocio sucio *or* fraudulento; **he runs a cut-price ticket racket** = tiene un chanchullo de billetes a precio reducido

◊ **racketeer** [rækə'tɪə] *noun* chantajista *mf or* estafador, -ra *or* timador, -ra

◊ **racketeering** [rækə'tɪərɪŋ] *noun* negocio ilícito o deshonesto

rag trade ['ræg 'treɪd] *noun (informal)* industria *f* del vestido

raid [reɪd] *noun* **dawn raid** = compra masiva de acciones de una compañía al principio de la sesión del día; **bear raid** = venta masiva de acciones para hacer bajar los precios en la bolsa

◊ **raider** ['reɪdə] *noun* especulador, -ra *or* compañía que compra acciones de otra antes de intentar su adquisición

QUOTE bear raiding involves trying to depress a target company's share price by heavy selling of its shares, spreading adverse rumours or a combination of the two. As an added refinement, the raiders may sell short. The aim is to push down the price so that the raiders can buy back the shares they sold at a lower price
Guardian

rail [reɪl] *noun* ferrocarril *m*; **six million commuters travel to work by rail each day** = seis millones de personas van al trabajo en tren todos los días; **we ship all our goods by rail** = enviamos todas las mercancías por ferrocarril; **rail travellers are complaining about rising fares** = los usuarios del tren se quejan del aumento de las tarifas; **rail travel is cheaper than air travel** = es más barato viajar en tren que en avión; **free on rail (FOR)** = franco vagón FF.CC.

◊ **railhead** ['reɪlhed] *noun* estación *f* terminal *or* cabeza *f* de línea; **the goods will be sent to the railhead by lorry** = las mercancías se enviarán a la estación terminal por camión

◊ **railway** *or* US **railroad** ['reɪlweɪ *or* 'reɪlrəʊd] *noun* ferrocarril *m*; **a railway station** = estación de ferrocarril; **a railway line** = línea de ferrocarril; **the British railway network** = la red británica de ferrocarriles

raise [reɪz] **1** *noun* US aumento *m* de sueldo; **he asked the boss for a raise** = pidió un aumento de sueldo al patrón; **she is pleased - she has had her raise** = está contenta - ha recibido un aumento de sueldo (NOTE: GB English is **rise**) **2** *verb* **(a)** *(bring up)* plantear; **to raise a question** *or* **a point at a meeting** = plantear una cuestión *or* un asunto en una reunión; **in answer to the questions raised by Mr Smith** = en relación a las cuestiones planteadas por el señor Smith; **the chairman tried to prevent the question of redundancies being raised** = el presidente intentó evitar que se planteara la cuestión de los despidos **(b) to raise an invoice** = preparar una factura **(c)** *(to increase)* aumentar *or* subir; **the government has raised taxes** = el gobierno ha subido los impuestos; **air fares will be raised on June 1st** = los billetes de avión subirán el 1 de junio; **the company raised its dividend by 10%** = la compañía incrementó su dividendo en un 10%; **when the company raised its prices, it lost half of its share of the market** = después de subir sus precios, la empresa perdió la mitad de su participación en el mercado **(d)** *(to obtain money or a loan)* conseguir *or* obtener; **the company is trying to raise the capital to fund its expansion programme** = la compañía está intentando conseguir capital para financiar su programa de expansión; **the government raises more money by indirect taxation than by direct** = el gobierno obtiene más dinero con los impuestos indirectos que con los directos; **where will he raise the money from to start up his business?** = ¿de dónde conseguirá el dinero para empezar su negocio?

QUOTE the company said yesterday that its recent share issue has been oversubscribed, raising A$225.5m
Financial Times

QUOTE investment trusts can raise capital, but this has to be done as a company does, by a rights issue of equity
Investors Chronicle

QUOTE over the past few weeks, companies raising new loans from international banks have been forced to pay more
Financial Times

rake in ['reɪk 'ɪn] *verb* amasar; **to rake in cash** *or* **to rake it in** = ganar mucho dinero

◊ **rake-off** ['reɪkɒf] *noun* comisión *f or* tajada *f*; **the group gets a rake-off on all the company's sales** = el grupo saca una tajada de todas las ventas de la compañía; **he got a £100,000 rake-off for introducing the new business** = se llevó una comisión de £100.000 por haber establecido contacto con la nueva compañía (NOTE: plural is **rake-offs**)

rally ['ræli] **1** *noun* recuperación *f* (de precios después de un periodo de baja); **shares staged a rally on the Stock Exchange** = el precio de las acciones en bolsa se recuperó; **after a brief rally shares fell back to a new low** = después de una breve recuperación, las acciones descendieron a sus precios más bajos **2** *verb* recuperarse; **shares rallied on the news of the latest government figures** = las

acciones se recuperaron al anunciarse los últimos
resultados del gobierno

```
QUOTE when Japan rallied, it had no
difficulty in surpassing its previous all-
time high, and this really stretched the
price-earnings     ratios     into     the
stratosphere
                          Money Observer
```

```
QUOTE bad news for the U.S. economy
ultimately may have been the cause of a
late rally in stock prices yesterday
                          Wall Street Journal
```

RAM [ræm] = RANDOM ACCESS MEMORY

ramp [ræmp] *noun* rampa *f or* desnivel *m*; **loading
ramp** = rampa de carga

rand [rænd] *noun (currency of South Africa and
Namibia)* rand *m*

random ['rændəm] *adjective* al azar *or* aleatorio,
-ria; **random access memory (RAM)** = memoria de
acceso al azar; **random check** = chequeo al azar;
random error = error aleatorio; **random sample** =
muestra aleatoria; **random sampling** = muestreo
aleatorio; **at random** = al azar; **the chairman
picked out two salesmen's reports at random** = el
presidente eligió al azar los informes de dos
vendedores

range [reɪn(d)ʒ] **1** *noun* **(a)** *(series of items to
choose from)* gama *f or* surtido *m*; **we offer a wide
range of sizes** *or* **range of styles** = ofrecemos un
amplio surtido de tallas *or* una amplia gama de
estilos; **their range of products** *or* **product range is
too narrow** = su gama de productos es demasiado
limitada; **we have the most modern range of
models** *or* **model range on the market** = nuestra
gama de modelos es la más moderna del mercado **(b)**
(variation from small to large) escala *f*; **I am
looking for something in the £2 - £3 price range** =
busco algo que cueste entre £2 y £3; **we make shoes
in a wide range of prices** = fabricamos zapatos
dentro de una amplia escala de precios **(c)** *(type of
variety)* ámbito *m*; **this falls within the company's
range of activities** = esto entra dentro del ámbito de
actividades de la compañía **2** *verb* oscilar *or* variar;
**the company sells products ranging from the
cheap down-market pens to imported luxury
items** = la empresa vende desde bolígrafos baratos a
artículos de importación lujosos; **the company's
salary scale ranges from £5,000 for a trainee to
£50,000 for the managing director** = la escala
salarial de la empresa oscila entre las £5.000 para un
aprendiz y las £50.000 para el director gerente; **our
activities range from mining in the USA to
computer servicing in Scotland** = nuestras
actividades abarcan desde minas en los EE UU a
servicios de revisión de ordenadores en Escocia

rank [ræŋk] **1** *noun* grado *m or* categoría *f*; **all
managers are of equal rank** = todos los directores
tienen la misma categoría; **in rank order** = en orden
de importancia **2** *verb* **(a)** *(to classify in order of
importance)* clasificar; **candidates are ranked in
order of appearance** = los candidatos están
clasificados por orden de aparición **(b)** *(to be in a
certain position)* clasificarse; **the non-voting shares
rank equally with the voting shares** = las acciones
sin derecho a voto tienen tanta importancia como las
que tienen derecho a voto; **all managers rank**

equally = todos los directores tienen la misma
categoría

◊ **rank and file** ['ræŋk ənd 'faɪl] *noun* base *f* (de
un sindicato); **the rank and file of the trade union
membership** = los afiliados de base del sindicato;
the decision was not liked by the rank and file = la
decisión no gustó a las bases; **rank-and-file
members** = socios ordinarios

◊ **ranking** ['ræŋkɪŋ] *adjective* de categoría
determinada; **high-ranking official** = un oficial *or*
delegado *or* representante de alta categoría; **he is the
top-ranking** *or* **the senior-ranking official in the
delegation** = es el delegado *or* representante
principal de la delegación

rapid ['ræpɪd] *adjective* rápido, -da; **we offer 5%
discount for rapid settlement** = ofrecemos un 5%
de descuento por pago al contado

◊ **rapidly** ['ræpɪdli] *adverb* rápidamente *or*
vertiginosamente; **the company rapidly ran up
debts of over £1m** = la compañía contrajo
rápidamente deudas de más de £1 millón; **the new
clothes shop rapidly increased sales** = la nueva
tienda de ropa aumentó sus ventas en poco tiempo

rare [reə] *adjective* raro, -ra *or* excepcional *or* poco
frecuente; **experienced salesmen are rare these
days** = los vendedores con experiencia son poco
frecuentes hoy en día; **it is rare to find a small
business with good cash flow** = es excepcional
encontrar una empresa pequeña con una buena
situación de flujo de caja

◊ **rarely** ['reəli] *adverb* raramente *or* con poca
frecuencia *or* casi nunca; **the company's shares are
rarely sold on the Stock Exchange** = las acciones
de la compañía se venden raramente en la bolsa; **the
chairman is rarely in his office on Friday
afternoons** = el presidente casi nunca está en su
oficina los viernes por la tarde

rata ['rɑːtə] *see* PRO RATA

rate [reɪt] **1** *noun* **(a)** *(price)* tasa *f or* precio *m or* tipo
m or porcentaje *m or* cuota *f*; **all-in rate** = precio todo
incluido *or* total; **fixed rate** = tipo fijo; **flat rate** =
tanto alzado *or* porcentaje *or* cuota fija; **a flat-rate
increase of 10%** = un aumento fijo de un 10%; **we
pay a flat rate for electricity each quarter** =
pagamos una cuota fija de luz cada trimestre; **he is
paid a flat rate of £2 per thousand** = se le paga un
tanto fijo de £2 por mil; **freight rates** = cuotas *or*
tarifas de flete; **full rate** = precio íntegro *or* sin
descuento; **the going rate** = la tarifa *or* el precio
vigente; **the going rate for offices is £15 per square
metre** = el precio normal de oficinas es de £15 por
metro cuadrado; **letter rate** *or* **parcel rate** = tarifa de
cartas *or* tarifa de paquetes; **it is more expensive to
send a packet letter rate but it will get there
quicker** = sale más caro enviar un paquete con tarifa
de carta pero llegará antes; **the market rate** = el
precio *or* la tarifa del mercado; **we pay the going
rate** *or* **the market rate for typists** = pagamos a los
mecanógrafos la tarifa corriente *or* en vigor; **night
rate** = tarifa nocturna; **reduced rate** = precio
reducido *or* tarifa reducida; **rate card** = tarifa de
anuncios publicitarios **(b)** **discount rate** = tipo de
descuento; **insurance rates** = tarifas de seguros;
interest rate *or* **rate of interest** = tipo de interés;
rate of return = tasa de rentabilidad *or* de
rendimiento; **tax rate** = tipo impositivo *or* de

gravamen **(c) bank base rates** = tipos base de interés bancario; **cross rate** = tipo de cambio de dos divisas expresado en una tercera; **exchange rate** or **rate of exchange** = tipo de cambio or tasa de cambio; **what is today's rate** or **the current rate for the dollar?** = ¿A cuánto está el dólar? or ¿cuál es el cambio actual del dólar?; **fixed exchange rate** = cambio fijo; **to calculate costs on a fixed exchange rate** = calcular costes tomando como base un tipo de cambio fijo; **floating rate of exchange** = cambio flotante; **forward rate** = tipo de cambio para operaciones a plazo **(d)** *(amount* or *number* or *speed compared with something else)* tasa *f* or cantidad *f* or cuota *f* or coeficiente *m* or indice *m*; **the rate of increase in redundancies** = la tasa de aumento or coeficiente de incremento de los despidos; **the rate of absenteeism** or **the absenteeism rate always increases in fine weather** = el índice de absentismo siempre aumenta con el buen tiempo; **birth rate** = indice or tasa de natalidad; **call rate** = número de visitas hechas por un representante durante un tiempo determinado; **depreciation rate** = coeficiente or tasa de amortización or depreciación; **error rate** = tasa de errores; **rate of sales** = ritmo de ventas **(e)** *(formerly British local taxes on property)* **the rates** = impuestos *mpl* municipales sobre la propiedad (NOTE: now replaced by **council tax**; the US equivalent is **local property tax**) **(uniform) business rate (UBR)** = impuesto municipal abonado por comerciantes o empresas; **water rate** = canon *m* de agua **2** *verb* **(a) to rate someone highly** = tener un gran concepto de una persona **(b) highly-rated part of London** = distrito de Londres con impuestos municipales elevados

◊ **rateable** ['reɪtəbl] *adjective* **rateable value** = valor imponible de la propiedad

◊ **ratepayer** ['reɪtpeɪə] *noun* contribuyente *mf* municipal; **business ratepayer** = contribuyente que paga los impuestos municipales sobre su empresa

QUOTE state-owned banks cut their prime rate a percentage point to 11%
Wall Street Journal

QUOTE the unions had argued that public sector pay rates had slipped behind rates applying in private sector employment
Australian Financial Review

QUOTE royalties have been levied at a rate of 12.5% of full production
Lloyd's List

ratify ['rætɪfaɪ] *verb* ratificar; **the agreement has to be ratified by the board** = el convenio tiene que ser ratificado por el consejo de administración

◊ **ratification** [rætɪfɪ'keɪʃən] *noun* ratificación *f*; **the agreement has to go to the board for ratification** = el convenio tiene que obtener la ratificación del consejo de administración

rating ['reɪtɪŋ] *noun* **(a)** *(property)* tasación *f* or valoración *f*; **rating officer** = tasador municipal **(b)** *(classification)* clasificación *f* or valoración *f* **credit rating** = clasificación crediticia; **merit rating** = valoración de méritos; **performance rating** = valoración de resultados **(c)** *(estimated audience)* **ratings** = nivel de audiencia de los programas televisivos; **the show is high in the ratings, which means it will attract good publicity** = el programa

tiene un alto nivel de audiencia y por tanto atraerá mucha publicidad

ratio ['reɪʃɪəʊ] *noun* razón *f* or relación *f*; **the ratio of successes to failures** = la relación entre éxitos y fracasos; **our product outsells theirs by a ratio of two to one** = nuestro producto se vende dos veces más que el suyo; **price/earnings ratio (P/E ratio)** = relación precio-ganancias; **the shares sell at a P/E ratio of 7** = el precio de las acciones implica una relación precio-ganancias de 7

ration ['ræʃən] *verb* racionar or dosificar or limitar; **to ration investment capital** or **to ration funds for investment** = limitar el capital destinado a la inversión; **to ration mortgages** = limitar los fondos disponibles para hipotecas; **mortgages are rationed for first-time buyers** = los préstamos para las primeras hipotecas están limitados

◊ **rationing** ['ræʃənɪŋ] *noun* racionamiento *m*; **there may be a period of food rationing this winter** = es posible que este invierno haya un periodo de racionamiento de víveres; **building societies are warning of mortgage rationing** = las sociedades de crédito hipotecario advierten de la posibilidad de restringir hipotecas

rationale [ræʃə'nɑːl] *noun* lógica *f*; **I do not understand the rationale behind the decision to sell the warehouse** = no entiendo la lógica de la decisión de vender el almacén

rationalization [ræʃnəlaɪ'zeɪʃən] *noun* racionalización *f*

◊ **rationalize** ['ræʃnəlaɪz] *verb* racionalizar; **the rail company is trying to rationalize its freight services** = la compañía de ferrocarriles está intentando racionalizar su servicio de carga

rat race ['ræt 'reɪs] *noun* competición *f* or lucha *f* agresiva por el éxito profesional; **he decided to get out of the rat race and buy a small farm** = decidió abandonar la lucha incesante del mundo profesional y se compró una pequeña granja

raw [rɔː] *adjective* crudo, -da or sin refinar; **raw data** = datos sin analizar; **raw materials** = materias primas

QUOTE it makes sense for them to produce goods for sale back home in the US from plants in Britain where raw materials are relatively cheap
Duns Business Month

R/D = REFER TO DRAWER

re [riː] *preposition* ref. or con referencia a; **re your inquiry of May 29th** = con referencia a su petición de información del 29 de mayo; **re: Smith's memo of yesterday** = ref.: memorandum de ayer del Sr. Smith; **re: the agenda for the AGM** = ref.1m: orden del día de la junta anual

re- [riː] *prefix* re-

reach [riːtʃ] **1** *noun* alcance *m*; **to be within reach** = estar al alcance **2** *verb* **(a)** *(to arrive at a place* or *at a point)* llegar or alcanzar; **the plane reaches Hong Kong at midday** = el avión llega a Hong Kong a mediodía; **sales reached £1m in the first four months of the year** = las ventas alcanzaron £1 millón en los primeros cuatro meses del año; **I did not reply because your letter never reached me** =

no respondí porque no recibí su carta **(b)** *(to come to)* llegar a; **to reach an agreement** = llegar a un acuerdo; **to reach an accommodation with creditors** = llegar a un acuerdo con los acreedores; **to reach a decision** = adoptar *or* tomar una decisión *or* una resolución; **an agreement has been reached between the management and the trade unions** = se ha llegado a un acuerdo entre la dirección y los sindicatos; **the two parties reached an agreement over the terms for the contract** = las dos partes llegaron a un acuerdo respecto a los términos del contrato; **the board reached a decision about closing the factory** = el consejo de administración llegó a un acuerdo respecto al cierre de la fábrica

react [rɪ'ækt] *verb* **to react to** = reaccionar ante; **shares reacted sharply to the fall in the exchange rate** = las acciones reaccionaron acusadamente ante la caída del tipo de cambio; **how will the chairman react when we tell him the news?** = ¿cómo reaccionará el presidente cuando le informemos de la noticia?

◇ **reaction** [rɪ'ækʃən] *noun* reacción *f*; **the reaction of the shares to the news of the takeover bid** = la reacción de las acciones ante la noticia de la oferta de adquisición

read [riːd] *verb* leer; **the terms and conditions are printed in very small letters so that they are difficult to read** = las condiciones se imprimen en letra muy pequeña para que sean difíciles de leer; **has the managing director read your report on sales in India?** = ¿ha leído el director gerente tu informe sobre las ventas en la India?; **can the computer read this information?** = ¿puede el ordenador leer esta información?

◇ **readable** ['riːdəbl] *adjective* legible; **machine-readable codes** = códigos legibles por la máquina; **the data has to be presented in computer-readable form** = los datos deben presentarse en forma legible por el ordenador

◇ **read only memory (ROM)** [riːd 'əʊnlɪ 'memərɪ] *noun (computer memory)* memoria de lectura solamente

readjust [riːə'dʒʌst] *verb* reajustar; **to readjust prices to take account of the rise in the costs of raw materials** = reajustar los precios para tener en cuenta el aumento del costo de materias primas; **shares prices readjusted quickly to the news of the devaluation** = los precios de las acciones se reajustaron rápidamente ante la noticia de la devaluación

◇ **readjustment** [riːə'dʒʌstmənt] *noun* reajuste *m*; **a readjustment in pricing** = un reajuste de precios; **after the devaluation there was a period of readjustment in the exchange rates** = después de la devaluación hubo un periodo de reajuste de los tipos de cambio

readvertise ['riːˈædvətaɪz] *verb* volver a anunciar; **to readvertise a post** = volver a anunciar una vacante; **all the candidates failed the test, so we will just have to readvertise** = ninguno de los aspirantes superó la prueba, por lo que tendremos que volver a anunciar el puesto

◇ **readvertisement** ['riːəd'vɜːtɪsmənt] *noun* segundo anuncio

ready ['redɪ] *adjective* **(a)** listo, -ta *or* preparado, -da; **the order will be ready for delivery next week** = el pedido estará listo para su entrega la semana que viene; **the driver had to wait because the shipment was not ready** = el chófer tuvo que esperar porque la mercancía no estaba preparada; **make-ready time** = tiempo necesario de preparación de una máquina antes de que pueda funcionar **(b) ready cash** = efectivo; **these items find a ready sale in the Middle East** = estos artículos se venden muy bien en el Oriente Próximo

◇ **ready-made** *or* **ready-to-wear** ['redɪˈmeɪd *or* 'redɪtə'weə] *adjective* de confección *or* confeccionado, -da; **the ready-to-wear trade has suffered from foreign competition** = el negocio de la confección ha sido víctima de la competencia extranjera

real [rɪəl] *adjective* **(a)** *(authentic)* real *or* verdadero, -ra *or* auténtico, -ca *or* genuino, -na; **his case is made of real leather** *or* **he has a real leather case** = su maleta es de cuero auténtico *or* tiene una maleta de cuero auténtico; **that car is a real bargain at £300** = al precio de £300 ese coche es una verdadera ganga **(b)** *(adjusted for inflation)* **real income** *or* **real wages** = ingreso real *or* salarios reales; **in real terms** = en términos reales *or* en realidad; **wages have gone up by 3% but with inflation running at 5% that is a fall in real terms** = los salarios han subido un 3% pero con una inflación del 5% supone un deterioro en términos reales **(c)** *(computer)* **real time** = tiempo real (de ordenador); **real-time system** = sistema de ordenador a tiempo real **(d) real estate** = bienes raíces *or* propiedad inmobiliaria; **he made his money from real estate deals in the 1970s** = hizo su fortuna durante los años 70 en transacciones inmobiliarias; **real estate management** = administración de bienes inmuebles; *US* **real estate agent** = agente inmobiliario

◇ **really** ['rɪəlɪ] *adverb* realmente *or* de hecho *or* en realidad; **these goods are really cheap** = estos artículos son realmente baratos; **the company is really making an acceptable profit** = la compañía en realidad está ganando unos beneficios aceptables; **the office building really belongs to the chairman's father** = el edificio de oficinas pertenece de hecho al padre del presidente; **the shop is really a bookshop, though it does carry some records** = la tienda es en realidad una librería, aunque también vende algunos discos

QUOTE real wages have been held down dramatically: they have risen as an annual rate of only 1% in the last two years
Sunday Times

QUOTE sterling M3 rose by 13.5% in the year to August - seven percentage points faster than the rate of inflation and the biggest increase in real terms since 1972-3
Economist

QUOTE on top of the cost of real estate, the investment in inventory and equipment to open a typical warehouse comes to around $5 million
Duns Business Month

QUOTE Japan's gross national product for the April-June quarter dropped 0.4% in real terms from the previous quarter
Nikkei Weekly

realign [riːə'laɪn] *verb* reordenar; **to realign currencies** = reordenar las divisas

◊ **realignment** [rɪə'laɪnmənt] *noun* reordenación *f*; **a realignment of currencies** *or* **a currency realignment** = una reordenación de divisas

realize ['rɪəlaɪz] *verb* **(a)** *(to understand clearly)* darse cuenta; **he soon realized the meeting was going to vote against his proposal** = pronto se dio cuenta de que los asistentes a la reunión iban a votar en contra de su propuesta; **the small shopkeepers realized that the hypermarket would take away some of their trade** = los pequeños comerciantes se dieron cuenta de que el hipermercado les quitaría una parte de su clientela; **when she went into the manager's office she did not realize she was going to be promoted** = cuando entró en la oficina del director no sabía que iba a ser ascendida **(b)** *(to make something become real)* **to realize a project** *or* **a plan** = realizar un proyecto *or* un plan **(c)** *(to sell for money)* realizar *or* liquidar; **to realize property** *or* **assets** = liquidar propiedades *or* activos; **the sale realized £100,000** = la venta produjo £100.000

◊ **realizable** [rɪə'laɪzəbl] *adjective* **realizable assets** = activo realizable

◊ **realization** [rɪəlaɪ'zeɪʃən] *noun* **(a)** *(gradual understanding)* comprensión *f* *or* toma de conciencia; **the chairman's realization that he was going to be outvoted** = el hecho de que el presidente comprendiera que iba a perder la votación **(b)** *(making real)* realización *f*; **the realization of a project** = realización de un proyecto; **the plan moved a stage nearer realization when the contracts were signed** = el plan avanzó hacia su realización cuando se firmaron los contratos **(c)** **realization of assets** = liquidación de activo

realtor ['rɪəltə] *noun US* agente *mf* de la propiedad inmobiliaria *or* corredor, -ra de fincas

◊ **realty** ['rɪəlti] *noun* propiedad *f* inmobiliaria *or* bienes *mpl* inmuebles

reapply [riːə'plaɪ] *verb* volver a presentarse *or* a solicitar; **when he saw that the job had still not been filled, he reapplied for it** = cuando vió que todavía no había sido asignado el puesto de trabajo, volvió a presentarse

◊ **reapplication** ['riːæplɪ'keɪʃən] *noun* nueva *or* segunda solicitud *f*

reappoint ['riːə'pɔɪnt] *verb* volver a nombrar; **he was reappointed chairman for a further three-year period** = le nombraron de nuevo presidente por otro periodo de tres años

◊ **reappointment** ['riːə'pɔɪntmənt] *noun* nuevo nombramiento *m*

reason ['riːzn] *noun* razón *f* *or* causa *f* *or* motivo *m*; **the airline gave no reason for the plane's late arrival** = la compañía aérea no explicó la causa del retraso en la llegada del avión; **the personnel officer asked him for the reason why he was late again** = el jefe de personal le preguntó el motivo de su nuevo retraso; **the chairman was asked for his reasons for closing the factory** = le pidieron al presidente que expusiera sus razones para el cierre de la fábrica

◊ **reasonable** ['riːzənəbl] *adjective* **(a)** *(sensible or not annoyed)* razonable *or* tolerante *or* comprensivo, -va; **the manager of the shop was very reasonable when she tried to explain that she had left her credit cards at home** = el encargado de la tienda fue muy comprensivo cuando ella trató de explicar que se había dejado sus tarjetas de crédito en casa; **no reasonable offer refused** = se acepta cualquier oferta razonable **(b)** *(not expensive)* moderado, -da; **the restaurant offers good food at reasonable prices** = el restaurante ofrece buena comida a precios moderados

reassess [riːə'ses] *verb* revaluar

◊ **reassessment** [riːə'sesmənt] *noun* revaluación *f*

reassign [riːə'saɪn] *verb* reasignar

◊ **reassignment** [riːə'saɪnmənt] *noun* reasignación *f*

reassure [riːə'ʃʊə] *verb* **(a)** *(make someone calm)* tranquilizar; **the markets were reassured by the government statement on import controls** = los mercados se tranquilizaron ante el anuncio del gobierno sobre el control de las importaciones; **the manager tried to reassure her that she would not lose her job** = el director intentó tranquilizarla, diciéndole que no iba a perder su trabajo **(b)** *(reinsure)* reasegurar

◊ **reassurance** [riːə'ʃʊərəns] *noun* **(a)** *(making someone calm)* alivio *m* **(b)** *(reinsurance)* reaseguros *mpl*

rebate ['riːbeɪt] *noun* **(a)** *(price reduction)* rebaja *f* *or* descuento *m*; **to offer a 10% rebate on selected goods** = ofrecer un descuento del 10% sobre determinadas mercancías **(b)** *(money back)* desgravación *f* *or* bonificación *f* *or* reembolso *m*; **he got a tax rebate at the end of the year** = consiguió una desgravación fiscal a fin de año

rebound [rɪ'baʊnd] *verb* rebotar *or* repercutir; **the market rebounded on the news of the government's decision** = la noticia de la decisión del gobierno repercutió favorablemente en el mercado

recall [rɪ'kɒl] *verb* *(defective products)* retirar *(productos defectuosos)*; **they recalled 10,000 washing machines because of a faulty electrical connection** = retiraron 10.000 lavadoras porque tenían una conexión eléctrica defectuosa

recd = RECEIVED

receipt [rɪ'siːt] **1** *noun* **(a)** *(for money paid)* recibo *m* *or* justificante *m* *or* resguardo *m* *or* comprobante *m*; **customs receipt** = recibo de aduana; **rent receipt** = recibo del alquiler; **sales receipt** = comprobante de caja; **receipt for items purchased** = recibo de compra; **please produce your receipt if you want to exchange items** = en caso de que quiera cambiar los artículos comprados se ruega presentar el recibo; **receipt book** *or* **book of receipts** = libro de recibos **(b)** *(act of receiving something)* recibo *m* *or* recepción *f*; **to acknowledge receipt of a letter** = acusar recibo de una carta; **we acknowledge receipt of your letter of the 15th** = acusamos recibo de su carta del día 15; **goods will be supplied within thirty days of receipt of order** = las mercancías se entregarán en el plazo de treinta días después de recibir el pedido; **invoices are payable within thirty days of receipt** = las facturas son pagaderas en el plazo de treinta días a partir de la fecha de recibo; **on receipt of the notification, the company lodged an appeal** = al recibir la notificación, la compañía presentó una apelación **(c) receipts** = ingresos *mpl*; **to itemize receipts and expenditure** = detallar los ingresos y los gastos; **receipts are down against the same period of last year** = los ingresos son inferiores a los del año pasado en el mismo periodo **2** *verb* firmar un recibo *or* una factura

QUOTE the public sector borrowing requirement is kept low by treating the receipts from selling public assets as a reduction in borrowing

Economist

QUOTE gross wool receipts for the selling season to end June appear likely to top $2 billion

Australian Financial Review

receive [rɪ'siːv] *verb* recibir; **we received the payment ten days ago** = recibimos el pago hace diez días; **the workers have not received any salary for six months** = los trabajadores llevan seis meses sin cobrar; **the goods were received in good condition** = las mercancías se recibieron en buen estado; **'received with thanks'** = 'recibí'

◊ **receivable** [rɪ'siːvəbl] *adjective* admisible *or* por cobrar *or* a cobrar; **accounts receivable** = cuentas por cobrar *or* a cobrar; **bills receivable** = letras por cobrar

◊ **receivables** [rɪ'siːvəblz] *plural noun* efectos *mpl* por cobrar

◊ **receiver** [rɪ'siːvə] *noun* **(a)** *(person who receives something)* destinatario, -ria; **the receiver of the shipment** = el destinatario del envío **(b)** **official receiver** = administrador, -ra judicial de la quiebra *or* síndico *m*; **the court appointed a receiver for the company** = el tribunal nombró un administrador judicial para la liquidación de la compañía; **the company is in the hands of the receiver** = la compañía está en liquidación *or* en manos del administrador judicial **(c)** *(apparatus)* receptor *m*

◊ **receivership** [rɪ'siːvəʃɪp] *noun* **the company went into receivership** = la compañía entró en liquidación *or* fue intervenida judicialmente por quiebra

◊ **receiving** [rɪ'siːvɪŋ] *noun* **(a)** *(a delivery)* recepción *f* de mercancías; **receiving clerk** = recepcionista; **receiving department** = servicio de recepción; **receiving office** = oficina de recepción **(b)** **receiving order** = mandato *m* por el que se designa un administrador judicial a una empresa

recent ['riːsnt] *adjective* reciente; **the company's recent acquisition of a chain of shoe shops** = la reciente adquisición por parte de la compañía de una cadena de zapaterías; **his recent appointment to the board** = su reciente nombramiento al consejo de administración; **we will mail you our most recent catalogue** = le enviaremos nuestro último catálogo

◊ **recently** ['riːsntli] *adverb* recientemente; **the company recently started on an expansion programme** = la empresa inició hace poco un programa de expansión; **they recently decided to close the branch office in Australia** = decidieron recientemente cerrar la sucursal de Australia

reception [rɪ'sepʃən] *noun* recepción *f*; **reception clerk** = recepcionista *mf*; **reception desk** = recepción

◊ **receptionist** [rɪ'sepʃənɪst] *noun* recepcionista *mf*

recession [rɪ'seʃən] *noun* recesión *f*; **the recession has reduced profits in many companies** = la recesión ha reducido los beneficios de muchas compañías; **several firms have closed factories because of the recession** = varias empresas han cerrado sus fábricas debido a la recesión

COMMENT: there are various ways of deciding if a recession is taking place: the usual one is when the GNP falls for three consecutive quarters

recipient [rɪ'sɪpɪənt] *noun* receptor, -ra *or* beneficiario, -ria *or* destinatario, -ria; **the recipient of an allowance** = el beneficiario de un subsidio

reciprocal [rɪ'sɪprəkəl] *adjective* recíproco, -ca; **reciprocal agreement** = acuerdo recíproco; **reciprocal contract** = contrato recíproco; **reciprocal holdings** = tenencia recíproca de acciones; **reciprocal trade** = comercio recíproco

◊ **reciprocate** [rɪ'sɪprəkeɪt] *verb* corresponder; **they offered us an exclusive agency for their cars and we reciprocated with an offer of the agency for our buses** = nos ofrecieron la representación exclusiva de sus coches y nosotros correspondimos ofreciéndoles la representación de nuestros autobuses

◊ **reciprocity** [resɪ'prɒsɪti] *noun* reciprocidad *f*

QUOTE in 1934 Congress authorized President Roosevelt to seek lower tariffs with any country willing to reciprocate

Duns Business Month

reckon ['rekən] *verb* **(a)** *(calculate)* calcular *or* estimar; **to reckon the costs at £25,000** = estimar los costes en £25.000; **we reckon the loss to be over £1m** = calculamos que la pérdida es superior a £1 millón; **they reckon the insurance costs to be too high** = consideran que el precio del seguro es demasiado alto **(b)** **to reckon on** = contar con; **they reckon on being awarded the contract** = cuentan con que se les adjudique el contrato; **he can reckon on the support of the managing director** = puede contar con el apoyo del director gerente

reclaim [rɪ'kleɪm] *verb* reclamar; **after he stopped paying the hire purchase instalments, the finance company tried to reclaim his car** = cuando dejó de pagar los plazos, la sociedad financiera intentó reclamarle el coche

recognize ['rekəgnaɪz] *verb* **(a)** reconocer; **I recognized his voice before he said who he was** = reconocí su voz antes de que dijera quién era; **do you recognize the handwriting on the letter?** = ¿reconoces la letra del autor de la carta? **(b)** **to recognize a union** = reconocer a un sindicato; **although all the staff had joined the union, the management refused to recognize it** = aunque todo el personal se había afiliado al sindicato, la patronal se negó a reconocerlo; **recognized agent** = agente acreditado

◊ **recognition** [rekəg'nɪʃən] *noun* reconocimiento *m*; **brand recognition** = reconocimiento de marca; **to grant a trade union**

recognition = reconocer un sindicato; **recognition of qualifications** = convalidación *f* de títulos

recommend [rekə'mend] *verb* **(a)** *(suggest action)* recomendar; **the investment adviser recommended buying shares in aircraft companies** = el asesor de inversiones recomendó comprar acciones de compañías aeronáuticas; **we do not recommend bank shares as a safe investment** = no recomendamos las acciones de los bancos como una inversión segura; **the board meeting recommended a dividend of 10p a share** = el consejo de administración recomendó repartir un dividendo de 10p por acción; **manufacturer's recommended price (MRP)** *or* **recommended retail price (RRP)** = precio recomendado por el fabricante para la venta al por menor; **'all typewriters - 20% off MRP'** = 'para todas las máquinas de escribir - descuento del 20% sobre el precio recomendado' **(b)** *(someone or something)* recomendar; **he recommended a shop in the High Street for shoes** = recomendó una zapatería en High Street; **I certainly would not recommend Miss Smith for the job** = ciertamente yo nunca recomendaría a la señorita Smith para el trabajo; **can you recommend a good hotel in Amsterdam?** = ¿puedes recomendar un buen hotel en Amsterdam?

◊ **recommendation** [rekəmen'deɪʃən] *noun* recomendación *f*; **we appointed him on the recommendation of his former employer** = le nombramos por la recomendación de su antiguo jefe

reconcile ['rekənsaɪl] *verb* cuadrar; **to reconcile one account with another** = cuadrar una cuenta con otra; **to reconcile the accounts** = cuadrar las cuentas

◊ **reconciliation** [rekənsɪlɪ'eɪʃən] *noun* reconciliación *f* *or* concertación *f*; **reconciliation statement** = estado de reconciliación; **reconciliation of accounts** = conciliación de cuentas

reconstruction [ri:kən'strʌkʃən] *noun* **(a)** *(building)* reconstrucción *f*; **the economic reconstruction of an area after a disaster** = la reconstrucción económica de una zona después de una catástrofe **(b)** *(financial)* reorganización *f*; **the reconstruction of a company** = la reorganización de una compañía

record 1 ['rekɔ:d] *noun* **(a)** *(report of something which has happened)* testimonio *m* *or* expresión *f* *or* informe *m*; **the chairman signed the minutes as a true record of the last meeting** = el presidente firmó el acta como expresión fiel de la última reunión; **for the record** *or* **to keep the record straight** = para que conste *or* para dejar las cosas en claro; **for the record, I would like these sales figures to be noted in the minutes** = quisiera dejar constancia de estas cifras de ventas consignándolas en el acta; **on record** = oficialmente; **the chairman is on record as saying that profits are set to rise** = el presidente ha dicho oficialmente que las ganancias van a aumentar; **off the record** = extraoficialmente *or* en privado; **he made some remarks off the record about the disastrous home sales figures** = hizo unas observaciones extraoficiales referentes a las desastrosas cifras de las ventas nacionales **(b)** **records** = archivos *mpl*; **the names of customers are kept in the company's records** = los nombres de los clientes se guardan en los archivos de la compañía; **we find from our records that our**

invoice number 1234 has not been paid = se desprende de nuestros libros que la factura número 1234 no ha sido pagada **(c)** *(description of what has happened)* historial *m* *or* expediente *m*; **the salesman's record of service** *or* **service record** = el historial del vendedor; **the company's record in industrial relations** = el historial de la empresa en el campo de las relaciones laborales; **criminal record** = antecedentes penales; **track record** = antecedentes *mpl* *or* experiencia *f*; **he has a good track record as a salesman** = tiene buenos antecedentes como vendedor; **the company has no track record in the computer market** = la empresa no tiene experiencia en el mercado de ordenadores **(d)** *(better than anything before)* récord *m*; **record sales** *or* **record losses** *or* **record profits** = récord de ventas *or* récord de pérdidas *or* récord de ganancias; **last year was a record year for the company** = el año pasado fue un año récord para la compañía; **sales for 1996 equalled the record of 1992** = las ventas en 1996 igualaron el récord de 1992; **our top salesman has set a new record for sales per call** = nuestro mejor vendedor ha establecido un nuevo récord de ventas por visita; **we broke our record for June** = hemos batido nuestro récord de junio **2** [rɪ'kɔ:d] *verb* registrar *or* anotar; **the company has recorded another year of increased sales** = la empresa ha registrado en otro año consecutivo un aumento de ventas; **your complaint has been recorded and will be investigated** = su queja ha sido anotada y será investigada; **recorded delivery** = correo certificado

◊ **record-breaking** ['rekɔ:d'breɪkɪŋ] *adjective* récord; **we are proud of our record-breaking profits** = estamos orgullosos de nuestros beneficios récord

◊ **recording** [rɪ'kɔ:dɪŋ] *noun* anotación *f*; **the recording of an order** *or* **of a complaint** = anotación de un pedido *or* de una queja

recoup [rɪ'ku:p] *verb* **to recoup one's losses** = recuperar las pérdidas

recourse [rɪ'kɔ:s] *noun* **to decide to have recourse to the courts** = decidir recurrir a los tribunales

recover [rɪ'kʌvə] *verb* **(a)** *(to get back)* recuperar; **he never recovered his money** = nunca recuperó su dinero; **the initial investment was never recovered** = la inversión inicial nunca fue recuperada; **to recover damages from the driver of the car** = obtener daños y perjuicios del conductor del coche; **to start a court action to recover property** = iniciar un proceso judicial para recuperar unos bienes **(b)** *(to get better or to rise)* recuperarse *or* mejorar; **the market has not recovered from the rise in oil prices** = el mercado no se ha recuperado de la subida de los precios del petróleo; **the stock market fell in the morning, but recovered during the afternoon** = la bolsa bajó por la mañana, pero mejoró durante la tarde

◊ **recoverable** [rɪ'kʌvərəbl] *adjective* recuperable

◊ **recovery** [rɪ'kʌvri] *noun* **(a)** *(getting back something which has been lost)* recuperación *f*; **we are aiming for the complete recovery of the money invested** = nuestro objetivo es la recuperación total del dinero invertido; **to start an action for recovery of property** = iniciar un proceso para la recuperación de bienes **(b)** *(movement upwards)* reactivación *f or* mejoría *f*; **the economy staged a recovery** = la economía experimentó una mejoría; **the recovery of the economy after a slump** = la reactivación de la economía después de una recesión; **recovery shares** = acciones en vías de recuperación

recruit [rɪ'kruːt] *verb* **to recruit new staff** = reclutar *or* contratar personal; **we are recruiting staff for our new store** = estamos contratando personal para nuestro nuevo almacén

◇ **recruitment** *or* **recruiting** [rɪ'kruːtmənt *or* rɪ'kruːtɪŋ] *noun* reclutamiento *m or* contratación *f*; **the recruitment of new staff** = contratación de nuevo personal; **graduate recruitment** = contratación de personal graduado *or* titulado

QUOTE some companies are still able to meet most of their needs by recruiting experienced people already in the industry
Personnel Management

QUOTE employers were asked about the nature of the jobs on offer and of the people they recruited to fill them
Employment Gazette

rectify ['rektɪfaɪ] *verb* corregir *or* rectificar; **to rectify an entry** = rectificar un asiento

◇ **rectification** [rektɪfɪ'keɪʃən] *noun* rectificación *f*

recurrent [rɪ'kʌrənt] *adjective* que se repite *or* repetido *or* constante; **a recurrent item of expenditure** = un gasto constante; **there is a recurrent problem in supplying this part** = hay un problema constante en el suministro de esta pieza de repuesto

recycle [riː'saɪkl] *verb* reciclar; **recycled paper** = papel reciclado

red [red] *noun* **in the red** = en números rojos *or* al descubierto; **my bank account is in the red** = mi cuenta bancaria está al descubierto; **the company went into the red in 1990** = la compañía entró en déficit en 1990; **the company is out of the red for the first time since 1950** = la compañía ha liquidado sus deudas por primera vez desde 1950

◇ **red tape** ['red 'teɪp] *noun* burocracia *f or* formalidades burocráticas *or* trámites burocráticos *or* papeleo *m*; **the Australian joint venture has been held up by government red tape** = los trámites gubernamentales han retrasado la operación conjunta de Australia

QUOTE he understood that little companies disliked red tape as much as big companies did and would pay to be relieved of the burden
Forbes Magazine

redeem [rɪ'diːm] *verb* **(a)** amortizar *or* pagar; **to redeem a mortgage** = amortizar una hipoteca; **to redeem a debt** = pagar una deuda **(b) to redeem a bond** = vender un bono

◇ **redeemable** [rɪ'diːməbl] *adjective* rescatable *or* amortizable

redemption [rɪ'dem(p)ʃən] *noun* **(a)** *(repayment of a loan)* amortización *f* de una deuda *or* rescate *m* de

un empréstito; **redemption date** = fecha de amortización *or* de rescate; **redemption before due date** = amortización anticipada *or* rescate anticipado; **redemption value** = valor de rescate; **redemption yield** = beneficio hasta la fecha de rescate **(b)** *(repayment of a debt)* reembolso *m or* cancelación *f* de una deuda; **redemption of a mortgage** = amortización de una hipoteca

redeploy [riːdɪ'plɔɪ] *verb* trasladar personal *or* adscribir el personal a una clase de trabajo diferente; **we closed the design department and redeployed the workforce in the publicity and sales departments** = cerramos el departamento de diseño y adscribimos el personal a los departamentos de publicidad y ventas

◇ **redeployment** [riːdɪ'plɔɪmənt] *noun* reorganización *f*

redevelop [riːdɪ'veləp] *verb* renovar

◇ **redevelopment** [riːdɪ'veləpmənt] *noun* renovación *f* urbana; **the redevelopment plan was rejected by the planning committee** = el plan de renovación urbana fue rechazado por la comisión de planificación

redistribute [riːdɪs'trɪbjʊt] *verb* redistribuir; **the government aims to redistribute wealth by taxing the rich and giving grants to the poor** = el gobierno pretende redistribuir la riqueza a través de impuestos a los ricos y subsidios a los pobres; **the orders have been redistributed among the company's factories** = los pedidos han sido redistribuidos entre las fábricas de la compañía

◇ **redistribution** ['riːdɪstrɪ'bjuːʃən] *noun* **redistribution of wealth** = redistribución *f* de la riqueza

redraft [riː'drɑːft] *verb* volver a redactar; **the whole contract had to be redrafted to take in the objections from the chairman** = hubo que volver a redactar todo el contrato para incluir las objeciones del presidente

reduce [rɪ'djuːs] *verb* reducir *or* rebajar *or* acortar *or* recortar *or* disminuir; **to reduce expenditure** = reducir gastos; **to reduce a price** = reducir un precio; **to reduce taxes** = reducir los impuestos; **we have made some staff redundant to reduce overmanning** = hemos despedido a algunos trabajadores para reducir el exceso de plantilla; **prices have been reduced by 15%** = los precios han sido reducidos en un 15%; **carpets are reduced from £100 to £50** = el precio de las alfombras ha sido rebajado de £100 a £50; **the company reduced output because of a fall in demand** = la empresa ha recortado su producción debido a la caída de la demanda; **the government's policy is to reduce inflation to 5%** = la política del gobierno es reducir la inflación al 5%; **to reduce staff** = reducir la plantilla

◇ **reduced** [rɪ'djuːst] *adjective* reducido, -da *or* rebajado, -da; **reduced prices have increased unit sales** = la rebaja de los precios ha aumentado el volumen de ventas; **prices have fallen due to a reduced demand for the goods** = los precios han bajado como consecuencia de una demanda reducida de los artículos

reduction [rɪ'dʌkʃən] *noun* reducción *f or* rebaja *f* (de precios); **price reductions** = rebajas de precios;

tax reductions = reducción de los impuestos; **staff reductions** = reducciones de personal; **reduction of expenditure** = recorte de gastos; **reduction in demand** = reducción de la demanda; **the company was forced to make job reductions** = la empresa se vió obligada a reducir la plantilla

redundancy [rı'dʌndənsi] *noun* despido *m or* pérdida *f* del puesto de trabajo *or* excedente de plantilla; **redundancy package** = paquete de indemnización por despido; **redundancy payment** = indemnización *or* compensación por despido; **voluntary redundancy** = baja incentivada *or* baja voluntaria con derecho a indemnización; **the takeover caused 250 redundancies** = la adquisición resultó en 250 despidos

◇ **redundant** [rı'dʌndənt] *adjective* **(a)** *(more than is needed)* excesivo, -va *or* redundante *or* sobrante *or* innecesario, -ria; **redundant capital** = capital sobrante; **redundant clause in a contract** = cláusula innecesaria de un contrato; **the new legislation has made clause 6 redundant** = debido a la nueva ley la cláusula 6 resulta innecesaria **(b) to make someone redundant** = despedir a un trabajador por exceso de plantilla; **redundant staff** = personal despedido por exceso de plantilla

> QUOTE when Mrs C. was made redundant at the age of 59 and 10 months, she lost ten-twelfths of her redundancy pay
> **Personnel Management**

re-elect [riː'lekt] *verb* reelegir; **he was re-elected chairman** = fue reelegido presidente; **the outgoing chairman is certain to be re-elected** = la reelección del presidente saliente está asegurada

◇ **re-election** [riː'lekʃən] *noun* reelección *f*; **to stand for re-election** = presentarse a reelección; **she is eligible to stand for re-election** = tiene derecho a presentarse a reelección

re-employ [riːım'plɔı] *verb* emplear de nuevo

◇ **re-employment** [riːım'plɔımənt] *noun* reempleo *m*

re-engage [riːın'geıdʒ] *verb* **to re-engage staff** = volver a contratar a personal

re-entry [riː'entri] *noun* reingreso *m or* segunda *or* nueva entrada *f*; **re-entry visa** *or* **permit** = visado que permite salir de un país y volver a entrar

re-establish [ˈriːıs'tæblıʃ] *verb* restablecer

re-examine [riːıg'zæmın] *verb* reexaminar

◇ **re-examination** [riːıgzæmı'neıʃən] *noun* nuevo examen *m*

re-export 1 [ˈriː'ekspɔːt] *noun* reexportación *f*; **re-export trade** = comercio de reexportación; **import wool for re-export** = importamos lana para reexportarla; **the value of re-exports has increased** = el valor de las reexportaciones ha subido **2** [riːeks'pɔːt] *verb* reexportar

◇ **re-exportation** [ˈriːekspɔː'teıʃən] *noun* reexportación *f*

ref [ref] = REFERENCE

refer [rı'fɜː] *verb* **(a)** *(mention)* referirse *or* mencionar; **we refer to your estimate of May 26th** = nos referimos a su estimación del 26 de mayo; **he referred to an article which he had seen in the 'Times'** = se refirió a un artículo que había visto en el 'Times'; **referring to your letter of June 4th** = con referencia a su carta del 4 de junio **(b)** *(to hand on to someone else)* remitir; **to refer a question to a committee** = remitir una cuestión a un comité; **we have referred your complaint to our supplier** = hemos remitido su queja a nuestro suministrador **(c)** *(to return)* **'refer to drawer' (R/D)** = 'remitir al librador'; **the bank referred the cheque to drawer** = el banco remitió el cheque al librador (NOTE: **referring - referred**)

◇ **referee** [refə'riː] *noun* persona *f* que da referencias *or* informes de otra; **to give someone's name as referee** = dar el nombre de alguien como referencia; **she gave the name of her boss as a referee** = dio el nombre de su jefe como referencia; **when applying please give the names of three referees** = al presentar las solicitudes, se ruega indicar los nombres de las tres personas que puedan proporcionar referencias

◇ **reference** [ˈrefərəns] *noun* **(a) terms of reference** = mandato *m*; **under the terms of reference of the committee, it cannot investigate complaints from the public** = conforme a su mandato, el comité no puede investigar quejas del público; **the committee's terms of reference do not cover exports** = las exportaciones no se incluyen en el mandato del comité **(b)** *(dealing with)* referencia *f*; **with reference to your letter of May 25th** = con referencia *or* con relación a su carta del 25 de mayo **(c)** *(numbers or letters which identify a document)* referencia; **our reference** *or* **our ref.** = nuestra referencia *or* n/ref.; **your reference** *or* **your ref.** = su referencia *or* s/ref.; **our reference: PC/MS 1234** = nuestra referencia: PC/MS 1234; **thank you for your letter (reference 1234)** = le agredecemos su carta (referencia 1234); **please quote this reference in all correspondence** = sírvanse indicar esta referencia en su correspondencia; **when replying please quote reference 1234** = sírvanse indicar la referencia 1234 en su respuesta **(d)** *(written report on someone's character or ability)* referencias; **to write someone a reference** *or* **to give someone a reference** = dar referencias a alguien; **to ask applicants to supply references** = pedir a los solicitantes que proporcionen referencias; **to ask a company for trade references** *or* **for bank references** = pedirle a una empresa referencias comerciales *or* referencias bancarias; **letter of reference** = carta de recomendación; **he enclosed letters of reference from his two previous employers** = adjuntó cartas de recomendación de sus dos jefes anteriores **(e)** *(person who reports on someone's character or ability)* persona *f* que da una referencia de otra *or* referencia; **to give someone's name as reference** = dar el nombre de alguien que pueda proporcionar una referencia; **please use me as a reference if you wish** = puedes dar mi nombre como referencia, si quieres

> QUOTE a reference has to be accurate and opinion must be clearly separated from the facts
> **Personnel Management**

refinance [riː'faınæns] *verb* refinanciar *or* renovar la financiación

◇ **refinancing** [ˈriːfaı'nænsıŋ] *noun* **refinancing of a loan** = refinanciación *f*

refit 1 ['riːfɪt] *noun* reparación *f or* reforma *f*; **the reopening of a store after a refit** = la reapertura de una tienda después de reformas **2** [riː'fɪt] *verb* reparar *or* reformar (NOTE: **refitting - refitted**)

◊ **refitting** [riː'fɪtɪŋ] *noun* reformas *fpl*

reflate [rɪ'fleɪt] *verb* **to reflate the economy** = reflacionar la economía; **the government's attempts to reflate the economy were not successful** = los esfuerzos del gobierno para reflacionar la economía no tuvieron éxito

◊ **reflation** [rɪ'fleɪʃən] *noun* reflación *f*

◊ **reflationary measures** [rɪ'fleɪʃnəri 'meʃəz] *noun* medidas reflacionarias

reform [rɪ'fɔːm] **1** *noun* reforma *f*; **tax reform** = reforma fiscal **2** *verb* reformar

refresher course [rɪ'freʃə 'kɔːs] *noun* curso *m* de reciclaje *or* actualización; **he went on a refresher course in bookkeeping** = asistió a un curso de reciclaje en contabilidad

refund 1 ['riːfʌnd] *noun* devolución *f or* reembolso *m*; **to ask for a refund** = exigir el reembolso; **she got a refund after she had complained to the manager** = consiguió que le reembolsaran después de quejarse al director; **full refund** *or* **refund in full** = reembolso total; **he got a full refund when he complained about the service** = reembolsaran el importe total cuando se quejó del servicio **2** [rɪ'fʌnd] *verb* reembolsar; **to refund the cost of postage** = reembolsar los gastos de correo; **all money will be refunded if the goods are not satisfactory** = en caso de que el producto no resulte satisfactorio se reembolsará el importe íntegro

◊ **refundable** [rɪ'fʌndəbl] *adjective* reembolsable; **refundable deposit** = depósito reembolsable; **the entrance fee is refundable if you purchase £5 worth of goods** = el precio de la entrada se devuelve si se compran mercancías por un valor de £5

◊ **refunding** [rɪ'fʌndɪŋ] *noun* **refunding of a loan** = conversión *f* de un préstamo

refuse [rɪ'fjuːz] *verb* rehusar *or* negar(se) *or* denegar *or* rechazar; **they refused to pay** = se negaron a pagar; **the bank refused to lend the company any more money** = el banco se negó a prestar más dinero a la compañía; **he asked for a rise but it was refused** = pidió un aumento de sueldo pero se le fue denegado; **the loan was refused by the bank** = el préstamo fue denegado por el banco; **the customer refused the goods** *or* **refused to accept the goods** = el cliente rechazó las mercancías *or* rehusó aceptar las mercancías (NOTE: you refuse **to do something** or refuse **something**)

◊ **refusal** [rɪ'fjuːzəl] *noun* denegación *f or* negativa *f or* rechazo *m*; **his request met with a refusal** = rechazaron su petición; **to give someone first refusal of something** = conceder una opción (de compra) a alguien; **blanket refusal** = rechazo *m* global

regard [rɪ'gɑːd] *noun* **with regard to** = con respecto a; **with regard to your request for unpaid leave** = con respecto a su solicitud de excedencia

◊ **regarding** [rɪ'gɑːdɪŋ] *preposition* relativo a *or* en cuanto a; **instructions regarding the shipment of goods to Africa** = instrucciones relativas al envío de mercancías a Africa

◊ **regardless** [rɪ'gɑːdləs] *adjective* **regardless of** = sin tener en cuenta; **the chairman furnished his office regardless of expense** = el presidente amuebló su oficina sin tener en cuenta el gasto

region ['riːdʒən] *noun* región *f*; **in the region of** = alrededor de; **he was earning a salary in the region of £25,000** = percibía un salario de alrededor de £25.000; **the house was sold for a price in the region of £100,000** = la casa se vendió por unas £100.000

◊ **regional** ['riːdʒənl] *adjective* regional; **regional planning** = planificación regional

register ['redʒɪstə] **1** *noun* **(a)** *(official list)* registro *m*; **to enter something in a register** = anotar algo en un registro; **to keep a register up to date** = mantener actualizado un registro; **companies' register** *or* **register of companies** = registro de compañías; **register of debentures** *or* **debenture register** = registro de títulos; **register of directors** = relación de directivos de una empresa; **land register** = catastro *or* registro de la propiedad; **Lloyd's register** = el registro de Lloyd's; **register of shareholders** *or* **share register** = libro registro de accionistas *or* acciones **(b)** *(large book)* libro de registro **(c) cash register** = caja registradora **2** *verb* **(a)** *(in an official list)* registrar *or* inscribir en un registro; **to register a company** = inscribir una compañía en un registro; **to register a sale** = registrar una venta; **to register a property** = registrar una propiedad; **to register a trademark** = registrar una marca comercial; **to register a ship** = abanderar **(b)** *(at a hotel or at a conference)* registrarse; **they registered at the hotel under the name of Macdonald** = se registraron en el hotel con el apellido Macdonald **(c)** *(post)* certificar; **I registered the letter, because it contained some money** = certifiqué la carta porque contenía dinero

◊ **registered** ['redʒɪstəd] *adjective* **(a)** *(official list)* registrado, -da *or* apuntado, -da oficialmente; **registered shares** = acciones nominativas; **registered share transaction** = transacción de acciones nominativas; **registered trademark** = marca registrada; **the company's registered office** = el domicilio social de la compañía **(b) registered letter** *or* **registered parcel** = carta certificada *or* paquete certificado; **registered post** *or* **registered mail** = correo certificado; **to send documents by registered mail** *or* **registered post** = enviar documentos por correo certificado

◊ **registrar** [redʒɪs'trɑː] *noun* (i) archivero, -ra *or* registrador, -ra; (ii) secretario, -ria general de una universidad; *(person who keep the share register of a company)* **the registrar of a company** = secretario *m or* registrador *m*; **Registrar of Companies** = (i) registrador mercantil; (ii) Registro *m* Mercantil

◊ **registration** [redʒɪs'treɪʃən] *noun* **(a)** *(noted on an official list)* registro *m or* inscripción *f or* matrícula *f*; **registration of a ship** = abanderamiento *m*; **registration of a trademark** *or* **of a share transaction** = registro de una marca comercial *or* de una transacción de acciones;

certificate of registration or **registration certificate** = certificado de inscripción; **registration fee** = cuota de inscripción or matrícula; **registration form** = boletín de inscripción; **registration number** = número de matrícula or de inscripción or de registro **(b) Companies Registration Office (CRO)** = Oficina del Registro Mercantil; **land registration** = catastro m or registro de la propiedad

◇ **registry** ['redʒɪstrɪ] noun **(a)** registro m; GB **land registry** = registro catastral or de la propiedad; **registry office** = oficina del registro civil **(b) port of registry** = puerto de registro **(c)** (of a ship) abanderamiento m

regressive taxation [rɪ'gresɪv tæk'seɪʃn] noun imposición f regresiva

regret [rɪ'gret] verb lamentar or sentir; **I regret having to make so many staff redundant** = siento tener que despedir a tanto personal; **we regret the delay in answering your letter** = lamentamos la demora en responder a su carta; **we regret to inform you of the death of the chairman** = lamentamos informarles de la muerte del presidente (NOTE: you **regret doing something** or **regret to do something** or **regret something**. Note also: **regretting** - **regretted**)

regular ['regjʊlə] adjective **(a)** (at the same time) regular; **his regular train is the 12.45** = normalmente viaja en el tren de las 12.45; **the regular flight to Athens leaves at 06.00** = el vuelo regular para Atenas sale a las 06.00; **regular customer** = cliente habitual; **regular income** = ingreso fijo; **she works freelance so she does not have a regular income** = trabaja por su cuenta y por eso no tiene unos ingresos fijos; **regular route** = ruta habitual; **regular staff** = personal fijo **(b)** (ordinary or standard) normal or ordinario, -ria or corriente; **the regular price is $1.25, but we are offering them at 99c** = el precio normal es de $1,25 pero los ofrecemos a 99c; **regular size** = tamaño normal

◇ **regularity** [regjʊ'lærɪtɪ] noun regularidad f

◇ **regularly** ['regjʊlɑlɪ] adverb regularmente or con regularidad; **the first train in the morning is regularly late** = el primer tren de la mañana suele llegar tarde

regulate ['regjʊleɪt] verb **(a)** (adjust) regular or ajustar **(b)** (according to law) regular or reglamentar; **prices are regulated by supply and demand** = los precios se regulan por la oferta y la demanda; **government-regulated price** = precio regulado por el gobierno

◇ **regulation** [regjʊ'leɪʃn] noun **(a)** (action) regulación f or reglamentación f; **the regulation of trading practices** = la regulación de las prácticas comerciales (NOTE: no plural in English) **(b)** (rule) regla f; **regulations** = normas fpl or disposiciones fpl or reglamento m; **the new government regulations on housing standards** = las nuevas disposiciones gubernamentales sobre la normalización de viviendas; **fire regulations** = reglamento sobre incendios; **safety regulations** = normas de seguridad; **regulations concerning imports and exports** = disposiciones sobre importación y exportación

◇ **regulator** ['regjʊleɪtə] noun regulador, -ra

◇ **regulatory** [regjʊ'leɪtərɪ] adjective reglamentario, -ra or según las normas establecidas;

regulatory power = poder reglamentario; see also SELF-REGULATORY

QUOTE EEC regulations which came into effect in July insist that customers can buy cars anywhere in the EEC at the local pre-tax price
Financial Times

QUOTE a unit trust is established under the regulations of the Department of Trade, with a trustee, a management company and a stock of units
Investors Chronicle

QUOTE the regulators have sought to protect investors and other market participants from the impact of a firm collapsing
Banking Technology

QUOTE fear of audit regulation, as much as financial pressures, is a major factor behind the increasing number of small accountancy firms deciding to sell their practices or merge with another firm
Accountancy

reimburse [riːɪm'bɜːs] verb reembolsar; **to reimburse someone his expenses** = reembolsarle los gastos a alguien; **you will be reimbursed for your expenses** or **your expenses will be reimbursed** = se le reembolsarán sus gastos or sus gastos serán reembolsados

◇ **reimbursement** ['riːɪm'bɜːsmənt] noun reembolso m; **reimbursement of expenses** = reembolso de gastos

reimport 1 [riː'ɪmpɔːt] noun reimportación f **2** ['riːɪm'pɔːt] verb reimportar

◇ **reimportation** ['riːɪmpɔː'teɪʃən] noun reimportación f

reinstate [riːɪn'steɪt] verb rehabilitar or reintegrar or restituir or readmitir; **the union demanded that the sacked workers should be reinstated** = el sindicato exigió que los trabajadores despedidos fueran readmitidos

◇ **reinstatement** ['riːɪn'steɪtmənt] noun restitución f or readmisión f

reinsure [riːɪn'ʃʊə] verb reasegurar

◇ **reinsurance** ['riːɪn'ʃʊərəns] noun reaseguro m

◇ **reinsurer** [riːɪn'ʃʊərə] noun reasegurador, -ra

reinvest [riːɪn'vest] verb reinvertir; **he reinvested the money in government stocks** = reinvirtió el dinero en títulos del Estado

◇ **reinvestment** ['riːɪn'vestmənt] noun reinversión f

QUOTE many large U.S. corporations offer shareholders the option of reinvesting their cash dividend payments in additional company stock at a discount to the market price. But to some big securities firms these discount reinvestment programs are an opportunity to turn a quick profit
Wall Street Journal

reissue [riː'ɪʃuː] **1** noun **(a)** (of shares) nueva emisión f (de títulos) **(b)** (of book) reedición f **2** verb

(a) *(shares)* emitir de nuevo **(b)** *(book)* reeditar; **the company reissued its catalogue with a new price list** = la empresa reeditó su catálogo con una nueva lista de precios

reject 1 ['ri:dʒekt] *noun* producto *m* defectuoso; **sale of rejects** *or* **of reject items** = venta de artículos defectuosos; **to sell off reject stock** = liquidar las existencias de artículos defectuosos; **reject shop** = tienda de artículos defectuosos **2** [rɪ'dʒekt] *verb* rechazar; **the union rejected the management's proposals** = el sindicato rechazó las propuestas de la dirección; **the company rejected the takeover bid** = la compañía rechazó la oferta de adquisición

◊ **rejection** [rɪ'dʒekʃən] *noun* rechazo *m*

related [rɪ'leɪtɪd] *adjective* relacionado, -da *or* afín; **related items on the agenda** = cuestiones afines en el orden del día; **related company** = compañía afiliada; **earnings-related pension** = pensión calculada en función del salario

◊ **relating to** [rɪ'leɪtɪŋ 'tʊ] *adverb* acerca de *or* referente a; **documents relating to the agreement** = documentos referentes al convenio

◊ **relation** [rɪ'leɪʃən] *noun* **(a) in relation to** = en relación con *or* referente a; **documents in relation to the agreement** = documentos referentes al convenio **(b) relations** = relaciones *fpl*; **we try to maintain good relations with our customers** = tratamos de mantener buenas relaciones con nuestros clientes; **to enter into relations with a company** = establecer relaciones con una compañía; **to break off relations with someone** = romper las relaciones con alguien; **industrial relations** *or* **labour relations** = relaciones laborales; **the company has a history of bad labour relations** = la empresa tiene un historial de malas relaciones laborales **(c) public relations (PR)** = relaciones *fpl* públicas (RP); **public relations department (PR department)** = departamento de relaciones públicas; **public relations officer (PRO)** = responsable de relaciones públicas

relative ['relətɪv] *adjective* relativo, -va; **relative error** = error relativo

◊ **relatively** ['relətɪvlɪ] *adverb* relativamente; **we have appointed a relatively new PR firm to handle our publicity** = hemos nombrado a una empresa de relaciones públicas relativamente nueva para dirigir nuestra publicidad

release [rɪ'li:s] **1** *noun* **(a)** *(setting free)* liberación *f*; **release from a contract** = rescisión de un contrato; **release of goods from customs** = despacho de mercancías de la aduana **(b) day release** = concesión de un día libre a la semana a un empleado para que asista a un curso; **the junior sales manager is attending a day release course** = el director adjunto de ventas asiste a un curso de formación personal un día por semana **(c) press release** = comunicado de prensa; **the company sent out** *or* **issued a press release about the launch of the new car** = la empresa emitió un comunicado de prensa sobre el lanzamiento del nuevo coche **(d) new releases** = novedades discográficas **2** *verb* **(a)** *(to free)* liberar; **to release goods from customs** = permitir la salida de mercancías de la aduana; **customs released the goods against payment of a fine** = la aduana permitió la salida de las mercancías previo pago de una multa; **to release someone from**

a debt = liberar a alguien de una deuda **(b)** *(to make something public)* divulgar; **the company released information about the new mine in Australia** = la empresa divulgó información sobre la nueva mina de Australia; **the government has refused to release figures for the number of unemployed women** = el gobierno se ha negado a revelar las cifras sobre el número de mujeres en paro **(c)** *(to put on the market)* poner a la venta; **to release a new CD** = poner un nuevo 'compact' a la venta; **to release dues** = despachar pedidos atrasados

QUOTE pressure to ease monetary policy mounted yesterday with the release of a set of pessimistic economic statistics
Financial Times

QUOTE the national accounts for the March quarter released by the Australian Bureau of Statistics showed a real increase in GDP
Australian Financial Review

relevant ['reləvənt] *adjective* apropiado, -da *or* pertinente; **which is the relevant government department?** = ¿a qué ministerio concierne?; **can you give me the relevant papers?** = ¿puedes darme los documentos pertinentes?

reliable [rɪ'laɪəbl] *adjective* fiable *or* de confianza *or* cumplidor, -ra; **reliable company** = compañía fiable; **the sales manager is completely reliable** = el director de ventas es una persona de absoluta confianza; **we have reliable information about our rival's sales** = tenemos información fiable *or* digna de crédito sobre las ventas de nuestro competidor; **the company makes a very reliable product** = la empresa fabrica un producto muy seguro

◊ **reliability** [rɪlaɪə'bɪlətɪ] *noun* fiabilidad *f*; **the product has passed its reliability tests** = el producto ha pasado las pruebas de fiabilidad

relief [rɪ'li:f] *noun* **(a)** *(comfort)* alivio *m* **(b)** ayuda *f*; **tax relief** = desgravación *f*; **there is full tax relief on mortgage interest payments** = la desgravación fiscal de los intereses hipotecarios es total; **mortgage relief** = desgravación fiscal de los intereses de la hipoteca; **relief shift** = turno de relevo

relocate [ri:lə'keɪt] *verb* trasladar *or* cambiar de sitio *or* desplazar; **the board decided to relocate the company in Scotland** = la junta decidió trasladar a la compañía a Escocia; **when the company moved its headquarters, 1500 people had to be relocated** = con el traslado de la sede, la compañía tuvo que desplazar a 1.500 personas

◊ **relocation** [ri:lə'keɪʃn] *noun* traslado *m* *or* cambio *m* de sitio

reluctant [rɪ'lʌktənt] *adjective* reacio, -cia; **he is reluctant to allow us to make any changes** = se muestra reacio a que hagamos ningún cambio

rely on [rɪ'laɪ 'ɒn] *verb* confiar en *or* contar con; **the chairman relies on the finance department for information on sales** = el presidente confía en el departamento de finanzas para la información sobre las ventas; **we rely on part-time staff for most of our mail-order business** = contamos con personal a tiempo parcial para la mayor parte de nuestro comercio por correo; **do not rely on the agents for accurate market reports** = no espere obtener de los representantes una información exacta del mercado

remain [rɪ'meɪn] *verb* **(a)** *(to be left)* quedar; **half the stock remained unsold** = la mitad de las existencias quedó sin vender; **we will sell off the old stock at half price and anything remaining will be thrown away** = liquidaremos las existencias antiguas a mitad de precio y tiraremos lo que quede **(b)** *(to stay)* quedarse *or* permanecer; **she remained behind at the office after 6.30 to finish her work** = se quedó en la oficina pasadas las 6.30 para terminar el trabajo

◊ **remainder** [rɪ'meɪndə] **1** *noun* **(a)** *(things left behind)* resto *m*; **the remainder of the stock will be sold off at half price** = el resto de las exitencias se liquidará a mitad de precio (NOTE: in this sense **remainder** is singular and usually written with the) **(b) remainders** = artículos no vendidos *or* saldos *or* restos de edición; **remainder merchant** = comerciante de restos de edición *or* de saldos **2** *verb* saldar; **to remainder books** = vender restos de edición a precios rebajados; **the shop was full of piles of remaindered books** = la librería estaba llena de restos de edición

remember [rɪ'membə] *verb* recordar *or* acordarse de; **do you remember the name of the Managing Director of Smith Ltd?** = ¿recuerdas el nombre del director gerente de Smith Ltd?; **I cannot remember the make of photocopier which he said was so good** = no consigo recordar la marca de la fotocopiadora que nos dijo era tan buena; **did you remember to ask the switchboard to put my calls through to the boardroom?** = ¿se acordó de pedir a la centralita que me pasara las llamadas a la sala de juntas?; **she remembered seeing the item in a supplier's catalogue** = se acordó de que había visto el artículo en el catálogo de un proveedor (NOTE: you **remember doing something** which you did in the past; you **remember to do something** in the future)

remind [rɪ'maɪnd] *verb* recordar; **I must remind my secretary to book the flight for New York** = tengo que recordarle a mi secretaria que haga una reserva en el vuelo a Nueva York; **he reminded the chairman that the meeting had to finish at 6.30** = recordó al presidente que la reunión tenía que terminar a las 6.30

◊ **reminder** [rɪ'maɪndə] *noun* **(a)** *(payment)* aviso *m* *or* notificación *f*; **to send someone a reminder** = enviar a alguien un aviso (de pago) **(b)** *(date)* recordatorio *m* **(c)** *(warning)* advertencia *f*

remission [rɪ'mɪʃən] *noun* **remission of taxes** = devolución *f* de impuestos

remit 1 ['ri:mɪt] *noun* *(task which someone is asked to deal with)* mandato *m* *or* cometido *m* *or* deber *m*; **the new MD was appointed with the remit to improve the company's performance** = el nuevo director gerente fue nombrado con el cometido de mejorar el rendimiento de la compañía **2** [rɪ'mɪt] *verb (to send money)* remitir; **to remit by cheque** = remitir por cheque (NOTE: **remitting - remitted**)

◊ **remittance** [rɪ'mɪtəns] *noun* envío *m* *or* giro *m* *or* transferencia *f* *or* remesa *f*; **please send remittances to the treasurer** = se ruega enviar los pagos al tesorero; **the family lives on a weekly remittance from their father in the USA** = la familia vive de un giro semanal que le envía el padre desde los EE UU

remnant ['remnənt] *noun* resto *m* *or* retal *m*;

remnant sale *or* **sale of remnants** = venta de retales *or* restos de serie

remote control [rɪ'məʊt kən'trəʊl] *noun* control *m* remoto; **by remote control** = por control remoto

remove [rɪ'mu:v] *verb* **(a)** *(take away)* quitar *or* borrar; **we can remove his name from the mailing list** = podemos borrar su nombre de la lista de destinatarios **(b)** *(lift)* levantar; **the government has removed the ban on imports from Japan** = el gobierno ha levantado el embargo sobre la importación de productos japoneses; **the minister has removed the embargo on the sale of computer equipment** = el ministro ha levantado el embargo sobre la venta de equipos informáticos **(c)** *(replace)* relevar *or* destituir; **two directors were removed from the board at the AGM** = dos consejeros fueron relevados del consejo de administración en la junta anual

◊ **removal** [rɪ'mu:vəl] *noun* **(a)** *(moving to a new house or office)* mudanza *f* *or* traslado *m*; **removal** *or* **removals company** = empresa de mudanzas *or* empresa de transporte **(b)** *(sacking someone)* destitución *f*; **the removal of the managing director is going to be very difficult** = va a ser muy difícil conseguir el cese del director general

remunerate [rɪ'mju:nəreɪt] *verb* remunerar; **to remunerate someone for their services** = remunerar a alguien por sus servicios

◊ **remuneration** [rɪmju:nə'reɪʃən] *noun* remuneración *f*; **she has a monthly remuneration of £400** = recibe una remuneración mensual de £400

◊ **remunerative** [rɪ'mju:nərətɪv] *adjective* remunerador, -ra *or* remunerativo, -va; **he is in a very remunerative job** = tiene un trabajo muy remunerativo

> COMMENT: remuneration can take several forms: the regular monthly salary cheque, a cheque or cash payment for hours worked or for work completed, etc.

render ['rendə] *verb* **to render an account** = presentar una cuenta *or* una factura; **payment for account rendered** = pago de la factura presentada; **please find enclosed payment per account rendered** = se adjunta pago por la factura presentada

renew [rɪ'nju:] *verb* renovar *or* prorrogar; **to renew a bill of exchange** *or* **to renew a lease** = renovar una letra de cambio *or* prorrogar un arrendamiento; **to renew a subscription** = renovar una suscripción *or* un abono; **to renew an insurance policy** = renovar una póliza de seguros

◊ **renewal** [rɪ'nju:əl] *noun* renovación *f* *or* prórroga *f*; **renewal of a lease** *or* **of a subscription** *or* **of a bill** = prórroga de un arrendamiento *or* renovación de una suscripción *or* de una letra; **the lease is up for renewal next month** = habrá que prorrogar el arrendamiento el mes que viene; **when is the renewal date of the bill?** = ¿cuál es la fecha de renovación de la letra?; **renewal notice** = notificación de renovación; **renewal premium** = prima de renovación

rent [rent] **1** *noun* alquiler *m* *or* renta *f*; **high rent** *or* **low rent** = alquiler elevado *or* alquiler barato; **rents are high in the centre of the town** = los alquileres son caros en el centro de la ciudad; **we cannot afford to pay High Street rents** = los alquileres del centro no están a nuestro alcance; **to pay three months' rent in advance** = pagar tres meses de alquiler por adelantado; **back rent** = alquiler atrasado; **the flat is let at an economic rent** = el piso se alquila a un precio económico; **ground rent** = renta de la tierra *or* del terreno *or* subsuelo; **nominal rent** = renta nominal; **rent collector** = cobrador de alquileres; **rent control** = control de rentas *or* alquileres; **income from rents** *or* **rent income** = ingresos *or* renta por alquiler **2** *verb* **(a)** *(pay money to hire something)* alquilar; **to rent an office** *or* **a car** = alquilar una oficina *or* un coche; **he rents an office in the centre of town** = alquila una oficina en el centro de la ciudad; **they were driving a rented car when they were stopped by the police** = conducían un coche alquilado cuando la policía les detuvo **(b)** *(receive money by hiring something)* **to rent (out)** = alquilar; **we rented part of the building to an American company** = alquilamos parte del edificio a una empresa norteamericana

◊ **rental** ['rentl] *noun* alquiler *m* (precio del alquiler); **the telephone rental bill comes to over £500 a quarter** = la factura del alquiler del teléfono sube a más de £500 al trimestre; **rental income** *or* **income from rentals** = ingresos por alquiler *or* renta por arrendamiento; **car rental firm** = empresa de alquiler de coches; **fleet rental** = alquiler de la flota de vehículos de una empresa

◊ **rent-free** [rent'fri:] *adverb* exento de alquiler *or* sin pagar alquiler

> QUOTE top quality office furniture: short or long-term rental 50% cheaper than any other rental company
> **Australian Financial Review**

> QUOTE until the vast acres of empty office space start to fill up with rent-paying tenants, rentals will continue to fall and so will values. Despite the very sluggish economic recovery under way, it is still difficult to see where the new tenants will come from
> **Australian Financial Review**

renunciation [rɪnʌnsɪ'eɪʃən] *noun* renuncia *f*; **letter of renunciation** = carta de renuncia

reopen [ri:'əupən] *verb* volver a abrir *or* reabrir; **the office will reopen soon after its refit** = la oficina volverá a abrir una vez concluidas las reformas

◊ **reopening** [ri:'əupənɪŋ] *noun* reapertura *f*; **the reopening of the store after refitting** = la reapertura del almacén después de las reformas

reorder [ri:'ɔ:də] **1** *noun* nuevo pedido *m or* pedido suplementario; **the product has only been on the market ten days and we are already getting reorders** = el producto ha estado a la venta sólo diez días y ya estamos recibiendo nuevos pedidos; **reorder level** = nivel de existencias que justifica nuevos pedidos; **reorder quantity** = cantidad de repetición de pedidos **2** *verb* renovar un pedido *or* hacer un pedido suplementario; **we must reorder these items because stock is getting low** = tenemos que hacer un pedido suplementario de estos artículos porque las existencias están bajando

reorganize [ri:'ɔ:gənaɪz] *verb* reorganizar

◊ **reorganization** [ri:ɔ:gənaɪ'zeɪʃən] *noun* **(a)** reorganización *f*; **his job was downgraded in the office reorganization** *or* **in the reorganization of**

the office = se le rebajó de categoría profesional a consecuencia de la reorganización de la oficina **(b)** *(financial)* **the reorganization of a company** *or* **a company reorganization** = la reorganización de una compañía

rep [rep] **1** *noun* = REPRESENTATIVE **to hold a reps' meeting** = celebrar una reunión de representantes; **our reps make on average six calls a day** = nuestros representantes hacen un promedio de seis visitas al día; **commission rep** = representante que trabaja a comisión **2** *verb* *(informal)* = REPRESENT **he reps for two firms on commission** = trabaja como representante a comisión para dos empresas (NOTE: **repping - repped**)

repack ['ri:'pæk] *verb* empaquetar *or* embalar de nuevo *or* volver a embalar

◊ **repacking** ['ri:'pækɪŋ] *noun* nuevo *m* embalaje

repair [rɪ'peə] **1** *noun* reparación *f*; **to carry out repairs to the machinery** = hacer reparaciones a la maquinaria; **his car is in the garage for repair** = su coche está en el garage para que lo reparen **2** *verb* reparar *or* componer; **the photocopier is being repaired** = la fotocopiadora está en reparación; **repairing lease** = arrendamiento en el que las reparaciones corren por cuenta del arrendatario

◊ **repairer** *or* **repair man** [rɪ'peərə *or* rɪ'peə mən] *noun* reparador *or* mecánico *m*; **the repair man has come to mend the photocopier** = ha llegado el mecánico para reparar la fotocopiadora

repay [rɪ'peɪ] *verb* pagar *or* reembolsar *or* devolver; **to repay money owed** = reembolsar una deuda; **the company had to cut back on expenditure in order to repay its debts** = la compañía tuvo que recortar los gastos para reembolsar sus deudas; **he repaid me in full** = me reembolsó íntegramente (NOTE: **repaying - repaid**)

◊ **repayable** [rɪ'peɪəbl] *adjective* reembolsable; **loan which is repayable over ten years** = un préstamo reembolsable en diez años

◊ **repayment** [rɪ'peɪmənt] *noun* reembolso *m or* pago *m*; **the loan is due for repayment next year** = el pago del préstamo vence el año que viene; **he fell behind with his mortgage repayments** = se ha retrasado en el pago de los plazos de la hipoteca; **repayment mortgage** = pago de hipoteca

repeat [rɪ'pi:t] *verb* **(a)** repetir; **he repeated his address slowly so that the salesgirl could write it down** = repitió su dirección despacio para que la vendedora pudiera apuntarla; **when asked what the company planned to do, the chairman repeated 'Nothing'** = cuando le preguntaron qué pensaba hacer la compañía, el presidente volvió a decir 'nada' **(b)** **to repeat an order** = renovar un pedido

◊ **repeat order** [rɪ'pi:t 'ɔ:də] *noun* pedido *m* suplementario; **the product has been on the market only ten days and we are already flooded with repeat orders** = el producto ha estado a la venta solamente durante diez días y ya estamos desbordados con pedidos suplementarios

replace [rɪ'pleɪs] *verb* reemplazar *or* sustituir *or* cambiar *or* reponer; **the cost of replacing damaged stock is very high** = el coste de reposición de las existencias dañadas es muy elevado; **the photocopier needs replacing** = hay que comprar una fotocopiadora nueva; **the company will replace any defective item free of charge** = la empresa cambiará cualquier artículo defectuoso gratuitamente; **we are replacing all our salaried staff with freelancers** = estamos sustituyendo a todos nuestros trabajadores asalariados por colaboradores autónomos

◊ **replacement** [rɪˈpleɪsmənt] *noun* **(a)** replacement cost *or* cost of replacement = coste de reposición; **replacement value** = valor de reposición; **the computer is insured at its replacement value** = el ordenador está asegurado por su valor de reposición **(b)** *(item)* reemplazo *m*; **we are out of stock and are waiting for replacements** = no nos quedan existencias y estamos esperando reposiciones **(c)** *(person)* sustituto, -ta; **my secretary leaves us next week, so we are advertising for a replacement** = mi secretaria se marcha la semana que viene, por lo que hemos puesto un anuncio para buscar una sustituta

reply [rɪˈplaɪ] **1** *noun* respuesta *f or* contestación *f*; **there was no reply to my letter** *or* **to my phone call** = no hubo respuesta a mi carta *or* a mi llamada telefónica; **I am writing in reply to your letter of the 24th** = escribo en contestación a su carta del 24; **the company's reply to the takeover bid** = la respuesta de la compañía a la oferta de adquisición; **reply coupon** = boletín de respuesta; **international postal reply coupon** = boletín de respuesta internacional; **he enclosed an international reply coupon with his letter** = adjuntó un boletín de respuesta internacional a su carta; **reply paid card** *or* **letter** = tarjeta postal *or* carta a franquear en destino **2** *verb* contestar *or* responder; **to reply to a letter** = contestar a una carta; **the company has replied to the takeover bid by offering the shareholders higher dividends** = la compañía ha respondido a la oferta de adquisición ofreciendo a los accionistas unos dividendos superiores

report [rɪˈpɔːt] **1** *noun* **(a)** *(document)* informe *m or* memoria *f*; **to draft a report** = redactar un informe; **to make a report** *or* **to present a report** *or* **to send in a report** = hacer un informe *or* presentar un informe *or* enviar un informe; **the sales manager reads all the reports from the sales team** = el director de ventas lee todos los informes de su equipo de vendedores; **the chairman has received a report from the insurance company** = el presidente ha recibido un informe de la compañía de seguros; **confidential report** = informe confidencial; **feasibility report** = informe de factibilidad *or* viabilidad; **financial report** = informe financiero; **progress report** = informe sobre la marcha de una actividad *or* situación; **the treasurer's report** = el informe del tesorero **(b)** **the company's annual report** *or* **the chairman's report** *or* **the directors' report** = el informe *or* la memoria anual de la compañía *or* el informe del presidente *or* el informe del consejo de administración **(c)** **a report in a newspaper** *or* **a newspaper report** = reportaje de un periódico; **can you confirm the report that the company is planning to close the factory?** = ¿puede confirmar el rumor según el cual la compañía tiene la intención de cerrar la fábrica? **(d)** *(from a government committee)* informe; **the government has issued a report on the credit problems of exporters** = el gobierno ha publicado un informe

sobre los problemas crediticios de los exportadores **2** *verb* **(a)** *(make a statement)* informar *or* comunicar *or* notificar; **the salesmen reported an increased demand for the product** = los vendedores comunicaron que la demanda del producto había aumentado; **he reported the damage to the insurance company** = notificó los daños a la compañía de seguros; **we asked the bank to report on his financial status** = le pedimos al banco que nos informara de su situación financiera; **he reported seeing the absentee in a shop** = comunicó que había visto al ausente en una tienda (NOTE: you **report something** or **report on something** or **report doing something**) **(b)** **to report to someone** = rendir cuentas a alguien *or* depender de alguien; **he reports direct to the managing director** = rinde cuentas directamente al director gerente; **the salesmen report to the sales director** = los vendedores dependen directamente del director de ventas **(c)** *(go to a place)* presentarse; **to report for an interview** = presentarse a una entrevista; **please report to our London office for training** = sírvanse presentarse en nuestra oficina de Londres para la capacitación

QUOTE a draft report on changes in the international monetary system
Wall Street Journal

QUOTE responsibilities include the production of premium quality business reports
Times

QUOTE the research director will manage a team of business analysts monitoring and reporting on the latest development in retail distribution
Times

QUOTE the successful candidate will report to the area director for profit responsibility for sales of leading brands
Times

repossess [riːpəˈzes] *verb (something bought on hire-purchase)* confiscar *or* recobrar por incumplimiento de los pagos; **when he fell behind with his mortgage payments, the bank repossessed his flat** = el banco confiscó su piso por incumplimiento de pagos

◊ **repossession** [riːpəˈzeʃn] *noun* recobro *m or* recuperación *f* (de bienes y propiedad) *or* confiscación *f*; **repossessions are increasing as people find it difficult to meet mortgage repayments** = el recobro de la propiedad ha aumentado dada la dificultad que la gente tiene en pagar las hipotecas

represent [reprɪˈzent] *verb* **(a)** *(selling goods for a company)* representar *or* ser agente de; **he represents an American car firm in Europe** = representa a una empresa norteamericana de automóviles en Europa; **our French distributor represents several other competing firms** = nuestro distribuidor francés también es el agente de varias empresas competidoras **(b)** *(to act for someone)* representar *or* actuar en nombre de; **he sent his solicitor and accountant to represent him at the meeting** = envió a su abogado y a su contable para que le representaran en la reunión; **three managers represent the workforce in discussions**

with the directors = tres encargados representan al personal en las negociaciones con la junta directiva

◊ **re-present** ['riːprɪ'zent] *verb* volver a presentar; **he re-presented the cheque two weeks later to try to get payment from the bank** = volvió a presentar el cheque dos semanas más tarde para intentar que el banco le pagase

◊ **representation** [reprɪzen'teɪʃən] *noun* **(a)** *(selling goods for a company)* representación *f*; **we offered them exclusive representation in Europe** = les ofrecimos la representación exclusiva en Europa; **they have no representation in the USA** = no tienen representación en los EE UU **(b)** *(acting on your behalf)* representación; **the minority shareholders want representation on the board** = los accionistas minoritarios quieren tener representación en el consejo de administración **(c)** *(complaint made on behalf of someone)* queja *f or* demanda *f*; **the managers made representations to the board on behalf of the hourly-paid members of staff** = los directores presentaron una demanda al consejo de administración en nombre del personal pagado por horas; *see also* WORKER

◊ **representative** [reprɪ'zentətɪv] **1** *adjective* representativo, -va; **we displayed a representative selection of our product range** = presentamos una selección representativa de nuestra gama de productos; **the sample chosen was not representative of the whole batch** = la muestra elegida no era representativa de la totalidad del lote **2** *noun* **(a)** *(person)* **sales representative** = representante *mf*; **we have six representatives in Europe** = tenemos seis representantes en Europa; **they have vacancies for representatives to call on accounts in the north of the country** = necesitan representantes para visitar clientes en el norte del país **(b)** *(company)* representante; **we have appointed Smith & Co our exclusive representatives in Europe** = hemos nombrado a Smith & Co. nuestros representantes exclusivos en Europa **(c)** *(acts on someone's behalf)* representante *or* apoderado, -da *or* mandatario *m*; **he sent his solicitor and accountant to act as his representatives at the meeting** = envió a su abogado y a su contable para que actuaran como sus representantes en la reunión; **the board refused to meet the representatives of the workforce** = el consejo de administración se negó a reunirse con los representantes del personal

reprice [riː'praɪs] *verb* fijar un nuevo precio *or* cambiar el precio (de un artículo)

repudiate [rɪ'pjuːdɪeɪt] *verb* repudiar *or* cancelar; **to repudiate an agreement** = negarse a cumplir un acuerdo

◊ **repudiation** [rɪpjuːdɪ'eɪʃən] *noun* repudio *m or* rechazo *m*

repurchase ['riː'pɜːtʃəs] *verb* volver a comprar *or* repetir

reputable ['repjʊtəbl] *adjective* acreditado, -da *or* de confianza *or* reputado, -da; **we only use reputable carriers** = solamente empleamos transportistas de confianza; **a reputable firm of accountants** = una empresa de contables acreditada

◊ **reputation** [repjʊ'teɪʃən] *noun* reputación *f or* fama *f*; **company with a reputation for quality** = empresa que se distingue por la calidad de sus

servicios; **he has a reputation for being difficult to negotiate with** = tiene fama de ser muy duro *or* muy difícil en las negociaciones

request [rɪ'kwest] **1** *noun* ruego *m or* petición *f or* solicitud *f*; *(for payment)* requerimiento *m*; **they put in a request for a government subsidy** = presentaron una solicitud para conseguir una subvención estatal; **his request for a loan was turned down by the bank** = su solicitud de préstamo fue rechazada por el banco; **on request** = a petición; **we will send samples on request** *or* **samples available on request** = enviaremos muestras a petición *or* muestras disponibles a petición de los interesados **2** *verb* pedir *or* solicitar; **to request assistance from the government** = pedir ayuda al Estado; **I am sending a catalogue as requested** = le envío el catálogo que había solicitado

require [rɪ'kwaɪə] *verb* **(a)** *(to demand something)* exigir; **to require a full explanation of expenditure** = exigir una explicación detallada de los gastos; **the law requires you to submit all income to the tax authorities** = la ley exige declarar todos los ingresos a las autoridades fiscales **(b)** *(to need)* necesitar *or* requerir; **the document requires careful study** = el documento requiere un examen cuidadoso; **to write the program requires a computer specialist** = para redactar el programa se necesita un especialista en informática

◊ **requirement** [rɪ'kwaɪəmənt] *noun* necesidad *f or* requisito *m*; **public sector borrowing requirement (PSBR)** = necesidades de endeudamiento del sector público

◊ **requirements** [rɪ'kwaɪəmənts] *plural noun* necesidades *fpl or* requisitos *mpl*; **to meet a customer's requirements** = satisfacer las necesidades de un cliente; **if you will supply us with a list of your requirements, we shall see if we can meet them** = si nos facilitan la lista de sus requisitos, veremos si les podemos satisfacer; **the requirements of a market** *or* **market requirements** = las necesidades de un mercado; **budgetary requirements** = necesidades presupuestarias; **manpower requirements** = necesidades de la mano de obra

requisition [rekwɪ'zɪʃən] **1** *noun* solicitud *f* oficial *or* demanda *f*; **what is the number of your latest requisition?** = ¿cuál es el número de su última solicitud oficial?; **cheque requisition** = solicitud oficial para que el departamento de contabilidad de una compañía pueda extender un cheque **2** *verb* solicitar *or* pedir *or* requerir

resale ['riː'seɪl] *noun* reventa *f*; **to purchase something for resale** = comprar algo para revenderlo; **the contract forbids resale of the goods to the USA** = el contrato prohibe la reventa de las mercancías a los EE UU; **resale price** = precio de reventa

◊ **resale price maintenance (RPM)** ['riː'seɪl 'praɪs 'meɪntənəns] *noun* mantenimiento del precio de reventa

reschedule [riː'ʃedjuːl] *verb* **(a)** *(to arrange a new timetable)* reprogramar *or* volver a programar; **he missed his plane, and all the meetings had to be rescheduled** = perdió el avión y todas las reuniones tuvieron que volver a ser programadas **(b)** *(to arrange new credit terms)* reestructurar; **some**

Third World countries asked for their loans to be **rescheduled** = algunos países del Tercer Mundo pidieron que se les reestructuraran los préstamos

rescind [rɪ'sɪnd] *verb* rescindir *or* anular; **to rescind a contract** *or* **an agreement** = rescindir un contrato *or* un acuerdo

rescue ['reskjuː] **1** *noun* rescate *m*; **rescue operation** = operación de rescate (de una compañía); **the banks planned a rescue operation for the company** = los bancos planearon una operación de rescate de la compañía **2** *verb* rescatar *or* salvar; **the company nearly collapsed, but was rescued by the banks** = la compañía estaba al borde de la ruina, pero fue rescatada por los bancos

research [rɪ'sɜːtʃ] **1** *noun* investigación *f or* estudio *m*; **consumer research** = estudio sobre el comportamiento del consumidor; **market research** = estudio *or* investigación de mercado; **research and development (R & D)** = investigación y desarrollo (I+D); **the company spends millions on research and development** = la compañía gasta millones en investigación y desarrollo; **research and development costs (R & D costs)** = costes de investigación y desarrollo; **scientific research** = la investigación científica; **he is engaged in research into the packaging of the new product line** = está estudiando las diferentes posibilidades de envase para la presentación de la nueva línea de productos; **the company is carrying out research into finding a medicine to cure colds** = la compañía está llevando a cabo trabajos de investigación para hallar una medicina que cure el resfriado; **research department** = departamento de investigación; **a research institute** *or* **organization** = un instituto *or* centro de investigación; **research unit** = unidad de investigación; **research worker** = investigador, -ra *or* persona *f* que hace trabajos de investigación **2** *verb* investigar *or* estudiar; **to research the market for a product** = hacer una investigación de mercado para un producto

◇ **researcher** [rɪ'sɜːtʃə] *noun* investigador, -ra

> COMMENT: research costs can be divided into (a) applied research, which is the cost of research leading to a specific aim, and (b) basic, or pure, research, which is research carried out without a specific aim in mind: these costs are written off in the year in which they are incurred. Development costs are the costs of making the commercial products based on the research

resell ['riː'sel] *verb* revender *or* volver a vender

◇ **reseller** [riː'selə] *noun* revendedor, -ra

reservation [rezə'veɪʃən] *noun* reserva *f*; **I want to make a reservation on the train to Plymouth tomorrow evening** = quiero reservar plaza en el tren de Plymouth de mañana por la tarde; **room reservations** = departamento *m* de reservas; **can you put me through to reservations?** = ¿puede ponerme con el departamento de reservas?

reserve [rɪ'zɜːv] **1** *noun* **(a)** *(money from profits not paid as dividend)* reserva *f or* provisión *f*; **bank reserves** = reservas bancarias *or* activo de caja; **capital reserves** = reservas de capital; **capitalization of reserves** = capitalización de reservas; **cash reserves** = reservas de caja *or* de efectivo; **the company was forced to fall back on its cash reserves** = la compañía se vio obligada a

recurrir a sus reservas de efectivo; **to have to draw on reserves to pay the dividend** = tener que recurrir a las reservas para pagar el dividendo; **contingency reserve** *or* **emergency reserves** = reservas para emergencias *or* imprevistos; **reserve for bad debts** = reserva para deudas incobrables; **hidden reserves** = reservas ocultas; **sums chargeable to the reserve** = cantidades imputables *or* a cargo de la reserva; **reserve fund** = fondo de reserva **(b)** **reserve currency** = divisas de reserva; **currency reserves** = reservas de divisas; **a country's foreign currency reserves** = las reservas de divisas de un país; **the UK's gold and dollar reserves fell by $200 million during the quarter** = las reservas de oro y de dólares del Reino Unido bajaron $200 millones durante el trimestre **(c)** **in reserve** = en reserva; **to keep something in reserve** = guardar algo en reserva; **we are keeping our new product in reserve until the launch date** = guardamos nuestro nuevo producto en reserva hasta la fecha de lanzamiento **(d)** *(supplies kept in case of need)* **reserves** = reservas; **our reserves of fuel fell during the winter** = nuestras reservas de combustible bajaron durante el invierno; **the country's reserves of gas** *or* **gas reserves are very large** = las reservas de gas del país son muy grandes; **research and development costs (R & D costs)** *(sic — see)* **reserve price** = precio mínimo aceptable (en una subasta); **the painting was withdrawn when it did not reach its reserve** = el cuadro fue retirado de la subasta por no alcanzar el precio mínimo **2** *verb* reservar; **to reserve a room** *or* **a table** *or* **a seat** = reservar una habitación *or* una mesa *or* un asiento; **I want to reserve a table for four people** = quiero reservar una mesa para cuatro personas; **can your secretary reserve a seat for me on the train to Glasgow?** = ¿puede su secretaria reservarme una plaza en el tren de Glasgow?

residence ['rezɪdəns] *noun* **(a)** *(place)* residencia *f or* domicilio *m*; **he has a country residence where he spends his weekends** = tiene una residencia en el campo donde pasa los fines de semana **(b)** *(act of living in a country)* **residence permit** = permiso de residencia; **he has applied for a residence permit** = ha solicitado un permiso de residencia; **she was granted a residence permit for one year** = se le concedió un permiso de residencia de un año

◇ **resident** ['rezɪdənt] **1** *noun* residente *mf or* habitante *mf* **2** *adjective* **the company is resident in France** = la compañía reside en Francia; **non-resident** = no residente; **he has a non-resident account with a French bank** = tiene una cuenta de no residente en un banco francés; **she was granted a non-resident visa** = se le concedió un visado de no residente

residue ['rezɪdjuː] *noun* residuo *m or* resto *m*; **after paying various bequests the residue of his estate was split between his children** = después de pagar varios legados el resto de la herencia se dividió entre sus hijos

◇ **residual** [rɪ'zɪdjʊəl] *adjective* residual *or* sobrante

resign [rɪ'zaɪn] *verb* dimitir; **he resigned from his post as treasurer** = dimitió de su cargo de tesorero; **he has resigned with effect from July 1st** = ha presentado su dimisión con efectos a partir del 1 de julio; **she resigned as finance director** = dimitió de su cargo de directora de finanzas

◇ **resignation** [rezɪg'neɪʃən] *noun* dimisión *f or*

renuncia *f*; **he wrote his letter of resignation to the chairman** = escribió su carta de renuncia al presidente del Consejo; **to hand in** *or* **to give in** *or* **to send in one's resignation** = presentar la dimisión

resist [rɪ'zɪst] *verb* resistir; **the chairman resisted all attempts to make him resign** = el presidente resistió todas las presiones para obligarle a dimitir; **the company is resisting the takeover bid** = la compañía se resiste a la oferta de adquisición

◊ **resistance** [rɪ'zɪstəns] *noun* resistencia *f*; **there was a lot of resistance from the shareholders to the new plan** = hubo mucha resistencia al nuevo plan por parte de los accionistas; **the chairman's proposal met with strong resistance from the banks** = la propuesta del presidente provocó una gran resistencia por parte de los bancos; **consumer resistance** = resistencia por parte del consumidor; **the new product met no consumer resistance even though the price was high** = el nuevo producto no encontró ninguna resistencia por parte de los consumidores a pesar de su elevado precio

resolution [rezə'lu:ʃən] *noun* resolución *f*; **to put a resolution to a meeting** = proponer una resolución a una reunión; **the meeting passed** *or* **carried** *or* **adopted a resolution to go on strike** = la asamblea aprobó la resolución de iniciar una huelga; **the meeting rejected the resolution** *or* **the resolution was defeated by ten votes to twenty** = la reunión rechazó la resolución *or* la resolución fue rechazada, por diez votos a favor y veinte en contra

COMMENT: there are three types or resolution which can be put to an AGM: the 'ordinary resolution', usually referring to some general procedural matter, and which requires a simple majority of votes, and the 'extraordinary resolution' and 'special resolution' such as a resolution to change a company's articles of association in some way, both of which need 75% of the votes before they can be carried

resolve [rɪ'zɒlv] *verb* optar *or* decidir *or* acordar; **the meeting resolved that a dividend should not be paid** = la junta decidió no pagar *or* optó por no pagar dividendos

resources [rɪ'sɔ:sɪz] *plural noun* (a) recursos *mpl*; **human resources** = recursos humanos; **natural resources** = recursos naturales; **the country is rich in natural resources** = el país es rico en recursos naturales; **we are looking for a site with good water resources** = buscamos un paraje con grandes recursos de agua (b) **financial resources** = recursos financieros; **the costs of the London office are a drain on the company's financial resources** = los costes de la sucursal de Londres son una sangría para los recursos financieros de la compañía; **the company's financial resources are not strong enough to support the cost of the research programme** = los recursos financieros de la compañía no son lo suficientemente fuertes como para soportar el coste del programa de investigación; **the cost of the new project is easily within our resources** = nuestros recursos son más que suficientes para pagar el coste del nuevo proyecto

respect [rɪs'pekt] **1** *noun* (a) *(to a person)* acatamiento *m* *or* respeto *m* *or* consideración *f* (b) *(concerning)* respecto *m*; **with respect to** = con respecto a **2** *verb* respetar *or* acatar; **to respect a**

clause in an agreement = respetar una cláusula de un acuerdo; **the company has not respected the terms of the contract** = la empresa no ha respetado los términos del contrato

◊ **respectively** [rɪs'pektɪvli] *adverb* respectivamente; **Mr Smith and Mr Jones are respectively MD and Sales Director of Smith Ltd** = el señor Smith y el señor Jones son director gerente y director comercial de Smith Ltd., respectivamente

response [rɪ'spɒns] *noun* respuesta *f or* reacción *f*; **there was no response to our mailing shot** = nuestros folletos de propaganda a domicilio no produjeron ninguna reacción; **we got very little response to our complaints** = nuestras reclamaciones tuvieron muy poca acogida

QUOTE forecasting consumer response is one problem which will never be finally solved
Marketing Week

responsibility [rɪspɒnsə'bɪləti] *noun* (a) responsabilidad *f*; **there is no responsibility on the company's part for loss of customers' property** = la empresa no asume ninguna responsabilidad por la pérdida de los objetos de los clientes; **the management accepts no responsibility for loss of goods in storage** = la dirección no acepta ninguna responsabilidad por la pérdida de las mercancías en depósito (b) **responsibilities** = oblicaciones *fpl*; **he finds the responsibilities of being managing director too heavy** = las obligaciones de su cargo como director gerente le parecen excesivas

◊ **responsible** [rɪ'spɒnsəbl] *adjective* (a) responsable; **responsible for** = responsable de; **he is responsible for all sales** = es responsable de todas las ventas; **she is responsible for a group of junior accountants** = es la encargada de un grupo de jóvenes contables (b) **responsible to someone** = que tiene que rendir cuentas a alguien; **he is directly responsible to the managing director** = rinde cuentas directamente al director gerente (c) **a responsible job** = un trabajo de responsabilidad; **he is looking for a responsible job in marketing** = está buscando un trabajo de responsabilidad en el ámbito del marketing

rest [rest] *noun* resto *m*; **the chairman went home, but the rest of the directors stayed in the boardroom** = el presidente se marchó a casa, pero los demás consejeros se quedaron en la sala de juntas; **we sold most of the stock before Christmas and hope to clear the rest in a sale** = vendimos la mayor parte de las existencias antes de Navidades y esperamos liquidar el resto con las rebajas; **the rest of the money is invested in gilts** = el resto del dinero está invertido en bonos del Estado

restaurant ['restrənt] *noun* restaurante *m*; **he runs a French restaurant in New York** = dirige un restaurante francés en Nueva York

◊ **restaurateur** [restərə'tɜ:] *noun* propietario, -ria de un restaurante *or* persona que dirige un restaurante

restitution [restɪ'tju:ʃən] *noun* (a) *(giving back)* restitución *f*; **the court ordered the restitution of assets to the company** = el tribunal decretó la restitución de los bienes a la compañía (b) *(compensation)* indemnización *f* (c) *(in the EU)* **export restitution** = restitución a la exportación

restock ['riː'stɒk] *verb* renovar existencias *or* repostar; **to restock after the Christmas sales =** renovar existencias después de las rebajas de Navidad

◊ **restocking** [riː'stɒkɪŋ] *noun* renovación *f* de existencias

restore [rɪs'tɔː] *verb* **(a)** *(return)* devolver *or* restituir **(b)** *(bring back)* rehabilitar *or* restablecer *or* restaurar; **to restore the value of a currency =** restaurar el valor de una moneda

restraint [rɪ'streɪnt] *noun* restricción *f*; **pay restraint** *or* **wage restraint =** moderación salarial

◊ **restraint of trade** [rɪ'streɪnt əv 'treɪd] *noun* **(a)** *(worker)* prohibición de utilizar información confidencial al cambiar de trabajo **(b)** *(price fixing)* restricción comercial

restrict [rɪ'strɪkt] *verb* restringir *or* limitar; **to restrict credit =** limitar el crédito; **we are restricted to twenty staff by the size of our offices =** el tamaño de nuestras oficinas nos obliga a limitar la plantilla a veinte empleados; **to restrict the flow of trade** *or* **to restrict imports =** restringir el flujo de comercio *or* limitar las importaciones; **to sell into a restricted market =** vender en un mercado limitado

◊ **restriction** [rɪ'strɪkʃən] *noun* restricción *f or* limitación *f*; **to impose restrictions on credit =** imponer restricciones al crédito; **to lift credit restrictions =** levantar las restricciones de crédito; **import restrictions** *or* **restrictions on imports =** restricción a las importaciones; **to impose restrictions on imports =** imponer restricciones a las importaciones

◊ **restrictive** [rɪ'strɪktɪv] *adjective* restrictivo, -va; **restrictive trade practices =** prácticas comerciales restrictivas

restructure ['riː'strʌktʃə] *verb* reestructurar

◊ **restructuring** ['riː'strʌktʃərɪŋ] *noun* reestructuración *f*; **restructuring of the company =** reestructuración de la compañía; **restructuring of a loan =** consolidación de un préstamo

result [rɪ'zʌlt] **1** *noun* **(a)** *(profit or loss)* resultados *mpl*; **the company's results for 1994 =** los resultados de la compañía en 1994 **(b)** *(consequence)* resultado *m or* consecuencia *f*; **what was the result of the price investigation? =** ¿cuál fue el resultado de la investigación de precios?; **the company doubled its sales force with the result that the sales rose by 26% =** la empresa duplicó su personal de ventas con el resultado de un aumento en las ventas del 26%; **the expansion programme has produced results =** el programa de expansión ha dado buenos resultados; **payment by results =** pago según resultados *or* producción *or* trabajo a destajo **2** *verb* **(a) to result in =** resultar *or* tener por *or* como resultado *or* dar lugar; **the doubling of the sales force resulted in increased sales =** la duplicación del personal de ventas produjo un aumento de las ventas; **the extra orders resulted in overtime work for all the factory staff =** los pedidos adicionales obligaron a todo el personal de la fábrica a hacer horas extraordinarias **(b) to result from =** resultar de *or* derivar de; **the increase in debt resulted from the expansion programme =** el aumento de la deuda fue una consecuencia del programa de expansión

resume [rɪ'zjuːm] *verb (to start again)* reanudar *or* comenzar de nuevo

résumé ['rezjʊmeɪ] *noun US* currículum *m* (NOTE: GB English is **curriculum vitae**)

resumption [rɪ'zʌm(p)ʃən] *noun* reanudación *f*; **we expect an early resumption of negotiations =** esperamos una pronta reanudación de las negociaciones

retail ['riːteɪl] **1** *noun* al por menor *or* venta al detalle *or* al detall; **retail dealer =** comerciante al por menor *or* minorista; **retail shop** *or* **retail outlet =** tienda *or* comercio al por menor; **the retail trade =** el comercio al por menor; **the goods in stock have a retail value of £1m =** las existencias tienen un valor al por menor de £1 millón **2** *adverb* **he sells retail and buys wholesale =** compra al por mayor y vende al por menor **3** *verb* **(a) to retail goods =** vender al por menor **(b)** *(to sell for a price)* vender *or* venderse al por menor; **these items retail at** *or* **for 125 ptas =** estos artículos se venden al por menor al precio de 125 ptas

◊ **retailer** ['riːteɪlə] *noun* vendedor, -ra al por menor *or* detallista *or* revendedor, -ra

◊ **retailing** ['riːteɪlɪŋ] *noun* comercio *m* al por menor; **from car retailing the company branched out into car leasing =** la compañía empezó vendiendo coches y después se extendió al ramo del alquiler

◊ **retail price** ['riːteɪl 'praɪs] *noun* precio *m* de venta al público (PVP); **retail price(s) index (RPI) =** índice de precios al comsumo

COMMENT: in the UK, the RPI is calculated on a group of essential goods and services; it includes both VAT and mortgage interest; the US equivalent is the Consumer Price Index

retain [rɪ'teɪn] *verb* **(a)** *(to keep)* retener *or* reservar; **out of the profits, the company has retained £50,000 as provision against bad debts =** la compañía ha reservado £50.000 de los beneficios como provisión para deudas incobrables; **retained income =** beneficios no distribuidos; **the balance sheet has £50,000 in retained income =** el balance incluye £50.000 de beneficios no distribuidos **(b)** *(contract)* ajustar; **to retain a lawyer to act for a company =** contratar a un abogado para que represente a una compañía

◊ **retainer** [rɪ'teɪnə] *noun* **we pay him a retainer of £1,000 =** reservamos el derecho a sus servicios por un pago de £1.000

retire [rɪ'taɪə] *verb* **(a)** *(to stop work and take a* *pension)* jubilarse; darse de baja; **she retired with a £6,000 pension** = se jubiló con una pensión de £6.000; **the founder of the company retired at the age of 85** = el fundador de la compañía se jubiló a los 85 años; **the shop is owned by a retired policeman** = la tienda es propiedad de un policía jubilado **(b)** *(to make a worker stop work and take a pension)* jubilar *or* obligar a jubilarse; **they decided to retire all staff over 50** = decidieron jubilar a todo el personal de más de 50 años **(c)** *(to come to the end of an elected term of office)* terminar un mandato; **the treasurer retires from the council after six years** = el tesorero termina su mandato en el consejo a los seis años

◊ **retiral** [rɪˈtaɪərəl] *noun US* = RETIREMENT

◊ **retirement** [rɪˈtaɪəmənt] *noun* jubilación *f or* retiro *m*; **to take early retirement** = tomar la jubilación anticipada *or* prematura; **retirement age** = edad de jubilación; **retirement pension** = pensión de jubilación *or* retiro

◊ **retiring** [rɪˈtaɪrɪŋ] *adjective* saliente; **two retiring directors offer themselves for re-election** = dos directores salientes se presentan a reelección

retrain [ˈriːˈtreɪn] *verb* reciclar

◊ **retraining** [ˈriːˈtreɪnɪŋ] *noun* reciclaje *m* profesional; **the shop is closed for staff retraining** = la tienda está cerrada por reciclaje del personal; **he had to attend a retraining session** = tuvo que asistir a una sesión de reciclaje

retrench [rɪˈtren(t)ʃ] *verb* reducir gastos *or* cercenar *or* frenar la expansión

◊ **retrenchment** [rɪˈtren(t)ʃmənt] *noun* reducción *f* de gastos *or* restricción *f* de planes; **the company is in for a period of retrenchment** = a la compañía le aguarda un periodo de economías *or* de reducción de gastos

retrieve [rɪˈtriːv] *verb* recuperar; **the company is fighting to retrieve its market share** = la empresa está luchando para recuperar su cuota de mercado; **all of the information was accidentally wiped off the computer so we cannot retrieve our sales figures for the last month** = no podemos recuperar nuestras cifras de ventas del mes pasado dado que toda la información se borró accidentalmente del ordenador

◊ **retrieval** [rɪˈtriːvəl] *noun* recuperación *f*; **data retrieval** *or* **information retrieval** = recuperación de datos; **retrieval system** = sistema de recuperación

retroactive [retrəʊˈæktɪv] *adjective* retroactivo, -va; **retroactive pay rise** = aumento retroactivo de salarios; **they got a pay rise retroactive to last January** = recibieron un aumento de sueldo con efecto retroactivo al mes de enero pasado

◊ **retroactively** [retrəʊˈæktɪvli] *adverb* retroactivamente

return [rɪˈtɜːn] **1** *noun* **(a)** *(going back)* vuelta *f or*
regreso *m*; **return journey** = viaje de vuelta; **a return ticket** *or* **a return** = un billete de ida y vuelta; **I want two returns to Edinburgh** = quiero dos billetes de ida y vuelta a Edimburgo; **return fare** = tarifa de ida y vuelta **(b)** *(sending back)* devolución *f*; **he replied by return of post** = respondió a vuelta de correo; **return address** = remite *m* **these goods are all on sale or return** = estos productos se devolverán en el caso de que no se vendan **(c)** *(profit)* ganancia *f or* beneficios *mpl or* rendimiento *m*; **to bring in a quick return** = producir una ganancia rápida; **what is the gross return on this line?** = ¿cuál es el beneficio bruto de estos productos?; **return on investment (ROI)** *or* **on capital employed (ROCE)** = rendimiento de la inversión *or* de capital; **rate of return** = tasa de rentabilidad *or* tasa de ganancia **(d)** **official return** = declaración *f* oficial; **to make a return to the tax office** *or* **to make an income tax return** = hacer una declaración a Hacienda *or* hacer una declaración de renta; **to fill in a VAT return** = hacer una declaración del IVA; **nil return** = declaración de ingresos nulos; **daily** *or* **weekly** *or* **quarterly sales return** = informe diario *or* semanal *or* trimestral de ventas **2** *verb* **(a)** *(to send back)* devolver; **to return unsold stock to the wholesaler** = devolver existencias no vendidas al mayorista; **to return a letter to sender** = devolver una carta al remitente; **returned empties** = envases vacíos devueltos **(b)** *(to make a statement)* declarar *or* hacer una declaración; **to return income of £15,000 to the tax authorities** = declarar unos ingresos de £15.000 al fisco **(c)** *(go back)* volver *or* regresar

◊ **returnable** [rɪˈtɜːnəbl] *adjective* retornable; **these bottles are not returnable** = estas botellas no son retornables

◊ **returns** [rɪˈtɜːnz] *plural noun* **(a)** *(profits)* ganancia *f or* beneficios *mpl*; **the company is looking for quick returns on its investment** = la compañía trata de conseguir beneficios rápidos de sus inversiones; **law of diminishing returns** = ley de rendimientos decrecientes **(b)** *(goods)* productos *mpl* devueltos al suministrador sin vender

revalue [riːˈvæljuː] *verb* revaluar; **the company's properties have been revalued** = las propiedades de la compañía han sido revaluadas; **the dollar has been revalued against all world currencies** = el dólar se ha revaluado frente a todas las demás monedas

◊ **revaluation** [riːˈvæljʊˈeɪʃən] *noun* revaluación *f*; **the balance sheet takes into account the revaluation of the company's properties** = el balance de situación tiene en cuenta la revaluación de las propiedades de la compañía; **the revaluation**

of the dollar against the peseta = la revaluación del dólar frente a la peseta

revenue ['revənju:] *noun* **(a)** *(money received)* ingreso *m*; **revenue from advertising** *or* **advertising revenue** = ingresos por publicidad; **oil revenues have risen with the rise in the dollar** = los ingresos por las ventas de petróleo han subido con el alza del dólar; **revenue accounts** = contabilidad de ingresos **(b)** *(tax)* recaudación *f* tributaria; **Inland Revenue** *US* **Internal Revenue Service** = fisco *m* *or* Hacienda Pública *f*; **revenue officer** = inspector, -ra *or* delegado, -da *or* funcionario, -ria de Hacienda

reversal [rɪ'vɜ:səl] *noun* inversión *f* *or* cambio *m* completo *or* revocación *f* *or* revés *m*; **the company suffered a reversal in the Far East** = la empresa sufrió un revés (de fortuna) en el Extremo Oriente

reverse [rɪ'vɜ:s] **1** *adjective* invertido, -da *or* opuesto, -ta; **reverse takeover** = adquisición de una compañía por otra más pequeña; **reverse charge call** = llamada a cobro revertido **2** *verb* **(a)** revocar; **the committee reversed its decision on import quotas** = el comité revocó su decisión sobre las cuotas de importación **(b)** **to reverse the charges** = llamar a cobro revertido

> QUOTE the trade balance sank $17 billion, reversing last fall's brief improvement
> **Fortune**

reversion [rɪ'vɜ:ʃən] *noun* reversión *f* *or* devolución *f*; **he has the reversion of the estate** = recuperará la propiedad al terminar el arrendamiento actual

◊ **reversionary** [rɪ'vɜ:ʃənəri] *adjective* (propiedad) que pasa a otro propietario al morir el actual; **reversionary annuity** = anualidad revertible *or* que se paga a una persona al morir otra

review [rɪ'vju:] **1** *noun* **(a)** *(examination)* revisión *f* *or* examen *m* general *or* análisis *m*; **to conduct a review of distributors** = hacer un análisis de los distribuidores; **financial review** = revisión financiera; **wage review** *or* **salary review** = revisión de salarios; **she had a salary review last April** = obtuvo una revisión del sueldo el pasado abril **(b)** *(magazine)* revista *f* **2** *verb* examinar *or* revisar; **to review salaries** = revisar los salarios; **his salary will be reviewed at the end of the year** = su salario se revisará a fin de año; **the company has decided to review freelance payments in the light of the rising cost of living** = la empresa ha decidido hacer una revisión de la remuneración de los trabajadores autónomos en vista del aumento del coste de la vida; **to review discounts** = revisar descuentos

revise [rɪ'vaɪz] *verb* revisar *or* corregir; **sales forecasts are revised annually** = las previsiones de ventas se revisan todos los años; **the chairman is revising his speech to the AGM** = el presidente está revisando su discurso para la junta general anual

revive [rɪ'vaɪv] *verb* reanimar; **the government is introducing measures to revive trade** = el gobierno está introduciendo medidas para reanimar el comercio; **industry is reviving after the recession** = la industria se está recuperando después de la recesión

◊ **revival** [rɪ'vaɪvəl] *noun* recuperación *f*; **revival of trade** = reactivación *f* del comercio

revoke [rɪ'vəʊk] *verb* revocar; **to revoke a clause in an agreement** = revocar una cláusula de un acuerdo; **the quota on luxury items has been revoked** = la cuota de los artículos de lujo ha sido revocada

revolving credit [rɪ'vɒlvɪŋ 'kredɪt] *noun* crédito renovable

reward [rɪ'wɔ:d] *noun* premio *m*

ribbon ['rɪbn] *noun* cinta *f*; **printer ribbon** = cinta de impresora; **typewriter ribbon** = cinta para máquina de escribir

rich [rɪtʃ] *adjective* **(a)** *(money)* rico, -ca; **a rich stockbroker** = un agente de bolsa rico; **a rich oil company** = una empresa petrolífera rica **(b)** *(resources)* rico, -ca; **the country is rich in minerals** = el país es rico en minerales; **oil-rich territory** = un territorio rico en petróleo

rid [rɪd] *verb* **to get rid of something** = deshacerse de algo; **the company is trying to get rid of all its old stock** = la empresa está intentando deshacerse de todas las existencias antiguas; **our department has been told to get rid of twenty staff** = el departamento ha recibido órdenes de deshacerse de veinte empleados (NOTE: **getting rid - got rid**)

rider ['raɪdə] *noun* cláusula *f* suplementaria *or* adicional; **to add a rider to a contract** = añadir una cláusula suplementaria a un contrato

rig [rɪg] **1** *noun* **oil rig** = torre *f* de perforación (petrolífera) **2** *verb* manipular; **they tried to rig the election of officers** = intentaron manipular la elección de los dirigentes de la compañía; **to rig the market** = manipular el mercado; **rigging of ballots** *or* **ballot-rigging** = manipulación de elecciones *or* pucherazo (NOTE: **rigging - rigged**)

right [raɪt] **1** *adjective* **(a)** *(correct)* correcto, -ta; *(person)* **to be right** = tener razón *or* estar en lo cierto; **the chairman was right when he said the figures did not add up** = el presidente estaba en lo cierto al decir que las cifras no cuadraban; **this is not the right plane for Paris** = éste no es el avión que va a París **(b)** *(not left)* derecho, -cha; **the credits are on the right side of the page** = el haber está en el lado derecho de la página **2** *noun* **(a)** *(title)* derecho *m*; **right of renewal of a contract** = derecho de renovación de un contrato; **she has a right to the property** = tiene derecho a la propiedad; **he has no right to the patent** = no tiene derechos sobre la patente; **the staff have a right to know how the company is doing** = el personal tiene derecho a conocer la marcha de la empresa; **foreign rights** = derechos de venta en el extranjero; **right to strike** = derecho de huelga; **right of way** = derecho de paso **(b)** **rights issue** = ampliación de capital en curso *or* emisión de derechos

◊ **rightful** ['raɪtfʊl] *adjective* legítimo, -ma; **rightful claimant** = derecho habiente; **rightful owner** = propietario, -ria legítimo, -ma

◊ **right-hand** ['raɪthænd] *adjective* *a* *or* de la derecha; **the credit side is the right-hand column in the accounts** = el haber es la columna de la derecha de las cuentas; **he keeps the address list in the right-hand drawer of his desk** = guarda la lista de direcciones en el cajón de la derecha de su mesa de trabajo; **right-hand man** = brazo derecho *or* hombre de confianza

ring [rɪŋ] **1** *noun* coalición *f or* cartel *m* de empresas que se ponen de acuerdo para fijar precios **2** *verb* llamar por teléfono; **he rang (up) his stockbroker** = llamó a su agente de bolsa (NOTE: **ringing - rang - has rung)**

◊ **ring back** ['rɪŋ 'bæk] *verb* volver a llamar; **the managing director rang - can you ring him back?** = llamó el director gerente ¿puedes volverle a llamar *or* devolverle la llamada?

◊ **ring binder** ['rɪŋ 'baɪndə] *noun* carpeta *f or* archivador *m* de anillas

ripe [raɪp] *adjective* maduro, -ra

rise [raɪz] **1** *noun* **(a)** *(increase)* alza *f or* subida *f or* aumento *m*; **rise in the price of raw materials** = subida del precio de las materias primas; **oil price rises brought about a recession in world trade** = la subida de los precios del petróleo produjo una recesión del comercio mundial; **there is a rise in sales of 10%** *or* **sales show a rise of 10%** = hay un aumento de ventas de un 10% *or* las ventas han aumentado en un 10%; **salaries are increasing to keep up with the rise in the cost of living** = los salarios aumentan para compensar el alza del coste de la vida; **the recent rise in interest rates has made mortgages dearer** = la subida reciente de los tipos de interés trae como consecuencia el encarecimiento de las hipotecas **(b)** *(in salary)* aumento (de salario); **she asked her boss for a rise** = pidió un aumento a su jefe; **he had a 6% rise in January** = recibió un aumento del 6% en enero (NOTE: US English for this is **raise) 2** *verb* subir *or* elevarse *or* aumentar; **prices are rising faster than inflation** = los precios suben más deprisa que la inflación; **interest rates have risen to 15%** = los tipos de interés han subido al 15% (NOTE: **rising - rose - has risen)**

risk [rɪsk] *noun* **(a)** *(possible harm or chance of danger)* riesgo *m*; **to run a risk** = correr un riesgo; **to take a risk** = arriesgarse; **financial risk** = riesgo financiero; **there is no financial risk in selling to East European countries on credit** = no existe riesgo financiero en vender a crédito a los países de Europa del Este; **he is running the risk of overspending his promotion budget** = corre el riesgo de rebasar su presupuesto de promoción; **the company is taking a considerable risk in manufacturing 25m units without doing any market research** = la empresa se arriesga seriamente al fabricar 25 millones de unidades sin haber hecho un estudio de mercado **(b) risk capital** = capital-riesgo *m* **(c) at owner's risk** = por cuenta y

riesgo del propietario; **goods left here are at owner's risk** = las mercancías se depositan aquí por cuenta y riesgo del propietario; **the shipment was sent at owner's risk** = el envío se hizo por cuenta y riesgo del propietario **(d)** *(loss or damage against which you are insured)* riesgo; **fire risk** = peligro *or* riesgo de incendio; **that warehouse full of paper is a fire risk** = ese almacén lleno de papel supone un peligro de incendio **(e) he is a good risk** = es una persona que presenta un bajo riesgo; **he is a bad risk** = es una persona que presenta un gran riesgo

◊ **risk-free** *or* US **riskless** ['rɪsk'fri: *or* 'rɪskləs] *adjective* sin riesgo; **a risk-free investment** = una inversión sin riesgo

◊ **risky** ['rɪski] *adjective* arriesgado, -da *or* peligroso, -sa; **he lost all his money in some risky ventures in South America** = perdió todo su dinero en actividades arriesgadas en América del Sur

rival ['raɪvəl] *noun* rival *mf or* competidor, -ra; **a rival company** = una empresa competidora; **to undercut a rival** = vender a precio más bajo que un rival; **we are analyzing the rival brands on the market** = estamos analizando las marcas competidoras del mercado

road [rəʊd] *noun* **(a)** carretera *f*; **the main office is in London Road** = la oficina principal está en London Road; **use the Park Road entrance to get to the buying department** = utilice la entrada de Park Road para ir a la sección de compras; **to send** *or* **to ship goods by road** = enviar mercancías por carretera; **road transport costs have risen** = los costos del transporte por carretera han subido; **road haulage** = transporte por carretera *or* rodado; **road haulier** = transportista *or* agencia de transportes; **road tax** = impuesto de viaje *or* viajante **(b) on the road** = de viaje *or* viajante; **the salesmen are on the road thirty weeks a year** = los vendedores viajan treinta semanas al año; **we have twenty salesmen on the road** = tenemos veinte viajantes

robot ['rəʊbɒt] *noun* robot *m*; **the car is made by robots** = el coche está fabricado por robots

◊ **robotics** [rəʊ'bɒtɪks] *noun* robótica *f* (NOTE: takes a singular verb)

ROCE = RETURN ON CAPITAL EMPLOYED

rock [rɒk] *noun* roca *f*; **the company is on the rocks** = la compañía tiene grandes dificultades financieras

◊ **rock bottom** ['rɒk 'bɒtəm] *noun* rock-bottom prices = precios reventados; **sales have reached rock bottom** = las ventas han llegado a su punto más bajo

> QUOTE investment companies took the view that secondhand prices had reached rock bottom and that levels could only go up
> **Lloyd's List**

rocket ['rɒkɪt] *verb* subir rápidamente; **rocketing prices** = precios que se disparan; **prices have rocketed** = los precios se han puesto por las nubes

ROI = RETURN ON INVESTMENT

roll [rəʊl] **1** *noun* rollo *m*; **the desk calculator uses a roll of paper** = la calculadora de mesa lleva un rollo de papel; **can you order some more rolls of fax paper?** = ¿puedes hacer un pedido de rollos de papel para el fax? **2** *verb* **(a)** *(to move on wheels)* mover; **they rolled the computer into position** = trasladaron el ordenador a su lugar **(b)** *(moving forward)* **rolling account** = ROLLING SETTLEMENT **rolling budget** = presupuesto periódicamente actualizado; **rolling plan** = plan periódicamente actualizado; **rolling settlement** = pago de acciones a plazos

◇ **roll on/roll off (Ro/Ro)** ['rəʊlɒnrəʊl'ɒf] *adjective* autopropulsado, -da

◇ **roll over** ['rəʊl 'əʊvə] *verb* **(a) to roll over credit** *or* **a debt** = refinanciar un crédito *or* una deuda **(b)** *US* **to roll over an IRA** = transferir un plan de jubilación a otra compañía de seguros

◇ **rolling stock** ['rəʊlɪŋ 'stɒk] *noun* material *m* rodante

> QUOTE at the IMF in Washington, officials are worried that Japanese and US banks might decline to roll over the principal of loans made in the 1980s to Southeast Asian and other developing countries
> **Far Eastern Economic Review**

ROM [rɒm] = READ ONLY MEMORY

Romania [ruː'meɪnɪə] *noun* Rumania *f*

◇ **Romanian** [ruː'meɪnɪən] *adjective & noun* rumano, -na
NOTE: capital: **Bucharest** (= Bucarest); currency: **Romanian leu** *or* **lei** = leu *or* lei rumano

room [ruːm] *noun* **(a)** *(in a building)* sala *f or* cuarto *m or* habitación *f*; **the chairman's room is at the end of the corridor** = el despacho del presidente está al final del pasillo; **conference room** = sala de juntas *or* conferencias; **mail room** = departamento de distribución del correo **(b)** *(in a hotel)* habitación; **I want a room with bath for two nights** = quiero una habitación con baño para dos noches; **double room** = habitación doble; **room service** = servicio de habitaciones de un hotel **(c)** *(space)* espacio *m*; **the filing cabinets take up a lot of room** = los archivadores ocupan mucho espacio; **there is no more room in the computer file** = no hay más espacio en el archivo del ordenador (NOTE: no plural for this meaning)

rotation [rəʊ'teɪʃən] *noun* rotación *f*; **to fill the post of chairman by rotation** = ocupar el cargo de presidente por turno; **two directors retire by rotation** = dos consejeros terminan su mandato por rotación

rouble *or* *US* **ruble** ['ruːbl] *noun (currency used in Russia)* rublo *m*

rough [rʌf] *adjective* **(a)** *(approximate)* aproximado, -da; **rough calculation** *or* **rough estimate** = cálculo aproximado; **I made some rough calculations on the back of an envelope** = hice unos cálculos aproximados al dorso de un sobre **(b)** *(not finished)* preliminar; **rough copy** = borrador *m*; **he made a rough draft of the new design** = preparó un borrador del nuevo diseño

◇ **roughly** ['rʌfli] *adverb* aproximadamente; **the turnover is roughly twice last year's** = el volumen de ventas es aproximadamente el doble del correspondiente al año pasado; **the development cost of the project will be roughly £25,000** = el costo de desarrollo del proyecto será aproximadamente de £25.000

◇ **rough out** ['rʌf 'aʊt] *verb* hacer un borrador *or* esbozar; **the finance director roughed out a plan of investment** = el director de finanzas hizo un borrador de un plan de inversiones

round [raʊnd] **1** *adjective* **(a) in round figures** = en números redondos **(b) round trip** = viaje de ida y vuelta; **round-trip ticket** = billete de ida y vuelta; **round-trip fare** = tarifa de ida y vuelta **2** *noun* *(series of meetings)* ronda *f or* tanda *f*; **pay round** = ronda salarial; **a round of pay negotiations** = una ronda de negociaciones salariales

◇ **round down** ['raʊnd 'daʊn] *verb* redondear por defecto

◇ **round up** ['raʊnd 'ʌp] *verb* redondear por exceso; **to round up the figures to the nearest pound** = redondear la cantidad hasta la siguiente cifra en libras

> QUOTE each cheque can be made out for the local equivalent of £100 rounded up to a convenient figure
> **Sunday Times**

route [ruːt] *noun* **(a)** ruta *f or* camino *m or* rumbo *m*; **air route** = línea aérea; **bus route** = ruta del autobús; **companies were warned that normal shipping routes were dangerous because of the war** = se advirtió a las compañías que las rutas marítimas normales eran peligrosas debido a la guerra **(b) en route** = en el camino de *or* de camino a; **the tanker sank when she was en route to the Gulf** = el petrolero se hundió durante el viaje al Golfo

routine [ruː'tiːn] **1** *noun* rutina *f or* costumbre *f*; **he follows a daily routine - he takes the 8.15 train to London, then the bus to his office, and returns by the same route in the evening** = sigue una rutina cotidiana - toma el tren de las 8.15 a Londres, luego el autobús a su oficina, y regresa siguiendo la misma ruta por la tarde; **refitting the conference room has disturbed the office routine** = las reformas de la sala de juntas han perturbado la rutina de la oficina **2** *adjective* rutinario, -ria *or* monótono, -na *or* habitual *or* periódico, -ca; **routine work** = trabajo rutinario *or* monótono; **routine call** = llamada rutinaria; **a routine check of the fire equipment** = un examen periódico del equipo contra incendios

row *noun* **(a)** [rəʊ] *(line)* fila *f*; **in a row** = uno detrás de otro *or* seguidos; **to be in the first row** = estar en primera fila **(b)** [raʊ] *(noise)* ruido *f or* escándalo *m*; **to kick up a row** = armar una bronca

(c) [raʊ] *(argument)* riña *f or* disputa *f*; **he had a row with his secretary** = tuvo una disputa con su secretaria

royalty ['rɔɪəlti] *noun* 'royalty' *m or* regalía *f or* derechos *mpl* de autor *or* de patente *or* canon *m*; **oil royalties** = cánones del petróleo; **he is receiving royalties from his invention** = recibe regalías por su invención

RPI ['ɑ:pi:'aɪ] = RETAIL PRICE(S) INDEX

RPM = RESALE PRICE MAINTENANCE

RRP = RECOMMENDED RETAIL PRICE

RSVP ['ɑ:esvi:'pi:] s.r.c. = REPONDEZ S'IL VOUS PLAIT se ruega contestación

rubber ['rʌbə] *noun* **(a)** *(material)* caucho *m*; **rubber band** = goma (elástica); **put a rubber band round the filing cards to stop them falling on the floor** = sujeta las fichas con una goma para que no caigan al suelo **(b)** *(eraser)* goma *f* (de borrar)

◊ **rubber check** ['rʌbə 'tʃek] *noun US* cheque sin fondos (NOTE: the British equivalent is a **bouncing cheque**)

◊ **rubber stamp** ['rʌbə 'stæmp] **1** *noun* sello *m*; **he stamped the invoice with the rubber stamp 'Paid'** = estampó la factura con el sello de 'Pagado' **2** *verb* dar visto bueno *or* aprobar sin debate *or* automáticamente; **the board simply rubber stamped the agreement** = la junta directiva aprobó el acuerdo sin debate previo

rule [ru:l] **1** *noun* **(a)** *(general way of conduct)* norma *f or* regla *f or* reglamento *m or* régimen *m*; **as a rule** = por regla general *or* por norma; **as a rule, we do not give discounts over 20%** = por regla general no damos descuentos por encima del 20%; **company rules** = normas de la empresa; **it is a company rule that smoking is not allowed in the offices** = es norma de la empresa que no se fume en las oficinas; **rule of thumb** = regla empírica **(b) to work to rule** = hacer huelga de celo *or* estar en paro técnico **2** *verb* **(a)** *(to give an official decision)* fallar *or* decidir; **the commission of inquiry ruled that the company was in breach of contract** = la comisión de investigación decidió que la compañía había incumplido el contrato; **the judge ruled that the documents had to be deposited with the court** = el juez falló que los documentos debían depositarse ante el tribunal **(b)** *(to be in force)* estar vigente; **prices which are ruling at the moment** = los precios vigentes en el momento actual

◊ **rulebook** ['ru:lbʊk] *noun (book of rules of a union)* libro *m* de normas *or* reglamentos *mpl* de un sindicato

ruler ['ru:lə] *noun* regla *f*

ruling ['ru:lɪŋ] **1** *adjective* vigente *or* corriente *or* actual; **we will invoice at ruling prices** = haremos las facturas a los precios corrientes *or* vigentes **2** *noun* decisión *f or* fallo *m*; **the inquiry gave a ruling on the case** = el tribunal pronunció el fallo sobre la causa; **according to the ruling of the court, the contract was illegal** = según el fallo del tribunal, el contrato era ilegal

run [rʌn] **1** *noun* **(a)** *(machine)* funcionamiento *m or* ciclo *m* de trabajo; **a cheque run** = serie de cheques

procesados por el ordenador; **a computer run** = periodo de trabajo del ordenador; **test run** = prueba de una máquina **(b)** *(rush to buy something)* mucha demanda *f*; **the Post Office reported a run on the new stamps** = la oficina de correos comunicó que había mucha demanda de los nuevos sellos; **a run on the bank** = retirada *f* masiva de fondos de un banco; **a run on the pound** = una venta apresurada de la libra **(c)** *(regular route of a bus or plane)* ruta *f* habitual **2** *verb* **(a)** *(to be in force)* durar *or* ser válido; **the lease runs for twenty years** = el arrendamiento tiene una duración de veinte años; **the lease has only six months to run** = el arrendamiento tiene solamente seis meses más de vigencia **(b)** *(to manage or organize)* dirigir *or* organizar; **she runs a mail-order business from home** = lleva un negocio de venta por correo desde su domicilio; **they run a staff sports club** = llevan la organización de un club deportivo del personal; **he is running a multimillion-pound company** = dirige una compañía multimillonaria **(c)** *(to work on a machine)* utilizar *or* hacer funcionar; **do not run the photocopier for more than four hours at a time** = no utilice la fotocopiadora más de cuatro horas consecutivas; **the computer was running invoices all night** = el ordenador estuvo preparando facturas toda la noche **(d)** *(of buses, trains etc.)* circular; **there is an evening plane running between Manchester and Paris** = hay un avión por la tarde entre Manchester y Paris; **this train runs on weekdays** = este tren circula los días laborables (NOTE: **running - ran - has run**)

◊ **runaway inflation** ['rʌnəweɪ ɪn'fleɪʃən] *noun* inflación *f* galopante

◊ **run down** ['rʌn 'daʊn] *verb* **(a)** *(gradual reduction)* reducir gradualmente; **to run down stocks** *or* **to let stocks run down** = reducir las existencias gradualmente *or* dejar que las existencias se reduzcan gradualmente **(b)** *(to slow down)* restringir la producción *or* reducir la actividad de una empresa antes de su cierre; **the company is being run down** = la empresa ha reducido sus actividades en preparación del cierre

◊ **run into** ['rʌn 'ɪntʊ] *verb* **(a) to run into debt** = endeudarse *or* adeudarse **(b)** *(to amount to)* ascender; **costs ran into thousands of pounds** = los costes ascendieron a miles de libras; **he has an income running into five figures** = sus ingresos ascienden a más de £10.000

◊ **running** ['rʌnɪŋ] *adjective* **(a) running total** = total acumulado **(b) running costs** *or* **running expenses** *or* **costs of running a business** = gastos de explotación *or* gastos corrientes *or* costes corrientes de una empresa **(c) the company has made a profit for six years running** = la compañía ha obtenido beneficios durante seis años consecutivos

◊ **run out of** ['rʌn 'aʊt əv] *verb* no quedar nada *or* agotar las existencias; **we have run out of headed notepaper** = se nos acabó el papel con membrete; **the printer has run out of paper** = la impresora se ha quedado sin papel *or* no hay papel en la impresora

◊ **run up** ['rʌn 'ʌp] *verb* contraer; **he quickly ran up a bill for £250** = contrajo rápidamente una deuda de £250

QUOTE applications for mortgages are running at a high level
Times

rupee [ruː'piː] *noun (currency used in India and some other countries)* rupia *f*

rush [rʌʃ] **1** *noun* prisa *f*; **rush hour** = hora punta *or* horas de mayor afluencia; **the taxi was delayed in the rush hour traffic** = el taxi se retrasó por el tráfico de la hora punta; **rush job** = trabajo urgente; **rush order** = pedido urgente **2** *verb* **(a)** *(to go fast)* precipitarse **(b)** *(to do something fast)* instar a hacer algo con rapidez *or* de forma inmediata; **to rush an**

order through the factory = instar a la fábrica a que despache el pedido con rapidez; **to rush a shipment to Africa** = expedir un envío a Africa a toda prisa

Russia ['rʌʃə] *noun* Rusia *f*

◇ **Russian** ['rʌʃn] *adjective & noun* ruso, -sa
NOTE: capital: **Moscow** (= Moscú); currency: **rouble (Rub)** = rublo (Rub)

Rwanda [rʊ'ændə] *noun* Ruanda *m or* Rwanda *m*

◇ **Rwandan** [rʊ'ændən] *adjective & noun* ruandés, -esa *or* rwandés, -esa
NOTE: capital: **Kigali;** currency: **Rwanda franc (RF)** = franco ruandés (FR)

Ss

sachet ['sæʃeɪ] *noun* bolsita *f*

sack [sæk] **1** *noun* **(a)** *(large bag)* saco *m*; **a sack of potatoes** = un saco de patatas; **we sell onions by the sack** = vendemos cebollas por sacos **(b) to get the sack** = ser despedido **2** *verb* **to sack someone** = despedir; **he was sacked after being late for work** = le despidieron por llegar tarde al trabajo

◊ **sacking** ['sækɪŋ] *noun* despido *m*; **his sacking triggered a strike** = su despido provocó una huelga; **the union protested against the sackings** = el sindicato protestó por los despidos

SAE *or* **s.a.e.** = STAMPED ADDRESSED ENVELOPE

safe [seɪf] **1** *noun* caja *f* fuerte *or* de caudales *or* arca *f*; **put the documents in the safe** = pon los documentos en la caja fuerte; **we keep the petty cash in the safe** = guardamos la caja para gastos menores en la caja de caudales; **fire-proof safe** = caja protegida contra incendios; **night safe** = caja nocturna; **wall safe** = caja de pared **2** *adjective* **(a)** *(out of danger)* seguro, -ra; **keep the documents in a safe place** = guarde los documentos en un lugar seguro; **safe keeping** = custodia *f*; **we put the documents into the bank for safe keeping** = guardamos los documentos en el banco para mayor seguridad **(b) safe investments** = inversiones seguras

◊ **safe deposit** ['seɪf dɪ'pɒzɪt] *noun* caja *f* de seguridad *or* caja fuerte

◊ **safe deposit box** ['seɪf dɪ'pɒzɪt bɒks] *noun* caja *f* de seguridad *or* caja fuerte

◊ **safely** ['seɪfli] *adverb* sin peligro *or* sin sufrir daños *or* con seguridad; **the cargo was unloaded safely from the sinking ship** = antes de hundirse el barco se descargó el cargamento sin sufrir daños

◊ **safeguard** ['seɪfgɑːd] *verb* proteger; **to safeguard the interests of the shareholders** = proteger los intereses de los accionistas

safety ['seɪfti] *noun* **(a)** seguridad *f*; **Health and Safety at Work Act** = ley de sanidad y seguridad en el trabajo; **safety margin** *or* **margin of safety** = margen de seguridad; **to take safety precautions** *or* **safety measures** = tomar precauciones *or* medidas de seguridad; **safety regulations** = normas de seguridad **(b) fire safety** = prevención de incendios; **fire safety officer** = responsable de la seguridad contra incendios **(c) for safety** = por razones de seguridad *or* para mayor seguridad; **put the documents in the cupboard for safety** = ponga los documentos en el armario para que estén seguros; **to take a copy of the disk for safety** = hacer una copia del disco para mayor seguridad

sail [seɪl] *verb* navegar *or* zarpar; **the ship sails at 12.00** = el barco zarpa a las 12.00

◊ **sailing** ['seɪlɪŋ] *noun* salida *f* (de un barco); **there are no sailings to Spain because of the strike** = no hay salidas a España debido a la huelga

salary ['sæləri] *noun* *(monthly)* sueldo *m or* salario *m*; **she got a salary increase in June** = recibió un aumento de sueldo en junio; **the company froze all salaries for a six-month period** = la empresa congeló los sueldos durante un periodo de seis meses; **basic salary** = sueldo base; **gross salary** = sueldo bruto; **minimum salary** = salario mínimo; **net salary** = sueldo neto; **starting salary** = sueldo inicial; **he was appointed at a starting salary of £10,000** = le nombraron con un sueldo inicial de £10.000; **salary cheque** = cheque de sueldo; **salary cut** = recorte salarial; **salary deductions** = deducciones salariales; **salary review** = revisión de sueldos; **she had a salary review last April** *or* **her salary was reviewed last April** = obtuvo una revisión salarial el pasado abril *or* su sueldo fue objeto de una revisión el pasado abril; **scale of salaries** *or* **salary scale** = escala salarial; **the company's salary structure** = la estructura salarial de la empresa

◊ **salaried** ['sælərɪd] *adjective* asalariado, -da; **the company has 250 salaried staff** = la empresa tiene 250 asalariados

QUOTE the union of hotel and personal service workers has demanded a new salary structure and uniform conditions of service for workers in the hotel and catering industry
Business Times (Lagos)

sale [seɪl] *noun* **(a)** venta *f*; **cash sale** = venta al contado; **credit card sale** = venta con tarjeta de crédito; **firm sale** = venta segura *or* en firme; **forced sale** = venta forzosa; **sale and lease-back** = venta y arrendamiento al comprador; **sale or return** = venta a prueba *or* en depósito; **we have taken 4,000 items on sale or return** = hemos tomado 4.000 artículos para vender a prueba; **bill of sale** = documento de venta; **conditions of sale** = condiciones de venta **(b) for sale** = en venta; **to offer something for sale** *or* **to put something up for sale** = poner algo en venta; **they put the factory up for sale** = pusieron la fábrica en venta; **his shop is for sale** = su tienda está en venta; **these items are not for sale to the general public** = estos artículos no están a la venta al público en general **(c) on sale** = a la venta; **these items are on sale in most chemists** = estos artículos están a la venta en la mayoría de las farmacias **(d)** *(selling at specially low prices)* liquidación *f or* saldo *m or* rebajas *fpl*; **the shop is having a sale to clear old stock** = la tienda ha organizado unas rebajas para liquidar las existencias antiguas; **the sale price is 50% of the normal price** = el precio rebajado es el 50% del precio normal; **bargain sale** = saldo *or* rebajas; **car boot sale** = venta de objetos usados expuestos en el maletero de un coche; **clearance sale** = liquidación; **garage sale** = venta de artículos de segunda mano en un garaje; **half-price sale** = rebajas a mitad de precio *or* al 50%; **jumble sale** = venta de artículos usados para recaudar fondos (con fines benéficos) *or* rastrillo

◊ **saleability** *or US* **salability** [seɪlə'bɪləti] *noun* facilidad *f* de venta

◊ **saleable** *or US* **salable** ['seɪləbl] *adjective* vendible

◊ **saleroom** ['seɪlrʊm] *noun* sala *f* de subastas

◊ **sales** [seɪlz] *noun* **(a)** *(selling of goods)* ventas; **sales have risen over the first quarter** = las ventas han subido durante el primer trimestre; **sales analysis** = análisis de ventas; **sales appeal** = atracción comercial; **sales book** = libro de ventas; **book sales** = las ventas registradas; **sales budget** = presupuesto de ventas; **sales campaign** = campaña de ventas; **sales conference** *or* **sales meeting** = reunión de ventas; **cost of sales** = coste de ventas; **sales day book (SDB)** *or* **sales journal** = libro *or* registro diario de ventas; **sales department** = sección *or* servicio de ventas; **the people from the sales department** = el personal de ventas; **domestic sales** *or* **home sales** = ventas nacionales; **sales drive** = promoción de ventas; **sales executive** = ejecutivo responsable de las ventas; **sales figures** = cifras de ventas; **sales force** = personal de ventas; **sales forecast** = previsión de ventas; **forward sales** = ventas a plazo *or* para entrega futura; **sales journal** = SALES DAY BOOK **sales ledger** = libro mayor de ventas; **sales ledger clerk** = encargado del libro de ventas; **sales literature** = información publicitaria; **sales manager** = director de ventas *or* comercial; **sales mix** = conjunto de ventas de los diferentes artículos de una compañía; **sales people** = el personal de ventas; **sales pitch** = rollo *m* publicitario; **sales promoter** = promotor *or* animador de ventas; **sales promotion** = campaña de promoción de ventas; **sales quota** = cupo de ventas; **sales receipt** *or* **sales slip** = comprobante de caja; **monthly sales report** = informe mensual de ventas; **in the sales reports all the European countries are bracketed together** = en los informes de ventas, todos los países europeos se incluyen en una categoría única; *US* **sales revenue** = ingresos de ventas *or* facturación (NOTE: GB English is **turnover**) **the sales staff** *or* **the sales people** = el personal de ventas; **sales tax** = impuesto sobre la venta; **sales volume** *or* **volume of sales** = volumen de ventas **(b)** **the sales** = las rebajas; **I bought this in the sales** *or* **at the sales** *or* **in the January sales** = compré esto en las rebajas *or* en las rebajas de enero

◊ **salesclerk** ['seɪlzklɑːk] *noun US* vendedor, -ra *or* dependiente, -ta

◊ **salesgirl** ['seɪlzgɜːl] *noun* dependienta *f or* vendedora *f*

◊ **saleslady** [seɪlzleɪdi] *noun* dependienta *f or* vendedora *f*

◊ **salesman** ['seɪlzmən] *noun* **(a)** *(to the public)* dependiente *m or* vendedor *m*; **he is the head salesman in the carpet department** = es el jefe de dependientes de la sección de alfombras y moquetas; **a used car salesman** = vendedor de coches usados; **door-to-door salesman** = vendedor a domicilio; **insurance salesman** = vendedor de seguros **(b)** *(to retail shops)* representante *m* comercial *or* comerciante *mf*; **we have six salesmen calling on accounts in central London** = seis de nuestros representantes visitan a los clientes del centro de Londres (NOTE: plural is **salesmen**)

◊ **salesmanship** ['seɪlzmənʃɪp] *noun* arte *f* de vender

◊ **saleswoman** ['seɪlzwʊmən] *noun* vendedora *f* (NOTE: plural is **saleswomen**)

El Salvador [el 'sælvədɔ:] *noun* El Salvador *m*

◊ **Salvadorian** [sælvə'dɔːriən] *adjective & noun* salvadoreño, -ña
NOTE: capital: **San Salvador**; currency: **Salvadorian colon (C)** = colón salvadoreño

salvage ['sælvɪdʒ] **1** *noun* **(a)** *(ship or cargo)* salvamento *m or* rescate *m*; **salvage money** = premio de salvamento; **salvage value** *or* **scrap value** = valor residual *or* precio de chatarra; **salvage vessel** = buque de salvamento **(b)** *(goods)* objetos *mpl* salvados; **a sale of flood salvage items** = liquidación de objetos salvados de una inundación **2** *verb* **(a)** *(contents of a ship)* salvar; **we are selling off a warehouse full of salvaged goods** = estamos liquidando un almacén lleno de objetos salvados de un siniestro **(b)** *(save from loss)* salvar; **the company is trying to salvage its reputation after the managing director was sent to prison for fraud** = la compañía está intentando salvar su reputación después del encarcelamiento del director gerente por fraude; **the receiver managed to salvage something from the collapse of the company** = el administrador judicial consiguió salvar algo de la ruina de la compañía

sample ['sɑːmpl] **1** *noun* **(a)** *(item)* muestra *f*; **a sample of the cloth** *or* **a cloth sample** = una muestra de la tela; **check sample** = muestra de control; **free sample** = muestra gratuita; **sample book** *or* **book of samples** = libro de muestras **(b)** *(survey)* selección *f*; **we interviewed a sample of potential customers** = entrevistamos a una muestra de clientes potenciales; **a random sample** = una muestra aleatoria *or* al azar **2** *verb* **(a)** probar; **to sample a product before buying it** = probar un producto antes de comprarlo **(b)** *(to ask a representative group of people questions)* hacer un muestreo; **they sampled 2,000 people at random to test the new drink** = hicieron un muestreo entre 2.000 personas escogidas al azar para probar la nueva bebida

◊ **sampling** ['sɑːmplɪŋ] *noun* **(a)** *(testing examples)* toma *f* de muestras *or* muestreo *m* por áreas; **sampling of EU produce** = muestreo de productos de la UE; **acceptance sampling** = muestra de aceptación **(b)** *(in statistics)* muestreo; **random sampling** = muestreo aleatorio *or* al azar; **sampling error** = error de muestreo

◊ **sanction** ['sæŋ(k)ʃən] **1** *noun* **(a)** permiso *m*; **you will need the sanction of the local authorities before you can knock down the office block** = necesitará el permiso de las autoridades locales para derribar el edificio de oficinas **(b)** **economic sanctions** = sanciones económicas; **to impose sanctions on a country** *or* **to lift sanctions** = imponer sanciones económicas a un país *or* levantar sanciones **2** *verb* aprobar; **the board sanctioned the expenditure of £1.2m on the development project** = el consejo de administración aprobó un presupuesto de £1,2 millones para el proyecto de expansión *or* desarrollo

QUOTE members of the new Association of Coffee Producing Countries voted to cut their exports by 20 per cent to try to raise prices. The Association voted also on ways to enforce the agreement and to implement sanctions if it is breached
Times

sandwich ['sændwɪtʃ] *noun* bocadillo *m or* sandwich *m* **sandwich boards** = carteles que lleva el hombre-anuncio; **sandwich course** = curso *m* de estudios que incluye un periodo de trabajo en una fábrica *or* oficina; **sandwich man** = hombre-anuncio *m*

satisfaction [sætɪs'fækʃən] *noun* satisfacción *f*; **customer satisfaction** = satisfacción del cliente; **job satisfaction** = satisfacción laboral *or* en el trabajo

◊ **satisfactory** [sætɪs'fæktri] *adjective* satisfactorio, -ria

◊ **satisfy** ['sætɪsfaɪ] *verb* **(a)** *(please)* satisfacer; **to satisfy a client** = satisfacer a un cliente; **a satisfied customer** = un cliente satisfecho **(b) to satisfy a demand** = satisfacer una demanda; **we cannot produce enough coal to satisfy the demand for the product** = no podemos producir carbón suficiente para satisfacer la demanda **(c)** *(convince)* convencer; **he is not satisfied with her explanation** = sus explicaciones no le convencen

saturation [sætʃə'reɪʃən] *noun* saturación *f*; **saturation of the market** *or* **market saturation** = saturación del mercado; **the market has reached saturation point** = el mercado ha llegado al punto de saturación; **saturation advertising** = campaña de publicidad intensiva

◊ **saturate** ['sætʃəreɪt] *verb* saturar; **to saturate the market** = saturar el mercado; **the market for home computers is saturated** = el mercado de ordenadores personales está saturado

Saudi Arabia ['saʊdi ə'reɪbiə] *noun* Arabia Saudita *f or* Arabia Saudí

◊ **Saudi (Arabian)** ['saʊdi (ə'reɪbiən)] *adjective & noun* árabe saudita *or* árabe saudí
NOTE: capital: **Riyadh**; currency: **Saudi Arabian riyal (SRls)** = riyal árabe saudita (SRls)

save [seɪv] *verb* **(a)** *(to keep money)* ahorrar; **he is trying to save money by walking to work** = está tratando de ahorrar dinero yendo al trabajo a pie; **she is saving to buy a house** = está ahorrando para comprar una casa **(b)** *(not to waste)* ahorrar *or* economizar; **to save time, let us continue the discussion in the taxi to the airport** = para ahorrar tiempo, continuaremos la conversación en el taxi mientras nos lleva al aeropuerto; **the government is encouraging companies to save energy** = el gobierno está alentando a las empresas para que ahorren energía **(c)** *(on a computer)* archivar *or* guardar *or* salvar; **do not forget to save your files when you have finished keyboarding them** = no olvides guardar tus archivos cuando los hayas pasado al ordenador

◊ **save-as-you-earn** **(SAYE)**

['seɪvæzju:'ɜːn] *noun GB* **save-as-you-earn scheme** = plan de ahorro mediante deducciones directas del salario

◊ **save on** ['seɪv 'ɒn] *verb* economizar *or* ahorrar; **by introducing shift work we find we can save on fuel** = el trabajo por turnos nos permite ahorrar combustible *or* energía

◊ **saver** ['seɪvə] *noun* ahorrador, -ra

◊ **save up** ['seɪv 'ʌp] *verb* ahorrar; **they are saving up for a holiday in the USA** = están ahorrando para ir de vacaciones a los EE UU

◊ **saving** ['seɪvɪŋ] **1** *noun* economía *f or* ahorro *m*; **we are aiming for a 10% saving in fuel** = nos proponemos ahorrar un 10% en combustible **2** *suffix* que ahorra; **an energy-saving** *or* **labour-saving device** = un mecanismo *or* dispositivo para ahorrar energía *or* trabajo; **time-saving** = que ahorra tiempo

◊ **savings** ['seɪvɪŋz] *plural noun* ahorros *mpl*; **he put all his savings into a deposit account** = puso todos sus ahorros en una cuenta a plazo fijo; *GB* **National Savings** = Caja de Ahorros; **savings certificate** *US* **savings bond** = bono de ahorro; **savings account** = cuenta de ahorro

◊ **savings and loan (association) (S&L)** ['seɪvɪŋz ən 'ləʊn (əsəʊsi'eɪʃən)] *noun US* sociedad *f* de crédito inmobiliario (NOTE: the S&Ls are also called **thrifts;** the UK equivalents are the building societies)

COMMENT: because of deregulation of interest rates in 1980, many S&Ls found that they were forced to raise interest on deposits to current market rates in order to secure funds, while at the same time they still were charging low fixed-interest rates on the mortgages granted to borrowers. This created considerable problems and many S&Ls had to be rescued by the Federal government

◊ **savings bank** ['seɪvɪŋz 'bæŋk] *noun* caja *f* de ahorros

say [seɪ] *verb* decir; **I am sorry to say that we are three months behind schdule** = siento decir que llevamos tres meses de retraso; **his secretary phoned to say he would be late** = su secretaria llamó para decir que él llegaría tarde

SAYE ['eseɪwaɪ'iː] = SAVE-AS-YOU-EARN

scab [skæb] *noun (informal) (worker who goes on working when there is a strike)* esquirol *m*

scale [skeɪl] **1** *noun* **(a)** *(graded system)* escala *f or* baremo *m*; **scale of charges** *or* **scale of prices** = escala de derechos *or* escala de precios; **fixed scale of charges** = escala de precios fija *or* baremo fijo; **scale of salaries** *or* **salary scale** = escala de salarios; **he was appointed at the top end of the salary scale** = le dieron el puesto con una asignación máxima en la escala de salarios; **incremental scale** = escala móvil del salarios **(b) large scale** *or* **small scale** = gran escala *or* pequeña escala; **to start in business on a small scale** = iniciar actividades comerciales a pequeña escala; **economies of scale** = economías de escala; **diseconomies of scale** = deseconomías de escala **(c)** *(machine for weighing)* **scales** = balanza *f* **2** *verb* **to scale down** *or* **to scale up** = reducir *or* aumentar proporcionalmente *or* a escala

scam [skæm] *noun US (informal)* fraude *m or* escándalo *m*

scandal ['skændl] *noun* escándalo *m*

scanner ['skænə] *noun* escáner *m*

scarce [skeəs] *adjective* escaso, -sa; **scarce raw materials** = materias primas escasas; **reliable trained staff are scarce** = el personal cualificado fiable es escaso

◇ **scarceness** *or* **scarcity** ['skeəsnəs *or* 'skeəsəti] *noun* escasez *f or* carestía *f*; **the scarceness of specialized workers** = la escasez de trabajadores profesionales; **there is a scarcity of trained staff** = hay escasez de personal cualificado; **scarcity value** = valor de escasez

scenario [se'nɑːriəʊ] *noun* pronóstico *m*

> QUOTE on the upside scenario, the outlook is reasonably optimistic, bankers say, the worst scenario being that a scheme of arrangement cannot be achieved, resulting in liquidation
> **Irish Times**

schedule ['ʃedjuːl] **1** *noun* **(a)** *(timetable or plan)* programa *m or* horario *m*; **schedule of events** = programa de actividades; **to be ahead of schedule** = ir adelantado; **to be on schedule** = ser puntual *or* cumplir los plazos *or* ir al ritmo previsto; **to be behind schedule** = ir atrasado *or* retrasado; **the project is on schedule** = el proyecto avanza de acuerdo con lo previsto; **the building was completed ahead of schedule** = el edificio se terminó antes de lo previsto; **I am sorry to say that we are three months behind schedule** = siento decir que llevamos tres meses de retraso; **the managing director has a busy schedule of appointments** = el director gerente tiene un programa de visitas muy apretado; **his secretary tried to fit me into his schedule** = su secretaria trató de hacerme un hueco en su horario **(b)** *(list)* lista *f*; **please find enclosed our schedule of charges** = adjuntamos nuestra lista de precios; **schedule of territories to which a contract applies** = lista de territorios en los que tiene validez un contrato; **see the attached schedule** *or* **as per the attached schedule** = véase la lista adjunta *or* según la lista adjunta **(c)** *GB* **tax schedules** = escalas impositivas **(d)** *(insurance)* relación de partidas aseguradas **2** *verb* **(a)** notificar oficialmente; **scheduled prices** *or* **scheduled charges** = precios *or* tarifas oficiales **(b)** proyectar *or* prever *or* programar *or* fijar; **the building is scheduled for completion in May** = está previsto que el edificio se termine en mayo; **scheduled flight** = vuelo regular; **he left for Helsinki on a scheduled flight** = partió para Helsinki en un vuelo regular

◇ **scheduling** ['ʃedjuːlɪŋ] *noun* programación *f*

scheme [skiːm] *noun* plan *m*; **bonus scheme** = plan de bonificación; **pension scheme** = plan de pensiones; **profit-sharing scheme** = programa de participación en los beneficios; **scheme of arrangement** = acuerdo preventivo *or* transacción previa a la quiebra

science ['saɪəns] *noun* ciencia *f*; **business science** *or* **management science** = ciencias empresariales; **he has a master's degree in business science** = tiene un master en ciencias empresariales; **science park** = parque tecnológico

scope [skəʊp] *noun* margen *m or* posibilidad *f or* alcance *m or* ámbito *m*; **there is scope for improvement in our sales performance** = hay margen para mejorar nuestras ventas; **there is considerable scope for expansion into the export market** = hay grandes posibilidades de extender las actividades al mercado de exportación

scrap [skræp] **1** *noun* chatarra *f*; **to sell a ship for scrap** = vender un barco como chatarra; **scrap value** = valor residual *or* precio de chatarra; **its scrap value is £2,500** = su valor como chatarra es de £2.500; **scrap dealer** *or* **scrap merchant** = comerciante de chatarra **2** *verb* **(a)** *(to stop working on)* abandonar; **to scrap plans for expansion** = abandonar los planes de expansión **(b)** *(to throw away as useless)* desguazar *or* tirar; **they had to scrap 10,000 spare parts** = tuvieron que tirar 10.000 repuestos (NOTE: **scrapping - scrapped**)

screen [skriːn] **1** *noun* pantalla *f*; **a TV screen** = una pantalla de televisión; **he brought up the information on the screen** = proyectó los datos en la pantalla **2** *verb* **to screen candidates** = seleccionar candidatos *or* pasar por la criba

◇ **screening** ['skriːnɪŋ] *noun* **the screening of candidates** = selección de candidatos *or* criba

scrip [skrɪp] *noun* **scrip issue** = emisión de acciones gratuitas a los accionistas

> QUOTE under the rule, brokers who fail to deliver stock within four days of a transaction are to be fined 1% of the transaction value for each day of missing scrip
> **Far Eastern Economic Review**

scroll [skrəʊl] *verb* desplazar *or* enrollar *or* mover el texto de arriba a abajo en una pantalla de ordenador

SDB = SALES DAY BOOK

SDRs = SPECIAL DRAWING RIGHTS derechos especiales de giro (DEG)

sea [siː] *noun* mar *m*; **to send a shipment by sea** = enviar algo por vía marítima; **by sea mail** = correo por vía marítima

◇ **seaport** ['siːpɔːt] *noun* puerto *m* marítimo

◇ **seaworthiness** ['siːwɜːðinəs] *noun* **certificate of seaworthiness** = certificado de navegabilidad

seal [siːl] **1** *noun* **(a)** **common seal** *or* **company's seal** = sello *m* de la compañía; **to attach the company's seal to a document** = poner el sello de la compañía a un documento; **contract under seal** = contrato sellado **(b)** *(piece of paper or metal or wax attached to close something)* precinto *m*; **customs seal** = precinto de aduana **2** *verb* **(a)** *(to close tightly)* cerrar *or* precintar; **the computer disks were sent in a sealed container** = los discos del ordenador fueron enviados en un paquete precintado; **sealed envelope** = sobre cerrado; **the information was sent in a sealed envelope** = se envió la información en sobre cerrado; **sealed tenders** = ofertas en pliego cerrado; **the company has asked for sealed bids for the warehouse** = la compañía ha pedido ofertas en pliego cerrado para el almacén **(b)** *(to attach a seal)* sellar *or* precintar; **the customs sealed the shipment** = la aduana precintó el envío

search [sɜːtʃ] **1** *noun* **(a)** *(inspection)* registro *m or* inspección *f* **(b)** *(a property for sale)* examen *m* del registro de la propiedad para ver las cargas que pesan sobre un inmueble **2** *verb* rastrear

season ['siːzn] *noun* **(a)** *(part of year)* estación *f* **(b)** *(period of time)* temporada *f*; **low season** *or* **high season** = temporada baja *or* temporada alta; **air fares are cheaper in the low season** = los vuelos en avión son más baratos en temporada baja; **tourist season** *or* **holiday season** = temporada turística *or* temporada de vacaciones; **busy season** *or* **slack season** = temporada de mucha actividad *or* temporada de poca actividad; **dead season** = temporada baja; **end of season sale** = rebajas de fin de temporada

◊ **seasonal** ['siːzənl] *adjective* estacional; **the demand for this item is very seasonal** = la demanda de este artículo es muy estacional; **seasonal variations in sales patterns** = variaciones de temporada en el régimen de ventas; **seasonal adjustments** = ajustes estacionales; **seasonal demand** = demanda estacional; **seasonal employment** = empleo estacional; **seasonal unemployment** = paro estacional

◊ **seasonally** ['siːznəli] *adverb* **seasonally adjusted figures** = cifras ajustadas estacionalmente

◊ **season ticket** ['siːzn 'tɪkɪt] *noun* abono *m*; **season ticket holder** = abonado, -da

sec [sek] = SECRETARY **hon sec** = secretario honorario *or* secretaria honoraria

SEC = SECURITIES & EXCHANGE COMMISSION

second 1 ['sekənd] *adjective* segundo, -da; **second half-year** = segundo semestre; **second mortgage** = segunda hipoteca; **second quarter** = segundo trimestre **2** ['sekənd] *verb* **(a) to second a motion** = apoyar una moción; **Mrs Smith seconded the motion** *or* **the motion was seconded by Mrs Smith** = la señora Smith apoyó la moción *or* la moción fue apoyada por la señora Smith **(b)** [sɪ'kɒnd] *(work)* trasladar temporalmente; **he was seconded to the Department of Trade for two years** = fue trasladado al Ministerio de Comercio por un periodo de dos años

◊ **secondary** ['sekəndri] *adjective* secundario, -ria; **secondary banks** = bancos subsidiarios; **secondary industry** = industria secundaria; **secondary picketing** = piquete subsidiario

◊ **second-class** [sekən(d)'klɑːs] **1** *adverb* en segunda clase; **to travel second-class** = viajar en segunda clase **2** *adjective* de segunda clase *or* categoría; **the price of a second-class ticket is half that of a first class** = el precio del billete de segunda clase es la mitad de primera; **I find second-class hotels are just as comfortable as the best ones** = los hoteles de segunda categoría me parecen tan confortables como los más lujosos; **second-class mail** = *GB* servicio de correos de segunda clase; *US* servicio de correos para periódicos y revistas; **a second-class letter is slower than a first-class** = una carta en correo de segunda clase tarda más que una en correo de primera; **send it second-class if it is not urgent** = envíalo por correo de segunda clase si no es urgente

◊ **seconder** ['sekəndə] *noun* persona *f* que apoya una moción; **there was no seconder for the motion**

so it was not put to the vote = no hubo nadie que apoyara la moción por lo que no fue sometida a votación

◊ **second half** ['sekənd 'hɑːf] *noun* segundo semestre *m* del año; **the figures for the second half are up on those for the first part of the year** = las cifras del segundo trimestre son superiores a las del primer trimestre

◊ **secondhand** [sekənd'hænd] **1** *adverb* de segunda mano *or* de ocasión; **to buy something secondhand** = comprar algo de segunda mano **2** *adjective* usado, -da *or* de segunda mano; **a secondhand car salesman** = un vendedor de coches usados; **the secondhand computer market** *or* **the market in secondhand computers** = el mercado de ordenadores usados *or* el mercado de ordenadores de segunda mano; **look at the prices of secondhand cars** *or* **look at secondhand car prices** = averigüe *or* compruebe los precios de los coches de segunda mano; **secondhand dealer** = comerciante de mercancías de segunda mano

◊ **secondment** [sɪ'kɒn(d)mənt] *noun* traslado *m* temporal (de un trabajo); **he is on three years' secondment to an Australian college** = ha sido trasladado a un colegio australiano por un periodo de tres años

◊ **second-rate** ['sekən(d)'reɪt] *adjective* de calidad inferior; **never buy anything second-rate** = no compre nunca nada de calidad inferior

◊ **seconds** ['sekəndz] *plural noun* artículos *mpl* de baja calidad *or* defectuosos; **the shop has a sale of seconds** = la tienda hace una liquidación de artículos defectuosos

secret ['siːkrət] **1** *noun* secreto *m*; **to keep a secret** = guardar un secreto **2** *adjective* secreto, -ta; **the MD kept the contract secret from the rest of the board** = el director gerente no reveló el contrato al resto del consejo de administración; **they signed a secret deal with their main rivals** = firmaron un acuerdo secreto con sus principales competidores

◊ **secretary** ['sekrətri] *noun* **(a)** *(office work)* secretario, -ria; **secretary and personal assistant** *or US* **executive secretary** = secretario y ayudante personal; **my secretary deals with incoming orders** = mi secretaria se ocupa de los pedidos recibidos; **his secretary phoned to say he would be late** = su secretaria llamó para decir que él llegaría tarde; **assistant secretary** = secretario adjunto; **private secretary** = secretario *or* secretaria particular; **secretary's office** = secretaría *f* **(b)** *(official of a company or society)* **company secretary** = secretario de una compañía; **honorary secretary** = secretario honorario; **he was elected secretary of the committee** *or* **committee secretary** = fue elegido secretario del comité; **membership secretary** = secretario que se ocupa de cuestiones de afiliación **(c)** *(member of the government in charge of a department)* ministro del gobierno; **Education Secretary** = ministro de Educación; **Foreign Secretary** = ministro de Asuntos Exteriores; *US* **Secretary of the Treasury** *or* **Treasury Secretary** = ministro de Hacienda

◊ **Secretary of State** ['sekrətri əv 'steɪt] *noun* **(a)** *GB* ministro, -tra (con cartera) **(b)** *US* ministro de Asuntos Exteriores (NOTE: the UK equivalent is the **Foreign Secretary**)

◊ **secretarial** [sekrə'teərɪəl] *adjective* de

secretario, -ria; **she is taking a secretarial course** = está haciendo un curso de secretariado; **he is looking for secretarial work** = está buscando trabajo de secretaría; **we need extra secretarial help to deal with the mailings** = necesitamos más secretarias para que se ocupen de los envíos por correo; **secretarial college** = escuela de secretariado

◇ **secretariat** [ˌsekrə'teərɪət] *noun* secretaría *f or* secretariado *m*; **the United Nations secretariat** = la secretaría de las Naciones Unidas

QUOTE a debate has been going on over the establishment of a general secretariat for the G7. Proponents argue that this would give the G7 a sense of direction and continuity
Times

section ['sekʃən] *noun* sección *f*; **legal section** = asesoría jurídica *or* departamento jurídico

sector ['sektə] *noun* sector *m*; **all sectors of the economy suffered from the fall in the exchange rate** = todos los sectores de la economía se vieron afectados por la caída del tipo de cambio; **technology is a booming sector of the economy** = la tecnología es un sector de la economía en alza; **public sector** = sector público; **public sector borrowing requirement (PSBR)** = necesidad de endeudamiento del sector público; **private sector** = sector privado; **the expansion is funded completely by the private sector** = la expansión está totalmente financiada por el sector privado; **salaries in the private sector have increased faster than in the public** = los salarios en el sector privado han subido con más rapidez que en el público

QUOTE government services form a large part of the tertiary or service sector
Sydney Morning Herald

QUOTE in the dry cargo sector, a total of 956 dry cargo vessels are laid up - 3% of world dry cargo tonnage
Lloyd's List

secure [sɪ'kjʊə] **1** *adjective* seguro, -ra *or* fijo, -ja; **secure job** = empleo seguro; **secure investment** = inversión segura **2** *verb* **(a)** **to secure a loan** = garantizar un préstamo **(b)** *(to get into your control)* conseguir; **to secure funds** = conseguir fondos; **he secured the backing of an Australian group** = consiguió el apoyo de un grupo australiano

◇ **secured** [sɪ'kjʊəd] *adjective* **secured creditor** = acreedor asegurado *or* con garantía; **secured debts** = deudas garantizadas; **secured loan** = préstamo garantizado

◇ **securities** [sɪ'kjʊərətɪz] *plural noun* títulos *mpl or* valores *mpl*; **gilt-edged securities** *or* **government securities** = títulos del Estado; **listed securities** = valores cotizables *or* bursátiles *or* acciones cotizables en bolsa; **the securities market** = el mercado *or* la bolsa de valores; **securities trader** = comerciante de valores; *US* **Securities and Exchange Commission (SEC)** *GB* **Securities and Investments Board (SIB)** = Comisión de Valores y Cambios *or* Comisión de Bolsa y Valores

◇ **security** [sɪ'kjʊərəti] *noun* **(a)** **job security** = seguridad *f* de empleo; **security of employment** = seguridad de permanencia en el empleo; **security of tenure** = derecho a conservar un puesto de trabajo *or* una vivienda alquilada **(b)** *(being protected)* **airport**

security = medidas de seguridad *or* personal de seguridad de un aeropuerto; **security guard** = guardia de seguridad; **office security** = medidas de seguridad *or* protección en una oficina **(c)** *(being secret)* seguridad; **security in this office is nil** = la seguridad en esta oficina es nula; **security printer** = impresor de seguridad para imprimir papel moneda o documentos secretos **(d)** **social security** = seguridad social; **he lives on social security payments** = vive de lo que le paga la seguridad social **(e)** *(guarantee)* fianza *f or* garantía *f*; **to stand security for someone** = avalar a alguien; **to give something as security for a debt** = garantizar una deuda; **to use a house as security for a loan** = dar una casa en garantía de un préstamo; **the bank lent him £20,000 without security** = el banco le prestó £20.000 sin fianza

see [siː] *verb* ver

◇ **see-safe** ['siː'seɪf] *noun* acuerdo *m* por el que un suministrador reintegra al comprador el valor de los bienes no vendidos al cabo de determinado tiempo; **we bought the stock see-safe** = compramos las existencias con el acuerdo de que se nos reintegrara el valor de los artículos no vendidos

seed capital *or* **seed money** *or* **seedcorn** ['siːd 'kæpitəl *or* 'siːd 'mʌni *or* 'siːdkɔːn] *noun* capital *m* inicial invertido en un proyecto

seek [siːk] *verb* pedir *or* solicitar; **they are seeking damages for loss of revenue** = piden una indemnización por la pérdida de ingresos; **to seek an interview** = solicitar una entrevista; **she sought an interview with the minister** = solicitó una entrevista con el ministro (NOTE: **seeking - sought**)

segment ['segmənt] *noun* segmento *m*

◇ **segmentation** [ˌsegmen'teɪʃn] *noun* segmentación *f*

seize [siːz] *verb* embargar *or* confiscar; **customs seized the shipment of books** = la aduana confiscó el envío de libros; **the court ordered the company's funds to be seized** = el tribunal ordenó el embargo de los fondos de la compañía

◇ **seizure** ['siːʒə] *noun* embargo *m or* incautación *f*; **the court ordered the seizure of the shipment** *or* **of the company's funds** = el tribunal ordenó la incautación del envío *or* de los fondos de la compañía

select [sɪ'lekt] **1** *adjective* selecto, -ta *or* de primera categoría; **our customers are very select** = nuestros clientes son muy selectos; **a select range of merchandise** = una gama de mercancías de primera categoría **2** *verb* escoger *or* elegir; **selected items are reduced by 25%** = ciertos artículos seleccionados tienen una rebaja del 25%

◇ **selection** [sɪ'lekʃn] *noun* surtido *m*; **a selection of our product line** = un surtido de nuestra línea de productos; **selection board** *or* **selection committee** = comité de selección; **selection procedure** = procedimiento de selección

◇ **selective** [sɪ'lektɪv] *adjective* selectivo, -va; **selective strikes** = huelgas selectivas

QUOTE engineering employers have been told they may have to revise their criteria for selecting trainees
Personnel Management

self [self] *pronoun* uno mismo *or* una misma; *(on cheques)* 'pay self' = (cheque) nominativo

◊ **self-** [self] *prefix* auto-

◊ **self-adhesive label** [selfəd'hi:zɪv 'leɪbl] *noun* etiqueta *f* autoadhesiva

◊ **self-contained office** [selfkən'teɪnd 'ɒfɪs] *noun* oficina *f* independiente

◊ **self-employed** [selfɪm'plɔɪd] **1** *adjective* autónomo, -ma *or* por cuenta propia *or* independiente; **a self-employed engineer** = un ingeniero independiente; **he worked for a bank for ten years but now is self-employed** = trabajó diez años en un banco pero ahora trabaja por su cuenta **2** *noun* **the self-employed** = los trabajadores autónomos (NOTE: in English, can be followed by a verb in the plural)

◊ **self-employment** [selfɪm'plɔɪmənt] *noun* autoempleo *m*

◊ **self-financed** [selffaɪ'nænst] *adjective* autofinanciado, -da; **the project is completely self-financed** = el proyecto se autofinancia completamente

◊ **self-financing** [selffaɪ'nænsɪŋ] **1** *noun* autofinanciación *f* **2** *adjective* **the company is completely self-financing** = la compañía se autofinancia completamente

◊ **self-made man** ['selfmeɪd 'mæn] *noun* hombre *m* que ha triunfado por sus propios esfuerzos

◊ **self-regulation** [selfregjʊ'leɪʃən] *noun* autoregulación *f*

◊ **self-regulatory** [selfregjʊ'leɪtəri] *adjective* autoregulado, -da

◊ **self-service** [self'sɜːvɪs] *adjective* **a self-service store** = autoservicio (comercio); **self-service petrol station** = autoservicio (gasolinera)

◊ **self-sufficiency** [selfsə'fɪʃənsi] *noun* autosuficiencia *f*

◊ **self-sufficient** [selfsə'fɪʃənt] *adjective* autosuficiente; **the country is self-sufficient in oil** = el país es autosuficiente en petróleo

◊ **self-supporting** [selfsə'pɔːtɪŋ] *adjective* independiente *or* autofinanciado, -da

sell [sel] **1** *noun* venta *f*; **to give a product the hard sell** = presionar al cliente para que compre; **he tried to give me the hard sell** = intentó presionarme para que comprara; **soft sell** = venta suave sin presionar al cliente **2** *verb* **(a)** *(in exchange for money)* vender; **to sell cars** *or* **to sell refrigerators** = vender coches *or* vender frigoríficos; **they have decided to sell their house** = han decidido vender la casa; **they tried to sell their house for £100,000** = intentaron vender la casa por £100.000; **to sell something on credit** = vender algo a crédito; **her house is difficult to sell** = su casa es difícil de vender; **their products are easy to sell** = sus productos son fáciles de vender; **to sell forward** = vender algo con entrega aplazada *or* a futuros **(b)** *(to be bought)* venderse; **these items sell well in the pre-Christmas period** = estos productos se venden bien en el periodo antes de Navidad; **those packs sell for £25 a dozen** = esos paquetes se venden a £25 la docena (NOTE: **selling - sold**)

◊ **sell-by date** ['selbaɪ 'deɪt] *noun* fecha *f* de caducidad

◊ **seller** ['selə] *noun* **(a)** *(person who sells)* vendedor, -ra; **there were few sellers in the market, so prices remained high** = había pocos vendedores en el mercado y por eso los precios se mantuvieron altos; **seller's market** = mercado de vendedores *or* favorable a los vendedores *or* de demanda **(b)** *(thing which sells)* producto *m* que se vende mucho; **this book is a steady seller** = este libro siempre se vende bien; **best-seller** = 'best-seller' *or* artículo de mayor venta

◊ **selling** ['selɪŋ] **1** *noun* **direct selling** = venta directa; **mail-order selling** = venta por correo; **selling costs** = costes de venta; **selling price** = precio de venta **2** *suffix* **fast-selling items** = artículos de venta rápida *or* fácil; **best-selling car** = coche en gran demanda

◊ **sell off** ['sel 'ɒf] *verb* liquidar

◊ **sell out** ['sel 'aʊt] *verb* **(a)** agotar *or* vender todas las existencias; **to sell out of an item** = agotar las existencias de un artículo; **to sell out of a product line** = agotar las existencias de una gama de productos; **we have sold out of electronic typewriters** = hemos agotado las existencias de máquinas de escribir; **this item has sold out** = este producto se ha agotado **(b)** **to sell out** = liquidar *or* vender un negocio; **he sold out and retired to the seaside** = vendió su negocio y se retiró a la costa

◊ **sellout** ['selaʊt] *noun* **this item has been a sellout** = este producto se ha agotado rápidamente

◊ **sell up** ['sel 'ʌp] *verb* venderlo todo *or* liquidar un negocio con todas sus existencias

semi- ['semi] *prefix* semi

◊ **semi-finished** [semi'fɪnɪʃt] *adjective* **semi-finished products** = productos semiacabados

◊ **semi-skilled** [semi'skɪld] *adjective* semicualificado, -da; **semi-skilled jobs** = trabajos semicualificados; **semi-skilled workers** = obreros semicualificados

send [send] *verb* enviar; **to send a letter** *or* **an order** *or* **a shipment** = enviar una carta *or* un pedido *or* un cargamento; **the company is sending him to Australia to be general manager of the Sydney office** = la compañía le envía a Australia en calidad de director general de la sucursal de Sydney; **send the letter airmail if you want it to arrive next week** = envía la carta por avión si quieres que llegue la semana que viene; **the shipment was sent by rail** = las mercancías se enviaron por ferrocarril (NOTE: **sending - sent**)

◊ **send away for** ['send ə'weɪ fɔː] *verb* solicitar algo por escrito; **we sent away for the new catalogue** = enviamos una carta solicitando el nuevo catálogo

◊ **sender** ['sendə] *noun* remitente *mf or* expedidor, -ra; **'return to sender'** = 'devolver al remitente'

◊ **send for** ['send 'fɔː] *verb* **(a)** *(someone for something)* llamar a alguien *or* mandar; **he sent for the chief accountant** = mandó llamar al jefe de contabilidad; **she sent for the papers on the contract** = mandó buscar los documentos del contrato **(b)** *US (to write to ask for something to be* *sent)* solicitar algo por escrito; **we sent for the new catalog** = enviamos una carta solicitando el nuevo catálogo (NOTE: GB English uses **send away for, send off for** in this meaning)

◊ **send in** ['send 'ɪn] *verb* enviar; **he sent in his resignation** = envió su dimisión; **to send in an application** = enviar una solicitud

◊ **send off** ['send 'ɒf] *verb* enviar *or* expedir

◊ **send off for** ['send 'ɒf fɔ:] *verb* solicitar el envío de algo; **we sent off for the new catalogue** = solicitamos el envío del nuevo catálogo

◊ **send on** ['send 'ɒn] *verb* remitir; **he sent the letter on to his brother** = remitió la carta a su hermano

Senegal [senɪ'gɑ:l] *noun* Senegal *m*

◊ **Senegalese** [senɪgə'li:z] *adjective & noun* senegalés, -esa
NOTE: capital: **Dakar;** currency: **CFA franc (CFAF)** = franco CFA (FCFA)

senior ['si:njə] *adjective* **(a)** *(older or more important)* mayor *or* más antiguo *or* superior; **senior manager** *or* **senior executive** = gerente *or* director principal; **senior partner** = socio principal; **John Smith, Senior** = John Smith, padre **(b)** *(debt which is repayable before others)* **senior debts** = deudas prioritarias

◊ **seniority** [si:nɪ'ɒrəti] *noun* antigüedad *f or* superioridad *f* (en rango) *or* autoridad *f*; **the managers were listed in order of seniority** = los nombres de los directores aparecían por orden de antigüedad *or* superioridad en el cargo desempeñado

sense [sens] *noun* **to make sense** = tener sentido; **it doesn't make sense** = no tiene ningún sentido

sensible ['sensɪbl] *adjective* sensato, -ta *or* razonable; **sensible prices** = precios razonables

sensitive ['sensətɪv] *adjective* sensible; **the market is very sensitive to the result of the elections** = el mercado es muy sensible al resultado de las elecciones; **price-sensitive product** = producto cuya demanda es muy sensible al precio

sentiment ['sentɪmənt] *noun (stock market)* **market sentiment** = opinión *or* sensación general sobre el mercado de valores

COMMENT: 'sentiment' (either optimistic or pessimistic) can be influenced by external factors, and affects the prices of shares or the volume of business transacted

separate 1 ['seprət] *adjective* separado, -da *or* aparte; **to send something under separate cover** = enviar algo por separado *or* por correo aparte **2** ['separeɪt] *verb* separar *or* dividir; **the personnel are separated into part-timers and full-time staff** = el personal está dividido en trabajadores a jornada parcial y a jornada completa

◊ **separately** ['seprətli] *adverb* separadamente *or* por separado; **each job was invoiced separately** = cada trabajo se facturó por separado

◊ **separation** [sepə'reɪʃən] *noun US* despido *m*

sequester *or* **sequestrate** [sɪ'kwestə *or* 'sekwəstreɪt] *verb* secuestrar *or* confiscar *or* embargar

◊ **sequestration** [sekwes'treɪʃən] *noun* embargo *m*

◊ **sequestrator** ['sekwəstreɪtə] *noun* embargador, -ra

Serbia ['sɜ:biə] *noun* Serbia

◊ **Serbian** ['sɜ:biən] *adjective & noun* serbio, -bia
NOTE: capital: **Belgrade** = Belgrado; currency: **dinar** = dinar

serial number ['sɪərɪəl 'nʌmbə] *noun* número *m* de serie; **this batch of shoes has the serial number 25-02** = este lote de zapatos lleva el número de serie 25-02

series ['sɪəri:z] *noun* serie *f*; **a series of successful takeovers made the company one of the largest in the trade** = una serie de adquisiciones favorables hicieron de la compañía una de las más grandes del sector (NOTE: plural is also **series)**

serious ['sɪərɪəs] *adjective* **(a)** *(bad)* serio, -ria *or* grave; **the storm caused serious damage** = la tormenta produjo daños graves; **the damage to the computer was not very serious** = los daños en el ordenador no fueron muy graves **(b)** *(thoughtful)* **the management is making serious attempts to improve working conditions** = la dirección está haciendo un intento serio *or* está haciendo lo posible por mejorar las condiciones de trabajo

◊ **seriously** ['sɪərɪəsli] *adverb* **(a)** *(badly)* seriamente *or* gravemente; **the cargo was seriously damaged by water** = la carga resultó gravemente dañada por el agua **(b)** *(in a thoughtful way)* en serio *or* seriamente; **we are taking the threat from our competitors very seriously** = tomamos la amenaza de los competidores muy en serio

servant ['sɜ:vənt] *noun* sirviente, -ta *or* criado, -da; **civil servant** = funcionario, -ria (del Estado)

serve [sɜ:v] *verb* servir *or* atender; **to serve a customer** = atender a un cliente; **to serve in a shop** *or* **in a restaurant** = ser dependiente en una tienda *or* ser camarero en un restaurante; **to serve someone with a writ** *or* **to serve a writ on someone** = entregar una orden judicial a alguien

service ['sɜ:vɪs] **1** *noun* **(a)** *(working for a company or in a shop)* servicio *m*; **length of service** = antigüedad *f*; **service agreement** *or* **service contract** = contrato de servicios **(b)** *(dealing with customers)* servicio; **the service in that restaurant is extremely slow** = el servicio en ese restaurante es extremadamente lento; **to add on 10% for service** = añadir el 10% por el servicio; **the bill includes service** = la cuenta incluye el servicio; **is the service included?** = ¿está el servicio incluído? **(c)** *(keeping a machine in good working order)* revisión *f*; **the machine has been sent in for service** = la máquina ha sido entregada para una revisión; **the routine service of equipment** = la revisión periódica del equipo; **service contract** = contrato de servicio de mantenimiento; **after-sales service** = servicio posventa; **service centre** = centro de revisión *or* de reparaciones; **service department** = sección *or* servicio de mantenimiento; **service engineer** = mecánico; **service handbook** *or* **service manual** = manual de mantenimiento; **service station** = gasolinera *or* estación de servicio **(d)** *(business or office which gives help)* servicio; **answering service** = servicio de contestación; **24-hour service** = servicio permanente; **service bureau** = oficina de servicios; **service department** = sección de servicios administrativos; **service industry** *or* **service sector** = industria de servicios **(e) to put a machine into service** = poner una máquina en funcionamiento **(f)** *(regular working of a public organization)* servicio; **the postal service is efficient** = el servicio de correos es eficiente; **the bus service is very irregular** = el servicio de autobuses es muy irregular; **we have a good train service to London** = tenemos un buen servicio de trenes a Londres; **the civil service** = la administración pública; **he has a job in the civil service** = tiene un trabajo en la administración; **civil service pensions are index-linked** = las pensiones de los funcionarios están ajustadas al coste de vida **2** *verb* **(a)** *(machine)* revisar; **the car needs to be serviced every six months** = el coche necesita una revisión cada seis meses; **the computer has gone back to the manufacturer for servicing** = el ordenador ha sido devuelto al fabricante para que sea revisado **(b)** *(debt)* pagar intereses; **to service a debt** = pagar los intereses de una deuda; **the company is having problems in servicing its debts** = la compañía tiene problemas para pagar los intereses de sus deudas

◇ **service charge** ['sɜːvɪs 'tʃɑːdʒ] *noun* **(a)** *(charge added to a bill)* servicio **(b)** *US (charges which a bank makes)* comisión bancaria *or* gastos bancarios (NOTE: the British English equivalent is **bank charges)**

session ['seʃən] *noun* sesión *f*; **the morning session** *or* **the afternoon session will be held in the conference room** = la sesión de la mañana *or* de la tarde tendrá lugar en la sala de reuniones; *(Stock Exchange)* **trading session** = sesión bursátil; **opening session** *or* **closing session** = sesión de apertura *or* sesión de clausura

set [set] **1** *noun* juego *m*; **set of tools** *or* **set of equipment** = juego de herramientas *or* juego de accesorios; **boxed set** = juego completo vendido en una caja de presentación **2** *adjective* fijo, -ja; **set price** = precio fijo; **set menu** = menú *or* menú del día **3** *verb* establecer *or* fijar; **we have to set a price for the new computer** = tenemos que fijar un precio para el nuevo ordenador; **the price of the calculator has been set low, so as to achieve maximum unit sales** = se ha fijado un precio bajo para la nueva calculadora con el fin de obtener un máximo de ventas; **the auction set a record for high prices** = la subasta estableció un record de precios (NOTE: **setting - set)**

◇ **set against** ['set ə'genst] *verb* compensar *or* deducir; **to set the costs against the sales** = hacer un balance de costes y ventas; **can you set the expenses against tax?** = ¿puedes deducir los gastos de la cantidad imponible?

◇ **set aside** ['set ə'saɪd] *verb* anular *or* dejar de lado *or* abandonar; **the arbitrator's award was set aside on appeal** = el fallo del árbitro se anuló en la apelación

◇ **set back** ['set 'bæk] *verb* retrasar; **the project was set back six weeks by bad weather** = el

proyecto sufrió un retraso de seis semanas debido al mal tiempo

◇ **setback** ['setbæk] *noun* revés *m*; **the company suffered a series of setbacks in 1994** = la compañía sufrió una serie de reveses en 1994; **the shares had a setback on the Stock Exchange** = las acciones sufrieron un revés en la bolsa

◇ **set out** ['set 'aʊt] *verb* exponer; **to set out the details in a report** = exponer los detalles en un informe

◇ **set up** ['set 'ʌp] *verb* **(a)** *(begin or organize)* hacer *or* crear *or* constituir; **to set up an inquiry** *or* **a working party** = iniciar una investigación *or* crear un grupo de trabajo; **to set up a company** = fundar una compañía **(b)** *(in business)* establecerse *or* poner; **to set up in business** = poner un negocio *or* establecerse; **he set up in business as an insurance broker** = se estableció como agente de seguros; **he set himself up as a tax adviser** = se estableció como asesor fiscal

◇ **setting up costs** *or* **setup costs** ['setɪŋ 'ʌp 'kɒsts *or* 'setʌp 'kɒsts] *plural noun* costes *mpl* de preparación de una máquina *or* fábrica para hacer un nuevo producto al terminar otro

◇ **setup** ['setʌp] *noun* **(a)** *(arrangement or organization)* sistema *m* *or* organización *f*; **the setup in the office** = el sistema de organización de la oficina **(b)** *(commercial firm)* empresa *f*; **he works for a PR setup** = trabaja para una empresa de relaciones públicas

settle ['setl] *verb* **(a)** *(in place)* establecerse **(b)** *(to pay)* saldar *or* ajustar; **to settle an account** = saldar una cuenta **(c)** *(to reach agreement)* arreglar *or* llegar a un arreglo; **to settle a claim** = pagar una reclamación; **the insurance company refused to settle his claim for storm damage** = la compañía de seguros se negó a pagar su reclamación de daños causados por la tormenta; **the two parties settled out of court** = las dos partes llegaron a un arreglo amistoso

◇ **settlement** ['setlmənt] *noun* **(a)** *(payment)* finiquito *m* *or* pago *m*; **settlement date** = fecha de liquidación; **settlement day** = día de liquidación; **our basic discount is 20% but we offer an extra 5% for rapid settlement** = nuestro descuento normal es de un 20% pero ofrecemos un 5% adicional por pronto pago; **settlement in cash** *or* **cash settlement** = pago en efectivo; **final settlement** = liquidación; **financial settlement** = ajuste financiero **(b)** *(agreement)* acuerdo *m* después de un conflicto; **to effect a settlement between two parties** = llevar a un acuerdo a las dos partes

◊ **settle on** ['setl 'ɒn] *verb* asignar; **he settled his property on his children** = asignó su propiedad a sus hijos

> QUOTE he emphasised that prompt settlement of all forms of industrial disputes would guarantee industrial peace in the country and ensure increased productivity
> **Business Times (Lagos)**

several ['sevrəl] *adjective* varios, -as *or* algunos, -as; **several managers are retiring this year** = varios directores se retiran este año; **several of our products sell well in Japan** = algunos de nuestros productos se venden bien en Japón

◊ **severally** ['sevrəli] *adverb* separadamente *or* respectivamente *or* por separado; **they are jointly and severally liable** = son responsables solidariamente *or* en grupo y por separado

severance pay ['sevərəns 'peɪ] *noun* indemnización *f* por despido

severe [sɪ'vɪə] *adjective* severo, -ra *or* grave; **the company suffered severe losses in the European market** = la empresa sufrió graves pérdidas en el mercado europeo; **the government imposed severe financial restrictions** = el gobierno impuso controles financieros rigurosos

◊ **severely** [sɪ'vɪəli] *adverb* severamente *or* gravemente *or* fuertemente; **train services have been severely affected by snow** = los servicios de trenes han sido severamente afectados por la nieve

shady ['ʃeɪdi] *adjective* sospechoso, -sa *or* turbio, -bia; **shady deal** = negocio sucio *or* transacción turbia

shake [ʃeɪk] *verb* **(a)** *(to move something quickly from side to side)* agitar; **to shake hands with someone** = dar la mano *or* estrechar la mano; **the two negotiating teams shook hands and sat down at the conference table** = las dos partes negociadoras se dieron la mano y a continuación se sentaron a la mesa de conferencias; **to shake hands on a deal** = cerrar un trato con un apretón de manos **(b)** *(to surprise or to shock)* perturbar *or* desconcertar; **the markets were shaken by the company's results** = los mercados se vieron perturbados por los resultados de la compañía (NOTE: **shaking - shook - has shaken**)

◊ **shakeout** ['ʃeɪkaʊt] *noun* reorganización *f or* reestructuración *f* (que implica la eliminación de algo o de alguien); **a shakeout in the top management** = una reorganización de la alta dirección; **only three companies were left after the shakeout in the computer market** = después de la reorganización del mercado de ordenadores solamente quedaron tres empresas

◊ **shakeup** ['ʃeɪkʌp] *noun* reorganización *f* total; **the managing director ordered a shakeup of the sales departments** = el director gerente ordenó una reorganización total de los servicios de ventas

◊ **shaky** ['ʃeɪki] *adjective* inseguro, -ra; **the year got off to a shaky start** = el año empezó lleno de incertidumbres

share [ʃeə] **1** *noun* **(a)** *(participation)* participación *f*; **to have a share in** = participar en; **to have a share in management decisions** = participar en las decisiones de la dirección; **market share** *or* **share of the market** = participación en el mercado *or* cuota de mercado; **the company hopes to boost its market share** = la empresa espera aumentar su participación en el mercado; **their share of the market has gone up by 10%** = su cuota de mercado ha subido en un 10% **(b)** *(part of a company's capital)* acción *f*; **he bought a block of shares in Marks and Spencer** = compró un paquete de acciones de Marks y Spencer; **shares fell on the London market** = las acciones bajaron en el mercado londinense; **the company offered 1.8m shares on the market** = la compañía ofreció 1,8 millones de acciones en el mercado; **'A' shares** = acciones de clase 'A', con derecho de voto limitado; **'B' shares** = acciones de clase 'B', con derecho de voto especial (normalmente propiedad del fundador y su familia); **bonus share** = acción prima *or* gratuita *or* liberada; **deferred shares** = acciones con derecho a dividendo en último lugar; **founder's shares** = acciones de fundador; **new share** = acción nueva; **ordinary shares** = acciones ordinarias; **preference shares** = acciones preferentes; **share allocation** *or* **share allotment** = asignación de acciones; **to allot shares** = asignar acciones; **share capital** = capital en acciones; **share certificate** = título *or* certificado de una acción; **share issue** = emisión de acciones (NOTE: British English often used the word **stock** where British English uses **share**. See the note at STOCK) **2** *verb* **(a)** *(to own or use something with someone else)* compartir; **to share a telephone** = compartir un teléfono; **to share an office** = compartir una oficina **(b)** *(to divide among several people)* dividir *or* compartir *or* repartir; **three companies share the market** = el mercado está repartido entre tres empresas; **to share computer time** = compartir el tiempo del ordenador; **to share the profits among the senior executives** = repartir los beneficios entre los directivos; **to share information** *or* **to share data** = compartir información *or* compartir datos

◊ **shareholder** ['ʃeəhəʊldə] *noun* accionista *mf or* tenedor, -ra de acciones; **to call a shareholders' meeting** = convocar una junta general de accionistas; **shareholders' equity** = capital de los accionistas; **majority** *or* **minority shareholder** = accionista mayoritario *or* minoritario; **the solicitor acting on behalf of the minority shareholders** = el abogado que actúa en nombre de los accionistas minoritarios (NOTE: American English is **stockholder**)

◊ **shareholding** ['ʃeəhəʊldɪŋ] *noun* tenencia *f* de acciones; **a majority shareholding** *or* **a minority shareholding** = una participación mayoritaria *or* minoritaria de las acciones; **he acquired a minority shareholding in the company** = adquirió una participación mayoritaria en la compañía; **she has sold all her shareholdings** = ha vendido todas sus acciones; **dilution of shareholding** = dilución del capital (NOTE: American English is **stockholding**)

◊ **shareout** ['ʃeəraʊt] *noun* reparto *m or* distribución *f*; **a shareout of the profits** = una distribución de los beneficios

◊ **sharing** ['ʃeərɪŋ] *noun* reparto *m or* participación *f*; **job sharing** = compartir un puesto de trabajo *or* trabajo a media jornada; **profit sharing** = participación en los beneficios; **the company operates a profit-sharing scheme** = la empresa tiene un plan de participación en los beneficios; **time-sharing** = *(owning a property in part)* multipropiedad; *(sharing a computer system)* tiempo compartido *or* utilización de un ordenador en tiempo compartido

> QUOTE falling profitability means falling share prices
> **Investors Chronicle**

> QUOTE the share of blue-collar occupations declined from 48 per cent to 43 per cent
> **Sydney Morning Herald**

> QUOTE as of last night the bank's shareholders no longer hold any rights to the bank's shares
> **South China Morning Post**

> QUOTE the company said that its recent issue of 10.5% convertible preference shares at A$8.50 has been oversubscribed, boosting shareholders' funds to A$700 million plus
> **Financial Times**

shark [ʃɑːk] *noun* tiburón *m*; **loan shark** = usurero *m*

sharp [ʃɑːp] *adjective* **(a)** *(sudden)* fuerte *or* repentino, -na *or* rápido, -da *or* brusco, -ca; **sharp rally on the stock market** = una recuperación rápida de la bolsa; **sharp drop in prices** = una caída acusada de los precios **(b)** *(person)* astuto, -ta; **sharp practice** = mañas *fpl or* métodos *mpl* poco escrupulosos *or* deshonestos (pero no ilegales)

◇ **sharply** [ʃɑːpli] *adverb* bruscamente *or* fuertemente *or* acusadamente; **shares dipped sharply in yesterday's trading** = los precios de las acciones bajaron fuertemente en la jornada de ayer; **the share price rose sharply** = el precio de las acciones subió acusadamente

sheet [ʃiːt] *noun* **(a)** **sheet of paper** = hoja *f* de papel; **sheet feed** = alimentador de papel; **sales sheet** = folleto publicitario; **time sheet** = hoja de asistencia *or* registro de horas trabajadas **(b)** **balance sheet** = balance; **the company's balance sheet for 1990** = el balance de la compañía para 1990; **the accountants prepared a balance sheet for the first half-year** = los contables prepararon un balance de situación del primer semestre

shelf [ʃelf] *noun* estantería *f or* anaquel *m*; **the shelves in the supermarket were full of items before the Christmas rush** = las estanterías del supermercado estaban repletas de artículos antes de las aglomeraciones de las Navidades; **shelf filler** = empleado encargado de mantener llenos los estantes; **shelf life of a product** = vida útil *or* periodo de conservación de un producto; **shelf space** = espacio en los estantes; **shelf talker** *or* **shelf wobbler** = tarjeta de promoción de un producto en una estantería; **off-the-shelf company** = compañía registrada disponible (NOTE: plural is **shelves**)

shell company [ʃel 'kʌmpəni] *noun* sociedad ficticia para la compra de acciones

shelter [ʃeltə] *noun* refugio *m*; **tax shelter** = amparo fiscal

shelve [ʃelv] *verb* aplazar; **the project was shelved** = el proyecto fue aplazado; **discussion of the problem has been shelved** = el debate sobre el problema ha sido aplazado

◇ **shelving** [ʃelvɪŋ] *noun* **(a)** *(rows of shelves)* estantería *f*; **we installed metal shelving in the household goods department** = instalamos estanterías metálicas en el departamento de enseres **(b)** *(postponing)* aplazamiento *m*; **the shelving of the project has resulted in six redundancies** = el aplazamiento del proyecto ha ocasionado seis despidos

shift [ʃɪft] **1** *noun* **(a)** *(working hours)* turno *m*; **day shift** = turno de día; **night shift** = turno de noche; **there are 150 men on the day shift** = hay 150 obreros en el turno de día; **he works the day shift** *or* **night shift** = trabaja en el turno de día *or* el turno de noche; **we work an 8-hour shift** = trabajamos por turnos de 8 horas; **the management is introducing a shift system** *or* **shift working** = la dirección va a introducir el trabajo por turnos; **they work double shifts** = trabajan en turnos dobles **(b)** *(movement or change)* cambio *m or* desplazamiento *m*; **a shift in the company's marketing strategy** = un cambio en la estrategia de comercialización de la empresa; **the company is taking advantage of a shift in the market towards higher priced goods** = la empresa está aprovechando un cambio de tendencia en el mercado hacia productos más caros **2** *verb* vender; **we shifted 20,000 items in one week** = vendimos 20.000 artículos en una semana

◇ **shift key** [ʃɪft 'kiː] *noun* tecla *f* de mayúsculas

◇ **shift work** [ʃɪft 'wɜːk] *noun* trabajo *m* por turnos

shilling [ʃɪlɪŋ] *noun (currency used in Kenya)* chelín *m*

ship [ʃɪp] **1** *noun* barco *m or* buque *m*; **cargo ship** = barco de carga; **container ship** = buque de contenedores; **ship chandler** = abastecedor de buques; **to jump ship** = desertar del barco en el que uno está enrolado **2** *verb* enviar *or* expedir; **to ship goods to the USA** = enviar mercancías a los EE UU; **we ship all our goods by rail** = enviamos toda nuestra mercancía por ferrocarril; **the consignment of cars was shipped abroad last week** = el envío de coches al extranjero se efectuó la semana pasada; **to drop ship** = enviar un pedido importante al cliente directamente (sin intermediario) (NOTE: **shipping - shipped**)

◇ **ship broker** [ʃɪp 'brəʊkə] *noun* consignatario, -ria

◇ **ship broking** [ʃɪp 'brəʊkɪŋ] *noun* corretaje marítimo

◇ **shipment** [ʃɪpmənt] *noun* envío *m or* carga *f or* partida *f*; **two shipments were lost in the fire** = dos envíos resultaron destruidos en el incendio; **a shipment of computers was damaged** = sufrió daños un envío de ordenadores; **we make two shipments a week to France** = hacemos dos envíos semanales a Francia; **bulk shipment** = envío de grandes cantidades *or* carga a granel; **consolidated shipment** = envío agrupado de mercancías; **drop shipment** = envío directo a un cliente de un pedido importante (sin intermediario)

◇ **shipper** [ʃɪpə] *noun* expedidor, -ra *or* remitente *mf or* transportista *mf*

◇ **shipping** [ʃɪpɪŋ] *noun* envío *m or* expedición *f*; **shipping charges** *or* **shipping costs** = costes de envío; **shipping agent** = agente *or* agencia de transportes; **shipping clerk** = empleado encargado de las expediciones *or* agente expedidor; **shipping company** *or* **shipping line** = compañía naviera *or* línea marítima; **shipping instructions** = instrucciones de envío; **shipping note** = nota de envío (NOTE: **shipping** does not always mean using a ship)

◊ **shipyard** ['ʃɪpjɑːd] *noun* astillero *m*

shoot up ['ʃuːt 'ʌp] *verb* subir rápidamente *or* dispararse; **prices have shot up during the strike** = durante la huelga los precios se han disparado (NOTE: **shooting - shot**)

shop [ʃɒp] **1** *noun* **(a)** *(store)* tienda *f*; **bookshop** = librería; **computer shop** = tienda de informática; **electrical goods shop** = tienda de artículos eléctricos; **he has bought a shoe shop in the centre of town** = ha comprado una zapatería en el centro de la ciudad; **she opened a women's wear shop** = abrió una tienda de ropa de señora; **all the shops in the centre of town close on Sundays** = todas las tiendas del centro de la ciudad cierran los domingos; **retail shop** = tienda al por menor; **the corner shop** = la tienda del barrio *or* la tienda de la esquina; **shop assistant** = vendedor, -ra *or* dependiente, -ta; **shop front** = fachada de la tienda; **shop steward** = delegado *or* enlace *or* representante sindical; **shop window** = escaparate *m* (NOTE: US English usually uses **store** where GB English uses **shop**) **(b)** *(workshop)* taller *m*; **machine shop** = taller mecánico; **repair shop** = taller de reparaciones; **on the shop floor** = en la fábrica *or* entre los obreros; **the feeling on the shop floor is that the manager does not know his job** = los obreros tienen la impresión que el director no sabe lo que (se) hace **(c)** **closed shop** = contratación exclusiva de obreros sindicados; **the union is asking the management to agree to a closed shop** = el sindicato pide a la dirección que emplee solamente a trabajadores sindicados **2** *verb* **to shop (for something)** = buscar en las tiendas (NOTE: **shopping - shopped**)

◊ **shop around** ['ʃɒp ə'raʊnd] *verb* comparar precios; **you should shop around before getting your car serviced** = deberías comparar precios antes de llevar tu coche a revisar; **he is shopping around for a new computer** = está comparando precios antes de comprar un nuevo ordenador; **it pays to shop around when you are planning to ask for a mortgage** = vale la pena comparar las opciones antes de solicitar una hipoteca

◊ **shopfront** ['ʃɒpfrʌnt] *noun* fachada de la tienda

◊ **shopkeeper** ['ʃɒpkiːpə] *noun* tendero, -ra *or* comerciante *mf*

◊ **shoplifter** ['ʃɒplɪftə] *noun* ratero, -ra de tiendas *or* mechera *f*

◊ **shoplifting** ['ʃɒplɪftɪŋ] *noun* robo *m or* hurto *m* en las tiendas

◊ **shopper** ['ʃɒpə] *noun* comprador, -ra; **the store stays open to midnight to cater for late-night shoppers** = la tienda está abierta hasta medianoche para atender a los compradores nocturnos; **shoppers' charter** = ley que protege los derechos del comprador

◊ **shopping** ['ʃɒpɪŋ] *noun* **(a)** compras *fpl*; **to go shopping** = ir de compras; **to buy one's shopping** *or* **to do one's shopping in the local supermarket** = hacer la compra en el supermercado del barrio;

window shopping = mirar los escaparates; **shopping around** = comparación de precios **(b)** **shopping basket** = cesta de la compra; **shopping centre** = centro comercial; *US* **shopping cart** = carrito de supermercado (NOTE: GB English is **supermarket trolley**) **shopping arcade** *or* **shopping mall** = centro comercial; **shopping precinct** = zona comercial peatonal

◊ **shop-soiled** ['ʃɒp'sɔɪld] *adjective* deteriorado, -da por haber estado expuesto en una tienda

◊ **shop steward** ['ʃɒp 'stjʊəd] *noun* delegado sindical

◊ **shopwalker** ['ʃɒpwɔːkə] *noun* empleado, -da de unos grandes almacenes que aconseja al cliente y supervisa a las dependientas

QUOTE these reforms hadn't changed conditions on the shop floor. Absenteeism was as high as 20% on some days
Business Week

short [ʃɔːt] **1** *adjective* **(a)** *(time)* breve *or* corto, -ta; **short credit** = crédito a corto plazo; **in the short term** = a corto plazo **(b)** *(not as much as should be)* insuficiente; **the shipment was three items short** = faltaban tres artículos en el envío; **when we cashed up we were £10 short** = cuando contamos el dinero nos faltaban £10; **to give short weight** = escatimar en el peso **(c)** **short of** = menos de lo necesario *or* escaso; **we are short of staff** *or* **short of money** = nos falta personal *or* dinero; **the company is short of new ideas** = a la empresa le faltan nuevas ideas **(d)** **to sell short** = vender al descubierto; **short selling** *or* **selling short** = venta al descubierto; **to borrow short** = tomar un préstamo a corto plazo **2** *noun* **shorts** = títulos *m* del Estado con fecha de vencimiento inferior a cinco años

◊ **shortage** ['ʃɔːtɪdʒ] *noun* escasez *f or* falta *f*; **a chronic shortage of skilled staff** = escasez crónica de personal cualificado; **we employ part-timers to make up for staff shortages** = empleamos personal a tiempo parcial para compensar la insuficiencia de plantilla; **the import controls have resulted in the shortage of spare parts** = el control a las importaciones ha provocado la falta de repuestos; **manpower shortage** *or* **shortage of manpower** = escasez de mano de obra; **there is no shortage of investment advice** = no hay falta de asesoramiento sobre inversiones

◊ **short-change** [ʃɔːt'tʃeɪn(d)ʒ] *verb* devolver de menos *or* defraudar

◊ **short-dated** [ʃɔːt'deɪtɪd] *adjective* **short-dated bills** = letras a cobrar en pocos días; **short-dated securities** = títulos del Estado con fecha de vencimiento inferior a cinco años

◊ **shorten** ['ʃɔːtn] *verb* reducir *or* abreviar; **to shorten a credit period** *or* **to shorten credit terms** = reducir el plazo de un crédito

◊ **shortfall** ['ʃɔːtfɔːl] *noun* déficit *m or* insuficiencia *f or* diferencia *f*; **we had to borrow money to cover the shortfall between expenditure and revenue** = tuvimos que tomar un préstamo para cubrir la diferencia entre los gastos y los ingresos

◊ **shorthand** ['ʃɔːthænd] *noun* taquigrafía *f*; **shorthand secretary** = secretario, -ria con taquigrafía; **shorthand typist** = taquimecanógrafo, -fa; **to take shorthand** = tomar taquigrafía; **he took** down the minutes in shorthand = tomó las actas en taquigrafía

◊ **shorthanded** [ʃɔːtˈhændɪd] *adjective* falto *or* escaso de personal; **we are rather shorthanded at the moment** = andamos bastante escasos de personal en este momento

◊ **short-haul flight** [ˈʃɔːthɔːfl ˈflaɪt] *noun* vuelo de corto recorrido

◊ **shortlist** [ˈʃɔːtlɪst] **1** *noun* preselección *f or* terna *f*; **to draw up a shortlist** = hacer una preselección; **he is on the shortlist for the job** = está en la lista de candidatos escogidos **2** *verb* preseleccionar *or* escoger; **four candidates have been shortlisted** = cuatro candidatos han sido preseleccionados; **shortlisted candidates will be asked for an interview** = los candidatos preseleccionados serán convocados para una entrevista

◊ **short-range** [ʃɔːtˈreɪnʒ] *adjective* **short-range forecast** = previsión a corto plazo

◊ **short-staffed** [ʃɔːtˈstɑːft] *adjective* falto de personal; **we are rather short-staffed at the moment** = nos falta bastante personal en este momento

◊ **short-term** [ʃɔːtˈtɜːm] *adjective* a corto plazo; **to place money on short-term deposit** = depositar dinero a corto plazo; **short-term contract** = contrato de corta duración; **on a short-term basis** = a corto plazo *or* para poco tiempo; **short-term debts** = deuda a corto plazo; **short-term forecast** = previsión a corto plazo; **short-term gains** = ganancias a corto plazo; **short-term loan** = préstamo a corto plazo

◊ **short time** [ˈʃɔːt ˈtaɪm] *noun* jornada *f* reducida; **to be on short time** = trabajar a jornada reducida; **the company has had to introduce short-time working because of lack of orders** = la empresa ha tenido que reducir la jornada por falta de pedidos

> QUOTE short-term interest rates have moved up quite a bit from year-ago levels
> **Forbes Magazine**

shot [ʃɒt] *noun* **mail shot** *or* **mailing shot** = propaganda enviada por correo

show [ʃəʊ] **1** *noun* **(a)** exposición *f or* feria *f*; **motor show** = salón *or* feria del automóvil; **computer show** = feria de la informática; **show house** *or* **show flat** = casa piloto *or* piso piloto **(b)** **show of hands** = votación a mano alzada; **the motion was carried on a show of hands** = la moción se aprobó a mano alzada **2** *verb* mostrar *or* indicar *or* arrojar *or* enseñar; **to show a gain** *or* **a fall** = indicar un aumento *or* una baja; **to show a profit** *or* **a loss** = arrojar una ganancia *or* una pérdida *or* mostrar un beneficio *or* una pérdida (NOTE: **showing - showed - has shown**)

◊ **showcard** [ˈʃəʊkɑːd] *noun* reclamo *m* de cartón *or* rótulo *m* publicitario

◊ **showcase** [ˈʃəʊkeɪs] *noun* vitrina *f or* expositor *m*

◊ **showroom** [ˈʃəʊruːm] *noun* sala *f* de exposición *or* exhibición; **car showroom** = sala de exhibición de automóviles

shred [ʃred] *verb (documents)* triturar; **they sent a pile of old invoices to be shredded** = mandaron un montón de facturas viejas para ser trituradas; **she told the police that the manager had told her to shred all the documents in the file** = declaró a la policía que el director le había mandado triturar todos los documentos del archivo

◊ **shredder** [ˈʃredə] *noun* trituradora *f*

shrink [ʃrɪŋk] *verb* mermar *or* disminuir *or* contraerse; **the market has shrunk by 20%** = el mercado se ha contraído en un 20%; **the company is having difficulty selling into a shrinking market** = la empresa tiene dificultades para vender en un mercado cada vez más pequeño (NOTE: **shrinking - shrank - has shrunk)**

◊ **shrinkage** [ˈʃrɪŋkɪdʒ] *noun* **(a)** *(smaller)* contracción *f or* encogimiento *m or* reducción *f*; **to allow for shrinkage** = dejar un margen por posibles reducciones *or* contracciones **(b)** *(losses)* pérdidas *fpl* por robos del personal

◊ **shrink-wrapped** [ˈʃrɪŋkræpt] *adjective* embalado, -da *or* empaquetado, -da al vacío

◊ **shrink-wrapping** [ˈʃrɪŋkˈræpɪŋ] *noun* embalaje *m* al vacío

shroff [ʃrɒf] *noun (in the Far East)* contable *mf*

shut [ʃʌt] **1** *adjective* cerrado, -da; **the office is shut on Saturdays** = la oficina está cerrada los sábados **2** *verb* cerrar; **to shut a shop** *or* **a warehouse** = cerrar una tienda *or* un almacén (NOTE: **shutting - shut)**

◊ **shut down** [ˈʃʌt ˈdaʊn] *verb* **to shut down a factory** = parar una fábrica; **the offices will shut down for Christmas** = las oficinas estarán cerradas en Navidades; **six factories have shut down this month** = seis fábricas han estado paradas durante este mes

◊ **shutdown** [ˈʃʌtdaʊn] *noun* cierre *m or* paro *m or* cese *m* de operaciones

◊ **shutout** [ˈʃʌtaʊt] *noun* cierre para impedir la entrada del personal

SIB = SECURITIES AND INVESTMENTS BOARD

sick [sɪk] *adjective* enfermo, -ma; **sick leave** = licencia de enfermedad *or* baja de enfermedad; **sick pay** = subsidio de enfermedad

◊ **sickness** [ˈsɪknəs] *noun* enfermedad *f*; **sickness benefit** = subsidio de enfermedad; **the sickness benefit is paid monthly** = el subsidio de enfermedad se paga mensualmente

side [saɪd] *noun* **(a)** *(part near edge)* lado *m*; **credit side** = columna del haber; **debit side** = columna del debe **(b)** *(one surface of a flat object)* lado *m or* cara *f*; **please write on one side of the paper only** = se ruega escribir por una cara del papel solamente **(c)** **on the side** = por cuenta propia *or* privadamente *or* extraoficialmente; **he works in an accountant's office, but he runs a construction company on the side** = trabaja en una oficina de contabilidad, pero lleva una empresa de construcción por su cuenta; **her salary is too small to live on, so the family lives on what she can make on the side** = su salario no le da para vivir y por eso la familia depende de lo que ella puede ganar por su cuenta

◊ **sideline** [ˈsaɪdlaɪn] *noun* negocio *m*

suplementario or actividad secundaria; **he runs a profitable sideline selling postcards to tourists** = lleva un rentable negocio suplementario de venta de postales a turistas

Sierra Leone [si'eərə lı'eəni] *noun* Sierra Leona *f*

◊ **Sierra Leonean** [si'eərə lı'eəniən] *adjective & noun* (habitante) de Sierra Leona
NOTE: capital: **Freetown;** currency: **Sierra Leonean leone (Le)** = leone de Sierra Leona (Le)

sight [saɪt] *noun* vista *f*; **bill payable at sight** = letra pagadera a la vista; **sight bill** or **sight draft** = letra or giro a la vista; **to buy something sight unseen** = comprar algo sin verlo

sign [saɪn] **1** *noun* pancarta *f* or rótulo *m* or letrero *m*; **they have asked for planning permission to put up a large red shop sign** = han solicitado permiso para colocar un gran rótulo rojo a la entrada de la tienda; **advertising signs cover most of the buildings in the centre of the town** = las vallas publicitarias cubren la mayor parte de los edificios del centro de la ciudad **2** *verb* firmar; **to sign a letter** or **a contract** or **a document** or **a cheque** = firmar una carta or un contrato or un documento or un cheque; **the letter is signed by the managing director** = la carta está firmada por el director gerente; **the cheque is not valid if it has not been signed by the finance director** = el cheque no es válido si no ha sido firmado por el director de finanzas; **the warehouse manager signed for the goods** = el jefe de almacén firmó la recepción de las mercancías; **he signed the goods in** or **he signed the goods out** = firmó la entrada de las mercancías or firmó la salida de las mercancías

◊ **signatory** ['sɪgnətri] *noun* signatario, -ria or firmante *mf*; **authorized signatory** = apoderado general; **you have to get the permission of all the signatories to the agreement if you want to change the terms** = si quieres cambiar las condiciones, tienes que conseguir el permiso de todos los firmantes del acuerdo

◊ **signature** ['sɪgnətʃə] *noun* firma *f*; **a pile of letters waiting for the managing director's signature** = un montón de cartas pendientes de la firma del director gerente; **he found a pile of cheques on his desk waiting for signature** = encontró un montón de cheques por firmar en su mesa; **all cheques need two signatures** = todos los cheques tienen que llevar dos firmas

◊ **sign on** ['saɪn 'ɒn] *verb* (at work) fichar a la entrada al trabajo; **to sign on for the dole** = darse de alta en el paro

signpost ['saɪnpəʊst] *verb* señalar

silent ['saɪlənt] *adjective* silencioso, -sa; **silent partner** = socio comanditario

simple interest ['sɪmpl 'ɪntrəst] *noun* interés *m* simple

sincerely [sɪn'sɪəli] *adverb* (on letters) **Yours sincerely** *US* **Sincerely yours** = atentamente or un saludo afectuoso

sine die ['siːni 'diːeɪ] *phrase* **to adjourn a case sine die** = suspender un juicio indefinidamente

Singapore [sɪŋgə'pɔː] *noun* Singapur *m*

◊ **Singaporean** [sɪŋgə'pɔːriən] *adjective & noun* (habitante) de Singapur
NOTE: currency: **Singapore dollar (S$)** = dólar de Singapur (S$)

single ['sɪŋgl] *adjective* único, -ca or sencillo, -lla **(a) single fare** or **single ticket** or **a single** = billete *m* de ida; **I want two singles to London** = quiero dos billetes de ida a Londres **(b) single currency** = moneda única; **single-entry bookkeeping** = contabilidad por partida única; **in single figures** = cifras de un solo dígito; **sales are down to single figures** = las ventas han descendido a una cifra de un solo dígito; **inflation is now in single figures** = la inflación es inferior al diez por ciento; **single-figure inflation** = inflación inferior al 10% anual; **single premium policy** = póliza de prima única; **single union agreement** = acuerdo entre la patronal y un sindicato único **(c)** *(EU)* **Single European Act** = Acta Unica Europea; **Single European Market** = Mercado Unico Europeo

> QUOTE to create a single market out of the EU member states, physical, technical and tax barriers to the free movement of trade between member states must be removed. Imposing VAT on importation of goods from other member states is seen as one such tax barrier. This will disappear with the abolition of national frontiers under the single market concept
>   **Accountancy**

sink [sɪŋk] *verb* **(a)** (in water) hundirse; **the ship sank in the storm and all the cargo was lost** = el barco se hundió con la tormenta y se perdió toda la carga **(b)** (to go down suddenly) bajar bruscamente; **prices sank at the news of the closure of the factory** = los precios bajaron bruscamente al hacerse público el cierre de la fábrica **(c)** (to invest money) invertir (dinero); **he sank all his savings into a car-hire business** = invirtió todos sus ahorros en un negocio de alquiler de coches (NOTE: **sinking - sank - sunk**)

◊ **sinking fund** ['sɪŋkɪŋ 'fʌnd] *noun* fondo *m* de amortización

sir [sɜː] *noun* (on letter) **'Dear Sir'** = 'Estimado Señor' or 'Muy señor mío or nuestro'; **'Dear Sirs'** = 'Estimados Señores' or 'Muy señores míos or nuestros'

sister ['sɪstə] *adjective* **sister company** = compañía asociada; **sister ship** = buque gemelo (de la misma flota)

sit-down ['sɪtdaʊn] *adjective* **sit-down protest** = sentada; **sit-down strike** = huelga de brazos caídos

◊ **sit-in** ['sɪtɪn] *noun* ocupación *f* or encierro *m* (en señal de protesta) (NOTE: plural is **sit-ins**)

site [saɪt] **1** *noun* sitio *m* or solar *m* or local *m* or precinto *m* or lugar *m*; **we have chosen a site for the new factory** = hemos elegido el solar para la nueva fábrica; **the supermarket is to be built on a site near the station** = el supermercado se va a construir en un solar cerca de la estación; **building site** or **construction site** = obra *f* or solar *m*; **all visitors to the site must wear safety helmets** = todos los visitantes de la obra tienen que llevar el casco de seguridad; **green field site** = solar no urbano para la construcción de una fabrica; **site engineer** =

ingeniero de obra **2** *verb* **to be sited** = estar situado; **the factory will be sited near the motorway** = la fábrica estará situada cerca de la autopista

sitting tenant ['sɪtɪŋ 'tenənt] *noun (tenant occupying a building when it is sold)* inquilino, -na en posesión

situated ['sɪtjʊeɪtɪd] *adjective* situado, -da; **the factory is situated on the edge of the town** = la fábrica está situada en las afueras de la ciudad; **the office is situated near the railway station** = la oficina está situada cerca de la estación de ferrocarriles

◊ **situation** [sɪtjʊ'eɪʃən] *noun* **(a)** *(state of affairs)* situación *f or* estado (de cosas) *m or* coyuntura *f*; **financial situation of a company** = la situación financiera de una compañía; **the general situation of the economy** = el estado general de la economía **(b)** *(job)* empleo *m or* trabajo *m*; **situations vacant** *or* **situations wanted** = ofertas de trabajo *or* demandas de trabajo **(c)** *(place where something is)* localización *f*; **the factory is in a very pleasant situation by the sea** = la fábrica se encuentra en un paraje muy agradable junto al mar

size [saɪz] *noun* tamaño *m or* dimensiones *fpl*; **what is the size of the container?** = ¿cuáles son las dimensiones del contenedor?; **large size** = talla grande; **medium size** = talla mediana; **small size** = talla pequeña; **the size of the staff has doubled in the last two years** = el personal se ha duplicado durante los últimos dos años; **this packet is the maximum size allowed by the post office** = este paquete es del tamaño máximo permitido por correos

skeleton staff ['skelɪtn 'stɑːf] *noun* personal reducido al mínimo

skill [skɪl] *noun* habilidad *f or* técnica *f or* destreza *f*; **she has acquired some very useful office management skills** = ha adquirido unas técnicas de gestión de oficinas muy útiles; **he will have to learn some new skills if he is going to direct the factory** = tiene que aprender nuevas técnicas si va a dirigir la fábrica

◊ **skilful** ['skɪlfʊl] *adjective* diestro, -tra *or* hábil

◊ **skilled** [skɪld] *adjective* cualificado, -da *or* especializado, -da; **skilled workers** *or* **skilled labour** = obreros cualificados *or* mano de obra cualificada *or* especializada

> QUOTE Britain's skills crisis has now reached such proportions that it is affecting the nation's economic growth
> **Personnel Today**

> QUOTE we aim to add the sensitivity of a new European to the broad skills of the new professional manager
> **Management Today**

slack [slæk] *adjective* flojo, -ja *or* débil; **business is slack at the end of the week** = la actividad comercial es floja durante el fin de semana; **January is always a slack period** = enero es siempre un periodo de poca actividad

◊ **slacken off** ['slækən 'ɒf] *verb* decaer; **trade has slackened off** = la actividad comercial ha decaído

slander ['slɑːndə] **1** *noun* calumnia *f or*

difamación *f*; **action for slander** *or* **slander action** = demanda por difamación **2** *verb* **to slander someone** = calumniar a alguien (NOTE: compare **LIBEL**)

slash [slæʃ] *verb* reducir drásticamente; **to slash prices** *or* **credit terms** = hacer rebajas drásticas de precios *or* de condiciones de crédito; **prices have been slashed in all departments** = los precios han sido drásticamente reducidos en todos los departamentos; **the bank has been forced to slash interest rates** = el banco se ha visto obligado a bajar considerablemente los tipos de interés

sleeper ['sliːpə] *noun* **(a)** *(share)* acción *f* de precio estable pero cuya cotización puede aumentar repentinamente **(b)** *(item)* artículo sin venta

◊ **sleeping partner** ['sliːpɪŋ 'pɑːtnə] *noun* socio comanditario

slide [slaɪd] *verb* bajar en picado; **prices slid after the company reported a loss** = los precios cayeron en picado al registrarse pérdidas en la compañía (NOTE: **sliding - slid**)

◊ **sliding** ['slaɪdɪŋ] *adjective* móvil; **a sliding scale of charges** = escala móvil de derechos

slight [slaɪt] *adjective* ligero, -ra *or* escaso, -sa *or* pequeño, -ña; **there was a slight improvement in the balance of trade** = la balanza comercial experimentó una escasa mejora; **we saw a slight increase in sales in February** = comprobamos un ligero aumento de las ventas en febrero

◊ **slightly** ['slaɪtli] *adverb* un poco *or* ligeramente; **sales fell slightly in the second quarter** = la ventas bajaron ligeramente durante el segundo trimestre; **the Swiss bank is offering slightly better terms** = el banco suizo ofrece condiciones un poco mejores

slip [slɪp] **1** *noun* **(a)** *(small piece of paper)* nota *f or* ficha *f or* recibo *m or* resguardo *m*; **compliments slip** = saluda *or* tarjeta de saludo; **deposit slip** = nota *or* recibo de depósito; **distribution slip** = lista *or* nota de distribución; **pay slip** = hoja *f* de sueldo *or* salario; **paying-in slip** = nota *or* recibo de depósito; **sales slip** = recibo; **goods can be exchanged only on production of a sales slip** = los artículos pueden cambiarse solamente si se presenta el recibo **(b)** *(mistake)* error *m*; **he made a couple of slips in calculating the discount** = hizo un par de errores al calcular el descuento **2** *verb* bajar; **profits slipped to £1.5m** = los beneficios bajaron a £1,5 millones; **shares slipped back at the close** = los precios de la bolsa volvieron a bajar al cierre (NOTE: **slipping - slipped**)

◊ **slip up** ['slɪp 'ʌp] *verb* equivocarse *or* cometer un error; **we slipped up badly in not signing the agreement with the Chinese company** = cometimos un grave error al no firmar el acuerdo con la empresa china

◊ **slip-up** ['slɪpʌp] *noun* error *m* (NOTE: plural is **slip-ups**)

> QUOTE the active December long gilt contract on the LIFFE slipped to close at 83-12 from the opening 83-24
> **Financial Times**

QUOTE with long-term fundamentals reasonably sound, the question for brokers is when does cheap become cheap enough? The Bangkok and Taipei exchanges offer lower p/e ratios than Jakarta, but if Jakarta p/e ratios slip to the 16-18 range, foreign investors would pay more attention to it
Far Eastern Economic Review

slogan ['sləʊgən] *noun* publicity slogan = consigna *f or* eslogan *m*; **we are using the same slogan on all our publicity** = empleamos el mismo eslogan en toda nuestra publicidad

slot [slɒt] *noun* **(a)** *(period of time)* periodo de tiempo **(b)** *(in a machine)* ranura *f*; **slot machine** = máquina *f* expendedora *or* tragaperras

Slovakia [sləˈvækiə] *noun* Eslovaquia

◊ **Slovak** ['sləʊvæk] *adjective & noun* eslovaco, -ca
NOTE: capital: **Bratislava;** currency: **koruna = corona**

Slovenia [sləˈviːniə] *noun* Eslovenia

◊ **Slovene** ['sləʊviːn] *adjective & noun* esloveno, -na
NOTE: capital: **Ljubljana;** currency: **tolar = tolar**

slow [sləʊ] **1** *adjective* lento, -ta; **a slow start to the day's trading** = un comienzo lento de las operaciones del día; **the sales got off to a slow start, but picked up later** = las ventas comenzaron despacio, pero se aceleraron más tarde; **business is always slow after Christmas** = hay siempre poca actividad comercial después de Navidades; **they were slow to reply** *or* **slow at replying to the customer's complaints** = se demoraron en contestar a las quejas del cliente; **the board is slow to come to a decision** = el consejo de administración es lento en tomar decisiones; **there was a slow improvement in sales in the first half of the year** = hubo una lenta mejora en las ventas durante el primer semestre del año **2** *adverb* **to go slow** = hacer huelga de celo

◊ **slow down** ['sləʊ 'daʊn] *verb* desacelerar *or* reducir *or* aflojar el paso *or* ralentizar; **inflation is slowing down** = la inflación se está reduciendo; **the fall in the exchange rate is slowing down** = la caída del tipo de cambio se está frenando; **the management decided to slow down production** = la dirección decidió reducir la tasa de producción

◊ **slowdown** ['sləʊdaʊn] *noun* desaceleración *f or* reducción *f or* ralentización *f*; **a slowdown in the company's expansion** = una reducción de la expansión de la compañía

◊ **slowly** ['sləʊli] *adverb* despacio *or* lentamente; **the company's sales slowly improved** = las ventas de la empresa mejoraron lentamente; **we are slowly increasing our market share** = estamos aumentando lentamente nuestra participación en el mercado

QUOTE a general price freeze succeeded in slowing the growth in consumer prices
Financial Times

QUOTE cash paid for stock: overstocked lines, factory seconds, slow sellers
Australian Financial Review

slump [slʌmp] **1** *noun* **(a)** *(rapid fall)* baja *f or* caída *f* repentina *or* caída en picado; **slump in sales** = caída de las ventas; **slump in profits** = baja repentina de beneficios; **slump in the value of the pound** = caída en el valor de la libra; **the pound's slump on the foreign exchange markets** = la caída de la libra en los mercados de divisas **(b)** *(period of economic collapse)* depresión *f or* crisis *f* económica *or* quiebra *f*; **we are experiencing slump conditions** = estamos viviendo una situación de depresión económica; **the Slump** = la crisis económica mundial de 1929 - 1933 **2** *verb* caer *or* bajar bruscamente *or* hundirse; **profits have slumped** = los beneficios han bajado bruscamente; **the pound slumped on the foreign exchange markets** = la libra ha sufrido un baja repentina en los mercados de divisas

QUOTE when gold began rising, after a long flat period in the fall of 1986, the dollar was slumping
Business Week

slush fund ['slʌʃ 'fʌnd] *noun* fondos *mpl* secretos *or* dinero *m* para sobornos *or* fondo de reptiles

small [smɔːl] *adjective* pequeño, -ña *or* menudo, -da; **small ads** = anuncios por palabras; **small businesses** = pequeñas empresas; **small businessman** = pequeño empresario; **small change** = moneda suelta *or* cambio *or* dinero suelto; *GB* **small claims court** = tribunal de instancia (que se ocupa de delitos menores); **the small investor** = el pequeño inversionista; **to read the small print on a contract** = leer la letra menuda *or* pequeña en un contrato; **small shareholders** = pequeños accionistas; **small shopkeepers** = pequeños comerciantes

◊ **small company** ['smɔːl 'kɒmpni] *noun* empresa *f* pequeña

COMMENT: a company with at least two of the following characteristics: turnover of less than £2.0m; fewer than 50 staff; net assets of less than £975,000 (small companies are allowed to file modified accounts with Companies House)

◊ **small-scale** ['smɔːlskeɪl] *adjective* a pequeña escala; **a small-scale enterprise** = empresa a pequeña escala

QUOTE running a small business is in many ways tougher and more disagreeable than being a top functionary in a large one
Forbes Magazine

smart [smɑːt] *adjective* **(a)** arreglado, -da; **his office looks very smart** = su oficina está muy bien arreglada **(b)** *(clever)* inteligente

◊ **smart card** ['smɑːt 'kɑːd] *noun* tarjeta *f* inteligente

smash [smæʃ] *verb* romper *or* batir; **to smash all production records** = batir todos los records de producción; **sales have smashed all records for the first half of the year** = las ventas han batido todos los records en el primer semestre del año

smokestack industry ['sməʊkstæk 'ɪndʌstrɪ] *noun* industria pesada

smuggle ['smʌgl] *verb* hacer contrabando; **they had to smuggle the spare parts into the country** = tuvieron que pasar los repuestos al país de contrabando

◊ **smuggler** ['smʌglə] *noun* contrabandista *mf*

◊ **smuggling** ['smʌglɪŋ] *noun* contrabando *m*; **he made his money in arms smuggling** = hizo su fortuna en el contrabando de armas

snake [sneɪk] *noun (EU)* serpiente *f*

snap [snæp] *adjective* repentino, -na *or* rápido, -da; **the board came to a snap decision** = el consejo de administración adoptó una decisión repentina; **they carried out a snap check** *or* **a snap inspection of the expense accounts** = hicieron una comprobación imprevista *or* sorpresa de las cuentas de gastos

◊ **snap up** ['snæp 'ʌp] *verb* comprar al instante; **to snap up a bargain** = arrebatar una ganga sin pensarlo; **he snapped up 15% of the company's shares** = compró al instante *or* inmediatamente el 15% de las acciones de la compañía (NOTE: **snapping - snapped)**

snip [snɪp] *noun (informal)* ganga *f*; **these typewriters are a snip at £50** = estas máquinas de escribir son una ganga a £50

soar [sɔ:] *verb* dispararse *or* remontarse; **food prices soared during the cold weather** = los precios de los alimentos se dispararon durante el periodo de frío; **share prices soared on the news of the takeover bid** *or* **the news of the takeover bid sent share prices soaring** = los precios de las acciones se dispararon al hacerse pública la noticia de la oferta de adquisición *or* la noticia de la oferta de adquisición hizo que los precios de las acciones se dispararan

social ['səʊʃəl] *adjective* social; **social costs** = costes sociales; **the report examines the social costs of building the factory in the middle of the town** = el informe examina los costes sociales de la construcción de la fábrica en el centro de la ciudad; **social security** = seguridad social; **he gets weekly social security payments** = recibe un subsidio semanal de la seguridad social; **the social system** = el sistema social

◊ **society** [sə'saɪəti] *noun* **(a)** *(way in which people are organized)* sociedad *f*; **consumer society** = sociedad de consumo; **the affluent society** = la sociedad opulenta **(b)** *(club or group of people)* club *m or* sociedad; **he has joined a computer society** = se ha afiliado a una sociedad de informática; **building society** = sociedad hipotecaria; **cooperative society** = sociedad cooperativa; **friendly society** = sociedad de socorro mutuo *or* mutualidad

◊ **socio-economic** ['səʊʃɪəʊɪkə'nɒmɪk] *adjective* socioeconómico, -ca; **the socio-economic system in capitalist countries** = el sistema socioeconómico en los países capitalistas; **socio-economic groups** = grupos socioeconómicos

Sod's Law ['sɒdz 'lɔ:] *noun see* MURPHY'S LAW

soft [sɒft] *adjective* flojo, -ja *or* blando, -da,; **soft currency** = moneda débil *or* no convertible; **soft landing** = *(economic measures)* medidas suaves para combatir la inflación; *(plane)* aterrizaje suave;

soft loan = crédito blando *or* préstamo sin interés; **to take the soft option** = decidirse por la opción más fácil; **soft sell** = venta realizada sin presionar al cliente

◊ **software** ['sɒftweə] *noun* 'software' *m or* programa *m* informático *or* soporte *m* lógico *or* componentes logicos

sole [səʊl] *adjective* único, -ca *or* exclusivo, -va; **sole agency** = representación exclusiva; **he has the sole agency for Ford cars** = tiene la representación exclusiva de los automóviles Ford; **sole agent** = representante *or* concesionario exclusivo; **sole distributor** = distribuidor exclusivo; **sole owner** *or* **sole proprietor** = propietario único; **sole trader** = comerciante exclusivo

solemn ['sɒləm] *solemne* **solemn and binding agreement** = acuerdo solemne y obligatorio

solicit [sə'lɪsɪt] *verb* pedir *or* solicitar; **to solicit orders** = solicitar pedidos

◊ **solicitor** [sə'lɪsɪtə] *noun GB* abogado, -da; **to instruct a solicitor** = dar instucciones a un abogado para que inicie un proceso legal en nombre de uno; **duty solicitor** = abogado de oficio

solus (advertisement) ['səʊləs (əd'vɜ:tɪsmənt)] *noun* anuncio *m* aislado

solution [sə'lu:ʃən] *noun* solución *f*; **to look for a solution to the financial problems** = buscar una solución a los problemas financieros; **the programmer came up with a solution to the systems problem** = el programador sugirió una solución al problema de los sistemas; **we think we have found a solution to the problem of getting skilled staff** = creemos que hemos encontrado la solución para resolver el problema de la falta de personal cualificado

solve [sɒlv] *verb* resolver; **to solve a problem** = resolver *or* solucionar un problema; **the loan will solve some of our short-term problems** = el crédito resolverá algunos de nuestros problemas a corto plazo

solvent ['sɒlvənt] *adjective* solvente; **when he bought the company it was barely solvent** = la compañía apenas era solvente cuando la compró

◊ **solvency** ['sɒlvənsi] *noun* solvencia *f*

Somalia [sə'mɑ:lɪə] *noun* Somalia *f*

◊ **Somali** [sə'mɑ:li] *adjective & noun* somalí
NOTE: capital: **Mogadishu** (= Mogadisio); currency: **Somali shilling (SoSh)** = chelín somalí (So.Sh.)

soon [su:n] *adverb* **as soon as possible (asap)** = tan pronto como sea posible *or* lo antes posible *or* enseguida

sort [sɔ:t] *verb* ordenar *or* clasificar; **she is sorting index cards into alphabetical order** = está clasificando fichas en orden alfabético

◊ **sort out** ['sɔ:t 'aʊt] *verb* arreglar *or* solucionar; **did you sort out the accounts problem with the auditors?** = ¿solucionaste el problema de las cuentas con los auditores?

sound [saʊnd] *adjective* sólido, -da *or* razonable *or* prudente; **the company's financial situation is very sound** = la situación financiera de la compañía es muy sólida; **he gave us some very sound advice** = nos dio un consejo muy acertado *or* nos dio muy buen consejo

◊ **soundness** ['saʊndnəs] *noun* solidez *f or* prudencia *f*

source [sɔːs] **1** *noun* fuente *f or* origen *m*; **source of income** = fuente de ingresos; **you must declare income from all sources to the tax office** = se tienen que declarar todas las fuentes de ingresos al fisco; **collection at source** = recaudación en el origen; **income which is taxed at source** = ingreso sujeto a retención en el origen **2** *verb* surtirse

◊ **sourcing** ['sɔːsɪŋ] *noun* suministro *m*; **the sourcing of spare parts can be diversified to suppliers outside Europe** = el suministro de piezas de repuesto puede diversificarse fuera de Europa; *see also* OUTSOURCING

South Africa [saʊθ 'æfrɪkə] *noun* Africa del Sur *or* Sudáfrica *f*

◊ **South African** [saʊθ 'æfrɪkən] *adjective & noun* sudafricano, -na
NOTE: capital: **Pretoria**; currency: **South African rand (R)** = rand sudafricano (R)

South America [saʊθ ə'merɪkə] *noun* América del Sur *or* Sudamérica *f*

◊ **South American** [saʊθ ə'merɪkən] *adjective & noun* sudamericano, -na

sovereign ['sɒvrɪn] *noun (gold coin)* soberano *m*

space [speɪs] *noun* espacio *m*; **advertising space** = espacio publicitario; **to take advertising space in a newspaper** = contratar espacio publicitario en un periódico; **floor space** = superficie útil; **office space** = espacio para oficinas; **we are looking for extra office space for our new accounts department** = estamos buscando espacio adicional para nuestro nuevo departamento de contabilidad

◊ **space bar** ['speɪs 'bɑː] *noun (key on typewriter or computer)* barra *f* espaciadora

◊ **space out** ['speɪs 'aʊt] *verb* espaciar; **the company name is written in spaced-out letters** = el nombre de la compañía está escrito en letras espaciadas; **payments can be spaced out over a period of ten years** = los pagos pueden escalonarse durante un periodo de diez años

Spain [speɪn] *noun* España *f*

◊ **Spaniard** ['spænjəd] *noun* español, -ola

◊ **Spanish** ['spænɪʃ] **1** *adjective* español **2** *noun* **the Spanish** = los españoles
NOTE: capital: **Madrid**; currency: **Spanish peseta (Ptas.)** = peseta española (Ptas)

spare [speə] *adjective* sobrante *or* disponible; **he has invested his spare capital in a computer shop** = ha invertido su capital disponible en una tienda de informática; **to use up spare capacity** = utilizar capacidad ociosa; **spare part** = pieza de recambio *or* de repuesto; **the photocopier will not work - it needs a spare part** = la fotocopiadora no funciona - le falta una pieza de repuesto; **spare time** = tiempo libre; **he built himself a car in his spare time** = se construyó un coche en su tiempo libre

spec [spek] *noun* **to buy something on spec** = comprar algo con fines especulativos

◊ **specs** [speks] *plural noun* = SPECIFICATIONS

special ['speʃəl] *adjective* especial; **he offered us special terms** = nos ofreció condiciones especiales; **the car is being offered at a special price** = el coche se ofrece a un precio especial; *(rapid postal service)* **special delivery** = entrega extraordinaria *or* reparto especial; **special deposits** = depósitos especiales; *(IMF)* **special drawing rights (SDRs)** ['speʃəl 'drɔːɪŋ raɪts] *noun* derechos especiales de giro (DEG)

| COMMENT: a unit of account used by the International Monetary Fund, allocated to each member country for use in loans and other international operations; their value is calculated daily on the weighted values of a group of currencies shown in dollars

◊ **specialist** ['speʃəlɪst] *noun* especialista *mf*; **you should go to a specialist in computers** *or* **to a computer specialist for advice** = tienes que consultar a un especialista en informática

◊ **speciality** *or* **specialty** [speʃɪ'ælətɪ *or* 'speʃəltɪ] *noun* especialidad *f*; **their speciality is computer programs** = su especialidad son los programas de ordenadores; *US* **specialty store** = tienda especializada

◊ **specialization** [speʃəlaɪ'zeɪʃən] *noun* especialización *f*; **the company's area of specialization is accounts packages for small businesses** = el campo de especialización de la compañía son los programas de contabilidad para empresas pequeñas

◊ **specialize** ['speʃəlaɪz] *verb* especializar; **the company specializes in electronic components** = la empresa está especializada en componentes electrónicos; **they have a specialized product line** = tienen una gama de productos especializados; **he sells very specialized equipment for the electronics industry** = vende equipos muy especializados para la industria electrónica

◊ **special resolution** ['speʃəl rezə'luːʃn] *noun* resolución *f* especial

| COMMENT: resolution of the members of a company which is only valid if it is approved by 75% of the votes cast at a meeting (a resolution concerning an important matter, such as a change to the company's articles of association). 21 days' notice must be given for a special resolution to be put to a meeting, as opposed to an 'extraordinary resolution' for which notice must be given, but no minimum period is specified by law. An extraordinary resolution could be a proposal to wind up a company voluntarily, but changes to the articles of association, such as a change of name, or of the objects of the company, or a reduction in share capital, need a special resolution

QUOTE the group specializes in the sale, lease and rental of new and second-user hardware
Financial Times

QUOTE airlines offer special stopover rates and hotel packages to attract customers to certain routes
Business Traveller

specie ['spiːʃiː] *plural noun (coins)* efectivo *m or* metálico *m*

specify ['spesɪfaɪ] *verb* especificar *or* precisar *or* indicar *or* concretar; **to specify full details of the**

goods ordered = precisar con todo detalle los artículos pedidos; **do not include VAT on the invoice unless specified** = no incluir el IVA en la factura a menos que se indique

◊ **specification** [spesɪfɪ'keɪʃən] *noun* especificación *f*; **specifications** = presupuesto *m*; **to detail the specifications of a computer system** = detallar las especificaciones de un sistema informático; **job specification** = perfil *or* requisitos del puesto de trabajo; **to work to standard specifications** = trabajar conforme a las normas establecidas; **the work is not up to specification** *or* **does not meet our specifications** = el trabajo no es de la calidad prevista *or* no cumple con nuestras especificaciones; **specification sheet** = ficha técnica

specimen ['spesɪmən] *noun* muestra *f or* espécimen *m*; **specimen signature** = muestra de firma; **to give specimen signatures on a bank mandate** = dar espécimen de firmas de una orden bancaria

speculate ['spekjʊleɪt] *verb* especular; **to speculate on the Stock Exchange** = especular en la bolsa *or* jugar a la bolsa

◊ **speculation** [spekjʊ'leɪʃən] *noun* especulación *f*; **he bought the company as a speculation** = compró la compañía con fines especulativos; **she lost all her money in Stock Exchange speculations** = perdió todo su dinero en especulaciones bursátiles

◊ **speculative** ['spekjʊlətɪv] *adjective* **speculative builder** = constructor especulativo; **speculative share** = acción especulativa

◊ **speculator** ['spekjʊleɪtə] *noun* especulador, -ra; **a property speculator** = un especulador inmobiliario; **a currency speculator** = un especulador en divisas; **a speculator on the Stock Exchange** *or* **a Stock Exchange speculator** = un especulador en bolsa

speed [spi:d] *noun* velocidad *f or* rapidez *f*; **dictation speed** = velocidad de dictado; **typing speed** = velocidad de mecanografiado

◊ **speed up** ['spi:d 'ʌp] *verb* acelerar *or* adelantar *or* activar; **we are aiming to speed up our delivery times** = pretendemos acelerar nuestros plazos de entrega

spend [spend] *verb* **(a)** *(money)* gastar; **they spent all their savings on buying the shop** = gastaron todos sus ahorros en comprar la tienda; **the company spends thousands of pounds on research** = la compañía gasta miles de libras en investigación **(b)** *(to use time)* pasar *or* dedicar; **the company spends hundreds of man-hours on meetings** = la compañía dedica centenares de horas/hombre a reuniones; **the chairman spent yesterday afternoon with the auditors** = el presidente pasó la tarde de ayer con los auditores (NOTE: **spending - spent**)

◊ **spending** ['spendɪŋ] *noun* gastos *mpl*; **cash spending** *or* **credit card spending** = gastos en efectivo *or* gastos (incurridos) con tarjetas de crédito; **consumer spending** = gastos de los consumidores; **spending money** = dinero para gastos personales; **spending power** = poder adquisitivo; **the spending power of the pound has fallen over the last ten years** = el poder adquisitivo de la libra ha bajado a lo

largo de los últimos diez años; **the spending power of the student market** = el poder adquisitivo del mercado estudiantil

sphere [sfɪə] *noun* esfera *f or* campo *m*; **sphere of activity** = campo de actividad; **sphere of influence** = esfera de influencia

spin off [spɪn'ɒf] *verb* **to spin off a subsidiary company** = convertir una parte de una compañía grande en una filial más pequeña (NOTE: **spinning - span - spun**)

◊ **spinoff** ['spɪnɒf] *noun* efecto *m* indirecto; **one of the spinoffs of the research programme has been the development of the electric car** = uno de los efectos indirectos del programa de investigación ha sido el desarrollo del automóvil eléctrico

spiral ['spaɪərəl] **1** *noun* espiral *f*; **the economy is in an inflationary spiral** = la economía está en una espiral inflacionaria; **wage-price spiral** = la espiral salarios-precios **2** *verb* subir en espiral; **a period of spiralling prices** = un periodo de subida en espiral de los precios; **spiralling inflation** = inflación galopante (NOTE: **spiralling - spiralled** but US English **spiraling - spiraled**)

split [splɪt] **1** *noun* **(a)** *(dividing)* división *f or* fraccionamiento *m or* escisión *f*; **share split** = fraccionamiento de acciones; **the company is proposing a five for one split** = la compañía propone el fraccionamiento de las acciones en cinco partes **(b)** *(lack of agreement)* ruptura *f*; **a split in the family shareholders** = una ruptura entre los accionistas pertenecientes a una familia **2** *verb* **(a)** **to split shares** = dividir acciones; **the shares were split five for one** = las acciones se dividieron en una proporción de cinco a una **(b) to split the difference** = partir la diferencia (NOTE: **splitting - split**) **3** *adjective* partido, -da *or* dividido, -da; **split commission** = comisión dividida; **split payment** = pago dividido; **split shift** jornada partida

COMMENT: a company may decide to split its shares if the share price becomes too 'heavy' (i.e., each share is priced at such a high level that small investors may be put off, and trading in the share is restricted); in the UK, a share price of £10.00 is considered 'heavy', though such prices are common on other stock markets

spoil [spɔɪl] *verb* estropear *or* echar a perder; **half the shipment was spoiled by water** = la mitad del envío se echó a perder por culpa del agua; **the company's results were spoiled by a disastrous last quarter** = los resultados de la compañía se echaron a perder por un último trimestre desastroso

sponsor ['spɒnsə] **1** *noun* **(a)** *(person or company)* patrocinador, -ra *or* padrino *m or* madrina *f* **(b)** *(company which advertises on TV)* patrocinador **2** *verb* patrocinar; **to sponsor a television programme** = patrocinar un programa de televisión; **the company has sponsored the football match** = la empresa ha patrocinado el partido de fútbol; **government-sponsored trade exhibition** = una feria comercial patrocinada por el gobierno

◊ **sponsorship** ['spɒnsəʃɪp] *noun* patrocinio *m*; **government sponsorship of overseas selling missions** = patrocinio gubernamental de misiones comerciales en el extranjero

spot [spɒt] *noun* **(a)** *(immediate)* compra *f* de

entrega inmediata *or* al contado; **spot cash** = pago *m* al contado *or* dinero *m* en mano; **the spot market in oil** = el mercado de entrega inmediata *or* 'spot' del petróleo; **spot price** *or* **spot rate** = precio *or* tarifa de entrega inmediata **(b)** *(place)* lugar *m*; **to be on the spot** = estar en el lugar mismo; **we have a man on the spot to deal with any problems which happen on the building site** = tenemos un representante en el lugar para ocuparse de cualquier problema que surja en la obra **(c)** **TV spot** = anuncio en la TV *or* espacio publicitario en la televisión; **we are running a series of TV spots over the next three weeks** = vamos a presentar una serie de anuncios publicitarios en la televisión durante las próximas tres semanas

QUOTE with most of the world's oil now traded on spot markets, Opec's official prices are much less significant than they once were
Economist

QUOTE the average spot price of Nigerian light crude oil for the month of July was 27.21 dollars per barrel
Business Times (Lagos)

spread [spred] **1** *noun* **(a)** *(range)* gama *f or* abanico *m*; **he has a wide spread of investments** *or* **of interests** = tiene una amplia gama de inversiones *or* de intereses **(b)** *(on the Stock Exchange)* diferencial *m* **2** *verb* extender; **to spread payments over several months** = distribuir los pagos a lo largo de varios meses; **to spread a risk** = repartir un riesgo (NOTE: **spreading - spread**)

◊ **spreadsheet** ['spredʃiːt] *noun (computer)* hoja *f* de cálculo

QUOTE dealers said markets were thin, with gaps between trades and wide spreads between bid and ask prices on the currencies
Wall Street Journal

QUOTE to ensure an average return you should hold a spread of different shares covering a wide cross-section of the market
Investors Chronicle

square [skweə] **1** *noun (shape)* cuadrado *m*; **graph paper is drawn with a series of small squares** = el papel cuadriculado presenta una serie de cuadrados pequeños **2** *adjective* **(a)** *(measurement of area)* cuadrado , -da; **the office is ten metres by twelve - its area is one hundred and twenty square metres** = las dimensiones de la oficina son de diez metros por doce - su área es de ciento veinte metros cuadrados; **square measure** = medida de superficie (NOTE: written with figures as ²: **10ft²** = ten square feet; **6m²** = six square metres) **(b)** *(informal)* igual; **now we're square** = ahora estamos en paz **3** *verb* US *(to pay a bill)* ajustar *or* pagar; **to square a bill** = pagar una cuenta; **to square away** = arreglar *or* ordenar (papeles)

◊ **squared paper** ['skweəd 'peɪpə] *noun* papel *m* cuadriculado

◊ **Square Mile** ['skweə 'maɪl] *noun (the City of London)* 'la City', centro financiero de Londres

squeeze [skwiːz] **1** *noun* restricción *f*; **credit squeeze** = restricciones de crédito; **profit squeeze** = reducción de la tasa de beneficio **2** *verb* apretar *or*

restringir; **to squeeze margins** *or* **profits** *or* **credit** = restringir los márgenes *or* beneficios *or* el crédito; **our margins have been squeezed by the competition** = nuestros márgenes se han visto reducidos por la competencia

QUOTE the real estate boom of the past three years has been based on the availability of easy credit. Today, money is tighter, so property should bear the brunt of the credit squeeze
Money Observer

Sri Lanka [sriː 'læŋkə] *noun* Sri Lanka *m*

◊ **Sri Lankan** [sriː 'læŋkən] *adjective & noun* cingalés, -esa
NOTE: capital: **Colombo**; currency: **Sri Lanka rupee (SL Rs)** = rupia de Sri Lanka (SL Rs)

SSP = STATUTORY SICK PAY

stability [stə'bɪləti] *noun* estabilidad *f*; **price stability** = estabilidad de los precios; **a period of economic stability** = un periodo de estabilidad económica; **the stability of the currency markets** = la estabilidad de los mercados de divisas

◊ **stabilization** [steɪbɪlaɪ'zeɪʃən] *noun* estabilización *f*; **stabilization of the economy** = estabilización de la economía

◊ **stabilize** ['steɪbɪlaɪz] *verb* estabilizar(se); **prices have stabilized** = los precios se han estabilizado; **to have a stabilizing effect on the economy** = tener un efecto estabilizador en la economía

◊ **stable** ['steɪbl] *adjective* estable; **stable prices** = precios estables; **stable exchange rate** = tipos de cambio estables; **stable currency** = moneda estable; **stable economy** = economía estable

stack [stæk] **1** *noun* montón *m*; **there is a stack of replies to our advertisement** = hemos recibido un montón de respuestas a nuestro anuncio **2** *verb* apilar *or* amontonar; **the boxes are stacked in the warehouse** = las cajas están apiladas en el almacén

staff [staːf] **1** *noun* personal *m or* plantilla *f*; **to be on the staff** *or* **a member of staff** *or* **a staff member** = ser un empleado fijo *or* estar en plantilla; **staff agency** = agencia de personal administrativo; **staff appointment** = empleo fijo; **staff association** = asociación del personal de una empresa; **accounts staff** = personal de contabilidad; **clerical staff** *or* **administrative staff** *or* **office staff** = personal administrativo; **counter staff** = personal de atención al público; **senior staff** *or* **junior staff** = personal de mayor categoría *or* antigüedad *or* de más edad *or* personal de menor categoría *or* antigüedad *or* de menos edad (NOTE: **staff** refers to a group of people and so is often followed by a verb in the plural) **2** *verb* contratar personal; **the business is staffed with skilled part-timers** = el personal de la empresa está compuesto de trabajadores cualificados contratados a tiempo parcial; **to have difficulty in staffing the factory** = tener dificultades en contratar personal para la fábrica

◊ **staffer** ['staːfə] *noun* US miembro *mf* de la plantilla permanente

◊ **staffing** ['staːfɪŋ] *noun* suministro *m or* dotación *f* de personal; **staffing levels** = niveles de dotación de personal *or* de plantilla; **the company's**

staffing policy = la política de personal de la empresa

stag [stæg] **1** *noun* **(a)** *(speculator)* especulador, -ra en nuevas emisiones de acciones **(b)** *(stock dealer)* US agente *mf* de bolsa autónomo, -ma **2** *verb* **to stag an issue** = comprar una acción nueva con fines especulativos (NOTE: **stagging - stagged**)

stage [steɪdʒ] **1** *noun* fase *f or* etapa *f or* trámite *m*; **the different stages of the production process** = las distintas etapas del proceso de producción; **the contract is still in the drafting stage** = el contrato está todavía en la etapa de preparación; **in stages** = por etapas; **the company has agreed to repay the loan in stages** = la compañía ha acordado devolver el préstamo por etapas **2** *verb* **(a)** *(organize a show)* organizar *or* presentar; **the exhibition is being staged in the conference centre** = la exposición tiene lugar en el palacio de congresos; **to stage a recovery** = experimentar una recuperación; **the company has staged a strong recovery from a point of near bankruptcy** = la compañía, que se encontraba al borde de la quiebra, ha experimentado una fuerte recuperación **(b) staged payments** = pagos por etapas

stagflation [stæɡˈfleɪʃən] *noun* estanflación *f or* estancamiento *m* con inflación

stagger [ˈstæɡə] *verb* escalonar; **staggered holidays help the tourist industry** = las vacaciones escalonadas ayudan a la industria del turismo; **we have to stagger the lunch hour so that there is always someone on the switchboard** = tenemos que escalonar la hora de comer *or* del almuerzo para que siempre haya alguien en la centralita de teléfonos

stagnant [ˈstæɡnənt] *adjective* estancado, -da; **turnover was stagnant for the first half of the year** = el volumen de ventas se estancó durante el primer trimestre del año; **a stagnant economy** = una economía estancada

◊ **stagnate** [stæɡˈneɪt] *verb* estancarse; **the economy is stagnating** = la economía está estancada; **after six hours the talks were stagnating** = después de seis horas las negociaciones se estancaron

◊ **stagnation** [stæɡˈneɪʃən] *noun* estancamiento *m*; **the country entered a period of stagnation** = el país entró en una fase de estancamiento; **economic stagnation** = estancamiento económico

stake [steɪk] **1** *noun* inversión *f or* participación *f*; **to have a stake in a business** = tener dinero invertido en un negocio; **to acquire a stake in a business** = adquirir una participación en un negocio; **he acquired a 25% stake in the business** = adquirió una participación de un 25% en el negocio **2** *verb* **to stake money on something** = arriesgar dinero en algo

stall [stɔːl] *noun* puesto *m* de mercado

◊ **stallholder** [ˈstɔːlhəʊldə] *noun* persona que tiene un puesto en el mercado

stamp [stæmp] **1** *noun* **(a)** *(device for making marks on documents)* estampilla *f or* sello *m or* timbre *m*; **the invoice has the stamp 'Received with thanks' on it** = la factura lleva el sello de 'recibí' *or* 'pagado' *or* 'cobrado'; **the customs officer looked at the stamps in his passport** = el funcionario de aduanas le miró los sellos del pasaporte; **date stamp** = fechador *m*; **rubber stamp** = sello *or* timbre *m*; **stamp pad** = tampón *m* **(b)** *(postage)* sello *m*; **a postage stamp** = sello de correos; **a £1 stamp** = un sello de £1 **(c) stamp duty** = derecho *or* impuesto del timbre **2** *verb* **(a)** *(put a mark on)* sellar *or* poner el sello; **to stamp an invoice 'Paid'** = poner el sello de 'recibí' en una factura; **the documents were stamped by the customs officials** = los funcionarios de la aduana sellaron los documentos **(b)** *(to put a postage stamp on)* poner un sello (en un sobre); **stamped addressed envelope (s.a.e.)** = sobre con el sello y la dirección del remitente; **send a stamped addressed envelope for further details and catalogue** = envíe un sobre franqueado y con sus señas para recibir más información y el catálogo

stand [stænd] **1** *noun (at an exhibition)* local *m* de exposición *or* 'stand' *m*; **display stand** = vitrina *f*; **news stand** = quiosco *m* **2** *verb* ser; **to stand liable for damages** = ser responsable de los daños; **the company's balance stands at £24,000** = el balance de la compañía es de £24.000 (NOTE: **standing - stood)**

◊ **stand down** [ˈstænd ˈdaʊn] *verb* retirarse (de una elección)

◊ **stand in for** [ˈstænd ˈɪn fɔː] *verb* sustituir; **Mr Smith is standing in for the chairman, who is ill** = el señor Smith sustituye al presidente que está enfermo

standard [ˈstændəd] **1** *noun* norma *f or* patrón *m or* modelo *m or* nivel *m*; **standard of living** *or* **living standards** = nivel *m* de vida; **production standards** = normas de producción; **up to standard** = conforme a la norma; **this batch is not up to standard** *or* **does not meet our standards** = este lote no alcanza el debido nivel *or* no cumple nuestras normas; **gold standard** = patrón-oro **2** *adjective* normal *or* estándar; **a standard model car** = un modelo de coche estándar; **we have a standard charge of £25 for a thirty-minute session** = nuestro precio normal es de £25 la sesión de media hora; **standard agreement** *or* **standard contract** = contrato-tipo; **standard letter** = carta tipo *or* estándar; **standard rate** = (i) tasa de impuesto normal; (ii) tipo de interés vigente

◊ **standardization** [stændədaɪˈzeɪʃən] *noun* estandarización *f or* normalización *f or* tipificación *f*; **standardization of design** = estandarización del diseño; **standardization of measurements** = normalización de medidas; **standardization of products** = normalización de productos

◊ **standardize** [ˈstændədaɪz] *verb* estandarizar *or* normalizar *or* tipificar

standby [ˈstæn(d)baɪ] *noun* **(a)** *(waiting list)* de reserva; **standby ticket** = billete en lista de espera; **standby fare** = tarifa de billete en lista de espera **(b)** *(IMF)* **standby arrangements** = planes de contingencia; **standby credit** = crédito contingente *or* 'stand by' *or* de apoyo

standing [ˈstændɪŋ] **1** *adjective* **standing order** =

domiciliación bancaria; **I pay my subscription by standing order** = pago mi suscripción por domiciliación bancaria *or* a través del banco **2** *noun* **(a) long-standing customer** *or* **customer of long standing** = cliente de toda la vida *or* cliente antiguo **(b)** fama *f or* reputación *f*; **the financial standing of a company** = la reputación financiera de la compañía; **company of good standing** = compañía acreditada

standstill ['stæn(d)stɪl] *noun* paro *m or* paralización *f*; **production is at a standstill** = la producción está paralizada; **the strike brought the factory to a standstill** = la huelga provocó la paralización de la fábrica

staple ['steɪpl] **1** *adjective* **(a) staple commodity** = producto básico *or* de primera necesidad; **staple industry** = industria principal; **staple product** = producto principal **(b)** *(for attaching papers together)* grapa *f*; **he used a pair of scissors to take the staples out of the documents** = empleó unas tijeras para desprender *or* quitar las grapas de los documentos **2** *verb* **to staple papers together** = grapar papeles; **he could not separate the pages, because the documents were stapled together** = no pudo separar las páginas porque los documentos estaban grapados *or* sujetos con grapas

◊ **stapler** ['steɪplə] *noun* grapadora *f*

star [stɑː] *noun* estrella *f*; **four star hotel** = hotel de cuatro estrellas

start [stɑːt] **1** *noun* comienzo *m or* principio *m or* inicio *m*; **cold start** = empezar un negocio a *or* desde cero; **house starts** *US* **housing starts** = número de viviendas que se han empezado a construir en un año **2** *verb* **to start a business from cold** *or* **from scratch** = empezar un negocio desde cero

◊ **starting** ['stɑːtɪŋ] **1** *adjective* inicial; **starting date** = fecha de comienzo; **starting salary** = salario inicial **2** *noun* comienzo *m or* puesta en marcha;

◊ **start-up** ['stɑːtʌp] *noun* inicio *m* (de un negocio); **start-up costs** = costes de puesta en marcha; **start-up financing** = financiación inicial (NOTE: plural is **start-ups**)

state [steɪt] **1** *noun* **(a)** *(country)* estado *m* **(b)** *(government)* estado *or* gobierno *m*; **state enterprise** = empresa estatal; **the bosses of state industries are appointed by the government** = los jefes de las empresas estatales son nombrados por el gobierno; **state ownership** = propiedad estatal **2** *verb* declarar *or* afirmar *or* indicar; **the document states that all revenue has to be declared to the tax office** = el documento indica que todo ingreso tiene que ser declarado al fisco

◊ **state-controlled** ['steɪtkən'trəʊld] *adjective* sujeto, -ta a control estatal; **state-controlled television** = televisión sujeta a control estatal

◊ **state-of-the-art** ['steɪtəvðɪ'ɑːt] *adjective* muy al día *or* novedoso, -da de la técnica más moderna; **state-of-the-art machine** = máquina dotada de la técnica más moderna

◊ **state-owned** ['steɪt'əʊnd] *adjective* estatal *or* de propiedad pública

statement ['steɪtmənt] *noun* **(a)** *(report)* declaración *f or* afirmación *f or* informe *m*; **to make a false statement** = hacer una declaración falsa; **statement of expenses** = relación de gastos **(b)** *(balance)* balance *m*; **financial statement** = balance general *or* estado de cuentas; **the accounts department have prepared a financial statement for the shareholders** = el departamento de contabilidad ha preparado un balance general para los accionistas **(c)** *(from supplier to customer)* **statement of account** = extracto de cuenta; **statement of expenses** = relación de gastos **(d) bank statement** = estado de cuentas; **monthly** *or* **quarterly statement** = estado de cuentas mensual *or* trimestral

static market ['stætɪk 'mɑːkɪt] *noun* *(market which does not increase or decrease)* mercado *m* estático *or* estancado

station ['steɪʃən] *noun* **(a)** *(train)* estación *f*; **the train leaves the Central Station at 14.15** = el tren sale de la estación central a las 14.15; **coach station** *or* **bus station** = estación de autobuses **(b)** TV **station** *or* **radio station** = estudios *or* canal de televisión *or* emisora de radio

stationery ['steɪʃənəri] *noun* objetos *mpl* de escritorio *or* papelería *f*; **continuous stationery** = papel continuo; **office stationery** = papel con membrete de la compañía *or* papel timbrado; **the letter was typed on his office stationery** = la carta estaba escrita a máquina en papel de la compañía; **stationery supplier** = proveedor, -ra de material de oficina *or* papelería

statistics [stə'tɪstɪks] *plural noun* *(study of figures)* estadística *f (figures)* estadísticas *fpl or* cifras *fpl or* números *mpl*; **to examine the sales statistics for the previous six months** = examinar las cifras de ventas del semestre anterior; **government trade statistics show an increase in imports** = las estadísticas oficiales muestran un aumento de las importaciones

◊ **statistical** [stə'tɪstɪkəl] *adjective* estadístico, -ca; **statistical analysis** = análisis estadístico; **statistical information** = información estadística; **statistical discrepancy** = discrepancia estadística

◊ **statistician** [,stætɪ'stɪʃən] *noun* estadístico, -ca

status ['steɪtəs] *noun* **(a)** *(importance or position in society)* status *m or* posición *f or* categoría *f*; **status symbols** = símbolos de posición social; **the chairman's car is a status symbol** = el coche del presidente es un signo externo de su categoría; **loss of status** = pérdida de posición **(b)** *(legal position)* **legal status** = condición *or* personalidad jurídica; *(checking on a customer's credit rating)* **status inquiry** = petición de informes sobre crédito

◊ **status quo** ['steɪtəs'kwəʊ] *noun* *(state of things as they are now)* statu quo *m*; **the contract** does not alter the status quo = el contrato no cambia el statu quo

statute ['stætjuːt] *noun (law made by parliament)* estatuto *m*; **statute book** = código de leyes; **statute of limitations** = ley de prescripción

◊ **statutory** ['stætjʊtəri] *adjective (fixed by law)* estatutario, -ria *or* reglamentario, -ria *or* legal; **there is a statutory period of probation of thirteen weeks** = hay un periodo reglamentario de prueba de trece semanas; **statutory holiday** = vacaciones reglamentarias *or* establecidas por ley; **statutory regulations** = normas estatutorias; **statutory sick pay (SSP)** = prestación por baja laboral

stay [steɪ] **1** *noun* **(a)** *(length of time)* estancia *f or* permanencia *f*; **the tourists were in town only for a short stay** = los turistas estuvieron en la ciudad sólo durante una breve estancia; **short-stay guests** = huéspedes por pocos días **(b)** *(temporary stopping of a legal order)* **stay of execution** = aplazamiento *m* de la ejecución de una sentencia; **the court granted the company a two-week stay of execution** = el tribunal otorgó a la compañía dos semanas de prórroga **2** *verb (to stop at a place)* quedarse *or* alojarse *or* permanecer; **the chairman is staying at the Hotel London** = el presidente se aloja en el Hotel Londres; **profits have stayed below 10% for two years** = los beneficios han permanecido por debajo del 10% durante dos años; **inflation has stayed high in spite of the government's efforts to bring it down** = la inflación sigue siendo alta a pesar de los esfuerzos del gobierno por reducirla

STD = SUBSCRIBER TRUNK DIALLING

steady ['stedi] **1** *adjective* estable *or* constante; **steady increase in profits** = un aumento constante de los beneficios; **the market stayed steady** = el mercado se mantuvo estable; **there is a steady demand for computers** = hay una demanda constante de ordenadores; **he's a steady worker** = es un hombre constante en su trabajo **2** *verb (to become firm or to stop fluctuating)* estabilizarse; **the markets steadied after last week's fluctuations** = los mercados se estabilizaron después de las fluctuaciones de la semana pasada; **prices steadied on the commodity markets** = los precios de los mercados de materias primas se estabilizaron; **the government's figures had a steadying influence on the exchange rate** = las cifras oficiales tuvieron un efecto estabilizador sobre el tipo de cambio

◊ **steadily** ['stedɪli] *adverb* constantemente; **output increased steadily over the last two quarters** = la producción aumentó constantemente durante los dos últimos trimestres; **the company has steadily increased its market share** = la empresa ha experimentado un aumento constante de su cuota de mercado

◊ **steadiness** ['stedɪnəs] *noun (being firm or not fluctuating)* estabilidad *f*; **the steadiness of the markets is due to the government's intervention** = la estabilidad de los mercados se debe a la intervención del gobierno

steal [stiːl] *verb* robar; **the rival company stole our best clients** = la empresa competidora nos robó nuestros mejores clientes; **one of our biggest problems is stealing in the wine department** = uno de nuestros mayores problemas son los robos en la sección de vinos (NOTE: **stealing - stole - has stolen**)

steep [stiːp] *adjective* fuerte *or* vertiginoso, -sa; **a steep increase in interest charges** = un fuerte aumento de los cargos en concepto de interés; **a steep decline in overseas sales** = una caída vertiginosa de las ventas en el extranjero

stencil ['stensl] *noun* plantilla *f or* cliché *m or* estarcido *m* de multicopista

stenographer [ste'nɒgrəfə] *noun (official person who can write in shorthand)* taquígrafo, -fa *or* estenógrafo, -fa

step [step] *noun* **(a)** *(type of action)* medida *f* *(measures)* gestión *f*; **some steps have been taken** = se han hecho gestiones; **the first step taken by the new MD was to analyse all the expenses** = la primera medida tomada por el nuevo director gerente fue analizar todos los gastos; **to take steps to prevent something happening** = tomar medidas para evitar que algo ocurra **(b)** *(movement)* paso *m*; **becoming assistant to the MD is a step up the promotion ladder** = ser nombrado ayudante del director gerente es un paso hacia adelante en la escalera de promoción; **in step with** = a la par que *or* al mismo ritmo; **the pound rose in step with the dollar** = la libra subió a la par con el dólar; **out of step with** = desfasado con respecto a; **the pound was out of step with other European currencies** = la libra estaba desfasada con respecto a las demás monedas europeas; **wages are out of step with the cost of living** = los salarios están desfasados con respecto al coste de la vida

◊ **step up** [step'ʌp] *verb (to increase)* aumentar *or* intensificar; **to step up industrial action** = intensificar la huelga; **the company has stepped up production of the latest models** = la empresa ha aumentado la producción de los últimos modelos (NOTE: **stepping - stepped**)

sterling ['stɜːlɪŋ] *noun (standard currency used in the United Kingdom)* libra *f* esterlina; **to quote prices in sterling** *or* **to quote sterling prices** = cotizar los precios en libras esterlinas; *(official term for the British currency)* **pound sterling** = libra esterlina; **sterling area** = zona de la libra esterlina; **sterling balances** = reservas de libras esterlinas; **sterling crisis** = crisis de la libra

QUOTE it is doubtful that British goods will price themselves back into world markets as long as sterling labour costs continue to rise faster than in competitor countries
Sunday Times

stevedore ['stiːvədɔː] *noun* estibador *m*

steward ['stjʊəd] *noun* **(a)** *(on a plane or ship)* auxiliar de vuelo *m or* camarero *m* **(b)** *(elected union representative for workers)* **shop steward** = delegado, -da *or* enlace *mf or* representante *mf* sindical

◊ **stewardess** [ˌstjʊə'des] *noun (on a plane)* azafata *f* (de avión)

stick [stɪk] *verb* **(a)** *(to glue)* pegar; **to stick a stamp on a letter** = pegar un sello a una carta; **they stuck a poster on the door** = pegaron un cartel en la puerta **(b)** *(to stay still or not to move)* quedarse; **sales have stuck at £2m for the last two years** = las ventas se han quedado fijas en £2 millones durante *or* en los últimos dos años (NOTE: **sticking - stuck**)

◇ **sticker** ['stɪkə] **1** *noun* pegatina *f or* etiqueta *f* adhesiva *or* engomada; **airmail sticker** = etiqueta de correo aéreo **2** *verb* pegar etiquetas; **we had to sticker all the stock** = tuvimos que pegar etiquetas en todas las existencias

stiff [stɪf] *adjective (strong or difficult)* duro, -ra *or* difícil; **stiff competition** = competencia dura; **he had to take a stiff test before he qualified** = tuvo que pasar una prueba difícil para sacar el título *or* conseguir la capacitación

stimulate ['stɪmjʊleɪt] *verb* **(a)** *(to encourage)* estimular; **to stimulate the economy** = estimular la economía; **to stimulate trade with the Middle East** = estimular el comercio con el Oriente Medio **(b)** *(market)* activar

◇ **stimulus** ['stɪmjʊləs] *noun* estímulo *m* (NOTE: plural is **stimuli**)

stipulate ['stɪpjʊleɪt] *verb* estipular; **to stipulate that the contract should run for five years** = estipular que el contrato tenga una validez de cinco años; **to pay the stipulated charges** = pagar los gastos estipulados; **the company failed to pay on the date stipulated in the contract** = la compañía no pagó en la fecha establecida por el contrato; **the contract stipulates that the seller pays the buyer's legal costs** = el contrato estipula que el vendedor pagará los gastos jurídicos del comprador

◇ **stipulation** [ˌstɪpjʊ'leɪʃən] *noun (condition in a contract)* estipulación *f*

stock [stɒk] **1** *adjective* común *or* corriente *or* en existencia; **butter is a stock item for any good grocer** = la mantequilla es un producto que se encuentra en cualquier tienda de alimentación bien surtida; **stock size** = talla *or* número *or* tamaño corriente; **we only carry stock sizes of shoes** = solamente vendemos los números de zapatos más corrientes **2** *noun* **(a)** *(raw materials)* reservas *fpl* de materias primas; **we have large stocks of oil** *or* **coal** = tenemos grandes reservas de petróleo *or* carbón; **the country's stocks of butter** *or* **sugar** = las reservas nacionales de mantequilla *or* azúcar **(b)** *(goods for sale)* existencias *fpl*; **opening stock** = existencias iniciales; **closing stock** = existencias finales; **stock code** = código de un producto; **stock control** = control de existencias; **stock control card** = ficha de almacén *or* de control de existencias; **stock depreciation** = depreciación de las existencias; **stock figures** = inventario de existencias; **stock in hand** = existencias disponibles; **stock level** = nivel de existencias; **we try to keep stock levels low during the summer** = tratamos de mantener bajos los niveles de existencias durante el verano; **stock turn** *or* **stock turnround** *or* **stock turnover** = rotación de existencias; **stock valuation** = valoración de existencias; **to buy a shop with stock at valuation** = comprar una tienda con las existencias según valoración; **to purchase stock at valuation** = comprar existencias según valoración; **building up of stock** = constitución de existencias **(c) in stock** *or* **out of stock** = (i) existencias disponibles *or* agotadas; (ii) número de acciones en propiedad; **to hold 2,000 lines in stock** = tenemos 2.000 productos en almacén; **the item went out of stock just before Christmas but came back into stock in the first week of January** = se agotaron las existencias del producto poco antes de Navidades pero estuvo disponible de nuevo durante la primera semana de enero; **we are out of stock of this item** = no nos quedan más existencias de este producto; **to take stock** = hacer un inventario de existencias (NOTE: the word 'inventory' is used in the USA where British English uses the word 'stock'. So, the British 'stock control' is 'inventory control' in American English) **(d) stocks and shares** = acciones *fpl or* valores *mpl* mobiliarios; **stock certificate** = título *or* certificado de una acción; **debenture stock** = obligaciones *mpl*; **dollar stocks** = acciones en compañías norteamericanas; **government stock** = títulos del Estado; **loan stock** = obligaciones de interés fijo; **convertible loan stock** = valores convertibles en acciones en una fecha futura; *US* **common stock** *or* **ordinary stock** = acciones ordinarias (NOTE: in the UK, the term **stocks** is generally applied to government stocks and debentures, and **shares** to shares of commercial companies. In the USA, shares in corporations are usually called **stocks** while government stocks are called **bonds**. In practice, **shares** and **stocks** are interchangeable terms, and this can lead to some confusion) **3** *verb (to hold goods for sale in a warehouse or store)* tener existencias; **to stock 200 lines** = tener existencias de 200 productos *or* tener 200 productos en almacén

◇ **stockbroker** ['stɒkbrəʊkə] *noun* corredor, -ra *or* agente *mf* de bolsa *or* agente bursátil; **stockbroker's commission** = comisión de corredor de bolsa

◇ **stockbroking** ['stɒkbrəʊkɪŋ] *noun* correduría *f* de bolsa *or* corretaje *m* **a stockbroking firm** = una sociedad de agentes de cambio y bolsa

◇ **stock controller** ['stɒkkən'trəʊlə] *noun* jefe de almacén

Stock Exchange ['stɒk ɪks'tʃeɪn(d)ʒ] *noun* bolsa *f*; **he works on the Stock Exchange** = trabaja en la bolsa; **shares in the company are traded on the Stock Exchange** = las acciones de la compañía se cotizan en la bolsa; **Stock Exchange listing** = derecho a cotizar en la bolsa; **the New York Stock Exchange** = la Bolsa de Nueva York (NOTE: capital letters are used when referring to a particular stock exchange: **the London Stock Exchange**; but **the Stock Exchange** is also generally used to refer to the local stock exchange of whichever country the speaker happens to be in)

stockholder ['stɒkhəʊldə] *noun* accionista *mf or* tenedor de acciones

◇ **stockholding** ['stɒkhəʊldɪŋ] *noun* tenencia *f* de acciones

◇ **stock-in-trade** [ˌstɒkɪn'treɪd] *noun (goods held by a business for sale)* existencias a la venta

◇ **stockist** ['stɒkɪst] *noun* distribuidor, -ra

◇ **stock jobber** ['stɒkdʒɒbə] *noun (formerly)* corredor intermediario en la bolsa *or* agiotista *mf*

◇ **stock jobbing** ['stɒkdʒɒbɪŋ] *noun (formerly)* corretaje *m* intermediario en la bolsa *or* agiotaje *m*

◇ **stocklist** ['stɒklɪst] *noun* lista *f* de existencias *or* inventario *m*

stock market ['stɒk 'mɑːkɪt] *noun* el mercado *or*

la bolsa de valores; **stock market price** *or* **price on the stock market** = cotización en el mercado bursátil; **stock market valuation** = valor bursátil de una compañía

◊ **stockout** ['stɒkaʊt] *noun* artículo sin existencias

◊ **stockpile** ['stɒkpaɪl] **1** *noun* reservas *fpl*; **a stockpile of raw materials** = reserva de materias primas **2** *verb (to buy items and keep them in case of need)* acumular; **to stockpile raw materials** = acumular materias primas

◊ **stockroom** ['stɒkrʊm] *noun (room where stores are kept)* almacén *m or* depósito *m*

◊ **stocktaking** ['stɒkteɪkɪŋ] *noun (at the end of an accounting period)* inventario *m*; **the warehouse is closed for the annual stocktaking** = el almacén está cerrado para hacer el inventario anual; **stocktaking sale** = liquidación de inventario

◊ **stock up** [stɒk'ʌp] *verb* acumular; **they stocked up with computer paper** = acumularon papel de ordenador

> QUOTE US crude oil stocks fell last week by nearly 2.5m barrels
>
> **Financial Times**

> QUOTE the stock rose to over $20 a share, higher than the $18 bid
>
> **Fortune**

> QUOTE the news was favourably received on the Sydney Stock Exchange, where the shares gained 40 cents to A$9.80
>
> **Financial Times**

stop [stɒp] **1** *noun* **(a)** *(end of an action)* parada *f or* alto *m or* interrupción *f*; **work came to a stop when the company could not pay the workers' wages** = el trabajo se interrumpió cuando la empresa no pudo pagar los salarios de los obreros; **the new finance director put a stop to the reps' expense claims** = el nuevo director de finanzas acabó con los gastos de representación **(b)** *(not supplying)* suspensión *f*; **account on stop** = cuenta bloqueada; **to put an account on stop** = bloquear una cuenta; **to put a stop on a cheque** = suspender el pago de un cheque **2** *verb* **(a)** *(put an end)* terminar *or* detener *or* suspender; **the shipment was stopped by customs** = el envío fue detenido por la aduana; **the government has stopped the import of cars** = el gobierno ha suspendido la importación de automóviles **(b)** *(not to do anything anymore)* interrumpir *or* parar *or* cesar *or* dejar; **the workforce stopped work when the company could not pay their wages** = el personal dejó de trabajar *or* cesó cuando la empresa no pudo pagar sus salarios; **the office staff stop work at 5.30** = el personal administrativo termina su trabajo a las 5.30; **we have stopped supplying Smith & Co.** = hemos dejado de suministrar a Smith & Co. **(c)** *(not to supply an account any more on credit)* **to stop an account** = suspender una cuenta; **to stop a cheque** *US* **to stop payment on a check** = suspender el pago de un cheque; **to stop payments** = suspender pagos **(d)** *(to take money out of someone's wages)* **to stop someone's wages** = descontar dinero del salario de alguien; **we stopped £25 from his pay because he was always late** = le descontamos £25 del salario por llegar siempre tarde **(e)** *(to call at)* hacer escala (NOTE: **stopping - stopped**)

◊ **stop over** [stɒp'əʊvə] *verb* hacer parada; **we**

stopped over in Hong Kong on the way to Australia = hicimos parada en Hong Kong en el viaje a Australia

◊ **stopover** ['stɒpəʊvə] *noun* parada *f or* escala *f*; **the ticket allows you two stopovers between London and Tokyo** = el billete permite dos paradas entre Londres y Tokio

◊ **stoppage** ['stɒpɪdʒ] *noun* **(a)** *(act of stopping)* suspensión *f or* paro *m or* cese *m*; **stoppage of deliveries** = suspensión de entregas; **stoppage of payments** = suspensión de pagos; **deliveries will be late because of stoppages on the production line** = las entregas se retrasarán debido a los paros de la cadena de producción **(b)** *(money taken from a worker's wage packet)* deducciones *fpl* del salario *or* retención *f* salarial

> QUOTE the commission noted that in the early 1960s there was an average of 203 stoppages each year arising out of dismissals
>
> **Employment Gazette**

storage ['stɔːrɪdʒ] *noun* **(a)** *(keeping in store or in a warehouse)* almacenaje *m or* depósito *m*; **we put our furniture into storage** = guardamos los muebles en depósito; **storage capacity** = capacidad de almacenaje; **storage company** = empresa de almacenaje; **storage facilities** = instalaciones de almacenaje; **storage unit** = unidad de almacenaje; **cold storage** = almacenaje frigorífico; **to put a plan into cold storage** = aplazar un plan indefinidamente **(b)** *(cost of keeping goods in store)* coste *m* de almacenaje; **storage was 10% of value, so we scrapped the stock** = nos deshicimos de las existencias ya que el coste de almacenaje representaba el 10% de su valor **(c)** *(facility for storing data in a computer)* almacenaje *m*; **disk with a storage capacity of 10Mb** = un disco con una capacidad de almacenaje de 10Mb; **disk storage** = almacenaje en disco; **backup storage** = almacenaje en reserva

◊ **store** [stɔː] **1** *noun* **(a)** *(place where goods are kept)* almacén *m or* depósito *m*; **cold store** = almacén frigorífico **(b)** *(quantity of items or materials kept)* reserva *f*; **I always keep a store of envelopes ready in my desk** = siempre guardo una reserva de sobres disponibles en mi mesa **(c)** *US* tienda *f or* almacén *m* **GB** *(large shop)* tienda importante *or* grandes almacenes; **a furniture store** = una tienda de muebles; **a big clothing store** = unos grandes almacenes de ropa *or* una gran tienda de confecciones; **store card** = tarjeta comercial; **chain store** = tienda que forma parte de una cadena; **department store** = grandes almacenes; **discount store** = tienda de rebajas; **general stores** = tiendas **2** *verb* **(a)** *(to keep in a warehouse)* almacenar; **to store goods for six months** = almacenar mercancías durante seis meses **(b)** *(to keep for future use)* guardar; **we store our pay records on computer** = guardamos nuestra información sobre salarios en el ordenador

◊ **storekeeper** *or* **storeman** ['stɔːkiːpə *or* 'stɔːmən] *noun* almacenero, -ra

◊ **storeroom** ['stɔːrʊm] *noun* almacén *m or* depósito *m*

straight line depreciation ['streɪt 'laɪn dɪpriːʃɪ'eɪʃn] *noun* amortización anual uniforme *or* lineal

COMMENT: depreciation calculated by dividing the cost of an asset, less its residual value, by the number of years it is likely to be used

stratagem [ˈstrætədʒəm] *noun* estratagema *f*

strategy [ˈstrætədʒi] *noun (plan of future action)* estrategia *f*; **business strategy** = estrategia comercial; **company strategy** = estrategia de la compañía; **marketing strategy** = estrategia de comercialización; **financial strategy** = estrategia financiera

◊ **strategic** [strəˈtiːdʒɪk] *adjective* estratégico, -ca; **strategic planning** = planificación estratégica

stream [striːm] *noun* flujo *m or* afluencia *f*; **we had a stream of customers on the first day of the sale** = tuvimos una gran afluencia de clientes el primer día de la liquidación; *(to start production)* **to come on stream** = empezar a producir

◊ **streamer** [ˈstriːmə] *noun (tape storage unit)* streamer *m* (unidad de almacenaje en cintas)

◊ **streamline** [ˈstriːmlaɪn] *verb* racionalizar; **to streamline the accounting system** = racionalizar el sistema de contabilidad; **to streamline distribution services** = racionalizar los servicios de distribución

◊ **streamlined** [ˈstriːmlaɪnd] *adjective (efficient or rapid)* racionalizado, -da *or* eficiente *or* rápido, -da; **streamlined production** = producción racionalizada; **the company introduced a streamlined system of distribution** = la empresa introdujo un sistema rápido de distribución

◊ **streamlining** [ˈstriːmlaɪnɪŋ] *noun* racionalización *f*

street [striːt] *noun* calle *f*; **High Street** = calle principal *or* calle mayor; **the High Street banks** = los bancos comerciales; **street directory** = (i) guía urbana; (ii) callejero *m*

strength [streŋθ] *noun* fuerza *f or* vigor *m*; **the company took advantage of the strength of the demand for home computers** = la empresa aprovechó la fuerte demanda de ordenadores personales; **the strength of the pound increases the possibility of high interest rates** = el vigor de la libra aumenta la posibilidad de mantener los tipos de interés elevados (NOTE: the opposite is **weakness)**

stress [stres] *noun* estrés *m or* tensión *f* **people in positions of responsibility suffer from stress-related illnesses** = personas en puestos de responsabilidad sufren enfermedades producidas por el estrés; **stress management** = medidas para combatir el estrés

◊ **stressful** [ˈstresfʊl] *adjective* estresante *or* tenso, -sa

QUOTE manual and clerical workers are more likely to suffer from stress-related diseases. Causes of stress include the introduction of new technology, job dissatisfaction, fear of job loss, poor working relations with the boss and colleagues, and bad working conditions
Personnel Management

stretch [stretʃ] *verb* extender *or* ampliar; **the investment programme has stretched the company's resources** = el programa de inversiones ha exigido la máxima utilización de los recursos de la compañía; **he is not fully stretched** = su trabajo no le exige un rendimiento *or* esfuerzo al máximo

strict [strɪkt] *adjective* estricto, -ta *or* exacto, -ta *or* riguroso, -sa; **in strict order of seniority** = por riguroso orden de antigüedad

◊ **strictly** [ˈstrɪktli] *adverb* estrictamente *or* exactamente *or* rigurosamente; **the company asks all staff to follow strictly the buying procedures** = la empresa exige al personal que observe rigurosamente los trámites de compra

strike [straɪk] **1** *noun* **(a)** *(stopping of work by the workers)* huelga *f*; **all-out strike** = huelga total; **general strike** = huelga general; **official strike** = huelga oficial; **protest strike** = huelga de protesta; **sit-down strike** = huelga de brazos caídos *f*; **sympathy strike** = huelga de solidaridad; **token strike** = huelga simbólica; **unofficial strike** = huelga ilegal *or* no aprobada por el sindicato; **wildcat strike** = huelga salvaje **(b)** **to take strike action** = declararse en huelga *or* ir a la huelga; **strike call** = convocatoria de huelga *or* llamada a la huelga; **no-strike agreement** *or* **no-strike clause** = acuerdo que prohibe la huelga; **strike fund** = fondo de huelga; **strike pay** = subsidio gremial; **strike ballot** *or* **strike vote** = votación para decidir si se hace huelga; **strike warning** *or* **notice of strike action** = aviso de huelga **(c)** **to come out on strike** *or* **to go on strike** = declararse en huelga *or* ir a la huelga; **the office workers are on strike for higher pay** = el personal administrativo está en huelga para conseguir un aumento salarial; **to call the workforce out on strike** = convocar una huelga; **the union called its members out on strike** = el sindicato llamó a sus afiliados a la huelga **2** *verb* **(a)** ir a la huelga *or* declararse en huelga; **to strike for higher wages** *or* **for shorter working hours** = declararse en huelga para conseguir aumentos salariales *or* una reducción de la jornada laboral; **to strike in protest against bad working conditions** = hacer huelga en protesta por las malas condiciones laborales; **to strike in sympathy with the postal workers** = declararse en huelga en solidaridad con los trabajadores de correos **(b)** *(to come to an agreement)* **to strike a bargain with someone** = llegar a un acuerdo; **a deal was struck at £25 a unit** = acordamos un precio de £25 la unidad (NOTE: **striking - struck)**

◊ **strikebound** [ˈstraɪkbaʊnd] *adjective* paralizado, -da por la huelga; **six ships are strikebound in the docks** = seis barcos están paralizados en el puerto debido a la huelga

◊ **strikebreaker** [ˈstraɪkbreɪkə] *noun* rompehuelgas *mf or* esquirol *m*

◊ **striker** [ˈstraɪkə] *noun* huelguista *mf*

stripper [ˈstrɪpə] *noun* **asset stripper** = persona que compra una compañía para realizar sus activos

◊ **stripping** [ˈstrɪpɪŋ] *noun* **asset stripping** = compra de una compañía para realizar sus activos

strong [strɒŋ] *adjective* fuerte *or* vigoroso, -sa *or* firme; **a strong demand for home computers** = una fuerte demanda de ordenadores personales; **the company needs a strong chairman** = la compañía necesita un presidente firme; **strong currency** = moneda *or* divisa fuerte; **strong pound** = libra fuerte

◊ **strongbox** [ˈstrɒŋbɒks] *noun* caja *f* fuerte

◊ **strongroom** ['strɒŋrʊm] *noun* cámara *f* acorazada

> QUOTE everybody blames the strong dollar for US trade problems
> **Duns Business Month**

> QUOTE in a world of floating exchange rates the dollar is strong because of capital inflows rather than weak because of the nation's trade deficit
> **Duns Business Month**

structure ['strʌktʃə] **1** *noun* estructura *f*; **the paper gives a diagram of the company's organizational structure** = el documento presenta un organigrama de la compañía; **the price structure in the small car market** = la estructura de precios en el mercado de automóviles utilitarios; **the career structure within a corporation** = la estructura profesional dentro de la corporación; **the company is reorganizing its discount structure** = la compañía está modificando la estructura de los descuentos; **capital structure of a company** = estructura de capital de una compañía; **the company's salary structure** = la estructura de salarios de la empresa **2** *verb (to arrange in a certain way)* estucturar; **to structure a meeting** = estructurar una reunión

◊ **structural** ['strʌktʃərəl] *adjective* estructural; **to make structural changes in a company** = hacer cambios estructurales en una compañía; **structural unemployment** = paro estructural

stub [stʌb] *noun* **cheque stub** = matriz *f* de un talonario

studio ['stju:dɪəʊ] *noun* estudio *m* or taller *m*; **design studio** = estudio de diseño

study ['stʌdi] **1** *noun (examining something carefully)* estudio *m*; **the company has asked the consultants to prepare a study of new production techniques** = la empresa ha pedido a los asesores que preparen un estudio de la nuevas técnicas de producción; **he has read the government study on sales opportunities** = ha leído el estudio del gobierno sobre las posibilidades de venta; **to carry out a feasibility study on a project** = llevar a cabo un estudio de viabilidad or factibilidad de un proyecto **2** *verb (to examine carefully)* estudiar; **we are studying the possibility of setting up an office in New York** = estamos estudiando la posibilidad de establecer una sucursal en Nueva York; **the government studied the committee's proposals for two months** = el gobierno estudió las propuestas del comité durante dos meses; **you will need to study the market carefully before deciding on the design of the product** = tendrá que estudiar el mercado cuidadosamente antes de decidir el diseño del producto

stuff [stʌf] *verb* llenar; **we pay casual workers £2 an hour for stuffing envelopes** or **for envelope stuffing** = pagamos a los trabajadores eventuales £2 la hora por llenar sobres

◊ **stuffer** ['stʌfə] *noun US (advertising paper to be put into an envelope for mailing)* folleto *m* publicitario

style [staɪl] *noun* estilo *m (taste)* gusto *m*; **a new style of product** = un nuevo estilo de producto; **old-style management techniques** = técnicas de gestión anticuadas

sub [sʌb] *noun* **(a)** *(wages paid in advance)* sueldo *m* pagado por adelantado **(b)** = SUBSCRIPTION

sub- [sʌb] *prefix* sub-

◊ **sub-agency** ['sʌb'eɪdʒənsi] *noun* subagencia *f*

◊ **sub-agent** ['sʌb'eɪdʒənt] *noun* subagente *mf*

◊ **subcommittee** ['sʌbkəmɪti] *noun* subcomité *m*; **the next item on the agenda is the report of the finance subcommittee** = la cuestión siguiente del orden del día trata sobre el informe del subcomité de finanzas

◊ **subcontract 1** [sʌb'kɒntrækt] *noun* subcontrato *m*; **they have been awarded the subcontract for all the electrical work in the new building** = les han concedido el subcontrato para toda la instalación eléctrica del nuevo edificio; **we will put the electrical work out to subcontract** = solicitaremos ofertas a subcontratistas para la instalación eléctrica **2** [sʌbkən'trækt] *verb* subcontratar [sʌbkən'træktə] **the electrical work has been subcontracted to Smith Ltd** = la instalación eléctrica ha sido subcontratada a Smith Ltd.

◊ **subcontractor** *noun* subcontratista *mf*

◊ **subdivision** ['sʌbdɪvɪʒən] *noun US (piece of land to be used for building)* subdivisión *f*

subject ['sʌbdʒekt] *noun (of a country)* súbdito, -ta de un país

◊ **subject to** ['sʌbdʒɪkt 'tʊ] *adjective* **(a)** *(depending on)* sujeto, -ta a; **the contract is subject to government approval** = el contrato está sujeto a la aprobación del gobierno; **agreement** or **sale subject to contract** = acuerdo sujeto a or venta sujeta a contrato; **offer subject to availability** = oferta según disponibilidad **(b)** **these articles are subject to import tax** = estos artículos están sujetos al impuesto sobre las importaciones

sub judice ['sʌb 'dʒu:dɪsi] *adverb (being considered by a court)* sub judice or en manos de los tribunales; **the papers cannot report the case because it is still sub judice** = los periódicos no pueden informar sobre el asunto porque está todavía sub judice

sublease 1 ['sʌbli:s] *noun* subarriendo *m* **2** [sʌb'li:s] *verb* subarrendar; **they subleased a small office in the centre of town** = subarrendaron una pequeña oficina en el centro de la ciudad

◊ **sublessee** [sʌble'si:] *noun* subarrendatario, -ria

◊ **sublessor** [sʌble'sɔ:] *noun* subarrendador, -ra

◊ **sublet** [sʌb'let] *verb* subarrendar; **we have sublet part of our office to a financial consultancy** = hemos subarrendado una parte de nuestra oficina a una asesoría financiera (NOTE: **subletting - sublet**)

subliminal advertising [sʌb'lɪmɪnəl 'ædvətaɪzɪŋ] *noun* publicidad subliminar

submit [səb'mɪt] *verb* presentar; **to submit a proposal to the committee** = presentar una propuesta al comité; **he submitted a claim to the insurers** = presentó una reclamación a los aseguradores; **the reps are asked to submit their expenses claims once a month** = se ruega a los representantes que presenten las notas de gastos una vez al mes (NOTE: **submitting - submitted**)

subordinate [sə'bɔːdɪnət] **1** *adjective (less important)* subordinado, -da; **subordinate to** = subordinado, -da a **2** *noun (member of staff)* subordinado, -da; **his subordinates find him difficult to work with** = a sus subordinados les resulta difícil trabajar con él

subpoena [səb'piːnə] **1** *noun* citación *f* judicial **2** *verb (to order someone to appear in court)* citar; **the finance director was subpoenaed by the prosecution** = el director de finanzas recibió una citación del fiscal

subscribe [səb'skraɪb] *verb* **(a)** *(magazine)* suscribirse *or* abonarse; **to subscribe to a magazine** = suscribirse a una revista **(b)** *(shares)* **to subscribe for shares** = suscribir acciones

◊ **subscriber** [səb'skraɪbə] *noun* **(a) subscriber to a magazine** *or* **magazine subscriber** = abonado, -da; **the extra issue is sent free to subscribers** = el número extra se envía gratuitamente a todos los abonados **(b) subscriber to a share issue** = suscriptor, -ra de una emisión de acciones **(c) telephone subscriber** = abonado telefónico; **subscriber trunk dialling (STD)** = servicio telefónico automático a larga distancia

◊ **subscription** [səb'skrɪpʃən] *noun* **(a)** *(money paid in advance)* abono *m* or cuota *f*; **did you remember to pay the subscription to the computer magazine?** = ¿te acordaste de pagar la suscripción a la revista de ordenadores?; **he forgot to renew his club subscription** = olvidó renovar su cuota del club; **to take out a subscription to a magazine** = suscribirse a una revista; **to cancel a subscription to a magazine** = darse de baja de una revista; **subscription rates** = tarifas de suscripción **(b)** *(shares)* **subscription to a new share issue** = suscribir una nueva emisión de acciones; **subscription list** = lista de suscriptores de valores; **the subscription lists close at 10.00 on September 24th** = las listas de suscriptores de valores cierran el 24 de septiembre a las 10.00

subsidiary [səb'sɪdjəri] **1** *adjective (less important)* subsidiario, -ria *or* secundario, -ria; **they agreed to most of the conditions in the contract but queried one or two subsidiary items** = estaban de acuerdo con la mayoría de las condiciones del contrato pero plantearon dudas sobre una o dos cuestiones secundarias; **subsidiary company** = compañía filial *or* subsidiaria **2** *noun* filial *f*; **most of the group profit was contributed by the subsidiaries in the Far East** = gran parte de los beneficios del grupo fueron debidos a las contribuciones de las filiales del Extremo Oriente

subsidize ['sʌbsɪdaɪz] *verb (to help by giving money)* subvencionar; **the government has refused to subsidize the car industry** = el gobierno se ha negado a subvencionar a la industria del automóvil; **subsidized accommodation** = vivienda subvencionada

◊ **subsidy** ['sʌbsɪdi] *noun* subsidio *m* or subvención *f*; **the industry exists on government subsidies** = la industria existe gracias a los subsidios del Estado; **the government has increased its subsidy to the car industry** = el gobierno ha aumentado su subsidio a la industria del automóvil; **the subsidy on butter** *or* **the butter subsidy** = la subvención a la mantequilla

subsistence [səb'sɪstəns] *noun* subsistencia *f*; **subsistence allowance** = dietas *fpl*; **to live at subsistence level** = vivir a nivel de subsistencia

substantial [səb'stænʃəl] *adjective (large or important)* sustancial *or* sustancioso, -sa; **she was awarded substantial damages** = recibió una indemnización sustanciosa; **to acquire a substantial interest in a company** = adquirir una participación sustancial en la compañía

substitute ['sʌbstɪtjuːt] **1** *noun* sustituto, -ta *or* suplente *mf* **2** *verb* sustituir

subtenancy [sʌb'tenənsi] *noun (agreement to sublet a property)* subarriendo *m*

◊ **subtenant** [sʌb'tenənt] *noun* subarrendatario, -ria

subtotal ['sʌbtəʊtl] *noun* total parcial *m*

subtract [səb'trækt] *verb (to take away from a total)* deducir *or* restar; **if the profits from the Far Eastern operations are subtracted, you will see that the group has not been profitable in the European market** = si se restan los beneficios de las operaciones en el Extremo Oriente, se dará cuenta que el grupo no ha sido rentable en el mercado europeo

◊ **subtraction** [səb'trækʃn] *noun* sustracción *f or* resta *f*

suburb *noun* barrio *m*

subvention [səb'venʃn] *noun (subsidy)* subvención *f*

succeed [sək'siːd] *verb* **(a)** *(to do well or to be profitable)* tener éxito *or* prosperar; **the company has succeeded best in the overseas markets** = la empresa ha cosechado los mayores éxitos en los mercados extranjeros; **his business has succeeded more than he had expected** = su negocio ha tenido más éxito de lo que esperaba **(b)** *(to do what was planned)* conseguir; **she succeeded in passing her shorthand test** = consiguió superar la prueba de taquigrafía; **they succeeded in putting their rivals out of business** = consiguieron arruinar a sus competidores **(c)** *(to follow someone)* suceder; **Mr Smith was succeeded as chairman by Mr Jones** = el señor Jones sucedió al señor Smith en el cargo de presidente

◊ **success** [sək'ses] *noun* **(a)** *(doing well)* éxito *m*; **the launch of the new model was a great success** = el lanzamiento del nuevo modelo fue un gran éxito; **the company has had great success in the Japanese market** = la empresa ha tenido un gran éxito en el mercado japonés **(b)** *(doing what was intended)* éxito *m or* resultado *m*; **we had no success in trying to sell the lease** = no conseguimos vender el arrendamiento; **he has been looking for a job for six months, but with no success** = ha estado buscando trabajo durante seis meses, pero sin resultado

◊ **successful** [sək'sesfʊl] *adjective (which does well)* con éxito *or* afortunado, -da *or* con resultados positivos; **a successful businessman** = un próspero hombre de negocios; **a successful selling trip to Germany** = un viaje comercial a Alemania con buenos resultados

◊ **successfully** [sək'sesfəli] *adverb* con éxito; **he successfully negotiated a new contract with the unions** = negoció con éxito un nuevo contrato con los sindicatos; **the new model was successfully launched last month** = el nuevo modelo fue lanzado con éxito el mes pasado

successive [sək'sesɪv] *adjective* sucesivo, -va *or* seguido, -da

successor *noun* [sək'sesə] sucesor, -ra; **Mr Smith's successor as chairman will be Mr Jones** = el sucesor del señor Smith en el cargo de presidente será el señor Jones

Sudan [su'da:n] *noun* Sudán *m*

◊ **Sudanese** [sudə'ni:z] *adjective & noun* sudanés, -esa
NOTE: capital: **Khartoum** (= Jartum); currency: **Sudanese pound (LSd)** = libra sudanesa (LSd)

sudden ['sʌdn] *adjective* brusco, -ca *or* repentino, -na

sue [su:] *verb* demandar; **to sue someone for damages** = demandar a alguien por daños y perjuicios; **he is suing the company for $50,000 compensation** = ha presentado una demanda de $50,000 contra la compañía

suffer ['sʌfə] *verb* **(a)** sufrir; **exports have suffered during the last six months** = las exportaciones han sufrido durante los últimos seis meses **(b) to suffer from something** = padecer *or* adolecer; **the company's products suffer from bad design** = los productos de la empresa adolecen de un mal diseño; **the group suffers from bad management** = el grupo se ve perjudicado por una mala gestión *or* administración

---

QUOTE the bank suffered losses to the extent that its capital has been wiped out
South China Morning Post

QUOTE the holding company has seen its earnings suffer from big writedowns in conjunction with its agricultural loan portfolio
Duns Business Month

---

sufficient [sə'fɪʃənt] *adjective* suficiente; **the company has sufficient funds to pay for its expansion programme** = la compañía tiene fondos suficientes para financiar su programa de expansión

suggest [sə'dʒest] *verb* sugerir *or* proponer; **the chairman suggested (that) the next meeting should be held in October** = el presidente sugirió que la próxima reunión se celebrara en octubre; **we suggested Mr Smith for the post of treasurer** = propusimos al señor Smith para el puesto de tesorero

◊ **suggestion** [sə'dʒestʃən] *noun* sugerencia *f or* propuesta *f*; **suggestion box** = buzón de sugerencias

suitable ['su:təbl] *adjective* adecuado, -da *or* apropiado, -da *or* conveniente *or* idóneo, -nea; **Wednesday is the most suitable day for board meetings** = el miércoles es el día más apropiado para las reuniones del consejo de administración; **we had to readvertise the job because there were no suitable candidates** = tuvimos que volver a convocar la plaza porque no se presentó ningún candidato idóneo *or* indicado

suitcase ['su:tkeɪs] *noun* maleta *f*; **the customs officer made him open his three suitcases** = el funcionario de la aduana le hizo abrir sus tres maletas

sum [sʌm] *noun* **(a)** *(of money)* cantidad *f or* suma *f*; **a sum of money was stolen from the personnel office** = robaron dinero de la oficina de personal; **he lost large sums on the Stock Exchange** = perdió grandes cantidades de dinero en la bolsa; **she received the sum of £500 in compensation** = recibió la cantidad de £500 como indemnización; **the sum insured** = la cantidad asegurada; **lump sum** = suma global *or* pago único *or* tanto alzado **(b)** *(total)* suma *f or* total *m*

summary ['sʌməri] *noun* resumen *m or* sumario *m*; **the chairman gave a summary of his discussions with the German trade delegation** = el presidente presentó un resumen de sus negociaciones con la delegación comercial alemana; **the sales department has given a summary of sales in Europe for the first six months** = la sección de ventas ha presentado un resumen de las ventas del primer semestre en Europa

summons ['sʌmənz] *noun* citación *f* judicial *or* emplazamiento *m*; **he threw away the summons and went on holiday to Spain** = tiró la citación y se marchó de vacaciones a España

Sunday ['sʌndeɪ] *noun* domingo *m*; **Sunday opening** *or* **trading** = comercio dominical; **Sunday trading laws** = [ˌsʌndɪ'treɪdɪŋ'lɔ:z] leyes que regulan el comercio dominical

sundry ['sʌndri] **1** *noun (various)* **sundries** = géneros *mpl or* artículos *mpl* diversos **2** *adjective (various)* varios, -as; **sundry items** = géneros *or* artículos diversos

sunrise industries ['sʌnraɪz 'ɪndʌstrɪz] *noun* industrias de alta tecnología *or* industrias del futuro

◊ **sunset industries** ['sʌnset 'ɪndʌstrɪz] *noun* industrias crepusculares

superannuation [su:pərænjʊ'eɪʃn] *noun* jubilación *f*; **superannuation plan** *or* **scheme** = plan de pensiones

superintend [su:pərɪn'tend] *verb* dirigir; **he superintends the company's overseas sales** = dirige las ventas de la empresa en el extranjero

◊ **superintendent** [ˌsu:pərɪn'tendənt] *noun* superintendente *mf or* supervisor, -ra

superior [su:'pɪərɪə] **1** *adjective (of better quality)* superior *or* mejor; **our product is superior to all competing products** = nuestro producto es superior a todos los de la competencia; **their sales are higher because of their superior distribution service** = venden más porque tienen un servicio de distribución mejor **2** *noun (more important person)* jefe, -fa; **each manager is responsible to his superior for accurate reporting of sales** = cada director de sección es reponsable de dar información exacta sobre las ventas a su superior

supermarket ['su:pəmɑ:kɪt] *noun* supermercado *m*; **sales in supermarkets** *or* **supermarket sales account for half the company's turnover** = las ventas en los supermercados representan la mitad del valor de las ventas de la empresa; **supermarket trolley** = carro *or* carrito de la compra (NOTE: the US English for this is **shopping cart**)

superstore ['su:pɔstɔ:] *noun* hipermercado *m*

supertanker ['su:pətæŋkə] *noun* superpetrolero *m*

supervise ['su:pəvaɪz] *verb* supervisar; **the move to the new offices was supervised by the administrative manager** = la mudanza a las nuevas oficinas fue supervisada por el director administrativo; **she supervises six girls in the accounts department** = supervisa a seis chicas en el departamento de contabilidad

◊ **supervision** [su:pə'vɪʒən] *noun* supervisión *f or* vigilancia *f*; **new staff work under supervision for the first three months** = el nuevo personal trabaja bajo supervisión durante los primeros tres meses; **she is very experienced and can be left to work without any supervision** = tiene mucha experiencia y puede trabajar sin supervisión; **the cash was counted under the supervision of the finance manager** = el dinero se contó bajo la supervisión del director de finanzas

◊ **supervisor** ['su:pəvaɪzə] *noun* supervisor, -ra

◊ **supervisory** [su:pə'vaɪzəri] *adjective* de supervisión *or* de control; **supervisory staff** = personal de supervisión; **he works in a supervisory capacity** = trabaja en calidad de supervisor

supplement ['sʌplɪmənt] **1** *noun* suplemento *m*; **the company gives him a supplement to his pension** = la empresa le concede un suplemento a su pensión **2** *verb (to add)* añadir; **we will supplement the warehouse staff with six part-timers during the Christmas rush** = añadiremos seis trabajadores eventuales al personal de almacén durante la campaña de Navidad

◊ **supplementary** [ˌsʌplɪ'mentəri] *adjective (in addition to)* suplementario, -ria; **supplementary benefit** = subsidio complementario

supply [sə'plaɪ] **1** *noun* **(a)** *(providing something which is needed)* oferta *f or* suministro *m or* abastecimiento *m*; **money supply** = oferta de dinero *or* monetaria; **supply price** = precio de oferta; **water supply** = abastecimiento de aguas; **supply and demand** = oferta y demanda; **the law of supply and demand** = la ley de la oferta y la demanda **(b) in short supply** = escaso, -sa; **spare parts are in short supply because of the strike** = los repuestos son escasos debido a la huelga **(c)** *(stock)* suministro *m or* reserva *f or* provisión *f*; **the factory is running short of supplies of coal** = a la fábrica se le están acabando

las reservas de carbón; **supplies of coal have been reduced** = los suministros de carbón han sido reducidos; **office supplies** = material *or* artículos de oficina **2** *verb (to provide something which is needed)* suministrar *or* abastecer *or* proveer *or* alimentar *or* proporcionar *or* aprovisionar; **to supply a factory with spare parts** = suministrar repuestos a una fábrica; **the finance department supplied the committee with the figures** = el departamento de finanzas suministró las cifras al comité; **details of staff addresses and phone numbers can be supplied by the personnel staff** = el departamento de personal puede proporcionar información detallada sobre las direcciones y los teléfonos de los trabajadores

◊ **supply side economics** [sə'plaɪˌsaɪdi:kə'nɒmɪks] *noun* economía *f* de oferta

◊ **supplier** [sə'plaɪə] *noun* suministrador, -ra *or* proveedor, -ra *or* abastecedor, -ra; **office equipment supplier** = suministrador de equipos de oficina; **they are major suppliers of spare parts to the car industry** = son abastecedores importantes de repuestos para la industria del automóvil

support [sə'pɔ:t] **1** *noun* **(a)** *(giving money to help)* apoyo *m or* ayuda *f or* sustento *m*; **the government has provided support to the electronics industry** = el gobierno ha prestado ayuda a la industria electrónica; **we have no financial support from the banks** = no recibimos ningún apoyo financiero de los bancos **(b)** *(agreement or encouragement)* apoyo *m*; **the chairman has the support of the committee** = el presidente tiene el apoyo del comité; *(in the EU)* **support price** = precio de subvención; *(with computers)* **support service** = servicio de asistencia técnica **2** *verb* **(a)** *(to give money to help)* ayudar *or* apoyar; **the central bank intervened to support the dollar** = el banco central intervino para respaldar el dólar; **the government is supporting the electronics industry to the tune of $2m per annum** = el gobierno ayuda a la industria electrónica a razón de $2 millones al año; **we hope the banks will support us during the expansion period** = esperamos que los bancos nos ayuden durante el periodo de expansión **(b)** *(to encourage or to agree with)* apoyar *or* soportar; **she hopes the other members of the committee will support her** = espera que los demás miembros del comité la apoyen; **the market will not support another price increase** = el mercado no soportará otra subida de precios

surcharge ['sɜ:tʃɑ:dʒ] *noun* sobretasa *f or* sobrecarga *f or* recargo *m*; **import surcharge** = sobretasa a la importación *or* recargo

surety ['ʃʊərəti] *noun* **(a)** *(person who guarantees)* garante *mf or* fiador, -ra; **to stand surety for someone** = actuar como fiador de alguien *or* salir garante de alguien **(b)** *(sum)* fianza *f or* garantía *f* **(c)** *(valuables deposited as security for a loan)* títulos *mpl* depositados en garantía de un préstamo

surface ['sɜ:fɪs] *noun* superficie *f*; **to send a package by surface mail** = enviar un paquete por correo terrestre *or* marítimo; **surface transport** = transporte terrestre *or* marítimo

Surinam [sʊərɪ'næm] *noun* Surinam

◊ **Surinamese** [suərɪnə'miːz] *adjective & noun*
surinamés, -esa
NOTE: capital: **Paramaribo**; currency: **Surinam guilder** = florín

surpass [sə'pɑːs] *verb* rebasar

surplus ['sɜːpləs] *noun* excedente *m or* exceso *m or* superávit *m*; **surplus government equipment** = equipos excedentes del Estado; **surplus butter is on sale in the shops** = los excedentes de mantequilla están a la venta en las tiendas; **we are holding a sale of surplus stock** = tenemos una liquidación de existencias sobrantes; **governments are trying to find ways of reducing the agricultural surpluses in the European Union** = los gobiernos están buscando la manera de eliminar los excedentes agrícolas en la Unión Europea; **we are trying to let surplus capacity in the warehouse** = estamos tratando de alquilar el espacio sobrante del almacén; **a budget surplus** = un superávit presupuestario; **these items are surplus to our requirements** = estos artículos exceden a nuestras necesidades; **to absorb a surplus** = absorber un superávit

QUOTE Both imports and exports reached record levels in the latest year. This generated a $371 million trade surplus in June, the seventh consecutive monthly surplus and close to market expectations
Dominion (Wellington, New Zealand)

surrender [sə'rendə] **1** *noun* rescate *m*; **surrender value** = valor de rescate **2** *verb* **to surrender a policy** = rescatar una póliza

surtax ['sɜːtæks] *noun* recargo *m* del impuesto sobre la renta *or* impuesto adicional

survey 1 ['sɜːveɪ] *noun* **(a)** *(report on a problem)* informe *m or* encuesta *f*; **the government has published a survey of population trends** = el gobierno ha publicado un informe sobre las tendencias demográficas; **we have asked the sales department to produce a survey of competing products** = hemos pedido al departamento de ventas que haga un informe de los productos competidores **(b)** *(professional examination)* inspección *f*; **we have asked for a survey of the house before buying it** = hemos pedido una inspección de la casa antes de comprarla; **the insurance company is carrying out a survey of the damage** = la compañía de seguros está llevando a cabo una inspección de los daños; **damage survey** = inspección de daños *or* de avería **(c)** *(measuring exactly)* medición *f*; **quantity survey** = cálculo de las cantidades de materiales y mano de obra necesarias para las obras de construcción **2** [sə'veɪ] *verb* examinar *or* inspeccionar

◊ **surveyor** [sə'veɪə] *noun* inspector, -ra de obra; **quantity surveyor** = aparejador, -ra

suspect 1 ['sʌspekt] *adjective* sospechoso, -sa **2** ['sʌspekt] *noun* sospechoso, -sa **3** [sə'spekt] *verb* sospechar

suspend [səs'pend] *verb* **(a)** *(to stop for a time)* suspender; **we have suspended payments while we are waiting for news from our agent** = hemos suspendido pagos a la espera de noticias de nuestro agente; **sailings have been suspended until the weather gets better** = se han suspendido las salidas en barco hasta que el tiempo mejore; **work on the**

construction project has been suspended = las obras del proyecto de construcción han sido suspendidas; **the management decided to suspend negotiations** = la dirección decidió suspender las negociaciones **(b)** *(to stop someone working for a time)* suspender a alguien; **he was suspended on full pay while the police investigations were going on** = le suspendieron de empleo y sueldo durante la investigación policial

◊ **suspension** [səs'penʃən] *noun* suspensión *f*; **suspension of payments** = suspensión de pagos; **suspension of deliveries** = suspensión de entregas

suspicious [sə'spɪʃəs] *adjective* sospechoso, -sa

swap [swɒp] **1** *noun* intercambio *m* **2** *verb* cambiar *or* intercambiar; **he swapped his old car for a new motorcycle** = cambió su coche viejo por una moto nueva; **they swapped jobs** = intercambiaron trabajos (NOTE: **swapping - swapped**)

swatch [swɒtʃ] *noun* muestra *f* pequeña; **colour swatch** = muestra de color (que deberá tener el producto acabado)

sweated labour ['swetɪd 'leɪbə] *noun* **(a)** *(people)* mano de obra muy mal pagada; **of course the firm makes a profit - it employs sweated labour** = claro que la empresa es rentable - paga muy mal a los obreros *or* utiliza mano de obra mal pagada **(b)** *(hard work)* trabajo muy mal pagado y en malas condiciones

◊ **sweatshop** ['swetʃɒp] *noun* fábrica que explota a su personal

Sweden [swiːdən] *noun* Suecia *f*

◊ **Swede** [swiːd] *noun* sueco, -ca

◊ **Swedish** ['swiːdɪʃ] *adjective* sueco, -ca
NOTE: capital: **Stockholm** (= Estocolmo); currency: **Swedish krona (SKr)** = corona sueca (SKr)

swipe [swaɪp] *verb* pasar la tarjeta de crédito por la máquina lectora

Swiss franc ['swɪs 'fræŋk] *noun* franco suizo

switch [swɪtʃ] *verb* *(to change from one thing to another)* cambiar *or* trasladar *or* transferir; **to switch funds from one investment to another** = trasladar fondos de una inversión a otra; **the job was switched from our British factory to the States** = el trabajo fue transferido de nuestra fábrica en Gran Bretaña a los EE UU

◊ **switchboard** ['swɪtʃbɔːd] *noun* centralita *f* de teléfonos; **switchboard operator** = telefonista *mf*

◊ **switch on** *verb* conectar *or* encender; *(engine)* poner en marcha

◊ **switch over to** [swɪtʃ'əʊvətə] *verb* cambiarse a *or* pasarse a; **we have switched over to a French supplier** = nos hemos pasado *or* cambiado a un suministrador francés; **the factory has switched over to gas for heating** = la fábrica ha cambiado la calefacción y ahora tiene gas

Switzerland ['swɪtsələnd] *noun* Suiza *f*

◊ **Swiss** [swɪs] *adjective & noun* suizo, -za
NOTE: capital: **Bern** (= Berna); currency: **Swiss franc (SwF)** = franco suizo (FS)

swop [swɒp] = SWAP

symbol ['sɪmbəl] *noun* símbolo *m*; **they use a bear as their advertising symbol** = tienen un oso como símbolo publicitario

sympathy ['sɪmpəθi] *noun* compasión *f*; **the manager had no sympathy for his secretary who complained of being overworked** = el director no quiso escuchar a su secretaria que se quejaba de tener demasiado trabajo; **sympathy strike** = huelga de solidaridad; **to strike in sympathy** = declarar una huelga de solidaridad; **the postal workers went on strike and the telephone engineers came out in sympathy** = los trabajadores de correos se declararon en huelga y los ingenieros de teléfonos declararon una huelga de solidaridad

◊ **sympathetic** [,sɪmpə'θetɪk] *adjective (person)* compasivo, -a *or* comprensivo, -va; **sympathetic strike** = huelga de solidaridad

syndicate 1 ['sɪndɪkət] *noun* sindicato *m or* consorcio *m*; **a German finance syndicate** = un consorcio financiero alemán; **arbitrage syndicate** = sindicato de arbitraje; **underwriting syndicate** = consorcio asegurador *or* emisor **2** ['sɪndɪkeɪt] *verb* publicar un trabajo en varios periódicos o revistas

> QUOTE over the past few weeks, companies raising new loans from international banks have been forced to pay more, and an unusually high number of attempts to syndicate loans among banks has failed
> **Financial Times**

◊ **syndicated** ['sɪndɪkeɪtɪd] *adjective* publicado, -da en varios periódicos o revistas; **he writes a syndicated column on personal finance** = escribe una columna sobre finanzas personales que se publica en varios periódicos

synergy ['sɪnədʒi] *noun* sinergia *f*

synthetic [sɪn'θetɪk] *adjective* sintético, -ca; **synthetic fibres** *or* **synthetic materials** = fibras sintéticas *or* materiales sintéticos

Syria ['sɪriə] *noun* Siria *f*

◊ **Syrian** ['sɪriən] *adjective & noun* sirio, -ria
NOTE: capital: **Damascus** (= Damasco); currency: **Syrian pound (LS)** = libra siria (LS)

system ['sɪstəm] *noun* **(a)** *(arrangement or organization)* sistema *m*; **our accounting system has worked well in spite of the large increase in orders** = nuestro sistema de contabilidad ha funcionado bien a pesar del gran aumento de pedidos; **decimal system** = sistema decimal; **filing system** = sistema de clasificación *or* archivo; **to operate a quota system** = utilizar un sistema de cupo; **we arrange our distribution using a quota system - each agent is allowed only a certain number of units** = organizamos nuestra distribución según un sistema de cupo - cada representante recibe solamente un número determinado de unidades; **tax system** = sistema fiscal **(b) computer system** = *(hardware)* sistema informático *or* equipo informático; *(software)* sistema operativo; **operating system** = sistema operativo; **real-time system** = sistema de tiempo real; **systems analysis** = análisis de sistemas; **systems analyst** = analista de sistemas

◊ **systematic** [,sɪstə'mætɪk] *adjective* sistemático, -ca; **he ordered a systematic report on the distribution service** = pidió un informe sistemático sobre el servicio de distribución

Tt

tab [tæb] *noun* = TABULATOR

table ['teɪbl] **1** *noun* **(a)** *(piece of furniture)* mesa *f;* **typing table** = mesa de la máquina de escribir **(b)** *(list of figures or facts)* cuadro *m or* tabla *f;* **table of contents** = índice de materias; **actuarial tables** = tabla de mortalidad **2** *verb* **(a)** *(put items before a meeting)* presentar; **the report of the finance committee was tabled** = se presentó el informe del comité de finanzas; **to table a motion** = presentar una moción **(b) to table a proposal** = *US* aplazar el examen de una moción; *GB* aplazar un proyecto

tabloid ['tæblɔɪd] *noun* **the tabloids** *or* **the tabloid press** = la prensa amarilla

tabular ['tæbjʊlə] *adjective* tabular; **in tabular form** = en forma de tabla

◊ **tabulate** ['tæbjʊleɪt] *verb* tabular *or* disponer datos en forma de tabla

◊ **tabulation** [tæbjʊ'leɪʃən] *noun* tabulación *f*

◊ **tabulator** ['tæbjʊleɪtə] *noun* tabulador, -ra

tachograph ['tækəgrɑːf] *noun* tacógrafo *m*

tacit ['tæsɪt] *adjective* tácito, -ta; **tacit approval** = aprobación tácita; **tacit agreement to a proposal** = acuerdo tácito a una propuesta

tactic ['tæktɪk] *noun* táctica *f;* **his usual tactic is to buy shares in a company, then mount a takeover bid, and sell out at a profit** = su táctica habitual es comprar acciones de una compañía, organizar una oferta de adquisición, y luego venderlas con beneficios; **the directors planned their tactics before going into the meeting with the union representatives** = los directores decidieron su táctica antes de ir a la reunión con los representantes del sindicato

tael [taɪl] *noun* medida de peso del oro usada en el Extremo Oriente (equivalente a 1,20 onzas)

tag [tæg] *noun* etiqueta *f;* **price tag** = etiqueta de precio; **name tag** = *(on branded item for sale)* etiqueta de marca

tailor ['teɪlə] *verb* adaptar; **press releases tailored to the reader interests of different newspapers** = comunicado de prensa adaptado a los intereses de los lectores de distintos periódicos

take [teɪk] **1** *noun (money received in a shop)* ingresos *mpl* de una tienda **2** *verb* **(a)** *(to receive or to get)* ingresar en caja *or* recibir *or* cobrar; **the shop takes £2,000 a week** = la tienda ingresa en caja £2.000 a la semana; **he takes home £250 a week** = su salario neto es de £250 a la semana **(b)** *(to do a certain action)* **to take action** = hacer algo *or* tomar medidas; **you must take immediate action if you want to stop thefts** = tienes que hacer algo inmediatamente si quieres evitar los robos; **to take a call** = recibir una llamada; **to take the chair** = presidir (una reunión); **in the absence of the chairman his deputy took the chair** = en ausencia del presidente presidió su adjunto; **to take dictation** = escribir al dictado; **the secretary was taking

dictation from the managing director** = la secretaria tomaba el dictado del director gerente; **to take stock** = hacer un inventario; **to take stock of a situation** = evaluar una situación **(c)** *(to need time or quantity)* tardar *or* llevar tiempo *or* hacer falta; **it took the factory six weeks** *or* **the factory took six weeks to clear the backlog of orders** = la fábrica tardó seis semanas en despachar los pedidos atrasados; **it will take her all morning to do my letters** = le llevará toda la mañana escribir mis cartas; **it took six men and a crane to get the computer into the office** = hicieron falta seis hombres y una grúa para instalar el ordenador en la oficina (NOTE: **taking - took - has taken**)

◊ **take away** ['teɪk ə'weɪ] *verb* **(a)** *(to remove one figure from a total)* sustraer *or* quitar *or* deducir; **if you take away the home sales, the total turnover is down** = si deducimos las ventas nacionales, el volumen de negocios total ha bajado **(b)** *(to remove)* retirar *or* llevarse; **we had to take the work away from the supplier because the quality was so bad** = la calidad del proveedor era tan mala que tuvimos que retirarle los pedidos *or* encargos; **the police took away piles of documents from the office** = la policía se llevó montones de documentos de la oficina; **sales of food to take away** = venta de comidas para llevar

◊ **takeaway** ['teɪkəweɪ] *noun* tienda *f* de comidas para llevar; **a takeaway meal** = una comida para llevar; **a Chinese takeaway** = (i) una tienda de comida china para llevar; (ii) una comida china para llevar

◊ **take back** ['teɪk 'bæk] *verb* **(a)** *(to return with something)* devolver; **when the watch went wrong, he took it back to the shop** = cuando el reloj se estropeó, lo devolvió a la tienda; **if you do not like the colour, you can take it back to change it** = si el color no te gusta, puedes devolverlo y cambiarlo **(b) to take back dismissed workers** = volver a emplear a obreros despedidos

◊ **take-home pay** ['teɪkhəʊm 'peɪ] *noun* salario *m* neto *or* líquido

◊ **take into** ['teɪk 'ɪntʊ] *verb* incorporar; **to take items into stock** *or* **into the warehouse** = incorporar artículos a las existencias *or* al almacén

◊ **take off** ['teɪk 'ɒf] *verb* **(a)** *(to remove or deduct)* rebajar *or* quitar; **he took £25 off the price** = rebajó el precio en £25 **(b)** *(to start to rise fast)* animarse; *(plane)* despegar; **sales took off after the TV commercials** = las ventas se animaron después de la publicidad en televisión **(c)** *(decide not to work)* **she took the day off** = se tomó el día libre

◊ **take on** ['teɪk 'ɒn] *verb* **(a)** *(to agree to do something)* asumir *or* aceptar; **she took on the job of preparing the VAT returns** = asumió la tarea de preparar las declaraciones del IVA; **he has taken on a lot of extra work** = ha aceptado mucho trabajo extra **(b)** *(to agree to employ someone)* emplear; **to take on more staff** = emplear más personal

◊ **take out** ['teɪk 'aʊt] *verb* **(a)** *(to remove)* sacar *or* extraer **(b) to take out a patent for an invention** = obtener una patente de invención; **to take out insurance against theft = hacerse un seguro contra robo

◊ **take over** ['teɪk 'əʊvə] *verb* **(a)** *(from someone else)* sustituir *or* hacerse cargo de *or* tomar posesión; **Miss Black took over from Mr Jones on May 1st** = la señorita Black sustituyó al señor Jones el 1 de mayo; **the new chairman takes over on July 1st** = el nuevo presidente toma posesión el 1 de julio; **the take-over period is always difficult** = el periodo de relevo es siempre difícil **(b) to take over a company** = adquirir una compañía; **the buyer takes over the company's liabilities** = el comprador asume el pasivo de la compañía; **the company was taken over by a large multinational** = la compañía fue adquirida por una gran multinacional

◊ **takeover** ['teɪkəʊvə] *noun (buying a business)* adquisición *f or* absorción *f*; **takeover bid** = oferta pública de adquisición (OPA); **to make a takeover bid for a company** = hacer una oferta de adquisición de una compañía; **to withdraw a takeover bid** = retirar una oferta de adquisición; **the company rejected the takeover bid** = la compañía rechazó la oferta de adquisición; **the disclosure of the takeover bid raised share prices** = la revelación de la oferta de adquisición hizo subir el precio de las acciones; **contested takeover** = oferta de adquisición disputada *or* rebatida; **takeover target** = objeto de una OPA

◊ **taker** ['teɪkə] *noun (person who wants to buy)* comprador, -ra; **there were no takers for the new shares** = no hubo compradores para las nuevas acciones

◊ **take up** ['teɪk 'ʌp] *verb* **(a) to take up an option** = suscribir una opción; **half the rights issue was not taken up by the shareholders** = la mitad de la emisión no fue suscrita por los accionistas; **take up rate** = porcentaje de suscripción **(b) our overheads have taken up all our profits** = los gastos generales han absorbido todos los beneficios

◊ **takings** ['teɪkɪŋz] *plural noun (money received in a shop or a business)* ingresos *mpl* de un negocio; **the week's takings were stolen from the cash desk** = robaron de la caja los ingresos de la semana

> QUOTE many takeovers result in the new managers/owners rationalizing the capital of the company through better asset management
>
> **Duns Business Month**

> QUOTE capital gains are not taxed, but money taken out in profits and dividends is taxed
>
> **Toronto Star**

tally ['tælɪ] **1** *noun (note of things counted or recorded)* cuenta *f or* registro *m*; **to keep a tally of stock movements** *or* **of expenses** = llevar la cuenta del movimiento de existencias *or* de gastos; **tally clerk** = persona que lleva la cuenta; **tally sheet** = hoja en que se lleva la cuenta **2** *verb (to agree or to be the same)* cuadrar *or* concordar; **the invoices do not tally** = las facturas no concuerdan; **the accounts department tried to make the figures tally** = el departamento de contabilidad intentó hacer cuadrar las cifras

tangible ['tæn(d)ʒəbl] *adjective* tangible *or* concreto, -ta; **tangible assets** *or* **property** = activo tangible; **tangible fixed assets** = bienes tangibles *or* fijos

tanker ['tæŋkə] *noun (ship)* buque *m* cisterna *or* petrolero *m (railway)* vagón *m* cisterna

Tanzania [tænzə'niːə] *noun* Tanzania *f*

◊ **Tanzanian** [tænzə'niːən] *adjective & noun* tanzano, -na *or* tanzaniano, -na
NOTE: capital: **Dodoma**; currency: **Tanzanian shilling (TS)** = chelín tanzano (TS)

tap [tæp] *noun GB (government stocks issued direct to the Bank of England)* emisión *f* de títulos del Estado adquiridos directamente por el Banco de Inglaterra

◊ **tap stock** ['tæp 'stɒk] *noun* emisión de títulos del Estado

tape [teɪp] *noun* cinta *f*; **magnetic tape** *or* **mag tape** = cinta magnética; **computer tape** = cinta de ordenador; **measuring tape** *or* **tape measure** = cinta métrica

tare [teə] *noun (allowance for weight)* tara *f*; **to allow for tare** = tener en cuenta la tara

target ['tɑːgɪt] **1** *noun* objetivo *m or* meta *f*; **monetary targets** = objetivos monetarios; **production targets** = objetivo de producción; **sales targets** = objetivo de ventas; *(company)* **takeover target** *or* **target company** = objeto de una OPA; **target market** = mercado previsto; **to set targets** = fijar objetivos; **to meet a target** = cumplir un objetivo *or* alcanzar una meta; **to miss a target** = no cumplir un objetivo *or* no alcanzar una meta; **they missed the target figure of £2m turnover** = no alcanzaron la cifra propuesta de £2 millones de ventas **2** *verb (to aim to sell)* tener como objetivo; **to target a market** = perseguir un mercado determinado

> QUOTE in a normal leveraged buyout the acquirer raises money by borrowing against the assets of the target company
>
> **Fortune**

> QUOTE the minister is persuading the oil, gas, electricity and coal industries to target their advertising towards energy efficiency
>
> **Times**

> QUOTE direct marketing is all about targeting the audience and getting a response
>
> **PR Week**

tariff ['tærɪf] *noun* **(a)** *(tax)* customs tariffs = aranceles *mpl* aduaneros; **tariff barriers** = barreras arancelarias; **to impose tariff barriers on** *or* **to lift tariff barriers from a product** = imponer *or* levantar barreras arancelarias a un producto; **differential tariffs** = tarifas diferenciales; **General Agreement on Tariffs and Trade (GATT)** = Acuerdo General sobre Aranceles Aduaneros y Comercio (NOTE: replaced by **World Trade Organization (WTO)** in 1995) **(b)** *(price)* tarifa *f or* precio *m*

task [tɑːsk] *noun* **(a)** *(work which has to be done)* tarea *f or* faena *f*; **to list task processes** = hacer una lista de las diferentes partes pendientes de un trabajo **(b) task force** = equipo *m* de trabajo especial

taste [teɪst] *noun* gusto *m*

tax [tæks] **1** *noun* **(a)** impuesto *m*; **airport tax** = tasas de aeropuerto; **capital gains tax (CGT)** = impuesto sobre las plusvalías; **capital transfer tax** = impuesto sobre las transferencias de capital; **corporation tax** = impuesto de sociedades; **advance corporation tax (ACT)** = pago anticipado sobre el impuesto de sociedades; **council tax** = contribución municipal; **excess profits tax** = impuesto sobre beneficios extraordinarios; **income tax** = impuesto sobre la renta; **land tax** = contribución territorial rústica; **mainstream corporation tax (MCT)** = impuesto de sociedades corriente; **road tax** = impuesto de circulación; **sales tax** = impuesto sobre la venta; **turnover tax** = impuesto sobre el volumen de negocios; **value added tax (VAT)** = impuesto sobre el valor añadido (IVA) **(b) ad valorem tax** = impuesto ad valorem; **back tax** = impuesto atrasado; **basic tax** = impuesto básico; **direct tax** = impuesto directo; **hidden tax** = impuesto encubierto; **indirect tax** = impuesto indirecto; **regressive tax** = impuesto regresivo; **to levy a tax** *or* **to impose a tax** = establecer un impuesto; **the government has imposed a 15% tax on petrol** = el gobierno ha establecido un impuesto del 15% sobre la gasolina; **to lift a tax** = suprimir un impuesto; **the tax on company profits has been lifted** = el impuesto sobre los beneficios de las sociedades ha sido suprimido; **exclusive of tax** = impuesto no incluido; **tax abatement** = reducción de un tipo impositivo; **tax adjustments** = ajuste impositivo; **border tax adjustment** = ajuste fiscal en frontera; **tax adviser** *or* **tax consultant** = asesor fiscal; **tax allowance** *or* **allowances against tax** = desgravación tributaria; **tax avoidance** = elusión de impuestos; **in the top tax bracket** = que paga la tasa máxima del impuesto sobre la renta; **tax code** = código impositivo *or* fiscal; **tax collector** = recaudador de impuestos; **tax concession** = desgravación impositiva *or* privilegio tributario; **tax credit** = crédito por impuestos pagados; **tax deductions** = retención fiscal; *US* desgravación impositiva por gastos; **tax deducted at source** = impuesto retenido en el origen; **tax disk** = placa del impuesto de circulación para los vehículos rodados; **tax evasion** = evasión fiscal; **tax exemption** = exención fiscal; *US* desgravación impositiva; **tax form** = formulario de declaración de la renta; **tax haven** = paraíso fiscal; **tax holiday** = periodo de exención fiscal concedido a una nueva empresa *or* franquicia fiscal; **tax inspector** *or* **inspector of taxes** = inspector de Hacienda; **tax loophole** = laguna fiscal; **tax loss** = pérdidaa a efectos fiscales; **tax rate** = tipo impositivo; **tax rebate** = desgravación fiscal; **tax relief** = desgravación fiscal; **tax return** *or* **tax declaration** = declaración de renta; **tax shelter** = exención fiscal para ciertos planes financieros; **tax system** = sistema tributario; **tax year** = año fiscal *or* ejercicio fiscal **2** *verb* gravar con un impuesto *or* sujetar a impuestos; **to tax businesses at 50%** = gravar las empresas con un impuesto del 50%; **income is taxed at 25%** = la renta tiene un impuesto del 25%; **luxury items are heavily taxed** = los artículos de lujo están sujetos a un impuesto elevado

◊ **taxable** ['tæksəbl] *adjective* sujeto, -ta a impuesto *or* imponible; **taxable earnings** = líquido imponible; **taxable items** = artículos sujetos a impuesto; **taxable income** = renta imponible

◊ **taxation** [tæk'seɪʃən] *noun* imposición *f or* impuestos *mpl*; **direct taxation** = impuestos directos; **graduated taxation** *or* **progressive taxation** = imposición progresiva *or* proporcional; **indirect taxation** = impuestos indirectos; **the government raises more money by indirect taxation than by direct** = el gobierno obtiene más ingresos de los impuestos indirectos que de los directos; **double taxation** = doble imposición; **double taxation agreement** = acuerdo de doble imposición; **regressive taxation** = imposición regresiva

◊ **tax-deductible** [tæksdɪ'dʌktəbl] *adjective* desgravable; **these expenses are not tax-deductible** = estos gastos no son desgravables

◊ **tax-exempt** [tæksɪg'zem(p)t] *adjective* exento, -ta de impuestos

◊ **tax-free** [tæks'friː] *adjective* libre de impuestos

◊ **taxpayer** ['tækspeɪə] *noun* contribuyente *mf*; **basic taxpayer** *or* **taxpayer at the basic rate** = contribuyente que paga el impuesto básico; **corporate taxpayer** = sociedad sujeta al pago de impuestos

◊ **tax point** ['tæks 'pɔɪnt] *noun (date when VAT becomes due)* punto *or* fecha de vencimiento del IVA

taxi ['tæksi] *noun* taxi *m*; **he took a taxi to the airport** = cogió un taxi para el aeropuerto; **taxi fares are very high in New York** = las tarifas de los taxis son muy elevadas en Nueva York

T-Bill ['tiː'bɪl] *US (informal)* = TREASURY BILL

teach [tiːtʃ] *verb* enseñar

team [tiːm] *noun* equipo *m*; **management team** = equipo directivo; **sales team** = equipo de ventas

◊ **teamster** ['tiːmstə] *noun US (truck driver)* camionero, -ra

◊ **teamwork** ['tiːmwɜːk] *noun* trabajo *m* en equipo

tear sheet ['teə 'ʃiːt] *noun* separata de un anuncio

teaser ['tiːzə] *noun* anuncio que provoca la curiosidad del cliente

technical ['teknɪkəl] *adjective* **(a)** *(machine)* técnico, -ca; **the document gives all the technical details on the new computer** = el documento explica todos los detalles técnicos del nuevo ordenador **(b)** *(change in a share price)* **technical correction** = ajuste técnico

technician [tek'nɪʃən] *noun* técnico *m*;

computer technician = técnico informático; **laboratory technician** = técnico de laboratorio

◊ **technique** [tek'ni:k] *noun* técnica *f or* método *m*; **the company has developed a new technique for processing steel** = la empresa ha inventado un método nuevo para la elaboración del acero; **he has a special technique for answering complaints from customers** = tiene una técnica especial para atender a las quejas de los clientes; **management techniques** = técnicas de dirección de empresas; **marketing techniques** = técnicas de comercialización

technology [tek'nɒlədʒi] *noun* tecnología *f or* técnica *f*; **information technology** = tecnología informática; **the introduction of new technology** = la introducción de nueva tecnología

◊ **technological** [teknə'lɒdʒɪkəl] *adjective* tecnológico, -ca *or* técnico, -ca; **the technological revolution** = la revolución tecnológica

tel = TELEPHONE tel. *or* telef.

telebanking [telɪ'bæŋkɪŋ] *noun* banca telefónica

telecommunications [telɪkəmju:nɪ'keɪʃənz] *plural noun* telecomunicaciones *fpl*

teleconference *or* **teleconferencing** [telɪ'kɒnfərəns] *noun* teleconferencia *f*

telegram ['telɪgræm] *noun* telegrama *m*; **to send an international telegram** = enviar un telegrama internacional

◊ **telegraph** ['telɪgrɑ:f] **1** *noun* telégrafo *m*; **to send a message by telegraph** = enviar un mensaje por telégrafo; **telegraph office** = oficina de telégrafos **2** *verb* enviar por telegrama; **to telegraph an order** = telegrafiar un pedido *or* hacer un pedido por telégrafo

◊ **telegraphic** [telɪ'græfɪk] *adjective* telegráfico, -ca; **telegraphic address** = dirección telegráfica; **telegraphic transfer** = [telɪgræfɪk'trɑ:nsfə] transferencia telegráfica

◊ **telemarketing** ['telɪmɑ:kɪtɪŋ] *noun* venta por teléfono *or* televenta

◊ **telemessage** ['telɪmesɪdʒ] *noun GB* mensaje *m* telegráfico

telephone ['telɪfəʊn] **1** *noun* teléfono *m*; **we had a new telephone system installed last week** = nos instalaron una nueva red telefónica la semana pasada; **to be on the telephone** = estar hablando por teléfono; **the managing director is on the telephone to Hong Kong** = el director gerente está hablando por teléfono con Hong Kong; **she has been on the telephone all day** = ha estado hablando por teléfono todo el día; **by telephone** = por teléfono; **to place an order by telephone** = hacer un pedido por teléfono; **to reserve a room by telephone** = reservar una habitación por teléfono; **cellular telephone** = teléfono celular *or* móvil; **cordless telephone** = teléfono inalámbrico; **house telephone** *or* **internal telephone** = teléfono interno; **telephone book** *or* **telephone directory** = guía telefónica; **he looked up the number of the company in the telephone book** = buscó el número de la compañía en la guía telefónica; **telephone call** = llamada telefónica; **to make a telephone call** = hacer una llamada telefónica; **to answer the telephone** *or* **to take a**

telephone call = contestar el teléfono *or* recibir una llamada; **telephone exchange** = centralita telefónica; **telephone number** = número de teléfono; **can you give me your telephone number?** = ¿puede darme su número de teléfono?; **telephone operator** = telefonista *mf*; **telephone orders** = pedidos realizados por teléfono; **since we mailed the catalogue we have received a large number of telephone orders** = después de enviar el catálogo hemos recibido un gran número de pedidos por teléfono; **telephone selling** = venta por teléfono *or* televenta; **telephone subscriber** = abonado telefónico; **telephone switchboard** = centralita telefónica **2** *verb* **to telephone a place** *or* **a person** = telefonear a *or* llamar a (Nueva York *or* Juan); **his secretary telephoned to say he would be late** = su secretaria llamó por teléfono para decir que llegaría tarde; **he telephoned the order through to the warehouse** = hizo el pedido al almacén por teléfono; **to telephone about something** = telefonear acerca de *or* sobre algo; **he telephoned about the January invoice** = llamó para hablar de la factura de enero; **to telephone for something** = pedir algo por teléfono; **he telephoned for a taxi** = llamó para pedir un taxi

◊ **telephonist** [tə'lefənɪst] *noun* telefonista *mf*

◊ **teleprinter** ['telɪprɪntə] *noun* teleimpresora *f or* teletipo *m*; **teleprinter operator** = teleimpresor, -ora

◊ **telesales** ['telɪseɪlz] *plural noun (sales made by telephone)* ventas *fpl* por teléfono *or* televenta *f*

◊ **teletype (TTY)** ['telɪ'taɪp] *noun* teleimpresor *m*

◊ **teletypewriter** ['telɪ'taɪpraɪtə] *noun US* = TELEPRINTER

telex ['teleks] **1** *noun* **(a)** *(system)* télex *m*; **to send information by telex** = enviar información por télex; **the order came by telex** = el pedido llegó por télex; **telex line** = línea de télex; **we cannot communicate with our Nigerian office because of the breakdown of the telex lines** = no podemos comunicarnos con nuestra oficina de Nigeria porque las líneas de télex están averiadas; **telex operator** = operador, -ra de télex; **telex subscriber** = abonado de télex **(b)** **a telex** = (i) una máquina télex *or* un télex; (ii) un mensaje por télex *or* un télex; **he sent a telex to his head office** = envió un télex a su oficina central; **we received his telex this morning** = recibimos su télex esta mañana **2** *verb* enviar por télex; **can you telex the Canadian office before they open?** = ¿puedes enviar un télex a la sucursal canadiense antes de que abran?; **he telexed the details of the contract to New York** = envió los detalles del contrato a Nueva York por télex

tell [tel] *verb* decir; **we had to tell him the truth** = tuvimos que decirle la verdad

teller ['telə] *noun* cajero, -ra de un banco

tem [tem] *see* PRO TEM

temp [temp] **1** *noun* secretario, -ria *f* eventual; **we have had two temps working in the office this week to clear the backlog of letters** = tenemos a dos secretarias eventuales trabajando en la oficina esta semana para despachar las cartas atrasadas; **temp agency** = agencia de trabajo temporal **2** *verb (to work as a temp)* hacer trabajo eventual *or* trabajar como empleado, -da eventual

◇ **temping** ['tempɪŋ] *noun* trabajar como empleado, -da eventual; **she can earn more money temping than from a full-time job** = puede ganar más en un trabajo eventual que en un trabajo a tiempo completo

temporary ['temprəri] *adjective* temporal *or* eventual *or* interino, -na *or* transitorio, -ria; **he was granted a temporary export licence** = recibió una licencia temporal de exportación; **to take temporary measures** = tomar medidas provisionales; **he has a temporary post with a construction company** = tiene un empleo eventual en una empresa de construcción; **he has a temporary job as a filing clerk** *or* **he has a job as a temporary filing clerk** = tiene trabajo eventual como archivero; **temporary employment** = empleo eventual *or* ocupación temporal; **temporary incapacity** = incapacidad transitoria; **temporary staff** = personal eventual

◇ **temporarily** ['temprərəli] *adverb* temporalmente

QUOTE regional analysis shows that the incidence of temporary jobs was slightly higher in areas where the rate of employment was above average
Employment Gazette

tenancy ['tenənsi] *noun* **(a)** *(agreement)* (acuerdo de) arrendamiento *m* **(b)** *(period)* (periodo de) arrendamiento

◇ **tenant** ['tenənt] *noun* inquilino, -na *or* arrendatario, -ria *or* habitante; **the tenant is liable for repairs** = el inquilino es responsable de las reparaciones; **sitting tenant** = inquilino, -na en posesión

tend [tend] *verb* tender *or* tener tendencia a; **he tends to appoint young girls to his staff** = tiene tendencia a emplear chicas jóvenes

◇ **tendency** ['tendənsi] *noun* tendencia *f or* propensión *f*; **to have a tendency towards** = tender a; **the market showed an upward tendency** = el mercado mostró una tendencia al alza; **there has been a downward tendency in the market for several days** = ha habido una tendencia a la baja en el mercado durante varios días; **the market showed a tendency to stagnate** = el mercado mostró una tendencia al estancamiento

tender ['tendə] **1** *noun* **(a)** *(offer to work)* oferta *f or* concurso *m* público *or* licitación *f*; **a successful tender** *or* **an unsuccessful tender** = oferta aceptada *or* oferta no aceptada; **to put a project out to tender** *or* **to ask for** *or* **to invite tenders for a project** = sacar un proyecto a contrata *or* a licitación *or* a concurso; **to put in a tender** *or* **to submit a tender** = presentar una oferta; **to sell shares by tender** = subastar acciones invitando ofertas por escrito; **sealed tenders** = ofertas cerradas **(b)** *(money)* **legal tender** = moneda de curso legal **2** *verb* **(a)** *(offer to do something for a price)* hacer una oferta; **to tender for a contract** = licitar para un contrato; **to tender for the construction of a hospital** = presentar una oferta para la construcción de un hospital **(b) to tender one's resignation** = presentar la dimisión **(c)** *(to offer money)* ofrecer en pago; **please tender the correct fare** = sírvase pagar el precio exacto

◇ **tenderer** ['tendərə] *noun* postor *m or* licitador *m*; **the company was the successful tenderer for the project** = la empresa obtuvo la asignación del proyecto

◇ **tendering** ['tendrɪŋ] *noun* oferta *f or* licitación *f*; **to be successful, you must follow the tendering procedure as laid out in the documents** = para tener éxito hay que seguir el procedimiento de licitación que se explica en los documentos

tentative ['tentətɪv] *adjective* provisional *or* en principio; **they reached a tentative agreement over the proposal** = llegaron a un acuerdo provisional sobre la propuesta; **we suggested Wednesday May 10th as a tentative date for the next meeting** = sugerimos el miércoles 10 de mayo como fecha provisional para la próxima reunión

◇ **tentatively** ['tentətɪvli] *adverb* provisionalmente; **we tentatively suggested Wednesday as the date for our next meeting** = sugerimos el miércoles provisionalmente como fecha para nuestra próxima reunión

tenure ['tenjə] *noun* **(a)** *(right to hold property or position)* tenencia *f or* posesión *f or* ocupación *f* de un cargo; **security of tenure** = derecho a conservar un puesto de trabajo *or* una vivienda alquilada **(b)** *(time when a position is held)* mandato *m*; **during his tenure of the office of chairman** = durante su mandato como presidente

term [tɜ:m] *noun* **(a)** *(period of time when something is legally valid)* vigencia *f or* plazo *m or* periodo *m or* duración *f*; **the term of a lease** = el plazo de un arrendamiento; **the term of the loan is fifteen years** = el plazo de amortización del préstamo es de quince años; **to have a loan for a term of fifteen years** = obtener un préstamo por un plazo de quince años; **during his term of office as chairman** = durante su mandato como presidente; **term deposit** = depósito a plazo; **term assurance** *or* **term insurance** = seguro temporal; **he took out a ten-year term insurance** = firmó un seguro temporal de diez años; **term loan** = préstamo a plazo fijo; **term shares** = depósito a plazo fijo (en una sociedad de crédito hipotecario) **(b)** **short-term** = corto plazo; **long-term** = largo plazo; **medium-term** = plazo medio **(c)** *(conditions or duties)* **terms** = condiciones *fpl or* términos *mpl*; **he refused to agree to some of the terms of the contract** = se negó a aceptar algunas de las condiciones del contrato; **by** *or* **under the terms of the contract, the company is responsible for all damage to the property** = según los términos del contrato, la compañía es responsable de todos los daños causados a la propiedad; **to negotiate for better terms** = negociar para obtener condiciones más favorables; **terms of payment** *or* **payment terms** = condiciones de pago; **terms of reference** = mandato *m*; **terms of sale** = condiciones de venta; **cash terms** = pago al contado; **'terms: cash with order'** = condiciones: el pago se hará efectivo al hacer el pedido; **easy terms** = facilidades de pago; **the shop is let on very easy terms** = la tienda se alquila con una renta baja; **to pay for something on easy terms** = pagar algo con facilidades de crédito; **on favourable terms** = en condiciones favorables; **the shop is let on very favourable terms** = la tienda se alquila en condiciones muy favorables; **trade terms** = descuento para comerciantes del sector **(d)** *(part of a legal or university year)* trimestre *m or* semestre *m* **(e) terms of employment** = condiciones de servicio

QUOTE companies have been improving communications, often as part of deals to cut down demarcation and to give everybody the same terms of employment

Economist

QUOTE the Federal Reserve Board has eased interest rates in the past year, but they are still at historically high levels in real terms

Sunday Times

terminal ['tɜ:mɪnl] **1** *noun* **(a) computer terminal** = terminal *m* de ordenador; **computer system consisting of a microprocessor and six terminals** = sistema de ordenador compuesto de un microprocesador y seis terminales **(b) air terminal** = terminal *f* aérea; **airport terminal** *or* **terminal building** = terminal de aeropuerto; **container terminal** = terminal de contenedores; **ocean terminal** = terminal marítima **2** *adjective (at the end)* terminal; **terminal bonus** = bonificación recibida al concluir un seguro

terminate ['tɜ:mɪneɪt] *verb* terminar *or* poner término a; **to terminate an agreement** = poner término a un acuerdo; **his employment was terminated** = su empleo se terminó; **the offer terminates on July 31st** = la oferta termina el 31 de julio; **the flight from Paris terminates in New York** = el vuelo de París termina en Nueva York

◊ **terminable** ['tɜ:mɪnəbl] *adjective* terminable

◊ **termination** [tɜ:mɪ'neɪʃən] *noun* **(a)** *(bringing to an end)* terminación *f or* expiración *f*; **termination clause** = cláusula resolutoria **(b)** *US (leaving a job)* dimisión *f or* despido *m*

terminus ['tɜ:mɪnəs] *noun* estación *f* terminal

territory ['terɪtri] *noun (area visited by a salesman)* territorio *m or* zona *f*; **a rep's territory** = zona de un representante; **his territory covers all the north of the country** = su zona incluye todo el norte del país

◊ **territorial waters** [terɪ'tɔ:rɪəl 'wɔ:təz] *noun* aguas territoriales *or* jurisdiccionales; **outside territorial waters** = fuera de las aguas territoriales

tertiary ['tɜ:ʃəri] *adjective* **tertiary industry** = industria terciaria *or* industria de los servicios; **tertiary sector** = sector terciario *or* sector de los servicios

test [test] **1** *noun* **(a)** *(examination)* examen *m or* ensayo *m or* prueba *f*; **test certificate** = certificado de aptitud *or* prueba; **blind test** = prueba a ciegas; **driving test** = examen para obtener el carnet de conducir; **feasibility test** = prueba de viabilidad *or* de factibilidad; **market test** = prueba de mercado **(b)** *(legal case)* **test case** = pleito cuya sentencia sentará precedente **2** *verb* probar *or* tantear *or* someter a prueba; **to test a computer system** = probar un sistema de ordenador; **to test the market for a product** = someter un producto a una prueba de mercado

◊ **test-drive** ['testdraɪv] *verb* **to test-drive a car** = someter un coche a una prueba de carretera

◊ **testing** ['testɪŋ] *noun* prueba *f*; **during the testing of the system several defects were corrected** = durante la prueba del sistema se rectificaron algunos defectos

◊ **test-market** ['test'mɑ:kɪt] *verb* **to test-market a product** = someter un producto a una prueba de mercado; **we are test-marketing the toothpaste in Scotland** = estamos sometiendo la pasta dentífrica a una prueba de mercado en Escocia

testament ['testəmənt] *noun* testamento *m*; **last will and testament** = última voluntad y testamento

◊ **testamentary** [testə'mentəri] *adjective* testamentario, -ria; **testamentary disposition** = disposición testamentaria

testate ['testeɪt] *adjective (having made a will)* testado, -da; **did he die testate?** = ¿dejó testamento? *or* ¿había hecho testamento?; *see also* INTESTATE

◊ **testator** [te'steɪtə] *noun (man who has made a will)* testador

◊ **testatrix** [te'steɪtrɪks] *noun (woman who has made a will)* testadora

testimonial [testɪ'məʊnjəl] *noun* certificado *m or* carta *f* de recomendación; **to write someone a testimonial** = escribir una carta de recomendación para alguien; **unsolicited testimonial** = recomendación no solicitada *or* testimonio espontáneo *or* no solicitado

text [tekst] *noun* texto *m*; **he wrote notes at the side of the text of the agreement** = escribió notas al margen del texto del acuerdo; **text processing** = procesamiento de textos

Thailand ['taɪlænd] *noun* Tailandia *f*

◊ **Thai** [taɪ] *adjective & noun* tailandés, -esa
NOTE: capital: **Bangkok;** currency: **Thai baht (B)** = baht tailandés (B)

thank [θæŋk] *verb* agradecer; **the committee thanked the retiring chairman for his work** = el comité agradeció al presidente saliente la labor realizada; **thank you for your letter of June 25th** = les agradecemos su carta del 25 de junio

◊ **thanks** [θæŋks] *plural noun* gracias *fpl*; **many thanks for your letter of June 25th** = agradecemos su carta del 25 de junio; **speech of thanks** = palabras de agradecimiento; **vote of thanks** = voto de gracias; **the meeting passed a vote of thanks to the organizing committee for their work in setting up the international conference** = la reunión adoptó un voto de gracias al comité organizador por su labor en la organización de la conferencia internacional

◊ **thanks to** ['θæŋks tə] *adverb (because of)* gracias a; **the company was able to continue trading thanks to a loan from the bank** = la compañía pudo continuar gracias a un préstamo del banco; **it was no thanks to the bank that we avoided making a loss** = no fue gracias al banco que evitamos tener pérdidas

theft [θeft] *noun* robo *m*; **we have brought in security guards to protect the store against theft** = hemos empleado guardias de seguridad para proteger la tienda contra los robos; **they are trying to cut their losses by theft** = están intentando reducir sus pérdidas por robo; **to take out insurance against theft** = hacerse un seguro contra robo

theory ['θɪəri] *noun* teoría *f*; **in theory the plan should work** = en teoría el plan debería funcionar

think tank ['θɪŋk 'tæŋk] *noun* grupo *m* de expertos

third [θɜːd] *noun* tercio *m or* tercera parte *f*; **to sell everything at one third off** = vender todos los artículos con un descuento de una tercera parte; **the company has two thirds of the total market** = la empresa tiene dos tercios del mercado total

◊ **third party** ['θɜːd 'pɑːti] *noun* tercero *m*; **third party insurance** *or* **third party policy** = seguro contra terceros; **the case is in the hands of a third party** = el asunto está en manos de un tercero

◊ **third quarter** ['θɜːd 'kwɔːtə] *noun (July to September)* tercer trimestre *m*

◊ **Third World** ['θɜːd 'wɜːld] *noun* Tercer Mundo *m*; **we sell tractors into the Third World** *or* **to Third World countries** = vendemos tractores al Tercer Mundo *or* a países del Tercer Mundo

three-part ['θriːpɑːt] *adjective* en tres partes; **three-part document** = tríptico *m*; **three-part invoices** = facturas por triplicado *or* facturas con original y dos copias; **three-part stationery** = papel con original y dos copias

threshold ['θreʃ(h)əʊld] *noun (limit or point at which something changes)* umbral *m*; **threshold agreement** = convenio de nivel crítico *or* acuerdo de ajuste salarial sobre el coste de la vida; *(in the EU)* **threshold price** = precio umbral *or* precio mínimo al que pueden venderse en la CE los productos agrícolas importados; **pay threshold** = nivel de inflación a partir del cual se aplica una subida salarial; **tax threshold** = nivel de ingresos en el que la tasa de impuestos cambia; **the government has raised the minimum tax threshold from £6,000 to £6,500** = el gobierno ha subido el nivel mínimo de la renta sujeta a impuestos de £6.000 a £6.500

thrift [θrɪft] *noun* **(a)** *(saving money)* ahorro *m* **(b)** *US (private local bank)* caja *f* de ahorros local

◊ **thrifty** ['θrɪfti] *adjective* ahorrador, -ra *or* ahorrativo, -va *or* frugal

```
QUOTE the thrift, which had grown from
$4.7 million in assets in 1980 to 1.5
billion this year, has ended in
liquidation
                                    Barrons
```

thrive [θraɪv] *verb (to grow well or to be profitable)* prosperar; **a thriving economy** = una economía próspera; **thriving black market in car radios** = un próspero mercado negro de radios para automóviles; **the company is thriving in spite of the recession** = la empresa prospera a pesar de la recesión

through [θruː] *preposition US* **the conference runs from 12 through** *or* **thru 16 June** = la conferencia *or* el congreso se celebra del 12 al 16 de junio

◊ **throughput** ['θruːpʊt] *noun* producción *f* por unidad de tiempo *or* rendimiento *m*; **we hope to increase our throughput by putting in two new machines** = esperamos aumentar nuestro rendimiento mediante la instalación de dos nuevas máquinas; **the invoice department has a throughput of 6,000 invoices a day** = el departamento de facturación tramita 6.000 facturas al día

throw out ['θrəʊ 'aʊt] *verb* **(a)** *(to reject or to refuse to accept)* rechazar; **the proposal was thrown out by the planning committee** = el comité

de planificación rechazó la propuesta; **the board threw out the draft contract submitted by the union** = el consejo de administración rechazó el proyecto de contrato propuesto por el sindicato **(b)** *(to get rid of something which is not wanted)* echar *or* deshacerse de *or* tirar; **we threw out the old telephones and installed a computerized system** = tiramos los teléfonos viejos e instalamos un sistema informatizado; **the AGM threw out the old board of directors** = la junta general anual expulsó al antiguo consejo de administración (NOTE: **throwing - threw - has thrown**)

thru [θruː] *US* = THROUGH

tick [tɪk] **1** *noun* **(a)** *(informal)* crédito *m*; **all the furniture in the house is bought on tick** = todos los muebles de la casa se compran a crédito **(b)** *(mark on paper to show approval)* señal *f or* marca *f*; **put a tick in the box marked 'R'** = ponga una señal en el espacio indicado con 'R' *or* marque la casilla indicada con una 'R' (NOTE: US English for this is **check) 2** *verb* **(a)** *(to mark to show that something is correct)* marcar; **tick the box marked 'R' if you require a receipt** = si necesita un recibo marque el espacio indicado con 'R' **(b)** **business is just ticking over** = el negocio va tirando simplemente

◊ **ticker** ['tɪkə] *noun US* teletipo *m* de cotizaciones de bolsa

ticket ['tɪkɪt] *noun* **(a)** *(which allows you to do something)* billete *m or* entrada *f*; **entrance ticket** *or* **admission ticket** = entrada *f*; **theatre ticket** = entrada de teatro **(b)** *(for travel)* billete; **train ticket** *or* **bus ticket** *or* **plane ticket** = billete de tren *or* de autobús *or* de avión; **season ticket** = billete de abono; **single ticket** *or US* **one-way ticket** = billete de ida; **return ticket** *or US* **round-trip ticket** = billete de ida y vuelta **(c)** **ticket agency** = agencia de venta de localidades de teatro; **ticket counter** = taquilla *or* ventanilla; **ticket machine** = máquina expendedora de billetes **(d)** *(paper which shows something)* billete *or* etiqueta *f*; **baggage ticket** = billete de consigna; **price ticket** = etiqueta de precio

tie [taɪ] *verb* atar; **he tied the parcel with thick string** = ató el paquete con cuerda gruesa; **she tied two labels on to the parcel** = ató dos etiquetas al paquete (NOTE: **tying - tied**)

◊ **tie-on label** ['taɪɒn 'leɪbl] *noun* etiqueta *f* colgante

◊ **tie up** ['taɪ 'ʌp] *verb* **(a)** *(fasten tightly)* atar *or* amarrar; **the parcel is tied up with string** = el paquete está sujeto con un cordel *or* una cuerda; **the ship was tied up to the quay** = el barco estaba amarrado en el muelle; **he is rather tied up at the moment** = está bastante ocupado en este momento **(b)** *(to invest money)* inmovilizar; **he has £100,000 tied up in long-dated gilts** = tiene £100.000 inmovilizadas en títulos del Estado a largo plazo; **the company has £250,000 tied up in stock which no one wants to buy** = la empresa tiene £250.000 inmovilizadas en existencias que nadie quiere comprar

◊ **tie-up** ['taɪʌp] *noun (connection)* enlace *m or* conexión *f or* vinculación *f*; **the company has a tie-up with a German distributor** = la empresa está vinculada a un distribuidor alemán (NOTE: plural is **tie-ups**)

tight [taɪt] *adjective* estirado, -da *or* apretado, -da; **the manager has a very tight schedule today - he cannot fit in any more appointments** = el director tiene un horario muy apretado hoy, no puede aceptar más citas; **expenses are kept under tight control** = los gastos están sujetos a un control riguroso; **tight money** = dinero escaso; **tight money policy** = política de dinero escaso

◊ **-tight** [taɪt] *suffix* **the computer is packed in a watertight case** = el ordenador está embalado en una caja hermética; **send the films in an airtight container** = envíen las películas en una caja hermética

◊ **tighten** ['taɪtn] *verb* apretar *or* reforzar; **the accounts department is tightening its control over departmental budgets** = el departamento de contabilidad está reforzando su control sobre los presupuestos departamentales; **to tighten one's belt** = apretarse el cinturón

◊ **tighten up on** ['taɪtn 'ʌp ɒn] *verb* intensificar el control; **the government is tightening up on tax evasion** = el gobierno está intensificando el control de la evasión de impuestos; **we must tighten up on the reps' expenses** = tenemos que intensificar el control de los gastos de los representantes

till [tɪl] *noun* cajón *m or* caja *f*; **cash till** = caja registradora; **there was not much money in the till at the end of the day** = no había mucho dinero en la caja al final del día

time [taɪm] *noun* **(a)** *(period when something takes place)* tiempo *m or* vez *f*; **computer time** = tiempo de funcionamiento *or* utilización de un ordenador (pagado por horas); **real time** = tiempo real; **time and motion study** = estudio de desplazamientos y tiempos; **time and motion expert** = experto en desplazamientos y tiempos **(b)** *(hour of the day)* hora *f*; **the time of arrival** *or* **the arrival time is indicated on the screen** = la hora de llegada está indicada en la pantalla; **departure times are delayed by up to fifteen minutes because of the volume of traffic** = el horario de salida puede llevar incluso quince minutos de retraso debido al volumen de tráfico; **on time** = a tiempo; **the plane was on time** = el avión llegó a tiempo; **you will have to hurry if you want to get to the meeting on time** *or* **if you want to be on time for the meeting** = tendrás

que darte prisa si quieres llegar a tiempo a la reunión; **opening time** *or* **closing time** = hora de apertura *or* hora de cierre **(c)** *(system of hours)* hora *f or* horario *m*; **Greenwich Mean Time (GMT)** = hora media de Greenwich; **Summer Time** *or* **Daylight Saving Time** = hora de verano; **Standard Time** = hora normal; **local time** = hora local; **she gets there at 4 pm local time** = llega allí a las 4 de la tarde, hora local **(d)** *(hours worked)* **he is paid time and a half on Sundays** = cobra paga y media *or* la mitad más los domingos; **full-time** = a tiempo completo *or* de jornada completa; **overtime** = horas extras *or* extraordinarias; **part-time** = a tiempo parcial *or* de media jornada **(e)** *(period before something happens)* plazo *m*; **time deposit** = depósito a plazo; **delivery time** = plazo de entrega; **lead time** = plazo de espera; **time limit** = plazo *or* término; **to keep within the time limits** *or* **within the time schedule** = cumplir el plazo estipulado

◊ **time-card** *or* US **time-clock card** ['taɪmkɑːd *or* 'taɪm'klɒk 'kɑːd] *noun* tarjeta *f* de control de entrada

◊ **time-keeping** ['taɪmkiːpɪŋ] *noun* puntualidad *f*; **he was warned for bad time-keeping** = recibió una advertencia por falta de puntualidad

◊ **time rate** ['taɪm 'reɪt] *noun* tarifa *f* horaria *or* por horas

◊ **time saving** ['taɪm 'seɪvɪŋ] **1** *adjective* que ahorra tiempo; **a time-saving device** = aparato que ahorra tiempo **2** *noun* ahorro *m* de tiempo; **the management is keen on time saving** = la dirección está muy interesada en ahorrar tiempo

◊ **time scale** ['taɪm 'skeɪl] *noun* programa *m or* calendario *m*; **our time scale is that all work should be completed by the end of August** = según nuestro programa, todo el trabajo debe terminarse antes de finales de agosto; **he is working to a strict time scale** = tiene que ceñirse a un calendario muy exigente

◊ **time share** ['taɪm 'ʃeə] *noun* multipropiedad *f or* copropiedad *f*

◊ **time-sharing** ['taɪmʃeərɪŋ] *noun* **(a)** = TIME SHARE **(b)** *(sharing a computer system)* utilización *f* colectiva (del ordenador)

◊ **time sheet** ['taɪm 'ʃiːt] *noun* hoja *f* de asistencia *or* registro *m* de horas trabajadas

◊ **timetable** ['taɪmteɪbl] **1** *noun* **(a)** *(trains or planes or buses)* horario *m*; **according to the timetable, there should be a train to London at 10.22** = según el horario debería haber un tren para Londres a las 10.22; **the bus company has brought out its winter timetable** = la compañía de autobuses ha sacado su horario de invierno **(b)** *(list of appointments or events)* horario *m or* programa *m*; **the manager has a very full timetable, so I doubt if he will be able to see you today** = el director tiene un programa muy apretado y dudo que pueda recibirle hoy; **conference timetable** = programa de un congreso **2** *verb (make a list of times)* preparar un horario *or* un programa

◊ **time work** ['taɪm 'wɜːk] *noun* trabajo *m* pagado por horas trabajadas

◊ **timing** ['taɪmɪŋ] *noun* cronometraje *m or* medida *f* del tiempo *or* fecha *f*; **the timing of the conference is very convenient, as it comes just before my annual holiday** = la fecha del congreso me va muy bien, dado que es inmediatamente antes de mis vacaciones anuales; **his arrival ten minutes after the meeting finished was very bad timing** = su llegada diez minutos después de que acabara la reunión fue muy inoportuna

tip [tɪp] **1** *noun* **(a)** *(money)* propina *f*; **I gave the taxi driver a 10 cent tip** = le di una propina de 10 centavos al taxista; **the staff are not allowed to accept tips** = el personal no está autorizado a aceptar propinas **(b)** *(advice)* aviso *m or* información *f* confidencial; **a stock market tip** = una información confidencial acerca de la bolsa; **he gave me a tip about a share which was likely to rise because of a takeover bid** = me dio información sobre acciones de una compañía que tenían posibilidades de subir debido a una oferta de adquisición; **tip sheet** = periódico que da consejos sobre la compra y venta de acciones **2** *verb* **(a)** *(to give money)* dar una propina; **he tipped the receptionist £5** = le dio £5 de propina al *or* a la recepcionista **(b)** *(to give advice)* dar un consejo *or* pronosticar; **two shares were tipped in the business section of the paper** = en la sección de negocios del periódico se pronosticaba una subida del precio de las acciones de dos compañías; **he is tipped to become the next chairman** = se perfila como el próximo presidente (NOTE: **tipping - tipped**)

TIR = TRANSPORTS INTERNATIONAUX ROUTIERS

title ['taɪtl] *noun* **(a)** *(right to own a property)* título *m or* derecho *m*; **she has no title to the property** = no tiene derecho a la propiedad; **he has a good title to the property** = tiene justo derecho a la propiedad; **title deeds** = escritura *or* título de propiedad **(b)** *(name given to a person in a certain job)* cargo *m*; **he has the title 'Chief Executive'** = tiene el cargo de 'Director General' **(c)** *(name of a book or film)* título *m*

Togo ['təɡəʊ] *noun* Togo *m*

◊ **Togolese** [təʊɡə'liːz] *adjective & noun* togolés, -esa
NOTE: capital: **Lomé**; currency: **CFA franc (CFAF)** = franco CFA (FCFA)

token ['təʊkən] *noun* **(a)** *(sign or symbol)* símbolo *m*; **token charge** = precio simbólico; **a token charge is made for heating** = hay un cargo simbólico de calefacción; **token payment** = pago simbólico; **token rent** = renta simbólica; **token strike** = huelga simbólica **(b)** **book token** *or* **flower token** *or* **gift token** = vale para comprar libros *or* flores *or* un regalo; **we gave her a gift token for her birthday** = le dimos un vale para un regalo por su aniversario

toll [təʊl] *noun* peaje *m*; **we had to cross a toll bridge to get to the island** = tuvimos que cruzar un puente de peaje para llegar a la isla; **you have to pay a toll to cross the bridge** = hay que pagar peaje para cruzar el puente

◊ **toll call** ['təʊl 'kɔːl] *noun US* llamada a larga distancia *or* interurbana

◊ **toll free** ['təʊl 'friː] *adverb US* **to call someone toll free** = hacer una llamada a cobro revertido; **toll free number** = número telefónico al que se llama gratuitamente (NOTE: GB English is **0800 number**, **Spanish is 009**)

tombstone ['tuːmstəʊn] *noun* *(informal)*

anuncio *m* oficial en la prensa de que se ha cubierto la suscripción de un empréstito

ton [tʌn] *noun (measure of weight)* tonelada *f* GB **long ton** = tonelada larga *or* británica (1016 kilos); *US* **short ton** = tonelada corta *or* norteamericana (907 kilos); **metric ton** = tonelada métrica (1000 kilos)

◊ **tonne** [tʌn] *noun* tonelada *f* métrica (NOTE: **ton** and **tonne** are usually written t after figures: **250t**)

◊ **tonnage** ['tʌnɪdʒ] *noun* tonelaje *m*; **gross tonnage** = tonelaje bruto; **deadweight tonnage** = peso muerto

QUOTE Canada agreed to the new duty-free quota of 600,000 tonnes a year
Globe and Mail (Toronto)

QUOTE in the dry cargo sector a total of 956 cargo vessels of 11.6m tonnes are laid up - 3% of world dry cargo tonnage
Lloyd's List

tone [təʊn] *noun* **dialling tone** = señal *f* de línea; **engaged tone** = señal de comunicar *or* de comunicando

toner ['təʊnə] *noun* virador *m*; **toner cartridge** = cartucho de virador; **the printer has run out of toner** = se ha acabado el virador de la impresora

tool [tuːl] *noun* herramienta *f or* útil *m*; **machine tools** = máquinas herramienta

◊ **tool up** ['tuːl 'ʌp] *verb* instalar la maquinaria en una fábrica

top [tɒp] **1** *noun* **(a)** *(upper surface or upper part)* parte *f* superior; **do not put coffee cups on top of the computer** = no ponga las tazas de café encima del ordenador **(b)** *(highest point or most important place)* cima *f or* cumbre *f* **2** *adjective* superior *or* mayor *or* primero, -ra; **the company is in the top six exporters** = la empresa es una de las seis principales exportadoras; **top copy** = original; **top-flight** *or* **top-ranking** = de primera categoría *or* clase; **top-flight managers can earn very high salaries** = los altos directivos *or* ejecutivos de alta dirección pueden ganar sueldos muy elevados; **he is the top-ranking official in the delegation** = es el funcionario más importante de la delegación; **top-grade** = de grado máximo; **the car only runs on top-grade petrol** = el coche marcha solamente con gasolina 'super'; **top management** = alta dirección; **to give something top priority** = dar prioridad absoluta a algo; **top quality** = alta calidad *or* calidad superior; **we specialize in top quality imported goods** = nuestra especialidad es la importación de mercancías de alta calidad **3** *verb (to go higher than)* superar; **sales topped £1m in the first quarter** = las ventas superaron £1 millón durante el primer trimestre (NOTE: **topping - topped**)

◊ **top-hat pension** [tɒp'hæt 'penʃən] *noun (special extra pension for senior managers)* pensión *f* de jubilación especial para ejecutivos

◊ **top-selling** ['tɒpselɪŋ] *adjective* más vendido, -da; **top-selling brands of toothpaste** = las marcas más vendidas de pasta dentífrica

◊ **top out** ['tɒp 'aʊt] **1** *noun US* periodo *m* de mayor demanda *or* cotización *f* más alta

◊ **top up** ['tɒp 'ʌp] *verb* llenar *or* completar; **to top** up stocks before the Christmas rush = completar las existencias antes del periodo de Navidades

> QUOTE gross wool receipts for the selling season appear likely to top $2 billion
> **Australian Financial Review**

> QUOTE the base lending rate, or prime rate, is the rate at which banks lend to their top corporate borrowers
> **Wall Street Journal**

> QUOTE fill huge warehouses with large quantities of top-brand, first-quality merchandise, sell the goods at rock-bottom prices
> **Duns Business Month**

topic ['tɒpɪk] *noun* tema *m or* asunto *m*; **the topic for discussion** = el tema de discusión *or* el asunto a discutir

tort [tɔːt] *noun (harm done, which can be the basis of a lawsuit)* agravio *m or* injusticia *f*

tot up ['tɒt 'ʌp] *verb* sumar; **he totted up the sales for the six months to December** = sumó las ventas de los seis meses anteriores a diciembre

total ['təʊtl] **1** *adjective* total; **total amount** = cantidad total; **total assets** = activos totales; **total cost** = coste total; **total expenditure** = gastos totales; **total income** = renta total; **total output** = producción total; **total revenue** = ingreso total; **the cargo was written off as a total loss** = la carga fue declarada siniestro total **2** *noun (amount)* total *m or* totalidad *f*; **the total of the charges comes to more than £1,000** = el total de los gastos asciende a más de £1.000; **grand total** = total general *or* global *or* suma *f* total **3** *verb* sumar *or* totalizar; **costs totalling more than £25,000** = costes que suman más de £25.000 (NOTE: **totalling - totalled** but US English **totaling - totaled**)

◇ **totally** ['təʊtli] *adverb* totalmente; **the factory was totally destroyed in the fire** = la fábrica quedó totalmente destruida por el incendio; **the cargo was totally ruined by water** = la carga quedó totalmente estropeada por el agua

tour [tʊə] *noun* viaje *m or* gira *f*; **the group went on a tour of Italy** = el grupo fue de viaje por Italia; **the minister went on a fact-finding tour of the region** = el ministro efectuó una gira de investigación por la región; **conducted tour** = excursión con guía; **package tour** = viaje de turismo organizado; **tour operator** = agente de viajes *or* agencia de viajes organizados; **to carry out a tour of inspection** = hacer una visita de inspección

◇ **tourism** ['tʊərɪzəm] *noun* turismo *m*

◇ **tourist** ['tʊərɪst] *noun* turista *mf*; **tourist bureau** *or* **tourist information office** = oficina de turismo *or* de información turística; **tourist class** = clase turística; **he always travels first class, because he says tourist class is too uncomfortable** = siempre viaja en primera clase porque dice que la clase turística es demasiado incómoda; **tourist trade** = turismo *m*; **tourist visa** = visado de turista

tout [taʊt] **1** *noun* revendedor, -ra **2** *verb* **(a) to tout for custom** = intentar atraer clientes **(b)** *US* vender presionando al cliente

trace [treɪs] *noun* rastro *m*; **without trace** *or* **leaving no trace(s)** = sin dejar rastro

track record ['træk 'rekɔːd] *noun* antecedentes *mpl*; **he has a good track record as a secondhand car salesman** = tiene buenos antecedentes como vendedor de coches de segunda mano; **the company has no track record in the computer market** = la empresa no tiene antecedentes en el mercado de ordenadores

trade [treɪd] **1** *noun* **(a)** *(business of buying and selling)* comercio *m*; **export trade** *or* **import trade** = comercio de exportación *or* comercio de importación; **foreign trade** *or* **overseas trade** *or* **external trade** = comercio exterior *or* comercio de ultramar; **domestic trade** *or* **home trade** = comercio interior; **invisible trade** = comercio invisible *or* de invisibles; **trade cycle** = ciclo económico; **balance of trade** *or* **trade balance** = balanza comercial; **adverse balance of trade** = balanza comercial con déficit *or* desfavorable *or* negativa; **the country had an adverse balance of trade for the second month running** = el país tuvo una balanza comercial negativa por segundo mes consecutivo; **favourable balance of trade** = balanza comercial favorable *or* con superávit; **trade deficit** *or* **trade gap** = déficit comercial; **trade surplus** = superávit *or* saldo comercial favorable *or* balance comercial favorable **(b) to do a good trade in a range of products** = vender bien una gama de productos; **fair trade** = sistema de comercio internacional con reciprocidad arancelaria; *US* = RESALE PRICE MAINTENANCE; **free trade** = libre comercio *or* libre cambio; **free trade area** = area de libre comercio; **free trade zone** = puerto franco *or* zona franca; **trade agreement** = acuerdo *or* tratado *or* convenio comercial; **trade bureau** = oficina de información comercial; **to impose trade barriers on** = imponer barreras comerciales sobre; **trade creditors** = acreedores comerciales; **trade debtors** = deudores comerciales; **trade description** = descripción comercial; *GB* **Trade Descriptions Act** = ley de Normativa para el comercio; **trade directory** = repertorio *or* guía comercial; **trade mission** = misión comercial **(c)** *(companies dealing in the same type of product)* he is in the secondhand car trade = se dedica a la compraventa de coches de segunda mano; **she is very well known in the clothing trade** = es muy conocida en la industria del vestido; **trade association** = asociación comercial *or* agrupación sectorial *or* de comerciantes y empresarios; **trade counter** = mostrador de venta para detallistas en una fábrica; **trade discount** *or* **trade terms** = descuento para comerciantes del sector *or* del ramo; **trade fair** = feria *or* exposición comercial; **there were two trade fairs running in London at the same time** = coincidieron dos ferias comerciales en Londres al mismo tiempo; **to organize** *or* **to run a trade fair** = organizar una feria comercial; **trade journal** *or* **trade magazine** *or* **trade paper** *or* **trade publication** = revista de una profesión o ramo determinados; **trade press** = publicaciones profesionales *or* del ramo; **trade price** = precio al detallista *or* al por mayor; **to ask a company to supply trade references** = pedir referencias comerciales a una empresa **2** *verb (to carry on a business)* comerciar *or* negociar; **to trade with another country** = comerciar con otro país; **to trade on the Stock Exchange** = negociar en bolsa; **the company has stopped trading** = la compañía ha cesado; **the company trades under the name 'Eeziphitt'** = la compañía opera bajo el nombre de 'Eeziphitt'

◇ **trade in** ['treɪd 'ɪn] *verb* **(a)** *(to buy and sell certain items)* comerciar; **the company trades in imported goods** = la empresa comercia con bienes importados; **he trades in French wine** = es comerciante de vino francés **(b)** *(to give in an old item as part of the payment for a new one)* ofrecer a cambio; **he got £500 when he traded in his old car for a new one** = al comprar un coche nuevo le ofrecieron £500 por el viejo; **the chairman traded in his old Rolls Royce for a new model** = el presidente entregó su antiguo Rolls Royce como pago parcial de un modelo nuevo

◇ **trade-in** ['treɪdɪn] *noun (old item as part of the payment for a new one)* artículo *m* usado entregado como pago parcial de uno nuevo; **to give the old car as a trade-in** = entregar el coche antiguo como parte del pago de uno nuevo; **trade-in price** = precio con entrega de artículo usado

◇ **trademark** *or* **trade name** ['treɪdmɑːk *or* 'treɪd 'neɪm] *noun* marca *f or* registrada *or* nombre *m* comercial; **you cannot call your beds 'Softn'kumfi' - it is a registered trademark** = no puede llamar a sus camas 'Softn'kumfi', es una marca registrada

◇ **trade-off** ['treɪdɒf] *noun* canje *m or* intercambio *m*

◇ **trader** ['treɪdə] *noun* comerciante *mf*; **commodity trader** = comerciante de materias primas; **free trader** = librecambista *mf or* partidario, -ria del libre comercio; **sole trader** = comerciante exclusivo

◇ **tradesman** ['treɪdzmən] *noun* **(a)** comerciante *mf or* tendero, -ra **(b)** *US* artesano, -na (NOTE: plural is **tradesmen**)

◇ **tradespeople** ['treɪdzpiːpl] *plural noun* comerciantes *mfpl or* negociantes *mfpl*

◇ **trade union** *or* **trades union** ['treɪd 'juːnjən *or* 'treɪdz 'juːnjən] *noun* sindicato *m*; **they are members of a trades union** *or* **they are trade union members** = están afiliados a un sindicato *or* son miembros del sindicato; **he has applied for trade union membership** *or* **he has applied to join a trades union** = ha solicitado la afiliación a un sindicato; **Trades Union Congress** = Confederación de Sindicatos (NOTE: although **Trades Union Congress** is the official name for the organization, **trade union** is commoner than **trades union** in GB English. US English is **labor union**)

◇ **trade unionist** [treɪd'juːnjənɪst] *noun* sindicalista *mf*

◇ **trade-weighted index** [treɪd'weɪtɪd 'ɪndeks] *noun* índice ponderado del valor de una divisa

trading ['treɪdɪŋ] *noun* comercio *m*; **trading account** = cuenta de explotación *or* de ejercicio; **trading area** = zona de comercio; **trading company** = sociedad comercial; **adverse trading conditions** = condiciones comerciales desfavorables; **trading estate** = zona industrial; *(Stock Exchange)* **trading floor** = parquet *or* patio de operaciones; **trading loss** = pérdida de ejercicio; **trading nation** = país *or* nación comerciante; **trading partner** = empresa que comercia con otra *or* país que comercia con otro; **trading profit** = beneficios de explotación; **trading stamp** = cupón con prima; **fair trading** = comercio justo; *GB* **Office of Fair Trading** = departamento de control de prácticas comerciales; **insider trading** = información privilegiada

traffic ['træfɪk] **1** *noun* **(a)** *(cars or planes, etc.)* circulación *f or* tráfico *m*; **air traffic** = tráfico aéreo; **road traffic** = tráfico vial *or* de carretera; **rail traffic** = tráfico ferroviario; **there is an increase in commuter traffic or goods traffic on the motorway** = hay un aumento de la circulación en la autopista a las horas de entrada y salida del trabajo *or* de vehículos de mercancías; **passenger traffic on the commuter lines has decreased during the summer** = ha disminuido el tráfico de pasajeros en las líneas de cercanías durante el verano; **air traffic controller** = controlador, -ra de tráfico aéreo **(b)** *(illegal trade)* tráfico; **drugs traffic** *or* **traffic in drugs** = tráfico de drogas **2** *verb (to deal illegally)* traficar; **they are trafficking in drugs** = trafican con drogas *or* son traficantes de drogas (NOTE: **trafficking - trafficked**)

train [treɪn] **1** *noun* tren *m*; **a passenger train** *or* **a goods train** = tren de pasajeros *or* tren de mercancías; **to take the 09.30 train to London** = coger el tren de las 9.30 para Londres; **he caught his train** *or* **he missed his train** = cogió el tren *or* perdió el tren; **to ship goods by train** = enviar mercancías por tren; **freight train** *or* **goods train** = tren de mercancías **2** *verb (to teach)* capacitar *or* formar; *(to learn)* estudiar *or* formarse; **he trained as an accountant** = estudió contabilidad; **the company only employs trained electricians** = la compañía sólo emplea electricistas capacitados

◇ **trainee** [treɪ'niː] *noun* aprendiz, -za *or* persona *f* en aprendizaje; **we employ a trainee accountant to help in the office at peak periods** = empleamos a un aprendiz de contabilidad en periodo de prácticas para ayudar en la oficina cuando hay mucho trabajo; **graduate trainees come to work in the laboratory when they have finished their courses at university** = algunos universitarios hacen un periodo de prácticas en el laboratorio al terminar su carrera; **management trainee** = joven en prácticas de dirección de empresas *or* aspirante a un puesto directivo

◊ **traineeship** [treɪˈniːʃɪp] *noun* aprendizaje *m*

◊ **training** [ˈtreɪnɪŋ] *noun* **(a)** *(work)* aprendizaje *m or* capacitación *f or* formación *f*; **there is a ten-week training period for new staff** = hay un periodo de formación de diez semanas para el personal de nueva contratación; **the shop is closed for staff training** = el negocio está cerrado porque el personal está realizando un cursillo de capacitación; **industrial training** = capacitación industrial; **intensive training course** = curso de formación profesional acelerada; **management training** = formación de mandos; **on-the-job training** = formación en el empleo; **off-the-job training** = formación fuera del empleo; **staff training** = capacitación *or* formación del personal; **training levy** = impuesto para financiar la formación profesional; **training officer** = director *or* responsable de capacitación; **training unit** = unidad de capacitación **(b)** *(sport)* entrenamiento *m*

> QUOTE trainee managers developed basic operational skills as well as acquiring a broad business education
> **Personnel Management**

tranche [trɑːnʃ] *noun* parte *f* (de un pago) *or* tramo *m*; **the second tranche of interest on the loan is now due for payment** = el segundo pago de los intereses sobre el préstamo ha vencido

transact [trænˈzækt] *verb* tramitar; **to transact business** = hacer negocios

◊ **transaction** [trænˈzækʃən] *noun* tramitación *f or* trámite *m*; **business transaction** = transacción *f or* operación *f* mercantil *or* negocio *m*; **cash transaction** = operación al contado; **a transaction on the Stock Exchange** = operación de bolsa; **the paper publishes a daily list of Stock Exchange transactions** = el periódico publica una lista diaria de las operaciones de bolsa; **exchange transaction** = operación de divisas; **fraudulent transaction** = operación fraudulenta

transfer 1 [ˈtrænsfə] *noun* **(a)** *(moving to a new place)* traslado *m or* transferencia *f*; **he applied for a transfer to our branch in Scotland** = solicitó el traslado a nuestra sucursal de Escocia; **transfer of property** *or* **transfer of shares** = transferencia de propiedad *or* transferencia de acciones; **airmail transfer** = transferencia entre bancos por vía aérea; **bank transfer** = transferencia bancaria; **credit transfer** *or* **transfer of funds** = transferencia de fondos; **stock transfer form** = formulario de transferencia de acciones *or* de transacciones bursátiles **(b)** *(changing to another form of transport)* transbordo *m*; **transfer passenger** = pasajero de transbordo **2** [trænsˈfɜː] *verb* **(a)** *(to move someone or something to a new place)* trasladar *or* transferir; **the accountant was transferred to our Scottish branch** = el contable fue trasladado a nuestra sucursal escocesa; **he transferred his shares to a family trust** = transfirió sus acciones a un fideicomiso familiar; **she transferred her**

money to a deposit account = transfirió su dinero a una cuenta de depósito **(b)** *(to change from one type of travel to another)* hacer transbordo; **when you get to London airport, you have to transfer onto an internal flight** = cuando llegas al aeropuerto de Londres, tienes que hacer transbordo a un vuelo nacional (NOTE: **transferring - transferred**)

◊ **transferable** [trænsˈfɜːrəbl] *adjective* transferible; **the season ticket is not transferable** = el billete de abono no es transferible

transform [trænzˈfɔːm] *verb* transformar

◊ **transformation** [trænzfəˈmeɪʃn] *noun* transformación *f*

tranship [trænˈʃɪp] *verb* *(to move cargo from one ship to another)* transbordar (NOTE: **transhipping - transhipped**)

transit [ˈtrænzɪt] *noun* **(a)** tránsito *m*; **to pay compensation for damage suffered in transit** *or* **for loss in transit** = pagar una indemnización por los daños sufridos en tránsito *or* por pérdidas en tránsito; **some of the goods were damaged in transit** = algunas de las mercancías fueron dañadas en el tránsito; **goods in transit** = mercancías en tránsito **(b)** **transit lounge** = sala para pasajeros en tránsito; **transit visa** *or* **transit permit** = visado *or* permiso de tránsito

translate [trænsˈleɪt] *verb* traducir; **he asked his secretary to translate the letter from the German agent** = pidió a su secretaria que tradujera la carta del agente alemán; **we have had the contract translated from Spanish into Japanese** = hemos hecho traducir el contrato del español al japonés

◊ **translation** [trænsˈleɪʃən] *noun* traducción *f*; **she passed the translation of the letter to the accounts department** = entregó la traducción de la carta al departamento de contabilidad; **translation bureau** = agencia de traducción

◊ **translator** [trænsˈleɪtə] *noun* traductor, -ra

transmission [trænzˈmɪʃən] *noun* transmisión *f*; **transmission of a message** = transmisión de un mensaje

◊ **transmit** [trænzˈmɪt] *verb* transmitir (un mensaje) (NOTE: **transmitting - transmitted**)

trans-national corporation [trænzˈnæʃnl kɔːpəˈreɪʃn] *noun* empresa *f or* compañía *f* multinacional

transport [ˈtrænspɔːt] **1** *noun* *(moving of goods or people)* transporte *m*; **air transport** *or* **transport by air** = transporte aéreo *or* transporte por vía aérea; **rail transport** *or* **transport by rail** = transporte por ferrocarril; **road transport** *or* **transport by road** = transporte por carretera; **passenger transport** *or* **the transport of passengers** = transporte de pasajeros; **the passenger transport services of British Rail** = los servicios de transporte de pasajeros de la British Rail; **what means of transport will you use to get to the factory?** = ¿qué medio de transporte empleará para llegar a la fábrica?; **he will be using private transport** = irá en *or* utilizará coche particular; **the visitors will be using public transport** = los visitantes utilizarán el transporte público; **public transport system** = sistema de transporte público (NOTE: no plural in English) **2** [trænsˈpɔːt] *verb* transportar *or* llevar; **the company transports**

millions of tons of goods by rail each year = la compañía transporta millones de toneladas de mercancías por tren cada año; **the visitors will be transported to the factory by air** *or* **by helicopter** *or* **by taxi** = los visitantes serán conducidos a la fábrica en avión *or* en helicóptero *or* en taxi

◊ **transportable** [trænsˈpɔːtəbl] *adjective* transportable

◊ **transportation** [trænspəˈteɪʃən] *noun* **(a)** *(action)* transporte *m* **(b)** *(vehicles used)* vehículos *mpl* de transporte; **the company will provide transportation to the airport** = la compañía proporcionará el transporte al aeropuerto; **ground transportation** = transporte terrestre

◊ **transporter** [trænsˈpɔːtə] *noun (company which transports goods)* transportista *mf*

◊ **Transports Internationaux Routiers (TIR)** [ˈtrɔːnspɔːz ænteˈnæsjənəʊ ˈruːtɪeɪ] *noun* Transporte Internacional por Carretera

travel [ˈtrævl] **1** *noun* viajes *mpl*; **business travel is a very important part of our overhead expenditure** = los viajes de trabajo son una parte importante de nuestros gastos generales; **travel agent** = agente de viajes; **travel agency** = agencia de viajes; **travel allowance** = dietas *fpl*; **travel magazine** = revista de viajes; **the travel trade** = la industria de los viajes (NOTE: no plural in English) **2** *verb* **(a)** *(journey)* viajar; **he travels to the States on business twice a year** = viaja a los Estados Unidos dos veces al año por negocios; **in her new job, she has to travel abroad at least ten times a year** = en su nuevo trabajo tiene que viajar al extranjero por lo menos diez veces al año **(b)** *(to act as representative)* ser viajante de comercio; **he travels in the north of the country for an insurance company** = es viajante de comercio en el norte del país para una compañía de seguros (NOTE: **travelling - travelled** but US **traveling - traveled**)

◊ **travelcard** [ˈtrævəkɑːd] *noun* tarjeta *f* de viaje; **weekly travelcard** = abono (de viaje) semanal

◊ **traveller** *or* US **traveler** [ˈtrævlə] *noun* **(a)** *(person who travels)* viajero, -ra; **business traveller** = viajero, -ra por razones de negocio; **traveller's cheques** *or* US **traveler's checks** = cheques de viaje **(b)** *(representative)* **commercial traveller** = viajante *mf* de comercio

◊ **travelling** [ˈtrævəlɪŋ] *noun* **travelling expenses** = gastos *mpl* de viaje; **travelling exhibition** = exposición ambulante; **travelling salesman** = representante de ventas

tray [treɪ] *noun* **filing tray** = bandeja *f* de documentos para archivar; **in tray** = bandeja de documentos por despachar; **out tray** = bandeja de documentos ya cumplimentados; **pending tray** = bandeja de asuntos pendientes

treasurer [ˈtreʒərə] *noun* **(a)** *(financial officer of a club or society)* tesorero, -ra; **honorary treasurer** = tesorero honorario **(b)** US *(main financial officer of a company)* director, -ra de finanzas de una compañía **(c)** *(Australia = finance minister)* ministro de (Economía) y Hacienda

◊ **treasury** [ˈtreʒəri] *noun* *(government department)* tesorería *f* *or* fisco *m*; **the Treasury** = el Tesoro *or* Hacienda *f* Pública; **treasury bill** *or* **T-Bill** = pagaré del Tesoro (a corto plazo) *or* letra del Tesoro; **treasury bonds** = bonos del Tesoro (a largo plazo); **treasury note** = pagaré *m or* cédula *f or* vale *m* de Tesorería; **treasury stocks** = acciones en cartera *or* valores del Tesoro (NOTE: also called **exchequer stocks)** US **Treasury Secretary** = ministro de Hacienda (NOTE: the equivalent of the **Finance Minister** in most countries, or of the **Chancellor of the Exchequer** in the UK) GB **Chief Secretary to the Treasury** = ministro de Hacienda (NOTE: in the USA, the equivalent is the **Director of the Budget)**

treaty [ˈtriːti] *noun* **(a)** *(agreement between countries)* tratado *m or* acuerdo *m*; **commercial treaty** = acuerdo comercial; **Treaty of Rome** = Tratado de Roma; **Treaty of the European Union** = Tratado de la Unión Europea (TUE) **(b)** *(agreement between individuals)* **to sell a house by private treaty** = vender una casa por acuerdo privado

treble [ˈtrebl] *verb* triplicar; **the company's borrowings have trebled** = los préstamos de la compañía se han triplicado

trend [trend] *noun* tendencia *f*; **there is a trend away from old-established food stores** = hay una tendencia en contra de las tiendas de alimentación tradiccionales; **a downward trend in investment** = una tendencia a la baja en las inversiones; **we notice a general trend to sell to the student market** = observamos una tendencia general a vender al mercado estudiantil; **the report points to inflationary trends in the economy** = el informe indica tendencias inflacionarias en la economía; **an upward trend in sales** = un tendencia alcista en las ventas; **economic trends** = tendencias económicas; **change in economic trends** = cambio en la coyuntura; **market trends** = tendencias del mercado; **population trends** = tendencias demográficas

trial [ˈtraɪəl] *noun* **(a)** *(court case)* proceso *m or* juicio *m*; **he is on trial** *or* **is standing trial for embezzlement** = está procesado por malversación; **trial court** = tribunal de primera instancia **(b)** *(test of a product)* prueba *f or* ensayo *m*; **on trial** = a prueba; **the product is on trial in our laboratories** = el producto está siendo sometido a prueba en nuestros laboratorios; **trial period** = periodo de prueba; **trial sample** = muestra de prueba *or* muestra de ensayo; **free trial** = prueba gratuita; **trial and error** = tanteo *m* **(c)** *(draft balance sheet)* **trial balance** = balance de comprobación

tribunal [traɪˈbjuːnl] *noun* tribunal *m or* juzgado *m*; **arbitration tribunal** = tribunal de arbitraje; **industrial tribunal** = magistratura de trabajo; **rent tribunal** = tribunal de rentas

trick [trɪk] *noun* trampa *f*; **confidence trick** = estafa *f*

◊ **trickster** [ˈtrɪkstə] *noun* **confidence trickster** = estafador, -ra

trigger [ˈtrɪgə] **1** *noun* activador *m or* disparador *m or* detonante *m* **2** *verb* accionar *or* disparar *or* poner en funcionamiento *or* desencadenar; **trigger point** = punto de arranque

COMMENT: if an individual or a company buys 5% of a company's shares, this shareholding must be declared to the company. If 15% is acquired it is assumed that a takeover bid will be made, and no more shares can be acquired for seven days to give the target company time to respond. There is no obligation to make a bid at this stage, but if the holding is increased to 30%, then a takeover bid must be made for the remaining 70%. If 90% of shares are owned, then the owner can purchase all outstanding shares compulsorily. These trigger points are often not crossed, and it is common to see that a company has acquired 14.9% or 29.9% of another company's shares

QUOTE the recovery is led by significant declines in short-term interest rates, which are forecast to be roughly 250 basis points below their previous peak in the second quarter of 1990. This should trigger a rebound in the housing markets and consumer spending on durables
Toronto Globe & Mail

trillion ['trɪljən] *noun* trillón *m*

COMMENT: British English now has the same meaning as American English; formerly in British English it meant one million million millions, and it is still sometimes used with this meaning; see also the note at BILLION

QUOTE if land is assessed at roughly half its current market value, the new tax could yield up to ¥10 trillion annually
Far Eastern Economic Review

Trinidad & Tobago ['trɪnɪdæd n tɒ'beɪgəʊ] *noun* Trinidad y Tobago *m*

◊ **Trinidadian** [trɪnɪ'dædɪən] *adjective & noun* (habitante) de Trinidad
NOTE: capital: **Port of Spain**; currency: **Trinidad and Tobago dollar (TT$)** = dólar de Trinidad y Tobago (TT$)

trinket ['trɪŋkɪt] *noun* quincalla *f*

trip [trɪp] *noun* viaje *m*; **business trip** = viaje de negocios

triple ['trɪpl] **1** *verb* triplicar; **the company's debts tripled in twelve months** = las deudas de la compañía se han triplicado en doce meses; **the acquisition of the chain of stores has tripled the group's turnover** = la adquisición de la cadena de tiendas ha triplicado el volumen de ventas del grupo **2** *adjective* triple; **the cost of airfreighting the goods is triple their manufacturing cost** = el coste del transporte aéreo de las mercancías es el triple de su coste de fabricación

triplicate ['trɪplɪkət] *noun* **in triplicate** = por triplicado; **to print an invoice in triplicate** = imprimir una factura por triplicado; **invoicing in triplicate** = facturación por triplicado

trolley ['trɒli] *noun* **airport trolley** = carrito *m* de aeropuerto *or* carrito del equipaje; **supermarket trolley** = carro *or* carrito de la compra *or* carrito de supermercado (NOTE: US English is **baggage cart, shopping cart**)

trouble ['trʌbl] *noun* problema *m or* dificultad *f*; **we are having some computer trouble** *or* **some trouble with the computer** = tenemos algunos problemas con el ordenador; **there was some trouble in the warehouse after the manager was**

fired = hubo dificultades en el almacén cuando el director fue despedido

◊ **troubleshoot** ['trʌblʃuːt] *verb* mediar en conflictos laborales

◊ **troubleshooter** ['trʌblʃuːtə] *noun* mediador, ra de conflictos laborales

trough [trɒf] *noun (low point in the economic cycle)* punto *m* más bajo

troy weight ['trɔɪ 'weɪt] *noun* peso *m* troy (oro y otros metales); **troy ounce** = onza troy (NOTE: in writing, often shortened to **troy oz.** after figures: **25.2 troy oz.**)

COMMENT: troy weight is divided into grains, pennyweights (24 grains = 1 pennyweight), ounces (20 pennyweights = 1 ounce) and pounds (12 troy ounces = 1 pound). Troy weights are slightly less than their avoirdupois equivalents; the troy pound equals 0.37kg or 0.82lb avoirdupois; see also AVOIRDUPOIS

truck [trʌk] *noun* **(a)** *(vehicle)* camión *m*; **fork-lift truck** = carretilla de horquilla elevadora **(b)** *(railway goods wagon)* vagón *m* (de ferrocarril)

◊ **trucker** ['trʌkə] *noun* camionero, -ra

◊ **trucking** ['trʌkɪŋ] *noun* acarreo *m or* transporte *m* de mercancías por carretera; **trucking firm** = compañía de transporte de mercancías por carretera

◊ **truckload** ['trʌkləʊd] *noun* carga *f* de un camión *or* camionada *f*

true [truː] *adjective* auténtico, -ca *or* verdadero, -ra *or* genuino, -na; **true copy** = compulsa *or* copia exacta; **I certify that this is a true copy** = certifico que esta es una copia exacta; **certified as a true copy** = compulsado, -da; **true and fair view** = balance real de la situación financiera de una compañía

truly ['truːli] *adverb (on letter)* **Yours truly** US **Truly yours** = atentamente

trunk call ['trʌŋk 'kɔːl] *noun* llamada *f or* conferencia *f* interurbana

trust [trʌst] **1** *noun* **(a)** *(being confident)* confianza *f*; **we took his statement on trust** = nos fiamos de sus afirmaciones **(b)** *(passing something to someone to look after)* depositar en confianza *or* a crédito; **he left his property in trust for his grandchildren** = dejó su propiedad en fideicomiso para ser entregada a sus nietos; **he was guilty of a breach of trust** = cometió un abuso de confianza; **he has a position of trust** = tiene un cargo de confianza **(c)** *(management of money or property for someone)* fideicomiso *m*; **they set up a family trust for their grandchildren** = establecieron un fideicomiso familiar para sus nietos; US **trust company** = compañía fiduciaria; **trust deed** = contrato de fideicomiso; **trust fund** = fondo de fideicomiso *or* fondo de custodia; **investment trust** = sociedad de inversión; **unit trust** = fondos de inversión (NOTE: the US equivalent is **mutual fund**) **(d)** US *(monopoly)* 'trust' *m or* consorcio *m* **2** *verb* **to trust someone with something** = confiar algo a alguien; **can he be trusted with all that cash?** = ¿se le puede confiar tanto dinero?

◊ **trustbusting** ['trʌstbʌstɪŋ] *noun* US disolución *f* de un monopolio para estimular la competencia

◇ **trustee** [trʌsˈtiː] *noun* administrador fiduciario; **the trustees of the pension fund** = los administradores del fondo de pensiones

◇ **trustworthy** [ˈtrʌstwɜːði] *adjective* de confianza *or* cumplidor, -ra; **our cashiers are completely trustworthy** = nuestros cajeros son de una confianza absoluta

TUC [ˈtiːjuːˈsiː] = TRADES UNION CONGRESS

tune [tjuːn] *noun (music)* melodía *f*; **the bank is backing him to the tune of £10,000** = el banco le apoya con un préstamo de £10.000

Tunisia [tjuːˈnɪziə] *noun* Túnez *m*

◇ **Tunisian** [tjuːˈnɪziən] *adjective & noun* tunecino, -na
NOTE: capital: **Tunis** (= Túnez); currency: **Tunisian dinar (D)** = dinar tunecino (D)

tunnel [ˈtʌnl] *noun* túnel *m*; **the Channel Tunnel** = el Eurotúnel

turkey [ˈtɜːki] *noun (informal)* mala inversión *f*

Turkey [ˈtɜːki] *noun* Turquía *f*

◇ **Turk** [tɜːk] *noun* turco, -ca *or* otomano, -na

◇ **Turkish** [ˈtɜːkɪʃ] *adjective* turco, -ca
NOTE: capital: **Ankara**; currency: **Turkish lira (LT)** = lira turca (LT)

turn [tɜːn] **1** *noun* **(a)** *(movement)* vuelta *f* **(b)** *(profit or commission)* ganancia *f*; **jobber's turn** = ganancias del corredor de bolsa **(c)** **stock turn** = rotación *f* de existencias; **the company has a stock turn of 6.7** = la empresa tiene una tasa de rotación de existencias del 6,7 **2** *verb* girar *or* volver *or* convertirse

◇ **turn down** [ˈtɜːn ˈdaʊn] *verb (to refuse)* rechazar; **the board turned down their takeover bid** = el consejo de administración rechazó su oferta de adquisición; **the bank turned down their request for a loan** = el banco rechazó su solicitud de préstamo; **the application for a licence was turned down** = la solicitud de licencia fue rechazada

◇ **turnkey** [ˈtɜːnkiː] *noun* **turnkey operation** = operación llaves en mano; **turnkey operator** = persona que realiza una operación llaves en mano

◇ **turn out** [ˈtɜːn ˈaʊt] *verb (to produce)* producir; **the factory turns out fifty units per day** = la fábrica produce cincuenta unidades al día

◇ **turn over** [ˈtɜːn ˈəʊvə] *verb (to have a certain amount of sales)* tener un volumen de ventas de; **we turn over £2,000 a week** = tenemos un volumen de ventas de más de £2.000 a la semana

◇ **turnover** [ˈtɜːnəʊvə] *noun* **(a)** *GB (amount of sales)* facturación *f or* volumen *m* de ventas *or* de negocios *or* cifra *f* de negocios; **the company's turnover has increased by 235%** = el volumen de ventas de la empresa ha aumentado en un 235%; **we based our calculations on the forecast turnover** = basamos nuestros cálculos en el volumen de ventas previsto; **gross turnover** = facturación *or* producción bruta; **net turnover** = facturación *or* producción neta; **stock turnover** = rotación *f* de existencias **(b)** *(changes in staff)* rotación *f*; **staff turnover** *or* **turnover of staff** = rotación de personal **(c)** *US (number of times something is sold in a period)* rotación

◇ **turn round** [ˈtɜːn ˈraʊnd] *verb* **(a)** *(to make profitable)* recuperar la rentabilidad de una empresa; **he turned the company round in less than a year** = convirtió la compañía en una empresa rentable en menos de un año **(b)** *(of person)* volverse

◇ **turnround** *or US* **turnaround** [ˈtɜːnraʊnd *or* ˈtɜːnəraʊnd] *noun* **(a)** *(ratio of value to goods sold)* rotación *f* de existencias **(b)** *(emptying a plane, etc., and getting it ready for another journey)* descarga de un avión *or* barco y su preparación para otro viaje **(c)** *(making a company profitable again)* recuperación *f or* reactivación

> QUOTE a 100,000 square foot warehouse can turn its inventory over 18 times a year, more than triple a discounter's turnover
> **Duns Business Month**

> QUOTE he is turning over his CEO title to one of his teammates, but will remain chairman for a year
> **Duns Business Month**

> QUOTE combined turnover for building and engineering was £692 million in 1986, up just 1.3% on the previous year
> **Management Today**

> QUOTE the US now accounts for more than half our world-wide sales; it has made a huge contribution to our earnings turnround
> **Duns Business Month**

(the) Twelve [ðəˈtwelv] *noun (EU up to 1995)* Los Doce (UE)

24-hour banking [ˈtwentiˈfɔːˈaʊə ˈbæŋkɪŋ] *noun* operaciones bancarias las 24 horas del día; **24-hour trading** = operaciones bursátiles las 24 horas del día

> QUOTE time-zone differences are an attraction for Asian speculators. In Hongkong, it is 5 p.m. when the London exchange opens and 9.30 or 10 p.m. when New York starts trading
> **Far Eastern Economic Review**

COMMENT: 24-hour trading is now possible because of instant communication to Stock Exchanges in different time zones; the Tokyo Stock Exchange closes about two hours before the London Stock Exchange opens; the New York Stock Exchange opens at the same time as the London one closes

two-bin system [ˈtuːbɪn ˈsɪstəm] *noun* sistema de inventario en dos depósitos

two-part [ˈtuːˈpɑːt] *noun* (papel) con copia; **two-part invoices** = facturas con copia; **two-part stationery** = papel de escribir con copia

two-way trade [ˈtuːweɪ ˈtreɪd] *noun* comercio *m* bilateral

tycoon [taɪˈkuːn] *noun* magnate *m*

type [taɪp] **1** *noun (printed letters)* tipo *m or* letra *f*; **did you read the small type on the back of the contract?** = ¿leíste la letra menuda *or* pequeña al dorso del contrato? **2** *verb (to write with a typewriter)* escribir a máquina *or* mecanografiar; **he**

can type quite fast = puede escribir a máquina bastante rápido; all his reports are typed on his portable typewriter = todos sus informes son mecanografiados en su máquina portátil

◊ **typewriter** ['taɪpraɪtə] *noun* máquina *f* de escribir; **portable typewriter** = máquina de escribir portátil; **electronic typewriter** = máquina de escribir electrónica

◊ **typewritten** ['taɪprɪtn] *adjective* escrito, -ta a máquina *or* mecanografiado, -da; **he sent in a typewritten job application** = envió una solicitud de trabajo escrita a máquina

◊ **typing** ['taɪpɪŋ] *noun* mecanografía *f*; **typing error** = error de impresión *or* mecanografía; **the secretary must have made a typing error** = la secretaria tiene que haber hecho un error de mecanografía *or* al pasarlo a máquina; **typing pool** = servicio de mecanografía; **copy typing** = (i) mecanografía *f* de copias; (ii) mecanografía de originales

◊ **typist** ['taɪpɪst] *noun* mecanógrafo, -fa; **copy typist** = mecanógrafo, -fa; **shorthand typist** = taquimecanógrafo, -fa

Uu

UBR = UNIFORM BUSINESS RATE

Uganda [ju:ˈgændə] *noun* Uganda *m*

◊ **Ugandan** [ju:ˈgændən] *adjective & noun* ugandés, -esa
NOTE: capital: **Kampala;** currency: **Uganda shilling (USh)** = chelín ugandés (USh)

UK = UNITED KINGDOM Reino Unido (R.U.)

Ukraine [ju:ˈkreɪn] *noun* Ucrania *f*

◊ **Ukrainian** [ju:ˈkreɪnɪən] *adjective & noun* ucranio, -nia
NOTE: capital: **Kiev** = currency: **Ukrainian rouble** = rublo ucranio

ultimate [ˈʌltɪmət] *adjective* último, -ma *or* final *or* definitivo, -va; **ultimate consumer** = consumidor final

◊ **ultimately** [ˈʌltɪmətli] *adverb* finalmente; **ultimately, the management had to agree to the demands of the union** = finalmente, la dirección tuvo que acceder a las demandas del sindicato

◊ **ultimatum** [ʌltɪˈmeɪtəm] *noun* ultimatum; **the union officials argued among themselves over the best way to deal with the ultimatum from the management** = los cargos sindicales discutieron entre ellos sobre la mejor manera de hacer frente al ultimatum de la dirección (NOTE: plural is **ultimatums** or **ultimata)**

umbrella organization [ʌmˈbrelə ˈɔːgənaɪzeɪʃn] *noun* organización *f* importante que comprende otras más pequeñas

UN [ˈjuːˈen] = THE UNITED NATIONS Organización de las Naciones Unidas (ONU)

unable [ʌnˈeɪbl] *adjective* incapaz; **the chairman was unable to come to the meeting** = el presidente no pudo *or* se vio en la imposibilidad de asistir a la reunión

unacceptable [ʌnəkˈseptəbl] *adjective* inaceptable; **the terms of the contract are quite unacceptable** = los términos del contrato son totalmente inaceptables

unaccounted for [ʌnəˈkaʊntɪd ˈfɔː] *adjective* inexplicado, -da *or* desaparecido, -da *or* sin figurar; **several thousand units are unaccounted for in the stocktaking** = hay varios miles de unidades que no figuran en el inventario

unanimous [juˈnænɪməs] *adjective* unánime; **there was a unanimous vote against the proposal** = hubo un voto unánime contra la propuesta; **they reached unanimous agreement** = alcanzaron un acuerdo unánime

◊ **unanimously** [juˈnænɪməsli] *adverb* unánimemente *or* por unanimidad; **the proposals were adopted unanimously** = las propuestas fueron adoptadas por unanimidad

unaudited [ʌnˈɔːdɪtɪd] *adjective* no verificado, -da; **unaudited accounts** = cuentas sin verificar

unauthorized [ʌnˈɔːθəraɪzd] *adjective* no autorizado, -da *or* desautorizado, -da; **unauthorized access to the company's records** = acceso no autorizado a los archivos de la compañía; **unauthorized expenditure** = gastos no autorizados; **no unauthorized persons are allowed into the laboratory** = no está permitida la entrada de personas no autorizadas en el laboratorio

unavailable [ʌnəˈveɪləbl] *adjective* no disponible *or* inasequible *or* agotado, -da; **the following items on your order are temporarily unavailable** = no disponemos en este momento de los artículos de su pedido que se indican a continuación

◊ **unavailability** [ʌnəveɪləˈbɪləti] *noun* indisponibilidad *f*

unavoidable [ʌnəˈvɔɪdəbl] *adjective* inevitable; **flights are subject to unavoidable delays** = los vuelos están sujetos a retrasos inevitables

unbalanced [ʌnˈbælənst] *adjective* (presupuesto) no equilibrado *or* desequilibrado

unbanked cheque [ʌnˈbæŋt ˈtʃek] *noun* cheque *m* por depositar

unblock [ʌnˈblɒk] *verb* descongelar *or* desbloquear

unbranded product [ʌnˈbrændɪd ˈprɒdʌkt] *noun* marca blanca

uncalled capital [ʌnˈkɔːld ˈkæpɪtəl] *noun* capital no desembolsado

uncashed [ʌnˈkæʃt] *adjective* sin cobrar; **uncashed cheques** = cheques sin cobrar

unchanged [ʌnˈtʃeɪn(d)ʒd] *adjective* inalterado, -da *or* invariable *or* igual

> QUOTE the dividend is unchanged at L90 per ordinary share
> **Financial Times**

unchecked [ʌnˈtʃekt] *adjective* sin comprobar *or* no comprobado, -da; **unchecked figures** = cifras sin comprobar

unclaimed [ʌnˈkleɪmd] *adjective* sin reclamar *or* no reclamado; **unclaimed baggage** = equipaje no reclamado; **unclaimed property** *or* **unclaimed baggage will be sold by auction after six months** = los objetos no reclamados se subastarán *or* el equipaje no reclamado se subastará a los seis meses

uncollected [ʌnkəˈlektɪd] *adjective* sin *or* por cobrar *or* no recaudado, -da; **uncollected subscriptions** = suscripciones por cobrar; **uncollected taxes** = impuestos sin cobrar *or* no recaudados

unconditional [ʌnkənˈdɪʃənl] *adjective* incondicional *or* sin condiciones; **unconditional acceptance of the offer by the board** = aceptación incondicional de la oferta por parte de la junta; **the offer went unconditional last Thursday** = la oferta perdió su carácter condicional el jueves pasado

◊ **unconditionally** [ʌnkən'dɪʃənli] *adverb* incondicionalmente; **the offer was accepted unconditionally by the trade union** = la oferta fue aceptada incondicionalmente por el sindicato

unconfirmed [ʌnkən'fɜːmd] *adjective* sin confirmar *or* no confirmado, -da; **there are unconfirmed reports that our agent has been arrested** = hay noticias sin confirmar de que nuestro representante ha sido detenido

unconstitutional [ʌnkɒnstɪ'tjuːʃənl] *adjective* inconstitucional; **the chairman ruled that the meeting was unconstitutional** = el presidente decidió que la reunión era inconstitucional

uncontrollable [ʌnkən'trəʊləbl] *adjective* incontrolable; **uncontrollable inflation** = inflación incontrolable

◊ **uncontrolled** [ʌnkən'trəʊld] *adjective* no controlado *or* sin control

uncrossed cheque ['ʌnkrɒst 'tʃek] *noun* cheque *m* no cruzado *or* sin cruzar

undated [ʌn'deɪtɪd] *adjective* sin fecha; **he tried to cash an undated cheque** = intentó hacer efectivo un cheque sin fecha; **undated bond** = obligación perpetua

undelivered [ʌndɪ'lɪvəd] *adjective (on letter)* **if undelivered, please return to** = en caso de no efectuarse la entrega, devuélvase *or* sírvanse a devolver a

under ['ʌndə] *preposition* **(a)** *(lower or less than)* por debajo de *or* menos de; **the interest rate is under 10%** = el tipo de interés está por debajo del 10%; **under half of the shareholders accepted the offer** = menos de la mitad de los accionistas aceptaron la oferta **(b)** *(according to)* conforme a *or* según *or* de conformidad con; **under the terms of the agreement, the goods should be delivered in October** = según los términos del acuerdo, la mercancía debe ser entregada en octubre; **he is acting under rule 23 of the union constitution** = actúa conforme a la norma 23 de los estatutos del sindicato *or* de la constitución sindical

◊ **under-** ['ʌndə] *prefix* menos que

◊ **underbid** [ʌndə'bɪd] *verb* ofrecer menos que (NOTE: **underbidding - underbid)**

◊ **underbidder** [ʌndə'bɪdə] *noun* persona *f* que ofrece menos

◊ **undercapitalized** [ʌndə'kæpɪtəlaɪzd] *adjective* infracapitalizado, -da *or* descapitalizado, -da; **the company is severely undercapitalized** = la compañía está muy descapitalizada

◊ **undercharge** [ʌndə'tʃɑːdʒ] *verb* cobrar de menos; **he undercharged us by £25** = nos cobró £25 de menos

◊ **undercut** [ʌndə'kʌt] *verb* vender más barato *or* trabajar por un sueldo inferior a los demás

◊ **underdeveloped** [ʌndədɪ'veləpt] *adjective* subdesarrollado, -da *or* poco desarrollado, -da; **Japan is an underdeveloped market for our products** = Japón es un mercado poco desarrollado para nuestros productos; **underdeveloped countries** = países subdesarrollados

◊ **underemployed** [ʌndərɪm'plɔɪd] *adjective* subempleado, -da *or* infrautilizado, -da; **the staff is underemployed because of the cutback in production** = el personal está insuficientemente utilizado debido al recorte sufrido en la producción; **underemployed capital** = capital subempleado

◊ **underemployment** [ʌndərɪm'plɔɪmənt] *noun* **(a)** *(in a company)* infraocupación *f* **(b)** *(in a country)* subempleo *m*

◊ **underequipped** [ʌndərɪ'kwɪpt] *adjective* mal equipado, -da

◊ **underestimate** [ʌndər'estɪmɪt] **1** *noun* infravaloración *f or* estimación baja; **the figure of £50,000 underestimate** = la cifra de un volumen de negocios de £50.000 fue una estimación muy baja **2** [ʌndər'estɪmeɪt] *verb* infravalorar *or* calcular por lo bajo *or* mal; **they underestimated the effects of the strike on their sales** = subestimaron los efectos de la huelga en las ventas; **he underestimated the amount of time needed to finish the work** = calculó por lo bajo el tiempo que se necesitaba para terminar el trabajo

◊ **underlease** ['ʌndəliːs] *noun* subarrendamiento *m or* subarriendo *m*

◊ **undermanned** [ʌndə'mænd] *adjective* falto de personal *or* mano de obra

◊ **undermanning** [ʌndə'mænɪŋ] *noun* insuficiencia de personal *or* mano de obra; **the company's production is affected by undermanning on the assembly line** = la producción de la empresa se ve afectada por la falta de mano de obra en la cadena de montaje

◊ **undermentioned** [ʌndə'menʃənd] *adjective* mencionado más abajo *or* citado a continuación

◊ **underpaid** [ʌndə'peɪd] *adjective* mal pagado, -da; **our staff say that they are underpaid and overworked** = nuestros empleados dicen que están mal pagados y tienen demasiado trabajo

underperform [ʌndəpə'fɔːm] *verb* actuar por debajo de las expectativas; **to underperform the market** = tener una actuación peor que el resto del mercado; **the hotel group has underperformed the sector this year** = el grupo hotelero no ha alcanzado la actuación del sector este año

QUOTE since mid-1989, Australia has been declining again. Because it has had such a long period of underperfomance, it is now not as vulnerable as other markets
Money Observer

underrate [ʌndə'reɪt] *verb* subestimar *or* menospreciar; **do not underrate the strength of the competition in the European market** = no subestime el poder de la competencia en el mercado europeo; **the power of the yen is underrated** = el poder del yen está subestimado

◊ **undersell** [ʌndə'sel] *verb* vender más barato; **to undersell a competitor** = vender más barato que un competidor; **the company is never undersold** = no hay otra compañía que venda más barato (NOTE: **underselling - undersold)**

◊ **undersigned** [ʌndə'saɪnd] *noun* abajo firmante *mf*; **we, the undersigned** = nosotros, los abajo firmantes (NOTE: can be followed by a plural verb: **the undersigned accept liability for the debt)**

◊ **underspend** [ʌndə'spend] *verb* gastar menos;

eq

he has underspent his budget = ha gastado menos de lo que había previsto (NOTE: **underspending - underspent**)

◇ **understaffed** [ʌndə'stɑ:ft] *adjective* falto, -ta de personal *or* escaso, -sa de personal

◇ **understand** [ʌndə'stænd] *verb* entender *or* comprender (NOTE: **understanding - understood**)

◇ **understanding** [ʌndə'stændɪŋ] **1** *adjective* *(person)* comprensivo, -va **2** *noun* **(a)** *(agreement)* acuerdo *m or* arreglo *m or* acomodo *m*; **to come to an understanding about the divisions of the market** = llegar a un arreglo sobre el reparto del mercado; **on the understanding that** = con tal que *or* siempre que *or* a condición de que; **we accept the terms of the contract, on the understanding that it has to be ratified by our main board** = aceptamos los términos del contrato con tal que sea ratificado por nuestra junta general **(b)** *(comprehension)* comprensión *f*

◇ **understate** [ʌndə'steɪt] *verb* subestimar *or* presentar algo de manera que parezca menor *or* quitar importancia; **the company accounts understate the real profit** = la contabilidad de la compañía presenta unos beneficios por debajo de los reales

◇ **undersubscribed** [ʌdəsʌb'skraɪbd] *adjective* **the new share issue was undersubscribed** = las acciones no fueron suscritas en su totalidad

◇ **undertake** [ʌndə'teɪk] *verb* emprender *or* encargarse de *or* comprometerse; **to undertake an investigation of the market** = emprender una investigación del mercado; **they have undertaken not to sell into our territory** = se han comprometido a no vender en nuestro territorio (NOTE: **undertaking - undertook - has undertaken**)

◇ **undertaking** [ʌndə'teɪkɪŋ] *noun* **(a)** *(company)* empresa *f* **(b)** *(task)* tarea *f*; **commercial undertaking** = una empresa comercial **(c)** *(promise)* compromiso *m or* promesa *f*; **they have given us a written undertaking not to sell their products in competition with ours** = se han comprometido por escrito a no hacernos la competencia con sus productos

◇ **underutilized** [ʌndə'ju:tɪlaɪzd] *adjective* infrautilizado, -da

undervalued [ʌndə'vælju:d] *adjective* infravalorado, -da *or* subestimado, -da; **the properties are undervalued on the balance sheet** = las propiedades están infravaloradas en el balance de situación; **the dollar is undervalued on the foreign exchanges** = el dólar está infravalorado en los mercados de divisas

◇ **undervaluation** [ʌndəvæljʊ'eɪʃən] *noun* infravaloración *f or* subestimación *f*

> QUOTE in terms of purchasing power, the dollar is considerably undervalued, while the US trade deficit is declining month by month
> **Financial Weekly**

underweight [ʌndə'weɪt] *adjective* de peso insuficiente; **the pack is twenty grams underweight** = faltan veinte gramos en el paquete

◇ **underworked** [ʌndə'wɜ:kt] *adjective* con poco trabajo; **the directors think our staff are overpaid and underworked** = los directores piensan que nuestro personal está excesivamente pagado y tiene poco trabajo

underwrite [ʌndə'raɪt] *verb* **(a)** *(accept responsability for)* garantizar *or* asegurar; **to underwrite a share issue** = garantizar una emisión de acciones (comprometiéndose a adquirir las que no hayan sido vendidas); **the issue was underwritten by three underwriting companies** = la emisión fue garantizada por tres empresas aseguradoras **(b)** *(insure)* avalar; **to underwrite an insurance policy** = avalar una póliza de seguros **(c)** *(guarantee payment)* garantizar el pago; **the government has underwritten the development costs of the project** = el gobierno ha garantizado el pago de los costes de desarrollo del proyecto (NOTE: **underwriting - underwrote - has underwritten**)

◇ **underwriter** ['ʌndəraɪtə] *noun* suscriptor, -ra *or* asegurador, -ra; **Lloyd's underwriter** = asegurador de Lloyd; **marine underwriter** = asegurador, -ra de riesgos marítimos

> COMMENT: when a major company flotation or share issue or loan is prepared, a group of companies (such as merchant banks) will form a syndicate to underwrite the flotation: the syndicate will be organized by the 'lead underwriter', together with a group of main underwriters; these in turn will ask others ('sub-underwriters') to share in the underwriting

> QUOTE under the new program, mortgage brokers are allowed to underwrite mortgages and get a much higher fee
> **Forbes Magazine**

undischarged bankrupt ['ʌndɪstʃɑ:dʒd 'bæŋkrʌpt] *noun* quebrado *m* no rehabilitado

undistributed profit [ʌndɪs'trɪbju:tɪd 'prɒfɪt] *noun* beneficio *m* no distribuido

unearned income ['ʌnɜ:nd 'ɪnkʌm] *noun* renta *f* no salarial *or* ingresos procedentes de intereses y dividendos; *compare* EARNED INCOME

uneconomic [ʌni:kə'nɒmɪk] *adjective* poco rentable *or* antieconómico, -ca; **it is an uneconomic proposition** = es una proposicón poco rentable; **uneconomic rent** = renta que no llega a cubrir los costes

unemployed [ʌnɪm'plɔɪd] **1** *adjective* en paro *or* parado, -da *or* desempleado, -da; **unemployed office workers** = oficinistas en paro **2** *noun* **the unemployed** = los parados *or* desempleados; **the long-term unemployed** = desempleados de larga duración

◇ **unemployment** [ʌnɪm'plɔɪmənt] *noun* paro *m or* desempleo *m*; **mass unemployment** = paro masivo; **seasonal unemployment** = desempleo *or* paro estacional; **unemployment benefit** *or US* **unemployment compensation** = subsidio *m* de paro *or* prestaciones por desempleo

> QUOTE unemployment fell by 33,000 in February to 2,531,000, the lowest figures for six years
> **Employment Gazette**

> QUOTE tax advantages directed toward small businesses will help create jobs and reduce the unemployment rate
> **Toronto Star**

unfair [ʌnˈfeə] *adjective* **unfair competition** = competencia desleal; **unfair dismissal** = despido injusto

unfavourable *or* *US* **unfavorable** [ʌnˈfeɪvərəbl] *adjective* desfavorable *or* adverso, -sa; **unfavourable balance of trade** = balanza comercial desfavorable; **unfavourable exchange rate** = tipo de cambio desfavorable; **the unfavourable exchange rate hit the country's exports** = el tipo de cambio desfavorable asestó un golpe a las exportaciones del país

unfulfilled order [ˈʌnfʊlfɪld ˈɔːdə] *noun* pedido no servido *or* por servir

ungeared [ʌnˈɡɪəd] *adjective* sin recurrir a préstamos

uniform business rate (UBR) [ˈjuːnɪfɔːm ˈbɪznəs reɪt] *noun* impuesto profesional

unilateral [juːnɪˈlætərəl] *adjective* unilateral; **they took the unilateral decision to cancel the contract** = tomaron la decisión unilateral de anular el contrato

◊ **unilaterally** [juːnɪˈlætərəli] *adverb* unilateralmente; **they cancelled the contract unilaterally** = anularon el contrato unilateralmente

uninsured [ʌnɪnˈʃʊəd] *adjective* sin asegurar *or* sin seguro *or* no asegurado

union [ˈjuːnjən] *noun* **(a) trade union** *or* **trades union** *or* *US* **labor union** = sindicato *m* de trabajadores; **union agreement** = acuerdo sindical; **union dues** *or* **union subscription** = cuota sindical *or* cuota de inscripción sindical; **union officials** = cargos sindicales; **union recognition** = reconocimiento de un sindicato; **union representative** = delegado *or* enlace *or* representante sindical **(b) customs union** = unión aduanera **(c) European Union** = Unión Europea

◊ **unionist** [ˈjuːnjənɪst] *noun* sindicalista *mf*

◊ **unionized** [ˈjuːnjənaɪzd] *adjective* sindicado, -da

> QUOTE in 1896 there were 1,358 unions and, apart from the few years after the First World War, the number has declined steadily over the last ninety years
> **Employment Gazette**

> QUOTE the blue-collar unions are the people who stand to lose most in terms of employment growth
> **Sydney Morning Herald**

> QUOTE after three days of tough negotiations, the company reached agreement with its 1,200 unionized workers
> **Toronto Star**

unique [juːˈniːk] *adjective* único, -ca; **unique selling point** *or* **unique selling proposition (USP)** = argumento de venta

unissued capital [ˈʌnɪʃuːd ˈkæpɪtl] *noun* capital *m* no emitido

unit [ˈjuːnɪt] *noun* **(a)** *(single product)* unidad *f*; **unit cost** = coste por unidad *or* coste unitario; **unit price** = precio por unidad **(b)** *(furniture)* elemento *m*

or unidad; **display unit** = escaparate *m* *or* vitrina *f* de exposición; **visual display unit** = unidad de representación visual *or* monitor *m* **(c)** *(building)* edificio *m* **factory unit** = fábrica *f*; **as production has increased, we have moved to a larger unit on the same estate** = dado el aumento de producción, nos hemos trasladado a un edificio más grande en el mismo polígono **(d)** *(group)* **production unit** = unidad de producción; **research unit** = unidad de investigación **(e) monetary unit** *or* **unit of currency** = moneda *f* *or* unidad monetaria; **unit of account** = unidad de cuenta **(f)** *(in unit trust)* acción *f* *or* título *m*

◊ **unit trust** [ˈjuːnɪt ˈtrʌst] *noun* sociedad *f* inversora por obligaciones *or* fondos *mpl* mutuos (NOTE: the US equivalent is **mutual fund**)

unite [juːˈnaɪt] *verb* unir; **the directors united with the managers to reject the takeover bid** = el cuerpo directivo se unió a la administración para rechazar la OPA

United Arab Emirates (UAE) [juːˈnaɪtɪd ærəb ˈemɪrəts] *noun* Emiratos Árabes Unidos (EAU) *mpl* NOTE: capital: **Abu Dhabi**; currency: **UAE dirham (Dh)** = dirham EAU (Dh)

United Kingdom (UK) [juːˈnaɪtɪd ˈkɪŋdəm] *noun* Reino Unido (RU) *m*

◊ **British** [ˈbrɪtɪʃ] *adjective & noun* británico, -ca *or* inglés, -esa NOTE: capital: **London** (= Londres); currency: **pound sterling (£** *or* **£stg)** = libra esterlina (£ *or* £est)

United Nations (UN) [juːˈnaɪtɪd ˈneɪʃnz] *noun* Organización de las Naciones Unidas (ONU)

United States of America (USA) [juːˈnaɪtɪd steɪts ʌv əˈmerɪkə] *noun* Estados Unidos de América (EE UU) *mpl*

◊ **American** *adjective & noun* estadounidense *mf* *or* norteamericano, -na NOTE: capital: **Washington**; currency: **US dollar ($** *or* **$US)** = dólar EE UU ($ *or* $US)

unladen [ʌnˈleɪdn] *adjective* sin cargamento *or* vacío, -cía

unlawful [ʌnˈlɔːfʊl] *adjective* ilegal *or* ilícito, -ta *or* ilegítimo, -ma

unlikely [ʌnˈlaɪkli] *adjective* difícil; **it's unlikely that I'll go to the meeting** = es difícil que vaya a la reunión

unlimited [ʌnˈlɪmɪtɪd] *adjective* ilimitado, -da; **the bank offered him unlimited credit** = el banco le ofreció un crédito ilimitado; **unlimited liability** = responsabilidad ilimitada

unlined [ʌnˈlaɪnd] *adjective* **unlined paper** = papel sin rayar *or* papel liso

unlisted [ʌnˈlɪstɪd] *adjective* **unlisted securities** = títulos no cotizados en bolsa; **unlisted securities market (USM)** = mercado de títulos no cotizados en bolsa

unload [ʌnˈləʊd] *verb* **(a)** *(goods)* descargar; **the ship is unloading at Hamburg** = el barco está descargando en Hamburgo; **we need a fork-lift truck to unload the lorry** = necesitamos una carretilla elevadora de horquilla para descargar el camión; **we unloaded the spare parts at Lagos** =

descargamos las piezas de recambio en Lagos; **there are no unloading facilities for container ships** = no hay instalaciones de descarga para los barcos portacontenedores **(b)** *(to get rid of)* deshacerse de; **we tried to unload our shareholding as soon as the company published its accounts** = intentamos deshacernos de nuestras acciones tan pronto como la sociedad hizo públicas sus cuentas

unobtainable [ʌnəb'teɪnəbl] *adjective* inalcanzable *or* imposible de conseguir

unofficial [ʌnə'fɪʃl] *adjective* extraoficial *or* no oficial *or* oficioso, -sa; **unofficial strike** = huelga no autorizada *or* aprobada por los sindicatos *or* huelga ilegal

◇ **unofficially** [ʌnə'fɪʃli] *adverb* extraoficialmente *or* oficiosamente; **the tax office told the company unofficially that it would be prosecuted** = la delegación de Hacienda le dijo extraoficialmente a la compañía que sería procesada

unpaid [ʌn'peɪd] *adjective* impagado, -da *or* sin pagar *or* no pagado, -da; **unpaid holiday** = vacaciones no pagadas; **unpaid invoices** = facturas impagadas

unprofitable [ʌn'prɒfɪtəbl] *adjective* no lucrativo, -va *or* no rentable

> QUOTE the airline has already eliminated a number of unprofitable flights
> **Duns Business Month**

unquoted shares ['ʌnkwəʊtɪd 'ʃeəz] *plural noun* acciones que no se cotizan en bolsa

unredeemed pledge [ʌnrɪ'diːmd 'pledʒ] *noun* prenda *f* no rescatada *or* sin desempeñar

unregistered [ʌn'redʒɪstəd] *adjective* *(company)* no registrado, -da *or* sin registrar

unreliable [ʌnrɪ'laɪəbl] *adjective* poco fiable *or* de poca confianza *or* poco seguro, -ra; **the postal service is very unreliable** = el servicio de correos es muy poco fiable

unsaleable [ʌn'seɪləbl] *adjective* invendible; **unsaleable item** = artículo invendible

unsealed envelope ['ʌnsiːld 'envələʊp] *noun* sobre abierto *or* sin cerrar

unsecured [ʌnsɪ'kjʊəd] *adjective* **unsecured creditor** = acreedor, -ra común *or* sin garantía; **unsecured debt** = deuda no garantizada; **unsecured loan** = préstamo sin garantía

unseen [ʌn'siːn] *adverb* inadvertido, -da *or* sin ser visto, -ta; **to buy something sight unseen** = comprar algo sin verlo

unsettled [ʌn'setld] *adjective* inestable *or* perturbado, -da *or* intranquilo, -la; **the market was unsettled by the news of the failure of the takeover bid** = el mercado se vió perturbado por la noticia del fracaso de la OPA

unskilled [ʌn'skɪld] *adjective* sin cualificar *or* no cualificado, -da *or* no especializado, -da; **unskilled labour** *or* **unskilled workforce** *or* **unskilled workers** = mano de obra sin cualificar *or* trabajadores no especializados

unsocial [ʌn'səʊʃl] *adjective* **to work unsocial hours** = trabajar a horas intempestivas *or* fuera de horas normales

unsold [ʌn'səʊld] *adjective* no vendido *or* sin vender *or* invendido, -da; **unsold items will be scrapped** = los artículos que no se hayan vendido se descartarán

unsolicited [ʌnsə'lɪsɪtɪd] *adjective* no solicitado, -da; **an unsolicited gift** = un regalo no solicitado; **unsolicited testimonial** = testimonio no solicitado

unstable [ʌn'steɪbl] *adjective* inestable; **unstable exchange rates** = tipos de cambio inestables

unsubsidized [ʌn'sʌbsɪdaɪzd] *adjective* sin subsidio *or* no subvencionado, -da

unsuccessful [ʌnsək'sesfʊl] *adjective* sin éxito *or* fracasado, -da; **an unsuccessful businessman** = un hombre de negocios fracasado; **the project was expensive and unsuccessful** = el proyecto era caro y no tuvo éxito

◇ **unsuccessfully** [ʌnsək'sesfəli] *adverb* sin éxito *or* infructuosamente; **the company unsuccessfully tried to break into the South American market** = la compañía intentó introducirse sin éxito en el mercado sudamericano

untrue [ʌn'truː] *adjective* falso, -sa

unused [ʌn'juːzd] *adjective* no usado, -da *or* sin usar *or* nuevo; **we are trying to sell off six unused typewriters** = estamos intentando vender tres máquinas de escribir nuevas

unwaged [ʌn'weɪdʒd] *adjective* **the unwaged** = las personas que no tienen un trabajo remunerado (NOTE: is followed by a plural verb)

unwritten agreement [ʌn'rɪtn ə'griːmənt] *noun* acuerdo *m* verbal

up [ʌp] *adverb & preposition* arriba *or* hacia arriba; **the inflation rate is going up steadily** = la inflación está subiendo sin parar; **shares were up slightly at the end of the day** = las acciones habían subido ligeramente al final de la sesión

◇ **up to** ['ʌp 'tuː] *adverb* hasta; **we will buy at prices up to £25** = compraremos hasta un precio máximo de £25

◇ **up to date** ['ʌp tə 'deɪt] **1** *adjective* actual *or* moderno, -na; **an up-to-date computer system** = un sistema informático moderno **2** *adverb* al día; **to bring something up to date** = poner algo al día *or* actualizar; **to keep something up to date** = mantener algo al día; **we spend a lot of time keeping our mailing list up to date** = empleamos mucho tiempo en mantener nuestra lista de direcciones al día

update ['ʌpdeɪt] **1** *noun* actualización *f* *or* modernización *f* **2** [ʌp'deɪt] *verb* actualizar *or* poner al día *or* modernizar; **the figures are updated annually** = las cifras se actualizan anualmente

up front ['ʌp 'frʌnt] *adverb* por adelantado; **money up front** = dinero por adelantado; **they are asking for £100,000 up front before they will consider the deal** = piden £100.000 por adelantado antes de estudiar la operación; **he had to put money up front before he could clinch the deal** = tuvo que dar dinero por adelantado antes de poder cerrar el trato

upgrade [ʌp'greɪd] *verb* ascender *or* mejorar; **his job has been upgraded to senior manager level** = su puesto de trabajo ha sido reclasificado dentro de la categoría de gerente principal

upkeep ['ʌpkiːp] *noun (cost)* coste *m* de mantenimiento *or* entretenimiento

uplift ['ʌplɪft] *noun* aumento *m*; **the contract provides for an annual uplift of charges** = el contrato estipula un aumento anual de los precios

up market ['ʌp 'maːkɪt] *adverb* de primera calidad; **the company has decided to move up market** = la compañía ha decidido lanzarse al mercado de artículos de primera calidad

> QUOTE prices of up market homes (costing $300,000 or more) are falling in many areas
> **Economist**

upset price ['ʌpset praɪs] *noun* precio *m* inicial *or* mínimo aceptable en una subasta

upside ['ʌpsaɪd] *noun* **upside potential** = potencial positivo (NOTE: the opposite is **downside)**

upturn ['ʌptɜːn] *noun* mejora *f or* reactivación *f*; **an upturn in the economy** = una reactivación de la economía; **an upturn in the market** = una reactivación del mercado

upward ['ʌpwəd] *adjective* alcista *or* ascendente *or* hacia arriba; **an upward movement** = un movimiento ascendente; **upward trend** = tendencia alcista

◊ **upwards** ['ʌpwədz] *adverb* ascendente *or* hacia arriba; **the market moved upwards after the news of the budget** = el mercado subió al hacerse público el presupuesto estatal (NOTE: US English uses **upward** as both adjective and adverb)

urban ['ɜːbən] *adjective* urbano, -na; **urban development** = urbanización *f*

urgency ['ɜːdʒənsi] *noun* urgencia *f*

◊ **urgent** ['ɜːdʒənt] *adjective* urgente

◊ **urgently** ['ɜːdʒəntli] *adverb* urgentemente; **to do something urgently** = hacer algo urgentemente

Uruguay ['juːrəgwaɪ] *noun* Uruguay *m*

◊ **Uruguayan** ['juːrəgwaɪən] *adjective & noun* uruguayo, -ya
NOTE: capital: **Montevideo;** currency: **new Uruguayan peso (NUr$)** = nuevo peso uruguayo (NUr$)

US *or* **USA** [juː'es *or* juːes'eɪ] = UNITED STATES OF AMERICA Estados Unidos de América (EE UU)

usage ['juːzɪdʒ] *noun* uso *m or* utilización *f*

use 1 [juːs] *noun* uso *m*; **directions for use** = instrucciones de uso *or* modo de empleo; **to make use of something** = hacer uso de algo; **in use** = en funcionamiento; **the computer is in use twenty-four hours a day** = el ordenador funciona *or* está en funcionamiento las veinticuatro horas del día; **items for personal use** = artículos de uso personal; **he has the use of a company car** = tiene un coche de la empresa para su uso personal; **land zoned for industrial use** = terreno destinado a uso industrial **2** [juːz] *verb* emplear *or* usar *or* utilizar; **we use airmail for all our overseas correspondence** = utilizamos el correo aéreo para toda la correspondencia con el extranjero; **the photocopier is being used all the time** = la fotocopiadora se usa continuamente; **they use freelancers for most of their work** = emplean a trabajadores independientes para la mayor parte de su trabajo

◊ **useful** ['juːsfʊl] *adjective* útil

◊ **usefulness** ['juːsfʊlnəs] *noun* utilidad *f*

◊ **useless** ['juːsləs] *adjective* inútil *or* inservible

◊ **user** ['juːzə] *noun* usuario, -ria; **end user** = usuario final; **user's guide** *or* **handbook** = guía del usuario *or* manual

◊ **user-friendly** ['juːzə'frendli] *adjective* fácil de usar *or* de fácil manejo *or* fácil para el usuario; **these programs are really user-friendly** = estos programas son realmente fáciles de usar; **user-friendly computer** = ordenador fácil de usar

USP = UNIQUE SELLING POINT, PROPOSITION

usual ['juːʒʊəl] *adjective* normal *or* usual *or* habitual; **our usual terms** *or* **usual conditions are thirty days' credit** = nuestras condiciones normales son treinta días de crédito; **the usual practice is to have the contract signed by the MD** = lo normal es que el contrato sea firmado por el director gerente; **the usual hours of work are from 9.30 to 5.30** = el horario normal de trabajo es de 9.30 a 5.30; **as usual** = como de costumbre

usury ['juːʒəri] *noun* usura *f*

◊ **usurer** ['juːzjʊrə] *noun* usurero, -ra

utilize ['juːtɪlaɪz] *verb* utilizar *or* usar *or* emplear

◊ **utilization** [juːtɪlaɪ'zeɪʃən] *noun* utilización *f or* uso *m or* empleo *m*; **capacity utilization** = empleo de la capacidad

> QUOTE control permits the manufacturer to react to changing conditions on the plant floor and to keep people and machines at a high level of utilization
> **Duns Business Month**

utility [juː'tɪlɪti] *noun* servicio *m* público

Vv

vacancy ['veɪkənsi] *noun* **(a)** *(job which is not filled)* plaza *f or* vacante *f*; **we advertised a vacancy in the local press** = hemos anunciado una vacante en la prensa local; **we have been unable to fill the vacancy for a skilled machinist** = no hemos podido cubrir la vacante de mecánico especializado; **they have a vacancy for a secretary** = tienen una vacante de secretaria; **to apply for a vacancy** = solicitar una plaza; **job vacancies** = ofertas de trabajo **(b)** *(empty rooms in a hotel)* **vacancy rate** = porcentaje de habitaciones no ocupadas; **vacancies** = habitaciones libres; **no vacancies** = 'completo' *or* no hay habitaciones libres *or* disponibles

◊ **vacant** ['veɪkənt] *adjective* vacante *or* libre *or* disponible; **vacant possession** = propiedad desocupada *or* libre de inquilinos *or* de ocupación inmediata; **the house is for sale with vacant possession** = la casa está en venta y libre de inquilinos; *(in a newspaper)* **situations vacant** *or* **appointments vacant** = ofertas de trabajo

QUOTE the official statistics on the number of vacancies at job centres at any one point in time represent about one third of total unfilled vacancies. The majority of vacancies are in small establishments
Employment Gazette

QUOTE the current vacancy rate in Tokyo stands at 7%. The supply of vacant office space, if new buildings are built at the current rate, is expected to take up to five years to absorb
Nikkei Weekly

vacate [və'keɪt] *verb* desocupar *or* desalojar; **to vacate the premises** = desalojar los locales; **rooms must be vacated before 12.00** = las habitaciones deben quedar libres antes de las 12.00

◊ **vacation** [və'keɪʃən] *noun* **(a)** *GB* días *mpl* inhábiles **(b)** *US* vacaciones *fpl*; **the CEO is on vacation in Florida** = el director general está de vacaciones en Florida

valid ['vælɪd] *adjective* **(a)** *(acceptable because true)* válido, -da; **that is not a valid argument** *or* **excuse** = no es un argumento válido *or* una excusa válida **(b)** *(which can be used lawfully)* válido, -da *or* valedero, -ra *or* en regla; **to be valid** = estar vigente *or* en vigencia; **the contract is not valid if it has not been witnessed** = el contrato no es válido si no ha sido firmado por un testigo; **ticket which is valid for three months** = billete valedero para tres meses; **he was carrying a valid passport** = llevaba un pasaporte en regla; **your passport is no longer valid** = tu pasaporte ha caducado

◊ **validate** ['vælɪdeɪt] *verb* **(a)** *(to check to see if something is correct)* validar *or* convalidar *or* comprobar la validez; **the document was validated by the bank** = el documento fue convalidado por el banco **(b)** *(to make something valid)* validar *or* dar validez a

◊ **validation** [vælɪ'deɪʃən] *noun* validación *f or* convalidación *f*

◊ **validity** [və'lɪdəti] *noun* validez *f*; **period of validity** = periodo de validez

valorem [və'lɔːrəm] *see* AD VALOREM

valuable ['væljʊbl] *adjective* valioso, -sa; **valuable property** *or* **valuables** = objetos *mpl* de valor

◊ **valuation** [væljʊ'eɪʃən] *noun* valoración *f or* evaluación *f or* tasación *f or* estimación *f*; **to ask for a valuation of a property before making an offer for it** = solicitar la valoración de una propiedad antes de hacer una oferta; **stock valuation** = valoración de existencias; **to buy a shop with stock at valuation** = comprar una tienda con las existencias tasadas; **stock market valuation** = valoración según la cotización en Bolsa

◊ **value** ['vælju:] **1** *noun* valor *m*; **he imported goods to the value of £250** = importó mercancías por valor de £250; **the fall in the value of sterling** = la caída *or* depreciación de la libra esterlina; **the valuer put the value of the stock at £25,000** = el tasador fijó el valor de las existencias en £25.000; **good value (for money)** = buen precio *m*; **that restaurant gives value for money** = ese restaurante está muy bien de precios *or* en ese restaurante se come bien y barato; **buy that computer now - it is very good value** = compre ese ordenador ahora - tiene un buen precio; **holidays in Italy are good value because of the exchange rate** = las vacaciones en Italia resultan muy ventajosas por el tipo de cambio; **to rise in value** *or* **to fall in value** = aumentar de valor *or* perder valor; **added value** *or* **value added** = valor añadido; *see also* VALUE ADDED TAX **asset value (of a company)** = valor de activo; **book value** = valor contable; **'sample only - of no commercial value'** = 'muestra gratuita - sin valor comercial'; **declared value** = valor declarado; **discounted value** = valor descontado; **face value** = valor nominal; **market value** = valor de mercado; **nominal value** = valor *or* importe nominal; **par value** = valor a la par; **present value** = valor actual; **scarcity value** = valor de escasez; *(of an insurance policy)* **surrender value** = valor de rescate **2** *verb* valorar *or* tasar *or* evaluar; **he valued the stock at £25,000** = valoró las existencias en £25.000; **we are having the jewellery valued for insurance** = nos están tasando las joyas para el seguro

◊ **Value Added Tax (VAT)** ['vælju: 'ædɪd tæks] *noun* impuesto *m* sobre el valor añadido (IVA); *see also* VAT

◊ **valuer** ['væljʊə] *noun* *(person who estimates value)* tasador, -ra *or* estimador, -ra *or* perito *m*

van [væn] *noun* camioneta *f*; **delivery van** = furgoneta de reparto

variable ['veərɪəbl] *adjective* variable; **variable costs** = costes variables

◊ **variability** [veərɪə'bɪləti] *noun* variabilidad *f*

◊ **variance** ['veərɪəns] *noun* desacuerdo *m or* discrepancia *f or* variación *f*; **budget variance** = variación presupuestaria; *(which does not agree)* **at variance with** = que difiere *or* que no concuerda; **the** actual sales are at variance with the sales reported by the reps = las ventas reales difieren de las ventas declaradas por los representantes

◊ **variation** [veərɪ'eɪʃən] *noun* variación *f*; **seasonal variations** = variaciones de temporada *or* estacionales; **seasonal variations in buying patterns** = variaciones estacionales del consumo

variety [və'raɪəti] *noun* variedad *f*; **the shop stocks a variety of goods** = la tienda tiene una variedad de mercancías; **we had a variety of visitors at the office today** = hoy hemos tenido una gran variedad de visitantes en la oficina; *US* **variety store** = tienda de artículos económicos y variados

◊ **vary** ['veəri] *verb* variar; **the gross margin varies from quarter to quarter** = el margen bruto varía de trimestre en trimestre; **we try to prevent the flow of production from varying in the factory** = intentamos evitar que varíe el flujo de producción de la fábrica

VAT ['viːeɪ'tiː *or* væt] = VALUE ADDED TAX impuesto sobre el valor añadido (IVA); **the invoice includes VAT at 15%** = la factura incluye el 15% de IVA; **the government is proposing to increase VAT to 17.5%** = el gobierno tiene la intención de aumentar el IVA al 17,5%; **some items (such as books) are zero-rated for VAT in Great Britain** = algunos artículos (tales como los libros) se gravan con un IVA del 0% en Gran Bretaña; **he does not charge VAT because he asks for payment in cash** = no cobra el IVA porque pide el pago al contado; **VAT declaration** = declaración del IVA; **VAT invoice** = factura con el IVA desglosado; **VAT invoicing** = facturación con IVA incluido; **VAT inspector** = inspector, -ra del IVA; **VAT office** = oficina del IVA

◊ **VATman** *or* **vatman** ['vætmæn] *noun* inspector *m* del IVA

COMMENT: In the UK, VAT is organized by the Customs and Excise Department, and not by the Treasury. It is applied at each stage in the process of making or selling a product or service. Company 'A' charges VAT for their work, which is bought by Company 'B', and pays the VAT collected from 'B' to the Customs and Excise; Company 'B' can reclaim the VAT element in Company 'A''s invoice from the Customs and Excise, but will charge VAT on their work in their invoice to Company 'C'. Each company along the line charges VAT and pays it to the Customs and Excise, but claims back any VAT charged to them. The final consumer pays a price which includes VAT, and which is the final VAT revenue paid to the Customs and Excise

QUOTE the directive means that the services of stockbrokers and managers of authorized unit trusts are now exempt from VAT; previously they were liable to VAT at the standard rate. Zero-rating for stockbrokers' services is still available as before, but only where the recipient of the service belongs outside the EC

Accountancy

VDU *or* **VDT** ['viːdiː'juː *or* 'viːdiː'tiː] = VISUAL DISPLAY UNIT *or* VISUAL DISPLAY TERMINAL unidad de despliegue visual (UDV) *or* unidad de presentación visual (UPV)

vehicle ['viːɪkl] *noun* vehículo *m*; **commercial vehicle** *or* **goods vehicle** = vehículo comercial *or*

vehículo de mercancías; **heavy goods vehicle (HGV)** = camión *m* de gran tonelaje; **goods vehicles can park in the loading bay** = los vehículos de mercancías pueden aparcar en la nave de carga

velocity [və'lɒsɪti] *noun* velocidad *f or* rapidez *f*

vending ['vendɪŋ] *noun* venta *f*; **(automatic) vending machine** = máquina expendedora automática *or* distribuidora automática

◊ **vendor** ['vendə] *noun* **(a)** *(person who is selling a property)* vendedor, -ra; **the solicitor acting on behalf of the vendor** = el abogado que actúa en nombre del vendedor **(b)** **street vendor** = buhonero, -ra *or* vendedor, -ra ambulante

Venezuela [venɪ'zweɪlə] *noun* Venezuela *f*

◊ **Venezuelan** [venɪ'zweɪlən] *adjective & noun* venezolano, -na
NOTE: capital: **Caracas**; currency: **Venezuelan bolivar (VBO)** = bolívar venezolano (VBO)

venture ['ventʃə] **1** *noun (business involving risk)* operación *f or* empresa *f*; **he lost money on several import ventures** = perdió dinero en varias operaciones de importación; **she has started a new venture - a computer shop** = ha lanzado una nueva empresa - una tienda de ordenadores; **joint venture** = empresa conjunta *or* negocio en participación *or* agrupación temporal de empresas; **venture capital** = capital riesgo **2** *verb* arriesgar

QUOTE along with the stock market boom of the 1980s, the venture capitalists piled more and more funds into the buyout business, backing bigger and bigger deals with ever more extravagant financing structures

Guardian

venue ['venjuː] *noun (of a meeting)* lugar *m or* punto *m* de reunión; **we have changed the venue for the conference** = hemos cambiado el lugar de la reunión; **what is the venue for the exhibition?** = ¿dónde tiene lugar la exposición?

verbal ['vɜːbəl] *adjective (using spoken words, not writing)* verbal; **verbal agreement** = acuerdo verbal

◊ **verbally** ['vɜːbəli] *adverb* verbalmente; **they agreed to the terms verbally, and then started to draft the contract** = llegaron a un acuerdo verbal sobre las condiciones y después empezaron a redactar el contrato

verify ['verɪfaɪ] *verb* verificar

◊ **verification** [verɪfɪ'keɪʃən] *noun* verificación *f or* comprobación *f*; **the shipment was allowed into the country after verification of the documents by customs** = se autorizó la entrada del cargamento en el país después de que la aduana verificara los documentos

vertical ['vɜːtɪkəl] *adjective* vertical; **vertical communication** = comunicación vertical; **vertical integration** = integración vertical

vessel ['vesl] *noun* buque *m or* barco *m*; **merchant vessel** = buque mercante

vested interest ['vestɪd 'ɪntrest] *noun (special interest in an existing state of affairs)* interés personal *or* intereses creados; **she has a vested interest in keeping the business working** = tiene un interés personal en que el negocio siga funcionando

vet [vet] *verb (to examine carefully)* someter a un examen riguroso *or* examinar rigurosamente; **all candidates have to be vetted by the managing director** = todos los candidatos tienen que ser rigurosamente examinados por el director gerente; **the contract has been sent to the legal department for vetting** = el contrato ha sido enviado a la asesoría jurídica para que lo sometan a un examen riguroso (NOTE: **vetting - vetted**)

veto ['vi:təʊ] **1** *noun* veto *m*; **right of veto** = derecho de veto **2** *verb* **to veto a decision** = vetar una decisión

via ['vaɪə] *preposition* por *or* vía; **the shipment is going via the Suez Canal** = el envío irá por el Canal de Suez; **we are sending the cheque via our office in New York** = enviaremos nuestro cheque vía nuestra oficina de Nueva York; **they sent the message via the telex line** = enviaron el mensaje por telex

viable ['vaɪəbl] *adjective* viable; **not commercially viable** = no viable comercialmente

◊ **viability** [vaɪə'bɪlətɪ] *noun* viabilidad *f*

vice- [vaɪs] *prefix* vice; **he is the vice-chairman of an industrial group** = es el vicepresidente de un grupo industrial; **she was appointed to the vice-chairmanship of the committee** = fue designada para que ocupara la vicepresidencia del comité

◊ **vice-president** [vaɪs'prezɪdənt] *noun* US vicepresidente, -ta; **senior vice-president** = director general adjunto *or* el vicepresidente principal *or* más antiguo

video ['vɪdɪəʊ] **1** *noun* vídeo *m*; **video camera** = cámara de vídeo *or* videocámara; **video cassette** = videocasete; **video recorder** = grabadora de vídeo *or* videograbadora; **video tape** = cinta de vídeo **2** *verb* hacer un vídeo *or* grabar en vídeo

◊ **videophone** ['vɪdɪəʊfəʊn] *noun* videófono *m*

Vietnam [vjet'næm *or* US vjet'nɑ:m] *noun* Vietnam *m*

◊ **Vietnamese** [vjetnə'mi:z] *adjective & noun* vietnamita
NOTE: capital: **Hanoi**; currency: **Vietnamese dong (D)** dong vietnamita (D)

view [vju:] *noun* opinión *f or* parecer *m*; **we asked the sales manager for his views on the reorganization of the reps' territories** = preguntamos al director de ventas su opinión sobre la reorganización de las zonas de los representantes; **the chairman takes the view that credit should never be longer than thirty days** = el presidente es de la opinión que el crédito no debería sobrepasar nunca los treinta días; **to take the long view** = planificar *or* pensar a largo plazo; **in view of** = en vista de *or* a la vista de; **in view of the falling exchange rate, we have redrafted our sales forecasts** = en vista de la caída del tipo de cambio, hemos vuelto a hacer nuestro proyecto de previsiones de ventas

vigilance ['vɪdʒɪləns] *noun* vigilancia *f*

vigorous ['vɪgərəs] *adjective* vigoroso, -sa *or* enérgico, -ca; **we are planning a vigorous publicity campaign** = estamos proyectando una enérgica campaña publicitaria

VIP ['vi:aɪ'pi:] = VERY IMPORTANT PERSON *(at airport)* **VIP lounge** = salón VIP *or* salón de personalidades; **we laid on VIP treatment for our visitors** *or* **we gave our visitors a VIP reception** = ofrecimos una recepción de categoría a nuestros visitantes

virement ['vaɪəmənt] *noun* transferencia *f*

visa ['vi:zə] *noun* visado *m*; **you will need a visa before you go to the USA** = necesitarás un visado para ir a los EE UU; **he filled in his visa application form** = rellenó el formulario de solicitud de visado; **entry visa** = visado de entrada; **multiple entry visa** = visado de entrada múltiple; **tourist visa** = visado turista; **transit visa** = visado de tránsito

visible ['vɪzəbl] *adjective* visible; **visible imports** *or* **exports** *or* **visibles** = importaciones *f or* exportaciones *f* visibles; **visible trade** = comercio de visibles

visit ['vɪzɪt] **1** *noun* visita *f or* viaje *m*; **we are expecting a visit from our German agents** = estamos esperando una visita de nuestros representantes alemanes; **he is on a business visit to London** = está de viaje de negocios en Londres; **we had a visit from the VAT inspector** = tuvimos una visita del inspector del IVA **2** *verb* visitar; **he spent a week in Scotland, visiting clients in Edinburgh and Glasgow** = pasó una semana en Escocia, visitando a clientes de Edimburgo y Glasgow; **the trade delegation visited the Ministry of Commerce** = la delegación comercial visitó el Ministerio de Comercio

◊ **visitor** ['vɪzɪtə] *noun* visitante *mf*; **the chairman showed the Japanese visitors round the factory** = el presidente enseñó la fábrica a los visistantes japoneses; **visitors' bureau** = despacho de visitantes

visual ['vɪʒuəl] *adjective* visual

◊ **visual display terminal (VDT)** *or* **visual display unit (VDU)** [,vɪzjuəldɪs'pleɪtɜ:mɪnəl *or* ,vɪzjuəldɪs'pleɪju:nɪt] *noun* unidad de despliegue *or* de representación visual *or* monitor *or* pantalla

vivos ['vaɪvɒs] *noun* **gift inter vivos** = donación *f* inter vivos

vocation [və(ʊ)'keɪʃən] *noun* vocación *f*; **he followed his vocation and became an accountant** = siguió su vocación y se hizo contable

◊ **vocational** [və(ʊ)'keɪʃənl] *adjective* profesional; **vocational guidance** = orientación profesional; **vocational training** = formación *or* capacitación profesional

void [vɔɪd] **1** *adjective (not legally valid)* nulo, -la *or* inválido, -da; **the contract was declared null and void** = el contrato fue declarado nulo y sin valor **2** *verb* **to void a contract** = invalidar *or* anular *or* rescindir un contrato

volume ['vɒlju:m] *noun* volumen *m*; **volume discount** = descuento por volumen; **volume of output** = volumen de producción; **volume of sales** *or* **sales volume** = volumen de ventas; **low** *or* **high**

volume of sales = volumen de ventas alto *or* bajo; **volume of trade** *or* **volume of business** = volumen comercial *or* volumen de negocios; **the company has maintained the same volume of business in spite of the recession** = la empresa ha mantenido el volumen de negocios a pesar de la recesión

voluntary ['vɒləntəri] *adjective* **(a)** *(done without being forced)* voluntario, -ria; **voluntary liquidation** = liquidación voluntaria; *(situation where a worker asks to be made redundant)* **voluntary redundancy** = baja incentivada *or* baja voluntaria con derecho a indemnización **(b)** *(done without being paid)* a título gratuito; **voluntary organization** = organización voluntaria *or* cuyo personal no percibe sueldo alguno

◊ **voluntarily** ['vɒləntərəli] *adverb* *(without being forced)* voluntariamente; *(without being paid)* sin percibir sueldo

vote [vəut] **1** *noun* voto *m* *or* votación *f*; **to take a vote on a proposal** *or* **to put a proposal to the vote** = someter una propuesta a votación; **block vote** = voto por representación *or* delegación; **casting vote** = voto de calidad; **the chairman has the casting vote** = el presidente tiene derecho al voto de calidad; **he used his casting vote to block the motion** = utilizó su voto de calidad para bloquear la moción; **postal vote** = voto por correo; **proxy vote** = voto por

poderes **2** *verb* votar; **the meeting voted to close the factory** = la reunión votó a favor del cierre de la fábrica; **52% of the members voted for Mr Smith as chairman** = el 52% de los socios votaron al Sr. Smith como presidente; **to vote for a proposal** *or* **to vote against a proposal** = votar a favor de *or* en contra de una propuesta; **two directors were voted off the board at the AGM** = en la junta general anual se votó a favor del cese de dos directores; **she was voted on to the committee** = fue elegida miembro del comité

◊ **voter** ['vəutə] *noun* votante *mf*

◊ **voting** ['vəutɪŋ] *noun* votación *f*; **voting paper** = papeleta (de voto); **voting rights** = derecho a voto; **voting share** = acción con derecho a voto; **non-voting shares** = acciones sin derecho a voto

voucher ['vautʃə] *noun* **(a)** *(paper given instead of money)* bono *m* *or* vale *m*; **cash voucher** = vale de caja; **with every £20 of purchases, the customer gets a cash voucher to the value of £2** = por cada £20 de compra, el cliente obtiene un vale de caja por un valor de £2; **gift voucher** = vale para un regalo; **luncheon voucher** = bono *or* vale de comida **(b)** *(written documennt from an auditor)* comprobante *m*

voyage ['vɔɪɪdʒ] *noun* travesía *f or* viaje *m* por mar *or* en barco

Ww

wage [weɪdʒ] *noun* sueldo *m or* salario *m or* jornal *m*; **she is earning a good wage** *or* **good wages in the supermarket** = gana un buen sueldo en el supermercado; **basic wage** = salario *or* sueldo base; **the basic wage is £110 a week, but you can expect to earn more than that with overtime** = el salario base es de £110 a la semana, pero se puede ganar más con horas extras; **hourly wage** *or* **wage per hour** = salario *or* sueldo *or* pago por hora; **minimum wage** = salario mínimo; **wage adjustments** = ajustes salariales; **index-linked wage agreement** = acuerdo *or* convenio de ajuste salarial sobre el coste de vida; **wage claim** = reivindicación salarial; **wages clerk** = empleado, -da que se ocupa del pago de salarios; **wage differentials** = diferencias salariales; **wage drift** = diferencial de salarios; **wage freeze** *or* **freeze on wages** = congelación de salarios; **wage levels** = niveles de salarios; **wage negotiations** = negociaciones salariales; **wage packet** = sobre de paga; **wages policy** = política salarial; **wage-price spiral** = espiral salarios-precios; **wage scale** = escala de salarios *or* escala salarial (NOTE: **wages** is more usual when referring to money earned, but **wage** is used before other nouns)

◊ **wage-earner** [ˈweɪdʒˈɜːnə] *noun* asalariado, -da

◊ **wage-earning** [ˈweɪdʒˈɜːnɪŋ] *adjective* **the wage-earning population** = la población asalariada

COMMENT: the term 'wages' refers to weekly or hourly pay for workers, usually paid in cash. For workers paid by a monthly cheque, the term used is 'salary'

QUOTE European economies are being held back by rigid labor markets and wage structures
Duns Business Month

QUOTE real wages have been held down dramatically: they have risen at an annual rate of only 1% in the last two years
Sunday Times

wagon *or* **waggon** [ˈwægn] *noun* vagón *m*

waive [weɪv] *verb* renunciar *or* desistir; **he waived his claim to the estate** = renunció a su derecho a la herencia; **to waive a payment** = renunciar a un pago

◊ **waiver** [ˈweɪvə] *noun (giving up a right)* renuncia *f or* desistimiento *m*; **if you want to work without a permit, you will have to apply for a waiver** = si quiere trabajar sin permiso, deberá solicitar una excepción; **waiver clause** = cláusula de renuncia

walk [wɔːk] *verb* andar *or* recorrer a pie; **he walks to the office every morning** = va a la oficina andando todas las mañanas; **the visitors walked round the factory** = los visitantes recorrieron la fábrica a pie

◊ **walk off** [ˈwɔːk ˈɒf] *verb (to go on strike)* declararse en huelga *or* abandonar el puesto de trabajo *or* parar; **the builders walked off the site because they said it was too dangerous** = los contratistas abandonaron la obra porque dijeron que era demasiado peligrosa

◊ **walk out** [ˈwɔːk ˈaʊt] *verb (to go on strike)* declararse en huelga *or* abandonar el puesto de trabajo *or* parar; **the whole workforce walked out in protest** = la totalidad del personal abandonó el trabajo en señal de protesta

◊ **walk-out** [ˈwɔːkaʊt] *noun* huelga *f or* paro *m or* plante *m*; **production has been held up by the walk-out of the workers** = la producción ha sido interrumpida por la huelga de los trabajadores (NOTE: plural is **walk-outs**)

Wall Street [ˈwɔːl ˈstriːt] *noun* Wall Street (centro financiero de Nueva York); **a Wall Street analyst** = un analista de Wall Street; **she writes the Wall Street column in the newspaper** = escribe la sección financiera *or* columna de Wall Street del periódico

wallet [ˈwɒlɪt] *noun* cartera *f or* billetera *f*; **wallet file** = carpeta *f*

want [wɒnt] *noun* falta *f or* necesidad *f or* carencia *f*; **want ads** = pequeños anuncios; **to draw up a wants list** = hacer una lista de cosas que faltan

war [wɔː] *noun* guerra *f*; **price war** = guerra de precios; **tariff war** = guerra de tarifas

warehouse [ˈweəhaʊs] **1** *noun* almacén *m*; **bonded warehouse** = depósito aduanero; **warehouse capacity** = capacidad de almacén; **price ex warehouse** = precio puesto en almacén *or* franco en almacén **2** *verb (to store in a warehouse)* almacenar

◊ **warehousing** [ˈweəhaʊzɪŋ] *noun* almacenaje *m*; **warehousing costs are rising rapidly** = los costes de almacenaje están aumentando vertiginosamente

◊ **warehouseman** [ˈweəhaʊsmən] *noun* almacenero, -ra *or* almacenista *mf*

warn [wɔːn] *verb* advertir *or* prevenir de *or* avisar de *or* anunciar; **he warned the shareholders that the dividend might be cut** = advirtió a los accionistas que el dividendo podía ser recortado; **the government warned of possible import duties** = el gobierno anunció que podrían aplicarse aranceles a la importación (NOTE: you warn someone **of** something, or **that** something may happen)

◊ **warning** [ˈwɔːnɪŋ] *noun* advertencia *f or* aviso *m*; **to issue a warning** = publicar un aviso; **warning notices were put up around the construction site** = se colocaron letreros *or* carteles de advertencia por toda la obra

warrant [ˈwɒrənt] **1** *noun (official document)* autorización *f*; **dividend warrant** = cheque *f* en pago de dividendos; **share warrant** = certificado *m or* documento *m* de posesión de acciones **2** *verb* **(a)** *(to guarantee)* garantizar; **all the spare parts are warranted** = todas las piezas de repuesto tienen garantía **(b)** *(to justify)* justificar; **the company's**

volume of trade with the USA does not warrant six trips a year to New York by the sales director = el volumen comercial que la empresa tiene con los EE UU no justifica los seis viajes anuales a Nueva York realizados por el director de ventas

◊ **warrantee** ['wɒrənti:] *noun* persona *f* que recibe una garantía

◊ **warrantor** ['wɒrəntɔ:] *noun (person who gives a warranty)* fiador, -ra *or* garante *mf*

◊ **warranty** ['wɒrənti] *noun* **(a)** *(legal guarantee)* garantía *f*; **the car is sold with a twelve-month warranty** = el coche se vende con una garantía de doce meses; **the warranty covers spare parts but not labour costs** = la garantía cubre las piezas de recambio pero no los costes de la mano de obra **(b)** *(promise in a contract)* garantía; **breach of warranty** = violación de garantía **(c)** *(statement that facts are true)* garantía

QUOTE the rights issue will grant shareholders free warrants to subscribe for further new shares
Financial Times

wastage ['weistidʒ] *noun* pérdida *f or* desperdicio *m*; **allow 10% extra material for wastage** = contar con un 10% de material de más para pérdidas; *(losing workers)* **natural wastage** = amortización de vacantes de una plantilla *or* reducción natural de la mano de obra por jubilación *o* baja voluntaria

◊ **waste** [weist] **1** *noun* desperdicio *m or* desecho *m or* vertido *m or* residuos *mpl*; **the company was fined for putting industrial waste into the river** = la empresa fue multada por echar residuos industriales al río; **it is a waste of time asking the chairman for a rise** = es una pérdida de tiempo pedirle al presidente un aumento de sueldo; **that computer is a waste of money - there are plenty of cheaper models which would do the work just as well** = comprar ese ordenador es desperdiciar el dinero - hay cantidad de modelos más baratos que harían el trabajo igual de bien **2** *adjective* de desecho; **waste materials** = materiales de desecho; **cardboard is made from recycled waste paper** = el cartón está hecho de papel reciclado; **waste paper basket** *US* **wastebasket** = ['weis(t)bɑ:skit] papelera *f* **3** *verb* desperdiciar *or* malgastar; **to waste money** *or* **paper** *or* **electricity** *or* **time** = despilfarrar *or* malgastar el dinero *or* desperdiciar el papel *or* la electricidad *or* perder el tiempo; **the MD does not like people wasting his time with minor details** = al director gerente no le gusta que le hagan perder el tiempo con pequeños detalles; **we turned off all the heating so as not to waste energy** = apagamos toda la calefacción para no desperdiciar energía

◊ **wastebasket** ['weis(t)bɑ:skit] *noun US* = WASTE PAPER BASKET

◊ **wasteful** ['weistful] *adjective* que gasta mucho; **this photocopier is very wasteful of paper** = esta fotocopiadora gasta mucho papel

◊ **wasting asset** ['weistiŋ 'æsit] *noun* activo consumible

waterproof ['wɔ:təpru:f] *adjective* impermeable; **the parts are sent in waterproof packing** = las piezas se envían en paquetes impermeables

way [wei] **1** *noun* **(a)** *(manner)* modo *m or* manera *f*; **in what way?** = ¿de qué modo? *or* ¿cómo? **(b)**

(direction) dirección *f*; **one-way street** = calle de dirección única

waybill ['weibil] *noun* carta *f* de porte *or* manifiesto *m* de carga

weak [wi:k] *adjective* débil *or* flojo, -ja; **weak market** = mercado débil *or* flojo; **share prices remained weak** = los precios de las acciones se mantuvieron flojos

◊ **weaken** ['wi:kən] *verb* debilitar; **the market weakened** = el mercado se debilitó

◊ **weakness** ['wi:knəs] *noun* debilidad *f*

QUOTE the Fed started to ease monetary policy months ago as the first stories appeared about weakening demand in manufacturing industry
Sunday Times

QUOTE indications of weakness in the US economy were contained in figures from the Fed on industrial production
Financial Times

wealth [welθ] *noun* riqueza *f or* patrimonio *m*; **wealth tax** = impuesto sobre el patrimonio

◊ **wealthy** ['welθi] *adjective* rico, -ca *or* acaudalado, -da

wear and tear ['weə ən 'teə] *noun* desgaste *m or* uso *m or* deterioro *m*; **fair wear and tear** = desgaste *m* natural *or* normal; **the insurance policy covers most damage but not fair wear and tear to the machine** = la póliza de seguros cubre la mayoría de los daños, pero no el desgaste natural de la máquina

week [wi:k] *noun* semana *f*; **to be paid by the week** = cobrar semanalmente; **he earns £500 a week** *or* **per week** = gana £500 a la semana *or* por semana; **she works thirty-five hours per week** *or* **she works a thirty-five-hour week** = trabaja treinta y cinco horas por semana

◊ **weekday** ['wi:kdei] *noun* día *m* laborable *or* de trabajo

◊ **weekly** ['wi:kli] *adjective* semanalmente; **the weekly rate for the job is £250** = el sueldo semanal por el trabajo es de £250; **a weekly magazine** *or* **a weekly** = revista *f* semanal

weigh [wei] *verb* **(a)** *(to measure weight)* pesar; **he weighed the packet at the post office** = pesó el paquete en la oficina de correos **(b)** *(to have a certain weight)* pesar; **the packet weighs twenty-five grams** = el paquete pesa veinticinco gramos

◊ **weighbridge** ['weibridʒ] *noun* báscula *f* puente *or* puente-báscula *m*

◊ **weighing machine** ['weiiŋ mə'ʃi:n] *noun* báscula *f or* balanza *f*

◊ **weight** [weit] *noun (measurement of how heavy something is)* peso *m*; **to sell fruit by weight** = vender fruta a peso; **false weight** = peso falso *or* escaso; **gross weight** = peso bruto; **net weight** = peso neto; **to give short weight** = dar el peso escaso; **inspector of weights and measures** = inspector, -ra de pesos y medidas

◊ **weighted** ['weitid] *adjective* **weighted average** = promedio ponderado; **weighted index** = índice ponderado

◊ **weighting** ['weitiŋ] *noun* gratificación *f or*

bonificación *f or* ponderación *f*; **salary plus a London weighting** = el sueldo más un subsidio por vivir en Londres

welfare ['welfeə] *noun* **(a)** *(looking after people)* bienestar *m or* asistencia *f* social; **the chairman is interested in the welfare of the workers' families** = el presidente está interesado en el bienestar de las familias de los trabajadores; **welfare state** = estado asistencial *or* benefactor *or* estado del bienestar **(b)** *(money paid by the government)* ayuda *f* del Estado

QUOTE California has become the latest state to enact a program forcing welfare recipients to work for their benefits
Fortune

well-known [wel'nəʊn] *adjective* muy conocido, -da *or* célebre

◊ **well-off** [wel'ɒf] *adjective* acaudalado, -da

◊ **well-paid** ['wel'peɪd] *adjective* bien pagado, -da; **well-paid job** = trabajo bien remunerado *or* empleo bien pagado

wharf [wɔ:f] *noun* muelle *m or* embarcadero *m* (NOTE: plural is **wharfs** or **wharves**)

◊ **wharfage** ['wɔ:fɪdʒ] *noun (charge for tying up at a wharf)* derechos *mpl* de muelle *or* muellaje *m*

◊ **wharfinger** ['wɔ:fɪŋgə] *noun* trabajador portuario *or* 'docker'

wheeler-dealer ['wi:lə'di:lə] *noun* comerciante *m* poco escrupuloso

whereas [weər'æz] *conjunction (legal)* considerando

◊ **whereof** [weər'ɒv] *adverb (formal)* **in witness whereof I sign my hand** = en fe de lo cual firmo (de mi puño y letra)

white [waɪt] *adjective* blanco, -ca; *(sale of sheets or towels, etc.)* **white sale** = rebajas de ropa blanca

◊ **white-collar** ['waɪtkɒlə] *adjective* oficinista *mf*; **white-collar crime** = delitos de oficinistas *or* administrativos; **white-collar union** = sindicato *m* de empleados de oficina; *(worker in an office)* **white-collar worker** = empleado, -da de oficina *or* administrativo, -va

◊ **white goods** ['waɪt 'gʊdz] *plural noun* **(a)** *(electric appliances)* electrodomésticos *mpl* **(b)** *(linen)* ropa blanca

◊ **white knight** ['waɪt 'naɪt] *noun* rescatador *m* de empresas

◊ **White Paper** ['waɪt 'peɪpə] *noun GB (report from the government)* libro blanco

QUOTE the share of white-collar occupations in total employment rose from 44 per cent to 49 per cent
Sydney Morning Herald

whole-life insurance *or* **assurance** ['həʊllaɪf ɪn'ʃʊərəns] *noun* seguro *m* corriente de vida

wholesale ['həʊlseɪl] **1** *noun* venta *f* al por mayor **2** *adjective* al por mayor; **wholesale discount** = descuento al por mayor; **wholesale shop** = tienda al por mayor; **wholesale dealer** = comerciante al por mayor *or* mayorista; **wholesale price index** = índice

de precios al por mayor **3** *adverb* **he buys wholesale and sells retail** = compra al por mayor y vende al por menor

◊ **wholesaler** ['həʊlseɪlə] *noun* mayorista *mf or* comerciante *mf* al por mayor; *US* **truck wholesaler** = mayorista sin almacén

wholly-owned subsidiary ['həʊlɪ'əʊnd səb'sɪdjəri] *noun* filial *f* en propiedad absoluta

wide [waɪd] *adjective* ancho, -cha

◊ **width** [wɪdθ] *noun* ancho *m*

wildcat strike ['waɪldkæt 'straɪk] *noun* huelga *f* salvaje

will [wɪl] *noun (legal document)* testamento *m*; **he wrote his will in 1984** = hizo testamento en 1984; **according to her will, all her property is left to her children** = según el testamento, todos los bienes pasan a sus hijos

COMMENT: a will should best be drawn up by a solicitor; it can also be written on a form which can be bought from a stationery shop. To be valid, a will must be dated and witnessed by a third party (i.e., by someone who is not mentioned in the will)

win [wɪn] *verb (to be successful)* ganar *or* conseguir *or* lograr; **to win a contract** = conseguir un contrato; **the company announced that it had won a contract worth £25m to supply buses and trucks** = la empresa anunció que había conseguido un contrato por un valor de £25 millones para suministrar autobuses y camiones (NOTE: **winning - won**)

windfall ['wɪn(d)fɔ:l] *noun (sudden profit which is not expected)* **windfall profit** = ganancia *f* inesperada; **windfall (profits) tax** = impuesto sobre los beneficios extraordinarios

wind up ['wɪnd 'ʌp] *verb* **(a)** *(to end a meeting)* terminar *or* concluir *or* clausurar; **he wound up the meeting with a vote of thanks to the committee** = clausuró la reunión dando las gracias al comité **(b)** *(to put a company into liquidation)* **to wind up a company** = liquidar una sociedad; **the court ordered the company to be wound up** = el tribunal ordenó que se liquidara la sociedad (NOTE: **winding - wound**)

◊ **winding up** ['waɪndɪŋ 'ʌp] *noun* liquidación *f*; **a compulsory winding up order** = orden forzosa de liquidación

window ['wɪndəʊ] *noun* **(a)** *(in a wall)* ventana *f*; **shop window** = escaparate *m*; **window display** = escaparate *or* objetos expuestos en un escaparate; **window envelope** = sobre de ventanilla; **window shopping** = ir de escaparates **(b)** *(short period)* **window of opportunity** = oportunidad *f or* apertura *f*

◊ **window dressing** ['wɪndəʊ 'dresɪŋ] *noun* **(a)** *(putting goods on display in a shop window)* decoración *f* de escaparates *or* escaparatismo *m* **(b)** *(pretending that a business is successful)* manipulación *f* engañosa del balance de situación de una empresa

WIP = WORK IN PROGRESS

wire ['waɪə] **1** *noun (telegram)* telegrama *f*; **to send someone a wire** = poner *or* enviar un telegrama a alguien **2** *verb* telegrafiar a alguien *or* poner un telegrama a alguien; **he wired the head office to say that the deal had been signed** = telegrafió a la oficina central para decir que se había firmado el trato

wise [waɪz] *adjective (prudent)* prudente; **a wise decision** = una decisión prudente

withdraw [wɪθ'drɔː] *verb* **(a)** *(to take money out of an account)* retirar *or* sacar; **to withdraw money from the bank** *or* **from your account** = sacar dinero del banco *or* de la cuenta propia; **you can withdraw up to £50 from any bank on presentation of a banker's card** = se pueden sacar hasta £50 de cualquier banco presentando una tarjeta bancaria *or* de crédito **(b)** *(to take back an offer)* retirar una oferta; **one of the company's backers has withdrawn** = uno de los capitalistas de la sociedad ha retirado su apoyo; **to withdraw a takeover bid** = retirar una oferta de adquisición; **the chairman asked him to withdraw the remarks he had made about the finance director** = el presidente le pidió que retirara las observaciones que había hecho sobre el director financiero (NOTE: **withdrawing - withdrew - has withdrawn)**

◊ **withdrawal** [wɪθ'drɔːəl] *noun* retirada *f or* retiro *m or* reintegro *m*; **withdrawal without penalty at seven days' notice** = retirada de fondos sin recargo siempre que se avise con siete días de antelación; **to give seven days' notice of withdrawal** = dar aviso de retirada de fondos con siete días de antelación

withholding tax [wɪθ'həʊldɪŋ 'tæks] *noun* **(a)** *(from interest or dividends)* retención de impuestos en origen **(b)** *US (from a worker's paycheck)* impuesto sobre la renta retenido en origen

within [wɪ'ðɪn] *preposition* dentro; **within a week** = dentro de una semana

without [wɪ'ðaʊt] *preposition* sin; **without a job** = sin trabajo

witness ['wɪtnəs] **1** *noun* testimonio *m or* testigo *mf*; **to act as a witness to a document** *or* **a signature** = actuar como testigo de la veracidad de un documento *or* firma; **the MD signed as a witness** = el director gerente firmó como testigo; **the contract has to be signed in front of two witnesses** = el contrato se ha de firmar en presencia de *or* ante dos testigos **2** *verb (to sign a document)* firmar como testigo; **to witness an agreement** *or* **a signature** = firmar como testigo de un acuerdo *or* ser testigo de una firma

wk = WEEK

wobbler ['wɒblə] *noun (card placed on the shelf in a shop to promote a product)* **shelf wobbler** = tarjeta de promoción de un producto en una estantería

wording ['wɜːdɪŋ] *noun* texto *m or* redacción *f*; **the wording of a contract** = la redacción de los términos de un contrato; **did you read the wording on the contract?** = ¿leyó Vd. el texto del contrato?

word-processing ['wɜːd'prəʊsesɪŋ] *noun* tratamiento *m* de textos; **load the word-processing program before you start keyboarding** = cargue el programa de tratamiento de textos antes de empezar a teclear; **word-processing bureau** = despacho de tratamiento de textos

◊ **word-processor** ['wɜːd'prəʊsesə] *noun* procesador *m* de textos

work [wɜːk] **1** *noun* **(a)** *(labour)* trabajo *m*; **casual work** = trabajo eventual; **clerical work** = trabajo de oficina; **manual work** = trabajo manual; **place of work** = lugar de trabajo **(b)** *(job)* trabajo *or* empleo *m*; **he goes to work by bus** = va al trabajo en autobús; **she never gets home from work before 8 p.m.** = nunca llega del trabajo antes de las 8 de la tarde; **his work involves a lot of travelling** = su empleo le exige viajar mucho; **he is still looking for work** = todavía está buscando trabajo; **she has been out of work for six months** = ha estado sin trabajar durante seis meses; **work permit** = permiso *m* de trabajo **(c)** *(piece of work)* obra *f*; **work in progress** (WIP) = obra en curso **2** *verb* **(a)** trabajar; **the factory is working hard to complete the order** = la fábrica está trabajando duramente para completar *or* terminar el pedido; **she works better now that she has been promoted** = ahora que ha sido ascendida trabaja mejor; **to work a machine** = manejar *or* hacer funcionar una máquina; **to work to rule** = hacer huelga de celo **(b)** *(to have a job)* trabajar; **she works in an office** = trabaja en una oficina; **he works at Smith's** = trabaja en Smith; **he is working as a cashier in a supermarket** = trabaja de cajero en un supermercado

◊ **workaholic** [wɜːkə'hɒlɪk] *noun* persona adicta al trabajo

◊ **workday** ['wɜːkdeɪ] *noun* día *m* laborable

◊ **worker** ['wɜːkə] *noun* **(a)** *(person who is employed)* trabajador, -ra *or* empleado, -da; **blue-collar worker** = obrero manual; **casual worker** = trabajador,-ra eventual *or* temporero, -ra; **clerical worker** = empleado de oficina; **factory worker** = obrero de fábrica; **farm worker** = trajador agrícola *or* granjero *or* agricultor; **hourly-paid worker** = trabajador por horas; **manual worker** = obrero manual; **white-collar worker** = empleado de oficina; **worker director** = delegado, -da del personal; **worker representation on the board** = representación del personal en el consejo de administración **(b)** *(person who works hard)* trabajador, -ra; **she's a real worker** = es una gran trabajadora

◊ **workforce** ['wɜːkfɔːs] *noun (all the workers)* mano *f* de obra *or* personal *m*

◊ **working** ['wɜːkɪŋ] *adjective* **(a)** trabajador, -ra *or* obrero, -ra; **hard-working** = muy trabajador; **the working population of a country** = la población activa *or* trabajadora de un país; **working partner** = socio activo; **working party** = grupo de trabajo; **the government set up a working party to examine the problem of computers in schools** = el gobierno creó un grupo de trabajo para estudiar el problema de los ordenadores en las escuelas **(b)** *(referring to work)* laborable *or* laboral *or* de trabajo; **working capital** = capital circulante; **working conditions** = condiciones de trabajo; **working day** = día útil *or* hábil; **in working order** = en marcha; **the normal working week** = semana laboral normal; **even though he is a freelance, he works a normal working week** = aunque es un trabajador independiente, hace una semana de trabajo normal

◊ **workload** ['wɜːkləʊd] *noun (amount of work to be done)* trabajo *m* asignado *or* carga *f* de trabajo;

he has difficulty in coping with his heavy workload = tiene dificultades en despachar el trabajo que se le ha asignado

◊ **workman** ['wɜːkmən] *noun* trabajador *or* obrero (NOTE: plural is **workmen**)

◊ **workmanship** ['wɜːkmənʃɪp] *noun* habilidad *f or* destreza *f*; **bad** *or* **shoddy workmanship** = trabajo mal realizado *or* mal hecho

◊ **work out** ['wɜːk 'aʊt] *verb* **(a)** *(to calculate)* calcular *or* hacer un cálculo; **he worked out the costs on the back of an envelope** = calculó los costes en el reverso de un sobre; **he worked out the discount at 15%** = calculó el descuento aplicando un 15%; **she worked out the discount on her calculator** = hizo el cálculo del descuento en su calculadora **(b)** he is working out his notice = está trabajando los últimos días que le quedan del contrato

◊ **workplace** ['wɜːkpleɪs] *noun* lugar *m* de trabajo

◊ **works** [wɜːks] *noun (factory)* fábrica *f*; **an industrial works** = fábrica industrial; **an engineering works** = fábrica de construcción de máquinas *or* de maquinaria; **the steel works is expanding** = se está ampliando la fábrica de acero; **works committee** *or* **works council** = comité de empresa; **price ex works** = precio en fábrica *or* franco en fábrica; **the works manager** = director, -ra de fábrica o taller (NOTE: **works** takes a singular verb)

◊ **work-sharing** ['wɜːk'ʃeərɪŋ] *noun* sistema de trabajo a horario compartido

◊ **workshop** ['wɜːkʃɒp] *noun* taller *m*

◊ **workspace** ['wɜːkspeɪs] *noun (space available on a computer)* memoria *f* de un ordenador para trabajos temporales *or* espacio *m* disponible

◊ **workstation** ['wɜːksteɪʃn] *noun (of a computer operator)* puesto *m* de trabajo *or* estación *f* de trabajo

◊ **work-to-rule** ['wɜːk tə 'ruːl] *noun* huelga *f* de celo *or* paro *m* técnico

◊ **workweek** ['wɜːkwiːk] *noun US* semana laboral (NOTE: GB English is **working week**)

world [wɜːld] *noun* **(a)** *(the earth)* mundo *m*; **the world market for steel** = el mercado mundial del acero; **he has world rights to a product** = tiene los derechos de venta del producto en todos los países; **world trade** = comercio mundial **(b)** *(people in a particular business)* mundo; **the world of big business** = el mundo de los grandes negocios; **the world of publishing** *or* **the publishing world** = el

mundo de las editoriales; **the world of lawyers** *or* **the legal world** = el mundo de los abogados

◊ **World Bank** ['wɜːld 'bæŋk] Banco Mundial

◊ **World Trade Organization (WTO)** ['wɜːld 'treɪd ɑːgənaɪ'zeɪʃn] Organización Mundial del Comercio (OMC)

| COMMENT: set up in 1995 to replace GATT

◊ **worldwide** [wɜːld'waɪd] **1** *adjective* mundial *or* global; **the company has a worldwide network of distributors** = la compañía tiene una red mundial de distribuidores; **worldwide sales** *or* **sales worldwide have topped two million units** = las ventas mundiales han superado la cifra de dos millones de unidades **2** *adverb* mundialmente *or* en todo el mundo; **this make of computer is available worldwide** = esta marca de ordenadores se vende en todo el mundo

worth [wɜːθ] **1** *adjective* que vale *or* que tiene; **do not get it repaired - it is worth only £25** = no lo hagas arreglar - sólo vale £25; **the car is worth £6,000 on the secondhand market** = el coche vale £6.000 en el mercado de ocasión; **he is worth £10m** = tiene £10 millones; **what are ten pounds worth in dollars?** = ¿cuánto son diez libras en dólares? (NOTE: always follows the verb **to be) 2** *noun (value)* valor *m*; **give me ten pounds' worth of petrol** = déme gasolina por valor de diez libras

◊ **worthless** ['wɜːθləs] *adjective* sin valor; **the cheque is worthless if it is not signed** = el cheque no tiene valor si no está firmado

wrap (up) ['ræp ('ʌp)] *verb* envolver; **he wrapped (up) the parcel in green paper** = envolvió el paquete con papel verde; **to gift-wrap a present** = envolver un obsequio con papel de regalo; **shrink-wrapped** = embalado, -da *or* empaquetado, -da al vacío (NOTE: **wrapping - wrapped**)

◊ **wrapper** ['ræpə] *noun* envoltura *f or* envoltorio *m or* envase *m*; **the biscuits are packed in plastic wrappers** = las galletas están empaquetadas en envoltorios de plástico

◊ **wrapping** ['ræpɪŋ] *noun* envoltorio *m or* envase *m*; **wrapping paper** = papel de envolver; **gift-wrapping** = (i) servicio *m* de paquetes para regalo; (ii) papel de envolver regalos; **gift-wrapping department** = sección *or* departamento de empaquetado *or* envoltorio de regalos; **shrink-wrapping** = embalaje al vacío

wreck [rek] **1** *noun* **(a)** *(ship)* naufragio *m or* restos *mpl* de un naufragio *or* de una colisión; **they saved the cargo from the wreck** = salvaron la carga del naufragio; **oil poured out of the wreck of the tanker** = el petróleo salió a raudales de los restos del petrolero **(b)** *(company which has collapsed)* empresa en ruinas *or* insolvente; **he managed to save some of his investment from the wreck of the company** = consiguió salvar algunas de sus inversiones en el hundimiento de la compañía; **investors lost thousands of pounds in the wreck of**

the investment company = los inversores perdieron miles de libras en el hundimiento de la sociedad de inversiones **2** *verb* naufragar *or* hundirse *or* fracasar; **they are trying to salvage the wrecked tanker** = están intentando salvar el petrolero que naufragó; **the negotiations were wrecked by the unions** = los sindicatos hicieron fracasar las negociaciones

writ [rɪt] *noun* orden *f or* mandato *m or* mandamiento *m*; **the court issued a writ to prevent the trade union from going on strike** = el tribunal dictó una orden para impedir que el sindicato fuera a la huelga; **to serve someone with a writ** *or* **to serve a writ on someone** = notificar un mandamiento judicial a alguien

write [raɪt] *verb* escribir; **she wrote a letter of complaint to the manager** = escribió una carta de reclamación al director; **the telephone number is written at the bottom of the notepaper** = el número de teléfono está escrito al pie de la nota (NOTE: **writing - wrote - has written**)

◊ **write down** ['raɪt 'daʊn] *verb (to note an asset at a lower value)* depreciar el valor de un activo; **written down value** = valor depreciado; **the car is written down in the company's books** = el valor del coche está depreciado en los libros de la compañía

◊ **writedown** ['raɪtdaʊn] *noun* depreciación *f* de un activo

◊ **write off** ['raɪt 'ɒf] *verb* anular *or* cancelar *or* eliminar; **to write off bad debts** = cancelar las deudas incobrables; **two cars were written off after the accident** = después del accidente los dos coches fueron declarados siniestros totales; **the cargo was written off as a total loss** = se declaró la pérdida total del cargamento

◊ **write-off** ['raɪtɒf] *noun* **(a)** *(bad debt)* deuda *f* incobrable *or* pérdida *f* total; **the car was a write-off** = el coche fue declarado siniestro total **(b)** *(of assets)* depreciación *f*; **to allow for write-offs in the yearly**

accounts = reservar una partida para depreciación en las cuentas anuales

◊ **write out** ['raɪt 'aʊt] *verb* pasar en limpio *or* escribir con todas las letras; **she wrote out the minutes of the meeting from her notes** = pasó en limpio sus notas de las actas de la reunión; **to write out a cheque** = extender un cheque

◊ **writing** ['raɪtɪŋ] *noun* escrito *m or* escritura *f or* letra *f*; **to put in writing** = poner por escrito *or* redactar; **to put the agreement in writing** = poner el acuerdo por escrito; **he has difficulty in reading my writing** = le cuesta leer mi letra

> QUOTE $30 million from usual company borrowings will either be amortized or written off in one sum
> *Australian Financial Review*

> QUOTE the holding company has seen its earnings suffer from big writedowns in conjunction with its $1 billion loan portfolio
> *Duns Business Month*

wrong [rɒŋ] *adjective (not right or not correct)* erróneo, -nea *or* equivocado, -da; **the total in the last column is wrong** = el total de la última columna está equivocado; **the sales director reported the wrong figures to the meeting** = las cifras que el director de ventas presentó a la reunión eran incorrectas; **I tried to phone, but I got the wrong number** = intenté llamar pero me equivoqué de número

◊ **wrongful dismissal** ['rɒŋfʊl dɪs'mɪsəl] *noun (unlawful)* despido *m* injusto

◊ **wrongly** ['rɒŋli] *adverb* erróneamente *or* equivocadamente; **he wrongly invoiced Smith Ltd for £250, when he should have credited them with the same amount** = facturó erróneamente a Smith Ltd. por un valor de £250, cuando hubiera tenido que abonarle la misma cantidad

WTO = WORLD TRADE ORGANIZATION

Xx Yy Zz

X = EXTENSION

brand X ['brænd 'eks] *noun* marca X (marca anónima utilizada en los anuncios televisivos)

Xerox ['zɪərɒks] **1** *noun* **(a)** *(trademark for a type of photocopier)* Xerox (nombre registrado) *f or* fotocopiadora *f;* **to make a xerox copy of a letter** = hacer una fotocopia de una carta; **we must order some more xerox paper for the copier** = tenemos que pedir más papel para la fotocopiadora; **we are having a new xerox machine installed tomorrow** = nos van a instalar una nueva fotocopiadora *or* máquina 'Xerox' mañana **(b)** *(photocopy made with a Xerox machine)* fotocopia *f;* **to send the other party a xerox of the contract** = enviar una fotocopia del contrato a la otra parte; **we have sent xeroxes to each of the agents** = hemos mandado fotocopias a cada uno de los representantes **2** *verb (to make a photocopy with a Xerox machine)* fotocopiar *or* hacer fotocopias; **to xerox a document** = fotocopiar un documento; **she xeroxed all the file** = fotocopió todo el fichero

yard [jɑːd] *noun* **(a)** *(measurement of length = 0.91 metres)* yarda *f* (NOTE: can be written **yd** after figures: **10yd**) **(b)** *(factory which builds ships)* astillero *m*

yd = YARD

year [jɜː] *noun* año *m;* **once a year** = una vez al año; **calendar year** = año civil; *(twelve month period for accounts)* **financial year** = ejercicio *m* financiero; *(in the UK April 6th to April 5th of the following year)* **fiscal year** = año *m* fiscal *or* ejercicio económico; **year end** = cierre *m* del ejercicio; **the accounts department has started work on the year-end accounts** = el departamento de contabilidad ha empezado a trabajar en las cuentas de cierre del ejercicio; **year-end adjustment** = ajuste por cierre de ejercicio; **year planner** = planificador anual *or* calendario de trabajo anual

◊ **yearbook** ['jɜːbʊk] *noun* anuario *m*

◊ **yearly** ['jɜːli] *adjective* anual; **yearly payment** = pago *m* anual; **yearly premium of £250** = prima *f* anual de £250

yellow pages ['jeləʊ 'peɪdʒɪz] *plural noun (section of a telephone directory)* páginas *fpl* amarillas

Yemen ['jemen] *noun* Yemen *m*

◊ **Yemeni** ['jemeni] *adjective & noun* yemenita
NOTE: capital: **San'a;** currency: **Yemeni rial (YRls)** *or* **Yemeni dinar (YD)** riyal del Yemen (YRls) *or* dinar yemení (YD)

yen [jen] *noun (money used in Japan)* yen *m* (NOTE: usually written **¥** before a figure: **¥2,700:** say 'two thousand seven hundred yen')

yield [jiːld] **1** *noun (return on an investment)* rendimiento *m or* rentabilidad *f or* producción *f;* **current yield** = rendimiento corriente; **share with a current yield of 5%** = acción con un rendimiento corriente del 5%; **dividend yield** = rentabilidad del dividendo; **earnings yield** = porcentaje de los dividendos repartidos en relación con el precio del mercado; **effective yield** = rendimiento efectivo; **fixed yield** = rendimiento fijo; **gross yield** = rendimiento bruto; **maturity yield** *US* **yield to maturity** = rentabilidad de una inversión a largo plazo **2** *verb (to produce interest, etc.)* devengar *or* dar *or* producir *or* rendir; **government stocks which yield a small interest** = títulos del Estado que devengan poco interés; **shares which yield 10%** = acciones que rinden un 10%

> QUOTE if you wish to cut your risks you should go for shares with yields higher than average
> **Investors Chronicle**

yuan [juˈæn] *noun (currency used in China)* yuan *m*

Zaire [zæˈiːə] *noun* Zaire *m*

◊ **Zairean** [zæˈiːəriən] *adjective & noun* zaireño, -ña *or* zairense
NOTE: capital: **Kinshasa;** currency: **zaïre (Z)** = zaire (Z)

Zambia ['zæmbiə] *noun* Zambia *f*

◊ **Zambian** ['zæmbiən] *adjective & noun* zambiano, -na
NOTE: capital: **Lusaka;** currency: **Zambian kwacha (K)** = kwacha zambiano (K)

zero ['zɪərəʊ] *noun* cero *m;* **in Britain, the code for international calls is zero zero (00)** = el prefijo para conferencias internacionales en Gran Bretaña es cero cero (00); **zero inflation** = inflación cero (NOTE: nought is also common in GB English)

◊ **zero-coupon bond** ['zɪərəʊkuːpɒn 'bɒnd] *noun* obligación *f* con cupón cero

◊ **zero-rated** [zɪərəʊˈreɪtɪd] *adjective (with a VAT rate of 0%)* con un IVA del 0%

◊ **zero-rating** [zɪərəʊˈreɪtɪŋ] *noun* imposición *f* del 0% de IVA

Zimbabwe [zɪmˈbæbwi] *noun* Zimbabue *or* Zimbabwe *m*

◊ **Zimbabwean** [zɪmˈbæbwiən] *adjective & noun* zimbabuo, -bua
NOTE: capital: **Harare;** currency: **Zimbabwe dollar (Z$)** = dólar de Zimbabwe (Z$)

ZIP code ['zɪpkəʊd] *noun US* código *m* postal (NOTE: the GB English for this is **postcode**)

zipper clause ['zɪpə 'klɔːz] *noun US* cláusula *f* de un contrato de trabajo que prohíbe solicitar la modificación de las condiciones de empleo durante la vigencia del contrato

zone [zəʊn] **1** *noun* distrito *m or* zona *f;* **development zone** *or* **enterprise zone** = zona *or* región de desarrollo; **free trade zone** = zona franca; **(customs) free zone** = área aduanera exenta **2** *verb* dividir en zonas; **land zoned for light industrial use** = terreno asignado para la industria ligera; **zoning regulations** *or US* **zoning ordinances** = ordenanzas sobre la planificación urbana de cada zona

SPECIALIST SPANISH DICTIONARIES

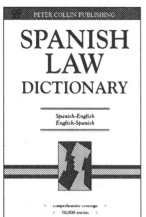

SPANISH LAW DICTIONARY
SPANISH-ENGLISH/ENGLISH-SPANISH

An up-to-date bilingual dictionary that provides accurate translations and comprehensive coverage of over 50,000 legal terms. Each entry includes part of speech and example sentences (that are also translated) to show how words are used in context.
 The legal terms cover British, American and Spanish law and cover subjects including criminal, civil, commercial and international law.

ISBN 1-901659-09-7   hardback   650pages

BUSINESS SPANISH DICTIONARY
SPANISH-ENGLISH/ENGLISH-SPANISH

The second edition of this respected dictionary. The dictionary is a fully bilingual edition that has been revised and updated to provide one of the most comprehensive and up-to-date dictionaries available. The dictionary includes accurate translation for over 50,000 terms that cover all aspects of business usage. Each entry includes example sentences, part of speech, grammar notes and comments.

ISBN 0-948549-90-4   hardback   680pages
ISBN 1-901659-23-2   paperback   680pages
ISBN 0-948549-42-4   CD-ROM   demo on our website

BUSINESS GLOSSARY SERIES

A range of bilingual business glossaries that provide accurate translations for over 5,000 business terms. Each glossary is in a convenient paperback format with 196 pages.

Spanish-English/English-Spanish   ISBN 0-948549-54-8
Spanish-Portuguese/Portuguese-Spanish   ISBN 1-901659-56-9
Spanish-German/German-Spanish   ISBN 0-948549-98-X
Catalan-English/English-Catalan   ISBN 0-948549-57-2

For full details of all our English and bilingual titles, please request a catalogue or visit our website.
tel: +44 020 8943 3386 fax: +44 020 8943 1673   email: info@petercollin.com
www.petercollin.com